The
HOLY BIBLE

ENGLISH STANDARD VERSION

Containing the Old and New Testaments

AMERICAN BIBLE SOCIETY

Philadelphia

www.americanbible.org

www.bibles.com

CONTENTS

THE BOOKS OF THE BIBLE IN ALPHABETICAL ORDER

PREFACE

The Bible

"This Book [is] the most valuable thing that this world affords. Here is Wisdom; this is the royal Law; these are the lively Oracles of God." With these words the Moderator of the Church of Scotland hands a Bible to the new monarch in Britain's coronation service. These words echo the King James Bible translators, who wrote in 1611, "God's sacred Word . . . is that inestimable treasure that excelleth all the riches of the earth." This assessment of the Bible is the motivating force behind the publication of the English Standard Version.

Translation Legacy

The English Standard Version (ESV) stands in the classic mainstream of English Bible translations over the past half-millennium. The fountainhead of that stream was William Tyndale's New Testament of 1526; marking its course were the King James Version of 1611 (KJV), the English Revised Version of 1885 (RV), the American Standard Version of 1901 (ASV), and the Revised Standard Version of 1952 and 1971 (RSV). In that stream, faithfulness to the text and vigorous pursuit of precision were combined with simplicity, beauty, and dignity of expression. Our goal has been to carry forward this legacy for this generation and generations to come.

To this end each word and phrase in the ESV has been carefully weighed against the original Hebrew, Aramaic, and Greek, to ensure the fullest accuracy and clarity and to avoid under-translating or overlooking any nuance of the original text. The words and phrases themselves grow out of the Tyndale–King James legacy, and most recently out of the RSV, with the 1971 RSV text providing the starting point for our work. Archaic language has been brought into line with current usage and significant corrections have been made in the translation of key texts. But throughout, our goal has been to retain the depth of meaning and enduring quality of language that have made their indelible mark on the English-speaking world and have defined the life and doctrine of its church over the last five centuries.

Translation Philosophy

The ESV is an "essentially literal" translation that seeks as far as possible to reproduce the precise wording of the original text and the personal style of each Bible writer. As such, its emphasis is on "word-for-word" correspondence, at the same time taking full account of differences in grammar, syntax, and idiom between current literary English and the original languages. Thus it seeks to be transparent to the original text, letting the reader see as directly as possible the structure and exact force of the original.

In contrast to the ESV, some Bible versions have followed a "thought-for-thought" rather than "word-for-word" translation philosophy, emphasizing "dynamic equivalence" rather than the "essentially literal" meaning of the original. A "thought-for-thought" translation is of necessity more inclined to reflect the interpretive views of the translator and the influences of contemporary culture.

Every translation is at many points a trade-off between literal precision and readability, between "formal equivalence" in expression and "functional equivalence" in communication, and the ESV is no exception. Within this framework we have sought to be "as literal as possible" while maintaining clarity of expression and literary excellence. Therefore, to the extent that plain English permits and the meaning in each case allows, we have sought to use the same English word for important recurring words in the original; and, as far as grammar and syntax allow, we have rendered Old Testament passages cited in the New in ways that show their correspondence. Thus in each of these areas, as well as throughout the Bible as a whole, we have sought to capture all the echoes and overtones of meaning that are so abundantly present in the original texts.

As an essentially literal translation, taking into account grammar and syntax, the ESV thus seeks to carry over every possible nuance of meaning in the original words of Scripture into our own language. As such, the ESV is ideally suited for in-depth study of the Bible. Indeed, with its commitment to literary excellence, the ESV is equally well suited for public reading and preaching, for private reading and reflection, for both academic and devotional study, and for Scripture memorization.

Translation Principles and Style

The ESV also carries forward classic translation principles in its literary style. Accordingly it retains theological terminology—words such as grace, faith, justification, sanctification, redemption, regeneration, reconciliation, propitiation—because of their central importance for Christian doctrine and also because the underlying Greek words were already becoming key words and technical terms among Christians in New Testament times.

The ESV lets the stylistic variety of the biblical writers fully express itself—from the exalted prose that opens Genesis, to the flowing narratives of the historical books, to the rich metaphors and dramatic imagery of the poetic books, to the ringing rhetoric in the prophetic books, to the smooth elegance of Luke, to the profound simplicities of John, and the closely reasoned logic of Paul.

In punctuating, paragraphing, dividing long sentences, and rendering connectives, the ESV follows the path that seems to make the ongoing flow of thought clearest in English. The biblical languages regularly connect sentences by frequent repetition of words such as "and," "but," and "for," in a way that goes beyond the conventions of current literary English. Effective translation, however, requires that these links in the original be reproduced so that the flow of the argument will be transparent to the reader. We have therefore normally translated these connectives, though occasionally we have varied the rendering by using alternatives (such as "also," "however," "now," "so," "then," or "thus") when they better express the linkage in specific instances.

In the area of gender language, the goal of the ESV is to render literally what is in the original. For example, "anyone" replaces "any man" where there is no word corresponding to "man" in the original languages, and "people" rather than "men" is regularly used where the original languages refer to both men and women. But the words "man" and "men" are retained where a male meaning component is part of the original Greek or Hebrew. Likewise, the word "man" has been retained where the original text intends to convey a clear contrast between "God" on the one hand and "man" on the other hand, with "man" being used in the collective sense of the whole human race (see Luke 2:52). Similarly, the English word "brothers" (translating the Greek word *adelphoi*) is retained as an important familial form of address between fellow-Jews and fellow-Christians in the first century. A recurring note is included to indicate that the term "brothers" (*adelphoi*) was often used in Greek to refer to both men and women, and to indicate the specific instances in the text where this is the case. In addition, the English word "sons" (translating the Greek word *huioi*) is retained in specific instances because the underlying Greek term usually includes a male meaning component and it was used as a legal term in the adoption and inheritance laws of first-century Rome. As used by the apostle Paul, this term refers to the status of all Christians, both men and women, who, having been adopted into God's family, now enjoy all the privileges, obligations, and inheritance rights of God's children.

The inclusive use of the generic "he" has also regularly been retained, because this is consistent with similar usage in the original languages and because an essentially literal translation would be impossible without it.

In each case the objective has been transparency to the original text, allowing the reader to understand the original on its own terms rather than in the terms of our present-day Western culture.

The Translation of Specialized Terms

In the translation of biblical terms referring to God, the ESV takes great care to convey the specific nuances of meaning of the original Hebrew and Greek words. First, concerning terms that refer to God in the Old Testament: God, the Maker of heaven and earth, introduced himself to the people of Israel with a special personal name, the consonants for which are YHWH (see Exodus 3:14–15). Scholars call this the "Tetragrammaton," a Greek term referring to the four Hebrew letters YHWH. The exact pronunciation of YHWH is uncertain, because the Jewish people considered the personal name of God to be so holy that it should never be spoken aloud. Instead of reading the word YHWH, therefore, they would normally read the Hebrew word *'adonay* ("Lord"), and the ancient translations into Greek, Syriac, and Aramaic also followed this practice. When the vowels of the word *'adonay* are placed with the consonants of YHWH, this results in the familiar word *Jehovah* that was used in some earlier English Bible translations. As is common among English translations today, the ESV usually renders the personal name of God (YHWH) by the word LORD (printed in small capitals). An exception to this is when the Hebrew word *'adonay* appears together with YHWH, in which case the two words are rendered together as "the Lord [in lowercase] GOD [in small capitals]." In contrast to the personal name for God (YHWH), the more general name for God in Old Testament Hebrew is *'elohim* and its related forms of *'el* or *'eloah*, all of which are normally translated "God" (in lowercase letters). The use of these different ways to translate the Hebrew words for God is especially beneficial to English readers, enabling them to see and understand the different ways that the *personal* name and the *general* name for God are both used to refer to the *One True God* of the Old Testament.

Second, in the New Testament, the Greek word *Christos* has been translated consistently as "Christ." Although the term originally meant simply "anointed," among Jews in New Testament times it had specifically come to designate the Messiah, the great Savior that God had promised to raise up. In other New Testament contexts, however, especially among Gentiles, *Christos* ("Christ") was on its way to becoming a proper name. It is important, therefore, to keep the context in mind in understanding the various ways that *Christos* ("Christ") is used in the New Testament. At the same time, in accord with its "essentially literal" translation philosophy, the ESV has retained consistency and concordance in the translation of *Christos* ("Christ") throughout the New Testament.

Third, a particular difficulty is presented when words in biblical Hebrew and Greek refer to ancient practices and institutions that do not correspond directly to those in the modern world. Such is the case in the translation of *'ebed* (Hebrew) and *doulos* (Greek), terms which are often rendered "slave." These terms, however, actually cover a range of relationships that requires a range of renderings—"slave," "bondservant," or "servant"—depending on the context. Further, the word "slave" currently carries associations with the often brutal and dehumanizing institution of slavery particularly in nineteenth-century America. For this reason, the ESV translation of the words ʿebed and doulos has been undertaken with particular attention to their meaning in each specific context. Thus in Old Testament times, one might enter slavery either voluntarily (e.g., to escape poverty or to pay off a debt) or involuntarily (e.g., by birth, by being captured in battle, or by judicial sentence). Protection for all in servitude in ancient Israel was provided by the Mosaic Law, including specific provisions for release from slavery. In New Testament times, a doulos is often best described as a "bondservant"—that is, someone in the Roman Empire officially bound under contract to serve his master for seven years (except for those in Caesar's household in Rome who were contracted for fourteen years). When the contract expired, the person was freed, given his wage that had been saved by the master, and officially declared a freedman. The ESV usage thus seeks to express the most fitting nuance of meaning in each context. Where absolute ownership by a master is envisaged (as in Romans 6), "slave" is used; where a more limited form of servitude is in view, "bondservant" is used (as in 1 Corinthians 7:21–24); where the context indicates a wide range of freedom (as in John 4:51), "servant" is preferred. Footnotes are generally provided to identify the Hebrew or Greek and the range of meaning that these terms may carry in each case. The issues involved in translating the Greek word doulos apply also to the Greek word sundoulos, translated in the text as "fellow servant."

Fourth, it is sometimes suggested that Bible translations should capitalize pronouns referring to deity. It has seemed best not to capitalize deity pronouns in the ESV, however, for the following reasons: first, there is nothing in the original Hebrew and Greek manuscripts that corresponds to such capitalization; second, the practice of capitalizing deity pronouns in English Bible translations is a recent innovation, which began only in the mid-twentieth century; and, third, such capitalization is absent from the KJV Bible and the whole stream of Bible translations that the ESV carries forward.

A fifth specialized term, the word "behold," usually has been retained as the most common translation for the Hebrew word hinneh and the Greek word idou. Both of these words mean something like "Pay careful attention to what follows! This is important!" Other than the word "behold," there is no single word in English that fits well in most contexts. Although "Look!" and "See!" and "Listen!" would be workable in some contexts, in many others these words lack sufficient weight and dignity. Given the principles of "essentially literal" translation, it is important not to leave hinneh and idou completely untranslated and so to lose the intended emphasis in the original languages. The older and more formal word "behold" has usually been retained, therefore, as the best available option for conveying the original weight of meaning.

Textual Basis and Resources

The ESV is based on the Masoretic text of the Hebrew Bible as found in Biblia Hebraica Stuttgartensia (5th ed., 1997), and on the Greek text in the 2014 editions of the Greek New Testament (5th corrected ed.), published by the United Bible Societies (UBS), and Novum Testamentum Graece (28th ed., 2012), edited by Nestle and Aland. The currently renewed respect among Old Testament scholars for the Masoretic text is reflected in the ESV's attempt, wherever possible, to translate difficult Hebrew passages as they stand in the Masoretic text rather than resorting to emendations or to finding an alternative reading in the ancient versions. In exceptional, difficult cases, the Dead Sea Scrolls, the Septuagint, the Samaritan Pentateuch, the Syriac Peshitta, the Latin Vulgate, and other sources were consulted to shed possible light on the text, or, if necessary, to support a divergence from the Masoretic text. Similarly, in a few difficult cases in the New Testament, the ESV has followed a Greek text different from the text given preference in the UBS/Nestle-Aland 28th edition. Throughout, the translation team has benefited greatly from the massive textual resources that have become readily available recently, from new insights into biblical laws and culture, and from current advances in Hebrew and Greek lexicography and grammatical understanding.

Textual Footnotes

The footnotes that are included in most editions of the ESV are therefore an integral part of the ESV translation, informing the reader of textual variations and difficulties and showing how these have been resolved by the ESV translation team. In addition to this, the footnotes indicate significant alternative readings and occasionally provide an explanation for technical terms or for a difficult reading in the text.

Publishing Team

The ESV publishing team has included more than a hundred people. The fourteen-member Translation Oversight Committee benefited from the work of more than fifty biblical experts serving as Translation Review Scholars and from the comments of the more than fifty members of the Advisory Council, all of which was carried out under the auspices of the Crossway Board of Directors. This hundred-plus-member team shares a common commitment to the truth of God's Word and to historic Christian orthodoxy and is international in scope, including leaders in many denominations.

To God's Honor and Praise

We know that no Bible translation is perfect; but we also know that God uses imperfect and inadequate things to his honor and praise. So to our triune God and to his people we offer what we have done, with our prayers that it may prove useful, with gratitude for much help given, and with ongoing wonder that our God should ever have entrusted to us so momentous a task.

Soli Deo Gloria!—To God alone be the glory!

The Translation Oversight Committee

EXPLANATION OF
FEATURES
INCLUDED IN THIS EDITION

The Thinline Edition of the ESV Bible includes a number of valuable features to encourage the reading and study of the Bible. A brief description is provided below explaining the purpose and use of these features.

SECTION HEADINGS

Section headings have been included throughout the text of the ESV Thinline Bible. While the headings are not part of the Bible text itself, they have been provided to help identify and locate important themes and topics throughout the Bible.

TEXTUAL FOOTNOTES

Several kinds of footnotes related to the ESV text are provided throughout the ESV Bible to assist the reader. These footnotes appear at the bottom of the page and are indicated in the ESV text by a superscript *number* that *follows* the word or phrase to which the footnote applies (e.g., "Isaac[2]"). Superscript *letters* that *precede* a word indicate cross-references (see explanation on the following page).

The footnotes included in the ESV Bible are an integral part of the text and provide important information concerning the understanding and translation of the text. The footnotes fall mainly into four categories, as illustrated in the examples below.

Types of Textual Footnotes

(1) *Alternative Translations*. Footnotes of this kind provide alternative translations for specific words or phrases when there is a strong possibility that such words or phrases could be translated in another way, such as: "Or *keep awake*" (see Matt. 26:38); and "Or *down payment*" (see Eph. 1:14). In such cases, the translation deemed to have the stronger support is in the text while other possible renderings are given in the note.

(2) *Explanation of Greek and Hebrew Terms*. Notes of this kind relate primarily to the meaning of specific Greek or Hebrew terms, as illustrated by the following examples:

(a) Notes about the meaning of names in the original languages, such as: "*Isaac* means *he laughs*" (see Gen. 17:19); and "*Simeon* sounds like the Hebrew for *heard*" (see Gen. 29:33).

(b) Notes that give the literal translation of a Greek or Hebrew word or phrase deemed too awkward to be used in the English text, such as: "Greek *girding up the loins of your mind*" (see 1 Pet. 1:13).

(c) Notes indicating that absolute certainty of the meaning of a word or phrase is not possible given our best understanding of the original language (e.g., Hebrew words occurring so infrequently in the Old Testament that their meaning cannot be determined with certainty). Such words are identified with a note stating that "The meaning of the Hebrew is uncertain" (see, e.g., Josh. 17:11).

(d) Notes that indicate the specialized use of a Greek word, such as: "brothers," translating the Greek word *adelphoi* (see, e.g., the extended note on Rom. 1:13, corresponding to the first occurrence of *adelphoi* in any New Testament book, and the abbreviated note, e.g., on Rom. 7:1, corresponding to subsequent occurrences of *adelphoi* in any New Testament book); and "sons," translating the

Greek word *huioi* (see, e.g., Rom. 8:14). See also the discussion of *adelphoi* and *huioi* in the Preface.

(3) *Other Explanatory Notes.* Footnotes of this kind provide clarifying information as illustrated by the following examples:

(a) Notes clarifying additional meanings that may not otherwise be apparent in the text, such as: "*Leprosy* was a term for several skin diseases; see Leviticus 13."

(b) Notes clarifying important grammatical points that would not otherwise be apparent in English, such as: "In Hebrew *you* is plural in verses 1–5" (see Gen. 3:1).

(c) Notes clarifying when the referent for a pronoun has been supplied in the English text, such as: "Greek *he*" (see, e.g., Mark 1:43).

(d) Notes giving English equivalents for weights, measures, and monetary values.

(4) *Technical Translation Notes.* Footnotes of this kind indicate how decisions have been made in the translation of difficult Hebrew and Greek passages. Such notes occasionally include technical terms. For an explanation of these terms the reader is referred to standard Bible study reference works. See further the section in the Preface on "Textual Basis and Resources" for an explanation of the original-language texts used in the translation of the ESV Bible and how the translation of difficult passages has been resolved.

CROSS-REFERENCE FOOTNOTES

In addition to the *numeric* (textual) footnotes, the New Testament portion of this edition of the ESV Bible includes two kinds of cross-reference notes. These are identified *alphabetically* and follow the numeric notes at the bottom of each page. These include (1) *direct quotations from the Old Testament* (indirect quotations and allusions are not included), and (2) *parallel passages in the four Gospels.* These cross-references are included to help the reader understand the relationship of the New Testament to the Old Testament, and the harmony of the Gospels in the New Testament.

The

OLD TESTAMENT

GENESIS

The Creation of the World

1 In the beginning, God created the heavens and the earth. [2] The earth was without form and void, and darkness was over the face of the deep. And the Spirit of God was hovering over the face of the waters.

[3] And God said, "Let there be light," and there was light. [4] And God saw that the light was good. And God separated the light from the darkness. [5] God called the light Day, and the darkness he called Night. And there was evening and there was morning, the first day.

[6] And God said, "Let there be an expanse[1] in the midst of the waters, and let it separate the waters from the waters." [7] And God made[2] the expanse and separated the waters that were under the expanse from the waters that were above the expanse. And it was so. [8] And God called the expanse Heaven.[3] And there was evening and there was morning, the second day.

[9] And God said, "Let the waters under the heavens be gathered together into one place, and let the dry land appear." And it was so. [10] God called the dry land Earth,[4] and the waters that were gathered together he called Seas. And God saw that it was good.

[11] And God said, "Let the earth sprout vegetation, plants[5] yielding seed, and fruit trees bearing fruit in which is their seed, each according to its kind, on the earth." And it was so. [12] The earth brought forth vegetation, plants yielding seed according to their own kinds, and trees bearing fruit in which is their seed, each according to its kind. And God saw that it was good. [13] And there was evening and there was morning, the third day.

[14] And God said, "Let there be lights in the expanse of the heavens to separate the day from the night. And let them be for signs and for seasons,[6] and for days and years, [15] and let them be lights in the expanse of the heavens to give light upon the earth." And it was so. [16] And God made the two great lights—the greater light to rule the day and the lesser light to rule the night—and the stars. [17] And God set them in the expanse of the heavens to give light on the earth, [18] to rule over the day and over the night, and to separate the light from the darkness. And God saw that it was good. [19] And there was evening and there was morning, the fourth day.

[20] And God said, "Let the waters swarm with swarms of living creatures, and let birds[7] fly above the earth across the expanse of the heavens." [21] So God created the great sea creatures and every living creature that moves, with which the waters swarm, according to their kinds, and every winged bird according to its kind. And God saw that it was good. [22] And God blessed them, saying, "Be fruitful and multiply and fill the waters in the seas, and let birds multiply on the earth." [23] And there was evening and there was morning, the fifth day.

[24] And God said, "Let the earth bring forth living creatures according to their kinds—livestock and creeping things and beasts of the earth according to their kinds." And it was so. [25] And God made the beasts of the earth according to their kinds and the livestock according to their kinds, and everything that creeps on the ground according to its kind. And God saw that it was good.

[26] Then God said, "Let us make man[8] in our image, after our likeness. And let them have dominion over the fish of the sea and over the birds of the heavens and over the livestock and over all the earth and over every creeping thing that creeps on the earth."

[27] So God created man in his own image,
in the image of God he created him;
male and female he created them.

[28] And God blessed them. And God said to them, "Be fruitful and multiply and fill the earth and subdue it, and have dominion over the fish of the sea and over the birds of the heavens and over every living thing that moves on the earth." [29] And God said, "Behold, I have given you every plant yielding seed that is on the face of all the earth, and every tree with seed in its fruit. You shall have them for food. [30] And to every beast of the earth and to every bird of the heavens and to everything that creeps on the earth, everything that has the breath of life, I have given every green plant for food." And

---

[1] Or *a canopy*; also verses 7, 8, 14, 15, 17, 20 [2] Or *fashioned*; also verse 16 [3] Or *Sky*; also verses 9, 14, 15, 17, 20, 26, 28, 30; 2:1 [4] Or *Land*; also verses 11, 12, 22, 24, 25, 26, 28, 30; 2:1 [5] Or *small plants*; also verses 12, 29 [6] Or *appointed times* [7] Or *flying things*; see Leviticus 11:19–20 [8] The Hebrew word for *man* (*adam*) is the generic term for mankind and becomes the proper name *Adam*

it was so. ³¹ And God saw everything that he had made, and behold, it was very good. And there was evening and there was morning, the sixth day.

The Seventh Day, God Rests

2 Thus the heavens and the earth were finished, and all the host of them. ² And on the seventh day God finished his work that he had done, and he rested on the seventh day from all his work that he had done. ³ So God blessed the seventh day and made it holy, because on it God rested from all his work that he had done in creation.

The Creation of Man and Woman

4 These are the generations
  of the heavens and the earth when they
        were created,
    in the day that the LORD God made the
        earth and the heavens.

⁵ When no bush of the field¹ was yet in the land² and no small plant of the field had yet sprung up—for the LORD God had not caused it to rain on the land, and there was no man to work the ground, ⁶ and a mist³ was going up from the land and was watering the whole face of the ground— ⁷ then the LORD God formed the man of dust from the ground and breathed into his nostrils the breath of life, and the man became a living creature. ⁸ And the LORD God planted a garden in Eden, in the east, and there he put the man whom he had formed. ⁹ And out of the ground the LORD God made to spring up every tree that is pleasant to the sight and good for food. The tree of life was in the midst of the garden, and the tree of the knowledge of good and evil.

¹⁰ A river flowed out of Eden to water the garden, and there it divided and became four rivers. ¹¹ The name of the first is the Pishon. It is the one that flowed around the whole land of Havilah, where there is gold. ¹² And the gold of that land is good; bdellium and onyx stone are there. ¹³ The name of the second river is the Gihon. It is the one that flowed around the whole land of Cush. ¹⁴ And the name of the third river is the Tigris, which flows east of Assyria. And the fourth river is the Euphrates.

¹⁵ The LORD God took the man and put him in the garden of Eden to work it and keep it. ¹⁶ And the LORD God commanded the man, saying, "You may surely eat of every tree of the garden, ¹⁷ but of the tree of the knowledge of good and evil you shall not eat, for in the day that you eat⁴ of it you shall surely die."

¹⁸ Then the LORD God said, "It is not good that the man should be alone; I will make him a helper fit for⁵ him." ¹⁹ Now out of the ground the LORD God had formed⁶ every beast of the field and every bird of the heavens and brought them to the man to see what he would call them. And whatever the man called every living creature, that was its name. ²⁰ The man gave names to all livestock and to the birds of the heavens and to every beast of the field. But for Adam⁷ there was not found a helper fit for him. ²¹ So the LORD God caused a deep sleep to fall upon the man, and while he slept took one of his ribs and closed up its place with flesh. ²² And the rib that the LORD God had taken from the man he made⁸ into a woman and brought her to the man. ²³ Then the man said,

"This at last is bone of my bones
    and flesh of my flesh;
  she shall be called Woman,
      because she was taken out of Man."⁹

²⁴ Therefore a man shall leave his father and his mother and hold fast to his wife, and they shall become one flesh. ²⁵ And the man and his wife were both naked and were not ashamed.

The Fall

3 Now the serpent was more crafty than any other beast of the field that the LORD God had made.

He said to the woman, "Did God actually say, 'You¹⁰ shall not eat of any tree in the garden'?" ² And the woman said to the serpent, "We may eat of the fruit of the trees in the garden, ³ but God said, 'You shall not eat of the fruit of the tree that is in the midst of the garden, neither shall you touch it, lest you die.'" ⁴ But the serpent said to the woman, "You will not surely die. ⁵ For God knows that when you eat of it your eyes will be opened, and you will be like God, knowing good and evil." ⁶ So when the woman saw that the tree was good for food, and that it was a delight to the eyes, and that the tree was to be desired to make one wise,¹¹ she took of its fruit and ate, and she also gave some to her husband who was with her, and he ate. ⁷ Then the eyes of both were opened, and they knew that they were naked. And they sewed fig leaves together and made themselves loincloths.

¹ Or open country ² Or earth; also verse 6 ³ Or spring ⁴ Or when you eat ⁵ Or corresponding to; also verse 20 ⁶ Or And out of the ground the LORD God formed ⁷ Or the man ⁸ Hebrew built ⁹ The Hebrew words for woman (ishshah) and man (ish) sound alike ¹⁰ In Hebrew you is plural in verses 1–5 ¹¹ Or to give insight

⁸And they heard the sound of the LORD God walking in the garden in the cool¹ of the day, and the man and his wife hid themselves from the presence of the LORD God among the trees of the garden. ⁹But the LORD God called to the man and said to him, "Where are you?"² ¹⁰And he said, "I heard the sound of you in the garden, and I was afraid, because I was naked, and I hid myself." ¹¹He said, "Who told you that you were naked? Have you eaten of the tree of which I commanded you not to eat?" ¹²The man said, "The woman whom you gave to be with me, she gave me fruit of the tree, and I ate." ¹³Then the LORD God said to the woman, "What is this that you have done?" The woman said, "The serpent deceived me, and I ate."

¹⁴The LORD God said to the serpent,

"Because you have done this,
 cursed are you above all livestock
 and above all beasts of the field;
on your belly you shall go,
 and dust you shall eat
 all the days of your life.
¹⁵ I will put enmity between you and the
  woman,
 and between your offspring³ and her
  offspring;
he shall bruise your head,
 and you shall bruise his heel."

¹⁶To the woman he said,

"I will surely multiply your pain in childbearing;
 in pain you shall bring forth children.
Your desire shall be contrary to⁴ your
  husband,
 but he shall rule over you."

¹⁷And to Adam he said,

"Because you have listened to the voice of
  your wife
 and have eaten of the tree
of which I commanded you,
 'You shall not eat of it,'
cursed is the ground because of you;
 in pain you shall eat of it all the days of
  your life;
¹⁸ thorns and thistles it shall bring forth for
  you;
 and you shall eat the plants of the field.

¹⁹ By the sweat of your face
 you shall eat bread,
till you return to the ground,
 for out of it you were taken;
for you are dust,
 and to dust you shall return."

²⁰The man called his wife's name Eve, because she was the mother of all living.⁵ ²¹And the LORD God made for Adam and for his wife garments of skins and clothed them.

²²Then the LORD God said, "Behold, the man has become like one of us in knowing good and evil. Now, lest he reach out his hand and take also of the tree of life and eat, and live forever—" ²³therefore the LORD God sent him out from the garden of Eden to work the ground from which he was taken. ²⁴He drove out the man, and at the east of the garden of Eden he placed the cherubim and a flaming sword that turned every way to guard the way to the tree of life.

Cain and Abel

4 Now Adam knew Eve his wife, and she conceived and bore Cain, saying, "I have gotten⁶ a man with the help of the LORD." ²And again, she bore his brother Abel. Now Abel was a keeper of sheep, and Cain a worker of the ground. ³In the course of time Cain brought to the LORD an offering of the fruit of the ground, ⁴and Abel also brought of the firstborn of his flock and of their fat portions. And the LORD had regard for Abel and his offering, ⁵but for Cain and his offering he had no regard. So Cain was very angry, and his face fell. ⁶The LORD said to Cain, "Why are you angry, and why has your face fallen? ⁷If you do well, will you not be accepted?⁷ And if you do not do well, sin is crouching at the door. Its desire is contrary to⁸ you, but you must rule over it."

⁸Cain spoke to Abel his brother.⁹ And when they were in the field, Cain rose up against his brother Abel and killed him. ⁹Then the LORD said to Cain, "Where is Abel your brother?" He said, "I do not know; am I my brother's keeper?" ¹⁰And the LORD said, "What have you done? The voice of your brother's blood is crying to me from the ground. ¹¹And now you are cursed from the ground, which has opened its mouth to receive your brother's blood from your hand. ¹²When you work the ground, it shall no longer

---

¹ Hebrew *wind* ² In Hebrew *you* is singular in verses 9 and 11 ³ Hebrew *seed*; so throughout Genesis ⁴ Or *shall be toward* (see 4:7) ⁵ *Eve* sounds like the Hebrew for *life-giver* and resembles the word for *living* ⁶ *Cain* sounds like the Hebrew for *gotten* ⁷ Hebrew *will there not be a lifting up* [of your face]? ⁸ Or *is toward* ⁹ Hebrew; Samaritan, Septuagint, Syriac, Vulgate add *Let us go out to the field*

yield to you its strength. You shall be a fugitive and a wanderer on the earth." [13] Cain said to the LORD, "My punishment is greater than I can bear.[1] [14] Behold, you have driven me today away from the ground, and from your face I shall be hidden. I shall be a fugitive and a wanderer on the earth, and whoever finds me will kill me." [15] Then the LORD said to him, "Not so! If anyone kills Cain, vengeance shall be taken on him sevenfold." And the LORD put a mark on Cain, lest any who found him should attack him. [16] Then Cain went away from the presence of the LORD and settled in the land of Nod,[2] east of Eden.

[17] Cain knew his wife, and she conceived and bore Enoch. When he built a city, he called the name of the city after the name of his son, Enoch. [18] To Enoch was born Irad, and Irad fathered Mehujael, and Mehujael fathered Methushael, and Methushael fathered Lamech. [19] And Lamech took two wives. The name of the one was Adah, and the name of the other Zillah. [20] Adah bore Jabal; he was the father of those who dwell in tents and have livestock. [21] His brother's name was Jubal; he was the father of all those who play the lyre and pipe. [22] Zillah also bore Tubal-cain; he was the forger of all instruments of bronze and iron. The sister of Tubal-cain was Naamah.

[23] Lamech said to his wives:

"Adah and Zillah, hear my voice;
    you wives of Lamech, listen to what I
    say:
I have killed a man for wounding me,
    a young man for striking me.
[24] If Cain's revenge is sevenfold,
    then Lamech's is seventy-sevenfold."

[25] And Adam knew his wife again, and she bore a son and called his name Seth, for she said, "God has appointed[3] for me another offspring instead of Abel, for Cain killed him." [26] To Seth also a son was born, and he called his name Enosh. At that time people began to call upon the name of the LORD.

Adam's Descendants to Noah

5 This is the book of the generations of Adam. When God created man, he made him in the likeness of God. [2] Male and female he created them, and he blessed them and named them Man[4] when they were created. [3] When Adam had lived 130 years, he fathered a son in his own likeness, after his image, and named

him Seth. [4] The days of Adam after he fathered Seth were 800 years; and he had other sons and daughters. [5] Thus all the days that Adam lived were 930 years, and he died.

[6] When Seth had lived 105 years, he fathered Enosh. [7] Seth lived after he fathered Enosh 807 years and had other sons and daughters. [8] Thus all the days of Seth were 912 years, and he died.

[9] When Enosh had lived 90 years, he fathered Kenan. [10] Enosh lived after he fathered Kenan 815 years and had other sons and daughters. [11] Thus all the days of Enosh were 905 years, and he died.

[12] When Kenan had lived 70 years, he fathered Mahalalel. [13] Kenan lived after he fathered Mahalalel 840 years and had other sons and daughters. [14] Thus all the days of Kenan were 910 years, and he died.

[15] When Mahalalel had lived 65 years, he fathered Jared. [16] Mahalalel lived after he fathered Jared 830 years and had other sons and daughters. [17] Thus all the days of Mahalalel were 895 years, and he died.

[18] When Jared had lived 162 years, he fathered Enoch. [19] Jared lived after he fathered Enoch 800 years and had other sons and daughters. [20] Thus all the days of Jared were 962 years, and he died.

[21] When Enoch had lived 65 years, he fathered Methuselah. [22] Enoch walked with God[5] after he fathered Methuselah 300 years and had other sons and daughters. [23] Thus all the days of Enoch were 365 years. [24] Enoch walked with God, and he was not,[6] for God took him.

[25] When Methuselah had lived 187 years, he fathered Lamech. [26] Methuselah lived after he fathered Lamech 782 years and had other sons and daughters. [27] Thus all the days of Methuselah were 969 years, and he died.

[28] When Lamech had lived 182 years, he fathered a son [29] and called his name Noah, saying, "Out of the ground that the LORD has cursed, this one shall bring us relief[7] from our work and from the painful toil of our hands." [30] Lamech lived after he fathered Noah 595 years and had other sons and daughters. [31] Thus all the days of Lamech were 777 years, and he died.

[32] After Noah was 500 years old, Noah fathered Shem, Ham, and Japheth.

[1] Or My guilt is too great to bear [2] Nod means wandering [3] Seth sounds like the Hebrew for he appointed [4] Hebrew adam [5] Septuagint pleased God; also verse 24 [6] Septuagint was not found [7] Noah sounds like the Hebrew for rest

Increasing Corruption on Earth

6 When man began to multiply on the face of the land and daughters were born to them, [2] the sons of God saw that the daughters of man were attractive. And they took as their wives any they chose. [3] Then the LORD said, "My Spirit shall not abide in[1] man forever, for he is flesh: his days shall be 120 years." [4] The Nephilim[2] were on the earth in those days, and also afterward, when the sons of God came in to the daughters of man and they bore children to them. These were the mighty men who were of old, the men of renown.

[5] The LORD saw that the wickedness of man was great in the earth, and that every intention of the thoughts of his heart was only evil continually. [6] And the LORD regretted that he had made man on the earth, and it grieved him to his heart. [7] So the LORD said, "I will blot out man whom I have created from the face of the land, man and animals and creeping things and birds of the heavens, for I am sorry that I have made them." [8] But Noah found favor in the eyes of the LORD.

Noah and the Flood

[9] These are the generations of Noah. Noah was a righteous man, blameless in his generation. Noah walked with God. [10] And Noah had three sons, Shem, Ham, and Japheth.

[11] Now the earth was corrupt in God's sight, and the earth was filled with violence. [12] And God saw the earth, and behold, it was corrupt, for all flesh had corrupted their way on the earth. [13] And God said to Noah, "I have determined to make an end of all flesh,[3] for the earth is filled with violence through them. Behold, I will destroy them with the earth. [14] Make yourself an ark of gopher wood.[4] Make rooms in the ark, and cover it inside and out with pitch. [15] This is how you are to make it: the length of the ark 300 cubits,[5] its breadth 50 cubits, and its height 30 cubits. [16] Make a roof[6] for the ark, and finish it to a cubit above, and set the door of the ark in its side. Make it with lower, second, and third decks. [17] For behold, I will bring a flood of waters upon the earth to destroy all flesh in which is the breath of life under heaven. Everything that is on the earth shall die. [18] But I will establish my covenant with you, and you shall come into the ark, you, your sons, your wife, and your sons' wives with you. [19] And of every living thing of all flesh, you shall bring two of every sort into the ark to keep them alive with you. They shall be male and female. [20] Of the birds according to their kinds, and of the animals according to their kinds, of every creeping thing of the ground, according to its kind, two of every sort shall come in to you to keep them alive. [21] Also take with you every sort of food that is eaten, and store it up. It shall serve as food for you and for them." [22] Noah did this; he did all that God commanded him.

7 Then the LORD said to Noah, "Go into the ark, you and all your household, for I have seen that you are righteous before me in this generation. [2] Take with you seven pairs of all clean animals,[7] the male and his mate, and a pair of the animals that are not clean, the male and his mate, [3] and seven pairs[8] of the birds of the heavens also, male and female, to keep their offspring alive on the face of all the earth. [4] For in seven days I will send rain on the earth forty days and forty nights, and every living thing[9] that I have made I will blot out from the face of the ground." [5] And Noah did all that the LORD had commanded him.

[6] Noah was six hundred years old when the flood of waters came upon the earth. [7] And Noah and his sons and his wife and his sons' wives with him went into the ark to escape the waters of the flood. [8] Of clean animals, and of animals that are not clean, and of birds, and of everything that creeps on the ground, [9] two and two, male and female, went into the ark with Noah, as God had commanded Noah. [10] And after seven days the waters of the flood came upon the earth.

[11] In the six hundredth year of Noah's life, in the second month, on the seventeenth day of the month, on that day all the fountains of the great deep burst forth, and the windows of the heavens were opened. [12] And rain fell upon the earth forty days and forty nights. [13] On the very same day Noah and his sons, Shem and Ham and Japheth, and Noah's wife and the three wives of his sons with them entered the ark, [14] they and every beast, according to its kind, and all the livestock according to their kinds, and every creeping thing that creeps on the earth, according to its kind, and every bird, according to its kind, every winged creature. [15] They went into the ark with Noah, two and two of all flesh in which there was the breath of life. [16] And those that entered, male and female

[1] Or My Spirit shall not contend with [2] Or giants [3] Hebrew The end of all flesh has come before me [4] An unknown kind of tree; transliterated from Hebrew [5] A cubit was about 18 inches or 45 centimeters [6] Or skylight [7] Or seven of each kind of clean animal [8] Or seven of each kind [9] Hebrew all existence; also verse 23

of all flesh, went in as God had commanded him. And the LORD shut him in.

[17] The flood continued forty days on the earth. The waters increased and bore up the ark, and it rose high above the earth. [18] The waters prevailed and increased greatly on the earth, and the ark floated on the face of the waters. [19] And the waters prevailed so mightily on the earth that all the high mountains under the whole heaven were covered. [20] The waters prevailed above the mountains, covering them fifteen cubits[1] deep. [21] And all flesh died that moved on the earth, birds, livestock, beasts, all swarming creatures that swarm on the earth, and all mankind. [22] Everything on the dry land in whose nostrils was the breath of life died. [23] He blotted out every living thing that was on the face of the ground, man and animals and creeping things and birds of the heavens. They were blotted out from the earth. Only Noah was left, and those who were with him in the ark. [24] And the waters prevailed on the earth 150 days.

The Flood Subsides

8 But God remembered Noah and all the beasts and all the livestock that were with him in the ark. And God made a wind blow over the earth, and the waters subsided. [2] The fountains of the deep and the windows of the heavens were closed, the rain from the heavens was restrained, [3] and the waters receded from the earth continually. At the end of 150 days the waters had abated, [4] and in the seventh month, on the seventeenth day of the month, the ark came to rest on the mountains of Ararat. [5] And the waters continued to abate until the tenth month; in the tenth month, on the first day of the month, the tops of the mountains were seen.

[6] At the end of forty days Noah opened the window of the ark that he had made [7] and sent forth a raven. It went to and fro until the waters were dried up from the earth. [8] Then he sent forth a dove from him, to see if the waters had subsided from the face of the ground. [9] But the dove found no place to set her foot, and she returned to him to the ark, for the waters were still on the face of the whole earth. So he put out his hand and took her and brought her into the ark with him. [10] He waited another seven days, and again he sent forth the dove out of the ark. [11] And the dove came back to him in the evening, and behold, in her mouth was a freshly plucked olive leaf. So Noah knew that the waters had subsided from the earth. [12] Then he waited another seven days and sent forth the dove, and she did not return to him anymore.

[13] In the six hundred and first year, in the first month, the first day of the month, the waters were dried from off the earth. And Noah removed the covering of the ark and looked, and behold, the face of the ground was dry. [14] In the second month, on the twenty-seventh day of the month, the earth had dried out. [15] Then God said to Noah, [16] "Go out from the ark, you and your wife, and your sons and your sons' wives with you. [17] Bring out with you every living thing that is with you of all flesh—birds and animals and every creeping thing that creeps on the earth—that they may swarm on the earth, and be fruitful and multiply on the earth." [18] So Noah went out, and his sons and his wife and his sons' wives with him. [19] Every beast, every creeping thing, and every bird, everything that moves on the earth, went out by families from the ark.

God's Covenant with Noah

[20] Then Noah built an altar to the LORD and took some of every clean animal and some of every clean bird and offered burnt offerings on the altar. [21] And when the LORD smelled the pleasing aroma, the LORD said in his heart, "I will never again curse[2] the ground because of man, for the intention of man's heart is evil from his youth. Neither will I ever again strike down every living creature as I have done. [22] While the earth remains, seedtime and harvest, cold and heat, summer and winter, day and night, shall not cease."

9 And God blessed Noah and his sons and said to them, "Be fruitful and multiply and fill the earth. [2] The fear of you and the dread of you shall be upon every beast of the earth and upon every bird of the heavens, upon everything that creeps on the ground and all the fish of the sea. Into your hand they are delivered. [3] Every moving thing that lives shall be food for you. And as I gave you the green plants, I give you everything. [4] But you shall not eat flesh with its life, that is, its blood. [5] And for your lifeblood I will require a reckoning: from every beast I will require it and from man. From his fellow man I will require a reckoning for the life of man.

[6]   "Whoever sheds the blood of man,
      by man shall his blood be shed,
      for God made man in his own image.

---

[1] A *cubit* was about 18 inches or 45 centimeters [2] Or *dishonor*

[7] And you,[1] be fruitful and multiply, increase greatly on the earth and multiply in it."

[8] Then God said to Noah and to his sons with him, [9] "Behold, I establish my covenant with you and your offspring after you, [10] and with every living creature that is with you, the birds, the livestock, and every beast of the earth with you, as many as came out of the ark; it is for every beast of the earth. [11] I establish my covenant with you, that never again shall all flesh be cut off by the waters of the flood, and never again shall there be a flood to destroy the earth." [12] And God said, "This is the sign of the covenant that I make between me and you and every living creature that is with you, for all future generations: [13] I have set my bow in the cloud, and it shall be a sign of the covenant between me and the earth. [14] When I bring clouds over the earth and the bow is seen in the clouds, [15] I will remember my covenant that is between me and you and every living creature of all flesh. And the waters shall never again become a flood to destroy all flesh. [16] When the bow is in the clouds, I will see it and remember the everlasting covenant between God and every living creature of all flesh that is on the earth." [17] God said to Noah, "This is the sign of the covenant that I have established between me and all flesh that is on the earth."

Noah's Descendants

[18] The sons of Noah who went forth from the ark were Shem, Ham, and Japheth. (Ham was the father of Canaan.) [19] These three were the sons of Noah, and from these the people of the whole earth were dispersed.[2]

[20] Noah began to be a man of the soil, and he planted a vineyard.[3] [21] He drank of the wine and became drunk and lay uncovered in his tent. [22] And Ham, the father of Canaan, saw the nakedness of his father and told his two brothers outside. [23] Then Shem and Japheth took a garment, laid it on both their shoulders, and walked backward and covered the nakedness of their father. Their faces were turned backward, and they did not see their father's nakedness. [24] When Noah awoke from his wine and knew what his youngest son had done to him, [25] he said,

> "Cursed be Canaan;
> a servant of servants shall he be to his brothers."

[26] He also said,

> "Blessed be the LORD, the God of Shem;
> and let Canaan be his servant.
> [27] May God enlarge Japheth,[4]
> and let him dwell in the tents of Shem,
> and let Canaan be his servant."

[28] After the flood Noah lived 350 years. [29] All the days of Noah were 950 years, and he died.

Nations Descended from Noah

10 These are the generations of the sons of Noah, Shem, Ham, and Japheth. Sons were born to them after the flood.

[2] The sons of Japheth: Gomer, Magog, Madai, Javan, Tubal, Meshech, and Tiras. [3] The sons of Gomer: Ashkenaz, Riphath, and Togarmah. [4] The sons of Javan: Elishah, Tarshish, Kittim, and Dodanim. [5] From these the coastland peoples spread in their lands, each with his own language, by their clans, in their nations.

[6] The sons of Ham: Cush, Egypt, Put, and Canaan. [7] The sons of Cush: Seba, Havilah, Sabtah, Raamah, and Sabteca. The sons of Raamah: Sheba and Dedan. [8] Cush fathered Nimrod; he was the first on earth to be a mighty man.[5] [9] He was a mighty hunter before the LORD. Therefore it is said, "Like Nimrod a mighty hunter before the LORD." [10] The beginning of his kingdom was Babel, Erech, Accad, and Calneh, in the land of Shinar. [11] From that land he went into Assyria and built Nineveh, Rehoboth-Ir, Calah, and [12] Resen between Nineveh and Calah; that is the great city. [13] Egypt fathered Ludim, Anamim, Lehabim, Naphtuhim, [14] Pathrusim, Casluhim (from whom[6] the Philistines came), and Caphtorim.

[15] Canaan fathered Sidon his firstborn and Heth, [16] and the Jebusites, the Amorites, the Girgashites, [17] the Hivites, the Arkites, the Sinites, [18] the Arvadites, the Zemarites, and the Hamathites. Afterward the clans of the Canaanites dispersed. [19] And the territory of the Canaanites extended from Sidon in the direction of Gerar as far as Gaza, and in the direction of Sodom, Gomorrah, Admah, and Zeboiim, as far as Lasha. [20] These are the sons of Ham, by their clans, their languages, their lands, and their nations.

[21] To Shem also, the father of all the children of Eber, the elder brother of Japheth, children were born. [22] The sons of Shem: Elam,

---

[1] In Hebrew you is plural　[2] Or from these the whole earth was populated　[3] Or Noah, a man of the soil, was the first to plant a vineyard　[4] Japheth sounds like the Hebrew for enlarge　[5] Or he began to be a mighty man on the earth　[6] Or from where

Asshur, Arpachshad, Lud, and Aram. [23] The sons of Aram: Uz, Hul, Gether, and Mash. [24] Arpachshad fathered Shelah; and Shelah fathered Eber. [25] To Eber were born two sons: the name of the one was Peleg,[1] for in his days the earth was divided, and his brother's name was Joktan. [26] Joktan fathered Almodad, Sheleph, Hazarmaveth, Jerah, [27] Hadoram, Uzal, Diklah, [28] Obal, Abimael, Sheba, [29] Ophir, Havilah, and Jobab; all these were the sons of Joktan. [30] The territory in which they lived extended from Mesha in the direction of Sephar to the hill country of the east. [31] These are the sons of Shem, by their clans, their languages, their lands, and their nations.

[32] These are the clans of the sons of Noah, according to their genealogies, in their nations, and from these the nations spread abroad on the earth after the flood.

The Tower of Babel

11 Now the whole earth had one language and the same words. [2] And as people migrated from the east, they found a plain in the land of Shinar and settled there. [3] And they said to one another, "Come, let us make bricks, and burn them thoroughly." And they had brick for stone, and bitumen for mortar. [4] Then they said, "Come, let us build ourselves a city and a tower with its top in the heavens, and let us make a name for ourselves, lest we be dispersed over the face of the whole earth." [5] And the LORD came down to see the city and the tower, which the children of man had built. [6] And the LORD said, "Behold, they are one people, and they have all one language, and this is only the beginning of what they will do. And nothing that they propose to do will now be impossible for them. [7] Come, let us go down and there confuse their language, so that they may not understand one another's speech." [8] So the LORD dispersed them from there over the face of all the earth, and they left off building the city. [9] Therefore its name was called Babel, because there the LORD confused[2] the language of all the earth. And from there the LORD dispersed them over the face of all the earth.

Shem's Descendants

[10] These are the generations of Shem. When Shem was 100 years old, he fathered Arpachshad two years after the flood. [11] And Shem lived after he fathered Arpachshad 500 years and had other sons and daughters.

[12] When Arpachshad had lived 35 years, he fathered Shelah. [13] And Arpachshad lived after he fathered Shelah 403 years and had other sons and daughters.

[14] When Shelah had lived 30 years, he fathered Eber. [15] And Shelah lived after he fathered Eber 403 years and had other sons and daughters.

[16] When Eber had lived 34 years, he fathered Peleg. [17] And Eber lived after he fathered Peleg 430 years and had other sons and daughters.

[18] When Peleg had lived 30 years, he fathered Reu. [19] And Peleg lived after he fathered Reu 209 years and had other sons and daughters.

[20] When Reu had lived 32 years, he fathered Serug. [21] And Reu lived after he fathered Serug 207 years and had other sons and daughters.

[22] When Serug had lived 30 years, he fathered Nahor. [23] And Serug lived after he fathered Nahor 200 years and had other sons and daughters.

[24] When Nahor had lived 29 years, he fathered Terah. [25] And Nahor lived after he fathered Terah 119 years and had other sons and daughters.

[26] When Terah had lived 70 years, he fathered Abram, Nahor, and Haran.

Terah's Descendants

[27] Now these are the generations of Terah. Terah fathered Abram, Nahor, and Haran; and Haran fathered Lot. [28] Haran died in the presence of his father Terah in the land of his kindred, in Ur of the Chaldeans. [29] And Abram and Nahor took wives. The name of Abram's wife was Sarai, and the name of Nahor's wife, Milcah, the daughter of Haran the father of Milcah and Iscah. [30] Now Sarai was barren; she had no child.

[31] Terah took Abram his son and Lot the son of Haran, his grandson, and Sarai his daughter-in-law, his son Abram's wife, and they went forth together from Ur of the Chaldeans to go into the land of Canaan, but when they came to Haran, they settled there. [32] The days of Terah were 205 years, and Terah died in Haran.

The Call of Abram

12 Now the LORD said[3] to Abram, "Go from your country[4] and your kindred and your father's house to the land that I will show you. [2] And I will make of you a great nation, and I will bless you and make your name great, so

---

[1] Peleg means division [2] Babel sounds like the Hebrew for confused [3] Or had said [4] Or land

that you will be a blessing. [3] I will bless those who bless you, and him who dishonors you I will curse, and in you all the families of the earth shall be blessed."[1]

[4] So Abram went, as the LORD had told him, and Lot went with him. Abram was seventy-five years old when he departed from Haran. [5] And Abram took Sarai his wife, and Lot his brother's son, and all their possessions that they had gathered, and the people that they had acquired in Haran, and they set out to go to the land of Canaan. When they came to the land of Canaan, [6] Abram passed through the land to the place at Shechem, to the oak[2] of Moreh. At that time the Canaanites were in the land. [7] Then the LORD appeared to Abram and said, "To your offspring I will give this land." So he built there an altar to the LORD, who had appeared to him. [8] From there he moved to the hill country on the east of Bethel and pitched his tent, with Bethel on the west and Ai on the east. And there he built an altar to the LORD and called upon the name of the LORD. [9] And Abram journeyed on, still going toward the Negeb.

Abram and Sarai in Egypt

[10] Now there was a famine in the land. So Abram went down to Egypt to sojourn there, for the famine was severe in the land. [11] When he was about to enter Egypt, he said to Sarai his wife, "I know that you are a woman beautiful in appearance, [12] and when the Egyptians see you, they will say, 'This is his wife.' Then they will kill me, but they will let you live. [13] Say you are my sister, that it may go well with me because of you, and that my life may be spared for your sake." [14] When Abram entered Egypt, the Egyptians saw that the woman was very beautiful. [15] And when the princes of Pharaoh saw her, they praised her to Pharaoh. And the woman was taken into Pharaoh's house. [16] And for her sake he dealt well with Abram; and he had sheep, oxen, male donkeys, male servants, female servants, female donkeys, and camels.

[17] But the LORD afflicted Pharaoh and his house with great plagues because of Sarai, Abram's wife. [18] So Pharaoh called Abram and said, "What is this you have done to me? Why did you not tell me that she was your wife? [19] Why did you say, 'She is my sister,' so that I took her for my wife? Now then, here is your wife; take her, and go." [20] And Pharaoh gave men orders concerning him, and they sent him away with his wife and all that he had.

Abram and Lot Separate

13 So Abram went up from Egypt, he and his wife and all that he had, and Lot with him, into the Negeb. [2] Now Abram was very rich in livestock, in silver, and in gold. [3] And he journeyed on from the Negeb as far as Bethel to the place where his tent had been at the beginning, between Bethel and Ai, [4] to the place where he had made an altar at the first. And there Abram called upon the name of the LORD. [5] And Lot, who went with Abram, also had flocks and herds and tents, [6] so that the land could not support both of them dwelling together; for their possessions were so great that they could not dwell together, [7] and there was strife between the herdsmen of Abram's livestock and the herdsmen of Lot's livestock. At that time the Canaanites and the Perizzites were dwelling in the land.

[8] Then Abram said to Lot, "Let there be no strife between you and me, and between your herdsmen and my herdsmen, for we are kinsmen.[3] [9] Is not the whole land before you? Separate yourself from me. If you take the left hand, then I will go to the right, or if you take the right hand, then I will go to the left." [10] And Lot lifted up his eyes and saw that the Jordan Valley was well watered everywhere like the garden of the LORD, like the land of Egypt, in the direction of Zoar. (This was before the LORD destroyed Sodom and Gomorrah.) [11] So Lot chose for himself all the Jordan Valley, and Lot journeyed east. Thus they separated from each other. [12] Abram settled in the land of Canaan, while Lot settled among the cities of the valley and moved his tent as far as Sodom. [13] Now the men of Sodom were wicked, great sinners against the LORD.

[14] The LORD said to Abram, after Lot had separated from him, "Lift up your eyes and look from the place where you are, northward and southward and eastward and westward, [15] for all the land that you see I will give to you and to your offspring forever. [16] I will make your offspring as the dust of the earth, so that if one can count the dust of the earth, your offspring also can be counted. [17] Arise, walk through the length and the breadth of the land, for I will

---

[1] Or by you all the families of the earth shall bless themselves [2] Or terebinth [3] Hebrew we are men, brothers

give it to you." ¹⁸ So Abram moved his tent and came and settled by the oaks¹ of Mamre, which are at Hebron, and there he built an altar to the Lord.

Abram Rescues Lot

14 In the days of Amraphel king of Shinar, Arioch king of Ellasar, Chedorlaomer king of Elam, and Tidal king of Goiim, ² these kings made war with Bera king of Sodom, Birsha king of Gomorrah, Shinab king of Admah, Shemeber king of Zeboiim, and the king of Bela (that is, Zoar). ³ And all these joined forces in the Valley of Siddim (that is, the Salt Sea). ⁴ Twelve years they had served Chedorlaomer, but in the thirteenth year they rebelled. ⁵ In the fourteenth year Chedorlaomer and the kings who were with him came and defeated the Rephaim in Ashteroth-karnaim, the Zuzim in Ham, the Emim in Shaveh-kiriathaim, ⁶ and the Horites in their hill country of Seir as far as El-paran on the border of the wilderness. ⁷ Then they turned back and came to En-mishpat (that is, Kadesh) and defeated all the country of the Amalekites, and also the Amorites who were dwelling in Hazazon-tamar.

⁸ Then the king of Sodom, the king of Gomorrah, the king of Admah, the king of Zeboiim, and the king of Bela (that is, Zoar) went out, and they joined battle in the Valley of Siddim ⁹ with Chedorlaomer king of Elam, Tidal king of Goiim, Amraphel king of Shinar, and Arioch king of Ellasar, four kings against five. ¹⁰ Now the Valley of Siddim was full of bitumen pits, and as the kings of Sodom and Gomorrah fled, some fell into them, and the rest fled to the hill country. ¹¹ So the enemy took all the possessions of Sodom and Gomorrah, and all their provisions, and went their way. ¹² They also took Lot, the son of Abram's brother, who was dwelling in Sodom, and his possessions, and went their way.

¹³ Then one who had escaped came and told Abram the Hebrew, who was living by the oaks² of Mamre the Amorite, brother of Eshcol and of Aner. These were allies of Abram. ¹⁴ When Abram heard that his kinsman had been taken captive, he led forth his trained men, born in his house, 318 of them, and went in pursuit as far as Dan. ¹⁵ And he divided his forces against them by night, he and his servants, and defeated them and

pursued them to Hobah, north of Damascus. ¹⁶ Then he brought back all the possessions, and also brought back his kinsman Lot with his possessions, and the women and the people.

Abram Blessed by Melchizedek

¹⁷ After his return from the defeat of Chedorlaomer and the kings who were with him, the king of Sodom went out to meet him at the Valley of Shaveh (that is, the King's Valley). ¹⁸ And Melchizedek king of Salem brought out bread and wine. (He was priest of God Most High.) ¹⁹ And he blessed him and said,

> "Blessed be Abram by God Most High,
>   Possessor³ of heaven and earth;
> 20 and blessed be God Most High,
>   who has delivered your enemies into
>   your hand!"

And Abram gave him a tenth of everything. ²¹ And the king of Sodom said to Abram, "Give me the persons, but take the goods for yourself." ²² But Abram said to the king of Sodom, "I have lifted my hand⁴ to the Lord, God Most High, Possessor of heaven and earth, ²³ that I would not take a thread or a sandal strap or anything that is yours, lest you should say, 'I have made Abram rich.' ²⁴ I will take nothing but what the young men have eaten, and the share of the men who went with me. Let Aner, Eshcol, and Mamre take their share."

God's Covenant with Abram

15 After these things the word of the Lord came to Abram in a vision: "Fear not, Abram, I am your shield; your reward shall be very great." ² But Abram said, "O Lord God, what will you give me, for I continue⁵ childless, and the heir of my house is Eliezer of Damascus?" ³ And Abram said, "Behold, you have given me no offspring, and a member of my household will be my heir." ⁴ And behold, the word of the Lord came to him: "This man shall not be your heir; your very own son⁶ shall be your heir." ⁵ And he brought him outside and said, "Look toward heaven, and number the stars, if you are able to number them." Then he said to him, "So shall your offspring be." ⁶ And he believed the Lord, and he counted it to him as righteousness.

⁷ And he said to him, "I am the Lord who brought you out from Ur of the Chaldeans to

---

¹ Or terebinths ² Or terebinths ³ Or Creator; also verse 22 ⁴ Or I have taken a solemn oath ⁵ Or I shall die ⁶ Hebrew what will come out of your own loins

give you this land to possess." ⁸But he said, "O Lord God, how am I to know that I shall possess it?" ⁹He said to him, "Bring me a heifer three years old, a female goat three years old, a ram three years old, a turtledove, and a young pigeon." ¹⁰And he brought him all these, cut them in half, and laid each half over against the other. But he did not cut the birds in half. ¹¹And when birds of prey came down on the carcasses, Abram drove them away.

¹²As the sun was going down, a deep sleep fell on Abram. And behold, dreadful and great darkness fell upon him. ¹³Then the Lord said to Abram, "Know for certain that your offspring will be sojourners in a land that is not theirs and will be servants there, and they will be afflicted for four hundred years. ¹⁴But I will bring judgment on the nation that they serve, and afterward they shall come out with great possessions. ¹⁵As for you, you shall go to your fathers in peace; you shall be buried in a good old age. ¹⁶And they shall come back here in the fourth generation, for the iniquity of the Amorites is not yet complete."

¹⁷When the sun had gone down and it was dark, behold, a smoking fire pot and a flaming torch passed between these pieces. ¹⁸On that day the Lord made a covenant with Abram, saying, "To your offspring I give¹ this land, from the river of Egypt to the great river, the river Euphrates, ¹⁹the land of the Kenites, the Kenizzites, the Kadmonites, ²⁰the Hittites, the Perizzites, the Rephaim, ²¹the Amorites, the Canaanites, the Girgashites and the Jebusites."

Sarai and Hagar

16 Now Sarai, Abram's wife, had borne him no children. She had a female Egyptian servant whose name was Hagar. ²And Sarai said to Abram, "Behold now, the Lord has prevented me from bearing children. Go in to my servant; it may be that I shall obtain children² by her." And Abram listened to the voice of Sarai. ³So, after Abram had lived ten years in the land of Canaan, Sarai, Abram's wife, took Hagar the Egyptian, her servant, and gave her to Abram her husband as a wife. ⁴And he went in to Hagar, and she conceived. And when she saw that she had conceived, she looked with contempt on her mistress.³ ⁵And Sarai said to Abram, "May the wrong done to me be on you! I gave my servant to your embrace, and when she

saw that she had conceived, she looked on me with contempt. May the Lord judge between you and me!" ⁶But Abram said to Sarai, "Behold, your servant is in your power; do to her as you please." Then Sarai dealt harshly with her, and she fled from her.

⁷The angel of the Lord found her by a spring of water in the wilderness, the spring on the way to Shur. ⁸And he said, "Hagar, servant of Sarai, where have you come from and where are you going?" She said, "I am fleeing from my mistress Sarai." ⁹The angel of the Lord said to her, "Return to your mistress and submit to her." ¹⁰The angel of the Lord also said to her, "I will surely multiply your offspring so that they cannot be numbered for multitude." ¹¹And the angel of the Lord said to her,

> "Behold, you are pregnant
>   and shall bear a son.
> You shall call his name Ishmael,⁴
>   because the Lord has listened to your
>   affliction.
> ¹² He shall be a wild donkey of a man,
>   his hand against everyone
>   and everyone's hand against him,
>   and he shall dwell over against all his kinsmen."

¹³So she called the name of the Lord who spoke to her, "You are a God of seeing,"⁵ for she said, "Truly here I have seen him who looks after me."⁶ ¹⁴Therefore the well was called Beer-lahai-roi;⁷ it lies between Kadesh and Bered.

¹⁵And Hagar bore Abram a son, and Abram called the name of his son, whom Hagar bore, Ishmael. ¹⁶Abram was eighty-six years old when Hagar bore Ishmael to Abram.

Abraham and the Covenant of Circumcision

17 When Abram was ninety-nine years old the Lord appeared to Abram and said to him, "I am God Almighty;⁸ walk before me, and be blameless, ²that I may make my covenant between me and you, and may multiply you greatly." ³Then Abram fell on his face. And God said to him, ⁴"Behold, my covenant is with you, and you shall be the father of a multitude of nations. ⁵No longer shall your name be called Abram,⁹ but your name shall be Abraham,¹⁰ for I have made you the father of a multitude of nations. ⁶I will make you exceedingly fruitful, and I will make you into nations, and kings

---

¹ Or *have given* ² Hebrew *be built up*, which sounds like the Hebrew for *children* ³ Hebrew *her mistress was dishonorable in her eyes*; similarly in verse 5 ⁴ *Ishmael* means *God hears* ⁵ Or *You are a God who sees me* ⁶ Hebrew *Have I really seen him here who sees me?* or *Would I have looked here for the one who sees me?* ⁷ *Beer-lahai-roi* means *the well of the Living One who sees me* ⁸ Hebrew *El Shaddai* ⁹ *Abram* means *exalted father* ¹⁰ *Abraham* means *father of a multitude*

shall come from you. ⁷ And I will establish my covenant between me and you and your offspring after you throughout their generations for an everlasting covenant, to be God to you and to your offspring after you. ⁸ And I will give to you and to your offspring after you the land of your sojournings, all the land of Canaan, for an everlasting possession, and I will be their God."

⁹ And God said to Abraham, "As for you, you shall keep my covenant, you and your offspring after you throughout their generations. ¹⁰ This is my covenant, which you shall keep, between me and you and your offspring after you: Every male among you shall be circumcised. ¹¹ You shall be circumcised in the flesh of your foreskins, and it shall be a sign of the covenant between me and you. ¹² He who is eight days old among you shall be circumcised. Every male throughout your generations, whether born in your house or bought with your money from any foreigner who is not of your offspring, ¹³ both he who is born in your house and he who is bought with your money, shall surely be circumcised. So shall my covenant be in your flesh an everlasting covenant. ¹⁴ Any uncircumcised male who is not circumcised in the flesh of his foreskin shall be cut off from his people; he has broken my covenant."

Isaac's Birth Promised

¹⁵ And God said to Abraham, "As for Sarai your wife, you shall not call her name Sarai, but Sarah¹ shall be her name. ¹⁶ I will bless her, and moreover, I will give² you a son by her. I will bless her, and she shall become nations; kings of peoples shall come from her." ¹⁷ Then Abraham fell on his face and laughed and said to himself, "Shall a child be born to a man who is a hundred years old? Shall Sarah, who is ninety years old, bear a child?" ¹⁸ And Abraham said to God, "Oh that Ishmael might live before you!" ¹⁹ God said, "No, but Sarah your wife shall bear you a son, and you shall call his name Isaac.³ I will establish my covenant with him as an everlasting covenant for his offspring after him. ²⁰ As for Ishmael, I have heard you; behold, I have blessed him and will make him fruitful and multiply him greatly. He shall father twelve princes, and I will make him into a great nation. ²¹ But I will establish my covenant with Isaac, whom Sarah shall bear to you at this time next year."

²² When he had finished talking with him, God went up from Abraham. ²³ Then Abraham took Ishmael his son and all those born in his house or bought with his money, every male among the men of Abraham's house, and he circumcised the flesh of their foreskins that very day, as God had said to him. ²⁴ Abraham was ninety-nine years old when he was circumcised in the flesh of his foreskin. ²⁵ And Ishmael his son was thirteen years old when he was circumcised in the flesh of his foreskin. ²⁶ That very day Abraham and his son Ishmael were circumcised. ²⁷ And all the men of his house, those born in the house and those bought with money from a foreigner, were circumcised with him.

18 And the LORD appeared to him by the oaks⁴ of Mamre, as he sat at the door of his tent in the heat of the day. ² He lifted up his eyes and looked, and behold, three men were standing in front of him. When he saw them, he ran from the tent door to meet them and bowed himself to the earth ³ and said, "O Lord,⁵ if I have found favor in your sight, do not pass by your servant. ⁴ Let a little water be brought, and wash your feet, and rest yourselves under the tree, ⁵ while I bring a morsel of bread, that you may refresh yourselves, and after that you may pass on—since you have come to your servant." So they said, "Do as you have said." ⁶ And Abraham went quickly into the tent to Sarah and said, "Quick! Three seahs⁶ of fine flour! Knead it, and make cakes." ⁷ And Abraham ran to the herd and took a calf, tender and good, and gave it to a young man, who prepared it quickly. ⁸ Then he took curds and milk and the calf that he had prepared, and set it before them. And he stood by them under the tree while they ate.

⁹ They said to him, "Where is Sarah your wife?" And he said, "She is in the tent." ¹⁰ The LORD said, "I will surely return to you about this time next year, and Sarah your wife shall have a son." And Sarah was listening at the tent door behind him. ¹¹ Now Abraham and Sarah were old, advanced in years. The way of women had ceased to be with Sarah. ¹² So Sarah laughed to herself, saying, "After I am worn out, and my lord is old, shall I have pleasure?" ¹³ The LORD said to Abraham, "Why did Sarah laugh and say, 'Shall I indeed bear a child, now that I am old?' ¹⁴ Is anything too hard⁷ for the LORD? At the appointed time I will return to you, about this time next year, and Sarah shall

---

¹ Sarai and Sarah mean princess ² Hebrew have given ³ Isaac means he laughs ⁴ Or terebinths ⁵ Or My lord ⁶ A seah was about 7 quarts or 7.3 liters ⁷ Or wonderful

have a son." [15] But Sarah denied it,[1] saying, "I did not laugh," for she was afraid. He said, "No, but you did laugh."

[16] Then the men set out from there, and they looked down toward Sodom. And Abraham went with them to set them on their way. [17] The LORD said, "Shall I hide from Abraham what I am about to do, [18] seeing that Abraham shall surely become a great and mighty nation, and all the nations of the earth shall be blessed in him? [19] For I have chosen[2] him, that he may command his children and his household after him to keep the way of the LORD by doing righteousness and justice, so that the LORD may bring to Abraham what he has promised him." [20] Then the LORD said, "Because the outcry against Sodom and Gomorrah is great and their sin is very grave, [21] I will go down to see whether they have done altogether[3] according to the outcry that has come to me. And if not, I will know."

Abraham Intercedes for Sodom

[22] So the men turned from there and went toward Sodom, but Abraham still stood before the LORD. [23] Then Abraham drew near and said, "Will you indeed sweep away the righteous with the wicked? [24] Suppose there are fifty righteous within the city. Will you then sweep away the place and not spare it for the fifty righteous who are in it? [25] Far be it from you to do such a thing, to put the righteous to death with the wicked, so that the righteous fare as the wicked! Far be that from you! Shall not the Judge of all the earth do what is just?" [26] And the LORD said, "If I find at Sodom fifty righteous in the city, I will spare the whole place for their sake."

[27] Abraham answered and said, "Behold, I have undertaken to speak to the Lord, I who am but dust and ashes. [28] Suppose five of the fifty righteous are lacking. Will you destroy the whole city for lack of five?" And he said, "I will not destroy it if I find forty-five there." [29] Again he spoke to him and said, "Suppose forty are found there." He answered, "For the sake of forty I will not do it." [30] Then he said, "Oh let not the Lord be angry, and I will speak. Suppose thirty are found there." He answered, "I will not do it, if I find thirty there." [31] He said, "Behold, I have undertaken to speak to the Lord. Suppose twenty are found there." He answered, "For the sake of twenty I will not destroy it." [32] Then he said, "Oh let not the Lord be angry, and I

will speak again but this once. Suppose ten are found there." He answered, "For the sake of ten I will not destroy it." [33] And the LORD went his way, when he had finished speaking to Abraham, and Abraham returned to his place.

God Rescues Lot

19 The two angels came to Sodom in the evening, and Lot was sitting in the gate of Sodom. When Lot saw them, he rose to meet them and bowed himself with his face to the earth [2] and said, "My lords, please turn aside to your servant's house and spend the night and wash your feet. Then you may rise up early and go on your way." They said, "No; we will spend the night in the town square." [3] But he pressed them strongly; so they turned aside to him and entered his house. And he made them a feast and baked unleavened bread, and they ate.

[4] But before they lay down, the men of the city, the men of Sodom, both young and old, all the people to the last man, surrounded the house. [5] And they called to Lot, "Where are the men who came to you tonight? Bring them out to us, that we may know them." [6] Lot went out to the men at the entrance, shut the door after him, [7] and said, "I beg you, my brothers, do not act so wickedly. [8] Behold, I have two daughters who have not known any man. Let me bring them out to you, and do to them as you please. Only do nothing to these men, for they have come under the shelter of my roof." [9] But they said, "Stand back!" And they said, "This fellow came to sojourn, and he has become the judge! Now we will deal worse with you than with them." Then they pressed hard against the man Lot, and drew near to break the door down. [10] But the men reached out their hands and brought Lot into the house with them and shut the door. [11] And they struck with blindness the men who were at the entrance of the house, both small and great, so that they wore themselves out groping for the door.

[12] Then the men said to Lot, "Have you anyone else here? Sons-in-law, sons, daughters, or anyone you have in the city, bring them out of the place. [13] For we are about to destroy this place, because the outcry against its people has become great before the LORD, and the LORD has sent us to destroy it." [14] So Lot went out and said to his sons-in-law, who were to marry his daughters, "Up! Get out of this place, for

[1] Or acted falsely [2] Hebrew known [3] Or they deserve destruction; Hebrew they have made a complete end

the LORD is about to destroy the city." But he seemed to his sons-in-law to be jesting.

¹⁵ As morning dawned, the angels urged Lot, saying, "Up! Take your wife and your two daughters who are here, lest you be swept away in the punishment of the city." ¹⁶ But he lingered. So the men seized him and his wife and his two daughters by the hand, the LORD being merciful to him, and they brought him out and set him outside the city. ¹⁷ And as they brought them out, one said, "Escape for your life. Do not look back or stop anywhere in the valley. Escape to the hills, lest you be swept away." ¹⁸ And Lot said to them, "Oh, no, my lords. ¹⁹ Behold, your servant has found favor in your sight, and you have shown me great kindness in saving my life. But I cannot escape to the hills, lest the disaster overtake me and I die. ²⁰ Behold, this city is near enough to flee to, and it is a little one. Let me escape there—is it not a little one?—and my life will be saved!" ²¹ He said to him, "Behold, I grant you this favor also, that I will not overthrow the city of which you have spoken. ²² Escape there quickly, for I can do nothing till you arrive there." Therefore the name of the city was called Zoar.¹

God Destroys Sodom

²³ The sun had risen on the earth when Lot came to Zoar. ²⁴ Then the LORD rained on Sodom and Gomorrah sulfur and fire from the LORD out of heaven. ²⁵ And he overthrew those cities, and all the valley, and all the inhabitants of the cities, and what grew on the ground. ²⁶ But Lot's wife, behind him, looked back, and she became a pillar of salt.

²⁷ And Abraham went early in the morning to the place where he had stood before the LORD. ²⁸ And he looked down toward Sodom and Gomorrah and toward all the land of the valley, and he looked and, behold, the smoke of the land went up like the smoke of a furnace.

²⁹ So it was that, when God destroyed the cities of the valley, God remembered Abraham and sent Lot out of the midst of the overthrow when he overthrew the cities in which Lot had lived.

Lot and His Daughters

³⁰ Now Lot went up out of Zoar and lived in the hills with his two daughters, for he was afraid to live in Zoar. So he lived in a cave with his two daughters. ³¹ And the firstborn said to the younger, "Our father is old, and there is not a man on earth to come in to us after the manner of all the earth. ³² Come, let us make our father drink wine, and we will lie with him, that we may preserve offspring from our father." ³³ So they made their father drink wine that night. And the firstborn went in and lay with her father. He did not know when she lay down or when she arose.

³⁴ The next day, the firstborn said to the younger, "Behold, I lay last night with my father. Let us make him drink wine tonight also. Then you go in and lie with him, that we may preserve offspring from our father." ³⁵ So they made their father drink wine that night also. And the younger arose and lay with him, and he did not know when she lay down or when she arose. ³⁶ Thus both the daughters of Lot became pregnant by their father. ³⁷ The first-born bore a son and called his name Moab.² He is the father of the Moabites to this day. ³⁸ The younger also bore a son and called his name Ben-ammi.³ He is the father of the Ammonites to this day.

Abraham and Abimelech

20 From there Abraham journeyed toward the territory of the Negeb and lived between Kadesh and Shur; and he sojourned in Gerar. ² And Abraham said of Sarah his wife, "She is my sister." And Abimelech king of Gerar sent and took Sarah. ³ But God came to Abimelech in a dream by night and said to him, "Behold, you are a dead man because of the woman whom you have taken, for she is a man's wife." ⁴ Now Abimelech had not approached her. So he said, "Lord, will you kill an innocent people? ⁵ Did he not himself say to me, 'She is my sister'? And she herself said, 'He is my brother.' In the integrity of my heart and the innocence of my hands I have done this." ⁶ Then God said to him in the dream, "Yes, I know that you have done this in the integrity of your heart, and it was I who kept you from sinning against me. Therefore I did not let you touch her. ⁷ Now then, return the man's wife, for he is a prophet, so that he will pray for you, and you shall live. But if you do not return her, know that you shall surely die, you and all who are yours."

⁸ So Abimelech rose early in the morning and called all his servants and told them all these things. And the men were very much

---

¹ *Zoar* means *little* ² *Moab* sounds like the Hebrew for *from father* ³ *Ben-ammi* means *son of my people*

afraid. ⁹Then Abimelech called Abraham and said to him, "What have you done to us? And how have I sinned against you, that you have brought on me and my kingdom a great sin? You have done to me things that ought not to be done." ¹⁰And Abimelech said to Abraham, "What did you see, that you did this thing?" ¹¹Abraham said, "I did it because I thought, 'There is no fear of God at all in this place, and they will kill me because of my wife.' ¹²Besides, she is indeed my sister, the daughter of my father though not the daughter of my mother, and she became my wife. ¹³And when God caused me to wander from my father's house, I said to her, 'This is the kindness you must do me: at every place to which we come, say of me, "He is my brother." ' "

¹⁴Then Abimelech took sheep and oxen, and male servants and female servants, and gave them to Abraham, and returned Sarah his wife to him. ¹⁵And Abimelech said, "Behold, my land is before you; dwell where it pleases you." ¹⁶To Sarah he said, "Behold, I have given your brother a thousand pieces of silver. It is a sign of your innocence in the eyes of all[1] who are with you, and before everyone you are vindicated." ¹⁷Then Abraham prayed to God, and God healed Abimelech, and also healed his wife and female slaves so that they bore children. ¹⁸For the LORD had closed all the wombs of the house of Abimelech because of Sarah, Abraham's wife.

The Birth of Isaac

21 The LORD visited Sarah as he had said, and the LORD did to Sarah as he had promised. ²And Sarah conceived and bore Abraham a son in his old age at the time of which God had spoken to him. ³Abraham called the name of his son who was born to him, whom Sarah bore him, Isaac.[2] ⁴And Abraham circumcised his son Isaac when he was eight days old, as God had commanded him. ⁵Abraham was a hundred years old when his son Isaac was born to him. ⁶And Sarah said, "God has made laughter for me; everyone who hears will laugh over me." ⁷And she said, "Who would have said to Abraham that Sarah would nurse children? Yet I have borne him a son in his old age."

God Protects Hagar and Ishmael

⁸And the child grew and was weaned. And Abraham made a great feast on the day that Isaac was weaned. ⁹But Sarah saw the son of Hagar the Egyptian, whom she had borne to Abraham, laughing.[3] ¹⁰So she said to Abraham, "Cast out this slave woman with her son, for the son of this slave woman shall not be heir with my son Isaac." ¹¹And the thing was very displeasing to Abraham on account of his son. ¹²But God said to Abraham, "Be not displeased because of the boy and because of your slave woman. Whatever Sarah says to you, do as she tells you, for through Isaac shall your offspring be named. ¹³And I will make a nation of the son of the slave woman also, because he is your offspring." ¹⁴So Abraham rose early in the morning and took bread and a skin of water and gave it to Hagar, putting it on her shoulder, along with the child, and sent her away. And she departed and wandered in the wilderness of Beersheba.

¹⁵When the water in the skin was gone, she put the child under one of the bushes. ¹⁶Then she went and sat down opposite him a good way off, about the distance of a bowshot, for she said, "Let me not look on the death of the child." And as she sat opposite him, she lifted up her voice and wept. ¹⁷And God heard the voice of the boy, and the angel of God called to Hagar from heaven and said to her, "What troubles you, Hagar? Fear not, for God has heard the voice of the boy where he is. ¹⁸Up! Lift up the boy, and hold him fast with your hand, for I will make him into a great nation." ¹⁹Then God opened her eyes, and she saw a well of water. And she went and filled the skin with water and gave the boy a drink. ²⁰And God was with the boy, and he grew up. He lived in the wilderness and became an expert with the bow. ²¹He lived in the wilderness of Paran, and his mother took a wife for him from the land of Egypt.

A Treaty with Abimelech

²²At that time Abimelech and Phicol the commander of his army said to Abraham, "God is with you in all that you do. ²³Now therefore swear to me here by God that you will not deal falsely with me or with my descendants or with my posterity, but as I have dealt kindly with you, so you will deal with me and with the land where you have sojourned." ²⁴And Abraham said, "I will swear."

²⁵When Abraham reproved Abimelech about a well of water that Abimelech's servants had seized, ²⁶Abimelech said, "I do not know who has done this thing; you did not

---

[1] Hebrew *It is a covering of eyes for all* [2] *Isaac* means *he laughs* [3] Possibly *laughing in mockery*

tell me, and I have not heard of it until today." ²⁷ So Abraham took sheep and oxen and gave them to Abimelech, and the two men made a covenant. ²⁸ Abraham set seven ewe lambs of the flock apart. ²⁹ And Abimelech said to Abraham, "What is the meaning of these seven ewe lambs that you have set apart?" ³⁰ He said, "These seven ewe lambs you will take from my hand, that this¹ may be a witness for me that I dug this well." ³¹ Therefore that place was called Beersheba,² because there both of them swore an oath. ³² So they made a covenant at Beersheba. Then Abimelech and Phicol the commander of his army rose up and returned to the land of the Philistines. ³³ Abraham planted a tamarisk tree in Beersheba and called there on the name of the LORD, the Everlasting God. ³⁴ And Abraham sojourned many days in the land of the Philistines.

The Sacrifice of Isaac

22 After these things God tested Abraham and said to him, "Abraham!" And he said, "Here I am." ² He said, "Take your son, your only son Isaac, whom you love, and go to the land of Moriah, and offer him there as a burnt offering on one of the mountains of which I shall tell you." ³ So Abraham rose early in the morning, saddled his donkey, and took two of his young men with him, and his son Isaac. And he cut the wood for the burnt offering and arose and went to the place of which God had told him. ⁴ On the third day Abraham lifted up his eyes and saw the place from afar. ⁵ Then Abraham said to his young men, "Stay here with the donkey; I and the boy³ will go over there and worship and come again to you." ⁶ And Abraham took the wood of the burnt offering and laid it on Isaac his son. And he took in his hand the fire and the knife. So they went both of them together. ⁷ And Isaac said to his father Abraham, "My father!" And he said, "Here I am, my son." He said, "Behold, the fire and the wood, but where is the lamb for a burnt offering?" ⁸ Abraham said, "God will provide for himself the lamb for a burnt offering, my son." So they went both of them together.

⁹ When they came to the place of which God had told him, Abraham built the altar there and laid the wood in order and bound Isaac his son and laid him on the altar, on top of the wood. ¹⁰ Then Abraham reached out his hand and took the knife to slaughter his son. ¹¹ But

the angel of the LORD called to him from heaven and said, "Abraham, Abraham!" And he said, "Here I am." ¹² He said, "Do not lay your hand on the boy or do anything to him, for now I know that you fear God, seeing you have not withheld your son, your only son, from me." ¹³ And Abraham lifted up his eyes and looked, and behold, behind him was a ram, caught in a thicket by his horns. And Abraham went and took the ram and offered it up as a burnt offering instead of his son. ¹⁴ So Abraham called the name of that place, "The LORD will provide";⁴ as it is said to this day, "On the mount of the LORD it shall be provided."⁵

¹⁵ And the angel of the LORD called to Abraham a second time from heaven ¹⁶ and said, "By myself I have sworn, declares the LORD, because you have done this and have not withheld your son, your only son, ¹⁷ I will surely bless you, and I will surely multiply your offspring as the stars of heaven and as the sand that is on the seashore. And your offspring shall possess the gate of his⁶ enemies, ¹⁸ and in your offspring shall all the nations of the earth be blessed, because you have obeyed my voice." ¹⁹ So Abraham returned to his young men, and they arose and went together to Beersheba. And Abraham lived at Beersheba.

²⁰ Now after these things it was told to Abraham, "Behold, Milcah also has borne children to your brother Nahor: ²¹ Uz his firstborn, Buz his brother, Kemuel the father of Aram, ²² Chesed, Hazo, Pildash, Jidlaph, and Bethuel." ²³ (Bethuel fathered Rebekah.) These eight Milcah bore to Nahor, Abraham's brother. ²⁴ Moreover, his concubine, whose name was Reumah, bore Tebah, Gaham, Tahash, and Maacah.

Sarah's Death and Burial

23 Sarah lived 127 years; these were the years of the life of Sarah. ² And Sarah died at Kiriath-arba (that is, Hebron) in the land of Canaan, and Abraham went in to mourn for Sarah and to weep for her. ³ And Abraham rose up from before his dead and said to the Hittites,⁷ ⁴ "I am a sojourner and foreigner among you; give me property among you for a burying place, that I may bury my dead out of my sight." ⁵ The Hittites answered Abraham, ⁶ "Hear us, my lord; you are a prince of God⁸ among us. Bury your dead in the choicest of our tombs. None of us will withhold from you his

¹ Or you ² Beersheba means well of seven or well of the oath ³ Or young man; also verse 12 ⁴ Or will see ⁵ Or he will be seen ⁶ Or their ⁷ Hebrew sons of Heth; also verses 5, 7, 10, 16, 18, 20 ⁸ Or a mighty prince

tomb to hinder you from burying your dead." [7] Abraham rose and bowed to the Hittites, the people of the land. [8] And he said to them, "If you are willing that I should bury my dead out of my sight, hear me and entreat for me Ephron the son of Zohar, [9] that he may give me the cave of Machpelah, which he owns; it is at the end of his field. For the full price let him give it to me in your presence as property for a burying place."

[10] Now Ephron was sitting among the Hittites, and Ephron the Hittite answered Abraham in the hearing of the Hittites, of all who went in at the gate of his city, [11] "No, my lord, hear me: I give you the field, and I give you the cave that is in it. In the sight of the sons of my people I give it to you. Bury your dead." [12] Then Abraham bowed down before the people of the land. [13] And he said to Ephron in the hearing of the people of the land, "But if you will, hear me: I give the price of the field. Accept it from me, that I may bury my dead there." [14] Ephron answered Abraham, [15] "My lord, listen to me: a piece of land worth four hundred shekels[1] of silver, what is that between you and me? Bury your dead." [16] Abraham listened to Ephron, and Abraham weighed out for Ephron the silver that he had named in the hearing of the Hittites, four hundred shekels of silver, according to the weights current among the merchants.

[17] So the field of Ephron in Machpelah, which was to the east of Mamre, the field with the cave that was in it and all the trees that were in the field, throughout its whole area, was made over [18] to Abraham as a possession in the presence of the Hittites, before all who went in at the gate of his city. [19] After this, Abraham buried Sarah his wife in the cave of the field of Machpelah east of Mamre (that is, Hebron) in the land of Canaan. [20] The field and the cave that is in it were made over to Abraham as property for a burying place by the Hittites.

Isaac and Rebekah

24 Now Abraham was old, well advanced in years. And the Lord had blessed Abraham in all things. [2] And Abraham said to his servant, the oldest of his household, who had charge of all that he had, "Put your hand under my thigh, [3] that I may make you swear by the Lord, the God of heaven and God of the earth, that you will not take a wife for my son from the daughters of the Canaanites, among whom I dwell, [4] but will go to my country and to my kindred, and take a wife for my son Isaac." [5] The servant said to him, "Perhaps the woman may not be willing to follow me to this land. Must I then take your son back to the land from which you came?" [6] Abraham said to him, "See to it that you do not take my son back there. [7] The Lord, the God of heaven, who took me from my father's house and from the land of my kindred, and who spoke to me and swore to me, 'To your offspring I will give this land,' he will send his angel before you, and you shall take a wife for my son from there. [8] But if the woman is not willing to follow you, then you will be free from this oath of mine; only you must not take my son back there." [9] So the servant put his hand under the thigh of Abraham his master and swore to him concerning this matter.

[10] Then the servant took ten of his master's camels and departed, taking all sorts of choice gifts from his master; and he arose and went to Mesopotamia[2] to the city of Nahor. [11] And he made the camels kneel down outside the city by the well of water at the time of evening, the time when women go out to draw water. [12] And he said, "O Lord, God of my master Abraham, please grant me success today and show steadfast love to my master Abraham. [13] Behold, I am standing by the spring of water, and the daughters of the men of the city are coming out to draw water. [14] Let the young woman to whom I shall say, 'Please let down your jar that I may drink,' and who shall say, 'Drink, and I will water your camels'—let her be the one whom you have appointed for your servant Isaac. By this[3] I shall know that you have shown steadfast love to my master."

[15] Before he had finished speaking, behold, Rebekah, who was born to Bethuel the son of Milcah, the wife of Nahor, Abraham's brother, came out with her water jar on her shoulder. [16] The young woman was very attractive in appearance, a maiden[4] whom no man had known. She went down to the spring and filled her jar and came up. [17] Then the servant ran to meet her and said, "Please give me a little water to drink from your jar." [18] She said, "Drink, my lord." And she quickly let down her jar upon her hand and gave him a drink. [19] When she had finished giving him a drink, she said, "I will draw water for your camels also, until

---

[1] A *shekel* was about 2/5 ounce or 11 grams [2] Hebrew *Aram-naharaim* [3] Or *By her* [4] Or *a woman of marriageable age*

they have finished drinking." ²⁰ So she quickly emptied her jar into the trough and ran again to the well to draw water, and she drew for all his camels. ²¹ The man gazed at her in silence to learn whether the LORD had prospered his journey or not.

²² When the camels had finished drinking, the man took a gold ring weighing a half shekel,¹ and two bracelets for her arms weighing ten gold shekels, ²³ and said, "Please tell me whose daughter you are. Is there room in your father's house for us to spend the night?" ²⁴ She said to him, "I am the daughter of Bethuel the son of Milcah, whom she bore to Nahor." ²⁵ She added, "We have plenty of both straw and fodder, and room to spend the night." ²⁶ The man bowed his head and worshiped the LORD ²⁷ and said, "Blessed be the LORD, the God of my master Abraham, who has not forsaken his steadfast love and his faithfulness toward my master. As for me, the LORD has led me in the way to the house of my master's kinsmen." ²⁸ Then the young woman ran and told her mother's household about these things.

²⁹ Rebekah had a brother whose name was Laban. Laban ran out toward the man, to the spring. ³⁰ As soon as he saw the ring and the bracelets on his sister's arms, and heard the words of Rebekah his sister, "Thus the man spoke to me," he went to the man. And behold, he was standing by the camels at the spring. ³¹ He said, "Come in, O blessed of the LORD. Why do you stand outside? For I have prepared the house and a place for the camels." ³² So the man came to the house and unharnessed the camels, and gave straw and fodder to the camels, and there was water to wash his feet and the feet of the men who were with him. ³³ Then food was set before him to eat. But he said, "I will not eat until I have said what I have to say." He said, "Speak on."

³⁴ So he said, "I am Abraham's servant. ³⁵ The LORD has greatly blessed my master, and he has become great. He has given him flocks and herds, silver and gold, male servants and female servants, camels and donkeys. ³⁶ And Sarah my master's wife bore a son to my master when she was old, and to him he has given all that he has. ³⁷ My master made me swear, saying, 'You shall not take a wife for my son from the daughters of the Canaanites, in whose land I dwell, ³⁸ but you shall go to my father's house and to my clan and take a wife for my son.' ³⁹ I said to my

master, 'Perhaps the woman will not follow me.' ⁴⁰ But he said to me, 'The LORD, before whom I have walked, will send his angel with you and prosper your way. You shall take a wife for my son from my clan and from my father's house. ⁴¹ Then you will be free from my oath, when you come to my clan. And if they will not give her to you, you will be free from my oath.'

⁴² "I came today to the spring and said, 'O LORD, the God of my master Abraham, if now you are prospering the way that I go, ⁴³ behold, I am standing by the spring of water. Let the virgin who comes out to draw water, to whom I shall say, "Please give me a little water from your jar to drink," ⁴⁴ and who will say to me, "Drink, and I will draw for your camels also," let her be the woman whom the LORD has appointed for my master's son.'

⁴⁵ "Before I had finished speaking in my heart, behold, Rebekah came out with her water jar on her shoulder, and she went down to the spring and drew water. I said to her, 'Please let me drink.' ⁴⁶ She quickly let down her jar from her shoulder and said, 'Drink, and I will give your camels drink also.' So I drank, and she gave the camels drink also. ⁴⁷ Then I asked her, 'Whose daughter are you?' She said, 'The daughter of Bethuel, Nahor's son, whom Milcah bore to him.' So I put the ring on her nose and the bracelets on her arms. ⁴⁸ Then I bowed my head and worshiped the LORD and blessed the LORD, the God of my master Abraham, who had led me by the right way² to take the daughter of my master's kinsman for his son. ⁴⁹ Now then, if you are going to show steadfast love and faithfulness to my master, tell me; and if not, tell me, that I may turn to the right hand or to the left."

⁵⁰ Then Laban and Bethuel answered and said, "The thing has come from the LORD; we cannot speak to you bad or good. ⁵¹ Behold, Rebekah is before you; take her and go, and let her be the wife of your master's son, as the LORD has spoken."

⁵² When Abraham's servant heard their words, he bowed himself to the earth before the LORD. ⁵³ And the servant brought out jewelry of silver and of gold, and garments, and gave them to Rebekah. He also gave to her brother and to her mother costly ornaments. ⁵⁴ And he and the men who were with him ate and drank, and they spent the night there. When they arose in the morning, he said, "Send me away

¹ A *shekel* was about 2/5 ounce or 11 grams ² Or *faithfully*

to my master." ⁵⁵Her brother and her mother said, "Let the young woman remain with us a while, at least ten days; after that she may go." ⁵⁶But he said to them, "Do not delay me, since the LORD has prospered my way. Send me away that I may go to my master." ⁵⁷They said, "Let us call the young woman and ask her." ⁵⁸And they called Rebekah and said to her, "Will you go with this man?" She said, "I will go." ⁵⁹So they sent away Rebekah their sister and her nurse, and Abraham's servant and his men. ⁶⁰And they blessed Rebekah and said to her,

> "Our sister, may you become
>   thousands of ten thousands,
>   and may your offspring possess
>   the gate of those who hate him!"¹

⁶¹Then Rebekah and her young women arose and rode on the camels and followed the man. Thus the servant took Rebekah and went his way.

⁶²Now Isaac had returned from Beer-lahai-roi and was dwelling in the Negeb. ⁶³And Isaac went out to meditate in the field toward evening. And he lifted up his eyes and saw, and behold, there were camels coming. ⁶⁴And Rebekah lifted up her eyes, and when she saw Isaac, she dismounted from the camel ⁶⁵and said to the servant, "Who is that man, walking in the field to meet us?" The servant said, "It is my master." So she took her veil and covered herself. ⁶⁶And the servant told Isaac all the things that he had done. ⁶⁷Then Isaac brought her into the tent of Sarah his mother and took Rebekah, and she became his wife, and he loved her. So Isaac was comforted after his mother's death.

Abraham's Death and His Descendants

25 Abraham took another wife, whose name was Keturah. ²She bore him Zimran, Jokshan, Medan, Midian, Ishbak, and Shuah. ³Jokshan fathered Sheba and Dedan. The sons of Dedan were Asshurim, Letushim, and Leummim. ⁴The sons of Midian were Ephah, Epher, Hanoch, Abida, and Eldaah. All these were the children of Keturah. ⁵Abraham gave all he had to Isaac. ⁶But to the sons of his concubines Abraham gave gifts, and while he was still living he sent them away from his son Isaac, eastward to the east country.

⁷These are the days of the years of Abraham's life, 175 years. ⁸Abraham breathed his last and died in a good old age, an old man and full of years, and was gathered to his people. ⁹Isaac and Ishmael his sons buried him in the cave of Machpelah, in the field of Ephron the son of Zohar the Hittite, east of Mamre, ¹⁰the field that Abraham purchased from the Hittites. There Abraham was buried, with Sarah his wife. ¹¹After the death of Abraham, God blessed Isaac his son. And Isaac settled at Beer-lahai-roi.

¹²These are the generations of Ishmael, Abraham's son, whom Hagar the Egyptian, Sarah's servant, bore to Abraham. ¹³These are the names of the sons of Ishmael, named in the order of their birth: Nebaioth, the firstborn of Ishmael; and Kedar, Adbeel, Mibsam, ¹⁴Mishma, Dumah, Massa, ¹⁵Hadad, Tema, Jetur, Naphish, and Kedemah. ¹⁶These are the sons of Ishmael and these are their names, by their villages and by their encampments, twelve princes according to their tribes. ¹⁷(These are the years of the life of Ishmael: 137 years. He breathed his last and died, and was gathered to his people.) ¹⁸They settled from Havilah to Shur, which is opposite Egypt in the direction of Assyria. He settled² over against all his kinsmen.

The Birth of Esau and Jacob

¹⁹These are the generations of Isaac, Abraham's son: Abraham fathered Isaac, ²⁰and Isaac was forty years old when he took Rebekah, the daughter of Bethuel the Aramean of Paddan-aram, the sister of Laban the Aramean, to be his wife. ²¹And Isaac prayed to the LORD for his wife, because she was barren. And the LORD granted his prayer, and Rebekah his wife conceived. ²²The children struggled together within her, and she said, "If it is thus, why is this happening to me?"³ So she went to inquire of the LORD. ²³And the LORD said to her,

> "Two nations are in your womb,
>   and two peoples from within you⁴ shall
>   be divided;
>   the one shall be stronger than the
>   other,
>   the older shall serve the younger."

²⁴When her days to give birth were completed, behold, there were twins in her womb. ²⁵The first came out red, all his body like a hairy cloak, so they called his name Esau.

¹ Or hate them ² Hebrew fell ³ Or why do I live? ⁴ Or from birth

[26] Afterward his brother came out with his hand holding Esau's heel, so his name was called Jacob.[1] Isaac was sixty years old when she bore them.

[27] When the boys grew up, Esau was a skillful hunter, a man of the field, while Jacob was a quiet man, dwelling in tents. [28] Isaac loved Esau because he ate of his game, but Rebekah loved Jacob.

Esau Sells His Birthright

[29] Once when Jacob was cooking stew, Esau came in from the field, and he was exhausted. [30] And Esau said to Jacob, "Let me eat some of that red stew, for I am exhausted!" (Therefore his name was called Edom.[2]) [31] Jacob said, "Sell me your birthright now." [32] Esau said, "I am about to die; of what use is a birthright to me?" [33] Jacob said, "Swear to me now." So he swore to him and sold his birthright to Jacob. [34] Then Jacob gave Esau bread and lentil stew, and he ate and drank and rose and went his way. Thus Esau despised his birthright.

God's Promise to Isaac

26 Now there was a famine in the land, besides the former famine that was in the days of Abraham. And Isaac went to Gerar to Abimelech king of the Philistines. [2] And the LORD appeared to him and said, "Do not go down to Egypt; dwell in the land of which I shall tell you. [3] Sojourn in this land, and I will be with you and will bless you, for to you and to your offspring I will give all these lands, and I will establish the oath that I swore to Abraham your father. [4] I will multiply your offspring as the stars of heaven and will give to your offspring all these lands. And in your offspring all the nations of the earth shall be blessed, [5] because Abraham obeyed my voice and kept my charge, my commandments, my statutes, and my laws."

Isaac and Abimelech

[6] So Isaac settled in Gerar. [7] When the men of the place asked him about his wife, he said, "She is my sister," for he feared to say, "My wife," thinking, "lest the men of the place should kill me because of Rebekah," because she was attractive in appearance. [8] When he had been there a long time, Abimelech king of the Philistines looked out of a window and saw Isaac laughing with[3] Rebekah his wife. [9] So Abimelech called Isaac and said, "Behold, she is your wife. How then could you say, 'She is my sister'?" Isaac said to him, "Because I thought, 'Lest I die because of her.'" [10] Abimelech said, "What is this you have done to us? One of the people might easily have lain with your wife, and you would have brought guilt upon us." [11] So Abimelech warned all the people, saying, "Whoever touches this man or his wife shall surely be put to death."

[12] And Isaac sowed in that land and reaped in the same year a hundredfold. The LORD blessed him, [13] and the man became rich, and gained more and more until he became very wealthy. [14] He had possessions of flocks and herds and many servants, so that the Philistines envied him. [15] (Now the Philistines had stopped and filled with earth all the wells that his father's servants had dug in the days of Abraham his father.) [16] And Abimelech said to Isaac, "Go away from us, for you are much mightier than we."

[17] So Isaac departed from there and encamped in the Valley of Gerar and settled there. [18] And Isaac dug again the wells of water that had been dug in the days of Abraham his father, which the Philistines had stopped after the death of Abraham. And he gave them the names that his father had given them. [19] But when Isaac's servants dug in the valley and found there a well of spring water, [20] the herdsmen of Gerar quarreled with Isaac's herdsmen, saying, "The water is ours." So he called the name of the well Esek,[4] because they contended with him. [21] Then they dug another well, and they quarreled over that also, so he called its name Sitnah.[5] [22] And he moved from there and dug another well, and they did not quarrel over it. So he called its name Rehoboth,[6] saying, "For now the LORD has made room for us, and we shall be fruitful in the land."

[23] From there he went up to Beersheba. [24] And the LORD appeared to him the same night and said, "I am the God of Abraham your father. Fear not, for I am with you and will bless you and multiply your offspring for my servant Abraham's sake." [25] So he built an altar there and called upon the name of the LORD and pitched his tent there. And there Isaac's servants dug a well.

[26] When Abimelech went to him from Gerar with Ahuzzath his adviser and Phicol the commander of his army, [27] Isaac said to them, "Why have you come to me, seeing that you hate

---

[1] Jacob means He takes by the heel, or He cheats [2] Edom sounds like the Hebrew for red [3] Hebrew may suggest an intimate relationship [4] Esek means contention [5] Sitnah means enmity [6] Rehoboth means broad places, or room

me and have sent me away from you?" **28** They said, "We see plainly that the LORD has been with you. So we said, let there be a sworn pact between us, between you and us, and let us make a covenant with you, **29** that you will do us no harm, just as we have not touched you and have done to you nothing but good and have sent you away in peace. You are now the blessed of the LORD." **30** So he made them a feast, and they ate and drank. **31** In the morning they rose early and exchanged oaths. And Isaac sent them on their way, and they departed from him in peace. **32** That same day Isaac's servants came and told him about the well that they had dug and said to him, "We have found water." **33** He called it Shibah;[1] therefore the name of the city is Beersheba to this day.

34 When Esau was forty years old, he took Judith the daughter of Beeri the Hittite to be his wife, and Basemath the daughter of Elon the Hittite, **35** and they made life bitter[2] for Isaac and Rebekah.

Isaac Blesses Jacob

27 When Isaac was old and his eyes were dim so that he could not see, he called Esau his older son and said to him, "My son"; and he answered, "Here I am." **2** He said, "Behold, I am old; I do not know the day of my death. **3** Now then, take your weapons, your quiver and your bow, and go out to the field and hunt game for me, **4** and prepare for me delicious food, such as I love, and bring it to me so that I may eat, that my soul may bless you before I die."

5 Now Rebekah was listening when Isaac spoke to his son Esau. So when Esau went to the field to hunt for game and bring it, **6** Rebekah said to her son Jacob, "I heard your father speak to your brother Esau, **7** 'Bring me game and prepare for me delicious food, that I may eat it and bless you before the LORD before I die.' **8** Now therefore, my son, obey my voice as I command you. **9** Go to the flock and bring me two good young goats, so that I may prepare from them delicious food for your father, such as he loves. **10** And you shall bring it to your father to eat, so that he may bless you before he dies." **11** But Jacob said to Rebekah his mother, "Behold, my brother Esau is a hairy man, and I am a smooth man. **12** Perhaps my father will feel me, and I shall seem to be mocking him and bring a curse upon myself and not a blessing." **13** His mother

said to him, "Let your curse be on me, my son; only obey my voice, and go, bring them to me."

14 So he went and took them and brought them to his mother, and his mother prepared delicious food, such as his father loved. **15** Then Rebekah took the best garments of Esau her older son, which were with her in the house, and put them on Jacob her younger son. **16** And the skins of the young goats she put on his hands and on the smooth part of his neck. **17** And she put the delicious food and the bread, which she had prepared, into the hand of her son Jacob.

18 So he went in to his father and said, "My father." And he said, "Here I am. Who are you, my son?" **19** Jacob said to his father, "I am Esau your firstborn. I have done as you told me; now sit up and eat of my game, that your soul may bless me." **20** But Isaac said to his son, "How is it that you have found it so quickly, my son?" He answered, "Because the LORD your God granted me success." **21** Then Isaac said to Jacob, "Please come near, that I may feel you, my son, to know whether you are really my son Esau or not." **22** So Jacob went near to Isaac his father, who felt him and said, "The voice is Jacob's voice, but the hands are the hands of Esau." **23** And he did not recognize him, because his hands were hairy like his brother Esau's hands. So he blessed him. **24** He said, "Are you really my son Esau?" He answered, "I am." **25** Then he said, "Bring it near to me, that I may eat of my son's game and bless you." So he brought it near to him, and he ate; and he brought him wine, and he drank. **26** Then his father Isaac said to him, "Come near and kiss me, my son." **27** So he came near and kissed him. And Isaac smelled the smell of his garments and blessed him and said,

> "See, the smell of my son
>   is as the smell of a field that the LORD
>   has blessed!
> **28** May God give you of the dew of heaven
>   and of the fatness of the earth
>   and plenty of grain and wine.
> **29** Let peoples serve you,
>   and nations bow down to you.
> Be lord over your brothers,
>   and may your mother's sons bow down
>   to you.
> Cursed be everyone who curses you,
>   and blessed be everyone who blesses
>   you!"

---

[1] *Shibah* sounds like the Hebrew for *oath* [2] Hebrew *they were bitterness of spirit*

³⁰ As soon as Isaac had finished blessing Jacob, when Jacob had scarcely gone out from the presence of Isaac his father, Esau his brother came in from his hunting. ³¹ He also prepared delicious food and brought it to his father. And he said to his father, "Let my father arise and eat of his son's game, that you may bless me." ³² His father Isaac said to him, "Who are you?" He answered, "I am your son, your firstborn, Esau." ³³ Then Isaac trembled very violently and said, "Who was it then that hunted game and brought it to me, and I ate it all before you came, and I have blessed him? Yes, and he shall be blessed." ³⁴ As soon as Esau heard the words of his father, he cried out with an exceedingly great and bitter cry and said to his father, "Bless me, even me also, O my father!" ³⁵ But he said, "Your brother came deceitfully, and he has taken away your blessing." ³⁶ Esau said, "Is he not rightly named Jacob?¹ For he has cheated me these two times. He took away my birthright, and behold, now he has taken away my blessing." Then he said, "Have you not reserved a blessing for me?" ³⁷ Isaac answered and said to Esau, "Behold, I have made him lord over you, and all his brothers I have given to him for servants, and with grain and wine I have sustained him. What then can I do for you, my son?" ³⁸ Esau said to his father, "Have you but one blessing, my father? Bless me, even me also, O my father." And Esau lifted up his voice and wept.

³⁹ Then Isaac his father answered and said to him:

"Behold, away from² the fatness of the earth
    shall your dwelling be,
  and away from³ the dew of heaven on
    high.
⁴⁰ By your sword you shall live,
    and you shall serve your brother;
  but when you grow restless
    you shall break his yoke from your
      neck."

⁴¹ Now Esau hated Jacob because of the blessing with which his father had blessed him, and Esau said to himself, "The days of mourning for my father are approaching; then I will kill my brother Jacob." ⁴² But the words of Esau her older son were told to Rebekah. So she sent and called Jacob her younger son and said to him, "Behold, your brother Esau comforts himself about you by planning to kill you. ⁴³ Now therefore, my son, obey my voice. Arise, flee to Laban my brother in Haran ⁴⁴ and stay with him a while, until your brother's fury turns away— ⁴⁵ until your brother's anger turns away from you, and he forgets what you have done to him. Then I will send and bring you from there. Why should I be bereft of you both in one day?"

⁴⁶ Then Rebekah said to Isaac, "I loathe my life because of the Hittite women.⁴ If Jacob marries one of the Hittite women like these, one of the women of the land, what good will my life be to me?"

Jacob Sent to Laban

28 Then Isaac called Jacob and blessed him and directed him, "You must not take a wife from the Canaanite women. ² Arise, go to Paddan-aram to the house of Bethuel your mother's father, and take as your wife from there one of the daughters of Laban your mother's brother. ³ God Almighty⁵ bless you and make you fruitful and multiply you, that you may become a company of peoples. ⁴ May he give the blessing of Abraham to you and to your offspring with you, that you may take possession of the land of your sojournings that God gave to Abraham!" ⁵ Thus Isaac sent Jacob away. And he went to Paddan-aram, to Laban, the son of Bethuel the Aramean, the brother of Rebekah, Jacob's and Esau's mother.

Esau Marries an Ishmaelite

⁶ Now Esau saw that Isaac had blessed Jacob and sent him away to Paddan-aram to take a wife from there, and that as he blessed him he directed him, "You must not take a wife from the Canaanite women," ⁷ and that Jacob had obeyed his father and his mother and gone to Paddan-aram. ⁸ So when Esau saw that the Canaanite women did not please Isaac his father, ⁹ Esau went to Ishmael and took as his wife, besides the wives he had, Mahalath the daughter of Ishmael, Abraham's son, the sister of Nebaioth.

Jacob's Dream

¹⁰ Jacob left Beersheba and went toward Haran. ¹¹ And he came to a certain place and stayed there that night, because the sun had set. Taking one of the stones of the place, he put it under his head and lay down in that place to sleep. ¹² And he dreamed, and behold, there was a ladder⁶ set up on the earth, and the top of it reached to heaven. And behold, the angels of God were ascending and descending on it!

¹ *Jacob means He takes by the heel, or He cheats* ² *Or Behold, of* ³ *Or and of* ⁴ *Hebrew daughters of Heth* ⁵ *Hebrew El Shaddai* ⁶ *Or a flight of steps*

[13] And behold, the LORD stood above it[1] and said, "I am the LORD, the God of Abraham your father and the God of Isaac. The land on which you lie I will give to you and to your offspring. [14] Your offspring shall be like the dust of the earth, and you shall spread abroad to the west and to the east and to the north and to the south, and in you and your offspring shall all the families of the earth be blessed. [15] Behold, I am with you and will keep you wherever you go, and will bring you back to this land. For I will not leave you until I have done what I have promised you." [16] Then Jacob awoke from his sleep and said, "Surely the LORD is in this place, and I did not know it." [17] And he was afraid and said, "How awesome is this place! This is none other than the house of God, and this is the gate of heaven."

[18] So early in the morning Jacob took the stone that he had put under his head and set it up for a pillar and poured oil on the top of it. [19] He called the name of that place Bethel,[2] but the name of the city was Luz at the first. [20] Then Jacob made a vow, saying, "If God will be with me and will keep me in this way that I go, and will give me bread to eat and clothing to wear, [21] so that I come again to my father's house in peace, then the LORD shall be my God, [22] and this stone, which I have set up for a pillar, shall be God's house. And of all that you give me I will give a full tenth to you."

Jacob Marries Leah and Rachel

29 Then Jacob went on his journey and came to the land of the people of the east. [2] As he looked, he saw a well in the field, and behold, three flocks of sheep lying beside it, for out of that well the flocks were watered. The stone on the well's mouth was large, [3] and when all the flocks were gathered there, the shepherds would roll the stone from the mouth of the well and water the sheep, and put the stone back in its place over the mouth of the well. [4] Jacob said to them, "My brothers, where do you come from?" They said, "We are from Haran." [5] He said to them, "Do you know Laban the son of Nahor?" They said, "We know him." [6] He said to them, "Is it well with him?" They said, "It is well; and see, Rachel his daughter is coming with the sheep!" [7] He said, "Behold, it is still high day; it is not time for the livestock to be gathered together. Water the sheep and go, pasture them." [8] But they said, "We cannot

until all the flocks are gathered together and the stone is rolled from the mouth of the well; then we water the sheep."

[9] While he was still speaking with them, Rachel came with her father's sheep, for she was a shepherdess. [10] Now as soon as Jacob saw Rachel the daughter of Laban his mother's brother, and the sheep of Laban his mother's brother, Jacob came near and rolled the stone from the well's mouth and watered the flock of Laban his mother's brother. [11] Then Jacob kissed Rachel and wept aloud. [12] And Jacob told Rachel that he was her father's kinsman, and that he was Rebekah's son, and she ran and told her father.

[13] As soon as Laban heard the news about Jacob, his sister's son, he ran to meet him and embraced him and kissed him and brought him to his house. Jacob told Laban all these things, [14] and Laban said to him, "Surely you are my bone and my flesh!" And he stayed with him a month.

[15] Then Laban said to Jacob, "Because you are my kinsman, should you therefore serve me for nothing? Tell me, what shall your wages be?" [16] Now Laban had two daughters. The name of the older was Leah, and the name of the younger was Rachel. [17] Leah's eyes were weak,[3] but Rachel was beautiful in form and appearance. [18] Jacob loved Rachel. And he said, "I will serve you seven years for your younger daughter Rachel." [19] Laban said, "It is better that I give her to you than that I should give her to any other man; stay with me." [20] So Jacob served seven years for Rachel, and they seemed to him but a few days because of the love he had for her.

[21] Then Jacob said to Laban, "Give me my wife that I may go in to her, for my time is completed." [22] So Laban gathered together all the people of the place and made a feast. [23] But in the evening he took his daughter Leah and brought her to Jacob, and he went in to her. [24] (Laban gave[4] his female servant Zilpah to his daughter Leah to be her servant.) [25] And in the morning, behold, it was Leah! And Jacob said to Laban, "What is this you have done to me? Did I not serve with you for Rachel? Why then have you deceived me?" [26] Laban said, "It is not so done in our country, to give the younger before the firstborn. [27] Complete the week of this one, and we will give you the other also in return for serving me another seven years."

[1] Or beside him [2] Bethel means the house of God [3] Or soft [4] Or had given; also verse 29

²⁸Jacob did so, and completed her week. Then Laban gave him his daughter Rachel to be his wife. ²⁹(Laban gave his female servant Bilhah to his daughter Rachel to be her servant.) ³⁰So Jacob went in to Rachel also, and he loved Rachel more than Leah, and served Laban for another seven years.

Jacob's Children

³¹When the LORD saw that Leah was hated, he opened her womb, but Rachel was barren. ³²And Leah conceived and bore a son, and she called his name Reuben,¹ for she said, "Because the LORD has looked upon my affliction; for now my husband will love me." ³³She conceived again and bore a son, and said, "Because the LORD has heard that I am hated, he has given me this son also." And she called his name Simeon.² ³⁴Again she conceived and bore a son, and said, "Now this time my husband will be attached to me, because I have borne him three sons." Therefore his name was called Levi.³ ³⁵And she conceived again and bore a son, and said, "This time I will praise the LORD." Therefore she called his name Judah.⁴ Then she ceased bearing.

30 When Rachel saw that she bore Jacob no children, she envied her sister. She said to Jacob, "Give me children, or I shall die!" ²Jacob's anger was kindled against Rachel, and he said, "Am I in the place of God, who has withheld from you the fruit of the womb?" ³Then she said, "Here is my servant Bilhah; go in to her, so that she may give birth on my behalf,⁵ that even I may have children⁶ through her." ⁴So she gave him her servant Bilhah as a wife, and Jacob went in to her. ⁵And Bilhah conceived and bore Jacob a son. ⁶Then Rachel said, "God has judged me, and has also heard my voice and given me a son." Therefore she called his name Dan.⁷ ⁷Rachel's servant Bilhah conceived again and bore Jacob a second son. ⁸Then Rachel said, "With mighty wrestlings⁸ I have wrestled with my sister and have prevailed." So she called his name Naphtali.⁹

⁹When Leah saw that she had ceased bearing children, she took her servant Zilpah and gave her to Jacob as a wife. ¹⁰Then Leah's servant Zilpah bore Jacob a son. ¹¹And Leah said, "Good fortune has come!" so she called his name Gad.¹⁰ ¹²Leah's servant Zilpah bore Jacob

a second son. ¹³And Leah said, "Happy am I! For women have called me happy." So she called his name Asher.¹¹

¹⁴In the days of wheat harvest Reuben went and found mandrakes in the field and brought them to his mother Leah. Then Rachel said to Leah, "Please give me some of your son's mandrakes." ¹⁵But she said to her, "Is it a small matter that you have taken away my husband? Would you take away my son's mandrakes also?" Rachel said, "Then he may lie with you tonight in exchange for your son's mandrakes." ¹⁶When Jacob came from the field in the evening, Leah went out to meet him and said, "You must come in to me, for I have hired you with my son's mandrakes." So he lay with her that night. ¹⁷And God listened to Leah, and she conceived and bore Jacob a fifth son. ¹⁸Leah said, "God has given me my wages because I gave my servant to my husband." So she called his name Issachar.¹²

¹⁹And Leah conceived again, and she bore Jacob a sixth son. ²⁰Then Leah said, "God has endowed me with a good endowment; now my husband will honor me, because I have borne him six sons." So she called his name Zebulun.¹³ ²¹Afterward she bore a daughter and called her name Dinah.

²²Then God remembered Rachel, and God listened to her and opened her womb. ²³She conceived and bore a son and said, "God has taken away my reproach." ²⁴And she called his name Joseph,¹⁴ saying, "May the LORD add to me another son!"

Jacob's Prosperity

²⁵As soon as Rachel had borne Joseph, Jacob said to Laban, "Send me away, that I may go to my own home and country. ²⁶Give me my wives and my children for whom I have served you, that I may go, for you know the service that I have given you." ²⁷But Laban said to him, "If I have found favor in your sight, I have learned by divination that¹⁵ the LORD has blessed me because of you. ²⁸Name your wages, and I will give it." ²⁹Jacob said to him, "You yourself know how I have served you, and how your livestock has fared with me. ³⁰For you had little before I came, and it has increased abundantly, and the LORD has blessed you wherever I turned. But now when shall I provide for my own house-

---

¹ Reuben means *See, a son* ² Simeon sounds like the Hebrew for *heard* ³ Levi sounds like the Hebrew for *attached* ⁴ Judah sounds like the Hebrew for *praise* ⁵ Hebrew *on my knees* ⁶ Hebrew *be built up*, which sounds like the Hebrew for *children* ⁷ Dan sounds like the Hebrew for *judged* ⁸ Hebrew *With wrestlings of God* ⁹ Naphtali sounds like the Hebrew for *wrestling* ¹⁰ Gad sounds like the Hebrew for *good fortune* ¹¹ Asher sounds like the Hebrew for *happy* ¹² Issachar sounds like the Hebrew for *wages, or hire* ¹³ Zebulun sounds like the Hebrew for *honor* ¹⁴ Joseph means *May he add*, and sounds like the Hebrew for *taken away* ¹⁵ Or *have become rich and*

hold also?" [31] He said, "What shall I give you?" Jacob said, "You shall not give me anything. If you will do this for me, I will again pasture your flock and keep it: [32] let me pass through all your flock today, removing from it every speckled and spotted sheep and every black lamb, and the spotted and speckled among the goats, and they shall be my wages. [33] So my honesty will answer for me later, when you come to look into my wages with you. Every one that is not speckled and spotted among the goats and black among the lambs, if found with me, shall be counted stolen." [34] Laban said, "Good! Let it be as you have said." [35] But that day Laban removed the male goats that were striped and spotted, and all the female goats that were speckled and spotted, every one that had white on it, and every lamb that was black, and put them in the charge of his sons. [36] And he set a distance of three days' journey between himself and Jacob, and Jacob pastured the rest of Laban's flock.

[37] Then Jacob took fresh sticks of poplar and almond and plane trees, and peeled white streaks in them, exposing the white of the sticks. [38] He set the sticks that he had peeled in front of the flocks in the troughs, that is, the watering places, where the flocks came to drink. And since they bred when they came to drink, [39] the flocks bred in front of the sticks and so the flocks brought forth striped, speckled, and spotted. [40] And Jacob separated the lambs and set the faces of the flocks toward the striped and all the black in the flock of Laban. He put his own droves apart and did not put them with Laban's flock. [41] Whenever the stronger of the flock were breeding, Jacob would lay the sticks in the troughs before the eyes of the flock, that they might breed among the sticks, [42] but for the feebler of the flock he would not lay them there. So the feebler would be Laban's, and the stronger Jacob's. [43] Thus the man increased greatly and had large flocks, female servants and male servants, and camels and donkeys.

Jacob Flees from Laban

31 Now Jacob heard that the sons of Laban were saying, "Jacob has taken all that was our father's, and from what was our father's he has gained all this wealth." [2] And Jacob saw that Laban did not regard him with favor as before.

[3] Then the LORD said to Jacob, "Return to the land of your fathers and to your kindred, and I will be with you."

[4] So Jacob sent and called Rachel and Leah into the field where his flock was [5] and said to them, "I see that your father does not regard me with favor as he did before. But the God of my father has been with me. [6] You know that I have served your father with all my strength, [7] yet your father has cheated me and changed my wages ten times. But God did not permit him to harm me. [8] If he said, 'The spotted shall be your wages,' then all the flock bore spotted; and if he said, 'The striped shall be your wages,' then all the flock bore striped. [9] Thus God has taken away the livestock of your father and given them to me. [10] In the breeding season of the flock I lifted up my eyes and saw in a dream that the goats that mated with the flock were striped, spotted, and mottled. [11] Then the angel of God said to me in the dream, 'Jacob,' and I said, 'Here I am!' [12] And he said, 'Lift up your eyes and see, all the goats that mate with the flock are striped, spotted, and mottled, for I have seen all that Laban is doing to you. [13] I am the God of Bethel, where you anointed a pillar and made a vow to me. Now arise, go out from this land and return to the land of your kindred.'" [14] Then Rachel and Leah answered and said to him, "Is there any portion or inheritance left to us in our father's house? [15] Are we not regarded by him as foreigners? For he has sold us, and he has indeed devoured our money. [16] All the wealth that God has taken away from our father belongs to us and to our children. Now then, whatever God has said to you, do."

[17] So Jacob arose and set his sons and his wives on camels. [18] He drove away all his livestock, all his property that he had gained, the livestock in his possession that he had acquired in Paddan-aram, to go to the land of Canaan to his father Isaac. [19] Laban had gone to shear his sheep, and Rachel stole her father's household gods. [20] And Jacob tricked[1] Laban the Aramean, by not telling him that he intended to flee. [21] He fled with all that he had and arose and crossed the Euphrates,[2] and set his face toward the hill country of Gilead.

[22] When it was told Laban on the third day that Jacob had fled, [23] he took his kinsmen with him and pursued him for seven days and

---

[1] Hebrew *stole the heart of*; also verses 26, 27　[2] Hebrew *the River*

followed close after him into the hill country of Gilead. 24 But God came to Laban the Aramean in a dream by night and said to him, "Be careful not to say anything to Jacob, either good or bad."

25 And Laban overtook Jacob. Now Jacob had pitched his tent in the hill country, and Laban with his kinsmen pitched tents in the hill country of Gilead. 26 And Laban said to Jacob, "What have you done, that you have tricked me and driven away my daughters like captives of the sword? 27 Why did you flee secretly and trick me, and did not tell me, so that I might have sent you away with mirth and songs, with tambourine and lyre? 28 And why did you not permit me to kiss my sons and my daughters farewell? Now you have done foolishly. 29 It is in my power to do you harm. But the God of your[1] father spoke to me last night, saying, 'Be careful not to say anything to Jacob, either good or bad.' 30 And now you have gone away because you longed greatly for your father's house, but why did you steal my gods?" 31 Jacob answered and said to Laban, "Because I was afraid, for I thought that you would take your daughters from me by force. 32 Anyone with whom you find your gods shall not live. In the presence of our kinsmen point out what I have that is yours, and take it." Now Jacob did not know that Rachel had stolen them.

33 So Laban went into Jacob's tent and into Leah's tent and into the tent of the two female servants, but he did not find them. And he went out of Leah's tent and entered Rachel's. 34 Now Rachel had taken the household gods and put them in the camel's saddle and sat on them. Laban felt all about the tent, but did not find them. 35 And she said to her father, "Let not my lord be angry that I cannot rise before you, for the way of women is upon me." So he searched but did not find the household gods.

36 Then Jacob became angry and berated Laban. Jacob said to Laban, "What is my offense? What is my sin, that you have hotly pursued me? 37 For you have felt through all my goods; what have you found of all your household goods? Set it here before my kinsmen and your kinsmen, that they may decide between us two. 38 These twenty years I have been with you. Your ewes and your female goats have not miscarried, and I have not eaten the rams of your flocks. 39 What was torn by wild beasts I did not bring to you. I bore the loss of it myself. From my hand you required it, whether stolen by day or stolen by night. 40 There I was: by day the heat consumed me, and the cold by night, and my sleep fled from my eyes. 41 These twenty years I have been in your house. I served you fourteen years for your two daughters, and six years for your flock, and you have changed my wages ten times. 42 If the God of my father, the God of Abraham and the Fear of Isaac, had not been on my side, surely now you would have sent me away empty-handed. God saw my affliction and the labor of my hands and rebuked you last night."

43 Then Laban answered and said to Jacob, "The daughters are my daughters, the children are my children, the flocks are my flocks, and all that you see is mine. But what can I do this day for these my daughters or for their children whom they have borne? 44 Come now, let us make a covenant, you and I. And let it be a witness between you and me." 45 So Jacob took a stone and set it up as a pillar. 46 And Jacob said to his kinsmen, "Gather stones." And they took stones and made a heap, and they ate there by the heap. 47 Laban called it Jegar-sahadutha,[2] but Jacob called it Galeed.[3] 48 Laban said, "This heap is a witness between you and me today." Therefore he named it Galeed, 49 and Mizpah,[4] for he said, "The Lord watch between you and me, when we are out of one another's sight. 50 If you oppress my daughters, or if you take wives besides my daughters, although no one is with us, see, God is witness between you and me."

51 Then Laban said to Jacob, "See this heap and the pillar, which I have set between you and me. 52 This heap is a witness, and the pillar is a witness, that I will not pass over this heap to you, and you will not pass over this heap and this pillar to me, to do harm. 53 The God of Abraham and the God of Nahor, the God of their father, judge between us." So Jacob swore by the Fear of his father Isaac, 54 and Jacob offered a sacrifice in the hill country and called his kinsmen to eat bread. They ate bread and spent the night in the hill country. 55 5 Early in the morning Laban arose and kissed his grandchildren and his daughters and blessed them. Then Laban departed and returned home.

[1] The Hebrew for *your* is plural here [2] Aramaic *the heap of witness* [3] Hebrew *the heap of witness* [4] *Mizpah* means *watchpost* [5] Ch 32:1 in Hebrew

Jacob Fears Esau

32 Jacob went on his way, and the angels of God met him. ²And when Jacob saw them he said, "This is God's camp!" So he called the name of that place Mahanaim.¹

³And Jacob sent² messengers before him to Esau his brother in the land of Seir, the country of Edom, ⁴instructing them, "Thus you shall say to my lord Esau: Thus says your servant Jacob, 'I have sojourned with Laban and stayed until now. ⁵I have oxen, donkeys, flocks, male servants, and female servants. I have sent to tell my lord, in order that I may find favor in your sight.'"

⁶And the messengers returned to Jacob, saying, "We came to your brother Esau, and he is coming to meet you, and there are four hundred men with him." ⁷Then Jacob was greatly afraid and distressed. He divided the people who were with him, and the flocks and herds and camels, into two camps, ⁸thinking, "If Esau comes to the one camp and attacks it, then the camp that is left will escape."

⁹And Jacob said, "O God of my father Abraham and God of my father Isaac, O LORD who said to me, 'Return to your country and to your kindred, that I may do you good,' ¹⁰I am not worthy of the least of all the deeds of steadfast love and all the faithfulness that you have shown to your servant, for with only my staff I crossed this Jordan, and now I have become two camps. ¹¹Please deliver me from the hand of my brother, from the hand of Esau, for I fear him, that he may come and attack me, the mothers with the children. ¹²But you said, 'I will surely do you good, and make your offspring as the sand of the sea, which cannot be numbered for multitude.'"

¹³So he stayed there that night, and from what he had with him he took a present for his brother Esau, ¹⁴two hundred female goats and twenty male goats, two hundred ewes and twenty rams, ¹⁵thirty milking camels and their calves, forty cows and ten bulls, twenty female donkeys and ten male donkeys. ¹⁶These he handed over to his servants, every drove by itself, and said to his servants, "Pass on ahead of me and put a space between drove and drove." ¹⁷He instructed the first, "When Esau my brother meets you and asks you, 'To whom do you belong? Where are you going? And whose are these ahead of you?' ¹⁸then you

shall say, 'They belong to your servant Jacob. They are a present sent to my lord Esau. And moreover, he is behind us.'" ¹⁹He likewise instructed the second and the third and all who followed the droves, "You shall say the same thing to Esau when you find him, ²⁰and you shall say, 'Moreover, your servant Jacob is behind us.'" For he thought, "I may appease him³ with the present that goes ahead of me, and afterward I shall see his face. Perhaps he will accept me."⁴ ²¹So the present passed on ahead of him, and he himself stayed that night in the camp.

Jacob Wrestles with God

²²The same night he arose and took his two wives, his two female servants, and his eleven children,⁵ and crossed the ford of the Jabbok. ²³He took them and sent them across the stream, and everything else that he had. ²⁴And Jacob was left alone. And a man wrestled with him until the breaking of the day. ²⁵When the man saw that he did not prevail against Jacob, he touched his hip socket, and Jacob's hip was put out of joint as he wrestled with him. ²⁶Then he said, "Let me go, for the day has broken." But Jacob said, "I will not let you go unless you bless me." ²⁷And he said to him, "What is your name?" And he said, "Jacob." ²⁸Then he said, "Your name shall no longer be called Jacob, but Israel,⁶ for you have striven with God and with men, and have prevailed." ²⁹Then Jacob asked him, "Please tell me your name." But he said, "Why is it that you ask my name?" And there he blessed him. ³⁰So Jacob called the name of the place Peniel,⁷ saying, "For I have seen God face to face, and yet my life has been delivered." ³¹The sun rose upon him as he passed Penuel, limping because of his hip. ³²Therefore to this day the people of Israel do not eat the sinew of the thigh that is on the hip socket, because he touched the socket of Jacob's hip on the sinew of the thigh.

Jacob Meets Esau

33 And Jacob lifted up his eyes and looked, and behold, Esau was coming, and four hundred men with him. So he divided the children among Leah and Rachel and the two female servants. ²And he put the servants with their children in front, then Leah with her children, and Rachel and Joseph last of all. ³He

---

¹ *Mahanaim* means *two camps* ² Or *had sent* ³ Hebrew *appease his face* ⁴ Hebrew *he will lift my face* ⁵ Or *sons* ⁶ *Israel* means *He strives with God,* or *God strives* ⁷ *Peniel* means *the face of God*

himself went on before them, bowing himself to the ground seven times, until he came near to his brother.

⁴ But Esau ran to meet him and embraced him and fell on his neck and kissed him, and they wept. ⁵ And when Esau lifted up his eyes and saw the women and children, he said, "Who are these with you?" Jacob said, "The children whom God has graciously given your servant." ⁶ Then the servants drew near, they and their children, and bowed down. ⁷ Leah likewise and her children drew near and bowed down. And last Joseph and Rachel drew near, and they bowed down. ⁸ Esau said, "What do you mean by all this company¹ that I met?" Jacob answered, "To find favor in the sight of my lord." ⁹ But Esau said, "I have enough, my brother; keep what you have for yourself." ¹⁰ Jacob said, "No, please, if I have found favor in your sight, then accept my present from my hand. For I have seen your face, which is like seeing the face of God, and you have accepted me. ¹¹ Please accept my blessing that is brought to you, because God has dealt graciously with me, and because I have enough." Thus he urged him, and he took it.

¹² Then Esau said, "Let us journey on our way, and I will go ahead of² you." ¹³ But Jacob said to him, "My lord knows that the children are frail, and that the nursing flocks and herds are a care to me. If they are driven hard for one day, all the flocks will die. ¹⁴ Let my lord pass on ahead of his servant, and I will lead on slowly, at the pace of the livestock that are ahead of me and at the pace of the children, until I come to my lord in Seir."

¹⁵ So Esau said, "Let me leave with you some of the people who are with me." But he said, "What need is there? Let me find favor in the sight of my lord." ¹⁶ So Esau returned that day on his way to Seir. ¹⁷ But Jacob journeyed to Succoth, and built himself a house and made booths for his livestock. Therefore the name of the place is called Succoth.³

¹⁸ And Jacob came safely⁴ to the city of Shechem, which is in the land of Canaan, on his way from Paddan-aram, and he camped before the city. ¹⁹ And from the sons of Hamor, Shechem's father, he bought for a hundred pieces of money⁵ the piece of land on which he had pitched his tent. ²⁰ There he erected an altar and called it El-Elohe-Israel.⁶

The Defiling of Dinah

34 Now Dinah the daughter of Leah, whom she had borne to Jacob, went out to see the women of the land. ² And when Shechem the son of Hamor the Hivite, the prince of the land, saw her, he seized her and lay with her and humiliated her. ³ And his soul was drawn to Dinah the daughter of Jacob. He loved the young woman and spoke tenderly to her. ⁴ So Shechem spoke to his father Hamor, saying, "Get me this girl for my wife."

⁵ Now Jacob heard that he had defiled his daughter Dinah. But his sons were with his livestock in the field, so Jacob held his peace until they came. ⁶ And Hamor the father of Shechem went out to Jacob to speak with him. ⁷ The sons of Jacob had come in from the field as soon as they heard of it, and the men were indignant and very angry, because he had done an outrageous thing in Israel by lying with Jacob's daughter, for such a thing must not be done.

⁸ But Hamor spoke with them, saying, "The soul of my son Shechem longs for your⁷ daughter. Please give her to him to be his wife. ⁹ Make marriages with us. Give your daughters to us, and take our daughters for yourselves. ¹⁰ You shall dwell with us, and the land shall be open to you. Dwell and trade in it, and get property in it." ¹¹ Shechem also said to her father and to her brothers, "Let me find favor in your eyes, and whatever you say to me I will give. ¹² Ask me for as great a bride-price⁸ and gift as you will, and I will give whatever you say to me. Only give me the young woman to be my wife."

¹³ The sons of Jacob answered Shechem and his father Hamor deceitfully, because he had defiled their sister Dinah. ¹⁴ They said to them, "We cannot do this thing, to give our sister to one who is uncircumcised, for that would be a disgrace to us. ¹⁵ Only on this condition will we agree with you—that you will become as we are by every male among you being circumcised. ¹⁶ Then we will give our daughters to you, and we will take your daughters to ourselves, and we will dwell with you and become one people. ¹⁷ But if you will not listen to us and be circumcised, then we will take our daughter, and we will be gone."

¹⁸ Their words pleased Hamor and Hamor's son Shechem. ¹⁹ And the young man did not delay to do the thing, because he delighted in Jacob's daughter. Now he was the most honored of all his father's house. ²⁰ So Hamor and his son

---

¹ Hebrew *camp* ² Or *along with* ³ *Succoth* means *booths* ⁴ Or *peacefully* ⁵ Hebrew *a hundred qesitah; a unit of money of unknown value* ⁶ *El-Elohe-Israel* means *God, the God of Israel* ⁷ The Hebrew for *your* is plural here ⁸ Or *engagement present*

Shechem came to the gate of their city and spoke to the men of their city, saying, 21 "These men are at peace with us; let them dwell in the land and trade in it, for behold, the land is large enough for them. Let us take their daughters as wives, and let us give them our daughters. 22 Only on this condition will the men agree to dwell with us to become one people—when every male among us is circumcised as they are circumcised. 23 Will not their livestock, their property and all their beasts be ours? Only let us agree with them, and they will dwell with us." 24 And all who went out of the gate of his city listened to Hamor and his son Shechem, and every male was circumcised, all who went out of the gate of his city.

25 On the third day, when they were sore, two of the sons of Jacob, Simeon and Levi, Dinah's brothers, took their swords and came against the city while it felt secure and killed all the males. 26 They killed Hamor and his son Shechem with the sword and took Dinah out of Shechem's house and went away. 27 The sons of Jacob came upon the slain and plundered the city, because they had defiled their sister. 28 They took their flocks and their herds, their donkeys, and whatever was in the city and in the field. 29 All their wealth, all their little ones and their wives, all that was in the houses, they captured and plundered.

30 Then Jacob said to Simeon and Levi, "You have brought trouble on me by making me stink to the inhabitants of the land, the Canaanites and the Perizzites. My numbers are few, and if they gather themselves against me and attack me, I shall be destroyed, both I and my household." 31 But they said, "Should he treat our sister like a prostitute?"

God Blesses and Renames Jacob

35 God said to Jacob, "Arise, go up to Bethel and dwell there. Make an altar there to the God who appeared to you when you fled from your brother Esau." 2 So Jacob said to his household and to all who were with him, "Put away the foreign gods that are among you and purify yourselves and change your garments. 3 Then let us arise and go up to Bethel, so that I may make there an altar to the God who answers me in the day of my distress and has been with me wherever I have gone." 4 So they gave to Jacob all the foreign gods that they had, and the rings that were in their ears. Jacob hid

them under the terebinth tree that was near Shechem.

5 And as they journeyed, a terror from God fell upon the cities that were around them, so that they did not pursue the sons of Jacob. 6 And Jacob came to Luz (that is, Bethel), which is in the land of Canaan, he and all the people who were with him, 7 and there he built an altar and called the place El-bethel,1 because there God had revealed himself to him when he fled from his brother. 8 And Deborah, Rebekah's nurse, died, and she was buried under an oak below Bethel. So he called its name Allon-bacuth.2

9 God appeared3 to Jacob again, when he came from Paddan-aram, and blessed him. 10 And God said to him, "Your name is Jacob; no longer shall your name be called Jacob, but Israel shall be your name." So he called his name Israel. 11 And God said to him, "I am God Almighty:4 be fruitful and multiply. A nation and a company of nations shall come from you, and kings shall come from your own body.5 12 The land that I gave to Abraham and Isaac I will give to you, and I will give the land to your offspring after you." 13 Then God went up from him in the place where he had spoken with him. 14 And Jacob set up a pillar in the place where he had spoken with him, a pillar of stone. He poured out a drink offering on it and poured oil on it. 15 So Jacob called the name of the place where God had spoken with him Bethel.

The Deaths of Rachel and Isaac

16 Then they journeyed from Bethel. When they were still some distance6 from Ephrath, Rachel went into labor, and she had hard labor. 17 And when her labor was at its hardest, the midwife said to her, "Do not fear, for you have another son." 18 And as her soul was departing (for she was dying), she called his name Ben-oni;7 but his father called him Benjamin.8 19 So Rachel died, and she was buried on the way to Ephrath (that is, Bethlehem), 20 and Jacob set up a pillar over her tomb. It is the pillar of Rachel's tomb, which is there to this day. 21 Israel journeyed on and pitched his tent beyond the tower of Eder.

22 While Israel lived in that land, Reuben went and lay with Bilhah his father's concubine. And Israel heard of it.

Now the sons of Jacob were twelve. 23 The sons of Leah: Reuben (Jacob's firstborn), Simeon, Levi, Judah, Issachar, and Zebulun. 24 The sons of Rachel: Joseph and Benjamin. 25 The sons

---

1 El-bethel means God of Bethel 2 Allon-bacuth means oak of weeping 3 Or had appeared 4 Hebrew El Shaddai 5 Hebrew from your loins 6 Or about two hours' distance 7 Ben-oni could mean son of my sorrow, or son of my strength 8 Benjamin means son of the right hand

of Bilhah, Rachel's servant: Dan and Naphtali. 26 The sons of Zilpah, Leah's servant: Gad and Asher. These were the sons of Jacob who were born to him in Paddan-aram.

27 And Jacob came to his father Isaac at Mamre, or Kiriath-arba (that is, Hebron), where Abraham and Isaac had sojourned. 28 Now the days of Isaac were 180 years. 29 And Isaac breathed his last, and he died and was gathered to his people, old and full of days. And his sons Esau and Jacob buried him.

Esau's Descendants

36 These are the generations of Esau (that is, Edom). 2 Esau took his wives from the Canaanites: Adah the daughter of Elon the Hittite, Oholibamah the daughter of Anah the daughter[1] of Zibeon the Hivite, 3 and Basemath, Ishmael's daughter, the sister of Nebaioth. 4 And Adah bore to Esau, Eliphaz; Basemath bore Reuel; 5 and Oholibamah bore Jeush, Jalam, and Korah. These are the sons of Esau who were born to him in the land of Canaan.

6 Then Esau took his wives, his sons, his daughters, and all the members of his household, his livestock, all his beasts, and all his property that he had acquired in the land of Canaan. He went into a land away from his brother Jacob. 7 For their possessions were too great for them to dwell together. The land of their sojournings could not support them because of their livestock. 8 So Esau settled in the hill country of Seir. (Esau is Edom.)

9 These are the generations of Esau the father of the Edomites in the hill country of Seir. 10 These are the names of Esau's sons: Eliphaz the son of Adah the wife of Esau, Reuel the son of Basemath the wife of Esau. 11 The sons of Eliphaz were Teman, Omar, Zepho, Gatam, and Kenaz. 12 (Timna was a concubine of Eliphaz, Esau's son; she bore Amalek to Eliphaz.) These are the sons of Adah, Esau's wife. 13 These are the sons of Reuel: Nahath, Zerah, Shammah, and Mizzah. These are the sons of Basemath, Esau's wife. 14 These are the sons of Oholibamah the daughter of Anah the daughter of Zibeon, Esau's wife: she bore to Esau Jeush, Jalam, and Korah.

15 These are the chiefs of the sons of Esau. The sons of Eliphaz the firstborn of Esau: the chiefs Teman, Omar, Zepho, Kenaz, 16 Korah, Gatam, and Amalek; these are the chiefs of Eliphaz in the land of Edom; these are the sons of Adah. 17 These are the sons of Reuel, Esau's son: the chiefs Nahath, Zerah, Shammah, and Mizzah; these are the chiefs of Reuel in the land of Edom; these are the sons of Basemath, Esau's wife. 18 These are the sons of Oholibamah, Esau's wife: the chiefs Jeush, Jalam, and Korah; these are the chiefs born of Oholibamah the daughter of Anah, Esau's wife. 19 These are the sons of Esau (that is, Edom), and these are their chiefs.

20 These are the sons of Seir the Horite, the inhabitants of the land: Lotan, Shobal, Zibeon, Anah, 21 Dishon, Ezer, and Dishan; these are the chiefs of the Horites, the sons of Seir in the land of Edom. 22 The sons of Lotan were Hori and Hemam; and Lotan's sister was Timna. 23 These are the sons of Shobal: Alvan, Manahath, Ebal, Shepho, and Onam. 24 These are the sons of Zibeon: Aiah and Anah; he is the Anah who found the hot springs in the wilderness, as he pastured the donkeys of Zibeon his father. 25 These are the children of Anah: Dishon and Oholibamah the daughter of Anah. 26 These are the sons of Dishon: Hemdan, Eshban, Ithran, and Cheran. 27 These are the sons of Ezer: Bilhan, Zaavan, and Akan. 28 These are the sons of Dishan: Uz and Aran. 29 These are the chiefs of the Horites: the chiefs Lotan, Shobal, Zibeon, Anah, 30 Dishon, Ezer, and Dishan; these are the chiefs of the Horites, chief by chief in the land of Seir.

31 These are the kings who reigned in the land of Edom, before any king reigned over the Israelites. 32 Bela the son of Beor reigned in Edom, the name of his city being Dinhabah. 33 Bela died, and Jobab the son of Zerah of Bozrah reigned in his place. 34 Jobab died, and Husham of the land of the Temanites reigned in his place. 35 Husham died, and Hadad the son of Bedad, who defeated Midian in the country of Moab, reigned in his place, the name of his city being Avith. 36 Hadad died, and Samlah of Masrekah reigned in his place. 37 Samlah died, and Shaul of Rehoboth on the Euphrates[2] reigned in his place. 38 Shaul died, and Baal-hanan the son of Achbor reigned in his place. 39 Baal-hanan the son of Achbor died, and Hadar reigned in his place, the name of his city being Pau; his wife's name was Mehetabel, the daughter of Matred, daughter of Mezahab.

40 These are the names of the chiefs of Esau, according to their clans and their dwelling places, by their names: the chiefs Timna, Alvah,

---

[1] Hebrew; Samaritan, Septuagint, Syriac *son; also verse 14* [2] Hebrew *the River*

Jetheth, [41] Oholibamah, Elah, Pinon, [42] Kenaz, Teman, Mibzar, [43] Magdiel, and Iram; these are the chiefs of Edom (that is, Esau, the father of Edom), according to their dwelling places in the land of their possession.

Joseph's Dreams

37 Jacob lived in the land of his father's sojournings, in the land of Canaan.
[2] These are the generations of Jacob.

Joseph, being seventeen years old, was pasturing the flock with his brothers. He was a boy with the sons of Bilhah and Zilpah, his father's wives. And Joseph brought a bad report of them to their father. [3] Now Israel loved Joseph more than any other of his sons, because he was the son of his old age. And he made him a robe of many colors.[1] [4] But when his brothers saw that their father loved him more than all his brothers, they hated him and could not speak peacefully to him.

[5] Now Joseph had a dream, and when he told it to his brothers they hated him even more. [6] He said to them, "Hear this dream that I have dreamed: [7] Behold, we were binding sheaves in the field, and behold, my sheaf arose and stood upright. And behold, your sheaves gathered around it and bowed down to my sheaf." [8] His brothers said to him, "Are you indeed to reign over us? Or are you indeed to rule over us?" So they hated him even more for his dreams and for his words.

[9] Then he dreamed another dream and told it to his brothers and said, "Behold, I have dreamed another dream. Behold, the sun, the moon, and eleven stars were bowing down to me." [10] But when he told it to his father and to his brothers, his father rebuked him and said to him, "What is this dream that you have dreamed? Shall I and your mother and your brothers indeed come to bow ourselves to the ground before you?" [11] And his brothers were jealous of him, but his father kept the saying in mind.

Joseph Sold by His Brothers

[12] Now his brothers went to pasture their father's flock near Shechem. [13] And Israel said to Joseph, "Are not your brothers pasturing the flock at Shechem? Come, I will send you to them." And he said to him, "Here I am." [14] So he said to him, "Go now, see if it is well with your brothers and with the flock, and bring

me word." So he sent him from the Valley of Hebron, and he came to Shechem. [15] And a man found him wandering in the fields. And the man asked him, "What are you seeking?" [16] "I am seeking my brothers," he said. "Tell me, please, where they are pasturing the flock." [17] And the man said, "They have gone away, for I heard them say, 'Let us go to Dothan.'" So Joseph went after his brothers and found them at Dothan.

[18] They saw him from afar, and before he came near to them they conspired against him to kill him. [19] They said to one another, "Here comes this dreamer. [20] Come now, let us kill him and throw him into one of the pits.[2] Then we will say that a fierce animal has devoured him, and we will see what will become of his dreams." [21] But when Reuben heard it, he rescued him out of their hands, saying, "Let us not take his life." [22] And Reuben said to them, "Shed no blood; throw him into this pit here in the wilderness, but do not lay a hand on him"— that he might rescue him out of their hand to restore him to his father. [23] So when Joseph came to his brothers, they stripped him of his robe, the robe of many colors that he wore. [24] And they took him and threw him into a pit. The pit was empty; there was no water in it.

[25] Then they sat down to eat. And looking up they saw a caravan of Ishmaelites coming from Gilead, with their camels bearing gum, balm, and myrrh, on their way to carry it down to Egypt. [26] Then Judah said to his brothers, "What profit is it if we kill our brother and conceal his blood? [27] Come, let us sell him to the Ishmaelites, and let not our hand be upon him, for he is our brother, our own flesh." And his brothers listened to him. [28] Then Midianite traders passed by. And they drew Joseph up and lifted him out of the pit, and sold him to the Ishmaelites for twenty shekels[3] of silver. They took Joseph to Egypt.

[29] When Reuben returned to the pit and saw that Joseph was not in the pit, he tore his clothes [30] and returned to his brothers and said, "The boy is gone, and I, where shall I go?" [31] Then they took Joseph's robe and slaughtered a goat and dipped the robe in the blood. [32] And they sent the robe of many colors and brought it to their father and said, "This we have found; please identify whether it is your son's robe or not." [33] And he identified it and said, "It is my

---

[1] See Septuagint, Vulgate; or (with Syriac) *a robe with long sleeves*. The meaning of the Hebrew is uncertain; also verses 23, 32 [2] Or *cisterns*; also verses 22, 24 [3] A *shekel* was about 2/5 ounce or 11 grams

son's robe. A fierce animal has devoured him. Joseph is without doubt torn to pieces." [34] Then Jacob tore his garments and put sackcloth on his loins and mourned for his son many days. [35] All his sons and all his daughters rose up to comfort him, but he refused to be comforted and said, "No, I shall go down to Sheol to my son, mourning." Thus his father wept for him. [36] Meanwhile the Midianites had sold him in Egypt to Potiphar, an officer of Pharaoh, the captain of the guard.

Judah and Tamar

38 It happened at that time that Judah went down from his brothers and turned aside to a certain Adullamite, whose name was Hirah. [2] There Judah saw the daughter of a certain Canaanite whose name was Shua. He took her and went in to her, [3] and she conceived and bore a son, and he called his name Er. [4] She conceived again and bore a son, and she called his name Onan. [5] Yet again she bore a son, and she called his name Shelah. Judah[1] was in Chezib when she bore him.

[6] And Judah took a wife for Er his firstborn, and her name was Tamar. [7] But Er, Judah's firstborn, was wicked in the sight of the LORD, and the LORD put him to death. [8] Then Judah said to Onan, "Go in to your brother's wife and perform the duty of a brother-in-law to her, and raise up offspring for your brother." [9] But Onan knew that the offspring would not be his. So whenever he went in to his brother's wife he would waste the semen on the ground, so as not to give offspring to his brother. [10] And what he did was wicked in the sight of the LORD, and he put him to death also. [11] Then Judah said to Tamar his daughter-in-law, "Remain a widow in your father's house, till Shelah my son grows up"—for he feared that he would die, like his brothers. So Tamar went and remained in her father's house.

[12] In the course of time the wife of Judah, Shua's daughter, died. When Judah was comforted, he went up to Timnah to his sheepshearers, he and his friend Hirah the Adullamite. [13] And when Tamar was told, "Your father-in-law is going up to Timnah to shear his sheep," [14] she took off her widow's garments and covered herself with a veil, wrapping herself up, and sat at the entrance to Enaim, which is on the road to Timnah. For she saw that Shelah was grown up, and she had not been given to

him in marriage. [15] When Judah saw her, he thought she was a prostitute, for she had covered her face. [16] He turned to her at the roadside and said, "Come, let me come in to you," for he did not know that she was his daughter-in-law. She said, "What will you give me, that you may come in to me?" [17] He answered, "I will send you a young goat from the flock." And she said, "If you give me a pledge, until you send it—" [18] He said, "What pledge shall I give you?" She replied, "Your signet and your cord and your staff that is in your hand." So he gave them to her and went in to her, and she conceived by him. [19] Then she arose and went away, and taking off her veil she put on the garments of her widowhood.

[20] When Judah sent the young goat by his friend the Adullamite to take back the pledge from the woman's hand, he did not find her. [21] And he asked the men of the place, "Where is the cult prostitute[2] who was at Enaim at the roadside?" And they said, "No cult prostitute has been here." [22] So he returned to Judah and said, "I have not found her. Also, the men of the place said, 'No cult prostitute has been here.'" [23] And Judah replied, "Let her keep the things as her own, or we shall be laughed at. You see, I sent this young goat, and you did not find her."

[24] About three months later Judah was told, "Tamar your daughter-in-law has been immoral.[3] Moreover, she is pregnant by immorality."[4] And Judah said, "Bring her out, and let her be burned." [25] As she was being brought out, she sent word to her father-in-law, "By the man to whom these belong, I am pregnant." And she said, "Please identify whose these are, the signet and the cord and the staff." [26] Then Judah identified them and said, "She is more righteous than I, since I did not give her to my son Shelah." And he did not know her again.

[27] When the time of her labor came, there were twins in her womb. [28] And when she was in labor, one put out a hand, and the midwife took and tied a scarlet thread on his hand, saying, "This one came out first." [29] But as he drew back his hand, behold, his brother came out. And she said, "What a breach you have made for yourself!" Therefore his name was called Perez.[5] [30] Afterward his brother came out with the scarlet thread on his hand, and his name was called Zerah.

---

[1] Hebrew *He* [2] Hebrew *sacred woman*; a woman who served a pagan deity by prostitution; also verse 22 [3] Or *has committed prostitution* [4] Or *by prostitution* [5] *Perez* means *a breach*

Joseph and Potiphar's Wife

39 Now Joseph had been brought down to Egypt, and Potiphar, an officer of Pharaoh, the captain of the guard, an Egyptian, had bought him from the Ishmaelites who had brought him down there. ²The LORD was with Joseph, and he became a successful man, and he was in the house of his Egyptian master. ³His master saw that the LORD was with him and that the LORD caused all that he did to succeed in his hands. ⁴So Joseph found favor in his sight and attended him, and he made him overseer of his house and put him in charge of all that he had. ⁵From the time that he made him overseer in his house and over all that he had, the LORD blessed the Egyptian's house for Joseph's sake; the blessing of the LORD was on all that he had, in house and field. ⁶So he left all that he had in Joseph's charge, and because of him he had no concern about anything but the food he ate.

Now Joseph was handsome in form and appearance. ⁷And after a time his master's wife cast her eyes on Joseph and said, "Lie with me." ⁸But he refused and said to his master's wife, "Behold, because of me my master has no concern about anything in the house, and he has put everything that he has in my charge. ⁹He is not greater in this house than I am, nor has he kept back anything from me except you, because you are his wife. How then can I do this great wickedness and sin against God?" ¹⁰And as she spoke to Joseph day after day, he would not listen to her, to lie beside her or to be with her.

¹¹But one day, when he went into the house to do his work and none of the men of the house was there in the house, ¹²she caught him by his garment, saying, "Lie with me." But he left his garment in her hand and fled and got out of the house. ¹³And as soon as she saw that he had left his garment in her hand and had fled out of the house, ¹⁴she called to the men of her household and said to them, "See, he has brought among us a Hebrew to laugh at us. He came in to me to lie with me, and I cried out with a loud voice. ¹⁵And as soon as he heard that I lifted up my voice and cried out, he left his garment beside me and fled and got out of the house." ¹⁶Then she laid up his garment by her until his master came home, ¹⁷and she told him the same story, saying, "The Hebrew servant, whom you have brought among us, came in to me to laugh at me. ¹⁸But as soon as I lifted up my voice and cried, he left his garment beside me and fled out of the house."

¹⁹As soon as his master heard the words that his wife spoke to him, "This is the way your servant treated me," his anger was kindled. ²⁰And Joseph's master took him and put him into the prison, the place where the king's prisoners were confined, and he was there in prison. ²¹But the LORD was with Joseph and showed him steadfast love and gave him favor in the sight of the keeper of the prison. ²²And the keeper of the prison put Joseph in charge of all the prisoners who were in the prison. Whatever was done there, he was the one who did it. ²³The keeper of the prison paid no attention to anything that was in Joseph's charge, because the LORD was with him. And whatever he did, the LORD made it succeed.

Joseph Interprets Two Prisoners' Dreams

40 Some time after this, the cupbearer of the king of Egypt and his baker committed an offense against their lord the king of Egypt. ²And Pharaoh was angry with his two officers, the chief cupbearer and the chief baker, ³and he put them in custody in the house of the captain of the guard, in the prison where Joseph was confined. ⁴The captain of the guard appointed Joseph to be with them, and he attended them. They continued for some time in custody.

⁵And one night they both dreamed—the cupbearer and the baker of the king of Egypt, who were confined in the prison—each his own dream, and each dream with its own interpretation. ⁶When Joseph came to them in the morning, he saw that they were troubled. ⁷So he asked Pharaoh's officers who were with him in custody in his master's house, "Why are your faces downcast today?" ⁸They said to him, "We have had dreams, and there is no one to interpret them." And Joseph said to them, "Do not interpretations belong to God? Please tell them to me."

⁹So the chief cupbearer told his dream to Joseph and said to him, "In my dream there was a vine before me, ¹⁰and on the vine there were three branches. As soon as it budded, its blossoms shot forth, and the clusters ripened into grapes. ¹¹Pharaoh's cup was in my hand, and I took the grapes and pressed them into Pharaoh's cup and placed the cup in Pharaoh's hand." ¹²Then Joseph said to him, "This is its

interpretation: the three branches are three days. [13] In three days Pharaoh will lift up your head and restore you to your office, and you shall place Pharaoh's cup in his hand as formerly, when you were his cupbearer. [14] Only remember me, when it is well with you, and please do me the kindness to mention me to Pharaoh, and so get me out of this house. [15] For I was indeed stolen out of the land of the Hebrews, and here also I have done nothing that they should put me into the pit."

[16] When the chief baker saw that the interpretation was favorable, he said to Joseph, "I also had a dream: there were three cake baskets on my head, [17] and in the uppermost basket there were all sorts of baked food for Pharaoh, but the birds were eating it out of the basket on my head." [18] And Joseph answered and said, "This is its interpretation: the three baskets are three days. [19] In three days Pharaoh will lift up your head—from you!—and hang you on a tree. And the birds will eat the flesh from you."

[20] On the third day, which was Pharaoh's birthday, he made a feast for all his servants and lifted up the head of the chief cupbearer and the head of the chief baker among his servants. [21] He restored the chief cupbearer to his position, and he placed the cup in Pharaoh's hand. [22] But he hanged the chief baker, as Joseph had interpreted to them. [23] Yet the chief cupbearer did not remember Joseph, but forgot him.

Joseph Interprets Pharaoh's Dreams

41 After two whole years, Pharaoh dreamed that he was standing by the Nile, [2] and behold, there came up out of the Nile seven cows, attractive and plump, and they fed in the reed grass. [3] And behold, seven other cows, ugly and thin, came up out of the Nile after them, and stood by the other cows on the bank of the Nile. [4] And the ugly, thin cows ate up the seven attractive, plump cows. And Pharaoh awoke. [5] And he fell asleep and dreamed a second time. And behold, seven ears of grain, plump and good, were growing on one stalk. [6] And behold, after them sprouted seven ears, thin and blighted by the east wind. [7] And the thin ears swallowed up the seven plump, full ears. And Pharaoh awoke, and behold, it was a dream. [8] So in the morning his spirit was troubled, and he sent and called for all the magicians of Egypt and all its wise men. Pharaoh told them his dreams, but there was none who could interpret them to Pharaoh.

[9] Then the chief cupbearer said to Pharaoh, "I remember my offenses today. [10] When Pharaoh was angry with his servants and put me and the chief baker in custody in the house of the captain of the guard, [11] we dreamed on the same night, he and I, each having a dream with its own interpretation. [12] A young Hebrew was there with us, a servant of the captain of the guard. When we told him, he interpreted our dreams to us, giving an interpretation to each man according to his dream. [13] And as he interpreted to us, so it came about. I was restored to my office, and the baker was hanged."

[14] Then Pharaoh sent and called Joseph, and they quickly brought him out of the pit. And when he had shaved himself and changed his clothes, he came in before Pharaoh. [15] And Pharaoh said to Joseph, "I have had a dream, and there is no one who can interpret it. I have heard it said of you that when you hear a dream you can interpret it." [16] Joseph answered Pharaoh, "It is not in me; God will give Pharaoh a favorable answer."[1] [17] Then Pharaoh said to Joseph, "Behold, in my dream I was standing on the banks of the Nile. [18] Seven cows, plump and attractive, came up out of the Nile and fed in the reed grass. [19] Seven other cows came up after them, poor and very ugly and thin, such as I had never seen in all the land of Egypt. [20] And the thin, ugly cows ate up the first seven plump cows, [21] but when they had eaten them no one would have known that they had eaten them, for they were still as ugly as at the beginning. Then I awoke. [22] I also saw in my dream seven ears growing on one stalk, full and good. [23] Seven ears, withered, thin, and blighted by the east wind, sprouted after them, [24] and the thin ears swallowed up the seven good ears. And I told it to the magicians, but there was no one who could explain it to me."

[25] Then Joseph said to Pharaoh, "The dreams of Pharaoh are one; God has revealed to Pharaoh what he is about to do. [26] The seven good cows are seven years, and the seven good ears are seven years; the dreams are one. [27] The seven lean and ugly cows that came up after them are seven years, and the seven empty ears blighted by the east wind are also seven years of famine. [28] It is as I told Pharaoh; God has shown to Pharaoh what he is about to do.

[1] Or (compare Samaritan, Septuagint) *Without God it is not possible to give Pharaoh an answer about his welfare*

[29] There will come seven years of great plenty throughout all the land of Egypt, [30] but after them there will arise seven years of famine, and all the plenty will be forgotten in the land of Egypt. The famine will consume the land, [31] and the plenty will be unknown in the land by reason of the famine that will follow, for it will be very severe. [32] And the doubling of Pharaoh's dream means that the thing is fixed by God, and God will shortly bring it about. [33] Now therefore let Pharaoh select a discerning and wise man, and set him over the land of Egypt. [34] Let Pharaoh proceed to appoint overseers over the land and take one-fifth of the produce of the land[1] of Egypt during the seven plentiful years. [35] And let them gather all the food of these good years that are coming and store up grain under the authority of Pharaoh for food in the cities, and let them keep it. [36] That food shall be a reserve for the land against the seven years of famine that are to occur in the land of Egypt, so that the land may not perish through the famine."

Joseph Rises to Power

[37] This proposal pleased Pharaoh and all his servants. [38] And Pharaoh said to his servants, "Can we find a man like this, in whom is the Spirit of God?"[2] [39] Then Pharaoh said to Joseph, "Since God has shown you all this, there is none so discerning and wise as you are. [40] You shall be over my house, and all my people shall order themselves as you command.[3] Only as regards the throne will I be greater than you." [41] And Pharaoh said to Joseph, "See, I have set you over all the land of Egypt." [42] Then Pharaoh took his signet ring from his hand and put it on Joseph's hand, and clothed him in garments of fine linen and put a gold chain about his neck. [43] And he made him ride in his second chariot. And they called out before him, "Bow the knee!"[4] Thus he set him over all the land of Egypt. [44] Moreover, Pharaoh said to Joseph, "I am Pharaoh, and without your consent no one shall lift up hand or foot in all the land of Egypt." [45] And Pharaoh called Joseph's name Zaphenath-paneah. And he gave him in marriage Asenath, the daughter of Potiphera priest of On. So Joseph went out over the land of Egypt.

[46] Joseph was thirty years old when he entered the service of Pharaoh king of Egypt. And Joseph went out from the presence of Pharaoh and went through all the land of Egypt. [47] During the seven plentiful years the earth produced abundantly, [48] and he gathered up all the food of these seven years, which occurred in the land of Egypt, and put the food in the cities. He put in every city the food from the fields around it. [49] And Joseph stored up grain in great abundance, like the sand of the sea, until he ceased to measure it, for it could not be measured.

[50] Before the year of famine came, two sons were born to Joseph. Asenath, the daughter of Potiphera priest of On, bore them to him. [51] Joseph called the name of the firstborn Manasseh. "For," he said, "God has made me forget all my hardship and all my father's house."[5] [52] The name of the second he called Ephraim, "For God has made me fruitful in the land of my affliction."[6]

[53] The seven years of plenty that occurred in the land of Egypt came to an end, [54] and the seven years of famine began to come, as Joseph had said. There was famine in all lands, but in all the land of Egypt there was bread. [55] When all the land of Egypt was famished, the people cried to Pharaoh for bread. Pharaoh said to all the Egyptians, "Go to Joseph. What he says to you, do." [56] So when the famine had spread over all the land, Joseph opened all the storehouses[7] and sold to the Egyptians, for the famine was severe in the land of Egypt. [57] Moreover, all the earth came to Egypt to Joseph to buy grain, because the famine was severe over all the earth.

Joseph's Brothers Go to Egypt

42 When Jacob learned that there was grain for sale in Egypt, he said to his sons, "Why do you look at one another?" [2] And he said, "Behold, I have heard that there is grain for sale in Egypt. Go down and buy grain for us there, that we may live and not die." [3] So ten of Joseph's brothers went down to buy grain in Egypt. [4] But Jacob did not send Benjamin, Joseph's brother, with his brothers, for he feared that harm might happen to him. [5] Thus the sons of Israel came to buy among the others who came, for the famine was in the land of Canaan.

[6] Now Joseph was governor over the land. He was the one who sold to all the people of the land. And Joseph's brothers came and bowed themselves before him with their faces

---

[1] Or over the land and organize the land [2] Or of the gods [3] Hebrew and according to your command all my people shall kiss the ground [4] Abrek, probably an Egyptian word, similar in sound to the Hebrew word meaning to kneel [5] Manasseh sounds like the Hebrew for making to forget [6] Ephraim sounds like the Hebrew for making fruitful [7] Hebrew all that was in them

to the ground. ⁷ Joseph saw his brothers and recognized them, but he treated them like strangers and spoke roughly to them. "Where do you come from?" he said. They said, "From the land of Canaan, to buy food." ⁸ And Joseph recognized his brothers, but they did not recognize him. ⁹ And Joseph remembered the dreams that he had dreamed of them. And he said to them, "You are spies; you have come to see the nakedness of the land." ¹⁰ They said to him, "No, my lord, your servants have come to buy food. ¹¹ We are all sons of one man. We are honest men. Your servants have never been spies."

¹² He said to them, "No, it is the nakedness of the land that you have come to see." ¹³ And they said, "We, your servants, are twelve brothers, the sons of one man in the land of Canaan, and behold, the youngest is this day with our father, and one is no more." ¹⁴ But Joseph said to them, "It is as I said to you. You are spies. ¹⁵ By this you shall be tested: by the life of Pharaoh, you shall not go from this place unless your youngest brother comes here. ¹⁶ Send one of you, and let him bring your brother, while you remain confined, that your words may be tested, whether there is truth in you. Or else, by the life of Pharaoh, surely you are spies." ¹⁷ And he put them all together in custody for three days.

¹⁸ On the third day Joseph said to them, "Do this and you will live, for I fear God: ¹⁹ if you are honest men, let one of your brothers remain confined where you are in custody, and let the rest go and carry grain for the famine of your households, ²⁰ and bring your youngest brother to me. So your words will be verified, and you shall not die." And they did so. ²¹ Then they said to one another, "In truth we are guilty concerning our brother, in that we saw the distress of his soul, when he begged us and we did not listen. That is why this distress has come upon us." ²² And Reuben answered them, "Did I not tell you not to sin against the boy? But you did not listen. So now there comes a reckoning for his blood." ²³ They did not know that Joseph understood them, for there was an interpreter between them. ²⁴ Then he turned away from them and wept. And he returned to them and spoke to them. And he took Simeon from them and bound him before their eyes. ²⁵ And Joseph gave orders to fill their bags with grain, and to replace every man's money in his sack, and to give them provisions for the journey. This was done for them.

²⁶ Then they loaded their donkeys with their grain and departed. ²⁷ And as one of them opened his sack to give his donkey fodder at the lodging place, he saw his money in the mouth of his sack. ²⁸ He said to his brothers, "My money has been put back; here it is in the mouth of my sack!" At this their hearts failed them, and they turned trembling to one another, saying, "What is this that God has done to us?"

²⁹ When they came to Jacob their father in the land of Canaan, they told him all that had happened to them, saying, ³⁰ "The man, the lord of the land, spoke roughly to us and took us to be spies of the land. ³¹ But we said to him, 'We are honest men; we have never been spies. ³² We are twelve brothers, sons of our father. One is no more, and the youngest is this day with our father in the land of Canaan.' ³³ Then the man, the lord of the land, said to us, 'By this I shall know that you are honest men: leave one of your brothers with me, and take grain for the famine of your households, and go your way. ³⁴ Bring your youngest brother to me. Then I shall know that you are not spies but honest men, and I will deliver your brother to you, and you shall trade in the land.'"

³⁵ As they emptied their sacks, behold, every man's bundle of money was in his sack. And when they and their father saw their bundles of money, they were afraid. ³⁶ And Jacob their father said to them, "You have bereaved me of my children: Joseph is no more, and Simeon is no more, and now you would take Benjamin. All this has come against me." ³⁷ Then Reuben said to his father, "Kill my two sons if I do not bring him back to you. Put him in my hands, and I will bring him back to you." ³⁸ But he said, "My son shall not go down with you, for his brother is dead, and he is the only one left. If harm should happen to him on the journey that you are to make, you would bring down my gray hairs with sorrow to Sheol."

Joseph's Brothers Return to Egypt

43 Now the famine was severe in the land. ² And when they had eaten the grain that they had brought from Egypt, their father said to them, "Go again, buy us a little food." ³ But Judah said to him, "The man solemnly warned us, saying, 'You shall not see my face unless your brother is with you.' ⁴ If you will send our brother with us, we will go down and buy you food. ⁵ But if you will not send him, we will not go down, for the man said to us, 'You shall not see my face, unless your brother is with you.' " ⁶ Israel said, "Why did you treat me so badly as to tell the man that you had another brother?" ⁷ They replied, "The man questioned us carefully about ourselves and our kindred, saying, 'Is your father still alive? Do you have another brother?' What we told him was in answer to these questions. Could we in any way know that he would say, 'Bring your brother down'?" ⁸ And Judah said to Israel his father, "Send the boy with me, and we will arise and go, that we may live and not die, both we and you and also our little ones. ⁹ I will be a pledge of his safety. From my hand you shall require him. If I do not bring him back to you and set him before you, then let me bear the blame forever. ¹⁰ If we had not delayed, we would now have returned twice."

¹¹ Then their father Israel said to them, "If it must be so, then do this: take some of the choice fruits of the land in your bags, and carry a present down to the man, a little balm and a little honey, gum, myrrh, pistachio nuts, and almonds. ¹² Take double the money with you. Carry back with you the money that was returned in the mouth of your sacks. Perhaps it was an oversight. ¹³ Take also your brother, and arise, go again to the man. ¹⁴ May God Almighty¹ grant you mercy before the man, and may he send back your other brother and Benjamin. And as for me, if I am bereaved of my children, I am bereaved."

¹⁵ So the men took this present, and they took double the money with them, and Benjamin. They arose and went down to Egypt and stood before Joseph.

¹⁶ When Joseph saw Benjamin with them, he said to the steward of his house, "Bring the men into the house, and slaughter an animal and make ready, for the men are to dine with me at noon." ¹⁷ The man did as Joseph told him and brought the men to Joseph's house. ¹⁸ And the men were afraid because they were brought to Joseph's house, and they said, "It is because of the money, which was replaced in our sacks the first time, that we are brought in, so that he may assault us and fall upon us to make us servants and seize our donkeys." ¹⁹ So they went up to the steward of Joseph's house and spoke with him at the door of the house, ²⁰ and said, "Oh, my lord, we came down the first time to buy food. ²¹ And when we came to the lodging place we opened our sacks, and there was each man's money in the mouth of his sack, our money in full weight. So we have brought it again with us, ²² and we have brought other money down with us to buy food. We do not know who put our money in our sacks." ²³ He replied, "Peace to you, do not be afraid. Your God and the God of your father has put treasure in your sacks for you. I received your money." Then he brought Simeon out to them. ²⁴ And when the man had brought the men into Joseph's house and given them water, and they had washed their feet, and when he had given their donkeys fodder, ²⁵ they prepared the present for Joseph's coming at noon, for they heard that they should eat bread there.

²⁶ When Joseph came home, they brought into the house to him the present that they had with them and bowed down to him to the ground. ²⁷ And he inquired about their welfare and said, "Is your father well, the old man of whom you spoke? Is he still alive?" ²⁸ They said, "Your servant our father is well; he is still alive." And they bowed their heads and prostrated themselves. ²⁹ And he lifted up his eyes and saw his brother Benjamin, his mother's son, and said, "Is this your youngest brother, of whom you spoke to me? God be gracious to you, my son!" ³⁰ Then Joseph hurried out, for his compassion grew warm for his brother, and he sought a place to weep. And he entered his chamber and wept there. ³¹ Then he washed his face and came out. And controlling himself he said, "Serve the food." ³² They served him by himself, and them by themselves, and the Egyptians who ate with him by themselves, because the Egyptians could not eat with the Hebrews, for that is an abomination to the Egyptians. ³³ And they sat before him, the firstborn according to his birthright and the youngest according to his youth. And the men looked at one another in amazement. ³⁴ Portions were taken to them from Joseph's table, but Benjamin's portion was five times as much as any of theirs. And they drank and were merry² with him.

¹ Hebrew El Shaddai ² Hebrew and became intoxicated

Joseph Tests His Brothers

44 Then he commanded the steward of his house, "Fill the men's sacks with food, as much as they can carry, and put each man's money in the mouth of his sack, ²and put my cup, the silver cup, in the mouth of the sack of the youngest, with his money for the grain." And he did as Joseph told him.

³As soon as the morning was light, the men were sent away with their donkeys. ⁴They had gone only a short distance from the city. Now Joseph said to his steward, "Up, follow after the men, and when you overtake them, say to them, 'Why have you repaid evil for good?¹ ⁵Is it not from this that my lord drinks, and by this that he practices divination? You have done evil in doing this.'"

⁶When he overtook them, he spoke to them these words. ⁷They said to him, "Why does my lord speak such words as these? Far be it from your servants to do such a thing! ⁸Behold, the money that we found in the mouths of our sacks we brought back to you from the land of Canaan. How then could we steal silver or gold from your lord's house? ⁹Whichever of your servants is found with it shall die, and we also will be my lord's servants." ¹⁰He said, "Let it be as you say: he who is found with it shall be my servant, and the rest of you shall be innocent." ¹¹Then each man quickly lowered his sack to the ground, and each man opened his sack. ¹²And he searched, beginning with the eldest and ending with the youngest. And the cup was found in Benjamin's sack. ¹³Then they tore their clothes, and every man loaded his donkey, and they returned to the city.

¹⁴When Judah and his brothers came to Joseph's house, he was still there. They fell before him to the ground. ¹⁵Joseph said to them, "What deed is this that you have done? Do you not know that a man like me can indeed practice divination?" ¹⁶And Judah said, "What shall we say to my lord? What shall we speak? Or how can we clear ourselves? God has found out the guilt of your servants; behold, we are my lord's servants, both we and he also in whose hand the cup has been found." ¹⁷But he said, "Far be it from me that I should do so! Only the man in whose hand the cup was found shall be my servant. But as for you, go up in peace to your father."

¹⁸Then Judah went up to him and said, "Oh, my lord, please let your servant speak a word in my lord's ears, and let not your anger burn against your servant, for you are like Pharaoh himself. ¹⁹My lord asked his servants, saying, 'Have you a father, or a brother?' ²⁰And we said to my lord, 'We have a father, an old man, and a young brother, the child of his old age. His brother is dead, and he alone is left of his mother's children, and his father loves him.' ²¹Then you said to your servants, 'Bring him down to me, that I may set my eyes on him.' ²²We said to my lord, 'The boy cannot leave his father, for if he should leave his father, his father would die.' ²³Then you said to your servants, 'Unless your youngest brother comes down with you, you shall not see my face again.'

²⁴"When we went back to your servant my father, we told him the words of my lord. ²⁵And when our father said, 'Go again, buy us a little food,' ²⁶we said, 'We cannot go down. If our youngest brother goes with us, then we will go down. For we cannot see the man's face unless our youngest brother is with us.' ²⁷Then your servant my father said to us, 'You know that my wife bore me two sons. ²⁸One left me, and I said, "Surely he has been torn to pieces," and I have never seen him since. ²⁹If you take this one also from me, and harm happens to him, you will bring down my gray hairs in evil to Sheol.'

³⁰"Now therefore, as soon as I come to your servant my father, and the boy is not with us, then, as his life is bound up in the boy's life, ³¹as soon as he sees that the boy is not with us, he will die, and your servants will bring down the gray hairs of your servant our father with sorrow to Sheol. ³²For your servant became a pledge of safety for the boy to my father, saying, 'If I do not bring him back to you, then I shall bear the blame before my father all my life.' ³³Now therefore, please let your servant remain instead of the boy as a servant to my lord, and let the boy go back with his brothers. ³⁴For how can I go back to my father if the boy is not with me? I fear to see the evil that would find my father."

Joseph Provides for His Brothers and Family

45 Then Joseph could not control himself before all those who stood by him. He cried, "Make everyone go out from me." So no one stayed with him when Joseph made himself

---

¹ Septuagint (compare Vulgate) adds *Why have you stolen my silver cup?*

known to his brothers. ²And he wept aloud, so that the Egyptians heard it, and the household of Pharaoh heard it. ³And Joseph said to his brothers, "I am Joseph! Is my father still alive?" But his brothers could not answer him, for they were dismayed at his presence.

⁴So Joseph said to his brothers, "Come near to me, please." And they came near. And he said, "I am your brother, Joseph, whom you sold into Egypt. ⁵And now do not be distressed or angry with yourselves because you sold me here, for God sent me before you to preserve life. ⁶For the famine has been in the land these two years, and there are yet five years in which there will be neither plowing nor harvest. ⁷And God sent me before you to preserve for you a remnant on earth, and to keep alive for you many survivors. ⁸So it was not you who sent me here, but God. He has made me a father to Pharaoh, and lord of all his house and ruler over all the land of Egypt. ⁹Hurry and go up to my father and say to him, 'Thus says your son Joseph, God has made me lord of all Egypt. Come down to me; do not tarry. ¹⁰You shall dwell in the land of Goshen, and you shall be near me, you and your children and your children's children, and your flocks, your herds, and all that you have. ¹¹There I will provide for you, for there are yet five years of famine to come, so that you and your household, and all that you have, do not come to poverty.' ¹²And now your eyes see, and the eyes of my brother Benjamin see, that it is my mouth that speaks to you. ¹³You must tell my father of all my honor in Egypt, and of all that you have seen. Hurry and bring my father down here." ¹⁴Then he fell upon his brother Benjamin's neck and wept, and Benjamin wept upon his neck. ¹⁵And he kissed all his brothers and wept upon them. After that his brothers talked with him.

¹⁶When the report was heard in Pharaoh's house, "Joseph's brothers have come," it pleased Pharaoh and his servants. ¹⁷And Pharaoh said to Joseph, "Say to your brothers, 'Do this: load your beasts and go back to the land of Canaan, ¹⁸and take your father and your households, and come to me, and I will give you the best of the land of Egypt, and you shall eat the fat of the land.' ¹⁹And you, Joseph, are commanded to say, 'Do this: take wagons from the land of Egypt for your little ones and for your wives, and bring your father, and come. ²⁰Have no concern for¹ your goods, for the best of all the land of Egypt is yours.' "

²¹The sons of Israel did so: and Joseph gave them wagons, according to the command of Pharaoh, and gave them provisions for the journey. ²²To each and all of them he gave a change of clothes, but to Benjamin he gave three hundred shekels² of silver and five changes of clothes. ²³To his father he sent as follows: ten donkeys loaded with the good things of Egypt, and ten female donkeys loaded with grain, bread, and provision for his father on the journey. ²⁴Then he sent his brothers away, and as they departed, he said to them, "Do not quarrel on the way."

²⁵So they went up out of Egypt and came to the land of Canaan to their father Jacob. ²⁶And they told him, "Joseph is still alive, and he is ruler over all the land of Egypt." And his heart became numb, for he did not believe them. ²⁷But when they told him all the words of Joseph, which he had said to them, and when he saw the wagons that Joseph had sent to carry him, the spirit of their father Jacob revived. ²⁸And Israel said, "It is enough; Joseph my son is still alive. I will go and see him before I die."

Joseph Brings His Family to Egypt

46 So Israel took his journey with all that he had and came to Beersheba, and offered sacrifices to the God of his father Isaac. ²And God spoke to Israel in visions of the night and said, "Jacob, Jacob." And he said, "Here I am." ³Then he said, "I am God, the God of your father. Do not be afraid to go down to Egypt, for there I will make you into a great nation. ⁴I myself will go down with you to Egypt, and I will also bring you up again, and Joseph's hand shall close your eyes."

⁵Then Jacob set out from Beersheba. The sons of Israel carried Jacob their father, their little ones, and their wives, in the wagons that Pharaoh had sent to carry him. ⁶They also took their livestock and their goods, which they had gained in the land of Canaan, and came into Egypt, Jacob and all his offspring with him, ⁷his sons, and his sons' sons with him, his daughters, and his sons' daughters. All his offspring he brought with him into Egypt.

⁸Now these are the names of the descendants of Israel, who came into Egypt, Jacob

¹ Hebrew *Let your eye not pity* ² A *shekel* was about 2/5 ounce or 11 grams

and his sons. Reuben, Jacob's firstborn, ⁹ and the sons of Reuben: Hanoch, Pallu, Hezron, and Carmi. ¹⁰ The sons of Simeon: Jemuel, Jamin, Ohad, Jachin, Zohar, and Shaul, the son of a Canaanite woman. ¹¹ The sons of Levi: Gershon, Kohath, and Merari. ¹² The sons of Judah: Er, Onan, Shelah, Perez, and Zerah (but Er and Onan died in the land of Canaan); and the sons of Perez were Hezron and Hamul. ¹³ The sons of Issachar: Tola, Puvah, Yob, and Shimron. ¹⁴ The sons of Zebulun: Sered, Elon, and Jahleel. ¹⁵ These are the sons of Leah, whom she bore to Jacob in Paddan-aram, together with his daughter Dinah; altogether his sons and his daughters numbered thirty-three.

¹⁶ The sons of Gad: Ziphion, Haggi, Shuni, Ezbon, Eri, Arodi, and Areli. ¹⁷ The sons of Asher: Imnah, Ishvah, Ishvi, Beriah, with Serah their sister. And the sons of Beriah: Heber and Malchiel. ¹⁸ These are the sons of Zilpah, whom Laban gave to Leah his daughter; and these she bore to Jacob—sixteen persons.

¹⁹ The sons of Rachel, Jacob's wife: Joseph and Benjamin. ²⁰ And to Joseph in the land of Egypt were born Manasseh and Ephraim, whom Asenath, the daughter of Potiphera the priest of On, bore to him. ²¹ And the sons of Benjamin: Bela, Becher, Ashbel, Gera, Naaman, Ehi, Rosh, Muppim, Huppim, and Ard. ²² These are the sons of Rachel, who were born to Jacob—fourteen persons in all.

²³ The son¹ of Dan: Hushim. ²⁴ The sons of Naphtali: Jahzeel, Guni, Jezer, and Shillem. ²⁵ These are the sons of Bilhah, whom Laban gave to Rachel his daughter, and these she bore to Jacob—seven persons in all.

²⁶ All the persons belonging to Jacob who came into Egypt, who were his own descendants, not including Jacob's sons' wives, were sixty-six persons in all. ²⁷ And the sons of Joseph, who were born to him in Egypt, were two. All the persons of the house of Jacob who came into Egypt were seventy.

Jacob and Joseph Reunited

²⁸ He had sent Judah ahead of him to Joseph to show the way before him in Goshen, and they came into the land of Goshen. ²⁹ Then Joseph prepared his chariot and went up to meet Israel his father in Goshen. He presented himself to him and fell on his neck and wept on his neck a good while. ³⁰ Israel said to Joseph, "Now let me

die, since I have seen your face and know that you are still alive." ³¹ Joseph said to his brothers and to his father's household, "I will go up and tell Pharaoh and will say to him, 'My brothers and my father's household, who were in the land of Canaan, have come to me. ³² And the men are shepherds, for they have been keepers of livestock, and they have brought their flocks and their herds and all that they have.' ³³ When Pharaoh calls you and says, 'What is your occupation?' ³⁴ you shall say, 'Your servants have been keepers of livestock from our youth even until now, both we and our fathers,' in order that you may dwell in the land of Goshen, for every shepherd is an abomination to the Egyptians."

Jacob's Family Settles in Goshen

47 So Joseph went in and told Pharaoh, "My father and my brothers, with their flocks and herds and all that they possess, have come from the land of Canaan. They are now in the land of Goshen." ² And from among his brothers he took five men and presented them to Pharaoh. ³ Pharaoh said to his brothers, "What is your occupation?" And they said to Pharaoh, "Your servants are shepherds, as our fathers were." ⁴ They said to Pharaoh, "We have come to sojourn in the land, for there is no pasture for your servants' flocks, for the famine is severe in the land of Canaan. And now, please let your servants dwell in the land of Goshen." ⁵ Then Pharaoh said to Joseph, "Your father and your brothers have come to you. ⁶ The land of Egypt is before you. Settle your father and your brothers in the best of the land. Let them settle in the land of Goshen, and if you know any able men among them, put them in charge of my livestock."

⁷ Then Joseph brought in Jacob his father and stood him before Pharaoh, and Jacob blessed Pharaoh. ⁸ And Pharaoh said to Jacob, "How many are the days of the years of your life?" ⁹ And Jacob said to Pharaoh, "The days of the years of my sojourning are 130 years. Few and evil have been the days of the years of my life, and they have not attained to the days of the years of the life of my fathers in the days of their sojourning." ¹⁰ And Jacob blessed Pharaoh and went out from the presence of Pharaoh. ¹¹ Then Joseph settled his father and his brothers and gave them a possession in the land of Egypt, in the best of the land, in the land of Rameses, as Pharaoh had commanded. ¹² And Joseph pro-

---

¹ Hebrew *sons*

vided his father, his brothers, and all his father's household with food, according to the number of their dependents.

Joseph and the Famine

[13] Now there was no food in all the land, for the famine was very severe, so that the land of Egypt and the land of Canaan languished by reason of the famine. [14] And Joseph gathered up all the money that was found in the land of Egypt and in the land of Canaan, in exchange for the grain that they bought. And Joseph brought the money into Pharaoh's house. [15] And when the money was all spent in the land of Egypt and in the land of Canaan, all the Egyptians came to Joseph and said, "Give us food. Why should we die before your eyes? For our money is gone." [16] And Joseph answered, "Give your livestock, and I will give you food in exchange for your livestock, if your money is gone." [17] So they brought their livestock to Joseph, and Joseph gave them food in exchange for the horses, the flocks, the herds, and the donkeys. He supplied them with food in exchange for all their livestock that year. [18] And when that year was ended, they came to him the following year and said to him, "We will not hide from my lord that our money is all spent. The herds of livestock are my lord's. There is nothing left in the sight of my lord but our bodies and our land. [19] Why should we die before your eyes, both we and our land? Buy us and our land for food, and we with our land will be servants to Pharaoh. And give us seed that we may live and not die, and that the land may not be desolate."

[20] So Joseph bought all the land of Egypt for Pharaoh, for all the Egyptians sold their fields, because the famine was severe on them. The land became Pharaoh's. [21] As for the people, he made servants of them[1] from one end of Egypt to the other. [22] Only the land of the priests he did not buy, for the priests had a fixed allowance from Pharaoh and lived on the allowance that Pharaoh gave them; therefore they did not sell their land.

[23] Then Joseph said to the people, "Behold, I have this day bought you and your land for Pharaoh. Now here is seed for you, and you shall sow the land. [24] And at the harvests you shall give a fifth to Pharaoh, and four fifths shall be your own, as seed for the field and as food for yourselves and your households, and as food for your little ones." [25] And they said, "You have saved our lives; may it please my lord, we will be servants to Pharaoh." [26] So Joseph made it a statute concerning the land of Egypt, and it stands to this day, that Pharaoh should have the fifth; the land of the priests alone did not become Pharaoh's.

[27] Thus Israel settled in the land of Egypt, in the land of Goshen. And they gained possessions in it, and were fruitful and multiplied greatly. [28] And Jacob lived in the land of Egypt seventeen years. So the days of Jacob, the years of his life, were 147 years.

[29] And when the time drew near that Israel must die, he called his son Joseph and said to him, "If now I have found favor in your sight, put your hand under my thigh and promise to deal kindly and truly with me. Do not bury me in Egypt, [30] but let me lie with my fathers. Carry me out of Egypt and bury me in their burying place." He answered, "I will do as you have said." [31] And he said, "Swear to me"; and he swore to him. Then Israel bowed himself upon the head of his bed.[2]

Jacob Blesses Ephraim and Manasseh

48 After this, Joseph was told, "Behold, your father is ill." So he took with him his two sons, Manasseh and Ephraim. [2] And it was told to Jacob, "Your son Joseph has come to you." Then Israel summoned his strength and sat up in bed. [3] And Jacob said to Joseph, "God Almighty[3] appeared to me at Luz in the land of Canaan and blessed me, [4] and said to me, 'Behold, I will make you fruitful and multiply you, and I will make of you a company of peoples and will give this land to your offspring after you for an everlasting possession.' [5] And now your two sons, who were born to you in the land of Egypt before I came to you in Egypt, are mine; Ephraim and Manasseh shall be mine, as Reuben and Simeon are. [6] And the children that you fathered after them shall be yours. They shall be called by the name of their brothers in their inheritance. [7] As for me, when I came from Paddan, to my sorrow Rachel died in the land of Canaan on the way, when there was still some distance[4] to go to Ephrath, and I buried her there on the way to Ephrath (that is, Bethlehem)."

[8] When Israel saw Joseph's sons, he said, "Who are these?" [9] Joseph said to his father, "They are my sons, whom God has given me here." And he said, "Bring them to me, please, that I may bless them." [10] Now the eyes of Israel

---

[1] Samaritan, Septuagint, Vulgate; Hebrew *he removed them to the cities* [2] Hebrew; Septuagint *staff* [3] Hebrew *El Shaddai* [4] Or *about two hours' distance*

were dim with age, so that he could not see. So Joseph brought them near him, and he kissed them and embraced them. ¹¹ And Israel said to Joseph, "I never expected to see your face; and behold, God has let me see your offspring also." ¹² Then Joseph removed them from his knees, and he bowed himself with his face to the earth. ¹³ And Joseph took them both, Ephraim in his right hand toward Israel's left hand, and Manasseh in his left hand toward Israel's right hand, and brought them near him. ¹⁴ And Israel stretched out his right hand and laid it on the head of Ephraim, who was the younger, and his left hand on the head of Manasseh, crossing his hands (for Manasseh was the firstborn). ¹⁵ And he blessed Joseph and said,

> "The God before whom my fathers
>   Abraham and Isaac walked,
>   the God who has been my shepherd all
>   my life long to this day,
> ¹⁶   the angel who has redeemed me from all
>   evil, bless the boys;
>   and in them let my name be carried
>   on, and the name of my fathers
>   Abraham and Isaac;
>   and let them grow into a multitude¹ in
>   the midst of the earth."

¹⁷ When Joseph saw that his father laid his right hand on the head of Ephraim, it displeased him, and he took his father's hand to move it from Ephraim's head to Manasseh's head. ¹⁸ And Joseph said to his father, "Not this way, my father; since this one is the firstborn, put your right hand on his head." ¹⁹ But his father refused and said, "I know, my son, I know. He also shall become a people, and he also shall be great. Nevertheless, his younger brother shall be greater than he, and his offspring shall become a multitude² of nations." ²⁰ So he blessed them that day, saying,

> "By you Israel will pronounce blessings, say-
>   ing,
>   'God make you as Ephraim and as
>   Manasseh.'"

Thus he put Ephraim before Manasseh. ²¹ Then Israel said to Joseph, "Behold, I am about to die, but God will be with you and will bring you again to the land of your fathers. ²² Moreover, I have given to you rather than to your brothers one mountain slope³ that I took from the hand of the Amorites with my sword and with my bow."

Jacob Blesses His Sons

49 Then Jacob called his sons and said, "Gather yourselves together, that I may tell you what shall happen to you in days to come.

² "Assemble and listen, O sons of Jacob,
>   listen to Israel your father.

³ "Reuben, you are my firstborn,
>   my might, and the firstfruits of my
>   strength,
>   preeminent in dignity and preeminent
>   in power.
⁴   Unstable as water, you shall not have pre-
>   eminence,
>   because you went up to your father's
>   bed;
>   then you defiled it—he went up to my
>   couch!

⁵ "Simeon and Levi are brothers;
>   weapons of violence are their swords.
⁶   Let my soul come not into their council;
>   O my glory, be not joined to their com-
>   pany.
>   For in their anger they killed men,
>   and in their willfulness they hamstrung
>   oxen.
⁷   Cursed be their anger, for it is fierce,
>   and their wrath, for it is cruel!
>   I will divide them in Jacob
>   and scatter them in Israel.

⁸ "Judah, your brothers shall praise you;
>   your hand shall be on the neck of your
>   enemies;
>   your father's sons shall bow down
>   before you.
⁹   Judah is a lion's cub;
>   from the prey, my son, you have gone up.
>   He stooped down; he crouched as a lion
>   and as a lioness; who dares rouse him?
¹⁰   The scepter shall not depart from Judah,
>   nor the ruler's staff from between his
>   feet,
>   until tribute comes to him;⁴
>   and to him shall be the obedience of the
>   peoples.
¹¹   Binding his foal to the vine
>   and his donkey's colt to the choice vine,

¹ Or let them be like fish for multitude ² Hebrew fullness ³ Or one portion of the land; Hebrew shekem, which sounds like the town and district called Shechem ⁴ By a slight revocalization; a slight emendation yields (compare Septuagint, Syriac, Targum) until he comes to whom it belongs; Hebrew until Shiloh comes, or until he comes to Shiloh

he has washed his garments in wine
and his vesture in the blood of grapes.
[12] His eyes are darker than wine,
and his teeth whiter than milk.

[13] "Zebulun shall dwell at the shore of the sea;
he shall become a haven for ships,
and his border shall be at Sidon.

[14] "Issachar is a strong donkey,
crouching between the sheepfolds.[1]
[15] He saw that a resting place was good,
and that the land was pleasant,
so he bowed his shoulder to bear,
and became a servant at forced labor.

[16] "Dan shall judge his people
as one of the tribes of Israel.
[17] Dan shall be a serpent in the way,
a viper by the path,
that bites the horse's heels
so that his rider falls backward.
[18] I wait for your salvation, O LORD.

[19] "Raiders shall raid Gad,[2]
but he shall raid at their heels.

[20] "Asher's food shall be rich,
and he shall yield royal delicacies.

[21] "Naphtali is a doe let loose
that bears beautiful fawns.[3]

[22] "Joseph is a fruitful bough,
a fruitful bough by a spring;
his branches run over the wall.[4]
[23] The archers bitterly attacked him,
shot at him, and harassed him severely,
[24] yet his bow remained unmoved;
his arms[5] were made agile
by the hands of the Mighty One of Jacob
(from there is the Shepherd,[6] the Stone
of Israel),
[25] by the God of your father who will help
you,
by the Almighty[7] who will bless you
with blessings of heaven above,
blessings of the deep that crouches
beneath,
blessings of the breasts and of the
womb.

[26] The blessings of your father
are mighty beyond the blessings of my
parents,
up to the bounties of the everlasting
hills.[8]
May they be on the head of Joseph,
and on the brow of him who was set
apart from his brothers.

[27] "Benjamin is a ravenous wolf,
in the morning devouring the prey
and at evening dividing the spoil."

Jacob's Death and Burial

[28] All these are the twelve tribes of Israel. This is what their father said to them as he blessed them, blessing each with the blessing suitable to him. [29] Then he commanded them and said to them, "I am to be gathered to my people; bury me with my fathers in the cave that is in the field of Ephron the Hittite, [30] in the cave that is in the field at Machpelah, to the east of Mamre, in the land of Canaan, which Abraham bought with the field from Ephron the Hittite to possess as a burying place. [31] There they buried Abraham and Sarah his wife. There they buried Isaac and Rebekah his wife, and there I buried Leah— [32] the field and the cave that is in it were bought from the Hittites." [33] When Jacob finished commanding his sons, he drew up his feet into the bed and breathed his last and was gathered to his people.

50 Then Joseph fell on his father's face and wept over him and kissed him. [2] And Joseph commanded his servants the physicians to embalm his father. So the physicians embalmed Israel. [3] Forty days were required for it, for that is how many are required for embalming. And the Egyptians wept for him seventy days.

[4] And when the days of weeping for him were past, Joseph spoke to the household of Pharaoh, saying, "If now I have found favor in your eyes, please speak in the ears of Pharaoh, saying, [5] 'My father made me swear, saying, "I am about to die: in my tomb that I hewed out for myself in the land of Canaan, there shall you bury me." Now therefore, let me please go up and bury my father. Then I will return.'" [6] And Pharaoh answered, "Go up, and bury your father, as he made you swear." [7] So Joseph went up to bury his father. With him went up all the servants of Pharaoh, the elders of his household, and all the elders of the land of Egypt, [8] as well

---

[1] Or between its saddlebags   [2] Gad sounds like the Hebrew for raiders and raid   [3] Or he gives beautiful words, or that bears fawns of the fold   [4] Or Joseph is a wild donkey, a wild donkey beside a spring, his wild colts beside the wall   [5] Hebrew the arms of his hands   [6] Or by the name of the Shepherd   [7] Hebrew Shaddai   [8] A slight emendation yields (compare Septuagint) the blessings of the eternal mountains, the bounties of the everlasting hills

as all the household of Joseph, his brothers, and his father's household. Only their children, their flocks, and their herds were left in the land of Goshen. [9] And there went up with him both chariots and horsemen. It was a very great company. [10] When they came to the threshing floor of Atad, which is beyond the Jordan, they lamented there with a very great and grievous lamentation, and he made a mourning for his father seven days. [11] When the inhabitants of the land, the Canaanites, saw the mourning on the threshing floor of Atad, they said, "This is a grievous mourning by the Egyptians." Therefore the place was named Abel-mizraim;[1] it is beyond the Jordan. [12] Thus his sons did for him as he had commanded them, [13] for his sons carried him to the land of Canaan and buried him in the cave of the field at Machpelah, to the east of Mamre, which Abraham bought with the field from Ephron the Hittite to possess as a burying place. [14] After he had buried his father, Joseph returned to Egypt with his brothers and all who had gone up with him to bury his father.

God's Good Purposes

[15] When Joseph's brothers saw that their father was dead, they said, "It may be that Joseph will hate us and pay us back for all the evil that we did to him." [16] So they sent a message to Joseph, saying, "Your father gave this command before he died: [17] 'Say to Joseph, "Please forgive the transgression of your brothers and their sin, because they did evil to you."' And now, please forgive the transgression of the servants of the God of your father." Joseph wept when they spoke to him. [18] His brothers also came and fell down before him and said, "Behold, we are your servants." [19] But Joseph said to them, "Do not fear, for am I in the place of God? [20] As for you, you meant evil against me, but God meant it for good, to bring it about that many people[2] should be kept alive, as they are today. [21] So do not fear; I will provide for you and your little ones." Thus he comforted them and spoke kindly to them.

The Death of Joseph

[22] So Joseph remained in Egypt, he and his father's house. Joseph lived 110 years. [23] And Joseph saw Ephraim's children of the third generation. The children also of Machir the son of Manasseh were counted as Joseph's own.[3] [24] And Joseph said to his brothers, "I am about to die, but God will visit you and bring you up out of this land to the land that he swore to Abraham, to Isaac, and to Jacob." [25] Then Joseph made the sons of Israel swear, saying, "God will surely visit you, and you shall carry up my bones from here." [26] So Joseph died, being 110 years old. They embalmed him, and he was put in a coffin in Egypt.

---

[1] Abel-mizraim means mourning (or meadow) of Egypt [2] Or a numerous people [3] Hebrew were born on Joseph's knees

EXODUS

Israel Increases Greatly in Egypt

1 These are the names of the sons of Israel who came to Egypt with Jacob, each with his household: ²Reuben, Simeon, Levi, and Judah, ³Issachar, Zebulun, and Benjamin, ⁴Dan and Naphtali, Gad and Asher. ⁵All the descendants of Jacob were seventy persons; Joseph was already in Egypt. ⁶Then Joseph died, and all his brothers and all that generation. ⁷But the people of Israel were fruitful and increased greatly; they multiplied and grew exceedingly strong, so that the land was filled with them.

Pharaoh Oppresses Israel

⁸Now there arose a new king over Egypt, who did not know Joseph. ⁹And he said to his people, "Behold, the people of Israel are too many and too mighty for us. ¹⁰Come, let us deal shrewdly with them, lest they multiply, and, if war breaks out, they join our enemies and fight against us and escape from the land." ¹¹Therefore they set taskmasters over them to afflict them with heavy burdens. They built for Pharaoh store cities, Pithom and Raamses. ¹²But the more they were oppressed, the more they multiplied and the more they spread abroad. And the Egyptians were in dread of the people of Israel. ¹³So they ruthlessly made the people of Israel work as slaves ¹⁴and made their lives bitter with hard service, in mortar and brick, and in all kinds of work in the field. In all their work they ruthlessly made them work as slaves.

¹⁵Then the king of Egypt said to the Hebrew midwives, one of whom was named Shiphrah and the other Puah, ¹⁶"When you serve as midwife to the Hebrew women and see them on the birthstool, if it is a son, you shall kill him, but if it is a daughter, she shall live." ¹⁷But the midwives feared God and did not do as the king of Egypt commanded them, but let the male children live. ¹⁸So the king of Egypt called the midwives and said to them, "Why have you done this, and let the male children live?" ¹⁹The midwives said to Pharaoh, "Because the Hebrew women are not like the Egyptian women, for they are vigorous and give birth before the midwife comes to them." ²⁰So God dealt well with the midwives. And the people multiplied and grew very strong. ²¹And because the midwives feared God, he gave them families. ²²Then Pharaoh commanded all his people, "Every son that is born to the Hebrews[1] you shall cast into the Nile, but you shall let every daughter live."

The Birth of Moses

2 Now a man from the house of Levi went and took as his wife a Levite woman. ²The woman conceived and bore a son, and when she saw that he was a fine child, she hid him three months. ³When she could hide him no longer, she took for him a basket made of bulrushes[2] and daubed it with bitumen and pitch. She put the child in it and placed it among the reeds by the river bank. ⁴And his sister stood at a distance to know what would be done to him. ⁵Now the daughter of Pharaoh came down to bathe at the river, while her young women walked beside the river. She saw the basket among the reeds and sent her servant woman, and she took it. ⁶When she opened it, she saw the child, and behold, the baby was crying. She took pity on him and said, "This is one of the Hebrews' children." ⁷Then his sister said to Pharaoh's daughter, "Shall I go and call you a nurse from the Hebrew women to nurse the child for you?" ⁸And Pharaoh's daughter said to her, "Go." So the girl went and called the child's mother. ⁹And Pharaoh's daughter said to her, "Take this child away and nurse him for me, and I will give you your wages." So the woman took the child and nursed him. ¹⁰When the child grew older, she brought him to Pharaoh's daughter, and he became her son. She named him Moses, "Because," she said, "I drew him out of the water."[3]

Moses Flees to Midian

¹¹One day, when Moses had grown up, he went out to his people and looked on their burdens, and he saw an Egyptian beating a Hebrew, one of his people.[4] ¹²He looked this way and that, and seeing no one, he struck down the Egyptian and hid him in the sand. ¹³When he went out the next day, behold, two Hebrews were struggling together. And he said to the man in the wrong, "Why do you strike your companion?" ¹⁴He answered, "Who made you a prince and a judge over us? Do you mean to kill me as you killed the Egyptian?" Then Moses was afraid, and thought, "Surely the

---

[1] Samaritan, Septuagint, Targum; Hebrew lacks *to the Hebrews*   [2] Hebrew *papyrus reeds*   [3] Moses sounds like the Hebrew for *draw out*   [4] Hebrew *brothers*

thing is known." [15] When Pharaoh heard of it, he sought to kill Moses. But Moses fled from Pharaoh and stayed in the land of Midian. And he sat down by a well.

[16] Now the priest of Midian had seven daughters, and they came and drew water and filled the troughs to water their father's flock. [17] The shepherds came and drove them away, but Moses stood up and saved them, and watered their flock. [18] When they came home to their father Reuel, he said, "How is it that you have come home so soon today?" [19] They said, "An Egyptian delivered us out of the hand of the shepherds and even drew water for us and watered the flock." [20] He said to his daughters, "Then where is he? Why have you left the man? Call him, that he may eat bread." [21] And Moses was content to dwell with the man, and he gave Moses his daughter Zipporah. [22] She gave birth to a son, and he called his name Gershom, for he said, "I have been a sojourner[1] in a foreign land."

God Hears Israel's Groaning

[23] During those many days the king of Egypt died, and the people of Israel groaned because of their slavery and cried out for help. Their cry for rescue from slavery came up to God. [24] And God heard their groaning, and God remembered his covenant with Abraham, with Isaac, and with Jacob. [25] God saw the people of Israel—and God knew.

The Burning Bush

3 Now Moses was keeping the flock of his father-in-law, Jethro, the priest of Midian, and he led his flock to the west side of the wilderness and came to Horeb, the mountain of God. [2] And the angel of the LORD appeared to him in a flame of fire out of the midst of a bush. He looked, and behold, the bush was burning, yet it was not consumed. [3] And Moses said, "I will turn aside to see this great sight, why the bush is not burned." [4] When the LORD saw that he turned aside to see, God called to him out of the bush, "Moses, Moses!" And he said, "Here I am." [5] Then he said, "Do not come near; take your sandals off your feet, for the place on which you are standing is holy ground." [6] And he said, "I am the God of your father, the God of Abraham, the God of Isaac, and the God of

Jacob." And Moses hid his face, for he was afraid to look at God.

[7] Then the LORD said, "I have surely seen the affliction of my people who are in Egypt and have heard their cry because of their taskmasters. I know their sufferings, [8] and I have come down to deliver them out of the hand of the Egyptians and to bring them up out of that land to a good and broad land, a land flowing with milk and honey, to the place of the Canaanites, the Hittites, the Amorites, the Perizzites, the Hivites, and the Jebusites. [9] And now, behold, the cry of the people of Israel has come to me, and I have also seen the oppression with which the Egyptians oppress them. [10] Come, I will send you to Pharaoh that you may bring my people, the children of Israel, out of Egypt." [11] But Moses said to God, "Who am I that I should go to Pharaoh and bring the children of Israel out of Egypt?" [12] He said, "But I will be with you, and this shall be the sign for you, that I have sent you: when you have brought the people out of Egypt, you shall serve God on this mountain."

[13] Then Moses said to God, "If I come to the people of Israel and say to them, 'The God of your fathers has sent me to you,' and they ask me, 'What is his name?' what shall I say to them?" [14] God said to Moses, "I AM WHO I AM."[2] And he said, "Say this to the people of Israel: 'I AM has sent me to you.'" [15] God also said to Moses, "Say this to the people of Israel: 'The LORD,[3] the God of your fathers, the God of Abraham, the God of Isaac, and the God of Jacob, has sent me to you.' This is my name forever, and thus I am to be remembered throughout all generations. [16] Go and gather the elders of Israel together and say to them, 'The LORD, the God of your fathers, the God of Abraham, of Isaac, and of Jacob, has appeared to me, saying, "I have observed you and what has been done to you in Egypt, [17] and I promise that I will bring you up out of the affliction of Egypt to the land of the Canaanites, the Hittites, the Amorites, the Perizzites, the Hivites, and the Jebusites, a land flowing with milk and honey."' [18] And they will listen to your voice, and you and the elders of Israel shall go to the king of Egypt and say to him, 'The LORD, the God of the Hebrews, has met with us; and now, please let us go a three days' journey into the wilderness, that

---

[1] Gershom sounds like the Hebrew for *sojourner* [2] Or *I AM WHAT I AM*, or *I WILL BE WHAT I WILL BE* [3] The word LORD, when spelled with capital letters, stands for the divine name, YHWH, which is here connected with the verb *hayah*, "to be" in verse 14

we may sacrifice to the LORD our God.' [19]But I know that the king of Egypt will not let you go unless compelled by a mighty hand.[1] [20]So I will stretch out my hand and strike Egypt with all the wonders that I will do in it; after that he will let you go. [21]And I will give this people favor in the sight of the Egyptians; and when you go, you shall not go empty, [22]but each woman shall ask of her neighbor, and any woman who lives in her house, for silver and gold jewelry, and for clothing. You shall put them on your sons and on your daughters. So you shall plunder the Egyptians."

Moses Given Powerful Signs

4 Then Moses answered, "But behold, they will not believe me or listen to my voice, for they will say, 'The LORD did not appear to you.'" [2]The LORD said to him, "What is that in your hand?" He said, "A staff." [3]And he said, "Throw it on the ground." So he threw it on the ground, and it became a serpent, and Moses ran from it. [4]But the LORD said to Moses, "Put out your hand and catch it by the tail"—so he put out his hand and caught it, and it became a staff in his hand— [5]"that they may believe that the LORD, the God of their fathers, the God of Abraham, the God of Isaac, and the God of Jacob, has appeared to you." [6]Again, the LORD said to him, "Put your hand inside your cloak."[2] And he put his hand inside his cloak, and when he took it out, behold, his hand was leprous[3] like snow. [7]Then God said, "Put your hand back inside your cloak." So he put his hand back inside his cloak, and when he took it out, behold, it was restored like the rest of his flesh. [8]"If they will not believe you," God said, "or listen to the first sign, they may believe the latter sign. [9]If they will not believe even these two signs or listen to your voice, you shall take some water from the Nile and pour it on the dry ground, and the water that you shall take from the Nile will become blood on the dry ground."

[10]But Moses said to the LORD, "Oh, my Lord, I am not eloquent, either in the past or since you have spoken to your servant, but I am slow of speech and of tongue." [11]Then the LORD said to him, "Who has made man's mouth? Who makes him mute, or deaf, or seeing, or blind? Is it not I, the LORD? [12]Now therefore go, and I will be with your mouth and teach you what you shall speak." [13]But he said, "Oh, my Lord,

please send someone else." [14]Then the anger of the LORD was kindled against Moses and he said, "Is there not Aaron, your brother, the Levite? I know that he can speak well. Behold, he is coming out to meet you, and when he sees you, he will be glad in his heart. [15]You shall speak to him and put the words in his mouth, and I will be with your mouth and with his mouth and will teach you both what to do. [16]He shall speak for you to the people, and he shall be your mouth, and you shall be as God to him. [17]And take in your hand this staff, with which you shall do the signs."

Moses Returns to Egypt

[18]Moses went back to Jethro his father-in-law and said to him, "Please let me go back to my brothers in Egypt to see whether they are still alive." And Jethro said to Moses, "Go in peace." [19]And the LORD said to Moses in Midian, "Go back to Egypt, for all the men who were seeking your life are dead." [20]So Moses took his wife and his sons and had them ride on a donkey, and went back to the land of Egypt. And Moses took the staff of God in his hand.

[21]And the LORD said to Moses, "When you go back to Egypt, see that you do before Pharaoh all the miracles that I have put in your power. But I will harden his heart, so that he will not let the people go. [22]Then you shall say to Pharaoh, 'Thus says the LORD, Israel is my firstborn son, [23]and I say to you, "Let my son go that he may serve me." If you refuse to let him go, behold, I will kill your firstborn son.'"

[24]At a lodging place on the way the LORD met him and sought to put him to death. [25]Then Zipporah took a flint and cut off her son's foreskin and touched Moses'[4] feet with it and said, "Surely you are a bridegroom of blood to me!" [26]So he let him alone. It was then that she said, "A bridegroom of blood," because of the circumcision.

[27]The LORD said to Aaron, "Go into the wilderness to meet Moses." So he went and met him at the mountain of God and kissed him. [28]And Moses told Aaron all the words of the LORD with which he had sent him to speak, and all the signs that he had commanded him to do. [29]Then Moses and Aaron went and gathered together all the elders of the people of Israel. [30]Aaron spoke all the words that the LORD had spoken to Moses and did the signs

---

[1] Septuagint, Vulgate; Hebrew *go, not by a mighty hand* [2] Hebrew *into your bosom*; also verse 7 [3] *Leprosy* was a term for several skin diseases; see Leviticus 13 [4] Hebrew *his*

in the sight of the people. [31] And the people believed; and when they heard that the LORD had visited the people of Israel and that he had seen their affliction, they bowed their heads and worshiped.

Making Bricks Without Straw

5 Afterward Moses and Aaron went and said to Pharaoh, "Thus says the LORD, the God of Israel, 'Let my people go, that they may hold a feast to me in the wilderness.'" [2] But Pharaoh said, "Who is the LORD, that I should obey his voice and let Israel go? I do not know the LORD, and moreover, I will not let Israel go." [3] Then they said, "The God of the Hebrews has met with us. Please let us go a three days' journey into the wilderness that we may sacrifice to the LORD our God, lest he fall upon us with pestilence or with the sword." [4] But the king of Egypt said to them, "Moses and Aaron, why do you take the people away from their work? Get back to your burdens." [5] And Pharaoh said, "Behold, the people of the land are now many,[1] and you make them rest from their burdens!" [6] The same day Pharaoh commanded the taskmasters of the people and their foremen, [7] "You shall no longer give the people straw to make bricks, as in the past; let them go and gather straw for themselves. [8] But the number of bricks that they made in the past you shall impose on them, you shall by no means reduce it, for they are idle. Therefore they cry, 'Let us go and offer sacrifice to our God.' [9] Let heavier work be laid on the men that they may labor at it and pay no regard to lying words."

[10] So the taskmasters and the foremen of the people went out and said to the people, "Thus says Pharaoh, 'I will not give you straw. [11] Go and get your straw yourselves wherever you can find it, but your work will not be reduced in the least.'" [12] So the people were scattered throughout all the land of Egypt to gather stubble for straw. [13] The taskmasters were urgent, saying, "Complete your work, your daily task each day, as when there was straw." [14] And the foremen of the people of Israel, whom Pharaoh's taskmasters had set over them, were beaten and were asked, "Why have you not done all your task of making bricks today and yesterday, as in the past?"

[15] Then the foremen of the people of Israel came and cried to Pharaoh, "Why do you treat your servants like this? [16] No straw is given to your servants, yet they say to us, 'Make bricks!' And behold, your servants are beaten; but the fault is in your own people." [17] But he said, "You are idle, you are idle; that is why you say, 'Let us go and sacrifice to the LORD.' [18] Go now and work. No straw will be given you, but you must still deliver the same number of bricks." [19] The foremen of the people of Israel saw that they were in trouble when they said, "You shall by no means reduce your number of bricks, your daily task each day." [20] They met Moses and Aaron, who were waiting for them, as they came out from Pharaoh; [21] and they said to them, "The LORD look on you and judge, because you have made us stink in the sight of Pharaoh and his servants, and have put a sword in their hand to kill us."

[22] Then Moses turned to the LORD and said, "O Lord, why have you done evil to this people? Why did you ever send me? [23] For since I came to Pharaoh to speak in your name, he has done evil to this people, and you have not delivered your people at all."

God Promises Deliverance

6 But the LORD said to Moses, "Now you shall see what I will do to Pharaoh; for with a strong hand he will send them out, and with a strong hand he will drive them out of his land."

[2] God spoke to Moses and said to him, "I am the LORD. [3] I appeared to Abraham, to Isaac, and to Jacob, as God Almighty,[2] but by my name the LORD I did not make myself known to them. [4] I also established my covenant with them to give them the land of Canaan, the land in which they lived as sojourners. [5] Moreover, I have heard the groaning of the people of Israel whom the Egyptians hold as slaves, and I have remembered my covenant. [6] Say therefore to the people of Israel, 'I am the LORD, and I will bring you out from under the burdens of the Egyptians, and I will deliver you from slavery to them, and I will redeem you with an outstretched arm and with great acts of judgment. [7] I will take you to be my people, and I will be your God, and you shall know that I am the LORD your God, who has brought you out from under the burdens of the Egyptians. [8] I will bring you into the land that I swore to give to Abraham, to Isaac, and to Jacob. I will give it to you for a possession. I am the LORD.'"

[1] Samaritan *they are now more numerous than the people of the land* [2] Hebrew *El Shaddai*

⁹Moses spoke thus to the people of Israel, but they did not listen to Moses, because of their broken spirit and harsh slavery.

¹⁰So the LORD said to Moses, ¹¹"Go in, tell Pharaoh king of Egypt to let the people of Israel go out of his land." ¹²But Moses said to the LORD, "Behold, the people of Israel have not listened to me. How then shall Pharaoh listen to me, for I am of uncircumcised lips?" ¹³But the LORD spoke to Moses and Aaron and gave them a charge about the people of Israel and about Pharaoh king of Egypt: to bring the people of Israel out of the land of Egypt.

The Genealogy of Moses and Aaron

¹⁴These are the heads of their fathers' houses: the sons of Reuben, the firstborn of Israel: Hanoch, Pallu, Hezron, and Carmi; these are the clans of Reuben. ¹⁵The sons of Simeon: Jemuel, Jamin, Ohad, Jachin, Zohar, and Shaul, the son of a Canaanite woman; these are the clans of Simeon. ¹⁶These are the names of the sons of Levi according to their generations: Gershon, Kohath, and Merari, the years of the life of Levi being 137 years. ¹⁷The sons of Gershon: Libni and Shimei, by their clans. ¹⁸The sons of Kohath: Amram, Izhar, Hebron, and Uzziel, the years of the life of Kohath being 133 years. ¹⁹The sons of Merari: Mahli and Mushi. These are the clans of the Levites according to their generations. ²⁰Amram took as his wife Jochebed his father's sister, and she bore him Aaron and Moses, the years of the life of Amram being 137 years. ²¹The sons of Izhar: Korah, Nepheg, and Zichri. ²²The sons of Uzziel: Mishael, Elzaphan, and Sithri. ²³Aaron took as his wife Elisheba, the daughter of Amminadab and the sister of Nahshon, and she bore him Nadab, Abihu, Eleazar, and Ithamar. ²⁴The sons of Korah: Assir, Elkanah, and Abiasaph; these are the clans of the Korahites. ²⁵Eleazar, Aaron's son, took as his wife one of the daughters of Putiel, and she bore him Phinehas. These are the heads of the fathers' houses of the Levites by their clans.

²⁶These are the Aaron and Moses to whom the LORD said: "Bring out the people of Israel from the land of Egypt by their hosts." ²⁷It was they who spoke to Pharaoh king of Egypt about bringing out the people of Israel from Egypt, this Moses and this Aaron.

²⁸On the day when the LORD spoke to Moses in the land of Egypt, ²⁹the LORD said to Moses, "I am the LORD; tell Pharaoh king of Egypt all that I say to you." ³⁰But Moses said to the LORD, "Behold, I am of uncircumcised lips. How will Pharaoh listen to me?"

Moses and Aaron Before Pharaoh

7 And the LORD said to Moses, "See, I have made you like God to Pharaoh, and your brother Aaron shall be your prophet. ²You shall speak all that I command you, and your brother Aaron shall tell Pharaoh to let the people of Israel go out of his land. ³But I will harden Pharaoh's heart, and though I multiply my signs and wonders in the land of Egypt, ⁴Pharaoh will not listen to you. Then I will lay my hand on Egypt and bring my hosts, my people the children of Israel, out of the land of Egypt by great acts of judgment. ⁵The Egyptians shall know that I am the LORD, when I stretch out my hand against Egypt and bring out the people of Israel from among them." ⁶Moses and Aaron did so; they did just as the LORD commanded them. ⁷Now Moses was eighty years old, and Aaron eighty-three years old, when they spoke to Pharaoh.

⁸Then the LORD said to Moses and Aaron, ⁹"When Pharaoh says to you, 'Prove yourselves by working a miracle,' then you shall say to Aaron, 'Take your staff and cast it down before Pharaoh, that it may become a serpent.'" ¹⁰So Moses and Aaron went to Pharaoh and did just as the LORD commanded. Aaron cast down his staff before Pharaoh and his servants, and it became a serpent. ¹¹Then Pharaoh summoned the wise men and the sorcerers, and they, the magicians of Egypt, also did the same by their secret arts. ¹²For each man cast down his staff, and they became serpents. But Aaron's staff swallowed up their staffs. ¹³Still Pharaoh's heart was hardened, and he would not listen to them, as the LORD had said.

The First Plague: Water Turned to Blood

¹⁴Then the LORD said to Moses, "Pharaoh's heart is hardened; he refuses to let the people go. ¹⁵Go to Pharaoh in the morning, as he is going out to the water. Stand on the bank of the Nile to meet him, and take in your hand the staff that turned into a serpent. ¹⁶And you shall say to him, 'The LORD, the God of the Hebrews, sent me to you, saying, "Let my people go, that they may serve me in the wilderness." But so far,

you have not obeyed. [17] Thus says the LORD, "By this you shall know that I am the LORD: behold, with the staff that is in my hand I will strike the water that is in the Nile, and it shall turn into blood. [18] The fish in the Nile shall die, and the Nile will stink, and the Egyptians will grow weary of drinking water from the Nile." ' " [19] And the LORD said to Moses, "Say to Aaron, 'Take your staff and stretch out your hand over the waters of Egypt, over their rivers, their canals, and their ponds, and all their pools of water, so that they may become blood, and there shall be blood throughout all the land of Egypt, even in vessels of wood and in vessels of stone.' "

[20] Moses and Aaron did as the LORD commanded. In the sight of Pharaoh and in the sight of his servants he lifted up the staff and struck the water in the Nile, and all the water in the Nile turned into blood. [21] And the fish in the Nile died, and the Nile stank, so that the Egyptians could not drink water from the Nile. There was blood throughout all the land of Egypt. [22] But the magicians of Egypt did the same by their secret arts. So Pharaoh's heart remained hardened, and he would not listen to them, as the LORD had said. [23] Pharaoh turned and went into his house, and he did not take even this to heart. [24] And all the Egyptians dug along the Nile for water to drink, for they could not drink the water of the Nile.

[25] Seven full days passed after the LORD had struck the Nile.

The Second Plague: Frogs

8 [1] Then the LORD said to Moses, "Go in to Pharaoh and say to him, 'Thus says the LORD, "Let my people go, that they may serve me. [2] But if you refuse to let them go, behold, I will plague all your country with frogs. [3] The Nile shall swarm with frogs that shall come up into your house and into your bedroom and on your bed and into the houses of your servants and your people,[2] and into your ovens and your kneading bowls. [4] The frogs shall come up on you and on your people and on all your servants." ' " [5] [3] And the LORD said to Moses, "Say to Aaron, 'Stretch out your hand with your staff over the rivers, over the canals and over the pools, and make frogs come up on the land of Egypt!' " [6] So Aaron stretched out his hand over the waters of Egypt, and the frogs came up and covered the land of Egypt. [7] But the magicians

did the same by their secret arts and made frogs come up on the land of Egypt.

[8] Then Pharaoh called Moses and Aaron and said, "Plead with the LORD to take away the frogs from me and from my people, and I will let the people go to sacrifice to the LORD." [9] Moses said to Pharaoh, "Be pleased to command me when I am to plead for you and for your servants and for your people, that the frogs be cut off from you and your houses and be left only in the Nile." [10] And he said, "Tomorrow." Moses said, "Be it as you say, so that you may know that there is no one like the LORD our God. [11] The frogs shall go away from you and your houses and your servants and your people. They shall be left only in the Nile." [12] So Moses and Aaron went out from Pharaoh, and Moses cried to the LORD about the frogs, as he had agreed with Pharaoh.[4] [13] And the LORD did according to the word of Moses. The frogs died out in the houses, the courtyards, and the fields. [14] And they gathered them together in heaps, and the land stank. [15] But when Pharaoh saw that there was a respite, he hardened his heart and would not listen to them, as the LORD had said.

The Third Plague: Gnats

[16] Then the LORD said to Moses, "Say to Aaron, 'Stretch out your staff and strike the dust of the earth, so that it may become gnats in all the land of Egypt.' " [17] And they did so. Aaron stretched out his hand with his staff and struck the dust of the earth, and there were gnats on man and beast. All the dust of the earth became gnats in all the land of Egypt. [18] The magicians tried by their secret arts to produce gnats, but they could not. So there were gnats on man and beast. [19] Then the magicians said to Pharaoh, "This is the finger of God." But Pharaoh's heart was hardened, and he would not listen to them, as the LORD had said.

The Fourth Plague: Flies

[20] Then the LORD said to Moses, "Rise up early in the morning and present yourself to Pharaoh, as he goes out to the water, and say to him, 'Thus says the LORD, "Let my people go, that they may serve me. [21] Or else, if you will not let my people go, behold, I will send swarms of flies on you and your servants and your people, and into your houses. And the houses of the Egyptians shall be filled with swarms of flies,

---

[1] Ch 7:26 in Hebrew [2] Or among your people [3] Ch 8:1 in Hebrew [4] Or which he had brought upon Pharaoh

and also the ground on which they stand. ²²But on that day I will set apart the land of Goshen, where my people dwell, so that no swarms of flies shall be there, that you may know that I am the LORD in the midst of the earth.¹ ²³Thus I will put a division² between my people and your people. Tomorrow this sign shall happen.'"" ²⁴And the LORD did so. There came great swarms of flies into the house of Pharaoh and into his servants' houses. Throughout all the land of Egypt the land was ruined by the swarms of flies.

²⁵Then Pharaoh called Moses and Aaron and said, "Go, sacrifice to your God within the land." ²⁶But Moses said, "It would not be right to do so, for the offerings we shall sacrifice to the LORD our God are an abomination to the Egyptians. If we sacrifice offerings abominable to the Egyptians before their eyes, will they not stone us? ²⁷We must go three days' journey into the wilderness and sacrifice to the LORD our God as he tells us." ²⁸So Pharaoh said, "I will let you go to sacrifice to the LORD your God in the wilderness; only you must not go very far away. Plead for me." ²⁹Then Moses said, "Behold, I am going out from you and I will plead with the LORD that the swarms of flies may depart from Pharaoh, from his servants, and from his people, tomorrow. Only let not Pharaoh cheat again by not letting the people go to sacrifice to the LORD." ³⁰So Moses went out from Pharaoh and prayed to the LORD. ³¹And the LORD did as Moses asked, and removed the swarms of flies from Pharaoh, from his servants, and from his people; not one remained. ³²But Pharaoh hardened his heart this time also, and did not let the people go.

The Fifth Plague: Egyptian Livestock Die

9 Then the LORD said to Moses, "Go in to Pharaoh and say to him, 'Thus says the LORD, the God of the Hebrews, "Let my people go, that they may serve me. ²For if you refuse to let them go and still hold them, ³behold, the hand of the LORD will fall with a very severe plague upon your livestock that are in the field, the horses, the donkeys, the camels, the herds, and the flocks. ⁴But the LORD will make a distinction between the livestock of Israel and the livestock of Egypt, so that nothing of all that belongs to the people of Israel shall die."'" ⁵And the LORD set a time, saying, "Tomorrow the LORD will do this thing in the land." ⁶And

the next day the LORD did this thing. All the livestock of the Egyptians died, but not one of the livestock of the people of Israel died. ⁷And Pharaoh sent, and behold, not one of the livestock of Israel was dead. But the heart of Pharaoh was hardened, and he did not let the people go.

The Sixth Plague: Boils

⁸And the LORD said to Moses and Aaron, "Take handfuls of soot from the kiln, and let Moses throw them in the air in the sight of Pharaoh. ⁹It shall become fine dust over all the land of Egypt, and become boils breaking out in sores on man and beast throughout all the land of Egypt." ¹⁰So they took soot from the kiln and stood before Pharaoh. And Moses threw it in the air, and it became boils breaking out in sores on man and beast. ¹¹And the magicians could not stand before Moses because of the boils, for the boils came upon the magicians and upon all the Egyptians. ¹²But the LORD hardened the heart of Pharaoh, and he did not listen to them, as the LORD had spoken to Moses.

The Seventh Plague: Hail

¹³Then the LORD said to Moses, "Rise up early in the morning and present yourself before Pharaoh and say to him, 'Thus says the LORD, the God of the Hebrews, "Let my people go, that they may serve me. ¹⁴For this time I will send all my plagues on you yourself,³ and on your servants and your people, so that you may know that there is none like me in all the earth. ¹⁵For by now I could have put out my hand and struck you and your people with pestilence, and you would have been cut off from the earth. ¹⁶But for this purpose I have raised you up, to show you my power, so that my name may be proclaimed in all the earth. ¹⁷You are still exalting yourself against my people and will not let them go. ¹⁸Behold, about this time tomorrow I will cause very heavy hail to fall, such as never has been in Egypt from the day it was founded until now. ¹⁹Now therefore send, get your livestock and all that you have in the field into safe shelter, for every man and beast that is in the field and is not brought home will die when the hail falls on them."'" ²⁰Then whoever feared the word of the LORD among the servants of Pharaoh hurried his slaves and his livestock into the houses, ²¹but whoever did not pay attention to the word of the LORD left his slaves and his livestock in the field.

¹ Or that I the LORD am in the land ² Septuagint, Vulgate; Hebrew set redemption ³ Hebrew on your heart

²² Then the LORD said to Moses, "Stretch out your hand toward heaven, so that there may be hail in all the land of Egypt, on man and beast and every plant of the field, in the land of Egypt." ²³ Then Moses stretched out his staff toward heaven, and the LORD sent thunder and hail, and fire ran down to the earth. And the LORD rained hail upon the land of Egypt. ²⁴ There was hail and fire flashing continually in the midst of the hail, very heavy hail, such as had never been in all the land of Egypt since it became a nation. ²⁵ The hail struck down everything that was in the field in all the land of Egypt, both man and beast. And the hail struck down every plant of the field and broke every tree of the field. ²⁶ Only in the land of Goshen, where the people of Israel were, was there no hail.

²⁷ Then Pharaoh sent and called Moses and Aaron and said to them, "This time I have sinned; the LORD is in the right, and I and my people are in the wrong. ²⁸ Plead with the LORD, for there has been enough of God's thunder and hail. I will let you go, and you shall stay no longer." ²⁹ Moses said to him, "As soon as I have gone out of the city, I will stretch out my hands to the LORD. The thunder will cease, and there will be no more hail, so that you may know that the earth is the LORD's. ³⁰ But as for you and your servants, I know that you do not yet fear the LORD God." ³¹ (The flax and the barley were struck down, for the barley was in the ear and the flax was in bud. ³² But the wheat and the emmer¹ were not struck down, for they are late in coming up.) ³³ So Moses went out of the city from Pharaoh and stretched out his hands to the LORD, and the thunder and the hail ceased, and the rain no longer poured upon the earth. ³⁴ But when Pharaoh saw that the rain and the hail and the thunder had ceased, he sinned yet again and hardened his heart, he and his servants. ³⁵ So the heart of Pharaoh was hardened, and he did not let the people of Israel go, just as the LORD had spoken through Moses.

The Eighth Plague: Locusts

10 Then the LORD said to Moses, "Go in to Pharaoh, for I have hardened his heart and the heart of his servants, that I may show these signs of mine among them, ² and that you may tell in the hearing of your son and of your grandson how I have dealt harshly with the Egyptians and what signs I have done among them, that you may know that I am the LORD."

³ So Moses and Aaron went in to Pharaoh and said to him, "Thus says the LORD, the God of the Hebrews, 'How long will you refuse to humble yourself before me? Let my people go, that they may serve me. ⁴ For if you refuse to let my people go, behold, tomorrow I will bring locusts into your country, ⁵ and they shall cover the face of the land, so that no one can see the land. And they shall eat what is left to you after the hail, and they shall eat every tree of yours that grows in the field, ⁶ and they shall fill your houses and the houses of all your servants and of all the Egyptians, as neither your fathers nor your grandfathers have seen, from the day they came on earth to this day.' " Then he turned and went out from Pharaoh.

⁷ Then Pharaoh's servants said to him, "How long shall this man be a snare to us? Let the men go, that they may serve the LORD their God. Do you not yet understand that Egypt is ruined?" ⁸ So Moses and Aaron were brought back to Pharaoh. And he said to them, "Go, serve the LORD your God. But which ones are to go?" ⁹ Moses said, "We will go with our young and our old. We will go with our sons and daughters and with our flocks and herds, for we must hold a feast to the LORD." ¹⁰ But he said to them, "The LORD be with you, if ever I let you and your little ones go! Look, you have some evil purpose in mind.² ¹¹ No! Go, the men among you, and serve the LORD, for that is what you are asking." And they were driven out from Pharaoh's presence.

¹² Then the LORD said to Moses, "Stretch out your hand over the land of Egypt for the locusts, so that they may come upon the land of Egypt and eat every plant in the land, all that the hail has left." ¹³ So Moses stretched out his staff over the land of Egypt, and the LORD brought an east wind upon the land all that day and all that night. When it was morning, the east wind had brought the locusts. ¹⁴ The locusts came up over all the land of Egypt and settled on the whole country of Egypt, such a dense swarm of locusts as had never been before, nor ever will be again. ¹⁵ They covered the face of the whole land, so that the land was darkened, and they ate all the plants in the land and all the fruit of the trees that the hail had left. Not a green thing remained, neither tree nor plant of the field, through all the land

¹ A type of wheat ² Hebrew *before your face*

of Egypt. [16] Then Pharaoh hastily called Moses and Aaron and said, "I have sinned against the LORD your God, and against you. [17] Now therefore, forgive my sin, please, only this once, and plead with the LORD your God only to remove this death from me." [18] So he went out from Pharaoh and pleaded with the LORD. [19] And the LORD turned the wind into a very strong west wind, which lifted the locusts and drove them into the Red Sea. Not a single locust was left in all the country of Egypt. [20] But the LORD hardened Pharaoh's heart, and he did not let the people of Israel go.

The Ninth Plague: Darkness

[21] Then the LORD said to Moses, "Stretch out your hand toward heaven, that there may be darkness over the land of Egypt, a darkness to be felt." [22] So Moses stretched out his hand toward heaven, and there was pitch darkness in all the land of Egypt three days. [23] They did not see one another, nor did anyone rise from his place for three days, but all the people of Israel had light where they lived. [24] Then Pharaoh called Moses and said, "Go, serve the LORD; your little ones also may go with you; only let your flocks and your herds remain behind." [25] But Moses said, "You must also let us have sacrifices and burnt offerings, that we may sacrifice to the LORD our God. [26] Our livestock also must go with us; not a hoof shall be left behind, for we must take of them to serve the LORD our God, and we do not know with what we must serve the LORD until we arrive there." [27] But the LORD hardened Pharaoh's heart, and he would not let them go. [28] Then Pharaoh said to him, "Get away from me; take care never to see my face again, for on the day you see my face you shall die." [29] Moses said, "As you say! I will not see your face again."

A Final Plague Threatened

11 The LORD said to Moses, "Yet one plague more I will bring upon Pharaoh and upon Egypt. Afterward he will let you go from here. When he lets you go, he will drive you away completely. [2] Speak now in the hearing of the people, that they ask, every man of his neighbor and every woman of her neighbor, for silver and gold jewelry." [3] And the LORD gave the people favor in the sight of the Egyptians. Moreover, the man Moses was very great in the land of Egypt, in the sight of Pharaoh's servants and in the sight of the people.

[4] So Moses said, "Thus says the LORD: 'About midnight I will go out in the midst of Egypt, [5] and every firstborn in the land of Egypt shall die, from the firstborn of Pharaoh who sits on his throne, even to the firstborn of the slave girl who is behind the handmill, and all the firstborn of the cattle. [6] There shall be a great cry throughout all the land of Egypt, such as there has never been, nor ever will be again. [7] But not a dog shall growl against any of the people of Israel, either man or beast, that you may know that the LORD makes a distinction between Egypt and Israel.' [8] And all these your servants shall come down to me and bow down to me, saying, 'Get out, you and all the people who follow you.' And after that I will go out." And he went out from Pharaoh in hot anger. [9] Then the LORD said to Moses, "Pharaoh will not listen to you, that my wonders may be multiplied in the land of Egypt."

[10] Moses and Aaron did all these wonders before Pharaoh, and the LORD hardened Pharaoh's heart, and he did not let the people of Israel go out of his land.

The Passover

12 The LORD said to Moses and Aaron in the land of Egypt, [2] "This month shall be for you the beginning of months. It shall be the first month of the year for you. [3] Tell all the congregation of Israel that on the tenth day of this month every man shall take a lamb according to their fathers' houses, a lamb for a household. [4] And if the household is too small for a lamb, then he and his nearest neighbor shall take according to the number of persons; according to what each can eat you shall make your count for the lamb. [5] Your lamb shall be without blemish, a male a year old. You may take it from the sheep or from the goats, [6] and you shall keep it until the fourteenth day of this month, when the whole assembly of the congregation of Israel shall kill their lambs at twilight.[1]

[7] "Then they shall take some of the blood and put it on the two doorposts and the lintel of the houses in which they eat it. [8] They shall eat the flesh that night, roasted on the fire; with unleavened bread and bitter herbs they shall eat it. [9] Do not eat any of it raw or boiled in water, but roasted, its head with its legs

[1] Hebrew *between the two evenings*

and its inner parts. ¹⁰ And you shall let none of it remain until the morning; anything that remains until the morning you shall burn. ¹¹ In this manner you shall eat it: with your belt fastened, your sandals on your feet, and your staff in your hand. And you shall eat it in haste. It is the LORD's Passover. ¹² For I will pass through the land of Egypt that night, and I will strike all the firstborn in the land of Egypt, both man and beast; and on all the gods of Egypt I will execute judgments: I am the LORD. ¹³ The blood shall be a sign for you, on the houses where you are. And when I see the blood, I will pass over you, and no plague will befall you to destroy you, when I strike the land of Egypt.

¹⁴ "This day shall be for you a memorial day, and you shall keep it as a feast to the LORD; throughout your generations, as a statute forever, you shall keep it as a feast. ¹⁵ Seven days you shall eat unleavened bread. On the first day you shall remove leaven out of your houses, for if anyone eats what is leavened, from the first day until the seventh day, that person shall be cut off from Israel. ¹⁶ On the first day you shall hold a holy assembly, and on the seventh day a holy assembly. No work shall be done on those days. But what everyone needs to eat, that alone may be prepared by you. ¹⁷ And you shall observe the Feast of Unleavened Bread, for on this very day I brought your hosts out of the land of Egypt. Therefore you shall observe this day, throughout your generations, as a statute forever. ¹⁸ In the first month, from the fourteenth day of the month at evening, you shall eat unleavened bread until the twenty-first day of the month at evening. ¹⁹ For seven days no leaven is to be found in your houses. If anyone eats what is leavened, that person will be cut off from the congregation of Israel, whether he is a sojourner or a native of the land. ²⁰ You shall eat nothing leavened; in all your dwelling places you shall eat unleavened bread."

²¹ Then Moses called all the elders of Israel and said to them, "Go and select lambs for yourselves according to your clans, and kill the Passover lamb. ²² Take a bunch of hyssop and dip it in the blood that is in the basin, and touch the lintel and the two doorposts with the blood that is in the basin. None of you shall go out of the door of his house until the morning. ²³ For the LORD will pass through to strike the Egyptians, and when he sees the blood on the lintel and on the two doorposts, the LORD will pass over the door and will not allow the destroyer to enter your houses to strike you. ²⁴ You shall observe this rite as a statute for you and for your sons forever. ²⁵ And when you come to the land that the LORD will give you, as he has promised, you shall keep this service. ²⁶ And when your children say to you, 'What do you mean by this service?' ²⁷ you shall say, 'It is the sacrifice of the LORD's Passover, for he passed over the houses of the people of Israel in Egypt, when he struck the Egyptians but spared our houses.'" And the people bowed their heads and worshiped.

²⁸ Then the people of Israel went and did so; as the LORD had commanded Moses and Aaron, so they did.

The Tenth Plague: Death of the Firstborn

²⁹ At midnight the LORD struck down all the firstborn in the land of Egypt, from the firstborn of Pharaoh who sat on his throne to the firstborn of the captive who was in the dungeon, and all the firstborn of the livestock. ³⁰ And Pharaoh rose up in the night, he and all his servants and all the Egyptians. And there was a great cry in Egypt, for there was not a house where someone was not dead. ³¹ Then he summoned Moses and Aaron by night and said, "Up, go out from among my people, both you and the people of Israel; and go, serve the LORD, as you have said. ³² Take your flocks and your herds, as you have said, and be gone, and bless me also!"

The Exodus

³³ The Egyptians were urgent with the people to send them out of the land in haste. For they said, "We shall all be dead." ³⁴ So the people took their dough before it was leavened, their kneading bowls being bound up in their cloaks on their shoulders. ³⁵ The people of Israel had also done as Moses told them, for they had asked the Egyptians for silver and gold jewelry and for clothing. ³⁶ And the LORD had given the people favor in the sight of the Egyptians, so that they let them have what they asked. Thus they plundered the Egyptians.

³⁷ And the people of Israel journeyed from Rameses to Succoth, about six hundred thousand men on foot, besides women and children. ³⁸ A mixed multitude also went up with them, and very much livestock, both flocks

and herds. [39] And they baked unleavened cakes of the dough that they had brought out of Egypt, for it was not leavened, because they were thrust out of Egypt and could not wait, nor had they prepared any provisions for themselves.

[40] The time that the people of Israel lived in Egypt was 430 years. [41] At the end of 430 years, on that very day, all the hosts of the LORD went out from the land of Egypt. [42] It was a night of watching by the LORD, to bring them out of the land of Egypt; so this same night is a night of watching kept to the LORD by all the people of Israel throughout their generations.

Institution of the Passover

[43] And the LORD said to Moses and Aaron, "This is the statute of the Passover: no foreigner shall eat of it, [44] but every slave[1] that is bought for money may eat of it after you have circumcised him. [45] No foreigner or hired worker may eat of it. [46] It shall be eaten in one house; you shall not take any of the flesh outside the house, and you shall not break any of its bones. [47] All the congregation of Israel shall keep it. [48] If a stranger shall sojourn with you and would keep the Passover to the LORD, let all his males be circumcised. Then he may come near and keep it; he shall be as a native of the land. But no uncircumcised person shall eat of it. [49] There shall be one law for the native and for the stranger who sojourns among you."

[50] All the people of Israel did just as the LORD commanded Moses and Aaron. [51] And on that very day the LORD brought the people of Israel out of the land of Egypt by their hosts.

Consecration of the Firstborn

13 The LORD said to Moses, [2] "Consecrate to me all the firstborn. Whatever is the first to open the womb among the people of Israel, both of man and of beast, is mine."

The Feast of Unleavened Bread

[3] Then Moses said to the people, "Remember this day in which you came out from Egypt, out of the house of slavery, for by a strong hand the LORD brought you out from this place. No leavened bread shall be eaten. [4] Today, in the month of Abib, you are going out. [5] And when the LORD brings you into the land of the Canaanites, the Hittites, the Amorites, the Hivites, and the Jebusites, which he swore to your fathers to give you, a land flowing with milk and honey, you shall keep this service in this month. [6] Seven days you shall eat unleavened bread, and on the seventh day there shall be a feast to the LORD. [7] Unleavened bread shall be eaten for seven days; no leavened bread shall be seen with you, and no leaven shall be seen with you in all your territory. [8] You shall tell your son on that day, 'It is because of what the LORD did for me when I came out of Egypt.' [9] And it shall be to you as a sign on your hand and as a memorial between your eyes, that the law of the LORD may be in your mouth. For with a strong hand the LORD has brought you out of Egypt. [10] You shall therefore keep this statute at its appointed time from year to year.

[11] "When the LORD brings you into the land of the Canaanites, as he swore to you and your fathers, and shall give it to you, [12] you shall set apart to the LORD all that first opens the womb. All the firstborn of your animals that are males shall be the LORD's. [13] Every firstborn of a donkey you shall redeem with a lamb, or if you will not redeem it you shall break its neck. Every firstborn of man among your sons you shall redeem. [14] And when in time to come your son asks you, 'What does this mean?' you shall say to him, 'By a strong hand the LORD brought us out of Egypt, from the house of slavery. [15] For when Pharaoh stubbornly refused to let us go, the LORD killed all the firstborn in the land of Egypt, both the firstborn of man and the firstborn of animals. Therefore I sacrifice to the LORD all the males that first open the womb, but all the firstborn of my sons I redeem.' [16] It shall be as a mark on your hand or frontlets between your eyes, for by a strong hand the LORD brought us out of Egypt."

Pillars of Cloud and Fire

[17] When Pharaoh let the people go, God did not lead them by way of the land of the Philistines, although that was near. For God said, "Lest the people change their minds when they see war and return to Egypt." [18] But God led the people around by the way of the wilderness toward the Red Sea. And the people of Israel went up out of the land of Egypt equipped for battle. [19] Moses took the bones of Joseph with him, for Joseph[2] had made the sons of Israel solemnly swear, saying, "God will surely visit you, and you shall carry up my bones with

---

[1] Or *servant*; the Hebrew term *'ebed* designates a range of social and economic roles (see Preface) [2] Samaritan, Septuagint; Hebrew *he*

you from here." ²⁰ And they moved on from Succoth and encamped at Etham, on the edge of the wilderness. ²¹ And the LORD went before them by day in a pillar of cloud to lead them along the way, and by night in a pillar of fire to give them light, that they might travel by day and by night. ²² The pillar of cloud by day and the pillar of fire by night did not depart from before the people.

Crossing the Red Sea

14 Then the LORD said to Moses, ² "Tell the people of Israel to turn back and encamp in front of Pi-hahiroth, between Migdol and the sea, in front of Baal-zephon; you shall encamp facing it, by the sea. ³ For Pharaoh will say of the people of Israel, 'They are wandering in the land; the wilderness has shut them in.' ⁴ And I will harden Pharaoh's heart, and he will pursue them, and I will get glory over Pharaoh and all his host, and the Egyptians shall know that I am the LORD." And they did so.

⁵ When the king of Egypt was told that the people had fled, the mind of Pharaoh and his servants was changed toward the people, and they said, "What is this we have done, that we have let Israel go from serving us?" ⁶ So he made ready his chariot and took his army with him, ⁷ and took six hundred chosen chariots and all the other chariots of Egypt with officers over all of them. ⁸ And the LORD hardened the heart of Pharaoh king of Egypt, and he pursued the people of Israel while the people of Israel were going out defiantly. ⁹ The Egyptians pursued them, all Pharaoh's horses and chariots and his horsemen and his army, and overtook them encamped at the sea, by Pi-hahiroth, in front of Baal-zephon.

¹⁰ When Pharaoh drew near, the people of Israel lifted up their eyes, and behold, the Egyptians were marching after them, and they feared greatly. And the people of Israel cried out to the LORD. ¹¹ They said to Moses, "Is it because there are no graves in Egypt that you have taken us away to die in the wilderness? What have you done to us in bringing us out of Egypt? ¹² Is not this what we said to you in Egypt: 'Leave us alone that we may serve the Egyptians'? For it would have been better for us to serve the Egyptians than to die in the wilderness." ¹³ And Moses said to the people, "Fear not, stand firm, and see the salvation of the LORD, which he will work for you today. For the Egyptians whom you see today, you shall never see again. ¹⁴ The LORD will fight for you, and you have only to be silent."

¹⁵ The LORD said to Moses, "Why do you cry to me? Tell the people of Israel to go forward. ¹⁶ Lift up your staff, and stretch out your hand over the sea and divide it, that the people of Israel may go through the sea on dry ground. ¹⁷ And I will harden the hearts of the Egyptians so that they shall go in after them, and I will get glory over Pharaoh and all his host, his chariots, and his horsemen. ¹⁸ And the Egyptians shall know that I am the LORD, when I have gotten glory over Pharaoh, his chariots, and his horsemen."

¹⁹ Then the angel of God who was going before the host of Israel moved and went behind them, and the pillar of cloud moved from before them and stood behind them, ²⁰ coming between the host of Egypt and the host of Israel. And there was the cloud and the darkness. And it lit up the night[1] without one coming near the other all night.

²¹ Then Moses stretched out his hand over the sea, and the LORD drove the sea back by a strong east wind all night and made the sea dry land, and the waters were divided. ²² And the people of Israel went into the midst of the sea on dry ground, the waters being a wall to them on their right hand and on their left. ²³ The Egyptians pursued and went in after them into the midst of the sea, all Pharaoh's horses, his chariots, and his horsemen. ²⁴ And in the morning watch the LORD in the pillar of fire and of cloud looked down on the Egyptian forces and threw the Egyptian forces into a panic, ²⁵ clogging[2] their chariot wheels so that they drove heavily. And the Egyptians said, "Let us flee from before Israel, for the LORD fights for them against the Egyptians."

²⁶ Then the LORD said to Moses, "Stretch out your hand over the sea, that the water may come back upon the Egyptians, upon their chariots, and upon their horsemen." ²⁷ So Moses stretched out his hand over the sea, and the sea returned to its normal course when the morning appeared. And as the Egyptians fled into it, the LORD threw[3] the Egyptians into the midst of the sea. ²⁸ The waters returned and covered the chariots and the horsemen; of all the host of Pharaoh that had followed them into the sea, not one of them remained. ²⁹ But the people of Israel walked on dry ground through the sea, the waters being a wall to them on their right hand and on their left.

---

[1] Septuagint *and the night passed* [2] Or *binding* (compare Samaritan, Septuagint, Syriac); Hebrew *removing* [3] Hebrew *shook off*

[30] Thus the LORD saved Israel that day from the hand of the Egyptians, and Israel saw the Egyptians dead on the seashore. [31] Israel saw the great power that the LORD used against the Egyptians, so the people feared the LORD, and they believed in the LORD and in his servant Moses.

The Song of Moses

15 Then Moses and the people of Israel sang this song to the LORD, saying,

"I will sing to the LORD, for he has triumphed gloriously;
     the horse and his rider[1] he has thrown into the sea.
[2] The LORD is my strength and my song,
     and he has become my salvation;
this is my God, and I will praise him,
     my father's God, and I will exalt him.
[3] The LORD is a man of war;
     the LORD is his name.

[4] "Pharaoh's chariots and his host he cast into the sea,
     and his chosen officers were sunk in the Red Sea.
[5] The floods covered them;
     they went down into the depths like a stone.
[6] Your right hand, O LORD, glorious in power,
     your right hand, O LORD, shatters the enemy.
[7] In the greatness of your majesty you overthrow your adversaries;
     you send out your fury; it consumes them like stubble.
[8] At the blast of your nostrils the waters piled up;
     the floods stood up in a heap;
     the deeps congealed in the heart of the sea.
[9] The enemy said, 'I will pursue, I will overtake,
     I will divide the spoil, my desire shall have its fill of them.
     I will draw my sword; my hand shall destroy them.'
[10] You blew with your wind; the sea covered them;
     they sank like lead in the mighty waters.

[11] "Who is like you, O LORD, among the gods?
     Who is like you, majestic in holiness,
awesome in glorious deeds, doing wonders?
[12] You stretched out your right hand;
     the earth swallowed them.

[13] "You have led in your steadfast love the people whom you have redeemed;
     you have guided them by your strength to your holy abode.
[14] The peoples have heard; they tremble;
     pangs have seized the inhabitants of Philistia.
[15] Now are the chiefs of Edom dismayed;
     trembling seizes the leaders of Moab;
     all the inhabitants of Canaan have melted away.
[16] Terror and dread fall upon them;
     because of the greatness of your arm, they are still as a stone,
till your people, O LORD, pass by,
     till the people pass by whom you have purchased.
[17] You will bring them in and plant them on your own mountain,
     the place, O LORD, which you have made for your abode,
     the sanctuary, O Lord, which your hands have established.
[18] The LORD will reign forever and ever."

[19] For when the horses of Pharaoh with his chariots and his horsemen went into the sea, the LORD brought back the waters of the sea upon them, but the people of Israel walked on dry ground in the midst of the sea. [20] Then Miriam the prophetess, the sister of Aaron, took a tambourine in her hand, and all the women went out after her with tambourines and dancing. [21] And Miriam sang to them:

"Sing to the LORD, for he has triumphed gloriously;
     the horse and his rider he has thrown into the sea."

Bitter Water Made Sweet

[22] Then Moses made Israel set out from the Red Sea, and they went into the wilderness of Shur. They went three days in the wilderness and found no water. [23] When they came to Marah, they could not drink the water of Marah because it was bitter; therefore it was named Marah.[2] [24] And the people grumbled against Moses, saying, "What shall we drink?" [25] And he cried to the LORD, and the LORD showed him

[1] Or its chariot; also verse 21 [2] Marah means bitterness

a log,[1] and he threw it into the water, and the water became sweet.

There the LORD[2] made for them a statute and a rule, and there he tested them, [26] saying, "If you will diligently listen to the voice of the LORD your God, and do that which is right in his eyes, and give ear to his commandments and keep all his statutes, I will put none of the diseases on you that I put on the Egyptians, for I am the LORD, your healer."

[27] Then they came to Elim, where there were twelve springs of water and seventy palm trees, and they encamped there by the water.

Bread from Heaven

16 They set out from Elim, and all the congregation of the people of Israel came to the wilderness of Sin, which is between Elim and Sinai, on the fifteenth day of the second month after they had departed from the land of Egypt. [2] And the whole congregation of the people of Israel grumbled against Moses and Aaron in the wilderness, [3] and the people of Israel said to them, "Would that we had died by the hand of the LORD in the land of Egypt, when we sat by the meat pots and ate bread to the full, for you have brought us out into this wilderness to kill this whole assembly with hunger."

[4] Then the LORD said to Moses, "Behold, I am about to rain bread from heaven for you, and the people shall go out and gather a day's portion every day, that I may test them, whether they will walk in my law or not. [5] On the sixth day, when they prepare what they bring in, it will be twice as much as they gather daily." [6] So Moses and Aaron said to all the people of Israel, "At evening you shall know that it was the LORD who brought you out of the land of Egypt, [7] and in the morning you shall see the glory of the LORD, because he has heard your grumbling against the LORD. For what are we, that you grumble against us?" [8] And Moses said, "When the LORD gives you in the evening meat to eat and in the morning bread to the full, because the LORD has heard your grumbling that you grumble against him—what are we? Your grumbling is not against us but against the LORD."

[9] Then Moses said to Aaron, "Say to the whole congregation of the people of Israel, 'Come near before the LORD, for he has heard your grumbling.'" [10] And as soon as Aaron spoke to the whole congregation of the people of Israel, they looked toward the wilderness, and behold, the glory of the LORD appeared in the cloud. [11] And the LORD said to Moses, [12] "I have heard the grumbling of the people of Israel. Say to them, 'At twilight you shall eat meat, and in the morning you shall be filled with bread. Then you shall know that I am the LORD your God.'"

[13] In the evening quail came up and covered the camp, and in the morning dew lay around the camp. [14] And when the dew had gone up, there was on the face of the wilderness a fine, flake-like thing, fine as frost on the ground. [15] When the people of Israel saw it, they said to one another, "What is it?"[3] For they did not know what it was. And Moses said to them, "It is the bread that the LORD has given you to eat. [16] This is what the LORD has commanded: 'Gather of it, each one of you, as much as he can eat. You shall each take an omer,[4] according to the number of the persons that each of you has in his tent.'" [17] And the people of Israel did so. They gathered, some more, some less. [18] But when they measured it with an omer, whoever gathered much had nothing left over, and whoever gathered little had no lack. Each of them gathered as much as he could eat. [19] And Moses said to them, "Let no one leave any of it over till the morning." [20] But they did not listen to Moses. Some left part of it till the morning, and it bred worms and stank. And Moses was angry with them. [21] Morning by morning they gathered it, each as much as he could eat; but when the sun grew hot, it melted.

[22] On the sixth day they gathered twice as much bread, two omers each. And when all the leaders of the congregation came and told Moses, [23] he said to them, "This is what the LORD has commanded: 'Tomorrow is a day of solemn rest, a holy Sabbath to the LORD; bake what you will bake and boil what you will boil, and all that is left over lay aside to be kept till the morning.'" [24] So they laid it aside till the morning, as Moses commanded them, and it did not stink, and there were no worms in it. [25] Moses said, "Eat it today, for today is a Sabbath to the LORD; today you will not find it in the field. [26] Six days you shall gather it, but on the seventh day, which is a Sabbath, there will be none."

[27] On the seventh day some of the people went out to gather, but they found none.

---

[1] Or tree [2] Hebrew he [3] Or "It is manna"; Hebrew man hu [4] An omer was about 2 quarts or 2 liters

²⁸ And the LORD said to Moses, "How long will you refuse to keep my commandments and my laws? ²⁹ See! The LORD has given you the Sabbath; therefore on the sixth day he gives you bread for two days. Remain each of you in his place; let no one go out of his place on the seventh day." ³⁰ So the people rested on the seventh day.

³¹ Now the house of Israel called its name manna. It was like coriander seed, white, and the taste of it was like wafers made with honey. ³² Moses said, "This is what the LORD has commanded: 'Let an omer of it be kept throughout your generations, so that they may see the bread with which I fed you in the wilderness, when I brought you out of the land of Egypt.'" ³³ And Moses said to Aaron, "Take a jar, and put an omer of manna in it, and place it before the LORD to be kept throughout your generations." ³⁴ As the LORD commanded Moses, so Aaron placed it before the testimony to be kept. ³⁵ The people of Israel ate the manna forty years, till they came to a habitable land. They ate the manna till they came to the border of the land of Canaan. ³⁶ (An omer is the tenth part of an ephah.)[1]

Water from the Rock

17 All the congregation of the people of Israel moved on from the wilderness of Sin by stages, according to the commandment of the LORD, and camped at Rephidim, but there was no water for the people to drink. ² Therefore the people quarreled with Moses and said, "Give us water to drink." And Moses said to them, "Why do you quarrel with me? Why do you test the LORD?" ³ But the people thirsted there for water, and the people grumbled against Moses and said, "Why did you bring us up out of Egypt, to kill us and our children and our livestock with thirst?" ⁴ So Moses cried to the LORD, "What shall I do with this people? They are almost ready to stone me." ⁵ And the LORD said to Moses, "Pass on before the people, taking with you some of the elders of Israel, and take in your hand the staff with which you struck the Nile, and go. ⁶ Behold, I will stand before you there on the rock at Horeb, and you shall strike the rock, and water shall come out of it, and the people will drink." And Moses did so, in the sight of the elders of Israel. ⁷ And he called the name of the place Massah[2] and Meribah,[3] because of the quarreling of the people of Israel, and because they tested the LORD by saying, "Is the LORD among us or not?"

Israel Defeats Amalek

⁸ Then Amalek came and fought with Israel at Rephidim. ⁹ So Moses said to Joshua, "Choose for us men, and go out and fight with Amalek. Tomorrow I will stand on the top of the hill with the staff of God in my hand." ¹⁰ So Joshua did as Moses told him, and fought with Amalek, while Moses, Aaron, and Hur went up to the top of the hill. ¹¹ Whenever Moses held up his hand, Israel prevailed, and whenever he lowered his hand, Amalek prevailed. ¹² But Moses' hands grew weary, so they took a stone and put it under him, and he sat on it, while Aaron and Hur held up his hands, one on one side, and the other on the other side. So his hands were steady until the going down of the sun. ¹³ And Joshua overwhelmed Amalek and his people with the sword.

¹⁴ Then the LORD said to Moses, "Write this as a memorial in a book and recite it in the ears of Joshua, that I will utterly blot out the memory of Amalek from under heaven." ¹⁵ And Moses built an altar and called the name of it, The LORD Is My Banner, ¹⁶ saying, "A hand upon the throne[4] of the LORD! The LORD will have war with Amalek from generation to generation."

Jethro's Advice

18 Jethro, the priest of Midian, Moses' father-in-law, heard of all that God had done for Moses and for Israel his people, how the LORD had brought Israel out of Egypt. ² Now Jethro, Moses' father-in-law, had taken Zipporah, Moses' wife, after he had sent her home, ³ along with her two sons. The name of the one was Gershom (for he said, "I have been a sojourner[5] in a foreign land"), ⁴ and the name of the other, Eliezer[6] (for he said, "The God of my father was my help, and delivered me from the sword of Pharaoh"). ⁵ Jethro, Moses' father-in-law, came with his sons and his wife to Moses in the wilderness where he was encamped at the mountain of God. ⁶ And when he sent word to Moses, "I,[7] your father-in-law Jethro, am coming to you with your wife and her two sons with her," ⁷ Moses went out to meet his father-in-law and bowed down and kissed him. And they asked each other of their welfare and went into

---

[1] An ephah was about 3/5 bushel or 22 liters [2] Massah means testing [3] Meribah means quarreling [4] A slight change would yield upon the banner [5] Gershom sounds like the Hebrew for sojourner [6] Eliezer means My God is help [7] Hebrew; Samaritan, Septuagint, Syriac behold

the tent. [8] Then Moses told his father-in-law all that the LORD had done to Pharaoh and to the Egyptians for Israel's sake, all the hardship that had come upon them in the way, and how the LORD had delivered them. [9] And Jethro rejoiced for all the good that the LORD had done to Israel, in that he had delivered them out of the hand of the Egyptians.

[10] Jethro said, "Blessed be the LORD, who has delivered you out of the hand of the Egyptians and out of the hand of Pharaoh and has delivered the people from under the hand of the Egyptians. [11] Now I know that the LORD is greater than all gods, because in this affair they dealt arrogantly with the people."[1] [12] And Jethro, Moses' father-in-law, brought a burnt offering and sacrifices to God; and Aaron came with all the elders of Israel to eat bread with Moses' father-in-law before God.

[13] The next day Moses sat to judge the people, and the people stood around Moses from morning till evening. [14] When Moses' father-in-law saw all that he was doing for the people, he said, "What is this that you are doing for the people? Why do you sit alone, and all the people stand around you from morning till evening?" [15] And Moses said to his father-in-law, "Because the people come to me to inquire of God; [16] when they have a dispute, they come to me and I decide between one person and another, and I make them know the statutes of God and his laws." [17] Moses' father-in-law said to him, "What you are doing is not good. [18] You and the people with you will certainly wear yourselves out, for the thing is too heavy for you. You are not able to do it alone. [19] Now obey my voice; I will give you advice, and God be with you! You shall represent the people before God and bring their cases to God, [20] and you shall warn them about the statutes and the laws, and make them know the way in which they must walk and what they must do. [21] Moreover, look for able men from all the people, men who fear God, who are trustworthy and hate a bribe, and place such men over the people as chiefs of thousands, of hundreds, of fifties, and of tens. [22] And let them judge the people at all times. Every great matter they shall bring to you, but any small matter they shall decide themselves. So it will be easier for you, and they will bear the burden with you. [23] If you do this, God will direct you, you will be able to endure, and all this people also will go to their place in peace."

[24] So Moses listened to the voice of his father-in-law and did all that he had said. [25] Moses chose able men out of all Israel and made them heads over the people, chiefs of thousands, of hundreds, of fifties, and of tens. [26] And they judged the people at all times. Any hard case they brought to Moses, but any small matter they decided themselves. [27] Then Moses let his father-in-law depart, and he went away to his own country.

Israel at Mount Sinai

19 On the third new moon after the people of Israel had gone out of the land of Egypt, on that day they came into the wilderness of Sinai. [2] They set out from Rephidim and came into the wilderness of Sinai, and they encamped in the wilderness. There Israel encamped before the mountain, [3] while Moses went up to God. The LORD called to him out of the mountain, saying, "Thus you shall say to the house of Jacob, and tell the people of Israel: [4] 'You yourselves have seen what I did to the Egyptians, and how I bore you on eagles' wings and brought you to myself. [5] Now therefore, if you will indeed obey my voice and keep my covenant, you shall be my treasured possession among all peoples, for all the earth is mine; [6] and you shall be to me a kingdom of priests and a holy nation.' These are the words that you shall speak to the people of Israel."

[7] So Moses came and called the elders of the people and set before them all these words that the LORD had commanded him. [8] All the people answered together and said, "All that the LORD has spoken we will do." And Moses reported the words of the people to the LORD. [9] And the LORD said to Moses, "Behold, I am coming to you in a thick cloud, that the people may hear when I speak with you, and may also believe you forever."

When Moses told the words of the people to the LORD, [10] the LORD said to Moses, "Go to the people and consecrate them today and tomorrow, and let them wash their garments [11] and be ready for the third day. For on the third day the LORD will come down on Mount Sinai in the sight of all the people. [12] And you shall set limits for the people all around, saying, 'Take care not to go up into the mountain or touch the edge of it. Whoever touches the mountain shall be put to death. [13] No hand shall touch him, but he shall be stoned or shot;[2] whether beast or man,

---

[1] Hebrew *with them* [2] That is, shot with an arrow

he shall not live.' When the trumpet sounds a long blast, they shall come up to the mountain." [14] So Moses went down from the mountain to the people and consecrated the people; and they washed their garments. [15] And he said to the people, "Be ready for the third day; do not go near a woman."

[16] On the morning of the third day there were thunders and lightnings and a thick cloud on the mountain and a very loud trumpet blast, so that all the people in the camp trembled. [17] Then Moses brought the people out of the camp to meet God, and they took their stand at the foot of the mountain. [18] Now Mount Sinai was wrapped in smoke because the LORD had descended on it in fire. The smoke of it went up like the smoke of a kiln, and the whole mountain trembled greatly. [19] And as the sound of the trumpet grew louder and louder, Moses spoke, and God answered him in thunder. [20] The LORD came down on Mount Sinai, to the top of the mountain. And the LORD called Moses to the top of the mountain, and Moses went up.

[21] And the LORD said to Moses, "Go down and warn the people, lest they break through to the LORD to look and many of them perish. [22] Also let the priests who come near to the LORD consecrate themselves, lest the LORD break out against them." [23] And Moses said to the LORD, "The people cannot come up to Mount Sinai, for you yourself warned us, saying, 'Set limits around the mountain and consecrate it.'" [24] And the LORD said to him, "Go down, and come up bringing Aaron with you. But do not let the priests and the people break through to come up to the LORD, lest he break out against them." [25] So Moses went down to the people and told them.

The Ten Commandments

20 And God spoke all these words, saying, [2] "I am the LORD your God, who brought you out of the land of Egypt, out of the house of slavery.

[3] "You shall have no other gods before[1] me.

[4] "You shall not make for yourself a carved image, or any likeness of anything that is in heaven above, or that is in the earth beneath, or that is in the water under the earth. [5] You shall not bow down to them or serve them, for I the LORD your God am a jealous God, visiting the iniquity of the fathers on the children to the third and the fourth generation of those who hate me, [6] but showing steadfast love to thousands[2] of those who love me and keep my commandments.

[7] "You shall not take the name of the LORD your God in vain, for the LORD will not hold him guiltless who takes his name in vain.

[8] "Remember the Sabbath day, to keep it holy. [9] Six days you shall labor, and do all your work, [10] but the seventh day is a Sabbath to the LORD your God. On it you shall not do any work, you, or your son, or your daughter, your male servant, or your female servant, or your livestock, or the sojourner who is within your gates. [11] For in six days the LORD made heaven and earth, the sea, and all that is in them, and rested on the seventh day. Therefore the LORD blessed the Sabbath day and made it holy.

[12] "Honor your father and your mother, that your days may be long in the land that the LORD your God is giving you.

[13] "You shall not murder.[3]

[14] "You shall not commit adultery.

[15] "You shall not steal.

[16] "You shall not bear false witness against your neighbor.

[17] "You shall not covet your neighbor's house; you shall not covet your neighbor's wife, or his male servant, or his female servant, or his ox, or his donkey, or anything that is your neighbor's."

[18] Now when all the people saw the thunder and the flashes of lightning and the sound of the trumpet and the mountain smoking, the people were afraid[4] and trembled, and they stood far off [19] and said to Moses, "You speak to us, and we will listen; but do not let God speak to us, lest we die." [20] Moses said to the people, "Do not fear, for God has come to test you, that the fear of him may be before you, that you may not sin." [21] The people stood far off, while Moses drew near to the thick darkness where God was.

Laws About Altars

[22] And the LORD said to Moses, "Thus you shall say to the people of Israel: 'You have seen for yourselves that I have talked with you from heaven. [23] You shall not make gods of silver to be with me, nor shall you make for yourselves gods of gold. [24] An altar of earth you shall make

---

[1] Or besides [2] Or to the thousandth generation [3] The Hebrew word also covers causing human death through carelessness or negligence [4] Samaritan, Septuagint, Syriac, Vulgate; Masoretic Text the people saw

for me and sacrifice on it your burnt offerings and your peace offerings, your sheep and your oxen. In every place where I cause my name to be remembered I will come to you and bless you. [25] If you make me an altar of stone, you shall not build it of hewn stones, for if you wield your tool on it you profane it. [26] And you shall not go up by steps to my altar, that your nakedness be not exposed on it.'

Laws About Slaves

21 "Now these are the rules that you shall set before them. [2] When you buy a Hebrew slave,[1] he shall serve six years, and in the seventh he shall go out free, for nothing. [3] If he comes in single, he shall go out single; if he comes in married, then his wife shall go out with him. [4] If his master gives him a wife and she bears him sons or daughters, the wife and her children shall be her master's, and he shall go out alone. [5] But if the slave plainly says, 'I love my master, my wife, and my children; I will not go out free,' [6] then his master shall bring him to God, and he shall bring him to the door or the doorpost. And his master shall bore his ear through with an awl, and he shall be his slave forever.

[7] "When a man sells his daughter as a slave, she shall not go out as the male slaves do. [8] If she does not please her master, who has designated her[2] for himself, then he shall let her be redeemed. He shall have no right to sell her to a foreign people, since he has broken faith with her. [9] If he designates her for his son, he shall deal with her as with a daughter. [10] If he takes another wife to himself, he shall not diminish her food, her clothing, or her marital rights. [11] And if he does not do these three things for her, she shall go out for nothing, without payment of money.

[12] "Whoever strikes a man so that he dies shall be put to death. [13] But if he did not lie in wait for him, but God let him fall into his hand, then I will appoint for you a place to which he may flee. [14] But if a man willfully attacks another to kill him by cunning, you shall take him from my altar, that he may die.

[15] "Whoever strikes his father or his mother shall be put to death.

[16] "Whoever steals a man and sells him, and anyone found in possession of him, shall be put to death.

[17] "Whoever curses[3] his father or his mother shall be put to death.

[18] "When men quarrel and one strikes the other with a stone or with his fist and the man does not die but takes to his bed, [19] then if the man rises again and walks outdoors with his staff, he who struck him shall be clear; only he shall pay for the loss of his time, and shall have him thoroughly healed.

[20] "When a man strikes his slave, male or female, with a rod and the slave dies under his hand, he shall be avenged. [21] But if the slave survives a day or two, he is not to be avenged, for the slave is his money.

[22] "When men strive together and hit a pregnant woman, so that her children come out, but there is no harm, the one who hit her shall surely be fined, as the woman's husband shall impose on him, and he shall pay as the judges determine. [23] But if there is harm,[4] then you shall pay life for life, [24] eye for eye, tooth for tooth, hand for hand, foot for foot, [25] burn for burn, wound for wound, stripe for stripe.

[26] "When a man strikes the eye of his slave, male or female, and destroys it, he shall let the slave go free because of his eye. [27] If he knocks out the tooth of his slave, male or female, he shall let the slave go free because of his tooth.

[28] "When an ox gores a man or a woman to death, the ox shall be stoned, and its flesh shall not be eaten, but the owner of the ox shall not be liable. [29] But if the ox has been accustomed to gore in the past, and its owner has been warned but has not kept it in, and it kills a man or a woman, the ox shall be stoned, and its owner also shall be put to death. [30] If a ransom is imposed on him, then he shall give for the redemption of his life whatever is imposed on him. [31] If it gores a man's son or daughter, he shall be dealt with according to this same rule. [32] If the ox gores a slave, male or female, the owner shall give to their master thirty shekels[5] of silver, and the ox shall be stoned.

Laws About Restitution

[33] "When a man opens a pit, or when a man digs a pit and does not cover it, and an ox or a donkey falls into it, [34] the owner of the pit shall make restoration. He shall give money to its owner, and the dead beast shall be his.

[35] "When one man's ox butts another's, so that it dies, then they shall sell the live ox and

---

[1] Or servant; the Hebrew term 'ebed designates a range of social and economic roles; also verses 5, 6, 7, 20, 21, 26, 27, 32 (see Preface) [2] Or so that he has not designated her [3] Or dishonors; Septuagint reviles [4] Or so that her children come out and it is clear who was to blame, he shall be fined as the woman's husband shall impose on him, and he alone shall pay. [23] If it is unclear who was to blame ... [5] A shekel was about 2/5 ounce or 11 grams

share its price, and the dead beast also they shall share. **36** Or if it is known that the ox has been accustomed to gore in the past, and its owner has not kept it in, he shall repay ox for ox, and the dead beast shall be his.

22 **1** "If a man steals an ox or a sheep, and kills it or sells it, he shall repay five oxen for an ox, and four sheep for a sheep. **2** If a thief is found breaking in and is struck so that he dies, there shall be no bloodguilt for him, **3** but if the sun has risen on him, there shall be bloodguilt for him. He[3] shall surely pay. If he has nothing, then he shall be sold for his theft. **4** If the stolen beast is found alive in his possession, whether it is an ox or a donkey or a sheep, he shall pay double.

5 "If a man causes a field or vineyard to be grazed over, or lets his beast loose and it feeds in another man's field, he shall make restitution from the best in his own field and in his own vineyard.

6 "If fire breaks out and catches in thorns so that the stacked grain or the standing grain or the field is consumed, he who started the fire shall make full restitution.

7 "If a man gives to his neighbor money or goods to keep safe, and it is stolen from the man's house, then, if the thief is found, he shall pay double. **8** If the thief is not found, the owner of the house shall come near to God to show whether or not he has put his hand to his neighbor's property. **9** For every breach of trust, whether it is for an ox, for a donkey, for a sheep, for a cloak, or for any kind of lost thing, of which one says, 'This is it,' the case of both parties shall come before God. The one whom God condemns shall pay double to his neighbor.

10 "If a man gives to his neighbor a donkey or an ox or a sheep or any beast to keep safe, and it dies or is injured or is driven away, without anyone seeing it, **11** an oath by the LORD shall be between them both to see whether or not he has put his hand to his neighbor's property. The owner shall accept the oath, and he shall not make restitution. **12** But if it is stolen from him, he shall make restitution to its owner. **13** If it is torn by beasts, let him bring it as evidence. He shall not make restitution for what has been torn.

14 "If a man borrows anything of his neighbor, and it is injured or dies, the owner not being with it, he shall make full restitution. **15** If the owner was with it, he shall not make restitution; if it was hired, it came for its hiring fee.[4]

Laws About Social Justice

16 "If a man seduces a virgin[5] who is not betrothed and lies with her, he shall give the bride-price[6] for her and make her his wife. **17** If her father utterly refuses to give her to him, he shall pay money equal to the bride-price for virgins.

18 "You shall not permit a sorceress to live.

19 "Whoever lies with an animal shall be put to death.

20 "Whoever sacrifices to any god, other than the LORD alone, shall be devoted to destruction.[7]

21 "You shall not wrong a sojourner or oppress him, for you were sojourners in the land of Egypt. **22** You shall not mistreat any widow or fatherless child. **23** If you do mistreat them, and they cry out to me, I will surely hear their cry, **24** and my wrath will burn, and I will kill you with the sword, and your wives shall become widows and your children fatherless.

25 "If you lend money to any of my people with you who is poor, you shall not be like a moneylender to him, and you shall not exact interest from him. **26** If ever you take your neighbor's cloak in pledge, you shall return it to him before the sun goes down, **27** for that is his only covering, and it is his cloak for his body; in what else shall he sleep? And if he cries to me, I will hear, for I am compassionate.

28 "You shall not revile God, nor curse a ruler of your people.

29 "You shall not delay to offer from the fullness of your harvest and from the outflow of your presses. The firstborn of your sons you shall give to me. **30** You shall do the same with your oxen and with your sheep: seven days it shall be with its mother; on the eighth day you shall give it to me.

31 "You shall be consecrated to me. Therefore you shall not eat any flesh that is torn by beasts in the field; you shall throw it to the dogs.

23 "You shall not spread a false report. You shall not join hands with a wicked man to be a malicious witness. **2** You shall not fall in with the many to do evil, nor shall you bear witness in a lawsuit, siding with the many, so as to pervert justice, **3** nor shall you be partial to a poor man in his lawsuit.

---

[1] Ch 21:37 in Hebrew   [2] Ch 22:1 in Hebrew   [3] That is, the thief   [4] Or it is reckoned in (Hebrew comes into) its hiring fee   [5] Or a girl of marriageable age; also verse 17
[6] Or engagement present; also verse 17   [7] That is, set apart (devoted) as an offering to the Lord (for destruction)

⁴ "If you meet your enemy's ox or his donkey going astray, you shall bring it back to him. ⁵ If you see the donkey of one who hates you lying down under its burden, you shall refrain from leaving him with it; you shall rescue it with him.

⁶ "You shall not pervert the justice due to your poor in his lawsuit. ⁷ Keep far from a false charge, and do not kill the innocent and righteous, for I will not acquit the wicked. ⁸ And you shall take no bribe, for a bribe blinds the clear-sighted and subverts the cause of those who are in the right.

⁹ "You shall not oppress a sojourner. You know the heart of a sojourner, for you were sojourners in the land of Egypt.

Laws About the Sabbath and Festivals

¹⁰ "For six years you shall sow your land and gather in its yield, ¹¹ but the seventh year you shall let it rest and lie fallow, that the poor of your people may eat; and what they leave the beasts of the field may eat. You shall do likewise with your vineyard, and with your olive orchard.

¹² "Six days you shall do your work, but on the seventh day you shall rest; that your ox and your donkey may have rest, and the son of your servant woman, and the alien, may be refreshed.

¹³ "Pay attention to all that I have said to you, and make no mention of the names of other gods, nor let it be heard on your lips.

¹⁴ "Three times in the year you shall keep a feast to me. ¹⁵ You shall keep the Feast of Unleavened Bread. As I commanded you, you shall eat unleavened bread for seven days at the appointed time in the month of Abib, for in it you came out of Egypt. None shall appear before me empty-handed. ¹⁶ You shall keep the Feast of Harvest, of the firstfruits of your labor, of what you sow in the field. You shall keep the Feast of Ingathering at the end of the year, when you gather in from the field the fruit of your labor. ¹⁷ Three times in the year shall all your males appear before the Lord GOD.

¹⁸ "You shall not offer the blood of my sacrifice with anything leavened, or let the fat of my feast remain until the morning.

¹⁹ "The best of the firstfruits of your ground you shall bring into the house of the LORD your God.

"You shall not boil a young goat in its mother's milk.

Conquest of Canaan Promised

²⁰ "Behold, I send an angel before you to guard you on the way and to bring you to the place that I have prepared. ²¹ Pay careful attention to him and obey his voice; do not rebel against him, for he will not pardon your transgression, for my name is in him. ²² "But if you carefully obey his voice and do all that I say, then I will be an enemy to your enemies and an adversary to your adversaries. ²³ "When my angel goes before you and brings you to the Amorites and the Hittites and the Perizzites and the Canaanites, the Hivites and the Jebusites, and I blot them out, ²⁴ you shall not bow down to their gods nor serve them, nor do as they do, but you shall utterly overthrow them and break their pillars in pieces. ²⁵ You shall serve the LORD your God, and he¹ will bless your bread and your water, and I will take sickness away from among you. ²⁶ None shall miscarry or be barren in your land; I will fulfill the number of your days. ²⁷ I will send my terror before you and will throw into confusion all the people against whom you shall come, and I will make all your enemies turn their backs to you. ²⁸ And I will send hornets² before you, which shall drive out the Hivites, the Canaanites, and the Hittites from before you. ²⁹ I will not drive them out from before you in one year, lest the land become desolate and the wild beasts multiply against you. ³⁰ Little by little I will drive them out from before you, until you have increased and possess the land. ³¹ And I will set your border from the Red Sea to the Sea of the Philistines, and from the wilderness to the Euphrates,³ for I will give the inhabitants of the land into your hand, and you shall drive them out before you. ³² You shall make no covenant with them and their gods. ³³ They shall not dwell in your land, lest they make you sin against me; for if you serve their gods, it will surely be a snare to you."

The Covenant Confirmed

24 Then he said to Moses, "Come up to the LORD, you and Aaron, Nadab, and Abihu, and seventy of the elders of Israel, and worship from afar. ² Moses alone shall come near to the LORD, but the others shall not come near, and the people shall not come up with him."

¹ Septuagint, Vulgate / ² Or the hornet ³ Hebrew the River

³Moses came and told the people all the words of the LORD and all the rules.¹ And all the people answered with one voice and said, "All the words that the LORD has spoken we will do." ⁴And Moses wrote down all the words of the LORD. He rose early in the morning and built an altar at the foot of the mountain, and twelve pillars, according to the twelve tribes of Israel. ⁵And he sent young men of the people of Israel, who offered burnt offerings and sacrificed peace offerings of oxen to the LORD. ⁶And Moses took half of the blood and put it in basins, and half of the blood he threw against the altar. ⁷Then he took the Book of the Covenant and read it in the hearing of the people. And they said, "All that the LORD has spoken we will do, and we will be obedient." ⁸And Moses took the blood and threw it on the people and said, "Behold the blood of the covenant that the LORD has made with you in accordance with all these words."

⁹Then Moses and Aaron, Nadab, and Abihu, and seventy of the elders of Israel went up, ¹⁰and they saw the God of Israel. There was under his feet as it were a pavement of sapphire stone, like the very heaven for clearness. ¹¹And he did not lay his hand on the chief men of the people of Israel; they beheld God, and ate and drank.

¹²The LORD said to Moses, "Come up to me on the mountain and wait there, that I may give you the tablets of stone, with the law and the commandment, which I have written for their instruction." ¹³So Moses rose with his assistant Joshua, and Moses went up into the mountain of God. ¹⁴And he said to the elders, "Wait here for us until we return to you. And behold, Aaron and Hur are with you. Whoever has a dispute, let him go to them."

¹⁵Then Moses went up on the mountain, and the cloud covered the mountain. ¹⁶The glory of the LORD dwelt on Mount Sinai, and the cloud covered it six days. And on the seventh day he called to Moses out of the midst of the cloud. ¹⁷Now the appearance of the glory of the LORD was like a devouring fire on the top of the mountain in the sight of the people of Israel. ¹⁸Moses entered the cloud and went up on the mountain. And Moses was on the mountain forty days and forty nights.

Contributions for the Sanctuary

25 The LORD said to Moses, ²"Speak to the people of Israel, that they take for me a contribution. From every man whose heart moves him you shall receive the contribution for me. ³And this is the contribution that you shall receive from them: gold, silver, and bronze, ⁴blue and purple and scarlet yarns and fine twined linen, goats' hair, ⁵tanned rams' skins, goatskins,² acacia wood, ⁶oil for the lamps, spices for the anointing oil and for the fragrant incense, ⁷onyx stones, and stones for setting, for the ephod and for the breastpiece. ⁸And let them make me a sanctuary, that I may dwell in their midst. ⁹Exactly as I show you concerning the pattern of the tabernacle, and of all its furniture, so you shall make it.

The Ark of the Covenant

¹⁰"They shall make an ark of acacia wood. Two cubits³ and a half shall be its length, a cubit and a half its breadth, and a cubit and a half its height. ¹¹You shall overlay it with pure gold, inside and outside shall you overlay it, and you shall make on it a molding of gold around it. ¹²You shall cast four rings of gold for it and put them on its four feet, two rings on the one side of it, and two rings on the other side of it. ¹³You shall make poles of acacia wood and overlay them with gold. ¹⁴And you shall put the poles into the rings on the sides of the ark to carry the ark by them. ¹⁵The poles shall remain in the rings of the ark; they shall not be taken from it. ¹⁶And you shall put into the ark the testimony that I shall give you.

¹⁷"You shall make a mercy seat⁴ of pure gold. Two cubits and a half shall be its length, and a cubit and a half its breadth. ¹⁸And you shall make two cherubim of gold; of hammered work shall you make them, on the two ends of the mercy seat. ¹⁹Make one cherub on the one end, and one cherub on the other end. Of one piece with the mercy seat shall you make the cherubim on its two ends. ²⁰The cherubim shall spread out their wings above, overshadowing the mercy seat with their wings, their faces one to another; toward the mercy seat shall the faces of the cherubim be. ²¹And you shall put the mercy seat on the top of the ark, and in the ark you shall put the testimony that I shall give you. ²²There I will meet with you, and from above the mercy seat, from between the two cherubim that are on the ark of the testimony, I will speak

¹ Or all the just decrees ² Uncertain; possibly dolphin skins, or dugong skins; compare 26:14 ³ A cubit was about 18 inches or 45 centimeters ⁴ Or cover

with you about all that I will give you in commandment for the people of Israel.

The Table for Bread

23 "You shall make a table of acacia wood. Two cubits shall be its length, a cubit its breadth, and a cubit and a half its height. 24 You shall overlay it with pure gold and make a molding of gold around it. 25 And you shall make a rim around it a handbreadth[1] wide, and a molding of gold around the rim. 26 And you shall make for it four rings of gold, and fasten the rings to the four corners at its four legs. 27 Close to the frame the rings shall lie, as holders for the poles to carry the table. 28 You shall make the poles of acacia wood, and overlay them with gold, and the table shall be carried with these. 29 And you shall make its plates and dishes for incense, and its flagons and bowls with which to pour drink offerings; you shall make them of pure gold. 30 And you shall set the bread of the Presence on the table before me regularly.

The Golden Lampstand

31 "You shall make a lampstand of pure gold. The lampstand shall be made of hammered work: its base, its stem, its cups, its calyxes, and its flowers shall be of one piece with it. 32 And there shall be six branches going out of its sides, three branches of the lampstand out of one side of it and three branches of the lampstand out of the other side of it; 33 three cups made like almond blossoms, each with calyx and flower, on one branch, and three cups made like almond blossoms, each with calyx and flower, on the other branch—so for the six branches going out of the lampstand. 34 And on the lampstand itself there shall be four cups made like almond blossoms, with their calyxes and flowers, 35 and a calyx of one piece with it under each pair of the six branches going out from the lampstand. 36 Their calyxes and their branches shall be of one piece with it, the whole of it a single piece of hammered work of pure gold. 37 You shall make seven lamps for it. And the lamps shall be set up so as to give light on the space in front of it. 38 Its tongs and their trays shall be of pure gold. 39 It shall be made, with all these utensils, out of a talent[2] of pure gold. 40 And see that you make them after the pattern for them, which is being shown you on the mountain.

The Tabernacle

26 "Moreover, you shall make the tabernacle with ten curtains of fine twined linen and blue and purple and scarlet yarns; you shall make them with cherubim skillfully worked into them. 2 The length of each curtain shall be twenty-eight cubits,[3] and the breadth of each curtain four cubits; all the curtains shall be the same size. 3 Five curtains shall be coupled to one another, and the other five curtains shall be coupled to one another. 4 And you shall make loops of blue on the edge of the outermost curtain in the first set. Likewise you shall make loops on the edge of the outermost curtain in the second set. 5 Fifty loops you shall make on the one curtain, and fifty loops you shall make on the edge of the curtain that is in the second set; the loops shall be opposite one another. 6 And you shall make fifty clasps of gold, and couple the curtains one to the other with the clasps, so that the tabernacle may be a single whole.

7 "You shall also make curtains of goats' hair for a tent over the tabernacle; eleven curtains shall you make. 8 The length of each curtain shall be thirty cubits, and the breadth of each curtain four cubits. The eleven curtains shall be the same size. 9 You shall couple five curtains by themselves, and six curtains by themselves, and the sixth curtain you shall double over at the front of the tent. 10 You shall make fifty loops on the edge of the curtain that is outermost in one set, and fifty loops on the edge of the curtain that is outermost in the second set.

11 "You shall make fifty clasps of bronze, and put the clasps into the loops, and couple the tent together that it may be a single whole. 12 And the part that remains of the curtains of the tent, the half curtain that remains, shall hang over the back of the tabernacle. 13 And the extra that remains in the length of the curtains, the cubit on the one side, and the cubit on the other side, shall hang over the sides of the tabernacle, on this side and that side, to cover it. 14 And you shall make for the tent a covering of tanned rams' skins[4] and a covering of goatskins on top.

15 "You shall make upright frames for the tabernacle of acacia wood. 16 Ten cubits shall be the length of a frame, and a cubit and a half the breadth of each frame. 17 There shall be two tenons in each frame, for fitting together. So shall you do for all the frames of the tabernacle.

---

[1] A handbreadth was about 3 inches or 7.5 centimeters [2] A talent was about 75 pounds or 34 kilograms [3] A cubit was about 18 inches or 45 centimeters [4] Or of rams' skins dyed red

[18] You shall make the frames for the tabernacle: twenty frames for the south side; [19] and forty bases of silver you shall make under the twenty frames, two bases under one frame for its two tenons, and two bases under the next frame for its two tenons; [20] and for the second side of the tabernacle, on the north side twenty frames, [21] and their forty bases of silver, two bases under one frame, and two bases under the next frame. [22] And for the rear of the tabernacle westward you shall make six frames. [23] And you shall make two frames for corners of the tabernacle in the rear; [24] they shall be separate beneath, but joined at the top, at the first ring. Thus shall it be with both of them; they shall form the two corners. [25] And there shall be eight frames, with their bases of silver, sixteen bases; two bases under one frame, and two bases under another frame.

[26] "You shall make bars of acacia wood, five for the frames of the one side of the tabernacle, [27] and five bars for the frames of the other side of the tabernacle, and five bars for the frames of the side of the tabernacle at the rear westward. [28] The middle bar, halfway up the frames, shall run from end to end. [29] You shall overlay the frames with gold and shall make their rings of gold for holders for the bars, and you shall overlay the bars with gold. [30] Then you shall erect the tabernacle according to the plan for it that you were shown on the mountain.

[31] "And you shall make a veil of blue and purple and scarlet yarns and fine twined linen. It shall be made with cherubim skillfully worked into it. [32] And you shall hang it on four pillars of acacia overlaid with gold, with hooks of gold, on four bases of silver. [33] And you shall hang the veil from the clasps, and bring the ark of the testimony in there within the veil. And the veil shall separate for you the Holy Place from the Most Holy. [34] You shall put the mercy seat on the ark of the testimony in the Most Holy Place. [35] And you shall set the table outside the veil, and the lampstand on the south side of the tabernacle opposite the table, and you shall put the table on the north side.

[36] "You shall make a screen for the entrance of the tent, of blue and purple and scarlet yarns and fine twined linen, embroidered with needlework. [37] And you shall make for the screen five pillars of acacia, and overlay them with gold. Their hooks shall be of gold, and you shall cast five bases of bronze for them.

The Bronze Altar

27 "You shall make the altar of acacia wood, five cubits[1] long and five cubits broad. The altar shall be square, and its height shall be three cubits. [2] And you shall make horns for it on its four corners; its horns shall be of one piece with it, and you shall overlay it with bronze. [3] You shall make pots for it to receive its ashes, and shovels and basins and forks and fire pans. You shall make all its utensils of bronze. [4] You shall also make for it a grating, a network of bronze, and on the net you shall make four bronze rings at its four corners. [5] And you shall set it under the ledge of the altar so that the net extends halfway down the altar. [6] And you shall make poles for the altar, poles of acacia wood, and overlay them with bronze. [7] And the poles shall be put through the rings, so that the poles are on the two sides of the altar when it is carried. [8] You shall make it hollow, with boards. As it has been shown you on the mountain, so shall it be made.

The Court of the Tabernacle

[9] "You shall make the court of the tabernacle. On the south side the court shall have hangings of fine twined linen a hundred cubits long for one side. [10] Its twenty pillars and their twenty bases shall be of bronze, but the hooks of the pillars and their fillets shall be of silver. [11] And likewise for its length on the north side there shall be hangings a hundred cubits long, its pillars twenty and their bases twenty, of bronze, but the hooks of the pillars and their fillets shall be of silver. [12] And for the breadth of the court on the west side there shall be hangings for fifty cubits, with ten pillars and ten bases. [13] The breadth of the court on the front to the east shall be fifty cubits. [14] The hangings for the one side of the gate shall be fifteen cubits, with their three pillars and three bases. [15] On the other side the hangings shall be fifteen cubits, with their three pillars and three bases. [16] For the gate of the court there shall be a screen twenty cubits long, of blue and purple and scarlet yarns and fine twined linen, embroidered with needlework. It shall have four pillars and with them four bases. [17] All the pillars around the court shall be filleted with silver. Their hooks shall be of silver, and their bases of bronze. [18] The length of the court shall be a hundred cubits, the breadth fifty, and the height five cubits, with hangings

[1] A *cubit* was about 18 inches or 45 centimeters

of fine twined linen and bases of bronze. [19] All the utensils of the tabernacle for every use, and all its pegs and all the pegs of the court, shall be of bronze.

Oil for the Lamp

[20] "You shall command the people of Israel that they bring to you pure beaten olive oil for the light, that a lamp may regularly be set up to burn. [21] In the tent of meeting, outside the veil that is before the testimony, Aaron and his sons shall tend it from evening to morning before the LORD. It shall be a statute forever to be observed throughout their generations by the people of Israel.

The Priests' Garments

28 "Then bring near to you Aaron your brother, and his sons with him, from among the people of Israel, to serve me as priests—Aaron and Aaron's sons, Nadab and Abihu, Eleazar and Ithamar. [2] And you shall make holy garments for Aaron your brother, for glory and for beauty. [3] You shall speak to all the skillful, whom I have filled with a spirit of skill, that they make Aaron's garments to consecrate him for my priesthood. [4] These are the garments that they shall make: a breastpiece, an ephod, a robe, a coat of checker work, a turban, and a sash. They shall make holy garments for Aaron your brother and his sons to serve me as priests. [5] They shall receive gold, blue and purple and scarlet yarns, and fine twined linen.

[6] "And they shall make the ephod of gold, of blue and purple and scarlet yarns, and of fine twined linen, skillfully worked. [7] It shall have two shoulder pieces attached to its two edges, so that it may be joined together. [8] And the skillfully woven band on it shall be made like it and be of one piece with it, of gold, blue and purple and scarlet yarns, and fine twined linen. [9] You shall take two onyx stones, and engrave on them the names of the sons of Israel, [10] six of their names on the one stone, and the names of the remaining six on the other stone, in the order of their birth. [11] As a jeweler engraves signets, so shall you engrave the two stones with the names of the sons of Israel. You shall enclose them in settings of gold filigree. [12] And you shall set the two stones on the shoulder pieces of the ephod, as stones of remembrance for the sons of Israel. And Aaron shall bear their names before the

LORD on his two shoulders for remembrance. [13] You shall make settings of gold filigree, [14] and two chains of pure gold, twisted like cords; and you shall attach the corded chains to the settings.

[15] "You shall make a breastpiece of judgment, in skilled work. In the style of the ephod you shall make it—of gold, blue and purple and scarlet yarns, and fine twined linen shall you make it. [16] It shall be square and doubled, a span[1] its length and a span its breadth. [17] You shall set in it four rows of stones. A row of sardius,[2] topaz, and carbuncle shall be the first row; [18] and the second row an emerald, a sapphire, and a diamond; [19] and the third row a jacinth, an agate, and an amethyst; [20] and the fourth row a beryl, an onyx, and a jasper. They shall be set in gold filigree. [21] There shall be twelve stones with their names according to the names of the sons of Israel. They shall be like signets, each engraved with its name, for the twelve tribes. [22] You shall make for the breastpiece twisted chains like cords, of pure gold. [23] And you shall make for the breastpiece two rings of gold, and put the two rings on the two edges of the breastpiece. [24] And you shall put the two cords of gold in the two rings at the edges of the breastpiece. [25] The two ends of the two cords you shall attach to the two settings of filigree, and so attach it in front to the shoulder pieces of the ephod. [26] You shall make two rings of gold, and put them at the two ends of the breastpiece, on its inside edge next to the ephod. [27] And you shall make two rings of gold, and attach them in front to the lower part of the two shoulder pieces of the ephod, at its seam above the skillfully woven band of the ephod. [28] And they shall bind the breastpiece by its rings to the rings of the ephod with a lace of blue, so that it may lie on the skillfully woven band of the ephod, so that the breastpiece shall not come loose from the ephod. [29] So Aaron shall bear the names of the sons of Israel in the breastpiece of judgment on his heart, when he goes into the Holy Place, to bring them to regular remembrance before the LORD. [30] And in the breastpiece of judgment you shall put the Urim and the Thummim, and they shall be on Aaron's heart, when he goes in before the LORD. Thus Aaron shall bear the judgment of the people of Israel on his heart before the LORD regularly.

---

[1] A *span* was about 9 inches or 22 centimeters [2] The identity of some of these stones is uncertain

31 "You shall make the robe of the ephod all of blue. **32** It shall have an opening for the head in the middle of it, with a woven binding around the opening, like the opening in a garment,[1] so that it may not tear. **33** On its hem you shall make pomegranates of blue and purple and scarlet yarns, around its hem, with bells of gold between them, **34** a golden bell and a pomegranate, a golden bell and a pomegranate, around the hem of the robe. **35** And it shall be on Aaron when he ministers, and its sound shall be heard when he goes into the Holy Place before the LORD, and when he comes out, so that he does not die.

36 "You shall make a plate of pure gold and engrave on it, like the engraving of a signet, 'Holy to the LORD.' **37** And you shall fasten it on the turban by a cord of blue. It shall be on the front of the turban. **38** It shall be on Aaron's forehead, and Aaron shall bear any guilt from the holy things that the people of Israel consecrate as their holy gifts. It shall regularly be on his forehead, that they may be accepted before the LORD.

39 "You shall weave the coat in checker work of fine linen, and you shall make a turban of fine linen, and you shall make a sash embroidered with needlework.

40 "For Aaron's sons you shall make coats and sashes and caps. You shall make them for glory and beauty. **41** And you shall put them on Aaron your brother, and on his sons with him, and shall anoint them and ordain them and consecrate them, that they may serve me as priests. **42** You shall make for them linen undergarments to cover their naked flesh. They shall reach from the hips to the thighs; **43** and they shall be on Aaron and on his sons when they go into the tent of meeting or when they come near the altar to minister in the Holy Place, lest they bear guilt and die. This shall be a statute forever for him and for his offspring after him.

Consecration of the Priests

29 "Now this is what you shall do to them to consecrate them, that they may serve me as priests. Take one bull of the herd and two rams without blemish, **2** and unleavened bread, unleavened cakes mixed with oil, and unleavened wafers smeared with oil. You shall make them of fine wheat flour. **3** You shall put them in one basket and bring them in the basket, and bring the bull and the two rams. **4** You shall

bring Aaron and his sons to the entrance of the tent of meeting and wash them with water. **5** Then you shall take the garments, and put on Aaron the coat and the robe of the ephod, and the ephod, and the breastpiece, and gird him with the skillfully woven band of the ephod. **6** And you shall set the turban on his head and put the holy crown on the turban. **7** You shall take the anointing oil and pour it on his head and anoint him. **8** Then you shall bring his sons and put coats on them, **9** and you shall gird Aaron and his sons with sashes and bind caps on them. And the priesthood shall be theirs by a statute forever. Thus you shall ordain Aaron and his sons.

10 "Then you shall bring the bull before the tent of meeting. Aaron and his sons shall lay their hands on the head of the bull. **11** Then you shall kill the bull before the LORD at the entrance of the tent of meeting, **12** and shall take part of the blood of the bull and put it on the horns of the altar with your finger, and the rest of[2] the blood you shall pour out at the base of the altar. **13** And you shall take all the fat that covers the entrails, and the long lobe of the liver, and the two kidneys with the fat that is on them, and burn them on the altar. **14** But the flesh of the bull and its skin and its dung you shall burn with fire outside the camp; it is a sin offering.

15 "Then you shall take one of the rams, and Aaron and his sons shall lay their hands on the head of the ram, **16** and you shall kill the ram and shall take its blood and throw it against the sides of the altar. **17** Then you shall cut the ram into pieces, and wash its entrails and its legs, and put them with its pieces and its head, **18** and burn the whole ram on the altar. It is a burnt offering to the LORD. It is a pleasing aroma, a food offering[3] to the LORD.

19 "You shall take the other ram, and Aaron and his sons shall lay their hands on the head of the ram, **20** and you shall kill the ram and take part of its blood and put it on the tip of the right ear of Aaron and on the tips of the right ears of his sons, and on the thumbs of their right hands and on the great toes of their right feet, and throw the rest of the blood against the sides of the altar. **21** Then you shall take part of the blood that is on the altar, and of the anointing oil, and sprinkle it on Aaron and his garments, and on his sons and his sons' garments with him. He and his garments shall be holy, and his sons and his sons' garments with him.

[1] The meaning of the Hebrew word is uncertain; possibly *coat of mail* [2] Hebrew *all* [3] Or *an offering by fire*; also verses 25, 41

22 "You shall also take the fat from the ram and the fat tail and the fat that covers the entrails, and the long lobe of the liver and the two kidneys with the fat that is on them, and the right thigh (for it is a ram of ordination), 23 and one loaf of bread and one cake of bread made with oil, and one wafer out of the basket of unleavened bread that is before the LORD. 24 You shall put all these on the palms of Aaron and on the palms of his sons, and wave them for a wave offering before the LORD. 25 Then you shall take them from their hands and burn them on the altar on top of the burnt offering, as a pleasing aroma before the LORD. It is a food offering to the LORD.

26 "You shall take the breast of the ram of Aaron's ordination and wave it for a wave offering before the LORD, and it shall be your portion. 27 And you shall consecrate the breast of the wave offering that is waved and the thigh of the priests' portion that is contributed from the ram of ordination, from what was Aaron's and his sons'. 28 It shall be for Aaron and his sons as a perpetual due from the people of Israel, for it is a contribution. It shall be a contribution from the people of Israel from their peace offerings, their contribution to the LORD.

29 "The holy garments of Aaron shall be for his sons after him; they shall be anointed in them and ordained in them. 30 The son who succeeds him as priest, who comes into the tent of meeting to minister in the Holy Place, shall wear them seven days.

31 "You shall take the ram of ordination and boil its flesh in a holy place. 32 And Aaron and his sons shall eat the flesh of the ram and the bread that is in the basket in the entrance of the tent of meeting. 33 They shall eat those things with which atonement was made at their ordination and consecration, but an outsider shall not eat of them, because they are holy. 34 And if any of the flesh for the ordination or of the bread remain until the morning, then you shall burn the remainder with fire. It shall not be eaten, because it is holy.

35 "Thus you shall do to Aaron and to his sons, according to all that I have commanded you. Through seven days shall you ordain them, 36 and every day you shall offer a bull as a sin offering for atonement. Also you shall purify the altar, when you make atonement for it, and shall anoint it to consecrate it. 37 Seven days you shall make atonement for the altar and

consecrate it, and the altar shall be most holy. Whatever touches the altar shall become holy.

38 "Now this is what you shall offer on the altar: two lambs a year old day by day regularly. 39 One lamb you shall offer in the morning, and the other lamb you shall offer at twilight. 40 And with the first lamb a tenth measure[1] of fine flour mingled with a fourth of a hin[2] of beaten oil, and a fourth of a hin of wine for a drink offering. 41 The other lamb you shall offer at twilight, and shall offer with it a grain offering and its drink offering, as in the morning, for a pleasing aroma, a food offering to the LORD. 42 It shall be a regular burnt offering throughout your generations at the entrance of the tent of meeting before the LORD, where I will meet with you, to speak to you there. 43 There I will meet with the people of Israel, and it shall be sanctified by my glory. 44 I will consecrate the tent of meeting and the altar. Aaron also and his sons I will consecrate to serve me as priests. 45 I will dwell among the people of Israel and will be their God. 46 And they shall know that I am the LORD their God, who brought them out of the land of Egypt that I might dwell among them. I am the LORD their God.

The Altar of Incense

30 "You shall make an altar on which to burn incense; you shall make it of acacia wood. 2 A cubit[3] shall be its length, and a cubit its breadth. It shall be square, and two cubits shall be its height. Its horns shall be of one piece with it. 3 You shall overlay it with pure gold, its top and around its sides and its horns. And you shall make a molding of gold around it. 4 And you shall make two golden rings for it. Under its molding on two opposite sides of it you shall make them, and they shall be holders for poles with which to carry it. 5 You shall make the poles of acacia wood and overlay them with gold. 6 And you shall put it in front of the veil that is above the ark of the testimony, in front of the mercy seat that is above the testimony, where I will meet with you. 7 And Aaron shall burn fragrant incense on it. Every morning when he dresses the lamps he shall burn it, 8 and when Aaron sets up the lamps at twilight, he shall burn it, a regular incense offering before the LORD throughout your generations. 9 You shall not offer unauthorized incense on it, or a burnt offering, or a grain offering, and you shall not pour a drink offering on it. 10 Aaron shall make atonement on its horns once a year.

[1] Possibly an ephah (about 3/5 bushel or 22 liters) [2] A *hin* was about 4 quarts or 3.5 liters [3] A *cubit* was about 18 inches or 45 centimeters

With the blood of the sin offering of atonement he shall make atonement for it once in the year throughout your generations. It is most holy to the LORD."

The Census Tax

[11] The LORD said to Moses, [12] "When you take the census of the people of Israel, then each shall give a ransom for his life to the LORD when you number them, that there be no plague among them when you number them. [13] Each one who is numbered in the census shall give this: half a shekel[1] according to the shekel of the sanctuary (the shekel is twenty gerahs),[2] half a shekel as an offering to the LORD. [14] Everyone who is numbered in the census, from twenty years old and upward, shall give the LORD's offering. [15] The rich shall not give more, and the poor shall not give less, than the half shekel, when you give the LORD's offering to make atonement for your lives. [16] You shall take the atonement money from the people of Israel and shall give it for the service of the tent of meeting, that it may bring the people of Israel to remembrance before the LORD, so as to make atonement for your lives."

The Bronze Basin

[17] The LORD said to Moses, [18] "You shall also make a basin of bronze, with its stand of bronze, for washing. You shall put it between the tent of meeting and the altar, and you shall put water in it, [19] with which Aaron and his sons shall wash their hands and their feet. [20] When they go into the tent of meeting, or when they come near the altar to minister, to burn a food offering[3] to the LORD, they shall wash with water, so that they may not die. [21] They shall wash their hands and their feet, so that they may not die. It shall be a statute forever to them, even to him and to his offspring throughout their generations."

The Anointing Oil and Incense

[22] The LORD said to Moses, [23] "Take the finest spices: of liquid myrrh 500 shekels, and of sweet-smelling cinnamon half as much, that is, 250, and 250 of aromatic cane, [24] and 500 of cassia, according to the shekel of the sanctuary, and a hin[4] of olive oil. [25] And you shall make of these a sacred anointing oil blended as by the perfumer; it shall be a holy anointing oil. [26] With it you shall anoint the tent of meeting and the ark of the testimony, [27] and the table

and all its utensils, and the lampstand and its utensils, and the altar of incense, [28] and the altar of burnt offering with all its utensils and the basin and its stand. [29] You shall consecrate them, that they may be most holy. Whatever touches them will become holy. [30] You shall anoint Aaron and his sons, and consecrate them, that they may serve me as priests. [31] And you shall say to the people of Israel, 'This shall be my holy anointing oil throughout your generations. [32] It shall not be poured on the body of an ordinary person, and you shall make no other like it in composition. It is holy, and it shall be holy to you. [33] Whoever compounds any like it or whoever puts any of it on an outsider shall be cut off from his people.'"

[34] The LORD said to Moses, "Take sweet spices, stacte, and onycha, and galbanum, sweet spices with pure frankincense (of each shall there be an equal part), [35] and make an incense blended as by the perfumer, seasoned with salt, pure and holy. [36] You shall beat some of it very small, and put part of it before the testimony in the tent of meeting where I shall meet with you. It shall be most holy for you. [37] And the incense that you shall make according to its composition, you shall not make for yourselves. It shall be for you holy to the LORD. [38] Whoever makes any like it to use as perfume shall be cut off from his people."

Oholiab and Bezalel

31 The LORD said to Moses, [2] "See, I have called by name Bezalel the son of Uri, son of Hur, of the tribe of Judah, [3] and I have filled him with the Spirit of God, with ability and intelligence, with knowledge and all craftsmanship, [4] to devise artistic designs, to work in gold, silver, and bronze, [5] in cutting stones for setting, and in carving wood, to work in every craft. [6] And behold, I have appointed with him Oholiab, the son of Ahisamach, of the tribe of Dan. And I have given to all able men ability, that they may make all that I have commanded you: [7] the tent of meeting, and the ark of the testimony, and the mercy seat that is on it, and all the furnishings of the tent, [8] the table and its utensils, and the pure lampstand with all its utensils, and the altar of incense, [9] and the altar of burnt offering with all its utensils, and the basin and its stand, [10] and the finely worked garments,[5] the holy garments for Aaron the priest and the garments of his sons, for their service as

---

[1] A *shekel* was about 2/5 ounce or 11 grams [2] A *gerah* was about 1/50 ounce or 0.6 gram [3] Or *an offering by fire* [4] A *hin* was about 4 quarts or 3.5 liters [5] Or *garments for worship*

priests, [11] and the anointing oil and the fragrant incense for the Holy Place. According to all that I have commanded you, they shall do."

The Sabbath

[12] And the LORD said to Moses, [13] "You are to speak to the people of Israel and say, 'Above all you shall keep my Sabbaths, for this is a sign between me and you throughout your generations, that you may know that I, the LORD, sanctify you. [14] You shall keep the Sabbath, because it is holy for you. Everyone who profanes it shall be put to death. Whoever does any work on it, that soul shall be cut off from among his people. [15] Six days shall work be done, but the seventh day is a Sabbath of solemn rest, holy to the LORD. Whoever does any work on the Sabbath day shall be put to death. [16] Therefore the people of Israel shall keep the Sabbath, observing the Sabbath throughout their generations, as a covenant forever. [17] It is a sign forever between me and the people of Israel that in six days the LORD made heaven and earth, and on the seventh day he rested and was refreshed.'"

[18] And he gave to Moses, when he had finished speaking with him on Mount Sinai, the two tablets of the testimony, tablets of stone, written with the finger of God.

The Golden Calf

32 When the people saw that Moses delayed to come down from the mountain, the people gathered themselves together to Aaron and said to him, "Up, make us gods who shall go before us. As for this Moses, the man who brought us up out of the land of Egypt, we do not know what has become of him." [2] So Aaron said to them, "Take off the rings of gold that are in the ears of your wives, your sons, and your daughters, and bring them to me." [3] So all the people took off the rings of gold that were in their ears and brought them to Aaron. [4] And he received the gold from their hand and fashioned it with a graving tool and made a golden[1] calf. And they said, "These are your gods, O Israel, who brought you up out of the land of Egypt!" [5] When Aaron saw this, he built an altar before it. And Aaron made a proclamation and said, "Tomorrow shall be a feast to the LORD." [6] And they rose up early the next day and offered burnt offerings and brought peace offerings. And the people sat down to eat and drink and rose up to play.

[7] And the LORD said to Moses, "Go down, for your people, whom you brought up out of the land of Egypt, have corrupted themselves. [8] They have turned aside quickly out of the way that I commanded them. They have made for themselves a golden calf and have worshiped it and sacrificed to it and said, 'These are your gods, O Israel, who brought you up out of the land of Egypt!'" [9] And the LORD said to Moses, "I have seen this people, and behold, it is a stiff-necked people. [10] Now therefore let me alone, that my wrath may burn hot against them and I may consume them, in order that I may make a great nation of you."

[11] But Moses implored the LORD his God and said, "O LORD, why does your wrath burn hot against your people, whom you have brought out of the land of Egypt with great power and with a mighty hand? [12] Why should the Egyptians say, 'With evil intent did he bring them out, to kill them in the mountains and to consume them from the face of the earth'? Turn from your burning anger and relent from this disaster against your people. [13] Remember Abraham, Isaac, and Israel, your servants, to whom you swore by your own self, and said to them, 'I will multiply your offspring as the stars of heaven, and all this land that I have promised I will give to your offspring, and they shall inherit it forever.'" [14] And the LORD relented from the disaster that he had spoken of bringing on his people.

[15] Then Moses turned and went down from the mountain with the two tablets of the testimony in his hand, tablets that were written on both sides; on the front and on the back they were written. [16] The tablets were the work of God, and the writing was the writing of God, engraved on the tablets. [17] When Joshua heard the noise of the people as they shouted, he said to Moses, "There is a noise of war in the camp." [18] But he said, "It is not the sound of shouting for victory, or the sound of the cry of defeat, but the sound of singing that I hear." [19] And as soon as he came near the camp and saw the calf and the dancing, Moses' anger burned hot, and he threw the tablets out of his hands and broke them at the foot of the mountain. [20] He took the calf that they had made and burned it with fire and ground it to powder and scattered it on the water and made the people of Israel drink it.

---

[1] Hebrew *cast metal*; also verse 8

[21] And Moses said to Aaron, "What did this people do to you that you have brought such a great sin upon them?" [22] And Aaron said, "Let not the anger of my lord burn hot. You know the people, that they are set on evil. [23] For they said to me, 'Make us gods who shall go before us. As for this Moses, the man who brought us up out of the land of Egypt, we do not know what has become of him.' [24] So I said to them, 'Let any who have gold take it off.' So they gave it to me, and I threw it into the fire, and out came this calf."

[25] And when Moses saw that the people had broken loose (for Aaron had let them break loose, to the derision of their enemies), [26] then Moses stood in the gate of the camp and said, "Who is on the LORD's side? Come to me." And all the sons of Levi gathered around him. [27] And he said to them, "Thus says the LORD God of Israel, 'Put your sword on your side each of you, and go to and fro from gate to gate throughout the camp, and each of you kill his brother and his companion and his neighbor.'" [28] And the sons of Levi did according to the word of Moses. And that day about three thousand men of the people fell. [29] And Moses said, "Today you have been ordained for the service of the LORD, each one at the cost of his son and of his brother, so that he might bestow a blessing upon you this day."

[30] The next day Moses said to the people, "You have sinned a great sin. And now I will go up to the LORD; perhaps I can make atonement for your sin." [31] So Moses returned to the LORD and said, "Alas, this people has sinned a great sin. They have made for themselves gods of gold. [32] But now, if you will forgive their sin—but if not, please blot me out of your book that you have written." [33] But the LORD said to Moses, "Whoever has sinned against me, I will blot out of my book. [34] But now go, lead the people to the place about which I have spoken to you; behold, my angel shall go before you. Nevertheless, in the day when I visit, I will visit their sin upon them."

[35] Then the LORD sent a plague on the people, because they made the calf, the one that Aaron made.

The Command to Leave Sinai

33 The LORD said to Moses, "Depart; go up from here, you and the people whom you have brought up out of the land of Egypt, to the land of which I swore to Abraham, Isaac, and Jacob, saying, 'To your offspring I will give it.' [2] I will send an angel before you, and I will drive out the Canaanites, the Amorites, the Hittites, the Perizzites, the Hivites, and the Jebusites. [3] Go up to a land flowing with milk and honey; but I will not go up among you, lest I consume you on the way, for you are a stiff-necked people."

[4] When the people heard this disastrous word, they mourned, and no one put on his ornaments. [5] For the LORD had said to Moses, "Say to the people of Israel, 'You are a stiff-necked people; if for a single moment I should go up among you, I would consume you. So now take off your ornaments, that I may know what to do with you.'" [6] Therefore the people of Israel stripped themselves of their ornaments, from Mount Horeb onward.

The Tent of Meeting

[7] Now Moses used to take the tent and pitch it outside the camp, far off from the camp, and he called it the tent of meeting. And everyone who sought the LORD would go out to the tent of meeting, which was outside the camp. [8] Whenever Moses went out to the tent, all the people would rise up, and each would stand at his tent door, and watch Moses until he had gone into the tent. [9] When Moses entered the tent, the pillar of cloud would descend and stand at the entrance of the tent, and the LORD[1] would speak with Moses. [10] And when all the people saw the pillar of cloud standing at the entrance of the tent, all the people would rise up and worship, each at his tent door. [11] Thus the LORD used to speak to Moses face to face, as a man speaks to his friend. When Moses turned again into the camp, his assistant Joshua the son of Nun, a young man, would not depart from the tent.

Moses' Intercession

[12] Moses said to the LORD, "See, you say to me, 'Bring up this people,' but you have not let me know whom you will send with me. Yet you have said, 'I know you by name, and you have also found favor in my sight.' [13] Now therefore, if I have found favor in your sight, please show me now your ways, that I may know you in order to find favor in your sight. Consider too that this nation is your people."

[1] Hebrew *he*

[14] And he said, "My presence will go with you, and I will give you rest." [15] And he said to him, "If your presence will not go with me, do not bring us up from here. [16] For how shall it be known that I have found favor in your sight, I and your people? Is it not in your going with us, so that we are distinct, I and your people, from every other people on the face of the earth?"

[17] And the LORD said to Moses, "This very thing that you have spoken I will do, for you have found favor in my sight, and I know you by name." [18] Moses said, "Please show me your glory." [19] And he said, "I will make all my goodness pass before you and will proclaim before you my name 'The LORD.' And I will be gracious to whom I will be gracious, and will show mercy on whom I will show mercy. [20] But," he said, "you cannot see my face, for man shall not see me and live." [21] And the LORD said, "Behold, there is a place by me where you shall stand on the rock, [22] and while my glory passes by I will put you in a cleft of the rock, and I will cover you with my hand until I have passed by. [23] Then I will take away my hand, and you shall see my back, but my face shall not be seen."

Moses Makes New Tablets

34 The LORD said to Moses, "Cut for yourself two tablets of stone like the first, and I will write on the tablets the words that were on the first tablets, which you broke. [2] Be ready by the morning, and come up in the morning to Mount Sinai, and present yourself there to me on the top of the mountain. [3] No one shall come up with you, and let no one be seen throughout all the mountain. Let no flocks or herds graze opposite that mountain." [4] So Moses cut two tablets of stone like the first. And he rose early in the morning and went up on Mount Sinai, as the LORD had commanded him, and took in his hand two tablets of stone. [5] The LORD descended in the cloud and stood with him there, and proclaimed the name of the LORD. [6] The LORD passed before him and proclaimed, "The LORD, the LORD, a God merciful and gracious, slow to anger, and abounding in steadfast love and faithfulness, [7] keeping steadfast love for thousands,[1] forgiving iniquity and transgression and sin, but who will by no means clear the guilty, visiting the iniquity of the fathers on the children and the children's children, to the third and the fourth

generation." [8] And Moses quickly bowed his head toward the earth and worshiped. [9] And he said, "If now I have found favor in your sight, O Lord, please let the Lord go in the midst of us, for it is a stiff-necked people, and pardon our iniquity and our sin, and take us for your inheritance."

The Covenant Renewed

[10] And he said, "Behold, I am making a covenant. Before all your people I will do marvels, such as have not been created in all the earth or in any nation. And all the people among whom you are shall see the work of the LORD, for it is an awesome thing that I will do with you.

[11] "Observe what I command you this day. Behold, I will drive out before you the Amorites, the Canaanites, the Hittites, the Perizzites, the Hivites, and the Jebusites. [12] Take care, lest you make a covenant with the inhabitants of the land to which you go, lest it become a snare in your midst. [13] You shall tear down their altars and break their pillars and cut down their Asherim [14] (for you shall worship no other god, for the LORD, whose name is Jealous, is a jealous God), [15] lest you make a covenant with the inhabitants of the land, and when they whore after their gods and sacrifice to their gods and you are invited, you eat of his sacrifice, [16] and you take of their daughters for your sons, and their daughters whore after their gods and make your sons whore after their gods.

[17] "You shall not make for yourself any gods of cast metal.

[18] "You shall keep the Feast of Unleavened Bread. Seven days you shall eat unleavened bread, as I commanded you, at the time appointed in the month Abib, for in the month Abib you came out from Egypt. [19] All that open the womb are mine, all your male[2] livestock, the firstborn of cow and sheep. [20] The firstborn of a donkey you shall redeem with a lamb, or if you will not redeem it you shall break its neck. All the firstborn of your sons you shall redeem. And none shall appear before me empty-handed.

[21] "Six days you shall work, but on the seventh day you shall rest. In plowing time and in harvest you shall rest. [22] You shall observe the Feast of Weeks, the firstfruits of wheat harvest, and the Feast of Ingathering at the year's end. [23] Three times in the year shall all your males appear before the LORD God, the God of Israel.

[1] Or to the thousandth generation [2] Septuagint, Theodotion, Vulgate, Targum; the meaning of the Hebrew is uncertain

[24] For I will cast out nations before you and enlarge your borders; no one shall covet your land, when you go up to appear before the LORD your God three times in the year.

[25] "You shall not offer the blood of my sacrifice with anything leavened, or let the sacrifice of the Feast of the Passover remain until the morning. [26] The best of the firstfruits of your ground you shall bring to the house of the LORD your God. You shall not boil a young goat in its mother's milk."

[27] And the LORD said to Moses, "Write these words, for in accordance with these words I have made a covenant with you and with Israel." [28] So he was there with the LORD forty days and forty nights. He neither ate bread nor drank water. And he wrote on the tablets the words of the covenant, the Ten Commandments.[1]

The Shining Face of Moses

[29] When Moses came down from Mount Sinai, with the two tablets of the testimony in his hand as he came down from the mountain, Moses did not know that the skin of his face shone because he had been talking with God.[2] [30] Aaron and all the people of Israel saw Moses, and behold, the skin of his face shone, and they were afraid to come near him. [31] But Moses called to them, and Aaron and all the leaders of the congregation returned to him, and Moses talked with them. [32] Afterward all the people of Israel came near, and he commanded them all that the LORD had spoken with him in Mount Sinai. [33] And when Moses had finished speaking with them, he put a veil over his face.

[34] Whenever Moses went in before the LORD to speak with him, he would remove the veil, until he came out. And when he came out and told the people of Israel what he was commanded, [35] the people of Israel would see the face of Moses, that the skin of Moses' face was shining. And Moses would put the veil over his face again, until he went in to speak with him.

Sabbath Regulations

35 Moses assembled all the congregation of the people of Israel and said to them, "These are the things that the LORD has commanded you to do. [2] Six days work shall be done, but on the seventh day you shall have a Sabbath of solemn rest, holy to the LORD. Whoever does any work on it shall be put to death. [3] You shall kindle no fire in all your dwelling places on the Sabbath day."

Contributions for the Tabernacle

[4] Moses said to all the congregation of the people of Israel, "This is the thing that the LORD has commanded. [5] Take from among you a contribution to the LORD. Whoever is of a generous heart, let him bring the LORD's contribution: gold, silver, and bronze; [6] blue and purple and scarlet yarns and fine twined linen; goats' hair, [7] tanned rams' skins, and goatskins;[3] acacia wood, [8] oil for the light, spices for the anointing oil and for the fragrant incense, [9] and onyx stones and stones for setting, for the ephod and for the breastpiece.

[10] "Let every skillful craftsman among you come and make all that the LORD has commanded: [11] the tabernacle, its tent and its covering, its hooks and its frames, its bars, its pillars, and its bases; [12] the ark with its poles, the mercy seat, and the veil of the screen; [13] the table with its poles and all its utensils, and the bread of the Presence; [14] the lampstand also for the light, with its utensils and its lamps, and the oil for the light; [15] and the altar of incense, with its poles, and the anointing oil and the fragrant incense, and the screen for the door, at the door of the tabernacle; [16] the altar of burnt offering, with its grating of bronze, its poles, and all its utensils, the basin and its stand; [17] the hangings of the court, its pillars and its bases, and the screen for the gate of the court; [18] the pegs of the tabernacle and the pegs of the court, and their cords; [19] the finely worked garments for ministering[4] in the Holy Place, the holy garments for Aaron the priest, and the garments of his sons, for their service as priests."

[20] Then all the congregation of the people of Israel departed from the presence of Moses. [21] And they came, everyone whose heart stirred him, and everyone whose spirit moved him, and brought the LORD's contribution to be used for the tent of meeting, and for all its service, and for the holy garments. [22] So they came, both men and women. All who were of a willing heart brought brooches and earrings and signet rings and armlets, all sorts of gold objects, every man dedicating an offering of gold to the LORD. [23] And every one who possessed blue or purple or scarlet yarns or fine linen or goats' hair or tanned rams' skins or

---

[1] Hebrew *the ten words* [2] Hebrew *him* [3] The meaning of the Hebrew word is uncertain; also verse 23; compare 25:5 [4] Or *garments for worship*; see 31:10

goatskins brought them. ²⁴ Everyone who could make a contribution of silver or bronze brought it as the LORD's contribution. And every one who possessed acacia wood of any use in the work brought it. ²⁵ And every skillful woman spun with her hands, and they all brought what they had spun in blue and purple and scarlet yarns and fine twined linen. ²⁶ All the women whose hearts stirred them to use their skill spun the goats' hair. ²⁷ And the leaders brought onyx stones and stones to be set, for the ephod and for the breastpiece, ²⁸ and spices and oil for the light, and for the anointing oil, and for the fragrant incense. ²⁹ All the men and women, the people of Israel, whose heart moved them to bring anything for the work that the LORD had commanded by Moses to be done brought it as a freewill offering to the LORD.

Construction of the Tabernacle

³⁰ Then Moses said to the people of Israel, "See, the LORD has called by name Bezalel the son of Uri, son of Hur, of the tribe of Judah; ³¹ and he has filled him with the Spirit of God, with skill, with intelligence, with knowledge, and with all craftsmanship, ³² to devise artistic designs, to work in gold and silver and bronze, ³³ in cutting stones for setting, and in carving wood, for work in every skilled craft. ³⁴ And he has inspired him to teach, both him and Oholiab the son of Ahisamach of the tribe of Dan. ³⁵ He has filled them with skill to do every sort of work done by an engraver or by a designer or by an embroiderer in blue and purple and scarlet yarns and fine twined linen, or by a weaver—by any sort of workman or skilled designer.

36 "Bezalel and Oholiab and every craftsman in whom the LORD has put skill and intelligence to know how to do any work in the construction of the sanctuary shall work in accordance with all that the LORD has commanded."

² And Moses called Bezalel and Oholiab and every craftsman in whose mind the LORD had put skill, everyone whose heart stirred him up to come to do the work. ³ And they received from Moses all the contribution that the people of Israel had brought for doing the work on the sanctuary. They still kept bringing him freewill offerings every morning, ⁴ so that all the craftsmen who were doing every sort of task on the sanctuary came, each from the task that

he was doing, ⁵ and said to Moses, "The people bring much more than enough for doing the work that the LORD has commanded us to do." ⁶ So Moses gave command, and word was proclaimed throughout the camp, "Let no man or woman do anything more for the contribution for the sanctuary." So the people were restrained from bringing, ⁷ for the material they had was sufficient to do all the work, and more.

⁸ And all the craftsmen among the workmen made the tabernacle with ten curtains. They were made of fine twined linen and blue and purple and scarlet yarns, with cherubim skillfully worked. ⁹ The length of each curtain was twenty-eight cubits,¹ and the breadth of each curtain four cubits. All the curtains were the same size.

¹⁰ He² coupled five curtains to one another, and the other five curtains he coupled to one another. ¹¹ He made loops of blue on the edge of the outermost curtain of the first set. Likewise he made them on the edge of the outermost curtain of the second set. ¹² He made fifty loops on the one curtain, and he made fifty loops on the edge of the curtain that was in the second set. The loops were opposite one another. ¹³ And he made fifty clasps of gold, and coupled the curtains one to the other with clasps. So the tabernacle was a single whole.

¹⁴ He also made curtains of goats' hair for a tent over the tabernacle. He made eleven curtains. ¹⁵ The length of each curtain was thirty cubits, and the breadth of each curtain four cubits. The eleven curtains were the same size. ¹⁶ He coupled five curtains by themselves, and six curtains by themselves. ¹⁷ And he made fifty loops on the edge of the outermost curtain of the one set, and fifty loops on the edge of the other connecting curtain. ¹⁸ And he made fifty clasps of bronze to couple the tent together that it might be a single whole. ¹⁹ And he made for the tent a covering of tanned rams' skins and goatskins.

²⁰ Then he made the upright frames for the tabernacle of acacia wood. ²¹ Ten cubits was the length of a frame, and a cubit and a half the breadth of each frame. ²² Each frame had two tenons for fitting together. He did this for all the frames of the tabernacle. ²³ The frames for the tabernacle he made thus: twenty frames for the south side. ²⁴ And he made forty bases of silver under the twenty frames, two bases under one frame for its two tenons, and two

---

¹ A *cubit* was about 18 inches or 45 centimeters ² Probably Bezalel (compare 35:30; 37:1)

bases under the next frame for its two tenons. [25] For the second side of the tabernacle, on the north side, he made twenty frames [26] and their forty bases of silver, two bases under one frame and two bases under the next frame. [27] For the rear of the tabernacle westward he made six frames. [28] He made two frames for corners of the tabernacle in the rear. [29] And they were separate beneath but joined at the top, at the first ring. He made two of them this way for the two corners. [30] There were eight frames with their bases of silver: sixteen bases, under every frame two bases.

[31] He made bars of acacia wood, five for the frames of the one side of the tabernacle, [32] and five bars for the frames of the other side of the tabernacle, and five bars for the frames of the tabernacle at the rear westward. [33] And he made the middle bar to run from end to end halfway up the frames. [34] And he overlaid the frames with gold, and made their rings of gold for holders for the bars, and overlaid the bars with gold.

[35] He made the veil of blue and purple and scarlet yarns and fine twined linen; with cherubim skillfully worked into it he made it. [36] And for it he made four pillars of acacia and overlaid them with gold. Their hooks were of gold, and he cast for them four bases of silver. [37] He also made a screen for the entrance of the tent, of blue and purple and scarlet yarns and fine twined linen, embroidered with needlework, [38] and its five pillars with their hooks. He overlaid their capitals, and their fillets were of gold, but their five bases were of bronze.

Making the Ark

37 Bezalel made the ark of acacia wood. Two cubits[1] and a half was its length, a cubit and a half its breadth, and a cubit and a half its height. [2] And he overlaid it with pure gold inside and outside, and made a molding of gold around it. [3] And he cast for it four rings of gold for its four feet, two rings on its one side and two rings on its other side. [4] And he made poles of acacia wood and overlaid them with gold [5] and put the poles into the rings on the sides of the ark to carry the ark. [6] And he made a mercy seat of pure gold. Two cubits and a half was its length, and a cubit and a half its breadth. [7] And he made two cherubim of gold. He made them of hammered work on the two ends of the mercy seat, [8] one cherub on the one end, and one cherub on the other end. Of one piece with

the mercy seat he made the cherubim on its two ends. [9] The cherubim spread out their wings above, overshadowing the mercy seat with their wings, with their faces one to another; toward the mercy seat were the faces of the cherubim.

Making the Table

[10] He also made the table of acacia wood. Two cubits was its length, a cubit its breadth, and a cubit and a half its height. [11] And he overlaid it with pure gold, and made a molding of gold around it. [12] And he made a rim around it a handbreadth[2] wide, and made a molding of gold around the rim. [13] He cast for it four rings of gold and fastened the rings to the four corners at its four legs. [14] Close to the frame were the rings, as holders for the poles to carry the table. [15] He made the poles of acacia wood to carry the table, and overlaid them with gold. [16] And he made the vessels of pure gold that were to be on the table, its plates and dishes for incense, and its bowls and flagons with which to pour drink offerings.

Making the Lampstand

[17] He also made the lampstand of pure gold. He made the lampstand of hammered work. Its base, its stem, its cups, its calyxes, and its flowers were of one piece with it. [18] And there were six branches going out of its sides, three branches of the lampstand out of one side of it and three branches of the lampstand out of the other side of it; [19] three cups made like almond blossoms, each with calyx and flower, on one branch, and three cups made like almond blossoms, each with calyx and flower, on the other branch—so for the six branches going out of the lampstand. [20] And on the lampstand itself were four cups made like almond blossoms, with their calyxes and flowers, [21] and a calyx of one piece with it under each pair of the six branches going out of it. [22] Their calyxes and their branches were of one piece with it. The whole of it was a single piece of hammered work of pure gold. [23] And he made its seven lamps and its tongs and its trays of pure gold. [24] He made it and all its utensils out of a talent[3] of pure gold.

Making the Altar of Incense

[25] He made the altar of incense of acacia wood. Its length was a cubit, and its breadth was a cubit. It was square, and two cubits was its height. Its horns were of one piece with it.

[1] A *cubit* was about 18 inches or 45 centimeters [2] A *handbreadth* was about 3 inches or 7.5 centimeters [3] A *talent* was about 75 pounds or 34 kilograms

26 He overlaid it with pure gold, its top and around its sides and its horns. And he made a molding of gold around it, 27 and made two rings of gold on it under its molding, on two opposite sides of it, as holders for the poles with which to carry it. 28 And he made the poles of acacia wood and overlaid them with gold.

29 He made the holy anointing oil also, and the pure fragrant incense, blended as by the perfumer.

Making the Altar of Burnt Offering

38 He made the altar of burnt offering of acacia wood. Five cubits[1] was its length, and five cubits its breadth. It was square, and three cubits was its height. 2 He made horns for it on its four corners. Its horns were of one piece with it, and he overlaid it with bronze. 3 And he made all the utensils of the altar, the pots, the shovels, the basins, the forks, and the fire pans. He made all its utensils of bronze. 4 And he made for the altar a grating, a network of bronze, under its ledge, extending halfway down. 5 He cast four rings on the four corners of the bronze grating as holders for the poles. 6 He made the poles of acacia wood and overlaid them with bronze. 7 And he put the poles through the rings on the sides of the altar to carry it with them. He made it hollow, with boards.

Making the Bronze Basin

8 He made the basin of bronze and its stand of bronze, from the mirrors of the ministering women who ministered in the entrance of the tent of meeting.

Making the Court

9 And he made the court. For the south side the hangings of the court were of fine twined linen, a hundred cubits; 10 their twenty pillars and their twenty bases were of bronze, but the hooks of the pillars and their fillets were of silver. 11 And for the north side there were hangings of a hundred cubits; their twenty pillars and their twenty bases were of bronze, but the hooks of the pillars and their fillets were of silver. 12 And for the west side were hangings of fifty cubits, their ten pillars, and their ten bases; the hooks of the pillars and their fillets were of silver. 13 And for the front to the east, fifty cubits. 14 The hangings for one side of the gate were fifteen cubits, with their three pillars and three bases. 15 And so for the other side. On both sides of the gate of the court were hangings of fifteen cubits, with their three pillars and their three bases. 16 All the hangings around the court were of fine twined linen. 17 And the bases for the pillars were of bronze, but the hooks of the pillars and their fillets were of silver. The overlaying of their capitals was also of silver, and all the pillars of the court were filleted with silver. 18 And the screen for the gate of the court was embroidered with needlework in blue and purple and scarlet yarns and fine twined linen. It was twenty cubits long and five cubits high in its breadth, corresponding to the hangings of the court. 19 And their pillars were four in number. Their four bases were of bronze, their hooks of silver, and the overlaying of their capitals and their fillets of silver. 20 And all the pegs for the tabernacle and for the court all around were of bronze.

Materials for the Tabernacle

21 These are the records of the tabernacle, the tabernacle of the testimony, as they were recorded at the commandment of Moses, the responsibility of the Levites under the direction of Ithamar the son of Aaron the priest. 22 Bezalel the son of Uri, son of Hur, of the tribe of Judah, made all that the LORD commanded Moses; 23 and with him was Oholiab the son of Ahisamach, of the tribe of Dan, an engraver and designer and embroiderer in blue and purple and scarlet yarns and fine twined linen.

24 All the gold that was used for the work, in all the construction of the sanctuary, the gold from the offering, was twenty-nine talents and 730 shekels,[2] by the shekel of the sanctuary. 25 The silver from those of the congregation who were recorded was a hundred talents and 1,775 shekels, by the shekel of the sanctuary: 26 a beka[3] a head (that is, half a shekel, by the shekel of the sanctuary), for everyone who was listed in the records, from twenty years old and upward, for 603,550 men. 27 The hundred talents of silver were for casting the bases of the sanctuary and the bases of the veil; a hundred bases for the hundred talents, a talent a base. 28 And of the 1,775 shekels he made hooks for the pillars and overlaid their capitals and made fillets for them. 29 The bronze that was offered was seventy talents and 2,400 shekels; 30 with it he made the bases for the entrance of the tent of meeting, the bronze altar and the bronze grating for it and all the utensils of the altar, 31 the bases around the court, and the bases of the gate

---

[1] A *cubit* was about 18 inches or 45 centimeters [2] A *talent* was about 75 pounds or 34 kilograms; a *shekel* was about 2/5 ounce or 11 grams [3] A *beka* was about 1/5 ounce or 5.5 grams

of the court, all the pegs of the tabernacle, and all the pegs around the court.

Making the Priestly Garments

39 From the blue and purple and scarlet yarns they made finely woven garments,[1] for ministering in the Holy Place. They made the holy garments for Aaron, as the LORD had commanded Moses.

[2] He made the ephod of gold, blue and purple and scarlet yarns, and fine twined linen. [3] And they hammered out gold leaf, and he cut it into threads to work into the blue and purple and the scarlet yarns, and into the fine twined linen, in skilled design. [4] They made for the ephod attaching shoulder pieces, joined to it at its two edges. [5] And the skillfully woven band on it was of one piece with it and made like it, of gold, blue and purple and scarlet yarns, and fine twined linen, as the LORD had commanded Moses.

[6] They made the onyx stones, enclosed in settings of gold filigree, and engraved like the engravings of a signet, according to the names of the sons of Israel. [7] And he set them on the shoulder pieces of the ephod to be stones of remembrance for the sons of Israel, as the LORD had commanded Moses.

[8] He made the breastpiece, in skilled work, in the style of the ephod, of gold, blue and purple and scarlet yarns, and fine twined linen. [9] It was square. They made the breastpiece doubled, a span[2] its length and a span its breadth when doubled. [10] And they set in it four rows of stones. A row of sardius, topaz, and carbuncle was the first row; [11] and the second row, an emerald, a sapphire, and a diamond; [12] and the third row, a jacinth, an agate, and an amethyst; [13] and the fourth row, a beryl, an onyx, and a jasper. They were enclosed in settings of gold filigree. [14] There were twelve stones with their names according to the names of the sons of Israel. They were like signets, each engraved with its name, for the twelve tribes. [15] And they made on the breastpiece twisted chains like cords, of pure gold. [16] And they made two settings of gold filigree and two gold rings, and put the two rings on the two edges of the breastpiece. [17] And they put the two cords of gold in the two rings at the edges of the breastpiece. [18] They attached the two ends of the two cords to the two settings of filigree. Thus they attached it in front to the shoulder pieces of the ephod. [19] Then they made two rings of gold, and put them at the two ends of the breastpiece,

on its inside edge next to the ephod. [20] And they made two rings of gold, and attached them in front to the lower part of the two shoulder pieces of the ephod, at its seam above the skillfully woven band of the ephod. [21] And they bound the breastpiece by its rings to the rings of the ephod with a lace of blue, so that it should lie on the skillfully woven band of the ephod, and that the breastpiece should not come loose from the ephod, as the LORD had commanded Moses.

[22] He also made the robe of the ephod woven all of blue, [23] and the opening of the robe in it was like the opening in a garment, with a binding around the opening, so that it might not tear. [24] On the hem of the robe they made pomegranates of blue and purple and scarlet yarns and fine twined linen. [25] They also made bells of pure gold, and put the bells between the pomegranates all around the hem of the robe, between the pomegranates— [26] a bell and a pomegranate, a bell and a pomegranate around the hem of the robe for ministering, as the LORD had commanded Moses.

[27] They also made the coats, woven of fine linen, for Aaron and his sons, [28] and the turban of fine linen, and the caps of fine linen, and the linen undergarments of fine twined linen, [29] and the sash of fine twined linen and of blue and purple and scarlet yarns, embroidered with needlework, as the LORD had commanded Moses.

[30] They made the plate of the holy crown of pure gold, and wrote on it an inscription, like the engraving of a signet, "Holy to the LORD." [31] And they tied to it a cord of blue to fasten it on the turban above, as the LORD had commanded Moses.

[32] Thus all the work of the tabernacle of the tent of meeting was finished, and the people of Israel did according to all that the LORD had commanded Moses; so they did. [33] Then they brought the tabernacle to Moses, the tent and all its utensils, its hooks, its frames, its bars, its pillars, and its bases; [34] the covering of tanned rams' skins and goatskins, and the veil of the screen; [35] the ark of the testimony with its poles and the mercy seat; [36] the table with all its utensils, and the bread of the Presence; [37] the lampstand of pure gold and its lamps with the lamps set and all its utensils, and the oil for the light; [38] the golden altar, the anointing oil and the fragrant incense, and the screen for the entrance of the tent; [39] the bronze altar, and its grating of bronze, its poles, and all its

[1] Or garments for worship [2] A span was about 9 inches or 22 centimeters

utensils; the basin and its stand; ⁴⁰ the hangings of the court, its pillars, and its bases, and the screen for the gate of the court, its cords, and its pegs; and all the utensils for the service of the tabernacle, for the tent of meeting; ⁴¹ the finely worked garments for ministering in the Holy Place, the holy garments for Aaron the priest, and the garments of his sons for their service as priests. ⁴² According to all that the LORD had commanded Moses, so the people of Israel had done all the work. ⁴³ And Moses saw all the work, and behold, they had done it; as the LORD had commanded, so had they done it. Then Moses blessed them.

The Tabernacle Erected

40 The LORD spoke to Moses, saying, ² "On the first day of the first month you shall erect the tabernacle of the tent of meeting. ³ And you shall put in it the ark of the testimony, and you shall screen the ark with the veil. ⁴ And you shall bring in the table and arrange it, and you shall bring in the lampstand and set up its lamps. ⁵ And you shall put the golden altar for incense before the ark of the testimony, and set up the screen for the door of the tabernacle. ⁶ You shall set the altar of burnt offering before the door of the tabernacle of the tent of meeting, ⁷ and place the basin between the tent of meeting and the altar, and put water in it. ⁸ And you shall set up the court all around, and hang up the screen for the gate of the court.

⁹ "Then you shall take the anointing oil and anoint the tabernacle and all that is in it, and consecrate it and all its furniture, so that it may become holy. ¹⁰ You shall also anoint the altar of burnt offering and all its utensils, and consecrate the altar, so that the altar may become most holy. ¹¹ You shall also anoint the basin and its stand, and consecrate it. ¹² Then you shall bring Aaron and his sons to the entrance of the tent of meeting and shall wash them with water ¹³ and put on Aaron the holy garments. And you shall anoint him and consecrate him, that he may serve me as priest. ¹⁴ You shall bring his sons also and put coats on them, ¹⁵ and anoint them, as you anointed their father, that they may serve me as priests. And their anointing shall admit them to a perpetual priesthood throughout their generations."

¹⁶ This Moses did; according to all that the LORD commanded him, so he did. ¹⁷ In the first month in the second year, on the first day of

the month, the tabernacle was erected. ¹⁸ Moses erected the tabernacle. He laid its bases, and set up its frames, and put in its poles, and raised up its pillars. ¹⁹ And he spread the tent over the tabernacle and put the covering of the tent over it, as the LORD had commanded Moses. ²⁰ He took the testimony and put it into the ark, and put the poles on the ark and set the mercy seat above on the ark. ²¹ And he brought the ark into the tabernacle and set up the veil of the screen, and screened the ark of the testimony, as the LORD had commanded Moses. ²² He put the table in the tent of meeting, on the north side of the tabernacle, outside the veil, ²³ and arranged the bread on it before the LORD, as the LORD had commanded Moses. ²⁴ He put the lampstand in the tent of meeting, opposite the table on the south side of the tabernacle, ²⁵ and set up the lamps before the LORD, as the LORD had commanded Moses. ²⁶ He put the golden altar in the tent of meeting before the veil, ²⁷ and burned fragrant incense on it, as the LORD had commanded Moses. ²⁸ He put in place the screen for the door of the tabernacle. ²⁹ And he set the altar of burnt offering at the entrance of the tabernacle of the tent of meeting, and offered on it the burnt offering and the grain offering, as the LORD had commanded Moses. ³⁰ He set the basin between the tent of meeting and the altar, and put water in it for washing, ³¹ with which Moses and Aaron and his sons washed their hands and their feet. ³² When they went into the tent of meeting, and when they approached the altar, they washed, as the LORD commanded Moses. ³³ And he erected the court around the tabernacle and the altar, and set up the screen of the gate of the court. So Moses finished the work.

The Glory of the LORD

³⁴ Then the cloud covered the tent of meeting, and the glory of the LORD filled the tabernacle. ³⁵ And Moses was not able to enter the tent of meeting because the cloud settled on it, and the glory of the LORD filled the tabernacle. ³⁶ Throughout all their journeys, whenever the cloud was taken up from over the tabernacle, the people of Israel would set out. ³⁷ But if the cloud was not taken up, then they did not set out till the day that it was taken up. ³⁸ For the cloud of the LORD was on the tabernacle by day, and fire was in it by night, in the sight of all the house of Israel throughout all their journeys.

LEVITICUS

Laws for Burnt Offerings

1 The LORD called Moses and spoke to him from the tent of meeting, saying, **2** "Speak to the people of Israel and say to them, When any one of you brings an offering to the LORD, you shall bring your offering of livestock from the herd or from the flock.

3 "If his offering is a burnt offering from the herd, he shall offer a male without blemish. He shall bring it to the entrance of the tent of meeting, that he may be accepted before the LORD. **4** He shall lay his hand on the head of the burnt offering, and it shall be accepted for him to make atonement for him. **5** Then he shall kill the bull before the LORD, and Aaron's sons the priests shall bring the blood and throw the blood against the sides of the altar that is at the entrance of the tent of meeting. **6** Then he shall flay the burnt offering and cut it into pieces, **7** and the sons of Aaron the priest shall put fire on the altar and arrange wood on the fire. **8** And Aaron's sons the priests shall arrange the pieces, the head, and the fat, on the wood that is on the fire on the altar; **9** but its entrails and its legs he shall wash with water. And the priest shall burn all of it on the altar, as a burnt offering, a food offering[1] with a pleasing aroma to the LORD.

10 "If his gift for a burnt offering is from the flock, from the sheep or goats, he shall bring a male without blemish, **11** and he shall kill it on the north side of the altar before the LORD, and Aaron's sons the priests shall throw its blood against the sides of the altar. **12** And he shall cut it into pieces, with its head and its fat, and the priest shall arrange them on the wood that is on the fire on the altar, **13** but the entrails and the legs he shall wash with water. And the priest shall offer all of it and burn it on the altar; it is a burnt offering, a food offering with a pleasing aroma to the LORD.

14 "If his offering to the LORD is a burnt offering of birds, then he shall bring his offering of turtledoves or pigeons. **15** And the priest shall bring it to the altar and wring off its head and burn it on the altar. Its blood shall be drained out on the side of the altar. **16** He shall remove its crop with its contents[2] and cast it beside the altar on the east side, in the place for ashes. **17** He shall tear it open by its wings, but shall not sever it completely. And the priest shall burn it on the altar, on the wood that is on the fire. It is a burnt offering, a food offering with a pleasing aroma to the LORD.

Laws for Grain Offerings

2 "When anyone brings a grain offering as an offering to the LORD, his offering shall be of fine flour. He shall pour oil on it and put frankincense on it **2** and bring it to Aaron's sons the priests. And he shall take from it a handful of the fine flour and oil, with all of its frankincense, and the priest shall burn this as its memorial portion on the altar, a food offering with a pleasing aroma to the LORD. **3** But the rest of the grain offering shall be for Aaron and his sons; it is a most holy part of the LORD's food offerings.

4 "When you bring a grain offering baked in the oven as an offering, it shall be unleavened loaves of fine flour mixed with oil or unleavened wafers smeared with oil. **5** And if your offering is a grain offering baked on a griddle, it shall be of fine flour unleavened, mixed with oil. **6** You shall break it in pieces and pour oil on it; it is a grain offering. **7** And if your offering is a grain offering cooked in a pan, it shall be made of fine flour with oil. **8** And you shall bring the grain offering that is made of these things to the LORD, and when it is presented to the priest, he shall bring it to the altar. **9** And the priest shall take from the grain offering its memorial portion and burn this on the altar, a food offering with a pleasing aroma to the LORD. **10** But the rest of the grain offering shall be for Aaron and his sons; it is a most holy part of the LORD's food offerings.

11 "No grain offering that you bring to the LORD shall be made with leaven, for you shall burn no leaven nor any honey as a food offering to the LORD. **12** As an offering of firstfruits you may bring them to the LORD, but they shall not be offered on the altar for a pleasing aroma. **13** You shall season all your grain offerings with salt. You shall not let the salt of the covenant with your God be missing from your grain offering; with all your offerings you shall offer salt.

14 "If you offer a grain offering of firstfruits to the LORD, you shall offer for the grain offering

---

[1] Or an offering by fire; so throughout Leviticus [2] Or feathers

of your firstfruits fresh ears, roasted with fire, crushed new grain. [15] And you shall put oil on it and lay frankincense on it; it is a grain offering. [16] And the priest shall burn as its memorial portion some of the crushed grain and some of the oil with all of its frankincense; it is a food offering to the LORD.

Laws for Peace Offerings

3 "If his offering is a sacrifice of peace offering, if he offers an animal from the herd, male or female, he shall offer it without blemish before the LORD. [2] And he shall lay his hand on the head of his offering and kill it at the entrance of the tent of meeting, and Aaron's sons the priests shall throw the blood against the sides of the altar. [3] And from the sacrifice of the peace offering, as a food offering to the LORD, he shall offer the fat covering the entrails and all the fat that is on the entrails, [4] and the two kidneys with the fat that is on them at the loins, and the long lobe of the liver that he shall remove with the kidneys. [5] Then Aaron's sons shall burn it on the altar on top of the burnt offering, which is on the wood on the fire; it is a food offering with a pleasing aroma to the LORD.

[6] "If his offering for a sacrifice of peace offering to the LORD is an animal from the flock, male or female, he shall offer it without blemish. [7] If he offers a lamb for his offering, then he shall offer it before the LORD, [8] lay his hand on the head of his offering, and kill it in front of the tent of meeting; and Aaron's sons shall throw its blood against the sides of the altar. [9] Then from the sacrifice of the peace offering he shall offer as a food offering to the LORD its fat; he shall remove the whole fat tail, cut off close to the backbone, and the fat that covers the entrails and all the fat that is on the entrails [10] and the two kidneys with the fat that is on them at the loins and the long lobe of the liver that he shall remove with the kidneys. [11] And the priest shall burn it on the altar as a food offering to the LORD.

[12] "If his offering is a goat, then he shall offer it before the LORD [13] and lay his hand on its head and kill it in front of the tent of meeting, and the sons of Aaron shall throw its blood against the sides of the altar. [14] Then he shall offer from it, as his offering for a food offering to the LORD, the fat covering the entrails and all the fat that is on the entrails [15] and the two kidneys with

the fat that is on them at the loins and the long lobe of the liver that he shall remove with the kidneys. [16] And the priest shall burn them on the altar as a food offering with a pleasing aroma. All fat is the LORD's. [17] It shall be a statute forever throughout your generations, in all your dwelling places, that you eat neither fat nor blood."

Laws for Sin Offerings

4 And the LORD spoke to Moses, saying, [2] "Speak to the people of Israel, saying, If anyone sins unintentionally[1] in any of the LORD's commandments about things not to be done, and does any one of them, [3] if it is the anointed priest who sins, thus bringing guilt on the people, then he shall offer for the sin that he has committed a bull from the herd without blemish to the LORD for a sin offering. [4] He shall bring the bull to the entrance of the tent of meeting before the LORD and lay his hand on the head of the bull and kill the bull before the LORD. [5] And the anointed priest shall take some of the blood of the bull and bring it into the tent of meeting, [6] and the priest shall dip his finger in the blood and sprinkle part of the blood seven times before the LORD in front of the veil of the sanctuary. [7] And the priest shall put some of the blood on the horns of the altar of fragrant incense before the LORD that is in the tent of meeting, and all the rest of the blood of the bull he shall pour out at the base of the altar of burnt offering that is at the entrance of the tent of meeting. [8] And all the fat of the bull of the sin offering he shall remove from it, the fat that covers the entrails and all the fat that is on the entrails [9] and the two kidneys with the fat that is on them at the loins and the long lobe of the liver that he shall remove with the kidneys [10] (just as these are taken from the ox of the sacrifice of the peace offerings); and the priest shall burn them on the altar of burnt offering. [11] But the skin of the bull and all its flesh, with its head, its legs, its entrails, and its dung— [12] all the rest of the bull—he shall carry outside the camp to a clean place, to the ash heap, and shall burn it up on a fire of wood. On the ash heap it shall be burned up.

[13] "If the whole congregation of Israel sins unintentionally[2] and the thing is hidden from the eyes of the assembly, and they do any one of the things that by the LORD's commandments ought not to be done, and they realize their guilt,[3] [14] when the sin which they have

[1] Or by mistake; so throughout Leviticus [2] Or makes a mistake [3] Or suffer for their guilt, or are guilty; also verses 22, 27, and chapter 5

committed becomes known, the assembly shall offer a bull from the herd for a sin offering and bring it in front of the tent of meeting. ¹⁵ And the elders of the congregation shall lay their hands on the head of the bull before the LORD, and the bull shall be killed before the LORD. ¹⁶ Then the anointed priest shall bring some of the blood of the bull into the tent of meeting, ¹⁷ and the priest shall dip his finger in the blood and sprinkle it seven times before the LORD in front of the veil. ¹⁸ And he shall put some of the blood on the horns of the altar that is in the tent of meeting before the LORD, and the rest of the blood he shall pour out at the base of the altar of burnt offering that is at the entrance of the tent of meeting. ¹⁹ And all its fat he shall take from it and burn on the altar. ²⁰ Thus shall he do with the bull. As he did with the bull of the sin offering, so shall he do with this. And the priest shall make atonement for them, and they shall be forgiven. ²¹ And he shall carry the bull outside the camp and burn it up as he burned the first bull; it is the sin offering for the assembly.

²² "When a leader sins, doing unintentionally any one of all the things that by the commandments of the LORD his God ought not to be done, and realizes his guilt, ²³ or the sin which he has committed is made known to him, he shall bring as his offering a goat, a male without blemish, ²⁴ and shall lay his hand on the head of the goat and kill it in the place where they kill the burnt offering before the LORD; it is a sin offering. ²⁵ Then the priest shall take some of the blood of the sin offering with his finger and put it on the horns of the altar of burnt offering and pour out the rest of its blood at the base of the altar of burnt offering. ²⁶ And all its fat he shall burn on the altar, like the fat of the sacrifice of peace offerings. So the priest shall make atonement for him for his sin, and he shall be forgiven.

²⁷ "If anyone of the common people sins unintentionally in doing any one of the things that by the LORD's commandments ought not to be done, and realizes his guilt, ²⁸ or the sin which he has committed is made known to him, he shall bring for his offering a goat, a female without blemish, for his sin which he has committed. ²⁹ And he shall lay his hand on the head of the sin offering and kill the sin offering in the place of burnt offering. ³⁰ And the priest shall take some of its blood with his finger and put it on the horns of the altar of burnt offering and pour out all the rest of its blood at the base of the altar. ³¹ And all its fat he shall remove, as the fat is removed from the peace offerings, and the priest shall burn it on the altar for a pleasing aroma to the LORD. And the priest shall make atonement for him, and he shall be forgiven.

³² "If he brings a lamb as his offering for a sin offering, he shall bring a female without blemish ³³ and lay his hand on the head of the sin offering and kill it for a sin offering in the place where they kill the burnt offering. ³⁴ Then the priest shall take some of the blood of the sin offering with his finger and put it on the horns of the altar of burnt offering and pour out all the rest of its blood at the base of the altar. ³⁵ And all its fat he shall remove as the fat of the lamb is removed from the sacrifice of peace offerings, and the priest shall burn it on the altar, on top of the LORD's food offerings. And the priest shall make atonement for him for the sin which he has committed, and he shall be forgiven.

5 "If anyone sins in that he hears a public adjuration to testify, and though he is a witness, whether he has seen or come to know the matter, yet does not speak, he shall bear his iniquity; ² or if anyone touches an unclean thing, whether a carcass of an unclean wild animal or a carcass of unclean livestock or a carcass of unclean swarming things, and it is hidden from him and he has become unclean, and he realizes his guilt; ³ or if he touches human uncleanness, of whatever sort the uncleanness may be with which one becomes unclean, and it is hidden from him, when he comes to know it, and realizes his guilt; ⁴ or if anyone utters with his lips a rash oath to do evil or to do good, any sort of rash oath that people swear, and it is hidden from him, when he comes to know it, and he realizes his guilt in any of these; ⁵ when he realizes his guilt in any of these and confesses the sin he has committed, ⁶ he shall bring to the LORD as his compensation¹ for the sin that he has committed, a female from the flock, a lamb or a goat, for a sin offering. And the priest shall make atonement for him for his sin.

⁷ "But if he cannot afford a lamb, then he shall bring to the LORD as his compensation for the sin that he has committed two turtledoves or two pigeons,² one for a sin offering and the other for a burnt offering. ⁸ He shall bring them to the priest, who shall offer first the one for

---

¹ Hebrew *his guilt penalty*; so throughout Leviticus ² Septuagint *two young pigeons*; also verse 11

the sin offering. He shall wring its head from its neck but shall not sever it completely, ⁹and he shall sprinkle some of the blood of the sin offering on the side of the altar, while the rest of the blood shall be drained out at the base of the altar; it is a sin offering. ¹⁰Then he shall offer the second for a burnt offering according to the rule. And the priest shall make atonement for him for the sin that he has committed, and he shall be forgiven.

¹¹ "But if he cannot afford two turtledoves or two pigeons, then he shall bring as his offering for the sin that he has committed a tenth of an ephah¹ of fine flour for a sin offering. He shall put no oil on it and shall put no frankincense on it, for it is a sin offering. ¹²And he shall bring it to the priest, and the priest shall take a handful of it as its memorial portion and burn this on the altar, on the LORD's food offerings; it is a sin offering. ¹³Thus the priest shall make atonement for him for the sin which he has committed in any one of these things, and he shall be forgiven. And the remainder² shall be for the priest, as in the grain offering."

Laws for Guilt Offerings

¹⁴The LORD spoke to Moses, saying, ¹⁵ "If anyone commits a breach of faith and sins unintentionally in any of the holy things of the LORD, he shall bring to the LORD as his compensation, a ram without blemish out of the flock, valued³ in silver shekels,⁴ according to the shekel of the sanctuary, for a guilt offering. ¹⁶He shall also make restitution for what he has done amiss in the holy thing and shall add a fifth to it and give it to the priest. And the priest shall make atonement for him with the ram of the guilt offering, and he shall be forgiven.

¹⁷ "If anyone sins, doing any of the things that by the LORD's commandments ought not to be done, though he did not know it, then realizes his guilt, he shall bear his iniquity. ¹⁸He shall bring to the priest a ram without blemish out of the flock, or its equivalent, for a guilt offering, and the priest shall make atonement for him for the mistake that he made unintentionally, and he shall be forgiven. ¹⁹It is a guilt offering; he has indeed incurred guilt before⁵ the LORD."

6 ⁶The LORD spoke to Moses, saying, ² "If anyone sins and commits a breach of faith against the LORD by deceiving his neighbor in a matter of deposit or security, or through robbery, or if he has oppressed his neighbor ³or has found something lost and lied about it, swearing falsely—in any of all the things that people do and sin thereby— ⁴if he has sinned and has realized his guilt and will restore what he took by robbery or what he got by oppression or the deposit that was committed to him or the lost thing that he found ⁵or anything about which he has sworn falsely, he shall restore it in full and shall add a fifth to it, and give it to him to whom it belongs on the day he realizes his guilt. ⁶And he shall bring to the priest as his compensation to the LORD a ram without blemish out of the flock, or its equivalent, for a guilt offering. ⁷And the priest shall make atonement for him before the LORD, and he shall be forgiven for any of the things that one may do and thereby become guilty."

The Priests and the Offerings

⁸⁷ The LORD spoke to Moses, saying, ⁹"Command Aaron and his sons, saying, This is the law of the burnt offering. The burnt offering shall be on the hearth on the altar all night until the morning, and the fire of the altar shall be kept burning on it. ¹⁰And the priest shall put on his linen garment and put his linen undergarment on his body, and he shall take up the ashes to which the fire has reduced the burnt offering on the altar and put them beside the altar. ¹¹Then he shall take off his garments and put on other garments and carry the ashes outside the camp to a clean place. ¹²The fire on the altar shall be kept burning on it; it shall not go out. The priest shall burn wood on it every morning, and he shall arrange the burnt offering on it and shall burn on it the fat of the peace offerings. ¹³Fire shall be kept burning on the altar continually; it shall not go out.

¹⁴ "And this is the law of the grain offering. The sons of Aaron shall offer it before the LORD in front of the altar. ¹⁵And one shall take from it a handful of the fine flour of the grain offering and its oil and all the frankincense that is on the grain offering and burn this as its memorial portion on the altar, a pleasing aroma to the LORD. ¹⁶And the rest of it Aaron and his sons shall eat. It shall be eaten unleavened in a holy place. In the court of the tent of meeting they shall eat it. ¹⁷It shall not be baked with leaven. I have given it as their portion of my food offerings. It is a thing most holy, like the sin offering

¹ An ephah was about 3/5 bushel or 22 liters ² Septuagint; Hebrew it ³ Or flock, or its equivalent ⁴ A shekel was about 2/5 ounce or 11 grams ⁵ Or he has paid full compensation to ⁶ Ch 5:20 in Hebrew ⁷ Ch 6:1 in Hebrew

and the guilt offering. [18] Every male among the children of Aaron may eat of it, as decreed forever throughout your generations, from the LORD's food offerings. Whatever touches them shall become holy."

[19] The LORD spoke to Moses, saying, [20] "This is the offering that Aaron and his sons shall offer to the LORD on the day when he is anointed: a tenth of an ephah[1] of fine flour as a regular grain offering, half of it in the morning and half in the evening. [21] It shall be made with oil on a griddle. You shall bring it well mixed, in baked[2] pieces like a grain offering, and offer it for a pleasing aroma to the LORD. [22] The priest from among Aaron's sons, who is anointed to succeed him, shall offer it to the LORD as decreed forever. The whole of it shall be burned. [23] Every grain offering of a priest shall be wholly burned. It shall not be eaten."

[24] The LORD spoke to Moses, saying, [25] "Speak to Aaron and his sons, saying, This is the law of the sin offering. In the place where the burnt offering is killed shall the sin offering be killed before the LORD; it is most holy. [26] The priest who offers it for sin shall eat it. In a holy place it shall be eaten, in the court of the tent of meeting. [27] Whatever touches its flesh shall be holy, and when any of its blood is splashed on a garment, you shall wash that on which it was splashed in a holy place. [28] And the earthenware vessel in which it is boiled shall be broken. But if it is boiled in a bronze vessel, that shall be scoured and rinsed in water. [29] Every male among the priests may eat of it; it is most holy. [30] But no sin offering shall be eaten from which any blood is brought into the tent of meeting to make atonement in the Holy Place; it shall be burned up with fire.

7 "This is the law of the guilt offering. It is most holy. [2] In the place where they kill the burnt offering they shall kill the guilt offering, and its blood shall be thrown against the sides of the altar. [3] And all its fat shall be offered, the fat tail, the fat that covers the entrails, [4] the two kidneys with the fat that is on them at the loins, and the long lobe of the liver that he shall remove with the kidneys. [5] The priest shall burn them on the altar as a food offering to the LORD; it is a guilt offering. [6] Every male among the priests may eat of it. It shall be eaten in a holy place. It is most holy. [7] The guilt offering is just like the sin offering; there is one law for

them. The priest who makes atonement with it shall have it. [8] And the priest who offers any man's burnt offering shall have for himself the skin of the burnt offering that he has offered. [9] And every grain offering baked in the oven and all that is prepared on a pan or a griddle shall belong to the priest who offers it. [10] And every grain offering, mixed with oil or dry, shall be shared equally among all the sons of Aaron.

[11] "And this is the law of the sacrifice of peace offerings that one may offer to the LORD. [12] If he offers it for a thanksgiving, then he shall offer with the thanksgiving sacrifice unleavened loaves mixed with oil, unleavened wafers smeared with oil, and loaves of fine flour well mixed with oil. [13] With the sacrifice of his peace offerings for thanksgiving he shall bring his offering with loaves of leavened bread. [14] And from it he shall offer one loaf from each offering, as a gift to the LORD. It shall belong to the priest who throws the blood of the peace offerings. [15] And the flesh of the sacrifice of his peace offerings for thanksgiving shall be eaten on the day of his offering. He shall not leave any of it until the morning. [16] But if the sacrifice of his offering is a vow offering or a freewill offering, it shall be eaten on the day that he offers his sacrifice, and on the next day what remains of it shall be eaten. [17] But what remains of the flesh of the sacrifice on the third day shall be burned up with fire. [18] If any of the flesh of the sacrifice of his peace offering is eaten on the third day, he who offers it shall not be accepted, neither shall it be credited to him. It is tainted, and he who eats of it shall bear his iniquity.

[19] "Flesh that touches any unclean thing shall not be eaten. It shall be burned up with fire. All who are clean may eat flesh, [20] but the person who eats of the flesh of the sacrifice of the LORD's peace offerings while an uncleanness is on him, that person shall be cut off from his people. [21] And if anyone touches an unclean thing, whether human uncleanness or an unclean beast or any unclean detestable creature, and then eats some flesh from the sacrifice of the LORD's peace offerings, that person shall be cut off from his people."

[22] The LORD spoke to Moses, saying, [23] "Speak to the people of Israel, saying, You shall eat no fat, of ox or sheep or goat. [24] The fat of an animal that dies of itself and the fat of one that is torn by beasts may be put to any other use, but on

[1] An ephah was about 3/5 bushel or 22 liters [2] The meaning of the Hebrew is uncertain

no account shall you eat it. ²⁵For every person who eats of the fat of an animal of which a food offering may be made to the LORD shall be cut off from his people. ²⁶Moreover, you shall eat no blood whatever, whether of fowl or of animal, in any of your dwelling places. ²⁷Whoever eats any blood, that person shall be cut off from his people."

²⁸The LORD spoke to Moses, saying, ²⁹"Speak to the people of Israel, saying, Whoever offers the sacrifice of his peace offerings to the LORD shall bring his offering to the LORD from the sacrifice of his peace offerings. ³⁰His own hands shall bring the LORD's food offerings. He shall bring the fat with the breast, that the breast may be waved as a wave offering before the LORD. ³¹The priest shall burn the fat on the altar, but the breast shall be for Aaron and his sons. ³²And the right thigh you shall give to the priest as a contribution from the sacrifice of your peace offerings. ³³Whoever among the sons of Aaron offers the blood of the peace offerings and the fat shall have the right thigh for a portion. ³⁴For the breast that is waved and the thigh that is contributed I have taken from the people of Israel, out of the sacrifices of their peace offerings, and have given them to Aaron the priest and to his sons, as a perpetual due from the people of Israel. ³⁵This is the portion of Aaron and of his sons from the LORD's food offerings, from the day they were presented to serve as priests of the LORD. ³⁶The LORD commanded this to be given them by the people of Israel, from the day that he anointed them. It is a perpetual due throughout their generations."

³⁷This is the law of the burnt offering, of the grain offering, of the sin offering, of the guilt offering, of the ordination offering, and of the peace offering, ³⁸which the LORD commanded Moses on Mount Sinai, on the day that he commanded the people of Israel to bring their offerings to the LORD, in the wilderness of Sinai.

Consecration of Aaron and His Sons

8 The LORD spoke to Moses, saying, ²"Take Aaron and his sons with him, and the garments and the anointing oil and the bull of the sin offering and the two rams and the basket of unleavened bread. ³And assemble all the congregation at the entrance of the tent of meeting." ⁴And Moses did as the LORD commanded him, and the congregation was assembled at the entrance of the tent of meeting.

⁵And Moses said to the congregation, "This is the thing that the LORD has commanded to be done." ⁶And Moses brought Aaron and his sons and washed them with water. ⁷And he put the coat on him and tied the sash around his waist and clothed him with the robe and put the ephod on him and tied the skillfully woven band of the ephod around him, binding it to him with the band.[1] ⁸And he placed the breastpiece on him, and in the breastpiece he put the Urim and the Thummim. ⁹And he set the turban on his head, and on the turban, in front, he set the golden plate, the holy crown, as the LORD commanded Moses.

¹⁰Then Moses took the anointing oil and anointed the tabernacle and all that was in it, and consecrated them. ¹¹And he sprinkled some of it on the altar seven times, and anointed the altar and all its utensils and the basin and its stand, to consecrate them. ¹²And he poured some of the anointing oil on Aaron's head and anointed him to consecrate him. ¹³And Moses brought Aaron's sons and clothed them with coats and tied sashes around their waists and bound caps on them, as the LORD commanded Moses.

¹⁴Then he brought the bull of the sin offering, and Aaron and his sons laid their hands on the head of the bull of the sin offering. ¹⁵And he[2] killed it, and Moses took the blood, and with his finger put it on the horns of the altar around it and purified the altar and poured out the blood at the base of the altar and consecrated it to make atonement for it. ¹⁶And he took all the fat that was on the entrails and the long lobe of the liver and the two kidneys with their fat, and Moses burned them on the altar. ¹⁷But the bull and its skin and its flesh and its dung he burned up with fire outside the camp, as the LORD commanded Moses.

¹⁸Then he presented the ram of the burnt offering, and Aaron and his sons laid their hands on the head of the ram. ¹⁹And he killed it, and Moses threw the blood against the sides of the altar. ²⁰He cut the ram into pieces, and Moses burned the head and the pieces and the fat. ²¹He washed the entrails and the legs with water, and Moses burned the whole ram on the altar. It was a burnt offering with a pleasing aroma, a food offering for the LORD, as the LORD commanded Moses.

[1] Hebrew *with it* [2] Probably Aaron or his representative; possibly Moses; also verses 16–23

²²Then he presented the other ram, the ram of ordination, and Aaron and his sons laid their hands on the head of the ram. ²³And he killed it, and Moses took some of its blood and put it on the lobe of Aaron's right ear and on the thumb of his right hand and on the big toe of his right foot. ²⁴Then he presented Aaron's sons, and Moses put some of the blood on the lobes of their right ears and on the thumbs of their right hands and on the big toes of their right feet. And Moses threw the blood against the sides of the altar. ²⁵Then he took the fat and the fat tail and all the fat that was on the entrails and the long lobe of the liver and the two kidneys with their fat and the right thigh, ²⁶and out of the basket of unleavened bread that was before the Lord he took one unleavened loaf and one loaf of bread with oil and one wafer and placed them on the pieces of fat and on the right thigh. ²⁷And he put all these in the hands of Aaron and in the hands of his sons and waved them as a wave offering before the Lord. ²⁸Then Moses took them from their hands and burned them on the altar with the burnt offering. This was an ordination offering with a pleasing aroma, a food offering to the Lord. ²⁹And Moses took the breast and waved it for a wave offering before the Lord. It was Moses' portion of the ram of ordination, as the Lord commanded Moses.

³⁰Then Moses took some of the anointing oil and of the blood that was on the altar and sprinkled it on Aaron and his garments, and also on his sons and his sons' garments. So he consecrated Aaron and his garments, and his sons and his sons' garments with him.

³¹And Moses said to Aaron and his sons, "Boil the flesh at the entrance of the tent of meeting, and there eat it and the bread that is in the basket of ordination offerings, as I commanded, saying, 'Aaron and his sons shall eat it.' ³²And what remains of the flesh and the bread you shall burn up with fire. ³³And you shall not go outside the entrance of the tent of meeting for seven days, until the days of your ordination are completed, for it will take seven days to ordain you. ³⁴As has been done today, the Lord has commanded to be done to make atonement for you. ³⁵At the entrance of the tent of meeting you shall remain day and night for seven days, performing what the Lord has charged, so that you do not die, for so I have been commanded." ³⁶And Aaron and his sons did all the things that the Lord commanded by Moses.

The Lord Accepts Aaron's Offering

9 On the eighth day Moses called Aaron and his sons and the elders of Israel, ²and he said to Aaron, "Take for yourself a bull calf for a sin offering and a ram for a burnt offering, both without blemish, and offer them before the Lord. ³And say to the people of Israel, 'Take a male goat for a sin offering, and a calf and a lamb, both a year old without blemish, for a burnt offering, ⁴and an ox and a ram for peace offerings, to sacrifice before the Lord, and a grain offering mixed with oil, for today the Lord will appear to you.'" ⁵And they brought what Moses commanded in front of the tent of meeting, and all the congregation drew near and stood before the Lord. ⁶And Moses said, "This is the thing that the Lord commanded you to do, that the glory of the Lord may appear to you." ⁷Then Moses said to Aaron, "Draw near to the altar and offer your sin offering and your burnt offering and make atonement for yourself and for the people, and bring the offering of the people and make atonement for them, as the Lord has commanded."

⁸So Aaron drew near to the altar and killed the calf of the sin offering, which was for himself. ⁹And the sons of Aaron presented the blood to him, and he dipped his finger in the blood and put it on the horns of the altar and poured out the blood at the base of the altar. ¹⁰But the fat and the kidneys and the long lobe of the liver from the sin offering he burned on the altar, as the Lord commanded Moses. ¹¹The flesh and the skin he burned up with fire outside the camp.

¹²Then he killed the burnt offering, and Aaron's sons handed him the blood, and he threw it against the sides of the altar. ¹³And they handed the burnt offering to him, piece by piece, and the head, and he burned them on the altar. ¹⁴And he washed the entrails and the legs and burned them with the burnt offering on the altar.

¹⁵Then he presented the people's offering and took the goat of the sin offering that was for the people and killed it and offered it as a sin offering, like the first one. ¹⁶And he presented the burnt offering and offered it according to the rule. ¹⁷And he presented the grain offering, took a handful of it, and burned it on the altar, besides the burnt offering of the morning.

¹⁸Then he killed the ox and the ram, the sacrifice of peace offerings for the people. And

Aaron's sons handed him the blood, and he threw it against the sides of the altar. ¹⁹ But the fat pieces of the ox and of the ram, the fat tail and that which covers the entrails and the kidneys and the long lobe of the liver— ²⁰ they put the fat pieces on the breasts, and he burned the fat pieces on the altar, ²¹ but the breasts and the right thigh Aaron waved for a wave offering before the LORD, as Moses commanded.

²² Then Aaron lifted up his hands toward the people and blessed them, and he came down from offering the sin offering and the burnt offering and the peace offerings. ²³ And Moses and Aaron went into the tent of meeting, and when they came out they blessed the people, and the glory of the LORD appeared to all the people. ²⁴ And fire came out from before the LORD and consumed the burnt offering and the pieces of fat on the altar, and when all the people saw it, they shouted and fell on their faces.

The Death of Nadab and Abihu

10 Now Nadab and Abihu, the sons of Aaron, each took his censer and put fire in it and laid incense on it and offered unauthorized[1] fire before the LORD, which he had not commanded them. ² And fire came out from before the LORD and consumed them, and they died before the LORD. ³ Then Moses said to Aaron, "This is what the LORD has said: 'Among those who are near me I will be sanctified, and before all the people I will be glorified.'" And Aaron held his peace.

⁴ And Moses called Mishael and Elzaphan, the sons of Uzziel the uncle of Aaron, and said to them, "Come near; carry your brothers away from the front of the sanctuary and out of the camp." ⁵ So they came near and carried them in their coats out of the camp, as Moses had said. ⁶ And Moses said to Aaron and to Eleazar and Ithamar his sons, "Do not let the hair of your heads hang loose, and do not tear your clothes, lest you die, and wrath come upon all the congregation; but let your brothers, the whole house of Israel, bewail the burning that the LORD has kindled. ⁷ And do not go outside the entrance of the tent of meeting, lest you die, for the anointing oil of the LORD is upon you." And they did according to the word of Moses.

⁸ And the LORD spoke to Aaron, saying, ⁹ "Drink no wine or strong drink, you or your sons with you, when you go into the tent of meeting, lest you die. It shall be a statute forever throughout your generations. ¹⁰ You are to distinguish between the holy and the common, and between the unclean and the clean, ¹¹ and you are to teach the people of Israel all the statutes that the LORD has spoken to them by Moses."

¹² Moses spoke to Aaron and to Eleazar and Ithamar, his surviving sons: "Take the grain offering that is left of the LORD's food offerings, and eat it unleavened beside the altar, for it is most holy. ¹³ You shall eat it in a holy place, because it is your due and your sons' due, from the LORD's food offerings, for so I am commanded. ¹⁴ But the breast that is waved and the thigh that is contributed you shall eat in a clean place, you and your sons and your daughters with you, for they are given as your due and your sons' due from the sacrifices of the peace offerings of the people of Israel. ¹⁵ The thigh that is contributed and the breast that is waved they shall bring with the food offerings of the fat pieces to wave for a wave offering before the LORD, and it shall be yours and your sons' with you as a due forever, as the LORD has commanded."

¹⁶ Now Moses diligently inquired about the goat of the sin offering, and behold, it was burned up! And he was angry with Eleazar and Ithamar, the surviving sons of Aaron, saying, ¹⁷ "Why have you not eaten the sin offering in the place of the sanctuary, since it is a thing most holy and has been given to you that you may bear the iniquity of the congregation, to make atonement for them before the LORD? ¹⁸ Behold, its blood was not brought into the inner part of the sanctuary. You certainly ought to have eaten it in the sanctuary, as I commanded." ¹⁹ And Aaron said to Moses, "Behold, today they have offered their sin offering and their burnt offering before the LORD, and yet such things as these have happened to me! If I had eaten the sin offering today, would the LORD have approved?" ²⁰ And when Moses heard that, he approved.

Clean and Unclean Animals

11 And the LORD spoke to Moses and Aaron, saying to them, ² "Speak to the people of Israel, saying, These are the living things that you may eat among all the animals that are on the earth. ³ Whatever parts the hoof and is cloven-footed and chews the cud, among the

---

[1] Or strange

animals, you may eat. [4] Nevertheless, among those that chew the cud or part the hoof, you shall not eat these: The camel, because it chews the cud but does not part the hoof, is unclean to you. [5] And the rock badger, because it chews the cud but does not part the hoof, is unclean to you. [6] And the hare, because it chews the cud but does not part the hoof, is unclean to you. [7] And the pig, because it parts the hoof and is cloven-footed but does not chew the cud, is unclean to you. [8] You shall not eat any of their flesh, and you shall not touch their carcasses; they are unclean to you.

[9] "These you may eat, of all that are in the waters. Everything in the waters that has fins and scales, whether in the seas or in the rivers, you may eat. [10] But anything in the seas or the rivers that does not have fins and scales, of the swarming creatures in the waters and of the living creatures that are in the waters, is detestable to you. [11] You shall regard them as detestable; you shall not eat any of their flesh, and you shall detest their carcasses. [12] Everything in the waters that does not have fins and scales is detestable to you.

[13] "And these you shall detest among the birds;[1] they shall not be eaten; they are detestable: the eagle,[2] the bearded vulture, the black vulture, [14] the kite, the falcon of any kind, [15] every raven of any kind, [16] the ostrich, the nighthawk, the sea gull, the hawk of any kind, [17] the little owl, the cormorant, the short-eared owl, [18] the barn owl, the tawny owl, the carrion vulture, [19] the stork, the heron of any kind, the hoopoe, and the bat.

[20] "All winged insects that go on all fours are detestable to you. [21] Yet among the winged insects that go on all fours you may eat those that have jointed legs above their feet, with which to hop on the ground. [22] Of them you may eat: the locust of any kind, the bald locust of any kind, the cricket of any kind, and the grasshopper of any kind. [23] But all other winged insects that have four feet are detestable to you.

[24] "And by these you shall become unclean. Whoever touches their carcass shall be unclean until the evening, [25] and whoever carries any part of their carcass shall wash his clothes and be unclean until the evening. [26] Every animal that parts the hoof but is not cloven-footed or does not chew the cud is unclean to you. Everyone who touches them shall be unclean.

[27] And all that walk on their paws, among the animals that go on all fours, are unclean to you. Whoever touches their carcass shall be unclean until the evening, [28] and he who carries their carcass shall wash his clothes and be unclean until the evening; they are unclean to you.

[29] "And these are unclean to you among the swarming things that swarm on the ground: the mole rat, the mouse, the great lizard of any kind, [30] the gecko, the monitor lizard, the lizard, the sand lizard, and the chameleon. [31] These are unclean to you among all that swarm. Whoever touches them when they are dead shall be unclean until the evening. [32] And anything on which any of them falls when they are dead shall be unclean, whether it is an article of wood or a garment or a skin or a sack, any article that is used for any purpose. It must be put into water, and it shall be unclean until the evening; then it shall be clean. [33] And if any of them falls into any earthenware vessel, all that is in it shall be unclean, and you shall break it. [34] Any food in it that could be eaten, on which water comes, shall be unclean. And all drink that could be drunk from every such vessel shall be unclean. [35] And everything on which any part of their carcass falls shall be unclean. Whether oven or stove, it shall be broken in pieces. They are unclean and shall remain unclean for you. [36] Nevertheless, a spring or a cistern holding water shall be clean, but whoever touches a carcass in them shall be unclean. [37] And if any part of their carcass falls upon any seed grain that is to be sown, it is clean, [38] but if water is put on the seed and any part of their carcass falls on it, it is unclean to you.

[39] "And if any animal which you may eat dies, whoever touches its carcass shall be unclean until the evening, [40] and whoever eats of its carcass shall wash his clothes and be unclean until the evening. And whoever carries the carcass shall wash his clothes and be unclean until the evening.

[41] "Every swarming thing that swarms on the ground is detestable; it shall not be eaten. [42] Whatever goes on its belly, and whatever goes on all fours, or whatever has many feet, any swarming thing that swarms on the ground, you shall not eat, for they are detestable. [43] You shall not make yourselves detestable with any swarming thing that swarms, and you shall not defile yourselves with them, and become

---

[1] Or *things that fly*; compare Genesis 1:20   [2] The identity of many of these birds is uncertain

unclean through them. ⁴⁴For I am the LORD your God. Consecrate yourselves therefore, and be holy, for I am holy. You shall not defile yourselves with any swarming thing that crawls on the ground. ⁴⁵For I am the LORD who brought you up out of the land of Egypt to be your God. You shall therefore be holy, for I am holy."

⁴⁶This is the law about beast and bird and every living creature that moves through the waters and every creature that swarms on the ground, ⁴⁷to make a distinction between the unclean and the clean and between the living creature that may be eaten and the living creature that may not be eaten.

Purification After Childbirth

12 The LORD spoke to Moses, saying, ²"Speak to the people of Israel, saying, If a woman conceives and bears a male child, then she shall be unclean seven days. As at the time of her menstruation, she shall be unclean. ³And on the eighth day the flesh of his foreskin shall be circumcised. ⁴Then she shall continue for thirty-three days in the blood of her purifying. She shall not touch anything holy, nor come into the sanctuary, until the days of her purifying are completed. ⁵But if she bears a female child, then she shall be unclean two weeks, as in her menstruation. And she shall continue in the blood of her purifying for sixty-six days.

⁶"And when the days of her purifying are completed, whether for a son or for a daughter, she shall bring to the priest at the entrance of the tent of meeting a lamb a year old for a burnt offering, and a pigeon or a turtledove for a sin offering, ⁷and he shall offer it before the LORD and make atonement for her. Then she shall be clean from the flow of her blood. This is the law for her who bears a child, either male or female. ⁸And if she cannot afford a lamb, then she shall take two turtledoves or two pigeons,¹ one for a burnt offering and the other for a sin offering. And the priest shall make atonement for her, and she shall be clean."

Laws About Leprosy

13 The LORD spoke to Moses and Aaron, saying, ²"When a person has on the skin of his body a swelling or an eruption or a spot, and it turns into a case of leprous² disease on the skin of his body, then he shall be brought to Aaron the priest or to one of his sons the priests, ³and the priest shall examine the diseased area

on the skin of his body. And if the hair in the diseased area has turned white and the disease appears to be deeper than the skin of his body, it is a case of leprous disease. When the priest has examined him, he shall pronounce him unclean. ⁴But if the spot is white in the skin of his body and appears no deeper than the skin, and the hair in it has not turned white, the priest shall shut up the diseased person for seven days. ⁵And the priest shall examine him on the seventh day, and if in his eyes the disease is checked and the disease has not spread in the skin, then the priest shall shut him up for another seven days. ⁶And the priest shall examine him again on the seventh day, and if the diseased area has faded and the disease has not spread in the skin, then the priest shall pronounce him clean; it is only an eruption. And he shall wash his clothes and be clean. ⁷But if the eruption spreads in the skin, after he has shown himself to the priest for his cleansing, he shall appear again before the priest. ⁸And the priest shall look, and if the eruption has spread in the skin, then the priest shall pronounce him unclean; it is a leprous disease.

⁹"When a man is afflicted with a leprous disease, he shall be brought to the priest, ¹⁰and the priest shall look. And if there is a white swelling in the skin that has turned the hair white, and there is raw flesh in the swelling, ¹¹it is a chronic leprous disease in the skin of his body, and the priest shall pronounce him unclean. He shall not shut him up, for he is unclean. ¹²And if the leprous disease breaks out in the skin, so that the leprous disease covers all the skin of the diseased person from head to foot, so far as the priest can see, ¹³then the priest shall look, and if the leprous disease has covered all his body, he shall pronounce him clean of the disease; it has all turned white, and he is clean. ¹⁴But when raw flesh appears on him, he shall be unclean. ¹⁵And the priest shall examine the raw flesh and pronounce him unclean. Raw flesh is unclean, for it is a leprous disease. ¹⁶But if the raw flesh recovers and turns white again, then he shall come to the priest, ¹⁷and the priest shall examine him, and if the disease has turned white, then the priest shall pronounce the diseased person clean; he is clean.

¹⁸"If there is in the skin of one's body a boil and it heals, ¹⁹and in the place of the boil there comes a white swelling or a reddish-white

¹ Septuagint *two young pigeons* ² *Leprosy* was a term for several skin diseases

spot, then it shall be shown to the priest. [20] And the priest shall look, and if it appears deeper than the skin and its hair has turned white, then the priest shall pronounce him unclean. It is a case of leprous disease that has broken out in the boil. [21] But if the priest examines it and there is no white hair in it and it is not deeper than the skin, but has faded, then the priest shall shut him up seven days. [22] And if it spreads in the skin, then the priest shall pronounce him unclean; it is a disease. [23] But if the spot remains in one place and does not spread, it is the scar of the boil, and the priest shall pronounce him clean.

[24] "Or, when the body has a burn on its skin and the raw flesh of the burn becomes a spot, reddish-white or white, [25] the priest shall examine it, and if the hair in the spot has turned white and it appears deeper than the skin, then it is a leprous disease. It has broken out in the burn, and the priest shall pronounce him unclean; it is a case of leprous disease. [26] But if the priest examines it and there is no white hair in the spot and it is no deeper than the skin, but has faded, the priest shall shut him up seven days, [27] and the priest shall examine him the seventh day. If it is spreading in the skin, then the priest shall pronounce him unclean; it is a case of leprous disease. [28] But if the spot remains in one place and does not spread in the skin, but has faded, it is a swelling from the burn, and the priest shall pronounce him clean, for it is the scar of the burn.

[29] "When a man or woman has a disease on the head or the beard, [30] the priest shall examine the disease. And if it appears deeper than the skin, and the hair in it is yellow and thin, then the priest shall pronounce him unclean. It is an itch, a leprous disease of the head or the beard. [31] And if the priest examines the itching disease and it appears no deeper than the skin and there is no black hair in it, then the priest shall shut up the person with the itching disease for seven days, [32] and on the seventh day the priest shall examine the disease. If the itch has not spread, and there is in it no yellow hair, and the itch appears to be no deeper than the skin, [33] then he shall shave himself, but the itch he shall not shave; and the priest shall shut up the person with the itching disease for another seven days. [34] And on the seventh day the priest shall examine the itch, and if the itch has not spread in the skin and it appears to be

no deeper than the skin, then the priest shall pronounce him clean. And he shall wash his clothes and be clean. [35] But if the itch spreads in the skin after his cleansing, [36] then the priest shall examine him, and if the itch has spread in the skin, the priest need not seek for the yellow hair; he is unclean. [37] But if in his eyes the itch is unchanged and black hair has grown in it, the itch is healed and he is clean, and the priest shall pronounce him clean.

[38] "When a man or a woman has spots on the skin of the body, white spots, [39] the priest shall look, and if the spots on the skin of the body are of a dull white, it is leukoderma that has broken out in the skin; he is clean.

[40] "If a man's hair falls out from his head, he is bald; he is clean. [41] And if a man's hair falls out from his forehead, he has baldness of the forehead; he is clean. [42] But if there is on the bald head or the bald forehead a reddish-white diseased area, it is a leprous disease breaking out on his bald head or his bald forehead. [43] Then the priest shall examine him, and if the diseased swelling is reddish-white on his bald head or on his bald forehead, like the appearance of leprous disease in the skin of the body, [44] he is a leprous man, he is unclean. The priest must pronounce him unclean; his disease is on his head.

[45] "The leprous person who has the disease shall wear torn clothes and let the hair of his head hang loose, and he shall cover his upper lip[1] and cry out, 'Unclean, unclean.' [46] He shall remain unclean as long as he has the disease. He is unclean. He shall live alone. His dwelling shall be outside the camp.

[47] "When there is a case of leprous disease in a garment, whether a woolen or a linen garment, [48] in warp or woof of linen or wool, or in a skin or in anything made of skin, [49] if the disease is greenish or reddish in the garment, or in the skin or in the warp or the woof or in any article made of skin, it is a case of leprous disease, and it shall be shown to the priest. [50] And the priest shall examine the disease and shut up that which has the disease for seven days. [51] Then he shall examine the disease on the seventh day. If the disease has spread in the garment, in the warp or the woof, or in the skin, whatever be the use of the skin, the disease is a persistent leprous disease; it is unclean. [52] And he shall burn the garment, or the warp or the woof, the wool or the linen, or any article made of skin

[1] Or mustache

that is diseased, for it is a persistent leprous disease. It shall be burned in the fire.

⁵³ "And if the priest examines, and if the disease has not spread in the garment, in the warp or the woof or in any article made of skin, ⁵⁴ then the priest shall command that they wash the thing in which is the disease, and he shall shut it up for another seven days. ⁵⁵ And the priest shall examine the diseased thing after it has been washed. And if the appearance of the diseased area has not changed, though the disease has not spread, it is unclean. You shall burn it in the fire, whether the rot is on the back or on the front.

⁵⁶ "But if the priest examines, and if the diseased area has faded after it has been washed, he shall tear it out of the garment or the skin or the warp or the woof. ⁵⁷ Then if it appears again in the garment, in the warp or the woof, or in any article made of skin, it is spreading. You shall burn with fire whatever has the disease. ⁵⁸ But the garment, or the warp or the woof, or any article made of skin from which the disease departs when you have washed it, shall then be washed a second time, and be clean."

⁵⁹ This is the law for a case of leprous disease in a garment of wool or linen, either in the warp or the woof, or in any article made of skin, to determine whether it is clean or unclean.

Laws for Cleansing Lepers

14 The LORD spoke to Moses, saying, ² "This shall be the law of the leprous person for the day of his cleansing. He shall be brought to the priest, ³ and the priest shall go out of the camp, and the priest shall look. Then, if the case of leprous disease is healed in the leprous person, ⁴ the priest shall command them to take for him who is to be cleansed two live¹ clean birds and cedarwood and scarlet yarn and hyssop. ⁵ And the priest shall command them to kill one of the birds in an earthenware vessel over fresh² water. ⁶ He shall take the live bird with the cedarwood and the scarlet yarn and the hyssop, and dip them and the live bird in the blood of the bird that was killed over the fresh water. ⁷ And he shall sprinkle it seven times on him who is to be cleansed of the leprous disease. Then he shall pronounce him clean and shall let the living bird go into the open field. ⁸ And he who is to be cleansed shall wash his clothes and shave off all his hair and bathe himself in water, and he shall be clean.

And after that he may come into the camp, but live outside his tent seven days. ⁹ And on the seventh day he shall shave off all his hair from his head, his beard, and his eyebrows. He shall shave off all his hair, and then he shall wash his clothes and bathe his body in water, and he shall be clean.

¹⁰ "And on the eighth day he shall take two male lambs without blemish, and one ewe lamb a year old without blemish, and a grain offering of three tenths of an ephah³ of fine flour mixed with oil, and one log⁴ of oil. ¹¹ And the priest who cleanses him shall set the man who is to be cleansed and these things before the LORD, at the entrance of the tent of meeting. ¹² And the priest shall take one of the male lambs and offer it for a guilt offering, along with the log of oil, and wave them for a wave offering before the LORD. ¹³ And he shall kill the lamb in the place where they kill the sin offering and the burnt offering, in the place of the sanctuary. For the guilt offering, like the sin offering, belongs to the priest; it is most holy. ¹⁴ The priest shall take some of the blood of the guilt offering, and the priest shall put it on the lobe of the right ear of him who is to be cleansed and on the thumb of his right hand and on the big toe of his right foot. ¹⁵ Then the priest shall take some of the log of oil and pour it into the palm of his own left hand ¹⁶ and dip his right finger in the oil that is in his left hand and sprinkle some oil with his finger seven times before the LORD. ¹⁷ And some of the oil that remains in his hand the priest shall put on the lobe of the right ear of him who is to be cleansed and on the thumb of his right hand and on the big toe of his right foot, on top of the blood of the guilt offering. ¹⁸ And the rest of the oil that is in the priest's hand he shall put on the head of him who is to be cleansed. Then the priest shall make atonement for him before the LORD. ¹⁹ The priest shall offer the sin offering, to make atonement for him who is to be cleansed from his uncleanness. And afterward he shall kill the burnt offering. ²⁰ And the priest shall offer the burnt offering and the grain offering on the altar. Thus the priest shall make atonement for him, and he shall be clean.

²¹ "But if he is poor and cannot afford so much, then he shall take one male lamb for a guilt offering to be waved, to make atonement for him, and a tenth of an ephah of fine flour mixed with oil for a grain offering, and a log

¹ Or *wild* ² Or *running*; Hebrew *living*; also verses 6, 50, 51, 52 ³ An *ephah* was about 3/5 bushel or 22 liters ⁴ A *log* was about 1/3 quart or 0.3 liter

of oil; [22] also two turtledoves or two pigeons, whichever he can afford. The one shall be a sin offering and the other a burnt offering. [23] And on the eighth day he shall bring them for his cleansing to the priest, to the entrance of the tent of meeting, before the LORD. [24] And the priest shall take the lamb of the guilt offering and the log of oil, and the priest shall wave them for a wave offering before the LORD. [25] And he shall kill the lamb of the guilt offering. And the priest shall take some of the blood of the guilt offering and put it on the lobe of the right ear of him who is to be cleansed, and on the thumb of his right hand and on the big toe of his right foot. [26] And the priest shall pour some of the oil into the palm of his own left hand, [27] and shall sprinkle with his right finger some of the oil that is in his left hand seven times before the LORD. [28] And the priest shall put some of the oil that is in his hand on the lobe of the right ear of him who is to be cleansed and on the thumb of his right hand and on the big toe of his right foot, in the place where the blood of the guilt offering was put. [29] And the rest of the oil that is in the priest's hand he shall put on the head of him who is to be cleansed, to make atonement for him before the LORD. [30] And he shall offer, of the turtledoves or pigeons, whichever he can afford, [31] one[1] for a sin offering and the other for a burnt offering, along with a grain offering. And the priest shall make atonement before the LORD for him who is being cleansed. [32] This is the law for him in whom is a case of leprous disease, who cannot afford the offerings for his cleansing."

Laws for Cleansing Houses

[33] The LORD spoke to Moses and Aaron, saying, [34] "When you come into the land of Canaan, which I give you for a possession, and I put a case of leprous disease in a house in the land of your possession, [35] then he who owns the house shall come and tell the priest, 'There seems to me to be some case of disease in my house.' [36] Then the priest shall command that they empty the house before the priest goes to examine the disease, lest all that is in the house be declared unclean. And afterward the priest shall go in to see the house. [37] And he shall examine the disease. And if the disease is in the walls of the house with greenish or reddish spots, and if it appears to be deeper than the surface, [38] then the priest shall go out of the house to the door of the house and shut up the house seven days. [39] And the priest shall come again on the seventh day, and look. If the disease has spread in the walls of the house, [40] then the priest shall command that they take out the stones in which is the disease and throw them into an unclean place outside the city. [41] And he shall have the inside of the house scraped all around, and the plaster that they scrape off they shall pour out in an unclean place outside the city. [42] Then they shall take other stones and put them in the place of those stones, and he shall take other plaster and plaster the house.

[43] "If the disease breaks out again in the house, after he has taken out the stones and scraped the house and plastered it, [44] then the priest shall go and look. And if the disease has spread in the house, it is a persistent leprous disease in the house; it is unclean. [45] And he shall break down the house, its stones and timber and all the plaster of the house, and he shall carry them out of the city to an unclean place. [46] Moreover, whoever enters the house while it is shut up shall be unclean until the evening, [47] and whoever sleeps in the house shall wash his clothes, and whoever eats in the house shall wash his clothes.

[48] "But if the priest comes and looks, and if the disease has not spread in the house after the house was plastered, then the priest shall pronounce the house clean, for the disease is healed. [49] And for the cleansing of the house he shall take two small birds, with cedarwood and scarlet yarn and hyssop, [50] and shall kill one of the birds in an earthenware vessel over fresh water [51] and shall take the cedarwood and the hyssop and the scarlet yarn, along with the live bird, and dip them in the blood of the bird that was killed and in the fresh water and sprinkle the house seven times. [52] Thus he shall cleanse the house with the blood of the bird and with the fresh water and with the live bird and with the cedarwood and hyssop and scarlet yarn. [53] And he shall let the live bird go out of the city into the open country. So he shall make atonement for the house, and it shall be clean."

[54] This is the law for any case of leprous disease: for an itch, [55] for leprous disease in a garment or in a house, [56] and for a swelling or an eruption or a spot, [57] to show when it is unclean and when it is clean. This is the law for leprous disease.

---

[1] Septuagint, Syriac; Hebrew *afford,* [31]*such as he can afford, one*

Laws About Bodily Discharges

15 The LORD spoke to Moses and Aaron, saying, [2] "Speak to the people of Israel and say to them, When any man has a discharge from his body,[1] his discharge is unclean. [3] And this is the law of his uncleanness for a discharge: whether his body runs with his discharge, or his body is blocked up by his discharge, it is his uncleanness. [4] Every bed on which the one with the discharge lies shall be unclean, and everything on which he sits shall be unclean. [5] And anyone who touches his bed shall wash his clothes and bathe himself in water and be unclean until the evening. [6] And whoever sits on anything on which the one with the discharge has sat shall wash his clothes and bathe himself in water and be unclean until the evening. [7] And whoever touches the body of the one with the discharge shall wash his clothes and bathe himself in water and be unclean until the evening. [8] And if the one with the discharge spits on someone who is clean, then he shall wash his clothes and bathe himself in water and be unclean until the evening. [9] And any saddle on which the one with the discharge rides shall be unclean. [10] And whoever touches anything that was under him shall be unclean until the evening. And whoever carries such things shall wash his clothes and bathe himself in water and be unclean until the evening. [11] Anyone whom the one with the discharge touches without having rinsed his hands in water shall wash his clothes and bathe himself in water and be unclean until the evening. [12] And an earthenware vessel that the one with the discharge touches shall be broken, and every vessel of wood shall be rinsed in water.

[13] "And when the one with a discharge is cleansed of his discharge, then he shall count for himself seven days for his cleansing, and wash his clothes. And he shall bathe his body in fresh water and shall be clean. [14] And on the eighth day he shall take two turtledoves or two pigeons and come before the LORD to the entrance of the tent of meeting and give them to the priest. [15] And the priest shall use them, one for a sin offering and the other for a burnt offering. And the priest shall make atonement for him before the LORD for his discharge.

[16] "If a man has an emission of semen, he shall bathe his whole body in water and be unclean until the evening. [17] And every garment and every skin on which the semen comes shall be washed with water and be unclean until the evening. [18] If a man lies with a woman and has an emission of semen, both of them shall bathe themselves in water and be unclean until the evening.

[19] "When a woman has a discharge, and the discharge in her body is blood, she shall be in her menstrual impurity for seven days, and whoever touches her shall be unclean until the evening. [20] And everything on which she lies during her menstrual impurity shall be unclean. Everything also on which she sits shall be unclean. [21] And whoever touches her bed shall wash his clothes and bathe himself in water and be unclean until the evening. [22] And whoever touches anything on which she sits shall wash his clothes and bathe himself in water and be unclean until the evening. [23] Whether it is the bed or anything on which she sits, when he touches it he shall be unclean until the evening. [24] And if any man lies with her and her menstrual impurity comes upon him, he shall be unclean seven days, and every bed on which he lies shall be unclean.

[25] "If a woman has a discharge of blood for many days, not at the time of her menstrual impurity, or if she has a discharge beyond the time of her impurity, all the days of the discharge she shall continue in uncleanness. As in the days of her impurity, she shall be unclean. [26] Every bed on which she lies, all the days of her discharge, shall be to her as the bed of her impurity. And everything on which she sits shall be unclean, as in the uncleanness of her menstrual impurity. [27] And whoever touches these things shall be unclean, and shall wash his clothes and bathe himself in water and be unclean until the evening. [28] But if she is cleansed of her discharge, she shall count for herself seven days, and after that she shall be clean. [29] And on the eighth day she shall take two turtledoves or two pigeons and bring them to the priest, to the entrance of the tent of meeting. [30] And the priest shall use one for a sin offering and the other for a burnt offering. And the priest shall make atonement for her before the LORD for her unclean discharge.

[31] "Thus you shall keep the people of Israel separate from their uncleanness, lest they die in their uncleanness by defiling my tabernacle that is in their midst."

---

[1] Hebrew *flesh*; also verse 3

³²This is the law for him who has a discharge and for him who has an emission of semen, becoming unclean thereby; ³³also for her who is unwell with her menstrual impurity, that is, for anyone, male or female, who has a discharge, and for the man who lies with a woman who is unclean.

The Day of Atonement

16 The LORD spoke to Moses after the death of the two sons of Aaron, when they drew near before the LORD and died, ²and the LORD said to Moses, "Tell Aaron your brother not to come at any time into the Holy Place inside the veil, before the mercy seat that is on the ark, so that he may not die. For I will appear in the cloud over the mercy seat. ³But in this way Aaron shall come into the Holy Place: with a bull from the herd for a sin offering and a ram for a burnt offering. ⁴He shall put on the holy linen coat and shall have the linen undergarment on his body, and he shall tie the linen sash around his waist, and wear the linen turban; these are the holy garments. He shall bathe his body in water and then put them on. ⁵And he shall take from the congregation of the people of Israel two male goats for a sin offering, and one ram for a burnt offering.

⁶"Aaron shall offer the bull as a sin offering for himself and shall make atonement for himself and for his house. ⁷Then he shall take the two goats and set them before the LORD at the entrance of the tent of meeting. ⁸And Aaron shall cast lots over the two goats, one lot for the LORD and the other lot for Azazel.¹ ⁹And Aaron shall present the goat on which the lot fell for the LORD and use it as a sin offering, ¹⁰but the goat on which the lot fell for Azazel shall be presented alive before the LORD to make atonement over it, that it may be sent away into the wilderness to Azazel.

¹¹"Aaron shall present the bull as a sin offering for himself, and shall make atonement for himself and for his house. He shall kill the bull as a sin offering for himself. ¹²And he shall take a censer full of coals of fire from the altar before the LORD, and two handfuls of sweet incense beaten small, and he shall bring it inside the veil ¹³and put the incense on the fire before the LORD, that the cloud of the incense may cover the mercy seat that is over the testimony, so that he does not die. ¹⁴And he shall take some of the blood of the bull and sprinkle it with his finger on the front of the mercy seat on the east side, and in front of the mercy seat he shall sprinkle some of the blood with his finger seven times.

¹⁵"Then he shall kill the goat of the sin offering that is for the people and bring its blood inside the veil and do with its blood as he did with the blood of the bull, sprinkling it over the mercy seat and in front of the mercy seat. ¹⁶Thus he shall make atonement for the Holy Place, because of the uncleannesses of the people of Israel and because of their transgressions, all their sins. And so he shall do for the tent of meeting, which dwells with them in the midst of their uncleannesses. ¹⁷No one may be in the tent of meeting from the time he enters to make atonement in the Holy Place until he comes out and has made atonement for himself and for his house and for all the assembly of Israel. ¹⁸Then he shall go out to the altar that is before the LORD and make atonement for it, and shall take some of the blood of the bull and some of the blood of the goat, and put it on the horns of the altar all around. ¹⁹And he shall sprinkle some of the blood on it with his finger seven times, and cleanse it and consecrate it from the uncleannesses of the people of Israel.

²⁰"And when he has made an end of atoning for the Holy Place and the tent of meeting and the altar, he shall present the live goat. ²¹And Aaron shall lay both his hands on the head of the live goat, and confess over it all the iniquities of the people of Israel, and all their transgressions, all their sins. And he shall put them on the head of the goat and send it away into the wilderness by the hand of a man who is in readiness. ²²The goat shall bear all their iniquities on itself to a remote area, and he shall let the goat go free in the wilderness.

²³"Then Aaron shall come into the tent of meeting and shall take off the linen garments that he put on when he went into the Holy Place and shall leave them there. ²⁴And he shall bathe his body in water in a holy place and put on his garments and come out and offer his burnt offering and the burnt offering of the people and make atonement for himself and for the people. ²⁵And the fat of the sin offering he shall burn on the altar. ²⁶And he who lets the goat go to Azazel shall wash his clothes and bathe his body in water, and afterward he may come into the camp. ²⁷And the bull for the sin offering and the goat for the sin offering, whose blood was brought in to make

¹ The meaning of *Azazel* is uncertain; possibly the name of a place or a demon, traditionally a scapegoat; also verses 10, 26

atonement in the Holy Place, shall be carried outside the camp. Their skin and their flesh and their dung shall be burned up with fire. ²⁸ And he who burns them shall wash his clothes and bathe his body in water, and afterward he may come into the camp.

²⁹ "And it shall be a statute to you forever that in the seventh month, on the tenth day of the month, you shall afflict yourselves¹ and shall do no work, either the native or the stranger who sojourns among you. ³⁰ For on this day shall atonement be made for you to cleanse you. You shall be clean before the LORD from all your sins. ³¹ It is a Sabbath of solemn rest to you, and you shall afflict yourselves; it is a statute forever. ³² And the priest who is anointed and consecrated as priest in his father's place shall make atonement, wearing the holy linen garments. ³³ He shall make atonement for the holy sanctuary, and he shall make atonement for the tent of meeting and for the altar, and he shall make atonement for the priests and for all the people of the assembly. ³⁴ And this shall be a statute forever for you, that atonement may be made for the people of Israel once in the year because of all their sins." And Aaron² did as the LORD commanded Moses.

The Place of Sacrifice

17 And the LORD spoke to Moses, saying, ² "Speak to Aaron and his sons and to all the people of Israel and say to them, This is the thing that the LORD has commanded. ³ If any one of the house of Israel kills an ox or a lamb or a goat in the camp, or kills it outside the camp, ⁴ and does not bring it to the entrance of the tent of meeting to offer it as a gift to the LORD in front of the tabernacle of the LORD, bloodguilt shall be imputed to that man. He has shed blood, and that man shall be cut off from among his people. ⁵ This is to the end that the people of Israel may bring their sacrifices that they sacrifice in the open field, that they may bring them to the LORD, to the priest at the entrance of the tent of meeting, and sacrifice them as sacrifices of peace offerings to the LORD. ⁶ And the priest shall throw the blood on the altar of the LORD at the entrance of the tent of meeting and burn the fat for a pleasing aroma to the LORD. ⁷ So they shall no more sacrifice their sacrifices to goat demons, after whom they whore. This shall be a statute forever for them throughout their generations.

⁸ "And you shall say to them, Any one of the house of Israel, or of the strangers who sojourn among them, who offers a burnt offering or sacrifice ⁹ and does not bring it to the entrance of the tent of meeting to offer it to the LORD, that man shall be cut off from his people.

Laws Against Eating Blood

¹⁰ "If any one of the house of Israel or of the strangers who sojourn among them eats any blood, I will set my face against that person who eats blood and will cut him off from among his people. ¹¹ For the life of the flesh is in the blood, and I have given it for you on the altar to make atonement for your souls, for it is the blood that makes atonement by the life. ¹² Therefore I have said to the people of Israel, No person among you shall eat blood, neither shall any stranger who sojourns among you eat blood.

¹³ "Any one also of the people of Israel, or of the strangers who sojourn among them, who takes in hunting any beast or bird that may be eaten shall pour out its blood and cover it with earth. ¹⁴ For the life of every creature³ is its blood: its blood is its life.⁴ Therefore I have said to the people of Israel, You shall not eat the blood of any creature, for the life of every creature is its blood. Whoever eats it shall be cut off. ¹⁵ And every person who eats what dies of itself or what is torn by beasts, whether he is a native or a sojourner, shall wash his clothes and bathe himself in water and be unclean until the evening; then he shall be clean. ¹⁶ But if he does not wash them or bathe his flesh, he shall bear his iniquity."

Unlawful Sexual Relations

18 And the LORD spoke to Moses, saying, ² "Speak to the people of Israel and say to them, I am the LORD your God. ³ You shall not do as they do in the land of Egypt, where you lived, and you shall not do as they do in the land of Canaan, to which I am bringing you. You shall not walk in their statutes. ⁴ You shall follow my rules⁵ and keep my statutes and walk in them. I am the LORD your God. ⁵ You shall therefore keep my statutes and my rules; if a person does them, he shall live by them: I am the LORD.

⁶ "None of you shall approach any one of his close relatives to uncover nakedness. I am the LORD. ⁷ You shall not uncover the nakedness of your father, which is the nakedness of your mother; she is your mother, you shall not

---

¹ Or *shall fast*; also verse 31 ² Hebrew *he* ³ Hebrew *all flesh* ⁴ Hebrew *it is in its life* ⁵ Or *my just decrees*; also verse 5

uncover her nakedness. [8] You shall not uncover the nakedness of your father's wife; it is your father's nakedness. [9] You shall not uncover the nakedness of your sister, your father's daughter or your mother's daughter, whether brought up in the family or in another home. [10] You shall not uncover the nakedness of your son's daughter or of your daughter's daughter, for their nakedness is your own nakedness. [11] You shall not uncover the nakedness of your father's wife's daughter, brought up in your father's family, since she is your sister. [12] You shall not uncover the nakedness of your father's sister; she is your father's relative. [13] You shall not uncover the nakedness of your mother's sister, for she is your mother's relative. [14] You shall not uncover the nakedness of your father's brother, that is, you shall not approach his wife; she is your aunt. [15] You shall not uncover the nakedness of your daughter-in-law; she is your son's wife, you shall not uncover her nakedness. [16] You shall not uncover the nakedness of your brother's wife; it is your brother's nakedness. [17] You shall not uncover the nakedness of a woman and of her daughter, and you shall not take her son's daughter or her daughter's daughter to uncover her nakedness; they are relatives; it is depravity. [18] And you shall not take a woman as a rival wife to her sister, uncovering her nakedness while her sister is still alive.

[19] "You shall not approach a woman to uncover her nakedness while she is in her menstrual uncleanness. [20] And you shall not lie sexually with your neighbor's wife and so make yourself unclean with her. [21] You shall not give any of your children to offer them[1] to Molech, and so profane the name of your God: I am the LORD. [22] You shall not lie with a male as with a woman; it is an abomination. [23] And you shall not lie with any animal and so make yourself unclean with it, neither shall any woman give herself to an animal to lie with it: it is perversion.

[24] "Do not make yourselves unclean by any of these things, for by all these the nations I am driving out before you have become unclean, [25] and the land became unclean, so that I punished its iniquity, and the land vomited out its inhabitants. [26] But you shall keep my statutes and my rules and do none of these abominations, either the native or the stranger who sojourns among you [27] (for the people of the land, who were before you, did all of these abominations, so that the land became unclean), [28] lest the land vomit you out when you make it unclean, as it vomited out the nation that was before you. [29] For everyone who does any of these abominations, the persons who do them shall be cut off from among their people. [30] So keep my charge never to practice any of these abominable customs that were practiced before you, and never to make yourselves unclean by them: I am the LORD your God."

The LORD Is Holy

19 And the LORD spoke to Moses, saying, [2] "Speak to all the congregation of the people of Israel and say to them, You shall be holy, for I the LORD your God am holy. [3] Every one of you shall revere his mother and his father, and you shall keep my Sabbaths: I am the LORD your God. [4] Do not turn to idols or make for yourselves any gods of cast metal: I am the LORD your God.

[5] "When you offer a sacrifice of peace offerings to the LORD, you shall offer it so that you may be accepted. [6] It shall be eaten the same day you offer it or on the day after, and anything left over until the third day shall be burned up with fire. [7] If it is eaten at all on the third day, it is tainted; it will not be accepted, [8] and everyone who eats it shall bear his iniquity, because he has profaned what is holy to the LORD, and that person shall be cut off from his people.

Love Your Neighbor as Yourself

[9] "When you reap the harvest of your land, you shall not reap your field right up to its edge, neither shall you gather the gleanings after your harvest. [10] And you shall not strip your vineyard bare, neither shall you gather the fallen grapes of your vineyard. You shall leave them for the poor and for the sojourner: I am the LORD your God.

[11] "You shall not steal; you shall not deal falsely; you shall not lie to one another. [12] You shall not swear by my name falsely, and so profane the name of your God: I am the LORD.

[13] "You shall not oppress your neighbor or rob him. The wages of a hired worker shall not remain with you all night until the morning. [14] You shall not curse the deaf or put a stumbling block before the blind, but you shall fear your God: I am the LORD.

[1] Hebrew *to make them pass through* [the fire]

¹⁵ "You shall do no injustice in court. You shall not be partial to the poor or defer to the great, but in righteousness shall you judge your neighbor. ¹⁶ You shall not go around as a slanderer among your people, and you shall not stand up against the life¹ of your neighbor: I am the LORD.

¹⁷ "You shall not hate your brother in your heart, but you shall reason frankly with your neighbor, lest you incur sin because of him. ¹⁸ You shall not take vengeance or bear a grudge against the sons of your own people, but you shall love your neighbor as yourself: I am the LORD.

You Shall Keep My Statutes

¹⁹ "You shall keep my statutes. You shall not let your cattle breed with a different kind. You shall not sow your field with two kinds of seed, nor shall you wear a garment of cloth made of two kinds of material.

²⁰ "If a man lies sexually with a woman who is a slave, assigned to another man and not yet ransomed or given her freedom, a distinction shall be made. They shall not be put to death, because she was not free; ²¹ but he shall bring his compensation to the LORD, to the entrance of the tent of meeting, a ram for a guilt offering. ²² And the priest shall make atonement for him with the ram of the guilt offering before the LORD for his sin that he has committed, and he shall be forgiven for the sin that he has committed.

²³ "When you come into the land and plant any kind of tree for food, then you shall regard its fruit as forbidden.² Three years it shall be forbidden to you; it must not be eaten. ²⁴ And in the fourth year all its fruit shall be holy, an offering of praise to the LORD. ²⁵ But in the fifth year you may eat of its fruit, to increase its yield for you: I am the LORD your God.

²⁶ "You shall not eat any flesh with the blood in it. You shall not interpret omens or tell fortunes. ²⁷ You shall not round off the hair on your temples or mar the edges of your beard. ²⁸ You shall not make any cuts on your body for the dead or tattoo yourselves: I am the LORD.

²⁹ "Do not profane your daughter by making her a prostitute, lest the land fall into prostitution and the land become full of depravity. ³⁰ You shall keep my Sabbaths and reverence my sanctuary: I am the LORD.

³¹ "Do not turn to mediums or necromancers; do not seek them out, and so make yourselves unclean by them: I am the LORD your God.

³² "You shall stand up before the gray head and honor the face of an old man, and you shall fear your God: I am the LORD.

³³ "When a stranger sojourns with you in your land, you shall not do him wrong. ³⁴ You shall treat the stranger who sojourns with you as the native among you, and you shall love him as yourself, for you were strangers in the land of Egypt: I am the LORD your God.

³⁵ "You shall do no wrong in judgment, in measures of length or weight or quantity. ³⁶ You shall have just balances, just weights, a just ephah, and a just hin:³ I am the LORD your God, who brought you out of the land of Egypt. ³⁷ And you shall observe all my statutes and all my rules, and do them: I am the LORD."

Punishment for Child Sacrifice

20 The LORD spoke to Moses, saying, ² "Say to the people of Israel, Any one of the people of Israel or of the strangers who sojourn in Israel who gives any of his children to Molech shall surely be put to death. The people of the land shall stone him with stones. ³ I myself will set my face against that man and will cut him off from among his people, because he has given one of his children to Molech, to make my sanctuary unclean and to profane my holy name. ⁴ And if the people of the land do at all close their eyes to that man when he gives one of his children to Molech, and do not put him to death, ⁵ then I will set my face against that man and against his clan and will cut them off from among their people, him and all who follow him in whoring after Molech.

⁶ "If a person turns to mediums and necromancers, whoring after them, I will set my face against that person and will cut him off from among his people. ⁷ Consecrate yourselves, therefore, and be holy, for I am the LORD your God. ⁸ Keep my statutes and do them; I am the LORD who sanctifies you. ⁹ For anyone who curses his father or his mother shall surely be put to death; he has cursed his father or his mother; his blood is upon him.

Punishments for Sexual Immorality

¹⁰ "If a man commits adultery with the wife of⁴ his neighbor, both the adulterer and the adulteress shall surely be put to death. ¹¹ If a man lies with his father's wife, he has uncovered

---

¹ Hebrew *blood* ² Hebrew *as its uncircumcision* ³ An *ephah* was about 3/5 bushel or 22 liters; a *hin* was about 4 quarts or 3.5 liters ⁴ Hebrew repeats *if a man commits adultery with the wife of*

his father's nakedness; both of them shall surely be put to death; their blood is upon them. ¹²If a man lies with his daughter-in-law, both of them shall surely be put to death; they have committed perversion; their blood is upon them. ¹³If a man lies with a male as with a woman, both of them have committed an abomination; they shall surely be put to death; their blood is upon them. ¹⁴If a man takes a woman and her mother also, it is depravity; he and they shall be burned with fire, that there may be no depravity among you. ¹⁵If a man lies with an animal, he shall surely be put to death, and you shall kill the animal. ¹⁶If a woman approaches any animal and lies with it, you shall kill the woman and the animal; they shall surely be put to death; their blood is upon them.

¹⁷"If a man takes his sister, a daughter of his father or a daughter of his mother, and sees her nakedness, and she sees his nakedness, it is a disgrace, and they shall be cut off in the sight of the children of their people. He has uncovered his sister's nakedness, and he shall bear his iniquity. ¹⁸If a man lies with a woman during her menstrual period and uncovers her nakedness, he has made naked her fountain, and she has uncovered the fountain of her blood. Both of them shall be cut off from among their people. ¹⁹You shall not uncover the nakedness of your mother's sister or of your father's sister, for that is to make naked one's relative; they shall bear their iniquity. ²⁰If a man lies with his uncle's wife, he has uncovered his uncle's nakedness; they shall bear their sin; they shall die childless. ²¹If a man takes his brother's wife, it is impurity.¹ He has uncovered his brother's nakedness; they shall be childless.

You Shall Be Holy

²²"You shall therefore keep all my statutes and all my rules and do them, that the land where I am bringing you to live may not vomit you out. ²³And you shall not walk in the customs of the nation that I am driving out before you, for they did all these things, and therefore I detested them. ²⁴But I have said to you, 'You shall inherit their land, and I will give it to you to possess, a land flowing with milk and honey.' I am the LORD your God, who has separated you from the peoples. ²⁵You shall therefore separate the clean beast from the unclean, and the unclean bird

from the clean. You shall not make yourselves detestable by beast or by bird or by anything with which the ground crawls, which I have set apart for you to hold unclean. ²⁶You shall be holy to me, for I the LORD am holy and have separated you from the peoples, that you should be mine.

²⁷"A man or a woman who is a medium or a necromancer shall surely be put to death. They shall be stoned with stones; their blood shall be upon them."

Holiness and the Priests

21 And the LORD said to Moses, "Speak to the priests, the sons of Aaron, and say to them, No one shall make himself unclean for the dead among his people, ²except for his closest relatives, his mother, his father, his son, his daughter, his brother, ³or his virgin sister (who is near to him because she has had no husband; for her he may make himself unclean). ⁴He shall not make himself unclean as a husband among his people and so profane himself. ⁵They shall not make bald patches on their heads, nor shave off the edges of their beards, nor make any cuts on their body. ⁶They shall be holy to their God and not profane the name of their God. For they offer the LORD's food offerings, the bread of their God; therefore they shall be holy. ⁷They shall not marry a prostitute or a woman who has been defiled, neither shall they marry a woman divorced from her husband, for the priest is holy to his God. ⁸You shall sanctify him, for he offers the bread of your God. He shall be holy to you, for I, the LORD, who sanctify you, am holy. ⁹And the daughter of any priest, if she profanes herself by whoring, profanes her father; she shall be burned with fire.

¹⁰"The priest who is chief among his brothers, on whose head the anointing oil is poured and who has been consecrated to wear the garments, shall not let the hair of his head hang loose nor tear his clothes. ¹¹He shall not go in to any dead bodies nor make himself unclean, even for his father or for his mother. ¹²He shall not go out of the sanctuary, lest he profane the sanctuary of his God, for the consecration of the anointing oil of his God is on him: I am the LORD. ¹³And he shall take a wife in her virginity.² ¹⁴A widow, or a divorced woman, or a woman who has been defiled, or a prostitute, these he shall not marry. But he shall take as his wife a virgin³

¹ Literally menstrual impurity ² Or a young wife ³ Hebrew young woman

of his own people, [15] that he may not profane his offspring among his people, for I am the LORD who sanctifies him."

[16] And the LORD spoke to Moses, saying, [17] "Speak to Aaron, saying, None of your offspring throughout their generations who has a blemish may approach to offer the bread of his God. [18] For no one who has a blemish shall draw near, a man blind or lame, or one who has a mutilated face or a limb too long, [19] or a man who has an injured foot or an injured hand, [20] or a hunchback or a dwarf or a man with a defect in his sight or an itching disease or scabs or crushed testicles. [21] No man of the offspring of Aaron the priest who has a blemish shall come near to offer the LORD's food offerings; since he has a blemish, he shall not come near to offer the bread of his God. [22] He may eat the bread of his God, both of the most holy and of the holy things, [23] but he shall not go through the veil or approach the altar, because he has a blemish, that he may not profane my sanctuaries,[1] for I am the LORD who sanctifies them." [24] So Moses spoke to Aaron and to his sons and to all the people of Israel.

22 And the LORD spoke to Moses, saying, [2] "Speak to Aaron and his sons so that they abstain from the holy things of the people of Israel, which they dedicate to me, so that they do not profane my holy name: I am the LORD. [3] Say to them, 'If any one of all your offspring throughout your generations approaches the holy things that the people of Israel dedicate to the LORD, while he has an uncleanness, that person shall be cut off from my presence: I am the LORD. [4] None of the offspring of Aaron who has a leprous disease or a discharge may eat of the holy things until he is clean. Whoever touches anything that is unclean through contact with the dead or a man who has had an emission of semen, [5] and whoever touches a swarming thing by which he may be made unclean or a person from whom he may take uncleanness, whatever his uncleanness may be— [6] the person who touches such a thing shall be unclean until the evening and shall not eat of the holy things unless he has bathed his body in water. [7] When the sun goes down he shall be clean, and afterward he may eat of the holy things, because they are his food. [8] He shall not eat what dies of itself or is torn by beasts, and so make himself unclean by it: I am the LORD.' [9] They shall therefore keep my charge, lest they bear sin for it and die thereby when they profane it: I am the LORD who sanctifies them.

[10] "A lay person shall not eat of a holy thing; no foreign guest of the priest or hired worker shall eat of a holy thing, [11] but if a priest buys a slave[2] as his property for money, the slave[3] may eat of it, and anyone born in his house may eat of his food. [12] If a priest's daughter marries a layman, she shall not eat of the contribution of the holy things. [13] But if a priest's daughter is widowed or divorced and has no child and returns to her father's house, as in her youth, she may eat of her father's food; yet no lay person shall eat of it. [14] And if anyone eats of a holy thing unintentionally, he shall add the fifth of its value to it and give the holy thing to the priest. [15] They shall not profane the holy things of the people of Israel, which they contribute to the LORD, [16] and so cause them to bear iniquity and guilt, by eating their holy things: for I am the LORD who sanctifies them."

Acceptable Offerings

[17] And the LORD spoke to Moses, saying, [18] "Speak to Aaron and his sons and all the people of Israel and say to them, When any one of the house of Israel or of the sojourners in Israel presents a burnt offering as his offering, for any of their vows or freewill offerings that they offer to the LORD, [19] if it is to be accepted for you it shall be a male without blemish, of the bulls or the sheep or the goats. [20] You shall not offer anything that has a blemish, for it will not be acceptable for you. [21] And when anyone offers a sacrifice of peace offerings to the LORD to fulfill a vow or as a freewill offering from the herd or from the flock, to be accepted it must be perfect; there shall be no blemish in it. [22] Animals blind or disabled or mutilated or having a discharge or an itch or scabs you shall not offer to the LORD or give them to the LORD as a food offering on the altar. [23] You may present a bull or a lamb that has a part too long or too short for a freewill offering, but for a vow offering it cannot be accepted. [24] Any animal that has its testicles bruised or crushed or torn or cut you shall not offer to the LORD; you shall not do it within your land, [25] neither shall you offer as the bread of your God any such animals gotten from a foreigner. Since there is a blemish in them, because of their mutilation, they will not be accepted for you."

---

[1] Or *my holy precincts* [2] Or *servant*; twice in this verse [3] Hebrew *he*

²⁶ And the LORD spoke to Moses, saying, ²⁷ "When an ox or sheep or goat is born, it shall remain seven days with its mother, and from the eighth day on it shall be acceptable as a food offering to the LORD. ²⁸ But you shall not kill an ox or a sheep and her young in one day. ²⁹ And when you sacrifice a sacrifice of thanksgiving to the LORD, you shall sacrifice it so that you may be accepted. ³⁰ It shall be eaten on the same day; you shall leave none of it until morning: I am the LORD.

³¹ "So you shall keep my commandments and do them: I am the LORD. ³² And you shall not profane my holy name, that I may be sanctified among the people of Israel. I am the LORD who sanctifies you, ³³ who brought you out of the land of Egypt to be your God: I am the LORD."

Feasts of the LORD

23 The LORD spoke to Moses, saying, ² "Speak to the people of Israel and say to them, These are the appointed feasts of the LORD that you shall proclaim as holy convocations; they are my appointed feasts.

The Sabbath

³ "Six days shall work be done, but on the seventh day is a Sabbath of solemn rest, a holy convocation. You shall do no work. It is a Sabbath to the LORD in all your dwelling places.

The Passover

⁴ "These are the appointed feasts of the LORD, the holy convocations, which you shall proclaim at the time appointed for them. ⁵ In the first month, on the fourteenth day of the month at twilight,[1] is the LORD's Passover. ⁶ And on the fifteenth day of the same month is the Feast of Unleavened Bread to the LORD; for seven days you shall eat unleavened bread. ⁷ On the first day you shall have a holy convocation; you shall not do any ordinary work. ⁸ But you shall present a food offering to the LORD for seven days. On the seventh day is a holy convocation; you shall not do any ordinary work."

The Feast of Firstfruits

⁹ And the LORD spoke to Moses, saying, ¹⁰ "Speak to the people of Israel and say to them, When you come into the land that I give you and reap its harvest, you shall bring the sheaf of the firstfruits of your harvest to the priest, ¹¹ and he shall wave the sheaf before the LORD, so that you may be accepted. On the day after the Sabbath the priest shall wave it. ¹² And on the day when you wave the sheaf, you shall offer a male lamb a year old without blemish as a burnt offering to the LORD. ¹³ And the grain offering with it shall be two tenths of an ephah[2] of fine flour mixed with oil, a food offering to the LORD with a pleasing aroma, and the drink offering with it shall be of wine, a fourth of a hin.[3] ¹⁴ And you shall eat neither bread nor grain parched or fresh until this same day, until you have brought the offering of your God: it is a statute forever throughout your generations in all your dwellings.

The Feast of Weeks

¹⁵ "You shall count seven full weeks from the day after the Sabbath, from the day that you brought the sheaf of the wave offering. ¹⁶ You shall count fifty days to the day after the seventh Sabbath. Then you shall present a grain offering of new grain to the LORD. ¹⁷ You shall bring from your dwelling places two loaves of bread to be waved, made of two tenths of an ephah. They shall be of fine flour, and they shall be baked with leaven, as firstfruits to the LORD. ¹⁸ And you shall present with the bread seven lambs a year old without blemish, and one bull from the herd and two rams. They shall be a burnt offering to the LORD, with their grain offering and their drink offerings, a food offering with a pleasing aroma to the LORD. ¹⁹ And you shall offer one male goat for a sin offering, and two male lambs a year old as a sacrifice of peace offerings. ²⁰ And the priest shall wave them with the bread of the firstfruits as a wave offering before the LORD, with the two lambs. They shall be holy to the LORD for the priest. ²¹ And you shall make a proclamation on the same day. You shall hold a holy convocation. You shall not do any ordinary work. It is a statute forever in all your dwelling places throughout your generations.

²² "And when you reap the harvest of your land, you shall not reap your field right up to its edge, nor shall you gather the gleanings after your harvest. You shall leave them for the poor and for the sojourner: I am the LORD your God."

The Feast of Trumpets

²³ And the LORD spoke to Moses, saying, ²⁴ "Speak to the people of Israel, saying, In the seventh month, on the first day of the month, you shall observe a day of solemn rest, a memorial proclaimed with blast of trumpets, a holy

---

[1] Hebrew *between the two evenings* [2] An *ephah* was about 3/5 bushel or 22 liters [3] A *hin* was about 4 quarts or 3.5 liters

convocation. [25] You shall not do any ordinary work, and you shall present a food offering to the LORD."

The Day of Atonement

[26] And the LORD spoke to Moses, saying, [27] "Now on the tenth day of this seventh month is the Day of Atonement. It shall be for you a time of holy convocation, and you shall afflict yourselves[1] and present a food offering to the LORD. [28] And you shall not do any work on that very day, for it is a Day of Atonement, to make atonement for you before the LORD your God. [29] For whoever is not afflicted[2] on that very day shall be cut off from his people. [30] And whoever does any work on that very day, that person I will destroy from among his people. [31] You shall not do any work. It is a statute forever throughout your generations in all your dwelling places. [32] It shall be to you a Sabbath of solemn rest, and you shall afflict yourselves. On the ninth day of the month beginning at evening, from evening to evening shall you keep your Sabbath."

The Feast of Booths

[33] And the LORD spoke to Moses, saying, [34] "Speak to the people of Israel, saying, On the fifteenth day of this seventh month and for seven days is the Feast of Booths[3] to the LORD. [35] On the first day shall be a holy convocation; you shall not do any ordinary work. [36] For seven days you shall present food offerings to the LORD. On the eighth day you shall hold a holy convocation and present a food offering to the LORD. It is a solemn assembly; you shall not do any ordinary work.

[37] "These are the appointed feasts of the LORD, which you shall proclaim as times of holy convocation, for presenting to the LORD food offerings, burnt offerings and grain offerings, sacrifices and drink offerings, each on its proper day, [38] besides the LORD's Sabbaths and besides your gifts and besides all your vow offerings and besides all your freewill offerings, which you give to the LORD.

[39] "On the fifteenth day of the seventh month, when you have gathered in the produce of the land, you shall celebrate the feast of the LORD seven days. On the first day shall be a solemn rest, and on the eighth day shall be a solemn rest. [40] And you shall take on the first day the fruit of splendid trees, branches of palm trees and boughs of leafy trees and willows of the brook, and you shall rejoice before the LORD your God seven days. [41] You shall celebrate it as a feast to the LORD for seven days in the year. It is a statute forever throughout your generations; you shall celebrate it in the seventh month. [42] You shall dwell in booths for seven days. All native Israelites shall dwell in booths, [43] that your generations may know that I made the people of Israel dwell in booths when I brought them out of the land of Egypt: I am the LORD your God."

[44] Thus Moses declared to the people of Israel the appointed feasts of the LORD.

The Lamps

24 The LORD spoke to Moses, saying, [2] "Command the people of Israel to bring you pure oil from beaten olives for the lamp, that a light may be kept burning regularly. [3] Outside the veil of the testimony, in the tent of meeting, Aaron shall arrange it from evening to morning before the LORD regularly. It shall be a statute forever throughout your generations. [4] He shall arrange the lamps on the lampstand of pure gold[4] before the LORD regularly.

Bread for the Tabernacle

[5] "You shall take fine flour and bake twelve loaves from it; two tenths of an ephah[5] shall be in each loaf. [6] And you shall set them in two piles, six in a pile, on the table of pure gold[6] before the LORD. [7] And you shall put pure frankincense on each pile, that it may go with the bread as a memorial portion as a food offering to the LORD. [8] Every Sabbath day Aaron shall arrange it before the LORD regularly; it is from the people of Israel as a covenant forever. [9] And it shall be for Aaron and his sons, and they shall eat it in a holy place, since it is for him a most holy portion out of the LORD's food offerings, a perpetual due."

Punishment for Blasphemy

[10] Now an Israelite woman's son, whose father was an Egyptian, went out among the people of Israel. And the Israelite woman's son and a man of Israel fought in the camp, [11] and the Israelite woman's son blasphemed the Name, and cursed. Then they brought him to Moses. His mother's name was Shelomith, the daughter of Dibri, of the tribe of Dan. [12] And they put him in custody, till the will of the LORD should be clear to them.

[1] Or shall fast; also verse 32 [2] Or is not fasting [3] Or Tabernacles [4] Hebrew the pure lampstand [5] An ephah was about 3/5 bushel or 22 liters [6] Hebrew the pure table

[13] Then the LORD spoke to Moses, saying, [14] "Bring out of the camp the one who cursed, and let all who heard him lay their hands on his head, and let all the congregation stone him. [15] And speak to the people of Israel, saying, Whoever curses his God shall bear his sin. [16] Whoever blasphemes the name of the LORD shall surely be put to death. All the congregation shall stone him. The sojourner as well as the native, when he blasphemes the Name, shall be put to death.

An Eye for an Eye

[17] "Whoever takes a human life shall surely be put to death. [18] Whoever takes an animal's life shall make it good, life for life. [19] If anyone injures his neighbor, as he has done it shall be done to him, [20] fracture for fracture, eye for eye, tooth for tooth; whatever injury he has given a person shall be given to him. [21] Whoever kills an animal shall make it good, and whoever kills a person shall be put to death. [22] You shall have the same rule for the sojourner and for the native, for I am the LORD your God." [23] So Moses spoke to the people of Israel, and they brought out of the camp the one who had cursed and stoned him with stones. Thus the people of Israel did as the LORD commanded Moses.

The Sabbath Year

25 The LORD spoke to Moses on Mount Sinai, saying, [2] "Speak to the people of Israel and say to them, When you come into the land that I give you, the land shall keep a Sabbath to the LORD. [3] For six years you shall sow your field, and for six years you shall prune your vineyard and gather in its fruits, [4] but in the seventh year there shall be a Sabbath of solemn rest for the land, a Sabbath to the LORD. You shall not sow your field or prune your vineyard. [5] You shall not reap what grows of itself in your harvest, or gather the grapes of your undressed vine. It shall be a year of solemn rest for the land. [6] The Sabbath of the land[1] shall provide food for you, for yourself and for your male and female slaves[2] and for your hired worker and the sojourner who lives with you, [7] and for your cattle and for the wild animals that are in your land: all its yield shall be for food.

The Year of Jubilee

[8] "You shall count seven weeks[3] of years, seven times seven years, so that the time of the seven weeks of years shall give you forty-nine years. [9] Then you shall sound the loud trumpet on the tenth day of the seventh month. On the Day of Atonement you shall sound the trumpet throughout all your land. [10] And you shall consecrate the fiftieth year, and proclaim liberty throughout the land to all its inhabitants. It shall be a jubilee for you, when each of you shall return to his property and each of you shall return to his clan. [11] That fiftieth year shall be a jubilee for you; in it you shall neither sow nor reap what grows of itself nor gather the grapes from the undressed vines. [12] For it is a jubilee. It shall be holy to you. You may eat the produce of the field.[4]

[13] "In this year of jubilee each of you shall return to his property. [14] And if you make a sale to your neighbor or buy from your neighbor, you shall not wrong one another. [15] You shall pay your neighbor according to the number of years after the jubilee, and he shall sell to you according to the number of years for crops. [16] If the years are many, you shall increase the price, and if the years are few, you shall reduce the price, for it is the number of the crops that he is selling to you. [17] You shall not wrong one another, but you shall fear your God, for I am the LORD your God.

[18] "Therefore you shall do my statutes and keep my rules and perform them, and then you will dwell in the land securely. [19] The land will yield its fruit, and you will eat your fill and dwell in it securely. [20] And if you say, 'What shall we eat in the seventh year, if we may not sow or gather in our crop?' [21] I will command my blessing on you in the sixth year, so that it will produce a crop sufficient for three years. [22] When you sow in the eighth year, you will be eating some of the old crop; you shall eat the old until the ninth year, when its crop arrives.

Redemption of Property

[23] "The land shall not be sold in perpetuity, for the land is mine. For you are strangers and sojourners with me. [24] And in all the country you possess, you shall allow a redemption of the land.

[25] "If your brother becomes poor and sells part of his property, then his nearest redeemer shall come and redeem what his brother has sold. [26] If a man has no one to redeem it and then himself becomes prosperous and finds sufficient means to redeem it, [27] let him calculate the years since he sold it and pay back the

---

[1] That is, the Sabbath produce of the land [2] Or servants [3] Or Sabbaths [4] Or countryside

balance to the man to whom he sold it, and then return to his property. [28] But if he does not have sufficient means to recover it, then what he sold shall remain in the hand of the buyer until the year of jubilee. In the jubilee it shall be released, and he shall return to his property.

[29] "If a man sells a dwelling house in a walled city, he may redeem it within a year of its sale. For a full year he shall have the right of redemption. [30] If it is not redeemed within a full year, then the house in the walled city shall belong in perpetuity to the buyer, throughout his generations; it shall not be released in the jubilee. [31] But the houses of the villages that have no wall around them shall be classified with the fields of the land. They may be redeemed, and they shall be released in the jubilee. [32] As for the cities of the Levites, the Levites may redeem at any time the houses in the cities they possess. [33] And if one of the Levites exercises his right of redemption, then the house that was sold in a city they possess shall be released in the jubilee. For the houses in the cities of the Levites are their possession among the people of Israel. [34] But the fields of pastureland belonging to their cities may not be sold, for that is their possession forever.

Kindness for Poor Brothers

[35] "If your brother becomes poor and cannot maintain himself with you, you shall support him as though he were a stranger and a sojourner, and he shall live with you. [36] Take no interest from him or profit, but fear your God, that your brother may live beside you. [37] You shall not lend him your money at interest, nor give him your food for profit. [38] I am the LORD your God, who brought you out of the land of Egypt to give you the land of Canaan, and to be your God.

[39] "If your brother becomes poor beside you and sells himself to you, you shall not make him serve as a slave: [40] he shall be with you as a hired worker and as a sojourner. He shall serve with you until the year of the jubilee. [41] Then he shall go out from you, he and his children with him, and go back to his own clan and return to the possession of his fathers. [42] For they are my servants,[1] whom I brought out of the land of Egypt; they shall not be sold as slaves. [43] You shall not rule over him ruthlessly but shall fear your God. [44] As for your male and female slaves whom you may have: you may buy male and female slaves from among the nations that are around you. [45] You may also buy from among the strangers who sojourn with you and their clans that are with you, who have been born in your land, and they may be your property. [46] You may bequeath them to your sons after you to inherit as a possession forever. You may make slaves of them, but over your brothers the people of Israel you shall not rule, one over another ruthlessly.

Redeeming a Poor Man

[47] "If a stranger or sojourner with you becomes rich, and your brother beside him becomes poor and sells himself to the stranger or sojourner with you or to a member of the stranger's clan, [48] then after he is sold he may be redeemed. One of his brothers may redeem him, [49] or his uncle or his cousin may redeem him, or a close relative from his clan may redeem him. Or if he grows rich he may redeem himself. [50] He shall calculate with his buyer from the year when he sold himself to him until the year of jubilee, and the price of his sale shall vary with the number of years. The time he was with his owner shall be rated as the time of a hired worker. [51] If there are still many years left, he shall pay proportionately for his redemption some of his sale price. [52] If there remain but a few years until the year of jubilee, he shall calculate and pay for his redemption in proportion to his years of service. [53] He shall treat him as a worker hired year by year. He shall not rule ruthlessly over him in your sight. [54] And if he is not redeemed by these means, then he and his children with him shall be released in the year of jubilee. [55] For it is to me that the people of Israel are servants.[2] They are my servants whom I brought out of the land of Egypt: I am the LORD your God.

Blessings for Obedience

26 "You shall not make idols for yourselves or erect an image or pillar, and you shall not set up a figured stone in your land to bow down to it, for I am the LORD your God. [2] You shall keep my Sabbaths and reverence my sanctuary: I am the LORD.

[3] "If you walk in my statutes and observe my commandments and do them, [4] then I will give you your rains in their season, and the land shall yield its increase, and the trees of the field shall yield their fruit. [5] Your threshing shall last to the time of the grape harvest, and the grape

---

[1] Hebrew slaves [2] Or slaves

harvest shall last to the time for sowing. And you shall eat your bread to the full and dwell in your land securely. [6] I will give peace in the land, and you shall lie down, and none shall make you afraid. And I will remove harmful beasts from the land, and the sword shall not go through your land. [7] You shall chase your enemies, and they shall fall before you by the sword. [8] Five of you shall chase a hundred, and a hundred of you shall chase ten thousand, and your enemies shall fall before you by the sword. [9] I will turn to you and make you fruitful and multiply you and will confirm my covenant with you. [10] You shall eat old store long kept, and you shall clear out the old to make way for the new. [11] I will make my dwelling[1] among you, and my soul shall not abhor you. [12] And I will walk among you and will be your God, and you shall be my people. [13] I am the LORD your God, who brought you out of the land of Egypt, that you should not be their slaves. And I have broken the bars of your yoke and made you walk erect.

Punishment for Disobedience

[14] "But if you will not listen to me and will not do all these commandments, [15] if you spurn my statutes, and if your soul abhors my rules, so that you will not do all my commandments, but break my covenant, [16] then I will do this to you: I will visit you with panic, with wasting disease and fever that consume the eyes and make the heart ache. And you shall sow your seed in vain, for your enemies shall eat it. [17] I will set my face against you, and you shall be struck down before your enemies. Those who hate you shall rule over you, and you shall flee when none pursues you. [18] And if in spite of this you will not listen to me, then I will discipline you again sevenfold for your sins, [19] and I will break the pride of your power, and I will make your heavens like iron and your earth like bronze. [20] And your strength shall be spent in vain, for your land shall not yield its increase, and the trees of the land shall not yield their fruit.

[21] "Then if you walk contrary to me and will not listen to me, I will continue striking you, sevenfold for your sins. [22] And I will let loose the wild beasts against you, which shall bereave you of your children and destroy your livestock and make you few in number, so that your roads shall be deserted.

[23] "And if by this discipline you are not turned to me but walk contrary to me, [24] then I also will walk contrary to you, and I myself will strike you sevenfold for your sins. [25] And I will bring a sword upon you, that shall execute vengeance for the covenant. And if you gather within your cities, I will send pestilence among you, and you shall be delivered into the hand of the enemy. [26] When I break your supply[2] of bread, ten women shall bake your bread in a single oven and shall dole out your bread again by weight, and you shall eat and not be satisfied.

[27] "But if in spite of this you will not listen to me, but walk contrary to me, [28] then I will walk contrary to you in fury, and I myself will discipline you sevenfold for your sins. [29] You shall eat the flesh of your sons, and you shall eat the flesh of your daughters. [30] And I will destroy your high places and cut down your incense altars and cast your dead bodies upon the dead bodies of your idols, and my soul will abhor you. [31] And I will lay your cities waste and will make your sanctuaries desolate, and I will not smell your pleasing aromas. [32] And I myself will devastate the land, so that your enemies who settle in it shall be appalled at it. [33] And I will scatter you among the nations, and I will unsheathe the sword after you, and your land shall be a desolation, and your cities shall be a waste.

[34] "Then the land shall enjoy[3] its Sabbaths as long as it lies desolate, while you are in your enemies' land; then the land shall rest, and enjoy its Sabbaths. [35] As long as it lies desolate it shall have rest, the rest that it did not have on your Sabbaths when you were dwelling in it. [36] And as for those of you who are left, I will send faintness into their hearts in the lands of their enemies. The sound of a driven leaf shall put them to flight, and they shall flee as one flees from the sword, and they shall fall when none pursues. [37] They shall stumble over one another, as if to escape a sword, though none pursues. And you shall have no power to stand before your enemies. [38] And you shall perish among the nations, and the land of your enemies shall eat you up. [39] And those of you who are left shall rot away in your enemies' lands because of their iniquity, and also because of the iniquities of their fathers they shall rot away like them.

[40] "But if they confess their iniquity and the iniquity of their fathers in their treachery that they committed against me, and also in walking contrary to me, [41] so that I walked contrary to

[1] Hebrew *tabernacle* [2] Hebrew *staff* [3] Or *pay for*; twice in this verse; also verse 43

them and brought them into the land of their enemies—if then their uncircumcised heart is humbled and they make amends for their iniquity, ⁴²then I will remember my covenant with Jacob, and I will remember my covenant with Isaac and my covenant with Abraham, and I will remember the land. ⁴³But the land shall be abandoned by them and enjoy its Sabbaths while it lies desolate without them, and they shall make amends for their iniquity, because they spurned my rules and their soul abhorred my statutes. ⁴⁴Yet for all that, when they are in the land of their enemies, I will not spurn them, neither will I abhor them so as to destroy them utterly and break my covenant with them, for I am the Lord their God. ⁴⁵But I will for their sake remember the covenant with their forefathers, whom I brought out of the land of Egypt in the sight of the nations, that I might be their God: I am the Lord."

⁴⁶These are the statutes and rules and laws that the Lord made between himself and the people of Israel through Moses on Mount Sinai.

Laws About Vows

27 The Lord spoke to Moses, saying, ²"Speak to the people of Israel and say to them, If anyone makes a special vow to the Lord involving the valuation of persons, ³then the valuation of a male from twenty years old up to sixty years old shall be fifty shekels[1] of silver, according to the shekel of the sanctuary. ⁴If the person is a female, the valuation shall be thirty shekels. ⁵If the person is from five years old up to twenty years old, the valuation shall be for a male twenty shekels, and for a female ten shekels. ⁶If the person is from a month old up to five years old, the valuation shall be for a male five shekels of silver, and for a female the valuation shall be three shekels of silver. ⁷And if the person is sixty years old or over, then the valuation for a male shall be fifteen shekels, and for a female ten shekels. ⁸And if someone is too poor to pay the valuation, then he shall be made to stand before the priest, and the priest shall value him; the priest shall value him according to what the vower can afford.

⁹"If the vow[2] is an animal that may be offered as an offering to the Lord, all of it that he gives to the Lord is holy. ¹⁰He shall not exchange it or make a substitute for it, good for bad, or bad for good; and if he does in fact substitute one animal for another, then both it and the sub-

stitute shall be holy. ¹¹And if it is any unclean animal that may not be offered as an offering to the Lord, then he shall stand the animal before the priest, ¹²and the priest shall value it as either good or bad; as the priest values it, so it shall be. ¹³But if he wishes to redeem it, he shall add a fifth to the valuation.

¹⁴"When a man dedicates his house as a holy gift to the Lord, the priest shall value it as either good or bad; as the priest values it, so it shall stand. ¹⁵And if the donor wishes to redeem his house, he shall add a fifth to the valuation price, and it shall be his.

¹⁶"If a man dedicates to the Lord part of the land that is his possession, then the valuation shall be in proportion to its seed. A homer[3] of barley seed shall be valued at fifty shekels of silver. ¹⁷If he dedicates his field from the year of jubilee, the valuation shall stand, ¹⁸but if he dedicates his field after the jubilee, then the priest shall calculate the price according to the years that remain until the year of jubilee, and a deduction shall be made from the valuation. ¹⁹And if he who dedicates the field wishes to redeem it, then he shall add a fifth to its valuation price, and it shall remain his. ²⁰But if he does not wish to redeem the field, or if he has sold the field to another man, it shall not be redeemed anymore. ²¹But the field, when it is released in the jubilee, shall be a holy gift to the Lord, like a field that has been devoted. The priest shall be in possession of it. ²²If he dedicates to the Lord a field that he has bought, which is not a part of his possession, ²³then the priest shall calculate the amount of the valuation for it up to the year of jubilee, and the man shall give the valuation on that day as a holy gift to the Lord. ²⁴In the year of jubilee the field shall return to him from whom it was bought, to whom the land belongs as a possession. ²⁵Every valuation shall be according to the shekel of the sanctuary: twenty gerahs[4] shall make a shekel.

²⁶"But a firstborn of animals, which as a firstborn belongs to the Lord, no man may dedicate; whether ox or sheep, it is the Lord's. ²⁷And if it is an unclean animal, then he shall buy it back at the valuation, and add a fifth to it; or, if it is not redeemed, it shall be sold at the valuation.

²⁸"But no devoted thing that a man devotes to the Lord, of anything that he has, whether man or beast, or of his inherited field, shall be

---

[1] A *shekel* was about 2/5 ounce or 11 grams [2] Hebrew *it* [3] A *homer* was about 6 bushels or 220 liters [4] A *gerah* was about 1/50 ounce or 0.6 gram

sold or redeemed; every devoted thing is most holy to the LORD. [29] No one devoted, who is to be devoted for destruction[1] from mankind, shall be ransomed; he shall surely be put to death.

[30] "Every tithe of the land, whether of the seed of the land or of the fruit of the trees, is the LORD's; it is holy to the LORD. [31] If a man wishes to redeem some of his tithe, he shall add a fifth to it. [32] And every tithe of herds and flocks, every tenth animal of all that pass under the herdsman's staff, shall be holy to the LORD. [33] One shall not differentiate between good or bad, neither shall he make a substitute for it; and if he does substitute for it, then both it and the substitute shall be holy; it shall not be redeemed."

[34] These are the commandments that the LORD commanded Moses for the people of Israel on Mount Sinai.

---

[1] That is, set apart (devoted) as an offering to the Lord (for destruction)

NUMBERS

A Census of Israel's Warriors

1 The LORD spoke to Moses in the wilderness of Sinai, in the tent of meeting, on the first day of the second month, in the second year after they had come out of the land of Egypt, saying, 2 "Take a census of all the congregation of the people of Israel, by clans, by fathers' houses, according to the number of names, every male, head by head. 3 From twenty years old and upward, all in Israel who are able to go to war, you and Aaron shall list them, company by company. 4 And there shall be with you a man from each tribe, each man being the head of the house of his fathers. 5 And these are the names of the men who shall assist you. From Reuben, Elizur the son of Shedeur; 6 from Simeon, Shelumiel the son of Zurishaddai; 7 from Judah, Nahshon the son of Amminadab; 8 from Issachar, Nethanel the son of Zuar; 9 from Zebulun, Eliab the son of Helon; 10 from the sons of Joseph, from Ephraim, Elishama the son of Ammihud, and from Manasseh, Gamaliel the son of Pedahzur; 11 from Benjamin, Abidan the son of Gideoni; 12 from Dan, Ahiezer the son of Ammishaddai; 13 from Asher, Pagiel the son of Ochran; 14 from Gad, Eliasaph the son of Deuel; 15 from Naphtali, Ahira the son of Enan." 16 These were the ones chosen from the congregation, the chiefs of their ancestral tribes, the heads of the clans of Israel.

17 Moses and Aaron took these men who had been named, 18 and on the first day of the second month, they assembled the whole congregation together, who registered themselves by clans, by fathers' houses, according to the number of names from twenty years old and upward, head by head, 19 as the LORD commanded Moses. So he listed them in the wilderness of Sinai.

20 The people of Reuben, Israel's firstborn, their generations, by their clans, by their fathers' houses, according to the number of names, head by head, every male from twenty years old and upward, all who were able to go to war: 21 those listed of the tribe of Reuben were 46,500.

22 Of the people of Simeon, their generations, by their clans, by their fathers' houses, those of them who were listed, according to the number of names, head by head, every male from twenty years old and upward, all who were able to go to war: 23 those listed of the tribe of Simeon were 59,300.

24 Of the people of Gad, their generations, by their clans, by their fathers' houses, according to the number of the names, from twenty years old and upward, all who were able to go to war: 25 those listed of the tribe of Gad were 45,650.

26 Of the people of Judah, their generations, by their clans, by their fathers' houses, according to the number of names, from twenty years old and upward, every man able to go to war: 27 those listed of the tribe of Judah were 74,600.

28 Of the people of Issachar, their generations, by their clans, by their fathers' houses, according to the number of names, from twenty years old and upward, every man able to go to war: 29 those listed of the tribe of Issachar were 54,400.

30 Of the people of Zebulun, their generations, by their clans, by their fathers' houses, according to the number of names, from twenty years old and upward, every man able to go to war: 31 those listed of the tribe of Zebulun were 57,400.

32 Of the people of Joseph, namely, of the people of Ephraim, their generations, by their clans, by their fathers' houses, according to the number of names, from twenty years old and upward, every man able to go to war: 33 those listed of the tribe of Ephraim were 40,500.

34 Of the people of Manasseh, their generations, by their clans, by their fathers' houses, according to the number of names, from twenty years old and upward, every man able to go to war: 35 those listed of the tribe of Manasseh were 32,200.

36 Of the people of Benjamin, their generations, by their clans, by their fathers' houses, according to the number of names, from twenty years old and upward, every man able to go to war: 37 those listed of the tribe of Benjamin were 35,400.

38 Of the people of Dan, their generations, by their clans, by their fathers' houses, according to the number of names, from twenty years

old and upward, every man able to go to war: [39] those listed of the tribe of Dan were 62,700.

[40] Of the people of Asher, their generations, by their clans, by their fathers' houses, according to the number of names, from twenty years old and upward, every man able to go to war: [41] those listed of the tribe of Asher were 41,500.

[42] Of the people of Naphtali, their generations, by their clans, by their fathers' houses, according to the number of names, from twenty years old and upward, every man able to go to war: [43] those listed of the tribe of Naphtali were 53,400.

[44] These are those who were listed, whom Moses and Aaron listed with the help of the chiefs of Israel, twelve men, each representing his fathers' house. [45] So all those listed of the people of Israel, by their fathers' houses, from twenty years old and upward, every man able to go to war in Israel— [46] all those listed were 603,550.

Levites Exempted

[47] But the Levites were not listed along with them by their ancestral tribe. [48] For the LORD spoke to Moses, saying, [49] "Only the tribe of Levi you shall not list, and you shall not take a census of them among the people of Israel. [50] But appoint the Levites over the tabernacle of the testimony, and over all its furnishings, and over all that belongs to it. They are to carry the tabernacle and all its furnishings, and they shall take care of it and shall camp around the tabernacle. [51] When the tabernacle is to set out, the Levites shall take it down, and when the tabernacle is to be pitched, the Levites shall set it up. And if any outsider comes near, he shall be put to death. [52] The people of Israel shall pitch their tents by their companies, each man in his own camp and each man by his own standard. [53] But the Levites shall camp around the tabernacle of the testimony, so that there may be no wrath on the congregation of the people of Israel. And the Levites shall keep guard over the tabernacle of the testimony." [54] Thus did the people of Israel; they did according to all that the LORD commanded Moses.

Arrangement of the Camp

2 The LORD spoke to Moses and Aaron, saying, [2] "The people of Israel shall camp each by his own standard, with the banners of their fathers' houses. They shall camp facing the tent of meeting on every side. [3] Those to camp on the east side toward the sunrise shall be of the standard of the camp of Judah by their companies, the chief of the people of Judah being Nahshon the son of Amminadab, [4] his company as listed being 74,600. [5] Those to camp next to him shall be the tribe of Issachar, the chief of the people of Issachar being Nethanel the son of Zuar, [6] his company as listed being 54,400. [7] Then the tribe of Zebulun, the chief of the people of Zebulun being Eliab the son of Helon, [8] his company as listed being 57,400. [9] All those listed of the camp of Judah, by their companies, were 186,400. They shall set out first on the march.

[10] "On the south side shall be the standard of the camp of Reuben by their companies, the chief of the people of Reuben being Elizur the son of Shedeur, [11] his company as listed being 46,500. [12] And those to camp next to him shall be the tribe of Simeon, the chief of the people of Simeon being Shelumiel the son of Zurishaddai, [13] his company as listed being 59,300. [14] Then the tribe of Gad, the chief of the people of Gad being Eliasaph the son of Reuel, [15] his company as listed being 45,650. [16] All those listed of the camp of Reuben, by their companies, were 151,450. They shall set out second.

[17] "Then the tent of meeting shall set out, with the camp of the Levites in the midst of the camps; as they camp, so shall they set out, each in position, standard by standard.

[18] "On the west side shall be the standard of the camp of Ephraim by their companies, the chief of the people of Ephraim being Elishama the son of Ammihud, [19] his company as listed being 40,500. [20] And next to him shall be the tribe of Manasseh, the chief of the people of Manasseh being Gamaliel the son of Pedahzur, [21] his company as listed being 32,200. [22] Then the tribe of Benjamin, the chief of the people of Benjamin being Abidan the son of Gideoni, [23] his company as listed being 35,400. [24] All those listed of the camp of Ephraim, by their companies, were 108,100. They shall set out third on the march.

[25] "On the north side shall be the standard of the camp of Dan by their companies, the chief of the people of Dan being Ahiezer the son of Ammishaddai, [26] his company as listed being 62,700. [27] And those to camp next to him shall be the tribe of Asher, the chief of the people of Asher being Pagiel the son of Ochran,

[28] his company as listed being 41,500. [29] Then the tribe of Naphtali, the chief of the people of Naphtali being Ahira the son of Enan, [30] his company as listed being 53,400. [31] All those listed of the camp of Dan were 157,600. They shall set out last, standard by standard."

[32] These are the people of Israel as listed by their fathers' houses. All those listed in the camps by their companies were 603,550. [33] But the Levites were not listed among the people of Israel, as the LORD commanded Moses.

[34] Thus did the people of Israel. According to all that the LORD commanded Moses, so they camped by their standards, and so they set out, each one in his clan, according to his fathers' house.

The Sons of Aaron

3 These are the generations of Aaron and Moses at the time when the LORD spoke with Moses on Mount Sinai. [2] These are the names of the sons of Aaron: Nadab the firstborn, and Abihu, Eleazar, and Ithamar. [3] These are the names of the sons of Aaron, the anointed priests, whom he ordained to serve as priests. [4] But Nadab and Abihu died before the LORD when they offered unauthorized fire before the LORD in the wilderness of Sinai, and they had no children. So Eleazar and Ithamar served as priests in the lifetime of Aaron their father.

Duties of the Levites

[5] And the LORD spoke to Moses, saying, [6] "Bring the tribe of Levi near, and set them before Aaron the priest, that they may minister to him. [7] They shall keep guard over him and over the whole congregation before the tent of meeting, as they minister at the tabernacle. [8] They shall guard all the furnishings of the tent of meeting, and keep guard over the people of Israel as they minister at the tabernacle. [9] And you shall give the Levites to Aaron and his sons; they are wholly given to him from among the people of Israel. [10] And you shall appoint Aaron and his sons, and they shall guard their priesthood. But if any outsider comes near, he shall be put to death."

[11] And the LORD spoke to Moses, saying, [12] "Behold, I have taken the Levites from among the people of Israel instead of every firstborn who opens the womb among the people of Israel. The Levites shall be mine, [13] for all the firstborn are mine. On the day that I struck down all the firstborn in the land of Egypt, I consecrated for my own all the firstborn in Israel, both of man and of beast. They shall be mine: I am the LORD."

[14] And the LORD spoke to Moses in the wilderness of Sinai, saying, [15] "List the sons of Levi, by fathers' houses and by clans; every male from a month old and upward you shall list." [16] So Moses listed them according to the word of the LORD, as he was commanded. [17] And these were the sons of Levi by their names: Gershon and Kohath and Merari. [18] And these are the names of the sons of Gershon by their clans: Libni and Shimei. [19] And the sons of Kohath by their clans: Amram, Izhar, Hebron, and Uzziel. [20] And the sons of Merari by their clans: Mahli and Mushi. These are the clans of the Levites, by their fathers' houses.

[21] To Gershon belonged the clan of the Libnites and the clan of the Shimeites; these were the clans of the Gershonites. [22] Their listing according to the number of all the males from a month old and upward was[1] 7,500. [23] The clans of the Gershonites were to camp behind the tabernacle on the west, [24] with Eliasaph, the son of Lael as chief of the fathers' house of the Gershonites. [25] And the guard duty of the sons of Gershon in the tent of meeting involved the tabernacle, the tent with its covering, the screen for the entrance of the tent of meeting, [26] the hangings of the court, the screen for the door of the court that is around the tabernacle and the altar, and its cords—all the service connected with these.

[27] To Kohath belonged the clan of the Amramites and the clan of the Izharites and the clan of the Hebronites and the clan of the Uzzielites; these are the clans of the Kohathites. [28] According to the number of all the males, from a month old and upward, there were 8,600, keeping guard over the sanctuary. [29] The clans of the sons of Kohath were to camp on the south side of the tabernacle, [30] with Elizaphan the son of Uzziel as chief of the fathers' house of the clans of the Kohathites. [31] And their guard duty involved the ark, the table, the lampstand, the altars, the vessels of the sanctuary with which the priests minister, and the screen; all the service connected with these. [32] And Eleazar the son of Aaron the priest was to be chief over the chiefs of the Levites, and to have oversight of those who kept guard over the sanctuary.

[1] Hebrew *their listing was*

[33] To Merari belonged the clan of the Mahlites and the clan of the Mushites: these are the clans of Merari. [34] Their listing according to the number of all the males from a month old and upward was 6,200. [35] And the chief of the fathers' house of the clans of Merari was Zuriel the son of Abihail. They were to camp on the north side of the tabernacle. [36] And the appointed guard duty of the sons of Merari involved the frames of the tabernacle, the bars, the pillars, the bases, and all their accessories; all the service connected with these; [37] also the pillars around the court, with their bases and pegs and cords.

[38] Those who were to camp before the tabernacle on the east, before the tent of meeting toward the sunrise, were Moses and Aaron and his sons, guarding the sanctuary itself, to protect[1] the people of Israel. And any outsider who came near was to be put to death. [39] All those listed among the Levites, whom Moses and Aaron listed at the commandment of the LORD, by clans, all the males from a month old and upward, were 22,000.

Redemption of the Firstborn

[40] And the LORD said to Moses, "List all the firstborn males of the people of Israel, from a month old and upward, taking the number of their names. [41] And you shall take the Levites for me—I am the LORD—instead of all the firstborn among the people of Israel, and the cattle of the Levites instead of all the firstborn among the cattle of the people of Israel." [42] So Moses listed all the firstborn among the people of Israel, as the LORD commanded him. [43] And all the firstborn males, according to the number of names, from a month old and upward as listed were 22,273.

[44] And the LORD spoke to Moses, saying, [45] "Take the Levites instead of all the firstborn among the people of Israel, and the cattle of the Levites instead of their cattle. The Levites shall be mine: I am the LORD. [46] And as the redemption price for the 273 of the firstborn of the people of Israel, over and above the number of the male Levites, [47] you shall take five shekels[2] per head; you shall take them according to the shekel of the sanctuary (the shekel of twenty gerahs[3]), [48] and give the money to Aaron and his sons as the redemption price for those who are over." [49] So Moses took the redemption money from those who were over and above those redeemed by the Levites. [50] From the firstborn of the people of Israel he took the money, 1,365 shekels, by the shekel of the sanctuary. [51] And Moses gave the redemption money to Aaron and his sons, according to the word of the LORD, as the LORD commanded Moses.

Duties of the Kohathites, Gershonites, and Merarites

4 The LORD spoke to Moses and Aaron, saying, [2] "Take a census of the sons of Kohath from among the sons of Levi, by their clans and their fathers' houses, [3] from thirty years old up to fifty years old, all who can come on duty, to do the work in the tent of meeting. [4] This is the service of the sons of Kohath in the tent of meeting: the most holy things. [5] When the camp is to set out, Aaron and his sons shall go in and take down the veil of the screen and cover the ark of the testimony with it. [6] Then they shall put on it a covering of goatskin[4] and spread on top of that a cloth all of blue, and shall put in its poles. [7] And over the table of the bread of the Presence they shall spread a cloth of blue and put on it the plates, the dishes for incense, the bowls, and the flagons for the drink offering; the regular showbread also shall be on it. [8] Then they shall spread over them a cloth of scarlet and cover the same with a covering of goatskin, and shall put in its poles. [9] And they shall take a cloth of blue and cover the lampstand for the light, with its lamps, its tongs, its trays, and all the vessels for oil with which it is supplied. [10] And they shall put it with all its utensils in a covering of goatskin and put it on the carrying frame. [11] And over the golden altar they shall spread a cloth of blue and cover it with a covering of goatskin, and shall put in its poles. [12] And they shall take all the vessels of the service that are used in the sanctuary and put them in a cloth of blue and cover them with a covering of goatskin and put them on the carrying frame. [13] And they shall take away the ashes from the altar and spread a purple cloth over it. [14] And they shall put on it all the utensils of the altar, which are used for the service there, the fire pans, the forks, the shovels, and the basins, all the utensils of the altar; and they shall spread on it a covering of goatskin, and shall put in its poles. [15] And when Aaron and his sons have finished covering the sanctuary and all the furnishings of the sanctuary, as the camp sets out, after that the sons of Kohath shall come to carry these, but they must not touch the holy things, lest they die. These

---

[1] Hebrew *guard*　[2] A *shekel* was about 2/5 ounce or 11 grams　[3] A *gerah* was about 1/50 ounce or 0.6 gram　[4] The meaning of the Hebrew word is uncertain; compare Exodus 25:5

are the things of the tent of meeting that the sons of Kohath are to carry.

[16] "And Eleazar the son of Aaron the priest shall have charge of the oil for the light, the fragrant incense, the regular grain offering, and the anointing oil, with the oversight of the whole tabernacle and all that is in it, of the sanctuary and its vessels."

[17] The LORD spoke to Moses and Aaron, saying, [18] "Let not the tribe of the clans of the Kohathites be destroyed from among the Levites, [19] but deal thus with them, that they may live and not die when they come near to the most holy things: Aaron and his sons shall go in and appoint them each to his task and to his burden, [20] but they shall not go in to look on the holy things even for a moment, lest they die."

[21] The LORD spoke to Moses, saying, [22] "Take a census of the sons of Gershon also, by their fathers' houses and by their clans. [23] From thirty years old up to fifty years old, you shall list them, all who can come to do duty, to do service in the tent of meeting. [24] This is the service of the clans of the Gershonites, in serving and bearing burdens: [25] they shall carry the curtains of the tabernacle and the tent of meeting with its covering and the covering of goatskin that is on top of it and the screen for the entrance of the tent of meeting [26] and the hangings of the court and the screen for the entrance of the gate of the court that is around the tabernacle and the altar, and their cords and all the equipment for their service. And they shall do all that needs to be done with regard to them. [27] All the service of the sons of the Gershonites shall be at the command of Aaron and his sons, in all that they are to carry and in all that they have to do. And you shall assign to their charge all that they are to carry. [28] This is the service of the clans of the sons of the Gershonites in the tent of meeting, and their guard duty is to be under the direction of Ithamar the son of Aaron the priest.

[29] "As for the sons of Merari, you shall list them by their clans and their fathers' houses. [30] From thirty years old up to fifty years old, you shall list them, everyone who can come on duty, to do the service of the tent of meeting. [31] And this is what they are charged to carry, as the whole of their service in the tent of meeting: the frames of the tabernacle, with its bars, pillars, and bases, [32] and the pillars around the court with their bases, pegs, and cords, with all their equipment and all their accessories. And you shall list by name the objects that they are required to carry. [33] This is the service of the clans of the sons of Merari, the whole of their service in the tent of meeting, under the direction of Ithamar the son of Aaron the priest."

[34] And Moses and Aaron and the chiefs of the congregation listed the sons of the Kohathites, by their clans and their fathers' houses, [35] from thirty years old up to fifty years old, everyone who could come on duty, for service in the tent of meeting; [36] and those listed by clans were 2,750. [37] This was the list of the clans of the Kohathites, all who served in the tent of meeting, whom Moses and Aaron listed according to the commandment of the LORD by Moses.

[38] Those listed of the sons of Gershon, by their clans and their fathers' houses, [39] from thirty years old up to fifty years old, everyone who could come on duty for service in the tent of meeting— [40] those listed by their clans and their fathers' houses were 2,630. [41] This was the list of the clans of the sons of Gershon, all who served in the tent of meeting, whom Moses and Aaron listed according to the commandment of the LORD.

[42] Those listed of the clans of the sons of Merari, by their clans and their fathers' houses, [43] from thirty years old up to fifty years old, everyone who could come on duty, for service in the tent of meeting— [44] those listed by clans were 3,200. [45] This was the list of the clans of the sons of Merari, whom Moses and Aaron listed according to the commandment of the LORD by Moses.

[46] All those who were listed of the Levites, whom Moses and Aaron and the chiefs of Israel listed, by their clans and their fathers' houses, [47] from thirty years old up to fifty years old, everyone who could come to do the service of ministry and the service of bearing burdens in the tent of meeting, [48] those listed were 8,580. [49] According to the commandment of the LORD through Moses they were listed, each one with his task of serving or carrying. Thus they were listed by him, as the LORD commanded Moses.

Unclean People

5 The LORD spoke to Moses, saying, [2] "Command the people of Israel that they put out of the camp everyone who is leprous[1] or has a discharge and everyone who is unclean

---

[1] Leprosy was a term for several skin diseases; see Leviticus 13

through contact with the dead. ³You shall put out both male and female, putting them outside the camp, that they may not defile their camp, in the midst of which I dwell." ⁴And the people of Israel did so, and put them outside the camp; as the LORD said to Moses, so the people of Israel did.

Confession and Restitution

⁵And the LORD spoke to Moses, saying, ⁶"Speak to the people of Israel, When a man or woman commits any of the sins that people commit by breaking faith with the LORD, and that person realizes his guilt, ⁷he shall confess his sin that he has committed.¹ And he shall make full restitution for his wrong, adding a fifth to it and giving it to him to whom he did the wrong. ⁸But if the man has no next of kin to whom restitution may be made for the wrong, the restitution for wrong shall go to the LORD for the priest, in addition to the ram of atonement with which atonement is made for him. ⁹And every contribution, all the holy donations of the people of Israel, which they bring to the priest, shall be his. ¹⁰Each one shall keep his holy donations: whatever anyone gives to the priest shall be his."

A Test for Adultery

¹¹And the LORD spoke to Moses, saying, ¹²"Speak to the people of Israel, If any man's wife goes astray and breaks faith with him, ¹³if a man lies with her sexually, and it is hidden from the eyes of her husband, and she is undetected though she has defiled herself, and there is no witness against her, since she was not taken in the act, ¹⁴and if the spirit of jealousy comes over him and he is jealous of his wife who has defiled herself, or if the spirit of jealousy comes over him and he is jealous of his wife, though she has not defiled herself, ¹⁵then the man shall bring his wife to the priest and bring the offering required of her, a tenth of an ephah² of barley flour. He shall pour no oil on it and put no frankincense on it, for it is a grain offering of jealousy, a grain offering of remembrance, bringing iniquity to remembrance.

¹⁶"And the priest shall bring her near and set her before the LORD. ¹⁷And the priest shall take holy water in an earthenware vessel and take some of the dust that is on the floor of the tabernacle and put it into the water. ¹⁸And the priest shall set the woman before the LORD and unbind the hair of the woman's head and place in her hands the grain offering of remembrance, which is the grain offering of jealousy. And in his hand the priest shall have the water of bitterness that brings the curse. ¹⁹Then the priest shall make her take an oath, saying, 'If no man has lain with you, and if you have not turned aside to uncleanness while you were under your husband's authority, be free from this water of bitterness that brings the curse. ²⁰But if you have gone astray, though you are under your husband's authority, and if you have defiled yourself, and some man other than your husband has lain with you, ²¹then' (let the priest make the woman take the oath of the curse, and say to the woman) 'the LORD make you a curse and an oath among your people, when the LORD makes your thigh fall away and your body swell. ²²May this water that brings the curse pass into your bowels and make your womb swell and your thigh fall away.' And the woman shall say, 'Amen, Amen.'

²³"Then the priest shall write these curses in a book and wash them off into the water of bitterness. ²⁴And he shall make the woman drink the water of bitterness that brings the curse, and the water that brings the curse shall enter into her and cause bitter pain. ²⁵And the priest shall take the grain offering of jealousy out of the woman's hand and shall wave the grain offering before the LORD and bring it to the altar. ²⁶And the priest shall take a handful of the grain offering, as its memorial portion, and burn it on the altar, and afterward shall make the woman drink the water. ²⁷And when he has made her drink the water, then, if she has defiled herself and has broken faith with her husband, the water that brings the curse shall enter into her and cause bitter pain, and her womb shall swell, and her thigh shall fall away, and the woman shall become a curse among her people. ²⁸But if the woman has not defiled herself and is clean, then she shall be free and shall conceive children.

²⁹"This is the law in cases of jealousy, when a wife, though under her husband's authority, goes astray and defiles herself, ³⁰or when the spirit of jealousy comes over a man and he is jealous of his wife. Then he shall set the woman before the LORD, and the priest shall carry out for her all this law. ³¹The man shall be free from iniquity, but the woman shall bear her iniquity."

---

¹ Hebrew *they shall confess their sin that they have committed* ² An *ephah* was about 3/5 bushel or 22 liters

The Nazirite Vow

6 And the LORD spoke to Moses, saying, [2] "Speak to the people of Israel and say to them, When either a man or a woman makes a special vow, the vow of a Nazirite,[1] to separate himself to the LORD, [3] he shall separate himself from wine and strong drink. He shall drink no vinegar made from wine or strong drink and shall not drink any juice of grapes or eat grapes, fresh or dried. [4] All the days of his separation[2] he shall eat nothing that is produced by the grapevine, not even the seeds or the skins.

[5] "All the days of his vow of separation, no razor shall touch his head. Until the time is completed for which he separates himself to the LORD, he shall be holy. He shall let the locks of hair of his head grow long.

[6] "All the days that he separates himself to the LORD he shall not go near a dead body. [7] Not even for his father or for his mother, for brother or sister, if they die, shall he make himself unclean, because his separation to God is on his head. [8] All the days of his separation he is holy to the LORD.

[9] "And if any man dies very suddenly beside him and he defiles his consecrated head, then he shall shave his head on the day of his cleansing; on the seventh day he shall shave it. [10] On the eighth day he shall bring two turtledoves or two pigeons to the priest to the entrance of the tent of meeting, [11] and the priest shall offer one for a sin offering and the other for a burnt offering, and make atonement for him, because he sinned by reason of the dead body. And he shall consecrate his head that same day [12] and separate himself to the LORD for the days of his separation and bring a male lamb a year old for a guilt offering. But the previous period shall be void, because his separation was defiled.

[13] "And this is the law for the Nazirite, when the time of his separation has been completed: he shall be brought to the entrance of the tent of meeting, [14] and he shall bring his gift to the LORD, one male lamb a year old without blemish for a burnt offering, and one ewe lamb a year old without blemish as a sin offering, and one ram without blemish as a peace offering, [15] and a basket of unleavened bread, loaves of fine flour mixed with oil, and unleavened wafers smeared with oil, and their grain offering and their drink offerings. [16] And the priest shall bring them before the LORD and offer his sin offering and his burnt offering,

[17] and he shall offer the ram as a sacrifice of peace offering to the LORD, with the basket of unleavened bread. The priest shall offer also its grain offering and its drink offering. [18] And the Nazirite shall shave his consecrated head at the entrance of the tent of meeting and shall take the hair from his consecrated head and put it on the fire that is under the sacrifice of the peace offering. [19] And the priest shall take the shoulder of the ram, when it is boiled, and one unleavened loaf out of the basket and one unleavened wafer, and shall put them on the hands of the Nazirite, after he has shaved the hair of his consecration, [20] and the priest shall wave them for a wave offering before the LORD. They are a holy portion for the priest, together with the breast that is waved and the thigh that is contributed. And after that the Nazirite may drink wine.

[21] "This is the law of the Nazirite. But if he vows an offering to the LORD above his Nazirite vow, as he can afford, in exact accordance with the vow that he takes, then he shall do in addition to the law of the Nazirite."

Aaron's Blessing

[22] The LORD spoke to Moses, saying, [23] "Speak to Aaron and his sons, saying, Thus you shall bless the people of Israel: you shall say to them,

[24]   The LORD bless you and keep you;
[25]   the LORD make his face to shine upon you
          and be gracious to you;
[26]   the LORD lift up his countenance[3] upon
          you and give you peace.

[27] "So shall they put my name upon the people of Israel, and I will bless them."

Offerings at the Tabernacle's Consecration

7 On the day when Moses had finished setting up the tabernacle and had anointed and consecrated it with all its furnishings and had anointed and consecrated the altar with all its utensils, [2] the chiefs of Israel, heads of their fathers' houses, who were the chiefs of the tribes, who were over those who were listed, approached [3] and brought their offerings before the LORD, six wagons and twelve oxen, a wagon for every two of the chiefs, and for each one an ox. They brought them before the tabernacle. [4] Then the LORD said to Moses, [5] "Accept these from them, that they may be used in the service of the tent of meeting, and give them to the Levites, to each man according to his ser-

---

[1] *Nazirite means one separated, or one consecrated* [2] Or *Naziriteship* [3] Or *face*

vice." [6] So Moses took the wagons and the oxen and gave them to the Levites. [7] Two wagons and four oxen he gave to the sons of Gershon, according to their service. [8] And four wagons and eight oxen he gave to the sons of Merari, according to their service, under the direction of Ithamar the son of Aaron the priest. [9] But to the sons of Kohath he gave none, because they were charged with the service of the holy things that had to be carried on the shoulder. [10] And the chiefs offered offerings for the dedication of the altar on the day it was anointed; and the chiefs offered their offering before the altar. [11] And the LORD said to Moses, "They shall offer their offerings, one chief each day, for the dedication of the altar."

[12] He who offered his offering the first day was Nahshon the son of Amminadab, of the tribe of Judah. [13] And his offering was one silver plate whose weight was 130 shekels,[1] one silver basin of 70 shekels, according to the shekel of the sanctuary, both of them full of fine flour mixed with oil for a grain offering; [14] one golden dish of 10 shekels, full of incense; [15] one bull from the herd, one ram, one male lamb a year old, for a burnt offering; [16] one male goat for a sin offering; [17] and for the sacrifice of peace offerings, two oxen, five rams, five male goats, and five male lambs a year old. This was the offering of Nahshon the son of Amminadab.

[18] On the second day Nethanel the son of Zuar, the chief of Issachar, made an offering. [19] He offered for his offering one silver plate whose weight was 130 shekels, one silver basin of 70 shekels, according to the shekel of the sanctuary, both of them full of fine flour mixed with oil for a grain offering; [20] one golden dish of 10 shekels, full of incense; [21] one bull from the herd, one ram, one male lamb a year old, for a burnt offering; [22] one male goat for a sin offering; [23] and for the sacrifice of peace offerings, two oxen, five rams, five male goats, and five male lambs a year old. This was the offering of Nethanel the son of Zuar.

[24] On the third day Eliab the son of Helon, the chief of the people of Zebulun: [25] his offering was one silver plate whose weight was 130 shekels, one silver basin of 70 shekels, according to the shekel of the sanctuary, both of them full of fine flour mixed with oil for a grain offering; [26] one golden dish of 10 shekels, full of incense; [27] one bull from the herd, one ram, one male lamb a year old, for a burnt offering; [28] one male goat for a sin offering; [29] and for the sacrifice of peace offerings, two oxen, five rams, five male goats, and five male lambs a year old. This was the offering of Eliab the son of Helon.

[30] On the fourth day Elizur the son of Shedeur, the chief of the people of Reuben: [31] his offering was one silver plate whose weight was 130 shekels, one silver basin of 70 shekels, according to the shekel of the sanctuary, both of them full of fine flour mixed with oil for a grain offering; [32] one golden dish of 10 shekels, full of incense; [33] one bull from the herd, one ram, one male lamb a year old, for a burnt offering; [34] one male goat for a sin offering; [35] and for the sacrifice of peace offerings, two oxen, five rams, five male goats, and five male lambs a year old. This was the offering of Elizur the son of Shedeur.

[36] On the fifth day Shelumiel the son of Zurishaddai, the chief of the people of Simeon: [37] his offering was one silver plate whose weight was 130 shekels, one silver basin of 70 shekels, according to the shekel of the sanctuary, both of them full of fine flour mixed with oil for a grain offering; [38] one golden dish of 10 shekels, full of incense; [39] one bull from the herd, one ram, one male lamb a year old, for a burnt offering; [40] one male goat for a sin offering; [41] and for the sacrifice of peace offerings, two oxen, five rams, five male goats, and five male lambs a year old. This was the offering of Shelumiel the son of Zurishaddai.

[42] On the sixth day Eliasaph the son of Deuel, the chief of the people of Gad: [43] his offering was one silver plate whose weight was 130 shekels, one silver basin of 70 shekels, according to the shekel of the sanctuary, both of them full of fine flour mixed with oil for a grain offering; [44] one golden dish of 10 shekels, full of incense; [45] one bull from the herd, one ram, one male lamb a year old, for a burnt offering; [46] one male goat for a sin offering; [47] and for the sacrifice of peace offerings, two oxen, five rams, five male goats, and five male lambs a year old. This was the offering of Eliasaph the son of Deuel.

[48] On the seventh day Elishama the son of Ammihud, the chief of the people of Ephraim: [49] his offering was one silver plate whose weight was 130 shekels, one silver basin of 70 shekels, according to the shekel of the sanctuary, both

---

[1] A *shekel* was about 2/5 ounce or 11 grams

of them full of fine flour mixed with oil for a grain offering; [50] one golden dish of 10 shekels, full of incense; [51] one bull from the herd, one ram, one male lamb a year old, for a burnt offering; [52] one male goat for a sin offering; [53] and for the sacrifice of peace offerings, two oxen, five rams, five male goats, and five male lambs a year old. This was the offering of Elishama the son of Ammihud.

[54] On the eighth day Gamaliel the son of Pedahzur, the chief of the people of Manasseh: [55] his offering was one silver plate whose weight was 130 shekels, one silver basin of 70 shekels, according to the shekel of the sanctuary, both of them full of fine flour mixed with oil for a grain offering; [56] one golden dish of 10 shekels, full of incense; [57] one bull from the herd, one ram, one male lamb a year old, for a burnt offering; [58] one male goat for a sin offering; [59] and for the sacrifice of peace offerings, two oxen, five rams, five male goats, and five male lambs a year old. This was the offering of Gamaliel the son of Pedahzur.

[60] On the ninth day Abidan the son of Gideoni, the chief of the people of Benjamin: [61] his offering was one silver plate whose weight was 130 shekels, one silver basin of 70 shekels, according to the shekel of the sanctuary, both of them full of fine flour mixed with oil for a grain offering; [62] one golden dish of 10 shekels, full of incense; [63] one bull from the herd, one ram, one male lamb a year old, for a burnt offering; [64] one male goat for a sin offering; [65] and for the sacrifice of peace offerings, two oxen, five rams, five male goats, and five male lambs a year old. This was the offering of Abidan the son of Gideoni.

[66] On the tenth day Ahiezer the son of Ammishaddai, the chief of the people of Dan: [67] his offering was one silver plate whose weight was 130 shekels, one silver basin of 70 shekels, according to the shekel of the sanctuary, both of them full of fine flour mixed with oil for a grain offering; [68] one golden dish of 10 shekels, full of incense; [69] one bull from the herd, one ram, one male lamb a year old, for a burnt offering; [70] one male goat for a sin offering; [71] and for the sacrifice of peace offerings, two oxen, five rams, five male goats, and five male lambs a year old. This was the offering of Ahiezer the son of Ammishaddai.

[72] On the eleventh day Pagiel the son of Ochran, the chief of the people of Asher: [73] his offering was one silver plate whose weight was 130 shekels, one silver basin of 70 shekels, according to the shekel of the sanctuary, both of them full of fine flour mixed with oil for a grain offering; [74] one golden dish of 10 shekels, full of incense; [75] one bull from the herd, one ram, one male lamb a year old, for a burnt offering; [76] one male goat for a sin offering; [77] and for the sacrifice of peace offerings, two oxen, five rams, five male goats, and five male lambs a year old. This was the offering of Pagiel the son of Ochran.

[78] On the twelfth day Ahira the son of Enan, the chief of the people of Naphtali: [79] his offering was one silver plate whose weight was 130 shekels, one silver basin of 70 shekels, according to the shekel of the sanctuary, both of them full of fine flour mixed with oil for a grain offering; [80] one golden dish of 10 shekels, full of incense; [81] one bull from the herd, one ram, one male lamb a year old, for a burnt offering; [82] one male goat for a sin offering; [83] and for the sacrifice of peace offerings, two oxen, five rams, five male goats, and five male lambs a year old. This was the offering of Ahira the son of Enan.

[84] This was the dedication offering for the altar on the day when it was anointed, from the chiefs of Israel: twelve silver plates, twelve silver basins, twelve golden dishes, [85] each silver plate weighing 130 shekels and each basin 70, all the silver of the vessels 2,400 shekels according to the shekel of the sanctuary, [86] the twelve golden dishes, full of incense, weighing 10 shekels apiece according to the shekel of the sanctuary, all the gold of the dishes being 120 shekels; [87] all the cattle for the burnt offering twelve bulls, twelve rams, twelve male lambs a year old, with their grain offering; and twelve male goats for a sin offering; [88] and all the cattle for the sacrifice of peace offerings twenty-four bulls, the rams sixty, the male goats sixty, the male lambs a year old sixty. This was the dedication offering for the altar after it was anointed.

[89] And when Moses went into the tent of meeting to speak with the LORD, he heard the voice speaking to him from above the mercy seat that was on the ark of the testimony, from between the two cherubim; and it spoke to him.

The Seven Lamps

8 Now the LORD spoke to Moses, saying, ²"Speak to Aaron and say to him, When you set up the lamps, the seven lamps shall give light in front of the lampstand." ³And Aaron did so: he set up its lamps in front of the lampstand, as the LORD commanded Moses. ⁴And this was the workmanship of the lampstand, hammered work of gold. From its base to its flowers, it was hammered work; according to the pattern that the LORD had shown Moses, so he made the lampstand.

Cleansing of the Levites

⁵And the LORD spoke to Moses, saying, ⁶"Take the Levites from among the people of Israel and cleanse them. ⁷Thus you shall do to them to cleanse them: sprinkle the water of purification upon them, and let them go with a razor over all their body, and wash their clothes and cleanse themselves. ⁸Then let them take a bull from the herd and its grain offering of fine flour mixed with oil, and you shall take another bull from the herd for a sin offering. ⁹And you shall bring the Levites before the tent of meeting and assemble the whole congregation of the people of Israel. ¹⁰When you bring the Levites before the LORD, the people of Israel shall lay their hands on the Levites, ¹¹and Aaron shall offer the Levites before the LORD as a wave offering from the people of Israel, that they may do the service of the LORD. ¹²Then the Levites shall lay their hands on the heads of the bulls, and you shall offer the one for a sin offering and the other for a burnt offering to the LORD to make atonement for the Levites. ¹³And you shall set the Levites before Aaron and his sons, and shall offer them as a wave offering to the LORD.

¹⁴"Thus you shall separate the Levites from among the people of Israel, and the Levites shall be mine. ¹⁵And after that the Levites shall go in to serve at the tent of meeting, when you have cleansed them and offered them as a wave offering. ¹⁶For they are wholly given to me from among the people of Israel. Instead of all who open the womb, the firstborn of all the people of Israel, I have taken them for myself. ¹⁷For all the firstborn among the people of Israel are mine, both of man and of beast. On the day that I struck down all the firstborn in the land of Egypt I conse-crated them for myself, ¹⁸and I have taken the Levites instead of all the firstborn among the people of Israel. ¹⁹And I have given the Levites as a gift to Aaron and his sons from among the people of Israel, to do the service for the people of Israel at the tent of meeting and to make atonement for the people of Israel, that there may be no plague among the people of Israel when the people of Israel come near the sanctuary."

²⁰Thus did Moses and Aaron and all the congregation of the people of Israel to the Levites. According to all that the LORD commanded Moses concerning the Levites, the people of Israel did to them. ²¹And the Levites purified themselves from sin and washed their clothes, and Aaron offered them as a wave offering before the LORD, and Aaron made atonement for them to cleanse them. ²²And after that the Levites went in to do their service in the tent of meeting before Aaron and his sons; as the LORD had commanded Moses concerning the Levites, so they did to them.

Retirement of the Levites

²³And the LORD spoke to Moses, saying, ²⁴"This applies to the Levites: from twenty-five years old and upward they¹ shall come to do duty in the service of the tent of meeting. ²⁵And from the age of fifty years they shall withdraw from the duty of the service and serve no more. ²⁶They minister² to their brothers in the tent of meeting by keeping guard, but they shall do no service. Thus shall you do to the Levites in assigning their duties."

The Passover Celebrated

9 And the LORD spoke to Moses in the wilderness of Sinai, in the first month of the second year after they had come out of the land of Egypt, saying, ²"Let the people of Israel keep the Passover at its appointed time. ³On the fourteenth day of this month, at twilight, you shall keep it at its appointed time; according to all its statutes and all its rules you shall keep it." ⁴So Moses told the people of Israel that they should keep the Passover. ⁵And they kept the Passover in the first month, on the fourteenth day of the month, at twilight, in the wilderness of Sinai; according to all that the LORD commanded Moses, so the people of Israel did. ⁶And there were certain men who were unclean through touching a dead body, so that they could not keep the Passover on that day, and they came

¹ Hebrew *he*; also verses 25, 26 ² Hebrew *He ministers*

before Moses and Aaron on that day. [7] And those men said to him, "We are unclean through touching a dead body. Why are we kept from bringing the LORD's offering at its appointed time among the people of Israel?" [8] And Moses said to them, "Wait, that I may hear what the LORD will command concerning you."

[9] The LORD spoke to Moses, saying, [10] "Speak to the people of Israel, saying, If any one of you or of your descendants is unclean through touching a dead body, or is on a long journey, he shall still keep the Passover to the LORD. [11] In the second month on the fourteenth day at twilight they shall keep it. They shall eat it with unleavened bread and bitter herbs. [12] They shall leave none of it until the morning, nor break any of its bones; according to all the statute for the Passover they shall keep it. [13] But if anyone who is clean and is not on a journey fails to keep the Passover, that person shall be cut off from his people because he did not bring the LORD's offering at its appointed time; that man shall bear his sin. [14] And if a stranger sojourns among you and would keep the Passover to the LORD, according to the statute of the Passover and according to its rule, so shall he do. You shall have one statute, both for the sojourner and for the native."

The Cloud Covering the Tabernacle

[15] On the day that the tabernacle was set up, the cloud covered the tabernacle, the tent of the testimony. And at evening it was over the tabernacle like the appearance of fire until morning. [16] So it was always: the cloud covered it by day[1] and the appearance of fire by night. [17] And whenever the cloud lifted from over the tent, after that the people of Israel set out, and in the place where the cloud settled down, there the people of Israel camped. [18] At the command of the LORD the people of Israel set out, and at the command of the LORD they camped. As long as the cloud rested over the tabernacle, they remained in camp. [19] Even when the cloud continued over the tabernacle many days, the people of Israel kept the charge of the LORD and did not set out. [20] Sometimes the cloud was a few days over the tabernacle, and according to the command of the LORD they remained in camp; then according to the command of the LORD they set out. [21] And sometimes the cloud remained from evening until morning. And

when the cloud lifted in the morning, they set out, or if it continued for a day and a night, when the cloud lifted they set out. [22] Whether it was two days, or a month, or a longer time, that the cloud continued over the tabernacle, abiding there, the people of Israel remained in camp and did not set out, but when it lifted they set out. [23] At the command of the LORD they camped, and at the command of the LORD they set out. They kept the charge of the LORD, at the command of the LORD by Moses.

The Silver Trumpets

10 The LORD spoke to Moses, saying, [2] "Make two silver trumpets. Of hammered work you shall make them, and you shall use them for summoning the congregation and for breaking camp. [3] And when both are blown, all the congregation shall gather themselves to you at the entrance of the tent of meeting. [4] But if they blow only one, then the chiefs, the heads of the tribes of Israel, shall gather themselves to you. [5] When you blow an alarm, the camps that are on the east side shall set out. [6] And when you blow an alarm the second time, the camps that are on the south side shall set out. An alarm is to be blown whenever they are to set out. [7] But when the assembly is to be gathered together, you shall blow a long blast, but you shall not sound an alarm. [8] And the sons of Aaron, the priests, shall blow the trumpets. The trumpets shall be to you for a perpetual statute throughout your generations. [9] And when you go to war in your land against the adversary who oppresses you, then you shall sound an alarm with the trumpets, that you may be remembered before the LORD your God, and you shall be saved from your enemies. [10] On the day of your gladness also, and at your appointed feasts and at the beginnings of your months, you shall blow the trumpets over your burnt offerings and over the sacrifices of your peace offerings. They shall be a reminder of you before your God: I am the LORD your God."

Israel Leaves Sinai

[11] In the second year, in the second month, on the twentieth day of the month, the cloud lifted from over the tabernacle of the testimony, [12] and the people of Israel set out by stages from the wilderness of Sinai. And the cloud settled down in the wilderness of Paran. [13] They set out for the first time at the command of the LORD

---

[1] Septuagint, Syriac, Vulgate; Hebrew lacks *by day*

by Moses. [14] The standard of the camp of the people of Judah set out first by their companies, and over their company was Nahshon the son of Amminadab. [15] And over the company of the tribe of the people of Issachar was Nethanel the son of Zuar. [16] And over the company of the tribe of the people of Zebulun was Eliab the son of Helon.

[17] And when the tabernacle was taken down, the sons of Gershon and the sons of Merari, who carried the tabernacle, set out. [18] And the standard of the camp of Reuben set out by their companies, and over their company was Elizur the son of Shedeur. [19] And over the company of the tribe of the people of Simeon was Shelumiel the son of Zurishaddai. [20] And over the company of the tribe of the people of Gad was Eliasaph the son of Deuel.

[21] Then the Kohathites set out, carrying the holy things, and the tabernacle was set up before their arrival. [22] And the standard of the camp of the people of Ephraim set out by their companies, and over their company was Elishama the son of Ammihud. [23] And over the company of the tribe of the people of Manasseh was Gamaliel the son of Pedahzur. [24] And over the company of the tribe of the people of Benjamin was Abidan the son of Gideoni.

[25] Then the standard of the camp of the people of Dan, acting as the rear guard of all the camps, set out by their companies, and over their company was Ahiezer the son of Ammishaddai. [26] And over the company of the tribe of the people of Asher was Pagiel the son of Ochran. [27] And over the company of the tribe of the people of Naphtali was Ahira the son of Enan. [28] This was the order of march of the people of Israel by their companies, when they set out.

[29] And Moses said to Hobab the son of Reuel the Midianite, Moses' father-in-law, "We are setting out for the place of which the LORD said, 'I will give it to you.' Come with us, and we will do good to you, for the LORD has promised good to Israel." [30] But he said to him, "I will not go. I will depart to my own land and to my kindred." [31] And he said, "Please do not leave us, for you know where we should camp in the wilderness, and you will serve as eyes for us. [32] And if you do go with us, whatever good the LORD will do to us, the same will we do to you."

[33] So they set out from the mount of the LORD three days' journey. And the ark of the covenant of the LORD went before them three days' journey, to seek out a resting place for them. [34] And the cloud of the LORD was over them by day, whenever they set out from the camp.

[35] And whenever the ark set out, Moses said, "Arise, O LORD, and let your enemies be scattered, and let those who hate you flee before you." [36] And when it rested, he said, "Return, O LORD, to the ten thousand thousands of Israel."

The People Complain

11 And the people complained in the hearing of the LORD about their misfortunes, and when the LORD heard it, his anger was kindled, and the fire of the LORD burned among them and consumed some outlying parts of the camp. [2] Then the people cried out to Moses, and Moses prayed to the LORD, and the fire died down. [3] So the name of that place was called Taberah,[1] because the fire of the LORD burned among them.

[4] Now the rabble that was among them had a strong craving. And the people of Israel also wept again and said, "Oh that we had meat to eat! [5] We remember the fish we ate in Egypt that cost nothing, the cucumbers, the melons, the leeks, the onions, and the garlic. [6] But now our strength is dried up, and there is nothing at all but this manna to look at."

[7] Now the manna was like coriander seed, and its appearance like that of bdellium. [8] The people went about and gathered it and ground it in handmills or beat it in mortars and boiled it in pots and made cakes of it. And the taste of it was like the taste of cakes baked with oil. [9] When the dew fell upon the camp in the night, the manna fell with it.

[10] Moses heard the people weeping throughout their clans, everyone at the door of his tent. And the anger of the LORD blazed hotly, and Moses was displeased. [11] Moses said to the LORD, "Why have you dealt ill with your servant? And why have I not found favor in your sight, that you lay the burden of all this people on me? [12] Did I conceive all this people? Did I give them birth, that you should say to me, 'Carry them in your bosom, as a nurse carries a nursing child,' to the land that you swore to give their fathers? [13] Where am I to get meat to give to all this people? For they weep before

---

[1] Taberah means burning

me and say, 'Give us meat, that we may eat.' ¹⁴I am not able to carry all this people alone; the burden is too heavy for me. ¹⁵If you will treat me like this, kill me at once, if I find favor in your sight, that I may not see my wretchedness."

Elders Appointed to Aid Moses

¹⁶Then the LORD said to Moses, "Gather for me seventy men of the elders of Israel, whom you know to be the elders of the people and officers over them, and bring them to the tent of meeting, and let them take their stand there with you. ¹⁷And I will come down and talk with you there. And I will take some of the Spirit that is on you and put it on them, and they shall bear the burden of the people with you, so that you may not bear it yourself alone. ¹⁸And say to the people, 'Consecrate yourselves for tomorrow, and you shall eat meat, for you have wept in the hearing of the LORD, saying, "Who will give us meat to eat? For it was better for us in Egypt." Therefore the LORD will give you meat, and you shall eat. ¹⁹You shall not eat just one day, or two days, or five days, or ten days, or twenty days, ²⁰but a whole month, until it comes out at your nostrils and becomes loathsome to you, because you have rejected the LORD who is among you and have wept before him, saying, "Why did we come out of Egypt?"'" ²¹But Moses said, "The people among whom I am number six hundred thousand on foot, and you have said, 'I will give them meat, that they may eat a whole month!' ²²Shall flocks and herds be slaughtered for them, and be enough for them? Or shall all the fish of the sea be gathered together for them, and be enough for them?" ²³And the LORD said to Moses, "Is the LORD's hand shortened? Now you shall see whether my word will come true for you or not."

²⁴So Moses went out and told the people the words of the LORD. And he gathered seventy men of the elders of the people and placed them around the tent. ²⁵Then the LORD came down in the cloud and spoke to him, and took some of the Spirit that was on him and put it on the seventy elders. And as soon as the Spirit rested on them, they prophesied. But they did not continue doing it.

²⁶Now two men remained in the camp, one named Eldad, and the other named Medad, and the Spirit rested on them. They were among those registered, but they had not gone out to the tent, and so they prophesied in the camp.

²⁷And a young man ran and told Moses, "Eldad and Medad are prophesying in the camp." ²⁸And Joshua the son of Nun, the assistant of Moses from his youth, said, "My lord Moses, stop them." ²⁹But Moses said to him, "Are you jealous for my sake? Would that all the LORD's people were prophets, that the LORD would put his Spirit on them!" ³⁰And Moses and the elders of Israel returned to the camp.

Quail and a Plague

³¹Then a wind from the LORD sprang up, and it brought quail from the sea and let them fall beside the camp, about a day's journey on this side and a day's journey on the other side, around the camp, and about two cubits¹ above the ground. ³²And the people rose all that day and all night and all the next day, and gathered the quail. Those who gathered least gathered ten homers.² And they spread them out for themselves all around the camp. ³³While the meat was yet between their teeth, before it was consumed, the anger of the LORD was kindled against the people, and the LORD struck down the people with a very great plague. ³⁴Therefore the name of that place was called Kibroth-hattaavah,³ because there they buried the people who had the craving. ³⁵From Kibroth-hattaavah the people journeyed to Hazeroth, and they remained at Hazeroth.

Miriam and Aaron Oppose Moses

12 Miriam and Aaron spoke against Moses because of the Cushite woman whom he had married, for he had married a Cushite woman. ²And they said, "Has the LORD indeed spoken only through Moses? Has he not spoken through us also?" And the LORD heard it. ³Now the man Moses was very meek, more than all people who were on the face of the earth. ⁴And suddenly the LORD said to Moses and to Aaron and Miriam, "Come out, you three, to the tent of meeting." And the three of them came out. ⁵And the LORD came down in a pillar of cloud and stood at the entrance of the tent and called Aaron and Miriam, and they both came forward. ⁶And he said, "Hear my words: If there is a prophet among you, I the LORD make myself known to him in a vision; I speak with him in a dream. ⁷Not so with my servant Moses. He is faithful in all my house. ⁸With him I speak mouth to mouth, clearly, and not in riddles, and he beholds the form of the LORD. Why then were you not afraid to speak against my

¹ A cubit was about 18 inches or 45 centimeters ² A homer was about 6 bushels or 220 liters ³ Kibroth-hattaavah means graves of craving

servant Moses?" [9] And the anger of the LORD was kindled against them, and he departed.

[10] When the cloud removed from over the tent, behold, Miriam was leprous,[1] like snow. And Aaron turned toward Miriam, and behold, she was leprous. [11] And Aaron said to Moses, "Oh, my lord, do not punish us[2] because we have done foolishly and have sinned. [12] Let her not be as one dead, whose flesh is half eaten away when he comes out of his mother's womb." [13] And Moses cried to the LORD, "O God, please heal her—please." [14] But the LORD said to Moses, "If her father had but spit in her face, should she not be shamed seven days? Let her be shut outside the camp seven days, and after that she may be brought in again." [15] So Miriam was shut outside the camp seven days, and the people did not set out on the march till Miriam was brought in again. [16] After that the people set out from Hazeroth, and camped in the wilderness of Paran.

Spies Sent into Canaan

13 The LORD spoke to Moses, saying, [2] "Send men to spy out the land of Canaan, which I am giving to the people of Israel. From each tribe of their fathers you shall send a man, every one a chief among them." [3] So Moses sent them from the wilderness of Paran, according to the command of the LORD, all of them men who were heads of the people of Israel. [4] And these were their names: From the tribe of Reuben, Shammua the son of Zaccur; [5] from the tribe of Simeon, Shaphat the son of Hori; [6] from the tribe of Judah, Caleb the son of Jephunneh; [7] from the tribe of Issachar, Igal the son of Joseph; [8] from the tribe of Ephraim, Hoshea the son of Nun; [9] from the tribe of Benjamin, Palti the son of Raphu; [10] from the tribe of Zebulun, Gaddiel the son of Sodi; [11] from the tribe of Joseph (that is, from the tribe of Manasseh), Gaddi the son of Susi; [12] from the tribe of Dan, Ammiel the son of Gemalli; [13] from the tribe of Asher, Sethur the son of Michael; [14] from the tribe of Naphtali, Nahbi the son of Vophsi; [15] from the tribe of Gad, Geuel the son of Machi. [16] These were the names of the men whom Moses sent to spy out the land. And Moses called Hoshea the son of Nun Joshua.

[17] Moses sent them to spy out the land of Canaan and said to them, "Go up into the Negeb and go up into the hill country, [18] and see what the land is, and whether the people who dwell in it are strong or weak, whether they are few or many, [19] and whether the land that they dwell in is good or bad, and whether the cities that they dwell in are camps or strongholds, [20] and whether the land is rich or poor, and whether there are trees in it or not. Be of good courage and bring some of the fruit of the land." Now the time was the season of the first ripe grapes.

[21] So they went up and spied out the land from the wilderness of Zin to Rehob, near Lebo-hamath. [22] They went up into the Negeb and came to Hebron. Ahiman, Sheshai, and Talmai, the descendants of Anak, were there. (Hebron was built seven years before Zoan in Egypt.) [23] And they came to the Valley of Eshcol and cut down from there a branch with a single cluster of grapes, and they carried it on a pole between two of them; they also brought some pomegranates and figs. [24] That place was called the Valley of Eshcol,[3] because of the cluster that the people of Israel cut down from there.

Report of the Spies

[25] At the end of forty days they returned from spying out the land. [26] And they came to Moses and Aaron and to all the congregation of the people of Israel in the wilderness of Paran, at Kadesh. They brought back word to them and to all the congregation, and showed them the fruit of the land. [27] And they told him, "We came to the land to which you sent us. It flows with milk and honey, and this is its fruit. [28] However, the people who dwell in the land are strong, and the cities are fortified and very large. And besides, we saw the descendants of Anak there. [29] The Amalekites dwell in the land of the Negeb. The Hittites, the Jebusites, and the Amorites dwell in the hill country. And the Canaanites dwell by the sea, and along the Jordan."

[30] But Caleb quieted the people before Moses and said, "Let us go up at once and occupy it, for we are well able to overcome it." [31] Then the men who had gone up with him said, "We are not able to go up against the people, for they are stronger than we are." [32] So they brought to the people of Israel a bad report of the land that they had spied out, saying, "The land, through which we have gone to spy it out, is a land that devours its inhabitants, and all the people that

---

[1] *Leprosy was a term for several skin diseases; see Leviticus 13* [2] *Hebrew do not lay sin upon us* [3] *Eshcol means cluster*

we saw in it are of great height. ³³And there we saw the Nephilim (the sons of Anak, who come from the Nephilim), and we seemed to ourselves like grasshoppers, and so we seemed to them."

The People Rebel

14 Then all the congregation raised a loud cry, and the people wept that night. ²And all the people of Israel grumbled against Moses and Aaron. The whole congregation said to them, "Would that we had died in the land of Egypt! Or would that we had died in this wilderness! ³Why is the Lord bringing us into this land, to fall by the sword? Our wives and our little ones will become a prey. Would it not be better for us to go back to Egypt?" ⁴And they said to one another, "Let us choose a leader and go back to Egypt."

⁵Then Moses and Aaron fell on their faces before all the assembly of the congregation of the people of Israel. ⁶And Joshua the son of Nun and Caleb the son of Jephunneh, who were among those who had spied out the land, tore their clothes ⁷and said to all the congregation of the people of Israel, "The land, which we passed through to spy it out, is an exceedingly good land. ⁸If the Lord delights in us, he will bring us into this land and give it to us, a land that flows with milk and honey. ⁹Only do not rebel against the Lord. And do not fear the people of the land, for they are bread for us. Their protection is removed from them, and the Lord is with us; do not fear them." ¹⁰Then all the congregation said to stone them with stones. But the glory of the Lord appeared at the tent of meeting to all the people of Israel.

¹¹And the Lord said to Moses, "How long will this people despise me? And how long will they not believe in me, in spite of all the signs that I have done among them? ¹²I will strike them with the pestilence and disinherit them, and I will make of you a nation greater and mightier than they."

Moses Intercedes for the People

¹³But Moses said to the Lord, "Then the Egyptians will hear of it, for you brought up this people in your might from among them, ¹⁴and they will tell the inhabitants of this land. They have heard that you, O Lord, are in the midst of this people. For you, O Lord, are seen face to face, and your cloud stands over them and you go before them, in a pillar of cloud by day and in a pillar of fire by night. ¹⁵Now if you kill this people as one man, then the nations who have heard your fame will say, ¹⁶'It is because the Lord was not able to bring this people into the land that he swore to give to them that he has killed them in the wilderness.' ¹⁷And now, please let the power of the Lord be great as you have promised, saying, ¹⁸'The Lord is slow to anger and abounding in steadfast love, forgiving iniquity and transgression, but he will by no means clear the guilty, visiting the iniquity of the fathers on the children, to the third and the fourth generation.' ¹⁹Please pardon the iniquity of this people, according to the greatness of your steadfast love, just as you have forgiven this people, from Egypt until now."

God Promises Judgment

²⁰Then the Lord said, "I have pardoned, according to your word. ²¹But truly, as I live, and as all the earth shall be filled with the glory of the Lord, ²²none of the men who have seen my glory and my signs that I did in Egypt and in the wilderness, and yet have put me to the test these ten times and have not obeyed my voice, ²³shall see the land that I swore to give to their fathers. And none of those who despised me shall see it. ²⁴But my servant Caleb, because he has a different spirit and has followed me fully, I will bring into the land into which he went, and his descendants shall possess it. ²⁵Now, since the Amalekites and the Canaanites dwell in the valleys, turn tomorrow and set out for the wilderness by the way to the Red Sea."

²⁶And the Lord spoke to Moses and to Aaron, saying, ²⁷"How long shall this wicked congregation grumble against me? I have heard the grumblings of the people of Israel, which they grumble against me. ²⁸Say to them, 'As I live, declares the Lord, what you have said in my hearing I will do to you: ²⁹your dead bodies shall fall in this wilderness, and of all your number, listed in the census from twenty years old and upward, who have grumbled against me, ³⁰not one shall come into the land where I swore that I would make you dwell, except Caleb the son of Jephunneh and Joshua the son of Nun. ³¹But your little ones, who you said would become a prey, I will bring in, and they shall know the land that you have rejected. ³²But as for you, your dead

bodies shall fall in this wilderness. ³³ And your children shall be shepherds in the wilderness forty years and shall suffer for your faithlessness, until the last of your dead bodies lies in the wilderness. ³⁴ According to the number of the days in which you spied out the land, forty days, a year for each day, you shall bear your iniquity forty years, and you shall know my displeasure.' ³⁵ I, the Lord, have spoken. Surely this will I do to all this wicked congregation who are gathered together against me: in this wilderness they shall come to a full end, and there they shall die."

³⁶ And the men whom Moses sent to spy out the land, who returned and made all the congregation grumble against him by bringing up a bad report about the land— ³⁷ the men who brought up a bad report of the land—died by plague before the Lord. ³⁸ Of those men who went to spy out the land, only Joshua the son of Nun and Caleb the son of Jephunneh remained alive.

Israel Defeated in Battle

³⁹ When Moses told these words to all the people of Israel, the people mourned greatly. ⁴⁰ And they rose early in the morning and went up to the heights of the hill country, saying, "Here we are. We will go up to the place that the Lord has promised, for we have sinned." ⁴¹ But Moses said, "Why now are you transgressing the command of the Lord, when that will not succeed? ⁴² Do not go up, for the Lord is not among you, lest you be struck down before your enemies. ⁴³ For there the Amalekites and the Canaanites are facing you, and you shall fall by the sword. Because you have turned back from following the Lord, the Lord will not be with you." ⁴⁴ But they presumed to go up to the heights of the hill country, although neither the ark of the covenant of the Lord nor Moses departed out of the camp. ⁴⁵ Then the Amalekites and the Canaanites who lived in that hill country came down and defeated them and pursued them, even to Hormah.

Laws About Sacrifices

15 The Lord spoke to Moses, saying, ² "Speak to the people of Israel and say to them, When you come into the land you are to inhabit, which I am giving you, ³ and you offer to the Lord from the herd or from the flock a food offering¹ or a burnt offering or a

sacrifice, to fulfill a vow or as a freewill offering or at your appointed feasts, to make a pleasing aroma to the Lord, ⁴ then he who brings his offering shall offer to the Lord a grain offering of a tenth of an ephah² of fine flour, mixed with a quarter of a hin³ of oil; ⁵ and you shall offer with the burnt offering, or for the sacrifice, a quarter of a hin of wine for the drink offering for each lamb. ⁶ Or for a ram, you shall offer for a grain offering two tenths of an ephah of fine flour mixed with a third of a hin of oil. ⁷ And for the drink offering you shall offer a third of a hin of wine, a pleasing aroma to the Lord. ⁸ And when you offer a bull as a burnt offering or sacrifice, to fulfill a vow or for peace offerings to the Lord, ⁹ then one shall offer with the bull a grain offering of three tenths of an ephah of fine flour, mixed with half a hin of oil. ¹⁰ And you shall offer for the drink offering half a hin of wine, as a food offering, a pleasing aroma to the Lord.

¹¹ "Thus it shall be done for each bull or ram, or for each lamb or young goat. ¹² As many as you offer, so shall you do with each one, as many as there are. ¹³ Every native Israelite shall do these things in this way, in offering a food offering, with a pleasing aroma to the Lord. ¹⁴ And if a stranger is sojourning with you, or anyone is living permanently among you, and he wishes to offer a food offering, with a pleasing aroma to the Lord, he shall do as you do. ¹⁵ For the assembly, there shall be one statute for you and for the stranger who sojourns with you, a statute forever throughout your generations. You and the sojourner shall be alike before the Lord. ¹⁶ One law and one rule shall be for you and for the stranger who sojourns with you."

¹⁷ The Lord spoke to Moses, saying, ¹⁸ "Speak to the people of Israel and say to them, When you come into the land to which I bring you ¹⁹ and when you eat of the bread of the land, you shall present a contribution to the Lord. ²⁰ Of the first of your dough you shall present a loaf as a contribution; like a contribution from the threshing floor, so shall you present it. ²¹ Some of the first of your dough you shall give to the Lord as a contribution throughout your generations.

Laws About Unintentional Sins

²² "But if you sin unintentionally,⁴ and do not observe all these commandments that the Lord has spoken to Moses, ²³ all that the Lord

¹ Or an offering by fire; so throughout Numbers ² An ephah was about 3/5 bushel or 22 liters ³ A hin was about 4 quarts or 3.5 liters ⁴ Or by mistake; also verses 24, 27, 28, 29

has commanded you by Moses, from the day that the LORD gave commandment, and onward throughout your generations, [24] then if it was done unintentionally without the knowledge of the congregation, all the congregation shall offer one bull from the herd for a burnt offering, a pleasing aroma to the LORD, with its grain offering and its drink offering, according to the rule, and one male goat for a sin offering. [25] And the priest shall make atonement for all the congregation of the people of Israel, and they shall be forgiven, because it was a mistake, and they have brought their offering, a food offering to the LORD, and their sin offering before the LORD for their mistake. [26] And all the congregation of the people of Israel shall be forgiven, and the stranger who sojourns among them, because the whole population was involved in the mistake.

[27] "If one person sins unintentionally, he shall offer a female goat a year old for a sin offering. [28] And the priest shall make atonement before the LORD for the person who makes a mistake, when he sins unintentionally, to make atonement for him, and he shall be forgiven. [29] You shall have one law for him who does anything unintentionally, for him who is native among the people of Israel and for the stranger who sojourns among them. [30] But the person who does anything with a high hand, whether he is native or a sojourner, reviles the LORD, and that person shall be cut off from among his people. [31] Because he has despised the word of the LORD and has broken his commandment, that person shall be utterly cut off; his iniquity shall be on him."

A Sabbathbreaker Executed

[32] While the people of Israel were in the wilderness, they found a man gathering sticks on the Sabbath day. [33] And those who found him gathering sticks brought him to Moses and Aaron and to all the congregation. [34] They put him in custody, because it had not been made clear what should be done to him. [35] And the LORD said to Moses, "The man shall be put to death; all the congregation shall stone him with stones outside the camp." [36] And all the congregation brought him outside the camp and stoned him to death with stones, as the LORD commanded Moses.

Tassels on Garments

[37] The LORD said to Moses, [38] "Speak to the people of Israel, and tell them to make tassels on the corners of their garments throughout their generations, and to put a cord of blue on the tassel of each corner. [39] And it shall be a tassel for you to look at and remember all the commandments of the LORD, to do them, not to follow[1] after your own heart and your own eyes, which you are inclined to whore after. [40] So you shall remember and do all my commandments, and be holy to your God. [41] I am the LORD your God, who brought you out of the land of Egypt to be your God: I am the LORD your God."

Korah's Rebellion

16 Now Korah the son of Izhar, son of Kohath, son of Levi, and Dathan and Abiram the sons of Eliab, and On the son of Peleth, sons of Reuben, took men. [2] And they rose up before Moses, with a number of the people of Israel, 250 chiefs of the congregation, chosen from the assembly, well-known men. [3] They assembled themselves together against Moses and against Aaron and said to them, "You have gone too far! For all in the congregation are holy, every one of them, and the LORD is among them. Why then do you exalt yourselves above the assembly of the LORD?" [4] When Moses heard it, he fell on his face, [5] and he said to Korah and all his company, "In the morning the LORD will show who is his,[2] and who is holy, and will bring him near to him. The one whom he chooses he will bring near to him. [6] Do this: take censers, Korah and all his company; [7] put fire in them and put incense on them before the LORD tomorrow, and the man whom the LORD chooses shall be the holy one. You have gone too far, sons of Levi!" [8] And Moses said to Korah, "Hear now, you sons of Levi: [9] is it too small a thing for you that the God of Israel has separated you from the congregation of Israel, to bring you near to himself, to do service in the tabernacle of the LORD and to stand before the congregation to minister to them, [10] and that he has brought you near him, and all your brothers the sons of Levi with you? And would you seek the priesthood also? [11] Therefore it is against the LORD that you and all your company have gathered together. What is Aaron that you grumble against him?"

[12] And Moses sent to call Dathan and Abiram the sons of Eliab, and they said, "We will not come up. [13] Is it a small thing that you have brought us up out of a land flowing with milk and honey, to kill us in the wilderness, that

[1] Hebrew to spy out [2] Septuagint The LORD knows those who are his

you must also make yourself a prince over us? [14] Moreover, you have not brought us into a land flowing with milk and honey, nor given us inheritance of fields and vineyards. Will you put out the eyes of these men? We will not come up." [15] And Moses was very angry and said to the LORD, "Do not respect their offering. I have not taken one donkey from them, and I have not harmed one of them."

[16] And Moses said to Korah, "Be present, you and all your company, before the LORD, you and they, and Aaron, tomorrow. [17] And let every one of you take his censer and put incense on it, and every one of you bring before the LORD his censer, 250 censers; you also, and Aaron, each his censer." [18] So every man took his censer and put fire in them and laid incense on them and stood at the entrance of the tent of meeting with Moses and Aaron. [19] Then Korah assembled all the congregation against them at the entrance of the tent of meeting. And the glory of the LORD appeared to all the congregation.

[20] And the LORD spoke to Moses and to Aaron, saying, [21] "Separate yourselves from among this congregation, that I may consume them in a moment." [22] And they fell on their faces and said, "O God, the God of the spirits of all flesh, shall one man sin, and will you be angry with all the congregation?" [23] And the LORD spoke to Moses, saying, [24] "Say to the congregation, Get away from the dwelling of Korah, Dathan, and Abiram."

[25] Then Moses rose and went to Dathan and Abiram, and the elders of Israel followed him. [26] And he spoke to the congregation, saying, "Depart, please, from the tents of these wicked men, and touch nothing of theirs, lest you be swept away with all their sins." [27] So they got away from the dwelling of Korah, Dathan, and Abiram. And Dathan and Abiram came out and stood at the door of their tents, together with their wives, their sons, and their little ones. [28] And Moses said, "Hereby you shall know that the LORD has sent me to do all these works, and that it has not been of my own accord. [29] If these men die as all men die, or if they are visited by the fate of all mankind, then the LORD has not sent me. [30] But if the LORD creates something new, and the ground opens its mouth and swallows them up with all that belongs to them, and they go down alive into Sheol, then you shall know that these men have despised the LORD."

[31] And as soon as he had finished speaking all these words, the ground under them split apart. [32] And the earth opened its mouth and swallowed them up, with their households and all the people who belonged to Korah and all their goods. [33] So they and all that belonged to them went down alive into Sheol, and the earth closed over them, and they perished from the midst of the assembly. [34] And all Israel who were around them fled at their cry, for they said, "Lest the earth swallow us up!" [35] And fire came out from the LORD and consumed the 250 men offering the incense.

[36] [1] Then the LORD spoke to Moses, saying, [37] "Tell Eleazar the son of Aaron the priest to take up the censers out of the blaze. Then scatter the fire far and wide, for they have become holy. [38] As for the censers of these men who have sinned at the cost of their lives, let them be made into hammered plates as a covering for the altar, for they offered them before the LORD, and they became holy. Thus they shall be a sign to the people of Israel." [39] So Eleazar the priest took the bronze censers, which those who were burned had offered, and they were hammered out as a covering for the altar, [40] to be a reminder to the people of Israel, so that no outsider, who is not of the descendants of Aaron, should draw near to burn incense before the LORD, lest he become like Korah and his company—as the LORD said to him through Moses.

[41] But on the next day all the congregation of the people of Israel grumbled against Moses and against Aaron, saying, "You have killed the people of the LORD." [42] And when the congregation had assembled against Moses and against Aaron, they turned toward the tent of meeting. And behold, the cloud covered it, and the glory of the LORD appeared. [43] And Moses and Aaron came to the front of the tent of meeting, [44] and the LORD spoke to Moses, saying, [45] "Get away from the midst of this congregation, that I may consume them in a moment." And they fell on their faces. [46] And Moses said to Aaron, "Take your censer, and put fire on it from off the altar and lay incense on it and carry it quickly to the congregation and make atonement for them, for wrath has gone out from the LORD; the plague has begun." [47] So Aaron took it as Moses said and ran into the midst of the assembly. And behold, the plague had already begun among the people. And he put on the incense

[1] Ch 17:1 in Hebrew

and made atonement for the people. [48] And he stood between the dead and the living, and the plague was stopped. [49] Now those who died in the plague were 14,700, besides those who died in the affair of Korah. [50] And Aaron returned to Moses at the entrance of the tent of meeting, when the plague was stopped.

Aaron's Staff Buds

17[1] The Lord spoke to Moses, saying, [2] "Speak to the people of Israel, and get from them staffs, one for each fathers' house, from all their chiefs according to their fathers' houses, twelve staffs. Write each man's name on his staff, [3] and write Aaron's name on the staff of Levi. For there shall be one staff for the head of each fathers' house. [4] Then you shall deposit them in the tent of meeting before the testimony, where I meet with you. [5] And the staff of the man whom I choose shall sprout. Thus I will make to cease from me the grumblings of the people of Israel, which they grumble against you." [6] Moses spoke to the people of Israel. And all their chiefs gave him staffs, one for each chief, according to their fathers' houses, twelve staffs. And the staff of Aaron was among their staffs. [7] And Moses deposited the staffs before the Lord in the tent of the testimony.

[8] On the next day Moses went into the tent of the testimony, and behold, the staff of Aaron for the house of Levi had sprouted and put forth buds and produced blossoms, and it bore ripe almonds. [9] Then Moses brought out all the staffs from before the Lord to all the people of Israel. And they looked, and each man took his staff. [10] And the Lord said to Moses, "Put back the staff of Aaron before the testimony, to be kept as a sign for the rebels, that you may make an end of their grumblings against me, lest they die." [11] Thus did Moses; as the Lord commanded him, so he did.

[12] And the people of Israel said to Moses, "Behold, we perish, we are undone, we are all undone. [13] Everyone who comes near, who comes near to the tabernacle of the Lord, shall die. Are we all to perish?"

Duties of Priests and Levites

18 So the Lord said to Aaron, "You and your sons and your father's house with you shall bear iniquity connected with the sanctuary, and you and your sons with you shall bear iniquity connected with your priesthood. [2] And with you bring your brothers also, the tribe of Levi, the tribe of your father, that they may join you and minister to you while you and your sons with you are before the tent of the testimony. [3] They shall keep guard over you and over the whole tent, but shall not come near to the vessels of the sanctuary or to the altar lest they, and you, die. [4] They shall join you and keep guard over the tent of meeting for all the service of the tent, and no outsider shall come near you. [5] And you shall keep guard over the sanctuary and over the altar, that there may never again be wrath on the people of Israel. [6] And behold, I have taken your brothers the Levites from among the people of Israel. They are a gift to you, given to the Lord, to do the service of the tent of meeting. [7] And you and your sons with you shall guard your priesthood for all that concerns the altar and that is within the veil; and you shall serve. I give your priesthood as a gift,[2] and any outsider who comes near shall be put to death."

[8] Then the Lord spoke to Aaron, "Behold, I have given you charge of the contributions made to me, all the consecrated things of the people of Israel. I have given them to you as a portion and to your sons as a perpetual due. [9] This shall be yours of the most holy things, reserved from the fire: every offering of theirs, every grain offering of theirs and every sin offering of theirs and every guilt offering of theirs, which they render to me, shall be most holy to you and to your sons. [10] In a most holy place shall you eat it. Every male may eat it; it is holy to you. [11] This also is yours: the contribution of their gift, all the wave offerings of the people of Israel. I have given them to you, and to your sons and daughters with you, as a perpetual due. Everyone who is clean in your house may eat it. [12] All the best of the oil and all the best of the wine and of the grain, the firstfruits of what they give to the Lord, I give to you. [13] The first ripe fruits of all that is in their land, which they bring to the Lord, shall be yours. Everyone who is clean in your house may eat it. [14] Every devoted thing in Israel shall be yours. [15] Everything that opens the womb of all flesh, whether man or beast, which they offer to the Lord, shall be yours. Nevertheless, the firstborn of man you shall redeem, and the firstborn of unclean animals you shall redeem.

[1] Ch 17:16 in Hebrew [2] Hebrew *service of gift*

¹⁶ And their redemption price (at a month old you shall redeem them) you shall fix at five shekels¹ in silver, according to the shekel of the sanctuary, which is twenty gerahs. ¹⁷ But the firstborn of a cow, or the firstborn of a sheep, or the firstborn of a goat, you shall not redeem; they are holy. You shall sprinkle their blood on the altar and shall burn their fat as a food offering, with a pleasing aroma to the LORD. ¹⁸ But their flesh shall be yours, as the breast that is waved and as the right thigh are yours. ¹⁹ All the holy contributions that the people of Israel present to the LORD I give to you, and to your sons and daughters with you, as a perpetual due. It is a covenant of salt forever before the LORD for you and for your offspring with you." ²⁰ And the LORD said to Aaron, "You shall have no inheritance in their land, neither shall you have any portion among them. I am your portion and your inheritance among the people of Israel.

²¹ "To the Levites I have given every tithe in Israel for an inheritance, in return for their service that they do, their service in the tent of meeting, ²² so that the people of Israel do not come near the tent of meeting, lest they bear sin and die. ²³ But the Levites shall do the service of the tent of meeting, and they shall bear their iniquity. It shall be a perpetual statute throughout your generations, and among the people of Israel they shall have no inheritance. ²⁴ For the tithe of the people of Israel, which they present as a contribution to the LORD, I have given to the Levites for an inheritance. Therefore I have said of them that they shall have no inheritance among the people of Israel."

²⁵ And the LORD spoke to Moses, saying, ²⁶ "Moreover, you shall speak and say to the Levites, 'When you take from the people of Israel the tithe that I have given you from them for your inheritance, then you shall present a contribution from it to the LORD, a tithe of the tithe. ²⁷ And your contribution shall be counted to you as though it were the grain of the threshing floor, and as the fullness of the winepress. ²⁸ So you shall also present a contribution to the LORD from all your tithes, which you receive from the people of Israel. And from it you shall give the LORD's contribution to Aaron the priest. ²⁹ Out of all the gifts to you, you shall present every contribution due to the LORD; from each its best part is to be dedicated.' ³⁰ Therefore you shall say to them,

'When you have offered from it the best of it, then the rest shall be counted to the Levites as produce of the threshing floor, and as produce of the winepress. ³¹ And you may eat it in any place, you and your households, for it is your reward in return for your service in the tent of meeting. ³² And you shall bear no sin by reason of it, when you have contributed the best of it. But you shall not profane the holy things of the people of Israel, lest you die.'"

Laws for Purification

19 Now the LORD spoke to Moses and to Aaron, saying, ² "This is the statute of the law that the LORD has commanded: Tell the people of Israel to bring you a red heifer without defect, in which there is no blemish, and on which a yoke has never come. ³ And you shall give it to Eleazar the priest, and it shall be taken outside the camp and slaughtered before him. ⁴ And Eleazar the priest shall take some of its blood with his finger, and sprinkle some of its blood toward the front of the tent of meeting seven times. ⁵ And the heifer shall be burned in his sight. Its skin, its flesh, and its blood, with its dung, shall be burned. ⁶ And the priest shall take cedarwood and hyssop and scarlet yarn, and throw them into the fire burning the heifer. ⁷ Then the priest shall wash his clothes and bathe his body in water, and afterward he may come into the camp. But the priest shall be unclean until evening. ⁸ The one who burns the heifer shall wash his clothes in water and bathe his body in water and shall be unclean until evening. ⁹ And a man who is clean shall gather up the ashes of the heifer and deposit them outside the camp in a clean place. And they shall be kept for the water for impurity for the congregation of the people of Israel; it is a sin offering. ¹⁰ And the one who gathers the ashes of the heifer shall wash his clothes and be unclean until evening. And this shall be a perpetual statute for the people of Israel, and for the stranger who sojourns among them.

¹¹ "Whoever touches the dead body of any person shall be unclean seven days. ¹² He shall cleanse himself with the water on the third day and on the seventh day, and so be clean. But if he does not cleanse himself on the third day and on the seventh day, he will not become clean. ¹³ Whoever touches a dead person, the body of anyone who has died, and does not cleanse himself, defiles the tabernacle of the LORD, and that

---

¹ A *shekel* was about 2/5 ounce or 11 grams

person shall be cut off from Israel; because the water for impurity was not thrown on him, he shall be unclean. His uncleanness is still on him.

[14] "This is the law when someone dies in a tent: everyone who comes into the tent and everyone who is in the tent shall be unclean seven days. [15] And every open vessel that has no cover fastened on it is unclean. [16] Whoever in the open field touches someone who was killed with a sword or who died naturally, or touches a human bone or a grave, shall be unclean seven days. [17] For the unclean they shall take some ashes of the burnt sin offering, and fresh[1] water shall be added in a vessel. [18] Then a clean person shall take hyssop and dip it in the water and sprinkle it on the tent and on all the furnishings and on the persons who were there and on whoever touched the bone, or the slain or the dead or the grave. [19] And the clean person shall sprinkle it on the unclean on the third day and on the seventh day. Thus on the seventh day he shall cleanse him, and he shall wash his clothes and bathe himself in water, and at evening he shall be clean.

[20] "If the man who is unclean does not cleanse himself, that person shall be cut off from the midst of the assembly, since he has defiled the sanctuary of the LORD. Because the water for impurity has not been thrown on him, he is unclean. [21] And it shall be a statute forever for them. The one who sprinkles the water for impurity shall wash his clothes, and the one who touches the water for impurity shall be unclean until evening. [22] And whatever the unclean person touches shall be unclean, and anyone who touches it shall be unclean until evening."

The Death of Miriam

20 And the people of Israel, the whole congregation, came into the wilderness of Zin in the first month, and the people stayed in Kadesh. And Miriam died there and was buried there.

The Waters of Meribah

[2] Now there was no water for the congregation. And they assembled themselves together against Moses and against Aaron. [3] And the people quarreled with Moses and said, "Would that we had perished when our brothers perished before the LORD! [4] Why have you brought the assembly of the LORD into this wilderness, that we should die here, both we and our cattle?

[5] And why have you made us come up out of Egypt to bring us to this evil place? It is no place for grain or figs or vines or pomegranates, and there is no water to drink." [6] Then Moses and Aaron went from the presence of the assembly to the entrance of the tent of meeting and fell on their faces. And the glory of the LORD appeared to them, [7] and the LORD spoke to Moses, saying, [8] "Take the staff, and assemble the congregation, you and Aaron your brother, and tell the rock before their eyes to yield its water. So you shall bring water out of the rock for them and give drink to the congregation and their cattle." [9] And Moses took the staff from before the LORD, as he commanded him.

Moses Strikes the Rock

[10] Then Moses and Aaron gathered the assembly together before the rock, and he said to them, "Hear now, you rebels: shall we bring water for you out of this rock?" [11] And Moses lifted up his hand and struck the rock with his staff twice, and water came out abundantly, and the congregation drank, and their livestock. [12] And the LORD said to Moses and Aaron, "Because you did not believe in me, to uphold me as holy in the eyes of the people of Israel, therefore you shall not bring this assembly into the land that I have given them." [13] These are the waters of Meribah,[2] where the people of Israel quarreled with the LORD, and through them he showed himself holy.

Edom Refuses Passage

[14] Moses sent messengers from Kadesh to the king of Edom: "Thus says your brother Israel: You know all the hardship that we have met: [15] how our fathers went down to Egypt, and we lived in Egypt a long time. And the Egyptians dealt harshly with us and our fathers. [16] And when we cried to the LORD, he heard our voice and sent an angel and brought us out of Egypt. And here we are in Kadesh, a city on the edge of your territory. [17] Please let us pass through your land. We will not pass through field or vineyard, or drink water from a well. We will go along the King's Highway. We will not turn aside to the right hand or to the left until we have passed through your territory." [18] But Edom said to him, "You shall not pass through, lest I come out with the sword against you." [19] And the people of Israel said to him, "We will go up by the highway, and if we drink of your water, I and my livestock, then I will pay for it. Let

---

[1] Hebrew *living* [2] *Meribah* means *quarreling*

me only pass through on foot, nothing more." [20]But he said, "You shall not pass through." And Edom came out against them with a large army and with a strong force. [21]Thus Edom refused to give Israel passage through his territory, so Israel turned away from him.

The Death of Aaron

[22]And they journeyed from Kadesh, and the people of Israel, the whole congregation, came to Mount Hor. [23]And the LORD said to Moses and Aaron at Mount Hor, on the border of the land of Edom, [24]"Let Aaron be gathered to his people, for he shall not enter the land that I have given to the people of Israel, because you rebelled against my command at the waters of Meribah. [25]Take Aaron and Eleazar his son and bring them up to Mount Hor. [26]And strip Aaron of his garments and put them on Eleazar his son. And Aaron shall be gathered to his people and shall die there." [27]Moses did as the LORD commanded. And they went up Mount Hor in the sight of all the congregation. [28]And Moses stripped Aaron of his garments and put them on Eleazar his son. And Aaron died there on the top of the mountain. Then Moses and Eleazar came down from the mountain. [29]And when all the congregation saw that Aaron had perished, all the house of Israel wept for Aaron thirty days.

Arad Destroyed

21 When the Canaanite, the king of Arad, who lived in the Negeb, heard that Israel was coming by the way of Atharim, he fought against Israel, and took some of them captive. [2]And Israel vowed a vow to the LORD and said, "If you will indeed give this people into my hand, then I will devote their cities to destruction."[1] [3]And the LORD heeded the voice of Israel and gave over the Canaanites, and they devoted them and their cities to destruction. So the name of the place was called Hormah.[2]

The Bronze Serpent

[4]From Mount Hor they set out by the way to the Red Sea, to go around the land of Edom. And the people became impatient on the way. [5]And the people spoke against God and against Moses, "Why have you brought us up out of Egypt to die in the wilderness? For there is no food and no water, and we loathe this worthless food." [6]Then the LORD sent fiery serpents among the people, and they bit the people, so that many people of Israel died. [7]And the people came to Moses and said, "We have sinned, for we have spoken against the LORD and against you. Pray to the LORD, that he take away the serpents from us." So Moses prayed for the people. [8]And the LORD said to Moses, "Make a fiery serpent and set it on a pole, and everyone who is bitten, when he sees it, shall live." [9]So Moses made a bronze[3] serpent and set it on a pole. And if a serpent bit anyone, he would look at the bronze serpent and live.

The Song of the Well

[10]And the people of Israel set out and camped in Oboth. [11]And they set out from Oboth and camped at Iye-abarim, in the wilderness that is opposite Moab, toward the sunrise. [12]From there they set out and camped in the Valley of Zered. [13]From there they set out and camped on the other side of the Arnon, which is in the wilderness that extends from the border of the Amorites, for the Arnon is the border of Moab, between Moab and the Amorites. [14]Therefore it is said in the Book of the Wars of the LORD,

> "Waheb in Suphah, and the valleys of the
> Arnon,
> [15] and the slope of the valleys
> that extends to the seat of Ar,
> and leans to the border of Moab."

[16]And from there they continued to Beer;[4] that is the well of which the LORD said to Moses, "Gather the people together, so that I may give them water." [17]Then Israel sang this song:

> "Spring up, O well!—Sing to it!—
> [18] the well that the princes made,
> that the nobles of the people dug,
> with the scepter and with their staffs."

And from the wilderness they went on to Mattanah, [19]and from Mattanah to Nahaliel, and from Nahaliel to Bamoth, [20]and from Bamoth to the valley lying in the region of Moab by the top of Pisgah that looks down on the desert.[5]

King Sihon Defeated

[21]Then Israel sent messengers to Sihon king of the Amorites, saying, [22]"Let me pass through your land. We will not turn aside into field or

---

[1] That is, set apart (devote) as an offering to the Lord (for destruction); also verse 3 [2] *Hormah* means *destruction* [3] Or *copper* [4] *Beer* means *well* [5] Or *Jeshimon*

vineyard. We will not drink the water of a well. We will go by the King's Highway until we have passed through your territory." ²³ But Sihon would not allow Israel to pass through his territory. He gathered all his people together and went out against Israel to the wilderness and came to Jahaz and fought against Israel. ²⁴ And Israel defeated him with the edge of the sword and took possession of his land from the Arnon to the Jabbok, as far as to the Ammonites, for the border of the Ammonites was strong. ²⁵ And Israel took all these cities, and Israel settled in all the cities of the Amorites, in Heshbon, and in all its villages. ²⁶ For Heshbon was the city of Sihon the king of the Amorites, who had fought against the former king of Moab and taken all his land out of his hand, as far as the Arnon. ²⁷ Therefore the ballad singers say,

> "Come to Heshbon, let it be built;
>   let the city of Sihon be established.
> ²⁸ For fire came out from Heshbon,
>   flame from the city of Sihon.
> It devoured Ar of Moab,
>   and swallowed¹ the heights of the
>   Arnon.
> ²⁹ Woe to you, O Moab!
>   You are undone, O people of
>   Chemosh!
> He has made his sons fugitives,
>   and his daughters captives,
>   to an Amorite king, Sihon.
> ³⁰ So we overthrew them;
>   Heshbon, as far as Dibon, perished;
>   and we laid waste as far as Nophah;
>   fire spread as far as Medeba."²

King Og Defeated

³¹ Thus Israel lived in the land of the Amorites. ³² And Moses sent to spy out Jazer, and they captured its villages and dispossessed the Amorites who were there. ³³ Then they turned and went up by the way to Bashan. And Og the king of Bashan came out against them, he and all his people, to battle at Edrei. ³⁴ But the LORD said to Moses, "Do not fear him, for I have given him into your hand, and all his people, and his land. And you shall do to him as you did to Sihon king of the Amorites, who lived at Heshbon." ³⁵ So they defeated him and his sons and all his people, until he had no survivor left. And they possessed his land.

Balak Summons Balaam

22 Then the people of Israel set out and camped in the plains of Moab beyond the Jordan at Jericho. ² And Balak the son of Zippor saw all that Israel had done to the Amorites. ³ And Moab was in great dread of the people, because they were many. Moab was overcome with fear of the people of Israel. ⁴ And Moab said to the elders of Midian, "This horde will now lick up all that is around us, as the ox licks up the grass of the field." So Balak the son of Zippor, who was king of Moab at that time, ⁵ sent messengers to Balaam the son of Beor at Pethor, which is near the River³ in the land of the people of Amaw,⁴ to call him, saying, "Behold, a people has come out of Egypt. They cover the face of the earth, and they are dwelling opposite me. ⁶ Come now, curse this people for me, since they are too mighty for me. Perhaps I shall be able to defeat them and drive them from the land, for I know that he whom you bless is blessed, and he whom you curse is cursed."

⁷ So the elders of Moab and the elders of Midian departed with the fees for divination in their hand. And they came to Balaam and gave him Balak's message. ⁸ And he said to them, "Lodge here tonight, and I will bring back word to you, as the LORD speaks to me." So the princes of Moab stayed with Balaam. ⁹ And God came to Balaam and said, "Who are these men with you?" ¹⁰ And Balaam said to God, "Balak the son of Zippor, king of Moab, has sent to me, saying, ¹¹ 'Behold, a people has come out of Egypt, and it covers the face of the earth. Now come, curse them for me. Perhaps I shall be able to fight against them and drive them out.'" ¹² God said to Balaam, "You shall not go with them. You shall not curse the people, for they are blessed." ¹³ So Balaam rose in the morning and said to the princes of Balak, "Go to your own land, for the LORD has refused to let me go with you." ¹⁴ So the princes of Moab rose and went to Balak and said, "Balaam refuses to come with us."

¹⁵ Once again Balak sent princes, more in number and more honorable than these. ¹⁶ And they came to Balaam and said to him, "Thus says Balak the son of Zippor: 'Let nothing hinder you from coming to me, ¹⁷ for I will surely do you great honor, and whatever you say to me I will do. Come, curse this people for me.'" ¹⁸ But Balaam answered and said to the servants of Balak, "Though Balak were to give me his

¹ Septuagint; Hebrew *the lords of* ² Compare Samaritan and Septuagint; Hebrew *and we laid waste as far as Nophah, which is as far as Medeba* ³ That is, the Euphrates ⁴ Or *the people of his kindred*

house full of silver and gold, I could not go beyond the command of the LORD my God to do less or more. [19] So you, too, please stay here tonight, that I may know what more the LORD will say to me." [20] And God came to Balaam at night and said to him, "If the men have come to call you, rise, go with them; but only do what I tell you." [21] So Balaam rose in the morning and saddled his donkey and went with the princes of Moab.

Balaam's Donkey and the Angel

[22] But God's anger was kindled because he went, and the angel of the LORD took his stand in the way as his adversary. Now he was riding on the donkey, and his two servants were with him. [23] And the donkey saw the angel of the LORD standing in the road, with a drawn sword in his hand. And the donkey turned aside out of the road and went into the field. And Balaam struck the donkey, to turn her into the road. [24] Then the angel of the LORD stood in a narrow path between the vineyards, with a wall on either side. [25] And when the donkey saw the angel of the LORD, she pushed against the wall and pressed Balaam's foot against the wall. So he struck her again. [26] Then the angel of the LORD went ahead and stood in a narrow place, where there was no way to turn either to the right or to the left. [27] When the donkey saw the angel of the LORD, she lay down under Balaam. And Balaam's anger was kindled, and he struck the donkey with his staff. [28] Then the LORD opened the mouth of the donkey, and she said to Balaam, "What have I done to you, that you have struck me these three times?" [29] And Balaam said to the donkey, "Because you have made a fool of me. I wish I had a sword in my hand, for then I would kill you." [30] And the donkey said to Balaam, "Am I not your donkey, on which you have ridden all your life long to this day? Is it my habit to treat you this way?" And he said, "No."

[31] Then the LORD opened the eyes of Balaam, and he saw the angel of the LORD standing in the way, with his drawn sword in his hand. And he bowed down and fell on his face. [32] And the angel of the LORD said to him, "Why have you struck your donkey these three times? Behold, I have come out to oppose you because your way is perverse[1] before me. [33] The donkey saw me and turned aside before me these three times. If she had not turned aside from me, surely just now I would have killed you and let her live."

[34] Then Balaam said to the angel of the LORD, "I have sinned, for I did not know that you stood in the road against me. Now therefore, if it is evil in your sight, I will turn back." [35] And the angel of the LORD said to Balaam, "Go with the men, but speak only the word that I tell you." So Balaam went on with the princes of Balak.

[36] When Balak heard that Balaam had come, he went out to meet him at the city of Moab, on the border formed by the Arnon, at the extremity of the border. [37] And Balak said to Balaam, "Did I not send to you to call you? Why did you not come to me? Am I not able to honor you?" [38] Balaam said to Balak, "Behold, I have come to you! Have I now any power of my own to speak anything? The word that God puts in my mouth, that must I speak." [39] Then Balaam went with Balak, and they came to Kiriath-huzoth. [40] And Balak sacrificed oxen and sheep, and sent for Balaam and for the princes who were with him.

[41] And in the morning Balak took Balaam and brought him up to Bamoth-baal, and from there he saw a fraction of the people.

Balaam's First Oracle

23 And Balaam said to Balak, "Build for me here seven altars, and prepare for me here seven bulls and seven rams." [2] Balak did as Balaam had said. And Balak and Balaam offered on each altar a bull and a ram. [3] And Balaam said to Balak, "Stand beside your burnt offering, and I will go. Perhaps the LORD will come to meet me, and whatever he shows me I will tell you." And he went to a bare height, [4] and God met Balaam. And Balaam said to him, "I have arranged the seven altars and I have offered on each altar a bull and a ram." [5] And the LORD put a word in Balaam's mouth and said, "Return to Balak, and thus you shall speak." [6] And he returned to him, and behold, he and all the princes of Moab were standing beside his burnt offering. [7] And Balaam took up his discourse and said,

> "From Aram Balak has brought me,
>   the king of Moab from the eastern
>   mountains:
> 'Come, curse Jacob for me,
>   and come, denounce Israel!'
> [8] How can I curse whom God has not
>   cursed?
>   How can I denounce whom the LORD
>   has not denounced?

---

[1] Or reckless

⁹ For from the top of the crags I see him,
    from the hills I behold him;
behold, a people dwelling alone,
    and not counting itself among the
        nations!
¹⁰ Who can count the dust of Jacob
    or number the fourth part[1] of Israel?
Let me die the death of the upright,
    and let my end be like his!"

¹¹ And Balak said to Balaam, "What have you done to me? I took you to curse my enemies, and behold, you have done nothing but bless them." ¹² And he answered and said, "Must I not take care to speak what the LORD puts in my mouth?"

Balaam's Second Oracle

¹³ And Balak said to him, "Please come with me to another place, from which you may see them. You shall see only a fraction of them and shall not see them all. Then curse them for me from there." ¹⁴ And he took him to the field of Zophim, to the top of Pisgah, and built seven altars and offered a bull and a ram on each altar. ¹⁵ Balaam said to Balak, "Stand here beside your burnt offering, while I meet the LORD over there." ¹⁶ And the LORD met Balaam and put a word in his mouth and said, "Return to Balak, and thus shall you speak." ¹⁷ And he came to him, and behold, he was standing beside his burnt offering, and the princes of Moab with him. And Balak said to him, "What has the LORD spoken?" ¹⁸ And Balaam took up his discourse and said,

"Rise, Balak, and hear;
    give ear to me, O son of Zippor:
¹⁹ God is not man, that he should lie,
    or a son of man, that he should change
        his mind.
Has he said, and will he not do it?
    Or has he spoken, and will he not fulfill
        it?
²⁰ Behold, I received a command to bless:
    he has blessed, and I cannot revoke it.
²¹ He has not beheld misfortune in Jacob,
    nor has he seen trouble in Israel.
The LORD their God is with them,
    and the shout of a king is among them.
²² God brings them out of Egypt
    and is for them like the horns of the
        wild ox.

²³ For there is no enchantment against Jacob,
    no divination against Israel;
now it shall be said of Jacob and Israel,
    'What has God wrought!'
²⁴ Behold, a people! As a lioness it rises up
    and as a lion it lifts itself;
it does not lie down until it has devoured
        the prey
    and drunk the blood of the slain."

²⁵ And Balak said to Balaam, "Do not curse them at all, and do not bless them at all." ²⁶ But Balaam answered Balak, "Did I not tell you, 'All that the LORD says, that I must do'?" ²⁷ And Balak said to Balaam, "Come now, I will take you to another place. Perhaps it will please God that you may curse them for me from there." ²⁸ So Balak took Balaam to the top of Peor, which overlooks the desert.[2] ²⁹ And Balaam said to Balak, "Build for me here seven altars and prepare for me here seven bulls and seven rams." ³⁰ And Balak did as Balaam had said, and offered a bull and a ram on each altar.

Balaam's Third Oracle

24 When Balaam saw that it pleased the LORD to bless Israel, he did not go, as at other times, to look for omens, but set his face toward the wilderness. ² And Balaam lifted up his eyes and saw Israel camping tribe by tribe. And the Spirit of God came upon him, ³ and he took up his discourse and said,

"The oracle of Balaam the son of Beor,
    the oracle of the man whose eye is
        opened,[3]
⁴ the oracle of him who hears the words of
        God,
who sees the vision of the Almighty,
    falling down with his eyes uncovered:
⁵ How lovely are your tents, O Jacob,
    your encampments, O Israel!
⁶ Like palm groves[4] that stretch afar,
    like gardens beside a river,
like aloes that the LORD has planted,
    like cedar trees beside the waters.
⁷ Water shall flow from his buckets,
    and his seed shall be in many waters;
his king shall be higher than Agag,
    and his kingdom shall be exalted.
⁸ God brings him out of Egypt
    and is for him like the horns of the wild
        ox;

---

[1] Or dust clouds [2] Or Jeshimon [3] Or closed, or perfect; also verse 15 [4] Or valleys

he shall eat up the nations, his adversaries,
and shall break their bones in pieces
and pierce them through with his
arrows.

9 He crouched, he lay down like a lion
and like a lioness; who will rouse him
up?

Blessed are those who bless you,
and cursed are those who curse you."

10 And Balak's anger was kindled against Balaam, and he struck his hands together. And Balak said to Balaam, "I called you to curse my enemies, and behold, you have blessed them these three times. 11 Therefore now flee to your own place. I said, 'I will certainly honor you,' but the Lord has held you back from honor." 12 And Balaam said to Balak, "Did I not tell your messengers whom you sent to me, 13 'If Balak should give me his house full of silver and gold, I would not be able to go beyond the word of the Lord, to do either good or bad of my own will. What the Lord speaks, that will I speak'? 14 And now, behold, I am going to my people. Come, I will let you know what this people will do to your people in the latter days."

Balaam's Final Oracle

15 And he took up his discourse and said,

"The oracle of Balaam the son of Beor,
the oracle of the man whose eye is
opened,

16 the oracle of him who hears the words of
God,
and knows the knowledge of the Most
High,

who sees the vision of the Almighty,
falling down with his eyes uncovered:

17 I see him, but not now;
I behold him, but not near:
a star shall come out of Jacob,
and a scepter shall rise out of Israel;
it shall crush the forehead[1] of Moab
and break down all the sons of Sheth.

18 Edom shall be dispossessed;
Seir also, his enemies, shall be dispossessed.

Israel is doing valiantly.

19 And one from Jacob shall exercise dominion
and destroy the survivors of cities!"

20 Then he looked on Amalek and took up his discourse and said,

"Amalek was the first among the nations,
but its end is utter destruction."

21 And he looked on the Kenite, and took up his discourse and said,

"Enduring is your dwelling place,
and your nest is set in the rock.

22 Nevertheless, Kain shall be burned
when Asshur takes you away captive."

23 And he took up his discourse and said,

"Alas, who shall live when God does this?

24 But ships shall come from Kittim
and shall afflict Asshur and Eber;
and he too shall come to utter destruction."

25 Then Balaam rose and went back to his place. And Balak also went his way.

Baal Worship at Peor

25 While Israel lived in Shittim, the people began to whore with the daughters of Moab. 2 These invited the people to the sacrifices of their gods, and the people ate and bowed down to their gods. 3 So Israel yoked himself to Baal of Peor. And the anger of the Lord was kindled against Israel. 4 And the Lord said to Moses, "Take all the chiefs of the people and hang[2] them in the sun before the Lord, that the fierce anger of the Lord may turn away from Israel." 5 And Moses said to the judges of Israel, "Each of you kill those of his men who have yoked themselves to Baal of Peor."

6 And behold, one of the people of Israel came and brought a Midianite woman to his family, in the sight of Moses and in the sight of the whole congregation of the people of Israel, while they were weeping in the entrance of the tent of meeting. 7 When Phinehas the son of Eleazar, son of Aaron the priest, saw it, he rose and left the congregation and took a spear in his hand 8 and went after the man of Israel into the chamber and pierced both of them, the man of Israel and the woman through her belly. Thus the plague on the people of Israel was stopped. 9 Nevertheless, those who died by the plague were twenty-four thousand.

The Zeal of Phinehas

10 And the Lord said to Moses, 11 "Phinehas the son of Eleazar, son of Aaron the priest, has turned back my wrath from the people of Israel, in that he was jealous with my jealousy among

---

[1] Hebrew corners [of the head] [2] Or impale

them, so that I did not consume the people of Israel in my jealousy. ¹²Therefore say, 'Behold, I give to him my covenant of peace, ¹³and it shall be to him and to his descendants after him the covenant of a perpetual priesthood, because he was jealous for his God and made atonement for the people of Israel.'"

¹⁴The name of the slain man of Israel, who was killed with the Midianite woman, was Zimri the son of Salu, chief of a father's house belonging to the Simeonites. ¹⁵And the name of the Midianite woman who was killed was Cozbi the daughter of Zur, who was the tribal head of a father's house in Midian.

¹⁶And the LORD spoke to Moses, saying, ¹⁷"Harass the Midianites and strike them down, ¹⁸for they have harassed you with their wiles, with which they beguiled you in the matter of Peor, and in the matter of Cozbi, the daughter of the chief of Midian, their sister, who was killed on the day of the plague on account of Peor."

Census of the New Generation

26 After the plague, the LORD said to Moses and to Eleazar the son of Aaron, the priest, ²"Take a census of all the congregation of the people of Israel, from twenty years old and upward, by their fathers' houses, all in Israel who are able to go to war." ³And Moses and Eleazar the priest spoke with them in the plains of Moab by the Jordan at Jericho, saying, ⁴"Take a census of the people,¹ from twenty years old and upward," as the LORD commanded Moses. The people of Israel who came out of the land of Egypt were:

⁵Reuben, the firstborn of Israel; the sons of Reuben: of Hanoch, the clan of the Hanochites; of Pallu, the clan of the Palluites; ⁶of Hezron, the clan of the Hezronites; of Carmi, the clan of the Carmites. ⁷These are the clans of the Reubenites, and those listed were 43,730. ⁸And the sons of Pallu: Eliab. ⁹The sons of Eliab: Nemuel, Dathan, and Abiram. These are the Dathan and Abiram, chosen from the congregation, who contended against Moses and Aaron in the company of Korah, when they contended against the LORD ¹⁰and the earth opened its mouth and swallowed them up together with Korah, when that company died, when the fire devoured 250 men, and they became a warning. ¹¹But the sons of Korah did not die.

¹²The sons of Simeon according to their clans: of Nemuel, the clan of the Nemuelites; of Jamin, the clan of the Jaminites; of Jachin, the clan of the Jachinites; ¹³of Zerah, the clan of the Zerahites; of Shaul, the clan of the Shaulites. ¹⁴These are the clans of the Simeonites, 22,200.

¹⁵The sons of Gad according to their clans: of Zephon, the clan of the Zephonites; of Haggi, the clan of the Haggites; of Shuni, the clan of the Shunites; ¹⁶of Ozni, the clan of the Oznites; of Eri, the clan of the Erites; ¹⁷of Arod, the clan of the Arodites; of Areli, the clan of the Arelites. ¹⁸These are the clans of the sons of Gad as they were listed, 40,500.

¹⁹The sons of Judah were Er and Onan; and Er and Onan died in the land of Canaan. ²⁰And the sons of Judah according to their clans were: of Shelah, the clan of the Shelanites; of Perez, the clan of the Perezites; of Zerah, the clan of the Zerahites. ²¹And the sons of Perez were: of Hezron, the clan of the Hezronites; of Hamul, the clan of the Hamulites. ²²These are the clans of Judah as they were listed, 76,500.

²³The sons of Issachar according to their clans: of Tola, the clan of the Tolaites; of Puvah, the clan of the Punites; ²⁴of Jashub, the clan of the Jashubites; of Shimron, the clan of the Shimronites. ²⁵These are the clans of Issachar as they were listed, 64,300.

²⁶The sons of Zebulun, according to their clans: of Sered, the clan of the Seredites; of Elon, the clan of the Elonites; of Jahleel, the clan of the Jahleelites. ²⁷These are the clans of the Zebulunites as they were listed, 60,500.

²⁸The sons of Joseph according to their clans: Manasseh and Ephraim. ²⁹The sons of Manasseh: of Machir, the clan of the Machirites; and Machir was the father of Gilead; of Gilead, the clan of the Gileadites. ³⁰These are the sons of Gilead: of Iezer, the clan of the Iezerites; of Helek, the clan of the Helekites; ³¹and of Asriel, the clan of the Asrielites; and of Shechem, the clan of the Shechemites; ³²and of Shemida, the clan of the Shemidaites; and of Hepher, the clan of the Hepherites. ³³Now Zelophehad the son of Hepher had no sons, but daughters. And the names of the daughters of Zelophehad were Mahlah, Noah, Hoglah, Milcah, and Tirzah. ³⁴These are the clans of Manasseh, and those listed were 52,700.

³⁵These are the sons of Ephraim according to their clans: of Shuthelah, the clan of the Shuthelahites; of Becher, the clan of the Becherites; of Tahan, the clan of the Tahanites.

---

¹ *Take a census of the people* is implied (compare verse 2)

[36] And these are the sons of Shuthelah: of Eran, the clan of the Eranites. [37] These are the clans of the sons of Ephraim as they were listed, 32,500. These are the sons of Joseph according to their clans.

[38] The sons of Benjamin according to their clans: of Bela, the clan of the Belaites; of Ashbel, the clan of the Ashbelites; of Ahiram, the clan of the Ahiramites; [39] of Shephupham, the clan of the Shuphamites; of Hupham, the clan of the Huphamites. [40] And the sons of Bela were Ard and Naaman: of Ard, the clan of the Ardites; of Naaman, the clan of the Naamites. [41] These are the sons of Benjamin according to their clans, and those listed were 45,600.

[42] These are the sons of Dan according to their clans: of Shuham, the clan of the Shuhamites. These are the clans of Dan according to their clans. [43] All the clans of the Shuhamites, as they were listed, were 64,400.

[44] The sons of Asher according to their clans: of Imnah, the clan of the Imnites; of Ishvi, the clan of the Ishvites; of Beriah, the clan of the Beriites. [45] Of the sons of Beriah: of Heber, the clan of the Heberites; of Malchiel, the clan of the Malchielites. [46] And the name of the daughter of Asher was Serah. [47] These are the clans of the sons of Asher as they were listed, 53,400.

[48] The sons of Naphtali according to their clans: of Jahzeel, the clan of the Jahzeelites; of Guni, the clan of the Gunites; [49] of Jezer, the clan of the Jezerites; of Shillem, the clan of the Shillemites. [50] These are the clans of Naphtali according to their clans, and those listed were 45,400.

[51] This was the list of the people of Israel, 601,730.

[52] The LORD spoke to Moses, saying, [53] "Among these the land shall be divided for inheritance according to the number of names. [54] To a large tribe you shall give a large inheritance, and to a small tribe you shall give a small inheritance; every tribe shall be given its inheritance in proportion to its list. [55] But the land shall be divided by lot. According to the names of the tribes of their fathers they shall inherit. [56] Their inheritance shall be divided according to lot between the larger and the smaller."

[57] This was the list of the Levites according to their clans: of Gershon, the clan of the Gershonites; of Kohath, the clan of the Kohathites; of Merari, the clan of the Merarites.

[58] These are the clans of Levi: the clan of the Libnites, the clan of the Hebronites, the clan of the Mahlites, the clan of the Mushites, the clan of the Korahites. And Kohath was the father of Amram. [59] The name of Amram's wife was Jochebed the daughter of Levi, who was born to Levi in Egypt. And she bore to Amram Aaron and Moses and Miriam their sister. [60] And to Aaron were born Nadab, Abihu, Eleazar, and Ithamar. [61] But Nadab and Abihu died when they offered unauthorized fire before the LORD. [62] And those listed were 23,000, every male from a month old and upward. For they were not listed among the people of Israel, because there was no inheritance given to them among the people of Israel.

[63] These were those listed by Moses and Eleazar the priest, who listed the people of Israel in the plains of Moab by the Jordan at Jericho. [64] But among these there was not one of those listed by Moses and Aaron the priest, who had listed the people of Israel in the wilderness of Sinai. [65] For the LORD had said of them, "They shall die in the wilderness." Not one of them was left, except Caleb the son of Jephunneh and Joshua the son of Nun.

The Daughters of Zelophehad

27 Then drew near the daughters of Zelophehad the son of Hepher, son of Gilead, son of Machir, son of Manasseh, from the clans of Manasseh the son of Joseph. The names of his daughters were: Mahlah, Noah, Hoglah, Milcah, and Tirzah. [2] And they stood before Moses and before Eleazar the priest and before the chiefs and all the congregation, at the entrance of the tent of meeting, saying, [3] "Our father died in the wilderness. He was not among the company of those who gathered themselves together against the LORD in the company of Korah, but died for his own sin. And he had no sons. [4] Why should the name of our father be taken away from his clan because he had no son? Give to us a possession among our father's brothers."

[5] Moses brought their case before the LORD. [6] And the LORD said to Moses, [7] "The daughters of Zelophehad are right. You shall give them possession of an inheritance among their father's brothers and transfer the inheritance of their father to them. [8] And you shall speak to the people of Israel, saying, 'If a man dies and has no son, then you shall transfer his

inheritance to his daughter. [9] And if he has no daughter, then you shall give his inheritance to his brothers. [10] And if he has no brothers, then you shall give his inheritance to his father's brothers. [11] And if his father has no brothers, then you shall give his inheritance to the nearest kinsman of his clan, and he shall possess it. And it shall be for the people of Israel a statute and rule, as the LORD commanded Moses.' "

Joshua to Succeed Moses

[12] The LORD said to Moses, "Go up into this mountain of Abarim and see the land that I have given to the people of Israel. [13] When you have seen it, you also shall be gathered to your people, as your brother Aaron was, [14] because you rebelled against my word in the wilderness of Zin when the congregation quarreled, failing to uphold me as holy at the waters before their eyes." (These are the waters of Meribah of Kadesh in the wilderness of Zin.) [15] Moses spoke to the LORD, saying, [16] "Let the LORD, the God of the spirits of all flesh, appoint a man over the congregation [17] who shall go out before them and come in before them, who shall lead them out and bring them in, that the congregation of the LORD may not be as sheep that have no shepherd." [18] So the LORD said to Moses, "Take Joshua the son of Nun, a man in whom is the Spirit, and lay your hand on him. [19] Make him stand before Eleazar the priest and all the congregation, and you shall commission him in their sight. [20] You shall invest him with some of your authority, that all the congregation of the people of Israel may obey. [21] And he shall stand before Eleazar the priest, who shall inquire for him by the judgment of the Urim before the LORD. At his word they shall go out, and at his word they shall come in, both he and all the people of Israel with him, the whole congregation." [22] And Moses did as the LORD commanded him. He took Joshua and made him stand before Eleazar the priest and the whole congregation, [23] and he laid his hands on him and commissioned him as the LORD directed through Moses.

Daily Offerings

28 The LORD spoke to Moses, saying, [2] "Command the people of Israel and say to them, 'My offering, my food for my food offerings, my pleasing aroma, you shall be careful to offer to me at its appointed time.' [3] And

you shall say to them, This is the food offering that you shall offer to the LORD: two male lambs a year old without blemish, day by day, as a regular offering. [4] The one lamb you shall offer in the morning, and the other lamb you shall offer at twilight; [5] also a tenth of an ephah[1] of fine flour for a grain offering, mixed with a quarter of a hin[2] of beaten oil. [6] It is a regular burnt offering, which was ordained at Mount Sinai for a pleasing aroma, a food offering to the LORD. [7] Its drink offering shall be a quarter of a hin for each lamb. In the Holy Place you shall pour out a drink offering of strong drink to the LORD. [8] The other lamb you shall offer at twilight. Like the grain offering of the morning, and like its drink offering, you shall offer it as a food offering, with a pleasing aroma to the LORD.

Sabbath Offerings

[9] "On the Sabbath day, two male lambs a year old without blemish, and two tenths of an ephah of fine flour for a grain offering, mixed with oil, and its drink offering: [10] this is the burnt offering of every Sabbath, besides the regular burnt offering and its drink offering.

Monthly Offerings

[11] "At the beginnings of your months, you shall offer a burnt offering to the LORD: two bulls from the herd, one ram, seven male lambs a year old without blemish; [12] also three tenths of an ephah of fine flour for a grain offering, mixed with oil, for each bull, and two tenths of fine flour for a grain offering, mixed with oil, for the one ram; [13] and a tenth of fine flour mixed with oil as a grain offering for every lamb; for a burnt offering with a pleasing aroma, a food offering to the LORD. [14] Their drink offerings shall be half a hin of wine for a bull, a third of a hin for a ram, and a quarter of a hin for a lamb. This is the burnt offering of each month throughout the months of the year. [15] Also one male goat for a sin offering to the LORD; it shall be offered besides the regular burnt offering and its drink offering.

Passover Offerings

[16] "On the fourteenth day of the first month is the LORD's Passover, [17] and on the fifteenth day of this month is a feast. Seven days shall unleavened bread be eaten. [18] On the first day there shall be a holy convocation. You shall

[1] An *ephah* was about 3/5 bushel or 22 liters [2] A *hin* was about 4 quarts or 3.5 liters

not do any ordinary work, [19] but offer a food offering, a burnt offering to the LORD: two bulls from the herd, one ram, and seven male lambs a year old; see that they are without blemish; [20] also their grain offering of fine flour mixed with oil; three tenths of an ephah shall you offer for a bull, and two tenths for a ram; [21] a tenth shall you offer for each of the seven lambs; [22] also one male goat for a sin offering, to make atonement for you. [23] You shall offer these besides the burnt offering of the morning, which is for a regular burnt offering. [24] In the same way you shall offer daily, for seven days, the food of a food offering, with a pleasing aroma to the LORD. It shall be offered besides the regular burnt offering and its drink offering. [25] And on the seventh day you shall have a holy convocation. You shall not do any ordinary work.

Offerings for the Feast of Weeks

[26] "On the day of the firstfruits, when you offer a grain offering of new grain to the LORD at your Feast of Weeks, you shall have a holy convocation. You shall not do any ordinary work, [27] but offer a burnt offering, with a pleasing aroma to the LORD: two bulls from the herd, one ram, seven male lambs a year old; [28] also their grain offering of fine flour mixed with oil, three tenths of an ephah for each bull, two tenths for one ram, [29] a tenth for each of the seven lambs; [30] with one male goat, to make atonement for you. [31] Besides the regular burnt offering and its grain offering, you shall offer them and their drink offering. See that they are without blemish.

Offerings for the Feast of Trumpets

29 "On the first day of the seventh month you shall have a holy convocation. You shall not do any ordinary work. It is a day for you to blow the trumpets, [2] and you shall offer a burnt offering, for a pleasing aroma to the LORD: one bull from the herd, one ram, seven male lambs a year old without blemish; [3] also their grain offering of fine flour mixed with oil, three tenths of an ephah[1] for the bull, two tenths for the ram, [4] and one tenth for each of the seven lambs; [5] with one male goat for a sin offering, to make atonement for you; [6] besides the burnt offering of the new moon, and its grain offering, and the regular burnt offering and its grain offering, and their drink offering,

according to the rule for them, for a pleasing aroma, a food offering to the LORD.

Offerings for the Day of Atonement

[7] "On the tenth day of this seventh month you shall have a holy convocation and afflict yourselves.[2] You shall do no work, [8] but you shall offer a burnt offering to the LORD, a pleasing aroma: one bull from the herd, one ram, seven male lambs a year old: see that they are without blemish. [9] And their grain offering shall be of fine flour mixed with oil, three tenths of an ephah for the bull, two tenths for the one ram, [10] a tenth for each of the seven lambs: [11] also one male goat for a sin offering, besides the sin offering of atonement, and the regular burnt offering and its grain offering, and their drink offerings.

Offerings for the Feast of Booths

[12] "On the fifteenth day of the seventh month you shall have a holy convocation. You shall not do any ordinary work, and you shall keep a feast to the LORD seven days. [13] And you shall offer a burnt offering, a food offering, with a pleasing aroma to the LORD, thirteen bulls from the herd, two rams, fourteen male lambs a year old; they shall be without blemish; [14] and their grain offering of fine flour mixed with oil, three tenths of an ephah for each of the thirteen bulls, two tenths for each of the two rams, [15] and a tenth for each of the fourteen lambs; [16] also one male goat for a sin offering, besides the regular burnt offering, its grain offering and its drink offering.

[17] "On the second day twelve bulls from the herd, two rams, fourteen male lambs a year old without blemish, [18] with the grain offering and the drink offerings for the bulls, for the rams, and for the lambs, in the prescribed quantities; [19] also one male goat for a sin offering, besides the regular burnt offering and its grain offering, and their drink offerings.

[20] "On the third day eleven bulls, two rams, fourteen male lambs a year old without blemish, [21] with the grain offering and the drink offerings for the bulls, for the rams, and for the lambs, in the prescribed quantities; [22] also one male goat for a sin offering, besides the regular burnt offering and its grain offering and its drink offering.

[23] "On the fourth day ten bulls, two rams, fourteen male lambs a year old without blemish, [24] with the grain offering and the drink offerings for the bulls, for the rams, and for the lambs, in the prescribed quantities; [25] also one male

[1] An ephah was about 3/5 bushel or 22 liters [2] Or and fast

goat for a sin offering, besides the regular burnt offering, its grain offering and its drink offering.

[26] "On the fifth day nine bulls, two rams, fourteen male lambs a year old without blemish, [27] with the grain offering and the drink offerings for the bulls, for the rams, and for the lambs, in the prescribed quantities; [28] also one male goat for a sin offering; besides the regular burnt offering and its grain offering and its drink offering.

[29] "On the sixth day eight bulls, two rams, fourteen male lambs a year old without blemish, [30] with the grain offering and the drink offerings for the bulls, for the rams, and for the lambs, in the prescribed quantities; [31] also one male goat for a sin offering; besides the regular burnt offering, its grain offering, and its drink offerings.

[32] "On the seventh day seven bulls, two rams, fourteen male lambs a year old without blemish, [33] with the grain offering and the drink offerings for the bulls, for the rams, and for the lambs, in the prescribed quantities; [34] also one male goat for a sin offering; besides the regular burnt offering, its grain offering, and its drink offering.

[35] "On the eighth day you shall have a solemn assembly. You shall not do any ordinary work, [36] but you shall offer a burnt offering, a food offering, with a pleasing aroma to the LORD: one bull, one ram, seven male lambs a year old without blemish, [37] and the grain offering and the drink offerings for the bull, for the ram, and for the lambs, in the prescribed quantities; [38] also one male goat for a sin offering; besides the regular burnt offering and its grain offering and its drink offering.

[39] "These you shall offer to the LORD at your appointed feasts, in addition to your vow offerings and your freewill offerings, for your burnt offerings, and for your grain offerings, and for your drink offerings, and for your peace offerings."

[40] [1] So Moses told the people of Israel everything just as the LORD had commanded Moses.

Men and Vows

30 Moses spoke to the heads of the tribes of the people of Israel, saying, "This is what the LORD has commanded. [2] If a man vows a vow to the LORD, or swears an oath to bind himself by a pledge, he shall not break his word.

He shall do according to all that proceeds out of his mouth.

Women and Vows

[3] "If a woman vows a vow to the LORD and binds herself by a pledge, while within her father's house in her youth, [4] and her father hears of her vow and of her pledge by which she has bound herself and says nothing to her, then all her vows shall stand, and every pledge by which she has bound herself shall stand. [5] But if her father opposes her on the day that he hears of it, no vow of hers, no pledge by which she has bound herself shall stand. And the LORD will forgive her, because her father opposed her.

[6] "If she marries a husband, while under her vows or any thoughtless utterance of her lips by which she has bound herself, [7] and her husband hears of it and says nothing to her on the day that he hears, then her vows shall stand, and her pledges by which she has bound herself shall stand. [8] But if, on the day that her husband comes to hear of it, he opposes her, then he makes void her vow that was on her, and the thoughtless utterance of her lips by which she bound herself. And the LORD will forgive her. [9] (But any vow of a widow or of a divorced woman, anything by which she has bound herself, shall stand against her.) [10] And if she vowed in her husband's house or bound herself by a pledge with an oath, [11] and her husband heard of it and said nothing to her and did not oppose her, then all her vows shall stand, and every pledge by which she bound herself shall stand. [12] But if her husband makes them null and void on the day that he hears them, then whatever proceeds out of her lips concerning her vows or concerning her pledge of herself shall not stand. Her husband has made them void, and the LORD will forgive her. [13] Any vow and any binding oath to afflict herself,[2] her husband may establish,[3] or her husband may make void. [14] But if her husband says nothing to her from day to day, then he establishes all her vows or all her pledges that are upon her. He has established them, because he said nothing to her on the day that he heard of them. [15] But if he makes them null and void after he has heard of them, then he shall bear her iniquity."

[16] These are the statutes that the LORD commanded Moses about a man and his wife and

[1] Ch 30:1 in Hebrew [2] Or to fast [3] Or may allow to stand

about a father and his daughter while she is in her youth within her father's house.

Vengeance on Midian

31 The Lord spoke to Moses, saying, [2] "Avenge the people of Israel on the Midianites. Afterward you shall be gathered to your people." [3] So Moses spoke to the people, saying, "Arm men from among you for the war, that they may go against Midian to execute the Lord's vengeance on Midian. [4] You shall send a thousand from each of the tribes of Israel to the war." [5] So there were provided, out of the thousands of Israel, a thousand from each tribe, twelve thousand armed for war. [6] And Moses sent them to the war, a thousand from each tribe, together with Phinehas the son of Eleazar the priest, with the vessels of the sanctuary and the trumpets for the alarm in his hand. [7] They warred against Midian, as the Lord commanded Moses, and killed every male. [8] They killed the kings of Midian with the rest of their slain, Evi, Rekem, Zur, Hur, and Reba, the five kings of Midian. And they also killed Balaam the son of Beor with the sword. [9] And the people of Israel took captive the women of Midian and their little ones, and they took as plunder all their cattle, their flocks, and all their goods. [10] All their cities in the places where they lived, and all their encampments, they burned with fire, [11] and took all the spoil and all the plunder, both of man and of beast. [12] Then they brought the captives and the plunder and the spoil to Moses, and to Eleazar the priest, and to the congregation of the people of Israel, at the camp on the plains of Moab by the Jordan at Jericho.

[13] Moses and Eleazar the priest and all the chiefs of the congregation went to meet them outside the camp. [14] And Moses was angry with the officers of the army, the commanders of thousands and the commanders of hundreds, who had come from service in the war. [15] Moses said to them, "Have you let all the women live? [16] Behold, these, on Balaam's advice, caused the people of Israel to act treacherously against the Lord in the incident of Peor, and so the plague came among the congregation of the Lord. [17] Now therefore, kill every male among the little ones, and kill every woman who has known man by lying with him. [18] But all the young girls who have not known man by lying with him keep alive for yourselves. [19] Encamp outside the camp seven days. Whoever of you

has killed any person and whoever has touched any slain, purify yourselves and your captives on the third day and on the seventh day. [20] You shall purify every garment, every article of skin, all work of goats' hair, and every article of wood."

[21] Then Eleazar the priest said to the men in the army who had gone to battle: "This is the statute of the law that the Lord has commanded Moses: [22] only the gold, the silver, the bronze, the iron, the tin, and the lead, [23] everything that can stand the fire, you shall pass through the fire, and it shall be clean. Nevertheless, it shall also be purified with the water for impurity. And whatever cannot stand the fire, you shall pass through the water. [24] You must wash your clothes on the seventh day, and you shall be clean. And afterward you may come into the camp."

[25] The Lord said to Moses, [26] "Take the count of the plunder that was taken, both of man and of beast, you and Eleazar the priest and the heads of the fathers' houses of the congregation, [27] and divide the plunder into two parts between the warriors who went out to battle and all the congregation. [28] And levy for the Lord a tribute from the men of war who went out to battle, one out of five hundred, of the people and of the oxen and of the donkeys and of the flocks. [29] Take it from their half and give it to Eleazar the priest as a contribution to the Lord. [30] And from the people of Israel's half you shall take one drawn out of every fifty, of the people, of the oxen, of the donkeys, and of the flocks, of all the cattle, and give them to the Levites who keep guard over the tabernacle of the Lord." [31] And Moses and Eleazar the priest did as the Lord commanded Moses.

[32] Now the plunder remaining of the spoil that the army took was 675,000 sheep, [33] 72,000 cattle, [34] 61,000 donkeys, [35] and 32,000 persons in all, women who had not known man by lying with him. [36] And the half, the portion of those who had gone out in the army, numbered 337,500 sheep, [37] and the Lord's tribute of sheep was 675. [38] The cattle were 36,000, of which the Lord's tribute was 72. [39] The donkeys were 30,500, of which the Lord's tribute was 61. [40] The persons were 16,000, of which the Lord's tribute was 32 persons. [41] And Moses gave the tribute, which was the contribution for the Lord, to Eleazar the priest, as the Lord commanded Moses.

[42] From the people of Israel's half, which

Moses separated from that of the men who had served in the army— [43] now the congregation's half was 337,500 sheep, [44] 36,000 cattle, [45] and 30,500 donkeys, [46] and 16,000 persons— [47] from the people of Israel's half Moses took one of every 50, both of persons and of beasts, and gave them to the Levites who kept guard over the tabernacle of the LORD, as the LORD commanded Moses.

[48] Then the officers who were over the thousands of the army, the commanders of thousands and the commanders of hundreds, came near to Moses [49] and said to Moses, "Your servants have counted the men of war who are under our command, and there is not a man missing from us. [50] And we have brought the LORD's offering, what each man found, articles of gold, armlets and bracelets, signet rings, earrings, and beads, to make atonement for ourselves before the LORD." [51] And Moses and Eleazar the priest received from them the gold, all crafted articles. [52] And all the gold of the contribution that they presented to the LORD, from the commanders of thousands and the commanders of hundreds, was 16,750 shekels.[1] [53] (The men in the army had each taken plunder for himself.) [54] And Moses and Eleazar the priest received the gold from the commanders of thousands and of hundreds, and brought it into the tent of meeting, as a memorial for the people of Israel before the LORD.

Reuben and Gad Settle in Gilead

32 Now the people of Reuben and the people of Gad had a very great number of livestock. And they saw the land of Jazer and the land of Gilead, and behold, the place was a place for livestock. [2] So the people of Gad and the people of Reuben came and said to Moses and to Eleazar the priest and to the chiefs of the congregation, [3] "Ataroth, Dibon, Jazer, Nimrah, Heshbon, Elealeh, Sebam, Nebo, and Beon, [4] the land that the LORD struck down before the congregation of Israel, is a land for livestock, and your servants have livestock." [5] And they said, "If we have found favor in your sight, let this land be given to your servants for a possession. Do not take us across the Jordan."

[6] But Moses said to the people of Gad and to the people of Reuben, "Shall your brothers go to the war while you sit here? [7] Why will you discourage the heart of the people of Israel from going over into the land that the LORD

has given them? [8] Your fathers did this, when I sent them from Kadesh-barnea to see the land. [9] For when they went up to the Valley of Eshcol and saw the land, they discouraged the heart of the people of Israel from going into the land that the LORD had given them. [10] And the LORD's anger was kindled on that day, and he swore, saying, [11] 'Surely none of the men who came up out of Egypt, from twenty years old and upward, shall see the land that I swore to give to Abraham, to Isaac, and to Jacob, because they have not wholly followed me, [12] none except Caleb the son of Jephunneh the Kenizzite and Joshua the son of Nun, for they have wholly followed the LORD.' [13] And the LORD's anger was kindled against Israel, and he made them wander in the wilderness forty years, until all the generation that had done evil in the sight of the LORD was gone. [14] And behold, you have risen in your fathers' place, a brood of sinful men, to increase still more the fierce anger of the LORD against Israel! [15] For if you turn away from following him, he will again abandon them in the wilderness, and you will destroy all this people."

[16] Then they came near to him and said, "We will build sheepfolds here for our livestock, and cities for our little ones, [17] but we will take up arms, ready to go before the people of Israel, until we have brought them to their place. And our little ones shall live in the fortified cities because of the inhabitants of the land. [18] We will not return to our homes until each of the people of Israel has gained his inheritance. [19] For we will not inherit with them on the other side of the Jordan and beyond, because our inheritance has come to us on this side of the Jordan to the east." [20] So Moses said to them, "If you will do this, if you will take up arms to go before the LORD for the war, [21] and every armed man of you will pass over the Jordan before the LORD, until he has driven out his enemies from before him [22] and the land is subdued before the LORD; then after that you shall return and be free of obligation to the LORD and to Israel, and this land shall be your possession before the LORD. [23] But if you will not do so, behold, you have sinned against the LORD, and be sure your sin will find you out. [24] Build cities for your little ones and folds for your sheep, and do what you have promised." [25] And the people of Gad and the people of Reuben said to Moses, "Your

[1] A *shekel* was about 2/5 ounce or 11 grams

servants will do as my lord commands. ²⁶ Our little ones, our wives, our livestock, and all our cattle shall remain there in the cities of Gilead, ²⁷ but your servants will pass over, every man who is armed for war, before the LORD to battle, as my lord orders."

²⁸ So Moses gave command concerning them to Eleazar the priest and to Joshua the son of Nun and to the heads of the fathers' houses of the tribes of the people of Israel. ²⁹ And Moses said to them, "If the people of Gad and the people of Reuben, every man who is armed to battle before the LORD, will pass with you over the Jordan and the land shall be subdued before you, then you shall give them the land of Gilead for a possession. ³⁰ However, if they will not pass over with you armed, they shall have possessions among you in the land of Canaan." ³¹ And the people of Gad and the people of Reuben answered, "What the LORD has said to your servants, we will do. ³² We will pass over armed before the LORD into the land of Canaan, and the possession of our inheritance shall remain with us beyond the Jordan."

³³ And Moses gave to them, to the people of Gad and to the people of Reuben and to the half-tribe of Manasseh the son of Joseph, the kingdom of Sihon king of the Amorites and the kingdom of Og king of Bashan, the land and its cities with their territories, the cities of the land throughout the country. ³⁴ And the people of Gad built Dibon, Ataroth, Aroer, ³⁵ Atroth-shophan, Jazer, Jogbehah, ³⁶ Beth-nimrah and Beth-haran, fortified cities, and folds for sheep. ³⁷ And the people of Reuben built Heshbon, Elealeh, Kiriathaim, ³⁸ Nebo, and Baal-meon (their names were changed), and Sibmah. And they gave other names to the cities that they built. ³⁹ And the sons of Machir the son of Manasseh went to Gilead and captured it, and dispossessed the Amorites who were in it. ⁴⁰ And Moses gave Gilead to Machir the son of Manasseh, and he settled in it. ⁴¹ And Jair the son of Manasseh went and captured their villages, and called them Havvoth-jair.¹ ⁴² And Nobah went and captured Kenath and its villages, and called it Nobah, after his own name.

Recounting Israel's Journey

33 These are the stages of the people of Israel, when they went out of the land of Egypt by their companies under the leadership of Moses and Aaron. ² Moses wrote down their starting places, stage by stage, by command of the LORD, and these are their stages according to their starting places. ³ They set out from Rameses in the first month, on the fifteenth day of the first month. On the day after the Passover, the people of Israel went out triumphantly in the sight of all the Egyptians, ⁴ while the Egyptians were burying all their firstborn, whom the LORD had struck down among them. On their gods also the LORD executed judgments.

⁵ So the people of Israel set out from Rameses and camped at Succoth. ⁶ And they set out from Succoth and camped at Etham, which is on the edge of the wilderness. ⁷ And they set out from Etham and turned back to Pi-hahiroth, which is east of Baal-zephon, and they camped before Migdol. ⁸ And they set out from before Hahiroth² and passed through the midst of the sea into the wilderness, and they went a three days' journey in the wilderness of Etham and camped at Marah. ⁹ And they set out from Marah and came to Elim; at Elim there were twelve springs of water and seventy palm trees, and they camped there. ¹⁰ And they set out from Elim and camped by the Red Sea. ¹¹ And they set out from the Red Sea and camped in the wilderness of Sin. ¹² And they set out from the wilderness of Sin and camped at Dophkah. ¹³ And they set out from Dophkah and camped at Alush. ¹⁴ And they set out from Alush and camped at Rephidim, where there was no water for the people to drink. ¹⁵ And they set out from Rephidim and camped in the wilderness of Sinai. ¹⁶ And they set out from the wilderness of Sinai and camped at Kibroth-hattaavah. ¹⁷ And they set out from Kibroth-hattaavah and camped at Hazeroth. ¹⁸ And they set out from Hazeroth and camped at Rithmah. ¹⁹ And they set out from Rithmah and camped at Rimmon-perez. ²⁰ And they set out from Rimmon-perez and camped at Libnah. ²¹ And they set out from Libnah and camped at Rissah. ²² And they set out from Rissah and camped at Kehelathah. ²³ And they set out from Kehelathah and camped at Mount Shepher. ²⁴ And they set out from Mount Shepher and camped at Haradah. ²⁵ And they set out from Haradah and camped at Makheloth. ²⁶ And they set out from Makheloth and camped at Tahath. ²⁷ And they set out from Tahath and camped at Terah. ²⁸ And they set out from Terah

---

¹ *Havvoth-jair* means *the villages of Jair* ² Some manuscripts and versions *Pi-hahiroth*

and camped at Mithkah. 29 And they set out from Mithkah and camped at Hashmonah. 30 And they set out from Hashmonah and camped at Moseroth. 31 And they set out from Moseroth and camped at Bene-jaakan. 32 And they set out from Bene-jaakan and camped at Hor-haggidgad. 33 And they set out from Hor-haggidgad and camped at Jotbathah. 34 And they set out from Jotbathah and camped at Abronah. 35 And they set out from Abronah and camped at Ezion-geber. 36 And they set out from Ezion-geber and camped in the wilderness of Zin (that is, Kadesh). 37 And they set out from Kadesh and camped at Mount Hor, on the edge of the land of Edom.

38 And Aaron the priest went up Mount Hor at the command of the LORD and died there, in the fortieth year after the people of Israel had come out of the land of Egypt, on the first day of the fifth month. 39 And Aaron was 123 years old when he died on Mount Hor.

40 And the Canaanite, the king of Arad, who lived in the Negeb in the land of Canaan, heard of the coming of the people of Israel.

41 And they set out from Mount Hor and camped at Zalmonah. 42 And they set out from Zalmonah and camped at Punon. 43 And they set out from Punon and camped at Oboth. 44 And they set out from Oboth and camped at Iye-abarim, in the territory of Moab. 45 And they set out from Iyim and camped at Dibon-gad. 46 And they set out from Dibon-gad and camped at Almon-diblathaim. 47 And they set out from Almon-diblathaim and camped in the mountains of Abarim, before Nebo. 48 And they set out from the mountains of Abarim and camped in the plains of Moab by the Jordan at Jericho; 49 they camped by the Jordan from Beth-jeshimoth as far as Abel-shittim in the plains of Moab.

Drive Out the Inhabitants

50 And the LORD spoke to Moses in the plains of Moab by the Jordan at Jericho, saying, 51 "Speak to the people of Israel and say to them, When you pass over the Jordan into the land of Canaan, 52 then you shall drive out all the inhabitants of the land from before you and destroy all their figured stones and destroy all their metal images and demolish all their high places. 53 And you shall take possession of the land and settle in it, for I have given the land to you to possess it. 54 You

shall inherit the land by lot according to your clans. To a large tribe you shall give a large inheritance, and to a small tribe you shall give a small inheritance. Wherever the lot falls for anyone, that shall be his. According to the tribes of your fathers you shall inherit. 55 But if you do not drive out the inhabitants of the land from before you, then those of them whom you let remain shall be as barbs in your eyes and thorns in your sides, and they shall trouble you in the land where you dwell. 56 And I will do to you as I thought to do to them."

Boundaries of the Land

34 The LORD spoke to Moses, saying, 2 "Command the people of Israel, and say to them, When you enter the land of Canaan (this is the land that shall fall to you for an inheritance, the land of Canaan as defined by its borders), 3 your south side shall be from the wilderness of Zin alongside Edom, and your southern border shall run from the end of the Salt Sea on the east. 4 And your border shall turn south of the ascent of Akrabbim, and cross to Zin, and its limit shall be south of Kadesh-barnea. Then it shall go on to Hazar-addar, and pass along to Azmon. 5 And the border shall turn from Azmon to the Brook of Egypt, and its limit shall be at the sea.

6 "For the western border, you shall have the Great Sea and its[1] coast. This shall be your western border.

7 "This shall be your northern border: from the Great Sea you shall draw a line to Mount Hor. 8 From Mount Hor you shall draw a line to Lebo-hamath, and the limit of the border shall be at Zedad. 9 Then the border shall extend to Ziphron, and its limit shall be at Hazar-enan. This shall be your northern border.

10 "You shall draw a line for your eastern border from Hazar-enan to Shepham. 11 And the border shall go down from Shepham to Riblah on the east side of Ain. And the border shall go down and reach to the shoulder of the Sea of Chinnereth on the east. 12 And the border shall go down to the Jordan, and its limit shall be at the Salt Sea. This shall be your land as defined by its borders all around."

13 Moses commanded the people of Israel, saying, "This is the land that you shall inherit by lot, which the LORD has commanded to give

---

[1] Syriac; Hebrew lacks *its*

to the nine tribes and to the half-tribe. [14] For the tribe of the people of Reuben by fathers' houses and the tribe of the people of Gad by their fathers' houses have received their inheritance, and also the half-tribe of Manasseh. [15] The two tribes and the half-tribe have received their inheritance beyond the Jordan east of Jericho, toward the sunrise."

List of Tribal Chiefs

[16] The LORD spoke to Moses, saying, [17] "These are the names of the men who shall divide the land to you for inheritance: Eleazar the priest and Joshua the son of Nun. [18] You shall take one chief from every tribe to divide the land for inheritance. [19] These are the names of the men: Of the tribe of Judah, Caleb the son of Jephunneh. [20] Of the tribe of the people of Simeon, Shemuel the son of Ammihud. [21] Of the tribe of Benjamin, Elidad the son of Chislon. [22] Of the tribe of the people of Dan a chief, Bukki the son of Jogli. [23] Of the people of Joseph: of the tribe of the people of Manasseh a chief, Hanniel the son of Ephod. [24] And of the tribe of the people of Ephraim a chief, Kemuel the son of Shiphtan. [25] Of the tribe of the people of Zebulun a chief, Elizaphan the son of Parnach. [26] Of the tribe of the people of Issachar a chief, Paltiel the son of Azzan. [27] And of the tribe of the people of Asher a chief, Ahihud the son of Shelomi. [28] Of the tribe of the people of Naphtali a chief, Pedahel the son of Ammihud." [29] These are the men whom the LORD commanded to divide the inheritance for the people of Israel in the land of Canaan.

Cities for the Levites

35 The LORD spoke to Moses in the plains of Moab by the Jordan at Jericho, saying, [2] "Command the people of Israel to give to the Levites some of the inheritance of their possession as cities for them to dwell in. And you shall give to the Levites pasturelands around the cities. [3] The cities shall be theirs to dwell in, and their pasturelands shall be for their cattle and for their livestock and for all their beasts. [4] The pasturelands of the cities, which you shall give to the Levites, shall reach from the wall of the city outward a thousand cubits[1] all around. [5] And you shall measure, outside the city, on the east side two thousand cubits, and on the south side two thousand cubits, and on the west side two thousand cubits, and on the north side two thousand cubits, the city being in the middle.

This shall belong to them as pastureland for their cities.

[6] "The cities that you give to the Levites shall be the six cities of refuge, where you shall permit the manslayer to flee, and in addition to them you shall give forty-two cities. [7] All the cities that you give to the Levites shall be forty-eight, with their pasturelands. [8] And as for the cities that you shall give from the possession of the people of Israel, from the larger tribes you shall take many, and from the smaller tribes you shall take few; each, in proportion to the inheritance that it inherits, shall give of its cities to the Levites."

Cities of Refuge

[9] And the LORD spoke to Moses, saying, [10] "Speak to the people of Israel and say to them, When you cross the Jordan into the land of Canaan, [11] then you shall select cities to be cities of refuge for you, that the manslayer who kills any person without intent may flee there. [12] The cities shall be for you a refuge from the avenger, that the manslayer may not die until he stands before the congregation for judgment. [13] And the cities that you give shall be your six cities of refuge. [14] You shall give three cities beyond the Jordan, and three cities in the land of Canaan, to be cities of refuge. [15] These six cities shall be for refuge for the people of Israel, and for the stranger and for the sojourner among them, that anyone who kills any person without intent may flee there.

[16] "But if he struck him down with an iron object, so that he died, he is a murderer. The murderer shall be put to death. [17] And if he struck him down with a stone tool that could cause death, and he died, he is a murderer. The murderer shall be put to death. [18] Or if he struck him down with a wooden tool that could cause death, and he died, he is a murderer. The murderer shall be put to death. [19] The avenger of blood shall himself put the murderer to death; when he meets him, he shall put him to death. [20] And if he pushed him out of hatred or hurled something at him, lying in wait, so that he died, [21] or in enmity struck him down with his hand, so that he died, then he who struck the blow shall be put to death. He is a murderer. The avenger of blood shall put the murderer to death when he meets him.

[22] "But if he pushed him suddenly without enmity, or hurled anything on him without

[1] A *cubit* was about 18 inches or 45 centimeters

lying in wait [23] or used a stone that could cause death, and without seeing him dropped it on him, so that he died, though he was not his enemy and did not seek his harm, [24] then the congregation shall judge between the manslayer and the avenger of blood, in accordance with these rules. [25] And the congregation shall rescue the manslayer from the hand of the avenger of blood, and the congregation shall restore him to his city of refuge to which he had fled, and he shall live in it until the death of the high priest who was anointed with the holy oil. [26] But if the manslayer shall at any time go beyond the boundaries of his city of refuge to which he fled, [27] and the avenger of blood finds him outside the boundaries of his city of refuge, and the avenger of blood kills the manslayer, he shall not be guilty of blood. [28] For he must remain in his city of refuge until the death of the high priest, but after the death of the high priest the manslayer may return to the land of his possession. [29] And these things shall be for a statute and rule for you throughout your generations in all your dwelling places.

[30] "If anyone kills a person, the murderer shall be put to death on the evidence of witnesses. But no person shall be put to death on the testimony of one witness. [31] Moreover, you shall accept no ransom for the life of a murderer, who is guilty of death, but he shall be put to death. [32] And you shall accept no ransom for him who has fled to his city of refuge, that he may return to dwell in the land before the death of the high priest. [33] You shall not pollute the land in which you live, for blood pollutes the land, and no atonement can be made for the land for the blood that is shed in it, except by the blood of the one who shed it. [34] You shall not defile the land in which you live, in the midst of which I dwell, for I the LORD dwell in the midst of the people of Israel."

Marriage of Female Heirs

36 The heads of the fathers' houses of the clan of the people of Gilead the son of Machir, son of Manasseh, from the clans of the people of Joseph, came near and spoke before Moses and before the chiefs, the heads of the fathers' houses of the people of Israel. [2] They said, "The LORD commanded my lord to give the land for inheritance by lot to the people of Israel, and my lord was commanded by the LORD to give the inheritance of Zelophehad our brother to his daughters. [3] But if they are married to any of the sons of the other tribes of the people of Israel, then their inheritance will be taken from the inheritance of our fathers and added to the inheritance of the tribe into which they marry. So it will be taken away from the lot of our inheritance. [4] And when the jubilee of the people of Israel comes, then their inheritance will be added to the inheritance of the tribe into which they marry, and their inheritance will be taken from the inheritance of the tribe of our fathers."

[5] And Moses commanded the people of Israel according to the word of the LORD, saying, "The tribe of the people of Joseph is right. [6] This is what the LORD commands concerning the daughters of Zelophehad: 'Let them marry whom they think best, only they shall marry within the clan of the tribe of their father. [7] The inheritance of the people of Israel shall not be transferred from one tribe to another, for every one of the people of Israel shall hold on to the inheritance of the tribe of his fathers. [8] And every daughter who possesses an inheritance in any tribe of the people of Israel shall be wife to one of the clan of the tribe of her father, so that every one of the people of Israel may possess the inheritance of his fathers. [9] So no inheritance shall be transferred from one tribe to another, for each of the tribes of the people of Israel shall hold on to its own inheritance.'"

[10] The daughters of Zelophehad did as the LORD commanded Moses, [11] for Mahlah, Tirzah, Hoglah, Milcah, and Noah, the daughters of Zelophehad, were married to sons of their father's brothers. [12] They were married into the clans of the people of Manasseh the son of Joseph, and their inheritance remained in the tribe of their father's clan.

[13] These are the commandments and the rules that the LORD commanded through Moses to the people of Israel in the plains of Moab by the Jordan at Jericho.

DEUTERONOMY

The Command to Leave Horeb

1 These are the words that Moses spoke to all Israel beyond the Jordan in the wilderness, in the Arabah opposite Suph, between Paran and Tophel, Laban, Hazeroth, and Dizahab. ²It is eleven days' journey from Horeb by the way of Mount Seir to Kadesh-barnea. ³In the fortieth year, on the first day of the eleventh month, Moses spoke to the people of Israel according to all that the LORD had given him in commandment to them, ⁴after he had defeated Sihon the king of the Amorites, who lived in Heshbon, and Og the king of Bashan, who lived in Ashtaroth and in Edrei. ⁵Beyond the Jordan, in the land of Moab, Moses undertook to explain this law, saying, ⁶"The LORD our God said to us in Horeb, 'You have stayed long enough at this mountain. ⁷Turn and take your journey, and go to the hill country of the Amorites and to all their neighbors in the Arabah, in the hill country and in the lowland and in the Negeb and by the seacoast, the land of the Canaanites, and Lebanon, as far as the great river, the river Euphrates. ⁸See, I have set the land before you. Go in and take possession of the land that the LORD swore to your fathers, to Abraham, to Isaac, and to Jacob, to give to them and to their offspring after them.'

Leaders Appointed

⁹"At that time I said to you, 'I am not able to bear you by myself. ¹⁰The LORD your God has multiplied you, and behold, you are today as numerous as the stars of heaven. ¹¹May the LORD, the God of your fathers, make you a thousand times as many as you are and bless you, as he has promised you! ¹²How can I bear by myself the weight and burden of you and your strife? ¹³Choose for your tribes wise, understanding, and experienced men, and I will appoint them as your heads.' ¹⁴And you answered me, 'The thing that you have spoken is good for us to do.' ¹⁵So I took the heads of your tribes, wise and experienced men, and set them as heads over you, commanders of thousands, commanders of hundreds, commanders of fifties, commanders of tens, and officers, throughout your tribes. ¹⁶And I charged your judges at that time, 'Hear the cases between your brothers, and judge righteously between a man and his brother or the alien who is with him. ¹⁷You shall not be partial in judgment. You shall hear the small and the great alike. You shall not be intimidated by anyone, for the judgment is God's. And the case that is too hard for you, you shall bring to me, and I will hear it.' ¹⁸And I commanded you at that time all the things that you should do.

Israel's Refusal to Enter the Land

¹⁹"Then we set out from Horeb and went through all that great and terrifying wilderness that you saw, on the way to the hill country of the Amorites, as the LORD our God commanded us. And we came to Kadesh-barnea. ²⁰And I said to you, 'You have come to the hill country of the Amorites, which the LORD our God is giving us. ²¹See, the LORD your God has set the land before you. Go up, take possession, as the LORD, the God of your fathers, has told you. Do not fear or be dismayed.' ²²Then all of you came near me and said, 'Let us send men before us, that they may explore the land for us and bring us word again of the way by which we must go up and the cities into which we shall come.' ²³The thing seemed good to me, and I took twelve men from you, one man from each tribe. ²⁴And they turned and went up into the hill country, and came to the Valley of Eshcol and spied it out. ²⁵And they took in their hands some of the fruit of the land and brought it down to us, and brought us word again and said, 'It is a good land that the LORD our God is giving us.'

²⁶"Yet you would not go up, but rebelled against the command of the LORD your God. ²⁷And you murmured in your tents and said, 'Because the LORD hated us he has brought us out of the land of Egypt, to give us into the hand of the Amorites, to destroy us. ²⁸Where are we going up? Our brothers have made our hearts melt, saying, "The people are greater and taller than we. The cities are great and fortified up to heaven. And besides, we have seen the sons of the Anakim there."' ²⁹Then I said to you, 'Do not be in dread or afraid of them. ³⁰The LORD your God who goes before you will himself fight for you, just as he did for you in Egypt before your eyes, ³¹and in the wilderness, where you have seen how the LORD your God carried

you, as a man carries his son, all the way that you went until you came to this place.' ³²Yet in spite of this word you did not believe the LORD your God, ³³who went before you in the way to seek you out a place to pitch your tents, in fire by night and in the cloud by day, to show you by what way you should go.

The Penalty for Israel's Rebellion

³⁴"And the LORD heard your words and was angered, and he swore, ³⁵'Not one of these men of this evil generation shall see the good land that I swore to give to your fathers, ³⁶except Caleb the son of Jephunneh. He shall see it, and to him and to his children I will give the land on which he has trodden, because he has wholly followed the LORD!' ³⁷Even with me the LORD was angry on your account and said, 'You also shall not go in there. ³⁸Joshua the son of Nun, who stands before you, he shall enter. Encourage him, for he shall cause Israel to inherit it. ³⁹And as for your little ones, who you said would become a prey, and your children, who today have no knowledge of good or evil, they shall go in there. And to them I will give it, and they shall possess it. ⁴⁰But as for you, turn, and journey into the wilderness in the direction of the Red Sea.'

⁴¹"Then you answered me, 'We have sinned against the LORD. We ourselves will go up and fight, just as the LORD our God commanded us.' And every one of you fastened on his weapons of war and thought it easy to go up into the hill country. ⁴²And the LORD said to me, 'Say to them, Do not go up or fight, for I am not in your midst, lest you be defeated before your enemies.' ⁴³So I spoke to you, and you would not listen; but you rebelled against the command of the LORD and presumptuously went up into the hill country. ⁴⁴Then the Amorites who lived in that hill country came out against you and chased you as bees do and beat you down in Seir as far as Hormah. ⁴⁵And you returned and wept before the LORD, but the LORD did not listen to your voice or give ear to you. ⁴⁶So you remained at Kadesh many days, the days that you remained there.

The Wilderness Years

2 "Then we turned and journeyed into the wilderness in the direction of the Red Sea, as the LORD told me. And for many days we traveled around Mount Seir. ²Then the LORD said

to me, ³'You have been traveling around this mountain country long enough. Turn northward ⁴and command the people, "You are about to pass through the territory of your brothers, the people of Esau, who live in Seir; and they will be afraid of you. So be very careful. ⁵Do not contend with them, for I will not give you any of their land, no, not so much as for the sole of the foot to tread on, because I have given Mount Seir to Esau as a possession. ⁶You shall purchase food from them with money, that you may eat, and you shall also buy water from them with money, that you may drink. ⁷For the LORD your God has blessed you in all the work of your hands. He knows your going through this great wilderness. These forty years the LORD your God has been with you. You have lacked nothing."' ⁸So we went on, away from our brothers, the people of Esau, who live in Seir, away from the Arabah road from Elath and Ezion-geber.

"And we turned and went in the direction of the wilderness of Moab. ⁹And the LORD said to me, 'Do not harass Moab or contend with them in battle, for I will not give you any of their land for a possession, because I have given Ar to the people of Lot for a possession.' ¹⁰(The Emim formerly lived there, a people great and many, and tall as the Anakim. ¹¹Like the Anakim they are also counted as Rephaim, but the Moabites call them Emim. ¹²The Horites also lived in Seir formerly, but the people of Esau dispossessed them and destroyed them from before them and settled in their place, as Israel did to the land of their possession, which the LORD gave to them.) ¹³'Now rise up and go over the brook Zered.' So we went over the brook Zered. ¹⁴And the time from our leaving Kadesh-barnea until we crossed the brook Zered was thirty-eight years, until the entire generation, that is, the men of war, had perished from the camp, as the LORD had sworn to them. ¹⁵For indeed the hand of the LORD was against them, to destroy them from the camp, until they had perished.

¹⁶"So as soon as all the men of war had perished and were dead from among the people, ¹⁷the LORD said to me, ¹⁸'Today you are to cross the border of Moab at Ar. ¹⁹And when you approach the territory of the people of Ammon, do not harass them or contend with them, for I will not give you any of the land of the people of Ammon as a possession, because I have given it to the sons of Lot for

a possession.' [20] (It is also counted as a land of Rephaim. Rephaim formerly lived there—but the Ammonites call them Zamzummim— [21] a people great and many, and tall as the Anakim; but the LORD destroyed them before the Ammonites,[1] and they dispossessed them and settled in their place, [22] as he did for the people of Esau, who live in Seir, when he destroyed the Horites before them and they dispossessed them and settled in their place even to this day. [23] As for the Avvim, who lived in villages as far as Gaza, the Caphtorim, who came from Caphtor, destroyed them and settled in their place.) [24] 'Rise up, set out on your journey and go over the Valley of the Arnon. Behold, I have given into your hand Sihon the Amorite, king of Heshbon, and his land. Begin to take possession, and contend with him in battle. [25] This day I will begin to put the dread and fear of you on the peoples who are under the whole heaven, who shall hear the report of you and shall tremble and be in anguish because of you.'

The Defeat of King Sihon

[26] "So I sent messengers from the wilderness of Kedemoth to Sihon the king of Heshbon, with words of peace, saying, [27] 'Let me pass through your land. I will go only by the road; I will turn aside neither to the right nor to the left. [28] You shall sell me food for money, that I may eat, and give me water for money, that I may drink. Only let me pass through on foot, [29] as the sons of Esau who live in Seir and the Moabites who live in Ar did for me, until I go over the Jordan into the land that the LORD our God is giving to us.' [30] But Sihon the king of Heshbon would not let us pass by him, for the LORD your God hardened his spirit and made his heart obstinate, that he might give him into your hand, as he is this day. [31] And the LORD said to me, 'Behold, I have begun to give Sihon and his land over to you. Begin to take possession, that you may occupy his land.' [32] Then Sihon came out against us, he and all his people, to battle at Jahaz. [33] And the LORD our God gave him over to us, and we defeated him and his sons and all his people. [34] And we captured all his cities at that time and devoted to destruction[2] every city, men, women, and children. We left no survivors. [35] Only the livestock we took as spoil for ourselves, with the plunder of the cities that we captured. [36] From Aroer, which is on the edge of the Valley of the Arnon, and from the city that is in the valley, as far as Gilead, there was not a city too high for us. The LORD our God gave all into our hands. [37] Only to the land of the sons of Ammon you did not draw near, that is, to all the banks of the river Jabbok and the cities of the hill country, whatever the LORD our God had forbidden us.

The Defeat of King Og

3 "Then we turned and went up the way to Bashan. And Og the king of Bashan came out against us, he and all his people, to battle at Edrei. [2] But the LORD said to me, 'Do not fear him, for I have given him and all his people and his land into your hand. And you shall do to him as you did to Sihon the king of the Amorites, who lived at Heshbon.' [3] So the LORD our God gave into our hand Og also, the king of Bashan, and all his people, and we struck him down until he had no survivor left. [4] And we took all his cities at that time—there was not a city that we did not take from them—sixty cities, the whole region of Argob, the kingdom of Og in Bashan. [5] All these were cities fortified with high walls, gates, and bars, besides very many unwalled villages. [6] And we devoted them to destruction,[3] as we did to Sihon the king of Heshbon, devoting to destruction every city, men, women, and children. [7] But all the livestock and the spoil of the cities we took as our plunder. [8] So we took the land at that time out of the hand of the two kings of the Amorites who were beyond the Jordan, from the Valley of the Arnon to Mount Hermon [9] (the Sidonians call Hermon Sirion, while the Amorites call it Senir), [10] all the cities of the tableland and all Gilead and all Bashan, as far as Salecah and Edrei, cities of the kingdom of Og in Bashan. [11] (For only Og the king of Bashan was left of the remnant of the Rephaim. Behold, his bed was a bed of iron. Is it not in Rabbah of the Ammonites? Nine cubits[4] was its length, and four cubits its breadth, according to the common cubit.[5])

[12] "When we took possession of this land at that time, I gave to the Reubenites and the Gadites the territory beginning at Aroer, which is on the edge of the Valley of the Arnon, and half the hill country of Gilead with its cities. [13] The rest of Gilead, and all Bashan, the kingdom of Og, that is, all the region of Argob, I gave to the half-tribe of Manasseh. (All that

---

[1] Hebrew them [2] That is, set apart (devoted) as an offering to the Lord (for destruction) [3] That is, set apart (devoted) as an offering to the Lord (for destruction); twice in this verse [4] A cubit was about 18 inches or 45 centimeters [5] Hebrew cubit of a man

portion of Bashan is called the land of Rephaim. [14] Jair the Manassite took all the region of Argob, that is, Bashan, as far as the border of the Geshurites and the Maacathites, and called the villages after his own name, Havvoth-jair, as it is to this day.) [15] To Machir I gave Gilead, [16] and to the Reubenites and the Gadites I gave the territory from Gilead as far as the Valley of the Arnon, with the middle of the valley as a border, as far over as the river Jabbok, the border of the Ammonites; [17] the Arabah also, with the Jordan as the border, from Chinnereth as far as the Sea of the Arabah, the Salt Sea, under the slopes of Pisgah on the east.

[18] "And I commanded you at that time, saying, 'The LORD your God has given you this land to possess. All your men of valor shall cross over armed before your brothers, the people of Israel. [19] Only your wives, your little ones, and your livestock (I know that you have much livestock) shall remain in the cities that I have given you, [20] until the LORD gives rest to your brothers, as to you, and they also occupy the land that the LORD your God gives them beyond the Jordan. Then each of you may return to his possession which I have given you.' [21] And I commanded Joshua at that time, 'Your eyes have seen all that the LORD your God has done to these two kings. So will the LORD do to all the kingdoms into which you are crossing. [22] You shall not fear them, for it is the LORD your God who fights for you.'

Moses Forbidden to Enter the Land

[23] "And I pleaded with the LORD at that time, saying, [24] 'O Lord GOD, you have only begun to show your servant your greatness and your mighty hand. For what god is there in heaven or on earth who can do such works and mighty acts as yours? [25] Please let me go over and see the good land beyond the Jordan, that good hill country and Lebanon.' [26] But the LORD was angry with me because of you and would not listen to me. And the LORD said to me, 'Enough from you; do not speak to me of this matter again. [27] Go up to the top of Pisgah and lift up your eyes westward and northward and southward and eastward, and look at it with your eyes, for you shall not go over this Jordan. [28] But charge Joshua, and encourage and strengthen him, for he shall go over at the head of this people, and he shall put them in possession of the land that you shall see.' [29] So we remained in the valley opposite Beth-peor.

Moses Commands Obedience

4 "And now, O Israel, listen to the statutes and the rules[1] that I am teaching you, and do them, that you may live, and go in and take possession of the land that the LORD, the God of your fathers, is giving you. [2] You shall not add to the word that I command you, nor take from it, that you may keep the commandments of the LORD your God that I command you. [3] Your eyes have seen what the LORD did at Baal-peor, for the LORD your God destroyed from among you all the men who followed the Baal of Peor. [4] But you who held fast to the LORD your God are all alive today. [5] See, I have taught you statutes and rules, as the LORD my God commanded me, that you should do them in the land that you are entering to take possession of it. [6] Keep them and do them, for that will be your wisdom and your understanding in the sight of the peoples, who, when they hear all these statutes, will say, 'Surely this great nation is a wise and understanding people.' [7] For what great nation is there that has a god so near to it as the LORD our God is to us, whenever we call upon him? [8] And what great nation is there, that has statutes and rules so righteous as all this law that I set before you today?

[9] "Only take care, and keep your soul diligently, lest you forget the things that your eyes have seen, and lest they depart from your heart all the days of your life. Make them known to your children and your children's children— [10] how on the day that you stood before the LORD your God at Horeb, the LORD said to me, 'Gather the people to me, that I may let them hear my words, so that they may learn to fear me all the days that they live on the earth, and that they may teach their children so.' [11] And you came near and stood at the foot of the mountain, while the mountain burned with fire to the heart of heaven, wrapped in darkness, cloud, and gloom. [12] Then the LORD spoke to you out of the midst of the fire. You heard the sound of words, but saw no form; there was only a voice. [13] And he declared to you his covenant, which he commanded you to perform, that is, the Ten Commandments,[2] and he wrote them on two tablets of stone. [14] And the LORD commanded me at that time to teach

---

[1] Or *just decrees*; also verses 5, 8, 14, 45 [2] Hebrew *the ten words*

you statutes and rules, that you might do them in the land that you are going over to possess.

Idolatry Forbidden

15 "Therefore watch yourselves very carefully. Since you saw no form on the day that the LORD spoke to you at Horeb out of the midst of the fire, 16 beware lest you act corruptly by making a carved image for yourselves, in the form of any figure, the likeness of male or female, 17 the likeness of any animal that is on the earth, the likeness of any winged bird that flies in the air, 18 the likeness of anything that creeps on the ground, the likeness of any fish that is in the water under the earth. 19 And beware lest you raise your eyes to heaven, and when you see the sun and the moon and the stars, all the host of heaven, you be drawn away and bow down to them and serve them, things that the LORD your God has allotted to all the peoples under the whole heaven. 20 But the LORD has taken you and brought you out of the iron furnace, out of Egypt, to be a people of his own inheritance, as you are this day. 21 Furthermore, the LORD was angry with me because of you, and he swore that I should not cross the Jordan, and that I should not enter the good land that the LORD your God is giving you for an inheritance. 22 For I must die in this land; I must not go over the Jordan. But you shall go over and take possession of that good land. 23 Take care, lest you forget the covenant of the LORD your God, which he made with you, and make a carved image, the form of anything that the LORD your God has forbidden you. 24 For the LORD your God is a consuming fire, a jealous God.

25 "When you father children and children's children, and have grown old in the land, if you act corruptly by making a carved image in the form of anything, and by doing what is evil in the sight of the LORD your God, so as to provoke him to anger, 26 I call heaven and earth to witness against you today, that you will soon utterly perish from the land that you are going over the Jordan to possess. You will not live long in it, but will be utterly destroyed. 27 And the LORD will scatter you among the peoples, and you will be left few in number among the nations where the LORD will drive you. 28 And there you will serve gods of wood and stone, the work of human hands, that neither see, nor hear, nor eat, nor smell. 29 But from there you will seek the LORD your God and you will find him, if you search after him with all your heart and with all your soul. 30 When you are in tribulation, and all these things come upon you in the latter days, you will return to the LORD your God and obey his voice. 31 For the LORD your God is a merciful God. He will not leave you or destroy you or forget the covenant with your fathers that he swore to them.

The LORD Alone Is God

32 "For ask now of the days that are past, which were before you, since the day that God created man on the earth, and ask from one end of heaven to the other, whether such a great thing as this has ever happened or was ever heard of. 33 Did any people ever hear the voice of a god speaking out of the midst of the fire, as you have heard, and still live? 34 Or has any god ever attempted to go and take a nation for himself from the midst of another nation, by trials, by signs, by wonders, and by war, by a mighty hand and an outstretched arm, and by great deeds of terror, all of which the LORD your God did for you in Egypt before your eyes? 35 To you it was shown, that you might know that the LORD is God; there is no other besides him. 36 Out of heaven he let you hear his voice, that he might discipline you. And on earth he let you see his great fire, and you heard his words out of the midst of the fire. 37 And because he loved your fathers and chose their offspring after them[1] and brought you out of Egypt with his own presence, by his great power, 38 driving out before you nations greater and mightier than you, to bring you in, to give you their land for an inheritance, as it is this day, 39 know therefore today, and lay it to your heart, that the LORD is God in heaven above and on the earth beneath; there is no other. 40 Therefore you shall keep his statutes and his commandments, which I command you today, that it may go well with you and with your children after you, and that you may prolong your days in the land that the LORD your God is giving you for all time."

Cities of Refuge

41 Then Moses set apart three cities in the east beyond the Jordan, 42 that the manslayer might flee there, anyone who kills his neighbor unintentionally, without being at enmity with him in time past; he may flee to one of these cities and save his life: 43 Bezer in the wilderness on the tableland for the Reubenites, Ramoth in

---

[1] Hebrew *his offspring after him*

Gilead for the Gadites, and Golan in Bashan for the Manassites.

Introduction to the Law

[44] This is the law that Moses set before the people of Israel. [45] These are the testimonies, the statutes, and the rules, which Moses spoke to the people of Israel when they came out of Egypt, [46] beyond the Jordan in the valley opposite Beth-peor, in the land of Sihon the king of the Amorites, who lived at Heshbon, whom Moses and the people of Israel defeated when they came out of Egypt. [47] And they took possession of his land and the land of Og, the king of Bashan, the two kings of the Amorites, who lived to the east beyond the Jordan; [48] from Aroer, which is on the edge of the Valley of the Arnon, as far as Mount Sirion[1] (that is, Hermon), [49] together with all the Arabah on the east side of the Jordan as far as the Sea of the Arabah, under the slopes of Pisgah.

The Ten Commandments

5 And Moses summoned all Israel and said to them, "Hear, O Israel, the statutes and the rules that I speak in your hearing today, and you shall learn them and be careful to do them. [2] The Lord our God made a covenant with us in Horeb. [3] Not with our fathers did the Lord make this covenant, but with us, who are all of us here alive today. [4] The Lord spoke with you face to face at the mountain, out of the midst of the fire, [5] while I stood between the Lord and you at that time, to declare to you the word of the Lord. For you were afraid because of the fire, and you did not go up into the mountain. He said:

[6] " 'I am the Lord your God, who brought you out of the land of Egypt, out of the house of slavery.

[7] " 'You shall have no other gods before[2] me.

[8] " 'You shall not make for yourself a carved image, or any likeness of anything that is in heaven above, or that is on the earth beneath, or that is in the water under the earth. [9] You shall not bow down to them or serve them; for I the Lord your God am a jealous God, visiting the iniquity of the fathers on the children to the third and fourth generation of those who hate me, [10] but showing steadfast love to thousands[3] of those who love me and keep my commandments.

[11] " 'You shall not take the name of the Lord your God in vain, for the Lord will not hold him guiltless who takes his name in vain.

[12] " 'Observe the Sabbath day, to keep it holy, as the Lord your God commanded you. [13] Six days you shall labor and do all your work, [14] but the seventh day is a Sabbath to the Lord your God. On it you shall not do any work, you or your son or your daughter or your male servant or your female servant, or your ox or your donkey or any of your livestock, or the sojourner who is within your gates, that your male servant and your female servant may rest as well as you. [15] You shall remember that you were a slave[4] in the land of Egypt, and the Lord your God brought you out from there with a mighty hand and an outstretched arm. Therefore the Lord your God commanded you to keep the Sabbath day.

[16] " 'Honor your father and your mother, as the Lord your God commanded you, that your days may be long, and that it may go well with you in the land that the Lord your God is giving you.

[17] " 'You shall not murder.[5]

[18] " 'And you shall not commit adultery.

[19] " 'And you shall not steal.

[20] " 'And you shall not bear false witness against your neighbor.

[21] " 'And you shall not covet your neighbor's wife. And you shall not desire your neighbor's house, his field, or his male servant, or his female servant, his ox, or his donkey, or anything that is your neighbor's.'

[22] "These words the Lord spoke to all your assembly at the mountain out of the midst of the fire, the cloud, and the thick darkness, with a loud voice; and he added no more. And he wrote them on two tablets of stone and gave them to me. [23] And as soon as you heard the voice out of the midst of the darkness, while the mountain was burning with fire, you came near to me, all the heads of your tribes, and your elders. [24] And you said, 'Behold, the Lord our God has shown us his glory and greatness, and we have heard his voice out of the midst of the fire. This day we have seen God speak with man, and man still live. [25] Now therefore why should we die? For this great fire will consume us. If we hear the voice of the Lord our God any more, we shall die. [26] For who is there of all flesh, that has heard the voice of the living God speaking out of the midst of fire as we have,

---

[1] Syriac; Hebrew *Sion* [2] Or *besides* [3] Or *to the thousandth generation* [4] Or *servant* [5] The Hebrew word also covers causing human death through carelessness or negligence

and has still lived? ²⁷ Go near and hear all that the LORD our God will say, and speak to us all that the LORD our God will speak to you, and we will hear and do it.'

²⁸ "And the LORD heard your words, when you spoke to me. And the LORD said to me, 'I have heard the words of this people, which they have spoken to you. They are right in all that they have spoken. ²⁹ Oh that they had such a heart as this always, to fear me and to keep all my commandments, that it might go well with them and with their descendants[1] forever! ³⁰ Go and say to them, "Return to your tents." ³¹ But you, stand here by me, and I will tell you the whole commandment and the statutes and the rules that you shall teach them, that they may do them in the land that I am giving them to possess.' ³² You shall be careful therefore to do as the LORD your God has commanded you. You shall not turn aside to the right hand or to the left. ³³ You shall walk in all the way that the LORD your God has commanded you, that you may live, and that it may go well with you, and that you may live long in the land that you shall possess.

The Greatest Commandment

6 "Now this is the commandment—the statutes and the rules[2]—that the LORD your God commanded me to teach you, that you may do them in the land to which you are going over, to possess it, ² that you may fear the LORD your God, you and your son and your son's son, by keeping all his statutes and his commandments, which I command you, all the days of your life, and that your days may be long. ³ Hear therefore, O Israel, and be careful to do them, that it may go well with you, and that you may multiply greatly, as the LORD, the God of your fathers, has promised you, in a land flowing with milk and honey.

⁴ "Hear, O Israel: The LORD our God, the LORD is one.[3] ⁵ You shall love the LORD your God with all your heart and with all your soul and with all your might. ⁶ And these words that I command you today shall be on your heart. ⁷ You shall teach them diligently to your children, and shall talk of them when you sit in your house, and when you walk by the way, and when you lie down, and when you rise. ⁸ You shall bind them as a sign on your hand, and they shall be as frontlets between your eyes. ⁹ You shall write them on the doorposts of your house and on your gates.

¹⁰ "And when the LORD your God brings you into the land that he swore to your fathers, to Abraham, to Isaac, and to Jacob, to give you— with great and good cities that you did not build, ¹¹ and houses full of all good things that you did not fill, and cisterns that you did not dig, and vineyards and olive trees that you did not plant—and when you eat and are full, ¹² then take care lest you forget the LORD, who brought you out of the land of Egypt, out of the house of slavery. ¹³ It is the LORD your God you shall fear. Him you shall serve and by his name you shall swear. ¹⁴ You shall not go after other gods, the gods of the peoples who are around you— ¹⁵ for the LORD your God in your midst is a jealous God—lest the anger of the LORD your God be kindled against you, and he destroy you from off the face of the earth.

¹⁶ "You shall not put the LORD your God to the test, as you tested him at Massah. ¹⁷ You shall diligently keep the commandments of the LORD your God, and his testimonies and his statutes, which he has commanded you. ¹⁸ And you shall do what is right and good in the sight of the LORD, that it may go well with you, and that you may go in and take possession of the good land that the LORD swore to give to your fathers ¹⁹ by thrusting out all your enemies from before you, as the LORD has promised.

²⁰ "When your son asks you in time to come, 'What is the meaning of the testimonies and the statutes and the rules that the LORD our God has commanded you?' ²¹ then you shall say to your son, 'We were Pharaoh's slaves in Egypt. And the LORD brought us out of Egypt with a mighty hand. ²² And the LORD showed signs and wonders, great and grievous, against Egypt and against Pharaoh and all his household, before our eyes. ²³ And he brought us out from there, that he might bring us in and give us the land that he swore to give to our fathers. ²⁴ And the LORD commanded us to do all these statutes, to fear the LORD our God, for our good always, that he might preserve us alive, as we are this day. ²⁵ And it will be righteousness for us, if we are careful to do all this commandment before the LORD our God, as he has commanded us.'

A Chosen People

7 "When the LORD your God brings you into the land that you are entering to take possession of it, and clears away many nations before you, the Hittites, the Girgashites, the

---

[1] Or sons [2] Or just decrees; also verse 20 [3] Or The LORD our God is one LORD; or The LORD is our God, the LORD is one; or The LORD is our God, the LORD alone

Amorites, the Canaanites, the Perizzites, the Hivites, and the Jebusites, seven nations more numerous and mightier than you, [2] and when the LORD your God gives them over to you, and you defeat them, then you must devote them to complete destruction.[1] You shall make no covenant with them and show no mercy to them. [3] You shall not intermarry with them, giving your daughters to their sons or taking their daughters for your sons, [4] for they would turn away your sons from following me, to serve other gods. Then the anger of the LORD would be kindled against you, and he would destroy you quickly. [5] But thus shall you deal with them: you shall break down their altars and dash in pieces their pillars and chop down their Asherim and burn their carved images with fire.

[6] "For you are a people holy to the LORD your God. The LORD your God has chosen you to be a people for his treasured possession, out of all the peoples who are on the face of the earth. [7] It was not because you were more in number than any other people that the LORD set his love on you and chose you, for you were the fewest of all peoples, [8] but it is because the LORD loves you and is keeping the oath that he swore to your fathers, that the LORD has brought you out with a mighty hand and redeemed you from the house of slavery, from the hand of Pharaoh king of Egypt. [9] Know therefore that the LORD your God is God, the faithful God who keeps covenant and steadfast love with those who love him and keep his commandments, to a thousand generations, [10] and repays to their face those who hate him, by destroying them. He will not be slack with one who hates him. He will repay him to his face. [11] You shall therefore be careful to do the commandment and the statutes and the rules that I command you today.

[12] "And because you listen to these rules and keep and do them, the LORD your God will keep with you the covenant and the steadfast love that he swore to your fathers. [13] He will love you, bless you, and multiply you. He will also bless the fruit of your womb and the fruit of your ground, your grain and your wine and your oil, the increase of your herds and the young of your flock, in the land that he swore to your fathers to give you. [14] You shall be blessed above all peoples. There shall not be male or female barren among you or among your livestock.

[15] And the LORD will take away from you all sickness, and none of the evil diseases of Egypt, which you knew, will he inflict on you, but he will lay them on all who hate you. [16] And you shall consume all the peoples that the LORD your God will give over to you. Your eye shall not pity them, neither shall you serve their gods, for that would be a snare to you.

[17] "If you say in your heart, 'These nations are greater than I. How can I dispossess them?' [18] you shall not be afraid of them but you shall remember what the LORD your God did to Pharaoh and to all Egypt, [19] the great trials that your eyes saw, the signs, the wonders, the mighty hand, and the outstretched arm, by which the LORD your God brought you out. So will the LORD your God do to all the peoples of whom you are afraid. [20] Moreover, the LORD your God will send hornets among them, until those who are left and hide themselves from you are destroyed. [21] You shall not be in dread of them, for the LORD your God is in your midst, a great and awesome God. [22] The LORD your God will clear away these nations before you little by little. You may not make an end of them at once,[2] lest the wild beasts grow too numerous for you. [23] But the LORD your God will give them over to you and throw them into great confusion, until they are destroyed. [24] And he will give their kings into your hand, and you shall make their name perish from under heaven. No one shall be able to stand against you until you have destroyed them. [25] The carved images of their gods you shall burn with fire. You shall not covet the silver or the gold that is on them or take it for yourselves, lest you be ensnared by it, for it is an abomination to the LORD your God. [26] And you shall not bring an abominable thing into your house and become devoted to destruction[3] like it. You shall utterly detest and abhor it, for it is devoted to destruction.

Remember the LORD Your God

8 "The whole commandment that I command you today you shall be careful to do, that you may live and multiply, and go in and possess the land that the LORD swore to give to your fathers. [2] And you shall remember the whole way that the LORD your God has led you these forty years in the wilderness, that he might humble you, testing you to know what was in your heart, whether you would keep his

---

[1] That is, set apart (devote) as an offering to the Lord (for destruction) [2] Or *quickly* [3] That is, set apart (devoted) as an offering to the Lord (for destruction); twice in this verse

commandments or not. [3] And he humbled you and let you hunger and fed you with manna, which you did not know, nor did your fathers know, that he might make you know that man does not live by bread alone, but man lives by every word[1] that comes from the mouth of the LORD. [4] Your clothing did not wear out on you and your foot did not swell these forty years. [5] Know then in your heart that, as a man disciplines his son, the LORD your God disciplines you. [6] So you shall keep the commandments of the LORD your God by walking in his ways and by fearing him. [7] For the LORD your God is bringing you into a good land, a land of brooks of water, of fountains and springs, flowing out in the valleys and hills, [8] a land of wheat and barley, of vines and fig trees and pomegranates, a land of olive trees and honey, [9] a land in which you will eat bread without scarcity, in which you will lack nothing, a land whose stones are iron, and out of whose hills you can dig copper. [10] And you shall eat and be full, and you shall bless the LORD your God for the good land he has given you.

[11] "Take care lest you forget the LORD your God by not keeping his commandments and his rules and his statutes, which I command you today, [12] lest, when you have eaten and are full and have built good houses and live in them, [13] and when your herds and flocks multiply and your silver and gold is multiplied and all that you have is multiplied, [14] then your heart be lifted up, and you forget the LORD your God, who brought you out of the land of Egypt, out of the house of slavery, [15] who led you through the great and terrifying wilderness, with its fiery serpents and scorpions and thirsty ground where there was no water, who brought you water out of the flinty rock, [16] who fed you in the wilderness with manna that your fathers did not know, that he might humble you and test you, to do you good in the end. [17] Beware lest you say in your heart, 'My power and the might of my hand have gotten me this wealth.' [18] You shall remember the LORD your God, for it is he who gives you power to get wealth, that he may confirm his covenant that he swore to your fathers, as it is this day. [19] And if you forget the LORD your God and go after other gods and serve them and worship them, I solemnly warn you today that you shall surely perish. [20] Like the nations that the LORD

makes to perish before you, so shall you perish, because you would not obey the voice of the LORD your God.

Not Because of Righteousness

9 "Hear, O Israel: you are to cross over the Jordan today, to go in to dispossess nations greater and mightier than you, cities great and fortified up to heaven, [2] a people great and tall, the sons of the Anakim, whom you know, and of whom you have heard it said, 'Who can stand before the sons of Anak?' [3] Know therefore today that he who goes over before you as a consuming fire is the LORD your God. He will destroy them and subdue them before you. So you shall drive them out and make them perish quickly, as the LORD has promised you.

[4] "Do not say in your heart, after the LORD your God has thrust them out before you, 'It is because of my righteousness that the LORD has brought me in to possess this land,' whereas it is because of the wickedness of these nations that the LORD is driving them out before you. [5] Not because of your righteousness or the uprightness of your heart are you going in to possess their land, but because of the wickedness of these nations the LORD your God is driving them out from before you, and that he may confirm the word that the LORD swore to your fathers, to Abraham, to Isaac, and to Jacob.

[6] "Know, therefore, that the LORD your God is not giving you this good land to possess because of your righteousness, for you are a stubborn people. [7] Remember and do not forget how you provoked the LORD your God to wrath in the wilderness. From the day you came out of the land of Egypt until you came to this place, you have been rebellious against the LORD. [8] Even at Horeb you provoked the LORD to wrath, and the LORD was so angry with you that he was ready to destroy you. [9] When I went up the mountain to receive the tablets of stone, the tablets of the covenant that the LORD made with you, I remained on the mountain forty days and forty nights. I neither ate bread nor drank water. [10] And the LORD gave me the two tablets of stone written with the finger of God, and on them were all the words that the LORD had spoken with you on the mountain out of the midst of the fire on the day of the

[1] Hebrew by all

assembly. [11] And at the end of forty days and forty nights the LORD gave me the two tablets of stone, the tablets of the covenant. [12] Then the LORD said to me, 'Arise, go down quickly from here, for your people whom you have brought from Egypt have acted corruptly. They have turned aside quickly out of the way that I commanded them; they have made themselves a metal image.'

The Golden Calf

[13] "Furthermore, the LORD said to me, 'I have seen this people, and behold, it is a stubborn people. [14] Let me alone, that I may destroy them and blot out their name from under heaven. And I will make of you a nation mightier and greater than they.' [15] So I turned and came down from the mountain, and the mountain was burning with fire. And the two tablets of the covenant were in my two hands. [16] And I looked, and behold, you had sinned against the LORD your God. You had made yourselves a golden[1] calf. You had turned aside quickly from the way that the LORD had commanded you. [17] So I took hold of the two tablets and threw them out of my two hands and broke them before your eyes. [18] Then I lay prostrate before the LORD as before, forty days and forty nights. I neither ate bread nor drank water, because of all the sin that you had committed, in doing what was evil in the sight of the LORD to provoke him to anger. [19] For I was afraid of the anger and hot displeasure that the LORD bore against you, so that he was ready to destroy you. But the LORD listened to me that time also. [20] And the LORD was so angry with Aaron that he was ready to destroy him. And I prayed for Aaron also at the same time. [21] Then I took the sinful thing, the calf that you had made, and burned it with fire and crushed it, grinding it very small, until it was as fine as dust. And I threw the dust of it into the brook that ran down from the mountain.

[22] "At Taberah also, and at Massah and at Kibroth-hattaavah you provoked the LORD to wrath. [23] And when the LORD sent you from Kadesh-barnea, saying, 'Go up and take possession of the land that I have given you,' then you rebelled against the commandment of the LORD your God and did not believe him or obey his voice. [24] You have been rebellious against the LORD from the day that I knew you.

[25] "So I lay prostrate before the LORD for these forty days and forty nights, because the LORD had said he would destroy you. [26] And I prayed to the LORD, 'O Lord GOD, do not destroy your people and your heritage, whom you have redeemed through your greatness, whom you have brought out of Egypt with a mighty hand. [27] Remember your servants, Abraham, Isaac, and Jacob. Do not regard the stubbornness of this people, or their wickedness or their sin, [28] lest the land from which you brought us say, "Because the LORD was not able to bring them into the land that he promised them, and because he hated them, he has brought them out to put them to death in the wilderness." [29] For they are your people and your heritage, whom you brought out by your great power and by your outstretched arm.'

New Tablets of Stone

10 "At that time the LORD said to me, 'Cut for yourself two tablets of stone like the first, and come up to me on the mountain and make an ark of wood. [2] And I will write on the tablets the words that were on the first tablets that you broke, and you shall put them in the ark.' [3] So I made an ark of acacia wood, and cut two tablets of stone like the first, and went up the mountain with the two tablets in my hand. [4] And he wrote on the tablets, in the same writing as before, the Ten Commandments[2] that the LORD had spoken to you on the mountain out of the midst of the fire on the day of the assembly. And the LORD gave them to me. [5] Then I turned and came down from the mountain and put the tablets in the ark that I had made. And there they are, as the LORD commanded me."

[6] (The people of Israel journeyed from Beeroth Bene-jaakan[3] to Moserah. There Aaron died, and there he was buried. And his son Eleazar ministered as priest in his place. [7] From there they journeyed to Gudgodah, and from Gudgodah to Jotbathah, a land with brooks of water. [8] At that time the LORD set apart the tribe of Levi to carry the ark of the covenant of the LORD to stand before the LORD to minister to him and to bless in his name, to this day. [9] Therefore Levi has no portion or inheritance with his brothers. The LORD is his inheritance, as the LORD your God said to him.)

[10] "I myself stayed on the mountain, as at the first time, forty days and forty nights, and the LORD listened to me that time also. The LORD

---

[1] Hebrew *cast metal* [2] Hebrew *the ten words* [3] Or *the wells of the Bene-jaakan*

was unwilling to destroy you. [11] And the LORD said to me, 'Arise, go on your journey at the head of the people, so that they may go in and possess the land, which I swore to their fathers to give them.'

Circumcise Your Heart

[12] "And now, Israel, what does the LORD your God require of you, but to fear the LORD your God, to walk in all his ways, to love him, to serve the LORD your God with all your heart and with all your soul, [13] and to keep the commandments and statutes of the LORD, which I am commanding you today for your good? [14] Behold, to the LORD your God belong heaven and the heaven of heavens, the earth with all that is in it. [15] Yet the LORD set his heart in love on your fathers and chose their offspring after them, you above all peoples, as you are this day. [16] Circumcise therefore the foreskin of your heart, and be no longer stubborn. [17] For the LORD your God is God of gods and Lord of lords, the great, the mighty, and the awesome God, who is not partial and takes no bribe. [18] He executes justice for the fatherless and the widow, and loves the sojourner, giving him food and clothing. [19] Love the sojourner, therefore, for you were sojourners in the land of Egypt. [20] You shall fear the LORD your God. You shall serve him and hold fast to him, and by his name you shall swear. [21] He is your praise. He is your God, who has done for you these great and terrifying things that your eyes have seen. [22] Your fathers went down to Egypt seventy persons, and now the LORD your God has made you as numerous as the stars of heaven.

Love and Serve the LORD

11 "You shall therefore love the LORD your God and keep his charge, his statutes, his rules, and his commandments always. [2] And consider today (since I am not speaking to your children who have not known or seen it), consider the discipline[1] of the LORD your God, his greatness, his mighty hand and his outstretched arm, [3] his signs and his deeds that he did in Egypt to Pharaoh the king of Egypt and to all his land, [4] and what he did to the army of Egypt, to their horses and to their chariots, how he made the water of the Red Sea flow over them as they pursued after you, and how the LORD has destroyed them to this day, [5] and what he did to you in the wilderness, until you came to this place, [6] and what he did to Dathan

and Abiram the sons of Eliab, son of Reuben, how the earth opened its mouth and swallowed them up, with their households, their tents, and every living thing that followed them, in the midst of all Israel. [7] For your eyes have seen all the great work of the LORD that he did.

[8] "You shall therefore keep the whole commandment that I command you today, that you may be strong, and go in and take possession of the land that you are going over to possess, [9] and that you may live long in the land that the LORD swore to your fathers to give to them and to their offspring, a land flowing with milk and honey. [10] For the land that you are entering to take possession of it is not like the land of Egypt, from which you have come, where you sowed your seed and irrigated it,[2] like a garden of vegetables. [11] But the land that you are going over to possess is a land of hills and valleys, which drinks water by the rain from heaven, [12] a land that the LORD your God cares for. The eyes of the LORD your God are always upon it, from the beginning of the year to the end of the year.

[13] "And if you will indeed obey my commandments that I command you today, to love the LORD your God, and to serve him with all your heart and with all your soul, [14] he[3] will give the rain for your land in its season, the early rain and the later rain, that you may gather in your grain and your wine and your oil. [15] And he will give grass in your fields for your livestock, and you shall eat and be full. [16] Take care lest your heart be deceived, and you turn aside and serve other gods and worship them; [17] then the anger of the LORD will be kindled against you, and he will shut up the heavens, so that there will be no rain, and the land will yield no fruit, and you will perish quickly off the good land that the LORD is giving you.

[18] "You shall therefore lay up these words of mine in your heart and in your soul, and you shall bind them as a sign on your hand, and they shall be as frontlets between your eyes. [19] You shall teach them to your children, talking of them when you are sitting in your house, and when you are walking by the way, and when you lie down, and when you rise. [20] You shall write them on the doorposts of your house and on your gates, [21] that your days and the days of your children may be multiplied in the land that the LORD swore to your fathers to give them, as long as the heave

[1] Or instruction   [2] Hebrew *watered it with your feet*   [3] Samaritan, Septuagint, Vulgate; Hebrew *I*; also verse 15

are above the earth. [22] For if you will be careful to do all this commandment that I command you to do, loving the LORD your God, walking in all his ways, and holding fast to him, [23] then the LORD will drive out all these nations before you, and you will dispossess nations greater and mightier than you. [24] Every place on which the sole of your foot treads shall be yours. Your territory shall be from the wilderness to[1] the Lebanon and from the River, the river Euphrates, to the western sea. [25] No one shall be able to stand against you. The LORD your God will lay the fear of you and the dread of you on all the land that you shall tread, as he promised you.

[26] "See, I am setting before you today a blessing and a curse: [27] the blessing, if you obey the commandments of the LORD your God, which I command you today, [28] and the curse, if you do not obey the commandments of the LORD your God, but turn aside from the way that I am commanding you today, to go after other gods that you have not known. [29] And when the LORD your God brings you into the land that you are entering to take possession of it, you shall set the blessing on Mount Gerizim and the curse on Mount Ebal. [30] Are they not beyond the Jordan, west of the road, toward the going down of the sun, in the land of the Canaanites who live in the Arabah, opposite Gilgal, beside the oak[2] of Moreh? [31] For you are to cross over the Jordan to go in to take possession of the land that the LORD your God is giving you. And when you possess it and live in it, [32] you shall be careful to do all the statutes and the rules that I am setting before you today.

The LORD's Chosen Place of Worship

12 "These are the statutes and rules that you shall be careful to do in the land that the LORD, the God of your fathers, has given you to possess, all the days that you live on the earth. [2] You shall surely destroy all the places where the nations whom you shall dispossess served their gods, on the high mountains and on the hills and under every green tree. [3] You shall tear down their altars and dash in pieces their pillars and burn their Asherim with fire. You shall chop down the carved images of their gods and destroy their name out of that place. [4] You shall not worship the LORD your God in that way. [5] But you shall seek the place that the LORD your God

will choose out of all your tribes to put his name and make his habitation[3] there. There you shall go, [6] and there you shall bring your burnt offerings and your sacrifices, your tithes and the contribution that you present, your vow offerings, your freewill offerings, and the firstborn of your herd and of your flock. [7] And there you shall eat before the LORD your God, and you shall rejoice, you and your households, in all that you undertake, in which the LORD your God has blessed you.

[8] "You shall not do according to all that we are doing here today, everyone doing whatever is right in his own eyes, [9] for you have not as yet come to the rest and to the inheritance that the LORD your God is giving you. [10] But when you go over the Jordan and live in the land that the LORD your God is giving you to inherit, and when he gives you rest from all your enemies around, so that you live in safety, [11] then to the place that the LORD your God will choose, to make his name dwell there, there you shall bring all that I command you: your burnt offerings and your sacrifices, your tithes and the contribution that you present, and all your finest vow offerings that you vow to the LORD. [12] And you shall rejoice before the LORD your God, you and your sons and your daughters, your male servants and your female servants, and the Levite that is within your towns, since he has no portion or inheritance with you. [13] Take care that you do not offer your burnt offerings at any place that you see, [14] but at the place that the LORD will choose in one of your tribes, there you shall offer your burnt offerings, and there you shall do all that I am commanding you.

[15] "However, you may slaughter and eat meat within any of your towns, as much as you desire, according to the blessing of the LORD your God that he has given you. The unclean and the clean may eat of it, as of the gazelle and as of the deer. [16] Only you shall not eat the blood; you shall pour it out on the earth like water. [17] You may not eat within your towns the tithe of your grain or of your wine or of your oil, or the firstborn of your herd or of your flock, or any of your vow offerings that you vow, or your freewill offerings or the contribution that you present, [18] but you shall eat them before the LORD your God in the place that the LORD your God will choose, you and your son and your daughter, your male servant and your female

[1] Hebrew *and* [2] Septuagint, Syriac; see Genesis 12:6. Hebrew *oaks,* or *terebinths* [3] Or *name as its habitation*

servant, and the Levite who is within your towns. And you shall rejoice before the LORD your God in all that you undertake. [19] Take care that you do not neglect the Levite as long as you live in your land.

[20] "When the LORD your God enlarges your territory, as he has promised you, and you say, 'I will eat meat,' because you crave meat, you may eat meat whenever you desire. [21] If the place that the LORD your God will choose to put his name there is too far from you, then you may kill any of your herd or your flock, which the LORD has given you, as I have commanded you, and you may eat within your towns whenever you desire. [22] Just as the gazelle or the deer is eaten, so you may eat of it. The unclean and the clean alike may eat of it. [23] Only be sure that you do not eat the blood, for the blood is the life, and you shall not eat the life with the flesh. [24] You shall not eat it; you shall pour it out on the earth like water. [25] You shall not eat it, that all may go well with you and with your children after you, when you do what is right in the sight of the LORD. [26] But the holy things that are due from you, and your vow offerings, you shall take, and you shall go to the place that the LORD will choose, [27] and offer your burnt offerings, the flesh and the blood, on the altar of the LORD your God. The blood of your sacrifices shall be poured out on the altar of the LORD your God, but the flesh you may eat. [28] Be careful to obey all these words that I command you, that it may go well with you and with your children after you forever, when you do what is good and right in the sight of the LORD your God.

Warning Against Idolatry

[29] "When the LORD your God cuts off before you the nations whom you go in to dispossess, and you dispossess them and dwell in their land, [30] take care that you be not ensnared to follow them, after they have been destroyed before you, and that you do not inquire about their gods, saying, 'How did these nations serve their gods?—that I also may do the same.' [31] You shall not worship the LORD your God in that way, for every abominable thing that the LORD hates they have done for their gods, for they even burn their sons and their daughters in the fire to their gods.

[32][1] "Everything that I command you, you shall be careful to do. You shall not add to it or take from it.

13 "If a prophet or a dreamer of dreams arises among you and gives you a sign or a wonder, [2] and the sign or wonder that he tells you comes to pass, and if he says, 'Let us go after other gods,' which you have not known, 'and let us serve them,' [3] you shall not listen to the words of that prophet or that dreamer of dreams. For the LORD your God is testing you, to know whether you love the LORD your God with all your heart and with all your soul. [4] You shall walk after the LORD your God and fear him and keep his commandments and obey his voice, and you shall serve him and hold fast to him. [5] But that prophet or that dreamer of dreams shall be put to death, because he has taught rebellion against the LORD your God, who brought you out of the land of Egypt and redeemed you out of the house of slavery, to make you leave the way in which the LORD your God commanded you to walk. So you shall purge the evil[2] from your midst.

[6] "If your brother, the son of your mother, or your son or your daughter or the wife you embrace[3] or your friend who is as your own soul entices you secretly, saying, 'Let us go and serve other gods,' which neither you nor your fathers have known, [7] some of the gods of the peoples who are around you, whether near you or far off from you, from the one end of the earth to the other, [8] you shall not yield to him or listen to him, nor shall your eye pity him, nor shall you spare him, nor shall you conceal him. [9] But you shall kill him. Your hand shall be first against him to put him to death, and afterward the hand of all the people. [10] You shall stone him to death with stones, because he sought to draw you away from the LORD your God, who brought you out of the land of Egypt, out of the house of slavery. [11] And all Israel shall hear and fear and never again do any such wickedness as this among you.

[12] "If you hear in one of your cities, which the LORD your God is giving you to dwell there, [13] that certain worthless fellows have gone out among you and have drawn away the inhabitants of their city, saying, 'Let us go and serve other gods,' which you have not known, [14] then you shall inquire and make search and ask diligently. And behold, if it be true and certain that such an abomination has been done among you, [15] you shall surely put the inhabitants of that city to the sword, devoting it to destruction,[4] all who are in it and its cattle, with the

---

[1] Ch 13:1 in Hebrew   [2] Or *evil person*   [3] Hebrew *the wife of your bosom*   [4] That is, setting apart (devoting) as an offering to the Lord (for destruction)

edge of the sword. [16] You shall gather all its spoil into the midst of its open square and burn the city and all its spoil with fire, as a whole burnt offering to the LORD your God. It shall be a heap forever. It shall not be built again. [17] None of the devoted things shall stick to your hand, that the LORD may turn from the fierceness of his anger and show you mercy and have compassion on you and multiply you, as he swore to your fathers, [18] if you obey the voice of the LORD your God, keeping all his commandments that I am commanding you today, and doing what is right in the sight of the LORD your God.

Clean and Unclean Food

14 "You are the sons of the LORD your God. You shall not cut yourselves or make any baldness on your foreheads for the dead. [2] For you are a people holy to the LORD your God, and the LORD has chosen you to be a people for his treasured possession, out of all the peoples who are on the face of the earth.

[3] "You shall not eat any abomination. [4] These are the animals you may eat: the ox, the sheep, the goat, [5] the deer, the gazelle, the roebuck, the wild goat, the ibex,[1] the antelope, and the mountain sheep. [6] Every animal that parts the hoof and has the hoof cloven in two and chews the cud, among the animals, you may eat. [7] Yet of those that chew the cud or have the hoof cloven you shall not eat these: the camel, the hare, and the rock badger, because they chew the cud but do not part the hoof, are unclean for you. [8] And the pig, because it parts the hoof but does not chew the cud, is unclean for you. Their flesh you shall not eat, and their carcasses you shall not touch.

[9] "Of all that are in the waters you may eat these: whatever has fins and scales you may eat. [10] And whatever does not have fins and scales you shall not eat; it is unclean for you.

[11] "You may eat all clean birds. [12] But these are the ones that you shall not eat: the eagle,[2] the bearded vulture, the black vulture, [13] the kite, the falcon of any kind; [14] every raven of any kind; [15] the ostrich, the nighthawk, the sea gull, the hawk of any kind; [16] the little owl and the short-eared owl, the barn owl [17] and the tawny owl, the carrion vulture and the cormorant, [18] the stork, the heron of any kind; the hoopoe and the bat. [19] And all winged insects are unclean for you; they shall not be eaten. [20] All clean winged things you may eat.

[21] "You shall not eat anything that has died naturally. You may give it to the sojourner who is within your towns, that he may eat it, or you may sell it to a foreigner. For you are a people holy to the LORD your God.

"You shall not boil a young goat in its mother's milk.

Tithes

[22] "You shall tithe all the yield of your seed that comes from the field year by year. [23] And before the LORD your God, in the place that he will choose, to make his name dwell there, you shall eat the tithe of your grain, of your wine, and of your oil, and the firstborn of your herd and flock, that you may learn to fear the LORD your God always. [24] And if the way is too long for you, so that you are not able to carry the tithe, when the LORD your God blesses you, because the place is too far from you, which the LORD your God chooses, to set his name there, [25] then you shall turn it into money and bind up the money in your hand and go to the place that the LORD your God chooses [26] and spend the money for whatever you desire—oxen or sheep or wine or strong drink, whatever your appetite craves. And you shall eat there before the LORD your God and rejoice, you and your household. [27] And you shall not neglect the Levite who is within your towns, for he has no portion or inheritance with you.

[28] "At the end of every three years you shall bring out all the tithe of your produce in the same year and lay it up within your towns. [29] And the Levite, because he has no portion or inheritance with you, and the sojourner, the fatherless, and the widow, who are within your towns, shall come and eat and be filled, that the LORD your God may bless you in all the work of your hands that you do.

The Sabbatical Year

15 "At the end of every seven years you shall grant a release. [2] And this is the manner of the release: every creditor shall release what he has lent to his neighbor. He shall not exact it of his neighbor, his brother, because the LORD's release has been proclaimed. [3] Of a foreigner you may exact it, but whatever of yours is with your brother your hand shall release. [4] But there will be no poor among you; for the LORD will bless you in the land that the LORD your God is giv-

ing you for an inheritance to possess—⁵if only you will strictly obey the voice of the LORD your God, being careful to do all this commandment that I command you today. ⁶For the LORD your God will bless you, as he promised you, and you shall lend to many nations, but you shall not borrow, and you shall rule over many nations, but they shall not rule over you.

⁷"If among you, one of your brothers should become poor, in any of your towns within your land that the LORD your God is giving you, you shall not harden your heart or shut your hand against your poor brother, ⁸but you shall open your hand to him and lend him sufficient for his need, whatever it may be. ⁹Take care lest there be an unworthy thought in your heart and you say, 'The seventh year, the year of release is near,' and your eye look grudgingly¹ on your poor brother, and you give him nothing, and he cry to the LORD against you, and you be guilty of sin. ¹⁰You shall give to him freely, and your heart shall not be grudging when you give to him, because for this the LORD your God will bless you in all your work and in all that you undertake. ¹¹For there will never cease to be poor in the land. Therefore I command you, 'You shall open wide your hand to your brother, to the needy and to the poor, in your land.'

¹²"If your brother, a Hebrew man or a Hebrew woman, is sold² to you, he shall serve you six years, and in the seventh year you shall let him go free from you. ¹³And when you let him go free from you, you shall not let him go empty-handed. ¹⁴You shall furnish him liberally out of your flock, out of your threshing floor, and out of your winepress. As the LORD your God has blessed you, you shall give to him. ¹⁵You shall remember that you were a slave in the land of Egypt, and the LORD your God redeemed you; therefore I command you this today. ¹⁶But if he says to you, 'I will not go out from you,' because he loves you and your household, since he is well-off with you, ¹⁷then you shall take an awl, and put it through his ear into the door, and he shall be your slave³ forever. And to your female slave⁴ you shall do the same. ¹⁸It shall not seem hard to you when you let him go free from you, for at half the cost of a hired worker he has served you six years. So the LORD your God will bless you in all that you do.

¹⁹"All the firstborn males that are born of your herd and flock you shall dedicate to the LORD your God. You shall do no work with the firstborn of your herd, nor shear the firstborn of your flock. ²⁰You shall eat it, you and your household, before the LORD your God year by year at the place that the LORD will choose. ²¹But if it has any blemish, if it is lame or blind or has any serious blemish whatever, you shall not sacrifice it to the LORD your God. ²²You shall eat it within your towns. The unclean and the clean alike may eat it, as though it were a gazelle or a deer. ²³Only you shall not eat its blood; you shall pour it out on the ground like water.

Passover

16 "Observe the month of Abib and keep the Passover to the LORD your God, for in the month of Abib the LORD your God brought you out of Egypt by night. ²And you shall offer the Passover sacrifice to the LORD your God, from the flock or the herd, at the place that the LORD will choose, to make his name dwell there. ³You shall eat no leavened bread with it. Seven days you shall eat it with unleavened bread, the bread of affliction—for you came out of the land of Egypt in haste—that all the days of your life you may remember the day when you came out of the land of Egypt. ⁴No leaven shall be seen with you in all your territory for seven days, nor shall any of the flesh that you sacrifice on the evening of the first day remain all night until morning. ⁵You may not offer the Passover sacrifice within any of your towns that the LORD your God is giving you, ⁶but at the place that the LORD your God will choose, to make his name dwell in it, there you shall offer the Passover sacrifice, in the evening at sunset, at the time you came out of Egypt. ⁷And you shall cook it and eat it at the place that the LORD your God will choose. And in the morning you shall turn and go to your tents. ⁸For six days you shall eat unleavened bread, and on the seventh day there shall be a solemn assembly to the LORD your God. You shall do no work on it.

The Feast of Weeks

⁹"You shall count seven weeks. Begin to count the seven weeks from the time the sickle is first put to the standing grain. ¹⁰Then you shall keep the Feast of Weeks to the LORD your God with the tribute of a freewill offering from your hand, which you shall give as

---

¹ Or *be evil*; also verse 10 ² Or *sells himself* ³ Or *servant*; the Hebrew term *'ebed* designates a range of social and economic roles (see Preface) ⁴ Or *servant*

the LORD your God blesses you. [11] And you shall rejoice before the LORD your God, you and your son and your daughter, your male servant and your female servant, the Levite who is within your towns, the sojourner, the fatherless, and the widow who are among you, at the place that the LORD your God will choose, to make his name dwell there. [12] You shall remember that you were a slave in Egypt; and you shall be careful to observe these statutes.

The Feast of Booths

[13] "You shall keep the Feast of Booths seven days, when you have gathered in the produce from your threshing floor and your winepress. [14] You shall rejoice in your feast, you and your son and your daughter, your male servant and your female servant, the Levite, the sojourner, the fatherless, and the widow who are within your towns. [15] For seven days you shall keep the feast to the LORD your God at the place that the LORD will choose, because the LORD your God will bless you in all your produce and in all the work of your hands, so that you will be altogether joyful.

[16] "Three times a year all your males shall appear before the LORD your God at the place that he will choose: at the Feast of Unleavened Bread, at the Feast of Weeks, and at the Feast of Booths. They shall not appear before the LORD empty-handed. [17] Every man shall give as he is able, according to the blessing of the LORD your God that he has given you.

Justice

[18] "You shall appoint judges and officers in all your towns that the LORD your God is giving you, according to your tribes, and they shall judge the people with righteous judgment. [19] You shall not pervert justice. You shall not show partiality, and you shall not accept a bribe, for a bribe blinds the eyes of the wise and subverts the cause of the righteous. [20] Justice, and only justice, you shall follow, that you may live and inherit the land that the LORD your God is giving you.

Forbidden Forms of Worship

[21] "You shall not plant any tree as an Asherah beside the altar of the LORD your God that you shall make. [22] And you shall not set up a pillar, which the LORD your God hates.

17 "You shall not sacrifice to the LORD your God an ox or a sheep in which is a blemish, any defect whatever, for that is an abomination to the LORD your God.

[2] "If there is found among you, within any of your towns that the LORD your God is giving you, a man or woman who does what is evil in the sight of the LORD your God, in transgressing his covenant, [3] and has gone and served other gods and worshiped them, or the sun or the moon or any of the host of heaven, which I have forbidden, [4] and it is told you and you hear of it, then you shall inquire diligently, and if it is true and certain that such an abomination has been done in Israel, [5] then you shall bring out to your gates that man or woman who has done this evil thing, and you shall stone that man or woman to death with stones. [6] On the evidence of two witnesses or of three witnesses the one who is to die shall be put to death; a person shall not be put to death on the evidence of one witness. [7] The hand of the witnesses shall be first against him to put him to death, and afterward the hand of all the people. So you shall purge[1] the evil[2] from your midst.

Legal Decisions by Priests and Judges

[8] "If any case arises requiring decision between one kind of homicide and another, one kind of legal right and another, or one kind of assault and another, any case within your towns that is too difficult for you, then you shall arise and go up to the place that the LORD your God will choose. [9] And you shall come to the Levitical priests and to the judge who is in office in those days, and you shall consult them, and they shall declare to you the decision. [10] Then you shall do according to what they declare to you from that place that the LORD will choose. And you shall be careful to do according to all that they direct you. [11] According to the instructions that they give you, and according to the decision which they pronounce to you, you shall do. You shall not turn aside from the verdict that they declare to you, either to the right hand or to the left. [12] The man who acts presumptuously by not obeying the priest who stands to minister there before the LORD your God, or the judge, that man shall die. So you shall purge the evil from Israel. [13] And all the people shall hear and fear and not act presumptuously again.

---

[1] Septuagint *drive out*; also verse 12 [2] Or *evil person*; also verse 12

Laws Concerning Israel's Kings

14 "When you come to the land that the LORD your God is giving you, and you possess it and dwell in it and then say, 'I will set a king over me, like all the nations that are around me,' 15 you may indeed set a king over you whom the LORD your God will choose. One from among your brothers you shall set as king over you. You may not put a foreigner over you, who is not your brother. 16 Only he must not acquire many horses for himself or cause the people to return to Egypt in order to acquire many horses, since the LORD has said to you, 'You shall never return that way again.' 17 And he shall not acquire many wives for himself, lest his heart turn away, nor shall he acquire for himself excessive silver and gold.

18 "And when he sits on the throne of his kingdom, he shall write for himself in a book a copy of this law, approved by[1] the Levitical priests. 19 And it shall be with him, and he shall read in it all the days of his life, that he may learn to fear the LORD his God by keeping all the words of this law and these statutes, and doing them, 20 that his heart may not be lifted up above his brothers, and that he may not turn aside from the commandment, either to the right hand or to the left, so that he may continue long in his kingdom, he and his children, in Israel.

Provision for Priests and Levites

18 "The Levitical priests, all the tribe of Levi, shall have no portion or inheritance with Israel. They shall eat the LORD's food offerings[2] as their[3] inheritance. 2 They shall have no inheritance among their brothers; the LORD is their inheritance, as he promised them. 3 And this shall be the priests' due from the people, from those offering a sacrifice, whether an ox or a sheep: they shall give to the priest the shoulder and the two cheeks and the stomach. 4 The firstfruits of your grain, of your wine and of your oil, and the first fleece of your sheep, you shall give him. 5 For the LORD your God has chosen him out of all your tribes to stand and minister in the name of the LORD, him and his sons for all time.

6 "And if a Levite comes from any of your towns out of all Israel, where he lives—and he may come when he desires[4]—to the place that the LORD will choose, 7 and ministers in the name of the LORD his God, like all his fellow Levites who stand to minister there before the LORD, 8 then he may have equal portions to eat, besides what he receives from the sale of his patrimony.[5]

Abominable Practices

9 "When you come into the land that the LORD your God is giving you, you shall not learn to follow the abominable practices of those nations. 10 There shall not be found among you anyone who burns his son or his daughter as an offering,[6] anyone who practices divination or tells fortunes or interprets omens, or a sorcerer 11 or a charmer or a medium or a necromancer or one who inquires of the dead, 12 for whoever does these things is an abomination to the LORD. And because of these abominations the LORD your God is driving them out before you. 13 You shall be blameless before the LORD your God, 14 for these nations, which you are about to dispossess, listen to fortune-tellers and to diviners. But as for you, the LORD your God has not allowed you to do this.

A New Prophet like Moses

15 "The LORD your God will raise up for you a prophet like me from among you, from your brothers—it is to him you shall listen— 16 just as you desired of the LORD your God at Horeb on the day of the assembly, when you said, 'Let me not hear again the voice of the LORD my God or see this great fire any more, lest I die.' 17 And the LORD said to me, 'They are right in what they have spoken. 18 I will raise up for them a prophet like you from among their brothers. And I will put my words in his mouth, and he shall speak to them all that I command him. 19 And whoever will not listen to my words that he shall speak in my name, I myself will require it of him. 20 But the prophet who presumes to speak a word in my name that I have not commanded him to speak, or[7] who speaks in the name of other gods, that same prophet shall die.' 21 And if you say in your heart, 'How may we know the word that the LORD has not spoken?'— 22 when a prophet speaks in the name of the LORD, if the word does not come to pass or come true, that is a word that the LORD has not spoken; the prophet has spoken it presumptuously. You need not be afraid of him.

---

[1] Hebrew from before [2] Or the offerings by fire to the LORD [3] Hebrew his [4] Or lives—if he comes enthusiastically [5] The meaning of the Hebrew is uncertain [6] Hebrew makes his son or his daughter pass through the fire [7] Or and

Laws Concerning Cities of Refuge

19 "When the LORD your God cuts off the nations whose land the LORD your God is giving you, and you dispossess them and dwell in their cities and in their houses, ²you shall set apart three cities for yourselves in the land that the LORD your God is giving you to possess. ³You shall measure the distances¹ and divide into three parts the area of the land that the LORD your God gives you as a possession, so that any manslayer can flee to them.

⁴"This is the provision for the manslayer, who by fleeing there may save his life. If anyone kills his neighbor unintentionally without having hated him in the past— ⁵as when someone goes into the forest with his neighbor to cut wood, and his hand swings the axe to cut down a tree, and the head slips from the handle and strikes his neighbor so that he dies—he may flee to one of these cities and live, ⁶lest the avenger of blood in hot anger pursue the manslayer and overtake him, because the way is long, and strike him fatally, though the man did not deserve to die, since he had not hated his neighbor in the past. ⁷Therefore I command you, You shall set apart three cities. ⁸And if the LORD your God enlarges your territory, as he has sworn to your fathers, and gives you all the land that he promised to give to your fathers— ⁹provided you are careful to keep all this commandment, which I command you today, by loving the LORD your God and by walking ever in his ways—then you shall add three other cities to these three, ¹⁰lest innocent blood be shed in your land that the LORD your God is giving you for an inheritance, and so the guilt of bloodshed be upon you.

¹¹"But if anyone hates his neighbor and lies in wait for him and attacks him and strikes him fatally so that he dies, and he flees into one of these cities, ¹²then the elders of his city shall send and take him from there, and hand him over to the avenger of blood, so that he may die. ¹³Your eye shall not pity him, but you shall purge the guilt of innocent blood² from Israel, so that it may be well with you.

Property Boundaries

¹⁴"You shall not move your neighbor's landmark, which the men of old have set, in the inheritance that you will hold in the land that the LORD your God is giving you to possess.

Laws Concerning Witnesses

¹⁵"A single witness shall not suffice against a person for any crime or for any wrong in connection with any offense that he has committed. Only on the evidence of two witnesses or of three witnesses shall a charge be established. ¹⁶If a malicious witness arises to accuse a person of wrongdoing, ¹⁷then both parties to the dispute shall appear before the LORD, before the priests and the judges who are in office in those days. ¹⁸The judges shall inquire diligently, and if the witness is a false witness and has accused his brother falsely, ¹⁹then you shall do to him as he had meant to do to his brother. So you shall purge the evil³ from your midst. ²⁰And the rest shall hear and fear, and shall never again commit any such evil among you. ²¹Your eye shall not pity. It shall be life for life, eye for eye, tooth for tooth, hand for hand, foot for foot.

Laws Concerning Warfare

20 "When you go out to war against your enemies, and see horses and chariots and an army larger than your own, you shall not be afraid of them, for the LORD your God is with you, who brought you up out of the land of Egypt. ²And when you draw near to the battle, the priest shall come forward and speak to the people ³and shall say to them, 'Hear, O Israel, today you are drawing near for battle against your enemies: let not your heart faint. Do not fear or panic or be in dread of them, ⁴for the LORD your God is he who goes with you to fight for you against your enemies, to give you the victory.' ⁵Then the officers shall speak to the people, saying, 'Is there any man who has built a new house and has not dedicated it? Let him go back to his house, lest he die in the battle and another man dedicate it. ⁶And is there any man who has planted a vineyard and has not enjoyed its fruit? Let him go back to his house, lest he die in the battle and another man enjoy its fruit. ⁷And is there any man who has betrothed a wife and has not taken her? Let him go back to his house, lest he die in the battle and another man take her.' ⁸And the officers shall speak further to the people, and say, 'Is there any man who is fearful and fainthearted? Let him go back to his house, lest he make the heart of his fellows melt like his own.' ⁹And when the officers have finished speaking to the people, then commanders shall be appointed at the head of the people.

¹ Hebrew *road* ² *Or the blood of the innocent* ³ *Or evil person*

[10] "When you draw near to a city to fight against it, offer terms of peace to it. [11] And if it responds to you peaceably and it opens to you, then all the people who are found in it shall do forced labor for you and shall serve you. [12] But if it makes no peace with you, but makes war against you, then you shall besiege it. [13] And when the LORD your God gives it into your hand, you shall put all its males to the sword, [14] but the women and the little ones, the livestock, and everything else in the city, all its spoil, you shall take as plunder for yourselves. And you shall enjoy the spoil of your enemies, which the LORD your God has given you. [15] Thus you shall do to all the cities that are very far from you, which are not cities of the nations here. [16] But in the cities of these peoples that the LORD your God is giving you for an inheritance, you shall save alive nothing that breathes, [17] but you shall devote them to complete destruction,[1] the Hittites and the Amorites, the Canaanites and the Perizzites, the Hivites and the Jebusites, as the LORD your God has commanded, [18] that they may not teach you to do according to all their abominable practices that they have done for their gods, and so you sin against the LORD your God.

[19] "When you besiege a city for a long time, making war against it in order to take it, you shall not destroy its trees by wielding an axe against them. You may eat from them, but you shall not cut them down. Are the trees in the field human, that they should be besieged by you? [20] Only the trees that you know are not trees for food you may destroy and cut down, that you may build siegeworks against the city that makes war with you, until it falls.

Atonement for Unsolved Murders

21 "If in the land that the LORD your God is giving you to possess someone is found slain, lying in the open country, and it is not known who killed him, [2] then your elders and your judges shall come out, and they shall measure the distance to the surrounding cities. [3] And the elders of the city that is nearest to the slain man shall take a heifer that has never been worked and that has not pulled in a yoke. [4] And the elders of that city shall bring the heifer down to a valley with running water, which is neither plowed nor sown, and shall break the heifer's neck there in the valley. [5] Then the priests, the sons of Levi, shall come forward,

for the LORD your God has chosen them to minister to him and to bless in the name of the LORD, and by their word every dispute and every assault shall be settled. [6] And all the elders of that city nearest to the slain man shall wash their hands over the heifer whose neck was broken in the valley, [7] and they shall testify, 'Our hands did not shed this blood, nor did our eyes see it shed. [8] Accept atonement, O LORD, for your people Israel, whom you have redeemed, and do not set the guilt of innocent blood in the midst of your people Israel, so that their blood guilt be atoned for.' [9] So you shall purge the guilt of innocent blood from your midst, when you do what is right in the sight of the LORD.

Marrying Female Captives

[10] "When you go out to war against your enemies, and the LORD your God gives them into your hand and you take them captive, [11] and you see among the captives a beautiful woman, and you desire to take her to be your wife, [12] and you bring her home to your house, she shall shave her head and pare her nails. [13] And she shall take off the clothes in which she was captured and shall remain in your house and lament her father and her mother a full month. After that you may go in to her and be her husband, and she shall be your wife. [14] But if you no longer delight in her, you shall let her go where she wants. But you shall not sell her for money, nor shall you treat her as a slave, since you have humiliated her.

Inheritance Rights of the Firstborn

[15] "If a man has two wives, the one loved and the other unloved, and both the loved and the unloved have borne him children, and if the firstborn son belongs to the unloved,[2] [16] then on the day when he assigns his possessions as an inheritance to his sons, he may not treat the son of the loved as the firstborn in preference to the son of the unloved, who is the firstborn, [17] but he shall acknowledge the firstborn, the son of the unloved, by giving him a double portion of all that he has, for he is the firstfruits of his strength. The right of the firstborn is his.

A Rebellious Son

[18] "If a man has a stubborn and rebellious son who will not obey the voice of his father or the voice of his mother, and, though they discipline him, will not listen to them, [19] then his father

---

[1] That is, set apart (devote) as an offering to the Lord (for destruction) [2] Or *hated*; also verses 16, 17

and his mother shall take hold of him and bring him out to the elders of his city at the gate of the place where he lives, **20** and they shall say to the elders of his city, 'This our son is stubborn and rebellious; he will not obey our voice; he is a glutton and a drunkard.' **21** Then all the men of the city shall stone him to death with stones. So you shall purge the evil from your midst, and all Israel shall hear, and fear.

A Man Hanged on a Tree Is Cursed

22 "And if a man has committed a crime punishable by death and he is put to death, and you hang him on a tree, **23** his body shall not remain all night on the tree, but you shall bury him the same day, for a hanged man is cursed by God. You shall not defile your land that the LORD your God is giving you for an inheritance.

Various Laws

22 "You shall not see your brother's ox or his sheep going astray and ignore them. You shall take them back to your brother. **2** And if he does not live near you and you do not know who he is, you shall bring it home to your house, and it shall stay with you until your brother seeks it. Then you shall restore it to him. **3** And you shall do the same with his donkey or with his garment, or with any lost thing of your brother's, which he loses and you find; you may not ignore it. **4** You shall not see your brother's donkey or his ox fallen down by the way and ignore them. You shall help him to lift them up again.

5 "A woman shall not wear a man's garment, nor shall a man put on a woman's cloak, for whoever does these things is an abomination to the LORD your God.

6 "If you come across a bird's nest in any tree or on the ground, with young ones or eggs and the mother sitting on the young or on the eggs, you shall not take the mother with the young. **7** You shall let the mother go, but the young you may take for yourself, that it may go well with you, and that you may live long.

8 "When you build a new house, you shall make a parapet for your roof, that you may not bring the guilt of blood upon your house, if anyone should fall from it.

9 "You shall not sow your vineyard with two kinds of seed, lest the whole yield be forfeited,[1] the crop that you have sown and the yield of the vineyard. **10** You shall not plow with an ox and a donkey together. **11** You shall not wear cloth of wool and linen mixed together.

12 "You shall make yourself tassels on the four corners of the garment with which you cover yourself.

Laws Concerning Sexual Immorality

13 "If any man takes a wife and goes in to her and then hates her **14** and accuses her of misconduct and brings a bad name upon her, saying, 'I took this woman, and when I came near her, I did not find in her evidence of virginity,' **15** then the father of the young woman and her mother shall take and bring out the evidence of her virginity to the elders of the city in the gate. **16** And the father of the young woman shall say to the elders, 'I gave my daughter to this man to marry, and he hates her; **17** and behold, he has accused her of misconduct, saying, "I did not find in your daughter evidence of virginity." And yet this is the evidence of my daughter's virginity.' And they shall spread the cloak before the elders of the city. **18** Then the elders of that city shall take the man and whip[2] him, **19** and they shall fine him a hundred shekels[3] of silver and give them to the father of the young woman, because he has brought a bad name upon a virgin[4] of Israel. And she shall be his wife. He may not divorce her all his days. **20** But if the thing is true, that evidence of virginity was not found in the young woman, **21** then they shall bring out the young woman to the door of her father's house, and the men of her city shall stone her to death with stones, because she has done an outrageous thing in Israel by whoring in her father's house. So you shall purge the evil from your midst.

22 "If a man is found lying with the wife of another man, both of them shall die, the man who lay with the woman, and the woman. So you shall purge the evil from Israel.

23 "If there is a betrothed virgin, and a man meets her in the city and lies with her, **24** then you shall bring them both out to the gate of that city, and you shall stone them to death with stones, the young woman because she did not cry for help though she was in the city, and the man because he violated his neighbor's wife. So you shall purge the evil from your midst.

25 "But if in the open country a man meets a young woman who is betrothed, and the man seizes her and lies with her, then only the man

---

[1] Hebrew *become holy* [2] Or *discipline* [3] A *shekel* was about 2/5 ounce or 11 grams [4] Or *girl of marriageable age*

who lay with her shall die. ²⁶But you shall do nothing to the young woman; she has committed no offense punishable by death. For this case is like that of a man attacking and murdering his neighbor, ²⁷because he met her in the open country, and though the betrothed young woman cried for help there was no one to rescue her.

²⁸"If a man meets a virgin who is not betrothed, and seizes her and lies with her, and they are found, ²⁹then the man who lay with her shall give to the father of the young woman fifty shekels of silver, and she shall be his wife, because he has violated her. He may not divorce her all his days.

³⁰ ¹"A man shall not take his father's wife, so that he does not uncover his father's nakedness.²

Those Excluded from the Assembly

23 "No one whose testicles are crushed or whose male organ is cut off shall enter the assembly of the Lord.

²"No one born of a forbidden union may enter the assembly of the Lord. Even to the tenth generation, none of his descendants may enter the assembly of the Lord.

³"No Ammonite or Moabite may enter the assembly of the Lord. Even to the tenth generation, none of them may enter the assembly of the Lord forever, ⁴because they did not meet you with bread and with water on the way, when you came out of Egypt, and because they hired against you Balaam the son of Beor from Pethor of Mesopotamia, to curse you. ⁵But the Lord your God would not listen to Balaam; instead the Lord your God turned the curse into a blessing for you, because the Lord your God loved you. ⁶You shall not seek their peace or their prosperity all your days forever.

⁷"You shall not abhor an Edomite, for he is your brother. You shall not abhor an Egyptian, because you were a sojourner in his land. ⁸Children born to them in the third generation may enter the assembly of the Lord.

Uncleanness in the Camp

⁹"When you are encamped against your enemies, then you shall keep yourself from every evil thing.

¹⁰"If any man among you becomes unclean because of a nocturnal emission, then he shall go outside the camp. He shall not come inside the camp, ¹¹but when evening comes, he shall

bathe himself in water, and as the sun sets, he may come inside the camp.

¹²"You shall have a place outside the camp, and you shall go out to it. ¹³And you shall have a trowel with your tools, and when you sit down outside, you shall dig a hole with it and turn back and cover up your excrement. ¹⁴Because the Lord your God walks in the midst of your camp, to deliver you and to give up your enemies before you, therefore your camp must be holy, so that he may not see anything indecent among you and turn away from you.

Miscellaneous Laws

¹⁵"You shall not give up to his master a slave³ who has escaped from his master to you. ¹⁶He shall dwell with you, in your midst, in the place that he shall choose within one of your towns, wherever it suits him. You shall not wrong him.

¹⁷"None of the daughters of Israel shall be a cult prostitute, and none of the sons of Israel shall be a cult prostitute. ¹⁸You shall not bring the fee of a prostitute or the wages of a dog⁴ into the house of the Lord your God in payment for any vow, for both of these are an abomination to the Lord your God.

¹⁹"You shall not charge interest on loans to your brother, interest on money, interest on food, interest on anything that is lent for interest. ²⁰You may charge a foreigner interest, but you may not charge your brother interest, that the Lord your God may bless you in all that you undertake in the land that you are entering to take possession of it.

²¹"If you make a vow to the Lord your God, you shall not delay fulfilling it, for the Lord your God will surely require it of you, and you will be guilty of sin. ²²But if you refrain from vowing, you will not be guilty of sin. ²³You shall be careful to do what has passed your lips, for you have voluntarily vowed to the Lord your God what you have promised with your mouth.

²⁴"If you go into your neighbor's vineyard, you may eat your fill of grapes, as many as you wish, but you shall not put any in your bag. ²⁵If you go into your neighbor's standing grain, you may pluck the ears with your hand, but you shall not put a sickle to your neighbor's standing grain.

Laws Concerning Divorce

24 "When a man takes a wife and marries her, if then she finds no favor in his eyes because he has found some indecency in

---

¹ Ch 23:1 in Hebrew ² Hebrew *uncover his father's skirt* ³ Or *servant*; the Hebrew term *'ebed* designates a range of social and economic roles (see Preface) ⁴ Or *male prostitute*

her, and he writes her a certificate of divorce and puts it in her hand and sends her out of his house, and she departs out of his house, ² and if she goes and becomes another man's wife, ³ and the latter man hates her and writes her a certificate of divorce and puts it in her hand and sends her out of his house, or if the latter man dies, who took her to be his wife, ⁴ then her former husband, who sent her away, may not take her again to be his wife, after she has been defiled, for that is an abomination before the LORD. And you shall not bring sin upon the land that the LORD your God is giving you for an inheritance.

Miscellaneous Laws

⁵ "When a man is newly married, he shall not go out with the army or be liable for any other public duty. He shall be free at home one year to be happy with his wife[1] whom he has taken.

⁶ "No one shall take a mill or an upper millstone in pledge, for that would be taking a life in pledge.

⁷ "If a man is found stealing one of his brothers of the people of Israel, and if he treats him as a slave or sells him, then that thief shall die. So you shall purge the evil from your midst.

⁸ "Take care, in a case of leprous[2] disease, to be very careful to do according to all that the Levitical priests shall direct you. As I commanded them, so you shall be careful to do. ⁹ Remember what the LORD your God did to Miriam on the way as you came out of Egypt.

¹⁰ "When you make your neighbor a loan of any sort, you shall not go into his house to collect his pledge. ¹¹ You shall stand outside, and the man to whom you make the loan shall bring the pledge out to you. ¹² And if he is a poor man, you shall not sleep in his pledge. ¹³ You shall restore to him the pledge as the sun sets, that he may sleep in his cloak and bless you. And it shall be righteousness for you before the LORD your God.

¹⁴ "You shall not oppress a hired worker who is poor and needy, whether he is one of your brothers or one of the sojourners who are in your land within your towns. ¹⁵ You shall give him his wages on the same day, before the sun sets (for he is poor and counts on it), lest he cry against you to the LORD, and you be guilty of sin.

¹⁶ "Fathers shall not be put to death because of their children, nor shall children be put to death because of their fathers. Each one shall be put to death for his own sin.

¹⁷ "You shall not pervert the justice due to the sojourner or to the fatherless, or take a widow's garment in pledge, ¹⁸ but you shall remember that you were a slave in Egypt and the LORD your God redeemed you from there; therefore I command you to do this.

¹⁹ "When you reap your harvest in your field and forget a sheaf in the field, you shall not go back to get it. It shall be for the sojourner, the fatherless, and the widow, that the LORD your God may bless you in all the work of your hands. ²⁰ When you beat your olive trees, you shall not go over them again. It shall be for the sojourner, the fatherless, and the widow. ²¹ When you gather the grapes of your vineyard, you shall not strip it afterward. It shall be for the sojourner, the fatherless, and the widow. ²² You shall remember that you were a slave in the land of Egypt; therefore I command you to do this.

25 "If there is a dispute between men and they come into court and the judges decide between them, acquitting the innocent and condemning the guilty, ² then if the guilty man deserves to be beaten, the judge shall cause him to lie down and be beaten in his presence with a number of stripes in proportion to his offense. ³ Forty stripes may be given him, but not more, lest, if one should go on to beat him with more stripes than these, your brother be degraded in your sight.

⁴ "You shall not muzzle an ox when it is treading out the grain.

Laws Concerning Levirate Marriage

⁵ "If brothers dwell together, and one of them dies and has no son, the wife of the dead man shall not be married outside the family to a stranger. Her husband's brother shall go in to her and take her as his wife and perform the duty of a husband's brother to her. ⁶ And the first son whom she bears shall succeed to the name of his dead brother, that his name may not be blotted out of Israel. ⁷ And if the man does not wish to take his brother's wife, then his brother's wife shall go up to the gate to the elders and say, 'My husband's brother refuses to perpetuate his brother's name in Israel; he will not perform the duty of a husband's brother to me.' ⁸ Then the elders of his city shall call him and speak to him, and if he persists, saying, 'I do not wish

[1] Or to make happy his wife [2] Leprosy was a term for several skin diseases; see Leviticus 13

to take her,' [9] then his brother's wife shall go up to him in the presence of the elders and pull his sandal off his foot and spit in his face. And she shall answer and say, 'So shall it be done to the man who does not build up his brother's house.' [10] And the name of his house[1] shall be called in Israel, 'The house of him who had his sandal pulled off.'

Miscellaneous Laws

[11] "When men fight with one another and the wife of the one draws near to rescue her husband from the hand of him who is beating him and puts out her hand and seizes him by the private parts, [12] then you shall cut off her hand. Your eye shall have no pity.

[13] "You shall not have in your bag two kinds of weights, a large and a small. [14] You shall not have in your house two kinds of measures, a large and a small. [15] A full and fair[2] weight you shall have, a full and fair measure you shall have, that your days may be long in the land that the LORD your God is giving you. [16] For all who do such things, all who act dishonestly, are an abomination to the LORD your God.

[17] "Remember what Amalek did to you on the way as you came out of Egypt, [18] how he attacked you on the way when you were faint and weary, and cut off your tail, those who were lagging behind you, and he did not fear God. [19] Therefore when the LORD your God has given you rest from all your enemies around you, in the land that the LORD your God is giving you for an inheritance to possess, you shall blot out the memory of Amalek from under heaven; you shall not forget.

Offerings of Firstfruits and Tithes

26 "When you come into the land that the LORD your God is giving you for an inheritance and have taken possession of it and live in it, [2] you shall take some of the first of all the fruit of the ground, which you harvest from your land that the LORD your God is giving you, and you shall put it in a basket, and you shall go to the place that the LORD your God will choose, to make his name to dwell there. [3] And you shall go to the priest who is in office at that time and say to him, 'I declare today to the LORD your God that I have come into the land that the LORD swore to our fathers to give us.' [4] Then the priest shall take the basket from your hand and set it down before the altar of the LORD your God.

[5] "And you shall make response before the LORD your God, 'A wandering Aramean was my father. And he went down into Egypt and sojourned there, few in number, and there he became a nation, great, mighty, and populous. [6] And the Egyptians treated us harshly and humiliated us and laid on us hard labor. [7] Then we cried to the LORD, the God of our fathers, and the LORD heard our voice and saw our affliction, our toil, and our oppression. [8] And the LORD brought us out of Egypt with a mighty hand and an outstretched arm, with great deeds of terror,[3] with signs and wonders. [9] And he brought us into this place and gave us this land, a land flowing with milk and honey. [10] And behold, now I bring the first of the fruit of the ground, which you, O LORD, have given me.' And you shall set it down before the LORD your God and worship before the LORD your God. [11] And you shall rejoice in all the good that the LORD your God has given to you and to your house, you, and the Levite, and the sojourner who is among you.

[12] "When you have finished paying all the tithe of your produce in the third year, which is the year of tithing, giving it to the Levite, the sojourner, the fatherless, and the widow, so that they may eat within your towns and be filled, [13] then you shall say before the LORD your God, 'I have removed the sacred portion out of my house, and moreover, I have given it to the Levite, the sojourner, the fatherless, and the widow, according to all your commandment that you have commanded me. I have not transgressed any of your commandments, nor have I forgotten them. [14] I have not eaten of the tithe while I was mourning, or removed any of it while I was unclean, or offered any of it to the dead. I have obeyed the voice of the LORD my God. I have done according to all that you have commanded me. [15] Look down from your holy habitation, from heaven, and bless your people Israel and the ground that you have given us, as you swore to our fathers, a land flowing with milk and honey.'

[16] "This day the LORD your God commands you to do these statutes and rules. You shall therefore be careful to do them with all your heart and with all your soul. [17] You have declared today that the LORD is your God, and that you will walk in his ways, and keep

---

[1] Hebrew *its name* [2] Or *just, or righteous*; twice in this verse [3] Hebrew *with great terror*

his statutes and his commandments and his rules, and will obey his voice. [18] And the LORD has declared today that you are a people for his treasured possession, as he has promised you, and that you are to keep all his commandments, [19] and that he will set you in praise and in fame and in honor high above all nations that he has made, and that you shall be a people holy to the LORD your God, as he promised."

The Altar on Mount Ebal

27 Now Moses and the elders of Israel commanded the people, saying, "Keep the whole commandment that I command you today. [2] And on the day you cross over the Jordan to the land that the LORD your God is giving you, you shall set up large stones and plaster them with plaster. [3] And you shall write on them all the words of this law, when you cross over to enter the land that the LORD your God is giving you, a land flowing with milk and honey, as the LORD, the God of your fathers, has promised you. [4] And when you have crossed over the Jordan, you shall set up these stones, concerning which I command you today, on Mount Ebal, and you shall plaster them with plaster. [5] And there you shall build an altar to the LORD your God, an altar of stones. You shall wield no iron tool on them; [6] you shall build an altar to the LORD your God of uncut[1] stones. And you shall offer burnt offerings on it to the LORD your God, [7] and you shall sacrifice peace offerings and shall eat there, and you shall rejoice before the LORD your God. [8] And you shall write on the stones all the words of this law very plainly."

Curses from Mount Ebal

[9] Then Moses and the Levitical priests said to all Israel, "Keep silence and hear, O Israel: this day you have become the people of the LORD your God. [10] You shall therefore obey the voice of the LORD your God, keeping his commandments and his statutes, which I command you today."

[11] That day Moses charged the people, saying, [12] "When you have crossed over the Jordan, these shall stand on Mount Gerizim to bless the people: Simeon, Levi, Judah, Issachar, Joseph, and Benjamin. [13] And these shall stand on Mount Ebal for the curse: Reuben, Gad, Asher, Zebulun, Dan, and Naphtali. [14] And the Levites shall declare to all the men of Israel in a loud voice:

[15] "'Cursed be the man who makes a carved or cast metal image, an abomination to the LORD, a thing made by the hands of a craftsman, and sets it up in secret.' And all the people shall answer and say, 'Amen.'

[16] "'Cursed be anyone who dishonors his father or his mother.' And all the people shall say, 'Amen.'

[17] "'Cursed be anyone who moves his neighbor's landmark.' And all the people shall say, 'Amen.'

[18] "'Cursed be anyone who misleads a blind man on the road.' And all the people shall say, 'Amen.'

[19] "'Cursed be anyone who perverts the justice due to the sojourner, the fatherless, and the widow.' And all the people shall say, 'Amen.'

[20] "'Cursed be anyone who lies with his father's wife, because he has uncovered his father's nakedness.'[2] And all the people shall say, 'Amen.'

[21] "'Cursed be anyone who lies with any kind of animal.' And all the people shall say, 'Amen.'

[22] "'Cursed be anyone who lies with his sister, whether the daughter of his father or the daughter of his mother.' And all the people shall say, 'Amen.'

[23] "'Cursed be anyone who lies with his mother-in-law.' And all the people shall say, 'Amen.'

[24] "'Cursed be anyone who strikes down his neighbor in secret.' And all the people shall say, 'Amen.'

[25] "'Cursed be anyone who takes a bribe to shed innocent blood.' And all the people shall say, 'Amen.'

[26] "'Cursed be anyone who does not confirm the words of this law by doing them.' And all the people shall say, 'Amen.'

Blessings for Obedience

28 "And if you faithfully obey the voice of the LORD your God, being careful to do all his commandments that I command you today, the LORD your God will set you high above all the nations of the earth. [2] And all these blessings shall come upon you and overtake you, if you obey the voice of the LORD your God. [3] Blessed shall you be in the city, and blessed shall you be in the field. [4] Blessed shall be the fruit of your womb and the fruit of your ground and the fruit of your cattle, the increase of your herds and the young of your flock. [5] Blessed shall be your basket and your knead-

---

[1] Hebrew *whole*   [2] Hebrew *uncovered his father's skirt*

ing bowl. [6] Blessed shall you be when you come in, and blessed shall you be when you go out.

[7] "The LORD will cause your enemies who rise against you to be defeated before you. They shall come out against you one way and flee before you seven ways. [8] The LORD will command the blessing on you in your barns and in all that you undertake. And he will bless you in the land that the LORD your God is giving you. [9] The LORD will establish you as a people holy to himself, as he has sworn to you, if you keep the commandments of the LORD your God and walk in his ways. [10] And all the peoples of the earth shall see that you are called by the name of the LORD, and they shall be afraid of you. [11] And the LORD will make you abound in prosperity, in the fruit of your womb and in the fruit of your livestock and in the fruit of your ground, within the land that the LORD swore to your fathers to give you. [12] The LORD will open to you his good treasury, the heavens, to give the rain to your land in its season and to bless all the work of your hands. And you shall lend to many nations, but you shall not borrow. [13] And the LORD will make you the head and not the tail, and you shall only go up and not down, if you obey the commandments of the LORD your God, which I command you today, being careful to do them, [14] and if you do not turn aside from any of the words that I command you today, to the right hand or to the left, to go after other gods to serve them.

Curses for Disobedience

[15] "But if you will not obey the voice of the LORD your God or be careful to do all his commandments and his statutes that I command you today, then all these curses shall come upon you and overtake you. [16] Cursed shall you be in the city, and cursed shall you be in the field. [17] Cursed shall be your basket and your kneading bowl. [18] Cursed shall be the fruit of your womb and the fruit of your ground, the increase of your herds and the young of your flock. [19] Cursed shall you be when you come in, and cursed shall you be when you go out.

[20] "The LORD will send on you curses, confusion, and frustration in all that you undertake to do, until you are destroyed and perish quickly on account of the evil of your deeds, because you have forsaken me. [21] The LORD will make the pestilence stick to you until he has consumed you off the land that you are entering to take possession of it. [22] The LORD will strike you with wasting disease and with fever, inflammation and fiery heat, and with drought[1] and with blight and with mildew. They shall pursue you until you perish. [23] And the heavens over your head shall be bronze, and the earth under you shall be iron. [24] The LORD will make the rain of your land powder. From heaven dust shall come down on you until you are destroyed.

[25] "The LORD will cause you to be defeated before your enemies. You shall go out one way against them and flee seven ways before them. And you shall be a horror to all the kingdoms of the earth. [26] And your dead body shall be food for all birds of the air and for the beasts of the earth, and there shall be no one to frighten them away. [27] The LORD will strike you with the boils of Egypt, and with tumors and scabs and itch, of which you cannot be healed. [28] The LORD will strike you with madness and blindness and confusion of mind, [29] and you shall grope at noonday, as the blind grope in darkness, and you shall not prosper in your ways.[2] And you shall be only oppressed and robbed continually, and there shall be no one to help you. [30] You shall betroth a wife, but another man shall ravish her. You shall build a house, but you shall not dwell in it. You shall plant a vineyard, but you shall not enjoy its fruit. [31] Your ox shall be slaughtered before your eyes, but you shall not eat any of it. Your donkey shall be seized before your face, but shall not be restored to you. Your sheep shall be given to your enemies, but there shall be no one to help you. [32] Your sons and your daughters shall be given to another people, while your eyes look on and fail with longing for them all day long, but you shall be helpless. [33] A nation that you have not known shall eat up the fruit of your ground and of all your labors, and you shall be only oppressed and crushed continually, [34] so that you are driven mad by the sights that your eyes see. [35] The LORD will strike you on the knees and on the legs with grievous boils of which you cannot be healed, from the sole of your foot to the crown of your head.

[36] "The LORD will bring you and your king whom you set over you to a nation that neither you nor your fathers have known. And there you shall serve other gods of wood and stone. [37] And you shall become a horror, a proverb, and a byword among all the peoples where the

---

[1] Or sword   [2] Or shall not succeed in finding your ways

LORD will lead you away. [38] You shall carry much seed into the field and shall gather in little, for the locust shall consume it. [39] You shall plant vineyards and dress them, but you shall neither drink of the wine nor gather the grapes, for the worm shall eat them. [40] You shall have olive trees throughout all your territory, but you shall not anoint yourself with the oil, for your olives shall drop off. [41] You shall father sons and daughters, but they shall not be yours, for they shall go into captivity. [42] The cricket[1] shall possess all your trees and the fruit of your ground. [43] The sojourner who is among you shall rise higher and higher above you, and you shall come down lower and lower. [44] He shall lend to you, and you shall not lend to him. He shall be the head, and you shall be the tail.

[45] "All these curses shall come upon you and pursue you and overtake you till you are destroyed, because you did not obey the voice of the LORD your God, to keep his commandments and his statutes that he commanded you. [46] They shall be a sign and a wonder against you and your offspring forever. [47] Because you did not serve the LORD your God with joyfulness and gladness of heart, because of the abundance of all things, [48] therefore you shall serve your enemies whom the LORD will send against you, in hunger and thirst, in nakedness, and lacking everything. And he will put a yoke of iron on your neck until he has destroyed you. [49] The LORD will bring a nation against you from far away, from the end of the earth, swooping down like the eagle, a nation whose language you do not understand, [50] a hard-faced nation who shall not respect the old or show mercy to the young. [51] It shall eat the offspring of your cattle and the fruit of your ground, until you are destroyed; it also shall not leave you grain, wine, or oil, the increase of your herds or the young of your flock, until they have caused you to perish.

[52] "They shall besiege you in all your towns, until your high and fortified walls, in which you trusted, come down throughout all your land. And they shall besiege you in all your towns throughout all your land, which the LORD your God has given you. [53] And you shall eat the fruit of your womb, the flesh of your sons and daughters, whom the LORD your God has given you, in the siege and in the distress with which your enemies shall distress you. [54] The man who is the most tender and refined among you will begrudge food to his brother, to the wife he embraces,[2] and to the last of the children whom he has left, [55] so that he will not give to any of them any of the flesh of his children whom he is eating, because he has nothing else left, in the siege and in the distress with which your enemy shall distress you in all your towns. [56] The most tender and refined woman among you, who would not venture to set the sole of her foot on the ground because she is so delicate and tender, will begrudge to the husband she embraces,[3] to her son and to her daughter, [57] her afterbirth that comes out from between her feet and her children whom she bears, because lacking everything she will eat them secretly, in the siege and in the distress with which your enemy shall distress you in your towns.

[58] "If you are not careful to do all the words of this law that are written in this book, that you may fear this glorious and awesome name, the LORD your God, [59] then the LORD will bring on you and your offspring extraordinary afflictions, afflictions severe and lasting, and sicknesses grievous and lasting. [60] And he will bring upon you again all the diseases of Egypt, of which you were afraid, and they shall cling to you. [61] Every sickness also and every affliction that is not recorded in the book of this law, the LORD will bring upon you, until you are destroyed. [62] Whereas you were as numerous as the stars of heaven, you shall be left few in number, because you did not obey the voice of the LORD your God. [63] And as the LORD took delight in doing you good and multiplying you, so the LORD will take delight in bringing ruin upon you and destroying you. And you shall be plucked off the land that you are entering to take possession of it.

[64] "And the LORD will scatter you among all peoples, from one end of the earth to the other, and there you shall serve other gods of wood and stone, which neither you nor your fathers have known. [65] And among these nations you shall find no respite, and there shall be no resting place for the sole of your foot, but the LORD will give you there a trembling heart and failing eyes and a languishing soul. [66] Your life shall hang in doubt before you. Night and day you shall be in dread and have no assurance of your life. [67] In the morning you shall say, 'If only it were evening!' and at evening you shall say, 'If only it were morning!' because of the dread that your heart shall feel, and the sights that

[1] Identity uncertain [2] Hebrew *the wife of his bosom* [3] Hebrew *the husband of her bosom*

your eyes shall see. ⁶⁸ And the LORD will bring you back in ships to Egypt, a journey that I promised that you should never make again; and there you shall offer yourselves for sale to your enemies as male and female slaves, but there will be no buyer."

The Covenant Renewed in Moab

29 ¹These are the words of the covenant that the LORD commanded Moses to make with the people of Israel in the land of Moab, besides the covenant that he had made with them at Horeb.

^{2 2} And Moses summoned all Israel and said to them: "You have seen all that the LORD did before your eyes in the land of Egypt, to Pharaoh and to all his servants and to all his land, ³ the great trials that your eyes saw, the signs, and those great wonders. ⁴ But to this day the LORD has not given you a heart to understand or eyes to see or ears to hear. ⁵ I have led you forty years in the wilderness. Your clothes have not worn out on you, and your sandals have not worn off your feet. ⁶ You have not eaten bread, and you have not drunk wine or strong drink, that you may know that I am the LORD your God. ⁷ And when you came to this place, Sihon the king of Heshbon and Og the king of Bashan came out against us to battle, but we defeated them. ⁸ We took their land and gave it for an inheritance to the Reubenites, the Gadites, and the half-tribe of the Manassites. ⁹ Therefore keep the words of this covenant and do them, that you may prosper³ in all that you do.

¹⁰ "You are standing today, all of you, before the LORD your God: the heads of your tribes,⁴ your elders, and your officers, all the men of Israel, ¹¹ your little ones, your wives, and the sojourner who is in your camp, from the one who chops your wood to the one who draws your water, ¹² so that you may enter into the sworn covenant of the LORD your God, which the LORD your God is making with you today, ¹³ that he may establish you today as his people, and that he may be your God, as he promised you, and as he swore to your fathers, to Abraham, to Isaac, and to Jacob. ¹⁴ It is not with you alone that I am making this sworn covenant, ¹⁵ but with whoever is standing here with us today before the LORD our God, and with whoever is not here with us today.

¹⁶ "You know how we lived in the land of Egypt, and how we came through the midst of the nations through which you passed. ¹⁷ And you have seen their detestable things, their idols of wood and stone, of silver and gold, which were among them. ¹⁸ Beware lest there be among you a man or woman or clan or tribe whose heart is turning away today from the LORD our God to go and serve the gods of those nations. Beware lest there be among you a root bearing poisonous and bitter fruit, ¹⁹ one who, when he hears the words of this sworn covenant, blesses himself in his heart, saying, 'I shall be safe, though I walk in the stubbornness of my heart.' This will lead to the sweeping away of moist and dry alike. ²⁰ The LORD will not be willing to forgive him, but rather the anger of the LORD and his jealousy will smoke against that man, and the curses written in this book will settle upon him, and the LORD will blot out his name from under heaven. ²¹ And the LORD will single him out from all the tribes of Israel for calamity, in accordance with all the curses of the covenant written in this Book of the Law. ²² And the next generation, your children who rise up after you, and the foreigner who comes from a far land, will say, when they see the afflictions of that land and the sicknesses with which the LORD has made it sick— ²³ the whole land burned out with brimstone and salt, nothing sown and nothing growing, where no plant can sprout, an overthrow like that of Sodom and Gomorrah, Admah, and Zeboiim, which the LORD overthrew in his anger and wrath— ²⁴ all the nations will say, 'Why has the LORD done thus to this land? What caused the heat of this great anger?' ²⁵ Then people will say, 'It is because they abandoned the covenant of the LORD, the God of their fathers, which he made with them when he brought them out of the land of Egypt, ²⁶ and went and served other gods and worshiped them, gods whom they had not known and whom he had not allotted to them. ²⁷ Therefore the anger of the LORD was kindled against this land, bringing upon it all the curses written in this book, ²⁸ and the LORD uprooted them from their land in anger and fury and great wrath, and cast them into another land, as they are this day.'

²⁹ "The secret things belong to the LORD our God, but the things that are revealed belong to us and to our children forever, that we may do all the words of this law.

¹ Ch 28:69 in Hebrew ² Ch 29:1 in Hebrew ³ Or *deal wisely* ⁴ Septuagint, Syriac; Hebrew *your heads, your tribes*

Repentance and Forgiveness

30 "And when all these things come upon you, the blessing and the curse, which I have set before you, and you call them to mind among all the nations where the LORD your God has driven you, ² and return to the LORD your God, you and your children, and obey his voice in all that I command you today, with all your heart and with all your soul, ³ then the LORD your God will restore your fortunes and have mercy on you, and he will gather you again from all the peoples where the LORD your God has scattered you. ⁴ If your outcasts are in the uttermost parts of heaven, from there the LORD your God will gather you, and from there he will take you. ⁵ And the LORD your God will bring you into the land that your fathers possessed, that you may possess it. And he will make you more prosperous and numerous than your fathers. ⁶ And the LORD your God will circumcise your heart and the heart of your offspring, so that you will love the LORD your God with all your heart and with all your soul, that you may live. ⁷ And the LORD your God will put all these curses on your foes and enemies who persecuted you. ⁸ And you shall again obey the voice of the LORD and keep all his commandments that I command you today. ⁹ The LORD your God will make you abundantly prosperous in all the work of your hand, in the fruit of your womb and in the fruit of your cattle and in the fruit of your ground. For the LORD will again take delight in prospering you, as he took delight in your fathers, ¹⁰ when you obey the voice of the LORD your God, to keep his commandments and his statutes that are written in this Book of the Law, when you turn to the LORD your God with all your heart and with all your soul.

The Choice of Life and Death

¹¹ "For this commandment that I command you today is not too hard for you, neither is it far off. ¹² It is not in heaven, that you should say, 'Who will ascend to heaven for us and bring it to us, that we may hear it and do it?' ¹³ Neither is it beyond the sea, that you should say, 'Who will go over the sea for us and bring it to us, that we may hear it and do it?' ¹⁴ But the word is very near you. It is in your mouth and in your heart, so that you can do it.

¹⁵ "See, I have set before you today life and good, death and evil. ¹⁶ If you obey the commandments of the LORD your God[1] that I command you today, by loving the LORD your God, by walking in his ways, and by keeping his commandments and his statutes and his rules,[2] then you shall live and multiply, and the LORD your God will bless you in the land that you are entering to take possession of it. ¹⁷ But if your heart turns away, and you will not hear, but are drawn away to worship other gods and serve them, ¹⁸ I declare to you today, that you shall surely perish. You shall not live long in the land that you are going over the Jordan to enter and possess. ¹⁹ I call heaven and earth to witness against you today, that I have set before you life and death, blessing and curse. Therefore choose life, that you and your offspring may live, ²⁰ loving the LORD your God, obeying his voice and holding fast to him, for he is your life and length of days, that you may dwell in the land that the LORD swore to your fathers, to Abraham, to Isaac, and to Jacob, to give them."

Joshua to Succeed Moses

31 So Moses continued to speak these words to all Israel. ² And he said to them, "I am 120 years old today. I am no longer able to go out and come in. The LORD has said to me, 'You shall not go over this Jordan.' ³ The LORD your God himself will go over before you. He will destroy these nations before you, so that you shall dispossess them, and Joshua will go over at your head, as the LORD has spoken. ⁴ And the LORD will do to them as he did to Sihon and Og, the kings of the Amorites, and to their land, when he destroyed them. ⁵ And the LORD will give them over to you, and you shall do to them according to the whole commandment that I have commanded you. ⁶ Be strong and courageous. Do not fear or be in dread of them, for it is the LORD your God who goes with you. He will not leave you or forsake you."

⁷ Then Moses summoned Joshua and said to him in the sight of all Israel, "Be strong and courageous, for you shall go with this people into the land that the LORD has sworn to their fathers to give them, and you shall put them in possession of it. ⁸ It is the LORD who goes before you. He will be with you; he will not leave you or forsake you. Do not fear or be dismayed."

¹ Septuagint; Hebrew lacks *If you obey the commandments of the LORD your God* ² Or *his just decrees*

The Reading of the Law

9 Then Moses wrote this law and gave it to the priests, the sons of Levi, who carried the ark of the covenant of the LORD, and to all the elders of Israel. 10 And Moses commanded them, "At the end of every seven years, at the set time in the year of release, at the Feast of Booths, 11 when all Israel comes to appear before the LORD your God at the place that he will choose, you shall read this law before all Israel in their hearing. 12 Assemble the people, men, women, and little ones, and the sojourner within your towns, that they may hear and learn to fear the LORD your God, and be careful to do all the words of this law, 13 and that their children, who have not known it, may hear and learn to fear the LORD your God, as long as you live in the land that you are going over the Jordan to possess."

Joshua Commissioned to Lead Israel

14 And the LORD said to Moses, "Behold, the days approach when you must die. Call Joshua and present yourselves in the tent of meeting, that I may commission him." And Moses and Joshua went and presented themselves in the tent of meeting. 15 And the LORD appeared in the tent in a pillar of cloud. And the pillar of cloud stood over the entrance of the tent.

16 And the LORD said to Moses, "Behold, you are about to lie down with your fathers. Then this people will rise and whore after the foreign gods among them in the land that they are entering, and they will forsake me and break my covenant that I have made with them. 17 Then my anger will be kindled against them in that day, and I will forsake them and hide my face from them, and they will be devoured. And many evils and troubles will come upon them, so that they will say in that day, 'Have not these evils come upon us because our God is not among us?' 18 And I will surely hide my face in that day because of all the evil that they have done, because they have turned to other gods. 19 "Now therefore write this song and teach it to the people of Israel. Put it in their mouths, that this song may be a witness for me against the people of Israel. 20 For when I have brought them into the land flowing with milk and honey, which I swore to give to their fathers, and they have eaten and are full and grown fat, they will turn to other gods and serve them, and despise me and break my covenant. 21 And when

many evils and troubles have come upon them, this song shall confront them as a witness (for it will live unforgotten in the mouths of their offspring). For I know what they are inclined to do even today, before I have brought them into the land that I swore to give." 22 So Moses wrote this song the same day and taught it to the people of Israel.

23 And the LORD[1] commissioned Joshua the son of Nun and said, "Be strong and courageous, for you shall bring the people of Israel into the land that I swore to give them. I will be with you."

24 When Moses had finished writing the words of this law in a book to the very end, 25 Moses commanded the Levites who carried the ark of the covenant of the LORD, 26 "Take this Book of the Law and put it by the side of the ark of the covenant of the LORD your God, that it may be there for a witness against you. 27 For I know how rebellious and stubborn you are. Behold, even today while I am yet alive with you, you have been rebellious against the LORD. How much more after my death! 28 Assemble to me all the elders of your tribes and your officers, that I may speak these words in their ears and call heaven and earth to witness against them. 29 For I know that after my death you will surely act corruptly and turn aside from the way that I have commanded you. And in the days to come evil will befall you, because you will do what is evil in the sight of the LORD, provoking him to anger through the work of your hands."

The Song of Moses

30 Then Moses spoke the words of this song until they were finished, in the ears of all the assembly of Israel:

32 "Give ear, O heavens, and I will speak,
　　and let the earth hear the words of my mouth.
2　May my teaching drop as the rain,
　　my speech distill as the dew,
　like gentle rain upon the tender grass,
　　and like showers upon the herb.
3　For I will proclaim the name of the LORD;
　　ascribe greatness to our God!

4　"The Rock, his work is perfect,
　　for all his ways are justice.
　A God of faithfulness and without iniquity,
　　just and upright is he.

1 Hebrew he

5 They have dealt corruptly with him;
  they are no longer his children because
    they are blemished;
  they are a crooked and twisted genera-
    tion.
6 Do you thus repay the LORD,
  you foolish and senseless people?
  Is not he your father, who created you,
    who made you and established you?
7 Remember the days of old;
  consider the years of many generations;
  ask your father, and he will show you,
    your elders, and they will tell you.
8 When the Most High gave to the nations
    their inheritance,
  when he divided mankind,
  he fixed the borders[1] of the peoples
    according to the number of the sons of
    God.[2]
9 But the LORD's portion is his people,
  Jacob his allotted heritage.

10 "He found him in a desert land,
    and in the howling waste of the wilder-
      ness;
  he encircled him, he cared for him,
    he kept him as the apple of his eye.
11 Like an eagle that stirs up its nest,
    that flutters over its young,
  spreading out its wings, catching them,
    bearing them on its pinions,
12 the LORD alone guided him,
    no foreign god was with him.
13 He made him ride on the high places of
    the land,
  and he ate the produce of the field,
  and he suckled him with honey out of the
    rock,
    and oil out of the flinty rock.
14 Curds from the herd, and milk from the
    flock,
    with fat[3] of lambs,
  rams of Bashan and goats,
    with the very finest[4] of the wheat—
    and you drank foaming wine made
      from the blood of the grape.

15 "But Jeshurun grew fat, and kicked;
    you grew fat, stout, and sleek;
  then he forsook God who made him
    and scoffed at the Rock of his salvation.

16 They stirred him to jealousy with strange
    gods;
  with abominations they provoked him
    to anger.
17 They sacrificed to demons that were no
    gods,
  to gods they had never known,
  to new gods that had come recently,
    whom your fathers had never dreaded.
18 You were unmindful of the Rock that bore[5]
    you,
  and you forgot the God who gave you
    birth.

19 "The LORD saw it and spurned them,
    because of the provocation of his sons
      and his daughters.
20 And he said, 'I will hide my face from them;
    I will see what their end will be,
  for they are a perverse generation,
    children in whom is no faithfulness.
21 They have made me jealous with what is
    no god;
    they have provoked me to anger with
      their idols.
  So I will make them jealous with those
    who are no people;
    I will provoke them to anger with a
      foolish nation.
22 For a fire is kindled by my anger,
    and it burns to the depths of Sheol,
  devours the earth and its increase,
    and sets on fire the foundations of the
      mountains.

23 "'And I will heap disasters upon them;
    I will spend my arrows on them;
24 they shall be wasted with hunger,
    and devoured by plague
    and poisonous pestilence;
  I will send the teeth of beasts against them,
    with the venom of things that crawl in
      the dust.
25 Outdoors the sword shall bereave,
    and indoors terror,
  for young man and woman alike,
    the nursing child with the man of gray
      hairs.
26 I would have said, "I will cut them to
      pieces;
    I will wipe them from human memory,"
27 had I not feared provocation by the enemy,
    lest their adversaries should misunder-
      stand,

[1] Or territories [2] Compare Dead Sea Scroll, Septuagint; Masoretic Text sons of Israel [3] That is, with the best [4] Hebrew with the kidney fat [5] Or fathered

lest they should say, "Our hand is triumphant,
   it was not the LORD who did all this."'

28 "For they are a nation void of counsel,
      and there is no understanding in them.
29 If they were wise, they would understand this;
      they would discern their latter end!
30 How could one have chased a thousand,
      and two have put ten thousand to flight,
   unless their Rock had sold them,
      and the LORD had given them up?
31 For their rock is not as our Rock;
      our enemies are by themselves.
32 For their vine comes from the vine of Sodom
      and from the fields of Gomorrah;
   their grapes are grapes of poison;
      their clusters are bitter;
33 their wine is the poison of serpents
      and the cruel venom of asps.

34 "'Is not this laid up in store with me,
      sealed up in my treasuries?
35 Vengeance is mine, and recompense,[1]
      for the time when their foot shall slip;
   for the day of their calamity is at hand,
      and their doom comes swiftly.'
36 For the LORD will vindicate[2] his people
      and have compassion on his servants,
   when he sees that their power is gone
      and there is none remaining, bond or free.
37 Then he will say, 'Where are their gods,
      the rock in which they took refuge,
38 who ate the fat of their sacrifices
      and drank the wine of their drink offering?
   Let them rise up and help you;
      let them be your protection!

39 "'See now that I, even I, am he,
      and there is no god beside me;
   I kill and I make alive;
      I wound and I heal;
      and there is none that can deliver out of my hand.
40 For I lift up my hand to heaven
      and swear, As I live forever,
41 if I sharpen my flashing sword[3]
      and my hand takes hold on judgment,

I will take vengeance on my adversaries
      and will repay those who hate me.
42 I will make my arrows drunk with blood,
      and my sword shall devour flesh—
   with the blood of the slain and the captives,
      from the long-haired heads of the enemy.'

43 "Rejoice with him, O heavens;[4]
      bow down to him, all gods,[5]
   for he avenges the blood of his children[6]
      and takes vengeance on his adversaries.
   He repays those who hate him[7]
      and cleanses[8] his people's land."[9]

44 Moses came and recited all the words of this song in the hearing of the people, he and Joshua[10] the son of Nun. 45 And when Moses had finished speaking all these words to all Israel, 46 he said to them, "Take to heart all the words by which I am warning you today, that you may command them to your children, that they may be careful to do all the words of this law. 47 For it is no empty word for you, but your very life, and by this word you shall live long in the land that you are going over the Jordan to possess."

Moses' Death Foretold

48 That very day the LORD spoke to Moses, 49 "Go up this mountain of the Abarim, Mount Nebo, which is in the land of Moab, opposite Jericho, and view the land of Canaan, which I am giving to the people of Israel for a possession. 50 And die on the mountain which you go up, and be gathered to your people, as Aaron your brother died in Mount Hor and was gathered to his people, 51 because you broke faith with me in the midst of the people of Israel at the waters of Meribah-kadesh, in the wilderness of Zin, and because you did not treat me as holy in the midst of the people of Israel. 52 For you shall see the land before you, but you shall not go there, into the land that I am giving to the people of Israel."

Moses' Final Blessing on Israel

33 This is the blessing with which Moses the man of God blessed the people of Israel before his death. 2 He said,

   "The LORD came from Sinai
      and dawned from Seir upon us;[11]
   he shone forth from Mount Paran;

---

[1] Septuagint *and I will repay* [2] Septuagint *judge* [3] Hebrew *the lightning of my sword* [4] Dead Sea Scroll, Septuagint; Masoretic Text *Rejoice his people, O nations* [5] Masoretic Text lacks *bow down to him, all gods* [6] Dead Sea Scroll, Septuagint; Masoretic Text *servants* [7] Dead Sea Scroll, Septuagint; Masoretic Text lacks *He repays those who hate him* [8] Or *atones for* [9] Septuagint, Vulgate; Hebrew *his land his people* [10] Septuagint, Syriac, Vulgate; Hebrew *Hoshea* [11] Septuagint, Syriac, Vulgate; Hebrew *them*

he came from the ten thousands of holy
  ones,
    with flaming fire[1] at his right hand.
3 Yes, he loved his people,[2]
      all his holy ones were in his[3] hand;
    so they followed[4] in your steps,
      receiving direction from you,
4 when Moses commanded us a law,
      as a possession for the assembly of Jacob.
5 Thus the LORD[5] became king in Jeshurun,
      when the heads of the people were
        gathered,
      all the tribes of Israel together.

6 "Let Reuben live, and not die,
      but let his men be few."

7 And this he said of Judah:

  "Hear, O LORD, the voice of Judah,
      and bring him in to his people.
    With your hands contend[6] for him,
      and be a help against his adversaries."

8 And of Levi he said,

  "Give to Levi[7] your Thummim,
      and your Urim to your godly one,
    whom you tested at Massah,
      with whom you quarreled at the waters
        of Meribah;
9 who said of his father and mother,
      'I regard them not';
    he disowned his brothers
      and ignored his children.
    For they observed your word
      and kept your covenant.
10 They shall teach Jacob your rules
      and Israel your law;
    they shall put incense before you
      and whole burnt offerings on your altar.
11 Bless, O LORD, his substance,
      and accept the work of his hands;
    crush the loins of his adversaries,
      of those who hate him, that they rise
        not again."

12 Of Benjamin he said,

  "The beloved of the LORD dwells in safety.
    The High God[8] surrounds him all day
      long,
      and dwells between his shoulders."

13 And of Joseph he said,

"Blessed by the LORD be his land,
    with the choicest gifts of heaven above,[9]
    and of the deep that crouches
      beneath,
14 with the choicest fruits of the sun
      and the rich yield of the months,
15 with the finest produce of the ancient
        mountains
      and the abundance of the everlasting
        hills,
16 with the best gifts of the earth and its full-
        ness
      and the favor of him who dwells in the
        bush.
    May these rest on the head of Joseph,
      on the pate of him who is prince among
        his brothers.
17 A firstborn bull[10]—he has majesty,
      and his horns are the horns of a wild óx;
    with them he shall gore the peoples,
      all of them, to the ends of the earth;
    they are the ten thousands of Ephraim,
      and they are the thousands of
        Manasseh."

18 And of Zebulun he said,

"Rejoice, Zebulun, in your going out,
      and Issachar, in your tents.
19 They shall call peoples to their moun-
        tain;
      there they offer right sacrifices;
    for they draw from the abundance of the
        seas
      and the hidden treasures of the sand."

20 And of Gad he said,

"Blessed be he who enlarges Gad!
    Gad crouches like a lion;
      he tears off arm and scalp.
21 He chose the best of the land for himself,
      for there a commander's portion was
        reserved;
    and he came with the heads of the peo-
        ple,
      with Israel he executed the justice of the
        LORD,
      and his judgments for Israel."

22 And of Dan he said,

"Dan is a lion's cub
      that leaps from Bashan."

---

[1] The meaning of the Hebrew word is uncertain [2] Septuagint; Hebrew *peoples* [3] Hebrew *your* [4] The meaning of the Hebrew word is uncertain [5] Hebrew *Thus he* [6] Probable reading; Hebrew *With his hands he contended* [7] Dead Sea Scroll, Septuagint; Masoretic Text lacks *Give to Levi* [8] Septuagint; Hebrew *dwells in safety by him. He* [9] Two Hebrew manuscripts and Targum; Hebrew *with the dew* [10] Dead Sea Scroll, Septuagint, Samaritan; Masoretic Text *His firstborn bull*

[23] And of Naphtali he said,

> "O Naphtali, sated with favor,
>> and full of the blessing of the LORD,
>> possess the lake[1] and the south."

[24] And of Asher he said,

> "Most blessed of sons be Asher;
>> let him be the favorite of his brothers,
>> and let him dip his foot in oil.
>
> [25] Your bars shall be iron and bronze,
>> and as your days, so shall your strength
>> be.
>
> [26] "There is none like God, O Jeshurun,
>> who rides through the heavens to your
>> help,
>> through the skies in his majesty.
>
> [27] The eternal God is your dwelling place,[2]
>> and underneath are the everlasting
>> arms.[3]
>> And he thrust out the enemy before you
>> and said, 'Destroy.'
>
> [28] So Israel lived in safety,
>> Jacob lived alone,[4]
>> in a land of grain and wine,
>> whose heavens drop down dew.
>
> [29] Happy are you, O Israel! Who is like you,
>> a people saved by the LORD,
>> the shield of your help,
>> and the sword of your triumph!
>> Your enemies shall come fawning to you,
>> and you shall tread upon their backs."

The Death of Moses

34 Then Moses went up from the plains of Moab to Mount Nebo, to the top of Pisgah, which is opposite Jericho. And the LORD showed him all the land, Gilead as far as Dan, [2] all Naphtali, the land of Ephraim and Manasseh, all the land of Judah as far as the western sea, [3] the Negeb, and the Plain, that is, the Valley of Jericho the city of palm trees, as far as Zoar. [4] And the LORD said to him, "This is the land of which I swore to Abraham, to Isaac, and to Jacob, 'I will give it to your offspring.' I have let you see it with your eyes, but you shall not go over there." [5] So Moses the servant of the LORD died there in the land of Moab, according to the word of the LORD, [6] and he buried him in the valley in the land of Moab opposite Beth-peor; but no one knows the place of his burial to this day. [7] Moses was 120 years old when he died. His eye was undimmed, and his vigor unabated. [8] And the people of Israel wept for Moses in the plains of Moab thirty days. Then the days of weeping and mourning for Moses were ended.

[9] And Joshua the son of Nun was full of the spirit of wisdom, for Moses had laid his hands on him. So the people of Israel obeyed him and did as the LORD had commanded Moses. [10] And there has not arisen a prophet since in Israel like Moses, whom the LORD knew face to face, [11] none like him for all the signs and the wonders that the LORD sent him to do in the land of Egypt, to Pharaoh and to all his servants and to all his land, [12] and for all the mighty power and all the great deeds of terror that Moses did in the sight of all Israel.

---

[1] Or west [2] Or a dwelling place [3] Revocalization of verse 27 yields He subdues the ancient gods, and shatters the forces of old [4] Hebrew the abode of Jacob was alone

JOSHUA

God Commissions Joshua

1 After the death of Moses the servant of the Lord, the Lord said to Joshua the son of Nun, Moses' assistant, [2] "Moses my servant is dead. Now therefore arise, go over this Jordan, you and all this people, into the land that I am giving to them, to the people of Israel. [3] Every place that the sole of your foot will tread upon I have given to you, just as I promised to Moses. [4] From the wilderness and this Lebanon as far as the great river, the river Euphrates, all the land of the Hittites to the Great Sea toward the going down of the sun shall be your territory. [5] No man shall be able to stand before you all the days of your life. Just as I was with Moses, so I will be with you. I will not leave you or forsake you. [6] Be strong and courageous, for you shall cause this people to inherit the land that I swore to their fathers to give them. [7] Only be strong and very courageous, being careful to do according to all the law that Moses my servant commanded you. Do not turn from it to the right hand or to the left, that you may have good success[1] wherever you go. [8] This Book of the Law shall not depart from your mouth, but you shall meditate on it day and night, so that you may be careful to do according to all that is written in it. For then you will make your way prosperous, and then you will have good success. [9] Have I not commanded you? Be strong and courageous. Do not be frightened, and do not be dismayed, for the Lord your God is with you wherever you go."

Joshua Assumes Command

[10] And Joshua commanded the officers of the people, [11] "Pass through the midst of the camp and command the people, 'Prepare your provisions, for within three days you are to pass over this Jordan to go in to take possession of the land that the Lord your God is giving you to possess.'"

[12] And to the Reubenites, the Gadites, and the half-tribe of Manasseh Joshua said, [13] "Remember the word that Moses the servant of the Lord commanded you, saying, 'The Lord your God is providing you a place of rest and will give you this land.' [14] Your wives, your little ones, and your livestock shall remain in the land that Moses gave you beyond the Jordan, but all the men of valor among you shall pass over armed before your brothers and shall help them, [15] until the Lord gives rest to your brothers as he has to you, and they also take possession of the land that the Lord your God is giving them. Then you shall return to the land of your possession and shall possess it, the land that Moses the servant of the Lord gave you beyond the Jordan toward the sunrise."

[16] And they answered Joshua, "All that you have commanded us we will do, and wherever you send us we will go. [17] Just as we obeyed Moses in all things, so we will obey you. Only may the Lord your God be with you, as he was with Moses! [18] Whoever rebels against your commandment and disobeys your words, whatever you command him, shall be put to death. Only be strong and courageous."

Rahab Hides the Spies

2 And Joshua the son of Nun sent[2] two men secretly from Shittim as spies, saying, "Go, view the land, especially Jericho." And they went and came into the house of a prostitute whose name was Rahab and lodged there. [2] And it was told to the king of Jericho, "Behold, men of Israel have come here tonight to search out the land." [3] Then the king of Jericho sent to Rahab, saying, "Bring out the men who have come to you, who entered your house, for they have come to search out all the land." [4] But the woman had taken the two men and hidden them. And she said, "True, the men came to me, but I did not know where they were from. [5] And when the gate was about to be closed at dark, the men went out. I do not know where the men went. Pursue them quickly, for you will overtake them." [6] But she had brought them up to the roof and hid them with the stalks of flax that she had laid in order on the roof. [7] So the men pursued after them on the way to the Jordan as far as the fords. And the gate was shut as soon as the pursuers had gone out.

[8] Before the men[3] lay down, she came up to them on the roof [9] and said to the men, "I know that the Lord has given you the land, and that the fear of you has fallen upon us, and that all the inhabitants of the land melt

---

[1] Or may act wisely [2] Or had sent [3] Hebrew they

away before you. ¹⁰ For we have heard how the LORD dried up the water of the Red Sea before you when you came out of Egypt, and what you did to the two kings of the Amorites who were beyond the Jordan, to Sihon and Og, whom you devoted to destruction.¹ ¹¹ And as soon as we heard it, our hearts melted, and there was no spirit left in any man because of you, for the LORD your God, he is God in the heavens above and on the earth beneath. ¹² Now then, please swear to me by the LORD that, as I have dealt kindly with you, you also will deal kindly with my father's house, and give me a sure sign ¹³ that you will save alive my father and mother, my brothers and sisters, and all who belong to them, and deliver our lives from death." ¹⁴ And the men said to her, "Our life for yours even to death! If you do not tell this business of ours, then when the LORD gives us the land we will deal kindly and faithfully with you."

¹⁵ Then she let them down by a rope through the window, for her house was built into the city wall, so that she lived in the wall. ¹⁶ And she said² to them, "Go into the hills, or the pursuers will encounter you, and hide there three days until the pursuers have returned. Then afterward you may go your way." ¹⁷ The men said to her, "We will be guiltless with respect to this oath of yours that you have made us swear. ¹⁸ Behold, when we come into the land, you shall tie this scarlet cord in the window through which you let us down, and you shall gather into your house your father and mother, your brothers, and all your father's household. ¹⁹ Then if anyone goes out of the doors of your house into the street, his blood shall be on his own head, and we shall be guiltless. But if a hand is laid on anyone who is with you in the house, his blood shall be on our head. ²⁰ But if you tell this business of ours, then we shall be guiltless with respect to your oath that you have made us swear." ²¹ And she said, "According to your words, so be it." Then she sent them away, and they departed. And she tied the scarlet cord in the window.

²² They departed and went into the hills and remained there three days until the pursuers returned, and the pursuers searched all along the way and found nothing. ²³ Then the two men returned. They came down from the hills and passed over and came to Joshua the son of Nun, and they told him all that had happened to them. ²⁴ And they said to Joshua, "Truly the LORD has given all the land into our hands. And also, all the inhabitants of the land melt away because of us."

Israel Crosses the Jordan

3 Then Joshua rose early in the morning and they set out from Shittim. And they came to the Jordan, he and all the people of Israel, and lodged there before they passed over. ² At the end of three days the officers went through the camp ³ and commanded the people, "As soon as you see the ark of the covenant of the LORD your God being carried by the Levitical priests, then you shall set out from your place and follow it. ⁴ Yet there shall be a distance between you and it, about 2,000 cubits³ in length. Do not come near it, in order that you may know the way you shall go, for you have not passed this way before." ⁵ Then Joshua said to the people, "Consecrate yourselves, for tomorrow the LORD will do wonders among you." ⁶ And Joshua said to the priests, "Take up the ark of the covenant and pass on before the people." So they took up the ark of the covenant and went before the people.

⁷ The LORD said to Joshua, "Today I will begin to exalt you in the sight of all Israel, that they may know that, as I was with Moses, so I will be with you. ⁸ And as for you, command the priests who bear the ark of the covenant, 'When you come to the brink of the waters of the Jordan, you shall stand still in the Jordan.'" ⁹ And Joshua said to the people of Israel, "Come here and listen to the words of the LORD your God." ¹⁰ And Joshua said, "Here is how you shall know that the living God is among you and that he will without fail drive out from before you the Canaanites, the Hittites, the Hivites, the Perizzites, the Girgashites, the Amorites, and the Jebusites. ¹¹ Behold, the ark of the covenant of the Lord of all the earth⁴ is passing over before you into the Jordan. ¹² Now therefore take twelve men from the tribes of Israel, from each tribe a man. ¹³ And when the soles of the feet of the priests bearing the ark of the LORD, the Lord of all the earth, shall rest in the waters of the Jordan, the waters of the Jordan shall be cut off from flowing, and the waters coming down from above shall stand in one heap."

¹⁴ So when the people set out from their tents to pass over the Jordan with the priests bearing

---

¹ That is, set apart (devoted) as an offering to the Lord (for destruction) ² Or had said ³ A cubit was about 18 inches or 45 centimeters ⁴ Hebrew the ark of the covenant, the Lord of all the earth

the ark of the covenant before the people, [15] and as soon as those bearing the ark had come as far as the Jordan, and the feet of the priests bearing the ark were dipped in the brink of the water (now the Jordan overflows all its banks throughout the time of harvest), [16] the waters coming down from above stood and rose up in a heap very far away, at Adam, the city that is beside Zarethan, and those flowing down toward the Sea of the Arabah, the Salt Sea, were completely cut off. And the people passed over opposite Jericho. [17] Now the priests bearing the ark of the covenant of the LORD stood firmly on dry ground in the midst of the Jordan, and all Israel was passing over on dry ground until all the nation finished passing over the Jordan.

Twelve Memorial Stones from the Jordan

4 When all the nation had finished passing over the Jordan, the LORD said to Joshua, [2] "Take twelve men from the people, from each tribe a man, [3] and command them, saying, 'Take twelve stones from here out of the midst of the Jordan, from the very place where the priests' feet stood firmly, and bring them over with you and lay them down in the place where you lodge tonight.'" [4] Then Joshua called the twelve men from the people of Israel, whom he had appointed, a man from each tribe. [5] And Joshua said to them, "Pass on before the ark of the LORD your God into the midst of the Jordan, and take up each of you a stone upon his shoulder, according to the number of the tribes of the people of Israel, [6] that this may be a sign among you. When your children ask in time to come, 'What do those stones mean to you?' [7] then you shall tell them that the waters of the Jordan were cut off before the ark of the covenant of the LORD. When it passed over the Jordan, the waters of the Jordan were cut off. So these stones shall be to the people of Israel a memorial forever."

[8] And the people of Israel did just as Joshua commanded and took up twelve stones out of the midst of the Jordan, according to the number of the tribes of the people of Israel, just as the LORD told Joshua. And they carried them over with them to the place where they lodged and laid them down[1] there. [9] And Joshua set up[2] twelve stones in the midst of the Jordan, in the place where the feet of the priests bearing the ark of the covenant had stood; and they are there to this day. [10] For the priests bearing the

ark stood in the midst of the Jordan until everything was finished that the LORD commanded Joshua to tell the people, according to all that Moses had commanded Joshua.

The people passed over in haste. [11] And when all the people had finished passing over, the ark of the LORD and the priests passed over before the people. [12] The sons of Reuben and the sons of Gad and the half-tribe of Manasseh passed over armed before the people of Israel, as Moses had told them. [13] About 40,000 ready for war passed over before the LORD for battle, to the plains of Jericho. [14] On that day the LORD exalted Joshua in the sight of all Israel, and they stood in awe of him just as they had stood in awe of Moses, all the days of his life.

[15] And the LORD said to Joshua, [16] "Command the priests bearing the ark of the testimony to come up out of the Jordan." [17] So Joshua commanded the priests, "Come up out of the Jordan." [18] And when the priests bearing the ark of the covenant of the LORD came up from the midst of the Jordan, and the soles of the priests' feet were lifted up on dry ground, the waters of the Jordan returned to their place and overflowed all its banks, as before.

[19] The people came up out of the Jordan on the tenth day of the first month, and they encamped at Gilgal on the east border of Jericho. [20] And those twelve stones, which they took out of the Jordan, Joshua set up at Gilgal. [21] And he said to the people of Israel, "When your children ask their fathers in times to come, 'What do these stones mean?' [22] then you shall let your children know, 'Israel passed over this Jordan on dry ground.' [23] For the LORD your God dried up the waters of the Jordan for you until you passed over, as the LORD your God did to the Red Sea, which he dried up for us until we passed over, [24] so that all the peoples of the earth may know that the hand of the LORD is mighty, that you may fear the LORD your God forever."[3]

The New Generation Circumcised

5 As soon as all the kings of the Amorites who were beyond the Jordan to the west, and all the kings of the Canaanites who were by the sea, heard that the LORD had dried up the waters of the Jordan for the people of Israel until they had crossed over, their hearts melted and there was no longer any spirit in them because of the people of Israel.

[1] Or to rest [2] Or Joshua had set up [3] Or all the days

²At that time the LORD said to Joshua, "Make flint knives and circumcise the sons of Israel a second time." ³So Joshua made flint knives and circumcised the sons of Israel at Gibeath-haaraloth.¹ ⁴And this is the reason why Joshua circumcised them: all the males of the people who came out of Egypt, all the men of war, had died in the wilderness on the way after they had come out of Egypt. ⁵Though all the people who came out had been circumcised, yet all the people who were born on the way in the wilderness after they had come out of Egypt had not been circumcised. ⁶For the people of Israel walked forty years in the wilderness, until all the nation, the men of war who came out of Egypt, perished, because they did not obey the voice of the LORD; the LORD swore to them that he would not let them see the land that the LORD had sworn to their fathers to give to us, a land flowing with milk and honey. ⁷So it was their children, whom he raised up in their place, that Joshua circumcised. For they were uncircumcised, because they had not been circumcised on the way.

⁸When the circumcising of the whole nation was finished, they remained in their places in the camp until they were healed. ⁹And the LORD said to Joshua, "Today I have rolled away the reproach of Egypt from you." And so the name of that place is called Gilgal² to this day.

First Passover in Canaan

¹⁰While the people of Israel were encamped at Gilgal, they kept the Passover on the fourteenth day of the month in the evening on the plains of Jericho. ¹¹And the day after the Passover, on that very day, they ate of the produce of the land, unleavened cakes and parched grain. ¹²And the manna ceased the day after they ate of the produce of the land. And there was no longer manna for the people of Israel, but they ate of the fruit of the land of Canaan that year.

The Commander of the LORD's Army

¹³When Joshua was by Jericho, he lifted up his eyes and looked, and behold, a man was standing before him with his drawn sword in his hand. And Joshua went to him and said to him, "Are you for us, or for our adversaries?" ¹⁴And he said, "No; but I am the commander of the army of the LORD. Now I have come." And Joshua fell on his face to the earth and worshiped³ and said to him, "What does my lord say to his servant?" ¹⁵And the commander of the LORD's army said to Joshua, "Take off your sandals from your feet, for the place where you are standing is holy." And Joshua did so.

The Fall of Jericho

6 Now Jericho was shut up inside and outside because of the people of Israel. None went out, and none came in. ²And the LORD said to Joshua, "See, I have given Jericho into your hand, with its king and mighty men of valor. ³You shall march around the city, all the men of war going around the city once. Thus shall you do for six days. ⁴Seven priests shall bear seven trumpets of rams' horns before the ark. On the seventh day you shall march around the city seven times, and the priests shall blow the trumpets. ⁵And when they make a long blast with the ram's horn, when you hear the sound of the trumpet, then all the people shall shout with a great shout, and the wall of the city will fall down flat,⁴ and the people shall go up, everyone straight before him." ⁶So Joshua the son of Nun called the priests and said to them, "Take up the ark of the covenant and let seven priests bear seven trumpets of rams' horns before the ark of the LORD." ⁷And he said to the people, "Go forward. March around the city and let the armed men pass on before the ark of the LORD."

⁸And just as Joshua had commanded the people, the seven priests bearing the seven trumpets of rams' horns before the LORD went forward, blowing the trumpets, with the ark of the covenant of the LORD following them. ⁹The armed men were walking before the priests who were blowing the trumpets, and the rear guard was walking after the ark, while the trumpets blew continually. ¹⁰But Joshua commanded the people, "You shall not shout or make your voice heard, neither shall any word go out of your mouth, until the day I tell you to shout. Then you shall shout." ¹¹So he caused the ark of the LORD to circle the city, going about it once. And they came into the camp and spent the night in the camp.

¹²Then Joshua rose early in the morning, and the priests took up the ark of the LORD. ¹³And the seven priests bearing the seven trumpets of rams' horns before the ark of the LORD walked on, and they blew the trumpets continually. And the armed men were walking before them, and the rear guard was walking after the ark of

---

¹ *Gibeath-haaraloth* means *the hill of the foreskins* ² *Gilgal* sounds like the Hebrew for *to roll* ³ Or *and paid homage* ⁴ Hebrew *under itself*; also verse 20

the LORD, while the trumpets blew continually. [14] And the second day they marched around the city once, and returned into the camp. So they did for six days.

[15] On the seventh day they rose early, at the dawn of day, and marched around the city in the same manner seven times. It was only on that day that they marched around the city seven times. [16] And at the seventh time, when the priests had blown the trumpets, Joshua said to the people, "Shout, for the LORD has given you the city. [17] And the city and all that is within it shall be devoted to the LORD for destruction.[1] Only Rahab the prostitute and all who are with her in her house shall live, because she hid the messengers whom we sent. [18] But you, keep yourselves from the things devoted to destruction, lest when you have devoted them you take any of the devoted things and make the camp of Israel a thing for destruction and bring trouble upon it. [19] But all silver and gold, and every vessel of bronze and iron, are holy to the LORD; they shall go into the treasury of the LORD." [20] So the people shouted, and the trumpets were blown. As soon as the people heard the sound of the trumpet, the people shouted a great shout, and the wall fell down flat, so that the people went up into the city, every man straight before him, and they captured the city. [21] Then they devoted all in the city to destruction, both men and women, young and old, oxen, sheep, and donkeys, with the edge of the sword.

[22] But to the two men who had spied out the land, Joshua said, "Go into the prostitute's house and bring out from there the woman and all who belong to her, as you swore to her." [23] So the young men who had been spies went in and brought out Rahab and her father and mother and brothers and all who belonged to her. And they brought all her relatives and put them outside the camp of Israel. [24] And they burned the city with fire, and everything in it. Only the silver and gold, and the vessels of bronze and of iron, they put into the treasury of the house of the LORD. [25] But Rahab the prostitute and her father's household and all who belonged to her, Joshua saved alive. And she has lived in Israel to this day, because she hid the messengers whom Joshua sent to spy out Jericho.

[26] Joshua laid an oath on them at that time, saying, "Cursed before the LORD be the man who rises up and rebuilds this city, Jericho.

" At the cost of his firstborn shall he
　　lay its foundation,
　and at the cost of his youngest son
　　shall he set up its gates."

[27] So the LORD was with Joshua, and his fame was in all the land.

Israel Defeated at Ai

7 But the people of Israel broke faith in regard to the devoted things, for Achan the son of Carmi, son of Zabdi, son of Zerah, of the tribe of Judah, took some of the devoted things. And the anger of the LORD burned against the people of Israel.

[2] Joshua sent men from Jericho to Ai, which is near Beth-aven, east of Bethel, and said to them, "Go up and spy out the land." And the men went up and spied out Ai. [3] And they returned to Joshua and said to him, "Do not have all the people go up, but let about two or three thousand men go up and attack Ai. Do not make the whole people toil up there, for they are few." [4] So about three thousand men went up there from the people. And they fled before the men of Ai, [5] and the men of Ai killed about thirty-six of their men and chased them before the gate as far as Shebarim and struck them at the descent. And the hearts of the people melted and became as water.

[6] Then Joshua tore his clothes and fell to the earth on his face before the ark of the LORD until the evening, he and the elders of Israel. And they put dust on their heads. [7] And Joshua said, "Alas, O Lord GOD, why have you brought this people over the Jordan at all, to give us into the hands of the Amorites, to destroy us? Would that we had been content to dwell beyond the Jordan! [8] O Lord, what can I say, when Israel has turned their backs before their enemies! [9] For the Canaanites and all the inhabitants of the land will hear of it and will surround us and cut off our name from the earth. And what will you do for your great name?"

The Sin of Achan

[10] The LORD said to Joshua, "Get up! Why have you fallen on your face? [11] Israel has sinned; they have transgressed my covenant that I commanded them; they have taken some of the devoted things; they have stolen and lied and put them among their own

---

[1] That is, set apart (devoted) as an offering to the Lord (for destruction); also verses 18, 21

belongings. [12] Therefore the people of Israel cannot stand before their enemies. They turn their backs before their enemies, because they have become devoted for destruction.[1] I will be with you no more, unless you destroy the devoted things from among you. [13] Get up! Consecrate the people and say, 'Consecrate yourselves for tomorrow; for thus says the LORD, God of Israel, "There are devoted things in your midst, O Israel. You cannot stand before your enemies until you take away the devoted things from among you." [14] In the morning therefore you shall be brought near by your tribes. And the tribe that the LORD takes by lot shall come near by clans. And the clan that the LORD takes shall come near by households. And the household that the LORD takes shall come near man by man. [15] And he who is taken with the devoted things shall be burned with fire, he and all that he has, because he has transgressed the covenant of the LORD, and because he has done an outrageous thing in Israel.'"

[16] So Joshua rose early in the morning and brought Israel near tribe by tribe, and the tribe of Judah was taken. [17] And he brought near the clans of Judah, and the clan of the Zerahites was taken. And he brought near the clan of the Zerahites man by man, and Zabdi was taken. [18] And he brought near his household man by man, and Achan the son of Carmi, son of Zabdi, son of Zerah, of the tribe of Judah, was taken. [19] Then Joshua said to Achan, "My son, give glory to the LORD God of Israel and give praise[2] to him. And tell me now what you have done; do not hide it from me." [20] And Achan answered Joshua, "Truly I have sinned against the LORD God of Israel, and this is what I did: [21] when I saw among the spoil a beautiful cloak from Shinar, and 200 shekels of silver, and a bar of gold weighing 50 shekels,[3] then I coveted them and took them. And see, they are hidden in the earth inside my tent, with the silver underneath."

[22] So Joshua sent messengers, and they ran to the tent; and behold, it was hidden in his tent with the silver underneath. [23] And they took them out of the tent and brought them to Joshua and to all the people of Israel. And they laid them down before the LORD. [24] And Joshua and all Israel with him took Achan the son of Zerah, and the silver and the cloak and the bar of gold, and his sons and daughters

and his oxen and donkeys and sheep and his tent and all that he had. And they brought them up to the Valley of Achor. [25] And Joshua said, "Why did you bring trouble on us? The LORD brings trouble on you today." And all Israel stoned him with stones. They burned them with fire and stoned them with stones. [26] And they raised over him a great heap of stones that remains to this day. Then the LORD turned from his burning anger. Therefore, to this day the name of that place is called the Valley of Achor.[4]

The Fall of Ai

8 And the LORD said to Joshua, "Do not fear and do not be dismayed. Take all the fighting men with you, and arise, go up to Ai. See, I have given into your hand the king of Ai, and his people, his city, and his land. [2] And you shall do to Ai and its king as you did to Jericho and its king. Only its spoil and its livestock you shall take as plunder for yourselves. Lay an ambush against the city, behind it."

[3] So Joshua and all the fighting men arose to go up to Ai. And Joshua chose 30,000 mighty men of valor and sent them out by night. [4] And he commanded them, "Behold, you shall lie in ambush against the city, behind it. Do not go very far from the city, but all of you remain ready. [5] And I and all the people who are with me will approach the city. And when they come out against us just as before, we shall flee before them. [6] And they will come out after us, until we have drawn them away from the city. For they will say, 'They are fleeing from us, just as before.' So we will flee before them. [7] Then you shall rise up from the ambush and seize the city, for the LORD your God will give it into your hand. [8] And as soon as you have taken the city, you shall set the city on fire. You shall do according to the word of the LORD. See, I have commanded you." [9] So Joshua sent them out. And they went to the place of ambush and lay between Bethel and Ai, to the west of Ai, but Joshua spent that night among the people.

[10] Joshua arose early in the morning and mustered the people and went up, he and the elders of Israel, before the people to Ai. [11] And all the fighting men who were with him went up and drew near before the city and encamped on the north side of Ai, with a ravine between them and Ai. [12] He took about 5,000 men and set them in ambush between Bethel and Ai,

---

[1] That is, set apart (devoted) as an offering to the Lord (for destruction) [2] Or *and make confession* [3] A *shekel* was about 2/5 ounce or 11 grams [4] *Achor* means *trouble*

to the west of the city. [13] So they stationed the forces, the main encampment that was north of the city and its rear guard west of the city. But Joshua spent that night in the valley. [14] And as soon as the king of Ai saw this, he and all his people, the men of the city, hurried and went out early to the appointed place[1] toward the Arabah to meet Israel in battle. But he did not know that there was an ambush against him behind the city. [15] And Joshua and all Israel pretended to be beaten before them and fled in the direction of the wilderness. [16] So all the people who were in the city were called together to pursue them, and as they pursued Joshua they were drawn away from the city. [17] Not a man was left in Ai or Bethel who did not go out after Israel. They left the city open and pursued Israel.

[18] Then the LORD said to Joshua, "Stretch out the javelin that is in your hand toward Ai, for I will give it into your hand." And Joshua stretched out the javelin that was in his hand toward the city. [19] And the men in the ambush rose quickly out of their place, and as soon as he had stretched out his hand, they ran and entered the city and captured it. And they hurried to set the city on fire. [20] So when the men of Ai looked back, behold, the smoke of the city went up to heaven, and they had no power to flee this way or that, for the people who fled to the wilderness turned back against the pursuers. [21] And when Joshua and all Israel saw that the ambush had captured the city, and that the smoke of the city went up, then they turned back and struck down the men of Ai. [22] And the others came out from the city against them, so they were in the midst of Israel, some on this side, and some on that side. And Israel struck them down, until there was left none that survived or escaped. [23] But the king of Ai they took alive, and brought him near to Joshua.

[24] When Israel had finished killing all the inhabitants of Ai in the open wilderness where they pursued them, and all of them to the very last had fallen by the edge of the sword, all Israel returned to Ai and struck it down with the edge of the sword. [25] And all who fell that day, both men and women, were 12,000, all the people of Ai. [26] But Joshua did not draw back his hand with which he stretched out the javelin until he had devoted all the inhabitants of Ai to destruction.[2] [27] Only the livestock and the spoil of that city Israel took as their plunder, according to the word of the LORD that he commanded Joshua. [28] So Joshua burned Ai and made it forever a heap of ruins, as it is to this day. [29] And he hanged the king of Ai on a tree until evening. And at sunset Joshua commanded, and they took his body down from the tree and threw it at the entrance of the gate of the city and raised over it a great heap of stones, which stands there to this day.

Joshua Renews the Covenant

[30] At that time Joshua built an altar to the LORD, the God of Israel, on Mount Ebal, [31] just as Moses the servant of the LORD had commanded the people of Israel, as it is written in the Book of the Law of Moses, "an altar of uncut stones, upon which no man has wielded an iron tool." And they offered on it burnt offerings to the LORD and sacrificed peace offerings. [32] And there, in the presence of the people of Israel, he wrote on the stones a copy of the law of Moses, which he had written. [33] And all Israel, sojourner as well as native born, with their elders and officers and their judges, stood on opposite sides of the ark before the Levitical priests who carried the ark of the covenant of the LORD, half of them in front of Mount Gerizim and half of them in front of Mount Ebal, just as Moses the servant of the LORD had commanded at the first, to bless the people of Israel. [34] And afterward he read all the words of the law, the blessing and the curse, according to all that is written in the Book of the Law. [35] There was not a word of all that Moses commanded that Joshua did not read before all the assembly of Israel, and the women, and the little ones, and the sojourners who lived[3] among them.

The Gibeonite Deception

9 As soon as all the kings who were beyond the Jordan in the hill country and in the lowland all along the coast of the Great Sea toward Lebanon, the Hittites, the Amorites, the Canaanites, the Perizzites, the Hivites, and the Jebusites, heard of this, [2] they gathered together as one to fight against Joshua and Israel.

[3] But when the inhabitants of Gibeon heard what Joshua had done to Jericho and to Ai, [4] they on their part acted with cunning and went and made ready provisions and took worn-out sacks for their donkeys, and wineskins, worn-out and torn and mended, [5] with worn-out, patched sandals on their feet, and worn-out clothes. And all their provisions were dry and crumbly. [6] And

---

[1] Hebrew *appointed time* [2] That is, set apart (devoted) as an offering to the Lord (for destruction) [3] Or *traveled*

they went to Joshua in the camp at Gilgal and said to him and to the men of Israel, "We have come from a distant country, so now make a covenant with us." ⁷But the men of Israel said to the Hivites, "Perhaps you live among us; then how can we make a covenant with you?" ⁸They said to Joshua, "We are your servants." And Joshua said to them, "Who are you? And where do you come from?" ⁹They said to him, "From a very distant country your servants have come, because of the name of the LORD your God. For we have heard a report of him, and all that he did in Egypt, ¹⁰and all that he did to the two kings of the Amorites who were beyond the Jordan, to Sihon the king of Heshbon, and to Og king of Bashan, who lived in Ashtaroth. ¹¹So our elders and all the inhabitants of our country said to us, 'Take provisions in your hand for the journey and go to meet them and say to them, "We are your servants. Come now, make a covenant with us." ' ¹²Here is our bread. It was still warm when we took it from our houses as our food for the journey on the day we set out to come to you, but now, behold, it is dry and crumbly. ¹³These wineskins were new when we filled them, and behold, they have burst. And these garments and sandals of ours are worn out from the very long journey." ¹⁴So the men took some of their provisions, but did not ask counsel from the LORD. ¹⁵And Joshua made peace with them and made a covenant with them, to let them live, and the leaders of the congregation swore to them.

¹⁶At the end of three days after they had made a covenant with them, they heard that they were their neighbors and that they lived among them. ¹⁷And the people of Israel set out and reached their cities on the third day. Now their cities were Gibeon, Chephirah, Beeroth, and Kiriath-jearim. ¹⁸But the people of Israel did not attack them, because the leaders of the congregation had sworn to them by the LORD, the God of Israel. Then all the congregation murmured against the leaders. ¹⁹But all the leaders said to all the congregation, "We have sworn to them by the LORD, the God of Israel, and now we may not touch them. ²⁰This we will do to them: let them live, lest wrath be upon us, because of the oath that we swore to them." ²¹And the leaders said to them, "Let them live." So they became cutters of wood and drawers of

water for all the congregation, just as the leaders had said of them.

²²Joshua summoned them, and he said to them, "Why did you deceive us, saying, 'We are very far from you,' when you dwell among us? ²³Now therefore you are cursed, and some of you shall never be anything but servants, cutters of wood and drawers of water for the house of my God." ²⁴They answered Joshua, "Because it was told to your servants for a certainty that the LORD your God had commanded his servant Moses to give you all the land and to destroy all the inhabitants of the land from before you—so we feared greatly for our lives because of you and did this thing. ²⁵And now, behold, we are in your hand. Whatever seems good and right in your sight to do to us, do it." ²⁶So he did this to them and delivered them out of the hand of the people of Israel, and they did not kill them. ²⁷But Joshua made them that day cutters of wood and drawers of water for the congregation and for the altar of the LORD, to this day, in the place that he should choose.

The Sun Stands Still

10 As soon as Adoni-zedek, king of Jerusalem, heard how Joshua had captured Ai and had devoted it to destruction,¹ doing to Ai and its king as he had done to Jericho and its king, and how the inhabitants of Gibeon had made peace with Israel and were among them, ²he² feared greatly, because Gibeon was a great city, like one of the royal cities, and because it was greater than Ai, and all its men were warriors. ³So Adoni-zedek king of Jerusalem sent to Hoham king of Hebron, to Piram king of Jarmuth, to Japhia king of Lachish, and to Debir king of Eglon, saying, ⁴"Come up to me and help me, and let us strike Gibeon. For it has made peace with Joshua and with the people of Israel." ⁵Then the five kings of the Amorites, the king of Jerusalem, the king of Hebron, the king of Jarmuth, the king of Lachish, and the king of Eglon, gathered their forces and went up with all their armies and encamped against Gibeon and made war against it.

⁶And the men of Gibeon sent to Joshua at the camp in Gilgal, saying, "Do not relax your hand from your servants. Come up to us quickly and save us and help us, for all the kings of the Amorites who dwell in the hill

---

¹ That is, set apart (devoted) as an offering to the Lord (for destruction); also verses 28, 35, 37, 39, 40   ² One Hebrew manuscript, Vulgate (compare Syriac); most Hebrew manuscripts *they*

country are gathered against us." [7] So Joshua went up from Gilgal, he and all the people of war with him, and all the mighty men of valor. [8] And the LORD said to Joshua, "Do not fear them, for I have given them into your hands. Not a man of them shall stand before you." [9] So Joshua came upon them suddenly, having marched up all night from Gilgal. [10] And the LORD threw them into a panic before Israel, who[1] struck them with a great blow at Gibeon and chased them by the way of the ascent of Beth-horon and struck them as far as Azekah and Makkedah. [11] And as they fled before Israel, while they were going down the ascent of Beth-horon, the LORD threw down large stones from heaven on them as far as Azekah, and they died. There were more who died because of the hailstones than the sons of Israel killed with the sword.

[12] At that time Joshua spoke to the LORD in the day when the LORD gave the Amorites over to the sons of Israel, and he said in the sight of Israel,

> "Sun, stand still at Gibeon,
> and moon, in the Valley of Aijalon."
> [13] And the sun stood still, and the moon stopped,
> until the nation took vengeance on
> their enemies.

Is this not written in the Book of Jashar? The sun stopped in the midst of heaven and did not hurry to set for about a whole day. [14] There has been no day like it before or since, when the LORD heeded the voice of a man, for the LORD fought for Israel.

[15] So Joshua returned, and all Israel with him, to the camp at Gilgal.

Five Amorite Kings Executed

[16] These five kings fled and hid themselves in the cave at Makkedah. [17] And it was told to Joshua, "The five kings have been found, hidden in the cave at Makkedah." [18] And Joshua said, "Roll large stones against the mouth of the cave and set men by it to guard them, [19] but do not stay there yourselves. Pursue your enemies; attack their rear guard. Do not let them enter their cities, for the LORD your God has given them into your hand." [20] When Joshua and the sons of Israel had finished striking them with a great blow until they were wiped out, and when the remnant that remained of them had

entered into the fortified cities, [21] then all the people returned safe to Joshua in the camp at Makkedah. Not a man moved his tongue against any of the people of Israel.

[22] Then Joshua said, "Open the mouth of the cave and bring those five kings out to me from the cave." [23] And they did so, and brought those five kings out to him from the cave, the king of Jerusalem, the king of Hebron, the king of Jarmuth, the king of Lachish, and the king of Eglon. [24] And when they brought those kings out to Joshua, Joshua summoned all the men of Israel and said to the chiefs of the men of war who had gone with him, "Come near; put your feet on the necks of these kings." Then they came near and put their feet on their necks. [25] And Joshua said to them, "Do not be afraid or dismayed; be strong and courageous. For thus the LORD will do to all your enemies against whom you fight." [26] And afterward Joshua struck them and put them to death, and he hanged them on five trees. And they hung on the trees until evening. [27] But at the time of the going down of the sun, Joshua commanded, and they took them down from the trees and threw them into the cave where they had hidden themselves, and they set large stones against the mouth of the cave, which remain to this very day.

[28] As for Makkedah, Joshua captured it on that day and struck it, and its king, with the edge of the sword. He devoted to destruction every person in it; he left none remaining. And he did to the king of Makkedah just as he had done to the king of Jericho.

Conquest of Southern Canaan

[29] Then Joshua and all Israel with him passed on from Makkedah to Libnah and fought against Libnah. [30] And the LORD gave it also and its king into the hand of Israel. And he struck it with the edge of the sword, and every person in it; he left none remaining in it. And he did to its king as he had done to the king of Jericho.

[31] Then Joshua and all Israel with him passed on from Libnah to Lachish and laid siege to it and fought against it. [32] And the LORD gave Lachish into the hand of Israel, and he captured it on the second day and struck it with the edge of the sword, and every person in it, as he had done to Libnah.

[33] Then Horam king of Gezer came up to

---

[1] Or *and he*

help Lachish. And Joshua struck him and his people, until he left none remaining.

[34] Then Joshua and all Israel with him passed on from Lachish to Eglon. And they laid siege to it and fought against it. [35] And they captured it on that day, and struck it with the edge of the sword. And he devoted every person in it to destruction that day, as he had done to Lachish.

[36] Then Joshua and all Israel with him went up from Eglon to Hebron. And they fought against it [37] and captured it and struck it with the edge of the sword, and its king and its towns, and every person in it. He left none remaining, as he had done to Eglon, and devoted it to destruction and every person in it.

[38] Then Joshua and all Israel with him turned back to Debir and fought against it [39] and he captured it with its king and all its towns. And they struck them with the edge of the sword and devoted to destruction every person in it; he left none remaining. Just as he had done to Hebron and to Libnah and its king, so he did to Debir and to its king.

[40] So Joshua struck the whole land, the hill country and the Negeb and the lowland and the slopes, and all their kings. He left none remaining, but devoted to destruction all that breathed, just as the LORD God of Israel commanded. [41] And Joshua struck them from Kadesh-barnea as far as Gaza, and all the country of Goshen, as far as Gibeon. [42] And Joshua captured all these kings and their land at one time, because the LORD God of Israel fought for Israel. [43] Then Joshua returned, and all Israel with him, to the camp at Gilgal.

Conquests in Northern Canaan

11 When Jabin, king of Hazor, heard of this, he sent to Jobab king of Madon, and to the king of Shimron, and to the king of Achshaph, [2] and to the kings who were in the northern hill country, and in the Arabah south of Chinneroth, and in the lowland, and in Naphoth-dor on the west, [3] to the Canaanites in the east and the west, the Amorites, the Hittites, the Perizzites, and the Jebusites in the hill country, and the Hivites under Hermon in the land of Mizpah. [4] And they came out with all their troops, a great horde, in number like the sand that is on the seashore, with very many horses and chariots. [5] And all these kings joined their forces and came and encamped together at the waters of Merom to fight against Israel.

[6] And the LORD said to Joshua, "Do not be afraid of them, for tomorrow at this time I will give over all of them, slain, to Israel. You shall hamstring their horses and burn their chariots with fire." [7] So Joshua and all his warriors came suddenly against them by the waters of Merom and fell upon them. [8] And the LORD gave them into the hand of Israel, who struck them and chased them as far as Great Sidon and Misrephoth-maim, and eastward as far as the Valley of Mizpeh. And they struck them until he left none remaining. [9] And Joshua did to them just as the LORD said to him: he hamstrung their horses and burned their chariots with fire.

[10] And Joshua turned back at that time and captured Hazor and struck its king with the sword, for Hazor formerly was the head of all those kingdoms. [11] And they struck with the sword all who were in it, devoting them to destruction;[1] there was none left that breathed. And he burned Hazor with fire. [12] And all the cities of those kings, and all their kings, Joshua captured, and struck them with the edge of the sword, devoting them to destruction, just as Moses the servant of the LORD had commanded. [13] But none of the cities that stood on mounds did Israel burn, except Hazor alone; that Joshua burned. [14] And all the spoil of these cities and the livestock, the people of Israel took for their plunder. But every person they struck with the edge of the sword until they had destroyed them, and they did not leave any who breathed. [15] Just as the LORD had commanded Moses his servant, so Moses commanded Joshua, and so Joshua did. He left nothing undone of all that the LORD had commanded Moses.

[16] So Joshua took all that land, the hill country and all the Negeb and all the land of Goshen and the lowland and the Arabah and the hill country of Israel and its lowland [17] from Mount Halak, which rises toward Seir, as far as Baal-gad in the Valley of Lebanon below Mount Hermon. And he captured all their kings and struck them and put them to death. [18] Joshua made war a long time with all those kings. [19] There was not a city that made peace with the people of Israel except the Hivites, the inhabitants of Gibeon. They took them all in battle. [20] For it was the LORD's doing to harden their hearts that they should come against Israel in battle, in order that they should be devoted to destruction and should receive no mercy but be destroyed, just as the LORD commanded Moses.

---

[1] That is, setting apart (devoting) as an offering to the Lord (for destruction); also verses 12, 20, 21

²¹ And Joshua came at that time and cut off the Anakim from the hill country, from Hebron, from Debir, from Anab, and from all the hill country of Judah, and from all the hill country of Israel. Joshua devoted them to destruction with their cities. ²² There was none of the Anakim left in the land of the people of Israel. Only in Gaza, in Gath, and in Ashdod did some remain. ²³ So Joshua took the whole land, according to all that the LORD had spoken to Moses. And Joshua gave it for an inheritance to Israel according to their tribal allotments. And the land had rest from war.

Kings Defeated by Moses

12 Now these are the kings of the land whom the people of Israel defeated and took possession of their land beyond the Jordan toward the sunrise, from the Valley of the Arnon to Mount Hermon, with all the Arabah eastward: ² Sihon king of the Amorites who lived at Heshbon and ruled from Aroer, which is on the edge of the Valley of the Arnon, and from the middle of the valley as far as the river Jabbok, the boundary of the Ammonites, that is, half of Gilead, ³ and the Arabah to the Sea of Chinneroth eastward, and in the direction of Beth-jeshimoth, to the Sea of the Arabah, the Salt Sea, southward to the foot of the slopes of Pisgah; ⁴ and Og¹ king of Bashan, one of the remnant of the Rephaim, who lived at Ashtaroth and at Edrei ⁵ and ruled over Mount Hermon and Salecah and all Bashan to the boundary of the Geshurites and the Maacathites, and over half of Gilead to the boundary of Sihon king of Heshbon. ⁶ Moses, the servant of the LORD, and the people of Israel defeated them. And Moses the servant of the LORD gave their land for a possession to the Reubenites and the Gadites and the half-tribe of Manasseh.

Kings Defeated by Joshua

⁷ And these are the kings of the land whom Joshua and the people of Israel defeated on the west side of the Jordan, from Baal-gad in the Valley of Lebanon to Mount Halak, that rises toward Seir (and Joshua gave their land to the tribes of Israel as a possession according to their allotments, ⁸ in the hill country, in the lowland, in the Arabah, in the slopes, in the wilderness, and in the Negeb, the land of the Hittites, the Amorites, the Canaanites, the Perizzites, the Hivites, and the Jebusites): ⁹ the king of Jericho, one; the king of Ai, which

is beside Bethel, one; ¹⁰ the king of Jerusalem, one; the king of Hebron, one; ¹¹ the king of Jarmuth, one; the king of Lachish, one; ¹² the king of Eglon, one; the king of Gezer, one; ¹³ the king of Debir, one; the king of Geder, one; ¹⁴ the king of Hormah, one; the king of Arad, one; ¹⁵ the king of Libnah, one; the king of Adullam, one; ¹⁶ the king of Makkedah, one; the king of Bethel, one; ¹⁷ the king of Tappuah, one; the king of Hepher, one; ¹⁸ the king of Aphek, one; the king of Lasharon, one; ¹⁹ the king of Madon, one; the king of Hazor, one; ²⁰ the king of Shimron-meron, one; the king of Achshaph, one; ²¹ the king of Taanach, one; the king of Megiddo, one; ²² the king of Kedesh, one; the king of Jokneam in Carmel, one; ²³ the king of Dor in Naphath-dor, one; the king of Goiim in Galilee,² one; ²⁴ the king of Tirzah, one: in all, thirty-one kings.

Land Still to Be Conquered

13 Now Joshua was old and advanced in years, and the LORD said to him, "You are old and advanced in years, and there remains yet very much land to possess. ² This is the land that yet remains: all the regions of the Philistines, and all those of the Geshurites ³ (from the Shihor, which is east of Egypt, northward to the boundary of Ekron, it is counted as Canaanite; there are five rulers of the Philistines, those of Gaza, Ashdod, Ashkelon, Gath, and Ekron), and those of the Avvim, ⁴ in the south, all the land of the Canaanites, and Mearah that belongs to the Sidonians, to Aphek, to the boundary of the Amorites, ⁵ and the land of the Gebalites, and all Lebanon, toward the sunrise, from Baal-gad below Mount Hermon to Lebo-hamath, ⁶ all the inhabitants of the hill country from Lebanon to Misrephoth-maim, even all the Sidonians. I myself will drive them out from before the people of Israel. Only allot the land to Israel for an inheritance, as I have commanded you. ⁷ Now therefore divide this land for an inheritance to the nine tribes and half the tribe of Manasseh."

The Inheritance East of the Jordan

⁸ With the other half of the tribe of Manasseh³ the Reubenites and the Gadites received their inheritance, which Moses gave them, beyond the Jordan eastward, as Moses the servant of the LORD gave them: ⁹ from Aroer, which is on the edge of the Valley of the Arnon, and the city that is in the middle of the valley, and all

---

¹ Septuagint; Hebrew *the boundary of Og* ² Septuagint; Hebrew *Gilgal* ³ Hebrew *With it*

the tableland of Medeba as far as Dibon; ¹⁰ and all the cities of Sihon king of the Amorites, who reigned in Heshbon, as far as the boundary of the Ammonites; ¹¹ and Gilead, and the region of the Geshurites and Maacathites, and all Mount Hermon, and all Bashan to Salecah; ¹² all the kingdom of Og in Bashan, who reigned in Ashtaroth and in Edrei (he alone was left of the remnant of the Rephaim); these Moses had struck and driven out. ¹³ Yet the people of Israel did not drive out the Geshurites or the Maacathites, but Geshur and Maacath dwell in the midst of Israel to this day.

¹⁴ To the tribe of Levi alone Moses gave no inheritance. The offerings by fire to the LORD God of Israel are their inheritance, as he said to him.

¹⁵ And Moses gave an inheritance to the tribe of the people of Reuben according to their clans. ¹⁶ So their territory was from Aroer, which is on the edge of the Valley of the Arnon, and the city that is in the middle of the valley, and all the tableland by Medeba; ¹⁷ with Heshbon, and all its cities that are in the tableland; Dibon, and Bamoth-baal, and Beth-baal-meon, ¹⁸ and Jahaz, and Kedemoth, and Mephaath, ¹⁹ and Kiriathaim, and Sibmah, and Zereth-shahar on the hill of the valley, ²⁰ and Beth-peor, and the slopes of Pisgah, and Beth-jeshimoth, ²¹ that is, all the cities of the tableland, and all the kingdom of Sihon king of the Amorites, who reigned in Heshbon, whom Moses defeated with the leaders of Midian, Evi and Rekem and Zur and Hur and Reba, the princes of Sihon, who lived in the land. ²² Balaam also, the son of Beor, the one who practiced divination, was killed with the sword by the people of Israel among the rest of their slain. ²³ And the border of the people of Reuben was the Jordan as a boundary. This was the inheritance of the people of Reuben, according to their clans with their cities and villages.

²⁴ Moses gave an inheritance also to the tribe of Gad, to the people of Gad, according to their clans. ²⁵ Their territory was Jazer, and all the cities of Gilead, and half the land of the Ammonites, to Aroer, which is east of Rabbah, ²⁶ and from Heshbon to Ramath-mizpeh and Betonim, and from Mahanaim to the territory of Debir,¹ ²⁷ and in the valley Beth-haram, Beth-nimrah, Succoth, and Zaphon, the rest of the kingdom of Sihon king of Heshbon, having the Jordan as a boundary, to the lower end of the Sea of Chinnereth, eastward beyond the Jordan. ²⁸ This is the inheritance of the people of Gad according to their clans, with their cities and villages.

²⁹ And Moses gave an inheritance to the half-tribe of Manasseh. It was allotted to the half-tribe of the people of Manasseh according to their clans. ³⁰ Their region extended from Mahanaim, through all Bashan, the whole kingdom of Og king of Bashan, and all the towns of Jair, which are in Bashan, sixty cities, ³¹ and half Gilead, and Ashtaroth, and Edrei, the cities of the kingdom of Og in Bashan. These were allotted to the people of Machir the son of Manasseh for the half of the people of Machir according to their clans.

³² These are the inheritances that Moses distributed in the plains of Moab, beyond the Jordan east of Jericho. ³³ But to the tribe of Levi Moses gave no inheritance; the LORD God of Israel is their inheritance, just as he said to them.

The Inheritance West of the Jordan

14 These are the inheritances that the people of Israel received in the land of Canaan, which Eleazar the priest and Joshua the son of Nun and the heads of the fathers' houses of the tribes of the people of Israel gave them to inherit. ² Their inheritance was by lot, just as the LORD had commanded by the hand of Moses for the nine and one-half tribes. ³ For Moses had given an inheritance to the two and one-half tribes beyond the Jordan, but to the Levites he gave no inheritance among them. ⁴ For the people of Joseph were two tribes, Manasseh and Ephraim. And no portion was given to the Levites in the land, but only cities to dwell in, with their pasturelands for their livestock and their substance. ⁵ The people of Israel did as the LORD commanded Moses; they allotted the land.

Caleb's Request and Inheritance

⁶ Then the people of Judah came to Joshua at Gilgal. And Caleb the son of Jephunneh the Kenizzite said to him, "You know what the LORD said to Moses the man of God in Kadesh-barnea concerning you and me. ⁷ I was forty years old when Moses the servant of the LORD sent me from Kadesh-barnea to spy out the land, and I brought him word again as it was in my heart. ⁸ But my brothers who went up with me made the heart of the people melt;

---

¹ Septuagint, Syriac, Vulgate; Hebrew *Lidebir*

yet I wholly followed the LORD my God. [9] And Moses swore on that day, saying, 'Surely the land on which your foot has trodden shall be an inheritance for you and your children forever, because you have wholly followed the LORD my God.' [10] And now, behold, the LORD has kept me alive, just as he said, these forty-five years since the time that the LORD spoke this word to Moses, while Israel walked in the wilderness. And now, behold, I am this day eighty-five years old. [11] I am still as strong today as I was in the day that Moses sent me; my strength now is as my strength was then, for war and for going and coming. [12] So now give me this hill country of which the LORD spoke on that day, for you heard on that day how the Anakim were there, with great fortified cities. It may be that the LORD will be with me, and I shall drive them out just as the LORD said."

[13] Then Joshua blessed him, and he gave Hebron to Caleb the son of Jephunneh for an inheritance. [14] Therefore Hebron became the inheritance of Caleb the son of Jephunneh the Kenizzite to this day, because he wholly followed the LORD, the God of Israel. [15] Now the name of Hebron formerly was Kiriath-arba.[1] (Arba[2] was the greatest man among the Anakim.) And the land had rest from war.

The Allotment for Judah

15 The allotment for the tribe of the people of Judah according to their clans reached southward to the boundary of Edom, to the wilderness of Zin at the farthest south. [2] And their south boundary ran from the end of the Salt Sea, from the bay that faces southward. [3] It goes out southward of the ascent of Akrabbim, passes along to Zin, and goes up south of Kadesh-barnea, along by Hezron, up to Addar, turns about to Karka, [4] passes along to Azmon, goes out by the Brook of Egypt, and comes to its end at the sea. This shall be your south boundary. [5] And the east boundary is the Salt Sea, to the mouth of the Jordan. And the boundary on the north side runs from the bay of the sea at the mouth of the Jordan. [6] And the boundary goes up to Beth-hoglah and passes along north of Beth-arabah. And the boundary goes up to the stone of Bohan the son of Reuben. [7] And the boundary goes up to Debir from the Valley of Achor, and so northward, turning toward Gilgal, which is opposite the ascent of Adummim, which is on the south side of the

valley. And the boundary passes along to the waters of En-shemesh and ends at En-rogel. [8] Then the boundary goes up by the Valley of the Son of Hinnom at the southern shoulder of the Jebusite (that is, Jerusalem). And the boundary goes up to the top of the mountain that lies over against the Valley of Hinnom, on the west, at the northern end of the Valley of Rephaim. [9] Then the boundary extends from the top of the mountain to the spring of the waters of Nephtoah, and from there to the cities of Mount Ephron. Then the boundary bends around to Baalah (that is, Kiriath-jearim). [10] And the boundary circles west of Baalah to Mount Seir, passes along to the northern shoulder of Mount Jearim (that is, Chesalon), and goes down to Beth-shemesh and passes along by Timnah. [11] The boundary goes out to the shoulder of the hill north of Ekron, then the boundary bends around to Shikkeron and passes along to Mount Baalah and goes out to Jabneel. Then the boundary comes to an end at the sea. [12] And the west boundary was the Great Sea with its coastline. This is the boundary around the people of Judah according to their clans.

[13] According to the commandment of the LORD to Joshua, he gave to Caleb the son of Jephunneh a portion among the people of Judah, Kiriath-arba, that is, Hebron (Arba was the father of Anak). [14] And Caleb drove out from there the three sons of Anak, Sheshai and Ahiman and Talmai, the descendants of Anak. [15] And he went up from there against the inhabitants of Debir. Now the name of Debir formerly was Kiriath-sepher. [16] And Caleb said, "Whoever strikes Kiriath-sepher and captures it, to him will I give Achsah my daughter as wife." [17] And Othniel the son of Kenaz, the brother of Caleb, captured it. And he gave him Achsah his daughter as wife. [18] When she came to him, she urged him to ask her father for a field. And she got off her donkey, and Caleb said to her, "What do you want?" [19] She said to him, "Give me a blessing. Since you have given me the land of the Negeb, give me also springs of water." And he gave her the upper springs and the lower springs.

[20] This is the inheritance of the tribe of the people of Judah according to their clans. [21] The cities belonging to the tribe of the people of Judah in the extreme south, toward the boundary of Edom, were Kabzeel, Eder, Jagur, [22] Kinah, Dimonah, Adadah, [23] Kedesh, Hazor, Ithnan, [24] Ziph, Telem, Bealoth, [25] Hazor-hadattah,

---

[1] *Kiriath-arba* means *the city of Arba* [2] Hebrew *He*

Kerioth-hezron (that is, Hazor), ²⁶ Amam, Shema, Moladah, ²⁷ Hazar-gaddah, Heshmon, Beth-pelet, ²⁸ Hazar-shual, Beersheba, Biziothiah, ²⁹ Baalah, Iim, Ezem, ³⁰ Eltolad, Chesil, Hormah, ³¹ Ziklag, Madmannah, Sansannah, ³² Lebaoth, Shilhim, Ain, and Rimmon: in all, twenty-nine cities with their villages.

³³ And in the lowland, Eshtaol, Zorah, Ashnah, ³⁴ Zanoah, En-gannim, Tappuah, Enam, ³⁵ Jarmuth, Adullam, Socoh, Azekah, ³⁶ Shaaraim, Adithaim, Gederah, Gederothaim: fourteen cities with their villages.

³⁷ Zenan, Hadashah, Migdal-gad, ³⁸ Dilean, Mizpeh, Joktheel, ³⁹ Lachish, Bozkath, Eglon, ⁴⁰ Cabbon, Lahmam, Chitlish, ⁴¹ Gederoth, Beth-dagon, Naamah, and Makkedah: sixteen cities with their villages.

⁴² Libnah, Ether, Ashan, ⁴³ Iphtah, Ashnah, Nezib, ⁴⁴ Keilah, Achzib, and Mareshah: nine cities with their villages.

⁴⁵ Ekron, with its towns and its villages; ⁴⁶ from Ekron to the sea, all that were by the side of Ashdod, with their villages.

⁴⁷ Ashdod, its towns and its villages; Gaza, its towns and its villages; to the Brook of Egypt, and the Great Sea with its coastline.

⁴⁸ And in the hill country, Shamir, Jattir, Socoh, ⁴⁹ Dannah, Kiriath-sannah (that is, Debir), ⁵⁰ Anab, Eshtemoh, Anim, ⁵¹ Goshen, Holon, and Giloh: eleven cities with their villages.

⁵² Arab, Dumah, Eshan, ⁵³ Janim, Beth-tappuah, Aphekah, ⁵⁴ Humtah, Kiriath-arba (that is, Hebron), and Zior: nine cities with their villages.

⁵⁵ Maon, Carmel, Ziph, Juttah, ⁵⁶ Jezreel, Jokdeam, Zanoah, ⁵⁷ Kain, Gibeah, and Timnah: ten cities with their villages.

⁵⁸ Halhul, Beth-zur, Gedor, ⁵⁹ Maarath, Beth-anoth, and Eltekon: six cities with their villages.

⁶⁰ Kiriath-baal (that is, Kiriath-jearim), and Rabbah: two cities with their villages.

⁶¹ In the wilderness, Beth-arabah, Middin, Secacah, ⁶² Nibshan, the City of Salt, and Engedi: six cities with their villages.

⁶³ But the Jebusites, the inhabitants of Jerusalem, the people of Judah could not drive out, so the Jebusites dwell with the people of Judah at Jerusalem to this day.

The Allotment for Ephraim and Manasseh

16 The allotment of the people of Joseph went from the Jordan by Jericho, east of the waters of Jericho, into the wilderness, going up from Jericho into the hill country to Bethel. ² Then going from Bethel to Luz, it passes along to Ataroth, the territory of the Archites. ³ Then it goes down westward to the territory of the Japhletites, as far as the territory of Lower Beth-horon, then to Gezer, and it ends at the sea.

⁴ The people of Joseph, Manasseh and Ephraim, received their inheritance.

⁵ The territory of the people of Ephraim by their clans was as follows: the boundary of their inheritance on the east was Ataroth-addar as far as Upper Beth-horon, ⁶ and the boundary goes from there to the sea. On the north is Michmethath. Then on the east the boundary turns around toward Taanath-shiloh and passes along beyond it on the east to Janoah, ⁷ then it goes down from Janoah to Ataroth and to Naarah, and touches Jericho, ending at the Jordan. ⁸ From Tappuah the boundary goes westward to the brook Kanah and ends at the sea. Such is the inheritance of the tribe of the people of Ephraim by their clans, ⁹ together with the towns that were set apart for the people of Ephraim within the inheritance of the Manassites, all those towns with their villages. ¹⁰ However, they did not drive out the Canaanites who lived in Gezer, so the Canaanites have lived in the midst of Ephraim to this day but have been made to do forced labor.

17 Then allotment was made to the people of Manasseh, for he was the firstborn of Joseph. To Machir the firstborn of Manasseh, the father of Gilead, were allotted Gilead and Bashan, because he was a man of war. ² And allotments were made to the rest of the people of Manasseh by their clans, Abiezer, Helek, Asriel, Shechem, Hepher, and Shemida. These were the male descendants of Manasseh the son of Joseph, by their clans.

³ Now Zelophehad the son of Hepher, son of Gilead, son of Machir, son of Manasseh, had no sons, but only daughters, and these are the names of his daughters: Mahlah, Noah, Hoglah, Milcah, and Tirzah. ⁴ They approached Eleazar the priest and Joshua the son of Nun and the leaders and said, "The LORD commanded Moses to give us an inheritance along with our brothers." So according to the mouth of the LORD he gave them an inheritance among the brothers of their father. ⁵ Thus there fell to Manasseh ten portions, besides the land of Gilead and Bashan, which is on the other side of the Jordan, ⁶ because the daughters of Manasseh received

an inheritance along with his sons. The land of Gilead was allotted to the rest of the people of Manasseh.

⁷ The territory of Manasseh reached from Asher to Michmethath, which is east of Shechem. Then the boundary goes along southward to the inhabitants of En-tappuah. ⁸ The land of Tappuah belonged to Manasseh, but the town of Tappuah on the boundary of Manasseh belonged to the people of Ephraim. ⁹ Then the boundary went down to the brook Kanah. These cities, to the south of the brook, among the cities of Manasseh, belong to Ephraim. Then the boundary of Manasseh goes on the north side of the brook and ends at the sea, ¹⁰ the land to the south being Ephraim's and that to the north being Manasseh's, with the sea forming its boundary. On the north Asher is reached, and on the east Issachar. ¹¹ Also in Issachar and in Asher Manasseh had Beth-shean and its villages, and Ibleam and its villages, and the inhabitants of Dor and its villages, and the inhabitants of En-dor and its villages, and the inhabitants of Taanach and its villages, and the inhabitants of Megiddo and its villages; the third is Naphath.[1] ¹² Yet the people of Manasseh could not take possession of those cities, but the Canaanites persisted in dwelling in that land. ¹³ Now when the people of Israel grew strong, they put the Canaanites to forced labor, but did not utterly drive them out.

¹⁴ Then the people of Joseph spoke to Joshua, saying, "Why have you given me but one lot and one portion as an inheritance, although I am a numerous people, since all along the LORD has blessed me?" ¹⁵ And Joshua said to them, "If you are a numerous people, go up by yourselves to the forest, and there clear ground for yourselves in the land of the Perizzites and the Rephaim, since the hill country of Ephraim is too narrow for you." ¹⁶ The people of Joseph said, "The hill country is not enough for us. Yet all the Canaanites who dwell in the plain have chariots of iron, both those in Beth-shean and its villages and those in the Valley of Jezreel." ¹⁷ Then Joshua said to the house of Joseph, to Ephraim and Manasseh, "You are a numerous people and have great power. You shall not have one allotment only, ¹⁸ but the hill country shall be yours, for though it is a forest, you shall clear it and possess it to its farthest borders. For you shall drive out the Canaanites,

though they have chariots of iron, and though they are strong."

Allotment of the Remaining Land

18 Then the whole congregation of the people of Israel assembled at Shiloh and set up the tent of meeting there. The land lay subdued before them.

² There remained among the people of Israel seven tribes whose inheritance had not yet been apportioned. ³ So Joshua said to the people of Israel, "How long will you put off going in to take possession of the land, which the LORD, the God of your fathers, has given you? ⁴ Provide three men from each tribe, and I will send them out that they may set out and go up and down the land. They shall write a description of it with a view to their inheritances, and then come to me. ⁵ They shall divide it into seven portions. Judah shall continue in his territory on the south, and the house of Joseph shall continue in their territory on the north. ⁶ And you shall describe the land in seven divisions and bring the description here to me. And I will cast lots for you here before the LORD our God. ⁷ The Levites have no portion among you, for the priesthood of the LORD is their heritage. And Gad and Reuben and half the tribe of Manasseh have received their inheritance beyond the Jordan eastward, which Moses the servant of the LORD gave them."

⁸ So the men arose and went, and Joshua charged those who went to write the description of the land, saying, "Go up and down in the land and write a description and return to me. And I will cast lots for you here before the LORD in Shiloh." ⁹ So the men went and passed up and down in the land and wrote in a book a description of it by towns in seven divisions. Then they came to Joshua to the camp at Shiloh, ¹⁰ and Joshua cast lots for them in Shiloh before the LORD. And there Joshua apportioned the land to the people of Israel, to each his portion.

The Inheritance for Benjamin

¹¹ The lot of the tribe of the people of Benjamin according to its clans came up, and the territory allotted to it fell between the people of Judah and the people of Joseph. ¹² On the north side their boundary began at the Jordan. Then the boundary goes up to the shoulder north of Jericho, then up through the hill country westward, and it ends at the wilderness of

---

[1] The meaning of the Hebrew is uncertain

Beth-aven. [13] From there the boundary passes along southward in the direction of Luz, to the shoulder of Luz (that is, Bethel), then the boundary goes down to Ataroth-addar, on the mountain that lies south of Lower Beth-horon. [14] Then the boundary goes in another direction, turning on the western side southward from the mountain that lies to the south, opposite Beth-horon, and it ends at Kiriath-baal (that is, Kiriath-jearim), a city belonging to the people of Judah. This forms the western side. [15] And the southern side begins at the outskirts of Kiriath-jearim. And the boundary goes from there to Ephron,[1] to the spring of the waters of Nephtoah. [16] Then the boundary goes down to the border of the mountain that overlooks the Valley of the Son of Hinnom, which is at the north end of the Valley of Rephaim. And it then goes down the Valley of Hinnom, south of the shoulder of the Jebusites, and downward to En-rogel. [17] Then it bends in a northerly direction going on to En-shemesh, and from there goes to Geliloth, which is opposite the ascent of Adummim. Then it goes down to the stone of Bohan the son of Reuben, [18] and passing on to the north of the shoulder of Beth-arabah[2] it goes down to the Arabah. [19] Then the boundary passes on to the north of the shoulder of Beth-hoglah. And the boundary ends at the northern bay of the Salt Sea, at the south end of the Jordan: this is the southern border. [20] The Jordan forms its boundary on the eastern side. This is the inheritance of the people of Benjamin, according to their clans, boundary by boundary all around.

[21] Now the cities of the tribe of the people of Benjamin according to their clans were Jericho, Beth-hoglah, Emek-keziz, [22] Beth-arabah, Zemaraim, Bethel, [23] Avvim, Parah, Ophrah, [24] Chephar-ammoni, Ophni, Geba—twelve cities with their villages: [25] Gibeon, Ramah, Beeroth, [26] Mizpeh, Chephirah, Mozah, [27] Rekem, Irpeel, Taralah, [28] Zela, Haeleph, Jebus[3] (that is, Jerusalem), Gibeah[4] and Kiriath-jearim[5]—fourteen cities with their villages. This is the inheritance of the people of Benjamin according to its clans.

The Inheritance for Simeon

19 The second lot came out for Simeon, for the tribe of the people of Simeon, according to their clans, and their inheritance was in the midst of the inheritance of the people of Judah. [2] And they had for their inheritance Beersheba, Sheba, Moladah, [3] Hazar-shual, Balah, Ezem, [4] Eltolad, Bethul, Hormah, [5] Ziklag, Beth-marcaboth, Hazar-susah, [6] Beth-lebaoth, and Sharuhen—thirteen cities with their villages; [7] Ain, Rimmon, Ether, and Ashan—four cities with their villages, [8] together with all the villages around these cities as far as Baalath-beer, Ramah of the Negeb. This was the inheritance of the tribe of the people of Simeon according to their clans. [9] The inheritance of the people of Simeon formed part of the territory of the people of Judah. Because the portion of the people of Judah was too large for them, the people of Simeon obtained an inheritance in the midst of their inheritance.

The Inheritance for Zebulun

[10] The third lot came up for the people of Zebulun, according to their clans. And the territory of their inheritance reached as far as Sarid. [11] Then their boundary goes up westward and on to Mareal and touches Dabbesheth, then the brook that is east of Jokneam. [12] From Sarid it goes in the other direction eastward toward the sunrise to the boundary of Chisloth-tabor. From there it goes to Daberath, then up to Japhia. [13] From there it passes along on the east toward the sunrise to Gath-hepher, to Eth-kazin, and going on to Rimmon it bends toward Neah, [14] then on the north the boundary turns about to Hannathon, and it ends at the Valley of Iphtahel; [15] and Kattath, Nahalal, Shimron, Idalah, and Bethlehem—twelve cities with their villages. [16] This is the inheritance of the people of Zebulun, according to their clans—these cities with their villages.

The Inheritance for Issachar

[17] The fourth lot came out for Issachar, for the people of Issachar, according to their clans. [18] Their territory included Jezreel, Chesulloth, Shunem, [19] Hapharaim, Shion, Anaharath, [20] Rabbith, Kishion, Ebez, [21] Remeth, En-gannim, En-haddah, Beth-pazzez. [22] The boundary also touches Tabor, Shahazumah, and Beth-shemesh, and its boundary ends at the Jordan—sixteen cities with their villages. [23] This is the inheritance of the tribe of the people of Issachar, according to their clans—the cities with their villages.

[1] See 15:9; Hebrew *westward* [2] Septuagint; Hebrew *to the shoulder over against the Arabah* [3] Septuagint, Syriac, Vulgate; Hebrew *the Jebusite* [4] Hebrew *Gibeath* [5] Septuagint; Hebrew *Kiriath*

The Inheritance for Asher

24 The fifth lot came out for the tribe of the people of Asher according to their clans. 25 Their territory included Helkath, Hali, Beten, Achshaph, 26 Allammelech, Amad, and Mishal. On the west it touches Carmel and Shihor-libnath, 27 then it turns eastward, it goes to Beth-dagon, and touches Zebulun and the Valley of Iphtahel northward to Beth-emek and Neiel. Then it continues in the north to Cabul, 28 Ebron, Rehob, Hammon, Kanah, as far as Sidon the Great. 29 Then the boundary turns to Ramah, reaching to the fortified city of Tyre. Then the boundary turns to Hosah, and it ends at the sea; Mahalab,1 Achzib, 30 Ummah, Aphek and Rehob—twenty-two cities with their villages. 31 This is the inheritance of the tribe of the people of Asher according to their clans—these cities with their villages.

The Inheritance for Naphtali

32 The sixth lot came out for the people of Naphtali, for the people of Naphtali, according to their clans. 33 And their boundary ran from Heleph, from the oak in Zaanannim, and Adami-nekeb, and Jabneel, as far as Lakkum, and it ended at the Jordan. 34 Then the boundary turns westward to Aznoth-tabor and goes from there to Hukkok, touching Zebulun at the south and Asher on the west and Judah on the east at the Jordan. 35 The fortified cities are Ziddim, Zer, Hammath, Rakkath, Chinnereth, 36 Adamah, Ramah, Hazor, 37 Kedesh, Edrei, En-hazor, 38 Yiron, Migdal-el, Horem, Beth-anath, and Beth-shemesh—nineteen cities with their villages. 39 This is the inheritance of the tribe of the people of Naphtali according to their clans—the cities with their villages.

The Inheritance for Dan

40 The seventh lot came out for the tribe of the people of Dan, according to their clans. 41 And the territory of its inheritance included Zorah, Eshtaol, Ir-shemesh, 42 Shaalabbin, Aijalon, Ithlah, 43 Elon, Timnah, Ekron, 44 Eltekeh, Gibbethon, Baalath, 45 Jehud, Bene-berak, Gath-rimmon, 46 and Me-jarkon and Rakkon with the territory over against Joppa. 47 When the territory of the people of Dan was lost to them, the people of Dan went up and fought against Leshem, and after capturing it and striking it with the sword they took possession of it and settled in it, calling Leshem, Dan, after the name of Dan their ancestor. 48 This is the inheritance of the tribe of the people of Dan, according to their clans—these cities with their villages.

The Inheritance for Joshua

49 When they had finished distributing the several territories of the land as inheritances, the people of Israel gave an inheritance among them to Joshua the son of Nun. 50 By command of the LORD they gave him the city that he asked, Timnath-serah in the hill country of Ephraim. And he rebuilt the city and settled in it.

51 These are the inheritances that Eleazar the priest and Joshua the son of Nun and the heads of the fathers' houses of the tribes of the people of Israel distributed by lot at Shiloh before the LORD, at the entrance of the tent of meeting. So they finished dividing the land.

The Cities of Refuge

20 Then the LORD said to Joshua, 2 "Say to the people of Israel, 'Appoint the cities of refuge, of which I spoke to you through Moses, 3 that the manslayer who strikes any person without intent or unknowingly may flee there. They shall be for you a refuge from the avenger of blood. 4 He shall flee to one of these cities and shall stand at the entrance of the gate of the city and explain his case to the elders of that city. Then they shall take him into the city and give him a place, and he shall remain with them. 5 And if the avenger of blood pursues him, they shall not give up the manslayer into his hand, because he struck his neighbor unknowingly, and did not hate him in the past. 6 And he shall remain in that city until he has stood before the congregation for judgment, until the death of him who is high priest at the time. Then the manslayer may return to his own town and his own home, to the town from which he fled.' "

7 So they set apart Kedesh in Galilee in the hill country of Naphtali, and Shechem in the hill country of Ephraim, and Kiriath-arba (that is, Hebron) in the hill country of Judah. 8 And beyond the Jordan east of Jericho, they appointed Bezer in the wilderness on the tableland, from the tribe of Reuben, and Ramoth in Gilead, from the tribe of Gad, and Golan in Bashan, from the tribe of Manasseh. 9 These were the cities designated for all the people of Israel and for the stranger sojourning among them, that anyone who killed a person without

1 Compare Septuagint; Hebrew *Mehebel*

intent could flee there, so that he might not die by the hand of the avenger of blood, till he stood before the congregation.

Cities and Pasturelands Allotted to Levi

21 Then the heads of the fathers' houses of the Levites came to Eleazar the priest and to Joshua the son of Nun and to the heads of the fathers' houses of the tribes of the people of Israel. ² And they said to them at Shiloh in the land of Canaan, "The LORD commanded through Moses that we be given cities to dwell in, along with their pasturelands for our livestock." ³ So by command of the LORD the people of Israel gave to the Levites the following cities and pasturelands out of their inheritance.

⁴ The lot came out for the clans of the Kohathites. So those Levites who were descendants of Aaron the priest received by lot from the tribes of Judah, Simeon, and Benjamin, thirteen cities.

⁵ And the rest of the Kohathites received by lot from the clans of the tribe of Ephraim, from the tribe of Dan and the half-tribe of Manasseh, ten cities.

⁶ The Gershonites received by lot from the clans of the tribe of Issachar, from the tribe of Asher, from the tribe of Naphtali, and from the half-tribe of Manasseh in Bashan, thirteen cities.

⁷ The Merarites according to their clans received from the tribe of Reuben, the tribe of Gad, and the tribe of Zebulun, twelve cities.

⁸ These cities and their pasturelands the people of Israel gave by lot to the Levites, as the LORD had commanded through Moses.

⁹ Out of the tribe of the people of Judah and the tribe of the people of Simeon they gave the following cities mentioned by name, ¹⁰ which went to the descendants of Aaron, one of the clans of the Kohathites who belonged to the people of Levi; since the lot fell to them first. ¹¹ They gave them Kiriath-arba (Arba being the father of Anak), that is Hebron, in the hill country of Judah, along with the pasturelands around it. ¹² But the fields of the city and its villages had been given to Caleb the son of Jephunneh as his possession.

¹³ And to the descendants of Aaron the priest they gave Hebron, the city of refuge for the manslayer, with its pasturelands, Libnah with its pasturelands, ¹⁴ Jattir with its pasturelands, Eshtemoa with its pasturelands, ¹⁵ Holon with its pasturelands, Debir with its pasturelands,

¹⁶ Ain with its pasturelands, Juttah with its pasturelands, Beth-shemesh with its pasturelands—nine cities out of these two tribes; ¹⁷ then out of the tribe of Benjamin, Gibeon with its pasturelands, Geba with its pasturelands, ¹⁸ Anathoth with its pasturelands, and Almon with its pasturelands—four cities. ¹⁹ The cities of the descendants of Aaron, the priests, were in all thirteen cities with their pasturelands.

²⁰ As to the rest of the Kohathites belonging to the Kohathite clans of the Levites, the cities allotted to them were out of the tribe of Ephraim. ²¹ To them were given Shechem, the city of refuge for the manslayer, with its pasturelands in the hill country of Ephraim, Gezer with its pasturelands, ²² Kibzaim with its pasturelands, Beth-horon with its pasturelands—four cities; ²³ and out of the tribe of Dan, Elteke with its pasturelands, Gibbethon with its pasturelands, ²⁴ Aijalon with its pasturelands, Gath-rimmon with its pasturelands—four cities; ²⁵ and out of the half-tribe of Manasseh, Taanach with its pasturelands, and Gath-rimmon with its pasturelands—two cities. ²⁶ The cities of the clans of the rest of the Kohathites were ten in all with their pasturelands.

²⁷ And to the Gershonites, one of the clans of the Levites, were given out of the half-tribe of Manasseh, Golan in Bashan with its pasturelands, the city of refuge for the manslayer, and Beeshterah with its pasturelands—two cities; ²⁸ and out of the tribe of Issachar, Kishion with its pasturelands, Daberath with its pasturelands, ²⁹ Jarmuth with its pasturelands, En-gannim with its pasturelands—four cities; ³⁰ and out of the tribe of Asher, Mishal with its pasturelands, Abdon with its pasturelands, ³¹ Helkath with its pasturelands, and Rehob with its pasturelands—four cities; ³² and out of the tribe of Naphtali, Kedesh in Galilee with its pasturelands, the city of refuge for the manslayer, Hammoth-dor with its pasturelands, and Kartan with its pasturelands—three cities. ³³ The cities of the several clans of the Gershonites were in all thirteen cities with their pasturelands.

³⁴ And to the rest of the Levites, the Merarite clans, were given out of the tribe of Zebulun, Jokneam with its pasturelands, Kartah with its pasturelands, ³⁵ Dimnah with its pasturelands, Nahalal with its pasturelands—four cities; ³⁶ and out of the tribe of Reuben, Bezer with its pasturelands, Jahaz with its pasturelands,

[37] Kedemoth with its pasturelands, and Mephaath with its pasturelands—four cities; [38] and out of the tribe of Gad, Ramoth in Gilead with its pasturelands, the city of refuge for the manslayer, Mahanaim with its pasturelands, [39] Heshbon with its pasturelands, Jazer with its pasturelands—four cities in all. [40] As for the cities of the several Merarite clans, that is, the remainder of the clans of the Levites, those allotted to them were in all twelve cities.

[41] The cities of the Levites in the midst of the possession of the people of Israel were in all forty-eight cities with their pasturelands. [42] These cities each had its pasturelands around it. So it was with all these cities.

[43] Thus the LORD gave to Israel all the land that he swore to give to their fathers. And they took possession of it, and they settled there. [44] And the LORD gave them rest on every side just as he had sworn to their fathers. Not one of all their enemies had withstood them, for the LORD had given all their enemies into their hands. [45] Not one word of all the good promises that the LORD had made to the house of Israel had failed; all came to pass.

The Eastern Tribes Return Home

22 At that time Joshua summoned the Reubenites and the Gadites and the half-tribe of Manasseh, [2] and said to them, "You have kept all that Moses the servant of the LORD commanded you and have obeyed my voice in all that I have commanded you. [3] You have not forsaken your brothers these many days, down to this day, but have been careful to keep the charge of the LORD your God. [4] And now the LORD your God has given rest to your brothers, as he promised them. Therefore turn and go to your tents in the land where your possession lies, which Moses the servant of the LORD gave you on the other side of the Jordan. [5] Only be very careful to observe the commandment and the law that Moses the servant of the LORD commanded you, to love the LORD your God, and to walk in all his ways and to keep his commandments and to cling to him and to serve him with all your heart and with all your soul." [6] So Joshua blessed them and sent them away, and they went to their tents.

[7] Now to the one half of the tribe of Manasseh Moses had given a possession in Bashan, but to the other half Joshua had given a possession beside their brothers in the land west of the Jordan. And when Joshua sent them away to their homes and blessed them, [8] he said to them, "Go back to your tents with much wealth and with very much livestock, with silver, gold, bronze, and iron, and with much clothing. Divide the spoil of your enemies with your brothers." [9] So the people of Reuben and the people of Gad and the half-tribe of Manasseh returned home, parting from the people of Israel at Shiloh, which is in the land of Canaan, to go to the land of Gilead, their own land of which they had possessed themselves by command of the LORD through Moses.

The Eastern Tribes' Altar of Witness

[10] And when they came to the region of the Jordan that is in the land of Canaan, the people of Reuben and the people of Gad and the half-tribe of Manasseh built there an altar by the Jordan, an altar of imposing size. [11] And the people of Israel heard it said, "Behold, the people of Reuben and the people of Gad and the half-tribe of Manasseh have built the altar at the frontier of the land of Canaan, in the region about the Jordan, on the side that belongs to the people of Israel." [12] And when the people of Israel heard of it, the whole assembly of the people of Israel gathered at Shiloh to make war against them.

[13] Then the people of Israel sent to the people of Reuben and the people of Gad and the half-tribe of Manasseh, in the land of Gilead, Phinehas the son of Eleazar the priest, [14] and with him ten chiefs, one from each of the tribal families of Israel, every one of them the head of a family among the clans of Israel. [15] And they came to the people of Reuben, the people of Gad, and the half-tribe of Manasseh, in the land of Gilead, and they said to them, [16] "Thus says the whole congregation of the LORD, 'What is this breach of faith that you have committed against the God of Israel in turning away this day from following the LORD by building yourselves an altar this day in rebellion against the LORD? [17] Have we not had enough of the sin at Peor from which even yet we have not cleansed ourselves, and for which there came a plague upon the congregation of the LORD, [18] that you too must turn away this day from following the LORD? And if you too rebel against the LORD today then tomorrow he will be angry with the whole congregation of Israel. [19] But now, if the land of your possession is unclean, pass over

into the LORD's land where the LORD's tabernacle stands, and take for yourselves a possession among us. Only do not rebel against the LORD or make us as rebels by building for yourselves an altar other than the altar of the LORD our God. ²⁰ Did not Achan the son of Zerah break faith in the matter of the devoted things, and wrath fell upon all the congregation of Israel? And he did not perish alone for his iniquity.'"

²¹ Then the people of Reuben, the people of Gad, and the half-tribe of Manasseh said in answer to the heads of the families of Israel, ²² "The Mighty One, God, the LORD! The Mighty One, God, the LORD! He knows; and let Israel itself know! If it was in rebellion or in breach of faith against the LORD, do not spare us today ²³ for building an altar to turn away from following the LORD. Or if we did so to offer burnt offerings or grain offerings or peace offerings on it, may the LORD himself take vengeance. ²⁴ No, but we did it from fear that in time to come your children might say to our children, 'What have you to do with the LORD, the God of Israel? ²⁵ For the LORD has made the Jordan a boundary between us and you, you people of Reuben and people of Gad. You have no portion in the LORD.' So your children might make our children cease to worship the LORD. ²⁶ Therefore we said, 'Let us now build an altar, not for burnt offering, nor for sacrifice, ²⁷ but to be a witness between us and you, and between our generations after us, that we do perform the service of the LORD in his presence with our burnt offerings and sacrifices and peace offerings, so your children will not say to our children in time to come, "You have no portion in the LORD."' ²⁸ And we thought, 'If this should be said to us or to our descendants in time to come, we should say, "Behold, the copy of the altar of the LORD, which our fathers made, not for burnt offerings, nor for sacrifice, but to be a witness between us and you."' ²⁹ Far be it from us that we should rebel against the LORD and turn away this day from following the LORD by building an altar for burnt offering, grain offering, or sacrifice, other than the altar of the LORD our God that stands before his tabernacle!"

³⁰ When Phinehas the priest and the chiefs of the congregation, the heads of the families of Israel who were with him, heard the words that the people of Reuben and the people of

Gad and the people of Manasseh spoke, it was good in their eyes. ³¹ And Phinehas the son of Eleazar the priest said to the people of Reuben and the people of Gad and the people of Manasseh, "Today we know that the LORD is in our midst, because you have not committed this breach of faith against the LORD. Now you have delivered the people of Israel from the hand of the LORD."

³² Then Phinehas the son of Eleazar the priest, and the chiefs, returned from the people of Reuben and the people of Gad in the land of Gilead to the land of Canaan, to the people of Israel, and brought back word to them. ³³ And the report was good in the eyes of the people of Israel. And the people of Israel blessed God and spoke no more of making war against them to destroy the land where the people of Reuben and the people of Gad were settled. ³⁴ The people of Reuben and the people of Gad called the altar Witness, "For," they said, "it is a witness between us that the LORD is God."

Joshua's Charge to Israel's Leaders

23 A long time afterward, when the LORD had given rest to Israel from all their surrounding enemies, and Joshua was old and well advanced in years, ² Joshua summoned all Israel, its elders and heads, its judges and officers, and said to them, "I am now old and well advanced in years. ³ And you have seen all that the LORD your God has done to all these nations for your sake, for it is the LORD your God who has fought for you. ⁴ Behold, I have allotted to you as an inheritance for your tribes those nations that remain, along with all the nations that I have already cut off, from the Jordan to the Great Sea in the west. ⁵ The LORD your God will push them back before you and drive them out of your sight. And you shall possess their land, just as the LORD your God promised you. ⁶ Therefore, be very strong to keep and to do all that is written in the Book of the Law of Moses, turning aside from it neither to the right hand nor to the left, ⁷ that you may not mix with these nations remaining among you or make mention of the names of their gods or swear by them or serve them or bow down to them, ⁸ but you shall cling to the LORD your God just as you have done to this day. ⁹ For the LORD has driven out before you great and strong nations. And as for you, no man has been able to stand

before you to this day. [10] One man of you puts to flight a thousand, since it is the LORD your God who fights for you, just as he promised you. [11] Be very careful, therefore, to love the LORD your God. [12] For if you turn back and cling to the remnant of these nations remaining among you and make marriages with them, so that you associate with them and they with you, [13] know for certain that the LORD your God will no longer drive out these nations before you, but they shall be a snare and a trap for you, a whip on your sides and thorns in your eyes, until you perish from off this good ground that the LORD your God has given you.

[14] "And now I am about to go the way of all the earth, and you know in your hearts and souls, all of you, that not one word has failed of all the good things[1] that the LORD your God promised concerning you. All have come to pass for you; not one of them has failed. [15] But just as all the good things that the LORD your God promised concerning you have been fulfilled for you, so the LORD will bring upon you all the evil things, until he has destroyed you from off this good land that the LORD your God has given you, [16] if you transgress the covenant of the LORD your God, which he commanded you, and go and serve other gods and bow down to them. Then the anger of the LORD will be kindled against you, and you shall perish quickly from off the good land that he has given to you."

The Covenant Renewal at Shechem

24 Joshua gathered all the tribes of Israel to Shechem and summoned the elders, the heads, the judges, and the officers of Israel. And they presented themselves before God. [2] And Joshua said to all the people, "Thus says the LORD, the God of Israel, 'Long ago, your fathers lived beyond the Euphrates,[2] Terah, the father of Abraham and of Nahor; and they served other gods. [3] Then I took your father Abraham from beyond the River[3] and led him through all the land of Canaan, and made his offspring many. I gave him Isaac. [4] And to Isaac I gave Jacob and Esau. And I gave Esau the hill country of Seir to possess, but Jacob and his children went down to Egypt. [5] And I sent Moses and Aaron, and I plagued Egypt with what I did in the midst of it, and afterward I brought you out.

[6] " 'Then I brought your fathers out of Egypt,

and you came to the sea. And the Egyptians pursued your fathers with chariots and horsemen to the Red Sea. [7] And when they cried to the LORD, he put darkness between you and the Egyptians and made the sea come upon them and cover them; and your eyes saw what I did in Egypt. And you lived in the wilderness a long time. [8] Then I brought you to the land of the Amorites, who lived on the other side of the Jordan. They fought with you, and I gave them into your hand, and you took possession of their land, and I destroyed them before you. [9] Then Balak the son of Zippor, king of Moab, arose and fought against Israel. And he sent and invited Balaam the son of Beor to curse you, [10] but I would not listen to Balaam. Indeed, he blessed you. So I delivered you out of his hand. [11] And you went over the Jordan and came to Jericho, and the leaders of Jericho fought against you, and also the Amorites, the Perizzites, the Canaanites, the Hittites, the Girgashites, the Hivites, and the Jebusites. And I gave them into your hand. [12] And I sent the hornet before you, which drove them out before you, the two kings of the Amorites; it was not by your sword or by your bow. [13] I gave you a land on which you had not labored and cities that you had not built, and you dwell in them. You eat the fruit of vineyards and olive orchards that you did not plant.'

Choose Whom You Will Serve

[14] "Now therefore fear the LORD and serve him in sincerity and in faithfulness. Put away the gods that your fathers served beyond the River and in Egypt, and serve the LORD. [15] And if it is evil in your eyes to serve the LORD, choose this day whom you will serve, whether the gods your fathers served in the region beyond the River, or the gods of the Amorites in whose land you dwell. But as for me and my house, we will serve the LORD."

[16] Then the people answered, "Far be it from us that we should forsake the LORD to serve other gods, [17] for it is the LORD our God who brought us and our fathers up from the land of Egypt, out of the house of slavery, and who did those great signs in our sight and preserved us in all the way that we went, and among all the peoples through whom we passed. [18] And the LORD drove out before us all the peoples, the Amorites who lived in the land. Therefore we also will serve the LORD, for he is our God."

[1] Or words; also twice in verse 15 [2] Hebrew the River [3] That is, the Euphrates; also verses 14, 15

¹⁹ But Joshua said to the people, "You are not able to serve the LORD, for he is a holy God. He is a jealous God; he will not forgive your transgressions or your sins. ²⁰ If you forsake the LORD and serve foreign gods, then he will turn and do you harm and consume you, after having done you good." ²¹ And the people said to Joshua, "No, but we will serve the LORD." ²² Then Joshua said to the people, "You are witnesses against yourselves that you have chosen the LORD, to serve him." And they said, "We are witnesses." ²³ He said, "Then put away the foreign gods that are among you, and incline your heart to the LORD, the God of Israel." ²⁴ And the people said to Joshua, "The LORD our God we will serve, and his voice we will obey." ²⁵ So Joshua made a covenant with the people that day, and put in place statutes and rules for them at Shechem. ²⁶ And Joshua wrote these words in the Book of the Law of God. And he took a large stone and set it up there under the terebinth that was by the sanctuary of the LORD. ²⁷ And Joshua said to all the people, "Behold, this stone shall be a witness against us, for it has heard all the words of the LORD that he spoke to us. Therefore it shall be a witness against you, lest you deal falsely with your God." ²⁸ So Joshua sent the people away, every man to his inheritance.

Joshua's Death and Burial

²⁹ After these things Joshua the son of Nun, the servant of the LORD, died, being 110 years old. ³⁰ And they buried him in his own inheritance at Timnath-serah, which is in the hill country of Ephraim, north of the mountain of Gaash.

³¹ Israel served the LORD all the days of Joshua, and all the days of the elders who outlived Joshua and had known all the work that the LORD did for Israel.

³² As for the bones of Joseph, which the people of Israel brought up from Egypt, they buried them at Shechem, in the piece of land that Jacob bought from the sons of Hamor the father of Shechem for a hundred pieces of money.[1] It became an inheritance of the descendants of Joseph.

³³ And Eleazar the son of Aaron died, and they buried him at Gibeah, the town of Phinehas his son, which had been given him in the hill country of Ephraim.

---

[1] Hebrew *for a hundred qesitah*; a unit of money of unknown value

JUDGES

The Continuing Conquest of Canaan

1 After the death of Joshua, the people of Israel inquired of the LORD, "Who shall go up first for us against the Canaanites, to fight against them?" ² The LORD said, "Judah shall go up; behold, I have given the land into his hand." ³ And Judah said to Simeon his brother, "Come up with me into the territory allotted to me, that we may fight against the Canaanites. And I likewise will go with you into the territory allotted to you." So Simeon went with him. ⁴ Then Judah went up and the LORD gave the Canaanites and the Perizzites into their hand, and they defeated 10,000 of them at Bezek. ⁵ They found Adoni-bezek at Bezek and fought against him and defeated the Canaanites and the Perizzites. ⁶ Adoni-bezek fled, but they pursued him and caught him and cut off his thumbs and his big toes. ⁷ And Adoni-bezek said, "Seventy kings with their thumbs and their big toes cut off used to pick up scraps under my table. As I have done, so God has repaid me." And they brought him to Jerusalem, and he died there.

⁸ And the men of Judah fought against Jerusalem and captured it and struck it with the edge of the sword and set the city on fire. ⁹ And afterward the men of Judah went down to fight against the Canaanites who lived in the hill country, in the Negeb, and in the lowland. ¹⁰ And Judah went against the Canaanites who lived in Hebron (now the name of Hebron was formerly Kiriath-arba), and they defeated Sheshai and Ahiman and Talmai.

¹¹ From there they went against the inhabitants of Debir. The name of Debir was formerly Kiriath-sepher. ¹² And Caleb said, "He who attacks Kiriath-sepher and captures it, I will give him Achsah my daughter for a wife." ¹³ And Othniel the son of Kenaz, Caleb's younger brother, captured it. And he gave him Achsah his daughter for a wife. ¹⁴ When she came to him, she urged him to ask her father for a field. And she dismounted from her donkey, and Caleb said to her, "What do you want?" ¹⁵ She said to him, "Give me a blessing. Since you have set me in the land of the Negeb, give me also springs of water." And Caleb gave her the upper springs and the lower springs.

¹⁶ And the descendants of the Kenite, Moses' father-in-law, went up with the people of Judah from the city of palms into the wilderness of Judah, which lies in the Negeb near Arad, and they went and settled with the people. ¹⁷ And Judah went with Simeon his brother, and they defeated the Canaanites who inhabited Zephath and devoted it to destruction. So the name of the city was called Hormah.¹ ¹⁸ Judah also captured Gaza with its territory, and Ashkelon with its territory, and Ekron with its territory. ¹⁹ And the LORD was with Judah, and he took possession of the hill country, but he could not drive out the inhabitants of the plain because they had chariots of iron. ²⁰ And Hebron was given to Caleb, as Moses had said. And he drove out from it the three sons of Anak. ²¹ But the people of Benjamin did not drive out the Jebusites who lived in Jerusalem, so the Jebusites have lived with the people of Benjamin in Jerusalem to this day.

²² The house of Joseph also went up against Bethel, and the LORD was with them. ²³ And the house of Joseph scouted out Bethel. (Now the name of the city was formerly Luz.) ²⁴ And the spies saw a man coming out of the city, and they said to him, "Please show us the way into the city, and we will deal kindly with you." ²⁵ And he showed them the way into the city. And they struck the city with the edge of the sword, but they let the man and all his family go. ²⁶ And the man went to the land of the Hittites and built a city and called its name Luz. That is its name to this day.

Failure to Complete the Conquest

²⁷ Manasseh did not drive out the inhabitants of Beth-shean and its villages, or Taanach and its villages, or the inhabitants of Dor and its villages, or the inhabitants of Ibleam and its villages, or the inhabitants of Megiddo and its villages, for the Canaanites persisted in dwelling in that land. ²⁸ When Israel grew strong, they put the Canaanites to forced labor, but did not drive them out completely.

²⁹ And Ephraim did not drive out the Canaanites who lived in Gezer, so the Canaanites lived in Gezer among them.

³⁰ Zebulun did not drive out the inhabitants of Kitron, or the inhabitants of Nahalol, so the

---

¹ Hormah means utter destruction

Canaanites lived among them, but became subject to forced labor.

[31] Asher did not drive out the inhabitants of Acco, or the inhabitants of Sidon or of Ahlab or of Achzib or of Helbah or of Aphik or of Rehob, [32] so the Asherites lived among the Canaanites, the inhabitants of the land, for they did not drive them out.

[33] Naphtali did not drive out the inhabitants of Beth-shemesh, or the inhabitants of Beth-anath, so they lived among the Canaanites, the inhabitants of the land. Nevertheless, the inhabitants of Beth-shemesh and of Beth-anath became subject to forced labor for them.

[34] The Amorites pressed the people of Dan back into the hill country, for they did not allow them to come down to the plain. [35] The Amorites persisted in dwelling in Mount Heres, in Aijalon, and in Shaalbim, but the hand of the house of Joseph rested heavily on them, and they became subject to forced labor. [36] And the border of the Amorites ran from the ascent of Akrabbim, from Sela and upward.

Israel's Disobedience

2 Now the angel of the LORD went up from Gilgal to Bochim. And he said, "I brought you up from Egypt and brought you into the land that I swore to give to your fathers. I said, 'I will never break my covenant with you, [2] and you shall make no covenant with the inhabitants of this land; you shall break down their altars.' But you have not obeyed my voice. What is this you have done? [3] So now I say, I will not drive them out before you, but they shall become thorns in your sides, and their gods shall be a snare to you." [4] As soon as the angel of the LORD spoke these words to all the people of Israel, the people lifted up their voices and wept. [5] And they called the name of that place Bochim.[1] And they sacrificed there to the LORD.

The Death of Joshua

[6] When Joshua dismissed the people, the people of Israel went each to his inheritance to take possession of the land. [7] And the people served the LORD all the days of Joshua, and all the days of the elders who outlived Joshua, who had seen all the great work that the LORD had done for Israel. [8] And Joshua the son of Nun, the servant of the LORD, died at the age of 110 years. [9] And they buried him within the boundaries of his inheritance in Timnath-heres, in the hill country of Ephraim, north of the mountain of Gaash. [10] And all that generation also were gathered to their fathers. And there arose another generation after them who did not know the LORD or the work that he had done for Israel.

Israel's Unfaithfulness

[11] And the people of Israel did what was evil in the sight of the LORD and served the Baals. [12] And they abandoned the LORD, the God of their fathers, who had brought them out of the land of Egypt. They went after other gods, from among the gods of the peoples who were around them, and bowed down to them. And they provoked the LORD to anger. [13] They abandoned the LORD and served the Baals and the Ashtaroth. [14] So the anger of the LORD was kindled against Israel, and he gave them over to plunderers, who plundered them. And he sold them into the hand of their surrounding enemies, so that they could no longer withstand their enemies. [15] Whenever they marched out, the hand of the LORD was against them for harm, as the LORD had warned, and as the LORD had sworn to them. And they were in terrible distress.

The LORD Raises Up Judges

[16] Then the LORD raised up judges, who saved them out of the hand of those who plundered them. [17] Yet they did not listen to their judges, for they whored after other gods and bowed down to them. They soon turned aside from the way in which their fathers had walked, who had obeyed the commandments of the LORD, and they did not do so. [18] Whenever the LORD raised up judges for them, the LORD was with the judge, and he saved them from the hand of their enemies all the days of the judge. For the LORD was moved to pity by their groaning because of those who afflicted and oppressed them. [19] But whenever the judge died, they turned back and were more corrupt than their fathers, going after other gods, serving them and bowing down to them. They did not drop any of their practices or their stubborn ways. [20] So the anger of the LORD was kindled against Israel, and he said, "Because this people have transgressed my covenant that I commanded their fathers and have not obeyed my voice, [21] I will no longer drive out before them any of the nations that Joshua left when he died, [22] in order to test Israel by them, whether they will take care to walk in the way of the LORD as their fathers did, or not."

---

[1] Bochim means weepers

²³ So the LORD left those nations, not driving them out quickly, and he did not give them into the hand of Joshua.

3 Now these are the nations that the LORD left, to test Israel by them, that is, all in Israel who had not experienced all the wars in Canaan. ² It was only in order that the generations of the people of Israel might know war, to teach war to those who had not known it before. ³ These are the nations: the five lords of the Philistines and all the Canaanites and the Sidonians and the Hivites who lived on Mount Lebanon, from Mount Baal-hermon as far as Lebo-hamath. ⁴ They were for the testing of Israel, to know whether Israel would obey the commandments of the LORD, which he commanded their fathers by the hand of Moses. ⁵ So the people of Israel lived among the Canaanites, the Hittites, the Amorites, the Perizzites, the Hivites, and the Jebusites. ⁶ And their daughters they took to themselves for wives, and their own daughters they gave to their sons, and they served their gods.

Othniel

⁷ And the people of Israel did what was evil in the sight of the LORD. They forgot the LORD their God and served the Baals and the Asheroth. ⁸ Therefore the anger of the LORD was kindled against Israel, and he sold them into the hand of Cushan-rishathaim king of Mesopotamia. And the people of Israel served Cushan-rishathaim eight years. ⁹ But when the people of Israel cried out to the LORD, the LORD raised up a deliverer for the people of Israel, who saved them, Othniel the son of Kenaz, Caleb's younger brother. ¹⁰ The Spirit of the LORD was upon him, and he judged Israel. He went out to war, and the LORD gave Cushan-rishathaim king of Mesopotamia into his hand. And his hand prevailed over Cushan-rishathaim. ¹¹ So the land had rest forty years. Then Othniel the son of Kenaz died.

Ehud

¹² And the people of Israel again did what was evil in the sight of the LORD, and the LORD strengthened Eglon the king of Moab against Israel, because they had done what was evil in the sight of the LORD. ¹³ He gathered to himself the Ammonites and the Amalekites, and went and defeated Israel. And they took possession of the city of palms. ¹⁴ And the people of Israel served Eglon the king of Moab eighteen years.

¹⁵ Then the people of Israel cried out to the LORD, and the LORD raised up for them a deliverer, Ehud, the son of Gera, the Benjaminite, a left-handed man. The people of Israel sent tribute by him to Eglon the king of Moab. ¹⁶ And Ehud made for himself a sword with two edges, a cubit[1] in length, and he bound it on his right thigh under his clothes. ¹⁷ And he presented the tribute to Eglon king of Moab. Now Eglon was a very fat man. ¹⁸ And when Ehud had finished presenting the tribute, he sent away the people who carried the tribute. ¹⁹ But he himself turned back at the idols near Gilgal and said, "I have a secret message for you, O king." And he commanded, "Silence." And all his attendants went out from his presence. ²⁰ And Ehud came to him as he was sitting alone in his cool roof chamber. And Ehud said, "I have a message from God for you." And he arose from his seat. ²¹ And Ehud reached with his left hand, took the sword from his right thigh, and thrust it into his belly. ²² And the hilt also went in after the blade, and the fat closed over the blade, for he did not pull the sword out of his belly; and the dung came out. ²³ Then Ehud went out into the porch[2] and closed the doors of the roof chamber behind him and locked them.

²⁴ When he had gone, the servants came, and when they saw that the doors of the roof chamber were locked, they thought, "Surely he is relieving himself in the closet of the cool chamber." ²⁵ And they waited till they were embarrassed. But when he still did not open the doors of the roof chamber, they took the key and opened them, and there lay their lord dead on the floor.

²⁶ Ehud escaped while they delayed, and he passed beyond the idols and escaped to Seirah. ²⁷ When he arrived, he sounded the trumpet in the hill country of Ephraim. Then the people of Israel went down with him from the hill country, and he was their leader. ²⁸ And he said to them, "Follow after me, for the LORD has given your enemies the Moabites into your hand." So they went down after him and seized the fords of the Jordan against the Moabites and did not allow anyone to pass over. ²⁹ And they killed at that time about 10,000 of the Moabites, all strong, able-bodied men; not a man escaped.

---

[1] A *cubit* was about 18 inches or 45 centimeters [2] The meaning of the Hebrew word is uncertain

[30] So Moab was subdued that day under the hand of Israel. And the land had rest for eighty years.

Shamgar

[31] After him was Shamgar the son of Anath, who killed 600 of the Philistines with an oxgoad, and he also saved Israel.

Deborah and Barak

4 And the people of Israel again did what was evil in the sight of the LORD after Ehud died. [2] And the LORD sold them into the hand of Jabin king of Canaan, who reigned in Hazor. The commander of his army was Sisera, who lived in Harosheth-hagoyim. [3] Then the people of Israel cried out to the LORD for help, for he had 900 chariots of iron and he oppressed the people of Israel cruelly for twenty years.

[4] Now Deborah, a prophetess, the wife of Lappidoth, was judging Israel at that time. [5] She used to sit under the palm of Deborah between Ramah and Bethel in the hill country of Ephraim, and the people of Israel came up to her for judgment. [6] She sent and summoned Barak the son of Abinoam from Kedesh-naphtali and said to him, "Has not the LORD, the God of Israel, commanded you, 'Go, gather your men at Mount Tabor, taking 10,000 from the people of Naphtali and the people of Zebulun. [7] And I will draw out Sisera, the general of Jabin's army, to meet you by the river Kishon with his chariots and his troops, and I will give him into your hand'?" [8] Barak said to her, "If you will go with me, I will go, but if you will not go with me, I will not go." [9] And she said, "I will surely go with you. Nevertheless, the road on which you are going will not lead to your glory, for the LORD will sell Sisera into the hand of a woman." Then Deborah arose and went with Barak to Kedesh. [10] And Barak called out Zebulun and Naphtali to Kedesh. And 10,000 men went up at his heels, and Deborah went up with him.

[11] Now Heber the Kenite had separated from the Kenites, the descendants of Hobab the father-in-law of Moses, and had pitched his tent as far away as the oak in Zaanannim, which is near Kedesh.

[12] When Sisera was told that Barak the son of Abinoam had gone up to Mount Tabor, [13] Sisera called out all his chariots, 900 chariots of iron, and all the men who were with him, from Harosheth-hagoyim to the river Kishon. [14] And Deborah said to Barak, "Up! For this is the day in which the LORD has given Sisera into your hand. Does not the LORD go out before you?" So Barak went down from Mount Tabor with 10,000 men following him. [15] And the LORD routed Sisera and all his chariots and all his army before Barak by the edge of the sword. And Sisera got down from his chariot and fled away on foot. [16] And Barak pursued the chariots and the army to Harosheth-hagoyim, and all the army of Sisera fell by the edge of the sword; not a man was left.

[17] But Sisera fled away on foot to the tent of Jael, the wife of Heber the Kenite, for there was peace between Jabin the king of Hazor and the house of Heber the Kenite. [18] And Jael came out to meet Sisera and said to him, "Turn aside, my lord; turn aside to me; do not be afraid." So he turned aside to her into the tent, and she covered him with a rug. [19] And he said to her, "Please give me a little water to drink, for I am thirsty." So she opened a skin of milk and gave him a drink and covered him. [20] And he said to her, "Stand at the opening of the tent, and if any man comes and asks you, 'Is anyone here?' say, 'No.'" [21] But Jael the wife of Heber took a tent peg, and took a hammer in her hand. Then she went softly to him and drove the peg into his temple until it went down into the ground while he was lying fast asleep from weariness. So he died. [22] And behold, as Barak was pursuing Sisera, Jael went out to meet him and said to him, "Come, and I will show you the man whom you are seeking." So he went in to her tent, and there lay Sisera dead, with the tent peg in his temple.

[23] So on that day God subdued Jabin the king of Canaan before the people of Israel. [24] And the hand of the people of Israel pressed harder and harder against Jabin the king of Canaan, until they destroyed Jabin king of Canaan.

The Song of Deborah and Barak

5 Then sang Deborah and Barak the son of Abinoam on that day:

[2] "That the leaders took the lead in Israel,
　　that the people offered themselves will-
　　　ingly,
　　bless the LORD!

[3] "Hear, O kings; give ear, O princes;
　　to the LORD I will sing;
　　I will make melody to the LORD, the
　　　God of Israel.

4 "LORD, when you went out from Seir,
    when you marched from the region of
        Edom,
the earth trembled
    and the heavens dropped,
    yes, the clouds dropped water.
5 The mountains quaked before the LORD,
    even Sinai before the LORD,[1] the God
        of Israel.

6 "In the days of Shamgar, son of Anath,
    in the days of Jael, the highways were
        abandoned,
    and travelers kept to the byways.
7 The villagers ceased in Israel;
    they ceased to be until I arose;
    I, Deborah, arose as a mother in Israel.
8 When new gods were chosen,
    then war was in the gates.
Was shield or spear to be seen
    among forty thousand in Israel?
9 My heart goes out to the commanders of
        Israel
    who offered themselves willingly
        among the people.
    Bless the LORD.

10 "Tell of it, you who ride on white donkeys,
    you who sit on rich carpets[2]
    and you who walk by the way.
11 To the sound of musicians[3] at the watering
        places,
    there they repeat the righteous tri-
        umphs of the LORD,
    the righteous triumphs of his villagers
        in Israel.

"Then down to the gates marched the
    people of the LORD.
12 "Awake, awake, Deborah!
    Awake, awake, break out in a song!
Arise, Barak, lead away your captives,
    O son of Abinoam.
13 Then down marched the remnant of the
        noble;
    the people of the LORD marched down
        for me against the mighty.
14 From Ephraim their root they marched
        down into the valley,[4]
    following you, Benjamin, with your
        kinsmen;

from Machir marched down the com-
        manders,
    and from Zebulun those who bear the
        lieutenant's[5] staff;
15 the princes of Issachar came with Deborah,
    and Issachar faithful to Barak;
    into the valley they rushed at his heels.
Among the clans of Reuben
    there were great searchings of heart.
16 Why did you sit still among the sheepfolds,
    to hear the whistling for the flocks?
Among the clans of Reuben
    there were great searchings of heart.
17 Gilead stayed beyond the Jordan;
    and Dan, why did he stay with the
        ships?
Asher sat still at the coast of the sea,
    staying by his landings.
18 Zebulun is a people who risked their lives
        to the death;
    Naphtali, too, on the heights of the
        field.

19 "The kings came, they fought;
    then fought the kings of Canaan,
at Taanach, by the waters of Megiddo;
    they got no spoils of silver.
20 From heaven the stars fought,
    from their courses they fought against
        Sisera.
21 The torrent Kishon swept them away,
    the ancient torrent, the torrent Kishon.
    March on, my soul, with might!

22 "Then loud beat the horses' hoofs
    with the galloping, galloping of his
        steeds.

23 "Curse Meroz, says the angel of the LORD,
    curse its inhabitants thoroughly,
because they did not come to the help of
        the LORD,
    to the help of the LORD against the
        mighty.

24 "Most blessed of women be Jael,
    the wife of Heber the Kenite,
    of tent-dwelling women most blessed.
25 He asked for water and she gave him milk;
    she brought him curds in a noble's
        bowl.
26 She sent her hand to the tent peg
    and her right hand to the workmen's
        mallet;

[1] Or before the LORD, the One of Sinai, before the LORD [2] The meaning of the Hebrew word is uncertain; it may connote saddle blankets [3] Or archers; the meaning of the Hebrew word is uncertain [4] Septuagint; Hebrew in Amalek [5] Hebrew commander's

she struck Sisera;
she crushed his head;
she shattered and pierced his temple.
27 Between her feet
he sank, he fell, he lay still;
between her feet
he sank, he fell;
where he sank,
there he fell—dead.

28 "Out of the window she peered,
the mother of Sisera wailed through the
lattice:
'Why is his chariot so long in coming?
Why tarry the hoofbeats of his chariots?'
29 Her wisest princesses answer,
indeed, she answers herself,
30 'Have they not found and divided the
spoil?—
A womb or two for every man;
spoil of dyed materials for Sisera,
spoil of dyed materials embroidered,
two pieces of dyed work embroidered
for the neck as spoil?'

31 "So may all your enemies perish, O LORD!
But your friends be like the sun as he
rises in his might."

And the land had rest for forty years.

Midian Oppresses Israel

6 The people of Israel did what was evil in
the sight of the LORD, and the LORD gave
them into the hand of Midian seven years. 2 And
the hand of Midian overpowered Israel, and
because of Midian the people of Israel made for
themselves the dens that are in the mountains
and the caves and the strongholds. 3 For whenever the Israelites planted crops, the Midianites
and the Amalekites and the people of the East
would come up against them. 4 They would
encamp against them and devour the produce
of the land, as far as Gaza, and leave no suste-
nance in Israel and no sheep or ox or donkey.
5 For they would come up with their livestock
and their tents; they would come like locusts in
number—both they and their camels could not
be counted—so that they laid waste the land
as they came in. 6 And Israel was brought very
low because of Midian. And the people of Israel
cried out for help to the LORD.

7 When the people of Israel cried out to the
LORD on account of the Midianites, 8 the LORD

sent a prophet to the people of Israel. And he
said to them, "Thus says the LORD, the God of
Israel: I led you up from Egypt and brought
you out of the house of slavery. 9 And I delivered
you from the hand of the Egyptians and from
the hand of all who oppressed you, and drove
them out before you and gave you their land.
10 And I said to you, 'I am the LORD your God;
you shall not fear the gods of the Amorites in
whose land you dwell.' But you have not obeyed
my voice."

The Call of Gideon

11 Now the angel of the LORD came and sat
under the terebinth at Ophrah, which belonged
to Joash the Abiezrite, while his son Gideon was
beating out wheat in the winepress to hide it
from the Midianites. 12 And the angel of the
LORD appeared to him and said to him, "The
LORD is with you, O mighty man of valor."
13 And Gideon said to him, "Please, my lord, if
the LORD is with us, why then has all this happened to us? And where are all his wonderful
deeds that our fathers recounted to us, saying,
'Did not the LORD bring us up from Egypt?' But
now the LORD has forsaken us and given us into
the hand of Midian." 14 And the LORD[1] turned
to him and said, "Go in this might of yours
and save Israel from the hand of Midian; do
not I send you?" 15 And he said to him, "Please,
Lord, how can I save Israel? Behold, my clan is
the weakest in Manasseh, and I am the least in
my father's house." 16 And the LORD said to him,
"But I will be with you, and you shall strike the
Midianites as one man." 17 And he said to him,
"If now I have found favor in your eyes, then
show me a sign that it is you who speak with
me. 18 Please do not depart from here until I
come to you and bring out my present and
set it before you." And he said, "I will stay till
you return."

19 So Gideon went into his house and prepared a young goat and unleavened cakes from
an ephah[2] of flour. The meat he put in a basket,
and the broth he put in a pot, and brought
them to him under the terebinth and presented
them. 20 And the angel of God said to him,
"Take the meat and the unleavened cakes, and
put them on this rock, and pour the broth over
them." And he did so. 21 Then the angel of the
LORD reached out the tip of the staff that was in
his hand and touched the meat and the unleavened cakes. And fire sprang up from the rock

1 Septuagint the angel of the LORD; also verse 16 2 An ephah was about 3/5 bushel or 22 liters

and consumed the meat and the unleavened cakes. And the angel of the LORD vanished from his sight. ²²Then Gideon perceived that he was the angel of the LORD. And Gideon said, "Alas, O Lord GOD! For now I have seen the angel of the LORD face to face." ²³But the LORD said to him, "Peace be to you. Do not fear; you shall not die." ²⁴Then Gideon built an altar there to the LORD and called it, The LORD Is Peace. To this day it still stands at Ophrah, which belongs to the Abiezrites.

²⁵That night the LORD said to him, "Take your father's bull, and the second bull seven years old, and pull down the altar of Baal that your father has, and cut down the Asherah that is beside it ²⁶and build an altar to the LORD your God on the top of the stronghold here, with stones laid in due order. Then take the second bull and offer it as a burnt offering with the wood of the Asherah that you shall cut down." ²⁷So Gideon took ten men of his servants and did as the LORD had told him. But because he was too afraid of his family and the men of the town to do it by day, he did it by night.

Gideon Destroys the Altar of Baal

²⁸When the men of the town rose early in the morning, behold, the altar of Baal was broken down, and the Asherah beside it was cut down, and the second bull was offered on the altar that had been built. ²⁹And they said to one another, "Who has done this thing?" And after they had searched and inquired, they said, "Gideon the son of Joash has done this thing." ³⁰Then the men of the town said to Joash, "Bring out your son, that he may die, for he has broken down the altar of Baal and cut down the Asherah beside it." ³¹But Joash said to all who stood against him, "Will you contend for Baal? Or will you save him? Whoever contends for him shall be put to death by morning. If he is a god, let him contend for himself, because his altar has been broken down." ³²Therefore on that day Gideon[1] was called Jerubbaal, that is to say, "Let Baal contend against him," because he broke down his altar.

³³Now all the Midianites and the Amalekites and the people of the East came together, and they crossed the Jordan and encamped in the Valley of Jezreel. ³⁴But the Spirit of the LORD clothed Gideon, and he sounded the trumpet, and the Abiezrites were called out to follow him. ³⁵And he sent messengers throughout all Manasseh, and they too were called out to follow him. And he sent messengers to Asher, Zebulun, and Naphtali, and they went up to meet them.

The Sign of the Fleece

³⁶Then Gideon said to God, "If you will save Israel by my hand, as you have said, ³⁷behold, I am laying a fleece of wool on the threshing floor. If there is dew on the fleece alone, and it is dry on all the ground, then I shall know that you will save Israel by my hand, as you have said." ³⁸And it was so. When he rose early next morning and squeezed the fleece, he wrung enough dew from the fleece to fill a bowl with water. ³⁹Then Gideon said to God, "Let not your anger burn against me; let me speak just once more. Please let me test just once more with the fleece. Please let it be dry on the fleece only, and on all the ground let there be dew." ⁴⁰And God did so that night; and it was dry on the fleece only, and on all the ground there was dew.

Gideon's Three Hundred Men

7 Then Jerubbaal (that is, Gideon) and all the people who were with him rose early and encamped beside the spring of Harod. And the camp of Midian was north of them, by the hill of Moreh, in the valley.

²The LORD said to Gideon, "The people with you are too many for me to give the Midianites into their hand, lest Israel boast over me, saying, 'My own hand has saved me.' ³Now therefore proclaim in the ears of the people, saying, 'Whoever is fearful and trembling, let him return home and hurry away from Mount Gilead.'" Then 22,000 of the people returned, and 10,000 remained.

⁴And the LORD said to Gideon, "The people are still too many. Take them down to the water, and I will test them for you there, and anyone of whom I say to you, 'This one shall go with you,' shall go with you, and anyone of whom I say to you, 'This one shall not go with you,' shall not go." ⁵So he brought the people down to the water. And the LORD said to Gideon, "Every one who laps the water with his tongue, as a dog laps, you shall set by himself. Likewise, every one who kneels down to drink." ⁶And the number of those who lapped, putting their hands to their mouths, was 300 men, but all the rest of the people knelt down

---

[1] Hebrew he

to drink water. [7] And the LORD said to Gideon, "With the 300 men who lapped I will save you and give the Midianites into your hand, and let all the others go every man to his home." [8] So the people took provisions in their hands, and their trumpets. And he sent all the rest of Israel every man to his tent, but retained the 300 men. And the camp of Midian was below him in the valley.

[9] That same night the LORD said to him, "Arise, go down against the camp, for I have given it into your hand. [10] But if you are afraid to go down, go down to the camp with Purah your servant. [11] And you shall hear what they say, and afterward your hands shall be strengthened to go down against the camp." Then he went down with Purah his servant to the outposts of the armed men who were in the camp. [12] And the Midianites and the Amalekites and all the people of the East lay along the valley like locusts in abundance, and their camels were without number, as the sand that is on the seashore in abundance. [13] When Gideon came, behold, a man was telling a dream to his comrade. And he said, "Behold, I dreamed a dream, and behold, a cake of barley bread tumbled into the camp of Midian and came to the tent and struck it so that it fell and turned it upside down, so that the tent lay flat." [14] And his comrade answered, "This is no other than the sword of Gideon the son of Joash, a man of Israel; God has given into his hand Midian and all the camp."

[15] As soon as Gideon heard the telling of the dream and its interpretation, he worshiped. And he returned to the camp of Israel and said, "Arise, for the LORD has given the host of Midian into your hand." [16] And he divided the 300 men into three companies and put trumpets into the hands of all of them and empty jars, with torches inside the jars. [17] And he said to them, "Look at me, and do likewise. When I come to the outskirts of the camp, do as I do. [18] When I blow the trumpet, I and all who are with me, then blow the trumpets also on every side of all the camp and shout, 'For the LORD and for Gideon.'"

Gideon Defeats Midian

[19] So Gideon and the hundred men who were with him came to the outskirts of the camp at the beginning of the middle watch, when they had just set the watch. And they blew the trumpets and smashed the jars that were in their hands. [20] Then the three companies blew the trumpets and broke the jars. They held in their left hands the torches, and in their right hands the trumpets to blow. And they cried out, "A sword for the LORD and for Gideon!" [21] Every man stood in his place around the camp, and all the army ran. They cried out and fled. [22] When they blew the 300 trumpets, the LORD set every man's sword against his comrade and against all the army. And the army fled as far as Beth-shittah toward Zererah,[1] as far as the border of Abel-meholah, by Tabbath. [23] And the men of Israel were called out from Naphtali and from Asher and from all Manasseh, and they pursued after Midian.

[24] Gideon sent messengers throughout all the hill country of Ephraim, saying, "Come down against the Midianites and capture the waters against them, as far as Beth-barah, and also the Jordan." So all the men of Ephraim were called out, and they captured the waters as far as Beth-barah, and also the Jordan. [25] And they captured the two princes of Midian, Oreb and Zeeb. They killed Oreb at the rock of Oreb, and Zeeb they killed at the winepress of Zeeb. Then they pursued Midian, and they brought the heads of Oreb and Zeeb to Gideon across the Jordan.

Gideon Defeats Zebah and Zalmunna

8 Then the men of Ephraim said to him, "What is this that you have done to us, not to call us when you went to fight against Midian?" And they accused him fiercely. [2] And he said to them, "What have I done now in comparison with you? Is not the gleaning of the grapes of Ephraim better than the grape harvest of Abiezer? [3] God has given into your hands the princes of Midian, Oreb and Zeeb. What have I been able to do in comparison with you?" Then their anger[2] against him subsided when he said this.

[4] And Gideon came to the Jordan and crossed over, he and the 300 men who were with him, exhausted yet pursuing. [5] So he said to the men of Succoth, "Please give loaves of bread to the people who follow me, for they are exhausted, and I am pursuing after Zebah and Zalmunna, the kings of Midian." [6] And the officials of Succoth said, "Are the hands of Zebah and Zalmunna already in your hand, that we

[1] Some Hebrew manuscripts *Zeredah* [2] Hebrew *their spirit*

should give bread to your army?" ⁷ So Gideon said, "Well then, when the LORD has given Zebah and Zalmunna into my hand, I will flail your flesh with the thorns of the wilderness and with briers." ⁸ And from there he went up to Penuel, and spoke to them in the same way, and the men of Penuel answered him as the men of Succoth had answered. ⁹ And he said to the men of Penuel, "When I come again in peace, I will break down this tower."

¹⁰ Now Zebah and Zalmunna were in Karkor with their army, about 15,000 men, all who were left of all the army of the people of the East, for there had fallen 120,000 men who drew the sword. ¹¹ And Gideon went up by the way of the tent dwellers east of Nobah and Jogbehah and attacked the army, for the army felt secure. ¹² And Zebah and Zalmunna fled, and he pursued them and captured the two kings of Midian, Zebah and Zalmunna, and he threw all the army into a panic.

¹³ Then Gideon the son of Joash returned from the battle by the ascent of Heres. ¹⁴ And he captured a young man of Succoth and questioned him. And he wrote down for him the officials and elders of Succoth, seventy-seven men. ¹⁵ And he came to the men of Succoth and said, "Behold Zebah and Zalmunna, about whom you taunted me, saying, 'Are the hands of Zebah and Zalmunna already in your hand, that we should give bread to your men who are exhausted?'" ¹⁶ And he took the elders of the city, and he took thorns of the wilderness and briers and with them taught the men of Succoth a lesson. ¹⁷ And he broke down the tower of Penuel and killed the men of the city.

¹⁸ Then he said to Zebah and Zalmunna, "Where are the men whom you killed at Tabor?" They answered, "As you are, so were they. Every one of them resembled the son of a king." ¹⁹ And he said, "They were my brothers, the sons of my mother. As the LORD lives, if you had saved them alive, I would not kill you." ²⁰ So he said to Jether his firstborn, "Rise and kill them!" But the young man did not draw his sword, for he was afraid, because he was still a young man. ²¹ Then Zebah and Zalmunna said, "Rise yourself and fall upon us, for as the man is, so is his strength." And Gideon arose and killed Zebah and Zalmunna, and he took the crescent ornaments that were on the necks of their camels.

Gideon's Ephod

²² Then the men of Israel said to Gideon, "Rule over us, you and your son and your grandson also, for you have saved us from the hand of Midian." ²³ Gideon said to them, "I will not rule over you, and my son will not rule over you; the LORD will rule over you." ²⁴ And Gideon said to them, "Let me make a request of you: every one of you give me the earrings from his spoil." (For they had golden earrings, because they were Ishmaelites.) ²⁵ And they answered, "We will willingly give them." And they spread a cloak, and every man threw in it the earrings of his spoil. ²⁶ And the weight of the golden earrings that he requested was 1,700 shekels[1] of gold, besides the crescent ornaments and the pendants and the purple garments worn by the kings of Midian, and besides the collars that were around the necks of their camels. ²⁷ And Gideon made an ephod of it and put it in his city, in Ophrah. And all Israel whored after it there, and it became a snare to Gideon and to his family. ²⁸ So Midian was subdued before the people of Israel, and they raised their heads no more. And the land had rest forty years in the days of Gideon.

The Death of Gideon

²⁹ Jerubbaal the son of Joash went and lived in his own house. ³⁰ Now Gideon had seventy sons, his own offspring,[2] for he had many wives. ³¹ And his concubine who was in Shechem also bore him a son, and he called his name Abimelech. ³² And Gideon the son of Joash died in a good old age and was buried in the tomb of Joash his father, at Ophrah of the Abiezrites.

³³ As soon as Gideon died, the people of Israel turned again and whored after the Baals and made Baal-berith their god. ³⁴ And the people of Israel did not remember the LORD their God, who had delivered them from the hand of all their enemies on every side, ³⁵ and they did not show steadfast love to the family of Jerubbaal (that is, Gideon) in return for all the good that he had done to Israel.

Abimelech's Conspiracy

9 Now Abimelech the son of Jerubbaal went to Shechem to his mother's relatives and said to them and to the whole clan of his mother's family, ² "Say in the ears of all the leaders of Shechem, 'Which is better for you, that all seventy of the sons of Jerubbaal rule over you,

---

[1] A *shekel* was about 2/5 ounce or 11 grams [2] Hebrew *who came from his own loins*

or that one rule over you?' Remember also that I am your bone and your flesh."

³ And his mother's relatives spoke all these words on his behalf in the ears of all the leaders of Shechem, and their hearts inclined to follow Abimelech, for they said, "He is our brother." ⁴ And they gave him seventy pieces of silver out of the house of Baal-berith with which Abimelech hired worthless and reckless fellows, who followed him. ⁵ And he went to his father's house at Ophrah and killed his brothers the sons of Jerubbaal, seventy men, on one stone. But Jotham the youngest son of Jerubbaal was left, for he hid himself. ⁶ And all the leaders of Shechem came together, and all Beth-millo, and they went and made Abimelech king, by the oak of the pillar at Shechem.

⁷ When it was told to Jotham, he went and stood on top of Mount Gerizim and cried aloud and said to them, "Listen to me, you leaders of Shechem, that God may listen to you. ⁸ The trees once went out to anoint a king over them, and they said to the olive tree, 'Reign over us.' ⁹ But the olive tree said to them, 'Shall I leave my abundance, by which gods and men are honored, and go hold sway over the trees?' ¹⁰ And the trees said to the fig tree, 'You come and reign over us.' ¹¹ But the fig tree said to them, 'Shall I leave my sweetness and my good fruit and go hold sway over the trees?' ¹² And the trees said to the vine, 'You come and reign over us.' ¹³ But the vine said to them, 'Shall I leave my wine that cheers God and men and go hold sway over the trees?' ¹⁴ Then all the trees said to the bramble, 'You come and reign over us.' ¹⁵ And the bramble said to the trees, 'If in good faith you are anointing me king over you, then come and take refuge in my shade, but if not, let fire come out of the bramble and devour the cedars of Lebanon.'

¹⁶ "Now therefore, if you acted in good faith and integrity when you made Abimelech king, and if you have dealt well with Jerubbaal and his house and have done to him as his deeds deserved— ¹⁷ for my father fought for you and risked his life and delivered you from the hand of Midian, ¹⁸ and you have risen up against my father's house this day and have killed his sons, seventy men on one stone, and have made Abimelech, the son of his female servant, king over the leaders of Shechem, because he is your relative— ¹⁹ if you then have acted in good faith and integrity with Jerubbaal and with his house this day, then rejoice in Abimelech, and let him also rejoice in you. ²⁰ But if not, let fire come out from Abimelech and devour the leaders of Shechem and Beth-millo; and let fire come out from the leaders of Shechem and from Beth-millo and devour Abimelech." ²¹ And Jotham ran away and fled and went to Beer and lived there, because of Abimelech his brother.

The Downfall of Abimelech

²² Abimelech ruled over Israel three years. ²³ And God sent an evil spirit between Abimelech and the leaders of Shechem, and the leaders of Shechem dealt treacherously with Abimelech, ²⁴ that the violence done to the seventy sons of Jerubbaal might come, and their blood be laid on Abimelech their brother, who killed them, and on the men of Shechem, who strengthened his hands to kill his brothers. ²⁵ And the leaders of Shechem put men in ambush against him on the mountaintops, and they robbed all who passed by them along that way. And it was told to Abimelech.

²⁶ And Gaal the son of Ebed moved into Shechem with his relatives, and the leaders of Shechem put confidence in him. ²⁷ And they went out into the field and gathered the grapes from their vineyards and trod them and held a festival; and they went into the house of their god and ate and drank and reviled Abimelech. ²⁸ And Gaal the son of Ebed said, "Who is Abimelech, and who are we of Shechem, that we should serve him? Is he not the son of Jerubbaal, and is not Zebul his officer? Serve the men of Hamor the father of Shechem; but why should we serve him? ²⁹ Would that this people were under my hand! Then I would remove Abimelech. I would say¹ to Abimelech, 'Increase your army, and come out.'"

³⁰ When Zebul the ruler of the city heard the words of Gaal the son of Ebed, his anger was kindled. ³¹ And he sent messengers to Abimelech secretly,² saying, "Behold, Gaal the son of Ebed and his relatives have come to Shechem, and they are stirring up³ the city against you. ³² Now therefore, go by night, you and the people who are with you, and set an ambush in the field. ³³ Then in the morning, as soon as the sun is up, rise early and rush upon the city. And when he and the people who are with him come out against you, you may do to them as your hand finds to do."

¹ Septuagint; Hebrew *and he said* ² Or at Tormah ³ Hebrew *besieging,* or *closing up*

[34] So Abimelech and all the men who were with him rose up by night and set an ambush against Shechem in four companies. [35] And Gaal the son of Ebed went out and stood in the entrance of the gate of the city, and Abimelech and the people who were with him rose from the ambush. [36] And when Gaal saw the people, he said to Zebul, "Look, people are coming down from the mountaintops!" And Zebul said to him, "You mistake[1] the shadow of the mountains for men." [37] Gaal spoke again and said, "Look, people are coming down from the center of the land, and one company is coming from the direction of the Diviners' Oak." [38] Then Zebul said to him, "Where is your mouth now, you who said, 'Who is Abimelech, that we should serve him?' Are not these the people whom you despised? Go out now and fight with them." [39] And Gaal went out at the head of the leaders of Shechem and fought with Abimelech. [40] And Abimelech chased him, and he fled before him. And many fell wounded, up to the entrance of the gate. [41] And Abimelech lived at Arumah, and Zebul drove out Gaal and his relatives, so that they could not dwell at Shechem.

[42] On the following day, the people went out into the field, and Abimelech was told. [43] He took his people and divided them into three companies and set an ambush in the fields. And he looked and saw the people coming out of the city. So he rose against them and killed them. [44] Abimelech and the company that was with him rushed forward and stood at the entrance of the gate of the city, while the two companies rushed upon all who were in the field and killed them. [45] And Abimelech fought against the city all that day. He captured the city and killed the people who were in it, and he razed the city and sowed it with salt.

[46] When all the leaders of the Tower of Shechem heard of it, they entered the stronghold of the house of El-berith. [47] Abimelech was told that all the leaders of the Tower of Shechem were gathered together. [48] And Abimelech went up to Mount Zalmon, he and all the people who were with him. And Abimelech took an axe in his hand and cut down a bundle of brushwood and took it up and laid it on his shoulder. And he said to the men who were with him, "What you have seen me do, hurry and do as I have done." [49] So every one of the people cut down his bundle and following Abimelech put it against the stronghold, and they set the stronghold on fire over them, so that all the people of the Tower of Shechem also died, about 1,000 men and women.

[50] Then Abimelech went to Thebez and encamped against Thebez and captured it. [51] But there was a strong tower within the city, and all the men and women and all the leaders of the city fled to it and shut themselves in, and they went up to the roof of the tower. [52] And Abimelech came to the tower and fought against it and drew near to the door of the tower to burn it with fire. [53] And a certain woman threw an upper millstone on Abimelech's head and crushed his skull. [54] Then he called quickly to the young man his armor-bearer and said to him, "Draw your sword and kill me, lest they say of me, 'A woman killed him.'" And his young man thrust him through, and he died. [55] And when the men of Israel saw that Abimelech was dead, everyone departed to his home. [56] Thus God returned the evil of Abimelech, which he committed against his father in killing his seventy brothers. [57] And God also made all the evil of the men of Shechem return on their heads, and upon them came the curse of Jotham the son of Jerubbaal.

Tola and Jair

10 After Abimelech there arose to save Israel Tola the son of Puah, son of Dodo, a man of Issachar, and he lived at Shamir in the hill country of Ephraim. [2] And he judged Israel twenty-three years. Then he died and was buried at Shamir.

[3] After him arose Jair the Gileadite, who judged Israel twenty-two years. [4] And he had thirty sons who rode on thirty donkeys, and they had thirty cities, called Havvoth-jair to this day, which are in the land of Gilead. [5] And Jair died and was buried in Kamon.

Further Disobedience and Oppression

[6] The people of Israel again did what was evil in the sight of the LORD and served the Baals and the Ashtaroth, the gods of Syria, the gods of Sidon, the gods of Moab, the gods of the Ammonites, and the gods of the Philistines. And they forsook the LORD and did not serve him. [7] So the anger of the LORD was kindled against Israel, and he sold them into the hand of the Philistines and into the hand of the

---

[1] Hebrew You see

Ammonites, [8] and they crushed and oppressed the people of Israel that year. For eighteen years they oppressed all the people of Israel who were beyond the Jordan in the land of the Amorites, which is in Gilead. [9] And the Ammonites crossed the Jordan to fight also against Judah and against Benjamin and against the house of Ephraim, so that Israel was severely distressed.

[10] And the people of Israel cried out to the LORD, saying, "We have sinned against you, because we have forsaken our God and have served the Baals." [11] And the LORD said to the people of Israel, "Did I not save you from the Egyptians and from the Amorites, from the Ammonites and from the Philistines? [12] The Sidonians also, and the Amalekites and the Maonites oppressed you, and you cried out to me, and I saved you out of their hand. [13] Yet you have forsaken me and served other gods; therefore I will save you no more. [14] Go and cry out to the gods whom you have chosen; let them save you in the time of your distress." [15] And the people of Israel said to the LORD, "We have sinned; do to us whatever seems good to you. Only please deliver us this day." [16] So they put away the foreign gods from among them and served the LORD, and he became impatient over the misery of Israel.

[17] Then the Ammonites were called to arms, and they encamped in Gilead. And the people of Israel came together, and they encamped at Mizpah. [18] And the people, the leaders of Gilead, said one to another, "Who is the man who will begin to fight against the Ammonites? He shall be head over all the inhabitants of Gilead."

Jephthah Delivers Israel

11 Now Jephthah the Gileadite was a mighty warrior, but he was the son of a prostitute. Gilead was the father of Jephthah. [2] And Gilead's wife also bore him sons. And when his wife's sons grew up, they drove Jephthah out and said to him, "You shall not have an inheritance in our father's house, for you are the son of another woman." [3] Then Jephthah fled from his brothers and lived in the land of Tob, and worthless fellows collected around Jephthah and went out with him.

[4] After a time the Ammonites made war against Israel. [5] And when the Ammonites made war against Israel, the elders of Gilead went to bring Jephthah from the land of Tob. [6] And they said to Jephthah, "Come and be our leader, that we may fight against the Ammonites." [7] But Jephthah said to the elders of Gilead, "Did you not hate me and drive me out of my father's house? Why have you come to me now when you are in distress?" [8] And the elders of Gilead said to Jephthah, "That is why we have turned to you now, that you may go with us and fight against the Ammonites and be our head over all the inhabitants of Gilead." [9] Jephthah said to the elders of Gilead, "If you bring me home again to fight against the Ammonites, and the LORD gives them over to me, I will be your head." [10] And the elders of Gilead said to Jephthah, "The LORD will be witness between us, if we do not do as you say." [11] So Jephthah went with the elders of Gilead, and the people made him head and leader over them. And Jephthah spoke all his words before the LORD at Mizpah.

[12] Then Jephthah sent messengers to the king of the Ammonites and said, "What do you have against me, that you have come to me to fight against my land?" [13] And the king of the Ammonites answered the messengers of Jephthah, "Because Israel on coming up from Egypt took away my land, from the Arnon to the Jabbok and to the Jordan; now therefore restore it peaceably." [14] Jephthah again sent messengers to the king of the Ammonites [15] and said to him, "Thus says Jephthah: Israel did not take away the land of Moab or the land of the Ammonites, [16] but when they came up from Egypt, Israel went through the wilderness to the Red Sea and came to Kadesh. [17] Israel then sent messengers to the king of Edom, saying, 'Please let us pass through your land,' but the king of Edom would not listen. And they sent also to the king of Moab, but he would not consent. So Israel remained at Kadesh. [18] "Then they journeyed through the wilderness and went around the land of Edom and the land of Moab and arrived on the east side of the land of Moab and camped on the other side of the Arnon. But they did not enter the territory of Moab, for the Arnon was the boundary of Moab. [19] Israel then sent messengers to Sihon king of the Amorites, king of Heshbon, and Israel said to him, 'Please let us pass through your land to our country,' [20] but Sihon did not trust Israel to pass through his territory, so Sihon gathered all his people together and encamped at Jahaz and fought

with Israel. [21] And the LORD, the God of Israel, gave Sihon and all his people into the hand of Israel, and they defeated them. So Israel took possession of all the land of the Amorites, who inhabited that country. [22] And they took possession of all the territory of the Amorites from the Arnon to the Jabbok and from the wilderness to the Jordan. [23] So then the LORD, the God of Israel, dispossessed the Amorites from before his people Israel; and are you to take possession of them? [24] Will you not possess what Chemosh your god gives you to possess? And all that the LORD our God has dispossessed before us, we will possess. [25] Now are you any better than Balak the son of Zippor, king of Moab? Did he ever contend against Israel, or did he ever go to war with them? [26] While Israel lived in Heshbon and its villages, and in Aroer and its villages, and in all the cities that are on the banks of the Arnon, 300 years, why did you not deliver them within that time? [27] I therefore have not sinned against you, and you do me wrong by making war on me. The LORD, the Judge, decide this day between the people of Israel and the people of Ammon." [28] But the king of the Ammonites did not listen to the words of Jephthah that he sent to him.

Jephthah's Tragic Vow

[29] Then the Spirit of the LORD was upon Jephthah, and he passed through Gilead and Manasseh and passed on to Mizpah of Gilead, and from Mizpah of Gilead he passed on to the Ammonites. [30] And Jephthah made a vow to the LORD and said, "If you will give the Ammonites into my hand, [31] then whatever[1] comes out from the doors of my house to meet me when I return in peace from the Ammonites shall be the LORD's, and I will offer it[2] up for a burnt offering." [32] So Jephthah crossed over to the Ammonites to fight against them, and the LORD gave them into his hand. [33] And he struck them from Aroer to the neighborhood of Minnith, twenty cities, and as far as Abel-keramim, with a great blow. So the Ammonites were subdued before the people of Israel.

[34] Then Jephthah came to his home at Mizpah. And behold, his daughter came out to meet him with tambourines and with dances. She was his only child; besides her he had neither son nor daughter. [35] And as soon as he saw her, he tore his clothes and said, "Alas, my daughter! You have brought me very low, and you have become the cause of great trouble to me. For I have opened my mouth to the LORD, and I cannot take back my vow." [36] And she said to him, "My father, you have opened your mouth to the LORD; do to me according to what has gone out of your mouth, now that the LORD has avenged you on your enemies, on the Ammonites." [37] So she said to her father, "Let this thing be done for me: leave me alone two months, that I may go up and down on the mountains and weep for my virginity, I and my companions." [38] So he said, "Go." Then he sent her away for two months, and she departed, she and her companions, and wept for her virginity on the mountains. [39] And at the end of two months, she returned to her father, who did with her according to his vow that he had made. She had never known a man, and it became a custom in Israel [40] that the daughters of Israel went year by year to lament the daughter of Jephthah the Gileadite four days in the year.

Jephthah's Conflict with Ephraim

12 The men of Ephraim were called to arms, and they crossed to Zaphon and said to Jephthah, "Why did you cross over to fight against the Ammonites and did not call us to go with you? We will burn your house over you with fire." [2] And Jephthah said to them, "I and my people had a great dispute with the Ammonites, and when I called you, you did not save me from their hand. [3] And when I saw that you would not save me, I took my life in my hand and crossed over against the Ammonites, and the LORD gave them into my hand. Why then have you come up to me this day to fight against me?" [4] Then Jephthah gathered all the men of Gilead and fought with Ephraim. And the men of Gilead struck Ephraim, because they said, "You are fugitives of Ephraim, you Gileadites, in the midst of Ephraim and Manasseh." [5] And the Gileadites captured the fords of the Jordan against the Ephraimites. And when any of the fugitives of Ephraim said, "Let me go over," the men of Gilead said to him, "Are you an Ephraimite?" When he said, "No," [6] they said to him, "Then say Shibboleth," and he said, "Sibboleth," for he could not pronounce it right. Then they seized him and slaughtered him at the fords of the Jordan. At that time 42,000 of the Ephraimites fell.

[1] Or whoever [2] Or him

[7] Jephthah judged Israel six years. Then Jephthah the Gileadite died and was buried in his city in Gilead.[1]

Ibzan, Elon, and Abdon

[8] After him Ibzan of Bethlehem judged Israel. [9] He had thirty sons, and thirty daughters he gave in marriage outside his clan, and thirty daughters he brought in from outside for his sons. And he judged Israel seven years. [10] Then Ibzan died and was buried at Bethlehem.

[11] After him Elon the Zebulunite judged Israel, and he judged Israel ten years. [12] Then Elon the Zebulunite died and was buried at Aijalon in the land of Zebulun.

[13] After him Abdon the son of Hillel the Pirathonite judged Israel. [14] He had forty sons and thirty grandsons, who rode on seventy donkeys, and he judged Israel eight years. [15] Then Abdon the son of Hillel the Pirathonite died and was buried at Pirathon in the land of Ephraim, in the hill country of the Amalekites.

The Birth of Samson

13 And the people of Israel again did what was evil in the sight of the LORD, so the LORD gave them into the hand of the Philistines for forty years.

[2] There was a certain man of Zorah, of the tribe of the Danites, whose name was Manoah. And his wife was barren and had no children. [3] And the angel of the LORD appeared to the woman and said to her, "Behold, you are barren and have not borne children, but you shall conceive and bear a son. [4] Therefore be careful and drink no wine or strong drink, and eat nothing unclean, [5] for behold, you shall conceive and bear a son. No razor shall come upon his head, for the child shall be a Nazirite to God from the womb, and he shall begin to save Israel from the hand of the Philistines." [6] Then the woman came and told her husband, "A man of God came to me, and his appearance was like the appearance of the angel of God, very awesome. I did not ask him where he was from, and he did not tell me his name, [7] but he said to me, 'Behold, you shall conceive and bear a son. So then drink no wine or strong drink, and eat nothing unclean, for the child shall be a Nazirite to God from the womb to the day of his death.'"

[8] Then Manoah prayed to the LORD and said,

"O Lord, please let the man of God whom you sent come again to us and teach us what we are to do with the child who will be born." [9] And God listened to the voice of Manoah, and the angel of God came again to the woman as she sat in the field. But Manoah her husband was not with her. [10] So the woman ran quickly and told her husband, "Behold, the man who came to me the other day has appeared to me." [11] And Manoah arose and went after his wife and came to the man and said to him, "Are you the man who spoke to this woman?" And he said, "I am." [12] And Manoah said, "Now when your words come true, what is to be the child's manner of life, and what is his mission?" [13] And the angel of the LORD said to Manoah, "Of all that I said to the woman let her be careful. [14] She may not eat of anything that comes from the vine, neither let her drink wine or strong drink, or eat any unclean thing. All that I commanded her let her observe."

[15] Manoah said to the angel of the LORD, "Please let us detain you and prepare a young goat for you." [16] And the angel of the LORD said to Manoah, "If you detain me, I will not eat of your food. But if you prepare a burnt offering, then offer it to the LORD." (For Manoah did not know that he was the angel of the LORD.) [17] And Manoah said to the angel of the LORD, "What is your name, so that, when your words come true, we may honor you?" [18] And the angel of the LORD said to him, "Why do you ask my name, seeing it is wonderful?" [19] So Manoah took the young goat with the grain offering, and offered it on the rock to the LORD, to the one who works[2] wonders, and Manoah and his wife were watching. [20] And when the flame went up toward heaven from the altar, the angel of the LORD went up in the flame of the altar. Now Manoah and his wife were watching, and they fell on their faces to the ground.

[21] The angel of the LORD appeared no more to Manoah and to his wife. Then Manoah knew that he was the angel of the LORD. [22] And Manoah said to his wife, "We shall surely die, for we have seen God." [23] But his wife said to him, "If the LORD had meant to kill us, he would not have accepted a burnt offering and a grain offering at our hands, or shown us all these things, or now announced to us such things as these." [24] And the woman bore a son and called his name Samson. And the young

---

[1] Septuagint; Hebrew *in the cities of Gilead*   [2] Septuagint, Vulgate; Hebrew *LORD, and working*

man grew, and the LORD blessed him. 25 And the Spirit of the LORD began to stir him in Mahaneh-dan, between Zorah and Eshtaol.

Samson's Marriage

14 Samson went down to Timnah, and at Timnah he saw one of the daughters of the Philistines. 2 Then he came up and told his father and mother, "I saw one of the daughters of the Philistines at Timnah. Now get her for me as my wife." 3 But his father and mother said to him, "Is there not a woman among the daughters of your relatives, or among all our people, that you must go to take a wife from the uncircumcised Philistines?" But Samson said to his father, "Get her for me, for she is right in my eyes."

4 His father and mother did not know that it was from the LORD, for he was seeking an opportunity against the Philistines. At that time the Philistines ruled over Israel.

5 Then Samson went down with his father and mother to Timnah, and they came to the vineyards of Timnah. And behold, a young lion came toward him roaring. 6 Then the Spirit of the LORD rushed upon him, and although he had nothing in his hand, he tore the lion in pieces as one tears a young goat. But he did not tell his father or his mother what he had done. 7 Then he went down and talked with the woman, and she was right in Samson's eyes.

8 After some days he returned to take her. And he turned aside to see the carcass of the lion, and behold, there was a swarm of bees in the body of the lion, and honey. 9 He scraped it out into his hands and went on, eating as he went. And he came to his father and mother and gave some to them, and they ate. But he did not tell them that he had scraped the honey from the carcass of the lion.

10 His father went down to the woman, and Samson prepared a feast there, for so the young men used to do. 11 As soon as the people saw him, they brought thirty companions to be with him. 12 And Samson said to them, "Let me now put a riddle to you. If you can tell me what it is, within the seven days of the feast, and find it out, then I will give you thirty linen garments and thirty changes of clothes, 13 but if you cannot tell me what it is, then you shall give me thirty linen garments and thirty changes of clothes." And they said to him, "Put your riddle, that we may hear it." 14 And he said to them,

"Out of the eater came something to eat.
Out of the strong came something
       sweet."

And in three days they could not solve the riddle.

15 On the fourth[1] day they said to Samson's wife, "Entice your husband to tell us what the riddle is, lest we burn you and your father's house with fire. Have you invited us here to impoverish us?" 16 And Samson's wife wept over him and said, "You only hate me; you do not love me. You have put a riddle to my people, and you have not told me what it is." And he said to her, "Behold, I have not told my father nor my mother, and shall I tell you?" 17 She wept before him the seven days that their feast lasted, and on the seventh day he told her, because she pressed him hard. Then she told the riddle to her people. 18 And the men of the city said to him on the seventh day before the sun went down,

"What is sweeter than honey?
 What is stronger than a lion?"

And he said to them,

"If you had not plowed with my heifer,
 you would not have found out my riddle."

19 And the Spirit of the LORD rushed upon him, and he went down to Ashkelon and struck down thirty men of the town and took their spoil and gave the garments to those who had told the riddle. In hot anger he went back to his father's house. 20 And Samson's wife was given to his companion, who had been his best man.

Samson Defeats the Philistines

15 After some days, at the time of wheat harvest, Samson went to visit his wife with a young goat. And he said, "I will go in to my wife in the chamber." But her father would not allow him to go in. 2 And her father said, "I really thought that you utterly hated her, so I gave her to your companion. Is not her younger sister more beautiful than she? Please take her instead." 3 And Samson said to them, "This time I shall be innocent in regard to the Philistines, when I do them harm." 4 So Samson went and caught 300 foxes and took torches. And he turned them tail to tail and put a torch between each pair of tails. 5 And when he had set fire to the torches, he let the foxes go into the standing grain of the Philistines and set fire to the stacked grain and the standing grain, as well as

[1] Septuagint, Syriac; Hebrew *seventh*

the olive orchards. [6] Then the Philistines said, "Who has done this?" And they said, "Samson, the son-in-law of the Timnite, because he has taken his wife and given her to his companion." And the Philistines came up and burned her and her father with fire. [7] And Samson said to them, "If this is what you do, I swear I will be avenged on you, and after that I will quit." [8] And he struck them hip and thigh with a great blow, and he went down and stayed in the cleft of the rock of Etam.

[9] Then the Philistines came up and encamped in Judah and made a raid on Lehi. [10] And the men of Judah said, "Why have you come up against us?" They said, "We have come up to bind Samson, to do to him as he did to us." [11] Then 3,000 men of Judah went down to the cleft of the rock of Etam, and said to Samson, "Do you not know that the Philistines are rulers over us? What then is this that you have done to us?" And he said to them, "As they did to me, so have I done to them." [12] And they said to him, "We have come down to bind you, that we may give you into the hands of the Philistines." And Samson said to them, "Swear to me that you will not attack me yourselves." [13] They said to him, "No; we will only bind you and give you into their hands. We will surely not kill you." So they bound him with two new ropes and brought him up from the rock.

[14] When he came to Lehi, the Philistines came shouting to meet him. Then the Spirit of the LORD rushed upon him, and the ropes that were on his arms became as flax that has caught fire, and his bonds melted off his hands. [15] And he found a fresh jawbone of a donkey, and put out his hand and took it, and with it he struck 1,000 men. [16] And Samson said,

"With the jawbone of a donkey,
　　heaps upon heaps,
　with the jawbone of a donkey
　　have I struck down a thousand men."

[17] As soon as he had finished speaking, he threw away the jawbone out of his hand. And that place was called Ramath-lehi.[1]

[18] And he was very thirsty, and he called upon the LORD and said, "You have granted this great salvation by the hand of your servant, and shall I now die of thirst and fall into the hands of the uncircumcised?" [19] And God split open the hollow place that is at Lehi, and water came out from it. And when he drank, his spirit

returned, and he revived. Therefore the name of it was called En-hakkore;[2] it is at Lehi to this day. [20] And he judged Israel in the days of the Philistines twenty years.

Samson and Delilah

16 Samson went to Gaza, and there he saw a prostitute, and he went in to her. [2] The Gazites were told, "Samson has come here." And they surrounded the place and set an ambush for him all night at the gate of the city. They kept quiet all night, saying, "Let us wait till the light of the morning; then we will kill him." [3] But Samson lay till midnight, and at midnight he arose and took hold of the doors of the gate of the city and the two posts, and pulled them up, bar and all, and put them on his shoulders and carried them to the top of the hill that is in front of Hebron.

[4] After this he loved a woman in the Valley of Sorek, whose name was Delilah. [5] And the lords of the Philistines came up to her and said to her, "Seduce him, and see where his great strength lies, and by what means we may overpower him, that we may bind him to humble him. And we will each give you 1,100 pieces of silver." [6] So Delilah said to Samson, "Please tell me where your great strength lies, and how you might be bound, that one could subdue you."

[7] Samson said to her, "If they bind me with seven fresh bowstrings that have not been dried, then I shall become weak and be like any other man." [8] Then the lords of the Philistines brought up to her seven fresh bowstrings that had not been dried, and she bound him with them. [9] Now she had men lying in ambush in an inner chamber. And she said to him, "The Philistines are upon you, Samson!" But he snapped the bowstrings, as a thread of flax snaps when it touches the fire. So the secret of his strength was not known.

[10] Then Delilah said to Samson, "Behold, you have mocked me and told me lies. Please tell me how you might be bound." [11] And he said to her, "If they bind me with new ropes that have not been used, then I shall become weak and be like any other man." [12] So Delilah took new ropes and bound him with them and said to him, "The Philistines are upon you, Samson!" And the men lying in ambush were in an inner chamber. But he snapped the ropes off his arms like a thread.

---

[1] *Ramath-lehi means the hill of the jawbone* [2] *En-hakkore means the spring of him who called*

[13] Then Delilah said to Samson, "Until now you have mocked me and told me lies. Tell me how you might be bound." And he said to her, "If you weave the seven locks of my head with the web and fasten it tight with the pin, then I shall become weak and be like any other man." [14] So while he slept, Delilah took the seven locks of his head and wove them into the web.[1] And she made them tight with the pin and said to him, "The Philistines are upon you, Samson!" But he awoke from his sleep and pulled away the pin, the loom, and the web.

[15] And she said to him, "How can you say, 'I love you,' when your heart is not with me? You have mocked me these three times, and you have not told me where your great strength lies." [16] And when she pressed him hard with her words day after day, and urged him, his soul was vexed to death. [17] And he told her all his heart, and said to her, "A razor has never come upon my head, for I have been a Nazirite to God from my mother's womb. If my head is shaved, then my strength will leave me, and I shall become weak and be like any other man."

[18] When Delilah saw that he had told her all his heart, she sent and called the lords of the Philistines, saying, "Come up again, for he has told me all his heart." Then the lords of the Philistines came up to her and brought the money in their hands. [19] She made him sleep on her knees. And she called a man and had him shave off the seven locks of his head. Then she began to torment him, and his strength left him. [20] And she said, "The Philistines are upon you, Samson!" And he awoke from his sleep and said, "I will go out as at other times and shake myself free." But he did not know that the LORD had left him. [21] And the Philistines seized him and gouged out his eyes and brought him down to Gaza and bound him with bronze shackles. And he ground at the mill in the prison. [22] But the hair of his head began to grow again after it had been shaved.

The Death of Samson

[23] Now the lords of the Philistines gathered to offer a great sacrifice to Dagon their god and to rejoice, and they said, "Our god has given Samson our enemy into our hand." [24] And when the people saw him, they praised their god. For they said, "Our god has given our enemy into our hand, the ravager of our country, who has killed many of us."[2] [25] And when their hearts were merry, they said, "Call Samson, that he may entertain us." So they called Samson out of the prison, and he entertained them. They made him stand between the pillars. [26] And Samson said to the young man who held him by the hand, "Let me feel the pillars on which the house rests, that I may lean against them." [27] Now the house was full of men and women. All the lords of the Philistines were there, and on the roof there were about 3,000 men and women, who looked on while Samson entertained.

[28] Then Samson called to the LORD and said, "O Lord GOD, please remember me and please strengthen me only this once, O God, that I may be avenged on the Philistines for my two eyes." [29] And Samson grasped the two middle pillars on which the house rested, and he leaned his weight against them, his right hand on the one and his left hand on the other. [30] And Samson said, "Let me die with the Philistines." Then he bowed with all his strength, and the house fell upon the lords and upon all the people who were in it. So the dead whom he killed at his death were more than those whom he had killed during his life. [31] Then his brothers and all his family came down and took him and brought him up and buried him between Zorah and Eshtaol in the tomb of Manoah his father. He had judged Israel twenty years.

Micah and the Levite

17 There was a man of the hill country of Ephraim, whose name was Micah. [2] And he said to his mother, "The 1,100 pieces of silver that were taken from you, about which you uttered a curse, and also spoke it in my ears, behold, the silver is with me; I took it." And his mother said, "Blessed be my son by the LORD." [3] And he restored the 1,100 pieces of silver to his mother. And his mother said, "I dedicate the silver to the LORD from my hand for my son, to make a carved image and a metal image. Now therefore I will restore it to you." [4] So when he restored the money to his mother, his mother took 200 pieces of silver and gave it to the silversmith, who made it into a carved image and a metal image. And it was in the house of Micah.

---

[1] Compare Septuagint; Hebrew lacks *and fasten it tight . . . into the web*　[2] Or *who has multiplied our slain*

[5] And the man Micah had a shrine, and he made an ephod and household gods, and ordained[1] one of his sons, who became his priest. [6] In those days there was no king in Israel. Everyone did what was right in his own eyes.

[7] Now there was a young man of Bethlehem in Judah, of the family of Judah, who was a Levite, and he sojourned there. [8] And the man departed from the town of Bethlehem in Judah to sojourn where he could find a place. And as he journeyed, he came to the hill country of Ephraim to the house of Micah. [9] And Micah said to him, "Where do you come from?" And he said to him, "I am a Levite of Bethlehem in Judah, and I am going to sojourn where I may find a place." [10] And Micah said to him, "Stay with me, and be to me a father and a priest, and I will give you ten pieces of silver a year and a suit of clothes and your living." And the Levite went in. [11] And the Levite was content to dwell with the man, and the young man became to him like one of his sons. [12] And Micah ordained the Levite, and the young man became his priest, and was in the house of Micah. [13] Then Micah said, "Now I know that the LORD will prosper me, because I have a Levite as priest."

Danites Take the Levite and the Idol

18 In those days there was no king in Israel. And in those days the tribe of the people of Dan was seeking for itself an inheritance to dwell in, for until then no inheritance among the tribes of Israel had fallen to them. [2] So the people of Dan sent five able men from the whole number of their tribe, from Zorah and from Eshtaol, to spy out the land and to explore it. And they said to them, "Go and explore the land." And they came to the hill country of Ephraim, to the house of Micah, and lodged there. [3] When they were by the house of Micah, they recognized the voice of the young Levite. And they turned aside and said to him, "Who brought you here? What are you doing in this place? What is your business here?" [4] And he said to them, "This is how Micah dealt with me: he has hired me, and I have become his priest." [5] And they said to him, "Inquire of God, please, that we may know whether the journey on which we are setting out will succeed." [6] And the priest said to them, "Go in peace. The journey on which you go is under the eye of the LORD."

[7] Then the five men departed and came to Laish and saw the people who were there, how they lived in security, after the manner of the Sidonians, quiet and unsuspecting, lacking[2] nothing that is in the earth and possessing wealth, and how they were far from the Sidonians and had no dealings with anyone. [8] And when they came to their brothers at Zorah and Eshtaol, their brothers said to them, "What do you report?" [9] They said, "Arise, and let us go up against them, for we have seen the land, and behold, it is very good. And will you do nothing? Do not be slow to go, to enter in and possess the land. [10] As soon as you go, you will come to an unsuspecting people. The land is spacious, for God has given it into your hands, a place where there is no lack of anything that is in the earth."

[11] So 600 men of the tribe of Dan, armed with weapons of war, set out from Zorah and Eshtaol, [12] and went up and encamped at Kiriath-jearim in Judah. On this account that place is called Mahaneh-dan[3] to this day; behold, it is west of Kiriath-jearim. [13] And they passed on from there to the hill country of Ephraim, and came to the house of Micah.

[14] Then the five men who had gone to scout out the country of Laish said to their brothers, "Do you know that in these houses there are an ephod, household gods, a carved image, and a metal image? Now therefore consider what you will do." [15] And they turned aside there and came to the house of the young Levite, at the home of Micah, and asked him about his welfare. [16] Now the 600 men of the Danites, armed with their weapons of war, stood by the entrance of the gate. [17] And the five men who had gone to scout out the land went up and entered and took the carved image, the ephod, the household gods, and the metal image, while the priest stood by the entrance of the gate with the 600 men armed with weapons of war. [18] And when these went into Micah's house and took the carved image, the ephod, the household gods, and the metal image, the priest said to them, "What are you doing?" [19] And they said to him, "Keep quiet; put your hand on your mouth and come with us and be to us a father and a priest. Is it better for you to be priest to the house of one man, or to be priest to a tribe and clan

---

[1] Hebrew *filled the hand of*; also verse 12 [2] Compare 18:10; the meaning of the Hebrew word is uncertain [3] *Mahaneh-dan* means *camp of Dan*

in Israel?" ²⁰ And the priest's heart was glad. He took the ephod and the household gods and the carved image and went along with the people.

²¹ So they turned and departed, putting the little ones and the livestock and the goods in front of them. ²² When they had gone a distance from the home of Micah, the men who were in the houses near Micah's house were called out, and they overtook the people of Dan. ²³ And they shouted to the people of Dan, who turned around and said to Micah, "What is the matter with you, that you come with such a company?" ²⁴ And he said, "You take my gods that I made and the priest, and go away, and what have I left? How then do you ask me, 'What is the matter with you?'" ²⁵ And the people of Dan said to him, "Do not let your voice be heard among us, lest angry fellows fall upon you, and you lose your life with the lives of your household." ²⁶ Then the people of Dan went their way. And when Micah saw that they were too strong for him, he turned and went back to his home.

²⁷ But the people of Dan took what Micah had made, and the priest who belonged to him, and they came to Laish, to a people quiet and unsuspecting, and struck them with the edge of the sword and burned the city with fire. ²⁸ And there was no deliverer because it was far from Sidon, and they had no dealings with anyone. It was in the valley that belongs to Beth-rehob. Then they rebuilt the city and lived in it. ²⁹ And they named the city Dan, after the name of Dan their ancestor, who was born to Israel; but the name of the city was Laish at the first. ³⁰ And the people of Dan set up the carved image for themselves, and Jonathan the son of Gershom, son of Moses,[1] and his sons were priests to the tribe of the Danites until the day of the captivity of the land. ³¹ So they set up Micah's carved image that he made, as long as the house of God was at Shiloh.

A Levite and His Concubine

19 In those days, when there was no king in Israel, a certain Levite was sojourning in the remote parts of the hill country of Ephraim, who took to himself a concubine from Bethlehem in Judah. ² And his concubine was unfaithful to[2] him, and she went away from him to her father's house at Bethlehem in Judah, and was there some four months. ³ Then her husband arose and went after her, to speak kindly to her and bring her back. He had with him his servant and a couple of donkeys. And she brought him into her father's house. And when the girl's father saw him, he came with joy to meet him. ⁴ And his father-in-law, the girl's father, made him stay, and he remained with him three days. So they ate and drank and spent the night there. ⁵ And on the fourth day they arose early in the morning, and he prepared to go, but the girl's father said to his son-in-law, "Strengthen your heart with a morsel of bread, and after that you may go." ⁶ So the two of them sat and ate and drank together. And the girl's father said to the man, "Be pleased to spend the night, and let your heart be merry." ⁷ And when the man rose up to go, his father-in-law pressed him, till he spent the night there again. ⁸ And on the fifth day he arose early in the morning to depart. And the girl's father said, "Strengthen your heart and wait until the day declines." So they ate, both of them. ⁹ And when the man and his concubine and his servant rose up to depart, his father-in-law, the girl's father, said to him, "Behold, now the day has waned toward evening. Please, spend the night. Behold, the day draws to its close. Lodge here and let your heart be merry, and tomorrow you shall arise early in the morning for your journey, and go home."

¹⁰ But the man would not spend the night. He rose up and departed and arrived opposite Jebus (that is, Jerusalem). He had with him a couple of saddled donkeys, and his concubine was with him. ¹¹ When they were near Jebus, the day was nearly over, and the servant said to his master, "Come now, let us turn aside to this city of the Jebusites and spend the night in it." ¹² And his master said to him, "We will not turn aside into the city of foreigners, who do not belong to the people of Israel, but we will pass on to Gibeah." ¹³ And he said to his young man, "Come and let us draw near to one of these places and spend the night at Gibeah or at Ramah." ¹⁴ So they passed on and went their way. And the sun went down on them near Gibeah, which belongs to Benjamin, ¹⁵ and they turned aside there, to go in and spend the night at Gibeah. And he went in and sat down in the open square of the city, for no one took them into his house to spend the night.

¹⁶ And behold, an old man was coming from his work in the field at evening. The man was from the hill country of Ephraim, and he was

¹ Or Manasseh   ² Septuagint, Old Latin *became angry with*

sojourning in Gibeah. The men of the place were Benjaminites. [17] And he lifted up his eyes and saw the traveler in the open square of the city. And the old man said, "Where are you going? And where do you come from?" [18] And he said to him, "We are passing from Bethlehem in Judah to the remote parts of the hill country of Ephraim, from which I come. I went to Bethlehem in Judah, and I am going to the house of the LORD,[1] but no one has taken me into his house. [19] We have straw and feed for our donkeys, with bread and wine for me and your female servant and the young man with your servants. There is no lack of anything." [20] And the old man said, "Peace be to you; I will care for all your wants. Only, do not spend the night in the square." [21] So he brought him into his house and gave the donkeys feed. And they washed their feet, and ate and drank.

Gibeah's Crime

[22] As they were making their hearts merry, behold, the men of the city, worthless fellows, surrounded the house, beating on the door. And they said to the old man, the master of the house, "Bring out the man who came into your house, that we may know him." [23] And the man, the master of the house, went out to them and said to them, "No, my brothers, do not act so wickedly; since this man has come into my house, do not do this vile thing. [24] Behold, here are my virgin daughter and his concubine. Let me bring them out now. Violate them and do with them what seems good to you, but against this man do not do this outrageous thing." [25] But the men would not listen to him. So the man seized his concubine and made her go out to them. And they knew her and abused her all night until the morning. And as the dawn began to break, they let her go. [26] And as morning appeared, the woman came and fell down at the door of the man's house where her master was, until it was light.

[27] And her master rose up in the morning, and when he opened the doors of the house and went out to go on his way, behold, there was his concubine lying at the door of the house, with her hands on the threshold. [28] He said to her, "Get up, let us be going." But there was no answer. Then he put her on the donkey, and the man rose up and went away to his home. [29] And when he entered his house, he took a knife, and taking hold of his concubine he divided her,

limb by limb, into twelve pieces, and sent her throughout all the territory of Israel. [30] And all who saw it said, "Such a thing has never happened or been seen from the day that the people of Israel came up out of the land of Egypt until this day; consider it, take counsel, and speak."

Israel's War with the Tribe of Benjamin

20 Then all the people of Israel came out, from Dan to Beersheba, including the land of Gilead, and the congregation assembled as one man to the LORD at Mizpah. [2] And the chiefs of all the people, of all the tribes of Israel, presented themselves in the assembly of the people of God, 400,000 men on foot that drew the sword. [3] (Now the people of Benjamin heard that the people of Israel had gone up to Mizpah.) And the people of Israel said, "Tell us, how did this evil happen?" [4] And the Levite, the husband of the woman who was murdered, answered and said, "I came to Gibeah that belongs to Benjamin, I and my concubine, to spend the night. [5] And the leaders of Gibeah rose against me and surrounded the house against me by night. They meant to kill me, and they violated my concubine, and she is dead. [6] So I took hold of my concubine and cut her in pieces and sent her throughout all the country of the inheritance of Israel, for they have committed abomination and outrage in Israel. [7] Behold, you people of Israel, all of you, give your advice and counsel here."

[8] And all the people arose as one man, saying, "None of us will go to his tent, and none of us will return to his house. [9] But now this is what we will do to Gibeah: we will go up against it by lot, [10] and we will take ten men of a hundred throughout all the tribes of Israel, and a hundred of a thousand, and a thousand of ten thousand, to bring provisions for the people, that when they come they may repay Gibeah of Benjamin for all the outrage that they have committed in Israel." [11] So all the men of Israel gathered against the city, united as one man.

[12] And the tribes of Israel sent men through all the tribe of Benjamin, saying, "What evil is this that has taken place among you? [13] Now therefore give up the men, the worthless fellows in Gibeah, that we may put them to death and purge evil from Israel." But the Benjaminites would not listen to the voice of their brothers, the people of Israel. [14] Then the people of Benjamin came together out of the

---

[1] Septuagint *my home*; compare verse 29

cities to Gibeah to go out to battle against the people of Israel. [15] And the people of Benjamin mustered out of their cities on that day 26,000 men who drew the sword, besides the inhabitants of Gibeah, who mustered 700 chosen men. [16] Among all these were 700 chosen men who were left-handed; every one could sling a stone at a hair and not miss. [17] And the men of Israel, apart from Benjamin, mustered 400,000 men who drew the sword; all these were men of war.

[18] The people of Israel arose and went up to Bethel and inquired of God, "Who shall go up first for us to fight against the people of Benjamin?" And the LORD said, "Judah shall go up first."

[19] Then the people of Israel rose in the morning and encamped against Gibeah. [20] And the men of Israel went out to fight against Benjamin, and the men of Israel drew up the battle line against them at Gibeah. [21] The people of Benjamin came out of Gibeah and destroyed on that day 22,000 men of the Israelites. [22] But the people, the men of Israel, took courage, and again formed the battle line in the same place where they had formed it on the first day. [23] And the people of Israel went up and wept before the LORD until the evening. And they inquired of the LORD, "Shall we again draw near to fight against our brothers, the people of Benjamin?" And the LORD said, "Go up against them."

[24] So the people of Israel came near against the people of Benjamin the second day. [25] And Benjamin went against them out of Gibeah the second day, and destroyed 18,000 men of the people of Israel. All these were men who drew the sword. [26] Then all the people of Israel, the whole army, went up and came to Bethel and wept. They sat there before the LORD and fasted that day until evening, and offered burnt offerings and peace offerings before the LORD. [27] And the people of Israel inquired of the LORD (for the ark of the covenant of God was there in those days, [28] and Phinehas the son of Eleazar, son of Aaron, ministered before it in those days), saying, "Shall we go out once more to battle against our brothers, the people of Benjamin, or shall we cease?" And the LORD said, "Go up, for tomorrow I will give them into your hand."

[29] So Israel set men in ambush around Gibeah. [30] And the people of Israel went up against the people of Benjamin on the third day and set themselves in array against Gibeah, as at other times. [31] And the people of Benjamin went out against the people and were drawn away from the city. And as at other times they began to strike and kill some of the people in the highways, one of which goes up to Bethel and the other to Gibeah, and in the open country, about thirty men of Israel. [32] And the people of Benjamin said, "They are routed before us, as at the first." But the people of Israel said, "Let us flee and draw them away from the city to the highways." [33] And all the men of Israel rose up out of their place and set themselves in array at Baal-tamar, and the men of Israel who were in ambush rushed out of their place from Maareh-geba.[1] [34] And there came against Gibeah 10,000 chosen men out of all Israel, and the battle was hard, but the Benjaminites did not know that disaster was close upon them. [35] And the LORD defeated Benjamin before Israel, and the people of Israel destroyed 25,100 men of Benjamin that day. All these were men who drew the sword. [36] So the people of Benjamin saw that they were defeated.

The men of Israel gave ground to Benjamin, because they trusted the men in ambush whom they had set against Gibeah. [37] Then the men in ambush hurried and rushed against Gibeah; the men in ambush moved out and struck all the city with the edge of the sword. [38] Now the appointed signal between the men of Israel and the men in the main ambush was that when they made a great cloud of smoke rise up out of the city [39] the men of Israel should turn in battle. Now Benjamin had begun to strike and kill about thirty men of Israel. They said, "Surely they are defeated before us, as in the first battle." [40] But when the signal began to rise out of the city in a column of smoke, the Benjaminites looked behind them, and behold, the whole of the city went up in smoke to heaven. [41] Then the men of Israel turned, and the men of Benjamin were dismayed, for they saw that disaster was close upon them. [42] Therefore they turned their backs before the men of Israel in the direction of the wilderness, but the battle overtook them. And those who came out of the cities were destroying them in

---

[1] Some Septuagint manuscripts place west of Geba

their midst. [43] Surrounding the Benjaminites, they pursued them and trod them down from Nohah[1] as far as opposite Gibeah on the east. [44] Eighteen thousand men of Benjamin fell, all of them men of valor. [45] And they turned and fled toward the wilderness to the rock of Rimmon. Five thousand men of them were cut down in the highways. And they were pursued hard to Gidom, and 2,000 men of them were struck down. [46] So all who fell that day of Benjamin were 25,000 men who drew the sword, all of them men of valor. [47] But 600 men turned and fled toward the wilderness to the rock of Rimmon and remained at the rock of Rimmon four months. [48] And the men of Israel turned back against the people of Benjamin and struck them with the edge of the sword, the city, men and beasts and all that they found. And all the towns that they found they set on fire.

Wives Provided for the Tribe of Benjamin

21 Now the men of Israel had sworn at Mizpah, "No one of us shall give his daughter in marriage to Benjamin." [2] And the people came to Bethel and sat there till evening before God, and they lifted up their voices and wept bitterly. [3] And they said, "O LORD, the God of Israel, why has this happened in Israel, that today there should be one tribe lacking in Israel?" [4] And the next day the people rose early and built there an altar and offered burnt offerings and peace offerings. [5] And the people of Israel said, "Which of all the tribes of Israel did not come up in the assembly to the LORD?" For they had taken a great oath concerning him who did not come up to the LORD to Mizpah, saying, "He shall surely be put to death." [6] And the people of Israel had compassion for Benjamin their brother and said, "One tribe is cut off from Israel this day. [7] What shall we do for wives for those who are left, since we have sworn by the LORD that we will not give them any of our daughters for wives?"

[8] And they said, "What one is there of the tribes of Israel that did not come up to the LORD to Mizpah?" And behold, no one had come to the camp from Jabesh-gilead, to the assembly. [9] For when the people were mustered, behold, not one of the inhabitants of Jabesh-gilead was there. [10] So the congregation sent 12,000 of their bravest men there and commanded them, "Go and strike the inhabitants of Jabesh-gilead with the edge of the sword; also the women and the little ones. [11] This is what you shall do: every male and every woman that has lain with a male you shall devote to destruction." [12] And they found among the inhabitants of Jabesh-gilead 400 young virgins who had not known a man by lying with him, and they brought them to the camp at Shiloh, which is in the land of Canaan.

[13] Then the whole congregation sent word to the people of Benjamin who were at the rock of Rimmon and proclaimed peace to them. [14] And Benjamin returned at that time. And they gave them the women whom they had saved alive of the women of Jabesh-gilead, but they were not enough for them. [15] And the people had compassion on Benjamin because the LORD had made a breach in the tribes of Israel.

[16] Then the elders of the congregation said, "What shall we do for wives for those who are left, since the women are destroyed out of Benjamin?" [17] And they said, "There must be an inheritance for the survivors of Benjamin, that a tribe not be blotted out from Israel. [18] Yet we cannot give them wives from our daughters." For the people of Israel had sworn, "Cursed be he who gives a wife to Benjamin." [19] So they said, "Behold, there is the yearly feast of the LORD at Shiloh, which is north of Bethel, on the east of the highway that goes up from Bethel to Shechem, and south of Lebonah." [20] And they commanded the people of Benjamin, saying, "Go and lie in ambush in the vineyards [21] and watch. If the daughters of Shiloh come out to dance in the dances, then come out of the vineyards and snatch each man his wife from the daughters of Shiloh, and go to the land of Benjamin. [22] And when their fathers or their brothers come to complain to us, we will say to them, 'Grant them graciously to us, because we did not take for each man of them his wife in battle, neither did you give them to them, else you would now be guilty.'" [23] And the people of Benjamin did so and took their wives, according to their number, from the dancers whom they carried off. Then they went and returned to their inheritance and rebuilt the towns and lived in them. [24] And the people of Israel departed from there at that time, every man to his tribe and family, and they went out from there every man to his inheritance.

[25] In those days there was no king in Israel. Everyone did what was right in his own eyes.

---

[1] Septuagint; Hebrew [at their] *resting place*

RUTH

Naomi Widowed

1 In the days when the judges ruled there was a famine in the land, and a man of Bethlehem in Judah went to sojourn in the country of Moab, he and his wife and his two sons. ² The name of the man was Elimelech and the name of his wife Naomi, and the names of his two sons were Mahlon and Chilion. They were Ephrathites from Bethlehem in Judah. They went into the country of Moab and remained there. ³ But Elimelech, the husband of Naomi, died, and she was left with her two sons. ⁴ These took Moabite wives; the name of the one was Orpah and the name of the other Ruth. They lived there about ten years, ⁵ and both Mahlon and Chilion died, so that the woman was left without her two sons and her husband.

Ruth's Loyalty to Naomi

⁶ Then she arose with her daughters-in-law to return from the country of Moab, for she had heard in the fields of Moab that the LORD had visited his people and given them food. ⁷ So she set out from the place where she was with her two daughters-in-law, and they went on the way to return to the land of Judah. ⁸ But Naomi said to her two daughters-in-law, "Go, return each of you to her mother's house. May the LORD deal kindly with you, as you have dealt with the dead and with me. ⁹ The LORD grant that you may find rest, each of you in the house of her husband!" Then she kissed them, and they lifted up their voices and wept. ¹⁰ And they said to her, "No, we will return with you to your people." ¹¹ But Naomi said, "Turn back, my daughters; why will you go with me? Have I yet sons in my womb that they may become your husbands? ¹² Turn back, my daughters; go your way, for I am too old to have a husband. If I should say I have hope, even if I should have a husband this night and should bear sons, ¹³ would you therefore wait till they were grown? Would you therefore refrain from marrying? No, my daughters, for it is exceedingly bitter to me for your sake that the hand of the LORD has gone out against me." ¹⁴ Then they lifted up their voices and wept again. And Orpah kissed her mother-in-law, but Ruth clung to her.

¹⁵ And she said, "See, your sister-in-law has gone back to her people and to her gods; return after your sister-in-law." ¹⁶ But Ruth said, "Do not urge me to leave you or to return from following you. For where you go I will go, and where you lodge I will lodge. Your people shall be my people, and your God my God. ¹⁷ Where you die I will die, and there will I be buried. May the LORD do so to me and more also if anything but death parts me from you." ¹⁸ And when Naomi saw that she was determined to go with her, she said no more.

Naomi and Ruth Return

¹⁹ So the two of them went on until they came to Bethlehem. And when they came to Bethlehem, the whole town was stirred because of them. And the women said, "Is this Naomi?" ²⁰ She said to them, "Do not call me Naomi;¹ call me Mara,² for the Almighty has dealt very bitterly with me. ²¹ I went away full, and the LORD has brought me back empty. Why call me Naomi, when the LORD has testified against me and the Almighty has brought calamity upon me?"

²² So Naomi returned, and Ruth the Moabite her daughter-in-law with her, who returned from the country of Moab. And they came to Bethlehem at the beginning of barley harvest.

Ruth Meets Boaz

2 Now Naomi had a relative of her husband's, a worthy man of the clan of Elimelech, whose name was Boaz. ² And Ruth the Moabite said to Naomi, "Let me go to the field and glean among the ears of grain after him in whose sight I shall find favor." And she said to her, "Go, my daughter." ³ So she set out and went and gleaned in the field after the reapers, and she happened to come to the part of the field belonging to Boaz, who was of the clan of Elimelech. ⁴ And behold, Boaz came from Bethlehem. And he said to the reapers, "The LORD be with you!" And they answered, "The LORD bless you." ⁵ Then Boaz said to his young man who was in charge of the reapers, "Whose young woman is this?" ⁶ And the servant who was in charge of the reapers answered, "She is the young Moabite woman, who came back

---

¹ *Naomi means pleasant* ² *Mara means bitter*

with Naomi from the country of Moab. [7] She said, 'Please let me glean and gather among the sheaves after the reapers.' So she came, and she has continued from early morning until now, except for a short rest."[1]

[8] Then Boaz said to Ruth, "Now, listen, my daughter, do not go to glean in another field or leave this one, but keep close to my young women. [9] Let your eyes be on the field that they are reaping, and go after them. Have I not charged the young men not to touch you? And when you are thirsty, go to the vessels and drink what the young men have drawn." [10] Then she fell on her face, bowing to the ground, and said to him, "Why have I found favor in your eyes, that you should take notice of me, since I am a foreigner?" [11] But Boaz answered her, "All that you have done for your mother-in-law since the death of your husband has been fully told to me, and how you left your father and mother and your native land and came to a people that you did not know before. [12] The LORD repay you for what you have done, and a full reward be given you by the LORD, the God of Israel, under whose wings you have come to take refuge!" [13] Then she said, "I have found favor in your eyes, my lord, for you have comforted me and spoken kindly to your servant, though I am not one of your servants."

[14] And at mealtime Boaz said to her, "Come here and eat some bread and dip your morsel in the wine." So she sat beside the reapers, and he passed to her roasted grain. And she ate until she was satisfied, and she had some left over. [15] When she rose to glean, Boaz instructed his young men, saying, "Let her glean even among the sheaves, and do not reproach her. [16] And also pull out some from the bundles for her and leave it for her to glean, and do not rebuke her."

[17] So she gleaned in the field until evening. Then she beat out what she had gleaned, and it was about an ephah[2] of barley. [18] And she took it up and went into the city. Her mother-in-law saw what she had gleaned. She also brought out and gave her what food she had left over after being satisfied. [19] And her mother-in-law said to her, "Where did you glean today? And where have you worked? Blessed be the man who took notice of you." So she told her mother-in-law with whom she had worked and said, "The man's name with whom I worked today is Boaz." [20] And Naomi said to her daughter-in-law, "May he be blessed by the LORD, whose kindness has not forsaken the living or the dead!" Naomi also said to her, "The man is a close relative of ours, one of our redeemers." [21] And Ruth the Moabite said, "Besides, he said to me, 'You shall keep close by my young men until they have finished all my harvest.'" [22] And Naomi said to Ruth, her daughter-in-law, "It is good, my daughter, that you go out with his young women, lest in another field you be assaulted." [23] So she kept close to the young women of Boaz, gleaning until the end of the barley and wheat harvests. And she lived with her mother-in-law.

Ruth and Boaz at the Threshing Floor

3 Then Naomi her mother-in-law said to her, "My daughter, should I not seek rest for you, that it may be well with you? [2] Is not Boaz our relative, with whose young women you were? See, he is winnowing barley tonight at the threshing floor. [3] Wash therefore and anoint yourself, and put on your cloak and go down to the threshing floor, but do not make yourself known to the man until he has finished eating and drinking. [4] But when he lies down, observe the place where he lies. Then go and uncover his feet and lie down, and he will tell you what to do." [5] And she replied, "All that you say I will do."

[6] So she went down to the threshing floor and did just as her mother-in-law had commanded her. [7] And when Boaz had eaten and drunk, and his heart was merry, he went to lie down at the end of the heap of grain. Then she came softly and uncovered his feet and lay down. [8] At midnight the man was startled and turned over, and behold, a woman lay at his feet! [9] He said, "Who are you?" And she answered, "I am Ruth, your servant. Spread your wings[3] over your servant, for you are a redeemer." [10] And he said, "May you be blessed by the LORD, my daughter. You have made this last kindness greater than the first in that you have not gone after young men, whether poor or rich. [11] And now, my daughter, do not fear. I will do for you all that you ask, for all my fellow townsmen know that you are a worthy woman. [12] And now it is true that I am a redeemer. Yet there is a redeemer nearer than I. [13] Remain tonight, and in the morning, if he will redeem you, good; let him do it. But if he is not willing to redeem you, then, as the LORD lives, I will redeem you. Lie down until the morning."

---

[1] Compare Septuagint, Vulgate; the meaning of the Hebrew phrase is uncertain   [2] An *ephah* was about 3/5 bushel or 22 liters   [3] Compare 2:12; the word for *wings* can also mean *corners of a garment*

[14]So she lay at his feet until the morning, but arose before one could recognize another. And he said, "Let it not be known that the woman came to the threshing floor." [15]And he said, "Bring the garment you are wearing and hold it out." So she held it, and he measured out six measures of barley and put it on her. Then she went into the city. [16]And when she came to her mother-in-law, she said, "How did you fare, my daughter?" Then she told her all that the man had done for her, [17]saying, "These six measures of barley he gave to me, for he said to me, 'You must not go back empty-handed to your mother-in-law.'" [18]She replied, "Wait, my daughter, until you learn how the matter turns out, for the man will not rest but will settle the matter today."

Boaz Redeems Ruth

4 Now Boaz had gone up to the gate and sat down there. And behold, the redeemer, of whom Boaz had spoken, came by. So Boaz said, "Turn aside, friend; sit down here." And he turned aside and sat down. [2]And he took ten men of the elders of the city and said, "Sit down here." So they sat down. [3]Then he said to the redeemer, "Naomi, who has come back from the country of Moab, is selling the parcel of land that belonged to our relative Elimelech. [4]So I thought I would tell you of it and say, 'Buy it in the presence of those sitting here and in the presence of the elders of my people.' If you will redeem it, redeem it. But if you[1] will not, tell me, that I may know, for there is no one besides you to redeem it, and I come after you." And he said, "I will redeem it." [5]Then Boaz said, "The day you buy the field from the hand of Naomi, you also acquire Ruth[2] the Moabite, the widow of the dead, in order to perpetuate the name of the dead in his inheritance." [6]Then the redeemer said, "I cannot redeem it for myself, lest I impair my own inheritance. Take my right of redemption yourself, for I cannot redeem it."

[7]Now this was the custom in former times in Israel concerning redeeming and exchanging: to confirm a transaction, the one drew off his sandal and gave it to the other, and this was the manner of attesting in Israel. [8]So when the redeemer said to Boaz, "Buy it for yourself," he drew off his sandal. [9]Then Boaz said to the elders and all the people, "You are witnesses this day that I have bought from the hand of Naomi all that belonged to Elimelech and all that belonged to Chilion and to Mahlon. [10]Also Ruth the Moabite, the widow of Mahlon, I have bought to be my wife, to perpetuate the name of the dead in his inheritance, that the name of the dead may not be cut off from among his brothers and from the gate of his native place. You are witnesses this day." [11]Then all the people who were at the gate and the elders said, "We are witnesses. May the LORD make the woman, who is coming into your house, like Rachel and Leah, who together built up the house of Israel. May you act worthily in Ephrathah and be renowned in Bethlehem, [12]and may your house be like the house of Perez, whom Tamar bore to Judah, because of the offspring that the LORD will give you by this young woman."

Ruth and Boaz Marry

[13]So Boaz took Ruth, and she became his wife. And he went in to her, and the LORD gave her conception, and she bore a son. [14]Then the women said to Naomi, "Blessed be the LORD, who has not left you this day without a redeemer, and may his name be renowned in Israel! [15]He shall be to you a restorer of life and a nourisher of your old age, for your daughter-in-law who loves you, who is more to you than seven sons, has given birth to him." [16]Then Naomi took the child and laid him on her lap and became his nurse. [17]And the women of the neighborhood gave him a name, saying, "A son has been born to Naomi." They named him Obed. He was the father of Jesse, the father of David.

The Genealogy of David

[18]Now these are the generations of Perez: Perez fathered Hezron, [19]Hezron fathered Ram, Ram fathered Amminadab, [20]Amminadab fathered Nahshon, Nahshon fathered Salmon, [21]Salmon fathered Boaz, Boaz fathered Obed, [22]Obed fathered Jesse, and Jesse fathered David.

---

[1] Hebrew *he* [2] Masoretic Text *you also buy it from* Ruth

1 SAMUEL

The Birth of Samuel

1 There was a certain man of Ramathaim-zophim of the hill country of Ephraim whose name was Elkanah the son of Jeroham, son of Elihu, son of Tohu, son of Zuph, an Ephrathite. [2] He had two wives. The name of the one was Hannah, and the name of the other, Peninnah. And Peninnah had children, but Hannah had no children.

[3] Now this man used to go up year by year from his city to worship and to sacrifice to the LORD of hosts at Shiloh, where the two sons of Eli, Hophni and Phinehas, were priests of the LORD. [4] On the day when Elkanah sacrificed, he would give portions to Peninnah his wife and to all her sons and daughters. [5] But to Hannah he gave a double portion, because he loved her, though the LORD had closed her womb.[1] [6] And her rival used to provoke her grievously to irritate her, because the LORD had closed her womb. [7] So it went on year by year. As often as she went up to the house of the LORD, she used to provoke her. Therefore Hannah wept and would not eat. [8] And Elkanah, her husband, said to her, "Hannah, why do you weep? And why do you not eat? And why is your heart sad? Am I not more to you than ten sons?"

[9] After they had eaten and drunk in Shiloh, Hannah rose. Now Eli the priest was sitting on the seat beside the doorpost of the temple of the LORD. [10] She was deeply distressed and prayed to the LORD and wept bitterly. [11] And she vowed a vow and said, "O LORD of hosts, if you will indeed look on the affliction of your servant and remember me and not forget your servant, but will give to your servant a son, then I will give him to the LORD all the days of his life, and no razor shall touch his head."

[12] As she continued praying before the LORD, Eli observed her mouth. [13] Hannah was speaking in her heart; only her lips moved, and her voice was not heard. Therefore Eli took her to be a drunken woman. [14] And Eli said to her, "How long will you go on being drunk? Put your wine away from you." [15] But Hannah answered, "No, my lord, I am a woman troubled in spirit. I have drunk neither wine nor strong drink, but I have been pouring out my soul before the LORD.

[16] Do not regard your servant as a worthless woman, for all along I have been speaking out of my great anxiety and vexation." [17] Then Eli answered, "Go in peace, and the God of Israel grant your petition that you have made to him." [18] And she said, "Let your servant find favor in your eyes." Then the woman went her way and ate, and her face was no longer sad.

[19] They rose early in the morning and worshiped before the LORD; then they went back to their house at Ramah. And Elkanah knew Hannah his wife, and the LORD remembered her. [20] And in due time Hannah conceived and bore a son, and she called his name Samuel, for she said, "I have asked for him from the LORD."[2]

Samuel Given to the LORD

[21] The man Elkanah and all his house went up to offer to the LORD the yearly sacrifice and to pay his vow. [22] But Hannah did not go up, for she said to her husband, "As soon as the child is weaned, I will bring him, so that he may appear in the presence of the LORD and dwell there forever." [23] Elkanah her husband said to her, "Do what seems best to you; wait until you have weaned him; only, may the LORD establish his word." So the woman remained and nursed her son until she weaned him. [24] And when she had weaned him, she took him up with her, along with a three-year-old bull,[3] an ephah[4] of flour, and a skin of wine, and she brought him to the house of the LORD at Shiloh. And the child was young. [25] Then they slaughtered the bull, and they brought the child to Eli. [26] And she said, "Oh, my lord! As you live, my lord, I am the woman who was standing here in your presence, praying to the LORD. [27] For this child I prayed, and the LORD has granted me my petition that I made to him. [28] Therefore I have lent him to the LORD. As long as he lives, he is lent to the LORD."

And he worshiped the LORD there.

Hannah's Prayer

2 And Hannah prayed and said,

" My heart exults in the LORD;
my horn is exalted in the LORD.

---

[1] Syriac; the meaning of the Hebrew is uncertain. Septuagint *And, although he loved Hannah, he would give Hannah only one portion, because the LORD had closed her womb* [2] *Samuel* sounds like the Hebrew for *heard of God* [3] Dead Sea Scroll, Septuagint, Syriac; Masoretic Text *three bulls* [4] An ephah was about 3/5 bushel or 22 liters

My mouth derides my enemies,
    because I rejoice in your salvation.

2 "There is none holy like the LORD:
    for there is none besides you;
    there is no rock like our God.
3 Talk no more so very proudly,
    let not arrogance come from your
      mouth;
  for the LORD is a God of knowledge,
    and by him actions are weighed.
4 The bows of the mighty are broken,
    but the feeble bind on strength.
5 Those who were full have hired themselves
      out for bread,
  but those who were hungry have ceased
    to hunger.
  The barren has borne seven,
    but she who has many children is for-
      lorn.
6 The LORD kills and brings to life;
    he brings down to Sheol and raises up.
7 The LORD makes poor and makes rich;
    he brings low and he exalts.
8 He raises up the poor from the dust;
    he lifts the needy from the ash heap
  to make them sit with princes
    and inherit a seat of honor.
  For the pillars of the earth are the
    LORD's,
    and on them he has set the world.

9 "He will guard the feet of his faithful
      ones,
  but the wicked shall be cut off in dark-
      ness,
  for not by might shall a man prevail.
10 The adversaries of the LORD shall be bro-
      ken to pieces;
  against them he will thunder in
    heaven.
  The LORD will judge the ends of the earth;
    he will give strength to his king
    and exalt the horn of his anointed."

11 Then Elkanah went home to Ramah. And the boy[1] was ministering to the LORD in the presence of Eli the priest.

Eli's Worthless Sons

12 Now the sons of Eli were worthless men. They did not know the LORD. 13 The custom of the priests with the people was that when any man offered sacrifice, the priest's servant would come, while the meat was boiling, with a three-pronged fork in his hand, 14 and he would thrust it into the pan or kettle or cauldron or pot. All that the fork brought up the priest would take for himself. This is what they did at Shiloh to all the Israelites who came there. 15 Moreover, before the fat was burned, the priest's servant would come and say to the man who was sacrificing, "Give meat for the priest to roast, for he will not accept boiled meat from you but only raw." 16 And if the man said to him, "Let them burn the fat first, and then take as much as you wish," he would say, "No, you must give it now, and if not, I will take it by force." 17 Thus the sin of the young men was very great in the sight of the LORD, for the men treated the offering of the LORD with contempt.

18 Samuel was ministering before the LORD, a boy clothed with a linen ephod. 19 And his mother used to make for him a little robe and take it to him each year when she went up with her husband to offer the yearly sacrifice. 20 Then Eli would bless Elkanah and his wife, and say, "May the LORD give you children by this woman for the petition she asked of the LORD." So then they would return to their home. 21 Indeed the LORD visited Hannah, and she conceived and bore three sons and two daughters. And the boy Samuel grew in the presence of the LORD.

Eli Rebukes His Sons

22 Now Eli was very old, and he kept hearing all that his sons were doing to all Israel, and how they lay with the women who were serving at the entrance to the tent of meeting. 23 And he said to them, "Why do you do such things? For I hear of your evil dealings from all these people. 24 No, my sons; it is no good report that I hear the people of the LORD spreading abroad. 25 If someone sins against a man, God will mediate for him, but if someone sins against the LORD, who can intercede for him?" But they would not listen to the voice of their father, for it was the will of the LORD to put them to death.

26 Now the boy Samuel continued to grow both in stature and in favor with the LORD and also with man.

The LORD Rejects Eli's Household

27 And there came a man of God to Eli and said to him, "Thus says the LORD, 'Did

---

[1] Hebrew *na'ar* can be rendered *boy* (2:11, 18, 21, 26; 3:1, 8), *servant* (2:13, 15), or *young man* (2:17), depending on the context

I indeed reveal myself to the house of your father when they were in Egypt subject to the house of Pharaoh? [28] Did I choose him out of all the tribes of Israel to be my priest, to go up to my altar, to burn incense, to wear an ephod before me? I gave to the house of your father all my offerings by fire from the people of Israel. [29] Why then do you scorn[1] my sacrifices and my offerings that I commanded for my dwelling, and honor your sons above me by fattening yourselves on the choicest parts of every offering of my people Israel?' [30] Therefore the LORD, the God of Israel, declares: 'I promised that your house and the house of your father should go in and out before me forever,' but now the LORD declares: 'Far be it from me, for those who honor me I will honor, and those who despise me shall be lightly esteemed. [31] Behold, the days are coming when I will cut off your strength and the strength of your father's house, so that there will not be an old man in your house. [32] Then in distress you will look with envious eye on all the prosperity that shall be bestowed on Israel, and there shall not be an old man in your house forever. [33] The only one of you whom I shall not cut off from my altar shall be spared to weep his[2] eyes out to grieve his heart, and all the descendants[3] of your house shall die by the sword of men.[4] [34] And this that shall come upon your two sons, Hophni and Phinehas, shall be the sign to you: both of them shall die on the same day. [35] And I will raise up for myself a faithful priest, who shall do according to what is in my heart and in my mind. And I will build him a sure house, and he shall go in and out before my anointed forever. [36] And everyone who is left in your house shall come to implore him for a piece of silver or a loaf of bread and shall say, "Please put me in one of the priests' places, that I may eat a morsel of bread."'"

The LORD Calls Samuel

3 Now the boy Samuel was ministering to the LORD in the presence of Eli. And the word of the LORD was rare in those days; there was no frequent vision.

[2] At that time Eli, whose eyesight had begun to grow dim so that he could not see, was lying down in his own place. [3] The lamp of God had not yet gone out, and Samuel was lying down in the temple of the LORD, where the ark of God was.

[4] Then the LORD called Samuel, and he said, "Here I am!" [5] and ran to Eli and said, "Here I am, for you called me." But he said, "I did not call; lie down again." So he went and lay down.

[6] And the LORD called again, "Samuel!" and Samuel arose and went to Eli and said, "Here I am, for you called me." But he said, "I did not call, my son; lie down again." [7] Now Samuel did not yet know the LORD, and the word of the LORD had not yet been revealed to him.

[8] And the LORD called Samuel again the third time. And he arose and went to Eli and said, "Here I am, for you called me." Then Eli perceived that the LORD was calling the boy. [9] Therefore Eli said to Samuel, "Go, lie down, and if he calls you, you shall say, 'Speak, LORD, for your servant hears.'" So Samuel went and lay down in his place.

[10] And the LORD came and stood, calling as at other times, "Samuel! Samuel!" And Samuel said, "Speak, for your servant hears." [11] Then the LORD said to Samuel, "Behold, I am about to do a thing in Israel at which the two ears of everyone who hears it will tingle. [12] On that day I will fulfill against Eli all that I have spoken concerning his house, from beginning to end. [13] And I declare to him that I am about to punish his house forever, for the iniquity that he knew, because his sons were blaspheming God,[5] and he did not restrain them. [14] Therefore I swear to the house of Eli that the iniquity of Eli's house shall not be atoned for by sacrifice or offering forever."

[15] Samuel lay until morning; then he opened the doors of the house of the LORD. And Samuel was afraid to tell the vision to Eli. [16] But Eli called Samuel and said, "Samuel, my son." And he said, "Here I am." [17] And Eli said, "What was it that he told you? Do not hide it from me. May God do so to you and more also if you hide anything from me of all that he told you." [18] So Samuel told him everything and hid nothing from him. And he said, "It is the LORD. Let him do what seems good to him."

[19] And Samuel grew, and the LORD was with him and let none of his words fall to the ground. [20] And all Israel from Dan to Beersheba knew that Samuel was established as a prophet of the LORD. [21] And the LORD appeared again at Shiloh, for the LORD revealed himself to Samuel at Shiloh by the word of the LORD.

---

[1] Hebrew kick at [2] Septuagint; Hebrew your; twice in this verse [3] Hebrew increase [4] Septuagint; Hebrew die as men [5] Or blaspheming for themselves

The Philistines Capture the Ark

4 And the word of Samuel came to all Israel. Now Israel went out to battle against the Philistines. They encamped at Ebenezer, and the Philistines encamped at Aphek. ² The Philistines drew up in line against Israel, and when the battle spread, Israel was defeated before the Philistines, who killed about four thousand men on the field of battle. ³ And when the people came to the camp, the elders of Israel said, "Why has the LORD defeated us today before the Philistines? Let us bring the ark of the covenant of the LORD here from Shiloh, that it¹ may come among us and save us from the power of our enemies." ⁴ So the people sent to Shiloh and brought from there the ark of the covenant of the LORD of hosts, who is enthroned on the cherubim. And the two sons of Eli, Hophni and Phinehas, were there with the ark of the covenant of God.

⁵ As soon as the ark of the covenant of the LORD came into the camp, all Israel gave a mighty shout, so that the earth resounded. ⁶ And when the Philistines heard the noise of the shouting, they said, "What does this great shouting in the camp of the Hebrews mean?" And when they learned that the ark of the LORD had come to the camp, ⁷ the Philistines were afraid, for they said, "A god has come into the camp." And they said, "Woe to us! For nothing like this has happened before. ⁸ Woe to us! Who can deliver us from the power of these mighty gods? These are the gods who struck the Egyptians with every sort of plague in the wilderness. ⁹ Take courage, and be men, O Philistines, lest you become slaves to the Hebrews as they have been to you; be men and fight."

¹⁰ So the Philistines fought, and Israel was defeated, and they fled, every man to his home. And there was a very great slaughter, for thirty thousand foot soldiers of Israel fell. ¹¹ And the ark of God was captured, and the two sons of Eli, Hophni and Phinehas, died.

The Death of Eli

¹² A man of Benjamin ran from the battle line and came to Shiloh the same day, with his clothes torn and with dirt on his head. ¹³ When he arrived, Eli was sitting on his seat by the road watching, for his heart trembled for the ark of God. And when the man came into the city and told the news, all the city cried out. ¹⁴ When Eli

heard the sound of the outcry, he said, "What is this uproar?" Then the man hurried and came and told Eli. ¹⁵ Now Eli was ninety-eight years old and his eyes were set so that he could not see. ¹⁶ And the man said to Eli, "I am he who has come from the battle; I fled from the battle today." And he said, "How did it go, my son?" ¹⁷ He who brought the news answered and said, "Israel has fled before the Philistines, and there has also been a great defeat among the people. Your two sons also, Hophni and Phinehas, are dead, and the ark of God has been captured." ¹⁸ As soon as he mentioned the ark of God, Eli fell over backward from his seat by the side of the gate, and his neck was broken and he died, for the man was old and heavy. He had judged Israel forty years.

¹⁹ Now his daughter-in-law, the wife of Phinehas, was pregnant, about to give birth. And when she heard the news that the ark of God was captured, and that her father-in-law and her husband were dead, she bowed and gave birth, for her pains came upon her. ²⁰ And about the time of her death the women attending her said to her, "Do not be afraid, for you have borne a son." But she did not answer or pay attention. ²¹ And she named the child Ichabod, saying, "The glory has departed² from Israel!" because the ark of God had been captured and because of her father-in-law and her husband. ²² And she said, "The glory has departed from Israel, for the ark of God has been captured."

The Philistines and the Ark

5 When the Philistines captured the ark of God, they brought it from Ebenezer to Ashdod. ² Then the Philistines took the ark of God and brought it into the house of Dagon and set it up beside Dagon. ³ And when the people of Ashdod rose early the next day, behold, Dagon had fallen face downward on the ground before the ark of the LORD. So they took Dagon and put him back in his place. ⁴ But when they rose early on the next morning, behold, Dagon had fallen face downward on the ground before the ark of the LORD, and the head of Dagon and both his hands were lying cut off on the threshold. Only the trunk of Dagon was left to him. ⁵ This is why the priests of Dagon and all who enter the house of Dagon do not tread on the threshold of Dagon in Ashdod to this day.

¹ Or he ² Or gone into exile; also verse 22

⁶ The hand of the LORD was heavy against the people of Ashdod, and he terrified and afflicted them with tumors, both Ashdod and its territory. ⁷ And when the men of Ashdod saw how things were, they said, "The ark of the God of Israel must not remain with us, for his hand is hard against us and against Dagon our god." ⁸ So they sent and gathered together all the lords of the Philistines and said, "What shall we do with the ark of the God of Israel?" They answered, "Let the ark of the God of Israel be brought around to Gath." So they brought the ark of the God of Israel there. ⁹ But after they had brought it around, the hand of the LORD was against the city, causing a very great panic, and he afflicted the men of the city, both young and old, so that tumors broke out on them. ¹⁰ So they sent the ark of God to Ekron. But as soon as the ark of God came to Ekron, the people of Ekron cried out, "They have brought around to us the ark of the God of Israel to kill us and our people." ¹¹ They sent therefore and gathered together all the lords of the Philistines and said, "Send away the ark of the God of Israel, and let it return to its own place, that it may not kill us and our people." For there was a deathly panic throughout the whole city. The hand of God was very heavy there. ¹² The men who did not die were struck with tumors, and the cry of the city went up to heaven.

The Ark Returned to Israel

6 The ark of the LORD was in the country of the Philistines seven months. ² And the Philistines called for the priests and the diviners and said, "What shall we do with the ark of the LORD? Tell us with what we shall send it to its place." ³ They said, "If you send away the ark of the God of Israel, do not send it empty, but by all means return him a guilt offering. Then you will be healed, and it will be known to you why his hand does not turn away from you." ⁴ And they said, "What is the guilt offering that we shall return to him?" They answered, "Five golden tumors and five golden mice, according to the number of the lords of the Philistines, for the same plague was on all of you and on your lords. ⁵ So you must make images of your tumors and images of your mice that ravage the land, and give glory to the God of Israel. Perhaps he will lighten his hand from off you and your gods and your land. ⁶ Why should

you harden your hearts as the Egyptians and Pharaoh hardened their hearts? After he had dealt severely with them, did they not send the people away, and they departed? ⁷ Now then, take and prepare a new cart and two milk cows on which there has never come a yoke, and yoke the cows to the cart, but take their calves home, away from them. ⁸ And take the ark of the LORD and place it on the cart and put in a box at its side the figures of gold, which you are returning to him as a guilt offering. Then send it off and let it go its way ⁹ and watch. If it goes up on the way to its own land, to Beth-shemesh, then it is he who has done us this great harm, but if not, then we shall know that it is not his hand that struck us; it happened to us by coincidence."

¹⁰ The men did so, and took two milk cows and yoked them to the cart and shut up their calves at home. ¹¹ And they put the ark of the LORD on the cart and the box with the golden mice and the images of their tumors. ¹² And the cows went straight in the direction of Beth-shemesh along one highway, lowing as they went. They turned neither to the right nor to the left, and the lords of the Philistines went after them as far as the border of Beth-shemesh. ¹³ Now the people of Beth-shemesh were reaping their wheat harvest in the valley. And when they lifted up their eyes and saw the ark, they rejoiced to see it. ¹⁴ The cart came into the field of Joshua of Beth-shemesh and stopped there. A great stone was there. And they split up the wood of the cart and offered the cows as a burnt offering to the LORD. ¹⁵ And the Levites took down the ark of the LORD and the box that was beside it, in which were the golden figures, and set them upon the great stone. And the men of Beth-shemesh offered burnt offerings and sacrificed sacrifices on that day to the LORD. ¹⁶ And when the five lords of the Philistines saw it, they returned that day to Ekron.

¹⁷ These are the golden tumors that the Philistines returned as a guilt offering to the LORD: one for Ashdod, one for Gaza, one for Ashkelon, one for Gath, one for Ekron, ¹⁸ and the golden mice, according to the number of all the cities of the Philistines belonging to the five lords, both fortified cities and unwalled villages. The great stone beside which they set down the ark of the LORD is a witness to this day in the field of Joshua of Beth-shemesh.

¹⁹ And he struck some of the men of

Beth-shemesh, because they looked upon the ark of the Lord. He struck seventy men of them,[1] and the people mourned because the Lord had struck the people with a great blow. [20] Then the men of Beth-shemesh said, "Who is able to stand before the Lord, this holy God? And to whom shall he go up away from us?" [21] So they sent messengers to the inhabitants of Kiriath-jearim, saying, "The Philistines have returned the ark of the Lord. Come down and take it up to you."

7 And the men of Kiriath-jearim came and took up the ark of the Lord and brought it to the house of Abinadab on the hill. And they consecrated his son Eleazar to have charge of the ark of the Lord. [2] From the day that the ark was lodged at Kiriath-jearim, a long time passed, some twenty years, and all the house of Israel lamented after the Lord.

Samuel Judges Israel

[3] And Samuel said to all the house of Israel, "If you are returning to the Lord with all your heart, then put away the foreign gods and the Ashtaroth from among you and direct your heart to the Lord and serve him only, and he will deliver you out of the hand of the Philistines." [4] So the people of Israel put away the Baals and the Ashtaroth, and they served the Lord only.

[5] Then Samuel said, "Gather all Israel at Mizpah, and I will pray to the Lord for you." [6] So they gathered at Mizpah and drew water and poured it out before the Lord and fasted on that day and said there, "We have sinned against the Lord." And Samuel judged the people of Israel at Mizpah. [7] Now when the Philistines heard that the people of Israel had gathered at Mizpah, the lords of the Philistines went up against Israel. And when the people of Israel heard of it, they were afraid of the Philistines. [8] And the people of Israel said to Samuel, "Do not cease to cry out to the Lord our God for us, that he may save us from the hand of the Philistines." [9] So Samuel took a nursing lamb and offered it as a whole burnt offering to the Lord. And Samuel cried out to the Lord for Israel, and the Lord answered him. [10] As Samuel was offering up the burnt offering, the Philistines drew near to attack Israel. But the Lord thundered with a mighty sound that day against the Philistines and threw them into confusion, and they were defeated before Israel.

[11] And the men of Israel went out from Mizpah and pursued the Philistines and struck them, as far as below Beth-car.

[12] Then Samuel took a stone and set it up between Mizpah and Shen[2] and called its name Ebenezer;[3] for he said, "Till now the Lord has helped us." [13] So the Philistines were subdued and did not again enter the territory of Israel. And the hand of the Lord was against the Philistines all the days of Samuel. [14] The cities that the Philistines had taken from Israel were restored to Israel, from Ekron to Gath, and Israel delivered their territory from the hand of the Philistines. There was peace also between Israel and the Amorites.

[15] Samuel judged Israel all the days of his life. [16] And he went on a circuit year by year to Bethel, Gilgal, and Mizpah. And he judged Israel in all these places. [17] Then he would return to Ramah, for his home was there, and there also he judged Israel. And he built there an altar to the Lord.

Israel Demands a King

8 When Samuel became old, he made his sons judges over Israel. [2] The name of his firstborn son was Joel, and the name of his second, Abijah; they were judges in Beersheba. [3] Yet his sons did not walk in his ways but turned aside after gain. They took bribes and perverted justice.

[4] Then all the elders of Israel gathered together and came to Samuel at Ramah [5] and said to him, "Behold, you are old and your sons do not walk in your ways. Now appoint for us a king to judge us like all the nations." [6] But the thing displeased Samuel when they said, "Give us a king to judge us." And Samuel prayed to the Lord. [7] And the Lord said to Samuel, "Obey the voice of the people in all that they say to you, for they have not rejected you, but they have rejected me from being king over them. [8] According to all the deeds that they have done, from the day I brought them up out of Egypt even to this day, forsaking me and serving other gods, so they are also doing to you. [9] Now then, obey their voice; only you shall solemnly warn them and show them the ways of the king who shall reign over them."

Samuel's Warning Against Kings

[10] So Samuel told all the words of the Lord to the people who were asking for a king from him. [11] He said, "These will be the ways of the

---

[1] Most Hebrew manuscripts *struck of the people seventy men, fifty thousand men*   [2] Hebrew; Septuagint, Syriac *Jeshanah*   [3] *Ebenezer* means *stone of help*

king who will reign over you: he will take your sons and appoint them to his chariots and to be his horsemen and to run before his chariots. [12] And he will appoint for himself commanders of thousands and commanders of fifties, and some to plow his ground and to reap his harvest, and to make his implements of war and the equipment of his chariots. [13] He will take your daughters to be perfumers and cooks and bakers. [14] He will take the best of your fields and vineyards and olive orchards and give them to his servants. [15] He will take the tenth of your grain and of your vineyards and give it to his officers and to his servants. [16] He will take your male servants and female servants and the best of your young men[1] and your donkeys, and put them to his work. [17] He will take the tenth of your flocks, and you shall be his slaves. [18] And in that day you will cry out because of your king, whom you have chosen for yourselves, but the LORD will not answer you in that day."

The LORD Grants Israel's Request

[19] But the people refused to obey the voice of Samuel. And they said, "No! But there shall be a king over us, [20] that we also may be like all the nations, and that our king may judge us and go out before us and fight our battles." [21] And when Samuel had heard all the words of the people, he repeated them in the ears of the LORD. [22] And the LORD said to Samuel, "Obey their voice and make them a king." Samuel then said to the men of Israel, "Go every man to his city."

Saul Chosen to Be King

9 There was a man of Benjamin whose name was Kish, the son of Abiel, son of Zeror, son of Becorath, son of Aphiah, a Benjaminite, a man of wealth. [2] And he had a son whose name was Saul, a handsome young man. There was not a man among the people of Israel more handsome than he. From his shoulders upward he was taller than any of the people.

[3] Now the donkeys of Kish, Saul's father, were lost. So Kish said to Saul his son, "Take one of the young men with you, and arise, go and look for the donkeys." [4] And he passed through the hill country of Ephraim and passed through the land of Shalishah, but they did not find them. And they passed through the land of Shaalim, but they were not there. Then they passed through the land of Benjamin, but did not find them. [5] When they came to the land of Zuph, Saul

said to his servant[2] who was with him, "Come, let us go back, lest my father cease to care about the donkeys and become anxious about us." [6] But he said to him, "Behold, there is a man of God in this city, and he is a man who is held in honor; all that he says comes true. So now let us go there. Perhaps he can tell us the way we should go." [7] Then Saul said to his servant, "But if we go, what can we bring the man? For the bread in our sacks is gone, and there is no present to bring to the man of God. What do we have?" [8] The servant answered Saul again, "Here, I have with me a quarter of a shekel[3] of silver, and I will give it to the man of God to tell us our way." [9] (Formerly in Israel, when a man went to inquire of God, he said, "Come, let us go to the seer," for today's "prophet" was formerly called a seer.) [10] And Saul said to his servant, "Well said; come, let us go." So they went to the city where the man of God was.

[11] As they went up the hill to the city, they met young women coming out to draw water and said to them, "Is the seer here?" [12] They answered, "He is; behold, he is just ahead of you. Hurry. He has come just now to the city, because the people have a sacrifice today on the high place. [13] As soon as you enter the city you will find him, before he goes up to the high place to eat. For the people will not eat till he comes, since he must bless the sacrifice; afterward those who are invited will eat. Now go up, for you will meet him immediately." [14] So they went up to the city. As they were entering the city, they saw Samuel coming out toward them on his way up to the high place.

[15] Now the day before Saul came, the LORD had revealed to Samuel: [16] "Tomorrow about this time I will send to you a man from the land of Benjamin, and you shall anoint him to be prince[4] over my people Israel. He shall save my people from the hand of the Philistines. For I have seen[5] my people, because their cry has come to me." [17] When Samuel saw Saul, the LORD told him, "Here is the man of whom I spoke to you! He it is who shall restrain my people." [18] Then Saul approached Samuel in the gate and said, "Tell me where is the house of the seer?" [19] Samuel answered Saul, "I am the seer. Go up before me to the high place, for today you shall eat with me, and in the morning I will let you go and will tell you all that is on your mind. [20] As for your donkeys that were lost three days ago, do not set your mind on them,

---

[1] Septuagint *cattle* [2] Hebrew *young man*; also verses 7, 8, 10, 27 [3] A *shekel* was about 2/5 ounce or 11 grams [4] Or *leader* [5] Septuagint adds *the affliction of*

for they have been found. And for whom is all that is desirable in Israel? Is it not for you and for all your father's house?" [21] Saul answered, "Am I not a Benjaminite, from the least of the tribes of Israel? And is not my clan the humblest of all the clans of the tribe of Benjamin? Why then have you spoken to me in this way?"

[22] Then Samuel took Saul and his young man and brought them into the hall and gave them a place at the head of those who had been invited, who were about thirty persons. [23] And Samuel said to the cook, "Bring the portion I gave you, of which I said to you, 'Put it aside.'" [24] So the cook took up the leg and what was on it and set them before Saul. And Samuel said, "See, what was kept is set before you. Eat, because it was kept for you until the hour appointed, that you might eat with the guests."[1]

So Saul ate with Samuel that day. [25] And when they came down from the high place into the city, a bed was spread for Saul on the roof, and he lay down to sleep.[2] [26] Then at the break of dawn[3] Samuel called to Saul on the roof, "Up, that I may send you on your way." So Saul arose, and both he and Samuel went out into the street.

[27] As they were going down to the outskirts of the city, Samuel said to Saul, "Tell the servant to pass on before us, and when he has passed on, stop here yourself for a while, that I may make known to you the word of God."

Saul Anointed King

10 Then Samuel took a flask of oil and poured it on his head and kissed him and said, "Has not the LORD anointed you to be prince[4] over his people Israel? And you shall reign over the people of the LORD and you will save them from the hand of their surrounding enemies. And this shall be the sign to you that the LORD has anointed you to be prince[5] over his heritage. [2] When you depart from me today, you will meet two men by Rachel's tomb in the territory of Benjamin at Zelzah, and they will say to you, 'The donkeys that you went to seek are found, and now your father has ceased to care about the donkeys and is anxious about you, saying, "What shall I do about my son?"' [3] Then you shall go on from there farther and come to the oak of Tabor. Three men going up to God at Bethel will meet you there, one carrying three young goats, another carrying three loaves of bread, and another carrying a skin of wine. [4] And

they will greet you and give you two loaves of bread, which you shall accept from their hand. [5] After that you shall come to Gibeath-elohim,[6] where there is a garrison of the Philistines. And there, as soon as you come to the city, you will meet a group of prophets coming down from the high place with harp, tambourine, flute, and lyre before them, prophesying. [6] Then the Spirit of the LORD will rush upon you, and you will prophesy with them and be turned into another man. [7] Now when these signs meet you, do what your hand finds to do, for God is with you. [8] Then go down before me to Gilgal. And behold, I am coming down to you to offer burnt offerings and to sacrifice peace offerings. Seven days you shall wait, until I come to you and show you what you shall do."

[9] When he turned his back to leave Samuel, God gave him another heart. And all these signs came to pass that day. [10] When they came to Gibeah,[7] behold, a group of prophets met him, and the Spirit of God rushed upon him, and he prophesied among them. [11] And when all who knew him previously saw how he prophesied with the prophets, the people said to one another, "What has come over the son of Kish? Is Saul also among the prophets?" [12] And a man of the place answered, "And who is their father?" Therefore it became a proverb, "Is Saul also among the prophets?" [13] When he had finished prophesying, he came to the high place.

[14] Saul's uncle said to him and to his servant, "Where did you go?" And he said, "To seek the donkeys. And when we saw they were not to be found, we went to Samuel." [15] And Saul's uncle said, "Please tell me what Samuel said to you." [16] And Saul said to his uncle, "He told us plainly that the donkeys had been found." But about the matter of the kingdom, of which Samuel had spoken, he did not tell him anything.

Saul Proclaimed King

[17] Now Samuel called the people together to the LORD at Mizpah. [18] And he said to the people of Israel, "Thus says the LORD, the God of Israel, 'I brought up Israel out of Egypt, and I delivered you from the hand of the Egyptians and from the hand of all the kingdoms that were oppressing you.' [19] But today you have rejected your God, who saves you from all your calamities and your distresses, and you have said to him, 'Set a king over us.' Now therefore present

---

[1] Hebrew *appointed, saying, 'I have invited the people'* [2] Septuagint; Hebrew *city, he spoke with Saul on the roof* [3] Septuagint; Hebrew *And they arose early, and at the break of dawn* [4] Or *leader* [5] Septuagint; Hebrew lacks *over his people Israel? And you shall. . . . to be prince* [6] *Gibeath-elohim* means *the hill of God* [7] *Gibeah* means *the hill*

yourselves before the LORD by your tribes and by your thousands."

²⁰ Then Samuel brought all the tribes of Israel near, and the tribe of Benjamin was taken by lot. ²¹ He brought the tribe of Benjamin near by its clans, and the clan of the Matrites was taken by lot;[1] and Saul the son of Kish was taken by lot. But when they sought him, he could not be found. ²² So they inquired again of the LORD, "Is there a man still to come?" and the LORD said, "Behold, he has hidden himself among the baggage." ²³ Then they ran and took him from there. And when he stood among the people, he was taller than any of the people from his shoulders upward. ²⁴ And Samuel said to all the people, "Do you see him whom the LORD has chosen? There is none like him among all the people." And all the people shouted, "Long live the king!"

²⁵ Then Samuel told the people the rights and duties of the kingship, and he wrote them in a book and laid it up before the LORD. Then Samuel sent all the people away, each one to his home. ²⁶ Saul also went to his home at Gibeah, and with him went men of valor whose hearts God had touched. ²⁷ But some worthless fellows said, "How can this man save us?" And they despised him and brought him no present. But he held his peace.

Saul Defeats the Ammonites

11 Then Nahash the Ammonite went up and besieged Jabesh-gilead, and all the men of Jabesh said to Nahash, "Make a treaty with us, and we will serve you." ² But Nahash the Ammonite said to them, "On this condition I will make a treaty with you, that I gouge out all your right eyes, and thus bring disgrace on all Israel." ³ The elders of Jabesh said to him, "Give us seven days' respite that we may send messengers through all the territory of Israel. Then, if there is no one to save us, we will give ourselves up to you." ⁴ When the messengers came to Gibeah of Saul, they reported the matter in the ears of the people, and all the people wept aloud.

⁵ Now, behold, Saul was coming from the field behind the oxen. And Saul said, "What is wrong with the people, that they are weeping?" So they told him the news of the men of Jabesh. ⁶ And the Spirit of God rushed upon Saul when he heard these words, and his anger

was greatly kindled. ⁷ He took a yoke of oxen and cut them in pieces and sent them throughout all the territory of Israel by the hand of the messengers, saying, "Whoever does not come out after Saul and Samuel, so shall it be done to his oxen!" Then the dread of the LORD fell upon the people, and they came out as one man. ⁸ When he mustered them at Bezek, the people of Israel were three hundred thousand, and the men of Judah thirty thousand. ⁹ And they said to the messengers who had come, "Thus shall you say to the men of Jabesh-gilead: 'Tomorrow, by the time the sun is hot, you shall have salvation.'" When the messengers came and told the men of Jabesh, they were glad. ¹⁰ Therefore the men of Jabesh said, "Tomorrow we will give ourselves up to you, and you may do to us whatever seems good to you." ¹¹ And the next day Saul put the people in three companies. And they came into the midst of the camp in the morning watch and struck down the Ammonites until the heat of the day. And those who survived were scattered, so that no two of them were left together.

The Kingdom Is Renewed

¹² Then the people said to Samuel, "Who is it that said, 'Shall Saul reign over us?' Bring the men, that we may put them to death." ¹³ But Saul said, "Not a man shall be put to death this day, for today the LORD has worked salvation in Israel." ¹⁴ Then Samuel said to the people, "Come, let us go to Gilgal and there renew the kingdom." ¹⁵ So all the people went to Gilgal, and there they made Saul king before the LORD in Gilgal. There they sacrificed peace offerings before the LORD, and there Saul and all the men of Israel rejoiced greatly.

Samuel's Farewell Address

12 And Samuel said to all Israel, "Behold, I have obeyed your voice in all that you have said to me and have made a king over you. ² And now, behold, the king walks before you, and I am old and gray; and behold, my sons are with you. I have walked before you from my youth until this day. ³ Here I am; testify against me before the LORD and before his anointed. Whose ox have I taken? Or whose donkey have I taken? Or whom have I defrauded? Whom have I oppressed? Or from whose hand have I taken a bribe to blind my eyes with it? Testify

---

[1] Septuagint adds *finally he brought the family of the Matrites near, man by man*

against me[1] and I will restore it to you." [4]They said, "You have not defrauded us or oppressed us or taken anything from any man's hand." [5]And he said to them, "The LORD is witness against you, and his anointed is witness this day, that you have not found anything in my hand." And they said, "He is witness."

[6]And Samuel said to the people, "The LORD is witness,[2] who appointed Moses and Aaron and brought your fathers up out of the land of Egypt. [7]Now therefore stand still that I may plead with you before the LORD concerning all the righteous deeds of the LORD that he performed for you and for your fathers. [8]When Jacob went into Egypt, and the Egyptians oppressed them,[3] then your fathers cried out to the LORD and the LORD sent Moses and Aaron, who brought your fathers out of Egypt and made them dwell in this place. [9]But they forgot the LORD their God. And he sold them into the hand of Sisera, commander of the army of Hazor,[4] and into the hand of the Philistines, and into the hand of the king of Moab. And they fought against them. [10]And they cried out to the LORD and said, 'We have sinned, because we have forsaken the LORD and have served the Baals and the Ashtaroth. But now deliver us out of the hand of our enemies, that we may serve you.' [11]And the LORD sent Jerubbaal and Barak[5] and Jephthah and Samuel and delivered you out of the hand of your enemies on every side, and you lived in safety. [12]And when you saw that Nahash the king of the Ammonites came against you, you said to me, 'No, but a king shall reign over us,' when the LORD your God was your king. [13]And now behold the king whom you have chosen, for whom you have asked; behold, the LORD has set a king over you. [14]If you will fear the LORD and serve him and obey his voice and not rebel against the commandment of the LORD, and if both you and the king who reigns over you will follow the LORD your God, it will be well. [15]But if you will not obey the voice of the LORD, but rebel against the commandment of the LORD, then the hand of the LORD will be against you and your king.[6] [16]Now therefore stand still and see this great thing that the LORD will do before your eyes. [17]Is it not wheat harvest today? I will call upon the LORD, that he may send thunder and rain. And you shall know and see that your wickedness is great, which you have done in the sight of the LORD, in asking for yourselves a king." [18]So Samuel called upon the LORD, and the LORD sent thunder and rain that day, and all the people greatly feared the LORD and Samuel.

[19]And all the people said to Samuel, "Pray for your servants to the LORD your God, that we may not die, for we have added to all our sins this evil, to ask for ourselves a king." [20]And Samuel said to the people, "Do not be afraid; you have done all this evil. Yet do not turn aside from following the LORD, but serve the LORD with all your heart. [21]And do not turn aside after empty things that cannot profit or deliver, for they are empty. [22]For the LORD will not forsake his people, for his great name's sake, because it has pleased the LORD to make you a people for himself. [23]Moreover, as for me, far be it from me that I should sin against the LORD by ceasing to pray for you, and I will instruct you in the good and the right way. [24]Only fear the LORD and serve him faithfully with all your heart. For consider what great things he has done for you. [25]But if you still do wickedly, you shall be swept away, both you and your king."

Saul Fights the Philistines

13 Saul lived for one year and then became king, and when he had reigned for two years over Israel,[7] [2]Saul chose three thousand men of Israel. Two thousand were with Saul in Michmash and the hill country of Bethel, and a thousand were with Jonathan in Gibeah of Benjamin. The rest of the people he sent home, every man to his tent. [3]Jonathan defeated the garrison of the Philistines that was at Geba, and the Philistines heard of it. And Saul blew the trumpet throughout all the land, saying, "Let the Hebrews hear." [4]And all Israel heard it said that Saul had defeated the garrison of the Philistines, and also that Israel had become a stench to the Philistines. And the people were called out to join Saul at Gilgal.

[5]And the Philistines mustered to fight with Israel, thirty thousand chariots and six thousand horsemen and troops like the sand on the seashore in multitude. They came up and encamped in Michmash, to the east of Beth-aven. [6]When the men of Israel saw that they were in trouble (for the people were hard pressed), the people hid themselves in caves and in holes and in rocks and in tombs and in cis-

---

[1] Septuagint; Hebrew lacks *Testify against me* [2] Septuagint; Hebrew lacks *is witness* [3] Septuagint; Hebrew lacks *and the Egyptians oppressed them* [4] Septuagint *the army of Jabin king of Hazor* [5] Septuagint, Syriac; Hebrew *Bedan* [6] Septuagint; Hebrew *fathers* [7] Hebrew *Saul was one year old when he became king, and he reigned two years over Israel*; some Greek manuscripts give Saul's age when he began to reign as thirty years

terns, [7] and some Hebrews crossed the fords of the Jordan to the land of Gad and Gilead. Saul was still at Gilgal, and all the people followed him trembling.

Saul's Unlawful Sacrifice

[8] He waited seven days, the time appointed by Samuel. But Samuel did not come to Gilgal, and the people were scattering from him. [9] So Saul said, "Bring the burnt offering here to me, and the peace offerings." And he offered the burnt offering. [10] As soon as he had finished offering the burnt offering, behold, Samuel came. And Saul went out to meet him and greet him. [11] Samuel said, "What have you done?" And Saul said, "When I saw that the people were scattering from me, and that you did not come within the days appointed, and that the Philistines had mustered at Michmash, [12] I said, 'Now the Philistines will come down against me at Gilgal, and I have not sought the favor of the LORD.' So I forced myself, and offered the burnt offering." [13] And Samuel said to Saul, "You have done foolishly. You have not kept the command of the LORD your God, with which he commanded you. For then the LORD would have established your kingdom over Israel forever. [14] But now your kingdom shall not continue. The LORD has sought out a man after his own heart, and the LORD has commanded him to be prince[1] over his people, because you have not kept what the LORD commanded you." [15] And Samuel arose and went up from Gilgal. The rest of the people went up after Saul to meet the army; they went up from Gilgal[2] to Gibeah of Benjamin.

And Saul numbered the people who were present with him, about six hundred men. [16] And Saul and Jonathan his son and the people who were present with them stayed in Geba of Benjamin, but the Philistines encamped in Michmash. [17] And raiders came out of the camp of the Philistines in three companies. One company turned toward Ophrah, to the land of Shual; [18] another company turned toward Beth-horon; and another company turned toward the border that looks down on the Valley of Zeboim toward the wilderness.

[19] Now there was no blacksmith to be found throughout all the land of Israel, for the Philistines said, "Lest the Hebrews make themselves swords or spears." [20] But every one of the Israelites went down to the Philistines to sharpen his plowshare, his mattock, his axe, or his sickle,[3] [21] and the charge was two-thirds of a shekel[4] for the plowshares and for the mattocks, and a third of a shekel[5] for sharpening the axes and for setting the goads.[6] [22] So on the day of the battle there was neither sword nor spear found in the hand of any of the people with Saul and Jonathan, but Saul and Jonathan his son had them. [23] And the garrison of the Philistines went out to the pass of Michmash.

Jonathan Defeats the Philistines

14 One day Jonathan the son of Saul said to the young man who carried his armor, "Come, let us go over to the Philistine garrison on the other side." But he did not tell his father. [2] Saul was staying in the outskirts of Gibeah in the pomegranate cave[7] at Migron. The people who were with him were about six hundred men, [3] including Ahijah the son of Ahitub, Ichabod's brother, son of Phinehas, son of Eli, the priest of the LORD in Shiloh, wearing an ephod. And the people did not know that Jonathan had gone. [4] Within the passes, by which Jonathan sought to go over to the Philistine garrison, there was a rocky crag on the one side and a rocky crag on the other side. The name of the one was Bozez, and the name of the other Seneh. [5] The one crag rose on the north in front of Michmash, and the other on the south in front of Geba.

[6] Jonathan said to the young man who carried his armor, "Come, let us go over to the garrison of these uncircumcised. It may be that the LORD will work for us, for nothing can hinder the LORD from saving by many or by few." [7] And his armor-bearer said to him, "Do all that is in your heart. Do as you wish.[8] Behold, I am with you heart and soul." [8] Then Jonathan said, "Behold, we will cross over to the men, and we will show ourselves to them. [9] If they say to us, 'Wait until we come to you,' then we will stand still in our place, and we will not go up to them. [10] But if they say, 'Come up to us,' then we will go up, for the LORD has given them into our hand. And this shall be the sign to us." [11] So both of them showed themselves to the garrison of the Philistines. And the Philistines said, "Look, Hebrews are coming out of the holes where they have

---

[1] Or leader [2] Septuagint; Hebrew lacks The rest of the people . . . from Gilgal [3] Septuagint; Hebrew plowshare [4] Hebrew was a pim [5] A shekel was about 2/5 ounce or 11 grams [6] The meaning of the Hebrew verse is uncertain [7] Or under the pomegranate [tree] [8] Septuagint Do all that your mind inclines to

hidden themselves." [12] And the men of the garrison hailed Jonathan and his armor-bearer and said, "Come up to us, and we will show you a thing." And Jonathan said to his armor-bearer, "Come up after me, for the LORD has given them into the hand of Israel." [13] Then Jonathan climbed up on his hands and feet, and his armor-bearer after him. And they fell before Jonathan, and his armor-bearer killed them after him. [14] And that first strike, which Jonathan and his armor-bearer made, killed about twenty men within as it were half a furrow's length in an acre[1] of land. [15] And there was a panic in the camp, in the field, and among all the people. The garrison and even the raiders trembled, the earth quaked, and it became a very great panic.[2]

[16] And the watchmen of Saul in Gibeah of Benjamin looked, and behold, the multitude was dispersing here and there.[3] [17] Then Saul said to the people who were with him, "Count and see who has gone from us." And when they had counted, behold, Jonathan and his armor-bearer were not there. [18] So Saul said to Ahijah, "Bring the ark of God here." For the ark of God went at that time with the people[4] of Israel. [19] Now while Saul was talking to the priest, the tumult in the camp of the Philistines increased more and more. So Saul said to the priest, "Withdraw your hand." [20] Then Saul and all the people who were with him rallied and went into the battle. And behold, every Philistine's sword was against his fellow, and there was very great confusion. [21] Now the Hebrews who had been with the Philistines before that time and who had gone up with them into the camp, even they also turned to be with the Israelites who were with Saul and Jonathan. [22] Likewise, when all the men of Israel who had hidden themselves in the hill country of Ephraim heard that the Philistines were fleeing, they too followed hard after them in the battle. [23] So the LORD saved Israel that day. And the battle passed beyond Beth-aven.

Saul's Rash Vow

[24] And the men of Israel had been hard pressed that day, so Saul had laid an oath on the people, saying, "Cursed be the man who eats food until it is evening and I am avenged on my enemies." So none of the people had tasted food. [25] Now when all the people[5] came to the forest, behold, there was honey on the ground. [26] And when the people entered the forest, behold, the honey was dropping, but no one put his hand to his mouth, for the people feared the oath. [27] But Jonathan had not heard his father charge the people with the oath, so he put out the tip of the staff that was in his hand and dipped it in the honeycomb and put his hand to his mouth, and his eyes became bright. [28] Then one of the people said, "Your father strictly charged the people with an oath, saying, 'Cursed be the man who eats food this day.'" And the people were faint. [29] Then Jonathan said, "My father has troubled the land. See how my eyes have become bright because I tasted a little of this honey. [30] How much better if the people had eaten freely today of the spoil of their enemies that they found. For now the defeat among the Philistines has not been great."

[31] They struck down the Philistines that day from Michmash to Aijalon. And the people were very faint. [32] The people pounced on the spoil and took sheep and oxen and calves and slaughtered them on the ground. And the people ate them with the blood. [33] Then they told Saul, "Behold, the people are sinning against the LORD by eating with the blood." And he said, "You have dealt treacherously; roll a great stone to me here."[6] [34] And Saul said, "Disperse yourselves among the people and say to them, 'Let every man bring his ox or his sheep and slaughter them here and eat, and do not sin against the LORD by eating with the blood.'" So every one of the people brought his ox with him that night and they slaughtered them there. [35] And Saul built an altar to the LORD; it was the first altar that he built to the LORD.

[36] Then Saul said, "Let us go down after the Philistines by night and plunder them until the morning light; let us not leave a man of them." And they said, "Do whatever seems good to you." But the priest said, "Let us draw near to God here." [37] And Saul inquired of God, "Shall I go down after the Philistines? Will you give them into the hand of Israel?" But he did not answer him that day. [38] And Saul said, "Come here, all you leaders of the people, and know and see how this sin has arisen today. [39] For as the LORD lives who saves Israel, though it be in Jonathan my son, he shall surely die." But there was not a man among all the people who answered him. [40] Then he

---

[1] Hebrew *a yoke* [2] Or *became a panic from God* [3] Septuagint; Hebrew *they went here and there* [4] Hebrew; Septuagint *"Bring the ephod." For at that time he wore the ephod before the people* [5] Hebrew *land* [6] Septuagint; Hebrew *this day*

said to all Israel, "You shall be on one side, and I and Jonathan my son will be on the other side." And the people said to Saul, "Do what seems good to you." **41** Therefore Saul said, "O LORD God of Israel, why have you not answered your servant this day? If this guilt is in me or in Jonathan my son, O LORD, God of Israel, give Urim. But if this guilt is in your people Israel, give Thummim."**1** And Jonathan and Saul were taken, but the people escaped. **42** Then Saul said, "Cast the lot between me and my son Jonathan." And Jonathan was taken.

43 Then Saul said to Jonathan, "Tell me what you have done." And Jonathan told him, "I tasted a little honey with the tip of the staff that was in my hand. Here I am; I will die." **44** And Saul said, "God do so to me and more also; you shall surely die, Jonathan." **45** Then the people said to Saul, "Shall Jonathan die, who has worked this great salvation in Israel? Far from it! As the LORD lives, there shall not one hair of his head fall to the ground, for he has worked with God this day." So the people ransomed Jonathan, so that he did not die. **46** Then Saul went up from pursuing the Philistines, and the Philistines went to their own place.

Saul Fights Israel's Enemies

47 When Saul had taken the kingship over Israel, he fought against all his enemies on every side, against Moab, against the Ammonites, against Edom, against the kings of Zobah, and against the Philistines. Wherever he turned he routed them. **48** And he did valiantly and struck the Amalekites and delivered Israel out of the hands of those who plundered them.

49 Now the sons of Saul were Jonathan, Ishvi, and Malchi-shua. And the names of his two daughters were these: the name of the firstborn was Merab, and the name of the younger Michal. **50** And the name of Saul's wife was Ahinoam the daughter of Ahimaaz. And the name of the commander of his army was Abner the son of Ner, Saul's uncle. **51** Kish was the father of Saul, and Ner the father of Abner was the son of Abiel.

52 There was hard fighting against the Philistines all the days of Saul. And when Saul saw any strong man, or any valiant man, he attached him to himself.

The LORD Rejects Saul

15 And Samuel said to Saul, "The LORD sent me to anoint you king over his people Israel; now therefore listen to the words of the LORD. **2** Thus says the LORD of hosts, 'I have noted what Amalek did to Israel in opposing them on the way when they came up out of Egypt. **3** Now go and strike Amalek and devote to destruction**2** all that they have. Do not spare them, but kill both man and woman, child and infant, ox and sheep, camel and donkey.'"

4 So Saul summoned the people and numbered them in Telaim, two hundred thousand men on foot, and ten thousand men of Judah. **5** And Saul came to the city of Amalek and lay in wait in the valley. **6** Then Saul said to the Kenites, "Go, depart; go down from among the Amalekites, lest I destroy you with them. For you showed kindness to all the people of Israel when they came up out of Egypt." So the Kenites departed from among the Amalekites. **7** And Saul defeated the Amalekites from Havilah as far as Shur, which is east of Egypt. **8** And he took Agag the king of the Amalekites alive and devoted to destruction all the people with the edge of the sword. **9** But Saul and the people spared Agag and the best of the sheep and of the oxen and of the fattened calves**3** and the lambs, and all that was good, and would not utterly destroy them. All that was despised and worthless they devoted to destruction.

10 The word of the LORD came to Samuel: **11** "I regret**4** that I have made Saul king, for he has turned back from following me and has not performed my commandments." And Samuel was angry, and he cried to the LORD all night. **12** And Samuel rose early to meet Saul in the morning. And it was told Samuel, "Saul came to Carmel, and behold, he set up a monument for himself and turned and passed on and went down to Gilgal." **13** And Samuel came to Saul, and Saul said to him, "Blessed be you to the LORD. I have performed the commandment of the LORD." **14** And Samuel said, "What then is this bleating of the sheep in my ears and the lowing of the oxen that I hear?" **15** Saul said, "They have brought them from the Amalekites, for the people spared the best of the sheep and of the oxen to sacrifice to the LORD your God, and the rest we have devoted to destruction." **16** Then Samuel said to Saul, "Stop! I will tell

---

1 Vulgate and Septuagint; Hebrew *Therefore Saul said to the LORD, the God of Israel, "Give Thummim."* **2** That is, set apart (devote) as an offering to the Lord (for destruction); also verses 8, 9, 15, 18, 20, 21 **3** The meaning of the Hebrew term is uncertain **4** See also verses 29, 35

you what the LORD said to me this night." And he said to him, "Speak."

¹⁷ And Samuel said, "Though you are little in your own eyes, are you not the head of the tribes of Israel? The LORD anointed you king over Israel. ¹⁸ And the LORD sent you on a mission and said, 'Go, devote to destruction the sinners, the Amalekites, and fight against them until they are consumed.' ¹⁹ Why then did you not obey the voice of the LORD? Why did you pounce on the spoil and do what was evil in the sight of the LORD?" ²⁰ And Saul said to Samuel, "I have obeyed the voice of the LORD. I have gone on the mission on which the LORD sent me. I have brought Agag the king of Amalek, and I have devoted the Amalekites to destruction. ²¹ But the people took of the spoil, sheep and oxen, the best of the things devoted to destruction, to sacrifice to the LORD your God in Gilgal." ²² And Samuel said,

"Has the LORD as great delight in burnt
        offerings and sacrifices,
    as in obeying the voice of the LORD?
Behold, to obey is better than sacrifice,
    and to listen than the fat of rams.
²³ For rebellion is as the sin of divination,
        and presumption is as iniquity and
        idolatry.
Because you have rejected the word of the
        LORD,
    he has also rejected you from being
        king."

²⁴ Saul said to Samuel, "I have sinned, for I have transgressed the commandment of the LORD and your words, because I feared the people and obeyed their voice. ²⁵ Now therefore, please pardon my sin and return with me that I may bow before the LORD." ²⁶ And Samuel said to Saul, "I will not return with you. For you have rejected the word of the LORD, and the LORD has rejected you from being king over Israel." ²⁷ As Samuel turned to go away, Saul seized the skirt of his robe, and it tore. ²⁸ And Samuel said to him, "The LORD has torn the kingdom of Israel from you this day and has given it to a neighbor of yours, who is better than you. ²⁹ And also the Glory of Israel will not lie or have regret, for he is not a man, that he should have regret." ³⁰ Then he said, "I have sinned; yet honor me now before the elders of my people and

before Israel, and return with me, that I may bow before the LORD your God." ³¹ So Samuel turned back after Saul, and Saul bowed before the LORD.

³² Then Samuel said, "Bring here to me Agag the king of the Amalekites." And Agag came to him cheerfully.[1] Agag said, "Surely the bitterness of death is past." ³³ And Samuel said, "As your sword has made women childless, so shall your mother be childless among women." And Samuel hacked Agag to pieces before the LORD in Gilgal.

³⁴ Then Samuel went to Ramah, and Saul went up to his house in Gibeah of Saul. ³⁵ And Samuel did not see Saul again until the day of his death, but Samuel grieved over Saul. And the LORD regretted that he had made Saul king over Israel.

David Anointed King

16 The LORD said to Samuel, "How long will you grieve over Saul, since I have rejected him from being king over Israel? Fill your horn with oil, and go. I will send you to Jesse the Bethlehemite, for I have provided for myself a king among his sons." ² And Samuel said, "How can I go? If Saul hears it, he will kill me." And the LORD said, "Take a heifer with you and say, 'I have come to sacrifice to the LORD.' ³ And invite Jesse to the sacrifice, and I will show you what you shall do. And you shall anoint for me him whom I declare to you." ⁴ Samuel did what the LORD commanded and came to Bethlehem. The elders of the city came to meet him trembling and said, "Do you come peaceably?" ⁵ And he said, "Peaceably; I have come to sacrifice to the LORD. Consecrate yourselves, and come with me to the sacrifice." And he consecrated Jesse and his sons and invited them to the sacrifice.

⁶ When they came, he looked on Eliab and thought, "Surely the LORD's anointed is before him." ⁷ But the LORD said to Samuel, "Do not look on his appearance or on the height of his stature, because I have rejected him. For the LORD sees not as man sees: man looks on the outward appearance, but the LORD looks on the heart." ⁸ Then Jesse called Abinadab and made him pass before Samuel. And he said, "Neither has the LORD chosen this one." ⁹ Then Jesse made Shammah pass by. And he said, "Neither has the LORD chosen this one." ¹⁰ And Jesse made seven of his sons pass before Samuel. And Samuel said to Jesse, "The LORD

---

[1] Or *haltingly* (compare Septuagint); the Hebrew is uncertain

has not chosen these." ¹¹ Then Samuel said to Jesse, "Are all your sons here?" And he said, "There remains yet the youngest,¹ but behold, he is keeping the sheep." And Samuel said to Jesse, "Send and get him, for we will not sit down till he comes here." ¹² And he sent and brought him in. Now he was ruddy and had beautiful eyes and was handsome. And the LORD said, "Arise, anoint him, for this is he." ¹³ Then Samuel took the horn of oil and anointed him in the midst of his brothers. And the Spirit of the LORD rushed upon David from that day forward. And Samuel rose up and went to Ramah.

David in Saul's Service

¹⁴ Now the Spirit of the LORD departed from Saul, and a harmful spirit from the LORD tormented him. ¹⁵ And Saul's servants said to him, "Behold now, a harmful spirit from God is tormenting you. ¹⁶ Let our lord now command your servants who are before you to seek out a man who is skillful in playing the lyre, and when the harmful spirit from God is upon you, he will play it, and you will be well." ¹⁷ So Saul said to his servants, "Provide for me a man who can play well and bring him to me." ¹⁸ One of the young men answered, "Behold, I have seen a son of Jesse the Bethlehemite, who is skillful in playing, a man of valor, a man of war, prudent in speech, and a man of good presence, and the LORD is with him." ¹⁹ Therefore Saul sent messengers to Jesse and said, "Send me David your son, who is with the sheep." ²⁰ And Jesse took a donkey laden with bread and a skin of wine and a young goat and sent them by David his son to Saul. ²¹ And David came to Saul and entered his service. And Saul loved him greatly, and he became his armor-bearer. ²² And Saul sent to Jesse, saying, "Let David remain in my service, for he has found favor in my sight." ²³ And whenever the harmful spirit from God was upon Saul, David took the lyre and played it with his hand. So Saul was refreshed and was well, and the harmful spirit departed from him.

David and Goliath

17 Now the Philistines gathered their armies for battle. And they were gathered at Socoh, which belongs to Judah, and encamped between Socoh and Azekah, in Ephes-dammim. ² And Saul and the men of Israel were gathered, and encamped in the Valley of Elah, and drew up in line of battle against the Philistines. ³ And the Philistines stood on the mountain on the one side, and Israel stood on the mountain on the other side, with a valley between them. ⁴ And there came out from the camp of the Philistines a champion named Goliath of Gath, whose height was six² cubits³ and a span. ⁵ He had a helmet of bronze on his head, and he was armed with a coat of mail, and the weight of the coat was five thousand shekels⁴ of bronze. ⁶ And he had bronze armor on his legs, and a javelin of bronze slung between his shoulders. ⁷ The shaft of his spear was like a weaver's beam, and his spear's head weighed six hundred shekels of iron. And his shield-bearer went before him. ⁸ He stood and shouted to the ranks of Israel, "Why have you come out to draw up for battle? Am I not a Philistine, and are you not servants of Saul? Choose a man for yourselves, and let him come down to me. ⁹ If he is able to fight with me and kill me, then we will be your servants. But if I prevail against him and kill him, then you shall be our servants and serve us." ¹⁰ And the Philistine said, "I defy the ranks of Israel this day. Give me a man, that we may fight together." ¹¹ When Saul and all Israel heard these words of the Philistine, they were dismayed and greatly afraid.

¹² Now David was the son of an Ephrathite of Bethlehem in Judah, named Jesse, who had eight sons. In the days of Saul the man was already old and advanced in years.⁵ ¹³ The three oldest sons of Jesse had followed Saul to the battle. And the names of his three sons who went to the battle were Eliab the firstborn, and next to him Abinadab, and the third Shammah. ¹⁴ David was the youngest. The three eldest followed Saul, ¹⁵ but David went back and forth from Saul to feed his father's sheep at Bethlehem. ¹⁶ For forty days the Philistine came forward and took his stand, morning and evening.

¹⁷ And Jesse said to David his son, "Take for your brothers an ephah⁶ of this parched grain, and these ten loaves, and carry them quickly to the camp to your brothers. ¹⁸ Also take these ten cheeses to the commander of their thousand. See if your brothers are well, and bring some token from them."

¹⁹ Now Saul and they and all the men of Israel were in the Valley of Elah, fighting with the Philistines. ²⁰ And David rose early in the

---

¹ Or *smallest* ² Hebrew; Septuagint, Dead Sea Scroll and Josephus *four* ³ A *cubit* was about 18 inches or 45 centimeters ⁴ A *shekel* was about 2/5 ounce or 11 grams ⁵ Septuagint, Syriac; Hebrew *advanced among men* ⁶ An *ephah* was about 3/5 bushel or 22 liters

morning and left the sheep with a keeper and took the provisions and went, as Jesse had commanded him. And he came to the encampment as the host was going out to the battle line, shouting the war cry. ²¹ And Israel and the Philistines drew up for battle, army against army. ²² And David left the things in charge of the keeper of the baggage and ran to the ranks and went and greeted his brothers. ²³ As he talked with them, behold, the champion, the Philistine of Gath, Goliath by name, came up out of the ranks of the Philistines and spoke the same words as before. And David heard him.

²⁴ All the men of Israel, when they saw the man, fled from him and were much afraid. ²⁵ And the men of Israel said, "Have you seen this man who has come up? Surely he has come up to defy Israel. And the king will enrich the man who kills him with great riches and will give him his daughter and make his father's house free in Israel." ²⁶ And David said to the men who stood by him, "What shall be done for the man who kills this Philistine and takes away the reproach from Israel? For who is this uncircumcised Philistine, that he should defy the armies of the living God?" ²⁷ And the people answered him in the same way, "So shall it be done to the man who kills him."

²⁸ Now Eliab his eldest brother heard when he spoke to the men. And Eliab's anger was kindled against David, and he said, "Why have you come down? And with whom have you left those few sheep in the wilderness? I know your presumption and the evil of your heart, for you have come down to see the battle." ²⁹ And David said, "What have I done now? Was it not but a word?" ³⁰ And he turned away from him toward another, and spoke in the same way, and the people answered him again as before.

³¹ When the words that David spoke were heard, they repeated them before Saul, and he sent for him. ³² And David said to Saul, "Let no man's heart fail because of him. Your servant will go and fight with this Philistine." ³³ And Saul said to David, "You are not able to go against this Philistine to fight with him, for you are but a youth, and he has been a man of war from his youth." ³⁴ But David said to Saul, "Your servant used to keep sheep for his father. And when there came a lion, or a bear, and took a lamb from the flock, ³⁵ I went after him and struck him and delivered it out of his mouth. And if he arose against me, I caught him by his beard and struck him and killed him. ³⁶ Your servant has struck down both lions and bears, and this uncircumcised Philistine shall be like one of them, for he has defied the armies of the living God." ³⁷ And David said, "The LORD who delivered me from the paw of the lion and from the paw of the bear will deliver me from the hand of this Philistine." And Saul said to David, "Go, and the LORD be with you!"

³⁸ Then Saul clothed David with his armor. He put a helmet of bronze on his head and clothed him with a coat of mail, ³⁹ and David strapped his sword over his armor. And he tried in vain to go, for he had not tested them. Then David said to Saul, "I cannot go with these, for I have not tested them." So David put them off. ⁴⁰ Then he took his staff in his hand and chose five smooth stones from the brook and put them in his shepherd's pouch. His sling was in his hand, and he approached the Philistine.

⁴¹ And the Philistine moved forward and came near to David, with his shield-bearer in front of him. ⁴² And when the Philistine looked and saw David, he disdained him, for he was but a youth, ruddy and handsome in appearance. ⁴³ And the Philistine said to David, "Am I a dog, that you come to me with sticks?" And the Philistine cursed David by his gods. ⁴⁴ The Philistine said to David, "Come to me, and I will give your flesh to the birds of the air and to the beasts of the field." ⁴⁵ Then David said to the Philistine, "You come to me with a sword and with a spear and with a javelin, but I come to you in the name of the LORD of hosts, the God of the armies of Israel, whom you have defied. ⁴⁶ This day the LORD will deliver you into my hand, and I will strike you down and cut off your head. And I will give the dead bodies of the host of the Philistines this day to the birds of the air and to the wild beasts of the earth, that all the earth may know that there is a God in Israel, ⁴⁷ and that all this assembly may know that the LORD saves not with sword and spear. For the battle is the LORD's, and he will give you into our hand."

⁴⁸ When the Philistine arose and came and drew near to meet David, David ran quickly toward the battle line to meet the Philistine. ⁴⁹ And David put his hand in his bag and took out a stone and slung it and struck the Philistine on his forehead. The stone sank into his forehead, and he fell on his face to the ground.

[50] So David prevailed over the Philistine with a sling and with a stone, and struck the Philistine and killed him. There was no sword in the hand of David. [51] Then David ran and stood over the Philistine and took his sword and drew it out of its sheath and killed him and cut off his head with it. When the Philistines saw that their champion was dead, they fled. [52] And the men of Israel and Judah rose with a shout and pursued the Philistines as far as Gath[1] and the gates of Ekron, so that the wounded Philistines fell on the way from Shaaraim as far as Gath and Ekron. [53] And the people of Israel came back from chasing the Philistines, and they plundered their camp. [54] And David took the head of the Philistine and brought it to Jerusalem, but he put his armor in his tent.

[55] As soon as Saul saw David go out against the Philistine, he said to Abner, the commander of the army, "Abner, whose son is this youth?" And Abner said, "As your soul lives, O king, I do not know." [56] And the king said, "Inquire whose son the boy is." [57] And as soon as David returned from the striking down of the Philistine, Abner took him, and brought him before Saul with the head of the Philistine in his hand. [58] And Saul said to him, "Whose son are you, young man?" And David answered, "I am the son of your servant Jesse the Bethlehemite."

David and Jonathan's Friendship

18 As soon as he had finished speaking to Saul, the soul of Jonathan was knit to the soul of David, and Jonathan loved him as his own soul. [2] And Saul took him that day and would not let him return to his father's house. [3] Then Jonathan made a covenant with David, because he loved him as his own soul. [4] And Jonathan stripped himself of the robe that was on him and gave it to David, and his armor, and even his sword and his bow and his belt. [5] And David went out and was successful wherever Saul sent him, so that Saul set him over the men of war. And this was good in the sight of all the people and also in the sight of Saul's servants.

Saul's Jealousy of David

[6] As they were coming home, when David returned from striking down the Philistine, the women came out of all the cities of Israel, singing and dancing, to meet King Saul, with tambourines, with songs of joy, and with musical instruments.[2] [7] And the women sang to one another as they celebrated,

> "Saul has struck down his thousands,
> and David his ten thousands."

[8] And Saul was very angry, and this saying displeased him. He said, "They have ascribed to David ten thousands, and to me they have ascribed thousands, and what more can he have but the kingdom?" [9] And Saul eyed David from that day on.

[10] The next day a harmful spirit from God rushed upon Saul, and he raved within his house while David was playing the lyre, as he did day by day. Saul had his spear in his hand. [11] And Saul hurled the spear, for he thought, "I will pin David to the wall." But David evaded him twice.

[12] Saul was afraid of David because the LORD was with him but had departed from Saul. [13] So Saul removed him from his presence and made him a commander of a thousand. And he went out and came in before the people. [14] And David had success in all his undertakings, for the LORD was with him. [15] And when Saul saw that he had great success, he stood in fearful awe of him. [16] But all Israel and Judah loved David, for he went out and came in before them.

David Marries Michal

[17] Then Saul said to David, "Here is my elder daughter Merab. I will give her to you for a wife. Only be valiant for me and fight the LORD's battles." For Saul thought, "Let not my hand be against him, but let the hand of the Philistines be against him." [18] And David said to Saul, "Who am I, and who are my relatives, my father's clan in Israel, that I should be son-in-law to the king?" [19] But at the time when Merab, Saul's daughter, should have been given to David, she was given to Adriel the Meholathite for a wife.

[20] Now Saul's daughter Michal loved David. And they told Saul, and the thing pleased him. [21] Saul thought, "Let me give her to him, that she may be a snare for him and that the hand of the Philistines may be against him." Therefore Saul said to David a second time,[3] "You shall now be my son-in-law." [22] And Saul commanded his servants, "Speak to David in private and say, 'Behold, the king has delight in you, and all his servants love you. Now then

---

[1] Septuagint; Hebrew *Gai* [2] Or *triangles, or three-stringed instruments* [3] Hebrew *by two*

become the king's son-in-law.'" ²³ And Saul's servants spoke those words in the ears of David. And David said, "Does it seem to you a little thing to become the king's son-in-law, since I am a poor man and have no reputation?" ²⁴ And the servants of Saul told him, "Thus and so did David speak." ²⁵ Then Saul said, "Thus shall you say to David, 'The king desires no bride-price except a hundred foreskins of the Philistines, that he may be avenged of the king's enemies.'" Now Saul thought to make David fall by the hand of the Philistines. ²⁶ And when his servants told David these words, it pleased David well to be the king's son-in-law. Before the time had expired, ²⁷ David arose and went, along with his men, and killed two hundred of the Philistines. And David brought their foreskins, which were given in full number to the king, that he might become the king's son-in-law. And Saul gave him his daughter Michal for a wife. ²⁸ But when Saul saw and knew that the LORD was with David, and that Michal, Saul's daughter, loved him, ²⁹ Saul was even more afraid of David. So Saul was David's enemy continually.

³⁰ Then the commanders of the Philistines came out to battle, and as often as they came out David had more success than all the servants of Saul, so that his name was highly esteemed.

Saul Tries to Kill David

19 And Saul spoke to Jonathan his son and to all his servants, that they should kill David. But Jonathan, Saul's son, delighted much in David. ² And Jonathan told David, "Saul my father seeks to kill you. Therefore be on your guard in the morning. Stay in a secret place and hide yourself. ³ And I will go out and stand beside my father in the field where you are, and I will speak to my father about you. And if I learn anything I will tell you." ⁴ And Jonathan spoke well of David to Saul his father and said to him, "Let not the king sin against his servant David, because he has not sinned against you, and because his deeds have brought good to you. ⁵ For he took his life in his hand and he struck down the Philistine, and the LORD worked a great salvation for all Israel. You saw it, and rejoiced. Why then will you sin against innocent blood by killing David without cause?" ⁶ And Saul listened to the voice of Jonathan. Saul swore, "As the LORD lives, he shall not be put to death." ⁷ And Jonathan called

David, and Jonathan reported to him all these things. And Jonathan brought David to Saul, and he was in his presence as before.

⁸ And there was war again. And David went out and fought with the Philistines and struck them with a great blow, so that they fled before him. ⁹ Then a harmful spirit from the LORD came upon Saul, as he sat in his house with his spear in his hand. And David was playing the lyre. ¹⁰ And Saul sought to pin David to the wall with the spear, but he eluded Saul, so that he struck the spear into the wall. And David fled and escaped that night.

¹¹ Saul sent messengers to David's house to watch him, that he might kill him in the morning. But Michal, David's wife, told him, "If you do not escape with your life tonight, tomorrow you will be killed." ¹² So Michal let David down through the window, and he fled away and escaped. ¹³ Michal took an image¹ and laid it on the bed and put a pillow of goats' hair at its head and covered it with the clothes. ¹⁴ And when Saul sent messengers to take David, she said, "He is sick." ¹⁵ Then Saul sent the messengers to see David, saying, "Bring him up to me in the bed, that I may kill him." ¹⁶ And when the messengers came in, behold, the image was in the bed, with the pillow of goats' hair at its head. ¹⁷ Saul said to Michal, "Why have you deceived me thus and let my enemy go, so that he has escaped?" And Michal answered Saul, "He said to me, 'Let me go. Why should I kill you?'"

¹⁸ Now David fled and escaped, and he came to Samuel at Ramah and told him all that Saul had done to him. And he and Samuel went and lived at Naioth. ¹⁹ And it was told Saul, "Behold, David is at Naioth in Ramah." ²⁰ Then Saul sent messengers to take David, and when they saw the company of the prophets prophesying, and Samuel standing as head over them, the Spirit of God came upon the messengers of Saul, and they also prophesied. ²¹ When it was told Saul, he sent other messengers, and they also prophesied. And Saul sent messengers again the third time, and they also prophesied. ²² Then he himself went to Ramah and came to the great well that is in Secu. And he asked, "Where are Samuel and David?" And one said, "Behold, they are at Naioth in Ramah." ²³ And he went there to Naioth in Ramah. And the Spirit of God came upon him also, and as he went he prophesied until he came to Naioth in Ramah.

¹ Or *a household god*

²⁴ And he too stripped off his clothes, and he too prophesied before Samuel and lay naked all that day and all that night. Thus it is said, "Is Saul also among the prophets?"

Jonathan Warns David

20 Then David fled from Naioth in Ramah and came and said before Jonathan, "What have I done? What is my guilt? And what is my sin before your father, that he seeks my life?" ² And he said to him, "Far from it! You shall not die. Behold, my father does nothing either great or small without disclosing it to me. And why should my father hide this from me? It is not so." ³ But David vowed again, saying, "Your father knows well that I have found favor in your eyes, and he thinks, 'Do not let Jonathan know this, lest he be grieved.' But truly, as the LORD lives and as your soul lives, there is but a step between me and death." ⁴ Then Jonathan said to David, "Whatever you say, I will do for you." ⁵ David said to Jonathan, "Behold, tomorrow is the new moon, and I should not fail to sit at table with the king. But let me go, that I may hide myself in the field till the third day at evening. ⁶ If your father misses me at all, then say, 'David earnestly asked leave of me to run to Bethlehem his city, for there is a yearly sacrifice there for all the clan.' ⁷ If he says, 'Good!' it will be well with your servant, but if he is angry, then know that harm is determined by him. ⁸ Therefore deal kindly with your servant, for you have brought your servant into a covenant of the LORD with you. But if there is guilt in me, kill me yourself, for why should you bring me to your father?" ⁹ And Jonathan said, "Far be it from you! If I knew that it was determined by my father that harm should come to you, would I not tell you?" ¹⁰ Then David said to Jonathan, "Who will tell me if your father answers you roughly?" ¹¹ And Jonathan said to David, "Come, let us go out into the field." So they both went out into the field.

¹² And Jonathan said to David, "The LORD, the God of Israel, be witness!¹ When I have sounded out my father, about this time tomorrow, or the third day, behold, if he is well disposed toward David, shall I not then send and disclose it to you? ¹³ But should it please my father to do you harm, the LORD do so to Jonathan and more also if I do not disclose it

to you and send you away, that you may go in safety. May the LORD be with you, as he has been with my father. ¹⁴ If I am still alive, show me the steadfast love of the LORD, that I may not die; ¹⁵ and do not cut off² your steadfast love from my house forever, when the LORD cuts off every one of the enemies of David from the face of the earth." ¹⁶ And Jonathan made a covenant with the house of David, saying, "May³ the LORD take vengeance on David's enemies." ¹⁷ And Jonathan made David swear again by his love for him, for he loved him as he loved his own soul.

¹⁸ Then Jonathan said to him, "Tomorrow is the new moon, and you will be missed, because your seat will be empty. ¹⁹ On the third day go down quickly to the place where you hid yourself when the matter was in hand, and remain beside the stone heap.⁴ ²⁰ And I will shoot three arrows to the side of it, as though I shot at a mark. ²¹ And behold, I will send the boy, saying, 'Go, find the arrows.' If I say to the boy, 'Look, the arrows are on this side of you, take them,' then you are to come, for, as the LORD lives, it is safe for you and there is no danger. ²² But if I say to the youth, 'Look, the arrows are beyond you,' then go, for the LORD has sent you away. ²³ And as for the matter of which you and I have spoken, behold, the LORD is between you and me forever."

²⁴ So David hid himself in the field. And when the new moon came, the king sat down to eat food. ²⁵ The king sat on his seat, as at other times, on the seat by the wall. Jonathan sat opposite,⁵ and Abner sat by Saul's side, but David's place was empty.

²⁶ Yet Saul did not say anything that day, for he thought, "Something has happened to him. He is not clean; surely he is not clean." ²⁷ But on the second day, the day after the new moon, David's place was empty. And Saul said to Jonathan his son, "Why has not the son of Jesse come to the meal, either yesterday or today?" ²⁸ Jonathan answered Saul, "David earnestly asked leave of me to go to Bethlehem. ²⁹ He said, 'Let me go, for our clan holds a sacrifice in the city, and my brother has commanded me to be there. So now, if I have found favor in your eyes, let me get away and see my brothers.' For this reason he has not come to the king's table."

¹ Hebrew lacks *be witness* ² Or *but if I die, do not cut off* ³ Septuagint *earth*, ¹⁶*let not the name of Jonathan be cut off from the house of David. And may* ⁴ Septuagint; Hebrew *the stone Ezel* ⁵ Compare Septuagint; Hebrew *stood up*

30 Then Saul's anger was kindled against Jonathan, and he said to him, "You son of a perverse, rebellious woman, do I not know that you have chosen the son of Jesse to your own shame, and to the shame of your mother's nakedness? 31 For as long as the son of Jesse lives on the earth, neither you nor your kingdom shall be established. Therefore send and bring him to me, for he shall surely die." 32 Then Jonathan answered Saul his father, "Why should he be put to death? What has he done?" 33 But Saul hurled his spear at him to strike him. So Jonathan knew that his father was determined to put David to death. 34 And Jonathan rose from the table in fierce anger and ate no food the second day of the month, for he was grieved for David, because his father had disgraced him.

35 In the morning Jonathan went out into the field to the appointment with David, and with him a little boy. 36 And he said to his boy, "Run and find the arrows that I shoot." As the boy ran, he shot an arrow beyond him. 37 And when the boy came to the place of the arrow that Jonathan had shot, Jonathan called after the boy and said, "Is not the arrow beyond you?" 38 And Jonathan called after the boy, "Hurry! Be quick! Do not stay!" So Jonathan's boy gathered up the arrows and came to his master. 39 But the boy knew nothing. Only Jonathan and David knew the matter. 40 And Jonathan gave his weapons to his boy and said to him, "Go and carry them to the city." 41 And as soon as the boy had gone, David rose from beside the stone heap[1] and fell on his face to the ground and bowed three times. And they kissed one another and wept with one another, David weeping the most. 42 Then Jonathan said to David, "Go in peace, because we have sworn both of us in the name of the LORD, saying, 'The LORD shall be between me and you, and between my offspring and your offspring, forever.'" And he rose and departed, and Jonathan went into the city.[2]

David and the Holy Bread

21 [3] Then David came to Nob, to Ahimelech the priest. And Ahimelech came to meet David, trembling, and said to him, "Why are you alone, and no one with you?" 2 And David said to Ahimelech the priest, "The king has charged me with a matter and said to me, 'Let no one know anything of the matter about which I send you, and with which I have charged you.'

I have made an appointment with the young men for such and such a place. 3 Now then, what do you have on hand? Give me five loaves of bread, or whatever is here." 4 And the priest answered David, "I have no common bread on hand, but there is holy bread—if the young men have kept themselves from women." 5 And David answered the priest, "Truly women have been kept from us as always when I go on an expedition. The vessels of the young men are holy even when it is an ordinary journey. How much more today will their vessels be holy?" 6 So the priest gave him the holy bread, for there was no bread there but the bread of the Presence, which is removed from before the LORD, to be replaced by hot bread on the day it is taken away.

7 Now a certain man of the servants of Saul was there that day, detained before the LORD. His name was Doeg the Edomite, the chief of Saul's herdsmen.

8 Then David said to Ahimelech, "Then have you not here a spear or a sword at hand? For I have brought neither my sword nor my weapons with me, because the king's business required haste." 9 And the priest said, "The sword of Goliath the Philistine, whom you struck down in the Valley of Elah, behold, it is here wrapped in a cloth behind the ephod. If you will take that, take it, for there is none but that here." And David said, "There is none like that; give it to me."

David Flees to Gath

10 And David rose and fled that day from Saul and went to Achish the king of Gath. 11 And the servants of Achish said to him, "Is not this David the king of the land? Did they not sing to one another of him in dances,

'Saul has struck down his thousands,
    and David his ten thousands'?"

12 And David took these words to heart and was much afraid of Achish the king of Gath. 13 So he changed his behavior before them and pretended to be insane in their hands and made marks on the doors of the gate and let his spittle run down his beard. 14 Then Achish said to his servants, "Behold, you see the man is mad. Why then have you brought him to me? 15 Do I lack madmen, that you have brought this fellow to behave as a madman in my presence? Shall this fellow come into my house?"

[1] Septuagint; Hebrew from beside the south [2] This sentence is 21:1 in Hebrew [3] Ch 21:2 in Hebrew

David at the Cave of Adullam

22 David departed from there and escaped to the cave of Adullam. And when his brothers and all his father's house heard it, they went down there to him. ² And everyone who was in distress, and everyone who was in debt, and everyone who was bitter in soul,¹ gathered to him. And he became commander over them. And there were with him about four hundred men.

³ And David went from there to Mizpeh of Moab. And he said to the king of Moab, "Please let my father and my mother stay² with you, till I know what God will do for me." ⁴ And he left them with the king of Moab, and they stayed with him all the time that David was in the stronghold. ⁵ Then the prophet Gad said to David, "Do not remain in the stronghold; depart, and go into the land of Judah." So David departed and went into the forest of Hereth.

Saul Kills the Priests at Nob

⁶ Now Saul heard that David was discovered, and the men who were with him. Saul was sitting at Gibeah under the tamarisk tree on the height with his spear in his hand, and all his servants were standing about him. ⁷ And Saul said to his servants who stood about him, "Hear now, people of Benjamin; will the son of Jesse give every one of you fields and vineyards, will he make you all commanders of thousands and commanders of hundreds, ⁸ that all of you have conspired against me? No one discloses to me when my son makes a covenant with the son of Jesse. None of you is sorry for me or discloses to me that my son has stirred up my servant against me, to lie in wait, as at this day." ⁹ Then answered Doeg the Edomite, who stood by the servants of Saul, "I saw the son of Jesse coming to Nob, to Ahimelech the son of Ahitub, ¹⁰ and he inquired of the LORD for him and gave him provisions and gave him the sword of Goliath the Philistine."

¹¹ Then the king sent to summon Ahimelech the priest, the son of Ahitub, and all his father's house, the priests who were at Nob, and all of them came to the king. ¹² And Saul said, "Hear now, son of Ahitub." And he answered, "Here I am, my lord." ¹³ And Saul said to him, "Why have you conspired against me, you and the son of Jesse, in that you have given him bread and a sword and have inquired of God for him, so that he has risen against me, to lie in wait, as at this day?" ¹⁴ Then Ahimelech answered the

king, "And who among all your servants is so faithful as David, who is the king's son-in-law, and captain over³ your bodyguard, and honored in your house? ¹⁵ Is today the first time that I have inquired of God for him? No! Let not the king impute anything to his servant or to all the house of my father, for your servant has known nothing of all this, much or little." ¹⁶ And the king said, "You shall surely die, Ahimelech, you and all your father's house." ¹⁷ And the king said to the guard who stood about him, "Turn and kill the priests of the LORD, because their hand also is with David, and they knew that he fled and did not disclose it to me." But the servants of the king would not put out their hand to strike the priests of the LORD. ¹⁸ Then the king said to Doeg, "You turn and strike the priests." And Doeg the Edomite turned and struck down the priests, and he killed on that day eighty-five persons who wore the linen ephod. ¹⁹ And Nob, the city of the priests, he put to the sword; both man and woman, child and infant, ox, donkey and sheep, he put to the sword.

²⁰ But one of the sons of Ahimelech the son of Ahitub, named Abiathar, escaped and fled after David. ²¹ And Abiathar told David that Saul had killed the priests of the LORD. ²² And David said to Abiathar, "I knew on that day, when Doeg the Edomite was there, that he would surely tell Saul. I have occasioned the death of all the persons of your father's house. ²³ Stay with me; do not be afraid, for he who seeks my life seeks your life. With me you shall be in safekeeping."

David Saves the City of Keilah

23 Now they told David, "Behold, the Philistines are fighting against Keilah and are robbing the threshing floors." ² Therefore David inquired of the LORD, "Shall I go and attack these Philistines?" And the LORD said to David, "Go and attack the Philistines and save Keilah." ³ But David's men said to him, "Behold, we are afraid here in Judah; how much more then if we go to Keilah against the armies of the Philistines?" ⁴ Then David inquired of the LORD again. And the LORD answered him, "Arise, go down to Keilah, for I will give the Philistines into your hand." ⁵ And David and his men went to Keilah and fought with the Philistines and brought away their livestock and struck them with a great blow. So David saved the inhabitants of Keilah.

¹ Or discontented ² Syriac, Vulgate; Hebrew go out ³ Septuagint, Targum; Hebrew and has turned aside to

⁶When Abiathar the son of Ahimelech had fled to David to Keilah, he had come down with an ephod in his hand. ⁷Now it was told Saul that David had come to Keilah. And Saul said, "God has given him into my hand, for he has shut himself in by entering a town that has gates and bars." ⁸And Saul summoned all the people to war, to go down to Keilah, to besiege David and his men. ⁹David knew that Saul was plotting harm against him. And he said to Abiathar the priest, "Bring the ephod here." ¹⁰Then David said, "O LORD, the God of Israel, your servant has surely heard that Saul seeks to come to Keilah, to destroy the city on my account. ¹¹Will the men of Keilah surrender me into his hand? Will Saul come down, as your servant has heard? O LORD, the God of Israel, please tell your servant." And the LORD said, "He will come down." ¹²Then David said, "Will the men of Keilah surrender me and my men into the hand of Saul?" And the LORD said, "They will surrender you." ¹³Then David and his men, who were about six hundred, arose and departed from Keilah, and they went wherever they could go. When Saul was told that David had escaped from Keilah, he gave up the expedition. ¹⁴And David remained in the strongholds in the wilderness, in the hill country of the wilderness of Ziph. And Saul sought him every day, but God did not give him into his hand.

Saul Pursues David

¹⁵David saw that Saul had come out to seek his life. David was in the wilderness of Ziph at Horesh. ¹⁶And Jonathan, Saul's son, rose and went to David at Horesh, and strengthened his hand in God. ¹⁷And he said to him, "Do not fear, for the hand of Saul my father shall not find you. You shall be king over Israel, and I shall be next to you. Saul my father also knows this." ¹⁸And the two of them made a covenant before the LORD. David remained at Horesh, and Jonathan went home.

¹⁹Then the Ziphites went up to Saul at Gibeah, saying, "Is not David hiding among us in the strongholds at Horesh, on the hill of Hachilah, which is south of Jeshimon? ²⁰Now come down, O king, according to all your heart's desire to come down, and our part shall be to surrender him into the king's hand." ²¹And Saul said, "May you be blessed by the

LORD, for you have had compassion on me. ²²Go, make yet more sure. Know and see the place where his foot is, and who has seen him there, for it is told me that he is very cunning. ²³See therefore and take note of all the lurking places where he hides, and come back to me with sure information. Then I will go with you. And if he is in the land, I will search him out among all the thousands of Judah." ²⁴And they arose and went to Ziph ahead of Saul.

Now David and his men were in the wilderness of Maon, in the Arabah to the south of Jeshimon. ²⁵And Saul and his men went to seek him. And David was told, so he went down to the rock and lived in the wilderness of Maon. And when Saul heard that, he pursued after David in the wilderness of Maon. ²⁶Saul went on one side of the mountain, and David and his men on the other side of the mountain. And David was hurrying to get away from Saul. As Saul and his men were closing in on David and his men to capture them, ²⁷a messenger came to Saul, saying, "Hurry and come, for the Philistines have made a raid against the land." ²⁸So Saul returned from pursuing after David and went against the Philistines. Therefore that place was called the Rock of Escape.¹ ²⁹²And David went up from there and lived in the strongholds of Engedi.

David Spares Saul's Life

24 ³When Saul returned from following the Philistines, he was told, "Behold, David is in the wilderness of Engedi." ²Then Saul took three thousand chosen men out of all Israel and went to seek David and his men in front of the Wildgoats' Rocks. ³And he came to the sheepfolds by the way, where there was a cave, and Saul went in to relieve himself.⁴ Now David and his men were sitting in the innermost parts of the cave. ⁴And the men of David said to him, "Here is the day of which the LORD said to you, 'Behold, I will give your enemy into your hand, and you shall do to him as it shall seem good to you.'" Then David arose and stealthily cut off a corner of Saul's robe. ⁵And afterward David's heart struck him, because he had cut off a corner of Saul's robe. ⁶He said to his men, "The LORD forbid that I should do this thing to my lord, the LORD's anointed, to put out my hand against him, seeing he is the

¹ Or Rock of Divisions ² Ch 24:1 in Hebrew ³ Ch 24:2 in Hebrew ⁴ Hebrew cover his feet

LORD's anointed." [7] So David persuaded his men with these words and did not permit them to attack Saul. And Saul rose up and left the cave and went on his way.

[8] Afterward David also arose and went out of the cave, and called after Saul, "My lord the king!" And when Saul looked behind him, David bowed with his face to the earth and paid homage. [9] And David said to Saul, "Why do you listen to the words of men who say, 'Behold, David seeks your harm'? [10] Behold, this day your eyes have seen how the LORD gave you today into my hand in the cave. And some told me to kill you, but I spared you.[1] I said, 'I will not put out my hand against my lord, for he is the LORD's anointed.' [11] See, my father, see the corner of your robe in my hand. For by the fact that I cut off the corner of your robe and did not kill you, you may know and see that there is no wrong or treason in my hands. I have not sinned against you, though you hunt my life to take it. [12] May the LORD judge between me and you, may the LORD avenge me against you, but my hand shall not be against you. [13] As the proverb of the ancients says, 'Out of the wicked comes wickedness.' But my hand shall not be against you. [14] After whom has the king of Israel come out? After whom do you pursue? After a dead dog! After a flea! [15] May the LORD therefore be judge and give sentence between me and you, and see to it and plead my cause and deliver me from your hand."

[16] As soon as David had finished speaking these words to Saul, Saul said, "Is this your voice, my son David?" And Saul lifted up his voice and wept. [17] He said to David, "You are more righteous than I, for you have repaid me good, whereas I have repaid you evil. [18] And you have declared this day how you have dealt well with me, in that you did not kill me when the LORD put me into your hands. [19] For if a man finds his enemy, will he let him go away safe? So may the LORD reward you with good for what you have done to me this day. [20] And now, behold, I know that you shall surely be king, and that the kingdom of Israel shall be established in your hand. [21] Swear to me therefore by the LORD that you will not cut off my offspring after me, and that you will not destroy my name out of my father's house." [22] And David swore this to Saul. Then Saul went home, but David and his men went up to the stronghold.

The Death of Samuel

25 Now Samuel died. And all Israel assembled and mourned for him, and they buried him in his house at Ramah.

David and Abigail

Then David rose and went down to the wilderness of Paran. [2] And there was a man in Maon whose business was in Carmel. The man was very rich; he had three thousand sheep and a thousand goats. He was shearing his sheep in Carmel. [3] Now the name of the man was Nabal, and the name of his wife Abigail. The woman was discerning and beautiful, but the man was harsh and badly behaved; he was a Calebite. [4] David heard in the wilderness that Nabal was shearing his sheep. [5] So David sent ten young men. And David said to the young men, "Go up to Carmel, and go to Nabal and greet him in my name. [6] And thus you shall greet him: 'Peace be to you, and peace be to your house, and peace be to all that you have. [7] I hear that you have shearers. Now your shepherds have been with us, and we did them no harm, and they missed nothing all the time they were in Carmel. [8] Ask your young men, and they will tell you. Therefore let my young men find favor in your eyes, for we come on a feast day. Please give whatever you have at hand to your servants and to your son David.'"

[9] When David's young men came, they said all this to Nabal in the name of David, and then they waited. [10] And Nabal answered David's servants, "Who is David? Who is the son of Jesse? There are many servants these days who are breaking away from their masters. [11] Shall I take my bread and my water and my meat that I have killed for my shearers and give it to men who come from I do not know where?" [12] So David's young men turned away and came back and told him all this. [13] And David said to his men, "Every man strap on his sword!" And every man of them strapped on his sword. David also strapped on his sword. And about four hundred men went up after David, while two hundred remained with the baggage.

[14] But one of the young men told Abigail, Nabal's wife, "Behold, David sent messengers out of the wilderness to greet our master, and he railed at them. [15] Yet the men were very good to us, and we suffered no harm, and we did not miss anything when we were in the fields, as long as we went with them. [16] They were a wall

---

[1] Septuagint, Syriac, Targum; Hebrew *it* [my eye] *spared you*

to us both by night and by day, all the while we were with them keeping the sheep. [17] Now therefore know this and consider what you should do, for harm is determined against our master and against all his house, and he is such a worthless man that one cannot speak to him."

[18] Then Abigail made haste and took two hundred loaves and two skins of wine and five sheep already prepared and five seahs[1] of parched grain and a hundred clusters of raisins and two hundred cakes of figs, and laid them on donkeys. [19] And she said to her young men, "Go on before me; behold, I come after you." But she did not tell her husband Nabal. [20] And as she rode on the donkey and came down under cover of the mountain, behold, David and his men came down toward her, and she met them. [21] Now David had said, "Surely in vain have I guarded all that this fellow has in the wilderness, so that nothing was missed of all that belonged to him, and he has returned me evil for good. [22] God do so to the enemies of David[2] and more also, if by morning I leave so much as one male of all who belong to him."

[23] When Abigail saw David, she hurried and got down from the donkey and fell before David on her face and bowed to the ground. [24] She fell at his feet and said, "On me alone, my lord, be the guilt. Please let your servant speak in your ears, and hear the words of your servant. [25] Let not my lord regard this worthless fellow, Nabal, for as his name is, so is he. Nabal[3] is his name, and folly is with him. But I your servant did not see the young men of my lord, whom you sent. [26] Now then, my lord, as the LORD lives, and as your soul lives, because the LORD has restrained you from bloodguilt and from saving with your own hand, now then let your enemies and those who seek to do evil to my lord be as Nabal. [27] And now let this present that your servant has brought to my lord be given to the young men who follow my lord. [28] Please forgive the trespass of your servant. For the LORD will certainly make my lord a sure house, because my lord is fighting the battles of the LORD, and evil shall not be found in you so long as you live. [29] If men rise up to pursue you and to seek your life, the life of my lord shall be bound in the bundle of the living in the care of the LORD your God. And the lives of your enemies he shall sling out as from the hollow of a sling. [30] And when the LORD has done to my lord according to all the good that he has spoken concerning you and has appointed you prince[4] over Israel, [31] my lord shall have no cause of grief or pangs of conscience for having shed blood without cause or for my lord working salvation himself. And when the LORD has dealt well with my lord, then remember your servant."

[32] And David said to Abigail, "Blessed be the LORD, the God of Israel, who sent you this day to meet me! [33] Blessed be your discretion, and blessed be you, who have kept me this day from bloodguilt and from working salvation with my own hand! [34] For as surely as the LORD, the God of Israel, lives, who has restrained me from hurting you, unless you had hurried and come to meet me, truly by morning there had not been left to Nabal so much as one male." [35] Then David received from her hand what she had brought him. And he said to her, "Go up in peace to your house. See, I have obeyed your voice, and I have granted your petition."

[36] And Abigail came to Nabal, and behold, he was holding a feast in his house, like the feast of a king. And Nabal's heart was merry within him, for he was very drunk. So she told him nothing at all until the morning light. [37] In the morning, when the wine had gone out of Nabal, his wife told him these things, and his heart died within him, and he became as a stone. [38] And about ten days later the LORD struck Nabal, and he died.

[39] When David heard that Nabal was dead, he said, "Blessed be the LORD who has avenged the insult I received at the hand of Nabal, and has kept back his servant from wrongdoing. The LORD has returned the evil of Nabal on his own head." Then David sent and spoke to Abigail, to take her as his wife. [40] When the servants of David came to Abigail at Carmel, they said to her, "David has sent us to you to take you to him as his wife." [41] And she rose and bowed with her face to the ground and said, "Behold, your handmaid is a servant to wash the feet of the servants of my lord." [42] And Abigail hurried and rose and mounted a donkey, and her five young women attended her. She followed the messengers of David and became his wife.

[43] David also took Ahinoam of Jezreel, and both of them became his wives. [44] Saul had given Michal his daughter, David's wife, to Palti the son of Laish, who was of Gallim.

---

[1] A *seah* was about 7 quarts or 7.3 liters [2] Septuagint *to David* [3] *Nabal* means *fool* [4] Or *leader*

David Spares Saul Again

26 Then the Ziphites came to Saul at Gibeah, saying, "Is not David hiding himself on the hill of Hachilah, which is on the east of Jeshimon?" ²So Saul arose and went down to the wilderness of Ziph with three thousand chosen men of Israel to seek David in the wilderness of Ziph. ³And Saul encamped on the hill of Hachilah, which is beside the road on the east of Jeshimon. But David remained in the wilderness. When he saw that Saul came after him into the wilderness, ⁴David sent out spies and learned that Saul had indeed come. ⁵Then David rose and came to the place where Saul had encamped. And David saw the place where Saul lay, with Abner the son of Ner, the commander of his army. Saul was lying within the encampment, while the army was encamped around him.

⁶Then David said to Ahimelech the Hittite, and to Joab's brother Abishai the son of Zeruiah, "Who will go down with me into the camp to Saul?" And Abishai said, "I will go down with you." ⁷So David and Abishai went to the army by night. And there lay Saul sleeping within the encampment, with his spear stuck in the ground at his head, and Abner and the army lay around him. ⁸Then Abishai said to David, "God has given your enemy into your hand this day. Now please let me pin him to the earth with one stroke of the spear, and I will not strike him twice." ⁹But David said to Abishai, "Do not destroy him, for who can put out his hand against the LORD's anointed and be guiltless?" ¹⁰And David said, "As the LORD lives, the LORD will strike him, or his day will come to die, or he will go down into battle and perish. ¹¹The LORD forbid that I should put out my hand against the LORD's anointed. But take now the spear that is at his head and the jar of water, and let us go." ¹²So David took the spear and the jar of water from Saul's head, and they went away. No man saw it or knew it, nor did any awake, for they were all asleep, because a deep sleep from the LORD had fallen upon them.

¹³Then David went over to the other side and stood far off on the top of the hill, with a great space between them. ¹⁴And David called to the army, and to Abner the son of Ner, saying, "Will you not answer, Abner?" Then Abner answered, "Who are you who calls to the king?" ¹⁵And David said to Abner, "Are you not a man? Who is like you in Israel? Why then have you not kept watch over your lord the king? For one of the people came in to destroy the king your lord. ¹⁶This thing that you have done is not good. As the LORD lives, you deserve to die, because you have not kept watch over your lord, the LORD's anointed. And now see where the king's spear is and the jar of water that was at his head."

¹⁷Saul recognized David's voice and said, "Is this your voice, my son David?" And David said, "It is my voice, my lord, O king." ¹⁸And he said, "Why does my lord pursue after his servant? For what have I done? What evil is on my hands? ¹⁹Now therefore let my lord the king hear the words of his servant. If it is the LORD who has stirred you up against me, may he accept an offering, but if it is men, may they be cursed before the LORD, for they have driven me out this day that I should have no share in the heritage of the LORD, saying, 'Go, serve other gods.' ²⁰Now therefore, let not my blood fall to the earth away from the presence of the LORD, for the king of Israel has come out to seek a single flea like one who hunts a partridge in the mountains."

²¹Then Saul said, "I have sinned. Return, my son David, for I will no more do you harm, because my life was precious in your eyes this day. Behold, I have acted foolishly, and have made a great mistake." ²²And David answered and said, "Here is the spear, O king! Let one of the young men come over and take it. ²³The LORD rewards every man for his righteousness and his faithfulness, for the LORD gave you into my hand today, and I would not put out my hand against the LORD's anointed. ²⁴Behold, as your life was precious this day in my sight, so may my life be precious in the sight of the LORD, and may he deliver me out of all tribulation." ²⁵Then Saul said to David, "Blessed be you, my son David! You will do many things and will succeed in them." So David went his way, and Saul returned to his place.

David Flees to the Philistines

27 Then David said in his heart, "Now I shall perish one day by the hand of Saul. There is nothing better for me than that I should escape to the land of the Philistines. Then Saul will despair of seeking me any longer within the borders of Israel, and I shall escape out of his hand." ²So David arose and went over, he and the six hundred men who were with him, to Achish the son of Maoch, king of Gath.

³And David lived with Achish at Gath, he and his men, every man with his household, and David with his two wives, Ahinoam of Jezreel, and Abigail of Carmel, Nabal's widow. ⁴And when it was told Saul that David had fled to Gath, he no longer sought him.

⁵Then David said to Achish, "If I have found favor in your eyes, let a place be given me in one of the country towns, that I may dwell there. For why should your servant dwell in the royal city with you?" ⁶So that day Achish gave him Ziklag. Therefore Ziklag has belonged to the kings of Judah to this day. ⁷And the number of the days that David lived in the country of the Philistines was a year and four months.

⁸Now David and his men went up and made raids against the Geshurites, the Girzites, and the Amalekites, for these were the inhabitants of the land from of old, as far as Shur, to the land of Egypt. ⁹And David would strike the land and would leave neither man nor woman alive, but would take away the sheep, the oxen, the donkeys, the camels, and the garments, and come back to Achish. ¹⁰When Achish asked, "Where have you made a raid today?" David would say, "Against the Negeb of Judah," or, "Against the Negeb of the Jerahmeelites," or, "Against the Negeb of the Kenites." ¹¹And David would leave neither man nor woman alive to bring news to Gath, thinking, "lest they should tell about us and say, 'So David has done.'" Such was his custom all the while he lived in the country of the Philistines. ¹²And Achish trusted David, thinking, "He has made himself an utter stench to his people Israel; therefore he shall always be my servant."

Saul and the Medium of En-dor

28 In those days the Philistines gathered their forces for war, to fight against Israel. And Achish said to David, "Understand that you and your men are to go out with me in the army." ²David said to Achish, "Very well, you shall know what your servant can do." And Achish said to David, "Very well, I will make you my bodyguard for life."

³Now Samuel had died, and all Israel had mourned for him and buried him in Ramah, his own city. And Saul had put the mediums and the necromancers out of the land. ⁴The Philistines assembled and came and encamped at Shunem. And Saul gathered all Israel, and they encamped at Gilboa. ⁵When Saul saw the army of the Philistines, he was afraid, and his heart trembled greatly. ⁶And when Saul inquired of the LORD, the LORD did not answer him, either by dreams, or by Urim, or by prophets. ⁷Then Saul said to his servants, "Seek out for me a woman who is a medium, that I may go to her and inquire of her." And his servants said to him, "Behold, there is a medium at En-dor."

⁸So Saul disguised himself and put on other garments and went, he and two men with him. And they came to the woman by night. And he said, "Divine for me by a spirit and bring up for me whomever I shall name to you." ⁹The woman said to him, "Surely you know what Saul has done, how he has cut off the mediums and the necromancers from the land. Why then are you laying a trap for my life to bring about my death?" ¹⁰But Saul swore to her by the LORD, "As the LORD lives, no punishment shall come upon you for this thing." ¹¹Then the woman said, "Whom shall I bring up for you?" He said, "Bring up Samuel for me." ¹²When the woman saw Samuel, she cried out with a loud voice. And the woman said to Saul, "Why have you deceived me? You are Saul." ¹³The king said to her, "Do not be afraid. What do you see?" And the woman said to Saul, "I see a god coming up out of the earth." ¹⁴He said to her, "What is his appearance?" And she said, "An old man is coming up, and he is wrapped in a robe." And Saul knew that it was Samuel, and he bowed with his face to the ground and paid homage.

¹⁵Then Samuel said to Saul, "Why have you disturbed me by bringing me up?" Saul answered, "I am in great distress, for the Philistines are warring against me, and God has turned away from me and answers me no more, either by prophets or by dreams. Therefore I have summoned you to tell me what I shall do." ¹⁶And Samuel said, "Why then do you ask me, since the LORD has turned from you and become your enemy? ¹⁷The LORD has done to you as he spoke by me, for the LORD has torn the kingdom out of your hand and given it to your neighbor, David. ¹⁸Because you did not obey the voice of the LORD and did not carry out his fierce wrath against Amalek, therefore the LORD has done this thing to you this day. ¹⁹Moreover, the LORD will give Israel also with you into the hand of the Philistines, and tomorrow you and your sons shall be with me. The LORD will give the army of Israel also into the hand of the Philistines."

²⁰ Then Saul fell at once full length on the ground, filled with fear because of the words of Samuel. And there was no strength in him, for he had eaten nothing all day and all night. ²¹ And the woman came to Saul, and when she saw that he was terrified, she said to him, "Behold, your servant has obeyed you. I have taken my life in my hand and have listened to what you have said to me. ²² Now therefore, you also obey your servant. Let me set a morsel of bread before you; and eat, that you may have strength when you go on your way." ²³ He refused and said, "I will not eat." But his servants, together with the woman, urged him, and he listened to their words. So he arose from the earth and sat on the bed. ²⁴ Now the woman had a fattened calf in the house, and she quickly killed it, and she took flour and kneaded it and baked unleavened bread of it, ²⁵ and she put it before Saul and his servants, and they ate. Then they rose and went away that night.

The Philistines Reject David

29 Now the Philistines had gathered all their forces at Aphek. And the Israelites were encamped by the spring that is in Jezreel. ² As the lords of the Philistines were passing on by hundreds and by thousands, and David and his men were passing on in the rear with Achish, ³ the commanders of the Philistines said, "What are these Hebrews doing here?" And Achish said to the commanders of the Philistines, "Is this not David, the servant of Saul, king of Israel, who has been with me now for days and years, and since he deserted to me I have found no fault in him to this day." ⁴ But the commanders of the Philistines were angry with him. And the commanders of the Philistines said to him, "Send the man back, that he may return to the place to which you have assigned him. He shall not go down with us to battle, lest in the battle he become an adversary to us. For how could this fellow reconcile himself to his lord? Would it not be with the heads of the men here? ⁵ Is not this David, of whom they sing to one another in dances,

'Saul has struck down his thousands,
   and David his ten thousands'?"

⁶ Then Achish called David and said to him, "As the LORD lives, you have been honest, and to me it seems right that you should march out and in with me in the campaign. For I have found nothing wrong in you from the day of your coming to me to this day. Nevertheless, the lords do not approve of you. ⁷ So go back now; and go peaceably, that you may not displease the lords of the Philistines." ⁸ And David said to Achish, "But what have I done? What have you found in your servant from the day I entered your service until now, that I may not go and fight against the enemies of my lord the king?" ⁹ And Achish answered David and said, "I know that you are as blameless in my sight as an angel of God. Nevertheless, the commanders of the Philistines have said, 'He shall not go up with us to the battle.' ¹⁰ Now then rise early in the morning with the servants of your lord who came with you, and start early in the morning, and depart as soon as you have light." ¹¹ So David set out with his men early in the morning to return to the land of the Philistines. But the Philistines went up to Jezreel.

David's Wives Are Captured

30 Now when David and his men came to Ziklag on the third day, the Amalekites had made a raid against the Negeb and against Ziklag. They had overcome Ziklag and burned it with fire ² and taken captive the women and all¹ who were in it, both small and great. They killed no one, but carried them off and went their way. ³ And when David and his men came to the city, they found it burned with fire, and their wives and sons and daughters taken captive. ⁴ Then David and the people who were with him raised their voices and wept until they had no more strength to weep. ⁵ David's two wives also had been taken captive, Ahinoam of Jezreel and Abigail the widow of Nabal of Carmel. ⁶ And David was greatly distressed, for the people spoke of stoning him, because all the people were bitter in soul,² each for his sons and daughters. But David strengthened himself in the LORD his God.

⁷ And David said to Abiathar the priest, the son of Ahimelech, "Bring me the ephod." So Abiathar brought the ephod to David. ⁸ And David inquired of the LORD, "Shall I pursue after this band? Shall I overtake them?" He answered him, "Pursue, for you shall surely

---

¹ Septuagint; Hebrew lacks *and all* ² Compare 22:2

overtake and shall surely rescue." [9] So David set out, and the six hundred men who were with him, and they came to the brook Besor, where those who were left behind stayed. [10] But David pursued, he and four hundred men. Two hundred stayed behind, who were too exhausted to cross the brook Besor.

[11] They found an Egyptian in the open country and brought him to David. And they gave him bread and he ate. They gave him water to drink, [12] and they gave him a piece of a cake of figs and two clusters of raisins. And when he had eaten, his spirit revived, for he had not eaten bread or drunk water for three days and three nights. [13] And David said to him, "To whom do you belong? And where are you from?" He said, "I am a young man of Egypt, servant to an Amalekite, and my master left me behind because I fell sick three days ago. [14] We had made a raid against the Negeb of the Cherethites and against that which belongs to Judah and against the Negeb of Caleb, and we burned Ziklag with fire." [15] And David said to him, "Will you take me down to this band?" And he said, "Swear to me by God that you will not kill me or deliver me into the hands of my master, and I will take you down to this band."

David Defeats the Amalekites

[16] And when he had taken him down, behold, they were spread abroad over all the land, eating and drinking and dancing, because of all the great spoil they had taken from the land of the Philistines and from the land of Judah. [17] And David struck them down from twilight until the evening of the next day, and not a man of them escaped, except four hundred young men, who mounted camels and fled. [18] David recovered all that the Amalekites had taken, and David rescued his two wives. [19] Nothing was missing, whether small or great, sons or daughters, spoil or anything that had been taken. David brought back all. [20] David also captured all the flocks and herds, and the people drove the livestock before him,[1] and said, "This is David's spoil."

[21] Then David came to the two hundred men who had been too exhausted to follow David, and who had been left at the brook Besor. And they went out to meet David and to meet the people who were with him. And when David came near to the people he greeted

them. [22] Then all the wicked and worthless fellows among the men who had gone with David said, "Because they did not go with us, we will not give them any of the spoil that we have recovered, except that each man may lead away his wife and children, and depart." [23] But David said, "You shall not do so, my brothers, with what the Lord has given us. He has preserved us and given into our hand the band that came against us. [24] Who would listen to you in this matter? For as his share is who goes down into the battle, so shall his share be who stays by the baggage. They shall share alike." [25] And he made it a statute and a rule for Israel from that day forward to this day.

[26] When David came to Ziklag, he sent part of the spoil to his friends, the elders of Judah, saying, "Here is a present for you from the spoil of the enemies of the Lord." [27] It was for those in Bethel, in Ramoth of the Negeb, in Jattir, [28] in Aroer, in Siphmoth, in Eshtemoa, [29] in Racal, in the cities of the Jerahmeelites, in the cities of the Kenites, [30] in Hormah, in Bor-ashan, in Athach, [31] in Hebron, for all the places where David and his men had roamed.

The Death of Saul

31 Now the Philistines were fighting against Israel, and the men of Israel fled before the Philistines and fell slain on Mount Gilboa. [2] And the Philistines overtook Saul and his sons, and the Philistines struck down Jonathan and Abinadab and Malchi-shua, the sons of Saul. [3] The battle pressed hard against Saul, and the archers found him, and he was badly wounded by the archers. [4] Then Saul said to his armor-bearer, "Draw your sword, and thrust me through with it, lest these uncircumcised come and thrust me through, and mistreat me." But his armor-bearer would not, for he feared greatly. Therefore Saul took his own sword and fell upon it. [5] And when his armor-bearer saw that Saul was dead, he also fell upon his sword and died with him. [6] Thus Saul died, and his three sons, and his armor-bearer, and all his men, on the same day together. [7] And when the men of Israel who were on the other side of the valley and those beyond the Jordan saw that the men of Israel had fled and that Saul and his sons were dead, they abandoned their cities and fled. And the Philistines came and lived in them.

[8] The next day, when the Philistines came to

---

[1] The meaning of the Hebrew clause is uncertain

strip the slain, they found Saul and his three sons fallen on Mount Gilboa. ⁹ So they cut off his head and stripped off his armor and sent messengers throughout the land of the Philistines, to carry the good news to the house of their idols and to the people. ¹⁰ They put his armor in the temple of Ashtaroth, and they fastened his body to the wall of Beth-shan. ¹¹ But when the inhabitants of Jabesh-gilead heard what the Philistines had done to Saul, ¹² all the valiant men arose and went all night and took the body of Saul and the bodies of his sons from the wall of Beth-shan, and they came to Jabesh and burned them there. ¹³ And they took their bones and buried them under the tamarisk tree in Jabesh and fasted seven days.

2 SAMUEL

David Hears of Saul's Death

1 After the death of Saul, when David had returned from striking down the Amalekites, David remained two days in Ziklag. ²And on the third day, behold, a man came from Saul's camp, with his clothes torn and dirt on his head. And when he came to David, he fell to the ground and paid homage. ³David said to him, "Where do you come from?" And he said to him, "I have escaped from the camp of Israel." ⁴And David said to him, "How did it go? Tell me." And he answered, "The people fled from the battle, and also many of the people have fallen and are dead, and Saul and his son Jonathan are also dead." ⁵Then David said to the young man who told him, "How do you know that Saul and his son Jonathan are dead?" ⁶And the young man who told him said, "By chance I happened to be on Mount Gilboa, and there was Saul leaning on his spear, and behold, the chariots and the horsemen were close upon him. ⁷And when he looked behind him, he saw me, and called to me. And I answered, 'Here I am.' ⁸And he said to me, 'Who are you?' I answered him, 'I am an Amalekite.' ⁹And he said to me, 'Stand beside me and kill me, for anguish has seized me, and yet my life still lingers.' ¹⁰So I stood beside him and killed him, because I was sure that he could not live after he had fallen. And I took the crown that was on his head and the armlet that was on his arm, and I have brought them here to my lord."

¹¹Then David took hold of his clothes and tore them, and so did all the men who were with him. ¹²And they mourned and wept and fasted until evening for Saul and for Jonathan his son and for the people of the LORD and for the house of Israel, because they had fallen by the sword. ¹³And David said to the young man who told him, "Where do you come from?" And he answered, "I am the son of a sojourner, an Amalekite." ¹⁴David said to him, "How is it you were not afraid to put out your hand to destroy the LORD's anointed?" ¹⁵Then David called one of the young men and said, "Go, execute him." And he struck him down so that he died. ¹⁶And David said to him, "Your blood be on your head, for your own mouth has testified against you, saying, 'I have killed the LORD's anointed.'"

David's Lament for Saul and Jonathan

¹⁷And David lamented with this lamentation over Saul and Jonathan his son, ¹⁸and he said it[1] should be taught to the people of Judah; behold, it is written in the Book of Jashar.[2] He said:

¹⁹ "Your glory, O Israel, is slain on your high
        places!
      How the mighty have fallen!
²⁰   Tell it not in Gath,
        publish it not in the streets of Ashkelon,
      lest the daughters of the Philistines rejoice,
        lest the daughters of the uncircumcised
          exult.

²¹ "You mountains of Gilboa,
        let there be no dew or rain upon you,
        nor fields of offerings![3]
      For there the shield of the mighty was
          defiled,
        the shield of Saul, not anointed with oil.

²² "From the blood of the slain,
        from the fat of the mighty,
      the bow of Jonathan turned not back,
        and the sword of Saul returned not
          empty.

²³ "Saul and Jonathan, beloved and lovely!
      In life and in death they were not
          divided;
      they were swifter than eagles;
        they were stronger than lions.

²⁴ "You daughters of Israel, weep over Saul,
        who clothed you luxuriously in scar-
          let,
      who put ornaments of gold on your
          apparel.

²⁵ "How the mighty have fallen
        in the midst of the battle!

   "Jonathan lies slain on your high places.
²⁶   I am distressed for you, my brother
          Jonathan;
      very pleasant have you been to me;
        your love to me was extraordinary,
          surpassing the love of women.

---

[1] Septuagint; Hebrew *the Bow*, which may be the name of the lament's tune [2] Or *of the upright* [3] Septuagint *firstfruits*

[27] "How the mighty have fallen,
    and the weapons of war perished!"

David Anointed King of Judah

2 After this David inquired of the LORD,
"Shall I go up into any of the cities of
Judah?" And the LORD said to him, "Go up."
David said, "To which shall I go up?" And he
said, "To Hebron." [2] So David went up there,
and his two wives also, Ahinoam of Jezreel and
Abigail the widow of Nabal of Carmel. [3] And
David brought up his men who were with him,
everyone with his household, and they lived in
the towns of Hebron. [4] And the men of Judah
came, and there they anointed David king over
the house of Judah.

When they told David, "It was the men of
Jabesh-gilead who buried Saul," [5] David sent
messengers to the men of Jabesh-gilead and
said to them, "May you be blessed by the LORD,
because you showed this loyalty to Saul your
lord and buried him. [6] Now may the LORD
show steadfast love and faithfulness to you.
And I will do good to you because you have
done this thing. [7] Now therefore let your hands
be strong, and be valiant, for Saul your lord is
dead, and the house of Judah has anointed me
king over them."

Ish-bosheth Made King of Israel

[8] But Abner the son of Ner, commander of
Saul's army, took Ish-bosheth the son of Saul
and brought him over to Mahanaim, [9] and he
made him king over Gilead and the Ashurites
and Jezreel and Ephraim and Benjamin and all
Israel. [10] Ish-bosheth, Saul's son, was forty years
old when he began to reign over Israel, and he
reigned two years. But the house of Judah followed David. [11] And the time that David was
king in Hebron over the house of Judah was
seven years and six months.

The Battle of Gibeon

[12] Abner the son of Ner, and the servants of
Ish-bosheth the son of Saul, went out from
Mahanaim to Gibeon. [13] And Joab the son of
Zeruiah and the servants of David went out
and met them at the pool of Gibeon. And
they sat down, the one on the one side of
the pool, and the other on the other side of
the pool. [14] And Abner said to Joab, "Let the
young men arise and compete before us." And
Joab said, "Let them arise." [15] Then they arose
and passed over by number, twelve for Ben-

jamin and Ish-bosheth the son of Saul, and
twelve of the servants of David. [16] And each
caught his opponent by the head and thrust
his sword in his opponent's side, so they fell
down together. Therefore that place was called
Helkath-hazzurim,[1] which is at Gibeon. [17] And
the battle was very fierce that day. And Abner
and the men of Israel were beaten before the
servants of David.

[18] And the three sons of Zeruiah were there,
Joab, Abishai, and Asahel. Now Asahel was as
swift of foot as a wild gazelle. [19] And Asahel pursued Abner, and as he went, he turned neither
to the right hand nor to the left from following
Abner. [20] Then Abner looked behind him and
said, "Is it you, Asahel?" And he answered, "It
is I." [21] Abner said to him, "Turn aside to your
right hand or to your left, and seize one of
the young men and take his spoil." But Asahel
would not turn aside from following him.
[22] And Abner said again to Asahel, "Turn aside
from following me. Why should I strike you to
the ground? How then could I lift up my face
to your brother Joab?" [23] But he refused to turn
aside. Therefore Abner struck him in the stomach with the butt of his spear, so that the spear
came out at his back. And he fell there and died
where he was. And all who came to the place
where Asahel had fallen and died, stood still.

[24] But Joab and Abishai pursued Abner. And
as the sun was going down they came to the hill
of Ammah, which lies before Giah on the way to
the wilderness of Gibeon. [25] And the people of
Benjamin gathered themselves together behind
Abner and became one group and took their
stand on the top of a hill. [26] Then Abner called
to Joab, "Shall the sword devour forever? Do
you not know that the end will be bitter? How
long will it be before you tell your people to
turn from the pursuit of their brothers?" [27] And
Joab said, "As God lives, if you had not spoken,
surely the men would not have given up the
pursuit of their brothers until the morning."
[28] So Joab blew the trumpet, and all the men
stopped and pursued Israel no more, nor did
they fight anymore.

[29] And Abner and his men went all that night
through the Arabah. They crossed the Jordan,
and marching the whole morning, they came
to Mahanaim. [30] Joab returned from the pursuit of Abner. And when he had gathered all
the people together, there were missing from
David's servants nineteen men besides Asahel.

[1] Helkath-hazzurim means the field of sword-edges

[31] But the servants of David had struck down of Benjamin 360 of Abner's men. [32] And they took up Asahel and buried him in the tomb of his father, which was at Bethlehem. And Joab and his men marched all night, and the day broke upon them at Hebron.

Abner Joins David

3 There was a long war between the house of Saul and the house of David. And David grew stronger and stronger, while the house of Saul became weaker and weaker.

[2] And sons were born to David at Hebron: his firstborn was Amnon, of Ahinoam of Jezreel; [3] and his second, Chileab, of Abigail the widow of Nabal of Carmel; and the third, Absalom the son of Maacah the daughter of Talmai king of Geshur; [4] and the fourth, Adonijah the son of Haggith; and the fifth, Shephatiah the son of Abital; [5] and the sixth, Ithream, of Eglah, David's wife. These were born to David in Hebron.

[6] While there was war between the house of Saul and the house of David, Abner was making himself strong in the house of Saul. [7] Now Saul had a concubine whose name was Rizpah, the daughter of Aiah. And Ish-bosheth said to Abner, "Why have you gone in to my father's concubine?" [8] Then Abner was very angry over the words of Ish-bosheth and said, "Am I a dog's head of Judah? To this day I keep showing steadfast love to the house of Saul your father, to his brothers, and to his friends, and have not given you into the hand of David. And yet you charge me today with a fault concerning a woman. [9] God do so to Abner and more also, if I do not accomplish for David what the LORD has sworn to him, [10] to transfer the kingdom from the house of Saul and set up the throne of David over Israel and over Judah, from Dan to Beersheba." [11] And Ish-bosheth could not answer Abner another word, because he feared him.

[12] And Abner sent messengers to David on his behalf,[1] saying, "To whom does the land belong? Make your covenant with me, and behold, my hand shall be with you to bring over all Israel to you." [13] And he said, "Good; I will make a covenant with you. But one thing I require of you; that is, you shall not see my face unless you first bring Michal, Saul's daughter, when you come to see my face." [14] Then David sent messengers to Ish-bosheth, Saul's son, saying, "Give me my wife Michal, for whom I paid the bridal price of a hundred foreskins of the Philistines." [15] And Ish-bosheth sent and took her from her husband Paltiel the son of Laish. [16] But her husband went with her, weeping after her all the way to Bahurim. Then Abner said to him, "Go, return." And he returned.

[17] And Abner conferred with the elders of Israel, saying, "For some time past you have been seeking David as king over you. [18] Now then bring it about, for the LORD has promised David, saying, 'By the hand of my servant David I will save my people Israel from the hand of the Philistines, and from the hand of all their enemies.'" [19] Abner also spoke to Benjamin. And then Abner went to tell David at Hebron all that Israel and the whole house of Benjamin thought good to do.

[20] When Abner came with twenty men to David at Hebron, David made a feast for Abner and the men who were with him. [21] And Abner said to David, "I will arise and go and will gather all Israel to my lord the king, that they may make a covenant with you, and that you may reign over all that your heart desires." So David sent Abner away, and he went in peace.

[22] Just then the servants of David arrived with Joab from a raid, bringing much spoil with them. But Abner was not with David at Hebron, for he had sent him away, and he had gone in peace. [23] When Joab and all the army that was with him came, it was told Joab, "Abner the son of Ner came to the king, and he has let him go, and he has gone in peace." [24] Then Joab went to the king and said, "What have you done? Behold, Abner came to you. Why is it that you have sent him away, so that he is gone? [25] You know that Abner the son of Ner came to deceive you and to know your going out and your coming in, and to know all that you are doing."

Joab Murders Abner

[26] When Joab came out from David's presence, he sent messengers after Abner, and they brought him back from the cistern of Sirah. But David did not know about it. [27] And when Abner returned to Hebron, Joab took him aside into the midst of the gate to speak with him privately, and there he struck him in the stomach, so that he died, for the blood of Asahel his brother. [28] Afterward, when David heard of it, he said, "I and my kingdom are forever guiltless before the LORD for the blood

---

[1] Or where he was; Septuagint at Hebron

of Abner the son of Ner. ²⁹May it fall upon the head of Joab and upon all his father's house, and may the house of Joab never be without one who has a discharge or who is leprous or who holds a spindle or who falls by the sword or who lacks bread!" ³⁰So Joab and Abishai his brother killed Abner, because he had put their brother Asahel to death in the battle at Gibeon.

David Mourns Abner

³¹Then David said to Joab and to all the people who were with him, "Tear your clothes and put on sackcloth and mourn before Abner." And King David followed the bier. ³²They buried Abner at Hebron. And the king lifted up his voice and wept at the grave of Abner, and all the people wept. ³³And the king lamented for Abner, saying,

"Should Abner die as a fool dies?
³⁴   Your hands were not bound;
        your feet were not fettered;
    as one falls before the wicked
        you have fallen."

And all the people wept again over him. ³⁵Then all the people came to persuade David to eat bread while it was yet day. But David swore, saying, "God do so to me and more also, if I taste bread or anything else till the sun goes down!" ³⁶And all the people took notice of it, and it pleased them, as everything that the king did pleased all the people. ³⁷So all the people and all Israel understood that day that it had not been the king's will to put to death Abner the son of Ner. ³⁸And the king said to his servants, "Do you not know that a prince and a great man has fallen this day in Israel? ³⁹And I was gentle today, though anointed king. These men, the sons of Zeruiah, are more severe than I. The LORD repay the evildoer according to his wickedness!"

Ish-bosheth Murdered

4 When Ish-bosheth, Saul's son, heard that Abner had died at Hebron, his courage failed, and all Israel was dismayed. ²Now Saul's son had two men who were captains of raiding bands; the name of the one was Baanah, and the name of the other Rechab, sons of Rimmon a man of Benjamin from Beeroth (for Beeroth also is counted part of Benjamin; ³the Beerothites fled to Gittaim and have been sojourners there to this day).

⁴Jonathan, the son of Saul, had a son who was crippled in his feet. He was five years old when the news about Saul and Jonathan came from Jezreel, and his nurse took him up and fled, and as she fled in her haste, he fell and became lame. And his name was Mephibosheth.

⁵Now the sons of Rimmon the Beerothite, Rechab and Baanah, set out, and about the heat of the day they came to the house of Ish-bosheth as he was taking his noonday rest. ⁶And they came into the midst of the house as if to get wheat, and they stabbed him in the stomach. Then Rechab and Baanah his brother escaped.[1] ⁷When they came into the house, as he lay on his bed in his bedroom, they struck him and put him to death and beheaded him. They took his head and went by the way of the Arabah all night, ⁸and brought the head of Ish-bosheth to David at Hebron. And they said to the king, "Here is the head of Ish-bosheth, the son of Saul, your enemy, who sought your life. The LORD has avenged my lord the king this day on Saul and on his offspring." ⁹But David answered Rechab and Baanah his brother, the sons of Rimmon the Beerothite, "As the LORD lives, who has redeemed my life out of every adversity, ¹⁰when one told me, 'Behold, Saul is dead,' and thought he was bringing good news, I seized him and killed him at Ziklag, which was the reward I gave him for his news. ¹¹How much more, when wicked men have killed a righteous man in his own house on his bed, shall I not now require his blood at your hand and destroy you from the earth?" ¹²And David commanded his young men, and they killed them and cut off their hands and feet and hanged them beside the pool at Hebron. But they took the head of Ish-bosheth and buried it in the tomb of Abner at Hebron.

David Anointed King of Israel

5 Then all the tribes of Israel came to David at Hebron and said, "Behold, we are your bone and flesh. ²In times past, when Saul was king over us, it was you who led out and brought in Israel. And the LORD said to you, 'You shall be shepherd of my people Israel, and you shall be prince[2] over Israel.'" ³So all the elders of Israel came to the king at Hebron, and King David made a covenant with them at Hebron before the LORD, and they anointed David king over

[1] Septuagint And behold, the doorkeeper of the house had been cleaning wheat, but she grew drowsy and slept. So Rechab and Baanah his brother slipped in [2] Or leader

Israel. ⁴David was thirty years old when he began to reign, and he reigned forty years. ⁵At Hebron he reigned over Judah seven years and six months, and at Jerusalem he reigned over all Israel and Judah thirty-three years.¹

⁶And the king and his men went to Jerusalem against the Jebusites, the inhabitants of the land, who said to David, "You will not come in here, but the blind and the lame will ward you off"—thinking, "David cannot come in here." ⁷Nevertheless, David took the stronghold of Zion, that is, the city of David. ⁸And David said on that day, "Whoever would strike the Jebusites, let him get up the water shaft to attack 'the lame and the blind,' who are hated by David's soul." Therefore it is said, "The blind and the lame shall not come into the house." ⁹And David lived in the stronghold and called it the city of David. And David built the city all around from the Millo inward. ¹⁰And David became greater and greater, for the LORD, the God of hosts, was with him.

¹¹And Hiram king of Tyre sent messengers to David, and cedar trees, also carpenters and masons who built David a house. ¹²And David knew that the LORD had established him king over Israel, and that he had exalted his kingdom for the sake of his people Israel.

¹³And David took more concubines and wives from Jerusalem, after he came from Hebron, and more sons and daughters were born to David. ¹⁴And these are the names of those who were born to him in Jerusalem: Shammua, Shobab, Nathan, Solomon, ¹⁵Ibhar, Elishua, Nepheg, Japhia, ¹⁶Elishama, Eliada, and Eliphelet.

David Defeats the Philistines

¹⁷When the Philistines heard that David had been anointed king over Israel, all the Philistines went up to search for David. But David heard of it and went down to the stronghold. ¹⁸Now the Philistines had come and spread out in the Valley of Rephaim. ¹⁹And David inquired of the LORD, "Shall I go up against the Philistines? Will you give them into my hand?" And the LORD said to David, "Go up, for I will certainly give the Philistines into your hand." ²⁰And David came to Baal-perazim, and David defeated them there. And he said, "The LORD has broken through my enemies before me like a breaking flood." Therefore the name of that place is called Baal-perazim.² ²¹And the

Philistines left their idols there, and David and his men carried them away.

²²And the Philistines came up yet again and spread out in the Valley of Rephaim. ²³And when David inquired of the LORD, he said, "You shall not go up; go around to their rear, and come against them opposite the balsam trees. ²⁴And when you hear the sound of marching in the tops of the balsam trees, then rouse yourself, for then the LORD has gone out before you to strike down the army of the Philistines." ²⁵And David did as the LORD commanded him, and struck down the Philistines from Geba to Gezer.

The Ark Brought to Jerusalem

6 David again gathered all the chosen men of Israel, thirty thousand. ²And David arose and went with all the people who were with him from Baale-judah to bring up from there the ark of God, which is called by the name of the LORD of hosts who sits enthroned on the cherubim. ³And they carried the ark of God on a new cart and brought it out of the house of Abinadab, which was on the hill. And Uzzah and Ahio,³ the sons of Abinadab, were driving the new cart, ⁴with the ark of God,⁴ and Ahio went before the ark.

Uzzah and the Ark

⁵And David and all the house of Israel were celebrating before the LORD, with songs⁵ and lyres and harps and tambourines and castanets and cymbals. ⁶And when they came to the threshing floor of Nacon, Uzzah put out his hand to the ark of God and took hold of it, for the oxen stumbled. ⁷And the anger of the LORD was kindled against Uzzah, and God struck him down there because of his error, and he died there beside the ark of God. ⁸And David was angry because the LORD had broken out against Uzzah. And that place is called Perez-uzzah⁶ to this day. ⁹And David was afraid of the LORD that day, and he said, "How can the ark of the LORD come to me?" ¹⁰So David was not willing to take the ark of the LORD into the city of David. But David took it aside to the house of Obed-edom the Gittite. ¹¹And the ark of the LORD remained in the house of Obed-edom the Gittite three months, and the LORD blessed Obed-edom and all his household.

¹²And it was told King David, "The LORD has blessed the household of Obed-edom and all that belongs to him, because of the ark of

¹ Dead Sea Scroll lacks verses 4–5 ² Baal-perazim means Lord of breaking through ³ Or and his brother; also verse 4 ⁴ Compare Septuagint; Hebrew the new cart, ⁴and brought it out of the house of Abinadab, which was on the hill, with the ark of God ⁵ Septuagint, 1 Chronicles 13:8; Hebrew fir trees ⁶ Perez-uzzah means the breaking out against Uzzah

God." So David went and brought up the ark of God from the house of Obed-edom to the city of David with rejoicing. [13]And when those who bore the ark of the LORD had gone six steps, he sacrificed an ox and a fattened animal. [14]And David danced before the LORD with all his might. And David was wearing a linen ephod. [15]So David and all the house of Israel brought up the ark of the LORD with shouting and with the sound of the horn.

David and Michal

[16]As the ark of the LORD came into the city of David, Michal the daughter of Saul looked out of the window and saw King David leaping and dancing before the LORD, and she despised him in her heart. [17]And they brought in the ark of the LORD and set it in its place, inside the tent that David had pitched for it. And David offered burnt offerings and peace offerings before the LORD. [18]And when David had finished offering the burnt offerings and the peace offerings, he blessed the people in the name of the LORD of hosts [19]and distributed among all the people, the whole multitude of Israel, both men and women, a cake of bread, a portion of meat,[1] and a cake of raisins to each one. Then all the people departed, each to his house.

[20]And David returned to bless his household. But Michal the daughter of Saul came out to meet David and said, "How the king of Israel honored himself today, uncovering himself today before the eyes of his servants' female servants, as one of the vulgar fellows shamelessly uncovers himself!" [21]And David said to Michal, "It was before the LORD, who chose me above your father and above all his house, to appoint me as prince[2] over Israel, the people of the LORD—and I will celebrate before the LORD. [22]I will make myself yet more contemptible than this, and I will be abased in your[3] eyes. But by the female servants of whom you have spoken, by them I shall be held in honor." [23]And Michal the daughter of Saul had no child to the day of her death.

The LORD's Covenant with David

7 Now when the king lived in his house and the LORD had given him rest from all his surrounding enemies, [2]the king said to Nathan the prophet, "See now, I dwell in a house of cedar, but the ark of God dwells in a tent." [3]And Nathan said to the king, "Go, do all that is in your heart, for the LORD is with you."

[4]But that same night the word of the LORD came to Nathan, [5]"Go and tell my servant David, 'Thus says the LORD: Would you build me a house to dwell in? [6]I have not lived in a house since the day I brought up the people of Israel from Egypt to this day, but I have been moving about in a tent for my dwelling. [7]In all places where I have moved with all the people of Israel, did I speak a word with any of the judges[4] of Israel, whom I commanded to shepherd my people Israel, saying, "Why have you not built me a house of cedar?"' [8]Now, therefore, thus you shall say to my servant David, 'Thus says the LORD of hosts, I took you from the pasture, from following the sheep, that you should be prince[5] over my people Israel. [9]And I have been with you wherever you went and have cut off all your enemies from before you. And I will make for you a great name, like the name of the great ones of the earth. [10]And I will appoint a place for my people Israel and will plant them, so that they may dwell in their own place and be disturbed no more. And violent men shall afflict them no more, as formerly, [11]from the time that I appointed judges over my people Israel. And I will give you rest from all your enemies. Moreover, the LORD declares to you that the LORD will make you a house. [12]When your days are fulfilled and you lie down with your fathers, I will raise up your offspring after you, who shall come from your body, and I will establish his kingdom. [13]He shall build a house for my name, and I will establish the throne of his kingdom forever. [14]I will be to him a father, and he shall be to me a son. When he commits iniquity, I will discipline him with the rod of men, with the stripes of the sons of men, [15]but my steadfast love will not depart from him, as I took it from Saul, whom I put away from before you. [16]And your house and your kingdom shall be made sure forever before me.[6] Your throne shall be established forever.'" [17]In accordance with all these words, and in accordance with all this vision, Nathan spoke to David.

David's Prayer of Gratitude

[18]Then King David went in and sat before the LORD and said, "Who am I, O Lord GOD, and what is my house, that you have brought me thus far? [19]And yet this was a small thing in your eyes, O Lord GOD. You have spoken also of your servant's house for a great while

---

[1] Vulgate; the meaning of the Hebrew term is uncertain [2] Or *leader* [3] Septuagint; Hebrew *my* [4] Compare 1 Chronicles 17:6; Hebrew *tribes* [5] Or *leader* [6] Septuagint; Hebrew *you*

to come, and this is instruction for mankind, O Lord GOD! [20] And what more can David say to you? For you know your servant, O Lord GOD! [21] Because of your promise, and according to your own heart, you have brought about all this greatness, to make your servant know it. [22] Therefore you are great, O LORD God. For there is none like you, and there is no God besides you, according to all that we have heard with our ears. [23] And who is like your people Israel, the one nation on earth whom God went to redeem to be his people, making himself a name and doing for them[1] great and awesome things by driving out before your people,[2] whom you redeemed for yourself from Egypt, a nation and its gods? [24] And you established for yourself your people Israel to be your people forever. And you, O LORD, became their God. [25] And now, O LORD God, confirm forever the word that you have spoken concerning your servant and concerning his house, and do as you have spoken. [26] And your name will be magnified forever, saying, 'The LORD of hosts is God over Israel,' and the house of your servant David will be established before you. [27] For you, O LORD of hosts, the God of Israel, have made this revelation to your servant, saying, 'I will build you a house.' Therefore your servant has found courage to pray this prayer to you. [28] And now, O Lord GOD, you are God, and your words are true, and you have promised this good thing to your servant. [29] Now therefore may it please you to bless the house of your servant, so that it may continue forever before you. For you, O Lord GOD, have spoken, and with your blessing shall the house of your servant be blessed forever."

David's Victories

8 After this David defeated the Philistines and subdued them, and David took Methegammah out of the hand of the Philistines. [2] And he defeated Moab and he measured them with a line, making them lie down on the ground. Two lines he measured to be put to death, and one full line to be spared. And the Moabites became servants to David and brought tribute.

[3] David also defeated Hadadezer the son of Rehob, king of Zobah, as he went to restore his power at the river Euphrates. [4] And David took from him 1,700 horsemen, and 20,000 foot soldiers. And David hamstrung all the chariot horses but left enough for 100 chariots. [5] And when the Syrians of Damascus came to help Hadadezer king of Zobah, David struck down 22,000 men of the Syrians. [6] Then David put garrisons in Aram of Damascus, and the Syrians became servants to David and brought tribute. And the LORD gave victory to David wherever he went. [7] And David took the shields of gold that were carried by the servants of Hadadezer and brought them to Jerusalem. [8] And from Betah and from Berothai, cities of Hadadezer, King David took very much bronze.

[9] When Toi king of Hamath heard that David had defeated the whole army of Hadadezer, [10] Toi sent his son Joram to King David, to ask about his health and to bless him because he had fought against Hadadezer and defeated him, for Hadadezer had often been at war with Toi. And Joram brought with him articles of silver, of gold, and of bronze. [11] These also King David dedicated to the LORD, together with the silver and gold that he dedicated from all the nations he subdued, [12] from Edom, Moab, the Ammonites, the Philistines, Amalek, and from the spoil of Hadadezer the son of Rehob, king of Zobah.

[13] And David made a name for himself when he returned from striking down 18,000 Edomites in the Valley of Salt. [14] Then he put garrisons in Edom; throughout all Edom he put garrisons, and all the Edomites became David's servants. And the LORD gave victory to David wherever he went.

David's Officials

[15] So David reigned over all Israel. And David administered justice and equity to all his people. [16] Joab the son of Zeruiah was over the army, and Jehoshaphat the son of Ahilud was recorder, [17] and Zadok the son of Ahitub and Ahimelech the son of Abiathar were priests, and Seraiah was secretary, [18] and Benaiah the son of Jehoiada was over[3] the Cherethites and the Pelethites, and David's sons were priests.

David's Kindness to Mephibosheth

9 And David said, "Is there still anyone left of the house of Saul, that I may show him kindness for Jonathan's sake?" [2] Now there was a servant of the house of Saul whose name was Ziba, and they called him to David. And

---

[1] With a few Targums, Vulgate, Syriac; Hebrew you [2] Septuagint (compare 1 Chronicles 17:21); Hebrew *awesome things for your land, before your people* [3] Compare 20:23, 1 Chronicles 18:17, Syriac, Targum, Vulgate; Hebrew lacks *was over*

the king said to him, "Are you Ziba?" And he said, "I am your servant." [3] And the king said, "Is there not still someone of the house of Saul, that I may show the kindness of God to him?" Ziba said to the king, "There is still a son of Jonathan; he is crippled in his feet." [4] The king said to him, "Where is he?" And Ziba said to the king, "He is in the house of Machir the son of Ammiel, at Lo-debar." [5] Then King David sent and brought him from the house of Machir the son of Ammiel, at Lo-debar. [6] And Mephibosheth the son of Jonathan, son of Saul, came to David and fell on his face and paid homage. And David said, "Mephibosheth!" And he answered, "Behold, I am your servant." [7] And David said to him, "Do not fear, for I will show you kindness for the sake of your father Jonathan, and I will restore to you all the land of Saul your father, and you shall eat at my table always." [8] And he paid homage and said, "What is your servant, that you should show regard for a dead dog such as I?"

[9] Then the king called Ziba, Saul's servant, and said to him, "All that belonged to Saul and to all his house I have given to your master's grandson. [10] And you and your sons and your servants shall till the land for him and shall bring in the produce, that your master's grandson may have bread to eat. But Mephibosheth your master's grandson shall always eat at my table." Now Ziba had fifteen sons and twenty servants. [11] Then Ziba said to the king, "According to all that my lord the king commands his servant, so will your servant do." So Mephibosheth ate at David's[1] table, like one of the king's sons. [12] And Mephibosheth had a young son, whose name was Mica. And all who lived in Ziba's house became Mephibosheth's servants. [13] So Mephibosheth lived in Jerusalem, for he ate always at the king's table. Now he was lame in both his feet.

David Defeats Ammon and Syria

10 After this the king of the Ammonites died, and Hanun his son reigned in his place. [2] And David said, "I will deal loyally[2] with Hanun the son of Nahash, as his father dealt loyally with me." So David sent by his servants to console him concerning his father. And David's servants came into the land of the Ammonites. [3] But the princes of the Ammonites said to Hanun their lord, "Do you think, because David

has sent comforters to you, that he is honoring your father? Has not David sent his servants to you to search the city and to spy it out and to overthrow it?" [4] So Hanun took David's servants and shaved off half the beard of each and cut off their garments in the middle, at their hips, and sent them away. [5] When it was told David, he sent to meet them, for the men were greatly ashamed. And the king said, "Remain at Jericho until your beards have grown and then return."

[6] When the Ammonites saw that they had become a stench to David, the Ammonites sent and hired the Syrians of Beth-rehob, and the Syrians of Zobah, 20,000 foot soldiers, and the king of Maacah with 1,000 men, and the men of Tob, 12,000 men. [7] And when David heard of it, he sent Joab and all the host of the mighty men. [8] And the Ammonites came out and drew up in battle array at the entrance of the gate, and the Syrians of Zobah and of Rehob and the men of Tob and Maacah were by themselves in the open country.

[9] When Joab saw that the battle was set against him both in front and in the rear, he chose some of the best men of Israel and arrayed them against the Syrians. [10] The rest of his men he put in the charge of Abishai his brother, and he arrayed them against the Ammonites. [11] And he said, "If the Syrians are too strong for me, then you shall help me, but if the Ammonites are too strong for you, then I will come and help you. [12] Be of good courage, and let us be courageous for our people, and for the cities of our God, and may the Lord do what seems good to him." [13] So Joab and the people who were with him drew near to battle against the Syrians, and they fled before him. [14] And when the Ammonites saw that the Syrians fled, they likewise fled before Abishai and entered the city. Then Joab returned from fighting against the Ammonites and came to Jerusalem.

[15] But when the Syrians saw that they had been defeated by Israel, they gathered themselves together. [16] And Hadadezer sent and brought out the Syrians who were beyond the Euphrates.[3] They came to Helam, with Shobach the commander of the army of Hadadezer at their head. [17] And when it was told David, he gathered all Israel together and crossed the Jordan and came to Helam. The

---

[1] Septuagint; Hebrew *my* [2] Or *kindly*; twice in this verse [3] Hebrew *the River*

Syrians arrayed themselves against David and fought with him. [18] And the Syrians fled before Israel, and David killed of the Syrians the men of 700 chariots, and 40,000 horsemen, and wounded Shobach the commander of their army, so that he died there. [19] And when all the kings who were servants of Hadadezer saw that they had been defeated by Israel, they made peace with Israel and became subject to them. So the Syrians were afraid to save the Ammonites anymore.

David and Bathsheba

11 In the spring of the year, the time when kings go out to battle, David sent Joab, and his servants with him, and all Israel. And they ravaged the Ammonites and besieged Rabbah. But David remained at Jerusalem.

[2] It happened, late one afternoon, when David arose from his couch and was walking on the roof of the king's house, that he saw from the roof a woman bathing; and the woman was very beautiful. [3] And David sent and inquired about the woman. And one said, "Is not this Bathsheba, the daughter of Eliam, the wife of Uriah the Hittite?" [4] So David sent messengers and took her, and she came to him, and he lay with her. (Now she had been purifying herself from her uncleanness.) Then she returned to her house. [5] And the woman conceived, and she sent and told David, "I am pregnant."

[6] So David sent word to Joab, "Send me Uriah the Hittite." And Joab sent Uriah to David. [7] When Uriah came to him, David asked how Joab was doing and how the people were doing and how the war was going. [8] Then David said to Uriah, "Go down to your house and wash your feet." And Uriah went out of the king's house, and there followed him a present from the king. [9] But Uriah slept at the door of the king's house with all the servants of his lord, and did not go down to his house. [10] When they told David, "Uriah did not go down to his house," David said to Uriah, "Have you not come from a journey? Why did you not go down to your house?" [11] Uriah said to David, "The ark and Israel and Judah dwell in booths, and my lord Joab and the servants of my lord are camping in the open field. Shall I then go to my house, to eat and to drink and to lie with my wife? As you live, and as your soul lives, I will not do this thing." [12] Then David said to

Uriah, "Remain here today also, and tomorrow I will send you back." So Uriah remained in Jerusalem that day and the next. [13] And David invited him, and he ate in his presence and drank, so that he made him drunk. And in the evening he went out to lie on his couch with the servants of his lord, but he did not go down to his house.

[14] In the morning David wrote a letter to Joab and sent it by the hand of Uriah. [15] In the letter he wrote, "Set Uriah in the forefront of the hardest fighting, and then draw back from him, that he may be struck down, and die." [16] And as Joab was besieging the city, he assigned Uriah to the place where he knew there were valiant men. [17] And the men of the city came out and fought with Joab, and some of the servants of David among the people fell. Uriah the Hittite also died. [18] Then Joab sent and told David all the news about the fighting. [19] And he instructed the messenger, "When you have finished telling all the news about the fighting to the king, [20] then, if the king's anger rises, and if he says to you, 'Why did you go so near the city to fight? Did you not know that they would shoot from the wall? [21] Who killed Abimelech the son of Jerubbesheth? Did not a woman cast an upper millstone on him from the wall, so that he died at Thebez? Why did you go so near the wall?' then you shall say, 'Your servant Uriah the Hittite is dead also.'"

[22] So the messenger went and came and told David all that Joab had sent him to tell. [23] The messenger said to David, "The men gained an advantage over us and came out against us in the field, but we drove them back to the entrance of the gate. [24] Then the archers shot at your servants from the wall. Some of the king's servants are dead, and your servant Uriah the Hittite is dead also." [25] David said to the messenger, "Thus shall you say to Joab, 'Do not let this matter displease you, for the sword devours now one and now another. Strengthen your attack against the city and overthrow it.' And encourage him."

[26] When the wife of Uriah heard that Uriah her husband was dead, she lamented over her husband. [27] And when the mourning was over, David sent and brought her to his house, and she became his wife and bore him a son. But the thing that David had done displeased the LORD.

Nathan Rebukes David

12 And the LORD sent Nathan to David. He came to him and said to him, "There were two men in a certain city, the one rich and the other poor. ² The rich man had very many flocks and herds, ³ but the poor man had nothing but one little ewe lamb, which he had bought. And he brought it up, and it grew up with him and with his children. It used to eat of his morsel and drink from his cup and lie in his arms,¹ and it was like a daughter to him. ⁴ Now there came a traveler to the rich man, and he was unwilling to take one of his own flock or herd to prepare for the guest who had come to him, but he took the poor man's lamb and prepared it for the man who had come to him." ⁵ Then David's anger was greatly kindled against the man, and he said to Nathan, "As the LORD lives, the man who has done this deserves to die, ⁶ and he shall restore the lamb fourfold, because he did this thing, and because he had no pity."

⁷ Nathan said to David, "You are the man! Thus says the LORD, the God of Israel, 'I anointed you king over Israel, and I delivered you out of the hand of Saul. ⁸ And I gave you your master's house and your master's wives into your arms and gave you the house of Israel and of Judah. And if this were too little, I would add to you as much more. ⁹ Why have you despised the word of the LORD, to do what is evil in his sight? You have struck down Uriah the Hittite with the sword and have taken his wife to be your wife and have killed him with the sword of the Ammonites. ¹⁰ Now therefore the sword shall never depart from your house, because you have despised me and have taken the wife of Uriah the Hittite to be your wife.' ¹¹ Thus says the LORD, 'Behold, I will raise up evil against you out of your own house. And I will take your wives before your eyes and give them to your neighbor, and he shall lie with your wives in the sight of this sun. ¹² For you did it secretly, but I will do this thing before all Israel and before the sun.'" ¹³ David said to Nathan, "I have sinned against the LORD." And Nathan said to David, "The LORD also has put away your sin; you shall not die. ¹⁴ Nevertheless, because by this deed you have utterly scorned the LORD,² the child who is born to you shall die." ¹⁵ Then Nathan went to his house.

David's Child Dies

And the LORD afflicted the child that Uriah's wife bore to David, and he became sick. ¹⁶ David therefore sought God on behalf of the child. And David fasted and went in and lay all night on the ground. ¹⁷ And the elders of his house stood beside him, to raise him from the ground, but he would not, nor did he eat food with them. ¹⁸ On the seventh day the child died. And the servants of David were afraid to tell him that the child was dead, for they said, "Behold, while the child was yet alive, we spoke to him, and he did not listen to us. How then can we say to him the child is dead? He may do himself some harm." ¹⁹ But when David saw that his servants were whispering together, David understood that the child was dead. And David said to his servants, "Is the child dead?" They said, "He is dead." ²⁰ Then David arose from the earth and washed and anointed himself and changed his clothes. And he went into the house of the LORD and worshiped. He then went to his own house. And when he asked, they set food before him, and he ate. ²¹ Then his servants said to him, "What is this thing that you have done? You fasted and wept for the child while he was alive; but when the child died, you arose and ate food." ²² He said, "While the child was still alive, I fasted and wept, for I said, 'Who knows whether the LORD will be gracious to me, that the child may live?' ²³ But now he is dead. Why should I fast? Can I bring him back again? I shall go to him, but he will not return to me."

Solomon's Birth

²⁴ Then David comforted his wife, Bathsheba, and went in to her and lay with her, and she bore a son, and he called his name Solomon. And the LORD loved him ²⁵ and sent a message by Nathan the prophet. So he called his name Jedidiah,³ because of the LORD.

Rabbah Is Captured

²⁶ Now Joab fought against Rabbah of the Ammonites and took the royal city. ²⁷ And Joab sent messengers to David and said, "I have fought against Rabbah; moreover, I have taken the city of waters. ²⁸ Now then gather the rest of the people together and encamp against the city and take it, lest I take the city and it be called by my name." ²⁹ So David gathered all the people together and went

¹ Hebrew bosom; also verse 8 ² Masoretic Text the enemies of the LORD; Dead Sea Scroll the word of the LORD ³ Jedidiah means beloved of the LORD

to Rabbah and fought against it and took it. [30] And he took the crown of their king from his head. The weight of it was a talent[1] of gold, and in it was a precious stone, and it was placed on David's head. And he brought out the spoil of the city, a very great amount. [31] And he brought out the people who were in it and set them to labor with saws and iron picks and iron axes and made them toil at[2] the brick kilns. And thus he did to all the cities of the Ammonites. Then David and all the people returned to Jerusalem.

Amnon and Tamar

13 Now Absalom, David's son, had a beautiful sister, whose name was Tamar. And after a time Amnon, David's son, loved her. [2] And Amnon was so tormented that he made himself ill because of his sister Tamar, for she was a virgin, and it seemed impossible to Amnon to do anything to her. [3] But Amnon had a friend, whose name was Jonadab, the son of Shimeah, David's brother. And Jonadab was a very crafty man. [4] And he said to him, "O son of the king, why are you so haggard morning after morning? Will you not tell me?" Amnon said to him, "I love Tamar, my brother Absalom's sister." [5] Jonadab said to him, "Lie down on your bed and pretend to be ill. And when your father comes to see you, say to him, 'Let my sister Tamar come and give me bread to eat, and prepare the food in my sight, that I may see it and eat it from her hand.'" [6] So Amnon lay down and pretended to be ill. And when the king came to see him, Amnon said to the king, "Please let my sister Tamar come and make a couple of cakes in my sight, that I may eat from her hand."

[7] Then David sent home to Tamar, saying, "Go to your brother Amnon's house and prepare food for him." [8] So Tamar went to her brother Amnon's house, where he was lying down. And she took dough and kneaded it and made cakes in his sight and baked the cakes. [9] And she took the pan and emptied it out before him, but he refused to eat. And Amnon said, "Send out everyone from me." So everyone went out from him. [10] Then Amnon said to Tamar, "Bring the food into the chamber, that I may eat from your hand." And Tamar took the cakes she had made and brought them into the chamber to Amnon her brother. [11] But when she brought them near

him to eat, he took hold of her and said to her, "Come, lie with me, my sister." [12] She answered him, "No, my brother, do not violate[3] me, for such a thing is not done in Israel; do not do this outrageous thing. [13] As for me, where could I carry my shame? And as for you, you would be as one of the outrageous fools in Israel. Now therefore, please speak to the king, for he will not withhold me from you." [14] But he would not listen to her, and being stronger than she, he violated her and lay with her.

[15] Then Amnon hated her with very great hatred, so that the hatred with which he hated her was greater than the love with which he had loved her. And Amnon said to her, "Get up! Go!" [16] But she said to him, "No, my brother, for this wrong in sending me away is greater than the other that you did to me."[4] But he would not listen to her. [17] He called the young man who served him and said, "Put this woman out of my presence and bolt the door after her." [18] Now she was wearing a long robe with sleeves,[5] for thus were the virgin daughters of the king dressed. So his servant put her out and bolted the door after her. [19] And Tamar put ashes on her head and tore the long robe that she wore. And she laid her hand on her head and went away, crying aloud as she went.

[20] And her brother Absalom said to her, "Has Amnon your brother been with you? Now hold your peace, my sister. He is your brother; do not take this to heart." So Tamar lived, a desolate woman, in her brother Absalom's house. [21] When King David heard of all these things, he was very angry.[6] [22] But Absalom spoke to Amnon neither good nor bad, for Absalom hated Amnon, because he had violated his sister Tamar.

Absalom Murders Amnon

[23] After two full years Absalom had sheepshearers at Baal-hazor, which is near Ephraim, and Absalom invited all the king's sons. [24] And Absalom came to the king and said, "Behold, your servant has sheepshearers. Please let the king and his servants go with your servant." [25] But the king said to Absalom, "No, my son, let us not all go, lest we be burdensome to you." He pressed him, but he would not go but gave him his blessing. [26] Then Absalom said, "If not, please let my brother Amnon go with us." And the king said to him, "Why should he go

---

[1] A talent was about 75 pounds or 34 kilograms [2] Hebrew pass through [3] Or humiliate; also verses 14, 22, 32 [4] Compare Septuagint, Vulgate; the meaning of the Hebrew is uncertain [5] Or a robe of many colors (compare Genesis 37:3); compare long robe, verse 19 [6] Dead Sea Scroll, Septuagint add But he would not punish his son Amnon, because he loved him, since he was his firstborn

with you?" ²⁷ But Absalom pressed him until he let Amnon and all the king's sons go with him. ²⁸ Then Absalom commanded his servants, "Mark when Amnon's heart is merry with wine, and when I say to you, 'Strike Amnon,' then kill him. Do not fear; have I not commanded you? Be courageous and be valiant." ²⁹ So the servants of Absalom did to Amnon as Absalom had commanded. Then all the king's sons arose, and each mounted his mule and fled.

³⁰ While they were on the way, news came to David, "Absalom has struck down all the king's sons, and not one of them is left." ³¹ Then the king arose and tore his garments and lay on the earth. And all his servants who were standing by tore their garments. ³² But Jonadab the son of Shimeah, David's brother, said, "Let not my lord suppose that they have killed all the young men, the king's sons, for Amnon alone is dead. For by the command of Absalom this has been determined from the day he violated his sister Tamar. ³³ Now therefore let not my lord the king so take it to heart as to suppose that all the king's sons are dead, for Amnon alone is dead."

Absalom Flees to Geshur

³⁴ But Absalom fled. And the young man who kept the watch lifted up his eyes and looked, and behold, many people were coming from the road behind him[1] by the side of the mountain. ³⁵ And Jonadab said to the king, "Behold, the king's sons have come; as your servant said, so it has come about." ³⁶ And as soon as he had finished speaking, behold, the king's sons came and lifted up their voice and wept. And the king also and all his servants wept very bitterly.

³⁷ But Absalom fled and went to Talmai the son of Ammihud, king of Geshur. And David mourned for his son day after day. ³⁸ So Absalom fled and went to Geshur, and was there three years. ³⁹ And the spirit of the king[2] longed to go out[3] to Absalom, because he was comforted about Amnon, since he was dead.

Absalom Returns to Jerusalem

14 Now Joab the son of Zeruiah knew that the king's heart went out to Absalom. ² And Joab sent to Tekoa and brought from there a wise woman and said to her, "Pretend to be a mourner and put on mourning garments. Do not anoint yourself with oil, but behave like a woman who has been mourning many days for the dead. ³ Go to the king and speak thus to him." So Joab put the words in her mouth.

⁴ When the woman of Tekoa came to the king, she fell on her face to the ground and paid homage and said, "Save me, O king." ⁵ And the king said to her, "What is your trouble?" She answered, "Alas, I am a widow; my husband is dead. ⁶ And your servant had two sons, and they quarreled with one another in the field. There was no one to separate them, and one struck the other and killed him. ⁷ And now the whole clan has risen against your servant, and they say, 'Give up the man who struck his brother, that we may put him to death for the life of his brother whom he killed.' And so they would destroy the heir also. Thus they would quench my coal that is left and leave to my husband neither name nor remnant on the face of the earth."

⁸ Then the king said to the woman, "Go to your house, and I will give orders concerning you." ⁹ And the woman of Tekoa said to the king, "On me be the guilt, my lord the king, and on my father's house; let the king and his throne be guiltless." ¹⁰ The king said, "If anyone says anything to you, bring him to me, and he shall never touch you again." ¹¹ Then she said, "Please let the king invoke the LORD your God, that the avenger of blood kill no more, and my son be not destroyed." He said, "As the LORD lives, not one hair of your son shall fall to the ground."

¹² Then the woman said, "Please let your servant speak a word to my lord the king." He said, "Speak." ¹³ And the woman said, "Why then have you planned such a thing against the people of God? For in giving this decision the king convicts himself, inasmuch as the king does not bring his banished one home again. ¹⁴ We must all die; we are like water spilled on the ground, which cannot be gathered up again. But God will not take away life, and he devises means so that the banished one will not remain an outcast. ¹⁵ Now I have come to say this to my lord the king because the people have made me afraid, and your servant thought, 'I will speak to the king; it may be that the king will perform the request of his servant. ¹⁶ For the king will hear and deliver his servant from the hand of the man who would destroy me and my son together from the heritage of God.' ¹⁷ And your servant thought, 'The word of my lord the king will set me at rest,' for my lord the king is like

---

[1] Septuagint *the Horonaim Road* [2] Dead Sea Scroll, Septuagint; Hebrew *David* [3] Compare Vulgate *ceased to go out*

the angel of God to discern good and evil. The LORD your God be with you!"

[18] Then the king answered the woman, "Do not hide from me anything I ask you." And the woman said, "Let my lord the king speak." [19] The king said, "Is the hand of Joab with you in all this?" The woman answered and said, "As surely as you live, my lord the king, one cannot turn to the right hand or to the left from anything that my lord the king has said. It was your servant Joab who commanded me; it was he who put all these words in the mouth of your servant. [20] In order to change the course of things your servant Joab did this. But my lord has wisdom like the wisdom of the angel of God to know all things that are on the earth."

[21] Then the king said to Joab, "Behold now, I grant this; go, bring back the young man Absalom." [22] And Joab fell on his face to the ground and paid homage and blessed the king. And Joab said, "Today your servant knows that I have found favor in your sight, my lord the king, in that the king has granted the request of his servant." [23] So Joab arose and went to Geshur and brought Absalom to Jerusalem. [24] And the king said, "Let him dwell apart in his own house; he is not to come into my presence." So Absalom lived apart in his own house and did not come into the king's presence.

[25] Now in all Israel there was no one so much to be praised for his handsome appearance as Absalom. From the sole of his foot to the crown of his head there was no blemish in him. [26] And when he cut the hair of his head (for at the end of every year he used to cut it; when it was heavy on him, he cut it), he weighed the hair of his head, two hundred shekels[1] by the king's weight. [27] There were born to Absalom three sons, and one daughter whose name was Tamar. She was a beautiful woman.

[28] So Absalom lived two full years in Jerusalem, without coming into the king's presence. [29] Then Absalom sent for Joab, to send him to the king, but Joab would not come to him. And he sent a second time, but Joab would not come. [30] Then he said to his servants, "See, Joab's field is next to mine, and he has barley there; go and set it on fire." So Absalom's servants set the field on fire.[2] [31] Then Joab arose and went to Absalom at his house and said to him, "Why have your servants set my field on fire?" [32] Absalom answered Joab, "Behold, I sent word

to you, 'Come here, that I may send you to the king, to ask, "Why have I come from Geshur? It would be better for me to be there still." Now therefore let me go into the presence of the king, and if there is guilt in me, let him put me to death.'" [33] Then Joab went to the king and told him, and he summoned Absalom. So he came to the king and bowed himself on his face to the ground before the king, and the king kissed Absalom.

Absalom's Conspiracy

15 After this Absalom got himself a chariot and horses, and fifty men to run before him. [2] And Absalom used to rise early and stand beside the way of the gate. And when any man had a dispute to come before the king for judgment, Absalom would call to him and say, "From what city are you?" And when he said, "Your servant is of such and such a tribe in Israel," [3] Absalom would say to him, "See, your claims are good and right, but there is no man designated by the king to hear you." [4] Then Absalom would say, "Oh that I were judge in the land! Then every man with a dispute or cause might come to me, and I would give him justice." [5] And whenever a man came near to pay homage to him, he would put out his hand and take hold of him and kiss him. [6] Thus Absalom did to all of Israel who came to the king for judgment. So Absalom stole the hearts of the men of Israel.

[7] And at the end of four[3] years Absalom said to the king, "Please let me go and pay my vow, which I have vowed to the LORD, in Hebron. [8] For your servant vowed a vow while I lived at Geshur in Aram, saying, 'If the LORD will indeed bring me back to Jerusalem, then I will offer worship to[4] the LORD.'" [9] The king said to him, "Go in peace." So he arose and went to Hebron. [10] But Absalom sent secret messengers throughout all the tribes of Israel, saying, "As soon as you hear the sound of the trumpet, then say, 'Absalom is king at Hebron!'" [11] With Absalom went two hundred men from Jerusalem who were invited guests, and they went in their innocence and knew nothing. [12] And while Absalom was offering the sacrifices, he sent for[5] Ahithophel the Gilonite, David's counselor, from his city Giloh. And the conspiracy grew strong, and the people with Absalom kept increasing.

---

[1] A *shekel* was about 2/5 ounce or 11 grams [2] Septuagint, Dead Sea Scroll add *So Joab's servants came to him with their clothes torn, and they said to him, "The servants of Absalom have set your field on fire."* [3] Septuagint, Syriac; Hebrew *forty* [4] Or *will serve* [5] Or *sent*

David Flees Jerusalem

[13] And a messenger came to David, saying, "The hearts of the men of Israel have gone after Absalom." [14] Then David said to all his servants who were with him at Jerusalem, "Arise, and let us flee, or else there will be no escape for us from Absalom. Go quickly, lest he overtake us quickly and bring down ruin on us and strike the city with the edge of the sword." [15] And the king's servants said to the king, "Behold, your servants are ready to do whatever my lord the king decides." [16] So the king went out, and all his household after him. And the king left ten concubines to keep the house. [17] And the king went out, and all the people after him. And they halted at the last house.

[18] And all his servants passed by him, and all the Cherethites, and all the Pelethites, and all the six hundred Gittites who had followed him from Gath, passed on before the king. [19] Then the king said to Ittai the Gittite, "Why do you also go with us? Go back and stay with the king, for you are a foreigner and also an exile from your home. [20] You came only yesterday, and shall I today make you wander about with us, since I go I know not where? Go back and take your brothers with you, and may the LORD show[1] steadfast love and faithfulness to you." [21] But Ittai answered the king, "As the LORD lives, and as my lord the king lives, wherever my lord the king shall be, whether for death or for life, there also will your servant be." [22] And David said to Ittai, "Go then, pass on." So Ittai the Gittite passed on with all his men and all the little ones who were with him. [23] And all the land wept aloud as all the people passed by, and the king crossed the brook Kidron, and all the people passed on toward the wilderness.

[24] And Abiathar came up, and behold, Zadok came also with all the Levites, bearing the ark of the covenant of God. And they set down the ark of God until the people had all passed out of the city. [25] Then the king said to Zadok, "Carry the ark of God back into the city. If I find favor in the eyes of the LORD, he will bring me back and let me see both it and his dwelling place. [26] But if he says, 'I have no pleasure in you,' behold, here I am, let him do to me what seems good to him." [27] The king also said to Zadok the priest, "Are you not a seer? Go back[2] to the city in peace, with your two sons, Ahimaaz your son, and Jonathan the son of Abiathar. [28] See, I will wait at the fords of the wilderness until word comes from you to inform me." [29] So Zadok and Abiathar carried the ark of God back to Jerusalem, and they remained there.

[30] But David went up the ascent of the Mount of Olives, weeping as he went, barefoot and with his head covered. And all the people who were with him covered their heads, and they went up, weeping as they went. [31] And it was told David, "Ahithophel is among the conspirators with Absalom." And David said, "O LORD, please turn the counsel of Ahithophel into foolishness."

[32] While David was coming to the summit, where God was worshiped, behold, Hushai the Archite came to meet him with his coat torn and dirt on his head. [33] David said to him, "If you go on with me, you will be a burden to me. [34] But if you return to the city and say to Absalom, 'I will be your servant, O king; as I have been your father's servant in time past, so now I will be your servant,' then you will defeat for me the counsel of Ahithophel. [35] Are not Zadok and Abiathar the priests with you there? So whatever you hear from the king's house, tell it to Zadok and Abiathar the priests. [36] Behold, their two sons are with them there, Ahimaaz, Zadok's son, and Jonathan, Abiathar's son, and by them you shall send to me everything you hear." [37] So Hushai, David's friend, came into the city, just as Absalom was entering Jerusalem.

David and Ziba

16 When David had passed a little beyond the summit, Ziba the servant of Mephibosheth met him, with a couple of donkeys saddled, bearing two hundred loaves of bread, a hundred bunches of raisins, a hundred of summer fruits, and a skin of wine. [2] And the king said to Ziba, "Why have you brought these?" Ziba answered, "The donkeys are for the king's household to ride on, the bread and summer fruit for the young men to eat, and the wine for those who faint in the wilderness to drink." [3] And the king said, "And where is your master's son?" Ziba said to the king, "Behold, he remains in Jerusalem, for he said, 'Today the house of Israel will give me back the kingdom of my father.'" [4] Then the king said to Ziba, "Behold, all that belonged to Mephibosheth is now yours." And Ziba said, "I pay homage; let me ever find favor in your sight, my lord the king."

[1] Septuagint; Hebrew lacks *may the LORD show* [2] Septuagint *The king also said to Zadok the priest, "Look, go back*

Shimei Curses David

[5] When King David came to Bahurim, there came out a man of the family of the house of Saul, whose name was Shimei, the son of Gera, and as he came he cursed continually. [6] And he threw stones at David and at all the servants of King David, and all the people and all the mighty men were on his right hand and on his left. [7] And Shimei said as he cursed, "Get out, get out, you man of blood, you worthless man! [8] The LORD has avenged on you all the blood of the house of Saul, in whose place you have reigned, and the LORD has given the kingdom into the hand of your son Absalom. See, your evil is on you, for you are a man of blood."

[9] Then Abishai the son of Zeruiah said to the king, "Why should this dead dog curse my lord the king? Let me go over and take off his head." [10] But the king said, "What have I to do with you, you sons of Zeruiah? If he is cursing because the LORD has said to him, 'Curse David,' who then shall say, 'Why have you done so?'" [11] And David said to Abishai and to all his servants, "Behold, my own son seeks my life; how much more now may this Benjaminite! Leave him alone, and let him curse, for the LORD has told him to. [12] It may be that the LORD will look on the wrong done to me,[1] and that the LORD will repay me with good for his cursing today." [13] So David and his men went on the road, while Shimei went along on the hillside opposite him and cursed as he went and threw stones at him and flung dust. [14] And the king, and all the people who were with him, arrived weary at the Jordan.[2] And there he refreshed himself.

Absalom Enters Jerusalem

[15] Now Absalom and all the people, the men of Israel, came to Jerusalem, and Ahithophel with him. [16] And when Hushai the Archite, David's friend, came to Absalom, Hushai said to Absalom, "Long live the king! Long live the king!" [17] And Absalom said to Hushai, "Is this your loyalty to your friend? Why did you not go with your friend?" [18] And Hushai said to Absalom, "No, for whom the LORD and this people and all the men of Israel have chosen, his I will be, and with him I will remain. [19] And again, whom should I serve? Should it not be his son? As I have served your father, so I will serve you."

[20] Then Absalom said to Ahithophel, "Give your counsel. What shall we do?" [21] Ahithophel said to Absalom, "Go in to your father's concubines, whom he has left to keep the house, and all Israel will hear that you have made yourself a stench to your father, and the hands of all who are with you will be strengthened." [22] So they pitched a tent for Absalom on the roof. And Absalom went in to his father's concubines in the sight of all Israel. [23] Now in those days the counsel that Ahithophel gave was as if one consulted the word of God; so was all the counsel of Ahithophel esteemed, both by David and by Absalom.

Hushai Saves David

17 Moreover, Ahithophel said to Absalom, "Let me choose twelve thousand men, and I will arise and pursue David tonight. [2] I will come upon him while he is weary and discouraged and throw him into a panic, and all the people who are with him will flee. I will strike down only the king, [3] and I will bring all the people back to you as a bride comes home to her husband. You seek the life of only one man,[3] and all the people will be at peace." [4] And the advice seemed right in the eyes of Absalom and all the elders of Israel.

[5] Then Absalom said, "Call Hushai the Archite also, and let us hear what he has to say." [6] And when Hushai came to Absalom, Absalom said to him, "Thus has Ahithophel spoken; shall we do as he says? If not, you speak." [7] Then Hushai said to Absalom, "This time the counsel that Ahithophel has given is not good." [8] Hushai said, "You know that your father and his men are mighty men, and that they are enraged,[4] like a bear robbed of her cubs in the field. Besides, your father is expert in war; he will not spend the night with the people. [9] Behold, even now he has hidden himself in one of the pits or in some other place. And as soon as some of the people fall[5] at the first attack, whoever hears it will say, 'There has been a slaughter among the people who follow Absalom.' [10] Then even the valiant man, whose heart is like the heart of a lion, will utterly melt with fear, for all Israel knows that your father is a mighty man, and that those who are with him are valiant men. [11] But my counsel is that all Israel be gathered to you, from Dan to Beersheba, as the sand by the sea for multitude, and that you go to battle in person. [12] So we shall come upon him in some place where he is to be found, and we shall light upon him as the dew falls on the ground, and of

---

[1] Septuagint, Vulgate *will look upon my affliction* [2] Septuagint; Hebrew lacks *at the Jordan* [3] Septuagint; Hebrew *back to you. Like the return of the whole is the man whom you seek* [4] Hebrew *bitter of soul* [5] Or *And as he falls on them*

him and all the men with him not one will be left. [13] If he withdraws into a city, then all Israel will bring ropes to that city, and we shall drag it into the valley, until not even a pebble is to be found there." [14] And Absalom and all the men of Israel said, "The counsel of Hushai the Archite is better than the counsel of Ahithophel." For the Lord had ordained[1] to defeat the good counsel of Ahithophel, so that the Lord might bring harm upon Absalom.

[15] Then Hushai said to Zadok and Abiathar the priests, "Thus and so did Ahithophel counsel Absalom and the elders of Israel, and thus and so have I counseled. [16] Now therefore send quickly and tell David, 'Do not stay tonight at the fords of the wilderness, but by all means pass over, lest the king and all the people who are with him be swallowed up.'" [17] Now Jonathan and Ahimaaz were waiting at En-rogel. A female servant was to go and tell them, and they were to go and tell King David, for they were not to be seen entering the city. [18] But a young man saw them and told Absalom. So both of them went away quickly and came to the house of a man at Bahurim, who had a well in his courtyard. And they went down into it. [19] And the woman took and spread a covering over the well's mouth and scattered grain on it, and nothing was known of it. [20] When Absalom's servants came to the woman at the house, they said, "Where are Ahimaaz and Jonathan?" And the woman said to them, "They have gone over the brook[2] of water." And when they had sought and could not find them, they returned to Jerusalem.

[21] After they had gone, the men came up out of the well, and went and told King David. They said to David, "Arise, and go quickly over the water, for thus and so has Ahithophel counseled against you." [22] Then David arose, and all the people who were with him, and they crossed the Jordan. By daybreak not one was left who had not crossed the Jordan.

[23] When Ahithophel saw that his counsel was not followed, he saddled his donkey and went off home to his own city. He set his house in order and hanged himself, and he died and was buried in the tomb of his father. [24] Then David came to Mahanaim. And Absalom crossed the Jordan with all the men of Israel. [25] Now Absalom had set Amasa over the army instead of Joab. Amasa was the son of

a man named Ithra the Ishmaelite,[3] who had married Abigal the daughter of Nahash, sister of Zeruiah, Joab's mother. [26] And Israel and Absalom encamped in the land of Gilead.

[27] When David came to Mahanaim, Shobi the son of Nahash from Rabbah of the Ammonites, and Machir the son of Ammiel from Lo-debar, and Barzillai the Gileadite from Rogelim, [28] brought beds, basins, and earthen vessels, wheat, barley, flour, parched grain, beans and lentils,[4] [29] honey and curds and sheep and cheese from the herd, for David and the people with him to eat, for they said, "The people are hungry and weary and thirsty in the wilderness."

Absalom Killed

18 Then David mustered the men who were with him and set over them commanders of thousands and commanders of hundreds. [2] And David sent out the army, one third under the command of Joab, one third under the command of Abishai the son of Zeruiah, Joab's brother, and one third under the command of Ittai the Gittite. And the king said to the men, "I myself will also go out with you." [3] But the men said, "You shall not go out. For if we flee, they will not care about us. If half of us die, they will not care about us. But you are worth ten thousand of us. Therefore it is better that you send us help from the city." [4] The king said to them, "Whatever seems best to you I will do." So the king stood at the side of the gate, while all the army marched out by hundreds and by thousands. [5] And the king ordered Joab and Abishai and Ittai, "Deal gently for my sake with the young man Absalom." And all the people heard when the king gave orders to all the commanders about Absalom.

[6] So the army went out into the field against Israel, and the battle was fought in the forest of Ephraim. [7] And the men of Israel were defeated there by the servants of David, and the loss there was great on that day, twenty thousand men. [8] The battle spread over the face of all the country, and the forest devoured more people that day than the sword.

[9] And Absalom happened to meet the servants of David. Absalom was riding on his mule, and the mule went under the thick branches of a great oak,[5] and his head caught fast in the oak, and he was suspended between heaven and earth, while the mule that was

---

[1] Hebrew *commanded* [2] The meaning of the Hebrew word is uncertain [3] Compare 1 Chronicles 2:17; Hebrew *Israelite* [4] Hebrew adds *and parched grain* [5] Or *terebinth*; also verses 10, 14

under him went on. [10] And a certain man saw it and told Joab, "Behold, I saw Absalom hanging in an oak." [11] Joab said to the man who told him, "What, you saw him! Why then did you not strike him there to the ground? I would have been glad to give you ten pieces of silver and a belt." [12] But the man said to Joab, "Even if I felt in my hand the weight of a thousand pieces of silver, I would not reach out my hand against the king's son, for in our hearing the king commanded you and Abishai and Ittai, 'For my sake protect the young man Absalom.' [13] On the other hand, if I had dealt treacherously against his life[1] (and there is nothing hidden from the king), then you yourself would have stood aloof." [14] Joab said, "I will not waste time like this with you." And he took three javelins in his hand and thrust them into the heart of Absalom while he was still alive in the oak. [15] And ten young men, Joab's armor-bearers, surrounded Absalom and struck him and killed him.

[16] Then Joab blew the trumpet, and the troops came back from pursuing Israel, for Joab restrained them. [17] And they took Absalom and threw him into a great pit in the forest and raised over him a very great heap of stones. And all Israel fled every one to his own home. [18] Now Absalom in his lifetime had taken and set up for himself the pillar that is in the King's Valley, for he said, "I have no son to keep my name in remembrance." He called the pillar after his own name, and it is called Absalom's monument[2] to this day.

David Hears of Absalom's Death

[19] Then Ahimaaz the son of Zadok said, "Let me run and carry news to the king that the LORD has delivered him from the hand of his enemies." [20] And Joab said to him, "You are not to carry news today. You may carry news another day, but today you shall carry no news, because the king's son is dead." [21] Then Joab said to the Cushite, "Go, tell the king what you have seen." The Cushite bowed before Joab, and ran. [22] Then Ahimaaz the son of Zadok said again to Joab, "Come what may, let me also run after the Cushite." And Joab said, "Why will you run, my son, seeing that you will have no reward for the news?" [23] "Come what may," he said, "I will run." So he said to him, "Run." Then Ahimaaz ran by the way of the plain, and outran the Cushite.

[24] Now David was sitting between the two gates, and the watchman went up to the roof of the gate by the wall, and when he lifted up his eyes and looked, he saw a man running alone. [25] The watchman called out and told the king. And the king said, "If he is alone, there is news in his mouth." And he drew nearer and nearer. [26] The watchman saw another man running. And the watchman called to the gate and said, "See, another man running alone!" The king said, "He also brings news." [27] The watchman said, "I think the running of the first is like the running of Ahimaaz the son of Zadok." And the king said, "He is a good man and comes with good news."

[28] Then Ahimaaz cried out to the king, "All is well." And he bowed before the king with his face to the earth and said, "Blessed be the LORD your God, who has delivered up the men who raised their hand against my lord the king." [29] And the king said, "Is it well with the young man Absalom?" Ahimaaz answered, "When Joab sent the king's servant, your servant, I saw a great commotion, but I do not know what it was." [30] And the king said, "Turn aside and stand here." So he turned aside and stood still.

David's Grief

[31] And behold, the Cushite came, and the Cushite said, "Good news for my lord the king! For the LORD has delivered you this day from the hand of all who rose up against you." [32] The king said to the Cushite, "Is it well with the young man Absalom?" And the Cushite answered, "May the enemies of my lord the king and all who rise up against you for evil be like that young man." [33][3] And the king was deeply moved and went up to the chamber over the gate and wept. And as he went, he said, "O my son Absalom, my son, my son Absalom! Would I had died instead of you, O Absalom, my son, my son!"

Joab Rebukes David

19 It was told Joab, "Behold, the king is weeping and mourning for Absalom." [2] So the victory that day was turned into mourning for all the people, for the people heard that day, "The king is grieving for his son." [3] And the people stole into the city that day as people steal in who are ashamed when they flee in battle. [4] The king covered his face, and the king cried with a loud voice, "O my son Absalom,

O Absalom, my son, my son!" ⁵Then Joab came into the house to the king and said, "You have today covered with shame the faces of all your servants, who have this day saved your life and the lives of your sons and your daughters and the lives of your wives and your concubines, ⁶because you love those who hate you and hate those who love you. For you have made it clear today that commanders and servants are nothing to you, for today I know that if Absalom were alive and all of us were dead today, then you would be pleased. ⁷Now therefore arise, go out and speak kindly to your servants, for I swear by the LORD, if you do not go, not a man will stay with you this night, and this will be worse for you than all the evil that has come upon you from your youth until now." ⁸Then the king arose and took his seat in the gate. And the people were all told, "Behold, the king is sitting in the gate." And all the people came before the king.

David Returns to Jerusalem

Now Israel had fled every man to his own home. ⁹And all the people were arguing throughout all the tribes of Israel, saying, "The king delivered us from the hand of our enemies and saved us from the hand of the Philistines, and now he has fled out of the land from Absalom. ¹⁰But Absalom, whom we anointed over us, is dead in battle. Now therefore why do you say nothing about bringing the king back?"

¹¹And King David sent this message to Zadok and Abiathar the priests: "Say to the elders of Judah, 'Why should you be the last to bring the king back to his house, when the word of all Israel has come to the king?¹ ¹²You are my brothers; you are my bone and my flesh. Why then should you be the last to bring back the king?' ¹³And say to Amasa, 'Are you not my bone and my flesh? God do so to me and more also, if you are not commander of my army from now on in place of Joab.'" ¹⁴And he swayed the heart of all the men of Judah as one man, so that they sent word to the king, "Return, both you and all your servants." ¹⁵So the king came back to the Jordan, and Judah came to Gilgal to meet the king and to bring the king over the Jordan.

David Pardons His Enemies

¹⁶And Shimei the son of Gera, the Benjaminite, from Bahurim, hurried to come down with the men of Judah to meet King David.

¹⁷And with him were a thousand men from Benjamin. And Ziba the servant of the house of Saul, with his fifteen sons and his twenty servants, rushed down to the Jordan before the king, ¹⁸and they crossed the ford to bring over the king's household and to do his pleasure. And Shimei the son of Gera fell down before the king, as he was about to cross the Jordan, ¹⁹and said to the king, "Let not my lord hold me guilty or remember how your servant did wrong on the day my lord the king left Jerusalem. Do not let the king take it to heart. ²⁰For your servant knows that I have sinned. Therefore, behold, I have come this day, the first of all the house of Joseph to come down to meet my lord the king." ²¹Abishai the son of Zeruiah answered, "Shall not Shimei be put to death for this, because he cursed the LORD's anointed?" ²²But David said, "What have I to do with you, you sons of Zeruiah, that you should this day be as an adversary to me? Shall anyone be put to death in Israel this day? For do I not know that I am this day king over Israel?" ²³And the king said to Shimei, "You shall not die." And the king gave him his oath.

²⁴And Mephibosheth the son of Saul came down to meet the king. He had neither taken care of his feet nor trimmed his beard nor washed his clothes, from the day the king departed until the day he came back in safety. ²⁵And when he came to Jerusalem to meet the king, the king said to him, "Why did you not go with me, Mephibosheth?" ²⁶He answered, "My lord, O king, my servant deceived me, for your servant said to him, 'I will saddle a donkey for myself,² that I may ride on it and go with the king.' For your servant is lame. ²⁷He has slandered your servant to my lord the king. But my lord the king is like the angel of God; do therefore what seems good to you. ²⁸For all my father's house were but men doomed to death before my lord the king, but you set your servant among those who eat at your table. What further right have I, then, to cry to the king?" ²⁹And the king said to him, "Why speak any more of your affairs? I have decided: you and Ziba shall divide the land." ³⁰And Mephibosheth said to the king, "Oh, let him take it all, since my lord the king has come safely home."

³¹Now Barzillai the Gileadite had come down from Rogelim, and he went on with the king to the Jordan, to escort him over the Jordan.

¹ Septuagint; Hebrew to the king, to his house ² Septuagint, Syriac, Vulgate Saddle a donkey for me

³² Barzillai was a very aged man, eighty years old. He had provided the king with food while he stayed at Mahanaim, for he was a very wealthy man. ³³ And the king said to Barzillai, "Come over with me, and I will provide for you with me in Jerusalem." ³⁴ But Barzillai said to the king, "How many years have I still to live, that I should go up with the king to Jerusalem? ³⁵ I am this day eighty years old. Can I discern what is pleasant and what is not? Can your servant taste what he eats or what he drinks? Can I still listen to the voice of singing men and singing women? Why then should your servant be an added burden to my lord the king? ³⁶ Your servant will go a little way over the Jordan with the king. Why should the king repay me with such a reward? ³⁷ Please let your servant return, that I may die in my own city near the grave of my father and my mother. But here is your servant Chimham. Let him go over with my lord the king, and do for him whatever seems good to you." ³⁸ And the king answered, "Chimham shall go over with me, and I will do for him whatever seems good to you, and all that you desire of me I will do for you." ³⁹ Then all the people went over the Jordan, and the king went over. And the king kissed Barzillai and blessed him, and he returned to his own home. ⁴⁰ The king went on to Gilgal, and Chimham went on with him. All the people of Judah, and also half the people of Israel, brought the king on his way.

⁴¹ Then all the men of Israel came to the king and said to the king, "Why have our brothers the men of Judah stolen you away and brought the king and his household over the Jordan, and all David's men with him?" ⁴² All the men of Judah answered the men of Israel, "Because the king is our close relative. Why then are you angry over this matter? Have we eaten at all at the king's expense? Or has he given us any gift?" ⁴³ And the men of Israel answered the men of Judah, "We have ten shares in the king, and in David also we have more than you. Why then did you despise us? Were we not the first to speak of bringing back our king?" But the words of the men of Judah were fiercer than the words of the men of Israel.

The Rebellion of Sheba

20 Now there happened to be there a worthless man, whose name was Sheba, the son of Bichri, a Benjaminite. And he blew the trumpet and said,

> "We have no portion in David,
>   and we have no inheritance in the son of
>   Jesse;
>   every man to his tents, O Israel!"

² So all the men of Israel withdrew from David and followed Sheba the son of Bichri. But the men of Judah followed their king steadfastly from the Jordan to Jerusalem.

³ And David came to his house at Jerusalem. And the king took the ten concubines whom he had left to care for the house and put them in a house under guard and provided for them, but did not go in to them. So they were shut up until the day of their death, living as if in widowhood.

⁴ Then the king said to Amasa, "Call the men of Judah together to me within three days, and be here yourself." ⁵ So Amasa went to summon Judah, but he delayed beyond the set time that had been appointed him. ⁶ And David said to Abishai, "Now Sheba the son of Bichri will do us more harm than Absalom. Take your lord's servants and pursue him, lest he get himself to fortified cities and escape from us."[1] ⁷ And there went out after him Joab's men and the Cherethites and the Pelethites, and all the mighty men. They went out from Jerusalem to pursue Sheba the son of Bichri. ⁸ When they were at the great stone that is in Gibeon, Amasa came to meet them. Now Joab was wearing a soldier's garment, and over it was a belt with a sword in its sheath fastened on his thigh, and as he went forward it fell out. ⁹ And Joab said to Amasa, "Is it well with you, my brother?" And Joab took Amasa by the beard with his right hand to kiss him. ¹⁰ But Amasa did not observe the sword that was in Joab's hand. So Joab struck him with it in the stomach and spilled his entrails to the ground without striking a second blow, and he died.

Then Joab and Abishai his brother pursued Sheba the son of Bichri. ¹¹ And one of Joab's young men took his stand by Amasa and said, "Whoever favors Joab, and whoever is for David, let him follow Joab." ¹² And Amasa lay wallowing in his blood in the highway. And anyone who came by, seeing him, stopped. And when the man saw that all the people stopped, he carried Amasa out of the highway into the field and threw a garment over him. ¹³ When he was taken out of the highway, all the people went on after Joab to pursue Sheba the son of Bichri.

---

[1] Hebrew *and snatch away our eyes*

[14] And Sheba passed through all the tribes of Israel to Abel of Beth-maacah,[1] and all the Bichrites[2] assembled and followed him in. [15] And all the men who were with Joab came and besieged him in Abel of Beth-maacah. They cast up a mound against the city, and it stood against the rampart, and they were battering the wall to throw it down. [16] Then a wise woman called from the city, "Listen! Listen! Tell Joab, 'Come here, that I may speak to you.'" [17] And he came near her, and the woman said, "Are you Joab?" He answered, "I am." Then she said to him, "Listen to the words of your servant." And he answered, "I am listening." [18] Then she said, "They used to say in former times, 'Let them but ask counsel at Abel,' and so they settled a matter. [19] I am one of those who are peaceable and faithful in Israel. You seek to destroy a city that is a mother in Israel. Why will you swallow up the heritage of the LORD?" [20] Joab answered, "Far be it from me, far be it, that I should swallow up or destroy! [21] That is not true. But a man of the hill country of Ephraim, called Sheba the son of Bichri, has lifted up his hand against King David. Give up him alone, and I will withdraw from the city." And the woman said to Joab, "Behold, his head shall be thrown to you over the wall." [22] Then the woman went to all the people in her wisdom. And they cut off the head of Sheba the son of Bichri and threw it out to Joab. So he blew the trumpet, and they dispersed from the city, every man to his home. And Joab returned to Jerusalem to the king.

[23] Now Joab was in command of all the army of Israel; and Benaiah the son of Jehoiada was in command of the Cherethites and the Pelethites; [24] and Adoram was in charge of the forced labor; and Jehoshaphat the son of Ahilud was the recorder; [25] and Sheva was secretary; and Zadok and Abiathar were priests; [26] and Ira the Jairite was also David's priest.

David Avenges the Gibeonites

21 Now there was a famine in the days of David for three years, year after year. And David sought the face of the LORD. And the LORD said, "There is bloodguilt on Saul and on his house, because he put the Gibeonites to death." [2] So the king called the Gibeonites and spoke to them. Now the Gibeonites were not of the people of Israel but of the remnant of the Amorites. Although the people of Israel had sworn to spare them, Saul had sought to strike them down in his zeal for the people of Israel and Judah. [3] And David said to the Gibeonites, "What shall I do for you? And how shall I make atonement, that you may bless the heritage of the LORD?" [4] The Gibeonites said to him, "It is not a matter of silver or gold between us and Saul or his house; neither is it for us to put any man to death in Israel." And he said, "What do you say that I shall do for you?" [5] They said to the king, "The man who consumed us and planned to destroy us, so that we should have no place in all the territory of Israel, [6] let seven of his sons be given to us, so that we may hang them before the LORD at Gibeah of Saul, the chosen of the LORD." And the king said, "I will give them."

[7] But the king spared Mephibosheth, the son of Saul's son Jonathan, because of the oath of the LORD that was between them, between David and Jonathan the son of Saul. [8] The king took the two sons of Rizpah the daughter of Aiah, whom she bore to Saul, Armoni and Mephibosheth; and the five sons of Merab[3] the daughter of Saul, whom she bore to Adriel the son of Barzillai the Meholathite; [9] and he gave them into the hands of the Gibeonites, and they hanged them on the mountain before the LORD, and the seven of them perished together. They were put to death in the first days of harvest, at the beginning of barley harvest.

[10] Then Rizpah the daughter of Aiah took sackcloth and spread it for herself on the rock, from the beginning of harvest until rain fell upon them from the heavens. And she did not allow the birds of the air to come upon them by day, or the beasts of the field by night. [11] When David was told what Rizpah the daughter of Aiah, the concubine of Saul, had done, [12] David went and took the bones of Saul and the bones of his son Jonathan from the men of Jabesh-gilead, who had stolen them from the public square of Beth-shan, where the Philistines had hanged them, on the day the Philistines killed Saul on Gilboa. [13] And he brought up from there the bones of Saul and the bones of his son Jonathan; and they gathered the bones of those who were hanged. [14] And they buried the bones of Saul and his son Jonathan in the land of Benjamin in Zela, in the tomb of Kish his father. And they did all that the king commanded. And after that God responded to the plea for the land.

---

[1] Compare 20:15; Hebrew *and Beth-maacah* [2] Hebrew *Berites* [3] Two Hebrew manuscripts, Septuagint; most Hebrew manuscripts *Michal*

War with the Philistines

15 There was war again between the Philistines and Israel, and David went down together with his servants, and they fought against the Philistines. And David grew weary. **16** And Ishbi-benob, one of the descendants of the giants, whose spear weighed three hundred shekels[1] of bronze, and who was armed with a new sword, thought to kill David. **17** But Abishai the son of Zeruiah came to his aid and attacked the Philistine and killed him. Then David's men swore to him, "You shall no longer go out with us to battle, lest you quench the lamp of Israel."

18 After this there was again war with the Philistines at Gob. Then Sibbecai the Hushathite struck down Saph, who was one of the descendants of the giants. **19** And there was again war with the Philistines at Gob, and Elhanan the son of Jaare-oregim, the Bethlehemite, struck down Goliath the Gittite, the shaft of whose spear was like a weaver's beam.[2] **20** And there was again war at Gath, where there was a man of great stature, who had six fingers on each hand, and six toes on each foot, twenty-four in number, and he also was descended from the giants. **21** And when he taunted Israel, Jonathan the son of Shimei, David's brother, struck him down. **22** These four were descended from the giants in Gath, and they fell by the hand of David and by the hand of his servants.

David's Song of Deliverance

22 And David spoke to the LORD the words of this song on the day when the LORD delivered him from the hand of all his enemies, and from the hand of Saul. **2** He said,

"The LORD is my rock and my fortress and
my deliverer,
3   my[3] God, my rock, in whom I take refuge,
my shield, and the horn of my salvation,
my stronghold and my refuge,
my savior; you save me from violence.
4   I call upon the LORD, who is worthy to be
praised,
and I am saved from my enemies.

5   "For the waves of death encompassed me,
the torrents of destruction assailed me;[4]

6   the cords of Sheol entangled me;
the snares of death confronted me.

7   "In my distress I called upon the LORD;
to my God I called.
From his temple he heard my voice,
and my cry came to his ears.

8   "Then the earth reeled and rocked;
the foundations of the heavens trembled
and quaked, because he was angry.
9   Smoke went up from his nostrils,[5]
and devouring fire from his mouth;
glowing coals flamed forth from him.
10   He bowed the heavens and came down;
thick darkness was under his feet.
11   He rode on a cherub and flew;
he was seen on the wings of the wind.
12   He made darkness around him his canopy,
thick clouds, a gathering of water.
13   Out of the brightness before him
coals of fire flamed forth.
14   The LORD thundered from heaven,
and the Most High uttered his voice.
15   And he sent out arrows and scattered
them;
lightning, and routed them.
16   Then the channels of the sea were seen;
the foundations of the world were laid
bare,
at the rebuke of the LORD,
at the blast of the breath of his nostrils.

17   "He sent from on high, he took me;
he drew me out of many waters.
18   He rescued me from my strong enemy,
from those who hated me,
for they were too mighty for me.
19   They confronted me in the day of my
calamity,
but the LORD was my support.
20   He brought me out into a broad place;
he rescued me, because he delighted in
me.

21   "The LORD dealt with me according to my
righteousness;
according to the cleanness of my hands
he rewarded me.
22   For I have kept the ways of the LORD
and have not wickedly departed from
my God.

---

[1] A shekel was about 2/5 ounce or 11 grams [2] Contrast 1 Chronicles 20:5, which may preserve the original reading [3] Septuagint (compare Psalm 18:2); Hebrew lacks *my* [4] Or *terrified me* [5] Or *in his wrath*

²³ For all his rules were before me,
    and from his statutes I did not turn
        aside.
²⁴ I was blameless before him,
    and I kept myself from guilt.
²⁵ And the LORD has rewarded me accord-
        ing to my righteousness,
    according to my cleanness in his sight.

²⁶ "With the merciful you show yourself
        merciful;
    with the blameless man you show
        yourself blameless;
²⁷ with the purified you deal purely,
    and with the crooked you make your-
        self seem tortuous.
²⁸ You save a humble people,
    but your eyes are on the haughty to
        bring them down.
²⁹ For you are my lamp, O LORD,
    and my God lightens my darkness.
³⁰ For by you I can run against a troop,
    and by my God I can leap over a wall.
³¹ This God—his way is perfect;
    the word of the LORD proves true;
    he is a shield for all those who take ref-
        uge in him.

³² "For who is God, but the LORD?
    And who is a rock, except our God?
³³ This God is my strong refuge
    and has made my¹ way blameless.²
³⁴ He made my feet like the feet of a deer
    and set me secure on the heights.
³⁵ He trains my hands for war,
    so that my arms can bend a bow of
        bronze.
³⁶ You have given me the shield of your sal-
        vation,
    and your gentleness made me great.
³⁷ You gave a wide place for my steps under
        me,
    and my feet³ did not slip;
³⁸ I pursued my enemies and destroyed them,
    and did not turn back until they were
        consumed.
³⁹ I consumed them; I thrust them through,
    so that they did not rise;
    they fell under my feet.
⁴⁰ For you equipped me with strength for the
        battle;
    you made those who rise against me
        sink under me.

⁴¹ You made my enemies turn their backs to
        me,⁴
    those who hated me, and I destroyed
        them.
⁴² They looked, but there was none to save;
    they cried to the LORD, but he did not
        answer them.
⁴³ I beat them fine as the dust of the earth;
    I crushed them and stamped them
        down like the mire of the streets.

⁴⁴ "You delivered me from strife with my
        people;⁵
    you kept me as the head of the nations;
    people whom I had not known served
        me.
⁴⁵ Foreigners came cringing to me;
    as soon as they heard of me, they obeyed
        me.
⁴⁶ Foreigners lost heart
    and came trembling⁶ out of their for-
        tresses.

⁴⁷ "The LORD lives, and blessed be my rock,
    and exalted be my God, the rock of my
        salvation,
⁴⁸ the God who gave me vengeance
    and brought down peoples under me,
⁴⁹ who brought me out from my enemies;
    you exalted me above those who rose
        against me;
    you delivered me from men of violence.

⁵⁰ "For this I will praise you, O LORD, among
        the nations,
    and sing praises to your name.
⁵¹ Great salvation he brings⁷ to his king,
    and shows steadfast love to his anointed,
    to David and his offspring forever."

The Last Words of David

23 Now these are the last words of David:

The oracle of David, the son of Jesse,
    the oracle of the man who was raised on
        high,
the anointed of the God of Jacob,
    the sweet psalmist of Israel:⁸

² "The Spirit of the LORD speaks by me;
    his word is on my tongue.

---

¹ Or his; also verse 34 ² Compare Psalm 18:32; Hebrew he has blamelessly set my way free, or he has made my way spring up blamelessly ³ Hebrew ankles ⁴ Or You gave me my enemies' necks ⁵ Septuagint with the peoples ⁶ Compare Psalm 18:45; Hebrew equipped themselves ⁷ Or He is a tower of salvation ⁸ Or the favorite of the songs of Israel

3 The God of Israel has spoken;
   the Rock of Israel has said to me:
When one rules justly over men,
   ruling in the fear of God,
4 he dawns on them like the morning
     light,
   like the sun shining forth on a cloudless
     morning,
   like rain[1] that makes grass to sprout
     from the earth.

5 "For does not my house stand so with
     God?
   For he has made with me an everlasting
     covenant,
   ordered in all things and secure.
For will he not cause to prosper
   all my help and my desire?
6 But worthless men[2] are all like thorns that
     are thrown away,
   for they cannot be taken with the hand;
7 but the man who touches them
     arms himself with iron and the shaft of
     a spear,
   and they are utterly consumed with
     fire."[3]

David's Mighty Men

8 These are the names of the mighty men whom David had: Josheb-basshebeth a Tahchemonite; he was chief of the three.[4] He wielded his spear[5] against eight hundred whom he killed at one time.

9 And next to him among the three mighty men was Eleazar the son of Dodo, son of Ahohi. He was with David when they defied the Philistines who were gathered there for battle, and the men of Israel withdrew. 10 He rose and struck down the Philistines until his hand was weary, and his hand clung to the sword. And the LORD brought about a great victory that day, and the men returned after him only to strip the slain.

11 And next to him was Shammah, the son of Agee the Hararite. The Philistines gathered together at Lehi,[6] where there was a plot of ground full of lentils, and the men fled from the Philistines. 12 But he took his stand in the midst of the plot and defended it and struck down the Philistines, and the LORD worked a great victory.

13 And three of the thirty chief men went down and came about harvest time to David at the cave of Adullam, when a band of Philistines was encamped in the Valley of Rephaim. 14 David was then in the stronghold, and the garrison of the Philistines was then at Bethlehem. 15 And David said longingly, "Oh, that someone would give me water to drink from the well of Bethlehem that is by the gate!" 16 Then the three mighty men broke through the camp of the Philistines and drew water out of the well of Bethlehem that was by the gate and carried and brought it to David. But he would not drink of it. He poured it out to the LORD 17 and said, "Far be it from me, O LORD, that I should do this. Shall I drink the blood of the men who went at the risk of their lives?" Therefore he would not drink it. These things the three mighty men did.

18 Now Abishai, the brother of Joab, the son of Zeruiah, was chief of the thirty.[7] And he wielded his spear against three hundred men[8] and killed them and won a name beside the three. 19 He was the most renowned of the thirty[9] and became their commander, but he did not attain to the three.

20 And Benaiah the son of Jehoiada was a valiant man[10] of Kabzeel, a doer of great deeds. He struck down two ariels[11] of Moab. He also went down and struck down a lion in a pit on a day when snow had fallen. 21 And he struck down an Egyptian, a handsome man. The Egyptian had a spear in his hand, but Benaiah went down to him with a staff and snatched the spear out of the Egyptian's hand and killed him with his own spear. 22 These things did Benaiah the son of Jehoiada, and won a name beside the three mighty men. 23 He was renowned among the thirty, but he did not attain to the three. And David set him over his bodyguard.

24 Asahel the brother of Joab was one of the thirty; Elhanan the son of Dodo of Bethlehem, 25 Shammah of Harod, Elika of Harod, 26 Helez the Paltite, Ira the son of Ikkesh of Tekoa, 27 Abiezer of Anathoth, Mebunnai the Hushathite, 28 Zalmon the Ahohite, Maharai of Netophah, 29 Heleb the son of Baanah of Netophah, Ittai the son of Ribai of Gibeah of the people of Benjamin, 30 Benaiah of Pirathon, Hiddai of the brooks of Gaash, 31 Abialbon the Arbathite, Azmaveth of Bahurim, 32 Eliahba the Shaalbonite, the sons of Jashen, Jonathan, 33 Shammah the Hararite, Ahiam

---

[1] Hebrew *from rain* [2] Hebrew *worthlessness* [3] Hebrew *consumed with fire in the sitting* [4] Or *of the captains* [5] Compare 1 Chronicles 11:11; the meaning of the Hebrew expression is uncertain [6] Or *gathered together as a camp* [7] Two Hebrew manuscripts, Syriac; most Hebrew manuscripts *three* [8] Or *slain ones* [9] Compare 1 Chronicles 11:21; Hebrew *Was he the most renowned of the three?* [10] Or *the son of Ishhai* [11] The meaning of the word *ariel* is unknown

the son of Sharar the Hararite, ³⁴ Eliphelet the son of Ahasbai of Maacah, Eliam the son of Ahithophel the Gilonite, ³⁵ Hezro¹ of Carmel, Paarai the Arbite, ³⁶ Igal the son of Nathan of Zobah, Bani the Gadite, ³⁷ Zelek the Ammonite, Naharai of Beeroth, the armor-bearer of Joab the son of Zeruiah, ³⁸ Ira the Ithrite, Gareb the Ithrite, ³⁹ Uriah the Hittite: thirty-seven in all.

David's Census

24 Again the anger of the LORD was kindled against Israel, and he incited David against them, saying, "Go, number Israel and Judah." ² So the king said to Joab, the commander of the army,² who was with him, "Go through all the tribes of Israel, from Dan to Beersheba, and number the people, that I may know the number of the people." ³ But Joab said to the king, "May the LORD your God add to the people a hundred times as many as they are, while the eyes of my lord the king still see it, but why does my lord the king delight in this thing?" ⁴ But the king's word prevailed against Joab and the commanders of the army. So Joab and the commanders of the army went out from the presence of the king to number the people of Israel. ⁵ They crossed the Jordan and began from Aroer,³ and from the city that is in the middle of the valley, toward Gad and on to Jazer. ⁶ Then they came to Gilead, and to Kadesh in the land of the Hittites;⁴ and they came to Dan, and from Dan⁵ they went around to Sidon, ⁷ and came to the fortress of Tyre and to all the cities of the Hivites and Canaanites; and they went out to the Negeb of Judah at Beersheba. ⁸ So when they had gone through all the land, they came to Jerusalem at the end of nine months and twenty days. ⁹ And Joab gave the sum of the numbering of the people to the king: in Israel there were 800,000 valiant men who drew the sword, and the men of Judah were 500,000.

The LORD's Judgment of David's Sin

¹⁰ But David's heart struck him after he had numbered the people. And David said to the LORD, "I have sinned greatly in what I have done. But now, O LORD, please take away the iniquity of your servant, for I have done very foolishly." ¹¹ And when David arose in the morning, the word of the LORD came to the prophet Gad, David's seer, saying, ¹² "Go and say to David, 'Thus says the LORD, Three things I offer⁶ you. Choose one of them, that I may do it to you.'" ¹³ So Gad came to David and told him, and said to him, "Shall three⁷ years of famine come to you in your land? Or will you flee three months before your foes while they pursue you? Or shall there be three days' pestilence in your land? Now consider, and decide what answer I shall return to him who sent me." ¹⁴ Then David said to Gad, "I am in great distress. Let us fall into the hand of the LORD, for his mercy is great; but let me not fall into the hand of man."

¹⁵ So the LORD sent a pestilence on Israel from the morning until the appointed time. And there died of the people from Dan to Beersheba 70,000 men. ¹⁶ And when the angel stretched out his hand toward Jerusalem to destroy it, the LORD relented from the calamity and said to the angel who was working destruction among the people, "It is enough; now stay your hand." And the angel of the LORD was by the threshing floor of Araunah the Jebusite. ¹⁷ Then David spoke to the LORD when he saw the angel who was striking the people, and said, "Behold, I have sinned, and I have done wickedly. But these sheep, what have they done? Please let your hand be against me and against my father's house."

David Builds an Altar

¹⁸ And Gad came that day to David and said to him, "Go up, raise an altar to the LORD on the threshing floor of Araunah the Jebusite." ¹⁹ So David went up at Gad's word, as the LORD commanded. ²⁰ And when Araunah looked down, he saw the king and his servants coming on toward him. And Araunah went out and paid homage to the king with his face to the ground. ²¹ And Araunah said, "Why has my lord the king come to his servant?" David said, "To buy the threshing floor from you, in order to build an altar to the LORD, that the plague may be averted from the people." ²² Then Araunah said to David, "Let my lord the king take and offer up what seems good to him. Here are the oxen for the burnt offering and the threshing sledges and the yokes of the oxen for the wood. ²³ All this, O king, Araunah gives to the king." And Araunah said to the king, "May the LORD your God accept you." ²⁴ But the king said to Araunah, "No, but I will buy it from you for

---

¹ Or *Hezrai* ² Septuagint *to Joab and the commanders of the army* ³ Septuagint; Hebrew *encamped in Aroer* ⁴ Septuagint; Hebrew *to the land of Tahtim-hodshi* ⁵ Septuagint; Hebrew *they came to Dan-jaan and* ⁶ Or *hold over* ⁷ Compare 1 Chronicles 21:12, Septuagint; Hebrew *seven*

a price. I will not offer burnt offerings to the LORD my God that cost me nothing." So David bought the threshing floor and the oxen for fifty shekels[1] of silver. 25 And David built there an altar to the LORD and offered burnt offerings and peace offerings. So the LORD responded to the plea for the land, and the plague was averted from Israel.

1 KINGS

David in His Old Age

1 Now King David was old and advanced in years. And although they covered him with clothes, he could not get warm. [2] Therefore his servants said to him, "Let a young woman be sought for my lord the king, and let her wait on the king and be in his service. Let her lie in your arms,[1] that my lord the king may be warm." [3] So they sought for a beautiful young woman throughout all the territory of Israel, and found Abishag the Shunammite, and brought her to the king. [4] The young woman was very beautiful, and she was of service to the king and attended to him, but the king knew her not.

Adonijah Sets Himself Up as King

[5] Now Adonijah the son of Haggith exalted himself, saying, "I will be king." And he prepared for himself chariots and horsemen, and fifty men to run before him. [6] His father had never at any time displeased him by asking, "Why have you done thus and so?" He was also a very handsome man, and he was born next after Absalom. [7] He conferred with Joab the son of Zeruiah and with Abiathar the priest. And they followed Adonijah and helped him. [8] But Zadok the priest and Benaiah the son of Jehoiada and Nathan the prophet and Shimei and Rei and David's mighty men were not with Adonijah.

[9] Adonijah sacrificed sheep, oxen, and fattened cattle by the Serpent's Stone, which is beside En-rogel, and he invited all his brothers, the king's sons, and all the royal officials of Judah, [10] but he did not invite Nathan the prophet or Benaiah or the mighty men or Solomon his brother.

Nathan and Bathsheba Before David

[11] Then Nathan said to Bathsheba the mother of Solomon, "Have you not heard that Adonijah the son of Haggith has become king and David our lord does not know it? [12] Now therefore come, let me give you advice, that you may save your own life and the life of your son Solomon. [13] Go in at once to King David, and say to him, 'Did you not, my lord the king, swear to your servant, saying, "Solomon your son shall reign after me, and he shall sit on my throne"? Why then is Adonijah king?'

[14] Then while you are still speaking with the king, I also will come in after you and confirm[2] your words."

[15] So Bathsheba went to the king in his chamber (now the king was very old, and Abishag the Shunammite was attending to the king). [16] Bathsheba bowed and paid homage to the king, and the king said, "What do you desire?" [17] She said to him, "My lord, you swore to your servant by the LORD your God, saying, 'Solomon your son shall reign after me, and he shall sit on my throne.' [18] And now, behold, Adonijah is king, although you, my lord the king, do not know it. [19] He has sacrificed oxen, fattened cattle, and sheep in abundance, and has invited all the sons of the king, Abiathar the priest, and Joab the commander of the army, but Solomon your servant he has not invited. [20] And now, my lord the king, the eyes of all Israel are on you, to tell them who shall sit on the throne of my lord the king after him. [21] Otherwise it will come to pass, when my lord the king sleeps with his fathers, that I and my son Solomon will be counted offenders."

[22] While she was still speaking with the king, Nathan the prophet came in. [23] And they told the king, "Here is Nathan the prophet." And when he came in before the king, he bowed before the king, with his face to the ground. [24] And Nathan said, "My lord the king, have you said, 'Adonijah shall reign after me, and he shall sit on my throne'? [25] For he has gone down this day and has sacrificed oxen, fattened cattle, and sheep in abundance, and has invited all the king's sons, the commanders[3] of the army, and Abiathar the priest. And behold, they are eating and drinking before him, and saying, 'Long live King Adonijah!' [26] But me, your servant, and Zadok the priest, and Benaiah the son of Jehoiada, and your servant Solomon he has not invited. [27] Has this thing been brought about by my lord the king and you have not told your servants who should sit on the throne of my lord the king after him?"

Solomon Anointed King

[28] Then King David answered, "Call Bathsheba to me." So she came into the king's

---

[1] Or in your bosom [2] Or expand on [3] Hebrew; Septuagint *Joab the commander*

presence and stood before the king. [29] And the king swore, saying, "As the LORD lives, who has redeemed my soul out of every adversity, [30] as I swore to you by the LORD, the God of Israel, saying, 'Solomon your son shall reign after me, and he shall sit on my throne in my place,' even so will I do this day." [31] Then Bathsheba bowed with her face to the ground and paid homage to the king and said, "May my lord King David live forever!"

[32] King David said, "Call to me Zadok the priest, Nathan the prophet, and Benaiah the son of Jehoiada." So they came before the king. [33] And the king said to them, "Take with you the servants of your lord and have Solomon my son ride on my own mule, and bring him down to Gihon. [34] And let Zadok the priest and Nathan the prophet there anoint him king over Israel. Then blow the trumpet and say, 'Long live King Solomon!' [35] You shall then come up after him, and he shall come and sit on my throne, for he shall be king in my place. And I have appointed him to be ruler over Israel and over Judah." [36] And Benaiah the son of Jehoiada answered the king, "Amen! May the LORD, the God of my lord the king, say so. [37] As the LORD has been with my lord the king, even so may he be with Solomon, and make his throne greater than the throne of my lord King David."

[38] So Zadok the priest, Nathan the prophet, and Benaiah the son of Jehoiada, and the Cherethites and the Pelethites went down and had Solomon ride on King David's mule and brought him to Gihon. [39] There Zadok the priest took the horn of oil from the tent and anointed Solomon. Then they blew the trumpet, and all the people said, "Long live King Solomon!" [40] And all the people went up after him, playing on pipes, and rejoicing with great joy, so that the earth was split by their noise.

[41] Adonijah and all the guests who were with him heard it as they finished feasting. And when Joab heard the sound of the trumpet, he said, "What does this uproar in the city mean?" [42] While he was still speaking, behold, Jonathan the son of Abiathar the priest came. And Adonijah said, "Come in, for you are a worthy man and bring good news." [43] Jonathan answered Adonijah, "No, for our lord King David has made Solomon king, [44] and the king has sent with him Zadok the priest, Nathan the prophet, and Benaiah the son of Jehoiada, and the Cherethites and the Pelethites. And they had

him ride on the king's mule. [45] And Zadok the priest and Nathan the prophet have anointed him king at Gihon, and they have gone up from there rejoicing, so that the city is in an uproar. This is the noise that you have heard. [46] Solomon sits on the royal throne. [47] Moreover, the king's servants came to congratulate our lord King David, saying, 'May your God make the name of Solomon more famous than yours, and make his throne greater than your throne.' And the king bowed himself on the bed. [48] And the king also said, 'Blessed be the LORD, the God of Israel, who has granted someone[1] to sit on my throne this day, my own eyes seeing it.'"

[49] Then all the guests of Adonijah trembled and rose, and each went his own way. [50] And Adonijah feared Solomon. So he arose and went and took hold of the horns of the altar. [51] Then it was told Solomon, "Behold, Adonijah fears King Solomon, for behold, he has laid hold of the horns of the altar, saying, 'Let King Solomon swear to me first that he will not put his servant to death with the sword.'" [52] And Solomon said, "If he will show himself a worthy man, not one of his hairs shall fall to the earth, but if wickedness is found in him, he shall die." [53] So King Solomon sent, and they brought him down from the altar. And he came and paid homage to King Solomon, and Solomon said to him, "Go to your house."

David's Instructions to Solomon

2 When David's time to die drew near, he commanded Solomon his son, saying, [2] "I am about to go the way of all the earth. Be strong, and show yourself a man, [3] and keep the charge of the LORD your God, walking in his ways and keeping his statutes, his commandments, his rules, and his testimonies, as it is written in the Law of Moses, that you may prosper in all that you do and wherever you turn, [4] that the LORD may establish his word that he spoke concerning me, saying, 'If your sons pay close attention to their way, to walk before me in faithfulness with all their heart and with all their soul, you shall not lack[2] a man on the throne of Israel.'

[5] "Moreover, you also know what Joab the son of Zeruiah did to me, how he dealt with the two commanders of the armies of Israel, Abner the son of Ner, and Amasa the son of Jether, whom he killed, avenging[3] in time of peace for blood that had been shed in war, and putting

the blood of war[1] on the belt around his[2] waist and on the sandals on his feet. [6] Act therefore according to your wisdom, but do not let his gray head go down to Sheol in peace. [7] But deal loyally with the sons of Barzillai the Gileadite, and let them be among those who eat at your table, for with such loyalty[3] they met me when I fled from Absalom your brother. [8] And there is also with you Shimei the son of Gera, the Benjaminite from Bahurim, who cursed me with a grievous curse on the day when I went to Mahanaim. But when he came down to meet me at the Jordan, I swore to him by the LORD, saying, 'I will not put you to death with the sword.' [9] Now therefore do not hold him guiltless, for you are a wise man. You will know what you ought to do to him, and you shall bring his gray head down with blood to Sheol."

The Death of David

[10] Then David slept with his fathers and was buried in the city of David. [11] And the time that David reigned over Israel was forty years. He reigned seven years in Hebron and thirty-three years in Jerusalem. [12] So Solomon sat on the throne of David his father, and his kingdom was firmly established.

Solomon's Reign Established

[13] Then Adonijah the son of Haggith came to Bathsheba the mother of Solomon. And she said, "Do you come peacefully?" He said, "Peacefully." [14] Then he said, "I have something to say to you." She said, "Speak." [15] He said, "You know that the kingdom was mine, and that all Israel fully expected me to reign. However, the kingdom has turned about and become my brother's, for it was his from the LORD. [16] And now I have one request to make of you; do not refuse me." She said to him, "Speak." [17] And he said, "Please ask King Solomon—he will not refuse you—to give me Abishag the Shunammite as my wife." [18] Bathsheba said, "Very well; I will speak for you to the king."

[19] So Bathsheba went to King Solomon to speak to him on behalf of Adonijah. And the king rose to meet her and bowed down to her. Then he sat on his throne and had a seat brought for the king's mother, and she sat on his right. [20] Then she said, "I have one small request to make of you; do not refuse me." And the king said to her, "Make your request, my mother, for I will not refuse you." [21] She said, "Let Abishag the Shunammite be given to Adonijah your brother as his wife." [22] King Solomon answered his mother, "And why do you ask Abishag the Shunammite for Adonijah? Ask for him the kingdom also, for he is my older brother, and on his side are Abiathar[4] the priest and Joab the son of Zeruiah." [23] Then King Solomon swore by the LORD, saying, "God do so to me and more also if this word does not cost Adonijah his life! [24] Now therefore as the LORD lives, who has established me and placed me on the throne of David my father, and who has made me a house, as he promised, Adonijah shall be put to death today." [25] So King Solomon sent Benaiah the son of Jehoiada, and he struck him down, and he died.

[26] And to Abiathar the priest the king said, "Go to Anathoth, to your estate, for you deserve death. But I will not at this time put you to death, because you carried the ark of the Lord GOD before David my father, and because you shared in all my father's affliction." [27] So Solomon expelled Abiathar from being priest to the LORD, thus fulfilling the word of the LORD that he had spoken concerning the house of Eli in Shiloh.

[28] When the news came to Joab—for Joab had supported Adonijah although he had not supported Absalom—Joab fled to the tent of the LORD and caught hold of the horns of the altar. [29] And when it was told King Solomon, "Joab has fled to the tent of the LORD, and behold, he is beside the altar," Solomon sent Benaiah the son of Jehoiada, saying, "Go, strike him down." [30] So Benaiah came to the tent of the LORD and said to him, "The king commands, 'Come out.'" But he said, "No, I will die here." Then Benaiah brought the king word again, saying, "Thus said Joab, and thus he answered me." [31] The king replied to him, "Do as he has said, strike him down and bury him, and thus take away from me and from my father's house the guilt for the blood that Joab shed without cause. [32] The LORD will bring back his bloody deeds on his own head, because, without the knowledge of my father David, he attacked and killed with the sword two men more righteous and better than himself, Abner the son of Ner, commander of the army of Israel, and Amasa the son of Jether, commander of the army of Judah. [33] So shall their blood come back on the head of Joab and on the head of his descendants forever. But for David and for his descendants and for his house and for his throne there shall

---

[1] Septuagint *innocent blood* [2] Septuagint *my*; twice in this verse [3] Or *steadfast love* [4] Septuagint, Syriac, Vulgate; Hebrew *and for him and for Abiathar*

be peace from the LORD forevermore." ³⁴Then Benaiah the son of Jehoiada went up and struck him down and put him to death. And he was buried in his own house in the wilderness. ³⁵The king put Benaiah the son of Jehoiada over the army in place of Joab, and the king put Zadok the priest in the place of Abiathar.

³⁶ Then the king sent and summoned Shimei and said to him, "Build yourself a house in Jerusalem and dwell there, and do not go out from there to any place whatever. ³⁷For on the day you go out and cross the brook Kidron, know for certain that you shall die. Your blood shall be on your own head." ³⁸And Shimei said to the king, "What you say is good; as my lord the king has said, so will your servant do." So Shimei lived in Jerusalem many days.

³⁹ But it happened at the end of three years that two of Shimei's servants ran away to Achish, son of Maacah, king of Gath. And when it was told Shimei, "Behold, your servants are in Gath," ⁴⁰Shimei arose and saddled a donkey and went to Gath to Achish to seek his servants. Shimei went and brought his servants from Gath. ⁴¹And when Solomon was told that Shimei had gone from Jerusalem to Gath and returned, ⁴²the king sent and summoned Shimei and said to him, "Did I not make you swear by the LORD and solemnly warn you, saying, 'Know for certain that on the day you go out and go to any place whatever, you shall die'? And you said to me, 'What you say is good; I will obey.' ⁴³Why then have you not kept your oath to the LORD and the commandment with which I commanded you?" ⁴⁴The king also said to Shimei, "You know in your own heart all the harm that you did to David my father. So the LORD will bring back your harm on your own head. ⁴⁵But King Solomon shall be blessed, and the throne of David shall be established before the LORD forever." ⁴⁶Then the king commanded Benaiah the son of Jehoiada, and he went out and struck him down, and he died.

So the kingdom was established in the hand of Solomon.

Solomon's Prayer for Wisdom

3 Solomon made a marriage alliance with Pharaoh king of Egypt. He took Pharaoh's daughter and brought her into the city of David until he had finished building his own house

and the house of the LORD and the wall around Jerusalem. ²The people were sacrificing at the high places, however, because no house had yet been built for the name of the LORD.

³Solomon loved the LORD, walking in the statutes of David his father, only he sacrificed and made offerings at the high places. ⁴And the king went to Gibeon to sacrifice there, for that was the great high place. Solomon used to offer a thousand burnt offerings on that altar. ⁵At Gibeon the LORD appeared to Solomon in a dream by night, and God said, "Ask what I shall give you." ⁶And Solomon said, "You have shown great and steadfast love to your servant David my father, because he walked before you in faithfulness, in righteousness, and in uprightness of heart toward you. And you have kept for him this great and steadfast love and have given him a son to sit on his throne this day. ⁷And now, O LORD my God, you have made your servant king in place of David my father, although I am but a little child. I do not know how to go out or come in. ⁸And your servant is in the midst of your people whom you have chosen, a great people, too many to be numbered or counted for multitude. ⁹Give your servant therefore an understanding mind to govern your people, that I may discern between good and evil, for who is able to govern this your great people?"

¹⁰It pleased the Lord that Solomon had asked this. ¹¹And God said to him, "Because you have asked this, and have not asked for yourself long life or riches or the life of your enemies, but have asked for yourself understanding to discern what is right, ¹²behold, I now do according to your word. Behold, I give you a wise and discerning mind, so that none like you has been before you and none like you shall arise after you. ¹³I give you also what you have not asked, both riches and honor, so that no other king shall compare with you, all your days. ¹⁴And if you will walk in my ways, keeping my statutes and my commandments, as your father David walked, then I will lengthen your days."

¹⁵And Solomon awoke, and behold, it was a dream. Then he came to Jerusalem and stood before the ark of the covenant of the Lord, and offered up burnt offerings and peace offerings, and made a feast for all his servants.

Solomon's Wisdom

[16] Then two prostitutes came to the king and stood before him. [17] The one woman said, "Oh, my lord, this woman and I live in the same house, and I gave birth to a child while she was in the house. [18] Then on the third day after I gave birth, this woman also gave birth. And we were alone. There was no one else with us in the house; only we two were in the house. [19] And this woman's son died in the night, because she lay on him. [20] And she arose at midnight and took my son from beside me, while your servant slept, and laid him at her breast, and laid her dead son at my breast. [21] When I rose in the morning to nurse my child, behold, he was dead. But when I looked at him closely in the morning, behold, he was not the child that I had borne." [22] But the other woman said, "No, the living child is mine, and the dead child is yours." The first said, "No, the dead child is yours, and the living child is mine." Thus they spoke before the king.

[23] Then the king said, "The one says, 'This is my son that is alive, and your son is dead'; and the other says, 'No; but your son is dead, and my son is the living one.' " [24] And the king said, "Bring me a sword." So a sword was brought before the king. [25] And the king said, "Divide the living child in two, and give half to the one and half to the other." [26] Then the woman whose son was alive said to the king, because her heart yearned for her son, "Oh, my lord, give her the living child, and by no means put him to death." But the other said, "He shall be neither mine nor yours; divide him." [27] Then the king answered and said, "Give the living child to the first woman, and by no means put him to death; she is his mother." [28] And all Israel heard of the judgment that the king had rendered, and they stood in awe of the king, because they perceived that the wisdom of God was in him to do justice.

Solomon's Officials

4 King Solomon was king over all Israel, [2] and these were his high officials: Azariah the son of Zadok was the priest; [3] Elihoreph and Ahijah the sons of Shisha were secretaries; Jehoshaphat the son of Ahilud was recorder; [4] Benaiah the son of Jehoiada was in command of the army; Zadok and Abiathar were priests; [5] Azariah the son of Nathan was over the officers; Zabud the son of Nathan was priest and

king's friend; [6] Ahishar was in charge of the palace; and Adoniram the son of Abda was in charge of the forced labor.

[7] Solomon had twelve officers over all Israel, who provided food for the king and his household. Each man had to make provision for one month in the year. [8] These were their names: Ben-hur, in the hill country of Ephraim; [9] Ben-deker, in Makaz, Shaalbim, Beth-shemesh, and Elonbeth-hanan; [10] Benhesed, in Arubboth (to him belonged Socoh and all the land of Hepher); [11] Ben-abinadab, in all Naphath-dor (he had Taphath the daughter of Solomon as his wife); [12] Baana the son of Ahilud, in Taanach, Megiddo, and all Bethshean that is beside Zarethan below Jezreel, and from Beth-shean to Abel-meholah, as far as the other side of Jokmeam; [13] Ben-geber, in Ramoth-gilead (he had the villages of Jair the son of Manasseh, which are in Gilead, and he had the region of Argob, which is in Bashan, sixty great cities with walls and bronze bars); [14] Ahinadab the son of Iddo, in Mahanaim; [15] Ahimaaz, in Naphtali (he had taken Basemath the daughter of Solomon as his wife); [16] Baana the son of Hushai, in Asher and Bealoth; [17] Jehoshaphat the son of Paruah, in Issachar; [18] Shimei the son of Ela, in Benjamin; [19] Geber the son of Uri, in the land of Gilead, the country of Sihon king of the Amorites and of Og king of Bashan. And there was one governor who was over the land.

Solomon's Wealth and Wisdom

[20] Judah and Israel were as many as the sand by the sea. They ate and drank and were happy. [21] [1] Solomon ruled over all the kingdoms from the Euphrates[2] to the land of the Philistines and to the border of Egypt. They brought tribute and served Solomon all the days of his life. [22] Solomon's provision for one day was thirty cors[3] of fine flour and sixty cors of meal, [23] ten fat oxen, and twenty pasture-fed cattle, a hundred sheep, besides deer, gazelles, roebucks, and fattened fowl. [24] For he had dominion over all the region west of the Euphrates[4] from Tiphsah to Gaza, over all the kings west of the Euphrates. And he had peace on all sides around him. [25] And Judah and Israel lived in safety, from Dan even to Beersheba, every man under his vine and under his fig tree, all the days of Solomon. [26] Solomon also had 40,000[5] stalls of horses for his chariots, and 12,000

[1] Ch 5:1 in Hebrew [2] Hebrew the River [3] A cor was about 6 bushels or 220 liters [4] Hebrew the River; twice in this verse [5] Hebrew; one Hebrew manuscript (see 2 Chronicles 9:25 and Septuagint of 1 Kings 10:26) 4,000

horsemen. ²⁷ And those officers supplied provisions for King Solomon, and for all who came to King Solomon's table, each one in his month. They let nothing be lacking. ²⁸ Barley also and straw for the horses and swift steeds they brought to the place where it was required, each according to his duty.

²⁹ And God gave Solomon wisdom and understanding beyond measure, and breadth of mind like the sand on the seashore, ³⁰ so that Solomon's wisdom surpassed the wisdom of all the people of the east and all the wisdom of Egypt. ³¹ For he was wiser than all other men, wiser than Ethan the Ezrahite, and Heman, Calcol, and Darda, the sons of Mahol, and his fame was in all the surrounding nations. ³² He also spoke 3,000 proverbs, and his songs were 1,005. ³³ He spoke of trees, from the cedar that is in Lebanon to the hyssop that grows out of the wall. He spoke also of beasts, and of birds, and of reptiles, and of fish. ³⁴ And people of all nations came to hear the wisdom of Solomon, and from all the kings of the earth, who had heard of his wisdom.

Preparations for Building the Temple

5 ¹ Now Hiram king of Tyre sent his servants to Solomon when he heard that they had anointed him king in place of his father, for Hiram always loved David. ² And Solomon sent word to Hiram, ³ "You know that David my father could not build a house for the name of the Lord his God because of the warfare with which his enemies surrounded him, until the Lord put them under the soles of his feet. ⁴ But now the Lord my God has given me rest on every side. There is neither adversary nor misfortune. ⁵ And so I intend to build a house for the name of the Lord my God, as the Lord said to David my father, 'Your son, whom I will set on your throne in your place, shall build the house for my name.' ⁶ Now therefore command that cedars of Lebanon be cut for me. And my servants will join your servants, and I will pay you for your servants such wages as you set, for you know that there is no one among us who knows how to cut timber like the Sidonians."

⁷ As soon as Hiram heard the words of Solomon, he rejoiced greatly and said, "Blessed be the Lord this day, who has given to David a wise son to be over this great people." ⁸ And Hiram sent to Solomon, saying, "I have heard the message that you have sent to me. I am ready to do all you desire in the matter of cedar and cypress timber. ⁹ My servants shall bring it down to the sea from Lebanon, and I will make it into rafts to go by sea to the place you direct. And I will have them broken up there, and you shall receive it. And you shall meet my wishes by providing food for my household." ¹⁰ So Hiram supplied Solomon with all the timber of cedar and cypress that he desired, ¹¹ while Solomon gave Hiram 20,000 cors² of wheat as food for his household, and 20,000³ cors of beaten oil. Solomon gave this to Hiram year by year. ¹² And the Lord gave Solomon wisdom, as he promised him. And there was peace between Hiram and Solomon, and the two of them made a treaty.

¹³ King Solomon drafted forced labor out of all Israel, and the draft numbered 30,000 men. ¹⁴ And he sent them to Lebanon, 10,000 a month in shifts. They would be a month in Lebanon and two months at home. Adoniram was in charge of the draft. ¹⁵ Solomon also had 70,000 burden-bearers and 80,000 stonecutters in the hill country, ¹⁶ besides Solomon's 3,300 chief officers who were over the work, who had charge of the people who carried on the work. ¹⁷ At the king's command they quarried out great, costly stones in order to lay the foundation of the house with dressed stones. ¹⁸ So Solomon's builders and Hiram's builders and the men of Gebal did the cutting and prepared the timber and the stone to build the house.

Solomon Builds the Temple

6 In the four hundred and eightieth year after the people of Israel came out of the land of Egypt, in the fourth year of Solomon's reign over Israel, in the month of Ziv, which is the second month, he began to build the house of the Lord. ² The house that King Solomon built for the Lord was sixty cubits⁴ long, twenty cubits wide, and thirty cubits high. ³ The vestibule in front of the nave of the house was twenty cubits long, equal to the width of the house, and ten cubits deep in front of the house. ⁴ And he made for the house windows with recessed frames.⁵ ⁵ He also built a structure⁶ against the wall of the house, running around the walls of the house, both the nave and the inner sanctuary. And he made

---

¹ Ch 5:15 in Hebrew ² A *cor* was about 6 bushels or 220 liters ³ Septuagint; Hebrew *twenty* ⁴ A *cubit* was about 18 inches or 45 centimeters ⁵ Or *blocked lattice windows* ⁶ Or *platform*; also verse 10

side chambers all around. [6] The lowest story[1] was five cubits broad, the middle one was six cubits broad, and the third was seven cubits broad. For around the outside of the house he made offsets on the wall in order that the supporting beams should not be inserted into the walls of the house.

[7] When the house was built, it was with stone prepared at the quarry, so that neither hammer nor axe nor any tool of iron was heard in the house while it was being built.

[8] The entrance for the lowest[2] story was on the south side of the house, and one went up by stairs to the middle story, and from the middle story to the third. [9] So he built the house and finished it, and he made the ceiling of the house of beams and planks of cedar. [10] He built the structure against the whole house, five cubits high, and it was joined to the house with timbers of cedar.

[11] Now the word of the LORD came to Solomon, [12] "Concerning this house that you are building, if you will walk in my statutes and obey my rules and keep all my commandments and walk in them, then I will establish my word with you, which I spoke to David your father. [13] And I will dwell among the children of Israel and will not forsake my people Israel."

[14] So Solomon built the house and finished it. [15] He lined the walls of the house on the inside with boards of cedar. From the floor of the house to the walls of the ceiling, he covered them on the inside with wood, and he covered the floor of the house with boards of cypress. [16] He built twenty cubits of the rear of the house with boards of cedar from the floor to the walls, and he built this within as an inner sanctuary, as the Most Holy Place. [17] The house, that is, the nave in front of the inner sanctuary, was forty cubits long. [18] The cedar within the house was carved in the form of gourds and open flowers. All was cedar; no stone was seen. [19] The inner sanctuary he prepared in the innermost part of the house, to set there the ark of the covenant of the LORD. [20] The inner sanctuary[3] was twenty cubits long, twenty cubits wide, and twenty cubits high, and he overlaid it with pure gold. He also overlaid[4] an altar of cedar. [21] And Solomon overlaid the inside of the house with pure gold, and he drew chains of gold across, in front of the inner

sanctuary, and overlaid it with gold. [22] And he overlaid the whole house with gold, until all the house was finished. Also the whole altar that belonged to the inner sanctuary he overlaid with gold.

[23] In the inner sanctuary he made two cherubim of olivewood, each ten cubits high. [24] Five cubits was the length of one wing of the cherub, and five cubits the length of the other wing of the cherub; it was ten cubits from the tip of one wing to the tip of the other. [25] The other cherub also measured ten cubits; both cherubim had the same measure and the same form. [26] The height of one cherub was ten cubits, and so was that of the other cherub. [27] He put the cherubim in the innermost part of the house. And the wings of the cherubim were spread out so that a wing of one touched the one wall, and a wing of the other cherub touched the other wall; their other wings touched each other in the middle of the house. [28] And he overlaid the cherubim with gold.

[29] Around all the walls of the house he carved engraved figures of cherubim and palm trees and open flowers, in the inner and outer rooms. [30] The floor of the house he overlaid with gold in the inner and outer rooms.

[31] For the entrance to the inner sanctuary he made doors of olivewood; the lintel and the doorposts were five-sided.[5] [32] He covered the two doors of olivewood with carvings of cherubim, palm trees, and open flowers. He overlaid them with gold and spread gold on the cherubim and on the palm trees.

[33] So also he made for the entrance to the nave doorposts of olivewood, in the form of a square, [34] and two doors of cypress wood. The two leaves of the one door were folding, and the two leaves of the other door were folding. [35] On them he carved cherubim and palm trees and open flowers, and he overlaid them with gold evenly applied on the carved work. [36] He built the inner court with three courses of cut stone and one course of cedar beams.

[37] In the fourth year the foundation of the house of the LORD was laid, in the month of Ziv. [38] And in the eleventh year, in the month of Bul, which is the eighth month, the house was finished in all its parts, and according to all its specifications. He was seven years in building it.

---

[1] Septuagint; Hebrew *structure, or platform* [2] Septuagint, Targum; Hebrew *middle* [3] Vulgate; Hebrew *And before the inner sanctuary* [4] Septuagint *made* [5] The meaning of the Hebrew phrase is uncertain

Solomon Builds His Palace

7 Solomon was building his own house thirteen years, and he finished his entire house.

[2] He built the House of the Forest of Lebanon. Its length was a hundred cubits[1] and its breadth fifty cubits and its height thirty cubits, and it was built on four[2] rows of cedar pillars, with cedar beams on the pillars. [3] And it was covered with cedar above the chambers that were on the forty-five pillars, fifteen in each row. [4] There were window frames in three rows, and window opposite window in three tiers. [5] All the doorways and windows[3] had square frames, and window was opposite window in three tiers.

[6] And he made the Hall of Pillars; its length was fifty cubits, and its breadth thirty cubits. There was a porch in front with pillars, and a canopy in front of them.

[7] And he made the Hall of the Throne where he was to pronounce judgment, even the Hall of Judgment. It was finished with cedar from floor to rafters.[4]

[8] His own house where he was to dwell, in the other court back of the hall, was of like workmanship. Solomon also made a house like this hall for Pharaoh's daughter whom he had taken in marriage.

[9] All these were made of costly stones, cut according to measure, sawed with saws, back and front, even from the foundation to the coping, and from the outside to the great court. [10] The foundation was of costly stones, huge stones, stones of eight and ten cubits. [11] And above were costly stones, cut according to measurement, and cedar. [12] The great court had three courses of cut stone all around, and a course of cedar beams; so had the inner court of the house of the LORD and the vestibule of the house.

The Temple Furnishings

[13] And King Solomon sent and brought Hiram from Tyre. [14] He was the son of a widow of the tribe of Naphtali, and his father was a man of Tyre, a worker in bronze. And he was full of wisdom, understanding, and skill for making any work in bronze. He came to King Solomon and did all his work.

[15] He cast two pillars of bronze. Eighteen cubits was the height of one pillar, and a line of twelve cubits measured its circumference. It was hollow, and its thickness was four fingers. The second pillar was the same.[5] [16] He also made two capitals of cast bronze to set on the tops of the pillars. The height of the one capital was five cubits, and the height of the other capital was five cubits. [17] There were lattices of checker work with wreaths of chain work for the capitals on the tops of the pillars, a lattice[6] for the one capital and a lattice for the other capital. [18] Likewise he made pomegranates[7] in two rows around the one latticework to cover the capital that was on the top of the pillar, and he did the same with the other capital. [19] Now the capitals that were on the tops of the pillars in the vestibule were of lily-work, four cubits. [20] The capitals were on the two pillars and also above the rounded projection which was beside the latticework. There were two hundred pomegranates in two rows all around, and so with the other capital. [21] He set up the pillars at the vestibule of the temple. He set up the pillar on the south and called its name Jachin, and he set up the pillar on the north and called its name Boaz. [22] And on the tops of the pillars was lily-work. Thus the work of the pillars was finished.

[23] Then he made the sea of cast metal. It was round, ten cubits from brim to brim, and five cubits high, and a line of thirty cubits measured its circumference. [24] Under its brim were gourds, for ten cubits, compassing the sea all around. The gourds were in two rows, cast with it when it was cast. [25] It stood on twelve oxen, three facing north, three facing west, three facing south, and three facing east. The sea was set on them, and all their rear parts were inward. [26] Its thickness was a handbreadth,[8] and its brim was made like the brim of a cup, like the flower of a lily. It held two thousand baths.[9]

[27] He also made the ten stands of bronze. Each stand was four cubits long, four cubits wide, and three cubits high. [28] This was the construction of the stands: they had panels, and the panels were set in the frames, [29] and on the panels that were set in the frames were lions, oxen, and cherubim. On the frames, both above and below the lions and oxen, there were wreaths of beveled work. [30] Moreover, each stand had four bronze wheels and axles of bronze, and at the four corners were supports for a basin. The supports were cast with

---

[1] A *cubit* was about 18 inches or 45 centimeters [2] Septuagint *three* [3] Septuagint; Hebrew *posts* [4] Syriac, Vulgate; Hebrew *floor* [5] Targum, Syriac (compare Septuagint and Jeremiah 52:21); Hebrew *and a line of twelve cubits measured the circumference of the second pillar* [6] Septuagint; Hebrew *seven*; twice in this verse [7] Two manuscripts (compare Septuagint); Hebrew *pillars* [8] A *handbreadth* was about 3 inches or 7.5 centimeters [9] A *bath* was about 6 gallons or 22 liters

wreaths at the side of each. ³¹Its opening was within a crown that projected upward one cubit. Its opening was round, as a pedestal is made, a cubit and a half deep. At its opening there were carvings, and its panels were square, not round. ³²And the four wheels were underneath the panels. The axles of the wheels were of one piece with the stands, and the height of a wheel was a cubit and a half. ³³The wheels were made like a chariot wheel; their axles, their rims, their spokes, and their hubs were all cast. ³⁴There were four supports at the four corners of each stand. The supports were of one piece with the stands. ³⁵And on the top of the stand there was a round band half a cubit high; and on the top of the stand its stays and its panels were of one piece with it. ³⁶And on the surfaces of its stays and on its panels, he carved cherubim, lions, and palm trees, according to the space of each, with wreaths all around. ³⁷After this manner he made the ten stands. All of them were cast alike, of the same measure and the same form.

³⁸And he made ten basins of bronze. Each basin held forty baths, each basin measured four cubits, and there was a basin for each of the ten stands. ³⁹And he set the stands, five on the south side of the house, and five on the north side of the house. And he set the sea at the southeast corner of the house.

⁴⁰Hiram also made the pots, the shovels, and the basins. So Hiram finished all the work that he did for King Solomon on the house of the LORD: ⁴¹the two pillars, the two bowls of the capitals that were on the tops of the pillars, and the two latticeworks to cover the two bowls of the capitals that were on the tops of the pillars; ⁴²and the four hundred pomegranates for the two latticeworks, two rows of pomegranates for each latticework, to cover the two bowls of the capitals that were on the pillars; ⁴³the ten stands, and the ten basins on the stands; ⁴⁴and the one sea, and the twelve oxen underneath the sea.

⁴⁵Now the pots, the shovels, and the basins, all these vessels in the house of the LORD, which Hiram made for King Solomon, were of burnished bronze. ⁴⁶In the plain of the Jordan the king cast them, in the clay ground between Succoth and Zarethan. ⁴⁷And Solomon left all the vessels unweighed, because there were so many of them; the weight of the bronze was not ascertained.

⁴⁸So Solomon made all the vessels that were in the house of the LORD: the golden altar, the golden table for the bread of the Presence, ⁴⁹the lampstands of pure gold, five on the south side and five on the north, before the inner sanctuary; the flowers, the lamps, and the tongs, of gold; ⁵⁰the cups, snuffers, basins, dishes for incense, and fire pans, of pure gold; and the sockets of gold, for the doors of the innermost part of the house, the Most Holy Place, and for the doors of the nave of the temple.

⁵¹Thus all the work that King Solomon did on the house of the LORD was finished. And Solomon brought in the things that David his father had dedicated, the silver, the gold, and the vessels, and stored them in the treasuries of the house of the LORD.

The Ark Brought into the Temple

8 Then Solomon assembled the elders of Israel and all the heads of the tribes, the leaders of the fathers' houses of the people of Israel, before King Solomon in Jerusalem, to bring up the ark of the covenant of the LORD out of the city of David, which is Zion. ²And all the men of Israel assembled to King Solomon at the feast in the month Ethanim, which is the seventh month. ³And all the elders of Israel came, and the priests took up the ark. ⁴And they brought up the ark of the LORD, the tent of meeting, and all the holy vessels that were in the tent; the priests and the Levites brought them up. ⁵And King Solomon and all the congregation of Israel, who had assembled before him, were with him before the ark, sacrificing so many sheep and oxen that they could not be counted or numbered. ⁶Then the priests brought the ark of the covenant of the LORD to its place in the inner sanctuary of the house, in the Most Holy Place, underneath the wings of the cherubim. ⁷For the cherubim spread out their wings over the place of the ark, so that the cherubim overshadowed the ark and its poles. ⁸And the poles were so long that the ends of the poles were seen from the Holy Place before the inner sanctuary; but they could not be seen from outside. And they are there to this day. ⁹There was nothing in the ark except the two tablets of stone that Moses put there at Horeb, where the LORD made a covenant with the people of Israel, when they came out of the land of Egypt. ¹⁰And when the priests came out of the Holy Place, a cloud filled the house of the LORD, ¹¹so that the priests could not stand to minister because of the cloud, for the glory of the LORD filled the house of the LORD.

Solomon Blesses the LORD

[12] Then Solomon said, "The LORD[1] has said that he would dwell in thick darkness. [13] I have indeed built you an exalted house, a place for you to dwell in forever." [14] Then the king turned around and blessed all the assembly of Israel, while all the assembly of Israel stood. [15] And he said, "Blessed be the LORD, the God of Israel, who with his hand has fulfilled what he promised with his mouth to David my father, saying, [16] 'Since the day that I brought my people Israel out of Egypt, I chose no city out of all the tribes of Israel in which to build a house, that my name might be there. But I chose David to be over my people Israel.' [17] Now it was in the heart of David my father to build a house for the name of the LORD, the God of Israel. [18] But the LORD said to David my father, 'Whereas it was in your heart to build a house for my name, you did well that it was in your heart. [19] Nevertheless, you shall not build the house, but your son who shall be born to you shall build the house for my name.' [20] Now the LORD has fulfilled his promise that he made. For I have risen in the place of David my father, and sit on the throne of Israel, as the LORD promised, and I have built the house for the name of the LORD, the God of Israel. [21] And there I have provided a place for the ark, in which is the covenant of the LORD that he made with our fathers, when he brought them out of the land of Egypt."

Solomon's Prayer of Dedication

[22] Then Solomon stood before the altar of the LORD in the presence of all the assembly of Israel and spread out his hands toward heaven, [23] and said, "O LORD, God of Israel, there is no God like you, in heaven above or on earth beneath, keeping covenant and showing steadfast love to your servants who walk before you with all their heart; [24] you have kept with your servant David my father what you declared to him. You spoke with your mouth, and with your hand have fulfilled it this day. [25] Now therefore, O LORD, God of Israel, keep for your servant David my father what you have promised him, saying, 'You shall not lack a man to sit before me on the throne of Israel, if only your sons pay close attention to their way, to walk before me as you have walked before me.'

[26] Now therefore, O God of Israel, let your word be confirmed, which you have spoken to your servant David my father.

[27] "But will God indeed dwell on the earth? Behold, heaven and the highest heaven cannot contain you; how much less this house that I have built! [28] Yet have regard to the prayer of your servant and to his plea, O LORD my God, listening to the cry and to the prayer that your servant prays before you this day, [29] that your eyes may be open night and day toward this house, the place of which you have said, 'My name shall be there,' that you may listen to the prayer that your servant offers toward this place. [30] And listen to the plea of your servant and of your people Israel, when they pray toward this place. And listen in heaven your dwelling place, and when you hear, forgive.

[31] "If a man sins against his neighbor and is made to take an oath and comes and swears his oath before your altar in this house, [32] then hear in heaven and act and judge your servants, condemning the guilty by bringing his conduct on his own head, and vindicating the righteous by rewarding him according to his righteousness.

[33] "When your people Israel are defeated before the enemy because they have sinned against you, and if they turn again to you and acknowledge your name and pray and plead with you in this house, [34] then hear in heaven and forgive the sin of your people Israel and bring them again to the land that you gave to their fathers.

[35] "When heaven is shut up and there is no rain because they have sinned against you, if they pray toward this place and acknowledge your name and turn from their sin, when you afflict them, [36] then hear in heaven and forgive the sin of your servants, your people Israel, when you teach them the good way in which they should walk, and grant rain upon your land, which you have given to your people as an inheritance.

[37] "If there is famine in the land, if there is pestilence or blight or mildew or locust or caterpillar, if their enemy besieges them in the land at their gates,[2] whatever plague, whatever sickness there is, [38] whatever prayer, whatever plea is made by any man or by all your people Israel, each knowing the affliction of his own heart and stretching out his hands toward this house, [39] then hear in heaven your dwelling place and forgive and act and render to each

---

[1] Septuagint *The LORD has set the sun in the heavens, but* [2] Septuagint, Syriac *in any of their cities*

whose heart you know, according to all his ways (for you, you only, know the hearts of all the children of mankind), [40] that they may fear you all the days that they live in the land that you gave to our fathers.

[41] "Likewise, when a foreigner, who is not of your people Israel, comes from a far country for your name's sake [42] (for they shall hear of your great name and your mighty hand, and of your outstretched arm), when he comes and prays toward this house, [43] hear in heaven your dwelling place and do according to all for which the foreigner calls to you, in order that all the peoples of the earth may know your name and fear you, as do your people Israel, and that they may know that this house that I have built is called by your name.

[44] "If your people go out to battle against their enemy, by whatever way you shall send them, and they pray to the LORD toward the city that you have chosen and the house that I have built for your name, [45] then hear in heaven their prayer and their plea, and maintain their cause.

[46] "If they sin against you—for there is no one who does not sin—and you are angry with them and give them to an enemy, so that they are carried away captive to the land of the enemy, far off or near, [47] yet if they turn their heart in the land to which they have been carried captive, and repent and plead with you in the land of their captors, saying, 'We have sinned and have acted perversely and wickedly,' [48] if they repent with all their heart and with all their soul in the land of their enemies, who carried them captive, and pray to you toward their land, which you gave to their fathers, the city that you have chosen, and the house that I have built for your name, [49] then hear in heaven your dwelling place their prayer and their plea, and maintain their cause [50] and forgive your people who have sinned against you, and all their transgressions that they have committed against you, and grant them compassion in the sight of those who carried them captive, that they may have compassion on them [51] (for they are your people, and your heritage, which you brought out of Egypt, from the midst of the iron furnace). [52] Let your eyes be open to the plea of your servant and to the plea of your people Israel, giving ear to them whenever they call to you. [53] For you separated them from among all the peoples of the earth to be your heritage, as you declared through Moses your servant, when you brought our fathers out of Egypt, O Lord GOD."

Solomon's Benediction

[54] Now as Solomon finished offering all this prayer and plea to the LORD, he arose from before the altar of the LORD, where he had knelt with hands outstretched toward heaven. [55] And he stood and blessed all the assembly of Israel with a loud voice, saying, [56] "Blessed be the LORD who has given rest to his people Israel, according to all that he promised. Not one word has failed of all his good promise, which he spoke by Moses his servant. [57] The LORD our God be with us, as he was with our fathers. May he not leave us or forsake us, [58] that he may incline our hearts to him, to walk in all his ways and to keep his commandments, his statutes, and his rules, which he commanded our fathers. [59] Let these words of mine, with which I have pleaded before the LORD, be near to the LORD our God day and night, and may he maintain the cause of his servant and the cause of his people Israel, as each day requires, [60] that all the peoples of the earth may know that the LORD is God; there is no other. [61] Let your heart therefore be wholly true to the LORD our God, walking in his statutes and keeping his commandments, as at this day."

Solomon's Sacrifices

[62] Then the king, and all Israel with him, offered sacrifice before the LORD. [63] Solomon offered as peace offerings to the LORD 22,000 oxen and 120,000 sheep. So the king and all the people of Israel dedicated the house of the LORD. [64] The same day the king consecrated the middle of the court that was before the house of the LORD, for there he offered the burnt offering and the grain offering and the fat pieces of the peace offerings, because the bronze altar that was before the LORD was too small to receive the burnt offering and the grain offering and the fat pieces of the peace offerings.

[65] So Solomon held the feast at that time, and all Israel with him, a great assembly, from Lebo-hamath to the Brook of Egypt, before the LORD our God, seven days.[1] [66] On the eighth day he sent the people away, and they blessed the king and went to their homes joyful and glad of heart for all the goodness that the LORD

---

[1] Septuagint; Hebrew *seven days and seven days, fourteen days*

had shown to David his servant and to Israel his people.

The LORD Appears to Solomon

9 As soon as Solomon had finished building the house of the LORD and the king's house and all that Solomon desired to build, ² the LORD appeared to Solomon a second time, as he had appeared to him at Gibeon. ³ And the LORD said to him, "I have heard your prayer and your plea, which you have made before me. I have consecrated this house that you have built, by putting my name there forever. My eyes and my heart will be there for all time. ⁴ And as for you, if you will walk before me, as David your father walked, with integrity of heart and uprightness, doing according to all that I have commanded you, and keeping my statutes and my rules, ⁵ then I will establish your royal throne over Israel forever, as I promised David your father, saying, 'You shall not lack a man on the throne of Israel.' ⁶ But if you turn aside from following me, you or your children, and do not keep my commandments and my statutes that I have set before you, but go and serve other gods and worship them, ⁷ then I will cut off Israel from the land that I have given them, and the house that I have consecrated for my name I will cast out of my sight, and Israel will become a proverb and a byword among all peoples. ⁸ And this house will become a heap of ruins.[1] Everyone passing by it will be astonished and will hiss, and they will say, 'Why has the LORD done thus to this land and to this house?' ⁹ Then they will say, 'Because they abandoned the LORD their God who brought their fathers out of the land of Egypt and laid hold on other gods and worshiped them and served them. Therefore the LORD has brought all this disaster on them.'"

Solomon's Other Acts

¹⁰ At the end of twenty years, in which Solomon had built the two houses, the house of the LORD and the king's house, ¹¹ and Hiram king of Tyre had supplied Solomon with cedar and cypress timber and gold, as much as he desired, King Solomon gave to Hiram twenty cities in the land of Galilee. ¹² But when Hiram came from Tyre to see the cities that Solomon had given him, they did not please him. ¹³ Therefore he said, "What kind of cities are these that you have given me, my brother?" So they are called the land of Cabul to this

day. ¹⁴ Hiram had sent to the king 120 talents[2] of gold.

¹⁵ And this is the account of the forced labor that King Solomon drafted to build the house of the LORD and his own house and the Millo and the wall of Jerusalem and Hazor and Megiddo and Gezer ¹⁶ (Pharaoh king of Egypt had gone up and captured Gezer and burned it with fire, and had killed the Canaanites who lived in the city, and had given it as dowry to his daughter, Solomon's wife; ¹⁷ so Solomon rebuilt Gezer) and Lower Beth-horon ¹⁸ and Baalath and Tamar in the wilderness, in the land of Judah,[3] ¹⁹ and all the store cities that Solomon had, and the cities for his chariots, and the cities for his horsemen, and whatever Solomon desired to build in Jerusalem, in Lebanon, and in all the land of his dominion. ²⁰ All the people who were left of the Amorites, the Hittites, the Perizzites, the Hivites, and the Jebusites, who were not of the people of Israel— ²¹ their descendants who were left after them in the land, whom the people of Israel were unable to devote to destruction[4]—these Solomon drafted to be slaves, and so they are to this day. ²² But of the people of Israel Solomon made no slaves. They were the soldiers, they were his officials, his commanders, his captains, his chariot commanders and his horsemen.

²³ These were the chief officers who were over Solomon's work: 550 who had charge of the people who carried on the work.

²⁴ But Pharaoh's daughter went up from the city of David to her own house that Solomon had built for her. Then he built the Millo.

²⁵ Three times a year Solomon used to offer up burnt offerings and peace offerings on the altar that he built to the LORD, making offerings with it[5] before the LORD. So he finished the house.

²⁶ King Solomon built a fleet of ships at Ezion-geber, which is near Eloth on the shore of the Red Sea, in the land of Edom. ²⁷ And Hiram sent with the fleet his servants, seamen who were familiar with the sea, together with the servants of Solomon. ²⁸ And they went to Ophir and brought from there gold, 420 talents, and they brought it to King Solomon.

The Queen of Sheba

10 Now when the queen of Sheba heard of the fame of Solomon concerning the name of the LORD, she came to test him with

---

[1] Syriac, Old Latin; Hebrew *will become high* [2] A *talent* was about 75 pounds or 34 kilograms [3] Hebrew lacks *of Judah* [4] That is, set apart (devote) as an offering to the Lord (for destruction) [5] Septuagint lacks *with it*

hard questions. [2] She came to Jerusalem with a very great retinue, with camels bearing spices and very much gold and precious stones. And when she came to Solomon, she told him all that was on her mind. [3] And Solomon answered all her questions; there was nothing hidden from the king that he could not explain to her. [4] And when the queen of Sheba had seen all the wisdom of Solomon, the house that he had built, [5] the food of his table, the seating of his officials, and the attendance of his servants, their clothing, his cupbearers, and his burnt offerings that he offered at the house of the LORD, there was no more breath in her.

[6] And she said to the king, "The report was true that I heard in my own land of your words and of your wisdom, [7] but I did not believe the reports until I came and my own eyes had seen it. And behold, the half was not told me. Your wisdom and prosperity surpass the report that I heard. [8] Happy are your men! Happy are your servants, who continually stand before you and hear your wisdom! [9] Blessed be the LORD your God, who has delighted in you and set you on the throne of Israel! Because the LORD loved Israel forever, he has made you king, that you may execute justice and righteousness." [10] Then she gave the king 120 talents[1] of gold, and a very great quantity of spices and precious stones. Never again came such an abundance of spices as these that the queen of Sheba gave to King Solomon.

[11] Moreover, the fleet of Hiram, which brought gold from Ophir, brought from Ophir a very great amount of almug wood and precious stones. [12] And the king made of the almug wood supports for the house of the LORD and for the king's house, also lyres and harps for the singers. No such almug wood has come or been seen to this day.

[13] And King Solomon gave to the queen of Sheba all that she desired, whatever she asked besides what was given her by the bounty of King Solomon. So she turned and went back to her own land with her servants.

Solomon's Great Wealth

[14] Now the weight of gold that came to Solomon in one year was 666 talents of gold, [15] besides that which came from the explorers and from the business of the merchants, and from all the kings of the west and from the governors of the land. [16] King Solomon made 200 large shields of beaten gold; 600 shekels[2] of gold went into each shield. [17] And he made 300 shields of beaten gold; three minas[3] of gold went into each shield. And the king put them in the House of the Forest of Lebanon. [18] The king also made a great ivory throne and overlaid it with the finest gold. [19] The throne had six steps, and the throne had a round top,[4] and on each side of the seat were armrests and two lions standing beside the armrests, [20] while twelve lions stood there, one on each end of a step on the six steps. The like of it was never made in any kingdom. [21] All King Solomon's drinking vessels were of gold, and all the vessels of the House of the Forest of Lebanon were of pure gold. None were of silver; silver was not considered as anything in the days of Solomon. [22] For the king had a fleet of ships of Tarshish at sea with the fleet of Hiram. Once every three years the fleet of ships of Tarshish used to come bringing gold, silver, ivory, apes, and peacocks.[5]

[23] Thus King Solomon excelled all the kings of the earth in riches and in wisdom. [24] And the whole earth sought the presence of Solomon to hear his wisdom, which God had put into his mind. [25] Every one of them brought his present, articles of silver and gold, garments, myrrh,[6] spices, horses, and mules, so much year by year.

[26] And Solomon gathered together chariots and horsemen. He had 1,400 chariots and 12,000 horsemen, whom he stationed in the chariot cities and with the king in Jerusalem. [27] And the king made silver as common in Jerusalem as stone, and he made cedar as plentiful as the sycamore of the Shephelah. [28] And Solomon's import of horses was from Egypt and Kue, and the king's traders received them from Kue at a price. [29] A chariot could be imported from Egypt for 600 shekels of silver and a horse for 150, and so through the king's traders they were exported to all the kings of the Hittites and the kings of Syria.

Solomon Turns from the LORD

11 Now King Solomon loved many foreign women, along with the daughter of Pharaoh: Moabite, Ammonite, Edomite, Sidonian, and Hittite women, [2] from the nations concerning which the LORD had said to the people of Israel, "You shall not enter into marriage with them, neither shall they with you, for surely they will turn away your heart after their gods." Solomon clung to these

---

[1] A *talent* was about 75 pounds or 34 kilograms [2] A *shekel* was about 2/5 ounce or 11 grams [3] A *mina* was about 1 1/4 pounds or 0.6 kilogram [4] Or *and at the back of the throne was a calf's head* [5] Or *baboons* [6] Or *armor*

in love. [3] He had 700 wives, who were princesses, and 300 concubines. And his wives turned away his heart. [4] For when Solomon was old his wives turned away his heart after other gods, and his heart was not wholly true to the LORD his God, as was the heart of David his father. [5] For Solomon went after Ashtoreth the goddess of the Sidonians, and after Milcom the abomination of the Ammonites. [6] So Solomon did what was evil in the sight of the LORD and did not wholly follow the LORD, as David his father had done. [7] Then Solomon built a high place for Chemosh the abomination of Moab, and for Molech the abomination of the Ammonites, on the mountain east of Jerusalem. [8] And so he did for all his foreign wives, who made offerings and sacrificed to their gods.

The LORD Raises Adversaries

[9] And the LORD was angry with Solomon, because his heart had turned away from the LORD, the God of Israel, who had appeared to him twice [10] and had commanded him concerning this thing, that he should not go after other gods. But he did not keep what the LORD commanded. [11] Therefore the LORD said to Solomon, "Since this has been your practice and you have not kept my covenant and my statutes that I have commanded you, I will surely tear the kingdom from you and will give it to your servant. [12] Yet for the sake of David your father I will not do it in your days, but I will tear it out of the hand of your son. [13] However, I will not tear away all the kingdom, but I will give one tribe to your son, for the sake of David my servant and for the sake of Jerusalem that I have chosen."

[14] And the LORD raised up an adversary against Solomon, Hadad the Edomite. He was of the royal house in Edom. [15] For when David was in Edom, and Joab the commander of the army went up to bury the slain, he struck down every male in Edom [16] (for Joab and all Israel remained there six months, until he had cut off every male in Edom). [17] But Hadad fled to Egypt, together with certain Edomites of his father's servants, Hadad still being a little child. [18] They set out from Midian and came to Paran and took men with them from Paran and came to Egypt, to Pharaoh king of Egypt, who gave him a house and assigned him an allowance of food and gave him land. [19] And Hadad found great favor in the sight of Pharaoh, so that he gave him in marriage the sister of his own wife,

the sister of Tahpenes the queen. [20] And the sister of Tahpenes bore him Genubath his son, whom Tahpenes weaned in Pharaoh's house. And Genubath was in Pharaoh's house among the sons of Pharaoh. [21] But when Hadad heard in Egypt that David slept with his fathers and that Joab the commander of the army was dead, Hadad said to Pharaoh, "Let me depart, that I may go to my own country." [22] But Pharaoh said to him, "What have you lacked with me that you are now seeking to go to your own country?" And he said to him, "Only let me depart."

[23] God also raised up as an adversary to him, Rezon the son of Eliada, who had fled from his master Hadadezer king of Zobah. [24] And he gathered men about him and became leader of a marauding band, after the killing by David. And they went to Damascus and lived there and made him king in Damascus. [25] He was an adversary of Israel all the days of Solomon, doing harm as Hadad did. And he loathed Israel and reigned over Syria.

[26] Jeroboam the son of Nebat, an Ephraimite of Zeredah, a servant of Solomon, whose mother's name was Zeruah, a widow, also lifted up his hand against the king. [27] And this was the reason why he lifted up his hand against the king. Solomon built the Millo, and closed up the breach of the city of David his father. [28] The man Jeroboam was very able, and when Solomon saw that the young man was industrious he gave him charge over all the forced labor of the house of Joseph. [29] And at that time, when Jeroboam went out of Jerusalem, the prophet Ahijah the Shilonite found him on the road. Now Ahijah had dressed himself in a new garment, and the two of them were alone in the open country. [30] Then Ahijah laid hold of the new garment that was on him, and tore it into twelve pieces. [31] And he said to Jeroboam, "Take for yourself ten pieces, for thus says the LORD, the God of Israel, 'Behold, I am about to tear the kingdom from the hand of Solomon and will give you ten tribes [32] (but he shall have one tribe, for the sake of my servant David and for the sake of Jerusalem, the city that I have chosen out of all the tribes of Israel), [33] because they have[1] forsaken me and worshiped Ashtoreth the goddess of the Sidonians, Chemosh the god of Moab, and Milcom the god of the Ammonites, and they have not walked in my ways, doing what is right in my sight and keeping my statutes and my rules, as David his father did. [34] Nevertheless,

---

[1] Septuagint, Syriac, Vulgate *he has*; twice in this verse

I will not take the whole kingdom out of his hand, but I will make him ruler all the days of his life, for the sake of David my servant whom I chose, who kept my commandments and my statutes. ³⁵ But I will take the kingdom out of his son's hand and will give it to you, ten tribes. ³⁶ Yet to his son I will give one tribe, that David my servant may always have a lamp before me in Jerusalem, the city where I have chosen to put my name. ³⁷ And I will take you, and you shall reign over all that your soul desires, and you shall be king over Israel. ³⁸ And if you will listen to all that I command you, and will walk in my ways, and do what is right in my eyes by keeping my statutes and my commandments, as David my servant did, I will be with you and will build you a sure house, as I built for David, and I will give Israel to you. ³⁹ And I will afflict the offspring of David because of this, but not forever.'" ⁴⁰ Solomon sought therefore to kill Jeroboam. But Jeroboam arose and fled into Egypt, to Shishak king of Egypt, and was in Egypt until the death of Solomon.

⁴¹ Now the rest of the acts of Solomon, and all that he did, and his wisdom, are they not written in the Book of the Acts of Solomon? ⁴² And the time that Solomon reigned in Jerusalem over all Israel was forty years. ⁴³ And Solomon slept with his fathers and was buried in the city of David his father. And Rehoboam his son reigned in his place.

Rehoboam's Folly

12 Rehoboam went to Shechem, for all Israel had come to Shechem to make him king. ² And as soon as Jeroboam the son of Nebat heard of it (for he was still in Egypt, where he had fled from King Solomon), then Jeroboam returned from[1] Egypt. ³ And they sent and called him, and Jeroboam and all the assembly of Israel came and said to Rehoboam, ⁴ "Your father made our yoke heavy. Now therefore lighten the hard service of your father and his heavy yoke on us, and we will serve you." ⁵ He said to them, "Go away for three days, then come again to me." So the people went away.

⁶ Then King Rehoboam took counsel with the old men, who had stood before Solomon his father while he was yet alive, saying, "How do you advise me to answer this people?" ⁷ And they said to him, "If you will be a servant to this people today and serve them, and speak good words to them when you answer them, then they will be your servants forever." ⁸ But he abandoned the counsel that the old men gave him and took counsel with the young men who had grown up with him and stood before him. ⁹ And he said to them, "What do you advise that we answer this people who have said to me, 'Lighten the yoke that your father put on us'?" ¹⁰ And the young men who had grown up with him said to him, "Thus shall you speak to this people who said to you, 'Your father made our yoke heavy, but you lighten it for us,' thus shall you say to them, 'My little finger is thicker than my father's thighs. ¹¹ And now, whereas my father laid on you a heavy yoke, I will add to your yoke. My father disciplined you with whips, but I will discipline you with scorpions.'"

¹² So Jeroboam and all the people came to Rehoboam the third day, as the king said, "Come to me again the third day." ¹³ And the king answered the people harshly, and forsaking the counsel that the old men had given him, ¹⁴ he spoke to them according to the counsel of the young men, saying, "My father made your yoke heavy, but I will add to your yoke. My father disciplined you with whips, but I will discipline you with scorpions." ¹⁵ So the king did not listen to the people, for it was a turn of affairs brought about by the LORD that he might fulfill his word, which the LORD spoke by Ahijah the Shilonite to Jeroboam the son of Nebat.

The Kingdom Divided

¹⁶ And when all Israel saw that the king did not listen to them, the people answered the king, "What portion do we have in David? We have no inheritance in the son of Jesse. To your tents, O Israel! Look now to your own house, David." So Israel went to their tents. ¹⁷ But Rehoboam reigned over the people of Israel who lived in the cities of Judah. ¹⁸ Then King Rehoboam sent Adoram, who was taskmaster over the forced labor, and all Israel stoned him to death with stones. And King Rehoboam hurried to mount his chariot to flee to Jerusalem. ¹⁹ So Israel has been in rebellion against the

---

[1] Septuagint, Vulgate (compare 2 Chronicles 10:2); Hebrew *lived in*

house of David to this day. [20] And when all Israel heard that Jeroboam had returned, they sent and called him to the assembly and made him king over all Israel. There was none that followed the house of David but the tribe of Judah only.

[21] When Rehoboam came to Jerusalem, he assembled all the house of Judah and the tribe of Benjamin, 180,000 chosen warriors, to fight against the house of Israel, to restore the kingdom to Rehoboam the son of Solomon. [22] But the word of God came to Shemaiah the man of God: [23] "Say to Rehoboam the son of Solomon, king of Judah, and to all the house of Judah and Benjamin, and to the rest of the people, [24] 'Thus says the LORD, You shall not go up or fight against your relatives the people of Israel. Every man return to his home, for this thing is from me.'" So they listened to the word of the LORD and went home again, according to the word of the LORD.

Jeroboam's Golden Calves

[25] Then Jeroboam built Shechem in the hill country of Ephraim and lived there. And he went out from there and built Penuel. [26] And Jeroboam said in his heart, "Now the kingdom will turn back to the house of David. [27] If this people go up to offer sacrifices in the temple of the LORD at Jerusalem, then the heart of this people will turn again to their lord, to Rehoboam king of Judah, and they will kill me and return to Rehoboam king of Judah." [28] So the king took counsel and made two calves of gold. And he said to the people, "You have gone up to Jerusalem long enough. Behold your gods, O Israel, who brought you up out of the land of Egypt." [29] And he set one in Bethel, and the other he put in Dan. [30] Then this thing became a sin, for the people went as far as Dan to be before one.[1] [31] He also made temples on high places and appointed priests from among all the people, who were not of the Levites. [32] And Jeroboam appointed a feast on the fifteenth day of the eighth month like the feast that was in Judah, and he offered sacrifices on the altar. So he did in Bethel, sacrificing to the calves that he made. And he placed in Bethel the priests of the high places that he had made. [33] He went up to the altar that he had made in Bethel on the fifteenth day in the eighth month, in the month that he had devised from his own heart. And he instituted a feast for the people of Israel and went up to the altar to make offerings.

A Man of God Confronts Jeroboam

13 And behold, a man of God came out of Judah by the word of the LORD to Bethel. Jeroboam was standing by the altar to make offerings. [2] And the man cried against the altar by the word of the LORD and said, "O altar, altar, thus says the LORD: 'Behold, a son shall be born to the house of David, Josiah by name, and he shall sacrifice on you the priests of the high places who make offerings on you, and human bones shall be burned on you.'" [3] And he gave a sign the same day, saying, "This is the sign that the LORD has spoken: 'Behold, the altar shall be torn down, and the ashes that are on it shall be poured out.'" [4] And when the king heard the saying of the man of God, which he cried against the altar at Bethel, Jeroboam stretched out his hand from the altar, saying, "Seize him." And his hand, which he stretched out against him, dried up, so that he could not draw it back to himself. [5] The altar also was torn down, and the ashes poured out from the altar, according to the sign that the man of God had given by the word of the LORD. [6] And the king said to the man of God, "Entreat now the favor of the LORD your God, and pray for me, that my hand may be restored to me." And the man of God entreated the LORD, and the king's hand was restored to him and became as it was before. [7] And the king said to the man of God, "Come home with me, and refresh yourself, and I will give you a reward." [8] And the man of God said to the king, "If you give me half your house, I will not go in with you. And I will not eat bread or drink water in this place, [9] for so was it commanded me by the word of the LORD, saying, 'You shall neither eat bread nor drink water nor return by the way that you came.'" [10] So he went another way and did not return by the way that he came to Bethel.

The Prophet's Disobedience

[11] Now an old prophet lived in Bethel. And his sons[2] came and told him all that the man of God had done that day in Bethel. They also told to their father the words that he had spoken to the king. [12] And their father said to them, "Which way did he go?" And his sons showed him the way that the man of God who came from Judah had gone. [13] And he said to his sons, "Saddle the donkey for me." So they saddled the donkey for him and he mounted it. [14] And he went after the man of God and found him sit-

---

[1] Septuagint *went to the one at Bethel and to the other as far as Dan*   [2] Septuagint, Syriac, Vulgate; Hebrew *son*

ting under an oak. And he said to him, "Are you the man of God who came from Judah?" And he said, "I am." ¹⁵ Then he said to him, "Come home with me and eat bread." ¹⁶ And he said, "I may not return with you, or go in with you, neither will I eat bread nor drink water with you in this place, ¹⁷ for it was said to me by the word of the Lord, 'You shall neither eat bread nor drink water there, nor return by the way that you came.'" ¹⁸ And he said to him, "I also am a prophet as you are, and an angel spoke to me by the word of the Lord, saying, 'Bring him back with you into your house that he may eat bread and drink water.'" But he lied to him. ¹⁹ So he went back with him and ate bread in his house and drank water.

²⁰ And as they sat at the table, the word of the Lord came to the prophet who had brought him back. ²¹ And he cried to the man of God who came from Judah, "Thus says the Lord, 'Because you have disobeyed the word of the Lord and have not kept the command that the Lord your God commanded you, ²² but have come back and have eaten bread and drunk water in the place of which he said to you, "Eat no bread and drink no water," your body shall not come to the tomb of your fathers.'" ²³ And after he had eaten bread and drunk, he saddled the donkey for the prophet whom he had brought back. ²⁴ And as he went away a lion met him on the road and killed him. And his body was thrown in the road, and the donkey stood beside it; the lion also stood beside the body. ²⁵ And behold, men passed by and saw the body thrown in the road and the lion standing by the body. And they came and told it in the city where the old prophet lived.

²⁶ And when the prophet who had brought him back from the way heard of it, he said, "It is the man of God who disobeyed the word of the Lord; therefore the Lord has given him to the lion, which has torn him and killed him, according to the word that the Lord spoke to him." ²⁷ And he said to his sons, "Saddle the donkey for me." And they saddled it. ²⁸ And he went and found his body thrown in the road, and the donkey and the lion standing beside the body. The lion had not eaten the body or torn the donkey. ²⁹ And the prophet took up the body of the man of God and laid it on the donkey and brought it back to the city¹ to mourn and to bury him. ³⁰ And he laid the body in his own grave. And they mourned over him, saying,

"Alas, my brother!" ³¹ And after he had buried him, he said to his sons, "When I die, bury me in the grave in which the man of God is buried; lay my bones beside his bones. ³² For the saying that he called out by the word of the Lord against the altar in Bethel and against all the houses of the high places that are in the cities of Samaria shall surely come to pass."

³³ After this thing Jeroboam did not turn from his evil way, but made priests for the high places again from among all the people. Any who would, he ordained to be priests of the high places. ³⁴ And this thing became sin to the house of Jeroboam, so as to cut it off and to destroy it from the face of the earth.

Prophecy Against Jeroboam

14 At that time Abijah the son of Jeroboam fell sick. ² And Jeroboam said to his wife, "Arise, and disguise yourself, that it not be known that you are the wife of Jeroboam, and go to Shiloh. Behold, Ahijah the prophet is there, who said of me that I should be king over this people. ³ Take with you ten loaves, some cakes, and a jar of honey, and go to him. He will tell you what shall happen to the child."

⁴ Jeroboam's wife did so. She arose and went to Shiloh and came to the house of Ahijah. Now Ahijah could not see, for his eyes were dim because of his age. ⁵ And the Lord said to Ahijah, "Behold, the wife of Jeroboam is coming to inquire of you concerning her son, for he is sick. Thus and thus shall you say to her."

When she came, she pretended to be another woman. ⁶ But when Ahijah heard the sound of her feet, as she came in at the door, he said, "Come in, wife of Jeroboam. Why do you pretend to be another? For I am charged with unbearable news for you. ⁷ Go, tell Jeroboam, 'Thus says the Lord, the God of Israel: "Because I exalted you from among the people and made you leader over my people Israel ⁸ and tore the kingdom away from the house of David and gave it to you, and yet you have not been like my servant David, who kept my commandments and followed me with all his heart, doing only that which was right in my eyes, ⁹ but you have done evil above all who were before you and have gone and made for yourself other gods and metal images, provoking me to anger, and have cast me behind your back, ¹⁰ therefore behold, I will bring harm upon the house of Jeroboam and will cut off from Jeroboam every male,

¹ Septuagint; Hebrew *he came to the city of the old prophet*

both bond and free in Israel, and will burn up the house of Jeroboam, as a man burns up dung until it is all gone. [11] Anyone belonging to Jeroboam who dies in the city the dogs shall eat, and anyone who dies in the open country the birds of the heavens shall eat, for the LORD has spoken it.'' [12] Arise therefore, go to your house. When your feet enter the city, the child shall die. [13] And all Israel shall mourn for him and bury him, for he only of Jeroboam shall come to the grave, because in him there is found something pleasing to the LORD, the God of Israel, in the house of Jeroboam. [14] Moreover, the LORD will raise up for himself a king over Israel who shall cut off the house of Jeroboam today. And henceforth, [15] the LORD will strike Israel as a reed is shaken in the water, and root up Israel out of this good land that he gave to their fathers and scatter them beyond the Euphrates,[1] because they have made their Asherim, provoking the LORD to anger. [16] And he will give Israel up because of the sins of Jeroboam, which he sinned and made Israel to sin."

[17] Then Jeroboam's wife arose and departed and came to Tirzah. And as she came to the threshold of the house, the child died. [18] And all Israel buried him and mourned for him, according to the word of the LORD, which he spoke by his servant Ahijah the prophet.

The Death of Jeroboam

[19] Now the rest of the acts of Jeroboam, how he warred and how he reigned, behold, they are written in the Book of the Chronicles of the Kings of Israel. [20] And the time that Jeroboam reigned was twenty-two years. And he slept with his fathers, and Nadab his son reigned in his place.

Rehoboam Reigns in Judah

[21] Now Rehoboam the son of Solomon reigned in Judah. Rehoboam was forty-one years old when he began to reign, and he reigned seventeen years in Jerusalem, the city that the LORD had chosen out of all the tribes of Israel, to put his name there. His mother's name was Naamah the Ammonite. [22] And Judah did what was evil in the sight of the LORD, and they provoked him to jealousy with their sins that they committed, more than all that their fathers had done. [23] For they also built for themselves high places and pillars and Asherim on every high hill and under every green tree, [24] and there were

also male cult prostitutes in the land. They did according to all the abominations of the nations that the LORD drove out before the people of Israel.

[25] In the fifth year of King Rehoboam, Shishak king of Egypt came up against Jerusalem. [26] He took away the treasures of the house of the LORD and the treasures of the king's house. He took away everything. He also took away all the shields of gold that Solomon had made, [27] and King Rehoboam made in their place shields of bronze, and committed them to the hands of the officers of the guard, who kept the door of the king's house. [28] And as often as the king went into the house of the LORD, the guard carried them and brought them back to the guardroom.

[29] Now the rest of the acts of Rehoboam and all that he did, are they not written in the Book of the Chronicles of the Kings of Judah? [30] And there was war between Rehoboam and Jeroboam continually. [31] And Rehoboam slept with his fathers and was buried with his fathers in the city of David. His mother's name was Naamah the Ammonite. And Abijam his son reigned in his place.

Abijam Reigns in Judah

15 Now in the eighteenth year of King Jeroboam the son of Nebat, Abijam began to reign over Judah. [2] He reigned for three years in Jerusalem. His mother's name was Maacah the daughter of Abishalom. [3] And he walked in all the sins that his father did before him, and his heart was not wholly true to the LORD his God, as the heart of David his father. [4] Nevertheless, for David's sake the LORD his God gave him a lamp in Jerusalem, setting up his son after him, and establishing Jerusalem, [5] because David did what was right in the eyes of the LORD and did not turn aside from anything that he commanded him all the days of his life, except in the matter of Uriah the Hittite. [6] Now there was war between Rehoboam and Jeroboam all the days of his life. [7] The rest of the acts of Abijam and all that he did, are they not written in the Book of the Chronicles of the Kings of Judah? And there was war between Abijam and Jeroboam. [8] And Abijam slept with his fathers, and they buried him in the city of David. And Asa his son reigned in his place.

---

[1] Hebrew *the River*

Asa Reigns in Judah

⁹ In the twentieth year of Jeroboam king of Israel, Asa began to reign over Judah, ¹⁰ and he reigned forty-one years in Jerusalem. His mother's name was Maacah the daughter of Abishalom. ¹¹ And Asa did what was right in the eyes of the LORD, as David his father had done. ¹² He put away the male cult prostitutes out of the land and removed all the idols that his fathers had made. ¹³ He also removed Maacah his mother from being queen mother because she had made an abominable image for Asherah. And Asa cut down her image and burned it at the brook Kidron. ¹⁴ But the high places were not taken away. Nevertheless, the heart of Asa was wholly true to the LORD all his days. ¹⁵ And he brought into the house of the LORD the sacred gifts of his father and his own sacred gifts, silver, and gold, and vessels.

¹⁶ And there was war between Asa and Baasha king of Israel all their days. ¹⁷ Baasha king of Israel went up against Judah and built Ramah, that he might permit no one to go out or come in to Asa king of Judah. ¹⁸ Then Asa took all the silver and the gold that were left in the treasures of the house of the LORD and the treasures of the king's house and gave them into the hands of his servants. And King Asa sent them to Ben-hadad the son of Tabrimmon, the son of Hezion, king of Syria, who lived in Damascus, saying, ¹⁹ "Let there be a covenant¹ between me and you, as there was between my father and your father. Behold, I am sending to you a present of silver and gold. Go, break your covenant with Baasha king of Israel, that he may withdraw from me." ²⁰ And Ben-hadad listened to King Asa and sent the commanders of his armies against the cities of Israel and conquered Ijon, Dan, Abel-beth-maacah, and all Chinneroth, with all the land of Naphtali. ²¹ And when Baasha heard of it, he stopped building Ramah, and he lived in Tirzah. ²² Then King Asa made a proclamation to all Judah, none was exempt, and they carried away the stones of Ramah and its timber, with which Baasha had been building, and with them King Asa built Geba of Benjamin and Mizpah. ²³ Now the rest of all the acts of Asa, all his might, and all that he did, and the cities that he built, are they not written in the Book of the Chronicles of the Kings of Judah? But in his old age he was diseased in his feet. ²⁴ And Asa slept with his fathers and was buried with his fathers in the city of David his father, and Jehoshaphat his son reigned in his place.

Nadab Reigns in Israel

²⁵ Nadab the son of Jeroboam began to reign over Israel in the second year of Asa king of Judah, and he reigned over Israel two years. ²⁶ He did what was evil in the sight of the LORD and walked in the way of his father, and in his sin which he made Israel to sin.

²⁷ Baasha the son of Ahijah, of the house of Issachar, conspired against him. And Baasha struck him down at Gibbethon, which belonged to the Philistines, for Nadab and all Israel were laying siege to Gibbethon. ²⁸ So Baasha killed him in the third year of Asa king of Judah and reigned in his place. ²⁹ And as soon as he was king, he killed all the house of Jeroboam. He left to the house of Jeroboam not one that breathed, until he had destroyed it, according to the word of the LORD that he spoke by his servant Ahijah the Shilonite. ³⁰ It was for the sins of Jeroboam that he sinned and that he made Israel to sin, and because of the anger to which he provoked the LORD, the God of Israel.

³¹ Now the rest of the acts of Nadab and all that he did, are they not written in the Book of the Chronicles of the Kings of Israel? ³² And there was war between Asa and Baasha king of Israel all their days.

Baasha Reigns in Israel

³³ In the third year of Asa king of Judah, Baasha the son of Ahijah began to reign over all Israel at Tirzah, and he reigned twenty-four years. ³⁴ He did what was evil in the sight of the LORD and walked in the way of Jeroboam and in his sin which he made Israel to sin.

16 And the word of the LORD came to Jehu the son of Hanani against Baasha, saying, ² "Since I exalted you out of the dust and made you leader over my people Israel, and you have walked in the way of Jeroboam and have made my people Israel to sin, provoking me to anger with their sins, ³ behold, I will utterly sweep away Baasha and his house, and I will make your house like the house of Jeroboam the son of Nebat. ⁴ Anyone belonging to Baasha who dies in the city the dogs shall eat, and anyone of his who dies in the field the birds of the heavens shall eat."

⁵ Now the rest of the acts of Baasha and what he did, and his might, are they not written in the Book of the Chronicles of the Kings of

---

¹ Or treaty; twice in this verse

Israel? ⁶ And Baasha slept with his fathers and was buried at Tirzah, and Elah his son reigned in his place. ⁷ Moreover, the word of the LORD came by the prophet Jehu the son of Hanani against Baasha and his house, both because of all the evil that he did in the sight of the LORD, provoking him to anger with the work of his hands, in being like the house of Jeroboam, and also because he destroyed it.

Elah Reigns in Israel

⁸ In the twenty-sixth year of Asa king of Judah, Elah the son of Baasha began to reign over Israel in Tirzah, and he reigned two years. ⁹ But his servant Zimri, commander of half his chariots, conspired against him. When he was at Tirzah, drinking himself drunk in the house of Arza, who was over the household in Tirzah, ¹⁰ Zimri came in and struck him down and killed him, in the twenty-seventh year of Asa king of Judah, and reigned in his place.

¹¹ When he began to reign, as soon as he had seated himself on his throne, he struck down all the house of Baasha. He did not leave him a single male of his relatives or his friends. ¹² Thus Zimri destroyed all the house of Baasha, according to the word of the LORD, which he spoke against Baasha by Jehu the prophet, ¹³ for all the sins of Baasha and the sins of Elah his son, which they sinned and which they made Israel to sin, provoking the LORD God of Israel to anger with their idols. ¹⁴ Now the rest of the acts of Elah and all that he did, are they not written in the Book of the Chronicles of the Kings of Israel?

Zimri Reigns in Israel

¹⁵ In the twenty-seventh year of Asa king of Judah, Zimri reigned seven days in Tirzah. Now the troops were encamped against Gibbethon, which belonged to the Philistines, ¹⁶ and the troops who were encamped heard it said, "Zimri has conspired, and he has killed the king." Therefore all Israel made Omri, the commander of the army, king over Israel that day in the camp. ¹⁷ So Omri went up from Gibbethon, and all Israel with him, and they besieged Tirzah. ¹⁸ And when Zimri saw that the city was taken, he went into the citadel of the king's house and burned the king's house over him with fire and died, ¹⁹ because of his sins that he committed, doing evil in the sight of the LORD, walking in the way of Jeroboam, and for his sin which he committed, making Israel to sin. ²⁰ Now the rest of the acts of Zimri, and the conspiracy that he made, are they not written in the Book of the Chronicles of the Kings of Israel?

Omri Reigns in Israel

²¹ Then the people of Israel were divided into two parts. Half of the people followed Tibni the son of Ginath, to make him king, and half followed Omri. ²² But the people who followed Omri overcame the people who followed Tibni the son of Ginath. So Tibni died, and Omri became king. ²³ In the thirty-first year of Asa king of Judah, Omri began to reign over Israel, and he reigned for twelve years; six years he reigned in Tirzah. ²⁴ He bought the hill of Samaria from Shemer for two talents¹ of silver, and he fortified the hill and called the name of the city that he built Samaria, after the name of Shemer, the owner of the hill.

²⁵ Omri did what was evil in the sight of the LORD, and did more evil than all who were before him. ²⁶ For he walked in all the way of Jeroboam the son of Nebat, and in the sins that he made Israel to sin, provoking the LORD, the God of Israel, to anger by their idols. ²⁷ Now the rest of the acts of Omri that he did, and the might that he showed, are they not written in the Book of the Chronicles of the Kings of Israel? ²⁸ And Omri slept with his fathers and was buried in Samaria, and Ahab his son reigned in his place.

Ahab Reigns in Israel

²⁹ In the thirty-eighth year of Asa king of Judah, Ahab the son of Omri began to reign over Israel, and Ahab the son of Omri reigned over Israel in Samaria twenty-two years. ³⁰ And Ahab the son of Omri did evil in the sight of the LORD, more than all who were before him. ³¹ And as if it had been a light thing for him to walk in the sins of Jeroboam the son of Nebat, he took for his wife Jezebel the daughter of Ethbaal king of the Sidonians, and went and served Baal and worshiped him. ³² He erected an altar for Baal in the house of Baal, which he built in Samaria. ³³ And Ahab made an Asherah. Ahab did more to provoke the LORD, the God of Israel, to anger than all the kings of Israel who were before him. ³⁴ In his days Hiel of Bethel built Jericho. He laid its foundation at the cost of Abiram his firstborn, and set up its gates at the cost of his youngest son Segub, according to the word of the LORD, which he spoke by Joshua the son of Nun.

---

¹ A *talent* was about 75 pounds or 34 kilograms

Elijah Predicts a Drought

17 Now Elijah the Tishbite, of Tishbe[1] in Gilead, said to Ahab, "As the LORD, the God of Israel, lives, before whom I stand, there shall be neither dew nor rain these years, except by my word." [2] And the word of the LORD came to him: [3] "Depart from here and turn eastward and hide yourself by the brook Cherith, which is east of the Jordan. [4] You shall drink from the brook, and I have commanded the ravens to feed you there." [5] So he went and did according to the word of the LORD. He went and lived by the brook Cherith that is east of the Jordan. [6] And the ravens brought him bread and meat in the morning, and bread and meat in the evening, and he drank from the brook. [7] And after a while the brook dried up, because there was no rain in the land.

The Widow of Zarephath

[8] Then the word of the LORD came to him, [9] "Arise, go to Zarephath, which belongs to Sidon, and dwell there. Behold, I have commanded a widow there to feed you." [10] So he arose and went to Zarephath. And when he came to the gate of the city, behold, a widow was there gathering sticks. And he called to her and said, "Bring me a little water in a vessel, that I may drink." [11] And as she was going to bring it, he called to her and said, "Bring me a morsel of bread in your hand." [12] And she said, "As the LORD your God lives, I have nothing baked, only a handful of flour in a jar and a little oil in a jug. And now I am gathering a couple of sticks that I may go in and prepare it for myself and my son, that we may eat it and die." [13] And Elijah said to her, "Do not fear; go and do as you have said. But first make me a little cake of it and bring it to me, and afterward make something for yourself and your son. [14] For thus says the LORD, the God of Israel, 'The jar of flour shall not be spent, and the jug of oil shall not be empty, until the day that the LORD sends rain upon the earth.'" [15] And she went and did as Elijah said. And she and he and her household ate for many days. [16] The jar of flour was not spent, neither did the jug of oil become empty, according to the word of the LORD that he spoke by Elijah.

Elijah Raises the Widow's Son

[17] After this the son of the woman, the mistress of the house, became ill. And his illness was so severe that there was no breath left in him. [18] And she said to Elijah, "What have you against me, O man of God? You have come to me to bring my sin to remembrance and to cause the death of my son!" [19] And he said to her, "Give me your son." And he took him from her arms and carried him up into the upper chamber where he lodged, and laid him on his own bed. [20] And he cried to the LORD, "O LORD my God, have you brought calamity even upon the widow with whom I sojourn, by killing her son?" [21] Then he stretched himself upon the child three times and cried to the LORD, "O LORD my God, let this child's life[2] come into him again." [22] And the LORD listened to the voice of Elijah. And the life of the child came into him again, and he revived. [23] And Elijah took the child and brought him down from the upper chamber into the house and delivered him to his mother. And Elijah said, "See, your son lives." [24] And the woman said to Elijah, "Now I know that you are a man of God, and that the word of the LORD in your mouth is truth."

Elijah Confronts Ahab

18 After many days the word of the LORD came to Elijah, in the third year, saying, "Go, show yourself to Ahab, and I will send rain upon the earth." [2] So Elijah went to show himself to Ahab. Now the famine was severe in Samaria. [3] And Ahab called Obadiah, who was over the household. (Now Obadiah feared the LORD greatly, [4] and when Jezebel cut off the prophets of the LORD, Obadiah took a hundred prophets and hid them by fifties in a cave and fed them with bread and water.) [5] And Ahab said to Obadiah, "Go through the land to all the springs of water and to all the valleys. Perhaps we may find grass and save the horses and mules alive, and not lose some of the animals." [6] So they divided the land between them to pass through it. Ahab went in one direction by himself, and Obadiah went in another direction by himself.

[7] And as Obadiah was on the way, behold, Elijah met him. And Obadiah recognized him and fell on his face and said, "Is it you, my lord Elijah?" [8] And he answered him, "It is I. Go, tell your lord, 'Behold, Elijah is here.'" [9] And he said, "How have I sinned, that you would give your servant into the hand of Ahab, to kill me? [10] As the LORD your God lives, there is no nation or kingdom where my lord has not sent to

---

[1] Septuagint; Hebrew *of the settlers* [2] Or *soul*; also verse 22

seek you. And when they would say, 'He is not here,' he would take an oath of the kingdom or nation, that they had not found you. ¹¹And now you say, 'Go, tell your lord, "Behold, Elijah is here."' ¹²And as soon as I have gone from you, the Spirit of the LORD will carry you I know not where. And so, when I come and tell Ahab and he cannot find you, he will kill me, although I your servant have feared the LORD from my youth. ¹³Has it not been told my lord what I did when Jezebel killed the prophets of the LORD, how I hid a hundred men of the LORD's prophets by fifties in a cave and fed them with bread and water? ¹⁴And now you say, 'Go, tell your lord, "Behold, Elijah is here"'; and he will kill me." ¹⁵And Elijah said, "As the LORD of hosts lives, before whom I stand, I will surely show myself to him today." ¹⁶So Obadiah went to meet Ahab, and told him. And Ahab went to meet Elijah.

¹⁷When Ahab saw Elijah, Ahab said to him, "Is it you, you troubler of Israel?" ¹⁸And he answered, "I have not troubled Israel, but you have, and your father's house, because you have abandoned the commandments of the LORD and followed the Baals. ¹⁹Now therefore send and gather all Israel to me at Mount Carmel, and the 450 prophets of Baal and the 400 prophets of Asherah, who eat at Jezebel's table."

The Prophets of Baal Defeated

²⁰So Ahab sent to all the people of Israel and gathered the prophets together at Mount Carmel. ²¹And Elijah came near to all the people and said, "How long will you go limping between two different opinions? If the LORD is God, follow him; but if Baal, then follow him." And the people did not answer him a word. ²²Then Elijah said to the people, "I, even I only, am left a prophet of the LORD, but Baal's prophets are 450 men. ²³Let two bulls be given to us, and let them choose one bull for themselves and cut it in pieces and lay it on the wood, but put no fire to it. And I will prepare the other bull and lay it on the wood and put no fire to it. ²⁴And you call upon the name of your god, and I will call upon the name of the LORD, and the God who answers by fire, he is God." And all the people answered, "It is well spoken." ²⁵Then Elijah said to the prophets of Baal, "Choose for yourselves one bull and prepare it first, for you are many, and call upon the name of your god, but put no fire to it." ²⁶And they took the bull that was given

them, and they prepared it and called upon the name of Baal from morning until noon, saying, "O Baal, answer us!" But there was no voice, and no one answered. And they limped around the altar that they had made. ²⁷And at noon Elijah mocked them, saying, "Cry aloud, for he is a god. Either he is musing, or he is relieving himself, or he is on a journey, or perhaps he is asleep and must be awakened." ²⁸And they cried aloud and cut themselves after their custom with swords and lances, until the blood gushed out upon them. ²⁹And as midday passed, they raved on until the time of the offering of the oblation, but there was no voice. No one answered; no one paid attention.

³⁰Then Elijah said to all the people, "Come near to me." And all the people came near to him. And he repaired the altar of the LORD that had been thrown down. ³¹Elijah took twelve stones, according to the number of the tribes of the sons of Jacob, to whom the word of the LORD came, saying, "Israel shall be your name," ³²and with the stones he built an altar in the name of the LORD. And he made a trench about the altar, as great as would contain two seahs¹ of seed. ³³And he put the wood in order and cut the bull in pieces and laid it on the wood. And he said, "Fill four jars with water and pour it on the burnt offering and on the wood." ³⁴And he said, "Do it a second time." And they did it a second time. And he said, "Do it a third time." And they did it a third time. ³⁵And the water ran around the altar and filled the trench also with water.

³⁶And at the time of the offering of the oblation, Elijah the prophet came near and said, "O LORD, God of Abraham, Isaac, and Israel, let it be known this day that you are God in Israel, and that I am your servant, and that I have done all these things at your word. ³⁷Answer me, O LORD, answer me, that this people may know that you, O LORD, are God, and that you have turned their hearts back." ³⁸Then the fire of the LORD fell and consumed the burnt offering and the wood and the stones and the dust, and licked up the water that was in the trench. ³⁹And when all the people saw it, they fell on their faces and said, "The LORD, he is God; the LORD, he is God." ⁴⁰And Elijah said to them, "Seize the prophets of Baal; let not one of them escape." And they seized them. And Elijah brought them down to the brook Kishon and slaughtered them there.

---

¹ A *seah* was about 7 quarts or 7.3 liters

The LORD Sends Rain

41 And Elijah said to Ahab, "Go up, eat and drink, for there is a sound of the rushing of rain." **42** So Ahab went up to eat and to drink. And Elijah went up to the top of Mount Carmel. And he bowed himself down on the earth and put his face between his knees. **43** And he said to his servant, "Go up now, look toward the sea." And he went up and looked and said, "There is nothing." And he said, "Go again," seven times. **44** And at the seventh time he said, "Behold, a little cloud like a man's hand is rising from the sea." And he said, "Go up, say to Ahab, 'Prepare your chariot and go down, lest the rain stop you.'" **45** And in a little while the heavens grew black with clouds and wind, and there was a great rain. And Ahab rode and went to Jezreel. **46** And the hand of the LORD was on Elijah, and he gathered up his garment and ran before Ahab to the entrance of Jezreel.

Elijah Flees Jezebel

19 Ahab told Jezebel all that Elijah had done, and how he had killed all the prophets with the sword. **2** Then Jezebel sent a messenger to Elijah, saying, "So may the gods do to me and more also, if I do not make your life as the life of one of them by this time tomorrow." **3** Then he was afraid, and he arose and ran for his life and came to Beersheba, which belongs to Judah, and left his servant there.

4 But he himself went a day's journey into the wilderness and came and sat down under a broom tree. And he asked that he might die, saying, "It is enough; now, O LORD, take away my life, for I am no better than my fathers." **5** And he lay down and slept under a broom tree. And behold, an angel touched him and said to him, "Arise and eat." **6** And he looked, and behold, there was at his head a cake baked on hot stones and a jar of water. And he ate and drank and lay down again. **7** And the angel of the LORD came again a second time and touched him and said, "Arise and eat, for the journey is too great for you." **8** And he arose and ate and drank, and went in the strength of that food forty days and forty nights to Horeb, the mount of God.

The LORD Speaks to Elijah

9 There he came to a cave and lodged in it. And behold, the word of the LORD came to him, and he said to him, "What are you doing here, Elijah?" **10** He said, "I have been very jealous for the LORD, the God of hosts. For the people of Israel have forsaken your covenant, thrown down your altars, and killed your prophets with the sword, and I, even I only, am left, and they seek my life, to take it away." **11** And he said, "Go out and stand on the mount before the LORD." And behold, the LORD passed by, and a great and strong wind tore the mountains and broke in pieces the rocks before the LORD, but the LORD was not in the wind. And after the wind an earthquake, but the LORD was not in the earthquake. **12** And after the earthquake a fire, but the LORD was not in the fire. And after the fire the sound of a low whisper.[1] **13** And when Elijah heard it, he wrapped his face in his cloak and went out and stood at the entrance of the cave. And behold, there came a voice to him and said, "What are you doing here, Elijah?" **14** He said, "I have been very jealous for the LORD, the God of hosts. For the people of Israel have forsaken your covenant, thrown down your altars, and killed your prophets with the sword, and I, even I only, am left, and they seek my life, to take it away." **15** And the LORD said to him, "Go, return on your way to the wilderness of Damascus. And when you arrive, you shall anoint Hazael to be king over Syria. **16** And Jehu the son of Nimshi you shall anoint to be king over Israel, and Elisha the son of Shaphat of Abel-meholah you shall anoint to be prophet in your place. **17** And the one who escapes from the sword of Hazael shall Jehu put to death, and the one who escapes from the sword of Jehu shall Elisha put to death. **18** Yet I will leave seven thousand in Israel, all the knees that have not bowed to Baal, and every mouth that has not kissed him."

The Call of Elisha

19 So he departed from there and found Elisha the son of Shaphat, who was plowing with twelve yoke of oxen in front of him, and he was with the twelfth. Elijah passed by him and cast his cloak upon him. **20** And he left the oxen and ran after Elijah and said, "Let me kiss my father and my mother, and then I will follow you." And he said to him, "Go back again, for what have I done to you?" **21** And he returned from following him and took the yoke of oxen and sacrificed them and boiled their flesh with the yokes of the oxen and gave it to the people, and they ate. Then he arose and went after Elijah and assisted him.

---

[1] Or a sound, a thin silence

Ahab's Wars with Syria

20 Ben-hadad the king of Syria gathered all his army together. Thirty-two kings were with him, and horses and chariots. And he went up and closed in on Samaria and fought against it. ² And he sent messengers into the city to Ahab king of Israel and said to him, "Thus says Ben-hadad: ³ 'Your silver and your gold are mine; your best wives and children also are mine.'" ⁴ And the king of Israel answered, "As you say, my lord, O king, I am yours, and all that I have." ⁵ The messengers came again and said, "Thus says Ben-hadad: 'I sent to you, saying, "Deliver to me your silver and your gold, your wives and your children." ⁶ Nevertheless I will send my servants to you tomorrow about this time, and they shall search your house and the houses of your servants and lay hands on whatever pleases you and take it away.'"

⁷ Then the king of Israel called all the elders of the land and said, "Mark, now, and see how this man is seeking trouble, for he sent to me for my wives and my children, and for my silver and my gold, and I did not refuse him." ⁸ And all the elders and all the people said to him, "Do not listen or consent." ⁹ So he said to the messengers of Ben-hadad, "Tell my lord the king, 'All that you first demanded of your servant I will do, but this thing I cannot do.'" And the messengers departed and brought him word again. ¹⁰ Ben-hadad sent to him and said, "The gods do so to me and more also, if the dust of Samaria shall suffice for handfuls for all the people who follow me." ¹¹ And the king of Israel answered, "Tell him, 'Let not him who straps on his armor boast himself as he who takes it off.'" ¹² When Ben-hadad heard this message as he was drinking with the kings in the booths, he said to his men, "Take your positions." And they took their positions against the city.

Ahab Defeats Ben-hadad

¹³ And behold, a prophet came near to Ahab king of Israel and said, "Thus says the LORD, Have you seen all this great multitude? Behold, I will give it into your hand this day, and you shall know that I am the LORD." ¹⁴ And Ahab said, "By whom?" He said, "Thus says the LORD, By the servants of the governors of the districts." Then he said, "Who shall begin the battle?" He answered, "You." ¹⁵ Then he mustered the servants of the governors of the districts, and they were 232. And after them he mustered all the people of Israel, seven thousand.

¹⁶ And they went out at noon, while Ben-hadad was drinking himself drunk in the booths, he and the thirty-two kings who helped him. ¹⁷ The servants of the governors of the districts went out first. And Ben-hadad sent out scouts, and they reported to him, "Men are coming out from Samaria." ¹⁸ He said, "If they have come out for peace, take them alive. Or if they have come out for war, take them alive."

¹⁹ So these went out of the city, the servants of the governors of the districts and the army that followed them. ²⁰ And each struck down his man. The Syrians fled, and Israel pursued them, but Ben-hadad king of Syria escaped on a horse with horsemen. ²¹ And the king of Israel went out and struck the horses and chariots, and struck the Syrians with a great blow.

²² Then the prophet came near to the king of Israel and said to him, "Come, strengthen yourself, and consider well what you have to do, for in the spring the king of Syria will come up against you."

²³ And the servants of the king of Syria said to him, "Their gods are gods of the hills, and so they were stronger than we. But let us fight against them in the plain, and surely we shall be stronger than they. ²⁴ And do this: remove the kings, each from his post, and put commanders in their places, ²⁵ and muster an army like the army that you have lost, horse for horse, and chariot for chariot. Then we will fight against them in the plain, and surely we shall be stronger than they." And he listened to their voice and did so.

Ahab Defeats Ben-hadad Again

²⁶ In the spring, Ben-hadad mustered the Syrians and went up to Aphek to fight against Israel. ²⁷ And the people of Israel were mustered and were provisioned and went against them. The people of Israel encamped before them like two little flocks of goats, but the Syrians filled the country. ²⁸ And a man of God came near and said to the king of Israel, "Thus says the LORD, 'Because the Syrians have said, "The LORD is a god of the hills but he is not a god of the valleys," therefore I will give all this great multitude into your hand, and you shall know that I

am the LORD.'" ²⁹ And they encamped opposite one another seven days. Then on the seventh day the battle was joined. And the people of Israel struck down of the Syrians 100,000 foot soldiers in one day. ³⁰ And the rest fled into the city of Aphek, and the wall fell upon 27,000 men who were left.

Ben-hadad also fled and entered an inner chamber in the city. ³¹ And his servants said to him, "Behold now, we have heard that the kings of the house of Israel are merciful kings. Let us put sackcloth around our waists and ropes on our heads and go out to the king of Israel. Perhaps he will spare your life." ³² So they tied sackcloth around their waists and put ropes on their heads and went to the king of Israel and said, "Your servant Ben-hadad says, 'Please, let me live.'" And he said, "Does he still live? He is my brother." ³³ Now the men were watching for a sign, and they quickly took it up from him and said, "Yes, your brother Ben-hadad." Then he said, "Go and bring him." Then Ben-hadad came out to him, and he caused him to come up into the chariot. ³⁴ And Ben-hadad said to him, "The cities that my father took from your father I will restore, and you may establish bazaars for yourself in Damascus, as my father did in Samaria." And Ahab said, "I will let you go on these terms." So he made a covenant with him and let him go.

A Prophet Condemns Ben-hadad's Release

³⁵ And a certain man of the sons of the prophets said to his fellow at the command of the LORD, "Strike me, please." But the man refused to strike him. ³⁶ Then he said to him, "Because you have not obeyed the voice of the LORD, behold, as soon as you have gone from me, a lion shall strike you down." And as soon as he had departed from him, a lion met him and struck him down. ³⁷ Then he found another man and said, "Strike me, please." And the man struck him—struck him and wounded him. ³⁸ So the prophet departed and waited for the king by the way, disguising himself with a bandage over his eyes. ³⁹ And as the king passed, he cried to the king and said, "Your servant went out into the midst of the battle, and behold, a soldier turned and brought a man to me and said, 'Guard this man; if by any means he is missing, your life shall be for his life, or else you shall pay a tal-

ent¹ of silver.' ⁴⁰ And as your servant was busy here and there, he was gone." The king of Israel said to him, "So shall your judgment be; you yourself have decided it." ⁴¹ Then he hurried to take the bandage away from his eyes, and the king of Israel recognized him as one of the prophets. ⁴² And he said to him, "Thus says the LORD, 'Because you have let go out of your hand the man whom I had devoted to destruction,² therefore your life shall be for his life, and your people for his people.'" ⁴³ And the king of Israel went to his house vexed and sullen and came to Samaria.

Naboth's Vineyard

21 Now Naboth the Jezreelite had a vineyard in Jezreel, beside the palace of Ahab king of Samaria. ² And after this Ahab said to Naboth, "Give me your vineyard, that I may have it for a vegetable garden, because it is near my house, and I will give you a better vineyard for it; or, if it seems good to you, I will give you its value in money." ³ But Naboth said to Ahab, "The LORD forbid that I should give you the inheritance of my fathers." ⁴ And Ahab went into his house vexed and sullen because of what Naboth the Jezreelite had said to him, for he had said, "I will not give you the inheritance of my fathers." And he lay down on his bed and turned away his face and would eat no food.

⁵ But Jezebel his wife came to him and said to him, "Why is your spirit so vexed that you eat no food?" ⁶ And he said to her, "Because I spoke to Naboth the Jezreelite and said to him, 'Give me your vineyard for money, or else, if it please you, I will give you another vineyard for it.' And he answered, 'I will not give you my vineyard.'" ⁷ And Jezebel his wife said to him, "Do you now govern Israel? Arise and eat bread and let your heart be cheerful; I will give you the vineyard of Naboth the Jezreelite."

⁸ So she wrote letters in Ahab's name and sealed them with his seal, and she sent the letters to the elders and the leaders who lived with Naboth in his city. ⁹ And she wrote in the letters, "Proclaim a fast, and set Naboth at the head of the people. ¹⁰ And set two worthless men opposite him, and let them bring a charge against him, saying, 'You have cursed³ God and the king.' Then take him out and stone him to death." ¹¹ And the men of his city, the elders and the leaders who lived in his city, did as Jezebel had sent word to them. As it was written in

the letters that she had sent to them, [12] they proclaimed a fast and set Naboth at the head of the people. [13] And the two worthless men came in and sat opposite him. And the worthless men brought a charge against Naboth in the presence of the people, saying, "Naboth cursed God and the king." So they took him outside the city and stoned him to death with stones. [14] Then they sent to Jezebel, saying, "Naboth has been stoned; he is dead."

[15] As soon as Jezebel heard that Naboth had been stoned and was dead, Jezebel said to Ahab, "Arise, take possession of the vineyard of Naboth the Jezreelite, which he refused to give you for money, for Naboth is not alive, but dead." [16] And as soon as Ahab heard that Naboth was dead, Ahab arose to go down to the vineyard of Naboth the Jezreelite, to take possession of it.

The LORD Condemns Ahab

[17] Then the word of the LORD came to Elijah the Tishbite, saying, [18] "Arise, go down to meet Ahab king of Israel, who is in Samaria; behold, he is in the vineyard of Naboth, where he has gone to take possession. [19] And you shall say to him, 'Thus says the LORD, "Have you killed and also taken possession?" ' And you shall say to him, 'Thus says the LORD: "In the place where dogs licked up the blood of Naboth shall dogs lick your own blood." ' "

[20] Ahab said to Elijah, "Have you found me, O my enemy?" He answered, "I have found you, because you have sold yourself to do what is evil in the sight of the LORD. [21] Behold, I will bring disaster upon you. I will utterly burn you up, and will cut off from Ahab every male, bond or free, in Israel. [22] And I will make your house like the house of Jeroboam the son of Nebat, and like the house of Baasha the son of Ahijah, for the anger to which you have provoked me, and because you have made Israel to sin. [23] And of Jezebel the LORD also said, 'The dogs shall eat Jezebel within the walls of Jezreel.' [24] Anyone belonging to Ahab who dies in the city the dogs shall eat, and anyone of his who dies in the open country the birds of the heavens shall eat."

Ahab's Repentance

[25] (There was none who sold himself to do what was evil in the sight of the LORD like Ahab, whom Jezebel his wife incited. [26] He acted very abominably in going after idols, as the Amorites had done, whom the LORD cast out before the people of Israel.)

[27] And when Ahab heard those words, he tore his clothes and put sackcloth on his flesh and fasted and lay in sackcloth and went about dejectedly. [28] And the word of the LORD came to Elijah the Tishbite, saying, [29] "Have you seen how Ahab has humbled himself before me? Because he has humbled himself before me, I will not bring the disaster in his days; but in his son's days I will bring the disaster upon his house."

Ahab and the False Prophets

22 For three years Syria and Israel continued without war. [2] But in the third year Jehoshaphat the king of Judah came down to the king of Israel. [3] And the king of Israel said to his servants, "Do you know that Ramoth-gilead belongs to us, and we keep quiet and do not take it out of the hand of the king of Syria?" [4] And he said to Jehoshaphat, "Will you go with me to battle at Ramoth-gilead?" And Jehoshaphat said to the king of Israel, "I am as you are, my people as your people, my horses as your horses."

[5] And Jehoshaphat said to the king of Israel, "Inquire first for the word of the LORD." [6] Then the king of Israel gathered the prophets together, about four hundred men, and said to them, "Shall I go to battle against Ramoth-gilead, or shall I refrain?" And they said, "Go up, for the Lord will give it into the hand of the king." [7] But Jehoshaphat said, "Is there not here another prophet of the LORD of whom we may inquire?" [8] And the king of Israel said to Jehoshaphat, "There is yet one man by whom we may inquire of the LORD, Micaiah the son of Imlah, but I hate him, for he never prophesies good concerning me, but evil." And Jehoshaphat said, "Let not the king say so." [9] Then the king of Israel summoned an officer and said, "Bring quickly Micaiah the son of Imlah." [10] Now the king of Israel and Jehoshaphat the king of Judah were sitting on their thrones, arrayed in their robes, at the threshing floor at the entrance of the gate of Samaria, and all the prophets were prophesying before them. [11] And Zedekiah the son of Chenaanah made for himself horns of iron and said, "Thus says the LORD, 'With these you shall push the Syrians until they are destroyed.'" [12] And all the prophets prophesied so and said,

upon his own head. [5] He heard the sound of the trumpet and did not take warning; his blood shall be upon himself. But if he had taken warning, he would have saved his life. [6] But if the watchman sees the sword coming and does not blow the trumpet, so that the people are not warned, and the sword comes and takes any one of them, that person is taken away in his iniquity, but his blood I will require at the watchman's hand.

[7] "So you, son of man, I have made a watchman for the house of Israel. Whenever you hear a word from my mouth, you shall give them warning from me. [8] If I say to the wicked, O wicked one, you shall surely die, and you do not speak to warn the wicked to turn from his way, that wicked person shall die in his iniquity, but his blood I will require at your hand. [9] But if you warn the wicked to turn from his way, and he does not turn from his way, that person shall die in his iniquity, but you will have delivered your soul.

Why Will You Die, Israel?

[10] "And you, son of man, say to the house of Israel, Thus have you said: 'Surely our transgressions and our sins are upon us, and we rot away because of them. How then can we live?' [11] Say to them, As I live, declares the Lord GOD, I have no pleasure in the death of the wicked, but that the wicked turn from his way and live; turn back, turn back from your evil ways, for why will you die, O house of Israel?

[12] "And you, son of man, say to your people, The righteousness of the righteous shall not deliver him when he transgresses, and as for the wickedness of the wicked, he shall not fall by it when he turns from his wickedness, and the righteous shall not be able to live by his righteousness[1] when he sins. [13] Though I say to the righteous that he shall surely live, yet if he trusts in his righteousness and does injustice, none of his righteous deeds shall be remembered, but in his injustice that he has done he shall die. [14] Again, though I say to the wicked, 'You shall surely die,' yet if he turns from his sin and does what is just and right, [15] if the wicked restores the pledge, gives back what he has taken by robbery, and walks in the statutes of life, not doing injustice, he shall surely live; he shall not die. [16] None of the sins that he has committed shall be remembered against him.

He has done what is just and right; he shall surely live.

[17] "Yet your people say, 'The way of the Lord is not just,' when it is their own way that is not just. [18] When the righteous turns from his righteousness and does injustice, he shall die for it. [19] And when the wicked turns from his wickedness and does what is just and right, he shall live by this. [20] Yet you say, 'The way of the Lord is not just.' O house of Israel, I will judge each of you according to his ways."

Jerusalem Struck Down

[21] In the twelfth year of our exile, in the tenth month, on the fifth day of the month, a fugitive from Jerusalem came to me and said, "The city has been struck down." [22] Now the hand of the LORD had been upon me the evening before the fugitive came; and he had opened my mouth by the time the man came to me in the morning, so my mouth was opened, and I was no longer mute.

[23] The word of the LORD came to me: [24] "Son of man, the inhabitants of these waste places in the land of Israel keep saying, 'Abraham was only one man, yet he got possession of the land; but we are many; the land is surely given us to possess.' [25] Therefore say to them, Thus says the Lord GOD: You eat flesh with the blood and lift up your eyes to your idols and shed blood; shall you then possess the land? [26] You rely on the sword, you commit abominations, and each of you defiles his neighbor's wife; shall you then possess the land? [27] Say this to them, Thus says the Lord GOD: As I live, surely those who are in the waste places shall fall by the sword, and whoever is in the open field I will give to the beasts to be devoured, and those who are in strongholds and in caves shall die by pestilence. [28] And I will make the land a desolation and a waste, and her proud might shall come to an end, and the mountains of Israel shall be so desolate that none will pass through. [29] Then they will know that I am the LORD, when I have made the land a desolation and a waste because of all their abominations that they have committed.

[30] "As for you, son of man, your people who talk together about you by the walls and at the doors of the houses, say to one another, each to his brother, 'Come, and hear what the word is that comes from the LORD.' [31] And they come to you as people come, and they sit before you as my people, and they hear what you say but

---

[1] Hebrew by it

they will not do it; for with lustful talk in their mouths they act; their heart is set on their gain. [32] And behold, you are to them like one who sings lustful songs with a beautiful voice and plays[1] well on an instrument, for they hear what you say, but they will not do it. [33] When this comes—and come it will!—then they will know that a prophet has been among them."

Prophecy Against the Shepherds of Israel

34 The word of the LORD came to me: [2] "Son of man, prophesy against the shepherds of Israel; prophesy, and say to them, even to the shepherds, Thus says the Lord GOD: Ah, shepherds of Israel who have been feeding yourselves! Should not shepherds feed the sheep? [3] You eat the fat, you clothe yourselves with the wool, you slaughter the fat ones, but you do not feed the sheep. [4] The weak you have not strengthened, the sick you have not healed, the injured you have not bound up, the strayed you have not brought back, the lost you have not sought, and with force and harshness you have ruled them. [5] So they were scattered, because there was no shepherd, and they became food for all the wild beasts. My sheep were scattered; [6] they wandered over all the mountains and on every high hill. My sheep were scattered over all the face of the earth, with none to search or seek for them.

[7] "Therefore, you shepherds, hear the word of the LORD: [8] As I live, declares the Lord GOD, surely because my sheep have become a prey, and my sheep have become food for all the wild beasts, since there was no shepherd, and because my shepherds have not searched for my sheep, but the shepherds have fed themselves, and have not fed my sheep, [9] therefore, you shepherds, hear the word of the LORD: [10] Thus says the Lord GOD, Behold, I am against the shepherds, and I will require my sheep at their hand and put a stop to their feeding the sheep. No longer shall the shepherds feed themselves. I will rescue my sheep from their mouths, that they may not be food for them.

The Lord GOD Will Seek Them Out

[11] "For thus says the Lord GOD: Behold, I, I myself will search for my sheep and will seek them out. [12] As a shepherd seeks out his flock when he is among his sheep that have been scattered, so will I seek out my sheep, and I will rescue them from all places where they have been scattered on a day of clouds and thick

darkness. [13] And I will bring them out from the peoples and gather them from the countries, and will bring them into their own land. And I will feed them on the mountains of Israel, by the ravines, and in all the inhabited places of the country. [14] I will feed them with good pasture, and on the mountain heights of Israel shall be their grazing land. There they shall lie down in good grazing land, and on rich pasture they shall feed on the mountains of Israel. [15] I myself will be the shepherd of my sheep, and I myself will make them lie down, declares the Lord GOD. [16] I will seek the lost, and I will bring back the strayed, and I will bind up the injured, and I will strengthen the weak, and the fat and the strong I will destroy.[2] I will feed them in justice.

[17] "As for you, my flock, thus says the Lord GOD: Behold, I judge between sheep and sheep, between rams and male goats. [18] Is it not enough for you to feed on the good pasture, that you must tread down with your feet the rest of your pasture; and to drink of clear water, that you must muddy the rest of the water with your feet? [19] And must my sheep eat what you have trodden with your feet, and drink what you have muddied with your feet?

[20] "Therefore, thus says the Lord GOD to them: Behold, I, I myself will judge between the fat sheep and the lean sheep. [21] Because you push with side and shoulder, and thrust at all the weak with your horns, till you have scattered them abroad, [22] I will rescue[3] my flock; they shall no longer be a prey. And I will judge between sheep and sheep. [23] And I will set up over them one shepherd, my servant David, and he shall feed them: he shall feed them and be their shepherd. [24] And I, the LORD, will be their God, and my servant David shall be prince among them. I am the LORD; I have spoken.

The LORD's Covenant of Peace

[25] "I will make with them a covenant of peace and banish wild beasts from the land, so that they may dwell securely in the wilderness and sleep in the woods. [26] And I will make them and the places all around my hill a blessing, and I will send down the showers in their season; they shall be showers of blessing. [27] And the trees of the field shall yield their fruit, and the earth shall yield its increase, and they shall be secure in their land. And they shall know that I am the LORD, when I break the bars of their yoke, and deliver them from

---

[1] Hebrew *like the singing of lustful songs with a beautiful voice and one who plays* [2] Septuagint, Syriac, Vulgate *I will watch over* [3] Or *save*

the hand of those who enslaved them. ²⁸ They shall no more be a prey to the nations, nor shall the beasts of the land devour them. They shall dwell securely, and none shall make them afraid. ²⁹ And I will provide for them renowned plantations so that they shall no more be consumed with hunger in the land, and no longer suffer the reproach of the nations. ³⁰ And they shall know that I am the LORD their God with them, and that they, the house of Israel, are my people, declares the Lord GOD. ³¹ And you are my sheep, human sheep of my pasture, and I am your God, declares the Lord GOD."

Prophecy Against Mount Seir

35 The word of the LORD came to me: ² "Son of man, set your face against Mount Seir, and prophesy against it, ³ and say to it, Thus says the Lord GOD: Behold, I am against you, Mount Seir, and I will stretch out my hand against you, and I will make you a desolation and a waste. ⁴ I will lay your cities waste, and you shall become a desolation, and you shall know that I am the LORD. ⁵ Because you cherished perpetual enmity and gave over the people of Israel to the power of the sword at the time of their calamity, at the time of their final punishment, ⁶ therefore, as I live, declares the Lord GOD, I will prepare you for blood, and blood shall pursue you; because you did not hate bloodshed, therefore blood shall pursue you. ⁷ I will make Mount Seir a waste and a desolation, and I will cut off from it all who come and go. ⁸ And I will fill its mountains with the slain. On your hills and in your valleys and in all your ravines those slain with the sword shall fall. ⁹ I will make you a perpetual desolation, and your cities shall not be inhabited. Then you will know that I am the LORD.

¹⁰ "Because you said, 'These two nations and these two countries shall be mine, and we will take possession of them'—although the LORD was there— ¹¹ therefore, as I live, declares the Lord GOD, I will deal with you according to the anger and envy that you showed because of your hatred against them. And I will make myself known among them, when I judge you. ¹² And you shall know that I am the LORD.

"I have heard all the revilings that you uttered against the mountains of Israel, saying, 'They are laid desolate; they are given us to devour.' ¹³ And you magnified yourselves against me with your mouth, and multiplied your words against me; I heard it. ¹⁴ Thus says the Lord GOD: While the whole earth rejoices, I will make you desolate. ¹⁵ As you rejoiced over the inheritance of the house of Israel, because it was desolate, so I will deal with you; you shall be desolate, Mount Seir, and all Edom, all of it. Then they will know that I am the LORD.

Prophecy to the Mountains of Israel

36 "And you, son of man, prophesy to the mountains of Israel, and say, O mountains of Israel, hear the word of the LORD. ² Thus says the Lord GOD: Because the enemy said of you, 'Aha!' and, 'The ancient heights have become our possession,' ³ therefore prophesy, and say, Thus says the Lord GOD: Precisely because they made you desolate and crushed you from all sides, so that you became the possession of the rest of the nations, and you became the talk and evil gossip of the people, ⁴ therefore, O mountains of Israel, hear the word of the Lord GOD: Thus says the Lord GOD to the mountains and the hills, the ravines and the valleys, the desolate wastes and the deserted cities, which have become a prey and derision to the rest of the nations all around, ⁵ therefore thus says the Lord GOD: Surely I have spoken in my hot jealousy against the rest of the nations and against all Edom, who gave my land to themselves as a possession with wholehearted joy and utter contempt, that they might make its pasturelands a prey. ⁶ Therefore prophesy concerning the land of Israel, and say to the mountains and hills, to the ravines and valleys, Thus says the Lord GOD: Behold, I have spoken in my jealous wrath, because you have suffered the reproach of the nations. ⁷ Therefore thus says the Lord GOD: I swear that the nations that are all around you shall themselves suffer reproach.

⁸ "But you, O mountains of Israel, shall shoot forth your branches and yield your fruit to my people Israel, for they will soon come home. ⁹ For behold, I am for you, and I will turn to you, and you shall be tilled and sown. ¹⁰ And I will multiply people on you, the whole house of Israel, all of it. The cities shall be inhabited and the waste places rebuilt. ¹¹ And I will multiply on you man and beast, and they shall multiply and be fruitful. And I will cause you to be inhabited as in your former times, and will do more good to you than ever before. Then you will know that I

am the LORD. [12] I will let people walk on you, even my people Israel. And they shall possess you, and you shall be their inheritance, and you shall no longer bereave them of children. [13] Thus says the Lord GOD: Because they say to you, 'You devour people, and you bereave your nation of children,' [14] therefore you shall no longer devour people and no longer bereave your nation of children, declares the Lord GOD. [15] And I will not let you hear anymore the reproach of the nations, and you shall no longer bear the disgrace of the peoples and no longer cause your nation to stumble, declares the Lord GOD."

The LORD's Concern for His Holy Name

[16] The word of the LORD came to me: [17] "Son of man, when the house of Israel lived in their own land, they defiled it by their ways and their deeds. Their ways before me were like the uncleanness of a woman in her menstrual impurity. [18] So I poured out my wrath upon them for the blood that they had shed in the land, for the idols with which they had defiled it. [19] I scattered them among the nations, and they were dispersed through the countries. In accordance with their ways and their deeds I judged them. [20] But when they came to the nations, wherever they came, they profaned my holy name, in that people said of them, 'These are the people of the LORD, and yet they had to go out of his land.' [21] But I had concern for my holy name, which the house of Israel had profaned among the nations to which they came.

I Will Put My Spirit Within You

[22] "Therefore say to the house of Israel, Thus says the Lord GOD: It is not for your sake, O house of Israel, that I am about to act, but for the sake of my holy name, which you have profaned among the nations to which you came. [23] And I will vindicate the holiness of my great name, which has been profaned among the nations, and which you have profaned among them. And the nations will know that I am the LORD, declares the Lord GOD, when through you I vindicate my holiness before their eyes. [24] I will take you from the nations and gather you from all the countries and bring you into your own land. [25] I will sprinkle clean water on you, and you shall be clean from all your uncleannesses, and from all your idols I will cleanse you. [26] And I will give you a new heart,

and a new spirit I will put within you. And I will remove the heart of stone from your flesh and give you a heart of flesh. [27] And I will put my Spirit within you, and cause you to walk in my statutes and be careful to obey my rules.[1] [28] You shall dwell in the land that I gave to your fathers, and you shall be my people, and I will be your God. [29] And I will deliver you from all your uncleannesses. And I will summon the grain and make it abundant and lay no famine upon you. [30] I will make the fruit of the tree and the increase of the field abundant, that you may never again suffer the disgrace of famine among the nations. [31] Then you will remember your evil ways, and your deeds that were not good, and you will loathe yourselves for your iniquities and your abominations. [32] It is not for your sake that I will act, declares the Lord GOD; let that be known to you. Be ashamed and confounded for your ways, O house of Israel.

[33] "Thus says the Lord GOD: On the day that I cleanse you from all your iniquities, I will cause the cities to be inhabited, and the waste places shall be rebuilt. [34] And the land that was desolate shall be tilled, instead of being the desolation that it was in the sight of all who passed by. [35] And they will say, 'This land that was desolate has become like the garden of Eden, and the waste and desolate and ruined cities are now fortified and inhabited.' [36] Then the nations that are left all around you shall know that I am the LORD; I have rebuilt the ruined places and replanted that which was desolate. I am the LORD; I have spoken, and I will do it.

[37] "Thus says the Lord GOD: This also I will let the house of Israel ask me to do for them: to increase their people like a flock. [38] Like the flock for sacrifices,[2] like the flock at Jerusalem during her appointed feasts, so shall the waste cities be filled with flocks of people. Then they will know that I am the LORD."

The Valley of Dry Bones

37 The hand of the LORD was upon me, and he brought me out in the Spirit of the LORD and set me down in the middle of the valley;[3] it was full of bones. [2] And he led me around among them, and behold, there were very many on the surface of the valley, and behold, they were very dry. [3] And he said to me, "Son of man, can these bones live?" And I answered,

---

[1] Or my just decrees [2] Hebrew flock of holy things [3] Or plain; also verse 2

"O Lord GOD, you know." [4] Then he said to me, "Prophesy over these bones, and say to them, O dry bones, hear the word of the LORD. [5] Thus says the Lord GOD to these bones: Behold, I will cause breath[1] to enter you, and you shall live. [6] And I will lay sinews upon you, and will cause flesh to come upon you, and cover you with skin, and put breath in you, and you shall live, and you shall know that I am the LORD."

[7] So I prophesied as I was commanded. And as I prophesied, there was a sound, and behold, a rattling,[2] and the bones came together, bone to its bone. [8] And I looked, and behold, there were sinews on them, and flesh had come upon them, and skin had covered them. But there was no breath in them. [9] Then he said to me, "Prophesy to the breath; prophesy, son of man, and say to the breath, Thus says the Lord GOD: Come from the four winds, O breath, and breathe on these slain, that they may live." [10] So I prophesied as he commanded me, and the breath came into them, and they lived and stood on their feet, an exceedingly great army.

[11] Then he said to me, "Son of man, these bones are the whole house of Israel. Behold, they say, 'Our bones are dried up, and our hope is lost; we are indeed cut off.' [12] Therefore prophesy, and say to them, Thus says the Lord GOD: Behold, I will open your graves and raise you from your graves, O my people. And I will bring you into the land of Israel. [13] And you shall know that I am the LORD, when I open your graves, and raise you from your graves, O my people. [14] And I will put my Spirit within you, and you shall live, and I will place you in your own land. Then you shall know that I am the LORD; I have spoken, and I will do it, declares the LORD."

I Will Be Their God; They Shall Be My People

[15] The word of the LORD came to me: [16] "Son of man, take a stick[3] and write on it, 'For Judah, and the people of Israel associated with him'; then take another stick and write on it, 'For Joseph (the stick of Ephraim) and all the house of Israel associated with him.' [17] And join them one to another into one stick, that they may become one in your hand. [18] And when your people say to you, 'Will you not tell us what you mean by these?' [19] say to them, Thus says the Lord GOD: Behold, I am about to take the stick of Joseph (that is in the hand of Ephraim) and the tribes of Israel associated with him. And I will join with it the stick of Judah,[4] and make them one stick, that they may be one in my hand. [20] When the sticks on which you write are in your hand before their eyes, [21] then say to them, Thus says the Lord GOD: Behold, I will take the people of Israel from the nations among which they have gone, and will gather them from all around, and bring them to their own land. [22] And I will make them one nation in the land, on the mountains of Israel. And one king shall be king over them all; and they shall be no longer two nations, and no longer divided into two kingdoms. [23] They shall not defile themselves anymore with their idols and their detestable things, or with any of their transgressions. But I will save them from all the backslidings[5] in which they have sinned, and will cleanse them; and they shall be my people, and I will be their God.

[24] "My servant David shall be king over them, and they shall all have one shepherd. They shall walk in my rules and be careful to obey my statutes. [25] They shall dwell in the land that I gave to my servant Jacob, where your fathers lived. They and their children and their children's children shall dwell there forever, and David my servant shall be their prince forever. [26] I will make a covenant of peace with them. It shall be an everlasting covenant with them. And I will set them in their land[6] and multiply them, and will set my sanctuary in their midst forevermore. [27] My dwelling place shall be with them, and I will be their God, and they shall be my people. [28] Then the nations will know that I am the LORD who sanctifies Israel, when my sanctuary is in their midst forevermore."

Prophecy Against Gog

38
The word of the LORD came to me: [2] "Son of man, set your face toward Gog, of the land of Magog, the chief prince of Meshech[7] and Tubal, and prophesy against him [3] and say, Thus says the Lord GOD: Behold, I am against you, O Gog, chief prince of Meshech[8] and Tubal. [4] And I will turn you about and put hooks into your jaws, and I will bring you out, and all your army, horses and horsemen, all of them clothed in full armor, a great host, all of them with buckler and shield, wielding swords. [5] Persia, Cush, and Put are with them, all of

them with shield and helmet; ⁶ Gomer and all his hordes; Beth-togarmah from the uttermost parts of the north with all his hordes—many peoples are with you.

⁷ "Be ready and keep ready, you and all your hosts that are assembled about you, and be a guard for them. ⁸ After many days you will be mustered. In the latter years you will go against the land that is restored from war, the land whose people were gathered from many peoples upon the mountains of Israel, which had been a continual waste. Its people were brought out from the peoples and now dwell securely, all of them. ⁹ You will advance, coming on like a storm. You will be like a cloud covering the land, you and all your hordes, and many peoples with you.

¹⁰ "Thus says the Lord GOD: On that day, thoughts will come into your mind, and you will devise an evil scheme ¹¹ and say, 'I will go up against the land of unwalled villages. I will fall upon the quiet people who dwell securely, all of them dwelling without walls, and having no bars or gates,' ¹² to seize spoil and carry off plunder, to turn your hand against the waste places that are now inhabited, and the people who were gathered from the nations, who have acquired livestock and goods, who dwell at the center of the earth. ¹³ Sheba and Dedan and the merchants of Tarshish and all its leaders¹ will say to you, 'Have you come to seize spoil? Have you assembled your hosts to carry off plunder, to carry away silver and gold, to take away livestock and goods, to seize great spoil?'

¹⁴ "Therefore, son of man, prophesy, and say to Gog, Thus says the Lord GOD: On that day when my people Israel are dwelling securely, will you not know it? ¹⁵ You will come from your place out of the uttermost parts of the north, you and many peoples with you, all of them riding on horses, a great host, a mighty army. ¹⁶ You will come up against my people Israel, like a cloud covering the land. In the latter days I will bring you against my land, that the nations may know me, when through you, O Gog, I vindicate my holiness before their eyes.

¹⁷ "Thus says the Lord GOD: Are you he of whom I spoke in former days by my servants the prophets of Israel, who in those days prophesied for years that I would bring you against them? ¹⁸ But on that day, the day that Gog shall come against the land of Israel, declares the Lord GOD, my wrath will be roused in my anger.

¹⁹ For in my jealousy and in my blazing wrath I declare, On that day there shall be a great earthquake in the land of Israel. ²⁰ The fish of the sea and the birds of the heavens and the beasts of the field and all creeping things that creep on the ground, and all the people who are on the face of the earth, shall quake at my presence. And the mountains shall be thrown down, and the cliffs shall fall, and every wall shall tumble to the ground. ²¹ I will summon a sword against Gog² on all my mountains, declares the Lord GOD. Every man's sword will be against his brother. ²² With pestilence and bloodshed I will enter into judgment with him, and I will rain upon him and his hordes and the many peoples who are with him torrential rains and hailstones, fire and sulfur. ²³ So I will show my greatness and my holiness and make myself known in the eyes of many nations. Then they will know that I am the LORD.

39 "And you, son of man, prophesy against Gog and say, Thus says the Lord GOD: Behold, I am against you, O Gog, chief prince of Meshech³ and Tubal. ² And I will turn you about and drive you forward,⁴ and bring you up from the uttermost parts of the north, and lead you against the mountains of Israel. ³ Then I will strike your bow from your left hand, and will make your arrows drop out of your right hand. ⁴ You shall fall on the mountains of Israel, you and all your hordes and the peoples who are with you. I will give you to birds of prey of every sort and to the beasts of the field to be devoured. ⁵ You shall fall in the open field, for I have spoken, declares the Lord GOD. ⁶ I will send fire on Magog and on those who dwell securely in the coastlands, and they shall know that I am the LORD.

⁷ "And my holy name I will make known in the midst of my people Israel, and I will not let my holy name be profaned anymore. And the nations shall know that I am the LORD, the Holy One in Israel. ⁸ Behold, it is coming and it will be brought about, declares the Lord GOD. That is the day of which I have spoken.

⁹ "Then those who dwell in the cities of Israel will go out and make fires of the weapons and burn them, shields and bucklers, bow and arrows, clubs⁵ and spears; and they will make fires of them for seven years, ¹⁰ so that they will not need to take wood out of the field or cut down any out of the forests, for they will make their fires of the weapons. They will seize the

---

¹ Hebrew *young lions* ² Hebrew *against him* ³ Or *Gog, prince of Rosh, Meshech* ⁴ Or *and drag you along* ⁵ Or *javelins*

spoil of those who despoiled them, and plunder those who plundered them, declares the Lord GOD.

¹¹ "On that day I will give to Gog a place for burial in Israel, the Valley of the Travelers, east of the sea. It will block the travelers, for there Gog and all his multitude will be buried. It will be called the Valley of Hamon-gog.¹ ¹² For seven months the house of Israel will be burying them, in order to cleanse the land. ¹³ All the people of the land will bury them, and it will bring them renown on the day that I show my glory, declares the Lord GOD. ¹⁴ They will set apart men to travel through the land regularly and bury those travelers remaining on the face of the land, so as to cleanse it. At² the end of seven months they will make their search. ¹⁵ And when these travel through the land and anyone sees a human bone, then he shall set up a sign by it, till the buriers have buried it in the Valley of Hamon-gog. ¹⁶ (Hamonah³ is also the name of the city.) Thus shall they cleanse the land.

¹⁷ "As for you, son of man, thus says the Lord GOD: Speak to the birds of every sort and to all beasts of the field: 'Assemble and come, gather from all around to the sacrificial feast that I am preparing for you, a great sacrificial feast on the mountains of Israel, and you shall eat flesh and drink blood. ¹⁸ You shall eat the flesh of the mighty, and drink the blood of the princes of the earth—of rams, of lambs, and of he-goats, of bulls, all of them fat beasts of Bashan. ¹⁹ And you shall eat fat till you are filled, and drink blood till you are drunk, at the sacrificial feast that I am preparing for you. ²⁰ And you shall be filled at my table with horses and charioteers, with mighty men and all kinds of warriors,' declares the Lord GOD.

²¹ "And I will set my glory among the nations, and all the nations shall see my judgment that I have executed, and my hand that I have laid on them. ²² The house of Israel shall know that I am the LORD their God, from that day forward. ²³ And the nations shall know that the house of Israel went into captivity for their iniquity, because they dealt so treacherously with me that I hid my face from them and gave them into the hand of their adversaries, and they all fell by the sword. ²⁴ I dealt with them according to their uncleanness and their transgressions, and hid my face from them.

The LORD Will Restore Israel

²⁵ "Therefore thus says the Lord GOD: Now I will restore the fortunes of Jacob and have mercy on the whole house of Israel, and I will be jealous for my holy name. ²⁶ They shall forget their shame and all the treachery they have practiced against me, when they dwell securely in their land with none to make them afraid, ²⁷ when I have brought them back from the peoples and gathered them from their enemies' lands, and through them have vindicated my holiness in the sight of many nations. ²⁸ Then they shall know that I am the LORD their God, because I sent them into exile among the nations and then assembled them into their own land. I will leave none of them remaining among the nations anymore. ²⁹ And I will not hide my face anymore from them, when I pour out my Spirit upon the house of Israel, declares the Lord GOD."

Vision of the New Temple

40 In the twenty-fifth year of our exile, at the beginning of the year, on the tenth day of the month, in the fourteenth year after the city was struck down, on that very day, the hand of the LORD was upon me, and he brought me to the city.⁴ ² In visions of God he brought me to the land of Israel, and set me down on a very high mountain, on which was a structure like a city to the south. ³ When he brought me there, behold, there was a man whose appearance was like bronze, with a linen cord and a measuring reed in his hand. And he was standing in the gateway. ⁴ And the man said to me, "Son of man, look with your eyes, and hear with your ears, and set your heart upon all that I shall show you, for you were brought here in order that I might show it to you. Declare all that you see to the house of Israel."

The East Gate to the Outer Court

⁵ And behold, there was a wall all around the outside of the temple area, and the length of the measuring reed in the man's hand was six long cubits, each being a cubit and a handbreadth⁵ in length. So he measured the thickness of the wall, one reed; and the height, one reed. ⁶ Then he went into the gateway facing east, going up its steps, and measured the threshold of the gate, one reed deep.⁶ ⁷ And the side rooms, one reed long and one reed broad; and the space between the side rooms, five cubits; and the

¹ Hamon-gog means the multitude of Gog ² Or Until ³ Hamonah means multitude ⁴ Hebrew brought me there ⁵ A cubit was about 18 inches or 45 centimeters; a handbreadth was about 3 inches or 7.5 centimeters ⁶ Hebrew deep, and one threshold, one reed deep

threshold of the gate by the vestibule of the gate at the inner end, one reed. [8] Then he measured the vestibule of the gateway, on the inside, one reed. [9] Then he measured the vestibule of the gateway, eight cubits; and its jambs, two cubits; and the vestibule of the gate was at the inner end. [10] And there were three side rooms on either side of the east gate. The three were of the same size, and the jambs on either side were of the same size. [11] Then he measured the width of the opening of the gateway, ten cubits; and the length of the gateway, thirteen cubits. [12] There was a barrier before the side rooms, one cubit on either side. And the side rooms were six cubits on either side. [13] Then he measured the gate from the ceiling of the one side room to the ceiling of the other, a breadth of twenty-five cubits; the openings faced each other. [14] He measured also the vestibule, sixty cubits. And around the vestibule of the gateway was the court.[1] [15] From the front of the gate at the entrance to the front of the inner vestibule of the gate was fifty cubits. [16] And the gateway had windows all around, narrowing inwards toward the side rooms and toward their jambs, and likewise the vestibule had windows all around inside, and on the jambs were palm trees.

The Outer Court

[17] Then he brought me into the outer court. And behold, there were chambers and a pavement, all around the court. Thirty chambers faced the pavement. [18] And the pavement ran along the side of the gates, corresponding to the length of the gates. This was the lower pavement. [19] Then he measured the distance from the inner front of the lower gate to the outer front of the inner court,[2] a hundred cubits on the east side and on the north side.[3]

The North Gate

[20] As for the gate that faced toward the north, belonging to the outer court, he measured its length and its breadth. [21] Its side rooms, three on either side, and its jambs and its vestibule were of the same size as those of the first gate. Its length was fifty cubits, and its breadth twenty-five cubits. [22] And its windows, its vestibule, and its palm trees were of the same size as those of the gate that faced toward the east. And by seven steps people would go up to it, and find its vestibule before them. [23] And

opposite the gate on the north, as on the east, was a gate to the inner court. And he measured from gate to gate, a hundred cubits.

The South Gate

[24] And he led me toward the south, and behold, there was a gate on the south. And he measured its jambs and its vestibule; they had the same size as the others. [25] Both it and its vestibule had windows all around, like the windows of the others. Its length was fifty cubits, and its breadth twenty-five cubits. [26] And there were seven steps leading up to it, and its vestibule was before them, and it had palm trees on its jambs, one on either side. [27] And there was a gate on the south of the inner court. And he measured from gate to gate toward the south, a hundred cubits.

The Inner Court

[28] Then he brought me to the inner court through the south gate, and he measured the south gate. It was of the same size as the others. [29] Its side rooms, its jambs, and its vestibule were of the same size as the others, and both it and its vestibule had windows all around. Its length was fifty cubits, and its breadth twenty-five cubits. [30] And there were vestibules all around, twenty-five cubits long and five cubits broad. [31] Its vestibule faced the outer court, and palm trees were on its jambs, and its stairway had eight steps.

[32] Then he brought me to the inner court on the east side, and he measured the gate. It was of the same size as the others. [33] Its side rooms, its jambs, and its vestibule were of the same size as the others, and both it and its vestibule had windows all around. Its length was fifty cubits, and its breadth twenty-five cubits. [34] Its vestibule faced the outer court, and it had palm trees on its jambs, on either side, and its stairway had eight steps.

[35] Then he brought me to the north gate, and he measured it. It had the same size as the others. [36] Its side rooms, its jambs, and its vestibule were of the same size as the others,[4] and it had windows all around. Its length was fifty cubits, and its breadth twenty-five cubits. [37] Its vestibule[5] faced the outer court, and it had palm trees on its jambs, on either side, and its stairway had eight steps.

[38] There was a chamber with its door in the vestibule of the gate,[6] where the burnt offering was to be washed. [39] And in the vestibule of the

---

[1] Text uncertain; Hebrew *And he made the jambs sixty cubits, and to the jamb of the court was the gateway all around* [2] Hebrew *distance from before the low gate before the inner court to the outside* [3] Or *cubits. So far the eastern gate; now to the northern gate* [4] One manuscript (compare verses 29 and 33); most manuscripts lack *were of the same size as the others* [5] Septuagint, Vulgate (compare verses 26, 31, 34); Hebrew *jambs* [6] Hebrew *at the jambs, the gates*

gate were two tables on either side, on which the burnt offering and the sin offering and the guilt offering were to be slaughtered. [40] And off to the side, on the outside as one goes up to the entrance of the north gate, were two tables; and off to the other side of the vestibule of the gate were two tables. [41] Four tables were on either side of the gate, eight tables, on which to slaughter. [42] And there were four tables of hewn stone for the burnt offering, a cubit and a half long, and a cubit and a half broad, and one cubit high, on which the instruments were to be laid with which the burnt offerings and the sacrifices were slaughtered. [43] And hooks,[1] a handbreadth long, were fastened all around within. And on the tables the flesh of the offering was to be laid.

Chambers for the Priests

[44] On the outside of the inner gateway there were two chambers[2] in the inner court, one[3] at the side of the north gate facing south, the other at the side of the south[4] gate facing north. [45] And he said to me, "This chamber that faces south is for the priests who have charge of the temple, [46] and the chamber that faces north is for the priests who have charge of the altar. These are the sons of Zadok, who alone[5] among the sons of Levi may come near to the LORD to minister to him." [47] And he measured the court, a hundred cubits long and a hundred cubits broad, a square. And the altar was in front of the temple.

The Vestibule of the Temple

[48] Then he brought me to the vestibule of the temple and measured the jambs of the vestibule, five cubits on either side. And the breadth of the gate was fourteen cubits, and the sidewalls of the gate[6] were three cubits on either side. [49] The length of the vestibule was twenty cubits, and the breadth twelve[7] cubits, and people would go up to it by ten steps.[8] And there were pillars beside the jambs, one on either side.

The Inner Temple

41 Then he brought me to the nave and measured the jambs. On each side six cubits[9] was the breadth of the jambs.[10] [2] And the breadth of the entrance was ten cubits, and the sidewalls of the entrance were five cubits on either side. And he measured the length of the nave,[11] forty cubits, and its breadth, twenty cubits. [3] Then he went into the inner room and measured the jambs of the entrance, two cubits; and the entrance, six cubits; and the sidewalls on either side[12] of the entrance, seven cubits. [4] And he measured the length of the room, twenty cubits, and its breadth, twenty cubits, across the nave. And he said to me, "This is the Most Holy Place."

[5] Then he measured the wall of the temple, six cubits thick, and the breadth of the side chambers, four cubits, all around the temple. [6] And the side chambers were in three stories, one over another, thirty in each story. There were offsets[13] all around the wall of the temple to serve as supports for the side chambers, so that they should not be supported by the wall of the temple. [7] And it became broader as it wound upward to the side chambers, because the temple was enclosed upward all around the temple. Thus the temple had a broad area upward, and so one went up from the lowest story to the top story through the middle story. [8] I saw also that the temple had a raised platform all around; the foundations of the side chambers measured a full reed of six long cubits. [9] The thickness of the outer wall of the side chambers was five cubits. The free space between the side chambers of the temple and the [10] other chambers was a breadth of twenty cubits all around the temple on every side. [11] And the doors of the side chambers opened on the free space, one door toward the north, and another door toward the south. And the breadth of the free space was five cubits all around.

[12] The building that was facing the separate yard on the west side was seventy cubits broad, and the wall of the building was five cubits thick all around, and its length ninety cubits.

[13] Then he measured the temple, a hundred cubits long; and the yard and the building with its walls, a hundred cubits long; [14] also the breadth of the east front of the temple and the yard, a hundred cubits.

[15] Then he measured the length of the building facing the yard that was at the back and its galleries[14] on either side, a hundred cubits.

The inside of the nave and the vestibules of the court, [16] the thresholds and the narrow windows and the galleries all around the three of them, opposite the threshold, were paneled

---

[1] Or shelves [2] Septuagint; Hebrew were chambers for singers [3] Hebrew lacks one [4] Septuagint; Hebrew east [5] Hebrew lacks alone [6] Septuagint; Hebrew lacks was fourteen cubits, and the sidewalls of the gate [7] Septuagint; Hebrew eleven [8] Septuagint; Hebrew and by steps that would go up to it [9] A cubit was about 18 inches or 45 centimeters [10] Compare Septuagint; Hebrew tent [11] Hebrew its length [12] Septuagint; Hebrew and the breadth [13] Septuagint, compare 1 Kings 6:6; the meaning of the Hebrew word is uncertain [14] The meaning of the Hebrew term is unknown; also verse 16

with wood all around, from the floor up to the windows (now the windows were covered), [17] to the space above the door, even to the inner room, and on the outside. And on all the walls all around, inside and outside, was a measured pattern.[1] [18] It was carved of cherubim and palm trees, a palm tree between cherub and cherub. Every cherub had two faces: [19] a human face toward the palm tree on the one side, and the face of a young lion toward the palm tree on the other side. They were carved on the whole temple all around. [20] From the floor to above the door, cherubim and palm trees were carved; similarly the wall of the nave.

[21] The doorposts of the nave were squared, and in front of the Holy Place was something resembling [22] an altar of wood, three cubits high, two cubits long, and two cubits broad.[2] Its corners, its base,[3] and its walls were of wood. He said to me, "This is the table that is before the LORD." [23] The nave and the Holy Place had each a double door. [24] The double doors had two leaves apiece, two swinging leaves for each door. [25] And on the doors of the nave were carved cherubim and palm trees, such as were carved on the walls. And there was a canopy[4] of wood in front of the vestibule outside. [26] And there were narrow windows and palm trees on either side, on the sidewalls of the vestibule, the side chambers of the temple, and the canopies.

The Temple's Chambers

42 Then he led me out into the outer court, toward the north, and he brought me to the chambers that were opposite the separate yard and opposite the building on the north. [2] The length of the building whose door faced north was a hundred cubits,[5] and the breadth fifty cubits. [3] Facing the twenty cubits that belonged to the inner court, and facing the pavement that belonged to the outer court, was gallery[6] against gallery in three stories. [4] And before the chambers was a passage inward, ten cubits wide and a hundred cubits long,[7] and their doors were on the north. [5] Now the upper chambers were narrower, for the galleries took more away from them than from the lower and middle chambers of the building. [6] For they were in three stories, and they had no pillars like the pillars of the courts. Thus the upper chambers were set back from the ground more than the lower and the middle

ones. [7] And there was a wall outside parallel to the chambers, toward the outer court, opposite the chambers, fifty cubits long. [8] For the chambers on the outer court were fifty cubits long, while those opposite the nave[8] were a hundred cubits long. [9] Below these chambers was an entrance on the east side, as one enters them from the outer court.

[10] In the thickness of the wall of the court, on the south[9] also, opposite the yard and opposite the building, there were chambers [11] with a passage in front of them. They were similar to the chambers on the north, of the same length and breadth, with the same exits[10] and arrangements and doors, [12] as were the entrances of the chambers on the south. There was an entrance at the beginning of the passage, the passage before the corresponding wall on the east as one enters them.[11]

[13] Then he said to me, "The north chambers and the south chambers opposite the yard are the holy chambers, where the priests who approach the LORD shall eat the most holy offerings. There they shall put the most holy offerings—the grain offering, the sin offering, and the guilt offering—for the place is holy. [14] When the priests enter the Holy Place, they shall not go out of it into the outer court without laying there the garments in which they minister, for these are holy. They shall put on other garments before they go near to that which is for the people."

[15] Now when he had finished measuring the interior of the temple area, he led me out by the gate that faced east, and measured the temple area all around. [16] He measured the east side with the measuring reed, 500 cubits by the measuring reed all around. [17] He measured the north side, 500 cubits by the measuring reed all around. [18] He measured the south side, 500 cubits by the measuring reed. [19] Then he turned to the west side and measured, 500 cubits by the measuring reed. [20] He measured it on the four sides. It had a wall around it, 500 cubits long and 500 cubits broad, to make a separation between the holy and the common.

The Glory of the LORD Fills the Temple

43 Then he led me to the gate, the gate facing east. [2] And behold, the glory of the God of Israel was coming from the east. And the sound of his coming was like the sound

---

[1] Hebrew *were measurements* [2] Septuagint; Hebrew lacks *two cubits broad* [3] Septuagint; Hebrew *length* [4] The meaning of the Hebrew word is unknown; also verse 26 [5] A cubit was about 18 inches or 45 centimeters [6] The meaning of the Hebrew word is unknown; also verse 5 [7] Septuagint, Syriac; Hebrew *and a way of one cubit* [8] Or temple [9] Septuagint; Hebrew *east* [10] Hebrew *and all their exits* [11] The meaning of the Hebrew verse is uncertain

of many waters, and the earth shone with his glory. [3] And the vision I saw was just like the vision that I had seen when he[1] came to destroy the city, and just like the vision that I had seen by the Chebar canal. And I fell on my face. [4] As the glory of the LORD entered the temple by the gate facing east, [5] the Spirit lifted me up and brought me into the inner court; and behold, the glory of the LORD filled the temple.

[6] While the man was standing beside me, I heard one speaking to me out of the temple, [7] and he said to me, "Son of man, this is the place of my throne and the place of the soles of my feet, where I will dwell in the midst of the people of Israel forever. And the house of Israel shall no more defile my holy name, neither they, nor their kings, by their whoring and by the dead bodies[2] of their kings at their high places,[3] [8] by setting their threshold by my threshold and their doorposts beside my doorposts, with only a wall between me and them. They have defiled my holy name by their abominations that they have committed, so I have consumed them in my anger. [9] Now let them put away their whoring and the dead bodies of their kings far from me, and I will dwell in their midst forever.

[10] "As for you, son of man, describe to the house of Israel the temple, that they may be ashamed of their iniquities; and they shall measure the plan. [11] And if they are ashamed of all that they have done, make known to them the design of the temple, its arrangement, its exits and its entrances, that is, its whole design; and make known to them as well all its statutes and its whole design and all its laws, and write it down in their sight, so that they may observe all its laws and all its statutes and carry them out. [12] This is the law of the temple: the whole territory on the top of the mountain all around shall be most holy. Behold, this is the law of the temple.

The Altar

[13] "These are the measurements of the altar by cubits (the cubit being a cubit and a handbreadth):[4] its base shall be one cubit high[5] and one cubit broad, with a rim of one span[6] around its edge. And this shall be the height of the altar: [14] from the base on the ground to the lower ledge, two cubits, with a breadth of one cubit; and from the smaller ledge to the larger ledge, four cubits, with a breadth of one cubit;

[15] and the altar hearth, four cubits; and from the altar hearth projecting upward, four horns. [16] The altar hearth shall be square, twelve cubits long by twelve broad. [17] The ledge also shall be square, fourteen cubits long by fourteen broad, with a rim around it half a cubit broad, and its base one cubit all around. The steps of the altar shall face east."

[18] And he said to me, "Son of man, thus says the Lord GOD: These are the ordinances for the altar: On the day when it is erected for offering burnt offerings upon it and for throwing blood against it, [19] you shall give to the Levitical priests of the family of Zadok, who draw near to me to minister to me, declares the Lord GOD, a bull from the herd for a sin offering. [20] And you shall take some of its blood and put it on the four horns of the altar and on the four corners of the ledge and upon the rim all around. Thus you shall purify the altar and make atonement for it. [21] You shall also take the bull of the sin offering, and it shall be burned in the appointed place belonging to the temple, outside the sacred area. [22] And on the second day you shall offer a male goat without blemish for a sin offering; and the altar shall be purified, as it was purified with the bull. [23] When you have finished purifying it, you shall offer a bull from the herd without blemish and a ram from the flock without blemish. [24] You shall present them before the LORD, and the priests shall sprinkle salt on them and offer them up as a burnt offering to the LORD. [25] For seven days you shall provide daily a male goat for a sin offering; also, a bull from the herd and a ram from the flock, without blemish, shall be provided. [26] Seven days shall they make atonement for the altar and cleanse it, and so consecrate it.[7] [27] And when they have completed these days, then from the eighth day onward the priests shall offer on the altar your burnt offerings and your peace offerings, and I will accept you, declares the Lord GOD."

The Gate for the Prince

44 Then he brought me back to the outer gate of the sanctuary, which faces east. And it was shut. [2] And the LORD said to me, "This gate shall remain shut; it shall not be opened, and no one shall enter by it, for the LORD, the God of Israel, has entered by it. Therefore it shall remain shut. [3] Only the prince

---

[1] Some Hebrew manuscripts and Vulgate; most Hebrew manuscripts when I [2] Or the monuments; also verse 9 [3] Or at their deaths [4] A cubit was about 18 inches or 45 centimeters; a handbreadth was about 3 inches or 7.5 centimeters [5] Or its gutter shall be one cubit deep [6] A span was about 9 inches or 22 centimeters [7] Hebrew fill its hand

may sit in it to eat bread before the LORD. He shall enter by way of the vestibule of the gate, and shall go out by the same way."

[4] Then he brought me by way of the north gate to the front of the temple, and I looked, and behold, the glory of the LORD filled the temple of the LORD. And I fell on my face. [5] And the LORD said to me, "Son of man, mark well, see with your eyes, and hear with your ears all that I shall tell you concerning all the statutes of the temple of the LORD and all its laws. And mark well the entrance to the temple and all the exits from the sanctuary. [6] And say to the rebellious house,[1] to the house of Israel, Thus says the Lord GOD: O house of Israel, enough of all your abominations, [7] in admitting foreigners, uncircumcised in heart and flesh, to be in my sanctuary, profaning my temple, when you offer to me my food, the fat and the blood. You[2] have broken my covenant, in addition to all your abominations. [8] And you have not kept charge of my holy things, but you have set others to keep my charge for you in my sanctuary.

[9] "Thus says the Lord GOD: No foreigner, uncircumcised in heart and flesh, of all the foreigners who are among the people of Israel, shall enter my sanctuary. [10] But the Levites who went far from me, going astray from me after their idols when Israel went astray, shall bear their punishment.[3] [11] They shall be ministers in my sanctuary, having oversight at the gates of the temple and ministering in the temple. They shall slaughter the burnt offering and the sacrifice for the people, and they shall stand before the people, to minister to them. [12] Because they ministered to them before their idols and became a stumbling block of iniquity to the house of Israel, therefore I have sworn concerning them, declares the Lord GOD, and they shall bear their punishment. [13] They shall not come near to me, to serve me as priest, nor come near any of my holy things and the things that are most holy, but they shall bear their shame and the abominations that they have committed. [14] Yet I will appoint them to keep charge of the temple, to do all its service and all that is to be done in it.

Rules for Levitical Priests

[15] "But the Levitical priests, the sons of Zadok, who kept the charge of my sanctuary when the people of Israel went astray from me, shall come near to me to minister to me. And they

shall stand before me to offer me the fat and the blood, declares the Lord GOD. [16] They shall enter my sanctuary, and they shall approach my table, to minister to me, and they shall keep my charge. [17] When they enter the gates of the inner court, they shall wear linen garments. They shall have nothing of wool on them, while they minister at the gates of the inner court, and within. [18] They shall have linen turbans on their heads, and linen undergarments around their waists. They shall not bind themselves with anything that causes sweat. [19] And when they go out into the outer court to the people, they shall put off the garments in which they have been ministering and lay them in the holy chambers. And they shall put on other garments, lest they transmit holiness to the people with their garments. [20] They shall not shave their heads or let their locks grow long; they shall surely trim the hair of their heads. [21] No priest shall drink wine when he enters the inner court. [22] They shall not marry a widow or a divorced woman, but only virgins of the offspring of the house of Israel, or a widow who is the widow of a priest. [23] They shall teach my people the difference between the holy and the common, and show them how to distinguish between the unclean and the clean. [24] In a dispute, they shall act as judges, and they shall judge it according to my judgments. They shall keep my laws and my statutes in all my appointed feasts, and they shall keep my Sabbaths holy. [25] They shall not defile themselves by going near to a dead person. However, for father or mother, for son or daughter, for brother or unmarried sister they may defile themselves. [26] After he[4] has become clean, they shall count seven days for him. [27] And on the day that he goes into the Holy Place, into the inner court, to minister in the Holy Place, he shall offer his sin offering, declares the Lord GOD.

[28] "This shall be their inheritance: I am their inheritance: and you shall give them no possession in Israel; I am their possession. [29] They shall eat the grain offering, the sin offering, and the guilt offering, and every devoted thing in Israel shall be theirs. [30] And the first of all the firstfruits of all kinds, and every offering of all kinds from all your offerings, shall belong to the priests. You shall also give to the priests the first of your dough, that a blessing may rest on your house. [31] The priests shall not eat of anything, whether bird or beast, that has died of itself or is torn by wild animals.

---

[1] Septuagint; Hebrew lacks *house* [2] Septuagint, Syriac, Vulgate; Hebrew *They* [3] Or *iniquity; also verse 12* [4] That is, a priest

The Holy District

45 "When you allot the land as an inheritance, you shall set apart for the Lord a portion of the land as a holy district, 25,000 cubits[1] long and 20,000[2] cubits broad. It shall be holy throughout its whole extent. [2] Of this a square plot of 500 by 500 cubits shall be for the sanctuary, with fifty cubits for an open space around it. [3] And from this measured district you shall measure off a section 25,000 cubits long and 10,000 broad, in which shall be the sanctuary, the Most Holy Place. [4] It shall be the holy portion of the land. It shall be for the priests, who minister in the sanctuary and approach the Lord to minister to him, and it shall be a place for their houses and a holy place for the sanctuary. [5] Another section, 25,000 cubits long and 10,000 cubits broad, shall be for the Levites who minister at the temple, as their possession for cities to live in.[3]

[6] "Alongside the portion set apart as the holy district you shall assign for the property of the city an area 5,000 cubits broad and 25,000 cubits long. It shall belong to the whole house of Israel.

The Portion for the Prince

[7] "And to the prince shall belong the land on both sides of the holy district and the property of the city, alongside the holy district and the property of the city, on the west and on the east, corresponding in length to one of the tribal portions, and extending from the western to the eastern boundary [8] of the land. It is to be his property in Israel. And my princes shall no more oppress my people, but they shall let the house of Israel have the land according to their tribes.

[9] "Thus says the Lord God: Enough, O princes of Israel! Put away violence and oppression, and execute justice and righteousness. Cease your evictions of my people, declares the Lord God. [10] "You shall have just balances, a just ephah, and a just bath.[4] [11] The ephah and the bath shall be of the same measure, the bath containing one tenth of a homer,[5] and the ephah one tenth of a homer; the homer shall be the standard measure. [12] The shekel shall be twenty gerahs;[6] twenty shekels plus twenty-five shekels plus fifteen shekels shall be your mina.[7]

[13] "This is the offering that you shall make: one sixth of an ephah from each homer of wheat, and one sixth of an ephah from each homer of barley, [14] and as the fixed portion of oil, measured in baths, one tenth of a bath from each cor[8] (the cor, like the homer, contains ten baths).[9] [15] And one sheep from every flock of two hundred, from the watering places of Israel for grain offering, burnt offering, and peace offerings, to make atonement for them, declares the Lord God. [16] All the people of the land shall be obliged to give this offering to the prince in Israel. [17] It shall be the prince's duty to furnish the burnt offerings, grain offerings, and drink offerings, at the feasts, the new moons, and the Sabbaths, all the appointed feasts of the house of Israel: he shall provide the sin offerings, grain offerings, burnt offerings, and peace offerings, to make atonement on behalf of the house of Israel.

[18] "Thus says the Lord God: In the first month, on the first day of the month, you shall take a bull from the herd without blemish, and purify the sanctuary. [19] The priest shall take some of the blood of the sin offering and put it on the doorposts of the temple, the four corners of the ledge of the altar, and the posts of the gate of the inner court. [20] You shall do the same on the seventh day of the month for anyone who has sinned through error or ignorance; so you shall make atonement for the temple.

[21] "In the first month, on the fourteenth day of the month, you shall celebrate the Feast of the Passover, and for seven days unleavened bread shall be eaten. [22] On that day the prince shall provide for himself and all the people of the land a young bull for a sin offering. [23] And on the seven days of the festival he shall provide as a burnt offering to the Lord seven young bulls and seven rams without blemish, on each of the seven days; and a male goat daily for a sin offering. [24] And he shall provide as a grain offering an ephah for each bull, an ephah for each ram, and a hin[10] of oil to each ephah. [25] In the seventh month, on the fifteenth day of the month and for the seven days of the feast, he shall make the same provision for sin offerings, burnt offerings, and grain offerings, and for the oil.

---

[1] A *cubit* was about 18 inches or 45 centimeters [2] Septuagint; Hebrew *10,000* [3] Septuagint; Hebrew *as their possession, twenty chambers* [4] An *ephah* was about 3/5 of a bushel or 22 liters; a *bath* was about 6 gallons or 22 liters [5] A *homer* was about 6 bushels or 220 liters [6] A *shekel* was about 2/5 ounce or 11 grams; a *gerah* was about 1/50 ounce or 0.6 gram [7] A *mina* was about 1 1/4 pounds or 0.6 kilogram [8] A *cor* was about 6 bushels or 220 liters [9] See Vulgate; Hebrew *(ten baths are a homer, for ten baths are a homer)* [10] A *hin* was about 4 quarts or 3.5 liters

The Prince and the Feasts

46 "Thus says the Lord GOD: The gate of the inner court that faces east shall be shut on the six working days, but on the Sabbath day it shall be opened, and on the day of the new moon it shall be opened. ²The prince shall enter by the vestibule of the gate from outside, and shall take his stand by the post of the gate. The priests shall offer his burnt offering and his peace offerings, and he shall worship at the threshold of the gate. Then he shall go out, but the gate shall not be shut until evening. ³The people of the land shall bow down at the entrance of that gate before the LORD on the Sabbaths and on the new moons. ⁴The burnt offering that the prince offers to the LORD on the Sabbath day shall be six lambs without blemish and a ram without blemish. ⁵And the grain offering with the ram shall be an ephah,¹ and the grain offering with the lambs shall be as much as he is able, together with a hin² of oil to each ephah. ⁶On the day of the new moon he shall offer a bull from the herd without blemish, and six lambs and a ram, which shall be without blemish. ⁷As a grain offering he shall provide an ephah with the bull and an ephah with the ram, and with the lambs as much as he is able, together with a hin of oil to each ephah. ⁸When the prince enters, he shall enter by the vestibule of the gate, and he shall go out by the same way.

⁹"When the people of the land come before the LORD at the appointed feasts, he who enters by the north gate to worship shall go out by the south gate, and he who enters by the south gate shall go out by the north gate: no one shall return by way of the gate by which he entered, but each shall go out straight ahead. ¹⁰When they enter, the prince shall enter with them, and when they go out, he shall go out.

¹¹"At the feasts and the appointed festivals, the grain offering with a young bull shall be an ephah, and with a ram an ephah, and with the lambs as much as one is able to give, together with a hin of oil to an ephah. ¹²When the prince provides a freewill offering, either a burnt offering or peace offerings as a freewill offering to the LORD, the gate facing east shall be opened for him. And he shall offer his burnt offering or his peace offerings as he does on the Sabbath day. Then he shall go out, and after he has gone out the gate shall be shut.

¹³"You shall provide a lamb a year old without blemish for a burnt offering to the LORD daily; morning by morning you shall provide it. ¹⁴And you shall provide a grain offering with it morning by morning, one sixth of an ephah, and one third of a hin of oil to moisten the flour, as a grain offering to the LORD. This is a perpetual statute. ¹⁵Thus the lamb and the meal offering and the oil shall be provided, morning by morning, for a regular burnt offering.

¹⁶"Thus says the Lord GOD: If the prince makes a gift to any of his sons as his inheritance, it shall belong to his sons. It is their property by inheritance. ¹⁷But if he makes a gift out of his inheritance to one of his servants, it shall be his to the year of liberty. Then it shall revert to the prince; surely it is his inheritance—it shall belong to his sons. ¹⁸The prince shall not take any of the inheritance of the people, thrusting them out of their property. He shall give his sons their inheritance out of his own property, so that none of my people shall be scattered from his property."

Boiling Places for Offerings

¹⁹Then he brought me through the entrance, which was at the side of the gate, to the north row of the holy chambers for the priests, and behold, a place was there at the extreme western end of them. ²⁰And he said to me, "This is the place where the priests shall boil the guilt offering and the sin offering, and where they shall bake the grain offering, in order not to bring them out into the outer court and so transmit holiness to the people."

²¹Then he brought me out to the outer court and led me around to the four corners of the court. And behold, in each corner of the court there was another court— ²²in the four corners of the court were small³ courts, forty cubits⁴ long and thirty broad; the four were of the same size. ²³On the inside, around each of the four courts was a row of masonry, with hearths made at the bottom of the rows all around. ²⁴Then he said to me, "These are the kitchens where those who minister at the temple shall boil the sacrifices of the people."

Water Flowing from the Temple

47 Then he brought me back to the door of the temple, and behold, water was issuing from below the threshold of the temple toward the east (for the temple faced east). The

¹ An *ephah* was about 3/5 bushel or 22 liters ² A *hin* was about 4 quarts or 3.5 liters ³ Septuagint, Syriac, Vulgate; the meaning of the Hebrew word is uncertain ⁴ A *cubit* was about 18 inches or 45 centimeters

water was flowing down from below the south end of the threshold of the temple, south of the altar. [2] Then he brought me out by way of the north gate and led me around on the outside to the outer gate that faces toward the east; and behold, the water was trickling out on the south side.

[3] Going on eastward with a measuring line in his hand, the man measured a thousand cubits,[1] and then led me through the water, and it was ankle-deep. [4] Again he measured a thousand, and led me through the water, and it was knee-deep. Again he measured a thousand, and led me through the water, and it was waist-deep. [5] Again he measured a thousand, and it was a river that I could not pass through, for the water had risen. It was deep enough to swim in, a river that could not be passed through. [6] And he said to me, "Son of man, have you seen this?"

Then he led me back to the bank of the river. [7] As I went back, I saw on the bank of the river very many trees on the one side and on the other. [8] And he said to me, "This water flows toward the eastern region and goes down into the Arabah, and enters the sea;[2] when the water flows into the sea, the water will become fresh.[3] [9] And wherever the river goes,[4] every living creature that swarms will live, and there will be very many fish. For this water goes there, that the waters of the sea[5] may become fresh; so everything will live where the river goes. [10] Fishermen will stand beside the sea. From Engedi to Eneglaim it will be a place for the spreading of nets. Its fish will be of very many kinds, like the fish of the Great Sea.[6] [11] But its swamps and marshes will not become fresh; they are to be left for salt. [12] And on the banks, on both sides of the river, there will grow all kinds of trees for food. Their leaves will not wither, nor their fruit fail, but they will bear fresh fruit every month, because the water for them flows from the sanctuary. Their fruit will be for food, and their leaves for healing."

Division of the Land

[13] Thus says the Lord God: "This is the boundary[7] by which you shall divide the land for inheritance among the twelve tribes of Israel. Joseph shall have two portions. [14] And you shall divide equally what I swore to give to your fathers. This land shall fall to you as your inheritance.

[15] "This shall be the boundary of the land: On the north side, from the Great Sea by way of Hethlon to Lebo-hamath, and on to Zedad,[8] [16] Berothah, Sibraim (which lies on the border between Damascus and Hamath), as far as Hazer-hatticon, which is on the border of Hauran. [17] So the boundary shall run from the sea to Hazar-enan, which is on the northern border of Damascus, with the border of Hamath to the north.[9] This shall be the north side.[10]

[18] "On the east side, the boundary shall run between Hauran and Damascus; along the Jordan between Gilead and the land of Israel; to the eastern sea and as far as Tamar.[11] This shall be the east side.

[19] "On the south side, it shall run from Tamar as far as the waters of Meribah-kadesh, from there along the Brook of Egypt[12] to the Great Sea. This shall be the south side.

[20] "On the west side, the Great Sea shall be the boundary to a point opposite Lebo-hamath. This shall be the west side.

[21] "So you shall divide this land among you according to the tribes of Israel. [22] You shall allot it as an inheritance for yourselves and for the sojourners who reside among you and have had children among you. They shall be to you as native-born children of Israel. With you they shall be allotted an inheritance among the tribes of Israel. [23] In whatever tribe the sojourner resides, there you shall assign him his inheritance, declares the Lord God.

48 "These are the names of the tribes: Beginning at the northern extreme, beside the way of Hethlon to Lebo-hamath, as far as Hazar-enan (which is on the northern border of Damascus over against Hamath), and extending[13] from the east side to the west,[14] Dan, one portion. [2] Adjoining the territory of Dan, from the east side to the west, Asher, one portion. [3] Adjoining the territory of Asher, from the east side to the west, Naphtali, one portion. [4] Adjoining the territory of Naphtali, from the east side to the west, Manasseh, one portion. [5] Adjoining the territory of Manasseh, from the east side to the west, Ephraim, one portion. [6] Adjoining the territory of Ephraim, from the east side to the west, Reuben, one portion. [7] Adjoining the territory of Reuben, from the east side to the west, Judah, one portion.

[1] A cubit was about 18 inches or 45 centimeters [2] That is, the Dead Sea [3] Hebrew will be healed; also verses 9, 11 [4] Septuagint, Syriac, Vulgate, Targum; Hebrew the two rivers go [5] Hebrew lacks the waters of the sea [6] That is, the Mediterranean Sea; also verses 15, 19, 20 [7] Probable reading; Hebrew The valley of the boundary [8] Septuagint; Hebrew the entrance of Zedad, Hamath [9] The meaning of the Hebrew is uncertain [10] Probable reading; Hebrew and as for the north side [11] Compare Syriac; Hebrew to the eastern sea you shall measure [12] Hebrew lacks of Egypt [13] Probable reading; Hebrew and they shall be his [14] Septuagint (compare verses 2–8); Hebrew the east side the west

8 "Adjoining the territory of Judah, from the east side to the west, shall be the portion which you shall set apart, 25,000 cubits[1] in breadth, and in length equal to one of the tribal portions, from the east side to the west, with the sanctuary in the midst of it. 9 The portion that you shall set apart for the LORD shall be 25,000 cubits in length, and 20,000[2] in breadth. 10 These shall be the allotments of the holy portion: the priests shall have an allotment measuring 25,000 cubits on the northern side, 10,000 cubits in breadth on the western side, 10,000 in breadth on the eastern side, and 25,000 in length on the southern side, with the sanctuary of the LORD in the midst of it. 11 This shall be for the consecrated priests, the sons of Zadok, who kept my charge, who did not go astray when the people of Israel went astray, as the Levites did. 12 And it shall belong to them as a special portion from the holy portion of the land, a most holy place, adjoining the territory of the Levites. 13 And alongside the territory of the priests, the Levites shall have an allotment 25,000 cubits in length and 10,000 in breadth. The whole length shall be 25,000 cubits and the breadth 20,000.[3] 14 They shall not sell or exchange any of it. They shall not alienate this choice portion of the land, for it is holy to the LORD.

15 "The remainder, 5,000 cubits in breadth and 25,000 in length, shall be for common use for the city, for dwellings and for open country. In the midst of it shall be the city, 16 and these shall be its measurements: the north side 4,500 cubits, the south side 4,500, the east side 4,500, and the west side 4,500. 17 And the city shall have open land: on the north 250 cubits, on the south 250, on the east 250, and on the west 250. 18 The remainder of the length alongside the holy portion shall be 10,000 cubits to the east, and 10,000 to the west, and it shall be alongside the holy portion. Its produce shall be food for the workers of the city. 19 And the workers of the city, from all the tribes of Israel, shall till it. 20 The whole portion that you shall set apart shall be 25,000 cubits square, that is, the holy portion together with the property of the city.

21 "What remains on both sides of the holy portion and of the property of the city shall belong to the prince. Extending from the 25,000 cubits of the holy portion to the east border, and westward from the 25,000 cubits to the west border, parallel to the tribal portions, it shall belong to the prince. The holy portion with the sanctuary of the temple shall be in its midst. 22 It shall be separate from the property of the Levites and the property of the city, which are in the midst of that which belongs to the prince. The portion of the prince shall lie between the territory of Judah and the territory of Benjamin.

23 "As for the rest of the tribes: from the east side to the west, Benjamin, one portion. 24 Adjoining the territory of Benjamin, from the east side to the west, Simeon, one portion. 25 Adjoining the territory of Simeon, from the east side to the west, Issachar, one portion. 26 Adjoining the territory of Issachar, from the east side to the west, Zebulun, one portion. 27 Adjoining the territory of Zebulun, from the east side to the west, Gad, one portion. 28 And adjoining the territory of Gad to the south, the boundary shall run from Tamar to the waters of Meribah-kadesh, from there along the Brook of Egypt[4] to the Great Sea.[5] 29 This is the land that you shall allot as an inheritance among the tribes of Israel, and these are their portions, declares the Lord GOD.

The Gates of the City

30 "These shall be the exits of the city: On the north side, which is to be 4,500 cubits by measure, 31 three gates, the gate of Reuben, the gate of Judah, and the gate of Levi, the gates of the city being named after the tribes of Israel. 32 On the east side, which is to be 4,500 cubits, three gates, the gate of Joseph, the gate of Benjamin, and the gate of Dan. 33 On the south side, which is to be 4,500 cubits by measure, three gates, the gate of Simeon, the gate of Issachar, and the gate of Zebulun. 34 On the west side, which is to be 4,500 cubits, three gates,[6] the gate of Gad, the gate of Asher, and the gate of Naphtali. 35 The circumference of the city shall be 18,000 cubits. And the name of the city from that time on shall be, The LORD Is There."

---

[1] A cubit was about 18 inches or 45 centimeters [2] Compare 45:1; Hebrew *10,000* [3] Septuagint; Hebrew *10,000* [4] Hebrew lacks *of Egypt* [5] That is, the Mediterranean Sea [6] One Hebrew manuscript, Syriac (compare Septuagint); most Hebrew manuscripts *their gates three*

DANIEL

Daniel Taken to Babylon

1 In the third year of the reign of Jehoiakim king of Judah, Nebuchadnezzar king of Babylon came to Jerusalem and besieged it. ² And the Lord gave Jehoiakim king of Judah into his hand, with some of the vessels of the house of God. And he brought them to the land of Shinar, to the house of his god, and placed the vessels in the treasury of his god. ³ Then the king commanded Ashpenaz, his chief eunuch, to bring some of the people of Israel, both of the royal family[1] and of the nobility, ⁴ youths without blemish, of good appearance and skillful in all wisdom, endowed with knowledge, understanding learning, and competent to stand in the king's palace, and to teach them the literature and language of the Chaldeans. ⁵ The king assigned them a daily portion of the food that the king ate, and of the wine that he drank. They were to be educated for three years, and at the end of that time they were to stand before the king. ⁶ Among these were Daniel, Hananiah, Mishael, and Azariah of the tribe of Judah. ⁷ And the chief of the eunuchs gave them names: Daniel he called Belteshazzar, Hananiah he called Shadrach, Mishael he called Meshach, and Azariah he called Abednego.

Daniel's Faithfulness

⁸ But Daniel resolved that he would not defile himself with the king's food, or with the wine that he drank. Therefore he asked the chief of the eunuchs to allow him not to defile himself. ⁹ And God gave Daniel favor and compassion in the sight of the chief of the eunuchs, ¹⁰ and the chief of the eunuchs said to Daniel, "I fear my lord the king, who assigned your food and your drink; for why should he see that you were in worse condition than the youths who are of your own age? So you would endanger my head with the king." ¹¹ Then Daniel said to the steward whom the chief of the eunuchs had assigned over Daniel, Hananiah, Mishael, and Azariah, ¹² "Test your servants for ten days; let us be given vegetables to eat and water to drink. ¹³ Then let our appearance and the appearance of the youths who eat the king's food be observed by you, and deal with your servants according to what you see." ¹⁴ So he listened to them in this matter, and tested them for ten days. ¹⁵ At the end of ten days it was seen that they were better in appearance and fatter in flesh than all the youths who ate the king's food. ¹⁶ So the steward took away their food and the wine they were to drink, and gave them vegetables.

¹⁷ As for these four youths, God gave them learning and skill in all literature and wisdom, and Daniel had understanding in all visions and dreams. ¹⁸ At the end of the time, when the king had commanded that they should be brought in, the chief of the eunuchs brought them in before Nebuchadnezzar. ¹⁹ And the king spoke with them, and among all of them none was found like Daniel, Hananiah, Mishael, and Azariah. Therefore they stood before the king. ²⁰ And in every matter of wisdom and understanding about which the king inquired of them, he found them ten times better than all the magicians and enchanters that were in all his kingdom. ²¹ And Daniel was there until the first year of King Cyrus.

Nebuchadnezzar's Dream

2 In the second year of the reign of Nebuchadnezzar, Nebuchadnezzar had dreams; his spirit was troubled, and his sleep left him. ² Then the king commanded that the magicians, the enchanters, the sorcerers, and the Chaldeans be summoned to tell the king his dreams. So they came in and stood before the king. ³ And the king said to them, "I had a dream, and my spirit is troubled to know the dream." ⁴ Then the Chaldeans said to the king in Aramaic,[2] "O king, live forever! Tell your servants the dream, and we will show the interpretation." ⁵ The king answered and said to the Chaldeans, "The word from me is firm: if you do not make known to me the dream and its interpretation, you shall be torn limb from limb, and your houses shall be laid in ruins. ⁶ But if you show the dream and its interpretation, you shall receive from me gifts and rewards and great honor. Therefore show me the dream and its interpretation." ⁷ They answered a second time and said, "Let the king tell his servants the dream, and we will show its

[1] Hebrew *of the seed of the kingdom* [2] The text from this point to the end of chapter 7 is in Aramaic

interpretation." [8] The king answered and said, "I know with certainty that you are trying to gain time, because you see that the word from me is firm— [9] if you do not make the dream known to me, there is but one sentence for you. You have agreed to speak lying and corrupt words before me till the times change. Therefore tell me the dream, and I shall know that you can show me its interpretation." [10] The Chaldeans answered the king and said, "There is not a man on earth who can meet the king's demand, for no great and powerful king has asked such a thing of any magician or enchanter or Chaldean. [11] The thing that the king asks is difficult, and no one can show it to the king except the gods, whose dwelling is not with flesh."

[12] Because of this the king was angry and very furious, and commanded that all the wise men of Babylon be destroyed. [13] So the decree went out, and the wise men were about to be killed; and they sought Daniel and his companions, to kill them. [14] Then Daniel replied with prudence and discretion to Arioch, the captain of the king's guard, who had gone out to kill the wise men of Babylon. [15] He declared[1] to Arioch, the king's captain, "Why is the decree of the king so urgent?" Then Arioch made the matter known to Daniel. [16] And Daniel went in and requested the king to appoint him a time, that he might show the interpretation to the king.

God Reveals Nebuchadnezzar's Dream

[17] Then Daniel went to his house and made the matter known to Hananiah, Mishael, and Azariah, his companions, [18] and told them to seek mercy from the God of heaven concerning this mystery, so that Daniel and his companions might not be destroyed with the rest of the wise men of Babylon. [19] Then the mystery was revealed to Daniel in a vision of the night. Then Daniel blessed the God of heaven. [20] Daniel answered and said:

"Blessed be the name of God forever and ever,
to whom belong wisdom and might.
[21] He changes times and seasons;
he removes kings and sets up kings;
he gives wisdom to the wise
and knowledge to those who have understanding;
[22] he reveals deep and hidden things;
he knows what is in the darkness,
and the light dwells with him.

[23] To you, O God of my fathers,
I give thanks and praise,
for you have given me wisdom and might,
and have now made known to me what we asked of you,
for you have made known to us the king's matter."

[24] Therefore Daniel went in to Arioch, whom the king had appointed to destroy the wise men of Babylon. He went and said thus to him: "Do not destroy the wise men of Babylon; bring me in before the king, and I will show the king the interpretation."

[25] Then Arioch brought in Daniel before the king in haste and said thus to him: "I have found among the exiles from Judah a man who will make known to the king the interpretation." [26] The king declared to Daniel, whose name was Belteshazzar, "Are you able to make known to me the dream that I have seen and its interpretation?" [27] Daniel answered the king and said, "No wise men, enchanters, magicians, or astrologers can show to the king the mystery that the king has asked, [28] but there is a God in heaven who reveals mysteries, and he has made known to King Nebuchadnezzar what will be in the latter days. Your dream and the visions of your head as you lay in bed are these: [29] To you, O king, as you lay in bed came thoughts of what would be after this, and he who reveals mysteries made known to you what is to be. [30] But as for me, this mystery has been revealed to me, not because of any wisdom that I have more than all the living, but in order that the interpretation may be made known to the king, and that you may know the thoughts of your mind.

Daniel Interprets the Dream

[31] "You saw, O king, and behold, a great image. This image, mighty and of exceeding brightness, stood before you, and its appearance was frightening. [32] The head of this image was of fine gold, its chest and arms of silver, its middle and thighs of bronze, [33] its legs of iron, its feet partly of iron and partly of clay. [34] As you looked, a stone was cut out by no human hand, and it struck the image on its feet of iron and clay, and broke them in pieces. [35] Then the iron, the clay, the bronze, the silver, and the gold, all together were broken in pieces, and became like the chaff of the summer threshing floors; and the wind carried them away, so that not a trace of them could be found. But the stone that

---

[1] Aramaic *answered and said*; also verse 26

struck the image became a great mountain and filled the whole earth.

36 "This was the dream. Now we will tell the king its interpretation. 37 You, O king, the king of kings, to whom the God of heaven has given the kingdom, the power, and the might, and the glory, 38 and into whose hand he has given, wherever they dwell, the children of man, the beasts of the field, and the birds of the heavens, making you rule over them all—you are the head of gold. 39 Another kingdom inferior to you shall arise after you, and yet a third kingdom of bronze, which shall rule over all the earth. 40 And there shall be a fourth kingdom, strong as iron, because iron breaks to pieces and shatters all things. And like iron that crushes, it shall break and crush all these. 41 And as you saw the feet and toes, partly of potter's clay and partly of iron, it shall be a divided kingdom, but some of the firmness of iron shall be in it, just as you saw iron mixed with the soft clay. 42 And as the toes of the feet were partly iron and partly clay, so the kingdom shall be partly strong and partly brittle. 43 As you saw the iron mixed with soft clay, so they will mix with one another in marriage,[1] but they will not hold together, just as iron does not mix with clay. 44 And in the days of those kings the God of heaven will set up a kingdom that shall never be destroyed, nor shall the kingdom be left to another people. It shall break in pieces all these kingdoms and bring them to an end, and it shall stand forever, 45 just as you saw that a stone was cut from a mountain by no human hand, and that it broke in pieces the iron, the bronze, the clay, the silver, and the gold. A great God has made known to the king what shall be after this. The dream is certain, and its interpretation sure."

Daniel Is Promoted

46 Then King Nebuchadnezzar fell upon his face and paid homage to Daniel, and commanded that an offering and incense be offered up to him. 47 The king answered and said to Daniel, "Truly, your God is God of gods and Lord of kings, and a revealer of mysteries, for you have been able to reveal this mystery." 48 Then the king gave Daniel high honors and many great gifts, and made him ruler over the whole province of Babylon and chief prefect over all the wise men of Babylon. 49 Daniel made a request of the king, and he appointed Shadrach, Meshach, and Abednego over the affairs of the province of Babylon. But Daniel remained at the king's court.

Nebuchadnezzar's Golden Image

3 King Nebuchadnezzar made an image of gold, whose height was sixty cubits[2] and its breadth six cubits. He set it up on the plain of Dura, in the province of Babylon. 2 Then King Nebuchadnezzar sent to gather the satraps, the prefects, and the governors, the counselors, the treasurers, the justices, the magistrates, and all the officials of the provinces to come to the dedication of the image that King Nebuchadnezzar had set up. 3 Then the satraps, the prefects, and the governors, the counselors, the treasurers, the justices, the magistrates, and all the officials of the provinces gathered for the dedication of the image that King Nebuchadnezzar had set up. And they stood before the image that Nebuchadnezzar had set up. 4 And the herald proclaimed aloud, "You are commanded, O peoples, nations, and languages, 5 that when you hear the sound of the horn, pipe, lyre, trigon, harp, bagpipe, and every kind of music, you are to fall down and worship the golden image that King Nebuchadnezzar has set up. 6 And whoever does not fall down and worship shall immediately be cast into a burning fiery furnace." 7 Therefore, as soon as all the peoples heard the sound of the horn, pipe, lyre, trigon, harp, bagpipe, and every kind of music, all the peoples, nations, and languages fell down and worshiped the golden image that King Nebuchadnezzar had set up.

The Fiery Furnace

8 Therefore at that time certain Chaldeans came forward and maliciously accused the Jews. 9 They declared[3] to King Nebuchadnezzar, "O king, live forever! 10 You, O king, have made a decree, that every man who hears the sound of the horn, pipe, lyre, trigon, harp, bagpipe, and every kind of music, shall fall down and worship the golden image. 11 And whoever does not fall down and worship shall be cast into a burning fiery furnace. 12 There are certain Jews whom you have appointed over the affairs of the province of Babylon: Shadrach, Meshach, and Abednego. These men, O king, pay no attention to you; they do not serve your gods or worship the golden image that you have set up."

---

[1] Aramaic *by the seed of men*   [2] A cubit was about 18 inches or 45 centimeters   [3] Aramaic *answered and said*; also verses 24, 26

13 Then Nebuchadnezzar in furious rage commanded that Shadrach, Meshach, and Abednego be brought. So they brought these men before the king. **14** Nebuchadnezzar answered and said to them, "Is it true, O Shadrach, Meshach, and Abednego, that you do not serve my gods or worship the golden image that I have set up? **15** Now if you are ready when you hear the sound of the horn, pipe, lyre, trigon, harp, bagpipe, and every kind of music, to fall down and worship the image that I have made, well and good.¹ But if you do not worship, you shall immediately be cast into a burning fiery furnace. And who is the god who will deliver you out of my hands?"

16 Shadrach, Meshach, and Abednego answered and said to the king, "O Nebuchadnezzar, we have no need to answer you in this matter. **17** If this be so, our God whom we serve is able to deliver us from the burning fiery furnace, and he will deliver us out of your hand, O king.² **18** But if not, be it known to you, O king, that we will not serve your gods or worship the golden image that you have set up."

19 Then Nebuchadnezzar was filled with fury, and the expression of his face was changed against Shadrach, Meshach, and Abednego. He ordered the furnace heated seven times more than it was usually heated. **20** And he ordered some of the mighty men of his army to bind Shadrach, Meshach, and Abednego, and to cast them into the burning fiery furnace. **21** Then these men were bound in their cloaks, their tunics,³ their hats, and their other garments, and they were thrown into the burning fiery furnace. **22** Because the king's order was urgent and the furnace overheated, the flame of the fire killed those men who took up Shadrach, Meshach, and Abednego. **23** And these three men, Shadrach, Meshach, and Abednego, fell bound into the burning fiery furnace.

24 Then King Nebuchadnezzar was astonished and rose up in haste. He declared to his counselors, "Did we not cast three men bound into the fire?" They answered and said to the king, "True, O king." **25** He answered and said, "But I see four men unbound, walking in the midst of the fire, and they are not hurt; and the appearance of the fourth is like a son of the gods."

26 Then Nebuchadnezzar came near to the door of the burning fiery furnace; he declared, "Shadrach, Meshach, and Abednego, servants of the Most High God, come out, and come here!" Then Shadrach, Meshach, and Abednego came out from the fire. **27** And the satraps, the prefects, the governors, and the king's counselors gathered together and saw that the fire had not had any power over the bodies of those men. The hair of their heads was not singed, their cloaks were not harmed, and no smell of fire had come upon them. **28** Nebuchadnezzar answered and said, "Blessed be the God of Shadrach, Meshach, and Abednego, who has sent his angel and delivered his servants, who trusted in him, and set aside⁴ the king's command, and yielded up their bodies rather than serve and worship any god except their own God. **29** Therefore I make a decree: Any people, nation, or language that speaks anything against the God of Shadrach, Meshach, and Abednego shall be torn limb from limb, and their houses laid in ruins, for there is no other god who is able to rescue in this way." **30** Then the king promoted Shadrach, Meshach, and Abednego in the province of Babylon.

Nebuchadnezzar Praises God

4 **5** King Nebuchadnezzar to all peoples, nations, and languages, that dwell in all the earth: Peace be multiplied to you! **2** It has seemed good to me to show the signs and wonders that the Most High God has done for me.

3   How great are his signs,
         how mighty his wonders!
     His kingdom is an everlasting kingdom,
         and his dominion endures from generation to generation.

Nebuchadnezzar's Second Dream

4 **6** I, Nebuchadnezzar, was at ease in my house and prospering in my palace. **5** I saw a dream that made me afraid. As I lay in bed the fancies and the visions of my head alarmed me. **6** So I made a decree that all the wise men of Babylon should be brought before me, that they might make known to me the interpretation of the dream. **7** Then the magicians, the enchanters, the Chaldeans, and the astrologers came in, and I told them the dream, but they could not make known to me its interpretation. **8** At last Daniel came in before me—he who was named Belteshazzar after the name of my god, and in

¹ Aramaic lacks *well and good*   ² Or *If our God whom we serve is able to deliver us, he will deliver us from the burning fiery furnace and out of your hand, O king*   ³ The meaning of the Aramaic words rendered *cloaks* and *tunics* is uncertain; also verse 27   ⁴ Aramaic *and changed*   ⁵ Ch 3:31 in Aramaic   ⁶ Ch 4:1 in Aramaic

whom is the spirit of the holy gods[1]—and I told him the dream, saying, [9] "O Belteshazzar, chief of the magicians, because I know that the spirit of the holy gods is in you and that no mystery is too difficult for you, tell me the visions of my dream that I saw and their interpretation. [10] The visions of my head as I lay in bed were these: I saw, and behold, a tree in the midst of the earth, and its height was great. [11] The tree grew and became strong, and its top reached to heaven, and it was visible to the end of the whole earth. [12] Its leaves were beautiful and its fruit abundant, and in it was food for all. The beasts of the field found shade under it, and the birds of the heavens lived in its branches, and all flesh was fed from it.

[13] "I saw in the visions of my head as I lay in bed, and behold, a watcher, a holy one, came down from heaven. [14] He proclaimed aloud and said thus: 'Chop down the tree and lop off its branches, strip off its leaves and scatter its fruit. Let the beasts flee from under it and the birds from its branches. [15] But leave the stump of its roots in the earth, bound with a band of iron and bronze, amid the tender grass of the field. Let him be wet with the dew of heaven. Let his portion be with the beasts in the grass of the earth. [16] Let his mind be changed from a man's, and let a beast's mind be given to him; and let seven periods of time pass over him. [17] The sentence is by the decree of the watchers, the decision by the word of the holy ones, to the end that the living may know that the Most High rules the kingdom of men and gives it to whom he will and sets over it the lowliest of men.' [18] This dream I, King Nebuchadnezzar, saw. And you, O Belteshazzar, tell me the interpretation, because all the wise men of my kingdom are not able to make known to me the interpretation, but you are able, for the spirit of the holy gods is in you."

Daniel Interprets the Second Dream

[19] Then Daniel, whose name was Belteshazzar, was dismayed for a while, and his thoughts alarmed him. The king answered and said, "Belteshazzar, let not the dream or the interpretation alarm you." Belteshazzar answered and said, "My lord, may the dream be for those who hate you and its interpretation for your enemies! [20] The tree you saw, which grew and became strong, so that its top reached to heaven, and it was visible to the end of the whole earth, [21] whose leaves were beautiful and its fruit abundant, and in which was food for all, under which beasts of the field found shade, and in whose branches the birds of the heavens lived— [22] it is you, O king, who have grown and become strong. Your greatness has grown and reaches to heaven, and your dominion to the ends of the earth. [23] And because the king saw a watcher, a holy one, coming down from heaven and saying, 'Chop down the tree and destroy it, but leave the stump of its roots in the earth, bound with a band of iron and bronze, in the tender grass of the field, and let him be wet with the dew of heaven, and let his portion be with the beasts of the field, till seven periods of time pass over him,' [24] this is the interpretation, O king: It is a decree of the Most High, which has come upon my lord the king, [25] that you shall be driven from among men, and your dwelling shall be with the beasts of the field. You shall be made to eat grass like an ox, and you shall be wet with the dew of heaven, and seven periods of time shall pass over you, till you know that the Most High rules the kingdom of men and gives it to whom he will. [26] And as it was commanded to leave the stump of the roots of the tree, your kingdom shall be confirmed for you from the time that you know that Heaven rules. [27] Therefore, O king, let my counsel be acceptable to you: break off your sins by practicing righteousness, and your iniquities by showing mercy to the oppressed, that there may perhaps be a lengthening of your prosperity."

Nebuchadnezzar's Humiliation

[28] All this came upon King Nebuchadnezzar. [29] At the end of twelve months he was walking on the roof of the royal palace of Babylon, [30] and the king answered and said, "Is not this great Babylon, which I have built by my mighty power as a royal residence and for the glory of my majesty?" [31] While the words were still in the king's mouth, there fell a voice from heaven, "O King Nebuchadnezzar, to you it is spoken: The kingdom has departed from you, [32] and you shall be driven from among men, and your dwelling shall be with the beasts of the field. And you shall be made to eat grass like an ox, and seven periods of time shall pass over you, until you know that the Most High rules the kingdom of men and gives it to whom he will." [33] Immediately the word was fulfilled against Nebuchadnezzar. He was driven from among

---

[1] Or *Spirit of the holy God*; also verses 9, 18

men and ate grass like an ox, and his body was wet with the dew of heaven till his hair grew as long as eagles' feathers, and his nails were like birds' claws.

Nebuchadnezzar Restored

34 At the end of the days I, Nebuchadnezzar, lifted my eyes to heaven, and my reason returned to me, and I blessed the Most High, and praised and honored him who lives forever,

> for his dominion is an everlasting dominion,
> and his kingdom endures from generation to generation;
> **35** all the inhabitants of the earth are accounted as nothing,
> and he does according to his will among the host of heaven
> and among the inhabitants of the earth;
> and none can stay his hand
> or say to him, "What have you done?"

36 At the same time my reason returned to me, and for the glory of my kingdom, my majesty and splendor returned to me. My counselors and my lords sought me, and I was established in my kingdom, and still more greatness was added to me. **37** Now I, Nebuchadnezzar, praise and extol and honor the King of heaven, for all his works are right and his ways are just; and those who walk in pride he is able to humble.

The Handwriting on the Wall

5 King Belshazzar made a great feast for a thousand of his lords and drank wine in front of the thousand. **2** Belshazzar, when he tasted the wine, commanded that the vessels of gold and of silver that Nebuchadnezzar his father[1] had taken out of the temple in Jerusalem be brought, that the king and his lords, his wives, and his concubines might drink from them. **3** Then they brought in the golden vessels that had been taken out of the temple, the house of God in Jerusalem, and the king and his lords, his wives, and his concubines drank from them. **4** They drank wine and praised the gods of gold and silver, bronze, iron, wood, and stone.

5 Immediately the fingers of a human hand appeared and wrote on the plaster of the wall of the king's palace, opposite the lampstand. And the king saw the hand as it wrote. **6** Then the king's color changed, and his thoughts alarmed him; his limbs gave way, and his knees knocked

together. **7** The king called loudly to bring in the enchanters, the Chaldeans, and the astrologers. The king declared[2] to the wise men of Babylon, "Whoever reads this writing, and shows me its interpretation, shall be clothed with purple and have a chain of gold around his neck and shall be the third ruler in the kingdom." **8** Then all the king's wise men came in, but they could not read the writing or make known to the king the interpretation. **9** Then King Belshazzar was greatly alarmed, and his color changed, and his lords were perplexed.

10 The queen,[3] because of the words of the king and his lords, came into the banqueting hall, and the queen declared, "O king, live forever! Let not your thoughts alarm you or your color change. **11** There is a man in your kingdom in whom is the spirit of the holy gods.[4] In the days of your father, light and understanding and wisdom like the wisdom of the gods were found in him, and King Nebuchadnezzar, your father—your father the king—made him chief of the magicians, enchanters, Chaldeans, and astrologers, **12** because an excellent spirit, knowledge, and understanding to interpret dreams, explain riddles, and solve problems were found in this Daniel, whom the king named Belteshazzar. Now let Daniel be called, and he will show the interpretation."

Daniel Interprets the Handwriting

13 Then Daniel was brought in before the king. The king answered and said to Daniel, "You are that Daniel, one of the exiles of Judah, whom the king my father brought from Judah. **14** I have heard of you that the spirit of the gods[5] is in you, and that light and understanding and excellent wisdom are found in you. **15** Now the wise men, the enchanters, have been brought in before me to read this writing and make known to me its interpretation, but they could not show the interpretation of the matter. **16** But I have heard that you can give interpretations and solve problems. Now if you can read the writing and make known to me its interpretation, you shall be clothed with purple and have a chain of gold around your neck and shall be the third ruler in the kingdom."

17 Then Daniel answered and said before the king, "Let your gifts be for yourself, and give

---

[1] Or predecessor; also verses 11, 13, 18   [2] Aramaic answered and said; also verse 10   [3] Or queen mother; twice in this verse   [4] Or Spirit of the holy God   [5] Or Spirit of God

your rewards to another. Nevertheless, I will read the writing to the king and make known to him the interpretation. ¹⁸O king, the Most High God gave Nebuchadnezzar your father kingship and greatness and glory and majesty. ¹⁹And because of the greatness that he gave him, all peoples, nations, and languages trembled and feared before him. Whom he would, he killed, and whom he would, he kept alive; whom he would, he raised up, and whom he would, he humbled. ²⁰But when his heart was lifted up and his spirit was hardened so that he dealt proudly, he was brought down from his kingly throne, and his glory was taken from him. ²¹He was driven from among the children of mankind, and his mind was made like that of a beast, and his dwelling was with the wild donkeys. He was fed grass like an ox, and his body was wet with the dew of heaven, until he knew that the Most High God rules the kingdom of mankind and sets over it whom he will. ²²And you his son,¹ Belshazzar, have not humbled your heart, though you knew all this, ²³but you have lifted up yourself against the Lord of heaven. And the vessels of his house have been brought in before you, and you and your lords, your wives, and your concubines have drunk wine from them. And you have praised the gods of silver and gold, of bronze, iron, wood, and stone, which do not see or hear or know, but the God in whose hand is your breath, and whose are all your ways, you have not honored.

²⁴"Then from his presence the hand was sent, and this writing was inscribed. ²⁵And this is the writing that was inscribed: MENE, MENE, TEKEL, and PARSIN. ²⁶This is the interpretation of the matter: MENE, God has numbered² the days of your kingdom and brought it to an end; ²⁷TEKEL, you have been weighed³ in the balances and found wanting; ²⁸PERES, your kingdom is divided and given to the Medes and Persians."⁴

²⁹Then Belshazzar gave the command, and Daniel was clothed with purple, a chain of gold was put around his neck, and a proclamation was made about him, that he should be the third ruler in the kingdom.

³⁰That very night Belshazzar the Chaldean king was killed. ³¹ ⁵And Darius the Mede received the kingdom, being about sixty-two years old.

Daniel and the Lions' Den

6 It pleased Darius to set over the kingdom 120 satraps, to be throughout the whole kingdom; ²and over them three high officials, of whom Daniel was one, to whom these satraps should give account, so that the king might suffer no loss. ³Then this Daniel became distinguished above all the other high officials and satraps, because an excellent spirit was in him. And the king planned to set him over the whole kingdom. ⁴Then the high officials and the satraps sought to find a ground for complaint against Daniel with regard to the kingdom, but they could find no ground for complaint or any fault, because he was faithful, and no error or fault was found in him. ⁵Then these men said, "We shall not find any ground for complaint against this Daniel unless we find it in connection with the law of his God."

⁶Then these high officials and satraps came by agreement⁶ to the king and said to him, "O King Darius, live forever! ⁷All the high officials of the kingdom, the prefects and the satraps, the counselors and the governors are agreed that the king should establish an ordinance and enforce an injunction, that whoever makes petition to any god or man for thirty days, except to you, O king, shall be cast into the den of lions. ⁸Now, O king, establish the injunction and sign the document, so that it cannot be changed, according to the law of the Medes and the Persians, which cannot be revoked." ⁹Therefore King Darius signed the document and injunction.

¹⁰When Daniel knew that the document had been signed, he went to his house where he had windows in his upper chamber open toward Jerusalem. He got down on his knees three times a day and prayed and gave thanks before his God, as he had done previously. ¹¹Then these men came by agreement and found Daniel making petition and plea before his God. ¹²Then they came near and said before the king, concerning the injunction, "O king! Did you not sign an injunction, that anyone who makes petition to any god or man within thirty days except to you, O king, shall be cast into the den of lions?" The king answered and said, "The thing stands fast, according to the law of the Medes and Persians, which cannot be revoked." ¹³Then they answered and said before the king, "Daniel, who is one of the exiles from

¹ Or successor ² MENE sounds like the Aramaic for numbered ³ TEKEL sounds like the Aramaic for weighed ⁴ PERES (the singular of Parsin) sounds like the Aramaic for divided and for Persia ⁵ Ch 6:1 in Aramaic ⁶ Or came thronging; also verses 11, 15

Judah, pays no attention to you, O king, or the injunction you have signed, but makes his petition three times a day."

¹⁴ Then the king, when he heard these words, was much distressed and set his mind to deliver Daniel. And he labored till the sun went down to rescue him. ¹⁵ Then these men came by agreement to the king and said to the king, "Know, O king, that it is a law of the Medes and Persians that no injunction or ordinance that the king establishes can be changed."

¹⁶ Then the king commanded, and Daniel was brought and cast into the den of lions. The king declared[1] to Daniel, "May your God, whom you serve continually, deliver you!" ¹⁷ And a stone was brought and laid on the mouth of the den, and the king sealed it with his own signet and with the signet of his lords, that nothing might be changed concerning Daniel. ¹⁸ Then the king went to his palace and spent the night fasting; no diversions were brought to him, and sleep fled from him.

¹⁹ Then, at break of day, the king arose and went in haste to the den of lions. ²⁰ As he came near to the den where Daniel was, he cried out in a tone of anguish. The king declared to Daniel, "O Daniel, servant of the living God, has your God, whom you serve continually, been able to deliver you from the lions?" ²¹ Then Daniel said to the king, "O king, live forever! ²² My God sent his angel and shut the lions' mouths, and they have not harmed me, because I was found blameless before him; and also before you, O king, I have done no harm." ²³ Then the king was exceedingly glad, and commanded that Daniel be taken up out of the den. So Daniel was taken up out of the den, and no kind of harm was found on him, because he had trusted in his God. ²⁴ And the king commanded, and those men who had maliciously accused Daniel were brought and cast into the den of lions—they, their children, and their wives. And before they reached the bottom of the den, the lions overpowered them and broke all their bones in pieces.

²⁵ Then King Darius wrote to all the peoples, nations, and languages that dwell in all the earth: "Peace be multiplied to you. ²⁶ I make a decree, that in all my royal dominion people are to tremble and fear before the God of Daniel,

for he is the living God,
    enduring forever;
his kingdom shall never be destroyed,
    and his dominion shall be to the end.
²⁷ He delivers and rescues;
    he works signs and wonders
    in heaven and on earth,
he who has saved Daniel
    from the power of the lions."

²⁸ So this Daniel prospered during the reign of Darius and the reign of Cyrus the Persian.

Daniel's Vision of the Four Beasts

7 In the first year of Belshazzar king of Babylon, Daniel saw a dream and visions of his head as he lay in his bed. Then he wrote down the dream and told the sum of the matter. ² Daniel declared,[2] "I saw in my vision by night, and behold, the four winds of heaven were stirring up the great sea. ³ And four great beasts came up out of the sea, different from one another. ⁴ The first was like a lion and had eagles' wings. Then as I looked its wings were plucked off, and it was lifted up from the ground and made to stand on two feet like a man, and the mind of a man was given to it. ⁵ And behold, another beast, a second one, like a bear. It was raised up on one side. It had three ribs in its mouth between its teeth; and it was told, 'Arise, devour much flesh.' ⁶ After this I looked, and behold, another, like a leopard, with four wings of a bird on its back. And the beast had four heads, and dominion was given to it. ⁷ After this I saw in the night visions, and behold, a fourth beast, terrifying and dreadful and exceedingly strong. It had great iron teeth; it devoured and broke in pieces and stamped what was left with its feet. It was different from all the beasts that were before it, and it had ten horns. ⁸ I considered the horns, and behold, there came up among them another horn, a little one, before which three of the first horns were plucked up by the roots. And behold, in this horn were eyes like the eyes of a man, and a mouth speaking great things.

The Ancient of Days Reigns

⁹ "As I looked,

thrones were placed,
    and the Ancient of Days took his seat;
his clothing was white as snow,
    and the hair of his head like pure wool;
his throne was fiery flames;
    its wheels were burning fire.

---

[1] Aramaic *answered and said*; also verse 20 [2] Aramaic *answered and said*

[10] A stream of fire issued
    and came out from before him;
a thousand thousands served him,
    and ten thousand times ten thousand
        stood before him;
the court sat in judgment,
    and the books were opened.

[11] "I looked then because of the sound of the great words that the horn was speaking. And as I looked, the beast was killed, and its body destroyed and given over to be burned with fire. [12] As for the rest of the beasts, their dominion was taken away, but their lives were prolonged for a season and a time.

The Son of Man Is Given Dominion

[13] "I saw in the night visions,

and behold, with the clouds of heaven
    there came one like a son of man,
and he came to the Ancient of Days
    and was presented before him.
[14] And to him was given dominion
    and glory and a kingdom,
that all peoples, nations, and languages
    should serve him;
his dominion is an everlasting dominion,
    which shall not pass away,
and his kingdom one
    that shall not be destroyed.

Daniel's Vision Interpreted

[15] "As for me, Daniel, my spirit within me[1] was anxious, and the visions of my head alarmed me. [16] I approached one of those who stood there and asked him the truth concerning all this. So he told me and made known to me the interpretation of the things. [17] 'These four great beasts are four kings who shall arise out of the earth. [18] But the saints of the Most High shall receive the kingdom and possess the kingdom forever, forever and ever.'

[19] "Then I desired to know the truth about the fourth beast, which was different from all the rest, exceedingly terrifying, with its teeth of iron and claws of bronze, and which devoured and broke in pieces and stamped what was left with its feet, [20] and about the ten horns that were on its head, and the other horn that came up and before which three of them fell, the horn that had eyes and a mouth that spoke great things, and that seemed greater than its companions. [21] As I looked, this horn made war with the saints and prevailed over them, [22] until the

Ancient of Days came, and judgment was given for the saints of the Most High, and the time came when the saints possessed the kingdom. [23] "Thus he said: 'As for the fourth beast,

there shall be a fourth kingdom on earth,
    which shall be different from all the
        kingdoms,
and it shall devour the whole earth,
    and trample it down, and break it to
        pieces.
[24] As for the ten horns,
out of this kingdom ten kings shall arise,
    and another shall arise after them;
he shall be different from the former ones,
    and shall put down three kings.
[25] He shall speak words against the Most
        High,
    and shall wear out the saints of the
        Most High,
    and shall think to change the times and
        the law;
and they shall be given into his hand
    for a time, times, and half a time.
[26] But the court shall sit in judgment,
    and his dominion shall be taken away,
    to be consumed and destroyed to the
        end.
[27] And the kingdom and the dominion
    and the greatness of the kingdoms
        under the whole heaven
    shall be given to the people of the saints
        of the Most High;
his kingdom shall be an everlasting king-
        dom,
    and all dominions shall serve and obey
        him.'[2]

[28] "Here is the end of the matter. As for me, Daniel, my thoughts greatly alarmed me, and my color changed, but I kept the matter in my heart."

Daniel's Vision of the Ram and the Goat

8 In the third year of the reign of King Belshazzar a vision appeared to me, Daniel, after that which appeared to me at the first. [2] And I saw in the vision; and when I saw, I was in Susa the citadel, which is in the province of Elam. And I saw in the vision, and I was at the Ulai canal. [3] I raised my eyes and saw, and behold, a ram standing on the bank of the canal. It had two horns, and both horns were high, but one was higher than the other, and the higher

---

[1] Aramaic *within its sheath* [2] Or *their kingdom shall be an everlasting kingdom, and all dominions shall serve and obey them*

one came up last. ⁴I saw the ram charging westward and northward and southward. No beast could stand before him, and there was no one who could rescue from his power. He did as he pleased and became great.

⁵As I was considering, behold, a male goat came from the west across the face of the whole earth, without touching the ground. And the goat had a conspicuous horn between his eyes. ⁶He came to the ram with the two horns, which I had seen standing on the bank of the canal, and he ran at him in his powerful wrath. ⁷I saw him come close to the ram, and he was enraged against him and struck the ram and broke his two horns. And the ram had no power to stand before him, but he cast him down to the ground and trampled on him. And there was no one who could rescue the ram from his power. ⁸Then the goat became exceedingly great, but when he was strong, the great horn was broken, and instead of it there came up four conspicuous horns toward the four winds of heaven.

⁹Out of one of them came a little horn, which grew exceedingly great toward the south, toward the east, and toward the glorious land. ¹⁰It grew great, even to the host of heaven. And some of the host and some¹ of the stars it threw down to the ground and trampled on them. ¹¹It became great, even as great as the Prince of the host. And the regular burnt offering was taken away from him, and the place of his sanctuary was overthrown. ¹²And a host will be given over to it together with the regular burnt offering because of transgression,² and it will throw truth to the ground, and it will act and prosper. ¹³Then I heard a holy one speaking, and another holy one said to the one who spoke, "For how long is the vision concerning the regular burnt offering, the transgression that makes desolate, and the giving over of the sanctuary and host to be trampled underfoot?" ¹⁴And he said to me,³ "For 2,300 evenings and mornings. Then the sanctuary shall be restored to its rightful state."

The Interpretation of the Vision

¹⁵When I, Daniel, had seen the vision, I sought to understand it. And behold, there stood before me one having the appearance of a man. ¹⁶And I heard a man's voice between the banks of the Ulai, and it called, "Gabriel, make this man understand the vision." ¹⁷So he came near where I stood. And when he came, I was frightened and fell on my face. But he said to me, "Understand, O son of man, that the vision is for the time of the end."

¹⁸And when he had spoken to me, I fell into a deep sleep with my face to the ground. But he touched me and made me stand up. ¹⁹He said, "Behold, I will make known to you what shall be at the latter end of the indignation, for it refers to the appointed time of the end. ²⁰As for the ram that you saw with the two horns, these are the kings of Media and Persia. ²¹And the goat⁴ is the king of Greece. And the great horn between his eyes is the first king. ²²As for the horn that was broken, in place of which four others arose, four kingdoms shall arise from his⁵ nation, but not with his power. ²³And at the latter end of their kingdom, when the transgressors have reached their limit, a king of bold face, one who understands riddles, shall arise. ²⁴His power shall be great—but not by his own power; and he shall cause fearful destruction and shall succeed in what he does, and destroy mighty men and the people who are the saints. ²⁵By his cunning he shall make deceit prosper under his hand, and in his own mind he shall become great. Without warning he shall destroy many. And he shall even rise up against the Prince of princes, and he shall be broken—but by no human hand. ²⁶The vision of the evenings and the mornings that has been told is true, but seal up the vision, for it refers to many days from now."

²⁷And I, Daniel, was overcome and lay sick for some days. Then I rose and went about the king's business, but I was appalled by the vision and did not understand it.

Daniel's Prayer for His People

9 In the first year of Darius the son of Ahasuerus, by descent a Mede, who was made king over the realm of the Chaldeans—²in the first year of his reign, I, Daniel, perceived in the books the number of years that, according to the word of the LORD to Jeremiah the prophet, must pass before the end of the desolations of Jerusalem, namely, seventy years.

³Then I turned my face to the Lord God, seeking him by prayer and pleas for mercy with fasting and sackcloth and ashes. ⁴I prayed to the LORD my God and made confession, saying, "O Lord, the great and awesome God, who keeps covenant and steadfast love with those who love

---

¹ Or host, that is, some ² Or in an act of rebellion ³ Hebrew; Septuagint, Theodotion, Vulgate to him ⁴ Or the shaggy goat ⁵ Theodotion, Septuagint, Vulgate; Hebrew a

him and keep his commandments, [5] we have sinned and done wrong and acted wickedly and rebelled, turning aside from your commandments and rules. [6] We have not listened to your servants the prophets, who spoke in your name to our kings, our princes, and our fathers, and to all the people of the land. [7] To you, O Lord, belongs righteousness, but to us open shame, as at this day, to the men of Judah, to the inhabitants of Jerusalem, and to all Israel, those who are near and those who are far away, in all the lands to which you have driven them, because of the treachery that they have committed against you. [8] To us, O LORD, belongs open shame, to our kings, to our princes, and to our fathers, because we have sinned against you. [9] To the Lord our God belong mercy and forgiveness, for we have rebelled against him [10] and have not obeyed the voice of the LORD our God by walking in his laws, which he set before us by his servants the prophets. [11] All Israel has transgressed your law and turned aside, refusing to obey your voice. And the curse and oath that are written in the Law of Moses the servant of God have been poured out upon us, because we have sinned against him. [12] He has confirmed his words, which he spoke against us and against our rulers who ruled us,[1] by bringing upon us a great calamity. For under the whole heaven there has not been done anything like what has been done against Jerusalem. [13] As it is written in the Law of Moses, all this calamity has come upon us; yet we have not entreated the favor of the LORD our God, turning from our iniquities and gaining insight by your truth. [14] Therefore the LORD has kept ready the calamity and has brought it upon us, for the LORD our God is righteous in all the works that he has done, and we have not obeyed his voice. [15] And now, O Lord our God, who brought your people out of the land of Egypt with a mighty hand, and have made a name for yourself, as at this day, we have sinned, we have done wickedly.

[16] "O Lord, according to all your righteous acts, let your anger and your wrath turn away from your city Jerusalem, your holy hill, because for our sins, and for the iniquities of our fathers, Jerusalem and your people have become a byword among all who are around us. [17] Now therefore, O our God, listen to the prayer of your servant and to his pleas for mercy, and for your own sake, O Lord,[2] make your face to shine upon your sanctuary, which is desolate. [18] O my God, incline your ear and hear. Open your eyes and see our desolations, and the city that is called by your name. For we do not present our pleas before you because of our righteousness, but because of your great mercy. [19] O Lord, hear; O Lord, forgive. O Lord, pay attention and act. Delay not, for your own sake, O my God, because your city and your people are called by your name."

Gabriel Brings an Answer

[20] While I was speaking and praying, confessing my sin and the sin of my people Israel, and presenting my plea before the LORD my God for the holy hill of my God, [21] while I was speaking in prayer, the man Gabriel, whom I had seen in the vision at the first, came to me in swift flight at the time of the evening sacrifice. [22] He made me understand, speaking with me and saying, "O Daniel, I have now come out to give you insight and understanding. [23] At the beginning of your pleas for mercy a word went out, and I have come to tell it to you, for you are greatly loved. Therefore consider the word and understand the vision.

The Seventy Weeks

[24] "Seventy weeks[3] are decreed about your people and your holy city, to finish the transgression, to put an end to sin, and to atone for iniquity, to bring in everlasting righteousness, to seal both vision and prophet, and to anoint a most holy place.[4] [25] Know therefore and understand that from the going out of the word to restore and build Jerusalem to the coming of an anointed one, a prince, there shall be seven weeks. Then for sixty-two weeks it shall be built again[5] with squares and moat, but in a troubled time. [26] And after the sixty-two weeks, an anointed one shall be cut off and shall have nothing. And the people of the prince who is to come shall destroy the city and the sanctuary. Its[6] end shall come with a flood, and to the end there shall be war. Desolations are decreed. [27] And he shall make a strong covenant with many for one week,[7] and for half of the week he shall put an end to sacrifice and offering. And on the wing of abominations shall come one who makes desolate, until the decreed end is poured out on the desolator."

---

[1] Or our judges who judged us [2] Hebrew for the Lord's sake [3] Or sevens; also twice in verse 25 and once in verse 26 [4] Or thing, or one [5] Or there shall be seven weeks and sixty-two weeks. It shall be built again [6] Or His [7] Or seven; twice in this verse

Daniel's Terrifying Vision of a Man

10 In the third year of Cyrus king of Persia a word was revealed to Daniel, who was named Belteshazzar. And the word was true, and it was a great conflict.[1] And he understood the word and had understanding of the vision.

2 In those days I, Daniel, was mourning for three weeks. 3 I ate no delicacies, no meat or wine entered my mouth, nor did I anoint myself at all, for the full three weeks. 4 On the twenty-fourth day of the first month, as I was standing on the bank of the great river (that is, the Tigris) 5 I lifted up my eyes and looked, and behold, a man clothed in linen, with a belt of fine gold from Uphaz around his waist. 6 His body was like beryl, his face like the appearance of lightning, his eyes like flaming torches, his arms and legs like the gleam of burnished bronze, and the sound of his words like the sound of a multitude. 7 And I, Daniel, alone saw the vision, for the men who were with me did not see the vision, but a great trembling fell upon them, and they fled to hide themselves. 8 So I was left alone and saw this great vision, and no strength was left in me. My radiant appearance was fearfully changed,[2] and I retained no strength. 9 Then I heard the sound of his words, and as I heard the sound of his words, I fell on my face in deep sleep with my face to the ground.

10 And behold, a hand touched me and set me trembling on my hands and knees. 11 And he said to me, "O Daniel, man greatly loved, understand the words that I speak to you, and stand upright, for now I have been sent to you." And when he had spoken this word to me, I stood up trembling. 12 Then he said to me, "Fear not, Daniel, for from the first day that you set your heart to understand and humbled yourself before your God, your words have been heard, and I have come because of your words. 13 The prince of the kingdom of Persia withstood me twenty-one days, but Michael, one of the chief princes, came to help me, for I was left there with the kings of Persia, 14 and came to make you understand what is to happen to your people in the latter days. For the vision is for days yet to come."

15 When he had spoken to me according to these words, I turned my face toward the ground and was mute. 16 And behold, one in the likeness of the children of man touched my lips. Then I opened my mouth and spoke. I said to him who stood before me, "O my lord, by reason of the vision pains have come upon me, and I retain no strength. 17 How can my lord's servant talk with my lord? For now no strength remains in me, and no breath is left in me."

18 Again one having the appearance of a man touched me and strengthened me. 19 And he said, "O man greatly loved, fear not, peace be with you; be strong and of good courage." And as he spoke to me, I was strengthened and said, "Let my lord speak, for you have strengthened me." 20 Then he said, "Do you know why I have come to you? But now I will return to fight against the prince of Persia; and when I go out, behold, the prince of Greece will come. 21 But I will tell you what is inscribed in the book of truth: there is none who contends by my side against these except Michael, your prince.

The Kings of the South and the North

11 "And as for me, in the first year of Darius the Mede, I stood up to confirm and strengthen him.

2 "And now I will show you the truth. Behold, three more kings shall arise in Persia, and a fourth shall be far richer than all of them. And when he has become strong through his riches, he shall stir up all against the kingdom of Greece. 3 Then a mighty king shall arise, who shall rule with great dominion and do as he wills. 4 And as soon as he has arisen, his kingdom shall be broken and divided toward the four winds of heaven, but not to his posterity, nor according to the authority with which he ruled, for his kingdom shall be plucked up and go to others besides these.

5 "Then the king of the south shall be strong, but one of his princes shall be stronger than he and shall rule, and his authority shall be a great authority. 6 After some years they shall make an alliance, and the daughter of the king of the south shall come to the king of the north to make an agreement. But she shall not retain the strength of her arm, and he and his arm shall not endure, but she shall be given up, and her attendants, he who fathered her, and he who supported[3] her in those times.

7 "And from a branch from her roots one shall arise in his place. He shall come against the army and enter the fortress of the king of the north, and he shall deal with them and

---

1 Or and it was about a great conflict 2 Hebrew My splendor was changed to ruin 3 Or obtained

shall prevail. [8] He shall also carry off to Egypt their gods with their metal images and their precious vessels of silver and gold, and for some years he shall refrain from attacking the king of the north. [9] Then the latter shall come into the realm of the king of the south but shall return to his own land.

[10] "His sons shall wage war and assemble a multitude of great forces, which shall keep coming and overflow and pass through, and again shall carry the war as far as his fortress. [11] Then the king of the south, moved with rage, shall come out and fight against the king of the north. And he shall raise a great multitude, but it shall be given into his hand. [12] And when the multitude is taken away, his heart shall be exalted, and he shall cast down tens of thousands, but he shall not prevail. [13] For the king of the north shall again raise a multitude, greater than the first. And after some years[1] he shall come on with a great army and abundant supplies.

[14] "In those times many shall rise against the king of the south, and the violent among your own people shall lift themselves up in order to fulfill the vision, but they shall fail. [15] Then the king of the north shall come and throw up siegeworks and take a well-fortified city. And the forces of the south shall not stand, or even his best troops, for there shall be no strength to stand. [16] But he who comes against him shall do as he wills, and none shall stand before him. And he shall stand in the glorious land, with destruction in his hand. [17] He shall set his face to come with the strength of his whole kingdom, and he shall bring terms of an agreement and perform them. He shall give him the daughter of women to destroy the kingdom,[2] but it shall not stand or be to his advantage. [18] Afterward he shall turn his face to the coastlands and shall capture many of them, but a commander shall put an end to his insolence. Indeed,[3] he shall turn his insolence back upon him. [19] Then he shall turn his face back toward the fortresses of his own land, but he shall stumble and fall, and shall not be found.

[20] "Then shall arise in his place one who shall send an exactor of tribute for the glory of the kingdom. But within a few days he shall be broken, neither in anger nor in battle. [21] In his place shall arise a contemptible person to whom royal majesty has not been given. He shall come in without warning and obtain the kingdom by flatteries. [22] Armies shall be utterly swept away before him and broken, even the prince of the covenant. [23] And from the time that an alliance is made with him he shall act deceitfully, and he shall become strong with a small people. [24] Without warning he shall come into the richest parts[4] of the province, and he shall do what neither his fathers nor his fathers' fathers have done, scattering among them plunder, spoil, and goods. He shall devise plans against strongholds, but only for a time. [25] And he shall stir up his power and his heart against the king of the south with a great army. And the king of the south shall wage war with an exceedingly great and mighty army, but he shall not stand, for plots shall be devised against him. [26] Even those who eat his food shall break him. His army shall be swept away, and many shall fall down slain. [27] And as for the two kings, their hearts shall be bent on doing evil. They shall speak lies at the same table, but to no avail, for the end is yet to be at the time appointed. [28] And he shall return to his land with great wealth, but his heart shall be set against the holy covenant. And he shall work his will and return to his own land.

[29] "At the time appointed he shall return and come into the south, but it shall not be this time as it was before. [30] For ships of Kittim shall come against him, and he shall be afraid and withdraw, and shall turn back and be enraged and take action against the holy covenant. He shall turn back and pay attention to those who forsake the holy covenant. [31] Forces from him shall appear and profane the temple and fortress, and shall take away the regular burnt offering. And they shall set up the abomination that makes desolate. [32] He shall seduce with flattery those who violate the covenant, but the people who know their God shall stand firm and take action. [33] And the wise among the people shall make many understand, though for some days they shall stumble by sword and flame, by captivity and plunder. [34] When they stumble, they shall receive a little help. And many shall join themselves to them with flattery, [35] and some of the wise shall stumble, so that they may be refined, purified, and made white, until the time of the end, for it still awaits the appointed time.

[36] "And the king shall do as he wills. He shall exalt himself and magnify himself above every god, and shall speak astonishing things against the God of gods. He shall prosper till the indignation is accomplished; for what is

---

[1] Hebrew *at the end of the times* [2] Hebrew *her, or it* [3] The meaning of the Hebrew is uncertain [4] Or *among the richest men*

decreed shall be done. [37] He shall pay no attention to the gods of his fathers, or to the one beloved by women. He shall not pay attention to any other god, for he shall magnify himself above all. [38] He shall honor the god of fortresses instead of these. A god whom his fathers did not know he shall honor with gold and silver, with precious stones and costly gifts. [39] He shall deal with the strongest fortresses with the help of a foreign god. Those who acknowledge him he shall load with honor. He shall make them rulers over many and shall divide the land for a price.[1]

[40] "At the time of the end, the king of the south shall attack[2] him, but the king of the north shall rush upon him like a whirlwind, with chariots and horsemen, and with many ships. And he shall come into countries and shall overflow and pass through. [41] He shall come into the glorious land. And tens of thousands shall fall, but these shall be delivered out of his hand: Edom and Moab and the main part of the Ammonites. [42] He shall stretch out his hand against the countries, and the land of Egypt shall not escape. [43] He shall become ruler of the treasures of gold and of silver, and all the precious things of Egypt, and the Libyans and the Cushites shall follow in his train. [44] But news from the east and the north shall alarm him, and he shall go out with great fury to destroy and devote many to destruction. [45] And he shall pitch his palatial tents between the sea and the glorious holy mountain. Yet he shall come to his end, with none to help him.

The Time of the End

12 "At that time shall arise Michael, the great prince who has charge of your people. And there shall be a time of trouble, such as never has been since there was a nation till that time. But at that time your people shall be delivered, everyone whose name shall be found written in the book. [2] And many of those who sleep in the dust of the earth shall awake, some to everlasting life, and some to shame and everlasting contempt. [3] And those who are wise shall shine like the brightness of the sky above;[3] and those who turn many to righteousness, like the stars forever and ever. [4] But you, Daniel, shut up the words and seal the book, until the time of the end. Many shall run to and fro, and knowledge shall increase."

[5] Then I, Daniel, looked, and behold, two others stood, one on this bank of the stream and one on that bank of the stream. [6] And someone said to the man clothed in linen, who was above the waters of the stream,[4] "How long shall it be till the end of these wonders?" [7] And I heard the man clothed in linen, who was above the waters of the stream; he raised his right hand and his left hand toward heaven and swore by him who lives forever that it would be for a time, times, and half a time, and that when the shattering of the power of the holy people comes to an end all these things would be finished. [8] I heard, but I did not understand. Then I said, "O my lord, what shall be the outcome of these things?" [9] He said, "Go your way, Daniel, for the words are shut up and sealed until the time of the end. [10] Many shall purify themselves and make themselves white and be refined, but the wicked shall act wickedly. And none of the wicked shall understand, but those who are wise shall understand. [11] And from the time that the regular burnt offering is taken away and the abomination that makes desolate is set up, there shall be 1,290 days. [12] Blessed is he who waits and arrives at the 1,335 days. [13] But go your way till the end. And you shall rest and shall stand in your allotted place at the end of the days."

---

[1] Or land as payment [2] Hebrew thrust at [3] Hebrew the expanse; compare Genesis 1:6–8 [4] Or who was upstream; also verse 7

HOSEA

1 The word of the LORD that came to Hosea, the son of Beeri, in the days of Uzziah, Jotham, Ahaz, and Hezekiah, kings of Judah, and in the days of Jeroboam the son of Joash, king of Israel.

Hosea's Wife and Children

2 When the LORD first spoke through Hosea, the LORD said to Hosea, "Go, take to yourself a wife of whoredom and have children of whoredom, for the land commits great whoredom by forsaking the LORD." 3 So he went and took Gomer, the daughter of Diblaim, and she conceived and bore him a son.

4 And the LORD said to him, "Call his name Jezreel, for in just a little while I will punish the house of Jehu for the blood of Jezreel, and I will put an end to the kingdom of the house of Israel. 5 And on that day I will break the bow of Israel in the Valley of Jezreel."

6 She conceived again and bore a daughter. And the LORD said to him, "Call her name No Mercy,[1] for I will no more have mercy on the house of Israel, to forgive them at all. 7 But I will have mercy on the house of Judah, and I will save them by the LORD their God. I will not save them by bow or by sword or by war or by horses or by horsemen."

8 When she had weaned No Mercy, she conceived and bore a son. 9 And the LORD said, "Call his name Not My People,[2] for you are not my people, and I am not your God."[3]

10 [4] Yet the number of the children of Israel shall be like the sand of the sea, which cannot be measured or numbered. And in the place where it was said to them, "You are not my people," it shall be said to them, "Children[5] of the living God." 11 And the children of Judah and the children of Israel shall be gathered together, and they shall appoint for themselves one head. And they shall go up from the land, for great shall be the day of Jezreel.

Israel's Unfaithfulness Punished

2 [6] Say to your brothers, "You are my people,"[7] and to your sisters, "You have received mercy."[8]

2 "Plead with your mother, plead—
   for she is not my wife,
   and I am not her husband—
that she put away her whoring from her face,
   and her adultery from between her breasts;
3 lest I strip her naked
   and make her as in the day she was born,
and make her like a wilderness,
   and make her like a parched land,
   and kill her with thirst.
4 Upon her children also I will have no mercy,
   because they are children of whoredom.
5 For their mother has played the whore;
   she who conceived them has acted shamefully.
For she said, 'I will go after my lovers,
   who give me my bread and my water,
   my wool and my flax, my oil and my drink.'
6 Therefore I will hedge up her[9] way with thorns,
   and I will build a wall against her,
   so that she cannot find her paths.
7 She shall pursue her lovers
   but not overtake them,
and she shall seek them
   but shall not find them.
Then she shall say,
   'I will go and return to my first husband,
   for it was better for me then than now.'
8 And she did not know
   that it was I who gave her
   the grain, the wine, and the oil,
and who lavished on her silver and gold,
   which they used for Baal.
9 Therefore I will take back
   my grain in its time,
   and my wine in its season,
and I will take away my wool and my flax,
   which were to cover her nakedness.
10 Now I will uncover her lewdness
   in the sight of her lovers,
   and no one shall rescue her out of my hand.

---

[1] Hebrew Lo-ruhama, which means she has not received mercy [2] Hebrew Lo-ammi, which means not my people [3] Hebrew I am not yours. [4] Ch 2:1 in Hebrew [5] Or Sons [6] Ch 2:3 in Hebrew [7] Hebrew ammi, which means my people [8] Hebrew ruhama, which means she has received mercy [9] Hebrew your

11   And I will put an end to all her mirth,
          her feasts, her new moons, her Sabbaths,
          and all her appointed feasts.
12   And I will lay waste her vines and her fig
              trees,
          of which she said,
       'These are my wages,
          which my lovers have given me.'
       I will make them a forest,
          and the beasts of the field shall devour
              them.
13   And I will punish her for the feast days of
              the Baals
          when she burned offerings to them
       and adorned herself with her ring and jew-
              elry,
          and went after her lovers
          and forgot me, declares the LORD.

The LORD's Mercy on Israel

14   "Therefore, behold, I will allure her,
          and bring her into the wilderness,
          and speak tenderly to her.
15   And there I will give her her vineyards
          and make the Valley of Achor[1] a door of
              hope.
       And there she shall answer as in the days of
              her youth,
          as at the time when she came out of the
              land of Egypt.

16"And in that day, declares the LORD, you will call me 'My Husband,' and no longer will you call me 'My Baal.' 17For I will remove the names of the Baals from her mouth, and they shall be remembered by name no more. 18And I will make for them a covenant on that day with the beasts of the field, the birds of the heavens, and the creeping things of the ground. And I will abolish[2] the bow, the sword, and war from the land, and I will make you lie down in safety. 19And I will betroth you to me forever. I will betroth you to me in righteousness and in justice, in steadfast love and in mercy. 20I will betroth you to me in faithfulness. And you shall know the LORD.

21   "And in that day I will answer, declares the
              LORD,
       I will answer the heavens,
          and they shall answer the earth,
22   and the earth shall answer the grain, the
              wine, and the oil,
          and they shall answer Jezreel,[3]
23   and I will sow her for myself in the land.

And I will have mercy on No Mercy,[4]
   and I will say to Not My People,[5] 'You
       are my people';
   and he shall say, 'You are my God.' "

Hosea Redeems His Wife

3 And the LORD said to me, "Go again, love a woman who is loved by another man and is an adulteress, even as the LORD loves the children of Israel, though they turn to other gods and love cakes of raisins." 2So I bought her for fifteen shekels of silver and a homer and a lethech[6] of barley. 3And I said to her, "You must dwell as mine for many days. You shall not play the whore, or belong to another man; so will I also be to you." 4For the children of Israel shall dwell many days without king or prince, without sacrifice or pillar, without ephod or household gods. 5Afterward the children of Israel shall return and seek the LORD their God, and David their king, and they shall come in fear to the LORD and to his goodness in the latter days.

The LORD Accuses Israel

4 Hear the word of the LORD, O children of Israel,
          for the LORD has a controversy with the
              inhabitants of the land.
       There is no faithfulness or steadfast love,
          and no knowledge of God in the land;
2   there is swearing, lying, murder, stealing,
              and committing adultery;
          they break all bounds, and bloodshed
              follows bloodshed.
3   Therefore the land mourns,
          and all who dwell in it languish,
       and also the beasts of the field
          and the birds of the heavens,
          and even the fish of the sea are taken
              away.

4   Yet let no one contend,
          and let none accuse,
          for with you is my contention, O priest.[7]
5   You shall stumble by day;
          the prophet also shall stumble with you
              by night;
          and I will destroy your mother.
6   My people are destroyed for lack of knowl-
              edge;
          because you have rejected knowledge,
          I reject you from being a priest to me.

---

[1] Achor means trouble; compare Joshua 7:26 [2] Hebrew break [3] Jezreel means God will sow [4] Hebrew Lo-ruhama [5] Hebrew Lo-ammi [6] A shekel was about 2/5 ounce or 11 grams; a homer was about 6 bushels or 220 liters; a lethech was about 3 bushels or 110 liters [7] Or for your people are like those who contend with the priest

And since you have forgotten the law of
　　your God,
　　I also will forget your children.

7 The more they increased,
　　the more they sinned against me;
　　I will change their glory into shame.
8 They feed on the sin[1] of my people;
　　they are greedy for their iniquity.
9 And it shall be like people, like priest;
　　I will punish them for their ways
　　and repay them for their deeds.
10 They shall eat, but not be satisfied;
　　they shall play the whore, but not mul-
　　　tiply,
　　because they have forsaken the LORD
　　to cherish 11 whoredom, wine, and new
　　　wine,
　　which take away the understanding.
12 My people inquire of a piece of wood,
　　and their walking staff gives them
　　　oracles.
　　For a spirit of whoredom has led them
　　　astray,
　　and they have left their God to play the
　　　whore.
13 They sacrifice on the tops of the mountains
　　and burn offerings on the hills,
　　under oak, poplar, and terebinth,
　　because their shade is good.
　　Therefore your daughters play the whore,
　　and your brides commit adultery.
14 I will not punish your daughters when
　　　they play the whore,
　　nor your brides when they commit
　　　adultery;
　　for the men themselves go aside with pros-
　　　titutes
　　and sacrifice with cult prostitutes,
　　and a people without understanding shall
　　　come to ruin.

15 Though you play the whore, O Israel,
　　let not Judah become guilty.
　　Enter not into Gilgal,
　　nor go up to Beth-aven,
　　and swear not, "As the LORD lives."
16 Like a stubborn heifer,
　　Israel is stubborn;
　　can the LORD now feed them
　　like a lamb in a broad pasture?

17 Ephraim is joined to idols;
　　leave him alone.

18 When their drink is gone, they give them-
　　　selves to whoring;
　　their rulers[2] dearly love shame.
19 A wind has wrapped them[3] in its wings,
　　and they shall be ashamed because of
　　　their sacrifices.

Punishment Coming for Israel and Judah

5 Hear this, O priests!
　　Pay attention, O house of Israel!
　Give ear, O house of the king!
　　For the judgment is for you;
　for you have been a snare at Mizpah
　　and a net spread upon Tabor.
2 And the revolters have gone deep into
　　　slaughter,
　　but I will discipline all of them.

3 I know Ephraim,
　　and Israel is not hidden from me;
　for now, O Ephraim, you have played the
　　　whore;
　　Israel is defiled.
4 Their deeds do not permit them
　　to return to their God.
　For the spirit of whoredom is within them,
　　and they know not the LORD.

5 The pride of Israel testifies to his face;[4]
　　Israel and Ephraim shall stumble in his
　　　guilt;
　　Judah also shall stumble with them.
6 With their flocks and herds they shall go
　　to seek the LORD,
　but they will not find him;
　　he has withdrawn from them.
7 They have dealt faithlessly with the LORD;
　　for they have borne alien children.
　　Now the new moon shall devour them
　　　with their fields.

8 Blow the horn in Gibeah,
　　the trumpet in Ramah.
　Sound the alarm at Beth-aven;
　　we follow you,[5] O Benjamin!
9 Ephraim shall become a desolation
　　in the day of punishment;
　among the tribes of Israel
　　I make known what is sure.
10 The princes of Judah have become
　　like those who move the landmark;
　upon them I will pour out
　　my wrath like water.

---

[1] Or sin offering [2] Hebrew shields [3] Hebrew her [4] Or in his presence [5] Or after you

11   Ephraim is oppressed, crushed in judg-
          ment,
        because he was determined to go after
            filth.[1]
12   But I am like a moth to Ephraim,
        and like dry rot to the house of Judah.

13   When Ephraim saw his sickness,
        and Judah his wound,
      then Ephraim went to Assyria,
        and sent to the great king.[2]
      But he is not able to cure you
        or heal your wound.
14   For I will be like a lion to Ephraim,
        and like a young lion to the house of
            Judah.
      I, even I, will tear and go away;
        I will carry off, and no one shall rescue.

15   I will return again to my place,
        until they acknowledge their guilt and
            seek my face,
        and in their distress earnestly seek me.

Israel and Judah Are Unrepentant

6   "Come, let us return to the LORD;
      for he has torn us, that he may heal us;
        he has struck us down, and he will bind
            us up.
2   After two days he will revive us;
        on the third day he will raise us up,
        that we may live before him.
3   Let us know; let us press on to know the
          LORD;
        his going out is sure as the dawn;
      he will come to us as the showers,
        as the spring rains that water the earth."

4   What shall I do with you, O Ephraim?
        What shall I do with you, O Judah?
      Your love is like a morning cloud,
        like the dew that goes early away.
5   Therefore I have hewn them by the proph-
          ets;
        I have slain them by the words of my
            mouth,
        and my judgment goes forth as the light.
6   For I desire steadfast love[3] and not sacrifice,
        the knowledge of God rather than
            burnt offerings.

7   But like Adam they transgressed the cov-
          enant;
        there they dealt faithlessly with me.

8   Gilead is a city of evildoers,
        tracked with blood.
9   As robbers lie in wait for a man,
        so the priests band together;
      they murder on the way to Shechem;
        they commit villainy.
10   In the house of Israel I have seen a horrible
            thing;
        Ephraim's whoredom is there; Israel is
            defiled.

11   For you also, O Judah, a harvest is
          appointed.

      When I restore the fortunes of my people,

7   when I would heal Israel,
        the iniquity of Ephraim is revealed,
          and the evil deeds of Samaria,
      for they deal falsely;
        the thief breaks in,
        and the bandits raid outside.
2   But they do not consider
        that I remember all their evil.
      Now their deeds surround them;
        they are before my face.
3   By their evil they make the king glad,
        and the princes by their treachery.
4   They are all adulterers;
        they are like a heated oven
      whose baker ceases to stir the fire,
        from the kneading of the dough
        until it is leavened.
5   On the day of our king, the princes
        became sick with the heat of wine;
        he stretched out his hand with mockers.
6   For with hearts like an oven they approach
            their intrigue;
        all night their anger smolders;
        in the morning it blazes like a flaming
            fire.
7   All of them are hot as an oven,
        and they devour their rulers.
      All their kings have fallen,
        and none of them calls upon me.

8   Ephraim mixes himself with the peoples;
        Ephraim is a cake not turned.
9   Strangers devour his strength,
        and he knows it not;
      gray hairs are sprinkled upon him,
        and he knows it not.
10   The pride of Israel testifies to his face;[4]
        yet they do not return to the LORD their
            God,
        nor seek him, for all this.

[1] Or to follow human precepts [2] Or to King Jareb [3] Septuagint mercy [4] Or in his presence

11 Ephraim is like a dove,
      silly and without sense,
      calling to Egypt, going to Assyria.
12 As they go, I will spread over them my net;
      I will bring them down like birds of the
         heavens;
      I will discipline them according to the
         report made to their congregation.
13 Woe to them, for they have strayed from
      me!
      Destruction to them, for they have
         rebelled against me!
   I would redeem them,
      but they speak lies against me.

14 They do not cry to me from the heart,
      but they wail upon their beds;
   for grain and wine they gash themselves;
      they rebel against me.
15 Although I trained and strengthened their
         arms,
      yet they devise evil against me.
16 They return, but not upward;[1]
      they are like a treacherous bow;
   their princes shall fall by the sword
      because of the insolence of their tongue.
   This shall be their derision in the land of
      Egypt.

Israel Will Reap the Whirlwind

8 Set the trumpet to your lips!
   One like a vulture is over the house of the
      LORD,
   because they have transgressed my cov-
      enant
      and rebelled against my law.
2 To me they cry,
   "My God, we—Israel—know you."
3 Israel has spurned the good;
      the enemy shall pursue him.

4 They made kings, but not through me.
      They set up princes, but I knew it not.
   With their silver and gold they made idols
      for their own destruction.
5 I have[2] spurned your calf, O Samaria.
      My anger burns against them.
   How long will they be incapable of inno-
      cence?
6 For it is from Israel;
   a craftsman made it;
      it is not God.
   The calf of Samaria
      shall be broken to pieces.[3]

7 For they sow the wind,
      and they shall reap the whirlwind.
   The standing grain has no heads;
      it shall yield no flour;
   if it were to yield,
      strangers would devour it.
8 Israel is swallowed up;
      already they are among the nations
         as a useless vessel.
9 For they have gone up to Assyria,
      a wild donkey wandering alone;
      Ephraim has hired lovers.
10 Though they hire allies among the nations,
      I will soon gather them up.
   And the king and princes shall soon writhe
      because of the tribute.

11 Because Ephraim has multiplied altars for
         sinning,
      they have become to him altars for sin-
         ning.
12 Were I to write for him my laws by the ten
         thousands,
      they would be regarded as a strange
         thing.
13 As for my sacrificial offerings,
      they sacrifice meat and eat it,
      but the LORD does not accept them.
   Now he will remember their iniquity
      and punish their sins;
      they shall return to Egypt.
14 For Israel has forgotten his Maker
      and built palaces,
   and Judah has multiplied fortified cities;
      so I will send a fire upon his cities,
      and it shall devour her strongholds.

The LORD Will Punish Israel

9 Rejoice not, O Israel!
   Exult not like the peoples;
   for you have played the whore, forsaking
      your God.
      You have loved a prostitute's wages
         on all threshing floors.
2 Threshing floor and wine vat shall not feed
      them,
      and the new wine shall fail them.
3 They shall not remain in the land of the
      LORD,
      but Ephraim shall return to Egypt,
      and they shall eat unclean food in
         Assyria.

[1] Or to the Most High [2] Hebrew He has [3] Or shall go up in flames

4 They shall not pour drink offerings of wine
        to the LORD,
    and their sacrifices shall not please him.
  It shall be like mourners' bread to them;
    all who eat of it shall be defiled;
  for their bread shall be for their hunger
        only;
      it shall not come to the house of the
        LORD.

5 What will you do on the day of the
        appointed festival,
    and on the day of the feast of the LORD?
6 For behold, they are going away from
        destruction;
      but Egypt shall gather them;
      Memphis shall bury them.
  Nettles shall possess their precious things
        of silver;
    thorns shall be in their tents.

7 The days of punishment have come;
    the days of recompense have come;
    Israel shall know it.
  The prophet is a fool;
    the man of the spirit is mad,
  because of your great iniquity
    and great hatred.
8 The prophet is the watchman of Ephraim
        with my God;
    yet a fowler's snare is on all his ways,
    and hatred in the house of his God.
9 They have deeply corrupted themselves
        as in the days of Gibeah:
    he will remember their iniquity;
    he will punish their sins.

10 Like grapes in the wilderness,
      I found Israel.
   Like the first fruit on the fig tree
      in its first season,
      I saw your fathers.
   But they came to Baal-peor
      and consecrated themselves to the thing
        of shame,
      and became detestable like the thing
        they loved.
11 Ephraim's glory shall fly away like a bird—
      no birth, no pregnancy, no conception!
12 Even if they bring up children,
      I will bereave them till none is left.
   Woe to them
      when I depart from them!

13 Ephraim, as I have seen, was like a young
        palm[1] planted in a meadow;
    but Ephraim must lead his children out
        to slaughter.[2]
14 Give them, O LORD—
      what will you give?
   Give them a miscarrying womb
      and dry breasts.

15 Every evil of theirs is in Gilgal;
      there I began to hate them.
   Because of the wickedness of their deeds
      I will drive them out of my house.
   I will love them no more;
      all their princes are rebels.
16 Ephraim is stricken;
      their root is dried up;
      they shall bear no fruit.
   Even though they give birth,
      I will put their beloved children to
        death.
17 My God will reject them
      because they have not listened to him;
      they shall be wanderers among the
        nations.

10 Israel is a luxuriant vine
        that yields its fruit.
   The more his fruit increased,
      the more altars he built;
   as his country improved,
      he improved his pillars.
2 Their heart is false;
      now they must bear their guilt.
   The LORD[3] will break down their altars
      and destroy their pillars.

3 For now they will say:
   "We have no king,
   for we do not fear the LORD;
      and a king—what could he do for us?"
4 They utter mere words;
      with empty[4] oaths they make cov-
        enants;
   so judgment springs up like poisonous
        weeds
      in the furrows of the field.
5 The inhabitants of Samaria tremble
      for the calf[5] of Beth-aven.
   Its people mourn for it, and so do its idola-
        trous priests—
      those who rejoiced over it and over its
        glory—
      for it has departed[6] from them.

[1] Or like Tyre [2] Hebrew to him who slaughters [3] Hebrew He [4] Or vain (see Exodus 20:7) [5] Or calves [6] Or has gone into exile

6   The thing itself shall be carried to Assyria
        as tribute to the great king.[1]
    Ephraim shall be put to shame,
        and Israel shall be ashamed of his idol.[2]

7   Samaria's king shall perish
        like a twig on the face of the waters.
8   The high places of Aven, the sin of Israel,
        shall be destroyed.
    Thorn and thistle shall grow up
        on their altars,
    and they shall say to the mountains, "Cover
        us,"
        and to the hills, "Fall on us."

9   From the days of Gibeah, you have sinned,
        O Israel;
        there they have continued.
    Shall not the war against the unjust[3]
        overtake them in Gibeah?
10 When I please, I will discipline them,
        and nations shall be gathered against
        them
        when they are bound up for their
        double iniquity.

11 Ephraim was a trained calf
        that loved to thresh,
        and I spared her fair neck;
    but I will put Ephraim to the yoke;
        Judah must plow;
        Jacob must harrow for himself.
12 Sow for yourselves righteousness;
        reap steadfast love;
        break up your fallow ground,
    for it is the time to seek the LORD,
        that he may come and rain righteous-
        ness upon you.

13 You have plowed iniquity;
        you have reaped injustice;
        you have eaten the fruit of lies.
    Because you have trusted in your own way
        and in the multitude of your warriors,
14 therefore the tumult of war shall arise
        among your people,
        and all your fortresses shall be
        destroyed,
    as Shalman destroyed Beth-arbel on the
        day of battle;
        mothers were dashed in pieces with
        their children.
15 Thus it shall be done to you, O Bethel,
        because of your great evil.

    At dawn the king of Israel
        shall be utterly cut off.

The LORD's Love for Israel

11 When Israel was a child, I loved him,
        and out of Egypt I called my son.
2   The more they were called,
        the more they went away;
    they kept sacrificing to the Baals
        and burning offerings to idols.

3   Yet it was I who taught Ephraim to walk;
        I took them up by their arms,
        but they did not know that I healed
        them.
4   I led them with cords of kindness,[4]
        with the bands of love,
    and I became to them as one who eases the
        yoke on their jaws,
        and I bent down to them and fed them.

5   They shall not[5] return to the land of Egypt,
        but Assyria shall be their king,
        because they have refused to return to
        me.
6   The sword shall rage against their cities,
        consume the bars of their gates,
        and devour them because of their own
        counsels.
7   My people are bent on turning away from
        me,
        and though they call out to the Most
        High,
        he shall not raise them up at all.

8   How can I give you up, O Ephraim?
        How can I hand you over, O Israel?
    How can I make you like Admah?
        How can I treat you like Zeboiim?
    My heart recoils within me;
        my compassion grows warm and ten-
        der.
9   I will not execute my burning anger;
        I will not again destroy Ephraim;
    for I am God and not a man,
        the Holy One in your midst,
        and I will not come in wrath.[6]

10 They shall go after the LORD;
        he will roar like a lion;
    when he roars,
        his children shall come trembling from
        the west;

---

[1] Or to King Jareb [2] Or counsel [3] Hebrew the children of injustice [4] Or humaneness; Hebrew man [5] Or surely [6] Or into the city

¹¹ they shall come trembling like birds from
Egypt,
    and like doves from the land of Assyria,
    and I will return them to their homes,
    declares the LORD.

^{12 1} Ephraim has surrounded me with lies,
    and the house of Israel with deceit,
but Judah still walks with God
    and is faithful to the Holy One.

12 Ephraim feeds on the wind
    and pursues the east wind all day
    long;
they multiply falsehood and violence;
    they make a covenant with Assyria,
    and oil is carried to Egypt.

The LORD's Indictment of Israel and Judah

² The LORD has an indictment against Judah
    and will punish Jacob according to his
    ways;
    he will repay him according to his
    deeds.
³ In the womb he took his brother by the
    heel,
    and in his manhood he strove with God.
⁴ He strove with the angel and prevailed;
    he wept and sought his favor.
He met God² at Bethel,
    and there God spoke with us—
⁵ the LORD, the God of hosts,
    the LORD is his memorial name:
⁶ "So you, by the help of your God, return,
    hold fast to love and justice,
    and wait continually for your God."

⁷ A merchant, in whose hands are false bal-
    ances,
    he loves to oppress.
⁸ Ephraim has said, "Ah, but I am rich;
    I have found wealth for myself;
in all my labors they cannot find in me
    iniquity or sin."
⁹ I am the LORD your God
    from the land of Egypt;
I will again make you dwell in tents,
    as in the days of the appointed feast.

¹⁰ I spoke to the prophets;
    it was I who multiplied visions,
    and through the prophets gave para-
    bles.
¹¹ If there is iniquity in Gilead,
    they shall surely come to nothing:

in Gilgal they sacrifice bulls;
    their altars also are like stone heaps
    on the furrows of the field.
¹² Jacob fled to the land of Aram;
    there Israel served for a wife,
    and for a wife he guarded sheep.
¹³ By a prophet the LORD brought Israel up
    from Egypt,
    and by a prophet he was guarded.
¹⁴ Ephraim has given bitter provocation;
    so his Lord will leave his bloodguilt on
    him
    and will repay him for his disgraceful
    deeds.

The LORD's Relentless Judgment on Israel

13 When Ephraim spoke, there was
trembling;
    he was exalted in Israel,
    but he incurred guilt through Baal and
    died.
² And now they sin more and more,
    and make for themselves metal
    images,
idols skillfully made of their silver,
    all of them the work of craftsmen.
It is said of them,
    "Those who offer human sacrifice kiss
    calves!"
³ Therefore they shall be like the morning
    mist
    or like the dew that goes early away,
like the chaff that swirls from the thresh-
    ing floor
    or like smoke from a window.

⁴ But I am the LORD your God
    from the land of Egypt;
you know no God but me,
    and besides me there is no savior.
⁵ It was I who knew you in the wilderness,
    in the land of drought;
⁶ but when they had grazed,³ they became
    full,
    they were filled, and their heart was
    lifted up;
    therefore they forgot me.
⁷ So I am to them like a lion;
    like a leopard I will lurk beside the
    way.
⁸ I will fall upon them like a bear robbed of
    her cubs;
    I will tear open their breast,

¹ Ch 12:1 in Hebrew ² Hebrew him ³ Hebrew according to their pasture

and there I will devour them like a lion,
  as a wild beast would rip them open.

9 He destroys[1] you, O Israel,
    for you are against me, against your
      helper.
10 Where now is your king, to save you in all
      your cities?
    Where are all your rulers—
  those of whom you said,
    "Give me a king and princes"?
11 I gave you a king in my anger,
    and I took him away in my wrath.

12 The iniquity of Ephraim is bound up;
    his sin is kept in store.
13 The pangs of childbirth come for him,
    but he is an unwise son,
  for at the right time he does not present
      himself
    at the opening of the womb.

14 I shall ransom them from the power of
      Sheol;
    I shall redeem them from Death.[2]
  O Death, where are your plagues?
    O Sheol, where is your sting?
    Compassion is hidden from my eyes.

15 Though he may flourish among his broth-
      ers,
    the east wind, the wind of the LORD,
      shall come,
    rising from the wilderness,
  and his fountain shall dry up;
    his spring shall be parched;
  it shall strip his treasury
    of every precious thing.
16[3] Samaria shall bear her guilt,
    because she has rebelled against her
      God;
  they shall fall by the sword;
    their little ones shall be dashed in
      pieces,
    and their pregnant women ripped
      open.

A Plea to Return to the LORD

14 Return, O Israel, to the LORD your
      God,
    for you have stumbled because of your
      iniquity.
2 Take with you words
    and return to the LORD;
  say to him,
    "Take away all iniquity;
  accept what is good,
    and we will pay with bulls
    the vows[4] of our lips.
3 Assyria shall not save us;
    we will not ride on horses;
  and we will say no more, 'Our God,'
    to the work of our hands.
  In you the orphan finds mercy."

4 I will heal their apostasy;
    I will love them freely,
    for my anger has turned from them.
5 I will be like the dew to Israel;
    he shall blossom like the lily;
    he shall take root like the trees of
      Lebanon;
6 his shoots shall spread out;
    his beauty shall be like the olive,
    and his fragrance like Lebanon.
7 They shall return and dwell beneath my[5]
      shadow;
    they shall flourish like the grain;
  they shall blossom like the vine;
    their fame shall be like the wine of
      Lebanon.

8 O Ephraim, what have I to do with idols?
    It is I who answer and look after you.[6]
  I am like an evergreen cypress;
    from me comes your fruit.

9 Whoever is wise, let him understand these
      things;
    whoever is discerning, let him know
      them;
  for the ways of the LORD are right,
    and the upright walk in them,
    but transgressors stumble in them.

---

[1] Or *I will destroy* [2] Or *Shall I ransom them from the power of Sheol? Shall I redeem them from Death?* [3] Ch 14:1 in Hebrew [4] Septuagint, Syriac *pay the fruit* [5] Hebrew *his*
[6] Hebrew *him*

JOEL

1 The word of the Lord that came to Joel, the son of Pethuel:

An Invasion of Locusts

2 Hear this, you elders;
>   give ear, all inhabitants of the land!
>   Has such a thing happened in your days,
>   or in the days of your fathers?
3 Tell your children of it,
>   and let your children tell their children,
>   and their children to another generation.

4 What the cutting locust left,
>   the swarming locust has eaten.
>   What the swarming locust left,
>   the hopping locust has eaten,
>   and what the hopping locust left,
>   the destroying locust has eaten.

5 Awake, you drunkards, and weep,
>   and wail, all you drinkers of wine,
>   because of the sweet wine,
>   for it is cut off from your mouth.
6 For a nation has come up against my land,
>   powerful and beyond number;
>   its teeth are lions' teeth,
>   and it has the fangs of a lioness.
7 It has laid waste my vine
>   and splintered my fig tree;
>   it has stripped off their bark and thrown it down;
>   their branches are made white.

8 Lament like a virgin[1] wearing sackcloth
>   for the bridegroom of her youth.
9 The grain offering and the drink offering
>   are cut off
>   from the house of the Lord.
>   The priests mourn,
>   the ministers of the Lord.
10 The fields are destroyed,
>   the ground mourns,
>   because the grain is destroyed,
>   the wine dries up,
>   the oil languishes.

11 Be ashamed,[2] O tillers of the soil;
>   wail, O vinedressers,
>   for the wheat and the barley,
>   because the harvest of the field has perished.
12 The vine dries up;
>   the fig tree languishes.
>   Pomegranate, palm, and apple,
>   all the trees of the field are dried up,
>   and gladness dries up
>   from the children of man.

A Call to Repentance

13 Put on sackcloth and lament, O priests;
>   wail, O ministers of the altar.
>   Go in, pass the night in sackcloth,
>   O ministers of my God!
>   Because grain offering and drink offering
>   are withheld from the house of your
>   God.

14 Consecrate a fast;
>   call a solemn assembly.
>   Gather the elders
>   and all the inhabitants of the land
>   to the house of the Lord your God,
>   and cry out to the Lord.

15 Alas for the day!
>   For the day of the Lord is near,
>   and as destruction from the Almighty[3]
>   it comes.
16 Is not the food cut off
>   before our eyes,
>   joy and gladness
>   from the house of our God?

17 The seed shrivels under the clods;[4]
>   the storehouses are desolate;
>   the granaries are torn down
>   because the grain has dried up.
18 How the beasts groan!
>   The herds of cattle are perplexed
>   because there is no pasture for them;
>   even the flocks of sheep suffer.[5]

19 To you, O Lord, I call.
>   For fire has devoured
>   the pastures of the wilderness,
>   and flame has burned
>   all the trees of the field.
20 Even the beasts of the field pant for you
>   because the water brooks are dried up,

---

[1] Or young woman [2] The Hebrew words for dry up and be ashamed in verses 10–12, 17 sound alike [3] Destruction sounds like the Hebrew for Almighty [4] The meaning of the Hebrew line is uncertain [5] Or are made desolate

and fire has devoured
　　the pastures of the wilderness.

The Day of the LORD

2 Blow a trumpet in Zion;
　　sound an alarm on my holy mountain!
Let all the inhabitants of the land tremble,
　　for the day of the LORD is coming; it is
　　　　near,
2 a day of darkness and gloom,
　　a day of clouds and thick darkness!
Like blackness there is spread upon the
　　mountains
　　a great and powerful people;
their like has never been before,
　　nor will be again after them
　　through the years of all generations.

3 Fire devours before them,
　　and behind them a flame burns.
The land is like the garden of Eden before
　　them,
　　but behind them a desolate wilderness,
　　and nothing escapes them.

4 Their appearance is like the appearance of
　　horses,
　　and like war horses they run.
5 As with the rumbling of chariots,
　　they leap on the tops of the mountains,
like the crackling of a flame of fire
　　devouring the stubble,
like a powerful army
　　drawn up for battle.

6 Before them peoples are in anguish;
　　all faces grow pale.
7 Like warriors they charge;
　　like soldiers they scale the wall.
They march each on his way;
　　they do not swerve from their paths.
8 They do not jostle one another;
　　each marches in his path;
they burst through the weapons
　　and are not halted.
9 They leap upon the city,
　　they run upon the walls,
they climb up into the houses,
　　they enter through the windows like a
　　　　thief.

10 The earth quakes before them;
　　the heavens tremble.
The sun and the moon are darkened,
　　and the stars withdraw their shining.

11 The LORD utters his voice
　　before his army,
for his camp is exceedingly great;
　　he who executes his word is powerful.
For the day of the LORD is great and very
　　awesome;
　　who can endure it?

Return to the LORD

12 "Yet even now," declares the LORD,
　　"return to me with all your heart,
with fasting, with weeping, and with
　　mourning;
13 and rend your hearts and not your gar-
　　ments."
Return to the LORD your God,
　　for he is gracious and merciful,
slow to anger, and abounding in steadfast
　　love;
　　and he relents over disaster.
14 Who knows whether he will not turn and
　　relent,
　　and leave a blessing behind him,
a grain offering and a drink offering
　　for the LORD your God?

15 Blow the trumpet in Zion;
　　consecrate a fast;
call a solemn assembly;
16 gather the people.
Consecrate the congregation;
　　assemble the elders;
gather the children,
　　even nursing infants.
Let the bridegroom leave his room,
　　and the bride her chamber.

17 Between the vestibule and the altar
　　let the priests, the ministers of the
　　　　LORD, weep
and say, "Spare your people, O LORD,
　　and make not your heritage a reproach,
　　a byword among the nations.[1]
Why should they say among the peoples,
　　'Where is their God?'"

The LORD Had Pity

18 Then the LORD became jealous for his land
　　and had pity on his people.
19 The LORD answered and said to his people,
　　"Behold, I am sending to you
　　　　grain, wine, and oil,
　　　　and you will be satisfied;
and I will no more make you
　　a reproach among the nations.

[1] Or reproach, that the nations should rule over them

20 "I will remove the northerner far from
        you,
    and drive him into a parched and deso-
        late land,
    his vanguard¹ into the eastern sea,
    and his rear guard² into the western
        sea;
    the stench and foul smell of him will rise,
        for he has done great things.

21 "Fear not, O land;
    be glad and rejoice,
        for the LORD has done great things!
22 Fear not, you beasts of the field,
    for the pastures of the wilderness are
        green;
    the tree bears its fruit;
        the fig tree and vine give their full
            yield.

23 "Be glad, O children of Zion,
    and rejoice in the LORD your God,
    for he has given the early rain for your vin-
        dication;
    he has poured down for you abundant
        rain,
        the early and the latter rain, as before.

24 "The threshing floors shall be full of
        grain;
        the vats shall overflow with wine and
            oil.
25 I will restore³ to you the years
        that the swarming locust has eaten,
    the hopper, the destroyer, and the cutter,
        my great army, which I sent among
            you.

26 "You shall eat in plenty and be satisfied,
        and praise the name of the LORD your
            God,
    who has dealt wondrously with you.
    And my people shall never again be put to
        shame.
27 You shall know that I am in the midst of
        Israel,
    and that I am the LORD your God and
        there is none else.
    And my people shall never again be put to
        shame.

The LORD Will Pour Out His Spirit

28 4 "And it shall come to pass afterward,
        that I will pour out my Spirit on all
            flesh;

    your sons and your daughters shall proph-
        esy,
    your old men shall dream dreams,
        and your young men shall see visions.
29   Even on the male and female servants
        in those days I will pour out my Spirit.

30 "And I will show wonders in the heavens
and on the earth, blood and fire and columns
of smoke. 31 The sun shall be turned to darkness, and the moon to blood, before the great
and awesome day of the LORD comes. 32 And it
shall come to pass that everyone who calls on
the name of the LORD shall be saved. For in
Mount Zion and in Jerusalem there shall be
those who escape, as the LORD has said, and
among the survivors shall be those whom the
LORD calls.

The LORD Judges the Nations

3 5"For behold, in those days and at that time,
    when I restore the fortunes of Judah and
Jerusalem, ² I will gather all the nations and
bring them down to the Valley of Jehoshaphat.
And I will enter into judgment with them
there, on behalf of my people and my heritage
Israel, because they have scattered them among
the nations and have divided up my land, ³ and
have cast lots for my people, and have traded
a boy for a prostitute, and have sold a girl for
wine and have drunk it.

⁴ "What are you to me, O Tyre and Sidon,
and all the regions of Philistia? Are you paying
me back for something? If you are paying me
back, I will return your payment on your own
head swiftly and speedily. ⁵ For you have taken
my silver and my gold, and have carried my
rich treasures into your temples.⁶ ⁶ You have
sold the people of Judah and Jerusalem to the
Greeks in order to remove them far from their
own border. ⁷ Behold, I will stir them up from
the place to which you have sold them, and I
will return your payment on your own head.
⁸ I will sell your sons and your daughters into
the hand of the people of Judah, and they will
sell them to the Sabeans, to a nation far away,
for the LORD has spoken."

9   Proclaim this among the nations:
        Consecrate for war;⁷
            stir up the mighty men.
        Let all the men of war draw near;
            let them come up.

¹ Hebrew face ² Hebrew his end ³ Or pay back ⁴ Ch 3:1 in Hebrew ⁵ Ch 4:1 in Hebrew ⁶ Or palaces ⁷ Or Consecrate a war

¹⁰ Beat your plowshares into swords,
  and your pruning hooks into spears;
  let the weak say, "I am a warrior."

¹¹ Hasten and come,
  all you surrounding nations,
  and gather yourselves there.
  Bring down your warriors, O LORD.
¹² Let the nations stir themselves up
  and come up to the Valley of
    Jehoshaphat;
  for there I will sit to judge
  all the surrounding nations.

¹³ Put in the sickle,
  for the harvest is ripe.
  Go in, tread,
  for the winepress is full.
  The vats overflow,
  for their evil is great.

¹⁴ Multitudes, multitudes,
  in the valley of decision!
  For the day of the LORD is near
  in the valley of decision.
¹⁵ The sun and the moon are darkened,
  and the stars withdraw their shining.
¹⁶ The LORD roars from Zion,
  and utters his voice from Jerusalem,
  and the heavens and the earth quake.

But the LORD is a refuge to his people,
  a stronghold to the people of Israel.

The Glorious Future of Judah

¹⁷ "So you shall know that I am the LORD your
    God,
  who dwells in Zion, my holy mountain.
  And Jerusalem shall be holy,
  and strangers shall never again pass
    through it.

¹⁸ "And in that day
  the mountains shall drip sweet wine,
  and the hills shall flow with milk,
  and all the streambeds of Judah
  shall flow with water;
  and a fountain shall come forth from the
    house of the LORD
  and water the Valley of Shittim.

¹⁹ "Egypt shall become a desolation
  and Edom a desolate wilderness,
  for the violence done to the people of
    Judah,
  because they have shed innocent blood
    in their land.
²⁰ But Judah shall be inhabited forever,
  and Jerusalem to all generations.
²¹ I will avenge their blood,
  blood I have not avenged,[1]
  for the LORD dwells in Zion."

---

[1] Or *I will acquit their bloodguilt that I have not acquitted*

AMOS

1 The words of Amos, who was among the shepherds[1] of Tekoa, which he saw concerning Israel in the days of Uzziah king of Judah and in the days of Jeroboam the son of Joash, king of Israel, two years[2] before the earthquake.

Judgment on Israel's Neighbors

2 And he said:

"The LORD roars from Zion
and utters his voice from Jerusalem;
the pastures of the shepherds mourn,
and the top of Carmel withers."

3 Thus says the LORD:

"For three transgressions of Damascus,
and for four, I will not revoke the punishment,[3]
because they have threshed Gilead
with threshing sledges of iron.
4 So I will send a fire upon the house of Hazael,
and it shall devour the strongholds of Ben-hadad.
5 I will break the gate-bar of Damascus,
and cut off the inhabitants from the Valley of Aven,[4]
and him who holds the scepter from Beth-eden;
and the people of Syria shall go into exile to Kir,"
says the LORD.

6 Thus says the LORD:

"For three transgressions of Gaza,
and for four, I will not revoke the punishment,
because they carried into exile a whole people
to deliver them up to Edom.
7 So I will send a fire upon the wall of Gaza,
and it shall devour her strongholds.
8 I will cut off the inhabitants from Ashdod,
and him who holds the scepter from Ashkelon;
I will turn my hand against Ekron,
and the remnant of the Philistines shall perish,"
says the Lord GOD.

9 Thus says the LORD:

"For three transgressions of Tyre,
and for four, I will not revoke the punishment,
because they delivered up a whole people to Edom,
and did not remember the covenant of brotherhood.
10 So I will send a fire upon the wall of Tyre,
and it shall devour her strongholds."

11 Thus says the LORD:

"For three transgressions of Edom,
and for four, I will not revoke the punishment,
because he pursued his brother with the sword
and cast off all pity,
and his anger tore perpetually,
and he kept his wrath forever.
12 So I will send a fire upon Teman,
and it shall devour the strongholds of Bozrah."

13 Thus says the LORD:

"For three transgressions of the Ammonites,
and for four, I will not revoke the punishment,
because they have ripped open pregnant women in Gilead,
that they might enlarge their border.
14 So I will kindle a fire in the wall of Rabbah,
and it shall devour her strongholds,
with shouting on the day of battle,
with a tempest in the day of the whirlwind;
15 and their king shall go into exile,
he and his princes[5] together,"
says the LORD.

2 Thus says the LORD:

"For three transgressions of Moab,
and for four, I will not revoke the punishment,[6]
because he burned to lime
the bones of the king of Edom.

---

[1] Or sheep breeders [2] Or during two years [3] Hebrew I will not turn it back; also verses 6, 9, 11, 13 [4] Or On [5] Or officials [6] Hebrew I will not turn it back; also verses 4, 6

2 So I will send a fire upon Moab,
    and it shall devour the strongholds of
        Kerioth,
    and Moab shall die amid uproar,
        amid shouting and the sound of the
            trumpet;
3 I will cut off the ruler from its midst,
    and will kill all its princes[1] with him,"
                            says the LORD.

Judgment on Judah

4 Thus says the LORD:

"For three transgressions of Judah,
    and for four, I will not revoke the pun-
        ishment,
    because they have rejected the law of the
        LORD,
    and have not kept his statutes,
    but their lies have led them astray,
        those after which their fathers walked.
5 So I will send a fire upon Judah,
    and it shall devour the strongholds of
        Jerusalem."

Judgment on Israel

6 Thus says the LORD:

"For three transgressions of Israel,
    and for four, I will not revoke the pun-
        ishment,
    because they sell the righteous for silver,
    and the needy for a pair of sandals—
7 those who trample the head of the poor
        into the dust of the earth
    and turn aside the way of the afflicted;
    a man and his father go in to the same girl,
    so that my holy name is profaned;
8 they lay themselves down beside every altar
        on garments taken in pledge,
    and in the house of their God they drink
        the wine of those who have been fined.

9 "Yet it was I who destroyed the Amorite
        before them,
    whose height was like the height of the
        cedars
    and who was as strong as the oaks;
    I destroyed his fruit above
    and his roots beneath.
10 Also it was I who brought you up out of
        the land of Egypt
    and led you forty years in the wilder-
        ness,
    to possess the land of the Amorite.

11 And I raised up some of your sons for
        prophets,
    and some of your young men for
        Nazirites.
    Is it not indeed so, O people of Israel?"
                            declares the LORD.

12 "But you made the Nazirites drink wine,
    and commanded the prophets,
    saying, 'You shall not prophesy.'

13 "Behold, I will press you down in your place,
    as a cart full of sheaves presses down.
14 Flight shall perish from the swift,
    and the strong shall not retain his
        strength,
    nor shall the mighty save his life;
15 he who handles the bow shall not stand,
    and he who is swift of foot shall not
        save himself,
    nor shall he who rides the horse save his
        life;
16 and he who is stout of heart among the
        mighty
    shall flee away naked in that day,"
                            declares the LORD.

Israel's Guilt and Punishment

3 Hear this word that the LORD has spoken
    against you, O people of Israel, against the
whole family that I brought up out of the land
of Egypt:

2 "You only have I known
        of all the families of the earth;
    therefore I will punish you
        for all your iniquities.

3 "Do two walk together,
        unless they have agreed to meet?
4 Does a lion roar in the forest,
        when he has no prey?
    Does a young lion cry out from his den,
        if he has taken nothing?
5 Does a bird fall in a snare on the earth,
        when there is no trap for it?
    Does a snare spring up from the ground,
        when it has taken nothing?
6 Is a trumpet blown in a city,
        and the people are not afraid?
    Does disaster come to a city,
        unless the LORD has done it?

7 "For the Lord GOD does nothing
        without revealing his secret
    to his servants the prophets.

[1] Or officials

8 The lion has roared;
　　who will not fear?
　The Lord GOD has spoken;
　　who can but prophesy?"

9 Proclaim to the strongholds in Ashdod
　　and to the strongholds in the land of
　　　Egypt,
　and say, "Assemble yourselves on the
　　mountains of Samaria,
　and see the great tumults within her,
　and the oppressed in her midst."

10 "They do not know how to do right,"
　　declares the LORD,
　　"those who store up violence and rob-
　　bery in their strongholds."

11 Therefore thus says the Lord GOD:

　"An adversary shall surround the land
　　and bring down[1] your defenses from
　　you,
　and your strongholds shall be plun-
　　dered."

12 Thus says the LORD: "As the shepherd rescues from the mouth of the lion two legs, or a
piece of an ear, so shall the people of Israel who
dwell in Samaria be rescued, with the corner of
a couch and part[2] of a bed.

13 "Hear, and testify against the house of
　　Jacob,"
　　declares the Lord GOD, the God of hosts,
14 "that on the day I punish Israel for his trans-
　　gressions,
　I will punish the altars of Bethel,
　and the horns of the altar shall be cut off
　　and fall to the ground.
15 I will strike the winter house along with
　　the summer house,
　and the houses of ivory shall perish,
　and the great houses[3] shall come to an
　　end,"
　　　declares the LORD.

4 "Hear this word, you cows of Bashan,
　　who are on the mountain of Samaria,
　who oppress the poor, who crush the
　　needy,
　who say to your husbands, 'Bring, that
　　we may drink!'
2 The Lord GOD has sworn by his holiness
　　that, behold, the days are coming upon
　　you,

when they shall take you away with hooks,
　even the last of you with fishhooks.
3 And you shall go out through the breaches,
　　each one straight ahead;
　and you shall be cast out into Harmon,"
　　　declares the LORD.

4 "Come to Bethel, and transgress;
　　to Gilgal, and multiply transgression;
　bring your sacrifices every morning,
　　your tithes every three days;
5 offer a sacrifice of thanksgiving of that
　　which is leavened,
　and proclaim freewill offerings, publish
　　them;
　for so you love to do, O people of Israel!"
　　　declares the Lord GOD.

Israel Has Not Returned to the LORD

6 "I gave you cleanness of teeth in all your cit-
　　ies,
　and lack of bread in all your places,
　yet you did not return to me,"
　　　declares the LORD.

7 "I also withheld the rain from you
　　when there were yet three months to
　　　the harvest;
　I would send rain on one city,
　　and send no rain on another city;
　one field would have rain,
　　and the field on which it did not rain
　　　would wither;
8 so two or three cities would wander to
　　another city
　　to drink water, and would not be satis-
　　　fied;
　yet you did not return to me,"
　　　declares the LORD.

9 "I struck you with blight and mildew;
　　your many gardens and your vineyards,
　　your fig trees and your olive trees the
　　　locust devoured;
　yet you did not return to me,"
　　　declares the LORD.

10 "I sent among you a pestilence after the
　　manner of Egypt;
　I killed your young men with the
　　sword,
　and carried away your horses,[4]
　　and I made the stench of your camp go
　　　up into your nostrils;

---

[1] Hebrew *An adversary, one who surrounds the land—he shall bring down* [2] The meaning of the Hebrew word is uncertain [3] Or *and many houses* [4] Hebrew *along with the captivity of your horses*

yet you did not return to me,"
>> declares the LORD.

11 "I overthrew some of you,
>> as when God overthrew Sodom and
>> Gomorrah,
>> and you were as a brand[1] plucked out of
>> the burning;
>> yet you did not return to me,"
>> declares the LORD.

12 "Therefore thus I will do to you, O Israel;
>> because I will do this to you,
>> prepare to meet your God, O Israel!"

13 For behold, he who forms the mountains
>> and creates the wind,
>> and declares to man what is his
>> thought,
>> who makes the morning darkness,
>> and treads on the heights of the earth—
>> the LORD, the God of hosts, is his name!

Seek the LORD and Live

5 Hear this word that I take up over you in
lamentation, O house of Israel:

2 "Fallen, no more to rise,
>> is the virgin Israel;
>> forsaken on her land,
>> with none to raise her up."

3 For thus says the Lord GOD:

"The city that went out a thousand
>> shall have a hundred left,
>> and that which went out a hundred
>> shall have ten left
>> to the house of Israel."

4 For thus says the LORD to the house of Israel:

"Seek me and live;
5 but do not seek Bethel,
>> and do not enter into Gilgal
>> or cross over to Beersheba;
>> for Gilgal shall surely go into exile,
>> and Bethel shall come to nothing."

6 Seek the LORD and live,
>> lest he break out like fire in the house of
>> Joseph,
>> and it devour, with none to quench it
>> for Bethel,
7 O you who turn justice to wormwood[2]
>> and cast down righteousness to the
>> earth!

8 He who made the Pleiades and Orion,
>> and turns deep darkness into the morn-
>> ing
>> and darkens the day into night,
>> who calls for the waters of the sea
>> and pours them out on the surface of
>> the earth,
>> the LORD is his name;
9 who makes destruction flash forth against
>> the strong,
>> so that destruction comes upon the for-
>> tress.

10 They hate him who reproves in the gate,
>> and they abhor him who speaks the
>> truth.
11 Therefore because you trample on[3] the
>> poor
>> and you exact taxes of grain from him,
>> you have built houses of hewn stone,
>> but you shall not dwell in them;
>> you have planted pleasant vineyards,
>> but you shall not drink their wine.
12 For I know how many are your transgres-
>> sions
>> and how great are your sins—
>> you who afflict the righteous, who take a
>> bribe,
>> and turn aside the needy in the gate.
13 Therefore he who is prudent will keep
>> silent in such a time,
>> for it is an evil time.

14 Seek good, and not evil,
>> that you may live;
>> and so the LORD, the God of hosts, will be
>> with you,
>> as you have said.
15 Hate evil, and love good,
>> and establish justice in the gate;
>> it may be that the LORD, the God of
>> hosts,
>> will be gracious to the remnant of
>> Joseph.

16 Therefore thus says the LORD, the God of
hosts, the Lord:

"In all the squares there shall be wailing,
>> and in all the streets they shall say, 'Alas!
>> Alas!'
>> They shall call the farmers to mourning
>> and to wailing those who are skilled in
>> lamentation,

---

[1] That is, a burning stick [2] Or to bitter fruit [3] Or you tax

¹⁷ and in all vineyards there shall be wailing,
for I will pass through your midst,"
                    says the LORD.

Let Justice Roll Down

¹⁸ Woe to you who desire the day of the
        LORD!
    Why would you have the day of the
        LORD?
    It is darkness, and not light,
¹⁹ as if a man fled from a lion,
    and a bear met him,
    or went into the house and leaned his hand
        against the wall,
    and a serpent bit him.
²⁰ Is not the day of the LORD darkness, and
        not light,
    and gloom with no brightness in it?

²¹ "I hate, I despise your feasts,
    and I take no delight in your solemn
        assemblies.
²² Even though you offer me your burnt
        offerings and grain offerings,
    I will not accept them;
    and the peace offerings of your fattened
        animals,
    I will not look upon them.
²³ Take away from me the noise of your
        songs;
    to the melody of your harps I will not
        listen.
²⁴ But let justice roll down like waters,
    and righteousness like an ever-flowing
        stream.

²⁵ "Did you bring to me sacrifices and offerings during the forty years in the wilderness, O house of Israel? ²⁶ You shall take up Sikkuth your king, and Kiyyun your star-god—your images that you made for yourselves, ²⁷ and I will send you into exile beyond Damascus," says the LORD, whose name is the God of hosts.

Woe to Those at Ease in Zion

6 "Woe to those who are at ease in Zion,
    and to those who feel secure on the mountain of Samaria,
    the notable men of the first of the nations,
    to whom the house of Israel comes!
² Pass over to Calneh, and see,
    and from there go to Hamath the great;
    then go down to Gath of the Philistines.

Are you better than these kingdoms?
    Or is their territory greater than your
        territory?
³ O you who put far away the day of disaster
    and bring near the seat of violence?

⁴ "Woe to those who lie on beds of ivory
    and stretch themselves out on their
        couches,
    and eat lambs from the flock
    and calves from the midst of the stall,
⁵ who sing idle songs to the sound of the
        harp
    and like David invent for themselves
        instruments of music,
⁶ who drink wine in bowls
    and anoint themselves with the finest
        oils,
    but are not grieved over the ruin of
        Joseph!
⁷ Therefore they shall now be the first of
        those who go into exile,
    and the revelry of those who stretch
        themselves out shall pass away."

⁸ The Lord GOD has sworn by himself, declares the LORD, the God of hosts:

"I abhor the pride of Jacob
    and hate his strongholds,
    and I will deliver up the city and all that
        is in it."

⁹ And if ten men remain in one house, they shall die. ¹⁰ And when one's relative, the one who anoints him for burial, shall take him up to bring the bones out of the house, and shall say to him who is in the innermost parts of the house, "Is there still anyone with you?" he shall say, "No"; and he shall say, "Silence! We must not mention the name of the LORD."

¹¹ For behold, the LORD commands,
    and the great house shall be struck
        down into fragments,
    and the little house into bits.
¹² Do horses run on rocks?
    Does one plow there[1] with oxen?
    But you have turned justice into poison
    and the fruit of righteousness into
        wormwood[2]—
¹³ you who rejoice in Lo-debar,[3]
    who say, "Have we not by our own
        strength
    captured Karnaim[4] for ourselves?"

---

[1] Or the sea [2] Or into bitter fruit [3] Lo-debar means nothing [4] Karnaim means horns (a symbol of strength)

14 "For behold, I will raise up against you a
nation,
  O house of Israel," declares the LORD,
    the God of hosts;
"and they shall oppress you from Lebo-
hamath
  to the Brook of the Arabah."

Warning Visions

7 This is what the Lord GOD showed me:
behold, he was forming locusts when the
latter growth was just beginning to sprout, and
behold, it was the latter growth after the king's
mowings. ²When they had finished eating the
grass of the land, I said,

"O Lord GOD, please forgive!
  How can Jacob stand?
  He is so small!"
3   The LORD relented concerning this:
  "It shall not be," said the LORD.

⁴This is what the Lord GOD showed me:
behold, the Lord GOD was calling for a judgment by fire, and it devoured the great deep and
was eating up the land. ⁵Then I said,

"O Lord GOD, please cease!
  How can Jacob stand?
  He is so small!"
6   The LORD relented concerning this:
  "This also shall not be," said the Lord
  GOD.

⁷This is what he showed me: behold, the
Lord was standing beside a wall built with a
plumb line, with a plumb line in his hand. ⁸And
the LORD said to me, "Amos, what do you see?"
And I said, "A plumb line." Then the Lord said,

"Behold, I am setting a plumb line
  in the midst of my people Israel;
  I will never again pass by them;
9   the high places of Isaac shall be made desolate,
  and the sanctuaries of Israel shall be laid
waste,
  and I will rise against the house of
    Jeroboam with the sword."

Amos Accused

¹⁰Then Amaziah the priest of Bethel sent to
Jeroboam king of Israel, saying, "Amos has conspired against you in the midst of the house of
Israel. The land is not able to bear all his words.
¹¹For thus Amos has said,

"'Jeroboam shall die by the sword,
  and Israel must go into exile
  away from his land.'"

¹²And Amaziah said to Amos, "O seer, go, flee
away to the land of Judah, and eat bread there,
and prophesy there, ¹³but never again prophesy
at Bethel, for it is the king's sanctuary, and it is
a temple of the kingdom."

¹⁴Then Amos answered and said to Amaziah,
"I was[1] no prophet, nor a prophet's son, but I
was a herdsman and a dresser of sycamore figs.
¹⁵But the LORD took me from following the
flock, and the LORD said to me, 'Go, prophesy
to my people Israel.' ¹⁶Now therefore hear the
word of the LORD.

"You say, 'Do not prophesy against Israel,
  and do not preach against the house of
    Isaac.'

¹⁷Therefore thus says the LORD:

"'Your wife shall be a prostitute in the city,
  and your sons and your daughters shall
    fall by the sword,
  and your land shall be divided up with
    a measuring line;
you yourself shall die in an unclean land,
  and Israel shall surely go into exile away
    from its land.'"

The Coming Day of Bitter Mourning

8 This is what the Lord GOD showed me:
behold, a basket of summer fruit. ²And
he said, "Amos, what do you see?" And I said,
"A basket of summer fruit." Then the LORD
said to me,

"The end[2] has come upon my people Israel;
  I will never again pass by them.
3   The songs of the temple[3] shall become
    wailings[4] in that day,"
        declares the Lord GOD.
"So many dead bodies!"
"They are thrown everywhere!"
"Silence!"

4   Hear this, you who trample on the needy
    and bring the poor of the land to an
    end,
5   saying, "When will the new moon be over,
    that we may sell grain?
  And the Sabbath,
    that we may offer wheat for sale,

¹ Or am; twice in this verse ² The Hebrew words for end and summer fruit sound alike ³ Or palace ⁴ Or The singing women of the palace shall wail

that we may make the ephah small and the
    shekel[1] great
  and deal deceitfully with false balances,
6 that we may buy the poor for silver
    and the needy for a pair of sandals
    and sell the chaff of the wheat?"

7 The LORD has sworn by the pride of Jacob:
  "Surely I will never forget any of their deeds.
8 Shall not the land tremble on this account,
    and everyone mourn who dwells in it,
  and all of it rise like the Nile,
    and be tossed about and sink again, like
    the Nile of Egypt?"

9 "And on that day," declares the Lord GOD,
  "I will make the sun go down at noon
    and darken the earth in broad daylight.
10 I will turn your feasts into mourning
    and all your songs into lamentation;
  I will bring sackcloth on every waist
    and baldness on every head;
  I will make it like the mourning for an
    only son
    and the end of it like a bitter day.

11 "Behold, the days are coming," declares the
    Lord GOD,
  "when I will send a famine on the
    land—
  not a famine of bread, nor a thirst for
    water,
  but of hearing the words of the LORD.
12 They shall wander from sea to sea,
    and from north to east;
  they shall run to and fro, to seek the word
    of the LORD,
  but they shall not find it.

13 "In that day the lovely virgins and the
    young men
    shall faint for thirst.
14 Those who swear by the Guilt of Samaria,
    and say, 'As your god lives, O Dan,'
  and, 'As the Way of Beersheba lives,'
    they shall fall, and never rise again."

The Destruction of Israel

9 I saw the Lord standing beside[2] the altar,
  and he said:

  "Strike the capitals until the thresholds
    shake,
    and shatter them on the heads of all the
    people;[3]

and those who are left of them I will kill
    with the sword;
  not one of them shall flee away;
  not one of them shall escape.

2 "If they dig into Sheol,
    from there shall my hand take them;
  if they climb up to heaven,
    from there I will bring them down.
3 If they hide themselves on the top of
    Carmel,
    from there I will search them out and
    take them;
  and if they hide from my sight at the bot-
    tom of the sea,
    there I will command the serpent, and
    it shall bite them.
4 And if they go into captivity before their
    enemies,
    there I will command the sword, and it
    shall kill them;
  and I will fix my eyes upon them
    for evil and not for good."

5 The Lord GOD of hosts,
  he who touches the earth and it melts,
    and all who dwell in it mourn,
  and all of it rises like the Nile,
    and sinks again, like the Nile of Egypt;
6 who builds his upper chambers in the
    heavens
    and founds his vault upon the earth;
  who calls for the waters of the sea
    and pours them out upon the surface of
    the earth—
  the LORD is his name.

7 "Are you not like the Cushites to me,
    O people of Israel?" declares the LORD.
  "Did I not bring up Israel from the land of
    Egypt,
    and the Philistines from Caphtor and
    the Syrians from Kir?
8 Behold, the eyes of the Lord GOD are upon
    the sinful kingdom,
    and I will destroy it from the surface of
    the ground,
    except that I will not utterly destroy the
    house of Jacob,"
                        declares the LORD.

9 "For behold, I will command,
    and shake the house of Israel among all
    the nations

---

[1] An *ephah* was about 3/5 bushel or 22 liters; a *shekel* was about 2/5 ounce or 11 grams [2] Or *on* [3] Hebrew *all of them*

as one shakes with a sieve,
    but no pebble shall fall to the earth.
10 All the sinners of my people shall die by
    the sword,
    who say, 'Disaster shall not overtake or
    meet us.'

The Restoration of Israel

11 "In that day I will raise up
    the booth of David that is fallen
and repair its breaches,
    and raise up its ruins
    and rebuild it as in the days of old,
12 that they may possess the remnant of
    Edom
    and all the nations who are called by my
    name,"[1]
    declares the LORD who does this.

13 "Behold, the days are coming," declares the
    LORD,

"when the plowman shall overtake the
    reaper
    and the treader of grapes him who sows
    the seed;
the mountains shall drip sweet wine,
    and all the hills shall flow with it.
14 I will restore the fortunes of my people
    Israel,
    and they shall rebuild the ruined cities
    and inhabit them;
they shall plant vineyards and drink their
    wine,
    and they shall make gardens and eat
    their fruit.
15 I will plant them on their land,
    and they shall never again be
    uprooted
    out of the land that I have given
    them,"
                says the LORD your God.

---

[1] Hebrew; Septuagint (compare Acts 15:17) *that the remnant of mankind and all the nations who are called by my name may seek the Lord*

OBADIAH

[1] The vision of Obadiah.

Edom Will Be Humbled

Thus says the Lord GOD concerning Edom:
We have heard a report from the LORD,
and a messenger has been sent among
the nations:
"Rise up! Let us rise against her for battle!"
[2] Behold, I will make you small among the
nations;
you shall be utterly despised.[1]
[3] The pride of your heart has deceived you,
you who live in the clefts of the rock,[2]
in your lofty dwelling,
who say in your heart,
"Who will bring me down to the
ground?"
[4] Though you soar aloft like the eagle,
though your nest is set among the stars,
from there I will bring you down,
declares the LORD.

[5] If thieves came to you,
if plunderers came by night—
how you have been destroyed!—
would they not steal only enough for
themselves?
If grape gatherers came to you,
would they not leave gleanings?
[6] How Esau has been pillaged,
his treasures sought out!
[7] All your allies have driven you to your border;
those at peace with you have deceived
you;
they have prevailed against you;
those who eat your bread[3] have set a
trap beneath you—
you have[4] no understanding.

[8] Will I not on that day, declares the LORD,
destroy the wise men out of Edom,
and understanding out of Mount Esau?
[9] And your mighty men shall be dismayed,
O Teman,
so that every man from Mount Esau
will be cut off by slaughter.

Edom's Violence Against Jacob

[10] Because of the violence done to your
brother Jacob,
shame shall cover you,
and you shall be cut off forever.
[11] On the day that you stood aloof,
on the day that strangers carried off his
wealth
and foreigners entered his gates
and cast lots for Jerusalem,
you were like one of them.
[12] But do not gloat over the day of your
brother
in the day of his misfortune;
do not rejoice over the people of Judah
in the day of their ruin;
do not boast[5]
in the day of distress.
[13] Do not enter the gate of my people
in the day of their calamity;
do not gloat over his disaster
in the day of his calamity;
do not loot his wealth
in the day of his calamity.
[14] Do not stand at the crossroads
to cut off his fugitives;
do not hand over his survivors
in the day of distress.

The Day of the LORD Is Near

[15] For the day of the LORD is near upon all
the nations.
As you have done, it shall be done to you;
your deeds shall return on your own
head.
[16] For as you have drunk on my holy mountain,
so all the nations shall drink continually;
they shall drink and swallow,
and shall be as though they had never
been.
[17] But in Mount Zion there shall be those
who escape,
and it shall be holy,
and the house of Jacob shall possess their
own possessions.
[18] The house of Jacob shall be a fire,
and the house of Joseph a flame,
and the house of Esau stubble;

---

[1] Or Behold, I have made you small among the nations; you are utterly despised [2] Or of Sela [3] Hebrew lacks those who eat [4] Hebrew he has [5] Hebrew do not enlarge your mouth

they shall burn them and consume them,
and there shall be no survivor for the
house of Esau,

for the LORD has spoken.

The Kingdom of the LORD

19 Those of the Negeb shall possess Mount
Esau,
and those of the Shephelah shall possess
the land of the Philistines;
they shall possess the land of Ephraim and
the land of Samaria,

and Benjamin shall possess Gilead.
20 The exiles of this host of the people of
Israel
shall possess the land of the Canaanites
as far as Zarephath,
and the exiles of Jerusalem who are in
Sepharad
shall possess the cities of the Negeb.
21 Saviors shall go up to Mount Zion
to rule Mount Esau,
and the kingdom shall be the LORD's.

JONAH

Jonah Flees the Presence of the LORD

1 Now the word of the LORD came to Jonah the son of Amittai, saying, ²"Arise, go to Nineveh, that great city, and call out against it, for their evil¹ has come up before me." ³But Jonah rose to flee to Tarshish from the presence of the LORD. He went down to Joppa and found a ship going to Tarshish. So he paid the fare and went down into it, to go with them to Tarshish, away from the presence of the LORD.

⁴But the LORD hurled a great wind upon the sea, and there was a mighty tempest on the sea, so that the ship threatened to break up. ⁵Then the mariners were afraid, and each cried out to his god. And they hurled the cargo that was in the ship into the sea to lighten it for them. But Jonah had gone down into the inner part of the ship and had lain down and was fast asleep. ⁶So the captain came and said to him, "What do you mean, you sleeper? Arise, call out to your god! Perhaps the god will give a thought to us, that we may not perish."

Jonah Is Thrown into the Sea

⁷And they said to one another, "Come, let us cast lots, that we may know on whose account this evil has come upon us." So they cast lots, and the lot fell on Jonah. ⁸Then they said to him, "Tell us on whose account this evil has come upon us. What is your occupation? And where do you come from? What is your country? And of what people are you?" ⁹And he said to them, "I am a Hebrew, and I fear the LORD, the God of heaven, who made the sea and the dry land." ¹⁰Then the men were exceedingly afraid and said to him, "What is this that you have done!" For the men knew that he was fleeing from the presence of the LORD, because he had told them.

¹¹Then they said to him, "What shall we do to you, that the sea may quiet down for us?" For the sea grew more and more tempestuous. ¹²He said to them, "Pick me up and hurl me into the sea; then the sea will quiet down for you, for I know it is because of me that this great tempest has come upon you." ¹³Nevertheless, the men rowed hard² to get back to dry land, but they could not, for the sea grew more and more tempestuous against them. ¹⁴Therefore they called out to the LORD, "O LORD, let us not perish for this man's life, and lay not on us innocent blood, for you, O LORD, have done as it pleased you." ¹⁵So they picked up Jonah and hurled him into the sea, and the sea ceased from its raging. ¹⁶Then the men feared the LORD exceedingly, and they offered a sacrifice to the LORD and made vows.

A Great Fish Swallows Jonah

¹⁷³And the LORD appointed⁴ a great fish to swallow up Jonah. And Jonah was in the belly of the fish three days and three nights.

Jonah's Prayer

2 Then Jonah prayed to the LORD his God from the belly of the fish, ²saying,

"I called out to the LORD, out of my distress,
    and he answered me;
out of the belly of Sheol I cried,
    and you heard my voice.
³ For you cast me into the deep,
    into the heart of the seas,
    and the flood surrounded me;
all your waves and your billows
    passed over me.
⁴ Then I said, 'I am driven away
    from your sight;
yet I shall again look
    upon your holy temple.'
⁵ The waters closed in over me to take my
        life;
    the deep surrounded me;
weeds were wrapped about my head
⁶   at the roots of the mountains.
I went down to the land
    whose bars closed upon me forever;
yet you brought up my life from the pit,
    O LORD my God.
⁷ When my life was fainting away,
    I remembered the LORD,
and my prayer came to you,
    into your holy temple.
⁸ Those who pay regard to vain idols
    forsake their hope of steadfast love.
⁹ But I with the voice of thanksgiving
    will sacrifice to you;
what I have vowed I will pay.
    Salvation belongs to the LORD!"

¹ The same Hebrew word can mean evil or disaster, depending on the context; so throughout Jonah ² Hebrew the men dug in [their oars] ³ Ch 2:1 in Hebrew ⁴ Or had appointed

10 And the Lord spoke to the fish, and it vomited Jonah out upon the dry land.

Jonah Goes to Nineveh

3 Then the word of the Lord came to Jonah the second time, saying, 2 "Arise, go to Nineveh, that great city, and call out against it the message that I tell you." 3 So Jonah arose and went to Nineveh, according to the word of the Lord. Now Nineveh was an exceedingly great city,[1] three days' journey in breadth.[2] 4 Jonah began to go into the city, going a day's journey. And he called out, "Yet forty days, and Nineveh shall be overthrown!" 5 And the people of Nineveh believed God. They called for a fast and put on sackcloth, from the greatest of them to the least of them.

The People of Nineveh Repent

6 The word reached[3] the king of Nineveh, and he arose from his throne, removed his robe, covered himself with sackcloth, and sat in ashes. 7 And he issued a proclamation and published through Nineveh, "By the decree of the king and his nobles: Let neither man nor beast, herd nor flock, taste anything. Let them not feed or drink water, 8 but let man and beast be covered with sackcloth, and let them call out mightily to God. Let everyone turn from his evil way and from the violence that is in his hands. 9 Who knows? God may turn and relent and turn from his fierce anger, so that we may not perish."

10 When God saw what they did, how they turned from their evil way, God relented of the disaster that he had said he would do to them, and he did not do it.

Jonah's Anger and the Lord's Compassion

4 But it displeased Jonah exceedingly,[4] and he was angry. 2 And he prayed to the Lord and said, "O Lord, is not this what I said when I was yet in my country? That is why I made haste to flee to Tarshish; for I knew that you are a gracious God and merciful, slow to anger and abounding in steadfast love, and relenting from disaster. 3 Therefore now, O Lord, please take my life from me, for it is better for me to die than to live." 4 And the Lord said, "Do you do well to be angry?"

5 Jonah went out of the city and sat to the east of the city and made a booth for himself there. He sat under it in the shade, till he should see what would become of the city. 6 Now the Lord God appointed a plant[5] and made it come up over Jonah, that it might be a shade over his head, to save him from his discomfort.[6] So Jonah was exceedingly glad because of the plant. 7 But when dawn came up the next day, God appointed a worm that attacked the plant, so that it withered. 8 When the sun rose, God appointed a scorching east wind, and the sun beat down on the head of Jonah so that he was faint. And he asked that he might die and said, "It is better for me to die than to live." 9 But God said to Jonah, "Do you do well to be angry for the plant?" And he said, "Yes, I do well to be angry, angry enough to die." 10 And the Lord said, "You pity the plant, for which you did not labor, nor did you make it grow, which came into being in a night and perished in a night. 11 And should not I pity Nineveh, that great city, in which there are more than 120,000 persons who do not know their right hand from their left, and also much cattle?"

---

1 Hebrew *a great city to God* 2 Or *a visit was a three days' journey* 3 Or *had reached* 4 Hebrew *it was exceedingly evil to Jonah* 5 Hebrew *qiqayon,* probably the castor oil plant; also verses 7, 9, 10 6 Or *his evil*

MICAH

The word of the LORD that came to Micah of Moresheth in the days of Jotham, Ahaz, and Hezekiah, kings of Judah, which he saw concerning Samaria and Jerusalem.

The Coming Destruction

2 Hear, you peoples, all of you;[1]
    pay attention, O earth, and all that is in it,
and let the Lord GOD be a witness against you,
    the Lord from his holy temple.
3 For behold, the LORD is coming out of his place,
    and will come down and tread upon the high places of the earth.
4 And the mountains will melt under him,
    and the valleys will split open,
like wax before the fire,
    like waters poured down a steep place.
5 All this is for the transgression of Jacob
    and for the sins of the house of Israel.
What is the transgression of Jacob?
    Is it not Samaria?
And what is the high place of Judah?
    Is it not Jerusalem?
6 Therefore I will make Samaria a heap in the open country,
    a place for planting vineyards,
and I will pour down her stones into the valley
    and uncover her foundations.
7 All her carved images shall be beaten to pieces,
    all her wages shall be burned with fire,
    and all her idols I will lay waste,
for from the fee of a prostitute she gathered them,
    and to the fee of a prostitute they shall return.

8 For this I will lament and wail;
    I will go stripped and naked;
I will make lamentation like the jackals,
    and mourning like the ostriches.
9 For her wound is incurable,
    and it has come to Judah;
it has reached to the gate of my people,
    to Jerusalem.
10 Tell it not in Gath;
    weep not at all;
in Beth-le-aphrah
    roll yourselves in the dust.
11 Pass on your way,
    inhabitants of Shaphir,
    in nakedness and shame;
the inhabitants of Zaanan
    do not come out;
the lamentation of Beth-ezel
    shall take away from you its standing place.
12 For the inhabitants of Maroth
    wait anxiously for good,
because disaster has come down from the LORD
    to the gate of Jerusalem.
13 Harness the steeds to the chariots,
    inhabitants of Lachish;
it was the beginning of sin
    to the daughter of Zion,
for in you were found
    the transgressions of Israel.
14 Therefore you shall give parting gifts[2]
    to Moresheth-gath;
the houses of Achzib shall be a deceitful thing
    to the kings of Israel.
15 I will again bring a conqueror to you,
    inhabitants of Mareshah;
the glory of Israel
    shall come to Adullam.
16 Make yourselves bald and cut off your hair,
    for the children of your delight;
make yourselves as bald as the eagle,
    for they shall go from you into exile.

Woe to the Oppressors

2 Woe to those who devise wickedness
    and work evil on their beds!
When the morning dawns, they perform it,
    because it is in the power of their hand.
2 They covet fields and seize them,
    and houses, and take them away;
they oppress a man and his house,
    a man and his inheritance.

[1] Hebrew *all of them* [2] Or *give dowry*

3 Therefore thus says the LORD:
behold, against this family I am devising
disaster,[1]
from which you cannot remove your
necks,
and you shall not walk haughtily,
for it will be a time of disaster.
4 In that day they shall take up a taunt song
against you
and moan bitterly,
and say, "We are utterly ruined;
he changes the portion of my people;
how he removes it from me!
To an apostate he allots our fields."
5 Therefore you will have none to cast the
line by lot
in the assembly of the LORD.

6 "Do not preach"—thus they preach—
"one should not preach of such things;
disgrace will not overtake us."
7 Should this be said, O house of Jacob?
Has the LORD grown impatient?[2]
Are these his deeds?
Do not my words do good
to him who walks uprightly?
8 But lately my people have risen up as an
enemy;
you strip the rich robe from those who pass
by trustingly
with no thought of war.[3]
9 The women of my people you drive out
from their delightful houses;
from their young children you take away
my splendor forever.
10 Arise and go,
for this is no place to rest,
because of uncleanness that destroys
with a grievous destruction.
11 If a man should go about and utter wind
and lies,
saying, "I will preach to you of wine and
strong drink,"
he would be the preacher for this people!
12 I will surely assemble all of you, O Jacob;
I will gather the remnant of Israel;
I will set them together
like sheep in a fold,
like a flock in its pasture,
a noisy multitude of men.

13 He who opens the breach goes up before
them;
they break through and pass the gate,
going out by it.
Their king passes on before them,
the LORD at their head.

Rulers and Prophets Denounced

3 And I said:
Hear, you heads of Jacob
and rulers of the house of Israel!
Is it not for you to know justice?—
2 you who hate the good and love the evil,
who tear the skin from off my people[4]
and their flesh from off their bones,
3 who eat the flesh of my people,
and flay their skin from off them,
and break their bones in pieces
and chop them up like meat in a pot,
like flesh in a cauldron.

4 Then they will cry to the LORD,
but he will not answer them;
he will hide his face from them at that time,
because they have made their deeds evil.

5 Thus says the LORD concerning the prophets
who lead my people astray,
who cry "Peace"
when they have something to eat,
but declare war against him
who puts nothing into their mouths.
6 Therefore it shall be night to you, without
vision,
and darkness to you, without divination.
The sun shall go down on the prophets,
and the day shall be black over them;
7 the seers shall be disgraced,
and the diviners put to shame;
they shall all cover their lips,
for there is no answer from God.
8 But as for me, I am filled with power,
with the Spirit of the LORD,
and with justice and might,
to declare to Jacob his transgression
and to Israel his sin.

9 Hear this, you heads of the house of Jacob
and rulers of the house of Israel,
who detest justice
and make crooked all that is straight,
10 who build Zion with blood
and Jerusalem with iniquity.

---

[1] The same Hebrew word can mean *evil* or *disaster*, depending on the context [2] Hebrew *Has the spirit of the LORD grown short?* [3] Or *returning from war* [4] Hebrew *from off them*

11 Its heads give judgment for a bribe;
    its priests teach for a price;
    its prophets practice divination for
        money;
yet they lean on the LORD and say,
    "Is not the LORD in the midst of us?
    No disaster shall come upon us."
12 Therefore because of you
    Zion shall be plowed as a field;
Jerusalem shall become a heap of ruins,
    and the mountain of the house a
        wooded height.

The Mountain of the LORD

4 It shall come to pass in the latter days
    that the mountain of the house of the
        LORD
shall be established as the highest of the
    mountains,
    and it shall be lifted up above the hills;
and peoples shall flow to it,
2   and many nations shall come, and say:
"Come, let us go up to the mountain of the
    LORD,
to the house of the God of Jacob,
that he may teach us his ways
    and that we may walk in his paths."
For out of Zion shall go forth the law,[1]
    and the word of the LORD from
        Jerusalem.
3 He shall judge between many peoples,
    and shall decide disputes for strong
        nations far away;
and they shall beat their swords into plow-
    shares,
    and their spears into pruning hooks;
nation shall not lift up sword against
    nation,
    neither shall they learn war anymore;
4 but they shall sit every man under his vine
    and under his fig tree,
    and no one shall make them afraid,
    for the mouth of the LORD of hosts has
        spoken.
5 For all the peoples walk
    each in the name of its god,
but we will walk in the name of the LORD
    our God
    forever and ever.

The LORD Shall Rescue Zion

6   In that day, declares the LORD,
    I will assemble the lame

and gather those who have been driven
    away
    and those whom I have afflicted;
7 and the lame I will make the remnant,
    and those who were cast off, a strong
        nation;
and the LORD will reign over them in
    Mount Zion
    from this time forth and forevermore.

8 And you, O tower of the flock,
    hill of the daughter of Zion,
to you shall it come,
    the former dominion shall come,
    kingship for the daughter of Jerusalem.

9 Now why do you cry aloud?
    Is there no king in you?
Has your counselor perished,
    that pain seized you like a woman in
        labor?
10 Writhe and groan,[2] O daughter of Zion,
    like a woman in labor,
for now you shall go out from the city
    and dwell in the open country;
    you shall go to Babylon.
There you shall be rescued;
    there the LORD will redeem you
    from the hand of your enemies.

11 Now many nations
    are assembled against you,
saying, "Let her be defiled,
    and let our eyes gaze upon Zion."
12 But they do not know
    the thoughts of the LORD;
they do not understand his plan,
    that he has gathered them as sheaves to
        the threshing floor.
13 Arise and thresh,
    O daughter of Zion,
for I will make your horn iron,
    and I will make your hoofs bronze;
you shall beat in pieces many peoples;
    and shall devote[3] their gain to the LORD,
    their wealth to the Lord of the whole
        earth.

The Ruler to Be Born in Bethlehem

5 [4] Now muster your troops, O daughter[5] of
    troops;
    siege is laid against us;
with a rod they strike the judge of Israel
    on the cheek.

---

[1] Or teaching [2] Or push [3] Hebrew devote to destruction [4] Ch 4:14 in Hebrew [5] That is, city

2 **1** But you, O Bethlehem Ephrathah,
    who are too little to be among the
      clans of Judah,
from you shall come forth for me
    one who is to be ruler in Israel,
whose coming forth is from of old,
    from ancient days.
3 Therefore he shall give them up until the
    time
    when she who is in labor has given
      birth;
then the rest of his brothers shall return
    to the people of Israel.
4 And he shall stand and shepherd his flock
    in the strength of the LORD,
    in the majesty of the name of the LORD
      his God.
And they shall dwell secure, for now he
    shall be great
    to the ends of the earth.
5 And he shall be their peace.

When the Assyrian comes into our land
    and treads in our palaces,
then we will raise against him seven shep-
    herds
    and eight princes of men;
6 they shall shepherd the land of Assyria
    with the sword,
    and the land of Nimrod at its entrances;
and he shall deliver us from the Assyrian
    when he comes into our land
    and treads within our border.

A Remnant Shall Be Delivered

7 Then the remnant of Jacob shall be
    in the midst of many peoples
like dew from the LORD,
    like showers on the grass,
which delay not for a man
    nor wait for the children of man.
8 And the remnant of Jacob shall be among
    the nations,
    in the midst of many peoples,
like a lion among the beasts of the forest,
    like a young lion among the flocks of
      sheep,
which, when it goes through, treads down
    and tears in pieces, and there is none to
    deliver.
9 Your hand shall be lifted up over your
    adversaries,
    and all your enemies shall be cut off.

10 And in that day, declares the LORD,
    I will cut off your horses from among
      you
    and will destroy your chariots;
11 and I will cut off the cities of your land
    and throw down all your strongholds;
12 and I will cut off sorceries from your hand,
    and you shall have no more tellers of
      fortunes;
13 and I will cut off your carved images
    and your pillars from among you,
and you shall bow down no more
    to the work of your hands;
14 and I will root out your Asherah images
    from among you
    and destroy your cities.
15 And in anger and wrath I will execute ven-
    geance
    on the nations that did not obey.

The Indictment of the LORD

6 Hear what the LORD says:
    Arise, plead your case before the moun-
      tains,
    and let the hills hear your voice.
2 Hear, you mountains, the indictment of
    the LORD,
    and you enduring foundations of the
      earth,
for the LORD has an indictment against his
    people,
    and he will contend with Israel.

3 "O my people, what have I done to you?
    How have I wearied you? Answer me!
4 For I brought you up from the land of
    Egypt
    and redeemed you from the house of
      slavery,
and I sent before you Moses,
    Aaron, and Miriam.
5 O my people, remember what Balak king
    of Moab devised,
    and what Balaam the son of Beor
      answered him,
and what happened from Shittim to
    Gilgal,
    that you may know the righteous acts
    of the LORD."

What Does the LORD Require?

6 "With what shall I come before the LORD,
    and bow myself before God on high?

1 Ch 5:1 in Hebrew

Shall I come before him with burnt offer-
    ings,
    with calves a year old?
7 Will the Lord be pleased with[1] thousands
    of rams,
    with ten thousands of rivers of oil?
Shall I give my firstborn for my transgres-
    sion,
    the fruit of my body for the sin of my
    soul?"

8 He has told you, O man, what is good;
    and what does the Lord require of you
but to do justice, and to love kindness,[2]
    and to walk humbly with your God?

Destruction of the Wicked

9 The voice of the Lord cries to the city—
    and it is sound wisdom to fear your
    name:
    "Hear of the rod and of him who appointed
    it![3]
10 Can I forget any longer the treasures[4]
    of wickedness in the house of the
    wicked,
    and the scant measure that is accursed?
11 Shall I acquit the man with wicked scales
    and with a bag of deceitful weights?
12 Your[5] rich men are full of violence;
    your inhabitants speak lies,
    and their tongue is deceitful in their
    mouth.
13 Therefore I strike you with a grievous blow,
    making you desolate because of your
    sins.
14 You shall eat, but not be satisfied,
    and there shall be hunger within you;
you shall put away, but not preserve,
    and what you preserve I will give to the
    sword.
15 You shall sow, but not reap;
    you shall tread olives, but not anoint
    yourselves with oil;
    you shall tread grapes, but not drink
    wine.
16 For you have kept the statutes of Omri,[6]
    and all the works of the house of Ahab;
    and you have walked in their counsels,
that I may make you a desolation, and
    your[7] inhabitants a hissing;
    so you shall bear the scorn of my peo-
    ple."

Wait for the God of Salvation

7 Woe is me! For I have become
    as when the summer fruit has been gath-
    ered,
    as when the grapes have been gleaned:
there is no cluster to eat,
    no first-ripe fig that my soul desires.
2 The godly has perished from the earth,
    and there is no one upright among
    mankind;
they all lie in wait for blood,
    and each hunts the other with a net.
3 Their hands are on what is evil, to do it
    well;
    the prince and the judge ask for a bribe,
and the great man utters the evil desire of
    his soul;
    thus they weave it together.
4 The best of them is like a brier,
    the most upright of them a thorn
    hedge.
The day of your watchmen, of your pun-
    ishment, has come;
    now their confusion is at hand.
5 Put no trust in a neighbor;
    have no confidence in a friend;
guard the doors of your mouth
    from her who lies in your arms;[8]
6 for the son treats the father with contempt,
    the daughter rises up against her
    mother,
the daughter-in-law against her mother-in-
    law;
    a man's enemies are the men of his own
    house.
7 But as for me, I will look to the Lord;
    I will wait for the God of my salvation;
    my God will hear me.

8 Rejoice not over me, O my enemy;
    when I fall, I shall rise;
when I sit in darkness,
    the Lord will be a light to me.
9 I will bear the indignation of the Lord
    because I have sinned against him,
until he pleads my cause
    and executes judgment for me.
He will bring me out to the light;
    I shall look upon his vindication.
10 Then my enemy will see,
    and shame will cover her who said to
    me,
    "Where is the Lord your God?"

[1] Or Will the Lord accept [2] Or steadfast love [3] The meaning of the Hebrew is uncertain [4] Or Are there still treasures [5] Hebrew whose [6] Hebrew For the statutes of Omri are kept [7] Hebrew its [8] Hebrew bosom

My eyes will look upon her;
  now she will be trampled down
  like the mire of the streets.

11 A day for the building of your walls!
  In that day the boundary shall be far
    extended.
12 In that day they[1] will come to you,
  from Assyria and the cities of Egypt,
and from Egypt to the River,[2]
  from sea to sea and from mountain to
    mountain.
13 But the earth will be desolate
  because of its inhabitants,
  for the fruit of their deeds.

14 Shepherd your people with your staff,
  the flock of your inheritance,
who dwell alone in a forest
  in the midst of a garden land;[3]
let them graze in Bashan and Gilead
  as in the days of old.
15 As in the days when you came out of the
    land of Egypt,
  I will show them[4] marvelous things.
16 The nations shall see and be ashamed of all
    their might;

they shall lay their hands on their
    mouths;
  their ears shall be deaf;
17 they shall lick the dust like a serpent,
  like the crawling things of the earth;
they shall come trembling out of their
    strongholds;
  they shall turn in dread to the LORD our
    God,
  and they shall be in fear of you.

God's Steadfast Love and Compassion

18 Who is a God like you, pardoning iniq-
    uity
  and passing over transgression
  for the remnant of his inheritance?
He does not retain his anger forever,
  because he delights in steadfast love.
19 He will again have compassion on us;
  he will tread our iniquities underfoot.
You will cast all our[5] sins
  into the depths of the sea.
20 You will show faithfulness to Jacob
  and steadfast love to Abraham,
as you have sworn to our fathers
  from the days of old.

---

[1] Hebrew *he* [2] That is, the Euphrates [3] Hebrew *of Carmel* [4] Hebrew *him* [5] Hebrew *their*

NAHUM

1 An oracle concerning Nineveh. The book of the vision of Nahum of Elkosh.

God's Wrath Against Nineveh

2 The LORD is a jealous and avenging God;
  the LORD is avenging and wrathful;
  the LORD takes vengeance on his adversaries
  and keeps wrath for his enemies.
3 The LORD is slow to anger and great in power,
  and the LORD will by no means clear the guilty.
His way is in whirlwind and storm,
  and the clouds are the dust of his feet.
4 He rebukes the sea and makes it dry;
  he dries up all the rivers;
Bashan and Carmel wither;
  the bloom of Lebanon withers.
5 The mountains quake before him;
  the hills melt;
the earth heaves before him,
  the world and all who dwell in it.

6 Who can stand before his indignation?
  Who can endure the heat of his anger?
His wrath is poured out like fire,
  and the rocks are broken into pieces by him.
7 The LORD is good,
  a stronghold in the day of trouble;
he knows those who take refuge in him.
8 But with an overflowing flood
  he will make a complete end of the adversaries,[1]
  and will pursue his enemies into darkness.

9 What do you plot against the LORD?
  He will make a complete end;
  trouble will not rise up a second time.
10 For they are like entangled thorns,
  like drunkards as they drink;
  they are consumed like stubble fully dried.
11 From you came one
  who plotted evil against the LORD,
  a worthless counselor.

12 Thus says the LORD,
  "Though they are at full strength and many,
  they will be cut down and pass away.

Though I have afflicted you,
  I will afflict you no more.
13 And now I will break his yoke from off you
  and will burst your bonds apart."

14 The LORD has given commandment about you:
  "No more shall your name be perpetuated;
from the house of your gods I will cut off
  the carved image and the metal image.
I will make your grave, for you are vile."

15 2 Behold, upon the mountains, the feet of him
  who brings good news,
  who publishes peace!
Keep your feasts, O Judah;
  fulfill your vows,
for never again shall the worthless pass through you;
  he is utterly cut off.

The Destruction of Nineveh

2 The scatterer has come up against you.
  Man the ramparts;
  watch the road;
dress for battle;[3]
  collect all your strength.

2 For the LORD is restoring the majesty of Jacob
  as the majesty of Israel,
for plunderers have plundered them
  and ruined their branches.

3 The shield of his mighty men is red;
  his soldiers are clothed in scarlet.
The chariots come with flashing metal
  on the day he musters them;
  the cypress spears are brandished.
4 The chariots race madly through the streets;
  they rush to and fro through the squares;
they gleam like torches;
  they dart like lightning.
5 He remembers his officers;
  they stumble as they go,
they hasten to the wall;
  the siege tower[4] is set up.

[1] Hebrew of her place [2] Ch 2:1 in Hebrew [3] Hebrew gird your loins [4] Or the mantelet

6 The river gates are opened;
    the palace melts away;
7 its mistress[1] is stripped;[2] she is carried off,
    her slave girls lamenting,
  moaning like doves
    and beating their breasts.
8 Nineveh is like a pool
    whose waters run away.[3]
  "Halt! Halt!" they cry,
    but none turns back.
9 Plunder the silver,
    plunder the gold!
  There is no end of the treasure
    or of the wealth of all precious things.

10 Desolate! Desolation and ruin!
    Hearts melt and knees tremble;
  anguish is in all loins;
    all faces grow pale!
11 Where is the lions' den,
    the feeding place of the young lions,
  where the lion and lioness went,
    where his cubs were, with none to dis-
      turb?
12 The lion tore enough for his cubs
    and strangled prey for his lionesses;
  he filled his caves with prey
    and his dens with torn flesh.

13 Behold, I am against you, declares the
LORD of hosts, and I will burn your[4] chariots
in smoke, and the sword shall devour your
young lions. I will cut off your prey from the
earth, and the voice of your messengers shall
no longer be heard.

Woe to Nineveh

3 Woe to the bloody city,
    all full of lies and plunder—
  no end to the prey!
2 The crack of the whip, and rumble of the
      wheel,
    galloping horse and bounding chariot!
3 Horsemen charging,
    flashing sword and glittering spear,
  hosts of slain,
    heaps of corpses,
  dead bodies without end—
    they stumble over the bodies!
4 And all for the countless whorings of the
      prostitute,
    graceful and of deadly charms,
  who betrays nations with her whorings,
    and peoples with her charms.

5 Behold, I am against you,
    declares the LORD of hosts,
    and will lift up your skirts over your
      face;
  and I will make nations look at your
      nakedness
    and kingdoms at your shame.
6 I will throw filth at you
    and treat you with contempt
    and make you a spectacle.
7 And all who look at you will shrink from
      you and say,
  "Wasted is Nineveh; who will grieve for
      her?"
    Where shall I seek comforters for you?

8 Are you better than Thebes[5]
    that sat by the Nile,
  with water around her,
    her rampart a sea,
    and water her wall?
9 Cush was her strength;
    Egypt too, and that without limit;
    Put and the Libyans were her[6] helpers.

10 Yet she became an exile;
    she went into captivity;
  her infants were dashed in pieces
    at the head of every street;
  for her honored men lots were cast,
    and all her great men were bound in
      chains.
11 You also will be drunken;
    you will go into hiding;
  you will seek a refuge from the enemy.
12 All your fortresses are like fig trees
    with first-ripe figs—
  if shaken they fall
    into the mouth of the eater.
13 Behold, your troops
    are women in your midst.
  The gates of your land
    are wide open to your enemies;
    fire has devoured your bars.

14 Draw water for the siege;
    strengthen your forts;
  go into the clay;
    tread the mortar;
    take hold of the brick mold!
15 There will the fire devour you;
    the sword will cut you off.
    It will devour you like the locust.

[1] The meaning of the Hebrew word rendered *its mistress* is uncertain [2] Or *exiled* [3] Compare Septuagint; the meaning of the Hebrew is uncertain [4] Hebrew *her* [5] Hebrew *No-amon* [6] Hebrew *your*

Multiply yourselves like the locust;
   multiply like the grasshopper!
16 You increased your merchants
   more than the stars of the heavens.
   The locust spreads its wings and flies
      away.

17 Your princes are like grasshoppers,
   your scribes[1] like clouds of locusts
settling on the fences
   in a day of cold—
when the sun rises, they fly away;
   no one knows where they are.

18 Your shepherds are asleep,
   O king of Assyria;
   your nobles slumber.
Your people are scattered on the mountains
   with none to gather them.
19 There is no easing your hurt;
   your wound is grievous.
All who hear the news about you
   clap their hands over you.
For upon whom has not come
   your unceasing evil?

[1] Or marshals

[13] Asa and the people who were with him pursued them as far as Gerar, and the Ethiopians fell until none remained alive, for they were broken before the LORD and his army. The men of Judah[1] carried away very much spoil. [14] And they attacked all the cities around Gerar, for the fear of the LORD was upon them. They plundered all the cities, for there was much plunder in them. [15] And they struck down the tents of those who had livestock and carried away sheep in abundance and camels. Then they returned to Jerusalem.

Asa's Religious Reforms

15 The Spirit of God came[2] upon Azariah the son of Oded, [2] and he went out to meet Asa and said to him, "Hear me, Asa, and all Judah and Benjamin: The LORD is with you while you are with him. If you seek him, he will be found by you, but if you forsake him, he will forsake you. [3] For a long time Israel was without the true God, and without a teaching priest and without law, [4] but when in their distress they turned to the LORD, the God of Israel, and sought him, he was found by them. [5] In those times there was no peace to him who went out or to him who came in, for great disturbances afflicted all the inhabitants of the lands. [6] They were broken in pieces. Nation was crushed by nation and city by city, for God troubled them with every sort of distress. [7] But you, take courage! Do not let your hands be weak, for your work shall be rewarded."

[8] As soon as Asa heard these words, the prophecy of Azariah the son of Oded, he took courage and put away the detestable idols from all the land of Judah and Benjamin and from the cities that he had taken in the hill country of Ephraim, and he repaired the altar of the LORD that was in front of the vestibule of the house of the LORD.[3] [9] And he gathered all Judah and Benjamin, and those from Ephraim, Manasseh, and Simeon who were residing with them, for great numbers had deserted to him from Israel when they saw that the LORD his God was with him. [10] They were gathered at Jerusalem in the third month of the fifteenth year of the reign of Asa. [11] They sacrificed to the LORD on that day from the spoil that they had brought 700 oxen and 7,000 sheep. [12] And they entered into a covenant to seek the LORD, the God of their fathers, with all their heart and with all their soul, [13] but that whoever would not seek the LORD, the God of Israel, should be put to death, whether young or old, man or woman. [14] They swore an oath to the LORD with a loud voice and with shouting and with trumpets and with horns. [15] And all Judah rejoiced over the oath, for they had sworn with all their heart and had sought him with their whole desire, and he was found by them, and the LORD gave them rest all around.

[16] Even Maacah, his mother, King Asa removed from being queen mother because she had made a detestable image for Asherah. Asa cut down her image, crushed it, and burned it at the brook Kidron. [17] But the high places were not taken out of Israel. Nevertheless, the heart of Asa was wholly true all his days. [18] And he brought into the house of God the sacred gifts of his father and his own sacred gifts, silver, and gold, and vessels. [19] And there was no more war until the thirty-fifth year of the reign of Asa.

Asa's Last Years

16 In the thirty-sixth year of the reign of Asa, Baasha king of Israel went up against Judah and built Ramah, that he might permit no one to go out or come in to Asa king of Judah. [2] Then Asa took silver and gold from the treasures of the house of the LORD and the king's house and sent them to Ben-hadad king of Syria, who lived in Damascus, saying, [3] "There is a covenant[4] between me and you, as there was between my father and your father. Behold, I am sending to you silver and gold. Go, break your covenant with Baasha king of Israel, that he may withdraw from me." [4] And Ben-hadad listened to King Asa and sent the commanders of his armies against the cities of Israel, and they conquered Ijon, Dan, Abel-maim, and all the store cities of Naphtali. [5] And when Baasha heard of it, he stopped building Ramah and let his work cease. [6] Then King Asa took all Judah, and they carried away the stones of Ramah and its timber, with which Baasha had been building, and with them he built Geba and Mizpah.

[7] At that time Hanani the seer came to Asa king of Judah and said to him, "Because you relied on the king of Syria, and did not rely on the LORD your God, the army of the king of Syria has escaped you. [8] Were not the Ethiopians and the Libyans a huge army with very many chariots and horsemen? Yet because you relied on the LORD, he gave them

---

[1] Hebrew *They* [2] Or *was* [3] Hebrew *the vestibule of the LORD* [4] Or *treaty*; twice in this verse

into your hand. ⁹For the eyes of the LORD run to and fro throughout the whole earth, to give strong support to those whose heart is blameless[1] toward him. You have done foolishly in this, for from now on you will have wars." ¹⁰Then Asa was angry with the seer and put him in the stocks in prison, for he was in a rage with him because of this. And Asa inflicted cruelties upon some of the people at the same time.

¹¹The acts of Asa, from first to last, are written in the Book of the Kings of Judah and Israel. ¹²In the thirty-ninth year of his reign Asa was diseased in his feet, and his disease became severe. Yet even in his disease he did not seek the LORD, but sought help from physicians. ¹³And Asa slept with his fathers, dying in the forty-first year of his reign. ¹⁴They buried him in the tomb that he had cut for himself in the city of David. They laid him on a bier that had been filled with various kinds of spices prepared by the perfumer's art, and they made a very great fire in his honor.

Jehoshaphat Reigns in Judah

17 Jehoshaphat his son reigned in his place and strengthened himself against Israel. ²He placed forces in all the fortified cities of Judah and set garrisons in the land of Judah, and in the cities of Ephraim that Asa his father had captured. ³The LORD was with Jehoshaphat, because he walked in the earlier ways of his father David. He did not seek the Baals, ⁴but sought the God of his father and walked in his commandments, and not according to the practices of Israel. ⁵Therefore the LORD established the kingdom in his hand. And all Judah brought tribute to Jehoshaphat, and he had great riches and honor. ⁶His heart was courageous in the ways of the LORD. And furthermore, he took the high places and the Asherim out of Judah.

⁷In the third year of his reign he sent his officials, Ben-hail, Obadiah, Zechariah, Nethanel, and Micaiah, to teach in the cities of Judah; ⁸and with them the Levites, Shemaiah, Nethaniah, Zebadiah, Asahel, Shemiramoth, Jehonathan, Adonijah, Tobijah, and Tobadonijah; and with these Levites, the priests Elishama and Jehoram. ⁹And they taught in Judah, having the Book of the Law of the LORD with them. They went about through all the cities of Judah and taught among the people.

¹⁰And the fear of the LORD fell upon all the kingdoms of the lands that were around Judah, and they made no war against Jehoshaphat. ¹¹Some of the Philistines brought Jehoshaphat presents and silver for tribute, and the Arabians also brought him 7,700 rams and 7,700 goats. ¹²And Jehoshaphat grew steadily greater. He built in Judah fortresses and store cities, ¹³and he had large supplies in the cities of Judah. He had soldiers, mighty men of valor, in Jerusalem. ¹⁴This was the muster of them by fathers' houses: Of Judah, the commanders of thousands: Adnah the commander, with 300,000 mighty men of valor; ¹⁵and next to him Jehohanan the commander, with 280,000; ¹⁶and next to him Amasiah the son of Zichri, a volunteer for the service of the LORD, with 200,000 mighty men of valor. ¹⁷Of Benjamin: Eliada, a mighty man of valor, with 200,000 men armed with bow and shield; ¹⁸and next to him Jehozabad with 180,000 armed for war. ¹⁹These were in the service of the king, besides those whom the king had placed in the fortified cities throughout all Judah.

Jehoshaphat Allies with Ahab

18 Now Jehoshaphat had great riches and honor, and he made a marriage alliance with Ahab. ²After some years he went down to Ahab in Samaria. And Ahab killed an abundance of sheep and oxen for him and for the people who were with him, and induced him to go up against Ramoth-gilead. ³Ahab king of Israel said to Jehoshaphat king of Judah, "Will you go with me to Ramoth-gilead?" He answered him, "I am as you are, my people as your people. We will be with you in the war."

⁴And Jehoshaphat said to the king of Israel, "Inquire first for the word of the LORD." ⁵Then the king of Israel gathered the prophets together, four hundred men, and said to them, "Shall we go to battle against Ramoth-gilead, or shall I refrain?" And they said, "Go up, for God will give it into the hand of the king." ⁶But Jehoshaphat said, "Is there not here another prophet of the LORD of whom we may inquire?" ⁷And the king of Israel said to Jehoshaphat, "There is yet one man by whom we may inquire of the LORD, Micaiah the son of Imlah; but I hate him, for he never prophesies good concerning me, but always evil." And Jehoshaphat said, "Let not the king say so." ⁸Then the king of Israel summoned an officer and said, "Bring

¹ Or whole

quickly Micaiah the son of Imlah." ⁹ Now the king of Israel and Jehoshaphat the king of Judah were sitting on their thrones, arrayed in their robes. And they were sitting at the threshing floor at the entrance of the gate of Samaria, and all the prophets were prophesying before them. ¹⁰ And Zedekiah the son of Chenaanah made for himself horns of iron and said, "Thus says the LORD, 'With these you shall push the Syrians until they are destroyed.'" ¹¹ And all the prophets prophesied so and said, "Go up to Ramoth-gilead and triumph. The LORD will give it into the hand of the king."

¹² And the messenger who went to summon Micaiah said to him, "Behold, the words of the prophets with one accord are favorable to the king. Let your word be like the word of one of them, and speak favorably." ¹³ But Micaiah said, "As the LORD lives, what my God says, that I will speak." ¹⁴ And when he had come to the king, the king said to him, "Micaiah, shall we go to Ramoth-gilead to battle, or shall I refrain?" And he answered, "Go up and triumph; they will be given into your hand." ¹⁵ But the king said to him, "How many times shall I make you swear that you speak to me nothing but the truth in the name of the LORD?" ¹⁶ And he said, "I saw all Israel scattered on the mountains, as sheep that have no shepherd. And the LORD said, 'These have no master; let each return to his home in peace.'" ¹⁷ And the king of Israel said to Jehoshaphat, "Did I not tell you that he would not prophesy good concerning me, but evil?" ¹⁸ And Micaiah said, "Therefore hear the word of the LORD: I saw the LORD sitting on his throne, and all the host of heaven standing on his right hand and on his left. ¹⁹ And the LORD said, 'Who will entice Ahab the king of Israel, that he may go up and fall at Ramoth-gilead?' And one said one thing, and another said another. ²⁰ Then a spirit came forward and stood before the LORD, saying, 'I will entice him.' And the LORD said to him, 'By what means?' ²¹ And he said, 'I will go out, and will be a lying spirit in the mouth of all his prophets.' And he said, 'You are to entice him, and you shall succeed; go out and do so.' ²² Now therefore behold, the LORD has put a lying spirit in the mouth of these your prophets. The LORD has declared disaster concerning you."

²³ Then Zedekiah the son of Chenaanah came near and struck Micaiah on the cheek and said, "Which way did the Spirit of the LORD go from me to speak to you?" ²⁴ And Micaiah said, "Behold, you shall see on that day when you go into an inner chamber to hide yourself." ²⁵ And the king of Israel said, "Seize Micaiah and take him back to Amon the governor of the city and to Joash the king's son, ²⁶ and say, 'Thus says the king, Put this fellow in prison and feed him with meager rations of bread and water until I return in peace.'" ²⁷ And Micaiah said, "If you return in peace, the LORD has not spoken by me." And he said, "Hear, all you peoples!"

The Defeat and Death of Ahab

²⁸ So the king of Israel and Jehoshaphat the king of Judah went up to Ramoth-gilead. ²⁹ And the king of Israel said to Jehoshaphat, "I will disguise myself and go into battle, but you wear your robes." And the king of Israel disguised himself, and they went into battle. ³⁰ Now the king of Syria had commanded the captains of his chariots, "Fight with neither small nor great, but only with the king of Israel." ³¹ As soon as the captains of the chariots saw Jehoshaphat, they said, "It is the king of Israel." So they turned to fight against him. And Jehoshaphat cried out, and the LORD helped him; God drew them away from him. ³² For as soon as the captains of the chariots saw that it was not the king of Israel, they turned back from pursuing him. ³³ But a certain man drew his bow at random¹ and struck the king of Israel between the scale armor and the breastplate. Therefore he said to the driver of his chariot, "Turn around and carry me out of the battle, for I am wounded." ³⁴ And the battle continued that day, and the king of Israel was propped up in his chariot facing the Syrians until evening. Then at sunset he died.

Jehoshaphat's Reforms

19 Jehoshaphat the king of Judah returned in safety to his house in Jerusalem. ² But Jehu the son of Hanani the seer went out to meet him and said to King Jehoshaphat, "Should you help the wicked and love those who hate the LORD? Because of this, wrath has gone out against you from the LORD. ³ Nevertheless, some good is found in you, for you destroyed the Asheroth out of the land, and have set your heart to seek God."

¹ Hebrew *in his innocence*

⁴ Jehoshaphat lived at Jerusalem. And he went out again among the people, from Beersheba to the hill country of Ephraim, and brought them back to the LORD, the God of their fathers. ⁵ He appointed judges in the land in all the fortified cities of Judah, city by city, ⁶ and said to the judges, "Consider what you do, for you judge not for man but for the LORD. He is with you in giving judgment. ⁷ Now then, let the fear of the LORD be upon you. Be careful what you do, for there is no injustice with the LORD our God, or partiality or taking bribes."

⁸ Moreover, in Jerusalem Jehoshaphat appointed certain Levites and priests and heads of families of Israel, to give judgment for the LORD and to decide disputed cases. They had their seat at Jerusalem. ⁹ And he charged them: "Thus you shall do in the fear of the LORD, in faithfulness, and with your whole heart: ¹⁰ whenever a case comes to you from your brothers who live in their cities, concerning bloodshed, law or commandment, statutes or rules, then you shall warn them, that they may not incur guilt before the LORD and wrath may not come upon you and your brothers. Thus you shall do, and you will not incur guilt. ¹¹ And behold, Amariah the chief priest is over you in all matters of the LORD; and Zebadiah the son of Ishmael, the governor of the house of Judah, in all the king's matters, and the Levites will serve you as officers. Deal courageously, and may the LORD be with the upright!"[1]

Jehoshaphat's Prayer

20 After this the Moabites and Ammonites, and with them some of the Meunites,[2] came against Jehoshaphat for battle. ² Some men came and told Jehoshaphat, "A great multitude is coming against you from Edom,[3] from beyond the sea; and, behold, they are in Hazazon-tamar" (that is, Engedi). ³ Then Jehoshaphat was afraid and set his face to seek the LORD, and proclaimed a fast throughout all Judah. ⁴ And Judah assembled to seek help from the LORD; from all the cities of Judah they came to seek the LORD.

⁵ And Jehoshaphat stood in the assembly of Judah and Jerusalem, in the house of the LORD, before the new court, ⁶ and said, "O LORD, God of our fathers, are you not God in heaven? You rule over all the kingdoms of the nations. In your hand are power and might, so that none is able to withstand you. ⁷ Did you not, our God, drive out the inhabitants of this land before your people Israel, and give it forever to the descendants of Abraham your friend? ⁸ And they have lived in it and have built for you in it a sanctuary for your name, saying, ⁹ 'If disaster comes upon us, the sword, judgment,[4] or pestilence, or famine, we will stand before this house and before you—for your name is in this house—and cry out to you in our affliction, and you will hear and save.' ¹⁰ And now behold, the men of Ammon and Moab and Mount Seir, whom you would not let Israel invade when they came from the land of Egypt, and whom they avoided and did not destroy— ¹¹ behold, they reward us by coming to drive us out of your possession, which you have given us to inherit. ¹² O our God, will you not execute judgment on them? For we are powerless against this great horde that is coming against us. We do not know what to do, but our eyes are on you."

¹³ Meanwhile all Judah stood before the LORD, with their little ones, their wives, and their children. ¹⁴ And the Spirit of the LORD came[5] upon Jahaziel the son of Zechariah, son of Benaiah, son of Jeiel, son of Mattaniah, a Levite of the sons of Asaph, in the midst of the assembly. ¹⁵ And he said, "Listen, all Judah and inhabitants of Jerusalem and King Jehoshaphat: Thus says the LORD to you, 'Do not be afraid and do not be dismayed at this great horde, for the battle is not yours but God's. ¹⁶ Tomorrow go down against them. Behold, they will come up by the ascent of Ziz. You will find them at the end of the valley, east of the wilderness of Jeruel. ¹⁷ You will not need to fight in this battle. Stand firm, hold your position, and see the salvation of the LORD on your behalf, O Judah and Jerusalem.' Do not be afraid and do not be dismayed. Tomorrow go out against them, and the LORD will be with you."

¹⁸ Then Jehoshaphat bowed his head with his face to the ground, and all Judah and the inhabitants of Jerusalem fell down before the LORD, worshiping the LORD. ¹⁹ And the Levites, of the Kohathites and the Korahites, stood up to praise the LORD, the God of Israel, with a very loud voice.

²⁰ And they rose early in the morning and went out into the wilderness of Tekoa. And when they went out, Jehoshaphat stood and said, "Hear me, Judah and inhabitants of Jerusalem!

---

[1] Hebrew *the good* [2] Compare 26:7; Hebrew *Ammonites* [3] One Hebrew manuscript; most Hebrew manuscripts *Aram* (Syria) [4] Or *the sword of judgment* [5] Or *was*

Believe in the LORD your God, and you will be established; believe his prophets, and you will succeed." [21] And when he had taken counsel with the people, he appointed those who were to sing to the LORD and praise him in holy attire, as they went before the army, and say,

"Give thanks to the LORD,
    for his steadfast love endures forever."

[22] And when they began to sing and praise, the LORD set an ambush against the men of Ammon, Moab, and Mount Seir, who had come against Judah, so that they were routed. [23] For the men of Ammon and Moab rose against the inhabitants of Mount Seir, devoting them to destruction, and when they had made an end of the inhabitants of Seir, they all helped to destroy one another.

The LORD Delivers Judah

[24] When Judah came to the watchtower of the wilderness, they looked toward the horde, and behold, there[1] were dead bodies lying on the ground; none had escaped. [25] When Jehoshaphat and his people came to take their spoil, they found among them, in great numbers, goods, clothing, and precious things, which they took for themselves until they could carry no more. They were three days in taking the spoil, it was so much. [26] On the fourth day they assembled in the Valley of Beracah,[2] for there they blessed the LORD. Therefore the name of that place has been called the Valley of Beracah to this day. [27] Then they returned, every man of Judah and Jerusalem, and Jehoshaphat at their head, returning to Jerusalem with joy, for the LORD had made them rejoice over their enemies. [28] They came to Jerusalem with harps and lyres and trumpets, to the house of the LORD. [29] And the fear of God came on all the kingdoms of the countries when they heard that the LORD had fought against the enemies of Israel. [30] So the realm of Jehoshaphat was quiet, for his God gave him rest all around.

[31] Thus Jehoshaphat reigned over Judah. He was thirty-five years old when he began to reign, and he reigned twenty-five years in Jerusalem. His mother's name was Azubah the daughter of Shilhi. [32] He walked in the way of Asa his father and did not turn aside from it, doing what was right in the sight of the LORD. [33] The high places, however, were not taken away; the people had not yet set their hearts upon the God of their fathers.

[34] Now the rest of the acts of Jehoshaphat, from first to last, are written in the chronicles of Jehu the son of Hanani, which are recorded in the Book of the Kings of Israel.

The End of Jehoshaphat's Reign

[35] After this Jehoshaphat king of Judah joined with Ahaziah king of Israel, who acted wickedly. [36] He joined him in building ships to go to Tarshish, and they built the ships in Eziongeber. [37] Then Eliezer the son of Dodavahu of Mareshah prophesied against Jehoshaphat, saying, "Because you have joined with Ahaziah, the LORD will destroy what you have made." And the ships were wrecked and were not able to go to Tarshish.

Jehoram Reigns in Judah

21 Jehoshaphat slept with his fathers and was buried with his fathers in the city of David, and Jehoram his son reigned in his place. [2] He had brothers, the sons of Jehoshaphat: Azariah, Jehiel, Zechariah, Azariah, Michael, and Shephatiah; all these were the sons of Jehoshaphat king of Israel.[3] [3] Their father gave them great gifts of silver, gold, and valuable possessions, together with fortified cities in Judah, but he gave the kingdom to Jehoram, because he was the firstborn. [4] When Jehoram had ascended the throne of his father and was established, he killed all his brothers with the sword, and also some of the princes of Israel. [5] Jehoram was thirty-two years old when he became king, and he reigned eight years in Jerusalem. [6] And he walked in the way of the kings of Israel, as the house of Ahab had done, for the daughter of Ahab was his wife. And he did what was evil in the sight of the LORD. [7] Yet the LORD was not willing to destroy the house of David, because of the covenant that he had made with David, and since he had promised to give a lamp to him and to his sons forever.

[8] In his days Edom revolted from the rule of Judah and set up a king of their own. [9] Then Jehoram passed over with his commanders and all his chariots, and he rose by night and struck the Edomites who had surrounded him and his chariot commanders. [10] So Edom revolted from the rule of Judah to this day. At that time Libnah also revolted from his rule, because he had forsaken the LORD, the God of his fathers. [11] Moreover, he made high places in the hill

---

[1] Hebrew they [2] Beracah means blessing [3] That is, Judah

country of Judah and led the inhabitants of Jerusalem into whoredom and made Judah go astray. [12] And a letter came to him from Elijah the prophet, saying, "Thus says the LORD, the God of David your father, 'Because you have not walked in the ways of Jehoshaphat your father, or in the ways of Asa king of Judah, [13] but have walked in the way of the kings of Israel and have enticed Judah and the inhabitants of Jerusalem into whoredom, as the house of Ahab led Israel into whoredom, and also you have killed your brothers, of your father's house, who were better than you, [14] behold, the LORD will bring a great plague on your people, your children, your wives, and all your possessions, [15] and you yourself will have a severe sickness with a disease of your bowels, until your bowels come out because of the disease, day by day.'"

[16] And the LORD stirred up against Jehoram the anger[1] of the Philistines and of the Arabians who are near the Ethiopians. [17] And they came up against Judah and invaded it and carried away all the possessions they found that belonged to the king's house, and also his sons and his wives, so that no son was left to him except Jehoahaz, his youngest son.

[18] And after all this the LORD struck him in his bowels with an incurable disease. [19] In the course of time, at the end of two years, his bowels came out because of the disease, and he died in great agony. His people made no fire in his honor, like the fires made for his fathers. [20] He was thirty-two years old when he began to reign, and he reigned eight years in Jerusalem. And he departed with no one's regret. They buried him in the city of David, but not in the tombs of the kings.

Ahaziah Reigns in Judah

22 And the inhabitants of Jerusalem made Ahaziah, his youngest son, king in his place, for the band of men that came with the Arabians to the camp had killed all the older sons. So Ahaziah the son of Jehoram king of Judah reigned. [2] Ahaziah was twenty-two[2] years old when he began to reign, and he reigned one year in Jerusalem. His mother's name was Athaliah, the granddaughter of Omri. [3] He also walked in the ways of the house of Ahab, for his mother was his counselor in doing wickedly. [4] He did what was evil in the sight of the LORD, as the house of Ahab had done. For after the death of his father they were his counselors, to

his undoing. [5] He even followed their counsel and went with Jehoram the son of Ahab king of Israel to make war against Hazael king of Syria at Ramoth-gilead. And the Syrians wounded Joram, [6] and he returned to be healed in Jezreel of the wounds that he had received at Ramah, when he fought against Hazael king of Syria. And Ahaziah the son of Jehoram king of Judah went down to see Joram the son of Ahab in Jezreel, because he was wounded.

[7] But it was ordained by[3] God that the downfall of Ahaziah should come about through his going to visit Joram. For when he came there, he went out with Jehoram to meet Jehu the son of Nimshi, whom the LORD had anointed to destroy the house of Ahab. [8] And when Jehu was executing judgment on the house of Ahab, he met the princes of Judah and the sons of Ahaziah's brothers, who attended Ahaziah, and he killed them. [9] He searched for Ahaziah, and he was captured while hiding in Samaria, and he was brought to Jehu and put to death. They buried him, for they said, "He is the grandson of Jehoshaphat, who sought the LORD with all his heart." And the house of Ahaziah had no one able to rule the kingdom.

Athaliah Reigns in Judah

[10] Now when Athaliah the mother of Ahaziah saw that her son was dead, she arose and destroyed all the royal family of the house of Judah. [11] But Jehoshabeath,[4] the daughter of the king, took Joash the son of Ahaziah and stole him away from among the king's sons who were about to be put to death, and she put him and his nurse in a bedroom. Thus Jehoshabeath, the daughter of King Jehoram and wife of Jehoiada the priest, because she was a sister of Ahaziah, hid him[5] from Athaliah, so that she did not put him to death. [12] And he remained with them six years, hidden in the house of God, while Athaliah reigned over the land.

Joash Made King

23 But in the seventh year Jehoiada took courage and entered into a covenant with the commanders of hundreds, Azariah the son of Jeroham, Ishmael the son of Jehohanan, Azariah the son of Obed, Maaseiah the son of Adaiah, and Elishaphat the son of Zichri. [2] And they went about through Judah and gathered the Levites from all the cities of Judah, and the heads of fathers' houses of Israel, and they came to Jerusalem. [3] And all the assembly made a cov-

---

[1] Hebrew *spirit* [2] See 2 Kings 8:26; Hebrew *forty-two*; Septuagint *twenty* [3] Hebrew *was from* [4] Spelled *Jehosheba* in 2 Kings 11:2 [5] That is, Joash

enant with the king in the house of God. And Jehoiada[1] said to them, "Behold, the king's son! Let him reign, as the Lord spoke concerning the sons of David. [4] This is the thing that you shall do: of you priests and Levites who come off duty on the Sabbath, one third shall be gatekeepers, [5] and one third shall be at the king's house and one third at the Gate of the Foundation. And all the people shall be in the courts of the house of the Lord. [6] Let no one enter the house of the Lord except the priests and ministering Levites. They may enter, for they are holy, but all the people shall keep the charge of the Lord. [7] The Levites shall surround the king, each with his weapons in his hand. And whoever enters the house shall be put to death. Be with the king when he comes in and when he goes out."

[8] The Levites and all Judah did according to all that Jehoiada the priest commanded, and they each brought his men, who were to go off duty on the Sabbath, with those who were to come on duty on the Sabbath, for Jehoiada the priest did not dismiss the divisions. [9] And Jehoiada the priest gave to the captains the spears and the large and small shields that had been King David's, which were in the house of God. [10] And he set all the people as a guard for the king, every man with his weapon in his hand, from the south side of the house to the north side of the house, around the altar and the house. [11] Then they brought out the king's son and put the crown on him and gave him the testimony. And they proclaimed him king, and Jehoiada and his sons anointed him, and they said, "Long live the king."

Athaliah Executed

[12] When Athaliah heard the noise of the people running and praising the king, she went into the house of the Lord to the people. [13] And when she looked, there was the king standing by his pillar at the entrance, and the captains and the trumpeters beside the king, and all the people of the land rejoicing and blowing trumpets, and the singers with their musical instruments leading in the celebration. And Athaliah tore her clothes and cried, "Treason! Treason!" [14] Then Jehoiada the priest brought out the captains who were set over the army, saying to them, "Bring her out between the ranks, and anyone who follows her is to be put to death with the sword." For the priest said,

"Do not put her to death in the house of the Lord." [15] So they laid hands on her,[2] and she went into the entrance of the horse gate of the king's house, and they put her to death there.

Jehoiada's Reforms

[16] And Jehoiada made a covenant between himself and all the people and the king that they should be the Lord's people. [17] Then all the people went to the house of Baal and tore it down; his altars and his images they broke in pieces, and they killed Mattan the priest of Baal before the altars. [18] And Jehoiada posted watchmen for the house of the Lord under the direction of the Levitical priests and the Levites whom David had organized to be in charge of the house of the Lord, to offer burnt offerings to the Lord, as it is written in the Law of Moses, with rejoicing and with singing, according to the order of David. [19] He stationed the gatekeepers at the gates of the house of the Lord so that no one should enter who was in any way unclean. [20] And he took the captains, the nobles, the governors of the people, and all the people of the land, and they brought the king down from the house of the Lord, marching through the upper gate to the king's house. And they set the king on the royal throne. [21] So all the people of the land rejoiced, and the city was quiet after Athaliah had been put to death with the sword.

Joash Repairs the Temple

24 Joash[3] was seven years old when he began to reign, and he reigned forty years in Jerusalem. His mother's name was Zibiah of Beersheba. [2] And Joash did what was right in the eyes of the Lord all the days of Jehoiada the priest. [3] Jehoiada got for him two wives, and he had sons and daughters.

[4] After this Joash decided to restore the house of the Lord. [5] And he gathered the priests and the Levites and said to them, "Go out to the cities of Judah and gather from all Israel money to repair the house of your God from year to year, and see that you act quickly." But the Levites did not act quickly. [6] So the king summoned Jehoiada the chief and said to him, "Why have you not required the Levites to bring in from Judah and Jerusalem the tax levied by Moses, the servant of the Lord, and the congregation of Israel for the tent of testimony?" [7] For the sons of Athaliah, that wicked woman, had broken into the house of God, and had also used all

[1] Hebrew he   [2] Or they made a passage for her   [3] Spelled Jehoash in 2 Kings 12:1

the dedicated things of the house of the LORD for the Baals.

⁸ So the king commanded, and they made a chest and set it outside the gate of the house of the LORD. ⁹ And proclamation was made throughout Judah and Jerusalem to bring in for the LORD the tax that Moses the servant of God laid on Israel in the wilderness. ¹⁰ And all the princes and all the people rejoiced and brought their tax and dropped it into the chest until they had finished.¹ ¹¹ And whenever the chest was brought to the king's officers by the Levites, when they saw that there was much money in it, the king's secretary and the officer of the chief priest would come and empty the chest and take it and return it to its place. Thus they did day after day, and collected money in abundance. ¹² And the king and Jehoiada gave it to those who had charge of the work of the house of the LORD, and they hired masons and carpenters to restore the house of the LORD, and also workers in iron and bronze to repair the house of the LORD. ¹³ So those who were engaged in the work labored, and the repairing went forward in their hands, and they restored the house of God to its proper condition and strengthened it. ¹⁴ And when they had finished, they brought the rest of the money before the king and Jehoiada, and with it were made utensils for the house of the LORD, both for the service and for the burnt offerings, and dishes for incense and vessels of gold and silver. And they offered burnt offerings in the house of the LORD regularly all the days of Jehoiada.

¹⁵ But Jehoiada grew old and full of days, and died. He was 130 years old at his death. ¹⁶ And they buried him in the city of David among the kings, because he had done good in Israel, and toward God and his house.

¹⁷ Now after the death of Jehoiada the princes of Judah came and paid homage to the king. Then the king listened to them. ¹⁸ And they abandoned the house of the LORD, the God of their fathers, and served the Asherim and the idols. And wrath came upon Judah and Jerusalem for this guilt of theirs. ¹⁹ Yet he sent prophets among them to bring them back to the LORD. These testified against them, but they would not pay attention.

Joash's Treachery

²⁰ Then the Spirit of God clothed Zechariah the son of Jehoiada the priest, and he stood above the people, and said to them, "Thus says God, 'Why do you break the commandments of the LORD, so that you cannot prosper? Because you have forsaken the LORD, he has forsaken you.'" ²¹ But they conspired against him, and by command of the king they stoned him with stones in the court of the house of the LORD. ²² Thus Joash the king did not remember the kindness that Jehoiada, Zechariah's father, had shown him, but killed his son. And when he was dying, he said, "May the LORD see and avenge!"²

Joash Assassinated

²³ At the end of the year the army of the Syrians came up against Joash. They came to Judah and Jerusalem and destroyed all the princes of the people from among the people and sent all their spoil to the king of Damascus. ²⁴ Though the army of the Syrians had come with few men, the LORD delivered into their hand a very great army, because Judah³ had forsaken the LORD, the God of their fathers. Thus they executed judgment on Joash.

²⁵ When they had departed from him, leaving him severely wounded, his servants conspired against him because of the blood of the son⁴ of Jehoiada the priest, and killed him on his bed. So he died, and they buried him in the city of David, but they did not bury him in the tombs of the kings. ²⁶ Those who conspired against him were Zabad the son of Shimeath the Ammonite, and Jehozabad the son of Shimrith the Moabite. ²⁷ Accounts of his sons and of the many oracles against him and of the rebuilding⁵ of the house of God are written in the Story⁶ of the Book of the Kings. And Amaziah his son reigned in his place.

Amaziah Reigns in Judah

25 Amaziah was twenty-five years old when he began to reign, and he reigned twenty-nine years in Jerusalem. His mother's name was Jehoaddan of Jerusalem. ² And he did what was right in the eyes of the LORD, yet not with a whole heart. ³ And as soon as the royal power was firmly his, he killed his servants who had struck down the king his father. ⁴ But he did not put their children to death, according to what is written in the Law, in the Book of Moses, where the LORD commanded, "Fathers shall not die because of their children, nor children die because of their fathers, but each one shall die for his own sin."

¹ Or until it was full ² Or and require it ³ Hebrew they ⁴ Septuagint, Vulgate; Hebrew sons ⁵ Hebrew founding ⁶ Or Exposition

Amaziah's Victories

[5] Then Amaziah assembled the men of Judah and set them by fathers' houses under commanders of thousands and of hundreds for all Judah and Benjamin. He mustered those twenty years old and upward, and found that they were 300,000 choice men, fit for war, able to handle spear and shield. [6] He hired also 100,000 mighty men of valor from Israel for 100 talents[1] of silver. [7] But a man of God came to him and said, "O king, do not let the army of Israel go with you, for the LORD is not with Israel, with all these Ephraimites. [8] But go, act, be strong for the battle. Why should you suppose that God will cast you down before the enemy? For God has power to help or to cast down." [9] And Amaziah said to the man of God, "But what shall we do about the hundred talents that I have given to the army of Israel?" The man of God answered, "The LORD is able to give you much more than this." [10] Then Amaziah discharged the army that had come to him from Ephraim to go home again. And they became very angry with Judah and returned home in fierce anger. [11] But Amaziah took courage and led out his people and went to the Valley of Salt and struck down 10,000 men of Seir. [12] The men of Judah captured another 10,000 alive and took them to the top of a rock and threw them down from the top of the rock, and they were all dashed to pieces. [13] But the men of the army whom Amaziah sent back, not letting them go with him to battle, raided the cities of Judah, from Samaria to Beth-horon, and struck down 3,000 people in them and took much spoil.

Amaziah's Idolatry

[14] After Amaziah came from striking down the Edomites, he brought the gods of the men of Seir and set them up as his gods and worshiped them, making offerings to them. [15] Therefore the LORD was angry with Amaziah and sent to him a prophet, who said to him, "Why have you sought the gods of a people who did not deliver their own people from your hand?" [16] But as he was speaking, the king said to him, "Have we made you a royal counselor? Stop! Why should you be struck down?" So the prophet stopped, but said, "I know that God has determined to destroy you, because you have done this and have not listened to my counsel."

Israel Defeats Amaziah

[17] Then Amaziah king of Judah took counsel and sent to Joash the son of Jehoahaz, son of Jehu, king of Israel, saying, "Come, let us look one another in the face." [18] And Joash the king of Israel sent word to Amaziah king of Judah, "A thistle on Lebanon sent to a cedar on Lebanon, saying, 'Give your daughter to my son for a wife,' and a wild beast of Lebanon passed by and trampled down the thistle. [19] You say, 'See, I[2] have struck down Edom,' and your heart has lifted you up in boastfulness. But now stay at home. Why should you provoke trouble so that you fall, you and Judah with you?"

[20] But Amaziah would not listen, for it was of God, in order that he might give them into the hand of their enemies, because they had sought the gods of Edom. [21] So Joash king of Israel went up, and he and Amaziah king of Judah faced one another in battle at Beth-shemesh, which belongs to Judah. [22] And Judah was defeated by Israel, and every man fled to his home. [23] And Joash king of Israel captured Amaziah king of Judah, the son of Joash, son of Ahaziah, at Beth-shemesh, and brought him to Jerusalem and broke down the wall of Jerusalem for 400 cubits,[3] from the Ephraim Gate to the Corner Gate. [24] And he seized all the gold and silver, and all the vessels that were found in the house of God, in the care of Obed-edom. He seized also the treasuries of the king's house, also hostages, and he returned to Samaria.

[25] Amaziah the son of Joash, king of Judah, lived fifteen years after the death of Joash the son of Jehoahaz, king of Israel. [26] Now the rest of the deeds of Amaziah, from first to last, are they not written in the Book of the Kings of Judah and Israel? [27] From the time when he turned away from the LORD they made a conspiracy against him in Jerusalem, and he fled to Lachish. But they sent after him to Lachish and put him to death there. [28] And they brought him upon horses, and he was buried with his fathers in the city of David.[4]

Uzziah Reigns in Judah

26 And all the people of Judah took Uzziah, who was sixteen years old, and made him king instead of his father Amaziah. [2] He built Eloth and restored it to Judah, after the king slept with his fathers. [3] Uzziah was sixteen years old when he began to reign, and he reigned fifty-two years in Jerusalem. His

---

[1] A *talent* was about 75 pounds or 34 kilograms [2] Hebrew *you* [3] A *cubit* was about 18 inches or 45 centimeters [4] Hebrew *of Judah*

mother's name was Jecoliah of Jerusalem. [4] And he did what was right in the eyes of the LORD, according to all that his father Amaziah had done. [5] He set himself to seek God in the days of Zechariah, who instructed him in the fear of God, and as long as he sought the LORD, God made him prosper.

[6] He went out and made war against the Philistines and broke through the wall of Gath and the wall of Jabneh and the wall of Ashdod, and he built cities in the territory of Ashdod and elsewhere among the Philistines. [7] God helped him against the Philistines and against the Arabians who lived in Gurbaal and against the Meunites. [8] The Ammonites paid tribute to Uzziah, and his fame spread even to the border of Egypt, for he became very strong. [9] Moreover, Uzziah built towers in Jerusalem at the Corner Gate and at the Valley Gate and at the Angle, and fortified them. [10] And he built towers in the wilderness and cut out many cisterns, for he had large herds, both in the Shephelah and in the plain, and he had farmers and vinedressers in the hills and in the fertile lands, for he loved the soil. [11] Moreover, Uzziah had an army of soldiers, fit for war, in divisions according to the numbers in the muster made by Jeiel the secretary and Maaseiah the officer, under the direction of Hananiah, one of the king's commanders. [12] The whole number of the heads of fathers' houses of mighty men of valor was 2,600. [13] Under their command was an army of 307,500, who could make war with mighty power, to help the king against the enemy. [14] And Uzziah prepared for all the army shields, spears, helmets, coats of mail, bows, and stones for slinging. [15] In Jerusalem he made machines, invented by skillful men, to be on the towers and the corners, to shoot arrows and great stones. And his fame spread far, for he was marvelously helped, till he was strong.

Uzziah's Pride and Punishment

[16] But when he was strong, he grew proud, to his destruction. For he was unfaithful to the LORD his God and entered the temple of the LORD to burn incense on the altar of incense. [17] But Azariah the priest went in after him, with eighty priests of the LORD who were men of valor, [18] and they withstood King Uzziah and said to him, "It is not for you, Uzziah, to burn incense to the LORD, but for the priests,

the sons of Aaron, who are consecrated to burn incense. Go out of the sanctuary, for you have done wrong, and it will bring you no honor from the LORD God." [19] Then Uzziah was angry. Now he had a censer in his hand to burn incense, and when he became angry with the priests, leprosy[1] broke out on his forehead in the presence of the priests in the house of the LORD, by the altar of incense. [20] And Azariah the chief priest and all the priests looked at him, and behold, he was leprous in his forehead! And they rushed him out quickly, and he himself hurried to go out, because the LORD had struck him. [21] And King Uzziah was a leper to the day of his death, and being a leper lived in a separate house, for he was excluded from the house of the LORD. And Jotham his son was over the king's household, governing the people of the land.

[22] Now the rest of the acts of Uzziah, from first to last, Isaiah the prophet the son of Amoz wrote. [23] And Uzziah slept with his fathers, and they buried him with his fathers in the burial field that belonged to the kings, for they said, "He is a leper." And Jotham his son reigned in his place.

Jotham Reigns in Judah

27 Jotham was twenty-five years old when he began to reign, and he reigned sixteen years in Jerusalem. His mother's name was Jerushah the daughter of Zadok. [2] And he did what was right in the eyes of the LORD according to all that his father Uzziah had done, except he did not enter the temple of the LORD. But the people still followed corrupt practices. [3] He built the upper gate of the house of the LORD and did much building on the wall of Ophel. [4] Moreover, he built cities in the hill country of Judah, and forts and towers on the wooded hills. [5] He fought with the king of the Ammonites and prevailed against them. And the Ammonites gave him that year 100 talents[2] of silver, and 10,000 cors[3] of wheat and 10,000 of barley. The Ammonites paid him the same amount in the second and the third years. [6] So Jotham became mighty, because he ordered his ways before the LORD his God. [7] Now the rest of the acts of Jotham, and all his wars and his ways, behold, they are written in the Book of the Kings of Israel and Judah. [8] He was twenty-five years old when he began to reign,

---

[1] Leprosy was a term for several skin diseases; see Leviticus 13 [2] A talent was about 75 pounds or 34 kilograms [3] A cor was about 6 bushels or 220 liters

and he reigned sixteen years in Jerusalem. [9] And Jotham slept with his fathers, and they buried him in the city of David, and Ahaz his son reigned in his place.

Ahaz Reigns in Judah

28 Ahaz was twenty years old when he began to reign, and he reigned sixteen years in Jerusalem. And he did not do what was right in the eyes of the LORD, as his father David had done, [2] but he walked in the ways of the kings of Israel. He even made metal images for the Baals, [3] and he made offerings in the Valley of the Son of Hinnom and burned his sons as an offering, [1] according to the abominations of the nations whom the LORD drove out before the people of Israel. [4] And he sacrificed and made offerings on the high places and on the hills and under every green tree.

Judah Defeated

[5] Therefore the LORD his God gave him into the hand of the king of Syria, who defeated him and took captive a great number of his people and brought them to Damascus. He was also given into the hand of the king of Israel, who struck him with great force. [6] For Pekah the son of Remaliah killed 120,000 from Judah in one day, all of them men of valor, because they had forsaken the LORD, the God of their fathers. [7] And Zichri, a mighty man of Ephraim, killed Maaseiah the king's son and Azrikam the commander of the palace and Elkanah the next in authority to the king.

[8] The men of Israel took captive 200,000 of their relatives, women, sons, and daughters. They also took much spoil from them and brought the spoil to Samaria. [9] But a prophet of the LORD was there, whose name was Oded, and he went out to meet the army that came to Samaria and said to them, "Behold, because the LORD, the God of your fathers, was angry with Judah, he gave them into your hand, but you have killed them in a rage that has reached up to heaven. [10] And now you intend to subjugate the people of Judah and Jerusalem, male and female, as your slaves. Have you not sins of your own against the LORD your God? [11] Now hear me, and send back the captives from your relatives whom you have taken, for the fierce wrath of the LORD is upon you."

[12] Certain chiefs also of the men of Ephraim, Azariah the son of Johanan, Berechiah the son of Meshillemoth, Jehizkiah the son of Shallum, and Amasa the son of Hadlai, stood up against those who were coming from the war [13] and said to them, "You shall not bring the captives in here, for you propose to bring upon us guilt against the LORD in addition to our present sins and guilt. For our guilt is already great, and there is fierce wrath against Israel." [14] So the armed men left the captives and the spoil before the princes and all the assembly. [15] And the men who have been mentioned by name rose and took the captives, and with the spoil they clothed all who were naked among them. They clothed them, gave them sandals, provided them with food and drink, and anointed them, and carrying all the feeble among them on donkeys, they brought them to their kinsfolk at Jericho, the city of palm trees. Then they returned to Samaria.

[16] At that time King Ahaz sent to the king[2] of Assyria for help. [17] For the Edomites had again invaded and defeated Judah and carried away captives. [18] And the Philistines had made raids on the cities in the Shephelah and the Negeb of Judah, and had taken Beth-shemesh, Aijalon, Gederoth, Soco with its villages, Timnah with its villages, and Gimzo with its villages. And they settled there. [19] For the LORD humbled Judah because of Ahaz king of Israel, for he had made Judah act sinfully[3] and had been very unfaithful to the LORD. [20] So Tiglath-pileser[4] king of Assyria came against him and afflicted him instead of strengthening him. [21] For Ahaz took a portion from the house of the LORD and the house of the king and of the princes, and gave tribute to the king of Assyria, but it did not help him.

Ahaz's Idolatry

[22] In the time of his distress he became yet more faithless to the LORD—this same King Ahaz. [23] For he sacrificed to the gods of Damascus that had defeated him and said, "Because the gods of the kings of Syria helped them, I will sacrifice to them that they may help me." But they were the ruin of him and of all Israel. [24] And Ahaz gathered together the vessels of the house of God and cut in pieces the vessels of the house of God, and he shut up the doors of the house of the LORD, and he made himself altars in every corner of Jerusalem. [25] In every city of Judah he made high places to make offerings to other gods, provoking to anger the LORD, the God of his fathers. [26] Now

---

[1] Hebrew *made his sons pass through the fire* [2] Septuagint, Syriac, Vulgate (compare 2 Kings 16:7); Hebrew *kings* [3] Or *wildly* [4] Hebrew *Tilgath-pilneser*

the rest of his acts and all his ways, from first to last, behold, they are written in the Book of the Kings of Judah and Israel. [27] And Ahaz slept with his fathers, and they buried him in the city, in Jerusalem, for they did not bring him into the tombs of the kings of Israel. And Hezekiah his son reigned in his place.

Hezekiah Reigns in Judah

29 Hezekiah began to reign when he was twenty-five years old, and he reigned twenty-nine years in Jerusalem. His mother's name was Abijah[1] the daughter of Zechariah. [2] And he did what was right in the eyes of the LORD, according to all that David his father had done.

Hezekiah Cleanses the Temple

[3] In the first year of his reign, in the first month, he opened the doors of the house of the LORD and repaired them. [4] He brought in the priests and the Levites and assembled them in the square on the east [5] and said to them, "Hear me, Levites! Now consecrate yourselves, and consecrate the house of the LORD, the God of your fathers, and carry out the filth[2] from the Holy Place. [6] For our fathers have been unfaithful and have done what was evil in the sight of the LORD our God. They have forsaken him and have turned away their faces from the habitation of the LORD and turned their backs. [7] They also shut the doors of the vestibule and put out the lamps and have not burned incense or offered burnt offerings in the Holy Place to the God of Israel. [8] Therefore the wrath of the LORD came on Judah and Jerusalem, and he has made them an object of horror, of astonishment, and of hissing, as you see with your own eyes. [9] For behold, our fathers have fallen by the sword, and our sons and our daughters and our wives are in captivity for this. [10] Now it is in my heart to make a covenant with the LORD, the God of Israel, in order that his fierce anger may turn away from us. [11] My sons, do not now be negligent, for the LORD has chosen you to stand in his presence, to minister to him and to be his ministers and make offerings to him."

[12] Then the Levites arose, Mahath the son of Amasai, and Joel the son of Azariah, of the sons of the Kohathites; and of the sons of Merari, Kish the son of Abdi, and Azariah the son of Jehallelel; and of the Gershonites, Joah the son of Zimmah, and Eden the son of Joah; [13] and of the sons of Elizaphan, Shimri and Jeuel; and of

the sons of Asaph, Zechariah and Mattaniah; [14] and of the sons of Heman, Jehuel and Shimei; and of the sons of Jeduthun, Shemaiah and Uzziel. [15] They gathered their brothers and consecrated themselves and went in as the king had commanded, by the words of the LORD, to cleanse the house of the LORD. [16] The priests went into the inner part of the house of the LORD to cleanse it, and they brought out all the uncleanness that they found in the temple of the LORD into the court of the house of the LORD. And the Levites took it and carried it out to the brook Kidron. [17] They began to consecrate on the first day of the first month, and on the eighth day of the month they came to the vestibule of the LORD. Then for eight days they consecrated the house of the LORD, and on the sixteenth day of the first month they finished. [18] Then they went in to Hezekiah the king and said, "We have cleansed all the house of the LORD, the altar of burnt offering and all its utensils, and the table for the showbread and all its utensils. [19] All the utensils that King Ahaz discarded in his reign when he was faithless, we have made ready and consecrated, and behold, they are before the altar of the LORD."

Hezekiah Restores Temple Worship

[20] Then Hezekiah the king rose early and gathered the officials of the city and went up to the house of the LORD. [21] And they brought seven bulls, seven rams, seven lambs, and seven male goats for a sin offering for the kingdom and for the sanctuary and for Judah. And he commanded the priests, the sons of Aaron, to offer them on the altar of the LORD. [22] So they slaughtered the bulls, and the priests received the blood and threw it against the altar. And they slaughtered the rams, and their blood was thrown against the altar. And they slaughtered the lambs, and their blood was thrown against the altar. [23] Then the goats for the sin offering were brought to the king and the assembly, and they laid their hands on them, [24] and the priests slaughtered them and made a sin offering with their blood on the altar, to make atonement for all Israel. For the king commanded that the burnt offering and the sin offering should be made for all Israel.

[25] And he stationed the Levites in the house of the LORD with cymbals, harps, and lyres, according to the commandment of David and of Gad the king's seer and of Nathan the

---

[1] Spelled *Abi* in 2 Kings 18:2 [2] Hebrew *impurity*

prophet, for the commandment was from the Lord through his prophets. ²⁶ The Levites stood with the instruments of David, and the priests with the trumpets. ²⁷ Then Hezekiah commanded that the burnt offering be offered on the altar. And when the burnt offering began, the song to the Lord began also, and the trumpets, accompanied by the instruments of David king of Israel. ²⁸ The whole assembly worshiped, and the singers sang, and the trumpeters sounded. All this continued until the burnt offering was finished. ²⁹ When the offering was finished, the king and all who were present with him bowed themselves and worshiped. ³⁰ And Hezekiah the king and the officials commanded the Levites to sing praises to the Lord with the words of David and of Asaph the seer. And they sang praises with gladness, and they bowed down and worshiped.

³¹ Then Hezekiah said, "You have now consecrated yourselves to¹ the Lord. Come near; bring sacrifices and thank offerings to the house of the Lord." And the assembly brought sacrifices and thank offerings, and all who were of a willing heart brought burnt offerings. ³² The number of the burnt offerings that the assembly brought was 70 bulls, 100 rams, and 200 lambs; all these were for a burnt offering to the Lord. ³³ And the consecrated offerings were 600 bulls and 3,000 sheep. ³⁴ But the priests were too few and could not flay all the burnt offerings, so until other priests had consecrated themselves, their brothers the Levites helped them, until the work was finished—for the Levites were more upright in heart than the priests in consecrating themselves. ³⁵ Besides the great number of burnt offerings, there was the fat of the peace offerings, and there were the drink offerings for the burnt offerings. Thus the service of the house of the Lord was restored. ³⁶ And Hezekiah and all the people rejoiced because God had provided for the people, for the thing came about suddenly.

Passover Celebrated

30 Hezekiah sent to all Israel and Judah, and wrote letters also to Ephraim and Manasseh, that they should come to the house of the Lord at Jerusalem to keep the Passover to the Lord, the God of Israel. ² For the king and his princes and all the assembly in Jerusalem had taken counsel to keep the Passover in the second month— ³ for they could not keep it at that time because the priests had not consecrated themselves in sufficient number, nor had the people assembled in Jerusalem— ⁴ and the plan seemed right to the king and all the assembly. ⁵ So they decreed to make a proclamation throughout all Israel, from Beersheba to Dan, that the people should come and keep the Passover to the Lord, the God of Israel, at Jerusalem, for they had not kept it as often as prescribed. ⁶ So couriers went throughout all Israel and Judah with letters from the king and his princes, as the king had commanded, saying, "O people of Israel, return to the Lord, the God of Abraham, Isaac, and Israel, that he may turn again to the remnant of you who have escaped from the hand of the kings of Assyria. ⁷ Do not be like your fathers and your brothers, who were faithless to the Lord God of their fathers, so that he made them a desolation, as you see. ⁸ Do not now be stiff-necked as your fathers were, but yield yourselves to the Lord and come to his sanctuary, which he has consecrated forever, and serve the Lord your God, that his fierce anger may turn away from you. ⁹ For if you return to the Lord, your brothers and your children will find compassion with their captors and return to this land. For the Lord your God is gracious and merciful and will not turn away his face from you, if you return to him."

¹⁰ So the couriers went from city to city through the country of Ephraim and Manasseh, and as far as Zebulun, but they laughed them to scorn and mocked them. ¹¹ However, some men of Asher, of Manasseh, and of Zebulun humbled themselves and came to Jerusalem. ¹² The hand of God was also on Judah to give them one heart to do what the king and the princes commanded by the word of the Lord.

¹³ And many people came together in Jerusalem to keep the Feast of Unleavened Bread in the second month, a very great assembly. ¹⁴ They set to work and removed the altars that were in Jerusalem, and all the altars for burning incense they took away and threw into the brook Kidron. ¹⁵ And they slaughtered the Passover lamb on the fourteenth day of the second month. And the priests and the Levites were ashamed, so that they consecrated themselves and brought burnt offerings into the house of the Lord. ¹⁶ They took their accustomed posts according to the Law of Moses the man of God. The priests threw the blood that

¹ Hebrew filled your hand for

they received from the hand of the Levites. [17] For there were many in the assembly who had not consecrated themselves. Therefore the Levites had to slaughter the Passover lamb for everyone who was not clean, to consecrate it to the LORD. [18] For a majority of the people, many of them from Ephraim, Manasseh, Issachar, and Zebulun, had not cleansed themselves, yet they ate the Passover otherwise than as prescribed. For Hezekiah had prayed for them, saying, "May the good LORD pardon everyone [19] who sets his heart to seek God, the LORD, the God of his fathers, even though not according to the sanctuary's rules of cleanness."[1] [20] And the LORD heard Hezekiah and healed the people. [21] And the people of Israel who were present at Jerusalem kept the Feast of Unleavened Bread seven days with great gladness, and the Levites and the priests praised the LORD day by day, singing with all their might[2] to the LORD. [22] And Hezekiah spoke encouragingly to all the Levites who showed good skill in the service of the LORD. So they ate the food of the festival for seven days, sacrificing peace offerings and giving thanks to the LORD, the God of their fathers.

[23] Then the whole assembly agreed together to keep the feast for another seven days. So they kept it for another seven days with gladness. [24] For Hezekiah king of Judah gave the assembly 1,000 bulls and 7,000 sheep for offerings, and the princes gave the assembly 1,000 bulls and 10,000 sheep. And the priests consecrated themselves in great numbers. [25] The whole assembly of Judah, and the priests and the Levites, and the whole assembly that came out of Israel, and the sojourners who came out of the land of Israel, and the sojourners who lived in Judah, rejoiced. [26] So there was great joy in Jerusalem, for since the time of Solomon the son of David king of Israel there had been nothing like this in Jerusalem. [27] Then the priests and the Levites arose and blessed the people, and their voice was heard, and their prayer came to his holy habitation in heaven.

Hezekiah Organizes the Priests

31 Now when all this was finished, all Israel who were present went out to the cities of Judah and broke in pieces the pillars and cut down the Asherim and broke down the high places and the altars throughout all Judah and Benjamin, and in Ephraim and Manasseh, until they had destroyed them all. Then all the people of Israel returned to their cities, every man to his possession.

[2] And Hezekiah appointed the divisions of the priests and of the Levites, division by division, each according to his service, the priests and the Levites, for burnt offerings and peace offerings, to minister in the gates of the camp of the LORD and to give thanks and praise. [3] The contribution of the king from his own possessions was for the burnt offerings: the burnt offerings of morning and evening, and the burnt offerings for the Sabbaths, the new moons, and the appointed feasts, as it is written in the Law of the LORD. [4] And he commanded the people who lived in Jerusalem to give the portion due to the priests and the Levites, that they might give themselves to the Law of the LORD. [5] As soon as the command was spread abroad, the people of Israel gave in abundance the firstfruits of grain, wine, oil, honey, and of all the produce of the field. And they brought in abundantly the tithe of everything. [6] And the people of Israel and Judah who lived in the cities of Judah also brought in the tithe of cattle and sheep, and the tithe of the dedicated things that had been dedicated to the LORD their God, and laid them in heaps. [7] In the third month they began to pile up the heaps, and finished them in the seventh month. [8] When Hezekiah and the princes came and saw the heaps, they blessed the LORD and his people Israel. [9] And Hezekiah questioned the priests and the Levites about the heaps. [10] Azariah the chief priest, who was of the house of Zadok, answered him, "Since they began to bring the contributions into the house of the LORD, we have eaten and had enough and have plenty left, for the LORD has blessed his people, so that we have this large amount left."

[11] Then Hezekiah commanded them to prepare chambers in the house of the LORD, and they prepared them. [12] And they faithfully brought in the contributions, the tithes, and the dedicated things. The chief officer in charge of them was Conaniah the Levite, with Shimei his brother as second, [13] while Jehiel, Azaziah, Nahath, Asahel, Jerimoth, Jozabad, Eliel, Ismachiah, Mahath, and Benaiah were overseers assisting Conaniah and Shimei his brother, by the appointment of Hezekiah the king and Azariah the chief officer of the house of God. [14] And Kore the son of Imnah the Levite, keeper of the east gate, was over the freewill

---

[1] Hebrew *not according to the cleanness of holiness* [2] Compare 1 Chronicles 13:8; Hebrew *with instruments of might*

offerings to God, to apportion the contribution reserved for the LORD and the most holy offerings. [15]Eden, Miniamin, Jeshua, Shemaiah, Amariah, and Shecaniah were faithfully assisting him in the cities of the priests, to distribute the portions to their brothers, old and young alike, by divisions, [16]except those enrolled by genealogy, males from three years old and upward—all who entered the house of the LORD as the duty of each day required—for their service according to their offices, by their divisions. [17]The enrollment of the priests was according to their fathers' houses; that of the Levites from twenty years old and upward was according to their offices, by their divisions. [18]They were enrolled with all their little children, their wives, their sons, and their daughters, the whole assembly, for they were faithful in keeping themselves holy. [19]And for the sons of Aaron, the priests, who were in the fields of common land belonging to their cities, there were men in the several cities who were designated by name to distribute portions to every male among the priests and to everyone among the Levites who was enrolled.

[20]Thus Hezekiah did throughout all Judah, and he did what was good and right and faithful before the LORD his God. [21]And every work that he undertook in the service of the house of God and in accordance with the law and the commandments, seeking his God, he did with all his heart, and prospered.

Sennacherib Invades Judah

32 After these things and these acts of faithfulness, Sennacherib king of Assyria came and invaded Judah and encamped against the fortified cities, thinking to win them for himself. [2]And when Hezekiah saw that Sennacherib had come and intended to fight against Jerusalem, [3]he planned with his officers and his mighty men to stop the water of the springs that were outside the city; and they helped him. [4]A great many people were gathered, and they stopped all the springs and the brook that flowed through the land, saying, "Why should the kings of Assyria come and find much water?" [5]He set to work resolutely and built up all the wall that was broken down and raised towers upon it,[1] and outside it he built another wall, and he strengthened the Millo in the city of David. He also made weapons and shields in abundance. [6]And he

set combat commanders over the people and gathered them together to him in the square at the gate of the city and spoke encouragingly to them, saying, [7]"Be strong and courageous. Do not be afraid or dismayed before the king of Assyria and all the horde that is with him, for there are more with us than with him. [8]With him is an arm of flesh, but with us is the LORD our God, to help us and to fight our battles." And the people took confidence from the words of Hezekiah king of Judah.

Sennacherib Blasphemes

[9]After this, Sennacherib king of Assyria, who was besieging Lachish with all his forces, sent his servants to Jerusalem to Hezekiah king of Judah and to all the people of Judah who were in Jerusalem, saying, [10]"Thus says Sennacherib king of Assyria, 'On what are you trusting, that you endure the siege in Jerusalem? [11]Is not Hezekiah misleading you, that he may give you over to die by famine and by thirst, when he tells you, "The LORD our God will deliver us from the hand of the king of Assyria"? [12]Has not this same Hezekiah taken away his high places and his altars and commanded Judah and Jerusalem, "Before one altar you shall worship, and on it you shall burn your sacrifices"? [13]Do you not know what I and my fathers have done to all the peoples of other lands? Were the gods of the nations of those lands at all able to deliver their lands out of my hand? [14]Who among all the gods of those nations that my fathers devoted to destruction was able to deliver his people from my hand, that your God should be able to deliver you from my hand? [15]Now, therefore, do not let Hezekiah deceive you or mislead you in this fashion, and do not believe him, for no god of any nation or kingdom has been able to deliver his people from my hand or from the hand of my fathers. How much less will your God deliver you out of my hand!'"

[16]And his servants said still more against the LORD God and against his servant Hezekiah. [17]And he wrote letters to cast contempt on the LORD, the God of Israel, and to speak against him, saying, "Like the gods of the nations of the lands who have not delivered their people from my hands, so the God of Hezekiah will not deliver his people from my hand." [18]And they shouted it with a loud voice in the language of Judah to the people of Jerusalem who were on the wall, to frighten and terrify them, in order

---

[1] Vulgate; Hebrew *and raised upon the towers*

that they might take the city. ¹⁹ And they spoke of the God of Jerusalem as they spoke of the gods of the peoples of the earth, which are the work of men's hands.

The LORD Delivers Jerusalem

²⁰ Then Hezekiah the king and Isaiah the prophet, the son of Amoz, prayed because of this and cried to heaven. ²¹ And the LORD sent an angel, who cut off all the mighty warriors and commanders and officers in the camp of the king of Assyria. So he returned with shame of face to his own land. And when he came into the house of his god, some of his own sons struck him down there with the sword. ²² So the LORD saved Hezekiah and the inhabitants of Jerusalem from the hand of Sennacherib king of Assyria and from the hand of all his enemies, and he provided for them on every side. ²³ And many brought gifts to the LORD to Jerusalem and precious things to Hezekiah king of Judah, so that he was exalted in the sight of all nations from that time onward.

Hezekiah's Pride and Achievements

²⁴ In those days Hezekiah became sick and was at the point of death, and he prayed to the LORD, and he answered him and gave him a sign. ²⁵ But Hezekiah did not make return according to the benefit done to him, for his heart was proud. Therefore wrath came upon him and Judah and Jerusalem. ²⁶ But Hezekiah humbled himself for the pride of his heart, both he and the inhabitants of Jerusalem, so that the wrath of the LORD did not come upon them in the days of Hezekiah.

²⁷ And Hezekiah had very great riches and honor, and he made for himself treasuries for silver, for gold, for precious stones, for spices, for shields, and for all kinds of costly vessels; ²⁸ storehouses also for the yield of grain, wine, and oil; and stalls for all kinds of cattle, and sheepfolds. ²⁹ He likewise provided cities for himself, and flocks and herds in abundance, for God had given him very great possessions. ³⁰ This same Hezekiah closed the upper outlet of the waters of Gihon and directed them down to the west side of the city of David. And Hezekiah prospered in all his works. ³¹ And so in the matter of the envoys of the princes of Babylon, who had been sent to him to inquire about the sign that had been done in the land,

God left him to himself, in order to test him and to know all that was in his heart.

³² Now the rest of the acts of Hezekiah and his good deeds, behold, they are written in the vision of Isaiah the prophet, the son of Amoz, in the Book of the Kings of Judah and Israel. ³³ And Hezekiah slept with his fathers, and they buried him in the upper part of the tombs of the sons of David, and all Judah and the inhabitants of Jerusalem did him honor at his death. And Manasseh his son reigned in his place.

Manasseh Reigns in Judah

33 Manasseh was twelve years old when he began to reign, and he reigned fifty-five years in Jerusalem. ² And he did what was evil in the sight of the LORD, according to the abominations of the nations whom the LORD drove out before the people of Israel. ³ For he rebuilt the high places that his father Hezekiah had broken down, and he erected altars to the Baals, and made Asheroth, and worshiped all the host of heaven and served them. ⁴ And he built altars in the house of the LORD, of which the LORD had said, "In Jerusalem shall my name be forever." ⁵ And he built altars for all the host of heaven in the two courts of the house of the LORD. ⁶ And he burned his sons as an offering in the Valley of the Son of Hinnom, and used fortune-telling and omens and sorcery, and dealt with mediums and with necromancers. He did much evil in the sight of the LORD, provoking him to anger. ⁷ And the carved image of the idol that he had made he set in the house of God, of which God said to David and to Solomon his son, "In this house, and in Jerusalem, which I have chosen out of all the tribes of Israel, I will put my name forever, ⁸ and I will no more remove the foot of Israel from the land that I appointed for your fathers, if only they will be careful to do all that I have commanded them, all the law, the statutes, and the rules given through Moses." ⁹ Manasseh led Judah and the inhabitants of Jerusalem astray, to do more evil than the nations whom the LORD destroyed before the people of Israel.

Manasseh's Repentance

¹⁰ The LORD spoke to Manasseh and to his people, but they paid no attention. ¹¹ Therefore the LORD brought upon them the commanders of the army of the king of Assyria, who captured Manasseh with hooks and bound

him with chains of bronze and brought him to Babylon. [12] And when he was in distress, he entreated the favor of the LORD his God and humbled himself greatly before the God of his fathers. [13] He prayed to him, and God was moved by his entreaty and heard his plea and brought him again to Jerusalem into his kingdom. Then Manasseh knew that the LORD was God.

[14] Afterward he built an outer wall for the city of David west of Gihon, in the valley, and for the entrance into the Fish Gate, and carried it around Ophel, and raised it to a very great height. He also put commanders of the army in all the fortified cities in Judah. [15] And he took away the foreign gods and the idol from the house of the LORD, and all the altars that he had built on the mountain of the house of the LORD and in Jerusalem, and he threw them outside of the city. [16] He also restored the altar of the LORD and offered on it sacrifices of peace offerings and of thanksgiving, and he commanded Judah to serve the LORD, the God of Israel. [17] Nevertheless, the people still sacrificed at the high places, but only to the LORD their God.

[18] Now the rest of the acts of Manasseh, and his prayer to his God, and the words of the seers who spoke to him in the name of the LORD, the God of Israel, behold, they are in the Chronicles of the Kings of Israel. [19] And his prayer, and how God was moved by his entreaty, and all his sin and his faithlessness, and the sites on which he built high places and set up the Asherim and the images, before he humbled himself, behold, they are written in the Chronicles of the Seers.[1] [20] So Manasseh slept with his fathers, and they buried him in his house, and Amon his son reigned in his place.

Amon's Reign and Death

[21] Amon was twenty-two years old when he began to reign, and he reigned two years in Jerusalem. [22] And he did what was evil in the sight of the LORD, as Manasseh his father had done. Amon sacrificed to all the images that Manasseh his father had made, and served them. [23] And he did not humble himself before the LORD, as Manasseh his father had humbled himself, but this Amon incurred guilt more and more. [24] And his servants conspired against him and put him to death in his house. [25] But the people of the land struck down all those who had conspired against King Amon. And

the people of the land made Josiah his son king in his place.

Josiah Reigns in Judah

34 Josiah was eight years old when he began to reign, and he reigned thirty-one years in Jerusalem. [2] And he did what was right in the eyes of the LORD, and walked in the ways of David his father; and he did not turn aside to the right hand or to the left. [3] For in the eighth year of his reign, while he was yet a boy, he began to seek the God of David his father, and in the twelfth year he began to purge Judah and Jerusalem of the high places, the Asherim, and the carved and the metal images. [4] And they chopped down the altars of the Baals in his presence, and he cut down the incense altars that stood above them. And he broke in pieces the Asherim and the carved and the metal images, and he made dust of them and scattered it over the graves of those who had sacrificed to them. [5] He also burned the bones of the priests on their altars and cleansed Judah and Jerusalem. [6] And in the cities of Manasseh, Ephraim, and Simeon, and as far as Naphtali, in their ruins[2] all around, [7] he broke down the altars and beat the Asherim and the images into powder and cut down all the incense altars throughout all the land of Israel. Then he returned to Jerusalem.

The Book of the Law Found

[8] Now in the eighteenth year of his reign, when he had cleansed the land and the house, he sent Shaphan the son of Azaliah, and Maaseiah the governor of the city, and Joah the son of Joahaz, the recorder, to repair the house of the LORD his God. [9] They came to Hilkiah the high priest and gave him the money that had been brought into the house of God, which the Levites, the keepers of the threshold, had collected from Manasseh and Ephraim and from all the remnant of Israel and from all Judah and Benjamin and from the inhabitants of Jerusalem. [10] And they gave it to the workmen who were working in the house of the LORD. And the workmen who were working in the house of the LORD gave it for repairing and restoring the house. [11] They gave it to the carpenters and the builders to buy quarried stone, and timber for binders and beams for the buildings that the kings of Judah had let go to ruin. [12] And the men did the work faithfully. Over them were set Jahath and Obadiah the Levites, of the sons of Merari, and Zechariah and

---

[1] One Hebrew manuscript, Septuagint; most Hebrew manuscripts of Hozai　[2] The meaning of the Hebrew is uncertain

Meshullam, of the sons of the Kohathites, to have oversight. The Levites, all who were skillful with instruments of music, [13] were over the burden-bearers and directed all who did work in every kind of service, and some of the Levites were scribes and officials and gatekeepers.

[14] While they were bringing out the money that had been brought into the house of the LORD, Hilkiah the priest found the Book of the Law of the LORD given through[1] Moses. [15] Then Hilkiah answered and said to Shaphan the secretary, "I have found the Book of the Law in the house of the LORD." And Hilkiah gave the book to Shaphan. [16] Shaphan brought the book to the king, and further reported to the king, "All that was committed to your servants they are doing. [17] They have emptied out the money that was found in the house of the LORD and have given it into the hand of the overseers and the workmen." [18] Then Shaphan the secretary told the king, "Hilkiah the priest has given me a book." And Shaphan read from it before the king.

[19] And when the king heard the words of the Law, he tore his clothes. [20] And the king commanded Hilkiah, Ahikam the son of Shaphan, Abdon the son of Micah, Shaphan the secretary, and Asaiah the king's servant, saying, [21] "Go, inquire of the LORD for me and for those who are left in Israel and in Judah, concerning the words of the book that has been found. For great is the wrath of the LORD that is poured out on us, because our fathers have not kept the word of the LORD, to do according to all that is written in this book."

Huldah Prophesies Disaster

[22] So Hilkiah and those whom the king had sent[2] went to Huldah the prophetess, the wife of Shallum the son of Tokhath, son of Hasrah, keeper of the wardrobe (now she lived in Jerusalem in the Second Quarter) and spoke to her to that effect. [23] And she said to them, "Thus says the LORD, the God of Israel: 'Tell the man who sent you to me, [24] Thus says the LORD, Behold, I will bring disaster upon this place and upon its inhabitants, all the curses that are written in the book that was read before the king of Judah. [25] Because they have forsaken me and have made offerings to other gods, that they might provoke me to anger with all the works of their hands, therefore my wrath will be poured out on this place and will not be quenched. [26] But to the king of Judah,

who sent you to inquire of the LORD, thus shall you say to him, Thus says the LORD, the God of Israel: Regarding the words that you have heard, [27] because your heart was tender and you humbled yourself before God when you heard his words against this place and its inhabitants, and you have humbled yourself before me and have torn your clothes and wept before me, I also have heard you, declares the LORD. [28] Behold, I will gather you to your fathers, and you shall be gathered to your grave in peace, and your eyes shall not see all the disaster that I will bring upon this place and its inhabitants.' " And they brought back word to the king.

[29] Then the king sent and gathered together all the elders of Judah and Jerusalem. [30] And the king went up to the house of the LORD, with all the men of Judah and the inhabitants of Jerusalem and the priests and the Levites, all the people both great and small. And he read in their hearing all the words of the Book of the Covenant that had been found in the house of the LORD. [31] And the king stood in his place and made a covenant before the LORD, to walk after the LORD and to keep his commandments and his testimonies and his statutes, with all his heart and all his soul, to perform the words of the covenant that were written in this book. [32] Then he made all who were present in Jerusalem and in Benjamin join in it. And the inhabitants of Jerusalem did according to the covenant of God, the God of their fathers. [33] And Josiah took away all the abominations from all the territory that belonged to the people of Israel and made all who were present in Israel serve the LORD their God. All his days they did not turn away from following the LORD, the God of their fathers.

Josiah Keeps the Passover

35 Josiah kept a Passover to the LORD in Jerusalem. And they slaughtered the Passover lamb on the fourteenth day of the first month. [2] He appointed the priests to their offices and encouraged them in the service of the house of the LORD. [3] And he said to the Levites who taught all Israel and who were holy to the LORD, "Put the holy ark in the house that Solomon the son of David, king of Israel, built. You need not carry it on your shoulders. Now serve the LORD your God and his people Israel. [4] Prepare yourselves according to your fathers' houses by your divisions, as prescribed in the

---

[1] Hebrew *by the hand of* [2] Syriac, Vulgate; Hebrew lacks *had sent*

writing of David king of Israel and the document of Solomon his son. [5] And stand in the Holy Place according to the groupings of the fathers' houses of your brothers the lay people, and according to the division of the Levites by fathers' household. [6] And slaughter the Passover lamb, and consecrate yourselves, and prepare for your brothers, to do according to the word of the LORD by[1] Moses."

[7] Then Josiah contributed to the lay people, as Passover offerings for all who were present, lambs and young goats from the flock to the number of 30,000, and 3,000 bulls; these were from the king's possessions. [8] And his officials contributed willingly to the people, to the priests, and to the Levites. Hilkiah, Zechariah, and Jehiel, the chief officers of the house of God, gave to the priests for the Passover offerings 2,600 Passover lambs and 300 bulls. [9] Conaniah also, and Shemaiah and Nethanel his brothers, and Hashabiah and Jeiel and Jozabad, the chiefs of the Levites, gave to the Levites for the Passover offerings 5,000 lambs and young goats and 500 bulls.

[10] When the service had been prepared for, the priests stood in their place, and the Levites in their divisions according to the king's command. [11] And they slaughtered the Passover lamb, and the priests threw the blood that they received from them while the Levites flayed the sacrifices. [12] And they set aside the burnt offerings that they might distribute them according to the groupings of the fathers' houses of the lay people, to offer to the LORD, as it is written in the Book of Moses. And so they did with the bulls. [13] And they roasted the Passover lamb with fire according to the rule; and they boiled the holy offerings in pots, in cauldrons, and in pans, and carried them quickly to all the lay people. [14] And afterward they prepared for themselves and for the priests, because the priests, the sons of Aaron, were offering the burnt offerings and the fat parts until night; so the Levites prepared for themselves and for the priests, the sons of Aaron. [15] The singers, the sons of Asaph, were in their place according to the command of David, and Asaph, and Heman, and Jeduthun the king's seer; and the gatekeepers were at each gate. They did not need to depart from their service, for their brothers the Levites prepared for them.

[16] So all the service of the LORD was prepared that day, to keep the Passover and to offer burnt offerings on the altar of the LORD, according to the command of King Josiah. [17] And the people of Israel who were present kept the Passover at that time, and the Feast of Unleavened Bread seven days. [18] No Passover like it had been kept in Israel since the days of Samuel the prophet. None of the kings of Israel had kept such a Passover as was kept by Josiah, and the priests and the Levites, and all Judah and Israel who were present, and the inhabitants of Jerusalem. [19] In the eighteenth year of the reign of Josiah this Passover was kept.

Josiah Killed in Battle

[20] After all this, when Josiah had prepared the temple, Neco king of Egypt went up to fight at Carchemish on the Euphrates, and Josiah went out to meet him. [21] But he sent envoys to him, saying, "What have we to do with each other, king of Judah? I am not coming against you this day, but against the house with which I am at war. And God has commanded me to hurry. Cease opposing God, who is with me, lest he destroy you." [22] Nevertheless, Josiah did not turn away from him, but disguised himself in order to fight with him. He did not listen to the words of Neco from the mouth of God, but came to fight in the plain of Megiddo. [23] And the archers shot King Josiah. And the king said to his servants, "Take me away, for I am badly wounded." [24] So his servants took him out of the chariot and carried him in his second chariot and brought him to Jerusalem. And he died and was buried in the tombs of his fathers. All Judah and Jerusalem mourned for Josiah. [25] Jeremiah also uttered a lament for Josiah; and all the singing men and singing women have spoken of Josiah in their laments to this day. They made these a rule in Israel; behold, they are written in the Laments. [26] Now the rest of the acts of Josiah, and his good deeds according to what is written in the Law of the LORD, [27] and his acts, first and last, behold, they are written in the Book of the Kings of Israel and Judah.

Judah's Decline

36 The people of the land took Jehoahaz the son of Josiah and made him king in his father's place in Jerusalem. [2] Jehoahaz was twenty-three years old when he began to reign, and he reigned three months in Jerusalem. [3] Then the king of Egypt deposed him in Jerusalem and laid on the land a tribute of a hundred talents of silver and a talent[2] of

[1] Hebrew *by the hand of* [2] A *talent* was about 75 pounds or 34 kilograms

gold. ⁴ And the king of Egypt made Eliakim his brother king over Judah and Jerusalem, and changed his name to Jehoiakim. But Neco took Jehoahaz his brother and carried him to Egypt.

⁵ Jehoiakim was twenty-five years old when he began to reign, and he reigned eleven years in Jerusalem. He did what was evil in the sight of the LORD his God. ⁶ Against him came up Nebuchadnezzar king of Babylon and bound him in chains to take him to Babylon. ⁷ Nebuchadnezzar also carried part of the vessels of the house of the LORD to Babylon and put them in his palace in Babylon. ⁸ Now the rest of the acts of Jehoiakim, and the abominations that he did, and what was found against him, behold, they are written in the Book of the Kings of Israel and Judah. And Jehoiachin his son reigned in his place.

⁹ Jehoiachin was eighteen¹ years old when he became king, and he reigned three months and ten days in Jerusalem. He did what was evil in the sight of the LORD. ¹⁰ In the spring of the year King Nebuchadnezzar sent and brought him to Babylon, with the precious vessels of the house of the LORD, and made his brother Zedekiah king over Judah and Jerusalem.

¹¹ Zedekiah was twenty-one years old when he began to reign, and he reigned eleven years in Jerusalem. ¹² He did what was evil in the sight of the LORD his God. He did not humble himself before Jeremiah the prophet, who spoke from the mouth of the LORD. ¹³ He also rebelled against King Nebuchadnezzar, who had made him swear by God. He stiffened his neck and hardened his heart against turning to the LORD, the God of Israel. ¹⁴ All the officers of the priests and the people likewise were exceedingly unfaithful, following all the abominations of the nations. And they polluted the house of the LORD that he had made holy in Jerusalem. ¹⁵ The LORD, the God of their fathers, sent persistently to them by his messengers, because

he had compassion on his people and on his dwelling place. ¹⁶ But they kept mocking the messengers of God, despising his words and scoffing at his prophets, until the wrath of the LORD rose against his people, until there was no remedy.

Jerusalem Captured and Burned

¹⁷ Therefore he brought up against them the king of the Chaldeans, who killed their young men with the sword in the house of their sanctuary and had no compassion on young man or virgin, old man or aged. He gave them all into his hand. ¹⁸ And all the vessels of the house of God, great and small, and the treasures of the house of the LORD, and the treasures of the king and of his princes, all these he brought to Babylon. ¹⁹ And they burned the house of God and broke down the wall of Jerusalem and burned all its palaces with fire and destroyed all its precious vessels. ²⁰ He took into exile in Babylon those who had escaped from the sword, and they became servants to him and to his sons until the establishment of the kingdom of Persia, ²¹ to fulfill the word of the LORD by the mouth of Jeremiah, until the land had enjoyed its Sabbaths. All the days that it lay desolate it kept Sabbath, to fulfill seventy years.

The Proclamation of Cyrus

²² Now in the first year of Cyrus king of Persia, that the word of the LORD by the mouth of Jeremiah might be fulfilled, the LORD stirred up the spirit of Cyrus king of Persia, so that he made a proclamation throughout all his kingdom and also put it in writing: ²³ "Thus says Cyrus king of Persia, 'The LORD, the God of heaven, has given me all the kingdoms of the earth, and he has charged me to build him a house at Jerusalem, which is in Judah. Whoever is among you of all his people, may the LORD his God be with him. Let him go up.'"

---

¹ Septuagint (compare 2 Kings 24:8); most Hebrew manuscripts eight

EZRA

The Proclamation of Cyrus

1 In the first year of Cyrus king of Persia, that the word of the LORD by the mouth of Jeremiah might be fulfilled, the LORD stirred up the spirit of Cyrus king of Persia, so that he made a proclamation throughout all his kingdom and also put it in writing:

2 "Thus says Cyrus king of Persia: The LORD, the God of heaven, has given me all the kingdoms of the earth, and he has charged me to build him a house at Jerusalem, which is in Judah. 3 Whoever is among you of all his people, may his God be with him, and let him go up to Jerusalem, which is in Judah, and rebuild the house of the LORD, the God of Israel— he is the God who is in Jerusalem. 4 And let each survivor, in whatever place he sojourns, be assisted by the men of his place with silver and gold, with goods and with beasts, besides freewill offerings for the house of God that is in Jerusalem."

5 Then rose up the heads of the fathers' houses of Judah and Benjamin, and the priests and the Levites, everyone whose spirit God had stirred to go up to rebuild the house of the LORD that is in Jerusalem. 6 And all who were about them aided them with vessels of silver, with gold, with goods, with beasts, and with costly wares, besides all that was freely offered. 7 Cyrus the king also brought out the vessels of the house of the LORD that Nebuchadnezzar had carried away from Jerusalem and placed in the house of his gods. 8 Cyrus king of Persia brought these out in the charge of Mithredath the treasurer, who counted them out to Sheshbazzar the prince of Judah. 9 And this was the number of them: 30 basins of gold, 1,000 basins of silver, 29 censers, 10 30 bowls of gold, 410 bowls of silver, and 1,000 other vessels; 11 all the vessels of gold and of silver were 5,400. All these did Sheshbazzar bring up, when the exiles were brought up from Babylonia to Jerusalem.

The Exiles Return

2 Now these were the people of the province who came up out of the captivity of those exiles whom Nebuchadnezzar the king of Babylon had carried captive to Babylonia. They returned to Jerusalem and Judah, each to his own town. 2 They came with Zerubbabel, Jeshua, Nehemiah, Seraiah, Reelaiah, Mordecai, Bilshan, Mispar, Bigvai, Rehum, and Baanah.

The number of the men of the people of Israel: 3 the sons of Parosh, 2,172. 4 The sons of Shephatiah, 372. 5 The sons of Arah, 775. 6 The sons of Pahath-moab, namely the sons of Jeshua and Joab, 2,812. 7 The sons of Elam, 1,254. 8 The sons of Zattu, 945. 9 The sons of Zaccai, 760. 10 The sons of Bani, 642. 11 The sons of Bebai, 623. 12 The sons of Azgad, 1,222. 13 The sons of Adonikam, 666. 14 The sons of Bigvai, 2,056. 15 The sons of Adin, 454. 16 The sons of Ater, namely of Hezekiah, 98. 17 The sons of Bezai, 323. 18 The sons of Jorah, 112. 19 The sons of Hashum, 223. 20 The sons of Gibbar, 95. 21 The sons of Bethlehem, 123. 22 The men of Netophah, 56. 23 The men of Anathoth, 128. 24 The sons of Azmaveth, 42. 25 The sons of Kiriath-arim, Chephirah, and Beeroth, 743. 26 The sons of Ramah and Geba, 621. 27 The men of Michmas, 122. 28 The men of Bethel and Ai, 223. 29 The sons of Nebo, 52. 30 The sons of Magbish, 156. 31 The sons of the other Elam, 1,254. 32 The sons of Harim, 320. 33 The sons of Lod, Hadid, and Ono, 725. 34 The sons of Jericho, 345. 35 The sons of Senaah, 3,630.

36 The priests: the sons of Jedaiah, of the house of Jeshua, 973. 37 The sons of Immer, 1,052. 38 The sons of Pashhur, 1,247. 39 The sons of Harim, 1,017.

40 The Levites: the sons of Jeshua and Kadmiel, of the sons of Hodaviah, 74. 41 The singers: the sons of Asaph, 128. 42 The sons of the gatekeepers: the sons of Shallum, the sons of Ater, the sons of Talmon, the sons of Akkub, the sons of Hatita, and the sons of Shobai, in all 139.

43 The temple servants: the sons of Ziha, the sons of Hasupha, the sons of Tabbaoth, 44 the sons of Keros, the sons of Siaha, the sons of Padon, 45 the sons of Lebanah, the sons of Hagabah, the sons of Akkub, 46 the sons of Hagab, the sons of Shamlai, the sons of Hanan, 47 the sons of Giddel, the sons of Gahar, the sons of Reaiah, 48 the sons of Rezin, the sons of Nekoda, the sons of Gazzam, 49 the sons of Uzza, the sons of Paseah, the sons of Besai, 50 the sons of Asnah, the sons of Meunim, the sons

of Nephisim, [51] the sons of Bakbuk, the sons of Hakupha, the sons of Harhur, [52] the sons of Bazluth, the sons of Mehida, the sons of Harsha, [53] the sons of Barkos, the sons of Sisera, the sons of Temah, [54] the sons of Neziah, and the sons of Hatipha.

[55] The sons of Solomon's servants: the sons of Sotai, the sons of Hassophereth, the sons of Peruda, [56] the sons of Jaalah, the sons of Darkon, the sons of Giddel, [57] the sons of Shephatiah, the sons of Hattil, the sons of Pochereth-hazzebaim, and the sons of Ami.

[58] All the temple servants and the sons of Solomon's servants were 392.

[59] The following were those who came up from Tel-melah, Tel-harsha, Cherub, Addan, and Immer, though they could not prove their fathers' houses or their descent, whether they belonged to Israel: [60] the sons of Delaiah, the sons of Tobiah, and the sons of Nekoda, 652. [61] Also, of the sons of the priests: the sons of Habaiah, the sons of Hakkoz, and the sons of Barzillai (who had taken a wife from the daughters of Barzillai the Gileadite, and was called by their name). [62] These sought their registration among those enrolled in the genealogies, but they were not found there, and so they were excluded from the priesthood as unclean. [63] The governor told them that they were not to partake of the most holy food, until there should be a priest to consult Urim and Thummim.

[64] The whole assembly together was 42,360, [65] besides their male and female servants, of whom there were 7,337, and they had 200 male and female singers. [66] Their horses were 736, their mules were 245, [67] their camels were 435, and their donkeys were 6,720.

[68] Some of the heads of families, when they came to the house of the LORD that is in Jerusalem, made freewill offerings for the house of God, to erect it on its site. [69] According to their ability they gave to the treasury of the work 61,000 darics[1] of gold, 5,000 minas[2] of silver, and 100 priests' garments.

[70] Now the priests, the Levites, some of the people, the singers, the gatekeepers, and the temple servants lived in their towns, and all the rest of Israel[3] in their towns.

Rebuilding the Altar

3 When the seventh month came, and the children of Israel were in the towns, the people gathered as one man to Jerusalem. [2] Then arose Jeshua the son of Jozadak, with his fellow priests, and Zerubbabel the son of Shealtiel with his kinsmen, and they built the altar of the God of Israel, to offer burnt offerings on it, as it is written in the Law of Moses the man of God. [3] They set the altar in its place, for fear was on them because of the peoples of the lands, and they offered burnt offerings on it to the LORD, burnt offerings morning and evening. [4] And they kept the Feast of Booths, as it is written, and offered the daily burnt offerings by number according to the rule, as each day required, [5] and after that the regular burnt offerings, the offerings at the new moon and at all the appointed feasts of the LORD, and the offerings of everyone who made a freewill offering to the LORD. [6] From the first day of the seventh month they began to offer burnt offerings to the LORD. But the foundation of the temple of the LORD was not yet laid. [7] So they gave money to the masons and the carpenters, and food, drink, and oil to the Sidonians and the Tyrians to bring cedar trees from Lebanon to the sea, to Joppa, according to the grant that they had from Cyrus king of Persia.

Rebuilding the Temple

[8] Now in the second year after their coming to the house of God at Jerusalem, in the second month, Zerubbabel the son of Shealtiel and Jeshua the son of Jozadak made a beginning, together with the rest of their kinsmen, the priests and the Levites and all who had come to Jerusalem from the captivity. They appointed the Levites, from twenty years old and upward, to supervise the work of the house of the LORD. [9] And Jeshua with his sons and his brothers, and Kadmiel and his sons, the sons of Judah, together supervised the workmen in the house of God, along with the sons of Henadad and the Levites, their sons and brothers.

[10] And when the builders laid the foundation of the temple of the LORD, the priests in their vestments came forward with trumpets, and the Levites, the sons of Asaph, with cymbals, to praise the LORD, according to the directions of David king of Israel. [11] And they sang responsively, praising and giving thanks to the LORD,

"For he is good,
    for his steadfast love endures forever
        toward Israel."

And all the people shouted with a great shout when they praised the LORD, because the foun-

---

[1] A *daric* was a coin weighing about 1/4 ounce or 8.5 grams [2] A *mina* was about 1 1/4 pounds or 0.6 kilogram [3] Hebrew *all Israel*

dation of the house of the LORD was laid. [12] But many of the priests and Levites and heads of fathers' houses, old men who had seen the first house, wept with a loud voice when they saw the foundation of this house being laid, though many shouted aloud for joy, [13] so that the people could not distinguish the sound of the joyful shout from the sound of the people's weeping, for the people shouted with a great shout, and the sound was heard far away.

Adversaries Oppose the Rebuilding

4 Now when the adversaries of Judah and Benjamin heard that the returned exiles were building a temple to the LORD, the God of Israel, [2] they approached Zerubbabel and the heads of fathers' houses and said to them, "Let us build with you, for we worship your God as you do, and we have been sacrificing to him ever since the days of Esarhaddon king of Assyria who brought us here." [3] But Zerubbabel, Jeshua, and the rest of the heads of fathers' houses in Israel said to them, "You have nothing to do with us in building a house to our God; but we alone will build to the LORD, the God of Israel, as King Cyrus the king of Persia has commanded us."

[4] Then the people of the land discouraged the people of Judah and made them afraid to build [5] and bribed counselors against them to frustrate their purpose, all the days of Cyrus king of Persia, even until the reign of Darius king of Persia.

[6] And in the reign of Ahasuerus, in the beginning of his reign, they wrote an accusation against the inhabitants of Judah and Jerusalem.

The Letter to King Artaxerxes

[7] In the days of Artaxerxes, Bishlam and Mithredath and Tabeel and the rest of their associates wrote to Artaxerxes king of Persia. The letter was written in Aramaic and translated.[1] [8] Rehum the commander and Shimshai the scribe wrote a letter against Jerusalem to Artaxerxes the king as follows: [9] Rehum the commander, Shimshai the scribe, and the rest of their associates, the judges, the governors, the officials, the Persians, the men of Erech, the Babylonians, the men of Susa, that is, the Elamites, [10] and the rest of the nations whom the great and noble Osnappar deported and settled in the cities of Samaria and in the rest of the province Beyond the River. [11] (This is a copy of the letter that they sent.) "To Artaxerxes the king: Your servants, the men of the province Beyond the River, send greeting. And now [12] be it known to the king that the Jews who came up from you to us have gone to Jerusalem. They are rebuilding that rebellious and wicked city. They are finishing the walls and repairing the foundations. [13] Now be it known to the king that if this city is rebuilt and the walls finished, they will not pay tribute, custom, or toll, and the royal revenue will be impaired. [14] Now because we eat the salt of the palace[2] and it is not fitting for us to witness the king's dishonor, therefore we send and inform the king, [15] in order that search may be made in the book of the records of your fathers. You will find in the book of the records and learn that this city is a rebellious city, hurtful to kings and provinces, and that sedition was stirred up in it from of old. That was why this city was laid waste. [16] We make known to the king that if this city is rebuilt and its walls finished, you will then have no possession in the province Beyond the River."

The King Orders the Work to Cease

[17] The king sent an answer: "To Rehum the commander and Shimshai the scribe and the rest of their associates who live in Samaria and in the rest of the province Beyond the River, greeting. And now [18] the letter that you sent to us has been plainly read before me. [19] And I made a decree, and search has been made, and it has been found that this city from of old has risen against kings, and that rebellion and sedition have been made in it. [20] And mighty kings have been over Jerusalem, who ruled over the whole province Beyond the River, to whom tribute, custom, and toll were paid. [21] Therefore make a decree that these men be made to cease, and that this city be not rebuilt, until a decree is made by me. [22] And take care not to be slack in this matter. Why should damage grow to the hurt of the king?"

[23] Then, when the copy of King Artaxerxes' letter was read before Rehum and Shimshai the scribe and their associates, they went in haste to the Jews at Jerusalem and by force and power made them cease. [24] Then the work on the house of God that is in Jerusalem stopped, and it ceased until the second year of the reign of Darius king of Persia.

---

[1] Hebrew *written in Aramaic and translated in Aramaic*, indicating that 4:8–6:18 is in Aramaic; another interpretation is *The letter was written in the Aramaic script and set forth in the Aramaic language* [2] Aramaic *because the salt of the palace is our salt*

Rebuilding Begins Anew

5 Now the prophets, Haggai and Zechariah the son of Iddo, prophesied to the Jews who were in Judah and Jerusalem, in the name of the God of Israel who was over them. ²Then Zerubbabel the son of Shealtiel and Jeshua the son of Jozadak arose and began to rebuild the house of God that is in Jerusalem, and the prophets of God were with them, supporting them.

³At the same time Tattenai the governor of the province Beyond the River and Shethar-bozenai and their associates came to them and spoke to them thus: "Who gave you a decree to build this house and to finish this structure?" ⁴They also asked them this:¹ "What are the names of the men who are building this building?" ⁵But the eye of their God was on the elders of the Jews, and they did not stop them until the report should reach Darius and then an answer be returned by letter concerning it.

Tattenai's Letter to King Darius

⁶This is a copy of the letter that Tattenai the governor of the province Beyond the River and Shethar-bozenai and his associates, the governors who were in the province Beyond the River, sent to Darius the king. ⁷They sent him a report, in which was written as follows: "To Darius the king, all peace. ⁸Be it known to the king that we went to the province of Judah, to the house of the great God. It is being built with huge stones, and timber is laid in the walls. This work goes on diligently and prospers in their hands. ⁹Then we asked those elders and spoke to them thus: 'Who gave you a decree to build this house and to finish this structure?' ¹⁰We also asked them their names, for your information, that we might write down the names of their leaders.² ¹¹And this was their reply to us: 'We are the servants of the God of heaven and earth, and we are rebuilding the house that was built many years ago, which a great king of Israel built and finished. ¹²But because our fathers had angered the God of heaven, he gave them into the hand of Nebuchadnezzar king of Babylon, the Chaldean, who destroyed this house and carried away the people to Babylonia. ¹³However, in the first year of Cyrus king of Babylon, Cyrus the king made a decree that this house of God should be rebuilt. ¹⁴And the gold and silver vessels of the house of God, which Nebuchadnezzar had taken out of the temple

that was in Jerusalem and brought into the temple of Babylon, these Cyrus the king took out of the temple of Babylon, and they were delivered to one whose name was Sheshbazzar, whom he had made governor; ¹⁵and he said to him, "Take these vessels, go and put them in the temple that is in Jerusalem, and let the house of God be rebuilt on its site." ¹⁶Then this Sheshbazzar came and laid the foundations of the house of God that is in Jerusalem, and from that time until now it has been in building, and it is not yet finished.' ¹⁷Therefore, if it seems good to the king, let search be made in the royal archives there in Babylon, to see whether a decree was issued by Cyrus the king for the rebuilding of this house of God in Jerusalem. And let the king send us his pleasure in this matter."

The Decree of Darius

6 Then Darius the king made a decree, and search was made in Babylonia, in the house of the archives where the documents were stored. ²And in Ecbatana, the citadel that is in the province of Media, a scroll was found on which this was written: "A record. ³In the first year of Cyrus the king, Cyrus the king issued a decree: Concerning the house of God at Jerusalem, let the house be rebuilt, the place where sacrifices were offered, and let its foundations be retained. Its height shall be sixty cubits³ and its breadth sixty cubits, ⁴with three layers of great stones and one layer of timber. Let the cost be paid from the royal treasury. ⁵And also let the gold and silver vessels of the house of God, which Nebuchadnezzar took out of the temple that is in Jerusalem and brought to Babylon, be restored and brought back to the temple that is in Jerusalem, each to its place. You shall put them in the house of God."

⁶"Now therefore, Tattenai, governor of the province Beyond the River, Shethar-bozenai, and your⁴ associates the governors who are in the province Beyond the River, keep away. ⁷Let the work on this house of God alone. Let the governor of the Jews and the elders of the Jews rebuild this house of God on its site. ⁸Moreover, I make a decree regarding what you shall do for these elders of the Jews for the rebuilding of this house of God. The cost is to be paid to these men in full and without delay from the royal revenue, the tribute of the province from Beyond the River. ⁹And whatever is needed—

---

¹ Septuagint, Syriac; Aramaic *Then we said to them,* ² Aramaic *of the men at their heads* ³ A cubit was about 18 inches or 45 centimeters ⁴ Aramaic *their*

bulls, rams, or sheep for burnt offerings to the God of heaven, wheat, salt, wine, or oil, as the priests at Jerusalem require—let that be given to them day by day without fail, [10] that they may offer pleasing sacrifices to the God of heaven and pray for the life of the king and his sons. [11] Also I make a decree that if anyone alters this edict, a beam shall be pulled out of his house, and he shall be impaled on it, and his house shall be made a dunghill. [12] May the God who has caused his name to dwell there overthrow any king or people who shall put out a hand to alter this, or to destroy this house of God that is in Jerusalem. I Darius make a decree; let it be done with all diligence."

The Temple Finished and Dedicated

[13] Then, according to the word sent by Darius the king, Tattenai, the governor of the province Beyond the River, Shethar-bozenai, and their associates did with all diligence what Darius the king had ordered. [14] And the elders of the Jews built and prospered through the prophesying of Haggai the prophet and Zechariah the son of Iddo. They finished their building by decree of the God of Israel and by decree of Cyrus and Darius and Artaxerxes king of Persia; [15] and this house was finished on the third day of the month of Adar, in the sixth year of the reign of Darius the king.

[16] And the people of Israel, the priests and the Levites, and the rest of the returned exiles, celebrated the dedication of this house of God with joy. [17] They offered at the dedication of this house of God 100 bulls, 200 rams, 400 lambs, and as a sin offering for all Israel 12 male goats, according to the number of the tribes of Israel. [18] And they set the priests in their divisions and the Levites in their divisions, for the service of God at Jerusalem, as it is written in the Book of Moses.

Passover Celebrated

[19] On the fourteenth day of the first month, the returned exiles kept the Passover. [20] For the priests and the Levites had purified themselves together; all of them were clean. So they slaughtered the Passover lamb for all the returned exiles, for their fellow priests, and for themselves. [21] It was eaten by the people of Israel who had returned from exile, and also by every one who had joined them and separated himself from the uncleanness of the peoples of the land to worship the LORD, the God of

Israel. [22] And they kept the Feast of Unleavened Bread seven days with joy, for the LORD had made them joyful and had turned the heart of the king of Assyria to them, so that he aided them in the work of the house of God, the God of Israel.

Ezra Sent to Teach the People

7 Now after this, in the reign of Artaxerxes king of Persia, Ezra the son of Seraiah, son of Azariah, son of Hilkiah, [2] son of Shallum, son of Zadok, son of Ahitub, [3] son of Amariah, son of Azariah, son of Meraioth, [4] son of Zerahiah, son of Uzzi, son of Bukki, [5] son of Abishua, son of Phinehas, son of Eleazar, son of Aaron the chief priest— [6] this Ezra went up from Babylonia. He was a scribe skilled in the Law of Moses that the LORD, the God of Israel, had given, and the king granted him all that he asked, for the hand of the LORD his God was on him.

[7] And there went up also to Jerusalem, in the seventh year of Artaxerxes the king, some of the people of Israel, and some of the priests and Levites, the singers and gatekeepers, and the temple servants. [8] And Ezra[1] came to Jerusalem in the fifth month, which was in the seventh year of the king. [9] For on the first day of the first month he began to go up from Babylonia, and on the first day of the fifth month he came to Jerusalem, for the good hand of his God was on him. [10] For Ezra had set his heart to study the Law of the LORD, and to do it and to teach his statutes and rules in Israel.

[11] This is a copy of the letter that King Artaxerxes gave to Ezra the priest, the scribe, a man learned in matters of the commandments of the LORD and his statutes for Israel: [12] "Artaxerxes, king of kings, to Ezra the priest, the scribe of the Law of the God of heaven. Peace.[2] And now [13] I make a decree that anyone of the people of Israel or their priests or Levites in my kingdom, who freely offers to go to Jerusalem, may go with you. [14] For you are sent by the king and his seven counselors to make inquiries about Judah and Jerusalem according to the Law of your God, which is in your hand, [15] and also to carry the silver and gold that the king and his counselors have freely offered to the God of Israel, whose dwelling is in Jerusalem, [16] with all the silver and gold that you shall find in the whole province of Babylonia, and with the freewill offerings of the people and the priests, vowed willingly

[1] Aramaic he [2] Aramaic Perfect (probably a greeting)

for the house of their God that is in Jerusalem. [17] With this money, then, you shall with all diligence buy bulls, rams, and lambs, with their grain offerings and their drink offerings, and you shall offer them on the altar of the house of your God that is in Jerusalem. [18] Whatever seems good to you and your brothers to do with the rest of the silver and gold, you may do, according to the will of your God. [19] The vessels that have been given you for the service of the house of your God, you shall deliver before the God of Jerusalem. [20] And whatever else is required for the house of your God, which it falls to you to provide, you may provide it out of the king's treasury.

[21] "And I, Artaxerxes the king, make a decree to all the treasurers in the province Beyond the River: Whatever Ezra the priest, the scribe of the Law of the God of heaven, requires of you, let it be done with all diligence, [22] up to 100 talents[1] of silver, 100 cors[2] of wheat, 100 baths[3] of wine, 100 baths of oil, and salt without prescribing how much. [23] Whatever is decreed by the God of heaven, let it be done in full for the house of the God of heaven, lest his wrath be against the realm of the king and his sons. [24] We also notify you that it shall not be lawful to impose tribute, custom, or toll on anyone of the priests, the Levites, the singers, the doorkeepers, the temple servants, or other servants of this house of God.

[25] "And you, Ezra, according to the wisdom of your God that is in your hand, appoint magistrates and judges who may judge all the people in the province Beyond the River, all such as know the laws of your God. And those who do not know them, you shall teach. [26] Whoever will not obey the law of your God and the law of the king, let judgment be strictly executed on him, whether for death or for banishment or for confiscation of his goods or for imprisonment."

[27] Blessed be the LORD, the God of our fathers, who put such a thing as this into the heart of the king, to beautify the house of the LORD that is in Jerusalem, [28] and who extended to me his steadfast love before the king and his counselors, and before all the king's mighty officers. I took courage, for the hand of the LORD my God was on me, and I gathered leading men from Israel to go up with me.

Genealogy of Those Who Returned with Ezra

8 These are the heads of their fathers' houses, and this is the genealogy of those who went up with me from Babylonia, in the reign of Artaxerxes the king: [2] Of the sons of Phinehas, Gershom. Of the sons of Ithamar, Daniel. Of the sons of David, Hattush. [3] Of the sons of Shecaniah, who was of the sons of Parosh, Zechariah, with whom were registered 150 men. [4] Of the sons of Pahath-moab, Eliehoenai the son of Zerahiah, and with him 200 men. [5] Of the sons of Zattu,[4] Shecaniah the son of Jahaziel, and with him 300 men. [6] Of the sons of Adin, Ebed the son of Jonathan, and with him 50 men. [7] Of the sons of Elam, Jeshaiah the son of Athaliah, and with him 70 men. [8] Of the sons of Shephatiah, Zebadiah the son of Michael, and with him 80 men. [9] Of the sons of Joab, Obadiah the son of Jehiel, and with him 218 men. [10] Of the sons of Bani,[5] Shelomith the son of Josiphiah, and with him 160 men. [11] Of the sons of Bebai, Zechariah, the son of Bebai, and with him 28 men. [12] Of the sons of Azgad, Johanan the son of Hakkatan, and with him 110 men. [13] Of the sons of Adonikam, those who came later, their names being Eliphelet, Jeuel, and Shemaiah, and with them 60 men. [14] Of the sons of Bigvai, Uthai and Zaccur, and with them 70 men.

Ezra Sends for Levites

[15] I gathered them to the river that runs to Ahava, and there we camped three days. As I reviewed the people and the priests, I found there none of the sons of Levi. [16] Then I sent for Eliezer, Ariel, Shemaiah, Elnathan, Jarib, Elnathan, Nathan, Zechariah, and Meshullam, leading men, and for Joiarib and Elnathan, who were men of insight, [17] and sent them to Iddo, the leading man at the place Casiphia, telling them what to say to Iddo and his brothers and[6] the temple servants at the place Casiphia, namely, to send us ministers for the house of our God. [18] And by the good hand of our God on us, they brought us a man of discretion, of the sons of Mahli the son of Levi, son of Israel, namely Sherebiah with his sons and kinsmen, 18; [19] also Hashabiah, and with him Jeshaiah of the sons of Merari, with his kinsmen and their sons, 20; [20] besides 220 of the temple servants, whom David and his officials had set apart to attend the Levites. These were all mentioned by name.

---

[1] A *talent* was about 75 pounds or 34 kilograms   [2] A *cor* was about 6 bushels or 220 liters   [3] A *bath* was about 6 gallons or 22 liters   [4] Septuagint; Hebrew lacks *of Zattu*
[5] Septuagint; Hebrew lacks *Bani*   [6] Hebrew lacks *and*

Fasting and Prayer for Protection

²¹ Then I proclaimed a fast there, at the river Ahava, that we might humble ourselves before our God, to seek from him a safe journey for ourselves, our children, and all our goods. ²² For I was ashamed to ask the king for a band of soldiers and horsemen to protect us against the enemy on our way, since we had told the king, "The hand of our God is for good on all who seek him, and the power of his wrath is against all who forsake him." ²³ So we fasted and implored our God for this, and he listened to our entreaty.

Priests to Guard Offerings

²⁴ Then I set apart twelve of the leading priests: Sherebiah, Hashabiah, and ten of their kinsmen with them. ²⁵ And I weighed out to them the silver and the gold and the vessels, the offering for the house of our God that the king and his counselors and his lords and all Israel there present had offered. ²⁶ I weighed out into their hand 650 talents[1] of silver, and silver vessels worth 200 talents,[2] and 100 talents of gold, ²⁷ 20 bowls of gold worth 1,000 darics,[3] and two vessels of fine bright bronze as precious as gold. ²⁸ And I said to them, "You are holy to the LORD, and the vessels are holy, and the silver and the gold are a freewill offering to the LORD, the God of your fathers. ²⁹ Guard them and keep them until you weigh them before the chief priests and the Levites and the heads of fathers' houses in Israel at Jerusalem, within the chambers of the house of the LORD." ³⁰ So the priests and the Levites took over the weight of the silver and the gold and the vessels, to bring them to Jerusalem, to the house of our God.

³¹ Then we departed from the river Ahava on the twelfth day of the first month, to go to Jerusalem. The hand of our God was on us, and he delivered us from the hand of the enemy and from ambushes by the way. ³² We came to Jerusalem, and there we remained three days. ³³ On the fourth day, within the house of our God, the silver and the gold and the vessels were weighed into the hands of Meremoth the priest, son of Uriah, and with him was Eleazar the son of Phinehas, and with them were the Levites, Jozabad the son of Jeshua and Noadiah the son of Binnui. ³⁴ The whole was counted and weighed, and the weight of everything was recorded.

³⁵ At that time those who had come from captivity, the returned exiles, offered burnt offerings to the God of Israel, twelve bulls for all Israel, ninety-six rams, seventy-seven lambs, and as a sin offering twelve male goats. All this was a burnt offering to the LORD. ³⁶ They also delivered the king's commissions to the king's satraps[4] and to the governors of the province Beyond the River, and they aided the people and the house of God.

Ezra Prays About Intermarriage

9 After these things had been done, the officials approached me and said, "The people of Israel and the priests and the Levites have not separated themselves from the peoples of the lands with their abominations, from the Canaanites, the Hittites, the Perizzites, the Jebusites, the Ammonites, the Moabites, the Egyptians, and the Amorites. ² For they have taken some of their daughters to be wives for themselves and for their sons, so that the holy race[5] has mixed itself with the peoples of the lands. And in this faithlessness the hand of the officials and chief men has been foremost." ³ As soon as I heard this, I tore my garment and my cloak and pulled hair from my head and beard and sat appalled. ⁴ Then all who trembled at the words of the God of Israel, because of the faithlessness of the returned exiles, gathered around me while I sat appalled until the evening sacrifice. ⁵ And at the evening sacrifice I rose from my fasting, with my garment and my cloak torn, and fell upon my knees and spread out my hands to the LORD my God, ⁶ saying:

"O my God, I am ashamed and blush to lift my face to you, my God, for our iniquities have risen higher than our heads, and our guilt has mounted up to the heavens. ⁷ From the days of our fathers to this day we have been in great guilt. And for our iniquities we, our kings, and our priests have been given into the hand of the kings of the lands, to the sword, to captivity, to plundering, and to utter shame, as it is today. ⁸ But now for a brief moment favor has been shown by the LORD our God, to leave us a remnant and to give us a secure hold[6] within his holy place, that our God may brighten our eyes and grant us a little reviving in our slavery. ⁹ For we are slaves. Yet our God has not forsaken us in our slavery, but has extended to us his steadfast love before the kings of Persia, to grant us some reviving to set up the house of our God,

---

[1] A *talent* was about 75 pounds or 34 kilograms [2] Revocalization; the number is missing in the Masoretic Text [3] A *daric* was a coin weighing about 1/4 ounce or 8.5 grams [4] A *satrap* was a Persian official [5] Hebrew *offspring* [6] Hebrew *nail*, or *tent-pin*

to repair its ruins, and to give us protection[1] in Judea and Jerusalem.

[10] "And now, O our God, what shall we say after this? For we have forsaken your commandments, [11] which you commanded by your servants the prophets, saying, 'The land that you are entering, to take possession of it, is a land impure with the impurity of the peoples of the lands, with their abominations that have filled it from end to end with their uncleanness. [12] Therefore do not give your daughters to their sons, neither take their daughters for your sons, and never seek their peace or prosperity, that you may be strong and eat the good of the land and leave it for an inheritance to your children forever.' [13] And after all that has come upon us for our evil deeds and for our great guilt, seeing that you, our God, have punished us less than our iniquities deserved and have given us such a remnant as this, [14] shall we break your commandments again and intermarry with the peoples who practice these abominations? Would you not be angry with us until you consumed us, so that there should be no remnant, nor any to escape? [15] O LORD, the God of Israel, you are just, for we are left a remnant that has escaped, as it is today. Behold, we are before you in our guilt, for none can stand before you because of this."

The People Confess Their Sin

10 While Ezra prayed and made confession, weeping and casting himself down before the house of God, a very great assembly of men, women, and children, gathered to him out of Israel, for the people wept bitterly. [2] And Shecaniah the son of Jehiel, of the sons of Elam, addressed Ezra: "We have broken faith with our God and have married foreign women from the peoples of the land, but even now there is hope for Israel in spite of this. [3] Therefore let us make a covenant with our God to put away all these wives and their children, according to the counsel of my lord[2] and of those who tremble at the commandment of our God, and let it be done according to the Law. [4] Arise, for it is your task, and we are with you; be strong and do it." [5] Then Ezra arose and made the leading priests and Levites and all Israel take an oath that they would do as had been said. So they took the oath. [6] Then Ezra withdrew from before the house of God and went to the chamber of Jehohanan

the son of Eliashib, where he spent the night,[3] neither eating bread nor drinking water, for he was mourning over the faithlessness of the exiles. [7] And a proclamation was made throughout Judah and Jerusalem to all the returned exiles that they should assemble at Jerusalem, [8] and that if anyone did not come within three days, by order of the officials and the elders all his property should be forfeited, and he himself banned from the congregation of the exiles.

[9] Then all the men of Judah and Benjamin assembled at Jerusalem within the three days. It was the ninth month, on the twentieth day of the month. And all the people sat in the open square before the house of God, trembling because of this matter and because of the heavy rain. [10] And Ezra the priest stood up and said to them, "You have broken faith and married foreign women, and so increased the guilt of Israel. [11] Now then make confession to the LORD, the God of your fathers and do his will. Separate yourselves from the peoples of the land and from the foreign wives." [12] Then all the assembly answered with a loud voice, "It is so; we must do as you have said. [13] But the people are many, and it is a time of heavy rain; we cannot stand in the open. Nor is this a task for one day or for two, for we have greatly transgressed in this matter. [14] Let our officials stand for the whole assembly. Let all in our cities who have taken foreign wives come at appointed times, and with them the elders and judges of every city, until the fierce wrath of our God over this matter is turned away from us." [15] Only Jonathan the son of Asahel and Jahzeiah the son of Tikvah opposed this, and Meshullam and Shabbethai the Levite supported them.

[16] Then the returned exiles did so. Ezra the priest selected men,[4] heads of fathers' houses, according to their fathers' houses, each of them designated by name. On the first day of the tenth month they sat down to examine the matter; [17] and by the first day of the first month they had come to the end of all the men who had married foreign women.

Those Guilty of Intermarriage

[18] Now there were found some of the sons of the priests who had married foreign women: Maaseiah, Eliezer, Jarib, and Gedaliah, some of the sons of Jeshua the son of Jozadak and his

[1] Hebrew a wall [2] Or of the Lord [3] Probable reading; Hebrew where he went [4] Syriac; Hebrew And there were selected Ezra...

brothers. [19] They pledged themselves to put away their wives, and their guilt offering was a ram of the flock for their guilt.[1] [20] Of the sons of Immer: Hanani and Zebadiah. [21] Of the sons of Harim: Maaseiah, Elijah, Shemaiah, Jehiel, and Uzziah. [22] Of the sons of Pashhur: Elioenai, Maaseiah, Ishmael, Nethanel, Jozabad, and Elasah.

[23] Of the Levites: Jozabad, Shimei, Kelaiah (that is, Kelita), Pethahiah, Judah, and Eliezer. [24] Of the singers: Eliashib. Of the gatekeepers: Shallum, Telem, and Uri.

[25] And of Israel: of the sons of Parosh: Ramiah, Izziah, Malchijah, Mijamin, Eleazar, Hashabiah,[2] and Benaiah. [26] Of the sons of Elam: Mattaniah, Zechariah, Jehiel, Abdi, Jeremoth, and Elijah. [27] Of the sons of Zattu: Elioenai, Eliashib, Mattaniah, Jeremoth, Zabad, and Aziza. [28] Of the sons of Bebai were Jehohanan, Hananiah, Zabbai, and Athlai. [29] Of the sons of Bani were Meshullam, Malluch, Adaiah, Jashub, Sheal, and Jeremoth. [30] Of the sons of Pahath-moab: Adna, Chelal, Benaiah, Maaseiah, Mattaniah, Bezalel, Binnui, and Manasseh. [31] Of the sons of Harim: Eliezer, Isshijah, Malchijah, Shemaiah, Shimeon, [32] Benjamin, Malluch, and Shemariah. [33] Of the sons of Hashum: Mattenai, Mattattah, Zabad, Eliphelet, Jeremai, Manasseh, and Shimei. [34] Of the sons of Bani: Maadai, Amram, Uel, [35] Benaiah, Bedeiah, Cheluhi, [36] Vaniah, Meremoth, Eliashib, [37] Mattaniah, Mattenai, Jaasu. [38] Of the sons of Binnui:[3] Shimei, [39] Shelemiah, Nathan, Adaiah, [40] Machnadebai, Shashai, Sharai, [41] Azarel, Shelemiah, Shemariah, [42] Shallum, Amariah, and Joseph. [43] Of the sons of Nebo: Jeiel, Mattithiah, Zabad, Zebina, Jaddai, Joel, and Benaiah. [44] All these had married foreign women, and some of the women had even borne children.[4]

---

[1] Or as their reparation [2] Septuagint; Hebrew *Malchijah* [3] Septuagint; Hebrew *Bani, Binnui* [4] Or and they put them away with their children

NEHEMIAH

Report from Jerusalem

1 The words of Nehemiah the son of Hacaliah.
Now it happened in the month of Chislev,
in the twentieth year, as I was in Susa the
citadel, ² that Hanani, one of my brothers,
came with certain men from Judah. And I
asked them concerning the Jews who escaped,
who had survived the exile, and concerning
Jerusalem. ³ And they said to me, "The remnant
there in the province who had survived the
exile is in great trouble and shame. The wall
of Jerusalem is broken down, and its gates are
destroyed by fire."

Nehemiah's Prayer

⁴ As soon as I heard these words I sat down
and wept and mourned for days, and I continued fasting and praying before the God of
heaven. ⁵ And I said, "O LORD God of heaven,
the great and awesome God who keeps covenant and steadfast love with those who love
him and keep his commandments, ⁶ let your
ear be attentive and your eyes open, to hear the
prayer of your servant that I now pray before
you day and night for the people of Israel your
servants, confessing the sins of the people of
Israel, which we have sinned against you. Even
I and my father's house have sinned. ⁷ We have
acted very corruptly against you and have not
kept the commandments, the statutes, and
the rules that you commanded your servant
Moses. ⁸ Remember the word that you commanded your servant Moses, saying, 'If you
are unfaithful, I will scatter you among the
peoples, ⁹ but if you return to me and keep my
commandments and do them, though your
outcasts are in the uttermost parts of heaven,
from there I will gather them and bring them
to the place that I have chosen, to make my
name dwell there.' ¹⁰ They are your servants
and your people, whom you have redeemed
by your great power and by your strong hand.
¹¹ O Lord, let your ear be attentive to the prayer
of your servant, and to the prayer of your servants who delight to fear your name, and give
success to your servant today, and grant him
mercy in the sight of this man."

Now I was cupbearer to the king.

Nehemiah Sent to Judah

2 In the month of Nisan, in the twentieth
year of King Artaxerxes, when wine was
before him, I took up the wine and gave it to the
king. Now I had not been sad in his presence.
² And the king said to me, "Why is your face sad,
seeing you are not sick? This is nothing but sadness of the heart." Then I was very much afraid.
³ I said to the king, "Let the king live forever!
Why should not my face be sad, when the city,
the place of my fathers' graves, lies in ruins, and
its gates have been destroyed by fire?" ⁴ Then the
king said to me, "What are you requesting?" So
I prayed to the God of heaven. ⁵ And I said to the
king, "If it pleases the king, and if your servant
has found favor in your sight, that you send
me to Judah, to the city of my fathers' graves,
that I may rebuild it." ⁶ And the king said to me
(the queen sitting beside him), "How long will
you be gone, and when will you return?" So it
pleased the king to send me when I had given
him a time. ⁷ And I said to the king, "If it pleases
the king, let letters be given me to the governors
of the province Beyond the River, that they may
let me pass through until I come to Judah, ⁸ and
a letter to Asaph, the keeper of the king's forest,
that he may give me timber to make beams for
the gates of the fortress of the temple, and for
the wall of the city, and for the house that I shall
occupy." And the king granted me what I asked,
for the good hand of my God was upon me.

Nehemiah Inspects Jerusalem's Walls

⁹ Then I came to the governors of the province Beyond the River and gave them the
king's letters. Now the king had sent with
me officers of the army and horsemen. ¹⁰ But
when Sanballat the Horonite and Tobiah the
Ammonite servant heard this, it displeased
them greatly that someone had come to seek
the welfare of the people of Israel.

¹¹ So I went to Jerusalem and was there three
days. ¹² Then I arose in the night, I and a few
men with me. And I told no one what my God
had put into my heart to do for Jerusalem.
There was no animal with me but the one on
which I rode. ¹³ I went out by night by the Valley
Gate to the Dragon Spring and to the Dung
Gate, and I inspected the walls of Jerusalem
that were broken down and its gates that had

been destroyed by fire. [14] Then I went on to the Fountain Gate and to the King's Pool, but there was no room for the animal that was under me to pass. [15] Then I went up in the night by the valley and inspected the wall, and I turned back and entered by the Valley Gate, and so returned. [16] And the officials did not know where I had gone or what I was doing, and I had not yet told the Jews, the priests, the nobles, the officials, and the rest who were to do the work.

[17] Then I said to them, "You see the trouble we are in, how Jerusalem lies in ruins with its gates burned. Come, let us build the wall of Jerusalem, that we may no longer suffer derision." [18] And I told them of the hand of my God that had been upon me for good, and also of the words that the king had spoken to me. And they said, "Let us rise up and build." So they strengthened their hands for the good work. [19] But when Sanballat the Horonite and Tobiah the Ammonite servant and Geshem the Arab heard of it, they jeered at us and despised us and said, "What is this thing that you are doing? Are you rebelling against the king?" [20] Then I replied to them, "The God of heaven will make us prosper, and we his servants will arise and build, but you have no portion or right or claim[1] in Jerusalem."

Rebuilding the Wall

3 Then Eliashib the high priest rose up with his brothers the priests, and they built the Sheep Gate. They consecrated it and set its doors. They consecrated it as far as the Tower of the Hundred, as far as the Tower of Hananel. [2] And next to him the men of Jericho built. And next to them[2] Zaccur the son of Imri built.

[3] The sons of Hassenaah built the Fish Gate. They laid its beams and set its doors, its bolts, and its bars. [4] And next to them Meremoth the son of Uriah, son of Hakkoz repaired. And next to them Meshullam the son of Berechiah, son of Meshezabel repaired. And next to them Zadok the son of Baana repaired. [5] And next to them the Tekoites repaired, but their nobles would not stoop to serve their Lord.[3]

[6] Joiada the son of Paseah and Meshullam the son of Besodeiah repaired the Gate of Yeshanah.[4] They laid its beams and set its doors, its bolts, and its bars. [7] And next to them repaired Melatiah the Gibeonite and Jadon

the Meronothite, the men of Gibeon and of Mizpah, the seat of the governor of the province Beyond the River. [8] Next to them Uzziel the son of Harhaiah, goldsmiths, repaired. Next to him Hananiah, one of the perfumers, repaired, and they restored Jerusalem as far as the Broad Wall. [9] Next to them Rephaiah the son of Hur, ruler of half the district of[5] Jerusalem, repaired. [10] Next to them Jedaiah the son of Harumaph repaired opposite his house. And next to him Hattush the son of Hashabneiah repaired. [11] Malchijah the son of Harim and Hasshub the son of Pahath-moab repaired another section and the Tower of the Ovens. [12] Next to him Shallum the son of Hallohesh, ruler of half the district of Jerusalem, repaired, he and his daughters.

[13] Hanun and the inhabitants of Zanoah repaired the Valley Gate. They rebuilt it and set its doors, its bolts, and its bars, and repaired a thousand cubits[6] of the wall, as far as the Dung Gate.

[14] Malchijah the son of Rechab, ruler of the district of Beth-haccherem, repaired the Dung Gate. He rebuilt it and set its doors, its bolts, and its bars.

[15] And Shallum the son of Col-hozeh, ruler of the district of Mizpah, repaired the Fountain Gate. He rebuilt it and covered it and set its doors, its bolts, and its bars. And he built the wall of the Pool of Shelah of the king's garden, as far as the stairs that go down from the city of David. [16] After him Nehemiah the son of Azbuk, ruler of half the district of Beth-zur, repaired to a point opposite the tombs of David, as far as the artificial pool, and as far as the house of the mighty men. [17] After him the Levites repaired: Rehum the son of Bani. Next to him Hashabiah, ruler of half the district of Keilah, repaired for his district. [18] After him their brothers repaired: Bavvai the son of Henadad, ruler of half the district of Keilah. [19] Next to him Ezer the son of Jeshua, ruler of Mizpah, repaired another section opposite the ascent to the armory at the buttress.[7] [20] After him Baruch the son of Zabbai repaired[8] another section from the buttress to the door of the house of Eliashib the high priest. [21] After him Meremoth the son of Uriah, son of Hakkoz repaired another section from the door of the house of Eliashib to the end of the house of Eliashib. [22] After him

---

[1] Or *memorial* [2] Hebrew *him* [3] Or *lords* [4] Or *of the old city* [5] Or *foreman of half the portion assigned to*; also verses 12, 14, 15, 16, 17, 18 [6] A *cubit* was about 18 inches or 45 centimeters [7] Or *corner*; also verses 20, 24, 25 [8] Some manuscripts *vigorously repaired*

the priests, the men of the surrounding area, repaired. [23] After them Benjamin and Hasshub repaired opposite their house. After them Azariah the son of Maaseiah, son of Ananiah repaired beside his own house. [24] After him Binnui the son of Henadad repaired another section, from the house of Azariah to the buttress and to the corner. [25] Palal the son of Uzai repaired opposite the buttress and the tower projecting from the upper house of the king at the court of the guard. After him Pedaiah the son of Parosh [26] and the temple servants living on Ophel repaired to a point opposite the Water Gate on the east and the projecting tower. [27] After him the Tekoites repaired another section opposite the great projecting tower as far as the wall of Ophel.

[28] Above the Horse Gate the priests repaired, each one opposite his own house. [29] After them Zadok the son of Immer repaired opposite his own house. After him Shemaiah the son of Shecaniah, the keeper of the East Gate, repaired. [30] After him Hananiah the son of Shelemiah and Hanun the sixth son of Zalaph repaired another section. After him Meshullam the son of Berechiah repaired opposite his chamber. [31] After him Malchijah, one of the goldsmiths, repaired as far as the house of the temple servants and of the merchants, opposite the Muster Gate,[1] and to the upper chamber of the corner. [32] And between the upper chamber of the corner and the Sheep Gate the goldsmiths and the merchants repaired.

Opposition to the Work

4 [2] Now when Sanballat heard that we were building the wall, he was angry and greatly enraged, and he jeered at the Jews. [2] And he said in the presence of his brothers and of the army of Samaria, "What are these feeble Jews doing? Will they restore it for themselves?[3] Will they sacrifice? Will they finish up in a day? Will they revive the stones out of the heaps of rubbish, and burned ones at that?" [3] Tobiah the Ammonite was beside him, and he said, "Yes, what they are building—if a fox goes up on it he will break down their stone wall!" [4] Hear, O our God, for we are despised. Turn back their taunt on their own heads and give them up to be plundered in a land where they are captives. [5] Do not cover their guilt, and let not their sin be blotted out from your sight, for they have

provoked you to anger in the presence of the builders.

[6] So we built the wall. And all the wall was joined together to half its height, for the people had a mind to work.

[7] [4] But when Sanballat and Tobiah and the Arabs and the Ammonites and the Ashdodites heard that the repairing of the walls of Jerusalem was going forward and that the breaches were beginning to be closed, they were very angry. [8] And they all plotted together to come and fight against Jerusalem and to cause confusion in it. [9] And we prayed to our God and set a guard as a protection against them day and night.

[10] In Judah it was said,[5] "The strength of those who bear the burdens is failing. There is too much rubble. By ourselves we will not be able to rebuild the wall." [11] And our enemies said, "They will not know or see till we come among them and kill them and stop the work." [12] At that time the Jews who lived near them came from all directions and said to us ten times, "You must return to us."[6] [13] So in the lowest parts of the space behind the wall, in open places, I stationed the people by their clans, with their swords, their spears, and their bows. [14] And I looked and arose and said to the nobles and to the officials and to the rest of the people, "Do not be afraid of them. Remember the Lord, who is great and awesome, and fight for your brothers, your sons, your daughters, your wives, and your homes."

The Work Resumes

[15] When our enemies heard that it was known to us and that God had frustrated their plan, we all returned to the wall, each to his work. [16] From that day on, half of my servants worked on construction, and half held the spears, shields, bows, and coats of mail. And the leaders stood behind the whole house of Judah, [17] who were building on the wall. Those who carried burdens were loaded in such a way that each labored on the work with one hand and held his weapon with the other. [18] And each of the builders had his sword strapped at his side while he built. The man who sounded the trumpet was beside me. [19] And I said to the nobles and to the officials and to the rest of the people, "The work is great and widely spread, and we are separated on the wall, far from one another. [20] In the place where you hear the sound of the trumpet, rally to us there. Our God will fight for us."

---

[1] Or *Hammiphkad Gate* [2] Ch 3:33 in Hebrew [3] Or *Will they commit themselves to God?* [4] Ch 4:1 in Hebrew [5] Hebrew *Judah said* [6] The meaning of the Hebrew is uncertain

[21] So we labored at the work, and half of them held the spears from the break of dawn until the stars came out. [22] I also said to the people at that time, "Let every man and his servant pass the night within Jerusalem, that they may be a guard for us by night and may labor by day." [23] So neither I nor my brothers nor my servants nor the men of the guard who followed me, none of us took off our clothes; each kept his weapon at his right hand.[1]

Nehemiah Stops Oppression of the Poor

5 Now there arose a great outcry of the people and of their wives against their Jewish brothers. [2] For there were those who said, "With our sons and our daughters, we are many. So let us get grain, that we may eat and keep alive." [3] There were also those who said, "We are mortgaging our fields, our vineyards, and our houses to get grain because of the famine." [4] And there were those who said, "We have borrowed money for the king's tax on our fields and our vineyards. [5] Now our flesh is as the flesh of our brothers, our children are as their children. Yet we are forcing our sons and our daughters to be slaves, and some of our daughters have already been enslaved, but it is not in our power to help it, for other men have our fields and our vineyards."

[6] I was very angry when I heard their outcry and these words. [7] I took counsel with myself, and I brought charges against the nobles and the officials. I said to them, "You are exacting interest, each from his brother." And I held a great assembly against them [8] and said to them, "We, as far as we are able, have bought back our Jewish brothers who have been sold to the nations, but you even sell your brothers that they may be sold to us!" They were silent and could not find a word to say. [9] So I said, "The thing that you are doing is not good. Ought you not to walk in the fear of our God to prevent the taunts of the nations our enemies? [10] Moreover, I and my brothers and my servants are lending them money and grain. Let us abandon this exacting of interest. [11] Return to them this very day their fields, their vineyards, their olive orchards, and their houses, and the percentage of money, grain, wine, and oil that you have been exacting from them." [12] Then they said, "We will restore these and require nothing from them. We will do as you say." And I called the priests and made them swear to do as they had promised. [13] I also shook out the fold[2] of my garment and said, "So may God shake out every man from his house and from his labor who does not keep this promise. So may he be shaken out and emptied." And all the assembly said "Amen" and praised the LORD. And the people did as they had promised.

Nehemiah's Generosity

[14] Moreover, from the time that I was appointed to be their governor in the land of Judah, from the twentieth year to the thirty-second year of Artaxerxes the king, twelve years, neither I nor my brothers ate the food allowance of the governor. [15] The former governors who were before me laid heavy burdens on the people and took from them for their daily ration[3] forty shekels[4] of silver. Even their servants lorded it over the people. But I did not do so, because of the fear of God. [16] I also persevered in the work on this wall, and we acquired no land, and all my servants were gathered there for the work. [17] Moreover, there were at my table 150 men, Jews and officials, besides those who came to us from the nations that were around us. [18] Now what was prepared at my expense[5] for each day was one ox and six choice sheep and birds, and every ten days all kinds of wine in abundance. Yet for all this I did not demand the food allowance of the governor, because the service was too heavy on this people. [19] Remember for my good, O my God, all that I have done for this people.

Conspiracy Against Nehemiah

6 Now when Sanballat and Tobiah and Geshem the Arab and the rest of our enemies heard that I had built the wall and that there was no breach left in it (although up to that time I had not set up the doors in the gates), [2] Sanballat and Geshem sent to me, saying, "Come and let us meet together at Hakkephirim in the plain of Ono." But they intended to do me harm. [3] And I sent messengers to them, saying, "I am doing a great work and I cannot come down. Why should the work stop while I leave it and come down to you?" [4] And they sent to me four times in this way, and I answered them in the same manner. [5] In the same way Sanballat for the fifth time sent his servant to me with an open letter in

---

[1] Or *his weapon when drinking*   [2] Hebrew *bosom*   [3] Compare Vulgate; Hebrew *took from them for food and wine after*   [4] A shekel was about 2/5 ounce or 11 grams
[5] Or *prepared for me*

his hand. [6] In it was written, "It is reported among the nations, and Geshem[1] also says it, that you and the Jews intend to rebel; that is why you are building the wall. And according to these reports you wish to become their king. [7] And you have also set up prophets to proclaim concerning you in Jerusalem, 'There is a king in Judah.' And now the king will hear of these reports. So now come and let us take counsel together." [8] Then I sent to him, saying, "No such things as you say have been done, for you are inventing them out of your own mind." [9] For they all wanted to frighten us, thinking, "Their hands will drop from the work, and it will not be done." But now, O God,[2] strengthen my hands.

[10] Now when I went into the house of Shemaiah the son of Delaiah, son of Mehetabel, who was confined to his home, he said, "Let us meet together in the house of God, within the temple. Let us close the doors of the temple, for they are coming to kill you. They are coming to kill you by night." [11] But I said, "Should such a man as I run away? And what man such as I could go into the temple and live?[3] I will not go in." [12] And I understood and saw that God had not sent him, but he had pronounced the prophecy against me because Tobiah and Sanballat had hired him. [13] For this purpose he was hired, that I should be afraid and act in this way and sin, and so they could give me a bad name in order to taunt me. [14] Remember Tobiah and Sanballat, O my God, according to these things that they did, and also the prophetess Noadiah and the rest of the prophets who wanted to make me afraid.

The Wall Is Finished

[15] So the wall was finished on the twenty-fifth day of the month Elul, in fifty-two days. [16] And when all our enemies heard of it, all the nations around us were afraid and fell greatly in their own esteem, for they perceived that this work had been accomplished with the help of our God. [17] Moreover, in those days the nobles of Judah sent many letters to Tobiah, and Tobiah's letters came to them. [18] For many in Judah were bound by oath to him, because he was the son-in-law of Shecaniah the son of Arah: and his son Jehohanan had taken the daughter of Meshullam the son of Berechiah as his wife. [19] Also they spoke of

his good deeds in my presence and reported my words to him. And Tobiah sent letters to make me afraid.

7 Now when the wall had been built and I had set up the doors, and the gatekeepers, the singers, and the Levites had been appointed, [2] I gave my brother Hanani and Hananiah the governor of the castle charge over Jerusalem, for he was a more faithful and God-fearing man than many. [3] And I said to them, "Let not the gates of Jerusalem be opened until the sun is hot. And while they are still standing guard, let them shut and bar the doors. Appoint guards from among the inhabitants of Jerusalem, some at their guard posts and some in front of their own homes." [4] The city was wide and large, but the people within it were few, and no houses had been rebuilt.

Lists of Returned Exiles

[5] Then my God put it into my heart to assemble the nobles and the officials and the people to be enrolled by genealogy. And I found the book of the genealogy of those who came up at the first, and I found written in it:

[6] These were the people of the province who came up out of the captivity of those exiles whom Nebuchadnezzar the king of Babylon had carried into exile. They returned to Jerusalem and Judah, each to his town. [7] They came with Zerubbabel, Jeshua, Nehemiah, Azariah, Raamiah, Nahamani, Mordecai, Bilshan, Mispereth, Bigvai, Nehum, Baanah.

The number of the men of the people of Israel: [8] the sons of Parosh, 2,172. [9] The sons of Shephatiah, 372. [10] The sons of Arah, 652. [11] The sons of Pahath-moab, namely the sons of Jeshua and Joab, 2,818. [12] The sons of Elam, 1,254. [13] The sons of Zattu, 845. [14] The sons of Zaccai, 760. [15] The sons of Binnui, 648. [16] The sons of Bebai, 628. [17] The sons of Azgad, 2,322. [18] The sons of Adonikam, 667. [19] The sons of Bigvai, 2,067. [20] The sons of Adin, 655. [21] The sons of Ater, namely of Hezekiah, 98. [22] The sons of Hashum, 328. [23] The sons of Bezai, 324. [24] The sons of Hariph, 112. [25] The sons of Gibeon, 95. [26] The men of Bethlehem and Netophah, 188. [27] The men of Anathoth, 128. [28] The men of Beth-azmaveth, 42. [29] The men of Kiriath-jearim, Chephirah, and Beeroth, 743. [30] The men of Ramah and Geba, 621. [31] The men of Michmas, 122. [32] The men of Bethel and Ai, 123. [33] The men of the other Nebo, 52.

---

[1] Hebrew *Gashmu*　[2] Hebrew lacks *O God*　[3] *Or would go into the temple to save his life*

³⁴ The sons of the other Elam, 1,254. ³⁵ The sons of Harim, 320. ³⁶ The sons of Jericho, 345. ³⁷ The sons of Lod, Hadid, and Ono, 721. ³⁸ The sons of Senaah, 3,930.

³⁹ The priests: the sons of Jedaiah, namely the house of Jeshua, 973. ⁴⁰ The sons of Immer, 1,052. ⁴¹ The sons of Pashhur, 1,247. ⁴² The sons of Harim, 1,017.

⁴³ The Levites: the sons of Jeshua, namely of Kadmiel of the sons of Hodevah, 74. ⁴⁴ The singers: the sons of Asaph, 148. ⁴⁵ The gatekeepers: the sons of Shallum, the sons of Ater, the sons of Talmon, the sons of Akkub, the sons of Hatita, the sons of Shobai, 138.

⁴⁶ The temple servants: the sons of Ziha, the sons of Hasupha, the sons of Tabbaoth, ⁴⁷ the sons of Keros, the sons of Sia, the sons of Padon, ⁴⁸ the sons of Lebana, the sons of Hagaba, the sons of Shalmai, ⁴⁹ the sons of Hanan, the sons of Giddel, the sons of Gahar, ⁵⁰ the sons of Reaiah, the sons of Rezin, the sons of Nekoda, ⁵¹ the sons of Gazzam, the sons of Uzza, the sons of Paseah, ⁵² the sons of Besai, the sons of Meunim, the sons of Nephushesim, ⁵³ the sons of Bakbuk, the sons of Hakupha, the sons of Harhur, ⁵⁴ the sons of Bazlith, the sons of Mehida, the sons of Harsha, ⁵⁵ the sons of Barkos, the sons of Sisera, the sons of Temah, ⁵⁶ the sons of Neziah, the sons of Hatipha.

⁵⁷ The sons of Solomon's servants: the sons of Sotai, the sons of Sophereth, the sons of Perida, ⁵⁸ the sons of Jaala, the sons of Darkon, the sons of Giddel, ⁵⁹ the sons of Shephatiah, the sons of Hattil, the sons of Pochereth-hazzebaim, the sons of Amon.

⁶⁰ All the temple servants and the sons of Solomon's servants were 392.

⁶¹ The following were those who came up from Tel-melah, Tel-harsha, Cherub, Addon, and Immer, but they could not prove their fathers' houses nor their descent, whether they belonged to Israel: ⁶² the sons of Delaiah, the sons of Tobiah, the sons of Nekoda, 642. ⁶³ Also, of the priests: the sons of Hobaiah, the sons of Hakkoz, the sons of Barzillai (who had taken a wife of the daughters of Barzillai the Gileadite and was called by their name). ⁶⁴ These sought their registration among those enrolled in the genealogies, but it was not found there, so they were excluded from the priesthood as unclean. ⁶⁵ The governor told them that they were not to partake of the most holy food until a priest with Urim and Thummim should arise.

Totals of People and Gifts

⁶⁶ The whole assembly together was 42,360, ⁶⁷ besides their male and female servants, of whom there were 7,337. And they had 245 singers, male and female. ⁶⁸ Their horses were 736, their mules 245,¹ ⁶⁹ their camels 435, and their donkeys 6,720.

⁷⁰ Now some of the heads of fathers' houses gave to the work. The governor gave to the treasury 1,000 darics² of gold, 50 basins, 30 priests' garments and 500 minas³ of silver.⁴ ⁷¹ And some of the heads of fathers' houses gave into the treasury of the work 20,000 darics of gold and 2,200 minas of silver. ⁷² And what the rest of the people gave was 20,000 darics of gold, 2,000 minas of silver, and 67 priests' garments.

⁷³ So the priests, the Levites, the gatekeepers, the singers, some of the people, the temple servants, and all Israel, lived in their towns.

And when the seventh month had come, the people of Israel were in their towns.

Ezra Reads the Law

8 And all the people gathered as one man into the square before the Water Gate. And they told Ezra the scribe to bring the Book of the Law of Moses that the LORD had commanded Israel. ² So Ezra the priest brought the Law before the assembly, both men and women and all who could understand what they heard, on the first day of the seventh month. ³ And he read from it facing the square before the Water Gate from early morning until midday, in the presence of the men and the women and those who could understand. And the ears of all the people were attentive to the Book of the Law. ⁴ And Ezra the scribe stood on a wooden platform that they had made for the purpose. And beside him stood Mattithiah, Shema, Anaiah, Uriah, Hilkiah, and Maaseiah on his right hand, and Pedaiah, Mishael, Malchijah, Hashum, Hashbaddanah, Zechariah, and Meshullam on his left hand. ⁵ And Ezra opened the book in the sight of all the people, for he was above all the people, and as he opened it all the people stood. ⁶ And Ezra blessed the LORD, the great God, and all the people answered, "Amen, Amen," lifting up their hands. And they bowed their heads and worshiped the LORD with their faces to the ground. [7] Also Jeshua, Bani, Sherebiah, Jamin, Akkub, Shabbethai, Hodiah, Maaseiah, Kelita, Azariah, Jozabad, Hanan, Pelaiah, the Levites,[1] helped the people to understand the Law, while the people remained in their places. [8] They read from the book, from the Law of God, clearly,[2] and they gave the sense, so that the people understood the reading.

This Day Is Holy

[9] And Nehemiah, who was the governor, and Ezra the priest and scribe, and the Levites who taught the people said to all the people, "This day is holy to the LORD your God; do not mourn or weep." For all the people wept as they heard the words of the Law. [10] Then he said to them, "Go your way. Eat the fat and drink sweet wine and send portions to anyone who has nothing ready, for this day is holy to our Lord. And do not be grieved, for the joy of the LORD is your strength." [11] So the Levites calmed all the people, saying, "Be quiet, for this day is holy; do not be grieved." [12] And all the people went their way to eat and drink and to send portions and to make great rejoicing, because they had understood the words that were declared to them.

Feast of Booths Celebrated

[13] On the second day the heads of fathers' houses of all the people, with the priests and the Levites, came together to Ezra the scribe in order to study the words of the Law. [14] And they found it written in the Law that the LORD had commanded by Moses that the people of Israel should dwell in booths[3] during the feast of the seventh month, [15] and that they should proclaim it and publish it in all their towns and in Jerusalem, "Go out to the hills and bring branches of olive, wild olive, myrtle, palm, and other leafy trees to make booths, as it is written." [16] So the people went out and brought them and made booths for themselves, each on his roof, and in their courts and in the courts of the house of God, and in the square at the Water Gate and in the square at the Gate of Ephraim. [17] And all the assembly of those who had returned from the captivity made booths and lived in the booths, for from the days of Jeshua the son of Nun to that day the people of Israel had not done so. And there was very great rejoicing. [18] And day by day, from the first day to the last day, he read from the Book of the Law of God. They kept the feast seven days, and on the eighth day there was a solemn assembly, according to the rule.

The People of Israel Confess Their Sin

9 Now on the twenty-fourth day of this month the people of Israel were assembled with fasting and in sackcloth, and with earth on their heads. [2] And the Israelites[4] separated themselves from all foreigners and stood and confessed their sins and the iniquities of their fathers. [3] And they stood up in their place and read from the Book of the Law of the LORD their God for a quarter of the day; for another quarter of it they made confession and worshiped the LORD their God. [4] On the stairs of the Levites stood Jeshua, Bani, Kadmiel, Shebaniah, Bunni, Sherebiah, Bani, and Chenani; and they cried with a loud voice to the LORD their God. [5] Then the Levites, Jeshua, Kadmiel, Bani, Hashabneiah, Sherebiah, Hodiah, Shebaniah, and Pethahiah, said, "Stand up and bless the LORD your God from everlasting to everlasting. Blessed be your glorious name, which is exalted above all blessing and praise.

[6] [5] "You are the LORD, you alone. You have made heaven, the heaven of heavens, with all their host, the earth and all that is on it, the seas and all that is in them; and you preserve all of them; and the host of heaven worships you. [7] You are the LORD, the God who chose Abram and brought him out of Ur of the Chaldeans and gave him the name Abraham. [8] You found his heart faithful before you, and made with him the covenant to give to his offspring the land of the Canaanite, the Hittite, the Amorite, the Perizzite, the Jebusite, and the Girgashite. And you have kept your promise, for you are righteous.

[9] "And you saw the affliction of our fathers in Egypt and heard their cry at the Red Sea, [10] and performed signs and wonders against Pharaoh and all his servants and all the people of his land, for you knew that they acted arrogantly against our fathers. And you made a name for yourself, as it is to this day. [11] And you divided the sea before them, so that they went through the midst of the sea on dry land, and you cast their pursuers into the depths, as a stone into mighty waters. [12] By a pillar of cloud you led them in the day, and by a pillar of fire in the night to light for them the way in which they should go. [13] You came down on Mount Sinai and spoke with them from heaven and gave

---

[1] Vulgate; Hebrew *and the Levites* [2] Or *with interpretation, or paragraph by paragraph* [3] Or *temporary shelters* [4] Hebrew *the offspring of Israel* [5] Septuagint adds *And Ezra said*

them right rules and true laws, good statutes and commandments, [14] and you made known to them your holy Sabbath and commanded them commandments and statutes and a law by Moses your servant. [15] You gave them bread from heaven for their hunger and brought water for them out of the rock for their thirst, and you told them to go in to possess the land that you had sworn to give them.

[16] "But they and our fathers acted presumptuously and stiffened their neck and did not obey your commandments. [17] They refused to obey and were not mindful of the wonders that you performed among them, but they stiffened their neck and appointed a leader to return to their slavery in Egypt.[1] But you are a God ready to forgive, gracious and merciful, slow to anger and abounding in steadfast love, and did not forsake them. [18] Even when they had made for themselves a golden[2] calf and said, 'This is your God who brought you up out of Egypt,' and had committed great blasphemies, [19] you in your great mercies did not forsake them in the wilderness. The pillar of cloud to lead them in the way did not depart from them by day, nor the pillar of fire by night to light for them the way by which they should go. [20] You gave your good Spirit to instruct them and did not withhold your manna from their mouth and gave them water for their thirst. [21] Forty years you sustained them in the wilderness, and they lacked nothing. Their clothes did not wear out and their feet did not swell.

[22] "And you gave them kingdoms and peoples and allotted to them every corner. So they took possession of the land of Sihon king of Heshbon and the land of Og king of Bashan. [23] You multiplied their children as the stars of heaven, and you brought them into the land that you had told their fathers to enter and possess. [24] So the descendants went in and possessed the land, and you subdued before them the inhabitants of the land, the Canaanites, and gave them into their hand, with their kings and the peoples of the land, that they might do with them as they would. [25] And they captured fortified cities and a rich land, and took possession of houses full of all good things, cisterns already hewn, vineyards, olive orchards and fruit trees in abundance. So they ate and were filled and became fat and delighted themselves in your great goodness.

[26] "Nevertheless, they were disobedient and rebelled against you and cast your law behind their back and killed your prophets, who had warned them in order to turn them back to you, and they committed great blasphemies. [27] Therefore you gave them into the hand of their enemies, who made them suffer. And in the time of their suffering they cried out to you and you heard them from heaven, and according to your great mercies you gave them saviors who saved them from the hand of their enemies. [28] But after they had rest they did evil again before you, and you abandoned them to the hand of their enemies, so that they had dominion over them. Yet when they turned and cried to you, you heard from heaven, and many times you delivered them according to your mercies. [29] And you warned them in order to turn them back to your law. Yet they acted presumptuously and did not obey your commandments, but sinned against your rules, which if a person does them, he shall live by them, and they turned a stubborn shoulder and stiffened their neck and would not obey. [30] Many years you bore with them and warned them by your Spirit through your prophets. Yet they would not give ear. Therefore you gave them into the hand of the peoples of the lands. [31] Nevertheless, in your great mercies you did not make an end of them or forsake them, for you are a gracious and merciful God.

[32] "Now, therefore, our God, the great, the mighty, and the awesome God, who keeps covenant and steadfast love, let not all the hardship seem little to you that has come upon us, upon our kings, our princes, our priests, our prophets, our fathers, and all your people, since the time of the kings of Assyria until this day. [33] Yet you have been righteous in all that has come upon us, for you have dealt faithfully and we have acted wickedly. [34] Our kings, our princes, our priests, and our fathers have not kept your law or paid attention to your commandments and your warnings that you gave them. [35] Even in their own kingdom, and amid your great goodness that you gave them, and in the large and rich land that you set before them, they did not serve you or turn from their wicked works. [36] Behold, we are slaves this day; in the land that you gave to our fathers to enjoy its fruit and its good gifts, behold, we are slaves. [37] And its rich yield goes to the kings whom you have set over us because of our sins. They rule over our bodies

[1] Some Hebrew manuscripts; many Hebrew manuscripts *and in their rebellion appointed a leader to return to their slavery* [2] Hebrew *metal*

and over our livestock as they please, and we are in great distress.

38 [1] "Because of all this we make a firm covenant in writing; on the sealed document are the names of [2] our princes, our Levites, and our priests.

The People Who Sealed the Covenant

10 3 "On the seals are the names of [4] Nehemiah the governor, the son of Hacaliah, Zedekiah, 2 Seraiah, Azariah, Jeremiah, 3 Pashhur, Amariah, Malchijah, 4 Hattush, Shebaniah, Malluch, 5 Harim, Meremoth, Obadiah, 6 Daniel, Ginnethon, Baruch, 7 Meshullam, Abijah, Mijamin, 8 Maaziah, Bilgai, Shemaiah; these are the priests. 9 And the Levites: Jeshua the son of Azaniah, Binnui of the sons of Henadad, Kadmiel; 10 and their brothers, Shebaniah, Hodiah, Kelita, Pelaiah, Hanan, 11 Mica, Rehob, Hashabiah, 12 Zaccur, Sherebiah, Shebaniah, 13 Hodiah, Bani, Beninu. 14 The chiefs of the people: Parosh, Pahath-moab, Elam, Zattu, Bani, 15 Bunni, Azgad, Bebai, 16 Adonijah, Bigvai, Adin, 17 Ater, Hezekiah, Azzur, 18 Hodiah, Hashum, Bezai, 19 Hariph, Anathoth, Nebai, 20 Magpiash, Meshullam, Hezir, 21 Meshezabel, Zadok, Jaddua, 22 Pelatiah, Hanan, Anaiah, 23 Hoshea, Hananiah, Hasshub, 24 Hallohesh, Pilha, Shobek, 25 Rehum, Hashabnah, Maaseiah, 26 Ahiah, Hanan, Anan, 27 Malluch, Harim, Baanah.

The Obligations of the Covenant

28 "The rest of the people, the priests, the Levites, the gatekeepers, the singers, the temple servants, and all who have separated themselves from the peoples of the lands to the Law of God, their wives, their sons, their daughters, all who have knowledge and understanding, 29 join with their brothers, their nobles, and enter into a curse and an oath to walk in God's Law that was given by Moses the servant of God, and to observe and do all the commandments of the LORD our Lord and his rules and his statutes. 30 We will not give our daughters to the peoples of the land or take their daughters for our sons. 31 And if the peoples of the land bring in goods or any grain on the Sabbath day to sell, we will not buy from them on the Sabbath or on a holy day. And we will forego the crops of the seventh year and the exaction of every debt.

32 "We also take on ourselves the obligation to give yearly a third part of a shekel [5] for the service of the house of our God: 33 for the showbread, the regular grain offering, the regular burnt offering, the Sabbaths, the new moons, the appointed feasts, the holy things, and the sin offerings to make atonement for Israel, and for all the work of the house of our God. 34 We, the priests, the Levites, and the people, have likewise cast lots for the wood offering, to bring it into the house of our God, according to our fathers' houses, at times appointed, year by year, to burn on the altar of the LORD our God, as it is written in the Law. 35 We obligate ourselves to bring the firstfruits of our ground and the firstfruits of all fruit of every tree, year by year, to the house of the LORD; 36 also to bring to the house of our God, to the priests who minister in the house of our God, the firstborn of our sons and of our cattle, as it is written in the Law, and the firstborn of our herds and of our flocks; 37 and to bring the first of our dough, and our contributions, the fruit of every tree, the wine and the oil, to the priests, to the chambers of the house of our God; and to bring to the Levites the tithes from our ground, for it is the Levites who collect the tithes in all our towns where we labor. 38 And the priest, the son of Aaron, shall be with the Levites when the Levites receive the tithes. And the Levites shall bring up the tithe of the tithes to the house of our God, to the chambers of the storehouse. 39 For the people of Israel and the sons of Levi shall bring the contribution of grain, wine, and oil to the chambers, where the vessels of the sanctuary are, as well as the priests who minister, and the gatekeepers and the singers. We will not neglect the house of our God."

The Leaders in Jerusalem

11 Now the leaders of the people lived in Jerusalem. And the rest of the people cast lots to bring one out of ten to live in Jerusalem the holy city, while nine out of ten [6] remained in the other towns. 2 And the people blessed all the men who willingly offered to live in Jerusalem.

3 These are the chiefs of the province who lived in Jerusalem; but in the towns of Judah everyone lived on his property in their towns: Israel, the priests, the Levites, the temple servants, and the descendants of Solomon's servants. 4 And in Jerusalem lived certain of the sons of Judah and of the sons of Benjamin. Of the sons of Judah: Athaiah the son of Uzziah, son of Zechariah, son of Amariah, son of

---

[1] Ch 10:1 in Hebrew [2] Hebrew lacks *the names of* [3] Ch 10:2 in Hebrew [4] Hebrew lacks *the names of* [5] A *shekel* was about 2/5 ounce or 11 grams [6] Hebrew *nine hands*

Shephatiah, son of Mahalalel, of the sons of Perez; [5] and Maaseiah the son of Baruch, son of Col-hozeh, son of Hazaiah, son of Adaiah, son of Joiarib, son of Zechariah, son of the Shilonite. [6] All the sons of Perez who lived in Jerusalem were 468 valiant men.

[7] And these are the sons of Benjamin: Sallu the son of Meshullam, son of Joed, son of Pedaiah, son of Kolaiah, son of Maaseiah, son of Ithiel, son of Jeshaiah, [8] and his brothers, men of valor, 928.[1] [9] Joel the son of Zichri was their overseer; and Judah the son of Hassenuah was second over the city.

[10] Of the priests: Jedaiah the son of Joiarib, Jachin, [11] Seraiah the son of Hilkiah, son of Meshullam, son of Zadok, son of Meraioth, son of Ahitub, ruler of the house of God, [12] and their brothers who did the work of the house, 822; and Adaiah the son of Jeroham, son of Pelaliah, son of Amzi, son of Zechariah, son of Pashhur, son of Malchijah, [13] and his brothers, heads of fathers' houses, 242; and Amashsai, the son of Azarel, son of Ahzai, son of Meshillemoth, son of Immer, [14] and their brothers, mighty men of valor, 128; their overseer was Zabdiel the son of Haggedolim.

[15] And of the Levites: Shemaiah the son of Hasshub, son of Azrikam, son of Hashabiah, son of Bunni; [16] and Shabbethai and Jozabad, of the chiefs of the Levites, who were over the outside work of the house of God; [17] and Mattaniah the son of Mica, son of Zabdi, son of Asaph, who was the leader of the praise,[2] who gave thanks, and Bakbukiah, the second among his brothers; and Abda the son of Shammua, son of Galal, son of Jeduthun. [18] All the Levites in the holy city were 284.

[19] The gatekeepers, Akkub, Talmon and their brothers, who kept watch at the gates, were 172. [20] And the rest of Israel, and of the priests and the Levites, were in all the towns of Judah, every one in his inheritance. [21] But the temple servants lived on Ophel; and Ziha and Gishpa were over the temple servants.

[22] The overseer of the Levites in Jerusalem was Uzzi the son of Bani, son of Hashabiah, son of Mattaniah, son of Mica, of the sons of Asaph, the singers, over the work of the house of God. [23] For there was a command from the king concerning them, and a fixed provision for the singers, as every day required. [24] And Pethahiah the son of Meshezabel, of the sons of Zerah the son of Judah, was at the king's side[3] in all matters concerning the people.

Villages Outside Jerusalem

[25] And as for the villages, with their fields, some of the people of Judah lived in Kiriath-arba and its villages, and in Dibon and its villages, and in Jekabzeel and its villages, [26] and in Jeshua and in Moladah and Beth-pelet, [27] in Hazar-shual, in Beersheba and its villages, [28] in Ziklag, in Meconah and its villages, [29] in En-rimmon, in Zorah, in Jarmuth, [30] Zanoah, Adullam, and their villages, Lachish and its fields, and Azekah and its villages. So they encamped from Beersheba to the Valley of Hinnom. [31] The people of Benjamin also lived from Geba onward, at Michmash, Aija, Bethel and its villages, [32] Anathoth, Nob, Ananiah, [33] Hazor, Ramah, Gittaim, [34] Hadid, Zeboim, Neballat, [35] Lod, and Ono, the valley of craftsmen. [36] And certain divisions of the Levites in Judah were assigned to Benjamin.

Priests and Levites

12 These are the priests and the Levites who came up with Zerubbabel the son of Shealtiel, and Jeshua: Seraiah, Jeremiah, Ezra, [2] Amariah, Malluch, Hattush, [3] Shecaniah, Rehum, Meremoth, [4] Iddo, Ginnethoi, Abijah, [5] Mijamin, Maadiah, Bilgah, [6] Shemaiah, Joiarib, Jedaiah, [7] Sallu, Amok, Hilkiah, Jedaiah. These were the chiefs of the priests and of their brothers in the days of Jeshua.

[8] And the Levites: Jeshua, Binnui, Kadmiel, Sherebiah, Judah, and Mattaniah, who with his brothers was in charge of the songs of thanksgiving. [9] And Bakbukiah and Unni and their brothers stood opposite them in the service. [10] And Jeshua was the father of Joiakim, Joiakim the father of Eliashib, Eliashib the father of Joiada, [11] Joiada the father of Jonathan, and Jonathan the father of Jaddua.

[12] And in the days of Joiakim were priests, heads of fathers' houses: of Seraiah, Meraiah; of Jeremiah, Hananiah; [13] of Ezra, Meshullam; of Amariah, Jehohanan; [14] of Malluchi, Jonathan; of Shebaniah, Joseph; [15] of Harim, Adna; of Meraioth, Helkai; [16] of Iddo, Zechariah; of Ginnethon, Meshullam; [17] of Abijah, Zichri; of Miniamin, of Moadiah, Piltai; [18] of Bilgah, Shammua; of Shemaiah, Jehonathan; [19] of

---

[1] Compare Septuagint; Hebrew *Jeshaiah, and after him Gabbai, Sallai, 928* [2] Compare Septuagint, Vulgate; Hebrew *beginning* [3] Hebrew *hand*

Joiarib, Mattenai; of Jedaiah, Uzzi; ²⁰ of Sallai, Kallai; of Amok, Eber; ²¹ of Hilkiah, Hashabiah; of Jedaiah, Nethanel.

²² In the days of Eliashib, Joiada, Johanan, and Jaddua, the Levites were recorded as heads of fathers' houses; so too were the priests in the reign of Darius the Persian. ²³ As for the sons of Levi, their heads of fathers' houses were written in the Book of the Chronicles until the days of Johanan the son of Eliashib. ²⁴ And the chiefs of the Levites: Hashabiah, Sherebiah, and Jeshua the son of Kadmiel, with their brothers who stood opposite them, to praise and to give thanks, according to the commandment of David the man of God, watch by watch. ²⁵ Mattaniah, Bakbukiah, Obadiah, Meshullam, Talmon, and Akkub were gatekeepers standing guard at the storehouses of the gates. ²⁶ These were in the days of Joiakim the son of Jeshua son of Jozadak, and in the days of Nehemiah the governor and of Ezra, the priest and scribe.

Dedication of the Wall

²⁷ And at the dedication of the wall of Jerusalem they sought the Levites in all their places, to bring them to Jerusalem to celebrate the dedication with gladness, with thanksgivings and with singing, with cymbals, harps, and lyres. ²⁸ And the sons of the singers gathered together from the district surrounding Jerusalem and from the villages of the Netophathites; ²⁹ also from Beth-gilgal and from the region of Geba and Azmaveth, for the singers had built for themselves villages around Jerusalem. ³⁰ And the priests and the Levites purified themselves, and they purified the people and the gates and the wall.

³¹ Then I brought the leaders of Judah up onto the wall and appointed two great choirs that gave thanks. One went to the south on the wall to the Dung Gate. ³² And after them went Hoshaiah and half of the leaders of Judah, ³³ and Azariah, Ezra, Meshullam, ³⁴ Judah, Benjamin, Shemaiah, and Jeremiah, ³⁵ and certain of the priests' sons with trumpets: Zechariah the son of Jonathan, son of Shemaiah, son of Mattaniah, son of Micaiah, son of Zaccur, son of Asaph; ³⁶ and his relatives, Shemaiah, Azarel, Milalai, Gilalai, Maai, Nethanel, Judah, and Hanani, with the musical instruments of David the man of God. And Ezra the scribe went before them. ³⁷ At the Fountain Gate they went up straight before them by the stairs of the city of David, at the ascent of the wall, above the house of David, to the Water Gate on the east.

³⁸ The other choir of those who gave thanks went to the north, and I followed them with half of the people, on the wall, above the Tower of the Ovens, to the Broad Wall, ³⁹ and above the Gate of Ephraim, and by the Gate of Yeshanah,¹ and by the Fish Gate and the Tower of Hananel and the Tower of the Hundred, to the Sheep Gate; and they came to a halt at the Gate of the Guard. ⁴⁰ So both choirs of those who gave thanks stood in the house of God, and I and half of the officials with me; ⁴¹ and the priests Eliakim, Maaseiah, Miniamin, Micaiah, Elioenai, Zechariah, and Hananiah, with trumpets; ⁴² and Maaseiah, Shemaiah, Eleazar, Uzzi, Jehohanan, Malchijah, Elam, and Ezer. And the singers sang with Jezrahiah as their leader. ⁴³ And they offered great sacrifices that day and rejoiced, for God had made them rejoice with great joy; the women and children also rejoiced. And the joy of Jerusalem was heard far away.

Service at the Temple

⁴⁴ On that day men were appointed over the storerooms, the contributions, the firstfruits, and the tithes, to gather into them the portions required by the Law for the priests and for the Levites according to the fields of the towns, for Judah rejoiced over the priests and the Levites who ministered. ⁴⁵ And they performed the service of their God and the service of purification, as did the singers and the gatekeepers, according to the command of David and his son Solomon. ⁴⁶ For long ago in the days of David and Asaph there were directors of the singers, and there were songs² of praise and thanksgiving to God. ⁴⁷ And all Israel in the days of Zerubbabel and in the days of Nehemiah gave the daily portions for the singers and the gatekeepers; and they set apart that which was for the Levites; and the Levites set apart that which was for the sons of Aaron.

Nehemiah's Final Reforms

13 On that day they read from the Book of Moses in the hearing of the people. And in it was found written that no Ammonite or Moabite should ever enter the assembly of God, ² for they did not meet the people of Israel with bread and water, but hired Balaam against them to curse them—yet our God turned the curse into a blessing. ³ As soon as the people

¹ Or of the old city ² Or leaders

heard the law, they separated from Israel all those of foreign descent.

[4] Now before this, Eliashib the priest, who was appointed over the chambers of the house of our God, and who was related to Tobiah, [5] prepared for Tobiah a large chamber where they had previously put the grain offering, the frankincense, the vessels, and the tithes of grain, wine, and oil, which were given by commandment to the Levites, singers, and gatekeepers, and the contributions for the priests. [6] While this was taking place, I was not in Jerusalem, for in the thirty-second year of Artaxerxes king of Babylon I went to the king. And after some time I asked leave of the king [7] and came to Jerusalem, and I then discovered the evil that Eliashib had done for Tobiah, preparing for him a chamber in the courts of the house of God. [8] And I was very angry, and I threw all the household furniture of Tobiah out of the chamber. [9] Then I gave orders, and they cleansed the chambers, and I brought back there the vessels of the house of God, with the grain offering and the frankincense.

[10] I also found out that the portions of the Levites had not been given to them, so that the Levites and the singers, who did the work, had fled each to his field. [11] So I confronted the officials and said, "Why is the house of God forsaken?" And I gathered them together and set them in their stations. [12] Then all Judah brought the tithe of the grain, wine, and oil into the storehouses. [13] And I appointed as treasurers over the storehouses Shelemiah the priest, Zadok the scribe, and Pedaiah of the Levites, and as their assistant Hanan the son of Zaccur, son of Mattaniah, for they were considered reliable, and their duty was to distribute to their brothers. [14] Remember me, O my God, concerning this, and do not wipe out my good deeds that I have done for the house of my God and for his service.

[15] In those days I saw in Judah people treading winepresses on the Sabbath, and bringing in heaps of grain and loading them on donkeys, and also wine, grapes, figs, and all kinds of loads, which they brought into Jerusalem on the Sabbath day. And I warned them on the day when they sold food. [16] Tyrians also, who lived in the city, brought in fish and all kinds of goods and sold them on the Sabbath to the people of Judah, in Jerusalem itself! [17] Then I confronted the nobles of Judah and said to them, "What is this evil thing that you are doing, profaning the Sabbath day? [18] Did not

your fathers act in this way, and did not our God bring all this disaster[1] on us and on this city? Now you are bringing more wrath on Israel by profaning the Sabbath."

[19] As soon as it began to grow dark at the gates of Jerusalem before the Sabbath, I commanded that the doors should be shut and gave orders that they should not be opened until after the Sabbath. And I stationed some of my servants at the gates, that no load might be brought in on the Sabbath day. [20] Then the merchants and sellers of all kinds of wares lodged outside Jerusalem once or twice. [21] But I warned them and said to them, "Why do you lodge outside the wall? If you do so again, I will lay hands on you." From that time on they did not come on the Sabbath. [22] Then I commanded the Levites that they should purify themselves and come and guard the gates, to keep the Sabbath day holy. Remember this also in my favor, O my God, and spare me according to the greatness of your steadfast love.

[23] In those days also I saw the Jews who had married women of Ashdod, Ammon, and Moab. [24] And half of their children spoke the language of Ashdod, and they could not speak the language of Judah, but only the language of each people. [25] And I confronted them and cursed them and beat some of them and pulled out their hair. And I made them take an oath in the name of God, saying, "You shall not give your daughters to their sons, or take their daughters for your sons or for yourselves. [26] Did not Solomon king of Israel sin on account of such women? Among the many nations there was no king like him, and he was beloved by his God, and God made him king over all Israel. Nevertheless, foreign women made even him to sin, [27] Shall we then listen to you and do all this great evil and act treacherously against our God by marrying foreign women?"

[28] And one of the sons of Jehoiada, the son of Eliashib the high priest, was the son-in-law of Sanballat the Horonite. Therefore I chased him from me. [29] Remember them, O my God, because they have desecrated the priesthood and the covenant of the priesthood and the Levites.

[30] Thus I cleansed them from everything foreign, and I established the duties of the priests and Levites, each in his work; [31] and I provided for the wood offering at appointed times, and for the firstfruits.

Remember me, O my God, for good.

---

[1] The Hebrew word can mean *evil*, *harm*, or *disaster*, depending on the context

ESTHER

The King's Banquets

1 Now in the days of Ahasuerus, the Ahasuerus who reigned from India to Ethiopia over 127 provinces, [2] in those days when King Ahasuerus sat on his royal throne in Susa, the citadel, [3] in the third year of his reign he gave a feast for all his officials and servants. The army of Persia and Media and the nobles and governors of the provinces were before him, [4] while he showed the riches of his royal glory and the splendor and pomp of his greatness for many days, 180 days. [5] And when these days were completed, the king gave for all the people present in Susa the citadel, both great and small, a feast lasting for seven days in the court of the garden of the king's palace. [6] There were white cotton curtains and violet hangings fastened with cords of fine linen and purple to silver rods[1] and marble pillars, and also couches of gold and silver on a mosaic pavement of porphyry, marble, mother-of-pearl, and precious stones. [7] Drinks were served in golden vessels, vessels of different kinds, and the royal wine was lavished according to the bounty of the king. [8] And drinking was according to this edict: "There is no compulsion." For the king had given orders to all the staff of his palace to do as each man desired. [9] Queen Vashti also gave a feast for the women in the palace that belonged to King Ahasuerus.

Queen Vashti's Refusal

[10] On the seventh day, when the heart of the king was merry with wine, he commanded Mehuman, Biztha, Harbona, Bigtha and Abagtha, Zethar and Carkas, the seven eunuchs who served in the presence of King Ahasuerus, [11] to bring Queen Vashti before the king with her royal crown,[2] in order to show the peoples and the princes her beauty, for she was lovely to look at. [12] But Queen Vashti refused to come at the king's command delivered by the eunuchs. At this the king became enraged, and his anger burned within him.

[13] Then the king said to the wise men who knew the times (for this was the king's procedure toward all who were versed in law and judgment, [14] the men next to him being Carshena, Shethar, Admatha, Tarshish, Meres, Marsena, and Memucan, the seven princes of Persia and Media, who saw the king's face, and sat first in the kingdom): [15] "According to the law, what is to be done to Queen Vashti, because she has not performed the command of King Ahasuerus delivered by the eunuchs?" [16] Then Memucan said in the presence of the king and the officials, "Not only against the king has Queen Vashti done wrong, but also against all the officials and all the peoples who are in all the provinces of King Ahasuerus. [17] For the queen's behavior will be made known to all women, causing them to look at their husbands with contempt,[3] since they will say, 'King Ahasuerus commanded Queen Vashti to be brought before him, and she did not come.' [18] This very day the noble women of Persia and Media who have heard of the queen's behavior will say the same to all the king's officials, and there will be contempt and wrath in plenty. [19] If it please the king, let a royal order go out from him, and let it be written among the laws of the Persians and the Medes so that it may not be repealed, that Vashti is never again to come before King Ahasuerus. And let the king give her royal position to another who is better than she. [20] So when the decree made by the king is proclaimed throughout all his kingdom, for it is vast, all women will give honor to their husbands, high and low alike." [21] This advice pleased the king and the princes, and the king did as Memucan proposed. [22] He sent letters to all the royal provinces, to every province in its own script and to every people in its own language, that every man be master in his own household and speak according to the language of his people.

Esther Chosen Queen

2 After these things, when the anger of King Ahasuerus had abated, he remembered Vashti and what she had done and what had been decreed against her. [2] Then the king's young men who attended him said, "Let beautiful young virgins be sought out for the king. [3] And let the king appoint officers in all the provinces of his kingdom to gather all the beautiful young virgins to the harem in Susa the citadel, under custody of Hegai, the king's eunuch, who is in charge of the women. Let their cosmetics be given them. [4] And let the

---

[1] Or rings [2] Or headdress [3] Hebrew to disdain their husbands in their eyes

young woman who pleases the king[1] be queen instead of Vashti." This pleased the king, and he did so.

[5] Now there was a Jew in Susa the citadel whose name was Mordecai, the son of Jair, son of Shimei, son of Kish, a Benjaminite, [6] who had been carried away from Jerusalem among the captives carried away with Jeconiah king of Judah, whom Nebuchadnezzar king of Babylon had carried away. [7] He was bringing up Hadassah, that is Esther, the daughter of his uncle, for she had neither father nor mother. The young woman had a beautiful figure and was lovely to look at, and when her father and her mother died, Mordecai took her as his own daughter. [8] So when the king's order and his edict were proclaimed, and when many young women were gathered in Susa the citadel in custody of Hegai, Esther also was taken into the king's palace and put in custody of Hegai, who had charge of the women. [9] And the young woman pleased him and won his favor. And he quickly provided her with her cosmetics and her portion of food, and with seven chosen young women from the king's palace, and advanced her and her young women to the best place in the harem. [10] Esther had not made known her people or kindred, for Mordecai had commanded her not to make it known. [11] And every day Mordecai walked in front of the court of the harem to learn how Esther was and what was happening to her.

[12] Now when the turn came for each young woman to go in to King Ahasuerus, after being twelve months under the regulations for the women, since this was the regular period of their beautifying, six months with oil of myrrh and six months with spices and ointments for women— [13] when the young woman went in to the king in this way, she was given whatever she desired to take with her from the harem to the king's palace. [14] In the evening she would go in, and in the morning she would return to the second harem in custody of Shaashgaz, the king's eunuch, who was in charge of the concubines. She would not go in to the king again, unless the king delighted in her and she was summoned by name.

[15] When the turn came for Esther the daughter of Abihail the uncle of Mordecai, who had taken her as his own daughter, to go in to the king, she asked for nothing except what Hegai the king's eunuch, who had charge of the women, advised. Now Esther was winning favor in the eyes of all who saw her. [16] And when Esther was taken to King Ahasuerus, into his royal palace, in the tenth month, which is the month of Tebeth, in the seventh year of his reign, [17] the king loved Esther more than all the women, and she won grace and favor in his sight more than all the virgins, so that he set the royal crown[2] on her head and made her queen instead of Vashti. [18] Then the king gave a great feast for all his officials and servants; it was Esther's feast. He also granted a remission of taxes to the provinces and gave gifts with royal generosity.

Mordecai Discovers a Plot

[19] Now when the virgins were gathered together the second time, Mordecai was sitting at the king's gate. [20] Esther had not made known her kindred or her people, as Mordecai had commanded her, for Esther obeyed Mordecai just as when she was brought up by him. [21] In those days, as Mordecai was sitting at the king's gate, Bigthan and Teresh, two of the king's eunuchs, who guarded the threshold, became angry and sought to lay hands on King Ahasuerus. [22] And this came to the knowledge of Mordecai, and he told it to Queen Esther, and Esther told the king in the name of Mordecai. [23] When the affair was investigated and found to be so, the men were both hanged on the gallows.[3] And it was recorded in the book of the chronicles in the presence of the king.

Haman Plots Against the Jews

3 After these things King Ahasuerus promoted Haman the Agagite, the son of Hammedatha, and advanced him and set his throne above all the officials who were with him. [2] And all the king's servants who were at the king's gate bowed down and paid homage to Haman, for the king had so commanded concerning him. But Mordecai did not bow down or pay homage. [3] Then the king's servants who were at the king's gate said to Mordecai, "Why do you transgress the king's command?" [4] And when they spoke to him day after day and he would not listen to them, they told Haman, in order to see whether Mordecai's words would stand, for he had told them that he was a Jew. [5] And when Haman saw that

---

[1] Hebrew who is good in the eyes of the king [2] Or headdress [3] Or wooden beam or stake; Hebrew tree or wood. This Persian execution practice involved affixing or impaling a person on a stake or pole (compare Ezra 6:11)

Mordecai did not bow down or pay homage to him, Haman was filled with fury. [6] But he disdained[1] to lay hands on Mordecai alone. So, as they had made known to him the people of Mordecai, Haman sought to destroy[2] all the Jews, the people of Mordecai, throughout the whole kingdom of Ahasuerus.

[7] In the first month, which is the month of Nisan, in the twelfth year of King Ahasuerus, they cast Pur (that is, they cast lots) before Haman day after day; and they cast it month after month till the twelfth month, which is the month of Adar. [8] Then Haman said to King Ahasuerus, "There is a certain people scattered abroad and dispersed among the peoples in all the provinces of your kingdom. Their laws are different from those of every other people, and they do not keep the king's laws, so that it is not to the king's profit to tolerate them. [9] If it please the king, let it be decreed that they be destroyed, and I will pay 10,000 talents[3] of silver into the hands of those who have charge of the king's business, that they may put it into the king's treasuries." [10] So the king took his signet ring from his hand and gave it to Haman the Agagite, the son of Hammedatha, the enemy of the Jews. [11] And the king said to Haman, "The money is given to you, the people also, to do with them as it seems good to you."

[12] Then the king's scribes were summoned on the thirteenth day of the first month, and an edict, according to all that Haman commanded, was written to the king's satraps and to the governors over all the provinces and to the officials of all the peoples, to every province in its own script and every people in its own language. It was written in the name of King Ahasuerus and sealed with the king's signet ring. [13] Letters were sent by couriers to all the king's provinces with instruction to destroy, to kill, and to annihilate all Jews, young and old, women and children, in one day, the thirteenth day of the twelfth month, which is the month of Adar, and to plunder their goods. [14] A copy of the document was to be issued as a decree in every province by proclamation to all the peoples to be ready for that day. [15] The couriers went out hurriedly by order of the king, and the decree was issued in Susa the citadel. And the king and Haman sat down to drink, but the city of Susa was thrown into confusion.

Esther Agrees to Help the Jews

4 When Mordecai learned all that had been done, Mordecai tore his clothes and put on sackcloth and ashes, and went out into the midst of the city, and he cried out with a loud and bitter cry. [2] He went up to the entrance of the king's gate, for no one was allowed to enter the king's gate clothed in sackcloth. [3] And in every province, wherever the king's command and his decree reached, there was great mourning among the Jews, with fasting and weeping and lamenting, and many of them lay in sackcloth and ashes.

[4] When Esther's young women and her eunuchs came and told her, the queen was deeply distressed. She sent garments to clothe Mordecai, so that he might take off his sackcloth, but he would not accept them. [5] Then Esther called for Hathach, one of the king's eunuchs, who had been appointed to attend her, and ordered him to go to Mordecai to learn what this was and why it was. [6] Hathach went out to Mordecai in the open square of the city in front of the king's gate, [7] and Mordecai told him all that had happened to him, and the exact sum of money that Haman had promised to pay into the king's treasuries for the destruction of the Jews. [8] Mordecai also gave him a copy of the written decree issued in Susa for their destruction,[4] that he might show it to Esther and explain it to her and command her to go to the king to beg his favor and plead with him[5] on behalf of her people. [9] And Hathach went and told Esther what Mordecai had said. [10] Then Esther spoke to Hathach and commanded him to go to Mordecai and say, [11] "All the king's servants and the people of the king's provinces know that if any man or woman goes to the king inside the inner court without being called, there is but one law—to be put to death, except the one to whom the king holds out the golden scepter so that he may live. But as for me, I have not been called to come in to the king these thirty days."

[12] And they told Mordecai what Esther had said. [13] Then Mordecai told them to reply to Esther, "Do not think to yourself that in the king's palace you will escape any more than all the other Jews. [14] For if you keep silent at this time, relief and deliverance will rise for the Jews from another place, but you and your father's house will perish. And who knows whether you have not come to the kingdom for such a time

---

[1] Hebrew *disdained in his eyes* [2] Or *annihilate* [3] A talent was about 75 pounds or 34 kilograms [4] Or *annihilation* [5] Hebrew *and seek from before his face*

as this?" [15] Then Esther told them to reply to Mordecai, [16] "Go, gather all the Jews to be found in Susa, and hold a fast on my behalf, and do not eat or drink for three days, night or day. I and my young women will also fast as you do. Then I will go to the king, though it is against the law, and if I perish, I perish." [1] [17] Mordecai then went away and did everything as Esther had ordered him.

Esther Prepares a Banquet

5 On the third day Esther put on her royal robes and stood in the inner court of the king's palace, in front of the king's quarters, while the king was sitting on his royal throne inside the throne room opposite the entrance to the palace. [2] And when the king saw Queen Esther standing in the court, she won favor in his sight, and he held out to Esther the golden scepter that was in his hand. Then Esther approached and touched the tip of the scepter. [3] And the king said to her, "What is it, Queen Esther? What is your request? It shall be given you, even to the half of my kingdom." [4] And Esther said, "If it please the king,[2] let the king and Haman come today to a feast that I have prepared for the king." [5] Then the king said, "Bring Haman quickly, so that we may do as Esther has asked." So the king and Haman came to the feast that Esther had prepared. [6] And as they were drinking wine after the feast, the king said to Esther, "What is your wish? It shall be granted you. And what is your request? Even to the half of my kingdom, it shall be fulfilled."[3] [7] Then Esther answered, "My wish and my request is: [8] If I have found favor in the sight of the king, and if it please the king[4] to grant my wish and fulfill my request, let the king and Haman come to the feast that I will prepare for them, and tomorrow I will do as the king has said."

Haman Plans to Hang Mordecai

[9] And Haman went out that day joyful and glad of heart. But when Haman saw Mordecai in the king's gate, that he neither rose nor trembled before him, he was filled with wrath against Mordecai. [10] Nevertheless, Haman restrained himself and went home, and he sent and brought his friends and his wife Zeresh. [11] And Haman recounted to them the splendor of his riches, the number of his sons, all the promotions with which the king had honored him, and how he had advanced him above the officials and the servants of the king. [12] Then Haman said, "Even Queen Esther let no one but me come with the king to the feast she prepared. And tomorrow also I am invited by her together with the king. [13] Yet all this is worth nothing to me, so long as I see Mordecai the Jew sitting at the king's gate." [14] Then his wife Zeresh and all his friends said to him, "Let a gallows[5] fifty cubits[6] high be made, and in the morning tell the king to have Mordecai hanged upon it. Then go joyfully with the king to the feast." This idea pleased Haman, and he had the gallows made.

The King Honors Mordecai

6 On that night the king could not sleep. And he gave orders to bring the book of memorable deeds, the chronicles, and they were read before the king. [2] And it was found written how Mordecai had told about Bigthana[7] and Teresh, two of the king's eunuchs, who guarded the threshold, and who had sought to lay hands on King Ahasuerus. [3] And the king said, "What honor or distinction has been bestowed on Mordecai for this?" The king's young men who attended him said, "Nothing has been done for him." [4] And the king said, "Who is in the court?" Now Haman had just entered the outer court of the king's palace to speak to the king about having Mordecai hanged on the gallows[8] that he had prepared for him. [5] And the king's young men told him, "Haman is there, standing in the court." And the king said, "Let him come in." [6] So Haman came in, and the king said to him, "What should be done to the man whom the king delights to honor?" And Haman said to himself, "Whom would the king delight to honor more than me?" [7] And Haman said to the king, "For the man whom the king delights to honor, [8] let royal robes be brought, which the king has worn, and the horse that the king has ridden, and on whose head a royal crown[9] is set. [9] And let the robes and the horse be handed over to one of the king's most noble officials. Let them dress the man whom the king delights to honor, and let them lead him on the horse through the square of the city, proclaiming before him: 'Thus shall it be done to the man whom the king delights to honor.'" [10] Then the king said to Haman, "Hurry; take the robes and the horse, as you have said, and do so to Mordecai the Jew, who sits at the king's gate. Leave out nothing that you have mentioned."

---

[1] Hebrew *if I am destroyed, then I will be destroyed* [2] Hebrew *If it is good to the king* [3] Or *done* [4] Hebrew *if it is good to the king* [5] Or *wooden beam*; twice in this verse (see note on 2:23) [6] A cubit was about 18 inches or 45 centimeters [7] *Bigthana* is an alternate spelling of *Bigthan* (see 2:21) [8] Or *wooden beam* (see note on 2:23) [9] Or *headdress*

¹¹So Haman took the robes and the horse, and he dressed Mordecai and led him through the square of the city, proclaiming before him, "Thus shall it be done to the man whom the king delights to honor."

¹²Then Mordecai returned to the king's gate. But Haman hurried to his house, mourning and with his head covered. ¹³And Haman told his wife Zeresh and all his friends everything that had happened to him. Then his wise men and his wife Zeresh said to him, "If Mordecai, before whom you have begun to fall, is of the Jewish people, you will not overcome him but will surely fall before him."

Esther Reveals Haman's Plot

¹⁴While they were yet talking with him, the king's eunuchs arrived and hurried to bring Haman to the feast that Esther had prepared. 7 So the king and Haman went in to feast with Queen Esther. ²And on the second day, as they were drinking wine after the feast, the king again said to Esther, "What is your wish, Queen Esther? It shall be granted you. And what is your request? Even to the half of my kingdom, it shall be fulfilled." ³Then Queen Esther answered, "If I have found favor in your sight, O king, and if it please the king, let my life be granted me for my wish, and my people for my request. ⁴For we have been sold, I and my people, to be destroyed, to be killed, and to be annihilated. If we had been sold merely as slaves, men and women, I would have been silent, for our affliction is not to be compared with the loss to the king." ⁵Then King Ahasuerus said to Queen Esther, "Who is he, and where is he, who has dared¹ to do this?" ⁶And Esther said, "A foe and enemy! This wicked Haman!" Then Haman was terrified before the king and the queen.

Haman Is Hanged

⁷And the king arose in his wrath from the wine-drinking and went into the palace garden, but Haman stayed to beg for his life from Queen Esther, for he saw that harm was determined against him by the king. ⁸And the king returned from the palace garden to the place where they were drinking wine, as Haman was falling on the couch where Esther was. And the king said, "Will he even assault the queen in my presence, in my own house?" As the word left the mouth of the king, they covered Haman's face. ⁹Then Harbona, one of

the eunuchs in attendance on the king, said, "Moreover, the gallows² that Haman has prepared for Mordecai, whose word saved the king, is standing at Haman's house, fifty cubits³ high." And the king said, "Hang him on that." ¹⁰So they hanged Haman on the gallows that he had prepared for Mordecai. Then the wrath of the king abated.

Esther Saves the Jews

8 On that day King Ahasuerus gave to Queen Esther the house of Haman, the enemy of the Jews. And Mordecai came before the king, for Esther had told what he was to her. ²And the king took off his signet ring, which he had taken from Haman, and gave it to Mordecai. And Esther set Mordecai over the house of Haman.

³Then Esther spoke again to the king. She fell at his feet and wept and pleaded with him to avert the evil plan of Haman the Agagite and the plot that he had devised against the Jews. ⁴When the king held out the golden scepter to Esther, Esther rose and stood before the king. ⁵And she said, "If it please the king, and if I have found favor in his sight, and if the thing seems right before the king, and I am pleasing in his eyes, let an order be written to revoke the letters devised by Haman the Agagite, the son of Hammedatha, which he wrote to destroy the Jews who are in all the provinces of the king. ⁶For how can I bear to see the calamity that is coming to my people? Or how can I bear to see the destruction of my kindred?" ⁷Then King Ahasuerus said to Queen Esther and to Mordecai the Jew, "Behold, I have given Esther the house of Haman, and they have hanged him on the gallows,⁴ because he intended to lay hands on the Jews. ⁸But you may write as you please with regard to the Jews, in the name of the king, and seal it with the king's ring, for an edict written in the name of the king and sealed with the king's ring cannot be revoked."

⁹The king's scribes were summoned at that time, in the third month, which is the month of Sivan, on the twenty-third day. And an edict was written, according to all that Mordecai commanded concerning the Jews, to the satraps and the governors and the officials of the provinces from India to Ethiopia, 127 provinces, to each province in its own script and to each people in its own language, and also to the Jews in their script and their language. ¹⁰And he wrote in

¹ Hebrew *whose heart has filled him* ² Or *wooden beam;* also verse 10 (see note on 2:23) ³ A *cubit* was about 18 inches or 45 centimeters ⁴ Or *wooden beam* (see note on 2:23)

the name of King Ahasuerus and sealed it with the king's signet ring. Then he sent the letters by mounted couriers riding on swift horses that were used in the king's service, bred from the royal stud, ¹¹ saying that the king allowed the Jews who were in every city to gather and defend their lives, to destroy, to kill, and to annihilate any armed force of any people or province that might attack them, children and women included, and to plunder their goods, ¹² on one day throughout all the provinces of King Ahasuerus, on the thirteenth day of the twelfth month, which is the month of Adar. ¹³ A copy of what was written was to be issued as a decree in every province, being publicly displayed to all peoples, and the Jews were to be ready on that day to take vengeance on their enemies. ¹⁴ So the couriers, mounted on their swift horses that were used in the king's service, rode out hurriedly, urged by the king's command. And the decree was issued in Susa the citadel.

¹⁵ Then Mordecai went out from the presence of the king in royal robes of blue and white, with a great golden crown[1] and a robe of fine linen and purple, and the city of Susa shouted and rejoiced. ¹⁶ The Jews had light and gladness and joy and honor. ¹⁷ And in every province and in every city, wherever the king's command and his edict reached, there was gladness and joy among the Jews, a feast and a holiday. And many from the peoples of the country declared themselves Jews, for fear of the Jews had fallen on them.

The Jews Destroy Their Enemies

9 Now in the twelfth month, which is the month of Adar, on the thirteenth day of the same, when the king's command and edict were about to be carried out, on the very day when the enemies of the Jews hoped to gain the mastery over them, the reverse occurred: the Jews gained mastery over those who hated them. ² The Jews gathered in their cities throughout all the provinces of King Ahasuerus to lay hands on those who sought their harm. And no one could stand against them, for the fear of them had fallen on all peoples. ³ All the officials of the provinces and the satraps and the governors and the royal agents also helped the Jews, for the fear of Mordecai had fallen on them. ⁴ For Mordecai was great in the king's house, and his fame spread throughout all the provinces, for the man Mordecai grew more and more power-

ful. ⁵ The Jews struck all their enemies with the sword, killing and destroying them, and did as they pleased to those who hated them. ⁶ In Susa the citadel itself the Jews killed and destroyed 500 men, ⁷ and also killed Parshandatha and Dalphon and Aspatha ⁸ and Poratha and Adalia and Aridatha ⁹ and Parmashta and Arisai and Aridai and Vaizatha, ¹⁰ the ten sons of Haman the son of Hammedatha, the enemy of the Jews, but they laid no hand on the plunder.

¹¹ That very day the number of those killed in Susa the citadel was reported to the king. ¹² And the king said to Queen Esther, "In Susa the citadel the Jews have killed and destroyed 500 men and also the ten sons of Haman. What then have they done in the rest of the king's provinces! Now what is your wish? It shall be granted you. And what further is your request? It shall be fulfilled." ¹³ And Esther said, "If it please the king, let the Jews who are in Susa be allowed tomorrow also to do according to this day's edict. And let the ten sons of Haman be hanged on the gallows."[2] ¹⁴ So the king commanded this to be done. A decree was issued in Susa, and the ten sons of Haman were hanged. ¹⁵ The Jews who were in Susa gathered also on the fourteenth day of the month of Adar and they killed 300 men in Susa, but they laid no hands on the plunder.

¹⁶ Now the rest of the Jews who were in the king's provinces also gathered to defend their lives, and got relief from their enemies and killed 75,000 of those who hated them, but they laid no hands on the plunder. ¹⁷ This was on the thirteenth day of the month of Adar, and on the fourteenth day they rested and made that a day of feasting and gladness. ¹⁸ But the Jews who were in Susa gathered on the thirteenth day and on the fourteenth, and rested on the fifteenth day, making that a day of feasting and gladness. ¹⁹ Therefore the Jews of the villages, who live in the rural towns, hold the fourteenth day of the month of Adar as a day for gladness and feasting, as a holiday, and as a day on which they send gifts of food to one another.

The Feast of Purim Inaugurated

²⁰ And Mordecai recorded these things and sent letters to all the Jews who were in all the provinces of King Ahasuerus, both near and far, ²¹ obliging them to keep the fourteenth day of the month Adar and also the fifteenth day of the same, year by year, ²² as the days on which

---

¹ Or *headdress* ² Or *wooden beam; also verse 25* (see note on 2:23)

the Jews got relief from their enemies, and as the month that had been turned for them from sorrow into gladness and from mourning into a holiday; that they should make them days of feasting and gladness, days for sending gifts of food to one another and gifts to the poor.

²³ So the Jews accepted what they had started to do, and what Mordecai had written to them. ²⁴ For Haman the Agagite, the son of Hammedatha, the enemy of all the Jews, had plotted against the Jews to destroy them, and had cast Pur (that is, cast lots), to crush and to destroy them. ²⁵ But when it came before the king, he gave orders in writing that his evil plan that he had devised against the Jews should return on his own head, and that he and his sons should be hanged on the gallows. ²⁶ Therefore they called these days Purim, after the term Pur. Therefore, because of all that was written in this letter, and of what they had faced in this matter, and of what had happened to them, ²⁷ the Jews firmly obligated themselves and their offspring and all who joined them, that without fail they would keep these two days according to what was written and at the time appointed every year, ²⁸ that these days should be remembered and kept throughout every generation, in every clan, province, and city, and that these days of Purim should never

fall into disuse among the Jews, nor should the commemoration of these days cease among their descendants.

²⁹ Then Queen Esther, the daughter of Abihail, and Mordecai the Jew gave full written authority, confirming this second letter about Purim. ³⁰ Letters were sent to all the Jews, to the 127 provinces of the kingdom of Ahasuerus, in words of peace and truth, ³¹ that these days of Purim should be observed at their appointed seasons, as Mordecai the Jew and Queen Esther obligated them, and as they had obligated themselves and their offspring, with regard to their fasts and their lamenting. ³² The command of Esther confirmed these practices of Purim, and it was recorded in writing.

The Greatness of Mordecai

10 King Ahasuerus imposed tax on the land and on the coastlands of the sea. ² And all the acts of his power and might, and the full account of the high honor of Mordecai, to which the king advanced him, are they not written in the Book of the Chronicles of the kings of Media and Persia? ³ For Mordecai the Jew was second in rank to King Ahasuerus, and he was great among the Jews and popular with the multitude of his brothers, for he sought the welfare of his people and spoke peace to all his people.

JOB

Job's Character and Wealth

1 There was a man in the land of Uz whose name was Job, and that man was blameless and upright, one who feared God and turned away from evil. ²There were born to him seven sons and three daughters. ³He possessed 7,000 sheep, 3,000 camels, 500 yoke of oxen, and 500 female donkeys, and very many servants, so that this man was the greatest of all the people of the east. ⁴His sons used to go and hold a feast in the house of each one on his day, and they would send and invite their three sisters to eat and drink with them. ⁵And when the days of the feast had run their course, Job would send and consecrate them, and he would rise early in the morning and offer burnt offerings according to the number of them all. For Job said, "It may be that my children have sinned, and cursed¹ God in their hearts." Thus Job did continually.

Satan Allowed to Test Job

⁶Now there was a day when the sons of God came to present themselves before the LORD, and Satan² also came among them. ⁷The LORD said to Satan, "From where have you come?" Satan answered the LORD and said, "From going to and fro on the earth, and from walking up and down on it." ⁸And the LORD said to Satan, "Have you considered my servant Job, that there is none like him on the earth, a blameless and upright man, who fears God and turns away from evil?" ⁹Then Satan answered the LORD and said, "Does Job fear God for no reason? ¹⁰Have you not put a hedge around him and his house and all that he has, on every side? You have blessed the work of his hands, and his possessions have increased in the land. ¹¹But stretch out your hand and touch all that he has, and he will curse you to your face." ¹²And the LORD said to Satan, "Behold, all that he has is in your hand. Only against him do not stretch out your hand." So Satan went out from the presence of the LORD.

Satan Takes Job's Property and Children

¹³Now there was a day when his sons and daughters were eating and drinking wine in their oldest brother's house, ¹⁴and there came a messenger to Job and said, "The oxen were plowing and the donkeys feeding beside them, ¹⁵and the Sabeans fell upon them and took them and struck down the servants³ with the edge of the sword, and I alone have escaped to tell you." ¹⁶While he was yet speaking, there came another and said, "The fire of God fell from heaven and burned up the sheep and the servants and consumed them, and I alone have escaped to tell you." ¹⁷While he was yet speaking, there came another and said, "The Chaldeans formed three groups and made a raid on the camels and took them and struck down the servants with the edge of the sword, and I alone have escaped to tell you." ¹⁸While he was yet speaking, there came another and said, "Your sons and daughters were eating and drinking wine in their oldest brother's house, ¹⁹and behold, a great wind came across the wilderness and struck the four corners of the house, and it fell upon the young people, and they are dead, and I alone have escaped to tell you."

²⁰Then Job arose and tore his robe and shaved his head and fell on the ground and worshiped. ²¹And he said, "Naked I came from my mother's womb, and naked shall I return. The LORD gave, and the LORD has taken away; blessed be the name of the LORD."

²²In all this Job did not sin or charge God with wrong.

Satan Attacks Job's Health

2 Again there was a day when the sons of God came to present themselves before the LORD, and Satan also came among them to present himself before the LORD. ²And the LORD said to Satan, "From where have you come?" Satan answered the LORD and said, "From going to and fro on the earth, and from walking up and down on it." ³And the LORD said to Satan, "Have you considered my servant Job, that there is none like him on the earth, a blameless and upright man, who fears God and turns away from evil? He still holds fast his integrity, although you incited me against him to destroy him without reason." ⁴Then Satan answered the LORD and said, "Skin for skin! All that a man has he will give for his life.

---

¹ The Hebrew word *bless* is used euphemistically for *curse* in 1:5, 11; 2:5, 9 ² Hebrew *the Accuser* or *the Adversary*; so throughout chapters 1–2 ³ Hebrew *the young men*; also verses 16, 17

⁵But stretch out your hand and touch his bone and his flesh, and he will curse you to your face." ⁶And the LORD said to Satan, "Behold, he is in your hand; only spare his life."

⁷So Satan went out from the presence of the LORD and struck Job with loathsome sores from the sole of his foot to the crown of his head. ⁸And he took a piece of broken pottery with which to scrape himself while he sat in the ashes.

⁹Then his wife said to him, "Do you still hold fast your integrity? Curse God and die." ¹⁰But he said to her, "You speak as one of the foolish women would speak. Shall we receive good from God, and shall we not receive evil?"¹ In all this Job did not sin with his lips.

Job's Three Friends

¹¹Now when Job's three friends heard of all this evil that had come upon him, they came each from his own place, Eliphaz the Temanite, Bildad the Shuhite, and Zophar the Naamathite. They made an appointment together to come to show him sympathy and comfort him. ¹²And when they saw him from a distance, they did not recognize him. And they raised their voices and wept, and they tore their robes and sprinkled dust on their heads toward heaven. ¹³And they sat with him on the ground seven days and seven nights, and no one spoke a word to him, for they saw that his suffering was very great.

Job Laments His Birth

3 After this Job opened his mouth and cursed the day of his birth. ²And Job said:

³   "Let the day perish on which I was born,
        and the night that said,
        'A man is conceived.'
⁴   Let that day be darkness!
        May God above not seek it,
        nor light shine upon it.
⁵   Let gloom and deep darkness claim it.
        Let clouds dwell upon it;
        let the blackness of the day terrify it.
⁶   That night—let thick darkness seize it!
        Let it not rejoice among the days of the
            year;
        let it not come into the number of the
            months.
⁷   Behold, let that night be barren;
        let no joyful cry enter it.
⁸   Let those curse it who curse the day,
        who are ready to rouse up Leviathan.

⁹   Let the stars of its dawn be dark;
        let it hope for light, but have none,
        nor see the eyelids of the morning,
¹⁰ because it did not shut the doors of my
            mother's womb,
        nor hide trouble from my eyes.

¹¹ "Why did I not die at birth,
        come out from the womb and expire?
¹² Why did the knees receive me?
        Or why the breasts, that I should nurse?
¹³ For then I would have lain down and been
            quiet;
        I would have slept; then I would have
            been at rest,
¹⁴ with kings and counselors of the earth
        who rebuilt ruins for themselves,
¹⁵ or with princes who had gold,
        who filled their houses with silver.
¹⁶ Or why was I not as a hidden stillborn
            child,
        as infants who never see the light?
¹⁷ There the wicked cease from troubling,
        and there the weary are at rest.
¹⁸ There the prisoners are at ease together;
        they hear not the voice of the taskmas-
            ter.
¹⁹ The small and the great are there,
        and the slave is free from his master.

²⁰ "Why is light given to him who is in misery,
        and life to the bitter in soul,
²¹ who long for death, but it comes not,
        and dig for it more than for hidden
            treasures,
²² who rejoice exceedingly
        and are glad when they find the grave?
²³ Why is light given to a man whose way is
            hidden,
        whom God has hedged in?
²⁴ For my sighing comes instead of² my bread,
        and my groanings are poured out like
            water.
²⁵ For the thing that I fear comes upon me,
        and what I dread befalls me.
²⁶ I am not at ease, nor am I quiet;
        I have no rest, but trouble comes."

Eliphaz Speaks: The Innocent Prosper

4 Then Eliphaz the Temanite answered and said:

²   "If one ventures a word with you, will you
            be impatient?
        Yet who can keep from speaking?

¹ Or disaster; also verse 11 ² Or like; Hebrew before

3 Behold, you have instructed many,
and you have strengthened the weak
hands.
4 Your words have upheld him who was
stumbling,
and you have made firm the feeble
knees.
5 But now it has come to you, and you are
impatient;
it touches you, and you are dismayed.
6 Is not your fear of God[1] your confidence,
and the integrity of your ways your
hope?

7 "Remember: who that was innocent ever
perished?
Or where were the upright cut off?
8 As I have seen, those who plow iniquity
and sow trouble reap the same.
9 By the breath of God they perish,
and by the blast of his anger they are
consumed.
10 The roar of the lion, the voice of the fierce
lion,
the teeth of the young lions are broken.
11 The strong lion perishes for lack of prey,
and the cubs of the lioness are scattered.

12 "Now a word was brought to me stealthily;
my ear received the whisper of it.
13 Amid thoughts from visions of the night,
when deep sleep falls on men,
14 dread came upon me, and trembling,
which made all my bones shake.
15 A spirit glided past my face;
the hair of my flesh stood up.
16 It stood still,
but I could not discern its appearance.
A form was before my eyes;
there was silence, then I heard a voice:
17 'Can mortal man be in the right before[2]
God?
Can a man be pure before his Maker?
18 Even in his servants he puts no trust,
and his angels he charges with error;
19 how much more those who dwell in
houses of clay,
whose foundation is in the dust,
who are crushed like[3] the moth.
20 Between morning and evening they are
beaten to pieces;
they perish forever without anyone
regarding it.

21 Is not their tent-cord plucked up within
them,
do they not die, and that without wisdom?'

5 "Call now; is there anyone who will answer
you?
To which of the holy ones will you
turn?
2 Surely vexation kills the fool,
and jealousy slays the simple.
3 I have seen the fool taking root,
but suddenly I cursed his dwelling.
4 His children are far from safety;
they are crushed in the gate,
and there is no one to deliver them.
5 The hungry eat his harvest,
and he takes it even out of thorns,[4]
and the thirsty pant[5] after his[6] wealth.
6 For affliction does not come from the dust,
nor does trouble sprout from the
ground,
7 but man is born to trouble
as the sparks fly upward.

8 "As for me, I would seek God,
and to God would I commit my cause,
9 who does great things and unsearchable,
marvelous things without number:
10 he gives rain on the earth
and sends waters on the fields;
11 he sets on high those who are lowly,
and those who mourn are lifted to
safety.
12 He frustrates the devices of the crafty,
so that their hands achieve no success.
13 He catches the wise in their own craftiness,
and the schemes of the wily are brought
to a quick end.
14 They meet with darkness in the daytime
and grope at noonday as in the night.
15 But he saves the needy from the sword of
their mouth
and from the hand of the mighty.
16 So the poor have hope,
and injustice shuts her mouth.

17 "Behold, blessed is the one whom God
reproves;
therefore despise not the discipline of
the Almighty.
18 For he wounds, but he binds up;
he shatters, but his hands heal.

---

[1] Hebrew lacks of God [2] Or more than; twice in this verse [3] Or before [4] The meaning of the Hebrew is uncertain [5] Aquila, Symmachus, Syriac, Vulgate; Hebrew could be read as and the snare pants [6] Hebrew their

19 He will deliver you from six troubles;
   in seven no evil[1] shall touch you.
20 In famine he will redeem you from
      death,
      and in war from the power of the
      sword.
21 You shall be hidden from the lash of the
      tongue,
      and shall not fear destruction when it
      comes.
22 At destruction and famine you shall laugh,
   and shall not fear the beasts of the earth.
23 For you shall be in league with the stones
      of the field,
      and the beasts of the field shall be at
      peace with you.
24 You shall know that your tent is at peace,
      and you shall inspect your fold and miss
      nothing.
25 You shall know also that your offspring
      shall be many,
      and your descendants as the grass of the
      earth.
26 You shall come to your grave in ripe old
      age,
      like a sheaf gathered up in its season.
27 Behold, this we have searched out; it is true.
   Hear, and know it for your good."[2]

Job Replies: My Complaint Is Just

6 Then Job answered and said:

2 "Oh that my vexation were weighed,
      and all my calamity laid in the balances!
3 For then it would be heavier than the sand
      of the sea;
      therefore my words have been rash.
4 For the arrows of the Almighty are in me;
      my spirit drinks their poison;
      the terrors of God are arrayed against
      me.
5 Does the wild donkey bray when he has
      grass,
      or the ox low over his fodder?
6 Can that which is tasteless be eaten with-
      out salt,
      or is there any taste in the juice of the
      mallow?[3]
7 My appetite refuses to touch them;
      they are as food that is loathsome to
      me.[4]

8 "Oh that I might have my request,
      and that God would fulfill my hope,
9 that it would please God to crush me,
      that he would let loose his hand and cut
      me off!
10 This would be my comfort;
      I would even exult[5] in pain unsparing,
      for I have not denied the words of the
      Holy One.
11 What is my strength, that I should wait?
      And what is my end, that I should be
      patient?
12 Is my strength the strength of stones, or is
      my flesh bronze?
13 Have I any help in me,
      when resource is driven from me?

14 "He who withholds[6] kindness from a friend
      forsakes the fear of the Almighty.
15 My brothers are treacherous as a torrent-
      bed,
      as torrential streams that pass away,
16 which are dark with ice,
      and where the snow hides itself.
17 When they melt, they disappear;
      when it is hot, they vanish from their
      place.
18 The caravans turn aside from their
      course;
      they go up into the waste and perish.
19 The caravans of Tema look,
      the travelers of Sheba hope.
20 They are ashamed because they were confi-
      dent;
      they come there and are disappointed.
21 For you have now become nothing;
      you see my calamity and are afraid.
22 Have I said, 'Make me a gift'?
      Or, 'From your wealth offer a bribe for
      me'?
23 Or, 'Deliver me from the adversary's hand'?
      Or, 'Redeem me from the hand of the
      ruthless'?

24 "Teach me, and I will be silent;
      make me understand how I have gone
      astray.
25 How forceful are upright words!
      But what does reproof from you
      reprove?

---

[1] Or disaster [2] Hebrew for yourself [3] The meaning of the Hebrew word is uncertain [4] The meaning of the Hebrew is uncertain [5] The meaning of the Hebrew word is uncertain
[6] Syriac, Vulgate (compare Targum); the meaning of the Hebrew word is uncertain

26 Do you think that you can reprove
        words,
            when the speech of a despairing man is
                wind?
27 You would even cast lots over the father-
        less,
            and bargain over your friend.

28 "But now, be pleased to look at me,
        for I will not lie to your face.
29 Please turn; let no injustice be done.
        Turn now; my vindication is at stake.
30 Is there any injustice on my tongue?
        Cannot my palate discern the cause of
            calamity?

Job Continues: My Life Has No Hope

7 "Has not man a hard service on earth,
        and are not his days like the days of a
            hired hand?
2 Like a slave who longs for the shadow,
        and like a hired hand who looks for his
            wages,
3 so I am allotted months of emptiness,
        and nights of misery are apportioned to
            me.
4 When I lie down I say, 'When shall I arise?'
        But the night is long,
        and I am full of tossing till the dawn.
5 My flesh is clothed with worms and dirt;
        my skin hardens, then breaks out
            afresh.
6 My days are swifter than a weaver's shuttle
        and come to their end without hope.

7 "Remember that my life is a breath;
        my eye will never again see good.
8 The eye of him who sees me will behold
        me no more;
            while your eyes are on me, I shall be
                gone.
9 As the cloud fades and vanishes,
        so he who goes down to Sheol does not
            come up;
10 he returns no more to his house,
        nor does his place know him anymore.

11 "Therefore I will not restrain my mouth;
        I will speak in the anguish of my spirit;
        I will complain in the bitterness of my
            soul.
12 Am I the sea, or a sea monster,
        that you set a guard over me?
13 When I say, 'My bed will comfort me,
        my couch will ease my complaint,'

14 then you scare me with dreams
        and terrify me with visions,
15 so that I would choose strangling
        and death rather than my bones.
16 I loathe my life; I would not live forever.
        Leave me alone, for my days are a
            breath.
17 What is man, that you make so much of
        him,
            and that you set your heart on him,
18 visit him every morning
        and test him every moment?
19 How long will you not look away from me,
        nor leave me alone till I swallow my
            spit?
20 If I sin, what do I do to you, you watcher of
        mankind?
            Why have you made me your mark?
            Why have I become a burden to you?
21 Why do you not pardon my transgres-
        sion
            and take away my iniquity?
        For now I shall lie in the earth;
            you will seek me, but I shall not be."

Bildad Speaks: Job Should Repent

8 Then Bildad the Shuhite answered and
    said:

2 "How long will you say these things,
        and the words of your mouth be a great
            wind?
3 Does God pervert justice?
        Or does the Almighty pervert the right?
4 If your children have sinned against him,
        he has delivered them into the hand of
            their transgression.
5 If you will seek God
        and plead with the Almighty for mercy,
6 if you are pure and upright,
        surely then he will rouse himself for
            you
        and restore your rightful habitation.
7 And though your beginning was small,
        your latter days will be very great.

8 "For inquire, please, of bygone ages,
        and consider what the fathers have
            searched out.
9 For we are but of yesterday and know
        nothing,
            for our days on earth are a shadow.

10 Will they not teach you and tell you
     and utter words out of their under-
       standing?

11 "Can papyrus grow where there is no marsh?
     Can reeds flourish where there is no
       water?
12 While yet in flower and not cut down,
     they wither before any other plant.
13 Such are the paths of all who forget God;
     the hope of the godless shall perish.
14 His confidence is severed,
     and his trust is a spider's web.[1]
15 He leans against his house, but it does not
       stand;
     he lays hold of it, but it does not endure.
16 He is a lush plant before the sun,
     and his shoots spread over his garden.
17 His roots entwine the stone heap;
     he looks upon a house of stones.
18 If he is destroyed from his place,
     then it will deny him, saying, 'I have
       never seen you.'
19 Behold, this is the joy of his way,
     and out of the soil others will spring.

20 "Behold, God will not reject a blameless man,
     nor take the hand of evildoers.
21 He will yet fill your mouth with laughter,
     and your lips with shouting.
22 Those who hate you will be clothed with
       shame,
     and the tent of the wicked will be no
       more."

Job Replies: There Is No Arbiter

9 Then Job answered and said:

2 "Truly I know that it is so:
     But how can a man be in the right
       before God?
3 If one wished to contend with him,
     one could not answer him once in a
       thousand times.
4 He is wise in heart and mighty in strength
     —who has hardened himself against
       him, and succeeded?—
5 he who removes mountains, and they
       know it not,
     when he overturns them in his anger,
6 who shakes the earth out of its place,
     and its pillars tremble;

7 who commands the sun, and it does not
       rise;
     who seals up the stars;
8 who alone stretched out the heavens
     and trampled the waves of the sea;
9 who made the Bear and Orion,
     the Pleiades and the chambers of the
       south;
10 who does great things beyond searching out,
     and marvelous things beyond number.
11 Behold, he passes by me, and I see him not;
     he moves on, but I do not perceive him.
12 Behold, he snatches away; who can turn
       him back?
     Who will say to him, 'What are you
       doing?'

13 "God will not turn back his anger;
     beneath him bowed the helpers of
       Rahab.
14 How then can I answer him,
     choosing my words with him?
15 Though I am in the right, I cannot answer
       him;
     I must appeal for mercy to my accuser.[2]
16 If I summoned him and he answered me,
     I would not believe that he was listen-
       ing to my voice.
17 For he crushes me with a tempest
     and multiplies my wounds without
       cause;
18 he will not let me get my breath,
     but fills me with bitterness.
19 If it is a contest of strength, behold, he is
       mighty!
     If it is a matter of justice, who can sum-
       mon him?[3]
20 Though I am in the right, my own mouth
       would condemn me;
     though I am blameless, he would prove
       me perverse.
21 I am blameless; I regard not myself;
     I loathe my life.
22 It is all one; therefore I say,
     'He destroys both the blameless and the
       wicked.'
23 When disaster brings sudden death,
     he mocks at the calamity[4] of the inno-
       cent.
24 The earth is given into the hand of the
       wicked;
     he covers the faces of its judges—
     if it is not he, who then is it?

---

[1] Hebrew house [2] Or to my judge [3] Or who can grant me a hearing? [4] The meaning of the Hebrew word is uncertain

25 "My days are swifter than a runner;
     they flee away; they see no good.
26 They go by like skiffs of reed,
     like an eagle swooping on the prey.
27 If I say, 'I will forget my complaint,
     I will put off my sad face, and be of
          good cheer,'
28 I become afraid of all my suffering,
     for I know you will not hold me inno-
          cent.
29 I shall be condemned;
     why then do I labor in vain?
30 If I wash myself with snow
     and cleanse my hands with lye,
31 yet you will plunge me into a pit,
     and my own clothes will abhor me.
32 For he is not a man, as I am, that I might
          answer him,
     that we should come to trial together.
33 There is no[1] arbiter between us,
     who might lay his hand on us both.
34 Let him take his rod away from me,
     and let not dread of him terrify me.
35 Then I would speak without fear of him,
     for I am not so in myself.

Job Continues: A Plea to God

10 "I loathe my life;
     I will give free utterance to my com-
          plaint;
     I will speak in the bitterness of my soul.
2 I will say to God, Do not condemn me;
     let me know why you contend against
          me.
3 Does it seem good to you to oppress,
     to despise the work of your hands
     and favor the designs of the wicked?
4 Have you eyes of flesh?
     Do you see as man sees?
5 Are your days as the days of man,
     or your years as a man's years,
6 that you seek out my iniquity
     and search for my sin,
7 although you know that I am not guilty,
     and there is none to deliver out of your
          hand?
8 Your hands fashioned and made me,
     and now you have destroyed me alto-
          gether.
9 Remember that you have made me like clay;
     and will you return me to the dust?
10 Did you not pour me out like milk
     and curdle me like cheese?

11 You clothed me with skin and flesh,
     and knit me together with bones and
          sinews.
12 You have granted me life and steadfast love,
     and your care has preserved my spirit.
13 Yet these things you hid in your heart;
     I know that this was your purpose.
14 If I sin, you watch me
     and do not acquit me of my iniquity.
15 If I am guilty, woe to me!
     If I am in the right, I cannot lift up my
          head,
     for I am filled with disgrace
     and look on my affliction.
16 And were my head lifted up,[2] you would
          hunt me like a lion
     and again work wonders against me.
17 You renew your witnesses against me
     and increase your vexation toward me;
     you bring fresh troops against me.

18 "Why did you bring me out from the womb?
     Would that I had died before any eye
          had seen me
19 and were as though I had not been,
     carried from the womb to the grave.
20 Are not my days few?
     Then cease, and leave me alone, that I
          may find a little cheer
21 before I go—and I shall not return—
     to the land of darkness and deep shadow,
22 the land of gloom like thick darkness,
     like deep shadow without any order,
     where light is as thick darkness."

Zophar Speaks: You Deserve Worse

11 Then Zophar the Naamathite answered
     and said:

2 "Should a multitude of words go unan-
          swered,
     and a man full of talk be judged right?
3 Should your babble silence men,
     and when you mock, shall no one
          shame you?
4 For you say, 'My doctrine is pure,
     and I am clean in God's[3] eyes.'
5 But oh, that God would speak
     and open his lips to you,
6 and that he would tell you the secrets of
          wisdom!
     For he is manifold in understanding.[4]
Know then that God exacts of you less
     than your guilt deserves.

---

[1] Or *Would that there were an* [2] Hebrew lacks *my head* [3] Hebrew *your* [4] The meaning of the Hebrew is uncertain

7 "Can you find out the deep things of
        God?
    Can you find out the limit of the
        Almighty?
8 It is higher than heaven[1]—what can you
        do?
    Deeper than Sheol—what can you
        know?
9 Its measure is longer than the earth
    and broader than the sea.
10 If he passes through and imprisons
    and summons the court, who can turn
        him back?
11 For he knows worthless men;
    when he sees iniquity, will he not con-
        sider it?
12 But a stupid man will get understanding
    when a wild donkey's colt is born a
        man!

13 "If you prepare your heart,
    you will stretch out your hands toward
        him.
14 If iniquity is in your hand, put it far
        away,
    and let not injustice dwell in your tents.
15 Surely then you will lift up your face with-
        out blemish;
    you will be secure and will not fear.
16 You will forget your misery;
    you will remember it as waters that
        have passed away.
17 And your life will be brighter than the
        noonday;
    its darkness will be like the morning.
18 And you will feel secure, because there is
        hope;
    you will look around and take your rest
        in security.
19 You will lie down, and none will make you
        afraid;
    many will court your favor.
20 But the eyes of the wicked will fail;
    all way of escape will be lost to
        them,
    and their hope is to breathe their
        last."

Job Replies: The LORD Has Done This

12 Then Job answered and said:

2 "No doubt you are the people,
    and wisdom will die with you.

3 But I have understanding as well as you;
    I am not inferior to you.
    Who does not know such things as
        these?
4 I am a laughingstock to my friends;
    I, who called to God and he answered
        me,
    a just and blameless man, am a laugh-
        ingstock.
5 In the thought of one who is at ease there
        is contempt for misfortune;
    it is ready for those whose feet slip.
6 The tents of robbers are at peace,
    and those who provoke God are
        secure,
    who bring their god in their hand.[2]

7 "But ask the beasts, and they will teach you;
    the birds of the heavens, and they will
        tell you;
8 or the bushes of the earth, and they will
        teach you;[3]
    and the fish of the sea will declare to
        you.
9 Who among all these does not know
    that the hand of the LORD has done
        this?
10 In his hand is the life of every living
        thing
    and the breath of all mankind.
11 Does not the ear test words
    as the palate tastes food?
12 Wisdom is with the aged,
    and understanding in length of days.

13 "With God[4] are wisdom and might;
    he has counsel and understanding.
14 If he tears down, none can rebuild;
    if he shuts a man in, none can open.
15 If he withholds the waters, they dry up;
    if he sends them out, they overwhelm
        the land.
16 With him are strength and sound wisdom;
    the deceived and the deceiver are his.
17 He leads counselors away stripped,
    and judges he makes fools.
18 He looses the bonds of kings
    and binds a waistcloth on their hips.
19 He leads priests away stripped
    and overthrows the mighty.
20 He deprives of speech those who are
        trusted
    and takes away the discernment of the
        elders.

---

[1] Hebrew *The heights of heaven* [2] The meaning of the Hebrew is uncertain [3] Or *or speak to the earth, and it will teach you* [4] Hebrew *him*

21 He pours contempt on princes
    and loosens the belt of the strong.
22 He uncovers the deeps out of darkness
    and brings deep darkness to light.
23 He makes nations great, and he destroys
        them;
    he enlarges nations, and leads them
        away.
24 He takes away understanding from the
        chiefs of the people of the earth
    and makes them wander in a trackless
        waste.
25 They grope in the dark without light,
    and he makes them stagger like a
        drunken man.

Job Continues: Still I Will Hope in God

13 "Behold, my eye has seen all this,
        my ear has heard and understood it.
2 What you know, I also know;
    I am not inferior to you.
3 But I would speak to the Almighty,
    and I desire to argue my case with God.
4 As for you, you whitewash with lies;
    worthless physicians are you all.
5 Oh that you would keep silent,
    and it would be your wisdom!
6 Hear now my argument
    and listen to the pleadings of my lips.
7 Will you speak falsely for God
    and speak deceitfully for him?
8 Will you show partiality toward him?
    Will you plead the case for God?
9 Will it be well with you when he searches
        you out?
    Or can you deceive him, as one deceives
        a man?
10 He will surely rebuke you
    if in secret you show partiality.
11 Will not his majesty terrify you,
    and the dread of him fall upon you?
12 Your maxims are proverbs of ashes;
    your defenses are defenses of clay.

13 "Let me have silence, and I will speak,
    and let come on me what may.
14 Why should I take my flesh in my teeth
    and put my life in my hand?
15 Though he slay me, I will hope in him;[1]
    yet I will argue my ways to his face.
16 This will be my salvation,
    that the godless shall not come before
        him.

17 Keep listening to my words,
    and let my declaration be in your ears.
18 Behold, I have prepared my case;
    I know that I shall be in the right.
19 Who is there who will contend with me?
    For then I would be silent and die.
20 Only grant me two things,
    then I will not hide myself from your
        face:
21 withdraw your hand far from me,
    and let not dread of you terrify me.
22 Then call, and I will answer;
    or let me speak, and you reply to me.
23 How many are my iniquities and my sins?
    Make me know my transgression and
        my sin.
24 Why do you hide your face
    and count me as your enemy?
25 Will you frighten a driven leaf
    and pursue dry chaff?
26 For you write bitter things against me
    and make me inherit the iniquities of
        my youth.
27 You put my feet in the stocks
    and watch all my paths;
    you set a limit for[2] the soles of my feet.
28 Man[3] wastes away like a rotten thing,
    like a garment that is moth-eaten.

Job Continues: Death Comes Soon to All

14 "Man who is born of a woman
        is few of days and full of trouble.
2 He comes out like a flower and withers;
    he flees like a shadow and continues not.
3 And do you open your eyes on such a one
    and bring me into judgment with you?
4 Who can bring a clean thing out of an
        unclean?
    There is not one.
5 Since his days are determined,
    and the number of his months is with
        you,
    and you have appointed his limits that
        he cannot pass,
6 look away from him and leave him alone,[4]
    that he may enjoy, like a hired hand, his
        day.

7 "For there is hope for a tree,
    if it be cut down, that it will sprout
        again,
    and that its shoots will not cease.
8 Though its root grow old in the earth,
    and its stump die in the soil,

---

1 Or *Behold, he will slay me; I have no hope* 2 Or *you marked* 3 Hebrew *He* 4 Probable reading; Hebrew *look away from him, that he may cease*

9   yet at the scent of water it will bud
        and put out branches like a young
            plant.
10 But a man dies and is laid low;
        man breathes his last, and where is
            he?
11 As waters fail from a lake
        and a river wastes away and dries up,
12 so a man lies down and rises not again;
        till the heavens are no more he will not
            awake
        or be roused out of his sleep.
13 Oh that you would hide me in Sheol,
        that you would conceal me until your
            wrath be past,
        that you would appoint me a set time,
            and remember me!
14 If a man dies, shall he live again?
        All the days of my service I would
            wait,
        till my renewal[1] should come.
15 You would call, and I would answer you;
        you would long for the work of your
            hands.
16 For then you would number my steps;
        you would not keep watch over my sin;
17 my transgression would be sealed up in a
            bag,
        and you would cover over my iniquity.

18 "But the mountain falls and crumbles away,
        and the rock is removed from its
            place;
19 the waters wear away the stones;
        the torrents wash away the soil of the
            earth;
        so you destroy the hope of man.
20 You prevail forever against him, and he
            passes;
        you change his countenance, and send
            him away.
21 His sons come to honor, and he does not
            know it;
        they are brought low, and he perceives it
            not.
22 He feels only the pain of his own body,
        and he mourns only for himself."

Eliphaz Accuses: Job Does Not Fear God

15 Then Eliphaz the Temanite answered
    and said:

2   "Should a wise man answer with windy
            knowledge,
        and fill his belly with the east wind?
3   Should he argue in unprofitable talk,
        or in words with which he can do no
            good?
4   But you are doing away with the fear of
            God[2]
        and hindering meditation before God.
5   For your iniquity teaches your mouth,
        and you choose the tongue of the crafty.
6   Your own mouth condemns you, and not I;
        your own lips testify against you.

7   "Are you the first man who was born?
        Or were you brought forth before the
            hills?
8   Have you listened in the council of God?
        And do you limit wisdom to yourself?
9   What do you know that we do not know?
        What do you understand that is not
            clear to us?
10 Both the gray-haired and the aged are
            among us,
        older than your father.
11 Are the comforts of God too small for you,
        or the word that deals gently with you?
12 Why does your heart carry you away,
        and why do your eyes flash,
13 that you turn your spirit against God
        and bring such words out of your
            mouth?
14 What is man, that he can be pure?
        Or he who is born of a woman, that he
            can be righteous?
15 Behold, God[3] puts no trust in his holy ones,
        and the heavens are not pure in his
            sight;
16 how much less one who is abominable and
            corrupt,
        a man who drinks injustice like water!

17 "I will show you; hear me,
        and what I have seen I will declare
18 (what wise men have told,
        without hiding it from their fathers,
19 to whom alone the land was given,
        and no stranger passed among them).
20 The wicked man writhes in pain all his
            days,
        through all the years that are laid up for
            the ruthless.

[1] Or relief [2] Hebrew lacks of God [3] Hebrew he

21 Dreadful sounds are in his ears;
    in prosperity the destroyer will come
      upon him.
22 He does not believe that he will return out
      of darkness,
    and he is marked for the sword.
23 He wanders abroad for bread, saying,
      'Where is it?'
    He knows that a day of darkness is
      ready at his hand;
24 distress and anguish terrify him;
    they prevail against him, like a king
      ready for battle.
25 Because he has stretched out his hand
      against God
    and defies the Almighty,
26 running stubbornly against him
    with a thickly bossed shield;
27 because he has covered his face with his
      fat
    and gathered fat upon his waist
28 and has lived in desolate cities,
    in houses that none should inhabit,
    which were ready to become heaps of
      ruins;
29 he will not be rich, and his wealth will not
      endure,
    nor will his possessions spread over
      the earth;[1]
30 he will not depart from darkness;
    the flame will dry up his shoots,
    and by the breath of his mouth he will
      depart.
31 Let him not trust in emptiness, deceiving
      himself,
    for emptiness will be his payment.
32 It will be paid in full before his time,
    and his branch will not be green.
33 He will shake off his unripe grape like the
      vine,
    and cast off his blossom like the olive
      tree.
34 For the company of the godless is barren,
    and fire consumes the tents of bribery.
35 They conceive trouble and give birth to
      evil,
    and their womb prepares deceit."

Job Replies: Miserable Comforters Are You

16 Then Job answered and said:

2 "I have heard many such things;
    miserable comforters are you all.

3 Shall windy words have an end?
    Or what provokes you that you answer?
4 I also could speak as you do,
    if you were in my place;
    I could join words together against you
      and shake my head at you.
5 I could strengthen you with my mouth,
    and the solace of my lips would assuage
      your pain.

6 "If I speak, my pain is not assuaged,
    and if I forbear, how much of it leaves
      me?
7 Surely now God has worn me out;
    he has[2] made desolate all my com-
      pany.
8 And he has shriveled me up,
    which is a witness against me,
    and my leanness has risen up against
      me;
    it testifies to my face.
9 He has torn me in his wrath and hated me;
    he has gnashed his teeth at me;
    my adversary sharpens his eyes against
      me.
10 Men have gaped at me with their mouth;
    they have struck me insolently on the
      cheek;
    they mass themselves together against
      me.
11 God gives me up to the ungodly
    and casts me into the hands of the
      wicked.
12 I was at ease, and he broke me apart;
    he seized me by the neck and dashed
      me to pieces;
    he set me up as his target;
13 his archers surround me.
    He slashes open my kidneys and does not
      spare;
    he pours out my gall on the ground.
14 He breaks me with breach upon breach;
    he runs upon me like a warrior.
15 I have sewed sackcloth upon my skin
    and have laid my strength in the dust.
16 My face is red with weeping,
    and on my eyelids is deep darkness,
17 although there is no violence in my
      hands,
    and my prayer is pure.

18 "O earth, cover not my blood,
    and let my cry find no resting place.

---

1 Or *nor will his produce bend down to the earth*   2 Hebrew *you have*; also verse 8

19 Even now, behold, my witness is in heaven,
    and he who testifies for me is on high.
20 My friends scorn me;
    my eye pours out tears to God,
21 that he would argue the case of a man with
        God,
    as¹ a son of man does with his neighbor.
22 For when a few years have come
    I shall go the way from which I shall not
        return.

Job Continues: Where Then Is My Hope?

17 "My spirit is broken; my days are
    extinct;
    the graveyard is ready for me.
2 Surely there are mockers about me,
    and my eye dwells on their provocation.

3 "Lay down a pledge for me with you;
    who is there who will put up security
        for me?
4 Since you have closed their hearts to under-
        standing,
    therefore you will not let them tri-
        umph.
5 He who informs against his friends to get a
        share of their property—
    the eyes of his children will fail.

6 "He has made me a byword of the peo-
        ples,
    and I am one before whom men spit.
7 My eye has grown dim from vexation,
    and all my members are like a
        shadow.
8 The upright are appalled at this,
    and the innocent stirs himself up
        against the godless.
9 Yet the righteous holds to his way,
    and he who has clean hands grows
        stronger and stronger.
10 But you, come on again, all of you,
    and I shall not find a wise man among
        you.
11 My days are past; my plans are broken
        off,
    the desires of my heart.
12 They make night into day:
    'The light,' they say, 'is near to the dark-
        ness.'²
13 If I hope for Sheol as my house,
    if I make my bed in darkness,

14 if I say to the pit, 'You are my father,'
    and to the worm, 'My mother,' or 'My
        sister,'
15 where then is my hope?
    Who will see my hope?
16 Will it go down to the bars of Sheol?
    Shall we descend together into the
        dust?"³

Bildad Speaks: God Punishes the Wicked

18 Then Bildad the Shuhite answered and
    said:

2 "How long will you hunt for words?
    Consider, and then we will speak.
3 Why are we counted as cattle?
    Why are we stupid in your sight?
4 You who tear yourself in your anger,
    shall the earth be forsaken for you,
    or the rock be removed out of its
        place?

5 "Indeed, the light of the wicked is put
        out,
    and the flame of his fire does not
        shine.
6 The light is dark in his tent,
    and his lamp above him is put out.
7 His strong steps are shortened,
    and his own schemes throw him down.
8 For he is cast into a net by his own feet,
    and he walks on its mesh.
9 A trap seizes him by the heel;
    a snare lays hold of him.
10 A rope is hidden for him in the ground,
    a trap for him in the path.
11 Terrors frighten him on every side,
    and chase him at his heels.
12 His strength is famished,
    and calamity is ready for his stumbling.
13 It consumes the parts of his skin;
    the firstborn of death consumes his
        limbs.
14 He is torn from the tent in which he
        trusted
    and is brought to the king of terrors.
15 In his tent dwells that which is none of his;
    sulfur is scattered over his habitation.
16 His roots dry up beneath,
    and his branches wither above.
17 His memory perishes from the earth,
    and he has no name in the street.
18 He is thrust from light into darkness,
    and driven out of the world.

¹ Hebrew *and* ² The meaning of the Hebrew is uncertain ³ Or *Will they go down to the bars of Sheol? Is rest to be found together in the dust?*

¹⁹ He has no posterity or progeny among his people,
and no survivor where he used to live.
²⁰ They of the west are appalled at his day,
and horror seizes them of the east.
²¹ Surely such are the dwellings of the unrighteous,
such is the place of him who knows not God."

Job Replies: My Redeemer Lives

19 Then Job answered and said:

² "How long will you torment me
and break me in pieces with words?
³ These ten times you have cast reproach upon me;
are you not ashamed to wrong me?
⁴ And even if it be true that I have erred,
my error remains with myself.
⁵ If indeed you magnify yourselves against me
and make my disgrace an argument against me,
⁶ know then that God has put me in the wrong
and closed his net about me.
⁷ Behold, I cry out, 'Violence!' but I am not answered;
I call for help, but there is no justice.
⁸ He has walled up my way, so that I cannot pass,
and he has set darkness upon my paths.
⁹ He has stripped from me my glory
and taken the crown from my head.
¹⁰ He breaks me down on every side, and I am gone,
and my hope has he pulled up like a tree.
¹¹ He has kindled his wrath against me
and counts me as his adversary.
¹² His troops come on together;
they have cast up their siege ramp[1] against me
and encamp around my tent.

¹³ "He has put my brothers far from me,
and those who knew me are wholly estranged from me.
¹⁴ My relatives have failed me,
my close friends have forgotten me.
¹⁵ The guests in my house and my maidservants count me as a stranger;
I have become a foreigner in their eyes.

¹⁶ I call to my servant, but he gives me no answer;
I must plead with him with my mouth for mercy.
¹⁷ My breath is strange to my wife,
and I am a stench to the children of my own mother.
¹⁸ Even young children despise me;
when I rise they talk against me.
¹⁹ All my intimate friends abhor me,
and those whom I loved have turned against me.
²⁰ My bones stick to my skin and to my flesh,
and I have escaped by the skin of my teeth.
²¹ Have mercy on me, have mercy on me,
O you my friends,
for the hand of God has touched me!
²² Why do you, like God, pursue me?
Why are you not satisfied with my flesh?

²³ "Oh that my words were written!
Oh that they were inscribed in a book!
²⁴ Oh that with an iron pen and lead
they were engraved in the rock forever!
²⁵ For I know that my Redeemer lives,
and at the last he will stand upon the earth.[2]
²⁶ And after my skin has been thus destroyed,
yet in[3] my flesh I shall see God,
²⁷ whom I shall see for myself,
and my eyes shall behold, and not another.
My heart faints within me!
²⁸ If you say, 'How we will pursue him!'
and, 'The root of the matter is found in him,'[4]
²⁹ be afraid of the sword,
for wrath brings the punishment of the sword,
that you may know there is a judgment."

Zophar Speaks: The Wicked Will Suffer

20 Then Zophar the Naamathite answered and said:

² "Therefore my thoughts answer me,
because of my haste within me.
³ I hear censure that insults me,
and out of my understanding a spirit answers me.

---

[1] Hebrew *their way* [2] Hebrew *dust* [3] Or *without* [4] Many Hebrew manuscripts *in me*

4 Do you not know this from of old,
  since man was placed on earth,
5 that the exulting of the wicked is short,
  and the joy of the godless but for a
  moment?
6 Though his height mount up to the heavens,
  and his head reach to the clouds,
7 he will perish forever like his own dung;
  those who have seen him will say,
  'Where is he?'
8 He will fly away like a dream and not be
  found;
  he will be chased away like a vision of
  the night.
9 The eye that saw him will see him no
  more,
  nor will his place any more behold him.
10 His children will seek the favor of the poor,
  and his hands will give back his
  wealth.
11 His bones are full of his youthful vigor,
  but it will lie down with him in the
  dust.

12 "Though evil is sweet in his mouth,
  though he hides it under his tongue,
13 though he is loath to let it go
  and holds it in his mouth,
14 yet his food is turned in his stomach;
  it is the venom of cobras within him.
15 He swallows down riches and vomits them
  up again;
  God casts them out of his belly.
16 He will suck the poison of cobras;
  the tongue of a viper will kill him.
17 He will not look upon the rivers,
  the streams flowing with honey and
  curds.
18 He will give back the fruit of his toil
  and will not swallow it down;
  from the profit of his trading
  he will get no enjoyment.
19 For he has crushed and abandoned the
  poor;
  he has seized a house that he did not
  build.
20 "Because he knew no contentment in his
  belly,
  he will not let anything in which he
  delights escape him.

21 There was nothing left after he had
  eaten;
  therefore his prosperity will not endure.
22 In the fullness of his sufficiency he will be
  in distress;
  the hand of everyone in misery will
  come against him.
23 To fill his belly to the full,
  God[1] will send his burning anger
  against him
  and rain it upon him into his body.
24 He will flee from an iron weapon;
  a bronze arrow will strike him through.
25 It is drawn forth and comes out of his
  body;
  the glittering point comes out of his
  gallbladder;
  terrors come upon him.
26 Utter darkness is laid up for his treasures;
  a fire not fanned will devour him;
  what is left in his tent will be consumed.
27 The heavens will reveal his iniquity,
  and the earth will rise up against him.
28 The possessions of his house will be carried
  away,
  dragged off in the day of God's[2]
  wrath.
29 This is the wicked man's portion from God,
  the heritage decreed for him by God."

Job Replies: The Wicked Do Prosper

21 Then Job answered and said:

2 "Keep listening to my words,
  and let this be your comfort.
3 Bear with me, and I will speak,
  and after I have spoken, mock on.
4 As for me, is my complaint against man?
  Why should I not be impatient?
5 Look at me and be appalled,
  and lay your hand over your mouth.
6 When I remember, I am dismayed,
  and shuddering seizes my flesh.
7 Why do the wicked live,
  reach old age, and grow mighty in
  power?
8 Their offspring are established in their
  presence,
  and their descendants before their
  eyes.
9 Their houses are safe from fear,
  and no rod of God is upon them.

---

[1] Hebrew he [2] Hebrew his

10 Their bull breeds without fail;
    their cow calves and does not miscarry.
11 They send out their little boys like a flock,
    and their children dance.
12 They sing to the tambourine and the lyre
    and rejoice to the sound of the pipe.
13 They spend their days in prosperity,
    and in peace they go down to Sheol.
14 They say to God, 'Depart from us!
    We do not desire the knowledge of your
    ways.
15 What is the Almighty, that we should serve
    him?
    And what profit do we get if we pray
    to him?'
16 Behold, is not their prosperity in their hand?
    The counsel of the wicked is far from me.

17 "How often is it that the lamp of the
    wicked is put out?
    That their calamity comes upon them?
    That God[1] distributes pains in his anger?
18 That they are like straw before the wind,
    and like chaff that the storm carries
    away?
19 You say, 'God stores up their iniquity for
    their children.'
    Let him pay it out to them, that they
    may know it.
20 Let their own eyes see their destruction,
    and let them drink of the wrath of the
    Almighty.
21 For what do they care for their houses after
    them,
    when the number of their months is cut
    off?
22 Will any teach God knowledge,
    seeing that he judges those who are on
    high?
23 One dies in his full vigor,
    being wholly at ease and secure,
24 his pails[2] full of milk
    and the marrow of his bones moist.
25 Another dies in bitterness of soul,
    never having tasted of prosperity.
26 They lie down alike in the dust,
    and the worms cover them.

27 "Behold, I know your thoughts
    and your schemes to wrong me.
28 For you say, 'Where is the house of the
    prince?
    Where is the tent in which the wicked
    lived?'
29 Have you not asked those who travel the
    roads,
    and do you not accept their testimony
30 that the evil man is spared in the day of
    calamity,
    that he is rescued in the day of wrath?
31 Who declares his way to his face,
    and who repays him for what he has
    done?
32 When he is carried to the grave,
    watch is kept over his tomb.
33 The clods of the valley are sweet to him;
    all mankind follows after him,
    and those who go before him are innu-
    merable.
34 How then will you comfort me with empty
    nothings?
    There is nothing left of your answers
    but falsehood."

Eliphaz Speaks: Job's Wickedness Is Great

22 Then Eliphaz the Temanite answered
    and said:

2 "Can a man be profitable to God?
    Surely he who is wise is profitable to
    himself.
3 Is it any pleasure to the Almighty if you are
    in the right,
    or is it gain to him if you make your
    ways blameless?
4 Is it for your fear of him that he reproves
    you
    and enters into judgment with you?
5 Is not your evil abundant?
    There is no end to your iniquities.
6 For you have exacted pledges of your
    brothers for nothing
    and stripped the naked of their clothing.
7 You have given no water to the weary to
    drink,
    and you have withheld bread from the
    hungry.
8 The man with power possessed the land,
    and the favored man lived in it.
9 You have sent widows away empty,
    and the arms of the fatherless were
    crushed.
10 Therefore snares are all around you,
    and sudden terror overwhelms you,
11 or darkness, so that you cannot see,
    and a flood of water covers you.

[1] Hebrew he [2] The meaning of the Hebrew word is uncertain

12 "Is not God high in the heavens?
   See the highest stars, how lofty they are!
13 But you say, 'What does God know?
   Can he judge through the deep darkness?
14 Thick clouds veil him, so that he does not see,
   and he walks on the vault of heaven.'
15 Will you keep to the old way
   that wicked men have trod?
16 They were snatched away before their time;
   their foundation was washed away.[1]
17 They said to God, 'Depart from us,'
   and 'What can the Almighty do to us?'[2]
18 Yet he filled their houses with good things—
   but the counsel of the wicked is far from me.
19 The righteous see it and are glad;
   the innocent one mocks at them,
20 saying, 'Surely our adversaries are cut off,
   and what they left the fire has consumed.'

21 "Agree with God, and be at peace;
   thereby good will come to you.
22 Receive instruction from his mouth,
   and lay up his words in your heart.
23 If you return to the Almighty you will be built up;
   if you remove injustice far from your tents,
24 if you lay gold in the dust,
   and gold of Ophir among the stones of the torrent-bed,
25 then the Almighty will be your gold
   and your precious silver.
26 For then you will delight yourself in the Almighty
   and lift up your face to God.
27 You will make your prayer to him, and he will hear you,
   and you will pay your vows.
28 You will decide on a matter, and it will be established for you,
   and light will shine on your ways.
29 For when they are humbled you say, 'It is because of pride';[3]
   but he saves the lowly.
30 He delivers even the one who is not innocent,
   who will be delivered through the cleanness of your hands."

Job Replies: Where Is God?

23 Then Job answered and said:

2 "Today also my complaint is bitter;[4]
   my hand is heavy on account of my groaning.
3 Oh, that I knew where I might find him,
   that I might come even to his seat!
4 I would lay my case before him
   and fill my mouth with arguments.
5 I would know what he would answer me
   and understand what he would say to me.
6 Would he contend with me in the greatness of his power?
   No; he would pay attention to me.
7 There an upright man could argue with him,
   and I would be acquitted forever by my judge.

8 "Behold, I go forward, but he is not there,
   and backward, but I do not perceive him;
9 on the left hand when he is working, I do not behold him;
   he turns to the right hand, but I do not see him.
10 But he knows the way that I take;
   when he has tried me, I shall come out as gold.
11 My foot has held fast to his steps;
   I have kept his way and have not turned aside.
12 I have not departed from the commandment of his lips;
   I have treasured the words of his mouth more than my portion of food.
13 But he is unchangeable,[5] and who can turn him back?
   What he desires, that he does.
14 For he will complete what he appoints for me,
   and many such things are in his mind.
15 Therefore I am terrified at his presence;
   when I consider, I am in dread of him.
16 God has made my heart faint;
   the Almighty has terrified me;
17 yet I am not silenced because of the darkness,
   nor because thick darkness covers my face.

[1] Or their foundation was poured out as a stream (or river) [2] Hebrew them [3] Or you say, 'It is exaltation' [4] Or defiant [5] Or one

24 "Why are not times of judgment kept
    by the Almighty,
      and why do those who know him never
        see his days?
2 Some move landmarks;
      they seize flocks and pasture them.
3 They drive away the donkey of the father-
      less;
      they take the widow's ox for a pledge.
4 They thrust the poor off the road;
      the poor of the earth all hide themselves.
5 Behold, like wild donkeys in the desert
      the poor[1] go out to their toil, seeking
        game;
      the wasteland yields food for their
        children.
6 They gather their[2] fodder in the field,
      and they glean the vineyard of the
        wicked man.
7 They lie all night naked, without clothing,
      and have no covering in the cold.
8 They are wet with the rain of the mountains
      and cling to the rock for lack of shelter.
9 (There are those who snatch the fatherless
      child from the breast,
      and they take a pledge against the poor.)
10 They go about naked, without clothing;
      hungry, they carry the sheaves;
11 among the olive rows of the wicked[3] they
      make oil;
      they tread the winepresses, but suffer
        thirst.
12 From out of the city the dying[4] groan,
      and the soul of the wounded cries for
        help;
      yet God charges no one with wrong.

13 "There are those who rebel against the light,
      who are not acquainted with its ways,
      and do not stay in its paths.
14 The murderer rises before it is light,
      that he may kill the poor and needy,
      and in the night he is like a thief.
15 The eye of the adulterer also waits for the
      twilight,
      saying, 'No eye will see me';
      and he veils his face.
16 In the dark they dig through houses;
      by day they shut themselves up;
      they do not know the light.
17 For deep darkness is morning to all of them;
      for they are friends with the terrors of
        deep darkness.

18 "You say, 'Swift are they on the face of the
      waters;
      their portion is cursed in the land;
      no treader turns toward their vineyards.
19 Drought and heat snatch away the snow
      waters;
      so does Sheol those who have sinned.
20 The womb forgets them;
      the worm finds them sweet;
      they are no longer remembered,
      so wickedness is broken like a tree.'

21 "They wrong the barren, childless woman,
      and do no good to the widow.
22 Yet God[5] prolongs the life of the mighty by
      his power;
      they rise up when they despair of life.
23 He gives them security, and they are sup-
      ported,
      and his eyes are upon their ways.
24 They are exalted a little while, and then are
      gone;
      they are brought low and gathered up
        like all others;
      they are cut off like the heads of grain.
25 If it is not so, who will prove me a liar
      and show that there is nothing in what
        I say?"

Bildad Speaks: Man Cannot Be Righteous

25 Then Bildad the Shuhite answered and
    said:

2 "Dominion and fear are with God;[6]
      he makes peace in his high heaven.
3 Is there any number to his armies?
      Upon whom does his light not arise?
4 How then can man be in the right before
      God?
      How can he who is born of woman be
        pure?
5 Behold, even the moon is not bright,
      and the stars are not pure in his eyes;
6 how much less man, who is a maggot,
      and the son of man, who is a worm!"

Job Replies: God's Majesty Is Unsearchable

26 Then Job answered and said:

2 "How you have helped him who has no
      power!
      How you have saved the arm that has
        no strength!

---

[1] Hebrew they [2] Hebrew his [3] Hebrew their olive rows [4] Or the men [5] Hebrew he [6] Hebrew him

3 How you have counseled him who has no
wisdom,
and plentifully declared sound knowledge!

4 With whose help have you uttered words,
and whose breath has come out from
you?

5 The dead tremble
under the waters and their inhabitants.

6 Sheol is naked before God,[1]
and Abaddon has no covering.

7 He stretches out the north over the void
and hangs the earth on nothing.

8 He binds up the waters in his thick clouds,
and the cloud is not split open under
them.

9 He covers the face of the full moon[2]
and spreads over it his cloud.

10 He has inscribed a circle on the face of the
waters
at the boundary between light and
darkness.

11 The pillars of heaven tremble
and are astounded at his rebuke.

12 By his power he stilled the sea;
by his understanding he shattered
Rahab.

13 By his wind the heavens were made fair;
his hand pierced the fleeing serpent.

14 Behold, these are but the outskirts of his
ways,
and how small a whisper do we hear of
him!
But the thunder of his power who can
understand?"

Job Continues: I Will Maintain My Integrity

27 And Job again took up his discourse,
and said:

2 "As God lives, who has taken away my right,
and the Almighty, who has made my
soul bitter,

3 as long as my breath is in me,
and the spirit of God is in my nostrils,

4 my lips will not speak falsehood,
and my tongue will not utter deceit.

5 Far be it from me to say that you are right;
till I die I will not put away my integrity
from me.

6 I hold fast my righteousness and will not
let it go;
my heart does not reproach me for any
of my days.

7 "Let my enemy be as the wicked,
and let him who rises up against me be
as the unrighteous.

8 For what is the hope of the godless when
God cuts him off,
when God takes away his life?

9 Will God hear his cry
when distress comes upon him?

10 Will he take delight in the Almighty?
Will he call upon God at all times?

11 I will teach you concerning the hand of
God;
what is with the Almighty I will not
conceal.

12 Behold, all of you have seen it yourselves;
why then have you become altogether
vain?

13 "This is the portion of a wicked man with
God,
and the heritage that oppressors receive
from the Almighty:

14 If his children are multiplied, it is for the
sword,
and his descendants have not enough
bread.

15 Those who survive him the pestilence buries,
and his widows do not weep.

16 Though he heap up silver like dust,
and pile up clothing like clay,

17 he may pile it up, but the righteous will
wear it,
and the innocent will divide the silver.

18 He builds his house like a moth's,
like a booth that a watchman makes.

19 He goes to bed rich, but will do so no more;
he opens his eyes, and his wealth is
gone.

20 Terrors overtake him like a flood;
in the night a whirlwind carries him off.

21 The east wind lifts him up and he is gone;
it sweeps him out of his place.

22 It[3] hurls at him without pity;
he flees from its[4] power in headlong
flight.

23 It claps its hands at him
and hisses at him from its place.

---

[1] Hebrew *him* [2] Or *his throne* [3] Or *He* (that is, God); also verse 23 [4] Or *his*; also verse 23

Job Continues: Where Is Wisdom?

28 "Surely there is a mine for silver,
  and a place for gold that they refine.
2 Iron is taken out of the earth,
  and copper is smelted from the ore.
3 Man puts an end to darkness
  and searches out to the farthest limit
  the ore in gloom and deep darkness.
4 He opens shafts in a valley away from
    where anyone lives;
  they are forgotten by travelers;
  they hang in the air, far away from
    mankind; they swing to and fro.
5 As for the earth, out of it comes bread,
  but underneath it is turned up as by fire.
6 Its stones are the place of sapphires,[1]
  and it has dust of gold.

7 "That path no bird of prey knows,
  and the falcon's eye has not seen it.
8 The proud beasts have not trodden it;
  the lion has not passed over it.

9 "Man puts his hand to the flinty rock
  and overturns mountains by the roots.
10 He cuts out channels in the rocks,
  and his eye sees every precious thing.
11 He dams up the streams so that they do
    not trickle,
  and the thing that is hidden he brings
    out to light.

12 "But where shall wisdom be found?
  And where is the place of understand-
    ing?
13 Man does not know its worth,
  and it is not found in the land of the
    living.
14 The deep says, 'It is not in me,'
  and the sea says, 'It is not with me.'
15 It cannot be bought for gold,
  and silver cannot be weighed as its price.
16 It cannot be valued in the gold of Ophir,
  in precious onyx or sapphire.
17 Gold and glass cannot equal it,
  nor can it be exchanged for jewels of
    fine gold.
18 No mention shall be made of coral or of
    crystal;
  the price of wisdom is above pearls.
19 The topaz of Ethiopia cannot equal it,
  nor can it be valued in pure gold.

20 "From where, then, does wisdom come?
  And where is the place of understand-
    ing?
21 It is hidden from the eyes of all living
  and concealed from the birds of the air.
22 Abaddon and Death say,
  'We have heard a rumor of it with our
    ears.'

23 "God understands the way to it,
  and he knows its place.
24 For he looks to the ends of the earth
  and sees everything under the heavens.
25 When he gave to the wind its weight
  and apportioned the waters by measure,
26 when he made a decree for the rain
  and a way for the lightning of the thun-
    der,
27 then he saw it and declared it;
  he established it, and searched it out.
28 And he said to man,
  'Behold, the fear of the Lord, that is wisdom,
  and to turn away from evil is under-
    standing.'"

Job's Summary Defense

29 And Job again took up his discourse,
  and said:

2 "Oh, that I were as in the months of old,
  as in the days when God watched over
    me,
3 when his lamp shone upon my head,
  and by his light I walked through dark-
    ness,
4 as I was in my prime,[2]
  when the friendship of God was upon
    my tent,
5 when the Almighty was yet with me,
  when my children were all around me,
6 when my steps were washed with butter,
  and the rock poured out for me streams
    of oil!
7 When I went out to the gate of the city,
  when I prepared my seat in the square,
8 the young men saw me and withdrew,
  and the aged rose and stood;
9 the princes refrained from talking
  and laid their hand on their mouth;
10 the voice of the nobles was hushed,
  and their tongue stuck to the roof of
    their mouth.
11 When the ear heard, it called me blessed,
  and when the eye saw, it approved,

[1] Or lapis lazuli; also verse 16 [2] Hebrew my autumn days

¹² because I delivered the poor who cried for
help,
and the fatherless who had none to help
him.
¹³ The blessing of him who was about to perish came upon me,
and I caused the widow's heart to sing
for joy.
¹⁴ I put on righteousness, and it clothed
me;
my justice was like a robe and a turban.
¹⁵ I was eyes to the blind
and feet to the lame.
¹⁶ I was a father to the needy,
and I searched out the cause of him
whom I did not know.
¹⁷ I broke the fangs of the unrighteous
and made him drop his prey from his
teeth.
¹⁸ Then I thought, 'I shall die in my nest,
and I shall multiply my days as the
sand,
¹⁹ my roots spread out to the waters,
with the dew all night on my
branches,
²⁰ my glory fresh with me,
and my bow ever new in my hand.'

²¹ "Men listened to me and waited
and kept silence for my counsel.
²² After I spoke they did not speak again,
and my word dropped upon them.
²³ They waited for me as for the rain,
and they opened their mouths as for the
spring rain.
²⁴ I smiled on them when they had no confidence,
and the light of my face they did not
cast down.
²⁵ I chose their way and sat as chief,
and I lived like a king among his troops,
like one who comforts mourners.

30

"But now they laugh at me,
men who are younger than I,
whose fathers I would have disdained
to set with the dogs of my flock.
² What could I gain from the strength of
their hands,
men whose vigor is gone?
³ Through want and hard hunger
they gnaw the dry ground by night in
waste and desolation;

⁴ they pick saltwort and the leaves of bushes,
and the roots of the broom tree for their
food.¹
⁵ They are driven out from human company;
they shout after them as after a thief.
⁶ In the gullies of the torrents they must
dwell,
in holes of the earth and of the rocks.
⁷ Among the bushes they bray;
under the nettles they huddle
together.
⁸ A senseless, a nameless brood,
they have been whipped out of the land.

⁹ "And now I have become their song;
I am a byword to them.
¹⁰ They abhor me; they keep aloof from
me;
they do not hesitate to spit at the sight
of me.
¹¹ Because God has loosed my cord and
humbled me,
they have cast off restraint² in my presence.
¹² On my right hand the rabble rise;
they push away my feet;
they cast up against me their ways of
destruction.
¹³ They break up my path;
they promote my calamity;
they need no one to help them.
¹⁴ As through a wide breach they come;
amid the crash they roll on.
¹⁵ Terrors are turned upon me;
my honor is pursued as by the wind,
and my prosperity has passed away like
a cloud.

¹⁶ "And now my soul is poured out within me;
days of affliction have taken hold of me.
¹⁷ The night racks my bones,
and the pain that gnaws me takes no
rest.
¹⁸ With great force my garment is disfigured;
it binds me about like the collar of my
tunic.
¹⁹ God³ has cast me into the mire,
and I have become like dust and ashes.
²⁰ I cry to you for help and you do not answer
me;
I stand, and you only look at me.

¹ Or warmth ² Hebrew the bridle ³ Hebrew He

21 You have turned cruel to me;
  with the might of your hand you perse-
    cute me.
22 You lift me up on the wind; you make me
    ride on it,
  and you toss me about in the roar of the
    storm.
23 For I know that you will bring me to death
  and to the house appointed for all liv-
    ing.

24 "Yet does not one in a heap of ruins stretch
    out his hand,
  and in his disaster cry for help?[1]
25 Did not I weep for him whose day was
    hard?
  Was not my soul grieved for the needy?
26 But when I hoped for good, evil came,
  and when I waited for light, darkness
    came.
27 My inward parts are in turmoil and never
    still;
  days of affliction come to meet me.
28 I go about darkened, but not by the sun;
  I stand up in the assembly and cry for
    help.
29 I am a brother of jackals
  and a companion of ostriches.
30 My skin turns black and falls from me,
  and my bones burn with heat.
31 My lyre is turned to mourning,
  and my pipe to the voice of those who
    weep.

Job's Final Appeal

31 "I have made a covenant with my eyes;
  how then could I gaze at a virgin?
2 What would be my portion from God
    above
  and my heritage from the Almighty on
    high?
3 Is not calamity for the unrighteous,
  and disaster for the workers of iniquity?
4 Does not he see my ways
  and number all my steps?

5 "If I have walked with falsehood
  and my foot has hastened to deceit;
6 (Let me be weighed in a just balance,
  and let God know my integrity!)
7 if my step has turned aside from the way
  and my heart has gone after my eyes,
  and if any spot has stuck to my hands,

8 then let me sow, and another eat,
  and let what grows for me[2] be rooted
    out.

9 "If my heart has been enticed toward a
    woman,
  and I have lain in wait at my neighbor's
    door,
10 then let my wife grind for another,
  and let others bow down on her.
11 For that would be a heinous crime;
  that would be an iniquity to be pun-
    ished by the judges;
12 for that would be a fire that consumes as
    far as Abaddon,
  and it would burn to the root all my
    increase.

13 "If I have rejected the cause of my manser-
    vant or my maidservant,
  when they brought a complaint
    against me,
14 what then shall I do when God rises up?
  When he makes inquiry, what shall I
    answer him?
15 Did not he who made me in the womb
    make him?
  And did not one fashion us in the
    womb?

16 "If I have withheld anything that the poor
    desired,
  or have caused the eyes of the widow to
    fail,
17 or have eaten my morsel alone,
  and the fatherless has not eaten of it
18 (for from my youth the fatherless[3] grew up
    with me as with a father,
  and from my mother's womb I guided
    the widow[4]),
19 if I have seen anyone perish for lack of
    clothing,
  or the needy without covering,
20 if his body has not blessed me,[5]
  and if he was not warmed with the
    fleece of my sheep,
21 if I have raised my hand against the father-
    less,
  because I saw my help in the gate,
22 then let my shoulder blade fall from my
    shoulder,
  and let my arm be broken from its
    socket.

---

[1] The meaning of the Hebrew is uncertain [2] Or *let my descendants* [3] Hebrew *he* [4] Hebrew *her* [5] Hebrew *if his loins have not blessed me*

23 For I was in terror of calamity from God,
   and I could not have faced his majesty.

24 "If I have made gold my trust
   or called fine gold my confidence,
25 if I have rejoiced because my wealth was
      abundant
   or because my hand had found much,
26 if I have looked at the sun[1] when it
      shone,
   or the moon moving in splendor,
27 and my heart has been secretly enticed,
   and my mouth has kissed my hand,
28 this also would be an iniquity to be pun-
      ished by the judges,
   for I would have been false to God
      above.

29 "If I have rejoiced at the ruin of him who
      hated me,
   or exulted when evil overtook him
30 (I have not let my mouth sin
   by asking for his life with a curse),
31 if the men of my tent have not said,
   'Who is there that has not been filled
      with his meat?'
32 (the sojourner has not lodged in the street;
   I have opened my doors to the traveler),
33 if I have concealed my transgressions as
      others do[2]
   by hiding my iniquity in my heart,
34 because I stood in great fear of the multi-
      tude,
   and the contempt of families terrified
      me,
   so that I kept silence, and did not go out
      of doors—
35 Oh, that I had one to hear me!
   (Here is my signature! Let the Almighty
      answer me!)
   Oh, that I had the indictment written
      by my adversary!
36 Surely I would carry it on my shoulder;
   I would bind it on me as a crown;
37 I would give him an account of all my
      steps;
   like a prince I would approach him.

38 "If my land has cried out against me
   and its furrows have wept together,
39 if I have eaten its yield without payment
   and made its owners breathe their
      last,

40 let thorns grow instead of wheat,
   and foul weeds instead of barley."

The words of Job are ended.

Elihu Rebukes Job's Three Friends

32 So these three men ceased to answer Job, because he was righteous in his own eyes. [2] Then Elihu the son of Barachel the Buzite, of the family of Ram, burned with anger. He burned with anger at Job because he justified himself rather than God. [3] He burned with anger also at Job's three friends because they had found no answer, although they had declared Job to be in the wrong. [4] Now Elihu had waited to speak to Job because they were older than he. [5] And when Elihu saw that there was no answer in the mouth of these three men, he burned with anger.

[6] And Elihu the son of Barachel the Buzite answered and said:

   "I am young in years,
      and you are aged;
   therefore I was timid and afraid
      to declare my opinion to you.
7 I said, 'Let days speak,
      and many years teach wisdom.'
8 But it is the spirit in man,
      the breath of the Almighty, that makes
         him understand.
9 It is not the old[3] who are wise,
      nor the aged who understand what is
         right.
10 Therefore I say, 'Listen to me;
      let me also declare my opinion.'

11 "Behold, I waited for your words,
      I listened for your wise sayings,
   while you searched out what to say.
12 I gave you my attention,
      and, behold, there was none among you
         who refuted Job
   or who answered his words.
13 Beware lest you say, 'We have found wis-
      dom;
   God may vanquish him, not a man.'
14 He has not directed his words against
      me,
   and I will not answer him with your
      speeches.

15 "They are dismayed; they answer no more;
   they have not a word to say.

---

[1] Hebrew *the light* [2] Or *as Adam did* [3] Hebrew *many* [in years]

16 And shall I wait, because they do not speak,
  because they stand there, and answer no
  more?

17 I also will answer with my share;
  I also will declare my opinion.

18 For I am full of words;
  the spirit within me constrains me.

19 Behold, my belly is like wine that has no
  vent;
  like new wineskins ready to burst.

20 I must speak, that I may find relief;
  I must open my lips and answer.

21 I will not show partiality to any man
  or use flattery toward any person.

22 For I do not know how to flatter,
  else my Maker would soon take me
  away.

Elihu Rebukes Job

33 "But now, hear my speech, O Job,
  and listen to all my words.

2 Behold, I open my mouth;
  the tongue in my mouth speaks.

3 My words declare the uprightness of my
  heart,
  and what my lips know they speak sincerely.

4 The Spirit of God has made me,
  and the breath of the Almighty gives
  me life.

5 Answer me, if you can;
  set your words in order before me;
  take your stand.

6 Behold, I am toward God as you are;
  I too was pinched off from a piece of
  clay.

7 Behold, no fear of me need terrify you;
  my pressure will not be heavy upon
  you.

8 "Surely you have spoken in my ears,
  and I have heard the sound of your
  words.

9 You say, 'I am pure, without transgression;
  I am clean, and there is no iniquity in
  me.

10 Behold, he finds occasions against me,
  he counts me as his enemy,

11 he puts my feet in the stocks
  and watches all my paths.'

12 "Behold, in this you are not right. I will
  answer you,
  for God is greater than man.

13 Why do you contend against him,
  saying, 'He will answer none of man's[1]
  words'?[2]

14 For God speaks in one way,
  and in two, though man does not perceive it.

15 In a dream, in a vision of the night,
  when deep sleep falls on men,
  while they slumber on their beds,

16 then he opens the ears of men
  and terrifies[3] them with warnings,

17 that he may turn man aside from his
  deed
  and conceal pride from a man;

18 he keeps back his soul from the pit,
  his life from perishing by the sword.

19 "Man is also rebuked with pain on his bed
  and with continual strife in his bones,

20 so that his life loathes bread,
  and his appetite the choicest food.

21 His flesh is so wasted away that it cannot
  be seen,
  and his bones that were not seen stick
  out.

22 His soul draws near the pit,
  and his life to those who bring death.

23 If there be for him an angel,
  a mediator, one of the thousand,
  to declare to man what is right for
  him,

24 and he is merciful to him, and says,
  'Deliver him from going down into the
  pit;
  I have found a ransom;

25 let his flesh become fresh with youth;
  let him return to the days of his youthful vigor';

26 then man[4] prays to God, and he accepts
  him;
  he sees his face with a shout of joy,
  and he restores to man his righteousness.

27 He sings before men and says:
  'I sinned and perverted what was right,
  and it was not repaid to me.

28 He has redeemed my soul from going
  down into the pit,
  and my life shall look upon the light.'

29 "Behold, God does all these things,
  twice, three times, with a man,

30 to bring back his soul from the pit,
  that he may be lighted with the light of
  life.

---

[1] Hebrew his [2] Or He will not answer for any of his own words [3] Or seals [4] Hebrew he

31 Pay attention, O Job, listen to me;
    be silent, and I will speak.
32 If you have any words, answer me;
    speak, for I desire to justify you.
33 If not, listen to me;
    be silent, and I will teach you wisdom."

Elihu Asserts God's Justice

34 Then Elihu answered and said:

2 "Hear my words, you wise men,
    and give ear to me, you who know;
3 for the ear tests words
    as the palate tastes food.
4 Let us choose what is right;
    let us know among ourselves what is
      good.
5 For Job has said, 'I am in the right,
    and God has taken away my right;
6 in spite of my right I am counted a liar;
    my wound is incurable, though I am
      without transgression.'
7 What man is like Job,
    who drinks up scoffing like water,
8 who travels in company with evildoers
    and walks with wicked men?
9 For he has said, 'It profits a man nothing
    that he should take delight in God.'

10 "Therefore, hear me, you men of under-
      standing:
    far be it from God that he should do
      wickedness,
    and from the Almighty that he should
      do wrong.
11 For according to the work of a man he will
      repay him,
    and according to his ways he will make
      it befall him.
12 Of a truth, God will not do wickedly,
    and the Almighty will not pervert justice.
13 Who gave him charge over the earth,
    and who laid on him[1] the whole world?
14 If he should set his heart to it
    and gather to himself his spirit and his
      breath,
15 all flesh would perish together,
    and man would return to dust.

16 "If you have understanding, hear this;
    listen to what I say.
17 Shall one who hates justice govern?
    Will you condemn him who is righ-
      teous and mighty,
18 who says to a king, 'Worthless one,'
    and to nobles, 'Wicked man,'
19 who shows no partiality to princes,
    nor regards the rich more than the poor,
    for they are all the work of his hands?
20 In a moment they die;
    at midnight the people are shaken and
      pass away,
    and the mighty are taken away by no
      human hand.

21 "For his eyes are on the ways of a man,
    and he sees all his steps.
22 There is no gloom or deep darkness
    where evildoers may hide themselves.
23 For God[2] has no need to consider a man
      further,
    that he should go before God in judg-
      ment.
24 He shatters the mighty without investiga-
      tion
    and sets others in their place.
25 Thus, knowing their works,
    he overturns them in the night, and
      they are crushed.
26 He strikes them for their wickedness
    in a place for all to see,
27 because they turned aside from following
      him
    and had no regard for any of his ways,
28 so that they caused the cry of the poor to
      come to him,
    and he heard the cry of the afflicted—
29 When he is quiet, who can condemn?
    When he hides his face, who can behold
      him,
    whether it be a nation or a man?—
30 that a godless man should not reign,
    that he should not ensnare the people.

31 "For has anyone said to God,
    'I have borne punishment; I will not
      offend any more;
32 teach me what I do not see;
    if I have done iniquity, I will do it no
      more'?
33 Will he then make repayment to suit you,
    because you reject it?
    For you must choose, and not I;
    therefore declare what you know.[3]
34 Men of understanding will say to me,
    and the wise man who hears me will
      say:

---

[1] Hebrew lacks *on him* [2] Hebrew *he* [3] The meaning of the Hebrew in verses 29–33 is uncertain

35 'Job speaks without knowledge;
     his words are without insight.'
36 Would that Job were tried to the end,
     because he answers like wicked men.
37 For he adds rebellion to his sin;
     he claps his hands among us
     and multiplies his words against God."

Elihu Condemns Job

35 And Elihu answered and said:

2 "Do you think this to be just?
     Do you say, 'It is my right before God,'
3 that you ask, 'What advantage have I?
     How am I better off than if I had sinned?'
4 I will answer you
     and your friends with you.
5 Look at the heavens, and see;
     and behold the clouds, which are higher
       than you.
6 If you have sinned, what do you accom-
       plish against him?
     And if your transgressions are multi-
       plied, what do you do to him?
7 If you are righteous, what do you give to
       him?
     Or what does he receive from your hand?
8 Your wickedness concerns a man like
       yourself,
     and your righteousness a son of man.

9 "Because of the multitude of oppressions
       people cry out;
     they call for help because of the arm of
       the mighty.[1]
10 But none says, 'Where is God my Maker,
     who gives songs in the night,
11 who teaches us more than the beasts of the
       earth
     and makes us wiser than the birds of
       the heavens?'
12 There they cry out, but he does not answer,
     because of the pride of evil men.
13 Surely God does not hear an empty cry,
     nor does the Almighty regard it.
14 How much less when you say that you do
       not see him,
     that the case is before him, and you are
       waiting for him!
15 And now, because his anger does not pun-
       ish,
     and he does not take much note of
       transgression,[2]

16 Job opens his mouth in empty talk;
     he multiplies words without knowl-
       edge."

Elihu Extols God's Greatness

36 And Elihu continued, and said:

2 "Bear with me a little, and I will show you,
     for I have yet something to say on
       God's behalf.
3 I will get my knowledge from afar
     and ascribe righteousness to my Maker.
4 For truly my words are not false;
     one who is perfect in knowledge is
       with you.

5 "Behold, God is mighty, and does not
       despise any;
     he is mighty in strength of understand-
       ing.
6 He does not keep the wicked alive,
     but gives the afflicted their right.
7 He does not withdraw his eyes from the
       righteous,
     but with kings on the throne
     he sets them forever, and they are exalted.
8 And if they are bound in chains
     and caught in the cords of affliction,
9 then he declares to them their work
     and their transgressions, that they are
       behaving arrogantly.
10 He opens their ears to instruction
     and commands that they return from
       iniquity.
11 If they listen and serve him,
     they complete their days in prosperity,
     and their years in pleasantness.
12 But if they do not listen, they perish by the
       sword
     and die without knowledge.

13 "The godless in heart cherish anger;
     they do not cry for help when he binds
       them.
14 They die in youth,
     and their life ends among the cult pros-
       titutes.
15 He delivers the afflicted by their affliction
     and opens their ear by adversity.
16 He also allured you out of distress
     into a broad place where there was no
       cramping,
     and what was set on your table was full
       of fatness.

[1] Or the many [2] Theodotion, Symmachus (compare Vulgate); the meaning of the Hebrew word is uncertain

17 "But you are full of the judgment on the
        wicked;
    judgment and justice seize you.
18 Beware lest wrath entice you into scoff-
        ing,
    and let not the greatness of the ransom
        turn you aside.
19 Will your cry for help avail to keep you
        from distress,
    or all the force of your strength?
20 Do not long for the night,
    when peoples vanish in their place.
21 Take care; do not turn to iniquity,
    for this you have chosen rather than
        affliction.
22 Behold, God is exalted in his power;
    who is a teacher like him?
23 Who has prescribed for him his way,
    or who can say, 'You have done
        wrong'?

24 "Remember to extol his work,
    of which men have sung.
25 All mankind has looked on it;
    man beholds it from afar.
26 Behold, God is great, and we know him
        not;
    the number of his years is unsearch-
        able.
27 For he draws up the drops of water;
    they distill his mist in rain,
28 which the skies pour down
    and drop on mankind abundantly.
29 Can anyone understand the spreading of
        the clouds,
    the thunderings of his pavilion?
30 Behold, he scatters his lightning about him
    and covers the roots of the sea.
31 For by these he judges peoples;
    he gives food in abundance.
32 He covers his hands with the lightning
    and commands it to strike the mark.
33 Its crashing declares his presence;[1]
    the cattle also declare that he rises.

Elihu Proclaims God's Majesty

37 "At this also my heart trembles
    and leaps out of its place.
2   Keep listening to the thunder of his
        voice
    and the rumbling that comes from his
        mouth.

3 Under the whole heaven he lets it go,
    and his lightning to the corners of the
        earth.
4 After it his voice roars;
    he thunders with his majestic voice,
    and he does not restrain the light-
        nings[2] when his voice is heard.
5 God thunders wondrously with his
        voice;
    he does great things that we cannot
        comprehend.
6 For to the snow he says, 'Fall on the
        earth,'
    likewise to the downpour, his mighty
        downpour.
7 He seals up the hand of every man,
    that all men whom he made may know
        it.
8 Then the beasts go into their lairs,
    and remain in their dens.
9 From its chamber comes the whirlwind,
    and cold from the scattering winds.
10 By the breath of God ice is given,
    and the broad waters are frozen fast.
11 He loads the thick cloud with moisture;
    the clouds scatter his lightning.
12 They turn around and around by his guid-
        ance,
    to accomplish all that he commands
        them
    on the face of the habitable world.
13 Whether for correction or for his land
    or for love, he causes it to happen.

14 "Hear this, O Job;
    stop and consider the wondrous works
        of God.
15 Do you know how God lays his command
        upon them
    and causes the lightning of his cloud to
        shine?
16 Do you know the balancings[3] of the clouds,
    the wondrous works of him who is per-
        fect in knowledge,
17 you whose garments are hot
    when the earth is still because of the
        south wind?
18 Can you, like him, spread out the skies,
    hard as a cast metal mirror?
19 Teach us what we shall say to him;
    we cannot draw up our case because of
        darkness.

[1] Hebrew *declares concerning him* [2] Hebrew *them* [3] Or *hoverings*

20 Shall it be told him that I would speak?
  Did a man ever wish that he would be
    swallowed up?

21 "And now no one looks on the light
    when it is bright in the skies,
    when the wind has passed and cleared
      them.

22 Out of the north comes golden splendor;
    God is clothed with awesome majesty.

23 The Almighty—we cannot find him;
    he is great in power;
    justice and abundant righteousness he
      will not violate.

24 Therefore men fear him;
    he does not regard any who are wise in
      their own conceit."[1]

The LORD Answers Job

38 Then the LORD answered Job out of the
    whirlwind and said:

2 "Who is this that darkens counsel by words
    without knowledge?

3 Dress for action[2] like a man;
    I will question you, and you make it
      known to me.

4 "Where were you when I laid the founda-
    tion of the earth?
    Tell me, if you have understanding.

5 Who determined its measurements—
    surely you know!
    Or who stretched the line upon it?

6 On what were its bases sunk,
    or who laid its cornerstone,

7 when the morning stars sang together
    and all the sons of God shouted for joy?

8 "Or who shut in the sea with doors
    when it burst out from the womb,

9 when I made clouds its garment
    and thick darkness its swaddling
      band,

10 and prescribed limits for it
    and set bars and doors,

11 and said, 'Thus far shall you come, and no
      farther,
    and here shall your proud waves be
      stayed'?

12 "Have you commanded the morning since
      your days began,
    and caused the dawn to know its place,

13 that it might take hold of the skirts of the
      earth,
    and the wicked be shaken out of it?

14 It is changed like clay under the seal,
    and its features stand out like a garment.

15 From the wicked their light is withheld,
    and their uplifted arm is broken.

16 "Have you entered into the springs of the
      sea,
    or walked in the recesses of the deep?

17 Have the gates of death been revealed to
      you,
    or have you seen the gates of deep dark-
      ness?

18 Have you comprehended the expanse of
      the earth?
    Declare, if you know all this.

19 "Where is the way to the dwelling of light,
    and where is the place of darkness,

20 that you may take it to its territory
    and that you may discern the paths to
      its home?

21 You know, for you were born then,
    and the number of your days is great!

22 "Have you entered the storehouses of the
      snow,
    or have you seen the storehouses of the
      hail,

23 which I have reserved for the time of
      trouble,
    for the day of battle and war?

24 What is the way to the place where the
      light is distributed,
    or where the east wind is scattered
      upon the earth?

25 "Who has cleft a channel for the torrents of
      rain
    and a way for the thunderbolt,

26 to bring rain on a land where no man is,
    on the desert in which there is no man,

27 to satisfy the waste and desolate land,
    and to make the ground sprout with
      grass?

28 "Has the rain a father,
    or who has begotten the drops of dew?

29 From whose womb did the ice come forth,
    and who has given birth to the frost of
      heaven?

30 The waters become hard like stone,
    and the face of the deep is frozen.

---

[1] Hebrew *in heart* [2] Hebrew *Gird up your loins*

31 "Can you bind the chains of the Pleiades
    or loose the cords of Orion?
32 Can you lead forth the Mazzaroth[1] in their
    season,
    or can you guide the Bear with its chil-
    dren?
33 Do you know the ordinances of the heav-
    ens?
    Can you establish their rule on the
    earth?

34 "Can you lift up your voice to the clouds,
    that a flood of waters may cover you?
35 Can you send forth lightnings, that they
    may go
    and say to you, 'Here we are'?
36 Who has put wisdom in the inward parts[2]
    or given understanding to the mind?[3]
37 Who can number the clouds by wisdom?
    Or who can tilt the waterskins of the
    heavens,
38 when the dust runs into a mass
    and the clods stick fast together?

39 "Can you hunt the prey for the lion,
    or satisfy the appetite of the young
    lions,
40 when they crouch in their dens
    or lie in wait in their thicket?
41 Who provides for the raven its prey,
    when its young ones cry to God for help,
    and wander about for lack of food?

39

"Do you know when the mountain
    goats give birth?
    Do you observe the calving of the does?
2 Can you number the months that they ful-
    fill,
    and do you know the time when they
    give birth,
3 when they crouch, bring forth their off-
    spring,
    and are delivered of their young?
4 Their young ones become strong; they
    grow up in the open;
    they go out and do not return to them.

5 "Who has let the wild donkey go free?
    Who has loosed the bonds of the swift
    donkey,
6 to whom I have given the arid plain for his
    home
    and the salt land for his dwelling place?
7 He scorns the tumult of the city;
    he hears not the shouts of the driver.

8 He ranges the mountains as his pasture,
    and he searches after every green thing.

9 "Is the wild ox willing to serve you?
    Will he spend the night at your man-
    ger?
10 Can you bind him in the furrow with
    ropes,
    or will he harrow the valleys after you?
11 Will you depend on him because his
    strength is great,
    and will you leave to him your labor?
12 Do you have faith in him that he will
    return your grain
    and gather it to your threshing floor?

13 "The wings of the ostrich wave proudly,
    but are they the pinions and plumage
    of love?[4]
14 For she leaves her eggs to the earth
    and lets them be warmed on the
    ground,
15 forgetting that a foot may crush them
    and that the wild beast may trample
    them.
16 She deals cruelly with her young, as if they
    were not hers;
    though her labor be in vain, yet she has
    no fear,
17 because God has made her forget wisdom
    and given her no share in understand-
    ing.
18 When she rouses herself to flee,[5]
    she laughs at the horse and his rider.

19 "Do you give the horse his might?
    Do you clothe his neck with a mane?
20 Do you make him leap like the locust?
    His majestic snorting is terrifying.
21 He paws[6] in the valley and exults in his
    strength;
    he goes out to meet the weapons.
22 He laughs at fear and is not dismayed;
    he does not turn back from the sword.
23 Upon him rattle the quiver,
    the flashing spear, and the javelin.
24 With fierceness and rage he swallows the
    ground;
    he cannot stand still at the sound of the
    trumpet.
25 When the trumpet sounds, he says 'Aha!'
    He smells the battle from afar,
    the thunder of the captains, and the
    shouting.

---

[1] Probably the name of a constellation   [2] Or *in the ibis*   [3] Or *rooster*   [4] The meaning of the Hebrew is uncertain   [5] The meaning of the Hebrew is uncertain   [6] Hebrew *They paw*

26 "Is it by your understanding that the hawk
      soars
   and spreads his wings toward the
      south?
27 Is it at your command that the eagle
      mounts up
   and makes his nest on high?
28 On the rock he dwells and makes his
      home,
   on the rocky crag and stronghold.
29 From there he spies out the prey;
   his eyes behold it from far away.
30 His young ones suck up blood,
   and where the slain are, there is he."

40 And the LORD said to Job:

2 " Shall a faultfinder contend with the
      Almighty?
   He who argues with God, let him
      answer it."

Job Promises Silence

3 Then Job answered the LORD and said:

4 "Behold, I am of small account; what shall I
      answer you?
   I lay my hand on my mouth.
5 I have spoken once, and I will not answer;
   twice, but I will proceed no further."

The LORD Challenges Job

6 Then the LORD answered Job out of the
whirlwind and said:

7 "Dress for action[1] like a man;
   I will question you, and you make it
      known to me.
8 Will you even put me in the wrong?
   Will you condemn me that you may be
      in the right?
9 Have you an arm like God,
   and can you thunder with a voice like
      his?

10 "Adorn yourself with majesty and dignity;
   clothe yourself with glory and splen-
      dor.
11 Pour out the overflowings of your anger,
   and look on everyone who is proud and
      abase him.
12 Look on everyone who is proud and bring
      him low
   and tread down the wicked where they
      stand.

13 Hide them all in the dust together;
   bind their faces in the world below.[2]
14 Then will I also acknowledge to you
   that your own right hand can save you.

15 "Behold, Behemoth,[3]
   which I made as I made you;
   he eats grass like an ox.
16 Behold, his strength in his loins,
   and his power in the muscles of his
      belly.
17 He makes his tail stiff like a cedar;
   the sinews of his thighs are knit
      together.
18 His bones are tubes of bronze,
   his limbs like bars of iron.

19 "He is the first of the works[4] of God;
   let him who made him bring near his
      sword!
20 For the mountains yield food for him
   where all the wild beasts play.
21 Under the lotus plants he lies,
   in the shelter of the reeds and in the
      marsh.
22 For his shade the lotus trees cover him;
   the willows of the brook surround
      him.
23 Behold, if the river is turbulent he is not
      frightened;
   he is confident though Jordan rushes
      against his mouth.
24 Can one take him by his eyes,[5]
   or pierce his nose with a snare?

41 6 "Can you draw out Leviathan[7] with a
      fishhook
   or press down his tongue with a cord?
2 Can you put a rope in his nose
   or pierce his jaw with a hook?
3 Will he make many pleas to you?
   Will he speak to you soft words?
4 Will he make a covenant with you
   to take him for your servant forever?
5 Will you play with him as with a bird,
   or will you put him on a leash for your
      girls?
6 Will traders bargain over him?
   Will they divide him up among the
      merchants?
7 Can you fill his skin with harpoons
   or his head with fishing spears?

[1] Hebrew *Gird up your loins* [2] Hebrew *in the hidden place* [3] A large animal, exact identity unknown [4] Hebrew *ways* [5] Or *in his sight* [6] Ch 40:25 in Hebrew [7] A large sea animal,
exact identity unknown

8 Lay your hands on him;
　　remember the battle—you will not do
　　　it again!

9 [1] Behold, the hope of a man is false;
　　he is laid low even at the sight of him.

10 No one is so fierce that he dares to stir him
　　up.
　　Who then is he who can stand before
　　　me?

11 Who has first given to me, that I should
　　repay him?
　　Whatever is under the whole heaven is
　　　mine.

12 "I will not keep silence concerning his
　　limbs,
　　or his mighty strength, or his goodly
　　　frame.

13 Who can strip off his outer garment?
　　Who would come near him with a
　　　bridle?

14 Who can open the doors of his face?
　　Around his teeth is terror.

15 His back is made of[2] rows of shields,
　　shut up closely as with a seal.

16 One is so near to another
　　that no air can come between them.

17 They are joined one to another;
　　they clasp each other and cannot be
　　　separated.

18 His sneezings flash forth light,
　　and his eyes are like the eyelids of the
　　　dawn.

19 Out of his mouth go flaming torches;
　　sparks of fire leap forth.

20 Out of his nostrils comes forth smoke,
　　as from a boiling pot and burning
　　　rushes.

21 His breath kindles coals,
　　and a flame comes forth from his
　　　mouth.

22 In his neck abides strength,
　　and terror dances before him.

23 The folds of his flesh stick together,
　　firmly cast on him and immovable.

24 His heart is hard as a stone,
　　hard as the lower millstone.

25 When he raises himself up, the mighty[3]
　　are afraid;
　　at the crashing they are beside them-
　　　selves.

26 Though the sword reaches him, it does not
　　avail,
　　nor the spear, the dart, or the javelin.

27 He counts iron as straw,
　　and bronze as rotten wood.

28 The arrow cannot make him flee;
　　for him, sling stones are turned to
　　　stubble.

29 Clubs are counted as stubble;
　　he laughs at the rattle of javelins.

30 His underparts are like sharp potsherds;
　　he spreads himself like a threshing
　　　sledge on the mire.

31 He makes the deep boil like a pot;
　　he makes the sea like a pot of ointment.

32 Behind him he leaves a shining wake;
　　one would think the deep to be white-
　　　haired.

33 On earth there is not his like,
　　a creature without fear.

34 He sees everything that is high;
　　he is king over all the sons of pride."

Job's Confession and Repentance

42 Then Job answered the LORD and said:

2 "I know that you can do all things,
　　and that no purpose of yours can be
　　　thwarted.

3 'Who is this that hides counsel without
　　knowledge?'
　　Therefore I have uttered what I did not
　　　understand,
　　things too wonderful for me, which I
　　　did not know.

4 'Hear, and I will speak;
　　I will question you, and you make it
　　　known to me.'

5 I had heard of you by the hearing of the
　　ear,
　　but now my eye sees you;

6 therefore I despise myself,
　　and repent[4] in dust and ashes."

The LORD Rebukes Job's Friends

7 After the LORD had spoken these words to Job, the LORD said to Eliphaz the Temanite: "My anger burns against you and against your two friends, for you have not spoken of me what is right, as my servant Job has. 8 Now therefore take seven bulls and seven rams and go to my servant Job and offer up a burnt offering for yourselves. And my servant Job shall pray for you, for I will accept his prayer not to deal

---

1 Ch 41:1 in Hebrew 2 Or *His pride is in his* 3 Or *gods* 4 Or *and am comforted*

with you according to your folly. For you have not spoken of me what is right, as my servant Job has." [9] So Eliphaz the Temanite and Bildad the Shuhite and Zophar the Naamathite went and did what the LORD had told them, and the LORD accepted Job's prayer.

The LORD Restores Job's Fortunes

[10] And the LORD restored the fortunes of Job, when he had prayed for his friends. And the LORD gave Job twice as much as he had before. [11] Then came to him all his brothers and sisters and all who had known him before, and ate bread with him in his house. And they showed him sympathy and comforted him for all the evil[1] that the LORD had brought upon him. And each of them gave him a piece of money[2] and a ring of gold.

[12] And the LORD blessed the latter days of Job more than his beginning. And he had 14,000 sheep, 6,000 camels, 1,000 yoke of oxen, and 1,000 female donkeys. [13] He had also seven sons and three daughters. [14] And he called the name of the first daughter Jemimah, and the name of the second Keziah, and the name of the third Keren-happuch. [15] And in all the land there were no women so beautiful as Job's daughters. And their father gave them an inheritance among their brothers. [16] And after this Job lived 140 years, and saw his sons, and his sons' sons, four generations. [17] And Job died, an old man, and full of days.

---

[1] Or disaster [2] Hebrew a qesitah; a unit of money of unknown value

THE PSALMS

BOOK ONE

The Way of the Righteous and the Wicked

1 Blessed is the man[1]
who walks not in the counsel of the wicked,
  nor stands in the way of sinners,
    nor sits in the seat of scoffers;

2   but his delight is in the law[2] of the LORD,
  and on his law he meditates day and
    night.

3   He is like a tree
  planted by streams of water
    that yields its fruit in its season,
      and its leaf does not wither.
  In all that he does, he prospers.

4   The wicked are not so,
    but are like chaff that the wind drives
      away.

5   Therefore the wicked will not stand in the
    judgment,
  nor sinners in the congregation of the
    righteous;

6   for the LORD knows the way of the righ-
    teous,
  but the way of the wicked will perish.

The Reign of the LORD's Anointed

2 Why do the nations rage[3]
  and the peoples plot in vain?

2   The kings of the earth set themselves,
  and the rulers take counsel together,
    against the LORD and against his
      Anointed, saying,

3   "Let us burst their bonds apart
  and cast away their cords from us."

4   He who sits in the heavens laughs;
  the Lord holds them in derision.

5   Then he will speak to them in his wrath,
  and terrify them in his fury, saying,

6   "As for me, I have set my King
  on Zion, my holy hill."

7   I will tell of the decree:
  The LORD said to me, "You are my Son;
    today I have begotten you.

8   Ask of me, and I will make the nations
    your heritage,
  and the ends of the earth your possession.

9   You shall break[4] them with a rod of iron
  and dash them in pieces like a potter's
    vessel."

10   Now therefore, O kings, be wise;
  be warned, O rulers of the earth.

11   Serve the LORD with fear,
  and rejoice with trembling.

12   Kiss the Son,
  lest he be angry, and you perish in the
    way,
  for his wrath is quickly kindled.
  Blessed are all who take refuge in him.

Save Me, O My God

3 A PSALM OF DAVID, WHEN HE FLED FROM
ABSALOM HIS SON.

1   O LORD, how many are my foes!
  Many are rising against me;

2   many are saying of my soul,
  "There is no salvation for him in God."
    Selah[5]

3   But you, O LORD, are a shield about me,
  my glory, and the lifter of my head.

4   I cried aloud to the LORD,
  and he answered me from his holy hill.
    Selah

5   I lay down and slept;
  I woke again, for the LORD sustained me.

6   I will not be afraid of many thousands of
    people
  who have set themselves against me all
    around.

7   Arise, O LORD!
  Save me, O my God!
  For you strike all my enemies on the cheek;
    you break the teeth of the wicked.

8   Salvation belongs to the LORD;
  your blessing be on your people! *Selah*

Answer Me When I Call

4 TO THE CHOIRMASTER: WITH STRINGED
INSTRUMENTS. A PSALM OF DAVID.

1   Answer me when I call, O God of my righ-
    teousness!
  You have given me relief when I was in
    distress.
  Be gracious to me and hear my prayer!

---

[1] The singular Hebrew word for *man* (*ish*) is used here to portray a representative example of a godly person; see Preface [2] Or *instruction* [3] Or *nations noisily assemble* [4] Revocalization yields (compare Septuagint) *You shall rule* [5] The meaning of the Hebrew word *Selah*, used frequently in the Psalms, is uncertain. It may be a musical or liturgical direction

2 O men,[1] how long shall my honor be
    turned into shame?
    How long will you love vain words and
      seek after lies?   *Selah*
3 But know that the LORD has set apart the
    godly for himself;
    the LORD hears when I call to him.

4 Be angry,[2] and do not sin;
    ponder in your own hearts on your
      beds, and be silent.   *Selah*
5 Offer right sacrifices,
    and put your trust in the LORD.

6 There are many who say, "Who will show
    us some good?
    Lift up the light of your face upon us,
      O LORD!"
7 You have put more joy in my heart
    than they have when their grain and
      wine abound.

8 In peace I will both lie down and sleep;
    for you alone, O LORD, make me dwell
      in safety.

Lead Me in Your Righteousness

5 To the choirmaster: for the flutes.
A Psalm of David.

1 Give ear to my words, O LORD;
    consider my groaning.
2 Give attention to the sound of my cry,
    my King and my God,
    for to you do I pray.
3 O LORD, in the morning you hear my
      voice;
    in the morning I prepare a sacrifice for
      you[3] and watch.

4 For you are not a God who delights in
      wickedness;
    evil may not dwell with you.
5 The boastful shall not stand before your
      eyes;
    you hate all evildoers.
6 You destroy those who speak lies;
    the LORD abhors the bloodthirsty and
      deceitful man.

7 But I, through the abundance of your
      steadfast love,
    will enter your house.
    I will bow down toward your holy tem-
      ple
    in the fear of you.

8 Lead me, O LORD, in your righteousness
    because of my enemies;
    make your way straight before me.

9 For there is no truth in their mouth;
    their inmost self is destruction;
    their throat is an open grave;
    they flatter with their tongue.
10 Make them bear their guilt, O God;
    let them fall by their own counsels;
    because of the abundance of their trans-
      gressions cast them out,
    for they have rebelled against you.

11 But let all who take refuge in you
      rejoice;
    let them ever sing for joy,
    and spread your protection over them,
    that those who love your name may
      exult in you.
12 For you bless the righteous, O LORD;
    you cover him with favor as with a
      shield.

O LORD, Deliver My Life

6 To the choirmaster: with stringed
instruments; according to The
Sheminith.[4] A Psalm of David.

1 O LORD, rebuke me not in your anger,
    nor discipline me in your wrath.
2 Be gracious to me, O LORD, for I am lan-
      guishing;
    heal me, O LORD, for my bones are
      troubled.
3 My soul also is greatly troubled.
    But you, O LORD—how long?

4 Turn, O LORD, deliver my life;
    save me for the sake of your steadfast
      love.
5 For in death there is no remembrance of
      you;
    in Sheol who will give you praise?

6 I am weary with my moaning;
    every night I flood my bed with
      tears;
    I drench my couch with my weeping.
7 My eye wastes away because of grief;
    it grows weak because of all my foes.

8 Depart from me, all you workers of evil,
    for the LORD has heard the sound of
      my weeping.

---

[1] Or *O men of rank*   [2] Or *Be agitated*   [3] Or *I direct my prayer to you*   [4] Probably a musical or liturgical term

9 The Lord has heard my plea;
  the Lord accepts my prayer.
10 All my enemies shall be ashamed and
   greatly troubled;
   they shall turn back and be put to
   shame in a moment.

In You Do I Take Refuge

7 A Shiggaion[1] of David, which he sang
to the Lord concerning the words of
Cush, a Benjaminite.

1 O Lord my God, in you do I take refuge;
  save me from all my pursuers and
  deliver me,
2 lest like a lion they tear my soul apart,
  rending it in pieces, with none to
  deliver.

3 O Lord my God, if I have done this,
  if there is wrong in my hands,
4 if I have repaid my friend[2] with evil
  or plundered my enemy without cause,
5 let the enemy pursue my soul and overtake
  it,
  and let him trample my life to the
  ground
  and lay my glory in the dust.   *Selah*

6 Arise, O Lord, in your anger;
  lift yourself up against the fury of my
  enemies;
  awake for me; you have appointed a
  judgment.
7 Let the assembly of the peoples be gathered
  about you;
  over it return on high.

8 The Lord judges the peoples;
  judge me, O Lord, according to my
  righteousness
  and according to the integrity that is in
  me.
9 Oh, let the evil of the wicked come to an
  end,
  and may you establish the righteous—
  you who test the minds and hearts,[3]
  O righteous God!
10 My shield is with God,
   who saves the upright in heart.
11 God is a righteous judge,
   and a God who feels indignation every
   day.

12 If a man[4] does not repent, God[5] will whet
   his sword;
   he has bent and readied his bow;
13 he has prepared for him his deadly weapons,
   making his arrows fiery shafts.
14 Behold, the wicked man conceives evil
   and is pregnant with mischief
   and gives birth to lies.
15 He makes a pit, digging it out,
   and falls into the hole that he has made.
16 His mischief returns upon his own head,
   and on his own skull his violence
   descends.

17 I will give to the Lord the thanks due to
   his righteousness,
   and I will sing praise to the name of the
   Lord, the Most High.

How Majestic Is Your Name

8 To the choirmaster: according to The
Gittith.[6] A Psalm of David.

1 O Lord, our Lord,
  how majestic is your name in all the
  earth!
  You have set your glory above the heavens.
2 Out of the mouth of babies and infants,
  you have established strength because of
  your foes,
  to still the enemy and the avenger.

3 When I look at your heavens, the work of
  your fingers,
  the moon and the stars, which you have
  set in place,
4 what is man that you are mindful of him,
  and the son of man that you care for
  him?
5 Yet you have made him a little lower than
  the heavenly beings[7]
  and crowned him with glory and honor.
6 You have given him dominion over the
  works of your hands;
  you have put all things under his feet,
7 all sheep and oxen,
  and also the beasts of the field,
8 the birds of the heavens, and the fish of the
  sea,
  whatever passes along the paths of the
  seas.

---

[1] Probably a musical or liturgical term [2] Hebrew *the one at peace with me* [3] Hebrew *the hearts and kidneys* [4] Hebrew *he* [5] Hebrew *he* [6] Probably a musical or liturgical term
[7] Or *than God*; Septuagint *than the angels*

⁹ O LORD, our Lord,
how majestic is your name in all the
earth!

I Will Recount Your Wonderful Deeds

9 ¹ TO THE CHOIRMASTER: ACCORDING TO
MUTH-LABBEN.² A PSALM OF DAVID.

¹ I will give thanks to the LORD with my
whole heart;
I will recount all of your wonderful
deeds.
² I will be glad and exult in you;
I will sing praise to your name, O Most
High.

³ When my enemies turn back,
they stumble and perish before³ your
presence.
⁴ For you have maintained my just cause;
you have sat on the throne, giving righteous judgment.

⁵ You have rebuked the nations; you have
made the wicked perish;
you have blotted out their name forever
and ever.
⁶ The enemy came to an end in everlasting
ruins;
their cities you rooted out;
the very memory of them has perished.

⁷ But the LORD sits enthroned forever;
he has established his throne for justice,
⁸ and he judges the world with righteousness;
he judges the peoples with uprightness.

⁹ The LORD is a stronghold for the
oppressed,
a stronghold in times of trouble.
¹⁰ And those who know your name put their
trust in you,
for you, O LORD, have not forsaken
those who seek you.

¹¹ Sing praises to the LORD, who sits
enthroned in Zion!
Tell among the peoples his deeds!
¹² For he who avenges blood is mindful of
them;
he does not forget the cry of the
afflicted.

¹³ Be gracious to me, O LORD!
See my affliction from those who hate
me,
O you who lift me up from the gates of
death,
¹⁴ that I may recount all your praises,
that in the gates of the daughter of Zion
I may rejoice in your salvation.

¹⁵ The nations have sunk in the pit that they
made;
in the net that they hid, their own foot
has been caught.
¹⁶ The LORD has made himself known; he
has executed judgment;
the wicked are snared in the work of
their own hands.   *Higgaion.*⁴ *Selah*

¹⁷ The wicked shall return to Sheol,
all the nations that forget God.

¹⁸ For the needy shall not always be forgotten,
and the hope of the poor shall not perish forever.

¹⁹ Arise, O LORD! Let not man prevail;
let the nations be judged before you!
²⁰ Put them in fear, O LORD!
Let the nations know that they are but
men!   *Selah*

Why Do You Hide Yourself?

10 Why, O LORD, do you stand far away?
Why do you hide yourself in times of
trouble?

² In arrogance the wicked hotly pursue the
poor;
let them be caught in the schemes that
they have devised.
³ For the wicked boasts of the desires of his
soul,
and the one greedy for gain curses⁵ and
renounces the LORD.
⁴ In the pride of his face⁶ the wicked does
not seek him;⁷
all his thoughts are, "There is no God."
⁵ His ways prosper at all times;
your judgments are on high, out of his
sight;
as for all his foes, he puffs at them.

¹ Psalms 9 and 10 together follow an acrostic pattern, each stanza beginning with the successive letters of the Hebrew alphabet. In the Septuagint they form one psalm
² Probably a musical or liturgical term ³ Or *because of* ⁴ Probably a musical or liturgical term ⁵ Or *and he blesses the one greedy for gain* ⁶ Or *of his anger* ⁷ Or *the wicked says, "He will not call to account"*

6 He says in his heart, "I shall not be moved;
    throughout all generations I shall not
      meet adversity."
7 His mouth is filled with cursing and deceit
    and oppression;
    under his tongue are mischief and iniq-
      uity.
8 He sits in ambush in the villages;
    in hiding places he murders the inno-
      cent.
  His eyes stealthily watch for the helpless;
9   he lurks in ambush like a lion in his
      thicket;
  he lurks that he may seize the poor;
    he seizes the poor when he draws him
      into his net.
10 The helpless are crushed, sink down,
    and fall by his might.
11 He says in his heart, "God has forgotten,
    he has hidden his face, he will never see
      it."

12 Arise, O LORD; O God, lift up your hand;
    forget not the afflicted.
13 Why does the wicked renounce God
    and say in his heart, "You will not call to
      account"?
14 But you do see, for you note mischief and
    vexation,
    that you may take it into your hands;
  to you the helpless commits himself;
    you have been the helper of the father-
      less.
15 Break the arm of the wicked and evildoer;
    call his wickedness to account till you
      find none.

16 The LORD is king forever and ever;
    the nations perish from his land.
17 O LORD, you hear the desire of the afflicted;
    you will strengthen their heart; you will
      incline your ear
18 to do justice to the fatherless and the
    oppressed,
    so that man who is of the earth may
      strike terror no more.

The LORD Is in His Holy Temple

11 TO THE CHOIRMASTER. OF DAVID.
  In the LORD I take refuge;
how can you say to my soul,
  "Flee like a bird to your mountain,

2 for behold, the wicked bend the bow;
    they have fitted their arrow to the string
    to shoot in the dark at the upright in
      heart;
3 if the foundations are destroyed, .
    what can the righteous do?"[1]

4 The LORD is in his holy temple;
    the LORD's throne is in heaven;
    his eyes see, his eyelids test the children
      of man.
5 The LORD tests the righteous,
    but his soul hates the wicked and the
      one who loves violence.
6 Let him rain coals on the wicked;
    fire and sulfur and a scorching wind
      shall be the portion of their cup.
7 For the LORD is righteous;
  he loves righteous deeds;
    the upright shall behold his face.

The Faithful Have Vanished

12 TO THE CHOIRMASTER: ACCORDING TO
THE SHEMINITH.[2] A PSALM OF DAVID.

1 Save, O LORD, for the godly one is gone;
    for the faithful have vanished from
      among the children of man.
2 Everyone utters lies to his neighbor;
    with flattering lips and a double heart
      they speak.

3 May the LORD cut off all flattering lips,
    the tongue that makes great boasts,
4 those who say, "With our tongue we will
    prevail,
    our lips are with us; who is master over
      us?"

5 "Because the poor are plundered, because
    the needy groan,
    I will now arise," says the LORD;
    "I will place him in the safety for which
      he longs."
6 The words of the LORD are pure words,
    like silver refined in a furnace on the
      ground,
    purified seven times.

7 You, O LORD, will keep them;
    you will guard us[3] from this generation
      forever.
8 On every side the wicked prowl,
    as vileness is exalted among the chil-
      dren of man.

---

[1] Or for the foundations will be destroyed; what has the righteous done? [2] Probably a musical or liturgical term [3] Or guard him

How Long, O Lord?

13
To the choirmaster. A Psalm of David.
How long, O Lord? Will you forget
me forever?
How long will you hide your face from
me?

2 How long must I take counsel in my
soul
and have sorrow in my heart all the
day?
How long shall my enemy be exalted over
me?

3 Consider and answer me, O Lord my God;
light up my eyes, lest I sleep the sleep of
death,
4 lest my enemy say, "I have prevailed over
him,"
lest my foes rejoice because I am shaken.

5 But I have trusted in your steadfast love;
my heart shall rejoice in your salvation.
6 I will sing to the Lord,
because he has dealt bountifully with
me.

The Fool Says, There Is No God

14
To the choirmaster. Of David.
The fool says in his heart, "There is no
God."
They are corrupt, they do abominable
deeds;
there is none who does good.

2 The Lord looks down from heaven on the
children of man,
to see if there are any who understand,[1]
who seek after God.

3 They have all turned aside; together they
have become corrupt;
there is none who does good,
not even one.

4 Have they no knowledge, all the evildoers
who eat up my people as they eat
bread
and do not call upon the Lord?

5 There they are in great terror,
for God is with the generation of the
righteous.

6 You would shame the plans of the poor,
but[2] the Lord is his refuge.

7 Oh, that salvation for Israel would come
out of Zion!
When the Lord restores the fortunes of
his people,
let Jacob rejoice, let Israel be glad.

Who Shall Dwell on Your Holy Hill?

15
A Psalm of David.
O Lord, who shall sojourn in your
tent?
Who shall dwell on your holy hill?

2 He who walks blamelessly and does what
is right
and speaks truth in his heart;
3 who does not slander with his tongue
and does no evil to his neighbor,
nor takes up a reproach against his
friend;
4 in whose eyes a vile person is despised,
but who honors those who fear the
Lord;
who swears to his own hurt and does not
change;
5 who does not put out his money at interest
and does not take a bribe against the
innocent.
He who does these things shall never be
moved.

You Will Not Abandon My Soul

16
A Miktam[3] of David.
Preserve me, O God, for in you I take
refuge.
2 I say to the Lord, "You are my Lord;
I have no good apart from you."

3 As for the saints in the land, they are the
excellent ones,
in whom is all my delight.[4]

4 The sorrows of those who run after[5]
another god shall multiply;
their drink offerings of blood I will not
pour out
or take their names on my lips.

5 The Lord is my chosen portion and my
cup;
you hold my lot.
6 The lines have fallen for me in pleasant
places;
indeed, I have a beautiful inheritance.

---

[1] Or that act wisely [2] Or for [3] Probably a musical or liturgical term [4] Or To the saints in the land, the excellent in whom is all my delight, I say: [5] Or who acquire

7 I bless the LORD who gives me counsel;
   in the night also my heart instructs me.[1]

8 I have set the LORD always before me;
   because he is at my right hand, I shall
      not be shaken.

9 Therefore my heart is glad, and my whole
   being[2] rejoices;
   my flesh also dwells secure.

10 For you will not abandon my soul to Sheol,
   or let your holy one see corruption.[3]

11 You make known to me the path of life;
   in your presence there is fullness of joy;
   at your right hand are pleasures forever-
      more.

In the Shadow of Your Wings

17 A PRAYER OF DAVID.
Hear a just cause, O LORD; attend to
   my cry!
   Give ear to my prayer from lips free of
      deceit!

2 From your presence let my vindication
   come!
   Let your eyes behold the right!

3 You have tried my heart, you have visited
   me by night,
   you have tested me, and you will find
      nothing;
   I have purposed that my mouth will not
      transgress.

4 With regard to the works of man, by the
   word of your lips
   I have avoided the ways of the violent.

5 My steps have held fast to your paths;
   my feet have not slipped.

6 I call upon you, for you will answer me,
   O God;
   incline your ear to me; hear my words.

7 Wondrously show[4] your steadfast love,
   O Savior of those who seek refuge
   from their adversaries at your right
      hand.

8 Keep me as the apple of your eye;
   hide me in the shadow of your wings,

9 from the wicked who do me violence,
   my deadly enemies who surround me.

10 They close their hearts to pity;
   with their mouths they speak arro-
      gantly.

11 They have now surrounded our steps;
   they set their eyes to cast us to the
      ground.

12 He is like a lion eager to tear,
   as a young lion lurking in ambush.

13 Arise, O LORD! Confront him, subdue
   him!
   Deliver my soul from the wicked by
      your sword,

14 from men by your hand, O LORD,
   from men of the world whose portion is
      in this life.[5]
You fill their womb with treasure;[6]
   they are satisfied with children,
   and they leave their abundance to their
      infants.

15 As for me, I shall behold your face in righteousness;
   when I awake, I shall be satisfied with
      your likeness.

The LORD Is My Rock and My Fortress

18 TO THE CHOIRMASTER. A PSALM OF
DAVID, THE SERVANT OF THE LORD, WHO
ADDRESSED THE WORDS OF THIS SONG TO
THE LORD ON THE DAY WHEN THE LORD
DELIVERED HIM FROM THE HAND OF ALL
HIS ENEMIES, AND FROM THE HAND OF
SAUL. HE SAID:

1 I love you, O LORD, my strength.

2 The LORD is my rock and my fortress and
   my deliverer,
   my God, my rock, in whom I take ref-
      uge,
   my shield, and the horn of my salvation,
      my stronghold.

3 I call upon the LORD, who is worthy to be
   praised,
   and I am saved from my enemies.

4 The cords of death encompassed me;
   the torrents of destruction assailed
      me;[7]

5 the cords of Sheol entangled me;
   the snares of death confronted me.

6 In my distress I called upon the LORD;
   to my God I cried for help.
   From his temple he heard my voice,
   and my cry to him reached his ears.

---

[1] Hebrew *my kidneys instruct me* [2] Hebrew *my glory* [3] Or *see the pit* [4] Or *Distinguish me by* [5] Or *from men whose portion in life is of the world* [6] Or *As for your treasured ones, you fill their womb* [7] Or *terrified me*

7 Then the earth reeled and rocked;
  the foundations also of the mountains
    trembled
  and quaked, because he was angry.
8 Smoke went up from his nostrils,[1]
  and devouring fire from his mouth;
  glowing coals flamed forth from him.
9 He bowed the heavens and came down;
  thick darkness was under his feet.
10 He rode on a cherub and flew;
   he came swiftly on the wings of the
     wind.
11 He made darkness his covering, his canopy
     around him,
   thick clouds dark with water.
12 Out of the brightness before him
   hailstones and coals of fire broke
     through his clouds.

13 The LORD also thundered in the heavens,
   and the Most High uttered his voice,
   hailstones and coals of fire.
14 And he sent out his arrows and scattered
     them;
   he flashed forth lightnings and routed
     them.
15 Then the channels of the sea were seen,
   and the foundations of the world were
     laid bare
   at your rebuke, O LORD,
   at the blast of the breath of your nostrils.

16 He sent from on high, he took me;
   he drew me out of many waters.
17 He rescued me from my strong enemy
   and from those who hated me,
   for they were too mighty for me.
18 They confronted me in the day of my
     calamity,
   but the LORD was my support.
19 He brought me out into a broad place;
   he rescued me, because he delighted in
     me.

20 The LORD dealt with me according to my
     righteousness;
   according to the cleanness of my hands
   he rewarded me.
21 For I have kept the ways of the LORD,
   and have not wickedly departed from
     my God.
22 For all his rules[2] were before me,
   and his statutes I did not put away from
     me.

23 I was blameless before him,
   and I kept myself from my guilt.
24 So the LORD has rewarded me according to
     my righteousness,
   according to the cleanness of my hands
     in his sight.

25 With the merciful you show yourself mer-
     ciful;
   with the blameless man you show your-
     self blameless;
26 with the purified you show yourself pure;
   and with the crooked you make your-
     self seem tortuous.
27 For you save a humble people,
   but the haughty eyes you bring down.
28 For it is you who light my lamp;
   the LORD my God lightens my darkness.
29 For by you I can run against a troop,
   and by my God I can leap over a wall.
30 This God—his way is perfect;[3]
   the word of the LORD proves true;
   he is a shield for all those who take ref-
     uge in him.

31 For who is God, but the LORD?
   And who is a rock, except our God?—
32 the God who equipped me with strength
   and made my way blameless.
33 He made my feet like the feet of a deer
   and set me secure on the heights.
34 He trains my hands for war,
   so that my arms can bend a bow of
     bronze.
35 You have given me the shield of your salva-
     tion,
   and your right hand supported me,
   and your gentleness made me great.
36 You gave a wide place for my steps under
     me,
   and my feet did not slip.
37 I pursued my enemies and overtook them,
   and did not turn back till they were
     consumed.
38 I thrust them through, so that they were
     not able to rise;
   they fell under my feet.
39 For you equipped me with strength for the
     battle;
   you made those who rise against me
     sink under me.
40 You made my enemies turn their backs to
     me,[4]
   and those who hated me I destroyed.

---

[1] Or in his wrath [2] Or just decrees [3] Or blameless [4] Or You gave me my enemies' necks

41 They cried for help, but there was none to
save;
they cried to the LORD, but he did not
answer them.
42 I beat them fine as dust before the wind;
I cast them out like the mire of the
streets.

43 You delivered me from strife with the
people;
you made me the head of the nations;
people whom I had not known served
me.
44 As soon as they heard of me they obeyed
me;
foreigners came cringing to me.
45 Foreigners lost heart
and came trembling out of their fortresses.

46 The LORD lives, and blessed be my rock,
and exalted be the God of my salvation—
47 the God who gave me vengeance
and subdued peoples under me,
48 who rescued me from my enemies;
yes, you exalted me above those who
rose against me;
you delivered me from the man of violence.

49 For this I will praise you, O LORD, among
the nations,
and sing to your name.
50 Great salvation he brings to his king,
and shows steadfast love to his
anointed,
to David and his offspring forever.

The Law of the LORD Is Perfect

19 To the choirmaster. A Psalm of David.
The heavens declare the glory of God,
and the sky above[1] proclaims his handiwork.
2 Day to day pours out speech,
and night to night reveals knowledge.
3 There is no speech, nor are there words,
whose voice is not heard.
4 Their voice[2] goes out through all the earth,
and their words to the end of the world.
In them he has set a tent for the sun,
5 which comes out like a bridegroom
leaving his chamber,
and, like a strong man, runs its course
with joy.

6 Its rising is from the end of the heavens,
and its circuit to the end of them,
and there is nothing hidden from its
heat.

7 The law of the LORD is perfect,[3]
reviving the soul;
the testimony of the LORD is sure,
making wise the simple;
8 the precepts of the LORD are right,
rejoicing the heart;
the commandment of the LORD is pure,
enlightening the eyes;
9 the fear of the LORD is clean,
enduring forever;
the rules[4] of the LORD are true,
and righteous altogether.
10 More to be desired are they than gold,
even much fine gold;
sweeter also than honey
and drippings of the honeycomb.
11 Moreover, by them is your servant warned;
in keeping them there is great reward.

12 Who can discern his errors?
Declare me innocent from hidden
faults.
13 Keep back your servant also from presumptuous sins;
let them not have dominion over me!
Then I shall be blameless,
and innocent of great transgression.

14 Let the words of my mouth and the meditation of my heart
be acceptable in your sight,
O LORD, my rock and my redeemer.

Trust in the Name of the LORD Our God

20 To the choirmaster. A Psalm of David.
1 May the LORD answer you in the day of
trouble!
May the name of the God of Jacob protect you!
2 May he send you help from the sanctuary
and give you support from Zion!
3 May he remember all your offerings
and regard with favor your burnt sacrifices!   *Selah*

4 May he grant you your heart's desire
and fulfill all your plans!

---

[1] Hebrew *the expanse*; compare Genesis 1:6–8 [2] Or *Their measuring line* [3] Or *blameless* [4] Or *just decrees*

⁵ May we shout for joy over your salvation,
  and in the name of our God set up our
    banners!
  May the LORD fulfill all your petitions!

⁶ Now I know that the LORD saves his
    anointed;
  he will answer him from his holy
    heaven
  with the saving might of his right hand.

⁷ Some trust in chariots and some in horses,
  but we trust in the name of the LORD
    our God.

⁸ They collapse and fall,
  but we rise and stand upright.

⁹ O LORD, save the king!
  May he answer us when we call.

The King Rejoices in the LORD's Strength

21 TO THE CHOIRMASTER. A PSALM OF DAVID.
  O LORD, in your strength the king
    rejoices,
  and in your salvation how greatly he
    exults!

² You have given him his heart's desire
  and have not withheld the request of
    his lips.   *Selah*

³ For you meet him with rich blessings;
  you set a crown of fine gold upon his
    head.

⁴ He asked life of you; you gave it to him,
  length of days forever and ever.

⁵ His glory is great through your salvation;
  splendor and majesty you bestow on
    him.

⁶ For you make him most blessed forever;[1]
  you make him glad with the joy of your
    presence.

⁷ For the king trusts in the LORD,
  and through the steadfast love of the
    Most High he shall not be moved.

⁸ Your hand will find out all your enemies;
  your right hand will find out those who
    hate you.

⁹ You will make them as a blazing oven
    when you appear.
  The LORD will swallow them up in his
    wrath,
  and fire will consume them.

¹⁰ You will destroy their descendants from
    the earth,
  and their offspring from among the
    children of man.

¹¹ Though they plan evil against you,
  though they devise mischief, they will
    not succeed.

¹² For you will put them to flight;
  you will aim at their faces with your
    bows.

¹³ Be exalted, O LORD, in your strength!
  We will sing and praise your power.

Why Have You Forsaken Me?

22 TO THE CHOIRMASTER: ACCORDING TO
  THE DOE OF THE DAWN. A PSALM OF
  DAVID.

¹ My God, my God, why have you forsaken
    me?
  Why are you so far from saving me,
    from the words of my groaning?

² O my God, I cry by day, but you do not
    answer,
  and by night, but I find no rest.

³ Yet you are holy,
  enthroned on the praises[2] of Israel.

⁴ In you our fathers trusted;
  they trusted, and you delivered them.

⁵ To you they cried and were rescued;
  in you they trusted and were not put to
    shame.

⁶ But I am a worm and not a man,
  scorned by mankind and despised by
    the people.

⁷ All who see me mock me;
  they make mouths at me; they wag
    their heads;

⁸ "He trusts in the LORD; let him deliver him;
  let him rescue him, for he delights in
    him!"

⁹ Yet you are he who took me from the
    womb;
  you made me trust you at my mother's
    breasts.

¹⁰ On you was I cast from my birth,
  and from my mother's womb you have
    been my God.

¹¹ Be not far from me,
  for trouble is near,
  and there is none to help.

¹² Many bulls encompass me;
  strong bulls of Bashan surround me;

¹³ they open wide their mouths at me,
  like a ravening and roaring lion.

---

[1] Or *make him a source of blessing forever* [2] Or *dwelling in the praises*

14 I am poured out like water,
    and all my bones are out of joint;
my heart is like wax;
    it is melted within my breast;
15 my strength is dried up like a potsherd,
    and my tongue sticks to my jaws;
    you lay me in the dust of death.

16 For dogs encompass me;
    a company of evildoers encircles me;
they have pierced my hands and feet[1]—
17 I can count all my bones—
    they stare and gloat over me;
18 they divide my garments among them,
    and for my clothing they cast lots.

19 But you, O Lord, do not be far off!
    O you my help, come quickly to my aid!
20 Deliver my soul from the sword,
    my precious life from the power of the
        dog!
21   Save me from the mouth of the lion!
You have rescued[2] me from the horns of
    the wild oxen!

22 I will tell of your name to my brothers;
    in the midst of the congregation I will
        praise you:
23 You who fear the Lord, praise him!
    All you offspring of Jacob, glorify him,
    and stand in awe of him, all you off-
        spring of Israel!
24 For he has not despised or abhorred
    the affliction of the afflicted,
and he has not hidden his face from him,
    but has heard, when he cried to him.

25 From you comes my praise in the great
        congregation;
    my vows I will perform before those
        who fear him.
26 The afflicted[3] shall eat and be satisfied;
    those who seek him shall praise the
        Lord!
    May your hearts live forever!

27 All the ends of the earth shall remember
    and turn to the Lord,
and all the families of the nations
    shall worship before you.
28 For kingship belongs to the Lord,
    and he rules over the nations.

29 All the prosperous of the earth eat and
        worship;
    before him shall bow all who go down
        to the dust,
    even the one who could not keep him-
        self alive.
30 Posterity shall serve him;
    it shall be told of the Lord to the coming
        generation;
31 they shall come and proclaim his righ-
    teousness to a people yet unborn,
    that he has done it.

The Lord Is My Shepherd

23 A Psalm of David.
    The Lord is my shepherd; I shall not
    want.
2   He makes me lie down in green pastures.
He leads me beside still waters.[4]
3   He restores my soul.
He leads me in paths of righteousness[5]
    for his name's sake.

4   Even though I walk through the valley of
        the shadow of death,[6]
    I will fear no evil,
for you are with me;
    your rod and your staff,
    they comfort me.

5   You prepare a table before me
    in the presence of my enemies;
you anoint my head with oil;
    my cup overflows.
6   Surely[7] goodness and mercy[8] shall follow
        me
    all the days of my life,
and I shall dwell[9] in the house of the Lord
    forever.[10]

The King of Glory

24 A Psalm of David.
    The earth is the Lord's and the full-
    ness thereof,[11]
    the world and those who dwell therein,
2   for he has founded it upon the seas
    and established it upon the rivers.

3   Who shall ascend the hill of the Lord?
    And who shall stand in his holy place?
4   He who has clean hands and a pure heart,
    who does not lift up his soul to what is
        false
    and does not swear deceitfully.

[1] Some Hebrew manuscripts, Septuagint, Vulgate, Syriac; most Hebrew manuscripts *like a lion* [they are at] *my hands and feet* [2] Hebrew *answered* [3] Or *The meek* [4] Hebrew *beside waters of rest* [5] Or *in right paths* [6] Or *the valley of deep darkness* [7] Or *Only* [8] Or *steadfast love* [9] Or *shall return to dwell* [10] Hebrew *for length of days* [11] Or *and all that fills it*

5 He will receive blessing from the Lord
    and righteousness from the God of his
        salvation.
6 Such is the generation of those who seek
    him,
    who seek the face of the God of Jacob.[1]
                                        Selah

7 Lift up your heads, O gates!
    And be lifted up, O ancient doors,
    that the King of glory may come in.
8 Who is this King of glory?
    The Lord, strong and mighty,
    the Lord, mighty in battle!
9 Lift up your heads, O gates!
    And lift them up, O ancient doors,
    that the King of glory may come in.
10 Who is this King of glory?
    The Lord of hosts,
    he is the King of glory!   *Selah*

Teach Me Your Paths

25 [2] Of David.
    To you, O Lord, I lift up my soul.
2 O my God, in you I trust;
    let me not be put to shame;
    let not my enemies exult over me.
3 Indeed, none who wait for you shall be put
    to shame;
    they shall be ashamed who are wan-
        tonly treacherous.

4 Make me to know your ways, O Lord;
    teach me your paths.
5 Lead me in your truth and teach me,
    for you are the God of my salvation;
    for you I wait all the day long.

6 Remember your mercy, O Lord, and your
    steadfast love,
    for they have been from of old.
7 Remember not the sins of my youth or my
    transgressions;
    according to your steadfast love remem-
        ber me,
    for the sake of your goodness, O Lord!

8 Good and upright is the Lord;
    therefore he instructs sinners in the way.
9 He leads the humble in what is right,
    and teaches the humble his way.
10 All the paths of the Lord are steadfast love
    and faithfulness,
    for those who keep his covenant and his
        testimonies.

11 For your name's sake, O Lord,
    pardon my guilt, for it is great.
12 Who is the man who fears the Lord?
    Him will he instruct in the way that he
        should choose.
13 His soul shall abide in well-being,
    and his offspring shall inherit the land.
14 The friendship[3] of the Lord is for those
    who fear him,
    and he makes known to them his cov-
        enant.
15 My eyes are ever toward the Lord,
    for he will pluck my feet out of the net.

16 Turn to me and be gracious to me,
    for I am lonely and afflicted.
17 The troubles of my heart are enlarged;
    bring me out of my distresses.
18 Consider my affliction and my trouble,
    and forgive all my sins.

19 Consider how many are my foes,
    and with what violent hatred they hate
        me.
20 Oh, guard my soul, and deliver me!
    Let me not be put to shame, for I take
        refuge in you.
21 May integrity and uprightness preserve me,
    for I wait for you.

22 Redeem Israel, O God,
    out of all his troubles.

I Will Bless the Lord

26 Of David.
    Vindicate me, O Lord,
    for I have walked in my integrity,
    and I have trusted in the Lord without
        wavering.
2 Prove me, O Lord, and try me;
    test my heart and my mind.[4]
3 For your steadfast love is before my eyes,
    and I walk in your faithfulness.

4 I do not sit with men of falsehood,
    nor do I consort with hypocrites.
5 I hate the assembly of evildoers,
    and I will not sit with the wicked.

6 I wash my hands in innocence
    and go around your altar, O Lord,
7 proclaiming thanksgiving aloud,
    and telling all your wondrous deeds.

[1] Septuagint, Syriac, and two Hebrew manuscripts; Masoretic Text *who seek your face, Jacob* [2] This psalm is an acrostic poem, each verse beginning with the successive letters of the Hebrew alphabet [3] Or *The secret counsel* [4] Hebrew *test my kidneys and my heart*

8 O LORD, I love the habitation of your house
    and the place where your glory dwells.
9 Do not sweep my soul away with sinners,
    nor my life with bloodthirsty men,
10 in whose hands are evil devices,
    and whose right hands are full of bribes.

11 But as for me, I shall walk in my integrity;
    redeem me, and be gracious to me.
12 My foot stands on level ground;
    in the great assembly I will bless the
    LORD.

The LORD Is My Light and My Salvation

27 OF DAVID.
    The LORD is my light and my salva-
    tion;
    whom shall I fear?
    The LORD is the stronghold[1] of my life;
    of whom shall I be afraid?

2 When evildoers assail me
    to eat up my flesh,
    my adversaries and foes,
    it is they who stumble and fall.

3 Though an army encamp against me,
    my heart shall not fear;
    though war arise against me,
    yet[2] I will be confident.

4 One thing have I asked of the LORD,
    that will I seek after:
    that I may dwell in the house of the LORD
    all the days of my life,
    to gaze upon the beauty of the LORD
    and to inquire[3] in his temple.

5 For he will hide me in his shelter
    in the day of trouble;
    he will conceal me under the cover of his
    tent;
    he will lift me high upon a rock.

6 And now my head shall be lifted up
    above my enemies all around me,
    and I will offer in his tent
    sacrifices with shouts of joy;
    I will sing and make melody to the LORD.

7 Hear, O LORD, when I cry aloud;
    be gracious to me and answer me!
8 You have said, "Seek[4] my face."
    My heart says to you,
    "Your face, LORD, do I seek."[5]
9   Hide not your face from me.

Turn not your servant away in anger,
    O you who have been my help.
Cast me not off; forsake me not,
    O God of my salvation!
10 For my father and my mother have for-
    saken me,
    but the LORD will take me in.

11 Teach me your way, O LORD,
    and lead me on a level path
    because of my enemies.
12 Give me not up to the will of my adversar-
    ies;
    for false witnesses have risen against
    me,
    and they breathe out violence.
13 I believe that I shall look[6] upon the good-
    ness of the LORD
    in the land of the living!
14 Wait for the LORD;
    be strong, and let your heart take cour-
    age;
    wait for the LORD!

The LORD Is My Strength and My Shield

28 OF DAVID.
    To you, O LORD, I call;
    my rock, be not deaf to me,
    lest, if you be silent to me,
    I become like those who go down to the
    pit.
2 Hear the voice of my pleas for mercy,
    when I cry to you for help,
    when I lift up my hands
    toward your most holy sanctuary.[7]

3 Do not drag me off with the wicked,
    with the workers of evil,
    who speak peace with their neighbors
    while evil is in their hearts.
4 Give to them according to their work
    and according to the evil of their deeds;
    give to them according to the work of their
    hands;
    render them their due reward.
5 Because they do not regard the works of
    the LORD
    or the work of his hands,
    he will tear them down and build them up
    no more.

---

[1] Or refuge [2] Or in this [3] Or meditate [4] The command (seek) is addressed to more than one person [5] The meaning of the Hebrew verse is uncertain [6] Other Hebrew manuscripts Oh! Had I not believed that I would look [7] Hebrew your innermost sanctuary

6 Blessed be the LORD!
       For he has heard the voice of my pleas
          for mercy.
7 The LORD is my strength and my shield;
       in him my heart trusts, and I am
          helped;
   my heart exults,
       and with my song I give thanks to him.

8 The LORD is the strength of his people;[1]
       he is the saving refuge of his anointed.
9 Oh, save your people and bless your heri-
          tage!
       Be their shepherd and carry them for-
          ever.

Ascribe to the LORD Glory

29 A PSALM OF DAVID.
   Ascribe to the LORD, O heavenly
       beings,[2]
   ascribe to the LORD glory and
       strength.
2 Ascribe to the LORD the glory due his
          name;
       worship the LORD in the splendor of
          holiness.[3]

3 The voice of the LORD is over the waters;
       the God of glory thunders,
       the LORD, over many waters.
4 The voice of the LORD is powerful;
       the voice of the LORD is full of majesty.

5 The voice of the LORD breaks the cedars;
       the LORD breaks the cedars of Lebanon.
6 He makes Lebanon to skip like a calf,
       and Sirion like a young wild ox.

7 The voice of the LORD flashes forth flames
          of fire.
8 The voice of the LORD shakes the wilder-
          ness;
       the LORD shakes the wilderness of
          Kadesh.

9 The voice of the LORD makes the deer give
          birth[4]
       and strips the forests bare,
       and in his temple all cry, "Glory!"

10 The LORD sits enthroned over the flood;
       the LORD sits enthroned as king forever.
11 May the LORD give strength to his people!
       May the LORD bless[5] his people with
          peace!

Joy Comes with the Morning

30 A PSALM OF DAVID. A SONG AT THE
   DEDICATION OF THE TEMPLE.

1 I will extol you, O LORD, for you have
          drawn me up
       and have not let my foes rejoice over me.
2 O LORD my God, I cried to you for help,
       and you have healed me.
3 O LORD, you have brought up my soul
          from Sheol;
       you restored me to life from among
          those who go down to the pit.[6]

4 Sing praises to the LORD, O you his
          saints,
       and give thanks to his holy name.[7]
5 For his anger is but for a moment,
       and his favor is for a lifetime.[8]
   Weeping may tarry for the night,
       but joy comes with the morning.

6 As for me, I said in my prosperity,
       "I shall never be moved."
7 By your favor, O LORD,
       you made my mountain stand
          strong;
   you hid your face;
       I was dismayed.

8 To you, O LORD, I cry,
       and to the Lord I plead for mercy:
9 "What profit is there in my death,[9]
       if I go down to the pit?[10]
   Will the dust praise you?
       Will it tell of your faithfulness?
10 Hear, O LORD, and be merciful to me!
       O LORD, be my helper!"

11 You have turned for me my mourning into
          dancing;
       you have loosed my sackcloth
       and clothed me with gladness,
12 that my glory may sing your praise and not
          be silent.
       O LORD my God, I will give thanks to
          you forever!

Into Your Hand I Commit My Spirit

31 TO THE CHOIRMASTER. A PSALM OF DAVID.
   In you, O LORD, do I take refuge;
       let me never be put to shame;
       in your righteousness deliver me!

---

[1] Some Hebrew manuscripts, Septuagint, Syriac; most Hebrew manuscripts *is their strength* [2] Hebrew *sons of God, or sons of might* [3] Or *in holy attire* [4] Revocalization yields makes the oaks to shake [5] Or *The LORD will give... The LORD will bless* [6] Or *to life, that I should not go down to the pit* [7] Hebrew *to the memorial of his holiness* (see Exodus 3:15) [8] Or *and in his favor is life* [9] Hebrew *in my blood* [10] Or *to corruption*

2 Incline your ear to me;
   rescue me speedily!
   Be a rock of refuge for me,
   a strong fortress to save me!

3 For you are my rock and my fortress;
   and for your name's sake you lead me
   and guide me;
4 you take me out of the net they have hidden for me,
   for you are my refuge.
5 Into your hand I commit my spirit;
   you have redeemed me, O LORD, faithful God.

6 I hate[1] those who pay regard to worthless
   idols,
   but I trust in the LORD.
7 I will rejoice and be glad in your steadfast
   love,
   because you have seen my affliction;
   you have known the distress of my soul,
8 and you have not delivered me into the
   hand of the enemy;
   you have set my feet in a broad place.

9 Be gracious to me, O LORD, for I am in distress;
   my eye is wasted from grief;
   my soul and my body also.
10 For my life is spent with sorrow,
   and my years with sighing;
   my strength fails because of my iniquity,
   and my bones waste away.

11 Because of all my adversaries I have
   become a reproach,
   especially to my neighbors,
   and an object of dread to my acquaintances;
   those who see me in the street flee from
   me.
12 I have been forgotten like one who is dead;
   I have become like a broken vessel.
13 For I hear the whispering of many—
   terror on every side!—
   as they scheme together against me,
   as they plot to take my life.

14 But I trust in you, O LORD;
   I say, "You are my God."
15 My times are in your hand;
   rescue me from the hand of my enemies
   and from my persecutors!
16 Make your face shine on your servant;
   save me in your steadfast love!

17 O LORD, let me not be put to shame,
   for I call upon you;
   let the wicked be put to shame;
   let them go silently to Sheol.
18 Let the lying lips be mute,
   which speak insolently against the righteous
   in pride and contempt.

19 Oh, how abundant is your goodness,
   which you have stored up for those who
   fear you
   and worked for those who take refuge in
   you,
   in the sight of the children of mankind!
20 In the cover of your presence you hide
   them
   from the plots of men;
   you store them in your shelter
   from the strife of tongues.

21 Blessed be the LORD,
   for he has wondrously shown his steadfast love to me
   when I was in a besieged city.
22 I had said in my alarm,[2]
   "I am cut off from your sight."
   But you heard the voice of my pleas for
   mercy
   when I cried to you for help.

23 Love the LORD, all you his saints!
   The LORD preserves the faithful
   but abundantly repays the one who acts
   in pride.
24 Be strong, and let your heart take courage,
   all you who wait for the LORD!

Blessed Are the Forgiven

32 A MASKIL[3] OF DAVID.
   Blessed is the one whose transgression
   is forgiven,
   whose sin is covered.
2 Blessed is the man against whom the LORD
   counts no iniquity,
   and in whose spirit there is no deceit.

3 For when I kept silent, my bones wasted
   away
   through my groaning all day long.
4 For day and night your hand was heavy
   upon me;
   my strength was dried up[4] as by the
   heat of summer.   *Selah*

---

[1] Masoretic Text; one Hebrew manuscript, Septuagint, Syriac, Jerome *You hate* [2] Or *in my haste* [3] Probably a musical or liturgical term [4] Hebrew *my vitality was changed*

5 I acknowledged my sin to you,
    and I did not cover my iniquity;
I said, "I will confess my transgressions to
    the LORD,"
    and you forgave the iniquity of my sin.
                Selah

6 Therefore let everyone who is godly
    offer prayer to you at a time when you
        may be found;
surely in the rush of great waters,
    they shall not reach him.

7 You are a hiding place for me;
    you preserve me from trouble;
    you surround me with shouts of deliv-
        erance.   *Selah*

8 I will instruct you and teach you in the way
    you should go;
    I will counsel you with my eye upon
        you.

9 Be not like a horse or a mule, without
    understanding,
    which must be curbed with bit and
        bridle,
    or it will not stay near you.

10 Many are the sorrows of the wicked,
    but steadfast love surrounds the one
        who trusts in the LORD.

11 Be glad in the LORD, and rejoice, O righ-
    teous,
    and shout for joy, all you upright in
        heart!

The Steadfast Love of the LORD

33 Shout for joy in the LORD, O you
            righteous!
    Praise befits the upright.

2 Give thanks to the LORD with the lyre;
    make melody to him with the harp of
        ten strings!

3 Sing to him a new song;
    play skillfully on the strings, with loud
        shouts.

4 For the word of the LORD is upright,
    and all his work is done in faithfulness.

5 He loves righteousness and justice;
    the earth is full of the steadfast love of
        the LORD.

6 By the word of the LORD the heavens were
    made,
    and by the breath of his mouth all their
        host.

7 He gathers the waters of the sea as a
    heap;
    he puts the deeps in storehouses.

8 Let all the earth fear the LORD;
    let all the inhabitants of the world stand
        in awe of him!

9 For he spoke, and it came to be;
    he commanded, and it stood firm.

10 The LORD brings the counsel of the nations
    to nothing;
    he frustrates the plans of the peoples.

11 The counsel of the LORD stands forever,
    the plans of his heart to all generations.

12 Blessed is the nation whose God is the
    LORD,
    the people whom he has chosen as his
        heritage!

13 The LORD looks down from heaven;
    he sees all the children of man;

14 from where he sits enthroned he looks out
    on all the inhabitants of the earth,

15 he who fashions the hearts of them all
    and observes all their deeds.

16 The king is not saved by his great army;
    a warrior is not delivered by his great
        strength.

17 The war horse is a false hope for salvation,
    and by its great might it cannot res-
        cue.

18 Behold, the eye of the LORD is on those
    who fear him,
    on those who hope in his steadfast love,

19 that he may deliver their soul from death
    and keep them alive in famine.

20 Our soul waits for the LORD;
    he is our help and our shield.

21 For our heart is glad in him,
    because we trust in his holy name.

22 Let your steadfast love, O LORD, be upon
    us,
    even as we hope in you.

Taste and See That the LORD Is Good

34   1 OF DAVID, WHEN HE CHANGED HIS
            BEHAVIOR BEFORE ABIMELECH, SO THAT
            HE DROVE HIM OUT, AND HE WENT AWAY.

1 I will bless the LORD at all times;
    his praise shall continually be in my
        mouth.

---

1 This psalm is an acrostic poem, each verse beginning with the successive letters of the Hebrew alphabet

2 My soul makes its boast in the LORD;
     let the humble hear and be glad.
3 Oh, magnify the LORD with me,
     and let us exalt his name together!

4 I sought the LORD, and he answered me
     and delivered me from all my fears.
5 Those who look to him are radiant,
     and their faces shall never be ashamed.
6 This poor man cried, and the LORD heard
       him
     and saved him out of all his troubles.
7 The angel of the LORD encamps
       around those who fear him, and deliv-
       ers them.

8 Oh, taste and see that the LORD is good!
     Blessed is the man who takes refuge in
       him!
9 Oh, fear the LORD, you his saints,
     for those who fear him have no lack!
10 The young lions suffer want and hunger;
     but those who seek the LORD lack no
       good thing.

11 Come, O children, listen to me;
     I will teach you the fear of the LORD.
12 What man is there who desires life
     and loves many days, that he may see
       good?
13 Keep your tongue from evil
     and your lips from speaking deceit.
14 Turn away from evil and do good;
     seek peace and pursue it.

15 The eyes of the LORD are toward the righ-
       teous
     and his ears toward their cry.
16 The face of the LORD is against those who
       do evil,
     to cut off the memory of them from the
       earth.
17 When the righteous cry for help, the LORD
       hears
     and delivers them out of all their trou-
       bles.
18 The LORD is near to the brokenhearted
     and saves the crushed in spirit.

19 Many are the afflictions of the righteous,
     but the LORD delivers him out of them
       all.
20 He keeps all his bones;
     not one of them is broken.

21 Affliction will slay the wicked,
     and those who hate the righteous will
       be condemned.
22 The LORD redeems the life of his servants;
     none of those who take refuge in him
       will be condemned.

Great Is the LORD

35 OF DAVID.
     Contend, O LORD, with those who
       contend with me;
     fight against those who fight against
       me!
2 Take hold of shield and buckler
     and rise for my help!
3 Draw the spear and javelin[1]
     against my pursuers!
   Say to my soul,
     "I am your salvation!"

4 Let them be put to shame and dishonor
     who seek after my life!
   Let them be turned back and disappointed
     who devise evil against me!
5 Let them be like chaff before the wind,
     with the angel of the LORD driving
       them away!
6 Let their way be dark and slippery,
     with the angel of the LORD pursuing
       them!

7 For without cause they hid their net for
       me;
     without cause they dug a pit for my
       life.[2]
8 Let destruction come upon him when he
       does not know it!
   And let the net that he hid ensnare him;
     let him fall into it—to his destruction!

9 Then my soul will rejoice in the LORD,
     exulting in his salvation.
10 All my bones shall say,
     "O LORD, who is like you,
   delivering the poor
     from him who is too strong for him,
     the poor and needy from him who robs
       him?"

11 Malicious[3] witnesses rise up;
     they ask me of things that I do not
       know.
12 They repay me evil for good;
     my soul is bereft.[4]

[1] Or *and close the way* [2] The word *pit* is transposed from the preceding line; Hebrew *For without cause they hid the pit of their net for me; without cause they dug for my life*
[3] Or *Violent* [4] Hebrew *it is bereavement to my soul*

13 But I, when they were sick—
    I wore sackcloth;
    I afflicted myself with fasting;
I prayed with head bowed[1] on my chest.
14   I went about as though I grieved for
        my friend or my brother;
as one who laments his mother,
    I bowed down in mourning.

15 But at my stumbling they rejoiced and
        gathered;
    they gathered together against me;
wretches whom I did not know
    tore at me without ceasing;
16 like profane mockers at a feast,[2]
    they gnash at me with their teeth.

17 How long, O Lord, will you look on?
    Rescue me from their destruction,
    my precious life from the lions!
18 I will thank you in the great congregation;
    in the mighty throng I will praise you.

19 Let not those rejoice over me
    who are wrongfully my foes,
and let not those wink the eye
    who hate me without cause.
20 For they do not speak peace,
    but against those who are quiet in the
        land
    they devise words of deceit.
21 They open wide their mouths against me;
    they say, "Aha, Aha!
    Our eyes have seen it!"

22 You have seen, O Lord; be not silent!
    O Lord, be not far from me!
23 Awake and rouse yourself for my vindica-
        tion,
    for my cause, my God and my Lord!
24 Vindicate me, O Lord, my God,
    according to your righteousness,
    and let them not rejoice over me!
25 Let them not say in their hearts,
    "Aha, our heart's desire!"
Let them not say, "We have swallowed him
    up."
26 Let them be put to shame and disap-
        pointed altogether
    who rejoice at my calamity!
Let them be clothed with shame and dis-
        honor
    who magnify themselves against me!

27 Let those who delight in my righteousness
    shout for joy and be glad
    and say evermore,
"Great is the Lord,
    who delights in the welfare of his ser-
        vant!"
28 Then my tongue shall tell of your righ-
    teousness
    and of your praise all the day long.

How Precious Is Your Steadfast Love

36 To the choirmaster. Of David, the servant of the Lord.

1 Transgression speaks to the wicked
    deep in his heart;[3]
there is no fear of God
    before his eyes.
2 For he flatters himself in his own eyes
    that his iniquity cannot be found out
        and hated.
3 The words of his mouth are trouble and
    deceit;
    he has ceased to act wisely and do good.
4 He plots trouble while on his bed;
    he sets himself in a way that is not good;
    he does not reject evil.

5 Your steadfast love, O Lord, extends to the
    heavens,
    your faithfulness to the clouds.
6 Your righteousness is like the mountains
    of God;
    your judgments are like the great deep;
    man and beast you save, O Lord.

7 How precious is your steadfast love, O God!
    The children of mankind take refuge in
        the shadow of your wings.
8 They feast on the abundance of your
    house,
    and you give them drink from the river
        of your delights.
9 For with you is the fountain of life;
    in your light do we see light.

10 Oh, continue your steadfast love to those
    who know you,
    and your righteousness to the upright
        of heart!
11 Let not the foot of arrogance come upon
    me,
    nor the hand of the wicked drive me
        away.

[1] Or *my prayer shall turn back* [2] The meaning of the Hebrew phrase is uncertain [3] Some Hebrew manuscripts, Syriac, Jerome (compare Septuagint); most Hebrew manuscripts *in my heart*

12 There the evildoers lie fallen;
　　they are thrust down, unable to rise.

He Will Not Forsake His Saints

37 [1] Of David.
　　Fret not yourself because of evildoers;
　　be not envious of wrongdoers!

2 For they will soon fade like the grass
　　and wither like the green herb.

3 Trust in the Lord, and do good;
　　dwell in the land and befriend faithful-
　　　ness.[2]

4 Delight yourself in the Lord,
　　and he will give you the desires of your
　　　heart.

5 Commit your way to the Lord;
　　trust in him, and he will act.

6 He will bring forth your righteousness as
　　　the light,
　　and your justice as the noonday.

7 Be still before the Lord and wait patiently
　　　for him;
　　fret not yourself over the one who pros-
　　　pers in his way,
　　over the man who carries out evil
　　　devices!

8 Refrain from anger, and forsake wrath!
　　Fret not yourself; it tends only to evil.

9 For the evildoers shall be cut off,
　　but those who wait for the Lord shall
　　　inherit the land.

10 In just a little while, the wicked will be no
　　　more;
　　though you look carefully at his place,
　　　he will not be there.

11 But the meek shall inherit the land
　　and delight themselves in abundant
　　　peace.

12 The wicked plots against the righteous
　　and gnashes his teeth at him,

13 but the Lord laughs at the wicked,
　　for he sees that his day is coming.

14 The wicked draw the sword and bend their
　　　bows
　　to bring down the poor and needy,
　　to slay those whose way is upright;

15 their sword shall enter their own heart,
　　and their bows shall be broken.

16 Better is the little that the righteous has
　　than the abundance of many wicked.

17 For the arms of the wicked shall be broken,
　　but the Lord upholds the righteous.

18 The Lord knows the days of the blameless,
　　and their heritage will remain for-
　　　ever;

19 they are not put to shame in evil times;
　　in the days of famine they have abun-
　　　dance.

20 But the wicked will perish;
　　the enemies of the Lord are like the
　　　glory of the pastures;
　　they vanish—like smoke they vanish
　　　away.

21 The wicked borrows but does not pay back,
　　but the righteous is generous and gives;

22 for those blessed by the Lord[3] shall inherit
　　　the land,
　　but those cursed by him shall be cut
　　　off.

23 The steps of a man are established by the
　　　Lord,
　　when he delights in his way;

24 though he fall, he shall not be cast head-
　　　long,
　　for the Lord upholds his hand.

25 I have been young, and now am old,
　　yet I have not seen the righteous for-
　　　saken
　　or his children begging for bread.

26 He is ever lending generously,
　　and his children become a blessing.

27 Turn away from evil and do good;
　　so shall you dwell forever.

28 For the Lord loves justice;
　　he will not forsake his saints.
　　They are preserved forever,
　　but the children of the wicked shall be
　　　cut off.

29 The righteous shall inherit the land
　　and dwell upon it forever.

30 The mouth of the righteous utters wis-
　　　dom,
　　and his tongue speaks justice.

31 The law of his God is in his heart;
　　his steps do not slip.

---

[1] This psalm is an acrostic poem, each stanza beginning with the successive letters of the Hebrew alphabet [2] Or *and feed on faithfulness*, or *and find safe pasture*
[3] Hebrew *by him*

32 The wicked watches for the righteous
   and seeks to put him to death.
33 The LORD will not abandon him to his
   power
   or let him be condemned when he is
   brought to trial.

34 Wait for the LORD and keep his way,
   and he will exalt you to inherit the land;
   you will look on when the wicked are
   cut off.

35 I have seen a wicked, ruthless man,
   spreading himself like a green laurel
   tree.[1]
36 But he passed away,[2] and behold, he was no
   more;
   though I sought him, he could not be
   found.

37 Mark the blameless and behold the upright,
   for there is a future for the man of peace.
38 But transgressors shall be altogether
   destroyed;
   the future of the wicked shall be cut off.

39 The salvation of the righteous is from the
   LORD;
   he is their stronghold in the time of
   trouble.
40 The LORD helps them and delivers them;
   he delivers them from the wicked and
   saves them,
   because they take refuge in him.

Do Not Forsake Me, O Lord

38

A PSALM OF DAVID, FOR THE MEMORIAL
OFFERING.

1 O LORD, rebuke me not in your anger,
   nor discipline me in your wrath!
2 For your arrows have sunk into me,
   and your hand has come down on me.

3 There is no soundness in my flesh
   because of your indignation;
   there is no health in my bones
   because of my sin.
4 For my iniquities have gone over my head;
   like a heavy burden, they are too heavy
   for me.

5 My wounds stink and fester
   because of my foolishness,
6 I am utterly bowed down and prostrate;
   all the day I go about mourning.

7 For my sides are filled with burning,
   and there is no soundness in my flesh.
8 I am feeble and crushed;
   I groan because of the tumult of my
   heart.

9 O Lord, all my longing is before you;
   my sighing is not hidden from you.
10 My heart throbs; my strength fails me,
   and the light of my eyes—it also has
   gone from me.
11 My friends and companions stand aloof
   from my plague,
   and my nearest kin stand far off.

12 Those who seek my life lay their snares;
   those who seek my hurt speak of ruin
   and meditate treachery all day long.
13 But I am like a deaf man; I do not hear,
   like a mute man who does not open his
   mouth.
14 I have become like a man who does not
   hear,
   and in whose mouth are no rebukes.

15 But for you, O LORD, do I wait;
   it is you, O Lord my God, who will
   answer.
16 For I said, "Only let them not rejoice over
   me,
   who boast against me when my foot
   slips!"

17 For I am ready to fall,
   and my pain is ever before me.
18 I confess my iniquity;
   I am sorry for my sin.
19 But my foes are vigorous, they are mighty,
   and many are those who hate me
   wrongfully.
20 Those who render me evil for good
   accuse me because I follow after good.

21 Do not forsake me, O LORD!
   O my God, be not far from me!
22 Make haste to help me,
   O Lord, my salvation!

What Is the Measure of My Days?

39

TO THE CHOIRMASTER: TO JEDUTHUN.
A PSALM OF DAVID.

1 I said, "I will guard my ways,
   that I may not sin with my tongue;

[1] The identity of this tree is uncertain [2] Or *But one passed by*

I will guard my mouth with a muzzle,
    so long as the wicked are in my presence."
2 I was mute and silent;
    I held my peace to no avail,
and my distress grew worse.
3   My heart became hot within me.
As I mused, the fire burned;
    then I spoke with my tongue:

4 "O LORD, make me know my end
    and what is the measure of my days;
    let me know how fleeting I am!
5 Behold, you have made my days a few
      handbreadths,
    and my lifetime is as nothing before you.
Surely all mankind stands as a mere
      breath!   *Selah*
6   Surely a man goes about as a shadow!
Surely for nothing[1] they are in turmoil;
    man heaps up wealth and does not
      know who will gather!

7 "And now, O Lord, for what do I wait?
    My hope is in you.
8 Deliver me from all my transgressions.
    Do not make me the scorn of the fool!
9 I am mute; I do not open my mouth,
    for it is you who have done it.
10 Remove your stroke from me;
    I am spent by the hostility of your hand.
11 When you discipline a man
    with rebukes for sin,
you consume like a moth what is dear to
      him;
    surely all mankind is a mere breath!
              Selah

12 "Hear my prayer, O LORD,
    and give ear to my cry;
    hold not your peace at my tears!
For I am a sojourner with you,
    a guest, like all my fathers.
13 Look away from me, that I may smile again,
    before I depart and am no more!"

My Help and My Deliverer

40

TO THE CHOIRMASTER. A PSALM OF
DAVID.

1 I waited patiently for the LORD;
    he inclined to me and heard my cry.
2 He drew me up from the pit of destruction,
    out of the miry bog,
and set my feet upon a rock,
    making my steps secure.

3 He put a new song in my mouth,
    a song of praise to our God.
Many will see and fear,
    and put their trust in the LORD.

4 Blessed is the man who makes
    the LORD his trust,
who does not turn to the proud,
    to those who go astray after a lie!
5 You have multiplied, O LORD my God,
    your wondrous deeds and your
      thoughts toward us;
    none can compare with you!
I will proclaim and tell of them,
    yet they are more than can be told.

6 In sacrifice and offering you have not
      delighted,
    but you have given me an open ear.[2]
Burnt offering and sin offering
    you have not required.
7 Then I said, "Behold, I have come;
    in the scroll of the book it is written of
      me:
8 I delight to do your will, O my God;
    your law is within my heart."

9 I have told the glad news of deliverance[3]
    in the great congregation;
behold, I have not restrained my lips,
    as you know, O LORD.
10 I have not hidden your deliverance within
      my heart;
    I have spoken of your faithfulness and
      your salvation;
I have not concealed your steadfast love
    and your faithfulness
from the great congregation.

11 As for you, O LORD, you will not restrain
    your mercy from me;
your steadfast love and your faithfulness will
    ever preserve me!
12 For evils have encompassed me
    beyond number;
my iniquities have overtaken me,
    and I cannot see;
they are more than the hairs of my head;
    my heart fails me.

13 Be pleased, O LORD, to deliver me!
    O LORD, make haste to help me!
14 Let those be put to shame and disap-
      pointed altogether
    who seek to snatch away my life;

---

[1] Hebrew *Surely as a breath* [2] Hebrew *ears you have dug for me* [3] Hebrew *righteousness*; also verse 10

let those be turned back and brought to
dishonor
who delight in my hurt!
15 Let those be appalled because of their
shame
who say to me, "Aha, Aha!"

16 But may all who seek you
rejoice and be glad in you;
may those who love your salvation
say continually, "Great is the LORD!"
17 As for me, I am poor and needy,
but the Lord takes thought for me.
You are my help and my deliverer;
do not delay, O my God!

O LORD, Be Gracious to Me

41

TO THE CHOIRMASTER. A PSALM OF DAVID.
Blessed is the one who considers the
poor![1]
In the day of trouble the LORD delivers
him;
2 the LORD protects him and keeps him
alive;
he is called blessed in the land;
you do not give him up to the will of
his enemies.
3 The LORD sustains him on his sickbed;
in his illness you restore him to full
health.[2]

4 As for me, I said, "O LORD, be gracious to
me;
heal me,[3] for I have sinned against you!"
5 My enemies say of me in malice,
"When will he die, and his name perish?"
6 And when one comes to see me, he utters
empty words,
while his heart gathers iniquity;
when he goes out, he tells it abroad.
7 All who hate me whisper together about
me;
they imagine the worst for me.[4]

8 They say, "A deadly thing is poured out[5] on
him;
he will not rise again from where he
lies."
9 Even my close friend in whom I trusted,
who ate my bread, has lifted his heel
against me.
10 But you, O LORD, be gracious to me,
and raise me up, that I may repay them!

11 By this I know that you delight in me:
my enemy will not shout in triumph
over me.
12 But you have upheld me because of my
integrity,
and set me in your presence forever.

13 Blessed be the LORD, the God of Israel,
from everlasting to everlasting!
Amen and Amen.

BOOK TWO

Why Are You Cast Down, O My Soul?

42

TO THE CHOIRMASTER. A MASKIL[6] OF
THE SONS OF KORAH.
1 As a deer pants for flowing streams,
so pants my soul for you, O God.
2 My soul thirsts for God,
for the living God.
When shall I come and appear before
God?[7]
3 My tears have been my food
day and night,
while they say to me all the day long,
"Where is your God?"
4 These things I remember,
as I pour out my soul:
how I would go with the throng
and lead them in procession to the
house of God
with glad shouts and songs of praise,
a multitude keeping festival.

5 Why are you cast down, O my soul,
and why are you in turmoil within me?
Hope in God; for I shall again praise
him,
my salvation[8] 6 and my God.

My soul is cast down within me;
therefore I remember you
from the land of Jordan and of Hermon,
from Mount Mizar.
7 Deep calls to deep
at the roar of your waterfalls;
all your breakers and your waves
have gone over me.
8 By day the LORD commands his steadfast
love,
and at night his song is with me,
a prayer to the God of my life.

---

[1] Or weak [2] Hebrew you turn all his bed [3] Hebrew my soul [4] Or they devise evil against me [5] Or has fastened [6] Probably a musical or liturgical term [7] Revocalization yields and
see the face of God [8] Hebrew the salvation of my face; also verse 11 and 43:5

9　I say to God, my rock:
　　"Why have you forgotten me?
　Why do I go mourning
　　　because of the oppression of the
　　　　enemy?"
10　As with a deadly wound in my bones,
　　　my adversaries taunt me,
　while they say to me all the day long,
　　"Where is your God?"

11　Why are you cast down, O my soul,
　　　and why are you in turmoil within
　　　　me?
　Hope in God; for I shall again praise him,
　　　my salvation and my God.

Send Out Your Light and Your Truth

43 Vindicate me, O God, and defend my
　　cause
　against an ungodly people,
　from the deceitful and unjust man
　　deliver me!
2　For you are the God in whom I take ref-
　　uge;
　　why have you rejected me?
　Why do I go about mourning
　　　because of the oppression of the
　　　　enemy?

3　Send out your light and your truth;
　　　let them lead me;
　let them bring me to your holy hill
　　　and to your dwelling!
4　Then I will go to the altar of God,
　　　to God my exceeding joy,
　and I will praise you with the lyre,
　　　O God, my God.

5　Why are you cast down, O my soul,
　　　and why are you in turmoil within me?
　Hope in God; for I shall again praise him,
　　　my salvation and my God.

Come to Our Help

44 To the choirmaster. A Maskil[1] of
　　the Sons of Korah.

1　O God, we have heard with our ears,
　　　our fathers have told us,
　what deeds you performed in their days,
　　　in the days of old:
2　you with your own hand drove out the
　　　nations,
　　　but them you planted;

you afflicted the peoples,
　　but them you set free;
3　for not by their own sword did they win
　　　the land,
　　　nor did their own arm save them,
　but your right hand and your arm,
　　　and the light of your face,
　　　for you delighted in them.

4　You are my King, O God;
　　　ordain salvation for Jacob!
5　Through you we push down our foes;
　　　through your name we tread down
　　　　those who rise up against us.
6　For not in my bow do I trust,
　　　nor can my sword save me.
7　But you have saved us from our foes
　　　and have put to shame those who hate
　　　　us.
8　In God we have boasted continually,
　　　and we will give thanks to your name
　　　　forever.　　　　　　　　　　*Selah*

9　But you have rejected us and disgraced us
　　　and have not gone out with our armies.
10　You have made us turn back from the foe,
　　　and those who hate us have gotten
　　　　spoil.
11　You have made us like sheep for slaughter
　　　and have scattered us among the
　　　　nations.
12　You have sold your people for a trifle,
　　　demanding no high price for them.
13　You have made us the taunt of our neigh-
　　　bors,
　　　the derision and scorn of those around
　　　　us.
14　You have made us a byword among the
　　　nations,
　　　a laughingstock[2] among the peoples.
15　All day long my disgrace is before me,
　　　and shame has covered my face
16　at the sound of the taunter and reviler,
　　　at the sight of the enemy and the
　　　　avenger.

17　All this has come upon us,
　　　though we have not forgotten you,
　　　and we have not been false to your cov-
　　　　enant.
18　Our heart has not turned back,
　　　nor have our steps departed from your
　　　　way;

---

[1] Probably a musical or liturgical term　[2] Hebrew *a shaking of the head*

19 yet you have broken us in the place of jackals
and covered us with the shadow of
death.
20 If we had forgotten the name of our God
or spread out our hands to a foreign god,
21 would not God discover this?
For he knows the secrets of the heart.
22 Yet for your sake we are killed all the day
long;
we are regarded as sheep to be slaughtered.

23 Awake! Why are you sleeping, O Lord?
Rouse yourself! Do not reject us forever!
24 Why do you hide your face?
Why do you forget our affliction and
oppression?
25 For our soul is bowed down to the dust;
our belly clings to the ground.
26 Rise up; come to our help!
Redeem us for the sake of your steadfast
love!

Your Throne, O God, Is Forever

45 To the choirmaster: according
to Lilies. A Maskil[1] of the Sons of
Korah; a love song.

1 My heart overflows with a pleasing theme;
I address my verses to the king;
my tongue is like the pen of a ready
scribe.

2 You are the most handsome of the sons of
men;
grace is poured upon your lips;
therefore God has blessed you forever.
3 Gird your sword on your thigh, O mighty
one,
in your splendor and majesty!

4 In your majesty ride out victoriously
for the cause of truth and meekness
and righteousness;
let your right hand teach you awesome deeds!
5 Your arrows are sharp
in the heart of the king's enemies;
the peoples fall under you.

6 Your throne, O God, is forever and ever.
The scepter of your kingdom is a scepter of uprightness;
7 you have loved righteousness and hated
wickedness.

Therefore God, your God, has anointed you
with the oil of gladness beyond your
companions;
8 your robes are all fragrant with myrrh
and aloes and cassia.
From ivory palaces stringed instruments
make you glad;
9 daughters of kings are among your
ladies of honor;
at your right hand stands the queen in
gold of Ophir.

10 Hear, O daughter, and consider, and incline
your ear:
forget your people and your father's
house,
11 and the king will desire your beauty.
Since he is your lord, bow to him.
12 The people[2] of Tyre will seek your favor
with gifts,
the richest of the people.[3]

13 All glorious is the princess in her chamber,
with robes interwoven with gold.
14 In many-colored robes she is led to the
king,
with her virgin companions following
behind her.
15 With joy and gladness they are led along
as they enter the palace of the king.

16 In place of your fathers shall be your sons;
you will make them princes in all the
earth.
17 I will cause your name to be remembered
in all generations;
therefore nations will praise you forever
and ever.

God Is Our Fortress

46 To the choirmaster. Of the Sons
of Korah. According to Alamoth.[4]
A Song.

1 God is our refuge and strength,
a very present[5] help in trouble.
2 Therefore we will not fear though the
earth gives way,
though the mountains be moved into
the heart of the sea,
3 though its waters roar and foam,
though the mountains tremble at its
swelling. *Selah*

---

[1] Probably a musical or liturgical term [2] Hebrew *daughter* [3] Or *The daughter of Tyre is here with gifts, the richest of people seek your favor* [4] Probably a musical or liturgical term
[5] Or *well proved*

4 There is a river whose streams make glad
　　the city of God,
　　the holy habitation of the Most High.
5 God is in the midst of her; she shall not be
　　moved;
　　God will help her when morning
　　dawns.
6 The nations rage, the kingdoms totter;
　　he utters his voice, the earth melts.
7 The LORD of hosts is with us;
　　the God of Jacob is our fortress.　　*Selah*

8 Come, behold the works of the LORD,
　　how he has brought desolations on the
　　earth.
9 He makes wars cease to the end of the
　　earth;
　　he breaks the bow and shatters the
　　spear;
　　he burns the chariots with fire.
10 "Be still, and know that I am God.
　　I will be exalted among the nations,
　　I will be exalted in the earth!"
11 The LORD of hosts is with us;
　　the God of Jacob is our fortress.　　*Selah*

God Is King over All the Earth

47 To the choirmaster. A Psalm of the
Sons of Korah.

1 Clap your hands, all peoples!
　　Shout to God with loud songs of joy!
2 For the LORD, the Most High, is to be
　　feared,
　　a great king over all the earth.
3 He subdued peoples under us,
　　and nations under our feet.
4 He chose our heritage for us,
　　the pride of Jacob whom he loves.
　　　　　　　　　　　　　　Selah

5 God has gone up with a shout,
　　the LORD with the sound of a trumpet.
6 Sing praises to God, sing praises!
　　Sing praises to our King, sing praises!
7 For God is the King of all the earth;
　　sing praises with a psalm![1]

8 God reigns over the nations;
　　God sits on his holy throne.
9 The princes of the peoples gather
　　as the people of the God of Abraham.
For the shields of the earth belong to God;
　　he is highly exalted!

Zion, the City of Our God

48 A Song. A Psalm of the Sons of Korah.
Great is the LORD and greatly to be
　　praised
　　in the city of our God!
His holy mountain, 2 beautiful in elevation,
　　is the joy of all the earth,
Mount Zion, in the far north,
　　the city of the great King.
3 Within her citadels God
　　has made himself known as a fortress.

4 For behold, the kings assembled;
　　they came on together.
5 As soon as they saw it, they were
　　astounded;
　　they were in panic; they took to flight.
6 Trembling took hold of them there,
　　anguish as of a woman in labor.
7 By the east wind you shattered
　　the ships of Tarshish.
8 As we have heard, so have we seen
　　in the city of the LORD of hosts,
in the city of our God,
　　which God will establish forever.　*Selah*

9 We have thought on your steadfast love,
　　O God,
　　in the midst of your temple.
10 As your name, O God,
　　so your praise reaches to the ends of the
　　earth.
Your right hand is filled with righteous-
　　ness.
11 　Let Mount Zion be glad!
Let the daughters of Judah rejoice
　　because of your judgments!

12 Walk about Zion, go around her,
　　number her towers,
13 consider well her ramparts,
　　go through her citadels,
that you may tell the next generation
14 　that this is God,
our God forever and ever.
　　He will guide us forever.[2]

Why Should I Fear in Times of Trouble?

49 To the choirmaster. A Psalm of the
Sons of Korah.

1 Hear this, all peoples!
　　Give ear, all inhabitants of the world,
2 both low and high,
　　rich and poor together!

---

[1] Hebrew *maskil*　[2] Septuagint; another reading is (compare Jerome, Syriac) *He will guide us beyond death*

3 My mouth shall speak wisdom;
      the meditation of my heart shall be
         understanding.
4 I will incline my ear to a proverb;
      I will solve my riddle to the music of
         the lyre.

5 Why should I fear in times of trouble,
      when the iniquity of those who cheat
         me surrounds me,
6 those who trust in their wealth
      and boast of the abundance of their
         riches?
7 Truly no man can ransom another,
      or give to God the price of his life,
8 for the ransom of their life is costly
      and can never suffice,
9 that he should live on forever
      and never see the pit.

10 For he sees that even the wise die;
      the fool and the stupid alike must per-
         ish
      and leave their wealth to others.
11 Their graves are their homes forever,[1]
      their dwelling places to all generations,
      though they called lands by their own
         names.
12 Man in his pomp will not remain;
      he is like the beasts that perish.

13 This is the path of those who have foolish
         confidence;
      yet after them people approve of their
         boasts.[2]   *Selah*
14 Like sheep they are appointed for Sheol;
      death shall be their shepherd,
   and the upright shall rule over them in the
         morning.
      Their form shall be consumed in Sheol,
         with no place to dwell.
15 But God will ransom my soul from the
         power of Sheol,
      for he will receive me.   *Selah*

16 Be not afraid when a man becomes rich,
      when the glory of his house increases.
17 For when he dies he will carry nothing
         away;
      his glory will not go down after him.
18 For though, while he lives, he counts
         himself blessed
      —and though you get praise when you
         do well for yourself—

19 his soul will go to the generation of his
         fathers,
      who will never again see light.
20 Man in his pomp yet without understand-
         ing is like the beasts that perish.

God Himself Is Judge

50 A Psalm of Asaph.
      The Mighty One, God the Lord,
      speaks and summons the earth
      from the rising of the sun to its setting.
2 Out of Zion, the perfection of beauty,
      God shines forth.

3 Our God comes; he does not keep silence;[3]
      before him is a devouring fire,
      around him a mighty tempest.
4 He calls to the heavens above
      and to the earth, that he may judge his
         people:
5 "Gather to me my faithful ones,
      who made a covenant with me by sacri-
         fice!"
6 The heavens declare his righteousness,
      for God himself is judge!   *Selah*

7 "Hear, O my people, and I will speak;
      O Israel, I will testify against you.
      I am God, your God.
8 Not for your sacrifices do I rebuke you;
      your burnt offerings are continually
         before me.
9 I will not accept a bull from your house
      or goats from your folds.
10 For every beast of the forest is mine,
      the cattle on a thousand hills.
11 I know all the birds of the hills,
      and all that moves in the field is mine.

12 "If I were hungry, I would not tell you,
      for the world and its fullness are mine.
13 Do I eat the flesh of bulls
      or drink the blood of goats?
14 Offer to God a sacrifice of thanksgiving,[4]
      and perform your vows to the Most
         High,
15 and call upon me in the day of trouble;
      I will deliver you, and you shall glorify
         me."

16 But to the wicked God says:
      "What right have you to recite my stat-
         utes
      or take my covenant on your lips?

---

[1] Septuagint, Syriac, Targum; Hebrew *Their inward thought was that their homes were forever* [2] Or *and of those after them who approve of their boasts* [3] Or *May our God come, and not keep silence* [4] Or *Make thanksgiving your sacrifice to God*

¹⁷ For you hate discipline,
    and you cast my words behind you.
¹⁸ If you see a thief, you are pleased with him,
    and you keep company with adulterers.

¹⁹ "You give your mouth free rein for evil,
    and your tongue frames deceit.
²⁰ You sit and speak against your brother;
    you slander your own mother's son.
²¹ These things you have done, and I have
        been silent;
    you thought that I¹ was one like your-
        self.
    But now I rebuke you and lay the charge
        before you.

²² "Mark this, then, you who forget God,
    lest I tear you apart, and there be none
        to deliver!
²³ The one who offers thanksgiving as his
        sacrifice glorifies me;
    to one who orders his way rightly
    I will show the salvation of God!"

Create in Me a Clean Heart, O God

51 To the choirmaster. A Psalm of David, when Nathan the prophet went to him, after he had gone in to Bathsheba.

¹ Have mercy on me,² O God,
    according to your steadfast love;
    according to your abundant mercy
        blot out my transgressions.
² Wash me thoroughly from my iniquity,
    and cleanse me from my sin!

³ For I know my transgressions,
    and my sin is ever before me.
⁴ Against you, you only, have I sinned
    and done what is evil in your sight,
    so that you may be justified in your words
    and blameless in your judgment.
⁵ Behold, I was brought forth in iniquity,
    and in sin did my mother conceive
        me.
⁶ Behold, you delight in truth in the inward
        being,
    and you teach me wisdom in the secret
        heart.
⁷ Purge me with hyssop, and I shall be clean;
    wash me, and I shall be whiter than
        snow.

⁸ Let me hear joy and gladness;
    let the bones that you have broken
        rejoice.
⁹ Hide your face from my sins,
    and blot out all my iniquities.
¹⁰ Create in me a clean heart, O God,
    and renew a right³ spirit within me.
¹¹ Cast me not away from your presence,
    and take not your Holy Spirit from me.
¹² Restore to me the joy of your salvation,
    and uphold me with a willing spirit.

¹³ Then I will teach transgressors your ways,
    and sinners will return to you.
¹⁴ Deliver me from bloodguiltiness, O God,
    O God of my salvation,
    and my tongue will sing aloud of your
        righteousness.
¹⁵ O Lord, open my lips,
    and my mouth will declare your praise.
¹⁶ For you will not delight in sacrifice, or I
        would give it;
    you will not be pleased with a burnt
        offering.
¹⁷ The sacrifices of God are a broken spirit;
    a broken and contrite heart, O God, you
        will not despise.

¹⁸ Do good to Zion in your good pleasure;
    build up the walls of Jerusalem;
¹⁹ then will you delight in right sacrifices,
    in burnt offerings and whole burnt
        offerings;
    then bulls will be offered on your altar.

The Steadfast Love of God Endures

52 To the choirmaster. A Maskil⁴ of David, when Doeg, the Edomite, came and told Saul, "David has come to the house of Ahimelech."

¹ Why do you boast of evil, O mighty man?
    The steadfast love of God endures all
        the day.
² Your tongue plots destruction,
    like a sharp razor, you worker of deceit.
³ You love evil more than good,
    and lying more than speaking what is
        right.   *Selah*
⁴ You love all words that devour,
    O deceitful tongue.

---

¹ Or that the I am ² Or Be gracious to me ³ Or steadfast ⁴ Probably a musical or liturgical term

⁵ But God will break you down forever;
    he will snatch and tear you from your
        tent;
    he will uproot you from the land of the
        living.   *Selah*
⁶ The righteous shall see and fear,
    and shall laugh at him, saying,
⁷ "See the man who would not make
      God his refuge,
    but trusted in the abundance of his riches
      and sought refuge in his own destruc-
        tion!"[1]

⁸ But I am like a green olive tree
    in the house of God.
    I trust in the steadfast love of God
      forever and ever.
⁹ I will thank you forever,
    because you have done it.
    I will wait for your name, for it is good,
      in the presence of the godly.

There Is None Who Does Good

53 TO THE CHOIRMASTER: ACCORDING TO MAHALATH. A MASKIL[2] OF DAVID.

¹ The fool says in his heart, "There is no
      God."
    They are corrupt, doing abominable
      iniquity;
    there is none who does good.

² God looks down from heaven
    on the children of man
    to see if there are any who understand,[3]
    who seek after God.

³ They have all fallen away;
    together they have become corrupt;
    there is none who does good,
      not even one.

⁴ Have those who work evil no knowledge,
    who eat up my people as they eat bread,
    and do not call upon God?

⁵ There they are, in great terror,
    where there is no terror!
    For God scatters the bones of him who
      encamps against you;
    you put them to shame, for God has
      rejected them.

⁶ Oh, that salvation for Israel would come
      out of Zion!
    When God restores the fortunes of his
      people,
    let Jacob rejoice, let Israel be glad.

The Lord Upholds My Life

54 TO THE CHOIRMASTER: WITH STRINGED INSTRUMENTS. A MASKIL[4] OF DAVID, WHEN THE ZIPHITES WENT AND TOLD SAUL, "IS NOT DAVID HIDING AMONG US?"

¹ O God, save me by your name,
    and vindicate me by your might.
² O God, hear my prayer;
    give ear to the words of my mouth.

³ For strangers[5] have risen against me;
    ruthless men seek my life;
    they do not set God before themselves.
           Selah

⁴ Behold, God is my helper;
    the Lord is the upholder of my life.
⁵ He will return the evil to my enemies;
    in your faithfulness put an end to them.

⁶ With a freewill offering I will sacrifice to
      you;
    I will give thanks to your name,
      O LORD, for it is good.
⁷ For he has delivered me from every trouble,
    and my eye has looked in triumph on
      my enemies.

Cast Your Burden on the LORD

55 TO THE CHOIRMASTER: WITH STRINGED INSTRUMENTS. A MASKIL[6] OF DAVID.

¹ Give ear to my prayer, O God,
    and hide not yourself from my plea for
      mercy!
² Attend to me, and answer me;
    I am restless in my complaint and I
      moan,
³ because of the noise of the enemy,
    because of the oppression of the wicked.
    For they drop trouble upon me,
    and in anger they bear a grudge against
      me.

⁴ My heart is in anguish within me;
    the terrors of death have fallen upon me.
⁵ Fear and trembling come upon me,
    and horror overwhelms me.

---

[1] Or *in his work of destruction* [2] Probably musical or liturgical terms [3] Or *who act wisely* [4] Probably a musical or liturgical term [5] Some Hebrew manuscripts and Targum *insolent men* (compare Psalm 86:14) [6] Probably a musical or liturgical term

6 And I say, "Oh, that I had wings like a dove!
   I would fly away and be at rest;
7 yes, I would wander far away;
   I would lodge in the wilderness;   *Selah*
8 I would hurry to find a shelter
   from the raging wind and tempest."

9 Destroy, O Lord, divide their tongues;
   for I see violence and strife in the city.
10 Day and night they go around it
   on its walls,
and iniquity and trouble are within it;
11   ruin is in its midst;
oppression and fraud
   do not depart from its marketplace.

12 For it is not an enemy who taunts me—
   then I could bear it;
it is not an adversary who deals insolently
   with me—
   then I could hide from him.
13 But it is you, a man, my equal,
   my companion, my familiar friend.
14 We used to take sweet counsel together;
   within God's house we walked in the
   throng.
15 Let death steal over them;
   let them go down to Sheol alive;
   for evil is in their dwelling place and in
   their heart.

16 But I call to God,
   and the LORD will save me.
17 Evening and morning and at noon
   I utter my complaint and moan,
   and he hears my voice.
18 He redeems my soul in safety
   from the battle that I wage,
   for many are arrayed against me.
19 God will give ear and humble them,
   he who is enthroned from of old,   *Selah*
because they do not change
   and do not fear God.

20 My companion[1] stretched out his hand
   against his friends;
   he violated his covenant.
21 His speech was smooth as butter,
   yet war was in his heart;
his words were softer than oil,
   yet they were drawn swords.

22 Cast your burden on the LORD,
   and he will sustain you;

he will never permit
   the righteous to be moved.

23 But you, O God, will cast them down
   into the pit of destruction;
men of blood and treachery
   shall not live out half their days.
But I will trust in you.

In God I Trust

56
TO THE CHOIRMASTER: ACCORDING TO
THE DOVE ON FAR-OFF TEREBINTHS.
A MIKTAM[2] OF DAVID, WHEN THE
PHILISTINES SEIZED HIM IN GATH.

1 Be gracious to me, O God, for man tramples on me;
   all day long an attacker oppresses me;
2 my enemies trample on me all day long,
   for many attack me proudly.
3 When I am afraid,
   I put my trust in you.
4 In God, whose word I praise,
   in God I trust; I shall not be afraid.
   What can flesh do to me?

5 All day long they injure my cause;[3]
   all their thoughts are against me for
   evil.
6 They stir up strife, they lurk;
   they watch my steps,
   as they have waited for my life.
7 For their crime will they escape?
   In wrath cast down the peoples, O God!

8 You have kept count of my tossings;[4]
   put my tears in your bottle.
   Are they not in your book?
9 Then my enemies will turn back
   in the day when I call.
   This I know, that[5] God is for me.
10 In God, whose word I praise,
   in the LORD, whose word I praise,
11 in God I trust; I shall not be afraid.
   What can man do to me?

12 I must perform my vows to you, O God;
   I will render thank offerings to you.
13 For you have delivered my soul from death,
   yes, my feet from falling,
that I may walk before God
   in the light of life.

[1] Hebrew *He* [2] Probably a musical or liturgical term [3] Or *they twist my words* [4] Or *wanderings* [5] Or *because*

Let Your Glory Be over All the Earth

57 TO THE CHOIRMASTER: ACCORDING TO
DO NOT DESTROY. A MIKTAM[1] OF DAVID,
WHEN HE FLED FROM SAUL, IN THE CAVE.

1 Be merciful to me, O God, be merciful to
me,
for in you my soul takes refuge;
in the shadow of your wings I will take
refuge,
till the storms of destruction pass by.
2 I cry out to God Most High,
to God who fulfills his purpose for
me.
3 He will send from heaven and save me;
he will put to shame him who tramples
on me.   *Selah*
God will send out his steadfast love and
his faithfulness!

4 My soul is in the midst of lions;
I lie down amid fiery beasts—
the children of man, whose teeth are
spears and arrows,
whose tongues are sharp swords.

5 Be exalted, O God, above the heavens!
Let your glory be over all the earth!

6 They set a net for my steps;
my soul was bowed down.
They dug a pit in my way,
but they have fallen into it themselves.
Selah

7 My heart is steadfast, O God,
my heart is steadfast!
I will sing and make melody!
8 Awake, my glory![2]
Awake, O harp and lyre!
I will awake the dawn!
9 I will give thanks to you, O Lord, among
the peoples;
I will sing praises to you among the
nations.
10 For your steadfast love is great to the heavens,
your faithfulness to the clouds.

11 Be exalted, O God, above the heavens!
Let your glory be over all the earth!

God Who Judges the Earth

58 TO THE CHOIRMASTER: ACCORDING TO
DO NOT DESTROY. A MIKTAM[3] OF DAVID.

1 Do you indeed decree what is right, you
gods?[4]

Do you judge the children of man
uprightly?
2 No, in your hearts you devise wrongs;
your hands deal out violence on earth.

3 The wicked are estranged from the
womb;
they go astray from birth, speaking
lies.
4 They have venom like the venom of a serpent,
like the deaf adder that stops its ear,
5 so that it does not hear the voice of
charmers
or of the cunning enchanter.

6 O God, break the teeth in their mouths;
tear out the fangs of the young lions,
O LORD!
7 Let them vanish like water that runs
away;
when he aims his arrows, let them be
blunted.
8 Let them be like the snail that dissolves
into slime,
like the stillborn child who never sees
the sun.
9 Sooner than your pots can feel the heat of
thorns,
whether green or ablaze, may he sweep
them away![5]

10 The righteous will rejoice when he sees the
vengeance;
he will bathe his feet in the blood of the
wicked.
11 Mankind will say, "Surely there is a reward
for the righteous;
surely there is a God who judges on
earth."

Deliver Me from My Enemies

59 TO THE CHOIRMASTER: ACCORDING TO
DO NOT DESTROY. A MIKTAM[6] OF DAVID,
WHEN SAUL SENT MEN TO WATCH HIS
HOUSE IN ORDER TO KILL HIM.

1 Deliver me from my enemies, O my God;
protect me from those who rise up
against me;
2 deliver me from those who work evil,
and save me from bloodthirsty men.

3 For behold, they lie in wait for my life;
fierce men stir up strife against me.

---

[1] Probably a musical or liturgical term [2] Or *my whole being* [3] Probably a musical or liturgical term [4] Or *you mighty lords* (by revocalization; Hebrew *in silence*) [5] The meaning of the Hebrew verse is uncertain [6] Probably a musical or liturgical term

4 For no transgression or sin of mine, O LORD,
    for no fault of mine, they run and make
        ready.
    Awake, come to meet me, and see!
5 You, LORD God of hosts, are God of
        Israel.
    Rouse yourself to punish all the nations;
        spare none of those who treacherously
            plot evil.   *Selah*

6 Each evening they come back,
        howling like dogs
        and prowling about the city.
7 There they are, bellowing with their mouths
        with swords in their lips—
        for "Who," they think,[1] "will hear us?"

8 But you, O LORD, laugh at them;
        you hold all the nations in derision.
9 O my Strength, I will watch for you,
        for you, O God, are my fortress.
10 My God in his steadfast love[2] will meet me;
        God will let me look in triumph on my
            enemies.

11 Kill them not, lest my people forget;
        make them totter[3] by your power and
            bring them down,
        O Lord, our shield!
12 For the sin of their mouths, the words of
            their lips,
        let them be trapped in their pride.
    For the cursing and lies that they utter,
13   consume them in wrath;
        consume them till they are no more,
    that they may know that God rules over
            Jacob
        to the ends of the earth.   *Selah*

14 Each evening they come back,
        howling like dogs
        and prowling about the city.
15 They wander about for food
        and growl if they do not get their fill.

16 But I will sing of your strength;
        I will sing aloud of your steadfast love
            in the morning.
    For you have been to me a fortress
        and a refuge in the day of my distress.
17 O my Strength, I will sing praises to you,
        for you, O God, are my fortress,
        the God who shows me steadfast love.

He Will Tread Down Our Foes

60 To the choirmaster: according to
Shushan Eduth. A Miktam[4] of David;
for instruction; when he strove
with Aram-naharaim and with Aram-
zobah, and when Joab on his return
struck down twelve thousand of
Edom in the Valley of Salt.

1 O God, you have rejected us, broken our
            defenses;
        you have been angry; oh, restore us.
2 You have made the land to quake; you have
            torn it open;
        repair its breaches, for it totters.
3 You have made your people see hard things;
        you have given us wine to drink that
            made us stagger.

4 You have set up a banner for those who
            fear you,
        that they may flee to it from the bow.[5]
                                    Selah
5 That your beloved ones may be delivered,
        give salvation by your right hand and
            answer us!

6 God has spoken in his holiness:[6]
        "With exultation I will divide up Shechem
        and portion out the Vale of Succoth.
7 Gilead is mine; Manasseh is mine;
        Ephraim is my helmet;
        Judah is my scepter.
8 Moab is my washbasin;
        upon Edom I cast my shoe;
        over Philistia I shout in triumph."[7]

9 Who will bring me to the fortified city?
        Who will lead me to Edom?
10 Have you not rejected us, O God?
        You do not go forth, O God, with our
            armies.
11 Oh, grant us help against the foe,
        for vain is the salvation of man!
12 With God we shall do valiantly;
        it is he who will tread down our foes.

Lead Me to the Rock

61 To the choirmaster: with stringed
instruments. Of David.

1 Hear my cry, O God,
        listen to my prayer;
2 from the end of the earth I call to you
        when my heart is faint.

[1] Hebrew lacks *they think* [2] Or *The God who shows me steadfast love* [3] Or *wander* [4] Probably musical or liturgical terms [5] Or *that it may be displayed because of truth*
[6] Or *sanctuary* [7] Revocalization (compare Psalm 108:10); Masoretic Text *over me, O Philistia, shout in triumph*

Lead me to the rock
 that is higher than I,
3 for you have been my refuge,
 a strong tower against the enemy.

4 Let me dwell in your tent forever!
 Let me take refuge under the shelter of
  your wings!   *Selah*
5 For you, O God, have heard my vows;
 you have given me the heritage of those
  who fear your name.

6 Prolong the life of the king;
 may his years endure to all generations!
7 May he be enthroned forever before God;
 appoint steadfast love and faithfulness
  to watch over him!

8 So will I ever sing praises to your name,
 as I perform my vows day after day.

My Soul Waits for God Alone

62 To the choirmaster: according to
Jeduthun. A Psalm of David.

1 For God alone my soul waits in silence;
 from him comes my salvation.
2 He alone is my rock and my salvation,
 my fortress; I shall not be greatly
  shaken.

3 How long will all of you attack a man
 to batter him,
 like a leaning wall, a tottering fence?
4 They only plan to thrust him down from
  his high position.
 They take pleasure in falsehood.
 They bless with their mouths,
  but inwardly they curse. *Selah*

5 For God alone, O my soul, wait in silence,
 for my hope is from him.
6 He only is my rock and my salvation,
 my fortress; I shall not be shaken.
7 On God rests my salvation and my glory;
 my mighty rock, my refuge is God.

8 Trust in him at all times, O people;
 pour out your heart before him;
 God is a refuge for us. *Selah*

9 Those of low estate are but a breath;
 those of high estate are a delusion;
 in the balances they go up;
 they are together lighter than a breath.

10 Put no trust in extortion;
 set no vain hopes on robbery;
 if riches increase, set not your heart on
  them.

11 Once God has spoken;
 twice have I heard this:
 that power belongs to God,
12 and that to you, O Lord, belongs steadfast love.
 For you will render to a man
  according to his work.

My Soul Thirsts for You

63 A Psalm of David, when he was in the
wilderness of Judah.

1 O God, you are my God; earnestly I seek
  you;
 my soul thirsts for you;
 my flesh faints for you,
  as in a dry and weary land where there
   is no water.
2 So I have looked upon you in the sanctuary,
 beholding your power and glory.
3 Because your steadfast love is better than
  life,
 my lips will praise you.
4 So I will bless you as long as I live;
 in your name I will lift up my hands.

5 My soul will be satisfied as with fat and
  rich food,
 and my mouth will praise you with joyful lips,
6 when I remember you upon my bed,
 and meditate on you in the watches of
  the night;
7 for you have been my help,
 and in the shadow of your wings I will
  sing for joy.
8 My soul clings to you;
 your right hand upholds me.

9 But those who seek to destroy my life
 shall go down into the depths of the
  earth;
10 they shall be given over to the power of the
  sword;
 they shall be a portion for jackals.
11 But the king shall rejoice in God;
 all who swear by him shall exult,
 for the mouths of liars will be stopped.

Hide Me from the Wicked

64 To the choirmaster. A Psalm of David.

1 Hear my voice, O God, in my complaint;
    preserve my life from dread of the
        enemy.
2 Hide me from the secret plots of the
        wicked,
    from the throng of evildoers,
3 who whet their tongues like swords,
    who aim bitter words like arrows,
4 shooting from ambush at the blameless,
    shooting at him suddenly and without
        fear.
5 They hold fast to their evil purpose;
    they talk of laying snares secretly,
thinking, "Who can see them?"
6   They search out injustice,
    saying, "We have accomplished a diligent
        search."
    For the inward mind and heart of a
        man are deep.

7 But God shoots his arrow at them;
    they are wounded suddenly.
8 They are brought to ruin, with their own
        tongues turned against them;
    all who see them will wag their heads.
9 Then all mankind fears;
    they tell what God has brought about
    and ponder what he has done.

10 Let the righteous one rejoice in the Lord
    and take refuge in him!
    Let all the upright in heart exult!

O God of Our Salvation

65 To the choirmaster. A Psalm of David. A Song.

1 Praise is due to you,[1] O God, in Zion,
    and to you shall vows be performed.
2 O you who hear prayer,
    to you shall all flesh come.
3 When iniquities prevail against me,
    you atone for our transgressions.
4 Blessed is the one you choose and bring
        near,
    to dwell in your courts!
    We shall be satisfied with the goodness of
        your house,
    the holiness of your temple!

5 By awesome deeds you answer us with
        righteousness,
    O God of our salvation,
the hope of all the ends of the earth
    and of the farthest seas;
6 the one who by his strength established
        the mountains,
    being girded with might;
7 who stills the roaring of the seas,
    the roaring of their waves,
    the tumult of the peoples,
8 so that those who dwell at the ends of the
        earth are in awe at your signs.
    You make the going out of the morning
        and the evening to shout for joy.

9 You visit the earth and water it;[2]
    you greatly enrich it;
the river of God is full of water;
    you provide their grain,
    for so you have prepared it.
10 You water its furrows abundantly,
        settling its ridges,
    softening it with showers,
    and blessing its growth.
11 You crown the year with your bounty;
    your wagon tracks overflow with abun-
        dance.
12 The pastures of the wilderness overflow,
    the hills gird themselves with joy,
13 the meadows clothe themselves with
        flocks,
    the valleys deck themselves with grain,
    they shout and sing together for joy.

How Awesome Are Your Deeds

66 To the choirmaster. A Song. A Psalm.
    Shout for joy to God, all the earth;
2   sing the glory of his name;
    give to him glorious praise!
3 Say to God, "How awesome are your deeds!
    So great is your power that your ene-
        mies come cringing to you.
4 All the earth worships you
    and sings praises to you;
    they sing praises to your name."   Selah

5 Come and see what God has done:
    he is awesome in his deeds toward the
        children of man.
6 He turned the sea into dry land;
    they passed through the river on foot.
There did we rejoice in him,
7   who rules by his might forever,

[1] Or Praise waits for you in silence [2] Or and make it overflow

whose eyes keep watch on the nations—
 let not the rebellious exalt themselves.
         Selah

8 Bless our God, O peoples;
 let the sound of his praise be heard,
9 who has kept our soul among the living
 and has not let our feet slip.
10 For you, O God, have tested us;
 you have tried us as silver is tried.
11 You brought us into the net;
 you laid a crushing burden on our
  backs;
12 you let men ride over our heads;
 we went through fire and through
  water;
 yet you have brought us out to a place of
  abundance.

13 I will come into your house with burnt
  offerings;
 I will perform my vows to you,
14 that which my lips uttered
 and my mouth promised when I was in
  trouble.
15 I will offer to you burnt offerings of fattened animals,
 with the smoke of the sacrifice of rams;
 I will make an offering of bulls and goats.
         Selah

16 Come and hear, all you who fear God,
 and I will tell what he has done for my
  soul.
17 I cried to him with my mouth,
 and high praise was on[1] my tongue.[2]
18 If I had cherished iniquity in my heart,
 the Lord would not have listened.
19 But truly God has listened;
 he has attended to the voice of my
  prayer.
20 Blessed be God,
 because he has not rejected my prayer
 or removed his steadfast love from me!

Make Your Face Shine upon Us

67 To the choirmaster: with stringed
instruments. A Psalm. A Song.

1 May God be gracious to us and bless us
 and make his face to shine upon us,
         Selah
2 that your way may be known on earth,
 your saving power among all nations.
3 Let the peoples praise you, O God;
 let all the peoples praise you!

4 Let the nations be glad and sing for joy,
 for you judge the peoples with equity
 and guide the nations upon earth.
         Selah
5 Let the peoples praise you, O God;
 let all the peoples praise you!

6 The earth has yielded its increase;
 God, our God, shall bless us.
7 God shall bless us;
 let all the ends of the earth fear him!

God Shall Scatter His Enemies

68 To the choirmaster. A Psalm of
David. A Song.

1 God shall arise, his enemies shall be scattered;
 and those who hate him shall flee
  before him!
2 As smoke is driven away, so you shall
  drive them away;
 as wax melts before fire,
 so the wicked shall perish before God!
3 But the righteous shall be glad;
 they shall exult before God;
 they shall be jubilant with joy!

4 Sing to God, sing praises to his name;
 lift up a song to him who rides through
  the deserts;
 his name is the LORD;
 exult before him!
5 Father of the fatherless and protector of
  widows
 is God in his holy habitation.
6 God settles the solitary in a home;
 he leads out the prisoners to prosperity,
 but the rebellious dwell in a parched
  land.

7 O God, when you went out before your
  people,
 when you marched through the wilderness,   *Selah*
8 the earth quaked, the heavens poured
  down rain,
 before God, the One of Sinai,
 before God,[3] the God of Israel.
9 Rain in abundance, O God, you shed
  abroad;
 you restored your inheritance as it languished;
10 your flock[4] found a dwelling in it;
 in your goodness, O God, you provided
  for the needy.

---

[1] Hebrew *under* [2] Or *and he was exalted with my tongue* [3] Or *before God, even Sinai before God* [4] Or *your congregation*

11 The Lord gives the word;
    the women who announce the news are
        a great host:
12 "The kings of the armies—they flee, they
        flee!"
    The women at home divide the spoil—
13 though you men lie among the sheep-
        folds—
    the wings of a dove covered with silver,
        its pinions with shimmering gold.
14 When the Almighty scatters kings there,
        let snow fall on Zalmon.

15 O mountain of God, mountain of Bashan;
    O many-peaked[1] mountain, mountain
        of Bashan!
16 Why do you look with hatred, O many-
        peaked mountain,
    at the mount that God desired for his
        abode,
    yes, where the LORD will dwell forever?
17 The chariots of God are twice ten thou-
        sand,
    thousands upon thousands;
    the Lord is among them; Sinai is now in
        the sanctuary.
18 You ascended on high,
    leading a host of captives in your train
    and receiving gifts among men,
    even among the rebellious, that the LORD
        God may dwell there.

19 Blessed be the Lord,
    who daily bears us up;
    God is our salvation.   *Selah*
20 Our God is a God of salvation,
    and to GOD, the Lord, belong deliver-
        ances from death.
21 But God will strike the heads of his ene-
        mies,
    the hairy crown of him who walks in
        his guilty ways.
22 The Lord said,
    "I will bring them back from Bashan,
    I will bring them back from the depths of
        the sea,
23 that you may strike your feet in their
        blood,
    that the tongues of your dogs may have
        their portion from the foe."

24 Your procession is[2] seen, O God,
    the procession of my God, my King,
        into the sanctuary—

25 the singers in front, the musicians last,
    between them virgins playing tambou-
        rines:
26 "Bless God in the great congregation,
    the LORD, O you[3] who are of Israel's
        fountain!"
27 There is Benjamin, the least of them, in the
        lead,
    the princes of Judah in their throng,
    the princes of Zebulun, the princes of
        Naphtali.

28 Summon your power, O God,[4]
    the power, O God, by which you have
        worked for us.
29 Because of your temple at Jerusalem
    kings shall bear gifts to you.
30 Rebuke the beasts that dwell among the
        reeds,
    the herd of bulls with the calves of the
        peoples.
    Trample underfoot those who lust after
        tribute;
    scatter the peoples who delight in war.[5]
31 Nobles shall come from Egypt;
    Cush shall hasten to stretch out her
        hands to God.

32 O kingdoms of the earth, sing to God;
    sing praises to the Lord,   *Selah*
33 to him who rides in the heavens, the
        ancient heavens;
    behold, he sends out his voice, his
        mighty voice.
34 Ascribe power to God,
    whose majesty is over Israel,
    and whose power is in the skies.
35 Awesome is God from his[6] sanctuary;
    the God of Israel—he is the one who
        gives power and strength to his
        people.
    Blessed be God!

Save Me, O God

69 TO THE CHOIRMASTER: ACCORDING TO
        LILIES. OF DAVID.

1 Save me, O God!
    For the waters have come up to my
        neck.[7]
2 I sink in deep mire,
    where there is no foothold;
    I have come into deep waters,
    and the flood sweeps over me.

---

[1] Or *hunch-backed*; also verse 16 [2] Or *has been* [3] The Hebrew for *you* is plural here [4] By revocalization (compare Septuagint); Hebrew *Your God has summoned your power*
[5] The meaning of the Hebrew verse is uncertain [6] Septuagint; Hebrew *your* [7] Or *waters threaten my life*

3 I am weary with my crying out;
   my throat is parched.
My eyes grow dim
   with waiting for my God.

4 More in number than the hairs of my
      head
   are those who hate me without cause;
mighty are those who would destroy me,
   those who attack me with lies.
What I did not steal
   must I now restore?

5 O God, you know my folly;
   the wrongs I have done are not hidden
      from you.

6 Let not those who hope in you be put to
      shame through me,
   O Lord GOD of hosts;
let not those who seek you be brought to
      dishonor through me,
   O God of Israel.

7 For it is for your sake that I have borne
      reproach,
   that dishonor has covered my face.

8 I have become a stranger to my brothers,
   an alien to my mother's sons.

9 For zeal for your house has consumed
      me,
   and the reproaches of those who
      reproach you have fallen on me.

10 When I wept and humbled[1] my soul with
      fasting,
   it became my reproach.

11 When I made sackcloth my clothing,
   I became a byword to them.

12 I am the talk of those who sit in the gate,
   and the drunkards make songs about
      me.

13 But as for me, my prayer is to you,
   O LORD.
   At an acceptable time, O God,
   in the abundance of your steadfast love
      answer me in your saving faithful-
      ness.

14 Deliver me
   from sinking in the mire;
let me be delivered from my enemies
   and from the deep waters.

15 Let not the flood sweep over me,
   or the deep swallow me up,
   or the pit close its mouth over me.

16 Answer me, O LORD, for your steadfast love
      is good;
   according to your abundant mercy, turn
      to me.

17 Hide not your face from your servant,
   for I am in distress; make haste to
      answer me.

18 Draw near to my soul, redeem me;
   ransom me because of my enemies!

19 You know my reproach,
   and my shame and my dishonor;
   my foes are all known to you.

20 Reproaches have broken my heart,
   so that I am in despair.
I looked for pity, but there was none,
   and for comforters, but I found none.

21 They gave me poison for food,
   and for my thirst they gave me sour
      wine to drink.

22 Let their own table before them become a
      snare;
   and when they are at peace, let it
      become a trap.[2]

23 Let their eyes be darkened, so that they
      cannot see,
   and make their loins tremble continu-
      ally.

24 Pour out your indignation upon them,
   and let your burning anger overtake
      them.

25 May their camp be a desolation;
   let no one dwell in their tents.

26 For they persecute him whom you have
      struck down,
   and they recount the pain of those you
      have wounded.

27 Add to them punishment upon punish-
      ment;
   may they have no acquittal from you.[3]

28 Let them be blotted out of the book of the
      living;
   let them not be enrolled among the
      righteous.

29 But I am afflicted and in pain;
   let your salvation, O God, set me on
      high!

30 I will praise the name of God with a song;
   I will magnify him with thanksgiving.

31 This will please the LORD more than an ox
   or a bull with horns and hoofs.

---

[1] Hebrew lacks and humbled [2] Hebrew; a slight revocalization yields (compare Septuagint, Syriac, Jerome) a snare, and retribution and a trap [3] Hebrew may they not come into your righteousness

32 When the humble see it they will be
glad;
    you who seek God, let your hearts
    revive.
33 For the LORD hears the needy
    and does not despise his own people
    who are prisoners.

34 Let heaven and earth praise him,
    the seas and everything that moves in
    them.
35 For God will save Zion
    and build up the cities of Judah,
    and people shall dwell there and possess it;
36   the offspring of his servants shall
    inherit it,
        and those who love his name shall
        dwell in it.

O LORD, Do Not Delay

70 TO THE CHOIRMASTER. OF DAVID, FOR
THE MEMORIAL OFFERING.

1   Make haste, O God, to deliver me!
        O LORD, make haste to help me!
2   Let them be put to shame and confusion
        who seek my life!
    Let them be turned back and brought to
        dishonor
        who delight in my hurt!
3   Let them turn back because of their shame
        who say, "Aha, Aha!"

4   May all who seek you
        rejoice and be glad in you!
    May those who love your salvation
        say evermore, "God is great!"
5   But I am poor and needy;
        hasten to me, O God!
    You are my help and my deliverer;
        O LORD, do not delay!

Forsake Me Not When My Strength Is Spent

71 In you, O LORD, do I take refuge;
        let me never be put to shame!
2   In your righteousness deliver me and res-
        cue me;
        incline your ear to me, and save me!
3   Be to me a rock of refuge,
        to which I may continually come;
    you have given the command to save me,
        for you are my rock and my fortress.

4   Rescue me, O my God, from the hand of
        the wicked,
        from the grasp of the unjust and cruel
        man.
5   For you, O Lord, are my hope,
        my trust, O LORD, from my youth.
6   Upon you I have leaned from before my
        birth;
        you are he who took me from my moth-
        er's womb.
    My praise is continually of you.

7   I have been as a portent to many,
        but you are my strong refuge.
8   My mouth is filled with your praise,
        and with your glory all the day.
9   Do not cast me off in the time of old age;
        forsake me not when my strength is
        spent.
10 For my enemies speak concerning me;
        those who watch for my life consult
        together
11 and say, "God has forsaken him;
        pursue and seize him,
        for there is none to deliver him."

12 O God, be not far from me;
        O my God, make haste to help me!
13 May my accusers be put to shame and con-
        sumed;
        with scorn and disgrace may they be
        covered
        who seek my hurt.
14 But I will hope continually
        and will praise you yet more and
        more.
15 My mouth will tell of your righteous
        acts,
        of your deeds of salvation all the day,
        for their number is past my knowledge.
16 With the mighty deeds of the Lord GOD I
        will come;
        I will remind them of your righteous-
        ness, yours alone.

17 O God, from my youth you have taught
        me,
        and I still proclaim your wondrous
        deeds.
18 So even to old age and gray hairs,
        O God, do not forsake me,
    until I proclaim your might to another
        generation,
        your power to all those to come.

19 Your righteousness, O God,
 reaches the high heavens.
You who have done great things,
 O God, who is like you?
20 You who have made me see many troubles
  and calamities
 will revive me again;
from the depths of the earth
 you will bring me up again.
21 You will increase my greatness
 and comfort me again.

22 I will also praise you with the harp
 for your faithfulness, O my God;
I will sing praises to you with the lyre,
 O Holy One of Israel.
23 My lips will shout for joy,
 when I sing praises to you;
 my soul also, which you have redeemed.
24 And my tongue will talk of your righteous help all the day long,
for they have been put to shame and disappointed
 who sought to do me hurt.

Give the King Your Justice

72 OF SOLOMON.
 Give the king your justice, O God,
 and your righteousness to the royal son!
2 May he judge your people with righteousness,
 and your poor with justice!
3 Let the mountains bear prosperity for the
  people,
 and the hills, in righteousness!
4 May he defend the cause of the poor of the
  people,
 give deliverance to the children of the
  needy,
 and crush the oppressor!
5 May they fear you[1] while the sun endures,
 and as long as the moon, throughout all
  generations!
6 May he be like rain that falls on the
  mown grass,
 like showers that water the earth!
7 In his days may the righteous flourish,
 and peace abound, till the moon be no
  more!

8 May he have dominion from sea to sea,
 and from the River[2] to the ends of the
  earth!
9 May desert tribes bow down before him,
 and his enemies lick the dust!

10 May the kings of Tarshish and of the coastlands
 render him tribute;
may the kings of Sheba and Seba
 bring gifts!
11 May all kings fall down before him,
 all nations serve him!

12 For he delivers the needy when he calls,
 the poor and him who has no helper.
13 He has pity on the weak and the needy,
 and saves the lives of the needy.
14 From oppression and violence he redeems
  their life,
 and precious is their blood in his sight.

15 Long may he live;
 may gold of Sheba be given to him!
May prayer be made for him continually,
 and blessings invoked for him all the
  day!
16 May there be abundance of grain in the
  land;
 on the tops of the mountains may it
  wave;
 may its fruit be like Lebanon;
and may people blossom in the cities
 like the grass of the field!
17 May his name endure forever,
 his fame continue as long as the sun!
May people be blessed in him,
 all nations call him blessed!

18 Blessed be the LORD, the God of Israel,
 who alone does wondrous things.
19 Blessed be his glorious name forever;
 may the whole earth be filled with his
  glory!
   Amen and Amen!

20 The prayers of David, the son of Jesse, are
 ended.

BOOK THREE

God Is My Strength and Portion Forever

73 A PSALM OF ASAPH.
 Truly God is good to Israel,
 to those who are pure in heart.
2 But as for me, my feet had almost stumbled,
 my steps had nearly slipped.
3 For I was envious of the arrogant
 when I saw the prosperity of the
  wicked.

---

[1] Septuagint *He shall endure* [2] That is, the Euphrates

4 For they have no pangs until death;
    their bodies are fat and sleek.
5 They are not in trouble as others are;
    they are not stricken like the rest of
      mankind.
6 Therefore pride is their necklace;
    violence covers them as a garment.
7 Their eyes swell out through fatness;
    their hearts overflow with follies.
8 They scoff and speak with malice;
    loftily they threaten oppression.
9 They set their mouths against the heavens,
    and their tongue struts through the
      earth.
10 Therefore his people turn back to them,
    and find no fault in them.[1]
11 And they say, "How can God know?
    Is there knowledge in the Most High?"
12 Behold, these are the wicked;
    always at ease, they increase in riches.
13 All in vain have I kept my heart clean
    and washed my hands in innocence.
14 For all the day long I have been stricken
    and rebuked every morning.
15 If I had said, "I will speak thus,"
    I would have betrayed the generation of
      your children.
16 But when I thought how to understand
      this,
    it seemed to me a wearisome task,
17 until I went into the sanctuary of God;
    then I discerned their end.

18 Truly you set them in slippery places;
    you make them fall to ruin.
19 How they are destroyed in a moment,
    swept away utterly by terrors!
20 Like a dream when one awakes,
    O Lord, when you rouse yourself, you
      despise them as phantoms.
21 When my soul was embittered,
    when I was pricked in heart,
22 I was brutish and ignorant;
    I was like a beast toward you.
23 Nevertheless, I am continually with you;
    you hold my right hand.
24 You guide me with your counsel,
    and afterward you will receive me to
      glory.
25 Whom have I in heaven but you?
    And there is nothing on earth that I
      desire besides you.

26 My flesh and my heart may fail,
    but God is the strength[2] of my heart
    and my portion forever.
27 For behold, those who are far from you
      shall perish;
    you put an end to everyone who is
      unfaithful to you.
28 But for me it is good to be near God;
    I have made the Lord GOD my refuge,
    that I may tell of all your works.

Arise, O God, Defend Your Cause

74 A MASKIL[3] OF ASAPH.
    O God, why do you cast us off forever?
    Why does your anger smoke against the
      sheep of your pasture?
2 Remember your congregation, which you
      have purchased of old,
    which you have redeemed to be the
      tribe of your heritage!
    Remember Mount Zion, where you
      have dwelt.
3 Direct your steps to the perpetual ruins;
    the enemy has destroyed everything in
      the sanctuary!

4 Your foes have roared in the midst of your
      meeting place;
    they set up their own signs for signs.
5 They were like those who swing axes
    in a forest of trees.[4]
6 And all its carved wood
    they broke down with hatchets and
      hammers.
7 They set your sanctuary on fire;
    they profaned the dwelling place of
      your name,
    bringing it down to the ground.
8 They said to themselves, "We will utterly
      subdue them";
    they burned all the meeting places of
      God in the land.

9 We do not see our signs;
    there is no longer any prophet,
    and there is none among us who knows
      how long.
10 How long, O God, is the foe to scoff?
    Is the enemy to revile your name forever?
11 Why do you hold back your hand, your
      right hand?
    Take it from the fold of your garment[5]
    and destroy them!

[1] Probable reading; Hebrew *the waters of a full cup are drained by them* [2] Hebrew *rock* [3] Probably a musical or liturgical term [4] The meaning of the Hebrew is uncertain
[5] Hebrew *from your bosom*

12 Yet God my King is from of old,
　　working salvation in the midst of the
　　　earth.
13 You divided the sea by your might;
　　you broke the heads of the sea mon-
　　　sters[1] on the waters.
14 You crushed the heads of Leviathan;
　　you gave him as food for the creatures
　　　of the wilderness.
15 You split open springs and brooks;
　　you dried up ever-flowing streams.
16 Yours is the day, yours also the night;
　　you have established the heavenly lights
　　　and the sun.
17 You have fixed all the boundaries of the
　　　earth;
　　you have made summer and winter.

18 Remember this, O LORD, how the enemy
　　　scoffs,
　　and a foolish people reviles your name.
19 Do not deliver the soul of your dove to the
　　　wild beasts;
　　do not forget the life of your poor forever.

20 Have regard for the covenant,
　　for the dark places of the land are full
　　　of the habitations of violence.
21 Let not the downtrodden turn back in
　　　shame;
　　let the poor and needy praise your name.

22 Arise, O God, defend your cause;
　　remember how the foolish scoff at you
　　　all the day!
23 Do not forget the clamor of your foes,
　　the uproar of those who rise against
　　　you, which goes up continually!

God Will Judge with Equity

75 TO THE CHOIRMASTER: ACCORDING TO
DO NOT DESTROY. A PSALM OF ASAPH.
A SONG.

1 We give thanks to you, O God;
　　we give thanks, for your name is near.
　　We[2] recount your wondrous deeds.

2 "At the set time that I appoint
　　I will judge with equity.
3 When the earth totters, and all its inhabi-
　　　tants,
　　it is I who keep steady its pillars.　Selah
4 I say to the boastful, 'Do not boast,'
　　and to the wicked, 'Do not lift up your
　　　horn;

5 do not lift up your horn on high,
　　or speak with haughty neck.'"

6 For not from the east or from the west
　　and not from the wilderness comes lift-
　　　ing up,
7 but it is God who executes judgment,
　　putting down one and lifting up
　　　another.
8 For in the hand of the LORD there is a cup
　　with foaming wine, well mixed,
　　and he pours out from it,
　　　and all the wicked of the earth
　　　shall drain it down to the dregs.

9 But I will declare it forever;
　　I will sing praises to the God of Jacob.
10 All the horns of the wicked I will cut off,
　　but the horns of the righteous shall be
　　　lifted up.

Who Can Stand Before You?

76 TO THE CHOIRMASTER: WITH STRINGED
INSTRUMENTS. A PSALM OF ASAPH.
A SONG.

1 In Judah God is known;
　　his name is great in Israel.
2 His abode has been established in Salem,
　　his dwelling place in Zion.
3 There he broke the flashing arrows,
　　the shield, the sword, and the weapons
　　　of war.　　　　　　　　Selah

4 Glorious are you, more majestic
　　than the mountains full of prey.
5 The stouthearted were stripped of their
　　　spoil;
　　they sank into sleep;
　　all the men of war
　　　were unable to use their hands.
6 At your rebuke, O God of Jacob,
　　both rider and horse lay stunned.

7 But you, you are to be feared!
　　Who can stand before you
　　　when once your anger is roused?
8 From the heavens you uttered judgment;
　　the earth feared and was still,
9 when God arose to establish judgment,
　　to save all the humble of the earth.　　　　　　　　　　　　　　　　Selah

10 Surely the wrath of man shall praise you;
　　the remnant[3] of wrath you will put on
　　　like a belt.

---

[1] Or the great sea creatures　[2] Hebrew They　[3] Or extremity

11 Make your vows to the LORD your God
　　　and perform them;
　　let all around him bring gifts
　　to him who is to be feared,
12 who cuts off the spirit of princes,
　　who is to be feared by the kings of the
　　　earth.

In the Day of Trouble I Seek the Lord

77 TO THE CHOIRMASTER: ACCORDING TO
JEDUTHUN. A PSALM OF ASAPH.

1 I cry aloud to God,
　　aloud to God, and he will hear me.
2 In the day of my trouble I seek the Lord;
　　in the night my hand is stretched out
　　　without wearying;
　　my soul refuses to be comforted.
3 When I remember God, I moan;
　　when I meditate, my spirit faints. *Selah*

4 You hold my eyelids open;
　　I am so troubled that I cannot speak.
5 I consider the days of old,
　　the years long ago.
6 I said,[1] "Let me remember my song in the
　　　night;
　　let me meditate in my heart."
　　Then my spirit made a diligent search:
7 "Will the Lord spurn forever,
　　and never again be favorable?
8 Has his steadfast love forever ceased?
　　Are his promises at an end for all
　　　time?
9 Has God forgotten to be gracious?
　　Has he in anger shut up his compas-
　　　sion?" *Selah*

10 Then I said, "I will appeal to this,
　　to the years of the right hand of the
　　　Most High."[2]

11 I will remember the deeds of the LORD;
　　yes, I will remember your wonders of
　　　old.
12 I will ponder all your work,
　　and meditate on your mighty deeds.
13 Your way, O God, is holy.
　　What god is great like our God?
14 You are the God who works wonders;
　　you have made known your might
　　　among the peoples.
15 You with your arm redeemed your people,
　　the children of Jacob and Joseph. *Selah*

16 When the waters saw you, O God,
　　when the waters saw you, they were
　　　afraid;
　　indeed, the deep trembled.
17 The clouds poured out water;
　　the skies gave forth thunder;
　　your arrows flashed on every side.
18 The crash of your thunder was in the
　　　whirlwind;
　　your lightnings lighted up the world;
　　the earth trembled and shook.
19 Your way was through the sea,
　　your path through the great waters;
　　yet your footprints were unseen.[3]
20 You led your people like a flock
　　by the hand of Moses and Aaron.

Tell the Coming Generation

78 A MASKIL[4] OF ASAPH.
Give ear, O my people, to my teaching;
incline your ears to the words of my
　　　mouth!
2 I will open my mouth in a parable;
　　I will utter dark sayings from of old,
3 things that we have heard and known,
　　that our fathers have told us.
4 We will not hide them from their chil-
　　　dren,
　　but tell to the coming generation
the glorious deeds of the LORD, and his
　　　might,
　　and the wonders that he has done.

5 He established a testimony in Jacob
　　and appointed a law in Israel,
which he commanded our fathers
　　to teach to their children,
6 that the next generation might know
　　　them,
　　the children yet unborn,
and arise and tell them to their children,
7 so that they should set their hope in
　　　God
and not forget the works of God,
　　but keep his commandments;
8 and that they should not be like their
　　　fathers,
　　a stubborn and rebellious generation,
a generation whose heart was not steadfast,
　　whose spirit was not faithful to God.

9 The Ephraimites, armed with[5] the bow,
　　turned back on the day of battle.

[1] Hebrew lacks *I said* [2] Or *This is my grief: that the right hand of the Most High has changed* [3] Hebrew *unknown* [4] Probably a musical or liturgical term [5] Hebrew *armed and shooting*

10 They did not keep God's covenant,
　　but refused to walk according to his law.
11 They forgot his works
　　and the wonders that he had shown
　　　them.
12 In the sight of their fathers he performed
　　　wonders
　　in the land of Egypt, in the fields of
　　　Zoan.
13 He divided the sea and let them pass
　　　through it,
　　and made the waters stand like a
　　　heap.
14 In the daytime he led them with a cloud,
　　and all the night with a fiery light.
15 He split rocks in the wilderness
　　and gave them drink abundantly as
　　　from the deep.
16 He made streams come out of the rock
　　and caused waters to flow down like riv-
　　　ers.

17 Yet they sinned still more against him,
　　rebelling against the Most High in the
　　　desert.
18 They tested God in their heart
　　by demanding the food they craved.
19 They spoke against God, saying,
　　"Can God spread a table in the wilder-
　　　ness?
20 He struck the rock so that water gushed
　　　out
　　and streams overflowed.
　　Can he also give bread
　　　or provide meat for his people?"

21 Therefore, when the LORD heard, he was
　　　full of wrath;
　　a fire was kindled against Jacob;
　　his anger rose against Israel,
22 because they did not believe in God
　　and did not trust his saving power.
23 Yet he commanded the skies above
　　and opened the doors of heaven,
24 and he rained down on them manna to
　　　eat
　　and gave them the grain of heaven.
25 Man ate of the bread of the angels;
　　he sent them food in abundance.
26 He caused the east wind to blow in the
　　　heavens,
　　and by his power he led out the south
　　　wind;

27 he rained meat on them like dust,
　　winged birds like the sand of the seas;
28 he let them fall in the midst of their
　　　camp,
　　all around their dwellings.
29 And they ate and were well filled,
　　for he gave them what they craved.
30 But before they had satisfied their craving,
　　while the food was still in their mouths,
31 the anger of God rose against them,
　　and he killed the strongest of them
　　and laid low the young men of Israel.

32 In spite of all this, they still sinned;
　　despite his wonders, they did not
　　　believe.
33 So he made their days vanish like[1] a
　　　breath,[2]
　　and their years in terror.
34 When he killed them, they sought him;
　　they repented and sought God ear-
　　　nestly.
35 They remembered that God was their rock,
　　the Most High God their redeemer.
36 But they flattered him with their
　　　mouths;
　　they lied to him with their tongues.
37 Their heart was not steadfast toward
　　　him;
　　they were not faithful to his covenant.
38 Yet he, being compassionate,
　　atoned for their iniquity
　　and did not destroy them;
　　he restrained his anger often
　　and did not stir up all his wrath.
39 He remembered that they were but flesh,
　　a wind that passes and comes not
　　　again.
40 How often they rebelled against him in the
　　　wilderness
　　and grieved him in the desert!
41 They tested God again and again
　　and provoked the Holy One of Israel.
42 They did not remember his power[3]
　　or the day when he redeemed them
　　　from the foe,
43 when he performed his signs in Egypt
　　and his marvels in the fields of Zoan.
44 He turned their rivers to blood,
　　so that they could not drink of their
　　　streams.

[1] Hebrew *in*　[2] Or *vapor*　[3] Hebrew *hand*

45 He sent among them swarms of flies,
    which devoured them,
    and frogs, which destroyed them.
46 He gave their crops to the destroying locust
    and the fruit of their labor to the locust.
47 He destroyed their vines with hail
    and their sycamores with frost.
48 He gave over their cattle to the hail
    and their flocks to thunderbolts.
49 He let loose on them his burning anger,
    wrath, indignation, and distress,
    a company of destroying angels.
50 He made a path for his anger;
    he did not spare them from death,
    but gave their lives over to the plague.
51 He struck down every firstborn in Egypt,
    the firstfruits of their strength in the
    tents of Ham.
52 Then he led out his people like sheep
    and guided them in the wilderness like
    a flock.
53 He led them in safety, so that they were not
    afraid,
    but the sea overwhelmed their enemies.
54 And he brought them to his holy land,
    to the mountain which his right hand
    had won.
55 He drove out nations before them;
    he apportioned them for a possession
    and settled the tribes of Israel in their
    tents.

56 Yet they tested and rebelled against the
    Most High God
    and did not keep his testimonies,
57 but turned away and acted treacherously
    like their fathers;
    they twisted like a deceitful bow.
58 For they provoked him to anger with their
    high places;
    they moved him to jealousy with their
    idols.
59 When God heard, he was full of wrath,
    and he utterly rejected Israel.
60 He forsook his dwelling at Shiloh,
    the tent where he dwelt among man-
    kind,
61 and delivered his power to captivity,
    his glory to the hand of the foe.
62 He gave his people over to the sword
    and vented his wrath on his heritage.

63 Fire devoured their young men,
    and their young women had no mar-
    riage song.
64 Their priests fell by the sword,
    and their widows made no lamentation.
65 Then the Lord awoke as from sleep,
    like a strong man shouting because of
    wine.
66 And he put his adversaries to rout;
    he put them to everlasting shame.

67 He rejected the tent of Joseph;
    he did not choose the tribe of Ephraim,
68 but he chose the tribe of Judah,
    Mount Zion, which he loves.
69 He built his sanctuary like the high heav-
    ens,
    like the earth, which he has founded
    forever.
70 He chose David his servant
    and took him from the sheepfolds;
71 from following the nursing ewes he
    brought him
    to shepherd Jacob his people,
    Israel his inheritance.
72 With upright heart he shepherded them
    and guided them with his skillful hand.

How Long, O Lord?

79 A Psalm of Asaph.
    O God, the nations have come into
    your inheritance;
    they have defiled your holy temple;
    they have laid Jerusalem in ruins.
2 They have given the bodies of your ser-
    vants
    to the birds of the heavens for food,
    the flesh of your faithful to the beasts of
    the earth.
3 They have poured out their blood like
    water
    all around Jerusalem,
    and there was no one to bury them.
4 We have become a taunt to our neighbors,
    mocked and derided by those around
    us.

5 How long, O Lord? Will you be angry for-
    ever?
    Will your jealousy burn like fire?
6 Pour out your anger on the nations
    that do not know you,
    and on the kingdoms
    that do not call upon your name!

7 For they have devoured Jacob
   and laid waste his habitation.

8 Do not remember against us our former
      iniquities;[1]
   let your compassion come speedily to
      meet us,
   for we are brought very low.

9 Help us, O God of our salvation,
      for the glory of your name;
   deliver us, and atone for our sins,
      for your name's sake!

10 Why should the nations say,
   "Where is their God?"
   Let the avenging of the outpoured blood of
      your servants
   be known among the nations before
      our eyes!

11 Let the groans of the prisoners come
      before you;
   according to your great power, preserve
      those doomed to die!

12 Return sevenfold into the lap of our
      neighbors
   the taunts with which they have
      taunted you, O Lord!

13 But we your people, the sheep of your pas-
      ture,
   will give thanks to you forever;
   from generation to generation we will
      recount your praise.

Restore Us, O God

80 To the choirmaster: according to
   Lilies. A Testimony. Of Asaph, a Psalm.

1 Give ear, O Shepherd of Israel,
   you who lead Joseph like a flock.
   You who are enthroned upon the cheru-
      bim, shine forth.

2 Before Ephraim and Benjamin and
      Manasseh,
   stir up your might
   and come to save us!

3 Restore us,[2] O God;
   let your face shine, that we may be
      saved!

4 O Lord God of hosts,
   how long will you be angry with your
      people's prayers?

5 You have fed them with the bread of tears
   and given them tears to drink in full
      measure.

6 You make us an object of contention for
      our neighbors,
   and our enemies laugh among them-
      selves.

7 Restore us, O God of hosts;
   let your face shine, that we may be
      saved!

8 You brought a vine out of Egypt;
   you drove out the nations and planted
      it.

9 You cleared the ground for it;
   it took deep root and filled the land.

10 The mountains were covered with its
      shade,
   the mighty cedars with its branches.

11 It sent out its branches to the sea
   and its shoots to the River.[3]

12 Why then have you broken down its walls,
   so that all who pass along the way pluck
      its fruit?

13 The boar from the forest ravages it,
   and all that move in the field feed on it.

14 Turn again, O God of hosts!
   Look down from heaven, and see;
   have regard for this vine,

15 the stock that your right hand
      planted,
   and for the son whom you made strong
      for yourself.

16 They have burned it with fire; they have
      cut it down;
   may they perish at the rebuke of your
      face!

17 But let your hand be on the man of your
      right hand,
   the son of man whom you have made
      strong for yourself!

18 Then we shall not turn back from you;
   give us life, and we will call upon your
      name!

19 Restore us, O Lord God of hosts!
   Let your face shine, that we may be
      saved!

Oh, That My People Would Listen to Me

81 To the choirmaster: according to
   The Gittith.[4] Of Asaph.

1 Sing aloud to God our strength;
   shout for joy to the God of Jacob!

2 Raise a song; sound the tambourine,
   the sweet lyre with the harp.

---

[1] Or the iniquities of former generations [2] Or Turn us again; also verses 7, 19 [3] That is, the Euphrates [4] Probably a musical or liturgical term

3 Blow the trumpet at the new moon,
   at the full moon, on our feast day.

4 For it is a statute for Israel,
   a rule[1] of the God of Jacob.

5 He made it a decree in Joseph
   when he went out over[2] the land of
      Egypt.
   I hear a language I had not known:

6 "I relieved your[3] shoulder of the burden;
   your hands were freed from the bas-
      ket.

7 In distress you called, and I delivered
      you;
   I answered you in the secret place of
      thunder;
   I tested you at the waters of Meribah.
                                    Selah

8 Hear, O my people, while I admonish you!
   O Israel, if you would but listen to me!

9 There shall be no strange god among
      you;
   you shall not bow down to a foreign
      god.

10 I am the LORD your God,
   who brought you up out of the land of
      Egypt.
   Open your mouth wide, and I will fill it.

11 "But my people did not listen to my voice;
   Israel would not submit to me.

12 So I gave them over to their stubborn
      hearts,
   to follow their own counsels.

13 Oh, that my people would listen to me,
   that Israel would walk in my ways!

14 I would soon subdue their enemies
   and turn my hand against their foes.

15 Those who hate the LORD would cringe
      toward him,
   and their fate would last forever.

16 But he would feed you[4] with the finest of
      the wheat,
   and with honey from the rock I would
      satisfy you."

Rescue the Weak and Needy

82 A PSALM OF ASAPH.
   God has taken his place in the divine
      council;
   in the midst of the gods he holds judg-
      ment:

2 "How long will you judge unjustly
   and show partiality to the wicked?
                                    Selah

3 Give justice to the weak and the fatherless;
   maintain the right of the afflicted and
      the destitute.

4 Rescue the weak and the needy;
   deliver them from the hand of the
      wicked."

5 They have neither knowledge nor under-
      standing,
   they walk about in darkness;
   all the foundations of the earth are
      shaken.

6 I said, "You are gods,
   sons of the Most High, all of you;

7 nevertheless, like men you shall die,
   and fall like any prince."[5]

8 Arise, O God, judge the earth;
   for you shall inherit all the nations!

O God, Do Not Keep Silence

83 A SONG. A PSALM OF ASAPH.
   O God, do not keep silence;
   do not hold your peace or be still,
      O God!

2 For behold, your enemies make an uproar;
   those who hate you have raised their
      heads.

3 They lay crafty plans against your people;
   they consult together against your trea-
      sured ones.

4 They say, "Come, let us wipe them out as a
      nation;
   let the name of Israel be remembered
      no more!"

5 For they conspire with one accord;
   against you they make a covenant—

6 the tents of Edom and the Ishmaelites,
   Moab and the Hagrites,

7 Gebal and Ammon and Amalek,
   Philistia with the inhabitants of Tyre;

8 Asshur also has joined them;
   they are the strong arm of the children
      of Lot.   *Selah*

9 Do to them as you did to Midian,
   as to Sisera and Jabin at the river
      Kishon,

10 who were destroyed at En-dor,
   who became dung for the ground.

---

[1] Or *just decree* [2] Or *against* [3] Hebrew *his; also next line* [4] That is, Israel; Hebrew *him* [5] Or *fall as one man, O princes*

11 Make their nobles like Oreb and Zeeb,
   all their princes like Zebah and
   Zalmunna,
12 who said, "Let us take possession for ourselves
   of the pastures of God."

13 O my God, make them like whirling dust,[1]
   like chaff before the wind.
14 As fire consumes the forest,
   as the flame sets the mountains ablaze,
15 so may you pursue them with your tempest
   and terrify them with your hurricane!
16 Fill their faces with shame,
   that they may seek your name,
   O LORD.
17 Let them be put to shame and dismayed
   forever;
   let them perish in disgrace,
18 that they may know that you alone,
   whose name is the LORD,
   are the Most High over all the earth.

My Soul Longs for the Courts of the LORD

84 TO THE CHOIRMASTER: ACCORDING TO
THE GITTITH.[2] A PSALM OF THE SONS OF
KORAH.

1 How lovely is your dwelling place,
   O LORD of hosts!
2 My soul longs, yes, faints
   for the courts of the LORD;
   my heart and flesh sing for joy
   to the living God.

3 Even the sparrow finds a home,
   and the swallow a nest for herself,
   where she may lay her young,
   at your altars, O LORD of hosts,
   my King and my God.
4 Blessed are those who dwell in your
   house,
   ever singing your praise! *Selah*

5 Blessed are those whose strength is in you,
   in whose heart are the highways to
   Zion.[3]
6 As they go through the Valley of Baca
   they make it a place of springs;
   the early rain also covers it with pools.
7 They go from strength to strength;
   each one appears before God in Zion.

8 O LORD God of hosts, hear my prayer;
   give ear, O God of Jacob! *Selah*

9 Behold our shield, O God;
   look on the face of your anointed!
10 For a day in your courts is better
   than a thousand elsewhere.
   I would rather be a doorkeeper in the
   house of my God
   than dwell in the tents of wickedness.
11 For the LORD God is a sun and shield;
   the LORD bestows favor and honor.
   No good thing does he withhold
   from those who walk uprightly.
12 O LORD of hosts,
   blessed is the one who trusts in you!

Revive Us Again

85 TO THE CHOIRMASTER. A PSALM OF THE
SONS OF KORAH.

1 LORD, you were favorable to your land;
   you restored the fortunes of Jacob.
2 You forgave the iniquity of your people;
   you covered all their sin. *Selah*
3 You withdrew all your wrath;
   you turned from your hot anger.

4 Restore us again, O God of our salvation,
   and put away your indignation
   toward us!
5 Will you be angry with us forever?
   Will you prolong your anger to all
   generations?
6 Will you not revive us again,
   that your people may rejoice in you?
7 Show us your steadfast love, O LORD,
   and grant us your salvation.

8 Let me hear what God the LORD will
   speak,
   for he will speak peace to his people, to
   his saints;
   but let them not turn back to folly.
9 Surely his salvation is near to those who
   fear him,
   that glory may dwell in our land.

10 Steadfast love and faithfulness meet;
   righteousness and peace kiss each
   other.
11 Faithfulness springs up from the ground,
   and righteousness looks down from the
   sky.
12 Yes, the LORD will give what is good,
   and our land will yield its increase.
13 Righteousness will go before him
   and make his footsteps a way.

---

[1] Or *like a tumbleweed* [2] Probably a musical or liturgical term [3] Hebrew lacks *to Zion*

Great Is Your Steadfast Love

86 A PRAYER OF DAVID.
Incline your ear, O LORD, and answer me,
for I am poor and needy.

2 Preserve my life, for I am godly;
save your servant, who trusts in you—
you are my God.
3 Be gracious to me, O Lord,
for to you do I cry all the day.
4 Gladden the soul of your servant,
for to you, O Lord, do I lift up my soul.
5 For you, O Lord, are good and forgiving,
abounding in steadfast love to all who call upon you.
6 Give ear, O LORD, to my prayer;
listen to my plea for grace.
7 In the day of my trouble I call upon you,
for you answer me.

8 There is none like you among the gods, O Lord,
nor are there any works like yours.
9 All the nations you have made shall come and worship before you, O Lord,
and shall glorify your name.
10 For you are great and do wondrous things;
you alone are God.
11 Teach me your way, O LORD,
that I may walk in your truth;
unite my heart to fear your name.
12 I give thanks to you, O Lord my God, with my whole heart,
and I will glorify your name forever.
13 For great is your steadfast love toward me;
you have delivered my soul from the depths of Sheol.

14 O God, insolent men have risen up against me;
a band of ruthless men seeks my life,
and they do not set you before them.
15 But you, O Lord, are a God merciful and gracious,
slow to anger and abounding in steadfast love and faithfulness.
16 Turn to me and be gracious to me;
give your strength to your servant,
and save the son of your maidservant.

17 Show me a sign of your favor,
that those who hate me may see and be put to shame
because you, LORD, have helped me and comforted me.

Glorious Things of You Are Spoken

87 A PSALM OF THE SONS OF KORAH. A SONG.
On the holy mount stands the city he founded;
2 the LORD loves the gates of Zion
more than all the dwelling places of Jacob.
3 Glorious things of you are spoken,
O city of God. *Selah*

4 Among those who know me I mention Rahab and Babylon;
behold, Philistia and Tyre, with Cush[1]—
"This one was born there," they say.
5 And of Zion it shall be said,
"This one and that one were born in her";
for the Most High himself will establish her.
6 The LORD records as he registers the peoples,
"This one was born there." *Selah*

7 Singers and dancers alike say,
"All my springs are in you."

I Cry Out Day and Night Before You

88 A SONG. A PSALM OF THE SONS OF KORAH.
TO THE CHOIRMASTER: ACCORDING TO
MAHALATH LEANNOTH. A MASKIL[2] OF
HEMAN THE EZRAHITE.

1 O LORD, God of my salvation,
I cry out day and night before you.
2 Let my prayer come before you;
incline your ear to my cry!

3 For my soul is full of troubles,
and my life draws near to Sheol.
4 I am counted among those who go down to the pit;
I am a man who has no strength,
5 like one set loose among the dead,
like the slain that lie in the grave,
like those whom you remember no more,
for they are cut off from your hand.
6 You have put me in the depths of the pit,
in the regions dark and deep.

---

[1] Probably *Nubia* [2] Probably musical or liturgical terms

7 Your wrath lies heavy upon me,
　　and you overwhelm me with all your
　　　　waves.　　　　　　　　　*Selah*

8 You have caused my companions to shun
　　me;
　　you have made me a horror[1] to them.
I am shut in so that I cannot escape;
9　　my eye grows dim through sorrow.
Every day I call upon you, O LORD;
　　I spread out my hands to you.

10 Do you work wonders for the dead?
　　Do the departed rise up to praise you?
　　　　　　　　　　　　　　Selah

11 Is your steadfast love declared in the grave,
　　or your faithfulness in Abaddon?
12 Are your wonders known in the darkness,
　　or your righteousness in the land of for-
　　　getfulness?

13 But I, O LORD, cry to you;
　　in the morning my prayer comes before
　　　you.
14 O LORD, why do you cast my soul away?
　　Why do you hide your face from me?
15 Afflicted and close to death from my youth
　　up,
　　I suffer your terrors; I am helpless.[2]
16 Your wrath has swept over me;
　　your dreadful assaults destroy me.
17 They surround me like a flood all day
　　long;
　　they close in on me together.
18 You have caused my beloved and my friend
　　to shun me;
　　my companions have become darkness.[3]

I Will Sing of the Steadfast Love of the LORD

89 A MASKIL[4] OF ETHAN THE EZRAHITE.
I will sing of the steadfast love of the
　　LORD, forever;
　　with my mouth I will make known
　　　your faithfulness to all genera-
　　　tions.
2 For I said, "Steadfast love will be built up
　　forever;
　　in the heavens you will establish your
　　　faithfulness."
3 You have said, "I have made a covenant
　　with my chosen one;
　　I have sworn to David my servant:
4 'I will establish your offspring forever,
　　and build your throne for all genera-
　　　tions.'"　　　　　　　　*Selah*

5 Let the heavens praise your wonders,
　　O LORD,
　　your faithfulness in the assembly of the
　　　holy ones!
6 For who in the skies can be compared to
　　the LORD?
　　Who among the heavenly beings[5] is
　　　like the LORD,
7 a God greatly to be feared in the council of
　　the holy ones,
　　and awesome above all who are
　　　around him?
8 O LORD God of hosts,
　　who is mighty as you are, O LORD,
　　with your faithfulness all around you?
9 You rule the raging of the sea;
　　when its waves rise, you still them.
10 You crushed Rahab like a carcass;
　　you scattered your enemies with your
　　　mighty arm.
11 The heavens are yours; the earth also is
　　yours;
　　the world and all that is in it, you have
　　　founded them.
12 The north and the south, you have cre-
　　ated them;
　　Tabor and Hermon joyously praise
　　　your name.
13 You have a mighty arm;
　　strong is your hand, high your right
　　　hand.
14 Righteousness and justice are the founda-
　　tion of your throne;
　　steadfast love and faithfulness go before
　　　you.
15 Blessed are the people who know the fes-
　　tal shout,
　　who walk, O LORD, in the light of your
　　　face,
16 who exult in your name all the day
　　and in your righteousness are exalted.
17 For you are the glory of their strength;
　　by your favor our horn is exalted.
18 For our shield belongs to the LORD,
　　our king to the Holy One of Israel.

19 Of old you spoke in a vision to your godly
　　one,[6] and said:
　　"I have granted help to one who is
　　　mighty;
　　I have exalted one chosen from the
　　　people.

---

[1] Or *an abomination*　[2] The meaning of the Hebrew word is uncertain　[3] Or *darkness has become my only companion*　[4] Probably a musical or liturgical term　[5] Hebrew *the sons of God, or the sons of might*　[6] Some Hebrew manuscripts *godly ones*

20 I have found David, my servant;
    with my holy oil I have anointed him,
21 so that my hand shall be established with
        him;
    my arm also shall strengthen him.
22 The enemy shall not outwit him;
    the wicked shall not humble him.
23 I will crush his foes before him
    and strike down those who hate him.
24 My faithfulness and my steadfast love shall
        be with him,
    and in my name shall his horn be
        exalted.
25 I will set his hand on the sea
    and his right hand on the rivers.
26 He shall cry to me, 'You are my Father,
    my God, and the Rock of my salvation.'
27 And I will make him the firstborn,
    the highest of the kings of the earth.
28 My steadfast love I will keep for him for-
        ever,
    and my covenant will stand firm[1] for
        him.
29 I will establish his offspring forever
    and his throne as the days of the heav-
        ens.
30 If his children forsake my law
    and do not walk according to my rules,[2]
31 if they violate my statutes
    and do not keep my commandments,
32 then I will punish their transgression with
        the rod
    and their iniquity with stripes,
33 but I will not remove from him my stead-
        fast love
    or be false to my faithfulness.
34 I will not violate my covenant
    or alter the word that went forth from
        my lips.
35 Once for all I have sworn by my holiness;
    I will not lie to David.
36 His offspring shall endure forever,
    his throne as long as the sun before me.
37 Like the moon it shall be established for-
        ever,
    a faithful witness in the skies."   *Selah*

38 But now you have cast off and rejected;
    you are full of wrath against your
        anointed.
39 You have renounced the covenant with
        your servant;
    you have defiled his crown in the dust.

40 You have breached all his walls;
    you have laid his strongholds in ruins.
41 All who pass by plunder him;
    he has become the scorn of his neigh-
        bors.
42 You have exalted the right hand of his foes;
    you have made all his enemies rejoice.
43 You have also turned back the edge of his
        sword,
    and you have not made him stand in
        battle.
44 You have made his splendor to cease
    and cast his throne to the ground.
45 You have cut short the days of his youth;
    you have covered him with shame.
                                            Selah

46 How long, O LORD? Will you hide yourself
        forever?
    How long will your wrath burn like
        fire?
47 Remember how short my time is!
    For what vanity you have created all the
        children of man!
48 What man can live and never see death?
    Who can deliver his soul from the
        power of Sheol?   *Selah*

49 Lord, where is your steadfast love of old,
    which by your faithfulness you swore to
        David?
50 Remember, O Lord, how your servants are
        mocked,
    and how I bear in my heart the insults[3]
        of all the many nations,
51 with which your enemies mock, O LORD,
    with which they mock the footsteps of
        your anointed.

52 Blessed be the LORD forever!
    Amen and Amen.

BOOK FOUR

From Everlasting to Everlasting

90 A PRAYER OF MOSES, THE MAN OF GOD.
    Lord, you have been our dwelling
        place[4]
    in all generations.
2 Before the mountains were brought forth,
    or ever you had formed the earth and
        the world,
    from everlasting to everlasting you are
        God.

[1] Or *will remain faithful* [2] Or *my just decrees* [3] Hebrew lacks *the insults* [4] Some Hebrew manuscripts (compare Septuagint) *our refuge*

3 You return man to dust
    and say, "Return, O children of man!"[1]
4 For a thousand years in your sight
    are but as yesterday when it is past,
    or as a watch in the night.

5 You sweep them away as with a flood; they
        are like a dream,
    like grass that is renewed in the morn-
        ing:
6 in the morning it flourishes and is
        renewed;
    in the evening it fades and withers.

7 For we are brought to an end by your
        anger;
    by your wrath we are dismayed.
8 You have set our iniquities before you,
    our secret sins in the light of your pres-
        ence.

9 For all our days pass away under your
        wrath;
    we bring our years to an end like a sigh.
10 The years of our life are seventy,
    or even by reason of strength eighty;
    yet their span[2] is but toil and trouble;
    they are soon gone, and we fly away.
11 Who considers the power of your anger,
    and your wrath according to the fear of
        you?

12 So teach us to number our days
    that we may get a heart of wisdom.
13 Return, O LORD! How long?
    Have pity on your servants!
14 Satisfy us in the morning with your
        steadfast love,
    that we may rejoice and be glad all our
        days.
15 Make us glad for as many days as you
        have afflicted us,
    and for as many years as we have seen
        evil.
16 Let your work be shown to your servants,
    and your glorious power to their chil-
        dren.
17 Let the favor[3] of the Lord our God be
        upon us,
    and establish the work of our hands
        upon us;
    yes, establish the work of our hands!

My Refuge and My Fortress

91 He who dwells in the shelter of the
        Most High
    will abide in the shadow of the
        Almighty.
2 I will say[4] to the LORD, "My refuge and my
        fortress,
    my God, in whom I trust."

3 For he will deliver you from the snare of
        the fowler
    and from the deadly pestilence.
4 He will cover you with his pinions,
    and under his wings you will find ref-
        uge;
    his faithfulness is a shield and buckler.
5 You will not fear the terror of the night,
    nor the arrow that flies by day,
6 nor the pestilence that stalks in darkness,
    nor the destruction that wastes at
        noonday.

7 A thousand may fall at your side,
    ten thousand at your right hand,
    but it will not come near you.
8 You will only look with your eyes
    and see the recompense of the wicked.

9 Because you have made the LORD your
        dwelling place—
    the Most High, who is my refuge[5]—
10 no evil shall be allowed to befall you,
    no plague come near your tent.

11 For he will command his angels concern-
        ing you
    to guard you in all your ways.
12 On their hands they will bear you up,
    lest you strike your foot against a stone.
13 You will tread on the lion and the adder;
    the young lion and the serpent you
        will trample underfoot.

14 "Because he holds fast to me in love, I will
        deliver him;
    I will protect him, because he knows
        my name.
15 When he calls to me, I will answer him;
    I will be with him in trouble;
    I will rescue him and honor him.
16 With long life I will satisfy him
    and show him my salvation."

[1] Or of Adam [2] Or pride [3] Or beauty [4] Septuagint *He will say* [5] Or *For you, O LORD, are my refuge! You have made the Most High your dwelling place*

How Great Are Your Works

92 A PSALM. A SONG FOR THE SABBATH.
It is good to give thanks to the LORD,
to sing praises to your name, O Most
High;

2 to declare your steadfast love in the morning,
and your faithfulness by night,

3 to the music of the lute and the harp,
to the melody of the lyre.

4 For you, O LORD, have made me glad by
your work;
at the works of your hands I sing for joy.

5 How great are your works, O LORD!
Your thoughts are very deep!

6 The stupid man cannot know;
the fool cannot understand this:

7 that though the wicked sprout like grass
and all evildoers flourish,
they are doomed to destruction forever;

8 but you, O LORD, are on high forever.

9 For behold, your enemies, O LORD,
for behold, your enemies shall perish;
all evildoers shall be scattered.

10 But you have exalted my horn like that of
the wild ox;
you have poured over me[1] fresh oil.

11 My eyes have seen the downfall of my
enemies;
my ears have heard the doom of my evil
assailants.

12 The righteous flourish like the palm tree
and grow like a cedar in Lebanon.

13 They are planted in the house of the LORD;
they flourish in the courts of our God.

14 They still bear fruit in old age;
they are ever full of sap and green,

15 to declare that the LORD is upright;
he is my rock, and there is no unrighteousness in him.

The LORD Reigns

93 The LORD reigns; he is robed in
majesty;
the LORD is robed; he has put on
strength as his belt.
Yes, the world is established; it shall never
be moved.

2 Your throne is established from of old;
you are from everlasting.

3 The floods have lifted up, O LORD,
the floods have lifted up their voice;
the floods lift up their roaring.

4 Mightier than the thunders of many
waters,
mightier than the waves of the sea,
the LORD on high is mighty!

5 Your decrees are very trustworthy;
holiness befits your house,
O LORD, forevermore.

The LORD Will Not Forsake His People

94 O LORD, God of vengeance,
O God of vengeance, shine forth!

2 Rise up, O judge of the earth;
repay to the proud what they deserve!

3 O LORD, how long shall the wicked,
how long shall the wicked exult?

4 They pour out their arrogant words;
all the evildoers boast.

5 They crush your people, O LORD,
and afflict your heritage.

6 They kill the widow and the sojourner,
and murder the fatherless;

7 and they say, "The LORD does not see;
the God of Jacob does not perceive."

8 Understand, O dullest of the people!
Fools, when will you be wise?

9 He who planted the ear, does he not hear?
He who formed the eye, does he not see?

10 He who disciplines the nations, does he not
rebuke?
He who teaches man knowledge—

11 the LORD—knows the thoughts of
man,
that they are but a breath.[2]

12 Blessed is the man whom you discipline,
O LORD,
and whom you teach out of your law,

13 to give him rest from days of trouble,
until a pit is dug for the wicked.

14 For the LORD will not forsake his people;
he will not abandon his heritage;

15 for justice will return to the righteous,
and all the upright in heart will follow
it.

16 Who rises up for me against the wicked?
Who stands up for me against evildoers?

17 If the LORD had not been my help,
my soul would soon have lived in the
land of silence.

---

[1] Compare Syriac; the meaning of the Hebrew is uncertain [2] Septuagint *they are futile*

18 When I thought, "My foot slips,"
  your steadfast love, O LORD, held me
  up.
19 When the cares of my heart are many,
  your consolations cheer my soul.
20 Can wicked rulers be allied with you,
  those who frame[1] injustice by statute?
21 They band together against the life of the
  righteous
  and condemn the innocent to death.[2]
22 But the LORD has become my stronghold,
  and my God the rock of my refuge.
23 He will bring back on them their iniquity
  and wipe them out for their wickedness;
  the LORD our God will wipe them out.

Let Us Sing Songs of Praise

95 Oh come, let us sing to the LORD;
  let us make a joyful noise to the rock
  of our salvation!
2 Let us come into his presence with thanksgiving;
  let us make a joyful noise to him with
  songs of praise!
3 For the LORD is a great God,
  and a great King above all gods.
4 In his hand are the depths of the earth;
  the heights of the mountains are his
  also.
5 The sea is his, for he made it,
  and his hands formed the dry land.

6 Oh come, let us worship and bow down;
  let us kneel before the LORD, our
  Maker!
7 For he is our God,
  and we are the people of his pasture,
  and the sheep of his hand.
  Today, if you hear his voice,
8   do not harden your hearts, as at
  Meribah,
  as on the day at Massah in the wilderness,
9 when your fathers put me to the test
  and put me to the proof, though they
  had seen my work.
10 For forty years I loathed that generation
  and said, "They are a people who go
  astray in their heart,
  and they have not known my ways."

11 Therefore I swore in my wrath,
  "They shall not enter my rest."

Worship in the Splendor of Holiness

96 Oh sing to the LORD a new song;
  sing to the LORD, all the earth!
2 Sing to the LORD, bless his name;
  tell of his salvation from day to day.
3 Declare his glory among the nations,
  his marvelous works among all the
  peoples!
4 For great is the LORD, and greatly to be
  praised;
  he is to be feared above all gods.
5 For all the gods of the peoples are worthless idols,
  but the LORD made the heavens.
6 Splendor and majesty are before him;
  strength and beauty are in his sanctuary.

7 Ascribe to the LORD, O families of the
  peoples,
  ascribe to the LORD glory and strength!
8 Ascribe to the LORD the glory due his
  name;
  bring an offering, and come into his
  courts!
9 Worship the LORD in the splendor of holiness;[3]
  tremble before him, all the earth!

10 Say among the nations, "The LORD
  reigns!
  Yes, the world is established; it shall
  never be moved;
  he will judge the peoples with equity."

11 Let the heavens be glad, and let the earth
  rejoice;
  let the sea roar, and all that fills it;
12   let the field exult, and everything in it!
  Then shall all the trees of the forest sing for
  joy
13   before the LORD, for he comes,
  for he comes to judge the earth.
  He will judge the world in righteousness,
  and the peoples in his faithfulness.

The LORD Reigns

97 The LORD reigns, let the earth rejoice;
  let the many coastlands be glad!
2 Clouds and thick darkness are all around
  him;
  righteousness and justice are the foundation of his throne.

[1] Or fashion [2] Hebrew condemn innocent blood [3] Or in holy attire

³ Fire goes before him
  and burns up his adversaries all around.
⁴ His lightnings light up the world;
  the earth sees and trembles.
⁵ The mountains melt like wax before the
    LORD,
  before the Lord of all the earth.

⁶ The heavens proclaim his righteousness,
  and all the peoples see his glory.
⁷ All worshipers of images are put to shame,
  who make their boast in worthless
    idols;
  worship him, all you gods!

⁸ Zion hears and is glad,
  and the daughters of Judah rejoice,
  because of your judgments, O LORD.
⁹ For you, O LORD, are most high over all the
    earth;
  you are exalted far above all gods.

¹⁰ O you who love the LORD, hate evil!
  He preserves the lives of his saints;
  he delivers them from the hand of the
    wicked.
¹¹ Light is sown¹ for the righteous,
  and joy for the upright in heart.
¹² Rejoice in the LORD, O you righteous,
  and give thanks to his holy name!

Make a Joyful Noise to the LORD

98 A PSALM.
  Oh sing to the LORD a new song,
  for he has done marvelous things!
His right hand and his holy arm
  have worked salvation for him.
² The LORD has made known his salvation;
  he has revealed his righteousness in the
    sight of the nations.
³ He has remembered his steadfast love and
    faithfulness
  to the house of Israel.
All the ends of the earth have seen
  the salvation of our God.

⁴ Make a joyful noise to the LORD, all the
    earth;
  break forth into joyous song and sing
    praises!
⁵ Sing praises to the LORD with the lyre,
  with the lyre and the sound of melody!

⁶ With trumpets and the sound of the
    horn
  make a joyful noise before the King, the
    LORD!

⁷ Let the sea roar, and all that fills it;
  the world and those who dwell in it!
⁸ Let the rivers clap their hands;
  let the hills sing for joy together
⁹ before the LORD, for he comes
  to judge the earth.
He will judge the world with righteous-
    ness,
  and the peoples with equity.

The LORD Our God Is Holy

99 The LORD reigns; let the peoples
    tremble!
  He sits enthroned upon the cherubim;
  let the earth quake!
² The LORD is great in Zion;
  he is exalted over all the peoples.
³ Let them praise your great and awesome
    name!
  Holy is he!
⁴ The King in his might loves justice.²
  You have established equity;
  you have executed justice
  and righteousness in Jacob.
⁵ Exalt the LORD our God;
  worship at his footstool!
  Holy is he!

⁶ Moses and Aaron were among his priests,
  Samuel also was among those who
    called upon his name.
  They called to the LORD, and he
    answered them.
⁷ In the pillar of the cloud he spoke to them;
  they kept his testimonies
  and the statute that he gave them.

⁸ O LORD our God, you answered them;
  you were a forgiving God to them,
  but an avenger of their wrongdoings.
⁹ Exalt the LORD our God,
  and worship at his holy mountain;
  for the LORD our God is holy!

His Steadfast Love Endures Forever

100 A PSALM FOR GIVING THANKS.
  Make a joyful noise to the LORD,
    all the earth!
² Serve the LORD with gladness!
  Come into his presence with singing!

---

¹ Most Hebrew manuscripts; one Hebrew manuscript, Septuagint, Syriac, Jerome *Light dawns* ² Or *The might of the King loves justice*

³ Know that the Lord, he is God!
    It is he who made us, and we are his;[1]
    we are his people, and the sheep of his
        pasture.

⁴ Enter his gates with thanksgiving,
    and his courts with praise!
    Give thanks to him; bless his name!

⁵ For the Lord is good;
    his steadfast love endures forever,
    and his faithfulness to all generations.

I Will Walk with Integrity

101
A Psalm of David.
I will sing of steadfast love and jus-
    tice;
    to you, O Lord, I will make music.

² I will ponder the way that is blameless.
    Oh when will you come to me?
    I will walk with integrity of heart
        within my house;

³ I will not set before my eyes
    anything that is worthless.
    I hate the work of those who fall away;
    it shall not cling to me.

⁴ A perverse heart shall be far from me;
    I will know nothing of evil.

⁵ Whoever slanders his neighbor secretly
    I will destroy.
    Whoever has a haughty look and an arro-
        gant heart
    I will not endure.

⁶ I will look with favor on the faithful in the
        land,
    that they may dwell with me;
    he who walks in the way that is blameless
        shall minister to me.

⁷ No one who practices deceit
    shall dwell in my house;
    no one who utters lies
    shall continue before my eyes.

⁸ Morning by morning I will destroy
    all the wicked in the land,
    cutting off all the evildoers
    from the city of the Lord.

Do Not Hide Your Face from Me

102
A Prayer of one afflicted, when
he is faint and pours out his
complaint before the Lord.

¹ Hear my prayer, O Lord;
    let my cry come to you!

² Do not hide your face from me
    in the day of my distress!
    Incline your ear to me;
    answer me speedily in the day when I
        call!

³ For my days pass away like smoke,
    and my bones burn like a furnace.

⁴ My heart is struck down like grass and
        has withered;
    I forget to eat my bread.

⁵ Because of my loud groaning
    my bones cling to my flesh.

⁶ I am like a desert owl of the wilderness,
    like an owl[2] of the waste places;

⁷ I lie awake;
    I am like a lonely sparrow on the house-
        top.

⁸ All the day my enemies taunt me;
    those who deride me use my name for
        a curse.

⁹ For I eat ashes like bread
    and mingle tears with my drink,

¹⁰ because of your indignation and anger;
    for you have taken me up and thrown
        me down.

¹¹ My days are like an evening shadow;
    I wither away like grass.

¹² But you, O Lord, are enthroned forever;
    you are remembered throughout all
        generations.

¹³ You will arise and have pity on Zion;
    it is the time to favor her;
    the appointed time has come.

¹⁴ For your servants hold her stones dear
    and have pity on her dust.

¹⁵ Nations will fear the name of the Lord,
    and all the kings of the earth will fear
        your glory.

¹⁶ For the Lord builds up Zion;
    he appears in his glory;

¹⁷ he regards the prayer of the destitute
    and does not despise their prayer.

¹⁸ Let this be recorded for a generation to
        come,
    so that a people yet to be created may
        praise the Lord:

¹⁹ that he looked down from his holy
        height;
    from heaven the Lord looked at the
        earth,

²⁰ to hear the groans of the prisoners,
    to set free those who were doomed to
        die,

[1] Or *and not we ourselves* [2] The precise identity of these birds is uncertain

21 that they may declare in Zion the name of
the LORD,
and in Jerusalem his praise,
22 when peoples gather together,
and kingdoms, to worship the LORD.

23 He has broken my strength in midcourse;
he has shortened my days.
24 "O my God," I say, "take me not away
in the midst of my days—
you whose years endure
throughout all generations!"

25 Of old you laid the foundation of the earth,
and the heavens are the work of your
hands.
26 They will perish, but you will remain;
they will all wear out like a garment.
You will change them like a robe, and they
will pass away,
27 but you are the same, and your years
have no end.
28 The children of your servants shall dwell
secure;
their offspring shall be established
before you.

Bless the LORD, O My Soul

103
OF DAVID.
Bless the LORD, O my soul,
and all that is within me,
bless his holy name!
2 Bless the LORD, O my soul,
and forget not all his benefits,
3 who forgives all your iniquity,
who heals all your diseases,
4 who redeems your life from the pit,
who crowns you with steadfast love and
mercy,
5 who satisfies you with good
so that your youth is renewed like the
eagle's.

6 The LORD works righteousness
and justice for all who are oppressed.
7 He made known his ways to Moses,
his acts to the people of Israel.
8 The LORD is merciful and gracious,
slow to anger and abounding in steadfast love.
9 He will not always chide,
nor will he keep his anger forever.
10 He does not deal with us according to our
sins,
nor repay us according to our iniquities.

11 For as high as the heavens are above the
earth,
so great is his steadfast love toward
those who fear him;
12 as far as the east is from the west,
so far does he remove our transgressions from us.
13 As a father shows compassion to his children,
so the LORD shows compassion to those
who fear him.
14 For he knows our frame;[1]
he remembers that we are dust.

15 As for man, his days are like grass;
he flourishes like a flower of the field;
16 for the wind passes over it, and it is gone,
and its place knows it no more.
17 But the steadfast love of the LORD is from
everlasting to everlasting on those
who fear him,
and his righteousness to children's children,
18 to those who keep his covenant
and remember to do his commandments.
19 The LORD has established his throne in the
heavens,
and his kingdom rules over all.

20 Bless the LORD, O you his angels,
you mighty ones who do his word,
obeying the voice of his word!
21 Bless the LORD, all his hosts,
his ministers, who do his will!
22 Bless the LORD, all his works,
in all places of his dominion.
Bless the LORD, O my soul!

O LORD My God, You Are Very Great

104
Bless the LORD, O my soul!
O LORD my God, you are very
great!
You are clothed with splendor and majesty,
2 covering yourself with light as with a
garment,
stretching out the heavens like a tent.
3 He lays the beams of his chambers on the
waters;
he makes the clouds his chariot;
he rides on the wings of the wind;
4 he makes his messengers winds,
his ministers a flaming fire.

[1] Or knows how we are formed

5 He set the earth on its foundations,
   so that it should never be moved.
6 You covered it with the deep as with a garment;
   the waters stood above the mountains.
7 At your rebuke they fled;
   at the sound of your thunder they took to flight.
8 The mountains rose, the valleys sank down
   to the place that you appointed for them.
9 You set a boundary that they may not pass,
   so that they might not again cover the earth.

10 You make springs gush forth in the valleys;
   they flow between the hills;
11 they give drink to every beast of the field;
   the wild donkeys quench their thirst.
12 Beside them the birds of the heavens dwell;
   they sing among the branches.
13 From your lofty abode you water the mountains;
   the earth is satisfied with the fruit of your work.

14 You cause the grass to grow for the livestock
   and plants for man to cultivate,
   that he may bring forth food from the earth
15 and wine to gladden the heart of man,
   oil to make his face shine
   and bread to strengthen man's heart.

16 The trees of the Lord are watered abundantly,
   the cedars of Lebanon that he planted.
17 In them the birds build their nests;
   the stork has her home in the fir trees.
18 The high mountains are for the wild goats;
   the rocks are a refuge for the rock badgers.

19 He made the moon to mark the seasons;[1]
   the sun knows its time for setting.
20 You make darkness, and it is night,
   when all the beasts of the forest creep about.
21 The young lions roar for their prey,
   seeking their food from God.

22 When the sun rises, they steal away
   and lie down in their dens.
23 Man goes out to his work
   and to his labor until the evening.

24 O Lord, how manifold are your works!
   In wisdom have you made them all;
   the earth is full of your creatures.
25 Here is the sea, great and wide,
   which teems with creatures innumerable,
   living things both small and great.
26 There go the ships,
   and Leviathan, which you formed to play in it.[2]

27 These all look to you,
   to give them their food in due season.
28 When you give it to them, they gather it up;
   when you open your hand, they are filled with good things.
29 When you hide your face, they are dismayed;
   when you take away their breath, they die
   and return to their dust.
30 When you send forth your Spirit,[3] they are created,
   and you renew the face of the ground.

31 May the glory of the Lord endure forever;
   may the Lord rejoice in his works,
32 who looks on the earth and it trembles,
   who touches the mountains and they smoke!
33 I will sing to the Lord as long as I live;
   I will sing praise to my God while I have being.
34 May my meditation be pleasing to him,
   for I rejoice in the Lord.
35 Let sinners be consumed from the earth,
   and let the wicked be no more!
   Bless the Lord, O my soul!
   Praise the Lord!

Tell of All His Wondrous Works

105 Oh give thanks to the Lord; call upon his name;
   make known his deeds among the peoples!
2 Sing to him, sing praises to him;
   tell of all his wondrous works!

[1] Or the appointed times (compare Genesis 1:14) [2] Or you formed to play with [3] Or breath

3 Glory in his holy name;
   let the hearts of those who seek the
      LORD rejoice!
4 Seek the LORD and his strength;
   seek his presence continually!
5 Remember the wondrous works that he
      has done,
   his miracles, and the judgments he
      uttered,
6 O offspring of Abraham, his servant,
   children of Jacob, his chosen ones!

7 He is the LORD our God;
   his judgments are in all the earth.
8 He remembers his covenant forever,
   the word that he commanded, for a
      thousand generations,
9 the covenant that he made with
      Abraham,
   his sworn promise to Isaac,
10 which he confirmed to Jacob as a statute,
   to Israel as an everlasting covenant,
11 saying, "To you I will give the land of
      Canaan
   as your portion for an inheritance."

12 When they were few in number,
   of little account, and sojourners in it,
13 wandering from nation to nation,
   from one kingdom to another people,
14 he allowed no one to oppress them;
   he rebuked kings on their account,
15 saying, "Touch not my anointed ones,
   do my prophets no harm!"

16 When he summoned a famine on the
      land
   and broke all supply[1] of bread,
17 he had sent a man ahead of them,
   Joseph, who was sold as a slave.
18 His feet were hurt with fetters;
   his neck was put in a collar of iron;
19 until what he had said came to pass,
   the word of the LORD tested him.
20 The king sent and released him;
   the ruler of the peoples set him free;
21 he made him lord of his house
   and ruler of all his possessions,
22 to bind[2] his princes at his pleasure
   and to teach his elders wisdom.

23 Then Israel came to Egypt;
   Jacob sojourned in the land of Ham.

24 And the LORD made his people very fruit-
      ful
   and made them stronger than their foes.
25 He turned their hearts to hate his people,
   to deal craftily with his servants.

26 He sent Moses, his servant,
   and Aaron, whom he had chosen.
27 They performed his signs among them
   and miracles in the land of Ham.
28 He sent darkness, and made the land dark;
   they did not rebel[3] against his words.
29 He turned their waters into blood
   and caused their fish to die.
30 Their land swarmed with frogs,
   even in the chambers of their kings.
31 He spoke, and there came swarms of
      flies,
   and gnats throughout their country.
32 He gave them hail for rain,
   and fiery lightning bolts through their
      land.
33 He struck down their vines and fig trees,
   and shattered the trees of their coun-
      try.
34 He spoke, and the locusts came,
   young locusts without number,
35 which devoured all the vegetation in their
      land
   and ate up the fruit of their ground.
36 He struck down all the firstborn in their
      land,
   the firstfruits of all their strength.

37 Then he brought out Israel with silver and
      gold,
   and there was none among his tribes
      who stumbled.
38 Egypt was glad when they departed,
   for dread of them had fallen upon it.

39 He spread a cloud for a covering,
   and fire to give light by night.
40 They asked, and he brought quail,
   and gave them bread from heaven in
      abundance.
41 He opened the rock, and water gushed out;
   it flowed through the desert like a river.
42 For he remembered his holy promise,
   and Abraham, his servant.

43 So he brought his people out with joy,
   his chosen ones with singing.

[1] Hebrew *staff* [2] Septuagint, Syriac, Jerome *instruct* [3] Septuagint, Syriac omit *not*

44 And he gave them the lands of the nations,
      and they took possession of the fruit of
         the peoples' toil,
45 that they might keep his statutes
      and observe his laws.
   Praise the LORD!

Give Thanks to the LORD, for He Is Good

106 Praise the LORD!
      Oh give thanks to the LORD, for he
         is good,
      for his steadfast love endures forever!
2 Who can utter the mighty deeds of the
      LORD,
      or declare all his praise?
3 Blessed are they who observe justice,
      who do righteousness at all times!

4 Remember me, O LORD, when you show
      favor to your people;
      help me when you save them,[1]
5 that I may look upon the prosperity of
      your chosen ones,
      that I may rejoice in the gladness of
         your nation,
      that I may glory with your inheri-
         tance.

6 Both we and our fathers have sinned;
      we have committed iniquity; we have
         done wickedness.
7 Our fathers, when they were in Egypt,
      did not consider your wondrous works;
   they did not remember the abundance of
         your steadfast love,
      but rebelled by the sea, at the Red Sea.
8 Yet he saved them for his name's sake,
      that he might make known his mighty
         power.
9 He rebuked the Red Sea, and it became dry,
      and he led them through the deep as
         through a desert.
10 So he saved them from the hand of the foe
      and redeemed them from the power of
         the enemy.
11 And the waters covered their adversaries;
      not one of them was left.
12 Then they believed his words;
      they sang his praise.

13 But they soon forgot his works;
      they did not wait for his counsel.
14 But they had a wanton craving in the wil-
         derness,
      and put God to the test in the desert;

15 he gave them what they asked,
      but sent a wasting disease among them.

16 When men in the camp were jealous of
      Moses
      and Aaron, the holy one of the LORD,
17 the earth opened and swallowed up
      Dathan,
      and covered the company of Abiram.
18 Fire also broke out in their company;
      the flame burned up the wicked.

19 They made a calf in Horeb
      and worshiped a metal image.
20 They exchanged the glory of God[2]
      for the image of an ox that eats grass.
21 They forgot God, their Savior,
      who had done great things in Egypt,
22 wondrous works in the land of Ham,
      and awesome deeds by the Red Sea.
23 Therefore he said he would destroy
         them—
      had not Moses, his chosen one,
   stood in the breach before him,
      to turn away his wrath from destroying
         them.

24 Then they despised the pleasant land,
      having no faith in his promise.
25 They murmured in their tents,
      and did not obey the voice of the
         LORD.
26 Therefore he raised his hand and swore to
      them
      that he would make them fall in the
         wilderness,
27 and would make their offspring fall
         among the nations,
      scattering them among the lands.

28 Then they yoked themselves to the Baal of
      Peor,
      and ate sacrifices offered to the dead;
29 they provoked the LORD to anger with
      their deeds,
      and a plague broke out among them.
30 Then Phinehas stood up and intervened,
      and the plague was stayed.
31 And that was counted to him as righteous-
         ness
      from generation to generation forever.

[1] Or Remember me, O LORD, with the favor you show to your people; help me with your salvation [2] Hebrew exchanged their glory

32 They angered him at the waters of
     Meribah,
     and it went ill with Moses on their
          account,
33 for they made his spirit bitter,[1]
     and he spoke rashly with his lips.

34 They did not destroy the peoples,
     as the LORD commanded them,
35 but they mixed with the nations
     and learned to do as they did.
36 They served their idols,
     which became a snare to them.
37 They sacrificed their sons
     and their daughters to the demons;
38 they poured out innocent blood,
     the blood of their sons and daughters,
     whom they sacrificed to the idols of
          Canaan,
     and the land was polluted with blood.
39 Thus they became unclean by their acts,
     and played the whore in their deeds.

40 Then the anger of the LORD was kindled
          against his people,
     and he abhorred his heritage;
41 he gave them into the hand of the
          nations,
     so that those who hated them ruled
          over them.
42 Their enemies oppressed them,
     and they were brought into subjection
          under their power.
43 Many times he delivered them,
     but they were rebellious in their pur-
          poses
     and were brought low through their
          iniquity.

44 Nevertheless, he looked upon their dis-
          tress,
     when he heard their cry.
45 For their sake he remembered his cov-
          enant,
     and relented according to the abun-
          dance of his steadfast love.
46 He caused them to be pitied
     by all those who held them captive.

47 Save us, O LORD our God,
     and gather us from among the
          nations,
     that we may give thanks to your holy
          name
     and glory in your praise.

48 Blessed be the LORD, the God of Israel,
     from everlasting to everlasting!
     And let all the people say, "Amen!"
     Praise the LORD!

BOOK FIVE

Let the Redeemed of the LORD Say So

107 Oh give thanks to the LORD, for he
     is good,
     for his steadfast love endures forever!
2 Let the redeemed of the LORD say so,
     whom he has redeemed from trouble[2]
3 and gathered in from the lands,
     from the east and from the west,
     from the north and from the south.

4 Some wandered in desert wastes,
     finding no way to a city to dwell in;
5 hungry and thirsty,
     their soul fainted within them.
6 Then they cried to the LORD in their trou-
          ble,
     and he delivered them from their dis-
          tress.
7 He led them by a straight way
     till they reached a city to dwell in.
8 Let them thank the LORD for his steadfast
          love,
     for his wondrous works to the children
          of man!
9 For he satisfies the longing soul,
     and the hungry soul he fills with good
          things.

10 Some sat in darkness and in the shadow of
          death,
     prisoners in affliction and in irons,
11 for they had rebelled against the words of
          God,
     and spurned the counsel of the Most
          High.
12 So he bowed their hearts down with hard
          labor;
     they fell down, with none to help.
13 Then they cried to the LORD in their trou-
          ble,
     and he delivered them from their dis-
          tress.
14 He brought them out of darkness and the
          shadow of death,
     and burst their bonds apart.
15 Let them thank the LORD for his steadfast
          love,

---

[1] Or they rebelled against God's Spirit [2] Or from the hand of the foe

for his wondrous works to the children
of man!

16 For he shatters the doors of bronze
and cuts in two the bars of iron.

17 Some were fools through their sinful ways,
and because of their iniquities suffered
affliction;

18 they loathed any kind of food,
and they drew near to the gates of
death.

19 Then they cried to the LORD in their trouble,
and he delivered them from their distress.

20 He sent out his word and healed them,
and delivered them from their destruction.

21 Let them thank the LORD for his steadfast
love,
for his wondrous works to the children
of man!

22 And let them offer sacrifices of thanksgiving,
and tell of his deeds in songs of joy!

23 Some went down to the sea in ships,
doing business on the great waters;

24 they saw the deeds of the LORD,
his wondrous works in the deep.

25 For he commanded and raised the stormy
wind,
which lifted up the waves of the sea.

26 They mounted up to heaven; they went
down to the depths;
their courage melted away in their evil
plight;

27 they reeled and staggered like drunken
men
and were at their wits' end.[1]

28 Then they cried to the LORD in their trouble,
and he delivered them from their distress.

29 He made the storm be still,
and the waves of the sea were hushed.

30 Then they were glad that the waters[2] were
quiet,
and he brought them to their desired
haven.

31 Let them thank the LORD for his steadfast
love,
for his wondrous works to the children
of man!

32 Let them extol him in the congregation of
the people,
and praise him in the assembly of the
elders.

33 He turns rivers into a desert,
springs of water into thirsty ground,

34 a fruitful land into a salty waste,
because of the evil of its inhabitants.

35 He turns a desert into pools of water,
a parched land into springs of water.

36 And there he lets the hungry dwell,
and they establish a city to live in;

37 they sow fields and plant vineyards
and get a fruitful yield.

38 By his blessing they multiply greatly,
and he does not let their livestock
diminish.

39 When they are diminished and brought
low
through oppression, evil, and sorrow,

40 he pours contempt on princes
and makes them wander in trackless
wastes;

41 but he raises up the needy out of affliction
and makes their families like flocks.

42 The upright see it and are glad,
and all wickedness shuts its mouth.

43 Whoever is wise, let him attend to these
things;
let them consider the steadfast love of
the LORD.

With God We Shall Do Valiantly

108 A SONG. A PSALM OF DAVID.
My heart is steadfast, O God!
I will sing and make melody with all
my being![3]

2 Awake, O harp and lyre!
I will awake the dawn!

3 I will give thanks to you, O LORD, among
the peoples;
I will sing praises to you among the
nations.

4 For your steadfast love is great above the
heavens;
your faithfulness reaches to the clouds.

5 Be exalted, O God, above the heavens!
Let your glory be over all the earth!

6 That your beloved ones may be delivered,
give salvation by your right hand and
answer me!

[1] Hebrew and all their wisdom was swallowed up　[2] Hebrew they　[3] Hebrew with my glory

7 God has promised in his holiness:[1]
  "With exultation I will divide up
      Shechem
    and portion out the Valley of Succoth.
8 Gilead is mine; Manasseh is mine;
    Ephraim is my helmet,
    Judah my scepter.
9 Moab is my washbasin;
    upon Edom I cast my shoe;
    over Philistia I shout in triumph."

10 Who will bring me to the fortified city?
    Who will lead me to Edom?
11 Have you not rejected us, O God?
    You do not go out, O God, with our
      armies.
12 Oh grant us help against the foe,
    for vain is the salvation of man!
13 With God we shall do valiantly;
    it is he who will tread down our foes.

Help Me, O Lord My God

109

To the choirmaster. A Psalm of David.

1 Be not silent, O God of my praise!
2 For wicked and deceitful mouths are
      opened against me,
    speaking against me with lying tongues.
3 They encircle me with words of hate,
    and attack me without cause.
4 In return for my love they accuse me,
    but I give myself to prayer.[2]
5 So they reward me evil for good,
    and hatred for my love.

6 Appoint a wicked man against him;
    let an accuser stand at his right hand.
7 When he is tried, let him come forth guilty;
    let his prayer be counted as sin!
8 May his days be few;
    may another take his office!
9 May his children be fatherless
    and his wife a widow!
10 May his children wander about and beg,
    seeking food far from the ruins they
      inhabit!
11 May the creditor seize all that he has;
    may strangers plunder the fruits of his
      toil!
12 Let there be none to extend kindness to
      him,
    nor any to pity his fatherless children!

13 May his posterity be cut off;
    may his name be blotted out in the sec-
      ond generation!
14 May the iniquity of his fathers be remem-
      bered before the Lord,
    and let not the sin of his mother be blot-
      ted out!
15 Let them be before the Lord continually,
    that he may cut off the memory of them
      from the earth!

16 For he did not remember to show kind-
      ness,
    but pursued the poor and needy
    and the brokenhearted, to put them to
      death.
17 He loved to curse; let curses come[3] upon
      him!
    He did not delight in blessing; may it be
      far[4] from him!
18 He clothed himself with cursing as his
      coat;
    may it soak[5] into his body like water,
    like oil into his bones!
19 May it be like a garment that he wraps
      around him,
    like a belt that he puts on every day!
20 May this be the reward of my accusers
      from the Lord,
    of those who speak evil against my life!

21 But you, O God my Lord,
    deal on my behalf for your name's sake;
    because your steadfast love is good,
      deliver me!
22 For I am poor and needy,
    and my heart is stricken within me.
23 I am gone like a shadow at evening;
    I am shaken off like a locust.
24 My knees are weak through fasting;
    my body has become gaunt, with no fat.
25 I am an object of scorn to my accusers;
    when they see me, they wag their heads.

26 Help me, O Lord my God!
    Save me according to your steadfast
      love!
27 Let them know that this is your hand;
    you, O Lord, have done it!
28 Let them curse, but you will bless!
    They arise and are put to shame, but
      your servant will be glad!

---

[1] Or sanctuary [2] Hebrew but I am prayer [3] Revocalization; Masoretic Text curses have come [4] Revocalization; Masoretic Text it is far [5] Revocalization; Masoretic Text it has soaked

29 May my accusers be clothed with dishonor;
   may they be wrapped in their own
      shame as in a cloak!

30 With my mouth I will give great thanks to
      the LORD;
   I will praise him in the midst of the
      throng.

31 For he stands at the right hand of the
      needy one,
   to save him from those who condemn
      his soul to death.

Sit at My Right Hand

110 A PSALM OF DAVID.
   The LORD says to my Lord:
"Sit at my right hand,
until I make your enemies your footstool."

2 The LORD sends forth from Zion
   your mighty scepter.
   Rule in the midst of your enemies!

3 Your people will offer themselves freely
   on the day of your power,[1]
   in holy garments;[2]
from the womb of the morning,
   the dew of your youth will be yours.[3]

4 The LORD has sworn
   and will not change his mind,
"You are a priest forever
   after the order of Melchizedek."

5 The Lord is at your right hand;
   he will shatter kings on the day of his
      wrath.

6 He will execute judgment among the
      nations,
   filling them with corpses;
he will shatter chiefs[4]
   over the wide earth.

7 He will drink from the brook by the way;
   therefore he will lift up his head.

Great Are the LORD's Works

111 [5] Praise the LORD!
   I will give thanks to the LORD with
      my whole heart,
   in the company of the upright, in the
      congregation.

2 Great are the works of the LORD,
   studied by all who delight in them.

3 Full of splendor and majesty is his work,
   and his righteousness endures forever.

4 He has caused his wondrous works to be
      remembered;
   the LORD is gracious and merciful.

5 He provides food for those who fear him;
   he remembers his covenant forever.

6 He has shown his people the power of his
      works,
   in giving them the inheritance of the
      nations.

7 The works of his hands are faithful and
      just;
   all his precepts are trustworthy;

8 they are established forever and ever,
   to be performed with faithfulness and
      uprightness.

9 He sent redemption to his people;
   he has commanded his covenant forever.
   Holy and awesome is his name!

10 The fear of the LORD is the beginning of
      wisdom;
   all those who practice it have a good
      understanding.
   His praise endures forever!

The Righteous Will Never Be Moved

112 [6] Praise the LORD!
   Blessed is the man who fears the
      LORD,
   who greatly delights in his command-
      ments!

2 His offspring will be mighty in the land;
   the generation of the upright will be
      blessed.

3 Wealth and riches are in his house,
   and his righteousness endures forever.

4 Light dawns in the darkness for the
      upright;
   he is gracious, merciful, and righteous.

5 It is well with the man who deals gener-
      ously and lends;
   who conducts his affairs with justice.

6 For the righteous will never be moved;
   he will be remembered forever.

7 He is not afraid of bad news;
   his heart is firm, trusting in the LORD.

8 His heart is steady;[7] he will not be afraid,
   until he looks in triumph on his adver-
      saries.

9 He has distributed freely; he has given to
      the poor;
   his righteousness endures forever;
   his horn is exalted in honor.

---

[1] Or on the day you lead your forces [2] Masoretic Text; some Hebrew manuscripts and Jerome on the holy mountains [3] The meaning of the Hebrew is uncertain [4] Or the head [5] This psalm is an acrostic poem, each line beginning with the successive letters of the Hebrew alphabet [6] This psalm is an acrostic poem, each line beginning with the successive letters of the Hebrew alphabet [7] Or established (compare 111:8)

10 The wicked man sees it and is angry;
   he gnashes his teeth and melts away;
   the desire of the wicked will perish!

Who Is like the LORD Our God?

113 Praise the LORD!
   Praise, O servants of the LORD,
   praise the name of the LORD!

2 Blessed be the name of the LORD
   from this time forth and forevermore!
3 From the rising of the sun to its setting,
   the name of the LORD is to be praised!

4 The LORD is high above all nations,
   and his glory above the heavens!
5 Who is like the LORD our God,
   who is seated on high,
6 who looks far down
   on the heavens and the earth?
7 He raises the poor from the dust
   and lifts the needy from the ash heap,
8 to make them sit with princes,
   with the princes of his people.
9 He gives the barren woman a home,
   making her the joyous mother of children.
   Praise the LORD!

Tremble at the Presence of the Lord

114 When Israel went out from Egypt,
   the house of Jacob from a people of
   strange language,
2 Judah became his sanctuary,
   Israel his dominion.

3 The sea looked and fled;
   Jordan turned back.
4 The mountains skipped like rams,
   the hills like lambs.

5 What ails you, O sea, that you flee?
   O Jordan, that you turn back?
6 O mountains, that you skip like rams?
   O hills, like lambs?

7 Tremble, O earth, at the presence of the
   Lord,
   at the presence of the God of Jacob,
8 who turns the rock into a pool of water,
   the flint into a spring of water.

To Your Name Give Glory

115 Not to us, O LORD, not to us, but to
   your name give glory,
   for the sake of your steadfast love and
   your faithfulness!

2 Why should the nations say,
   "Where is their God?"
3 Our God is in the heavens;
   he does all that he pleases.

4 Their idols are silver and gold,
   the work of human hands.
5 They have mouths, but do not speak;
   eyes, but do not see.
6 They have ears, but do not hear;
   noses, but do not smell.
7 They have hands, but do not feel;
   feet, but do not walk;
   and they do not make a sound in their
   throat.
8 Those who make them become like them;
   so do all who trust in them.

9 O Israel,[1] trust in the LORD!
   He is their help and their shield.
10 O house of Aaron, trust in the LORD!
   He is their help and their shield.
11 You who fear the LORD, trust in the LORD!
   He is their help and their shield.

12 The LORD has remembered us; he will
   bless us;
   he will bless the house of Israel;
   he will bless the house of Aaron;
13 he will bless those who fear the LORD,
   both the small and the great.

14 May the LORD give you increase,
   you and your children!
15 May you be blessed by the LORD,
   who made heaven and earth!
16 The heavens are the LORD's heavens,
   but the earth he has given to the children of man.
17 The dead do not praise the LORD,
   nor do any who go down into silence.
18 But we will bless the LORD
   from this time forth and forevermore.
   Praise the LORD!

I Love the LORD

116 I love the LORD, because he has
   heard
   my voice and my pleas for mercy.
2 Because he inclined his ear to me,
   therefore I will call on him as long as I
   live.
3 The snares of death encompassed me;
   the pangs of Sheol laid hold on me;
   I suffered distress and anguish.

[1] Masoretic Text; many Hebrew manuscripts, Septuagint, Syriac *O house of Israel*

4 Then I called on the name of the LORD:
   "O LORD, I pray, deliver my soul!"

5 Gracious is the LORD, and righteous;
   our God is merciful.

6 The LORD preserves the simple;
   when I was brought low, he saved me.

7 Return, O my soul, to your rest;
   for the LORD has dealt bountifully with
   you.

8 For you have delivered my soul from death,
   my eyes from tears,
   my feet from stumbling;

9 I will walk before the LORD
   in the land of the living.

10 I believed, even when[1] I spoke:
   "I am greatly afflicted";

11 I said in my alarm,
   "All mankind are liars."

12 What shall I render to the LORD
   for all his benefits to me?

13 I will lift up the cup of salvation
   and call on the name of the LORD,

14 I will pay my vows to the LORD
   in the presence of all his people.

15 Precious in the sight of the LORD
   is the death of his saints.

16 O LORD, I am your servant;
   I am your servant, the son of your maid-
   servant.
   You have loosed my bonds.

17 I will offer to you the sacrifice of thanksgiving
   and call on the name of the LORD.

18 I will pay my vows to the LORD
   in the presence of all his people,

19 in the courts of the house of the LORD,
   in your midst, O Jerúsalem.
   Praise the LORD!

The LORD's Faithfulness Endures Forever

117
Praise the LORD, all nations!
   Extol him, all peoples!
2 For great is his steadfast love toward us,
   and the faithfulness of the LORD
   endures forever.
   Praise the LORD!

His Steadfast Love Endures Forever

118
Oh give thanks to the LORD, for he is
   good;
   for his steadfast love endures forever!

2 Let Israel say,
   "His steadfast love endures forever."

3 Let the house of Aaron say,
   "His steadfast love endures forever."

4 Let those who fear the LORD say,
   "His steadfast love endures forever."

5 Out of my distress I called on the LORD;
   the LORD answered me and set me free.

6 The LORD is on my side; I will not fear.
   What can man do to me?

7 The LORD is on my side as my helper;
   I shall look in triumph on those who
   hate me.

8 It is better to take refuge in the LORD
   than to trust in man.

9 It is better to take refuge in the LORD
   than to trust in princes.

10 All nations surrounded me;
   in the name of the LORD I cut them off!

11 They surrounded me, surrounded me on
   every side;
   in the name of the LORD I cut them off!

12 They surrounded me like bees;
   they went out like a fire among thorns;
   in the name of the LORD I cut them
   off!

13 I was pushed hard,[2] so that I was falling,
   but the LORD helped me.

14 The LORD is my strength and my song;
   he has become my salvation.

15 Glad songs of salvation
   are in the tents of the righteous:
   "The right hand of the LORD does valiantly,

16 the right hand of the LORD exalts,
   the right hand of the LORD does valiantly!"

17 I shall not die, but I shall live,
   and recount the deeds of the LORD.

18 The LORD has disciplined me severely,
   but he has not given me over to death.

19 Open to me the gates of righteousness,
   that I may enter through them
   and give thanks to the LORD.

20 This is the gate of the LORD;
   the righteous shall enter through it.

21 I thank you that you have answered me
   and have become my salvation.

22 The stone that the builders rejected
   has become the cornerstone.[3]

---

[1] Or believed, indeed; Septuagint believed, therefore [2] Hebrew You (that is, the enemy) pushed me hard [3] Hebrew the head of the corner

²³ This is the LORD's doing;
    it is marvelous in our eyes.
²⁴ This is the day that the LORD has made;
    let us rejoice and be glad in it.

²⁵ Save us, we pray, O LORD!
    O LORD, we pray, give us success!

²⁶ Blessed is he who comes in the name of the
    LORD!
    We bless you from the house of the
    LORD.
²⁷ The LORD is God,
    and he has made his light to shine upon
    us.
    Bind the festal sacrifice with cords,
    up to the horns of the altar!

²⁸ You are my God, and I will give thanks to
    you;
    you are my God; I will extol you.
²⁹ Oh give thanks to the LORD, for he is good;
    for his steadfast love endures forever!

Your Word Is a Lamp to My Feet

ALEPH

119
¹ Blessed are those whose way is
    blameless,
    who walk in the law of the LORD!
² Blessed are those who keep his testimonies,
    who seek him with their whole heart,
³ who also do no wrong,
    but walk in his ways!
⁴ You have commanded your precepts
    to be kept diligently.
⁵ Oh that my ways may be steadfast
    in keeping your statutes!
⁶ Then I shall not be put to shame,
    having my eyes fixed on all your com-
    mandments.
⁷ I will praise you with an upright heart,
    when I learn your righteous rules.²
⁸ I will keep your statutes;
    do not utterly forsake me!

BETH

⁹ How can a young man keep his way pure?
    By guarding it according to your word.
¹⁰ With my whole heart I seek you;
    let me not wander from your com-
    mandments!
¹¹ I have stored up your word in my heart,
    that I might not sin against you.

¹² Blessed are you, O LORD;
    teach me your statutes!
¹³ With my lips I declare
    all the rules³ of your mouth.
¹⁴ In the way of your testimonies I delight
    as much as in all riches.
¹⁵ I will meditate on your precepts
    and fix my eyes on your ways.
¹⁶ I will delight in your statutes;
    I will not forget your word.

GIMEL

¹⁷ Deal bountifully with your servant,
    that I may live and keep your word.
¹⁸ Open my eyes, that I may behold
    wondrous things out of your law.
¹⁹ I am a sojourner on the earth;
    hide not your commandments from
    me!
²⁰ My soul is consumed with longing
    for your rules⁴ at all times.
²¹ You rebuke the insolent, accursed ones,
    who wander from your command-
    ments.
²² Take away from me scorn and contempt,
    for I have kept your testimonies.
²³ Even though princes sit plotting against
    me,
    your servant will meditate on your stat-
    utes.
²⁴ Your testimonies are my delight;
    they are my counselors.

DALETH

²⁵ My soul clings to the dust;
    give me life according to your word!
²⁶ When I told of my ways, you answered me;
    teach me your statutes!
²⁷ Make me understand the way of your pre-
    cepts,
    and I will meditate on your wondrous
    works.
²⁸ My soul melts away for sorrow;
    strengthen me according to your word!
²⁹ Put false ways far from me
    and graciously teach me your law!
³⁰ I have chosen the way of faithfulness;
    I set your rules before me.
³¹ I cling to your testimonies, O LORD;
    let me not be put to shame!
³² I will run in the way of your command-
    ments
    when you enlarge my heart!⁵

---

¹ This psalm is an acrostic poem of twenty-two stanzas, following the letters of the Hebrew alphabet; within a stanza, each verse begins with the same Hebrew letter ² Or your just and righteous decrees; also verses 62, 106, 160, 164 ³ Or all the just decrees ⁴ Or your just decrees; also verses 30, 39, 43, 52, 75, 102, 108, 137, 156, 175 ⁵ Or for you set my heart free

HE

33 Teach me, O LORD, the way of your statutes;
    and I will keep it to the end.[1]
34 Give me understanding, that I may keep
        your law
    and observe it with my whole heart.
35 Lead me in the path of your command-
        ments,
    for I delight in it.
36 Incline my heart to your testimonies,
    and not to selfish gain!
37 Turn my eyes from looking at worthless
        things;
    and give me life in your ways.
38 Confirm to your servant your promise,
    that you may be feared.
39 Turn away the reproach that I dread,
    for your rules are good.
40 Behold, I long for your precepts;
    in your righteousness give me life!

WAW

41 Let your steadfast love come to me, O LORD,
    your salvation according to your prom-
        ise;
42 then shall I have an answer for him who
        taunts me,
    for I trust in your word.
43 And take not the word of truth utterly out
        of my mouth,
    for my hope is in your rules.
44 I will keep your law continually,
    forever and ever,
45 and I shall walk in a wide place,
    for I have sought your precepts.
46 I will also speak of your testimonies before
        kings
    and shall not be put to shame,
47 for I find my delight in your command-
        ments,
    which I love.
48 I will lift up my hands toward your com-
        mandments, which I love,
    and I will meditate on your statutes.

ZAYIN

49 Remember your word to your servant,
    in which you have made me hope.
50 This is my comfort in my affliction,
    that your promise gives me life.
51 The insolent utterly deride me,
    but I do not turn away from your law.
52 When I think of your rules from of old,
    I take comfort, O LORD.

53 Hot indignation seizes me because of the
        wicked,
    who forsake your law.
54 Your statutes have been my songs
    in the house of my sojourning.
55 I remember your name in the night,
        O LORD,
    and keep your law.
56 This blessing has fallen to me,
    that I have kept your precepts.

HETH

57 The LORD is my portion;
    I promise to keep your words.
58 I entreat your favor with all my heart;
    be gracious to me according to your
        promise.
59 When I think on my ways,
    I turn my feet to your testimonies;
60 I hasten and do not delay
    to keep your commandments.
61 Though the cords of the wicked ensnare me,
    I do not forget your law.
62 At midnight I rise to praise you,
    because of your righteous rules.
63 I am a companion of all who fear you,
    of those who keep your precepts.
64 The earth, O LORD, is full of your steadfast
        love;
    teach me your statutes!

TETH

65 You have dealt well with your servant,
    O LORD, according to your word.
66 Teach me good judgment and knowledge,
    for I believe in your commandments.
67 Before I was afflicted I went astray,
    but now I keep your word.
68 You are good and do good;
    teach me your statutes.
69 The insolent smear me with lies,
    but with my whole heart I keep your
        precepts;
70 their heart is unfeeling like fat,
    but I delight in your law.
71 It is good for me that I was afflicted,
    that I might learn your statutes.
72 The law of your mouth is better to me
    than thousands of gold and silver pieces.

YODH

73 Your hands have made and fashioned
        me;
    give me understanding that I may
        learn your commandments.

---

[1] Or *keep it as my reward*

74 Those who fear you shall see me and
rejoice,
because I have hoped in your word.
75 I know, O LORD, that your rules are righteous,
and that in faithfulness you have
afflicted me.
76 Let your steadfast love comfort me
according to your promise to your servant.
77 Let your mercy come to me, that I may live;
for your law is my delight.
78 Let the insolent be put to shame,
because they have wronged me with
falsehood;
as for me, I will meditate on your precepts.
79 Let those who fear you turn to me,
that they may know your testimonies.
80 May my heart be blameless in your statutes,
that I may not be put to shame!

KAPH

81 My soul longs for your salvation;
I hope in your word.
82 My eyes long for your promise;
I ask, "When will you comfort me?"
83 For I have become like a wineskin in the
smoke,
yet I have not forgotten your statutes.
84 How long must your servant endure?[1]
When will you judge those who persecute me?
85 The insolent have dug pitfalls for me;
they do not live according to your law.
86 All your commandments are sure;
they persecute me with falsehood; help
me!
87 They have almost made an end of me on
earth,
but I have not forsaken your precepts.
88 In your steadfast love give me life,
that I may keep the testimonies of your
mouth.

LAMEDH

89 Forever, O LORD, your word
is firmly fixed in the heavens.
90 Your faithfulness endures to all generations;
you have established the earth, and it
stands fast.

91 By your appointment they stand this
day,
for all things are your servants.
92 If your law had not been my delight,
I would have perished in my affliction.
93 I will never forget your precepts,
for by them you have given me life.
94 I am yours; save me,
for I have sought your precepts.
95 The wicked lie in wait to destroy me,
but I consider your testimonies.
96 I have seen a limit to all perfection,
but your commandment is exceedingly
broad.

MEM

97 Oh how I love your law!
It is my meditation all the day.
98 Your commandment makes me wiser than
my enemies,
for it is ever with me.
99 I have more understanding than all my
teachers,
for your testimonies are my meditation.
100 I understand more than the aged,[2]
for I keep your precepts.
101 I hold back my feet from every evil way,
in order to keep your word.
102 I do not turn aside from your rules,
for you have taught me.
103 How sweet are your words to my taste,
sweeter than honey to my mouth!
104 Through your precepts I get understanding;
therefore I hate every false way.

NUN

105 Your word is a lamp to my feet
and a light to my path.
106 I have sworn an oath and confirmed it,
to keep your righteous rules.
107 I am severely afflicted;
give me life, O LORD, according to your
word!
108 Accept my freewill offerings of praise,
O LORD,
and teach me your rules.
109 I hold my life in my hand continually,
but I do not forget your law.
110 The wicked have laid a snare for me,
but I do not stray from your precepts.

[1] Hebrew *How many are the days of your servant?* [2] Or *the elders*

111 Your testimonies are my heritage for-
　　ever,
　　　for they are the joy of my heart.
112 I incline my heart to perform your statutes
　　forever, to the end.[1]

Samekh

113 I hate the double-minded,
　　　but I love your law.
114 You are my hiding place and my shield;
　　　I hope in your word.
115 Depart from me, you evildoers,
　　　that I may keep the commandments of
　　　my God.
116 Uphold me according to your promise,
　　that I may live,
　　　and let me not be put to shame in my
　　　hope!
117 Hold me up, that I may be safe
　　　and have regard for your statutes con-
　　　tinually!
118 You spurn all who go astray from your
　　statutes,
　　　for their cunning is in vain.
119 All the wicked of the earth you discard like
　　dross,
　　　therefore I love your testimonies.
120 My flesh trembles for fear of you,
　　　and I am afraid of your judgments.

Ayin

121 I have done what is just and right;
　　　do not leave me to my oppressors.
122 Give your servant a pledge of good;
　　　let not the insolent oppress me.
123 My eyes long for your salvation
　　　and for the fulfillment of your righ-
　　　teous promise.
124 Deal with your servant according to your
　　steadfast love,
　　　and teach me your statutes.
125 I am your servant; give me understand-
　　ing,
　　　that I may know your testimonies!
126 It is time for the Lord to act,
　　　for your law has been broken.
127 Therefore I love your commandments
　　　above gold, above fine gold.
128 Therefore I consider all your precepts to be
　　right;
　　　I hate every false way.

Pe

129 Your testimonies are wonderful;
　　　therefore my soul keeps them.

130 The unfolding of your words gives light;
　　　it imparts understanding to the sim-
　　　ple.
131 I open my mouth and pant,
　　　because I long for your commandments.
132 Turn to me and be gracious to me,
　　　as is your way with those who love your
　　　name.
133 Keep steady my steps according to your
　　promise,
　　　and let no iniquity get dominion over
　　　me.
134 Redeem me from man's oppression,
　　　that I may keep your precepts.
135 Make your face shine upon your servant,
　　　and teach me your statutes.
136 My eyes shed streams of tears,
　　　because people do not keep your law.

Tsadhe

137 Righteous are you, O Lord,
　　　and right are your rules.
138 You have appointed your testimonies in
　　righteousness
　　　and in all faithfulness.
139 My zeal consumes me,
　　　because my foes forget your words.
140 Your promise is well tried,
　　　and your servant loves it.
141 I am small and despised,
　　　yet I do not forget your precepts.
142 Your righteousness is righteous forever,
　　　and your law is true.
143 Trouble and anguish have found me out,
　　　but your commandments are my
　　　delight.
144 Your testimonies are righteous forever;
　　　give me understanding that I may
　　　live.

Qoph

145 With my whole heart I cry; answer me,
　　O Lord!
　　　I will keep your statutes.
146 I call to you; save me,
　　　that I may observe your testimonies.
147 I rise before dawn and cry for help;
　　　I hope in your words.
148 My eyes are awake before the watches of
　　the night,
　　　that I may meditate on your promise.

---

[1] Or statutes; the reward is eternal

149 Hear my voice according to your steadfast
          love;
     O LORD, according to your justice give
          me life.
150 They draw near who persecute me with
          evil purpose;
     they are far from your law.
151 But you are near, O LORD,
     and all your commandments are true.
152 Long have I known from your testimonies
     that you have founded them forever.

RESH

153 Look on my affliction and deliver me,
     for I do not forget your law.
154 Plead my cause and redeem me;
     give me life according to your promise!
155 Salvation is far from the wicked,
     for they do not seek your statutes.
156 Great is your mercy, O LORD;
     give me life according to your rules.
157 Many are my persecutors and my adversar-
          ies,
     but I do not swerve from your testimo-
          nies.
158 I look at the faithless with disgust,
     because they do not keep your com-
          mands.
159 Consider how I love your precepts!
     Give me life according to your steadfast
          love.
160 The sum of your word is truth,
     and every one of your righteous rules
          endures forever.

SIN AND SHIN

161 Princes persecute me without cause,
     but my heart stands in awe of your
          words.
162 I rejoice at your word
     like one who finds great spoil.
163 I hate and abhor falsehood,
     but I love your law.
164 Seven times a day I praise you
     for your righteous rules.
165 Great peace have those who love your law;
     nothing can make them stumble.
166 I hope for your salvation, O LORD,
     and I do your commandments.
167 My soul keeps your testimonies;
     I love them exceedingly.
168 I keep your precepts and testimonies,
     for all my ways are before you.

TAW

169 Let my cry come before you, O LORD;
     give me understanding according to
          your word!
170 Let my plea come before you;
     deliver me according to your word.
171 My lips will pour forth praise,
     for you teach me your statutes.
172 My tongue will sing of your word,
     for all your commandments are right.
173 Let your hand be ready to help me,
     for I have chosen your precepts.
174 I long for your salvation, O LORD,
     and your law is my delight.
175 Let my soul live and praise you,
     and let your rules help me.
176 I have gone astray like a lost sheep; seek
          your servant,
     for I do not forget your commandments.

Deliver Me, O LORD

120 A SONG OF ASCENTS.
     In my distress I called to the LORD,
     and he answered me.
2 Deliver me, O LORD,
     from lying lips,
     from a deceitful tongue.

3 What shall be given to you,
     and what more shall be done to you,
     you deceitful tongue?
4 A warrior's sharp arrows,
     with glowing coals of the broom tree!

5 Woe to me, that I sojourn in Meshech,
     that I dwell among the tents of Kedar!
6 Too long have I had my dwelling
     among those who hate peace.
7 I am for peace,
     but when I speak, they are for war!

My Help Comes from the LORD

121 A SONG OF ASCENTS.
     I lift up my eyes to the hills.
     From where does my help come?
2 My help comes from the LORD,
     who made heaven and earth.

3 He will not let your foot be moved;
     he who keeps you will not slumber.
4 Behold, he who keeps Israel
     will neither slumber nor sleep.

5 The LORD is your keeper;
     the LORD is your shade on your right
          hand.

6   The sun shall not strike you by day,
      nor the moon by night.

7   The LORD will keep you from all evil;
      he will keep your life.

8   The LORD will keep
      your going out and your coming in
      from this time forth and forevermore.

Let Us Go to the House of the LORD

122 A SONG OF ASCENTS. OF DAVID.
      I was glad when they said to me,
   "Let us go to the house of the LORD!"

2   Our feet have been standing
      within your gates, O Jerusalem!

3   Jerusalem—built as a city
      that is bound firmly together,

4   to which the tribes go up,
      the tribes of the LORD,
   as was decreed for[1] Israel,
      to give thanks to the name of the LORD.

5   There thrones for judgment were set,
      the thrones of the house of David.

6   Pray for the peace of Jerusalem!
   "May they be secure who love you!

7   Peace be within your walls
      and security within your towers!"

8   For my brothers and companions' sake
      I will say, "Peace be within you!"

9   For the sake of the house of the LORD our
      God,
      I will seek your good.

Our Eyes Look to the LORD Our God

123 A SONG OF ASCENTS.
      To you I lift up my eyes,
   O you who are enthroned in the heav-
      ens!

2   Behold, as the eyes of servants
      look to the hand of their master,
   as the eyes of a maidservant
      to the hand of her mistress,
   so our eyes look to the LORD our God,
      till he has mercy upon us.

3   Have mercy upon us, O LORD, have mercy
      upon us,
      for we have had more than enough of
      contempt.

4   Our soul has had more than enough
      of the scorn of those who are at ease,
      of the contempt of the proud.

Our Help Is in the Name of the LORD

124 A SONG OF ASCENTS. OF DAVID.
      If it had not been the LORD who
      was on our side—
   let Israel now say—

2   if it had not been the LORD who was on
      our side
      when people rose up against us,

3   then they would have swallowed us up
      alive,
      when their anger was kindled against
      us;

4   then the flood would have swept us away,
      the torrent would have gone over us;

5   then over us would have gone
      the raging waters.

6   Blessed be the LORD,
      who has not given us
      as prey to their teeth!

7   We have escaped like a bird
      from the snare of the fowlers;
   the snare is broken,
      and we have escaped!

8   Our help is in the name of the LORD,
      who made heaven and earth.

The LORD Surrounds His People

125 A SONG OF ASCENTS.
      Those who trust in the LORD are
      like Mount Zion,
      which cannot be moved, but abides for-
      ever.

2   As the mountains surround Jerusalem,
      so the LORD surrounds his people,
      from this time forth and forevermore.

3   For the scepter of wickedness shall not rest
      on the land allotted to the righteous,
      lest the righteous stretch out
      their hands to do wrong.

4   Do good, O LORD, to those who are good,
      and to those who are upright in their
      hearts!

5   But those who turn aside to their crooked
      ways
      the LORD will lead away with evildoers!
      Peace be upon Israel!

Restore Our Fortunes, O LORD

126 A SONG OF ASCENTS.
      When the LORD restored the for-
      tunes of Zion,
      we were like those who dream.

---

[1] Or as a testimony for

2 Then our mouth was filled with laughter,
    and our tongue with shouts of joy;
  then they said among the nations,
    "The LORD has done great things for
      them."

3 The LORD has done great things for us;
    we are glad.

4 Restore our fortunes, O LORD,
    like streams in the Negeb!

5 Those who sow in tears
    shall reap with shouts of joy!

6 He who goes out weeping,
    bearing the seed for sowing,
  shall come home with shouts of joy,
    bringing his sheaves with him.

Unless the LORD Builds the House

127 A SONG OF ASCENTS. OF SOLOMON.
    Unless the LORD builds the house,
    those who build it labor in vain.
  Unless the LORD watches over the city,
    the watchman stays awake in vain.

2 It is in vain that you rise up early
    and go late to rest,
  eating the bread of anxious toil;
    for he gives to his beloved sleep.

3 Behold, children are a heritage from the
      LORD,
    the fruit of the womb a reward.

4 Like arrows in the hand of a warrior
    are the children[1] of one's youth.

5 Blessed is the man
    who fills his quiver with them!
  He shall not be put to shame
    when he speaks with his enemies in the
      gate.[2]

Blessed Is Everyone Who Fears the LORD

128 A SONG OF ASCENTS.
    Blessed is everyone who fears the
      LORD,
    who walks in his ways!

2 You shall eat the fruit of the labor of your
      hands;
    you shall be blessed, and it shall be well
      with you.

3 Your wife will be like a fruitful vine
    within your house;
  your children will be like olive shoots
    around your table.

4 Behold, thus shall the man be blessed
    who fears the LORD.

5 The LORD bless you from Zion!
    May you see the prosperity of Jerusalem
    all the days of your life!

6 May you see your children's children!
    Peace be upon Israel!

They Have Afflicted Me from My Youth

129 A SONG OF ASCENTS.
    "Greatly[3] have they afflicted me
      from my youth"—
    let Israel now say—

2 "Greatly have they afflicted me from my
      youth,
    yet they have not prevailed against me.

3 The plowers plowed upon my back;
    they made long their furrows."

4 The LORD is righteous;
    he has cut the cords of the wicked.

5 May all who hate Zion
    be put to shame and turned backward!

6 Let them be like the grass on the house-
      tops,
    which withers before it grows up,

7 with which the reaper does not fill his
      hand
    nor the binder of sheaves his arms,

8 nor do those who pass by say,
    "The blessing of the LORD be upon
      you!
    We bless you in the name of the LORD!"

My Soul Waits for the Lord

130 A SONG OF ASCENTS.
    Out of the depths I cry to you,
      O LORD!

2 O Lord, hear my voice!
  Let your ears be attentive
    to the voice of my pleas for mercy!

3 If you, O LORD, should mark iniquities,
    O Lord, who could stand?

4 But with you there is forgiveness,
    that you may be feared.

5 I wait for the LORD, my soul waits,
    and in his word I hope;

6 my soul waits for the Lord
    more than watchmen for the morning,
    more than watchmen for the morning.

7 O Israel, hope in the LORD!
    For with the LORD there is steadfast
      love,
    and with him is plentiful redemption.

---

1 Or sons 2 Or They shall not be put to shame when they speak with their enemies in the gate 3 Or Often; also verse 2

8 And he will redeem Israel
from all his iniquities.

I Have Calmed and Quieted My Soul

131 A Song of Ascents. Of David.
O Lord, my heart is not lifted up;
my eyes are not raised too high;
I do not occupy myself with things
too great and too marvelous for me.
2 But I have calmed and quieted my soul,
like a weaned child with its mother;
like a weaned child is my soul within
me.

3 O Israel, hope in the Lord
from this time forth and forevermore.

The Lord Has Chosen Zion

132 A Song of Ascents.
Remember, O Lord, in David's
favor,
all the hardships he endured,
2 how he swore to the Lord
and vowed to the Mighty One of Jacob,
3 "I will not enter my house
or get into my bed,
4 I will not give sleep to my eyes
or slumber to my eyelids,
5 until I find a place for the Lord,
a dwelling place for the Mighty One of
Jacob."

6 Behold, we heard of it in Ephrathah;
we found it in the fields of Jaar.
7 "Let us go to his dwelling place;
let us worship at his footstool!"

8 Arise, O Lord, and go to your resting place,
you and the ark of your might.
9 Let your priests be clothed with righteousness,
and let your saints shout for joy.
10 For the sake of your servant David,
do not turn away the face of your
anointed one.

11 The Lord swore to David a sure oath
from which he will not turn back:
"One of the sons of your body[1]
I will set on your throne.
12 If your sons keep my covenant
and my testimonies that I shall teach
them,
their sons also forever
shall sit on your throne."

13 For the Lord has chosen Zion;
he has desired it for his dwelling place:
14 "This is my resting place forever;
here I will dwell, for I have desired it.
15 I will abundantly bless her provisions;
I will satisfy her poor with bread.
16 Her priests I will clothe with salvation,
and her saints will shout for joy.
17 There I will make a horn to sprout for
David;
I have prepared a lamp for my anointed.
18 His enemies I will clothe with shame,
but on him his crown will shine."

When Brothers Dwell in Unity

133 A Song of Ascents. Of David.
Behold, how good and pleasant
it is
when brothers dwell in unity![2]
2 It is like the precious oil on the head,
running down on the beard,
on the beard of Aaron,
running down on the collar of his robes!
3 It is like the dew of Hermon,
which falls on the mountains of Zion!
For there the Lord has commanded the
blessing,
life forevermore.

Come, Bless the Lord

134 A Song of Ascents.
Come, bless the Lord, all you servants of the Lord,
who stand by night in the house of the
Lord!
2 Lift up your hands to the holy place
and bless the Lord!

3 May the Lord bless you from Zion,
he who made heaven and earth!

Your Name, O Lord, Endures Forever

135 Praise the Lord!
Praise the name of the Lord,
give praise, O servants of the Lord,
2 who stand in the house of the Lord,
in the courts of the house of our God!
3 Praise the Lord, for the Lord is good;
sing to his name, for it is pleasant![3]
4 For the Lord has chosen Jacob for himself,
Israel as his own possession.

5 For I know that the Lord is great,
and that our Lord is above all gods.

[1] Hebrew of your fruit of the womb [2] Or dwell together [3] Or for he is beautiful

⁶ Whatever the LORD pleases, he does,
    in heaven and on earth,
    in the seas and all deeps.
⁷ He it is who makes the clouds rise at the
    end of the earth,
    who makes lightnings for the rain
    and brings forth the wind from his
    storehouses.

⁸ He it was who struck down the firstborn of
    Egypt,
    both of man and of beast;
⁹ who in your midst, O Egypt,
    sent signs and wonders
    against Pharaoh and all his servants;
¹⁰ who struck down many nations
    and killed mighty kings,
¹¹ Sihon, king of the Amorites,
    and Og, king of Bashan,
    and all the kingdoms of Canaan,
¹² and gave their land as a heritage,
    a heritage to his people Israel.

¹³ Your name, O LORD, endures forever,
    your renown,[1] O LORD, throughout all
    ages.
¹⁴ For the LORD will vindicate his people
    and have compassion on his servants.

¹⁵ The idols of the nations are silver and gold,
    the work of human hands.
¹⁶ They have mouths, but do not speak;
    they have eyes, but do not see;
¹⁷ they have ears, but do not hear,
    nor is there any breath in their mouths.
¹⁸ Those who make them become like
    them,
    so do all who trust in them.

¹⁹ O house of Israel, bless the LORD!
    O house of Aaron, bless the LORD!
²⁰ O house of Levi, bless the LORD!
    You who fear the LORD, bless the LORD!
²¹ Blessed be the LORD from Zion,
    he who dwells in Jerusalem!
    Praise the LORD!

His Steadfast Love Endures Forever

136 Give thanks to the LORD, for he is
    good,
    for his steadfast love endures forever.
² Give thanks to the God of gods,
    for his steadfast love endures forever.
³ Give thanks to the Lord of lords,
    for his steadfast love endures forever;

⁴ to him who alone does great wonders,
    for his steadfast love endures forever;
⁵ to him who by understanding made the
    heavens,
    for his steadfast love endures forever;
⁶ to him who spread out the earth above the
    waters,
    for his steadfast love endures forever;
⁷ to him who made the great lights,
    for his steadfast love endures forever;
⁸ the sun to rule over the day,
    for his steadfast love endures forever;
⁹ the moon and stars to rule over the
    night,
    for his steadfast love endures forever;

¹⁰ to him who struck down the firstborn of
    Egypt,
    for his steadfast love endures forever;
¹¹ and brought Israel out from among
    them,
    for his steadfast love endures forever;
¹² with a strong hand and an outstretched
    arm,
    for his steadfast love endures forever;
¹³ to him who divided the Red Sea in two,
    for his steadfast love endures forever;
¹⁴ and made Israel pass through the midst of
    it,
    for his steadfast love endures forever;
¹⁵ but overthrew[2] Pharaoh and his host in the
    Red Sea,
    for his steadfast love endures forever;
¹⁶ to him who led his people through the wil-
    derness,
    for his steadfast love endures forever;

¹⁷ to him who struck down great kings,
    for his steadfast love endures forever;
¹⁸ and killed mighty kings,
    for his steadfast love endures forever;
¹⁹ Sihon, king of the Amorites,
    for his steadfast love endures forever;
²⁰ and Og, king of Bashan,
    for his steadfast love endures forever;
²¹ and gave their land as a heritage,
    for his steadfast love endures forever;
²² a heritage to Israel his servant,
    for his steadfast love endures forever.

²³ It is he who remembered us in our low
    estate,
    for his steadfast love endures forever;

[1] Or remembrance [2] Hebrew *shook off*

24 and rescued us from our foes,
 for his steadfast love endures forever;
25 he who gives food to all flesh,
 for his steadfast love endures forever.

26 Give thanks to the God of heaven,
 for his steadfast love endures forever.

How Shall We Sing the LORD's Song?

137 By the waters of Babylon,
 there we sat down and wept,
when we remembered Zion.
2 On the willows[1] there
 we hung up our lyres.
3 For there our captors
 required of us songs,
and our tormentors, mirth, saying,
 "Sing us one of the songs of Zion!"

4 How shall we sing the LORD's song
 in a foreign land?
5 If I forget you, O Jerusalem,
 let my right hand forget its skill!
6 Let my tongue stick to the roof of my
 mouth,
 if I do not remember you,
if I do not set Jerusalem
 above my highest joy!

7 Remember, O LORD, against the Edomites
 the day of Jerusalem,
how they said, "Lay it bare, lay it bare,
 down to its foundations!"
8 O daughter of Babylon, doomed to be
 destroyed,
 blessed shall he be who repays you
 with what you have done to us!
9 Blessed shall he be who takes your little
 ones
 and dashes them against the rock!

Give Thanks to the LORD

138 OF DAVID.
 I give you thanks, O LORD, with
 my whole heart;
before the gods I sing your praise;
2 I bow down toward your holy temple
 and give thanks to your name for your
  steadfast love and your faithfulness,
 for you have exalted above all things
 your name and your word.[2]
3 On the day I called, you answered me;
 my strength of soul you increased.[3]

4 All the kings of the earth shall give you
 thanks, O LORD,
 for they have heard the words of your
  mouth,
5 and they shall sing of the ways of the
 LORD,
 for great is the glory of the LORD.
6 For though the LORD is high, he regards
 the lowly,
 but the haughty he knows from afar.

7 Though I walk in the midst of trouble,
 you preserve my life;
you stretch out your hand against the
 wrath of my enemies,
 and your right hand delivers me.
8 The LORD will fulfill his purpose for me;
 your steadfast love, O LORD, endures
 forever.
 Do not forsake the work of your hands.

Search Me, O God, and Know My Heart

139 TO THE CHOIRMASTER. A PSALM OF
 DAVID.

1 O LORD, you have searched me and known
 me!
2 You know when I sit down and when I rise
 up;
 you discern my thoughts from afar.
3 You search out my path and my lying
 down
 and are acquainted with all my ways.
4 Even before a word is on my tongue,
 behold, O LORD, you know it altogether.
5 You hem me in, behind and before,
 and lay your hand upon me.
6 Such knowledge is too wonderful for me;
 it is high; I cannot attain it.

7 Where shall I go from your Spirit?
 Or where shall I flee from your presence?
8 If I ascend to heaven, you are there!
 If I make my bed in Sheol, you are
  there!
9 If I take the wings of the morning
 and dwell in the uttermost parts of the
  sea,
10 even there your hand shall lead me,
 and your right hand shall hold me.
11 If I say, "Surely the darkness shall cover me,
 and the light about me be night,"

---

[1] Or poplars [2] Or you have exalted your word above all your name [3] Hebrew you made me bold in my soul with strength

¹² even the darkness is not dark to you;
　　the night is bright as the day,
　　for darkness is as light with you.

¹³ For you formed my inward parts;
　　you knitted me together in my mother's
　　　womb.
¹⁴ I praise you, for I am fearfully and wonder-
　　fully made.¹
　Wonderful are your works;
　　my soul knows it very well.
¹⁵ My frame was not hidden from you,
　when I was being made in secret,
　　intricately woven in the depths of the
　　　earth.
¹⁶ Your eyes saw my unformed substance;
　in your book were written, every one of
　　them,
　　the days that were formed for me,
　　when as yet there was none of them.

¹⁷ How precious to me are your thoughts,
　　O God!
　　How vast is the sum of them!
¹⁸ If I would count them, they are more than
　　the sand.
　I awake, and I am still with you.

¹⁹ Oh that you would slay the wicked, O God!
　O men of blood, depart from me!
²⁰ They speak against you with malicious
　　intent;
　　your enemies take your name in vain.²
²¹ Do I not hate those who hate you, O Lord?
　And do I not loathe those who rise up
　　against you?
²² I hate them with complete hatred;
　I count them my enemies.

²³ Search me, O God, and know my heart!
　Try me and know my thoughts!³
²⁴ And see if there be any grievous way in me,
　and lead me in the way everlasting!⁴

Deliver Me, O Lord, from Evil Men

140

To the choirmaster. A Psalm of
David.

¹ Deliver me, O Lord, from evil men;
　preserve me from violent men,
² who plan evil things in their heart
　and stir up wars continually.
³ They make their tongue sharp as a ser-
　　pent's,
　and under their lips is the venom of
　　asps.   *Selah*

⁴ Guard me, O Lord, from the hands of the
　　wicked;
　　preserve me from violent men,
　　who have planned to trip up my feet.
⁵ The arrogant have hidden a trap for me,
　and with cords they have spread a
　　net;⁵
　　beside the way they have set snares for
　　me.   *Selah*

⁶ I say to the Lord, You are my God;
　give ear to the voice of my pleas for
　　mercy, O Lord!
⁷ O Lord, my Lord, the strength of my salva-
　　tion,
　　you have covered my head in the day of
　　battle.
⁸ Grant not, O Lord, the desires of the
　　wicked;
　　do not further their⁶ evil plot, or they
　　　will be exalted!   *Selah*

⁹ As for the head of those who surround
　　me,
　　let the mischief of their lips overwhelm
　　them!
¹⁰ Let burning coals fall upon them!
　Let them be cast into fire,
　into miry pits, no more to rise!
¹¹ Let not the slanderer be established in the
　　land;
　　let evil hunt down the violent man
　　speedily!

¹² I know that the Lord will maintain the
　　cause of the afflicted,
　　and will execute justice for the needy.
¹³ Surely the righteous shall give thanks to
　　your name;
　　the upright shall dwell in your presence.

Give Ear to My Voice

141

A Psalm of David.
O Lord, I call upon you; hasten to
me!
　Give ear to my voice when I call to
　　you!
² Let my prayer be counted as incense before
　　you,
　　and the lifting up of my hands as the
　　evening sacrifice!

³ Set a guard, O Lord, over my mouth;
　keep watch over the door of my lips!

---

¹ Or for I am fearfully set apart ² Hebrew lacks your name ³ Or cares ⁴ Or in the ancient way (compare Jeremiah 6:16) ⁵ Or they have spread cords as a net ⁶ Hebrew his

4 Do not let my heart incline to any evil,
   to busy myself with wicked deeds
 in company with men who work iniquity,
   and let me not eat of their delicacies!

5 Let a righteous man strike me—it is a
      kindness;
   let him rebuke me—it is oil for my head;
   let my head not refuse it.
 Yet my prayer is continually against their
      evil deeds.

6 When their judges are thrown over the
      cliff,[1]
   then they shall hear my words, for they
      are pleasant.

7 As when one plows and breaks up the earth,
   so shall our bones be scattered at the
      mouth of Sheol.[2]

8 But my eyes are toward you, O GOD, my
      Lord;
   in you I seek refuge; leave me not
      defenseless![3]

9 Keep me from the trap that they have laid
      for me
   and from the snares of evildoers!

10 Let the wicked fall into their own nets,
    while I pass by safely.

You Are My Refuge

142
A MASKIL[4] OF DAVID, WHEN HE WAS
IN THE CAVE. A PRAYER.

1 With my voice I cry out to the LORD;
   with my voice I plead for mercy to the
      LORD.

2 I pour out my complaint before him;
   I tell my trouble before him.

3 When my spirit faints within me,
   you know my way!
 In the path where I walk
   they have hidden a trap for me.

4 Look to the right and see:
   there is none who takes notice of me;
 no refuge remains to me;
   no one cares for my soul.

5 I cry to you, O LORD;
   I say, "You are my refuge,
   my portion in the land of the living."

6 Attend to my cry,
   for I am brought very low!
 Deliver me from my persecutors,
   for they are too strong for me!

7 Bring me out of prison,
   that I may give thanks to your name!
 The righteous will surround me,
   for you will deal bountifully with me.

My Soul Thirsts for You

143
A PSALM OF DAVID.
Hear my prayer, O LORD;
   give ear to my pleas for mercy!
 In your faithfulness answer me, in your
      righteousness!

2 Enter not into judgment with your servant,
   for no one living is righteous before you.

3 For the enemy has pursued my soul;
   he has crushed my life to the ground;
   he has made me sit in darkness like
      those long dead.

4 Therefore my spirit faints within me;
   my heart within me is appalled.

5 I remember the days of old;
   I meditate on all that you have done;
   I ponder the work of your hands.

6 I stretch out my hands to you;
   my soul thirsts for you like a parched
      land.   *Selah*

7 Answer me quickly, O LORD!
   My spirit fails!
 Hide not your face from me,
   lest I be like those who go down to the
      pit.

8 Let me hear in the morning of your stead-
      fast love,
   for in you I trust.
 Make me know the way I should go,
   for to you I lift up my soul.

9 Deliver me from my enemies, O LORD!
   I have fled to you for refuge.[5]

10 Teach me to do your will,
    for you are my God!
 Let your good Spirit lead me
    on level ground!

11 For your name's sake, O LORD, preserve my
       life!
    In your righteousness bring my soul
       out of trouble!

12 And in your steadfast love you will cut off
       my enemies,
    and you will destroy all the adversaries
       of my soul,
    for I am your servant.

---

[1] Or *When their judges fall into the hands of the Rock* [2] The meaning of the Hebrew in verses 6, 7 is uncertain [3] Hebrew *refuge; do not pour out my life!* [4] Probably a musical or liturgical term [5] One Hebrew manuscript, Septuagint; most Hebrew manuscripts *To you I have covered*

My Rock and My Fortress

144 Of David.

Blessed be the LORD, my rock,
  who trains my hands for war,
  and my fingers for battle;
2 he is my steadfast love and my fortress,
  my stronghold and my deliverer,
  my shield and he in whom I take refuge,
  who subdues peoples[1] under me.

3 O LORD, what is man that you regard him,
  or the son of man that you think of
    him?
4 Man is like a breath;
  his days are like a passing shadow.

5 Bow your heavens, O LORD, and come
    down!
  Touch the mountains so that they
    smoke!
6 Flash forth the lightning and scatter them;
  send out your arrows and rout them!
7 Stretch out your hand from on high;
  rescue me and deliver me from the
    many waters,
  from the hand of foreigners,
8 whose mouths speak lies
  and whose right hand is a right hand of
    falsehood.

9 I will sing a new song to you, O God;
  upon a ten-stringed harp I will play to
    you,
10 who gives victory to kings,
  who rescues David his servant from the
    cruel sword.
11 Rescue me and deliver me
  from the hand of foreigners,
  whose mouths speak lies
  and whose right hand is a right hand of
    falsehood.

12 May our sons in their youth
  be like plants full grown,
  our daughters like corner pillars
    cut for the structure of a palace;
13 may our granaries be full,
  providing all kinds of produce;
  may our sheep bring forth thousands
    and ten thousands in our fields;
14 may our cattle be heavy with young,
  suffering no mishap or failure in bear-
    ing;[2]

may there be no cry of distress in our
    streets!
15 Blessed are the people to whom such bless-
    ings fall!
  Blessed are the people whose God is the
    LORD!

Great Is the LORD

145[3] A Song of Praise. Of David.

I will extol you, my God and King,
  and bless your name forever and ever.
2 Every day I will bless you
  and praise your name forever and ever.
3 Great is the LORD, and greatly to be
    praised,
  and his greatness is unsearchable.

4 One generation shall commend your
    works to another,
  and shall declare your mighty acts.
5 On the glorious splendor of your majesty,
  and on your wondrous works, I will
    meditate.
6 They shall speak of the might of your awe-
    some deeds,
  and I will declare your greatness.
7 They shall pour forth the fame of your
    abundant goodness
  and shall sing aloud of your righteous-
    ness.

8 The LORD is gracious and merciful,
  slow to anger and abounding in stead-
    fast love.
9 The LORD is good to all,
  and his mercy is over all that he has
    made.

10 All your works shall give thanks to you,
    O LORD,
  and all your saints shall bless you!
11 They shall speak of the glory of your king-
    dom
  and tell of your power,
12 to make known to the children of man
    your[4] mighty deeds,
  and the glorious splendor of your king-
    dom.
13 Your kingdom is an everlasting kingdom,
  and your dominion endures through-
    out all generations.

[The LORD is faithful in all his words
  and kind in all his works.][5]

---

[1] Many Hebrew manuscripts, Dead Sea Scroll, Jerome, Syriac, Aquila; most Hebrew manuscripts *subdues my people* [2] Hebrew *with no breaking in or going out* [3] This psalm is an acrostic poem, each verse beginning with the successive letters of the Hebrew alphabet [4] Hebrew *his*; also next line [5] These two lines are supplied by one Hebrew manuscript, Septuagint, Syriac (compare Dead Sea Scroll)

14 The LORD upholds all who are falling
        and raises up all who are bowed
            down.
15 The eyes of all look to you,
        and you give them their food in due
            season.
16 You open your hand;
        you satisfy the desire of every living
            thing.
17 The LORD is righteous in all his ways
        and kind in all his works.
18 The LORD is near to all who call on him,
        to all who call on him in truth.
19 He fulfills the desire of those who fear him;
        he also hears their cry and saves them.
20 The LORD preserves all who love him,
        but all the wicked he will destroy.

21 My mouth will speak the praise of the
        LORD,
        and let all flesh bless his holy name for-
            ever and ever.

Put Not Your Trust in Princes

146 Praise the LORD!
        Praise the LORD, O my soul!
2 I will praise the LORD as long as I live;
        I will sing praises to my God while I
            have my being.

3 Put not your trust in princes,
        in a son of man, in whom there is no
            salvation.
4 When his breath departs, he returns to the
        earth;
        on that very day his plans perish.

5 Blessed is he whose help is the God of
        Jacob,
        whose hope is in the LORD his God,
6 who made heaven and earth,
        the sea, and all that is in them,
    who keeps faith forever;
7   who executes justice for the
            oppressed,
        who gives food to the hungry.

    The LORD sets the prisoners free;
8   the LORD opens the eyes of the blind.
    The LORD lifts up those who are bowed
            down;
        the LORD loves the righteous.

9 The LORD watches over the sojourners;
        he upholds the widow and the father-
            less,
        but the way of the wicked he brings to
            ruin.

10 The LORD will reign forever,
        your God, O Zion, to all generations.
    Praise the LORD!

He Heals the Brokenhearted

147 Praise the LORD!
        For it is good to sing praises to our
            God;
        for it is pleasant,[1] and a song of praise is
            fitting.
2 The LORD builds up Jerusalem;
        he gathers the outcasts of Israel.
3 He heals the brokenhearted
        and binds up their wounds.
4 He determines the number of the stars;
        he gives to all of them their names.
5 Great is our Lord, and abundant in
        power;
        his understanding is beyond measure.
6 The LORD lifts up the humble;[2]
        he casts the wicked to the ground.

7 Sing to the LORD with thanksgiving;
        make melody to our God on the lyre!
8 He covers the heavens with clouds;
        he prepares rain for the earth;
        he makes grass grow on the hills.
9 He gives to the beasts their food,
        and to the young ravens that cry.
10 His delight is not in the strength of the
        horse,
        nor his pleasure in the legs of a man,
11 but the LORD takes pleasure in those who
        fear him,
        in those who hope in his steadfast
            love.

12 Praise the LORD, O Jerusalem!
        Praise your God, O Zion!
13 For he strengthens the bars of your gates;
        he blesses your children within you.
14 He makes peace in your borders;
        he fills you with the finest of the wheat.
15 He sends out his command to the earth;
        his word runs swiftly.
16 He gives snow like wool;
        he scatters frost like ashes.

[1] Or for he is beautiful [2] Or afflicted

17 He hurls down his crystals of ice like
     crumbs;
   who can stand before his cold?
18 He sends out his word, and melts them;
   he makes his wind blow and the waters
     flow.
19 He declares his word to Jacob,
   his statutes and rules[1] to Israel.
20 He has not dealt thus with any other
     nation;
   they do not know his rules.[2]
   Praise the LORD!

Praise the Name of the LORD

148 Praise the LORD!
   Praise the LORD from the heavens;
   praise him in the heights!
2 Praise him, all his angels;
   praise him, all his hosts!

3 Praise him, sun and moon,
   praise him, all you shining stars!
4 Praise him, you highest heavens,
   and you waters above the heavens!

5 Let them praise the name of the LORD!
   For he commanded and they were cre-
     ated.
6 And he established them forever and ever;
   he gave a decree, and it shall not pass
     away.[3]

7 Praise the LORD from the earth,
   you great sea creatures and all deeps,
8 fire and hail, snow and mist,
   stormy wind fulfilling his word!

9 Mountains and all hills,
   fruit trees and all cedars!
10 Beasts and all livestock,
   creeping things and flying birds!

11 Kings of the earth and all peoples,
   princes and all rulers of the earth!
12 Young men and maidens together,
   old men and children!

13 Let them praise the name of the LORD,
   for his name alone is exalted;
   his majesty is above earth and heaven.

14 He has raised up a horn for his people,
   praise for all his saints,
   for the people of Israel who are near to
     him.
   Praise the LORD!

Sing to the LORD a New Song

149 Praise the LORD!
   Sing to the LORD a new song,
   his praise in the assembly of the godly!
2 Let Israel be glad in his Maker;
   let the children of Zion rejoice in their
     King!
3 Let them praise his name with dancing,
   making melody to him with tambou-
     rine and lyre!
4 For the LORD takes pleasure in his people;
   he adorns the humble with salvation.
5 Let the godly exult in glory;
   let them sing for joy on their beds.
6 Let the high praises of God be in their
     throats
   and two-edged swords in their hands,
7 to execute vengeance on the nations
   and punishments on the peoples,
8 to bind their kings with chains
   and their nobles with fetters of iron,
9 to execute on them the judgment written!
   This is honor for all his godly ones.
   Praise the LORD!

Let Everything Praise the LORD

150 Praise the LORD!
   Praise God in his sanctuary;
   praise him in his mighty heavens![4]
2 Praise him for his mighty deeds;
   praise him according to his excellent
     greatness!

3 Praise him with trumpet sound;
   praise him with lute and harp!
4 Praise him with tambourine and dance;
   praise him with strings and pipe!
5 Praise him with sounding cymbals;
   praise him with loud clashing cymbals!
6 Let everything that has breath praise the
     LORD!
   Praise the LORD!

---

[1] Or *and just decrees* [2] Or *his just decrees* [3] Or *it shall not be transgressed* [4] Hebrew *expanse* (compare Genesis 1:6–8)

PROVERBS

The Beginning of Knowledge

1 The proverbs of Solomon, son of David, king of Israel:

2 To know wisdom and instruction,
    to understand words of insight,
3 to receive instruction in wise dealing,
    in righteousness, justice, and equity;
4 to give prudence to the simple,
    knowledge and discretion to the youth—
5 Let the wise hear and increase in learning,
    and the one who understands obtain guidance,
6 to understand a proverb and a saying,
    the words of the wise and their riddles.

7 The fear of the LORD is the beginning of knowledge;
    fools despise wisdom and instruction.

The Enticement of Sinners

8 Hear, my son, your father's instruction,
    and forsake not your mother's teaching,
9 for they are a graceful garland for your head
    and pendants for your neck.
10 My son, if sinners entice you,
    do not consent.
11 If they say, "Come with us, let us lie in wait for blood;
    let us ambush the innocent without reason;
12 like Sheol let us swallow them alive,
    and whole, like those who go down to the pit;
13 we shall find all precious goods,
    we shall fill our houses with plunder;
14 throw in your lot among us;
    we will all have one purse"—
15 my son, do not walk in the way with them;
    hold back your foot from their paths,
16 for their feet run to evil,
    and they make haste to shed blood.
17 For in vain is a net spread
    in the sight of any bird,
18 but these men lie in wait for their own blood;
    they set an ambush for their own lives.
19 Such are the ways of everyone who is greedy for unjust gain;
    it takes away the life of its possessors.

The Call of Wisdom

20 Wisdom cries aloud in the street,
    in the markets she raises her voice;
21 at the head of the noisy streets she cries out;
    at the entrance of the city gates she speaks:
22 "How long, O simple ones, will you love being simple?
    How long will scoffers delight in their scoffing
    and fools hate knowledge?
23 If you turn at my reproof,[1]
    behold, I will pour out my spirit to you;
    I will make my words known to you.
24 Because I have called and you refused to listen,
    have stretched out my hand and no one has heeded,
25 because you have ignored all my counsel
    and would have none of my reproof,
26 I also will laugh at your calamity;
    I will mock when terror strikes you,
27 when terror strikes you like a storm
    and your calamity comes like a whirlwind,
    when distress and anguish come upon you.
28 Then they will call upon me, but I will not answer;
    they will seek me diligently but will not find me.
29 Because they hated knowledge
    and did not choose the fear of the LORD,
30 would have none of my counsel
    and despised all my reproof,
31 therefore they shall eat the fruit of their way,
    and have their fill of their own devices.
32 For the simple are killed by their turning away,
    and the complacency of fools destroys them;

---

[1] Or Will you turn away at my reproof?

33 but whoever listens to me will dwell secure
     and will be at ease, without dread of
        disaster."

The Value of Wisdom

2 My son, if you receive my words
     and treasure up my commandments with
        you,
2 making your ear attentive to wisdom
     and inclining your heart to understand-
        ing;
3 yes, if you call out for insight
     and raise your voice for understand-
        ing,
4 if you seek it like silver
     and search for it as for hidden treasures,
5 then you will understand the fear of the
        LORD
     and find the knowledge of God.
6 For the LORD gives wisdom;
     from his mouth come knowledge and
        understanding;
7 he stores up sound wisdom for the
        upright;
     he is a shield to those who walk in
        integrity,
8 guarding the paths of justice
     and watching over the way of his saints.
9 Then you will understand righteousness
        and justice
     and equity, every good path;
10 for wisdom will come into your heart,
     and knowledge will be pleasant to your
        soul;
11 discretion will watch over you,
     understanding will guard you,
12 delivering you from the way of evil,
     from men of perverted speech,
13 who forsake the paths of uprightness
     to walk in the ways of darkness,
14 who rejoice in doing evil
     and delight in the perverseness of evil,
15 men whose paths are crooked,
     and who are devious in their ways.

16 So you will be delivered from the forbid-
        den[1] woman,
     from the adulteress[2] with her smooth
        words,
17 who forsakes the companion of her
        youth
     and forgets the covenant of her God;
18 for her house sinks down to death,
     and her paths to the departed;[3]

19 none who go to her come back,
     nor do they regain the paths of life.
20 So you will walk in the way of the good
     and keep to the paths of the righ-
        teous.
21 For the upright will inhabit the land,
     and those with integrity will remain in
        it,
22 but the wicked will be cut off from the
        land,
     and the treacherous will be rooted out
        of it.

Trust in the LORD with All Your Heart

3 My son, do not forget my teaching,
     but let your heart keep my command-
        ments,
2 for length of days and years of life
     and peace they will add to you.

3 Let not steadfast love and faithfulness for-
        sake you;
     bind them around your neck;
     write them on the tablet of your heart.
4 So you will find favor and good success[4]
     in the sight of God and man.

5 Trust in the LORD with all your heart,
     and do not lean on your own under-
        standing.
6 In all your ways acknowledge him,
     and he will make straight your paths.
7 Be not wise in your own eyes;
     fear the LORD, and turn away from evil.
8 It will be healing to your flesh[5]
     and refreshment[6] to your bones.

9 Honor the LORD with your wealth
     and with the firstfruits of all your pro-
        duce;
10 then your barns will be filled with plenty,
     and your vats will be bursting with
        wine.

11 My son, do not despise the LORD's disci-
        pline
     or be weary of his reproof,
12 for the LORD reproves him whom he loves,
     as a father the son in whom he delights.

Blessed Is the One Who Finds Wisdom

13 Blessed is the one who finds wisdom,
     and the one who gets understanding,

---

[1] Hebrew strange [2] Hebrew foreign woman [3] Hebrew to the Rephaim [4] Or repute [5] Hebrew navel [6] Or medicine

14 for the gain from her is better than gain
 from silver
 and her profit better than gold.
15 She is more precious than jewels,
 and nothing you desire can compare
 with her.
16 Long life is in her right hand;
 in her left hand are riches and honor.
17 Her ways are ways of pleasantness,
 and all her paths are peace.
18 She is a tree of life to those who lay hold of
 her;
 those who hold her fast are called
 blessed.

19 The LORD by wisdom founded the earth;
 by understanding he established the
 heavens;
20 by his knowledge the deeps broke open,
 and the clouds drop down the dew.

21 My son, do not lose sight of these—
 keep sound wisdom and discretion,
22 and they will be life for your soul
 and adornment for your neck.
23 Then you will walk on your way securely,
 and your foot will not stumble.
24 If you lie down, you will not be afraid;
 when you lie down, your sleep will be
 sweet.
25 Do not be afraid of sudden terror
 or of the ruin[1] of the wicked, when it
 comes,
26 for the LORD will be your confidence
 and will keep your foot from being
 caught.

27 Do not withhold good from those to
 whom it is due,[2]
 when it is in your power to do it.
28 Do not say to your neighbor, "Go, and
 come again,
 tomorrow I will give it"—when you
 have it with you.
29 Do not plan evil against your neighbor,
 who dwells trustingly beside you.
30 Do not contend with a man for no reason,
 when he has done you no harm.
31 Do not envy a man of violence
 and do not choose any of his ways,
32 for the devious person is an abomination
 to the LORD,
 but the upright are in his confidence.

33 The LORD's curse is on the house of the
 wicked,
 but he blesses the dwelling of the righteous.
34 Toward the scorners he is scornful,
 but to the humble he gives favor.[3]
35 The wise will inherit honor,
 but fools get[4] disgrace.

A Father's Wise Instruction

4 Hear, O sons, a father's instruction,
 and be attentive, that you may gain[5]
 insight,
2 for I give you good precepts;
 do not forsake my teaching.
3 When I was a son with my father,
 tender, the only one in the sight of my
 mother,
4 he taught me and said to me,
 "Let your heart hold fast my words;
 keep my commandments, and live.
5 Get wisdom; get insight;
 do not forget, and do not turn away
 from the words of my mouth.
6 Do not forsake her, and she will keep you;
 love her, and she will guard you.
7 The beginning of wisdom is this: Get wisdom,
 and whatever you get, get insight.
8 Prize her highly, and she will exalt you;
 she will honor you if you embrace her.
9 She will place on your head a graceful garland;
 she will bestow on you a beautiful
 crown."

10 Hear, my son, and accept my words,
 that the years of your life may be many.
11 I have taught you the way of wisdom;
 I have led you in the paths of uprightness.
12 When you walk, your step will not be ham-
 pered,
 and if you run, you will not stumble.
13 Keep hold of instruction; do not let go;
 guard her, for she is your life.
14 Do not enter the path of the wicked,
 and do not walk in the way of the evil.
15 Avoid it; do not go on it;
 turn away from it and pass on.
16 For they cannot sleep unless they have
 done wrong;
 they are robbed of sleep unless they
 have made someone stumble.

---

[1] Hebrew *storm*   [2] Hebrew *Do not withhold good from its owners*   [3] Or *grace*   [4] The meaning of the Hebrew word is uncertain   [5] Hebrew *know*

17 For they eat the bread of wickedness
   and drink the wine of violence.
18 But the path of the righteous is like the
       light of dawn,
     which shines brighter and brighter
       until full day.
19 The way of the wicked is like deep dark-
       ness;
     they do not know over what they stum-
       ble.

20 My son, be attentive to my words;
     incline your ear to my sayings.
21 Let them not escape from your sight;
     keep them within your heart.
22 For they are life to those who find them,
     and healing to all their[1] flesh.
23 Keep your heart with all vigilance,
     for from it flow the springs of life.
24 Put away from you crooked speech,
     and put devious talk far from you.
25 Let your eyes look directly forward,
     and your gaze be straight before you.
26 Ponder[2] the path of your feet;
     then all your ways will be sure.
27 Do not swerve to the right or to the left;
     turn your foot away from evil.

Warning Against Adultery

5 My son, be attentive to my wisdom;
   incline your ear to my understanding,
2 that you may keep discretion,
     and your lips may guard knowledge.
3 For the lips of a forbidden[3] woman drip
       honey,
     and her speech[4] is smoother than oil,
4 but in the end she is bitter as wormwood,
     sharp as a two-edged sword.
5 Her feet go down to death;
     her steps follow the path to[5] Sheol;
6 she does not ponder the path of life;
     her ways wander, and she does not
       know it.

7 And now, O sons, listen to me,
     and do not depart from the words of
       my mouth.
8 Keep your way far from her,
     and do not go near the door of her
       house,
9 lest you give your honor to others
     and your years to the merciless,

10 lest strangers take their fill of your
       strength,
     and your labors go to the house of a for-
       eigner,
11 and at the end of your life you groan,
     when your flesh and body are con-
       sumed,
12 and you say, "How I hated discipline,
     and my heart despised reproof!
13 I did not listen to the voice of my teachers
     or incline my ear to my instructors.
14 I am at the brink of utter ruin
     in the assembled congregation."

15 Drink water from your own cistern,
     flowing water from your own well.
16 Should your springs be scattered abroad,
     streams of water in the streets?
17 Let them be for yourself alone,
     and not for strangers with you.
18 Let your fountain be blessed,
     and rejoice in the wife of your youth,
19 a lovely deer, a graceful doe.
   Let her breasts fill you at all times with
       delight;
     be intoxicated[6] always in her love.
20 Why should you be intoxicated, my son,
       with a forbidden woman
     and embrace the bosom of an adulter-
       ess?[7]
21 For a man's ways are before the eyes of the
       LORD,
     and he ponders[8] all his paths.
22 The iniquities of the wicked ensnare him,
     and he is held fast in the cords of his sin.
23 He dies for lack of discipline,
     and because of his great folly he is led
       astray.

Practical Warnings

6 My son, if you have put up security for
   your neighbor,
     have given your pledge for a stranger,
2 if you are snared in the words of your
       mouth,
     caught in the words of your mouth,
3 then do this, my son, and save yourself,
     for you have come into the hand of your
       neighbor:
     go, hasten,[9] and plead urgently with
       your neighbor.
4 Give your eyes no sleep
     and your eyelids no slumber;

---

[1] Hebrew his [2] Or Make level [3] Hebrew strange; also verse 20 [4] Hebrew palate [5] Hebrew lay hold of [6] Hebrew be led astray; also verse 20 [7] Hebrew a foreign woman [8] Or makes level [9] Or humble yourself

5 save yourself like a gazelle from the hand
of the hunter,[1]
like a bird from the hand of the fowler.

6 Go to the ant, O sluggard;
consider her ways, and be wise.
7 Without having any chief,
officer, or ruler,
8 she prepares her bread in summer
and gathers her food in harvest.
9 How long will you lie there, O sluggard?
When will you arise from your sleep?
10 A little sleep, a little slumber,
a little folding of the hands to rest,
11 and poverty will come upon you like a robber,
and want like an armed man.

12 A worthless person, a wicked man,
goes about with crooked speech,
13 winks with his eyes, signals[2] with his feet,
points with his finger,
14 with perverted heart devises evil,
continually sowing discord;
15 therefore calamity will come upon him
suddenly;
in a moment he will be broken beyond
healing.

16 There are six things that the LORD hates,
seven that are an abomination to him:
17 haughty eyes, a lying tongue,
and hands that shed innocent blood,
18 a heart that devises wicked plans,
feet that make haste to run to evil,
19 a false witness who breathes out lies,
and one who sows discord among
brothers.

Warnings Against Adultery

20 My son, keep your father's commandment,
and forsake not your mother's teaching.
21 Bind them on your heart always;
tie them around your neck.
22 When you walk, they[3] will lead you;
when you lie down, they will watch
over you;
and when you awake, they will talk
with you.
23 For the commandment is a lamp and the
teaching a light,
and the reproofs of discipline are the
way of life,

24 to preserve you from the evil woman,[4]
from the smooth tongue of the adulteress.[5]
25 Do not desire her beauty in your heart,
and do not let her capture you with her
eyelashes;
26 for the price of a prostitute is only a loaf of
bread,[6]
but a married woman[7] hunts down a
precious life.
27 Can a man carry fire next to his chest
and his clothes not be burned?
28 Or can one walk on hot coals
and his feet not be scorched?
29 So is he who goes in to his neighbor's wife;
none who touches her will go unpunished.
30 People do not despise a thief if he steals
to satisfy his appetite when he is hungry,
31 but if he is caught, he will pay sevenfold;
he will give all the goods of his house.
32 He who commits adultery lacks sense;
he who does it destroys himself.
33 He will get wounds and dishonor,
and his disgrace will not be wiped away.
34 For jealousy makes a man furious,
and he will not spare when he takes
revenge.
35 He will accept no compensation;
he will refuse though you multiply gifts.

Warning Against the Adulteress

7 My son, keep my words
and treasure up my commandments with
you;
2 keep my commandments and live;
keep my teaching as the apple of your
eye;
3 bind them on your fingers;
write them on the tablet of your heart.
4 Say to wisdom, "You are my sister,"
and call insight your intimate friend,
5 to keep you from the forbidden[8] woman,
from the adulteress[9] with her smooth
words.

6 For at the window of my house
I have looked out through my lattice,
7 and I have seen among the simple,
I have perceived among the youths,
a young man lacking sense,

---

[1] Hebrew lacks *of the hunter* [2] Hebrew *scrapes* [3] Hebrew *it*; three times in this verse [4] Revocalization (compare Septuagint) yields *from the wife of a neighbor* [5] Hebrew *the foreign woman* [6] Or (compare Septuagint, Syriac, Vulgate) *for a prostitute leaves a man with nothing but a loaf of bread* [7] Hebrew *a man's wife* [8] Hebrew *strange* [9] Hebrew *the foreign woman*

8 passing along the street near her corner,
     taking the road to her house
9 in the twilight, in the evening,
     at the time of night and darkness.

10 And behold, the woman meets him,
     dressed as a prostitute, wily of heart.[1]
11 She is loud and wayward;
     her feet do not stay at home;
12 now in the street, now in the market,
     and at every corner she lies in wait.
13 She seizes him and kisses him,
     and with bold face she says to him,
14 "I had to offer sacrifices,[2]
     and today I have paid my vows;
15 so now I have come out to meet you,
     to seek you eagerly, and I have found
     you.
16 I have spread my couch with coverings,
     colored linens from Egyptian linen;
17 I have perfumed my bed with myrrh,
     aloes, and cinnamon.
18 Come, let us take our fill of love till morn-
     ing;
     let us delight ourselves with love.
19 For my husband is not at home;
     he has gone on a long journey;
20 he took a bag of money with him;
     at full moon he will come home."

21 With much seductive speech she persuades
     him;
     with her smooth talk she compels him.
22 All at once he follows her,
     as an ox goes to the slaughter,
     or as a stag is caught fast[3]
23   till an arrow pierces its liver;
     as a bird rushes into a snare;
     he does not know that it will cost him
     his life.

24 And now, O sons, listen to me,
     and be attentive to the words of my
     mouth.
25 Let not your heart turn aside to her ways;
     do not stray into her paths,
26 for many a victim has she laid low,
     and all her slain are a mighty throng.
27 Her house is the way to Sheol,
     going down to the chambers of death.

The Blessings of Wisdom

8 Does not wisdom call?
     Does not understanding raise her voice?
2 On the heights beside the way,
     at the crossroads she takes her stand;
3 beside the gates in front of the town,
     at the entrance of the portals she cries
     aloud:
4 "To you, O men, I call,
     and my cry is to the children of man.
5 O simple ones, learn prudence;
     O fools, learn sense.
6 Hear, for I will speak noble things,
     and from my lips will come what is
     right,
7 for my mouth will utter truth;
     wickedness is an abomination to my
     lips.
8 All the words of my mouth are righteous;
     there is nothing twisted or crooked in
     them.
9 They are all straight to him who under-
     stands,
     and right to those who find knowledge.
10 Take my instruction instead of silver,
     and knowledge rather than choice gold,
11 for wisdom is better than jewels,
     and all that you may desire cannot com-
     pare with her.

12 "I, wisdom, dwell with prudence,
     and I find knowledge and discretion.
13 The fear of the Lord is hatred of evil.
     Pride and arrogance and the way of evil
     and perverted speech I hate.
14 I have counsel and sound wisdom;
     I have insight; I have strength.
15 By me kings reign,
     and rulers decree what is just;
16 by me princes rule,
     and nobles, all who govern justly.[4]
17 I love those who love me,
     and those who seek me diligently find
     me.
18 Riches and honor are with me,
     enduring wealth and righteousness.
19 My fruit is better than gold, even fine gold,
     and my yield than choice silver.
20 I walk in the way of righteousness,
     in the paths of justice,
21 granting an inheritance to those who love
     me,
     and filling their treasuries.

[1] Hebrew guarded in heart [2] Hebrew peace offerings [3] Probable reading (compare Septuagint, Vulgate, Syriac); Hebrew as a chain to discipline a fool [4] Most Hebrew manuscripts; many Hebrew manuscripts, Septuagint govern the earth

22 "The LORD possessed[1] me at the beginning
     of his work,[2]
       the first of his acts of old.
23 Ages ago I was set up,
       at the first, before the beginning of the
         earth.
24 When there were no depths I was
       brought forth,
       when there were no springs abounding
         with water.
25 Before the mountains had been shaped,
       before the hills, I was brought forth,
26 before he had made the earth with its fields,
       or the first of the dust of the world.
27 When he established the heavens, I was
       there;
       when he drew a circle on the face of
         the deep,
28 when he made firm the skies above,
       when he established[3] the fountains of
         the deep,
29 when he assigned to the sea its limit,
       so that the waters might not trans-
         gress his command,
       when he marked out the foundations of
         the earth,
30   then I was beside him, like a master
         workman,
     and I was daily his[4] delight,
       rejoicing before him always,
31 rejoicing in his inhabited world
       and delighting in the children of man.

32 "And now, O sons, listen to me:
       blessed are those who keep my ways.
33 Hear instruction and be wise,
       and do not neglect it.
34 Blessed is the one who listens to me,
       watching daily at my gates,
       waiting beside my doors.
35 For whoever finds me finds life
       and obtains favor from the LORD,
36 but he who fails to find me injures himself;
       all who hate me love death."

The Way of Wisdom

9 Wisdom has built her house;
     she has hewn her seven pillars.
2   She has slaughtered her beasts; she has
       mixed her wine;
       she has also set her table.
3   She has sent out her young women to call
       from the highest places in the town,

4   "Whoever is simple, let him turn in here!"
       To him who lacks sense she says,
5   "Come, eat of my bread
       and drink of the wine I have mixed.
6   Leave your simple ways,[5] and live,
       and walk in the way of insight."

7   Whoever corrects a scoffer gets himself
       abuse,
       and he who reproves a wicked man
         incurs injury.
8   Do not reprove a scoffer, or he will hate you;
       reprove a wise man, and he will love
         you.
9   Give instruction[6] to a wise man, and he will
       be still wiser;
       teach a righteous man, and he will
         increase in learning.
10   The fear of the LORD is the beginning of
       wisdom,
       and the knowledge of the Holy One is
         insight.
11   For by me your days will be multiplied,
       and years will be added to your life.
12   If you are wise, you are wise for yourself;
       if you scoff, you alone will bear it.

The Way of Folly

13   The woman Folly is loud;
       she is seductive[7] and knows nothing.
14   She sits at the door of her house;
       she takes a seat on the highest places of
         the town,
15   calling to those who pass by,
       who are going straight on their way,
16   "Whoever is simple, let him turn in here!"
       And to him who lacks sense she says,
17   "Stolen water is sweet,
       and bread eaten in secret is pleasant."
18   But he does not know that the dead[8] are
       there,
       that her guests are in the depths of
         Sheol.

The Proverbs of Solomon

10 The proverbs of Solomon.

     A wise son makes a glad father,
       but a foolish son is a sorrow to his
         mother.
2   Treasures gained by wickedness do not
       profit,
       but righteousness delivers from death.

[1] Or fathered; Septuagint created [2] Hebrew way [3] The meaning of the Hebrew is uncertain [4] Or daily filled with [5] Or Leave the company of the simple [6] Hebrew lacks instruction [7] Or full of simpleness [8] Hebrew Rephaim

3 The LORD does not let the righteous go
hungry,
but he thwarts the craving of the
wicked.
4 A slack hand causes poverty,
but the hand of the diligent makes rich.
5 He who gathers in summer is a prudent
son,
but he who sleeps in harvest is a son
who brings shame.
6 Blessings are on the head of the righteous,
but the mouth of the wicked conceals
violence.[1]
7 The memory of the righteous is a blessing,
but the name of the wicked will rot.
8 The wise of heart will receive commandments,
but a babbling fool will come to ruin.
9 Whoever walks in integrity walks
securely,
but he who makes his ways crooked
will be found out.
10 Whoever winks the eye causes trouble,
and a babbling fool will come to ruin.
11 The mouth of the righteous is a fountain
of life,
but the mouth of the wicked conceals
violence.
12 Hatred stirs up strife,
but love covers all offenses.
13 On the lips of him who has understanding,
wisdom is found,
but a rod is for the back of him who
lacks sense.
14 The wise lay up knowledge,
but the mouth of a fool brings ruin
near.
15 A rich man's wealth is his strong city;
the poverty of the poor is their ruin.
16 The wage of the righteous leads to life,
the gain of the wicked to sin.
17 Whoever heeds instruction is on the path
to life,
but he who rejects reproof leads others
astray.
18 The one who conceals hatred has lying lips,
and whoever utters slander is a fool.
19 When words are many, transgression is not
lacking,
but whoever restrains his lips is prudent.

20 The tongue of the righteous is choice silver;
the heart of the wicked is of little worth.
21 The lips of the righteous feed many,
but fools die for lack of sense.
22 The blessing of the LORD makes rich,
and he adds no sorrow with it.[2]
23 Doing wrong is like a joke to a fool,
but wisdom is pleasure to a man of
understanding.
24 What the wicked dreads will come upon
him,
but the desire of the righteous will be
granted.
25 When the tempest passes, the wicked is no
more,
but the righteous is established forever.
26 Like vinegar to the teeth and smoke to the
eyes,
so is the sluggard to those who send
him.
27 The fear of the LORD prolongs life,
but the years of the wicked will be short.
28 The hope of the righteous brings joy,
but the expectation of the wicked will
perish.
29 The way of the LORD is a stronghold to the
blameless,
but destruction to evildoers.
30 The righteous will never be removed,
but the wicked will not dwell in the
land.
31 The mouth of the righteous brings forth
wisdom,
but the perverse tongue will be cut
off.
32 The lips of the righteous know what is
acceptable,
but the mouth of the wicked, what is
perverse.

11 A false balance is an abomination to
the LORD,
but a just weight is his delight.
2 When pride comes, then comes disgrace,
but with the humble is wisdom.
3 The integrity of the upright guides
them,
but the crookedness of the treacherous
destroys them.
4 Riches do not profit in the day of wrath,
but righteousness delivers from death.

[1] Or but violence covers the mouth of the wicked; also verse 11 [2] Or and toil adds nothing to it

5 The righteousness of the blameless keeps
      his way straight,
    but the wicked falls by his own wick-
      edness.
6 The righteousness of the upright delivers
      them,
    but the treacherous are taken captive
      by their lust.
7 When the wicked dies, his hope will perish,
    and the expectation of wealth[1] per-
      ishes too.
8 The righteous is delivered from trouble,
    and the wicked walks into it instead.
9 With his mouth the godless man would
      destroy his neighbor,
    but by knowledge the righteous are
      delivered.
10 When it goes well with the righteous, the
      city rejoices,
    and when the wicked perish there are
      shouts of gladness.
11 By the blessing of the upright a city is
      exalted,
    but by the mouth of the wicked it is
      overthrown.
12 Whoever belittles his neighbor lacks
      sense,
    but a man of understanding remains
      silent.
13 Whoever goes about slandering reveals
      secrets,
    but he who is trustworthy in spirit
      keeps a thing covered.
14 Where there is no guidance, a people
      falls,
    but in an abundance of counselors
      there is safety.
15 Whoever puts up security for a stranger
      will surely suffer harm,
    but he who hates striking hands in
      pledge is secure.
16 A gracious woman gets honor,
    and violent men get riches.
17 A man who is kind benefits himself,
    but a cruel man hurts himself.
18 The wicked earns deceptive wages,
    but one who sows righteousness gets a
      sure reward.
19 Whoever is steadfast in righteousness will
      live,
    but he who pursues evil will die.

20 Those of crooked heart are an abomination
      to the Lord,
    but those of blameless ways are his
      delight.
21 Be assured, an evil person will not go
      unpunished,
    but the offspring of the righteous will
      be delivered.
22 Like a gold ring in a pig's snout
    is a beautiful woman without discre-
      tion.
23 The desire of the righteous ends only in
      good,
    the expectation of the wicked in wrath.
24 One gives freely, yet grows all the richer;
    another withholds what he should give,
      and only suffers want.
25 Whoever brings blessing will be enriched,
    and one who waters will himself be
      watered.
26 The people curse him who holds back
      grain,
    but a blessing is on the head of him
      who sells it.
27 Whoever diligently seeks good seeks favor,[2]
    but evil comes to him who searches for
      it.
28 Whoever trusts in his riches will fall,
    but the righteous will flourish like a
      green leaf.
29 Whoever troubles his own household will
      inherit the wind,
    and the fool will be servant to the wise
      of heart.
30 The fruit of the righteous is a tree of life,
    and whoever captures souls is wise.
31 If the righteous is repaid on earth,
    how much more the wicked and the
      sinner!

12 Whoever loves discipline loves
      knowledge,
    but he who hates reproof is stupid.
2 A good man obtains favor from the Lord,
    but a man of evil devices he condemns.
3 No one is established by wickedness,
    but the root of the righteous will never
      be moved.
4 An excellent wife is the crown of her hus-
      band,
    but she who brings shame is like rotten-
      ness in his bones.
5 The thoughts of the righteous are just;
    the counsels of the wicked are deceitful.

[1] Or of his strength, or of iniquity [2] Or acceptance

6 The words of the wicked lie in wait for
blood,
but the mouth of the upright delivers
them.
7 The wicked are overthrown and are no
more,
but the house of the righteous will
stand.
8 A man is commended according to his
good sense,
but one of twisted mind is despised.
9 Better to be lowly and have a servant
than to play the great man and lack
bread.
10 Whoever is righteous has regard for the life
of his beast,
but the mercy of the wicked is cruel.
11 Whoever works his land will have plenty of
bread,
but he who follows worthless pursuits
lacks sense.
12 Whoever is wicked covets the spoil of evildoers,
but the root of the righteous bears fruit.
13 An evil man is ensnared by the transgression of his lips,[1]
but the righteous escapes from trouble.
14 From the fruit of his mouth a man is satisfied with good,
and the work of a man's hand comes
back to him.
15 The way of a fool is right in his own eyes,
but a wise man listens to advice.
16 The vexation of a fool is known at once,
but the prudent ignores an insult.
17 Whoever speaks[2] the truth gives honest
evidence,
but a false witness utters deceit.
18 There is one whose rash words are like
sword thrusts,
but the tongue of the wise brings healing.
19 Truthful lips endure forever,
but a lying tongue is but for a moment.
20 Deceit is in the heart of those who devise
evil,
but those who plan peace have joy.
21 No ill befalls the righteous,
but the wicked are filled with trouble.
22 Lying lips are an abomination to the LORD,
but those who act faithfully are his
delight.

23 A prudent man conceals knowledge,
but the heart of fools proclaims folly.
24 The hand of the diligent will rule,
while the slothful will be put to forced
labor.
25 Anxiety in a man's heart weighs him down,
but a good word makes him glad.
26 One who is righteous is a guide to his
neighbor,[3]
but the way of the wicked leads them
astray.
27 Whoever is slothful will not roast his game,
but the diligent man will get precious
wealth.[4]
28 In the path of righteousness is life,
and in its pathway there is no death.

13 A wise son hears his father's
instruction,
but a scoffer does not listen to
rebuke.
2 From the fruit of his mouth a man eats
what is good,
but the desire of the treacherous is for
violence.
3 Whoever guards his mouth preserves his
life;
he who opens wide his lips comes to
ruin.
4 The soul of the sluggard craves and gets
nothing,
while the soul of the diligent is richly
supplied.
5 The righteous hates falsehood,
but the wicked brings shame[5] and disgrace.
6 Righteousness guards him whose way is
blameless,
but sin overthrows the wicked.
7 One pretends to be rich,[6] yet has nothing;
another pretends to be poor,[7] yet has
great wealth.
8 The ransom of a man's life is his wealth,
but a poor man hears no threat.
9 The light of the righteous rejoices,
but the lamp of the wicked will be put
out.
10 By insolence comes nothing but strife,
but with those who take advice is wisdom.
11 Wealth gained hastily[8] will dwindle,
but whoever gathers little by little will
increase it.

---

[1] Or In the transgression of the lips, there is an evil snare [2] Hebrew breathes out [3] Or The righteous chooses his friends carefully [4] Or but diligence is precious wealth [5] Or stench [6] Or One makes himself rich [7] Or another makes himself poor [8] Or by fraud

12 Hope deferred makes the heart sick,
    but a desire fulfilled is a tree of life.
13 Whoever despises the word[1] brings
    destruction on himself,
    but he who reveres the command-
    ment[2] will be rewarded.
14 The teaching of the wise is a fountain of
    life,
    that one may turn away from the
    snares of death.
15 Good sense wins favor,
    but the way of the treacherous is their
    ruin.[3]
16 Every prudent man acts with knowledge,
    but a fool flaunts his folly.
17 A wicked messenger falls into trouble,
    but a faithful envoy brings healing.
18 Poverty and disgrace come to him who
    ignores instruction,
    but whoever heeds reproof is honored.
19 A desire fulfilled is sweet to the soul,
    but to turn away from evil is an abomi-
    nation to fools.
20 Whoever walks with the wise becomes
    wise,
    but the companion of fools will suffer
    harm.
21 Disaster[4] pursues sinners,
    but the righteous are rewarded with
    good.
22 A good man leaves an inheritance to his
    children's children,
    but the sinner's wealth is laid up for
    the righteous.
23 The fallow ground of the poor would
    yield much food,
    but it is swept away through injustice.
24 Whoever spares the rod hates his son,
    but he who loves him is diligent to
    discipline him.[5]
25 The righteous has enough to satisfy his
    appetite,
    but the belly of the wicked suffers want.

14 The wisest of women builds her
    house,
    but folly with her own hands tears it
    down.
2 Whoever walks in uprightness fears the
    LORD,
    but he who is devious in his ways
    despises him.

3 By the mouth of a fool comes a rod for his
    back,[6]
    but the lips of the wise will preserve
    them.
4 Where there are no oxen, the manger is
    clean,
    but abundant crops come by the
    strength of the ox.
5 A faithful witness does not lie,
    but a false witness breathes out lies.
6 A scoffer seeks wisdom in vain,
    but knowledge is easy for a man of
    understanding.
7 Leave the presence of a fool,
    for there you do not meet words of
    knowledge.
8 The wisdom of the prudent is to discern
    his way,
    but the folly of fools is deceiving.
9 Fools mock at the guilt offering,
    but the upright enjoy acceptance.[7]
10 The heart knows its own bitterness,
    and no stranger shares its joy.
11 The house of the wicked will be destroyed,
    but the tent of the upright will flourish.
12 There is a way that seems right to a man,
    but its end is the way to death.[8]
13 Even in laughter the heart may ache,
    and the end of joy may be grief.
14 The backslider in heart will be filled with
    the fruit of his ways,
    and a good man will be filled with the
    fruit of his ways.
15 The simple believes everything,
    but the prudent gives thought to his
    steps.
16 One who is wise is cautious[9] and turns
    away from evil,
    but a fool is reckless and careless.
17 A man of quick temper acts foolishly,
    and a man of evil devices is hated.
18 The simple inherit folly,
    but the prudent are crowned with
    knowledge.
19 The evil bow down before the good,
    the wicked at the gates of the righteous.
20 The poor is disliked even by his neighbor,
    but the rich has many friends.
21 Whoever despises his neighbor is a sinner,
    but blessed is he who is generous to the
    poor.

---

[1] Or a word [2] Or a commandment [3] Probable reading (compare Septuagint, Syriac, Vulgate); Hebrew is rugged, or is an enduring rut [4] Or Evil [5] Or who loves him disciplines him early [6] Or In the mouth of a fool is a rod of pride [7] Hebrew but among the upright is acceptance [8] Hebrew ways of death [9] Or fears [the LORD]

22 Do they not go astray who devise evil?
　　Those who devise good meet[1] steadfast
　　love and faithfulness.

23 In all toil there is profit,
　　but mere talk tends only to poverty.

24 The crown of the wise is their wealth,
　　but the folly of fools brings folly.

25 A truthful witness saves lives,
　　but one who breathes out lies is deceitful.

26 In the fear of the LORD one has strong con-
　　fidence,
　　and his children will have a refuge.

27 The fear of the LORD is a fountain of life,
　　that one may turn away from the snares
　　of death.

28 In a multitude of people is the glory of a
　　king,
　　but without people a prince is ruined.

29 Whoever is slow to anger has great under-
　　standing,
　　but he who has a hasty temper exalts
　　folly.

30 A tranquil[2] heart gives life to the flesh,
　　but envy[3] makes the bones rot.

31 Whoever oppresses a poor man insults his
　　Maker,
　　but he who is generous to the needy
　　honors him.

32 The wicked is overthrown through his evil-
　　doing,
　　but the righteous finds refuge in his
　　death.

33 Wisdom rests in the heart of a man of
　　understanding,
　　but it makes itself known even in the
　　midst of fools.[4]

34 Righteousness exalts a nation,
　　but sin is a reproach to any people.

35 A servant who deals wisely has the king's
　　favor,
　　but his wrath falls on one who acts
　　shamefully.

15 A soft answer turns away wrath,
　　but a harsh word stirs up anger.

2 The tongue of the wise commends knowl-
　　edge,
　　but the mouths of fools pour out folly.

3 The eyes of the LORD are in every place,
　　keeping watch on the evil and the good.

4 A gentle[5] tongue is a tree of life,
　　but perverseness in it breaks the spirit.

5 A fool despises his father's instruction,
　　but whoever heeds reproof is prudent.

6 In the house of the righteous there is much
　　treasure,
　　but trouble befalls the income of the
　　wicked.

7 The lips of the wise spread knowledge;
　　not so the hearts of fools.[6]

8 The sacrifice of the wicked is an abomina-
　　tion to the LORD,
　　but the prayer of the upright is accept-
　　able to him.

9 The way of the wicked is an abomination
　　to the LORD,
　　but he loves him who pursues righ-
　　teousness.

10 There is severe discipline for him who for-
　　sakes the way;
　　whoever hates reproof will die.

11 Sheol and Abaddon lie open before the
　　LORD;
　　how much more the hearts of the chil-
　　dren of man!

12 A scoffer does not like to be reproved;
　　he will not go to the wise.

13 A glad heart makes a cheerful face,
　　but by sorrow of heart the spirit is
　　crushed.

14 The heart of him who has understanding
　　seeks knowledge,
　　but the mouths of fools feed on folly.

15 All the days of the afflicted are evil,
　　but the cheerful of heart has a continual
　　feast.

16 Better is a little with the fear of the LORD
　　than great treasure and trouble with it.

17 Better is a dinner of herbs where love is
　　than a fattened ox and hatred with it.

18 A hot-tempered man stirs up strife,
　　but he who is slow to anger quiets con-
　　tention.

19 The way of a sluggard is like a hedge of
　　thorns,
　　but the path of the upright is a level
　　highway.

20 A wise son makes a glad father,
　　but a foolish man despises his mother.

21 Folly is a joy to him who lacks sense,
　　but a man of understanding walks
　　straight ahead.

22 Without counsel plans fail,
　　but with many advisers they succeed.

23 To make an apt answer is a joy to a man,
　　and a word in season, how good it is!

---

[1] Or show [2] Or healing [3] Or jealousy [4] Or Wisdom rests quietly in the heart of a man of understanding, but makes itself known in the midst of fools [5] Or healing [6] Or the hearts of fools are not steadfast

24 The path of life leads upward for the prudent,
    that he may turn away from Sheol beneath.

25 The LORD tears down the house of the proud
    but maintains the widow's boundaries.

26 The thoughts of the wicked are an abomination to the LORD,
    but gracious words are pure.

27 Whoever is greedy for unjust gain troubles his own household,
    but he who hates bribes will live.

28 The heart of the righteous ponders how to answer,
    but the mouth of the wicked pours out evil things.

29 The LORD is far from the wicked,
    but he hears the prayer of the righteous.

30 The light of the eyes rejoices the heart,
    and good news refreshes[1] the bones.

31 The ear that listens to life-giving reproof will dwell among the wise.

32 Whoever ignores instruction despises himself,
    but he who listens to reproof gains intelligence.

33 The fear of the LORD is instruction in wisdom,
    and humility comes before honor.

16

The plans of the heart belong to man,
    but the answer of the tongue is from the LORD.

2 All the ways of a man are pure in his own eyes,
    but the LORD weighs the spirit.[2]

3 Commit your work to the LORD,
    and your plans will be established.

4 The LORD has made everything for its purpose,
    even the wicked for the day of trouble.

5 Everyone who is arrogant in heart is an abomination to the LORD;
    be assured, he will not go unpunished.

6 By steadfast love and faithfulness iniquity is atoned for,
    and by the fear of the LORD one turns away from evil.

7 When a man's ways please the LORD,
    he makes even his enemies to be at peace with him.

8 Better is a little with righteousness
    than great revenues with injustice.

9 The heart of man plans his way,
    but the LORD establishes his steps.

10 An oracle is on the lips of a king;
    his mouth does not sin in judgment.

11 A just balance and scales are the LORD's;
    all the weights in the bag are his work.

12 It is an abomination to kings to do evil,
    for the throne is established by righteousness.

13 Righteous lips are the delight of a king,
    and he loves him who speaks what is right.

14 A king's wrath is a messenger of death,
    and a wise man will appease it.

15 In the light of a king's face there is life,
    and his favor is like the clouds that bring the spring rain.

16 How much better to get wisdom than gold!
    To get understanding is to be chosen rather than silver.

17 The highway of the upright turns aside from evil;
    whoever guards his way preserves his life.

18 Pride goes before destruction,
    and a haughty spirit before a fall.

19 It is better to be of a lowly spirit with the poor
    than to divide the spoil with the proud.

20 Whoever gives thought to the word[3] will discover good,
    and blessed is he who trusts in the LORD.

21 The wise of heart is called discerning,
    and sweetness of speech increases persuasiveness.

22 Good sense is a fountain of life to him who has it,
    but the instruction of fools is folly.

23 The heart of the wise makes his speech judicious
    and adds persuasiveness to his lips.

24 Gracious words are like a honeycomb,
    sweetness to the soul and health to the body.

25 There is a way that seems right to a man,
    but its end is the way to death.[4]

26 A worker's appetite works for him;
    his mouth urges him on.

---

[1] Hebrew *makes fat* [2] Or *spirits* [3] Or *to a matter* [4] Hebrew *ways of death*

27 A worthless man plots evil,
  and his speech[1] is like a scorching fire.
28 A dishonest man spreads strife,
  and a whisperer separates close friends.
29 A man of violence entices his neighbor
  and leads him in a way that is not good.
30 Whoever winks his eyes plans[2] dishonest
  things;
  he who purses his lips brings evil to
  pass.
31 Gray hair is a crown of glory;
  it is gained in a righteous life.
32 Whoever is slow to anger is better than the
  mighty,
  and he who rules his spirit than he who
  takes a city.
33 The lot is cast into the lap,
  but its every decision is from the LORD.

17 Better is a dry morsel with quiet
  than a house full of feasting[3] with
  strife.
2 A servant who deals wisely will rule over a
  son who acts shamefully
  and will share the inheritance as one of
  the brothers.
3 The crucible is for silver, and the furnace is
  for gold,
  and the LORD tests hearts.
4 An evildoer listens to wicked lips,
  and a liar gives ear to a mischievous
  tongue.
5 Whoever mocks the poor insults his Maker;
  he who is glad at calamity will not go
  unpunished.
6 Grandchildren are the crown of the aged,
  and the glory of children is their fathers.
7 Fine speech is not becoming to a fool;
  still less is false speech to a prince.
8 A bribe is like a magic[4] stone in the eyes
  of the one who gives it;
  wherever he turns he prospers.
9 Whoever covers an offense seeks love,
  but he who repeats a matter separates
  close friends.
10 A rebuke goes deeper into a man of understanding
  than a hundred blows into a fool.
11 An evil man seeks only rebellion,
  and a cruel messenger will be sent
  against him.
12 Let a man meet a she-bear robbed of her
  cubs
  rather than a fool in his folly.

13 If anyone returns evil for good,
  evil will not depart from his house.
14 The beginning of strife is like letting out
  water,
  so quit before the quarrel breaks out.
15 He who justifies the wicked and he who
  condemns the righteous
  are both alike an abomination to the
  LORD.
16 Why should a fool have money in his hand
  to buy wisdom
  when he has no sense?
17 A friend loves at all times,
  and a brother is born for adversity.
18 One who lacks sense gives a pledge
  and puts up security in the presence of
  his neighbor.
19 Whoever loves transgression loves strife;
  he who makes his door high seeks
  destruction.
20 A man of crooked heart does not discover
  good,
  and one with a dishonest tongue falls
  into calamity.
21 He who sires a fool gets himself sorrow,
  and the father of a fool has no joy.
22 A joyful heart is good medicine,
  but a crushed spirit dries up the bones.
23 The wicked accepts a bribe in secret[5]
  to pervert the ways of justice.
24 The discerning sets his face toward wisdom,
  but the eyes of a fool are on the ends of
  the earth.
25 A foolish son is a grief to his father
  and bitterness to her who bore him.
26 To impose a fine on a righteous man is not
  good,
  nor to strike the noble for their uprightness.
27 Whoever restrains his words has knowledge,
  and he who has a cool spirit is a man of
  understanding.
28 Even a fool who keeps silent is considered
  wise;
  when he closes his lips, he is deemed
  intelligent.

18 Whoever isolates himself seeks his
  own desire;
  he breaks out against all sound judgment.

---

[1] Hebrew *what is on his lips* [2] Hebrew *to plan* [3] Hebrew *sacrifices* [4] Or *precious* [5] Hebrew *a bribe from the bosom*

2 A fool takes no pleasure in understanding,
  but only in expressing his opinion.

3 When wickedness comes, contempt comes
    also,
  and with dishonor comes disgrace.

4 The words of a man's mouth are deep
    waters;
  the fountain of wisdom is a bubbling
    brook.

5 It is not good to be partial to[1] the wicked
  or to deprive the righteous of justice.

6 A fool's lips walk into a fight,
  and his mouth invites a beating.

7 A fool's mouth is his ruin,
  and his lips are a snare to his soul.

8 The words of a whisperer are like delicious
    morsels;
  they go down into the inner parts of
    the body.

9 Whoever is slack in his work
  is a brother to him who destroys.

10 The name of the LORD is a strong tower;
  the righteous man runs into it and is
    safe.

11 A rich man's wealth is his strong city,
  and like a high wall in his imagination.

12 Before destruction a man's heart is
    haughty,
  but humility comes before honor.

13 If one gives an answer before he hears,
  it is his folly and shame.

14 A man's spirit will endure sickness,
  but a crushed spirit who can bear?

15 An intelligent heart acquires knowledge,
  and the ear of the wise seeks knowl-
    edge.

16 A man's gift makes room for him
  and brings him before the great.

17 The one who states his case first seems
    right,
  until the other comes and examines
    him.

18 The lot puts an end to quarrels
  and decides between powerful contend-
    ers.

19 A brother offended is more unyielding
    than a strong city,
  and quarreling is like the bars of a
    castle.

20 From the fruit of a man's mouth his stom-
    ach is satisfied;
  he is satisfied by the yield of his lips.

21 Death and life are in the power of the
    tongue,
  and those who love it will eat its fruits.

22 He who finds a wife finds a good thing
  and obtains favor from the LORD.

23 The poor use entreaties,
  but the rich answer roughly.

24 A man of many companions may come to
    ruin,
  but there is a friend who sticks closer
    than a brother.

19 Better is a poor person who walks in
    his integrity
  than one who is crooked in speech and
    is a fool.

2 Desire[2] without knowledge is not good,
  and whoever makes haste with his feet
    misses his way.

3 When a man's folly brings his way to
    ruin,
  his heart rages against the LORD.

4 Wealth brings many new friends,
  but a poor man is deserted by his friend.

5 A false witness will not go unpunished,
  and he who breathes out lies will not
    escape.

6 Many seek the favor of a generous man,[3]
  and everyone is a friend to a man who
    gives gifts.

7 All a poor man's brothers hate him;
  how much more do his friends go far
    from him!
He pursues them with words, but does not
    have them.[4]

8 Whoever gets sense loves his own soul;
  he who keeps understanding will dis-
    cover good.

9 A false witness will not go unpunished,
  and he who breathes out lies will perish.

10 It is not fitting for a fool to live in luxury,
  much less for a slave to rule over princes.

11 Good sense makes one slow to anger,
  and it is his glory to overlook an offense.

12 A king's wrath is like the growling of a
    lion,
  but his favor is like dew on the grass.

13 A foolish son is ruin to his father,
  and a wife's quarreling is a continual
    dripping of rain.

14 House and wealth are inherited from
    fathers,
  but a prudent wife is from the LORD.

[1] Hebrew to lift the face of [2] Or A soul [3] Or of a noble [4] The meaning of the Hebrew sentence is uncertain

15 Slothfulness casts into a deep sleep,
   and an idle person will suffer hunger.
16 Whoever keeps the commandment keeps
   his life;
   he who despises his ways will die.
17 Whoever is generous to the poor lends to
   the LORD,
   and he will repay him for his deed.
18 Discipline your son, for there is hope;
   do not set your heart on putting him to
   death.
19 A man of great wrath will pay the penalty,
   for if you deliver him, you will only
   have to do it again.
20 Listen to advice and accept instruction,
   that you may gain wisdom in the
   future.
21 Many are the plans in the mind of a man,
   but it is the purpose of the LORD that
   will stand.
22 What is desired in a man is steadfast love,
   and a poor man is better than a liar.
23 The fear of the LORD leads to life,
   and whoever has it rests satisfied;
   he will not be visited by harm.
24 The sluggard buries his hand in the dish
   and will not even bring it back to his
   mouth.
25 Strike a scoffer, and the simple will learn
   prudence;
   reprove a man of understanding, and
   he will gain knowledge.
26 He who does violence to his father and
   chases away his mother
   is a son who brings shame and
   reproach.
27 Cease to hear instruction, my son,
   and you will stray from the words of
   knowledge.
28 A worthless witness mocks at justice,
   and the mouth of the wicked devours
   iniquity.
29 Condemnation is ready for scoffers,
   and beating for the backs of fools.

20 Wine is a mocker, strong drink a
   brawler,
   and whoever is led astray by it is not
   wise.[1]
2 The terror of a king is like the growling of
   a lion;
   whoever provokes him to anger forfeits
   his life.

3 It is an honor for a man to keep aloof from
   strife,
   but every fool will be quarreling.
4 The sluggard does not plow in the
   autumn;
   he will seek at harvest and have nothing.
5 The purpose in a man's heart is like deep
   water,
   but a man of understanding will draw
   it out.
6 Many a man proclaims his own steadfast
   love,
   but a faithful man who can find?
7 The righteous who walks in his integrity—
   blessed are his children after him!
8 A king who sits on the throne of judgment
   winnows all evil with his eyes.
9 Who can say, "I have made my heart pure;
   I am clean from my sin"?
10 Unequal[2] weights and unequal measures
   are both alike an abomination to the
   LORD.
11 Even a child makes himself known by his
   acts,
   by whether his conduct is pure and
   upright.[3]
12 The hearing ear and the seeing eye,
   the LORD has made them both.
13 Love not sleep, lest you come to poverty;
   open your eyes, and you will have
   plenty of bread.
14 "Bad, bad," says the buyer,
   but when he goes away, then he boasts.
15 There is gold and abundance of costly
   stones,
   but the lips of knowledge are a precious
   jewel.
16 Take a man's garment when he has put up
   security for a stranger,
   and hold it in pledge when he puts up
   security for foreigners.[4]
17 Bread gained by deceit is sweet to a man,
   but afterward his mouth will be full of
   gravel.
18 Plans are established by counsel;
   by wise guidance wage war.
19 Whoever goes about slandering reveals
   secrets;
   therefore do not associate with a simple
   babbler.[5]

[1] Or will not become wise [2] Or Two kinds of; also verse 23 [3] Or Even a child can dissemble in his actions, though his conduct seems pure and upright [4] Or for an adulteress (compare 27:13) [5] Hebrew with one who is simple in his lips

20 If one curses his father or his mother,
  his lamp will be put out in utter dark-
    ness.
21 An inheritance gained hastily in the begin-
    ning
  will not be blessed in the end.
22 Do not say, "I will repay evil";
  wait for the LORD, and he will deliver
    you.
23 Unequal weights are an abomination to
    the LORD,
  and false scales are not good.
24 A man's steps are from the LORD;
  how then can man understand his way?
25 It is a snare to say rashly, "It is holy,"
  and to reflect only after making vows.
26 A wise king winnows the wicked
  and drives the wheel over them.
27 The spirit[1] of man is the lamp of the
    LORD,
  searching all his innermost parts.
28 Steadfast love and faithfulness preserve
    the king,
  and by steadfast love his throne is
    upheld.
29 The glory of young men is their strength,
  but the splendor of old men is their
    gray hair.
30 Blows that wound cleanse away evil;
  strokes make clean the innermost parts.

21 The king's heart is a stream of water in
    the hand of the LORD;
  he turns it wherever he will.
2 Every way of a man is right in his own
    eyes,
  but the LORD weighs the heart.
3 To do righteousness and justice
  is more acceptable to the LORD than
    sacrifice.
4 Haughty eyes and a proud heart,
  the lamp[2] of the wicked, are sin.
5 The plans of the diligent lead surely to
    abundance,
  but everyone who is hasty comes only
    to poverty.
6 The getting of treasures by a lying
    tongue
  is a fleeting vapor and a snare of
    death.[3]
7 The violence of the wicked will sweep
    them away,
  because they refuse to do what is just.

8 The way of the guilty is crooked,
  but the conduct of the pure is upright.
9 It is better to live in a corner of the house-
    top
  than in a house shared with a quarrel-
    some wife.
10 The soul of the wicked desires evil;
  his neighbor finds no mercy in his eyes.
11 When a scoffer is punished, the simple
    becomes wise;
  when a wise man is instructed, he gains
    knowledge.
12 The Righteous One observes the house of
    the wicked;
  he throws the wicked down to ruin.
13 Whoever closes his ear to the cry of the
    poor
  will himself call out and not be
    answered.
14 A gift in secret averts anger,
  and a concealed bribe,[4] strong wrath.
15 When justice is done, it is a joy to the righ-
    teous
  but terror to evildoers.
16 One who wanders from the way of good
    sense
  will rest in the assembly of the dead.
17 Whoever loves pleasure will be a poor man;
  he who loves wine and oil will not be
    rich.
18 The wicked is a ransom for the righteous,
  and the traitor for the upright.
19 It is better to live in a desert land
  than with a quarrelsome and fretful
    woman.
20 Precious treasure and oil are in a wise
    man's dwelling,
  but a foolish man devours it.
21 Whoever pursues righteousness and kind-
    ness
  will find life, righteousness, and honor.
22 A wise man scales the city of the mighty
  and brings down the stronghold in
    which they trust.
23 Whoever keeps his mouth and his tongue
  keeps himself out of trouble.
24 "Scoffer" is the name of the arrogant,
    haughty man
  who acts with arrogant pride.
25 The desire of the sluggard kills him,
  for his hands refuse to labor.

[1] Hebrew breath [2] Or the plowing [3] Some Hebrew manuscripts, Septuagint, Latin; most Hebrew manuscripts vapor for those who seek death [4] Hebrew a bribe in the bosom

26 All day long he craves and craves,
　　but the righteous gives and does not
　　　hold back.
27 The sacrifice of the wicked is an abomina-
　　tion;
　　how much more when he brings it with
　　　evil intent.
28 A false witness will perish,
　　but the word of a man who hears will
　　　endure.
29 A wicked man puts on a bold face,
　　but the upright gives thought to[1] his
　　　ways.
30 No wisdom, no understanding, no counsel
　　can avail against the LORD.
31 The horse is made ready for the day of
　　battle,
　　but the victory belongs to the LORD.

22 A good name is to be chosen rather
　　than great riches,
　　and favor is better than silver or gold.
2 The rich and the poor meet together;
　　the LORD is the Maker of them all.
3 The prudent sees danger and hides him-
　　self,
　　but the simple go on and suffer for it.
4 The reward for humility and fear of the
　　LORD
　　is riches and honor and life.[2]
5 Thorns and snares are in the way of the
　　crooked;
　　whoever guards his soul will keep far
　　　from them.
6 Train up a child in the way he should go;
　　even when he is old he will not depart
　　　from it.
7 The rich rules over the poor,
　　and the borrower is the slave of the
　　　lender.
8 Whoever sows injustice will reap calamity,
　　and the rod of his fury will fail.
9 Whoever has a bountiful[3] eye will be
　　blessed,
　　for he shares his bread with the poor.
10 Drive out a scoffer, and strife will go out,
　　and quarreling and abuse will cease.
11 He who loves purity of heart,
　　and whose speech is gracious, will have
　　　the king as his friend.
12 The eyes of the LORD keep watch over
　　knowledge,
　　but he overthrows the words of the trai-
　　　tor.

13 The sluggard says, "There is a lion outside!
　　I shall be killed in the streets!"
14 The mouth of forbidden[4] women is a deep
　　pit;
　　he with whom the LORD is angry will
　　　fall into it.
15 Folly is bound up in the heart of a child,
　　but the rod of discipline drives it far
　　　from him.
16 Whoever oppresses the poor to increase his
　　own wealth,
　　or gives to the rich, will only come to
　　　poverty.

Words of the Wise

17 Incline your ear, and hear the words of the
　　wise,
　　and apply your heart to my knowledge,
18 for it will be pleasant if you keep them
　　within you,
　　if all of them are ready on your lips.
19 That your trust may be in the LORD,
　　I have made them known to you today,
　　　even to you.
20 Have I not written for you thirty sayings
　　of counsel and knowledge,
21 to make you know what is right and true,
　　that you may give a true answer to those
　　　who sent you?

22 Do not rob the poor, because he is poor,
　　or crush the afflicted at the gate,
23 for the LORD will plead their cause
　　and rob of life those who rob them.
24 Make no friendship with a man given to
　　anger,
　　nor go with a wrathful man,
25 lest you learn his ways
　　and entangle yourself in a snare.
26 Be not one of those who give pledges,
　　who put up security for debts.
27 If you have nothing with which to pay,
　　why should your bed be taken from
　　　under you?
28 Do not move the ancient landmark
　　that your fathers have set.
29 Do you see a man skillful in his work?
　　He will stand before kings;
　　he will not stand before obscure men.

23 When you sit down to eat with a ruler,
　　observe carefully what[5] is before you,
2 and put a knife to your throat
　　if you are given to appetite.

---

[1] Or establishes [2] Or The reward for humility is the fear of the LORD, riches and honor and life [3] Hebrew good [4] Hebrew strange [5] Or who

3 Do not desire his delicacies,
  for they are deceptive food.
4 Do not toil to acquire wealth;
  be discerning enough to desist.
5 When your eyes light on it, it is gone,
  for suddenly it sprouts wings,
  flying like an eagle toward heaven.
6 Do not eat the bread of a man who is stingy;[1]
  do not desire his delicacies,
7 for he is like one who is inwardly calculating.[2]
  "Eat and drink!" he says to you,
  but his heart is not with you.
8 You will vomit up the morsels that you
  have eaten,
  and waste your pleasant words.
9 Do not speak in the hearing of a fool,
  for he will despise the good sense of
  your words.
10 Do not move an ancient landmark
   or enter the fields of the fatherless,
11 for their Redeemer is strong;
   he will plead their cause against you.
12 Apply your heart to instruction
   and your ear to words of knowledge.
13 Do not withhold discipline from a child;
   if you strike him with a rod, he will not
   die.
14 If you strike him with the rod,
   you will save his soul from Sheol.
15 My son, if your heart is wise,
   my heart too will be glad.
16 My inmost being[3] will exult
   when your lips speak what is right.
17 Let not your heart envy sinners,
   but continue in the fear of the LORD all
   the day.
18 Surely there is a future,
   and your hope will not be cut off.

19 Hear, my son, and be wise,
   and direct your heart in the way.
20 Be not among drunkards[4]
   or among gluttonous eaters of meat,
21 for the drunkard and the glutton will
   come to poverty,
   and slumber will clothe them with rags.

22 Listen to your father who gave you life,
   and do not despise your mother when
   she is old.
23 Buy truth, and do not sell it;
   buy wisdom, instruction, and understanding.

24 The father of the righteous will greatly
   rejoice;
   he who fathers a wise son will be glad in
   him.
25 Let your father and mother be glad;
   let her who bore you rejoice.

26 My son, give me your heart,
   and let your eyes observe[5] my ways.
27 For a prostitute is a deep pit;
   an adulteress[6] is a narrow well.
28 She lies in wait like a robber
   and increases the traitors among mankind.

29 Who has woe? Who has sorrow?
   Who has strife? Who has complaining?
   Who has wounds without cause?
   Who has redness of eyes?
30 Those who tarry long over wine;
   those who go to try mixed wine.
31 Do not look at wine when it is red,
   when it sparkles in the cup
   and goes down smoothly.
32 In the end it bites like a serpent
   and stings like an adder.
33 Your eyes will see strange things,
   and your heart utter perverse things.
34 You will be like one who lies down in the
   midst of the sea,
   like one who lies on the top of a mast.[7]
35 "They struck me," you will say,[8] "but I was
   not hurt;
   they beat me, but I did not feel it.
   When shall I awake?
   I must have another drink."

24 Be not envious of evil men,
   nor desire to be with them,
2 for their hearts devise violence,
  and their lips talk of trouble.

3 By wisdom a house is built,
  and by understanding it is established;
4 by knowledge the rooms are filled
  with all precious and pleasant riches.
5 A wise man is full of strength,
  and a man of knowledge enhances his
  might,
6 for by wise guidance you can wage your
  war,
  and in abundance of counselors there is
  victory.

[1] Hebrew whose eye is evil [2] Or for as he calculates in his soul, so is he [3] Hebrew My kidneys [4] Hebrew those who drink too much wine [5] Or delight in [6] Hebrew a foreign woman [7] Or of the rigging [8] Hebrew lacks you will say

7 Wisdom is too high for a fool;
    in the gate he does not open his mouth.

8 Whoever plans to do evil
    will be called a schemer.
9 The devising[1] of folly is sin,
    and the scoffer is an abomination to
      mankind.

10 If you faint in the day of adversity,
    your strength is small.
11 Rescue those who are being taken away to
      death;
    hold back those who are stumbling to
      the slaughter.
12 If you say, "Behold, we did not know this,"
    does not he who weighs the heart per-
      ceive it?
    Does not he who keeps watch over your
      soul know it,
    and will he not repay man according to
      his work?

13 My son, eat honey, for it is good,
    and the drippings of the honeycomb
      are sweet to your taste.
14 Know that wisdom is such to your soul;
    if you find it, there will be a future,
    and your hope will not be cut off.

15 Lie not in wait as a wicked man against the
      dwelling of the righteous;
    do no violence to his home;
16 for the righteous falls seven times and rises
      again,
    but the wicked stumble in times of
      calamity.

17 Do not rejoice when your enemy falls,
    and let not your heart be glad when he
      stumbles,
18 lest the LORD see it and be displeased,
    and turn away his anger from him.

19 Fret not yourself because of evildoers,
    and be not envious of the wicked,
20 for the evil man has no future;
    the lamp of the wicked will be put out.

21 My son, fear the LORD and the king,
    and do not join with those who do oth-
      erwise,
22 for disaster will arise suddenly from them,
    and who knows the ruin that will come
      from them both?

More Sayings of the Wise

23 These also are sayings of the wise.

    Partiality in judging is not good.
24 Whoever says to the wicked, "You are in
      the right,"
    will be cursed by peoples, abhorred by
      nations,
25 but those who rebuke the wicked will have
      delight,
    and a good blessing will come upon
      them.
26 Whoever gives an honest answer
    kisses the lips.

27 Prepare your work outside;
    get everything ready for yourself in the
      field,
    and after that build your house.

28 Be not a witness against your neighbor
      without cause,
    and do not deceive with your lips.
29 Do not say, "I will do to him as he has done
      to me;
    I will pay the man back for what he has
      done."

30 I passed by the field of a sluggard,
    by the vineyard of a man lacking sense,
31 and behold, it was all overgrown with
      thorns;
    the ground was covered with nettles,
    and its stone wall was broken down.
32 Then I saw and considered it;
    I looked and received instruction.
33 A little sleep, a little slumber,
    a little folding of the hands to rest,
34 and poverty will come upon you like a rob-
      ber,
    and want like an armed man.

More Proverbs of Solomon

25 These also are proverbs of Solomon
which the men of Hezekiah king of
Judah copied.

2 It is the glory of God to conceal things,
    but the glory of kings is to search things
      out.
3 As the heavens for height, and the earth for
      depth,
    so the heart of kings is unsearchable.
4 Take away the dross from the silver,
    and the smith has material for a vessel;

---

[1] Or scheming

5 take away the wicked from the presence
of the king,
and his throne will be established in
righteousness.
6 Do not put yourself forward in the king's
presence
or stand in the place of the great,
7 for it is better to be told, "Come up here,"
than to be put lower in the presence of a
noble.

What your eyes have seen
8 do not hastily bring into court,[1]
for[2] what will you do in the end,
when your neighbor puts you to
shame?
9 Argue your case with your neighbor himself,
and do not reveal another's secret,
10 lest he who hears you bring shame upon
you,
and your ill repute have no end.

11 A word fitly spoken
is like apples of gold in a setting of silver.
12 Like a gold ring or an ornament of gold
is a wise reprover to a listening ear.
13 Like the cold of snow in the time of harvest
is a faithful messenger to those who
send him;
he refreshes the soul of his masters.
14 Like clouds and wind without rain
is a man who boasts of a gift he does
not give.

15 With patience a ruler may be persuaded,
and a soft tongue will break a bone.
16 If you have found honey, eat only enough
for you,
lest you have your fill of it and vomit
it.
17 Let your foot be seldom in your neighbor's house,
lest he have his fill of you and hate
you.
18 A man who bears false witness against his
neighbor
is like a war club, or a sword, or a sharp
arrow.
19 Trusting in a treacherous man in time of
trouble
is like a bad tooth or a foot that slips.

20 Whoever sings songs to a heavy heart
is like one who takes off a garment on a
cold day,
and like vinegar on soda.
21 If your enemy is hungry, give him bread
to eat,
and if he is thirsty, give him water to
drink,
22 for you will heap burning coals on his
head,
and the LORD will reward you.
23 The north wind brings forth rain,
and a backbiting tongue, angry looks.
24 It is better to live in a corner of the housetop
than in a house shared with a quarrelsome wife.
25 Like cold water to a thirsty soul,
so is good news from a far country.
26 Like a muddied spring or a polluted fountain
is a righteous man who gives way
before the wicked.
27 It is not good to eat much honey,
nor is it glorious to seek one's own
glory.[3]
28 A man without self-control
is like a city broken into and left without walls.

26 Like snow in summer or rain in
harvest,
so honor is not fitting for a fool.
2 Like a sparrow in its flitting, like a swallow
in its flying,
a curse that is causeless does not alight.
3 A whip for the horse, a bridle for the donkey,
and a rod for the back of fools.
4 Answer not a fool according to his folly,
lest you be like him yourself.
5 Answer a fool according to his folly,
lest he be wise in his own eyes.
6 Whoever sends a message by the hand of a
fool
cuts off his own feet and drinks violence.
7 Like a lame man's legs, which hang useless,
is a proverb in the mouth of fools.
8 Like one who binds the stone in the sling
is one who gives honor to a fool.
9 Like a thorn that goes up into the hand of
a drunkard
is a proverb in the mouth of fools.

---

[1] Or presence of a noble, as your eyes have seen. [8] Do not go hastily out to court [2] Hebrew or else [3] The meaning of the Hebrew line is uncertain

10 Like an archer who wounds everyone
    is one who hires a passing fool or
        drunkard.[1]

11 Like a dog that returns to his vomit
    is a fool who repeats his folly.

12 Do you see a man who is wise in his own
        eyes?
    There is more hope for a fool than for
        him.

13 The sluggard says, "There is a lion in the
        road!
    There is a lion in the streets!"

14 As a door turns on its hinges,
    so does a sluggard on his bed.

15 The sluggard buries his hand in the dish;
    it wears him out to bring it back to his
        mouth.

16 The sluggard is wiser in his own eyes
        than seven men who can answer sensi-
        bly.

17 Whoever meddles in a quarrel not his own
    is like one who takes a passing dog by
        the ears.

18 Like a madman who throws firebrands,
        arrows, and death

19 is the man who deceives his neighbor
    and says, "I am only joking!"

20 For lack of wood the fire goes out,
    and where there is no whisperer, quar-
        reling ceases.

21 As charcoal to hot embers and wood to fire,
    so is a quarrelsome man for kindling
        strife.

22 The words of a whisperer are like delicious
        morsels;
    they go down into the inner parts of the
        body.

23 Like the glaze[2] covering an earthen vessel
    are fervent lips with an evil heart.

24 Whoever hates disguises himself with his
        lips
    and harbors deceit in his heart;

25 when he speaks graciously, believe him not,
    for there are seven abominations in his
        heart;

26 though his hatred be covered with decep-
        tion,
    his wickedness will be exposed in the
        assembly.

27 Whoever digs a pit will fall into it,
    and a stone will come back on him who
        starts it rolling.

28 A lying tongue hates its victims,
    and a flattering mouth works ruin.

27 Do not boast about tomorrow,
    for you do not know what a day may
        bring.

2 Let another praise you, and not your own
        mouth;
    a stranger, and not your own lips.

3 A stone is heavy, and sand is weighty,
    but a fool's provocation is heavier than
        both.

4 Wrath is cruel, anger is overwhelming,
    but who can stand before jealousy?

5 Better is open rebuke
    than hidden love.

6 Faithful are the wounds of a friend;
    profuse are the kisses of an enemy.

7 One who is full loathes honey,
    but to one who is hungry everything
        bitter is sweet.

8 Like a bird that strays from its nest
    is a man who strays from his home.

9 Oil and perfume make the heart glad,
    and the sweetness of a friend comes
        from his earnest counsel.[3]

10 Do not forsake your friend and your
        father's friend,
    and do not go to your brother's house in
        the day of your calamity.
    Better is a neighbor who is near
        than a brother who is far away.

11 Be wise, my son, and make my heart glad,
    that I may answer him who reproaches
        me.

12 The prudent sees danger and hides him-
        self,
    but the simple go on and suffer for it.

13 Take a man's garment when he has put up
        security for a stranger,
    and hold it in pledge when he puts up
        security for an adulteress.[4]

14 Whoever blesses his neighbor with a loud
        voice,
    rising early in the morning,
    will be counted as cursing.

15 A continual dripping on a rainy day
    and a quarrelsome wife are alike;

16 to restrain her is to restrain the wind
    or to grasp[5] oil in one's right hand.

17 Iron sharpens iron,
    and one man sharpens another.[6]

[1] Or hires a fool or passersby [2] By revocalization; Hebrew silver of dross [3] Or and so does the sweetness of a friend that comes from his earnest counsel [4] Hebrew a foreign woman; a slight emendation yields (compare Vulgate; see also 20:16) foreigners [5] Hebrew to meet with [6] Hebrew sharpens the face of another

18 Whoever tends a fig tree will eat its fruit,
  and he who guards his master will be
    honored.

19 As in water face reflects face,
  so the heart of man reflects the man.

20 Sheol and Abaddon are never satisfied,
  and never satisfied are the eyes of man.

21 The crucible is for silver, and the furnace
    is for gold,
  and a man is tested by his praise.

22 Crush a fool in a mortar with a pestle
    along with crushed grain,
  yet his folly will not depart from him.

23 Know well the condition of your flocks,
  and give attention to your herds,

24 for riches do not last forever;
  and does a crown endure to all genera-
    tions?

25 When the grass is gone and the new
    growth appears
  and the vegetation of the mountains is
    gathered,

26 the lambs will provide your clothing,
  and the goats the price of a field.

27 There will be enough goats' milk for your
    food,
  for the food of your household
  and maintenance for your girls.

28

The wicked flee when no one
  pursues,
  but the righteous are bold as a lion.

2 When a land transgresses, it has many rulers,
  but with a man of understanding and
    knowledge,
  its stability will long continue.

3 A poor man who oppresses the poor
  is a beating rain that leaves no food.

4 Those who forsake the law praise the
    wicked,
  but those who keep the law strive
    against them.

5 Evil men do not understand justice,
  but those who seek the LORD under-
    stand it completely.

6 Better is a poor man who walks in his
    integrity
  than a rich man who is crooked in his
    ways.

7 The one who keeps the law is a son with
    understanding,
  but a companion of gluttons shames his
    father.

8 Whoever multiplies his wealth by inter-
    est and profit[1]
  gathers it for him who is generous to
    the poor.

9 If one turns away his ear from hearing the
    law,
  even his prayer is an abomination.

10 Whoever misleads the upright into an
    evil way
  will fall into his own pit,
  but the blameless will have a goodly
    inheritance.

11 A rich man is wise in his own eyes,
  but a poor man who has understanding
    will find him out.

12 When the righteous triumph, there is
    great glory,
  but when the wicked rise, people hide
    themselves.

13 Whoever conceals his transgressions will
    not prosper,
  but he who confesses and forsakes them
    will obtain mercy.

14 Blessed is the one who fears the LORD[2]
    always,
  but whoever hardens his heart will fall
    into calamity.

15 Like a roaring lion or a charging bear
  is a wicked ruler over a poor people.

16 A ruler who lacks understanding is a cruel
    oppressor,
  but he who hates unjust gain will pro-
    long his days.

17 If one is burdened with the blood of
    another,
  he will be a fugitive until death;[3]
  let no one help him.

18 Whoever walks in integrity will be delivered,
  but he who is crooked in his ways will
    suddenly fall.

19 Whoever works his land will have plenty of
    bread,
  but he who follows worthless pursuits
    will have plenty of poverty.

20 A faithful man will abound with blessings,
  but whoever hastens to be rich will not
    go unpunished.

21 To show partiality is not good,
  but for a piece of bread a man will do
    wrong.

22 A stingy man[4] hastens after wealth
  and does not know that poverty will
    come upon him.

---

[1] That is, profit that comes from charging interest to the poor   [2] Hebrew lacks *the LORD*   [3] Hebrew *until the pit*   [4] Hebrew *A man whose eye is evil*

23 Whoever rebukes a man will afterward
        find more favor
    than he who flatters with his tongue.
24 Whoever robs his father or his mother
        and says, "That is no transgression,"
    is a companion to a man who
        destroys.
25 A greedy man stirs up strife,
    but the one who trusts in the LORD will
        be enriched.
26 Whoever trusts in his own mind is a fool,
    but he who walks in wisdom will be
        delivered.
27 Whoever gives to the poor will not want,
    but he who hides his eyes will get many
        a curse.
28 When the wicked rise, people hide them-
        selves,
    but when they perish, the righteous
        increase.

29 He who is often reproved, yet stiffens
        his neck,
    will suddenly be broken beyond heal-
        ing.
2 When the righteous increase, the people
        rejoice,
    but when the wicked rule, the people
        groan.
3 He who loves wisdom makes his father
        glad,
    but a companion of prostitutes squan-
        ders his wealth.
4 By justice a king builds up the land,
    but he who exacts gifts[1] tears it down.
5 A man who flatters his neighbor
    spreads a net for his feet.
6 An evil man is ensnared in his transgres-
        sion,
    but a righteous man sings and
        rejoices.
7 A righteous man knows the rights of the
        poor;
    a wicked man does not understand such
        knowledge.
8 Scoffers set a city aflame,
    but the wise turn away wrath.
9 If a wise man has an argument with a fool,
    the fool only rages and laughs, and
        there is no quiet.
10 Bloodthirsty men hate one who is blame-
        less
    and seek the life of the upright.[2]

11 A fool gives full vent to his spirit,
    but a wise man quietly holds it back.
12 If a ruler listens to falsehood,
    all his officials will be wicked.
13 The poor man and the oppressor meet
        together;
    the LORD gives light to the eyes of both.
14 If a king faithfully judges the poor,
    his throne will be established forever.
15 The rod and reproof give wisdom,
    but a child left to himself brings shame
        to his mother.
16 When the wicked increase, transgression
        increases,
    but the righteous will look upon their
        downfall.
17 Discipline your son, and he will give you
        rest;
    he will give delight to your heart.
18 Where there is no prophetic vision the
        people cast off restraint,[3]
    but blessed is he who keeps the law.
19 By mere words a servant is not disciplined,
    for though he understands, he will not
        respond.
20 Do you see a man who is hasty in his
        words?
    There is more hope for a fool than for
        him.
21 Whoever pampers his servant from child-
        hood
    will in the end find him his heir.[4]
22 A man of wrath stirs up strife,
    and one given to anger causes much
        transgression.
23 One's pride will bring him low,
    but he who is lowly in spirit will obtain
        honor.
24 The partner of a thief hates his own life;
    he hears the curse, but discloses noth-
        ing.
25 The fear of man lays a snare,
    but whoever trusts in the LORD is safe.
26 Many seek the face of a ruler,
    but it is from the LORD that a man gets
        justice.
27 An unjust man is an abomination to the
        righteous,
    but one whose way is straight is an
        abomination to the wicked.

---

[1] Or who taxes heavily [2] Or but the upright seek his soul [3] Or the people are discouraged [4] The meaning of the Hebrew word rendered his heir is uncertain

The Words of Agur

30

The words of Agur son of Jakeh. The oracle.[1]

The man declares, I am weary, O God;
  I am weary, O God, and worn out.[2]
2 Surely I am too stupid to be a man.
  I have not the understanding of a man.
3 I have not learned wisdom,
  nor have I knowledge of the Holy One.
4 Who has ascended to heaven and come
    down?
  Who has gathered the wind in his
    fists?
  Who has wrapped up the waters in a gar-
    ment?
  Who has established all the ends of the
    earth?
  What is his name, and what is his son's
    name?
  Surely you know!

5 Every word of God proves true;
  he is a shield to those who take refuge
    in him.
6 Do not add to his words,
  lest he rebuke you and you be found a
    liar.

7 Two things I ask of you;
  deny them not to me before I die:
8 Remove far from me falsehood and lying;
  give me neither poverty nor riches;
  feed me with the food that is needful
    for me,
9 lest I be full and deny you
  and say, "Who is the LORD?"
  or lest I be poor and steal
  and profane the name of my God.

10 Do not slander a servant to his master,
  lest he curse you, and you be held
    guilty.

11 There are those[3] who curse their fathers
  and do not bless their mothers.
12 There are those who are clean in their
    own eyes
  but are not washed of their filth.
13 There are those—how lofty are their eyes,
  how high their eyelids lift!
14 There are those whose teeth are swords,
  whose fangs are knives,

to devour the poor from off the earth,
  the needy from among mankind.

15 The leech has two daughters:
  Give and Give.[4]
Three things are never satisfied;
  four never say, "Enough":
16 Sheol, the barren womb,
  the land never satisfied with water,
  and the fire that never says, "Enough."

17 The eye that mocks a father
  and scorns to obey a mother
will be picked out by the ravens of the
    valley
  and eaten by the vultures.

18 Three things are too wonderful for me;
  four I do not understand:
19 the way of an eagle in the sky,
  the way of a serpent on a rock,
the way of a ship on the high seas,
  and the way of a man with a virgin.

20 This is the way of an adulteress:
  she eats and wipes her mouth
  and says, "I have done no wrong."

21 Under three things the earth trembles;
  under four it cannot bear up:
22 a slave when he becomes king,
  and a fool when he is filled with food;
23 an unloved woman when she gets a hus-
    band,
  and a maidservant when she displaces
    her mistress.

24 Four things on earth are small,
  but they are exceedingly wise:
25 the ants are a people not strong,
  yet they provide their food in the sum-
    mer;
26 the rock badgers are a people not mighty,
  yet they make their homes in the cliffs;
27 the locusts have no king,
  yet all of them march in rank;
28 the lizard you can take in your hands,
  yet it is in kings' palaces.

29 Three things are stately in their tread;
  four are stately in their stride:
30 the lion, which is mightiest among beasts
  and does not turn back before any;
31 the strutting rooster,[5] the he-goat,
  and a king whose army is with him.[6]

---

[1] Or *Jakeh, the man of Massa* [2] Revocalization; Hebrew *The man declares to Ithiel, to Ithiel and Ucal* [3] Hebrew *There is a generation;* also verses 12, 13, 14 [4] Or *"Give, give," they cry* [5] Or *the magpie,* or *the greyhound;* Hebrew *girt-of-loins* [6] Or *against whom there is no rising up*

32 If you have been foolish, exalting yourself,
    or if you have been devising evil,
    put your hand on your mouth.
33 For pressing milk produces curds,
    pressing the nose produces blood,
    and pressing anger produces strife.

The Words of King Lemuel

31 The words of King Lemuel. An oracle that his mother taught him:

2 What are you doing, my son?[1] What are
        you doing, son of my womb?
    What are you doing, son of my vows?
3 Do not give your strength to women,
    your ways to those who destroy kings.
4 It is not for kings, O Lemuel,
        it is not for kings to drink wine,
        or for rulers to take strong drink,
5 lest they drink and forget what has been
        decreed
    and pervert the rights of all the afflicted.
6 Give strong drink to the one who is perish-
        ing,
    and wine to those in bitter distress;[2]
7 let them drink and forget their poverty
    and remember their misery no more.
8 Open your mouth for the mute,
    for the rights of all who are destitute.[3]
9 Open your mouth, judge righteously,
    defend the rights of the poor and needy.

The Woman Who Fears the LORD

10[4] An excellent wife who can find?
    She is far more precious than jewels.
11 The heart of her husband trusts in her,
    and he will have no lack of gain.
12 She does him good, and not harm,
    all the days of her life.
13 She seeks wool and flax,
    and works with willing hands.
14 She is like the ships of the merchant;
    she brings her food from afar.

15 She rises while it is yet night
    and provides food for her household
    and portions for her maidens.
16 She considers a field and buys it;
    with the fruit of her hands she plants a
        vineyard.
17 She dresses herself[5] with strength
    and makes her arms strong.
18 She perceives that her merchandise is prof-
        itable.
    Her lamp does not go out at night.
19 She puts her hands to the distaff,
    and her hands hold the spindle.
20 She opens her hand to the poor
    and reaches out her hands to the needy.
21 She is not afraid of snow for her house-
        hold,
    for all her household are clothed in scar-
        let.[6]
22 She makes bed coverings for herself;
    her clothing is fine linen and purple.
23 Her husband is known in the gates
    when he sits among the elders of the
        land.
24 She makes linen garments and sells them;
    she delivers sashes to the merchant.
25 Strength and dignity are her clothing,
    and she laughs at the time to come.
26 She opens her mouth with wisdom,
    and the teaching of kindness is on her
        tongue.
27 She looks well to the ways of her house-
        hold
    and does not eat the bread of idleness.
28 Her children rise up and call her blessed;
    her husband also, and he praises her:
29 "Many women have done excellently,
    but you surpass them all."
30 Charm is deceitful, and beauty is vain,
    but a woman who fears the LORD is to
        be praised.
31 Give her of the fruit of her hands,
    and let her works praise her in the gates.

---

[1] Hebrew *What, my son?* [2] Hebrew *those bitter in soul* [3] Hebrew *are sons of passing away* [4] Verses 10–31 are an acrostic poem, each verse beginning with the successive letters of the Hebrew alphabet [5] Hebrew *She girds her loins* [6] Or *in double thickness*

ECCLESIASTES

All Is Vanity

1 The words of the Preacher,[1] the son of David, king in Jerusalem.

2 Vanity[2] of vanities, says the Preacher,
   vanity of vanities! All is vanity.
3 What does man gain by all the toil
   at which he toils under the sun?
4 A generation goes, and a generation comes,
   but the earth remains forever.
5 The sun rises, and the sun goes down,
   and hastens[3] to the place where it rises.
6 The wind blows to the south
   and goes around to the north;
   around and around goes the wind,
   and on its circuits the wind returns.
7 All streams run to the sea,
   but the sea is not full;
   to the place where the streams flow,
   there they flow again.
8 All things are full of weariness;
   a man cannot utter it;
   the eye is not satisfied with seeing,
   nor the ear filled with hearing.
9 What has been is what will be,
   and what has been done is what will be done,
   and there is nothing new under the sun.
10 Is there a thing of which it is said,
   "See, this is new"?
   It has been already
   in the ages before us.
11 There is no remembrance of former things,[4]
   nor will there be any remembrance
   of later things[5] yet to be
   among those who come after.

The Vanity of Wisdom

12 I the Preacher have been king over Israel in Jerusalem. 13 And I applied my heart[6] to seek and to search out by wisdom all that is done under heaven. It is an unhappy business that God has given to the children of man to be busy with. 14 I have seen everything that is done under the sun, and behold, all is vanity[7] and a striving after wind.[8]

15 What is crooked cannot be made
   straight,
   and what is lacking cannot be
   counted.

16 I said in my heart, "I have acquired great wisdom, surpassing all who were over Jerusalem before me, and my heart has had great experience of wisdom and knowledge." 17 And I applied my heart to know wisdom and to know madness and folly. I perceived that this also is but a striving after wind.

18 For in much wisdom is much vexation,
   and he who increases knowledge
   increases sorrow.

The Vanity of Self-Indulgence

2 I said in my heart, "Come now, I will test you with pleasure; enjoy yourself." But behold, this also was vanity.[9] 2 I said of laughter, "It is mad," and of pleasure, "What use is it?" 3 I searched with my heart how to cheer my body with wine—my heart still guiding me with wisdom—and how to lay hold on folly, till I might see what was good for the children of man to do under heaven during the few days of their life. 4 I made great works. I built houses and planted vineyards for myself. 5 I made myself gardens and parks, and planted in them all kinds of fruit trees. 6 I made myself pools from which to water the forest of growing trees. 7 I bought male and female slaves, and had slaves who were born in my house. I had also great possessions of herds and flocks, more than any who had been before me in Jerusalem. 8 I also gathered for myself silver and gold and the treasure of kings and provinces. I got singers, both men and women, and many concubines,[10] the delight of the sons of man.

9 So I became great and surpassed all who were before me in Jerusalem. Also my wisdom remained with me. 10 And whatever my eyes desired I did not keep from them. I kept my heart from no pleasure, for my heart found pleasure in all my toil, and this was my reward for all my toil. 11 Then I considered all that my hands had done and the toil I had expended

---

[1] Or *Convener*, or *Collector*; Hebrew *Qoheleth* (so throughout Ecclesiastes) [2] The Hebrew term *hebel*, translated *vanity* or *vain*, refers concretely to a "mist," "vapor," or "mere breath," and metaphorically to something that is fleeting or elusive (with different nuances depending on the context). It appears five times in this verse and in 29 other verses in Ecclesiastes. [3] Or *and returns panting* [4] Or *former people* [5] Or *later people* [6] The Hebrew term denotes the center of one's inner life, including mind, will, and emotions [7] The Hebrew term *hebel* can refer to a "vapor" or "mere breath" (see note on 1:2) [8] Or *a feeding on wind*; compare Hosea 12:1 (also in Ecclesiastes 1:17; 2:11, 17, 26; 4:4, 6, 16; 6:9) [9] The Hebrew term *hebel* can refer to a "vapor" or "mere breath"; also verses 11, 15, 17, 19, 21, 23, 26 (see note on 1:2) [10] The meaning of the Hebrew word is uncertain

in doing it, and behold, all was vanity and a striving after wind, and there was nothing to be gained under the sun.

The Vanity of Living Wisely

[12] So I turned to consider wisdom and madness and folly. For what can the man do who comes after the king? Only what has already been done. [13] Then I saw that there is more gain in wisdom than in folly, as there is more gain in light than in darkness. [14] The wise person has his eyes in his head, but the fool walks in darkness. And yet I perceived that the same event happens to all of them. [15] Then I said in my heart, "What happens to the fool will happen to me also. Why then have I been so very wise?" And I said in my heart that this also is vanity. [16] For of the wise as of the fool there is no enduring remembrance, seeing that in the days to come all will have been long forgotten. How the wise dies just like the fool! [17] So I hated life, because what is done under the sun was grievous to me, for all is vanity and a striving after wind.

The Vanity of Toil

[18] I hated all my toil in which I toil under the sun, seeing that I must leave it to the man who will come after me, [19] and who knows whether he will be wise or a fool? Yet he will be master of all for which I toiled and used my wisdom under the sun. This also is vanity. [20] So I turned about and gave my heart up to despair over all the toil of my labors under the sun, [21] because sometimes a person who has toiled with wisdom and knowledge and skill must leave everything to be enjoyed by someone who did not toil for it. This also is vanity and a great evil. [22] What has a man from all the toil and striving of heart with which he toils beneath the sun? [23] For all his days are full of sorrow, and his work is a vexation. Even in the night his heart does not rest. This also is vanity.

[24] There is nothing better for a person than that he should eat and drink and find enjoyment[1] in his toil. This also, I saw, is from the hand of God, [25] for apart from him[2] who can eat or who can have enjoyment? [26] For to the one who pleases him God has given wisdom and knowledge and joy, but to the sinner he has given the business of gathering and collecting, only to give to one who pleases God. This also is vanity and a striving after wind.

A Time for Everything

3 For everything there is a season, and a time for every matter under heaven:

[2] a time to be born, and a time to die;
a time to plant, and a time to pluck up
what is planted;
[3] a time to kill, and a time to heal;
a time to break down, and a time to build
up;
[4] a time to weep, and a time to laugh;
a time to mourn, and a time to dance;
[5] a time to cast away stones, and a time to
gather stones together;
a time to embrace, and a time to refrain
from embracing;
[6] a time to seek, and a time to lose;
a time to keep, and a time to cast away;
[7] a time to tear, and a time to sew;
a time to keep silence, and a time to
speak;
[8] a time to love, and a time to hate;
a time for war, and a time for peace.

The God-Given Task

[9] What gain has the worker from his toil? [10] I have seen the business that God has given to the children of man to be busy with. [11] He has made everything beautiful in its time. Also, he has put eternity into man's heart, yet so that he cannot find out what God has done from the beginning to the end. [12] I perceived that there is nothing better for them than to be joyful and to do good as long as they live; [13] also that everyone should eat and drink and take pleasure in all his toil—this is God's gift to man.

[14] I perceived that whatever God does endures forever; nothing can be added to it, nor anything taken from it. God has done it, so that people fear before him. [15] That which is, already has been; that which is to be, already has been; and God seeks what has been driven away.[3]

From Dust to Dust

[16] Moreover, I saw under the sun that in the place of justice, even there was wickedness, and in the place of righteousness, even there was wickedness. [17] I said in my heart, God will judge the righteous and the wicked, for there is a time for every matter and for every work. [18] I said in my heart with regard to the children of man that God is testing them that they may see that they themselves are but beasts. [19] For

[1] Or and make his soul see good   [2] Some Hebrew manuscripts, Septuagint, Syriac; most Hebrew manuscripts apart from me   [3] Hebrew what has been pursued

what happens to the children of man and what happens to the beasts is the same; as one dies, so dies the other. They all have the same breath, and man has no advantage over the beasts, for all is vanity.[1] [20] All go to one place. All are from the dust, and to dust all return. [21] Who knows whether the spirit of man goes upward and the spirit of the beast goes down into the earth? [22] So I saw that there is nothing better than that a man should rejoice in his work, for that is his lot. Who can bring him to see what will be after him?

Evil Under the Sun

4 Again I saw all the oppressions that are done under the sun. And behold, the tears of the oppressed, and they had no one to comfort them! On the side of their oppressors there was power, and there was no one to comfort them. [2] And I thought the dead who are already dead more fortunate than the living who are still alive. [3] But better than both is he who has not yet been and has not seen the evil deeds that are done under the sun.

[4] Then I saw that all toil and all skill in work come from a man's envy of his neighbor. This also is vanity[2] and a striving after wind.

[5] The fool folds his hands and eats his own flesh.

[6] Better is a handful of quietness than two hands full of toil and a striving after wind.

[7] Again, I saw vanity under the sun: [8] one person who has no other, either son or brother, yet there is no end to all his toil, and his eyes are never satisfied with riches, so that he never asks, "For whom am I toiling and depriving myself of pleasure?" This also is vanity and an unhappy business.

[9] Two are better than one, because they have a good reward for their toil. [10] For if they fall, one will lift up his fellow. But woe to him who is alone when he falls and has not another to lift him up! [11] Again, if two lie together, they keep warm, but how can one keep warm alone? [12] And though a man might prevail against one who is alone, two will withstand him—a threefold cord is not quickly broken.

[13] Better was a poor and wise youth than an old and foolish king who no longer knew how to take advice. [14] For he went from prison to the throne, though in his own kingdom he had been born poor. [15] I saw all the living who move about

under the sun, along with that[3] youth who was to stand in the king's[4] place. [16] There was no end of all the people, all of whom he led. Yet those who come later will not rejoice in him. Surely this also is vanity and a striving after wind.

Fear God

5 [5] Guard your steps when you go to the house of God. To draw near to listen is better than to offer the sacrifice of fools, for they do not know that they are doing evil. [2] [6] Be not rash with your mouth, nor let your heart be hasty to utter a word before God, for God is in heaven and you are on earth. Therefore let your words be few. [3] For a dream comes with much business, and a fool's voice with many words.

[4] When you vow a vow to God, do not delay paying it, for he has no pleasure in fools. Pay what you vow. [5] It is better that you should not vow than that you should vow and not pay. [6] Let not your mouth lead you[7] into sin, and do not say before the messenger[8] that it was a mistake. Why should God be angry at your voice and destroy the work of your hands? [7] For when dreams increase and words grow many, there is vanity;[9] but[10] God is the one you must fear.

The Vanity of Wealth and Honor

[8] If you see in a province the oppression of the poor and the violation of justice and righteousness, do not be amazed at the matter, for the high official is watched by a higher, and there are yet higher ones over them. [9] But this is gain for a land in every way: a king committed to cultivated fields.[11]

[10] He who loves money will not be satisfied with money, nor he who loves wealth with his income; this also is vanity. [11] When goods increase, they increase who eat them, and what advantage has their owner but to see them with his eyes? [12] Sweet is the sleep of a laborer, whether he eats little or much, but the full stomach of the rich will not let him sleep.

[13] There is a grievous evil that I have seen under the sun: riches were kept by their owner to his hurt, [14] and those riches were lost in a bad venture. And he is father of a son, but he has nothing in his hand. [15] As he came from his mother's womb he shall go again, naked as he came, and shall take nothing for his toil that he may carry away in his hand. [16] This also is a grievous evil: just as he came, so shall he go,

---

[1] The Hebrew term *hebel* can refer to a "vapor" or "mere breath" (see note on 1:2)   [2] The Hebrew term *hebel* can refer to a "vapor" or "mere breath"; also verses 7, 8, 16 (see note on 1:2)   [3] Hebrew *the second*   [4] Hebrew *his*   [5] Ch 4:17 in Hebrew   [6] Ch 5:1 in Hebrew   [7] Hebrew *your flesh*   [8] Or *angel*   [9] The Hebrew term *hebel* can refer to a "vapor" or "mere breath"; also verse 10 (see note on 1:2)   [10] Or *For when dreams and vanities increase, words also grow many; but*   [11] The meaning of the Hebrew verse is uncertain

and what gain is there to him who toils for the wind? [17] Moreover, all his days he eats in darkness in much vexation and sickness and anger.

[18] Behold, what I have seen to be good and fitting is to eat and drink and find enjoyment[1] in all the toil with which one toils under the sun the few days of his life that God has given him, for this is his lot. [19] Everyone also to whom God has given wealth and possessions and power to enjoy them, and to accept his lot and rejoice in his toil—this is the gift of God. [20] For he will not much remember the days of his life because God keeps him occupied with joy in his heart.

6 There is an evil that I have seen under the sun, and it lies heavy on mankind: [2] a man to whom God gives wealth, possessions, and honor, so that he lacks nothing of all that he desires, yet God does not give him power to enjoy them, but a stranger enjoys them. This is vanity;[2] it is a grievous evil. [3] If a man fathers a hundred children and lives many years, so that the days of his years are many, but his soul is not satisfied with life's good things, and he also has no burial, I say that a stillborn child is better off than he. [4] For it comes in vanity and goes in darkness, and in darkness its name is covered. [5] Moreover, it has not seen the sun or known anything, yet it finds rest rather than he. [6] Even though he should live a thousand years twice over, yet enjoy[3] no good—do not all go to the one place?

[7] All the toil of man is for his mouth, yet his appetite is not satisfied.[4] [8] For what advantage has the wise man over the fool? And what does the poor man have who knows how to conduct himself before the living? [9] Better is the sight of the eyes than the wandering of the appetite: this also is vanity and a striving after wind.

[10] Whatever has come to be has already been named, and it is known what man is, and that he is not able to dispute with one stronger than he. [11] The more words, the more vanity, and what is the advantage to man? [12] For who knows what is good for man while he lives the few days of his vain[5] life, which he passes like a shadow? For who can tell man what will be after him under the sun?

The Contrast of Wisdom and Folly

7 A good name is better than precious ointment,
> and the day of death than the day of birth.

[2] It is better to go to the house of mourning
> than to go to the house of feasting,
for this is the end of all mankind,
> and the living will lay it to heart.

[3] Sorrow is better than laughter,
> for by sadness of face the heart is made glad.

[4] The heart of the wise is in the house of mourning,
> but the heart of fools is in the house of mirth.

[5] It is better for a man to hear the rebuke of the wise
> than to hear the song of fools.

[6] For as the crackling of thorns under a pot,
> so is the laughter of the fools;
> this also is vanity.[6]

[7] Surely oppression drives the wise into madness,
> and a bribe corrupts the heart.

[8] Better is the end of a thing than its beginning,
> and the patient in spirit is better than the proud in spirit.

[9] Be not quick in your spirit to become angry,
> for anger lodges in the heart[7] of fools.

[10] Say not, "Why were the former days better than these?"
> For it is not from wisdom that you ask this.

[11] Wisdom is good with an inheritance,
> an advantage to those who see the sun.

[12] For the protection of wisdom is like the protection of money,
> and the advantage of knowledge is that wisdom preserves the life of him who has it.

[13] Consider the work of God:
> who can make straight what he has made crooked?

[14] In the day of prosperity be joyful, and in the day of adversity consider: God has made the one as well as the other, so that man may not find out anything that will be after him.

[15] In my vain[8] life I have seen everything. There is a righteous man who perishes in his righteousness, and there is a wicked man who prolongs his life in his evildoing. [16] Be not overly righteous, and do not make yourself too wise.

---

[1] Or and see good [2] The Hebrew term hebel can refer to a "vapor" or "mere breath"; also verses 4, 9, 11 (see note on 1:2) [3] Or see [4] Hebrew filled [5] The Hebrew term hebel can refer to a "vapor" or "mere breath" (see note on 1:2) [6] The Hebrew term hebel can refer to a "vapor" or "mere breath" (see note on 1:2) [7] Hebrew in the bosom [8] The Hebrew term hebel can refer to a "vapor" or "mere breath" (see note on 1:2)

Why should you destroy yourself? [17] Be not overly wicked, neither be a fool. Why should you die before your time? [18] It is good that you should take hold of this, and from that withhold not your hand, for the one who fears God shall come out from both of them.

[19] Wisdom gives strength to the wise man more than ten rulers who are in a city.

[20] Surely there is not a righteous man on earth who does good and never sins.

[21] Do not take to heart all the things that people say, lest you hear your servant cursing you. [22] Your heart knows that many times you yourself have cursed others.

[23] All this I have tested by wisdom. I said, "I will be wise," but it was far from me. [24] That which has been is far off, and deep, very deep; who can find it out?

[25] I turned my heart to know and to search out and to seek wisdom and the scheme of things, and to know the wickedness of folly and the foolishness that is madness. [26] And I find something more bitter than death: the woman whose heart is snares and nets, and whose hands are fetters. He who pleases God escapes her, but the sinner is taken by her. [27] Behold, this is what I found, says the Preacher, while adding one thing to another to find the scheme of things— [28] which my soul has sought repeatedly, but I have not found. One man among a thousand I found, but a woman among all these I have not found. [29] See, this alone I found, that God made man upright, but they have sought out many schemes.

Keep the King's Command

8 Who is like the wise?
And who knows the interpretation of a thing?
A man's wisdom makes his face shine,
and the hardness of his face is changed.

[2] I say:[1] Keep the king's command, because of God's oath to him.[2] [3] Be not hasty to go from his presence. Do not take your stand in an evil cause, for he does whatever he pleases. [4] For the word of the king is supreme, and who may say to him, "What are you doing?" [5] Whoever keeps a command will know no evil thing, and the wise heart will know the proper time and the just way.[3] [6] For there is a time and a way for everything, although man's trouble[4] lies heavy on him. [7] For he does not know what is to be, for

who can tell him how it will be? [8] No man has power to retain the spirit, or power over the day of death. There is no discharge from war, nor will wickedness deliver those who are given to it. [9] All this I observed while applying my heart to all that is done under the sun, when man had power over man to his hurt.

Those Who Fear God Will Do Well

[10] Then I saw the wicked buried. They used to go in and out of the holy place and were praised[5] in the city where they had done such things. This also is vanity.[6] [11] Because the sentence against an evil deed is not executed speedily, the heart of the children of man is fully set to do evil. [12] Though a sinner does evil a hundred times and prolongs his life, yet I know that it will be well with those who fear God, because they fear before him. [13] But it will not be well with the wicked, neither will he prolong his days like a shadow, because he does not fear before God.

Man Cannot Know God's Ways

[14] There is a vanity that takes place on earth, that there are righteous people to whom it happens according to the deeds of the wicked, and there are wicked people to whom it happens according to the deeds of the righteous. I said that this also is vanity. [15] And I commend joy, for man has nothing better under the sun but to eat and drink and be joyful, for this will go with him in his toil through the days of his life that God has given him under the sun.

[16] When I applied my heart to know wisdom, and to see the business that is done on earth, how neither day nor night do one's eyes see sleep, [17] then I saw all the work of God, that man cannot find out the work that is done under the sun. However much man may toil in seeking, he will not find it out. Even though a wise man claims to know, he cannot find it out.

Death Comes to All

9 But all this I laid to heart, examining it all, how the righteous and the wise and their deeds are in the hand of God. Whether it is love or hate, man does not know; both are before him. [2] It is the same for all, since the same event happens to the righteous and the wicked, to the good and the evil,[7] to the clean and the unclean, to him who sacrifices and him who does not sacrifice. As the good one is, so is the

---

[1] Hebrew lacks *say* [2] Or *because of your oath to God* [3] Or *and judgment* [4] Or *evil* [5] Some Hebrew manuscripts, Septuagint, Vulgate; most Hebrew manuscripts *forgotten*
[6] The Hebrew term *hebel* can refer to a "vapor" or "mere breath"; also twice in verse 14 (see note on 1:2) [7] Septuagint, Syriac, Vulgate; Hebrew lacks *and the evil*

sinner, and he who swears is as he who shuns an oath. ³This is an evil in all that is done under the sun, that the same event happens to all. Also, the hearts of the children of man are full of evil, and madness is in their hearts while they live, and after that they go to the dead. ⁴But he who is joined with all the living has hope, for a living dog is better than a dead lion. ⁵For the living know that they will die, but the dead know nothing, and they have no more reward, for the memory of them is forgotten. ⁶Their love and their hate and their envy have already perished, and forever they have no more share in all that is done under the sun.

Enjoy Life with the One You Love

⁷Go, eat your bread with joy, and drink your wine with a merry heart, for God has already approved what you do.

⁸Let your garments be always white. Let not oil be lacking on your head.

⁹Enjoy life with the wife whom you love, all the days of your vain[1] life that he has given you under the sun, because that is your portion in life and in your toil at which you toil under the sun. ¹⁰Whatever your hand finds to do, do it with your might,[2] for there is no work or thought or knowledge or wisdom in Sheol, to which you are going.

Wisdom Better Than Folly

¹¹Again I saw that under the sun the race is not to the swift, nor the battle to the strong, nor bread to the wise, nor riches to the intelligent, nor favor to those with knowledge, but time and chance happen to them all. ¹²For man does not know his time. Like fish that are taken in an evil net, and like birds that are caught in a snare, so the children of man are snared at an evil time, when it suddenly falls upon them.

¹³I have also seen this example of wisdom under the sun, and it seemed great to me. ¹⁴There was a little city with few men in it, and a great king came against it and besieged it, building great siegeworks against it. ¹⁵But there was found in it a poor, wise man, and he by his wisdom delivered the city. Yet no one remembered that poor man. ¹⁶But I say that wisdom is better than might, though the poor man's wisdom is despised and his words are not heard.

¹⁷The words of the wise heard in quiet are better than the shouting of a ruler among fools.

¹⁸Wisdom is better than weapons of war, but one sinner destroys much good.

10 Dead flies make the perfumer's
    ointment give off a stench;
    so a little folly outweighs wisdom and
        honor.
² A wise man's heart inclines him to the
        right,
    but a fool's heart to the left.
³ Even when the fool walks on the road, he
        lacks sense,
    and he says to everyone that he is a fool.
⁴ If the anger of the ruler rises against you,
        do not leave your place,
    for calmness[3] will lay great offenses to
        rest.

⁵There is an evil that I have seen under the sun, as it were an error proceeding from the ruler: ⁶folly is set in many high places, and the rich sit in a low place. ⁷I have seen slaves on horses, and princes walking on the ground like slaves.

⁸ He who digs a pit will fall into it,
    and a serpent will bite him who breaks
        through a wall.
⁹ He who quarries stones is hurt by them,
    and he who splits logs is endangered by
        them.
¹⁰ If the iron is blunt, and one does not
        sharpen the edge,
    he must use more strength,
    but wisdom helps one to succeed.[4]
¹¹ If the serpent bites before it is charmed,
    there is no advantage to the charmer.

¹² The words of a wise man's mouth win him
        favor,[5]
    but the lips of a fool consume him.
¹³ The beginning of the words of his mouth
        is foolishness,
    and the end of his talk is evil madness.
¹⁴ A fool multiplies words,
    though no man knows what is to be,
    and who can tell him what will be after
        him?
¹⁵ The toil of a fool wearies him,
    for he does not know the way to the city.

¹⁶ Woe to you, O land, when your king is a
        child,
    and your princes feast in the morning!

[1] The Hebrew term *hebel* can refer to a "vapor" or "mere breath" (see note on 1:2) [2] Or *finds to do with your might, do it* [3] Hebrew *healing* [4] Or *wisdom is an advantage for success*
[5] Or *are gracious*

17 Happy are you, O land, when your king is
    the son of the nobility,
  and your princes feast at the proper
    time,
  for strength, and not for drunkenness!
18 Through sloth the roof sinks in,
  and through indolence the house
    leaks.
19 Bread is made for laughter,
  and wine gladdens life,
  and money answers everything.
20 Even in your thoughts, do not curse the
    king,
  nor in your bedroom curse the rich,
  for a bird of the air will carry your voice,
  or some winged creature tell the matter.

Cast Your Bread upon the Waters

11 Cast your bread upon the waters,
  for you will find it after many days.
2 Give a portion to seven, or even to eight,
  for you know not what disaster may
    happen on earth.
3 If the clouds are full of rain,
  they empty themselves on the earth,
  and if a tree falls to the south or to the
    north,
    in the place where the tree falls, there it
      will lie.
4 He who observes the wind will not sow,
  and he who regards the clouds will not
    reap.

5 As you do not know the way the spirit
comes to the bones in the womb[1] of a woman
with child, so you do not know the work of God
who makes everything.
6 In the morning sow your seed, and at
evening withhold not your hand, for you do
not know which will prosper, this or that, or
whether both alike will be good.
7 Light is sweet, and it is pleasant for the eyes
to see the sun.
8 So if a person lives many years, let him
rejoice in them all; but let him remember that
the days of darkness will be many. All that
comes is vanity.[2]
9 Rejoice, O young man, in your youth, and
let your heart cheer you in the days of your
youth. Walk in the ways of your heart and the
sight of your eyes. But know that for all these
things God will bring you into judgment.
10 Remove vexation from your heart, and put
away pain[3] from your body, for youth and the
dawn of life are vanity.

Remember Your Creator in Your Youth

12 Remember also your Creator in the days
of your youth, before the evil days come
and the years draw near of which you will say,
"I have no pleasure in them"; 2 before the sun
and the light and the moon and the stars are
darkened and the clouds return after the rain,
3 in the day when the keepers of the house
tremble, and the strong men are bent, and the
grinders cease because they are few, and those
who look through the windows are dimmed,
4 and the doors on the street are shut—when
the sound of the grinding is low, and one rises
up at the sound of a bird, and all the daughters
of song are brought low— 5 they are afraid also
of what is high, and terrors are in the way; the
almond tree blossoms, the grasshopper drags
itself along,[4] and desire fails, because man is
going to his eternal home, and the mourners
go about the streets— 6 before the silver cord is
snapped, or the golden bowl is broken, or the
pitcher is shattered at the fountain, or the wheel
broken at the cistern, 7 and the dust returns to
the earth as it was, and the spirit returns to
God who gave it. 8 Vanity[5] of vanities, says the
Preacher; all is vanity.

Fear God and Keep His Commandments

9 Besides being wise, the Preacher also taught
the people knowledge, weighing and studying
and arranging many proverbs with great care.
10 The Preacher sought to find words of delight,
and uprightly he wrote words of truth.
11 The words of the wise are like goads, and
like nails firmly fixed are the collected sayings;
they are given by one Shepherd. 12 My son,
beware of anything beyond these. Of making
many books there is no end, and much study
is a weariness of the flesh.
13 The end of the matter; all has been heard.
Fear God and keep his commandments, for this
is the whole duty of man.[6] 14 For God will bring
every deed into judgment, with[7] every secret
thing, whether good or evil.

---

[1] Some Hebrew manuscripts, Targum; most Hebrew manuscripts *As you do not know the way of the wind, or how the bones grow in the womb* [2] The Hebrew term *hebel* can refer
to a "vapor" or "mere breath"; also verse 10 (see note on 1:2) [3] *Or evil* [4] *Or is a burden* [5] The Hebrew term *hebel* can refer to a "vapor" or "mere breath" (three times in this verse);
see note on 1:2 [6] *Or the duty of all mankind* [7] *Or into the judgment on*

THE SONG OF SOLOMON

1 The Song of Songs, which is Solomon's.

The Bride Confesses Her Love

SHE[1]

2 Let him kiss me with the kisses of his
     mouth!
For your love is better than wine;
3   your anointing oils are fragrant;
your name is oil poured out;
     therefore virgins love you.
4 Draw me after you; let us run.
     The king has brought me into his
     chambers.

OTHERS

We will exult and rejoice in you;
     we will extol your love more than wine;
rightly do they love you.

SHE

5 I am very dark, but lovely,
     O daughters of Jerusalem,
like the tents of Kedar,
     like the curtains of Solomon.
6 Do not gaze at me because I am dark,
     because the sun has looked upon me.
My mother's sons were angry with me;
     they made me keeper of the vine-
     yards,
     but my own vineyard I have not kept!
7 Tell me, you whom my soul loves,
     where you pasture your flock,
     where you make it lie down at noon;
for why should I be like one who veils her-
     self
     beside the flocks of your companions?

Solomon and His Bride Delight in Each Other

HE

8 If you do not know,
     O most beautiful among women,
follow in the tracks of the flock,
     and pasture your young goats
     beside the shepherds' tents.

9 I compare you, my love,
     to a mare among Pharaoh's chariots.
10 Your cheeks are lovely with ornaments,
     your neck with strings of jewels.

OTHERS

11 We will make for you[2] ornaments of
     gold,
     studded with silver.

SHE

12 While the king was on his couch,
     my nard gave forth its fragrance.
13 My beloved is to me a sachet of myrrh
     that lies between my breasts.
14 My beloved is to me a cluster of henna
     blossoms
     in the vineyards of Engedi.

HE

15 Behold, you are beautiful, my love;
     behold, you are beautiful;
     your eyes are doves.

SHE

16 Behold, you are beautiful, my beloved,
     truly delightful.
Our couch is green;
17   the beams of our house are cedar;
     our rafters are pine.

2 I am a rose[3] of Sharon,
     a lily of the valleys.

HE

2 As a lily among brambles,
     so is my love among the young
     women.

SHE

3 As an apple tree among the trees of the for-
     est,
     so is my beloved among the young men.
With great delight I sat in his shadow,
     and his fruit was sweet to my taste.
4 He brought me to the banqueting
     house,[4]
     and his banner over me was love.
5 Sustain me with raisins;
     refresh me with apples,
     for I am sick with love.
6 His left hand is under my head,
     and his right hand embraces me!
7 I adjure you,[5] O daughters of Jerusalem,
     by the gazelles or the does of the field,
that you not stir up or awaken love
     until it pleases.

---

[1] The translators have added speaker identifications based on the gender and number of the Hebrew words [2] The Hebrew for *you* is feminine singular [3] Probably a bulb, such as a crocus, asphodel, or narcissus [4] Hebrew *the house of wine* [5] That is, I put you on oath; so throughout the Song

The Bride Adores Her Beloved

8 The voice of my beloved!
    Behold, he comes,
    leaping over the mountains,
        bounding over the hills.

9 My beloved is like a gazelle
        or a young stag.
    Behold, there he stands
        behind our wall,
    gazing through the windows,
        looking through the lattice.

10 My beloved speaks and says to me:
    "Arise, my love, my beautiful one,
        and come away,

11 for behold, the winter is past;
        the rain is over and gone.

12 The flowers appear on the earth,
        the time of singing[1] has come,
    and the voice of the turtledove
        is heard in our land.

13 The fig tree ripens its figs,
        and the vines are in blossom;
        they give forth fragrance.
    Arise, my love, my beautiful one,
        and come away.

14 O my dove, in the clefts of the rock,
        in the crannies of the cliff,
    let me see your face,
        let me hear your voice,
    for your voice is sweet,
        and your face is lovely.

15 Catch the foxes[2] for us,
        the little foxes
    that spoil the vineyards,
        for our vineyards are in blossom."

16 My beloved is mine, and I am his;
        he grazes[3] among the lilies.

17 Until the day breathes
        and the shadows flee,
    turn, my beloved, be like a gazelle
        or a young stag on cleft mountains.[4]

The Bride's Dream

3 On my bed by night
    I sought him whom my soul loves;
        I sought him, but found him not.

2 I will rise now and go about the city,
        in the streets and in the squares;
    I will seek him whom my soul loves.
        I sought him, but found him not.

3 The watchmen found me
        as they went about in the city.
    "Have you seen him whom my soul loves?"

4 Scarcely had I passed them
        when I found him whom my soul loves.
    I held him, and would not let him go
        until I had brought him into my moth-
            er's house,
        and into the chamber of her who con-
            ceived me.

5 I adjure you, O daughters of Jerusalem,
        by the gazelles or the does of the field,
    that you not stir up or awaken love
        until it pleases.

Solomon Arrives for the Wedding

6 What is that coming up from the wilderness
        like columns of smoke,
    perfumed with myrrh and frankincense,
        with all the fragrant powders of a mer-
            chant?

7 Behold, it is the litter[5] of Solomon!
    Around it are sixty mighty men,
        some of the mighty men of Israel,

8 all of them wearing swords
        and expert in war,
    each with his sword at his thigh,
        against terror by night.

9 King Solomon made himself a carriage[6]
        from the wood of Lebanon.

10 He made its posts of silver,
        its back of gold, its seat of purple;
    its interior was inlaid with love
        by the daughters of Jerusalem.

11 Go out, O daughters of Zion,
        and look upon King Solomon,
    with the crown with which his mother
            crowned him
        on the day of his wedding,
        on the day of the gladness of his heart.

Solomon Admires His Bride's Beauty

HE

4 Behold, you are beautiful, my love,
        behold, you are beautiful!
    Your eyes are doves
        behind your veil.
    Your hair is like a flock of goats
        leaping down the slopes of Gilead.

2 Your teeth are like a flock of shorn ewes
        that have come up from the washing,
    all of which bear twins,
        and not one among them has lost its
            young.

3 Your lips are like a scarlet thread,
        and your mouth is lovely.

---

[1] Or pruning [2] Or jackals [3] Or he pastures his flock [4] Or mountains of Bether [5] That is, the couch on which servants carry a king [6] Or sedan chair

Your cheeks are like halves of a pomegranate
behind your veil.
4 Your neck is like the tower of David,
built in rows of stone;[1]
on it hang a thousand shields,
all of them shields of warriors.
5 Your two breasts are like two fawns,
twins of a gazelle,
that graze among the lilies.
6 Until the day breathes
and the shadows flee,
I will go away to the mountain of myrrh
and the hill of frankincense.
7 You are altogether beautiful, my love;
there is no flaw in you.
8 Come with me from Lebanon, my bride;
come with me from Lebanon.
Depart[2] from the peak of Amana,
from the peak of Senir and Hermon,
from the dens of lions,
from the mountains of leopards.

9 You have captivated my heart, my sister,
my bride;
you have captivated my heart with one
glance of your eyes,
with one jewel of your necklace.
10 How beautiful is your love, my sister, my
bride!
How much better is your love than
wine,
and the fragrance of your oils than any
spice!
11 Your lips drip nectar, my bride;
honey and milk are under your tongue;
the fragrance of your garments is like
the fragrance of Lebanon.
12 A garden locked is my sister, my bride,
a spring locked, a fountain sealed.
13 Your shoots are an orchard of pomegranates
with all choicest fruits,
henna with nard,
14 nard and saffron, calamus and cinnamon,
with all trees of frankincense,
myrrh and aloes,
with all choice spices—
15 a garden fountain, a well of living water,
and flowing streams from Lebanon.

16 Awake, O north wind,
and come, O south wind!
Blow upon my garden,
let its spices flow.

Together in the Garden of Love

She

Let my beloved come to his garden,
and eat its choicest fruits.

He

5 I came to my garden, my sister, my bride,
I gathered my myrrh with my spice,
I ate my honeycomb with my honey,
I drank my wine with my milk.

Others

Eat, friends, drink,
and be drunk with love!

The Bride Searches for Her Beloved

She

2 I slept, but my heart was awake.
A sound! My beloved is knocking.
"Open to me, my sister, my love,
my dove, my perfect one,
for my head is wet with dew,
my locks with the drops of the night."
3 I had put off my garment;
how could I put it on?
I had bathed my feet;
how could I soil them?
4 My beloved put his hand to the latch,
and my heart was thrilled within me.
5 I arose to open to my beloved,
and my hands dripped with myrrh,
my fingers with liquid myrrh,
on the handles of the bolt.
6 I opened to my beloved,
but my beloved had turned and gone.
My soul failed me when he spoke.
I sought him, but found him not;
I called him, but he gave no answer.
7 The watchmen found me
as they went about in the city;
they beat me, they bruised me,
they took away my veil,
those watchmen of the walls.
8 I adjure you, O daughters of Jerusalem,
if you find my beloved,
that you tell him
I am sick with love.

Others

9 What is your beloved more than another
beloved,
O most beautiful among women?
What is your beloved more than another
beloved,
that you thus adjure us?

---

1 The meaning of the Hebrew word is uncertain 2 Or *Look*

The Bride Praises Her Beloved

SHE

10 My beloved is radiant and ruddy,
  distinguished among ten thousand.
11 His head is the finest gold;
  his locks are wavy,
  black as a raven.
12 His eyes are like doves
  beside streams of water,
 bathed in milk,
  sitting beside a full pool.[1]
13 His cheeks are like beds of spices,
  mounds of sweet-smelling herbs.
 His lips are lilies,
  dripping liquid myrrh.
14 His arms are rods of gold,
  set with jewels.
 His body is polished ivory,[2]
  bedecked with sapphires.[3]
15 His legs are alabaster columns,
  set on bases of gold.
 His appearance is like Lebanon,
  choice as the cedars.
16 His mouth[4] is most sweet,
  and he is altogether desirable.
 This is my beloved and this is my friend,
  O daughters of Jerusalem.

OTHERS

6 Where has your beloved gone,
  O most beautiful among women?
 Where has your beloved turned,
  that we may seek him with you?

Together in the Garden of Love

SHE

2 My beloved has gone down to his garden
  to the beds of spices,
 to graze[5] in the gardens
  and to gather lilies.
3 I am my beloved's and my beloved is mine;
  he grazes among the lilies.

Solomon and His Bride Delight
in Each Other

HE

4 You are beautiful as Tirzah, my love,
  lovely as Jerusalem,
  awesome as an army with banners.
5 Turn away your eyes from me,
  for they overwhelm me—
 Your hair is like a flock of goats
  leaping down the slopes of Gilead.

6 Your teeth are like a flock of ewes
  that have come up from the washing;
 all of them bear twins;
  not one among them has lost its
  young.
7 Your cheeks are like halves of a pomegranate
  behind your veil.
8 There are sixty queens and eighty concubines,
  and virgins without number.
9 My dove, my perfect one, is the only one,
  the only one of her mother,
  pure to her who bore her.
 The young women saw her and called her
  blessed;
  the queens and concubines also, and
  they praised her.

10 "Who is this who looks down like the
  dawn,
  beautiful as the moon, bright as the
  sun,
  awesome as an army with banners?"

SHE

11 I went down to the nut orchard
  to look at the blossoms of the valley,
 to see whether the vines had budded,
  whether the pomegranates were in
  bloom.
12 Before I was aware, my desire set me
  among the chariots of my kinsman, a
  prince.[6]

OTHERS

13 7 Return, return, O Shulammite,
  return, return, that we may look upon
  you.

HE

Why should you look upon the
  Shulammite,
  as upon a dance before two armies?[8]

7 How beautiful are your feet in sandals,
  O noble daughter!
 Your rounded thighs are like jewels,
  the work of a master hand.
2 Your navel is a rounded bowl
  that never lacks mixed wine.
 Your belly is a heap of wheat,
  encircled with lilies.
3 Your two breasts are like two fawns,
  twins of a gazelle.

---

[1] The meaning of the Hebrew is uncertain [2] The meaning of the Hebrew word is uncertain [3] Hebrew *lapis lazuli* [4] Hebrew *palate* [5] Or *to pasture his flock; also verse 3* [6] Or *chariots of Ammi-Nadib* [7] Ch 7:1 in Hebrew [8] Or *dance of Mahanaim*

4 Your neck is like an ivory tower.
   Your eyes are pools in Heshbon,
      by the gate of Bath-rabbim.
   Your nose is like a tower of Lebanon,
      which looks toward Damascus.
5 Your head crowns you like Carmel,
      and your flowing locks are like purple;
      a king is held captive in the tresses.

6 How beautiful and pleasant you are,
      O loved one, with all your delights![1]
7 Your stature is like a palm tree,
      and your breasts are like its clusters.
8 I say I will climb the palm tree
      and lay hold of its fruit.
   Oh may your breasts be like clusters of the
      vine,
      and the scent of your breath like apples,
9 and your mouth[2] like the best wine.

SHE
   It goes down smoothly for my beloved,
      gliding over lips and teeth.[3]

10 I am my beloved's,
      and his desire is for me.

The Bride Gives Her Love
11 Come, my beloved,
      let us go out into the fields
      and lodge in the villages;[4]
12 let us go out early to the vineyards
      and see whether the vines have bud-
         ded,
      whether the grape blossoms have opened
      and the pomegranates are in bloom.
   There I will give you my love.
13 The mandrakes give forth fragrance,
      and beside our doors are all choice
         fruits,
   new as well as old,
      which I have laid up for you, O my
         beloved.

Longing for Her Beloved
8 Oh that you were like a brother to me
      who nursed at my mother's breasts!
   If I found you outside, I would kiss you,
      and none would despise me.
2 I would lead you and bring you
      into the house of my mother—
      she who used to teach me.
   I would give you spiced wine to drink,
      the juice of my pomegranate.

3 His left hand is under my head,
      and his right hand embraces me!
4 I adjure you, O daughters of Jerusalem,
      that you not stir up or awaken love
      until it pleases.

5 Who is that coming up from the wilder-
         ness,
      leaning on her beloved?

   Under the apple tree I awakened you.
   There your mother was in labor with you;
      there she who bore you was in labor.

6 Set me as a seal upon your heart,
      as a seal upon your arm,
   for love is strong as death,
      jealousy[5] is fierce as the grave.[6]
   Its flashes are flashes of fire,
      the very flame of the LORD.
7 Many waters cannot quench love,
      neither can floods drown it.
   If a man offered for love
      all the wealth of his house,
      he[7] would be utterly despised.

Final Advice
OTHERS
8 We have a little sister,
      and she has no breasts.
   What shall we do for our sister
      on the day when she is spoken for?
9 If she is a wall,
      we will build on her a battlement of
         silver,
   but if she is a door,
      we will enclose her with boards of cedar.

SHE
10 I was a wall,
      and my breasts were like towers;
   then I was in his eyes
      as one who finds[8] peace.

11 Solomon had a vineyard at Baal-hamon;
      he let out the vineyard to keepers;
      each one was to bring for its fruit a
         thousand pieces of silver.
12 My vineyard, my very own, is before me;
      you, O Solomon, may have the thou-
         sand,
      and the keepers of the fruit two hun-
         dred.

[1] Or among delights [2] Hebrew palate [3] Septuagint, Syriac, Vulgate; Hebrew causing the lips of sleepers to speak, or gliding over the lips of those who sleep [4] Or among the henna plants [5] Or ardor [6] Hebrew as Sheol [7] Or it [8] Or brings out

He

13 O you who dwell in the gardens,
  with companions listening for your
    voice;
  let me hear it.

She

14 Make haste, my beloved,
  and be like a gazelle
  or a young stag
    on the mountains of spices.

ISAIAH

1 The vision of Isaiah the son of Amoz, which he saw concerning Judah and Jerusalem in the days of Uzziah, Jotham, Ahaz, and Hezekiah, kings of Judah.

The Wickedness of Judah

2 Hear, O heavens, and give ear, O earth;
    for the LORD has spoken:
"Children[1] have I reared and brought up,
    but they have rebelled against me.
3 The ox knows its owner,
    and the donkey its master's crib,
but Israel does not know,
    my people do not understand."

4 Ah, sinful nation,
    a people laden with iniquity,
offspring of evildoers,
    children who deal corruptly!
They have forsaken the LORD,
    they have despised the Holy One of
        Israel,
    they are utterly estranged.

5 Why will you still be struck down?
    Why will you continue to rebel?
The whole head is sick,
    and the whole heart faint.
6 From the sole of the foot even to the head,
    there is no soundness in it,
but bruises and sores
    and raw wounds;
they are not pressed out or bound up
    or softened with oil.

7 Your country lies desolate;
    your cities are burned with fire;
in your very presence
    foreigners devour your land;
    it is desolate, as overthrown by foreigners.
8 And the daughter of Zion is left
    like a booth in a vineyard,
like a lodge in a cucumber field,
    like a besieged city.

9 If the LORD of hosts
    had not left us a few survivors,
we should have been like Sodom,
    and become like Gomorrah.

10 Hear the word of the LORD,
    you rulers of Sodom!
Give ear to the teaching[2] of our God,
    you people of Gomorrah!
11 "What to me is the multitude of your sacrifices?
    says the LORD;
I have had enough of burnt offerings of
    rams
    and the fat of well-fed beasts;
I do not delight in the blood of bulls,
    or of lambs, or of goats.

12 "When you come to appear before me,
    who has required of you
    this trampling of my courts?
13 Bring no more vain offerings;
    incense is an abomination to me.
New moon and Sabbath and the calling of
    convocations—
    I cannot endure iniquity and solemn
        assembly.
14 Your new moons and your appointed
        feasts
    my soul hates;
they have become a burden to me;
    I am weary of bearing them.
15 When you spread out your hands,
    I will hide my eyes from you;
even though you make many prayers,
    I will not listen;
    your hands are full of blood.
16 Wash yourselves; make yourselves clean;
    remove the evil of your deeds from
        before my eyes;
cease to do evil,
17   learn to do good;
seek justice,
    correct oppression;
bring justice to the fatherless,
    plead the widow's cause.

18 "Come now, let us reason[3] together, says the
        LORD:
though your sins are like scarlet,
    they shall be as white as snow;
though they are red like crimson,
    they shall become like wool.
19 If you are willing and obedient,
    you shall eat the good of the land;

[1] Or Sons; also verse 4 [2] Or law [3] Or dispute

²⁰ but if you refuse and rebel,
    you shall be eaten by the sword;
    for the mouth of the LORD has spoken."

The Unfaithful City

²¹ How the faithful city
    has become a whore,[1]
    she who was full of justice!
Righteousness lodged in her,
    but now murderers.
²² Your silver has become dross,
    your best wine mixed with water.
²³ Your princes are rebels
    and companions of thieves.
Everyone loves a bribe
    and runs after gifts.
They do not bring justice to the fatherless,
    and the widow's cause does not come to
        them.

²⁴ Therefore the Lord declares,
    the LORD of hosts,
    the Mighty One of Israel:
"Ah, I will get relief from my enemies
    and avenge myself on my foes.
²⁵ I will turn my hand against you
    and will smelt away your dross as with
        lye
    and remove all your alloy.
²⁶ And I will restore your judges as at the
        first,
    and your counselors as at the beginning.
Afterward you shall be called the city of
        righteousness,
    the faithful city."

²⁷ Zion shall be redeemed by justice,
    and those in her who repent, by righ-
        teousness.
²⁸ But rebels and sinners shall be broken
        together,
    and those who forsake the LORD shall
        be consumed.
²⁹ For they[2] shall be ashamed of the oaks
    that you desired;
and you shall blush for the gardens
    that you have chosen.
³⁰ For you shall be like an oak
    whose leaf withers,
    and like a garden without water.
³¹ And the strong shall become tinder,
    and his work a spark,
    and both of them shall burn together,
        with none to quench them.

The Mountain of the LORD

2 The word that Isaiah the son of Amoz saw
    concerning Judah and Jerusalem.

² It shall come to pass in the latter days
    that the mountain of the house of the
        LORD
shall be established as the highest of the
        mountains,
    and shall be lifted up above the hills;
and all the nations shall flow to it,
    and many peoples shall come, and say:
"Come, let us go up to the mountain of the
        LORD,
    to the house of the God of Jacob,
that he may teach us his ways
    and that we may walk in his paths."
For out of Zion shall go forth the law,[3]
    and the word of the LORD from
        Jerusalem.
⁴ He shall judge between the nations,
    and shall decide disputes for many
        peoples;
and they shall beat their swords into plow-
        shares,
    and their spears into pruning hooks;
nation shall not lift up sword against
        nation,
    neither shall they learn war anymore.

⁵ O house of Jacob,
    come, let us walk
    in the light of the LORD.

The Day of the LORD

⁶ For you have rejected your people,
    the house of Jacob,
because they are full of things from the
        east
    and of fortune-tellers like the
        Philistines,
    and they strike hands with the children
        of foreigners.
⁷ Their land is filled with silver and gold,
    and there is no end to their treasures;
their land is filled with horses,
    and there is no end to their chariots.
⁸ Their land is filled with idols;
    they bow down to the work of their
        hands,
    to what their own fingers have made.
⁹ So man is humbled,
    and each one is brought low—
    do not forgive them!

[1] Or become unchaste [2] Some Hebrew manuscripts you [3] Or teaching

10 Enter into the rock
     and hide in the dust
   from before the terror of the LORD,
     and from the splendor of his majesty.
11 The haughty looks of man shall be
       brought low,
     and the lofty pride of men shall be
       humbled,
   and the LORD alone will be exalted in that
     .day.

12 For the LORD of hosts has a day
     against all that is proud and lofty,
     against all that is lifted up—and it shall
       be brought low;
13 against all the cedars of Lebanon,
     lofty and lifted up;
   and against all the oaks of Bashan;
14 against all the lofty mountains,
     and against all the uplifted hills;
15 against every high tower,
     and against every fortified wall;
16 against all the ships of Tarshish,
     and against all the beautiful craft.
17 And the haughtiness of man shall be
       humbled, ·
     and the lofty pride of men shall be
       brought low,
   and the LORD alone will be exalted in
     that day.
18 And the idols shall utterly pass away.
19 And people shall enter the caves of the
     rocks
     and the holes of the ground,[1]
   from before the terror of the LORD,
     and from the splendor of his majesty,
     when he rises to terrify the earth.

20 In that day mankind will cast away
     their idols of silver and their idols of
       gold,
   which they made for themselves to
     worship,
     to the moles and to the bats,
21 to enter the caverns of the rocks
     and the clefts of the cliffs,
   from before the terror of the LORD,
     and from the splendor of his majesty,
     when he rises to terrify the earth.
22 Stop regarding man
     in whose nostrils is breath,
     for of what account is he?

Judgment on Judah and Jerusalem

3 For behold, the Lord GOD of hosts
   is taking away from Jerusalem and from
     Judah
   support and supply,[2]
     all support of bread,
     and all support of water;
2 the mighty man and the soldier,
     the judge and the prophet,
     the diviner and the elder,
3 the captain of fifty
     and the man of rank,
   the counselor and the skillful magician
     and the expert in charms.
4 And I will make boys their princes,
     and infants[3] shall rule over them.
5 And the people will oppress one another,
     every one his fellow
     and every one his neighbor;
   the youth will be insolent to the elder,
     and the despised to the honorable.

6 For a man will take hold of his brother
     in the house of his father, saying:
   "You have a cloak;
     you shall be our leader,
   and this heap of ruins
     shall be under your rule";
7 in that day he will speak out, saying:
   "I will not be a healer;[4]
     in my house there is neither bread nor
       cloak;
   you shall not make me
     leader of the people."
8 For Jerusalem has stumbled,
     and Judah has fallen,
   because their speech and their deeds are
     against the LORD,
   defying his glorious presence.[5]

9 For the look on their faces bears witness
     against them;
   they proclaim their sin like Sodom;
     they do not hide it.
   Woe to them!
     For they have brought evil on themselves.
10 Tell the righteous that it shall be well with
     them,
     for they shall eat the fruit of their deeds.
11 Woe to the wicked! It shall be ill with him,
     for what his hands have dealt out shall
       be done to him.
12 My people—infants are their oppressors,
     and women rule over them.

---

[1] Hebrew dust [2] Hebrew staff [3] Or caprice [4] Hebrew binder of wounds [5] Hebrew the eyes of his glory

O my people, your guides mislead you
  and they have swallowed up[1] the course
    of your paths.

13 The LORD has taken his place to contend;
  he stands to judge peoples.
14 The LORD will enter into judgment
  with the elders and princes of his peo-
    ple:
"It is you who have devoured[2] the vineyard,
  the spoil of the poor is in your houses.
15 What do you mean by crushing my people,
  by grinding the face of the poor?"
    declares the Lord GOD of hosts.

16 The LORD said:
Because the daughters of Zion are haughty
  and walk with outstretched necks,
  glancing wantonly with their eyes,
  mincing along as they go,
  tinkling with their feet,
17 therefore the Lord will strike with a scab
  the heads of the daughters of Zion,
  and the LORD will lay bare their secret
    parts.

18 In that day the Lord will take away the finery of the anklets, the headbands, and the crescents; 19 the pendants, the bracelets, and the scarves; 20 the headdresses, the armlets, the sashes, the perfume boxes, and the amulets; 21 the signet rings and nose rings; 22 the festal robes, the mantles, the cloaks, and the handbags; 23 the mirrors, the linen garments, the turbans, and the veils.

24 Instead of perfume there will be rotten-
    ness;
  and instead of a belt, a rope;
  and instead of well-set hair, baldness;
  and instead of a rich robe, a skirt of
    sackcloth;
  and branding instead of beauty.
25 Your men shall fall by the sword
  and your mighty men in battle.
26 And her gates shall lament and mourn;
  empty, she shall sit on the ground.

4 And seven women shall take hold of one man in that day, saying, "We will eat our own bread and wear our own clothes, only let us be called by your name; take away our reproach."

The Branch of the LORD Glorified

2 In that day the branch of the LORD shall be beautiful and glorious, and the fruit of the land shall be the pride and honor of the survivors of Israel. 3 And he who is left in Zion and remains in Jerusalem will be called holy, everyone who has been recorded for life in Jerusalem, 4 when the Lord shall have washed away the filth of the daughters of Zion and cleansed the bloodstains of Jerusalem from its midst by a spirit of judg-ment and by a spirit of burning.[3] 5 Then the LORD will create over the whole site of Mount Zion and over her assemblies a cloud by day, and smoke and the shining of a flaming fire by night; for over all the glory there will be a canopy. 6 There will be a booth for shade by day from the heat, and for a refuge and a shelter from the storm and rain.

The Vineyard of the LORD Destroyed

5 Let me sing for my beloved
  my love song concerning his vineyard:
My beloved had a vineyard
  on a very fertile hill.
2 He dug it and cleared it of stones,
  and planted it with choice vines;
he built a watchtower in the midst of it,
  and hewed out a wine vat in it;
and he looked for it to yield grapes,
  but it yielded wild grapes.

3 And now, O inhabitants of Jerusalem
  and men of Judah,
judge between me and my vineyard.
4 What more was there to do for my vine-
    yard,
  that I have not done in it?
When I looked for it to yield grapes,
  why did it yield wild grapes?

5 And now I will tell you
  what I will do to my vineyard.
I will remove its hedge,
  and it shall be devoured;[4]
I will break down its wall,
  and it shall be trampled down.
6 I will make it a waste;
  it shall not be pruned or hoed,
  and briers and thorns shall grow up;
I will also command the clouds
  that they rain no rain upon it.

7 For the vineyard of the LORD of hosts
  is the house of Israel,

---

[1] Or they have confused [2] Or grazed over; compare Exodus 22:5 [3] Or purging [4] Or grazed over; compare Exodus 22:5

and the men of Judah
are his pleasant planting;
and he looked for justice,
but behold, bloodshed;[1]
for righteousness,
but behold, an outcry![2]

Woe to the Wicked

8 Woe to those who join house to house,
who add field to field,
until there is no more room,
and you are made to dwell alone
in the midst of the land.

9 The LORD of hosts has sworn in my hearing:
"Surely many houses shall be desolate,
large and beautiful houses, without
inhabitant.

10 For ten acres[3] of vineyard shall yield but
one bath,
and a homer of seed shall yield but an
ephah."[4]

11 Woe to those who rise early in the morning,
that they may run after strong drink,
who tarry late into the evening
as wine inflames them!

12 They have lyre and harp,
tambourine and flute and wine at their
feasts,
but they do not regard the deeds of the
LORD,
or see the work of his hands.

13 Therefore my people go into exile
for lack of knowledge;[5]
their honored men go hungry,[6]
and their multitude is parched with
thirst.

14 Therefore Sheol has enlarged its appetite
and opened its mouth beyond measure,
and the nobility of Jerusalem[7] and her multitude will go down,
her revelers and he who exults in her.

15 Man is humbled, and each one is brought
low,
and the eyes of the haughty[8] are
brought low.

16 But the LORD of hosts is exalted[9] in justice,
and the Holy God shows himself holy
in righteousness.

17 Then shall the lambs graze as in their pasture,
and nomads shall eat among the ruins
of the rich.

18 Woe to those who draw iniquity with cords
of falsehood,
who draw sin as with cart ropes,

19 who say: "Let him be quick,
let him speed his work
that we may see it;
let the counsel of the Holy One of Israel
draw near,
and let it come, that we may know it!"

20 Woe to those who call evil good
and good evil,
who put darkness for light
and light for darkness,
who put bitter for sweet
and sweet for bitter!

21 Woe to those who are wise in their own
eyes,
and shrewd in their own sight!

22 Woe to those who are heroes at drinking
wine,
and valiant men in mixing strong drink,

23 who acquit the guilty for a bribe,
and deprive the innocent of his right!

24 Therefore, as the tongue of fire devours the
stubble,
and as dry grass sinks down in the
flame,
so their root will be as rottenness,
and their blossom go up like dust;
for they have rejected the law of the LORD
of hosts,
and have despised the word of the Holy
One of Israel.

25 Therefore the anger of the LORD was
kindled against his people,
and he stretched out his hand against
them and struck them,
and the mountains quaked;
and their corpses were as refuse
in the midst of the streets.
For all this his anger has not turned away,
and his hand is stretched out still.

26 He will raise a signal for nations far away,
and whistle for them from the ends of
the earth;
and behold, quickly, speedily they come!

---

[1] The Hebrew words for *justice* and *bloodshed* sound alike　[2] The Hebrew words for *righteous* and *outcry* sound alike　[3] Hebrew *ten yoke*, the area ten yoke of oxen can plow in a day　[4] A *bath* was about 6 gallons or 22 liters; a *homer* was about 6 bushels or 220 liters; an *ephah* was about 3/5 bushel or 22 liters　[5] Or *without their knowledge*　[6] Or *die of hunger*　[7] Hebrew *her nobility*　[8] Hebrew *high*　[9] Hebrew *high*

27 None is weary, none stumbles,
 none slumbers or sleeps,
not a waistband is loose,
 not a sandal strap broken;
28 their arrows are sharp,
 all their bows bent,
their horses' hoofs seem like flint,
 and their wheels like the whirlwind.
29 Their roaring is like a lion,
 like young lions they roar;
they growl and seize their prey;
 they carry it off, and none can rescue.
30 They will growl over it on that day,
 like the growling of the sea.
And if one looks to the land,
 behold, darkness and distress;
and the light is darkened by its clouds.

Isaiah's Vision of the Lord

6 In the year that King Uzziah died I saw the Lord sitting upon a throne, high and lifted up; and the train[1] of his robe filled the temple. [2] Above him stood the seraphim. Each had six wings: with two he covered his face, and with two he covered his feet, and with two he flew. [3] And one called to another and said:

"Holy, holy, holy is the LORD of hosts;
 the whole earth is full of his glory!"[2]

[4] And the foundations of the thresholds shook at the voice of him who called, and the house was filled with smoke. [5] And I said: "Woe is me! For I am lost; for I am a man of unclean lips, and I dwell in the midst of a people of unclean lips; for my eyes have seen the King, the LORD of hosts!"

[6] Then one of the seraphim flew to me, having in his hand a burning coal that he had taken with tongs from the altar. [7] And he touched my mouth and said: "Behold, this has touched your lips; your guilt is taken away, and your sin atoned for."

Isaiah's Commission from the Lord

[8] And I heard the voice of the Lord saying, "Whom shall I send, and who will go for us?" Then I said, "Here I am! Send me." [9] And he said, "Go, and say to this people:

"'Keep on hearing,[3] but do not understand;
 keep on seeing,[4] but do not perceive.'

10 Make the heart of this people dull,[5]
 and their ears heavy,
 and blind their eyes;
lest they see with their eyes,
 and hear with their ears,
and understand with their hearts,
 and turn and be healed."
11 Then I said, "How long, O Lord?"
 And he said:
"Until cities lie waste
 without inhabitant,
and houses without people,
 and the land is a desolate waste,
12 and the LORD removes people far away,
 and the forsaken places are many in the
  midst of the land.
13 And though a tenth remain in it,
 it will be burned[6] again,
like a terebinth or an oak,
 whose stump remains
 when it is felled."
The holy seed[7] is its stump.

Isaiah Sent to King Ahaz

7 In the days of Ahaz the son of Jotham, son of Uzziah, king of Judah, Rezin the king of Syria and Pekah the son of Remaliah the king of Israel came up to Jerusalem to wage war against it, but could not yet mount an attack against it. [2] When the house of David was told, "Syria is in league with[8] Ephraim," the heart of Ahaz[9] and the heart of his people shook as the trees of the forest shake before the wind.

[3] And the LORD said to Isaiah, "Go out to meet Ahaz, you and Shear-jashub[10] your son, at the end of the conduit of the upper pool on the highway to the Washer's Field. [4] And say to him, 'Be careful, be quiet, do not fear, and do not let your heart be faint because of these two smoldering stumps of firebrands, at the fierce anger of Rezin and Syria and the son of Remaliah. [5] Because Syria, with Ephraim and the son of Remaliah, has devised evil against you, saying, [6] "Let us go up against Judah and terrify it, and let us conquer it[11] for ourselves, and set up the son of Tabeel as king in the midst of it," [7] thus says the Lord GOD:

"'It shall not stand,
 and it shall not come to pass.
8 For the head of Syria is Damascus,
 and the head of Damascus is Rezin.

[1] Or hem [2] Or may his glory fill the whole earth [3] Or Hear indeed [4] Or see indeed [5] Hebrew fat [6] Or purged [7] Or offspring [8] Hebrew Syria has rested upon [9] Hebrew his heart [10] Shear-jashub means A remnant shall return [11] Hebrew let us split it open

And within sixty-five years
> Ephraim will be shattered from being a
> people.
9 And the head of Ephraim is Samaria,
> and the head of Samaria is the son of
> Remaliah.
> If you[1] are not firm in faith,
> you will not be firm at all.'"

The Sign of Immanuel

[10] Again the LORD spoke to Ahaz: [11] "Ask a sign of the LORD your[2] God; let it be deep as Sheol or high as heaven." [12] But Ahaz said, "I will not ask, and I will not put the LORD to the test." [13] And he[3] said, "Hear then, O house of David! Is it too little for you to weary men, that you weary my God also? [14] Therefore the Lord himself will give you a sign. Behold, the virgin shall conceive and bear a son, and shall call his name Immanuel.[4] [15] He shall eat curds and honey when he knows how to refuse the evil and choose the good. [16] For before the boy knows how to refuse the evil and choose the good, the land whose two kings you dread will be deserted. [17] The LORD will bring upon you and upon your people and upon your father's house such days as have not come since the day that Ephraim departed from Judah—the king of Assyria!"

[18] In that day the LORD will whistle for the fly that is at the end of the streams of Egypt, and for the bee that is in the land of Assyria. [19] And they will all come and settle in the steep ravines, and in the clefts of the rocks, and on all the thornbushes, and on all the pastures.[5]

[20] In that day the Lord will shave with a razor that is hired beyond the River[6]—with the king of Assyria—the head and the hair of the feet, and it will sweep away the beard also.

[21] In that day a man will keep alive a young cow and two sheep, [22] and because of the abundance of milk that they give, he will eat curds, for everyone who is left in the land will eat curds and honey.

[23] In that day every place where there used to be a thousand vines, worth a thousand shekels[7] of silver, will become briers and thorns. [24] With bow and arrows a man will come there, for all the land will be briers and thorns. [25] And as for all the hills that used to be hoed with a hoe, you will not come there for fear of briers and thorns, but they will become a place where cattle are let loose and where sheep tread.

The Coming Assyrian Invasion

8 Then the LORD said to me, "Take a large tablet and write on it in common characters,[8] 'Belonging to Maher-shalal-hash-baz.'[9] [2] And I will get reliable witnesses, Uriah the priest and Zechariah the son of Jeberechiah, to attest for me."

[3] And I went to the prophetess, and she conceived and bore a son. Then the LORD said to me, "Call his name Maher-shalal-hash-baz; [4] for before the boy knows how to cry 'My father' or 'My mother,' the wealth of Damascus and the spoil of Samaria will be carried away before the king of Assyria."

[5] The LORD spoke to me again: [6] "Because this people has refused the waters of Shiloah that flow gently, and rejoice over Rezin and the son of Remaliah, [7] therefore, behold, the Lord is bringing up against them the waters of the River,[10] mighty and many, the king of Assyria and all his glory. And it will rise over all its channels and go over all its banks, [8] and it will sweep on into Judah, it will overflow and pass on, reaching even to the neck, and its outspread wings will fill the breadth of your land, O Immanuel."

9 Be broken,[11] you peoples, and be shattered;[12]
> give ear, all you far countries;
> strap on your armor and be shattered;
> strap on your armor and be shattered.
10 Take counsel together, but it will come to
> nothing;
> speak a word, but it will not stand,
> for God is with us.[13]

Fear God, Wait for the LORD

[11] For the LORD spoke thus to me with his strong hand upon me, and warned me not to walk in the way of this people, saying: [12] "Do not call conspiracy all that this people calls conspiracy, and do not fear what they fear, nor be in dread. [13] But the LORD of hosts, him you shall honor as holy. Let him be your fear, and let him be your dread. [14] And he will become a sanctuary and a stone of offense and a rock of stumbling to both houses of Israel, a trap and a snare to the inhabitants of Jerusalem. [15] And many shall stumble on it. They shall fall and be broken; they shall be snared and taken."

[16] Bind up the testimony; seal the teaching[14] among my disciples. [17] I will wait for the LORD,

---

[1] The Hebrew for *you* is plural in verses 9, 13, 14   [2] The Hebrew for *you* and *your* is singular in verses 11, 16, 17   [3] That is, Isaiah   [4] *Immanuel* means *God is with us*   [5] Or *watering holes, or brambles*   [6] That is, the Euphrates   [7] A *shekel* was about 2/5 ounce or 11 grams   [8] Hebrew *with a man's stylus*   [9] *Maher-shalal-hash-baz* means *The spoil speeds, the prey hastens*   [10] That is, the Euphrates   [11] Or *Be evil*   [12] Or *dismayed*   [13] The Hebrew for *God is with us* is *Immanuel*   [14] Or *law*; also verse 20

who is hiding his face from the house of Jacob, and I will hope in him. [18] Behold, I and the children whom the LORD has given me are signs and portents in Israel from the LORD of hosts, who dwells on Mount Zion. [19] And when they say to you, "Inquire of the mediums and the necromancers who chirp and mutter," should not a people inquire of their God? Should they inquire of the dead on behalf of the living? [20] To the teaching and to the testimony! If they will not speak according to this word, it is because they have no dawn. [21] They will pass through the land,[1] greatly distressed and hungry. And when they are hungry, they will be enraged and will speak contemptuously against[2] their king and their God, and turn their faces upward. [22] And they will look to the earth, but behold, distress and darkness, the gloom of anguish. And they will be thrust into thick darkness.

For to Us a Child Is Born

9 [3] But there will be no gloom for her who was in anguish. In the former time he brought into contempt the land of Zebulun and the land of Naphtali, but in the latter time he has made glorious the way of the sea, the land beyond the Jordan, Galilee of the nations.[4]

[2] [5] The people who walked in darkness
  have seen a great light;
those who dwelt in a land of deep darkness,
  on them has light shone.
[3] You have multiplied the nation;
  you have increased its joy;
they rejoice before you
  as with joy at the harvest,
  as they are glad when they divide the spoil.
[4] For the yoke of his burden,
  and the staff for his shoulder,
  the rod of his oppressor,
  you have broken as on the day of Midian.
[5] For every boot of the tramping warrior in battle tumult
  and every garment rolled in blood
  will be burned as fuel for the fire.
[6] For to us a child is born,
  to us a son is given;
and the government shall be upon[6] his shoulder,
  and his name shall be called[7]

Wonderful Counselor, Mighty God,
  Everlasting Father, Prince of Peace.
[7] Of the increase of his government and of peace
  there will be no end,
on the throne of David and over his kingdom,
  to establish it and to uphold it
with justice and with righteousness
  from this time forth and forevermore.
The zeal of the LORD of hosts will do this.

Judgment on Arrogance and Oppression

[8] The Lord has sent a word against Jacob,
  and it will fall on Israel;
[9] and all the people will know,
  Ephraim and the inhabitants of Samaria,
  who say in pride and in arrogance of heart:
[10] "The bricks have fallen,
  but we will build with dressed stones;
the sycamores have been cut down,
  but we will put cedars in their place."
[11] But the LORD raises the adversaries of Rezin against him,
  and stirs up his enemies.
[12] The Syrians on the east and the Philistines on the west
  devour Israel with open mouth.
For all this his anger has not turned away,
  and his hand is stretched out still.

[13] The people did not turn to him who struck them,
  nor inquire of the LORD of hosts.
[14] So the LORD cut off from Israel head and tail,
  palm branch and reed in one day—
[15] the elder and honored man is the head,
  and the prophet who teaches lies is the tail;
[16] for those who guide this people have been leading them astray,
  and those who are guided by them are swallowed up.
[17] Therefore the Lord does not rejoice over their young men,
  and has no compassion on their fatherless and widows;
for everyone is godless and an evildoer,
  and every mouth speaks folly.[8]
For all this his anger has not turned away,
  and his hand is stretched out still.

[1] Hebrew it [2] Or speak contemptuously by [3] Ch 8:23 in Hebrew [4] Or of the Gentiles [5] Ch 9:1 in Hebrew [6] Or is upon [7] Or is called [8] Or speaks disgraceful things

18 For wickedness burns like a fire;
        it consumes briers and thorns;
    it kindles the thickets of the forest,
        and they roll upward in a column of
            smoke.
19 Through the wrath of the LORD of hosts
        the land is scorched,
    and the people are like fuel for the fire;
        no one spares another.
20 They slice meat on the right, but are still
            hungry,
        and they devour on the left, but are not
            satisfied;
    each devours the flesh of his own arm,
21 Manasseh devours Ephraim, and Ephraim
            devours Manasseh;
        together they are against Judah.
    For all this his anger has not turned away,
        and his hand is stretched out still.

10 Woe to those who decree iniquitous
            decrees,
        and the writers who keep writing
            oppression,
2   to turn aside the needy from justice
        and to rob the poor of my people of
            their right,
    that widows may be their spoil,
        and that they may make the fatherless
            their prey!
3   What will you do on the day of punish-
            ment,
        in the ruin that will come from afar?
    To whom will you flee for help,
        and where will you leave your wealth?
4   Nothing remains but to crouch among the
            prisoners
        or fall among the slain.
    For all this his anger has not turned away,
        and his hand is stretched out still.

Judgment on Arrogant Assyria

5   Woe to Assyria, the rod of my anger;
        the staff in their hands is my fury!
6   Against a godless nation I send him,
        and against the people of my wrath I
            command him,
    to take spoil and seize plunder,
        and to tread them down like the mire of
            the streets.
7   But he does not so intend,
        and his heart does not so think;
    but it is in his heart to destroy,
        and to cut off nations not a few;

8   for he says:
    "Are not my commanders all kings?
9   Is not Calno like Carchemish?
        Is not Hamath like Arpad?
        Is not Samaria like Damascus?
10 As my hand has reached to the kingdoms
            of the idols,
        whose carved images were greater than
            those of Jerusalem and Samaria,
11 shall I not do to Jerusalem and her idols
        as I have done to Samaria and her
            images?"

12 When the Lord has finished all his work on
Mount Zion and on Jerusalem, he[1] will punish
the speech[2] of the arrogant heart of the king
of Assyria and the boastful look in his eyes.
13 For he says:

    "By the strength of my hand I have done it,
        and by my wisdom, for I have under-
            standing;
    I remove the boundaries of peoples,
        and plunder their treasures;
        like a bull I bring down those who sit
            on thrones.
14 My hand has found like a nest
        the wealth of the peoples;
    and as one gathers eggs that have been for-
            saken,
        so I have gathered all the earth;
    and there was none that moved a wing
        or opened the mouth or chirped."

15 Shall the axe boast over him who hews
            with it,
        or the saw magnify itself against him
            who wields it?
    As if a rod should wield him who lifts it,
        or as if a staff should lift him who is not
            wood!
16 Therefore the Lord GOD of hosts
        will send wasting sickness among his
            stout warriors,
    and under his glory a burning will be
            kindled,
        like the burning of fire.
17 The light of Israel will become a fire,
        and his Holy One a flame,
    and it will burn and devour
        his thorns and briers in one day.

---

1 Hebrew *I*   2 Hebrew *fruit*

18   The glory of his forest and of his fruitful
         land
      the LORD will destroy, both soul and
         body,
      and it will be as when a sick man wastes
         away.
19   The remnant of the trees of his forest will
         be so few
      that a child can write them down.

The Remnant of Israel Will Return

20 In that day the remnant of Israel and the
survivors of the house of Jacob will no more
lean on him who struck them, but will lean
on the LORD, the Holy One of Israel, in truth.
21 A remnant will return, the remnant of Jacob,
to the mighty God. 22 For though your people
Israel be as the sand of the sea, only a remnant
of them will return. Destruction is decreed,
overflowing with righteousness. 23 For the Lord
GOD of hosts will make a full end, as decreed,
in the midst of all the earth.

24 Therefore thus says the Lord GOD of hosts:
"O my people, who dwell in Zion, be not afraid
of the Assyrians when they strike with the
rod and lift up their staff against you as the
Egyptians did. 25 For in a very little while my
fury will come to an end, and my anger will be
directed to their destruction. 26 And the LORD of
hosts will wield against them a whip, as when
he struck Midian at the rock of Oreb. And his
staff will be over the sea, and he will lift it as
he did in Egypt. 27 And in that day his burden
will depart from your shoulder, and his yoke
from your neck; and the yoke will be broken
because of the fat."[1]

28   He has come to Aiath;
      he has passed through Migron;
         at Michmash he stores his baggage;
29   they have crossed over the pass;
         at Geba they lodge for the night;
      Ramah trembles;
         Gibeah of Saul has fled.
30   Cry aloud, O daughter of Gallim!
         Give attention, O Laishah!
         O poor Anathoth!
31   Madmenah is in flight;
         the inhabitants of Gebim flee for safety.
32   This very day he will halt at Nob;
         he will shake his fist
      at the mount of the daughter of Zion,
         the hill of Jerusalem.

33   Behold, the Lord GOD of hosts
         will lop the boughs with terrifying
            power;
      the great in height will be hewn down,
         and the lofty will be brought low.
34   He will cut down the thickets of the forest
         with an axe,
      and Lebanon will fall by the Majestic
         One.

The Righteous Reign of the Branch

11 There shall come forth a shoot from
      the stump of Jesse,
      and a branch from his roots shall bear
         fruit.
2   And the Spirit of the LORD shall rest upon
         him,
      the Spirit of wisdom and understand-
         ing,
      the Spirit of counsel and might,
      the Spirit of knowledge and the fear of
         the LORD.
3   And his delight shall be in the fear of the
         LORD.
      He shall not judge by what his eyes see,
         or decide disputes by what his ears hear,
4   but with righteousness he shall judge the
         poor,
      and decide with equity for the meek of
         the earth;
      and he shall strike the earth with the rod of
         his mouth,
      and with the breath of his lips he shall
         kill the wicked.
5   Righteousness shall be the belt of his waist,
      and faithfulness the belt of his loins.

6   The wolf shall dwell with the lamb,
      and the leopard shall lie down with the
         young goat,
      and the calf and the lion and the fattened
         calf together;
      and a little child shall lead them.
7   The cow and the bear shall graze;
         their young shall lie down together;
      and the lion shall eat straw like the ox.
8   The nursing child shall play over the hole
         of the cobra,
      and the weaned child shall put his hand
         on the adder's den.
9   They shall not hurt or destroy
         in all my holy mountain;

[1] The meaning of the Hebrew is uncertain

for the earth shall be full of the knowledge
   of the Lord
     as the waters cover the sea.

[10] In that day the root of Jesse, who shall stand as a signal for the peoples—of him shall the nations inquire, and his resting place shall be glorious.

[11] In that day the Lord will extend his hand yet a second time to recover the remnant that remains of his people, from Assyria, from Egypt, from Pathros, from Cush,[1] from Elam, from Shinar, from Hamath, and from the coastlands of the sea.

[12] He will raise a signal for the nations
    and will assemble the banished of Israel,
and gather the dispersed of Judah
    from the four corners of the earth.
[13] The jealousy of Ephraim shall depart,
    and those who harass Judah shall be cut
      off;
Ephraim shall not be jealous of Judah,
    and Judah shall not harass Ephraim.
[14] But they shall swoop down on the shoulder of the Philistines in the west,
    and together they shall plunder the
      people of the east.
They shall put out their hand against
    Edom and Moab,
    and the Ammonites shall obey them.
[15] And the Lord will utterly destroy[2]
    the tongue of the Sea of Egypt,
and will wave his hand over the River[3]
    with his scorching breath,[4]
and strike it into seven channels,
    and he will lead people across in sandals.
[16] And there will be a highway from Assyria
    for the remnant that remains of his
      people,
as there was for Israel
    when they came up from the land of
      Egypt.

The Lord Is My Strength and My Song

12 You[5] will say in that day:
   "I will give thanks to you, O Lord,
    for though you were angry with me,
   your anger turned away,
    that you might comfort me.

[2] "Behold, God is my salvation;
   I will trust, and will not be afraid;
   for the Lord God[6] is my strength and my
     song,
   and he has become my salvation."

[3] With joy you[7] will draw water from the wells of salvation. [4] And you will say in that day:

"Give thanks to the Lord,
   call upon his name,
make known his deeds among the peoples,
   proclaim that his name is exalted.

[5] "Sing praises to the Lord, for he has done
     gloriously;
   let this be made known[8] in all the earth.
[6] Shout, and sing for joy, O inhabitant of
     Zion,
   for great in your[9] midst is the Holy One
     of Israel."

The Judgment of Babylon

13 The oracle concerning Babylon which Isaiah the son of Amoz saw.

[2] On a bare hill raise a signal;
   cry aloud to them;
wave the hand for them to enter
   the gates of the nobles.
[3] I myself have commanded my consecrated
     ones,
   and have summoned my mighty men
    to execute my anger,
   my proudly exulting ones.[10]

[4] The sound of a tumult is on the mountains
   as of a great multitude!
The sound of an uproar of kingdoms,
   of nations gathering together!
The Lord of hosts is mustering
   a host for battle.
[5] They come from a distant land,
   from the end of the heavens,
the Lord and the weapons of his indignation,
   to destroy the whole land.[11]

[6] Wail, for the day of the Lord is near;
   as destruction from the Almighty[12] it
    will come!
[7] Therefore all hands will be feeble,
   and every human heart will melt.

---

[1] Probably *Nubia* [2] Hebrew *devote to destruction* [3] That is, the Euphrates [4] Or *wind* [5] The Hebrew for *you* is singular in verse 1 [6] Hebrew *for Yah, the Lord* [7] The Hebrew for *you* is plural in verses 3, 4 [8] Or *this is made known* [9] The Hebrew for *your* in verse 6 is singular, referring to the *inhabitant of Zion* [10] Or *those who exult in my majesty* [11] Or *earth;* also verse 9 [12] The Hebrew words for *destruction* and *almighty* sound alike

8 They will be dismayed:
  pangs and agony will seize them;
  they will be in anguish like a woman
    in labor.
They will look aghast at one another;
  their faces will be aflame.

9 Behold, the day of the LORD comes,
  cruel, with wrath and fierce anger,
to make the land a desolation
  and to destroy its sinners from it.

10 For the stars of the heavens and their con-
    stellations
  will not give their light;
the sun will be dark at its rising,
  and the moon will not shed its light.

11 I will punish the world for its evil,
  and the wicked for their iniquity;
I will put an end to the pomp of the arro-
    gant,
  and lay low the pompous pride of the
    ruthless.

12 I will make people more rare than fine
    gold,
  and mankind than the gold of Ophir.

13 Therefore I will make the heavens tremble,
  and the earth will be shaken out of its
    place,
at the wrath of the LORD of hosts
  in the day of his fierce anger.

14 And like a hunted gazelle,
  or like sheep with none to gather them,
each will turn to his own people,
  and each will flee to his own land.

15 Whoever is found will be thrust through,
  and whoever is caught will fall by the
    sword.

16 Their infants will be dashed in pieces
  before their eyes;
their houses will be plundered
  and their wives ravished.

17 Behold, I am stirring up the Medes against
    them,
  who have no regard for silver
  and do not delight in gold.

18 Their bows will slaughter[1] the young men;
  they will have no mercy on the fruit of
    the womb;
  their eyes will not pity children.

19 And Babylon, the glory of kingdoms,
  the splendor and pomp of the
    Chaldeans,

will be like Sodom and Gomorrah
  when God overthrew them.

20 It will never be inhabited
  or lived in for all generations;
no Arab will pitch his tent there;
  no shepherds will make their flocks lie
    down there.

21 But wild animals will lie down there,
  and their houses will be full of howling
    creatures;
there ostriches[2] will dwell,
  and there wild goats will dance.

22 Hyenas[3] will cry in its towers,
  and jackals in the pleasant palaces;
its time is close at hand
  and its days will not be prolonged.

The Restoration of Jacob

14 For the LORD will have compassion on
Jacob and will again choose Israel, and
will set them in their own land, and sojourners
will join them and will attach themselves to
the house of Jacob. [2] And the peoples will take
them and bring them to their place, and the
house of Israel will possess them in the LORD's
land as male and female slaves.[4] They will take
captive those who were their captors, and rule
over those who oppressed them.

Israel's Remnant Taunts Babylon

[3] When the LORD has given you rest from
your pain and turmoil and the hard service
with which you were made to serve, [4] you will
take up this taunt against the king of Babylon:

"How the oppressor has ceased,
  the insolent fury[5] ceased!
5 The LORD has broken the staff of the
    wicked,
  the scepter of rulers,
6 that struck the peoples in wrath
  with unceasing blows,
that ruled the nations in anger
  with unrelenting persecution.
7 The whole earth is at rest and quiet;
  they break forth into singing.
8 The cypresses rejoice at you,
  the cedars of Lebanon, saying,
'Since you were laid low,
  no woodcutter comes up against us.'
9 Sheol beneath is stirred up
  to meet you when you come;
it rouses the shades to greet you,
  all who were leaders of the earth;

[1] Hebrew dash in pieces [2] Or owls [3] Or foxes [4] Or servants [5] Dead Sea Scroll (compare Septuagint, Syriac, Vulgate); the meaning of the word in the Masoretic Text is uncertain

it raises from their thrones
   all who were kings of the nations.
10 All of them will answer
   and say to you:
'You too have become as weak as we!
   You have become like us!'
11 Your pomp is brought down to Sheol,
   the sound of your harps;
maggots are laid as a bed beneath you,
   and worms are your covers.

12 "How you are fallen from heaven,
   O Day Star, son of Dawn!
How you are cut down to the ground,
   you who laid the nations low!
13 You said in your heart,
   'I will ascend to heaven;
above the stars of God
   I will set my throne on high;
I will sit on the mount of assembly
   in the far reaches of the north;[1]
14 I will ascend above the heights of the
   clouds;
   I will make myself like the Most High.'
15 But you are brought down to Sheol,
   to the far reaches of the pit.
16 Those who see you will stare at you
   and ponder over you:
'Is this the man who made the earth tremble,
   who shook kingdoms,
17 who made the world like a desert
   and overthrew its cities,
   who did not let his prisoners go home?'
18 All the kings of the nations lie in glory,
   each in his own tomb;[2]
19 but you are cast out, away from your grave,
   like a loathed branch,
clothed with the slain, those pierced by the
   sword,
   who go down to the stones of the pit,
   like a dead body trampled underfoot.
20 You will not be joined with them in burial,
   because you have destroyed your land,
   you have slain your people.

"May the offspring of evildoers
   nevermore be named!
21 Prepare slaughter for his sons
   because of the guilt of their fathers,
lest they rise and possess the earth,
   and fill the face of the world with cities."

22 "I will rise up against them," declares the
LORD of hosts, "and will cut off from Babylon
name and remnant, descendants and posterity,"
declares the LORD. 23 "And I will make it a possession of the hedgehog,[3] and pools of water,
and I will sweep it with the broom of destruction," declares the LORD of hosts.

An Oracle Concerning Assyria
24   The LORD of hosts has sworn:
"As I have planned,
   so shall it be,
and as I have purposed,
   so shall it stand,
25 that I will break the Assyrian in my land,
   and on my mountains trample him
      underfoot;
and his yoke shall depart from them,
   and his burden from their shoulder."

26 This is the purpose that is purposed
   concerning the whole earth,
and this is the hand that is stretched out
   over all the nations.
27 For the LORD of hosts has purposed,
   and who will annul it?
His hand is stretched out,
   and who will turn it back?

An Oracle Concerning Philistia
28 In the year that King Ahaz died came this
oracle:

29 Rejoice not, O Philistia, all of you,
   that the rod that struck you is broken,
for from the serpent's root will come forth
   an adder,
   and its fruit will be a flying fiery ser-
      pent.
30 And the firstborn of the poor will graze,
   and the needy lie down in safety;
but I will kill your root with famine,
   and your remnant it will slay.
31 Wail, O gate; cry out, O city;
   melt in fear, O Philistia, all of you!
For smoke comes out of the north,
   and there is no straggler in his ranks.
32 What will one answer the messengers of
   the nation?
"The LORD has founded Zion,
   and in her the afflicted of his people
      find refuge."

---

[1] Or in the remote parts of Zaphon [2] Hebrew house [3] Possibly porcupine, or owl

An Oracle Concerning Moab

15 An oracle concerning Moab.

Because Ar of Moab is laid waste in a
    night,
    Moab is undone;
because Kir of Moab is laid waste in a
    night,
    Moab is undone.
2 He has gone up to the temple,[1] and to
    Dibon,
    to the high places[2] to weep;
over Nebo and over Medeba
    Moab wails.
On every head is baldness;
    every beard is shorn;
3 in the streets they wear sackcloth;
    on the housetops and in the squares
    everyone wails and melts in tears.
4 Heshbon and Elealeh cry out;
    their voice is heard as far as Jahaz;
therefore the armed men of Moab cry
    aloud;
    his soul trembles.
5 My heart cries out for Moab;
    her fugitives flee to Zoar,
    to Eglath-shelishiyah.
For at the ascent of Luhith
    they go up weeping;
on the road to Horonaim
    they raise a cry of destruction;
6 the waters of Nimrim
    are a desolation;
the grass is withered, the vegetation fails,
    the greenery is no more.
7 Therefore the abundance they have
    gained
    and what they have laid up
they carry away
    over the Brook of the Willows.
8 For a cry has gone
    around the land of Moab;
her wailing reaches to Eglaim;
    her wailing reaches to Beer-elim.
9 For the waters of Dibon[3] are full of blood;
    for I will bring upon Dibon even more,
a lion for those of Moab who escape,
    for the remnant of the land.

16 Send the lamb to the ruler of the land,
    from Sela, by way of the desert,
    to the mount of the daughter of Zion.

2 Like fleeing birds,
    like a scattered nest,
so are the daughters of Moab
    at the fords of the Arnon.

3 "Give counsel;
    grant justice;
make your shade like night
    at the height of noon;
shelter the outcasts;
    do not reveal the fugitive;
4 let the outcasts of Moab
    sojourn among you;
be a shelter to them[4]
    from the destroyer.
When the oppressor is no more,
    and destruction has ceased,
and he who tramples underfoot has van-
    ished from the land,
5 then a throne will be established in stead-
    fast love,
    and on it will sit in faithfulness
    in the tent of David
one who judges and seeks justice
    and is swift to do righteousness."

6 We have heard of the pride of Moab—
    how proud he is!—
of his arrogance, his pride, and his inso-
    lence;
    in his idle boasting he is not right.
7 Therefore let Moab wail for Moab,
    let everyone wail.
Mourn, utterly stricken,
    for the raisin cakes of Kir-hareseth.

8 For the fields of Heshbon languish,
    and the vine of Sibmah;
the lords of the nations
    have struck down its branches,
which reached to Jazer
    and strayed to the desert;
its shoots spread abroad
    and passed over the sea.
9 Therefore I weep with the weeping of Jazer
    for the vine of Sibmah;
I drench you with my tears,
    O Heshbon and Elealeh;
for over your summer fruit and your har-
    vest
    the shout has ceased.
10 And joy and gladness are taken away from
    the fruitful field,

---

[1] Hebrew *the house* [2] Or *temple, even Dibon to the high places* [3] Dead Sea Scroll, Vulgate (compare Syriac); Masoretic Text *Dimon*; twice in this verse [4] Some Hebrew manuscripts, Septuagint, Syriac; Masoretic Text *let my outcasts sojourn among you; as for Moab, be a shelter to them*

and in the vineyards no songs are sung,
   no cheers are raised;
no treader treads out wine in the presses;
   I have put an end to the shouting.
[11] Therefore my inner parts moan like a lyre
   for Moab,
     and my inmost self for Kir-hareseth.

[12] And when Moab presents himself, when he wearies himself on the high place, when he comes to his sanctuary to pray, he will not prevail. [13] This is the word that the LORD spoke concerning Moab in the past. [14] But now the LORD has spoken, saying, "In three years, like the years of a hired worker, the glory of Moab will be brought into contempt, in spite of all his great multitude, and those who remain will be very few and feeble."

An Oracle Concerning Damascus

17 An oracle concerning Damascus.

Behold, Damascus will cease to be a city
   and will become a heap of ruins.
[2] The cities of Aroer are deserted;
   they will be for flocks,
     which will lie down, and none will
       make them afraid.
[3] The fortress will disappear from Ephraim,
   and the kingdom from Damascus;
and the remnant of Syria will be
   like the glory of the children of Israel,
       declares the LORD of hosts.

[4] And in that day the glory of Jacob will be
   brought low,
   and the fat of his flesh will grow lean.
[5] And it shall be as when the reaper gathers
   standing grain
   and his arm harvests the ears,
and as when one gleans the ears of grain
   in the Valley of Rephaim.
[6] Gleanings will be left in it,
   as when an olive tree is beaten—
two or three berries
   in the top of the highest bough,
four or five
   on the branches of a fruit tree,
       declares the LORD God of Israel.

[7] In that day man will look to his Maker, and his eyes will look on the Holy One of Israel. [8] He will not look to the altars, the work of his hands, and he will not look on what his own fingers have made, either the Asherim or the altars of incense.

[9] In that day their strong cities will be like the deserted places of the wooded heights and the hilltops, which they deserted because of the children of Israel, and there will be desolation.

[10] For you have forgotten the God of your
   salvation
   and have not remembered the Rock of
     your refuge;
therefore, though you plant pleasant
   plants
   and sow the vine-branch of a stranger,
[11] though you make them grow[1] on the day
     that you plant them,
   and make them blossom in the morn-
     ing that you sow,
yet the harvest will flee away[2]
   in a day of grief and incurable pain.

[12] Ah, the thunder of many peoples;
   they thunder like the thundering of the
     sea!
Ah, the roar of nations;
   they roar like the roaring of mighty
     waters!
[13] The nations roar like the roaring of many
   waters,
   but he will rebuke them, and they will
     flee far away,
chased like chaff on the mountains before
   the wind
   and whirling dust before the storm.
[14] At evening time, behold, terror!
   Before morning, they are no more!
This is the portion of those who loot us,
   and the lot of those who plunder us.

An Oracle Concerning Cush

18 Ah, land of whirring wings
   that is beyond the rivers of Cush,[3]
[2] which sends ambassadors by the sea,
   in vessels of papyrus on the waters!
Go, you swift messengers,
   to a nation tall and smooth,
to a people feared near and far,
   a nation mighty and conquering,
   whose land the rivers divide.

[3] All you inhabitants of the world,
   you who dwell on the earth,
when a signal is raised on the mountains,
   look!
When a trumpet is blown, hear!

---

[1] Or *though you carefully fence them* [2] Or *will be a heap* [3] Probably *Nubia*

⁴ For thus the Lord said to me:
"I will quietly look from my dwelling
        like clear heat in sunshine,
        like a cloud of dew in the heat of har-
            vest."
⁵ For before the harvest, when the blossom is
        over,
    and the flower becomes a ripening
        grape,
    he cuts off the shoots with pruning hooks,
        and the spreading branches he lops off
            and clears away.
⁶ They shall all of them be left
        to the birds of prey of the mountains
        and to the beasts of the earth.
    And the birds of prey will summer on
        them,
        and all the beasts of the earth will
            winter on them.

    ⁷ At that time tribute will be brought to the
Lord of hosts

    from a people tall and smooth,
        from a people feared near and far,
    a nation mighty and conquering,
        whose land the rivers divide,

to Mount Zion, the place of the name of the
Lord of hosts.

An Oracle Concerning Egypt

19 An oracle concerning Egypt.

    Behold, the Lord is riding on a swift
        cloud
        and comes to Egypt;
    and the idols of Egypt will tremble at his
        presence,
    and the heart of the Egyptians will melt
        within them.
² And I will stir up Egyptians against
        Egyptians,
    and they will fight, each against
        another
    and each against his neighbor,
        city against city, kingdom against king-
            dom;
³ and the spirit of the Egyptians within
        them will be emptied out,
    and I will confound¹ their counsel;
    and they will inquire of the idols and the
        sorcerers,
        and the mediums and the necroman-
            cers;

⁴ and I will give over the Egyptians
        into the hand of a hard master,
    and a fierce king will rule over them,
        declares the Lord God of hosts.

⁵ And the waters of the sea will be dried up,
        and the river will be dry and parched,
⁶ and its canals will become foul,
        and the branches of Egypt's Nile will
            diminish and dry up,
        reeds and rushes will rot away.
⁷ There will be bare places by the Nile,
        on the brink of the Nile,
    and all that is sown by the Nile will be
        parched,
        will be driven away, and will be no
            more.
⁸ The fishermen will mourn and lament,
        all who cast a hook in the Nile;
    and they will languish
        who spread nets on the water.
⁹ The workers in combed flax will be in
        despair,
        and the weavers of white cotton.
¹⁰ Those who are the pillars of the land will
        be crushed,
        and all who work for pay will be
            grieved.

¹¹ The princes of Zoan are utterly foolish;
        the wisest counselors of Pharaoh give
            stupid counsel.
    How can you say to Pharaoh,
    "I am a son of the wise,
        a son of ancient kings"?
¹² Where then are your wise men?
        Let them tell you
        that they might know what the Lord of
            hosts has purposed against Egypt.
¹³ The princes of Zoan have become fools,
        and the princes of Memphis are
            deluded;
    those who are the cornerstones of her
        tribes
        have made Egypt stagger.
¹⁴ The Lord has mingled within her a spirit
        of confusion,
    and they will make Egypt stagger in all its
        deeds,
        as a drunken man staggers in his vomit.
¹⁵ And there will be nothing for Egypt
        that head or tail, palm branch or reed,
            may do.

¹ Or I will swallow up

Egypt, Assyria, Israel Blessed

16 In that day the Egyptians will be like women, and tremble with fear before the hand that the LORD of hosts shakes over them. 17 And the land of Judah will become a terror to the Egyptians. Everyone to whom it is mentioned will fear because of the purpose that the LORD of hosts has purposed against them.

18 In that day there will be five cities in the land of Egypt that speak the language of Canaan and swear allegiance to the LORD of hosts. One of these will be called the City of Destruction.[1]

19 In that day there will be an altar to the LORD in the midst of the land of Egypt, and a pillar to the LORD at its border. 20 It will be a sign and a witness to the LORD of hosts in the land of Egypt. When they cry to the LORD because of oppressors, he will send them a savior and defender, and deliver them. 21 And the LORD will make himself known to the Egyptians, and the Egyptians will know the LORD in that day and worship with sacrifice and offering, and they will make vows to the LORD and perform them. 22 And the LORD will strike Egypt, striking and healing, and they will return to the LORD, and he will listen to their pleas for mercy and heal them.

23 In that day there will be a highway from Egypt to Assyria, and Assyria will come into Egypt, and Egypt into Assyria, and the Egyptians will worship with the Assyrians.

24 In that day Israel will be the third with Egypt and Assyria, a blessing in the midst of the earth, 25 whom the LORD of hosts has blessed, saying, "Blessed be Egypt my people, and Assyria the work of my hands, and Israel my inheritance."

A Sign Against Egypt and Cush

20 In the year that the commander in chief, who was sent by Sargon the king of Assyria, came to Ashdod and fought against it and captured it— 2 at that time the LORD spoke by Isaiah the son of Amoz, saying, "Go, and loose the sackcloth from your waist and take off your sandals from your feet," and he did so, walking naked and barefoot.

3 Then the LORD said, "As my servant Isaiah has walked naked and barefoot for three years as a sign and a portent against Egypt and Cush,[2] 4 so shall the king of Assyria lead away the Egyptian captives and the Cushite exiles, both the young and the old, naked and barefoot, with buttocks uncovered, the nakedness of Egypt. 5 Then they shall be dismayed and ashamed because of Cush their hope and of Egypt their boast. 6 And the inhabitants of this coastland will say in that day, 'Behold, this is what has happened to those in whom we hoped and to whom we fled for help to be delivered from the king of Assyria! And we, how shall we escape?'"

Fallen, Fallen Is Babylon

21 The oracle concerning the wilderness of the sea.

As whirlwinds in the Negeb sweep on,
    it comes from the wilderness,
    from a terrible land.
2 A stern vision is told to me;
    the traitor betrays,
    and the destroyer destroys.
Go up, O Elam;
    lay siege, O Media;
all the sighing she has caused
    I bring to an end.
3 Therefore my loins are filled with
       anguish;
    pangs have seized me,
    like the pangs of a woman in labor;
I am bowed down so that I cannot hear;
    I am dismayed so that I cannot see.
4 My heart staggers; horror has appalled me;
    the twilight I longed for
    has been turned for me into trem-
       bling.
5 They prepare the table,
    they spread the rugs,[3]
    they eat, they drink.
Arise, O princes;
    oil the shield!
6 For thus the Lord said to me:
"Go, set a watchman;
    let him announce what he sees.
7 When he sees riders, horsemen in pairs,
    riders on donkeys, riders on camels,
let him listen diligently,
    very diligently."
8 Then he who saw cried out:[4]
"Upon a watchtower I stand, O Lord,
    continually by day,
    and at my post I am stationed
    whole nights.

---

[1] Dead Sea Scroll and some other manuscripts *City of the Sun* [2] Probably *Nubia* [3] Or *they set the watchman* [4] Dead Sea Scroll, Syriac; Masoretic Text *Then a lion cried out*, or *Then he cried out like a lion*

9 And behold, here come riders,
  horsemen in pairs!"
And he answered,
  "Fallen, fallen is Babylon;
and all the carved images of her gods
  he has shattered to the ground."
10 O my threshed and winnowed one,
  what I have heard from the LORD of
    hosts,
  the God of Israel, I announce to you.

11 The oracle concerning Dumah.

One is calling to me from Seir,
  "Watchman, what time of the night?
  Watchman, what time of the night?"
12 The watchman says:
  "Morning comes, and also the night.
  If you will inquire, inquire;
  come back again."

13 The oracle concerning Arabia.

In the thickets in Arabia you will lodge,
  O caravans of Dedanites.
14 To the thirsty bring water;
  meet the fugitive with bread,
  O inhabitants of the land of Tema.
15 For they have fled from the swords,
  from the drawn sword,
from the bent bow,
  and from the press of battle.

16 For thus the Lord said to me, "Within a year, according to the years of a hired worker, all the glory of Kedar will come to an end. 17 And the remainder of the archers of the mighty men of the sons of Kedar will be few, for the LORD, the God of Israel, has spoken."

An Oracle Concerning Jerusalem

22 The oracle concerning the valley of vision.

What do you mean that you have gone
  up,
  all of you, to the housetops,
2 you who are full of shoutings,
  tumultuous city, exultant town?
Your slain are not slain with the sword
  or dead in battle.
3 All your leaders have fled together;
  without the bow they were captured.
All of you who were found were cap-
    tured,
  though they had fled far away.

4 Therefore I said:
  "Look away from me;
  let me weep bitter tears;
  do not labor to comfort me
  concerning the destruction of the
    daughter of my people."

5 For the Lord GOD of hosts has a day
  of tumult and trampling and confusion
  in the valley of vision,
a battering down of walls
  and a shouting to the mountains.
6 And Elam bore the quiver
  with chariots and horsemen,
  and Kir uncovered the shield.
7 Your choicest valleys were full of chari-
    ots,
  and the horsemen took their stand at
    the gates.
8 He has taken away the covering of
    Judah.

In that day you looked to the weapons of the House of the Forest, 9 and you saw that the breaches of the city of David were many. You collected the waters of the lower pool, 10 and you counted the houses of Jerusalem, and you broke down the houses to fortify the wall. 11 You made a reservoir between the two walls for the water of the old pool. But you did not look to him who did it, or see him who planned it long ago.

12 In that day the Lord GOD of hosts
  called for weeping and mourning,
  for baldness and wearing sackcloth;
13 and behold, joy and gladness,
  killing oxen and slaughtering sheep,
  eating flesh and drinking wine.
"Let us eat and drink,
  for tomorrow we die."
14 The LORD of hosts has revealed himself in
    my ears:
  "Surely this iniquity will not be atoned for
    you until you die,"
  says the Lord GOD of hosts.

15 Thus says the Lord GOD of hosts, "Come, go to this steward, to Shebna, who is over the household, and say to him: 16 What have you to do here, and whom have you here, that you have cut out here a tomb for yourself, you who cut out a tomb on the height and carve a dwelling for yourself in the rock? 17 Behold, the LORD will hurl you away violently, O you

strong man. He will seize firm hold on you
[18] and whirl you around and around, and
throw you like a ball into a wide land. There
you shall die, and there shall be your glorious
chariots, you shame of your master's house.
[19] I will thrust you from your office, and you
will be pulled down from your station. [20] In
that day I will call my servant Eliakim the
son of Hilkiah, [21] and I will clothe him with
your robe, and will bind your sash on him,
and will commit your authority to his hand.
And he shall be a father to the inhabitants of
Jerusalem and to the house of Judah. [22] And I
will place on his shoulder the key of the house
of David. He shall open, and none shall shut;
and he shall shut, and none shall open. [23] And I
will fasten him like a peg in a secure place, and
he will become a throne of honor to his father's
house. [24] And they will hang on him the whole
honor of his father's house, the offspring and
issue, every small vessel, from the cups to all
the flagons. [25] In that day, declares the LORD
of hosts, the peg that was fastened in a secure
place will give way, and it will be cut down and
fall, and the load that was on it will be cut off,
for the LORD has spoken."

An Oracle Concerning Tyre and Sidon

23
The oracle concerning Tyre.

Wail, O ships of Tarshish,
for Tyre is laid waste, without house or
harbor!
From the land of Cyprus[1]
it is revealed to them.
[2] Be still, O inhabitants of the coast;
the merchants of Sidon, who cross the
sea, have filled you.
[3] And on many waters
your revenue was the grain of Shihor,
the harvest of the Nile;
you were the merchant of the nations.
[4] Be ashamed, O Sidon, for the sea has spoken,
the stronghold of the sea, saying:
"I have neither labored nor given birth,
I have neither reared young men
nor brought up young women."
[5] When the report comes to Egypt,
they will be in anguish[2] over the report
about Tyre.
[6] Cross over to Tarshish;
wail, O inhabitants of the coast!

[7] Is this your exultant city
whose origin is from days of old,
whose feet carried her
to settle far away?
[8] Who has purposed this
against Tyre, the bestower of crowns,
whose merchants were princes,
whose traders were the honored of the
earth?
[9] The LORD of hosts has purposed it,
to defile the pompous pride of all glory,[3]
to dishonor all the honored of the earth.
[10] Cross over your land like the Nile,
O daughter of Tarshish;
there is no restraint anymore.
[11] He has stretched out his hand over the sea;
he has shaken the kingdoms;
the LORD has given command concerning
Canaan
to destroy its strongholds.
[12] And he said:
"You will no more exult,
O oppressed virgin daughter of Sidon;
arise, cross over to Cyprus,
even there you will have no rest."

[13] Behold the land of the Chaldeans! This is
the people that was not;[4] Assyria destined it
for wild beasts. They erected their siege towers, they stripped her palaces bare, they made
her a ruin.

[14] Wail, O ships of Tarshish,
for your stronghold is laid waste.

[15] In that day Tyre will be forgotten for seventy
years, like the days[5] of one king. At the end of
seventy years, it will happen to Tyre as in the
song of the prostitute:

[16] "Take a harp;
go about the city,
O forgotten prostitute!
Make sweet melody;
sing many songs,
that you may be remembered."

[17] At the end of seventy years, the LORD will visit
Tyre, and she will return to her wages and will
prostitute herself with all the kingdoms of the
world on the face of the earth. [18] Her merchandise and her wages will be holy to the LORD.
It will not be stored or hoarded, but her merchandise will supply abundant food and fine
clothing for those who dwell before the LORD.

---

[1] Hebrew *Kittim*; also verse 12 [2] Hebrew *they will have labor pains* [3] The Hebrew words for *glory* and *hosts* sound alike [4] Or *that has become nothing* [5] Or *lifetime*

Judgment on the Whole Earth

24 Behold, the LORD will empty the
earth[1] and make it desolate,
and he will twist its surface and scatter
its inhabitants.
2 And it shall be, as with the people, so
with the priest;
as with the slave, so with his master;
as with the maid, so with her mistress;
as with the buyer, so with the seller;
as with the lender, so with the borrower;
as with the creditor, so with the debtor.
3 The earth shall be utterly empty and
utterly plundered;
for the LORD has spoken this word.

4 The earth mourns and withers;
the world languishes and withers;
the highest people of the earth languish.
5 The earth lies defiled
under its inhabitants;
for they have transgressed the laws,
violated the statutes,
broken the everlasting covenant.
6 Therefore a curse devours the earth,
and its inhabitants suffer for their
guilt;
therefore the inhabitants of the earth are
scorched,
and few men are left.
7 The wine mourns,
the vine languishes,
all the merry-hearted sigh.
8 The mirth of the tambourines is stilled,
the noise of the jubilant has ceased,
the mirth of the lyre is stilled.
9 No more do they drink wine with singing;
strong drink is bitter to those who
drink it.
10 The wasted city is broken down;
every house is shut up so that none
can enter.
11 There is an outcry in the streets for lack of
wine;
all joy has grown dark;
the gladness of the earth is banished.
12 Desolation is left in the city;
the gates are battered into ruins.
13 For thus it shall be in the midst of the earth
among the nations,

as when an olive tree is beaten,
as at the gleaning when the grape harvest is done.
14 They lift up their voices, they sing for joy;
over the majesty of the LORD they shout
from the west.[2]
15 Therefore in the east[3] give glory to the
LORD;
in the coastlands of the sea, give glory
to the name of the LORD, the God of
Israel.
16 From the ends of the earth we hear songs
of praise,
of glory to the Righteous One.
But I say, "I waste away,
I waste away. Woe is me!
For the traitors have betrayed,
with betrayal the traitors have
betrayed."

17 Terror and the pit and the snare[4]
are upon you, O inhabitant of the earth!
18 He who flees at the sound of the terror
shall fall into the pit,
and he who climbs out of the pit
shall be caught in the snare.
For the windows of heaven are opened,
and the foundations of the earth tremble.
19 The earth is utterly broken,
the earth is split apart,
the earth is violently shaken.
20 The earth staggers like a drunken man;
it sways like a hut;
its transgression lies heavy upon it,
and it falls, and will not rise again.

21 On that day the LORD will punish
the host of heaven, in heaven,
and the kings of the earth, on the earth.
22 They will be gathered together
as prisoners in a pit;
they will be shut up in a prison,
and after many days they will be punished.
23 Then the moon will be confounded
and the sun ashamed,
for the LORD of hosts reigns
on Mount Zion and in Jerusalem,
and his glory will be before his elders.

[1] Or *land*; also throughout this chapter [2] Hebrew *from the sea* [3] Hebrew *in the realm of light*, or *with the fires* [4] The Hebrew words for *terror, pit,* and *snare* sound alike

God Will Swallow Up Death Forever

25 O LORD, you are my God;
I will exalt you; I will praise your
name,
for you have done wonderful things,
plans formed of old, faithful and sure.
[2] For you have made the city a heap,
the fortified city a ruin;
the foreigners' palace is a city no more;
it will never be rebuilt.
[3] Therefore strong peoples will glorify you;
cities of ruthless nations will fear you.
[4] For you have been a stronghold to the
poor,
a stronghold to the needy in his distress,
a shelter from the storm and a shade
from the heat;
for the breath of the ruthless is like a storm
against a wall,
[5] like heat in a dry place.
You subdue the noise of the foreigners;
as heat by the shade of a cloud,
so the song of the ruthless is put down.

[6] On this mountain the LORD of hosts will
make for all peoples
a feast of rich food, a feast of well-aged
wine,
of rich food full of marrow, of aged
wine well refined.
[7] And he will swallow up on this mountain
the covering that is cast over all peoples,
the veil that is spread over all nations.
[8] He will swallow up death forever;
and the Lord GOD will wipe away tears
from all faces,
and the reproach of his people he will
take away from all the earth,
for the LORD has spoken.
[9] It will be said on that day,
"Behold, this is our God; we have waited
for him, that he might save us.
This is the LORD; we have waited for
him;
let us be glad and rejoice in his salvation."
[10] For the hand of the LORD will rest on this
mountain,
and Moab shall be trampled down in
his place,
as straw is trampled down in a dunghill.[1]

[11] And he will spread out his hands in the
midst of it
as a swimmer spreads his hands out to
swim,
but the LORD will lay low his pompous
pride together with the skill[2] of his
hands.
[12] And the high fortifications of his walls he
will bring down,
lay low, and cast to the ground, to the
dust.

You Keep Him in Perfect Peace

26 In that day this song will be sung in the
land of Judah:

"We have a strong city;
he sets up salvation
as walls and bulwarks.
[2] Open the gates,
that the righteous nation that keeps
faith may enter in.
[3] You keep him in perfect peace
whose mind is stayed on you,
because he trusts in you.
[4] Trust in the LORD forever,
for the LORD GOD is an everlasting rock.
[5] For he has humbled
the inhabitants of the height,
the lofty city.
He lays it low, lays it low to the ground,
casts it to the dust.
[6] The foot tramples it,
the feet of the poor,
the steps of the needy."

[7] The path of the righteous is level;
you make level the way of the righteous.
[8] In the path of your judgments,
O LORD, we wait for you;
your name and remembrance
are the desire of our soul.
[9] My soul yearns for you in the night;
my spirit within me earnestly seeks you.
For when your judgments are in the earth,
the inhabitants of the world learn righteousness.
[10] If favor is shown to the wicked,
he does not learn righteousness;
in the land of uprightness he deals corruptly
and does not see the majesty of the
LORD.

[1] The Hebrew words for *dunghill* and for the Moabite town *Madmen* (Jeremiah 48:2) sound alike [2] Or *in spite of the skill*

¹¹ O Lord, your hand is lifted up,
     but they do not see it.
Let them see your zeal for your people, and
     be ashamed.
     Let the fire for your adversaries con-
     sume them.
¹² O Lord, you will ordain peace for us,
     for you have indeed done for us all our
     works.
¹³ O Lord our God,
     other lords besides you have ruled over
     us,
     but your name alone we bring to
     remembrance.
¹⁴ They are dead, they will not live;
     they are shades, they will not arise;
to that end you have visited them with
     destruction
     and wiped out all remembrance of
     them.
¹⁵ But you have increased the nation, O Lord,
     you have increased the nation; you are
     glorified;
     you have enlarged all the borders of the
     land.

¹⁶ O Lord, in distress they sought you;
     they poured out a whispered prayer
     when your discipline was upon them.
¹⁷ Like a pregnant woman
     who writhes and cries out in her pangs
     when she is near to giving birth,
so were we because of you, O Lord;
¹⁸   we were pregnant, we writhed,
     but we have given birth to wind.
We have accomplished no deliverance in
     the earth,
     and the inhabitants of the world have
     not fallen.
¹⁹ Your dead shall live; their bodies shall rise.
     You who dwell in the dust, awake and
     sing for joy!
For your dew is a dew of light,
     and the earth will give birth to the dead.

²⁰ Come, my people, enter your chambers,
     and shut your doors behind you;
hide yourselves for a little while
     until the fury has passed by.
²¹ For behold, the Lord is coming out from
     his place
     to punish the inhabitants of the earth
     for their iniquity,

and the earth will disclose the blood shed
     on it,
     and will no more cover its slain.

The Redemption of Israel

27 In that day the Lord with his hard and great and strong sword will punish Leviathan the fleeing serpent, Leviathan the twisting serpent, and he will slay the dragon that is in the sea.

²   In that day,
"A pleasant vineyard,[1] sing of it!
³   I, the Lord, am its keeper;
     every moment I water it.
     Lest anyone punish it,
I keep it night and day;
⁴   I have no wrath.
Would that I had thorns and briers to
     battle!
     I would march against them,
     I would burn them up together.
⁵   Or let them lay hold of my protection,
     let them make peace with me,
     let them make peace with me."

⁶   In days to come[2] Jacob shall take root,
     Israel shall blossom and put forth
     shoots
     and fill the whole world with fruit.

⁷   Has he struck them as he struck those who
     struck them?
     Or have they been slain as their slayers
     were slain?
⁸   Measure by measure,[3] by exile you con-
     tended with them;
     he removed them with his fierce breath[4]
     in the day of the east wind.
⁹   Therefore by this the guilt of Jacob will be
     atoned for,
     and this will be the full fruit of the
     removal of his sin:[5]
when he makes all the stones of the altars
     like chalkstones crushed to pieces,
     no Asherim or incense altars will
     remain standing.
¹⁰   For the fortified city is solitary,
     a habitation deserted and forsaken, like
     the wilderness;
there the calf grazes;
     there it lies down and strips its
     branches.

[1] Many Hebrew manuscripts *A vineyard of wine* [2] Hebrew *In those come* [3] Or *By driving her away*; the meaning of the Hebrew word is uncertain [4] Or *wind* [5] Septuagint *and this is the blessing when I take away his sin*

¹¹ When its boughs are dry, they are broken;
 women come and make a fire of them.
For this is a people without discernment;
 therefore he who made them will not
  have compassion on them;
 he who formed them will show them
  no favor.

¹² In that day from the river Euphrates¹ to the Brook of Egypt the LORD will thresh out the grain, and you will be gleaned one by one, O people of Israel. ¹³ And in that day a great trumpet will be blown, and those who were lost in the land of Assyria and those who were driven out to the land of Egypt will come and worship the LORD on the holy mountain at Jerusalem.

Judgment on Ephraim and Jerusalem

28 Ah, the proud crown of the drunkards
 of Ephraim,
 and the fading flower of its glorious
  beauty,
 which is on the head of the rich valley of
  those overcome with wine!
² Behold, the Lord has one who is mighty
  and strong;
 like a storm of hail, a destroying tempest,
 like a storm of mighty, overflowing waters,
 he casts down to the earth with his
  hand.
³ The proud crown of the drunkards of
  Ephraim
 will be trodden underfoot;
⁴ and the fading flower of its glorious
  beauty,
 which is on the head of the rich valley,
 will be like a first-ripe fig² before the
  summer:
 when someone sees it, he swallows it
  as soon as it is in his hand.
⁵ In that day the LORD of hosts will be a
  crown of glory,³
 and a diadem of beauty, to the remnant
  of his people,
⁶ and a spirit of justice to him who sits in
  judgment,
 and strength to those who turn back
  the battle at the gate.
⁷ These also reel with wine
 and stagger with strong drink;

the priest and the prophet reel with strong
 drink,
 they are swallowed by⁴ wine,
 they stagger with strong drink,
they reel in vision,
 they stumble in giving judgment.
⁸ For all tables are full of filthy vomit,
 with no space left.

⁹ "To whom will he teach knowledge,
 and to whom will he explain the message?
Those who are weaned from the milk,
 those taken from the breast?
¹⁰ For it is precept upon precept, precept
  upon precept,
 line upon line, line upon line,
 here a little, there a little."

¹¹ For by people of strange lips
 and with a foreign tongue
the LORD will speak to this people,
¹² to whom he has said,
"This is rest;
 give rest to the weary;
and this is repose";
 yet they would not hear.
¹³ And the word of the LORD will be to them
 precept upon precept, precept upon precept,
 line upon line, line upon line,
 here a little, there a little,
that they may go, and fall backward,
 and be broken, and snared, and taken.

A Cornerstone in Zion

¹⁴ Therefore hear the word of the LORD, you
  scoffers,
 who rule this people in Jerusalem!
¹⁵ Because you have said, "We have made a
  covenant with death,
 and with Sheol we have an agreement,
when the overwhelming whip passes
  through
 it will not come to us,
for we have made lies our refuge,
 and in falsehood we have taken shelter";
¹⁶ therefore thus says the Lord GOD,
"Behold, I am the one who has laid⁵ as a
  foundation in Zion,
 a stone, a tested stone,
a precious cornerstone, of a sure foundation:
 'Whoever believes will not be in haste.'

¹ Hebrew *from the River* ² Or *fruit* ³ The Hebrew words for *glory* and *hosts* sound alike ⁴ Or *confused by* ⁵ Dead Sea Scroll *I am laying*

17 And I will make justice the line,
　　and righteousness the plumb line;
and hail will sweep away the refuge of
　　lies,
　　and waters will overwhelm the shelter."
18 Then your covenant with death will be
　　annulled,
　　and your agreement with Sheol will not
　　stand;
when the overwhelming scourge passes
　　through,
　　you will be beaten down by it.
19 As often as it passes through it will take
　　you;
　　for morning by morning it will pass
　　through,
　　by day and by night;
and it will be sheer terror to understand
　　the message.
20 For the bed is too short to stretch oneself
　　on,
　　and the covering too narrow to wrap
　　oneself in.
21 For the LORD will rise up as on Mount
　　Perazim;
　　as in the Valley of Gibeon he will be
　　roused;
to do his deed—strange is his deed!
　　and to work his work—alien is his
　　work!
22 Now therefore do not scoff,
　　lest your bonds be made strong;
for I have heard a decree of destruction
　　from the Lord GOD of hosts against
　　the whole land.

23 Give ear, and hear my voice;
　　give attention, and hear my speech.
24 Does he who plows for sowing plow con-
　　tinually?
　　Does he continually open and harrow
　　his ground?
25 When he has leveled its surface,
　　does he not scatter dill, sow cumin,
and put in wheat in rows
　　and barley in its proper place,
　　and emmer[1] as the border?
26 For he is rightly instructed;
　　his God teaches him.
27 Dill is not threshed with a threshing
　　sledge,
　　nor is a cart wheel rolled over cumin,

but dill is beaten out with a stick,
　　and cumin with a rod.
28 Does one crush grain for bread?
　　No, he does not thresh it forever;[2]
when he drives his cart wheel over it
　　with his horses, he does not crush it.
29 This also comes from the LORD of hosts;
　　he is wonderful in counsel
　　and excellent in wisdom.

The Siege of Jerusalem

29 Ah, Ariel, Ariel,
　　the city where David encamped!
Add year to year;
　　let the feasts run their round.
2 Yet I will distress Ariel,
　　and there shall be moaning and lamen-
　　tation,
　　and she shall be to me like an Ariel.[3]
3 And I will encamp against you all
　　around,
　　and will besiege you with towers
　　and I will raise siegeworks against
　　you.
4 And you will be brought low; from the
　　earth you shall speak,
　　and from the dust your speech will be
　　bowed down;
your voice shall come from the ground
　　like the voice of a ghost,
　　and from the dust your speech shall
　　whisper.

5 But the multitude of your foreign foes
　　shall be like small dust,
　　and the multitude of the ruthless like
　　passing chaff.
And in an instant, suddenly,
6 　　you will be visited by the LORD of hosts
with thunder and with earthquake and
　　great noise,
　　with whirlwind and tempest, and the
　　flame of a devouring fire.
7 And the multitude of all the nations that
　　fight against Ariel,
　　all that fight against her and her strong-
　　hold and distress her,
　　shall be like a dream, a vision of the
　　night.
8 As when a hungry man dreams, and
　　behold, he is eating,
　　and awakes with his hunger not satis-
　　fied,

---

[1] A type of wheat [2] Or Grain is crushed for bread; he will surely thresh it, but not forever [3] Ariel could mean lion of God, or hero (2 Samuel 23:20), or altar hearth (Ezekiel 43:15–16)

or as when a thirsty man dreams, and
    behold, he is drinking,
and awakes faint, with his thirst not
    quenched,
so shall the multitude of all the
    nations be
that fight against Mount Zion.

9 Astonish yourselves[1] and be astonished;
    blind yourselves and be blind!
Be drunk,[2] but not with wine;
    stagger,[3] but not with strong drink!
10 For the LORD has poured out upon you
    a spirit of deep sleep,
and has closed your eyes (the prophets),
    and covered your heads (the seers).

11 And the vision of all this has become to you like the words of a book that is sealed. When men give it to one who can read, saying, "Read this," he says, "I cannot, for it is sealed." 12 And when they give the book to one who cannot read, saying, "Read this," he says, "I cannot read."

13 And the Lord said:
"Because this people draw near with their
    mouth
    and honor me with their lips,
    while their hearts are far from me,
and their fear of me is a commandment
    taught by men,
14 therefore, behold, I will again
    do wonderful things with this people,
    with wonder upon wonder;
and the wisdom of their wise men shall
    perish,
    and the discernment of their discerning
    men shall be hidden."

15 Ah, you who hide deep from the LORD
    your counsel,
    whose deeds are in the dark,
and who say, "Who sees us? Who knows
    us?"
16 You turn things upside down!
Shall the potter be regarded as the clay,
that the thing made should say of its
    maker,
    "He did not make me";
or the thing formed say of him who
    formed it,
    "He has no understanding"?

17 Is it not yet a very little while
    until Lebanon shall be turned into a
    fruitful field,
    and the fruitful field shall be regarded
    as a forest?
18 In that day the deaf shall hear
    the words of a book,
and out of their gloom and darkness
    the eyes of the blind shall see.
19 The meek shall obtain fresh joy in the LORD,
    and the poor among mankind shall
    exult in the Holy One of Israel.
20 For the ruthless shall come to nothing
    and the scoffer cease,
    and all who watch to do evil shall be cut
    off,
21 who by a word make a man out to be an
    offender,
    and lay a snare for him who reproves in
    the gate,
    and with an empty plea turn aside him
    who is in the right.

22 Therefore thus says the LORD, who redeemed Abraham, concerning the house of Jacob:

"Jacob shall no more be ashamed,
    no more shall his face grow pale.
23 For when he sees his children,
    the work of my hands, in his midst,
    they will sanctify my name;
they will sanctify the Holy One of Jacob
    and will stand in awe of the God of Israel.
24 And those who go astray in spirit will come
    to understanding,
    and those who murmur will accept
    instruction."

Do Not Go Down to Egypt

30 "Ah, stubborn children," declares the
    LORD,
"who carry out a plan, but not mine,
    and who make an alliance,[4] but not of my
    Spirit,
    that they may add sin to sin;
2 who set out to go down to Egypt,
    without asking for my direction,
to take refuge in the protection of Pharaoh
    and to seek shelter in the shadow of
    Egypt!
3 Therefore shall the protection of Pharaoh
    turn to your shame,
    and the shelter in the shadow of Egypt
    to your humiliation.

[1] Or Linger awhile [2] Or They are drunk [3] Or they stagger [4] Hebrew who weave a web

4 For though his officials are at Zoan
   and his envoys reach Hanes,
5 everyone comes to shame
   through a people that cannot profit
     them,
that brings neither help nor profit,
   but shame and disgrace."

6 An oracle on the beasts of the Negeb.

Through a land of trouble and anguish,
   from where come the lioness and the
     lion,
   the adder and the flying fiery serpent,
they carry their riches on the backs of don-
     keys,
   and their treasures on the humps of
     camels,
to a people that cannot profit them.
7 Egypt's help is worthless and empty;
   therefore I have called her
   "Rahab who sits still."

A Rebellious People

8 And now, go, write it before them on a tab-
     let
   and inscribe it in a book,
that it may be for the time to come
   as a witness forever.[1]
9 For they are a rebellious people,
   lying children,
children unwilling to hear
   the instruction of the LORD;
10 who say to the seers, "Do not see,"
   and to the prophets, "Do not prophesy
     to us what is right;
speak to us smooth things,
   prophesy illusions,
11 leave the way, turn aside from the path,
   let us hear no more about the Holy
     One of Israel."

12 Therefore thus says the Holy One of Israel,
"Because you despise this word
   and trust in oppression and perverse-
     ness
   and rely on them,
13 therefore this iniquity shall be to you
   like a breach in a high wall, bulging out
     and about to collapse,
   whose breaking comes suddenly, in an
     instant;
14 and its breaking is like that of a potter's
     vessel
   that is smashed so ruthlessly

that among its fragments not a shard is
     found
   with which to take fire from the hearth,
   or to dip up water out of the cistern."

15 For thus said the Lord GOD, the Holy One
     of Israel,
"In returning[2] and rest you shall be saved;
   in quietness and in trust shall be your
     strength."
But you were unwilling, 16 and you said,
"No! We will flee upon horses";
   therefore you shall flee away;
and, "We will ride upon swift steeds";
   therefore your pursuers shall be swift.
17 A thousand shall flee at the threat of one;
   at the threat of five you shall flee,
till you are left
   like a flagstaff on the top of a moun-
     tain,
   like a signal on a hill.

The LORD Will Be Gracious

18 Therefore the LORD waits to be gracious to
     you,
   and therefore he exalts himself to show
     mercy to you.
For the LORD is a God of justice;
   blessed are all those who wait for him.

19 For a people shall dwell in Zion, in Jerusalem; you shall weep no more. He will surely be gracious to you at the sound of your cry. As soon as he hears it, he answers you. 20 And though the Lord give you the bread of adversity and the water of affliction, yet your Teacher will not hide himself anymore, but your eyes shall see your Teacher. 21 And your ears shall hear a word behind you, saying, "This is the way, walk in it," when you turn to the right or when you turn to the left. 22 Then you will defile your carved idols overlaid with silver and your gold-plated metal images. You will scatter them as unclean things. You will say to them, "Be gone!"

23 And he will give rain for the seed with which you sow the ground, and bread, the produce of the ground, which will be rich and plenteous. In that day your livestock will graze in large pastures, 24 and the oxen and the donkeys that work the ground will eat seasoned fodder, which has been winnowed with shovel and fork. 25 And on every lofty mountain and every high hill there will be brooks running with water, in the day of the great slaughter,

---

[1] Some Hebrew manuscripts, Syriac, Targum, Vulgate, and Greek versions; Masoretic Text *forever and ever* [2] Or *repentance*

when the towers fall. [26] Moreover, the light of the moon will be as the light of the sun, and the light of the sun will be sevenfold, as the light of seven days, in the day when the LORD binds up the brokenness of his people, and heals the wounds inflicted by his blow.

[27] Behold, the name of the LORD comes from afar,
    burning with his anger, and in thick rising smoke;[1]
his lips are full of fury,
    and his tongue is like a devouring fire;
[28] his breath is like an overflowing stream
    that reaches up to the neck;
to sift the nations with the sieve of destruction,
    and to place on the jaws of the peoples a bridle that leads astray.

[29] You shall have a song as in the night when a holy feast is kept, and gladness of heart, as when one sets out to the sound of the flute to go to the mountain of the LORD, to the Rock of Israel. [30] And the LORD will cause his majestic voice to be heard and the descending blow of his arm to be seen, in furious anger and a flame of devouring fire, with a cloudburst and storm and hailstones. [31] The Assyrians will be terror-stricken at the voice of the LORD, when he strikes with his rod. [32] And every stroke of the appointed staff that the LORD lays on them will be to the sound of tambourines and lyres. Battling with brandished arm, he will fight with them. [33] For a burning place[2] has long been prepared; indeed, for the king it is made ready, its pyre made deep and wide, with fire and wood in abundance; the breath of the LORD, like a stream of sulfur, kindles it.

Woe to Those Who Go Down to Egypt

31 Woe[3] to those who go down to Egypt for help
    and rely on horses,
who trust in chariots because they are many
    and in horsemen because they are very strong,
but do not look to the Holy One of Israel
    or consult the LORD!
[2] And yet he is wise and brings disaster;
    he does not call back his words,

but will arise against the house of the evildoers
    and against the helpers of those who work iniquity.
[3] The Egyptians are man, and not God,
    and their horses are flesh, and not spirit.
When the LORD stretches out his hand,
    the helper will stumble, and he who is helped will fall,
    and they will all perish together.

[4] For thus the LORD said to me,
"As a lion or a young lion growls over his prey,
    and when a band of shepherds is called out against him
he is not terrified by their shouting
    or daunted at their noise,
so the LORD of hosts will come down
    to fight[4] on Mount Zion and on its hill.
[5] Like birds hovering, so the LORD of hosts
    will protect Jerusalem;
he will protect and deliver it;
    he will spare and rescue it."

[6] Turn to him from whom people[5] have deeply revolted, O children of Israel. [7] For in that day everyone shall cast away his idols of silver and his idols of gold, which your hands have sinfully made for you.

[8] "And the Assyrian shall fall by a sword, not of man;
    and a sword, not of man, shall devour him;
and he shall flee from the sword,
    and his young men shall be put to forced labor.
[9] His rock shall pass away in terror,
    and his officers desert the standard in panic,"
declares the LORD, whose fire is in Zion,
    and whose furnace is in Jerusalem.

A King Will Reign in Righteousness

32 Behold, a king will reign in righteousness,
    and princes will rule in justice.
[2] Each will be like a hiding place from the wind,
    a shelter from the storm,
like streams of water in a dry place,
    like the shade of a great rock in a weary land.

---

[1] Hebrew *in weight of uplifted clouds* [2] Or *For Topheth* [3] Or *Ah,* [4] The Hebrew words for *hosts* and *to fight* sound alike [5] Hebrew *they*

3 Then the eyes of those who see will not be
closed,
   and the ears of those who hear will give
   attention.
4 The heart of the hasty will understand and
know,
   and the tongue of the stammerers will
   hasten to speak distinctly.
5 The fool will no more be called noble,
   nor the scoundrel said to be honorable.
6 For the fool speaks folly,
   and his heart is busy with iniquity,
to practice ungodliness,
   to utter error concerning the LORD,
to leave the craving of the hungry unsatis-
fied,
   and to deprive the thirsty of drink.
7 As for the scoundrel—his devices are evil;
   he plans wicked schemes
to ruin the poor with lying words,
   even when the plea of the needy is right.
8 But he who is noble plans noble things,
   and on noble things he stands.

Complacent Women Warned of Disaster

9 Rise up, you women who are at ease, hear
my voice;
   you complacent daughters, give ear to
   my speech.
10 In little more than a year
   you will shudder, you complacent
   women;
for the grape harvest fails,
   the fruit harvest will not come.
11 Tremble, you women who are at ease,
   shudder, you complacent ones;
strip, and make yourselves bare,
   and tie sackcloth around your waist.
12 Beat your breasts for the pleasant fields,
   for the fruitful vine,
13 for the soil of my people
   growing up in thorns and briers,
yes, for all the joyous houses
   in the exultant city.
14 For the palace is forsaken,
   the populous city deserted;
the hill and the watchtower
   will become dens forever,
a joy of wild donkeys,
   a pasture of flocks;

15 until the Spirit is poured upon us from
on high,
   and the wilderness becomes a fruitful
   field,
   and the fruitful field is deemed a forest.
16 Then justice will dwell in the wilderness,
   and righteousness abide in the fruitful
   field.
17 And the effect of righteousness will be
peace,
   and the result of righteousness, quietness and trust[1] forever.
18 My people will abide in a peaceful habitation,
   in secure dwellings, and in quiet resting
   places.
19 And it will hail when the forest falls down,
   and the city will be utterly laid low.
20 Happy are you who sow beside all waters,
   who let the feet of the ox and the donkey range free.

O LORD, Be Gracious to Us

33 Ah, you destroyer,
   who yourself have not been destroyed,
you traitor,
   whom none has betrayed!
When you have ceased to destroy,
   you will be destroyed;
and when you have finished betraying,
   they will betray you.

2 O LORD, be gracious to us; we wait for you.
   Be our arm every morning,
   our salvation in the time of trouble.
3 At the tumultuous noise peoples flee;
   when you lift yourself up, nations are
   scattered,
4 and your spoil is gathered as the caterpillar gathers;
   as locusts leap, it is leapt upon.

5 The LORD is exalted, for he dwells on
high;
   he will fill Zion with justice and righteousness,
6 and he will be the stability of your times,
   abundance of salvation, wisdom, and
   knowledge;
   the fear of the LORD is Zion's[2] treasure.

7 Behold, their heroes cry in the streets;
   the envoys of peace weep bitterly.
8 The highways lie waste;
   the traveler ceases.

[1] Or security [2] Hebrew his

Covenants are broken;
   cities[1] are despised;
   there is no regard for man.
9 The land mourns and languishes;
   Lebanon is confounded and withers
     away;
   Sharon is like a desert,
   and Bashan and Carmel shake off their
     leaves.

10 "Now I will arise," says the LORD,
   "now I will lift myself up;
   now I will be exalted.
11 You conceive chaff; you give birth to stubble;
   your breath is a fire that will consume
     you.
12 And the peoples will be as if burned to
   lime,
   like thorns cut down, that are burned in
     the fire."

13 Hear, you who are far off, what I have done;
   and you who are near, acknowledge my
     might.
14 The sinners in Zion are afraid;
   trembling has seized the godless:
  "Who among us can dwell with the con-
     suming fire?
   Who among us can dwell with everlast-
     ing burnings?"
15 He who walks righteously and speaks
   uprightly,
   who despises the gain of oppressions,
   who shakes his hands, lest they hold a
     bribe,
   who stops his ears from hearing of
     bloodshed
   and shuts his eyes from looking on evil,
16 he will dwell on the heights;
   his place of defense will be the fortresses
     of rocks;
   his bread will be given him; his water
     will be sure.

17 Your eyes will behold the king in his
   beauty;
   they will see a land that stretches afar.
18 Your heart will muse on the terror:
  "Where is he who counted, where is he
     who weighed the tribute?
   Where is he who counted the towers?"

19 You will see no more the insolent people,
   the people of an obscure speech that
     you cannot comprehend,
   stammering in a tongue that you can-
     not understand.
20 Behold Zion, the city of our appointed
   feasts!
   Your eyes will see Jerusalem,
   an untroubled habitation, an immov-
     able tent,
  whose stakes will never be plucked up,
   nor will any of its cords be broken.
21 But there the LORD in majesty will be
   for us
   a place of broad rivers and streams,
  where no galley with oars can go,
   nor majestic ship can pass.
22 For the LORD is our judge; the LORD is our
   lawgiver;
   the LORD is our king; he will save us.

23 Your cords hang loose;
   they cannot hold the mast firm in its
     place
   or keep the sail spread out.
  Then prey and spoil in abundance will be
   divided;
   even the lame will take the prey.
24 And no inhabitant will say, "I am sick";
   the people who dwell there will be for-
     given their iniquity.

Judgment on the Nations

34 Draw near, O nations, to hear,
   and give attention, O peoples!
  Let the earth hear, and all that fills it;
   the world, and all that comes from it.
2 For the LORD is enraged against all the
   nations,
   and furious against all their host;
   he has devoted them to destruction,[2]
     has given them over for slaughter.
3 Their slain shall be cast out,
   and the stench of their corpses shall rise;
   the mountains shall flow with their
     blood.
4 All the host of heaven shall rot away,
   and the skies roll up like a scroll.
  All their host shall fall,
   as leaves fall from the vine,
   like leaves falling from the fig tree.

[1] Masoretic Text; Dead Sea Scroll *witnesses* [2] That is, set apart (devoted) as an offering to the Lord (for destruction); also verse 5

5 For my sword has drunk its fill in the heavens;
 behold, it descends for judgment upon
 Edom,
 upon the people I have devoted to
 destruction.
6 The LORD has a sword; it is sated with
 blood;
 it is gorged with fat,
 with the blood of lambs and goats,
 with the fat of the kidneys of rams.
 For the LORD has a sacrifice in Bozrah,
 a great slaughter in the land of Edom.
7 Wild oxen shall fall with them,
 and young steers with the mighty bulls.
 Their land shall drink its fill of blood,
 and their soil shall be gorged with fat.

8 For the LORD has a day of vengeance,
 a year of recompense for the cause of
 Zion.
9 And the streams of Edom[1] shall be turned
 into pitch,
 and her soil into sulfur;
 her land shall become burning pitch.
10 Night and day it shall not be quenched;
 its smoke shall go up forever.
 From generation to generation it shall lie
 waste;
 none shall pass through it forever and
 ever.
11 But the hawk and the porcupine[2] shall
 possess it,
 the owl and the raven shall dwell in it.
 He shall stretch the line of confusion[3]
 over it,
 and the plumb line of emptiness.
12 Its nobles—there is no one there to call it
 a kingdom,
 and all its princes shall be nothing.

13 Thorns shall grow over its strongholds,
 nettles and thistles in its fortresses.
 It shall be the haunt of jackals,
 an abode for ostriches.[4]
14 And wild animals shall meet with hyenas;
 the wild goat shall cry to his fellow;
 indeed, there the night bird[5] settles
 and finds for herself a resting place.
15 There the owl nests and lays
 and hatches and gathers her young in
 her shadow;

indeed, there the hawks are gathered,
 each one with her mate.
16 Seek and read from the book of the LORD:
 Not one of these shall be missing;
 none shall be without her mate.
 For the mouth of the LORD has commanded,
 and his Spirit has gathered them.
17 He has cast the lot for them;
 his hand has portioned it out to them
 with the line;
 they shall possess it forever;
 from generation to generation they
 shall dwell in it.

The Ransomed Shall Return

35 The wilderness and the dry land shall
 be glad;
 the desert shall rejoice and blossom
 like the crocus;
2 it shall blossom abundantly
 and rejoice with joy and singing.
 The glory of Lebanon shall be given to it,
 the majesty of Carmel and Sharon.
 They shall see the glory of the LORD,
 the majesty of our God.

3 Strengthen the weak hands,
 and make firm the feeble knees.
4 Say to those who have an anxious heart,
 "Be strong; fear not!
 Behold, your God
 will come with vengeance,
 with the recompense of God.
 He will come and save you."

5 Then the eyes of the blind shall be opened,
 and the ears of the deaf unstopped;
6 then shall the lame man leap like a deer,
 and the tongue of the mute sing for
 joy.
 For waters break forth in the wilderness,
 and streams in the desert;
7 the burning sand shall become a pool,
 and the thirsty ground springs of
 water;
 in the haunt of jackals, where they lie
 down,
 the grass shall become reeds and rushes.

8 And a highway shall be there,
 and it shall be called the Way of
 Holiness;

[1] Hebrew *her streams* [2] The identity of the animals rendered *hawk* and *porcupine* is uncertain [3] Hebrew *formlessness* [4] Or *owls* [5] Identity uncertain

the unclean shall not pass over it.
  It shall belong to those who walk on the
    way;
    even if they are fools, they shall not go
      astray.[1]
9 No lion shall be there,
     nor shall any ravenous beast come up
       on it;
   they shall not be found there,
     but the redeemed shall walk there.
10 And the ransomed of the LORD shall
       return
     and come to Zion with singing;
   everlasting joy shall be upon their heads;
     they shall obtain gladness and joy,
     and sorrow and sighing shall flee away.

Sennacherib Invades Judah

36 In the fourteenth year of King Hezekiah, Sennacherib king of Assyria came up against all the fortified cities of Judah and took them. [2] And the king of Assyria sent the Rabshakeh[2] from Lachish to King Hezekiah at Jerusalem, with a great army. And he stood by the conduit of the upper pool on the highway to the Washer's Field. [3] And there came out to him Eliakim the son of Hilkiah, who was over the household, and Shebna the secretary, and Joah the son of Asaph, the recorder.

[4] And the Rabshakeh said to them, "Say to Hezekiah, 'Thus says the great king, the king of Assyria: On what do you rest this trust of yours? [5] Do you think that mere words are strategy and power for war? In whom do you now trust, that you have rebelled against me? [6] Behold, you are trusting in Egypt, that broken reed of a staff, which will pierce the hand of any man who leans on it. Such is Pharaoh king of Egypt to all who trust in him. [7] But if you say to me, "We trust in the LORD our God," is it not he whose high places and altars Hezekiah has removed, saying to Judah and to Jerusalem, "You shall worship before this altar"? [8] Come now, make a wager with my master the king of Assyria: I will give you two thousand horses, if you are able on your part to set riders on them. [9] How then can you repulse a single captain among the least of my master's servants, when you trust in Egypt for chariots and for horsemen? [10] Moreover, is it without the LORD that I have come up against this land to destroy it? The LORD said to me, "Go up against this land and destroy it." ' "

[11] Then Eliakim, Shebna, and Joah said to the Rabshakeh, "Please speak to your servants in Aramaic, for we understand it. Do not speak to us in the language of Judah within the hearing of the people who are on the wall." [12] But the Rabshakeh said, "Has my master sent me to speak these words to your master and to you, and not to the men sitting on the wall, who are doomed with you to eat their own dung and drink their own urine?"

[13] Then the Rabshakeh stood and called out in a loud voice in the language of Judah: "Hear the words of the great king, the king of Assyria! [14] Thus says the king: 'Do not let Hezekiah deceive you, for he will not be able to deliver you. [15] Do not let Hezekiah make you trust in the LORD by saying, "The LORD will surely deliver us. This city will not be given into the hand of the king of Assyria." [16] Do not listen to Hezekiah. For thus says the king of Assyria: Make your peace with me[3] and come out to me. Then each one of you will eat of his own vine, and each one of his own fig tree, and each one of you will drink the water of his own cistern, [17] until I come and take you away to a land like your own land, a land of grain and wine, a land of bread and vineyards. [18] Beware lest Hezekiah mislead you by saying, "The LORD will deliver us." Has any of the gods of the nations delivered his land out of the hand of the king of Assyria? [19] Where are the gods of Hamath and Arpad? Where are the gods of Sepharvaim? Have they delivered Samaria out of my hand? [20] Who among all the gods of these lands have delivered their lands out of my hand, that the LORD should deliver Jerusalem out of my hand?' "

[21] But they were silent and answered him not a word, for the king's command was, "Do not answer him." [22] Then Eliakim the son of Hilkiah, who was over the household, and Shebna the secretary, and Joah the son of Asaph, the recorder, came to Hezekiah with their clothes torn, and told him the words of the Rabshakeh.

Hezekiah Seeks Isaiah's Help

37 As soon as King Hezekiah heard it, he tore his clothes and covered himself with sackcloth and went into the house of the LORD. [2] And he sent Eliakim, who was over the household, and Shebna the secretary, and the senior priests, covered with sackcloth, to the prophet Isaiah the son of Amoz. [3] They said to him, "Thus says Hezekiah, 'This day is a day of

---

[1] Or if they are fools, they shall not wander in it   [2] Rabshakeh is the title of a high-ranking Assyrian military officer   [3] Hebrew Make a blessing with me

distress, of rebuke, and of disgrace; children have come to the point of birth, and there is no strength to bring them forth. **4** It may be that the LORD your God will hear the words of the Rabshakeh, whom his master the king of Assyria has sent to mock the living God, and will rebuke the words that the LORD your God has heard; therefore lift up your prayer for the remnant that is left.' "

5 When the servants of King Hezekiah came to Isaiah, **6** Isaiah said to them, "Say to your master, 'Thus says the LORD: Do not be afraid because of the words that you have heard, with which the young men of the king of Assyria have reviled me. **7** Behold, I will put a spirit in him, so that he shall hear a rumor and return to his own land, and I will make him fall by the sword in his own land.' "

8 The Rabshakeh returned, and found the king of Assyria fighting against Libnah, for he had heard that the king had left Lachish. **9** Now the king heard concerning Tirhakah king of Cush,[1] "He has set out to fight against you." And when he heard it, he sent messengers to Hezekiah, saying, **10** "Thus shall you speak to Hezekiah king of Judah: 'Do not let your God in whom you trust deceive you by promising that Jerusalem will not be given into the hand of the king of Assyria. **11** Behold, you have heard what the kings of Assyria have done to all lands, devoting them to destruction. And shall you be delivered? **12** Have the gods of the nations delivered them, the nations that my fathers destroyed, Gozan, Haran, Rezeph, and the people of Eden who were in Telassar? **13** Where is the king of Hamath, the king of Arpad, the king of the city of Sepharvaim, the king of Hena, or the king of Ivvah?' "

Hezekiah's Prayer for Deliverance

14 Hezekiah received the letter from the hand of the messengers, and read it; and Hezekiah went up to the house of the LORD, and spread it before the LORD. **15** And Hezekiah prayed to the LORD: **16** "O LORD of hosts, God of Israel, enthroned above the cherubim, you are the God, you alone, of all the kingdoms of the earth; you have made heaven and earth. **17** Incline your ear, O LORD, and hear; open your eyes, O LORD, and see; and hear all the words of Sennacherib, which he has sent to mock the living God. **18** Truly, O LORD, the kings of Assyria have laid waste all the nations and their lands, **19** and have

cast their gods into the fire. For they were no gods, but the work of men's hands, wood and stone. Therefore they were destroyed. **20** So now, O LORD our God, save us from his hand, that all the kingdoms of the earth may know that you alone are the LORD."

Sennacherib's Fall

21 Then Isaiah the son of Amoz sent to Hezekiah, saying, "Thus says the LORD, the God of Israel: Because you have prayed to me concerning Sennacherib king of Assyria, **22** this is the word that the LORD has spoken concerning him:

" 'She despises you, she scorns you—
　　the virgin daughter of Zion;
she wags her head behind you—
　　the daughter of Jerusalem.

23 " 'Whom have you mocked and reviled?
　　Against whom have you raised your
　　　　voice
and lifted your eyes to the heights?
　　Against the Holy One of Israel!
24 By your servants you have mocked the
　　　　Lord,
　　and you have said, With my many
　　　　chariots
I have gone up the heights of the moun-
　　　　tains,
　　to the far recesses of Lebanon,
to cut down its tallest cedars,
　　its choicest cypresses,
to come to its remotest height,
　　its most fruitful forest.
25 I dug wells
　　and drank waters,
to dry up with the sole of my foot
　　all the streams of Egypt.

26 " 'Have you not heard
　　that I determined it long ago?
I planned from days of old
　　what now I bring to pass,
that you should make fortified cities
　　crash into heaps of ruins,
27 while their inhabitants, shorn of strength,
　　are dismayed and confounded,
and have become like plants of the field
　　and like tender grass,
like grass on the housetops,
　　blighted[2] before it is grown.

---

[1] Probably *Nubia*　[2] Some Hebrew manuscripts and 2 Kings 19:26; most Hebrew manuscripts *a field*

28 " 'I know your sitting down
   and your going out and coming in,
   and your raging against me.
29 Because you have raged against me
   and your complacency has come to my
      ears,
   I will put my hook in your nose
      and my bit in your mouth,
   and I will turn you back on the way
      by which you came.'

30 "And this shall be the sign for you: this year you shall eat what grows of itself, and in the second year what springs from that. Then in the third year sow and reap, and plant vineyards, and eat their fruit. 31 And the surviving remnant of the house of Judah shall again take root downward and bear fruit upward. 32 For out of Jerusalem shall go a remnant, and out of Mount Zion a band of survivors. The zeal of the LORD of hosts will do this.

33 "Therefore thus says the LORD concerning the king of Assyria: He shall not come into this city or shoot an arrow there or come before it with a shield or cast up a siege mound against it. 34 By the way that he came, by the same he shall return, and he shall not come into this city, declares the LORD. 35 For I will defend this city to save it, for my own sake and for the sake of my servant David."

36 And the angel of the LORD went out and struck down 185,000 in the camp of the Assyrians. And when people arose early in the morning, behold, these were all dead bodies. 37 Then Sennacherib king of Assyria departed and returned home and lived at Nineveh. 38 And as he was worshiping in the house of Nisroch his god, Adrammelech and Sharezer, his sons, struck him down with the sword. And after they escaped into the land of Ararat, Esarhaddon his son reigned in his place.

Hezekiah's Sickness and Recovery

38 In those days Hezekiah became sick and was at the point of death. And Isaiah the prophet the son of Amoz came to him, and said to him, "Thus says the LORD: Set your house in order, for you shall die, you shall not recover."[1]. 2 Then Hezekiah turned his face to the wall and prayed to the LORD, 3 and said, "Please, O LORD, remember how I have walked before you in faithfulness and with a whole heart, and have done what is good in your sight." And Hezekiah wept bitterly.

4 Then the word of the LORD came to Isaiah: 5 "Go and say to Hezekiah, Thus says the LORD, the God of David your father: I have heard your prayer; I have seen your tears. Behold, I will add fifteen years to your life.[2] 6 I will deliver you and this city out of the hand of the king of Assyria, and will defend this city.

7 "This shall be the sign to you from the LORD, that the LORD will do this thing that he has promised: 8 Behold, I will make the shadow cast by the declining sun on the dial of Ahaz turn back ten steps." So the sun turned back on the dial the ten steps by which it had declined.[3]

9 A writing of Hezekiah king of Judah, after he had been sick and had recovered from his sickness:

10 I said, In the middle[4] of my days
      I must depart;
   I am consigned to the gates of Sheol
      for the rest of my years.
11 I said, I shall not see the LORD,
      the LORD in the land of the living;
   I shall look on man no more
      among the inhabitants of the world.
12 My dwelling is plucked up and removed
         from me
      like a shepherd's tent;
   like a weaver I have rolled up my life;
      he cuts me off from the loom;
   from day to night you bring me to an
         end;
13 I calmed myself[5] until morning;
   like a lion he breaks all my bones;
      from day to night you bring me to an
         end.

14 Like a swallow or a crane I chirp;
      I moan like a dove.
   My eyes are weary with looking upward.
      O Lord, I am oppressed; be my pledge of
         safety!
15 What shall I say? For he has spoken to
         me,
      and he himself has done it.
   I walk slowly all my years
      because of the bitterness of my soul.

16 O Lord, by these things men live,
      and in all these is the life of my spirit.
   Oh restore me to health and make me
         live!

---

1 Or live; also verses 9, 21 2 Hebrew to your days 3 The meaning of the Hebrew verse is uncertain 4 Or In the quiet 5 Or (with Targum) I cried for help

17 Behold, it was for my welfare
      that I had great bitterness;
  but in love you have delivered my life
      from the pit of destruction,
  for you have cast all my sins
      behind your back.
18 For Sheol does not thank you;
      death does not praise you;
  those who go down to the pit do not
      hope
      for your faithfulness.
19 The living, the living, he thanks you,
      as I do this day;
  the father makes known to the children
      your faithfulness.

20 The LORD will save me,
      and we will play my music on stringed
          instruments
  all the days of our lives,
      at the house of the LORD.

21 Now Isaiah had said, "Let them take a cake of figs and apply it to the boil, that he may recover." 22 Hezekiah also had said, "What is the sign that I shall go up to the house of the LORD?"

Envoys from Babylon

39 At that time Merodach-baladan the son of Baladan, king of Babylon, sent envoys with letters and a present to Hezekiah, for he heard that he had been sick and had recovered. 2 And Hezekiah welcomed them gladly. And he showed them his treasure house, the silver, the gold, the spices, the precious oil, his whole armory, all that was found in his storehouses. There was nothing in his house or in all his realm that Hezekiah did not show them. 3 Then Isaiah the prophet came to King Hezekiah, and said to him, "What did these men say? And from where did they come to you?" Hezekiah said, "They have come to me from a far country, from Babylon." 4 He said, "What have they seen in your house?" Hezekiah answered, "They have seen all that is in my house. There is nothing in my storehouses that I did not show them."

5 Then Isaiah said to Hezekiah, "Hear the word of the LORD of hosts: 6 Behold, the days are coming, when all that is in your house, and that which your fathers have stored up till this day, shall be carried to Babylon. Nothing shall be left, says the LORD. 7 And some of your own sons, who will come from you, whom you will father, shall be taken away, and they shall be

eunuchs in the palace of the king of Babylon." 8 Then Hezekiah said to Isaiah, "The word of the LORD that you have spoken is good." For he thought, "There will be peace and security in my days."

Comfort for God's People

40 Comfort, comfort my people, says
          your God.
2 Speak tenderly to Jerusalem,
      and cry to her
  that her warfare[1] is ended,
      that her iniquity is pardoned,
  that she has received from the LORD's hand
      double for all her sins.

3 A voice cries:[2]
  "In the wilderness prepare the way of the
      LORD;
      make straight in the desert a highway
          for our God.
4 Every valley shall be lifted up,
      and every mountain and hill be made
          low;
  the uneven ground shall become level,
      and the rough places a plain.
5 And the glory of the LORD shall be
          revealed,
      and all flesh shall see it together,
  for the mouth of the LORD has spoken."

The Word of God Stands Forever

6 A voice says, "Cry!"
      And I said,[3] "What shall I cry?"
  All flesh is grass,
      and all its beauty[4] is like the flower of
          the field.
7 The grass withers, the flower fades
      when the breath of the LORD blows on
          it;
      surely the people are grass.
8 The grass withers, the flower fades,
      but the word of our God will stand
          forever.

The Greatness of God

9 Go on up to a high mountain,
      O Zion, herald of good news;[5]
  lift up your voice with strength,
      O Jerusalem, herald of good news;[6]
      lift it up, fear not;
  say to the cities of Judah,
      "Behold your God!"

1 Or hardship 2 Or A voice of one crying 3 Revocalization based on Dead Sea Scroll, Septuagint, Vulgate; Masoretic Text And someone says 4 Or all its constancy 5 Or O herald of good news to Zion 6 Or O herald of good news to Jerusalem

10 Behold, the Lord GOD comes with might,
    and his arm rules for him;
behold, his reward is with him,
    and his recompense before him.

11 He will tend his flock like a shepherd;
    he will gather the lambs in his arms;
he will carry them in his bosom,
    and gently lead those that are with
      young.

12 Who has measured the waters in the hol-
    low of his hand
    and marked off the heavens with a
      span,
enclosed the dust of the earth in a measure
    and weighed the mountains in scales
    and the hills in a balance?

13 Who has measured[1] the Spirit of the LORD,
    or what man shows him his counsel?

14 Whom did he consult,
    and who made him understand?
Who taught him the path of justice,
    and taught him knowledge,
    and showed him the way of under-
      standing?

15 Behold, the nations are like a drop from a
    bucket,
    and are accounted as the dust on the
      scales;
    behold, he takes up the coastlands like
      fine dust.

16 Lebanon would not suffice for fuel,
    nor are its beasts enough for a burnt
      offering.

17 All the nations are as nothing before
    him,
    they are accounted by him as less than
      nothing and emptiness.

18 To whom then will you liken God,
    or what likeness compare with him?

19 An idol! A craftsman casts it,
    and a goldsmith overlays it with gold
    and casts for it silver chains.

20 He who is too impoverished for an offering
    chooses wood[2] that will not rot;
he seeks out a skillful craftsman
    to set up an idol that will not move.

21 Do you not know? Do you not hear?
    Has it not been told you from the
      beginning?
    Have you not understood from the
      foundations of the earth?

22 It is he who sits above the circle of the
    earth,
    and its inhabitants are like grasshop-
      pers;
who stretches out the heavens like a
    curtain,
    and spreads them like a tent to dwell in;

23 who brings princes to nothing,
    and makes the rulers of the earth as
      emptiness.

24 Scarcely are they planted, scarcely sown,
    scarcely has their stem taken root in the
      earth,
when he blows on them, and they
    wither,
    and the tempest carries them off like
      stubble.

25 To whom then will you compare me,
    that I should be like him? says the Holy
      One.

26 Lift up your eyes on high and see:
    who created these?
He who brings out their host by number,
    calling them all by name;
by the greatness of his might
    and because he is strong in power,
    not one is missing.

27 Why do you say, O Jacob,
    and speak, O Israel,
"My way is hidden from the LORD,
    and my right is disregarded by my
      God"?

28 Have you not known? Have you not
    heard?
The LORD is the everlasting God,
    the Creator of the ends of the earth.
He does not faint or grow weary;
    his understanding is unsearchable.

29 He gives power to the faint,
    and to him who has no might he
      increases strength.

30 Even youths shall faint and be weary,
    and young men shall fall exhausted;

31 but they who wait for the LORD shall
    renew their strength;
    they shall mount up with wings like
      eagles;
they shall run and not be weary;
    they shall walk and not faint.

[1] Or has directed [2] Or He chooses valuable wood

Fear Not, for I Am with You

41 Listen to me in silence, O coastlands;
　　let the peoples renew their strength;
let them approach, then let them speak;
　　let us together draw near for judgment.

2 Who stirred up one from the east
　　whom victory meets at every step?[1]
He gives up nations before him,
　　so that he tramples kings underfoot;
he makes them like dust with his sword,
　　like driven stubble with his bow.
3 He pursues them and passes on safely,
　　by paths his feet have not trod.
4 Who has performed and done this,
　　calling the generations from the beginning?
I, the LORD, the first,
　　and with the last; I am he.

5 The coastlands have seen and are afraid;
　　the ends of the earth tremble;
　　they have drawn near and come.
6 Everyone helps his neighbor
　　and says to his brother, "Be strong!"
7 The craftsman strengthens the goldsmith,
　　and he who smooths with the hammer him who strikes the anvil,
saying of the soldering, "It is good";
　　and they strengthen it with nails so that
　　it cannot be moved.

8 But you, Israel, my servant,
　　Jacob, whom I have chosen,
　　the offspring of Abraham, my friend;
9 you whom I took from the ends of the
　　earth,
　　and called from its farthest corners,
saying to you, "You are my servant,
　　I have chosen you and not cast you
　　off";
10 fear not, for I am with you;
　　be not dismayed, for I am your God;
I will strengthen you, I will help you,
　　I will uphold you with my righteous
　　right hand.

11 Behold, all who are incensed against you
　　shall be put to shame and confounded;
those who strive against you
　　shall be as nothing and shall perish.

12 You shall seek those who contend with
　　you,
　　but you shall not find them;
those who war against you
　　shall be as nothing at all.
13 For I, the LORD your God,
　　hold your right hand;
it is I who say to you, "Fear not,
　　I am the one who helps you."

14 Fear not, you worm Jacob,
　　you men of Israel!
I am the one who helps you, declares the
　　LORD;
　　your Redeemer is the Holy One of
　　Israel.
15 Behold, I make of you a threshing sledge,
　　new, sharp, and having teeth;
you shall thresh the mountains and crush
　　them,
　　and you shall make the hills like chaff;
16 you shall winnow them, and the wind
　　shall carry them away,
　　and the tempest shall scatter them.
And you shall rejoice in the LORD;
　　in the Holy One of Israel you shall
　　glory.

17 When the poor and needy seek water,
　　and there is none,
　　and their tongue is parched with thirst,
I the LORD will answer them;
　　I the God of Israel will not forsake
　　them.
18 I will open rivers on the bare heights,
　　and fountains in the midst of the valleys.
I will make the wilderness a pool of
　　water,
　　and the dry land springs of water.
19 I will put in the wilderness the cedar,
　　the acacia, the myrtle, and the olive.
I will set in the desert the cypress,
　　the plane and the pine together,
20 that they may see and know,
　　may consider and understand together,
that the hand of the LORD has done this,
　　the Holy One of Israel has created it.

The Futility of Idols

21 Set forth your case, says the LORD;
　　bring your proofs, says the King of
　　Jacob.

[1] Or whom righteousness calls to follow?

22 Let them bring them, and tell us
      what is to happen.
   Tell us the former things, what they are,
      that we may consider them,
   that we may know their outcome;
      or declare to us the things to come.
23 Tell us what is to come hereafter,
      that we may know that you are gods;
   do good, or do harm,
      that we may be dismayed and terrified.[1]
24 Behold, you are nothing,
      and your work is less than nothing;
      an abomination is he who chooses
         you.

25 I stirred up one from the north, and he has
         come,
      from the rising of the sun, and he shall
         call upon my name;
   he shall trample on rulers as on mortar,
      as the potter treads clay.
26 Who declared it from the beginning, that
         we might know,
      and beforehand, that we might say, "He
         is right"?
   There was none who declared it, none who
         proclaimed,
      none who heard your words.
27 I was the first to say[2] to Zion, "Behold, here
         they are!"
      and I give to Jerusalem a herald of good
         news.
28 But when I look, there is no one;
      among these there is no counselor
      who, when I ask, gives an answer.
29 Behold, they are all a delusion;
      their works are nothing;
      their metal images are empty wind.

The LORD's Chosen Servant

42 Behold my servant, whom I uphold,
      my chosen, in whom my soul delights;
   I have put my Spirit upon him;
      he will bring forth justice to the nations.
2   He will not cry aloud or lift up his voice,
      or make it heard in the street;
3   a bruised reed he will not break,
      and a faintly burning wick he will not
         quench;
      he will faithfully bring forth justice.
4   He will not grow faint or be discouraged[3]
      till he has established justice in the
         earth;
      and the coastlands wait for his law.

5 Thus says God, the LORD,
      who created the heavens and stretched
         them out,
      who spread out the earth and what
         comes from it,
   who gives breath to the people on it
      and spirit to those who walk in it:
6 "I am the LORD; I have called you[4] in righ-
         teousness;
      I will take you by the hand and keep
         you;
   I will give you as a covenant for the people,
      a light for the nations,
7   to open the eyes that are blind,
   to bring out the prisoners from the dun-
         geon,
      from the prison those who sit in dark-
         ness.
8 I am the LORD; that is my name;
      my glory I give to no other,
      nor my praise to carved idols.
9 Behold, the former things have come to
         pass,
      and new things I now declare;
   before they spring forth
      I tell you of them."

Sing to the LORD a New Song

10 Sing to the LORD a new song,
      his praise from the end of the earth,
   you who go down to the sea, and all that
         fills it,
      the coastlands and their inhabitants.
11 Let the desert and its cities lift up their
         voice,
      the villages that Kedar inhabits;
   let the habitants of Sela sing for joy,
      let them shout from the top of the
         mountains.
12 Let them give glory to the LORD,
      and declare his praise in the coast-
         lands.
13 The LORD goes out like a mighty man,
      like a man of war he stirs up his zeal;
   he cries out, he shouts aloud,
      he shows himself mighty against his
         foes.

14 For a long time I have held my peace;
      I have kept still and restrained
         myself;
   now I will cry out like a woman in labor;
      I will gasp and pant.

[1] Or that we may both be dismayed and see [2] Or Formerly I said [3] Or bruised [4] The Hebrew for you is singular; four times in this verse

15 I will lay waste mountains and hills,
     and dry up all their vegetation;
I will turn the rivers into islands,[1]
     and dry up the pools.

16 And I will lead the blind
     in a way that they do not know,
in paths that they have not known
     I will guide them.
I will turn the darkness before them into
     light,
     the rough places into level ground.
These are the things I do,
     and I do not forsake them.

17 They are turned back and utterly put to
     shame,
     who trust in carved idols,
who say to metal images,
     "You are our gods."

Israel's Failure to Hear and See

18 Hear, you deaf,
     and look, you blind, that you may see!

19 Who is blind but my servant,
     or deaf as my messenger whom I send?
Who is blind as my dedicated one,[2]
     or blind as the servant of the LORD?

20 He sees many things, but does not observe
     them;
     his ears are open, but he does not hear.

21 The LORD was pleased, for his righteous-
     ness' sake,
     to magnify his law and make it glorious.

22 But this is a people plundered and
     looted;
     they are all of them trapped in holes
     and hidden in prisons;
they have become plunder with none to
     rescue,
     spoil with none to say, "Restore!"

23 Who among you will give ear to this,
     will attend and listen for the time to
     come?

24 Who gave up Jacob to the looter,
     and Israel to the plunderers?
Was it not the LORD, against whom we
     have sinned,
     in whose ways they would not walk,
     and whose law they would not obey?

25 So he poured on him the heat of his anger
     and the might of battle;

it set him on fire all around, but he did not
     understand;
     it burned him up, but he did not take it
     to heart.

Israel's Only Savior

43 But now thus says the LORD,
     he who created you, O Jacob,
     he who formed you, O Israel:
"Fear not, for I have redeemed you;
     I have called you by name, you are
     mine.

2 When you pass through the waters, I will
     be with you;
     and through the rivers, they shall not
     overwhelm you;
when you walk through fire you shall not
     be burned,
     and the flame shall not consume you.

3 For I am the LORD your God,
     the Holy One of Israel, your Savior.
I give Egypt as your ransom,
     Cush and Seba in exchange for you.

4 Because you are precious in my eyes,
     and honored, and I love you,
I give men in return for you,
     peoples in exchange for your life.

5 Fear not, for I am with you;
     I will bring your offspring from the
     east,
     and from the west I will gather you.

6 I will say to the north, Give up,
     and to the south, Do not withhold;
bring my sons from afar
     and my daughters from the end of the
     earth,

7 everyone who is called by my name,
     whom I created for my glory,
     whom I formed and made."

8 Bring out the people who are blind, yet
     have eyes,
     who are deaf, yet have ears!

9 All the nations gather together,
     and the peoples assemble.
Who among them can declare this,
     and show us the former things?
Let them bring their witnesses to prove
     them right,
     and let them hear and say, It is true.

10 "You are my witnesses," declares the LORD,
     "and my servant whom I have chosen,
that you may know and believe me
     and understand that I am he.

---

[1] Or into coastlands [2] Or as the one at peace with me

Before me no god was formed,
  nor shall there be any after me.
11 I, I am the LORD,
    and besides me there is no savior.
12 I declared and saved and proclaimed,
    when there was no strange god among
      you;
    and you are my witnesses," declares the
      LORD, "and I am God.
13 Also henceforth I am he;
    there is none who can deliver from my
      hand;
    I work, and who can turn it back?"

14 Thus says the LORD,
    your Redeemer, the Holy One of Israel:
  "For your sake I send to Babylon
    and bring them all down as fugitives,
    even the Chaldeans, in the ships in
      which they rejoice.
15 I am the LORD, your Holy One,
    the Creator of Israel, your King."

16 Thus says the LORD,
    who makes a way in the sea,
    a path in the mighty waters,
17 who brings forth chariot and horse,
    army and warrior;
  they lie down, they cannot rise,
    they are extinguished, quenched like a
      wick:
18 "Remember not the former things,
    nor consider the things of old.
19 Behold, I am doing a new thing;
    now it springs forth, do you not per-
      ceive it?
  I will make a way in the wilderness
    and rivers in the desert.
20 The wild beasts will honor me,
    the jackals and the ostriches,
  for I give water in the wilderness,
    rivers in the desert,
  to give drink to my chosen people,
21   the people whom I formed for myself
  that they might declare my praise.

22 "Yet you did not call upon me, O Jacob;
    but you have been weary of me, O Israel!
23 You have not brought me your sheep for
      burnt offerings,
    or honored me with your sacrifices.
  I have not burdened you with offerings,
    or wearied you with frankincense.

24 You have not bought me sweet cane with
      money,
    or satisfied me with the fat of your sacri-
      fices.
  But you have burdened me with your sins;
    you have wearied me with your iniqui-
      ties.

25 "I, I am he
    who blots out your transgressions for
      my own sake,
    and I will not remember your sins.
26 Put me in remembrance; let us argue
      together;
    set forth your case, that you may be
      proved right.
27 Your first father sinned,
    and your mediators transgressed
      against me.
28 Therefore I will profane the princes of the
      sanctuary,
    and deliver Jacob to utter destruction
    and Israel to reviling.

Israel the LORD's Chosen

44 "But now hear, O Jacob my servant,
    Israel whom I have chosen!
2 Thus says the LORD who made you,
    who formed you from the womb and
      will help you:
  Fear not, O Jacob my servant,
    Jeshurun whom I have chosen.
3 For I will pour water on the thirsty land,
    and streams on the dry ground;
  I will pour my Spirit upon your offspring,
    and my blessing on your descendants.
4 They shall spring up among the grass
    like willows by flowing streams.
5 This one will say, 'I am the LORD's,'
    another will call on the name of Jacob,
  and another will write on his hand, 'The
      LORD's,'
    and name himself by the name of
      Israel."

Besides Me There Is No God

6 Thus says the LORD, the King of Israel
    and his Redeemer, the LORD of hosts:
  "I am the first and I am the last;
    besides me there is no god.
7 Who is like me? Let him proclaim it.[1]
    Let him declare and set it before me,

---

[1] Or Who like me can proclaim it?

since I appointed an ancient people.
Let them declare what is to come, and
what will happen.
8 Fear not, nor be afraid;
have I not told you from of old and
declared it?
And you are my witnesses!
Is there a God besides me?
There is no Rock; I know not any."

The Folly of Idolatry

9 All who fashion idols are nothing, and the things they delight in do not profit. Their witnesses neither see nor know, that they may be put to shame. 10 Who fashions a god or casts an idol that is profitable for nothing? 11 Behold, all his companions shall be put to shame, and the craftsmen are only human. Let them all assemble, let them stand forth. They shall be terrified; they shall be put to shame together.

12 The ironsmith takes a cutting tool and works it over the coals. He fashions it with hammers and works it with his strong arm. He becomes hungry, and his strength fails; he drinks no water and is faint. 13 The carpenter stretches a line; he marks it out with a pencil.[1] He shapes it with planes and marks it with a compass. He shapes it into the figure of a man, with the beauty of a man, to dwell in a house. 14 He cuts down cedars, or he chooses a cypress tree or an oak and lets it grow strong among the trees of the forest. He plants a cedar and the rain nourishes it. 15 Then it becomes fuel for a man. He takes a part of it and warms himself; he kindles a fire and bakes bread. Also he makes a god and worships it; he makes it an idol and falls down before it. 16 Half of it he burns in the fire. Over the half he eats meat; he roasts it and is satisfied. Also he warms himself and says, "Aha, I am warm, I have seen the fire!" 17 And the rest of it he makes into a god, his idol, and falls down to it and worships it. He prays to it and says, "Deliver me, for you are my god!"

18 They know not, nor do they discern, for he has shut their eyes, so that they cannot see, and their hearts, so that they cannot understand. 19 No one considers, nor is there knowledge or discernment to say, "Half of it I burned in the fire; I also baked bread on its coals; I roasted meat and have eaten. And shall I make the rest of it an abomination? Shall I fall down before a block of wood?" 20 He feeds on ashes; a deluded heart has led him astray, and he cannot deliver himself or say, "Is there not a lie in my right hand?"

The Lord Redeems Israel

21 Remember these things, O Jacob,
and Israel, for you are my servant;
I formed you; you are my servant;
O Israel, you will not be forgotten by
me.
22 I have blotted out your transgressions
like a cloud
and your sins like mist;
return to me, for I have redeemed you.

23 Sing, O heavens, for the Lord has done it;
shout, O depths of the earth;
break forth into singing, O mountains,
O forest, and every tree in it!
For the Lord has redeemed Jacob,
and will be glorified[2] in Israel.

24 Thus says the Lord, your Redeemer,
who formed you from the womb:
"I am the Lord, who made all things,
who alone stretched out the heavens,
who spread out the earth by myself,
25 who frustrates the signs of liars
and makes fools of diviners,
who turns wise men back
and makes their knowledge foolish,
26 who confirms the word of his servant
and fulfills the counsel of his messengers,
who says of Jerusalem, 'She shall be
inhabited,'
and of the cities of Judah, 'They shall
be built,
and I will raise up their ruins';
27 who says to the deep, 'Be dry;
I will dry up your rivers';
28 who says of Cyrus, 'He is my shepherd,
and he shall fulfill all my purpose';
saying of Jerusalem, 'She shall be built,'
and of the temple, 'Your foundation
shall be laid.'"

Cyrus, God's Instrument

45 Thus says the Lord to his anointed, to Cyrus,
whose right hand I have grasped,
to subdue nations before him
and to loose the belts of kings,
to open doors before him
that gates may not be closed:
2 "I will go before you
and level the exalted places,[3]

---

[1] Hebrew *stylus* [2] Or *will display his beauty* [3] Masoretic Text; Dead Sea Scroll, Septuagint *level the mountains*

I will break in pieces the doors of bronze
and cut through the bars of iron,
3 I will give you the treasures of darkness
and the hoards in secret places,
that you may know that it is I, the LORD,
the God of Israel, who call you by your
name.
4 For the sake of my servant Jacob,
and Israel my chosen,
I call you by your name,
I name you, though you do not know
me.
5 I am the LORD, and there is no other,
besides me there is no God;
I equip you, though you do not know
me,
6 that people may know, from the rising of
the sun
and from the west, that there is none
besides me;
I am the LORD, and there is no other.
7 I form light and create darkness;
I make well-being and create calamity;
I am the LORD, who does all these
things.

8 "Shower, O heavens, from above,
and let the clouds rain down righteousness;
let the earth open, that salvation and righteousness may bear fruit;
let the earth cause them both to sprout;
I the LORD have created it.

9 "Woe to him who strives with him who
formed him,
a pot among earthen pots!
Does the clay say to him who forms it,
'What are you making?'
or 'Your work has no handles'?
10 Woe to him who says to a father, 'What are
you begetting?'
or to a woman, 'With what are you in
labor?'"

11 Thus says the LORD,
the Holy One of Israel, and the one who
formed him:
"Ask me of things to come;
will you command me concerning
my children and the work of my
hands?[1]
12 I made the earth
and created man on it;

it was my hands that stretched out the
heavens,
and I commanded all their host.
13 I have stirred him up in righteousness,
and I will make all his ways level;
he shall build my city
and set my exiles free,
not for price or reward,"
says the LORD of hosts.

The LORD, the Only Savior

14 Thus says the LORD:
"The wealth of Egypt and the merchandise
of Cush,
and the Sabeans, men of stature,
shall come over to you and be yours;
they shall follow you;
they shall come over in chains and bow
down to you.
They will plead with you, saying:
'Surely God is in you, and there is no
other,
no god besides him.'"

15 Truly, you are a God who hides himself,
O God of Israel, the Savior.
16 All of them are put to shame and confounded;
the makers of idols go in confusion
together.
17 But Israel is saved by the LORD
with everlasting salvation;
you shall not be put to shame or confounded
to all eternity.

18 For thus says the LORD,
who created the heavens
(he is God!),
who formed the earth and made it
(he established it;
he did not create it empty,
he formed it to be inhabited!):
"I am the LORD, and there is no other.
19 I did not speak in secret,
in a land of darkness;
I did not say to the offspring of Jacob,
'Seek me in vain.'[2]
I the LORD speak the truth;
I declare what is right.

20 "Assemble yourselves and come;
draw near together,
you survivors of the nations!

---

[1] A slight emendation yields will you question me about my children, or command me concerning the work of my hands?   [2] Hebrew in emptiness

They have no knowledge
who carry about their wooden idols,
and keep on praying to a god
that cannot save.
[21] Declare and present your case;
let them take counsel together!
Who told this long ago?
Who declared it of old?
Was it not I, the LORD?
And there is no other god besides me,
a righteous God and a Savior;
there is none besides me.

[22] "Turn to me and be saved,
all the ends of the earth!
For I am God, and there is no other.
[23] By myself I have sworn;
from my mouth has gone out in righteousness
a word that shall not return:
'To me every knee shall bow,
every tongue shall swear allegiance.'[1]

[24] "Only in the LORD, it shall be said of me,
are righteousness and strength;
to him shall come and be ashamed
all who were incensed against him.
[25] In the LORD all the offspring of Israel
shall be justified and shall glory."

The Idols of Babylon and the One True God

46 Bel bows down; Nebo stoops;
their idols are on beasts and livestock;
these things you carry are borne
as burdens on weary beasts.
[2] They stoop; they bow down together;
they cannot save the burden,
but themselves go into captivity.

[3] "Listen to me, O house of Jacob,
all the remnant of the house of Israel,
who have been borne by me from before
your birth,
carried from the womb;
[4] even to your old age I am he,
and to gray hairs I will carry you.
I have made, and I will bear;
I will carry and will save.

[5] "To whom will you liken me and make me
equal,
and compare me, that we may be alike?
[6] Those who lavish gold from the purse,
and weigh out silver in the scales,

hire a goldsmith, and he makes it into a
god;
then they fall down and worship!
[7] They lift it to their shoulders, they carry it,
they set it in its place, and it stands
there;
it cannot move from its place.
If one cries to it, it does not answer
or save him from his trouble.

[8] "Remember this and stand firm,
recall it to mind, you transgressors,
[9] remember the former things of old;
for I am God, and there is no other;
I am God, and there is none like me,
[10] declaring the end from the beginning
and from ancient times things not yet
done,
saying, 'My counsel shall stand,
and I will accomplish all my purpose,'
[11] calling a bird of prey from the east,
the man of my counsel from a far country.
I have spoken, and I will bring it to pass;
I have purposed, and I will do it.

[12] "Listen to me, you stubborn of heart,
you who are far from righteousness:
[13] I bring near my righteousness; it is not far
off,
and my salvation will not delay;
I will put salvation in Zion,
for Israel my glory."

The Humiliation of Babylon

47 Come down and sit in the dust,
O virgin daughter of Babylon;
sit on the ground without a throne,
O daughter of the Chaldeans!
For you shall no more be called
tender and delicate.
[2] Take the millstones and grind flour,
put off your veil,
strip off your robe, uncover your legs,
pass through the rivers.
[3] Your nakedness shall be uncovered,
and your disgrace shall be seen.
I will take vengeance,
and I will spare no one.
[4] Our Redeemer—the LORD of hosts is his
name—
is the Holy One of Israel.

[5] Sit in silence, and go into darkness,
O daughter of the Chaldeans;

[1] Septuagint every tongue shall confess to God

for you shall no more be called
the mistress of kingdoms.
6 I was angry with my people;
I profaned my heritage;
I gave them into your hand;
you showed them no mercy;
on the aged you made your yoke exceedingly heavy.
7 You said, "I shall be mistress forever,"
so that you did not lay these things to
heart
or remember their end.

8 Now therefore hear this, you lover of pleasures,
who sit securely,
who say in your heart,
"I am, and there is no one besides me;
I shall not sit as a widow
or know the loss of children":
9 These two things shall come to you
in a moment, in one day;
the loss of children and widowhood
shall come upon you in full measure,
in spite of your many sorceries
and the great power of your enchantments.

10 You felt secure in your wickedness;
you said, "No one sees me";
your wisdom and your knowledge led you
astray,
and you said in your heart,
"I am, and there is no one besides me."
11 But evil shall come upon you,
which you will not know how to charm
away;
disaster shall fall upon you,
for which you will not be able to atone;
and ruin shall come upon you suddenly,
of which you know nothing.

12 Stand fast in your enchantments
and your many sorceries,
with which you have labored from your
youth;
perhaps you may be able to succeed;
perhaps you may inspire terror.
13 You are wearied with your many counsels;
let them stand forth and save you,
those who divide the heavens,
who gaze at the stars,
who at the new moons make known
what shall come upon you.

14 Behold, they are like stubble;
the fire consumes them;
they cannot deliver themselves
from the power of the flame.
No coal for warming oneself is this,
no fire to sit before!
15 Such to you are those with whom you have
labored,
who have done business with you from
your youth;
they wander about, each in his own direction;
there is no one to save you.

Israel Refined for God's Glory

48 Hear this, O house of Jacob,
who are called by the name of Israel,
and who came from the waters of Judah,
who swear by the name of the LORD
and confess the God of Israel,
but not in truth or right.
2 For they call themselves after the holy city,
and stay themselves on the God of Israel;
the LORD of hosts is his name.

3 "The former things I declared of old;
they went out from my mouth, and I
announced them;
then suddenly I did them, and they
came to pass.
4 Because I know that you are obstinate,
and your neck is an iron sinew
and your forehead brass,
5 I declared them to you from of old,
before they came to pass I announced
them to you,
lest you should say, 'My idol did them,
my carved image and my metal image
commanded them.'

6 "You have heard; now see all this;
and will you not declare it?
From this time forth I announce to you
new things,
hidden things that you have not known.
7 They are created now, not long ago;
before today you have never heard of
them,
lest you should say, 'Behold, I knew
them.'
8 You have never heard, you have never
known,
from of old your ear has not been
opened.

For I knew that you would surely deal
  treacherously,
    and that from before birth you were
    called a rebel.

9 "For my name's sake I defer my anger;
    for the sake of my praise I restrain it for
    you,
    that I may not cut you off.
10 Behold, I have refined you, but not as sil-
    ver;
    I have tried[1] you in the furnace of afflic-
    tion.
11 For my own sake, for my own sake, I do it,
    for how should my name[2] be profaned?
    My glory I will not give to another.

The LORD's Call to Israel

12 "Listen to me, O Jacob,
    and Israel, whom I called!
    I am he; I am the first,
    and I am the last.
13 My hand laid the foundation of the earth,
    and my right hand spread out the heav-
    ens;
    when I call to them,
    they stand forth together.

14 "Assemble, all of you, and listen!
    Who among them has declared these
    things?
    The LORD loves him;
    he shall perform his purpose on
    Babylon,
    and his arm shall be against the
    Chaldeans.
15 I, even I, have spoken and called him;
    I have brought him, and he will prosper
    in his way.
16 Draw near to me, hear this:
    from the beginning I have not spoken
    in secret,
    from the time it came to be I have been
    there."
    And now the Lord GOD has sent me, and
    his Spirit.

17 Thus says the LORD,
    your Redeemer, the Holy One of Israel:
    "I am the LORD your God,
    who teaches you to profit,
    who leads you in the way you should
    go.

18 Oh that you had paid attention to my com-
    mandments!
    Then your peace would have been like a
    river,
    and your righteousness like the waves
    of the sea;
19 your offspring would have been like the
    sand,
    and your descendants like its grains;
    their name would never be cut off
    or destroyed from before me."

20 Go out from Babylon, flee from Chaldea,
    declare this with a shout of joy, pro-
    claim it,
    send it out to the end of the earth;
    say, "The LORD has redeemed his ser-
    vant Jacob!"
21 They did not thirst when he led them
    through the deserts;
    he made water flow for them from the
    rock;
    he split the rock and the water gushed
    out.

22 "There is no peace," says the LORD, "for the
    wicked."

The Servant of the LORD

49 Listen to me, O coastlands,
    and give attention, you peoples from
    afar.
    The LORD called me from the womb,
    from the body of my mother he named
    my name.
2 He made my mouth like a sharp sword;
    in the shadow of his hand he hid me;
    he made me a polished arrow;
    in his quiver he hid me away.
3 And he said to me, "You are my servant,
    Israel, in whom I will be glorified."[3]
4 But I said, "I have labored in vain;
    I have spent my strength for nothing
    and vanity;
    yet surely my right is with the LORD,
    and my recompense with my God."

5 And now the LORD says,
    he who formed me from the womb to
    be his servant,
    to bring Jacob back to him;
    and that Israel might be gathered to
    him—
    for I am honored in the eyes of the LORD,
    and my God has become my strength—

---

[1] Or *I have chosen* [2] Hebrew lacks *my name* [3] Or *I will display my beauty*

6 he says:

"It is too light a thing that you should be
my servant
to raise up the tribes of Jacob
and to bring back the preserved of
Israel;
I will make you as a light for the nations,
that my salvation may reach to the end
of the earth."

7 Thus says the LORD,
the Redeemer of Israel and his Holy
One,
to one deeply despised, abhorred by the
nation,
the servant of rulers:
"Kings shall see and arise;
princes, and they shall prostrate themselves;
because of the LORD, who is faithful,
the Holy One of Israel, who has chosen
you."

The Restoration of Israel

8 Thus says the LORD:
"In a time of favor I have answered you;
in a day of salvation I have helped you;
I will keep you and give you
as a covenant to the people,
to establish the land,
to apportion the desolate heritages,
9 saying to the prisoners, 'Come out,'
to those who are in darkness, 'Appear.'
They shall feed along the ways;
on all bare heights shall be their pasture;
10 they shall not hunger or thirst,
neither scorching wind nor sun shall
strike them,
for he who has pity on them will lead
them,
and by springs of water will guide
them.
11 And I will make all my mountains a road,
and my highways shall be raised up.
12 Behold, these shall come from afar,
and behold, these from the north and
from the west,[1]
and these from the land of Syene."[2]

13 Sing for joy, O heavens, and exult, O earth;
break forth, O mountains, into singing!

For the LORD has comforted his people
and will have compassion on his
afflicted.

14 But Zion said, "The LORD has forsaken me;
my Lord has forgotten me."

15 "Can a woman forget her nursing child,
that she should have no compassion on
the son of her womb?
Even these may forget,
yet I will not forget you.
16 Behold, I have engraved you on the palms
of my hands;
your walls are continually before me.
17 Your builders make haste;[3]
your destroyers and those who laid you
waste go out from you.
18 Lift up your eyes around and see;
they all gather, they come to you.
As I live, declares the LORD,
you shall put them all on as an ornament;
you shall bind them on as a bride does.

19 "Surely your waste and your desolate places
and your devastated land—
surely now you will be too narrow for your
inhabitants,
and those who swallowed you up will
be far away.
20 The children of your bereavement
will yet say in your ears:
'The place is too narrow for me;
make room for me to dwell in.'
21 Then you will say in your heart:
'Who has borne me these?
I was bereaved and barren,
exiled and put away,
but who has brought up these?
Behold, I was left alone;
from where have these come?'"

22 Thus says the Lord GOD:
"Behold, I will lift up my hand to the
nations,
and raise my signal to the peoples;
and they shall bring your sons in their
arms,[4]
and your daughters shall be carried on
their shoulders.
23 Kings shall be your foster fathers,
and their queens your nursing mothers.

[1] Hebrew from the sea [2] Dead Sea Scroll; Masoretic Text Sinim [3] Dead Sea Scroll; Masoretic Text Your children make haste [4] Hebrew in their bosom

With their faces to the ground they shall
    bow down to you,
  and lick the dust of your feet.
Then you will know that I am the LORD;
  those who wait for me shall not be put
    to shame."

24 Can the prey be taken from the mighty,
  or the captives of a tyrant[1] be rescued?
25 For thus says the LORD:
"Even the captives of the mighty shall be
  taken,
  and the prey of the tyrant be rescued,
for I will contend with those who contend
  with you,
  and I will save your children.
26 I will make your oppressors eat their own
  flesh,
  and they shall be drunk with their own
  blood as with wine.
Then all flesh shall know
  that I am the LORD your Savior,
  and your Redeemer, the Mighty One of
  Jacob."

Israel's Sin and the Servant's Obedience

50 Thus says the LORD:
  "Where is your mother's certificate of
  divorce,
  with which I sent her away?
Or which of my creditors is it
  to whom I have sold you?
Behold, for your iniquities you were sold,
  and for your transgressions your
  mother was sent away.
2 Why, when I came, was there no man;
  why, when I called, was there no one to
  answer?
Is my hand shortened, that it cannot
  redeem?
  Or have I no power to deliver?
Behold, by my rebuke I dry up the sea,
  I make the rivers a desert;
their fish stink for lack of water
  and die of thirst.
3 I clothe the heavens with blackness
  and make sackcloth their covering."

4 The Lord GOD has given me
  the tongue of those who are taught,
that I may know how to sustain with a word
  him who is weary.
Morning by morning he awakens;
  he awakens my ear
  to hear as those who are taught.

5 The Lord GOD has opened my ear,
  and I was not rebellious;
  I turned not backward.
6 I gave my back to those who strike,
  and my cheeks to those who pull out
  the beard;
I hid not my face
  from disgrace and spitting.

7 But the Lord GOD helps me;
  therefore I have not been disgraced;
therefore I have set my face like a flint,
  and I know that I shall not be put to
  shame.
8 He who vindicates me is near.
Who will contend with me?
  Let us stand up together.
Who is my adversary?
  Let him come near to me.
9 Behold, the Lord GOD helps me;
  who will declare me guilty?
Behold, all of them will wear out like a garment;
  the moth will eat them up.

10 Who among you fears the LORD
  and obeys the voice of his servant?
Let him who walks in darkness
  and has no light
trust in the name of the LORD
  and rely on his God.
11 Behold, all you who kindle a fire,
  who equip yourselves with burning
  torches!
Walk by the light of your fire,
  and by the torches that you have kindled!
This you have from my hand:
  you shall lie down in torment.

The LORD's Comfort for Zion

51 "Listen to me, you who pursue
  righteousness,
  you who seek the LORD:
look to the rock from which you were hewn,
  and to the quarry from which you
  were dug.
2 Look to Abraham your father
  and to Sarah who bore you;
for he was but one when I called him,
  that I might bless him and multiply
  him.
3 For the LORD comforts Zion;
  he comforts all her waste places
and makes her wilderness like Eden,
  her desert like the garden of the LORD;

[1] Dead Sea Scroll, Syriac, Vulgate (see also verse 25); Masoretic Text of *a righteous man*

joy and gladness will be found in her,
   thanksgiving and the voice of song.

4 "Give attention to me, my people,
   and give ear to me, my nation;
for a law[1] will go out from me,
   and I will set my justice for a light to the
     peoples.
5 My righteousness draws near,
   my salvation has gone out,
   and my arms will judge the peoples;
the coastlands hope for me,
   and for my arm they wait.
6 Lift up your eyes to the heavens,
   and look at the earth beneath;
for the heavens vanish like smoke,
   the earth will wear out like a garment,
   and they who dwell in it will die in like
     manner;[2]
but my salvation will be forever,
   and my righteousness will never be dis-
     mayed.

7 "Listen to me, you who know righteousness,
   the people in whose heart is my law;
fear not the reproach of man,
   nor be dismayed at their revilings.
8 For the moth will eat them up like a gar-
     ment,
   and the worm will eat them like wool,
but my righteousness will be forever,
   and my salvation to all generations."

9 Awake, awake, put on strength,
   O arm of the LORD;
awake, as in days of old,
   the generations of long ago.
Was it not you who cut Rahab in pieces,
   who pierced the dragon?
10 Was it not you who dried up the sea,
   the waters of the great deep,
who made the depths of the sea a way
   for the redeemed to pass over?
11 And the ransomed of the LORD shall return
   and come to Zion with singing;
everlasting joy shall be upon their heads;
   they shall obtain gladness and joy,
   and sorrow and sighing shall flee
     away.

12 "I, I am he who comforts you;
   who are you that you are afraid of man
     who dies,
   of the son of man who is made like
     grass,

13 and have forgotten the LORD, your
     Maker,
   who stretched out the heavens
   and laid the foundations of the earth,
and you fear continually all the day
   because of the wrath of the oppressor,
when he sets himself to destroy?
   And where is the wrath of the oppres-
     sor?
14 He who is bowed down shall speedily be
     released;
   he shall not die and go down to the
     pit,
   neither shall his bread be lacking.
15 I am the LORD your God,
   who stirs up the sea so that its waves
     roar—
   the LORD of hosts is his name.
16 And I have put my words in your mouth
   and covered you in the shadow of my
     hand,
establishing[3] the heavens
   and laying the foundations of the earth,
   and saying to Zion, 'You are my peo-
     ple.' "

17 Wake yourself, wake yourself,
   stand up, O Jerusalem,
you who have drunk from the hand of the
     LORD
   the cup of his wrath,
who have drunk to the dregs
   the bowl, the cup of staggering.
18 There is none to guide her
   among all the sons she has borne;
there is none to take her by the hand
   among all the sons she has brought
     up.
19 These two things have happened to you—
   who will console you?—
devastation and destruction, famine and
     sword;
   who will comfort you?[4]
20 Your sons have fainted;
   they lie at the head of every street
   like an antelope in a net;
they are full of the wrath of the LORD,
   the rebuke of your God.

21 Therefore hear this, you who are
     afflicted,
   who are drunk, but not with wine:

---

[1] Or for teaching; also verse 7 [2] Or will die like gnats [3] Or planting [4] Dead Sea Scroll, Septuagint, Syriac, Vulgate; Masoretic Text how shall I comfort you

22 Thus says your Lord, the LORD,
  your God who pleads the cause of his
    people:
  "Behold, I have taken from your hand the
    cup of staggering;
  the bowl of my wrath you shall drink no
    more;
23 and I will put it into the hand of your tor-
    mentors,
    who have said to you,
    'Bow down, that we may pass over';
  and you have made your back like the
    ground
    and like the street for them to pass
      over."

The LORD's Coming Salvation

52 Awake, awake,
    put on your strength, O Zion;
  put on your beautiful garments,
    O Jerusalem, the holy city;
  for there shall no more come into you
    the uncircumcised and the unclean.
2 Shake yourself from the dust and arise;
    be seated, O Jerusalem;
  loose the bonds from your neck,
    O captive daughter of Zion.

3 For thus says the LORD: "You were sold
for nothing, and you shall be redeemed without money." 4 For thus says the Lord GOD: "My
people went down at the first into Egypt to
sojourn there, and the Assyrian oppressed them
for nothing.[1] 5 Now therefore what have I here,"
declares the LORD, "seeing that my people are
taken away for nothing? Their rulers wail,"
declares the LORD, "and continually all the day
my name is despised. 6 Therefore my people
shall know my name. Therefore in that day they
shall know that it is I who speak; here I am."

7 How beautiful upon the mountains
    are the feet of him who brings good
      news,
  who publishes peace, who brings good
    news of happiness,
    who publishes salvation,
    who says to Zion, "Your God reigns."
8 The voice of your watchmen—they lift up
      their voice;
    together they sing for joy;
  for eye to eye they see
    the return of the LORD to Zion.

9 Break forth together into singing,
    you waste places of Jerusalem,
  for the LORD has comforted his people;
    he has redeemed Jerusalem.
10 The LORD has bared his holy arm
    before the eyes of all the nations,
  and all the ends of the earth shall see
    the salvation of our God.

11 Depart, depart, go out from there;
    touch no unclean thing;
  go out from the midst of her; purify your-
      selves,
    you who bear the vessels of the
      LORD.
12 For you shall not go out in haste,
    and you shall not go in flight,
  for the LORD will go before you,
    and the God of Israel will be your rear
      guard.

He Was Pierced for Our Transgressions

13 Behold, my servant shall act wisely;[2]
    he shall be high and lifted up,
    and shall be exalted.
14 As many were astonished at you—
    his appearance was so marred, beyond
      human semblance,
    and his form beyond that of the chil-
      dren of mankind—
15 so shall he sprinkle[3] many nations.
    Kings shall shut their mouths because
      of him,
  for that which has not been told them they
      see,
    and that which they have not heard
      they understand.

53 Who has believed what he has heard
    from us?[4]
  And to whom has the arm of the LORD
    been revealed?
2 For he grew up before him like a young
    plant,
    and like a root out of dry ground;
  he had no form or majesty that we should
    look at him,
    and no beauty that we should desire
      him.
3 He was despised and rejected[5] by men,
    a man of sorrows[6] and acquainted with[7]
      grief;[8]

---

[1] Or the Assyrian has oppressed them of late [2] Or shall prosper [3] Or startle [4] Or Who has believed what we have heard? [5] Or forsaken [6] Or pains; also verse 4 [7] Or and knowing
[8] Or sickness; also verse 4

and as one from whom men hide their
    faces[1]
  he was despised, and we esteemed him
    not.

4 Surely he has borne our griefs
    and carried our sorrows;
  yet we esteemed him stricken,
    smitten by God, and afflicted.
5 But he was pierced for our transgressions;
    he was crushed for our iniquities;
  upon him was the chastisement that
    brought us peace,
    and with his wounds we are healed.
6 All we like sheep have gone astray;
    we have turned—every one—to his
    own way;
  and the LORD has laid on him
    the iniquity of us all.

7 He was oppressed, and he was afflicted,
    yet he opened not his mouth;
  like a lamb that is led to the slaughter,
    and like a sheep that before its shearers
    is silent,
  so he opened not his mouth.
8 By oppression and judgment he was taken
    away;
    and as for his generation, who consid-
    ered
  that he was cut off out of the land of the
    living,
    stricken for the transgression of my
    people?
9 And they made his grave with the wicked
    and with a rich man in his death,
  although he had done no violence,
    and there was no deceit in his mouth.

10 Yet it was the will of the LORD to crush
    him;
    he has put him to grief;[2]
  when his soul makes[3] an offering for guilt,
    he shall see his offspring; he shall pro-
    long his days;
  the will of the LORD shall prosper in his
    hand.
11 Out of the anguish of his soul he shall see[4]
    and be satisfied;
  by his knowledge shall the righteous one,
    my servant,
    make many to be accounted righteous,
    and he shall bear their iniquities.

12 Therefore I will divide him a portion with
    the many,[5]
    and he shall divide the spoil with the
    strong,[6]
  because he poured out his soul to death
    and was numbered with the transgres-
    sors;
  yet he bore the sin of many,
    and makes intercession for the trans-
    gressors.

The Eternal Covenant of Peace

54 "Sing, O barren one, who did not bear;
    break forth into singing and cry aloud,
    you who have not been in labor!
  For the children of the desolate one will be
    more
    than the children of her who is mar-
    ried," says the LORD.
2 "Enlarge the place of your tent,
    and let the curtains of your habitations
    be stretched out;
  do not hold back; lengthen your cords
    and strengthen your stakes.
3 For you will spread abroad to the right and
    to the left,
    and your offspring will possess the
    nations
    and will people the desolate cities.

4 "Fear not, for you will not be ashamed;
    be not confounded, for you will not be
    disgraced;
  for you will forget the shame of your
    youth,
    and the reproach of your widowhood
    you will remember no more.
5 For your Maker is your husband,
    the LORD of hosts is his name;
  and the Holy One of Israel is your
    Redeemer,
    the God of the whole earth he is called.
6 For the LORD has called you
    like a wife deserted and grieved in
    spirit,
  like a wife of youth when she is cast off,
    says your God.
7 For a brief moment I deserted you,
    but with great compassion I will gather
    you.
8 In overflowing anger for a moment
    I hid my face from you,

---

[1] Or as one who hides his face from us [2] Or he has made him sick [3] Or when you make his soul [4] Masoretic Text; Dead Sea Scroll he shall see light [5] Or with the great [6] Or with the numerous

but with everlasting love I will have compassion on you,"
says the LORD, your Redeemer.

9 "This is like the days of Noah[1] to me:
as I swore that the waters of Noah
should no more go over the earth,
so I have sworn that I will not be angry
with you,
and will not rebuke you.

10 For the mountains may depart
and the hills be removed,
but my steadfast love shall not depart from
you,
and my covenant of peace shall not be
removed,"
says the LORD, who has compassion on
you.

11 "O afflicted one, storm-tossed and not comforted,
behold, I will set your stones in anti-
mony,
and lay your foundations with sapphires.[2]

12 I will make your pinnacles of agate,[3]
your gates of carbuncles,[4]
and all your wall of precious stones.

13 All your children shall be taught by the
LORD,
and great shall be the peace of your children.

14 In righteousness you shall be established;
you shall be far from oppression, for
you shall not fear;
and from terror, for it shall not come
near you.

15 If anyone stirs up strife,
it is not from me;
whoever stirs up strife with you
shall fall because of you.

16 Behold, I have created the smith
who blows the fire of coals
and produces a weapon for its purpose.
I have also created the ravager to destroy;

17 no weapon that is fashioned against you
shall succeed,
and you shall refute every tongue that
rises against you in judgment.
This is the heritage of the servants of the
LORD
and their vindication[5] from me, declares
the LORD."

The Compassion of the LORD

55 "Come, everyone who thirsts,
come to the waters;
and he who has no money,
come, buy and eat!
Come, buy wine and milk
without money and without price.

2 Why do you spend your money for that
which is not bread,
and your labor for that which does not
satisfy?
Listen diligently to me, and eat what is
good,
and delight yourselves in rich food.

3 Incline your ear, and come to me;
hear, that your soul may live;
and I will make with you an everlasting
covenant,
my steadfast, sure love for David.

4 Behold, I made him a witness to the
peoples,
a leader and commander for the peoples.

5 Behold, you shall call a nation that you do
not know,
and a nation that did not know you
shall run to you,
because of the LORD your God, and of the
Holy One of Israel,
for he has glorified you.

6 "Seek the LORD while he may be found;
call upon him while he is near;

7 let the wicked forsake his way,
and the unrighteous man his thoughts;
let him return to the LORD, that he may
have compassion on him,
and to our God, for he will abundantly
pardon.

8 For my thoughts are not your thoughts,
neither are your ways my ways, declares
the LORD.

9 For as the heavens are higher than the
earth,
so are my ways higher than your ways
and my thoughts than your thoughts.

10 "For as the rain and the snow come down
from heaven
and do not return there but water the
earth,
making it bring forth and sprout,
giving seed to the sower and bread to
the eater,

[1] Some manuscripts *For this is as the waters of Noah* [2] Or *lapis lazuli* [3] Or *jasper, or ruby* [4] Or *crystal* [5] Or *righteousness*

11 so shall my word be that goes out from my
mouth;
it shall not return to me empty,
but it shall accomplish that which I purpose,
and shall succeed in the thing for which
I sent it.

12 "For you shall go out in joy
and be led forth in peace;
the mountains and the hills before you
shall break forth into singing,
and all the trees of the field shall clap
their hands.
13 Instead of the thorn shall come up the
cypress;
instead of the brier shall come up the
myrtle;
and it shall make a name for the LORD,
an everlasting sign that shall not be cut
off."

Salvation for Foreigners

56 Thus says the LORD:
"Keep justice, and do righteousness,
for soon my salvation will come,
and my righteousness be revealed.
2 Blessed is the man who does this,
and the son of man who holds it fast,
who keeps the Sabbath, not profaning it,
and keeps his hand from doing any evil."

3 Let not the foreigner who has joined himself to the LORD say,
"The LORD will surely separate me from
his people";
and let not the eunuch say,
"Behold, I am a dry tree."
4 For thus says the LORD:
"To the eunuchs who keep my Sabbaths,
who choose the things that please me
and hold fast my covenant,
5 I will give in my house and within my walls
a monument and a name
better than sons and daughters;
I will give them an everlasting name
that shall not be cut off.

6 "And the foreigners who join themselves to
the LORD,
to minister to him, to love the name of
the LORD,
and to be his servants,
everyone who keeps the Sabbath and does
not profane it,
and holds fast my covenant—

7 these I will bring to my holy mountain,
and make them joyful in my house of
prayer;
their burnt offerings and their sacrifices
will be accepted on my altar;
for my house shall be called a house of
prayer
for all peoples."
8 The Lord GOD,
who gathers the outcasts of Israel,
declares,
"I will gather yet others to him
besides those already gathered."

Israel's Irresponsible Leaders

9 All you beasts of the field, come to devour—
all you beasts in the forest.
10 His watchmen are blind;
they are all without knowledge;
they are all silent dogs;
they cannot bark,
dreaming, lying down,
loving to slumber.
11 The dogs have a mighty appetite;
they never have enough.
But they are shepherds who have no
understanding;
they have all turned to their own way,
each to his own gain, one and all.
12 "Come," they say, "let me get wine;
let us fill ourselves with strong drink;
and tomorrow will be like this day,
great beyond measure."

Israel's Futile Idolatry

57 The righteous man perishes,
and no one lays it to heart;
devout men are taken away,
while no one understands.
For the righteous man is taken away from
calamity;
2 he enters into peace;
they rest in their beds
who walk in their uprightness.
3 But you, draw near,
sons of the sorceress,
offspring of the adulterer and the loose
woman.
4 Whom are you mocking?
Against whom do you open your
mouth wide
and stick out your tongue?
Are you not children of transgression,
the offspring of deceit,

5 you who burn with lust among the oaks,[1]
   under every green tree,
who slaughter your children in the valleys,
   under the clefts of the rocks?
6 Among the smooth stones of the valley is
      your portion;
   they, they, are your lot;
to them you have poured out a drink offer-
      ing,
   you have brought a grain offering.
   Shall I relent for these things?
7 On a high and lofty mountain
   you have set your bed,
   and there you went up to offer sacri-
      fice.
8 Behind the door and the doorpost
   you have set up your memorial;
for, deserting me, you have uncovered your
      bed,
   you have gone up to it,
   you have made it wide;
and you have made a covenant for yourself
      with them,
   you have loved their bed,
   you have looked on nakedness.[2]
9 You journeyed to the king with oil
   and multiplied your perfumes;
you sent your envoys far off,
   and sent down even to Sheol.
10 You were wearied with the length of your
      way,
   but you did not say, "It is hopeless";
you found new life for your strength,
   and so you were not faint.[3]

11 Whom did you dread and fear,
   so that you lied,
and did not remember me,
   did not lay it to heart?
Have I not held my peace, even for a long
      time,
   and you do not fear me?
12 I will declare your righteousness and your
      deeds,
   but they will not profit you.
13 When you cry out, let your collection of
      idols deliver you!
   The wind will carry them all off,
   a breath will take them away.
But he who takes refuge in me shall pos-
      sess the land
   and shall inherit my holy mountain.

Comfort for the Contrite

14 And it shall be said,
"Build up, build up, prepare the way,
   remove every obstruction from my
      people's way."
15 For thus says the One who is high and
      lifted up,
   who inhabits eternity, whose name is
      Holy:
"I dwell in the high and holy place,
   and also with him who is of a contrite
      and lowly spirit,
to revive the spirit of the lowly,
   and to revive the heart of the contrite.
16 For I will not contend forever,
   nor will I always be angry;
for the spirit would grow faint before me,
   and the breath of life that I made.
17 Because of the iniquity of his unjust gain I
      was angry,
   I struck him; I hid my face and was
      angry,
   but he went on backsliding in the way
      of his own heart.
18 I have seen his ways, but I will heal him;
   I will lead him and restore comfort to
      him and his mourners,
19   creating the fruit of the lips.
Peace, peace, to the far and to the near," says
      the LORD,
   "and I will heal him.
20 But the wicked are like the tossing sea;
   for it cannot be quiet,
   and its waters toss up mire and dirt.
21 There is no peace," says my God, "for the
      wicked."

True and False Fasting

58 "Cry aloud; do not hold back;
      lift up your voice like a trumpet;
declare to my people their transgression,
   to the house of Jacob their sins.
2 Yet they seek me daily
   and delight to know my ways,
as if they were a nation that did righ-
      teousness
   and did not forsake the judgment of
      their God;
they ask of me righteous judgments;
   they delight to draw near to God.
3 'Why have we fasted, and you see it not?
   Why have we humbled ourselves, and
      you take no knowledge of it?'

---

[1] Or among the terebinths [2] Or on a monument (see 56:5); Hebrew on a hand [3] Hebrew and so you were not sick

Behold, in the day of your fast you seek
 your own pleasure,[1]
and oppress all your workers.
4 Behold, you fast only to quarrel and to
 fight
 and to hit with a wicked fist.
Fasting like yours this day
 will not make your voice to be heard on
 high.
5 Is such the fast that I choose,
 a day for a person to humble himself?
Is it to bow down his head like a reed,
 and to spread sackcloth and ashes under
 him?
Will you call this a fast,
 and a day acceptable to the LORD?

6 "Is not this the fast that I choose:
 to loose the bonds of wickedness,
 to undo the straps of the yoke,
to let the oppressed[2] go free,
 and to break every yoke?
7 Is it not to share your bread with the hungry
 and bring the homeless poor into your
 house;
when you see the naked, to cover him,
 and not to hide yourself from your own
 flesh?
8 Then shall your light break forth like the
 dawn,
 and your healing shall spring up speedily;
your righteousness shall go before you;
 the glory of the LORD shall be your rear
 guard.
9 Then you shall call, and the LORD will
 answer;
 you shall cry, and he will say, 'Here I am.'
If you take away the yoke from your midst,
 the pointing of the finger, and speaking
 wickedness,
10 if you pour yourself out for the hungry
 and satisfy the desire of the afflicted,
then shall your light rise in the darkness
 and your gloom be as the noonday.
11 And the LORD will guide you continually
 and satisfy your desire in scorched
 places
 and make your bones strong;
and you shall be like a watered garden,
 like a spring of water,
 whose waters do not fail.

12 And your ancient ruins shall be rebuilt;
 you shall raise up the foundations of
 many generations;
you shall be called the repairer of the
 breach,
 the restorer of streets to dwell in.

13 "If you turn back your foot from the
 Sabbath,
 from doing your pleasure[3] on my holy
 day,
and call the Sabbath a delight
 and the holy day of the LORD honorable;
if you honor it, not going your own ways,
 or seeking your own pleasure,[4] or talking idly;[5]
14 then you shall take delight in the LORD,
 and I will make you ride on the heights
 of the earth;[6]
I will feed you with the heritage of Jacob
 your father,
 for the mouth of the LORD has spoken."

Evil and Oppression

59 Behold, the LORD's hand is not
 shortened, that it cannot save,
 or his ear dull, that it cannot hear;
2 but your iniquities have made a separation
 between you and your God,
and your sins have hidden his face from
 you
 so that he does not hear.
3 For your hands are defiled with blood
 and your fingers with iniquity;
your lips have spoken lies;
 your tongue mutters wickedness.
4 No one enters suit justly;
 no one goes to law honestly;
they rely on empty pleas, they speak lies,
 they conceive mischief and give birth to
 iniquity.
5 They hatch adders' eggs;
 they weave the spider's web;
he who eats their eggs dies,
 and from one that is crushed a viper is
 hatched.
6 Their webs will not serve as clothing;
 men will not cover themselves with
 what they make.
Their works are works of iniquity,
 and deeds of violence are in their hands.

[1] Or pursue your own business [2] Or bruised [3] Or business [4] Or pursuing your own business [5] Hebrew or speaking a word [6] Or of the land

⁷ Their feet run to evil,
  and they are swift to shed innocent
    blood;
their thoughts are thoughts of iniquity;
  desolation and destruction are in their
    highways.
⁸ The way of peace they do not know,
  and there is no justice in their paths;
they have made their roads crooked;
  no one who treads on them knows
    peace.

⁹ Therefore justice is far from us,
  and righteousness does not overtake us;
we hope for light, and behold, darkness,
  and for brightness, but we walk in
    gloom.
¹⁰ We grope for the wall like the blind;
  we grope like those who have no eyes;
we stumble at noon as in the twilight,
  among those in full vigor we are like
    dead men.
¹¹ We all growl like bears;
  we moan and moan like doves;
we hope for justice, but there is none;
  for salvation, but it is far from us.
¹² For our transgressions are multiplied
    before you,
  and our sins testify against us;
for our transgressions are with us,
  and we know our iniquities:
¹³ transgressing, and denying the LORD,
  and turning back from following our
    God,
speaking oppression and revolt,
  conceiving and uttering from the heart
    lying words.

Judgment and Redemption
¹⁴ Justice is turned back,
  and righteousness stands far away;
for truth has stumbled in the public
    squares,
  and uprightness cannot enter.
¹⁵ Truth is lacking,
  and he who departs from evil makes
    himself a prey.

The LORD saw it, and it displeased him[1]
    that there was no justice.
¹⁶ He saw that there was no man,
  and wondered that there was no one to
    intercede;

then his own arm brought him salvation,
  and his righteousness upheld him.
¹⁷ He put on righteousness as a breastplate,
  and a helmet of salvation on his head;
he put on garments of vengeance for cloth-
    ing,
  and wrapped himself in zeal as a cloak.
¹⁸ According to their deeds, so will he repay,
  wrath to his adversaries, repayment to
    his enemies;
to the coastlands he will render repay-
    ment.
¹⁹ So they shall fear the name of the LORD
    from the west,
  and his glory from the rising of the sun;
for he will come like a rushing stream,[2]
  which the wind of the LORD drives.

²⁰ "And a Redeemer will come to Zion,
  to those in Jacob who turn from trans-
    gression," declares the LORD.

²¹ "And as for me, this is my covenant with
them," says the LORD: "My Spirit that is upon
you, and my words that I have put in your
mouth, shall not depart out of your mouth, or
out of the mouth of your offspring, or out of
the mouth of your children's offspring," says the
LORD, "from this time forth and forevermore."

The Future Glory of Israel
60 Arise, shine, for your light has come,
      and the glory of the LORD has risen
        upon you.
² For behold, darkness shall cover the earth,
    and thick darkness the peoples;
but the LORD will arise upon you,
    and his glory will be seen upon you.
³ And nations shall come to your light,
    and kings to the brightness of your ris-
      ing.

⁴ Lift up your eyes all around, and see;
    they all gather together, they come to
      you;
your sons shall come from afar,
    and your daughters shall be carried on
      the hip.
⁵ Then you shall see and be radiant;
    your heart shall thrill and exult,[3]
because the abundance of the sea shall be
      turned to you,
    the wealth of the nations shall come to
      you.

---

[1] Hebrew *and it was evil in his eyes* [2] Hebrew *a narrow river* [3] Hebrew *your heart shall tremble and grow wide*

6 A multitude of camels shall cover you,
    the young camels of Midian and Ephah;
    all those from Sheba shall come.
  They shall bring gold and frankincense,
    and shall bring good news, the praises
      of the LORD.
7 All the flocks of Kedar shall be gathered to
      you;
    the rams of Nebaioth shall minister to
      you;
  they shall come up with acceptance on my
      altar,
    and I will beautify my beautiful
      house.

8 Who are these that fly like a cloud,
    and like doves to their windows?
9 For the coastlands shall hope for me,
    the ships of Tarshish first,
  to bring your children from afar,
    their silver and gold with them,
  for the name of the LORD your God,
    and for the Holy One of Israel,
    because he has made you beautiful.

10 Foreigners shall build up your walls,
    and their kings shall minister to you;
  for in my wrath I struck you,
    but in my favor I have had mercy on
      you.
11 Your gates shall be open continually;
    day and night they shall not be shut,
  that people may bring to you the wealth of
      the nations,
    with their kings led in procession.
12 For the nation and kingdom
    that will not serve you shall perish;
    those nations shall be utterly laid waste.
13 The glory of Lebanon shall come to you,
    the cypress, the plane, and the pine,
  to beautify the place of my sanctuary,
    and I will make the place of my feet glo-
      rious.
14 The sons of those who afflicted you
    shall come bending low to you,
  and all who despised you
    shall bow down at your feet;
  they shall call you the City of the LORD,
    the Zion of the Holy One of Israel.

15 Whereas you have been forsaken and
      hated,
    with no one passing through,

I will make you majestic forever,
    a joy from age to age.
16 You shall suck the milk of nations;
    you shall nurse at the breast of kings;
  and you shall know that I, the LORD, am
      your Savior
    and your Redeemer, the Mighty One of
      Jacob.

17 Instead of bronze I will bring gold,
    and instead of iron I will bring silver;
  instead of wood, bronze,
    instead of stones, iron.
  I will make your overseers peace
    and your taskmasters righteousness.
18 Violence shall no more be heard in your
      land,
    devastation or destruction within your
      borders;
  you shall call your walls Salvation,
    and your gates Praise.

19 The sun shall be no more
    your light by day,
  nor for brightness shall the moon
    give you light;[1]
  but the LORD will be your everlasting light,
    and your God will be your glory.[2]
20 Your sun shall no more go down,
    nor your moon withdraw itself;
  for the LORD will be your everlasting light,
    and your days of mourning shall be
      ended.
21 Your people shall all be righteous;
    they shall possess the land forever,
  the branch of my planting, the work of my
      hands,
    that I might be glorified.[3]
22 The least one shall become a clan,
    and the smallest one a mighty nation;
  I am the LORD;
    in its time I will hasten it.

The Year of the LORD's Favor

61 The Spirit of the Lord GOD is upon
    me,
    because the LORD has anointed me
  to bring good news to the poor;[4]
    he has sent me to bind up the broken-
      hearted,
  to proclaim liberty to the captives,
    and the opening of the prison to those
      who are bound;[5]

---

[1] Masoretic Text; Dead Sea Scroll, Septuagint, Targum add by night [2] Or your beauty [3] Or that I might display my beauty [4] Or afflicted [5] Or the opening [of the eyes] to those who are blind; Septuagint and recovery of sight to the blind

² to proclaim the year of the Lord's favor,
    and the day of vengeance of our God;
    to comfort all who mourn;
³ to grant to those who mourn in Zion—
    to give them a beautiful headdress
        instead of ashes,
  the oil of gladness instead of mourning,
    the garment of praise instead of a faint
        spirit;
  that they may be called oaks of righteous-
        ness,
    the planting of the Lord, that he may
        be glorified.[1]
⁴ They shall build up the ancient ruins;
    they shall raise up the former devasta-
        tions;
  they shall repair the ruined cities,
    the devastations of many generations.

⁵ Strangers shall stand and tend your flocks;
    foreigners shall be your plowmen and
        vinedressers;
⁶ but you shall be called the priests of the
    Lord;
    they shall speak of you as the ministers
        of our God;
  you shall eat the wealth of the nations,
    and in their glory you shall boast.
⁷ Instead of your shame there shall be a
    double portion;
    instead of dishonor they shall rejoice in
        their lot;
  therefore in their land they shall possess a
    double portion;
    they shall have everlasting joy.

⁸ For I the Lord love justice;
    I hate robbery and wrong;[2]
  I will faithfully give them their recompense,
    and I will make an everlasting covenant
        with them.
⁹ Their offspring shall be known among the
    nations,
    and their descendants in the midst of
        the peoples;
  all who see them shall acknowledge them,
    that they are an offspring the Lord has
        blessed.

¹⁰ I will greatly rejoice in the Lord;
    my soul shall exult in my God,
  for he has clothed me with the garments of
    salvation;
    he has covered me with the robe of
        righteousness,

as a bridegroom decks himself like a priest
    with a beautiful headdress,
  and as a bride adorns herself with her
    jewels.
¹¹ For as the earth brings forth its sprouts,
    and as a garden causes what is sown in
        it to sprout up,
  so the Lord God will cause righteousness
    and praise
    to sprout up before all the nations.

Zion's Coming Salvation

62 For Zion's sake I will not keep silent,
    and for Jerusalem's sake I will not be
        quiet,
  until her righteousness goes forth as
    brightness,
    and her salvation as a burning torch.
² The nations shall see your righteousness,
    and all the kings your glory,
  and you shall be called by a new name
    that the mouth of the Lord will give.
³ You shall be a crown of beauty in the hand
    of the Lord,
    and a royal diadem in the hand of your
        God.
⁴ You shall no more be termed Forsaken,[3]
    and your land shall no more be termed
        Desolate,[4]
  but you shall be called My Delight Is in Her,[5]
    and your land Married;[6]
  for the Lord delights in you,
    and your land shall be married.
⁵ For as a young man marries a young
    woman,
    so shall your sons marry you,
  and as the bridegroom rejoices over the
    bride,
    so shall your God rejoice over you.

⁶ On your walls, O Jerusalem,
    I have set watchmen;
  all the day and all the night
    they shall never be silent.
  You who put the Lord in remembrance,
    take no rest,
⁷ and give him no rest
    until he establishes Jerusalem
    and makes it a praise in the earth.
⁸ The Lord has sworn by his right hand
    and by his mighty arm:
  "I will not again give your grain
    to be food for your enemies,

---

[1] Or that he may display his beauty [2] Or robbery with a burnt offering [3] Hebrew Azubah [4] Hebrew Shemamah [5] Hebrew Hephzibah [6] Hebrew Beulah

and foreigners shall not drink your wine
  for which you have labored;
⁹ but those who garner it shall eat it
    and praise the LORD,
  and those who gather it shall drink it
    in the courts of my sanctuary."¹

¹⁰ Go through, go through the gates;
    prepare the way for the people;
  build up, build up the highway;
    clear it of stones;
  lift up a signal over the peoples.
¹¹ Behold, the LORD has proclaimed
    to the end of the earth:
  Say to the daughter of Zion,
    "Behold, your salvation comes;
  behold, his reward is with him,
    and his recompense before him."
¹² And they shall be called The Holy People,
    The Redeemed of the LORD;
  and you shall be called Sought Out,
    A City Not Forsaken.

The LORD's Day of Vengeance

63 Who is this who comes from Edom,
    in crimsoned garments from Bozrah,
  he who is splendid in his apparel,
    marching in the greatness of his
      strength?
  "It is I, speaking in righteousness,
    mighty to save."

² Why is your apparel red,
    and your garments like his who treads
      in the winepress?

³ "I have trodden the winepress alone,
    and from the peoples no one was with
      me;
  I trod them in my anger
    and trampled them in my wrath;
  their lifeblood² spattered on my garments,
    and stained all my apparel.
⁴ For the day of vengeance was in my
      heart,
    and my year of redemption³ had come.
⁵ I looked, but there was no one to help;
    I was appalled, but there was no one to
      uphold;
  so my own arm brought me salvation,
    and my wrath upheld me.

⁶ I trampled down the peoples in my
      anger;
    I made them drunk in my wrath,
  and I poured out their lifeblood on the
      earth."

The LORD's Mercy Remembered

⁷ I will recount the steadfast love of the
      LORD,
    the praises of the LORD,
  according to all that the LORD has granted
      us,
    and the great goodness to the house of
      Israel
  that he has granted them according to his
      compassion,
    according to the abundance of his stead-
      fast love.
⁸ For he said, "Surely they are my people,
    children who will not deal falsely."
  And he became their Savior.
⁹ In all their affliction he was afflicted,⁴
    and the angel of his presence saved
      them;
  in his love and in his pity he redeemed
      them;
    he lifted them up and carried them all
      the days of old.

¹⁰ But they rebelled
    and grieved his Holy Spirit;
  therefore he turned to be their enemy,
    and himself fought against them.
¹¹ Then he remembered the days of old,
    of Moses and his people.⁵
  Where is he who brought them up out of
      the sea
    with the shepherds of his flock?
  Where is he who put in the midst of them
    his Holy Spirit,
¹² who caused his glorious arm
    to go at the right hand of Moses,
  who divided the waters before them
    to make for himself an everlasting
      name,
¹³ who led them through the depths?
  Like a horse in the desert,
    they did not stumble.
¹⁴ Like livestock that go down into the valley,
    the Spirit of the LORD gave them rest.
  So you led your people,
    to make for yourself a glorious name.

¹ Or in my holy courts ² Or their juice; also verse 6 ³ Or the year of my redeemed ⁴ Or he did not afflict ⁵ Or Then his people remembered the days of old, of Moses

Prayer for Mercy

15 Look down from heaven and see,
   from your holy and beautiful[1] habita-
      tion.
   Where are your zeal and your might?
   The stirring of your inner parts and
      your compassion
   are held back from me.
16 For you are our Father,
   though Abraham does not know us,
   and Israel does not acknowledge us;
   you, O LORD, are our Father,
   our Redeemer from of old is your name.
17 O LORD, why do you make us wander from
      your ways
   and harden our heart, so that we fear
      you not?
   Return for the sake of your servants,
   the tribes of your heritage.
18 Your holy people held possession for a little
      while;[2]
   our adversaries have trampled down
      your sanctuary.
19 We have become like those over whom you
      have never ruled,
   like those who are not called by your
      name.

64 Oh that you would rend the heavens
   and come down,
   that the mountains might quake at
      your presence—
2 3 as when fire kindles brushwood
   and the fire causes water to boil—
   to make your name known to your adver-
      saries,
   and that the nations might tremble at
      your presence!
3 When you did awesome things that we did
      not look for,
   you came down, the mountains quaked
      at your presence.
4 From of old no one has heard
   or perceived by the ear,
   no eye has seen a God besides you,
   who acts for those who wait for him.
5 You meet him who joyfully works righ-
      teousness,
   those who remember you in your ways.
   Behold, you were angry, and we sinned;
   in our sins we have been a long time,
   and shall we be saved?[4]

6 We have all become like one who is
      unclean,
   and all our righteous deeds are like a
      polluted garment.
   We all fade like a leaf,
   and our iniquities, like the wind, take us
      away.
7 There is no one who calls upon your name,
   who rouses himself to take hold of you;
   for you have hidden your face from us,
   and have made us melt in[5] the hand of
      our iniquities.

8 But now, O LORD, you are our Father;
   we are the clay, and you are our potter;
   we are all the work of your hand.
9 Be not so terribly angry, O LORD,
   and remember not iniquity forever.
   Behold, please look, we are all your
      people.
10 Your holy cities have become a wilderness;
   Zion has become a wilderness,
   Jerusalem a desolation.
11 Our holy and beautiful[6] house,
   where our fathers praised you,
   has been burned by fire,
   and all our pleasant places have become
      ruins.
12 Will you restrain yourself at these things,
      O LORD?
   Will you keep silent, and afflict us so
      terribly?

Judgment and Salvation

65 I was ready to be sought by those who
   did not ask for me;
   I was ready to be found by those who
      did not seek me.
   I said, "Here I am, here I am,"
   to a nation that was not called by[7] my
      name.
2 I spread out my hands all the day
   to a rebellious people,
   who walk in a way that is not good,
   following their own devices;
3 a people who provoke me
   to my face continually,
   sacrificing in gardens
   and making offerings on bricks;
4 who sit in tombs,
   and spend the night in secret places;

---

[1] Or *holy and glorious* [2] Or *They have dispossessed your holy people for a little while* [3] Ch 64:1 in Hebrew [4] Or *in your ways is continuance, that we might be saved* [5] Masoretic Text; Septuagint, Syriac, Targum *have delivered us into* [6] Or *holy and glorious* [7] Or *that did not call upon*

who eat pig's flesh,
   and broth of tainted meat is in their ves-
     sels;
5 who say, "Keep to yourself,
   do not come near me, for I am too holy
     for you."
These are a smoke in my nostrils,
   a fire that burns all the day.
6 Behold, it is written before me:
   "I will not keep silent, but I will repay;
I will indeed repay into their lap
7   both your iniquities and your fathers'
     iniquities together,
           says the LORD;
because they made offerings on the moun-
     tains
   and insulted me on the hills,
I will measure into their lap
   payment for their former deeds."[1]

8 Thus says the LORD:
"As the new wine is found in the cluster,
   and they say, 'Do not destroy it,
     for there is a blessing in it,'
so I will do for my servants' sake,
   and not destroy them all.
9 I will bring forth offspring from Jacob,
   and from Judah possessors of my
     mountains;
my chosen shall possess it,
   and my servants shall dwell there.
10 Sharon shall become a pasture for flocks,
   and the Valley of Achor a place for herds
     to lie down,
for my people who have sought me.
11 But you who forsake the LORD,
   who forget my holy mountain,
who set a table for Fortune
   and fill cups of mixed wine for
     Destiny,
12 I will destine you to the sword,
   and all of you shall bow down to the
     slaughter,
because, when I called, you did not answer;
   when I spoke, you did not listen,
but you did what was evil in my eyes
   and chose what I did not delight in."

13 Therefore thus says the Lord GOD:
"Behold, my servants shall eat,
   but you shall be hungry;
behold, my servants shall drink,
   but you shall be thirsty;

behold, my servants shall rejoice,
   but you shall be put to shame;
14 behold, my servants shall sing for gladness
     of heart,
   but you shall cry out for pain of heart
   and shall wail for breaking of spirit.
15 You shall leave your name to my chosen for
     a curse,
   and the Lord GOD will put you to death,
   but his servants he will call by another
     name,
16 so that he who blesses himself in the land
   shall bless himself by the God of
     truth,
and he who takes an oath in the land
   shall swear by the God of truth;
because the former troubles are forgot-
     ten
   and are hidden from my eyes.

New Heavens and a New Earth

17 "For behold, I create new heavens
   and a new earth,
and the former things shall not be remem-
     bered
   or come into mind.
18 But be glad and rejoice forever
   in that which I create;
for behold, I create Jerusalem to be a joy,
   and her people to be a gladness.
19 I will rejoice in Jerusalem
   and be glad in my people;
no more shall be heard in it the sound of
     weeping
   and the cry of distress.
20 No more shall there be in it
   an infant who lives but a few days,
   or an old man who does not fill out his
     days,
for the young man shall die a hundred
     years old,
   and the sinner a hundred years old shall
     be accursed.
21 They shall build houses and inhabit them;
   they shall plant vineyards and eat their
     fruit.
22 They shall not build and another inhabit;
   they shall not plant and another eat;
for like the days of a tree shall the days of
     my people be,
   and my chosen shall long enjoy[2] the
     work of their hands.

---

[1] Or I will first measure their payment into their lap   [2] Hebrew shall wear out

23 They shall not labor in vain
    or bear children for calamity,[1]
for they shall be the offspring of the
    blessed of the LORD,
    and their descendants with them.
24 Before they call I will answer;
    while they are yet speaking I will hear.
25 The wolf and the lamb shall graze
    together;
    the lion shall eat straw like the ox,
    and dust shall be the serpent's food.
They shall not hurt or destroy
    in all my holy mountain,"
                says the LORD.

The Humble and Contrite in Spirit

66 Thus says the LORD:
    "Heaven is my throne,
    and the earth is my footstool;
what is the house that you would build for
    me,
    and what is the place of my rest?
2 All these things my hand has made,
    and so all these things came to be,
             declares the LORD.
But this is the one to whom I will look:
    he who is humble and contrite in spirit
    and trembles at my word.

3 "He who slaughters an ox is like one who
    kills a man;
    he who sacrifices a lamb, like one who
    breaks a dog's neck;
    he who presents a grain offering, like one
    who offers pig's blood;
    he who makes a memorial offering of
    frankincense, like one who blesses
    an idol.
These have chosen their own ways,
    and their soul delights in their abomi-
    nations;
4 I also will choose harsh treatment for them
    and bring their fears upon them,
because when I called, no one answered,
    when I spoke, they did not listen;
but they did what was evil in my eyes
    and chose that in which I did not
    delight."

5 Hear the word of the LORD,
    you who tremble at his word:
"Your brothers who hate you
    and cast you out for my name's sake

have said, 'Let the LORD be glorified,
    that we may see your joy';
    but it is they who shall be put to shame.
6 "The sound of an uproar from the city!
    A sound from the temple!
The sound of the LORD,
    rendering recompense to his enemies!

Rejoice with Jerusalem

7 "Before she was in labor
    she gave birth;
before her pain came upon her
    she delivered a son.
8 Who has heard such a thing?
    Who has seen such things?
Shall a land be born in one day?
    Shall a nation be brought forth in one
    moment?
For as soon as Zion was in labor
    she brought forth her children.
9 Shall I bring to the point of birth and not
    cause to bring forth?"
    says the LORD;
"shall I, who cause to bring forth, shut the
    womb?"
    says your God.

10 "Rejoice with Jerusalem, and be glad for her,
    all you who love her;
rejoice with her in joy,
    all you who mourn over her;
11 that you may nurse and be satisfied
    from her consoling breast;
that you may drink deeply with delight
    from her glorious abundance."[2]

12 For thus says the LORD:
"Behold, I will extend peace to her like a
    river,
    and the glory of the nations like an
    overflowing stream;
and you shall nurse, you shall be carried
    upon her hip,
    and bounced upon her knees.
13 As one whom his mother comforts,
    so I will comfort you;
    you shall be comforted in Jerusalem.
14 You shall see, and your heart shall rejoice;
    your bones shall flourish like the grass;
and the hand of the LORD shall be known
    to his servants,
    and he shall show his indignation
    against his enemies.

[1] Or for sudden terror [2] Or breast

Final Judgment and Glory of the Lord

15 "For behold, the Lord will come in fire,
    and his chariots like the whirlwind,
to render his anger in fury,
    and his rebuke with flames of fire.
16 For by fire will the Lord enter into judgment,
    and by his sword, with all flesh;
and those slain by the Lord shall be many.

17 "Those who sanctify and purify themselves to go into the gardens, following one in the midst, eating pig's flesh and the abomination and mice, shall come to an end together, declares the Lord.

18 "For I know[1] their works and their thoughts, and the time is coming[2] to gather all nations and tongues. And they shall come and shall see my glory, 19 and I will set a sign among them. And from them I will send survivors to the nations, to Tarshish, Pul, and Lud, who draw the bow, to Tubal and Javan, to the coastlands far away, that have not heard my fame or seen my glory. And they shall declare my glory among the nations. 20 And they shall bring all your brothers from all the nations as an offering to the Lord, on horses and in chariots and in litters and on mules and on dromedaries, to my holy mountain Jerusalem, says the Lord, just as the Israelites bring their grain offering in a clean vessel to the house of the Lord. 21 And some of them also I will take for priests and for Levites, says the Lord.

22 "For as the new heavens and the new earth that I make
shall remain before me, says the Lord,
    so shall your offspring and your name remain.
23 From new moon to new moon,
    and from Sabbath to Sabbath,
all flesh shall come to worship before me,
declares the Lord.

24 "And they shall go out and look on the dead bodies of the men who have rebelled against me. For their worm shall not die, their fire shall not be quenched, and they shall be an abhorrence to all flesh."

---

[1] Septuagint, Syriac; Hebrew lacks *know* [2] Hebrew *and it is coming*

JEREMIAH

1 The words of Jeremiah, the son of Hilkiah, one of the priests who were in Anathoth in the land of Benjamin, ²to whom the word of the LORD came in the days of Josiah the son of Amon, king of Judah, in the thirteenth year of his reign. ³It came also in the days of Jehoiakim the son of Josiah, king of Judah, and until the end of the eleventh year of Zedekiah, the son of Josiah, king of Judah, until the captivity of Jerusalem in the fifth month.

The Call of Jeremiah

⁴Now the word of the LORD came to me, saying,

⁵ "Before I formed you in the womb I knew you,
   and before you were born I consecrated you;
   I appointed you a prophet to the nations."

⁶Then I said, "Ah, Lord GOD! Behold, I do not know how to speak, for I am only a youth." ⁷But the LORD said to me,

"Do not say, 'I am only a youth';
   for to all to whom I send you, you shall go,
   and whatever I command you, you shall speak.
⁸ Do not be afraid of them,
   for I am with you to deliver you,
                  declares the LORD."

⁹Then the LORD put out his hand and touched my mouth. And the LORD said to me,

"Behold, I have put my words in your mouth.
¹⁰ See, I have set you this day over nations and over kingdoms,
   to pluck up and to break down,
   to destroy and to overthrow,
   to build and to plant."

¹¹And the word of the LORD came to me, saying, "Jeremiah, what do you see?" And I said, "I see an almond[1] branch." ¹²Then the LORD said to me, "You have seen well, for I am watching over my word to perform it."

¹³The word of the LORD came to me a second time, saying, "What do you see?" And I said, "I see a boiling pot, facing away from the north." ¹⁴Then the LORD said to me, "Out of the north disaster[2] shall be let loose upon all the inhabitants of the land. ¹⁵For behold, I am calling all the tribes of the kingdoms of the north, declares the LORD, and they shall come, and every one shall set his throne at the entrance of the gates of Jerusalem, against all its walls all around and against all the cities of Judah. ¹⁶And I will declare my judgments against them, for all their evil in forsaking me. They have made offerings to other gods and worshiped the works of their own hands. ¹⁷But you, dress yourself for work;[3] arise, and say to them everything that I command you. Do not be dismayed by them, lest I dismay you before them. ¹⁸And I, behold, I make you this day a fortified city, an iron pillar, and bronze walls, against the whole land, against the kings of Judah, its officials, its priests, and the people of the land. ¹⁹They will fight against you, but they shall not prevail against you, for I am with you, declares the LORD, to deliver you."

Israel Forsakes the LORD

2 The word of the LORD came to me, saying, ²"Go and proclaim in the hearing of Jerusalem, Thus says the LORD,

"I remember the devotion of your youth,
   your love as a bride,
   how you followed me in the wilderness,
   in a land not sown.
³ Israel was holy to the LORD,
   the firstfruits of his harvest.
All who ate of it incurred guilt;
   disaster came upon them,
                  declares the LORD."

⁴Hear the word of the LORD, O house of Jacob, and all the clans of the house of Israel. ⁵Thus says the LORD:

"What wrong did your fathers find in me
   that they went far from me,
   and went after worthlessness, and became worthless?

---

[1] Almond sounds like the Hebrew for watching (compare verse 12) [2] The Hebrew word can mean evil, harm, or disaster, depending on the context; so throughout Jeremiah
[3] Hebrew gird up your loins

⁶ They did not say, 'Where is the LORD
    who brought us up from the land of
      Egypt,
  who led us in the wilderness,
    in a land of deserts and pits,
  in a land of drought and deep darkness,
    in a land that none passes through,
      where no man dwells?'
⁷ And I brought you into a plentiful land
    to enjoy its fruits and its good things.
  But when you came in, you defiled my
      land
    and made my heritage an abomina-
      tion.
⁸ The priests did not say, 'Where is the
      LORD?'
    Those who handle the law did not
      know me;
  the shepherds¹ transgressed against me;
    the prophets prophesied by Baal
    and went after things that do not profit.

⁹ "Therefore I still contend with you,
                    declares the LORD,
    and with your children's children I will
      contend.
¹⁰ For cross to the coasts of Cyprus and see,
    or send to Kedar and examine with care;
      see if there has been such a thing.
¹¹ Has a nation changed its gods,
    even though they are no gods?
  But my people have changed their glory
    for that which does not profit.
¹² Be appalled, O heavens, at this;
  be shocked, be utterly desolate,
                    declares the LORD,
¹³ for my people have committed two evils:
  they have forsaken me,
    the fountain of living waters,
  and hewed out cisterns for themselves,
    broken cisterns that can hold no
      water.

¹⁴ "Is Israel a slave? Is he a homeborn ser-
      vant?
    Why then has he become a prey?
¹⁵ The lions have roared against him;
    they have roared loudly.
  They have made his land a waste;
    his cities are in ruins, without inhabi-
      tant.
¹⁶ Moreover, the men of Memphis and
      Tahpanhes
    have shaved² the crown of your head.

¹⁷ Have you not brought this upon your-
      self
    by forsaking the LORD your God,
      when he led you in the way?
¹⁸ And now what do you gain by going to
      Egypt
    to drink the waters of the Nile?
  Or what do you gain by going to Assyria
    to drink the waters of the Euphrates?³
¹⁹ Your evil will chastise you,
    and your apostasy will reprove you.
  Know and see that it is evil and bitter
    for you to forsake the LORD your God;
      the fear of me is not in you,
                declares the Lord GOD of hosts.

²⁰ "For long ago I broke your yoke
    and burst your bonds;
      but you said, 'I will not serve.'
  Yes, on every high hill
    and under every green tree
      you bowed down like a whore.
²¹ Yet I planted you a choice vine,
    wholly of pure seed.
  How then have you turned degenerate
    and become a wild vine?
²² Though you wash yourself with lye
    and use much soap,
      the stain of your guilt is still before
        me,
                    declares the Lord GOD.
²³ How can you say, 'I am not unclean,
    I have not gone after the Baals'?
  Look at your way in the valley;
    know what you have done—
  a restless young camel running here and
        there,
²⁴   a wild donkey used to the wilderness,
  in her heat sniffing the wind!
    Who can restrain her lust?
  None who seek her need weary themselves;
    in her month they will find her.
²⁵ Keep your feet from going unshod
    and your throat from thirst.
  But you said, 'It is hopeless,
    for I have loved foreigners,
    and after them I will go.'

²⁶ "As a thief is shamed when caught,
    so the house of Israel shall be
        shamed:
  they, their kings, their officials,
    their priests, and their prophets,

¹ Or rulers ² Hebrew grazed ³ Hebrew the River

27 who say to a tree, 'You are my father,'
  and to a stone, 'You gave me birth.'
For they have turned their back to me,
  and not their face.
But in the time of their trouble they say,
  'Arise and save us!'
28 But where are your gods
  that you made for yourself?
Let them arise, if they can save you,
  in your time of trouble;
for as many as your cities
  are your gods, O Judah.

29 "Why do you contend with me?
  You have all transgressed against me,
      declares the LORD.
30 In vain have I struck your children;
  they took no correction;
your own sword devoured your prophets
  like a ravening lion.
31 And you, O generation, behold the word of
      the LORD.
  Have I been a wilderness to Israel,
    or a land of thick darkness?
Why then do my people say, 'We are free,
  we will come no more to you'?
32 Can a virgin forget her ornaments,
  or a bride her attire?
Yet my people have forgotten me
  days without number.

33 "How well you direct your course
    to seek love!
So that even to wicked women
  you have taught your ways.
34 Also on your skirts is found
    the lifeblood of the guiltless poor;
you did not find them breaking in.
  Yet in spite of all these things
35 you say, 'I am innocent;
    surely his anger has turned from me.'
Behold, I will bring you to judgment
  for saying, 'I have not sinned.'
36 How much you go about,
  changing your way!
You shall be put to shame by Egypt
  as you were put to shame by Assyria.
37 From it too you will come away
  with your hands on your head,
for the LORD has rejected those in whom
      you trust,
  and you will not prosper by them.

3 "If[1] a man divorces his wife
  and she goes from him
and becomes another man's wife,
  will he return to her?
Would not that land be greatly polluted?
You have played the whore with many lov-
    ers;
  and would you return to me?
              declares the LORD.
2 Lift up your eyes to the bare heights, and
    see!
  Where have you not been ravished?
By the waysides you have sat awaiting lov-
    ers
  like an Arab in the wilderness.
You have polluted the land
  with your vile whoredom.
3 Therefore the showers have been withheld,
    and the spring rain has not come;
yet you have the forehead of a whore;
  you refuse to be ashamed.
4 Have you not just now called to me,
  'My father, you are the friend of my
      youth—
5 will he be angry forever,
    will he be indignant to the end?'
Behold, you have spoken,
  but you have done all the evil that you
    could."

Faithless Israel Called to Repentance

6 The LORD said to me in the days of King
Josiah: "Have you seen what she did, that
faithless one, Israel, how she went up on every
high hill and under every green tree, and there
played the whore? 7 And I thought, 'After she
has done all this she will return to me,' but she
did not return, and her treacherous sister Judah
saw it. 8 She saw that for all the adulteries of
that faithless one, Israel, I had sent her away
with a decree of divorce. Yet her treacherous
sister Judah did not fear, but she too went and
played the whore. 9 Because she took her whoredom lightly, she polluted the land, committing
adultery with stone and tree. 10 Yet for all this
her treacherous sister Judah did not return
to me with her whole heart, but in pretense,
declares the LORD."

11 And the LORD said to me, "Faithless Israel
has shown herself more righteous than treacherous Judah. 12 Go, and proclaim these words
toward the north, and say,

[1] Septuagint, Syriac; Hebrew *Saying, "If*

"'Return, faithless Israel,
>> declares the LORD.
I will not look on you in anger,
>> for I am merciful,
>> declares the LORD;
I will not be angry forever.
13 Only acknowledge your guilt,
>> that you rebelled against the LORD your
>> God
>> and scattered your favors among foreigners
>> under every green tree,
>> and that you have not obeyed my voice,
>> declares the LORD.
14 Return, O faithless children,
>> declares the LORD;
>> for I am your master;
I will take you, one from a city and two
>> from a family,
>> and I will bring you to Zion.

15 "'And I will give you shepherds after my own heart, who will feed you with knowledge and understanding. 16 And when you have multiplied and been fruitful in the land, in those days, declares the LORD, they shall no more say, "The ark of the covenant of the LORD." It shall not come to mind or be remembered or missed; it shall not be made again. 17 At that time Jerusalem shall be called the throne of the LORD, and all nations shall gather to it, to the presence of the LORD in Jerusalem, and they shall no more stubbornly follow their own evil heart. 18 In those days the house of Judah shall join the house of Israel, and together they shall come from the land of the north to the land that I gave your fathers for a heritage.

19 "'I said,
>> How I would set you among my sons,
>> and give you a pleasant land,
>> a heritage most beautiful of all nations.
And I thought you would call me, My Father,
>> and would not turn from following me.
20 Surely, as a treacherous wife leaves her husband,
>> so have you been treacherous to me,
>> O house of Israel,
>> declares the LORD.'"

21 A voice on the bare heights is heard,
>> the weeping and pleading of Israel's sons
because they have perverted their way;
>> they have forgotten the LORD their God.
22 "Return, O faithless sons;
>> I will heal your faithlessness."

"Behold, we come to you,
>> for you are the LORD our God.
23 Truly the hills are a delusion,
>> the orgies[1] on the mountains.
Truly in the LORD our God
>> is the salvation of Israel.

24 "But from our youth the shameful thing has devoured all for which our fathers labored, their flocks and their herds, their sons and their daughters. 25 Let us lie down in our shame, and let our dishonor cover us. For we have sinned against the LORD our God, we and our fathers, from our youth even to this day, and we have not obeyed the voice of the LORD our God."

4 "If you return, O Israel,
>> declares the LORD,
>> to me you should return.
If you remove your detestable things from
>> my presence,
>> and do not waver,
2 and if you swear, 'As the LORD lives,'
>> in truth, in justice, and in righteousness,
>> then nations shall bless themselves in him,
>> and in him shall they glory."

3 For thus says the LORD to the men of Judah and Jerusalem:

"Break up your fallow ground,
>> and sow not among thorns.
4 Circumcise yourselves to the LORD;
>> remove the foreskin of your hearts,
>> O men of Judah and inhabitants of
>> Jerusalem;
lest my wrath go forth like fire,
>> and burn with none to quench it,
>> because of the evil of your deeds."

Disaster from the North

5 Declare in Judah, and proclaim in Jerusalem, and say,

"Blow the trumpet through the land;
>> cry aloud and say,
'Assemble, and let us go
>> into the fortified cities!'
6 Raise a standard toward Zion,
>> flee for safety, stay not,
for I bring disaster from the north,
>> and great destruction.
7 A lion has gone up from his thicket,
>> a destroyer of nations has set out;
>> he has gone out from his place

---

[1] Hebrew commotion

to make your land a waste;
   your cities will be ruins
   without inhabitant.
8 For this put on sackcloth,
   lament and wail,
   for the fierce anger of the LORD
   has not turned back from us."

9 "In that day, declares the LORD, courage shall fail both king and officials. The priests shall be appalled and the prophets astounded." 10 Then I said, "Ah, Lord GOD, surely you have utterly deceived this people and Jerusalem, saying, 'It shall be well with you,' whereas the sword has reached their very life."

11 At that time it will be said to this people and to Jerusalem, "A hot wind from the bare heights in the desert toward the daughter of my people, not to winnow or cleanse, 12 a wind too full for this comes for me. Now it is I who speak in judgment upon them."

13 Behold, he comes up like clouds;
   his chariots like the whirlwind;
   his horses are swifter than eagles—
   woe to us, for we are ruined!
14 O Jerusalem, wash your heart from evil,
   that you may be saved.
   How long shall your wicked thoughts
   lodge within you?
15 For a voice declares from Dan
   and proclaims trouble from Mount
     Ephraim.
16 Warn the nations that he is coming;
   announce to Jerusalem,
   "Besiegers come from a distant land;
   they shout against the cities of Judah.
17 Like keepers of a field are they against her
   all around,
   because she has rebelled against me,
     declares the LORD.
18 Your ways and your deeds
   have brought this upon you.
   This is your doom, and it is bitter;
   it has reached your very heart."

Anguish over Judah's Desolation

19 My anguish, my anguish! I writhe in pain!
   Oh the walls of my heart!
   My heart is beating wildly;
   I cannot keep silent,
   for I hear the sound of the trumpet,
   the alarm of war.

20 Crash follows hard on crash;
   the whole land is laid waste.
   Suddenly my tents are laid waste,
   my curtains in a moment.
21 How long must I see the standard
   and hear the sound of the trumpet?

22 "For my people are foolish;
   they know me not;
   they are stupid children;
   they have no understanding.
   They are 'wise'—in doing evil!
   But how to do good they know not."

23 I looked on the earth, and behold, it was
     without form and void;
   and to the heavens, and they had no
     light.
24 I looked on the mountains, and behold,
     they were quaking,
   and all the hills moved to and fro.
25 I looked, and behold, there was no man,
   and all the birds of the air had fled.
26 I looked, and behold, the fruitful land was
     a desert,
   and all its cities were laid in ruins
   before the LORD, before his fierce anger.

27 For thus says the LORD, "The whole land shall be a desolation; yet I will not make a full end.

28 "For this the earth shall mourn,
   and the heavens above be dark;
   for I have spoken; I have purposed;
   I have not relented, nor will I turn
     back."

29 At the noise of horseman and archer
   every city takes to flight;
   they enter thickets; they climb among
     rocks;
   all the cities are forsaken,
   and no man dwells in them.
30 And you, O desolate one,
   what do you mean that you dress in scarlet,
   that you adorn yourself with ornaments
     of gold,
   that you enlarge your eyes with paint?
   In vain you beautify yourself.
   Your lovers despise you;
   they seek your life.
31 For I heard a cry as of a woman in labor,
   anguish as of one giving birth to her
     first child,

the cry of the daughter of Zion gasping for
breath,
stretching out her hands,
"Woe is me! I am fainting before murderers."

Jerusalem Refused to Repent

5 Run to and fro through the streets of
Jerusalem,
look and take note!
Search her squares to see
if you can find a man,
one who does justice
and seeks truth,
that I may pardon her.
2 Though they say, "As the LORD lives,"
yet they swear falsely.
3 O LORD, do not your eyes look for truth?
You have struck them down,
but they felt no anguish;
you have consumed them,
but they refused to take correction.
They have made their faces harder than
rock;
they have refused to repent.

4 Then I said, "These are only the poor;
they have no sense;
for they do not know the way of the LORD,
the justice of their God.
5 I will go to the great
and will speak to them,
for they know the way of the LORD,
the justice of their God."
But they all alike had broken the yoke;
they had burst the bonds.

6 Therefore a lion from the forest shall strike
them down;
a wolf from the desert shall devastate
them.
A leopard is watching their cities;
everyone who goes out of them shall be
torn in pieces,
because their transgressions are many,
their apostasies are great.

7 "How can I pardon you?
Your children have forsaken me
and have sworn by those who are no
gods.
When I fed them to the full,
they committed adultery
and trooped to the houses of whores.
8 They were well-fed, lusty stallions,
each neighing for his neighbor's wife.

9 Shall I not punish them for these things?
declares the LORD;
and shall I not avenge myself
on a nation such as this?

10 "Go up through her vine rows and destroy,
but make not a full end;
strip away her branches,
for they are not the LORD's.
11 For the house of Israel and the house of
Judah
have been utterly treacherous to me,
declares the LORD.
12 They have spoken falsely of the LORD
and have said, 'He will do nothing;
no disaster will come upon us,
nor shall we see sword or famine.
13 The prophets will become wind;
the word is not in them.
Thus shall it be done to them!'"

The LORD Proclaims Judgment

14 Therefore thus says the LORD, the God of
hosts:
"Because you have spoken this word,
behold, I am making my words in your
mouth a fire,
and this people wood, and the fire shall
consume them.
15 Behold, I am bringing against you
a nation from afar, O house of Israel,
declares the LORD.
It is an enduring nation;
it is an ancient nation,
a nation whose language you do not know,
nor can you understand what they say.
16 Their quiver is like an open tomb;
they are all mighty warriors.
17 They shall eat up your harvest and your
food;
they shall eat up your sons and your
daughters;
they shall eat up your flocks and your herds;
they shall eat up your vines and your fig
trees;
your fortified cities in which you trust
they shall beat down with the sword."

18 "But even in those days, declares the LORD,
I will not make a full end of you. 19 And when
your people say, 'Why has the LORD our God
done all these things to us?' you shall say to
them, 'As you have forsaken me and served
foreign gods in your land, so you shall serve
foreigners in a land that is not yours.'"

20 Declare this in the house of Jacob;
proclaim it in Judah:

21 "Hear this, O foolish and senseless people,
   who have eyes, but see not,
   who have ears, but hear not.
22 Do you not fear me? declares the LORD.
   Do you not tremble before me?
   I placed the sand as the boundary for the
      sea,
      a perpetual barrier that it cannot pass;
   though the waves toss, they cannot pre-
      vail;
      though they roar, they cannot pass over
      it.
23 But this people has a stubborn and rebel-
      lious heart;
      they have turned aside and gone away.
24 They do not say in their hearts,
   'Let us fear the LORD our God,
   who gives the rain in its season,
      the autumn rain and the spring rain,
   and keeps for us
      the weeks appointed for the harvest.'
25 Your iniquities have turned these away,
   and your sins have kept good from
      you.
26 For wicked men are found among my
      people;
      they lurk like fowlers lying in wait.[1]
   They set a trap;
      they catch men.
27 Like a cage full of birds,
      their houses are full of deceit;
   therefore they have become great and
      rich;
28 they have grown fat and sleek.
   They know no bounds in deeds of evil;
      they judge not with justice
   the cause of the fatherless, to make it pros-
      per,
      and they do not defend the rights of the
      needy.
29 Shall I not punish them for these things?
                     declares the LORD,
      and shall I not avenge myself
      on a nation such as this?"

30 An appalling and horrible thing
      has happened in the land:
31 the prophets prophesy falsely,
      and the priests rule at their direction;
   my people love to have it so,
      but what will you do when the end
      comes?

Impending Disaster for Jerusalem

6 Flee for safety, O people of Benjamin,
   from the midst of Jerusalem!
   Blow the trumpet in Tekoa,
      and raise a signal on Beth-haccherem,
   for disaster looms out of the north,
      and great destruction.
2 The lovely and delicately bred I will
      destroy,
      the daughter of Zion.[2]
3 Shepherds with their flocks shall come
      against her;
      they shall pitch their tents around her;
      they shall pasture, each in his place.
4 "Prepare war against her;
      arise, and let us attack at noon!
   Woe to us, for the day declines,
      for the shadows of evening lengthen!
5 Arise, and let us attack by night
      and destroy her palaces!"

6 For thus says the LORD of hosts:
   "Cut down her trees;
      cast up a siege mound against
      Jerusalem.
   This is the city that must be punished;
      there is nothing but oppression within
      her.
7 As a well keeps its water fresh,
      so she keeps fresh her evil;
   violence and destruction are heard within
      her;
      sickness and wounds are ever before me.
8 Be warned, O Jerusalem,
      lest I turn from you in disgust,
   lest I make you a desolation,
      an uninhabited land."

9 Thus says the LORD of hosts:
   "They shall glean thoroughly as a vine
      the remnant of Israel;
   like a grape gatherer pass your hand again
      over its branches."
10 To whom shall I speak and give warning,
      that they may hear?
   Behold, their ears are uncircumcised,
      they cannot listen;
   behold, the word of the LORD is to them an
      object of scorn;
      they take no pleasure in it.
11 Therefore I am full of the wrath of the
      LORD;
      I am weary of holding it in.

[1] The meaning of the Hebrew is uncertain [2] Or I have likened the daughter of Zion to the loveliest pasture

"Pour it out upon the children in the street,
  and upon the gatherings of young men,
    also;
both husband and wife shall be taken,
  the elderly and the very aged.
12 Their houses shall be turned over to others,
  their fields and wives together,
for I will stretch out my hand
  against the inhabitants of the land,"
                    declares the LORD.
13 "For from the least to the greatest of them,
  everyone is greedy for unjust gain;
and from prophet to priest,
  everyone deals falsely.
14 They have healed the wound of my people
    lightly,
  saying, 'Peace, peace,'
  when there is no peace.
15 Were they ashamed when they committed
    abomination?
  No, they were not at all ashamed;
  they did not know how to blush.
Therefore they shall fall among those who
    fall;
  at the time that I punish them, they
    shall be overthrown,"
                    says the LORD.

16 Thus says the LORD:
"Stand by the roads, and look,
  and ask for the ancient paths,
where the good way is; and walk in it,
  and find rest for your souls.
But they said, 'We will not walk in it.'
17 I set watchmen over you, saying,
  'Pay attention to the sound of the trum-
    pet!'
But they said, 'We will not pay attention.'
18 Therefore hear, O nations,
  and know, O congregation, what will
    happen to them.
19 Hear, O earth; behold, I am bringing disas-
    ter upon this people,
  the fruit of their devices,
because they have not paid attention to my
    words;
  and as for my law, they have rejected
    it.
20 What use to me is frankincense that comes
    from Sheba,
  or sweet cane from a distant land?
Your burnt offerings are not acceptable,
  nor your sacrifices pleasing to me.

21 Therefore thus says the LORD:
'Behold, I will lay before this people
  stumbling blocks against which they
    shall stumble;
fathers and sons together,
  neighbor and friend shall perish.'"

22 Thus says the LORD:
"Behold, a people is coming from the north
    country,
  a great nation is stirring from the far-
    thest parts of the earth.
23 They lay hold on bow and javelin;
  they are cruel and have no mercy;
  the sound of them is like the roaring
    sea;
they ride on horses,
  set in array as a man for battle,
  against you, O daughter of Zion!"
24 We have heard the report of it;
  our hands fall helpless;
anguish has taken hold of us,
  pain as of a woman in labor.
25 Go not out into the field,
  nor walk on the road,
for the enemy has a sword;
  terror is on every side.
26 O daughter of my people, put on sackcloth,
    and roll in ashes;
make mourning as for an only son,
  most bitter lamentation,
for suddenly the destroyer
  will come upon us.

27 "I have made you a tester of metals among
    my people,
  that you may know and test their ways.
28 They are all stubbornly rebellious,
  going about with slanders;
they are bronze and iron;
  all of them act corruptly.
29 The bellows blow fiercely;
  the lead is consumed by the fire;
in vain the refining goes on,
  for the wicked are not removed.
30 Rejected silver they are called,
  for the LORD has rejected them."

Evil in the Land

7 The word that came to Jeremiah from the
LORD: [2] "Stand in the gate of the LORD's
house, and proclaim there this word, and say,
Hear the word of the LORD, all you men of
Judah who enter these gates to worship the

LORD. ³ Thus says the LORD of hosts, the God of Israel: Amend your ways and your deeds, and I will let you dwell in this place. ⁴ Do not trust in these deceptive words: 'This is the temple of the LORD, the temple of the LORD, the temple of the LORD.'

⁵ "For if you truly amend your ways and your deeds, if you truly execute justice one with another, ⁶ if you do not oppress the sojourner, the fatherless, or the widow, or shed innocent blood in this place, and if you do not go after other gods to your own harm, ⁷ then I will let you dwell in this place, in the land that I gave of old to your fathers forever.

⁸ "Behold, you trust in deceptive words to no avail. ⁹ Will you steal, murder, commit adultery, swear falsely, make offerings to Baal, and go after other gods that you have not known, ¹⁰ and then come and stand before me in this house, which is called by my name, and say, 'We are delivered!'—only to go on doing all these abominations? ¹¹ Has this house, which is called by my name, become a den of robbers in your eyes? Behold, I myself have seen it, declares the LORD. ¹² Go now to my place that was in Shiloh, where I made my name dwell at first, and see what I did to it because of the evil of my people Israel. ¹³ And now, because you have done all these things, declares the LORD, and when I spoke to you persistently you did not listen, and when I called you, you did not answer, ¹⁴ therefore I will do to the house that is called by my name, and in which you trust, and to the place that I gave to you and to your fathers, as I did to Shiloh. ¹⁵ And I will cast you out of my sight, as I cast out all your kinsmen, all the offspring of Ephraim.

¹⁶ "As for you, do not pray for this people, or lift up a cry or prayer for them, and do not intercede with me, for I will not hear you. ¹⁷ Do you not see what they are doing in the cities of Judah and in the streets of Jerusalem? ¹⁸ The children gather wood, the fathers kindle fire, and the women knead dough, to make cakes for the queen of heaven. And they pour out drink offerings to other gods, to provoke me to anger. ¹⁹ Is it I whom they provoke? declares the LORD. Is it not themselves, to their own shame? ²⁰ Therefore thus says the Lord GOD: Behold, my anger and my wrath will be poured out on this place, upon man and beast, upon the trees of the field and the fruit of the ground; it will burn and not be quenched."

²¹ Thus says the LORD of hosts, the God of Israel: "Add your burnt offerings to your sacrifices, and eat the flesh. ²² For in the day that I brought them out of the land of Egypt, I did not speak to your fathers or command them concerning burnt offerings and sacrifices. ²³ But this command I gave them: 'Obey my voice, and I will be your God, and you shall be my people. And walk in all the way that I command you, that it may be well with you.' ²⁴ But they did not obey or incline their ear, but walked in their own counsels and the stubbornness of their evil hearts, and went backward and not forward. ²⁵ From the day that your fathers came out of the land of Egypt to this day, I have persistently sent all my servants the prophets to them, day after day. ²⁶ Yet they did not listen to me or incline their ear, but stiffened their neck. They did worse than their fathers.

²⁷ "So you shall speak all these words to them, but they will not listen to you. You shall call to them, but they will not answer you. ²⁸ And you shall say to them, 'This is the nation that did not obey the voice of the LORD their God, and did not accept discipline; truth has perished; it is cut off from their lips.

²⁹ " 'Cut off your hair and cast it away;
    raise a lamentation on the bare heights,
  for the LORD has rejected and forsaken
    the generation of his wrath.'

The Valley of Slaughter

³⁰ "For the sons of Judah have done evil in my sight, declares the LORD. They have set their detestable things in the house that is called by my name, to defile it. ³¹ And they have built the high places of Topheth, which is in the Valley of the Son of Hinnom, to burn their sons and their daughters in the fire, which I did not command, nor did it come into my mind. ³² Therefore, behold, the days are coming, declares the LORD, when it will no more be called Topheth, or the Valley of the Son of Hinnom, but the Valley of Slaughter; for they will bury in Topheth, because there is no room elsewhere. ³³ And the dead bodies of this people will be food for the birds of the air, and for the beasts of the earth, and none will frighten them away. ³⁴ And I will silence in the cities of Judah and in the streets of Jerusalem the voice of mirth and the voice of gladness, the voice of the bridegroom and the voice of the bride, for the land shall become a waste.

8 "At that time, declares the Lord, the bones of the kings of Judah, the bones of its officials, the bones of the priests, the bones of the prophets, and the bones of the inhabitants of Jerusalem shall be brought out of their tombs. ² And they shall be spread before the sun and the moon and all the host of heaven, which they have loved and served, which they have gone after, and which they have sought and worshiped. And they shall not be gathered or buried. They shall be as dung on the surface of the ground. ³ Death shall be preferred to life by all the remnant that remains of this evil family in all the places where I have driven them, declares the Lord of hosts.

Sin and Treachery

4 "You shall say to them, Thus says the Lord:
When men fall, do they not rise again?
    If one turns away, does he not return?
5 Why then has this people turned away
    in perpetual backsliding?
They hold fast to deceit;
    they refuse to return.
6 I have paid attention and listened,
    but they have not spoken rightly;
no man relents of his evil,
    saying, 'What have I done?'
Everyone turns to his own course,
    like a horse plunging headlong into
      battle.
7 Even the stork in the heavens
    knows her times,
and the turtledove, swallow, and crane[1]
    keep the time of their coming,
but my people know not
    the rules[2] of the Lord.

8 "How can you say, 'We are wise,
    and the law of the Lord is with us'?
But behold, the lying pen of the scribes
    has made it into a lie.
9 The wise men shall be put to shame;
    they shall be dismayed and taken;
behold, they have rejected the word of the
    Lord,
    so what wisdom is in them?
10 Therefore I will give their wives to others
    and their fields to conquerors,
because from the least to the greatest
    everyone is greedy for unjust gain;
from prophet to priest,
    everyone deals falsely.
11 They have healed the wound of my people
    lightly,
saying, 'Peace, peace,'
    when there is no peace.
12 Were they ashamed when they committed
    abomination?
No, they were not at all ashamed;
    they did not know how to blush.
Therefore they shall fall among the fallen;
    when I punish them, they shall be over-
      thrown,
            says the Lord.
13 When I would gather them, declares the
    Lord,
there are no grapes on the vine,
    nor figs on the fig tree;
even the leaves are withered,
    and what I gave them has passed away
      from them."[3]

14 Why do we sit still?
Gather together; let us go into the fortified
    cities
    and perish there,
for the Lord our God has doomed us to
    perish
and has given us poisoned water to
    drink,
because we have sinned against the
    Lord.
15 We looked for peace, but no good came;
    for a time of healing, but behold, terror.

16 "The snorting of their horses is heard from
    Dan;
at the sound of the neighing of their
    stallions
    the whole land quakes.
They come and devour the land and all
    that fills it,
    the city and those who dwell in it.
17 For behold, I am sending among you ser-
    pents,
adders that cannot be charmed,
    and they shall bite you,"
           declares the Lord.

Jeremiah Grieves for His People

18 My joy is gone; grief is upon me;[4]
    my heart is sick within me.
19 Behold, the cry of the daughter of my
    people
from the length and breadth of the
    land:

---

[1] The meaning of the Hebrew word is uncertain [2] Or *just decrees* [3] The meaning of the Hebrew is uncertain [4] Compare Septuagint; the meaning of the Hebrew is uncertain

"Is the LORD not in Zion?
  Is her King not in her?"
"Why have they provoked me to anger with
    their carved images
  and with their foreign idols?"
20 "The harvest is past, the summer is ended,
  and we are not saved."
21 For the wound of the daughter of my
    people is my heart wounded;
  I mourn, and dismay has taken hold on
    me.

22 Is there no balm in Gilead?
  Is there no physician there?
  Why then has the health of the daughter of
    my people
    not been restored?

9 ¹ Oh that my head were waters,
    and my eyes a fountain of tears,
  that I might weep day and night
    for the slain of the daughter of my
    people!
² ² Oh that I had in the desert
    a travelers' lodging place,
  that I might leave my people
    and go away from them!
  For they are all adulterers,
    a company of treacherous men.
³ They bend their tongue like a bow;
    falsehood and not truth has grown
    strong³ in the land;
  for they proceed from evil to evil,
    and they do not know me, declares the
    LORD.
⁴ Let everyone beware of his neighbor,
    and put no trust in any brother,
  for every brother is a deceiver,
    and every neighbor goes about as a slan-
    derer.
⁵ Everyone deceives his neighbor,
    and no one speaks the truth;
  they have taught their tongue to speak lies;
    they weary themselves committing
    iniquity.
⁶ Heaping oppression upon oppression, and
    deceit upon deceit,
  they refuse to know me, declares the
    LORD.
⁷ Therefore thus says the LORD of hosts:
  "Behold, I will refine them and test them,
    for what else can I do, because of my
    people?

⁸ Their tongue is a deadly arrow;
    it speaks deceitfully;
  with his mouth each speaks peace to his
    neighbor,
    but in his heart he plans an ambush for
    him.
⁹ Shall I not punish them for these things?
    declares the LORD,
  and shall I not avenge myself
    on a nation such as this?

10 "I will take up weeping and wailing for the
    mountains,
  and a lamentation for the pastures of
    the wilderness,
  because they are laid waste so that no one
    passes through,
    and the lowing of cattle is not heard;
  both the birds of the air and the beasts
    have fled and are gone.
11 I will make Jerusalem a heap of ruins,
    a lair of jackals,
  and I will make the cities of Judah a desola-
    tion,
    without inhabitant."

12 Who is the man so wise that he can understand this? To whom has the mouth of the LORD
spoken, that he may declare it? Why is the land
ruined and laid waste like a wilderness, so that
no one passes through? 13 And the LORD says:
"Because they have forsaken my law that I set
before them, and have not obeyed my voice or
walked in accord with it, 14 but have stubbornly
followed their own hearts and have gone after the
Baals, as their fathers taught them. 15 Therefore
thus says the LORD of hosts, the God of Israel:
Behold, I will feed this people with bitter food, and
give them poisonous water to drink. 16 I will scatter them among the nations whom neither they
nor their fathers have known, and I will send the
sword after them, until I have consumed them."

17 Thus says the LORD of hosts:
  "Consider, and call for the mourning
    women to come;
    send for the skillful women to come;
18 let them make haste and raise a wailing
    over us,
  that our eyes may run down with tears
    and our eyelids flow with water.
19 For a sound of wailing is heard from Zion:
  'How we are ruined!
    We are utterly shamed,

¹ Ch 8:23 in Hebrew ² Ch 9:1 in Hebrew ³ Septuagint; Hebrew and not for truth they have grown strong

because we have left the land,
    because they have cast down our dwell-
        ings.'"

20 Hear, O women, the word of the LORD,
        and let your ear receive the word of his
            mouth;
    teach to your daughters a lament,
        and each to her neighbor a dirge.
21 For death has come up into our windows;
        it has entered our palaces,
    cutting off the children from the streets
        and the young men from the squares.
22 Speak: "Thus declares the LORD,
    'The dead bodies of men shall fall
        like dung upon the open field,
        like sheaves after the reaper,
        and none shall gather them.'"

23 Thus says the LORD: "Let not the wise man
boast in his wisdom, let not the mighty man
boast in his might, let not the rich man boast
in his riches, 24 but let him who boasts boast in
this, that he understands and knows me, that I
am the LORD who practices steadfast love, justice, and righteousness in the earth. For in these
things I delight, declares the LORD."

25 "Behold, the days are coming, declares the
LORD, when I will punish all those who are circumcised merely in the flesh— 26 Egypt, Judah,
Edom, the sons of Ammon, Moab, and all who
dwell in the desert who cut the corners of their
hair, for all these nations are uncircumcised,
and all the house of Israel are uncircumcised
in heart."

Idols and the Living God

10 Hear the word that the LORD speaks to
you, O house of Israel. 2 Thus says the
LORD:

"Learn not the way of the nations,
    nor be dismayed at the signs of the
        heavens
    because the nations are dismayed at
        them,
3 for the customs of the peoples are vanity.[1]
    A tree from the forest is cut down
        and worked with an axe by the hands of
            a craftsman.
4 They decorate it with silver and gold;
        they fasten it with hammer and nails
    so that it cannot move.

5 Their idols[2] are like scarecrows in a cucum-
        ber field,
    and they cannot speak;
    they have to be carried,
        for they cannot walk.
    Do not be afraid of them,
        for they cannot do evil,
        neither is it in them to do good."

6 There is none like you, O LORD;
    you are great, and your name is great in
        might.
7 Who would not fear you, O King of the
        nations?
    For this is your due;
    for among all the wise ones of the nations
        and in all their kingdoms
        there is none like you.
8 They are both stupid and foolish;
        the instruction of idols is but wood!
9 Beaten silver is brought from Tarshish,
        and gold from Uphaz.
    They are the work of the craftsman and of
        the hands of the goldsmith;
        their clothing is violet and purple;
        they are all the work of skilled men.
10 But the LORD is the true God;
        he is the living God and the everlasting
            King.
    At his wrath the earth quakes,
        and the nations cannot endure his
            indignation.

11 Thus shall you say to them: "The gods
who did not make the heavens and the earth
shall perish from the earth and from under the
heavens."[3]

12 It is he who made the earth by his power,
        who established the world by his wis-
            dom,
    and by his understanding stretched out
        the heavens.
13 When he utters his voice, there is a tumult
        of waters in the heavens,
    and he makes the mist rise from the
        ends of the earth.
    He makes lightning for the rain,
        and he brings forth the wind from his
            storehouses.
14 Every man is stupid and without knowl-
            edge;
        every goldsmith is put to shame by his
            idols,

---

[1] Or *vapor, or mist* [2] Hebrew *They* [3] This verse is in Aramaic

for his images are false,
and there is no breath in them.
15 They are worthless, a work of delusion;
at the time of their punishment they
shall perish.
16 Not like these is he who is the portion of
Jacob,
for he is the one who formed all things,
and Israel is the tribe of his inheritance;
the LORD of hosts is his name.

17 Gather up your bundle from the ground,
O you who dwell under siege!
18 For thus says the LORD:
"Behold, I am slinging out the inhabitants
of the land
at this time,
and I will bring distress on them,
that they may feel it."

19 Woe is me because of my hurt!
My wound is grievous.
But I said, "Truly this is an affliction,
and I must bear it."
20 My tent is destroyed,
and all my cords are broken;
my children have gone from me,
and they are not;
there is no one to spread my tent again
and to set up my curtains.
21 For the shepherds are stupid
and do not inquire of the LORD;
therefore they have not prospered,
and all their flock is scattered.
22 A voice, a rumor! Behold, it comes!—
a great commotion out of the north
country
to make the cities of Judah a desolation,
a lair of jackals.
23 I know, O LORD, that the way of man is not
in himself,
that it is not in man who walks to direct
his steps.
24 Correct me, O LORD, but in justice;
not in your anger, lest you bring me to
nothing.
25 Pour out your wrath on the nations that
know you not,
and on the peoples that call not on your
name,
for they have devoured Jacob;
they have devoured him and consumed
him,
and have laid waste his habitation.

The Broken Covenant

11 The word that came to Jeremiah from the LORD: ²"Hear the words of this covenant, and speak to the men of Judah and the inhabitants of Jerusalem. ³You shall say to them, Thus says the LORD, the God of Israel: Cursed be the man who does not hear the words of this covenant ⁴that I commanded your fathers when I brought them out of the land of Egypt, from the iron furnace, saying, Listen to my voice, and do all that I command you. So shall you be my people, and I will be your God, ⁵that I may confirm the oath that I swore to your fathers, to give them a land flowing with milk and honey, as at this day." Then I answered, "So be it, LORD."

⁶And the LORD said to me, "Proclaim all these words in the cities of Judah and in the streets of Jerusalem: Hear the words of this covenant and do them. ⁷For I solemnly warned your fathers when I brought them up out of the land of Egypt, warning them persistently, even to this day, saying, Obey my voice. ⁸Yet they did not obey or incline their ear, but everyone walked in the stubbornness of his evil heart. Therefore I brought upon them all the words of this covenant, which I commanded them to do, but they did not."

⁹Again the LORD said to me, "A conspiracy exists among the men of Judah and the inhabitants of Jerusalem. ¹⁰They have turned back to the iniquities of their forefathers, who refused to hear my words. They have gone after other gods to serve them. The house of Israel and the house of Judah have broken my covenant that I made with their fathers. ¹¹Therefore, thus says the LORD, Behold, I am bringing disaster upon them that they cannot escape. Though they cry to me, I will not listen to them. ¹²Then the cities of Judah and the inhabitants of Jerusalem will go and cry to the gods to whom they make offerings, but they cannot save them in the time of their trouble. ¹³For your gods have become as many as your cities, O Judah, and as many as the streets of Jerusalem are the altars you have set up to shame, altars to make offerings to Baal.

¹⁴"Therefore do not pray for this people, or lift up a cry or prayer on their behalf, for I will not listen when they call to me in the time of their trouble. ¹⁵What right has my beloved in my house, when she has done many vile deeds? Can even sacrificial flesh avert your doom? Can you then exult? ¹⁶The LORD once called you 'a green

olive tree, beautiful with good fruit.' But with the roar of a great tempest he will set fire to it, and its branches will be consumed. [17] The LORD of hosts, who planted you, has decreed disaster against you, because of the evil that the house of Israel and the house of Judah have done, provoking me to anger by making offerings to Baal."

[18] The LORD made it known to me and I
     knew;
     then you showed me their deeds.
[19] But I was like a gentle lamb
     led to the slaughter.
     I did not know it was against me
     they devised schemes, saying,
     "Let us destroy the tree with its fruit,
          let us cut him off from the land of the
               living,
          that his name be remembered no
               more."
[20] But, O LORD of hosts, who judges righ-
          teously,
          who tests the heart and the mind,
     let me see your vengeance upon them,
          for to you have I committed my cause.

[21] Therefore thus says the LORD concerning the men of Anathoth, who seek your life, and say, "Do not prophesy in the name of the LORD, or you will die by our hand"— [22] therefore thus says the LORD of hosts: "Behold, I will punish them. The young men shall die by the sword, their sons and their daughters shall die by famine, [23] and none of them shall be left. For I will bring disaster upon the men of Anathoth, the year of their punishment."

Jeremiah's Complaint

12 Righteous are you, O LORD,
          when I complain to you;
     yet I would plead my case before you.
     Why does the way of the wicked prosper?
          Why do all who are treacherous thrive?
[2] You plant them, and they take root;
          they grow and produce fruit;
     you are near in their mouth
          and far from their heart.
[3] But you, O LORD, know me;
          you see me, and test my heart toward
               you.
     Pull them out like sheep for the slaughter,
          and set them apart for the day of
               slaughter.

[4] How long will the land mourn
          and the grass of every field wither?
     For the evil of those who dwell in it
          the beasts and the birds are swept away,
          because they said, "He will not see our
               latter end."

The LORD Answers Jeremiah

[5] "If you have raced with men on foot, and
          they have wearied you,
     how will you compete with horses?
     And if in a safe land you are so trusting,
          what will you do in the thicket of the
               Jordan?
[6] For even your brothers and the house of
          your father,
          even they have dealt treacherously with
               you;
          they are in full cry after you;
     do not believe them,
          though they speak friendly words to
               you."

[7] "I have forsaken my house;
          I have abandoned my heritage;
     I have given the beloved of my soul
          into the hands of her enemies.
[8] My heritage has become to me
          like a lion in the forest;
     she has lifted up her voice against me;
          therefore I hate her.
[9] Is my heritage to me like a hyena's lair?
          Are the birds of prey against her all
               around?
     Go, assemble all the wild beasts;
          bring them to devour.
[10] Many shepherds have destroyed my vine-
               yard;
          they have trampled down my portion;
     they have made my pleasant portion
          a desolate wilderness.
[11] They have made it a desolation;
          desolate, it mourns to me.
     The whole land is made desolate,
          but no man lays it to heart.
[12] Upon all the bare heights in the desert
          destroyers have come,
     for the sword of the LORD devours
          from one end of the land to the other;
          no flesh has peace.
[13] They have sown wheat and have reaped
               thorns;
          they have tired themselves out but
               profit nothing.

They shall be ashamed of their[1] harvests
because of the fierce anger of the LORD."

[14] Thus says the LORD concerning all my evil neighbors who touch the heritage that I have given my people Israel to inherit: "Behold, I will pluck them up from their land, and I will pluck up the house of Judah from among them. [15] And after I have plucked them up, I will again have compassion on them, and I will bring them again each to his heritage and each to his land. [16] And it shall come to pass, if they will diligently learn the ways of my people, to swear by my name, 'As the LORD lives,' even as they taught my people to swear by Baal, then they shall be built up in the midst of my people. [17] But if any nation will not listen, then I will utterly pluck it up and destroy it, declares the LORD."

The Ruined Loincloth

13 Thus says the LORD to me, "Go and buy a linen loincloth and put it around your waist, and do not dip it in water." [2] So I bought a loincloth according to the word of the LORD, and put it around my waist. [3] And the word of the LORD came to me a second time, [4] "Take the loincloth that you have bought, which is around your waist, and arise, go to the Euphrates and hide it there in a cleft of the rock." [5] So I went and hid it by the Euphrates, as the LORD commanded me. [6] And after many days the LORD said to me, "Arise, go to the Euphrates, and take from there the loincloth that I commanded you to hide there." [7] Then I went to the Euphrates, and dug, and I took the loincloth from the place where I had hidden it. And behold, the loincloth was spoiled; it was good for nothing.

[8] Then the word of the LORD came to me: [9] "Thus says the LORD: Even so will I spoil the pride of Judah and the great pride of Jerusalem. [10] This evil people, who refuse to hear my words, who stubbornly follow their own heart and have gone after other gods to serve them and worship them, shall be like this loincloth, which is good for nothing. [11] For as the loincloth clings to the waist of a man, so I made the whole house of Israel and the whole house of Judah cling to me, declares the LORD, that they might be for me a people, a name, a praise, and a glory, but they would not listen.

The Jars Filled with Wine

[12] "You shall speak to them this word: 'Thus says the LORD, the God of Israel, "Every jar shall be filled with wine."' And they will say to you, 'Do we not indeed know that every jar will be filled with wine?' [13] Then you shall say to them, 'Thus says the LORD: Behold, I will fill with drunkenness all the inhabitants of this land: the kings who sit on David's throne, the priests, the prophets, and all the inhabitants of Jerusalem. [14] And I will dash them one against another, fathers and sons together, declares the LORD. I will not pity or spare or have compassion, that I should not destroy them.'"

Exile Threatened

[15] Hear and give ear; be not proud,
        for the LORD has spoken.
[16] Give glory to the LORD your God
        before he brings darkness,
      before your feet stumble
        on the twilight mountains,
      and while you look for light
        he turns it into gloom
        and makes it deep darkness.
[17] But if you will not listen,
        my soul will weep in secret for your
          pride;
      my eyes will weep bitterly and run down
          with tears,
        because the LORD's flock has been taken
          captive.

[18] Say to the king and the queen mother:
        "Take a lowly seat,
      for your beautiful crown
        has come down from your head."
[19] The cities of the Negeb are shut up,
        with none to open them;
      all Judah is taken into exile,
        wholly taken into exile.

[20] "Lift up your eyes and see
        those who come from the north.
      Where is the flock that was given you,
        your beautiful flock?
[21] What will you say when they set as head
          over you
        those whom you yourself have taught
          to be friends to you?
      Will not pangs take hold of you
        like those of a woman in labor?
[22] And if you say in your heart,
        'Why have these things come upon me?'
      it is for the greatness of your iniquity
        that your skirts are lifted up
        and you suffer violence.

[1] Hebrew your

²³ Can the Ethiopian change his skin
 or the leopard his spots?
Then also you can do good
 who are accustomed to do evil.
²⁴ I will scatter you[1] like chaff
 driven by the wind from the desert.
²⁵ This is your lot,
 the portion I have measured out to you,
 declares the LORD,
because you have forgotten me
 and trusted in lies.
²⁶ I myself will lift up your skirts over your
 face,
 and your shame will be seen.
²⁷ I have seen your abominations,
 your adulteries and neighings, your
 lewd whorings,
 on the hills in the field.
Woe to you, O Jerusalem!
 How long will it be before you are made
 clean?"

Famine, Sword, and Pestilence

14 The word of the LORD that came to Jeremiah concerning the drought:

² "Judah mourns,
 and her gates languish;
her people lament on the ground,
 and the cry of Jerusalem goes up.
³ Her nobles send their servants for
 water;
 they come to the cisterns;
they find no water;
 they return with their vessels empty;
they are ashamed and confounded
 and cover their heads.
⁴ Because of the ground that is dismayed,
 since there is no rain on the land,
the farmers are ashamed;
 they cover their heads.
⁵ Even the doe in the field forsakes her new-
 born fawn
 because there is no grass.
⁶ The wild donkeys stand on the bare
 heights;
 they pant for air like jackals;
their eyes fail
 because there is no vegetation.

⁷ "Though our iniquities testify against us,
 act, O LORD, for your name's sake;
for our backslidings are many;
 we have sinned against you.

⁸ O you hope of Israel,
 its savior in time of trouble,
why should you be like a stranger in the
 land,
 like a traveler who turns aside to tarry
 for a night?
⁹ Why should you be like a man confused,
 like a mighty warrior who cannot save?
Yet you, O LORD, are in the midst of us,
 and we are called by your name;
 do not leave us."

¹⁰ Thus says the LORD concerning this peo-
 ple:
"They have loved to wander thus;
 they have not restrained their feet;
therefore the LORD does not accept them;
 now he will remember their iniquity
 and punish their sins."

¹¹ The LORD said to me: "Do not pray for the welfare of this people. ¹² Though they fast, I will not hear their cry, and though they offer burnt offering and grain offering, I will not accept them. But I will consume them by the sword, by famine, and by pestilence."

Lying Prophets

¹³ Then I said: "Ah, Lord GOD, behold, the prophets say to them, 'You shall not see the sword, nor shall you have famine, but I will give you assured peace in this place.'" ¹⁴ And the LORD said to me: "The prophets are prophesying lies in my name. I did not send them, nor did I command them or speak to them. They are prophesying to you a lying vision, worthless divination, and the deceit of their own minds. ¹⁵ Therefore thus says the LORD concerning the prophets who prophesy in my name although I did not send them, and who say, 'Sword and famine shall not come upon this land': By sword and famine those prophets shall be consumed. ¹⁶ And the people to whom they prophesy shall be cast out in the streets of Jerusalem, victims of famine and sword, with none to bury them— them, their wives, their sons, and their daughters. For I will pour out their evil upon them.

¹⁷ "You shall say to them this word:
'Let my eyes run down with tears night and
 day,
 and let them not cease,
for the virgin daughter of my people is
 shattered with a great wound,
 with a very grievous blow.

[1] Hebrew *them*

18 If I go out into the field,
   behold, those pierced by the sword!
And if I enter the city,
   behold, the diseases of famine!
For both prophet and priest ply their
      trade through the land
      and have no knowledge.'"

19 Have you utterly rejected Judah?
   Does your soul loathe Zion?
Why have you struck us down
   so that there is no healing for us?
We looked for peace, but no good came;
   for a time of healing, but behold, ter-
      ror.
20 We acknowledge our wickedness,
      O LORD,
   and the iniquity of our fathers,
   for we have sinned against you.
21 Do not spurn us, for your name's sake;
   do not dishonor your glorious throne;
   remember and do not break your cov-
      enant with us.
22 Are there any among the false gods of the
      nations that can bring rain?
   Or can the heavens give showers?
Are you not he, O LORD our God?
   We set our hope on you,
   for you do all these things.

The LORD Will Not Relent

15 Then the LORD said to me, "Though Moses and Samuel stood before me, yet my heart would not turn toward this people. Send them out of my sight, and let them go! ²And when they ask you, 'Where shall we go?' you shall say to them, 'Thus says the LORD:

"'Those who are for pestilence, to pesti-
      lence,
      and those who are for the sword, to the
         sword;
   those who are for famine, to famine,
      and those who are for captivity, to cap-
         tivity.'

³I will appoint over them four kinds of destroyers, declares the LORD: the sword to kill, the
dogs to tear, and the birds of the air and the
beasts of the earth to devour and destroy. ⁴And
I will make them a horror to all the kingdoms
of the earth because of what Manasseh the son
of Hezekiah, king of Judah, did in Jerusalem.

5 "Who will have pity on you, O Jerusalem,
   or who will grieve for you?
Who will turn aside
   to ask about your welfare?
6 You have rejected me, declares the LORD;
   you keep going backward,
so I have stretched out my hand against
      you and destroyed you—
   I am weary of relenting.
7 I have winnowed them with a winnowing
      fork
   in the gates of the land;
I have bereaved them; I have destroyed my
      people;
   they did not turn from their ways.
8 I have made their widows more in number
   than the sand of the seas;
I have brought against the mothers of
      young men
   a destroyer at noonday;
I have made anguish and terror
   fall upon them suddenly.
9 She who bore seven has grown feeble;
   she has fainted away;
her sun went down while it was yet day;
   she has been shamed and disgraced.
And the rest of them I will give to the
      sword
   before their enemies,
                     declares the LORD."

Jeremiah's Complaint

10Woe is me, my mother, that you bore me, a
man of strife and contention to the whole land!
I have not lent, nor have I borrowed, yet all of
them curse me. ¹¹The LORD said, "Have I not[1]
set you free for their good? Have I not pleaded
for you before the enemy in the time of trouble
and in the time of distress? ¹²Can one break
iron, iron from the north, and bronze?
¹³ "Your wealth and your treasures I will
give as spoil, without price, for all your sins,
throughout all your territory. ¹⁴I will make
you serve your enemies in a land that you do
not know, for in my anger a fire is kindled that
shall burn forever."

15 O LORD, you know;
   remember me and visit me,
      and take vengeance for me on my perse-
         cutors.
In your forbearance take me not away;
   know that for your sake I bear reproach.

[1] The meaning of the Hebrew is uncertain

16 Your words were found, and I ate them,
      and your words became to me a joy
      and the delight of my heart,
   for I am called by your name,
      O LORD, God of hosts.
17 I did not sit in the company of revelers,
      nor did I rejoice;
   I sat alone, because your hand was upon
      me,
      for you had filled me with indignation.
18 Why is my pain unceasing,
      my wound incurable,
      refusing to be healed?
   Will you be to me like a deceitful brook,
      like waters that fail?

19 Therefore thus says the LORD:
   "If you return, I will restore you,
      and you shall stand before me.
   If you utter what is precious, and not what
      is worthless,
      you shall be as my mouth.
   They shall turn to you,
      but you shall not turn to them.
20 And I will make you to this people
      a fortified wall of bronze;
   they will fight against you,
      but they shall not prevail over you,
   for I am with you
      to save you and deliver you,
                         declares the LORD.
21 I will deliver you out of the hand of the
      wicked,
      and redeem you from the grasp of the
      ruthless."

Famine, Sword, and Death

16 The word of the LORD came to me: ²"You shall not take a wife, nor shall you have sons or daughters in this place. ³For thus says the LORD concerning the sons and daughters who are born in this place, and concerning the mothers who bore them and the fathers who fathered them in this land: ⁴They shall die of deadly diseases. They shall not be lamented, nor shall they be buried. They shall be as dung on the surface of the ground. They shall perish by the sword and by famine, and their dead bodies shall be food for the birds of the air and for the beasts of the earth.

⁵"For thus says the LORD: Do not enter the house of mourning, or go to lament or grieve for them, for I have taken away my peace from this people, my steadfast love and mercy,

declares the LORD. ⁶Both great and small shall die in this land. They shall not be buried, and no one shall lament for them or cut himself or make himself bald for them. ⁷No one shall break bread for the mourner, to comfort him for the dead, nor shall anyone give him the cup of consolation to drink for his father or his mother. ⁸You shall not go into the house of feasting to sit with them, to eat and drink. ⁹For thus says the LORD of hosts, the God of Israel: Behold, I will silence in this place, before your eyes and in your days, the voice of mirth and the voice of gladness, the voice of the bridegroom and the voice of the bride.

¹⁰"And when you tell this people all these words, and they say to you, 'Why has the LORD pronounced all this great evil against us? What is our iniquity? What is the sin that we have committed against the LORD our God?' ¹¹then you shall say to them: 'Because your fathers have forsaken me, declares the LORD, and have gone after other gods and have served and worshiped them, and have forsaken me and have not kept my law, ¹²and because you have done worse than your fathers, for behold, every one of you follows his stubborn, evil will, refusing to listen to me. ¹³Therefore I will hurl you out of this land into a land that neither you nor your fathers have known, and there you shall serve other gods day and night, for I will show you no favor.'

The LORD Will Restore Israel

¹⁴"Therefore, behold, the days are coming, declares the LORD, when it shall no longer be said, 'As the LORD lives who brought up the people of Israel out of the land of Egypt,' ¹⁵but 'As the LORD lives who brought up the people of Israel out of the north country and out of all the countries where he had driven them.' For I will bring them back to their own land that I gave to their fathers.

¹⁶"Behold, I am sending for many fishers, declares the LORD, and they shall catch them. And afterward I will send for many hunters, and they shall hunt them from every mountain and every hill, and out of the clefts of the rocks. ¹⁷For my eyes are on all their ways. They are not hidden from me, nor is their iniquity concealed from my eyes. ¹⁸But first I will doubly repay their iniquity and their sin, because they have polluted my land with the carcasses

of their detestable idols, and have filled my inheritance with their abominations."

19 O Lord, my strength and my stronghold,
    my refuge in the day of trouble,
to you shall the nations come
    from the ends of the earth and say:
"Our fathers have inherited nothing but
        lies,
    worthless things in which there is no
        profit.
20 Can man make for himself gods?
    Such are not gods!"

21 "Therefore, behold, I will make them know, this once I will make them know my power and my might, and they shall know that my name is the Lord."

The Sin of Judah

17 "The sin of Judah is written with a pen of iron; with a point of diamond it is engraved on the tablet of their heart, and on the horns of their altars, 2 while their children remember their altars and their Asherim, beside every green tree and on the high hills, 3 on the mountains in the open country. Your wealth and all your treasures I will give for spoil as the price of your high places for sin throughout all your territory. 4 You shall loosen your hand from your heritage that I gave to you, and I will make you serve your enemies in a land that you do not know, for in my anger a fire is kindled that shall burn forever."

5 Thus says the Lord:
"Cursed is the man who trusts in man
    and makes flesh his strength,[1]
    whose heart turns away from the Lord.
6 He is like a shrub in the desert,
    and shall not see any good come.
He shall dwell in the parched places of the
        wilderness,
    in an uninhabited salt land.
7 "Blessed is the man who trusts in the Lord,
    whose trust is the Lord.
8 He is like a tree planted by water,
    that sends out its roots by the stream,
and does not fear when heat comes,
    for its leaves remain green,
and is not anxious in the year of
        drought,
    for it does not cease to bear fruit."

9 The heart is deceitful above all things,
    and desperately sick;
    who can understand it?
10 "I the Lord search the heart
    and test the mind,[2]
to give every man according to his ways,
    according to the fruit of his deeds."

11 Like the partridge that gathers a brood that
        she did not hatch,
    so is he who gets riches but not by jus-
        tice;
in the midst of his days they will leave him,
    and at his end he will be a fool.

12 A glorious throne set on high from the
        beginning
    is the place of our sanctuary.
13 O Lord, the hope of Israel,
    all who forsake you shall be put to
        shame;
those who turn away from you[3] shall be
        written in the earth,
    for they have forsaken the Lord, the
        fountain of living water.

Jeremiah Prays for Deliverance

14 Heal me, O Lord, and I shall be healed;
    save me, and I shall be saved,
    for you are my praise.
15 Behold, they say to me,
    "Where is the word of the Lord?
    Let it come!"
16 I have not run away from being your shep-
        herd,
    nor have I desired the day of sickness.
You know what came out of my lips;
    it was before your face.
17 Be not a terror to me;
    you are my refuge in the day of disaster.
18 Let those be put to shame who persecute
        me,
    but let me not be put to shame;
let them be dismayed,
    but let me not be dismayed;
bring upon them the day of disaster;
    destroy them with double destruction!

Keep the Sabbath Holy

19 Thus said the Lord to me: "Go and stand in the People's Gate, by which the kings of Judah enter and by which they go out, and in all the gates of Jerusalem, 20 and say: 'Hear the word of the Lord, you kings of Judah, and all Judah, and all the inhabitants of Jerusalem, who enter

---

[1] Hebrew arm [2] Hebrew kidneys [3] Hebrew me

by these gates. ²¹Thus says the LORD: Take care for the sake of your lives, and do not bear a burden on the Sabbath day or bring it in by the gates of Jerusalem. ²²And do not carry a burden out of your houses on the Sabbath or do any work, but keep the Sabbath day holy, as I commanded your fathers. ²³Yet they did not listen or incline their ear, but stiffened their neck, that they might not hear and receive instruction.

²⁴ " 'But if you listen to me, declares the LORD, and bring in no burden by the gates of this city on the Sabbath day, but keep the Sabbath day holy and do no work on it, ²⁵then there shall enter by the gates of this city kings and princes who sit on the throne of David, riding in chariots and on horses, they and their officials, the men of Judah and the inhabitants of Jerusalem. And this city shall be inhabited forever. ²⁶And people shall come from the cities of Judah and the places around Jerusalem, from the land of Benjamin, from the Shephelah, from the hill country, and from the Negeb, bringing burnt offerings and sacrifices, grain offerings and frankincense, and bringing thank offerings to the house of the LORD. ²⁷But if you do not listen to me, to keep the Sabbath day holy, and not to bear a burden and enter by the gates of Jerusalem on the Sabbath day, then I will kindle a fire in its gates, and it shall devour the palaces of Jerusalem and shall not be quenched.' "

The Potter and the Clay

18 The word that came to Jeremiah from the LORD: ²"Arise, and go down to the potter's house, and there I will let you hear[1] my words." ³So I went down to the potter's house, and there he was working at his wheel. ⁴And the vessel he was making of clay was spoiled in the potter's hand, and he reworked it into another vessel, as it seemed good to the potter to do.

⁵Then the word of the LORD came to me: ⁶"O house of Israel, can I not do with you as this potter has done? declares the LORD. Behold, like the clay in the potter's hand, so are you in my hand, O house of Israel. ⁷If at any time I declare concerning a nation or a kingdom, that I will pluck up and break down and destroy it, ⁸and if that nation, concerning which I have spoken, turns from its evil, I will relent of the disaster that I intended to do to it. ⁹And if at any time I declare concerning a nation or a kingdom that

I will build and plant it, ¹⁰and if it does evil in my sight, not listening to my voice, then I will relent of the good that I had intended to do to it. ¹¹Now, therefore, say to the men of Judah and the inhabitants of Jerusalem: 'Thus says the LORD, Behold, I am shaping disaster against you and devising a plan against you. Return, every one from his evil way, and amend your ways and your deeds.'

¹²"But they say, 'That is in vain! We will follow our own plans, and will every one act according to the stubbornness of his evil heart.'

¹³ "Therefore thus says the LORD:
Ask among the nations,
   Who has heard the like of this?
The virgin Israel
   has done a very horrible thing.
¹⁴ Does the snow of Lebanon leave
   the crags of Sirion?[2]
Do the mountain waters run dry,[3]
   the cold flowing streams?
¹⁵ But my people have forgotten me;
   they make offerings to false gods;
they made them stumble in their ways,
   in the ancient roads,
and to walk into side roads,
   not the highway,
¹⁶ making their land a horror,
   a thing to be hissed at forever.
Everyone who passes by it is horrified
   and shakes his head.
¹⁷ Like the east wind I will scatter them
   before the enemy.
I will show them my back, not my face,
   in the day of their calamity."

¹⁸Then they said, "Come, let us make plots against Jeremiah, for the law shall not perish from the priest, nor counsel from the wise, nor the word from the prophet. Come, let us strike him with the tongue, and let us not pay attention to any of his words."

¹⁹ Hear me, O LORD,
   and listen to the voice of my adversaries.
²⁰ Should good be repaid with evil?
   Yet they have dug a pit for my life.
Remember how I stood before you
   to speak good for them,
   to turn away your wrath from them.

---

[1] Or will cause you to hear [2] Hebrew of the field [3] Hebrew Are foreign waters plucked up

21 Therefore deliver up their children to famine;
give them over to the power of the
sword;
let their wives become childless and widowed.
May their men meet death by pestilence,
their youths be struck down by the
sword in battle.
22 May a cry be heard from their houses,
when you bring the plunderer suddenly upon them!
For they have dug a pit to take me
and laid snares for my feet.
23 Yet you, O LORD, know
all their plotting to kill me.
Forgive not their iniquity,
nor blot out their sin from your sight.
Let them be overthrown before you;
deal with them in the time of your
anger.

The Broken Flask

19 Thus says the LORD, "Go, buy a potter's
earthenware flask, and take some of the
elders of the people and some of the elders of
the priests, ²and go out to the Valley of the Son
of Hinnom at the entry of the Potsherd Gate,
and proclaim there the words that I tell you.
³You shall say, 'Hear the word of the LORD, O
kings of Judah and inhabitants of Jerusalem.
Thus says the LORD of hosts, the God of Israel:
Behold, I am bringing such disaster upon this
place that the ears of everyone who hears of it
will tingle. ⁴Because the people have forsaken
me and have profaned this place by making
offerings in it to other gods whom neither they
nor their fathers nor the kings of Judah have
known; and because they have filled this place
with the blood of innocents, ⁵and have built
the high places of Baal to burn their sons in
the fire as burnt offerings to Baal, which I did
not command or decree, nor did it come into
my mind— ⁶therefore, behold, days are coming, declares the LORD, when this place shall
no more be called Topheth, or the Valley of the
Son of Hinnom, but the Valley of Slaughter.
⁷And in this place I will make void the plans
of Judah and Jerusalem, and will cause their
people to fall by the sword before their enemies,
and by the hand of those who seek their life. I
will give their dead bodies for food to the birds

of the air and to the beasts of the earth. ⁸And I
will make this city a horror, a thing to be hissed
at. Everyone who passes by it will be horrified
and will hiss because of all its wounds. ⁹And I
will make them eat the flesh of their sons and
their daughters, and everyone shall eat the flesh
of his neighbor in the siege and in the distress,
with which their enemies and those who seek
their life afflict them.'

¹⁰ "Then you shall break the flask in the
sight of the men who go with you, ¹¹and shall
say to them, 'Thus says the LORD of hosts: So
will I break this people and this city, as one
breaks a potter's vessel, so that it can never be
mended. Men shall bury in Topheth because
there will be no place else to bury. ¹²Thus will
I do to this place, declares the LORD, and to
its inhabitants, making this city like Topheth.
¹³The houses of Jerusalem and the houses of
the kings of Judah—all the houses on whose
roofs offerings have been offered to all the
host of heaven, and drink offerings have been
poured out to other gods—shall be defiled like
the place of Topheth.'"

¹⁴Then Jeremiah came from Topheth, where
the LORD had sent him to prophesy, and he
stood in the court of the LORD's house and
said to all the people: ¹⁵"Thus says the LORD
of hosts, the God of Israel, behold, I am bringing upon this city and upon all its towns all
the disaster that I have pronounced against it,
because they have stiffened their neck, refusing
to hear my words."

Jeremiah Persecuted by Pashhur

20 Now Pashhur the priest, the son of
Immer, who was chief officer in the
house of the LORD, heard Jeremiah prophesying these things. ²Then Pashhur beat Jeremiah
the prophet, and put him in the stocks that
were in the upper Benjamin Gate of the house
of the LORD. ³The next day, when Pashhur
released Jeremiah from the stocks, Jeremiah
said to him, "The LORD does not call your name
Pashhur, but Terror on Every Side. ⁴For thus
says the LORD: Behold, I will make you a terror to yourself and to all your friends. They
shall fall by the sword of their enemies while
you look on. And I will give all Judah into the
hand of the king of Babylon. He shall carry
them captive to Babylon, and shall strike them
down with the sword. ⁵Moreover, I will give all
the wealth of the city, all its gains, all its prized

belongings, and all the treasures of the kings of Judah into the hand of their enemies, who shall plunder them and seize them and carry them to Babylon. ⁶ And you, Pashhur, and all who dwell in your house, shall go into captivity. To Babylon you shall go, and there you shall die, and there you shall be buried, you and all your friends, to whom you have prophesied falsely."

7   O LORD, you have deceived me,
      and I was deceived;
  you are stronger than I,
      and you have prevailed.
  I have become a laughingstock all the day;
      everyone mocks me.
8   For whenever I speak, I cry out,
      I shout, "Violence and destruction!"
  For the word of the LORD has become
      for me
  a reproach and derision all day long.
9   If I say, "I will not mention him,
      or speak any more in his name,"
  there is in my heart as it were a burning fire
      shut up in my bones,
  and I am weary with holding it in,
      and I cannot.
10   For I hear many whispering.
      Terror is on every side!
  "Denounce him! Let us denounce him!"
      say all my close friends,
      watching for my fall.
  "Perhaps he will be deceived;
      then we can overcome him
      and take our revenge on him."
11   But the LORD is with me as a dread warrior;
      therefore my persecutors will stumble;
      they will not overcome me.
  They will be greatly shamed,
      for they will not succeed.
  Their eternal dishonor
      will never be forgotten.
12   O LORD of hosts, who tests the righteous,
      who sees the heart and the mind,[1]
  let me see your vengeance upon them,
      for to you have I committed my cause.

13   Sing to the LORD;
      praise the LORD!
  For he has delivered the life of the needy
      from the hand of evildoers.

14   Cursed be the day
      on which I was born!

  The day when my mother bore me,
      let it not be blessed!
15   Cursed be the man who brought the news
      to my father,
  "A son is born to you,"
      making him very glad.
16   Let that man be like the cities
      that the LORD overthrew without pity;
  let him hear a cry in the morning
      and an alarm at noon,
17   because he did not kill me in the womb;
      so my mother would have been my grave,
      and her womb forever great.
18   Why did I come out from the womb
      to see toil and sorrow,
      and spend my days in shame?

Jerusalem Will Fall to Nebuchadnezzar

21 This is the word that came to Jeremiah from the LORD, when King Zedekiah sent to him Pashhur the son of Malchiah and Zephaniah the priest, the son of Maaseiah, saying, ² "Inquire of the LORD for us, for Nebuchadnezzar[2] king of Babylon is making war against us. Perhaps the LORD will deal with us according to all his wonderful deeds and will make him withdraw from us."

³ Then Jeremiah said to them: "Thus you shall say to Zedekiah, ⁴ 'Thus says the LORD, the God of Israel: Behold, I will turn back the weapons of war that are in your hands and with which you are fighting against the king of Babylon and against the Chaldeans who are besieging you outside the walls. And I will bring them together into the midst of this city. ⁵ I myself will fight against you with outstretched hand and strong arm, in anger and in fury and in great wrath. ⁶ And I will strike down the inhabitants of this city, both man and beast. They shall die of a great pestilence. ⁷ Afterward, declares the LORD, I will give Zedekiah king of Judah and his servants and the people in this city who survive the pestilence, sword, and famine into the hand of Nebuchadnezzar king of Babylon and into the hand of their enemies, into the hand of those who seek their lives. He shall strike them down with the edge of the sword. He shall not pity them or spare them or have compassion.'

⁸ "And to this people you shall say: 'Thus says the LORD: Behold, I set before you the way of life and the way of death. ⁹ He who stays in this city shall die by the sword, by famine, and by

---

[1] Hebrew *kidneys* [2] Hebrew *Nebuchadrezzar*, an alternate spelling of *Nebuchadnezzar* (king of Babylon) occurring frequently from Jeremiah 21-52; this latter spelling is used throughout Jeremiah for consistency

pestilence, but he who goes out and surrenders to the Chaldeans who are besieging you shall live and shall have his life as a prize of war. ¹⁰ For I have set my face against this city for harm and not for good, declares the LORD: it shall be given into the hand of the king of Babylon, and he shall burn it with fire.'

Message to the House of David

¹¹ "And to the house of the king of Judah say, 'Hear the word of the LORD, ¹² O house of David! Thus says the LORD:

"'Execute justice in the morning,
    and deliver from the hand of the
        oppressor
him who has been robbed,
    lest my wrath go forth like fire,
    and burn with none to quench it,
    because of your evil deeds.'"

¹³ "Behold, I am against you, O inhabitant of
        the valley,
    O rock of the plain,
                    declares the LORD;
you who say, 'Who shall come down
        against us,
    or who shall enter our habitations?'
¹⁴ I will punish you according to the fruit of
        your deeds,
                    declares the LORD;
    I will kindle a fire in her forest,
    and it shall devour all that is around
        her."

22 Thus says the LORD: "Go down to the house of the king of Judah and speak there this word, ² and say, 'Hear the word of the LORD, O king of Judah, who sits on the throne of David, you, and your servants, and your people who enter these gates. ³ Thus says the LORD: Do justice and righteousness, and deliver from the hand of the oppressor him who has been robbed. And do no wrong or violence to the resident alien, the fatherless, and the widow, nor shed innocent blood in this place. ⁴ For if you will indeed obey this word, then there shall enter the gates of this house kings who sit on the throne of David, riding in chariots and on horses, they and their servants and their people. ⁵ But if you will not obey these words, I swear by myself, declares the LORD, that this house shall become a desolation. ⁶ For thus says the LORD concerning the house of the king of Judah:

"'You are like Gilead to me,
    like the summit of Lebanon,
yet surely I will make you a desert,
    an uninhabited city.¹
⁷ I will prepare destroyers against you,
    each with his weapons,
and they shall cut down your choicest
        cedars
    and cast them into the fire.

⁸ "'And many nations will pass by this city, and every man will say to his neighbor, "Why has the LORD dealt thus with this great city?" ⁹ And they will answer, "Because they have forsaken the covenant of the LORD their God and worshiped other gods and served them."'"

¹⁰   Weep not for him who is dead,
        nor grieve for him,
    but weep bitterly for him who goes
        away,
    for he shall return no more
    to see his native land.

Message to the Sons of Josiah

¹¹ For thus says the LORD concerning Shallum the son of Josiah, king of Judah, who reigned instead of Josiah his father, and who went away from this place: "He shall return here no more, ¹² but in the place where they have carried him captive, there shall he die, and he shall never see this land again."

¹³   "Woe to him who builds his house by
        unrighteousness,
    and his upper rooms by injustice,
    who makes his neighbor serve him for
        nothing
    and does not give him his wages,
¹⁴ who says, 'I will build myself a great
        house
    with spacious upper rooms,'
who cuts out windows for it,
    paneling it with cedar
    and painting it with vermilion.
¹⁵ Do you think you are a king
    because you compete in cedar?
Did not your father eat and drink
    and do justice and righteousness?
    Then it was well with him.
¹⁶ He judged the cause of the poor and needy;
    then it was well.
Is not this to know me?
    declares the LORD.

¹ Hebrew *cities*

17 But you have eyes and heart
        only for your dishonest gain,
    for shedding innocent blood,
        and for practicing oppression and vio-
        lence."

18 Therefore thus says the LORD concerning Jehoiakim the son of Josiah, king of Judah:

    "They shall not lament for him, saying,
        'Ah, my brother!' or 'Ah, sister!'
    They shall not lament for him, saying,
        'Ah, lord!' or 'Ah, his majesty!'
19 With the burial of a donkey he shall be
        buried,
        dragged and dumped beyond the gates
            of Jerusalem."

20 "Go up to Lebanon, and cry out,
        and lift up your voice in Bashan;
    cry out from Abarim,
        for all your lovers are destroyed.
21 I spoke to you in your prosperity,
        but you said, 'I will not listen.'
    This has been your way from your youth,
        that you have not obeyed my voice.
22 The wind shall shepherd all your shep-
        herds,
        and your lovers shall go into captivity;
    then you will be ashamed and confounded
        because of all your evil.
23 O inhabitant of Lebanon,
        nested among the cedars,
    how you will be pitied when pangs come
        upon you,
        pain as of a woman in labor!"

24 "As I live, declares the LORD, though Coniah the son of Jehoiakim, king of Judah, were the signet ring on my right hand, yet I would tear you off 25 and give you into the hand of those who seek your life, into the hand of those of whom you are afraid, even into the hand of Nebuchadnezzar king of Babylon and into the hand of the Chaldeans. 26 I will hurl you and the mother who bore you into another country, where you were not born, and there you shall die. 27 But to the land to which they will long to return, there they shall not return."

28 Is this man Coniah a despised, broken pot,
        a vessel no one cares for?
    Why are he and his children hurled and
        cast
        into a land that they do not know?

29 O land, land, land,
        hear the word of the LORD!
30 Thus says the LORD:
    "Write this man down as childless,
        a man who shall not succeed in his days,
    for none of his offspring shall succeed
        in sitting on the throne of David
        and ruling again in Judah."

The Righteous Branch

23 "Woe to the shepherds who destroy and scatter the sheep of my pasture!" declares the LORD. 2 Therefore thus says the LORD, the God of Israel, concerning the shepherds who care for my people: "You have scattered my flock and have driven them away, and you have not attended to them. Behold, I will attend to you for your evil deeds, declares the LORD. 3 Then I will gather the remnant of my flock out of all the countries where I have driven them, and I will bring them back to their fold, and they shall be fruitful and multiply. 4 I will set shepherds over them who will care for them, and they shall fear no more, nor be dismayed, neither shall any be missing, declares the LORD.

5 "Behold, the days are coming, declares the LORD, when I will raise up for David a righteous Branch, and he shall reign as king and deal wisely, and shall execute justice and righteousness in the land. 6 In his days Judah will be saved, and Israel will dwell securely. And this is the name by which he will be called: 'The LORD is our righteousness.'

7 "Therefore, behold, the days are coming, declares the LORD, when they shall no longer say, 'As the LORD lives who brought up the people of Israel out of the land of Egypt,' 8 but 'As the LORD lives who brought up and led the offspring of the house of Israel out of the north country and out of all the countries where he[1] had driven them.' Then they shall dwell in their own land."

Lying Prophets

9 Concerning the prophets:

    My heart is broken within me;
        all my bones shake;
    I am like a drunken man,
        like a man overcome by wine,
    because of the LORD
        and because of his holy words.

[1] Septuagint; Hebrew I

¹⁰ For the land is full of adulterers;
   because of the curse the land mourns,
   and the pastures of the wilderness are
      dried up.
Their course is evil,
   and their might is not right.
¹¹ "Both prophet and priest are ungodly;
   even in my house I have found their
      evil,
                        declares the LORD.
¹² Therefore their way shall be to them
   like slippery paths in the darkness,
   into which they shall be driven and fall,
for I will bring disaster upon them
   in the year of their punishment,
                        declares the LORD.
¹³ In the prophets of Samaria
   I saw an unsavory thing:
they prophesied by Baal
   and led my people Israel astray.
¹⁴ But in the prophets of Jerusalem
   I have seen a horrible thing:
they commit adultery and walk in lies;
   they strengthen the hands of evildo-
      ers,
   so that no one turns from his evil;
all of them have become like Sodom to me,
   and its inhabitants like Gomorrah."
¹⁵ Therefore thus says the LORD of hosts
   concerning the prophets:
"Behold, I will feed them with bitter food
   and give them poisoned water to drink,
for from the prophets of Jerusalem
   ungodliness has gone out into all the
      land."

¹⁶ Thus says the LORD of hosts: "Do not listen to the words of the prophets who prophesy to you, filling you with vain hopes. They
speak visions of their own minds, not from the
mouth of the LORD. ¹⁷ They say continually to
those who despise the word of the LORD, 'It
shall be well with you'; and to everyone who
stubbornly follows his own heart, they say, 'No
disaster shall come upon you.'"

¹⁸ For who among them has stood in the
      council of the LORD
   to see and to hear his word,
   or who has paid attention to his word
      and listened?
¹⁹ Behold, the storm of the LORD!
   Wrath has gone forth,

a whirling tempest;
   it will burst upon the head of the
      wicked.
²⁰ The anger of the LORD will not turn back
   until he has executed and accomplished
   the intents of his heart.
In the latter days you will understand it
   clearly.

²¹ "I did not send the prophets,
   yet they ran;
I did not speak to them,
   yet they prophesied.
²² But if they had stood in my council,
   then they would have proclaimed my
      words to my people,
and they would have turned them from
      their evil way,
   and from the evil of their deeds.

²³ "Am I a God at hand, declares the LORD,
and not a God far away? ²⁴ Can a man hide
himself in secret places so that I cannot see
him? declares the LORD. Do I not fill heaven
and earth? declares the LORD. ²⁵ I have heard
what the prophets have said who prophesy
lies in my name, saying, 'I have dreamed, I
have dreamed!' ²⁶ How long shall there be lies
in the heart of the prophets who prophesy
lies, and who prophesy the deceit of their own
heart, ²⁷ who think to make my people forget
my name by their dreams that they tell one
another, even as their fathers forgot my name
for Baal? ²⁸ Let the prophet who has a dream
tell the dream, but let him who has my word
speak my word faithfully. What has straw in
common with wheat? declares the LORD. ²⁹ Is
not my word like fire, declares the LORD, and
like a hammer that breaks the rock in pieces?
³⁰ Therefore, behold, I am against the prophets,
declares the LORD, who steal my words from
one another. ³¹ Behold, I am against the prophets, declares the LORD, who use their tongues
and declare, 'declares the LORD.' ³² Behold, I
am against those who prophesy lying dreams,
declares the LORD, and who tell them and lead
my people astray by their lies and their reck-
lessness, when I did not send them or charge
them. So they do not profit this people at all,
declares the LORD.

³³ "When one of this people, or a prophet
or a priest asks you, 'What is the burden of
the LORD?' you shall say to them, 'You are the
burden,¹ and I will cast you off, declares the

¹ Septuagint, Vulgate; Hebrew *What burden?*

LORD.' ³⁴ And as for the prophet, priest, or one of the people who says, 'The burden of the LORD,' I will punish that man and his household. ³⁵ Thus shall you say, every one to his neighbor and every one to his brother, 'What has the LORD answered?' or 'What has the LORD spoken?' ³⁶ But 'the burden of the LORD' you shall mention no more, for the burden is every man's own word, and you pervert the words of the living God, the LORD of hosts, our God. ³⁷ Thus you shall say to the prophet, 'What has the LORD answered you?' or 'What has the LORD spoken?' ³⁸ But if you say, 'The burden of the LORD,' thus says the LORD, 'Because you have said these words, "The burden of the LORD," when I sent to you, saying, "You shall not say, 'The burden of the LORD,'" ³⁹ therefore, behold, I will surely lift you up¹ and cast you away from my presence, you and the city that I gave to you and your fathers. ⁴⁰ And I will bring upon you everlasting reproach and perpetual shame, which shall not be forgotten.'"

The Good Figs and the Bad Figs

24 After Nebuchadnezzar king of Babylon had taken into exile from Jerusalem Jeconiah the son of Jehoiakim, king of Judah, together with the officials of Judah, the craftsmen, and the metal workers, and had brought them to Babylon, the LORD showed me this vision: behold, two baskets of figs placed before the temple of the LORD. ² One basket had very good figs, like first-ripe figs, but the other basket had very bad figs, so bad that they could not be eaten. ³ And the LORD said to me, "What do you see, Jeremiah?" I said, "Figs, the good figs very good, and the bad figs very bad, so bad that they cannot be eaten."

⁴ Then the word of the LORD came to me: ⁵ "Thus says the LORD, the God of Israel: Like these good figs, so I will regard as good the exiles from Judah, whom I have sent away from this place to the land of the Chaldeans. ⁶ I will set my eyes on them for good, and I will bring them back to this land. I will build them up, and not tear them down; I will plant them, and not pluck them up. ⁷ I will give them a heart to know that I am the LORD, and they shall be my people and I will be their God, for they shall return to me with their whole heart.

⁸ "But thus says the LORD: Like the bad figs that are so bad they cannot be eaten, so will I treat Zedekiah the king of Judah, his officials,

the remnant of Jerusalem who remain in this land, and those who dwell in the land of Egypt. ⁹ I will make them a horror² to all the kingdoms of the earth, to be a reproach, a byword, a taunt, and a curse in all the places where I shall drive them. ¹⁰ And I will send sword, famine, and pestilence upon them, until they shall be utterly destroyed from the land that I gave to them and their fathers."

Seventy Years of Captivity

25 The word that came to Jeremiah concerning all the people of Judah, in the fourth year of Jehoiakim the son of Josiah, king of Judah (that was the first year of Nebuchadnezzar king of Babylon), ² which Jeremiah the prophet spoke to all the people of Judah and all the inhabitants of Jerusalem: ³ "For twenty-three years, from the thirteenth year of Josiah the son of Amon, king of Judah, to this day, the word of the LORD has come to me, and I have spoken persistently to you, but you have not listened. ⁴ You have neither listened nor inclined your ears to hear, although the LORD persistently sent to you all his servants the prophets, ⁵ saying, 'Turn now, every one of you, from his evil way and evil deeds, and dwell upon the land that the LORD has given to you and your fathers from of old and forever. ⁶ Do not go after other gods to serve and worship them, or provoke me to anger with the work of your hands. Then I will do you no harm.' ⁷ Yet you have not listened to me, declares the LORD, that you might provoke me to anger with the work of your hands to your own harm.

⁸ "Therefore thus says the LORD of hosts: Because you have not obeyed my words, ⁹ behold, I will send for all the tribes of the north, declares the LORD, and for Nebuchadnezzar the king of Babylon, my servant, and I will bring them against this land and its inhabitants, and against all these surrounding nations. I will devote them to destruction, and make them a horror, a hissing, and an everlasting desolation. ¹⁰ Moreover, I will banish from them the voice of mirth and the voice of gladness, the voice of the bridegroom and the voice of the bride, the grinding of the millstones and the light of the lamp. ¹¹ This whole land shall become a ruin and a waste, and these nations shall serve the king of Babylon seventy years. ¹² Then after seventy years are completed, I will punish the king of Babylon and that nation, the land of

---

¹ Or surely forget you ² Compare Septuagint; Hebrew horror for evil

the Chaldeans, for their iniquity, declares the LORD, making the land an everlasting waste. [13] I will bring upon that land all the words that I have uttered against it, everything written in this book, which Jeremiah prophesied against all the nations. [14] For many nations and great kings shall make slaves even of them, and I will recompense them according to their deeds and the work of their hands."

The Cup of the LORD's Wrath

[15] Thus the LORD, the God of Israel, said to me: "Take from my hand this cup of the wine of wrath, and make all the nations to whom I send you drink it. [16] They shall drink and stagger and be crazed because of the sword that I am sending among them."

[17] So I took the cup from the LORD's hand, and made all the nations to whom the LORD sent me drink it: [18] Jerusalem and the cities of Judah, its kings and officials, to make them a desolation and a waste, a hissing and a curse, as at this day; [19] Pharaoh king of Egypt, his servants, his officials, all his people, [20] and all the mixed tribes among them; all the kings of the land of Uz and all the kings of the land of the Philistines (Ashkelon, Gaza, Ekron, and the remnant of Ashdod); [21] Edom, Moab, and the sons of Ammon; [22] all the kings of Tyre, all the kings of Sidon, and the kings of the coastland across the sea; [23] Dedan, Tema, Buz, and all who cut the corners of their hair; [24] all the kings of Arabia and all the kings of the mixed tribes who dwell in the desert; [25] all the kings of Zimri, all the kings of Elam, and all the kings of Media; [26] all the kings of the north, far and near, one after another, and all the kingdoms of the world that are on the face of the earth. And after them the king of Babylon[1] shall drink.

[27] "Then you shall say to them, 'Thus says the LORD of hosts, the God of Israel: Drink, be drunk and vomit, fall and rise no more, because of the sword that I am sending among you.'

[28] "And if they refuse to accept the cup from your hand to drink, then you shall say to them, 'Thus says the LORD of hosts: You must drink! [29] For behold, I begin to work disaster at the city that is called by my name, and shall you go unpunished? You shall not go unpunished, for I am summoning a sword against all the inhabitants of the earth, declares the LORD of hosts.'

[30] "You, therefore, shall prophesy against them all these words, and say to them:

"'The LORD will roar from on high,
    and from his holy habitation utter his
       voice;
he will roar mightily against his fold,
    and shout, like those who tread
       grapes,
    against all the inhabitants of the
       earth.
[31] The clamor will resound to the ends of
       the earth,
    for the LORD has an indictment against
       the nations;
he is entering into judgment with all flesh,
    and the wicked he will put to the sword,
           declares the LORD.'

[32] "Thus says the LORD of hosts:
Behold, disaster is going forth
    from nation to nation,
and a great tempest is stirring
    from the farthest parts of the earth!

[33] "And those pierced by the LORD on that day shall extend from one end of the earth to the other. They shall not be lamented, or gathered, or buried; they shall be dung on the surface of the ground.

[34] "Wail, you shepherds, and cry out,
    and roll in ashes, you lords of the
       flock,
for the days of your slaughter and dispersion have come,
    and you shall fall like a choice vessel.
[35] No refuge will remain for the shepherds,
    nor escape for the lords of the flock.
[36] A voice—the cry of the shepherds,
    and the wail of the lords of the flock!
For the LORD is laying waste their pasture,
[37]   and the peaceful folds are devastated
    because of the fierce anger of the
       LORD.
[38] Like a lion he has left his lair,
    for their land has become a waste
because of the sword of the oppressor,
    and because of his fierce anger."

Jeremiah Threatened with Death

26 In the beginning of the reign of Jehoiakim the son of Josiah, king of Judah, this word came from the LORD: [2] "Thus says the LORD: Stand in the court of the LORD's house, and speak to all the cities of Judah that come to worship in the house of the LORD all the words that I command you to speak to

[1] Hebrew *Sheshach*, a code name for Babylon

them; do not hold back a word. ³ It may be they will listen, and every one turn from his evil way, that I may relent of the disaster that I intend to do to them because of their evil deeds. ⁴ You shall say to them, 'Thus says the LORD: If you will not listen to me, to walk in my law that I have set before you, ⁵ and to listen to the words of my servants the prophets whom I send to you urgently, though you have not listened, ⁶ then I will make this house like Shiloh, and I will make this city a curse for all the nations of the earth.'"

⁷ The priests and the prophets and all the people heard Jeremiah speaking these words in the house of the LORD. ⁸ And when Jeremiah had finished speaking all that the LORD had commanded him to speak to all the people, then the priests and the prophets and all the people laid hold of him, saying, "You shall die! ⁹ Why have you prophesied in the name of the LORD, saying, 'This house shall be like Shiloh, and this city shall be desolate, without inhabitant'?" And all the people gathered around Jeremiah in the house of the LORD.

¹⁰ When the officials of Judah heard these things, they came up from the king's house to the house of the LORD and took their seat in the entry of the New Gate of the house of the LORD. ¹¹ Then the priests and the prophets said to the officials and to all the people, "This man deserves the sentence of death, because he has prophesied against this city, as you have heard with your own ears."

¹² Then Jeremiah spoke to all the officials and all the people, saying, "The LORD sent me to prophesy against this house and this city all the words you have heard. ¹³ Now therefore mend your ways and your deeds, and obey the voice of the LORD your God, and the LORD will relent of the disaster that he has pronounced against you. ¹⁴ But as for me, behold, I am in your hands. Do with me as seems good and right to you. ¹⁵ Only know for certain that if you put me to death, you will bring innocent blood upon yourselves and upon this city and its inhabitants, for in truth the LORD sent me to you to speak all these words in your ears."

Jeremiah Spared from Death

¹⁶ Then the officials and all the people said to the priests and the prophets, "This man

does not deserve the sentence of death, for he has spoken to us in the name of the LORD our God." ¹⁷ And certain of the elders of the land arose and spoke to all the assembled people, saying, ¹⁸ "Micah of Moresheth prophesied in the days of Hezekiah king of Judah, and said to all the people of Judah: 'Thus says the LORD of hosts,

"'Zion shall be plowed as a field;
    Jerusalem shall become a heap of
        ruins,
    and the mountain of the house a
        wooded height.'

¹⁹ Did Hezekiah king of Judah and all Judah put him to death? Did he not fear the LORD and entreat the favor of the LORD, and did not the LORD relent of the disaster that he had pronounced against them? But we are about to bring great disaster upon ourselves."

²⁰ There was another man who prophesied in the name of the LORD, Uriah the son of Shemaiah from Kiriath-jearim. He prophesied against this city and against this land in words like those of Jeremiah. ²¹ And when King Jehoiakim, with all his warriors and all the officials, heard his words, the king sought to put him to death. But when Uriah heard of it, he was afraid and fled and escaped to Egypt. ²² Then King Jehoiakim sent to Egypt certain men, Elnathan the son of Achbor and others with him, ²³ and they took Uriah from Egypt and brought him to King Jehoiakim, who struck him down with the sword and dumped his dead body into the burial place of the common people.

²⁴ But the hand of Ahikam the son of Shaphan was with Jeremiah so that he was not given over to the people to be put to death.

The Yoke of Nebuchadnezzar

27 In the beginning of the reign of Zedekiah¹ the son of Josiah, king of Judah, this word came to Jeremiah from the LORD. ² Thus the LORD said to me: "Make yourself straps and yoke-bars, and put them on your neck. ³ Send word² to the king of Edom, the king of Moab, the king of the sons of Ammon, the king of Tyre, and the king of Sidon by the hand of the envoys who have come to Jerusalem to Zedekiah king of Judah. ⁴ Give them this charge for their masters: 'Thus says the LORD of hosts, the God of Israel: This is what you shall

¹ Or Jehoiakim ² Hebrew Send them

say to your masters: [5] "It is I who by my great power and my outstretched arm have made the earth, with the men and animals that are on the earth, and I give it to whomever it seems right to me. [6] Now I have given all these lands into the hand of Nebuchadnezzar, the king of Babylon, my servant, and I have given him also the beasts of the field to serve him. [7] All the nations shall serve him and his son and his grandson, until the time of his own land comes. Then many nations and great kings shall make him their slave.

[8] " ' "But if any nation or kingdom will not serve this Nebuchadnezzar king of Babylon, and put its neck under the yoke of the king of Babylon, I will punish that nation with the sword, with famine, and with pestilence, declares the LORD, until I have consumed it by his hand. [9] So do not listen to your prophets, your diviners, your dreamers, your fortune-tellers, or your sorcerers, who are saying to you, 'You shall not serve the king of Babylon.' [10] For it is a lie that they are prophesying to you, with the result that you will be removed far from your land, and I will drive you out, and you will perish. [11] But any nation that will bring its neck under the yoke of the king of Babylon and serve him, I will leave on its own land, to work it and dwell there, declares the LORD." ' "

[12] To Zedekiah king of Judah I spoke in like manner: "Bring your necks under the yoke of the king of Babylon, and serve him and his people and live. [13] Why will you and your people die by the sword, by famine, and by pestilence, as the LORD has spoken concerning any nation that will not serve the king of Babylon? [14] Do not listen to the words of the prophets who are saying to you, 'You shall not serve the king of Babylon,' for it is a lie that they are prophesying to you. [15] I have not sent them, declares the LORD, but they are prophesying falsely in my name, with the result that I will drive you out and you will perish, you and the prophets who are prophesying to you."

[16] Then I spoke to the priests and to all this people, saying, "Thus says the LORD: Do not listen to the words of your prophets who are prophesying to you, saying, 'Behold, the vessels of the LORD's house will now shortly be brought back from Babylon,' for it is a lie that they are prophesying to you. [17] Do not listen to them; serve the king of Babylon and live. Why should this city become a desolation? [18] If they

are prophets, and if the word of the LORD is with them, then let them intercede with the LORD of hosts, that the vessels that are left in the house of the LORD, in the house of the king of Judah, and in Jerusalem may not go to Babylon. [19] For thus says the LORD of hosts concerning the pillars, the sea, the stands, and the rest of the vessels that are left in this city, [20] which Nebuchadnezzar king of Babylon did not take away, when he took into exile from Jerusalem to Babylon Jeconiah the son of Jehoiakim, king of Judah, and all the nobles of Judah and Jerusalem— [21] thus says the LORD of hosts, the God of Israel, concerning the vessels that are left in the house of the LORD, in the house of the king of Judah, and in Jerusalem: [22] They shall be carried to Babylon and remain there until the day when I visit them, declares the LORD. Then I will bring them back and restore them to this place."

Hananiah the False Prophet

28 In that same year, at the beginning of the reign of Zedekiah king of Judah, in the fifth month of the fourth year, Hananiah the son of Azzur, the prophet from Gibeon, spoke to me in the house of the LORD, in the presence of the priests and all the people, saying, [2] "Thus says the LORD of hosts, the God of Israel: I have broken the yoke of the king of Babylon. [3] Within two years I will bring back to this place all the vessels of the LORD's house, which Nebuchadnezzar king of Babylon took away from this place and carried to Babylon. [4] I will also bring back to this place Jeconiah the son of Jehoiakim, king of Judah, and all the exiles from Judah who went to Babylon, declares the LORD, for I will break the yoke of the king of Babylon."

[5] Then the prophet Jeremiah spoke to Hananiah the prophet in the presence of the priests and all the people who were standing in the house of the LORD, [6] and the prophet Jeremiah said, "Amen! May the LORD do so; may the LORD make the words that you have prophesied come true, and bring back to this place from Babylon the vessels of the house of the LORD, and all the exiles. [7] Yet hear now this word that I speak in your hearing and in the hearing of all the people. [8] The prophets who preceded you and me from ancient times prophesied war, famine, and pestilence against many countries and great kingdoms. [9] As for

the prophet who prophesies peace, when the word of that prophet comes to pass, then it will be known that the LORD has truly sent the prophet."

¹⁰ Then the prophet Hananiah took the yoke-bars from the neck of Jeremiah the prophet and broke them. ¹¹ And Hananiah spoke in the presence of all the people, saying, "Thus says the LORD: Even so will I break the yoke of Nebuchadnezzar king of Babylon from the neck of all the nations within two years." But Jeremiah the prophet went his way.

¹² Sometime after the prophet Hananiah had broken the yoke-bars from off the neck of Jeremiah the prophet, the word of the LORD came to Jeremiah: ¹³ "Go, tell Hananiah, 'Thus says the LORD: You have broken wooden bars, but you have made in their place bars of iron. ¹⁴ For thus says the LORD of hosts, the God of Israel: I have put upon the neck of all these nations an iron yoke to serve Nebuchadnezzar king of Babylon, and they shall serve him, for I have given to him even the beasts of the field.'" ¹⁵ And Jeremiah the prophet said to the prophet Hananiah, "Listen, Hananiah, the LORD has not sent you, and you have made this people trust in a lie. ¹⁶ Therefore thus says the LORD: 'Behold, I will remove you from the face of the earth. This year you shall die, because you have uttered rebellion against the LORD.'"

¹⁷ In that same year, in the seventh month, the prophet Hananiah died.

Jeremiah's Letter to the Exiles

29 These are the words of the letter that Jeremiah the prophet sent from Jerusalem to the surviving elders of the exiles, and to the priests, the prophets, and all the people, whom Nebuchadnezzar had taken into exile from Jerusalem to Babylon. ² This was after King Jeconiah and the queen mother, the eunuchs, the officials of Judah and Jerusalem, the craftsmen, and the metal workers had departed from Jerusalem. ³ The letter was sent by the hand of Elasah the son of Shaphan and Gemariah the son of Hilkiah, whom Zedekiah king of Judah sent to Babylon to Nebuchadnezzar king of Babylon. It said: ⁴ "Thus says the LORD of hosts, the God of Israel, to all the exiles whom I have sent into exile from Jerusalem to Babylon: ⁵ Build houses and live in them; plant gardens and eat their produce. ⁶ Take wives and have sons

and daughters; take wives for your sons, and give your daughters in marriage, that they may bear sons and daughters; multiply there, and do not decrease. ⁷ But seek the welfare of the city where I have sent you into exile, and pray to the LORD on its behalf, for in its welfare you will find your welfare. ⁸ For thus says the LORD of hosts, the God of Israel: Do not let your prophets and your diviners who are among you deceive you, and do not listen to the dreams that they dream,[1] ⁹ for it is a lie that they are prophesying to you in my name; I did not send them, declares the LORD.

¹⁰ "For thus says the LORD: When seventy years are completed for Babylon, I will visit you, and I will fulfill to you my promise and bring you back to this place. ¹¹ For I know the plans I have for you, declares the LORD, plans for welfare[2] and not for evil, to give you a future and a hope. ¹² Then you will call upon me and come and pray to me, and I will hear you. ¹³ You will seek me and find me, when you seek me with all your heart. ¹⁴ I will be found by you, declares the LORD, and I will restore your fortunes and gather you from all the nations and all the places where I have driven you, declares the LORD, and I will bring you back to the place from which I sent you into exile.

¹⁵ "Because you have said, 'The LORD has raised up prophets for us in Babylon,' ¹⁶ thus says the LORD concerning the king who sits on the throne of David, and concerning all the people who dwell in this city, your kinsmen who did not go out with you into exile: ¹⁷ 'Thus says the LORD of hosts, behold, I am sending on them sword, famine, and pestilence, and I will make them like vile figs that are so rotten they cannot be eaten. ¹⁸ I will pursue them with sword, famine, and pestilence, and will make them a horror to all the kingdoms of the earth, to be a curse, a terror, a hissing, and a reproach among all the nations where I have driven them, ¹⁹ because they did not pay attention to my words, declares the LORD, that I persistently sent to you by my servants the prophets, but you would not listen, declares the LORD.' ²⁰ Hear the word of the LORD, all you exiles whom I sent away from Jerusalem to Babylon: ²¹ 'Thus says the LORD of hosts, the God of Israel, concerning Ahab the son of Kolaiah and Zedekiah the son of Maaseiah, who are prophesying a lie to you in my name: Behold, I will deliver them into the hand of Nebuchadnezzar king of Babylon,

---

[1] Hebrew *your dreams, which you cause to dream* [2] Or *peace*

and he shall strike them down before your eyes. [22] Because of them this curse shall be used by all the exiles from Judah in Babylon: "The LORD make you like Zedekiah and Ahab, whom the king of Babylon roasted in the fire," [23] because they have done an outrageous thing in Israel, they have committed adultery with their neighbors' wives, and they have spoken in my name lying words that I did not command them. I am the one who knows, and I am witness, declares the LORD.'"

Shemaiah's False Prophecy

[24] To Shemaiah of Nehelam you shall say: [25] "Thus says the LORD of hosts, the God of Israel: You have sent letters in your name to all the people who are in Jerusalem, and to Zephaniah the son of Maaseiah the priest, and to all the priests, saying, [26] 'The LORD has made you priest instead of Jehoiada the priest, to have charge in the house of the LORD over every madman who prophesies, to put him in the stocks and neck irons. [27] Now why have you not rebuked Jeremiah of Anathoth who is prophesying to you? [28] For he has sent to us in Babylon, saying, "Your exile will be long; build houses and live in them, and plant gardens and eat their produce."'"

[29] Zephaniah the priest read this letter in the hearing of Jeremiah the prophet. [30] Then the word of the LORD came to Jeremiah: [31] "Send to all the exiles, saying, 'Thus says the LORD concerning Shemaiah of Nehelam: Because Shemaiah had prophesied to you when I did not send him, and has made you trust in a lie, [32] therefore thus says the LORD: Behold, I will punish Shemaiah of Nehelam and his descendants. He shall not have anyone living among this people, and he shall not see the good that I will do to my people, declares the LORD, for he has spoken rebellion against the LORD.'"

Restoration for Israel and Judah

30 The word that came to Jeremiah from the LORD: [2] "Thus says the LORD, the God of Israel: Write in a book all the words that I have spoken to you. [3] For behold, days are coming, declares the LORD, when I will restore the fortunes of my people, Israel and Judah, says the LORD, and I will bring them back to the land that I gave to their fathers, and they shall take possession of it."

[4] These are the words that the LORD spoke concerning Israel and Judah:

[5]   "Thus says the LORD:
       We have heard a cry of panic,
           of terror, and no peace.
[6]   Ask now, and see,
           can a man bear a child?
       Why then do I see every man
           with his hands on his stomach like a
               woman in labor?
       Why has every face turned pale?
[7]   Alas! That day is so great
           there is none like it;
       it is a time of distress for Jacob;
           yet he shall be saved out of it.

[8] "And it shall come to pass in that day, declares the LORD of hosts, that I will break his yoke from off your neck, and I will burst your bonds, and foreigners shall no more make a servant of him.[1] [9] But they shall serve the LORD their God and David their king, whom I will raise up for them.

[10]   "Then fear not, O Jacob my servant, declares
           the LORD,
           nor be dismayed, O Israel;
       for behold, I will save you from far away,
           and your offspring from the land of
               their captivity.
       Jacob shall return and have quiet and ease,
           and none shall make him afraid.
[11]   For I am with you to save you,
                       declares the LORD;
       I will make a full end of all the nations
           among whom I scattered you,
           but of you I will not make a full end.
       I will discipline you in just measure,
           and I will by no means leave you
               unpunished.

[12]   "For thus says the LORD:
       Your hurt is incurable,
           and your wound is grievous.
[13]   There is none to uphold your cause,
           no medicine for your wound,
           no healing for you.
[14]   All your lovers have forgotten you;
           they care nothing for you;
       for I have dealt you the blow of an enemy,
           the punishment of a merciless foe,
       because your guilt is great,
           because your sins are flagrant.
[15]   Why do you cry out over your hurt?
           Your pain is incurable.

[1] Or serve him

Because your guilt is great,
> because your sins are flagrant,
> I have done these things to you.
16 Therefore all who devour you shall be
> devoured,
> and all your foes, every one of them,
> shall go into captivity;
> those who plunder you shall be plundered,
> and all who prey on you I will make a
> prey.
17 For I will restore health to you,
> and your wounds I will heal,
> declares the LORD,
> because they have called you an outcast:
> 'It is Zion, for whom no one cares!'

18 "Thus says the LORD:
> Behold, I will restore the fortunes of the
> tents of Jacob
> and have compassion on his dwellings;
> the city shall be rebuilt on its mound,
> and the palace shall stand where it used
> to be.
19 Out of them shall come songs of thanks-
> giving,
> and the voices of those who celebrate.
> I will multiply them, and they shall not be
> few;
> I will make them honored, and they
> shall not be small.
20 Their children shall be as they were of old,
> and their congregation shall be estab-
> lished before me,
> and I will punish all who oppress them.
21 Their prince shall be one of themselves;
> their ruler shall come out from their
> midst;
> I will make him draw near, and he shall
> approach me,
> for who would dare of himself to
> approach me?
> declares the LORD.
22 And you shall be my people,
> and I will be your God."

23 Behold the storm of the LORD!
> Wrath has gone forth,
> a whirling tempest;
> it will burst upon the head of the
> wicked.

24 The fierce anger of the LORD will not turn
> back
> until he has executed and accomplished
> the intentions of his mind.
> In the latter days you will understand this.

The LORD Will Turn Mourning to Joy

31 "At that time, declares the LORD, I will be
the God of all the clans of Israel, and they
shall be my people."

2 Thus says the LORD:
> "The people who survived the sword
> found grace in the wilderness;
> when Israel sought for rest,
3 the LORD appeared to him[1] from far
> away.
> I have loved you with an everlasting love;
> therefore I have continued my faithful-
> ness to you.
4 Again I will build you, and you shall be
> built,
> O virgin Israel!
> Again you shall adorn yourself with tam-
> bourines
> and shall go forth in the dance of the
> merrymakers.
5 Again you shall plant vineyards
> on the mountains of Samaria;
> the planters shall plant
> and shall enjoy the fruit.
6 For there shall be a day when watchmen
> will call
> in the hill country of Ephraim:
> 'Arise, and let us go up to Zion,
> to the LORD our God.'"

7 For thus says the LORD:
> "Sing aloud with gladness for Jacob,
> and raise shouts for the chief of the
> nations;
> proclaim, give praise, and say,
> 'O LORD, save your people,
> the remnant of Israel.'
8 Behold, I will bring them from the north
> country
> and gather them from the farthest parts
> of the earth,
> among them the blind and the lame,
> the pregnant woman and she who is in
> labor, together;
> a great company, they shall return here.

[1] Septuagint; Hebrew *me*

9 With weeping they shall come,
    and with pleas for mercy I will lead
      them back,
I will make them walk by brooks of water,
    in a straight path in which they shall
      not stumble,
for I am a father to Israel,
    and Ephraim is my firstborn.

10 "Hear the word of the LORD, O nations,
    and declare it in the coastlands far away;
say, 'He who scattered Israel will gather him,
    and will keep him as a shepherd keeps
      his flock.'
11 For the LORD has ransomed Jacob
    and has redeemed him from hands
      too strong for him.
12 They shall come and sing aloud on the
      height of Zion,
    and they shall be radiant over the
      goodness of the LORD,
over the grain, the wine, and the oil,
    and over the young of the flock and the
      herd;
their life shall be like a watered garden,
    and they shall languish no more.
13 Then shall the young women rejoice in the
      dance,
    and the young men and the old shall be
      merry.
I will turn their mourning into joy;
    I will comfort them, and give them
      gladness for sorrow.
14 I will feast the soul of the priests with
      abundance,
    and my people shall be satisfied with
      my goodness,
                declares the LORD."

15 Thus says the LORD:
"A voice is heard in Ramah,
    lamentation and bitter weeping.
Rachel is weeping for her children;
    she refuses to be comforted for her
      children,
because they are no more."

16 Thus says the LORD:
"Keep your voice from weeping,
    and your eyes from tears,
for there is a reward for your work,
                declares the LORD,
    and they shall come back from the
      land of the enemy.

17 There is hope for your future,
                declares the LORD,
    and your children shall come back to
      their own country.
18 I have heard Ephraim grieving,
'You have disciplined me, and I was disci-
      plined,
    like an untrained calf;
bring me back that I may be restored,
    for you are the LORD my God.
19 For after I had turned away, I relented,
    and after I was instructed, I struck my
      thigh;
I was ashamed, and I was confounded,
    because I bore the disgrace of my youth.'
20 Is Ephraim my dear son?
    Is he my darling child?
For as often as I speak against him,
    I do remember him still.
Therefore my heart[1] yearns for him;
    I will surely have mercy on him,
                declares the LORD.

21 "Set up road markers for yourself;
    make yourself guideposts;
consider well the highway,
    the road by which you went.
Return, O virgin Israel,
    return to these your cities.
22 How long will you waver,
    O faithless daughter?
For the LORD has created a new thing on
      the earth:
    a woman encircles a man."

23 Thus says the LORD of hosts, the God of
Israel: "Once more they shall use these words in
the land of Judah and in its cities, when I restore
their fortunes:

"'The LORD bless you, O habitation of righ-
      teousness,
    O holy hill!'

24 And Judah and all its cities shall dwell there
together, and the farmers and those who wander
with their flocks. 25 For I will satisfy the weary
soul, and every languishing soul I will replenish."
26 At this I awoke and looked, and my sleep
was pleasant to me.
27 "Behold, the days are coming, declares the
LORD, when I will sow the house of Israel and
the house of Judah with the seed of man and
the seed of beast. 28 And it shall come to pass
that as I have watched over them to pluck up

1 Hebrew *bowels*

and break down, to overthrow, destroy, and bring harm, so I will watch over them to build and to plant, declares the LORD. ²⁹ In those days they shall no longer say:

"'The fathers have eaten sour grapes,
    and the children's teeth are set on edge.'

³⁰ But everyone shall die for his own iniquity. Each man who eats sour grapes, his teeth shall be set on edge.

The New Covenant

³¹ "Behold, the days are coming, declares the LORD, when I will make a new covenant with the house of Israel and the house of Judah, ³² not like the covenant that I made with their fathers on the day when I took them by the hand to bring them out of the land of Egypt, my covenant that they broke, though I was their husband, declares the LORD. ³³ For this is the covenant that I will make with the house of Israel after those days, declares the LORD: I will put my law within them, and I will write it on their hearts. And I will be their God, and they shall be my people. ³⁴ And no longer shall each one teach his neighbor and each his brother, saying, 'Know the LORD,' for they shall all know me, from the least of them to the greatest, declares the LORD. For I will forgive their iniquity, and I will remember their sin no more."

³⁵   Thus says the LORD,
        who gives the sun for light by day
            and the fixed order of the moon and the
                stars for light by night,
        who stirs up the sea so that its waves
            roar—
            the LORD of hosts is his name:
³⁶   "If this fixed order departs
        from before me, declares the LORD,
        then shall the offspring of Israel cease
            from being a nation before me forever."

³⁷   Thus says the LORD:
    "If the heavens above can be measured,
        and the foundations of the earth below
            can be explored,
        then I will cast off all the offspring of Israel
            for all that they have done,
                            declares the LORD."

³⁸ "Behold, the days are coming, declares the LORD, when the city shall be rebuilt for the LORD from the Tower of Hananel to the Corner Gate. ³⁹ And the measuring line shall go out farther, straight to the hill Gareb, and shall then turn to Goah. ⁴⁰ The whole valley of the dead bodies and the ashes, and all the fields as far as the brook Kidron, to the corner of the Horse Gate toward the east, shall be sacred to the LORD. It shall not be plucked up or overthrown anymore forever."

Jeremiah Buys a Field During the Siege

32 The word that came to Jeremiah from the LORD in the tenth year of Zedekiah king of Judah, which was the eighteenth year of Nebuchadnezzar. ² At that time the army of the king of Babylon was besieging Jerusalem, and Jeremiah the prophet was shut up in the court of the guard that was in the palace of the king of Judah. ³ For Zedekiah king of Judah had imprisoned him, saying, "Why do you prophesy and say, 'Thus says the LORD: Behold, I am giving this city into the hand of the king of Babylon, and he shall capture it; ⁴ Zedekiah king of Judah shall not escape out of the hand of the Chaldeans, but shall surely be given into the hand of the king of Babylon, and shall speak with him face to face and see him eye to eye. ⁵ And he shall take Zedekiah to Babylon, and there he shall remain until I visit him, declares the LORD. Though you fight against the Chaldeans, you shall not succeed'?"

⁶ Jeremiah said, "The word of the LORD came to me: ⁷ Behold, Hanamel the son of Shallum your uncle will come to you and say, 'Buy my field that is at Anathoth, for the right of redemption by purchase is yours.' ⁸ Then Hanamel my cousin came to me in the court of the guard, in accordance with the word of the LORD, and said to me, 'Buy my field that is at Anathoth in the land of Benjamin, for the right of possession and redemption is yours; buy it for yourself.' Then I knew that this was the word of the LORD.

⁹ "And I bought the field at Anathoth from Hanamel my cousin, and weighed out the money to him, seventeen shekels of silver. ¹⁰ I signed the deed, sealed it, got witnesses, and weighed the money on scales. ¹¹ Then I took the sealed deed of purchase, containing the terms and conditions and the open copy. ¹² And I gave the deed of purchase to Baruch the son of Neriah son of Mahseiah, in the presence of Hanamel my cousin, in the presence of the witnesses who signed the deed of purchase, and in

the presence of all the Judeans who were sitting in the court of the guard. ¹³I charged Baruch in their presence, saying, ¹⁴"Thus says the LORD of hosts, the God of Israel: Take these deeds, both this sealed deed of purchase and this open deed, and put them in an earthenware vessel, that they may last for a long time. ¹⁵For thus says the LORD of hosts, the God of Israel: Houses and fields and vineyards shall again be bought in this land.'

Jeremiah Prays for Understanding

¹⁶"After I had given the deed of purchase to Baruch the son of Neriah, I prayed to the LORD, saying: ¹⁷'Ah, Lord GOD! It is you who have made the heavens and the earth by your great power and by your outstretched arm! Nothing is too hard for you. ¹⁸You show steadfast love to thousands, but you repay the guilt of fathers to their children after them, O great and mighty God, whose name is the LORD of hosts, ¹⁹great in counsel and mighty in deed, whose eyes are open to all the ways of the children of man, rewarding each one according to his ways and according to the fruit of his deeds. ²⁰You have shown signs and wonders in the land of Egypt, and to this day in Israel and among all mankind, and have made a name for yourself, as at this day. ²¹You brought your people Israel out of the land of Egypt with signs and wonders, with a strong hand and outstretched arm, and with great terror. ²²And you gave them this land, which you swore to their fathers to give them, a land flowing with milk and honey. ²³And they entered and took possession of it. But they did not obey your voice or walk in your law. They did nothing of all you commanded them to do. Therefore you have made all this disaster come upon them. ²⁴Behold, the siege mounds have come up to the city to take it, and because of sword and famine and pestilence the city is given into the hands of the Chaldeans who are fighting against it. What you spoke has come to pass, and behold, you see it. ²⁵Yet you, O Lord GOD, have said to me, "Buy the field for money and get witnesses"—though the city is given into the hands of the Chaldeans.'"

²⁶The word of the LORD came to Jeremiah: ²⁷"Behold, I am the LORD, the God of all flesh. Is anything too hard for me? ²⁸Therefore, thus says the LORD: Behold, I am giving this city into the hands of the Chaldeans and into the hand of Nebuchadnezzar king of Babylon, and he shall capture it. ²⁹The Chaldeans who are fighting against this city shall come and set this city on fire and burn it, with the houses on whose roofs offerings have been made to Baal and drink offerings have been poured out to other gods, to provoke me to anger. ³⁰For the children of Israel and the children of Judah have done nothing but evil in my sight from their youth. The children of Israel have done nothing but provoke me to anger by the work of their hands, declares the LORD. ³¹This city has aroused my anger and wrath, from the day it was built to this day, so that I will remove it from my sight ³²because of all the evil of the children of Israel and the children of Judah that they did to provoke me to anger—their kings and their officials, their priests and their prophets, the men of Judah and the inhabitants of Jerusalem. ³³They have turned to me their back and not their face. And though I have taught them persistently, they have not listened to receive instruction. ³⁴They set up their abominations in the house that is called by my name, to defile it. ³⁵They built the high places of Baal in the Valley of the Son of Hinnom, to offer up their sons and daughters to Molech, though I did not command them, nor did it enter into my mind, that they should do this abomination, to cause Judah to sin.

They Shall Be My People; I Will Be Their God

³⁶"Now therefore thus says the LORD, the God of Israel, concerning this city of which you say, 'It is given into the hand of the king of Babylon by sword, by famine, and by pestilence': ³⁷Behold, I will gather them from all the countries to which I drove them in my anger and my wrath and in great indignation. I will bring them back to this place, and I will make them dwell in safety. ³⁸And they shall be my people, and I will be their God. ³⁹I will give them one heart and one way, that they may fear me forever, for their own good and the good of their children after them. ⁴⁰I will make with them an everlasting covenant, that I will not turn away from doing good to them. And I will put the fear of me in their hearts, that they may not turn from me. ⁴¹I will rejoice in doing them good, and I will plant them in this land in faithfulness, with all my heart and all my soul.

[42] "For thus says the LORD: Just as I have brought all this great disaster upon this people, so I will bring upon them all the good that I promise them. [43] Fields shall be bought in this land of which you are saying, 'It is a desolation, without man or beast; it is given into the hand of the Chaldeans.' [44] Fields shall be bought for money, and deeds shall be signed and sealed and witnessed, in the land of Benjamin, in the places about Jerusalem, and in the cities of Judah, in the cities of the hill country, in the cities of the Shephelah, and in the cities of the Negeb; for I will restore their fortunes, declares the LORD."

The LORD Promises Peace

33 The word of the LORD came to Jeremiah a second time, while he was still shut up in the court of the guard: [2] "Thus says the LORD who made the earth,[1] the LORD who formed it to establish it—the LORD is his name: [3] Call to me and I will answer you, and will tell you great and hidden things that you have not known. [4] For thus says the LORD, the God of Israel, concerning the houses of this city and the houses of the kings of Judah that were torn down to make a defense against the siege mounds and against the sword: [5] They are coming in to fight against the Chaldeans and to fill them[2] with the dead bodies of men whom I shall strike down in my anger and my wrath, for I have hidden my face from this city because of all their evil. [6] Behold, I will bring to it health and healing, and I will heal them and reveal to them abundance of prosperity and security. [7] I will restore the fortunes of Judah and the fortunes of Israel, and rebuild them as they were at first. [8] I will cleanse them from all the guilt of their sin against me, and I will forgive all the guilt of their sin and rebellion against me. [9] And this city[3] shall be to me a name of joy, a praise and a glory before all the nations of the earth who shall hear of all the good that I do for them. They shall fear and tremble because of all the good and all the prosperity I provide for it.

[10] "Thus says the LORD: In this place of which you say, 'It is a waste without man or beast,' in the cities of Judah and the streets of Jerusalem that are desolate, without man or inhabitant or beast, there shall be heard again [11] the voice of mirth and the voice of gladness, the voice of the bridegroom and the voice of the bride, the voices of those who sing, as they bring thank offerings to the house of the LORD:

" 'Give thanks to the LORD of hosts,
     for the LORD is good,
     for his steadfast love endures forever!'

For I will restore the fortunes of the land as at first, says the LORD.

[12] "Thus says the LORD of hosts: In this place that is waste, without man or beast, and in all of its cities, there shall again be habitations of shepherds resting their flocks. [13] In the cities of the hill country, in the cities of the Shephelah, and in the cities of the Negeb, in the land of Benjamin, the places about Jerusalem, and in the cities of Judah, flocks shall again pass under the hands of the one who counts them, says the LORD.

The LORD's Eternal Covenant with David

[14] "Behold, the days are coming, declares the LORD, when I will fulfill the promise I made to the house of Israel and the house of Judah. [15] In those days and at that time I will cause a righteous Branch to spring up for David, and he shall execute justice and righteousness in the land. [16] In those days Judah will be saved, and Jerusalem will dwell securely. And this is the name by which it will be called: 'The LORD is our righteousness.'

[17] "For thus says the LORD: David shall never lack a man to sit on the throne of the house of Israel, [18] and the Levitical priests shall never lack a man in my presence to offer burnt offerings, to burn grain offerings, and to make sacrifices forever."

[19] The word of the LORD came to Jeremiah: [20] "Thus says the LORD: If you can break my covenant with the day and my covenant with the night, so that day and night will not come at their appointed time, [21] then also my covenant with David my servant may be broken, so that he shall not have a son to reign on his throne, and my covenant with the Levitical priests my ministers. [22] As the host of heaven cannot be numbered and the sands of the sea cannot be measured, so I will multiply the offspring of David my servant, and the Levitical priests who minister to me."

[23] The word of the LORD came to Jeremiah: [24] "Have you not observed that these people are saying, 'The LORD has rejected the two clans that he chose'? Thus they have despised my people so that they are no longer a nation in their sight. [25] Thus says the LORD: If I have not established my covenant with day and night

---

[1] Septuagint; Hebrew *it* [2] That is, the torn-down houses [3] Hebrew *And it*

and the fixed order of heaven and earth, [26] then I will reject the offspring of Jacob and David my servant and will not choose one of his offspring to rule over the offspring of Abraham, Isaac, and Jacob. For I will restore their fortunes and will have mercy on them."

Zedekiah to Die in Babylon

34 The word that came to Jeremiah from the LORD, when Nebuchadnezzar king of Babylon and all his army and all the kingdoms of the earth under his dominion and all the peoples were fighting against Jerusalem and all of its cities: [2] "Thus says the LORD, the God of Israel: Go and speak to Zedekiah king of Judah and say to him, 'Thus says the LORD: Behold, I am giving this city into the hand of the king of Babylon, and he shall burn it with fire. [3] You shall not escape from his hand but shall surely be captured and delivered into his hand. You shall see the king of Babylon eye to eye and speak with him face to face. And you shall go to Babylon.' [4] Yet hear the word of the LORD, O Zedekiah king of Judah! Thus says the LORD concerning you: 'You shall not die by the sword. [5] You shall die in peace. And as spices were burned for your fathers, the former kings who were before you, so people shall burn spices for you and lament for you, saying, "Alas, lord!"' For I have spoken the word, declares the LORD."

[6] Then Jeremiah the prophet spoke all these words to Zedekiah king of Judah, in Jerusalem, [7] when the army of the king of Babylon was fighting against Jerusalem and against all the cities of Judah that were left, Lachish and Azekah, for these were the only fortified cities of Judah that remained.

[8] The word that came to Jeremiah from the LORD, after King Zedekiah had made a covenant with all the people in Jerusalem to make a proclamation of liberty to them, [9] that everyone should set free his Hebrew slaves, male and female, so that no one should enslave a Jew, his brother. [10] And they obeyed, all the officials and all the people who had entered into the covenant that everyone would set free his slave, male or female, so that they would not be enslaved again. They obeyed and set them free. [11] But afterward they turned around and took back the male and female slaves they had set free, and brought them into subjection as slaves. [12] The word of the LORD came to Jeremiah from the LORD: [13] "Thus says the LORD, the God of Israel: I myself made a covenant with your fathers when I brought them out of the land of Egypt, out of the house of slavery, saying, [14] 'At the end of seven years each of you must set free the fellow Hebrew who has been sold to you and has served you six years; you must set him free from your service.' But your fathers did not listen to me or incline their ears to me. [15] You recently repented and did what was right in my eyes by proclaiming liberty, each to his neighbor, and you made a covenant before me in the house that is called by my name, [16] but then you turned around and profaned my name when each of you took back his male and female slaves, whom you had set free according to their desire, and you brought them into subjection to be your slaves.

[17] "Therefore, thus says the LORD: You have not obeyed me by proclaiming liberty, every one to his brother and to his neighbor; behold, I proclaim to you liberty to the sword, to pestilence, and to famine, declares the LORD. I will make you a horror to all the kingdoms of the earth. [18] And the men who transgressed my covenant and did not keep the terms of the covenant that they made before me, I will make them like[1] the calf that they cut in two and passed between its parts— [19] the officials of Judah, the officials of Jerusalem, the eunuchs, the priests, and all the people of the land who passed between the parts of the calf. [20] And I will give them into the hand of their enemies and into the hand of those who seek their lives. Their dead bodies shall be food for the birds of the air and the beasts of the earth. [21] And Zedekiah king of Judah and his officials I will give into the hand of their enemies and into the hand of those who seek their lives, into the hand of the army of the king of Babylon which has withdrawn from you. [22] Behold, I will command, declares the LORD, and will bring them back to this city. And they will fight against it and take it and burn it with fire. I will make the cities of Judah a desolation without inhabitant."

The Obedience of the Rechabites

35 The word that came to Jeremiah from the LORD in the days of Jehoiakim the son of Josiah, king of Judah: [2] "Go to the house of the Rechabites and speak with them and bring them to the house of the LORD, into one of the chambers; then offer them wine to drink." [3] So I took Jaazaniah the son of Jeremiah,

---

[1] Hebrew lacks *them like*

son of Habazziniah and his brothers and all his sons and the whole house of the Rechabites. ⁴I brought them to the house of the LORD into the chamber of the sons of Hanan the son of Igdaliah, the man of God, which was near the chamber of the officials, above the chamber of Maaseiah the son of Shallum, keeper of the threshold. ⁵Then I set before the Rechabites pitchers full of wine, and cups, and I said to them, "Drink wine." ⁶But they answered, "We will drink no wine, for Jonadab the son of Rechab, our father, commanded us, 'You shall not drink wine, neither you nor your sons forever. ⁷You shall not build a house; you shall not sow seed; you shall not plant or have a vineyard; but you shall live in tents all your days, that you may live many days in the land where you sojourn.' ⁸We have obeyed the voice of Jonadab the son of Rechab, our father, in all that he commanded us, to drink no wine all our days, ourselves, our wives, our sons, or our daughters, ⁹and not to build houses to dwell in. We have no vineyard or field or seed, ¹⁰but we have lived in tents and have obeyed and done all that Jonadab our father commanded us. ¹¹But when Nebuchadnezzar king of Babylon came up against the land, we said, 'Come, and let us go to Jerusalem for fear of the army of the Chaldeans and the army of the Syrians.' So we are living in Jerusalem."

¹²Then the word of the LORD came to Jeremiah: ¹³"Thus says the LORD of hosts, the God of Israel: Go and say to the people of Judah and the inhabitants of Jerusalem, Will you not receive instruction and listen to my words? declares the LORD. ¹⁴The command that Jonadab the son of Rechab gave to his sons, to drink no wine, has been kept, and they drink none to this day, for they have obeyed their father's command. I have spoken to you persistently, but you have not listened to me. ¹⁵I have sent to you all my servants the prophets, sending them persistently, saying, 'Turn now every one of you from his evil way, and amend your deeds, and do not go after other gods to serve them, and then you shall dwell in the land that I gave to you and your fathers.' But you did not incline your ear or listen to me. ¹⁶The sons of Jonadab the son of Rechab have kept the command that their father gave them, but this people has not obeyed me. ¹⁷Therefore, thus says the LORD, the God of hosts, the God of Israel: Behold, I am bringing upon Judah and all the inhabitants of Jerusalem

all the disaster that I have pronounced against them, because I have spoken to them and they have not listened, I have called to them and they have not answered."

·¹⁸But to the house of the Rechabites Jeremiah said, "Thus says the LORD of hosts, the God of Israel: Because you have obeyed the command of Jonadab your father and kept all his precepts and done all that he commanded you, ¹⁹therefore thus says the LORD of hosts, the God of Israel: Jonadab the son of Rechab shall never lack a man to stand before me."

Jehoiakim Burns Jeremiah's Scroll

36 In the fourth year of Jehoiakim the son of Josiah, king of Judah, this word came to Jeremiah from the LORD: ²"Take a scroll and write on it all the words that I have spoken to you against Israel and Judah and all the nations, from the day I spoke to you, from the days of Josiah until today. ³It may be that the house of Judah will hear all the disaster that I intend to do to them, so that every one may turn from his evil way, and that I may forgive their iniquity and their sin."

⁴Then Jeremiah called Baruch the son of Neriah, and Baruch wrote on a scroll at the dictation of Jeremiah all the words of the LORD that he had spoken to him. ⁵And Jeremiah ordered Baruch, saying, "I am banned from going to the house of the LORD, ⁶so you are to go, and on a day of fasting in the hearing of all the people in the LORD's house you shall read the words of the LORD from the scroll that you have written at my dictation. You shall read them also in the hearing of all the men of Judah who come out of their cities. ⁷It may be that their plea for mercy will come before the LORD, and that every one will turn from his evil way, for great is the anger and wrath that the LORD has pronounced against this people." ⁸And Baruch the son of Neriah did all that Jeremiah the prophet ordered him about reading from the scroll the words of the LORD in the LORD's house.

⁹In the fifth year of Jehoiakim the son of Josiah, king of Judah, in the ninth month, all the people in Jerusalem and all the people who came from the cities of Judah to Jerusalem proclaimed a fast before the LORD. ¹⁰Then, in the hearing of all the people, Baruch read the words of Jeremiah from the scroll, in the house of the LORD, in the chamber of Gemariah the

son of Shaphan the secretary, which was in the upper court, at the entry of the New Gate of the Lord's house.

¹¹ When Micaiah the son of Gemariah, son of Shaphan, heard all the words of the Lord from the scroll, ¹² he went down to the king's house, into the secretary's chamber, and all the officials were sitting there: Elishama the secretary, Delaiah the son of Shemaiah, Elnathan the son of Achbor, Gemariah the son of Shaphan, Zedekiah the son of Hananiah, and all the officials. ¹³ And Micaiah told them all the words that he had heard, when Baruch read the scroll in the hearing of the people. ¹⁴ Then all the officials sent Jehudi the son of Nethaniah, son of Shelemiah, son of Cushi, to say to Baruch, "Take in your hand the scroll that you read in the hearing of the people, and come." So Baruch the son of Neriah took the scroll in his hand and came to them. ¹⁵ And they said to him, "Sit down and read it." So Baruch read it to them. ¹⁶ When they heard all the words, they turned one to another in fear. And they said to Baruch, "We must report all these words to the king." ¹⁷ Then they asked Baruch, "Tell us, please, how did you write all these words? Was it at his dictation?" ¹⁸ Baruch answered them, "He dictated all these words to me, while I wrote them with ink on the scroll." ¹⁹ Then the officials said to Baruch, "Go and hide, you and Jeremiah, and let no one know where you are."

²⁰ So they went into the court to the king, having put the scroll in the chamber of Elishama the secretary, and they reported all the words to the king. ²¹ Then the king sent Jehudi to get the scroll, and he took it from the chamber of Elishama the secretary. And Jehudi read it to the king and all the officials who stood beside the king. ²² It was the ninth month, and the king was sitting in the winter house, and there was a fire burning in the fire pot before him. ²³ As Jehudi read three or four columns, the king would cut them off with a knife and throw them into the fire in the fire pot, until the entire scroll was consumed in the fire that was in the fire pot. ²⁴ Yet neither the king nor any of his servants who heard all these words was afraid, nor did they tear their garments. ²⁵ Even when Elnathan and Delaiah and Gemariah urged the king not to burn the scroll, he would not listen to them. ²⁶ And the king commanded Jerahmeel the king's son and Seraiah the son of Azriel and Shelemiah the son of Abdeel to seize Baruch

the secretary and Jeremiah the prophet, but the Lord hid them.

²⁷ Now after the king had burned the scroll with the words that Baruch wrote at Jeremiah's dictation, the word of the Lord came to Jeremiah: ²⁸ "Take another scroll and write on it all the former words that were in the first scroll, which Jehoiakim the king of Judah has burned. ²⁹ And concerning Jehoiakim king of Judah you shall say, 'Thus says the Lord, You have burned this scroll, saying, "Why have you written in it that the king of Babylon will certainly come and destroy this land, and will cut off from it man and beast?" ³⁰ Therefore thus says the Lord concerning Jehoiakim king of Judah: He shall have none to sit on the throne of David, and his dead body shall be cast out to the heat by day and the frost by night. ³¹ And I will punish him and his offspring and his servants for their iniquity. I will bring upon them and upon the inhabitants of Jerusalem and upon the people of Judah all the disaster that I have pronounced against them, but they would not hear.' "

³² Then Jeremiah took another scroll and gave it to Baruch the scribe, the son of Neriah, who wrote on it at the dictation of Jeremiah all the words of the scroll that Jehoiakim king of Judah had burned in the fire. And many similar words were added to them.

Jeremiah Warns Zedekiah

37 Zedekiah the son of Josiah, whom Nebuchadnezzar king of Babylon made king in the land of Judah, reigned instead of Coniah the son of Jehoiakim. ² But neither he nor his servants nor the people of the land listened to the words of the Lord that he spoke through Jeremiah the prophet.

³ King Zedekiah sent Jehucal the son of Shelemiah, and Zephaniah the priest, the son of Maaseiah, to Jeremiah the prophet, saying, "Please pray for us to the Lord our God." ⁴ Now Jeremiah was still going in and out among the people, for he had not yet been put in prison. ⁵ The army of Pharaoh had come out of Egypt. And when the Chaldeans who were besieging Jerusalem heard news about them, they withdrew from Jerusalem.

⁶ Then the word of the Lord came to Jeremiah the prophet: ⁷ "Thus says the Lord, God of Israel: Thus shall you say to the king of Judah who sent you to me to inquire of me, 'Behold, Pharaoh's army that came to help you

is about to return to Egypt, to its own land. [8] And the Chaldeans shall come back and fight against this city. They shall capture it and burn it with fire. [9] Thus says the LORD, Do not deceive yourselves, saying, "The Chaldeans will surely go away from us," for they will not go away. [10] For even if you should defeat the whole army of Chaldeans who are fighting against you, and there remained of them only wounded men, every man in his tent, they would rise up and burn this city with fire.'"

Jeremiah Imprisoned

[11] Now when the Chaldean army had withdrawn from Jerusalem at the approach of Pharaoh's army, [12] Jeremiah set out from Jerusalem to go to the land of Benjamin to receive his portion there among the people. [13] When he was at the Benjamin Gate, a sentry there named Irijah the son of Shelemiah, son of Hananiah, seized Jeremiah the prophet, saying, "You are deserting to the Chaldeans." [14] And Jeremiah said, "It is a lie; I am not deserting to the Chaldeans." But Irijah would not listen to him, and seized Jeremiah and brought him to the officials. [15] And the officials were enraged at Jeremiah, and they beat him and imprisoned him in the house of Jonathan the secretary, for it had been made a prison.

[16] When Jeremiah had come to the dungeon cells and remained there many days, [17] King Zedekiah sent for him and received him. The king questioned him secretly in his house and said, "Is there any word from the LORD?" Jeremiah said, "There is." Then he said, "You shall be delivered into the hand of the king of Babylon." [18] Jeremiah also said to King Zedekiah, "What wrong have I done to you or your servants or this people, that you have put me in prison? [19] Where are your prophets who prophesied to you, saying, 'The king of Babylon will not come against you and against this land'? [20] Now hear, please, O my lord the king: let my humble plea come before you and do not send me back to the house of Jonathan the secretary, lest I die there." [21] So King Zedekiah gave orders, and they committed Jeremiah to the court of the guard. And a loaf of bread was given him daily from the bakers' street, until all the bread of the city was gone. So Jeremiah remained in the court of the guard.

Jeremiah Cast into the Cistern

38 Now Shephatiah the son of Mattan, Gedaliah the son of Pashhur, Jucal the son of Shelemiah, and Pashhur the son of Malchiah heard the words that Jeremiah was saying to all the people: [2] "Thus says the LORD: He who stays in this city shall die by the sword, by famine, and by pestilence, but he who goes out to the Chaldeans shall live. He shall have his life as a prize of war, and live. [3] Thus says the LORD: This city shall surely be given into the hand of the army of the king of Babylon and be taken." [4] Then the officials said to the king, "Let this man be put to death, for he is weakening the hands of the soldiers who are left in this city, and the hands of all the people, by speaking such words to them. For this man is not seeking the welfare of this people, but their harm." [5] King Zedekiah said, "Behold, he is in your hands, for the king can do nothing against you." [6] So they took Jeremiah and cast him into the cistern of Malchiah, the king's son, which was in the court of the guard, letting Jeremiah down by ropes. And there was no water in the cistern, but only mud, and Jeremiah sank in the mud.

Jeremiah Rescued from the Cistern

[7] When Ebed-melech the Ethiopian, a eunuch who was in the king's house, heard that they had put Jeremiah into the cistern—the king was sitting in the Benjamin Gate— [8] Ebed-melech went from the king's house and said to the king, [9] "My lord the king, these men have done evil in all that they did to Jeremiah the prophet by casting him into the cistern, and he will die there of hunger, for there is no bread left in the city." [10] Then the king commanded Ebed-melech the Ethiopian, "Take thirty men with you from here, and lift Jeremiah the prophet out of the cistern before he dies." [11] So Ebed-melech took the men with him and went to the house of the king, to a wardrobe in the storehouse, and took from there old rags and worn-out clothes, which he let down to Jeremiah in the cistern by ropes. [12] Then Ebed-melech the Ethiopian said to Jeremiah, "Put the rags and clothes between your armpits and the ropes." Jeremiah did so. [13] Then they drew Jeremiah up with ropes and lifted him out of the cistern. And Jeremiah remained in the court of the guard.

Jeremiah Warns Zedekiah Again

[14] King Zedekiah sent for Jeremiah the prophet and received him at the third entrance of the temple of the LORD. The king said to Jeremiah, "I will ask you a question; hide nothing from me." [15] Jeremiah said to Zedekiah, "If I tell you, will you not surely put me to death? And if I give you counsel, you will not listen to me." [16] Then King Zedekiah swore secretly to Jeremiah, "As the LORD lives, who made our souls, I will not put you to death or deliver you into the hand of these men who seek your life."

[17] Then Jeremiah said to Zedekiah, "Thus says the LORD, the God of hosts, the God of Israel: If you will surrender to the officials of the king of Babylon, then your life shall be spared, and this city shall not be burned with fire, and you and your house shall live. [18] But if you do not surrender to the officials of the king of Babylon, then this city shall be given into the hand of the Chaldeans, and they shall burn it with fire, and you shall not escape from their hand." [19] King Zedekiah said to Jeremiah, "I am afraid of the Judeans who have deserted to the Chaldeans, lest I be handed over to them and they deal cruelly with me." [20] Jeremiah said, "You shall not be given to them. Obey now the voice of the LORD in what I say to you, and it shall be well with you, and your life shall be spared. [21] But if you refuse to surrender, this is the vision which the LORD has shown to me: [22] Behold, all the women left in the house of the king of Judah were being led out to the officials of the king of Babylon and were saying,

> "'Your trusted friends have deceived you
>   and prevailed against you;
> now that your feet are sunk in the mud,
>   they turn away from you.'

[23] All your wives and your sons shall be led out to the Chaldeans, and you yourself shall not escape from their hand, but shall be seized by the king of Babylon, and this city shall be burned with fire."

[24] Then Zedekiah said to Jeremiah, "Let no one know of these words, and you shall not die. [25] If the officials hear that I have spoken with you and come to you and say to you, 'Tell us what you said to the king and what the king said to you; hide nothing from us and we will not put you to death,' [26] then you shall say to them, 'I made a humble plea to the king that he would not send me back to the house of Jonathan to die there.'" [27] Then all the officials came to Jeremiah and asked him, and he answered them as the king had instructed him. So they stopped speaking with him, for the conversation had not been overheard. [28] And Jeremiah remained in the court of the guard until the day that Jerusalem was taken.

The Fall of Jerusalem

39 In the ninth year of Zedekiah king of Judah, in the tenth month, Nebuchadnezzar king of Babylon and all his army came against Jerusalem and besieged it. [2] In the eleventh year of Zedekiah, in the fourth month, on the ninth day of the month, a breach was made in the city. [3] Then all the officials of the king of Babylon came and sat in the middle gate: Nergal-sar-ezer of Samgar, Nebu-sar-sekim the Rab-saris, Nergal-sar-ezer the Rab-mag, with all the rest of the officers of the king of Babylon. [4] When Zedekiah king of Judah and all the soldiers saw them, they fled, going out of the city at night by way of the king's garden through the gate between the two walls; and they went toward the Arabah. [5] But the army of the Chaldeans pursued them and overtook Zedekiah in the plains of Jericho. And when they had taken him, they brought him up to Nebuchadnezzar king of Babylon, at Riblah, in the land of Hamath; and he passed sentence on him. [6] The king of Babylon slaughtered the sons of Zedekiah at Riblah before his eyes, and the king of Babylon slaughtered all the nobles of Judah. [7] He put out the eyes of Zedekiah and bound him in chains to take him to Babylon. [8] The Chaldeans burned the king's house and the house of the people, and broke down the walls of Jerusalem. [9] Then Nebuzaradan, the captain of the guard, carried into exile to Babylon the rest of the people who were left in the city, those who had deserted to him, and the people who remained. [10] Nebuzaradan, the captain of the guard, left in the land of Judah some of the poor people who owned nothing, and gave them vineyards and fields at the same time.

The LORD Delivers Jeremiah

[11] Nebuchadnezzar king of Babylon gave command concerning Jeremiah through Nebuzaradan, the captain of the guard, saying,

[12] "Take him, look after him well, and do him no harm, but deal with him as he tells you." [13] So Nebuzaradan the captain of the guard, Nebushazban the Rab-saris, Nergal-sar-ezer the Rab-mag, and all the chief officers of the king of Babylon [14] sent and took Jeremiah from the court of the guard. They entrusted him to Gedaliah the son of Ahikam, son of Shaphan, that he should take him home. So he lived among the people.

[15] The word of the LORD came to Jeremiah while he was shut up in the court of the guard: [16] "Go, and say to Ebed-melech the Ethiopian, 'Thus says the LORD of hosts, the God of Israel: Behold, I will fulfill my words against this city for harm and not for good, and they shall be accomplished before you on that day. [17] But I will deliver you on that day, declares the LORD, and you shall not be given into the hand of the men of whom you are afraid. [18] For I will surely save you, and you shall not fall by the sword, but you shall have your life as a prize of war, because you have put your trust in me, declares the LORD.'"

Jeremiah Remains in Judah

40 The word that came to Jeremiah from the LORD after Nebuzaradan the captain of the guard had let him go from Ramah, when he took him bound in chains along with all the captives of Jerusalem and Judah who were being exiled to Babylon. [2] The captain of the guard took Jeremiah and said to him, "The LORD your God pronounced this disaster against this place. [3] The LORD has brought it about, and has done as he said. Because you sinned against the LORD and did not obey his voice, this thing has come upon you. [4] Now, behold, I release you today from the chains on your hands. If it seems good to you to come with me to Babylon, come, and I will look after you well, but if it seems wrong to you to come with me to Babylon, do not come. See, the whole land is before you; go wherever you think it good and right to go. [5] If you remain,[1] then return to Gedaliah the son of Ahikam, son of Shaphan, whom the king of Babylon appointed governor of the cities of Judah, and dwell with him among the people. Or go wherever you think it right to go." So the captain of the guard gave him an allowance of food and a present, and let him go. [6] Then Jeremiah went to Gedaliah the son of Ahikam, at Mizpah, and

lived with him among the people who were left in the land.

[7] When all the captains of the forces in the open country and their men heard that the king of Babylon had appointed Gedaliah the son of Ahikam governor in the land and had committed to him men, women, and children, those of the poorest of the land who had not been taken into exile to Babylon, [8] they went to Gedaliah at Mizpah—Ishmael the son of Nethaniah, Johanan the son of Kareah, Seraiah the son of Tanhumeth, the sons of Ephai the Netophathite, Jezaniah the son of the Maacathite, they and their men. [9] Gedaliah the son of Ahikam, son of Shaphan, swore to them and their men, saying, "Do not be afraid to serve the Chaldeans. Dwell in the land and serve the king of Babylon, and it shall be well with you. [10] As for me, I will dwell at Mizpah, to represent you before the Chaldeans who will come to us. But as for you, gather wine and summer fruits and oil, and store them in your vessels, and dwell in your cities that you have taken." [11] Likewise, when all the Judeans who were in Moab and among the Ammonites and in Edom and in other lands heard that the king of Babylon had left a remnant in Judah and had appointed Gedaliah the son of Ahikam, son of Shaphan, as governor over them, [12] then all the Judeans returned from all the places to which they had been driven and came to the land of Judah, to Gedaliah at Mizpah. And they gathered wine and summer fruits in great abundance.

[13] Now Johanan the son of Kareah and all the leaders of the forces in the open country came to Gedaliah at Mizpah [14] and said to him, "Do you know that Baalis the king of the Ammonites has sent Ishmael the son of Nethaniah to take your life?" But Gedaliah the son of Ahikam would not believe them. [15] Then Johanan the son of Kareah spoke secretly to Gedaliah at Mizpah, "Please let me go and strike down Ishmael the son of Nethaniah, and no one will know it. Why should he take your life, so that all the Judeans who are gathered about you would be scattered, and the remnant of Judah would perish?" [16] But Gedaliah the son of Ahikam said to Johanan the son of Kareah, "You shall not do this thing, for you are speaking falsely of Ishmael."

Gedaliah Murdered

41 In the seventh month, Ishmael the son of Nethaniah, son of Elishama, of the royal family, one of the chief officers of

---

[1] Syriac; the meaning of the Hebrew phrase is uncertain

the king, came with ten men to Gedaliah the son of Ahikam, at Mizpah. As they ate bread together there at Mizpah, ² Ishmael the son of Nethaniah and the ten men with him rose up and struck down Gedaliah the son of Ahikam, son of Shaphan, with the sword, and killed him, whom the king of Babylon had appointed governor in the land. ³ Ishmael also struck down all the Judeans who were with Gedaliah at Mizpah, and the Chaldean soldiers who happened to be there.

⁴ On the day after the murder of Gedaliah, before anyone knew of it, ⁵ eighty men arrived from Shechem and Shiloh and Samaria, with their beards shaved and their clothes torn, and their bodies gashed, bringing grain offerings and incense to present at the temple of the LORD. ⁶ And Ishmael the son of Nethaniah came out from Mizpah to meet them, weeping as he came. As he met them, he said to them, "Come in to Gedaliah the son of Ahikam." ⁷ When they came into the city, Ishmael the son of Nethaniah and the men with him slaughtered them and cast them into a cistern. ⁸ But there were ten men among them who said to Ishmael, "Do not put us to death, for we have stores of wheat, barley, oil, and honey hidden in the fields." So he refrained and did not put them to death with their companions.

⁹ Now the cistern into which Ishmael had thrown all the bodies of the men whom he had struck down along with¹ Gedaliah was the large cistern that King Asa had made for defense against Baasha king of Israel; Ishmael the son of Nethaniah filled it with the slain. ¹⁰ Then Ishmael took captive all the rest of the people who were in Mizpah, the king's daughters and all the people who were left at Mizpah, whom Nebuzaradan, the captain of the guard, had committed to Gedaliah the son of Ahikam. Ishmael the son of Nethaniah took them captive and set out to cross over to the Ammonites.

¹¹ But when Johanan the son of Kareah and all the leaders of the forces with him heard of all the evil that Ishmael the son of Nethaniah had done, ¹² they took all their men and went to fight against Ishmael the son of Nethaniah. They came upon him at the great pool that is in Gibeon. ¹³ And when all the people who were with Ishmael saw Johanan the son of Kareah and all the leaders of the forces with him, they rejoiced. ¹⁴ So all the people whom Ishmael had carried away captive from Mizpah

turned around and came back, and went to Johanan the son of Kareah. ¹⁵ But Ishmael the son of Nethaniah escaped from Johanan with eight men, and went to the Ammonites. ¹⁶ Then Johanan the son of Kareah and all the leaders of the forces with him took from Mizpah all the rest of the people whom he had recovered from Ishmael the son of Nethaniah, after he had struck down Gedaliah the son of Ahikam—soldiers, women, children, and eunuchs, whom Johanan brought back from Gibeon. ¹⁷ And they went and stayed at Geruth Chimham near Bethlehem, intending to go to Egypt ¹⁸ because of the Chaldeans. For they were afraid of them, because Ishmael the son of Nethaniah had struck down Gedaliah the son of Ahikam, whom the king of Babylon had made governor over the land.

Warning Against Going to Egypt

42 Then all the commanders of the forces, and Johanan the son of Kareah and Jezaniah the son of Hoshaiah, and all the people from the least to the greatest, came near ² and said to Jeremiah the prophet, "Let our plea for mercy come before you, and pray to the LORD your God for us, for all this remnant—because we are left with but a few, as your eyes see us— ³ that the LORD your God may show us the way we should go, and the thing that we should do." ⁴ Jeremiah the prophet said to them, "I have heard you. Behold, I will pray to the LORD your God according to your request, and whatever the LORD answers you I will tell you. I will keep nothing back from you." ⁵ Then they said to Jeremiah, "May the LORD be a true and faithful witness against us if we do not act according to all the word with which the LORD your God sends you to us. ⁶ Whether it is good or bad, we will obey the voice of the LORD our God to whom we are sending you, that it may be well with us when we obey the voice of the LORD our God."

⁷ At the end of ten days the word of the LORD came to Jeremiah. ⁸ Then he summoned Johanan the son of Kareah and all the commanders of the forces who were with him, and all the people from the least to the greatest, ⁹ and said to them, "Thus says the LORD, the God of Israel, to whom you sent me to present your plea for mercy before him: ¹⁰ If you will remain in this land, then I will build you up and not pull you down; I will plant you, and not

---

¹ Hebrew *by the hand of*

pluck you up; for I relent of the disaster that I did to you. [11] Do not fear the king of Babylon, of whom you are afraid. Do not fear him, declares the LORD, for I am with you, to save you and to deliver you from his hand. [12] I will grant you mercy, that he may have mercy on you and let you remain in your own land. [13] But if you say, 'We will not remain in this land,' disobeying the voice of the LORD your God [14] and saying, 'No, we will go to the land of Egypt, where we shall not see war or hear the sound of the trumpet or be hungry for bread, and we will dwell there,' [15] then hear the word of the LORD, O remnant of Judah. Thus says the LORD of hosts, the God of Israel: If you set your faces to enter Egypt and go to live there, [16] then the sword that you fear shall overtake you there in the land of Egypt, and the famine of which you are afraid shall follow close after you to Egypt, and there you shall die. [17] All the men who set their faces to go to Egypt to live there shall die by the sword, by famine, and by pestilence. They shall have no remnant or survivor from the disaster that I will bring upon them.

[18] "For thus says the LORD of hosts, the God of Israel: As my anger and my wrath were poured out on the inhabitants of Jerusalem, so my wrath will be poured out on you when you go to Egypt. You shall become an execration, a horror, a curse, and a taunt. You shall see this place no more. [19] The LORD has said to you, O remnant of Judah, 'Do not go to Egypt.' Know for a certainty that I have warned you this day [20] that you have gone astray at the cost of your lives. For you sent me to the LORD your God, saying, 'Pray for us to the LORD our God, and whatever the LORD our God says, declare to us and we will do it.' [21] And I have this day declared it to you, but you have not obeyed the voice of the LORD your God in anything that he sent me to tell you. [22] Now therefore know for a certainty that you shall die by the sword, by famine, and by pestilence in the place where you desire to go to live."

Jeremiah Taken to Egypt

43 When Jeremiah finished speaking to all the people all these words of the LORD their God, with which the LORD their God had sent him to them, [2] Azariah the son of Hoshaiah and Johanan the son of Kareah and all the insolent men said to Jeremiah, "You are telling a lie. The LORD our God did not send you

to say, 'Do not go to Egypt to live there,' [3] but Baruch the son of Neriah has set you against us, to deliver us into the hand of the Chaldeans, that they may kill us or take us into exile in Babylon." [4] So Johanan the son of Kareah and all the commanders of the forces and all the people did not obey the voice of the LORD, to remain in the land of Judah. [5] But Johanan the son of Kareah and all the commanders of the forces took all the remnant of Judah who had returned to live in the land of Judah from all the nations to which they had been driven— [6] the men, the women, the children, the princesses, and every person whom Nebuzaradan the captain of the guard had left with Gedaliah the son of Ahikam, son of Shaphan; also Jeremiah the prophet and Baruch the son of Neriah. [7] And they came into the land of Egypt, for they did not obey the voice of the LORD. And they arrived at Tahpanhes.

[8] Then the word of the LORD came to Jeremiah in Tahpanhes: [9] "Take in your hands large stones and hide them in the mortar in the pavement that is at the entrance to Pharaoh's palace in Tahpanhes, in the sight of the men of Judah, [10] and say to them, 'Thus says the LORD of hosts, the God of Israel: Behold, I will send and take Nebuchadnezzar the king of Babylon, my servant, and I will set his throne above these stones that I have hidden, and he will spread his royal canopy over them. [11] He shall come and strike the land of Egypt, giving over to the pestilence those who are doomed to the pestilence, to captivity those who are doomed to captivity, and to the sword those who are doomed to the sword. [12] I shall kindle a fire in the temples of the gods of Egypt, and he shall burn them and carry them away captive. And he shall clean the land of Egypt as a shepherd cleans his cloak of vermin, and he shall go away from there in peace. [13] He shall break the obelisks of Heliopolis, which is in the land of Egypt, and the temples of the gods of Egypt he shall burn with fire.'"

Judgment for Idolatry

44 The word that came to Jeremiah concerning all the Judeans who lived in the land of Egypt, at Migdol, at Tahpanhes, at Memphis, and in the land of Pathros, [2] "Thus says the LORD of hosts, the God of Israel: You have seen all the disaster that I brought upon Jerusalem and upon all the cities of Judah.

Behold, this day they are a desolation, and no one dwells in them, [3] because of the evil that they committed, provoking me to anger, in that they went to make offerings and serve other gods that they knew not, neither they, nor you, nor your fathers. [4] Yet I persistently sent to you all my servants the prophets, saying, 'Oh, do not do this abomination that I hate!' [5] But they did not listen or incline their ear, to turn from their evil and make no offerings to other gods. [6] Therefore my wrath and my anger were poured out and kindled in the cities of Judah and in the streets of Jerusalem, and they became a waste and a desolation, as at this day. [7] And now thus says the LORD God of hosts, the God of Israel: Why do you commit this great evil against yourselves, to cut off from you man and woman, infant and child, from the midst of Judah, leaving you no remnant? [8] Why do you provoke me to anger with the works of your hands, making offerings to other gods in the land of Egypt where you have come to live, so that you may be cut off and become a curse and a taunt among all the nations of the earth? [9] Have you forgotten the evil of your fathers, the evil of the kings of Judah, the evil of their[1] wives, your own evil, and the evil of your wives, which they committed in the land of Judah and in the streets of Jerusalem? [10] They have not humbled themselves even to this day, nor have they feared, nor walked in my law and my statutes that I set before you and before your fathers.

[11] "Therefore thus says the LORD of hosts, the God of Israel: Behold, I will set my face against you for harm, to cut off all Judah. [12] I will take the remnant of Judah who have set their faces to come to the land of Egypt to live, and they shall all be consumed. In the land of Egypt they shall fall; by the sword and by famine they shall be consumed. From the least to the greatest, they shall die by the sword and by famine, and they shall become an oath, a horror, a curse, and a taunt. [13] I will punish those who dwell in the land of Egypt, as I have punished Jerusalem, with the sword, with famine, and with pestilence, [14] so that none of the remnant of Judah who have come to live in the land of Egypt shall escape or survive or return to the land of Judah, to which they desire to return to dwell there. For they shall not return, except some fugitives."

[15] Then all the men who knew that their wives had made offerings to other gods, and all the women who stood by, a great assembly, all the people who lived in Pathros in the land of Egypt, answered Jeremiah: [16] "As for the word that you have spoken to us in the name of the LORD, we will not listen to you. [17] But we will do everything that we have vowed, make offerings to the queen of heaven and pour out drink offerings to her, as we did, both we and our fathers, our kings and our officials, in the cities of Judah and in the streets of Jerusalem. For then we had plenty of food, and prospered, and saw no disaster. [18] But since we left off making offerings to the queen of heaven and pouring out drink offerings to her, we have lacked everything and have been consumed by the sword and by famine." [19] And the women said,[2] "When we made offerings to the queen of heaven and poured out drink offerings to her, was it without our husbands' approval that we made cakes for her bearing her image and poured out drink offerings to her?"

[20] Then Jeremiah said to all the people, men and women, all the people who had given him this answer: [21] "As for the offerings that you offered in the cities of Judah and in the streets of Jerusalem, you and your fathers, your kings and your officials, and the people of the land, did not the LORD remember them? Did it not come into his mind? [22] The LORD could no longer bear your evil deeds and the abominations that you committed. Therefore your land has become a desolation and a waste and a curse, without inhabitant, as it is this day. [23] It is because you made offerings and because you sinned against the LORD and did not obey the voice of the LORD or walk in his law and in his statutes and in his testimonies that this disaster has happened to you, as at this day."

[24] Jeremiah said to all the people and all the women, "Hear the word of the LORD, all you of Judah who are in the land of Egypt. [25] Thus says the LORD of hosts, the God of Israel: You and your wives have declared with your mouths, and have fulfilled it with your hands, saying, 'We will surely perform our vows that we have made, to make offerings to the queen of heaven and to pour out drink offerings to her.' Then confirm your vows and perform your vows! [26] Therefore hear the word of the LORD, all you of Judah who dwell in the land of Egypt: Behold, I have sworn by my great name, says the LORD, that my name shall no more be invoked by the mouth of any man of Judah in all the land of Egypt, saying, 'As the Lord GOD lives.' [27] Behold, I am watching

[1] Hebrew *his* [2] Compare Syriac; Hebrew lacks *And the women said*

over them for disaster and not for good. All the men of Judah who are in the land of Egypt shall be consumed by the sword and by famine, until there is an end of them. ²⁸ And those who escape the sword shall return from the land of Egypt to the land of Judah, few in number; and all the remnant of Judah, who came to the land of Egypt to live, shall know whose word will stand, mine or theirs. ²⁹ This shall be the sign to you, declares the LORD, that I will punish you in this place, in order that you may know that my words will surely stand against you for harm: ³⁰ Thus says the LORD, Behold, I will give Pharaoh Hophra king of Egypt into the hand of his enemies and into the hand of those who seek his life, as I gave Zedekiah king of Judah into the hand of Nebuchadnezzar king of Babylon, who was his enemy and sought his life."

Message to Baruch

45 The word that Jeremiah the prophet spoke to Baruch the son of Neriah, when he wrote these words in a book at the dictation of Jeremiah, in the fourth year of Jehoiakim the son of Josiah, king of Judah: ²"Thus says the LORD, the God of Israel, to you, O Baruch: ³ You said, 'Woe is me! For the LORD has added sorrow to my pain. I am weary with my groaning, and I find no rest.' ⁴ Thus shall you say to him, Thus says the LORD: Behold, what I have built I am breaking down, and what I have planted I am plucking up—that is, the whole land. ⁵ And do you seek great things for yourself? Seek them not, for behold, I am bringing disaster upon all flesh, declares the LORD. But I will give you your life as a prize of war in all places to which you may go."

Judgment on Egypt

46 The word of the LORD that came to Jeremiah the prophet concerning the nations.

² About Egypt. Concerning the army of Pharaoh Neco, king of Egypt, which was by the river Euphrates at Carchemish and which Nebuchadnezzar king of Babylon defeated in the fourth year of Jehoiakim the son of Josiah, king of Judah:

³   "Prepare buckler and shield,
        and advance for battle!
⁴   Harness the horses;
        mount, O horsemen!

Take your stations with your helmets,
        polish your spears,
        put on your armor!
⁵   Why have I seen it?
They are dismayed
        and have turned backward.
Their warriors are beaten down
        and have fled in haste;
they look not back—
        terror on every side!
                        declares the LORD.

⁶   "The swift cannot flee away,
        nor the warrior escape;
in the north by the river Euphrates
        they have stumbled and fallen.

⁷   "Who is this, rising like the Nile,
        like rivers whose waters surge?
⁸   Egypt rises like the Nile,
        like rivers whose waters surge.
He said, 'I will rise, I will cover the earth,
        I will destroy cities and their inhabi-
        tants.'
⁹   Advance, O horses,
        and rage, O chariots!
Let the warriors go out:
        men of Cush and Put who handle the
        shield,
        men of Lud, skilled in handling the
        bow.
¹⁰ That day is the day of the Lord GOD of
        hosts,
        a day of vengeance,
        to avenge himself on his foes.
The sword shall devour and be sated
        and drink its fill of their blood.
For the Lord GOD of hosts holds a sacrifice
        in the north country by the river
        Euphrates.
¹¹ Go up to Gilead, and take balm,
        O virgin daughter of Egypt!
In vain you have used many medicines;
        there is no healing for you.
¹² The nations have heard of your shame,
        and the earth is full of your cry;
for warrior has stumbled against warrior;
        they have both fallen together."

¹³ The word that the LORD spoke to Jeremiah the prophet about the coming of Nebuchadnezzar king of Babylon to strike the land of Egypt:

14 "Declare in Egypt, and proclaim in Migdol;
    proclaim in Memphis and Tahpanhes;
say, 'Stand ready and be prepared,
    for the sword shall devour around you.'
15 Why are your mighty ones face down?
    They do not stand[1]
    because the LORD thrust them down.
16 He made many stumble, and they fell,
    and they said one to another,
'Arise, and let us go back to our own people
    and to the land of our birth,
    because of the sword of the oppressor.'
17 Call the name of Pharaoh, king of Egypt,
    'Noisy one who lets the hour go by.'

18 "As I live, declares the King,
    whose name is the LORD of hosts,
like Tabor among the mountains
    and like Carmel by the sea, shall one
    come.
19 Prepare yourselves baggage for exile,
    O inhabitants of Egypt!
For Memphis shall become a waste,
    a ruin, without inhabitant.

20 "A beautiful heifer is Egypt,
    but a biting fly from the north has come
    upon her.
21 Even her hired soldiers in her midst
    are like fattened calves;
yes, they have turned and fled together;
    they did not stand,
for the day of their calamity has come
    upon them,
    the time of their punishment.

22 "She makes a sound like a serpent gliding
    away;
    for her enemies march in force
and come against her with axes
    like those who fell trees.
23 They shall cut down her forest,
           declares the LORD,
    though it is impenetrable,
because they are more numerous than
    locusts;
    they are without number.
24 The daughter of Egypt shall be put to
    shame;
    she shall be delivered into the hand of a
    people from the north."

25 The LORD of hosts, the God of Israel, said:
"Behold, I am bringing punishment upon
Amon of Thebes, and Pharaoh and Egypt and
her gods and her kings, upon Pharaoh and
those who trust in him. 26 I will deliver them
into the hand of those who seek their life, into
the hand of Nebuchadnezzar king of Babylon
and his officers. Afterward Egypt shall be inhabited as in the days of old, declares the LORD.

27 "But fear not, O Jacob my servant,
    nor be dismayed, O Israel,
for behold, I will save you from far away,
    and your offspring from the land of
    their captivity.
Jacob shall return and have quiet and ease,
    and none shall make him afraid.
28 Fear not, O Jacob my servant,
           declares the LORD,
    for I am with you.
I will make a full end of all the nations
    to which I have driven you,
    but of you I will not make a full end.
I will discipline you in just measure,
    and I will by no means leave you
    unpunished."

Judgment on the Philistines

47 The word of the LORD that came to
Jeremiah the prophet concerning the
Philistines, before Pharaoh struck down Gaza.

2 "Thus says the LORD:
Behold, waters are rising out of the north,
    and shall become an overflowing tor-
    rent;
they shall overflow the land and all that
    fills it,
    the city and those who dwell in it.
Men shall cry out,
    and every inhabitant of the land shall
    wail.
3 At the noise of the stamping of the hoofs
    of his stallions,
    at the rushing of his chariots, at the
    rumbling of their wheels,
the fathers look not back to their children,
    so feeble are their hands,
4 because of the day that is coming to
    destroy
    all the Philistines,
to cut off from Tyre and Sidon
    every helper that remains.
For the LORD is destroying the Philistines,
    the remnant of the coastland of
    Caphtor.

[1] Hebrew He does not stand

5 Baldness has come upon Gaza;
    Ashkelon has perished.
  O remnant of their valley,
    how long will you gash yourselves?
6 Ah, sword of the LORD!
    How long till you are quiet?
  Put yourself into your scabbard;
    rest and be still!
7 How can it[1] be quiet
    when the LORD has given it a charge?
  Against Ashkelon and against the sea-
    shore
    he has appointed it."

Judgment on Moab

48 Concerning Moab.
    Thus says the LORD of hosts, the God
of Israel:

  "Woe to Nebo, for it is laid waste!
    Kiriathaim is put to shame, it is
      taken;
  the fortress is put to shame and broken
    down;
2   the renown of Moab is no more.
  In Heshbon they planned disaster against
    her:
    'Come, let us cut her off from being a
      nation!'
  You also, O Madmen, shall be brought to
    silence;
    the sword shall pursue you.

3 "A voice! A cry from Horonaim,
    'Desolation and great destruction!'
4 Moab is destroyed;
    her little ones have made a cry.
5 For at the ascent of Luhith
    they go up weeping;[2]
  for at the descent of Horonaim
    they have heard the distressed cry[3] of
      destruction.
6 Flee! Save yourselves!
    You will be like a juniper in the des-
      ert!
7 For, because you trusted in your works and
    your treasures,
    you also shall be taken;
  and Chemosh shall go into exile
    with his priests and his officials.
8 The destroyer shall come upon every city,
    and no city shall escape;

  the valley shall perish,
    and the plain shall be destroyed,
    as the LORD has spoken.
9 "Give wings to Moab,
    for she would fly away;
  her cities shall become a desolation,
    with no inhabitant in them.

10 "Cursed is he who does the work of the
LORD with slackness, and cursed is he who
keeps back his sword from bloodshed.

11 "Moab has been at ease from his youth
    and has settled on his dregs;
  he has not been emptied from vessel to ves-
    sel,
    nor has he gone into exile;
  so his taste remains in him,
    and his scent is not changed.

12 "Therefore, behold, the days are coming,
declares the LORD, when I shall send to him
pourers who will pour him, and empty his vessels and break his[4] jars in pieces. 13 Then Moab
shall be ashamed of Chemosh, as the house of
Israel was ashamed of Bethel, their confidence.

14 "How do you say, 'We are heroes
    and mighty men of war'?
15 The destroyer of Moab and his cities has
    come up,
  and the choicest of his young men have
    gone down to slaughter,
  declares the King, whose name is the
    LORD of hosts.
16 The calamity of Moab is near at hand,
    and his affliction hastens swiftly.
17 Grieve for him, all you who are around
    him,
  and all who know his name;
  say, 'How the mighty scepter is broken,
    the glorious staff.'

18 "Come down from your glory,
    and sit on the parched ground,
    O inhabitant of Dibon!
  For the destroyer of Moab has come up
    against you;
  he has destroyed your strongholds.
19 Stand by the way and watch,
    O inhabitant of Aroer!
  Ask him who flees and her who escapes;
    say, 'What has happened?'
20 Moab is put to shame, for it is broken;
    wail and cry!

[1] Septuagint, Vulgate; Hebrew *you* [2] Hebrew *weeping goes up with weeping* [3] Septuagint (compare Isaiah 15:5) *heard the cry* [4] Septuagint, Aquila; Hebrew *their*

Tell it beside the Arnon,
   that Moab is laid waste.

21 "Judgment has come upon the tableland, upon Holon, and Jahzah, and Mephaath, 22 and Dibon, and Nebo, and Beth-diblathaim, 23 and Kiriathaim, and Beth-gamul, and Beth-meon, 24 and Kerioth, and Bozrah, and all the cities of the land of Moab, far and near. 25 The horn of Moab is cut off, and his arm is broken, declares the LORD.

26 "Make him drunk, because he magnified himself against the LORD, so that Moab shall wallow in his vomit, and he too shall be held in derision. 27 Was not Israel a derision to you? Was he found among thieves, that whenever you spoke of him you wagged your head?

28   "Leave the cities, and dwell in the rock,
      O inhabitants of Moab!
   Be like the dove that nests
      in the sides of the mouth of a gorge.
29   We have heard of the pride of Moab—
      he is very proud—
   of his loftiness, his pride, and his arrogance,
      and the haughtiness of his heart.
30   I know his insolence, declares the LORD;
      his boasts are false,
      his deeds are false.
31   Therefore I wail for Moab;
      I cry out for all Moab;
      for the men of Kir-hareseth I mourn.
32   More than for Jazer I weep for you,
      O vine of Sibmah!
   Your branches passed over the sea,
      reached to the Sea of Jazer;
   on your summer fruits and your grapes
      the destroyer has fallen.
33   Gladness and joy have been taken away
      from the fruitful land of Moab;
   I have made the wine cease from the wine-
      presses;
      no one treads them with shouts of joy;
      the shouting is not the shout of joy.

34 "From the outcry at Heshbon even to Elealeh, as far as Jahaz they utter their voice, from Zoar to Horonaim and Eglath-shelishiyah. For the waters of Nimrim also have become desolate. 35 And I will bring to an end in Moab, declares the LORD, him who offers sacrifice in the high place and makes offerings to his god. 36 Therefore my heart moans for Moab like a flute, and my heart moans like a flute for the men of Kir-hareseth. Therefore the riches they gained have perished.

37 "For every head is shaved and every beard cut off. On all the hands are gashes, and around the waist is sackcloth. 38 On all the housetops of Moab and in the squares there is nothing but lamentation, for I have broken Moab like a vessel for which no one cares, declares the LORD. 39 How it is broken! How they wail! How Moab has turned his back in shame! So Moab has become a derision and a horror to all that are around him."

40   For thus says the LORD:
   "Behold, one shall fly swiftly like an eagle
      and spread his wings against Moab;
41   the cities shall be taken
      and the strongholds seized.
   The heart of the warriors of Moab shall be
      in that day
      like the heart of a woman in her birth
         pains;
42   Moab shall be destroyed and be no longer
      a people,
   because he magnified himself against
      the LORD.
43   Terror, pit, and snare
      are before you, O inhabitant of Moab!
                     declares the LORD.
44   He who flees from the terror
      shall fall into the pit,
   and he who climbs out of the pit
      shall be caught in the snare.
   For I will bring these things upon Moab,
      the year of their punishment,
                     declares the LORD.

45   "In the shadow of Heshbon
      fugitives stop without strength,
   for fire came out from Heshbon,
      flame from the house of Sihon;
   it has destroyed the forehead of Moab,
      the crown of the sons of tumult.
46   Woe to you, O Moab!
      The people of Chemosh are undone,
   for your sons have been taken captive,
      and your daughters into captivity.
47   Yet I will restore the fortunes of Moab
      in the latter days, declares the LORD."
   Thus far is the judgment on Moab.

Judgment on Ammon

49 Concerning the Ammonites.
   Thus says the LORD:

   "Has Israel no sons?
      Has he no heir?

Why then has Milcom[1] dispossessed Gad,
and his people settled in its cities?

2 Therefore, behold, the days are coming,
declares the LORD,
when I will cause the battle cry to be heard
against Rabbah of the Ammonites;
it shall become a desolate mound,
and its villages shall be burned with
fire;
then Israel shall dispossess those who dispossessed him,
says the LORD.

3 "Wail, O Heshbon, for Ai is laid waste!
Cry out, O daughters of Rabbah!
Put on sackcloth,
lament, and run to and fro among the
hedges!
For Milcom shall go into exile,
with his priests and his officials.

4 Why do you boast of your valleys,[2]
O faithless daughter,
who trusted in her treasures, saying,
'Who will come against me?'

5 Behold, I will bring terror upon you,
declares the Lord GOD of hosts,
from all who are around you,
and you shall be driven out, every man
straight before him,
with none to gather the fugitives.

6 "But afterward I will restore the fortunes of
the Ammonites, declares the LORD."

Judgment on Edom

7 Concerning Edom.
Thus says the LORD of hosts:

"Is wisdom no more in Teman?
Has counsel perished from the prudent?
Has their wisdom vanished?

8 Flee, turn back, dwell in the depths,
O inhabitants of Dedan!
For I will bring the calamity of Esau upon
him,
the time when I punish him.

9 If grape gatherers came to you,
would they not leave gleanings?
If thieves came by night,
would they not destroy only enough for
themselves?

10 But I have stripped Esau bare;
I have uncovered his hiding places,
and he is not able to conceal himself.

His children are destroyed, and his brothers,
and his neighbors; and he is no more.

11 Leave your fatherless children; I will keep
them alive;
and let your widows trust in me."

12 For thus says the LORD: "If those who did
not deserve to drink the cup must drink it, will
you go unpunished? You shall not go unpunished, but you must drink. 13 For I have sworn
by myself, declares the LORD, that Bozrah shall
become a horror, a taunt, a waste, and a curse,
and all her cities shall be perpetual wastes."

14 I have heard a message from the LORD,
and an envoy has been sent among the
nations:
"Gather yourselves together and come
against her,
and rise up for battle!

15 For behold, I will make you small among
the nations,
despised among mankind.

16 The horror you inspire has deceived you,
and the pride of your heart,
you who live in the clefts of the rock,[3]
who hold the height of the hill.
Though you make your nest as high as the
eagle's,
I will bring you down from there,
declares the LORD.

17 "Edom shall become a horror. Everyone
who passes by it will be horrified and will hiss
because of all its disasters. 18 As when Sodom
and Gomorrah and their neighboring cities were overthrown, says the LORD, no man
shall dwell there, no man shall sojourn in her.
19 Behold, like a lion coming up from the jungle
of the Jordan against a perennial pasture, I will
suddenly make him[4] run away from her. And I
will appoint over her whomever I choose. For
who is like me? Who will summon me? What
shepherd can stand before me? 20 Therefore hear
the plan that the LORD has made against Edom
and the purposes that he has formed against the
inhabitants of Teman: Even the little ones of
the flock shall be dragged away. Surely their fold
shall be appalled at their fate. 21 At the sound of
their fall the earth shall tremble; the sound of
their cry shall be heard at the Red Sea. 22 Behold,
one shall mount up and fly swiftly like an eagle
and spread his wings against Bozrah, and the

---

1 Or their king; also verse 3 2 Hebrew boast of your valleys, your valley flows 3 Or of Sela 4 Septuagint, Syriac them

heart of the warriors of Edom shall be in that day like the heart of a woman in her birth pains."

Judgment on Damascus

²³ Concerning Damascus:

"Hamath and Arpad are confounded,
    for they have heard bad news;
they melt in fear,
    they are troubled like the sea that cannot be quiet.
²⁴ Damascus has become feeble, she turned to flee,
    and panic seized her;
anguish and sorrows have taken hold of her,
    as of a woman in labor.
²⁵ How is the famous city not forsaken,
    the city of my joy?
²⁶ Therefore her young men shall fall in her squares,
    and all her soldiers shall be destroyed in that day,
                declares the LORD of hosts.
²⁷ And I will kindle a fire in the wall of Damascus,
    and it shall devour the strongholds of Ben-hadad."

Judgment on Kedar and Hazor

²⁸ Concerning Kedar and the kingdoms of Hazor that Nebuchadnezzar king of Babylon struck down.

Thus says the LORD:
"Rise up, advance against Kedar!
    Destroy the people of the east!
²⁹ Their tents and their flocks shall be taken,
    their curtains and all their goods;
their camels shall be led away from them,
    and men shall cry to them: 'Terror on every side!'
³⁰ Flee, wander far away, dwell in the depths,
    O inhabitants of Hazor!
                declares the LORD.
For Nebuchadnezzar king of Babylon
    has made a plan against you
    and formed a purpose against you.

³¹ "Rise up, advance against a nation at ease,
    that dwells securely,
                declares the LORD,
that has no gates or bars,
    that dwells alone.
³² Their camels shall become plunder,
    their herds of livestock a spoil.
I will scatter to every wind
    those who cut the corners of their hair,
and I will bring their calamity
    from every side of them,
                declares the LORD.
³³ Hazor shall become a haunt of jackals,
    an everlasting waste;
no man shall dwell there;
    no man shall sojourn in her."

Judgment on Elam

³⁴ The word of the LORD that came to Jeremiah the prophet concerning Elam, in the beginning of the reign of Zedekiah king of Judah.

³⁵ Thus says the LORD of hosts: "Behold, I will break the bow of Elam, the mainstay of their might. ³⁶ And I will bring upon Elam the four winds from the four quarters of heaven. And I will scatter them to all those winds, and there shall be no nation to which those driven out of Elam shall not come. ³⁷ I will terrify Elam before their enemies and before those who seek their life. I will bring disaster upon them, my fierce anger, declares the LORD. I will send the sword after them, until I have consumed them, ³⁸ and I will set my throne in Elam and destroy their king and officials, declares the LORD.

³⁹ "But in the latter days I will restore the fortunes of Elam, declares the LORD."

Judgment on Babylon

50 The word that the LORD spoke concerning Babylon, concerning the land of the Chaldeans, by Jeremiah the prophet:

² "Declare among the nations and proclaim,
    set up a banner and proclaim,
    conceal it not, and say:
'Babylon is taken,
    Bel is put to shame,
    Merodach is dismayed.
Her images are put to shame,
    her idols are dismayed.'

³ "For out of the north a nation has come up against her, which shall make her land a desolation, and none shall dwell in it; both man and beast shall flee away.

4 "In those days and in that time, declares the LORD, the people of Israel and the people of Judah shall come together, weeping as they come, and they shall seek the LORD their God. 5 They shall ask the way to Zion, with faces turned toward it, saying, 'Come, let us join ourselves to the LORD in an everlasting covenant that will never be forgotten.'

6 "My people have been lost sheep. Their shepherds have led them astray, turning them away on the mountains. From mountain to hill they have gone. They have forgotten their fold. 7 All who found them have devoured them, and their enemies have said, 'We are not guilty, for they have sinned against the LORD, their habitation of righteousness, the LORD, the hope of their fathers.'

8 "Flee from the midst of Babylon, and go out of the land of the Chaldeans, and be as male goats before the flock. 9 For behold, I am stirring up and bringing against Babylon a gathering of great nations, from the north country. And they shall array themselves against her. From there she shall be taken. Their arrows are like a skilled warrior who does not return empty-handed. 10 Chaldea shall be plundered; all who plunder her shall be sated, declares the LORD.

11 "Though you rejoice, though you exult,
   O plunderers of my heritage,
   though you frolic like a heifer in the pasture,
      and neigh like stallions,
12 your mother shall be utterly shamed,
      and she who bore you shall be disgraced.
   Behold, she shall be the last of the nations,
      a wilderness, a dry land, and a desert.
13 Because of the wrath of the LORD she shall not be inhabited
      but shall be an utter desolation;
   everyone who passes by Babylon shall be appalled,
      and hiss because of all her wounds.
14 Set yourselves in array against Babylon all around,
      all you who bend the bow;
   shoot at her, spare no arrows,
      for she has sinned against the LORD.
15 Raise a shout against her all around;
      she has surrendered;

her bulwarks have fallen;
      her walls are thrown down.
   For this is the vengeance of the LORD:
      take vengeance on her;
      do to her as she has done.
16 Cut off from Babylon the sower,
      and the one who handles the sickle in time of harvest;
   because of the sword of the oppressor,
      every one shall turn to his own people,
      and every one shall flee to his own land.

17 "Israel is a hunted sheep driven away by lions. First the king of Assyria devoured him, and now at last Nebuchadnezzar king of Babylon has gnawed his bones. 18 Therefore, thus says the LORD of hosts, the God of Israel: Behold, I am bringing punishment on the king of Babylon and his land, as I punished the king of Assyria. 19 I will restore Israel to his pasture, and he shall feed on Carmel and in Bashan, and his desire shall be satisfied on the hills of Ephraim and in Gilead. 20 In those days and in that time, declares the LORD, iniquity shall be sought in Israel, and there shall be none, and sin in Judah, and none shall be found, for I will pardon those whom I leave as a remnant.

21   "Go up against the land of Merathaim,[1]
      and against the inhabitants of Pekod.[2]
   Kill, and devote them to destruction,[3]
                              declares the LORD,
      and do all that I have commanded you.
22 The noise of battle is in the land,
      and great destruction!
23 How the hammer of the whole earth
      is cut down and broken!
   How Babylon has become
      a horror among the nations!
24 I set a snare for you and you were taken,
      O Babylon,
      and you did not know it;
   you were found and caught,
      because you opposed the LORD.
25 The LORD has opened his armory
      and brought out the weapons of his wrath,
   for the Lord GOD of hosts has a work to do
      in the land of the Chaldeans.
26 Come against her from every quarter;
      open her granaries;
   pile her up like heaps of grain, and devote her to destruction;
      let nothing be left of her.

[1] Merathaim means double rebellion [2] Pekod means punishment [3] That is, set apart (devote) as an offering to the Lord (for destruction)

27 Kill all her bulls;
　　let them go down to the slaughter.
　Woe to them, for their day has come,
　　the time of their punishment.

28 "A voice! They flee and escape from the land of Babylon, to declare in Zion the vengeance of the LORD our God, vengeance for his temple.
29 "Summon archers against Babylon, all those who bend the bow. Encamp around her; let no one escape. Repay her according to her deeds; do to her according to all that she has done. For she has proudly defied the LORD, the Holy One of Israel. 30 Therefore her young men shall fall in her squares, and all her soldiers shall be destroyed on that day, declares the LORD.

31 "Behold, I am against you, O proud one,
　　declares the Lord GOD of hosts,
　for your day has come,
　　the time when I will punish you.
32 The proud one shall stumble and fall,
　　with none to raise him up,
　and I will kindle a fire in his cities,
　　and it will devour all that is around
　　　him.

33 "Thus says the LORD of hosts: The people of Israel are oppressed, and the people of Judah with them. All who took them captive have held them fast; they refuse to let them go. 34 Their Redeemer is strong; the LORD of hosts is his name. He will surely plead their cause, that he may give rest to the earth, but unrest to the inhabitants of Babylon.

35 "A sword against the Chaldeans, declares
　　the LORD,
　　and against the inhabitants of
　　　Babylon,
　　and against her officials and her wise
　　　men!
36 A sword against the diviners,
　　that they may become fools!
　A sword against her warriors,
　　that they may be destroyed!
37 A sword against her horses and against her
　　chariots,
　　and against all the foreign troops in her
　　　midst,
　　that they may become women!
　A sword against all her treasures,
　　that they may be plundered!
38 A drought against her waters,
　　that they may be dried up!

For it is a land of images,
　　and they are mad over idols.

39 "Therefore wild beasts shall dwell with hyenas in Babylon,[1] and ostriches shall dwell in her. She shall never again have people, nor be inhabited for all generations. 40 As when God overthrew Sodom and Gomorrah and their neighboring cities, declares the LORD, so no man shall dwell there, and no son of man shall sojourn in her.

41 "Behold, a people comes from the north;
　　a mighty nation and many kings
　　are stirring from the farthest parts of
　　　the earth.
42 They lay hold of bow and spear;
　　they are cruel and have no mercy.
　The sound of them is like the roaring of
　　the sea;
　　they ride on horses,
　arrayed as a man for battle
　　against you, O daughter of Babylon!

43 "The king of Babylon heard the report of
　　them,
　　and his hands fell helpless;
　anguish seized him,
　　pain as of a woman in labor.

44 "Behold, like a lion coming up from the thicket of the Jordan against a perennial pasture, I will suddenly make them run away from her, and I will appoint over her whomever I choose. For who is like me? Who will summon me? What shepherd can stand before me? 45 Therefore hear the plan that the LORD has made against Babylon, and the purposes that he has formed against the land of the Chaldeans: Surely the little ones of their flock shall be dragged away; surely their fold shall be appalled at their fate. 46 At the sound of the capture of Babylon the earth shall tremble, and her cry shall be heard among the nations."

The Utter Destruction of Babylon

51 Thus says the LORD:
　"Behold, I will stir up the spirit of a
　　destroyer
　　against Babylon,
　　against the inhabitants of Leb-kamai,[2]
2 and I will send to Babylon winnowers,
　　and they shall winnow her,

---

[1] Hebrew lacks in Babylon [2] A code name for Chaldea

and they shall empty her land,
    when they come against her from every
      side
    on the day of trouble.

3 Let not the archer bend his bow,
    and let him not stand up in his armor.
Spare not her young men;
    devote to destruction[1] all her army.

4 They shall fall down slain in the land of the
    Chaldeans,
    and wounded in her streets.

5 For Israel and Judah have not been for-
    saken
    by their God, the LORD of hosts,
but the land of the Chaldeans[2] is full of
    guilt
    against the Holy One of Israel.

6 "Flee from the midst of Babylon;
    let every one save his life!
Be not cut off in her punishment,
    for this is the time of the LORD's ven-
      geance,
    the repayment he is rendering her.

7 Babylon was a golden cup in the LORD's
    hand,
    making all the earth drunken;
the nations drank of her wine;
    therefore the nations went mad.

8 Suddenly Babylon has fallen and been bro-
    ken;
    wail for her!
Take balm for her pain;
    perhaps she may be healed.

9 We would have healed Babylon,
    but she was not healed.
Forsake her, and let us go
    each to his own country,
for her judgment has reached up to heaven
    and has been lifted up even to the skies.

10 The LORD has brought about our vindica-
    tion;
    come, let us declare in Zion
    the work of the LORD our God.

11 "Sharpen the arrows!
    Take up the shields!

The LORD has stirred up the spirit of the kings
of the Medes, because his purpose concerning
Babylon is to destroy it, for that is the vengeance
of the LORD, the vengeance for his temple.

12 "Set up a standard against the walls of
    Babylon;
    make the watch strong;
set up watchmen;
    prepare the ambushes;
for the LORD has both planned and done
    what he spoke concerning the inhabi-
      tants of Babylon.

13 O you who dwell by many waters,
    rich in treasures,
your end has come;
    the thread of your life is cut.

14 The LORD of hosts has sworn by himself:
Surely I will fill you with men, as many as
    locusts,
    and they shall raise the shout of victory
      over you.

15 "It is he who made the earth by his power,
    who established the world by his wis-
      dom,
and by his understanding stretched out the
    heavens.

16 When he utters his voice there is a tumult
    of waters in the heavens,
    and he makes the mist rise from the
      ends of the earth.
He makes lightning for the rain,
    and he brings forth the wind from his
      storehouses.

17 Every man is stupid and without knowl-
    edge;
    every goldsmith is put to shame by his
      idols,
for his images are false,
    and there is no breath in them.

18 They are worthless, a work of delusion;
    at the time of their punishment they
      shall perish.

19 Not like these is he who is the portion of
    Jacob,
    for he is the one who formed all things,
and Israel is the tribe of his inheritance;
    the LORD of hosts is his name.

20 "You are my hammer and weapon of war:
    with you I break nations in pieces;
    with you I destroy kingdoms;

21 with you I break in pieces the horse and his
    rider;
    with you I break in pieces the chariot
    and the charioteer;

---

[1] That is, set apart (devote) as an offering to the Lord (for destruction) [2] Hebrew *their land*

²² with you I break in pieces man and
      woman;
        with you I break in pieces the old man
          and the youth;
        with you I break in pieces the young man
          and the young woman;
²³   with you I break in pieces the shepherd
          and his flock;
        with you I break in pieces the farmer and
          his team;
        with you I break in pieces governors
          and commanders.

²⁴ "I will repay Babylon and all the inhabitants of Chaldea before your very eyes for all
the evil that they have done in Zion, declares
the LORD.

²⁵ "Behold, I am against you, O destroying
      mountain,
                  declares the LORD,
        which destroys the whole earth;
      I will stretch out my hand against you,
        and roll you down from the crags,
        and make you a burnt mountain.
²⁶ No stone shall be taken from you for a cor-
      ner
        and no stone for a foundation,
      but you shall be a perpetual waste,
        declares the LORD.

²⁷ "Set up a standard on the earth;
        blow the trumpet among the nations;
      prepare the nations for war against her;
        summon against her the kingdoms,
        Ararat, Minni, and Ashkenaz;
      appoint a marshal against her;
        bring up horses like bristling locusts.
²⁸ Prepare the nations for war against her,
        the kings of the Medes, with their gov-
          ernors and deputies,
        and every land under their dominion.
²⁹ The land trembles and writhes in pain,
        for the LORD's purposes against Babylon
          stand,
      to make the land of Babylon a desolation,
        without inhabitant.
³⁰ The warriors of Babylon have ceased fight-
      ing;
        they remain in their strongholds;
      their strength has failed;
        they have become women;
      her dwellings are on fire;
        her bars are broken.

³¹ One runner runs to meet another,
        and one messenger to meet another,
      to tell the king of Babylon
        that his city is taken on every side;
³² the fords have been seized,
        the marshes are burned with fire,
        and the soldiers are in panic.
³³ For thus says the LORD of hosts, the God of
      Israel:
      The daughter of Babylon is like a thresh-
        ing floor
        at the time when it is trodden;
      yet a little while
        and the time of her harvest will come."

³⁴ "Nebuchadnezzar the king of Babylon has
      devoured me;
        he has crushed me;
      he has made me an empty vessel;
        he has swallowed me like a monster;
      he has filled his stomach with my delica-
        cies;
        he has rinsed me out.¹
³⁵ The violence done to me and to my kins-
      men be upon Babylon,"
        let the inhabitant of Zion say.
      "My blood be upon the inhabitants of
        Chaldea,"
        let Jerusalem say.
³⁶ Therefore thus says the LORD:
      "Behold, I will plead your cause
        and take vengeance for you.
      I will dry up her sea
        and make her fountain dry,
³⁷ and Babylon shall become a heap of ruins,
        the haunt of jackals,
      a horror and a hissing,
        without inhabitant.

³⁸ "They shall roar together like lions;
        they shall growl like lions' cubs.
³⁹ While they are inflamed I will prepare
        them a feast
        and make them drunk, that they may
          become merry,
      then sleep a perpetual sleep
        and not wake, declares the LORD.
⁴⁰ I will bring them down like lambs to the
        slaughter,
        like rams and male goats.

⁴¹ "How Babylon² is taken,
        the praise of the whole earth seized!

---

¹ Or *he has expelled me* ² Hebrew *Sheshach*, a code name for Babylon

How Babylon has become
   a horror among the nations!
42 The sea has come up on Babylon;
   she is covered with its tumultuous waves.
43 Her cities have become a horror,
   a land of drought and a desert,
a land in which no one dwells,
   and through which no son of man passes.
44 And I will punish Bel in Babylon,
   and take out of his mouth what he has
     swallowed.
The nations shall no longer flow to him;
   the wall of Babylon has fallen.

45 "Go out of the midst of her, my people!
   Let every one save his life
   from the fierce anger of the LORD!
46 Let not your heart faint, and be not fearful
   at the report heard in the land,
when a report comes in one year
   and afterward a report in another year,
and violence is in the land,
   and ruler is against ruler.

47 "Therefore, behold, the days are coming
   when I will punish the images of
     Babylon;
her whole land shall be put to shame,
   and all her slain shall fall in the midst of
     her.
48 Then the heavens and the earth,
   and all that is in them,
shall sing for joy over Babylon,
   for the destroyers shall come against
     them out of the north,
       declares the LORD.
49 Babylon must fall for the slain of Israel,
   just as for Babylon have fallen the slain
     of all the earth.

50 "You who have escaped from the sword,
   go, do not stand still!
Remember the LORD from far away,
   and let Jerusalem come into your mind:
51 'We are put to shame, for we have heard
    reproach;
   dishonor has covered our face,
for foreigners have come
   into the holy places of the LORD's house.'

52 "Therefore, behold, the days are coming,
    declares the LORD,
   when I will execute judgment upon her
     images,

and through all her land
   the wounded shall groan.
53 Though Babylon should mount up to
     heaven,
   and though she should fortify her
     strong height,
yet destroyers would come from me
    against her,
   declares the LORD.

54 "A voice! A cry from Babylon!
   The noise of great destruction from the
     land of the Chaldeans!
55 For the LORD is laying Babylon waste
   and stilling her mighty voice.
Their waves roar like many waters;
   the noise of their voice is raised,
56 for a destroyer has come upon her,
    upon Babylon;
her warriors are taken;
   their bows are broken in pieces,
for the LORD is a God of recompense;
   he will surely repay.
57 I will make drunk her officials and her
     wise men,
   her governors, her commanders, and
     her warriors;
they shall sleep a perpetual sleep and not
     wake,
   declares the King, whose name is the
     LORD of hosts.

58 "Thus says the LORD of hosts:
The broad wall of Babylon
   shall be leveled to the ground,
and her high gates
   shall be burned with fire.
The peoples labor for nothing,
   and the nations weary themselves only
     for fire."

59 The word that Jeremiah the prophet commanded Seraiah the son of Neriah, son of Mahseiah, when he went with Zedekiah king of Judah to Babylon, in the fourth year of his reign. Seraiah was the quartermaster. 60 Jeremiah wrote in a book all the disaster that should come upon Babylon, all these words that are written concerning Babylon. 61 And Jeremiah said to Seraiah: "When you come to Babylon, see that you read all these words, 62 and say, 'O LORD, you have said concerning this place that you will cut it off, so that nothing shall dwell in it, neither man nor beast, and it shall be desolate forever.' 63 When you finish reading this book, tie a stone

to it and cast it into the midst of the Euphrates, [64] and say, 'Thus shall Babylon sink, to rise no more, because of the disaster that I am bringing upon her, and they shall become exhausted.'"

Thus far are the words of Jeremiah.

The Fall of Jerusalem Recounted

52 Zedekiah was twenty-one years old when he became king, and he reigned eleven years in Jerusalem. His mother's name was Hamutal the daughter of Jeremiah of Libnah. [2] And he did what was evil in the sight of the LORD, according to all that Jehoiakim had done. [3] For because of the anger of the LORD it came to the point in Jerusalem and Judah that he cast them out from his presence.

And Zedekiah rebelled against the king of Babylon. [4] And in the ninth year of his reign, in the tenth month, on the tenth day of the month, Nebuchadnezzar king of Babylon came with all his army against Jerusalem, and laid siege to it. And they built siegeworks all around it. [5] So the city was besieged till the eleventh year of King Zedekiah. [6] On the ninth day of the fourth month the famine was so severe in the city that there was no food for the people of the land. [7] Then a breach was made in the city, and all the men of war fled and went out from the city by night by the way of a gate between the two walls, by the king's garden, and the Chaldeans were around the city. And they went in the direction of the Arabah. [8] But the army of the Chaldeans pursued the king and overtook Zedekiah in the plains of Jericho, and all his army was scattered from him. [9] Then they captured the king and brought him up to the king of Babylon at Riblah in the land of Hamath, and he passed sentence on him. [10] The king of Babylon slaughtered the sons of Zedekiah before his eyes, and also slaughtered all the officials of Judah at Riblah. [11] He put out the eyes of Zedekiah, and bound him in chains, and the king of Babylon took him to Babylon, and put him in prison till the day of his death.

The Temple Burned

[12] In the fifth month, on the tenth day of the month—that was the nineteenth year of King Nebuchadnezzar, king of Babylon—Nebuzaradan the captain of the bodyguard, who served the king of Babylon, entered Jerusalem. [13] And he burned the house of the LORD, and the king's house and all the houses of Jerusalem; every great house he burned down. [14] And all the army of the Chaldeans, who were with the captain of the guard, broke down all the walls around Jerusalem. [15] And Nebuzaradan the captain of the guard carried away captive some of the poorest of the people and the rest of the people who were left in the city and the deserters who had deserted to the king of Babylon, together with the rest of the artisans. [16] But Nebuzaradan the captain of the guard left some of the poorest of the land to be vinedressers and plowmen.

[17] And the pillars of bronze that were in the house of the LORD, and the stands and the bronze sea that were in the house of the LORD, the Chaldeans broke in pieces, and carried all the bronze to Babylon. [18] And they took away the pots and the shovels and the snuffers and the basins and the dishes for incense and all the vessels of bronze used in the temple service; [19] also the small bowls and the fire pans and the basins and the pots and the lampstands and the dishes for incense and the bowls for drink offerings. What was of gold the captain of the guard took away as gold, and what was of silver, as silver. [20] As for the two pillars, the one sea, the twelve bronze bulls that were under the sea,[1] and the stands, which Solomon the king had made for the house of the LORD, the bronze of all these things was beyond weight. [21] As for the pillars, the height of the one pillar was eighteen cubits,[2] its circumference was twelve cubits, and its thickness was four fingers, and it was hollow. [22] On it was a capital of bronze. The height of the one capital was five cubits. A network and pomegranates, all of bronze, were around the capital. And the second pillar had the same, with pomegranates. [23] There were ninety-six pomegranates on the sides; all the pomegranates were a hundred upon the network all around.

The People Exiled to Babylon

[24] And the captain of the guard took Seraiah the chief priest, and Zephaniah the second priest and the three keepers of the threshold; [25] and from the city he took an officer who had been in command of the men of war, and seven men of the king's council, who were found in the city; and the secretary of the commander of the army, who mustered the people of the land; and sixty men of the people of the land, who were found in the midst of the city. [26] And

---

[1] Hebrew lacks *the sea* [2] A *cubit* was about 18 inches or 45 centimeters

Nebuzaradan the captain of the guard took them and brought them to the king of Babylon at Riblah. ²⁷ And the king of Babylon struck them down and put them to death at Riblah in the land of Hamath. So Judah was taken into exile out of its land.

²⁸ This is the number of the people whom Nebuchadnezzar carried away captive: in the seventh year, 3,023 Judeans; ²⁹ in the eighteenth year of Nebuchadnezzar he carried away captive from Jerusalem 832 persons; ³⁰ in the twenty-third year of Nebuchadnezzar, Nebuzaradan the captain of the guard carried away captive of the Judeans 745 persons; all the persons were 4,600.

Jehoiachin Released from Prison

³¹ And in the thirty-seventh year of the exile of Jehoiachin king of Judah, in the twelfth month, on the twenty-fifth day of the month, Evil-merodach king of Babylon, in the year that he began to reign, graciously freed[1] Jehoiachin king of Judah and brought him out of prison. ³² And he spoke kindly to him and gave him a seat above the seats of the kings who were with him in Babylon. ³³ So Jehoiachin put off his prison garments. And every day of his life he dined regularly at the king's table, ³⁴ and for his allowance, a regular allowance was given him by the king, according to his daily needs, until the day of his death, as long as he lived.

---

[1] Hebrew reign, lifted up the head of

LAMENTATIONS

How Lonely Sits the City

1 How lonely sits the city
   that was full of people!
How like a widow has she become,
   she who was great among the nations!
She who was a princess among the provinces
   has become a slave.

2 She weeps bitterly in the night,
   with tears on her cheeks;
among all her lovers
   she has none to comfort her;
all her friends have dealt treacherously
      with her;
   they have become her enemies.

3 Judah has gone into exile because of affliction[1]
   and hard servitude;
she dwells now among the nations,
   but finds no resting place;
her pursuers have all overtaken her
   in the midst of her distress.[2]

4 The roads to Zion mourn,
   for none come to the festival;
all her gates are desolate;
   her priests groan;
her virgins have been afflicted,[3]
   and she herself suffers bitterly.

5 Her foes have become the head;
   her enemies prosper,
because the LORD has afflicted her
   for the multitude of her transgressions;
her children have gone away,
   captives before the foe.

6 From the daughter of Zion
   all her majesty has departed.
Her princes have become like deer
   that find no pasture;
they fled without strength
   before the pursuer.

7 Jerusalem remembers
   in the days of her affliction and wandering
all the precious things
   that were hers from days of old.
When her people fell into the hand of the
      foe,
   and there was none to help her,
her foes gloated over her;
   they mocked at her downfall.

8 Jerusalem sinned grievously;
   therefore she became filthy;
all who honored her despise her,
   for they have seen her nakedness;
she herself groans
   and turns her face away.

9 Her uncleanness was in her skirts;
   she took no thought of her future;[4]
therefore her fall is terrible;
   she has no comforter.
"O LORD, behold my affliction,
   for the enemy has triumphed!"

10 The enemy has stretched out his hands
   over all her precious things;
for she has seen the nations
   enter her sanctuary,
those whom you forbade
   to enter your congregation.

11 All her people groan
   as they search for bread;
they trade their treasures for food
   to revive their strength.
"Look, O LORD, and see,
   for I am despised."

12 "Is it nothing to you, all you who pass by?
   Look and see
if there is any sorrow like my sorrow,
   which was brought upon me,
which the LORD inflicted
   on the day of his fierce anger.

13 "From on high he sent fire;
   into my bones[5] he made it descend;
he spread a net for my feet;
   he turned me back;
he has left me stunned,
   faint all the day long.

14 "My transgressions were bound[6] into a
      yoke;
   by his hand they were fastened
      together;

---

[1] Or under affliction [2] Or in the narrow passes [3] Septuagint, Old Latin dragged away [4] Or end [5] Septuagint; Hebrew bones and [6] The meaning of the Hebrew is uncertain

they were set upon my neck;
  he caused my strength to fail;
the Lord gave me into the hands
  of those whom I cannot withstand.

15 "The Lord rejected
  all my mighty men in my midst;
he summoned an assembly against me
  to crush my young men;
the Lord has trodden as in a winepress
  the virgin daughter of Judah.

16 "For these things I weep;
  my eyes flow with tears;
for a comforter is far from me,
  one to revive my spirit;
my children are desolate,
  for the enemy has prevailed."

17 Zion stretches out her hands,
  but there is none to comfort her;
the LORD has commanded against Jacob
  that his neighbors should be his foes;
Jerusalem has become
  a filthy thing among them.

18 "The LORD is in the right,
  for I have rebelled against his word;
but hear, all you peoples,
  and see my suffering;
my young women and my young men
  have gone into captivity.

19 "I called to my lovers,
  but they deceived me;
my priests and elders
  perished in the city,
while they sought food
  to revive their strength.

20 "Look, O LORD, for I am in distress;
  my stomach churns;
my heart is wrung within me,
  because I have been very rebellious.
In the street the sword bereaves;
  in the house it is like death.

21 "They heard[1] my groaning,
  yet there is no one to comfort me.
All my enemies have heard of my trouble;
  they are glad that you have done it.
You have brought[2] the day you announced;
  now let them be as I am.

22 "Let all their evildoing come before you,
  and deal with them

as you have dealt with me
  because of all my transgressions;
for my groans are many,
  and my heart is faint."

The Lord Has Destroyed Without Pity

2 How the Lord in his anger
  has set the daughter of Zion under a
  cloud!
He has cast down from heaven to earth
  the splendor of Israel;
he has not remembered his footstool
  in the day of his anger.

2 The Lord has swallowed up without mercy
  all the habitations of Jacob;
in his wrath he has broken down
  the strongholds of the daughter of
  Judah;
he has brought down to the ground in dishonor
  the kingdom and its rulers.

3 He has cut down in fierce anger
  all the might of Israel;
he has withdrawn from them his right
  hand
  in the face of the enemy;
he has burned like a flaming fire in Jacob,
  consuming all around.

4 He has bent his bow like an enemy,
  with his right hand set like a foe;
and he has killed all who were delightful in
  our eyes
  in the tent of the daughter of Zion;
he has poured out his fury like fire.

5 The Lord has become like an enemy;
  he has swallowed up Israel;
he has swallowed up all its palaces;
  he has laid in ruins its strongholds,
and he has multiplied in the daughter of
  Judah
  mourning and lamentation.

6 He has laid waste his booth like a garden,
  laid in ruins his meeting place;
the LORD has made Zion forget
  festival and Sabbath,
and in his fierce indignation has spurned
  king and priest.

7 The Lord has scorned his altar,
  disowned his sanctuary;

---

[1] Septuagint, Syriac *Hear* [2] Syriac *Bring*

he has delivered into the hand of the enemy
   the walls of her palaces;
they raised a clamor in the house of the
   LORD
     as on the day of festival.

8   The LORD determined to lay in ruins
   the wall of the daughter of Zion;
he stretched out the measuring line;
   he did not restrain his hand from
     destroying;
he caused rampart and wall to lament;
   they languished together.

9   Her gates have sunk into the ground;
   he has ruined and broken her bars;
her king and princes are among the nations;
   the law is no more,
and her prophets find
   no vision from the LORD.

10   The elders of the daughter of Zion
   sit on the ground in silence;
they have thrown dust on their heads
   and put on sackcloth;
the young women of Jerusalem
   have bowed their heads to the ground.

11   My eyes are spent with weeping;
   my stomach churns;
my bile is poured out to the ground
   because of the destruction of the daugh-
     ter of my people,
because infants and babies faint
   in the streets of the city.

12   They cry to their mothers,
   "Where is bread and wine?"
as they faint like a wounded man
   in the streets of the city,
as their life is poured out
   on their mothers' bosom.

13   What can I say for you, to what compare
     you,
   O daughter of Jerusalem?
What can I liken to you, that I may comfort
     you,
   O virgin daughter of Zion?
For your ruin is vast as the sea;
   who can heal you?

14   Your prophets have seen for you
   false and deceptive visions;
they have not exposed your iniquity
   to restore your fortunes,

but have seen for you oracles
   that are false and misleading.

15   All who pass along the way
   clap their hands at you;
they hiss and wag their heads
   at the daughter of Jerusalem:
"Is this the city that was called
   the perfection of beauty,
   the joy of all the earth?"

16   All your enemies
   rail against you;
they hiss, they gnash their teeth,
   they cry: "We have swallowed her!
Ah, this is the day we longed for;
   now we have it; we see it!"

17   The LORD has done what he purposed;
   he has carried out his word,
which he commanded long ago;
   he has thrown down without pity;
he has made the enemy rejoice over you
   and exalted the might of your foes.

18   Their heart cried to the Lord.
   O wall of the daughter of Zion,
let tears stream down like a torrent
   day and night!
Give yourself no rest,
   your eyes no respite!

19   "Arise, cry out in the night,
   at the beginning of the night watches!
Pour out your heart like water
   before the presence of the Lord!
Lift your hands to him
   for the lives of your children,
who faint for hunger
   at the head of every street."

20   Look, O LORD, and see!
   With whom have you dealt thus?
Should women eat the fruit of their womb,
   the children of their tender care?
Should priest and prophet be killed
   in the sanctuary of the Lord?

21   In the dust of the streets
   lie the young and the old;
my young women and my young men
   have fallen by the sword;
you have killed them in the day of your
     anger,
   slaughtering without pity.

22   You summoned as if to a festival day
   my terrors on every side,

and on the day of the anger of the Lord
　　no one escaped or survived;
those whom I held and raised
　　my enemy destroyed.

Great Is Your Faithfulness

3 I am the man who has seen affliction
　　under the rod of his wrath;

2 he has driven and brought me
　　into darkness without any light;

3 surely against me he turns his hand
　　again and again the whole day long.

4 He has made my flesh and my skin waste
　　　away;
　　he has broken my bones;

5 he has besieged and enveloped me
　　with bitterness and tribulation;

6 he has made me dwell in darkness
　　like the dead of long ago.

7 He has walled me about so that I cannot
　　　escape;
　　he has made my chains heavy;

8 though I call and cry for help,
　　he shuts out my prayer;

9 he has blocked my ways with blocks of
　　　stones;
　　he has made my paths crooked.

10 He is a bear lying in wait for me,
　　a lion in hiding;

11 he turned aside my steps and tore me to
　　　pieces;
　　he has made me desolate;

12 he bent his bow and set me
　　as a target for his arrow.

13 He drove into my kidneys
　　the arrows of his quiver;

14 I have become the laughingstock of all
　　　peoples,
　　the object of their taunts all day long.

15 He has filled me with bitterness;
　　he has sated me with wormwood.

16 He has made my teeth grind on gravel,
　　and made me cower in ashes;

17 my soul is bereft of peace;
　　I have forgotten what happiness[1] is;

18 so I say, "My endurance has perished;
　　so has my hope from the Lord."

19 Remember my affliction and my wander-
　　　ings,
　　the wormwood and the gall!

20 My soul continually remembers it
　　and is bowed down within me.

21 But this I call to mind,
　　and therefore I have hope:

22 The steadfast love of the Lord never ceases;[2]
　　his mercies never come to an end;

23 they are new every morning;
　　great is your faithfulness.

24 "The Lord is my portion," says my soul,
　　"therefore I will hope in him."

25 The Lord is good to those who wait for
　　　him,
　　to the soul who seeks him.

26 It is good that one should wait quietly
　　for the salvation of the Lord.

27 It is good for a man that he bear
　　the yoke in his youth.

28 Let him sit alone in silence
　　when it is laid on him;

29 let him put his mouth in the dust—
　　there may yet be hope;

30 let him give his cheek to the one who strikes,
　　and let him be filled with insults.

31 For the Lord will not
　　cast off forever,

32 but, though he cause grief, he will have
　　　compassion
　　according to the abundance of his stead-
　　　fast love;

33 for he does not afflict from his heart
　　or grieve the children of men.

34 To crush underfoot
　　all the prisoners of the earth,

35 to deny a man justice
　　in the presence of the Most High,

36 to subvert a man in his lawsuit,
　　the Lord does not approve.

37 Who has spoken and it came to pass,
　　unless the Lord has commanded it?

38 Is it not from the mouth of the Most High
　　that good and bad come?

39 Why should a living man complain,
　　a man, about the punishment of his sins?

40 Let us test and examine our ways,
　　and return to the Lord!

41 Let us lift up our hearts and hands
　　to God in heaven:

42 "We have transgressed and rebelled,
　　and you have not forgiven.

---

[1] Hebrew good [2] Syriac, Targum; Hebrew *Because of the steadfast love of the Lord, we are not cut off*

43 "You have wrapped yourself with anger and
      pursued us,
    killing without pity;
44 you have wrapped yourself with a cloud
    so that no prayer can pass through.
45 You have made us scum and garbage
    among the peoples.

46 "All our enemies
    open their mouths against us;
47 panic and pitfall have come upon us,
    devastation and destruction;
48 my eyes flow with rivers of tears
    because of the destruction of the daugh-
      ter of my people.

49 "My eyes will flow without ceasing,
    without respite,
50 until the LORD from heaven
    looks down and sees;
51 my eyes cause me grief
    at the fate of all the daughters of my city.

52 "I have been hunted like a bird
    by those who were my enemies without
      cause;
53 they flung me alive into the pit
    and cast stones on me;
54 water closed over my head;
    I said, 'I am lost.'

55 "I called on your name, O LORD,
    from the depths of the pit;
56 you heard my plea, 'Do not close
    your ear to my cry for help!'
57 You came near when I called on you;
    you said, 'Do not fear!'

58 "You have taken up my cause, O Lord;
    you have redeemed my life.
59 You have seen the wrong done to me,
    O LORD;
    judge my cause.
60 You have seen all their vengeance,
    all their plots against me.

61 "You have heard their taunts, O LORD,
    all their plots against me.
62 The lips and thoughts of my assailants
    are against me all the day long.
63 Behold their sitting and their rising;
    I am the object of their taunts.

64 "You will repay them,[1] O LORD,
    according to the work of their hands.
65 You will give them[2] dullness of heart;
    your curse will be[3] on them.
66 You will pursue them[4] in anger and
    destroy them
    from under your heavens, O LORD."[5]

The Holy Stones Lie Scattered

4 How the gold has grown dim,
  how the pure gold is changed!
The holy stones lie scattered
    at the head of every street.

2 The precious sons of Zion,
    worth their weight in fine gold,
how they are regarded as earthen pots,
    the work of a potter's hands!

3 Even jackals offer the breast;
    they nurse their young;
but the daughter of my people has become
    cruel,
    like the ostriches in the wilderness.

4 The tongue of the nursing infant sticks
    to the roof of its mouth for thirst;
the children beg for food,
    but no one gives to them.

5 Those who once feasted on delicacies
    perish in the streets;
those who were brought up in purple
    embrace ash heaps.

6 For the chastisement[6] of the daughter of
    my people has been greater
    than the punishment[7] of Sodom,
which was overthrown in a moment,
    and no hands were wrung for her.[8]

7 Her princes were purer than snow,
    whiter than milk;
their bodies were more ruddy than coral,
    the beauty of their form[9] was like sap-
    phire.[10]

8 Now their face is blacker than soot;
    they are not recognized in the streets;
their skin has shriveled on their bones;
    it has become as dry as wood.

9 Happier were the victims of the sword
    than the victims of hunger,
who wasted away, pierced
    by lack of the fruits of the field.

10 The hands of compassionate women
    have boiled their own children;

---

[1] Or *Repay them* [2] Or *Give them* [3] Or *place your curse* [4] Or *Pursue them* [5] Syriac (compare Septuagint, Vulgate); Hebrew *the heavens of the LORD* [6] Or *iniquity* [7] Or *sin* [8] The meaning of the Hebrew is uncertain [9] The meaning of the Hebrew is uncertain [10] Hebrew *lapis lazuli*

they became their food
 during the destruction of the daughter
  of my people.

11 The LORD gave full vent to his wrath;
 he poured out his hot anger,
and he kindled a fire in Zion
 that consumed its foundations.

12 The kings of the earth did not believe,
 nor any of the inhabitants of the world,
that foe or enemy could enter
 the gates of Jerusalem.

13 This was for the sins of her prophets
 and the iniquities of her priests,
who shed in the midst of her
 the blood of the righteous.

14 They wandered, blind, through the streets;
 they were so defiled with blood
that no one was able to touch
 their garments.

15 "Away! Unclean!" people cried at them.
 "Away! Away! Do not touch!"
So they became fugitives and wanderers;
 people said among the nations,
 "They shall stay with us no longer."

16 The LORD himself[1] has scattered them;
 he will regard them no more;
no honor was shown to the priests,
 no favor to the elders.

17 Our eyes failed, ever watching
 vainly for help;
in our watching we watched
 for a nation which could not save.

18 They dogged our steps
 so that we could not walk in our streets;
our end drew near; our days were numbered,
 for our end had come.

19 Our pursuers were swifter
 than the eagles in the heavens;
they chased us on the mountains;
 they lay in wait for us in the wilderness.

20 The breath of our nostrils, the LORD's
  anointed,
 was captured in their pits,
of whom we said, "Under his shadow
 we shall live among the nations."

21 Rejoice and be glad, O daughter of Edom,

you who dwell in the land of Uz;
but to you also the cup shall pass;
 you shall become drunk and strip yourself bare.

22 The punishment of your iniquity,
 O daughter of Zion, is accomplished;
 he will keep you in exile no longer;[2]
but your iniquity, O daughter of Edom, he
 will punish;
 he will uncover your sins.

Restore Us to Yourself, O LORD

5 Remember, O LORD, what has befallen us;
 look, and see our disgrace!
2 Our inheritance has been turned over to
  strangers,
 our homes to foreigners.
3 We have become orphans, fatherless;
 our mothers are like widows.
4 We must pay for the water we drink;
 the wood we get must be bought.
5 Our pursuers are at our necks;
 we are weary; we are given no rest.
6 We have given the hand to Egypt, and to
  Assyria,
 to get bread enough.
7 Our fathers sinned, and are no more;
 and we bear their iniquities.
8 Slaves rule over us;
 there is none to deliver us from their
  hand.
9 We get our bread at the peril of our lives,
 because of the sword in the wilderness.
10 Our skin is hot as an oven
 with the burning heat of famine.
11 Women are raped in Zion,
 young women in the towns of Judah.
12 Princes are hung up by their hands;
 no respect is shown to the elders.
13 Young men are compelled to grind at the
  mill,
 and boys stagger under loads of wood.
14 The old men have left the city gate,
 the young men their music.
15 The joy of our hearts has ceased;
 our dancing has been turned to mourning.
16 The crown has fallen from our head;
 woe to us, for we have sinned!
17 For this our heart has become sick,
 for these things our eyes have grown
  dim,

---

[1] Hebrew *The face of the LORD* [2] Or *he will not exile you again*

18 for Mount Zion which lies desolate;
jackals prowl over it.
19 But you, O LORD, reign forever;
your throne endures to all generations.
20 Why do you forget us forever,
why do you forsake us for so many days?

21 Restore us to yourself, O LORD, that we
may be restored!
Renew our days as of old—
22 unless you have utterly rejected us,
and you remain exceedingly angry
with us.

EZEKIEL

Ezekiel in Babylon

1 In the thirtieth year, in the fourth month, on the fifth day of the month, as I was among the exiles by the Chebar canal, the heavens were opened, and I saw visions of God.[1] [2] On the fifth day of the month (it was the fifth year of the exile of King Jehoiachin), [3] the word of the LORD came to Ezekiel the priest, the son of Buzi, in the land of the Chaldeans by the Chebar canal, and the hand of the LORD was upon him there.

The Glory of the LORD

[4] As I looked, behold, a stormy wind came out of the north, and a great cloud, with brightness around it, and fire flashing forth continually, and in the midst of the fire, as it were gleaming metal.[2] [5] And from the midst of it came the likeness of four living creatures. And this was their appearance: they had a human likeness, [6] but each had four faces, and each of them had four wings. [7] Their legs were straight, and the soles of their feet were like the sole of a calf's foot. And they sparkled like burnished bronze. [8] Under their wings on their four sides they had human hands. And the four had their faces and their wings thus: [9] their wings touched one another. Each one of them went straight forward, without turning as they went. [10] As for the likeness of their faces, each had a human face. The four had the face of a lion on the right side, the four had the face of an ox on the left side, and the four had the face of an eagle. [11] Such were their faces. And their wings were spread out above. Each creature had two wings, each of which touched the wing of another, while two covered their bodies. [12] And each went straight forward. Wherever the spirit[3] would go, they went, without turning as they went. [13] As for the likeness of the living creatures, their appearance was like burning coals of fire, like the appearance of torches moving to and fro among the living creatures. And the fire was bright, and out of the fire went forth lightning. [14] And the living creatures darted to and fro, like the appearance of a flash of lightning.

[15] Now as I looked at the living creatures, I saw a wheel on the earth beside the living creatures, one for each of the four of them.[4] [16] As for the appearance of the wheels and their construction: their appearance was like the gleaming of beryl. And the four had the same likeness, their appearance and construction being as it were a wheel within a wheel. [17] When they went, they went in any of their four directions[5] without turning as they went. [18] And their rims were tall and awesome, and the rims of all four were full of eyes all around. [19] And when the living creatures went, the wheels went beside them; and when the living creatures rose from the earth, the wheels rose. [20] Wherever the spirit wanted to go, they went, and the wheels rose along with them, for the spirit of the living creatures[6] was in the wheels. [21] When those went, these went; and when those stood, these stood; and when those rose from the earth, the wheels rose along with them, for the spirit of the living creatures was in the wheels.

[22] Over the heads of the living creatures there was the likeness of an expanse, shining like awe-inspiring crystal, spread out above their heads. [23] And under the expanse their wings were stretched out straight, one toward another. And each creature had two wings covering its body. [24] And when they went, I heard the sound of their wings like the sound of many waters, like the sound of the Almighty, a sound of tumult like the sound of an army. When they stood still, they let down their wings. [25] And there came a voice from above the expanse over their heads. When they stood still, they let down their wings.

[26] And above the expanse over their heads there was the likeness of a throne, in appearance like sapphire;[7] and seated above the likeness of a throne was a likeness with a human appearance. [27] And upward from what had the appearance of his waist I saw as it were gleaming metal, like the appearance of fire enclosed all around. And downward from what had the appearance of his waist I saw as it were the appearance of fire, and there was brightness around him.[8] [28] Like the appearance of the bow that is in the cloud on the day of rain, so was the appearance of the brightness all around.

Such was the appearance of the likeness of the glory of the LORD. And when I saw it, I fell on my face, and I heard the voice of one speaking.

---

[1] Or *from God* [2] Or *amber*; also verse 27 [3] Or *Spirit*; also twice in verse 20 and once in verse 21 [4] Hebrew *of their faces* [5] Hebrew *on their four sides* [6] Or *the spirit of life*; also verse 21 [7] Or *lapis lazuli* [8] Or *it*

Ezekiel's Call

2 And he said to me, "Son of man,[1] stand on your feet, and I will speak with you." [2] And as he spoke to me, the Spirit entered into me and set me on my feet, and I heard him speaking to me. [3] And he said to me, "Son of man, I send you to the people of Israel, to nations of rebels, who have rebelled against me. They and their fathers have transgressed against me to this very day. [4] The descendants also are impudent and stubborn: I send you to them, and you shall say to them, 'Thus says the Lord God.' [5] And whether they hear or refuse to hear (for they are a rebellious house) they will know that a prophet has been among them. [6] And you, son of man, be not afraid of them, nor be afraid of their words, though briers and thorns are with you and you sit on scorpions.[2] Be not afraid of their words, nor be dismayed at their looks, for they are a rebellious house. [7] And you shall speak my words to them, whether they hear or refuse to hear, for they are a rebellious house.

[8] "But you, son of man, hear what I say to you. Be not rebellious like that rebellious house; open your mouth and eat what I give you." [9] And when I looked, behold, a hand was stretched out to me, and behold, a scroll of a book was in it. [10] And he spread it before me. And it had writing on the front and on the back, and there were written on it words of lamentation and mourning and woe.

3 And he said to me, "Son of man, eat whatever you find here. Eat this scroll, and go, speak to the house of Israel." [2] So I opened my mouth, and he gave me this scroll to eat. [3] And he said to me, "Son of man, feed your belly with this scroll that I give you and fill your stomach with it." Then I ate it, and it was in my mouth as sweet as honey.

[4] And he said to me, "Son of man, go to the house of Israel and speak with my words to them. [5] For you are not sent to a people of foreign speech and a hard language, but to the house of Israel— [6] not to many peoples of foreign speech and a hard language, whose words you cannot understand. Surely, if I sent you to such, they would listen to you. [7] But the house of Israel will not be willing to listen to you, for they are not willing to listen to me: because all the house of Israel have a hard forehead and a stubborn heart. [8] Behold, I have made your face as hard as their faces, and your forehead

as hard as their foreheads. [9] Like emery harder than flint have I made your forehead. Fear them not, nor be dismayed at their looks, for they are a rebellious house." [10] Moreover, he said to me, "Son of man, all my words that I shall speak to you receive in your heart, and hear with your ears. [11] And go to the exiles, to your people, and speak to them and say to them, 'Thus says the Lord God,' whether they hear or refuse to hear."

[12] Then the Spirit[3] lifted me up, and I heard behind me the voice[4] of a great earthquake: "Blessed be the glory of the Lord from its place!" [13] It was the sound of the wings of the living creatures as they touched one another, and the sound of the wheels beside them, and the sound of a great earthquake. [14] The Spirit lifted me up and took me away, and I went in bitterness in the heat of my spirit, the hand of the Lord being strong upon me. [15] And I came to the exiles at Tel-abib, who were dwelling by the Chebar canal, and I sat where they were dwelling.[5] And I sat there overwhelmed among them seven days.

A Watchman for Israel

[16] And at the end of seven days, the word of the Lord came to me: [17] "Son of man, I have made you a watchman for the house of Israel. Whenever you hear a word from my mouth, you shall give them warning from me. [18] If I say to the wicked, 'You shall surely die,' and you give him no warning, nor speak to warn the wicked from his wicked way, in order to save his life, that wicked person shall die for[6] his iniquity, but his blood I will require at your hand. [19] But if you warn the wicked, and he does not turn from his wickedness, or from his wicked way, he shall die for his iniquity, but you will have delivered your soul. [20] Again, if a righteous person turns from his righteousness and commits injustice, and I lay a stumbling block before him, he shall die. Because you have not warned him, he shall die for his sin, and his righteous deeds that he has done shall not be remembered, but his blood I will require at your hand. [21] But if you warn the righteous person not to sin, and he does not sin, he shall surely live, because he took warning, and you will have delivered your soul."

[22] And the hand of the Lord was upon me there. And he said to me, "Arise, go out into the

---

[1] Or *Son of Adam; so throughout Ezekiel* [2] Or *on scorpion plants* [3] Or *the wind; also verse 14* [4] Or *sound* [5] Or *Chebar, and to where they dwelt* [6] Or *in; also verses 19, 20*

valley,[1] and there I will speak with you." ²³So I arose and went out into the valley, and behold, the glory of the LORD stood there, like the glory that I had seen by the Chebar canal, and I fell on my face. ²⁴But the Spirit entered into me and set me on my feet, and he spoke with me and said to me, "Go, shut yourself within your house. ²⁵And you, O son of man, behold, cords will be placed upon you, and you shall be bound with them, so that you cannot go out among the people. ²⁶And I will make your tongue cling to the roof of your mouth, so that you shall be mute and unable to reprove them, for they are a rebellious house. ²⁷But when I speak with you, I will open your mouth, and you shall say to them, 'Thus says the Lord GOD.' He who will hear, let him hear; and he who will refuse to hear, let him refuse, for they are a rebellious house.

The Siege of Jerusalem Symbolized

4 "And you, son of man, take a brick and lay it before you, and engrave on it a city, even Jerusalem. ²And put siegeworks against it, and build a siege wall against it, and cast up a mound against it. Set camps also against it, and plant battering rams against it all around. ³And you, take an iron griddle, and place it as an iron wall between you and the city; and set your face toward it, and let it be in a state of siege, and press the siege against it. This is a sign for the house of Israel.

⁴"Then lie on your left side, and place the punishment[2] of the house of Israel upon it. For the number of the days that you lie on it, you shall bear their punishment. ⁵For I assign to you a number of days, 390 days, equal to the number of the years of their punishment. So long shall you bear the punishment of the house of Israel. ⁶And when you have completed these, you shall lie down a second time, but on your right side, and bear the punishment of the house of Judah. Forty days I assign you, a day for each year. ⁷And you shall set your face toward the siege of Jerusalem, with your arm bared, and you shall prophesy against the city. ⁸And behold, I will place cords upon you, so that you cannot turn from one side to the other, till you have completed the days of your siege.

⁹"And you, take wheat and barley, beans and lentils, millet and emmer,[3] and put them into a single vessel and make your bread from them. During the number of days that you lie on your side, 390 days, you shall eat it. ¹⁰And your food that you eat shall be by weight, twenty shekels[4] a day; from day to day[5] you shall eat it. ¹¹And water you shall drink by measure, the sixth part of a hin;[6] from day to day you shall drink. ¹²And you shall eat it as a barley cake, baking it in their sight on human dung." ¹³And the LORD said, "Thus shall the people of Israel eat their bread unclean, among the nations where I will drive them." ¹⁴Then I said, "Ah, Lord GOD! Behold, I have never defiled myself.[7] From my youth up till now I have never eaten what died of itself or was torn by beasts, nor has tainted meat come into my mouth." ¹⁵Then he said to me, "See, I assign to you cow's dung instead of human dung, on which you may prepare your bread." ¹⁶Moreover, he said to me, "Son of man, behold, I will break the supply[8] of bread in Jerusalem. They shall eat bread by weight and with anxiety, and they shall drink water by measure and in dismay. ¹⁷I will do this that they may lack bread and water, and look at one another in dismay, and rot away because of their punishment.

Jerusalem Will Be Destroyed

5 "And you, O son of man, take a sharp sword. Use it as a barber's razor and pass it over your head and your beard. Then take balances for weighing and divide the hair. ²A third part you shall burn in the fire in the midst of the city, when the days of the siege are completed. And a third part you shall take and strike with the sword all around the city. And a third part you shall scatter to the wind, and I will unsheathe the sword after them. ³And you shall take from these a small number and bind them in the skirts of your robe. ⁴And of these again you shall take some and cast them into the midst of the fire and burn them in the fire. From there a fire will come out into all the house of Israel.

⁵"Thus says the Lord GOD: This is Jerusalem. I have set her in the center of the nations, with countries all around her. ⁶And she has rebelled against my rules by doing wickedness more than the nations, and against my statutes more than the countries all around her; for they have rejected my rules and have not walked in my statutes. ⁷Therefore thus says the Lord GOD: Because you are more turbulent than the nations that are all around you, and have not walked in my statutes or obeyed my rules, and have not[9] even acted according to the rules of the nations that are all around you, ⁸therefore

---

¹ Or plain; also verse 23 ² Or iniquity; also verses 5, 6, 17 ³ A type of wheat ⁴ A shekel was about 2/5 ounce or 11 grams ⁵ Or at a set time daily; also verse 11 ⁶ A hin was about 4 quarts or 3.5 liters ⁷ Hebrew my soul (or throat) has never been made unclean ⁸ Hebrew staff ⁹ Some Hebrew manuscripts and Syriac lack not

thus says the Lord God: Behold, I, even I, am against you. And I will execute judgments[1] in your midst in the sight of the nations. [9] And because of all your abominations I will do with you what I have never yet done, and the like of which I will never do again. [10] Therefore fathers shall eat their sons in your midst, and sons shall eat their fathers. And I will execute judgments on you, and any of you who survive I will scatter to all the winds. [11] Therefore, as I live, declares the Lord God, surely, because you have defiled my sanctuary with all your detestable things and with all your abominations, therefore I will withdraw.[2] My eye will not spare, and I will have no pity. [12] A third part of you shall die of pestilence and be consumed with famine in your midst; a third part shall fall by the sword all around you; and a third part I will scatter to all the winds and will unsheathe the sword after them.

[13] "Thus shall my anger spend itself, and I will vent my fury upon them and satisfy myself. And they shall know that I am the Lord—that I have spoken in my jealousy—when I spend my fury upon them. [14] Moreover, I will make you a desolation and an object of reproach among the nations all around you and in the sight of all who pass by. [15] You shall be[3] a reproach and a taunt, a warning and a horror, to the nations all around you, when I execute judgments on you in anger and fury, and with furious rebukes—I am the Lord; I have spoken— [16] when I send against you[4] the deadly arrows of famine, arrows for destruction, which I will send to destroy you, and when I bring more and more famine upon you and break your supply[5] of bread. [17] I will send famine and wild beasts against you, and they will rob you of your children. Pestilence and blood shall pass through you, and I will bring the sword upon you. I am the Lord; I have spoken."

Judgment Against Idolatry

6 The word of the Lord came to me: [2] "Son of man, set your face toward the mountains of Israel, and prophesy against them, [3] and say, You mountains of Israel, hear the word of the Lord God! Thus says the Lord God to the mountains and the hills, to the ravines and the valleys: Behold, I, even I, will bring a sword upon you, and I will destroy your high places. [4] Your altars

shall become desolate, and your incense altars shall be broken, and I will cast down your slain before your idols. [5] And I will lay the dead bodies of the people of Israel before their idols, and I will scatter your bones around your altars. [6] Wherever you dwell, the cities shall be waste and the high places ruined, so that your altars will be waste and ruined,[6] your idols broken and destroyed, your incense altars cut down, and your works wiped out. [7] And the slain shall fall in your midst, and you shall know that I am the Lord.

[8] "Yet I will leave some of you alive. When you have among the nations some who escape the sword, and when you are scattered through the countries, [9] then those of you who escape will remember me among the nations where they are carried captive, how I have been broken over their whoring heart that has departed from me and over their eyes that go whoring after their idols. And they will be loathsome in their own sight for the evils that they have committed, for all their abominations. [10] And they shall know that I am the Lord. I have not said in vain that I would do this evil to them."

[11] Thus says the Lord God: "Clap your hands and stamp your foot and say, Alas, because of all the evil abominations of the house of Israel, for they shall fall by the sword, by famine, and by pestilence. [12] He who is far off shall die of pestilence, and he who is near shall fall by the sword, and he who is left and is preserved shall die of famine. Thus I will spend my fury upon them. [13] And you shall know that I am the Lord, when their slain lie among their idols around their altars, on every high hill, on all the mountaintops, under every green tree, and under every leafy oak, wherever they offered pleasing aroma to all their idols. [14] And I will stretch out my hand against them and make the land desolate and waste, in all their dwelling places, from the wilderness to Riblah.[7] Then they will know that I am the Lord."

The Day of the Wrath of the Lord

7 The word of the Lord came to me: [2] "And you, O son of man, thus says the Lord God to the land of Israel: An end! The end has come upon the four corners of the land.[8] [3] Now the end is upon you, and I will send my anger upon you; I will judge you according to your ways, and I will punish you for all your abominations.

---

[1] The same Hebrew expression can mean *obey rules*, or *execute judgments*, depending on the context [2] Some Hebrew manuscripts *I will cut you down* [3] Dead Sea Scroll, Septuagint, Syriac, Vulgate, Targum; Masoretic Text *And it shall be* [4] Hebrew *them* [5] Hebrew *staff* [6] Or *and punished* [7] Some Hebrew manuscripts; most Hebrew manuscripts *Diblah* [8] Or *earth*

4 And my eye will not spare you, nor will I have pity, but I will punish you for your ways, while your abominations are in your midst. Then you will know that I am the LORD.

5 "Thus says the Lord GOD: Disaster after disaster![1] Behold, it comes. 6 An end has come; the end has come; it has awakened against you. Behold, it comes. 7 Your doom[2] has come to you, O inhabitant of the land. The time has come; the day is near, a day of tumult, and not of joyful shouting on the mountains. 8 Now I will soon pour out my wrath upon you, and spend my anger against you, and judge you according to your ways, and I will punish you for all your abominations. 9 And my eye will not spare, nor will I have pity. I will punish you according to your ways, while your abominations are in your midst. Then you will know that I am the LORD, who strikes.

10 "Behold, the day! Behold, it comes! Your doom has come; the rod has blossomed; pride has budded. 11 Violence has grown up into a rod of wickedness. None of them shall remain, nor their abundance, nor their wealth; neither shall there be preeminence among them.[3] 12 The time has come; the day has arrived. Let not the buyer rejoice, nor the seller mourn, for wrath is upon all their multitude.[4] 13 For the seller shall not return to what he has sold, while they live. For the vision concerns all their multitude; it shall not turn back; and because of his iniquity, none can maintain his life.[5]

14 "They have blown the trumpet and made everything ready, but none goes to battle, for my wrath is upon all their multitude. 15 The sword is without; pestilence and famine are within. He who is in the field dies by the sword, and him who is in the city famine and pestilence devour. 16 And if any survivors escape, they will be on the mountains, like doves of the valleys, all of them moaning, each one over his iniquity. 17 All hands are feeble, and all knees turn to water. 18 They put on sackcloth, and horror covers them. Shame is on all faces, and baldness on all their heads. 19 They cast their silver into the streets, and their gold is like an unclean thing. Their silver and gold are not able to deliver them in the day of the wrath of the LORD. They cannot satisfy their hunger or fill their stomachs with it. For it was the stumbling block of their iniquity. 20 His beautiful ornament they used for

pride, and they made their abominable images and their detestable things of it. Therefore I make it an unclean thing to them. 21 And I will give it into the hands of foreigners for prey, and to the wicked of the earth for spoil, and they shall profane it. 22 I will turn my face from them, and they shall profane my treasured[6] place. Robbers shall enter and profane it.

23 "Forge a chain![7] For the land is full of bloody crimes and the city is full of violence. 24 I will bring the worst of the nations to take possession of their houses. I will put an end to the pride of the strong, and their holy places[8] shall be profaned. 25 When anguish comes, they will seek peace, but there shall be none. 26 Disaster comes upon disaster; rumor follows rumor. They seek a vision from the prophet, while the law[9] perishes from the priest and counsel from the elders. 27 The king mourns, the prince is wrapped in despair, and the hands of the people of the land are paralyzed by terror. According to their way I will do to them, and according to their judgments I will judge them, and they shall know that I am the LORD."

Abominations in the Temple

8 In the sixth year, in the sixth month, on the fifth day of the month, as I sat in my house, with the elders of Judah sitting before me, the hand of the Lord GOD fell upon me there. 2 Then I looked, and behold, a form that had the appearance of a man.[10] Below what appeared to be his waist was fire, and above his waist was something like the appearance of brightness, like gleaming metal.[11] 3 He put out the form of a hand and took me by a lock of my head, and the Spirit lifted me up between earth and heaven and brought me in visions of God to Jerusalem, to the entrance of the gateway of the inner court that faces north, where was the seat of the image of jealousy, which provokes to jealousy. 4 And behold, the glory of the God of Israel was there, like the vision that I saw in the valley.

5 Then he said to me, "Son of man, lift up your eyes now toward the north." So I lifted up my eyes toward the north, and behold, north of the altar gate, in the entrance, was this image of jealousy. 6 And he said to me, "Son of man, do you see what they are doing, the great abominations that the house of Israel are committing

---

[1] Some Hebrew manuscripts (compare Syriac, Targum); most Hebrew manuscripts *Disaster! A unique disaster!* [2] The meaning of the Hebrew word is uncertain; also verse 10 [3] The meaning of this last Hebrew sentence is uncertain [4] Or *abundance*; also verses 13, 14 [5] The meaning of this last Hebrew sentence is uncertain [6] Or *secret* [7] Probably refers to an instrument of captivity [8] By revocalization (compare Septuagint); Hebrew *and those who sanctify them* [9] Or *instruction* [10] By revocalization (compare Septuagint); Hebrew *of fire* [11] Or *amber*

here, to drive me far from my sanctuary? But you will see still greater abominations."

⁷And he brought me to the entrance of the court, and when I looked, behold, there was a hole in the wall. ⁸Then he said to me, "Son of man, dig in the wall." So I dug in the wall, and behold, there was an entrance. ⁹And he said to me, "Go in, and see the vile abominations that they are committing here." ¹⁰So I went in and saw. And there, engraved on the wall all around, was every form of creeping things and loathsome beasts, and all the idols of the house of Israel. ¹¹And before them stood seventy men of the elders of the house of Israel, with Jaazaniah the son of Shaphan standing among them. Each had his censer in his hand, and the smoke of the cloud of incense went up. ¹²Then he said to me, "Son of man, have you seen what the elders of the house of Israel are doing in the dark, each in his room of pictures? For they say, 'The LORD does not see us, the LORD has forsaken the land.'" ¹³He said also to me, "You will see still greater abominations that they commit."

¹⁴Then he brought me to the entrance of the north gate of the house of the LORD, and behold, there sat women weeping for Tammuz. ¹⁵Then he said to me, "Have you seen this, O son of man? You will see still greater abominations than these."

¹⁶And he brought me into the inner court of the house of the LORD. And behold, at the entrance of the temple of the LORD, between the porch and the altar, were about twenty-five men, with their backs to the temple of the LORD, and their faces toward the east, worshiping the sun toward the east. ¹⁷Then he said to me, "Have you seen this, O son of man? Is it too light a thing for the house of Judah to commit the abominations that they commit here, that they should fill the land with violence and provoke me still further to anger? Behold, they put the branch to their¹ nose. ¹⁸Therefore I will act in wrath. My eye will not spare, nor will I have pity. And though they cry in my ears with a loud voice, I will not hear them."

Idolaters Killed

9 Then he cried in my ears with a loud voice, saying, "Bring near the executioners of the city, each with his destroying weapon in his hand." ²And behold, six men came from the direction of the upper gate, which faces north,

each with his weapon for slaughter in his hand, and with them was a man clothed in linen, with a writing case at his waist. And they went in and stood beside the bronze altar.

³Now the glory of the God of Israel had gone up from the cherub on which it rested to the threshold of the house. And he called to the man clothed in linen, who had the writing case at his waist. ⁴And the LORD said to him, "Pass through the city, through Jerusalem, and put a mark on the foreheads of the men who sigh and groan over all the abominations that are committed in it." ⁵And to the others he said in my hearing, "Pass through the city after him, and strike. Your eye shall not spare, and you shall show no pity. ⁶Kill old men outright, young men and maidens, little children and women, but touch no one on whom is the mark. And begin at my sanctuary." So they began with the elders who were before the house. ⁷Then he said to them, "Defile the house, and fill the courts with the slain. Go out." So they went out and struck in the city. ⁸And while they were striking, and I was left alone, I fell upon my face, and cried, "Ah, Lord GOD! Will you destroy all the remnant of Israel in the outpouring of your wrath on Jerusalem?"

⁹Then he said to me, "The guilt of the house of Israel and Judah is exceedingly great. The land is full of blood, and the city full of injustice. For they say, 'The LORD has forsaken the land, and the LORD does not see.' ¹⁰As for me, my eye will not spare, nor will I have pity; I will bring their deeds upon their heads."

¹¹And behold, the man clothed in linen, with the writing case at his waist, brought back word, saying, "I have done as you commanded me."

The Glory of the LORD Leaves the Temple

10 Then I looked, and behold, on the expanse that was over the heads of the cherubim there appeared above them something like a sapphire,² in appearance like a throne. ²And he said to the man clothed in linen, "Go in among the whirling wheels underneath the cherubim. Fill your hands with burning coals from between the cherubim, and scatter them over the city."

And he went in before my eyes. ³Now the cherubim were standing on the south side of the house, when the man went in, and a cloud

¹ Or my ² Or lapis lazuli

filled the inner court. ⁴ And the glory of the LORD went up from the cherub to the threshold of the house, and the house was filled with the cloud, and the court was filled with the brightness of the glory of the LORD. ⁵ And the sound of the wings of the cherubim was heard as far as the outer court, like the voice of God Almighty when he speaks.

⁶ And when he commanded the man clothed in linen, "Take fire from between the whirling wheels, from between the cherubim," he went in and stood beside a wheel. ⁷ And a cherub stretched out his hand from between the cherubim to the fire that was between the cherubim, and took some of it and put it into the hands of the man clothed in linen, who took it and went out. ⁸ The cherubim appeared to have the form of a human hand under their wings.

⁹ And I looked, and behold, there were four wheels beside the cherubim, one beside each cherub, and the appearance of the wheels was like sparkling beryl. ¹⁰ And as for their appearance, the four had the same likeness, as if a wheel were within a wheel. ¹¹ When they went, they went in any of their four directions[1] without turning as they went, but in whatever direction the front wheel[2] faced, the others followed without turning as they went. ¹² And their whole body, their rims, and their spokes, their wings,[3] and the wheels were full of eyes all around—the wheels that the four of them had. ¹³ As for the wheels, they were called in my hearing "the whirling wheels." ¹⁴ And every one had four faces: the first face was the face of the cherub, and the second face was a human face, and the third the face of a lion, and the fourth the face of an eagle.

¹⁵ And the cherubim mounted up. These were the living creatures that I saw by the Chebar canal. ¹⁶ And when the cherubim went, the wheels went beside them. And when the cherubim lifted up their wings to mount up from the earth, the wheels did not turn from beside them. ¹⁷ When they stood still, these stood still, and when they mounted up, these mounted up with them, for the spirit of the living creatures[4] was in them.

¹⁸ Then the glory of the LORD went out from the threshold of the house, and stood over the cherubim. ¹⁹ And the cherubim lifted up their wings and mounted up from the earth before my eyes as they went out, with the wheels beside them. And they stood at the entrance of the east gate of the house of the LORD, and the glory of the God of Israel was over them.

²⁰ These were the living creatures that I saw underneath the God of Israel by the Chebar canal; and I knew that they were cherubim. ²¹ Each had four faces, and each four wings, and underneath their wings the likeness of human hands. ²² And as for the likeness of their faces, they were the same faces whose appearance I had seen by the Chebar canal. Each one of them went straight forward.

Judgment on Wicked Counselors

11 The Spirit lifted me up and brought me to the east gate of the house of the LORD, which faces east. And behold, at the entrance of the gateway there were twenty-five men. And I saw among them Jaazaniah the son of Azzur, and Pelatiah the son of Benaiah, princes of the people. ² And he said to me, "Son of man, these are the men who devise iniquity and who give wicked counsel in this city; ³ who say, 'The time is not near[5] to build houses. This city is the cauldron, and we are the meat.' ⁴ Therefore prophesy against them; prophesy, O son of man."

⁵ And the Spirit of the LORD fell upon me, and he said to me, "Say, Thus says the LORD: So you think, O house of Israel. For I know the things that come into your mind. ⁶ You have multiplied your slain in this city and have filled its streets with the slain. ⁷ Therefore thus says the Lord GOD: Your slain whom you have laid in the midst of it, they are the meat, and this city is the cauldron, but you shall be brought out of the midst of it. ⁸ You have feared the sword, and I will bring the sword upon you, declares the Lord GOD. ⁹ And I will bring you out of the midst of it, and give you into the hands of foreigners, and execute judgments upon you. ¹⁰ You shall fall by the sword. I will judge you at the border of Israel, and you shall know that I am the LORD. ¹¹ This city shall not be your cauldron, nor shall you be the meat in the midst of it. I will judge you at the border of Israel, ¹² and you shall know that I am the LORD. For you have not walked in my statutes, nor obeyed my rules, but have acted according to the rules of the nations that are around you."

¹³ And it came to pass, while I was prophesying, that Pelatiah the son of Benaiah died. Then I fell down on my face and cried out with a loud voice and said, "Ah, Lord GOD! Will you make a full end of the remnant of Israel?"

---

[1] Hebrew *to their four sides* [2] Hebrew *the head* [3] Or *their whole body, their backs, their hands, and their wings* [4] Or *spirit of life* [5] Or *Is not the time near...?*

Israel's New Heart and Spirit

14 And the word of the LORD came to me: **15** "Son of man, your brothers, even your brothers, your kinsmen,[1] the whole house of Israel, all of them, are those of whom the inhabitants of Jerusalem have said, 'Go far from the LORD; to us this land is given for a possession.' **16** Therefore say, 'Thus says the Lord GOD: Though I removed them far off among the nations, and though I scattered them among the countries, yet I have been a sanctuary to them for a while[2] in the countries where they have gone.' **17** Therefore say, 'Thus says the Lord GOD: I will gather you from the peoples and assemble you out of the countries where you have been scattered, and I will give you the land of Israel.' **18** And when they come there, they will remove from it all its detestable things and all its abominations. **19** And I will give them one heart, and a new spirit I will put within them. I will remove the heart of stone from their flesh and give them a heart of flesh, **20** that they may walk in my statutes and keep my rules and obey them. And they shall be my people, and I will be their God. **21** But as for those whose heart goes after their detestable things and their abominations, I will[3] bring their deeds upon their own heads, declares the Lord GOD."

22 Then the cherubim lifted up their wings, with the wheels beside them, and the glory of the God of Israel was over them. **23** And the glory of the LORD went up from the midst of the city and stood on the mountain that is on the east side of the city. **24** And the Spirit lifted me up and brought me in the vision by the Spirit of God into Chaldea, to the exiles. Then the vision that I had seen went up from me. **25** And I told the exiles all the things that the LORD had shown me.

Judah's Captivity Symbolized

12 The word of the LORD came to me: **2** "Son of man, you dwell in the midst of a rebellious house, who have eyes to see, but see not, who have ears to hear, but hear not, for they are a rebellious house. **3** As for you, son of man, prepare for yourself an exile's baggage, and go into exile by day in their sight. You shall go like an exile from your place to another place in their sight. Perhaps they will understand, though[4] they are a rebellious house. **4** You shall bring out your baggage by day in their sight, as baggage for exile, and you shall go out yourself at evening in their sight, as those who must go into exile. **5** In their sight dig through the wall, and bring your baggage out through it. **6** In their sight you shall lift the baggage upon your shoulder and carry it out at dusk. You shall cover your face that you may not see the land, for I have made you a sign for the house of Israel."

7 And I did as I was commanded. I brought out my baggage by day, as baggage for exile, and in the evening I dug through the wall with my own hands. I brought out my baggage at dusk, carrying it on my shoulder in their sight.

8 In the morning the word of the LORD came to me: **9** "Son of man, has not the house of Israel, the rebellious house, said to you, 'What are you doing?' **10** Say to them, 'Thus says the Lord GOD: This oracle concerns[5] the prince in Jerusalem and all the house of Israel who are in it.'[6] **11** Say, 'I am a sign for you: as I have done, so shall it be done to them. They shall go into exile, into captivity.' **12** And the prince who is among them shall lift his baggage upon his shoulder at dusk, and shall go out. They shall dig through the wall to bring him out through it. He shall cover his face, that he may not see the land with his eyes. **13** And I will spread my net over him, and he shall be taken in my snare. And I will bring him to Babylon, the land of the Chaldeans, yet he shall not see it, and he shall die there. **14** And I will scatter toward every wind all who are around him, his helpers and all his troops, and I will unsheathe the sword after them. **15** And they shall know that I am the LORD, when I disperse them among the nations and scatter them among the countries. **16** But I will let a few of them escape from the sword, from famine and pestilence, that they may declare all their abominations among the nations where they go, and may know that I am the LORD."

17 And the word of the LORD came to me: **18** "Son of man, eat your bread with quaking, and drink water with trembling and with anxiety. **19** And say to the people of the land, Thus says the Lord GOD concerning the inhabitants of Jerusalem in the land of Israel: They shall eat their bread with anxiety, and drink water in dismay. In this way her land will be stripped of all it contains, on account of the violence of

---

[1] Hebrew *the men of your redemption* [2] Or *in small measure* [3] Hebrew *To the heart of their detestable things and their abominations their heart goes; I will* [4] Or *will see that* [5] Or *This burden is* [6] Hebrew *in the midst of them*

all those who dwell in it. ²⁰ And the inhabited cities shall be laid waste, and the land shall become a desolation; and you shall know that I am the LORD."

²¹ And the word of the LORD came to me: ²² "Son of man, what is this proverb that you¹ have about the land of Israel, saying, 'The days grow long, and every vision comes to nothing'? ²³ Tell them therefore, 'Thus says the Lord GOD: I will put an end to this proverb, and they shall no more use it as a proverb in Israel.' But say to them, The days are near, and the fulfillment² of every vision. ²⁴ For there shall be no more any false vision or flattering divination within the house of Israel. ²⁵ For I am the LORD; I will speak the word that I will speak, and it will be performed. It will no longer be delayed, but in your days, O rebellious house, I will speak the word and perform it, declares the Lord GOD."

²⁶ And the word of the LORD came to me: ²⁷ "Son of man, behold, they of the house of Israel say, 'The vision that he sees is for many days from now, and he prophesies of times far off.' ²⁸ Therefore say to them, Thus says the Lord GOD: None of my words will be delayed any longer, but the word that I speak will be performed, declares the Lord GOD."

False Prophets Condemned

13 The word of the LORD came to me: ² "Son of man, prophesy against the prophets of Israel, who are prophesying, and say to those who prophesy from their own hearts: 'Hear the word of the LORD!' ³ Thus says the Lord GOD, Woe to the foolish prophets who follow their own spirit, and have seen nothing! ⁴ Your prophets have been like jackals among ruins, O Israel. ⁵ You have not gone up into the breaches, or built up a wall for the house of Israel, that it might stand in battle in the day of the LORD. ⁶ They have seen false visions and lying divinations. They say, 'Declares the LORD,' when the LORD has not sent them, and yet they expect him to fulfill their word. ⁷ Have you not seen a false vision and uttered a lying divination, whenever you have said, 'Declares the LORD,' although I have not spoken?"

⁸ Therefore thus says the Lord GOD: "Because you have uttered falsehood and seen lying visions, therefore behold, I am against you, declares the Lord GOD. ⁹ My hand will be against the prophets who see false visions and

who give lying divinations. They shall not be in the council of my people, nor be enrolled in the register of the house of Israel, nor shall they enter the land of Israel. And you shall know that I am the Lord GOD. ¹⁰ Precisely because they have misled my people, saying, 'Peace,' when there is no peace, and because, when the people build a wall, these prophets smear it with whitewash,³ ¹¹ say to those who smear it with whitewash that it shall fall! There will be a deluge of rain, and you, O great hailstones, will fall, and a stormy wind break out. ¹² And when the wall falls, will it not be said to you, 'Where is the coating with which you smeared it?' ¹³ Therefore thus says the Lord GOD: I will make a stormy wind break out in my wrath, and there shall be a deluge of rain in my anger, and great hailstones in wrath to make a full end. ¹⁴ And I will break down the wall that you have smeared with whitewash, and bring it down to the ground, so that its foundation will be laid bare. When it falls, you shall perish in the midst of it, and you shall know that I am the LORD. ¹⁵ Thus will I spend my wrath upon the wall and upon those who have smeared it with whitewash, and I will say to you, The wall is no more, nor those who smeared it, ¹⁶ the prophets of Israel who prophesied concerning Jerusalem and saw visions of peace for her, when there was no peace, declares the Lord GOD.

¹⁷ "And you, son of man, set your face against the daughters of your people, who prophesy out of their own hearts. Prophesy against them ¹⁸ and say, Thus says the Lord GOD: Woe to the women who sew magic bands upon all wrists, and make veils for the heads of persons of every stature, in the hunt for souls! Will you hunt down souls belonging to my people and keep your own souls alive? ¹⁹ You have profaned me among my people for handfuls of barley and for pieces of bread, putting to death souls who should not die and keeping alive souls who should not live, by your lying to my people, who listen to lies.

²⁰ "Therefore thus says the Lord GOD: Behold, I am against your magic bands with which you hunt the souls like birds, and I will tear them from your arms, and I will let the souls whom you hunt go free, the souls like birds. ²¹ Your veils also I will tear off and deliver my people out of your hand, and they shall be no more in your hand as prey, and you shall know that I am

---

¹ The Hebrew for *you* is plural ² Hebrew *word* ³ Or *plaster*; also verses 11, 14, 15

the LORD. [22] Because you have disheartened the righteous falsely, although I have not grieved him, and you have encouraged the wicked, that he should not turn from his evil way to save his life, [23] therefore you shall no more see false visions nor practice divination. I will deliver my people out of your hand. And you shall know that I am the LORD."

Idolatrous Elders Condemned

14 Then certain of the elders of Israel came to me and sat before me. [2] And the word of the LORD came to me: [3] "Son of man, these men have taken their idols into their hearts, and set the stumbling block of their iniquity before their faces. Should I indeed let myself be consulted by them? [4] Therefore speak to them and say to them, Thus says the Lord GOD: Any one of the house of Israel who takes his idols into his heart and sets the stumbling block of his iniquity before his face, and yet comes to the prophet, I the LORD will answer him as he comes with the multitude of his idols, [5] that I may lay hold of the hearts of the house of Israel, who are all estranged from me through their idols.

[6] "Therefore say to the house of Israel, Thus says the Lord GOD: Repent and turn away from your idols, and turn away your faces from all your abominations. [7] For any one of the house of Israel, or of the strangers who sojourn in Israel, who separates himself from me, taking his idols into his heart and putting the stumbling block of his iniquity before his face, and yet comes to a prophet to consult me through him, I the LORD will answer him myself. [8] And I will set my face against that man; I will make him a sign and a byword and cut him off from the midst of my people, and you shall know that I am the LORD. [9] And if the prophet is deceived and speaks a word, I, the LORD, have deceived that prophet, and I will stretch out my hand against him and will destroy him from the midst of my people Israel. [10] And they shall bear their punishment[1]—the punishment of the prophet and the punishment of the inquirer shall be alike— [11] that the house of Israel may no more go astray from me, nor defile themselves anymore with all their transgressions, but that they may be my people and I may be their God, declares the Lord GOD."

Jerusalem Will Not Be Spared

[12] And the word of the LORD came to me: [13] "Son of man, when a land sins against me by acting faithlessly, and I stretch out my hand against it and break its supply[2] of bread and send famine upon it, and cut off from it man and beast, [14] even if these three men, Noah, Daniel, and Job, were in it, they would deliver but their own lives by their righteousness, declares the Lord GOD.

[15] "If I cause wild beasts to pass through the land, and they ravage it, and it be made desolate, so that no one may pass through because of the beasts, [16] even if these three men were in it, as I live, declares the Lord GOD, they would deliver neither sons nor daughters. They alone would be delivered, but the land would be desolate.

[17] "Or if I bring a sword upon that land and say, Let a sword pass through the land, and I cut off from it man and beast, [18] though these three men were in it, as I live, declares the Lord GOD, they would deliver neither sons nor daughters, but they alone would be delivered.

[19] "Or if I send a pestilence into that land and pour out my wrath upon it with blood, to cut off from it man and beast, [20] even if Noah, Daniel, and Job were in it, as I live, declares the Lord GOD, they would deliver neither son nor daughter. They would deliver but their own lives by their righteousness.

[21] "For thus says the Lord GOD: How much more when I send upon Jerusalem my four disastrous acts of judgment, sword, famine, wild beasts, and pestilence, to cut off from it man and beast! [22] But behold, some survivors will be left in it, sons and daughters who will be brought out; behold, when they come out to you, and you see their ways and their deeds, you will be consoled for the disaster that I have brought upon Jerusalem, for all that I have brought upon it. [23] They will console you, when you see their ways and their deeds, and you shall know that I have not done without cause all that I have done in it, declares the Lord GOD."

Jerusalem, a Useless Vine

15 And the word of the LORD came to me: [2] "Son of man, how does the wood of the vine surpass any wood, the vine branch that is among the trees of the forest? [3] Is wood taken from it to make anything? Do people take a

---

[1] Or iniquity; three times in this verse [2] Hebrew staff

peg from it to hang any vessel on it? [4] Behold, it is given to the fire for fuel. When the fire has consumed both ends of it, and the middle of it is charred, is it useful for anything? [5] Behold, when it was whole, it was used for nothing. How much less, when the fire has consumed it and it is charred, can it ever be used for anything! [6] Therefore thus says the Lord God: Like the wood of the vine among the trees of the forest, which I have given to the fire for fuel, so have I given up the inhabitants of Jerusalem. [7] And I will set my face against them. Though they escape from the fire, the fire shall yet consume them, and you will know that I am the Lord, when I set my face against them. [8] And I will make the land desolate, because they have acted faithlessly, declares the Lord God."

The Lord's Faithless Bride

16 Again the word of the Lord came to me: [2] "Son of man, make known to Jerusalem her abominations, [3] and say, Thus says the Lord God to Jerusalem: Your origin and your birth are of the land of the Canaanites; your father was an Amorite and your mother a Hittite. [4] And as for your birth, on the day you were born your cord was not cut, nor were you washed with water to cleanse you, nor rubbed with salt, nor wrapped in swaddling cloths. [5] No eye pitied you, to do any of these things to you out of compassion for you, but you were cast out on the open field, for you were abhorred, on the day that you were born.

[6] "And when I passed by you and saw you wallowing in your blood, I said to you in your blood, 'Live!' I said to you in your blood, 'Live!' [7] I made you flourish like a plant of the field. And you grew up and became tall and arrived at full adornment. Your breasts were formed, and your hair had grown; yet you were naked and bare.

[8] "When I passed by you again and saw you, behold, you were at the age for love, and I spread the corner of my garment over you and covered your nakedness; I made my vow to you and entered into a covenant with you, declares the Lord God, and you became mine. [9] Then I bathed you with water and washed off your blood from you and anointed you with oil. [10] I clothed you also with embroidered cloth and shod you with fine leather. I wrapped you in fine linen and covered you with silk.[1] [11] And I adorned you with ornaments and put bracelets on your wrists and a chain on your neck. [12] And

I put a ring on your nose and earrings in your ears and a beautiful crown on your head. [13] Thus you were adorned with gold and silver, and your clothing was of fine linen and silk and embroidered cloth. You ate fine flour and honey and oil. You grew exceedingly beautiful and advanced to royalty. [14] And your renown went forth among the nations because of your beauty, for it was perfect through the splendor that I had bestowed on you, declares the Lord God.

[15] "But you trusted in your beauty and played the whore[2] because of your renown and lavished your whorings[3] on any passerby; your beauty[4] became his. [16] You took some of your garments and made for yourself colorful shrines, and on them played the whore. The like has never been, nor ever shall be.[5] [17] You also took your beautiful jewels of my gold and of my silver, which I had given you, and made for yourself images of men, and with them played the whore. [18] And you took your embroidered garments to cover them, and set my oil and my incense before them. [19] Also my bread that I gave you—I fed you with fine flour and oil and honey—you set before them for a pleasing aroma; and so it was, declares the Lord God. [20] And you took your sons and your daughters, whom you had borne to me, and these you sacrificed to them to be devoured. Were your whorings so small a matter [21] that you slaughtered my children and delivered them up as an offering by fire to them? [22] And in all your abominations and your whorings you did not remember the days of your youth, when you were naked and bare, wallowing in your blood.

[23] "And after all your wickedness (woe, woe to you! declares the Lord God), [24] you built yourself a vaulted chamber and made yourself a lofty place in every square. [25] At the head of every street you built your lofty place and made your beauty an abomination, offering yourself[6] to any passerby and multiplying your whoring. [26] You also played the whore with the Egyptians, your lustful neighbors, multiplying your whoring, to provoke me to anger. [27] Behold, therefore, I stretched out my hand against you and diminished your allotted portion and delivered you to the greed of your enemies, the daughters of the Philistines, who were ashamed of your lewd behavior. [28] You played the whore also with the Assyrians, because you were not satisfied; yes, you played the whore with them, and still you

---

[1] Or with rich fabric [2] Or were unfaithful; also verses 16, 17, 26, 28 [3] Or unfaithfulness; also verses 20, 22, 25, 26, 29, 33, 34, 36 [4] Hebrew it [5] The meaning of this Hebrew sentence is uncertain [6] Hebrew spreading your legs

were not satisfied. [29] You multiplied your whoring also with the trading land of Chaldea, and even with this you were not satisfied.

[30] "How sick is your heart,[1] declares the Lord GOD, because you did all these things, the deeds of a brazen prostitute, [31] building your vaulted chamber at the head of every street, and making your lofty place in every square. Yet you were not like a prostitute, because you scorned payment. [32] Adulterous wife, who receives strangers instead of her husband! [33] Men give gifts to all prostitutes, but you gave your gifts to all your lovers, bribing them to come to you from every side with your whorings. [34] So you were different from other women in your whorings. No one solicited you to play the whore, and you gave payment, while no payment was given to you; therefore you were different.

[35] "Therefore, O prostitute, hear the word of the LORD: [36] Thus says the Lord GOD, Because your lust was poured out and your nakedness uncovered in your whorings with your lovers, and with all your abominable idols, and because of the blood of your children that you gave to them, [37] therefore, behold, I will gather all your lovers with whom you took pleasure, all those you loved and all those you hated. I will gather them against you from every side and will uncover your nakedness to them, that they may see all your nakedness. [38] And I will judge you as women who commit adultery and shed blood are judged, and bring upon you the blood of wrath and jealousy. [39] And I will give you into their hands, and they shall throw down your vaulted chamber and break down your lofty places. They shall strip you of your clothes and take your beautiful jewels and leave you naked and bare. [40] They shall bring up a crowd against you, and they shall stone you and cut you to pieces with their swords. [41] And they shall burn your houses and execute judgments upon you in the sight of many women. I will make you stop playing the whore, and you shall also give payment no more. [42] So will I satisfy my wrath on you, and my jealousy shall depart from you. I will be calm and will no more be angry. [43] Because you have not remembered the days of your youth, but have enraged me with all these things, therefore, behold, I have returned your deeds upon your head, declares the Lord GOD. Have you not committed lewdness in addition to all your abominations?

[44] "Behold, everyone who uses proverbs will use this proverb about you: 'Like mother, like daughter.' [45] You are the daughter of your mother, who loathed her husband and her children; and you are the sister of your sisters, who loathed their husbands and their children. Your mother was a Hittite and your father an Amorite. [46] And your elder sister is Samaria, who lived with her daughters to the north of you; and your younger sister, who lived to the south of you, is Sodom with her daughters. [47] Not only did you walk in their ways and do according to their abominations; within a very little time you were more corrupt than they in all your ways. [48] As I live, declares the Lord GOD, your sister Sodom and her daughters have not done as you and your daughters have done. [49] Behold, this was the guilt of your sister Sodom: she and her daughters had pride, excess of food, and prosperous ease, but did not aid the poor and needy. [50] They were haughty and did an abomination before me. So I removed them, when I saw it. [51] Samaria has not committed half your sins. You have committed more abominations than they, and have made your sisters appear righteous by all the abominations that you have committed. [52] Bear your disgrace, you also, for you have intervened on behalf of your sisters. Because of your sins in which you acted more abominably than they, they are more in the right than you. So be ashamed, you also, and bear your disgrace, for you have made your sisters appear righteous.

[53] "I will restore their fortunes, both the fortunes of Sodom and her daughters, and the fortunes of Samaria and her daughters, and I will restore your own fortunes in their midst, [54] that you may bear your disgrace and be ashamed of all that you have done, becoming a consolation to them. [55] As for your sisters, Sodom and her daughters shall return to their former state, and Samaria and her daughters shall return to their former state, and you and your daughters shall return to your former state. [56] Was not your sister Sodom a byword in your mouth in the day of your pride, [57] before your wickedness was uncovered? Now you have become an object of reproach for the daughters of Syria[2] and all those around her, and for the daughters of the Philistines, those all around who despise you. [58] You bear the penalty of your lewdness and your abominations, declares the LORD.

---

[1] Revocalization yields *How I am filled with anger against you*   [2] Some manuscripts (compare Syriac) *of Edom*

The LORD's Everlasting Covenant

⁵⁹ "For thus says the Lord GOD: I will deal with you as you have done, you who have despised the oath in breaking the covenant, ⁶⁰ yet I will remember my covenant with you in the days of your youth, and I will establish for you an everlasting covenant. ⁶¹ Then you will remember your ways and be ashamed when you take your sisters, both your elder and your younger, and I give them to you as daughters, but not on account of¹ the covenant with you. ⁶² I will establish my covenant with you, and you shall know that I am the LORD, ⁶³ that you may remember and be confounded, and never open your mouth again because of your shame, when I atone for you for all that you have done, declares the Lord GOD."

Parable of Two Eagles and a Vine

17 The word of the LORD came to me: ² "Son of man, propound a riddle, and speak a parable to the house of Israel; ³ say, Thus says the Lord GOD: A great eagle with great wings and long pinions, rich in plumage of many colors, came to Lebanon and took the top of the cedar. ⁴ He broke off the topmost of its young twigs and carried it to a land of trade and set it in a city of merchants. ⁵ Then he took of the seed of the land and planted it in fertile soil.² He placed it beside abundant waters. He set it like a willow twig, ⁶ and it sprouted and became a low spreading vine, and its branches turned toward him, and its roots remained where it stood. So it became a vine and produced branches and put out boughs.

⁷ "And there was another great eagle with great wings and much plumage, and behold, this vine bent its roots toward him and shot forth its branches toward him from the bed where it was planted, that he might water it. ⁸ It had been planted on good soil by abundant waters, that it might produce branches and bear fruit and become a noble vine.

⁹ "Say, Thus says the Lord GOD: Will it thrive? Will he not pull up its roots and cut off its fruit, so that it withers, so that all its fresh sprouting leaves wither? It will not take a strong arm or many people to pull it from its roots. ¹⁰ Behold, it is planted; will it thrive? Will it not utterly wither when the east wind strikes it—wither away on the bed where it sprouted?"

¹¹ Then the word of the LORD came to me:

¹² "Say now to the rebellious house, Do you not know what these things mean? Tell them, behold, the king of Babylon came to Jerusalem, and took her king and her princes and brought them to him to Babylon. ¹³ And he took one of the royal offspring³ and made a covenant with him, putting him under oath (the chief men of the land he had taken away), ¹⁴ that the kingdom might be humble and not lift itself up, and keep his covenant that it might stand. ¹⁵ But he rebelled against him by sending his ambassadors to Egypt, that they might give him horses and a large army. Will he thrive? Can one escape who does such things? Can he break the covenant and yet escape?

¹⁶ "As I live, declares the Lord GOD, surely in the place where the king dwells who made him king, whose oath he despised, and whose covenant with him he broke, in Babylon he shall die. ¹⁷ Pharaoh with his mighty army and great company will not help him in war, when mounds are cast up and siege walls built to cut off many lives. ¹⁸ He despised the oath in breaking the covenant, and behold, he gave his hand and did all these things; he shall not escape. ¹⁹ Therefore thus says the Lord GOD: As I live, surely it is my oath that he despised, and my covenant that he broke. I will return it upon his head. ²⁰ I will spread my net over him, and he shall be taken in my snare, and I will bring him to Babylon and enter into judgment with him there for the treachery he has committed against me. ²¹ And all the pick⁴ of his troops shall fall by the sword, and the survivors shall be scattered to every wind, and you shall know that I am the LORD; I have spoken."

²² Thus says the Lord GOD: "I myself will take a sprig from the lofty top of the cedar and will set it out. I will break off from the topmost of its young twigs a tender one, and I myself will plant it on a high and lofty mountain. ²³ On the mountain height of Israel will I plant it, that it may bear branches and produce fruit and become a noble cedar. And under it will dwell every kind of bird; in the shade of its branches birds of every sort will nest. ²⁴ And all the trees of the field shall know that I am the LORD; I bring low the high tree, and make high the low tree, dry up the green tree, and make the dry tree flourish. I am the LORD; I have spoken, and I will do it."

---

¹ Or *not apart from* ² Hebrew *in a field of seed* ³ Hebrew *seed* ⁴ Some Hebrew manuscripts, Syriac, Targum; most Hebrew manuscripts *all the fugitives*

The Soul Who Sins Shall Die

18 The word of the LORD came to me: [2] "What do you[1] mean by repeating this proverb concerning the land of Israel, 'The fathers have eaten sour grapes, and the children's teeth are set on edge'? [3] As I live, declares the Lord GOD, this proverb shall no more be used by you in Israel. [4] Behold, all souls are mine; the soul of the father as well as the soul of the son is mine: the soul who sins shall die.

[5] "If a man is righteous and does what is just and right— [6] if he does not eat upon the mountains or lift up his eyes to the idols of the house of Israel, does not defile his neighbor's wife or approach a woman in her time of menstrual impurity, [7] does not oppress anyone, but restores to the debtor his pledge, commits no robbery, gives his bread to the hungry and covers the naked with a garment, [8] does not lend at interest or take any profit,[2] withholds his hand from injustice, executes true justice between man and man, [9] walks in my statutes, and keeps my rules by acting faithfully—he is righteous; he shall surely live, declares the Lord GOD.

[10] "If he fathers a son who is violent, a shedder of blood, who does any of these things [11] (though he himself did none of these things), who even eats upon the mountains, defiles his neighbor's wife, [12] oppresses the poor and needy, commits robbery, does not restore the pledge, lifts up his eyes to the idols, commits abomination, [13] lends at interest, and takes profit; shall he then live? He shall not live. He has done all these abominations; he shall surely die; his blood shall be upon himself.

[14] "Now suppose this man fathers a son who sees all the sins that his father has done; he sees, and does not do likewise: [15] he does not eat upon the mountains or lift up his eyes to the idols of the house of Israel, does not defile his neighbor's wife, [16] does not oppress anyone, exacts no pledge, commits no robbery, but gives his bread to the hungry and covers the naked with a garment, [17] withholds his hand from iniquity,[3] takes no interest or profit, obeys my rules, and walks in my statutes; he shall not die for his father's iniquity; he shall surely live. [18] As for his father, because he practiced extortion, robbed his brother, and did what is not good among his people, behold, he shall die for his iniquity.

[19] "Yet you say, 'Why should not the son suffer for the iniquity of the father?' When the son has done what is just and right, and has been careful to observe all my statutes, he shall surely live. [20] The soul who sins shall die. The son shall not suffer for the iniquity of the father, nor the father suffer for the iniquity of the son. The righteousness of the righteous shall be upon himself, and the wickedness of the wicked shall be upon himself.

[21] "But if a wicked person turns away from all his sins that he has committed and keeps all my statutes and does what is just and right, he shall surely live; he shall not die. [22] None of the transgressions that he has committed shall be remembered against him; for the righteousness that he has done he shall live. [23] Have I any pleasure in the death of the wicked, declares the Lord GOD, and not rather that he should turn from his way and live? [24] But when a righteous person turns away from his righteousness and does injustice and does the same abominations that the wicked person does, shall he live? None of the righteous deeds that he has done shall be remembered; for the treachery of which he is guilty and the sin he has committed, for them he shall die.

[25] "Yet you say, 'The way of the Lord is not just.' Hear now, O house of Israel: Is my way not just? Is it not your ways that are not just? [26] When a righteous person turns away from his righteousness and does injustice, he shall die for it; for the injustice that he has done he shall die. [27] Again, when a wicked person turns away from the wickedness he has committed and does what is just and right, he shall save his life. [28] Because he considered and turned away from all the transgressions that he had committed, he shall surely live; he shall not die. [29] Yet the house of Israel says, 'The way of the Lord is not just.' O house of Israel, are my ways not just? Is it not your ways that are not just?

[30] "Therefore I will judge you, O house of Israel, every one according to his ways, declares the Lord GOD. Repent and turn from all your transgressions, lest iniquity be your ruin.[4] [31] Cast away from you all the transgressions that you have committed, and make yourselves a new heart and a new spirit! Why will you die, O house of Israel? [32] For I have no pleasure in the death of anyone, declares the Lord GOD; so turn, and live."

[1] The Hebrew for *you* is plural [2] That is, profit that comes from charging interest to the poor; also verses 13, 17 (compare Leviticus 25:36) [3] Septuagint; Hebrew *from the poor* [4] Or *lest iniquity be your stumbling block*

A Lament for the Princes of Israel

19 And you, take up a lamentation for the princes of Israel, [2] and say:

What was your mother? A lioness!
Among lions she crouched;
in the midst of young lions
she reared her cubs.
[3] And she brought up one of her cubs;
he became a young lion,
and he learned to catch prey;
he devoured men.
[4] The nations heard about him;
he was caught in their pit,
and they brought him with hooks
to the land of Egypt.
[5] When she saw that she waited in vain,
that her hope was lost,
she took another of her cubs
and made him a young lion.
[6] He prowled among the lions;
he became a young lion,
and he learned to catch prey;
he devoured men,
[7] and seized[1] their widows.
He laid waste their cities,
and the land was appalled and all who
were in it
at the sound of his roaring.
[8] Then the nations set against him
from provinces on every side;
they spread their net over him;
he was taken in their pit.
[9] With hooks they put him in a cage[2]
and brought him to the king of Babylon;
they brought him into custody,
that his voice should no more be heard
on the mountains of Israel.

[10] Your mother was like a vine in a vineyard[3]
planted by the water,
fruitful and full of branches
by reason of abundant water.
[11] Its strong stems became
rulers' scepters;
it towered aloft
among the thick boughs;[4]
it was seen in its height
with the mass of its branches.
[12] But the vine was plucked up in fury,
cast down to the ground;
the east wind dried up its fruit;
they were stripped off and withered.

As for its strong stem,
fire consumed it.
[13] Now it is planted in the wilderness,
in a dry and thirsty land.
[14] And fire has gone out from the stem of its
shoots,
has consumed its fruit,
so that there remains in it no strong stem,
no scepter for ruling.

This is a lamentation and has become a lamentation.

Israel's Continuing Rebellion

20 In the seventh year, in the fifth month, on the tenth day of the month, certain of the elders of Israel came to inquire of the LORD, and sat before me. [2] And the word of the LORD came to me: [3] "Son of man, speak to the elders of Israel, and say to them, Thus says the Lord GOD, Is it to inquire of me that you come? As I live, declares the Lord GOD, I will not be inquired of by you. [4] Will you judge them, son of man, will you judge them? Let them know the abominations of their fathers, [5] and say to them, Thus says the Lord GOD: On the day when I chose Israel, I swore[5] to the offspring of the house of Jacob, making myself known to them in the land of Egypt; I swore to them, saying, I am the LORD your God. [6] On that day I swore to them that I would bring them out of the land of Egypt into a land that I had searched out for them, a land flowing with milk and honey, the most glorious of all lands. [7] And I said to them, 'Cast away the detestable things your eyes feast on, every one of you, and do not defile yourselves with the idols of Egypt; I am the LORD your God.' [8] But they rebelled against me and were not willing to listen to me. None of them cast away the detestable things their eyes feasted on, nor did they forsake the idols of Egypt.

"Then I said I would pour out my wrath upon them and spend my anger against them in the midst of the land of Egypt. [9] But I acted for the sake of my name, that it should not be profaned in the sight of the nations among whom they lived, in whose sight I made myself known to them in bringing them out of the land of Egypt. [10] So I led them out of the land of Egypt and brought them into the wilderness. [11] I gave them my statutes and made known to them my rules, by which, if a person does them, he shall live. [12] Moreover, I gave them my

[1] Hebrew *knew* [2] Or *in a wooden collar* [3] Some Hebrew manuscripts; most Hebrew manuscripts *in your blood* [4] Or *the clouds* [5] Hebrew *I lifted my hand*; twice in this verse; also verses 6, 15, 23, 28, 42

Sabbaths, as a sign between me and them, that they might know that I am the LORD who sanctifies them. [13] But the house of Israel rebelled against me in the wilderness. They did not walk in my statutes but rejected my rules, by which, if a person does them, he shall live; and my Sabbaths they greatly profaned.

"Then I said I would pour out my wrath upon them in the wilderness, to make a full end of them. [14] But I acted for the sake of my name, that it should not be profaned in the sight of the nations, in whose sight I had brought them out. [15] Moreover, I swore to them in the wilderness that I would not bring them into the land that I had given them, a land flowing with milk and honey, the most glorious of all lands, [16] because they rejected my rules and did not walk in my statutes, and profaned my Sabbaths; for their heart went after their idols. [17] Nevertheless, my eye spared them, and I did not destroy them or make a full end of them in the wilderness.

[18] "And I said to their children in the wilderness, 'Do not walk in the statutes of your fathers, nor keep their rules, nor defile yourselves with their idols. [19] I am the LORD your God; walk in my statutes, and be careful to obey my rules, [20] and keep my Sabbaths holy that they may be a sign between me and you, that you may know that I am the LORD your God.' [21] But the children rebelled against me. They did not walk in my statutes and were not careful to obey my rules, by which, if a person does them, he shall live; they profaned my Sabbaths.

"Then I said I would pour out my wrath upon them and spend my anger against them in the wilderness. [22] But I withheld my hand and acted for the sake of my name, that it should not be profaned in the sight of the nations, in whose sight I had brought them out. [23] Moreover, I swore to them in the wilderness that I would scatter them among the nations and disperse them through the countries, [24] because they had not obeyed my rules, but had rejected my statutes and profaned my Sabbaths, and their eyes were set on their fathers' idols. [25] Moreover, I gave them statutes that were not good and rules by which they could not have life, [26] and I defiled them through their very gifts in their offering up all their firstborn, that I might devastate them. I did it that they might know that I am the LORD.

[27] "Therefore, son of man, speak to the house of Israel and say to them, Thus says the Lord GOD: In this also your fathers blasphemed me, by dealing treacherously with me. [28] For when I had brought them into the land that I swore to give them, then wherever they saw any high hill or any leafy tree, there they offered their sacrifices and there they presented the provocation of their offering; there they sent up their pleasing aromas, and there they poured out their drink offerings. [29] (I said to them, 'What is the high place to which you go?' So its name is called Bamah[1] to this day.)

[30] "Therefore say to the house of Israel, Thus says the Lord GOD: Will you defile yourselves after the manner of your fathers and go whoring after their detestable things? [31] When you present your gifts and offer up your children in fire,[2] you defile yourselves with all your idols to this day. And shall I be inquired of by you, O house of Israel? As I live, declares the Lord GOD, I will not be inquired of by you.

[32] "What is in your mind shall never happen—the thought, 'Let us be like the nations, like the tribes of the countries, and worship wood and stone.'

The LORD Will Restore Israel

[33] "As I live, declares the Lord GOD, surely with a mighty hand and an outstretched arm and with wrath poured out I will be king over you. [34] I will bring you out from the peoples and gather you out of the countries where you are scattered, with a mighty hand and an outstretched arm, and with wrath poured out. [35] And I will bring you into the wilderness of the peoples, and there I will enter into judgment with you face to face. [36] As I entered into judgment with your fathers in the wilderness of the land of Egypt, so I will enter into judgment with you, declares the Lord GOD. [37] I will make you pass under the rod, and I will bring you into the bond of the covenant. [38] I will purge out the rebels from among you, and those who transgress against me. I will bring them out of the land where they sojourn, but they shall not enter the land of Israel. Then you will know that I am the LORD.

[39] "As for you, O house of Israel, thus says the Lord GOD: Go serve every one of you his idols, now and hereafter, if you will not listen to me; but my holy name you shall no more profane with your gifts and your idols.

---

[1] Bamah means high place [2] Hebrew and make your children pass through the fire

⁴⁰"For on my holy mountain, the mountain height of Israel, declares the Lord GOD, there all the house of Israel, all of them, shall serve me in the land. There I will accept them, and there I will require your contributions and the choicest of your gifts, with all your sacred offerings. ⁴¹As a pleasing aroma I will accept you, when I bring you out from the peoples and gather you out of the countries where you have been scattered. And I will manifest my holiness among you in the sight of the nations. ⁴²And you shall know that I am the LORD, when I bring you into the land of Israel, the country that I swore to give to your fathers. ⁴³And there you shall remember your ways and all your deeds with which you have defiled yourselves, and you shall loathe yourselves for all the evils that you have committed. ⁴⁴And you shall know that I am the LORD, when I deal with you for my name's sake, not according to your evil ways, nor according to your corrupt deeds, O house of Israel, declares the Lord GOD."

⁴⁵ ¹ And the word of the LORD came to me: ⁴⁶"Son of man, set your face toward the southland;² preach against the south, and prophesy against the forest land in the Negeb. ⁴⁷Say to the forest of the Negeb, Hear the word of the LORD: Thus says the Lord GOD, Behold, I will kindle a fire in you, and it shall devour every green tree in you and every dry tree. The blazing flame shall not be quenched, and all faces from south to north shall be scorched by it. ⁴⁸All flesh shall see that I the LORD have kindled it; it shall not be quenched." ⁴⁹Then I said, "Ah, Lord GOD! They are saying of me, 'Is he not a maker of parables?'"

The LORD Has Drawn His Sword

21 ³ The word of the LORD came to me: ²"Son of man, set your face toward Jerusalem and preach against the sanctuaries.⁴ Prophesy against the land of Israel ³and say to the land of Israel, Thus says the LORD: Behold, I am against you and will draw my sword from its sheath and will cut off from you both righteous and wicked. ⁴Because I will cut off from you both righteous and wicked, therefore my sword shall be drawn from its sheath against all flesh from south to north. ⁵And all flesh shall know that I am the LORD. I have drawn my sword from its sheath; it shall not be sheathed again.

⁶"As for you, son of man, groan; with breaking heart and bitter grief, groan before their eyes. ⁷And when they say to you, 'Why do you groan?' you shall say, 'Because of the news that it is coming. Every heart will melt, and all hands will be feeble; every spirit will faint, and all knees will be weak as water. Behold, it is coming, and it will be fulfilled,'" declares the Lord GOD.

⁸And the word of the LORD came to me: ⁹"Son of man, prophesy and say, Thus says the Lord, say:

"A sword, a sword is sharpened
    and also polished,
¹⁰   sharpened for slaughter,
        polished to flash like lightning!

(Or shall we rejoice? You have despised the rod, my son, with everything of wood.)⁵ ¹¹So the sword is given to be polished, that it may be grasped in the hand. It is sharpened and polished to be given into the hand of the slayer. ¹²Cry out and wail, son of man, for it is against my people. It is against all the princes of Israel. They are delivered over to the sword with my people. Strike therefore upon your thigh. ¹³For it will not be a testing—what could it do if you despise the rod?"⁶ declares the Lord GOD.

¹⁴"As for you, son of man, prophesy. Clap your hands and let the sword come down twice, yes, three times,⁷ the sword for those to be slain. It is the sword for the great slaughter, which surrounds them, ¹⁵that their hearts may melt, and many stumble.⁸ At all their gates I have given the glittering sword. Ah, it is made like lightning; it is taken up⁹ for slaughter. ¹⁶Cut sharply to the right; set yourself to the left, wherever your face is directed. ¹⁷I also will clap my hands, and I will satisfy my fury; I the LORD have spoken."

¹⁸The word of the LORD came to me again: ¹⁹"As for you, son of man, mark two ways for the sword of the king of Babylon to come. Both of them shall come from the same land. And make a signpost; make it at the head of the way to a city. ²⁰Mark a way for the sword to come to Rabbah of the Ammonites and to Judah, into Jerusalem the fortified. ²¹For the king of Babylon stands at the parting of the way, at the head of the two ways, to use divination. He shakes the arrows; he consults the teraphim;¹⁰ he looks at the liver. ²²Into his right hand comes

¹ Ch 21:1 in Hebrew ² Or toward Teman ³ Ch 21:6 in Hebrew ⁴ Some Hebrew manuscripts, compare Septuagint, Syriac against their sanctuary ⁵ Probable reading; Hebrew The rod of my son despises everything of wood ⁶ Or For it is a testing; and what if even the rod despises? It shall not be! ⁷ Hebrew its third ⁸ Hebrew many stumbling blocks ⁹ The meaning of the Hebrew word rendered taken up is uncertain ¹⁰ Or household idols

the divination for Jerusalem, to set battering rams, to open the mouth with murder, to lift up the voice with shouting, to set battering rams against the gates, to cast up mounds, to build siege towers. [23] But to them it will seem like a false divination. They have sworn solemn oaths, but he brings their guilt to remembrance, that they may be taken.

[24] "Therefore thus says the Lord GOD: Because you have made your guilt to be remembered, in that your transgressions are uncovered, so that in all your deeds your sins appear—because you have come to remembrance, you shall be taken in hand. [25] And you, O profane[1] wicked one, prince of Israel, whose day has come, the time of your final punishment, [26] thus says the Lord GOD: Remove the turban and take off the crown. Things shall not remain as they are. Exalt that which is low, and bring low that which is exalted. [27] A ruin, ruin, ruin I will make it. This also shall not be, until he comes, the one to whom judgment belongs, and I will give it to him.

[28] "And you, son of man, prophesy, and say, Thus says the Lord GOD concerning the Ammonites and concerning their reproach; say, A sword, a sword is drawn for the slaughter. It is polished to consume and to flash like lightning— [29] while they see for you false visions, while they divine lies for you—to place you on the necks of the profane wicked, whose day has come, the time of their final punishment. [30] Return it to its sheath. In the place where you were created, in the land of your origin, I will judge you. [31] And I will pour out my indignation upon you; I will blow upon you with the fire of my wrath, and I will deliver you into the hands of brutish men, skillful to destroy. [32] You shall be fuel for the fire. Your blood shall be in the midst of the land. You shall be no more remembered, for I the LORD have spoken."

Israel's Shedding of Blood

22 And the word of the LORD came to me, saying, [2] "And you, son of man, will you judge, will you judge the bloody city? Then declare to her all her abominations. [3] You shall say, Thus says the Lord GOD: A city that sheds blood in her midst, so that her time may come, and that makes idols to defile herself! [4] You have become guilty by the blood that you have shed, and defiled by the idols that you have made, and you have brought your days near,

the appointed time of[2] your years has come. Therefore I have made you a reproach to the nations, and a mockery to all the countries. [5] Those who are near and those who are far from you will mock you; your name is defiled; you are full of tumult.

[6] "Behold, the princes of Israel in you, every one according to his power, have been bent on shedding blood. [7] Father and mother are treated with contempt in you; the sojourner suffers extortion in your midst; the fatherless and the widow are wronged in you. [8] You have despised my holy things and profaned my Sabbaths. [9] There are men in you who slander to shed blood, and people in you who eat on the mountains; they commit lewdness in your midst. [10] In you men uncover their fathers' nakedness; in you they violate women who are unclean in their menstrual impurity. [11] One commits abomination with his neighbor's wife; another lewdly defiles his daughter-in-law; another in you violates his sister, his father's daughter. [12] In you they take bribes to shed blood; you take interest and profit[3] and make gain of your neighbors by extortion; but me you have forgotten, declares the Lord GOD.

[13] "Behold, I strike my hand at the dishonest gain that you have made, and at the blood that has been in your midst. [14] Can your courage endure, or can your hands be strong, in the days that I shall deal with you? I the LORD have spoken, and I will do it. [15] I will scatter you among the nations and disperse you through the countries, and I will consume your uncleanness out of you. [16] And you shall be profaned by your own doing in the sight of the nations, and you shall know that I am the LORD."

[17] And the word of the LORD came to me: [18] "Son of man, the house of Israel has become dross to me; all of them are bronze and tin and iron and lead in the furnace; they are dross of silver. [19] Therefore thus says the Lord GOD: Because you have all become dross, therefore, behold, I will gather you into the midst of Jerusalem. [20] As one gathers silver and bronze and iron and lead and tin into a furnace, to blow the fire on it in order to melt it, so I will gather you in my anger and in my wrath, and I will put you in and melt you. [21] I will gather you and blow on you with the fire of my wrath, and you shall be melted in the midst of it. [22] As silver is melted in a furnace, so you shall be melted in

---

[1] Or *slain*; also verse 29 [2] Some Hebrew manuscripts, Septuagint, Syriac, Vulgate, Targum; most Hebrew manuscripts *until* [3] That is, profit that comes from charging interest to the poor (compare Leviticus 25:36)

the midst of it, and you shall know that I am the LORD; I have poured out my wrath upon you."

23 And the word of the LORD came to me: 24 "Son of man, say to her, You are a land that is not cleansed or rained upon in the day of indignation. 25 The conspiracy of her prophets in her midst is like a roaring lion tearing the prey; they have devoured human lives; they have taken treasure and precious things; they have made many widows in her midst. 26 Her priests have done violence to my law and have profaned my holy things. They have made no distinction between the holy and the common, neither have they taught the difference between the unclean and the clean, and they have disregarded my Sabbaths, so that I am profaned among them. 27 Her princes in her midst are like wolves tearing the prey, shedding blood, destroying lives to get dishonest gain. 28 And her prophets have smeared whitewash for them, seeing false visions and divining lies for them, saying, 'Thus says the Lord GOD,' when the LORD has not spoken. 29 The people of the land have practiced extortion and committed robbery. They have oppressed the poor and needy, and have extorted from the sojourner without justice. 30 And I sought for a man among them who should build up the wall and stand in the breach before me for the land, that I should not destroy it, but I found none. 31 Therefore I have poured out my indignation upon them. I have consumed them with the fire of my wrath. I have returned their way upon their heads, declares the Lord GOD."

Oholah and Oholibah

23 The word of the LORD came to me: 2 "Son of man, there were two women, the daughters of one mother. 3 They played the whore in Egypt; they played the whore in their youth; there their breasts were pressed and their virgin bosoms[1] handled. 4 Oholah was the name of the elder and Oholibah the name of her sister. They became mine, and they bore sons and daughters. As for their names, Oholah is Samaria, and Oholibah is Jerusalem.

5 "Oholah played the whore while she was mine, and she lusted after her lovers the Assyrians, warriors 6 clothed in purple, governors and commanders, all of them desirable young men, horsemen riding on horses. 7 She bestowed her whoring upon them, the choicest men of Assyria all of them, and she

defiled herself with all the idols of everyone after whom she lusted. 8 She did not give up her whoring that she had begun in Egypt; for in her youth men had lain with her and handled her virgin bosom and poured out their whoring lust upon her. 9 Therefore I delivered her into the hands of her lovers, into the hands of the Assyrians, after whom she lusted. 10 These uncovered her nakedness; they seized her sons and her daughters; and as for her, they killed her with the sword; and she became a byword among women, when judgment had been executed on her.

11 "Her sister Oholibah saw this, and she became more corrupt than her sister[2] in her lust and in her whoring, which was worse than that of her sister. 12 She lusted after the Assyrians, governors and commanders, warriors clothed in full armor, horsemen riding on horses, all of them desirable young men. 13 And I saw that she was defiled; they both took the same way. 14 But she carried her whoring further. She saw men portrayed on the wall, the images of the Chaldeans portrayed in vermilion, 15 wearing belts on their waists, with flowing turbans on their heads, all of them having the appearance of officers, a likeness of Babylonians whose native land was Chaldea. 16 When she saw them, she lusted after them and sent messengers to them in Chaldea. 17 And the Babylonians came to her into the bed of love, and they defiled her with their whoring lust. And after she was defiled by them, she turned from them in disgust. 18 When she carried on her whoring so openly and flaunted her nakedness, I turned in disgust from her, as I had turned in disgust from her sister. 19 Yet she increased her whoring, remembering the days of her youth, when she played the whore in the land of Egypt 20 and lusted after her lovers there, whose members were like those of donkeys, and whose issue was like that of horses. 21 Thus you longed for the lewdness of your youth, when the Egyptians handled your bosom and pressed[3] your young breasts."

22 Therefore, O Oholibah, thus says the Lord GOD: "Behold, I will stir up against you your lovers from whom you turned in disgust, and I will bring them against you from every side: 23 the Babylonians and all the Chaldeans, Pekod and Shoa and Koa, and all the Assyrians with them, desirable young men, governors and commanders all of them, officers and men of

---

* [1] Hebrew *nipples*; also verses 8, 21 [2] Hebrew *than she* [3] Vulgate, Syriac; Hebrew *bosom for the sake of*

renown, all of them riding on horses. [24] And they shall come against you from the north[1] with chariots and wagons and a host of peoples. They shall set themselves against you on every side with buckler, shield, and helmet; and I will commit the judgment to them, and they shall judge you according to their judgments. [25] And I will direct my jealousy against you, that they may deal with you in fury. They shall cut off your nose and your ears, and your survivors shall fall by the sword. They shall seize your sons and your daughters, and your survivors shall be devoured by fire. [26] They shall also strip you of your clothes and take away your beautiful jewels. [27] Thus I will put an end to your lewdness and your whoring begun in the land of Egypt, so that you shall not lift up your eyes to them or remember Egypt anymore.

[28] "For thus says the Lord GOD: Behold, I will deliver you into the hands of those whom you hate, into the hands of those from whom you turned in disgust, [29] and they shall deal with you in hatred and take away all the fruit of your labor and leave you naked and bare, and the nakedness of your whoring shall be uncovered. Your lewdness and your whoring [30] have brought this upon you, because you played the whore with the nations and defiled yourself with their idols. [31] You have gone the way of your sister; therefore I will give her cup into your hand. [32] Thus says the Lord GOD:

"You shall drink your sister's cup
　　that is deep and large;
　you shall be laughed at and held in deri-
　　sion,
　　for it contains much;
[33]　you will be filled with drunkenness and
　　sorrow.
　A cup of horror and desolation,
　　the cup of your sister Samaria;
[34]　you shall drink it and drain it out,
　　and gnaw its shards,
　　and tear your breasts;

for I have spoken, declares the Lord GOD. [35] Therefore thus says the Lord GOD: Because you have forgotten me and cast me behind your back, you yourself must bear the consequences of your lewdness and whoring."

[36] The LORD said to me: "Son of man, will you judge Oholah and Oholibah? Declare to them their abominations. [37] For they have committed adultery, and blood is on their hands. With their idols they have committed adultery, and they have even offered up[2] to them for food the children whom they had borne to me. [38] Moreover, this they have done to me: they have defiled my sanctuary on the same day and profaned my Sabbaths. [39] For when they had slaughtered their children in sacrifice to their idols, on the same day they came into my sanctuary to profane it. And behold, this is what they did in my house. [40] They even sent for men to come from afar, to whom a messenger was sent; and behold, they came. For them you bathed yourself, painted your eyes, and adorned yourself with ornaments. [41] You sat on a stately couch, with a table spread before it on which you had placed my incense and my oil. [42] The sound of a carefree multitude was with her; and with men of the common sort, drunkards[3] were brought from the wilderness; and they put bracelets on the hands of the women, and beautiful crowns on their heads.

[43] "Then I said of her who was worn out by adultery, 'Now they will continue to use her for a whore, even her!'[4] [44] For they have gone in to her, as men go in to a prostitute. Thus they went in to Oholah and to Oholibah, lewd women! [45] But righteous men shall pass judgment on them with the sentence of adulteresses, and with the sentence of women who shed blood, because they are adulteresses, and blood is on their hands."

[46] For thus says the Lord GOD: "Bring up a vast host against them, and make them an object of terror and a plunder. [47] And the host shall stone them and cut them down with their swords. They shall kill their sons and their daughters, and burn up their houses. [48] Thus will I put an end to lewdness in the land, that all women may take warning and not commit lewdness as you have done. [49] And they shall return your lewdness upon you, and you shall bear the penalty for your sinful idolatry, and you shall know that I am the Lord GOD."

The Siege of Jerusalem

24 In the ninth year, in the tenth month, on the tenth day of the month, the word of the LORD came to me: [2] "Son of man, write down the name of this day, this very day. The king of Babylon has laid siege to Jerusalem this very day. [3] And utter a parable to the rebellious house and say to them, Thus says the Lord GOD:

---

[1] Septuagint; the meaning of the Hebrew word is unknown [2] Or have even made pass through the fire [3] Or Sabeans [4] The meaning of the Hebrew verse is uncertain

"Set on the pot, set it on;
　　pour in water also;
4　put in it the pieces of meat,
　　all the good pieces, the thigh and the
　　　shoulder;
　　fill it with choice bones.
5　Take the choicest one of the flock;
　　pile the logs[1] under it;
　　boil it well;
　　seethe also its bones in it.

6 "Therefore thus says the Lord GOD: Woe to the bloody city, to the pot whose corrosion is in it, and whose corrosion has not gone out of it! Take out of it piece after piece, without making any choice.[2] 7 For the blood she has shed is in her midst; she put it on the bare rock; she did not pour it out on the ground to cover it with dust. 8 To rouse my wrath, to take vengeance, I have set on the bare rock the blood she has shed, that it may not be covered. 9 Therefore thus says the Lord GOD: Woe to the bloody city! I also will make the pile great. 10 Heap on the logs, kindle the fire, boil the meat well, mix in the spices,[3] and let the bones be burned up. 11 Then set it empty upon the coals, that it may become hot, and its copper may burn, that its uncleanness may be melted in it, its corrosion consumed. 12 She has wearied herself with toil;[4] its abundant corrosion does not go out of it. Into the fire with its corrosion! 13 On account of your unclean lewdness, because I would have cleansed you and you were not cleansed from your uncleanness, you shall not be cleansed anymore till I have satisfied my fury upon you. 14 I am the LORD. I have spoken; it shall come to pass; I will do it. I will not go back; I will not spare; I will not relent; according to your ways and your deeds you will be judged, declares the Lord GOD."

Ezekiel's Wife Dies

15 The word of the LORD came to me: 16 "Son of man, behold, I am about to take the delight of your eyes away from you at a stroke; yet you shall not mourn or weep, nor shall your tears run down. 17 Sigh, but not aloud; make no mourning for the dead. Bind on your turban, and put your shoes on your feet; do not cover your lips, nor eat the bread of men." 18 So I spoke to the people in the morning, and at evening my wife died. And on the next morning I did as I was commanded.

19 And the people said to me, "Will you not tell us what these things mean for us, that you are acting thus?" 20 Then I said to them, "The word of the LORD came to me: 21 'Say to the house of Israel, Thus says the Lord GOD: Behold, I will profane my sanctuary, the pride of your power, the delight of your eyes, and the yearning of your soul, and your sons and your daughters whom you left behind shall fall by the sword. 22 And you shall do as I have done; you shall not cover your lips, nor eat the bread of men. 23 Your turbans shall be on your heads and your shoes on your feet; you shall not mourn or weep, but you shall rot away in your iniquities and groan to one another. 24 Thus shall Ezekiel be to you a sign; according to all that he has done you shall do. When this comes, then you will know that I am the Lord GOD.'

25 "As for you, son of man, surely on the day when I take from them their stronghold, their joy and glory, the delight of their eyes and their soul's desire, and also their sons and daughters, 26 on that day a fugitive will come to you to report to you the news. 27 On that day your mouth will be opened to the fugitive, and you shall speak and be no longer mute. So you will be a sign to them, and they will know that I am the LORD."

Prophecy Against Ammon

25 The word of the LORD came to me: 2 "Son of man, set your face toward the Ammonites and prophesy against them. 3 Say to the Ammonites, Hear the word of the Lord GOD: Thus says the Lord GOD, Because you said, 'Aha!' over my sanctuary when it was profaned, and over the land of Israel when it was made desolate, and over the house of Judah when they went into exile, 4 therefore behold, I am handing you over to the people of the East for a possession, and they shall set their encampments among you and make their dwellings in your midst. They shall eat your fruit, and they shall drink your milk. 5 I will make Rabbah a pasture for camels and Ammon[5] a fold for flocks. Then you will know that I am the LORD. 6 For thus says the Lord GOD: Because you have clapped your hands and stamped your feet and rejoiced with all the malice within your soul against the land of Israel, 7 therefore, behold, I have stretched out my hand against you, and will hand you over as plunder to the nations. And I will cut you off from the peoples and

---

[1] Compare verse 10; Hebrew *the bones* [2] Hebrew *no lot has fallen upon it* [3] Or *empty out the broth* [4] The meaning of the Hebrew is uncertain [5] Hebrew *and the Ammonites*

will make you perish out of the countries; I will destroy you. Then you will know that I am the Lord.

Prophecy Against Moab and Seir

[8] "Thus says the Lord God: Because Moab and Seir[1] said, 'Behold, the house of Judah is like all the other nations,' [9] therefore I will lay open the flank of Moab from the cities, from its cities on its frontier, the glory of the country, Beth-jeshimoth, Baal-meon, and Kiriathaim. [10] I will give it along with the Ammonites to the people of the East as a possession, that the Ammonites may be remembered no more among the nations, [11] and I will execute judgments upon Moab. Then they will know that I am the Lord.

Prophecy Against Edom

[12] "Thus says the Lord God: Because Edom acted revengefully against the house of Judah and has grievously offended in taking vengeance on them, [13] therefore thus says the Lord God, I will stretch out my hand against Edom and cut off from it man and beast. And I will make it desolate; from Teman even to Dedan they shall fall by the sword. [14] And I will lay my vengeance upon Edom by the hand of my people Israel, and they shall do in Edom according to my anger and according to my wrath, and they shall know my vengeance, declares the Lord God.

Prophecy Against Philistia

[15] "Thus says the Lord God: Because the Philistines acted revengefully and took vengeance with malice of soul to destroy in never-ending enmity, [16] therefore thus says the Lord God, Behold, I will stretch out my hand against the Philistines, and I will cut off the Cherethites and destroy the rest of the seacoast. [17] I will execute great vengeance on them with wrathful rebukes. Then they will know that I am the Lord, when I lay my vengeance upon them."

Prophecy Against Tyre

26 In the eleventh year, on the first day of the month, the word of the Lord came to me: [2] "Son of man, because Tyre said concerning Jerusalem, 'Aha, the gate of the peoples is broken; it has swung open to me. I shall be replenished, now that she is laid waste,' [3] therefore thus says the Lord God: Behold, I am against you, O Tyre, and will bring up many nations against you, as the sea brings up its waves. [4] They shall destroy the walls of Tyre and break down her towers, and I will scrape her soil from her and make her a bare rock. [5] She shall be in the midst of the sea a place for the spreading of nets, for I have spoken, declares the Lord God. And she shall become plunder for the nations, [6] and her daughters on the mainland shall be killed by the sword. Then they will know that I am the Lord.

[7] "For thus says the Lord God: Behold, I will bring against Tyre from the north Nebuchadnezzar[2] king of Babylon, king of kings, with horses and chariots, and with horsemen and a host of many soldiers. [8] He will kill with the sword your daughters on the mainland. He will set up a siege wall against you and throw up a mound against you, and raise a roof of shields against you. [9] He will direct the shock of his battering rams against your walls, and with his axes he will break down your towers. [10] His horses will be so many that their dust will cover you. Your walls will shake at the noise of the horsemen and wagons and chariots, when he enters your gates as men enter a city that has been breached. [11] With the hoofs of his horses he will trample all your streets. He will kill your people with the sword, and your mighty pillars will fall to the ground. [12] They will plunder your riches and loot your merchandise. They will break down your walls and destroy your pleasant houses. Your stones and timber and soil they will cast into the midst of the waters. [13] And I will stop the music of your songs, and the sound of your lyres shall be heard no more. [14] I will make you a bare rock. You shall be a place for the spreading of nets. You shall never be rebuilt, for I am the Lord; I have spoken, declares the Lord God.

[15] "Thus says the Lord God to Tyre: Will not the coastlands shake at the sound of your fall, when the wounded groan, when slaughter is made in your midst? [16] Then all the princes of the sea will step down from their thrones and remove their robes and strip off their embroidered garments. They will clothe themselves with trembling; they will sit on the ground and tremble every moment and be appalled at you. [17] And they will raise a lamentation over you and say to you,

"'How you have perished,
     you who were inhabited from the seas,

---

[1] Septuagint lacks *and Seir* [2] Hebrew *Nebuchadrezzar*, so throughout Ezekiel

O city renowned,
  who was mighty on the sea;
she and her inhabitants imposed their ter-
    ror
  on all her inhabitants!
18 Now the coastlands tremble
  on the day of your fall,
and the coastlands that are on the sea
  are dismayed at your passing.'

19 "For thus says the Lord GOD: When I make you a city laid waste, like the cities that are not inhabited, when I bring up the deep over you, and the great waters cover you, 20 then I will make you go down with those who go down to the pit, to the people of old, and I will make you to dwell in the world below, among ruins from of old, with those who go down to the pit, so that you will not be inhabited; but I will set beauty in the land of the living. 21 I will bring you to a dreadful end, and you shall be no more. Though you be sought for, you will never be found again, declares the Lord GOD."

A Lament for Tyre

27 The word of the LORD came to me: 2 "Now you, son of man, raise a lamentation over Tyre, 3 and say to Tyre, who dwells at the entrances to the sea, merchant of the peoples to many coastlands, thus says the Lord GOD:

"O Tyre, you have said,
  'I am perfect in beauty.'
4 Your borders are in the heart of the seas;
    your builders made perfect your beauty.
5 They made all your planks
    of fir trees from Senir;
  they took a cedar from Lebanon
    to make a mast for you.
6 Of oaks of Bashan
    they made your oars;
  they made your deck of pines
    from the coasts of Cyprus,
    inlaid with ivory.
7 Of fine embroidered linen from Egypt
    was your sail,
      serving as your banner;
  blue and purple from the coasts of Elishah
    was your awning.
8 The inhabitants of Sidon and Arvad
    were your rowers;
  your skilled men, O Tyre, were in you;
    they were your pilots.

9 The elders of Gebal and her skilled men
    were in you,
      caulking your seams;
  all the ships of the sea with their mariners
    were in you
    to barter for your wares.

10 "Persia and Lud and Put were in your army as your men of war. They hung the shield and helmet in you; they gave you splendor. 11 Men of Arvad and Helech were on your walls all around, and men of Gamad were in your towers. They hung their shields on your walls all around; they made perfect your beauty.

12 "Tarshish did business with you because of your great wealth of every kind; silver, iron, tin, and lead they exchanged for your wares. 13 Javan, Tubal, and Meshech traded with you; they exchanged human beings and vessels of bronze for your merchandise. 14 From Beth-togarmah they exchanged horses, war horses, and mules for your wares. 15 The men of Dedan[1] traded with you. Many coastlands were your own special markets; they brought you in payment ivory tusks and ebony. 16 Syria did business with you because of your abundant goods; they exchanged for your wares emeralds, purple, embroidered work, fine linen, coral, and ruby. 17 Judah and the land of Israel traded with you; they exchanged for your merchandise wheat of Minnith, meal,[2] honey, oil, and balm. 18 Damascus did business with you for your abundant goods, because of your great wealth of every kind; wine of Helbon and wool of Sahar 19 and casks of wine[3] from Uzal they exchanged for your wares; wrought iron, cassia, and calamus were bartered for your merchandise. 20 Dedan traded with you in saddlecloths for riding. 21 Arabia and all the princes of Kedar were your favored dealers in lambs, rams, and goats; in these they did business with you. 22 The traders of Sheba and Raamah traded with you; they exchanged for your wares the best of all kinds of spices and all precious stones and gold. 23 Haran, Canneh, Eden, traders of Sheba, Asshur, and Chilmad traded with you. 24 In your market these traded with you in choice garments, in clothes of blue and embroidered work, and in carpets of colored material, bound with cords and made secure. 25 The ships of Tarshish traveled for you with your merchandise. So you were filled and heavily laden in the heart of the seas.

---

[1] Hebrew; Septuagint *Rhodes* [2] The meaning of the Hebrew word is unknown [3] Probable reading; Hebrew *wool of Sahar* [19] *and Dan and Javan*

²⁶ "Your rowers have brought you out
     into the high seas.
The east wind has wrecked you
     in the heart of the seas.
²⁷ Your riches, your wares, your merchandise,
     your mariners and your pilots,
your caulkers, your dealers in merchandise,
     and all your men of war who are in
       you,
with all your crew
     that is in your midst,
sink into the heart of the seas
     on the day of your fall.
²⁸ At the sound of the cry of your pilots
     the countryside shakes,
²⁹ and down from their ships
     come all who handle the oar.
The mariners and all the pilots of the sea
     stand on the land
³⁰ and shout aloud over you
     and cry out bitterly.
They cast dust on their heads
     and wallow in ashes;
³¹ they make themselves bald for you
     and put sackcloth on their waist,
and they weep over you in bitterness of
       soul,
     with bitter mourning.
³² In their wailing they raise a lamentation
       for you
     and lament over you:
'Who is like Tyre,
     like one destroyed in the midst of the
       sea?
³³ When your wares came from the seas,
     you satisfied many peoples;
with your abundant wealth and mer-
       chandise
     you enriched the kings of the earth.
³⁴ Now you are wrecked by the seas,
     in the depths of the waters;
your merchandise and all your crew in
       your midst
     have sunk with you.
³⁵ All the inhabitants of the coastlands
     are appalled at you,
and the hair of their kings bristles with
       horror;
     their faces are convulsed.
³⁶ The merchants among the peoples hiss at
       you;
you have come to a dreadful end
     and shall be no more forever.' "

¹ The meaning of the Hebrew phrase is uncertain

Prophecy Against the Prince of Tyre

28 The word of the LORD came to me:
² "Son of man, say to the prince of Tyre,
Thus says the Lord GOD:

"Because your heart is proud,
     and you have said, 'I am a god,
I sit in the seat of the gods,
     in the heart of the seas,'
yet you are but a man, and no god,
     though you make your heart like the
       heart of a god—
³ you are indeed wiser than Daniel;
     no secret is hidden from you;
⁴ by your wisdom and your understanding
     you have made wealth for yourself,
and have gathered gold and silver
     into your treasuries;
⁵ by your great wisdom in your trade
     you have increased your wealth,
and your heart has become proud in
       your wealth—
⁶ therefore thus says the Lord GOD:
Because you make your heart
     like the heart of a god,
⁷ therefore, behold, I will bring foreigners
       upon you,
     the most ruthless of the nations;
and they shall draw their swords against
       the beauty of your wisdom
     and defile your splendor.
⁸ They shall thrust you down into the pit,
     and you shall die the death of the slain
     in the heart of the seas.
⁹ Will you still say, 'I am a god,'
     in the presence of those who kill you,
though you are but a man, and no god,
     in the hands of those who slay you?
¹⁰ You shall die the death of the uncircum-
       cised
     by the hand of foreigners;
     for I have spoken, declares the Lord
       GOD."

A Lament over the King of Tyre

¹¹ Moreover, the word of the LORD came to
me: ¹² "Son of man, raise a lamentation over
the king of Tyre, and say to him, Thus says the
Lord GOD:

"You were the signet of perfection,¹
     full of wisdom and perfect in beauty.
¹³ You were in Eden, the garden of God;
     every precious stone was your covering,

sardius, topaz, and diamond,
    beryl, onyx, and jasper,
sapphire,[1] emerald, and carbuncle;
    and crafted in gold were your settings
    and your engravings.[2]
On the day that you were created
    they were prepared.

14 You were an anointed guardian cherub.
    I placed you;[3] you were on the holy
      mountain of God;
    in the midst of the stones of fire you
      walked.

15 You were blameless in your ways
    from the day you were created,
    till unrighteousness was found in you.

16 In the abundance of your trade
    you were filled with violence in your
      midst, and you sinned;
so I cast you as a profane thing from the
      mountain of God,
    and I destroyed you,[4] O guardian
      cherub,
    from the midst of the stones of fire.

17 Your heart was proud because of your
      beauty;
    you corrupted your wisdom for the sake
      of your splendor.
I cast you to the ground;
    I exposed you before kings,
    to feast their eyes on you.

18 By the multitude of your iniquities,
    in the unrighteousness of your trade
    you profaned your sanctuaries;
so I brought fire out from your midst;
    it consumed you,
and I turned you to ashes on the earth
    in the sight of all who saw you.

19 All who know you among the peoples
    are appalled at you;
you have come to a dreadful end
    and shall be no more forever."

Prophecy Against Sidon

20 The word of the LORD came to me: 21 "Son of
man, set your face toward Sidon, and prophesy
against her 22 and say, Thus says the Lord GOD:

"Behold, I am against you, O Sidon,
    and I will manifest my glory in your
      midst.
And they shall know that I am the LORD
    when I execute judgments in her
    and manifest my holiness in her;

23 for I will send pestilence into her,
    and blood into her streets;
and the slain shall fall in her midst,
    by the sword that is against her on every
      side.
Then they will know that I am the LORD.

24 "And for the house of Israel there shall be
no more a brier to prick or a thorn to hurt them
among all their neighbors who have treated
them with contempt. Then they will know that
I am the Lord GOD.

Israel Gathered in Security

25 "Thus says the Lord GOD: When I gather
the house of Israel from the peoples among
whom they are scattered, and manifest my holiness in them in the sight of the nations, then
they shall dwell in their own land that I gave
to my servant Jacob. 26 And they shall dwell
securely in it, and they shall build houses and
plant vineyards. They shall dwell securely, when
I execute judgments upon all their neighbors
who have treated them with contempt. Then
they will know that I am the LORD their God."

Prophecy Against Egypt

29 In the tenth year, in the tenth month, on
the twelfth day of the month, the word
of the LORD came to me: 2 "Son of man, set your
face against Pharaoh king of Egypt, and prophesy against him and against all Egypt; 3 speak,
and say, Thus says the Lord GOD:

"Behold, I am against you,
    Pharaoh king of Egypt,
the great dragon that lies
    in the midst of his streams,
that says, 'My Nile is my own;
    I made it for myself.'
4 I will put hooks in your jaws,
    and make the fish of your streams stick
      to your scales;
and I will draw you up out of the midst of
      your streams,
    with all the fish of your streams
    that stick to your scales.
5 And I will cast you out into the wilderness,
    you and all the fish of your streams;
you shall fall on the open field,
    and not be brought together or gath-
      ered.
To the beasts of the earth and to the birds
      of the heavens
    I give you as food.

---

[1] Or lapis lazuli   [2] The meaning of the Hebrew phrase is uncertain   [3] The meaning of the Hebrew phrase is uncertain   [4] Or banished you

⁶Then all the inhabitants of Egypt shall know that I am the Lord.

"Because you[1] have been a staff of reed to the house of Israel, ⁷when they grasped you with the hand, you broke and tore all their shoulders; and when they leaned on you, you broke and made all their loins to shake.[2] ⁸Therefore thus says the Lord God: Behold, I will bring a sword upon you, and will cut off from you man and beast, ⁹and the land of Egypt shall be a desolation and a waste. Then they will know that I am the Lord.

"Because you[3] said, 'The Nile is mine, and I made it,' ¹⁰therefore, behold, I am against you and against your streams, and I will make the land of Egypt an utter waste and desolation, from Migdol to Syene, as far as the border of Cush. ¹¹No foot of man shall pass through it, and no foot of beast shall pass through it; it shall be uninhabited forty years. ¹²And I will make the land of Egypt a desolation in the midst of desolated countries, and her cities shall be a desolation forty years among cities that are laid waste. I will scatter the Egyptians among the nations, and disperse them through the countries.

¹³"For thus says the Lord God: At the end of forty years I will gather the Egyptians from the peoples among whom they were scattered, ¹⁴and I will restore the fortunes of Egypt and bring them back to the land of Pathros, the land of their origin, and there they shall be a lowly kingdom. ¹⁵It shall be the most lowly of the kingdoms, and never again exalt itself above the nations. And I will make them so small that they will never again rule over the nations. ¹⁶And it shall never again be the reliance of the house of Israel, recalling their iniquity, when they turn to them for aid. Then they will know that I am the Lord God."

¹⁷In the twenty-seventh year, in the first month, on the first day of the month, the word of the Lord came to me: ¹⁸"Son of man, Nebuchadnezzar king of Babylon made his army labor hard against Tyre. Every head was made bald, and every shoulder was rubbed bare, yet neither he nor his army got anything from Tyre to pay for the labor that he had performed against her. ¹⁹Therefore thus says the Lord God: Behold, I will give the land of Egypt to Nebuchadnezzar king of Babylon; and he shall carry off its wealth[4] and despoil it and plunder it; and it shall be the wages for his army. ²⁰I have

given him the land of Egypt as his payment for which he labored, because they worked for me, declares the Lord God.

²¹"On that day I will cause a horn to spring up for the house of Israel, and I will open your lips among them. Then they will know that I am the Lord."

A Lament for Egypt

30 The word of the Lord came to me: ²"Son of man, prophesy, and say, Thus says the Lord God:

"Wail, 'Alas for the day!'
3   For the day is near,
      the day of the Lord is near;
    it will be a day of clouds,
      a time of doom for[5] the nations.
4   A sword shall come upon Egypt,
      and anguish shall be in Cush,
    when the slain fall in Egypt,
      and her wealth[6] is carried away,
      and her foundations are torn down.

⁵Cush, and Put, and Lud, and all Arabia, and Libya,[7] and the people of the land that is in league,[8] shall fall with them by the sword.

6   "Thus says the Lord:
    Those who support Egypt shall fall,
      and her proud might shall come down;
    from Migdol to Syene
      they shall fall within her by the sword,
    declares the Lord God.
7   And they shall be desolated in the midst of
      desolated countries,
      and their cities shall be in the midst of
      cities that are laid waste.
8   Then they will know that I am the Lord,
      when I have set fire to Egypt,
      and all her helpers are broken.

⁹"On that day messengers shall go out from me in ships to terrify the unsuspecting people of Cush, and anguish shall come upon them on the day of Egypt's doom;[9] for, behold, it comes!

¹⁰"Thus says the Lord God:

"I will put an end to the wealth of Egypt,
      by the hand of Nebuchadnezzar king of
      Babylon.
11   He and his people with him, the most
      ruthless of nations,
      shall be brought in to destroy the
      land,

---

[1] Hebrew *they* [2] Syriac (compare Psalm 69:23); Hebrew *to stand* [3] Hebrew *they* [4] Or *multitude* [5] Hebrew lacks *doom for* [6] Or *multitude* [7] With Septuagint; Hebrew *Cub* [8] Hebrew *and the sons of the land of the covenant* [9] Hebrew *the day of Egypt*

and they shall draw their swords against
    Egypt
    and fill the land with the slain.
12 And I will dry up the Nile
    and will sell the land into the hand of
      evildoers;
    I will bring desolation upon the land and
      everything in it,
    by the hand of foreigners;
    I am the LORD; I have spoken.

13 "Thus says the Lord GOD:

  "I will destroy the idols
    and put an end to the images in
      Memphis;
  there shall no longer be a prince from the
    land of Egypt;
    so I will put fear in the land of Egypt.
14 I will make Pathros a desolation
    and will set fire to Zoan
    and will execute judgments on
      Thebes.
15 And I will pour out my wrath on Pelusium,
    the stronghold of Egypt,
    and cut off the multitude[1] of Thebes.
16 And I will set fire to Egypt;
    Pelusium shall be in great agony;
  Thebes shall be breached,
    and Memphis shall face enemies[2] by
      day.
17 The young men of On and of Pi-beseth
    shall fall by the sword,
    and the women[3] shall go into captiv-
      ity.
18 At Tehaphnehes the day shall be dark,
    when I break there the yoke bars of
      Egypt,
  and her proud might shall come to an end
    in her;
    she shall be covered by a cloud,
    and her daughters shall go into captiv-
      ity.
19 Thus I will execute judgments on Egypt.
    Then they will know that I am the
      LORD."

Egypt Shall Fall to Babylon

20 In the eleventh year, in the first month, on the seventh day of the month, the word of the LORD came to me: 21 "Son of man, I have broken the arm of Pharaoh king of Egypt, and behold, it has not been bound up, to heal it by binding it with a bandage, so that it may become strong

to wield the sword. 22 Therefore thus says the Lord GOD: Behold, I am against Pharaoh king of Egypt and will break his arms, both the strong arm and the one that was broken, and I will make the sword fall from his hand. 23 I will scatter the Egyptians among the nations and disperse them through the countries. 24 And I will strengthen the arms of the king of Babylon and put my sword in his hand, but I will break the arms of Pharaoh, and he will groan before him like a man mortally wounded. 25 I will strengthen the arms of the king of Babylon, but the arms of Pharaoh shall fall. Then they shall know that I am the LORD, when I put my sword into the hand of the king of Babylon and he stretches it out against the land of Egypt. 26 And I will scatter the Egyptians among the nations and disperse them throughout the countries. Then they will know that I am the LORD."

Pharaoh to Be Slain

31 In the eleventh year, in the third month, on the first day of the month, the word of the LORD came to me: 2 "Son of man, say to Pharaoh king of Egypt and to his multitude:

  "Whom are you like in your greatness?
3   Behold, Assyria was a cedar in Lebanon,
  with beautiful branches and forest shade,
    and of towering height,
    its top among the clouds.[4]
4 The waters nourished it;
    the deep made it grow tall,
  making its rivers flow
    around the place of its planting,
  sending forth its streams
    to all the trees of the field.
5 So it towered high
    above all the trees of the field;
  its boughs grew large
    and its branches long
    from abundant water in its shoots.
6 All the birds of the heavens
    made their nests in its boughs;
  under its branches all the beasts of the field
    gave birth to their young,
  and under its shadow
    lived all great nations.
7 It was beautiful in its greatness,
    in the length of its branches;
  for its roots went down
    to abundant waters.

---

[1] Or wealth [2] Or distress [3] Or the cities; Hebrew they [4] Or its top went through the thick boughs

8 The cedars in the garden of God could not
     rival it,
       nor the fir trees equal its boughs;
    neither were the plane trees
       like its branches;
    no tree in the garden of God
       was its equal in beauty.
9 I made it beautiful
       in the mass of its branches,
     and all the trees of Eden envied it,
       that were in the garden of God.

10 "Therefore thus says the Lord God:
Because it[1] towered high and set its top among
the clouds,[2] and its heart was proud of its
height, [11] I will give it into the hand of a mighty
one of the nations. He shall surely deal with it
as its wickedness deserves. I have cast it out.
12 Foreigners, the most ruthless of nations, have
cut it down and left it. On the mountains and
in all the valleys its branches have fallen, and its
boughs have been broken in all the ravines of
the land, and all the peoples of the earth have
gone away from its shadow and left it. [13] On its
fallen trunk dwell all the birds of the heavens,
and on its branches are all the beasts of the field.
14 All this is in order that no trees by the waters
may grow to towering height or set their tops
among the clouds,[3] and that no trees that drink
water may reach up to them in height. For they
are all given over to death, to the world below,
among the children of man,[4] with those who
go down to the pit.

15 "Thus says the Lord God: On the day the
cedar[5] went down to Sheol I caused mourning;
I closed the deep over it, and restrained its rivers, and many waters were stopped. I clothed
Lebanon in gloom for it, and all the trees of
the field fainted because of it. [16] I made the
nations quake at the sound of its fall, when I
cast it down to Sheol with those who go down
to the pit. And all the trees of Eden, the choice
and best of Lebanon, all that drink water, were
comforted in the world below. [17] They also went
down to Sheol with it, to those who are slain
by the sword; yes, those who were its arm, who
lived under its shadow among the nations.

18 "Whom are you thus like in glory and in
greatness among the trees of Eden? You shall
be brought down with the trees of Eden to the
world below. You shall lie among the uncircumcised, with those who are slain by the sword.

"This is Pharaoh and all his multitude,
declares the Lord God."

A Lament over Pharaoh and Egypt

32 In the twelfth year, in the twelfth
month, on the first day of the month,
the word of the Lord came to me: [2] "Son of
man, raise a lamentation over Pharaoh king of
Egypt and say to him:

"You consider yourself a lion of the nations,
     but you are like a dragon in the seas;
you burst forth in your rivers,
     trouble the waters with your feet,
     and foul their rivers.
3 Thus says the Lord God:
     I will throw my net over you
     with a host of many peoples,
     and they will haul you up in my drag-
       net.
4 And I will cast you on the ground;
     on the open field I will fling you,
and will cause all the birds of the heavens
       to settle on you,
     and I will gorge the beasts of the whole
       earth with you.
5 I will strew your flesh upon the mountains
     and fill the valleys with your carcass.[6]
6 I will drench the land even to the moun-
     tains
     with your flowing blood,
     and the ravines will be full of you.
7 When I blot you out, I will cover the heav-
     ens
     and make their stars dark;
I will cover the sun with a cloud,
     and the moon shall not give its light.
8 All the bright lights of heaven
     will I make dark over you,
     and put darkness on your land,
                declares the Lord God.

9 "I will trouble the hearts of many peoples,
when I bring your destruction among the
nations, into the countries that you have not
known. [10] I will make many peoples appalled
at you, and the hair of their kings shall bristle
with horror because of you, when I brandish
my sword before them. They shall tremble
every moment, every one for his own life, on
the day of your downfall.

11 "For thus says the Lord God: The sword
of the king of Babylon shall come upon you.
12 I will cause your multitude to fall by the

---

[1] Syriac, Vulgate; Hebrew you   [2] Or its top through the thick boughs   [3] Or their tops through the thick boughs   [4] Or of Adam   [5] Hebrew it   [6] Hebrew your height

swords of mighty ones, all of them most ruthless of nations.

"They shall bring to ruin the pride of Egypt,
   and all its multitude[1] shall perish.
13 I will destroy all its beasts
      from beside many waters;
   and no foot of man shall trouble them any-
      more,
   nor shall the hoofs of beasts trouble
      them.
14 Then I will make their waters clear,
      and cause their rivers to run like oil,
         declares the Lord GOD.
15 When I make the land of Egypt desolate,
      and when the land is desolate of all that
         fills it,
   when I strike down all who dwell in it,
      then they will know that I am the LORD.

16 This is a lamentation that shall be chanted;
the daughters of the nations shall chant it; over
Egypt, and over all her multitude, shall they
chant it, declares the Lord GOD."

17 In the twelfth year, in the twelfth month,[2]
on the fifteenth day of the month, the word of
the LORD came to me: 18 "Son of man, wail over
the multitude of Egypt, and send them down,
her and the daughters of majestic nations, to
the world below, to those who have gone down
to the pit:

19   'Whom do you surpass in beauty?
        Go down and be laid to rest with the
           uncircumcised.'

20 They shall fall amid those who are slain by
the sword. Egypt[3] is delivered to the sword;
drag her away, and all her multitudes. 21 The
mighty chiefs shall speak of them, with their
helpers, out of the midst of Sheol: 'They have
come down, they lie still, the uncircumcised,
slain by the sword.'

22 "Assyria is there, and all her company, its
graves all around it, all of them slain, fallen
by the sword, 23 whose graves are set in the
uttermost parts of the pit; and her company
is all around her grave, all of them slain, fallen
by the sword, who spread terror in the land of
the living.

24 "Elam is there, and all her multitude
around her grave; all of them slain, fallen by
the sword, who went down uncircumcised
into the world below, who spread their terror
in the land of the living; and they bear their

shame with those who go down to the pit.
25 They have made her a bed among the slain
with all her multitude, her graves all around it,
all of them uncircumcised, slain by the sword;
for terror of them was spread in the land of
the living, and they bear their shame with
those who go down to the pit; they are placed
among the slain.

26 "Meshech-Tubal is there, and all her multitude, her graves all around it, all of them uncircumcised, slain by the sword; for they spread
their terror in the land of the living. 27 And
they do not lie with the mighty, the fallen from
among the uncircumcised, who went down to
Sheol with their weapons of war, whose swords
were laid under their heads, and whose iniquities are upon their bones; for the terror of the
mighty men was in the land of the living. 28 But
as for you, you shall be broken and lie among
the uncircumcised, with those who are slain by
the sword.

29 "Edom is there, her kings and all her
princes, who for all their might are laid with
those who are killed by the sword; they lie with
the uncircumcised, with those who go down
to the pit.

30 "The princes of the north are there, all of
them, and all the Sidonians, who have gone
down in shame with the slain, for all the terror that they caused by their might; they lie
uncircumcised with those who are slain by the
sword, and bear their shame with those who go
down to the pit.

31 "When Pharaoh sees them, he will be
comforted for all his multitude, Pharaoh and
all his army, slain by the sword, declares the
Lord GOD. 32 For I spread terror in the land of
the living; and he shall be laid to rest among
the uncircumcised, with those who are slain
by the sword, Pharaoh and all his multitude,
declares the Lord GOD."

Ezekiel Is Israel's Watchman

33 The word of the LORD came to me:
2 "Son of man, speak to your people and
say to them, If I bring the sword upon a land,
and the people of the land take a man from
among them, and make him their watchman,
3 and if he sees the sword coming upon the land
and blows the trumpet and warns the people,
4 then if anyone who hears the sound of the
trumpet does not take warning, and the sword
comes and takes him away, his blood shall be

---

[1] Or wealth [2] Hebrew lacks *in the twelfth month* [3] Hebrew *She*

upon his own head. [5] He heard the sound of the trumpet and did not take warning; his blood shall be upon himself. But if he had taken warning, he would have saved his life. [6] But if the watchman sees the sword coming and does not blow the trumpet, so that the people are not warned, and the sword comes and takes any one of them, that person is taken away in his iniquity, but his blood I will require at the watchman's hand.

[7] "So you, son of man, I have made a watchman for the house of Israel. Whenever you hear a word from my mouth, you shall give them warning from me. [8] If I say to the wicked, O wicked one, you shall surely die, and you do not speak to warn the wicked to turn from his way, that wicked person shall die in his iniquity, but his blood I will require at your hand. [9] But if you warn the wicked to turn from his way, and he does not turn from his way, that person shall die in his iniquity, but you will have delivered your soul.

Why Will You Die, Israel?

[10] "And you, son of man, say to the house of Israel, Thus have you said: 'Surely our transgressions and our sins are upon us, and we rot away because of them. How then can we live?' [11] Say to them, As I live, declares the Lord GOD, I have no pleasure in the death of the wicked, but that the wicked turn from his way and live; turn back, turn back from your evil ways, for why will you die, O house of Israel?

[12] "And you, son of man, say to your people, The righteousness of the righteous shall not deliver him when he transgresses, and as for the wickedness of the wicked, he shall not fall by it when he turns from his wickedness, and the righteous shall not be able to live by his righteousness[1] when he sins. [13] Though I say to the righteous that he shall surely live, yet if he trusts in his righteousness and does injustice, none of his righteous deeds shall be remembered, but in his injustice that he has done he shall die. [14] Again, though I say to the wicked, 'You shall surely die,' yet if he turns from his sin and does what is just and right, [15] if the wicked restores the pledge, gives back what he has taken by robbery, and walks in the statutes of life, not doing injustice, he shall surely live; he shall not die. [16] None of the sins that he has committed shall be remembered against him.

He has done what is just and right; he shall surely live.

[17] "Yet your people say, 'The way of the Lord is not just,' when it is their own way that is not just. [18] When the righteous turns from his righteousness and does injustice, he shall die for it. [19] And when the wicked turns from his wickedness and does what is just and right, he shall live by this. [20] Yet you say, 'The way of the Lord is not just.' O house of Israel, I will judge each of you according to his ways."

Jerusalem Struck Down

[21] In the twelfth year of our exile, in the tenth month, on the fifth day of the month, a fugitive from Jerusalem came to me and said, "The city has been struck down." [22] Now the hand of the LORD had been upon me the evening before the fugitive came; and he had opened my mouth by the time the man came to me in the morning, so my mouth was opened, and I was no longer mute.

[23] The word of the LORD came to me: [24] "Son of man, the inhabitants of these waste places in the land of Israel keep saying, 'Abraham was only one man, yet he got possession of the land; but we are many; the land is surely given us to possess.' [25] Therefore say to them, Thus says the Lord GOD: You eat flesh with the blood and lift up your eyes to your idols and shed blood; shall you then possess the land? [26] You rely on the sword, you commit abominations, and each of you defiles his neighbor's wife; shall you then possess the land? [27] Say this to them, Thus says the Lord GOD: As I live, surely those who are in the waste places shall fall by the sword, and whoever is in the open field I will give to the beasts to be devoured, and those who are in strongholds and in caves shall die by pestilence. [28] And I will make the land a desolation and a waste, and her proud might shall come to an end, and the mountains of Israel shall be so desolate that none will pass through. [29] Then they will know that I am the LORD, when I have made the land a desolation and a waste because of all their abominations that they have committed.

[30] "As for you, son of man, your people who talk together about you by the walls and at the doors of the houses, say to one another, each to his brother, 'Come, and hear what the word is that comes from the LORD.' [31] And they come to you as people come, and they sit before you as my people, and they hear what you say but

[1] Hebrew by it

they will not do it; for with lustful talk in their mouths they act; their heart is set on their gain. [32] And behold, you are to them like one who sings lustful songs with a beautiful voice and plays[1] well on an instrument, for they hear what you say, but they will not do it. [33] When this comes—and come it will!—then they will know that a prophet has been among them."

Prophecy Against the Shepherds of Israel

34 The word of the LORD came to me: [2] "Son of man, prophesy against the shepherds of Israel; prophesy, and say to them, even to the shepherds, Thus says the Lord GOD: Ah, shepherds of Israel who have been feeding yourselves! Should not shepherds feed the sheep? [3] You eat the fat, you clothe yourselves with the wool, you slaughter the fat ones, but you do not feed the sheep. [4] The weak you have not strengthened, the sick you have not healed, the injured you have not bound up, the strayed you have not brought back, the lost you have not sought, and with force and harshness you have ruled them. [5] So they were scattered, because there was no shepherd, and they became food for all the wild beasts. My sheep were scattered; [6] they wandered over all the mountains and on every high hill. My sheep were scattered over all the face of the earth, with none to search or seek for them.

[7] "Therefore, you shepherds, hear the word of the LORD: [8] As I live, declares the Lord GOD, surely because my sheep have become a prey, and my sheep have become food for all the wild beasts, since there was no shepherd, and because my shepherds have not searched for my sheep, but the shepherds have fed themselves, and have not fed my sheep, [9] therefore, you shepherds, hear the word of the LORD: [10] Thus says the Lord GOD, Behold, I am against the shepherds, and I will require my sheep at their hand and put a stop to their feeding the sheep. No longer shall the shepherds feed themselves. I will rescue my sheep from their mouths, that they may not be food for them.

The Lord GOD Will Seek Them Out

[11] "For thus says the Lord GOD: Behold, I, I myself will search for my sheep and will seek them out. [12] As a shepherd seeks out his flock when he is among his sheep that have been scattered, so will I seek out my sheep, and I will rescue them from all places where they have been scattered on a day of clouds and thick

darkness. [13] And I will bring them out from the peoples and gather them from the countries, and will bring them into their own land. And I will feed them on the mountains of Israel, by the ravines, and in all the inhabited places of the country. [14] I will feed them with good pasture, and on the mountain heights of Israel shall be their grazing land. There they shall lie down in good grazing land, and on rich pasture they shall feed on the mountains of Israel. [15] I myself will be the shepherd of my sheep, and I myself will make them lie down, declares the Lord GOD. [16] I will seek the lost, and I will bring back the strayed, and I will bind up the injured, and I will strengthen the weak, and the fat and the strong I will destroy.[2] I will feed them in justice.

[17] "As for you, my flock, thus says the Lord GOD: Behold, I judge between sheep and sheep, between rams and male goats. [18] Is it not enough for you to feed on the good pasture, that you must tread down with your feet the rest of your pasture; and to drink of clear water, that you must muddy the rest of the water with your feet? [19] And must my sheep eat what you have trodden with your feet, and drink what you have muddied with your feet?

[20] "Therefore, thus says the Lord GOD to them: Behold, I, I myself will judge between the fat sheep and the lean sheep. [21] Because you push with side and shoulder, and thrust at all the weak with your horns, till you have scattered them abroad, [22] I will rescue[3] my flock; they shall no longer be a prey. And I will judge between sheep and sheep. [23] And I will set up over them one shepherd, my servant David, and he shall feed them: he shall feed them and be their shepherd. [24] And I, the LORD, will be their God, and my servant David shall be prince among them. I am the LORD; I have spoken.

The LORD's Covenant of Peace

[25] "I will make with them a covenant of peace and banish wild beasts from the land, so that they may dwell securely in the wilderness and sleep in the woods. [26] And I will make them and the places all around my hill a blessing, and I will send down the showers in their season; they shall be showers of blessing. [27] And the trees of the field shall yield their fruit, and the earth shall yield its increase, and they shall be secure in their land. And they shall know that I am the LORD, when I break the bars of their yoke, and deliver them from

---

[1] Hebrew *like the singing of lustful songs with a beautiful voice and one who plays* [2] Septuagint, Syriac, Vulgate *I will watch over* [3] Or *save*

the hand of those who enslaved them. ²⁸They shall no more be a prey to the nations, nor shall the beasts of the land devour them. They shall dwell securely, and none shall make them afraid. ²⁹And I will provide for them renowned plantations so that they shall no more be consumed with hunger in the land, and no longer suffer the reproach of the nations. ³⁰And they shall know that I am the Lᴏʀᴅ their God with them, and that they, the house of Israel, are my people, declares the Lord Gᴏᴅ. ³¹And you are my sheep, human sheep of my pasture, and I am your God, declares the Lord Gᴏᴅ."

Prophecy Against Mount Seir

35 The word of the Lᴏʀᴅ came to me: ²"Son of man, set your face against Mount Seir, and prophesy against it, ³and say to it, Thus says the Lord Gᴏᴅ: Behold, I am against you, Mount Seir, and I will stretch out my hand against you, and I will make you a desolation and a waste. ⁴I will lay your cities waste, and you shall become a desolation, and you shall know that I am the Lᴏʀᴅ. ⁵Because you cherished perpetual enmity and gave over the people of Israel to the power of the sword at the time of their calamity, at the time of their final punishment, ⁶therefore, as I live, declares the Lord Gᴏᴅ, I will prepare you for blood, and blood shall pursue you; because you did not hate bloodshed, therefore blood shall pursue you. ⁷I will make Mount Seir a waste and a desolation, and I will cut off from it all who come and go. ⁸And I will fill its mountains with the slain. On your hills and in your valleys and in all your ravines those slain with the sword shall fall. ⁹I will make you a perpetual desolation, and your cities shall not be inhabited. Then you will know that I am the Lᴏʀᴅ.

¹⁰"Because you said, 'These two nations and these two countries shall be mine, and we will take possession of them'—although the Lᴏʀᴅ was there— ¹¹therefore, as I live, declares the Lord Gᴏᴅ, I will deal with you according to the anger and envy that you showed because of your hatred against them. And I will make myself known among them, when I judge you. ¹²And you shall know that I am the Lᴏʀᴅ.

"I have heard all the revilings that you uttered against the mountains of Israel, saying, 'They are laid desolate; they are given us to devour.' ¹³And you magnified yourselves against me with your mouth, and multiplied your words against me; I heard it. ¹⁴Thus says the Lord Gᴏᴅ: While the whole earth rejoices, I will make you desolate. ¹⁵As you rejoiced over the inheritance of the house of Israel, because it was desolate, so I will deal with you; you shall be desolate, Mount Seir, and all Edom, all of it. Then they will know that I am the Lᴏʀᴅ.

Prophecy to the Mountains of Israel

36 "And you, son of man, prophesy to the mountains of Israel, and say, O mountains of Israel, hear the word of the Lᴏʀᴅ. ²Thus says the Lord Gᴏᴅ: Because the enemy said of you, 'Aha!' and, 'The ancient heights have become our possession,' ³therefore prophesy, and say, Thus says the Lord Gᴏᴅ: Precisely because they made you desolate and crushed you from all sides, so that you became the possession of the rest of the nations, and you became the talk and evil gossip of the people, ⁴therefore, O mountains of Israel, hear the word of the Lord Gᴏᴅ: Thus says the Lord Gᴏᴅ to the mountains and the hills, the ravines and the valleys, the desolate wastes and the deserted cities, which have become a prey and derision to the rest of the nations all around, ⁵therefore thus says the Lord Gᴏᴅ: Surely I have spoken in my hot jealousy against the rest of the nations and against all Edom, who gave my land to themselves as a possession with wholehearted joy and utter contempt, that they might make its pasturelands a prey. ⁶Therefore prophesy concerning the land of Israel, and say to the mountains and hills, to the ravines and valleys, Thus says the Lord Gᴏᴅ: Behold, I have spoken in my jealous wrath, because you have suffered the reproach of the nations. ⁷Therefore thus says the Lord Gᴏᴅ: I swear that the nations that are all around you shall themselves suffer reproach.

⁸"But you, O mountains of Israel, shall shoot forth your branches and yield your fruit to my people Israel, for they will soon come home. ⁹For behold, I am for you, and I will turn to you, and you shall be tilled and sown. ¹⁰And I will multiply people on you, the whole house of Israel, all of it. The cities shall be inhabited and the waste places rebuilt. ¹¹And I will multiply on you man and beast, and they shall multiply and be fruitful. And I will cause you to be inhabited as in your former times, and will do more good to you than ever before. Then you will know that I

am the LORD. [12] I will let people walk on you, even my people Israel. And they shall possess you, and you shall be their inheritance, and you shall no longer bereave them of children. [13] Thus says the Lord GOD: Because they say to you, 'You devour people, and you bereave your nation of children,' [14] therefore you shall no longer devour people and no longer bereave your nation of children, declares the Lord GOD. [15] And I will not let you hear anymore the reproach of the nations, and you shall no longer bear the disgrace of the peoples and no longer cause your nation to stumble, declares the Lord GOD."

The Lord's Concern for His Holy Name

[16] The word of the LORD came to me: [17] "Son of man, when the house of Israel lived in their own land, they defiled it by their ways and their deeds. Their ways before me were like the uncleanness of a woman in her menstrual impurity. [18] So I poured out my wrath upon them for the blood that they had shed in the land, for the idols with which they had defiled it. [19] I scattered them among the nations, and they were dispersed through the countries. In accordance with their ways and their deeds I judged them. [20] But when they came to the nations, wherever they came, they profaned my holy name, in that people said of them, 'These are the people of the LORD, and yet they had to go out of his land.' [21] But I had concern for my holy name, which the house of Israel had profaned among the nations to which they came.

I Will Put My Spirit Within You

[22] "Therefore say to the house of Israel, Thus says the Lord GOD: It is not for your sake, O house of Israel, that I am about to act, but for the sake of my holy name, which you have profaned among the nations to which you came. [23] And I will vindicate the holiness of my great name, which has been profaned among the nations, and which you have profaned among them. And the nations will know that I am the LORD, declares the Lord GOD, when through you I vindicate my holiness before their eyes. [24] I will take you from the nations and gather you from all the countries and bring you into your own land. [25] I will sprinkle clean water on you, and you shall be clean from all your uncleannesses, and from all your idols I will cleanse you. [26] And I will give you a new heart, and a new spirit I will put within you. And I will remove the heart of stone from your flesh and give you a heart of flesh. [27] And I will put my Spirit within you, and cause you to walk in my statutes and be careful to obey my rules.[1] [28] You shall dwell in the land that I gave to your fathers, and you shall be my people, and I will be your God. [29] And I will deliver you from all your uncleannesses. And I will summon the grain and make it abundant and lay no famine upon you. [30] I will make the fruit of the tree and the increase of the field abundant, that you may never again suffer the disgrace of famine among the nations. [31] Then you will remember your evil ways, and your deeds that were not good, and you will loathe yourselves for your iniquities and your abominations. [32] It is not for your sake that I will act, declares the Lord GOD; let that be known to you. Be ashamed and confounded for your ways, O house of Israel.

[33] "Thus says the Lord GOD: On the day that I cleanse you from all your iniquities, I will cause the cities to be inhabited, and the waste places shall be rebuilt. [34] And the land that was desolate shall be tilled, instead of being the desolation that it was in the sight of all who passed by. [35] And they will say, 'This land that was desolate has become like the garden of Eden, and the waste and desolate and ruined cities are now fortified and inhabited.' [36] Then the nations that are left all around you shall know that I am the LORD; I have rebuilt the ruined places and replanted that which was desolate. I am the LORD; I have spoken, and I will do it.

[37] "Thus says the Lord GOD: This also I will let the house of Israel ask me to do for them: to increase their people like a flock. [38] Like the flock for sacrifices,[2] like the flock at Jerusalem during her appointed feasts, so shall the waste cities be filled with flocks of people. Then they will know that I am the LORD."

The Valley of Dry Bones

37 The hand of the LORD was upon me, and he brought me out in the Spirit of the LORD and set me down in the middle of the valley;[3] it was full of bones. [2] And he led me around among them, and behold, there were very many on the surface of the valley, and behold, they were very dry. [3] And he said to me, "Son of man, can these bones live?" And I answered,

---

[1] Or my just decrees [2] Hebrew flock of holy things [3] Or plain; also verse 2

"O Lord God, you know." [4] Then he said to me, "Prophesy over these bones, and say to them, O dry bones, hear the word of the Lord. [5] Thus says the Lord God to these bones: Behold, I will cause breath[1] to enter you, and you shall live. [6] And I will lay sinews upon you, and will cause flesh to come upon you, and cover you with skin, and put breath in you, and you shall live, and you shall know that I am the Lord."

[7] So I prophesied as I was commanded. And as I prophesied, there was a sound, and behold, a rattling,[2] and the bones came together, bone to its bone. [8] And I looked, and behold, there were sinews on them, and flesh had come upon them, and skin had covered them. But there was no breath in them. [9] Then he said to me, "Prophesy to the breath; prophesy, son of man, and say to the breath, Thus says the Lord God: Come from the four winds, O breath, and breathe on these slain, that they may live." [10] So I prophesied as he commanded me, and the breath came into them, and they lived and stood on their feet, an exceedingly great army.

[11] Then he said to me, "Son of man, these bones are the whole house of Israel. Behold, they say, 'Our bones are dried up, and our hope is lost; we are indeed cut off.' [12] Therefore prophesy, and say to them, Thus says the Lord God: Behold, I will open your graves and raise you from your graves, O my people. And I will bring you into the land of Israel. [13] And you shall know that I am the Lord, when I open your graves, and raise you from your graves, O my people. [14] And I will put my Spirit within you, and you shall live, and I will place you in your own land. Then you shall know that I am the Lord; I have spoken, and I will do it, declares the Lord."

I Will Be Their God; They Shall Be My People

[15] The word of the Lord came to me: [16] "Son of man, take a stick[3] and write on it, 'For Judah, and the people of Israel associated with him'; then take another stick and write on it, 'For Joseph (the stick of Ephraim) and all the house of Israel associated with him.' [17] And join them one to another into one stick, that they may become one in your hand. [18] And when your people say to you, 'Will you not tell us what you mean by these?' [19] say to them, Thus says the Lord God: Behold, I am

about to take the stick of Joseph (that is in the hand of Ephraim) and the tribes of Israel associated with him. And I will join with it the stick of Judah,[4] and make them one stick, that they may be one in my hand. [20] When the sticks, on which you write are in your hand before their eyes, [21] then say to them, Thus says the Lord God: Behold, I will take the people of Israel from the nations among which they have gone, and will gather them from all around, and bring them to their own land. [22] And I will make them one nation in the land, on the mountains of Israel. And one king shall be king over them all, and they shall be no longer two nations, and no longer divided into two kingdoms. [23] They shall not defile themselves anymore with their idols and their detestable things, or with any of their transgressions. But I will save them from all the backslidings[5] in which they have sinned, and will cleanse them; and they shall be my people, and I will be their God.

[24] "My servant David shall be king over them, and they shall all have one shepherd. They shall walk in my rules and be careful to obey my statutes. [25] They shall dwell in the land that I gave to my servant Jacob, where your fathers lived. They and their children and their children's children shall dwell there forever, and David my servant shall be their prince forever. [26] I will make a covenant of peace with them. It shall be an everlasting covenant with them. And I will set them in their land[6] and multiply them, and will set my sanctuary in their midst forevermore. [27] My dwelling place shall be with them, and I will be their God, and they shall be my people. [28] Then the nations will know that I am the Lord who sanctifies Israel, when my sanctuary is in their midst forevermore."

Prophecy Against Gog

38 The word of the Lord came to me: [2] "Son of man, set your face toward Gog, of the land of Magog, the chief prince of Meshech[7] and Tubal, and prophesy against him [3] and say, Thus says the Lord God: Behold, I am against you, O Gog, chief prince of Meshech[8] and Tubal. [4] And I will turn you about and put hooks into your jaws, and I will bring you out, and all your army, horses and horsemen, all of them clothed in full armor, a great host, all of them with buckler and shield, wielding swords. [5] Persia, Cush, and Put are with them, all of

---

[1] Or spirit; also verses 6, 9, 10 [2] Or an earthquake (compare 3:12, 13) [3] One piece of wood; also verses 17, 19, 20 [4] Hebrew And I will place them on it, the stick of Judah [5] Many Hebrew manuscripts; other Hebrew manuscripts dwellings [6] Hebrew lacks in their land [7] Or Magog, the prince of Rosh, Meshech [8] Or Gog, prince of Rosh, Meshech

them with shield and helmet; [6] Gomer and all his hordes; Beth-togarmah from the uttermost parts of the north with all his hordes—many peoples are with you.

[7] "Be ready and keep ready, you and all your hosts that are assembled about you, and be a guard for them. [8] After many days you will be mustered. In the latter years you will go against the land that is restored from war, the land whose people were gathered from many peoples upon the mountains of Israel, which had been a continual waste. Its people were brought out from the peoples and now dwell securely, all of them. [9] You will advance, coming on like a storm. You will be like a cloud covering the land, you and all your hordes, and many peoples with you.

[10] "Thus says the Lord God: On that day, thoughts will come into your mind, and you will devise an evil scheme [11] and say, 'I will go up against the land of unwalled villages. I will fall upon the quiet people who dwell securely, all of them dwelling without walls, and having no bars or gates,' [12] to seize spoil and carry off plunder, to turn your hand against the waste places that are now inhabited, and the people who were gathered from the nations, who have acquired livestock and goods, who dwell at the center of the earth. [13] Sheba and Dedan and the merchants of Tarshish and all its leaders[1] will say to you, 'Have you come to seize spoil? Have you assembled your hosts to carry off plunder, to carry away silver and gold, to take away livestock and goods, to seize great spoil?'

[14] "Therefore, son of man, prophesy, and say to Gog, Thus says the Lord God: On that day when my people Israel are dwelling securely, will you not know it? [15] You will come from your place out of the uttermost parts of the north, you and many peoples with you, all of them riding on horses, a great host, a mighty army. [16] You will come up against my people Israel, like a cloud covering the land. In the latter days I will bring you against my land, that the nations may know me, when through you, O Gog, I vindicate my holiness before their eyes.

[17] "Thus says the Lord God: Are you he of whom I spoke in former days by my servants the prophets of Israel, who in those days prophesied for years that I would bring you against them? [18] But on that day, the day that Gog shall come against the land of Israel, declares the Lord God, my wrath will be roused in my anger.

[19] For in my jealousy and in my blazing wrath I declare, On that day there shall be a great earthquake in the land of Israel. [20] The fish of the sea and the birds of the heavens and the beasts of the field and all creeping things that creep on the ground, and all the people who are on the face of the earth, shall quake at my presence. And the mountains shall be thrown down, and the cliffs shall fall, and every wall shall tumble to the ground. [21] I will summon a sword against Gog[2] on all my mountains, declares the Lord God. Every man's sword will be against his brother. [22] With pestilence and bloodshed I will enter into judgment with him, and I will rain upon him and his hordes and the many peoples who are with him torrential rains and hailstones, fire and sulfur. [23] So I will show my greatness and my holiness and make myself known in the eyes of many nations. Then they will know that I am the Lord.

39 "And you, son of man, prophesy against Gog and say, Thus says the Lord God: Behold, I am against you, O Gog, chief prince of Meshech[3] and Tubal. [2] And I will turn you about and drive you forward,[4] and bring you up from the uttermost parts of the north, and lead you against the mountains of Israel. [3] Then I will strike your bow from your left hand, and will make your arrows drop out of your right hand. [4] You shall fall on the mountains of Israel, you and all your hordes and the peoples who are with you. I will give you to birds of prey of every sort and to the beasts of the field to be devoured. [5] You shall fall in the open field, for I have spoken, declares the Lord God. [6] I will send fire on Magog and on those who dwell securely in the coastlands, and they shall know that I am the Lord.

[7] "And my holy name I will make known in the midst of my people Israel, and I will not let my holy name be profaned anymore. And the nations shall know that I am the Lord, the Holy One in Israel. [8] Behold, it is coming and it will be brought about, declares the Lord God. That is the day of which I have spoken.

[9] "Then those who dwell in the cities of Israel will go out and make fires of the weapons and burn them, shields and bucklers, bow and arrows, clubs[5] and spears; and they will make fires of them for seven years, [10] so that they will not need to take wood out of the field or cut down any out of the forests, for they will make their fires of the weapons. They will seize the

---

[1] Hebrew young lions [2] Hebrew against him [3] Or Gog, prince of Rosh, Meshech [4] Or and drag you along [5] Or javelins

spoil of those who despoiled them, and plunder those who plundered them, declares the Lord GOD.

¹¹ "On that day I will give to Gog a place for burial in Israel, the Valley of the Travelers, east of the sea. It will block the travelers, for there Gog and all his multitude will be buried. It will be called the Valley of Hamon-gog.¹ ¹² For seven months the house of Israel will be burying them, in order to cleanse the land. ¹³ All the people of the land will bury them, and it will bring them renown on the day that I show my glory, declares the Lord GOD. ¹⁴ They will set apart men to travel through the land regularly and bury those travelers remaining on the face of the land, so as to cleanse it. At² the end of seven months they will make their search. ¹⁵ And when these travel through the land and anyone sees a human bone, then he shall set up a sign by it, till the buriers have buried it in the Valley of Hamon-gog. ¹⁶ (Hamonah³ is also the name of the city.) Thus shall they cleanse the land.

¹⁷ "As for you, son of man, thus says the Lord GOD: Speak to the birds of every sort and to all beasts of the field: 'Assemble and come, gather from all around to the sacrificial feast that I am preparing for you, a great sacrificial feast on the mountains of Israel, and you shall eat flesh and drink blood. ¹⁸ You shall eat the flesh of the mighty, and drink the blood of the princes of the earth—of rams, of lambs, and of he-goats, of bulls, all of them fat beasts of Bashan. ¹⁹ And you shall eat fat till you are filled, and drink blood till you are drunk, at the sacrificial feast that I am preparing for you. ²⁰ And you shall be filled at my table with horses and charioteers, with mighty men and all kinds of warriors,' declares the Lord GOD.

²¹ "And I will set my glory among the nations, and all the nations shall see my judgment that I have executed, and my hand that I have laid on them. ²² The house of Israel shall know that I am the LORD their God, from that day forward. ²³ And the nations shall know that the house of Israel went into captivity for their iniquity, because they dealt so treacherously with me that I hid my face from them and gave them into the hand of their adversaries, and they all fell by the sword. ²⁴ I dealt with them according to their uncleanness and their transgressions, and hid my face from them.

The LORD Will Restore Israel

²⁵ "Therefore thus says the Lord GOD: Now I will restore the fortunes of Jacob and have mercy on the whole house of Israel, and I will be jealous for my holy name. ²⁶ They shall forget their shame and all the treachery they have practiced against me, when they dwell securely in their land with none to make them afraid, ²⁷ when I have brought them back from the peoples and gathered them from their enemies' lands, and through them have vindicated my holiness in the sight of many nations. ²⁸ Then they shall know that I am the LORD their God, because I sent them into exile among the nations and then assembled them into their own land. I will leave none of them remaining among the nations anymore. ²⁹ And I will not hide my face anymore from them, when I pour out my Spirit upon the house of Israel, declares the Lord GOD."

Vision of the New Temple

40 In the twenty-fifth year of our exile, at the beginning of the year, on the tenth day of the month, in the fourteenth year after the city was struck down, on that very day, the hand of the LORD was upon me, and he brought me to the city.⁴ ² In visions of God he brought me to the land of Israel, and set me down on a very high mountain, on which was a structure like a city to the south. ³ When he brought me there, behold, there was a man whose appearance was like bronze, with a linen cord and a measuring reed in his hand. And he was standing in the gateway. ⁴ And the man said to me, "Son of man, look with your eyes, and hear with your ears, and set your heart upon all that I shall show you, for you were brought here in order that I might show it to you. Declare all that you see to the house of Israel."

The East Gate to the Outer Court

⁵ And behold, there was a wall all around the outside of the temple area, and the length of the measuring reed in the man's hand was six long cubits, each being a cubit and a handbreadth⁵ in length. So he measured the thickness of the wall, one reed; and the height, one reed. ⁶ Then he went into the gateway facing east, going up its steps, and measured the threshold of the gate, one reed deep.⁶ ⁷ And the side rooms, one reed long and one reed broad; and the space between the side rooms, five cubits; and the

threshold of the gate by the vestibule of the gate at the inner end, one reed. [8] Then he measured the vestibule of the gateway, on the inside, one reed. [9] Then he measured the vestibule of the gateway, eight cubits; and its jambs, two cubits; and the vestibule of the gate was at the inner end. [10] And there were three side rooms on either side of the east gate. The three were of the same size, and the jambs on either side were of the same size. [11] Then he measured the width of the opening of the gateway, ten cubits; and the length of the gateway, thirteen cubits. [12] There was a barrier before the side rooms, one cubit on either side. And the side rooms were six cubits on either side. [13] Then he measured the gate from the ceiling of the one side room to the ceiling of the other, a breadth of twenty-five cubits; the openings faced each other. [14] He measured also the vestibule, sixty cubits. And around the vestibule of the gateway was the court.[1] [15] From the front of the gate at the entrance to the front of the inner vestibule of the gate was fifty cubits. [16] And the gateway had windows all around, narrowing inwards toward the side rooms and toward their jambs, and likewise the vestibule had windows all around inside, and on the jambs were palm trees.

The Outer Court

[17] Then he brought me into the outer court. And behold, there were chambers and a pavement, all around the court. Thirty chambers faced the pavement. [18] And the pavement ran along the side of the gates, corresponding to the length of the gates. This was the lower pavement. [19] Then he measured the distance from the inner front of the lower gate to the outer front of the inner court,[2] a hundred cubits on the east side and on the north side.[3]

The North Gate

[20] As for the gate that faced toward the north, belonging to the outer court, he measured its length and its breadth. [21] Its side rooms, three on either side, and its jambs and its vestibule were of the same size as those of the first gate. Its length was fifty cubits, and its breadth twenty-five cubits. [22] And its windows, its vestibule, and its palm trees were of the same size as those of the gate that faced toward the east. And by seven steps people would go up to it, and find its vestibule before them. [23] And

opposite the gate on the north, as on the east, was a gate to the inner court. And he measured from gate to gate, a hundred cubits.

The South Gate

[24] And he led me toward the south, and behold, there was a gate on the south. And he measured its jambs and its vestibule; they had the same size as the others. [25] Both it and its vestibule had windows all around, like the windows of the others. Its length was fifty cubits, and its breadth twenty-five cubits. [26] And there were seven steps leading up to it, and its vestibule was before them, and it had palm trees on its jambs, one on either side. [27] And there was a gate on the south of the inner court. And he measured from gate to gate toward the south, a hundred cubits.

The Inner Court

[28] Then he brought me to the inner court through the south gate, and he measured the south gate. It was of the same size as the others. [29] Its side rooms, its jambs, and its vestibule were of the same size as the others, and both it and its vestibule had windows all around. Its length was fifty cubits, and its breadth twenty-five cubits. [30] And there were vestibules all around, twenty-five cubits long and five cubits broad. [31] Its vestibule faced the outer court, and palm trees were on its jambs, and its stairway had eight steps.

[32] Then he brought me to the inner court on the east side, and he measured the gate. It was of the same size as the others. [33] Its side rooms, its jambs, and its vestibule were of the same size as the others, and both it and its vestibule had windows all around. Its length was fifty cubits, and its breadth twenty-five cubits. [34] Its vestibule faced the outer court, and it had palm trees on its jambs, on either side, and its stairway had eight steps.

[35] Then he brought me to the north gate, and he measured it. It had the same size as the others. [36] Its side rooms, its jambs, and its vestibule were of the same size as the others,[4] and it had windows all around. Its length was fifty cubits, and its breadth twenty-five cubits. [37] Its vestibule[5] faced the outer court, and it had palm trees on its jambs, on either side, and its stairway had eight steps.

[38] There was a chamber with its door in the vestibule of the gate,[6] where the burnt offering was to be washed. [39] And in the vestibule of the

[1] Text uncertain; Hebrew *And he made the jambs sixty cubits, and to the jamb of the court was the gateway all around* [2] Hebrew *distance from before the low gate before the inner court to the outside* [3] Or *cubits. So far the eastern gate; now to the northern gate* [4] One manuscript (compare verses 29 and 33); most manuscripts lack *were of the same size as the others* [5] Septuagint, Vulgate (compare verses 26, 31, 34); Hebrew *jambs* [6] Hebrew *at the jambs, the gates*

gate were two tables on either side, on which the burnt offering and the sin offering and the guilt offering were to be slaughtered. [40] And off to the side, on the outside as one goes up to the entrance of the north gate, were two tables; and off to the other side of the vestibule of the gate were two tables. [41] Four tables were on either side of the gate, eight tables, on which to slaughter. [42] And there were four tables of hewn stone for the burnt offering, a cubit and a half long, and a cubit and a half broad, and one cubit high, on which the instruments were to be laid with which the burnt offerings and the sacrifices were slaughtered. [43] And hooks,[1] a handbreadth long, were fastened all around within. And on the tables the flesh of the offering was to be laid.

Chambers for the Priests

[44] On the outside of the inner gateway there were two chambers[2] in the inner court, one[3] at the side of the north gate facing south, the other at the side of the south[4] gate facing north. [45] And he said to me, "This chamber that faces south is for the priests who have charge of the temple, [46] and the chamber that faces north is for the priests who have charge of the altar. These are the sons of Zadok, who alone[5] among the sons of Levi may come near to the LORD to minister to him." [47] And he measured the court, a hundred cubits long and a hundred cubits broad, a square. And the altar was in front of the temple.

The Vestibule of the Temple

[48] Then he brought me to the vestibule of the temple and measured the jambs of the vestibule, five cubits on either side. And the breadth of the gate was fourteen cubits, and the sidewalls of the gate[6] were three cubits on either side. [49] The length of the vestibule was twenty cubits, and the breadth twelve[7] cubits, and people would go up to it by ten steps.[8] And there were pillars beside the jambs, one on either side.

The Inner Temple

41 Then he brought me to the nave and measured the jambs. On each side six cubits[9] was the breadth of the jambs.[10] [2] And the breadth of the entrance was ten cubits, and the sidewalls of the entrance were five cubits on either side. And he measured the length of the nave,[11] forty cubits, and its breadth, twenty cubits. [3] Then he went into the inner room and measured the jambs of the entrance, two cubits; and the entrance, six cubits; and the sidewalls on either side[12] of the entrance, seven cubits. [4] And he measured the length of the room, twenty cubits, and its breadth, twenty cubits, across the nave. And he said to me, "This is the Most Holy Place."

[5] Then he measured the wall of the temple, six cubits thick, and the breadth of the side chambers, four cubits, all around the temple. [6] And the side chambers were in three stories, one over another, thirty in each story. There were offsets[13] all around the wall of the temple to serve as supports for the side chambers, so that they should not be supported by the wall of the temple. [7] And it became broader as it wound upward to the side chambers, because the temple was enclosed upward all around the temple. Thus the temple had a broad area upward, and so one went up from the lowest story to the top story through the middle story. [8] I saw also that the temple had a raised platform all around; the foundations of the side chambers measured a full reed of six long cubits. [9] The thickness of the outer wall of the side chambers was five cubits. The free space between the side chambers of the temple and the [10] other chambers was a breadth of twenty cubits all around the temple on every side. [11] And the doors of the side chambers opened on the free space, one door toward the north, and another door toward the south. And the breadth of the free space was five cubits all around.

[12] The building that was facing the separate yard on the west side was seventy cubits broad, and the wall of the building was five cubits thick all around, and its length ninety cubits.

[13] Then he measured the temple, a hundred cubits long; and the yard and the building with its walls, a hundred cubits long; [14] also the breadth of the east front of the temple and the yard, a hundred cubits.

[15] Then he measured the length of the building facing the yard that was at the back and its galleries[14] on either side, a hundred cubits.

The inside of the nave and the vestibules of the court, [16] the thresholds and the narrow windows and the galleries all around the three of them, opposite the threshold, were paneled

---

[1] Or shelves [2] Septuagint; Hebrew were chambers for singers [3] Hebrew lacks one [4] Septuagint; Hebrew east [5] Hebrew lacks alone [6] Septuagint; Hebrew lacks was fourteen cubits, and the sidewalls of the gate [7] Septuagint; Hebrew eleven [8] Septuagint; Hebrew and by steps that would go up to it [9] A cubit was about 18 inches or 45 centimeters [10] Compare Septuagint; Hebrew tent [11] Hebrew its length [12] Septuagint; Hebrew and the breadth [13] Septuagint, compare 1 Kings 6:6; the meaning of the Hebrew word is uncertain [14] The meaning of the Hebrew term is unknown; also verse 16

with wood all around, from the floor up to the windows (now the windows were covered), [17] to the space above the door, even to the inner room, and on the outside. And on all the walls all around, inside and outside, was a measured pattern.[1] [18] It was carved of cherubim and palm trees, a palm tree between cherub and cherub. Every cherub had two faces: [19] a human face toward the palm tree on the one side, and the face of a young lion toward the palm tree on the other side. They were carved on the whole temple all around. [20] From the floor to above the door, cherubim and palm trees were carved; similarly the wall of the nave.

[21] The doorposts of the nave were squared, and in front of the Holy Place was something resembling [22] an altar of wood, three cubits high, two cubits long, and two cubits broad.[2] Its corners, its base,[3] and its walls were of wood. He said to me, "This is the table that is before the LORD." [23] The nave and the Holy Place had each a double door. [24] The double doors had two leaves apiece, two swinging leaves for each door. [25] And on the doors of the nave were carved cherubim and palm trees, such as were carved on the walls. And there was a canopy[4] of wood in front of the vestibule outside. [26] And there were narrow windows and palm trees on either side, on the sidewalls of the vestibule, the side chambers of the temple, and the canopies.

The Temple's Chambers

42 Then he led me out into the outer court, toward the north, and he brought me to the chambers that were opposite the separate yard and opposite the building on the north. [2] The length of the building whose door faced north was a hundred cubits,[5] and the breadth fifty cubits. [3] Facing the twenty cubits that belonged to the inner court, and facing the pavement that belonged to the outer court, was gallery[6] against gallery in three stories. [4] And before the chambers was a passage inward, ten cubits wide and a hundred cubits long,[7] and their doors were on the north. [5] Now the upper chambers were narrower, for the galleries took more away from them than from the lower and middle chambers of the building. [6] For they were in three stories, and they had no pillars like the pillars of the courts. Thus the upper chambers were set back from the ground more than the lower and the middle

ones. [7] And there was a wall outside parallel to the chambers, toward the outer court, opposite the chambers, fifty cubits long. [8] For the chambers on the outer court were fifty cubits long, while those opposite the nave[8] were a hundred cubits long. [9] Below these chambers was an entrance on the east side, as one enters them from the outer court.

[10] In the thickness of the wall of the court, on the south[9] also, opposite the yard and opposite the building, there were chambers [11] with a passage in front of them. They were similar to the chambers on the north, of the same length and breadth, with the same exits[10] and arrangements and doors, [12] as were the entrances of the chambers on the south. There was an entrance at the beginning of the passage, the passage before the corresponding wall on the east as one enters them.[11]

[13] Then he said to me, "The north chambers and the south chambers opposite the yard are the holy chambers, where the priests who approach the LORD shall eat the most holy offerings. There they shall put the most holy offerings—the grain offering, the sin offering, and the guilt offering—for the place is holy. [14] When the priests enter the Holy Place, they shall not go out of it into the outer court without laying there the garments in which they minister, for these are holy. They shall put on other garments before they go near to that which is for the people."

[15] Now when he had finished measuring the interior of the temple area, he led me out by the gate that faced east, and measured the temple area all around. [16] He measured the east side with the measuring reed, 500 cubits by the measuring reed all around. [17] He measured the north side, 500 cubits by the measuring reed all around. [18] He measured the south side, 500 cubits by the measuring reed. [19] Then he turned to the west side and measured, 500 cubits by the measuring reed. [20] He measured it on the four sides. It had a wall around it, 500 cubits long and 500 cubits broad, to make a separation between the holy and the common.

The Glory of the LORD Fills the Temple

43 Then he led me to the gate, the gate facing east. [2] And behold, the glory of the God of Israel was coming from the east. And the sound of his coming was like the sound

[1] Hebrew *were measurements* [2] Septuagint; Hebrew lacks *two cubits broad* [3] Septuagint; Hebrew *length* [4] The meaning of the Hebrew word is unknown; also verse 26 [5] A *cubit* was about 18 inches or 45 centimeters [6] The meaning of the Hebrew word is unknown; also verse 5 [7] Septuagint, Syriac; Hebrew *and a way of one cubit* [8] Or temple [9] Septuagint; Hebrew *east* [10] Hebrew *and all their exits* [11] The meaning of the Hebrew verse is uncertain

of many waters, and the earth shone with his glory. [3] And the vision I saw was just like the vision that I had seen when he[1] came to destroy the city, and just like the vision that I had seen by the Chebar canal. And I fell on my face. [4] As the glory of the LORD entered the temple by the gate facing east, [5] the Spirit lifted me up and brought me into the inner court; and behold, the glory of the LORD filled the temple.

[6] While the man was standing beside me, I heard one speaking to me out of the temple, [7] and he said to me, "Son of man, this is the place of my throne and the place of the soles of my feet, where I will dwell in the midst of the people of Israel forever. And the house of Israel shall no more defile my holy name, neither they, nor their kings, by their whoring and by the dead bodies[2] of their kings at their high places,[3] [8] by setting their threshold by my threshold and their doorposts beside my doorposts, with only a wall between me and them. They have defiled my holy name by their abominations that they have committed, so I have consumed them in my anger. [9] Now let them put away their whoring and the dead bodies of their kings far from me, and I will dwell in their midst forever.

[10] "As for you, son of man, describe to the house of Israel the temple, that they may be ashamed of their iniquities; and they shall measure the plan. [11] And if they are ashamed of all that they have done, make known to them the design of the temple, its arrangement, its exits and its entrances, that is, its whole design; and make known to them as well all its statutes and its whole design and all its laws, and write it down in their sight, so that they may observe all its laws and all its statutes and carry them out. [12] This is the law of the temple: the whole territory on the top of the mountain all around shall be most holy. Behold, this is the law of the temple.

The Altar

[13] "These are the measurements of the altar by cubits (the cubit being a cubit and a handbreadth):[4] its base shall be one cubit high[5] and one cubit broad, with a rim of one span[6] around its edge. And this shall be the height of the altar: [14] from the base on the ground to the lower ledge, two cubits, with a breadth of one cubit; and from the smaller ledge to the larger ledge, four cubits, with a breadth of one cubit;

[15] and the altar hearth, four cubits; and from the altar hearth projecting upward, four horns. [16] The altar hearth shall be square, twelve cubits long by twelve broad. [17] The ledge also shall be square, fourteen cubits long by fourteen broad, with a rim around it half a cubit broad, and its base one cubit all around. The steps of the altar shall face east."

[18] And he said to me, "Son of man, thus says the Lord GOD: These are the ordinances for the altar: On the day when it is erected for offering burnt offerings upon it and for throwing blood against it, [19] you shall give to the Levitical priests of the family of Zadok, who draw near to me to minister to me, declares the Lord GOD, a bull from the herd for a sin offering. [20] And you shall take some of its blood and put it on the four horns of the altar and on the four corners of the ledge and upon the rim all around. Thus you shall purify the altar and make atonement for it. [21] You shall also take the bull of the sin offering, and it shall be burned in the appointed place belonging to the temple, outside the sacred area. [22] And on the second day you shall offer a male goat without blemish for a sin offering; and the altar shall be purified, as it was purified with the bull. [23] When you have finished purifying it, you shall offer a bull from the herd without blemish and a ram from the flock without blemish. [24] You shall present them before the LORD, and the priests shall sprinkle salt on them and offer them up as a burnt offering to the LORD. [25] For seven days you shall provide daily a male goat for a sin offering; also, a bull from the herd and a ram from the flock, without blemish, shall be provided. [26] Seven days shall they make atonement for the altar and cleanse it, and so consecrate it.[7] [27] And when they have completed these days, then from the eighth day onward the priests shall offer on the altar your burnt offerings and your peace offerings, and I will accept you, declares the Lord GOD."

The Gate for the Prince

44 Then he brought me back to the outer gate of the sanctuary, which faces east. And it was shut. [2] And the LORD said to me, "This gate shall remain shut; it shall not be opened, and no one shall enter by it, for the LORD, the God of Israel, has entered by it. Therefore it shall remain shut. [3] Only the prince

---

[1] Some Hebrew manuscripts and Vulgate; most Hebrew manuscripts *when I* [2] Or *the monuments;* also verse 9 [3] Or *at their deaths* [4] A *cubit* was about 18 inches or 45 centimeters; a *handbreadth* was about 3 inches or 7.5 centimeters [5] Or *its gutter shall be one cubit deep* [6] A *span* was about 9 inches or 22 centimeters [7] Hebrew *fill its hand*

may sit in it to eat bread before the LORD. He shall enter by way of the vestibule of the gate, and shall go out by the same way."

4 Then he brought me by way of the north gate to the front of the temple, and I looked, and behold, the glory of the LORD filled the temple of the LORD. And I fell on my face. 5 And the LORD said to me, "Son of man, mark well, see with your eyes, and hear with your ears all that I shall tell you concerning all the statutes of the temple of the LORD and all its laws. And mark well the entrance to the temple and all the exits from the sanctuary. 6 And say to the rebellious house,[1] to the house of Israel, Thus says the Lord GOD: O house of Israel, enough of all your abominations, 7 in admitting foreigners, uncircumcised in heart and flesh, to be in my sanctuary, profaning my temple, when you offer to me my food, the fat and the blood. You[2] have broken my covenant, in addition to all your abominations. 8 And you have not kept charge of my holy things, but you have set others to keep my charge for you in my sanctuary.

9 "Thus says the Lord GOD: No foreigner, uncircumcised in heart and flesh, of all the foreigners who are among the people of Israel, shall enter my sanctuary. 10 But the Levites who went far from me, going astray from me after their idols when Israel went astray, shall bear their punishment.[3] 11 They shall be ministers in my sanctuary, having oversight at the gates of the temple and ministering in the temple. They shall slaughter the burnt offering and the sacrifice for the people, and they shall stand before the people, to minister to them. 12 Because they ministered to them before their idols and became a stumbling block of iniquity to the house of Israel, therefore I have sworn concerning them, declares the Lord GOD, and they shall bear their punishment. 13 They shall not come near to me, to serve me as priest, nor come near any of my holy things and the things that are most holy, but they shall bear their shame and the abominations that they have committed. 14 Yet I will appoint them to keep charge of the temple, to do all its service and all that is to be done in it.

Rules for Levitical Priests

15 "But the Levitical priests, the sons of Zadok, who kept the charge of my sanctuary when the people of Israel went astray from me, shall come near to me to minister to me. And they shall stand before me to offer me the fat and the blood, declares the Lord GOD. 16 They shall enter my sanctuary, and they shall approach my table, to minister to me, and they shall keep my charge. 17 When they enter the gates of the inner court, they shall wear linen garments. They shall have nothing of wool on them, while they minister at the gates of the inner court, and within. 18 They shall have linen turbans on their heads, and linen undergarments around their waists. They shall not bind themselves with anything that causes sweat. 19 And when they go out into the outer court to the people, they shall put off the garments in which they have been ministering and lay them in the holy chambers. And they shall put on other garments, lest they transmit holiness to the people with their garments. 20 They shall not shave their heads or let their locks grow long; they shall surely trim the hair of their heads. 21 No priest shall drink wine when he enters the inner court. 22 They shall not marry a widow or a divorced woman, but only virgins of the offspring of the house of Israel, or a widow who is the widow of a priest. 23 They shall teach my people the difference between the holy and the common, and show them how to distinguish between the unclean and the clean. 24 In a dispute, they shall act as judges, and they shall judge it according to my judgments. They shall keep my laws and my statutes in all my appointed feasts, and they shall keep my Sabbaths holy. 25 They shall not defile themselves by going near to a dead person. However, for father or mother, for son or daughter, for brother or unmarried sister they may defile themselves. 26 After he[4] has become clean, they shall count seven days for him. 27 And on the day that he goes into the Holy Place, into the inner court, to minister in the Holy Place, he shall offer his sin offering, declares the Lord GOD.

28 "This shall be their inheritance: I am their inheritance: and you shall give them no possession in Israel; I am their possession. 29 They shall eat the grain offering, the sin offering, and the guilt offering, and every devoted thing in Israel shall be theirs. 30 And the first of all the firstfruits of all kinds, and every offering of all kinds from all your offerings, shall belong to the priests. You shall also give to the priests the first of your dough, that a blessing may rest on your house. 31 The priests shall not eat of anything, whether bird or beast, that has died of itself or is torn by wild animals.

---

[1] Septuagint; Hebrew lacks *house* [2] Septuagint, Syriac, Vulgate; Hebrew *They* [3] Or *iniquity*; also verse 12 [4] That is, a priest

The Holy District

45 "When you allot the land as an inheritance, you shall set apart for the LORD a portion of the land as a holy district, 25,000 cubits[1] long and 20,000[2] cubits broad. It shall be holy throughout its whole extent. [2] Of this a square plot of 500 by 500 cubits shall be for the sanctuary, with fifty cubits for an open space around it. [3] And from this measured district you shall measure off a section 25,000 cubits long and 10,000 broad, in which shall be the sanctuary, the Most Holy Place. [4] It shall be the holy portion of the land. It shall be for the priests, who minister in the sanctuary and approach the LORD to minister to him, and it shall be a place for their houses and a holy place for the sanctuary. [5] Another section, 25,000 cubits long and 10,000 cubits broad, shall be for the Levites who minister at the temple, as their possession for cities to live in.[3]

[6] "Alongside the portion set apart as the holy district you shall assign for the property of the city an area 5,000 cubits broad and 25,000 cubits long. It shall belong to the whole house of Israel.

The Portion for the Prince

[7] "And to the prince shall belong the land on both sides of the holy district and the property of the city, alongside the holy district and the property of the city, on the west and on the east, corresponding in length to one of the tribal portions, and extending from the western to the eastern boundary [8] of the land. It is to be his property in Israel. And my princes shall no more oppress my people, but they shall let the house of Israel have the land according to their tribes.

[9] "Thus says the Lord GOD: Enough, O princes of Israel! Put away violence and oppression, and execute justice and righteousness. Cease your evictions of my people, declares the Lord GOD.

[10] "You shall have just balances, a just ephah, and a just bath.[4] [11] The ephah and the bath shall be of the same measure, the bath containing one tenth of a homer,[5] and the ephah one tenth of a homer; the homer shall be the standard measure. [12] The shekel shall be twenty gerahs;[6] twenty shekels plus twenty-five shekels plus fifteen shekels shall be your mina.[7]

[13] "This is the offering that you shall make: one sixth of an ephah from each homer of wheat, and one sixth of an ephah from each homer of barley, [14] and as the fixed portion of oil, measured in baths, one tenth of a bath from each cor[8] (the cor, like the homer, contains ten baths).[9] [15] And one sheep from every flock of two hundred, from the watering places of Israel for grain offering, burnt offering, and peace offerings, to make atonement for them, declares the Lord GOD. [16] All the people of the land shall be obliged to give this offering to the prince in Israel. [17] It shall be the prince's duty to furnish the burnt offerings, grain offerings, and drink offerings, at the feasts, the new moons, and the Sabbaths, all the appointed feasts of the house of Israel: he shall provide the sin offerings, grain offerings, burnt offerings, and peace offerings, to make atonement on behalf of the house of Israel.

[18] "Thus says the Lord GOD: In the first month, on the first day of the month, you shall take a bull from the herd without blemish, and purify the sanctuary. [19] The priest shall take some of the blood of the sin offering and put it on the doorposts of the temple, the four corners of the ledge of the altar, and the posts of the gate of the inner court. [20] You shall do the same on the seventh day of the month for anyone who has sinned through error or ignorance; so you shall make atonement for the temple.

[21] "In the first month, on the fourteenth day of the month, you shall celebrate the Feast of the Passover, and for seven days unleavened bread shall be eaten. [22] On that day the prince shall provide for himself and all the people of the land a young bull for a sin offering. [23] And on the seven days of the festival he shall provide as a burnt offering to the LORD seven young bulls and seven rams without blemish, on each of the seven days; and a male goat daily for a sin offering. [24] And he shall provide as a grain offering an ephah for each bull, an ephah for each ram, and a hin[10] of oil to each ephah. [25] In the seventh month, on the fifteenth day of the month and for the seven days of the feast, he shall make the same provision for sin offerings, burnt offerings, and grain offerings, and for the oil.

The Prince and the Feasts

46 "Thus says the Lord GOD: The gate of the inner court that faces east shall be shut on the six working days, but on the Sabbath day it shall be opened, and on the day of the new moon it shall be opened. ²The prince shall enter by the vestibule of the gate from outside, and shall take his stand by the post of the gate. The priests shall offer his burnt offering and his peace offerings, and he shall worship at the threshold of the gate. Then he shall go out, but the gate shall not be shut until evening. ³The people of the land shall bow down at the entrance of that gate before the LORD on the Sabbaths and on the new moons. ⁴The burnt offering that the prince offers to the LORD on the Sabbath day shall be six lambs without blemish and a ram without blemish. ⁵And the grain offering with the ram shall be an ephah,[1] and the grain offering with the lambs shall be as much as he is able, together with a hin[2] of oil to each ephah. ⁶On the day of the new moon he shall offer a bull from the herd without blemish, and six lambs and a ram, which shall be without blemish. ⁷As a grain offering he shall provide an ephah with the bull and an ephah with the ram, and with the lambs as much as he is able, together with a hin of oil to each ephah. ⁸When the prince enters, he shall enter by the vestibule of the gate, and he shall go out by the same way.

⁹"When the people of the land come before the LORD at the appointed feasts, he who enters by the north gate to worship shall go out by the south gate, and he who enters by the south gate shall go out by the north gate: no one shall return by way of the gate by which he entered, but each shall go out straight ahead. ¹⁰When they enter, the prince shall enter with them, and when they go out, he shall go out.

¹¹"At the feasts and the appointed festivals, the grain offering with a young bull shall be an ephah, and with a ram an ephah, and with the lambs as much as one is able to give, together with a hin of oil to an ephah. ¹²When the prince provides a freewill offering, either a burnt offering or peace offerings as a freewill offering to the LORD, the gate facing east shall be opened for him. And he shall offer his burnt offering or his peace offerings as he does on the Sabbath day. Then he shall go out, and after he has gone out the gate shall be shut.

¹³"You shall provide a lamb a year old without blemish for a burnt offering to the LORD daily; morning by morning you shall provide it. ¹⁴And you shall provide a grain offering with it morning by morning, one sixth of an ephah, and one third of a hin of oil to moisten the flour, as a grain offering to the LORD. This is a perpetual statute. ¹⁵Thus the lamb and the meal offering and the oil shall be provided, morning by morning, for a regular burnt offering.

¹⁶"Thus says the Lord GOD: If the prince makes a gift to any of his sons as his inheritance, it shall belong to his sons. It is their property by inheritance. ¹⁷But if he makes a gift out of his inheritance to one of his servants, it shall be his to the year of liberty. Then it shall revert to the prince; surely it is his inheritance—it shall belong to his sons. ¹⁸The prince shall not take any of the inheritance of the people, thrusting them out of their property. He shall give his sons their inheritance out of his own property, so that none of my people shall be scattered from his property."

Boiling Places for Offerings

¹⁹Then he brought me through the entrance, which was at the side of the gate, to the north row of the holy chambers for the priests, and behold, a place was there at the extreme western end of them. ²⁰And he said to me, "This is the place where the priests shall boil the guilt offering and the sin offering, and where they shall bake the grain offering, in order not to bring them out into the outer court and so transmit holiness to the people."

²¹Then he brought me out to the outer court and led me around to the four corners of the court. And behold, in each corner of the court there was another court— ²²in the four corners of the court were small[3] courts, forty cubits[4] long and thirty broad; the four were of the same size. ²³On the inside, around each of the four courts was a row of masonry, with hearths made at the bottom of the rows all around. ²⁴Then he said to me, "These are the kitchens where those who minister at the temple shall boil the sacrifices of the people."

Water Flowing from the Temple

47 Then he brought me back to the door of the temple, and behold, water was issuing from below the threshold of the temple toward the east (for the temple faced east). The

---

[1] An *ephah* was about 3/5 bushel or 22 liters [2] A *hin* was about 4 quarts or 3.5 liters [3] Septuagint, Syriac, Vulgate; the meaning of the Hebrew word is uncertain [4] A *cubit* was about 18 inches or 45 centimeters

water was flowing down from below the south end of the threshold of the temple, south of the altar. [2] Then he brought me out by way of the north gate and led me around on the outside to the outer gate that faces toward the east; and behold, the water was trickling out on the south side.

[3] Going on eastward with a measuring line in his hand, the man measured a thousand cubits,[1] and then led me through the water, and it was ankle-deep. [4] Again he measured a thousand, and led me through the water, and it was knee-deep. Again he measured a thousand, and led me through the water, and it was waist-deep. [5] Again he measured a thousand, and it was a river that I could not pass through, for the water had risen. It was deep enough to swim in, a river that could not be passed through. [6] And he said to me, "Son of man, have you seen this?"

Then he led me back to the bank of the river. [7] As I went back, I saw on the bank of the river very many trees on the one side and on the other. [8] And he said to me, "This water flows toward the eastern region and goes down into the Arabah, and enters the sea;[2] when the water flows into the sea, the water will become fresh.[3] [9] And wherever the river goes,[4] every living creature that swarms will live, and there will be very many fish. For this water goes there, that the waters of the sea[5] may become fresh; so everything will live where the river goes. [10] Fishermen will stand beside the sea. From Engedi to Eneglaim it will be a place for the spreading of nets. Its fish will be of very many kinds, like the fish of the Great Sea.[6] [11] But its swamps and marshes will not become fresh; they are to be left for salt. [12] And on the banks, on both sides of the river, there will grow all kinds of trees for food. Their leaves will not wither, nor their fruit fail, but they will bear fresh fruit every month, because the water for them flows from the sanctuary. Their fruit will be for food, and their leaves for healing."

Division of the Land

[13] Thus says the Lord GOD: "This is the boundary[7] by which you shall divide the land for inheritance among the twelve tribes of Israel. Joseph shall have two portions. [14] And you shall divide equally what I swore to give to your fathers. This land shall fall to you as your inheritance.

[15] "This shall be the boundary of the land: On the north side, from the Great Sea by way of Hethlon to Lebo-hamath, and on to Zedad,[8] [16] Berothah, Sibraim (which lies on the border between Damascus and Hamath), as far as Hazer-hatticon, which is on the border of Hauran. [17] So the boundary shall run from the sea to Hazar-enan, which is on the northern border of Damascus, with the border of Hamath to the north.[9] This shall be the north side.[10]

[18] "On the east side, the boundary shall run between Hauran and Damascus; along the Jordan between Gilead and the land of Israel; to the eastern sea and as far as Tamar.[11] This shall be the east side.

[19] "On the south side, it shall run from Tamar as far as the waters of Meribah-kadesh, from there along the Brook of Egypt[12] to the Great Sea. This shall be the south side.

[20] "On the west side, the Great Sea shall be the boundary to a point opposite Lebo-hamath. This shall be the west side.

[21] "So you shall divide this land among you according to the tribes of Israel. [22] You shall allot it as an inheritance for yourselves and for the sojourners who reside among you and have had children among you. They shall be to you as native-born children of Israel. With you they shall be allotted an inheritance among the tribes of Israel. [23] In whatever tribe the sojourner resides, there you shall assign him his inheritance, declares the Lord GOD.

48

"These are the names of the tribes: Beginning at the northern extreme, beside the way of Hethlon to Lebo-hamath, as far as Hazar-enan (which is on the northern border of Damascus over against Hamath), and extending[13] from the east side to the west,[14] Dan, one portion. [2] Adjoining the territory of Dan, from the east side to the west, Asher, one portion. [3] Adjoining the territory of Asher, from the east side to the west, Naphtali, one portion. [4] Adjoining the territory of Naphtali, from the east side to the west, Manasseh, one portion. [5] Adjoining the territory of Manasseh, from the east side to the west, Ephraim, one portion. [6] Adjoining the territory of Ephraim, from the east side to the west, Reuben, one portion. [7] Adjoining the territory of Reuben, from the east side to the west, Judah, one portion.

---

[1] A cubit was about 18 inches or 45 centimeters [2] That is, the Dead Sea [3] Hebrew will be healed; also verses 9, 11 [4] Septuagint, Syriac, Vulgate, Targum; Hebrew the two rivers go [5] Hebrew lacks the waters of the sea [6] That is, the Mediterranean Sea; also verses 15, 19, 20 [7] Probable reading; Hebrew The valley of the boundary [8] Septuagint; Hebrew the entrance of Zedad, Hamath [9] The meaning of the Hebrew is uncertain [10] Probable reading; Hebrew and as for the north side [11] Compare Syriac; Hebrew to the eastern sea you shall measure [12] Hebrew lacks of Egypt [13] Probable reading; Hebrew and they shall be his [14] Septuagint (compare verses 2–8); Hebrew the east side the west

8 "Adjoining the territory of Judah, from the east side to the west, shall be the portion which you shall set apart, 25,000 cubits[1] in breadth, and in length equal to one of the tribal portions, from the east side to the west, with the sanctuary in the midst of it. 9 The portion that you shall set apart for the LORD shall be 25,000 cubits in length, and 20,000[2] in breadth. 10 These shall be the allotments of the holy portion: the priests shall have an allotment measuring 25,000 cubits on the northern side, 10,000 cubits in breadth on the western side, 10,000 in breadth on the eastern side, and 25,000 in length on the southern side, with the sanctuary of the LORD in the midst of it. 11 This shall be for the consecrated priests, the sons of Zadok, who kept my charge, who did not go astray when the people of Israel went astray, as the Levites did. 12 And it shall belong to them as a special portion from the holy portion of the land, a most holy place, adjoining the territory of the Levites. 13 And alongside the territory of the priests, the Levites shall have an allotment 25,000 cubits in length and 10,000 in breadth. The whole length shall be 25,000 cubits and the breadth 20,000.[3] 14 They shall not sell or exchange any of it. They shall not alienate this choice portion of the land, for it is holy to the LORD.

15 "The remainder, 5,000 cubits in breadth and 25,000 in length, shall be for common use for the city, for dwellings and for open country. In the midst of it shall be the city, 16 and these shall be its measurements: the north side 4,500 cubits, the south side 4,500, the east side 4,500, and the west side 4,500. 17 And the city shall have open land: on the north 250 cubits, on the south 250, on the east 250, and on the west 250. 18 The remainder of the length alongside the holy portion shall be 10,000 cubits to the east, and 10,000 to the west, and it shall be alongside the holy portion. Its produce shall be food for the workers of the city. 19 And the workers of the city, from all the tribes of Israel, shall till it. 20 The whole portion that you shall set apart shall be 25,000 cubits square, that is, the holy portion together with the property of the city.

21 "What remains on both sides of the holy portion and of the property of the city shall belong to the prince. Extending from the 25,000 cubits of the holy portion to the east border, and westward from the 25,000 cubits to the west border, parallel to the tribal portions, it shall belong to the prince. The holy portion with the sanctuary of the temple shall be in its midst. 22 It shall be separate from the property of the Levites and the property of the city, which are in the midst of that which belongs to the prince. The portion of the prince shall lie between the territory of Judah and the territory of Benjamin.

23 "As for the rest of the tribes: from the east side to the west, Benjamin, one portion. 24 Adjoining the territory of Benjamin, from the east side to the west, Simeon, one portion. 25 Adjoining the territory of Simeon, from the east side to the west, Issachar, one portion. 26 Adjoining the territory of Issachar, from the east side to the west, Zebulun, one portion. 27 Adjoining the territory of Zebulun, from the east side to the west, Gad, one portion. 28 And adjoining the territory of Gad to the south, the boundary shall run from Tamar to the waters of Meribah-kadesh, from there along the Brook of Egypt[4] to the Great Sea.[5] 29 This is the land that you shall allot as an inheritance among the tribes of Israel, and these are their portions, declares the Lord GOD.

The Gates of the City

30 "These shall be the exits of the city: On the north side, which is to be 4,500 cubits by measure, 31 three gates, the gate of Reuben, the gate of Judah, and the gate of Levi, the gates of the city being named after the tribes of Israel. 32 On the east side, which is to be 4,500 cubits, three gates, the gate of Joseph, the gate of Benjamin, and the gate of Dan. 33 On the south side, which is to be 4,500 cubits by measure, three gates, the gate of Simeon, the gate of Issachar, and the gate of Zebulun. 34 On the west side, which is to be 4,500 cubits, three gates,[6] the gate of Gad, the gate of Asher, and the gate of Naphtali. 35 The circumference of the city shall be 18,000 cubits. And the name of the city from that time on shall be, The LORD Is There."

---

[1] A cubit was about 18 inches or 45 centimeters [2] Compare 45:1; Hebrew 10,000 [3] Septuagint; Hebrew 10,000 [4] Hebrew lacks of Egypt [5] That is, the Mediterranean Sea [6] One Hebrew manuscript, Syriac (compare Septuagint); most Hebrew manuscripts their gates three

DANIEL

Daniel Taken to Babylon

1 In the third year of the reign of Jehoiakim king of Judah, Nebuchadnezzar king of Babylon came to Jerusalem and besieged it. ²And the Lord gave Jehoiakim king of Judah into his hand, with some of the vessels of the house of God. And he brought them to the land of Shinar, to the house of his god, and placed the vessels in the treasury of his god. ³Then the king commanded Ashpenaz, his chief eunuch, to bring some of the people of Israel, both of the royal family[1] and of the nobility, ⁴youths without blemish, of good appearance and skillful in all wisdom, endowed with knowledge, understanding learning, and competent to stand in the king's palace, and to teach them the literature and language of the Chaldeans. ⁵The king assigned them a daily portion of the food that the king ate, and of the wine that he drank. They were to be educated for three years, and at the end of that time they were to stand before the king. ⁶Among these were Daniel, Hananiah, Mishael, and Azariah of the tribe of Judah. ⁷And the chief of the eunuchs gave them names: Daniel he called Belteshazzar, Hananiah he called Shadrach, Mishael he called Meshach, and Azariah he called Abednego.

Daniel's Faithfulness

⁸But Daniel resolved that he would not defile himself with the king's food, or with the wine that he drank. Therefore he asked the chief of the eunuchs to allow him not to defile himself. ⁹And God gave Daniel favor and compassion in the sight of the chief of the eunuchs, ¹⁰and the chief of the eunuchs said to Daniel, "I fear my lord the king, who assigned your food and your drink; for why should he see that you were in worse condition than the youths who are of your own age? So you would endanger my head with the king." ¹¹Then Daniel said to the steward whom the chief of the eunuchs had assigned over Daniel, Hananiah, Mishael, and Azariah, ¹²"Test your servants for ten days; let us be given vegetables to eat and water to drink. ¹³Then let our appearance and the appearance of the youths who eat the king's food be observed by you, and deal with your servants according to what you see." ¹⁴So he listened to them in this matter, and tested them for ten days. ¹⁵At the end of ten days it was seen that they were better in appearance and fatter in flesh than all the youths who ate the king's food. ¹⁶So the steward took away their food and the wine they were to drink, and gave them vegetables.

¹⁷As for these four youths, God gave them learning and skill in all literature and wisdom, and Daniel had understanding in all visions and dreams. ¹⁸At the end of the time, when the king had commanded that they should be brought in, the chief of the eunuchs brought them in before Nebuchadnezzar. ¹⁹And the king spoke with them, and among all of them none was found like Daniel, Hananiah, Mishael, and Azariah. Therefore they stood before the king. ²⁰And in every matter of wisdom and understanding about which the king inquired of them, he found them ten times better than all the magicians and enchanters that were in all his kingdom. ²¹And Daniel was there until the first year of King Cyrus.

Nebuchadnezzar's Dream

2 In the second year of the reign of Nebuchadnezzar, Nebuchadnezzar had dreams; his spirit was troubled, and his sleep left him. ²Then the king commanded that the magicians, the enchanters, the sorcerers, and the Chaldeans be summoned to tell the king his dreams. So they came in and stood before the king. ³And the king said to them, "I had a dream, and my spirit is troubled to know the dream." ⁴Then the Chaldeans said to the king in Aramaic,[2] "O king, live forever! Tell your servants the dream, and we will show the interpretation." ⁵The king answered and said to the Chaldeans, "The word from me is firm: if you do not make known to me the dream and its interpretation, you shall be torn limb from limb, and your houses shall be laid in ruins. ⁶But if you show the dream and its interpretation, you shall receive from me gifts and rewards and great honor. Therefore show me the dream and its interpretation." ⁷They answered a second time and said, "Let the king tell his servants the dream, and we will show its

---

[1] Hebrew *of the seed of the kingdom* [2] The text from this point to the end of chapter 7 is in Aramaic

interpretation." [8] The king answered and said, "I know with certainty that you are trying to gain time, because you see that the word from me is firm— [9] if you do not make the dream known to me, there is but one sentence for you. You have agreed to speak lying and corrupt words before me till the times change. Therefore tell me the dream, and I shall know that you can show me its interpretation." [10] The Chaldeans answered the king and said, "There is not a man on earth who can meet the king's demand, for no great and powerful king has asked such a thing of any magician or enchanter or Chaldean. [11] The thing that the king asks is difficult, and no one can show it to the king except the gods, whose dwelling is not with flesh."

[12] Because of this the king was angry and very furious, and commanded that all the wise men of Babylon be destroyed. [13] So the decree went out, and the wise men were about to be killed; and they sought Daniel and his companions, to kill them. [14] Then Daniel replied with prudence and discretion to Arioch, the captain of the king's guard, who had gone out to kill the wise men of Babylon. [15] He declared[1] to Arioch, the king's captain, "Why is the decree of the king so urgent?" Then Arioch made the matter known to Daniel. [16] And Daniel went in and requested the king to appoint him a time, that he might show the interpretation to the king.

God Reveals Nebuchadnezzar's Dream

[17] Then Daniel went to his house and made the matter known to Hananiah, Mishael, and Azariah, his companions, [18] and told them to seek mercy from the God of heaven concerning this mystery, so that Daniel and his companions might not be destroyed with the rest of the wise men of Babylon. [19] Then the mystery was revealed to Daniel in a vision of the night. Then Daniel blessed the God of heaven. [20] Daniel answered and said:

"Blessed be the name of God forever and
  ever,
  to whom belong wisdom and might.
[21] He changes times and seasons;
    he removes kings and sets up kings;
  he gives wisdom to the wise
    and knowledge to those who have
      understanding;
[22] he reveals deep and hidden things;
    he knows what is in the darkness,
    and the light dwells with him.

[23] To you, O God of my fathers,
    I give thanks and praise,
  for you have given me wisdom and might,
    and have now made known to me what
      we asked of you,
    for you have made known to us the
      king's matter."

[24] Therefore Daniel went in to Arioch, whom the king had appointed to destroy the wise men of Babylon. He went and said thus to him: "Do not destroy the wise men of Babylon; bring me in before the king, and I will show the king the interpretation."

[25] Then Arioch brought in Daniel before the king in haste and said thus to him: "I have found among the exiles from Judah a man who will make known to the king the interpretation." [26] The king declared to Daniel, whose name was Belteshazzar, "Are you able to make known to me the dream that I have seen and its interpretation?" [27] Daniel answered the king and said, "No wise men, enchanters, magicians, or astrologers can show to the king the mystery that the king has asked, [28] but there is a God in heaven who reveals mysteries, and he has made known to King Nebuchadnezzar what will be in the latter days. Your dream and the visions of your head as you lay in bed are these: [29] To you, O king, as you lay in bed came thoughts of what would be after this, and he who reveals mysteries made known to you what is to be. [30] But as for me, this mystery has been revealed to me, not because of any wisdom that I have more than all the living, but in order that the interpretation may be made known to the king, and that you may know the thoughts of your mind.

Daniel Interprets the Dream

[31] "You saw, O king, and behold, a great image. This image, mighty and of exceeding brightness, stood before you, and its appearance was frightening. [32] The head of this image was of fine gold, its chest and arms of silver, its middle and thighs of bronze, [33] its legs of iron, its feet partly of iron and partly of clay. [34] As you looked, a stone was cut out by no human hand, and it struck the image on its feet of iron and clay, and broke them in pieces. [35] Then the iron, the clay, the bronze, the silver, and the gold, all together were broken in pieces, and became like the chaff of the summer threshing floors; and the wind carried them away, so that not a trace of them could be found. But the stone that

---

[1] Aramaic *answered and said*; also verse 26

struck the image became a great mountain and filled the whole earth.

36 "This was the dream. Now we will tell the king its interpretation. 37 You, O king, the king of kings, to whom the God of heaven has given the kingdom, the power, and the might, and the glory, 38 and into whose hand he has given, wherever they dwell, the children of man, the beasts of the field, and the birds of the heavens, making you rule over them all—you are the head of gold. 39 Another kingdom inferior to you shall arise after you, and yet a third kingdom of bronze, which shall rule over all the earth. 40 And there shall be a fourth kingdom, strong as iron, because iron breaks to pieces and shatters all things. And like iron that crushes, it shall break and crush all these. 41 And as you saw the feet and toes, partly of potter's clay and partly of iron, it shall be a divided kingdom, but some of the firmness of iron shall be in it, just as you saw iron mixed with the soft clay. 42 And as the toes of the feet were partly iron and partly clay, so the kingdom shall be partly strong and partly brittle. 43 As you saw the iron mixed with soft clay, so they will mix with one another in marriage,[1] but they will not hold together, just as iron does not mix with clay. 44 And in the days of those kings the God of heaven will set up a kingdom that shall never be destroyed, nor shall the kingdom be left to another people. It shall break in pieces all these kingdoms and bring them to an end, and it shall stand forever, 45 just as you saw that a stone was cut from a mountain by no human hand, and that it broke in pieces the iron, the bronze, the clay, the silver, and the gold. A great God has made known to the king what shall be after this. The dream is certain, and its interpretation sure."

Daniel Is Promoted

46 Then King Nebuchadnezzar fell upon his face and paid homage to Daniel, and commanded that an offering and incense be offered up to him. 47 The king answered and said to Daniel, "Truly, your God is God of gods and Lord of kings, and a revealer of mysteries, for you have been able to reveal this mystery." 48 Then the king gave Daniel high honors and many great gifts, and made him ruler over the whole province of Babylon and chief prefect over all the wise men of Babylon. 49 Daniel made a request of the king, and he appointed Shadrach, Meshach, and Abednego over the affairs of the province of Babylon. But Daniel remained at the king's court.

Nebuchadnezzar's Golden Image

3 King Nebuchadnezzar made an image of gold, whose height was sixty cubits[2] and its breadth six cubits. He set it up on the plain of Dura, in the province of Babylon. 2 Then King Nebuchadnezzar sent to gather the satraps, the prefects, and the governors, the counselors, the treasurers, the justices, the magistrates, and all the officials of the provinces to come to the dedication of the image that King Nebuchadnezzar had set up. 3 Then the satraps, the prefects, and the governors, the counselors, the treasurers, the justices, the magistrates, and all the officials of the provinces gathered for the dedication of the image that King Nebuchadnezzar had set up. And they stood before the image that Nebuchadnezzar had set up. 4 And the herald proclaimed aloud, "You are commanded, O peoples, nations, and languages, 5 that when you hear the sound of the horn, pipe, lyre, trigon, harp, bagpipe, and every kind of music, you are to fall down and worship the golden image that King Nebuchadnezzar has set up. 6 And whoever does not fall down and worship shall immediately be cast into a burning fiery furnace." 7 Therefore, as soon as all the peoples heard the sound of the horn, pipe, lyre, trigon, harp, bagpipe, and every kind of music, all the peoples, nations, and languages fell down and worshiped the golden image that King Nebuchadnezzar had set up.

The Fiery Furnace

8 Therefore at that time certain Chaldeans came forward and maliciously accused the Jews. 9 They declared[3] to King Nebuchadnezzar, "O king, live forever! 10 You, O king, have made a decree, that every man who hears the sound of the horn, pipe, lyre, trigon, harp, bagpipe, and every kind of music, shall fall down and worship the golden image. 11 And whoever does not fall down and worship shall be cast into a burning fiery furnace. 12 There are certain Jews whom you have appointed over the affairs of the province of Babylon: Shadrach, Meshach, and Abednego. These men, O king, pay no attention to you; they do not serve your gods or worship the golden image that you have set up."

---

[1] Aramaic *by the seed of men* [2] A cubit was about 18 inches or 45 centimeters [3] Aramaic *answered and said*; also verses 24, 26

[13] Then Nebuchadnezzar in furious rage commanded that Shadrach, Meshach, and Abednego be brought. So they brought these men before the king. [14] Nebuchadnezzar answered and said to them, "Is it true, O Shadrach, Meshach, and Abednego, that you do not serve my gods or worship the golden image that I have set up? [15] Now if you are ready when you hear the sound of the horn, pipe, lyre, trigon, harp, bagpipe, and every kind of music, to fall down and worship the image that I have made, well and good.[1] But if you do not worship, you shall immediately be cast into a burning fiery furnace. And who is the god who will deliver you out of my hands?"

[16] Shadrach, Meshach, and Abednego answered and said to the king, "O Nebuchadnezzar, we have no need to answer you in this matter. [17] If this be so, our God whom we serve is able to deliver us from the burning fiery furnace, and he will deliver us out of your hand, O king.[2] [18] But if not, be it known to you, O king, that we will not serve your gods or worship the golden image that you have set up."

[19] Then Nebuchadnezzar was filled with fury, and the expression of his face was changed against Shadrach, Meshach, and Abednego. He ordered the furnace heated seven times more than it was usually heated. [20] And he ordered some of the mighty men of his army to bind Shadrach, Meshach, and Abednego, and to cast them into the burning fiery furnace. [21] Then these men were bound in their cloaks, their tunics,[3] their hats, and their other garments, and they were thrown into the burning fiery furnace. [22] Because the king's order was urgent and the furnace overheated, the flame of the fire killed those men who took up Shadrach, Meshach, and Abednego. [23] And these three men, Shadrach, Meshach, and Abednego, fell bound into the burning fiery furnace.

[24] Then King Nebuchadnezzar was astonished and rose up in haste. He declared to his counselors, "Did we not cast three men bound into the fire?" They answered and said to the king, "True, O king." [25] He answered and said, "But I see four men unbound, walking in the midst of the fire, and they are not hurt; and the appearance of the fourth is like a son of the gods."

[26] Then Nebuchadnezzar came near to the door of the burning fiery furnace; he declared, "Shadrach, Meshach, and Abednego, servants of the Most High God, come out, and come here!" Then Shadrach, Meshach, and Abednego came out from the fire. [27] And the satraps, the prefects, the governors, and the king's counselors gathered together and saw that the fire had not had any power over the bodies of those men. The hair of their heads was not singed, their cloaks were not harmed, and no smell of fire had come upon them. [28] Nebuchadnezzar answered and said, "Blessed be the God of Shadrach, Meshach, and Abednego, who has sent his angel and delivered his servants, who trusted in him, and set aside[4] the king's command, and yielded up their bodies rather than serve and worship any god except their own God. [29] Therefore I make a decree: Any people, nation, or language that speaks anything against the God of Shadrach, Meshach, and Abednego shall be torn limb from limb, and their houses laid in ruins, for there is no other god who is able to rescue in this way." [30] Then the king promoted Shadrach, Meshach, and Abednego in the province of Babylon.

Nebuchadnezzar Praises God

4 [5] King Nebuchadnezzar to all peoples, nations, and languages, that dwell in all the earth: Peace be multiplied to you! [2] It has seemed good to me to show the signs and wonders that the Most High God has done for me.

[3]   How great are his signs,
       how mighty his wonders!
    His kingdom is an everlasting kingdom,
       and his dominion endures from generation to generation.

Nebuchadnezzar's Second Dream

4 [6] I, Nebuchadnezzar, was at ease in my house and prospering in my palace. [5] I saw a dream that made me afraid. As I lay in bed the fancies and the visions of my head alarmed me. [6] So I made a decree that all the wise men of Babylon should be brought before me, that they might make known to me the interpretation of the dream. [7] Then the magicians, the enchanters, the Chaldeans, and the astrologers came in, and I told them the dream, but they could not make known to me its interpretation. [8] At last Daniel came in before me—he who was named Belteshazzar after the name of my god, and in

---

[1] Aramaic lacks *well and good*   [2] Or *If our God whom we serve is able to deliver us, he will deliver us from the burning fiery furnace and out of your hand, O king*   [3] The meaning of the Aramaic words rendered *cloaks* and *tunics* is uncertain; also verse 27   [4] Aramaic *and changed*   [5] Ch 3:31 in Aramaic   [6] Ch 4:1 in Aramaic

whom is the spirit of the holy gods[1]—and I told him the dream, saying, [9]"O Belteshazzar, chief of the magicians, because I know that the spirit of the holy gods is in you and that no mystery is too difficult for you, tell me the visions of my dream that I saw and their interpretation. [10]The visions of my head as I lay in bed were these: I saw, and behold, a tree in the midst of the earth, and its height was great. [11]The tree grew and became strong, and its top reached to heaven, and it was visible to the end of the whole earth. [12]Its leaves were beautiful and its fruit abundant, and in it was food for all. The beasts of the field found shade under it, and the birds of the heavens lived in its branches, and all flesh was fed from it.

[13]"I saw in the visions of my head as I lay in bed, and behold, a watcher, a holy one, came down from heaven. [14]He proclaimed aloud and said thus: 'Chop down the tree and lop off its branches, strip off its leaves and scatter its fruit. Let the beasts flee from under it and the birds from its branches. [15]But leave the stump of its roots in the earth, bound with a band of iron and bronze, amid the tender grass of the field. Let him be wet with the dew of heaven. Let his portion be with the beasts in the grass of the earth. [16]Let his mind be changed from a man's, and let a beast's mind be given to him; and let seven periods of time pass over him. [17]The sentence is by the decree of the watchers, the decision by the word of the holy ones, to the end that the living may know that the Most High rules the kingdom of men and gives it to whom he will and sets over it the lowliest of men.' [18]This dream I, King Nebuchadnezzar, saw. And you, O Belteshazzar, tell me the interpretation, because all the wise men of my kingdom are not able to make known to me the interpretation, but you are able, for the spirit of the holy gods is in you."

Daniel Interprets the Second Dream

[19] Then Daniel, whose name was Belteshazzar, was dismayed for a while, and his thoughts alarmed him. The king answered and said, "Belteshazzar, let not the dream or the interpretation alarm you." Belteshazzar answered and said, "My lord, may the dream be for those who hate you and its interpretation for your enemies! [20] The tree you saw, which grew and became strong, so that its top reached to heaven, and it was visible to the end of the

whole earth, [21] whose leaves were beautiful and its fruit abundant, and in which was food for all, under which beasts of the field found shade, and in whose branches the birds of the heavens lived— [22] it is you, O king, who have grown and become strong. Your greatness has grown and reaches to heaven, and your dominion to the ends of the earth. [23] And because the king saw a watcher, a holy one, coming down from heaven and saying, 'Chop down the tree and destroy it, but leave the stump of its roots in the earth, bound with a band of iron and bronze, in the tender grass of the field, and let him be wet with the dew of heaven, and let his portion be with the beasts of the field, till seven periods of time pass over him,' [24] this is the interpretation, O king: It is a decree of the Most High, which has come upon my lord the king, [25] that you shall be driven from among men, and your dwelling shall be with the beasts of the field. You shall be made to eat grass like an ox, and you shall be wet with the dew of heaven, and seven periods of time shall pass over you, till you know that the Most High rules the kingdom of men and gives it to whom he will. [26] And as it was commanded to leave the stump of the roots of the tree, your kingdom shall be confirmed for you from the time that you know that Heaven rules. [27] Therefore, O king, let my counsel be acceptable to you: break off your sins by practicing righteousness, and your iniquities by showing mercy to the oppressed, that there may perhaps be a lengthening of your prosperity."

Nebuchadnezzar's Humiliation

[28] All this came upon King Nebuchadnezzar. [29] At the end of twelve months he was walking on the roof of the royal palace of Babylon, [30] and the king answered and said, "Is not this great Babylon, which I have built by my mighty power as a royal residence and for the glory of my majesty?" [31] While the words were still in the king's mouth, there fell a voice from heaven, "O King Nebuchadnezzar, to you it is spoken: The kingdom has departed from you, [32] and you shall be driven from among men, and your dwelling shall be with the beasts of the field. And you shall be made to eat grass like an ox, and seven periods of time shall pass over you, until you know that the Most High rules the kingdom of men and gives it to whom he will." [33] Immediately the word was fulfilled against Nebuchadnezzar. He was driven from among

[1] Or *Spirit of the holy God*; also verses 9, 18

men and ate grass like an ox, and his body was wet with the dew of heaven till his hair grew as long as eagles' feathers, and his nails were like birds' claws.

Nebuchadnezzar Restored

34 At the end of the days I, Nebuchadnezzar, lifted my eyes to heaven, and my reason returned to me, and I blessed the Most High, and praised and honored him who lives forever,

for his dominion is an everlasting dominion,
and his kingdom endures from generation to generation;
35 all the inhabitants of the earth are accounted as nothing,
and he does according to his will among the host of heaven
and among the inhabitants of the earth;
and none can stay his hand
or say to him, "What have you done?"

36 At the same time my reason returned to me, and for the glory of my kingdom, my majesty and splendor returned to me. My counselors and my lords sought me, and I was established in my kingdom, and still more greatness was added to me. 37 Now I, Nebuchadnezzar, praise and extol and honor the King of heaven, for all his works are right and his ways are just; and those who walk in pride he is able to humble.

The Handwriting on the Wall

5 King Belshazzar made a great feast for a thousand of his lords and drank wine in front of the thousand. 2 Belshazzar, when he tasted the wine, commanded that the vessels of gold and of silver that Nebuchadnezzar his father[1] had taken out of the temple in Jerusalem be brought, that the king and his lords, his wives, and his concubines might drink from them. 3 Then they brought in the golden vessels that had been taken out of the temple, the house of God in Jerusalem, and the king and his lords, his wives, and his concubines drank from them. 4 They drank wine and praised the gods of gold and silver, bronze, iron, wood, and stone.

5 Immediately the fingers of a human hand appeared and wrote on the plaster of the wall of the king's palace, opposite the lampstand. And the king saw the hand as it wrote. 6 Then the king's color changed, and his thoughts alarmed him; his limbs gave way, and his knees knocked

together. 7 The king called loudly to bring in the enchanters, the Chaldeans, and the astrologers. The king declared[2] to the wise men of Babylon, "Whoever reads this writing, and shows me its interpretation, shall be clothed with purple and have a chain of gold around his neck and shall be the third ruler in the kingdom." 8 Then all the king's wise men came in, but they could not read the writing or make known to the king the interpretation. 9 Then King Belshazzar was greatly alarmed, and his color changed, and his lords were perplexed.

10 The queen,[3] because of the words of the king and his lords, came into the banqueting hall, and the queen declared, "O king, live forever! Let not your thoughts alarm you or your color change. 11 There is a man in your kingdom in whom is the spirit of the holy gods.[4] In the days of your father, light and understanding and wisdom like the wisdom of the gods were found in him, and King Nebuchadnezzar, your father—your father the king—made him chief of the magicians, enchanters, Chaldeans, and astrologers, 12 because an excellent spirit, knowledge, and understanding to interpret dreams, explain riddles, and solve problems were found in this Daniel, whom the king named Belteshazzar. Now let Daniel be called, and he will show the interpretation."

Daniel Interprets the Handwriting

13 Then Daniel was brought in before the king. The king answered and said to Daniel, "You are that Daniel, one of the exiles of Judah, whom the king my father brought from Judah. 14 I have heard of you that the spirit of the gods[5] is in you, and that light and understanding and excellent wisdom are found in you. 15 Now the wise men, the enchanters, have been brought in before me to read this writing and make known to me its interpretation, but they could not show the interpretation of the matter. 16 But I have heard that you can give interpretations and solve problems. Now if you can read the writing and make known to me its interpretation, you shall be clothed with purple and have a chain of gold around your neck and shall be the third ruler in the kingdom."

17 Then Daniel answered and said before the king, "Let your gifts be for yourself, and give

[1] Or predecessor; also verses 11, 13, 18　[2] Aramaic answered and said; also verse 10　[3] Or queen mother; twice in this verse　[4] Or Spirit of the holy God　[5] Or Spirit of God

your rewards to another. Nevertheless, I will read the writing to the king and make known to him the interpretation. [18] O king, the Most High God gave Nebuchadnezzar your father kingship and greatness and glory and majesty. [19] And because of the greatness that he gave him, all peoples, nations, and languages trembled and feared before him. Whom he would, he killed, and whom he would, he kept alive; whom he would, he raised up, and whom he would, he humbled. [20] But when his heart was lifted up and his spirit was hardened so that he dealt proudly, he was brought down from his kingly throne, and his glory was taken from him. [21] He was driven from among the children of mankind, and his mind was made like that of a beast, and his dwelling was with the wild donkeys. He was fed grass like an ox, and his body was wet with the dew of heaven, until he knew that the Most High God rules the kingdom of mankind and sets over it whom he will. [22] And you his son,[1] Belshazzar, have not humbled your heart, though you knew all this, [23] but you have lifted up yourself against the Lord of heaven. And the vessels of his house have been brought in before you, and you and your lords, your wives, and your concubines have drunk wine from them. And you have praised the gods of silver and gold, of bronze, iron, wood, and stone, which do not see or hear or know, but the God in whose hand is your breath, and whose are all your ways, you have not honored.

[24] "Then from his presence the hand was sent, and this writing was inscribed. [25] And this is the writing that was inscribed: MENE, MENE, TEKEL, and PARSIN. [26] This is the interpretation of the matter: MENE, God has numbered[2] the days of your kingdom and brought it to an end; [27] TEKEL, you have been weighed[3] in the balances and found wanting; [28] PERES, your kingdom is divided and given to the Medes and Persians."[4]

[29] Then Belshazzar gave the command, and Daniel was clothed with purple, a chain of gold was put around his neck, and a proclamation was made about him, that he should be the third ruler in the kingdom.

[30] That very night Belshazzar the Chaldean king was killed. [31] [5] And Darius the Mede received the kingdom, being about sixty-two years old.

Daniel and the Lions' Den

6 It pleased Darius to set over the kingdom 120 satraps, to be throughout the whole kingdom; [2] and over them three high officials, of whom Daniel was one, to whom these satraps should give account, so that the king might suffer no loss. [3] Then this Daniel became distinguished above all the other high officials and satraps, because an excellent spirit was in him. And the king planned to set him over the whole kingdom. [4] Then the high officials and the satraps sought to find a ground for complaint against Daniel with regard to the kingdom, but they could find no ground for complaint or any fault, because he was faithful, and no error or fault was found in him. [5] Then these men said, "We shall not find any ground for complaint against this Daniel unless we find it in connection with the law of his God."

[6] Then these high officials and satraps came by agreement[6] to the king and said to him, "O King Darius, live forever! [7] All the high officials of the kingdom, the prefects and the satraps, the counselors and the governors are agreed that the king should establish an ordinance and enforce an injunction, that whoever makes petition to any god or man for thirty days, except to you, O king, shall be cast into the den of lions. [8] Now, O king, establish the injunction and sign the document, so that it cannot be changed, according to the law of the Medes and the Persians, which cannot be revoked." [9] Therefore King Darius signed the document and injunction.

[10] When Daniel knew that the document had been signed, he went to his house where he had windows in his upper chamber open toward Jerusalem. He got down on his knees three times a day and prayed and gave thanks before his God, as he had done previously. [11] Then these men came by agreement and found Daniel making petition and plea before his God. [12] Then they came near and said before the king, concerning the injunction, "O king! Did you not sign an injunction, that anyone who makes petition to any god or man within thirty days except to you, O king, shall be cast into the den of lions?" The king answered and said, "The thing stands fast, according to the law of the Medes and Persians, which cannot be revoked." [13] Then they answered and said before the king, "Daniel, who is one of the exiles from

---

[1] Or successor [2] MENE sounds like the Aramaic for numbered [3] TEKEL sounds like the Aramaic for weighed [4] PERES (the singular of Parsin) sounds like the Aramaic for divided and for Persia [5] Ch 6:1 in Aramaic [6] Or came thronging; also verses 11, 15

Judah, pays no attention to you, O king, or the injunction you have signed, but makes his petition three times a day."

14 Then the king, when he heard these words, was much distressed and set his mind to deliver Daniel. And he labored till the sun went down to rescue him. 15 Then these men came by agreement to the king and said to the king, "Know, O king, that it is a law of the Medes and Persians that no injunction or ordinance that the king establishes can be changed."

16 Then the king commanded, and Daniel was brought and cast into the den of lions. The king declared[1] to Daniel, "May your God, whom you serve continually, deliver you!" 17 And a stone was brought and laid on the mouth of the den, and the king sealed it with his own signet and with the signet of his lords, that nothing might be changed concerning Daniel. 18 Then the king went to his palace and spent the night fasting; no diversions were brought to him, and sleep fled from him.

19 Then, at break of day, the king arose and went in haste to the den of lions. 20 As he came near to the den where Daniel was, he cried out in a tone of anguish. The king declared to Daniel, "O Daniel, servant of the living God, has your God, whom you serve continually, been able to deliver you from the lions?" 21 Then Daniel said to the king, "O king, live forever! 22 My God sent his angel and shut the lions' mouths, and they have not harmed me, because I was found blameless before him; and also before you, O king, I have done no harm." 23 Then the king was exceedingly glad, and commanded that Daniel be taken up out of the den. So Daniel was taken up out of the den, and no kind of harm was found on him, because he had trusted in his God. 24 And the king commanded, and those men who had maliciously accused Daniel were brought and cast into the den of lions—they, their children, and their wives. And before they reached the bottom of the den, the lions overpowered them and broke all their bones in pieces.

25 Then King Darius wrote to all the peoples, nations, and languages that dwell in all the earth: "Peace be multiplied to you. 26 I make a decree, that in all my royal dominion people are to tremble and fear before the God of Daniel,

for he is the living God,
enduring forever;

his kingdom shall never be destroyed,
and his dominion shall be to the end.
27 He delivers and rescues;
he works signs and wonders
in heaven and on earth,
he who has saved Daniel
from the power of the lions."

28 So this Daniel prospered during the reign of Darius and the reign of Cyrus the Persian.

Daniel's Vision of the Four Beasts

7 In the first year of Belshazzar king of Babylon, Daniel saw a dream and visions of his head as he lay in his bed. Then he wrote down the dream and told the sum of the matter. 2 Daniel declared,[2] "I saw in my vision by night, and behold, the four winds of heaven were stirring up the great sea. 3 And four great beasts came up out of the sea, different from one another. 4 The first was like a lion and had eagles' wings. Then as I looked its wings were plucked off, and it was lifted up from the ground and made to stand on two feet like a man, and the mind of a man was given to it. 5 And behold, another beast, a second one, like a bear. It was raised up on one side. It had three ribs in its mouth between its teeth; and it was told, 'Arise, devour much flesh.' 6 After this I looked, and behold, another, like a leopard, with four wings of a bird on its back. And the beast had four heads, and dominion was given to it. 7 After this I saw in the night visions, and behold, a fourth beast, terrifying and dreadful and exceedingly strong. It had great iron teeth; it devoured and broke in pieces and stamped what was left with its feet. It was different from all the beasts that were before it, and it had ten horns. 8 I considered the horns, and behold, there came up among them another horn, a little one, before which three of the first horns were plucked up by the roots. And behold, in this horn were eyes like the eyes of a man, and a mouth speaking great things.

The Ancient of Days Reigns

9 "As I looked,

thrones were placed,
and the Ancient of Days took his seat;
his clothing was white as snow,
and the hair of his head like pure wool;
his throne was fiery flames;
its wheels were burning fire.

---

[1] Aramaic *answered and said;* also verse 20 [2] Aramaic *answered and said*

[10] A stream of fire issued
   and came out from before him;
a thousand thousands served him,
   and ten thousand times ten thousand
      stood before him;
the court sat in judgment,
   and the books were opened.

[11] "I looked then because of the sound of the great words that the horn was speaking. And as I looked, the beast was killed, and its body destroyed and given over to be burned with fire. [12] As for the rest of the beasts, their dominion was taken away, but their lives were prolonged for a season and a time.

The Son of Man Is Given Dominion

[13] "I saw in the night visions,

and behold, with the clouds of heaven
   there came one like a son of man,
and he came to the Ancient of Days
   and was presented before him.
[14] And to him was given dominion
   and glory and a kingdom,
that all peoples, nations, and languages
   should serve him;
his dominion is an everlasting dominion,
   which shall not pass away,
and his kingdom one
   that shall not be destroyed.

Daniel's Vision Interpreted

[15] "As for me, Daniel, my spirit within me[1] was anxious, and the visions of my head alarmed me. [16] I approached one of those who stood there and asked him the truth concerning all this. So he told me and made known to me the interpretation of the things. [17] 'These four great beasts are four kings who shall arise out of the earth. [18] But the saints of the Most High shall receive the kingdom and possess the kingdom forever, forever and ever.'

[19] "Then I desired to know the truth about the fourth beast, which was different from all the rest, exceedingly terrifying, with its teeth of iron and claws of bronze, and which devoured and broke in pieces and stamped what was left with its feet, [20] and about the ten horns that were on its head, and the other horn that came up and before which three of them fell, the horn that had eyes and a mouth that spoke great things, and that seemed greater than its companions. [21] As I looked, this horn made war with the saints and prevailed over them, [22] until the Ancient of Days came, and judgment was given for the saints of the Most High, and the time came when the saints possessed the kingdom.

[23] "Thus he said: 'As for the fourth beast,

there shall be a fourth kingdom on earth,
   which shall be different from all the
      kingdoms,
and it shall devour the whole earth,
   and trample it down, and break it to
      pieces.
[24] As for the ten horns,
out of this kingdom ten kings shall arise,
   and another shall arise after them;
he shall be different from the former ones,
   and shall put down three kings.
[25] He shall speak words against the Most
      High,
   and shall wear out the saints of the
      Most High,
   and shall think to change the times and
      the law;
and they shall be given into his hand
   for a time, times, and half a time.
[26] But the court shall sit in judgment,
   and his dominion shall be taken away,
   to be consumed and destroyed to the
      end.
[27] And the kingdom and the dominion
   and the greatness of the kingdoms
      under the whole heaven
   shall be given to the people of the saints
      of the Most High;
his kingdom shall be an everlasting king-
      dom,
   and all dominions shall serve and obey
      him.'[2]

[28] "Here is the end of the matter. As for me, Daniel, my thoughts greatly alarmed me, and my color changed, but I kept the matter in my heart."

Daniel's Vision of the Ram and the Goat

8 In the third year of the reign of King Belshazzar a vision appeared to me, Daniel, after that which appeared to me at the first. [2] And I saw in the vision; and when I saw, I was in Susa the citadel, which is in the province of Elam. And I saw in the vision, and I was at the Ulai canal. [3] I raised my eyes and saw, and behold, a ram standing on the bank of the canal. It had two horns, and both horns were high, but one was higher than the other, and the higher

---

[1] Aramaic within its sheath [2] Or their kingdom shall be an everlasting kingdom, and all dominions shall serve and obey them

one came up last. [4] I saw the ram charging westward and northward and southward. No beast could stand before him, and there was no one who could rescue from his power. He did as he pleased and became great.

[5] As I was considering, behold, a male goat came from the west across the face of the whole earth, without touching the ground. And the goat had a conspicuous horn between his eyes. [6] He came to the ram with the two horns, which I had seen standing on the bank of the canal, and he ran at him in his powerful wrath. [7] I saw him come close to the ram, and he was enraged against him and struck the ram and broke his two horns. And the ram had no power to stand before him, but he cast him down to the ground and trampled on him. And there was no one who could rescue the ram from his power. [8] Then the goat became exceedingly great, but when he was strong, the great horn was broken, and instead of it there came up four conspicuous horns toward the four winds of heaven.

[9] Out of one of them came a little horn, which grew exceedingly great toward the south, toward the east, and toward the glorious land. [10] It grew great, even to the host of heaven. And some of the host and some[1] of the stars it threw down to the ground and trampled on them. [11] It became great, even as great as the Prince of the host. And the regular burnt offering was taken away from him, and the place of his sanctuary was overthrown. [12] And a host will be given over to it together with the regular burnt offering because of transgression,[2] and it will throw truth to the ground, and it will act and prosper. [13] Then I heard a holy one speaking, and another holy one said to the one who spoke, "For how long is the vision concerning the regular burnt offering, the transgression that makes desolate, and the giving over of the sanctuary and host to be trampled underfoot?" [14] And he said to me,[3] "For 2,300 evenings and mornings. Then the sanctuary shall be restored to its rightful state."

The Interpretation of the Vision

[15] When I, Daniel, had seen the vision, I sought to understand it. And behold, there stood before me one having the appearance of a man. [16] And I heard a man's voice between the banks of the Ulai, and it called, "Gabriel, make this man understand the vision." [17] So he came near where I stood. And when he came, I was frightened and fell on my face. But he said to me, "Understand, O son of man, that the vision is for the time of the end."

[18] And when he had spoken to me, I fell into a deep sleep with my face to the ground. But he touched me and made me stand up. [19] He said, "Behold, I will make known to you what shall be at the latter end of the indignation, for it refers to the appointed time of the end. [20] As for the ram that you saw with the two horns, these are the kings of Media and Persia. [21] And the goat[4] is the king of Greece. And the great horn between his eyes is the first king. [22] As for the horn that was broken, in place of which four others arose, four kingdoms shall arise from his[5] nation, but not with his power. [23] And at the latter end of their kingdom, when the transgressors have reached their limit, a king of bold face, one who understands riddles, shall arise. [24] His power shall be great—but not by his own power; and he shall cause fearful destruction and shall succeed in what he does, and destroy mighty men and the people who are the saints. [25] By his cunning he shall make deceit prosper under his hand, and in his own mind he shall become great. Without warning he shall destroy many. And he shall even rise up against the Prince of princes, and he shall be broken—but by no human hand. [26] The vision of the evenings and the mornings that has been told is true, but seal up the vision, for it refers to many days from now."

[27] And I, Daniel, was overcome and lay sick for some days. Then I rose and went about the king's business, but I was appalled by the vision and did not understand it.

Daniel's Prayer for His People

9 In the first year of Darius the son of Ahasuerus, by descent a Mede, who was made king over the realm of the Chaldeans— [2] in the first year of his reign, I, Daniel, perceived in the books the number of years that, according to the word of the LORD to Jeremiah the prophet, must pass before the end of the desolations of Jerusalem, namely, seventy years.

[3] Then I turned my face to the Lord God, seeking him by prayer and pleas for mercy with fasting and sackcloth and ashes. [4] I prayed to the LORD my God and made confession, saying, "O Lord, the great and awesome God, who keeps covenant and steadfast love with those who love

---

[1] Or host, that is, some   [2] Or in an act of rebellion   [3] Hebrew; Septuagint, Theodotion, Vulgate to him   [4] Or the shaggy goat   [5] Theodotion, Septuagint, Vulgate; Hebrew a

him and keep his commandments, [5] we have sinned and done wrong and acted wickedly and rebelled, turning aside from your commandments and rules. [6] We have not listened to your servants the prophets, who spoke in your name to our kings, our princes, and our fathers, and to all the people of the land. [7] To you, O Lord, belongs righteousness, but to us open shame, as at this day, to the men of Judah, to the inhabitants of Jerusalem, and to all Israel, those who are near and those who are far away, in all the lands to which you have driven them, because of the treachery that they have committed against you. [8] To us, O LORD, belongs open shame, to our kings, to our princes, and to our fathers, because we have sinned against you. [9] To the Lord our God belong mercy and forgiveness, for we have rebelled against him [10] and have not obeyed the voice of the LORD our God by walking in his laws, which he set before us by his servants the prophets. [11] All Israel has transgressed your law and turned aside, refusing to obey your voice. And the curse and oath that are written in the Law of Moses the servant of God have been poured out upon us, because we have sinned against him. [12] He has confirmed his words, which he spoke against us and against our rulers who ruled us,[1] by bringing upon us a great calamity. For under the whole heaven there has not been done anything like what has been done against Jerusalem. [13] As it is written in the Law of Moses, all this calamity has come upon us; yet we have not entreated the favor of the LORD our God, turning from our iniquities and gaining insight by your truth. [14] Therefore the LORD has kept ready the calamity and has brought it upon us, for the LORD our God is righteous in all the works that he has done, and we have not obeyed his voice. [15] And now, O Lord our God, who brought your people out of the land of Egypt with a mighty hand, and have made a name for yourself, as at this day, we have sinned, we have done wickedly.

[16] "O Lord, according to all your righteous acts, let your anger and your wrath turn away from your city Jerusalem, your holy hill, because for our sins, and for the iniquities of our fathers, Jerusalem and your people have become a byword among all who are around us. [17] Now therefore, O our God, listen to the prayer of your servant and to his pleas for mercy, and for your own sake, O Lord,[2] make your face to shine upon your sanctuary, which is desolate. [18] O my God, incline your ear and hear. Open your eyes and see our desolations, and the city that is called by your name. For we do not present our pleas before you because of our righteousness, but because of your great mercy. [19] O Lord, hear; O Lord, forgive. O Lord, pay attention and act. Delay not, for your own sake, O my God, because your city and your people are called by your name."

Gabriel Brings an Answer

[20] While I was speaking and praying, confessing my sin and the sin of my people Israel, and presenting my plea before the LORD my God for the holy hill of my God, [21] while I was speaking in prayer, the man Gabriel, whom I had seen in the vision at the first, came to me in swift flight at the time of the evening sacrifice. [22] He made me understand, speaking with me and saying, "O Daniel, I have now come out to give you insight and understanding. [23] At the beginning of your pleas for mercy a word went out, and I have come to tell it to you, for you are greatly loved. Therefore consider the word and understand the vision.

The Seventy Weeks

[24] "Seventy weeks[3] are decreed about your people and your holy city, to finish the transgression, to put an end to sin, and to atone for iniquity, to bring in everlasting righteousness, to seal both vision and prophet, and to anoint a most holy place.[4] [25] Know therefore and understand that from the going out of the word to restore and build Jerusalem to the coming of an anointed one, a prince, there shall be seven weeks. Then for sixty-two weeks it shall be built again[5] with squares and moat, but in a troubled time. [26] And after the sixty-two weeks, an anointed one shall be cut off and shall have nothing. And the people of the prince who is to come shall destroy the city and the sanctuary. Its[6] end shall come with a flood, and to the end there shall be war. Desolations are decreed. [27] And he shall make a strong covenant with many for one week,[7] and for half of the week he shall put an end to sacrifice and offering. And on the wing of abominations shall come one who makes desolate, until the decreed end is poured out on the desolator."

---

[1] Or our judges who judged us [2] Hebrew for the Lord's sake [3] Or sevens; also twice in verse 25 and once in verse 26 [4] Or thing, or one [5] Or there shall be seven weeks and sixty-two weeks. It shall be built again [6] Or His [7] Or seven; twice in this verse

Daniel's Terrifying Vision of a Man

10 In the third year of Cyrus king of Persia a word was revealed to Daniel, who was named Belteshazzar. And the word was true, and it was a great conflict.[1] And he understood the word and had understanding of the vision.

² In those days I, Daniel, was mourning for three weeks. ³ I ate no delicacies, no meat or wine entered my mouth, nor did I anoint myself at all, for the full three weeks. ⁴ On the twenty-fourth day of the first month, as I was standing on the bank of the great river (that is, the Tigris) ⁵ I lifted up my eyes and looked, and behold, a man clothed in linen, with a belt of fine gold from Uphaz around his waist. ⁶ His body was like beryl, his face like the appearance of lightning, his eyes like flaming torches, his arms and legs like the gleam of burnished bronze, and the sound of his words like the sound of a multitude. ⁷ And I, Daniel, alone saw the vision, for the men who were with me did not see the vision, but a great trembling fell upon them, and they fled to hide themselves. ⁸ So I was left alone and saw this great vision, and no strength was left in me. My radiant appearance was fearfully changed,[2] and I retained no strength. ⁹ Then I heard the sound of his words, and as I heard the sound of his words, I fell on my face in deep sleep with my face to the ground.

¹⁰ And behold, a hand touched me and set me trembling on my hands and knees. ¹¹ And he said to me, "O Daniel, man greatly loved, understand the words that I speak to you, and stand upright, for now I have been sent to you." And when he had spoken this word to me, I stood up trembling. ¹² Then he said to me, "Fear not, Daniel, for from the first day that you set your heart to understand and humbled yourself before your God, your words have been heard, and I have come because of your words. ¹³ The prince of the kingdom of Persia withstood me twenty-one days, but Michael, one of the chief princes, came to help me, for I was left there with the kings of Persia, ¹⁴ and came to make you understand what is to happen to your people in the latter days. For the vision is for days yet to come."

¹⁵ When he had spoken to me according to these words, I turned my face toward the ground and was mute. ¹⁶ And behold, one in the likeness of the children of man touched my lips. Then I opened my mouth and spoke. I said to him who stood before me, "O my lord, by reason of the vision pains have come upon me, and I retain no strength. ¹⁷ How can my lord's servant talk with my lord? For now no strength remains in me, and no breath is left in me."

¹⁸ Again one having the appearance of a man touched me and strengthened me. ¹⁹ And he said, "O man greatly loved, fear not, peace be with you; be strong and of good courage." And as he spoke to me, I was strengthened and said, "Let my lord speak, for you have strengthened me." ²⁰ Then he said, "Do you know why I have come to you? But now I will return to fight against the prince of Persia; and when I go out, behold, the prince of Greece will come. ²¹ But I will tell you what is inscribed in the book of truth: there is none who contends by my side against these except Michael, your prince.

The Kings of the South and the North

11 "And as for me, in the first year of Darius the Mede, I stood up to confirm and strengthen him.

² "And now I will show you the truth. Behold, three more kings shall arise in Persia, and a fourth shall be far richer than all of them. And when he has become strong through his riches, he shall stir up all against the kingdom of Greece. ³ Then a mighty king shall arise, who shall rule with great dominion and do as he wills. ⁴ And as soon as he has arisen, his kingdom shall be broken and divided toward the four winds of heaven, but not to his posterity, nor according to the authority with which he ruled, for his kingdom shall be plucked up and go to others besides these.

⁵ "Then the king of the south shall be strong, but one of his princes shall be stronger than he and shall rule, and his authority shall be a great authority. ⁶ After some years they shall make an alliance, and the daughter of the king of the south shall come to the king of the north to make an agreement. But she shall not retain the strength of her arm, and he and his arm shall not endure, but she shall be given up, and her attendants, he who fathered her, and he who supported[3] her in those times.

⁷ "And from a branch from her roots one shall arise in his place. He shall come against the army and enter the fortress of the king of the north, and he shall deal with them and

---

¹ Or *and it was about a great conflict* ² Hebrew *My splendor was changed to ruin* ³ Or *obtained*

shall prevail. [8] He shall also carry off to Egypt their gods with their metal images and their precious vessels of silver and gold, and for some years he shall refrain from attacking the king of the north. [9] Then the latter shall come into the realm of the king of the south but shall return to his own land.

[10] "His sons shall wage war and assemble a multitude of great forces, which shall keep coming and overflow and pass through, and again shall carry the war as far as his fortress. [11] Then the king of the south, moved with rage, shall come out and fight against the king of the north. And he shall raise a great multitude, but it shall be given into his hand. [12] And when the multitude is taken away, his heart shall be exalted, and he shall cast down tens of thousands, but he shall not prevail. [13] For the king of the north shall again raise a multitude, greater than the first. And after some years[1] he shall come on with a great army and abundant supplies.

[14] "In those times many shall rise against the king of the south, and the violent among your own people shall lift themselves up in order to fulfill the vision, but they shall fail. [15] Then the king of the north shall come and throw up siegeworks and take a well-fortified city. And the forces of the south shall not stand, or even his best troops, for there shall be no strength to stand. [16] But he who comes against him shall do as he wills, and none shall stand before him. And he shall stand in the glorious land, with destruction in his hand. [17] He shall set his face to come with the strength of his whole kingdom, and he shall bring terms of an agreement and perform them. He shall give him the daughter of women to destroy the kingdom,[2] but it shall not stand or be to his advantage. [18] Afterward he shall turn his face to the coastlands and shall capture many of them, but a commander shall put an end to his insolence. Indeed,[3] he shall turn his insolence back upon him. [19] Then he shall turn his face back toward the fortresses of his own land, but he shall stumble and fall, and shall not be found.

[20] "Then shall arise in his place one who shall send an exactor of tribute for the glory of the kingdom. But within a few days he shall be broken, neither in anger nor in battle. [21] In his place shall arise a contemptible person to whom royal majesty has not been given. He shall come in without warning and obtain the kingdom by flatteries. [22] Armies shall be utterly swept away before him and broken, even the prince of the covenant. [23] And from the time that an alliance is made with him he shall act deceitfully, and he shall become strong with a small people. [24] Without warning he shall come into the richest parts[4] of the province, and he shall do what neither his fathers nor his fathers' fathers have done, scattering among them plunder, spoil, and goods. He shall devise plans against strongholds, but only for a time. [25] And he shall stir up his power and his heart against the king of the south with a great army. And the king of the south shall wage war with an exceedingly great and mighty army, but he shall not stand, for plots shall be devised against him. [26] Even those who eat his food shall break him. His army shall be swept away, and many shall fall down slain. [27] And as for the two kings, their hearts shall be bent on doing evil. They shall speak lies at the same table, but to no avail, for the end is yet to be at the time appointed. [28] And he shall return to his land with great wealth, but his heart shall be set against the holy covenant. And he shall work his will and return to his own land.

[29] "At the time appointed he shall return and come into the south, but it shall not be this time as it was before. [30] For ships of Kittim shall come against him, and he shall be afraid and withdraw, and shall turn back and be enraged and take action against the holy covenant. He shall turn back and pay attention to those who forsake the holy covenant. [31] Forces from him shall appear and profane the temple and fortress, and shall take away the regular burnt offering. And they shall set up the abomination that makes desolate. [32] He shall seduce with flattery those who violate the covenant, but the people who know their God shall stand firm and take action. [33] And the wise among the people shall make many understand, though for some days they shall stumble by sword and flame, by captivity and plunder. [34] When they stumble, they shall receive a little help. And many shall join themselves to them with flattery, [35] and some of the wise shall stumble, so that they may be refined, purified, and made white, until the time of the end, for it still awaits the appointed time.

[36] "And the king shall do as he wills. He shall exalt himself and magnify himself above every god, and shall speak astonishing things against the God of gods. He shall prosper till the indignation is accomplished; for what is

---

[1] Hebrew *at the end of the times* [2] Hebrew *her, or it* [3] The meaning of the Hebrew is uncertain [4] Or *among the richest men*

decreed shall be done. [37] He shall pay no attention to the gods of his fathers, or to the one beloved by women. He shall not pay attention to any other god, for he shall magnify himself above all. [38] He shall honor the god of fortresses instead of these. A god whom his fathers did not know he shall honor with gold and silver, with precious stones and costly gifts. [39] He shall deal with the strongest fortresses with the help of a foreign god. Those who acknowledge him he shall load with honor. He shall make them rulers over many and shall divide the land for a price.[1]

[40] "At the time of the end, the king of the south shall attack[2] him, but the king of the north shall rush upon him like a whirlwind, with chariots and horsemen, and with many ships. And he shall come into countries and shall overflow and pass through. [41] He shall come into the glorious land. And tens of thousands shall fall, but these shall be delivered out of his hand: Edom and Moab and the main part of the Ammonites. [42] He shall stretch out his hand against the countries, and the land of Egypt shall not escape. [43] He shall become ruler of the treasures of gold and of silver, and all the precious things of Egypt, and the Libyans and the Cushites shall follow in his train. [44] But news from the east and the north shall alarm him, and he shall go out with great fury to destroy and devote many to destruction. [45] And he shall pitch his palatial tents between the sea and the glorious holy mountain. Yet he shall come to his end, with none to help him.

The Time of the End

12 "At that time shall arise Michael, the great prince who has charge of your people. And there shall be a time of trouble, such as never has been since there was a nation till that time. But at that time your people shall be delivered, everyone whose name shall be found written in the book. [2] And many of those who sleep in the dust of the earth shall awake, some to everlasting life, and some to shame and everlasting contempt. [3] And those who are wise shall shine like the brightness of the sky above;[3] and those who turn many to righteousness, like the stars forever and ever. [4] But you, Daniel, shut up the words and seal the book, until the time of the end. Many shall run to and fro, and knowledge shall increase."

[5] Then I, Daniel, looked, and behold, two others stood, one on this bank of the stream and one on that bank of the stream. [6] And someone said to the man clothed in linen, who was above the waters of the stream,[4] "How long shall it be till the end of these wonders?" [7] And I heard the man clothed in linen, who was above the waters of the stream; he raised his right hand and his left hand toward heaven and swore by him who lives forever that it would be for a time, times, and half a time, and that when the shattering of the power of the holy people comes to an end all these things would be finished. [8] I heard, but I did not understand. Then I said, "O my lord, what shall be the outcome of these things?" [9] He said, "Go your way, Daniel, for the words are shut up and sealed until the time of the end. [10] Many shall purify themselves and make themselves white and be refined, but the wicked shall act wickedly. And none of the wicked shall understand, but those who are wise shall understand. [11] And from the time that the regular burnt offering is taken away and the abomination that makes desolate is set up, there shall be 1,290 days. [12] Blessed is he who waits and arrives at the 1,335 days. [13] But go your way till the end. And you shall rest and shall stand in your allotted place at the end of the days."

---

[1] Or land as payment [2] Hebrew thrust at [3] Hebrew the expanse; compare Genesis 1:6–8 [4] Or who was upstream; also verse 7

HOSEA

1 The word of the LORD that came to Hosea,
the son of Beeri, in the days of Uzziah,
Jotham, Ahaz, and Hezekiah, kings of Judah,
and in the days of Jeroboam the son of Joash,
king of Israel.

Hosea's Wife and Children

2 When the LORD first spoke through Hosea,
the LORD said to Hosea, "Go, take to yourself a
wife of whoredom and have children of whoredom, for the land commits great whoredom
by forsaking the LORD." 3 So he went and took
Gomer, the daughter of Diblaim, and she conceived and bore him a son.

4 And the LORD said to him, "Call his name
Jezreel, for in just a little while I will punish
the house of Jehu for the blood of Jezreel, and
I will put an end to the kingdom of the house
of Israel. 5 And on that day I will break the bow
of Israel in the Valley of Jezreel."

6 She conceived again and bore a daughter.
And the LORD said to him, "Call her name No
Mercy,[1] for I will no more have mercy on the
house of Israel, to forgive them at all. 7 But I will
have mercy on the house of Judah, and I will
save them by the LORD their God. I will not save
them by bow or by sword or by war or by horses
or by horsemen."

8 When she had weaned No Mercy, she conceived and bore a son. 9 And the LORD said, "Call
his name Not My People,[2] for you are not my
people, and I am not your God."[3]

10 [4] Yet the number of the children of Israel
shall be like the sand of the sea, which cannot be
measured or numbered. And in the place where
it was said to them, "You are not my people," it
shall be said to them, "Children[5] of the living
God." 11 And the children of Judah and the
children of Israel shall be gathered together,
and they shall appoint for themselves one head.
And they shall go up from the land, for great
shall be the day of Jezreel.

Israel's Unfaithfulness Punished

2 [6] Say to your brothers, "You are my people,"[7]
and to your sisters, "You have received
mercy."[8]

2 "Plead with your mother, plead—
　　for she is not my wife,
　　and I am not her husband—
that she put away her whoring from her
　　　face,
　　and her adultery from between her
　　　breasts;
3 lest I strip her naked
　　and make her as in the day she was
　　　born,
and make her like a wilderness,
　　and make her like a parched land,
　　and kill her with thirst.
4 Upon her children also I will have no
　　　mercy,
　　because they are children of whoredom.
5 For their mother has played the whore;
　　she who conceived them has acted
　　　shamefully.
For she said, 'I will go after my lovers,
　　who give me my bread and my water,
　　my wool and my flax, my oil and my
　　　drink.'
6 Therefore I will hedge up her[9] way with
　　　thorns,
　　and I will build a wall against her,
　　so that she cannot find her paths.
7 She shall pursue her lovers
　　but not overtake them,
and she shall seek them
　　but shall not find them.
Then she shall say,
　　'I will go and return to my first husband,
　　for it was better for me then than now.'
8 And she did not know
　　that it was I who gave her
　　the grain, the wine, and the oil,
and who lavished on her silver and gold,
　　which they used for Baal.
9 Therefore I will take back
　　my grain in its time,
　　and my wine in its season,
and I will take away my wool and my flax,
　　which were to cover her nakedness.
10 Now I will uncover her lewdness
　　in the sight of her lovers,
　　and no one shall rescue her out of my
　　　hand.

---

[1] Hebrew *Lo-ruhama*, which means *she has not received mercy* [2] Hebrew *Lo-ammi*, which means *not my people* [3] Hebrew *I am not yours* [4] Ch 2:1 in Hebrew [5] Or *Sons* [6] Ch 2:3 in Hebrew [7] Hebrew *ammi*, which means *my people* [8] Hebrew *ruhama*, which means *she has received mercy* [9] Hebrew *your*

11 And I will put an end to all her mirth,
  her feasts, her new moons, her Sabbaths,
  and all her appointed feasts.
12 And I will lay waste her vines and her fig
    trees,
  of which she said,
  'These are my wages,
    which my lovers have given me.'
  I will make them a forest,
    and the beasts of the field shall devour
    them.
13 And I will punish her for the feast days of
    the Baals
  when she burned offerings to them
  and adorned herself with her ring and jew-
    elry,
  and went after her lovers
  and forgot me, declares the LORD.

The LORD's Mercy on Israel

14 "Therefore, behold, I will allure her,
  and bring her into the wilderness,
  and speak tenderly to her.
15 And there I will give her her vineyards
  and make the Valley of Achor[1] a door of
    hope.
  And there she shall answer as in the days of
    her youth,
  as at the time when she came out of the
    land of Egypt.

16 "And in that day, declares the LORD, you will call me 'My Husband,' and no longer will you call me 'My Baal.' 17 For I will remove the names of the Baals from her mouth, and they shall be remembered by name no more. 18 And I will make for them a covenant on that day with the beasts of the field, the birds of the heavens, and the creeping things of the ground. And I will abolish[2] the bow, the sword, and war from the land, and I will make you lie down in safety. 19 And I will betroth you to me forever. I will betroth you to me in righteousness and in justice, in steadfast love and in mercy. 20 I will betroth you to me in faithfulness. And you shall know the LORD.

21 "And in that day I will answer, declares the
    LORD,
  I will answer the heavens,
    and they shall answer the earth,
22 and the earth shall answer the grain, the
    wine, and the oil,
    and they shall answer Jezreel,[3]
23 and I will sow her for myself in the land.

And I will have mercy on No Mercy,[4]
  and I will say to Not My People,[5] 'You
    are my people';
  and he shall say, 'You are my God.'"

Hosea Redeems His Wife

3 And the LORD said to me, "Go again, love a woman who is loved by another man and is an adulteress, even as the LORD loves the children of Israel, though they turn to other gods and love cakes of raisins." 2 So I bought her for fifteen shekels of silver and a homer and a lethech[6] of barley. 3 And I said to her, "You must dwell as mine for many days. You shall not play the whore, or belong to another man; so will I also be to you." 4 For the children of Israel shall dwell many days without king or prince, without sacrifice or pillar, without ephod or household gods. 5 Afterward the children of Israel shall return and seek the LORD their God, and David their king, and they shall come in fear to the LORD and to his goodness in the latter days.

The LORD Accuses Israel

4 Hear the word of the LORD, O children of
    Israel,
  for the LORD has a controversy with the
    inhabitants of the land.
  There is no faithfulness or steadfast love,
    and no knowledge of God in the land;
2 there is swearing, lying, murder, stealing,
    and committing adultery;
  they break all bounds, and bloodshed
    follows bloodshed.
3 Therefore the land mourns,
    and all who dwell in it languish,
  and also the beasts of the field
    and the birds of the heavens,
    and even the fish of the sea are taken
    away.

4 Yet let no one contend,
    and let none accuse,
  for with you is my contention, O priest.[7]
5 You shall stumble by day;
    the prophet also shall stumble with you
    by night;
  and I will destroy your mother.
6 My people are destroyed for lack of knowl-
    edge;
  because you have rejected knowledge,
  I reject you from being a priest to me.

---

[1] Achor means trouble; compare Joshua 7:26 [2] Hebrew break [3] Jezreel means God will sow [4] Hebrew Lo-ruhama [5] Hebrew Lo-ammi [6] A shekel was about 2/5 ounce or 11 grams; a homer was about 6 bushels or 220 liters; a lethech was about 3 bushels or 110 liters [7] Or for your people are like those who contend with the priest

And since you have forgotten the law of
　　your God,
　　I also will forget your children.

7 The more they increased,
　　the more they sinned against me;
　　I will change their glory into shame.
8 They feed on the sin[1] of my people;
　　they are greedy for their iniquity.
9 And it shall be like people, like priest;
　　I will punish them for their ways
　　and repay them for their deeds.
10 They shall eat, but not be satisfied;
　　they shall play the whore, but not mul-
　　　tiply,
　　because they have forsaken the LORD
　　　to cherish [11] whoredom, wine, and new
　　　wine,
　　which take away the understanding.
12 My people inquire of a piece of wood,
　　and their walking staff gives them
　　　oracles.
　　For a spirit of whoredom has led them
　　　astray,
　　and they have left their God to play the
　　　whore.
13 They sacrifice on the tops of the mountains
　　and burn offerings on the hills,
　　under oak, poplar, and terebinth,
　　because their shade is good.
　　Therefore your daughters play the whore,
　　and your brides commit adultery.
14 I will not punish your daughters when
　　they play the whore,
　　nor your brides when they commit
　　　adultery;
　　for the men themselves go aside with pros-
　　　titutes
　　and sacrifice with cult prostitutes,
　　and a people without understanding shall
　　　come to ruin.

15 Though you play the whore, O Israel,
　　let not Judah become guilty.
　　Enter not into Gilgal,
　　nor go up to Beth-aven,
　　and swear not, "As the LORD lives."
16 Like a stubborn heifer,
　　Israel is stubborn;
　　can the LORD now feed them
　　like a lamb in a broad pasture?

17 Ephraim is joined to idols;
　　leave him alone.

18 When their drink is gone, they give them-
　　selves to whoring;
　　their rulers[2] dearly love shame.
19 A wind has wrapped them[3] in its wings,
　　and they shall be ashamed because of
　　　their sacrifices.

Punishment Coming for Israel and Judah

5 Hear this, O priests!
　Pay attention, O house of Israel!
Give ear, O house of the king!
　　For the judgment is for you;
for you have been a snare at Mizpah
　　and a net spread upon Tabor.
2 And the revolters have gone deep into
　　slaughter,
　　but I will discipline all of them.

3 I know Ephraim,
　　and Israel is not hidden from me;
　　for now, O Ephraim, you have played the
　　　whore;
　　Israel is defiled.
4 Their deeds do not permit them
　　to return to their God.
　　For the spirit of whoredom is within them,
　　and they know not the LORD.

5 The pride of Israel testifies to his face;[4]
　　Israel and Ephraim shall stumble in his
　　　guilt;
　　Judah also shall stumble with them.
6 With their flocks and herds they shall go
　　to seek the LORD,
　　but they will not find him;
　　he has withdrawn from them.
7 They have dealt faithlessly with the LORD;
　　for they have borne alien children.
　　Now the new moon shall devour them
　　　with their fields.

8 Blow the horn in Gibeah,
　　the trumpet in Ramah.
　　Sound the alarm at Beth-aven;
　　we follow you,[5] O Benjamin!
9 Ephraim shall become a desolation
　　in the day of punishment;
　　among the tribes of Israel
　　I make known what is sure.
10 The princes of Judah have become
　　like those who move the landmark;
　　upon them I will pour out
　　my wrath like water.

[1] Or sin offering　[2] Hebrew shields　[3] Hebrew her　[4] Or in his presence　[5] Or after you

11 Ephraim is oppressed, crushed in judg-
        ment,
        because he was determined to go after
            filth.[1]
12 But I am like a moth to Ephraim,
        and like dry rot to the house of Judah.

13 When Ephraim saw his sickness,
        and Judah his wound,
        then Ephraim went to Assyria,
            and sent to the great king.[2]
        But he is not able to cure you
            or heal your wound.
14 For I will be like a lion to Ephraim,
        and like a young lion to the house of
            Judah.
        I, even I, will tear and go away;
            I will carry off, and no one shall rescue.

15 I will return again to my place,
        until they acknowledge their guilt and
            seek my face,
        and in their distress earnestly seek me.

Israel and Judah Are Unrepentant

6 "Come, let us return to the LORD;
        for he has torn us, that he may heal us;
            he has struck us down, and he will bind
                us up.
2 After two days he will revive us;
        on the third day he will raise us up,
            that we may live before him.
3 Let us know; let us press on to know the
        LORD;
        his going out is sure as the dawn;
        he will come to us as the showers,
            as the spring rains that water the earth."

4 What shall I do with you, O Ephraim?
        What shall I do with you, O Judah?
        Your love is like a morning cloud,
            like the dew that goes early away.
5 Therefore I have hewn them by the proph-
        ets;
        I have slain them by the words of my
            mouth,
        and my judgment goes forth as the light.
6 For I desire steadfast love[3] and not sacrifice,
        the knowledge of God rather than
            burnt offerings.

7 But like Adam they transgressed the cov-
        enant;
        there they dealt faithlessly with me.

8 Gilead is a city of evildoers,
        tracked with blood.
9 As robbers lie in wait for a man,
        so the priests band together;
    they murder on the way to Shechem;
        they commit villainy.
10 In the house of Israel I have seen a horrible
        thing;
        Ephraim's whoredom is there; Israel is
            defiled.

11 For you also, O Judah, a harvest is
        appointed.

When I restore the fortunes of my people,
7 when I would heal Israel,
        the iniquity of Ephraim is revealed,
            and the evil deeds of Samaria,
    for they deal falsely;
        the thief breaks in,
        and the bandits raid outside.
2 But they do not consider
        that I remember all their evil.
    Now their deeds surround them;
        they are before my face.
3 By their evil they make the king glad,
        and the princes by their treachery.
4 They are all adulterers;
        they are like a heated oven
    whose baker ceases to stir the fire,
        from the kneading of the dough
            until it is leavened.
5 On the day of our king, the princes
        became sick with the heat of wine;
        he stretched out his hand with mockers.
6 For with hearts like an oven they approach
            their intrigue;
        all night their anger smolders;
        in the morning it blazes like a flaming
            fire.
7 All of them are hot as an oven,
        and they devour their rulers.
    All their kings have fallen,
        and none of them calls upon me.

8 Ephraim mixes himself with the peoples;
        Ephraim is a cake not turned.
9 Strangers devour his strength,
        and he knows it not;
    gray hairs are sprinkled upon him,
        and he knows it not.
10 The pride of Israel testifies to his face;[4]
        yet they do not return to the LORD their
            God,
        nor seek him, for all this.

[1] Or to follow human precepts [2] Or to King Jareb [3] Septuagint mercy [4] Or in his presence

11 Ephraim is like a dove,
        silly and without sense,
        calling to Egypt, going to Assyria.
12 As they go, I will spread over them my net;
        I will bring them down like birds of the
            heavens;
        I will discipline them according to the
            report made to their congregation.
13 Woe to them, for they have strayed from
        me!
        Destruction to them, for they have
            rebelled against me!
        I would redeem them,
            but they speak lies against me.

14 They do not cry to me from the heart,
        but they wail upon their beds;
        for grain and wine they gash themselves;
            they rebel against me.
15 Although I trained and strengthened their
        arms,
        yet they devise evil against me.
16 They return, but not upward;[1]
        they are like a treacherous bow;
        their princes shall fall by the sword
            because of the insolence of their tongue.
        This shall be their derision in the land of
            Egypt.

Israel Will Reap the Whirlwind

8 Set the trumpet to your lips!
        One like a vulture is over the house of the
            Lord,
        because they have transgressed my cov-
            enant
        and rebelled against my law.
2 To me they cry,
        "My God, we—Israel—know you."
3 Israel has spurned the good;
        the enemy shall pursue him.

4 They made kings, but not through me.
        They set up princes, but I knew it not.
        With their silver and gold they made idols
            for their own destruction.
5 I have[2] spurned your calf, O Samaria.
        My anger burns against them.
        How long will they be incapable of inno-
            cence?
6 For it is from Israel;
        a craftsman made it;
        it is not God.
        The calf of Samaria
            shall be broken to pieces.[3]

7 For they sow the wind,
        and they shall reap the whirlwind.
        The standing grain has no heads;
            it shall yield no flour;
        if it were to yield,
            strangers would devour it.
8 Israel is swallowed up;
        already they are among the nations
            as a useless vessel.
9 For they have gone up to Assyria,
        a wild donkey wandering alone;
        Ephraim has hired lovers.
10 Though they hire allies among the nations,
        I will soon gather them up.
        And the king and princes shall soon writhe
            because of the tribute.

11 Because Ephraim has multiplied altars for
        sinning,
        they have become to him altars for sin-
            ning.
12 Were I to write for him my laws by the ten
        thousands,
        they would be regarded as a strange
            thing.
13 As for my sacrificial offerings,
        they sacrifice meat and eat it,
        but the Lord does not accept them.
        Now he will remember their iniquity
            and punish their sins;
        they shall return to Egypt.
14 For Israel has forgotten his Maker
        and built palaces,
        and Judah has multiplied fortified cities;
        so I will send a fire upon his cities,
            and it shall devour her strongholds.

The Lord Will Punish Israel

9 Rejoice not, O Israel!
        Exult not like the peoples;
        for you have played the whore, forsaking
            your God.
        You have loved a prostitute's wages
            on all threshing floors.
2 Threshing floor and wine vat shall not feed
        them,
        and the new wine shall fail them.
3 They shall not remain in the land of the
        Lord,
        but Ephraim shall return to Egypt,
        and they shall eat unclean food in
            Assyria.

[1] Or to the Most High [2] Hebrew He has [3] Or shall go up in flames

⁴ They shall not pour drink offerings of wine
　　to the LORD,
　　and their sacrifices shall not please him.
It shall be like mourners' bread to them;
　　all who eat of it shall be defiled;
for their bread shall be for their hunger
　　only;
　　it shall not come to the house of the
　　LORD.

⁵ What will you do on the day of the
　　appointed festival,
　　and on the day of the feast of the LORD?
⁶ For behold, they are going away from
　　destruction;
　　but Egypt shall gather them;
　　Memphis shall bury them.
Nettles shall possess their precious things
　　of silver;
　　thorns shall be in their tents.

⁷ The days of punishment have come;
　　the days of recompense have come;
　　Israel shall know it.
The prophet is a fool;
　　the man of the spirit is mad,
because of your great iniquity
　　and great hatred.
⁸ The prophet is the watchman of Ephraim
　　with my God;
　　yet a fowler's snare is on all his ways,
　　and hatred in the house of his God.
⁹ They have deeply corrupted themselves
　　as in the days of Gibeah:
he will remember their iniquity;
　　he will punish their sins.

¹⁰ Like grapes in the wilderness,
　　I found Israel.
Like the first fruit on the fig tree
　　in its first season,
　　I saw your fathers.
But they came to Baal-peor
　　and consecrated themselves to the thing
　　of shame,
　　and became detestable like the thing
　　they loved.
¹¹ Ephraim's glory shall fly away like a bird—
　　no birth, no pregnancy, no conception!
¹² Even if they bring up children,
　　I will bereave them till none is left.
Woe to them
　　when I depart from them!

¹³ Ephraim, as I have seen, was like a young
　　palm[1] planted in a meadow;
　　but Ephraim must lead his children out
　　to slaughter.[2]
¹⁴ Give them, O LORD—
　　what will you give?
Give them a miscarrying womb
　　and dry breasts.

¹⁵ Every evil of theirs is in Gilgal;
　　there I began to hate them.
Because of the wickedness of their deeds
　　I will drive them out of my house.
I will love them no more;
　　all their princes are rebels.
¹⁶ Ephraim is stricken;
　　their root is dried up;
　　they shall bear no fruit.
Even though they give birth,
　　I will put their beloved children to
　　death.
¹⁷ My God will reject them
　　because they have not listened to him;
　　they shall be wanderers among the
　　nations.

10 Israel is a luxuriant vine
　　that yields its fruit.
The more his fruit increased,
　　the more altars he built;
as his country improved,
　　he improved his pillars.
² Their heart is false;
　　now they must bear their guilt.
The LORD[3] will break down their altars
　　and destroy their pillars.

³ For now they will say:
　　"We have no king,
for we do not fear the LORD;
　　and a king—what could he do for us?"
⁴ They utter mere words;
　　with empty[4] oaths they make cov-
　　enants;
so judgment springs up like poisonous
　　weeds
　　in the furrows of the field.
⁵ The inhabitants of Samaria tremble
　　for the calf[5] of Beth-aven.
Its people mourn for it, and so do its idola-
　　trous priests—
　　those who rejoiced over it and over its
　　glory—
　　for it has departed[6] from them.

6 The thing itself shall be carried to Assyria
    as tribute to the great king.[1]
Ephraim shall be put to shame,
    and Israel shall be ashamed of his idol.[2]

7 Samaria's king shall perish
    like a twig on the face of the waters.
8 The high places of Aven, the sin of Israel,
    shall be destroyed.
Thorn and thistle shall grow up
    on their altars,
and they shall say to the mountains, "Cover
    us,"
    and to the hills, "Fall on us."

9 From the days of Gibeah, you have sinned,
    O Israel;
    there they have continued.
    Shall not the war against the unjust[3]
    overtake them in Gibeah?
10 When I please, I will discipline them,
    and nations shall be gathered against
    them
    when they are bound up for their
    double iniquity.

11 Ephraim was a trained calf
    that loved to thresh,
    and I spared her fair neck;
but I will put Ephraim to the yoke;
    Judah must plow;
    Jacob must harrow for himself.
12 Sow for yourselves righteousness;
    reap steadfast love;
    break up your fallow ground,
for it is the time to seek the LORD,
    that he may come and rain righteous-
    ness upon you.

13 You have plowed iniquity;
    you have reaped injustice;
    you have eaten the fruit of lies.
Because you have trusted in your own way
    and in the multitude of your warriors,
14 therefore the tumult of war shall arise
    among your people,
    and all your fortresses shall be
    destroyed,
as Shalman destroyed Beth-arbel on the
    day of battle;
    mothers were dashed in pieces with
    their children.
15 Thus it shall be done to you, O Bethel,
    because of your great evil.

At dawn the king of Israel
    shall be utterly cut off.

The LORD's Love for Israel

11 When Israel was a child, I loved him,
    and out of Egypt I called my son.
2 The more they were called,
    the more they went away;
they kept sacrificing to the Baals
    and burning offerings to idols.

3 Yet it was I who taught Ephraim to walk;
    I took them up by their arms,
    but they did not know that I healed
    them.
4 I led them with cords of kindness,[4]
    with the bands of love,
and I became to them as one who eases the
    yoke on their jaws,
    and I bent down to them and fed them.

5 They shall not[5] return to the land of Egypt,
    but Assyria shall be their king,
    because they have refused to return to
    me.
6 The sword shall rage against their cities,
    consume the bars of their gates,
    and devour them because of their own
    counsels.
7 My people are bent on turning away from
    me,
    and though they call out to the Most
    High,
    he shall not raise them up at all.

8 How can I give you up, O Ephraim?
    How can I hand you over, O Israel?
How can I make you like Admah?
    How can I treat you like Zeboiim?
My heart recoils within me;
    my compassion grows warm and ten-
    der.
9 I will not execute my burning anger;
    I will not again destroy Ephraim;
for I am God and not a man,
    the Holy One in your midst,
    and I will not come in wrath.[6]

10 They shall go after the LORD;
    he will roar like a lion;
when he roars,
    his children shall come trembling from
    the west;

---

[1] Or to King Jareb [2] Or counsel [3] Hebrew the children of injustice [4] Or humaneness; Hebrew man [5] Or surely [6] Or into the city

11 they shall come trembling like birds from
      Egypt,
        and like doves from the land of Assyria,
        and I will return them to their homes,
          declares the LORD.
12 1 Ephraim has surrounded me with lies,
        and the house of Israel with deceit,
    but Judah still walks with God
      and is faithful to the Holy One.

12

Ephraim feeds on the wind
    and pursues the east wind all day
      long;
  they multiply falsehood and violence;
    they make a covenant with Assyria,
    and oil is carried to Egypt.

The LORD's Indictment of Israel and Judah

2   The LORD has an indictment against Judah
      and will punish Jacob according to his
        ways;
      he will repay him according to his
        deeds.
3   In the womb he took his brother by the
      heel,
      and in his manhood he strove with God.
4   He strove with the angel and prevailed;
      he wept and sought his favor.
    He met God[2] at Bethel,
      and there God spoke with us—
5   the LORD, the God of hosts,
        the LORD is his memorial name:
6   "So you, by the help of your God, return,
      hold fast to love and justice,
      and wait continually for your God."

7   A merchant, in whose hands are false bal-
      ances,
      he loves to oppress.
8   Ephraim has said, "Ah, but I am rich;
      I have found wealth for myself;
    in all my labors they cannot find in me
      iniquity or sin."
9   I am the LORD your God
      from the land of Egypt;
    I will again make you dwell in tents,
      as in the days of the appointed feast.
10 I spoke to the prophets;
      it was I who multiplied visions,
      and through the prophets gave para-
        bles.
11 If there is iniquity in Gilead,
      they shall surely come to nothing:

    in Gilgal they sacrifice bulls;
      their altars also are like stone heaps
        on the furrows of the field.
12 Jacob fled to the land of Aram;
      there Israel served for a wife,
      and for a wife he guarded sheep.
13 By a prophet the LORD brought Israel up
      from Egypt,
      and by a prophet he was guarded.
14 Ephraim has given bitter provocation;
      so his Lord will leave his bloodguilt on
        him
      and will repay him for his disgraceful
        deeds.

The LORD's Relentless Judgment on Israel

13

When Ephraim spoke, there was
  trembling;
    he was exalted in Israel,
    but he incurred guilt through Baal and
      died.
2   And now they sin more and more,
      and make for themselves metal
        images,
    idols skillfully made of their silver,
      all of them the work of craftsmen.
    It is said of them,
      "Those who offer human sacrifice kiss
        calves!"
3   Therefore they shall be like the morning
      mist
      or like the dew that goes early away,
    like the chaff that swirls from the thresh-
      ing floor
      or like smoke from a window.

4   But I am the LORD your God
      from the land of Egypt;
    you know no God but me,
      and besides me there is no savior.
5   It was I who knew you in the wilderness,
      in the land of drought;
6   but when they had grazed,[3] they became
      full,
      they were filled, and their heart was
        lifted up;
      therefore they forgot me.
7   So I am to them like a lion;
      like a leopard I will lurk beside the
        way.
8   I will fall upon them like a bear robbed of
      her cubs;
      I will tear open their breast,

---

1 Ch 12:1 in Hebrew 2 Hebrew *him* 3 Hebrew *according to their pasture*

and there I will devour them like a lion,
　　as a wild beast would rip them open.

9　He destroys[1] you, O Israel,
　　for you are against me, against your
　　　helper.

10　Where now is your king, to save you in all
　　　your cities?
　　Where are all your rulers—
　　those of whom you said,
　　　"Give me a king and princes"?

11　I gave you a king in my anger,
　　and I took him away in my wrath.

12　The iniquity of Ephraim is bound up;
　　his sin is kept in store.

13　The pangs of childbirth come for him,
　　but he is an unwise son,
　　for at the right time he does not present
　　　himself
　　at the opening of the womb.

14　I shall ransom them from the power of
　　　Sheol;
　　I shall redeem them from Death.[2]
　　O Death, where are your plagues?
　　O Sheol, where is your sting?
　　Compassion is hidden from my eyes.

15　Though he may flourish among his broth-
　　　ers,
　　the east wind, the wind of the LORD,
　　　shall come,
　　rising from the wilderness,
　　and his fountain shall dry up;
　　his spring shall be parched;
　　it shall strip his treasury
　　of every precious thing.

16 [3]　Samaria shall bear her guilt,
　　because she has rebelled against her
　　　God;
　　they shall fall by the sword;
　　their little ones shall be dashed in
　　　pieces,
　　and their pregnant women ripped
　　　open.

A Plea to Return to the LORD

14　Return, O Israel, to the LORD your
　　　God,
　　for you have stumbled because of your
　　　iniquity.

2　Take with you words
　　and return to the LORD;
　　say to him,
　　"Take away all iniquity;
　　accept what is good,
　　and we will pay with bulls
　　the vows[4] of our lips.

3　Assyria shall not save us;
　　we will not ride on horses;
　　and we will say no more, 'Our God,'
　　to the work of our hands.
　　In you the orphan finds mercy."

4　I will heal their apostasy;
　　I will love them freely,
　　for my anger has turned from them.

5　I will be like the dew to Israel;
　　he shall blossom like the lily;
　　he shall take root like the trees of
　　　Lebanon;

6　his shoots shall spread out;
　　his beauty shall be like the olive,
　　and his fragrance like Lebanon.

7　They shall return and dwell beneath my[5]
　　　shadow;
　　they shall flourish like the grain;
　　they shall blossom like the vine;
　　their fame shall be like the wine of
　　　Lebanon.

8　O Ephraim, what have I to do with idols?
　　It is I who answer and look after you.[6]
　　I am like an evergreen cypress;
　　from me comes your fruit.

9　Whoever is wise, let him understand these
　　　things;
　　whoever is discerning, let him know
　　　them;
　　for the ways of the LORD are right,
　　and the upright walk in them,
　　but transgressors stumble in them.

---

[1] Or I will destroy　[2] Or Shall I ransom them from the power of Sheol? Shall I redeem them from Death?　[3] Ch 14:1 in Hebrew　[4] Septuagint, Syriac pay the fruit　[5] Hebrew his
[6] Hebrew him

JOEL

1 The word of the LORD that came to Joel, the son of Pethuel:

An Invasion of Locusts

2 Hear this, you elders;
   give ear, all inhabitants of the land!
Has such a thing happened in your days,
   or in the days of your fathers?
3 Tell your children of it,
   and let your children tell their children,
   and their children to another generation.

4 What the cutting locust left,
   the swarming locust has eaten.
What the swarming locust left,
   the hopping locust has eaten,
and what the hopping locust left,
   the destroying locust has eaten.

5 Awake, you drunkards, and weep,
   and wail, all you drinkers of wine,
because of the sweet wine,
   for it is cut off from your mouth.
6 For a nation has come up against my land,
   powerful and beyond number;
its teeth are lions' teeth,
   and it has the fangs of a lioness.
7 It has laid waste my vine
   and splintered my fig tree;
it has stripped off their bark and thrown it
   down;
   their branches are made white.

8 Lament like a virgin[1] wearing sackcloth
   for the bridegroom of her youth.
9 The grain offering and the drink offering
   are cut off
   from the house of the LORD.
The priests mourn,
   the ministers of the LORD.
10 The fields are destroyed,
   the ground mourns,
because the grain is destroyed,
   the wine dries up,
   the oil languishes.

11 Be ashamed,[2] O tillers of the soil;
   wail, O vinedressers,
for the wheat and the barley,
   because the harvest of the field has perished.
12 The vine dries up;
   the fig tree languishes.
Pomegranate, palm, and apple,
   all the trees of the field are dried up,
and gladness dries up
   from the children of man.

A Call to Repentance

13 Put on sackcloth and lament, O priests;
   wail, O ministers of the altar.
Go in, pass the night in sackcloth,
   O ministers of my God!
Because grain offering and drink offering
   are withheld from the house of your
   God.

14 Consecrate a fast;
   call a solemn assembly.
Gather the elders
   and all the inhabitants of the land
to the house of the LORD your God,
   and cry out to the LORD.

15 Alas for the day!
For the day of the LORD is near,
   and as destruction from the Almighty[3]
   it comes.
16 Is not the food cut off
   before our eyes,
joy and gladness
   from the house of our God?

17 The seed shrivels under the clods;[4]
   the storehouses are desolate;
the granaries are torn down
   because the grain has dried up.
18 How the beasts groan!
   The herds of cattle are perplexed
because there is no pasture for them;
   even the flocks of sheep suffer.[5]

19 To you, O LORD, I call.
For fire has devoured
   the pastures of the wilderness,
and flame has burned
   all the trees of the field.
20 Even the beasts of the field pant for you
   because the water brooks are dried up,

[1] Or young woman [2] The Hebrew words for dry up and be ashamed in verses 10–12, 17 sound alike [3] Destruction sounds like the Hebrew for Almighty [4] The meaning of the Hebrew line is uncertain [5] Or are made desolate

and fire has devoured
  the pastures of the wilderness.

The Day of the LORD

2 Blow a trumpet in Zion;
  sound an alarm on my holy mountain!
Let all the inhabitants of the land tremble,
  for the day of the LORD is coming; it is
    near,

2 a day of darkness and gloom,
  a day of clouds and thick darkness!
Like blackness there is spread upon the
    mountains
  a great and powerful people;
their like has never been before,
  nor will be again after them
    through the years of all generations.

3 Fire devours before them,
  and behind them a flame burns.
The land is like the garden of Eden before
    them,
  but behind them a desolate wilderness,
    and nothing escapes them.

4 Their appearance is like the appearance of
    horses,
  and like war horses they run.

5 As with the rumbling of chariots,
  they leap on the tops of the mountains,
like the crackling of a flame of fire
  devouring the stubble,
like a powerful army
  drawn up for battle.

6 Before them peoples are in anguish;
  all faces grow pale.

7 Like warriors they charge;
  like soldiers they scale the wall.
They march each on his way;
  they do not swerve from their paths.

8 They do not jostle one another;
  each marches in his path;
they burst through the weapons
  and are not halted.

9 They leap upon the city,
  they run upon the walls,
they climb up into the houses,
  they enter through the windows like a
    thief.

10 The earth quakes before them;
  the heavens tremble.
The sun and the moon are darkened,
  and the stars withdraw their shining.

11 The LORD utters his voice
  before his army,
for his camp is exceedingly great;
  he who executes his word is powerful.
For the day of the LORD is great and very
    awesome;
  who can endure it?

Return to the LORD

12 "Yet even now," declares the LORD,
  "return to me with all your heart,
with fasting, with weeping, and with
    mourning;

13 and rend your hearts and not your gar-
    ments."
Return to the LORD your God,
  for he is gracious and merciful,
slow to anger, and abounding in steadfast
    love;
  and he relents over disaster.

14 Who knows whether he will not turn and
    relent,
  and leave a blessing behind him,
a grain offering and a drink offering
  for the LORD your God?

15 Blow the trumpet in Zion;
  consecrate a fast;
call a solemn assembly;

16 gather the people.
Consecrate the congregation;
  assemble the elders;
gather the children,
  even nursing infants.
Let the bridegroom leave his room,
  and the bride her chamber.

17 Between the vestibule and the altar
  let the priests, the ministers of the
    LORD, weep
and say, "Spare your people, O LORD,
  and make not your heritage a reproach,
a byword among the nations.[1]
Why should they say among the peoples,
  'Where is their God?'"

The LORD Had Pity

18 Then the LORD became jealous for his land
  and had pity on his people.

19 The LORD answered and said to his people,
  "Behold, I am sending to you
    grain, wine, and oil,
      and you will be satisfied;
and I will no more make you
  a reproach among the nations.

---

[1] Or reproach, that the nations should rule over them

20 "I will remove the northerner far from
        you,
      and drive him into a parched and deso-
        late land,
    his vanguard[1] into the eastern sea,
      and his rear guard[2] into the western
        sea;
    the stench and foul smell of him will rise,
      for he has done great things.

21 "Fear not, O land;
      be glad and rejoice,
      for the LORD has done great things!
22 Fear not, you beasts of the field,
      for the pastures of the wilderness are
        green;
    the tree bears its fruit;
      the fig tree and vine give their full
        yield.

23 "Be glad, O children of Zion,
      and rejoice in the LORD your God,
    for he has given the early rain for your vin-
        dication;
    he has poured down for you abundant
        rain,
      the early and the latter rain, as before.

24 "The threshing floors shall be full of
        grain;
      the vats shall overflow with wine and
        oil.
25 I will restore[3] to you the years
      that the swarming locust has eaten,
    the hopper, the destroyer, and the cutter,
      my great army, which I sent among
        you.

26 "You shall eat in plenty and be satisfied,
      and praise the name of the LORD your
        God,
      who has dealt wondrously with you.
    And my people shall never again be put to
        shame.
27 You shall know that I am in the midst of
        Israel,
      and that I am the LORD your God and
        there is none else.
    And my people shall never again be put to
        shame.

The LORD Will Pour Out His Spirit

28[4] "And it shall come to pass afterward,
      that I will pour out my Spirit on all
        flesh;

your sons and your daughters shall proph-
        esy,
    your old men shall dream dreams,
      and your young men shall see visions.
29 Even on the male and female servants
      in those days I will pour out my Spirit.

30 "And I will show wonders in the heavens and on the earth, blood and fire and columns of smoke. 31 The sun shall be turned to darkness, and the moon to blood, before the great and awesome day of the LORD comes. 32 And it shall come to pass that everyone who calls on the name of the LORD shall be saved. For in Mount Zion and in Jerusalem there shall be those who escape, as the LORD has said, and among the survivors shall be those whom the LORD calls.

The LORD Judges the Nations

3 5"For behold, in those days and at that time, when I restore the fortunes of Judah and Jerusalem, 2 I will gather all the nations and bring them down to the Valley of Jehoshaphat. And I will enter into judgment with them there, on behalf of my people and my heritage Israel, because they have scattered them among the nations and have divided up my land, 3 and have cast lots for my people, and have traded a boy for a prostitute, and have sold a girl for wine and have drunk it.

4 "What are you to me, O Tyre and Sidon, and all the regions of Philistia? Are you paying me back for something? If you are paying me back, I will return your payment on your own head swiftly and speedily. 5 For you have taken my silver and my gold, and have carried my rich treasures into your temples.[6] 6 You have sold the people of Judah and Jerusalem to the Greeks in order to remove them far from their own border. 7 Behold, I will stir them up from the place to which you have sold them, and I will return your payment on your own head. 8 I will sell your sons and your daughters into the hand of the people of Judah, and they will sell them to the Sabeans, to a nation far away, for the LORD has spoken."

9   Proclaim this among the nations:
      Consecrate for war;[7]
        stir up the mighty men.
      Let all the men of war draw near;
        let them come up.

---

[1] Hebrew face [2] Hebrew his end [3] Or pay back [4] Ch 3:1 in Hebrew [5] Ch 4:1 in Hebrew [6] Or palaces [7] Or Consecrate a war

10 Beat your plowshares into swords,
    and your pruning hooks into spears;
    let the weak say, "I am a warrior."

11 Hasten and come,
    all you surrounding nations,
    and gather yourselves there.
    Bring down your warriors, O LORD.
12 Let the nations stir themselves up
    and come up to the Valley of
      Jehoshaphat;
    for there I will sit to judge
    all the surrounding nations.

13 Put in the sickle,
    for the harvest is ripe.
    Go in, tread,
    for the winepress is full.
    The vats overflow,
    for their evil is great.

14 Multitudes, multitudes,
    in the valley of decision!
    For the day of the LORD is near
    in the valley of decision.
15 The sun and the moon are darkened,
    and the stars withdraw their shining.
16 The LORD roars from Zion,
    and utters his voice from Jerusalem,
    and the heavens and the earth quake.

But the LORD is a refuge to his people,
    a stronghold to the people of Israel.

The Glorious Future of Judah

17 "So you shall know that I am the LORD your
      God,
    who dwells in Zion, my holy mountain.
    And Jerusalem shall be holy,
    and strangers shall never again pass
      through it.

18 "And in that day
    the mountains shall drip sweet wine,
    and the hills shall flow with milk,
    and all the streambeds of Judah
    shall flow with water;
    and a fountain shall come forth from the
      house of the LORD
    and water the Valley of Shittim.

19 "Egypt shall become a desolation
    and Edom a desolate wilderness,
    for the violence done to the people of
      Judah,
    because they have shed innocent blood
      in their land.
20 But Judah shall be inhabited forever,
    and Jerusalem to all generations.
21 I will avenge their blood,
    blood I have not avenged,[1]
    for the LORD dwells in Zion."

---

[1] Or I will acquit their bloodguilt that I have not acquitted

AMOS

1 The words of Amos, who was among the shepherds[1] of Tekoa, which he saw concerning Israel in the days of Uzziah king of Judah and in the days of Jeroboam the son of Joash, king of Israel, two years[2] before the earthquake.

Judgment on Israel's Neighbors

2 And he said:

"The LORD roars from Zion
　　and utters his voice from Jerusalem;
　the pastures of the shepherds mourn,
　　and the top of Carmel withers."

3 Thus says the LORD:

"For three transgressions of Damascus,
　　and for four, I will not revoke the punishment,[3]
　because they have threshed Gilead
　　with threshing sledges of iron.
4 　So I will send a fire upon the house of Hazael,
　　and it shall devour the strongholds of Ben-hadad.
5 　I will break the gate-bar of Damascus,
　　and cut off the inhabitants from the Valley of Aven,[4]
　and him who holds the scepter from Beth-eden;
　　and the people of Syria shall go into exile to Kir,"
　　　　　　　　says the LORD.

6 Thus says the LORD:

"For three transgressions of Gaza,
　　and for four, I will not revoke the punishment,
　because they carried into exile a whole people
　　to deliver them up to Edom.
7 　So I will send a fire upon the wall of Gaza,
　　and it shall devour her strongholds.
8 　I will cut off the inhabitants from Ashdod,
　　and him who holds the scepter from Ashkelon;
　I will turn my hand against Ekron,
　　and the remnant of the Philistines shall perish,"
　　　　　　　　says the Lord GOD.

9 Thus says the LORD:

"For three transgressions of Tyre,
　　and for four, I will not revoke the punishment,
　because they delivered up a whole people to Edom,
　　and did not remember the covenant of brotherhood.
10 　So I will send a fire upon the wall of Tyre,
　　and it shall devour her strongholds."

11 Thus says the LORD:

"For three transgressions of Edom,
　　and for four, I will not revoke the punishment,
　because he pursued his brother with the sword
　　and cast off all pity,
　and his anger tore perpetually,
　　and he kept his wrath forever.
12 　So I will send a fire upon Teman,
　　and it shall devour the strongholds of Bozrah."

13 Thus says the LORD:

"For three transgressions of the Ammonites,
　　and for four, I will not revoke the punishment,
　because they have ripped open pregnant women in Gilead,
　　that they might enlarge their border.
14 　So I will kindle a fire in the wall of Rabbah,
　　and it shall devour her strongholds,
　with shouting on the day of battle,
　　with a tempest in the day of the whirlwind;
15 　and their king shall go into exile,
　　he and his princes[5] together,"
　　　　　　　　says the LORD.

2 Thus says the LORD:

"For three transgressions of Moab,
　　and for four, I will not revoke the punishment,[6]
　because he burned to lime
　　the bones of the king of Edom.

---

[1] Or sheep breeders [2] Or during two years [3] Hebrew I will not turn it back; also verses 6, 9, 11, 13 [4] Or On [5] Or officials [6] Hebrew I will not turn it back; also verses 4, 6

2 So I will send a fire upon Moab,
     and it shall devour the strongholds of
         Kerioth,
and Moab shall die amid uproar,
     amid shouting and the sound of the
         trumpet;
3 I will cut off the ruler from its midst,
     and will kill all its princes[1] with him,"
               says the LORD.

Judgment on Judah

4 Thus says the LORD:

"For three transgressions of Judah,
     and for four, I will not revoke the pun-
         ishment,
because they have rejected the law of the
     LORD,
     and have not kept his statutes,
but their lies have led them astray,
     those after which their fathers walked.
5 So I will send a fire upon Judah,
     and it shall devour the strongholds of
         Jerusalem."

Judgment on Israel

6 Thus says the LORD:

"For three transgressions of Israel,
     and for four, I will not revoke the pun-
         ishment,
because they sell the righteous for silver,
     and the needy for a pair of sandals—
7 those who trample the head of the poor
     into the dust of the earth
     and turn aside the way of the afflicted;
a man and his father go in to the same girl,
     so that my holy name is profaned;
8 they lay themselves down beside every altar
     on garments taken in pledge,
and in the house of their God they drink
     the wine of those who have been fined.

9 "Yet it was I who destroyed the Amorite
     before them,
     whose height was like the height of the
         cedars
     and who was as strong as the oaks;
I destroyed his fruit above
     and his roots beneath.
10 Also it was I who brought you up out of
     the land of Egypt
     and led you forty years in the wilder-
         ness,
     to possess the land of the Amorite.

11 And I raised up some of your sons for
     prophets,
     and some of your young men for
         Nazirites.
     Is it not indeed so, O people of Israel?"
               declares the LORD.

12 "But you made the Nazirites drink wine,
     and commanded the prophets,
     saying, 'You shall not prophesy.'

13 "Behold, I will press you down in your place,
     as a cart full of sheaves presses down.
14 Flight shall perish from the swift,
     and the strong shall not retain his
         strength,
     nor shall the mighty save his life;
15 he who handles the bow shall not stand,
     and he who is swift of foot shall not
         save himself,
     nor shall he who rides the horse save his
         life;
16 and he who is stout of heart among the
     mighty
     shall flee away naked in that day,"
               declares the LORD.

Israel's Guilt and Punishment

3 Hear this word that the LORD has spoken
against you, O people of Israel, against the
whole family that I brought up out of the land
of Egypt:

2 "You only have I known
     of all the families of the earth;
therefore I will punish you
     for all your iniquities.

3 "Do two walk together,
     unless they have agreed to meet?
4 Does a lion roar in the forest,
     when he has no prey?
Does a young lion cry out from his den,
     if he has taken nothing?
5 Does a bird fall in a snare on the earth,
     when there is no trap for it?
Does a snare spring up from the ground,
     when it has taken nothing?
6 Is a trumpet blown in a city,
     and the people are not afraid?
Does disaster come to a city,
     unless the LORD has done it?

7 "For the Lord GOD does nothing
     without revealing his secret
     to his servants the prophets.

[1] Or officials

8 The lion has roared;
    who will not fear?
The Lord GOD has spoken;
    who can but prophesy?"

9 Proclaim to the strongholds in Ashdod
    and to the strongholds in the land of
        Egypt,
    and say, "Assemble yourselves on the
        mountains of Samaria,
    and see the great tumults within her,
    and the oppressed in her midst."
10 "They do not know how to do right,"
        declares the LORD,
    "those who store up violence and rob-
        bery in their strongholds."

11 Therefore thus says the Lord GOD:

    "An adversary shall surround the land
        and bring down[1] your defenses from
            you,
        and your strongholds shall be plun-
            dered."

12 Thus says the LORD: "As the shepherd rescues from the mouth of the lion two legs, or a
piece of an ear, so shall the people of Israel who
dwell in Samaria be rescued, with the corner of
a couch and part[2] of a bed.

13 "Hear, and testify against the house of
        Jacob,"
    declares the Lord GOD, the God of hosts,
14 "that on the day I punish Israel for his trans-
        gressions,
    I will punish the altars of Bethel,
    and the horns of the altar shall be cut off
        and fall to the ground.
15 I will strike the winter house along with
        the summer house,
    and the houses of ivory shall perish,
    and the great houses[3] shall come to an
        end,"
        declares the LORD.

4 "Hear this word, you cows of Bashan,
    who are on the mountain of Samaria,
who oppress the poor, who crush the
    needy,
    who say to your husbands, 'Bring, that
        we may drink!'
2 The Lord GOD has sworn by his holiness
    that, behold, the days are coming upon
        you,

when they shall take you away with hooks,
    even the last of you with fishhooks.
3 And you shall go out through the breaches,
    each one straight ahead;
    and you shall be cast out into Harmon,"
        declares the LORD.

4 "Come to Bethel, and transgress;
    to Gilgal, and multiply transgression;
bring your sacrifices every morning,
    your tithes every three days;
5 offer a sacrifice of thanksgiving of that
        which is leavened,
    and proclaim freewill offerings, publish
        them;
    for so you love to do, O people of Israel!"
        declares the Lord GOD.

Israel Has Not Returned to the LORD

6 "I gave you cleanness of teeth in all your cit-
        ies,
    and lack of bread in all your places,
    yet you did not return to me,"
        declares the LORD.

7 "I also withheld the rain from you
    when there were yet three months to
        the harvest;
I would send rain on one city,
    and send no rain on another city;
one field would have rain,
    and the field on which it did not rain
        would wither;
8 so two or three cities would wander to
        another city
    to drink water, and would not be satis-
        fied;
    yet you did not return to me,"
        declares the LORD.

9 "I struck you with blight and mildew;
    your many gardens and your vineyards,
    your fig trees and your olive trees the
        locust devoured;
    yet you did not return to me,"
        declares the LORD.

10 "I sent among you a pestilence after the
        manner of Egypt;
    I killed your young men with the
        sword,
    and carried away your horses,[4]
        and I made the stench of your camp go
            up into your nostrils;

yet you did not return to me,"
          declares the LORD.

11 "I overthrew some of you,
    as when God overthrew Sodom and
      Gomorrah,
    and you were as a brand[1] plucked out of
      the burning;
    yet you did not return to me,"
          declares the LORD.

12 "Therefore thus I will do to you, O Israel;
    because I will do this to you,
    prepare to meet your God, O Israel!"

13 For behold, he who forms the mountains
    and creates the wind,
    and declares to man what is his
      thought,
  who makes the morning darkness,
    and treads on the heights of the earth—
    the LORD, the God of hosts, is his name!

Seek the LORD and Live

5 Hear this word that I take up over you in
lamentation, O house of Israel:

2 "Fallen, no more to rise,
    is the virgin Israel;
  forsaken on her land,
    with none to raise her up."

3 For thus says the Lord GOD:

"The city that went out a thousand
    shall have a hundred left,
  and that which went out a hundred
    shall have ten left
  to the house of Israel."

4 For thus says the LORD to the house of Israel:

"Seek me and live;
5   but do not seek Bethel,
  and do not enter into Gilgal
    or cross over to Beersheba;
  for Gilgal shall surely go into exile,
    and Bethel shall come to nothing."

6 Seek the LORD and live,
    lest he break out like fire in the house of
      Joseph,
    and it devour, with none to quench it
      for Bethel,
7 O you who turn justice to wormwood[2]
    and cast down righteousness to the
      earth!

8 He who made the Pleiades and Orion,
    and turns deep darkness into the morn-
      ing
    and darkens the day into night,
  who calls for the waters of the sea
    and pours them out on the surface of
      the earth,
  the LORD is his name;
9 who makes destruction flash forth against
    the strong,
    so that destruction comes upon the for-
      tress.

10 They hate him who reproves in the gate,
    and they abhor him who speaks the
      truth.
11 Therefore because you trample on[3] the
    poor
    and you exact taxes of grain from him,
  you have built houses of hewn stone,
    but you shall not dwell in them;
  you have planted pleasant vineyards,
    but you shall not drink their wine.
12 For I know how many are your transgres-
    sions
    and how great are your sins—
  you who afflict the righteous, who take a
    bribe,
    and turn aside the needy in the gate.
13 Therefore he who is prudent will keep
    silent in such a time,
    for it is an evil time.

14 Seek good, and not evil,
    that you may live;
  and so the LORD, the God of hosts, will be
    with you,
    as you have said.
15 Hate evil, and love good,
    and establish justice in the gate;
  it may be that the LORD, the God of
    hosts,
    will be gracious to the remnant of
    Joseph.

16 Therefore thus says the LORD, the God of
hosts, the Lord:

"In all the squares there shall be wailing,
    and in all the streets they shall say, 'Alas!
      Alas!'
They shall call the farmers to mourning
    and to wailing those who are skilled in
      lamentation,

---

[1] That is, a burning stick [2] Or to bitter fruit [3] Or you tax

17 and in all vineyards there shall be wailing,
    for I will pass through your midst,"
                says the LORD.

Let Justice Roll Down

18 Woe to you who desire the day of the
    LORD!
    Why would you have the day of the
      LORD?
  It is darkness, and not light,
19   as if a man fled from a lion,
    and a bear met him,
  or went into the house and leaned his hand
    against the wall,
    and a serpent bit him.
20 Is not the day of the LORD darkness, and
    not light,
  and gloom with no brightness in it?

21 "I hate, I despise your feasts,
    and I take no delight in your solemn
      assemblies.
22 Even though you offer me your burnt
    offerings and grain offerings,
  I will not accept them;
  and the peace offerings of your fattened
    animals,
  I will not look upon them.
23 Take away from me the noise of your
    songs;
  to the melody of your harps I will not
    listen.
24 But let justice roll down like waters,
    and righteousness like an ever-flowing
    stream.

25 "Did you bring to me sacrifices and offerings during the forty years in the wilderness, O house of Israel? 26 You shall take up Sikkuth your king, and Kiyyun your star-god—your images that you made for yourselves, 27 and I will send you into exile beyond Damascus," says the LORD, whose name is the God of hosts.

Woe to Those at Ease in Zion

6 "Woe to those who are at ease in Zion,
  and to those who feel secure on the mountain of Samaria,
  the notable men of the first of the nations,
  to whom the house of Israel comes!
2   Pass over to Calneh, and see,
    and from there go to Hamath the great;
    then go down to Gath of the Philistines.

  Are you better than these kingdoms?
    Or is their territory greater than your
      territory,
3 O you who put far away the day of disaster
    and bring near the seat of violence?

4 "Woe to those who lie on beds of ivory
    and stretch themselves out on their
      couches,
  and eat lambs from the flock
    and calves from the midst of the stall,
5 who sing idle songs to the sound of the
    harp
    and like David invent for themselves
      instruments of music,
6 who drink wine in bowls
    and anoint themselves with the finest
      oils,
  but are not grieved over the ruin of
    Joseph!
7 Therefore they shall now be the first of
    those who go into exile,
    and the revelry of those who stretch
      themselves out shall pass away."

8 The Lord GOD has sworn by himself, declares the LORD, the God of hosts:

"I abhor the pride of Jacob
    and hate his strongholds,
    and I will deliver up the city and all that
      is in it."

9 And if ten men remain in one house, they shall die. 10 And when one's relative, the one who anoints him for burial, shall take him up to bring the bones out of the house, and shall say to him who is in the innermost parts of the house, "Is there still anyone with you?" he shall say, "No"; and he shall say, "Silence! We must not mention the name of the LORD."

11 For behold, the LORD commands,
    and the great house shall be struck
      down into fragments,
    and the little house into bits.
12 Do horses run on rocks?
    Does one plow there[1] with oxen?
  But you have turned justice into poison
    and the fruit of righteousness into
      wormwood[2]—
13 you who rejoice in Lo-debar,[3]
    who say, "Have we not by our own
      strength
    captured Karnaim[4] for ourselves?"

---

1 Or the sea   2 Or into bitter fruit   3 Lo-debar means nothing   4 Karnaim means horns (a symbol of strength)

¹⁴ "For behold, I will raise up against you a
nation,
O house of Israel," declares the LORD,
the God of hosts;
"and they shall oppress you from Lebo-
hamath
to the Brook of the Arabah."

Warning Visions

7 This is what the Lord GOD showed me:
behold, he was forming locusts when the
latter growth was just beginning to sprout, and
behold, it was the latter growth after the king's
mowings. ² When they had finished eating the
grass of the land, I said,

"O Lord GOD, please forgive!
How can Jacob stand?
He is so small!"
³ The LORD relented concerning this:
"It shall not be," said the LORD.

⁴ This is what the Lord GOD showed me:
behold, the Lord GOD was calling for a judgment by fire, and it devoured the great deep and
was eating up the land. ⁵ Then I said,

"O Lord GOD, please cease!
How can Jacob stand?
He is so small!"
⁶ The LORD relented concerning this:
"This also shall not be," said the Lord
GOD.

⁷ This is what he showed me: behold, the
Lord was standing beside a wall built with a
plumb line, with a plumb line in his hand. ⁸ And
the LORD said to me, "Amos, what do you see?"
And I said, "A plumb line." Then the Lord said,

"Behold, I am setting a plumb line
in the midst of my people Israel;
I will never again pass by them;
⁹ the high places of Isaac shall be made deso-
late,
and the sanctuaries of Israel shall be laid
waste,
and I will rise against the house of
Jeroboam with the sword."

Amos Accused

¹⁰ Then Amaziah the priest of Bethel sent to
Jeroboam king of Israel, saying, "Amos has con-
spired against you in the midst of the house of
Israel. The land is not able to bear all his words.
¹¹ For thus Amos has said,

"'Jeroboam shall die by the sword,
and Israel must go into exile
away from his land.'"

¹² And Amaziah said to Amos, "O seer, go, flee
away to the land of Judah, and eat bread there,
and prophesy there, ¹³ but never again prophesy
at Bethel, for it is the king's sanctuary, and it is
a temple of the kingdom."

¹⁴ Then Amos answered and said to Amaziah,
"I was¹ no prophet, nor a prophet's son, but I
was a herdsman and a dresser of sycamore figs.
¹⁵ But the LORD took me from following the
flock, and the LORD said to me, 'Go, prophesy
to my people Israel.' ¹⁶ Now therefore hear the
word of the LORD.

"You say, 'Do not prophesy against Israel,
and do not preach against the house of
Isaac.'

¹⁷ Therefore thus says the LORD:

"'Your wife shall be a prostitute in the city,
and your sons and your daughters shall
fall by the sword,
and your land shall be divided up with
a measuring line;
you yourself shall die in an unclean land,
and Israel shall surely go into exile away
from its land.'"

The Coming Day of Bitter Mourning

8 This is what the Lord GOD showed me:
behold, a basket of summer fruit. ² And
he said, "Amos, what do you see?" And I said,
"A basket of summer fruit." Then the LORD
said to me,

"The end² has come upon my people Israel;
I will never again pass by them.
³ The songs of the temple³ shall become
wailings⁴ in that day,"
declares the Lord GOD.
"So many dead bodies!"
"They are thrown everywhere!"
"Silence!"

⁴ Hear this, you who trample on the needy
and bring the poor of the land to an
end,
⁵ saying, "When will the new moon be over,
that we may sell grain?
And the Sabbath,
that we may offer wheat for sale,

¹ Or *am*; twice in this verse ² The Hebrew words for *end* and *summer fruit* sound alike ³ Or *palace* ⁴ Or *The singing women of the palace shall wail*

that we may make the ephah small and the
    shekel[1] great
    and deal deceitfully with false balances,
6 that we may buy the poor for silver
    and the needy for a pair of sandals
    and sell the chaff of the wheat?"

7 The LORD has sworn by the pride of Jacob:
    "Surely I will never forget any of their deeds.
8 Shall not the land tremble on this account,
    and everyone mourn who dwells in it,
  and all of it rise like the Nile,
    and be tossed about and sink again, like
      the Nile of Egypt?"

9 "And on that day," declares the Lord GOD,
    "I will make the sun go down at noon
    and darken the earth in broad daylight.
10 I will turn your feasts into mourning
    and all your songs into lamentation;
  I will bring sackcloth on every waist
    and baldness on every head;
  I will make it like the mourning for an
    only son
    and the end of it like a bitter day.

11 "Behold, the days are coming," declares the
    Lord GOD,
    "when I will send a famine on the
      land—
  not a famine of bread, nor a thirst for
    water,
    but of hearing the words of the LORD.
12 They shall wander from sea to sea,
    and from north to east;
  they shall run to and fro, to seek the word
    of the LORD,
    but they shall not find it.
13 "In that day the lovely virgins and the
    young men
    shall faint for thirst.
14 Those who swear by the Guilt of Samaria,
    and say, 'As your god lives, O Dan,'
  and, 'As the Way of Beersheba lives,'
    they shall fall, and never rise again."

The Destruction of Israel

9 I saw the Lord standing beside[2] the altar,
  and he said:

"Strike the capitals until the thresholds
    shake,
    and shatter them on the heads of all the
    people;[3]

and those who are left of them I will kill
    with the sword;
  not one of them shall flee away;
  not one of them shall escape.
2 "If they dig into Sheol,
    from there shall my hand take them;
  if they climb up to heaven,
    from there I will bring them down.
3 If they hide themselves on the top of
    Carmel,
    from there I will search them out and
    take them;
  and if they hide from my sight at the bot-
    tom of the sea,
    there I will command the serpent, and
    it shall bite them.
4 And if they go into captivity before their
    enemies,
    there I will command the sword, and it
    shall kill them;
  and I will fix my eyes upon them
    for evil and not for good."

5 The Lord GOD of hosts,
  he who touches the earth and it melts,
    and all who dwell in it mourn,
  and all of it rises like the Nile,
    and sinks again, like the Nile of Egypt;
6 who builds his upper chambers in the
    heavens
    and founds his vault upon the earth;
  who calls for the waters of the sea
    and pours them out upon the surface of
    the earth—
  the LORD is his name.

7 "Are you not like the Cushites to me,
    O people of Israel?" declares the LORD.
  "Did I not bring up Israel from the land of
    Egypt,
    and the Philistines from Caphtor and
    the Syrians from Kir?
8 Behold, the eyes of the Lord GOD are upon
    the sinful kingdom,
    and I will destroy it from the surface of
    the ground,
    except that I will not utterly destroy the
    house of Jacob,"
             declares the LORD.

9 "For behold, I will command,
    and shake the house of Israel among all
    the nations

---

[1] An *ephah* was about 3/5 bushel or 22 liters; a *shekel* was about 2/5 ounce or 11 grams [2] Or *on* [3] Hebrew *all of them*

as one shakes with a sieve,
    but no pebble shall fall to the earth.
10 All the sinners of my people shall die by
    the sword,
    who say, 'Disaster shall not overtake or
    meet us.'

The Restoration of Israel

11 "In that day I will raise up
    the booth of David that is fallen
and repair its breaches,
    and raise up its ruins
    and rebuild it as in the days of old,
12 that they may possess the remnant of
    Edom
    and all the nations who are called by my
    name,"[1]
    declares the LORD who does this.

13 "Behold, the days are coming," declares
    the LORD,

"when the plowman shall overtake the
    reaper
    and the treader of grapes him who sows
    the seed;
the mountains shall drip sweet wine,
    and all the hills shall flow with it.
14 I will restore the fortunes of my people
    Israel,
    and they shall rebuild the ruined cities
    and inhabit them;
they shall plant vineyards and drink their
    wine,
    and they shall make gardens and eat
    their fruit.
15 I will plant them on their land,
    and they shall never again be
    uprooted
    out of the land that I have given
    them,"
           says the LORD your God.

---

[1] Hebrew; Septuagint (compare Acts 15:17) *that the remnant of mankind and all the nations who are called by my name may seek the Lord*

OBADIAH

¹The vision of Obadiah.

Edom Will Be Humbled

Thus says the Lord God concerning Edom:
We have heard a report from the Lord,
  and a messenger has been sent among
    the nations:
"Rise up! Let us rise against her for battle!"
² Behold, I will make you small among the
    nations;
  you shall be utterly despised.¹
³ The pride of your heart has deceived you,
  you who live in the clefts of the rock,²
in your lofty dwelling,
who say in your heart,
  "Who will bring me down to the
    ground?"
⁴ Though you soar aloft like the eagle,
  though your nest is set among the stars,
  from there I will bring you down,
                  declares the Lord.

⁵ If thieves came to you,
  if plunderers came by night—
  how you have been destroyed!—
  would they not steal only enough for
    themselves?
If grape gatherers came to you,
  would they not leave gleanings?
⁶ How Esau has been pillaged,
  his treasures sought out!
⁷ All your allies have driven you to your bor-
    der;
  those at peace with you have deceived
    you;
  they have prevailed against you;
  those who eat your bread³ have set a
    trap beneath you—
  you have⁴ no understanding.

⁸ Will I not on that day, declares the Lord,
  destroy the wise men out of Edom,
  and understanding out of Mount Esau?
⁹ And your mighty men shall be dismayed,
    O Teman,
  so that every man from Mount Esau
    will be cut off by slaughter.

Edom's Violence Against Jacob

¹⁰ Because of the violence done to your
      brother Jacob,
    shame shall cover you,
    and you shall be cut off forever.
¹¹ On the day that you stood aloof,
    on the day that strangers carried off his
      wealth
  and foreigners entered his gates
    and cast lots for Jerusalem,
    you were like one of them.
¹² But do not gloat over the day of your
      brother
    in the day of his misfortune;
  do not rejoice over the people of Judah
    in the day of their ruin;
  do not boast⁵
    in the day of distress.
¹³ Do not enter the gate of my people
    in the day of their calamity;
  do not gloat over his disaster
    in the day of his calamity;
  do not loot his wealth
    in the day of his calamity.
¹⁴ Do not stand at the crossroads
    to cut off his fugitives;
  do not hand over his survivors
    in the day of distress.

The Day of the Lord Is Near

¹⁵ For the day of the Lord is near upon all
      the nations.
  As you have done, it shall be done to you;
    your deeds shall return on your own
      head.
¹⁶ For as you have drunk on my holy moun-
      tain,
    so all the nations shall drink continually;
  they shall drink and swallow,
    and shall be as though they had never
      been.
¹⁷ But in Mount Zion there shall be those
      who escape,
    and it shall be holy,
  and the house of Jacob shall possess their
      own possessions.
¹⁸ The house of Jacob shall be a fire,
    and the house of Joseph a flame,
    and the house of Esau stubble;

¹ Or Behold, I have made you small among the nations; you are utterly despised ² Or of Sela ³ Hebrew lacks those who eat ⁴ Hebrew he has ⁵ Hebrew do not enlarge your mouth

they shall burn them and consume them,
and there shall be no survivor for the
house of Esau,
for the LORD has spoken.

The Kingdom of the LORD

19 Those of the Negeb shall possess Mount
Esau,
and those of the Shephelah shall possess
the land of the Philistines;
they shall possess the land of Ephraim and
the land of Samaria,

and Benjamin shall possess Gilead.
20 The exiles of this host of the people of
Israel
shall possess the land of the Canaanites
as far as Zarephath,
and the exiles of Jerusalem who are in
Sepharad
shall possess the cities of the Negeb.
21 Saviors shall go up to Mount Zion
to rule Mount Esau,
and the kingdom shall be the LORD's.

JONAH

Jonah Flees the Presence of the LORD

1 Now the word of the LORD came to Jonah the son of Amittai, saying, **2** "Arise, go to Nineveh, that great city, and call out against it, for their evil[1] has come up before me." **3** But Jonah rose to flee to Tarshish from the presence of the LORD. He went down to Joppa and found a ship going to Tarshish. So he paid the fare and went down into it, to go with them to Tarshish, away from the presence of the LORD.

4 But the LORD hurled a great wind upon the sea, and there was a mighty tempest on the sea, so that the ship threatened to break up. **5** Then the mariners were afraid, and each cried out to his god. And they hurled the cargo that was in the ship into the sea to lighten it for them. But Jonah had gone down into the inner part of the ship and had lain down and was fast asleep. **6** So the captain came and said to him, "What do you mean, you sleeper? Arise, call out to your god! Perhaps the god will give a thought to us, that we may not perish."

Jonah Is Thrown into the Sea

7 And they said to one another, "Come, let us cast lots, that we may know on whose account this evil has come upon us." So they cast lots, and the lot fell on Jonah. **8** Then they said to him, "Tell us on whose account this evil has come upon us. What is your occupation? And where do you come from? What is your country? And of what people are you?" **9** And he said to them, "I am a Hebrew, and I fear the LORD, the God of heaven, who made the sea and the dry land." **10** Then the men were exceedingly afraid and said to him, "What is this that you have done!" For the men knew that he was fleeing from the presence of the LORD, because he had told them.

11 Then they said to him, "What shall we do to you, that the sea may quiet down for us?" For the sea grew more and more tempestuous. **12** He said to them, "Pick me up and hurl me into the sea; then the sea will quiet down for you, for I know it is because of me that this great tempest has come upon you." **13** Nevertheless, the men rowed hard[2] to get back to dry land, but they could not, for the sea grew more and more tempestuous against them. **14** Therefore they called out to the LORD, "O LORD, let us not perish for this man's life, and lay not on us innocent blood, for you, O LORD, have done as it pleased you." **15** So they picked up Jonah and hurled him into the sea, and the sea ceased from its raging. **16** Then the men feared the LORD exceedingly, and they offered a sacrifice to the LORD and made vows.

A Great Fish Swallows Jonah

17[3] And the LORD appointed[4] a great fish to swallow up Jonah. And Jonah was in the belly of the fish three days and three nights.

Jonah's Prayer

2 Then Jonah prayed to the LORD his God from the belly of the fish, **2** saying,

"I called out to the LORD, out of my distress,
 and he answered me;
out of the belly of Sheol I cried,
 and you heard my voice.
3 For you cast me into the deep,
 into the heart of the seas,
 and the flood surrounded me;
all your waves and your billows
 passed over me.
4 Then I said, 'I am driven away
 from your sight;
yet I shall again look
 upon your holy temple.'
5 The waters closed in over me to take my
 life;
 the deep surrounded me;
weeds were wrapped about my head
6 at the roots of the mountains.
I went down to the land
 whose bars closed upon me forever;
yet you brought up my life from the pit,
 O LORD my God.
7 When my life was fainting away,
 I remembered the LORD,
and my prayer came to you,
 into your holy temple.
8 Those who pay regard to vain idols
 forsake their hope of steadfast love.
9 But I with the voice of thanksgiving
 will sacrifice to you;
what I have vowed I will pay.
 Salvation belongs to the LORD!"

---

[1] The same Hebrew word can mean *evil* or *disaster*, depending on the context; so throughout Jonah [2] Hebrew *the men dug in* [their oars] [3] Ch 2:1 in Hebrew [4] Or *had appointed*

[10] And the Lord spoke to the fish, and it vomited Jonah out upon the dry land.

Jonah Goes to Nineveh

3 Then the word of the Lord came to Jonah the second time, saying, [2] "Arise, go to Nineveh, that great city, and call out against it the message that I tell you." [3] So Jonah arose and went to Nineveh, according to the word of the Lord. Now Nineveh was an exceedingly great city,[1] three days' journey in breadth.[2] [4] Jonah began to go into the city, going a day's journey. And he called out, "Yet forty days, and Nineveh shall be overthrown!" [5] And the people of Nineveh believed God. They called for a fast and put on sackcloth, from the greatest of them to the least of them.

The People of Nineveh Repent

[6] The word reached[3] the king of Nineveh, and he arose from his throne, removed his robe, covered himself with sackcloth, and sat in ashes. [7] And he issued a proclamation and published through Nineveh, "By the decree of the king and his nobles: Let neither man nor beast, herd nor flock, taste anything. Let them not feed or drink water, [8] but let man and beast be covered with sackcloth, and let them call out mightily to God. Let everyone turn from his evil way and from the violence that is in his hands. [9] Who knows? God may turn and relent and turn from his fierce anger, so that we may not perish."

[10] When God saw what they did, how they turned from their evil way, God relented of the disaster that he had said he would do to them, and he did not do it.

Jonah's Anger and the Lord's Compassion

4 But it displeased Jonah exceedingly,[4] and he was angry. [2] And he prayed to the Lord and said, "O Lord, is not this what I said when I was yet in my country? That is why I made haste to flee to Tarshish; for I knew that you are a gracious God and merciful, slow to anger and abounding in steadfast love, and relenting from disaster. [3] Therefore now, O Lord, please take my life from me, for it is better for me to die than to live." [4] And the Lord said, "Do you do well to be angry?"

[5] Jonah went out of the city and sat to the east of the city and made a booth for himself there. He sat under it in the shade, till he should see what would become of the city. [6] Now the Lord God appointed a plant[5] and made it come up over Jonah, that it might be a shade over his head, to save him from his discomfort.[6] So Jonah was exceedingly glad because of the plant. [7] But when dawn came up the next day, God appointed a worm that attacked the plant, so that it withered. [8] When the sun rose, God appointed a scorching east wind, and the sun beat down on the head of Jonah so that he was faint. And he asked that he might die and said, "It is better for me to die than to live." [9] But God said to Jonah, "Do you do well to be angry for the plant?" And he said, "Yes, I do well to be angry, angry enough to die." [10] And the Lord said, "You pity the plant, for which you did not labor, nor did you make it grow, which came into being in a night and perished in a night. [11] And should not I pity Nineveh, that great city, in which there are more than 120,000 persons who do not know their right hand from their left, and also much cattle?"

---

[1] Hebrew *a great city to God*   [2] Or *a visit was a three days' journey*   [3] Or *had reached*   [4] Hebrew *it was exceedingly evil to Jonah*   [5] Hebrew *qiqayon, probably the castor oil plant; also verses 7, 9, 10*   [6] Or *his evil*

MICAH

1 The word of the LORD that came to Micah
of Moresheth in the days of Jotham, Ahaz,
and Hezekiah, kings of Judah, which he saw
concerning Samaria and Jerusalem.

The Coming Destruction

2 Hear, you peoples, all of you;[1]
> pay attention, O earth, and all that is in
> it,
> and let the Lord GOD be a witness against
> you,
> the Lord from his holy temple.

3 For behold, the LORD is coming out of his
place,
> and will come down and tread upon the
> high places of the earth.

4 And the mountains will melt under him,
> and the valleys will split open,
> like wax before the fire,
> like waters poured down a steep
> place.

5 All this is for the transgression of Jacob
> and for the sins of the house of Israel.
> What is the transgression of Jacob?
> Is it not Samaria?
> And what is the high place of Judah?
> Is it not Jerusalem?

6 Therefore I will make Samaria a heap in
> the open country,
> a place for planting vineyards,
> and I will pour down her stones into the
> valley
> and uncover her foundations.

7 All her carved images shall be beaten to
> pieces,
> all her wages shall be burned with
> fire,
> and all her idols I will lay waste,
> for from the fee of a prostitute she gath-
> ered them,
> and to the fee of a prostitute they shall
> return.

8 For this I will lament and wail;
> I will go stripped and naked;
> I will make lamentation like the jackals,
> and mourning like the ostriches.

9 For her wound is incurable,
> and it has come to Judah;

> it has reached to the gate of my people,
> to Jerusalem.

10 Tell it not in Gath;
> weep not at all;
> in Beth-le-aphrah
> roll yourselves in the dust.

11 Pass on your way,
> inhabitants of Shaphir,
> in nakedness and shame;
> the inhabitants of Zaanan
> do not come out;
> the lamentation of Beth-ezel
> shall take away from you its standing
> place.

12 For the inhabitants of Maroth
> wait anxiously for good,
> because disaster has come down from the
> LORD
> to the gate of Jerusalem.

13 Harness the steeds to the chariots,
> inhabitants of Lachish;
> it was the beginning of sin
> to the daughter of Zion,
> for in you were found
> the transgressions of Israel.

14 Therefore you shall give parting gifts[2]
> to Moresheth-gath;
> the houses of Achzib shall be a deceitful
> thing
> to the kings of Israel.

15 I will again bring a conqueror to you,
> inhabitants of Mareshah;
> the glory of Israel
> shall come to Adullam.

16 Make yourselves bald and cut off your hair,
> for the children of your delight;
> make yourselves as bald as the eagle,
> for they shall go from you into exile.

Woe to the Oppressors

2 Woe to those who devise wickedness
and work evil on their beds!
> When the morning dawns, they perform it,
> because it is in the power of their
> hand.

2 They covet fields and seize them,
> and houses, and take them away;
> they oppress a man and his house,
> a man and his inheritance.

---

[1] Hebrew *all of them* [2] Or *give dowry*

3 Therefore thus says the LORD:
behold, against this family I am devising
    disaster,[1]
    from which you cannot remove your
        necks,
and you shall not walk haughtily,
    for it will be a time of disaster.
4 In that day they shall take up a taunt song
        against you
    and moan bitterly,
and say, "We are utterly ruined;
    he changes the portion of my people;
how he removes it from me!
    To an apostate he allots our fields."
5 Therefore you will have none to cast the
        line by lot
    in the assembly of the LORD.

6 "Do not preach"—thus they preach—
    "one should not preach of such things;
        disgrace will not overtake us."
7 Should this be said, O house of Jacob?
    Has the LORD grown impatient?[2]
    Are these his deeds?
Do not my words do good
    to him who walks uprightly?
8 But lately my people have risen up as an
        enemy;
    you strip the rich robe from those who pass
        by trustingly
    with no thought of war.[3]
9 The women of my people you drive out
    from their delightful houses;
from their young children you take away
    my splendor forever.
10 Arise and go,
    for this is no place to rest,
because of uncleanness that destroys
    with a grievous destruction.
11 If a man should go about and utter wind
        and lies,
    saying, "I will preach to you of wine and
        strong drink,"
    he would be the preacher for this people!
12 I will surely assemble all of you, O Jacob;
    I will gather the remnant of Israel;
I will set them together
    like sheep in a fold,
like a flock in its pasture,
    a noisy multitude of men.

13 He who opens the breach goes up before
        them;
    they break through and pass the gate,
        going out by it.
Their king passes on before them,
    the LORD at their head.

Rulers and Prophets Denounced

3 And I said:
    Hear, you heads of Jacob
        and rulers of the house of Israel!
Is it not for you to know justice?—
2   you who hate the good and love the evil,
who tear the skin from off my people[4]
    and their flesh from off their bones,
3 who eat the flesh of my people,
    and flay their skin from off them,
and break their bones in pieces
    and chop them up like meat in a pot,
    like flesh in a cauldron.

4 Then they will cry to the LORD,
    but he will not answer them;
he will hide his face from them at that time,
    because they have made their deeds evil.

5 Thus says the LORD concerning the proph-
        ets
    who lead my people astray,
who cry "Peace"
    when they have something to eat,
but declare war against him
    who puts nothing into their mouths.
6 Therefore it shall be night to you, without
        vision,
    and darkness to you, without divination.
The sun shall go down on the prophets,
    and the day shall be black over them;
7 the seers shall be disgraced,
    and the diviners put to shame;
they shall all cover their lips,
    for there is no answer from God.
8 But as for me, I am filled with power,
    with the Spirit of the LORD,
    and with justice and might,
to declare to Jacob his transgression
    and to Israel his sin.

9 Hear this, you heads of the house of Jacob
    and rulers of the house of Israel,
who detest justice
    and make crooked all that is straight,
10 who build Zion with blood
    and Jerusalem with iniquity.

---

[1] The same Hebrew word can mean *evil* or *disaster*, depending on the context   [2] Hebrew *Has the spirit of the LORD grown short?*   [3] Or *returning from war*   [4] Hebrew *from off them*

11 Its heads give judgment for a bribe;
       its priests teach for a price;
       its prophets practice divination for
           money;
   yet they lean on the LORD and say,
       "Is not the LORD in the midst of us?
       No disaster shall come upon us."
12 Therefore because of you
       Zion shall be plowed as a field;
   Jerusalem shall become a heap of ruins,
       and the mountain of the house a
           wooded height.

The Mountain of the LORD

4 It shall come to pass in the latter days
   that the mountain of the house of the
       LORD
   shall be established as the highest of the
       mountains,
       and it shall be lifted up above the hills;
   and peoples shall flow to it,
2   and many nations shall come, and say:
   "Come, let us go up to the mountain of the
       LORD,
       to the house of the God of Jacob,
   that he may teach us his ways
       and that we may walk in his paths."
   For out of Zion shall go forth the law,[1]
       and the word of the LORD from
           Jerusalem.
3 He shall judge between many peoples,
       and shall decide disputes for strong
           nations far away;
   and they shall beat their swords into plow-
       shares,
       and their spears into pruning hooks;
   nation shall not lift up sword against
       nation,
       neither shall they learn war anymore;
4 but they shall sit every man under his vine
       and under his fig tree,
       and no one shall make them afraid,
   for the mouth of the LORD of hosts has
       spoken.
5 For all the peoples walk
       each in the name of its god,
   but we will walk in the name of the LORD
       our God
       forever and ever.

The LORD Shall Rescue Zion

6 In that day, declares the LORD,
       I will assemble the lame

and gather those who have been driven
       away
       and those whom I have afflicted;
7 and the lame I will make the remnant,
       and those who were cast off, a strong
           nation;
   and the LORD will reign over them in
       Mount Zion
       from this time forth and forevermore.

8 And you, O tower of the flock,
       hill of the daughter of Zion,
   to you shall it come,
       the former dominion shall come,
       kingship for the daughter of Jerusalem.

9 Now why do you cry aloud?
       Is there no king in you?
   Has your counselor perished,
       that pain seized you like a woman in
           labor?
10 Writhe and groan,[2] O daughter of Zion,
       like a woman in labor,
   for now you shall go out from the city
       and dwell in the open country;
       you shall go to Babylon.
   There you shall be rescued;
       there the LORD will redeem you
       from the hand of your enemies.

11 Now many nations
       are assembled against you,
   saying, "Let her be defiled,
       and let our eyes gaze upon Zion."
12 But they do not know
       the thoughts of the LORD;
   they do not understand his plan,
       that he has gathered them as sheaves to
           the threshing floor.
13 Arise and thresh,
       O daughter of Zion,
   for I will make your horn iron,
       and I will make your hoofs bronze;
   you shall beat in pieces many peoples;
       and shall devote[3] their gain to the LORD,
       their wealth to the Lord of the whole
           earth.

The Ruler to Be Born in Bethlehem

5 [4] Now muster your troops, O daughter[5] of
       troops;
       siege is laid against us;
   with a rod they strike the judge of Israel
       on the cheek.

---

[1] Or teaching [2] Or push [3] Hebrew devote to destruction [4] Ch 4:14 in Hebrew [5] That is, city

²¹ But you, O Bethlehem Ephrathah,
who are too little to be among the
clans of Judah,
from you shall come forth for me
one who is to be ruler in Israel,
whose coming forth is from of old,
from ancient days.
³ Therefore he shall give them up until the
time
when she who is in labor has given
birth;
then the rest of his brothers shall return
to the people of Israel.
⁴ And he shall stand and shepherd his flock
in the strength of the LORD,
in the majesty of the name of the LORD
his God.
And they shall dwell secure, for now he
shall be great
to the ends of the earth.
⁵ And he shall be their peace.

When the Assyrian comes into our land
and treads in our palaces,
then we will raise against him seven shepherds
and eight princes of men;
⁶ they shall shepherd the land of Assyria
with the sword,
and the land of Nimrod at its entrances;
and he shall deliver us from the Assyrian
when he comes into our land
and treads within our border.

A Remnant Shall Be Delivered

⁷ Then the remnant of Jacob shall be
in the midst of many peoples
like dew from the LORD,
like showers on the grass,
which delay not for a man
nor wait for the children of man.
⁸ And the remnant of Jacob shall be among
the nations,
in the midst of many peoples,
like a lion among the beasts of the forest,
like a young lion among the flocks of
sheep,
which, when it goes through, treads down
and tears in pieces, and there is none to
deliver.
⁹ Your hand shall be lifted up over your
adversaries,
and all your enemies shall be cut off.

¹⁰ And in that day, declares the LORD,
I will cut off your horses from among
you
and will destroy your chariots;
¹¹ and I will cut off the cities of your land
and throw down all your strongholds;
¹² and I will cut off sorceries from your hand,
and you shall have no more tellers of
fortunes;
¹³ and I will cut off your carved images
and your pillars from among you,
and you shall bow down no more
to the work of your hands;
¹⁴ and I will root out your Asherah images
from among you
and destroy your cities.
¹⁵ And in anger and wrath I will execute vengeance
on the nations that did not obey.

The Indictment of the LORD

6 Hear what the LORD says:
Arise, plead your case before the mountains,
and let the hills hear your voice.
² Hear, you mountains, the indictment of
the LORD,
and you enduring foundations of the
earth,
for the LORD has an indictment against his
people,
and he will contend with Israel.

³ "O my people, what have I done to you?
How have I wearied you? Answer me!
⁴ For I brought you up from the land of
Egypt
and redeemed you from the house of
slavery,
and I sent before you Moses,
Aaron, and Miriam.
⁵ O my people, remember what Balak king
of Moab devised,
and what Balaam the son of Beor
answered him,
and what happened from Shittim to
Gilgal,
that you may know the righteous acts
of the LORD."

What Does the LORD Require?

⁶ "With what shall I come before the LORD,
and bow myself before God on high?

¹ Ch 5:1 in Hebrew

Shall I come before him with burnt offerings,
  with calves a year old?
7 Will the LORD be pleased with[1] thousands
    of rams,
  with ten thousands of rivers of oil?
Shall I give my firstborn for my transgression,
  the fruit of my body for the sin of my
    soul?"
8 He has told you, O man, what is good;
  and what does the LORD require of you
but to do justice, and to love kindness,[2]
  and to walk humbly with your God?

Destruction of the Wicked

9 The voice of the LORD cries to the city—
  and it is sound wisdom to fear your
    name:
"Hear of the rod and of him who appointed
  it![3]
10 Can I forget any longer the treasures[4]
    of wickedness in the house of the
    wicked,
  and the scant measure that is accursed?
11 Shall I acquit the man with wicked scales
  and with a bag of deceitful weights?
12 Your[5] rich men are full of violence;
  your inhabitants speak lies,
  and their tongue is deceitful in their
    mouth.
13 Therefore I strike you with a grievous blow,
  making you desolate because of your
    sins.
14 You shall eat, but not be satisfied,
  and there shall be hunger within you;
you shall put away, but not preserve,
  and what you preserve I will give to the
    sword.
15 You shall sow, but not reap;
  you shall tread olives, but not anoint
    yourselves with oil;
  you shall tread grapes, but not drink
    wine.
16 For you have kept the statutes of Omri,[6]
  and all the works of the house of Ahab;
  and you have walked in their counsels,
that I may make you a desolation, and
  your[7] inhabitants a hissing;
  so you shall bear the scorn of my peo-
    ple."

Wait for the God of Salvation

7 Woe is me! For I have become
  as when the summer fruit has been gath-
    ered,
  as when the grapes have been gleaned:
there is no cluster to eat,
  no first-ripe fig that my soul desires.
2 The godly has perished from the earth,
  and there is no one upright among
    mankind;
they all lie in wait for blood,
  and each hunts the other with a net.
3 Their hands are on what is evil, to do it
    well;
  the prince and the judge ask for a bribe,
and the great man utters the evil desire of
    his soul;
  thus they weave it together.
4 The best of them is like a brier,
  the most upright of them a thorn
    hedge.
The day of your watchmen, of your pun-
    ishment, has come;
  now their confusion is at hand.
5 Put no trust in a neighbor;
  have no confidence in a friend;
guard the doors of your mouth
  from her who lies in your arms;[8]
6 for the son treats the father with contempt,
  the daughter rises up against her
    mother,
the daughter-in-law against her mother-in-
    law;
  a man's enemies are the men of his own
    house.
7 But as for me, I will look to the LORD;
  I will wait for the God of my salvation;
  my God will hear me.

8 Rejoice not over me, O my enemy;
  when I fall, I shall rise;
when I sit in darkness,
  the LORD will be a light to me.
9 I will bear the indignation of the LORD
  because I have sinned against him,
until he pleads my cause
  and executes judgment for me.
He will bring me out to the light;
  I shall look upon his vindication.
10 Then my enemy will see,
  and shame will cover her who said to
    me,
  "Where is the LORD your God?"

---

[1] Or Will the LORD accept [2] Or steadfast love [3] The meaning of the Hebrew is uncertain [4] Or Are there still treasures [5] Hebrew whose [6] Hebrew For the statutes of Omri are kept
[7] Hebrew its [8] Hebrew bosom

My eyes will look upon her;
>> now she will be trampled down
>> like the mire of the streets.

11 A day for the building of your walls!
>> In that day the boundary shall be far
>> extended.
12 In that day they[1] will come to you,
>> from Assyria and the cities of Egypt,
>> and from Egypt to the River,[2]
>>> from sea to sea and from mountain to
>>> mountain.
13 But the earth will be desolate
>> because of its inhabitants,
>> for the fruit of their deeds.

14 Shepherd your people with your staff,
>> the flock of your inheritance,
>> who dwell alone in a forest
>> in the midst of a garden land;[3]
>> let them graze in Bashan and Gilead
>> as in the days of old.
15 As in the days when you came out of the
>> land of Egypt,
>> I will show them[4] marvelous things.
16 The nations shall see and be ashamed of all
>> their might;

they shall lay their hands on their
>> mouths;
>> their ears shall be deaf;
17 they shall lick the dust like a serpent,
>> like the crawling things of the earth;
they shall come trembling out of their
>> strongholds;
>> they shall turn in dread to the LORD our
>> God,
>> and they shall be in fear of you.

God's Steadfast Love and Compassion

18 Who is a God like you, pardoning iniq-
>> uity
>> and passing over transgression
>> for the remnant of his inheritance?
He does not retain his anger forever,
>> because he delights in steadfast love.
19 He will again have compassion on us;
>> he will tread our iniquities underfoot.
You will cast all our[5] sins
>> into the depths of the sea.
20 You will show faithfulness to Jacob
>> and steadfast love to Abraham,
>> as you have sworn to our fathers
>> from the days of old.

---

[1] Hebrew *he* [2] That is, the Euphrates [3] Hebrew *of Carmel* [4] Hebrew *him* [5] Hebrew *their*

NAHUM

1 An oracle concerning Nineveh. The book of the vision of Nahum of Elkosh.

God's Wrath Against Nineveh

2 The Lord is a jealous and avenging God;
  the Lord is avenging and wrathful;
  the Lord takes vengeance on his adversaries
  and keeps wrath for his enemies.
3 The Lord is slow to anger and great in
    power,
  and the Lord will by no means clear the
    guilty.
  His way is in whirlwind and storm,
  and the clouds are the dust of his feet.
4 He rebukes the sea and makes it dry;
  he dries up all the rivers;
  Bashan and Carmel wither;
  the bloom of Lebanon withers.
5 The mountains quake before him;
  the hills melt;
  the earth heaves before him,
  the world and all who dwell in it.

6 Who can stand before his indignation?
  Who can endure the heat of his anger?
  His wrath is poured out like fire,
  and the rocks are broken into pieces by
    him.
7 The Lord is good,
  a stronghold in the day of trouble;
  he knows those who take refuge in him.
8 But with an overflowing flood
  he will make a complete end of the adversaries,[1]
  and will pursue his enemies into darkness.
9 What do you plot against the Lord?
  He will make a complete end;
  trouble will not rise up a second time.
10 For they are like entangled thorns,
  like drunkards as they drink;
  they are consumed like stubble fully
    dried.
11 From you came one
  who plotted evil against the Lord,
  a worthless counselor.

12 Thus says the Lord,
  "Though they are at full strength and many,
  they will be cut down and pass away.

Though I have afflicted you,
  I will afflict you no more.
13 And now I will break his yoke from off you
  and will burst your bonds apart."

14 The Lord has given commandment about
    you:
  "No more shall your name be perpetuated;
  from the house of your gods I will cut off
  the carved image and the metal image.
  I will make your grave, for you are vile."

15[2] Behold, upon the mountains, the feet of
    him
  who brings good news,
  who publishes peace!
  Keep your feasts, O Judah;
  fulfill your vows,
  for never again shall the worthless pass
    through you;
  he is utterly cut off.

The Destruction of Nineveh

2 The scatterer has come up against you.
  Man the ramparts;
  watch the road;
  dress for battle;[3]
  collect all your strength.

2 For the Lord is restoring the majesty of
    Jacob
  as the majesty of Israel,
  for plunderers have plundered them
  and ruined their branches.

3 The shield of his mighty men is red;
  his soldiers are clothed in scarlet.
  The chariots come with flashing metal
  on the day he musters them;
  the cypress spears are brandished.
4 The chariots race madly through the
    streets;
  they rush to and fro through the
    squares;
  they gleam like torches;
  they dart like lightning.
5 He remembers his officers;
  they stumble as they go,
  they hasten to the wall;
  the siege tower[4] is set up.

---

[1] Hebrew *of her place* [2] Ch 2:1 in Hebrew [3] Hebrew *gird your loins* [4] Or *the mantelet*

6 The river gates are opened;
    the palace melts away;
7 its mistress[1] is stripped;[2] she is carried off,
    her slave girls lamenting,
    moaning like doves
    and beating their breasts.
8 Nineveh is like a pool
    whose waters run away.[3]
"Halt! Halt!" they cry,
    but none turns back.
9 Plunder the silver,
    plunder the gold!
There is no end of the treasure
    or of the wealth of all precious things.

10 Desolate! Desolation and ruin!
    Hearts melt and knees tremble;
anguish is in all loins;
    all faces grow pale!
11 Where is the lions' den,
    the feeding place of the young lions,
where the lion and lioness went,
    where his cubs were, with none to disturb?
12 The lion tore enough for his cubs
    and strangled prey for his lionesses;
he filled his caves with prey
    and his dens with torn flesh.

13 Behold, I am against you, declares the LORD of hosts, and I will burn your[4] chariots in smoke, and the sword shall devour your young lions. I will cut off your prey from the earth, and the voice of your messengers shall no longer be heard.

Woe to Nineveh

3 Woe to the bloody city,
    all full of lies and plunder—
    no end to the prey!
2 The crack of the whip, and rumble of the
    wheel,
    galloping horse and bounding chariot!
3 Horsemen charging,
    flashing sword and glittering spear,
hosts of slain,
    heaps of corpses,
dead bodies without end—
    they stumble over the bodies!
4 And all for the countless whorings of the
    prostitute,
    graceful and of deadly charms,
who betrays nations with her whorings,
    and peoples with her charms.

5 Behold, I am against you,
    declares the LORD of hosts,
    and will lift up your skirts over your
    face;
and I will make nations look at your
    nakedness
    and kingdoms at your shame.
6 I will throw filth at you
    and treat you with contempt
    and make you a spectacle.
7 And all who look at you will shrink from
    you and say,
"Wasted is Nineveh; who will grieve for
    her?"
    Where shall I seek comforters for you?

8 Are you better than Thebes[5]
    that sat by the Nile,
with water around her,
    her rampart a sea,
    and water her wall?
9 Cush was her strength;
    Egypt too, and that without limit;
    Put and the Libyans were her[6] helpers.

10 Yet she became an exile;
    she went into captivity;
her infants were dashed in pieces
    at the head of every street;
for her honored men lots were cast,
    and all her great men were bound in
    chains.
11 You also will be drunken;
    you will go into hiding;
you will seek a refuge from the enemy.
12 All your fortresses are like fig trees
    with first-ripe figs—
if shaken they fall
    into the mouth of the eater.
13 Behold, your troops
    are women in your midst.
The gates of your land
    are wide open to your enemies;
    fire has devoured your bars.

14 Draw water for the siege;
    strengthen your forts;
go into the clay;
    tread the mortar;
    take hold of the brick mold!
15 There will the fire devour you;
    the sword will cut you off.
    It will devour you like the locust.

---

[1] The meaning of the Hebrew word rendered *its mistress* is uncertain [2] Or *exiled* [3] Compare Septuagint; the meaning of the Hebrew is uncertain [4] Hebrew *her* [5] Hebrew *No-amon* [6] Hebrew *your*

Multiply yourselves like the locust;
    multiply like the grasshopper!

16 You increased your merchants
    more than the stars of the heavens.
The locust spreads its wings and flies
    away.

17 Your princes are like grasshoppers,
    your scribes[1] like clouds of locusts
settling on the fences
    in a day of cold—
when the sun rises, they fly away;
    no one knows where they are.

18 Your shepherds are asleep,
    O king of Assyria;
    your nobles slumber.
Your people are scattered on the mountains
    with none to gather them.

19 There is no easing your hurt;
    your wound is grievous.
All who hear the news about you
    clap their hands over you.
For upon whom has not come
    your unceasing evil?

---

[1] Or marshals

HABAKKUK

1

The oracle that Habakkuk the prophet saw.

Habakkuk's Complaint

2 O LORD, how long shall I cry for help,
  and you will not hear?
  Or cry to you "Violence!"
  and you will not save?
3 Why do you make me see iniquity,
  and why do you idly look at wrong?
  Destruction and violence are before me;
  strife and contention arise.
4 So the law is paralyzed,
  and justice never goes forth.
  For the wicked surround the righteous;
  so justice goes forth perverted.

The LORD's Answer

5 "Look among the nations, and see;
  wonder and be astounded.
  For I am doing a work in your days
  that you would not believe if told.
6 For behold, I am raising up the Chaldeans,
  that bitter and hasty nation,
  who march through the breadth of the
  earth,
  to seize dwellings not their own.
7 They are dreaded and fearsome;
  their justice and dignity go forth from
  themselves.
8 Their horses are swifter than leopards,
  more fierce than the evening wolves;
  their horsemen press proudly on.
  Their horsemen come from afar;
  they fly like an eagle swift to devour.
9 They all come for violence,
  all their faces forward.
  They gather captives like sand.
10 At kings they scoff,
  and at rulers they laugh.
  They laugh at every fortress,
  for they pile up earth and take it.
11 Then they sweep by like the wind and go
  on,
  guilty men, whose own might is their
  god!"

Habakkuk's Second Complaint

12 Are you not from everlasting,
  O LORD my God, my Holy One?
  We shall not die.

O LORD, you have ordained them as a judgment,
  and you, O Rock, have established them
  for reproof.
13 You who are of purer eyes than to see evil
  and cannot look at wrong,
  why do you idly look at traitors
  and remain silent when the wicked
  swallows up
  the man more righteous than he?
14 You make mankind like the fish of the sea,
  like crawling things that have no ruler.
15 He[1] brings all of them up with a hook;
  he drags them out with his net;
  he gathers them in his dragnet;
  so he rejoices and is glad.
16 Therefore he sacrifices to his net
  and makes offerings to his dragnet;
  for by them he lives in luxury,[2]
  and his food is rich.
17 Is he then to keep on emptying his net
  and mercilessly killing nations forever?

2

I will take my stand at my watchpost
  and station myself on the tower,
  and look out to see what he will say to me,
  and what I will answer concerning my
  complaint.

The Righteous Shall Live by His Faith

2 And the LORD answered me:

"Write the vision;
  make it plain on tablets,
  so he may run who reads it.
3 For still the vision awaits its appointed
  time;
  it hastens to the end—it will not lie.
  If it seems slow, wait for it;
  it will surely come; it will not delay.

4 "Behold, his soul is puffed up; it is not
  upright within him,
  but the righteous shall live by his faith.[3]

5 "Moreover, wine[4] is a traitor,
  an arrogant man who is never at rest.[5]
  His greed is as wide as Sheol;
  like death he has never enough.
  He gathers for himself all nations
  and collects as his own all peoples."

[1] That is, the wicked foe [2] Hebrew *his portion is fat* [3] Or *faithfulness* [4] Masoretic Text; Dead Sea Scroll *wealth* [5] The meaning of the Hebrew of these two lines is uncertain

Woe to the Chaldeans

6 Shall not all these take up their taunt against
him, with scoffing and riddles for him, and say,

"Woe to him who heaps up what is not his
own—
for how long?—
and loads himself with pledges!"
7 Will not your debtors suddenly arise,
and those awake who will make you
tremble?
Then you will be spoil for them.
8 Because you have plundered many nations,
all the remnant of the peoples shall
plunder you,
for the blood of man and violence to the
earth,
to cities and all who dwell in them.

9 "Woe to him who gets evil gain for his house,
to set his nest on high,
to be safe from the reach of harm!
10 You have devised shame for your house
by cutting off many peoples;
you have forfeited your life.
11 For the stone will cry out from the wall,
and the beam from the woodwork
respond.

12 "Woe to him who builds a town with blood
and founds a city on iniquity!
13 Behold, is it not from the LORD of hosts
that peoples labor merely for fire,
and nations weary themselves for nothing?
14 For the earth will be filled
with the knowledge of the glory of the
LORD
as the waters cover the sea.

15 "Woe to him who makes his neighbors
drink—
you pour out your wrath and make
them drunk,
in order to gaze at their nakedness!
16 You will have your fill of shame instead of
glory.
Drink, yourself, and show your uncircumcision!
The cup in the LORD's right hand
will come around to you,
and utter shame will come upon your
glory!

17 The violence done to Lebanon will overwhelm you,
as will the destruction of the beasts that
terrified them,
for the blood of man and violence to the
earth,
to cities and all who dwell in them.

18 "What profit is an idol
when its maker has shaped it,
a metal image, a teacher of lies?
For its maker trusts in his own creation
when he makes speechless idols!
19 Woe to him who says to a wooden thing,
Awake;
to a silent stone, Arise!
Can this teach?
Behold, it is overlaid with gold and silver,
and there is no breath at all in it.
20 But the LORD is in his holy temple;
let all the earth keep silence before him."

Habakkuk's Prayer

3 A prayer of Habakkuk the prophet, according to Shigionoth.

2 O LORD, I have heard the report of you,
and your work, O LORD, do I fear.
In the midst of the years revive it;
in the midst of the years make it known;
in wrath remember mercy.
3 God came from Teman,
and the Holy One from Mount Paran.
Selah

His splendor covered the heavens,
and the earth was full of his praise.
4 His brightness was like the light;
rays flashed from his hand;
and there he veiled his power.
5 Before him went pestilence,
and plague followed at his heels.[1]
6 He stood and measured the earth;
he looked and shook the nations;
then the eternal mountains were scattered;
the everlasting hills sank low.
His were the everlasting ways.
7 I saw the tents of Cushan in affliction;
the curtains of the land of Midian did
tremble.
8 Was your wrath against the rivers,
O LORD?
Was your anger against the rivers,
or your indignation against the sea,

[1] Hebrew *feet*

when you rode on your horses,
 on your chariot of salvation?
9 You stripped the sheath from your bow,
 calling for many arrows.[1] *Selah*
You split the earth with rivers.
10 The mountains saw you and writhed;
 the raging waters swept on;
the deep gave forth its voice;
 it lifted its hands on high.
11 The sun and moon stood still in their
 place
  at the light of your arrows as they
  sped,
 at the flash of your glittering spear.
12 You marched through the earth in fury;
 you threshed the nations in anger.
13 You went out for the salvation of your
 people,
 for the salvation of your anointed.
You crushed the head of the house of the
 wicked,
 laying him bare from thigh to neck.[2]
         Selah
14 You pierced with his own arrows the heads
 of his warriors,
 who came like a whirlwind to scatter
 me,

rejoicing as if to devour the poor in
 secret.
15 You trampled the sea with your horses,
 the surging of mighty waters.

16 I hear, and my body trembles;
 my lips quiver at the sound;
rottenness enters into my bones;
 my legs tremble beneath me.
Yet I will quietly wait for the day of trouble
 to come upon people who invade us.

Habakkuk Rejoices in the LORD

17 Though the fig tree should not blossom,
 nor fruit be on the vines,
the produce of the olive fail
 and the fields yield no food,
the flock be cut off from the fold
 and there be no herd in the stalls,
18 yet I will rejoice in the LORD;
 I will take joy in the God of my salvation.
19 GOD, the Lord, is my strength;
 he makes my feet like the deer's;
 he makes me tread on my high places.

To the choirmaster: with stringed[3] instruments.

---

[1] The meaning of the Hebrew line is uncertain [2] The meaning of the Hebrew line is uncertain [3] Hebrew *my stringed*

ZEPHANIAH

1 The word of the LORD that came to Zephaniah the son of Cushi, son of Gedaliah, son of Amariah, son of Hezekiah, in the days of Josiah the son of Amon, king of Judah.

The Coming Judgment on Judah

2 "I will utterly sweep away everything
   from the face of the earth," declares the
      LORD.
3 "I will sweep away man and beast;
   I will sweep away the birds of the heavens
      and the fish of the sea,
   and the rubble[1] with the wicked.
   I will cut off mankind
      from the face of the earth," declares the
         LORD.
4 "I will stretch out my hand against Judah
   and against all the inhabitants of
      Jerusalem;
   and I will cut off from this place the remnant of Baal
      and the name of the idolatrous priests
         along with the priests,
5 those who bow down on the roofs
      to the host of the heavens,
   those who bow down and swear to the
      LORD
   and yet swear by Milcom,[2]
6 those who have turned back from following the LORD,
   who do not seek the LORD or inquire of
      him."

The Day of the LORD Is Near

7 Be silent before the Lord GOD!
   For the day of the LORD is near;
   the LORD has prepared a sacrifice
      and consecrated his guests.
8 And on the day of the LORD's sacrifice—
   "I will punish the officials and the king's
      sons
      and all who array themselves in foreign
         attire.
9 On that day I will punish
      everyone who leaps over the threshold,
   and those who fill their master's[3] house
      with violence and fraud.

10 "On that day," declares the LORD,
   "a cry will be heard from the Fish Gate,
   a wail from the Second Quarter,
      a loud crash from the hills.
11 Wail, O inhabitants of the Mortar!
      For all the traders[4] are no more;
   all who weigh out silver are cut off.
12 At that time I will search Jerusalem with
      lamps,
   and I will punish the men
   who are complacent,[5]
      those who say in their hearts,
   'The LORD will not do good,
      nor will he do ill.'
13 Their goods shall be plundered,
      and their houses laid waste.
   Though they build houses,
      they shall not inhabit them;
   though they plant vineyards,
      they shall not drink wine from them."

14 The great day of the LORD is near,
      near and hastening fast;
   the sound of the day of the LORD is bitter;
      the mighty man cries aloud there.
15 A day of wrath is that day,
      a day of distress and anguish,
   a day of ruin and devastation,
      a day of darkness and gloom,
   a day of clouds and thick darkness,
16   a day of trumpet blast and battle cry
   against the fortified cities
      and against the lofty battlements.

17 I will bring distress on mankind,
      so that they shall walk like the blind,
      because they have sinned against the
         LORD;
   their blood shall be poured out like dust,
      and their flesh like dung.
18 Neither their silver nor their gold
      shall be able to deliver them
      on the day of the wrath of the LORD.
   In the fire of his jealousy,
      all the earth shall be consumed;
   for a full and sudden end
      he will make of all the inhabitants of
         the earth.

---

[1] Or stumbling blocks (that is, idols) [2] Or their king [3] Or their Lord's [4] Or all the people of Canaan [5] Hebrew are thickening on the dregs [of their wine]

Judgment on Judah's Enemies

2 Gather together, yes, gather,
    O shameless nation,
² before the decree takes effect[1]
        —before the day passes away like
            chaff—
    before there comes upon you
        the burning anger of the LORD,
    before there comes upon you
        the day of the anger of the LORD.
³ Seek the LORD, all you humble of the land,
        who do his just commands;[2]
    seek righteousness; seek humility;
        perhaps you may be hidden
        on the day of the anger of the LORD.
⁴ For Gaza shall be deserted,
        and Ashkelon shall become a desola-
            tion;
    Ashdod's people shall be driven out at
        noon,
        and Ekron shall be uprooted.

⁵ Woe to you inhabitants of the seacoast,
        you nation of the Cherethites!
    The word of the LORD is against you,
        O Canaan, land of the Philistines;
        and I will destroy you until no inhabi-
            tant is left.
⁶ And you, O seacoast, shall be pastures,
        with meadows[3] for shepherds
        and folds for flocks.
⁷ The seacoast shall become the possession
        of the remnant of the house of Judah,
        on which they shall graze,
    and in the houses of Ashkelon
        they shall lie down at evening.
    For the LORD their God will be mindful of
        them
        and restore their fortunes.

⁸ "I have heard the taunts of Moab
        and the revilings of the Ammonites,
    how they have taunted my people
        and made boasts against their territory.
⁹ Therefore, as I live," declares the LORD of
        hosts,
        the God of Israel,
    "Moab shall become like Sodom,
        and the Ammonites like Gomorrah,
    a land possessed by nettles and salt pits,
        and a waste forever.

The remnant of my people shall plunder
    them,
    and the survivors of my nation shall
        possess them."
¹⁰ This shall be their lot in return for their
        pride,
    because they taunted and boasted
        against the people of the LORD of hosts.
¹¹ The LORD will be awesome against them;
    for he will famish all the gods of the
        earth,
    and to him shall bow down,
        each in its place,
        all the lands of the nations.

¹² You also, O Cushites,
        shall be slain by my sword.

¹³ And he will stretch out his hand against
            the north
        and destroy Assyria,
    and he will make Nineveh a desolation,
        a dry waste like the desert.
¹⁴ Herds shall lie down in her midst,
        all kinds of beasts;[4]
    even the owl and the hedgehog[5]
        shall lodge in her capitals;
    a voice shall hoot in the window;
        devastation will be on the threshold;
        for her cedar work will be laid bare.
¹⁵ This is the exultant city
        that lived securely,
    that said in her heart,
        "I am, and there is no one else."
    What a desolation she has become,
        a lair for wild beasts!
    Everyone who passes by her
        hisses and shakes his fist.

Judgment on Jerusalem and the Nations

3 Woe to her who is rebellious and defiled,
    the oppressing city!
² She listens to no voice;
        she accepts no correction.
    She does not trust in the LORD;
        she does not draw near to her God.

³ Her officials within her
        are roaring lions;
    her judges are evening wolves
        that leave nothing till the morning.
⁴ Her prophets are fickle, treacherous men;
    her priests profane what is holy;
        they do violence to the law.

---

[1] Hebrew gives birth [2] Or who carry out his judgment [3] Or caves [4] Hebrew beasts of every nation [5] The identity of the animals rendered owl and hedgehog is uncertain

5 The LORD within her is righteous;
  he does no injustice;
every morning he shows forth his justice;
  each dawn he does not fail;
  but the unjust knows no shame.

6 "I have cut off nations;
  their battlements are in ruins;
I have laid waste their streets
  so that no one walks in them;
their cities have been made desolate,
  without a man, without an inhabitant.

7 I said, 'Surely you will fear me;
  you will accept correction.
Then your[1] dwelling would not be cut off
  according to all that I have appointed
    against you.'[2]
But all the more they were eager
  to make all their deeds corrupt.

8 "Therefore wait for me," declares the LORD,
  "for the day when I rise up to seize the
    prey.
For my decision is to gather nations,
  to assemble kingdoms,
to pour out upon them my indignation,
  all my burning anger;
for in the fire of my jealousy
  all the earth shall be consumed.

The Conversion of the Nations

9 "For at that time I will change the speech of
    the peoples
  to a pure speech,
that all of them may call upon the name of
    the LORD
  and serve him with one accord.

10 From beyond the rivers of Cush
  my worshipers, the daughter of my dis-
    persed ones,
  shall bring my offering.

11 "On that day you shall not be put to shame
  because of the deeds by which you have
    rebelled against me;
for then I will remove from your midst
  your proudly exultant ones,
and you shall no longer be haughty
  in my holy mountain.

12 But I will leave in your midst
  a people humble and lowly.
They shall seek refuge in the name of the
    LORD,

13   those who are left in Israel;
they shall do no injustice
  and speak no lies,
nor shall there be found in their mouth
  a deceitful tongue.
For they shall graze and lie down,
  and none shall make them afraid."

Israel's Joy and Restoration

14 Sing aloud, O daughter of Zion;
  shout, O Israel!
Rejoice and exult with all your heart,
  O daughter of Jerusalem!

15 The LORD has taken away the judgments
    against you;
  he has cleared away your enemies.
The King of Israel, the LORD, is in your
    midst;
  you shall never again fear evil.

16 On that day it shall be said to Jerusalem:
"Fear not, O Zion;
  let not your hands grow weak.

17 The LORD your God is in your midst,
  a mighty one who will save;
he will rejoice over you with gladness;
  he will quiet you by his love;
he will exult over you with loud singing.

18 I will gather those of you who mourn for
    the festival,
  so that you will no longer suffer
    reproach.[3]

19 Behold, at that time I will deal
  with all your oppressors.
And I will save the lame
  and gather the outcast,
and I will change their shame into praise
  and renown in all the earth.

20 At that time I will bring you in,
  at the time when I gather you together;
for I will make you renowned and praised
  among all the peoples of the earth,
when I restore your fortunes
  before your eyes," says the LORD.

[1] Hebrew her [2] Hebrew her [3] The meaning of the Hebrew is uncertain

HAGGAI

The Command to Rebuild the Temple

1 In the second year of Darius the king, in the sixth month, on the first day of the month, the word of the LORD came by the hand of Haggai the prophet to Zerubbabel the son of Shealtiel, governor of Judah, and to Joshua the son of Jehozadak, the high priest: ²"Thus says the LORD of hosts: These people say the time has not yet come to rebuild the house of the LORD." ³Then the word of the LORD came by the hand of Haggai the prophet, ⁴"Is it a time for you yourselves to dwell in your paneled houses, while this house lies in ruins? ⁵Now, therefore, thus says the LORD of hosts: Consider your ways. ⁶You have sown much, and harvested little. You eat, but you never have enough; you drink, but you never have your fill. You clothe yourselves, but no one is warm. And he who earns wages does so to put them into a bag with holes.

⁷"Thus says the LORD of hosts: Consider your ways. ⁸Go up to the hills and bring wood and build the house, that I may take pleasure in it and that I may be glorified, says the LORD. ⁹You looked for much, and behold, it came to little. And when you brought it home, I blew it away. Why? declares the LORD of hosts. Because of my house that lies in ruins, while each of you busies himself with his own house. ¹⁰Therefore the heavens above you have withheld the dew, and the earth has withheld its produce. ¹¹And I have called for a drought on the land and the hills, on the grain, the new wine, the oil, on what the ground brings forth, on man and beast, and on all their labors."

The People Obey the LORD

¹²Then Zerubbabel the son of Shealtiel, and Joshua the son of Jehozadak, the high priest, with all the remnant of the people, obeyed the voice of the LORD their God, and the words of Haggai the prophet, as the LORD their God had sent him. And the people feared the LORD. ¹³Then Haggai, the messenger of the LORD, spoke to the people with the LORD's message, "I am with you, declares the LORD." ¹⁴And the LORD stirred up the spirit of Zerubbabel the son of Shealtiel, governor of Judah, and the spirit of Joshua the son of Jehozadak, the high priest, and the spirit of all the remnant of the people.

And they came and worked on the house of the LORD of hosts, their God, ¹⁵on the twenty-fourth day of the month, in the sixth month, in the second year of Darius the king.

The Coming Glory of the Temple

2 In the seventh month, on the twenty-first day of the month, the word of the LORD came by the hand of Haggai the prophet: ²"Speak now to Zerubbabel the son of Shealtiel, governor of Judah, and to Joshua the son of Jehozadak, the high priest, and to all the remnant of the people, and say, ³'Who is left among you who saw this house in its former glory? How do you see it now? Is it not as nothing in your eyes? ⁴Yet now be strong, O Zerubbabel, declares the LORD. Be strong, O Joshua, son of Jehozadak, the high priest. Be strong, all you people of the land, declares the LORD. Work, for I am with you, declares the LORD of hosts, ⁵according to the covenant that I made with you when you came out of Egypt. My Spirit remains in your midst. Fear not. ⁶For thus says the LORD of hosts: Yet once more, in a little while, I will shake the heavens and the earth and the sea and the dry land. ⁷And I will shake all nations, so that the treasures of all nations shall come in, and I will fill this house with glory, says the LORD of hosts. ⁸The silver is mine, and the gold is mine, declares the LORD of hosts. ⁹The latter glory of this house shall be greater than the former, says the LORD of hosts. And in this place I will give peace, declares the LORD of hosts.'"

Blessings for a Defiled People

¹⁰On the twenty-fourth day of the ninth month, in the second year of Darius, the word of the LORD came by Haggai the prophet, ¹¹"Thus says the LORD of hosts: Ask the priests about the law: ¹²'If someone carries holy meat in the fold of his garment and touches with his fold bread or stew or wine or oil or any kind of food, does it become holy?'" The priests answered and said, "No." ¹³Then Haggai said, "If someone who is unclean by contact with a dead body touches any of these, does it become unclean?" The priests answered and said, "It does become unclean."

14 Then Haggai answered and said, "So is it with this people, and with this nation before me, declares the LORD, and so with every work of their hands. And what they offer there is unclean. 15 Now then, consider from this day onward.[1] Before stone was placed upon stone in the temple of the LORD, 16 how did you fare? When[2] one came to a heap of twenty measures, there were but ten. When one came to the wine vat to draw fifty measures, there were but twenty. 17 I struck you and all the products of your toil with blight and with mildew and with hail, yet you did not turn to me, declares the LORD. 18 Consider from this day onward, from the twenty-fourth day of the ninth month. Since the day that the foundation of the LORD's temple was laid, consider: 19 Is the seed yet in the barn? Indeed, the vine, the fig tree, the pomegranate, and the olive tree have yielded nothing. But from this day on I will bless you."

Zerubbabel Chosen as a Signet

20 The word of the LORD came a second time to Haggai on the twenty-fourth day of the month, 21 "Speak to Zerubbabel, governor of Judah, saying, I am about to shake the heavens and the earth, 22 and to overthrow the throne of kingdoms. I am about to destroy the strength of the kingdoms of the nations, and overthrow the chariots and their riders. And the horses and their riders shall go down, every one by the sword of his brother. 23 On that day, declares the LORD of hosts, I will take you, O Zerubbabel my servant, the son of Shealtiel, declares the LORD, and make you like a[3] signet ring, for I have chosen you, declares the LORD of hosts."

---

[1] Or backward; also verse 18. [2] Probable reading (compare Septuagint); Hebrew LORD, since they were. When [3] Hebrew the

ZECHARIAH

A Call to Return to the LORD

1 In the eighth month, in the second year of Darius, the word of the LORD came to the prophet Zechariah, the son of Berechiah, son of Iddo, saying, ² "The LORD was very angry with your fathers. ³ Therefore say to them, Thus declares the LORD of hosts: Return to me, says the LORD of hosts, and I will return to you, says the LORD of hosts. ⁴ Do not be like your fathers, to whom the former prophets cried out, 'Thus says the LORD of hosts, Return from your evil ways and from your evil deeds.' But they did not hear or pay attention to me, declares the LORD. ⁵ Your fathers, where are they? And the prophets, do they live forever? ⁶ But my words and my statutes, which I commanded my servants the prophets, did they not overtake your fathers? So they repented and said, 'As the LORD of hosts purposed to deal with us for our ways and deeds, so has he dealt with us.'"

A Vision of a Horseman

⁷ On the twenty-fourth day of the eleventh month, which is the month of Shebat, in the second year of Darius, the word of the LORD came to the prophet Zechariah, the son of Berechiah, son of Iddo, saying, ⁸ "I saw in the night, and behold, a man riding on a red horse! He was standing among the myrtle trees in the glen, and behind him were red, sorrel, and white horses. ⁹ Then I said, 'What are these, my lord?' The angel who talked with me said to me, 'I will show you what they are.' ¹⁰ So the man who was standing among the myrtle trees answered, 'These are they whom the LORD has sent to patrol the earth.' ¹¹ And they answered the angel of the LORD who was standing among the myrtle trees, and said, 'We have patrolled the earth, and behold, all the earth remains at rest.' ¹² Then the angel of the LORD said, 'O LORD of hosts, how long will you have no mercy on Jerusalem and the cities of Judah, against which you have been angry these seventy years?' ¹³ And the LORD answered gracious and comforting words to the angel who talked with me. ¹⁴ So the angel who talked with me said to me, 'Cry out, Thus says the LORD of hosts: I am exceedingly jealous for Jerusalem and for Zion. ¹⁵ And I am exceedingly angry with the nations that are at ease; for while I was angry but a little, they furthered the disaster. ¹⁶ Therefore, thus says the LORD, I have returned to Jerusalem with mercy; my house shall be built in it, declares the LORD of hosts, and the measuring line shall be stretched out over Jerusalem. ¹⁷ Cry out again, Thus says the LORD of hosts: My cities shall again overflow with prosperity, and the LORD will again comfort Zion and again choose Jerusalem.'"

A Vision of Horns and Craftsmen

¹⁸ ¹ And I lifted my eyes and saw, and behold, four horns! ¹⁹ And I said to the angel who talked with me, "What are these?" And he said to me, "These are the horns that have scattered Judah, Israel, and Jerusalem." ²⁰ Then the LORD showed me four craftsmen. ²¹ And I said, "What are these coming to do?" He said, "These are the horns that scattered Judah, so that no one raised his head. And these have come to terrify them, to cast down the horns of the nations who lifted up their horns against the land of Judah to scatter it."

A Vision of a Man with a Measuring Line

2 ² And I lifted my eyes and saw, and behold, a man with a measuring line in his hand! ² Then I said, "Where are you going?" And he said to me, "To measure Jerusalem, to see what is its width and what is its length." ³ And behold, the angel who talked with me came forward, and another angel came forward to meet him ⁴ and said to him, "Run, say to that young man, 'Jerusalem shall be inhabited as villages without walls, because of the multitude of people and livestock in it. ⁵ And I will be to her a wall of fire all around, declares the LORD, and I will be the glory in her midst.'"

⁶ Up! Up! Flee from the land of the north, declares the LORD. For I have spread you abroad as the four winds of the heavens, declares the LORD. ⁷ Up! Escape to Zion, you who dwell with the daughter of Babylon. ⁸ For thus said the LORD of hosts, after his glory sent me³ to the nations who plundered you, for he who touches you touches the apple of his eye: ⁹ "Behold, I will shake my hand over them, and they shall become plunder for those who served them. Then you will know that the

---

¹ Ch 2:1 in Hebrew ² Ch 2:5 in Hebrew ³ Or he sent me after glory

LORD of hosts has sent me. ¹⁰ Sing and rejoice, O daughter of Zion, for behold, I come and I will dwell in your midst, declares the LORD. ¹¹ And many nations shall join themselves to the LORD in that day, and shall be my people. And I will dwell in your midst, and you shall know that the LORD of hosts has sent me to you. ¹² And the LORD will inherit Judah as his portion in the holy land, and will again choose Jerusalem."

¹³ Be silent, all flesh, before the LORD, for he has roused himself from his holy dwelling.

A Vision of Joshua the High Priest

3 Then he showed me Joshua the high priest standing before the angel of the LORD, and Satan[1] standing at his right hand to accuse him. ² And the LORD said to Satan, "The LORD rebuke you, O Satan! The LORD who has chosen Jerusalem rebuke you! Is not this a brand[2] plucked from the fire?" ³ Now Joshua was standing before the angel, clothed with filthy garments. ⁴ And the angel said to those who were standing before him, "Remove the filthy garments from him." And to him he said, "Behold, I have taken your iniquity away from you, and I will clothe you with pure vestments." ⁵ And I said, "Let them put a clean turban on his head." So they put a clean turban on his head and clothed him with garments. And the angel of the LORD was standing by.

⁶ And the angel of the LORD solemnly assured Joshua, ⁷ "Thus says the LORD of hosts: If you will walk in my ways and keep my charge, then you shall rule my house and have charge of my courts, and I will give you the right of access among those who are standing here. ⁸ Hear now, O Joshua the high priest, you and your friends who sit before you, for they are men who are a sign: behold, I will bring my servant the Branch. ⁹ For behold, on the stone that I have set before Joshua, on a single stone with seven eyes,[3] I will engrave its inscription, declares the LORD of hosts, and I will remove the iniquity of this land in a single day. ¹⁰ In that day, declares the LORD of hosts, every one of you will invite his neighbor to come under his vine and under his fig tree."

A Vision of a Golden Lampstand

4 And the angel who talked with me came again and woke me, like a man who is awakened out of his sleep. ² And he said to me,

"What do you see?" I said, "I see, and behold, a lampstand all of gold, with a bowl on the top of it, and seven lamps on it, with seven lips on each of the lamps that are on the top of it. ³ And there are two olive trees by it, one on the right of the bowl and the other on its left." ⁴ And I said to the angel who talked with me, "What are these, my lord?" ⁵ Then the angel who talked with me answered and said to me, "Do you not know what these are?" I said, "No, my lord." ⁶ Then he said to me, "This is the word of the LORD to Zerubbabel: Not by might, nor by power, but by my Spirit, says the LORD of hosts. ⁷ Who are you, O great mountain? Before Zerubbabel you shall become a plain. And he shall bring forward the top stone amid shouts of 'Grace, grace to it!'"

⁸ Then the word of the LORD came to me, saying, ⁹ "The hands of Zerubbabel have laid the foundation of this house; his hands shall also complete it. Then you will know that the LORD of hosts has sent me to you. ¹⁰ For whoever has despised the day of small things shall rejoice, and shall see the plumb line in the hand of Zerubbabel.

"These seven are the eyes of the LORD, which range through the whole earth." ¹¹ Then I said to him, "What are these two olive trees on the right and the left of the lampstand?" ¹² And a second time I answered and said to him, "What are these two branches of the olive trees, which are beside the two golden pipes from which the golden oil[4] is poured out?" ¹³ He said to me, "Do you not know what these are?" I said, "No, my lord." ¹⁴ Then he said, "These are the two anointed ones[5] who stand by the Lord of the whole earth."

A Vision of a Flying Scroll

5 Again I lifted my eyes and saw, and behold, a flying scroll! ² And he said to me, "What do you see?" I answered, "I see a flying scroll. Its length is twenty cubits, and its width ten cubits."[6] ³ Then he said to me, "This is the curse that goes out over the face of the whole land. For everyone who steals shall be cleaned out according to what is on one side, and everyone who swears falsely[7] shall be cleaned out according to what is on the other side. ⁴ I will send it out, declares the LORD of hosts, and it shall enter the house of the thief, and the house of him who swears falsely by my name. And it shall remain in his house and consume it, both timber and stones."

---

[1] Hebrew *the Accuser* or *the Adversary* [2] That is, a burning stick [3] Or *facets* [4] Hebrew lacks *oil* [5] Hebrew *two sons of new oil* [6] A *cubit* was about 18 inches or 45 centimeters
[7] Hebrew lacks *falsely* (supplied from verse 4)

A Vision of a Woman in a Basket

[5] Then the angel who talked with me came forward and said to me, "Lift your eyes and see what this is that is going out." [6] And I said, "What is it?" He said, "This is the basket[1] that is going out." And he said, "This is their iniquity[2] in all the land." [7] And behold, the leaden cover was lifted, and there was a woman sitting in the basket! [8] And he said, "This is Wickedness." And he thrust her back into the basket, and thrust down the leaden weight on its opening.

[9] Then I lifted my eyes and saw, and behold, two women coming forward! The wind was in their wings. They had wings like the wings of a stork, and they lifted up the basket between earth and heaven. [10] Then I said to the angel who talked with me, "Where are they taking the basket?" [11] He said to me, "To the land of Shinar, to build a house for it. And when this is prepared, they will set the basket down there on its base."

A Vision of Four Chariots

[6] Again I lifted my eyes and saw, and behold, four chariots came out from between two mountains. And the mountains were mountains of bronze. [2] The first chariot had red horses, the second black horses, [3] the third white horses, and the fourth chariot dappled horses—all of them strong.[3] [4] Then I answered and said to the angel who talked with me, "What are these, my lord?" [5] And the angel answered and said to me, "These are going out to the four winds of heaven, after presenting themselves before the Lord of all the earth. [6] The chariot with the black horses goes toward the north country, the white ones go after them, and the dappled ones go toward the south country." [7] When the strong horses came out, they were impatient to go and patrol the earth. And he said, "Go, patrol the earth." So they patrolled the earth. [8] Then he cried to me, "Behold, those who go toward the north country have set my Spirit at rest in the north country."

The Crown and the Temple

[9] And the word of the Lord came to me: [10] "Take from the exiles Heldai, Tobijah, and Jedaiah, who have arrived from Babylon, and go the same day to the house of Josiah, the son of Zephaniah. [11] Take from them silver and gold, and make a crown, and set it on the head of Joshua, the son of Jehozadak, the high priest. [12] And say to him, 'Thus says the Lord of hosts, "Behold, the man whose name is the Branch: for he shall branch out from his place, and he shall build the temple of the Lord. [13] It is he who shall build the temple of the Lord and shall bear royal honor, and shall sit and rule on his throne. And there[4] shall be a priest on his throne, and the counsel of peace shall be between them both."' [14] And the crown shall be in the temple of the Lord as a reminder to Helem,[5] Tobijah, Jedaiah, and Hen the son of Zephaniah.

[15] "And those who are far off shall come and help to build the temple of the Lord. And you shall know that the Lord of hosts has sent me to you. And this shall come to pass, if you will diligently obey the voice of the Lord your God."

A Call for Justice and Mercy

[7] In the fourth year of King Darius, the word of the Lord came to Zechariah on the fourth day of the ninth month, which is Chislev. [2] Now the people of Bethel had sent Sharezer and Regem-melech and their men to entreat the favor of the Lord, [3] saying to the priests of the house of the Lord of hosts and the prophets, "Should I weep and abstain in the fifth month, as I have done for so many years?"

[4] Then the word of the Lord of hosts came to me: [5] "Say to all the people of the land and the priests, 'When you fasted and mourned in the fifth month and in the seventh, for these seventy years, was it for me that you fasted? [6] And when you eat and when you drink, do you not eat for yourselves and drink for yourselves? [7] Were not these the words that the Lord proclaimed by the former prophets, when Jerusalem was inhabited and prosperous, with her cities around her, and the South and the lowland were inhabited?'"

[8] And the word of the Lord came to Zechariah, saying, [9] "Thus says the Lord of hosts, Render true judgments, show kindness and mercy to one another, [10] do not oppress the widow, the fatherless, the sojourner, or the poor, and let none of you devise evil against another in your heart." [11] But they refused to pay attention and turned a stubborn shoulder and stopped their ears that they might not

---

[1] Hebrew ephah; also verses 7-11. An ephah was about 3/5 bushel or 22 liters [2] One Hebrew manuscript, Septuagint, Syriac; most Hebrew manuscripts eye [3] Or and the fourth chariot strong dappled horses [4] Or he [5] An alternate spelling of Heldai (verse 10)

hear.[1] [12]They made their hearts diamond-hard lest they should hear the law and the words that the LORD of hosts had sent by his Spirit through the former prophets. Therefore great anger came from the LORD of hosts. [13]"As I[2] called, and they would not hear, so they called, and I would not hear," says the LORD of hosts, [14]"and I scattered them with a whirlwind among all the nations that they had not known. Thus the land they left was desolate, so that no one went to and fro, and the pleasant land was made desolate."

The Coming Peace and Prosperity of Zion

8 And the word of the LORD of hosts came, saying, [2]"Thus says the LORD of hosts: I am jealous for Zion with great jealousy, and I am jealous for her with great wrath. [3]Thus says the LORD: I have returned to Zion and will dwell in the midst of Jerusalem, and Jerusalem shall be called the faithful city, and the mountain of the LORD of hosts, the holy mountain. [4]Thus says the LORD of hosts: Old men and old women shall again sit in the streets of Jerusalem, each with staff in hand because of great age. [5]And the streets of the city shall be full of boys and girls playing in its streets. [6]Thus says the LORD of hosts: If it is marvelous in the sight of the remnant of this people in those days, should it also be marvelous in my sight, declares the LORD of hosts? [7]Thus says the LORD of hosts: Behold, I will save my people from the east country and from the west country, [8]and I will bring them to dwell in the midst of Jerusalem. And they shall be my people, and I will be their God, in faithfulness and in righteousness."

[9]Thus says the LORD of hosts: "Let your hands be strong, you who in these days have been hearing these words from the mouth of the prophets who were present on the day that the foundation of the house of the LORD of hosts was laid, that the temple might be built. [10]For before those days there was no wage for man or any wage for beast, neither was there any safety from the foe for him who went out or came in, for I set every man against his neighbor. [11]But now I will not deal with the remnant of this people as in the former days, declares the LORD of hosts. [12]For there shall be a sowing of peace. The vine shall give its fruit, and the ground shall give its produce, and the heavens shall give their dew. And I will cause the remnant of this people to possess all these things. [13]And as you have been a byword of cursing among the nations, O house of Judah and house of Israel, so will I save you, and you shall be a blessing. Fear not, but let your hands be strong."

[14]For thus says the LORD of hosts: "As I purposed to bring disaster to you when your fathers provoked me to wrath, and I did not relent, says the LORD of hosts, [15]so again have I purposed in these days to bring good to Jerusalem and to the house of Judah; fear not. [16]These are the things that you shall do: Speak the truth to one another; render in your gates judgments that are true and make for peace; [17]do not devise evil in your hearts against one another, and love no false oath, for all these things I hate, declares the LORD."

[18]And the word of the LORD of hosts came to me, saying, [19]"Thus says the LORD of hosts: The fast of the fourth month and the fast of the fifth and the fast of the seventh and the fast of the tenth shall be to the house of Judah seasons of joy and gladness and cheerful feasts. Therefore love truth and peace.

[20]"Thus says the LORD of hosts: Peoples shall yet come, even the inhabitants of many cities. [21]The inhabitants of one city shall go to another, saying, 'Let us go at once to entreat the favor of the LORD and to seek the LORD of hosts; I myself am going.' [22]Many peoples and strong nations shall come to seek the LORD of hosts in Jerusalem and to entreat the favor of the LORD. [23]Thus says the LORD of hosts: In those days ten men from the nations of every tongue shall take hold of the robe of a Jew, saying, 'Let us go with you, for we have heard that God is with you.'"

Judgment on Israel's Enemies

9 The oracle of the word of the LORD is
 against the land of Hadrach
 and Damascus is its resting place.
For the LORD has an eye on mankind
 and on all the tribes of Israel,[3]
[2] and on Hamath also, which borders on it,
 Tyre and Sidon, though they are very
 wise.
[3] Tyre has built herself a rampart
 and heaped up silver like dust,
 and fine gold like the mud of the streets.
[4] But behold, the Lord will strip her of her
 possessions
 and strike down her power on the sea,
 and she shall be devoured by fire.

---

[1] Hebrew and made their ears too heavy to hear [2] Hebrew he [3] Or For the eye of mankind, especially of all the tribes of Israel, is toward the LORD

5 Ashkelon shall see it, and be afraid;
Gaza too, and shall writhe in anguish;
Ekron also, because its hopes are confounded.
The king shall perish from Gaza;
Ashkelon shall be uninhabited;
6 a mixed people[1] shall dwell in Ashdod,
and I will cut off the pride of Philistia.
7 I will take away its blood from its mouth,
and its abominations from between its
teeth;
it too shall be a remnant for our God;
it shall be like a clan in Judah,
and Ekron shall be like the Jebusites.
8 Then I will encamp at my house as a guard,
so that none shall march to and fro;
no oppressor shall again march over them,
for now I see with my own eyes.

The Coming King of Zion

9 Rejoice greatly, O daughter of Zion!
Shout aloud, O daughter of
Jerusalem!
Behold, your king is coming to you;
righteous and having salvation is he,
humble and mounted on a donkey,
on a colt, the foal of a donkey.
10 I will cut off the chariot from Ephraim
and the war horse from Jerusalem;
and the battle bow shall be cut off,
and he shall speak peace to the nations;
his rule shall be from sea to sea,
and from the River[2] to the ends of the
earth.
11 As for you also, because of the blood of my
covenant with you,
I will set your prisoners free from the
waterless pit.
12 Return to your stronghold, O prisoners of
hope;
today I declare that I will restore to you
double.
13 For I have bent Judah as my bow;
I have made Ephraim its arrow.
I will stir up your sons, O Zion,
against your sons, O Greece,
and wield you like a warrior's sword.

The LORD Will Save His People

14 Then the LORD will appear over them,
and his arrow will go forth like lightning;

the Lord GOD will sound the trumpet
and will march forth in the whirlwinds
of the south.
15 The LORD of hosts will protect them,
and they shall devour, and tread down
the sling stones,
and they shall drink and roar as if drunk
with wine,
and be full like a bowl,
drenched like the corners of the altar.
16 On that day the LORD their God will save
them,
as the flock of his people;
for like the jewels of a crown
they shall shine on his land.
17 For how great is his goodness, and how
great his beauty!
Grain shall make the young men flourish,
and new wine the young women.

The Restoration for Judah and Israel

10 Ask rain from the LORD
in the season of the spring rain,
from the LORD who makes the storm
clouds,
and he will give them showers of rain,
to everyone the vegetation in the field.
2 For the household gods utter nonsense,
and the diviners see lies;
they tell false dreams
and give empty consolation.
Therefore the people wander like sheep;
they are afflicted for lack of a shepherd.

3 "My anger is hot against the shepherds,
and I will punish the leaders;[3]
for the LORD of hosts cares for his flock, the
house of Judah,
and will make them like his majestic
steed in battle.
4 From him shall come the cornerstone,
from him the tent peg,
from him the battle bow,
from him every ruler—all of them
together.
5 They shall be like mighty men in battle,
trampling the foe in the mud of the
streets;
they shall fight because the LORD is with
them,
and they shall put to shame the riders
on horses.

---

[1] Or a foreign people; Hebrew a bastard   [2] That is, the Euphrates   [3] Hebrew the male goats

6 "I will strengthen the house of Judah,
  and I will save the house of Joseph.
I will bring them back because I have com-
      passion on them,
  and they shall be as though I had not
      rejected them,
    for I am the LORD their God and I will
      answer them.
7 Then Ephraim shall become like a mighty
      warrior,
  and their hearts shall be glad as with
      wine.
  Their children shall see it and be glad;
    their hearts shall rejoice in the LORD.

8 "I will whistle for them and gather them in,
  for I have redeemed them,
    and they shall be as many as they were
      before.
9 Though I scattered them among the
      nations,
  yet in far countries they shall remember
      me,
    and with their children they shall live
      and return.
10 I will bring them home from the land of
      Egypt,
  and gather them from Assyria,
  and I will bring them to the land of Gilead
      and to Lebanon,
    till there is no room for them.
11 He shall pass through the sea of troubles
  and strike down the waves of the sea,
  and all the depths of the Nile shall be
      dried up.
  The pride of Assyria shall be laid low,
    and the scepter of Egypt shall depart.
12 I will make them strong in the LORD,
  and they shall walk in his name,"
                            declares the LORD.

The Flock Doomed to Slaughter

11 Open your doors, O Lebanon,
    that the fire may devour your cedars!
2 Wail, O cypress, for the cedar has fallen,
    for the glorious trees are ruined!
  Wail, oaks of Bashan,
    for the thick forest has been felled!
3 The sound of the wail of the shepherds,
    for their glory is ruined!
  The sound of the roar of the lions,
    for the thicket of the Jordan is ruined!

4 Thus said the LORD my God: "Become shepherd of the flock doomed to slaughter. 5 Those
who buy them slaughter them and go unpunished, and those who sell them say, 'Blessed be
the LORD, I have become rich,' and their own
shepherds have no pity on them. 6 For I will no
longer have pity on the inhabitants of this land,
declares the LORD. Behold, I will cause each of
them to fall into the hand of his neighbor, and
each into the hand of his king, and they shall
crush the land, and I will deliver none from
their hand."

7 So I became the shepherd of the flock
doomed to be slaughtered by the sheep traders. And I took two staffs, one I named Favor, the
other I named Union. And I tended the sheep.
8 In one month I destroyed the three shepherds.
But I became impatient with them, and they
also detested me. 9 So I said, "I will not be your
shepherd. What is to die, let it die. What is to be
destroyed, let it be destroyed. And let those who
are left devour the flesh of one another." 10 And
I took my staff Favor, and I broke it, annul-
ling the covenant that I had made with all the
peoples. 11 So it was annulled on that day, and
the sheep traders, who were watching me, knew
that it was the word of the LORD. 12 Then I said
to them, "If it seems good to you, give me my
wages; but if not, keep them." And they weighed
out as my wages thirty pieces of silver. 13 Then
the LORD said to me, "Throw it to the potter"—
the lordly price at which I was priced by them.
So I took the thirty pieces of silver and threw
them into the house of the LORD, to the potter.
14 Then I broke my second staff Union, annul-
ling the brotherhood between Judah and Israel.

15 Then the LORD said to me, "Take once more
the equipment of a foolish shepherd. 16 For
behold, I am raising up in the land a shepherd
who does not care for those being destroyed,
or seek the young or heal the maimed or nour-
ish the healthy, but devours the flesh of the fat
ones, tearing off even their hoofs.

17 "Woe to my worthless shepherd,
    who deserts the flock!
  May the sword strike his arm
    and his right eye!
  Let his arm be wholly withered,
    his right eye utterly blinded!"

The LORD Will Give Salvation

12 The oracle of the word of the LORD concerning Israel: Thus declares the LORD,
who stretched out the heavens and founded
the earth and formed the spirit of man within

him: [2]"Behold, I am about to make Jerusalem a cup of staggering to all the surrounding peoples. The siege of Jerusalem will also be against Judah. [3] On that day I will make Jerusalem a heavy stone for all the peoples. All who lift it will surely hurt themselves. And all the nations of the earth will gather against it. [4] On that day, declares the LORD, I will strike every horse with panic, and its rider with madness. But for the sake of the house of Judah I will keep my eyes open, when I strike every horse of the peoples with blindness. [5] Then the clans of Judah shall say to themselves, 'The inhabitants of Jerusalem have strength through the LORD of hosts, their God.'

[6] "On that day I will make the clans of Judah like a blazing pot in the midst of wood, like a flaming torch among sheaves. And they shall devour to the right and to the left all the surrounding peoples, while Jerusalem shall again be inhabited in its place, in Jerusalem.

[7] "And the LORD will give salvation to the tents of Judah first, that the glory of the house of David and the glory of the inhabitants of Jerusalem may not surpass that of Judah. [8] On that day the LORD will protect the inhabitants of Jerusalem, so that the feeblest among them on that day shall be like David, and the house of David shall be like God, like the angel of the LORD, going before them. [9] And on that day I will seek to destroy all the nations that come against Jerusalem.

Him Whom They Have Pierced

[10] "And I will pour out on the house of David and the inhabitants of Jerusalem a spirit of grace and pleas for mercy, so that, when they look on me, on him whom they have pierced, they shall mourn for him, as one mourns for an only child, and weep bitterly over him, as one weeps over a firstborn. [11] On that day the mourning in Jerusalem will be as great as the mourning for Hadad-rimmon in the plain of Megiddo. [12] The land shall mourn, each family[1] by itself: the family of the house of David by itself, and their wives by themselves; the family of the house of Nathan by itself, and their wives by themselves; [13] the family of the house of Levi by itself, and their wives by themselves; the family of the Shimeites by itself, and their wives by themselves; [14] and all the families that are left, each by itself, and their wives by themselves.

13 "On that day there shall be a fountain opened for the house of David and the inhabitants of Jerusalem, to cleanse them from sin and uncleanness.

Idolatry Cut Off

[2] "And on that day, declares the LORD of hosts, I will cut off the names of the idols from the land, so that they shall be remembered no more. And also I will remove from the land the prophets and the spirit of uncleanness. [3] And if anyone again prophesies, his father and mother who bore him will say to him, 'You shall not live, for you speak lies in the name of the LORD.' And his father and mother who bore him shall pierce him through when he prophesies.

[4] "On that day every prophet will be ashamed of his vision when he prophesies. He will not put on a hairy cloak in order to deceive, [5] but he will say, 'I am no prophet, I am a worker of the soil, for a man sold me in my youth.'[2] [6] And if one asks him, 'What are these wounds on your back?'[3] he will say, 'The wounds I received in the house of my friends.'

The Shepherd Struck

[7] "Awake, O sword, against my shepherd,
      against the man who stands next to
        me,"
              declares the LORD of hosts.

"Strike the shepherd, and the sheep will be
      scattered;
      I will turn my hand against the little
        ones.
[8] In the whole land, declares the LORD,
      two thirds shall be cut off and perish,
      and one third shall be left alive.
[9] And I will put this third into the fire,
      and refine them as one refines silver,
      and test them as gold is tested.
  They will call upon my name,
      and I will answer them.
  I will say, 'They are my people';
      and they will say, 'The LORD is my
        God.'"

The Coming Day of the LORD

14 Behold, a day is coming for the LORD, when the spoil taken from you will be divided in your midst. [2] For I will gather all the nations against Jerusalem to battle, and the city shall be taken and the houses plundered and the women raped. Half of the city shall go out into exile, but the rest of the people shall

---

[1] Or clan; throughout verses 12–14   [2] Or for the land has been my possession since my youth   [3] Or on your chest; Hebrew wounds between your hands

not be cut off from the city. ³ Then the LORD will go out and fight against those nations as when he fights on a day of battle. ⁴ On that day his feet shall stand on the Mount of Olives that lies before Jerusalem on the east, and the Mount of Olives shall be split in two from east to west by a very wide valley, so that one half of the Mount shall move northward, and the other half southward. ⁵ And you shall flee to the valley of my mountains, for the valley of the mountains shall reach to Azal. And you shall flee as you fled from the earthquake in the days of Uzziah king of Judah. Then the LORD my God will come, and all the holy ones with him.¹

⁶ On that day there shall be no light, cold, or frost.²⁷ And there shall be a unique³ day, which is known to the LORD, neither day nor night, but at evening time there shall be light.

⁸ On that day living waters shall flow out from Jerusalem, half of them to the eastern sea⁴ and half of them to the western sea.⁵ It shall continue in summer as in winter.

⁹ And the LORD will be king over all the earth. On that day the LORD will be one and his name one.

¹⁰ The whole land shall be turned into a plain from Geba to Rimmon south of Jerusalem. But Jerusalem shall remain aloft on its site from the Gate of Benjamin to the place of the former gate, to the Corner Gate, and from the Tower of Hananel to the king's winepresses. ¹¹ And it shall be inhabited, for there shall never again be a decree of utter destruction.⁶ Jerusalem shall dwell in security.

¹² And this shall be the plague with which the LORD will strike all the peoples that wage war against Jerusalem: their flesh will rot while they are still standing on their feet, their eyes will rot in their sockets, and their tongues will rot in their mouths.

¹³ And on that day a great panic from the LORD shall fall on them, so that each will seize the hand of another, and the hand of the one will be raised against the hand of the other. ¹⁴ Even Judah will fight at Jerusalem.⁷ And the wealth of all the surrounding nations shall be collected, gold, silver, and garments in great abundance. ¹⁵ And a plague like this plague shall fall on the horses, the mules, the camels, the donkeys, and whatever beasts may be in those camps.

¹⁶ Then everyone who survives of all the nations that have come against Jerusalem shall go up year after year to worship the King, the LORD of hosts, and to keep the Feast of Booths. ¹⁷ And if any of the families of the earth do not go up to Jerusalem to worship the King, the LORD of hosts, there will be no rain on them. ¹⁸ And if the family of Egypt does not go up and present themselves, then on them there shall be no rain;⁸ there shall be the plague with which the LORD afflicts the nations that do not go up to keep the Feast of Booths. ¹⁹ This shall be the punishment to Egypt and the punishment to all the nations that do not go up to keep the Feast of Booths.

²⁰ And on that day there shall be inscribed on the bells of the horses, "Holy to the LORD." And the pots in the house of the LORD shall be as the bowls before the altar. ²¹ And every pot in Jerusalem and Judah shall be holy to the LORD of hosts, so that all who sacrifice may come and take of them and boil the meat of the sacrifice in them. And there shall no longer be a trader⁹ in the house of the LORD of hosts on that day.

¹ Other Hebrew manuscripts *you* ² Compare Septuagint, Syriac, Vulgate, Targum; the meaning of the Hebrew is uncertain ³ Hebrew *one* ⁴ That is, the Dead Sea ⁵ That is, the Mediterranean Sea ⁶ The Hebrew term rendered *decree of utter destruction* refers to things devoted (or set apart) to the Lord (or by the Lord) for destruction ⁷ Or *against Jerusalem* ⁸ Hebrew lacks *rain* ⁹ Or *Canaanite*

MALACHI

1 The oracle of the word of the LORD to Israel by Malachi.[1]

The LORD's Love for Israel

2 "I have loved you," says the LORD. But you say, "How have you loved us?" "Is not Esau Jacob's brother?" declares the LORD. "Yet I have loved Jacob 3 but Esau I have hated. I have laid waste his hill country and left his heritage to jackals of the desert." 4 If Edom says, "We are shattered but we will rebuild the ruins," the LORD of hosts says, "They may build, but I will tear down, and they will be called 'the wicked country,' and 'the people with whom the LORD is angry forever.'" 5 Your own eyes shall see this, and you shall say, "Great is the LORD beyond the border of Israel!"

The Priests' Polluted Offerings

6 "A son honors his father, and a servant his master. If then I am a father, where is my honor? And if I am a master, where is my fear? says the LORD of hosts to you, O priests, who despise my name. But you say, 'How have we despised your name?' 7 By offering polluted food upon my altar. But you say, 'How have we polluted you?' By saying that the LORD's table may be despised. 8 When you offer blind animals in sacrifice, is that not evil? And when you offer those that are lame or sick, is that not evil? Present that to your governor; will he accept you or show you favor? says the LORD of hosts. 9 And now entreat the favor of God, that he may be gracious to us. With such a gift from your hand, will he show favor to any of you? says the LORD of hosts. 10 Oh that there were one among you who would shut the doors, that you might not kindle fire on my altar in vain! I have no pleasure in you, says the LORD of hosts, and I will not accept an offering from your hand. 11 For from the rising of the sun to its setting my name will be[2] great among the nations, and in every place incense will be offered to my name, and a pure offering. For my name will be great among the nations, says the LORD of hosts. 12 But you profane it when you say that the Lord's table is polluted, and its fruit, that is, its food may be despised. 13 But you say, 'What a weariness this is,' and you snort at it, says the LORD of hosts. You bring what has

been taken by violence or is lame or sick, and this you bring as your offering! Shall I accept that from your hand? says the LORD. 14 Cursed be the cheat who has a male in his flock, and vows it, and yet sacrifices to the Lord what is blemished. For I am a great King, says the LORD of hosts, and my name will be feared among the nations.

The LORD Rebukes the Priests

2 "And now, O priests, this command is for you. 2 If you will not listen, if you will not take it to heart to give honor to my name, says the LORD of hosts, then I will send the curse upon you and I will curse your blessings. Indeed, I have already cursed them, because you do not lay it to heart. 3 Behold, I will rebuke your offspring,[3] and spread dung on your faces, the dung of your offerings, and you shall be taken away with it. 4 So shall you know that I have sent this command to you, that my covenant with Levi may stand, says the LORD of hosts. 5 My covenant with him was one of life and peace, and I gave them to him. It was a covenant of fear, and he feared me. He stood in awe of my name. 6 True instruction[5] was in his mouth, and no wrong was found on his lips. He walked with me in peace and uprightness, and he turned many from iniquity. 7 For the lips of a priest should guard knowledge, and people[6] should seek instruction from his mouth, for he is the messenger of the LORD of hosts. 8 But you have turned aside from the way. You have caused many to stumble by your instruction. You have corrupted the covenant of Levi, says the LORD of hosts, 9 and so I make you despised and abased before all the people, inasmuch as you do not keep my ways but show partiality in your instruction."

Judah Profaned the Covenant

10 Have we not all one Father? Has not one God created us? Why then are we faithless to one another, profaning the covenant of our fathers? 11 Judah has been faithless, and abomination has been committed in Israel and in Jerusalem. For Judah has profaned the sanctuary of the LORD, which he loves, and has married the daughter of a foreign god.

[1] Malachi means my messenger [2] Or is (three times in verse 11; also verse 14) [3] Hebrew seed [4] Or to it [5] Or law; also verses 7, 8, 9 [6] Hebrew they

¹²May the LORD cut off from the tents of Jacob any descendant[1] of the man who does this, who brings an offering to the LORD of hosts!

¹³And this second thing you do. You cover the LORD's altar with tears, with weeping and groaning because he no longer regards the offering or accepts it with favor from your hand. ¹⁴But you say, "Why does he not?" Because the LORD was witness between you and the wife of your youth, to whom you have been faithless, though she is your companion and your wife by covenant. ¹⁵Did he not make them one, with a portion of the Spirit in their union?[2] And what was the one God[3] seeking?[4] Godly offspring. So guard yourselves[5] in your spirit, and let none of you be faithless to the wife of your youth. ¹⁶"For the man who does not love his wife but divorces her,[6] says the LORD, the God of Israel, covers[7] his garment with violence, says the LORD of hosts. So guard yourselves in your spirit, and do not be faithless."

The Messenger of the LORD

¹⁷You have wearied the LORD with your words. But you say, "How have we wearied him?" By saying, "Everyone who does evil is good in the sight of the LORD, and he delights in them." Or by asking, "Where is the God of justice?"

3 "Behold, I send my messenger, and he will prepare the way before me. And the Lord whom you seek will suddenly come to his temple; and the messenger of the covenant in whom you delight, behold, he is coming, says the LORD of hosts. ²But who can endure the day of his coming, and who can stand when he appears? For he is like a refiner's fire and like fullers' soap. ³He will sit as a refiner and purifier of silver, and he will purify the sons of Levi and refine them like gold and silver, and they will bring offerings in righteousness to the LORD.[8] ⁴Then the offering of Judah and Jerusalem will be pleasing to the LORD as in the days of old and as in former years.

⁵"Then I will draw near to you for judgment. I will be a swift witness against the sorcerers, against the adulterers, against those who swear falsely, against those who oppress the hired worker in his wages, the widow and the fatherless, against those who thrust aside the sojourner, and do not fear me, says the LORD of hosts.

Robbing God

⁶"For I the LORD do not change; therefore you, O children of Jacob, are not consumed. ⁷From the days of your fathers you have turned aside from my statutes and have not kept them. Return to me, and I will return to you, says the LORD of hosts. But you say, 'How shall we return?' ⁸Will man rob God? Yet you are robbing me. But you say, 'How have we robbed you?' In your tithes and contributions. ⁹You are cursed with a curse, for you are robbing me, the whole nation of you. ¹⁰Bring the full tithe into the storehouse, that there may be food in my house. And thereby put me to the test, says the LORD of hosts, if I will not open the windows of heaven for you and pour down for you a blessing until there is no more need. ¹¹I will rebuke the devourer[9] for you, so that it will not destroy the fruits of your soil, and your vine in the field shall not fail to bear, says the LORD of hosts. ¹²Then all nations will call you blessed, for you will be a land of delight, says the LORD of hosts.

¹³"Your words have been hard against me, says the LORD. But you say, 'How have we spoken against you?' ¹⁴You have said, 'It is vain to serve God. What is the profit of our keeping his charge or of walking as in mourning before the LORD of hosts? ¹⁵And now we call the arrogant blessed. Evildoers not only prosper but they put God to the test and they escape.'"

The Book of Remembrance

¹⁶Then those who feared the LORD spoke with one another. The LORD paid attention and heard them, and a book of remembrance was written before him of those who feared the LORD and esteemed his name. ¹⁷"They shall be mine, says the LORD of hosts, in the day when I make up my treasured possession, and I will spare them as a man spares his son who serves him. ¹⁸Then once more you shall see the distinction between the righteous and the wicked, between one who serves God and one who does not serve him.

The Great Day of the LORD

4 ¹⁰ "For behold, the day is coming, burning like an oven, when all the arrogant and all evildoers will be stubble. The day that is

---

[1] Hebrew any who wakes and answers [2] Hebrew in it [3] Hebrew the one [4] Or And not one has done this who has a portion of the Spirit. And what was that one seeking? [5] Or So take care; also verse 16 [6] Hebrew who hates and divorces [7] Probable meaning (compare Septuagint and Deuteronomy 24:1–4); or "The LORD, the God of Israel, says that he hates divorce, and him who covers [8] Or and they will belong to the LORD, bringers of an offering in righteousness [9] Probably a name for some crop-destroying pest or pests [10] Ch 4:1–6 is ch 3:19–24 in Hebrew

coming shall set them ablaze, says the LORD of hosts, so that it will leave them neither root nor branch. ²But for you who fear my name, the sun of righteousness shall rise with healing in its wings. You shall go out leaping like calves from the stall. ³And you shall tread down the wicked, for they will be ashes under the soles of your feet, on the day when I act, says the LORD of hosts.

⁴"Remember the law of my servant Moses, the statutes and rules¹ that I commanded him at Horeb for all Israel.

⁵"Behold, I will send you Elijah the prophet before the great and awesome day of the LORD comes. ⁶And he will turn the hearts of fathers to their children and the hearts of children to their fathers, lest I come and strike the land with a decree of utter destruction."²

---

¹ Or *and just decrees* ² The Hebrew term rendered *decree of utter destruction* refers to things devoted (or set apart) to the Lord (or by the Lord) for destruction

The

NEW TESTAMENT

MATTHEW

The Genealogy of Jesus Christ

1 The book of the genealogy of Jesus Christ, the son of David, the son of Abraham.

² Abraham was the father of Isaac, and Isaac the father of Jacob, and Jacob the father of Judah and his brothers, ³ and Judah the father of Perez and Zerah by Tamar, and Perez the father of Hezron, and Hezron the father of Ram,[1] ⁴ and Ram the father of Amminadab, and Amminadab the father of Nahshon, and Nahshon the father of Salmon, ⁵ and Salmon the father of Boaz by Rahab, and Boaz the father of Obed by Ruth, and Obed the father of Jesse, ⁶ and Jesse the father of David the king.

And David was the father of Solomon by the wife of Uriah, ⁷ and Solomon the father of Rehoboam, and Rehoboam the father of Abijah, and Abijah the father of Asaph,[2] ⁸ and Asaph the father of Jehoshaphat, and Jehoshaphat the father of Joram, and Joram the father of Uzziah, ⁹ and Uzziah the father of Jotham, and Jotham the father of Ahaz, and Ahaz the father of Hezekiah, ¹⁰ and Hezekiah the father of Manasseh, and Manasseh the father of Amos,[3] and Amos the father of Josiah, ¹¹ and Josiah the father of Jechoniah and his brothers, at the time of the deportation to Babylon.

¹² And after the deportation to Babylon: Jechoniah was the father of Shealtiel,[4] and Shealtiel the father of Zerubbabel, ¹³ and Zerubbabel the father of Abiud, and Abiud the father of Eliakim, and Eliakim the father of Azor, ¹⁴ and Azor the father of Zadok, and Zadok the father of Achim, and Achim the father of Eliud, ¹⁵ and Eliud the father of Eleazar, and Eleazar the father of Matthan, and Matthan the father of Jacob, ¹⁶ and Jacob the father of Joseph the husband of Mary, of whom Jesus was born, who is called Christ.

¹⁷ So all the generations from Abraham to David were fourteen generations, and from David to the deportation to Babylon fourteen generations, and from the deportation to Babylon to the Christ fourteen generations.

The Birth of Jesus Christ

¹⁸ Now the birth of Jesus Christ[5] took place in this way. When his mother Mary had been betrothed[6] to Joseph, before they came together she was found to be with child from the Holy Spirit. ¹⁹ And her husband Joseph, being a just man and unwilling to put her to shame, resolved to divorce her quietly. ²⁰ But as he considered these things, behold, an angel of the Lord appeared to him in a dream, saying, "Joseph, son of David, do not fear to take Mary as your wife, for that which is conceived in her is from the Holy Spirit. ²¹ She will bear a son, and you shall call his name Jesus, for he will save his people from their sins." ²² All this took place to fulfill what the Lord had spoken by the prophet:

²³ ᵃ"Behold, the virgin shall conceive and bear a
  son,
  and they shall call his name Immanuel"

(which means, God with us). ²⁴ When Joseph woke from sleep, he did as the angel of the Lord commanded him: he took his wife, ²⁵ but knew her not until she had given birth to a son. And he called his name Jesus.

The Visit of the Wise Men

2 Now after Jesus was born in Bethlehem of Judea in the days of Herod the king, behold, wise men[7] from the east came to Jerusalem, ² saying, "Where is he who has been born king of the Jews? For we saw his star when it rose[8] and have come to worship him." ³ When Herod the king heard this, he was troubled, and all Jerusalem with him; ⁴ and assembling all the chief priests and scribes of the people, he inquired of them where the Christ was to be born. ⁵ They told him, "In Bethlehem of Judea, for so it is written by the prophet:

⁶ ᵇ"'And you, O Bethlehem, in the land of
    Judah,
  are by no means least among the rulers
      of Judah;
  for from you shall come a ruler
    who will shepherd my people Israel.'"

⁷ Then Herod summoned the wise men secretly and ascertained from them what time the star had appeared. ⁸ And he sent them to Bethlehem, saying, "Go and search diligently for the child, and when you have found him,

---

[1] Greek Aram; also verse 4 [2] Asaph is probably an alternate spelling of Asa; some manuscripts Asa; also verse 8 [3] Amos is probably an alternate spelling of Amon; some manuscripts Amon; twice in this verse [4] Greek Salathiel; twice in this verse [5] Some manuscripts of the Christ [6] That is, legally pledged to be married [7] Greek magi; also verses 7, 16 [8] Or in the east; also verse 9 ᵃ Isa. 7:14 ᵇ Mic. 5:2

bring me word, that I too may come and worship him." [9] After listening to the king, they went on their way. And behold, the star that they had seen when it rose went before them until it came to rest over the place where the child was. [10] When they saw the star, they rejoiced exceedingly with great joy. [11] And going into the house, they saw the child with Mary his mother, and they fell down and worshiped him. Then, opening their treasures, they offered him gifts, gold and frankincense and myrrh. [12] And being warned in a dream not to return to Herod, they departed to their own country by another way.

The Flight to Egypt

[13] Now when they had departed, behold, an angel of the Lord appeared to Joseph in a dream and said, "Rise, take the child and his mother, and flee to Egypt, and remain there until I tell you, for Herod is about to search for the child, to destroy him." [14] And he rose and took the child and his mother by night and departed to Egypt [15] and remained there until the death of Herod. This was to fulfill what the Lord had spoken by the prophet, [a]"Out of Egypt I called my son."

Herod Kills the Children

[16] Then Herod, when he saw that he had been tricked by the wise men, became furious, and he sent and killed all the male children in Bethlehem and in all that region who were two years old or under, according to the time that he had ascertained from the wise men. [17] Then was fulfilled what was spoken by the prophet Jeremiah:

[18] [b]"A voice was heard in Ramah,
     weeping and loud lamentation,
Rachel weeping for her children;
     she refused to be comforted, because
         they are no more."

The Return to Nazareth

[19] But when Herod died, behold, an angel of the Lord appeared in a dream to Joseph in Egypt, [20] saying, "Rise, take the child and his mother and go to the land of Israel, for those who sought the child's life are dead." [21] And he rose and took the child and his mother and went to the land of Israel. [22] But when he heard that Archelaus was reigning over Judea in place of his father Herod, he was afraid to go there,

and being warned in a dream he withdrew to the district of Galilee. [23] And he went and lived in a city called Nazareth, so that what was spoken by the prophets might be fulfilled, that he would be called a Nazarene.

John the Baptist Prepares the Way

3 [1] In those days John the Baptist came preaching in the wilderness of Judea, [2] "Repent, for the kingdom of heaven is at hand."[1] [3] For this is he who was spoken of by the prophet Isaiah when he said,

[d]"The voice of one crying in the wilderness:
   'Prepare[2] the way of the Lord;
     make his paths straight.'"

[4] Now John wore a garment of camel's hair and a leather belt around his waist, and his food was locusts and wild honey. [5] Then Jerusalem and all Judea and all the region about the Jordan were going out to him, [6] and they were baptized by him in the river Jordan, confessing their sins.

[7] But when he saw many of the Pharisees and Sadducees coming to his baptism, he said to them, "You brood of vipers! Who warned you to flee from the wrath to come? [8] Bear fruit in keeping with repentance. [9] And do not presume to say to yourselves, 'We have Abraham as our father,' for I tell you, God is able from these stones to raise up children for Abraham. [10] Even now the axe is laid to the root of the trees. Every tree therefore that does not bear good fruit is cut down and thrown into the fire.

[11] "I baptize you with water for repentance, but he who is coming after me is mightier than I, whose sandals I am not worthy to carry. He will baptize you with the Holy Spirit and fire. [12] His winnowing fork is in his hand, and he will clear his threshing floor and gather his wheat into the barn, but the chaff he will burn with unquenchable fire."

The Baptism of Jesus

[13] [e] Then Jesus came from Galilee to the Jordan to John, to be baptized by him. [14] John would have prevented him, saying, "I need to be baptized by you, and do you come to me?" [15] But Jesus answered him, "Let it be so now, for thus it is fitting for us to fulfill all righteousness." Then he consented. [16] And when Jesus was baptized, immediately he went up from the water, and behold, the heavens were opened to him,[3] and he saw the Spirit of God descending like a

[1] Or the kingdom of heaven has come near   [2] Or crying: Prepare in the wilderness   [3] Some manuscripts omit to him   [a] Hos. 11:1   [b] Jer. 31:15   [c] For 3:1-12 see parallels Mark 1:2-8; Luke 3:1-17   [d] Isa. 40:3   [e] For 3:13-17 see parallels Mark 1:9-11; Luke 3:21, 22

dove and coming to rest on him; [17] and behold, a voice from heaven said, "This is my beloved Son,[1] with whom I am well pleased."

The Temptation of Jesus

4 [a]Then Jesus was led up by the Spirit into the wilderness to be tempted by the devil. [2] And after fasting forty days and forty nights, he was hungry. [3] And the tempter came and said to him, "If you are the Son of God, command these stones to become loaves of bread." [4] But he answered, "It is written,

[b]"'Man shall not live by bread alone,
    but by every word that comes from the
        mouth of God.'"

[5] Then the devil took him to the holy city and set him on the pinnacle of the temple [6] and said to him, "If you are the Son of God, throw yourself down, for it is written,

[c]"'He will command his angels concerning
    you,'

and

"'On their hands they will bear you up,
    lest you strike your foot against a stone.'"

[7] Jesus said to him, "Again it is written, [d]'You shall not put the Lord your God to the test.'" [8] Again, the devil took him to a very high mountain and showed him all the kingdoms of the world and their glory. [9] And he said to him, "All these I will give you, if you will fall down and worship me." [10] Then Jesus said to him, "Be gone, Satan! For it is written,

[e]"'You shall worship the Lord your God
    and him only shall you serve.'"

[11] Then the devil left him, and behold, angels came and were ministering to him.

Jesus Begins His Ministry

[12] Now when he heard that John had been arrested, he withdrew into Galilee. [13] And leaving Nazareth he went and lived in Capernaum by the sea, in the territory of Zebulun and Naphtali, [14] so that what was spoken by the prophet Isaiah might be fulfilled:

[15] [f]"The land of Zebulun and the land of
    Naphtali,
    the way of the sea, beyond the Jordan,
    Galilee of the Gentiles—

[16]   the people dwelling in darkness
    have seen a great light,
   and for those dwelling in the region and
    shadow of death,
   on them a light has dawned."

[17] From that time Jesus began to preach, saying, "Repent, for the kingdom of heaven is at hand."[2]

Jesus Calls the First Disciples

[18] [g]While walking by the Sea of Galilee, he saw two brothers, Simon (who is called Peter) and Andrew his brother, casting a net into the sea, for they were fishermen. [19] And he said to them, "Follow me, and I will make you fishers of men."[3] [20] Immediately they left their nets and followed him. [21] And going on from there he saw two other brothers, James the son of Zebedee and John his brother, in the boat with Zebedee their father, mending their nets, and he called them. [22] Immediately they left the boat and their father and followed him.

Jesus Ministers to Great Crowds

[23] And he went throughout all Galilee, teaching in their synagogues and proclaiming the gospel of the kingdom and healing every disease and every affliction among the people. [24] So his fame spread throughout all Syria, and they brought him all the sick, those afflicted with various diseases and pains, those oppressed by demons, those having seizures, and paralytics, and he healed them. [25] And great crowds followed him from Galilee and the Decapolis, and from Jerusalem and Judea, and from beyond the Jordan.

The Sermon on the Mount

5 Seeing the crowds, he went up on the mountain, and when he sat down, his disciples came to him.

The Beatitudes

[2] And he opened his mouth and taught them, saying:

[3] "Blessed are the poor in spirit, for theirs is the kingdom of heaven.

[4] "Blessed are those who mourn, for they shall be comforted.

[5] "Blessed are the meek, for they shall inherit the earth.

[6] "Blessed are those who hunger and thirst for righteousness, for they shall be satisfied.

[7] "Blessed are the merciful, for they shall receive mercy.

---

[1] Or my Son, my (or the) Beloved   [2] Or the kingdom of heaven has come near   [3] The Greek word anthropoi refers here to both men and women   [a] For 4:1-11 see parallels Mark 1:12, 13; Luke 4:1-13   [b] Deut. 8:3   [c] Ps. 91:11, 12   [d] Deut. 6:16   [e] Deut. 6:13   [f] Isa. 9:1, 2   [g] For 4:18-22 see parallel Mark 1:16-20

8"Blessed are the pure in heart, for they shall see God.

9"Blessed are the peacemakers, for they shall be called sons[1] of God.

10"Blessed are those who are persecuted for righteousness' sake, for theirs is the kingdom of heaven.

11"Blessed are you when others revile you and persecute you and utter all kinds of evil against you falsely on my account. 12Rejoice and be glad, for your reward is great in heaven, for so they persecuted the prophets who were before you.

Salt and Light

13"You are the salt of the earth, but if salt has lost its taste, how shall its saltiness be restored? It is no longer good for anything except to be thrown out and trampled under people's feet.

14"You are the light of the world. A city set on a hill cannot be hidden. 15Nor do people light a lamp and put it under a basket, but on a stand, and it gives light to all in the house. 16In the same way, let your light shine before others, so that[2] they may see your good works and give glory to your Father who is in heaven.

Christ Came to Fulfill the Law

17"Do not think that I have come to abolish the Law or the Prophets; I have not come to abolish them but to fulfill them. 18For truly, I say to you, until heaven and earth pass away, not an iota, not a dot, will pass from the Law until all is accomplished. 19Therefore whoever relaxes one of the least of these commandments and teaches others to do the same will be called least in the kingdom of heaven, but whoever does them and teaches them will be called great in the kingdom of heaven. 20For I tell you, unless your righteousness exceeds that of the scribes and Pharisees, you will never enter the kingdom of heaven.

Anger

21"You have heard that it was said to those of old, a'You shall not murder; and whoever murders will be liable to judgment.' 22But I say to you that everyone who is angry with his brother[3] will be liable to judgment; whoever insults[4] his brother will be liable to the council; and whoever says, 'You fool!' will be liable to the hell[5] of fire. 23So if you are offering your gift at the altar and there remember that your brother

has something against you, 24leave your gift there before the altar and go. First be reconciled to your brother, and then come and offer your gift. 25Come to terms quickly with your accuser while you are going with him to court, lest your accuser hand you over to the judge, and the judge to the guard, and you be put in prison. 26Truly, I say to you, you will never get out until you have paid the last penny.[6]

Lust

27"You have heard that it was said, b"You shall not commit adultery.' 28But I say to you that everyone who looks at a woman with lustful intent has already committed adultery with her in his heart. 29If your right eye causes you to sin, tear it out and throw it away. For it is better that you lose one of your members than that your whole body be thrown into hell. 30And if your right hand causes you to sin, cut it off and throw it away. For it is better that you lose one of your members than that your whole body go into hell.

Divorce

31"It was also said, c'Whoever divorces his wife, let him give her a certificate of divorce.' 32But I say to you that everyone who divorces his wife, except on the ground of sexual immorality, makes her commit adultery, and whoever marries a divorced woman commits adultery.

Oaths

33"Again you have heard that it was said to those of old, 'You shall not swear falsely, but shall perform to the Lord what you have sworn.' 34But I say to you, Do not take an oath at all, either by heaven, for it is the throne of God, 35or by the earth, for it is his footstool, or by Jerusalem, for it is the city of the great King. 36And do not take an oath by your head, for you cannot make one hair white or black. 37Let what you say be simply 'Yes' or 'No'; anything more than this comes from evil.[7]

Retaliation

38"You have heard that it was said, d'An eye for an eye and a tooth for a tooth.' 39But I say to you, Do not resist the one who is evil. But e if anyone slaps you on the right cheek, turn to him the other also. 40And if anyone would sue you and take your tunic,[8] let him have your

---

[1] Greek huioi; see Preface [2] Or house. *16Let your light so shine before others that* [3] Some manuscripts insert *without cause* [4] Greek *says Raca* (a term of abuse) [5] Greek *Gehenna*; also verses 29, 30 [6] Greek *kodrantes*, Roman copper coin (Latin *quadrans*) worth about 1/64 of a *denarius* (which was a day's wage for a laborer) [7] Or *the evil one* [8] Greek *chiton*, a long garment worn under the cloak next to the skin a Ex. 20:13; Deut. 5:17 b Ex. 20:14; Deut. 5:18 c Deut. 24:1 d Ex. 21:24; Lev. 24:20; Deut. 19:21 e For 5:39-42 see parallel Luke 6:29, 30

cloak as well. [41]And if anyone forces you to go one mile, go with him two miles. [42]Give to the one who begs from you, and do not refuse the one who would borrow from you.

Love Your Enemies

[43]"You have heard that it was said, [a]'You shall love your neighbor and hate your enemy.' [44]But I say to you, Love your enemies and pray for those who persecute you, [45]so that you may be sons of your Father who is in heaven. For he makes his sun rise on the evil and on the good, and sends rain on the just and on the unjust. [46]For if you love those who love you, what reward do you have? Do not even the tax collectors do the same? [47]And if you greet only your brothers,[1] what more are you doing than others? Do not even the Gentiles do the same? [48]You therefore must be perfect, as your heavenly Father is perfect.

Giving to the Needy

6 "Beware of practicing your righteousness before other people in order to be seen by them, for then you will have no reward from your Father who is in heaven.

[2]"Thus, when you give to the needy, sound no trumpet before you, as the hypocrites do in the synagogues and in the streets, that they may be praised by others. Truly, I say to you, they have received their reward. [3]But when you give to the needy, do not let your left hand know what your right hand is doing, [4]so that your giving may be in secret. And your Father who sees in secret will reward you.

The Lord's Prayer

[5]"And when you pray, you must not be like the hypocrites. For they love to stand and pray in the synagogues and at the street corners, that they may be seen by others. Truly, I say to you, they have received their reward. [6]But when you pray, go into your room and shut the door and pray to your Father who is in secret. And your Father who sees in secret will reward you.

[7]"And when you pray, do not heap up empty phrases as the Gentiles do, for they think that they will be heard for their many words. [8]Do not be like them, for your Father knows what you need before you ask him. [9]Pray then like this:

"Our Father in heaven,
   hallowed be your name.[2]
[10] Your kingdom come,
   your will be done,[3]
     on earth as it is in heaven.
[11] Give us this day our daily bread,[4]
[12] and forgive us our debts,
     as we also have forgiven our debtors.
[13] And lead us not into temptation,
     but deliver us from evil.[5]

[14]For if you forgive others their trespasses, your heavenly Father will also forgive you, [15]but if you do not forgive others their trespasses, neither will your Father forgive your trespasses.

Fasting

[16]"And when you fast, do not look gloomy like the hypocrites, for they disfigure their faces that their fasting may be seen by others. Truly, I say to you, they have received their reward. [17]But when you fast, anoint your head and wash your face, [18]that your fasting may not be seen by others but by your Father who is in secret. And your Father who sees in secret will reward you.

Lay Up Treasures in Heaven

[19]"Do not lay up for yourselves treasures on earth, where moth and rust[6] destroy and where thieves break in and steal, [20]but lay up for yourselves treasures in heaven, where neither moth nor rust destroys and where thieves do not break in and steal. [21]For where your treasure is, there your heart will be also.

[22]"The eye is the lamp of the body. So, if your eye is healthy, your whole body will be full of light, [23]but if your eye is bad, your whole body will be full of darkness. If then the light in you is darkness, how great is the darkness!

[24]"No one can serve two masters, for either he will hate the one and love the other, or he will be devoted to the one and despise the other. You cannot serve God and money.[7]

Do Not Be Anxious

[25b] "Therefore I tell you, do not be anxious about your life, what you will eat or what you will drink, nor about your body, what you will put on. Is not life more than food, and the body more than clothing? [26]Look at the birds of the air: they neither sow nor reap nor gather into barns, and yet your heavenly Father feeds

---

[1] Or brothers and sisters. In New Testament usage, depending on the context, the plural Greek word adelphoi (translated "brothers") may refer either to brothers or to brothers and sisters [2] Or Let your name be kept holy, or Let your name be treated with reverence [3] Or Let your kingdom come, let your will be done [4] Or our bread for tomorrow [5] Or the evil one; some manuscripts add For yours is the kingdom and the power and the glory, forever. Amen [6] Or worm; also verse 20 [7] Greek mammon, a Semitic word for money or possessions [a] Lev. 19:18 [b] For 6:25-33 see parallel Luke 12:22-31

them. Are you not of more value than they? [27]And which of you by being anxious can add a single hour to his span of life?[1] [28]And why are you anxious about clothing? Consider the lilies of the field, how they grow: they neither toil nor spin, [29]yet I tell you, even Solomon in all his glory was not arrayed like one of these. [30]But if God so clothes the grass of the field, which today is alive and tomorrow is thrown into the oven, will he not much more clothe you, O you of little faith? [31]Therefore do not be anxious, saying, 'What shall we eat?' or 'What shall we drink?' or 'What shall we wear?' [32]For the Gentiles seek after all these things, and your heavenly Father knows that you need them all. [33]But seek first the kingdom of God and his righteousness, and all these things will be added to you.

[34]"Therefore do not be anxious about tomorrow, for tomorrow will be anxious for itself. Sufficient for the day is its own trouble.

Judging Others

7 [a]"Judge not, that you be not judged. [2]For with the judgment you pronounce you will be judged, and with the measure you use it will be measured to you. [3]Why do you see the speck that is in your brother's eye, but do not notice the log that is in your own eye? [4]Or how can you say to your brother, 'Let me take the speck out of your eye,' when there is the log in your own eye? [5]You hypocrite, first take the log out of your own eye, and then you will see clearly to take the speck out of your brother's eye.

[6]"Do not give dogs what is holy, and do not throw your pearls before pigs, lest they trample them underfoot and turn to attack you.

Ask, and It Will Be Given

[7b]"Ask, and it will be given to you; seek, and you will find; knock, and it will be opened to you. [8]For everyone who asks receives, and the one who seeks finds, and to the one who knocks it will be opened. [9]Or which one of you, if his son asks him for bread, will give him a stone? [10]Or if he asks for a fish, will give him a serpent? [11]If you then, who are evil, know how to give good gifts to your children, how much more will your Father who is in heaven give good things to those who ask him!

The Golden Rule

[12]"So whatever you wish that others would do to you, do also to them, for this is the Law and the Prophets.

[13]"Enter by the narrow gate. For the gate is wide and the way is easy[2] that leads to destruction, and those who enter by it are many. [14]For the gate is narrow and the way is hard that leads to life, and those who find it are few.

A Tree and Its Fruit

[15]"Beware of false prophets, who come to you in sheep's clothing but inwardly are ravenous wolves. [16]You will recognize them by their fruits. Are grapes gathered from thornbushes, or figs from thistles? [17]So, every healthy tree bears good fruit, but the diseased tree bears bad fruit. [18]A healthy tree cannot bear bad fruit, nor can a diseased tree bear good fruit. [19]Every tree that does not bear good fruit is cut down and thrown into the fire. [20]Thus you will recognize them by their fruits.

I Never Knew You

[21]"Not everyone who says to me, 'Lord, Lord,' will enter the kingdom of heaven, but the one who does the will of my Father who is in heaven. [22]On that day many will say to me, 'Lord, Lord, did we not prophesy in your name, and cast out demons in your name, and do many mighty works in your name?' [23]And then will I declare to them, 'I never knew you; depart from me, you workers of lawlessness.'

Build Your House on the Rock

[24c]"Everyone then who hears these words of mine and does them will be like a wise man who built his house on the rock. [25]And the rain fell, and the floods came, and the winds blew and beat on that house, but it did not fall, because it had been founded on the rock. [26]And everyone who hears these words of mine and does not do them will be like a foolish man who built his house on the sand. [27]And the rain fell, and the floods came, and the winds blew and beat against that house, and it fell, and great was the fall of it."

The Authority of Jesus

[28]And when Jesus finished these sayings, the crowds were astonished at his teaching, [29]for he was teaching them as one who had authority, and not as their scribes.

---

[1] Or a single cubit to his stature; a cubit was about 18 inches or 45 centimeters [2] Some manuscripts For the way is wide and easy [a]For 7:1-5 see parallel Luke 6:37, 38, 41, 42 [b]For 7:7-11 see parallel Luke 11:9-13 [c]For 7:24-27 see parallel Luke 6:47-49

Jesus Cleanses a Leper

8 When he came down from the mountain, great crowds followed him. [2] [a] And behold, a leper[1] came to him and knelt before him, saying, "Lord, if you will, you can make me clean." [3] And Jesus[2] stretched out his hand and touched him, saying, "I will; be clean." And immediately his leprosy was cleansed. [4] And Jesus said to him, "See that you say nothing to anyone, but go, show yourself to the priest and offer the gift that Moses commanded, for a proof to them."

The Faith of a Centurion

[5] [b] When he had entered Capernaum, a centurion came forward to him, appealing to him, [6] "Lord, my servant is lying paralyzed at home, suffering terribly." [7] And he said to him, "I will come and heal him." [8] But the centurion replied, "Lord, I am not worthy to have you come under my roof, but only say the word, and my servant will be healed. [9] For I too am a man under authority, with soldiers under me. And I say to one, 'Go,' and he goes, and to another, 'Come,' and he comes, and to my servant,[3] 'Do this,' and he does it." [10] When Jesus heard this, he marveled and said to those who followed him, "Truly, I tell you, with no one in Israel[4] have I found such faith. [11] I tell you, many will come from east and west and recline at table with Abraham, Isaac, and Jacob in the kingdom of heaven, [12] while the sons of the kingdom will be thrown into the outer darkness. In that place there will be weeping and gnashing of teeth." [13] And to the centurion Jesus said, "Go; let it be done for you as you have believed." And the servant was healed at that very moment.

Jesus Heals Many

[14] [c] And when Jesus entered Peter's house, he saw his mother-in-law lying sick with a fever. [15] He touched her hand, and the fever left her, and she rose and began to serve him. [16] That evening they brought to him many who were oppressed by demons, and he cast out the spirits with a word and healed all who were sick. [17] This was to fulfill what was spoken by the prophet Isaiah: [d] "He took our illnesses and bore our diseases."

The Cost of Following Jesus

[18] Now when Jesus saw a crowd around him, he gave orders to go over to the other side. [19] [e] And a scribe came up and said to him, "Teacher, I will follow you wherever you go." [20] And Jesus said to him, "Foxes have holes, and birds of the air have nests, but the Son of Man has nowhere to lay his head." [21] Another of the disciples said to him, "Lord, let me first go and bury my father." [22] And Jesus said to him, "Follow me, and leave the dead to bury their own dead."

Jesus Calms a Storm

[23] [f] And when he got into the boat, his disciples followed him. [24] And behold, there arose a great storm on the sea, so that the boat was being swamped by the waves; but he was asleep. [25] And they went and woke him, saying, "Save us, Lord; we are perishing." [26] And he said to them, "Why are you afraid, O you of little faith?" Then he rose and rebuked the winds and the sea, and there was a great calm. [27] And the men marveled, saying, "What sort of man is this, that even winds and sea obey him?"

Jesus Heals Two Men with Demons

[28] [g] And when he came to the other side, to the country of the Gadarenes,[5] two demon-possessed[6] men met him, coming out of the tombs, so fierce that no one could pass that way. [29] And behold, they cried out, "What have you to do with us, O Son of God? Have you come here to torment us before the time?" [30] Now a herd of many pigs was feeding at some distance from them. [31] And the demons begged him, saying, "If you cast us out, send us away into the herd of pigs." [32] And he said to them, "Go." So they came out and went into the pigs, and behold, the whole herd rushed down the steep bank into the sea and drowned in the waters. [33] The herdsmen fled, and going into the city they told everything, especially what had happened to the demon-possessed men. [34] And behold, all the city came out to meet Jesus, and when they saw him, they begged him to leave their region.

Jesus Heals a Paralytic

9 And getting into a boat he crossed over and came to his own city. [2] [h] And behold, some people brought to him a paralytic, lying on a bed. And when Jesus saw their faith, he said to the paralytic, "Take heart, my son; your sins are forgiven." [3] And behold, some of the scribes said to themselves, "This man is blaspheming."

---

[1] Leprosy was a term for several skin diseases; see Leviticus 13　[2] Greek he　[3] Or bondservant　[4] Some manuscripts not even in Israel　[5] Some manuscripts Gergesenes; some Gerasenes　[6] Greek daimonizomai (demonized); also verse 33; elsewhere rendered oppressed by demons　[a] For 8:2-4 see parallels Mark 1:40-44; Luke 5:12-14　[b] For 8:5-13 see parallel Luke 7:1-10　[c] For 8:14-17 see parallels Mark 1:29-34; Luke 4:38-41　[d] Isa. 53:4　[e] For 8:19-22 see parallel Luke 9:57-62　[f] For 8:23-27 see parallels Mark 4:35-41; Luke 8:22-25　[g] For 8:28-34 see parallels Mark 5:1-21; Luke 8:26-39　[h] For 9:2-8 see parallels Mark 2:1-12; Luke 5:17-26

4 But Jesus, knowing[1] their thoughts, said, "Why do you think evil in your hearts? 5 For which is easier, to say, 'Your sins are forgiven,' or to say, 'Rise and walk'? 6 But that you may know that the Son of Man has authority on earth to forgive sins"—he then said to the paralytic—"Rise, pick up your bed and go home." 7 And he rose and went home. 8 When the crowds saw it, they were afraid, and they glorified God, who had given such authority to men.

Jesus Calls Matthew

9 a As Jesus passed on from there, he saw a man called Matthew sitting at the tax booth, and he said to him, "Follow me." And he rose and followed him.

10 And as Jesus[2] reclined at table in the house, behold, many tax collectors and sinners came and were reclining with Jesus and his disciples. 11 And when the Pharisees saw this, they said to his disciples, "Why does your teacher eat with tax collectors and sinners?" 12 But when he heard it, he said, "Those who are well have no need of a physician, but those who are sick. 13 Go and learn what this means: b 'I desire mercy, and not sacrifice.' For I came not to call the righteous, but sinners."

A Question About Fasting

14 Then the disciples of John came to him, saying, "Why do we and the Pharisees fast,[3] but your disciples do not fast?" 15 And Jesus said to them, "Can the wedding guests mourn as long as the bridegroom is with them? The days will come when the bridegroom is taken away from them, and then they will fast. 16 No one puts a piece of unshrunk cloth on an old garment, for the patch tears away from the garment, and a worse tear is made. 17 Neither is new wine put into old wineskins. If it is, the skins burst and the wine is spilled and the skins are destroyed. But new wine is put into fresh wineskins, and so both are preserved."

A Girl Restored to Life and a Woman Healed

18 c While he was saying these things to them, behold, a ruler came in and knelt before him, saying, "My daughter has just died, but come and lay your hand on her, and she will live." 19 And Jesus rose and followed him, with his disciples. 20 And behold, a woman who had suffered from a discharge of blood for twelve years came up behind him and touched the fringe of his garment, 21 for she said to herself, "If I only touch his garment, I will be made well." 22 Jesus turned, and seeing her he said, "Take heart, daughter; your faith has made you well." And instantly[4] the woman was made well. 23 And when Jesus came to the ruler's house and saw the flute players and the crowd making a commotion, 24 he said, "Go away, for the girl is not dead but sleeping." And they laughed at him. 25 But when the crowd had been put outside, he went in and took her by the hand, and the girl arose. 26 And the report of this went through all that district.

Jesus Heals Two Blind Men

27 And as Jesus passed on from there, two blind men followed him, crying aloud, "Have mercy on us, Son of David." 28 When he entered the house, the blind men came to him, and Jesus said to them, "Do you believe that I am able to do this?" They said to him, "Yes, Lord." 29 Then he touched their eyes, saying, "According to your faith be it done to you." 30 And their eyes were opened. And Jesus sternly warned them, "See that no one knows about it." 31 But they went away and spread his fame through all that district.

Jesus Heals a Man Unable to Speak

32 As they were going away, behold, a demon-oppressed man who was mute was brought to him. 33 And when the demon had been cast out, the mute man spoke. And the crowds marveled, saying, "Never was anything like this seen in Israel." 34 But the Pharisees said, "He casts out demons by the prince of demons."

The Harvest Is Plentiful, the Laborers Few

35 And Jesus went throughout all the cities and villages, teaching in their synagogues and proclaiming the gospel of the kingdom and healing every disease and every affliction. 36 When he saw the crowds, he had compassion for them, because they were harassed and helpless, like sheep without a shepherd. 37 Then he said to his disciples, "The harvest is plentiful, but the laborers are few; 38 therefore pray earnestly to the Lord of the harvest to send out laborers into his harvest."

The Twelve Apostles

10 And he called to him his twelve disciples and gave them authority over unclean spirits, to cast them out, and to heal every disease and every affliction. 2 d The names of the

---

[1] Some manuscripts *perceiving* [2] Greek *he* [3] Some manuscripts add *much,* or often [4] Greek *from that hour* [a] For 9:9-17 see parallels Mark 2:13-22; Luke 5:27-39 [b] Hos. 6:6 [c] For 9:18-26 see parallels Mark 5:21-43; Luke 8:40-56 [d] For 10:2-4 see parallels Mark 3:16-19; Luke 6:13-16

twelve apostles are these: first, Simon, who is called Peter, and Andrew his brother; James the son of Zebedee, and John his brother; [3] Philip and Bartholomew; Thomas and Matthew the tax collector; James the son of Alphaeus, and Thaddaeus;[1] [4] Simon the Zealot,[2] and Judas Iscariot, who betrayed him.

Jesus Sends Out the Twelve Apostles

[5] These twelve Jesus sent out, instructing them, "Go nowhere among the Gentiles and enter no town of the Samaritans, [6] but go rather to the lost sheep of the house of Israel. [7] And proclaim as you go, saying, 'The kingdom of heaven is at hand.'[3] [8] Heal the sick, raise the dead, cleanse lepers,[4] cast out demons. You received without paying; give without pay. [9a] Acquire no gold or silver or copper for your belts, [10] no bag for your journey, or two tunics[5] or sandals or a staff, for the laborer deserves his food. [11] And whatever town or village you enter, find out who is worthy in it and stay there until you depart. [12] As you enter the house, greet it. [13] And if the house is worthy, let your peace come upon it, but if it is not worthy, let your peace return to you. [14] And if anyone will not receive you or listen to your words, shake off the dust from your feet when you leave that house or town. [15] Truly, I say to you, it will be more bearable on the day of judgment for the land of Sodom and Gomorrah than for that town.

Persecution Will Come

[16] "Behold, I am sending you out as sheep in the midst of wolves, so be wise as serpents and innocent as doves. [17] Beware of men, for they will deliver you over to courts and flog you in their synagogues, [18] and you will be dragged before governors and kings for my sake, to bear witness before them and the Gentiles. [19] When they deliver you over, do not be anxious how you are to speak or what you are to say, for what you are to say will be given to you in that hour. [20] For it is not you who speak, but the Spirit of your Father speaking through you. [21] Brother will deliver brother over to death, and the father his child, and children will rise against parents and have them put to death, [22] and you will be hated by all for my name's sake. But the one who endures to the end will be saved. [23] When they persecute you in one town, flee to the next, for truly, I say to you, you will not have gone

through all the towns of Israel before the Son of Man comes.

[24] "A disciple is not above his teacher, nor a servant[6] above his master. [25] It is enough for the disciple to be like his teacher, and the servant like his master. If they have called the master of the house Beelzebul, how much more will they malign[7] those of his household.

Have No Fear

[26] "So have no fear of them, [b] for nothing is covered that will not be revealed, or hidden that will not be known. [27] What I tell you in the dark, say in the light, and what you hear whispered, proclaim on the housetops. [28] And do not fear those who kill the body but cannot kill the soul. Rather fear him who can destroy both soul and body in hell.[8] [29] Are not two sparrows sold for a penny?[9] And not one of them will fall to the ground apart from your Father. [30] But even the hairs of your head are all numbered. [31] Fear not, therefore; you are of more value than many sparrows. [32] So everyone who acknowledges me before men, I also will acknowledge before my Father who is in heaven, [33] but whoever denies me before men, I also will deny before my Father who is in heaven.

Not Peace, but a Sword

[34c] "Do not think that I have come to bring peace to the earth. I have not come to bring peace, but a sword. [35] For I have come to set a man against his father, and a daughter against her mother, and a daughter-in-law against her mother-in-law. [36] And a person's enemies will be those of his own household. [37] Whoever loves father or mother more than me is not worthy of me, and whoever loves son or daughter more than me is not worthy of me. [38] And whoever does not take his cross and follow me is not worthy of me. [39] Whoever finds his life will lose it, and whoever loses his life for my sake will find it.

Rewards

[40] "Whoever receives you receives me, and whoever receives me receives him who sent me. [41] The one who receives a prophet because he is a prophet will receive a prophet's reward, and the one who receives a righteous person because he is a righteous person will receive a righteous person's reward. [42] And whoever gives

---

[1] Some manuscripts *Lebbaeus*, or *Lebbaeus called Thaddaeus* [2] Greek *kananaios*, meaning *zealot* [3] Or *The kingdom of heaven has come near* [4] *Leprosy* was a term for several skin diseases; see Leviticus 13 [5] Greek *chiton*, a long garment worn under the cloak next to the skin [6] Or *bondservant*; also verse 25 [7] Greek lacks *will they malign* [8] Greek *Gehenna* [9] Greek *assarion*, Roman copper coin (Latin *quadrans*) worth about 1/16 of a *denarius* (which was a day's wage for a laborer) [a] For 10:9-15 see parallels Mark 6:8-11; Luke 9:3-5 [b] For 10:26-33 see parallel Luke 12:2-9 [c] For 10:34, 35 see parallel Luke 12:51-53

one of these little ones even a cup of cold water because he is a disciple, truly, I say to you, he will by no means lose his reward."

Messengers from John the Baptist

11 When Jesus had finished instructing his twelve disciples, he went on from there to teach and preach in their cities.

2 [a]Now when John heard in prison about the deeds of the Christ, he sent word by his disciples [3]and said to him, "Are you the one who is to come, or shall we look for another? [4]And Jesus answered them, "Go and tell John what you hear and see: [5]the blind receive their sight and the lame walk, lepers[1] are cleansed and the deaf hear, and the dead are raised up, and the poor have good news preached to them. [6]And blessed is the one who is not offended by me."

7 As they went away, Jesus began to speak to the crowds concerning John: "What did you go out into the wilderness to see? A reed shaken by the wind? [8]What then did you go out to see? A man[2] dressed in soft clothing? Behold, those who wear soft clothing are in kings' houses. [9]What then did you go out to see? A prophet?[3] Yes, I tell you, and more than a prophet. [10]This is he of whom it is written,

[b]"'Behold, I send my messenger before your
face,
who will prepare your way before you.'

11 Truly, I say to you, among those born of women there has arisen no one greater than John the Baptist. Yet the one who is least in the kingdom of heaven is greater than he. [12]From the days of John the Baptist until now the kingdom of heaven has suffered violence,[4] and the violent take it by force. [13]For all the Prophets and the Law prophesied until John, [14]and if you are willing to accept it, he is Elijah who is to come. [15]He who has ears to hear,[5] let him hear.

16 "But to what shall I compare this generation? It is like children sitting in the marketplaces and calling to their playmates,

17 "'We played the flute for you, and you did
not dance;
we sang a dirge, and you did not
mourn.'

18 For John came neither eating nor drinking, and they say, 'He has a demon.' [19]The Son of Man came eating and drinking, and they say, 'Look at him! A glutton and a drunkard, a friend of tax collectors and sinners!' Yet wisdom is justified by her deeds."[6]

Woe to Unrepentant Cities

20 Then he began to denounce the cities where most of his mighty works had been done, because they did not repent. [21][c]"Woe to you, Chorazin! Woe to you, Bethsaida! For if the mighty works done in you had been done in Tyre and Sidon, they would have repented long ago in sackcloth and ashes. [22]But I tell you, it will be more bearable on the day of judgment for Tyre and Sidon than for you. [23]And you, Capernaum, will you be exalted to heaven? You will be brought down to Hades. For if the mighty works done in you had been done in Sodom, it would have remained until this day. [24]But I tell you that it will be more tolerable on the day of judgment for the land of Sodom than for you."

Come to Me, and I Will Give You Rest

25 [d]At that time Jesus declared, "I thank you, Father, Lord of heaven and earth, that you have hidden these things from the wise and understanding and revealed them to little children; [26]yes, Father, for such was your gracious will.[7] [27]All things have been handed over to me by my Father, and no one knows the Son except the Father, and no one knows the Father except the Son and anyone to whom the Son chooses to reveal him. [28]Come to me, all who labor and are heavy laden, and I will give you rest. [29]Take my yoke upon you, and learn from me, for I am gentle and lowly in heart, and you will find rest for your souls. [30]For my yoke is easy, and my burden is light."

Jesus Is Lord of the Sabbath

12 At that time [e]Jesus went through the grainfields on the Sabbath. His disciples were hungry, and they began to pluck heads of grain and to eat. [2]But when the Pharisees saw it, they said to him, "Look, your disciples are doing what is not lawful to do on the Sabbath." [3]He said to them, "Have you not read what David did when he was hungry, and those who were with him: [4]how he entered the house of God and ate the bread of the Presence, which it was not lawful for him to eat nor for those who were with him, but only for the priests?

---

[1] Leprosy was a term for several skin diseases; see Leviticus 13 [2] Or Why then did you go out? To see a man … [3] Some manuscripts Why then did you go out? To see a prophet?
[4] Or has been coming violently [5] Some manuscripts omit to hear [6] Some manuscripts children (compare Luke 7:35) [7] Or for so it pleased you well [a]For 11:2-19 see parallel Luke 7:18-35 [b]Mal. 3:1 [c]For 11:21-24 see parallel Luke 10:13-15 [d]For 11:25-27 see parallel Luke 10:21, 22 [e]For 12:1-8 see parallels Mark 2:23-28; Luke 6:1-5

[5]Or have you not read in the Law how on the Sabbath the priests in the temple profane the Sabbath and are guiltless? [6]I tell you, something greater than the temple is here. [7]And if you had known what this means, [a]'I desire mercy, and not sacrifice,' you would not have condemned the guiltless. [8]For the Son of Man is lord of the Sabbath."

A Man with a Withered Hand

[9]He went on from there and [b]entered their synagogue. [10]And a man was there with a withered hand. And they asked him, "Is it lawful to heal on the Sabbath?"—so that they might accuse him. [11]He said to them, "Which one of you who has a sheep, if it falls into a pit on the Sabbath, will not take hold of it and lift it out? [12]Of how much more value is a man than a sheep! So it is lawful to do good on the Sabbath." [13]Then he said to the man, "Stretch out your hand." And the man stretched it out, and it was restored, healthy like the other. [14]But the Pharisees went out and conspired against him, how to destroy him.

God's Chosen Servant

[15]Jesus, aware of this, withdrew from there. And many followed him, and he healed them all [16]and ordered them not to make him known. [17]This was to fulfill what was spoken by the prophet Isaiah:

[18] [c]"Behold, my servant whom I have chosen,
    my beloved with whom my soul is well
      pleased.
  I will put my Spirit upon him,
    and he will proclaim justice to the
      Gentiles.
[19] He will not quarrel or cry aloud,
    nor will anyone hear his voice in the
      streets;
[20] a bruised reed he will not break,
    and a smoldering wick he will not
      quench,
  until he brings justice to victory;
[21]   and in his name the Gentiles will
      hope."

Blasphemy Against the Holy Spirit

[22][d]Then a demon-oppressed man who was blind and mute was brought to him, and he healed him, so that the man spoke and saw. [23]And all the people were amazed, and said, "Can this be the Son of David?" [24]But when

the Pharisees heard it, they said, "It is only by Beelzebul, the prince of demons, that this man casts out demons." [25]Knowing their thoughts, [e]he said to them, "Every kingdom divided against itself is laid waste, and no city or house divided against itself will stand. [26]And if Satan casts out Satan, he is divided against himself. How then will his kingdom stand? [27]And if I cast out demons by Beelzebul, by whom do your sons cast them out? Therefore they will be your judges. [28]But if it is by the Spirit of God that I cast out demons, then the kingdom of God has come upon you. [29]Or how can someone enter a strong man's house and plunder his goods, unless he first binds the strong man? Then indeed he may plunder his house. [30]Whoever is not with me is against me, and whoever does not gather with me scatters. [31][f]Therefore I tell you, every sin and blasphemy will be forgiven people, but the blasphemy against the Spirit will not be forgiven. [32]And whoever speaks a word against the Son of Man will be forgiven, but whoever speaks against the Holy Spirit will not be forgiven, either in this age or in the age to come.

A Tree Is Known by Its Fruit

[33]"Either make the tree good and its fruit good, or make the tree bad and its fruit bad, for the tree is known by its fruit. [34]You brood of vipers! How can you speak good, when you are evil? For out of the abundance of the heart the mouth speaks. [35]The good person out of his good treasure brings forth good, and the evil person out of his evil treasure brings forth evil. [36]I tell you, on the day of judgment people will give account for every careless word they speak, [37]for by your words you will be justified, and by your words you will be condemned."

The Sign of Jonah

[38]Then some of the scribes and Pharisees answered him, saying, "Teacher, we wish to see a sign from you." [39]But he answered them, [g]"An evil and adulterous generation seeks for a sign, but no sign will be given to it except the sign of the prophet Jonah. [40]For just as Jonah was three days and three nights in the belly of the great fish, so will the Son of Man be three days and three nights in the heart of the earth. [41]The men of Nineveh will rise up at the judgment with this generation and condemn it, for they repented at the preaching of Jonah, and

[a]Hos. 6:6 [b]For 12:9-14 see parallels Mark 3:1-6; Luke 6:6-11 [c]Isa. 42:1-3 [d]For 12:22-24 see parallel Luke 11:14, 15 [e]For 12:25-29 see parallels Mark 3:23-27; Luke 11:17-22 [f]For 12:31, 32 see parallel Mark 3:28-30 [g]For 12:39-42 see parallel Luke 11:29-32

behold, something greater than Jonah is here. [42]The queen of the South will rise up at the judgment with this generation and condemn it, for she came from the ends of the earth to hear the wisdom of Solomon, and behold, something greater than Solomon is here.

Return of an Unclean Spirit

[43]"When [a]the unclean spirit has gone out of a person, it passes through waterless places seeking rest, but finds none. [44]Then it says, 'I will return to my house from which I came.' And when it comes, it finds the house empty, swept, and put in order. [45]Then it goes and brings with it seven other spirits more evil than itself, and they enter and dwell there, and the last state of that person is worse than the first. So also will it be with this evil generation."

Jesus' Mother and Brothers

[46]While he was still speaking to the people, behold, [b]his mother and his brothers[1] stood outside, asking to speak to him.[2] [48]But he replied to the man who told him, "Who is my mother, and who are my brothers?" [49]And stretching out his hand toward his disciples, he said, "Here are my mother and my brothers! [50]For whoever does the will of my Father in heaven is my brother and sister and mother."

The Parable of the Sower

13 That same day Jesus went out of the house [c]and sat beside the sea. [2]And great crowds gathered about him, so that he got into a boat and sat down. And the whole crowd stood on the beach. [3]And he told them many things in parables, saying: "A sower went out to sow. [4]And as he sowed, some seeds fell along the path, and the birds came and devoured them. [5]Other seeds fell on rocky ground, where they did not have much soil, and immediately they sprang up, since they had no depth of soil, [6]but when the sun rose they were scorched. And since they had no root, they withered away. [7]Other seeds fell among thorns, and the thorns grew up and choked them. [8]Other seeds fell on good soil and produced grain, some a hundredfold, some sixty, some thirty. [9]He who has ears,[3] let him hear."

The Purpose of the Parables

[10]Then the disciples came and said to him, "Why do you speak to them in parables?" [11]And he answered them, "To you it has been given to know the secrets of the kingdom of heaven, but to them it has not been given. [12]For to the one who has, more will be given, and he will have an abundance, but from the one who has not, even what he has will be taken away. [13]This is why I speak to them in parables, because seeing they do not see, and hearing they do not hear, nor do they understand. [14]Indeed, in their case the prophecy of Isaiah is fulfilled that says:

[d]"'"You will indeed hear but never understand,
    and you will indeed see but never perceive."
[15] For this people's heart has grown dull,
    and with their ears they can barely hear,
    and their eyes they have closed,
  lest they should see with their eyes
    and hear with their ears
  and understand with their heart
    and turn, and I would heal them.'

[16]But blessed are your eyes, for they see, and your ears, for they hear. [17]For truly, I say to you, many prophets and righteous people longed to see what you see, and did not see it, and to hear what you hear, and did not hear it.

The Parable of the Sower Explained

[18e] "Hear then the parable of the sower: [19]When anyone hears the word of the kingdom and does not understand it, the evil one comes and snatches away what has been sown in his heart. This is what was sown along the path. [20]As for what was sown on rocky ground, this is the one who hears the word and immediately receives it with joy, [21]yet he has no root in himself, but endures for a while, and when tribulation or persecution arises on account of the word, immediately he falls away.[4] [22]As for what was sown among thorns, this is the one who hears the word, but the cares of the world and the deceitfulness of riches choke the word, and it proves unfruitful. [23]As for what was sown on good soil, this is the one who hears the word and understands it. He indeed bears fruit and yields, in one case a hundredfold, in another sixty, and in another thirty."

The Parable of the Weeds

[24]He put another parable before them, saying, "The kingdom of heaven may be compared

---

[1] Or brothers and sisters; also verses 48, 49 [2] Some manuscripts insert verse 47: Someone told him, "Your mother and your brothers are standing outside, asking to speak to you" [3] Some manuscripts add here and in verse 43 to hear [4] Or stumbles [a] For 12:43-45 see parallel Luke 11:24-26 [b] For 12:46-50 see parallels Mark 3:31-35; Luke 8:19-21 [c] For 13:1-15 see parallels Mark 4:1-12; Luke 8:4-10 [d] Isa. 6:9, 10 [e] For 13:18-23 see parallels Mark 4:13-20; Luke 8:11-15

to a man who sowed good seed in his field, [25]but while his men were sleeping, his enemy came and sowed weeds[1] among the wheat and went away. [26]So when the plants came up and bore grain, then the weeds appeared also. [27]And the servants[2] of the master of the house came and said to him, 'Master, did you not sow good seed in your field? How then does it have weeds?' [28]He said to them, 'An enemy has done this.' So the servants said to him, 'Then do you want us to go and gather them?' [29]But he said, 'No, lest in gathering the weeds you root up the wheat along with them. [30]Let both grow together until the harvest, and at harvest time I will tell the reapers, "Gather the weeds first and bind them in bundles to be burned, but gather the wheat into my barn." ' "

The Mustard Seed and the Leaven

[31] He put another parable before them, saying, [a]"The kingdom of heaven is like a grain of mustard seed that a man took and sowed in his field. [32]It is the smallest of all seeds, but when it has grown it is larger than all the garden plants and becomes a tree, so that the birds of the air come and make nests in its branches."

[33] He told them another parable. "The kingdom of heaven is like leaven that a woman took and hid in three measures of flour, till it was all leavened."

Prophecy and Parables

[34] All these things Jesus said to the crowds in parables; indeed, he said nothing to them without a parable. [35] This was to fulfill what was spoken by the prophet:[3]

[b]"I will open my mouth in parables;
  I will utter what has been hidden since
    the foundation of the world."

The Parable of the Weeds Explained

[36] Then he left the crowds and went into the house. And his disciples came to him, saying, "Explain to us the parable of the weeds of the field." [37] He answered, "The one who sows the good seed is the Son of Man. [38]The field is the world, and the good seed is the sons of the kingdom. The weeds are the sons of the evil one, [39]and the enemy who sowed them is the devil. The harvest is the end of the age, and the reapers are angels. [40]Just as the weeds are gathered and burned with fire, so will it be at the end of the age. [41]The Son of Man will send his angels, and

they will gather out of his kingdom all causes of sin and all law-breakers, [42]and throw them into the fiery furnace. In that place there will be weeping and gnashing of teeth. [43]Then the righteous will shine like the sun in the kingdom of their Father. He who has ears, let him hear.

The Parable of the Hidden Treasure

[44]"The kingdom of heaven is like treasure hidden in a field, which a man found and covered up. Then in his joy he goes and sells all that he has and buys that field.

The Parable of the Pearl of Great Value

[45]"Again, the kingdom of heaven is like a merchant in search of fine pearls, [46]who, on finding one pearl of great value, went and sold all that he had and bought it.

The Parable of the Net

[47]"Again, the kingdom of heaven is like a net that was thrown into the sea and gathered fish of every kind. [48]When it was full, men drew it ashore and sat down and sorted the good into containers but threw away the bad. [49]So it will be at the end of the age. The angels will come out and separate the evil from the righteous [50]and throw them into the fiery furnace. In that place there will be weeping and gnashing of teeth.

New and Old Treasures

[51]"Have you understood all these things?" They said to him, "Yes." [52]And he said to them, "Therefore every scribe who has been trained for the kingdom of heaven is like a master of a house, who brings out of his treasure what is new and what is old."

Jesus Rejected at Nazareth

[53] And when Jesus had finished these parables, he went away from there, [54][c] and coming to his hometown he taught them in their synagogue, so that they were astonished, and said, "Where did this man get this wisdom and these mighty works? [55]Is not this the carpenter's son? Is not his mother called Mary? And are not his brothers James and Joseph and Simon and Judas? [56]And are not all his sisters with us? Where then did this man get all these things?" [57]And they took offense at him. But Jesus said to them, "A prophet is not without honor except in his hometown and in his own household."

---

[1] Probably *darnel*, a wheat-like weed   [2] Or *bondservants*; also verse 28   [3] Some manuscripts *Isaiah the prophet*   [a] For 13:31, 32 see parallels Mark 4:30-32; Luke 13:18, 19
[b] Ps. 78:2   [c] For 13:54-58 see parallel Mark 6:1-6

58 And he did not do many mighty works there, because of their unbelief.

The Death of John the Baptist

14 ᵃAt that time Herod the tetrarch heard about the fame of Jesus, ² and he said to his servants, "This is John the Baptist. He has been raised from the dead; that is why these miraculous powers are at work in him." ³ For Herod had seized John and bound him and put him in prison for the sake of Herodias, his brother Philip's wife,¹ ⁴ because John had been saying to him, "It is not lawful for you to have her." ⁵ And though he wanted to put him to death, he feared the people, because they held him to be a prophet. ⁶ But when Herod's birthday came, the daughter of Herodias danced before the company and pleased Herod, ⁷ so that he promised with an oath to give her whatever she might ask. ⁸ Prompted by her mother, she said, "Give me the head of John the Baptist here on a platter." ⁹ And the king was sorry, but because of his oaths and his guests he commanded it to be given. ¹⁰ He sent and had John beheaded in the prison, ¹¹ and his head was brought on a platter and given to the girl, and she brought it to her mother. ¹² And his disciples came and took the body and buried it, and they went and told Jesus.

Jesus Feeds the Five Thousand

¹³ Now when Jesus heard this, ᵇhe withdrew from there in a boat to a desolate place by himself. But when the crowds heard it, they followed him on foot from the towns. ¹⁴ When he went ashore he saw a great crowd, and he had compassion on them and healed their sick. ¹⁵ Now when it was evening, the disciples came to him and said, "This is a desolate place, and the day is now over; send the crowds away to go into the villages and buy food for themselves." ¹⁶ But Jesus said, "They need not go away; you give them something to eat." ¹⁷ They said to him, "We have only five loaves here and two fish." ¹⁸ And he said, "Bring them here to me." ¹⁹ Then he ordered the crowds to sit down on the grass, and taking the five loaves and the two fish, he looked up to heaven and said a blessing. Then he broke the loaves and gave them to the disciples, and the disciples gave them to the crowds. ²⁰ And they all ate and were satisfied. And they took up twelve baskets full of the broken pieces left over. ²¹ And those who ate were about five thousand men, besides women and children.

Jesus Walks on the Water

²² ᶜImmediately he made the disciples get into the boat and go before him to the other side, while he dismissed the crowds. ²³ And after he had dismissed the crowds, he went up on the mountain by himself to pray. When evening came, he was there alone, ²⁴ but the boat by this time was a long way² from the land,³ beaten by the waves, for the wind was against them. ²⁵ And in the fourth watch of the night⁴ he came to them, walking on the sea. ²⁶ But when the disciples saw him walking on the sea, they were terrified, and said, "It is a ghost!" and they cried out in fear. ²⁷ But immediately Jesus spoke to them, saying, "Take heart; it is I. Do not be afraid."

²⁸ And Peter answered him, "Lord, if it is you, command me to come to you on the water." ²⁹ He said, "Come." So Peter got out of the boat and walked on the water and came to Jesus. ³⁰ But when he saw the wind,⁵ he was afraid, and beginning to sink he cried out, "Lord, save me." ³¹ Jesus immediately reached out his hand and took hold of him, saying to him, "O you of little faith, why did you doubt?" ³² And when they got into the boat, the wind ceased. ³³ And those in the boat worshiped him, saying, "Truly you are the Son of God."

Jesus Heals the Sick in Gennesaret

³⁴ ᵈAnd when they had crossed over, they came to land at Gennesaret. ³⁵ And when the men of that place recognized him, they sent around to all that region and brought to him all who were sick ³⁶ and implored him that they might only touch the fringe of his garment. And as many as touched it were made well.

Traditions and Commandments

15 ᵉThen Pharisees and scribes came to Jesus from Jerusalem and said, ² "Why do your disciples break the tradition of the elders? For they do not wash their hands when they eat." ³ He answered them, "And why do you break the commandment of God for the sake of your tradition? ⁴ For God commanded, ᶠ'Honor your father and your mother,' and, ᵍ'Whoever reviles

¹ Some manuscripts his brother's wife ² Greek many stadia, a stadion was about 607 feet or 185 meters ³ Some manuscripts was out on the sea ⁴ That is, between 3 A.M. and 6 A.M. ⁵ Some manuscripts strong wind ᵃFor 14:1-12 see parallels Mark 6:14-29; Luke 9:7-9 ᵇFor 14:13-21 see parallels Mark 6:32-44; Luke 9:10-17; John 6:1-13 ᶜFor 14:22-33 see parallels Mark 6:45-52; John 6:16-21 ᵈFor 14:34-36 see parallel Mark 6:53-56 ᵉFor 15:1-20 see parallel Mark 7:1-23 ᶠEx. 20:12 ᵍEx. 21:17

father or mother must surely die.' [5]But you say, 'If anyone tells his father or his mother, "What you would have gained from me is given to God,"[1] [6]he need not honor his father.' So for the sake of your tradition you have made void the word[2] of God. [7]You hypocrites! Well did Isaiah prophesy of you, when he said:

[8][a]" 'This people honors me with their lips,
　　 but their heart is far from me;
[9]　 in vain do they worship me,
　　 teaching as doctrines the command-
　　 ments of men.' "

What Defiles a Person

[10]And he called the people to him and said to them, "Hear and understand: [11]it is not what goes into the mouth that defiles a person, but what comes out of the mouth; this defiles a person." [12]Then the disciples came and said to him, "Do you know that the Pharisees were offended when they heard this saying?" [13]He answered, "Every plant that my heavenly Father has not planted will be rooted up. [14]Let them alone; they are blind guides.[3] And if the blind lead the blind, both will fall into a pit." [15]But Peter said to him, "Explain the parable to us." [16]And he said, "Are you also still without understanding? [17]Do you not see that whatever goes into the mouth passes into the stomach and is expelled?[4] [18]But what comes out of the mouth proceeds from the heart, and this defiles a person. [19]For out of the heart come evil thoughts, murder, adultery, sexual immorality, theft, false witness, slander. [20]These are what defile a person. But to eat with unwashed hands does not defile anyone."

The Faith of a Canaanite Woman

[21][b]And Jesus went away from there and withdrew to the district of Tyre and Sidon. [22]And behold, a Canaanite woman from that region came out and was crying, "Have mercy on me, O Lord, Son of David; my daughter is severely oppressed by a demon." [23]But he did not answer her a word. And his disciples came and begged him, saying, "Send her away, for she is crying out after us." [24]He answered, "I was sent only to the lost sheep of the house of Israel." [25]But she came and knelt before him, saying, "Lord, help me." [26]And he answered, "It is not right to take the children's bread and throw it to the dogs." [27]She said, "Yes, Lord, yet even the dogs eat the crumbs that fall from their masters' table." [28]Then Jesus answered her, "O woman, great is your faith! Be it done for you as you desire." And her daughter was healed instantly.[5]

Jesus Heals Many

[29]Jesus went on from there and walked beside the Sea of Galilee. And he went up on the mountain and sat down there. [30]And great crowds came to him, bringing with them the lame, the blind, the crippled, the mute, and many others, and they put them at his feet, and he healed them, [31]so that the crowd wondered, when they saw the mute speaking, the crippled healthy, the lame walking, and the blind seeing. And they glorified the God of Israel.

Jesus Feeds the Four Thousand

[32][c]Then Jesus called his disciples to him and said, "I have compassion on the crowd because they have been with me now three days and have nothing to eat. And I am unwilling to send them away hungry, lest they faint on the way." [33]And the disciples said to him, "Where are we to get enough bread in such a desolate place to feed so great a crowd?" [34]And Jesus said to them, "How many loaves do you have?" They said, "Seven, and a few small fish." [35]And directing the crowd to sit down on the ground, [36]he took the seven loaves and the fish, and having given thanks he broke them and gave them to the disciples, and the disciples gave them to the crowds. [37]And they all ate and were satisfied. And they took up seven baskets full of the broken pieces left over. [38]Those who ate were four thousand men, besides women and children. [39]And after sending away the crowds, he got into the boat and went to the region of Magadan.

The Pharisees and Sadducees Demand Signs

16 [d]And the Pharisees and Sadducees came, and to test him they asked him to show them a sign from heaven. [2]He answered them,[6] "When it is evening, you say, 'It will be fair weather, for the sky is red.' [3]And in the morning, 'It will be stormy today, for the sky is red and threatening.' You know how to interpret the appearance of the sky, but you cannot interpret the signs of the times. [4]An evil and adulterous generation seeks for a sign, but no sign will be given to it except the sign of Jonah." So he left them and departed.

---

[1] Or is an offering　[2] Some manuscripts law　[3] Some manuscripts add of the blind　[4] Greek is expelled into the latrine　[5] Greek from that hour　[6] Some manuscripts omit the following words to the end of verse 3　[a] Isa. 29:13　[b] For 15:21-28 see parallel Mark 7:24-30　[c] For 15:32-39 see parallel Mark 8:1-10　[d] For 16:1-12 see parallel Mark 8:11-21

The Leaven of the Pharisees and Sadducees

[5] When the disciples reached the other side, they had forgotten to bring any bread. [6] Jesus said to them, "Watch and beware of the leaven of the Pharisees and Sadducees." [7] And they began discussing it among themselves, saying, "We brought no bread." [8] But Jesus, aware of this, said, "O you of little faith, why are you discussing among yourselves the fact that you have no bread? [9] Do you not yet perceive? Do you not remember the five loaves for the five thousand, and how many baskets you gathered? [10] Or the seven loaves for the four thousand, and how many baskets you gathered? [11] How is it that you fail to understand that I did not speak about bread? Beware of the leaven of the Pharisees and Sadducees." [12] Then they understood that he did not tell them to beware of the leaven of bread, but of the teaching of the Pharisees and Sadducees.

Peter Confesses Jesus as the Christ

[13] [a] Now when Jesus came into the district of Caesarea Philippi, he asked his disciples, "Who do people say that the Son of Man is?" [14] And they said, "Some say John the Baptist, others say Elijah, and others Jeremiah or one of the prophets." [15] He said to them, "But who do you say that I am?" [16] Simon Peter replied, "You are the Christ, the Son of the living God." [17] And Jesus answered him, "Blessed are you, Simon Bar-Jonah! For flesh and blood has not revealed this to you, but my Father who is in heaven. [18] And I tell you, you are Peter, and on this rock[1] I will build my church, and the gates of hell[2] shall not prevail against it. [19] I will give you the keys of the kingdom of heaven, and whatever you bind on earth shall be bound in heaven, and whatever you loose on earth shall be loosed[3] in heaven." [20] Then he strictly charged the disciples to tell no one that he was the Christ.

Jesus Foretells His Death and Resurrection

[21] [b] From that time Jesus began to show his disciples that he must go to Jerusalem and suffer many things from the elders and chief priests and scribes, and be killed, and on the third day be raised. [22] And Peter took him aside and began to rebuke him, saying, "Far be it from you, Lord![4] This shall never happen to you." [23] But he turned and said to Peter, "Get behind me, Satan! You are a hindrance[5] to me. For you are not setting your mind on the things of God, but on the things of man."

Take Up Your Cross and Follow Jesus

[24] Then Jesus told his disciples, "If anyone would come after me, let him deny himself and take up his cross and follow me. [25] For whoever would save his life[6] will lose it, but whoever loses his life for my sake will find it. [26] For what will it profit a man if he gains the whole world and forfeits his soul? Or what shall a man give in return for his soul? [27] For the Son of Man is going to come with his angels in the glory of his Father, and then he will repay each person according to what he has done. [28] Truly, I say to you, there are some standing here who will not taste death until they see the Son of Man coming in his kingdom."

The Transfiguration

17 [c] And after six days Jesus took with him Peter and James, and John his brother, and led them up a high mountain by themselves. [2] And he was transfigured before them, and his face shone like the sun, and his clothes became white as light. [3] And behold, there appeared to them Moses and Elijah, talking with him. [4] And Peter said to Jesus, "Lord, it is good that we are here. If you wish, I will make three tents here, one for you and one for Moses and one for Elijah." [5] He was still speaking when, behold, a bright cloud overshadowed them, and a voice from the cloud said, "This is my beloved Son,[7] with whom I am well pleased; listen to him." [6] When the disciples heard this, they fell on their faces and were terrified. [7] But Jesus came and touched them, saying, "Rise, and have no fear." [8] And when they lifted up their eyes, they saw no one but Jesus only.

[9] [d] And as they were coming down the mountain, Jesus commanded them, "Tell no one the vision, until the Son of Man is raised from the dead." [10] And the disciples asked him, "Then why do the scribes say that first Elijah must come?" [11] He answered, "Elijah does come, and he will restore all things. [12] But I tell you that Elijah has already come, and they did not recognize him, but did to him whatever they pleased. So also the Son of Man will certainly suffer at their hands." [13] Then the disciples understood that he was speaking to them of John the Baptist.

Jesus Heals a Boy with a Demon

[14] [e] And when they came to the crowd, a man came up to him and, kneeling before him, [15] said, "Lord, have mercy on my son, for he has

---

[1] The Greek words for *Peter* and *rock* sound similar [2] Greek *the gates of Hades* [3] Or *shall have been bound . . . shall have been loosed* [4] Or "[May God be] *merciful to you, Lord!*" [5] Greek *stumbling block* [6] The same Greek word can mean either *soul* or *life*, depending on the context; twice in this verse and twice in verse 26 [7] Or *my Son, my* (or *the*) *Beloved* [a] For 16:13-16 see parallels Mark 8:27-29; Luke 9:18-20 [b] For 16:21-28 see parallels Mark 8:31–9:1; Luke 9:22-27 [c] For 17:1-8 see parallels Mark 9:2-8; Luke 9:28-36 [d] For 17:9-13 see parallel Mark 9:9-13 [e] For 17:14-19 see parallels Mark 9:14-28; Luke 9:37-42

seizures and he suffers terribly. For often he falls into the fire, and often into the water. [16]And I brought him to your disciples, and they could not heal him." [17]And Jesus answered, "O faithless and twisted generation, how long am I to be with you? How long am I to bear with you? Bring him here to me." [18]And Jesus rebuked the demon,[1] and it[2] came out of him, and the boy was healed instantly.[3] [19]Then the disciples came to Jesus privately and said, "Why could we not cast it out?" [20]He said to them, "Because of your little faith. For truly, I say to you, if you have faith like a grain of mustard seed, you will say to this mountain, 'Move from here to there,' and it will move, and nothing will be impossible for you."[4]

Jesus Again Foretells Death, Resurrection

[22][a]As they were gathering[5] in Galilee, Jesus said to them, "The Son of Man is about to be delivered into the hands of men, [23]and they will kill him, and he will be raised on the third day." And they were greatly distressed.

The Temple Tax

[24]When they came to Capernaum, the collectors of the two-drachma tax went up to Peter and said, "Does your teacher not pay the tax?" [25]He said, "Yes." And when he came into the house, Jesus spoke to him first, saying, "What do you think, Simon? From whom do kings of the earth take toll or tax? From their sons or from others?" [26]And when he said, "From others," Jesus said to him, "Then the sons are free. [27]However, not to give offense to them, go to the sea and cast a hook and take the first fish that comes up, and when you open its mouth you will find a shekel.[6] Take that and give it to them for me and for yourself."

Who Is the Greatest?

18 [b]At that time the disciples came to Jesus, saying, "Who is the greatest in the kingdom of heaven?" [2]And calling to him a child, he put him in the midst of them [3]and said, "Truly, I say to you, unless you turn and become like children, you will never enter the kingdom of heaven. [4]Whoever humbles himself like this child is the greatest in the kingdom of heaven. [5]"Whoever receives one such child in my name receives me, [6]but whoever causes one of these little ones who believe in me to sin,[7] it would be better for him to have a great

millstone fastened around his neck and to be drowned in the depth of the sea.

Temptations to Sin

[7]"Woe to the world for temptations to sin![8] For it is necessary that temptations come, but woe to the one by whom the temptation comes! [8]And if your hand or your foot causes you to sin, cut it off and throw it away. It is better for you to enter life crippled or lame than with two hands or two feet to be thrown into the eternal fire. [9]And if your eye causes you to sin, tear it out and throw it away. It is better for you to enter life with one eye than with two eyes to be thrown into the hell[9] of fire.

The Parable of the Lost Sheep

[10]"See that you do not despise one of these little ones. For I tell you that in heaven their angels always see the face of my Father who is in heaven.[10] [12]What do you think? If a man has a hundred sheep, and one of them has gone astray, does he not leave the ninety-nine on the mountains and go in search of the one that went astray? [13]And if he finds it, truly, I say to you, he rejoices over it more than over the ninety-nine that never went astray. [14]So it is not the will of my[11] Father who is in heaven that one of these little ones should perish.

If Your Brother Sins Against You

[15]"If your brother sins against you, go and tell him his fault, between you and him alone. If he listens to you, you have gained your brother. [16]But if he does not listen, take one or two others along with you, that every charge may be established by the evidence of two or three witnesses. [17]If he refuses to listen to them, tell it to the church. And if he refuses to listen even to the church, let him be to you as a Gentile and a tax collector. [18]Truly, I say to you, whatever you bind on earth shall be bound in heaven, and whatever you loose on earth shall be loosed[12] in heaven. [19]Again I say to you, if two of you agree on earth about anything they ask, it will be done for them by my Father in heaven. [20]For where two or three are gathered in my name, there am I among them."

The Parable of the Unforgiving Servant

[21]Then Peter came up and said to him, "Lord, how often will my brother sin against me, and

---

[1] Greek it [2] Greek the demon [3] Greek from that hour [4] Some manuscripts insert verse 21: *But this kind never comes out except by prayer and fasting* [5] Some manuscripts remained [6] Greek stater, a silver coin worth four drachmas or approximately one shekel [7] Greek causes . . . to stumble; also verses 8, 9 [8] Greek stumbling blocks [9] Greek Gehenna [10] Some manuscripts add verse 11: *For the Son of Man came to save the lost* [11] Some manuscripts your [12] Or shall have been bound . . . shall have been loosed [a] For 17:22, 23 see parallels Mark 9:30-32; Luke 9:43-45 [b] For 18:1-5 see parallels Mark 9:33-37; Luke 9:46-48

I forgive him? As many as seven times?" [22]Jesus said to him, "I do not say to you seven times, but seventy-seven times.

[23]"Therefore the kingdom of heaven may be compared to a king who wished to settle accounts with his servants.[1] [24]When he began to settle, one was brought to him who owed him ten thousand talents.[2] [25]And since he could not pay, his master ordered him to be sold, with his wife and children and all that he had, and payment to be made. [26]So the servant[3] fell on his knees, imploring him, 'Have patience with me, and I will pay you everything.' [27]And out of pity for him, the master of that servant released him and forgave him the debt. [28]But when that same servant went out, he found one of his fellow servants who owed him a hundred denarii,[4] and seizing him, he began to choke him, saying, 'Pay what you owe.' [29]So his fellow servant fell down and pleaded with him, 'Have patience with me, and I will pay you.' [30]He refused and went and put him in prison until he should pay the debt. [31]When his fellow servants saw what had taken place, they were greatly distressed, and they went and reported to their master all that had taken place. [32]Then his master summoned him and said to him, 'You wicked servant! I forgave you all that debt because you pleaded with me. [33]And should not you have had mercy on your fellow servant, as I had mercy on you?' [34]And in anger his master delivered him to the jailers,[5] until he should pay all his debt. [35]So also my heavenly Father will do to every one of you, if you do not forgive your brother from your heart."

Teaching About Divorce

19 Now when Jesus had finished these sayings, he went away from Galilee and [a]entered the region of Judea beyond the Jordan. [2]And large crowds followed him, and he healed them there.

[3]And Pharisees came up to him and tested him by asking, "Is it lawful to divorce one's wife for any cause?" [4]He answered, "Have you not read that he who created them from the beginning made them male and female, [5]and said, [b]'Therefore a man shall leave his father and his mother and hold fast to his wife, and the two shall become one flesh'? [6]So they are no longer two but one flesh. What therefore God has joined together, let not man separate." [7]They said to him, "Why then did Moses command one to give a certificate of divorce and to send her away?" [8]He said to them, "Because of your hardness of heart Moses allowed you to divorce your wives, but from the beginning it was not so. [9]And I say to you: whoever divorces his wife, except for sexual immorality, and marries another, commits adultery."[6]

[10]The disciples said to him, "If such is the case of a man with his wife, it is better not to marry." [11]But he said to them, "Not everyone can receive this saying, but only those to whom it is given. [12]For there are eunuchs who have been so from birth, and there are eunuchs who have been made eunuchs by men, and there are eunuchs who have made themselves eunuchs for the sake of the kingdom of heaven. Let the one who is able to receive this receive it."

Let the Children Come to Me

[13][c]Then children were brought to him that he might lay his hands on them and pray. The disciples rebuked the people, [14]but Jesus said, "Let the little children come to me and do not hinder them, for to such belongs the kingdom of heaven." [15]And he laid his hands on them and went away.

The Rich Young Man

[16][d]And behold, a man came up to him, saying, "Teacher, what good deed must I do to have eternal life?" [17]And he said to him, "Why do you ask me about what is good? There is only one who is good. If you would enter life, keep the commandments." [18]He said to him, "Which ones?" And Jesus said, [e]"You shall not murder, You shall not commit adultery, You shall not steal, You shall not bear false witness, [19]Honor your father and mother, and, [f]You shall love your neighbor as yourself." [20]The young man said to him, "All these I have kept. What do I still lack?" [21]Jesus said to him, "If you would be perfect, go, sell what you possess and give to the poor, and you will have treasure in heaven; and come, follow me." [22]When the young man heard this he went away sorrowful, for he had great possessions.

[23]And Jesus said to his disciples, "Truly, I say to you, only with difficulty will a rich person enter the kingdom of heaven. [24]Again I tell you,

---

[1] Or *bondservants*; also verses 28, 31 [2] A *talent* was a monetary unit worth about twenty years' wages for a laborer [3] Or *bondservant*; also verses 27, 28, 29, 32, 33 [4] A *denarius* was a day's wage for a laborer [5] Greek *torturers* [6] Some manuscripts add *and whoever marries a divorced woman commits adultery*; other manuscripts *except for sexual immorality, makes her commit adultery, and whoever marries a divorced woman commits adultery* [a] For 19:1-9 see parallel Mark 10:1-12 [b] Gen. 2:24 [c] For 19:13-15 see parallels Mark 10:13-16; Luke 18:15-17 [d] For 19:16-30 see parallels Mark 10:17-31; Luke 18:18-30 [e] Ex. 20:12-16; Deut. 5:16-20 [f] Lev. 19:18

it is easier for a camel to go through the eye of a needle than for a rich person to enter the kingdom of God." ²⁵ When the disciples heard this, they were greatly astonished, saying, "Who then can be saved?" ²⁶ But Jesus looked at them and said, "With man this is impossible, but with God all things are possible." ²⁷ Then Peter said in reply, "See, we have left everything and followed you. What then will we have?" ²⁸ Jesus said to them, "Truly, I say to you, in the new world,¹ when the Son of Man will sit on his glorious throne, you who have followed me will also sit on twelve thrones, judging the twelve tribes of Israel. ²⁹ And everyone who has left houses or brothers or sisters or father or mother or children or lands, for my name's sake, will receive a hundredfold² and will inherit eternal life. ³⁰ But many who are first will be last, and the last first.

Laborers in the Vineyard

20 "For the kingdom of heaven is like a master of a house who went out early in the morning to hire laborers for his vineyard. ²After agreeing with the laborers for a denarius³ a day, he sent them into his vineyard. ³And going out about the third hour he saw others standing idle in the marketplace, ⁴and to them he said, 'You go into the vineyard too, and whatever is right I will give you.' ⁵So they went. Going out again about the sixth hour and the ninth hour, he did the same. ⁶And about the eleventh hour he went out and found others standing. And he said to them, 'Why do you stand here idle all day?' ⁷They said to him, 'Because no one has hired us.' He said to them, 'You go into the vineyard too.' ⁸And when evening came, the owner of the vineyard said to his foreman, 'Call the laborers and pay them their wages, beginning with the last, up to the first.' ⁹And when those hired about the eleventh hour came, each of them received a denarius. ¹⁰Now when those hired first came, they thought they would receive more, but each of them also received a denarius. ¹¹And on receiving it they grumbled at the master of the house, ¹²saying, 'These last worked only one hour, and you have made them equal to us who have borne the burden of the day and the scorching heat.' ¹³But he replied to one of them, 'Friend, I am doing you no wrong. Did you not agree with me for a denarius? ¹⁴Take what belongs to you and go.

I choose to give to this last worker as I give to you. ¹⁵Am I not allowed to do what I choose with what belongs to me? Or do you begrudge my generosity?'⁴ ¹⁶So the last will be first, and the first last."

Jesus Foretells His Death a Third Time

¹⁷ᵃ And as Jesus was going up to Jerusalem, he took the twelve disciples aside, and on the way he said to them, ¹⁸"See, we are going up to Jerusalem. And the Son of Man will be delivered over to the chief priests and scribes, and they will condemn him to death ¹⁹and deliver him over to the Gentiles to be mocked and flogged and crucified, and he will be raised on the third day."

A Mother's Request

²⁰ᵇ Then the mother of the sons of Zebedee came up to him with her sons, and kneeling before him she asked him for something. ²¹ And he said to her, "What do you want?" She said to him, "Say that these two sons of mine are to sit, one at your right hand and one at your left, in your kingdom." ²² Jesus answered, "You do not know what you are asking. Are you able to drink the cup that I am to drink?" They said to him, "We are able." ²³ He said to them, "You will drink my cup, but to sit at my right hand and at my left is not mine to grant, but it is for those for whom it has been prepared by my Father." ²⁴ And when the ten heard it, they were indignant at the two brothers. ²⁵ But Jesus called them to him and said, "You know that the rulers of the Gentiles lord it over them, and their great ones exercise authority over them. ²⁶It shall not be so among you. But whoever would be great among you must be your servant,⁵ ²⁷and whoever would be first among you must be your slave,⁶ ²⁸even as the Son of Man came not to be served but to serve, and to give his life as a ransom for many."

Jesus Heals Two Blind Men

²⁹ᶜ And as they went out of Jericho, a great crowd followed him. ³⁰ And behold, there were two blind men sitting by the roadside, and when they heard that Jesus was passing by, they cried out, "Lord,⁷ have mercy on us, Son of David!" ³¹ The crowd rebuked them, telling them to be silent, but they cried out all the more, "Lord, have mercy on us, Son of David!"

¹ Greek *in the regeneration* ² Some manuscripts *manifold* ³ A *denarius* was a day's wage for a laborer ⁴ Or *is your eye bad because I am good?* ⁵ Greek *diakonos* ⁶ Or *bondservant, or servant* (for the contextual rendering of the Greek word *doulos*, see Preface) ⁷ Some manuscripts omit *Lord* ᵃ For 20:17-19 see parallels Mark 10:32-34; Luke 18:31-33
ᵇ For 20:20-28 see parallel Mark 10:35-45 ᶜ For 20:29-34 see parallels Mark 10:46-52; Luke 18:35-43

[32] And stopping, Jesus called them and said, "What do you want me to do for you?" [33] They said to him, "Lord, let our eyes be opened." [34] And Jesus in pity touched their eyes, and immediately they recovered their sight and followed him.

The Triumphal Entry

21 [a]Now when they drew near to Jerusalem and came to Bethphage, to the Mount of Olives, then Jesus sent two disciples, [2] saying to them, "Go into the village in front of you, and immediately you will find a donkey tied, and a colt with her. Untie them and bring them to me. [3] If anyone says anything to you, you shall say, 'The Lord needs them,' and he will send them at once." [4] This took place to fulfill what was spoken by the prophet, saying,

[5] [b]"Say to the daughter of Zion,
　'Behold, your king is coming to you,
　　humble, and mounted on a donkey,
　　on a colt,[1] the foal of a beast of bur-
　　den.'"

[6] The disciples went and did as Jesus had directed them. [7] They brought the donkey and the colt and put on them their cloaks, and he sat on them. [8] Most of the crowd spread their cloaks on the road, and others cut branches from the trees and spread them on the road. [9] And the crowds that went before him and that followed him were shouting, "Hosanna to the Son of David! Blessed is he who comes in the name of the Lord! Hosanna in the highest!" [10] And when he entered Jerusalem, the whole city was stirred up, saying, "Who is this?" [11] And the crowds said, "This is the prophet Jesus, from Nazareth of Galilee."

Jesus Cleanses the Temple

[12] [c]And Jesus entered the temple[2] and drove out all who sold and bought in the temple, and he overturned the tables of the money-changers and the seats of those who sold pigeons. [13] He said to them, "It is written, [d]'My house shall be called a house of prayer,' but you make it a den of robbers."

[14] And the blind and the lame came to him in the temple, and he healed them. [15] But when the chief priests and the scribes saw the wonderful things that he did, and the children crying out in the temple, "Hosanna to the Son of David!" they were indignant, [16] and they said to him,

"Do you hear what these are saying?" And Jesus said to them, "Yes; have you never read,

　[e]"'Out of the mouth of infants and nursing
　　babies
　　you have prepared praise'?"

[17] And leaving them, he went out of the city to Bethany and lodged there.

Jesus Curses the Fig Tree

[18] [f]In the morning, as he was returning to the city, he became hungry. [19] And seeing a fig tree by the wayside, he went to it and found nothing on it but only leaves. And he said to it, "May no fruit ever come from you again!" And the fig tree withered at once.

[20] When the disciples saw it, they marveled, saying, "How did the fig tree wither at once?" [21] And Jesus answered them, "Truly, I say to you, if you have faith and do not doubt, you will not only do what has been done to the fig tree, but even if you say to this mountain, 'Be taken up and thrown into the sea,' it will happen. [22] And whatever you ask in prayer, you will receive, if you have faith."

The Authority of Jesus Challenged

[23] [g]And when he entered the temple, the chief priests and the elders of the people came up to him as he was teaching, and said, "By what authority are you doing these things, and who gave you this authority?" [24] Jesus answered them, "I also will ask you one question, and if you tell me the answer, then I also will tell you by what authority I do these things. [25] The baptism of John, from where did it come? From heaven or from man?" And they discussed it among themselves, saying, "If we say, 'From heaven,' he will say to us, 'Why then did you not believe him?' [26] But if we say, 'From man,' we are afraid of the crowd, for they all hold that John was a prophet." [27] So they answered Jesus, "We do not know." And he said to them, "Neither will I tell you by what authority I do these things.

The Parable of the Two Sons

[28] "What do you think? A man had two sons. And he went to the first and said, 'Son, go and work in the vineyard today.' [29] And he answered, 'I will not,' but afterward he changed his mind and went. [30] And he went to the other son and said the same. And he answered, 'I go, sir,' but did not go. [31] Which of the two did the will of

---

[1] Or donkey, and on a colt [2] Some manuscripts add of God [a] For 21:1-9 see parallels Mark 11:1-10; Luke 19:28-38; John 12:12-15 [b] Zech. 9:9 [c] For 21:12-16 see parallels Mark 11:15-18; Luke 19:45-47 [d] Isa. 56:7 [e] Ps. 8:2 (Gk.) [f] For 21:18-22 see parallel Mark 11:12-14, 20-24 [g] For 21:23-27 see parallels Mark 11:27-33; Luke 20:1-8

his father?" They said, "The first." Jesus said to them, "Truly, I say to you, the tax collectors and the prostitutes go into the kingdom of God before you. [32]For John came to you in the way of righteousness, and you did not believe him, but the tax collectors and the prostitutes believed him. And even when you saw it, you did not afterward change your minds and believe him.

The Parable of the Tenants

[33]ᵃ"Hear another parable. There was a master of a house who planted a vineyard and put a fence around it and dug a winepress in it and built a tower and leased it to tenants, and went into another country. [34]When the season for fruit drew near, he sent his servants[1] to the tenants to get his fruit. [35]And the tenants took his servants and beat one, killed another, and stoned another. [36]Again he sent other servants, more than the first. And they did the same to them. [37]Finally he sent his son to them, saying, 'They will respect my son.' [38]But when the tenants saw the son, they said to themselves, 'This is the heir. Come, let us kill him and have his inheritance.' [39]And they took him and threw him out of the vineyard and killed him. [40]When therefore the owner of the vineyard comes, what will he do to those tenants?" [41]They said to him, "He will put those wretches to a miserable death and let out the vineyard to other tenants who will give him the fruits in their seasons."

[42]Jesus said to them, "Have you never read in the Scriptures:

ᵇ"'The stone that the builders rejected
   has become the cornerstone;[2]
this was the Lord's doing,
   and it is marvelous in our eyes'?

[43]Therefore I tell you, the kingdom of God will be taken away from you and given to a people producing its fruits. [44]And the one who falls on this stone will be broken to pieces; and when it falls on anyone, it will crush him."[3]

[45]When the chief priests and the Pharisees heard his parables, they perceived that he was speaking about them. [46]And although they were seeking to arrest him, they feared the crowds, because they held him to be a prophet.

The Parable of the Wedding Feast

22 And again Jesus spoke to them in parables, saying, [2]"The kingdom of heaven may be compared to a king who gave a wedding feast for his son, [3]and sent his servants[4] to call those who were invited to the wedding feast, but they would not come. [4]Again he sent other servants, saying, 'Tell those who are invited, "See, I have prepared my dinner, my oxen and my fat calves have been slaughtered, and everything is ready. Come to the wedding feast."' [5]But they paid no attention and went off, one to his farm, another to his business, [6]while the rest seized his servants, treated them shamefully, and killed them. [7]The king was angry, and he sent his troops and destroyed those murderers and burned their city. [8]Then he said to his servants, 'The wedding feast is ready, but those invited were not worthy. [9]Go therefore to the main roads and invite to the wedding feast as many as you find.' [10]And those servants went out into the roads and gathered all whom they found, both bad and good. So the wedding hall was filled with guests.

[11]"But when the king came in to look at the guests, he saw there a man who had no wedding garment. [12]And he said to him, 'Friend, how did you get in here without a wedding garment?' And he was speechless. [13]Then the king said to the attendants, 'Bind him hand and foot and cast him into the outer darkness. In that place there will be weeping and gnashing of teeth.' [14]For many are called, but few are chosen."

Paying Taxes to Caesar

[15]ᶜ Then the Pharisees went and plotted how to entangle him in his words. [16]And they sent their disciples to him, along with the Herodians, saying, "Teacher, we know that you are true and teach the way of God truthfully, and you do not care about anyone's opinion, for you are not swayed by appearances.[5] [17]Tell us, then, what you think. Is it lawful to pay taxes to Caesar, or not?" [18]But Jesus, aware of their malice, said, "Why put me to the test, you hypocrites? [19]Show me the coin for the tax." And they brought him a denarius.[6] [20]And Jesus said to them, "Whose likeness and inscription is this?" [21]They said, "Caesar's." Then he said to them, "Therefore render to Caesar the things that are Caesar's, and to God the things that

---

[1] Or bondservants; also verses 35, 36   [2] Greek the head of the corner   [3] Some manuscripts omit verse 44   [4] Or bondservants; also verses 4, 6, 8, 10   [5] Greek for you do not look at people's faces   [6] A denarius was a day's wage for a laborer   ᵈ For 21:33-46 see parallels Mark 12:1-12; Luke 20:9-18   ᵇ Ps. 118:22, 23   ᶜ For 22:15-32 see parallels Mark 12:13-27; Luke 20:20-38

are God's." [22] When they heard it, they marveled. And they left him and went away.

Sadducees Ask About the Resurrection

[23] The same day Sadducees came to him, who say that there is no resurrection, and they asked him a question, [24] saying, "Teacher, Moses said, 'If a man dies having no children, his brother must marry the widow and raise up offspring for his brother.' [25] Now there were seven brothers among us. The first married and died, and having no offspring left his wife to his brother. [26] So too the second and third, down to the seventh. [27] After them all, the woman died. [28] In the resurrection, therefore, of the seven, whose wife will she be? For they all had her."

[29] But Jesus answered them, "You are wrong, because you know neither the Scriptures nor the power of God. [30] For in the resurrection they neither marry nor are given in marriage, but are like angels in heaven. [31] And as for the resurrection of the dead, have you not read what was said to you by God: [32][a] 'I am the God of Abraham, and the God of Isaac, and the God of Jacob'? He is not God of the dead, but of the living." [33] And when the crowd heard it, they were astonished at his teaching.

The Great Commandment

[34][b] But when the Pharisees heard that he had silenced the Sadducees, they gathered together. [35] And one of them, a lawyer, asked him a question to test him. [36] "Teacher, which is the great commandment in the Law?" [37] And he said to him, "You shall love the Lord your God with all your heart and with all your soul and with all your mind. [38] This is the great and first commandment. [39] And a second is like it: You shall love your neighbor as yourself. [40] On these two commandments depend all the Law and the Prophets."

Whose Son Is the Christ?

[41][c] Now while the Pharisees were gathered together, Jesus asked them a question, [42] saying, "What do you think about the Christ? Whose son is he?" They said to him, "The son of David." [43] He said to them, "How is it then that David, in the Spirit, calls him Lord, saying,

[44][d] "'The Lord said to my Lord,
  "Sit at my right hand,
     until I put your enemies under your
        feet"'?

[45] If then David calls him Lord, how is he his son?" [46] And no one was able to answer him a word, nor from that day did anyone dare to ask him any more questions.

Seven Woes to the Scribes and Pharisees

23 Then Jesus [e] said to the crowds and to his disciples, [2] "The scribes and the Pharisees sit on Moses' seat, [3] so do and observe whatever they tell you, but not the works they do. For they preach, but do not practice. [4] They tie up heavy burdens, hard to bear,[1] and lay them on people's shoulders, but they themselves are not willing to move them with their finger. [5] They do all their deeds to be seen by others. For they make their phylacteries broad and their fringes long, [6] and they love the place of honor at feasts and the best seats in the synagogues [7] and greetings in the marketplaces and being called rabbi[2] by others. [8] But you are not to be called rabbi, for you have one teacher, and you are all brothers.[3] [9] And call no man your father on earth, for you have one Father, who is in heaven. [10] Neither be called instructors, for you have one instructor, the Christ. [11] The greatest among you shall be your servant. [12] Whoever exalts himself will be humbled, and whoever humbles himself will be exalted.

[13] "But woe to you, scribes and Pharisees, hypocrites! For you shut the kingdom of heaven in people's faces. For you neither enter yourselves nor allow those who would enter to go in.[4] [15] Woe to you, scribes and Pharisees, hypocrites! For you travel across sea and land to make a single proselyte, and when he becomes a proselyte, you make him twice as much a child of hell[5] as yourselves.

[16] "Woe to you, blind guides, who say, 'If anyone swears by the temple, it is nothing, but if anyone swears by the gold of the temple, he is bound by his oath.' [17] You blind fools! For which is greater, the gold or the temple that has made the gold sacred? [18] And you say, 'If anyone swears by the altar, it is nothing, but if anyone swears by the gift that is on the altar, he is bound by his oath.' [19] You blind men! For which is greater, the gift or the altar that makes the gift sacred? [20] So whoever swears by the altar swears by it and by everything on it. [21] And whoever swears by the

---

[1] Some manuscripts omit *hard to bear* [2] *Rabbi* means *my teacher*, or *my master*; also verse 8 [3] Or *brothers and sisters* [4] Some manuscripts add here (or after verse 12) verse 14: *Woe to you, scribes and Pharisees, hypocrites! For you devour widows' houses and for a pretense you make long prayers; therefore you will receive the greater condemnation* [5] Greek *Gehenna*; also verse 33 [a] Ex. 3:6 [b] For 22:34-40 see parallel Mark 12:28-33 [c] For 22:41-45 see parallels Mark 12:35-37; Luke 20:41-44 [d] Ps. 110:1 [e] For 23:1, 2, 5-7 see parallels Mark 12:38-40; Luke 20:45, 46

temple swears by it and by him who dwells in it. [22]And whoever swears by heaven swears by the throne of God and by him who sits upon it.

[23]"Woe to you, scribes and Pharisees, hypocrites! For you tithe mint and dill and cumin, and have neglected the weightier matters of the law: justice and mercy and faithfulness. These you ought to have done, without neglecting the others. [24]You blind guides, straining out a gnat and swallowing a camel!

[25]"Woe to you, scribes and Pharisees, hypocrites! For you clean the outside of the cup and the plate, but inside they are full of greed and self-indulgence. [26]You blind Pharisee! First clean the inside of the cup and the plate, that the outside also may be clean.

[27]"Woe to you, scribes and Pharisees, hypocrites! For you are like whitewashed tombs, which outwardly appear beautiful, but within are full of dead people's bones and all uncleanness. [28]So you also outwardly appear righteous to others, but within you are full of hypocrisy and lawlessness.

[29]"Woe to you, scribes and Pharisees, hypocrites! For you build the tombs of the prophets and decorate the monuments of the righteous, [30]saying, 'If we had lived in the days of our fathers, we would not have taken part with them in shedding the blood of the prophets.' [31]Thus you witness against yourselves that you are sons of those who murdered the prophets. [32]Fill up, then, the measure of your fathers. [33]You serpents, you brood of vipers, how are you to escape being sentenced to hell? [34]Therefore I send you prophets and wise men and scribes, some of whom you will kill and crucify, and some you will flog in your synagogues and persecute from town to town, [35]so that on you may come all the righteous blood shed on earth, from the blood of righteous Abel to the blood of Zechariah the son of Barachiah,[1] whom you murdered between the sanctuary and the altar. [36]Truly, I say to you, all these things will come upon this generation.

Lament over Jerusalem

[37a]"O Jerusalem, Jerusalem, the city that kills the prophets and stones those who are sent to it! How often would I have gathered your children together as a hen gathers her brood under her wings, and you were not willing! [38]See, your house is left to you desolate. [39]For I tell you, you will not see me again, until you say, [b]'Blessed is he who comes in the name of the Lord.'"

Jesus Foretells Destruction of the Temple

24 [1]Jesus left the temple and was going away, when his disciples came to point out to him the buildings of the temple. [2]But he answered them, "You see all these, do you not? Truly, I say to you, there will not be left here one stone upon another that will not be thrown down."

Signs of the End of the Age

[3]As he sat on the Mount of Olives, the disciples came to him privately, saying, "Tell us, when will these things be, and what will be the sign of your coming and of the end of the age?" [4]And Jesus answered them, "See that no one leads you astray. [5]For many will come in my name, saying, 'I am the Christ,' and they will lead many astray. [6]And you will hear of wars and rumors of wars. See that you are not alarmed, for this must take place, but the end is not yet. [7]For nation will rise against nation, and kingdom against kingdom, and there will be famines and earthquakes in various places. [8]All these are but the beginning of the birth pains.

[9]"Then they will deliver you up to tribulation and put you to death, and you will be hated by all nations for my name's sake. [10]And then many will fall away[2] and betray one another and hate one another. [11]And many false prophets will arise and lead many astray. [12]And because lawlessness will be increased, the love of many will grow cold. [13]But the one who endures to the end will be saved. [14]And this gospel of the kingdom will be proclaimed throughout the whole world as a testimony to all nations, and then the end will come.

The Abomination of Desolation

[15]"So when you see the abomination of desolation spoken of by the prophet Daniel, standing in the holy place (let the reader understand), [16]then let those who are in Judea flee to the mountains. [17]Let the one who is on the housetop not go down to take what is in his house, [18]and let the one who is in the field not turn back to take his cloak. [19]And alas for women who are pregnant and for those who are nursing infants in those days! [20]Pray that your flight may not be in winter or on a Sabbath. [21]For then there will be great tribulation, such as has not been from the beginning of the world until now, no, and never will be. [22]And if those days had not been cut short, no human being would be saved. But for the

[1] Some manuscripts omit the son of Barachiah [2] Or stumble [a]For 23:37-39 see parallel Luke 13:34, 35 [b]Ps. 118:26 [c]For 24:1-51 see parallels Mark 13:1-37; Luke 21:5-36

sake of the elect those days will be cut short. ²³Then if anyone says to you, 'Look, here is the Christ!' or 'There he is!' do not believe it. ²⁴For false christs and false prophets will arise and perform great signs and wonders, so as to lead astray, if possible, even the elect. ²⁵See, I have told you beforehand. ²⁶So, if they say to you, 'Look, he is in the wilderness,' do not go out. If they say, 'Look, he is in the inner rooms,' do not believe it. ²⁷For as the lightning comes from the east and shines as far as the west, so will be the coming of the Son of Man. ²⁸Wherever the corpse is, there the vultures will gather.

The Coming of the Son of Man

²⁹"Immediately after the tribulation of those days the sun will be darkened, and the moon will not give its light, and the stars will fall from heaven, and the powers of the heavens will be shaken. ³⁰Then will appear in heaven the sign of the Son of Man, and then all the tribes of the earth will mourn, and they will see the Son of Man coming on the clouds of heaven with power and great glory. ³¹And he will send out his angels with a loud trumpet call, and they will gather his elect from the four winds, from one end of heaven to the other.

The Lesson of the Fig Tree

³²"From the fig tree learn its lesson: as soon as its branch becomes tender and puts out its leaves, you know that summer is near. ³³So also, when you see all these things, you know that he is near, at the very gates. ³⁴Truly, I say to you, this generation will not pass away until all these things take place. ³⁵Heaven and earth will pass away, but my words will not pass away.

No One Knows That Day and Hour

³⁶"But concerning that day and hour no one knows, not even the angels of heaven, nor the Son,¹ but the Father only. ³⁷For as were the days of Noah, so will be the coming of the Son of Man. ³⁸For as in those days before the flood they were eating and drinking, marrying and giving in marriage, until the day when Noah entered the ark, ³⁹and they were unaware until the flood came and swept them all away, so will be the coming of the Son of Man. ⁴⁰Then two men will be in the field; one will be taken and one left. ⁴¹Two women will be grinding at the mill; one will be taken and one left. ⁴²Therefore, stay awake, for you do not know on what day

your Lord is coming. ⁴³But know this, that if the master of the house had known in what part of the night the thief was coming, he would have stayed awake and would not have let his house be broken into. ⁴⁴Therefore you also must be ready, for the Son of Man is coming at an hour you do not expect.

⁴⁵"Who then is the faithful and wise servant,² whom his master has set over his household, to give them their food at the proper time? ⁴⁶Blessed is that servant whom his master will find so doing when he comes. ⁴⁷Truly, I say to you, he will set him over all his possessions. ⁴⁸But if that wicked servant says to himself, 'My master is delayed,' ⁴⁹and begins to beat his fellow servants³ and eats and drinks with drunkards, ⁵⁰the master of that servant will come on a day when he does not expect him and at an hour he does not know ⁵¹and will cut him in pieces and put him with the hypocrites. In that place there will be weeping and gnashing of teeth.

The Parable of the Ten Virgins

25 "Then the kingdom of heaven will be like ten virgins who took their lamps⁴ and went to meet the bridegroom.⁵ ²Five of them were foolish, and five were wise. ³For when the foolish took their lamps, they took no oil with them, ⁴but the wise took flasks of oil with their lamps. ⁵As the bridegroom was delayed, they all became drowsy and slept. ⁶But at midnight there was a cry, 'Here is the bridegroom! Come out to meet him.' ⁷Then all those virgins rose and trimmed their lamps. ⁸And the foolish said to the wise, 'Give us some of your oil, for our lamps are going out.' ⁹But the wise answered, saying, 'Since there will not be enough for us and for you, go rather to the dealers and buy for yourselves.' ¹⁰And while they were going to buy, the bridegroom came, and those who were ready went in with him to the marriage feast, and the door was shut. ¹¹Afterward the other virgins came also, saying, 'Lord, lord, open to us.' ¹²But he answered, 'Truly, I say to you, I do not know you.' ¹³Watch therefore, for you know neither the day nor the hour.

The Parable of the Talents

¹⁴"For it will be like a man going on a journey, who called his servants⁶ and entrusted to them his property. ¹⁵To one he gave five talents,⁷ to

¹ Some manuscripts omit *nor the Son* ² Or *bondservant; also verses 46, 48, 50* ³ Or *bondservants* ⁴ Or *torches* ⁵ Some manuscripts add *and the bride* ⁶ Or *bondservants; also* verse 19 ⁷ A *talent* was a monetary unit worth about twenty years' wages for a laborer

another two, to another one, to each according to his ability. Then he went away. [16]He who had received the five talents went at once and traded with them, and he made five talents more. [17]So also he who had the two talents made two talents more. [18]But he who had received the one talent went and dug in the ground and hid his master's money. [19]Now after a long time the master of those servants came and settled accounts with them. [20]And he who had received the five talents came forward, bringing five talents more, saying, 'Master, you delivered to me five talents; here, I have made five talents more.' [21]His master said to him, 'Well done, good and faithful servant.[1] You have been faithful over a little; I will set you over much. Enter into the joy of your master.' [22]And he also who had the two talents came forward, saying, 'Master, you delivered to me two talents; here, I have made two talents more.' [23]His master said to him, 'Well done, good and faithful servant. You have been faithful over a little; I will set you over much. Enter into the joy of your master.' [24]He also who had received the one talent came forward, saying, 'Master, I knew you to be a hard man, reaping where you did not sow, and gathering where you scattered no seed, [25]so I was afraid, and I went and hid your talent in the ground. Here, you have what is yours.' [26]But his master answered him, 'You wicked and slothful servant! You knew that I reap where I have not sown and gather where I scattered no seed? [27]Then you ought to have invested my money with the bankers, and at my coming I should have received what was my own with interest. [28]So take the talent from him and give it to him who has the ten talents. [29]For to everyone who has will more be given, and he will have an abundance. But from the one who has not, even what he has will be taken away. [30]And cast the worthless servant into the outer darkness. In that place there will be weeping and gnashing of teeth.'

The Final Judgment

[31]"When the Son of Man comes in his glory, and all the angels with him, then he will sit on his glorious throne. [32]Before him will be gathered all the nations, and he will separate people one from another as a shepherd separates the sheep from the goats. [33]And he will place the sheep on his right, but the goats on the left. [34]Then the King will say to those on his right, 'Come, you who are blessed by my Father, inherit the kingdom prepared for you from the foundation of the world. [35]For I was hungry and you gave me food, I was thirsty and you gave me drink, I was a stranger and you welcomed me, [36]I was naked and you clothed me, I was sick and you visited me, I was in prison and you came to me.' [37]Then the righteous will answer him, saying, 'Lord, when did we see you hungry and feed you, or thirsty and give you drink? [38]And when did we see you a stranger and welcome you, or naked and clothe you? [39]And when did we see you sick or in prison and visit you?' [40]And the King will answer them, 'Truly, I say to you, as you did it to one of the least of these my brothers,[2] you did it to me.'

[41]"Then he will say to those on his left, 'Depart from me, you cursed, into the eternal fire prepared for the devil and his angels. [42]For I was hungry and you gave me no food, I was thirsty and you gave me no drink, [43]I was a stranger and you did not welcome me, naked and you did not clothe me, sick and in prison and you did not visit me.' [44]Then they also will answer, saying, 'Lord, when did we see you hungry or thirsty or a stranger or naked or sick or in prison, and did not minister to you?' [45]Then he will answer them, saying, 'Truly, I say to you, as you did not do it to one of the least of these, you did not do it to me.' [46]And these will go away into eternal punishment, but the righteous into eternal life."

The Plot to Kill Jesus

26 When Jesus had finished all these sayings, he said to his disciples, [2a]"You know that after two days the Passover is coming, and the Son of Man will be delivered up to be crucified."

[3]Then the chief priests and the elders of the people gathered in the palace of the high priest, whose name was Caiaphas, [4]and plotted together in order to arrest Jesus by stealth and kill him. [5]But they said, "Not during the feast, lest there be an uproar among the people."

Jesus Anointed at Bethany

[6b]Now when Jesus was at Bethany in the house of Simon the leper,[3] [7]a woman came up to him with an alabaster flask of very expensive ointment, and she poured it on his head as he

---

[1] Or bondservant; also verses 23, 26, 30   [2] Or brothers and sisters   [3] Leprosy was a term for several skin diseases; see Leviticus 13   [a]For 26:2-5 see parallels Mark 14:1, 2; Luke 22:1, 2   [b]For 26:6-13 see parallels Mark 14:3-9; John 12:1-8

reclined at table. [8] And when the disciples saw it, they were indignant, saying, "Why this waste? [9] For this could have been sold for a large sum and given to the poor." [10] But Jesus, aware of this, said to them, "Why do you trouble the woman? For she has done a beautiful thing to me. [11] For you always have the poor with you, but you will not always have me. [12] In pouring this ointment on my body, she has done it to prepare me for burial. [13] Truly, I say to you, wherever this gospel is proclaimed in the whole world, what she has done will also be told in memory of her."

Judas to Betray Jesus

[14] [a] Then one of the twelve, whose name was Judas Iscariot, went to the chief priests [15] and said, "What will you give me if I deliver him over to you?" And they paid him thirty pieces of silver. [16] And from that moment he sought an opportunity to betray him.

The Passover with the Disciples

[17] [b] Now on the first day of Unleavened Bread the disciples came to Jesus, saying, "Where will you have us prepare for you to eat the Passover?" [18] He said, "Go into the city to a certain man and say to him, 'The Teacher says, My time is at hand. I will keep the Passover at your house with my disciples.'" [19] And the disciples did as Jesus had directed them, and they prepared the Passover.

[20] [c] When it was evening, he reclined at table with the twelve.[1] [21] And as they were eating, he said, "Truly, I say to you, one of you will betray me." [22] And they were very sorrowful and began to say to him one after another, "Is it I, Lord?" [23] He answered, "He who has dipped his hand in the dish with me will betray me. [24] The Son of Man goes as it is written of him, but woe to that man by whom the Son of Man is betrayed! It would have been better for that man if he had not been born." [25] Judas, who would betray him, answered, "Is it I, Rabbi?" He said to him, "You have said so."

Institution of the Lord's Supper

[26] [d] Now as they were eating, Jesus took bread, and after blessing it broke it and gave it to the disciples, and said, "Take, eat; this is my body." [27] And he took a cup, and when he had given thanks he gave it to them, saying, "Drink of it, all of you, [28] for this is my blood of the[2] covenant, which is poured out for many for the forgiveness of sins. [29] I tell you I will not drink again of this fruit of the vine until that day when I drink it new with you in my Father's kingdom."

Jesus Foretells Peter's Denial

[30] [e] And when they had sung a hymn, they went out to the Mount of Olives. [31] Then Jesus said to them, "You will all fall away because of me this night. For it is written, 'I will [f] strike the shepherd, and the sheep of the flock will be scattered.' [32] But after I am raised up, I will go before you to Galilee." [33] Peter answered him, "Though they all fall away because of you, I will never fall away." [34] Jesus said to him, "Truly, I tell you, this very night, before the rooster crows, you will deny me three times." [35] Peter said to him, "Even if I must die with you, I will not deny you!" And all the disciples said the same.

Jesus Prays in Gethsemane

[36] [g] Then Jesus went with them to a place called Gethsemane, and he said to his disciples, "Sit here, while I go over there and pray." [37] And taking with him Peter and the two sons of Zebedee, he began to be sorrowful and troubled. [38] Then he said to them, "My soul is very sorrowful, even to death; remain here, and watch[3] with me." [39] And going a little farther he fell on his face and prayed, saying, "My Father, if it be possible, let this cup pass from me; nevertheless, not as I will, but as you will." [40] And he came to the disciples and found them sleeping. And he said to Peter, "So, could you not watch with me one hour? [41] Watch and pray that you may not enter into temptation. The spirit indeed is willing, but the flesh is weak." [42] Again, for the second time, he went away and prayed, "My Father, if this cannot pass unless I drink it, your will be done." [43] And again he came and found them sleeping, for their eyes were heavy. [44] So, leaving them again, he went away and prayed for the third time, saying the same words again. [45] Then he came to the disciples and said to them, "Sleep and take your rest later on.[4] See, the hour is at hand, and the Son of Man is betrayed into the hands of sinners. [46] Rise, let us be going; see, my betrayer is at hand."

---

[1] Some manuscripts add *disciples* [2] Some manuscripts insert *new* [3] Or *keep awake; also verses 40, 41* [4] Or *Are you still sleeping and taking your rest?* [a] For 26:14-16 see parallels Mark 14:10, 11; Luke 22:3-6 [b] For 26:17-19 see parallels Mark 14:12-16; Luke 22:7-13 [c] For 26:20-24 see parallel Mark 14:17-21 [d] For 26:26-29 see parallels Mark 14:22-25; Luke 22:18-20 [e] For 26:30-35 see parallel Mark 14:26-31 [f] Zech. 13:7 [g] For 26:36-46 see parallels Mark 14:32-42; Luke 22:39-46

Betrayal and Arrest of Jesus

47 ^a While he was still speaking, Judas came, one of the twelve, and with him a great crowd with swords and clubs, from the chief priests and the elders of the people. 48 Now the betrayer had given them a sign, saying, "The one I will kiss is the man; seize him." 49 And he came up to Jesus at once and said, "Greetings, Rabbi!" And he kissed him. 50 Jesus said to him, "Friend, do what you came to do."[1] Then they came up and laid hands on Jesus and seized him. 51 And behold, one of those who were with Jesus stretched out his hand and drew his sword and struck the servant[2] of the high priest and cut off his ear. 52 Then Jesus said to him, "Put your sword back into its place. For all who take the sword will perish by the sword. 53 Do you think that I cannot appeal to my Father, and he will at once send me more than twelve legions of angels? 54 But how then should the Scriptures be fulfilled, that it must be so?" 55 At that hour Jesus said to the crowds, "Have you come out as against a robber, with swords and clubs to capture me? Day after day I sat in the temple teaching, and you did not seize me. 56 But all this has taken place that the Scriptures of the prophets might be fulfilled." Then all the disciples left him and fled.

Jesus Before Caiaphas and the Council

57 Then ^b those who had seized Jesus led him to Caiaphas the high priest, where the scribes and the elders had gathered. 58 And Peter was following him at a distance, as far as the courtyard of the high priest, and going inside he sat with the guards to see the end. 59 Now the chief priests and the whole council[3] were seeking false testimony against Jesus that they might put him to death, 60 but they found none, though many false witnesses came forward. At last two came forward 61 and said, "This man said, 'I am able to destroy the temple of God, and to rebuild it in three days.'" 62 And the high priest stood up and said, "Have you no answer to make? What is it that these men testify against you?"[4] 63 But Jesus remained silent. And the high priest said to him, "I adjure you by the living God, tell us if you are the Christ, the Son of God." 64 Jesus said to him, "You have said so. But I tell you, from now on you will see the Son of Man seated at the right hand of Power and coming on the clouds of heaven."

65 Then the high priest tore his robes and said, "He has uttered blasphemy. What further witnesses do we need? You have now heard his blasphemy. 66 What is your judgment?" They answered, "He deserves death." 67 Then they spit in his face and struck him. And some slapped him, 68 saying, "Prophesy to us, you Christ! Who is it that struck you?"

Peter Denies Jesus

69 ^c Now Peter was sitting outside in the courtyard. And a servant girl came up to him and said, "You also were with Jesus the Galilean." 70 But he denied it before them all, saying, "I do not know what you mean." 71 And when he went out to the entrance, another servant girl saw him, and she said to the bystanders, "This man was with Jesus of Nazareth." 72 And again he denied it with an oath: "I do not know the man." 73 After a little while the bystanders came up and said to Peter, "Certainly you too are one of them, for your accent betrays you." 74 Then he began to invoke a curse on himself and to swear, "I do not know the man." And immediately the rooster crowed. 75 And Peter remembered the saying of Jesus, "Before the rooster crows, you will deny me three times." And he went out and wept bitterly.

Jesus Delivered to Pilate

27 When morning came, all the chief priests and the elders of the people took counsel against Jesus to put him to death. 2 And they bound him and led him away and delivered him over to Pilate the governor.

Judas Hangs Himself

3 Then when Judas, his betrayer, saw that Jesus[5] was condemned, he changed his mind and brought back the thirty pieces of silver to the chief priests and the elders, 4 saying, "I have sinned by betraying innocent blood." They said, "What is that to us? See to it yourself." 5 And throwing down the pieces of silver into the temple, he departed, and he went and hanged himself. 6 But the chief priests, taking the pieces of silver, said, "It is not lawful to put them into the treasury, since it is blood money." 7 So they took counsel and bought with them the potter's field as a burial place for strangers. 8 Therefore that field has been called the Field of Blood to this day. 9 Then was fulfilled what had been spoken by the prophet Jeremiah, saying,

---

[1] Or Friend, why are you here? [2] Or bondservant [3] Greek Sanhedrin [4] Or Have you no answer to what these men testify against you? [5] Greek he ^a For 26:47-56 see parallels Mark 14:43-50; Luke 22:47-53; John 18:3-11 ^b For 26:57-68 see parallel Mark 14:53-65 ^c For 26:69-75 see parallels Mark 14:66-72; Luke 22:55-62; John 18:16-18, 25-27

a"And they took the thirty pieces of silver, the price of him on whom a price had been set by some of the sons of Israel, [10] and they gave them for the potter's field, as the Lord directed me."

Jesus Before Pilate

[11] b Now Jesus stood before the governor, and the governor asked him, "Are you the King of the Jews?" Jesus said, "You have said so." [12] But when he was accused by the chief priests and elders, he gave no answer. [13] Then Pilate said to him, "Do you not hear how many things they testify against you?" [14] But he gave him no answer, not even to a single charge, so that the governor was greatly amazed.

The Crowd Chooses Barabbas

[15] c Now at the feast the governor was accustomed to release for the crowd any one prisoner whom they wanted. [16] And they had then a notorious prisoner called Barabbas. [17] So when they had gathered, Pilate said to them, "Whom do you want me to release for you: Barabbas, or Jesus who is called Christ?" [18] For he knew that it was out of envy that they had delivered him up. [19] Besides, while he was sitting on the judgment seat, his wife sent word to him, "Have nothing to do with that righteous man, for I have suffered much because of him today in a dream." [20] Now the chief priests and the elders persuaded the crowd to ask for Barabbas and destroy Jesus. [21] The governor again said to them, "Which of the two do you want me to release for you?" And they said, "Barabbas." [22] Pilate said to them, "Then what shall I do with Jesus who is called Christ?" They all said, "Let him be crucified!" [23] And he said, "Why? What evil has he done?" But they shouted all the more, "Let him be crucified!"

Pilate Delivers Jesus to Be Crucified

[24] So when Pilate saw that he was gaining nothing, but rather that a riot was beginning, he took water and washed his hands before the crowd, saying, "I am innocent of this man's blood;[1] see to it yourselves." [25] And all the people answered, "His blood be on us and on our children!" [26] Then he released for them Barabbas, and having scourged[2] Jesus, delivered him to be crucified.

Jesus Is Mocked

[27] d Then the soldiers of the governor took Jesus into the governor's headquarters,[3] and they gathered the whole battalion[4] before him. [28] And they stripped him and put a scarlet robe on him, [29] and twisting together a crown of thorns, they put it on his head and put a reed in his right hand. And kneeling before him, they mocked him, saying, "Hail, King of the Jews!" [30] And they spit on him and took the reed and struck him on the head. [31] And when they had mocked him, they stripped him of the robe and put his own clothes on him and led him away to crucify him.

The Crucifixion

[32] As they went out, they found a man of Cyrene, Simon by name. They compelled this man to carry his cross. [33] e And when they came to a place called Golgotha (which means Place of a Skull), [34] they offered him wine to drink, mixed with gall, but when he tasted it, he would not drink it. [35] And when they had crucified him, they divided his garments among them by casting lots. [36] Then they sat down and kept watch over him there. [37] And over his head they put the charge against him, which read, "This is Jesus, the King of the Jews." [38] Then two robbers were crucified with him, one on the right and one on the left. [39] And those who passed by derided him, wagging their heads [40] and saying, "You who would destroy the temple and rebuild it in three days, save yourself! If you are the Son of God, come down from the cross." [41] So also the chief priests, with the scribes and elders, mocked him, saying, [42] "He saved others; he cannot save himself. He is the King of Israel; let him come down now from the cross, and we will believe in him. [43] He trusts in God; let God deliver him now, if he desires him. For he said, 'I am the Son of God.'" [44] And the robbers who were crucified with him also reviled him in the same way.

The Death of Jesus

[45] Now from the sixth hour[5] there was darkness over all the land[6] until the ninth hour.[7] [46] And about the ninth hour Jesus cried out with a loud voice, saying, f "Eli, Eli, lema sabachthani?" that is, "My God, my God, why have you forsaken me?" [47] And some of the bystanders, hearing it, said, "This man is calling Elijah."

---

[1] Some manuscripts this righteous blood, or this righteous man's blood [2] A Roman judicial penalty, consisting of a severe beating with a multi-lashed whip containing embedded pieces of bone and metal [3] Greek the praetorium [4] Greek cohort; a tenth of a Roman legion, usually about 600 men [5] That is, noon [6] Or earth [7] That is, 3 P.M. a Zech. 11:13 b For 27:11-14 see parallels Mark 15:1-5; Luke 23:1-3; John 18:28-38 c For 27:15-26 see parallels Mark 15:6-15; Luke 23:18-25; John 18:39, 40; 19:16 d For 27:27-31 see parallels Mark 15:16-20; John 19:2, 3 e For 27:33-51 see parallels Mark 15:22-38; Luke 23:32-38, 44-46; John 19:17-19, 23, 24, 28-30 f Ps. 22:1

[48] And one of them at once ran and took a sponge, filled it with sour wine, and put it on a reed and gave it to him to drink. [49] But the others said, "Wait, let us see whether Elijah will come to save him." [50] And Jesus cried out again with a loud voice and yielded up his spirit.

[51] And behold, the curtain of the temple was torn in two, from top to bottom. And the earth shook, and the rocks were split. [52] The tombs also were opened. And many bodies of the saints who had fallen asleep were raised, [53] and coming out of the tombs after his resurrection they went into the holy city and appeared to many. [54][a] When the centurion and those who were with him, keeping watch over Jesus, saw the earthquake and what took place, they were filled with awe and said, "Truly this was the Son[1] of God!"

[55] There were also many women there, looking on from a distance, who had followed Jesus from Galilee, ministering to him, [56] among whom were Mary Magdalene and Mary the mother of James and Joseph and the mother of the sons of Zebedee.

Jesus Is Buried

[57][b] When it was evening, there came a rich man from Arimathea, named Joseph, who also was a disciple of Jesus. [58] He went to Pilate and asked for the body of Jesus. Then Pilate ordered it to be given to him. [59] And Joseph took the body and wrapped it in a clean linen shroud [60] and laid it in his own new tomb, which he had cut in the rock. And he rolled a great stone to the entrance of the tomb and went away. [61] Mary Magdalene and the other Mary were there, sitting opposite the tomb.

The Guard at the Tomb

[62] The next day, that is, after the day of Preparation, the chief priests and the Pharisees gathered before Pilate [63] and said, "Sir, we remember how that impostor said, while he was still alive, 'After three days I will rise.' [64] Therefore order the tomb to be made secure until the third day, lest his disciples go and steal him away and tell the people, 'He has risen from the dead,' and the last fraud will be worse than the first." [65] Pilate said to them, "You have a guard[2] of soldiers. Go, make it as secure as you can." [66] So they went and made the tomb secure by sealing the stone and setting a guard.

The Resurrection

28 [1] Now after the Sabbath, toward the dawn of the first day of the week, Mary Magdalene and the other Mary went to see the tomb. [2] And behold, there was a great earthquake, for an angel of the Lord descended from heaven and came and rolled back the stone and sat on it. [3] His appearance was like lightning, and his clothing white as snow. [4] And for fear of him the guards trembled and became like dead men. [5] But the angel said to the women, "Do not be afraid, for I know that you seek Jesus who was crucified. [6] He is not here, for he has risen, as he said. Come, see the place where he[3] lay. [7] Then go quickly and tell his disciples that he has risen from the dead, and behold, he is going before you to Galilee; there you will see him. See, I have told you." [8] So they departed quickly from the tomb with fear and great joy, and ran to tell his disciples. [9] And behold, Jesus met them and said, "Greetings!" And they came up and took hold of his feet and worshiped him. [10] Then Jesus said to them, "Do not be afraid; go and tell my brothers to go to Galilee, and there they will see me."

The Report of the Guard

[11] While they were going, behold, some of the guard went into the city and told the chief priests all that had taken place. [12] And when they had assembled with the elders and taken counsel, they gave a sufficient sum of money to the soldiers [13] and said, "Tell people, 'His disciples came by night and stole him away while we were asleep.' [14] And if this comes to the governor's ears, we will satisfy him and keep you out of trouble." [15] So they took the money and did as they were directed. And this story has been spread among the Jews to this day.

The Great Commission

[16] Now the eleven disciples went to Galilee, to the mountain to which Jesus had directed them. [17] And when they saw him they worshiped him, but some doubted. [18] And Jesus came and said to them, "All authority in heaven and on earth has been given to me. [19] Go therefore and make disciples of all nations, baptizing them in[4] the name of the Father and of the Son and of the Holy Spirit, [20] teaching them to observe all that I have commanded you. And behold, I am with you always, to the end of the age."

---

[1] Or a son   [2] Or Take a guard   [3] Some manuscripts the Lord   [4] Or into   [a] For 27:54-56 see parallels Mark 15:39-41; Luke 23:47, 49   [b] For 27:57-61 see parallels Mark 15:42-47; Luke 23:50-56; John 19:38-42   [c] For 28:1-8 see parallels Mark 16:1-8; Luke 24:1-10; John 20:1

THE GOSPEL ACCORDING TO
MARK

John the Baptist Prepares the Way

1 The beginning of the gospel of Jesus Christ, the Son of God.[1]

[2] [a]As it is written in Isaiah the prophet,[2]

[b]"Behold, I send my messenger before your face,
who will prepare your way,

[3] [c]the voice of one crying in the wilderness:
'Prepare[3] the way of the Lord,
make his paths straight,'"

[4] John appeared, baptizing in the wilderness and proclaiming a baptism of repentance for the forgiveness of sins. [5] And all the country of Judea and all Jerusalem were going out to him and were being baptized by him in the river Jordan, confessing their sins. [6] Now John was clothed with camel's hair and wore a leather belt around his waist and ate locusts and wild honey. [7] And he preached, saying, "After me comes he who is mightier than I, the strap of whose sandals I am not worthy to stoop down and untie. [8] I have baptized you with water, but he will baptize you with the Holy Spirit."

The Baptism of Jesus

[9] [d]In those days Jesus came from Nazareth of Galilee and was baptized by John in the Jordan. [10] And when he came up out of the water, immediately he saw the heavens being torn open and the Spirit descending on him like a dove. [11] And a voice came from heaven, "You are my beloved Son;[4] with you I am well pleased."

The Temptation of Jesus

[12] The Spirit immediately drove him out into the wilderness. [13] And he was in the wilderness forty days, being tempted by Satan. And he was with the wild animals, and the angels were ministering to him.

Jesus Begins His Ministry

[14] Now after John was arrested, Jesus came into Galilee, proclaiming the gospel of God, [15] and saying, "The time is fulfilled, and the kingdom of God is at hand;[5] repent and believe in the gospel."

Jesus Calls the First Disciples

[16] [e]Passing alongside the Sea of Galilee, he saw Simon and Andrew the brother of Simon casting a net into the sea, for they were fishermen. [17] And Jesus said to them, "Follow me, and I will make you become fishers of men."[6] [18] And immediately they left their nets and followed him. [19] And going on a little farther, he saw James the son of Zebedee and John his brother, who were in their boat mending the nets. [20] And immediately he called them, and they left their father Zebedee in the boat with the hired servants and followed him.

Jesus Heals a Man with an Unclean Spirit

[21] [f]And they went into Capernaum, and immediately on the Sabbath he entered the synagogue and was teaching. [22] And they were astonished at his teaching, for he taught them as one who had authority, and not as the scribes. [23] And immediately there was in their synagogue a man with an unclean spirit. And he cried out, [24] "What have you to do with us, Jesus of Nazareth? Have you come to destroy us? I know who you are—the Holy One of God." [25] But Jesus rebuked him, saying, "Be silent, and come out of him!" [26] And the unclean spirit, convulsing him and crying out with a loud voice, came out of him. [27] And they were all amazed, so that they questioned among themselves, saying, "What is this? A new teaching with authority! He commands even the unclean spirits, and they obey him." [28] And at once his fame spread everywhere throughout all the surrounding region of Galilee.

Jesus Heals Many

[29] [g]And immediately he[7] left the synagogue and entered the house of Simon and Andrew, with James and John. [30] Now Simon's mother-in-law lay ill with a fever, and immediately they told him about her. [31] And he came and took her by the hand and lifted her up, and the fever left her, and she began to serve them.

[32] That evening at sundown they brought to him all who were sick or oppressed by demons. [33] And the whole city was gathered together

---

at the door. [34] And he healed many who were sick with various diseases, and cast out many demons. And he would not permit the demons to speak, because they knew him.

Jesus Preaches in Galilee

[35][a] And rising very early in the morning, while it was still dark, he departed and went out to a desolate place, and there he prayed. [36] And Simon and those who were with him searched for him, [37] and they found him and said to him, "Everyone is looking for you." [38] And he said to them, "Let us go on to the next towns, that I may preach there also, for that is why I came out." [39] And he went throughout all Galilee, preaching in their synagogues and casting out demons.

Jesus Cleanses a Leper

[40][b] And a leper[1] came to him, imploring him, and kneeling said to him, "If you will, you can make me clean." [41] Moved with pity, he stretched out his hand and touched him and said to him, "I will; be clean." [42] And immediately the leprosy left him, and he was made clean. [43] And Jesus[2] sternly charged him and sent him away at once, [44] and said to him, "See that you say nothing to anyone, but go, show yourself to the priest and offer for your cleansing what Moses commanded, for a proof to them." [45] But he went out and began to talk freely about it, and to spread the news, so that Jesus could no longer openly enter a town, but was out in desolate places, and people were coming to him from every quarter.

Jesus Heals a Paralytic

2 And when he returned to Capernaum after some days, it was reported that he was at home. [2] And many were gathered together, so that there was no more room, not even at the door. And he was preaching the word to them. [3][c] And they came, bringing to him a paralytic carried by four men. [4] And when they could not get near him because of the crowd, they removed the roof above him, and when they had made an opening, they let down the bed on which the paralytic lay. [5] And when Jesus saw their faith, he said to the paralytic, "Son, your sins are forgiven." [6] Now some of the scribes were sitting there, questioning in their hearts, [7] "Why does this man speak like that? He is blaspheming! Who can forgive sins but God alone?" [8] And immediately Jesus, perceiving in his spirit

that they thus questioned within themselves, said to them, "Why do you question these things in your hearts? [9] Which is easier, to say to the paralytic, 'Your sins are forgiven,' or to say, 'Rise, take up your bed and walk'? [10] But that you may know that the Son of Man has authority on earth to forgive sins"—he said to the paralytic— [11] "I say to you, rise, pick up your bed, and go home." [12] And he rose and immediately picked up his bed and went out before them all, so that they were all amazed and glorified God, saying, "We never saw anything like this!"

Jesus Calls Levi

[13] He went out again beside the sea, and all the crowd was coming to him, and he was teaching them. [14][d] And as he passed by, he saw Levi the son of Alphaeus sitting at the tax booth, and he said to him, "Follow me." And he rose and followed him.

[15] And as he reclined at table in his house, many tax collectors and sinners were reclining with Jesus and his disciples, for there were many who followed him. [16] And the scribes of[3] the Pharisees, when they saw that he was eating with sinners and tax collectors, said to his disciples, "Why does he eat[4] with tax collectors and sinners?" [17] And when Jesus heard it, he said to them, "Those who are well have no need of a physician, but those who are sick. I came not to call the righteous, but sinners."

A Question About Fasting

[18] Now John's disciples and the Pharisees were fasting. And people came and said to him, "Why do John's disciples and the disciples of the Pharisees fast, but your disciples do not fast?" [19] And Jesus said to them, "Can the wedding guests fast while the bridegroom is with them? As long as they have the bridegroom with them, they cannot fast. [20] The days will come when the bridegroom is taken away from them, and then they will fast in that day. [21] No one sews a piece of unshrunk cloth on an old garment. If he does, the patch tears away from it, the new from the old, and a worse tear is made. [22] And no one puts new wine into old wineskins. If he does, the wine will burst the skins—and the wine is destroyed, and so are the skins. But new wine is for fresh wineskins."[5]

---

[1] Leprosy was a term for several skin diseases; see Leviticus 13 [2] Greek he; also verse 45 [3] Some manuscripts and [4] Some manuscripts add and drink [5] Some manuscripts omit But new wine is for fresh wineskins [a] For 1:35-38 see parallel Luke 4:42, 43 [b] For 1:40-44 see parallels Matt. 8:2-4; Luke 5:12-14 [c] For 2:3-12 see parallels Matt. 9:2-8; Luke 5:17-26 [d] For 2:14-22 see parallels Matt. 9:9-17; Luke 5:27-39

Jesus Is Lord of the Sabbath

23 [a] One Sabbath he was going through the grainfields, and as they made their way, his disciples began to pluck heads of grain. **24** And the Pharisees were saying to him, "Look, why are they doing what is not lawful on the Sabbath?" **25** And he said to them, "Have you never read what David did, when he was in need and was hungry, he and those who were with him: **26** how he entered the house of God, in the time of[1] Abiathar the high priest, and ate the bread of the Presence, which it is not lawful for any but the priests to eat, and also gave it to those who were with him?" **27** And he said to them, "The Sabbath was made for man, not man for the Sabbath. **28** So the Son of Man is lord even of the Sabbath."

A Man with a Withered Hand

3 [b] Again he entered the synagogue, and a man was there with a withered hand. **2** And they watched Jesus,[2] to see whether he would heal him on the Sabbath, so that they might accuse him. **3** And he said to the man with the withered hand, "Come here." **4** And he said to them, "Is it lawful on the Sabbath to do good or to do harm, to save life or to kill?" But they were silent. **5** And he looked around at them with anger, grieved at their hardness of heart, and said to the man, "Stretch out your hand." He stretched it out, and his hand was restored. **6** The Pharisees went out and immediately held counsel with the Herodians against him, how to destroy him.

A Great Crowd Follows Jesus

7 Jesus withdrew with his disciples to the sea, and a great crowd followed, from Galilee and Judea **8** and Jerusalem and Idumea and from beyond the Jordan and from around Tyre and Sidon. When the great crowd heard all that he was doing, they came to him. **9** And he told his disciples to have a boat ready for him because of the crowd, lest they crush him, **10** for he had healed many, so that all who had diseases pressed around him to touch him. **11** And whenever the unclean spirits saw him, they fell down before him and cried out, "You are the Son of God." **12** And he strictly ordered them not to make him known.

The Twelve Apostles

13 And he went up on the mountain and called to him those whom he desired, and they came to him. **14** And he appointed twelve (whom he also named apostles) so that they might be with him and he might send them out to preach **15** and have authority to cast out demons. **16** He appointed the twelve: Simon (to whom he gave the name Peter); **17** James the son of Zebedee and John the brother of James (to whom he gave the name Boanerges, that is, Sons of Thunder); **18** Andrew, and Philip, and Bartholomew, and Matthew, and Thomas, and James the son of Alphaeus, and Thaddaeus, and Simon the Zealot,[3] **19** and Judas Iscariot, who betrayed him.

20 Then he went home, and the crowd gathered again, so that they could not even eat. **21** And when his family heard it, they went out to seize him, for they were saying, "He is out of his mind."

Blasphemy Against the Holy Spirit

22 And the scribes who came down from Jerusalem were saying, "He is possessed by Beelzebul," and "by the prince of demons he casts out the demons." **23** [d] And he called them to him and said to them in parables, "How can Satan cast out Satan? **24** If a kingdom is divided against itself, that kingdom cannot stand. **25** And if a house is divided against itself, that house will not be able to stand. **26** And if Satan has risen up against himself and is divided, he cannot stand, but is coming to an end. **27** But no one can enter a strong man's house and plunder his goods, unless he first binds the strong man. Then indeed he may plunder his house.

28 "Truly, I say to you, all sins will be forgiven the children of man, and whatever blasphemies they utter, **29** but whoever blasphemes against the Holy Spirit never has forgiveness, but is guilty of an eternal sin"— **30** for they were saying, "He has an unclean spirit."

Jesus' Mother and Brothers

31 And his mother and his brothers came, and standing outside they sent to him and called him. **32** And a crowd was sitting around him, and they said to him, "Your mother and your brothers[4] are outside, seeking you." **33** And he answered them, "Who are my mother and my brothers?" **34** And looking about at those who sat around him, he said, "Here are my mother and my brothers! **35** For whoever does the will of God, he is my brother and sister and mother."

---

[1] Or *in the passage about* [2] Greek *him* [3] Greek *kananaios*, meaning *zealot* [4] Other manuscripts add *and your sisters* [a] For 2:23-28 see parallels Matt. 12:1-8; Luke 6:1-5 [b] For 3:1-6 see parallels Matt. 12:9-14; Luke 6:6-11 [c] For 3:16-19 see parallels Matt. 10:2-4; Luke 6:13-16 [d] For 3:23-27 see parallels Matt. 12:25-29; Luke 11:17-22 [e] For 3:28-30 see parallel Matt. 12:31, 32 [f] For 3:31-35 see parallels Matt. 12:46-50; Luke 8:19-21

The Parable of the Sower

4 Again [a]he began to teach beside the sea. And a very large crowd gathered about him, so that he got into a boat and sat in it on the sea, and the whole crowd was beside the sea on the land. [2]And he was teaching them many things in parables, and in his teaching he said to them: [3]"Listen! Behold, a sower went out to sow. [4]And as he sowed, some seed fell along the path, and the birds came and devoured it. [5]Other seed fell on rocky ground, where it did not have much soil, and immediately it sprang up, since it had no depth of soil. [6]And when the sun rose, it was scorched, and since it had no root, it withered away. [7]Other seed fell among thorns, and the thorns grew up and choked it, and it yielded no grain. [8]And other seeds fell into good soil and produced grain, growing up and increasing and yielding thirtyfold and sixtyfold and a hundredfold." [9]And he said, "He who has ears to hear, let him hear."

The Purpose of the Parables

[10]And when he was alone, those around him with the twelve asked him about the parables. [11]And he said to them, "To you has been given the secret of the kingdom of God, but for those outside everything is in parables, [12]so that

> " 'they may indeed see but not perceive,
>   and may indeed hear but not under-
>   stand,
>   lest they should turn and be forgiven.' "

[13][b]And he said to them, "Do you not understand this parable? How then will you understand all the parables? [14]The sower sows the word. [15]And these are the ones along the path, where the word is sown: when they hear, Satan immediately comes and takes away the word that is sown in them. [16]And these are the ones sown on rocky ground: the ones who, when they hear the word, immediately receive it with joy. [17]And they have no root in themselves, but endure for a while; then, when tribulation or persecution arises on account of the word, immediately they fall away.[1] [18]And others are the ones sown among thorns. They are those who hear the word, [19]but the cares of the world and the deceitfulness of riches and the desires for other things enter in and choke the word, and it proves unfruitful. [20]But those that were sown on the good soil are the ones who hear the

word and accept it and bear fruit, thirtyfold and sixtyfold and a hundredfold."

A Lamp Under a Basket

[21][c]And he said to them, "Is a lamp brought in to be put under a basket, or under a bed, and not on a stand? [22]For nothing is hidden except to be made manifest; nor is anything secret except to come to light. [23]If anyone has ears to hear, let him hear." [24]And he said to them, "Pay attention to what you hear: with the measure you use, it will be measured to you, and still more will be added to you. [25]For to the one who has, more will be given, and from the one who has not, even what he has will be taken away."

The Parable of the Seed Growing

[26]And he said, "The kingdom of God is as if a man should scatter seed on the ground. [27]He sleeps and rises night and day, and the seed sprouts and grows; he knows not how. [28]The earth produces by itself, first the blade, then the ear, then the full grain in the ear. [29]But when the grain is ripe, at once he puts in the sickle, because the harvest has come."

The Parable of the Mustard Seed

[30][d]And he said, "With what can we compare the kingdom of God, or what parable shall we use for it? [31]It is like a grain of mustard seed, which, when sown on the ground, is the smallest of all the seeds on earth, [32]yet when it is sown it grows up and becomes larger than all the garden plants and puts out large branches, so that the birds of the air can make nests in its shade."

[33]With many such parables he spoke the word to them, as they were able to hear it. [34]He did not speak to them without a parable, but privately to his own disciples he explained everything.

Jesus Calms a Storm

[35][e]On that day, when evening had come, he said to them, "Let us go across to the other side." [36]And leaving the crowd, they took him with them in the boat, just as he was. And other boats were with him. [37]And a great windstorm arose, and the waves were breaking into the boat, so that the boat was already filling. [38]But he was in the stern, asleep on the cushion. And they woke him and said to him, "Teacher, do you not care that we are perishing?" [39]And he awoke and rebuked the wind and said to the sea, "Peace!

---

[1] Or stumble [a]For 4:1-12 see parallels Matt. 13:1-15; Luke 8:4-10 [b]For 4:13-20 see parallels Matt. 13:18-23; Luke 8:11-15 [c]For 4:21-25 see parallel Luke 8:16-18 [d]For 4:30-32 see parallels Matt. 13:31, 32; Luke 13:18, 19 [e]For 4:35-41 see parallels Matt. 8:18, 23-27; Luke 8:22-25

Be still!" And the wind ceased, and there was a great calm. [40] He said to them, "Why are you so afraid? Have you still no faith?" [41] And they were filled with great fear and said to one another, "Who then is this, that even the wind and the sea obey him?"

Jesus Heals a Man with a Demon

5 [a]They came to the other side of the sea, to the country of the Gerasenes.[1] [2] And when Jesus[2] had stepped out of the boat, immediately there met him out of the tombs a man with an unclean spirit. [3] He lived among the tombs. And no one could bind him anymore, not even with a chain, [4] for he had often been bound with shackles and chains, but he wrenched the chains apart, and he broke the shackles in pieces. No one had the strength to subdue him. [5] Night and day among the tombs and on the mountains he was always crying out and cutting himself with stones. [6] And when he saw Jesus from afar, he ran and fell down before him. [7] And crying out with a loud voice, he said, "What have you to do with me, Jesus, Son of the Most High God? I adjure you by God, do not torment me." [8] For he was saying to him, "Come out of the man, you unclean spirit!" [9] And Jesus asked him, "What is your name?" He replied, "My name is Legion, for we are many." [10] And he begged him earnestly not to send them out of the country. [11] Now a great herd of pigs was feeding there on the hillside, [12] and they begged him, saying, "Send us to the pigs; let us enter them." [13] So he gave them permission. And the unclean spirits came out and entered the pigs; and the herd, numbering about two thousand, rushed down the steep bank into the sea and drowned in the sea.

[14] The herdsmen fled and told it in the city and in the country. And people came to see what it was that had happened. [15] And they came to Jesus and saw the demon-possessed[3] man, the one who had had the legion, sitting there, clothed and in his right mind, and they were afraid. [16] And those who had seen it described to them what had happened to the demon-possessed man and to the pigs. [17] And they began to beg Jesus[4] to depart from their region. [18] As he was getting into the boat, the man who had been possessed with demons begged him that he might be with him. [19] And he did not permit him but said to him, "Go home to your friends and tell them how much the Lord has done for

you, and how he has had mercy on you." [20] And he went away and began to proclaim in the Decapolis how much Jesus had done for him, and everyone marveled.

Jesus Heals a Woman and Jairus's Daughter

[21] And when Jesus had crossed again in the boat to the other side, a great crowd gathered about him, and he was beside the sea. [22] [b]Then came one of the rulers of the synagogue, Jairus by name, and seeing him, he fell at his feet [23] and implored him earnestly, saying, "My little daughter is at the point of death. Come and lay your hands on her, so that she may be made well and live." [24] And he went with him.

And a great crowd followed him and thronged about him. [25] And there was a woman who had had a discharge of blood for twelve years, [26] and who had suffered much under many physicians, and had spent all that she had, and was no better but rather grew worse. [27] She had heard the reports about Jesus and came up behind him in the crowd and touched his garment. [28] For she said, "If I touch even his garments, I will be made well." [29] And immediately the flow of blood dried up, and she felt in her body that she was healed of her disease. [30] And Jesus, perceiving in himself that power had gone out from him, immediately turned about in the crowd and said, "Who touched my garments?" [31] And his disciples said to him, "You see the crowd pressing around you, and yet you say, 'Who touched me?'" [32] And he looked around to see who had done it. [33] But the woman, knowing what had happened to her, came in fear and trembling and fell down before him and told him the whole truth. [34] And he said to her, "Daughter, your faith has made you well; go in peace, and be healed of your disease."

[35] While he was still speaking, there came from the ruler's house some who said, "Your daughter is dead. Why trouble the Teacher any further?" [36] But overhearing[5] what they said, Jesus said to the ruler of the synagogue, "Do not fear, only believe." [37] And he allowed no one to follow him except Peter and James and John the brother of James. [38] They came to the house of the ruler of the synagogue, and Jesus[6] saw a commotion, people weeping and wailing loudly. [39] And when he had entered, he said to them, "Why are you making a commotion and weeping? The child is not dead but sleep-

---

[1] Some manuscripts *Gergesenes*; some *Gadarenes* [2] Greek *he*; also verse 9 [3] Greek *daimonizomai* (demonized); also verses 16, 18; elsewhere rendered *oppressed by demons* [4] Greek *him* [5] Or *ignoring*; some manuscripts *hearing* [6] Greek *he* [a] For 5:1-20 see parallels Matt. 8:28-34; Luke 8:26-39 [b] For 5:22-43 see parallels Matt. 9:18-26; Luke 8:40-56

ing." [40] And they laughed at him. But he put them all outside and took the child's father and mother and those who were with him and went in where the child was. [41] Taking her by the hand he said to her, "Talitha cumi," which means, "Little girl, I say to you, arise." [42] And immediately the girl got up and began walking (for she was twelve years of age), and they were immediately overcome with amazement. [43] And he strictly charged them that no one should know this, and told them to give her something to eat.

Jesus Rejected at Nazareth

6 [a] He went away from there and came to his hometown, and his disciples followed him. [2] And on the Sabbath he began to teach in the synagogue, and many who heard him were astonished, saying, "Where did this man get these things? What is the wisdom given to him? How are such mighty works done by his hands? [3] Is not this the carpenter, the son of Mary and brother of James and Joses and Judas and Simon? And are not his sisters here with us?" And they took offense at him. [4] And Jesus said to them, "A prophet is not without honor, except in his hometown and among his relatives and in his own household." [5] And he could do no mighty work there, except that he laid his hands on a few sick people and healed them. [6] And he marveled because of their unbelief.

And he went about among the villages teaching.

Jesus Sends Out the Twelve Apostles

[7][b] And he called the twelve and began to send them out two by two, and gave them authority over the unclean spirits. [8] He charged them to take nothing for their journey except a staff—no bread, no bag, no money in their belts— [9] but to wear sandals and not put on two tunics.[1] [10] And he said to them, "Whenever you enter a house, stay there until you depart from there. [11] And if any place will not receive you and they will not listen to you, when you leave, shake off the dust that is on your feet as a testimony against them." [12] So they went out and proclaimed that people should repent. [13] And they cast out many demons and anointed with oil many who were sick and healed them.

The Death of John the Baptist

[14][c] King Herod heard of it, for Jesus'[2] name had become known. Some[3] said, "John the Baptist[4] has been raised from the dead. That is why these miraculous powers are at work in him." [15] But others said, "He is Elijah." And others said, "He is a prophet, like one of the prophets of old." [16] But when Herod heard of it, he said, "John, whom I beheaded, has been raised." [17] For it was Herod who had sent and seized John and bound him in prison for the sake of Herodias, his brother Philip's wife, because he had married her. [18] For John had been saying to Herod, "It is not lawful for you to have your brother's wife." [19] And Herodias had a grudge against him and wanted to put him to death. But she could not, [20] for Herod feared John, knowing that he was a righteous and holy man, and he kept him safe. When he heard him, he was greatly perplexed, and yet he heard him gladly.

[21] But an opportunity came when Herod on his birthday gave a banquet for his nobles and military commanders and the leading men of Galilee. [22] For when Herodias's daughter came in and danced, she pleased Herod and his guests. And the king said to the girl, "Ask me for whatever you wish, and I will give it to you." [23] And he vowed to her, "Whatever you ask me, I will give you, up to half of my kingdom." [24] And she went out and said to her mother, "For what should I ask?" And she said, "The head of John the Baptist." [25] And she came in immediately with haste to the king and asked, saying, "I want you to give me at once the head of John the Baptist on a platter." [26] And the king was exceedingly sorry, but because of his oaths and his guests he did not want to break his word to her. [27] And immediately the king sent an executioner with orders to bring John's[5] head. He went and beheaded him in the prison [28] and brought his head on a platter and gave it to the girl, and the girl gave it to her mother. [29] When his disciples heard of it, they came and took his body and laid it in a tomb.

Jesus Feeds the Five Thousand

[30] The apostles returned to Jesus and told him all that they had done and taught. [31] And he said to them, "Come away by yourselves to a desolate place and rest a while." For many were coming and going, and they had no leisure even to eat. [32][d] And they went away in the boat to a desolate place by themselves. [33] Now many saw

---

[1] Greek *chiton*, a long garment worn under the cloak next to the skin [2] Greek *his* [3] Some manuscripts *He* [4] Greek *baptizer*; also verse 24 [5] Greek *his* [a] For 6:1-6 see parallel Matt. 13:54-58 [b] For 6:7-11 see parallels Matt. 10:1, 5, 9-14; Luke 9:1, 3-5 [c] For 6:14-29 see parallels Matt. 14:1-12; Luke 9:7-9 [d] For 6:32-44 see parallels Matt. 14:13-21; Luke 9:10-17; John 6:1-13

them going and recognized them, and they ran there on foot from all the towns and got there ahead of them. [34] When he went ashore he saw a great crowd, and he had compassion on them, because they were like sheep without a shepherd. And he began to teach them many things. [35] And when it grew late, his disciples came to him and said, "This is a desolate place, and the hour is now late. [36] Send them away to go into the surrounding countryside and villages and buy themselves something to eat." [37] But he answered them, "You give them something to eat." And they said to him, "Shall we go and buy two hundred denarii[1] worth of bread and give it to them to eat?" [38] And he said to them, "How many loaves do you have? Go and see." And when they had found out, they said, "Five, and two fish." [39] Then he commanded them all to sit down in groups on the green grass. [40] So they sat down in groups, by hundreds and by fifties. [41] And taking the five loaves and the two fish, he looked up to heaven and said a blessing and broke the loaves and gave them to the disciples to set before the people. And he divided the two fish among them all. [42] And they all ate and were satisfied. [43] And they took up twelve baskets full of broken pieces and of the fish. [44] And those who ate the loaves were five thousand men.

Jesus Walks on the Water

[45] [d] Immediately he made his disciples get into the boat and go before him to the other side, to Bethsaida, while he dismissed the crowd. [46] And after he had taken leave of them, he went up on the mountain to pray. [47] And when evening came, the boat was out on the sea, and he was alone on the land. [48] And he saw that they were making headway painfully, for the wind was against them. And about the fourth watch of the night[2] he came to them, walking on the sea. He meant to pass by them, [49] but when they saw him walking on the sea they thought it was a ghost, and cried out, [50] for they all saw him and were terrified. But immediately he spoke to them and said, "Take heart; it is I. Do not be afraid." [51] And he got into the boat with them, and the wind ceased. And they were utterly astounded, [52] for they did not understand about the loaves, but their hearts were hardened.

Jesus Heals the Sick in Gennesaret

[53] [b] When they had crossed over, they came to land at Gennesaret and moored to the shore. [54] And when they got out of the boat, the people immediately recognized him [55] and ran about the whole region and began to bring the sick people on their beds to wherever they heard he was. [56] And wherever he came, in villages, cities, or countryside, they laid the sick in the marketplaces and implored him that they might touch even the fringe of his garment. And as many as touched it were made well.

Traditions and Commandments

7 [c] Now when the Pharisees gathered to him, with some of the scribes who had come from Jerusalem, [2] they saw that some of his disciples ate with hands that were defiled, that is, unwashed. [3] (For the Pharisees and all the Jews do not eat unless they wash their hands properly,[3] holding to the tradition of the elders, [4] and when they come from the marketplace, they do not eat unless they wash.[4] And there are many other traditions that they observe, such as the washing of cups and pots and copper vessels and dining couches.[5]) [5] And the Pharisees and the scribes asked him, "Why do your disciples not walk according to the tradition of the elders, but eat with defiled hands?" [6] And he said to them, "Well did Isaiah prophesy of you hypocrites, as it is written,

> [d] "'This people honors me with their lips,
>   but their heart is far from me;
> [7] in vain do they worship me,
>   teaching as doctrines the commandments of men.'

[8] You leave the commandment of God and hold to the tradition of men."

[9] And he said to them, "You have a fine way of rejecting the commandment of God in order to establish your tradition! [10] For Moses said, [e] 'Honor your father and your mother'; and, [f] 'Whoever reviles father or mother must surely die.' [11] But you say, 'If a man tells his father or his mother, "Whatever you would have gained from me is Corban"' (that is, given to God)[6]— [12] then you no longer permit him to do anything for his father or mother, [13] thus making void the word of God by your tradition that you have handed down. And many such things you do."

---

[1] A *denarius* was a day's wage for a laborer [2] That is, between 3 A.M. and 6 A.M. [3] Greek *unless they wash the hands with a fist*, probably indicating a kind of ceremonial washing [4] Greek *unless they baptize*; some manuscripts *unless they purify themselves* [5] Some manuscripts omit *and dining couches* [6] Or *an offering* [a] For 6:45-52 see parallels Matt. 14:22-33; John 6:16-21 [b] For 6:53-56 see parallel Matt. 14:34-36 [c] For 7:1-30 see parallel Matt. 15:1-28 [d] Isa. 29:13 [e] Ex. 20:12 [f] Ex. 21:17

What Defiles a Person

[14] And he called the people to him again and said to them, "Hear me, all of you, and understand: [15] There is nothing outside a person that by going into him can defile him, but the things that come out of a person are what defile him."[1] [17] And when he had entered the house and left the people, his disciples asked him about the parable. [18] And he said to them, "Then are you also without understanding? Do you not see that whatever goes into a person from outside cannot defile him, [19] since it enters not his heart but his stomach, and is expelled?"[2] (Thus he declared all foods clean.) [20] And he said, "What comes out of a person is what defiles him. [21] For from within, out of the heart of man, come evil thoughts, sexual immorality, theft, murder, adultery, [22] coveting, wickedness, deceit, sensuality, envy, slander, pride, foolishness. [23] All these evil things come from within, and they defile a person."

The Syrophoenician Woman's Faith

[24] And from there he arose and went away to the region of Tyre and Sidon.[3] And he entered a house and did not want anyone to know, yet he could not be hidden. [25] But immediately a woman whose little daughter had an unclean spirit heard of him and came and fell down at his feet. [26] Now the woman was a Gentile, a Syrophoenician by birth. And she begged him to cast the demon out of her daughter. [27] And he said to her, "Let the children be fed first, for it is not right to take the children's bread and throw it to the dogs." [28] But she answered him, "Yes, Lord; yet even the dogs under the table eat the children's crumbs." [29] And he said to her, "For this statement you may go your way; the demon has left your daughter." [30] And she went home and found the child lying in bed and the demon gone.

Jesus Heals a Deaf Man

[31] Then he returned from the region of Tyre and went through Sidon to the Sea of Galilee, in the region of the Decapolis. [32] And they brought to him a man who was deaf and had a speech impediment, and they begged him to lay his hand on him. [33] And taking him aside from the crowd privately, he put his fingers into his ears, and after spitting touched his tongue. [34] And looking up to heaven, he sighed and said to him, "Ephphatha," that is,

"Be opened." [35] And his ears were opened, his tongue was released, and he spoke plainly. [36] And Jesus[4] charged them to tell no one. But the more he charged them, the more zealously they proclaimed it. [37] And they were astonished beyond measure, saying, "He has done all things well. He even makes the deaf hear and the mute speak."

Jesus Feeds the Four Thousand

8 "In those days, when again a great crowd had gathered, and they had nothing to eat, he called his disciples to him and said to them, [2] "I have compassion on the crowd, because they have been with me now three days and have nothing to eat. [3] And if I send them away hungry to their homes, they will faint on the way. And some of them have come from far away." [4] And his disciples answered him, "How can one feed these people with bread here in this desolate place?" [5] And he asked them, "How many loaves do you have?" They said, "Seven." [6] And he directed the crowd to sit down on the ground. And he took the seven loaves, and having given thanks, he broke them and gave them to his disciples to set before the people; and they set them before the crowd. [7] And they had a few small fish. And having blessed them, he said that these also should be set before them. [8] And they ate and were satisfied. And they took up the broken pieces left over, seven baskets full. [9] And there were about four thousand people. And he sent them away. [10] And immediately he got into the boat with his disciples and went to the district of Dalmanutha.[5]

The Pharisees Demand a Sign

[11] [b] The Pharisees came and began to argue with him, seeking from him a sign from heaven to test him. [12] And he sighed deeply in his spirit and said, "Why does this generation seek a sign? Truly, I say to you, no sign will be given to this generation." [13] And he left them, got into the boat again, and went to the other side.

The Leaven of the Pharisees and Herod

[14] Now they had forgotten to bring bread, and they had only one loaf with them in the boat. [15] And he cautioned them, saying, "Watch out; beware of the leaven of the Pharisees and the leaven of Herod."[6] [16] And they began discussing with one another the fact that they

---

[1] Some manuscripts add verse 16: *If anyone has ears to hear, let him hear* [2] Greek *goes out into the latrine* [3] Some manuscripts omit *and Sidon* [4] Greek *he* [5] Some manuscripts *Magadan*, or *Magdala* [6] Some manuscripts *the Herodians* [a] For 8:1-10 see parallel Matt. 15:32-39 [b] For 8:11-21 see parallel Matt. 16:1-12

had no bread. [17] And Jesus, aware of this, said to them, "Why are you discussing the fact that you have no bread? Do you not yet perceive or understand? Are your hearts hardened? [18]Having eyes do you not see, and having ears do you not hear? And do you not remember? [19]When I broke the five loaves for the five thousand, how many baskets full of broken pieces did you take up?" They said to him, "Twelve." [20]"And the seven for the four thousand, how many baskets full of broken pieces did you take up?" And they said to him, "Seven." [21]And he said to them, "Do you not yet understand?"

Jesus Heals a Blind Man at Bethsaida

[22] And they came to Bethsaida. And some people brought to him a blind man and begged him to touch him. [23]And he took the blind man by the hand and led him out of the village, and when he had spit on his eyes and laid his hands on him, he asked him, "Do you see anything?" [24]And he looked up and said, "I see people, but they look like trees, walking." [25]Then Jesus[1] laid his hands on his eyes again; and he opened his eyes, his sight was restored, and he saw everything clearly. [26]And he sent him to his home, saying, "Do not even enter the village."

Peter Confesses Jesus as the Christ

[27][a]And Jesus went on with his disciples to the villages of Caesarea Philippi. And on the way he asked his disciples, "Who do people say that I am?" [28]And they told him, "John the Baptist; and others say, Elijah; and others, one of the prophets." [29]And he asked them, "But who do you say that I am?" Peter answered him, "You are the Christ." [30]And he strictly charged them to tell no one about him.

Jesus Foretells His Death and Resurrection

[31][b]And he began to teach them that the Son of Man must suffer many things and be rejected by the elders and the chief priests and the scribes and be killed, and after three days rise again. [32]And he said this plainly. And Peter took him aside and began to rebuke him. [33]But turning and seeing his disciples, he rebuked Peter and said, "Get behind me, Satan! For you are not setting your mind on the things of God, but on the things of man."

[34]And calling the crowd to him with his disciples, he said to them, "If anyone would come after me, let him deny himself and take up his

cross and follow me. [35]For whoever would save his life[2] will lose it, but whoever loses his life for my sake and the gospel's will save it. [36]For what does it profit a man to gain the whole world and forfeit his soul? [37]For what can a man give in return for his soul? [38]For whoever is ashamed of me and of my words in this adulterous and sinful generation, of him will the Son of Man also be ashamed when he comes in the glory of his Father with the holy angels."

9 And he said to them, "Truly, I say to you, there are some standing here who will not taste death until they see the kingdom of God after it has come with power."

The Transfiguration

[2][c] And after six days Jesus took with him Peter and James and John, and led them up a high mountain by themselves. And he was transfigured before them, [3]and his clothes became radiant, intensely white, as no one[3] on earth could bleach them. [4]And there appeared to them Elijah with Moses, and they were talking with Jesus. [5]And Peter said to Jesus, "Rabbi,[4] it is good that we are here. Let us make three tents, one for you and one for Moses and one for Elijah." [6]For he did not know what to say, for they were terrified. [7]And a cloud overshadowed them, and a voice came out of the cloud, "This is my beloved Son;[5] listen to him." [8]And suddenly, looking around, they no longer saw anyone with them but Jesus only.

[9][d]And as they were coming down the mountain, he charged them to tell no one what they had seen, until the Son of Man had risen from the dead. [10]So they kept the matter to themselves, questioning what this rising from the dead might mean. [11]And they asked him, "Why do the scribes say that first Elijah must come?" [12]And he said to them, "Elijah does come first to restore all things. And how is it written of the Son of Man that he should suffer many things and be treated with contempt? [13]But I tell you that Elijah has come, and they did to him whatever they pleased, as it is written of him."

Jesus Heals a Boy with an Unclean Spirit

[14][e]And when they came to the disciples, they saw a great crowd around them, and scribes arguing with them. [15]And immediately all the crowd, when they saw him, were greatly amazed and ran up to him and greeted him.

[1] Greek he [2] The same Greek word can mean either soul or life, depending on the context; twice in this verse and once in verse 36 and once in verse 37 [3] Greek launderer (gnapheus) [4] Rabbi means my teacher, or my master [5] Or my Son, my (or the) Beloved [a] For 8:27-29 see parallels Matt. 16:13-16; Luke 9:18-20 [b] For 8:31-9:1 see parallels Matt. 16:21-28; Luke 9:22-27 [c] For 9:2-8 see parallels Matt. 17:1-8; Luke 9:28-36 [d] For 9:9-13 see parallel Matt. 17:9-13 [e] For 9:14-28 see parallels Matt. 17:14-19; Luke 9:37-42

[16] And he asked them, "What are you arguing about with them?" [17] And someone from the crowd answered him, "Teacher, I brought my son to you, for he has a spirit that makes him mute. [18] And whenever it seizes him, it throws him down, and he foams and grinds his teeth and becomes rigid. So I asked your disciples to cast it out, and they were not able." [19] And he answered them, "O faithless generation, how long am I to be with you? How long am I to bear with you? Bring him to me." [20] And they brought the boy to him. And when the spirit saw him, immediately it convulsed the boy, and he fell on the ground and rolled about, foaming at the mouth. [21] And Jesus asked his father, "How long has this been happening to him?" And he said, "From childhood. [22] And it has often cast him into fire and into water, to destroy him. But if you can do anything, have compassion on us and help us." [23] And Jesus said to him, "'If you can'! All things are possible for one who believes." [24] Immediately the father of the child cried out[1] and said, "I believe; help my unbelief!" [25] And when Jesus saw that a crowd came running together, he rebuked the unclean spirit, saying to it, "You mute and deaf spirit, I command you, come out of him and never enter him again." [26] And after crying out and convulsing him terribly, it came out, and the boy was like a corpse, so that most of them said, "He is dead." [27] But Jesus took him by the hand and lifted him up, and he arose. [28] And when he had entered the house, his disciples asked him privately, "Why could we not cast it out?" [29] And he said to them, "This kind cannot be driven out by anything but prayer."[2]

Jesus Again Foretells Death, Resurrection

[30] [a] They went on from there and passed through Galilee. And he did not want anyone to know, [31] for he was teaching his disciples, saying to them, "The Son of Man is going to be delivered into the hands of men, and they will kill him. And when he is killed, after three days he will rise." [32] But they did not understand the saying, and were afraid to ask him.

Who Is the Greatest?

[33] And they came to Capernaum. And when he was in the house [b] he asked them, "What were you discussing on the way?" [34] But they kept silent, for on the way they had argued with one another about who was the greatest. [35] And he sat down and called the twelve. And he said to them, "If anyone would be first, he must be last of all and servant of all." [36] And he took a child and put him in the midst of them, and taking him in his arms, he said to them, [37] "Whoever receives one such child in my name receives me, and whoever receives me, receives not me but him who sent me."

Anyone Not Against Us Is for Us

[38] [c] John said to him, "Teacher, we saw someone casting out demons in your name,[3] and we tried to stop him, because he was not following us." [39] But Jesus said, "Do not stop him, for no one who does a mighty work in my name will be able soon afterward to speak evil of me. [40] For the one who is not against us is for us. [41] For truly, I say to you, whoever gives you a cup of water to drink because you belong to Christ will by no means lose his reward.

Temptations to Sin

[42] "Whoever causes one of these little ones who believe in me to sin,[4] it would be better for him if a great millstone were hung around his neck and he were thrown into the sea. [43] And if your hand causes you to sin, cut it off. It is better for you to enter life crippled than with two hands to go to hell,[5] to the unquenchable fire.[6] [45] And if your foot causes you to sin, cut it off. It is better for you to enter life lame than with two feet to be thrown into hell. [47] And if your eye causes you to sin, tear it out. It is better for you to enter the kingdom of God with one eye than with two eyes to be thrown into hell, [48] 'where their worm does not die and the fire is not quenched.' [49] For everyone will be salted with fire.[7] [50] Salt is good, but if the salt has lost its saltiness, how will you make it salty again? Have salt in yourselves, and be at peace with one another."

Teaching About Divorce

10 [d] And he left there and went to the region of Judea and beyond the Jordan, and crowds gathered to him again. And again, as was his custom, he taught them.

[2] And Pharisees came up and in order to test him asked, "Is it lawful for a man to divorce his wife?" [3] He answered them, "What did Moses

---

[1] Some manuscripts add *with tears* [2] Some manuscripts add *and fasting* [3] Some manuscripts add *who does not follow us* [4] Greek *to stumble*; also verses 43, 45, 47 [5] Greek *Gehenna*; also verse 47 [6] Some manuscripts add verses 44 and 46 (which are identical with verse 48) [7] Some manuscripts add *and every sacrifice will be salted with salt* [a] For 9:30-32 see parallels Matt. 17:22, 23; Luke 9:43-45 [b] For 9:33-37 see parallels Matt. 18:1-5; Luke 9:46-48 [c] For 9:38-40 see parallel Luke 9:49, 50 [d] For 10:1-12 see parallel Matt. 19:1-9

command you?" [4] They said, "Moses allowed a man to write a certificate of divorce and to send her away." [5] And Jesus said to them, "Because of your hardness of heart he wrote you this commandment. [6] But from the beginning of creation, 'God made them [d] male and female.' [7b] 'Therefore a man shall leave his father and mother and hold fast to his wife,[1] [8] and the two shall become one flesh.' So they are no longer two but one flesh. [9] What therefore God has joined together, let not man separate."

[10] And in the house the disciples asked him again about this matter. [11] And he said to them, "Whoever divorces his wife and marries another commits adultery against her, [12] and if she divorces her husband and marries another, she commits adultery."

Let the Children Come to Me

[13c] And they were bringing children to him that he might touch them, and the disciples rebuked them. [14] But when Jesus saw it, he was indignant and said to them, "Let the children come to me; do not hinder them, for to such belongs the kingdom of God. [15] Truly, I say to you, whoever does not receive the kingdom of God like a child shall not enter it." [16] And he took them in his arms and blessed them, laying his hands on them.

The Rich Young Man

[17d] And as he was setting out on his journey, a man ran up and knelt before him and asked him, "Good Teacher, what must I do to inherit eternal life?" [18] And Jesus said to him, "Why do you call me good? No one is good except God alone. [19] You know the commandments: 'Do not murder, Do not commit adultery, Do not steal, Do not bear false witness, Do not defraud, Honor your father and mother.'" [20] And he said to him, "Teacher, all these I have kept from my youth." [21] And Jesus, looking at him, loved him, and said to him, "You lack one thing: go, sell all that you have and give to the poor, and you will have treasure in heaven; and come, follow me." [22] Disheartened by the saying, he went away sorrowful, for he had great possessions.

[23] And Jesus looked around and said to his disciples, "How difficult it will be for those who have wealth to enter the kingdom of God!" [24] And the disciples were amazed at his words. But Jesus said to them again, "Children, how difficult it is[2] to enter the kingdom of God! [25] It is easier for a camel to go through the eye of a needle than for a rich person to enter the kingdom of God." [26] And they were exceedingly astonished, and said to him,[3] "Then who can be saved?" [27] Jesus looked at them and said, "With man it is impossible, but not with God. For all things are possible with God." [28] Peter began to say to him, "See, we have left everything and followed you." [29] Jesus said, "Truly, I say to you, there is no one who has left house or brothers or sisters or mother or father or children or lands, for my sake and for the gospel, [30] who will not receive a hundredfold now in this time, houses and brothers and sisters and mothers and children and lands, with persecutions, and in the age to come eternal life. [31] But many who are first will be last, and the last first."

Jesus Foretells His Death a Third Time

[32f] And they were on the road, going up to Jerusalem, and Jesus was walking ahead of them. And they were amazed, and those who followed were afraid. And taking the twelve again, he began to tell them what was to happen to him, [33] saying, "See, we are going up to Jerusalem, and the Son of Man will be delivered over to the chief priests and the scribes, and they will condemn him to death and deliver him over to the Gentiles. [34] And they will mock him and spit on him, and flog him and kill him. And after three days he will rise."

The Request of James and John

[35g] And James and John, the sons of Zebedee, came up to him and said to him, "Teacher, we want you to do for us whatever we ask of you." [36] And he said to them, "What do you want me to do for you?" [37] And they said to him, "Grant us to sit, one at your right hand and one at your left, in your glory." [38] Jesus said to them, "You do not know what you are asking. Are you able to drink the cup that I drink, or to be baptized with the baptism with which I am baptized?" [39] And they said to him, "We are able." And Jesus said to them, "The cup that I drink you will drink, and with the baptism with which I am baptized, you will be baptized, [40] but to sit at my right hand or at my left is not mine to grant, but it is for those for whom it has been prepared." [41] And when the ten heard it, they

---

[1] Some manuscripts omit *and hold fast to his wife* [2] Some manuscripts add *for those who trust in riches* [3] Some manuscripts *to one another* [a] Gen. 1:27; 5:2 [b] Gen. 2:24 [c] For 10:13-16 see parallels Matt. 19:13-15; Luke 18:15-17 [d] For 10:17-31 see parallels Matt. 19:16-30; Luke 18:18-30 [e] Ex. 20:12-16; Deut. 5:16-20 [f] For 10:32-34 see parallels Matt. 20:17-19; Luke 18:31-33 [g] For 10:35-45 see parallel Matt. 20:20-28

began to be indignant at James and John. [42] And Jesus called them to him and said to them, "You know that those who are considered rulers of the Gentiles lord it over them, and their great ones exercise authority over them. [43] But it shall not be so among you. But whoever would be great among you must be your servant,[1] [44] and whoever would be first among you must be slave[2] of all. [45] For even the Son of Man came not to be served but to serve, and to give his life as a ransom for many."

Jesus Heals Blind Bartimaeus

[46][a] And they came to Jericho. And as he was leaving Jericho with his disciples and a great crowd, Bartimaeus, a blind beggar, the son of Timaeus, was sitting by the roadside. [47] And when he heard that it was Jesus of Nazareth, he began to cry out and say, "Jesus, Son of David, have mercy on me!" [48] And many rebuked him, telling him to be silent. But he cried out all the more, "Son of David, have mercy on me!" [49] And Jesus stopped and said, "Call him." And they called the blind man, saying to him, "Take heart. Get up; he is calling you." [50] And throwing off his cloak, he sprang up and came to Jesus. [51] And Jesus said to him, "What do you want me to do for you?" And the blind man said to him, "Rabbi, let me recover my sight." [52] And Jesus said to him, "Go your way; your faith has made you well." And immediately he recovered his sight and followed him on the way.

The Triumphal Entry

11 [b] Now when they drew near to Jerusalem, to Bethphage and Bethany, at the Mount of Olives, Jesus[3] sent two of his disciples [2] and said to them, "Go into the village in front of you, and immediately as you enter it you will find a colt tied, on which no one has ever sat. Untie it and bring it. [3] If anyone says to you, 'Why are you doing this?' say, 'The Lord has need of it and will send it back here immediately.'" [4] And they went away and found a colt tied at a door outside in the street, and they untied it. [5] And some of those standing there said to them, "What are you doing, untying the colt?" [6] And they told them what Jesus had said, and they let them go. [7] And they brought the colt to Jesus and threw their cloaks on it, and he sat on it. [8] And many spread their cloaks on the road, and others spread leafy branches that they

had cut from the fields. [9] And those who went before and those who followed were shouting, "Hosanna! Blessed is he who comes in the name of the Lord! [10] Blessed is the coming kingdom of our father David! Hosanna in the highest!"

[11] And he entered Jerusalem and went into the temple. And when he had looked around at everything, as it was already late, he went out to Bethany with the twelve.

Jesus Curses the Fig Tree

[12] On the following day, when they came from Bethany, he was hungry. [13] And seeing in the distance a fig tree in leaf, he went to see if he could find anything on it. When he came to it, he found nothing but leaves, for it was not the season for figs. [14] And he said to it, "May no one ever eat fruit from you again." And his disciples heard it.

Jesus Cleanses the Temple

[15][c] And they came to Jerusalem. And he entered the temple and began to drive out those who sold and those who bought in the temple, and he overturned the tables of the money-changers and the seats of those who sold pigeons. [16] And he would not allow anyone to carry anything through the temple. [17] And he was teaching them and saying to them, "Is it not written, [d] 'My house shall be called a house of prayer for all the nations'? But you have made it a den of robbers." [18] And the chief priests and the scribes heard it and were seeking a way to destroy him, for they feared him, because all the crowd was astonished at his teaching. [19] And when evening came they[4] went out of the city.

The Lesson from the Withered Fig Tree

[20][e] As they passed by in the morning, they saw the fig tree withered away to its roots. [21] And Peter remembered and said to him, "Rabbi, look! The fig tree that you cursed has withered." [22] And Jesus answered them, "Have faith in God. [23] Truly, I say to you, whoever says to this mountain, 'Be taken up and thrown into the sea,' and does not doubt in his heart, but believes that what he says will come to pass, it will be done for him. [24] Therefore I tell you, whatever you ask in prayer, believe that you have received[5] it, and it will be yours. [25] And whenever you stand praying, forgive, if you have anything against anyone, so that your

---

[1] Greek *diakonos* [2] Or *bondservant*, or *servant* (for the contextual rendering of the Greek word *doulos*, see Preface) [3] Greek *he* [4] Some manuscripts *he* [5] Some manuscripts *are receiving* [a] For 10:46-52 see parallels Matt. 20:29-34; Luke 18:35-43 [b] For 11:1-10 see parallels Matt. 21:1-9; Luke 19:28-38; John 12:12-15 [c] For 11:15-18 see parallels Matt. 21:12-16; Luke 19:45-47 [d] Isa. 56:7 [e] For 11:20-24 see parallel Matt. 21:19-22

Father also who is in heaven may forgive you your trespasses."[1]

The Authority of Jesus Challenged

27 [a] And they came again to Jerusalem. And as he was walking in the temple, the chief priests and the scribes and the elders came to him, 28 and they said to him, "By what authority are you doing these things, or who gave you this authority to do them?" 29 Jesus said to them, "I will ask you one question; answer me, and I will tell you by what authority I do these things. 30 Was the baptism of John from heaven or from man? Answer me." 31 And they discussed it with one another, saying, "If we say, 'From heaven,' he will say, 'Why then did you not believe him?' 32 But shall we say, 'From man'?"—they were afraid of the people, for they all held that John really was a prophet. 33 So they answered Jesus, "We do not know." And Jesus said to them, "Neither will I tell you by what authority I do these things."

The Parable of the Tenants

12 [b] And he began to speak to them in parables. "A man planted a vineyard and put a fence around it and dug a pit for the winepress and built a tower, and leased it to tenants and went into another country. 2 When the season came, he sent a servant[2] to the tenants to get from them some of the fruit of the vineyard. 3 And they took him and beat him and sent him away empty-handed. 4 Again he sent to them another servant, and they struck him on the head and treated him shamefully. 5 And he sent another, and him they killed. And so with many others: some they beat, and some they killed. 6 He had still one other, a beloved son. Finally he sent him to them, saying, 'They will respect my son.' 7 But those tenants said to one another, 'This is the heir. Come, let us kill him, and the inheritance will be ours.' 8 And they took him and killed him and threw him out of the vineyard. 9 What will the owner of the vineyard do? He will come and destroy the tenants and give the vineyard to others. 10 Have you not read this Scripture:

[c] "'The stone that the builders rejected
     has become the cornerstone;[3]
11   this was the Lord's doing,
     and it is marvelous in our eyes'?"

12 And they were seeking to arrest him but feared the people, for they perceived that he had told the parable against them. So they left him and went away.

Paying Taxes to Caesar

13 [d] And they sent to him some of the Pharisees and some of the Herodians, to trap him in his talk. 14 And they came and said to him, "Teacher, we know that you are true and do not care about anyone's opinion. For you are not swayed by appearances,[4] but truly teach the way of God. Is it lawful to pay taxes to Caesar, or not? Should we pay them, or should we not?" 15 But, knowing their hypocrisy, he said to them, "Why put me to the test? Bring me a denarius[5] and let me look at it." 16 And they brought one. And he said to them, "Whose likeness and inscription is this?" They said to him, "Caesar's." 17 Jesus said to them, "Render to Caesar the things that are Caesar's, and to God the things that are God's." And they marveled at him.

The Sadducees Ask About the Resurrection

18 And Sadducees came to him, who say that there is no resurrection. And they asked him a question, saying, 19 "Teacher, Moses wrote for us that if a man's brother dies and leaves a wife, but leaves no child, the man[6] must take the widow and raise up offspring for his brother. 20 There were seven brothers; the first took a wife, and when he died left no offspring. 21 And the second took her, and died, leaving no offspring. And the third likewise. 22 And the seven left no offspring. Last of all the woman also died. 23 In the resurrection, when they rise again, whose wife will she be? For the seven had her as wife."

24 Jesus said to them, "Is this not the reason you are wrong, because you know neither the Scriptures nor the power of God? 25 For when they rise from the dead, they neither marry nor are given in marriage, but are like angels in heaven. 26 And as for the dead being raised, have you not read in the book of Moses, in the passage about the bush, how God spoke to him, saying, 'I am the God of Abraham, and the God of Isaac, and the God of Jacob'? 27 He is not God of the dead, but of the living. You are quite wrong."

The Great Commandment

28 [f] And one of the scribes came up and heard them disputing with one another, and seeing that he answered them well, asked him, "Which commandment is the most important of all?"

[1] Some manuscripts add verse 26: But if you do not forgive, neither will your Father who is in heaven forgive your trespasses [2] Or bondservant; also verse 4 [3] Greek the head of the corner [4] Greek you do not look at people's faces [5] A denarius was a day's wage for a laborer [6] Greek his brother [a] For 11:27-33 see parallels Matt. 21:23-27; Luke 20:1-8 [b] For 12:1-12 see parallels Matt. 21:33-46; Luke 20:9-18 [c] Ps. 118:22, 23 [d] For 12:13-27 see parallels Matt. 22:15-32; Luke 20:20-38 [e] Ex. 3:6 [f] For 12:28-34 see parallel Matt. 22:34-40, 46

29Jesus answered, "The most important is, *a*"Hear, O Israel: The Lord our God, the Lord is one. **30**And you shall love the Lord your God with all your heart and with all your soul and with all your mind and with all your strength.' **31**The second is this: *b*"You shall love your neighbor as yourself.' There is no other commandment greater than these." **32**And the scribe said to him, "You are right, Teacher. You have truly said that he is one, and there is no other besides him. **33**And to love him with all the heart and with all the understanding and with all the strength, and to love one's neighbor as oneself, is much more than all whole burnt offerings and sacrifices." **34**And when Jesus saw that he answered wisely, he said to him, "You are not far from the kingdom of God." And after that no one dared to ask him any more questions.

Whose Son Is the Christ?

35 *c*And as Jesus taught in the temple, he said, "How can the scribes say that the Christ is the son of David? **36**David himself, in the Holy Spirit, declared,

d"'The Lord said to my Lord,
  "Sit at my right hand,
      until I put your enemies under your
          feet."'

37David himself calls him Lord. So how is he his son?" And the great throng heard him gladly.

Beware of the Scribes

38 *e*And in his teaching he said, "Beware of the scribes, who like to walk around in long robes and like greetings in the marketplaces **39**and have the best seats in the synagogues and the places of honor at feasts, **40**who devour widows' houses and for a pretense make long prayers. They will receive the greater condemnation."

The Widow's Offering

41 *f*And he sat down opposite the treasury and watched the people putting money into the offering box. Many rich people put in large sums. **42**And a poor widow came and put in two small copper coins, which make a penny.[1] **43**And he called his disciples to him and said to them, "Truly, I say to you, this poor widow has put in more than all those who are contributing to the offering box. **44**For they all contributed out of their abundance, but she out of her poverty has put in everything she had, all she had to live on."

Jesus Foretells Destruction of the Temple

13 *g*And as he came out of the temple, one of his disciples said to him, "Look, Teacher, what wonderful stones and what wonderful buildings!" **2**And Jesus said to him, "Do you see these great buildings? There will not be left here one stone upon another that will not be thrown down."

Signs of the End of the Age

3And as he sat on the Mount of Olives opposite the temple, Peter and James and John and Andrew asked him privately, **4**"Tell us, when will these things be, and what will be the sign when all these things are about to be accomplished?" **5**And Jesus began to say to them, "See that no one leads you astray. **6**Many will come in my name, saying, 'I am he!' and they will lead many astray. **7**And when you hear of wars and rumors of wars, do not be alarmed. This must take place, but the end is not yet. **8**For nation will rise against nation, and kingdom against kingdom. There will be earthquakes in various places; there will be famines. These are but the beginning of the birth pains.

9"But be on your guard. For they will deliver you over to councils, and you will be beaten in synagogues, and you will stand before governors and kings for my sake, to bear witness before them. **10**And the gospel must first be proclaimed to all nations. **11**And when they bring you to trial and deliver you over, do not be anxious beforehand what you are to say, but say whatever is given you in that hour, for it is not you who speak, but the Holy Spirit. **12**And brother will deliver brother over to death, and the father his child, and children will rise against parents and have them put to death. **13**And you will be hated by all for my name's sake. But the one who endures to the end will be saved.

The Abomination of Desolation

14"But when you see the abomination of desolation standing where he ought not to be (let the reader understand), then let those who are in Judea flee to the mountains. **15**Let the one who is on the housetop not go down, nor enter his house, to take anything out, **16**and let the one who is in the field not turn back to take his cloak. **17**And alas for women who are pregnant and for those who are nursing infants in those days! **18**Pray that it may not happen in winter.

---

[1] Greek *two lepta*, which make a *kodrantes*; a *kodrantes* (Latin *quadrans*) was a Roman copper coin worth about 1/64 of a *denarius* (which was a day's wage for a laborer)
a Deut. 6:4, 5 *b* Lev. 19:18 *c* For 12:35-37 see parallels Matt. 22:41-45; Luke 20:41-44 *d* Ps. 110:1 *e* For 12:38-40 see parallels Matt. 23:1, 2, 5-7; Luke 20:45, 46 *f* For 12:41-44 see parallel Luke 21:1-4 *g* For 13:1-37 see parallels Matt. 24:1-51; Luke 21:5-36

¹⁹For in those days there will be such tribulation as has not been from the beginning of the creation that God created until now, and never will be. ²⁰And if the Lord had not cut short the days, no human being would be saved. But for the sake of the elect, whom he chose, he shortened the days. ²¹And then if anyone says to you, 'Look, here is the Christ!' or 'Look, there he is!' do not believe it. ²²For false christs and false prophets will arise and perform signs and wonders, to lead astray, if possible, the elect. ²³But be on guard; I have told you all things beforehand.

The Coming of the Son of Man

²⁴"But in those days, after that tribulation, the sun will be darkened, and the moon will not give its light, ²⁵and the stars will be falling from heaven, and the powers in the heavens will be shaken. ²⁶And then they will see the Son of Man coming in clouds with great power and glory. ²⁷And then he will send out the angels and gather his elect from the four winds, from the ends of the earth to the ends of heaven.

The Lesson of the Fig Tree

²⁸"From the fig tree learn its lesson: as soon as its branch becomes tender and puts out its leaves, you know that summer is near. ²⁹So also, when you see these things taking place, you know that he is near, at the very gates. ³⁰Truly, I say to you, this generation will not pass away until all these things take place. ³¹Heaven and earth will pass away, but my words will not pass away.

No One Knows That Day or Hour

³²"But concerning that day or that hour, no one knows, not even the angels in heaven, nor the Son, but only the Father. ³³Be on guard, keep awake.¹ For you do not know when the time will come. ³⁴It is like a man going on a journey, when he leaves home and puts his servants² in charge, each with his work, and commands the doorkeeper to stay awake. ³⁵Therefore stay awake—for you do not know when the master of the house will come, in the evening, or at midnight, or when the rooster crows,³ or in the morning— ³⁶lest he come suddenly and find you asleep. ³⁷And what I say to you I say to all: Stay awake."

The Plot to Kill Jesus

14 "It was now two days before the Passover and the Feast of Unleavened Bread. And the chief priests and the scribes were seeking how to arrest him by stealth and kill him, ²for they said, "Not during the feast, lest there be an uproar from the people."

Jesus Anointed at Bethany

³ᵇAnd while he was at Bethany in the house of Simon the leper,⁴ as he was reclining at table, a woman came with an alabaster flask of ointment of pure nard, very costly, and she broke the flask and poured it over his head. ⁴There were some who said to themselves indignantly, "Why was the ointment wasted like that? ⁵For this ointment could have been sold for more than three hundred denarii⁵ and given to the poor." And they scolded her. ⁶But Jesus said, "Leave her alone. Why do you trouble her? She has done a beautiful thing to me. ⁷For you always have the poor with you, and whenever you want, you can do good for them. But you will not always have me. ⁸She has done what she could; she has anointed my body beforehand for burial. ⁹And truly, I say to you, wherever the gospel is proclaimed in the whole world, what she has done will be told in memory of her."

Judas to Betray Jesus

¹⁰ᶜThen Judas Iscariot, who was one of the twelve, went to the chief priests in order to betray him to them. ¹¹And when they heard it, they were glad and promised to give him money. And he sought an opportunity to betray him.

The Passover with the Disciples

¹²ᵈAnd on the first day of Unleavened Bread, when they sacrificed the Passover lamb, his disciples said to him, "Where will you have us go and prepare for you to eat the Passover?" ¹³And he sent two of his disciples and said to them, "Go into the city, and a man carrying a jar of water will meet you. Follow him, ¹⁴and wherever he enters, say to the master of the house, 'The Teacher says, Where is my guest room, where I may eat the Passover with my disciples?' ¹⁵And he will show you a large upper room furnished and ready; there prepare for us." ¹⁶And the disciples set out and went to the city

and found it just as he had told them, and they prepared the Passover.

[17a] And when it was evening, he came with the twelve. [18] And as they were reclining at table and eating, Jesus said, "Truly, I say to you, one of you will betray me, one who is eating with me." [19] They began to be sorrowful and to say to him one after another, "Is it I?" [20] He said to them, "It is one of the twelve, one who is dipping bread into the dish with me. [21] For the Son of Man goes as it is written of him, but woe to that man by whom the Son of Man is betrayed! It would have been better for that man if he had not been born."

Institution of the Lord's Supper

[22b] And as they were eating, he took bread, and after blessing it broke it and gave it to them, and said, "Take; this is my body." [23] And he took a cup, and when he had given thanks he gave it to them, and they all drank of it. [24] And he said to them, "This is my blood of the[1] covenant, which is poured out for many. [25] Truly, I say to you, I will not drink again of the fruit of the vine until that day when I drink it new in the kingdom of God."

Jesus Foretells Peter's Denial

[26c] And when they had sung a hymn, they went out to the Mount of Olives. [27] And Jesus said to them, "You will all fall away, for it is written, 'I will [d]strike the shepherd, and the sheep will be scattered.' [28] But after I am raised up, I will go before you to Galilee." [29] Peter said to him, "Even though they all fall away, I will not." [30] And Jesus said to him, "Truly, I tell you, this very night, before the rooster crows twice, you will deny me three times." [31] But he said emphatically, "If I must die with you, I will not deny you." And they all said the same.

Jesus Prays in Gethsemane

[32e] And they went to a place called Gethsemane. And he said to his disciples, "Sit here while I pray." [33] And he took with him Peter and James and John, and began to be greatly distressed and troubled. [34] And he said to them, "My soul is very sorrowful, even to death. Remain here and watch."[2] [35] And going a little farther, he fell on the ground and prayed that, if it were possible, the hour might pass from him. [36] And he said, "Abba, Father, all things are possible for you. Remove this cup from me.

Yet not what I will, but what you will." [37] And he came and found them sleeping, and he said to Peter, "Simon, are you asleep? Could you not watch one hour? [38] Watch and pray that you may not enter into temptation. The spirit indeed is willing, but the flesh is weak." [39] And again he went away and prayed, saying the same words. [40] And again he came and found them sleeping, for their eyes were very heavy, and they did not know what to answer him. [41] And he came the third time and said to them, "Are you still sleeping and taking your rest? It is enough; the hour has come. The Son of Man is betrayed into the hands of sinners. [42] Rise, let us be going; see, my betrayer is at hand."

Betrayal and Arrest of Jesus

[43f] And immediately, while he was still speaking, Judas came, one of the twelve, and with him a crowd with swords and clubs, from the chief priests and the scribes and the elders. [44] Now the betrayer had given them a sign, saying, "The one I will kiss is the man. Seize him and lead him away under guard." [45] And when he came, he went up to him at once and said, "Rabbi!" And he kissed him. [46] And they laid hands on him and seized him. [47] But one of those who stood by drew his sword and struck the servant[3] of the high priest and cut off his ear. [48] And Jesus said to them, "Have you come out as against a robber, with swords and clubs to capture me? [49] Day after day I was with you in the temple teaching, and you did not seize me. But let the Scriptures be fulfilled." [50] And they all left him and fled.

A Young Man Flees

[51] And a young man followed him, with nothing but a linen cloth about his body. And they seized him, [52] but he left the linen cloth and ran away naked.

Jesus Before the Council

[53g] And they led Jesus to the high priest. And all the chief priests and the elders and the scribes came together. [54] And Peter had followed him at a distance, right into the courtyard of the high priest. And he was sitting with the guards and warming himself at the fire. [55] Now the chief priests and the whole council[4] were seeking testimony against Jesus to put him to death, but they found none. [56] For many bore false witness against him, but their testimony did not agree. [57] And some stood up and bore false

---

[1] Some manuscripts insert *new* [2] Or *keep awake*; also verses 37, 38 [3] Or *bondservant* [4] Greek *Sanhedrin* [a]For 14:17-21 see parallel Matt. 26:20-24 [b]For 14:22-25 see parallels Matt. 26:26-29; Luke 22:18-20 [c]For 14:26-31 see parallel Matt. 26:30-35 [d]Zech. 13:7 [e]For 14:32-42 see parallels Matt. 26:36-46; Luke 22:39-46 [f]For 14:43-50 see parallels Matt. 26:47-56; Luke 22:47-53; John 18:3-11 [g]For 14:53-65 see parallel Matt. 26:57-68

witness against him, saying, [58] "We heard him say, 'I will destroy this temple that is made with hands, and in three days I will build another, not made with hands.'" [59] Yet even about this their testimony did not agree. [60] And the high priest stood up in the midst and asked Jesus, "Have you no answer to make? What is it that these men testify against you?"[1] [61] But he remained silent and made no answer. Again the high priest asked him, "Are you the Christ, the Son of the Blessed?" [62] And Jesus said, "I am, and you will see the Son of Man seated at the right hand of Power, and coming with the clouds of heaven." [63] And the high priest tore his garments and said, "What further witnesses do we need? [64] You have heard his blasphemy. What is your decision?" And they all condemned him as deserving death. [65] And some began to spit on him and to cover his face and to strike him, saying to him, "Prophesy!" And the guards received him with blows.

Peter Denies Jesus

[66] [a] And as Peter was below in the courtyard, one of the servant girls of the high priest came, [67] and seeing Peter warming himself, she looked at him and said, "You also were with the Nazarene, Jesus." [68] But he denied it, saying, "I neither know nor understand what you mean." And he went out into the gateway[2] and the rooster crowed.[3] [69] And the servant girl saw him and began again to say to the bystanders, "This man is one of them." [70] But again he denied it. And after a little while the bystanders again said to Peter, "Certainly you are one of them, for you are a Galilean." [71] But he began to invoke a curse on himself and to swear, "I do not know this man of whom you speak." [72] And immediately the rooster crowed a second time. And Peter remembered how Jesus had said to him, "Before the rooster crows twice, you will deny me three times." And he broke down and wept.[4]

Jesus Delivered to Pilate

15 And as soon as it was morning, the chief priests held a consultation with the elders and scribes and the whole council. And they bound Jesus and led him away and delivered him over to Pilate. [2] [b] And Pilate asked him, "Are you the King of the Jews?" And he answered him, "You have said so." [3] And

the chief priests accused him of many things. [4] And Pilate again asked him, "Have you no answer to make? See how many charges they bring against you." [5] But Jesus made no further answer, so that Pilate was amazed.

Pilate Delivers Jesus to Be Crucified

[6] [c] Now at the feast he used to release for them one prisoner for whom they asked. [7] And among the rebels in prison, who had committed murder in the insurrection, there was a man called Barabbas. [8] And the crowd came up and began to ask Pilate to do as he usually did for them. [9] And he answered them, saying, "Do you want me to release for you the King of the Jews?" [10] For he perceived that it was out of envy that the chief priests had delivered him up. [11] But the chief priests stirred up the crowd to have him release for them Barabbas instead. [12] And Pilate again said to them, "Then what shall I do with the man you call the King of the Jews?" [13] And they cried out again, "Crucify him." [14] And Pilate said to them, "Why? What evil has he done?" But they shouted all the more, "Crucify him." [15] So Pilate, wishing to satisfy the crowd, released for them Barabbas, and having scourged[5] Jesus, he delivered him to be crucified.

Jesus Is Mocked

[16] [d] And the soldiers led him away inside the palace (that is, the governor's headquarters),[6] and they called together the whole battalion.[7] [17] And they clothed him in a purple cloak, and twisting together a crown of thorns, they put it on him. [18] And they began to salute him, "Hail, King of the Jews!" [19] And they were striking his head with a reed and spitting on him and kneeling down in homage to him. [20] And when they had mocked him, they stripped him of the purple cloak and put his own clothes on him. And they led him out to crucify him.

The Crucifixion

[21] And they compelled a passerby, Simon of Cyrene, who was coming in from the country, the father of Alexander and Rufus, to carry his cross. [22] [e] And they brought him to the place called Golgotha (which means Place of a Skull). [23] And they offered him wine mixed with myrrh, but he did not take it. [24] And they crucified him and divided his garments among

---

[1] Or Have you no answer to what these men testify against you? [2] Or forecourt [3] Some manuscripts omit and the rooster crowed [4] Or And when he had thought about it, he wept [5] A Roman judicial penalty, consisting of a severe beating with a multi-lashed whip containing embedded pieces of bone and metal [6] Greek the praetorium [7] Greek cohort; a tenth of a Roman legion, usually about 600 men   [a] For 14:66-72 see parallels Matt. 26:69-75; Luke 22:55-62; John 18:16-18, 25-27   [b] For 15:2-5 see parallels Matt. 27:11-14; Luke 23:1-3; John 18:28-38   [c] For 15:6-15 see parallels Matt. 27:15-26; Luke 23:18-25; John 18:39, 40; 19:16   [d] For 15:16-20 see parallels Matt. 27:27-31; John 19:2, 3   [e] For 15:22-38 see parallels Matt. 27:33-51; Luke 23:32-38, 44-46; John 19:17-19, 23, 24, 28-30

them, casting lots for them, to decide what each should take. ²⁵ And it was the third hour¹ when they crucified him. ²⁶ And the inscription of the charge against him read, "The King of the Jews." ²⁷ And with him they crucified two robbers, one on his right and one on his left.² ²⁹ And those who passed by derided him, wagging their heads and saying, "Aha! You who would destroy the temple and rebuild it in three days, ³⁰ save yourself, and come down from the cross!" ³¹ So also the chief priests with the scribes mocked him to one another, saying, "He saved others; he cannot save himself. ³² Let the Christ, the King of Israel, come down now from the cross that we may see and believe." Those who were crucified with him also reviled him.

The Death of Jesus

³³ And when the sixth hour³ had come, there was darkness over the whole land until the ninth hour.⁴ ³⁴ And at the ninth hour Jesus cried with a loud voice, ᵃ "Eloi, Eloi, lema sabachthani?" which means, "My God, my God, why have you forsaken me?" ³⁵ And some of the bystanders hearing it said, "Behold, he is calling Elijah." ³⁶ And someone ran and filled a sponge with sour wine, put it on a reed and gave it to him to drink, saying, "Wait, let us see whether Elijah will come to take him down." ³⁷ And Jesus uttered a loud cry and breathed his last. ³⁸ And the curtain of the temple was torn in two, from top to bottom. ³⁹ ᵇ And when the centurion, who stood facing him, saw that in this way he⁵ breathed his last, he said, "Truly this man was the Son⁶ of God!"

⁴⁰ There were also women looking on from a distance, among whom were Mary Magdalene and Mary the mother of James the younger and of Joses, and Salome. ⁴¹ When he was in Galilee, they followed him and ministered to him, and there were also many other women who came up with him to Jerusalem.

Jesus Is Buried

⁴² ᶜ And when evening had come, since it was the day of Preparation, that is, the day before the Sabbath, ⁴³ Joseph of Arimathea, a respected member of the council, who was also himself looking for the kingdom of God, took courage and went to Pilate and asked for the body of Jesus. ⁴⁴ Pilate was surprised to hear that he should have already died.⁷ And summoning the centurion, he asked him whether he was already dead. ⁴⁵ And when he learned from the centurion that he was dead, he granted the corpse to Joseph. ⁴⁶ And Joseph⁸ bought a linen shroud, and taking him down, wrapped him in the linen shroud and laid him in a tomb that had been cut out of the rock. And he rolled a stone against the entrance of the tomb. ⁴⁷ Mary Magdalene and Mary the mother of Joses saw where he was laid.

The Resurrection

16 ᵈ When the Sabbath was past, Mary Magdalene, Mary the mother of James, and Salome bought spices, so that they might go and anoint him. ² And very early on the first day of the week, when the sun had risen, they went to the tomb. ³ And they were saying to one another, "Who will roll away the stone for us from the entrance of the tomb?" ⁴ And looking up, they saw that the stone had been rolled back—it was very large. ⁵ And entering the tomb, they saw a young man sitting on the right side, dressed in a white robe, and they were alarmed. ⁶ And he said to them, "Do not be alarmed. You seek Jesus of Nazareth, who was crucified. He has risen; he is not here. See the place where they laid him. ⁷ But go, tell his disciples and Peter that he is going before you to Galilee. There you will see him, just as he told you." ⁸ And they went out and fled from the tomb, for trembling and astonishment had seized them, and they said nothing to anyone, for they were afraid.

[Some of the earliest manuscripts do not include 16:9–20.]⁹

Jesus Appears to Mary Magdalene

⁹ [[Now when he rose early on the first day of the week, he appeared first to Mary Magdalene, from whom he had cast out seven demons. ¹⁰ She went and told those who had been with him, as they mourned and wept. ¹¹ But when they heard that he was alive and had been seen by her, they would not believe it.

¹ That is, 9 A.M. ² Some manuscripts insert verse 28: And the Scripture was fulfilled that says, "He was numbered with the transgressors" ³ That is, noon ⁴ That is, 3 P.M. ⁵ Some manuscripts insert cried out and ⁶ Or a son ⁷ Or Pilate wondered whether he had already died ⁸ Greek he ⁹ Some manuscripts end the book with 16:8; others include verses 9–20 immediately after verse 8. At least one manuscript inserts additional material after verse 14; some manuscripts include after verse 8 the following: But they reported briefly to Peter and those with him all that they had been told. And after this, Jesus himself sent out by means of them, from east to west, the sacred and imperishable proclamation of eternal salvation. These manuscripts then continue with verses 9–20 ᵃPs. 22:1 ᵇFor 15:39-41 see parallels Matt. 27:54-56; Luke 23:47, 49 ᶜFor 15:42-47 see parallels Matt. 27:57-61; Luke 23:50-56; John 19:38-42 ᵈFor 16:1-8 see parallels Matt. 28:1-8; Luke 24:1-10; John 20:1

Jesus Appears to Two Disciples

[12] After these things he appeared in another form to two of them, as they were walking into the country. [13] And they went back and told the rest, but they did not believe them.

The Great Commission

[14] Afterward he appeared to the eleven themselves as they were reclining at table, and he rebuked them for their unbelief and hardness of heart, because they had not believed those who saw him after he had risen. [15] And he said to them, "Go into all the world and proclaim the gospel to the whole creation. [16] Whoever believes and is baptized will be saved, but whoever does not believe will be condemned. [17] And these signs will accompany those who believe: in my name they will cast out demons; they will speak in new tongues; [18] they will pick up serpents with their hands; and if they drink any deadly poison, it will not hurt them; they will lay their hands on the sick, and they will recover."

[19] So then the Lord Jesus, after he had spoken to them, was taken up into heaven and sat down at the right hand of God. [20] And they went out and preached everywhere, while the Lord worked with them and confirmed the message by accompanying signs.]]

LUKE

Dedication to Theophilus

1 Inasmuch as many have undertaken to compile a narrative of the things that have been accomplished among us, [2] just as those who from the beginning were eyewitnesses and ministers of the word have delivered them to us, [3] it seemed good to me also, having followed all things closely for some time past, to write an orderly account for you, most excellent Theophilus, [4] that you may have certainty concerning the things you have been taught.

Birth of John the Baptist Foretold

[5] In the days of Herod, king of Judea, there was a priest named Zechariah,[1] of the division of Abijah. And he had a wife from the daughters of Aaron, and her name was Elizabeth. [6] And they were both righteous before God, walking blamelessly in all the commandments and statutes of the Lord. [7] But they had no child, because Elizabeth was barren, and both were advanced in years.

[8] Now while he was serving as priest before God when his division was on duty, [9] according to the custom of the priesthood, he was chosen by lot to enter the temple of the Lord and burn incense. [10] And the whole multitude of the people were praying outside at the hour of incense. [11] And there appeared to him an angel of the Lord standing on the right side of the altar of incense. [12] And Zechariah was troubled when he saw him, and fear fell upon him. [13] But the angel said to him, "Do not be afraid, Zechariah, for your prayer has been heard, and your wife Elizabeth will bear you a son, and you shall call his name John. [14] And you will have joy and gladness, and many will rejoice at his birth, [15] for he will be great before the Lord. And he must not drink wine or strong drink, and he will be filled with the Holy Spirit, even from his mother's womb. [16] And he will turn many of the children of Israel to the Lord their God, [17] and he will go before him in the spirit and power of Elijah, to turn the hearts of the fathers to the children, and the disobedient to the wisdom of the just, to make ready for the Lord a people prepared."

[18] And Zechariah said to the angel, "How shall I know this? For I am an old man, and my wife is advanced in years." [19] And the angel answered him, "I am Gabriel. I stand in the presence of God, and I was sent to speak to you and to bring you this good news. [20] And behold, you will be silent and unable to speak until the day that these things take place, because you did not believe my words, which will be fulfilled in their time." [21] And the people were waiting for Zechariah, and they were wondering at his delay in the temple. [22] And when he came out, he was unable to speak to them, and they realized that he had seen a vision in the temple. And he kept making signs to them and remained mute. [23] And when his time of service was ended, he went to his home.

[24] After these days his wife Elizabeth conceived, and for five months she kept herself hidden, saying, [25] "Thus the Lord has done for me in the days when he looked on me, to take away my reproach among people."

Birth of Jesus Foretold

[26] In the sixth month the angel Gabriel was sent from God to a city of Galilee named Nazareth, [27] to a virgin betrothed[2] to a man whose name was Joseph, of the house of David. And the virgin's name was Mary. [28] And he came to her and said, "Greetings, O favored one, the Lord is with you!"[3] [29] But she was greatly troubled at the saying, and tried to discern what sort of greeting this might be. [30] And the angel said to her, "Do not be afraid, Mary, for you have found favor with God. [31] And behold, you will conceive in your womb and bear a son, and you shall call his name Jesus. [32] He will be great and will be called the Son of the Most High. And the Lord God will give to him the throne of his father David, [33] and he will reign over the house of Jacob forever, and of his kingdom there will be no end."

[34] And Mary said to the angel, "How will this be, since I am a virgin?"[4]

[35] And the angel answered her, "The Holy Spirit will come upon you, and the power of the Most High will overshadow you; therefore the child to be born[5] will be called holy—the Son of God. [36] And behold, your relative Elizabeth in her old age has also conceived a son, and this is the sixth month with her who was called

[1] Greek Zacharias [2] That is, legally pledged to be married [3] Some manuscripts add Blessed are you among women! [4] Greek since I do not know a man [5] Some manuscripts add of you

barren. [37] For nothing will be impossible with God." [38] And Mary said, "Behold, I am the servant[1] of the Lord; let it be to me according to your word." And the angel departed from her.

Mary Visits Elizabeth

[39] In those days Mary arose and went with haste into the hill country, to a town in Judah, [40] and she entered the house of Zechariah and greeted Elizabeth. [41] And when Elizabeth heard the greeting of Mary, the baby leaped in her womb. And Elizabeth was filled with the Holy Spirit, [42] and she exclaimed with a loud cry, "Blessed are you among women, and blessed is the fruit of your womb! [43] And why is this granted to me that the mother of my Lord should come to me? [44] For behold, when the sound of your greeting came to my ears, the baby in my womb leaped for joy. [45] And blessed is she who believed that there would be[2] a fulfillment of what was spoken to her from the Lord."

Mary's Song of Praise: The Magnificat

[46] And Mary said,

"My soul magnifies the Lord,
[47]   and my spirit rejoices in God my Savior,
[48]   for he has looked on the humble estate of
            his servant.
        For behold, from now on all generations
            will call me blessed;
[49]   for he who is mighty has done great things
            for me,
        and holy is his name.
[50]   And his mercy is for those who fear him
            from generation to generation.
[51]   He has shown strength with his arm;
            he has scattered the proud in the
                thoughts of their hearts;
[52]   he has brought down the mighty from
            their thrones
        and exalted those of humble estate;
[53]   he has filled the hungry with good
            things,
        and the rich he has sent away empty.
[54]   He has helped his servant Israel,
            in remembrance of his mercy,
[55]   as he spoke to our fathers,
            to Abraham and to his offspring for-
                ever."

[56] And Mary remained with her about three months and returned to her home.

The Birth of John the Baptist

[57] Now the time came for Elizabeth to give birth, and she bore a son. [58] And her neighbors and relatives heard that the Lord had shown great mercy to her, and they rejoiced with her. [59] And on the eighth day they came to circumcise the child. And they would have called him Zechariah after his father, [60] but his mother answered, "No; he shall be called John." [61] And they said to her, "None of your relatives is called by this name." [62] And they made signs to his father, inquiring what he wanted him to be called. [63] And he asked for a writing tablet and wrote, "His name is John." And they all wondered. [64] And immediately his mouth was opened and his tongue loosed, and he spoke, blessing God. [65] And fear came on all their neighbors. And all these things were talked about through all the hill country of Judea, [66] and all who heard them laid them up in their hearts, saying, "What then will this child be?" For the hand of the Lord was with him.

Zechariah's Prophecy

[67] And his father Zechariah was filled with the Holy Spirit and prophesied, saying,

[68] "Blessed be the Lord God of Israel,
            for he has visited and redeemed his
                people
[69]   and has raised up a horn of salvation for us
            in the house of his servant David,
[70]   as he spoke by the mouth of his holy
                prophets from of old,
[71]   that we should be saved from our ene-
                mies
        and from the hand of all who hate us;
[72]   to show the mercy promised to our
                fathers
        and to remember his holy covenant,
[73]   the oath that he swore to our father
                Abraham, to grant us
[74]   that we, being delivered from the hand
                of our enemies,
        might serve him without fear,
[75]   in holiness and righteousness before
                him all our days.
[76]   And you, child, will be called the prophet
                of the Most High;
        for you will go before the Lord to pre-
                pare his ways,

---

[1] Greek bondservant; also verse 48 [2] Or believed, for there will be

77 to give knowledge of salvation to his
        people
    in the forgiveness of their sins,
78 because of the tender mercy of our God,
        whereby the sunrise shall visit us[1] from
            on high
79 to give light to those who sit in darkness
        and in the shadow of death,
    to guide our feet into the way of
        peace."

80 And the child grew and became strong in spirit, and he was in the wilderness until the day of his public appearance to Israel.

The Birth of Jesus Christ

2 In those days a decree went out from Caesar Augustus that all the world should be registered. ²This was the first registration when[2] Quirinius was governor of Syria. ³And all went to be registered, each to his own town. ⁴And Joseph also went up from Galilee, from the town of Nazareth, to Judea, to the city of David, which is called Bethlehem, because he was of the house and lineage of David, ⁵to be registered with Mary, his betrothed,[3] who was with child. ⁶And while they were there, the time came for her to give birth. ⁷And she gave birth to her firstborn son and wrapped him in swaddling cloths and laid him in a manger, because there was no place for them in the inn.[4]

The Shepherds and the Angels

⁸And in the same region there were shepherds out in the field, keeping watch over their flock by night. ⁹And an angel of the Lord appeared to them, and the glory of the Lord shone around them, and they were filled with great fear. ¹⁰And the angel said to them, "Fear not, for behold, I bring you good news of great joy that will be for all the people. ¹¹For unto you is born this day in the city of David a Savior, who is Christ the Lord. ¹²And this will be a sign for you: you will find a baby wrapped in swaddling cloths and lying in a manger." ¹³And suddenly there was with the angel a multitude of the heavenly host praising God and saying,

14   "Glory to God in the highest,
        and on earth peace among those with
            whom he is pleased!"[5]

¹⁵When the angels went away from them into heaven, the shepherds said to one another,

"Let us go over to Bethlehem and see this thing that has happened, which the Lord has made known to us." ¹⁶And they went with haste and found Mary and Joseph, and the baby lying in a manger. ¹⁷And when they saw it, they made known the saying that had been told them concerning this child. ¹⁸And all who heard it wondered at what the shepherds told them. ¹⁹But Mary treasured up all these things, pondering them in her heart. ²⁰And the shepherds returned, glorifying and praising God for all they had heard and seen, as it had been told them.

²¹And at the end of eight days, when he was circumcised, he was called Jesus, the name given by the angel before he was conceived in the womb.

Jesus Presented at the Temple

²²And when the time came for their purification according to the Law of Moses, they brought him up to Jerusalem to present him to the Lord ²³(as it is written in the Law of the Lord, ᵃ"Every male who first opens the womb shall be called holy to the Lord") ²⁴and to offer a sacrifice according to what is said in the Law of the Lord, ᵇ"a pair of turtledoves, or two young pigeons." ²⁵Now there was a man in Jerusalem, whose name was Simeon, and this man was righteous and devout, waiting for the consolation of Israel, and the Holy Spirit was upon him. ²⁶And it had been revealed to him by the Holy Spirit that he would not see death before he had seen the Lord's Christ. ²⁷And he came in the Spirit into the temple, and when the parents brought in the child Jesus, to do for him according to the custom of the Law, ²⁸he took him up in his arms and blessed God and said,

29   "Lord, now you are letting your servant[6]
        depart in peace,
        according to your word;
30 for my eyes have seen your salvation
31   that you have prepared in the presence
            of all peoples,
32 a light for revelation to the Gentiles,
        and for glory to your people Israel."

³³And his father and his mother marveled at what was said about him. ³⁴And Simeon blessed them and said to Mary his mother, "Behold, this child is appointed for the fall and rising of many in Israel, and for a sign that is opposed

---

[1] Or when the sunrise shall dawn upon us; some manuscripts since the sunrise has visited us [2] Or This was the registration before [3] That is, one legally pledged to be married [4] Or guest room [5] Some manuscripts peace, good will among men [6] Or bondservant ᵃEx. 13:2, 12 ᵇLev. 12:8

[35] (and a sword will pierce through your own soul also), so that thoughts from many hearts may be revealed."

[36] And there was a prophetess, Anna, the daughter of Phanuel, of the tribe of Asher. She was advanced in years, having lived with her husband seven years from when she was a virgin, [37] and then as a widow until she was eighty-four.[1] She did not depart from the temple, worshiping with fasting and prayer night and day. [38] And coming up at that very hour she began to give thanks to God and to speak of him to all who were waiting for the redemption of Jerusalem.

The Return to Nazareth

[39] And when they had performed everything according to the Law of the Lord, they returned into Galilee, to their own town of Nazareth. [40] And the child grew and became strong, filled with wisdom. And the favor of God was upon him.

The Boy Jesus in the Temple

[41] Now his parents went to Jerusalem every year at the Feast of the Passover. [42] And when he was twelve years old, they went up according to custom. [43] And when the feast was ended, as they were returning, the boy Jesus stayed behind in Jerusalem. His parents did not know it, [44] but supposing him to be in the group they went a day's journey, but then they began to search for him among their relatives and acquaintances, [45] and when they did not find him, they returned to Jerusalem, searching for him. [46] After three days they found him in the temple, sitting among the teachers, listening to them and asking them questions. [47] And all who heard him were amazed at his understanding and his answers. [48] And when his parents[2] saw him, they were astonished. And his mother said to him, "Son, why have you treated us so? Behold, your father and I have been searching for you in great distress." [49] And he said to them, "Why were you looking for me? Did you not know that I must be in my Father's house?"[3] [50] And they did not understand the saying that he spoke to them. [51] And he went down with them and came to Nazareth and was submissive to them. And his mother treasured up all these things in her heart.

[52] And Jesus increased in wisdom and in stature[4] and in favor with God and man.

John the Baptist Prepares the Way

3 In the fifteenth year of the reign of Tiberius Caesar, Pontius Pilate being governor of Judea, and Herod being tetrarch of Galilee, and his brother Philip tetrarch of the region of Ituraea and Trachonitis, and Lysanias tetrarch of Abilene, [2] during the high priesthood of Annas and Caiaphas, [a] the word of God came to John the son of Zechariah in the wilderness. [3] And he went into all the region around the Jordan, proclaiming a baptism of repentance for the forgiveness of sins. [4] As it is written in the book of the words of Isaiah the prophet,

> [b] "The voice of one crying in the wilderness:
>   'Prepare the way of the Lord,[5]
>   make his paths straight.
> [5] Every valley shall be filled,
>   and every mountain and hill shall be made low,
>   and the crooked shall become straight,
>   and the rough places shall become level ways,
> [6]   and all flesh shall see the salvation of God.'"

[7] He said therefore to the crowds that came out to be baptized by him, "You brood of vipers! Who warned you to flee from the wrath to come? [8] Bear fruits in keeping with repentance. And do not begin to say to yourselves, 'We have Abraham as our father.' For I tell you, God is able from these stones to raise up children for Abraham. [9] Even now the axe is laid to the root of the trees. Every tree therefore that does not bear good fruit is cut down and thrown into the fire."

[10] And the crowds asked him, "What then shall we do?" [11] And he answered them, "Whoever has two tunics[6] is to share with him who has none, and whoever has food is to do likewise." [12] Tax collectors also came to be baptized and said to him, "Teacher, what shall we do?" [13] And he said to them, "Collect no more than you are authorized to do." [14] Soldiers also asked him, "And we, what shall we do?" And he said to them, "Do not extort money from anyone by threats or by false accusation, and be content with your wages."

[15] As the people were in expectation, and all were questioning in their hearts concerning John, whether he might be the Christ, [16] John answered them all, saying, "I baptize you with

---

[1] Or as a widow for eighty-four years [2] Greek they [3] Or about my Father's business [4] Or years [5] Or crying, Prepare in the wilderness the way of the Lord [6] Greek chiton, a long garment worn under the cloak next to the skin [a] For 3:2-17 see parallels Matt. 3:1-12; Mark 1:2-8 [b] Isa. 40:3-5

water, but he who is mightier than I is coming, the strap of whose sandals I am not worthy to untie. He will baptize you with the Holy Spirit and fire. [17] His winnowing fork is in his hand, to clear his threshing floor and to gather the wheat into his barn, but the chaff he will burn with unquenchable fire."

[18] So with many other exhortations he preached good news to the people. [19] But Herod the tetrarch, who had been reproved by him for Herodias, his brother's wife, and for all the evil things that Herod had done, [20] added this to them all, that he locked up John in prison.

[21] Now when all the people were baptized, and when [a] Jesus also had been baptized and was praying, the heavens were opened, [22] and the Holy Spirit descended on him in bodily form, like a dove; and a voice came from heaven, "You are my beloved Son;[1] with you I am well pleased."[2]

The Genealogy of Jesus Christ

[23] Jesus, when he began his ministry, was about thirty years of age, being the son (as was supposed) of Joseph, the son of Heli, [24] the son of Matthat, the son of Levi, the son of Melchi, the son of Jannai, the son of Joseph, [25] the son of Mattathias, the son of Amos, the son of Nahum, the son of Esli, the son of Naggai, [26] the son of Maath, the son of Mattathias, the son of Semein, the son of Josech, the son of Joda, [27] the son of Joanan, the son of Rhesa, the son of Zerubbabel, the son of Shealtiel,[3] the son of Neri, [28] the son of Melchi, the son of Addi, the son of Cosam, the son of Elmadam, the son of Er, [29] the son of Joshua, the son of Eliezer, the son of Jorim, the son of Matthat, the son of Levi, [30] the son of Simeon, the son of Judah, the son of Joseph, the son of Jonam, the son of Eliakim, [31] the son of Melea, the son of Menna, the son of Mattatha, the son of Nathan, the son of David, [32] the son of Jesse, the son of Obed, the son of Boaz, the son of Sala, the son of Nahshon, [33] the son of Amminadab, the son of Admin, the son of Arni, the son of Hezron, the son of Perez, the son of Judah, [34] the son of Jacob, the son of Isaac, the son of Abraham, the son of Terah, the son of Nahor, [35] the son of Serug, the son of Reu, the son of Peleg, the son of Eber, the son of Shelah, [36] the son of Cainan, the son of Arphaxad, the son of Shem, the son of Noah, the son of Lamech, [37] the son of

Methuselah, the son of Enoch, the son of Jared, the son of Mahalaleel, the son of Cainan, [38] the son of Enos, the son of Seth, the son of Adam, the son of God.

The Temptation of Jesus

4 [b] And Jesus, full of the Holy Spirit, returned from the Jordan and was led by the Spirit in the wilderness [2] for forty days, being tempted by the devil. And he ate nothing during those days. And when they were ended, he was hungry. [3] The devil said to him, "If you are the Son of God, command this stone to become bread." [4] And Jesus answered him, "It is written, 'Man shall not live by bread alone.'" [5] And the devil took him up and showed him all the kingdoms of the world in a moment of time, [6] and said to him, "To you I will give all this authority and their glory, for it has been delivered to me, and I give it to whom I will. [7] If you, then, will worship me, it will all be yours." [8] And Jesus answered him, "It is written,

[d] "'You shall worship the Lord your God,
　　and him only shall you serve.'"

[9] And he took him to Jerusalem and set him on the pinnacle of the temple and said to him, "If you are the Son of God, throw yourself down from here, [10] for it is written,

[e] "'He will command his angels concerning
　　you,
　　　to guard you,'

[11] and

[f] "'On their hands they will bear you up,
　　lest you strike your foot against a
　　stone.'"

[12] And Jesus answered him, "It is said, [g] 'You shall not put the Lord your God to the test.'" [13] And when the devil had ended every temptation, he departed from him until an opportune time.

Jesus Begins His Ministry

[14] And Jesus returned in the power of the Spirit to Galilee, and a report about him went out through all the surrounding country. [15] And he taught in their synagogues, being glorified by all.

Jesus Rejected at Nazareth

[16] And he came to Nazareth, where he had been brought up. And as was his custom, he

---

[1] Or my Son, my (or the) Beloved [2] Some manuscripts beloved Son; today I have begotten you [3] Greek Salathiel [a] For 3:21, 22 see parallels Matt. 3:13-17; Mark 1:9-11 [b] For 4:1-13 see parallels Matt. 4:1-11; Mark 1:12, 13 [c] Deut. 8:3 [d] Deut. 6:13 [e] Ps. 91:11 [f] Ps. 91:12 [g] Deut. 6:16

went to the synagogue on the Sabbath day, and he stood up to read. [17]And the scroll of the prophet Isaiah was given to him. He unrolled the scroll and found the place where it was written,

[18] [a]"The Spirit of the Lord is upon me,
    because he has anointed me
        to proclaim good news to the poor.
    He has sent me to proclaim liberty to the captives
        and recovering of sight to the blind,
        to set at liberty those who are oppressed,
[19]   to proclaim the year of the Lord's favor."

[20]And he rolled up the scroll and gave it back to the attendant and sat down. And the eyes of all in the synagogue were fixed on him. [21]And he began to say to them, "Today this Scripture has been fulfilled in your hearing." [22]And all spoke well of him and marveled at the gracious words that were coming from his mouth. And they said, "Is not this Joseph's son?" [23]And he said to them, "Doubtless you will quote to me this proverb, '"Physician, heal yourself." What we have heard you did at Capernaum, do here in your hometown as well.'" [24]And he said, "Truly, I say to you, no prophet is acceptable in his hometown. [25]But in truth, I tell you, there were many widows in Israel in the days of Elijah, when the heavens were shut up three years and six months, and a great famine came over all the land, [26]and Elijah was sent to none of them but only to Zarephath, in the land of Sidon, to a woman who was a widow. [27]And there were many lepers[1] in Israel in the time of the prophet Elisha, and none of them was cleansed, but only Naaman the Syrian." [28]When they heard these things, all in the synagogue were filled with wrath. [29]And they rose up and drove him out of the town and brought him to the brow of the hill on which their town was built, so that they could throw him down the cliff. [30]But passing through their midst, he went away.

Jesus Heals a Man with an Unclean Demon

[31] [b]And he went down to Capernaum, a city of Galilee. And he was teaching them on the Sabbath, [32]and they were astonished at his teaching, for his word possessed authority. [33]And in the synagogue there was a man who had the spirit of an unclean demon, and he cried out with a loud voice, [34]"Ha![2] What have you to do with us, Jesus of Nazareth? Have you

come to destroy us? I know who you are—the Holy One of God." [35]But Jesus rebuked him, saying, "Be silent and come out of him!" And when the demon had thrown him down in their midst, he came out of him, having done him no harm. [36]And they were all amazed and said to one another, "What is this word? For with authority and power he commands the unclean spirits, and they come out!" [37]And reports about him went out into every place in the surrounding region.

Jesus Heals Many

[38] [c]And he arose and left the synagogue and entered Simon's house. Now Simon's mother-in-law was ill with a high fever, and they appealed to him on her behalf. [39]And he stood over her and rebuked the fever, and it left her, and immediately she rose and began to serve them.

[40]Now when the sun was setting, all those who had any who were sick with various diseases brought them to him, and he laid his hands on every one of them and healed them. [41]And demons also came out of many, crying, "You are the Son of God!" But he rebuked them and would not allow them to speak, because they knew that he was the Christ.

Jesus Preaches in Synagogues

[42] [d]And when it was day, he departed and went into a desolate place. And the people sought him and came to him, and would have kept him from leaving them, [43]but he said to them, "I must preach the good news of the kingdom of God to the other towns as well; for I was sent for this purpose." [44]And he was preaching in the synagogues of Judea.[3]

Jesus Calls the First Disciples

5 On one occasion, while the crowd was pressing in on him to hear the word of God, he was standing by the lake of Gennesaret, [2]and he saw two boats by the lake, but the fishermen had gone out of them and were washing their nets. [3]Getting into one of the boats, which was Simon's, he asked him to put out a little from the land. And he sat down and taught the people from the boat. [4]And when he had finished speaking, he said to Simon, "Put out into the deep and let down your nets for a catch." [5]And Simon answered, "Master, we toiled all night and took nothing! But at your word I will let

---

[1] *Leprosy* was a term for several skin diseases; see Leviticus 13 [2] Or *Leave us alone* [3] Some manuscripts *Galilee* [a] Isa. 61:1, 2 [b] For 4:31-37 see parallel Mark 1:21-28 [c] For 4:38-41 see parallels Matt. 8:14-17; Mark 1:29-34 [d] For 4:42, 43 see parallel Mark 1:35-38

down the nets." [6] And when they had done this, they enclosed a large number of fish, and their nets were breaking. [7] They signaled to their partners in the other boat to come and help them. And they came and filled both the boats, so that they began to sink. [8] But when Simon Peter saw it, he fell down at Jesus' knees, saying, "Depart from me, for I am a sinful man, O Lord." [9] For he and all who were with him were astonished at the catch of fish that they had taken, [10] and so also were James and John, sons of Zebedee, who were partners with Simon. And Jesus said to Simon, "Do not be afraid; from now on you will be catching men."[1] [11] And when they had brought their boats to land, they left everything and followed him.

Jesus Cleanses a Leper

[12] While he was in one of the cities, [a] there came a man full of leprosy.[2] And when he saw Jesus, he fell on his face and begged him, "Lord, if you will, you can make me clean." [13] And Jesus[3] stretched out his hand and touched him, saying, "I will; be clean." And immediately the leprosy left him. [14] And he charged him to tell no one, but "go and show yourself to the priest, and make an offering for your cleansing, as Moses commanded, for a proof to them." [15] But now even more the report about him went abroad, and great crowds gathered to hear him and to be healed of their infirmities. [16] But he would withdraw to desolate places and pray.

Jesus Heals a Paralytic

[17] On one of those days, as he was teaching, Pharisees and teachers of the law were sitting there, who had come from every village of Galilee and Judea and from Jerusalem. And the power of the Lord was with him to heal.[4] [18] [b] And behold, some men were bringing on a bed a man who was paralyzed, and they were seeking to bring him in and lay him before Jesus, [19] but finding no way to bring him in, because of the crowd, they went up on the roof and let him down with his bed through the tiles into the midst before Jesus. [20] And when he saw their faith, he said, "Man, your sins are forgiven you." [21] And the scribes and the Pharisees began to question, saying, "Who is this who speaks blasphemies? Who can forgive sins but God alone?" [22] When Jesus perceived their thoughts, he answered them, "Why do you question in

your hearts? [23] Which is easier, to say, 'Your sins are forgiven you,' or to say, 'Rise and walk'? [24] But that you may know that the Son of Man has authority on earth to forgive sins"—he said to the man who was paralyzed—"I say to you, rise, pick up your bed and go home." [25] And immediately he rose up before them and picked up what he had been lying on and went home, glorifying God. [26] And amazement seized them all, and they glorified God and were filled with awe, saying, "We have seen extraordinary things today."

Jesus Calls Levi

[27] [c] After this he went out and saw a tax collector named Levi, sitting at the tax booth. And he said to him, "Follow me." [28] And leaving everything, he rose and followed him.

[29] And Levi made him a great feast in his house, and there was a large company of tax collectors and others reclining at table with them. [30] And the Pharisees and their scribes grumbled at his disciples, saying, "Why do you eat and drink with tax collectors and sinners?" [31] And Jesus answered them, "Those who are well have no need of a physician, but those who are sick. [32] I have not come to call the righteous but sinners to repentance."

A Question About Fasting

[33] And they said to him, "The disciples of John fast often and offer prayers, and so do the disciples of the Pharisees, but yours eat and drink." [34] And Jesus said to them, "Can you make wedding guests fast while the bridegroom is with them? [35] The days will come when the bridegroom is taken away from them, and then they will fast in those days." [36] He also told them a parable: "No one tears a piece from a new garment and puts it on an old garment. If he does, he will tear the new, and the piece from the new will not match the old. [37] And no one puts new wine into old wineskins. If he does, the new wine will burst the skins and it will be spilled, and the skins will be destroyed. [38] But new wine must be put into fresh wineskins. [39] And no one after drinking old wine desires new, for he says, 'The old is good.' "[5]

Jesus Is Lord of the Sabbath

6 [d] On a Sabbath,[6] while he was going through the grainfields, his disciples plucked and ate some heads of grain, rubbing

---

[1] The Greek word *anthropoi* refers here to both men and women [2] *Leprosy* was a term for several skin diseases; see Leviticus 13 [3] Greek *he* [4] Some manuscripts *was present to heal them* [5] Some manuscripts *better* [6] Some manuscripts *On the second first Sabbath* (that is, on the second Sabbath after the first) [a] For 5:12-14 see parallels Matt. 8:2-4; Mark 1:40-44 [b] For 5:18-26 see parallels Matt. 9:2-8; Mark 2:1-12 [c] For 5:27-38 see parallels Matt. 9:9-17; Mark 2:13-22 [d] For 6:1-5 see parallels Matt. 12:1-8; Mark 2:23-28

them in their hands. ²But some of the Pharisees said, "Why are you doing what is not lawful to do on the Sabbath?" ³And Jesus answered them, "Have you not read what David did when he was hungry, he and those who were with him: ⁴how he entered the house of God and took and ate the bread of the Presence, which is not lawful for any but the priests to eat, and also gave it to those with him?" ⁵And he said to them, "The Son of Man is lord of the Sabbath."

A Man with a Withered Hand

⁶On another Sabbath, ᵃhe entered the synagogue and was teaching, and a man was there whose right hand was withered. ⁷And the scribes and the Pharisees watched him, to see whether he would heal on the Sabbath, so that they might find a reason to accuse him. ⁸But he knew their thoughts, and he said to the man with the withered hand, "Come and stand here." And he rose and stood there. ⁹And Jesus said to them, "I ask you, is it lawful on the Sabbath to do good or to do harm, to save life or to destroy it?" ¹⁰And after looking around at them all he said to him, "Stretch out your hand." And he did so, and his hand was restored. ¹¹But they were filled with fury and discussed with one another what they might do to Jesus.

The Twelve Apostles

¹²In these days he went out to the mountain to pray, and all night he continued in prayer to God. ¹³And when day came, he called his disciples ᵇand chose from them twelve, whom he named apostles: ¹⁴Simon, whom he named Peter, and Andrew his brother, and James and John, and Philip, and Bartholomew, ¹⁵and Matthew, and Thomas, and James the son of Alphaeus, and Simon who was called the Zealot, ¹⁶and Judas the son of James, and Judas Iscariot, who became a traitor.

Jesus Ministers to a Great Multitude

¹⁷And he came down with them and stood on a level place, with a great crowd of his disciples and a great multitude of people from all Judea and Jerusalem and the seacoast of Tyre and Sidon, ¹⁸who came to hear him and to be healed of their diseases. And those who were troubled with unclean spirits were cured. ¹⁹And all the crowd sought to touch him, for power came out from him and healed them all.

The Beatitudes

²⁰And he lifted up his eyes on his disciples, and said:

"Blessed are you who are poor, for yours is the kingdom of God.

²¹"Blessed are you who are hungry now, for you shall be satisfied.

"Blessed are you who weep now, for you shall laugh.

²²"Blessed are you when people hate you and when they exclude you and revile you and spurn your name as evil, on account of the Son of Man! ²³Rejoice in that day, and leap for joy, for behold, your reward is great in heaven; for so their fathers did to the prophets.

Jesus Pronounces Woes

²⁴"But woe to you who are rich, for you have received your consolation.

²⁵"Woe to you who are full now, for you shall be hungry.

"Woe to you who laugh now, for you shall mourn and weep.

²⁶"Woe to you, when all people speak well of you, for so their fathers did to the false prophets.

Love Your Enemies

²⁷"But I say to you who hear, Love your enemies, do good to those who hate you, ²⁸bless those who curse you, pray for those who abuse you. ²⁹ᶜTo one who strikes you on the cheek, offer the other also, and from one who takes away your cloak do not withhold your tunic¹ either. ³⁰Give to everyone who begs from you, and from one who takes away your goods do not demand them back. ³¹And as you wish that others would do to you, do so to them.

³²"If you love those who love you, what benefit is that to you? For even sinners love those who love them. ³³And if you do good to those who do good to you, what benefit is that to you? For even sinners do the same. ³⁴And if you lend to those from whom you expect to receive, what credit is that to you? Even sinners lend to sinners, to get back the same amount. ³⁵But love your enemies, and do good, and lend, expecting nothing in return, and your reward will be great, and you will be sons of the Most High, for he is kind to the ungrateful and the evil. ³⁶Be merciful, even as your Father is merciful.

¹ Greek *chiton*, a long garment worn under the cloak next to the skin ᵃFor 6:6-11 see parallels Matt. 12:9-14; Mark 3:1-6 ᵇFor 6:13-16 see parallels Matt. 10:2-4; Mark 3:16-19 ᶜFor 6:29, 30 see parallel Matt. 5:39-42

Judging Others

37ᵃ "Judge not, and you will not be judged; condemn not, and you will not be condemned; forgive, and you will be forgiven; **38**give, and it will be given to you. Good measure, pressed down, shaken together, running over, will be put into your lap. For with the measure you use it will be measured back to you."

39 He also told them a parable: "Can a blind man lead a blind man? Will they not both fall into a pit? **40**A disciple is not above his teacher, but everyone when he is fully trained will be like his teacher. **41**Why do you see the speck that is in your brother's eye, but do not notice the log that is in your own eye? **42**How can you say to your brother, 'Brother, let me take out the speck that is in your eye,' when you yourself do not see the log that is in your own eye? You hypocrite, first take the log out of your own eye, and then you will see clearly to take out the speck that is in your brother's eye.

A Tree and Its Fruit

43 "For ᵇ no good tree bears bad fruit, nor again does a bad tree bear good fruit, **44**for each tree is known by its own fruit. For figs are not gathered from thornbushes, nor are grapes picked from a bramble bush. **45**The good person out of the good treasure of his heart produces good, and the evil person out of his evil treasure produces evil, for out of the abundance of the heart his mouth speaks.

Build Your House on the Rock

46 "Why do you call me 'Lord, Lord,' and not do what I tell you? **47**ᶜ Everyone who comes to me and hears my words and does them, I will show you what he is like: **48**he is like a man building a house, who dug deep and laid the foundation on the rock. And when a flood arose, the stream broke against that house and could not shake it, because it had been well built.¹ **49**But the one who hears and does not do them is like a man who built a house on the ground without a foundation. When the stream broke against it, immediately it fell, and the ruin of that house was great."

Jesus Heals a Centurion's Servant

7 After he had finished all his sayings in the hearing of the people, ᵈ he entered Capernaum. **2**Now a centurion had a servant² who was sick and at the point of death, who was highly valued by him. **3**When the centurion³ heard about Jesus, he sent to him elders of the Jews, asking him to come and heal his servant. **4**And when they came to Jesus, they pleaded with him earnestly, saying, "He is worthy to have you do this for him, **5**for he loves our nation, and he is the one who built us our synagogue." **6**And Jesus went with them. When he was not far from the house, the centurion sent friends, saying to him, "Lord, do not trouble yourself, for I am not worthy to have you come under my roof. **7**Therefore I did not presume to come to you. But say the word, and let my servant be healed. **8**For I too am a man set under authority, with soldiers under me: and I say to one, 'Go,' and he goes; and to another, 'Come,' and he comes; and to my servant, 'Do this,' and he does it." **9**When Jesus heard these things, he marveled at him, and turning to the crowd that followed him, said, "I tell you, not even in Israel have I found such faith." **10**And when those who had been sent returned to the house, they found the servant well.

Jesus Raises a Widow's Son

11 Soon afterward⁴ he went to a town called Nain, and his disciples and a great crowd went with him. **12**As he drew near to the gate of the town, behold, a man who had died was being carried out, the only son of his mother, and she was a widow, and a considerable crowd from the town was with her. **13**And when the Lord saw her, he had compassion on her and said to her, "Do not weep." **14**Then he came up and touched the bier, and the bearers stood still. And he said, "Young man, I say to you, arise." **15**And the dead man sat up and began to speak, and Jesus⁵ gave him to his mother. **16**Fear seized them all, and they glorified God, saying, "A great prophet has arisen among us!" and "God has visited his people!" **17**And this report about him spread through the whole of Judea and all the surrounding country.

Messengers from John the Baptist

18 ᵉ The disciples of John reported all these things to him. And John, **19**calling two of his disciples to him, sent them to the Lord, saying, "Are you the one who is to come, or shall we look for another?" **20**And when the men had come to him, they said, "John the Baptist has sent us to you, saying, 'Are you the one who is to

---

¹ Some manuscripts *founded upon the rock* ² Or *bondservant;* also verses 3, 8, 10 ³ Greek *he* ⁴ Some manuscripts *The next day* ⁵ Greek *he* ᵃFor 6:37, 38, 41, 42 see parallel Matt. 7:1-5 ᵇFor 6:43, 44 see parallel Matt. 7:16, 20 ᶜFor 6:47-49 see parallel Matt. 7:24-27 ᵈFor 7:1-10 see parallel Matt. 8:5-13 ᵉFor 7:18-35 see parallel Matt. 11:2-19

come, or shall we look for another?' " ²¹ In that hour he healed many people of diseases and plagues and evil spirits, and on many who were blind he bestowed sight. ²² And he answered them, "Go and tell John what you have seen and heard: the blind receive their sight, the lame walk, lepers¹ are cleansed, and the deaf hear, the dead are raised up, the poor have good news preached to them. ²³ And blessed is the one who is not offended by me."

²⁴ When John's messengers had gone, Jesus² began to speak to the crowds concerning John: "What did you go out into the wilderness to see? A reed shaken by the wind? ²⁵ What then did you go out to see? A man dressed in soft clothing? Behold, those who are dressed in splendid clothing and live in luxury are in kings' courts. ²⁶ What then did you go out to see? A prophet? Yes, I tell you, and more than a prophet. ²⁷ This is he of whom it is written,

ᵃ" 'Behold, I send my messenger before your
     face,
   who will prepare your way before
     you.'

²⁸ I tell you, among those born of women none is greater than John. Yet the one who is least in the kingdom of God is greater than he." ²⁹ (When all the people heard this, and the tax collectors too, they declared God just,³ having been baptized with the baptism of John, ³⁰ but the Pharisees and the lawyers rejected the purpose of God for themselves, not having been baptized by him.)

³¹ "To what then shall I compare the people of this generation, and what are they like? ³² They are like children sitting in the marketplace and calling to one another,

" 'We played the flute for you, and you did
     not dance;
   we sang a dirge, and you did not weep.'

³³ For John the Baptist has come eating no bread and drinking no wine, and you say, 'He has a demon.' ³⁴ The Son of Man has come eating and drinking, and you say, 'Look at him! A glutton and a drunkard, a friend of tax collectors and sinners!' ³⁵ Yet wisdom is justified by all her children."

A Sinful Woman Forgiven

³⁶ One of the Pharisees asked him to eat with him, and he went into the Pharisee's house and reclined at table. ³⁷ And behold, a woman of the city, who was a sinner, when she learned that he was reclining at table in the Pharisee's house, brought an alabaster flask of ointment, ³⁸ and standing behind him at his feet, weeping, she began to wet his feet with her tears and wiped them with the hair of her head and kissed his feet and anointed them with the ointment. ³⁹ Now when the Pharisee who had invited him saw this, he said to himself, "If this man were a prophet, he would have known who and what sort of woman this is who is touching him, for she is a sinner." ⁴⁰ And Jesus answering said to him, "Simon, I have something to say to you." And he answered, "Say it, Teacher."

⁴¹ "A certain moneylender had two debtors. One owed five hundred denarii, and the other fifty. ⁴² When they could not pay, he cancelled the debt of both. Now which of them will love him more?" ⁴³ Simon answered, "The one, I suppose, for whom he cancelled the larger debt." And he said to him, "You have judged rightly." ⁴⁴ Then turning toward the woman he said to Simon, "Do you see this woman? I entered your house; you gave me no water for my feet, but she has wet my feet with her tears and wiped them with her hair. ⁴⁵ You gave me no kiss, but from the time I came in she has not ceased to kiss my feet. ⁴⁶ You did not anoint my head with oil, but she has anointed my feet with ointment. ⁴⁷ Therefore I tell you, her sins, which are many, are forgiven—for she loved much. But he who is forgiven little, loves little." ⁴⁸ And he said to her, "Your sins are forgiven." ⁴⁹ Then those who were at table with him began to say among⁴ themselves, "Who is this, who even forgives sins?" ⁵⁰ And he said to the woman, "Your faith has saved you; go in peace."

Women Accompanying Jesus

8 Soon afterward he went on through cities and villages, proclaiming and bringing the good news of the kingdom of God. And the twelve were with him, ² and also some women who had been healed of evil spirits and infirmities: Mary, called Magdalene, from whom seven demons had gone out, ³ and Joanna, the wife of Chuza, Herod's household manager, and Susanna, and many others, who provided for them⁵ out of their means.

---

¹ Leprosy was a term for several skin diseases; see Leviticus 13 ² Greek *he* ³ Greek *they justified God* ⁴ Or *to* ⁵ Some manuscripts *him* ᵃ Mal. 3:1

The Parable of the Sower

4 [a] And when a great crowd was gathering and people from town after town came to him, he said in a parable, **5** "A sower went out to sow his seed. And as he sowed, some fell along the path and was trampled underfoot, and the birds of the air devoured it. **6** And some fell on the rock, and as it grew up, it withered away, because it had no moisture. **7** And some fell among thorns, and the thorns grew up with it and choked it. **8** And some fell into good soil and grew and yielded a hundredfold." As he said these things, he called out, "He who has ears to hear, let him hear."

The Purpose of the Parables

9 And when his disciples asked him what this parable meant, **10** he said, "To you it has been given to know the secrets of the kingdom of God, but for others they are in parables, so [b] that 'seeing they may not see, and hearing they may not understand.' **11** [c] Now the parable is this: The seed is the word of God. **12** The ones along the path are those who have heard; then the devil comes and takes away the word from their hearts, so that they may not believe and be saved. **13** And the ones on the rock are those who, when they hear the word, receive it with joy. But these have no root; they believe for a while, and in time of testing fall away. **14** And as for what fell among the thorns, they are those who hear, but as they go on their way they are choked by the cares and riches and pleasures of life, and their fruit does not mature. **15** As for that in the good soil, they are those who, hearing the word, hold it fast in an honest and good heart, and bear fruit with patience.

A Lamp Under a Jar

16 [d] "No one after lighting a lamp covers it with a jar or puts it under a bed, but puts it on a stand, so that those who enter may see the light. **17** For nothing is hidden that will not be made manifest, nor is anything secret that will not be known and come to light. **18** Take care then how you hear, for to the one who has, more will be given, and from the one who has not, even what he thinks that he has will be taken away."

Jesus' Mother and Brothers

19 Then his mother and his brothers [i] came to him, but they could not reach him because of the crowd. **20** And he was told, "Your mother and your brothers are standing outside, desiring to see you." **21** But he answered them, "My mother and my brothers are those who hear the word of God and do it."

Jesus Calms a Storm

22 [e] One day he got into a boat with his disciples, and he said to them, "Let us go across to the other side of the lake." So they set out, **23** and as they sailed he fell asleep. And a windstorm came down on the lake, and they were filling with water and were in danger. **24** And they went and woke him, saying, "Master, Master, we are perishing!" And he awoke and rebuked the wind and the raging waves, and they ceased, and there was a calm. **25** He said to them, "Where is your faith?" And they were afraid, and they marveled, saying to one another, "Who then is this, that he commands even winds and water, and they obey him?"

Jesus Heals a Man with a Demon

26 [g] Then they sailed to the country of the Gerasenes, [2] which is opposite Galilee. **27** When Jesus [3] had stepped out on land, there met him a man from the city who had demons. For a long time he had worn no clothes, and he had not lived in a house but among the tombs. **28** When he saw Jesus, he cried out and fell down before him and said with a loud voice, "What have you to do with me, Jesus, Son of the Most High God? I beg you, do not torment me." **29** For he had commanded the unclean spirit to come out of the man. (For many a time it had seized him. He was kept under guard and bound with chains and shackles, but he would break the bonds and be driven by the demon into the desert.) **30** Jesus then asked him, "What is your name?" And he said, "Legion," for many demons had entered him. **31** And they begged him not to command them to depart into the abyss. **32** Now a large herd of pigs was feeding there on the hillside, and they begged him to let them enter these. So he gave them permission. **33** Then the demons came out of the man and entered the pigs, and the herd rushed down the steep bank into the lake and drowned.

34 When the herdsmen saw what had happened, they fled and told it in the city and in the country. **35** Then people went out to see what had happened, and they came to Jesus

---

[1] Or brothers and sisters. In New Testament usage, depending on the context, the plural Greek word *adelphoi* (translated "brothers") may refer either to *brothers* or to *brothers and sisters*; also verses 20, 21 [2] Some manuscripts *Gadarenes*; others *Gergesenes*; also verse 37 [3] Greek *he*; also verses 38, 42 [a] For 8:4-10 see parallels Matt. 13:1-15; Mark 4:1-12 [b] Isa. 6:9, 10 [c] For 8:11-15 see parallels Matt. 13:18-23; Mark 4:13-20 [d] For 8:16-18 see parallel Mark 4:21-25 [e] For 8:19-21 see parallels Matt. 12:46-50; Mark 3:31-35 [f] For 8:22-25 see parallels Matt. 8:23-27; Mark 4:35-41 [g] For 8:26-39 see parallels Matt. 8:28-34; Mark 5:1-20

and found the man from whom the demons had gone, sitting at the feet of Jesus, clothed and in his right mind, and they were afraid. **36** And those who had seen it told them how the demon-possessed[1] man had been healed. **37** Then all the people of the surrounding country of the Gerasenes asked him to depart from them, for they were seized with great fear. So he got into the boat and returned. **38** The man from whom the demons had gone begged that he might be with him, but Jesus sent him away, saying, **39** "Return to your home, and declare how much God has done for you." And he went away, proclaiming throughout the whole city how much Jesus had done for him.

Jesus Heals a Woman and Jairus's Daughter

40 Now when Jesus returned, the crowd welcomed him, for they were all waiting for him. **41**[d] And there came a man named Jairus, who was a ruler of the synagogue. And falling at Jesus' feet, he implored him to come to his house, **42** for he had an only daughter, about twelve years of age, and she was dying.

As Jesus went, the people pressed around him. **43** And there was a woman who had had a discharge of blood for twelve years, and though she had spent all her living on physicians,[2] she could not be healed by anyone. **44** She came up behind him and touched the fringe of his garment, and immediately her discharge of blood ceased. **45** And Jesus said, "Who was it that touched me?" When all denied it, Peter[3] said, "Master, the crowds surround you and are pressing in on you!" **46** But Jesus said, "Someone touched me, for I perceive that power has gone out from me." **47** And when the woman saw that she was not hidden, she came trembling, and falling down before him declared in the presence of all the people why she had touched him, and how she had been immediately healed. **48** And he said to her, "Daughter, your faith has made you well; go in peace."

49 While he was still speaking, someone from the ruler's house came and said, "Your daughter is dead; do not trouble the Teacher any more." **50** But Jesus on hearing this answered him, "Do not fear; only believe, and she will be well." **51** And when he came to the house, he allowed no one to enter with him, except Peter and John and James, and the father and mother of the child. **52** And all were weeping and mourn-

ing for her, but he said, "Do not weep, for she is not dead but sleeping." **53** And they laughed at him, knowing that she was dead. **54** But taking her by the hand he called, saying, "Child, arise." **55** And her spirit returned, and she got up at once. And he directed that something should be given her to eat. **56** And her parents were amazed, but he charged them to tell no one what had happened.

Jesus Sends Out the Twelve Apostles

9 And he called the twelve together and gave them power and authority over all demons and to cure diseases, **2** and he sent them out to proclaim the kingdom of God and to heal. **3**[b] And he said to them, "Take nothing for your journey, no staff, nor bag, nor bread, nor money; and do not have two tunics.[4] **4** And whatever house you enter, stay there, and from there depart. **5** And wherever they do not receive you, when you leave that town shake off the dust from your feet as a testimony against them." **6** And they departed and went through the villages, preaching the gospel and healing everywhere.

Herod Is Perplexed by Jesus

7[c] Now Herod the tetrarch heard about all that was happening, and he was perplexed, because it was said by some that John had been raised from the dead, **8** by some that Elijah had appeared, and by others that one of the prophets of old had risen. **9** Herod said, "John I beheaded, but who is this about whom I hear such things?" And he sought to see him.

Jesus Feeds the Five Thousand

10 On their return the apostles told him all that they had done. [d] And he took them and withdrew apart to a town called Bethsaida. **11** When the crowds learned it, they followed him, and he welcomed them and spoke to them of the kingdom of God and cured those who had need of healing. **12** Now the day began to wear away, and the twelve came and said to him, "Send the crowd away to go into the surrounding villages and countryside to find lodging and get provisions, for we are here in a desolate place." **13** But he said to them, "You give them something to eat." They said, "We have no more than five loaves and two fish—unless we are to go and buy food for all these people." **14** For there were about five thousand men. And

---

[1] Greek daimonizomai (demonized); elsewhere rendered oppressed by demons [2] Some manuscripts omit and though she had spent all her living on physicians [3] Some manuscripts add and those who were with him [4] Greek chiton, a long garment worn under the cloak next to the skin [a] For 8:41-56 see parallels Matt. 9:18-26; Mark 5:21-43 [b] For 9:3-5 see parallels Matt. 10:9-15; Mark 6:8-11 [c] For 9:7-9 see parallels Matt. 14:1-12; Mark 6:14-29 [d] For 9:10-17 see parallels Matt. 14:13-21; Mark 6:32-44; John 6:1-13

he said to his disciples, "Have them sit down in groups of about fifty each." ¹⁵And they did so, and had them all sit down. ¹⁶And taking the five loaves and the two fish, he looked up to heaven and said a blessing over them. Then he broke the loaves and gave them to the disciples to set before the crowd. ¹⁷And they all ate and were satisfied. And what was left over was picked up, twelve baskets of broken pieces.

Peter Confesses Jesus as the Christ

¹⁸ᵃNow it happened that as he was praying alone, the disciples were with him. And he asked them, "Who do the crowds say that I am?" ¹⁹And they answered, "John the Baptist. But others say, Elijah, and others, that one of the prophets of old has risen." ²⁰Then he said to them, "But who do you say that I am?" And Peter answered, "The Christ of God."

Jesus Foretells His Death

²¹And he strictly charged and commanded them to tell this to no one, ²²ᵇsaying, "The Son of Man must suffer many things and be rejected by the elders and chief priests and scribes, and be killed, and on the third day be raised."

Take Up Your Cross and Follow Jesus

²³And he said to all, "If anyone would come after me, let him deny himself and take up his cross daily and follow me. ²⁴For whoever would save his life will lose it, but whoever loses his life for my sake will save it. ²⁵For what does it profit a man if he gains the whole world and loses or forfeits himself? ²⁶For whoever is ashamed of me and of my words, of him will the Son of Man be ashamed when he comes in his glory and the glory of the Father and of the holy angels. ²⁷But I tell you truly, there are some standing here who will not taste death until they see the kingdom of God."

The Transfiguration

²⁸Now about eight days after these sayings he took with him Peter and John and James and went up on the mountain to pray. ²⁹And as he was praying, the appearance of his face was altered, and his clothing became dazzling white. ³⁰And behold, two men were talking with him, Moses and Elijah, ³¹who appeared in glory and spoke of his departure,¹ which he was about to accomplish at Jerusalem. ³²Now Peter and those who were with him were heavy with sleep, but when they became fully awake they saw his glory and the two men who stood with him. ³³And as the men were parting from him, Peter said to Jesus, "Master, it is good that we are here. Let us make three tents, one for you and one for Moses and one for Elijah"—not knowing what he said. ³⁴As he was saying these things, a cloud came and overshadowed them, and they were afraid as they entered the cloud. ³⁵And a voice came out of the cloud, saying, "This is my Son, my Chosen One;² listen to him!" ³⁶And when the voice had spoken, Jesus was found alone. And they kept silent and told no one in those days anything of what they had seen.

Jesus Heals a Boy with an Unclean Spirit

³⁷On the next day, when they had come down from the mountain, a great crowd met him. ³⁸And behold, a man from the crowd cried out, "Teacher, I beg you to look at my son, for he is my only child. ³⁹And behold, a spirit seizes him, and he suddenly cries out. It convulses him so that he foams at the mouth, and shatters him, and will hardly leave him. ⁴⁰And I begged your disciples to cast it out, but they could not." ⁴¹Jesus answered, "O faithless and twisted generation, how long am I to be with you and bear with you? Bring your son here." ⁴²While he was coming, the demon threw him to the ground and convulsed him. But Jesus rebuked the unclean spirit and healed the boy, and gave him back to his father. ⁴³And all were astonished at the majesty of God.

Jesus Again Foretells His Death

But while they were all marveling at everything he was doing, Jesus³ said to his disciples, ⁴⁴"Let these words sink into your ears: The Son of Man is about to be delivered into the hands of men." ⁴⁵But they did not understand this saying, and it was concealed from them, so that they might not perceive it. And they were afraid to ask him about this saying.

Who Is the Greatest?

⁴⁶An argument arose among them as to which of them was the greatest. ⁴⁷But Jesus, knowing the reasoning of their hearts, took a child and put him by his side ⁴⁸and said to them, "Whoever receives this child in my name receives me, and whoever receives me receives him who sent me. For he who is least among you all is the one who is great."

---

¹ Greek exodus ² Some manuscripts my Beloved ³ Greek he ᵃFor 9:18-20 see parallels Matt. 16:13-16; Mark 8:27-29 ᵇFor 9:22-27 see parallels Matt. 16:21-28; Mark 8:31–9:1

Anyone Not Against Us Is For Us

[49] John answered, "Master, we saw someone casting out demons in your name, and we tried to stop him, because he does not follow with us." [50] But Jesus said to him, "Do not stop him, for the one who is not against you is for you."

A Samaritan Village Rejects Jesus

[51] When the days drew near for him to be taken up, he set his face to go to Jerusalem. [52] And he sent messengers ahead of him, who went and entered a village of the Samaritans, to make preparations for him. [53] But the people did not receive him, because his face was set toward Jerusalem. [54] And when his disciples James and John saw it, they said, "Lord, do you want us to tell fire to come down from heaven and consume them?"[1] [55] But he turned and rebuked them.[2] [56] And they went on to another village.

The Cost of Following Jesus

[57][a] As they were going along the road, someone said to him, "I will follow you wherever you go." [58] And Jesus said to him, "Foxes have holes, and birds of the air have nests, but the Son of Man has nowhere to lay his head." [59] To another he said, "Follow me." But he said, "Lord, let me first go and bury my father." [60] And Jesus[3] said to him, "Leave the dead to bury their own dead. But as for you, go and proclaim the kingdom of God." [61] Yet another said, "I will follow you, Lord, but let me first say farewell to those at my home." [62] Jesus said to him, "No one who puts his hand to the plow and looks back is fit for the kingdom of God."

Jesus Sends Out the Seventy-Two

10 After this the Lord appointed seventy-two[4] others and sent them on ahead of him, two by two, into every town and place where he himself was about to go. [2] And he said to them, "The harvest is plentiful, but the laborers are few. Therefore pray earnestly to the Lord of the harvest to send out laborers into his harvest. [3] Go your way; behold, I am sending you out as lambs in the midst of wolves. [4] Carry no moneybag, no knapsack, no sandals, and greet no one on the road. [5] Whatever house you enter, first say, 'Peace be to this house!' [6] And if a son of peace is there, your peace will rest upon him. But if not, it will return to you. [7] And remain in

the same house, eating and drinking what they provide, for the laborer deserves his wages. Do not go from house to house. [8] Whenever you enter a town and they receive you, eat what is set before you. [9] Heal the sick in it and say to them, 'The kingdom of God has come near to you.' [10] But whenever you enter a town and they do not receive you, go into its streets and say, [11] 'Even the dust of your town that clings to our feet we wipe off against you. Nevertheless know this, that the kingdom of God has come near.' [12] I tell you, it will be more bearable on that day for Sodom than for that town.

Woe to Unrepentant Cities

[13][b] "Woe to you, Chorazin! Woe to you, Bethsaida! For if the mighty works done in you had been done in Tyre and Sidon, they would have repented long ago, sitting in sackcloth and ashes. [14] But it will be more bearable in the judgment for Tyre and Sidon than for you. [15] And you, Capernaum, will you be exalted to heaven? You shall be brought down to Hades.

[16] "The one who hears you hears me, and the one who rejects you rejects me, and the one who rejects me rejects him who sent me."

The Return of the Seventy-Two

[17] The seventy-two returned with joy, saying, "Lord, even the demons are subject to us in your name!" [18] And he said to them, "I saw Satan fall like lightning from heaven. [19] Behold, I have given you authority to tread on serpents and scorpions, and over all the power of the enemy, and nothing shall hurt you. [20] Nevertheless, do not rejoice in this, that the spirits are subject to you, but rejoice that your names are written in heaven."

Jesus Rejoices in the Father's Will

[21][c] In that same hour he rejoiced in the Holy Spirit and said, "I thank you, Father, Lord of heaven and earth, that you have hidden these things from the wise and understanding and revealed them to little children; yes, Father, for such was your gracious will.[5] [22] All things have been handed over to me by my Father, and no one knows who the Son is except the Father, or who the Father is except the Son and anyone to whom the Son chooses to reveal him."

[23] Then turning to the disciples he said privately, "Blessed are the eyes that see what you

see! [24]For I tell you that many prophets and kings desired to see what you see, and did not see it, and to hear what you hear, and did not hear it."

The Parable of the Good Samaritan

[25]And behold, a lawyer stood up to put him to the test, saying, "Teacher, what shall I do to inherit eternal life?" [26]He said to him, "What is written in the Law? How do you read it?" [27]And he answered, [a]"You shall love the Lord your God with all your heart and with all your soul and with all your strength and with all your mind, and [b]your neighbor as yourself." [28]And he said to him, "You have answered correctly; do this, and you will live."

[29]But he, desiring to justify himself, said to Jesus, "And who is my neighbor?" [30]Jesus replied, "A man was going down from Jerusalem to Jericho, and he fell among robbers, who stripped him and beat him and departed, leaving him half dead. [31]Now by chance a priest was going down that road, and when he saw him he passed by on the other side. [32]So likewise a Levite, when he came to the place and saw him, passed by on the other side. [33]But a Samaritan, as he journeyed, came to where he was, and when he saw him, he had compassion. [34]He went to him and bound up his wounds, pouring on oil and wine. Then he set him on his own animal and brought him to an inn and took care of him. [35]And the next day he took out two denarii[1] and gave them to the innkeeper, saying, 'Take care of him, and whatever more you spend, I will repay you when I come back.' [36]Which of these three, do you think, proved to be a neighbor to the man who fell among the robbers?" [37]He said, "The one who showed him mercy." And Jesus said to him, "You go, and do likewise."

Martha and Mary

[38]Now as they went on their way, Jesus[2] entered a village. And a woman named Martha welcomed him into her house. [39]And she had a sister called Mary, who sat at the Lord's feet and listened to his teaching. [40]But Martha was distracted with much serving. And she went up to him and said, "Lord, do you not care that my sister has left me to serve alone? Tell her then to help me." [41]But the Lord answered her, "Martha, Martha, you are anxious and troubled about many things, [42]but one thing is necessary.[3] Mary has chosen the good portion, which will not be taken away from her."

The Lord's Prayer

11 Now Jesus[4] was praying in a certain place, and when he finished, one of his disciples said to him, "Lord, teach us to pray, as John taught his disciples." [2]And he said to them, "When you pray, say:

"Father, hallowed be your name.
 Your kingdom come.
[3] Give us each day our daily bread,[5]
[4] and forgive us our sins,
 for we ourselves forgive everyone who is indebted to us.
 And lead us not into temptation."

[5]And he said to them, "Which of you who has a friend will go to him at midnight and say to him, 'Friend, lend me three loaves, [6]for a friend of mine has arrived on a journey, and I have nothing to set before him'; [7]and he will answer from within, 'Do not bother me; the door is now shut, and my children are with me in bed. I cannot get up and give you anything'? [8]I tell you, though he will not get up and give him anything because he is his friend, yet because of his impudence[6] he will rise and give him whatever he needs. [9]And I tell you, [c]ask, and it will be given to you; seek, and you will find; knock, and it will be opened to you. [10]For everyone who asks receives, and the one who seeks finds, and to the one who knocks it will be opened. [11]What father among you, if his son asks for[7] a fish, will instead of a fish give him a serpent; [12]or if he asks for an egg, will give him a scorpion? [13]If you then, who are evil, know how to give good gifts to your children, how much more will the heavenly Father give the Holy Spirit to those who ask him!"

Jesus and Beelzebul

[14][d]Now he was casting out a demon that was mute. When the demon had gone out, the mute man spoke, and the people marveled. [15]But some of them said, "He casts out demons by Beelzebul, the prince of demons," [16]while others, to test him, kept seeking from him a sign from heaven. [17][e]But he, knowing their thoughts, said to them, "Every kingdom divided against itself is laid waste, and a divided household falls. [18]And if Satan also is divided

[1] A *denarius* was a day's wage for a laborer   [2] Greek *he*   [3] Some manuscripts *few things are necessary, or only one*   [4] Greek *he*   [5] Or *our bread for tomorrow*   [6] Or *persistence*   [7] Some manuscripts insert *bread, will give him a stone; or if he asks for*   [a] Deut. 6:5   [b] Lev. 19:18   [c] For 11:9-13 see parallel Matt. 7:7-11   [d] For 11:14, 15 see parallel Matt. 12:22-24   [e] For 11:17-22 see parallels Matt. 12:25-29; Mark 3:23-27

against himself, how will his kingdom stand? For you say that I cast out demons by Beelzebul. [19]And if I cast out demons by Beelzebul, by whom do your sons cast them out? Therefore they will be your judges. [20]But if it is by the finger of God that I cast out demons, then the kingdom of God has come upon you. [21]When a strong man, fully armed, guards his own palace, his goods are safe; [22]but when one stronger than he attacks him and overcomes him, he takes away his armor in which he trusted and divides his spoil. [23]Whoever is not with me is against me, and whoever does not gather with me scatters.

Return of an Unclean Spirit

[24a]"When the unclean spirit has gone out of a person, it passes through waterless places seeking rest, and finding none it says, 'I will return to my house from which I came.' [25]And when it comes, it finds the house swept and put in order. [26]Then it goes and brings seven other spirits more evil than itself, and they enter and dwell there. And the last state of that person is worse than the first."

True Blessedness

[27]As he said these things, a woman in the crowd raised her voice and said to him, "Blessed is the womb that bore you, and the breasts at which you nursed!" [28]But he said, "Blessed rather are those who hear the word of God and keep it!"

The Sign of Jonah

[29]When the crowds were increasing, he began to say, [b]"This generation is an evil generation. It seeks for a sign, but no sign will be given to it except the sign of Jonah. [30]For as Jonah became a sign to the people of Nineveh, so will the Son of Man be to this generation. [31]The queen of the South will rise up at the judgment with the men of this generation and condemn them, for she came from the ends of the earth to hear the wisdom of Solomon, and behold, something greater than Solomon is here. [32]The men of Nineveh will rise up at the judgment with this generation and condemn it, for they repented at the preaching of Jonah, and behold, something greater than Jonah is here.

The Light in You

[33]"No one after lighting a lamp puts it in a cellar or under a basket, but on a stand, so that those who enter may see the light. [34]Your eye is the lamp of your body. When your eye is healthy, your whole body is full of light, but when it is bad, your body is full of darkness. [35]Therefore be careful lest the light in you be darkness. [36]If then your whole body is full of light, having no part dark, it will be wholly bright, as when a lamp with its rays gives you light."

Woes to the Pharisees and Lawyers

[37]While Jesus[1] was speaking, a Pharisee asked him to dine with him, so he went in and reclined at table. [38]The Pharisee was astonished to see that he did not first wash before dinner. [39]And the Lord said to him, "Now you Pharisees cleanse the outside of the cup and of the dish, but inside you are full of greed and wickedness. [40]You fools! Did not he who made the outside make the inside also? [41]But give as alms those things that are within, and behold, everything is clean for you.

[42]"But woe to you Pharisees! For you tithe mint and rue and every herb, and neglect justice and the love of God. These you ought to have done, without neglecting the others. [43]Woe to you Pharisees! For you love the best seat in the synagogues and greetings in the marketplaces. [44]Woe to you! For you are like unmarked graves, and people walk over them without knowing it."

[45]One of the lawyers answered him, "Teacher, in saying these things you insult us also." [46]And he said, "Woe to you lawyers also! For you load people with burdens hard to bear, and you yourselves do not touch the burdens with one of your fingers. [47]Woe to you! For you build the tombs of the prophets whom your fathers killed. [48]So you are witnesses and you consent to the deeds of your fathers, for they killed them, and you build their tombs. [49]Therefore also the Wisdom of God said, 'I will send them prophets and apostles, some of whom they will kill and persecute,' [50]so that the blood of all the prophets, shed from the foundation of the world, may be charged against this generation, [51]from the blood of Abel to the blood of Zechariah, who perished between the altar and the sanctuary. Yes, I tell you, it will be required of this generation. [52]Woe to you lawyers! For you have taken away the key of knowledge. You did not enter yourselves, and you hindered those who were entering."

[53]As he went away from there, the scribes and the Pharisees began to press him hard and to provoke him to speak about many things,

[1] Greek he [a]For 11:24-26 see parallel Matt. 12:43-45 [b]For 11:29-32 see parallel Matt. 12:39-42

[54] lying in wait for him, to catch him in something he might say.

Beware of the Leaven of the Pharisees

12 In the meantime, when so many thousands of the people had gathered together that they were trampling one another, he began to say to his disciples first, "Beware of the leaven of the Pharisees, which is hypocrisy. [2a] Nothing is covered up that will not be revealed, or hidden that will not be known. [3] Therefore whatever you have said in the dark shall be heard in the light, and what you have whispered in private rooms shall be proclaimed on the housetops.

Have No Fear

[4] "I tell you, my friends, do not fear those who kill the body, and after that have nothing more that they can do. [5] But I will warn you whom to fear: fear him who, after he has killed, has authority to cast into hell.[1] Yes, I tell you, fear him! [6] Are not five sparrows sold for two pennies?[2] And not one of them is forgotten before God. [7] Why, even the hairs of your head are all numbered. Fear not; you are of more value than many sparrows.

Acknowledge Christ Before Men

[8] "And I tell you, everyone who acknowledges me before men, the Son of Man also will acknowledge before the angels of God, [9] but the one who denies me before men will be denied before the angels of God. [10] And everyone who speaks a word against the Son of Man will be forgiven, but the one who blasphemes against the Holy Spirit will not be forgiven. [11] And when they bring you before the synagogues and the rulers and the authorities, do not be anxious about how you should defend yourself or what you should say, [12] for the Holy Spirit will teach you in that very hour what you ought to say."

The Parable of the Rich Fool

[13] Someone in the crowd said to him, "Teacher, tell my brother to divide the inheritance with me." [14] But he said to him, "Man, who made me a judge or arbitrator over you?" [15] And he said to them, "Take care, and be on your guard against all covetousness, for one's life does not consist in the abundance of his possessions." [16] And he told them a parable, saying, "The land of a rich man produced plenti-

fully, [17] and he thought to himself, 'What shall I do, for I have nowhere to store my crops?' [18] And he said, 'I will do this: I will tear down my barns and build larger ones, and there I will store all my grain and my goods. [19] And I will say to my soul, "Soul, you have ample goods laid up for many years; relax, eat, drink, be merry."' [20] But God said to him, 'Fool! This night your soul is required of you, and the things you have prepared, whose will they be?' [21] So is the one who lays up treasure for himself and is not rich toward God."

Do Not Be Anxious

[22] And he said to his disciples, [b] "Therefore I tell you, do not be anxious about your life, what you will eat, nor about your body, what you will put on. [23] For life is more than food, and the body more than clothing. [24] Consider the ravens: they neither sow nor reap, they have neither storehouse nor barn, and yet God feeds them. Of how much more value are you than the birds! [25] And which of you by being anxious can add a single hour to his span of life?[3] [26] If then you are not able to do as small a thing as that, why are you anxious about the rest? [27] Consider the lilies, how they grow: they neither toil nor spin,[4] yet I tell you, even Solomon in all his glory was not arrayed like one of these. [28] But if God so clothes the grass, which is alive in the field today, and tomorrow is thrown into the oven, how much more will he clothe you, O you of little faith! [29] And do not seek what you are to eat and what you are to drink, nor be worried. [30] For all the nations of the world seek after these things, and your Father knows that you need them. [31] Instead, seek his[5] kingdom, and these things will be added to you.

[32] "Fear not, little flock, for it is your Father's good pleasure to give you the kingdom. [33] Sell your possessions, and give to the needy. Provide yourselves with moneybags that do not grow old, with a treasure in the heavens that does not fail, where no thief approaches and no moth destroys. [34] For where your treasure is, there will your heart be also.

You Must Be Ready

[35] "Stay dressed for action[6] and keep your lamps burning, [36] and be like men who are waiting for their master to come home from the wedding feast, so that they may open the

---

[1] Greek *Gehenna* [2] Greek *two assaria; an assarion* was a Roman copper coin worth about 1/16 of a *denarius* (which was a day's wage for a laborer) [3] Or *a single cubit to his stature; a cubit* was about 18 inches or 45 centimeters [4] Some manuscripts *Consider the lilies; they neither spin nor weave* [5] Some manuscripts *God's* [6] Greek *Let your loins stay girded;* compare Exodus 12:11 [a] For 12:2-9 see parallel Matt. 10:26-33 [b] For 12:22-31 see parallel Matt. 6:25-33

door to him at once when he comes and knocks. [37]Blessed are those servants[1] whom the master finds awake when he comes. Truly, I say to you, he will dress himself for service and have them recline at table, and he will come and serve them. [38]If he comes in the second watch, or in the third, and finds them awake, blessed are those servants! [39]But know this, that if the master of the house had known at what hour the thief was coming, he[2] would not have left his house to be broken into. [40]You also must be ready, for the Son of Man is coming at an hour you do not expect."

[41]Peter said, "Lord, are you telling this parable for us or for all?" [42]And the Lord said, "Who then is the faithful and wise manager, whom his master will set over his household, to give them their portion of food at the proper time? [43]Blessed is that servant[3] whom his master will find so doing when he comes. [44]Truly, I say to you, he will set him over all his possessions. [45]But if that servant says to himself, 'My master is delayed in coming,' and begins to beat the male and female servants, and to eat and drink and get drunk, [46]the master of that servant will come on a day when he does not expect him and at an hour he does not know, and will cut him in pieces and put him with the unfaithful. [47]And that servant who knew his master's will but did not get ready or act according to his will, will receive a severe beating. [48]But the one who did not know, and did what deserved a beating, will receive a light beating. Everyone to whom much was given, of him much will be required, and from him to whom they entrusted much, they will demand the more.

Not Peace, but Division

[49]"I came to cast fire on the earth, and would that it were already kindled! [50]I have a baptism to be baptized with, and how great is my distress until it is accomplished! [51a]Do you think that I have come to give peace on earth? No, I tell you, but rather division. [52]For from now on in one house there will be five divided, three against two and two against three. [53]They will be divided, father against son and son against father, mother against daughter and daughter against mother, mother-in-law against her daughter-in-law and daughter-in-law against mother-in-law."

Interpreting the Time

[54]He also said to the crowds, "When you see a cloud rising in the west, you say at once, 'A shower is coming.' And so it happens. [55]And when you see the south wind blowing, you say, 'There will be scorching heat,' and it happens. [56]You hypocrites! You know how to interpret the appearance of earth and sky, but why do you not know how to interpret the present time?

Settle with Your Accuser

[57]"And why do you not judge for yourselves what is right? [58]As you go with your accuser before the magistrate, make an effort to settle with him on the way, lest he drag you to the judge, and the judge hand you over to the officer, and the officer put you in prison. [59]I tell you, you will never get out until you have paid the very last penny."[4]

Repent or Perish

13 There were some present at that very time who told him about the Galileans whose blood Pilate had mingled with their sacrifices. [2]And he answered them, "Do you think that these Galileans were worse sinners than all the other Galileans, because they suffered in this way? [3]No, I tell you; but unless you repent, you will all likewise perish. [4]Or those eighteen on whom the tower in Siloam fell and killed them: do you think that they were worse offenders than all the others who lived in Jerusalem? [5]No, I tell you; but unless you repent, you will all likewise perish."

The Parable of the Barren Fig Tree

[6]And he told this parable: "A man had a fig tree planted in his vineyard, and he came seeking fruit on it and found none. [7]And he said to the vinedresser, 'Look, for three years now I have come seeking fruit on this fig tree, and I find none. Cut it down. Why should it use up the ground?' [8]And he answered him, 'Sir, let it alone this year also, until I dig around it and put on manure. [9]Then if it should bear fruit next year, well and good; but if not, you can cut it down.'"

A Woman with a Disabling Spirit

[10]Now he was teaching in one of the synagogues on the Sabbath. [11]And behold, there was a woman who had had a disabling spirit for eighteen years. She was bent over and could not fully straighten herself. [12]When Jesus saw her, he called her over and said to her, "Woman, you

---

[1] Or bondservants [2] Some manuscripts add would have stayed awake and [3] Or bondservant; also verses 45, 46, 47 [4] Greek lepton, a Jewish bronze or copper coin worth about 1/128 of a denarius (which was a day's wage for a laborer) [d] For 12:51-53 see parallel Matt. 10:34, 35

are freed from your disability." [13] And he laid his hands on her, and immediately she was made straight, and she glorified God. [14] But the ruler of the synagogue, indignant because Jesus had healed on the Sabbath, said to the people, "There are six days in which work ought to be done. Come on those days and be healed, and not on the Sabbath day." [15] Then the Lord answered him, "You hypocrites! Does not each of you on the Sabbath untie his ox or his donkey from the manger and lead it away to water it? [16] And ought not this woman, a daughter of Abraham whom Satan bound for eighteen years, be loosed from this bond on the Sabbath day?" [17] As he said these things, all his adversaries were put to shame, and all the people rejoiced at all the glorious things that were done by him.

The Mustard Seed and the Leaven

[18][a] He said therefore, "What is the kingdom of God like? And to what shall I compare it? [19] It is like a grain of mustard seed that a man took and sowed in his garden, and it grew and became a tree, and the birds of the air made nests in its branches."

[20] And again he said, "To what shall I compare the kingdom of God? [21] It is like leaven that a woman took and hid in three measures of flour, until it was all leavened."

The Narrow Door

[22] He went on his way through towns and villages, teaching and journeying toward Jerusalem. [23] And someone said to him, "Lord, will those who are saved be few?" And he said to them, [24] "Strive to enter through the narrow door. For many, I tell you, will seek to enter and will not be able. [25] When once the master of the house has risen and shut the door, and you begin to stand outside and to knock at the door, saying, 'Lord, open to us,' then he will answer you, 'I do not know where you come from.' [26] Then you will begin to say, 'We ate and drank in your presence, and you taught in our streets.' [27] But he will say, 'I tell you, I do not know where you come from. Depart from me, all you workers of evil!' [28] In that place there will be weeping and gnashing of teeth, when you see Abraham and Isaac and Jacob and all the prophets in the kingdom of God but you yourselves cast out. [29] And people will come from east and west, and from north and south, and recline at table in the kingdom of God. [30] And behold, some are last who will be first, and some are first who will be last."

Lament over Jerusalem

[31] At that very hour some Pharisees came and said to him, "Get away from here, for Herod wants to kill you." [32] And he said to them, "Go and tell that fox, 'Behold, I cast out demons and perform cures today and tomorrow, and the third day I finish my course. [33] Nevertheless, I must go on my way today and tomorrow and the day following, for it cannot be that a prophet should perish away from Jerusalem.' [34][b] O Jerusalem, Jerusalem, the city that kills the prophets and stones those who are sent to it! How often would I have gathered your children together as a hen gathers her brood under her wings, and you were not willing! [35] Behold, your house is forsaken. And I tell you, you will not see me until you say, 'Blessed is he who comes in the name of the Lord!'"

Healing of a Man on the Sabbath

14 One Sabbath, when he went to dine at the house of a ruler of the Pharisees, they were watching him carefully. [2] And behold, there was a man before him who had dropsy. [3] And Jesus responded to the lawyers and Pharisees, saying, "Is it lawful to heal on the Sabbath, or not?" [4] But they remained silent. Then he took him and healed him and sent him away. [5] And he said to them, "Which of you, having a son[1] or an ox that has fallen into a well on a Sabbath day, will not immediately pull him out?" [6] And they could not reply to these things.

The Parable of the Wedding Feast

[7] Now he told a parable to those who were invited, when he noticed how they chose the places of honor, saying to them, [8] "When you are invited by someone to a wedding feast, do not sit down in a place of honor, lest someone more distinguished than you be invited by him, [9] and he who invited you both will come and say to you, 'Give your place to this person,' and then you will begin with shame to take the lowest place. [10] But when you are invited, go and sit in the lowest place, so that when your host comes he may say to you, 'Friend, move up higher.' Then you will be honored in the presence of all who sit at table with you. [11] For everyone who exalts himself will be humbled, and he who humbles himself will be exalted."

---

[1] Some manuscripts *a donkey* [a] For 13:18, 19 see parallels Matt. 13:31, 32; Mark 4:30-32 [b] For 13:34, 35 see parallel Matt. 23:37-39 [c] Ps. 118:26

The Parable of the Great Banquet

[12] He said also to the man who had invited him, "When you give a dinner or a banquet, do not invite your friends or your brothers[1] or your relatives or rich neighbors, lest they also invite you in return and you be repaid. [13] But when you give a feast, invite the poor, the crippled, the lame, the blind, [14] and you will be blessed, because they cannot repay you. For you will be repaid at the resurrection of the just."

[15] When one of those who reclined at table with him heard these things, he said to him, "Blessed is everyone who will eat bread in the kingdom of God!" [16] But he said to him, "A man once gave a great banquet and invited many. [17] And at the time for the banquet he sent his servant[2] to say to those who had been invited, 'Come, for everything is now ready.' [18] But they all alike began to make excuses. The first said to him, 'I have bought a field, and I must go out and see it. Please have me excused.' [19] And another said, 'I have bought five yoke of oxen, and I go to examine them. Please have me excused.' [20] And another said, 'I have married a wife, and therefore I cannot come.' [21] So the servant came and reported these things to his master. Then the master of the house became angry and said to his servant, 'Go out quickly to the streets and lanes of the city, and bring in the poor and crippled and blind and lame.' [22] And the servant said, 'Sir, what you commanded has been done, and still there is room.' [23] And the master said to the servant, 'Go out to the highways and hedges and compel people to come in, that my house may be filled. [24] For I tell you,[3] none of those men who were invited shall taste my banquet.'"

The Cost of Discipleship

[25] Now great crowds accompanied him, and he turned and said to them, [26] "If anyone comes to me and does not hate his own father and mother and wife and children and brothers and sisters, yes, and even his own life, he cannot be my disciple. [27] Whoever does not bear his own cross and come after me cannot be my disciple. [28] For which of you, desiring to build a tower, does not first sit down and count the cost, whether he has enough to complete it? [29] Otherwise, when he has laid a foundation and is not able to finish, all who see it begin to mock him, [30] saying, 'This man began to build

and was not able to finish.' [31] Or what king, going out to encounter another king in war, will not sit down first and deliberate whether he is able with ten thousand to meet him who comes against him with twenty thousand? [32] And if not, while the other is yet a great way off, he sends a delegation and asks for terms of peace. [33] So therefore, any one of you who does not renounce all that he has cannot be my disciple.

Salt Without Taste Is Worthless

[34] "Salt is good, but if salt has lost its taste, how shall its saltiness be restored? [35] It is of no use either for the soil or for the manure pile. It is thrown away. He who has ears to hear, let him hear."

The Parable of the Lost Sheep

15 Now the tax collectors and sinners were all drawing near to hear him. [2] And the Pharisees and the scribes grumbled, saying, "This man receives sinners and eats with them."

[3] So he told them this parable: [4] "What man of you, having a hundred sheep, if he has lost one of them, does not leave the ninety-nine in the open country, and go after the one that is lost, until he finds it? [5] And when he has found it, he lays it on his shoulders, rejoicing. [6] And when he comes home, he calls together his friends and his neighbors, saying to them, 'Rejoice with me, for I have found my sheep that was lost.' [7] Just so, I tell you, there will be more joy in heaven over one sinner who repents than over ninety-nine righteous persons who need no repentance.

The Parable of the Lost Coin

[8] "Or what woman, having ten silver coins,[4] if she loses one coin, does not light a lamp and sweep the house and seek diligently until she finds it? [9] And when she has found it, she calls together her friends and neighbors, saying, 'Rejoice with me, for I have found the coin that I had lost.' [10] Just so, I tell you, there is joy before the angels of God over one sinner who repents."

The Parable of the Prodigal Son

[11] And he said, "There was a man who had two sons. [12] And the younger of them said to his father, 'Father, give me the share of property that is coming to me.' And he divided his

---

[1] Or your brothers and sisters [2] Or bondservant; also verses 21 (twice), 22, 23 [3] The Greek word for you here is plural [4] Greek ten drachmas; a drachma was a Greek coin approximately equal in value to a Roman denarius, worth about a day's wage for a laborer

property between them. ¹³Not many days later, the younger son gathered all he had and took a journey into a far country, and there he squandered his property in reckless living. ¹⁴And when he had spent everything, a severe famine arose in that country, and he began to be in need. ¹⁵So he went and hired himself out to¹ one of the citizens of that country, who sent him into his fields to feed pigs. ¹⁶And he was longing to be fed with the pods that the pigs ate, and no one gave him anything.

¹⁷"But when he came to himself, he said, 'How many of my father's hired servants have more than enough bread, but I perish here with hunger! ¹⁸I will arise and go to my father, and I will say to him, "Father, I have sinned against heaven and before you. ¹⁹I am no longer worthy to be called your son. Treat me as one of your hired servants."' ²⁰And he arose and came to his father. But while he was still a long way off, his father saw him and felt compassion, and ran and embraced him and kissed him. ²¹And the son said to him, 'Father, I have sinned against heaven and before you. I am no longer worthy to be called your son.'² ²²But the father said to his servants,³ 'Bring quickly the best robe, and put it on him, and put a ring on his hand, and shoes on his feet. ²³And bring the fattened calf and kill it, and let us eat and celebrate. ²⁴For this my son was dead, and is alive again; he was lost, and is found.' And they began to celebrate.

²⁵"Now his older son was in the field, and as he came and drew near to the house, he heard music and dancing. ²⁶And he called one of the servants and asked what these things meant. ²⁷And he said to him, 'Your brother has come, and your father has killed the fattened calf, because he has received him back safe and sound.' ²⁸But he was angry and refused to go in. His father came out and entreated him, ²⁹but he answered his father, 'Look, these many years I have served you, and I never disobeyed your command, yet you never gave me a young goat, that I might celebrate with my friends. ³⁰But when this son of yours came, who has devoured your property with prostitutes, you killed the fattened calf for him!' ³¹And he said to him, 'Son, you are always with me, and all that is mine is yours. ³²It was fitting to celebrate and be glad, for this your brother was dead, and is alive; he was lost, and is found.'"

The Parable of the Dishonest Manager

16 He also said to the disciples, "There was a rich man who had a manager, and charges were brought to him that this man was wasting his possessions. ²And he called him and said to him, 'What is this that I hear about you? Turn in the account of your management, for you can no longer be manager.' ³And the manager said to himself, 'What shall I do, since my master is taking the management away from me? I am not strong enough to dig, and I am ashamed to beg. ⁴I have decided what to do, so that when I am removed from management, people may receive me into their houses.' ⁵So, summoning his master's debtors one by one, he said to the first, 'How much do you owe my master?' ⁶He said, 'A hundred measures⁴ of oil.' He said to him, 'Take your bill, and sit down quickly and write fifty.' ⁷Then he said to another, 'And how much do you owe?' He said, 'A hundred measures⁵ of wheat.' He said to him, 'Take your bill, and write eighty.' ⁸The master commended the dishonest manager for his shrewdness. For the sons of this world⁶ are more shrewd in dealing with their own generation than the sons of light. ⁹And I tell you, make friends for yourselves by means of unrighteous wealth,⁷ so that when it fails they may receive you into the eternal dwellings.

¹⁰"One who is faithful in a very little is also faithful in much, and one who is dishonest in a very little is also dishonest in much. ¹¹If then you have not been faithful in the unrighteous wealth, who will entrust to you the true riches? ¹²And if you have not been faithful in that which is another's, who will give you that which is your own? ¹³No servant can serve two masters, for either he will hate the one and love the other, or he will be devoted to the one and despise the other. You cannot serve God and money."

The Law and the Kingdom of God

¹⁴The Pharisees, who were lovers of money, heard all these things, and they ridiculed him. ¹⁵And he said to them, "You are those who justify yourselves before men, but God knows your hearts. For what is exalted among men is an abomination in the sight of God.

¹⁶"The Law and the Prophets were until John; since then the good news of the kingdom of God is preached, and everyone forces his way into it.⁸ ¹⁷But it is easier for heaven and earth to pass away than for one dot of the Law to become void.

---

¹ Greek *joined himself to*   ² Some manuscripts add *treat me as one of your hired servants*   ³ Or *bondservants*   ⁴ About 875 gallons or 3,200 liters   ⁵ Between 1,000 and 1,200 bushels or 37,000 to 45,000 liters   ⁶ Greek *age*   ⁷ Greek *mammon*, a Semitic word for money or possessions; also verse 11; rendered *money* in verse 13   ⁸ Or *everyone is forcefully urged into it*

Divorce and Remarriage

¹⁸"Everyone who divorces his wife and marries another commits adultery, and he who marries a woman divorced from her husband commits adultery.

The Rich Man and Lazarus

¹⁹"There was a rich man who was clothed in purple and fine linen and who feasted sumptuously every day. ²⁰And at his gate was laid a poor man named Lazarus, covered with sores, ²¹who desired to be fed with what fell from the rich man's table. Moreover, even the dogs came and licked his sores. ²²The poor man died and was carried by the angels to Abraham's side.¹ The rich man also died and was buried, ²³and in Hades, being in torment, he lifted up his eyes and saw Abraham far off and Lazarus at his side. ²⁴And he called out, 'Father Abraham, have mercy on me, and send Lazarus to dip the end of his finger in water and cool my tongue, for I am in anguish in this flame.' ²⁵But Abraham said, 'Child, remember that you in your lifetime received your good things, and Lazarus in like manner bad things; but now he is comforted here, and you are in anguish. ²⁶And besides all this, between us and you a great chasm has been fixed, in order that those who would pass from here to you may not be able, and none may cross from there to us.' ²⁷And he said, 'Then I beg you, father, to send him to my father's house— ²⁸for I have five brothers—so that he may warn them, lest they also come into this place of torment.' ²⁹But Abraham said, 'They have Moses and the Prophets; let them hear them.' ³⁰And he said, 'No, father Abraham, but if someone goes to them from the dead, they will repent.' ³¹He said to him, 'If they do not hear Moses and the Prophets, neither will they be convinced if someone should rise from the dead.'"

Temptations to Sin

17 And he said to his disciples, "Temptations to sin² are sure to come, but woe to the one through whom they come! ²It would be better for him if a millstone were hung around his neck and he were cast into the sea than that he should cause one of these little ones to sin.³ ³Pay attention to yourselves! If your brother sins, rebuke him, and if he repents, forgive him, ⁴and if he sins against you seven times in the day, and turns to you seven times, saying, 'I repent,' you must forgive him."

Increase Our Faith

⁵The apostles said to the Lord, "Increase our faith!" ⁶And the Lord said, "If you had faith like a grain of mustard seed, you could say to this mulberry tree, 'Be uprooted and planted in the sea,' and it would obey you.

Unworthy Servants

⁷"Will any one of you who has a servant⁴ plowing or keeping sheep say to him when he has come in from the field, 'Come at once and recline at table'? ⁸Will he not rather say to him, 'Prepare supper for me, and dress properly,⁵ and serve me while I eat and drink, and afterward you will eat and drink'? ⁹Does he thank the servant because he did what was commanded? ¹⁰So you also, when you have done all that you were commanded, say, 'We are unworthy servants;⁶ we have only done what was our duty.'"

Jesus Cleanses Ten Lepers

¹¹On the way to Jerusalem he was passing along between Samaria and Galilee. ¹²And as he entered a village, he was met by ten lepers,⁷ who stood at a distance ¹³and lifted up their voices, saying, "Jesus, Master, have mercy on us." ¹⁴When he saw them he said to them, "Go and show yourselves to the priests." And as they went they were cleansed. ¹⁵Then one of them, when he saw that he was healed, turned back, praising God with a loud voice; ¹⁶and he fell on his face at Jesus' feet, giving him thanks. Now he was a Samaritan. ¹⁷Then Jesus answered, "Were not ten cleansed? Where are the nine? ¹⁸Was no one found to return and give praise to God except this foreigner?" ¹⁹And he said to him, "Rise and go your way; your faith has made you well."⁸

The Coming of the Kingdom

²⁰Being asked by the Pharisees when the kingdom of God would come, he answered them, "The kingdom of God is not coming in ways that can be observed, ²¹nor will they say, 'Look, here it is!' or 'There!' for behold, the kingdom of God is in the midst of you."⁹

²²And he said to the disciples, "The days are coming when you will desire to see one of the days of the Son of Man, and you will not see it. ²³And they will say to you, 'Look, there!' or 'Look, here!' Do not go out or follow them. ²⁴For as the lightning flashes and lights up the sky from one side to the other, so will the Son of Man be in his day.¹⁰ ²⁵But first he

must suffer many things and be rejected by this generation. [26]Just as it was in the days of Noah, so will it be in the days of the Son of Man. [27]They were eating and drinking and marrying and being given in marriage, until the day when Noah entered the ark, and the flood came and destroyed them all. [28]Likewise, just as it was in the days of Lot—they were eating and drinking, buying and selling, planting and building, [29]but on the day when Lot went out from Sodom, fire and sulfur rained from heaven and destroyed them all— [30]so will it be on the day when the Son of Man is revealed. [31]On that day, let the one who is on the housetop, with his goods in the house, not come down to take them away, and likewise let the one who is in the field not turn back. [32]Remember Lot's wife. [33]Whoever seeks to preserve his life will lose it, but whoever loses his life will keep it. [34]I tell you, in that night there will be two in one bed. One will be taken and the other left. [35]There will be two women grinding together. One will be taken and the other left."[1] [37]And they said to him, "Where, Lord?" He said to them, "Where the corpse[2] is, there the vultures[3] will gather."

The Parable of the Persistent Widow

18 And he told them a parable to the effect that they ought always to pray and not lose heart. [2]He said, "In a certain city there was a judge who neither feared God nor respected man. [3]And there was a widow in that city who kept coming to him and saying, 'Give me justice against my adversary.' [4]For a while he refused, but afterward he said to himself, 'Though I neither fear God nor respect man, [5]yet because this widow keeps bothering me, I will give her justice, so that she will not beat me down by her continual coming.'" [6]And the Lord said, "Hear what the unrighteous judge says. [7]And will not God give justice to his elect, who cry to him day and night? Will he delay long over them? [8]I tell you, he will give justice to them speedily. Nevertheless, when the Son of Man comes, will he find faith on earth?"

The Pharisee and the Tax Collector

[9]He also told this parable to some who trusted in themselves that they were righteous, and treated others with contempt: [10]"Two men went up into the temple to pray, one a Pharisee and the other a tax collector. [11]The Pharisee, standing by himself, prayed[4] thus: 'God, I thank you that I am not like other men, extortioners, unjust, adulterers, or even like this tax collector. [12]I fast twice a week; I give tithes of all that I get.' [13]But the tax collector, standing far off, would not even lift up his eyes to heaven, but beat his breast, saying, 'God, be merciful to me, a sinner!' [14]I tell you, this man went down to his house justified, rather than the other. For everyone who exalts himself will be humbled, but the one who humbles himself will be exalted."

Let the Children Come to Me

[15][a]Now they were bringing even infants to him that he might touch them. And when the disciples saw it, they rebuked them. [16]But Jesus called them to him, saying, "Let the children come to me, and do not hinder them, for to such belongs the kingdom of God. [17]Truly, I say to you, whoever does not receive the kingdom of God like a child shall not enter it."

The Rich Ruler

[18][b]And a ruler asked him, "Good Teacher, what must I do to inherit eternal life?" [19]And Jesus said to him, "Why do you call me good? No one is good except God alone. [20]You know the commandments: 'Do not commit adultery, Do not murder, Do not steal, Do not bear false witness, Honor your father and mother.'" [21]And he said, "All these I have kept from my youth." [22]When Jesus heard this, he said to him, "One thing you still lack. Sell all that you have and distribute to the poor, and you will have treasure in heaven; and come, follow me." [23]But when he heard these things, he became very sad, for he was extremely rich. [24]Jesus, seeing that he had become sad, said, "How difficult it is for those who have wealth to enter the kingdom of God! [25]For it is easier for a camel to go through the eye of a needle than for a rich person to enter the kingdom of God." [26]Those who heard it said, "Then who can be saved?" [27]But he said, "What is impossible with man is possible with God." [28]And Peter said, "See, we have left our homes and followed you." [29]And he said to them, "Truly, I say to you, there is no one who has left house or wife or brothers[5] or parents or children, for the sake of the kingdom of God, [30]who will not receive many times more in this time, and in the age to come eternal life."

---

[1] Some manuscripts add verse 36: *Two men will be in the field; one will be taken and the other left* [2] Greek *body* [3] Or *eagles* [4] Or *standing, prayed to himself* [5] Or *wife or brothers and sisters* [a] For 18:15-17 see parallels Matt. 19:13-15; Mark 10:13-16 [b] For 18:18-30 see parallels Matt. 19:16-30; Mark 10:17-31 [c] Ex. 20:12-16; Deut. 5:16-20

Jesus Foretells His Death a Third Time

31 ^a And taking the twelve, he said to them, "See, we are going up to Jerusalem, and everything that is written about the Son of Man by the prophets will be accomplished. 32 For he will be delivered over to the Gentiles and will be mocked and shamefully treated and spit upon. 33 And after flogging him, they will kill him, and on the third day he will rise." 34 But they understood none of these things. This saying was hidden from them, and they did not grasp what was said.

Jesus Heals a Blind Beggar

35 ^b As he drew near to Jericho, a blind man was sitting by the roadside begging. 36 And hearing a crowd going by, he inquired what this meant. 37 They told him, "Jesus of Nazareth is passing by." 38 And he cried out, "Jesus, Son of David, have mercy on me!" 39 And those who were in front rebuked him, telling him to be silent. But he cried out all the more, "Son of David, have mercy on me!" 40 And Jesus stopped and commanded him to be brought to him. And when he came near, he asked him, 41 "What do you want me to do for you?" He said, "Lord, let me recover my sight." 42 And Jesus said to him, "Recover your sight; your faith has made you well." 43 And immediately he recovered his sight and followed him, glorifying God. And all the people, when they saw it, gave praise to God.

Jesus and Zacchaeus

19 He entered Jericho and was passing through. 2 And behold, there was a man named Zacchaeus. He was a chief tax collector and was rich. 3 And he was seeking to see who Jesus was, but on account of the crowd he could not, because he was small in stature. 4 So he ran on ahead and climbed up into a sycamore tree to see him, for he was about to pass that way. 5 And when Jesus came to the place, he looked up and said to him, "Zacchaeus, hurry and come down, for I must stay at your house today." 6 So he hurried and came down and received him joyfully. 7 And when they saw it, they all grumbled, "He has gone in to be the guest of a man who is a sinner." 8 And Zacchaeus stood and said to the Lord, "Behold, Lord, the half of my goods I give to the poor. And if I have defrauded anyone of anything, I restore it fourfold." 9 And Jesus said to him,

"Today salvation has come to this house, since he also is a son of Abraham. 10 For the Son of Man came to seek and to save the lost."

The Parable of the Ten Minas

11 As they heard these things, he proceeded to tell a parable, because he was near to Jerusalem, and because they supposed that the kingdom of God was to appear immediately. 12 He said therefore, "A nobleman went into a far country to receive for himself a kingdom and then return. 13 Calling ten of his servants,[1] he gave them ten minas,[2] and said to them, 'Engage in business until I come.' 14 But his citizens hated him and sent a delegation after him, saying, 'We do not want this man to reign over us.' 15 When he returned, having received the kingdom, he ordered these servants to whom he had given the money to be called to him, that he might know what they had gained by doing business. 16 The first came before him, saying, 'Lord, your mina has made ten minas more.' 17 And he said to him, 'Well done, good servant![3] Because you have been faithful in a very little, you shall have authority over ten cities.' 18 And the second came, saying, 'Lord, your mina has made five minas.' 19 And he said to him, 'And you are to be over five cities.' 20 Then another came, saying, 'Lord, here is your mina, which I kept laid away in a handkerchief; 21 for I was afraid of you, because you are a severe man. You take what you did not deposit, and reap what you did not sow.' 22 He said to him, 'I will condemn you with your own words, you wicked servant! You knew that I was a severe man, taking what I did not deposit and reaping what I did not sow? 23 Why then did you not put my money in the bank, and at my coming I might have collected it with interest?' 24 And he said to those who stood by, 'Take the mina from him, and give it to the one who has the ten minas.' 25 And they said to him, 'Lord, he has ten minas!' 26 'I tell you that to everyone who has, more will be given, but from the one who has not, even what he has will be taken away. 27 But as for these enemies of mine, who did not want me to reign over them, bring them here and slaughter them before me.'"

The Triumphal Entry

28 And when he had said these things, he went on ahead, going up to Jerusalem. 29 ^c When he drew near to Bethphage and Bethany, at

[1] Or bondservants; also verse 15 [2] A mina was about three months' wages for a laborer [3] Or bondservant; also verse 22 [a] For 18:31-33 see parallels Matt. 20:17-19; Mark 10:32-34 [b] For 18:35-43 see parallels Matt. 20:29-34; Mark 10:46-52 [c] For 19:29-38 see parallels Matt. 21:1-9; Mark 11:1-10; John 12:12-15

the mount that is called Olivet, he sent two of the disciples, [30] saying, "Go into the village in front of you, where on entering you will find a colt tied, on which no one has ever yet sat. Untie it and bring it here. [31] If anyone asks you, 'Why are you untying it?' you shall say this: 'The Lord has need of it.'" [32] So those who were sent went away and found it just as he had told them. [33] And as they were untying the colt, its owners said to them, "Why are you untying the colt?" [34] And they said, "The Lord has need of it." [35] And they brought it to Jesus, and throwing their cloaks on the colt, they set Jesus on it. [36] And as he rode along, they spread their cloaks on the road. [37] As he was drawing near—already on the way down the Mount of Olives—the whole multitude of his disciples began to rejoice and praise God with a loud voice for all the mighty works that they had seen, [38] saying, "Blessed is the King who comes in the name of the Lord! Peace in heaven and glory in the highest!" [39] And some of the Pharisees in the crowd said to him, "Teacher, rebuke your disciples." [40] He answered, "I tell you, if these were silent, the very stones would cry out."

Jesus Weeps over Jerusalem

[41] And when he drew near and saw the city, he wept over it, [42] saying, "Would that you, even you, had known on this day the things that make for peace! But now they are hidden from your eyes. [43] For the days will come upon you, when your enemies will set up a barricade around you and surround you and hem you in on every side [44] and tear you down to the ground, you and your children within you. And they will not leave one stone upon another in you, because you did not know the time of your visitation."

Jesus Cleanses the Temple

[45] [a] And he entered the temple and began to drive out those who sold, [46] saying to them, "It is written, [b] 'My house shall be a house of prayer,' but you have made it a den of robbers."

[47] And he was teaching daily in the temple. The chief priests and the scribes and the principal men of the people were seeking to destroy him, [48] but they did not find anything they could do, for all the people were hanging on his words.

The Authority of Jesus Challenged

20 'One day, as Jesus[1] was teaching the people in the temple and preaching the gospel, the chief priests and the scribes with the elders came up [2] and said to him, "Tell us by what authority you do these things, or who it is that gave you this authority." [3] He answered them, "I also will ask you a question. Now tell me, [4] was the baptism of John from heaven or from man?" [5] And they discussed it with one another, saying, "If we say, 'From heaven,' he will say, 'Why did you not believe him?' [6] But if we say, 'From man,' all the people will stone us to death, for they are convinced that John was a prophet." [7] So they answered that they did not know where it came from. [8] And Jesus said to them, "Neither will I tell you by what authority I do these things."

The Parable of the Wicked Tenants

[9] [d] And he began to tell the people this parable: "A man planted a vineyard and let it out to tenants and went into another country for a long while. [10] When the time came, he sent a servant[2] to the tenants, so that they would give him some of the fruit of the vineyard. But the tenants beat him and sent him away empty-handed. [11] And he sent another servant. But they also beat and treated him shamefully, and sent him away empty-handed. [12] And he sent yet a third. This one also they wounded and cast out. [13] Then the owner of the vineyard said, 'What shall I do? I will send my beloved son; perhaps they will respect him.' [14] But when the tenants saw him, they said to themselves, 'This is the heir. Let us kill him, so that the inheritance may be ours.' [15] And they threw him out of the vineyard and killed him. What then will the owner of the vineyard do to them? [16] He will come and destroy those tenants and give the vineyard to others." When they heard this, they said, "Surely not!" [17] But he looked directly at them and said, "What then is this that is written:

[c] "'The stone that the builders rejected
    has become the cornerstone'?[3]

[18] Everyone who falls on that stone will be broken to pieces, and when it falls on anyone, it will crush him."

Paying Taxes to Caesar

[19] The scribes and the chief priests sought to lay hands on him at that very hour, for they

---

[1] Greek he [2] Or bondservant; also verse 11 [3] Greek the head of the corner [a] For 19:45-47 see parallels Matt. 21:12-16; Mark 11:15-18 [b] Isa. 56:7 [c] For 20:1-8 see parallels Matt. 21:23-27; Mark 11:27-33 [d] For 20:9-18 see parallels Matt. 21:33-46; Mark 12:1-12 [e] Ps. 118:22

perceived that he had told this parable against them, but they feared the people. 20 ᵃ So they watched him and sent spies, who pretended to be sincere, that they might catch him in something he said, so as to deliver him up to the authority and jurisdiction of the governor. 21 So they asked him, "Teacher, we know that you speak and teach rightly, and show no partiality,¹ but truly teach the way of God. 22 Is it lawful for us to give tribute to Caesar, or not?" 23 But he perceived their craftiness, and said to them, 24"Show me a denarius.² Whose likeness and inscription does it have?" They said, "Caesar's." 25 He said to them, "Then render to Caesar the things that are Caesar's, and to God the things that are God's." 26 And they were not able in the presence of the people to catch him in what he said, but marveling at his answer they became silent.

Sadducees Ask About the Resurrection

27 There came to him some Sadducees, those who deny that there is a resurrection, 28 and they asked him a question, saying, "Teacher, Moses wrote for us that if a man's brother dies, having a wife but no children, the man³ must take the widow and raise up offspring for his brother. 29 Now there were seven brothers. The first took a wife, and died without children. 30 And the second 31 and the third took her, and likewise all seven left no children and died. 32 Afterward the woman also died. 33 In the resurrection, therefore, whose wife will the woman be? For the seven had her as wife."

34 And Jesus said to them, "The sons of this age marry and are given in marriage, 35 but those who are considered worthy to attain to that age and to the resurrection from the dead neither marry nor are given in marriage, 36 for they cannot die anymore, because they are equal to angels and are sons of God, being sons⁴ of the resurrection. 37 But that the dead are raised, even Moses showed, in the passage about the bush, where he calls the Lord the God of Abraham and the God of Isaac and the God of Jacob. 38 Now he is not God of the dead, but of the living, for all live to him." 39 Then some of the scribes answered, "Teacher, you have spoken well." 40 For they no longer dared to ask him any question.

Whose Son Is the Christ?

41 ᵇ But he said to them, "How can they say that the Christ is David's son? 42 For David himself says in the Book of Psalms,

ᶜ "'The Lord said to my Lord,
  "Sit at my right hand,
43   until I make your enemies your footstool."'

44 David thus calls him Lord, so how is he his son?"

Beware of the Scribes

45 ᵈ And in the hearing of all the people he said to his disciples, 46"Beware of the scribes, who like to walk around in long robes, and love greetings in the marketplaces and the best seats in the synagogues and the places of honor at feasts, 47 who devour widows' houses and for a pretense make long prayers. They will receive the greater condemnation."

The Widow's Offering

21 ᵉ Jesus⁵ looked up and saw the rich putting their gifts into the offering box, 2 and he saw a poor widow put in two small copper coins.⁶ 3 And he said, "Truly, I tell you, this poor widow has put in more than all of them. 4 For they all contributed out of their abundance, but she out of her poverty put in all she had to live on."

Jesus Foretells Destruction of the Temple

5 ᶠ And while some were speaking of the temple, how it was adorned with noble stones and offerings, he said, 6"As for these things that you see, the days will come when there will not be left here one stone upon another that will not be thrown down." 7 And they asked him, "Teacher, when will these things be, and what will be the sign when these things are about to take place?" 8 And he said, "See that you are not led astray. For many will come in my name, saying, 'I am he!' and, 'The time is at hand!' Do not go after them. 9 And when you hear of wars and tumults, do not be terrified, for these things must first take place, but the end will not be at once."

Jesus Foretells Wars and Persecution

10 Then he said to them, "Nation will rise against nation, and kingdom against kingdom.

---

¹ Greek and do not receive a face ² A denarius was a day's wage for a laborer ³ Greek his brother ⁴ Greek huioi; see Preface ⁵ Greek He ⁶ Greek two lepta; a lepton was a Jewish bronze or copper coin worth about 1/128 of a denarius (which was a day's wage for a laborer) ᵃ For 20:20-38 see parallels Matt. 22:15-32; Mark 12:13-27 ᵇ For 20:41-44 see parallels Matt. 22:41-45; Mark 12:35-37 ᶜ Ps. 110:1 ᵈ For 20:45, 46 see parallels Matt. 23:1, 2, 5-7; Mark 12:38-40 ᵉ For 21:1-4 see parallel Mark 12:41-44 ᶠ For 21:5-36 see parallels Matt. 24:1-51; Mark 13:1-37

[11]There will be great earthquakes, and in various places famines and pestilences. And there will be terrors and great signs from heaven. [12]But before all this they will lay their hands on you and persecute you, delivering you up to the synagogues and prisons, and you will be brought before kings and governors for my name's sake. [13]This will be your opportunity to bear witness. [14]Settle it therefore in your minds not to meditate beforehand how to answer, [15]for I will give you a mouth and wisdom, which none of your adversaries will be able to withstand or contradict. [16]You will be delivered up even by parents and brothers[1] and relatives and friends, and some of you they will put to death. [17]You will be hated by all for my name's sake. [18]But not a hair of your head will perish. [19]By your endurance you will gain your lives.

Jesus Foretells Destruction of Jerusalem

[20]"But when you see Jerusalem surrounded by armies, then know that its desolation has come near. [21]Then let those who are in Judea flee to the mountains, and let those who are inside the city depart, and let not those who are out in the country enter it, [22]for these are days of vengeance, to fulfill all that is written. [23]Alas for women who are pregnant and for those who are nursing infants in those days! For there will be great distress upon the earth and wrath against this people. [24]They will fall by the edge of the sword and be led captive among all nations, and Jerusalem will be trampled underfoot by the Gentiles, until the times of the Gentiles are fulfilled.

The Coming of the Son of Man

[25]"And there will be signs in sun and moon and stars, and on the earth distress of nations in perplexity because of the roaring of the sea and the waves, [26]people fainting with fear and with foreboding of what is coming on the world. For the powers of the heavens will be shaken. [27]And then they will see the Son of Man coming in a cloud with power and great glory. [28]Now when these things begin to take place, straighten up and raise your heads, because your redemption is drawing near."

The Lesson of the Fig Tree

[29]And he told them a parable: "Look at the fig tree, and all the trees. [30]As soon as they come out in leaf, you see for yourselves and know that the summer is already near. [31]So also, when you see these things taking place, you know that the kingdom of God is near. [32]Truly, I say to you, this generation will not pass away until all has taken place. [33]Heaven and earth will pass away, but my words will not pass away.

Watch Yourselves

[34]"But watch yourselves lest your hearts be weighed down with dissipation and drunkenness and cares of this life, and that day come upon you suddenly like a trap. [35]For it will come upon all who dwell on the face of the whole earth. [36]But stay awake at all times, praying that you may have strength to escape all these things that are going to take place, and to stand before the Son of Man."

[37]And every day he was teaching in the temple, but at night he went out and lodged on the mount called Olivet. [38]And early in the morning all the people came to him in the temple to hear him.

The Plot to Kill Jesus

22 Now the Feast of Unleavened Bread drew near, which is called the Passover. [2]And the chief priests and the scribes were seeking how to put him to death, for they feared the people.

Judas to Betray Jesus

[3][a]Then Satan entered into Judas called Iscariot, who was of the number of the twelve. [4]He went away and conferred with the chief priests and officers how he might betray him to them. [5]And they were glad, and agreed to give him money. [6]So he consented and sought an opportunity to betray him to them in the absence of a crowd.

The Passover with the Disciples

[7][b]Then came the day of Unleavened Bread, on which the Passover lamb had to be sacrificed. [8]So Jesus[2] sent Peter and John, saying, "Go and prepare the Passover for us, that we may eat it." [9]They said to him, "Where will you have us prepare it?" [10]He said to them, "Behold, when you have entered the city, a man carrying a jar of water will meet you. Follow him into the house that he enters [11]and tell the master of the house, 'The Teacher says to you, Where is the guest room, where I may eat the Passover with my disciples?' [12]And he will show you a large upper room furnished; prepare it there." [13]And they went and found it just as he had told them, and they prepared the Passover.

---

[1] Or parents and brothers and sisters [2] Greek he [a] For 22:3-6 see parallels Matt. 26:14-16; Mark 14:10, 11 [b] For 22:7-13 see parallels Matt. 26:17-19; Mark 14:12-16

Institution of the Lord's Supper

14 And when the hour came, he reclined at table, and the apostles with him. **15** And he said to them, "I have earnestly desired to eat this Passover with you before I suffer. **16** For I tell you I will not eat it[1] until it is fulfilled in the kingdom of God." **17** And he took a cup, and when he had given thanks he said, "Take this, and divide it among yourselves. **18** For I tell you that from now on I will not drink of the fruit of the vine until the kingdom of God comes." **19**[a] And he took bread, and when he had given thanks, he broke it and gave it to them, saying, "This is my body, which is given for you. Do this in remembrance of me." **20** And likewise the cup after they had eaten, saying, "This cup that is poured out for you is the new covenant in my blood.[2] **21**[b] But behold, the hand of him who betrays me is with me on the table. **22** For the Son of Man goes as it has been determined, but woe to that man by whom he is betrayed!" **23** And they began to question one another, which of them it could be who was going to do this.

Who Is the Greatest?

24 A dispute also arose among them, as to which of them was to be regarded as the greatest. **25** And he said to them, "The kings of the Gentiles exercise lordship over them, and those in authority over them are called benefactors. **26** But not so with you. Rather, let the greatest among you become as the youngest, and the leader as one who serves. **27** For who is the greater, one who reclines at table or one who serves? Is it not the one who reclines at table? But I am among you as the one who serves.

28 "You are those who have stayed with me in my trials, **29** and I assign to you, as my Father assigned to me, a kingdom, **30** that you may eat and drink at my table in my kingdom and sit on thrones judging the twelve tribes of Israel.

Jesus Foretells Peter's Denial

31 "Simon, Simon, behold, Satan demanded to have you,[3] that he might sift you like wheat, **32** but I have prayed for you that your faith may not fail. And when you have turned again, strengthen your brothers." **33** Peter[4] said to him, "Lord, I am ready to go with you both to prison and to death." **34** Jesus[5] said, "I tell you, Peter, the rooster will not crow this day, until you deny three times that you know me."

Scripture Must Be Fulfilled in Jesus

35 And he said to them, "When I sent you out with no moneybag or knapsack or sandals, did you lack anything?" They said, "Nothing." **36** He said to them, "But now let the one who has a moneybag take it, and likewise a knapsack. And let the one who has no sword sell his cloak and buy one. **37** For I tell you that this Scripture must be fulfilled in me: 'And he was numbered with the transgressors.' For what is written about me has its fulfillment." **38** And they said, "Look, Lord, here are two swords." And he said to them, "It is enough."

Jesus Prays on the Mount of Olives

39 And he came out and went, as was his custom, to the Mount of Olives, and the disciples followed him. **40**[d] And when he came to the place, he said to them, "Pray that you may not enter into temptation." **41** And he withdrew from them about a stone's throw, and knelt down and prayed, **42** saying, "Father, if you are willing, remove this cup from me. Nevertheless, not my will, but yours, be done." **43** And there appeared to him an angel from heaven, strengthening him. **44** And being in agony he prayed more earnestly; and his sweat became like great drops of blood falling down to the ground.[6] **45** And when he rose from prayer, he came to the disciples and found them sleeping for sorrow, **46** and he said to them, "Why are you sleeping? Rise and pray that you may not enter into temptation."

Betrayal and Arrest of Jesus

47[e] While he was still speaking, there came a crowd, and the man called Judas, one of the twelve, was leading them. He drew near to Jesus to kiss him, **48** but Jesus said to him, "Judas, would you betray the Son of Man with a kiss?" **49** And when those who were around him saw what would follow, they said, "Lord, shall we strike with the sword?" **50** And one of them struck the servant[7] of the high priest and cut off his right ear. **51** But Jesus said, "No more of this!" And he touched his ear and healed him. **52** Then Jesus said to the chief priests and officers of the temple and elders, who had come

[1] Some manuscripts never eat it again [2] Some manuscripts omit, in whole or in part, verses 19b-20 (which is given . . . in my blood) [3] The Greek word for you (twice in this verse) is plural; in verse 32, all four instances are singular [4] Greek He [5] Greek He [6] Some manuscripts omit verses 43 and 44 [7] Or bondservant [a] For 22:19, 20 see parallels Matt. 26:26-28; Mark 14:22-24 [b] For 22:21-23 see parallels Matt. 26:21-24; Mark 14:18-21 [c] Isa. 53:12 [d] For 22:40-46 see parallels Matt. 26:36-46; Mark 14:32-42 [e] For 22:47-53 see parallels Matt. 26:47-56; Mark 14:43-50; John 18:3-11

out against him, "Have you come out as against a robber, with swords and clubs? [53] When I was with you day after day in the temple, you did not lay hands on me. But this is your hour, and the power of darkness."

Peter Denies Jesus

[54] Then they seized him and led him away, bringing him into the high priest's house, and Peter was following at a distance. [55] [a] And when they had kindled a fire in the middle of the courtyard and sat down together, Peter sat down among them. [56] Then a servant girl, seeing him as he sat in the light and looking closely at him, said, "This man also was with him." [57] But he denied it, saying, "Woman, I do not know him." [58] And a little later someone else saw him and said, "You also are one of them." But Peter said, "Man, I am not." [59] And after an interval of about an hour still another insisted, saying, "Certainly this man also was with him, for he too is a Galilean." [60] But Peter said, "Man, I do not know what you are talking about." And immediately, while he was still speaking, the rooster crowed. [61] And the Lord turned and looked at Peter. And Peter remembered the saying of the Lord, how he had said to him, "Before the rooster crows today, you will deny me three times." [62] And he went out and wept bitterly.

Jesus Is Mocked

[63] Now the men who were holding Jesus in custody were mocking him as they beat him. [64] They also blindfolded him and kept asking him, "Prophesy! Who is it that struck you?" [65] And they said many other things against him, blaspheming him.

Jesus Before the Council

[66] When day came, the assembly of the elders of the people gathered together, both chief priests and scribes. And they led him away to their council, and they said, [67] "If you are the Christ, tell us." But he said to them, "If I tell you, you will not believe, [68] and if I ask you, you will not answer. [69] But from now on the Son of Man shall be seated at the right hand of the power of God." [70] So they all said, "Are you the Son of God, then?" And he said to them, "You say that I am." [71] Then they said, "What further testimony do we need? We have heard it ourselves from his own lips."

Jesus Before Pilate

23 Then the whole company of them arose and brought him before Pilate. [2] And they began to accuse him, saying, "We found this man misleading our nation and forbidding us to give tribute to Caesar, and saying that he himself is Christ, a king." [3] And Pilate asked him, "Are you the King of the Jews?" And he answered him, "You have said so." [4] Then Pilate said to the chief priests and the crowds, "I find no guilt in this man." [5] But they were urgent, saying, "He stirs up the people, teaching throughout all Judea, from Galilee even to this place."

Jesus Before Herod

[6] When Pilate heard this, he asked whether the man was a Galilean. [7] And when he learned that he belonged to Herod's jurisdiction, he sent him over to Herod, who was himself in Jerusalem at that time. [8] When Herod saw Jesus, he was very glad, for he had long desired to see him, because he had heard about him, and he was hoping to see some sign done by him. [9] So he questioned him at some length, but he made no answer. [10] The chief priests and the scribes stood by, vehemently accusing him. [11] And Herod with his soldiers treated him with contempt and mocked him. Then, arraying him in splendid clothing, he sent him back to Pilate. [12] And Herod and Pilate became friends with each other that very day, for before this they had been at enmity with each other.

[13] Pilate then called together the chief priests and the rulers and the people, [14] and said to them, "You brought me this man as one who was misleading the people. And after examining him before you, behold, I did not find this man guilty of any of your charges against him. [15] Neither did Herod, for he sent him back to us. Look, nothing deserving death has been done by him. [16] I will therefore punish and release him." [1]

Pilate Delivers Jesus to Be Crucified

[18] [b] But they all cried out together, "Away with this man, and release to us Barabbas"— [19] a man who had been thrown into prison for an insurrection started in the city and for murder. [20] Pilate addressed them once more, desiring to release Jesus, [21] but they kept shouting, "Crucify, crucify him!" [22] A third time he said to them, "Why? What evil has he done? I have

---

[1] Here, or after verse 19, some manuscripts add verse 17: *Now he was obliged to release one man to them at the festival* [a] For 22:55-62 see parallels Matt. 26:69-75; Mark 14:66-72; John 18:16-18, 25-27 [b] For 23:18-25 see parallels Matt. 27:15-26; Mark 15:6-15; John 18:39, 40; 19:16

found in him no guilt deserving death. I will therefore punish and release him." [23] But they were urgent, demanding with loud cries that he should be crucified. And their voices prevailed. [24] So Pilate decided that their demand should be granted. [25] He released the man who had been thrown into prison for insurrection and murder, for whom they asked, but he delivered Jesus over to their will.

The Crucifixion

[26] And as they led him away, they seized one Simon of Cyrene, who was coming in from the country, and laid on him the cross, to carry it behind Jesus. [27] And there followed him a great multitude of the people and of women who were mourning and lamenting for him. [28] But turning to them Jesus said, "Daughters of Jerusalem, do not weep for me, but weep for yourselves and for your children. [29] For behold, the days are coming when they will say, 'Blessed are the barren and the wombs that never bore and the breasts that never nursed!' [30] Then they will begin to say to the mountains, 'Fall on us,' and to the hills, 'Cover us.' [31] For if they do these things when the wood is green, what will happen when it is dry?"

[32] Two others, who were criminals, were led away to be put to death with him. [33] And when they came to the place that is called The Skull, there they crucified him, and the criminals, one on his right and one on his left. [34] And Jesus said, "Father, forgive them, for they know not what they do."[1] And they cast lots to divide his garments. [35] And the people stood by, watching, but the rulers scoffed at him, saying, "He saved others; let him save himself, if he is the Christ of God, his Chosen One!" [36] The soldiers also mocked him, coming up and offering him sour wine [37] and saying, "If you are the King of the Jews, save yourself!" [38] There was also an inscription over him,[2] "This is the King of the Jews."

[39] One of the criminals who were hanged railed at him,[3] saying, "Are you not the Christ? Save yourself and us!" [40] But the other rebuked him, saying, "Do you not fear God, since you are under the same sentence of condemnation? [41] And we indeed justly, for we are receiving the due reward of our deeds; but this man has done nothing wrong." [42] And he said, "Jesus, remember me when you come into your kingdom." [43] And he said to him, "Truly, I say to you, today you will be with me in paradise."

The Death of Jesus

[44] It was now about the sixth hour,[4] and there was darkness over the whole land until the ninth hour,[5] [45] while the sun's light failed. And the curtain of the temple was torn in two. [46] Then Jesus, calling out with a loud voice, said, "Father, into your hands I commit my spirit!" And having said this he breathed his last. [47] Now when the centurion saw what had taken place, he praised God, saying, "Certainly this man was innocent!" [48] And all the crowds that had assembled for this spectacle, when they saw what had taken place, returned home beating their breasts. [49] And all his acquaintances and the women who had followed him from Galilee stood at a distance watching these things.

Jesus Is Buried

[50] [a] Now there was a man named Joseph, from the Jewish town of Arimathea. He was a member of the council, a good and righteous man, [51] who had not consented to their decision and action; and he was looking for the kingdom of God. [52] This man went to Pilate and asked for the body of Jesus. [53] Then he took it down and wrapped it in a linen shroud and laid him in a tomb cut in stone, where no one had ever yet been laid. [54] It was the day of Preparation, and the Sabbath was beginning.[6] [55] The women who had come with him from Galilee followed and saw the tomb and how his body was laid. [56] Then they returned and prepared spices and ointments.

On the Sabbath they rested according to the commandment.

The Resurrection

24 [b] But on the first day of the week, at early dawn, they went to the tomb, taking the spices they had prepared. [2] And they found the stone rolled away from the tomb, [3] but when they went in they did not find the body of the Lord Jesus. [4] While they were perplexed about this, behold, two men stood by them in dazzling apparel. [5] And as they were frightened and bowed their faces to the ground, the men said to them, "Why do you seek the living among the dead? [6] He is not here, but has risen. Remember how he told you, while he was still in Galilee, [7] that the Son of Man must be delivered into the hands of sinful men and be crucified and on the third day rise." [8] And they remembered his words, [9] and returning from the tomb they told all these things to the eleven and to all the

---

[1] Some manuscripts omit the sentence *And Jesus ... what they do* [2] Some manuscripts add *in letters of Greek and Latin and Hebrew* [3] Or *blasphemed him* [4] That is, noon [5] That is, 3 P.M. [6] Greek *was dawning* [a] For 23:50-56 see parallels Matt. 27:57-61; Mark 15:42-47; John 19:38-42 [b] For 24:1-10 see parallels Matt. 28:1-8; Mark 16:1-8; John 20:1

rest. [10] Now it was Mary Magdalene and Joanna and Mary the mother of James and the other women with them who told these things to the apostles, [11] but these words seemed to them an idle tale, and they did not believe them. [12] But Peter rose and ran to the tomb; stooping and looking in, he saw the linen cloths by themselves; and he went home marveling at what had happened.

On the Road to Emmaus

[13] That very day two of them were going to a village named Emmaus, about seven miles[1] from Jerusalem, [14] and they were talking with each other about all these things that had happened. [15] While they were talking and discussing together, Jesus himself drew near and went with them. [16] But their eyes were kept from recognizing him. [17] And he said to them, "What is this conversation that you are holding with each other as you walk?" And they stood still, looking sad. [18] Then one of them, named Cleopas, answered him, "Are you the only visitor to Jerusalem who does not know the things that have happened there in these days?" [19] And he said to them, "What things?" And they said to him, "Concerning Jesus of Nazareth, a man who was a prophet mighty in deed and word before God and all the people, [20] and how our chief priests and rulers delivered him up to be condemned to death, and crucified him. [21] But we had hoped that he was the one to redeem Israel. Yes, and besides all this, it is now the third day since these things happened. [22] Moreover, some women of our company amazed us. They were at the tomb early in the morning, [23] and when they did not find his body, they came back saying that they had even seen a vision of angels, who said that he was alive. [24] Some of those who were with us went to the tomb and found it just as the women had said, but him they did not see." [25] And he said to them, "O foolish ones, and slow of heart to believe all that the prophets have spoken! [26] Was it not necessary that the Christ should suffer these things and enter into his glory?" [27] And beginning with Moses and all the Prophets, he interpreted to them in all the Scriptures the things concerning himself.

[28] So they drew near to the village to which they were going. He acted as if he were going farther, [29] but they urged him strongly, saying, "Stay with us, for it is toward evening and the day is now far spent." So he went in to stay with them. [30] When he was at table with them, he took the bread and blessed and broke it and gave it to them. [31] And their eyes were opened, and they recognized him. And he vanished from their sight. [32] They said to each other, "Did not our hearts burn within us while he talked to us on the road, while he opened to us the Scriptures?" [33] And they rose that same hour and returned to Jerusalem. And they found the eleven and those who were with them gathered together, [34] saying, "The Lord has risen indeed, and has appeared to Simon!" [35] Then they told what had happened on the road, and how he was known to them in the breaking of the bread.

Jesus Appears to His Disciples

[36] As they were talking about these things, Jesus himself stood among them, and said to them, "Peace to you!" [37] But they were startled and frightened and thought they saw a spirit. [38] And he said to them, "Why are you troubled, and why do doubts arise in your hearts? [39] See my hands and my feet, that it is I myself. Touch me, and see. For a spirit does not have flesh and bones as you see that I have." [40] And when he had said this, he showed them his hands and his feet. [41] And while they still disbelieved for joy and were marveling, he said to them, "Have you anything here to eat?" [42] They gave him a piece of broiled fish,[2] [43] and he took it and ate before them.

[44] Then he said to them, "These are my words that I spoke to you while I was still with you, that everything written about me in the Law of Moses and the Prophets and the Psalms must be fulfilled." [45] Then he opened their minds to understand the Scriptures, [46] and said to them, "Thus it is written, that the Christ should suffer and on the third day rise from the dead, [47] and that repentance for[3] the forgiveness of sins should be proclaimed in his name to all nations, beginning from Jerusalem. [48] You are witnesses of these things. [49] And behold, I am sending the promise of my Father upon you. But stay in the city until you are clothed with power from on high."

The Ascension

[50] And he led them out as far as Bethany, and lifting up his hands he blessed them. [51] While he blessed them, he parted from them and was carried up into heaven. [52] And they worshiped him and returned to Jerusalem with great joy, [53] and were continually in the temple blessing God.

---

[1] Greek sixty stadia; a stadion was about 607 feet or 185 meters [2] Some manuscripts add and some honeycomb [3] Some manuscripts and

JOHN

The Word Became Flesh

1 In the beginning was the Word, and the Word was with God, and the Word was God. [2] He was in the beginning with God. [3] All things were made through him, and without him was not any thing made that was made. [4] In him was life,[1] and the life was the light of men. [5] The light shines in the darkness, and the darkness has not overcome it.

[6] There was a man sent from God, whose name was John. [7] He came as a witness, to bear witness about the light, that all might believe through him. [8] He was not the light, but came to bear witness about the light.

[9] The true light, which gives light to everyone, was coming into the world. [10] He was in the world, and the world was made through him, yet the world did not know him. [11] He came to his own,[2] and his own people[3] did not receive him. [12] But to all who did receive him, who believed in his name, he gave the right to become children of God, [13] who were born, not of blood nor of the will of the flesh nor of the will of man, but of God.

[14] And the Word became flesh and dwelt among us, and we have seen his glory, glory as of the only Son[4] from the Father, full of grace and truth. [15] (John bore witness about him, and cried out, "This was he of whom I said, 'He who comes after me ranks before me, because he was before me.'") [16] For from his fullness we have all received, grace upon grace.[5] [17] For the law was given through Moses; grace and truth came through Jesus Christ. [18] No one has ever seen God; the only God,[6] who is at the Father's side,[7] he has made him known.

The Testimony of John the Baptist

[19] And this is the testimony of John, when the Jews sent priests and Levites from Jerusalem to ask him, "Who are you?" [20] He confessed, and did not deny, but confessed, "I am not the Christ." [21] And they asked him, "What then? Are you Elijah?" He said, "I am not." "Are you the Prophet?" And he answered, "No." [22] So they said to him, "Who are you? We need to give an answer to those who sent us. What do you say about yourself?" [23] He said, "I am [a] the voice of one crying out in the wilderness, 'Make straight[8] the way of the Lord,' as the prophet Isaiah said."

[24] (Now they had been sent from the Pharisees.) [25] They asked him, "Then why are you baptizing, if you are neither the Christ, nor Elijah, nor the Prophet?" [26] John answered them, "I baptize with water, but among you stands one you do not know, [27] even he who comes after me, the strap of whose sandal I am not worthy to untie." [28] These things took place in Bethany across the Jordan, where John was baptizing.

Behold, the Lamb of God

[29] The next day he saw Jesus coming toward him, and said, "Behold, the Lamb of God, who takes away the sin of the world! [30] This is he of whom I said, 'After me comes a man who ranks before me, because he was before me.' [31] I myself did not know him, but for this purpose I came baptizing with water, that he might be revealed to Israel." [32] And John bore witness: "I saw the Spirit descend from heaven like a dove, and it remained on him. [33] I myself did not know him, but he who sent me to baptize with water said to me, 'He on whom you see the Spirit descend and remain, this is he who baptizes with the Holy Spirit.' [34] And I have seen and have borne witness that this is the Son[9] of God."

Jesus Calls the First Disciples

[35] The next day again John was standing with two of his disciples, [36] and he looked at Jesus as he walked by and said, "Behold, the Lamb of God!" [37] The two disciples heard him say this, and they followed Jesus. [38] Jesus turned and saw them following and said to them, "What are you seeking?" And they said to him, "Rabbi" (which means Teacher), "where are you staying?" [39] He said to them, "Come and you will see." So they came and saw where he was staying, and they stayed with him that day, for it was about the tenth hour.[10] [40] One of the two who heard John speak and followed Jesus[11] was Andrew, Simon Peter's brother. [41] He first found his own brother Simon and said to him, "We have found the Messiah"

---

[1] Or *was not any thing made. That which has been made was life in him* [2] Greek *to his own things; that is, to his own domain, or to his own people* [3] *People* is implied in Greek [4] Or *only One, or unique One* [5] Or *grace in place of grace* [6] Or *the Only One, who is God; some manuscripts the only Son* [7] Greek *in the bosom of the Father* [8] Or *crying out, 'In the wilderness make straight* [9] Some manuscripts *the Chosen One* [10] That is, about 4 P.M. [11] Greek *him* [a] Isa. 40:3

(which means Christ). [42] He brought him to Jesus. Jesus looked at him and said, "You are Simon the son of John. You shall be called Cephas" (which means Peter[1]).

Jesus Calls Philip and Nathanael

[43] The next day Jesus decided to go to Galilee. He found Philip and said to him, "Follow me." [44] Now Philip was from Bethsaida, the city of Andrew and Peter. [45] Philip found Nathanael and said to him, "We have found him of whom Moses in the Law and also the prophets wrote, Jesus of Nazareth, the son of Joseph." [46] Nathanael said to him, "Can anything good come out of Nazareth?" Philip said to him, "Come and see." [47] Jesus saw Nathanael coming toward him and said of him, "Behold, an Israelite indeed, in whom there is no deceit!" [48] Nathanael said to him, "How do you know me?" Jesus answered him, "Before Philip called you, when you were under the fig tree, I saw you." [49] Nathanael answered him, "Rabbi, you are the Son of God! You are the King of Israel!" [50] Jesus answered him, "Because I said to you, 'I saw you under the fig tree,' do you believe? You will see greater things than these." [51] And he said to him, "Truly, truly, I say to you,[2] you will see heaven opened, and the angels of God ascending and descending on the Son of Man."

The Wedding at Cana

2 On the third day there was a wedding at Cana in Galilee, and the mother of Jesus was there. [2] Jesus also was invited to the wedding with his disciples. [3] When the wine ran out, the mother of Jesus said to him, "They have no wine." [4] And Jesus said to her, "Woman, what does this have to do with me? My hour has not yet come." [5] His mother said to the servants, "Do whatever he tells you."

[6] Now there were six stone water jars there for the Jewish rites of purification, each holding twenty or thirty gallons.[3] [7] Jesus said to the servants, "Fill the jars with water." And they filled them up to the brim. [8] And he said to them, "Now draw some out and take it to the master of the feast." So they took it. [9] When the master of the feast tasted the water now become wine, and did not know where it came from (though the servants who had drawn the water knew), the master of the feast called the bridegroom [10] and said to him, "Everyone

serves the good wine first, and when people have drunk freely, then the poor wine. But you have kept the good wine until now." [11] This, the first of his signs, Jesus did at Cana in Galilee, and manifested his glory. And his disciples believed in him.

[12] After this he went down to Capernaum, with his mother and his brothers[4] and his disciples, and they stayed there for a few days.

Jesus Cleanses the Temple

[13] The Passover of the Jews was at hand, and Jesus went up to Jerusalem. [14] In the temple he found those who were selling oxen and sheep and pigeons, and the money-changers sitting there. [15] And making a whip of cords, he drove them all out of the temple, with the sheep and oxen. And he poured out the coins of the money-changers and overturned their tables. [16] And he told those who sold the pigeons, "Take these things away; do not make my Father's house a house of trade." [17] His disciples remembered that it was written, [a] "Zeal for your house will consume me."

[18] So the Jews said to him, "What sign do you show us for doing these things?" [19] Jesus answered them, "Destroy this temple, and in three days I will raise it up." [20] The Jews then said, "It has taken forty-six years to build this temple,[5] and will you raise it up in three days?" [21] But he was speaking about the temple of his body. [22] When therefore he was raised from the dead, his disciples remembered that he had said this, and they believed the Scripture and the word that Jesus had spoken.

Jesus Knows What Is in Man

[23] Now when he was in Jerusalem at the Passover Feast, many believed in his name when they saw the signs that he was doing. [24] But Jesus on his part did not entrust himself to them, because he knew all people [25] and needed no one to bear witness about man, for he himself knew what was in man.

You Must Be Born Again

3 Now there was a man of the Pharisees named Nicodemus, a ruler of the Jews. [2] This man came to Jesus[6] by night and said to him, "Rabbi, we know that you are a teacher come from God, for no one can do these signs that you do unless God is with him." [3] Jesus answered him, "Truly, truly, I say to you, unless

[1] Cephas and Peter are from the word for rock in Aramaic and Greek, respectively [2] The Greek for you is plural; twice in this verse [3] Greek two or three measures (metrētas); a metrētēs was about 10 gallons or 35 liters [4] Or brothers and sisters. In New Testament usage, depending on the context, the plural Greek word adelphoi (translated "brothers") may refer either to brothers or to brothers and sisters [5] Or This temple was built forty-six years ago [6] Greek him [a] Ps. 69:9

one is born again[1] he cannot see the kingdom of God." [4] Nicodemus said to him, "How can a man be born when he is old? Can he enter a second time into his mother's womb and be born?" [5] Jesus answered, "Truly, truly, I say to you, unless one is born of water and the Spirit, he cannot enter the kingdom of God. [6] That which is born of the flesh is flesh, and that which is born of the Spirit is spirit.[2] [7] Do not marvel that I said to you, 'You[3] must be born again.' [8] The wind[4] blows where it wishes, and you hear its sound, but you do not know where it comes from or where it goes. So it is with everyone who is born of the Spirit."

[9] Nicodemus said to him, "How can these things be?" [10] Jesus answered him, "Are you the teacher of Israel and yet you do not understand these things? [11] Truly, truly, I say to you, we speak of what we know, and bear witness to what we have seen, but you[5] do not receive our testimony. [12] If I have told you earthly things and you do not believe, how can you believe if I tell you heavenly things? [13] No one has ascended into heaven except he who descended from heaven, the Son of Man.[6] [14] And as Moses lifted up the serpent in the wilderness, so must the Son of Man be lifted up, [15] that whoever believes in him may have eternal life.[7]

For God So Loved the World

[16] "For God so loved the world,[8] that he gave his only Son, that whoever believes in him should not perish but have eternal life. [17] For God did not send his Son into the world to condemn the world, but in order that the world might be saved through him. [18] Whoever believes in him is not condemned, but whoever does not believe is condemned already, because he has not believed in the name of the only Son of God. [19] And this is the judgment: the light has come into the world, and people loved the darkness rather than the light because their works were evil. [20] For everyone who does wicked things hates the light and does not come to the light, lest his works should be exposed. [21] But whoever does what is true comes to the light, so that it may be clearly seen that his works have been carried out in God."

John the Baptist Exalts Christ

[22] After this Jesus and his disciples went into the Judean countryside, and he remained there with them and was baptizing. [23] John also was baptizing at Aenon near Salim, because water was plentiful there, and people were coming and being baptized [24] (for John had not yet been put in prison).

[25] Now a discussion arose between some of John's disciples and a Jew over purification. [26] And they came to John and said to him, "Rabbi, he who was with you across the Jordan, to whom you bore witness—look, he is baptizing, and all are going to him." [27] John answered, "A person cannot receive even one thing unless it is given him from heaven. [28] You yourselves bear me witness, that I said, 'I am not the Christ, but I have been sent before him.' [29] The one who has the bride is the bridegroom. The friend of the bridegroom, who stands and hears him, rejoices greatly at the bridegroom's voice. Therefore this joy of mine is now complete. [30] He must increase, but I must decrease."[9]

[31] He who comes from above is above all. He who is of the earth belongs to the earth and speaks in an earthly way. He who comes from heaven is above all. [32] He bears witness to what he has seen and heard, yet no one receives his testimony. [33] Whoever receives his testimony sets his seal to this, that God is true. [34] For he whom God has sent utters the words of God, for he gives the Spirit without measure. [35] The Father loves the Son and has given all things into his hand. [36] Whoever believes in the Son has eternal life; whoever does not obey the Son shall not see life, but the wrath of God remains on him.

Jesus and the Woman of Samaria

4 Now when Jesus learned that the Pharisees had heard that Jesus was making and baptizing more disciples than John [2] (although Jesus himself did not baptize, but only his disciples), [3] he left Judea and departed again for Galilee. [4] And he had to pass through Samaria. [5] So he came to a town of Samaria called Sychar, near the field that Jacob had given to his son Joseph. [6] Jacob's well was there; so Jesus, wearied as he was from his journey, was sitting beside the well. It was about the sixth hour.[10]

[7] A woman from Samaria came to draw water. Jesus said to her, "Give me a drink." [8] (For his disciples had gone away into the city to buy food.) [9] The Samaritan woman said to him, "How is

---

[1] Or *from above*; the Greek is purposely ambiguous and can mean both *again* and *from above*; also verse 7 [2] The same Greek word means both *wind* and *spirit* [3] The Greek for *you* is plural here [4] The same Greek word means both *wind* and *spirit* [5] The Greek for *you* is plural here; also four times in verse 12 [6] Some manuscripts add *who is in heaven* [7] Some interpreters hold that the quotation ends at verse 15 [8] Or *For this is how God loved the world* [9] Some interpreters hold that the quotation continues through verse 36 [10] That is, about noon

it that you, a Jew, ask for a drink from me, a woman of Samaria?" (For Jews have no dealings with Samaritans.) [10] Jesus answered her, "If you knew the gift of God, and who it is that is saying to you, 'Give me a drink,' you would have asked him, and he would have given you living water." [11] The woman said to him, "Sir, you have nothing to draw water with, and the well is deep. Where do you get that living water? [12] Are you greater than our father Jacob? He gave us the well and drank from it himself, as did his sons and his livestock." [13] Jesus said to her, "Everyone who drinks of this water will be thirsty again, [14] but whoever drinks of the water that I will give him will never be thirsty again.[1] The water that I will give him will become in him a spring of water welling up to eternal life." [15] The woman said to him, "Sir, give me this water, so that I will not be thirsty or have to come here to draw water."

[16] Jesus said to her, "Go, call your husband, and come here." [17] The woman answered him, "I have no husband." Jesus said to her, "You are right in saying, 'I have no husband'; [18] for you have had five husbands, and the one you now have is not your husband. What you have said is true." [19] The woman said to him, "Sir, I perceive that you are a prophet. [20] Our fathers worshiped on this mountain, but you say that in Jerusalem is the place where people ought to worship." [21] Jesus said to her, "Woman, believe me, the hour is coming when neither on this mountain nor in Jerusalem will you worship the Father. [22] You worship what you do not know; we worship what we know, for salvation is from the Jews. [23] But the hour is coming, and is now here, when the true worshipers will worship the Father in spirit and truth, for the Father is seeking such people to worship him. [24] God is spirit, and those who worship him must worship in spirit and truth." [25] The woman said to him, "I know that Messiah is coming (he who is called Christ). When he comes, he will tell us all things." [26] Jesus said to her, "I who speak to you am he."

[27] Just then his disciples came back. They marveled that he was talking with a woman, but no one said, "What do you seek?" or, "Why are you talking with her?" [28] So the woman left her water jar and went away into town and said to the people, [29] "Come, see a man who told me all that I ever did. Can this be the Christ?"

[30] They went out of the town and were coming to him.

[31] Meanwhile the disciples were urging him, saying, "Rabbi, eat." [32] But he said to them, "I have food to eat that you do not know about." [33] So the disciples said to one another, "Has anyone brought him something to eat?" [34] Jesus said to them, "My food is to do the will of him who sent me and to accomplish his work. [35] Do you not say, 'There are yet four months, then comes the harvest'? Look, I tell you, lift up your eyes, and see that the fields are white for harvest. [36] Already the one who reaps is receiving wages and gathering fruit for eternal life, so that sower and reaper may rejoice together. [37] For here the saying holds true, 'One sows and another reaps.' [38] I sent you to reap that for which you did not labor. Others have labored, and you have entered into their labor."

[39] Many Samaritans from that town believed in him because of the woman's testimony, "He told me all that I ever did." [40] So when the Samaritans came to him, they asked him to stay with them, and he stayed there two days. [41] And many more believed because of his word. [42] They said to the woman, "It is no longer because of what you said that we believe, for we have heard for ourselves, and we know that this is indeed the Savior of the world."

[43] After the two days he departed for Galilee. [44] (For Jesus himself had testified that a prophet has no honor in his own hometown.) [45] So when he came to Galilee, the Galileans welcomed him, having seen all that he had done in Jerusalem at the feast. For they too had gone to the feast.

Jesus Heals an Official's Son

[46] So he came again to Cana in Galilee, where he had made the water wine. And at Capernaum there was an official whose son was ill. [47] When this man heard that Jesus had come from Judea to Galilee, he went to him and asked him to come down and heal his son, for he was at the point of death. [48] So Jesus said to him, "Unless you[2] see signs and wonders you will not believe." [49] The official said to him, "Sir, come down before my child dies." [50] Jesus said to him, "Go; your son will live." The man believed the word that Jesus spoke to him and went on his way. [51] As he was going down, his servants[3] met him and told him that his son was recovering. [52] So he asked them the hour when he began to get better, and they said to him, "Yesterday

---

[1] Greek forever [2] The Greek for you is plural; twice in this verse [3] Or bondservants

at the seventh hour[1] the fever left him." [53]The father knew that was the hour when Jesus had said to him, "Your son will live." And he himself believed, and all his household. [54]This was now the second sign that Jesus did when he had come from Judea to Galilee.

The Healing at the Pool on the Sabbath

5 After this there was a feast of the Jews, and Jesus went up to Jerusalem.

[2]Now there is in Jerusalem by the Sheep Gate a pool, in Aramaic[2] called Bethesda,[3] which has five roofed colonnades. [3]In these lay a multitude of invalids—blind, lame, and paralyzed.[4] [5]One man was there who had been an invalid for thirty-eight years. [6]When Jesus saw him lying there and knew that he had already been there a long time, he said to him, "Do you want to be healed?" [7]The sick man answered him, "Sir, I have no one to put me into the pool when the water is stirred up, and while I am going another steps down before me." [8]Jesus said to him, "Get up, take up your bed, and walk." [9]And at once the man was healed, and he took up his bed and walked.

Now that day was the Sabbath.[5] [10]So the Jews[5] said to the man who had been healed, "It is the Sabbath, and it is not lawful for you to take up your bed." [11]But he answered them, "The man who healed me, that man said to me, 'Take up your bed, and walk.'" [12]They asked him, "Who is the man who said to you, 'Take up your bed and walk'?" [13]Now the man who had been healed did not know who it was, for Jesus had withdrawn, as there was a crowd in the place. [14]Afterward Jesus found him in the temple and said to him, "See, you are well! Sin no more, that nothing worse may happen to you." [15]The man went away and told the Jews that it was Jesus who had healed him. [16]And this was why the Jews were persecuting Jesus, because he was doing these things on the Sabbath. [17]But Jesus answered them, "My Father is working until now, and I am working."

Jesus Is Equal with God

[18]This was why the Jews were seeking all the more to kill him, because not only was he breaking the Sabbath, but he was even calling God his own Father, making himself equal with God.

The Authority of the Son

[19]So Jesus said to them, "Truly, truly, I say to you, the Son can do nothing of his own accord, but only what he sees the Father doing. For whatever the Father[6] does, that the Son does likewise. [20]For the Father loves the Son and shows him all that he himself is doing. And greater works than these will he show him, so that you may marvel. [21]For as the Father raises the dead and gives them life, so also the Son gives life to whom he will. [22]For the Father judges no one, but has given all judgment to the Son, [23]that all may honor the Son, just as they honor the Father. Whoever does not honor the Son does not honor the Father who sent him. [24]Truly, truly, I say to you, whoever hears my word and believes him who sent me has eternal life. He does not come into judgment, but has passed from death to life.

[25]"Truly, truly, I say to you, an hour is coming, and is now here, when the dead will hear the voice of the Son of God, and those who hear will live. [26]For as the Father has life in himself, so he has granted the Son also to have life in himself. [27]And he has given him authority to execute judgment, because he is the Son of Man. [28]Do not marvel at this, for an hour is coming when all who are in the tombs will hear his voice [29]and come out, those who have done good to the resurrection of life, and those who have done evil to the resurrection of judgment.

Witnesses to Jesus

[30]"I can do nothing on my own. As I hear, I judge, and my judgment is just, because I seek not my own will but the will of him who sent me. [31]If I alone bear witness about myself, my testimony is not true. [32]There is another who bears witness about me, and I know that the testimony that he bears about me is true. [33]You sent to John, and he has borne witness to the truth. [34]Not that the testimony that I receive is from man, but I say these things so that you may be saved. [35]He was a burning and shining lamp, and you were willing to rejoice for a while in his light. [36]But the testimony that I have is greater than that of John. For the works that the Father has given me to accomplish, the very works that I am doing, bear witness about me that the Father has sent me. [37]And the Father who sent me has himself borne witness about me. His voice you have never heard, his form you have never seen, [38]and you do not

[1] That is, at 1 P.M. [2] Or Hebrew [3] Some manuscripts Bethsaida [4] Some manuscripts insert, wholly or in part, waiting for the moving of the water; [4]for an angel of the Lord went down at certain seasons into the pool, and stirred the water: whoever stepped in first after the stirring of the water was healed of whatever disease he had [5] The Greek word Ioudaioi refers specifically here to Jewish religious leaders, and others under their influence, who opposed Jesus in that time; also verses 15, 16, 18 [6] Greek he

have his word abiding in you, for you do not believe the one whom he has sent. [39]You search the Scriptures because you think that in them you have eternal life; and it is they that bear witness about me, [40]yet you refuse to come to me that you may have life. [41]I do not receive glory from people. [42]But I know that you do not have the love of God within you. [43]I have come in my Father's name, and you do not receive me. If another comes in his own name, you will receive him. [44]How can you believe, when you receive glory from one another and do not seek the glory that comes from the only God? [45]Do not think that I will accuse you to the Father. There is one who accuses you: Moses, on whom you have set your hope. [46]For if you believed Moses, you would believe me; for he wrote of me. [47]But if you do not believe his writings, how will you believe my words?"

Jesus Feeds the Five Thousand

6 After this [a]Jesus went away to the other side of the Sea of Galilee, which is the Sea of Tiberias. [2]And a large crowd was following him, because they saw the signs that he was doing on the sick. [3]Jesus went up on the mountain, and there he sat down with his disciples. [4]Now the Passover, the feast of the Jews, was at hand. [5]Lifting up his eyes, then, and seeing that a large crowd was coming toward him, Jesus said to Philip, "Where are we to buy bread, so that these people may eat?" [6]He said this to test him, for he himself knew what he would do. [7]Philip answered him, "Two hundred denarii[1] worth of bread would not be enough for each of them to get a little." [8]One of his disciples, Andrew, Simon Peter's brother, said to him, [9]"There is a boy here who has five barley loaves and two fish, but what are they for so many?" [10]Jesus said, "Have the people sit down." Now there was much grass in the place. So the men sat down, about five thousand in number. [11]Jesus then took the loaves, and when he had given thanks, he distributed them to those who were seated. So also the fish, as much as they wanted. [12]And when they had eaten their fill, he told his disciples, "Gather up the leftover fragments, that nothing may be lost." [13]So they gathered them up and filled twelve baskets with fragments from the five barley loaves left by those who had eaten. [14]When the people saw the sign that he had done, they said, "This is indeed the Prophet who is to come into the world!"

[15]Perceiving then that they were about to come and take him by force to make him king, Jesus [b]withdrew again to the mountain by himself.

Jesus Walks on Water

[16]When evening came, his disciples went down to the sea, [17]got into a boat, and started across the sea to Capernaum. It was now dark, and Jesus had not yet come to them. [18]The sea became rough because a strong wind was blowing. [19]When they had rowed about three or four miles,[2] they saw Jesus walking on the sea and coming near the boat, and they were frightened. [20]But he said to them, "It is I; do not be afraid." [21]Then they were glad to take him into the boat, and immediately the boat was at the land to which they were going.

I Am the Bread of Life

[22]On the next day the crowd that remained on the other side of the sea saw that there had been only one boat there, and that Jesus had not entered the boat with his disciples, but that his disciples had gone away alone. [23]Other boats from Tiberias came near the place where they had eaten the bread after the Lord had given thanks. [24]So when the crowd saw that Jesus was not there, nor his disciples, they themselves got into the boats and went to Capernaum, seeking Jesus.

[25]When they found him on the other side of the sea, they said to him, "Rabbi, when did you come here?" [26]Jesus answered them, "Truly, truly, I say to you, you are seeking me, not because you saw signs, but because you ate your fill of the loaves. [27]Do not work for the food that perishes, but for the food that endures to eternal life, which the Son of Man will give to you. For on him God the Father has set his seal." [28]Then they said to him, "What must we do, to be doing the works of God?" [29]Jesus answered them, "This is the work of God, that you believe in him whom he has sent." [30]So they said to him, "Then what sign do you do, that we may see and believe you? What work do you perform? [31]Our fathers ate the manna in the wilderness; as it is written, 'He gave them bread from heaven to eat.'" [32]Jesus then said to them, "Truly, truly, I say to you, it was not Moses who gave you the bread from heaven, but my Father gives you the true bread from heaven. [33]For the bread of God is he

---

[1] A *denarius* was a day's wage for a laborer [2] Greek *twenty-five or thirty stadia; a stadion* was about 607 feet or 185 meters [a]For 6:1-13 see parallels Matt. 14:13-21; Mark 6:32-44; Luke 9:10-17 [b]For 6:15-21 see parallels Matt. 14:22-33; Mark 6:45-52 [c]Neh. 9:15

who comes down from heaven and gives life to the world." [34] They said to him, "Sir, give us this bread always."

[35] Jesus said to them, "I am the bread of life; whoever comes to me shall not hunger, and whoever believes in me shall never thirst. [36] But I said to you that you have seen me and yet do not believe. [37] All that the Father gives me will come to me, and whoever comes to me I will never cast out. [38] For I have come down from heaven, not to do my own will but the will of him who sent me. [39] And this is the will of him who sent me, that I should lose nothing of all that he has given me, but raise it up on the last day. [40] For this is the will of my Father, that everyone who looks on the Son and believes in him should have eternal life, and I will raise him up on the last day."

[41] So the Jews grumbled about him, because he said, "I am the bread that came down from heaven." [42] They said, "Is not this Jesus, the son of Joseph, whose father and mother we know? How does he now say, 'I have come down from heaven'?" [43] Jesus answered them, "Do not grumble among yourselves. [44] No one can come to me unless the Father who sent me draws him. And I will raise him up on the last day. [45] It is written in the Prophets, ᵃ'And they will all be taught by God.' Everyone who has heard and learned from the Father comes to me— [46] not that anyone has seen the Father except he who is from God; he has seen the Father. [47] Truly, truly, I say to you, whoever believes has eternal life. [48] I am the bread of life. [49] Your fathers ate the manna in the wilderness, and they died. [50] This is the bread that comes down from heaven, so that one may eat of it and not die. [51] I am the living bread that came down from heaven. If anyone eats of this bread, he will live forever. And the bread that I will give for the life of the world is my flesh."

[52] The Jews then disputed among themselves, saying, "How can this man give us his flesh to eat?" [53] So Jesus said to them, "Truly, truly, I say to you, unless you eat the flesh of the Son of Man and drink his blood, you have no life in you. [54] Whoever feeds on my flesh and drinks my blood has eternal life, and I will raise him up on the last day. [55] For my flesh is true food, and my blood is true drink. [56] Whoever feeds on my flesh and drinks my blood abides in me, and I in him. [57] As the living Father sent me, and I live because of the Father, so whoever feeds on me, he also will live because of me. [58] This is the bread that came down from heaven, not like the bread¹ the fathers ate, and died. Whoever feeds on this bread will live forever." [59] Jesus² said these things in the synagogue, as he taught at Capernaum.

The Words of Eternal Life

[60] When many of his disciples heard it, they said, "This is a hard saying; who can listen to it?" [61] But Jesus, knowing in himself that his disciples were grumbling about this, said to them, "Do you take offense at this? [62] Then what if you were to see the Son of Man ascending to where he was before? [63] It is the Spirit who gives life; the flesh is no help at all. The words that I have spoken to you are spirit and life. [64] But there are some of you who do not believe." (For Jesus knew from the beginning who those were who did not believe, and who it was who would betray him.) [65] And he said, "This is why I told you that no one can come to me unless it is granted him by the Father."

[66] After this many of his disciples turned back and no longer walked with him. [67] So Jesus said to the twelve, "Do you want to go away as well?" [68] Simon Peter answered him, "Lord, to whom shall we go? You have the words of eternal life, [69] and we have believed, and have come to know, that you are the Holy One of God." [70] Jesus answered them, "Did I not choose you, the twelve? And yet one of you is a devil." [71] He spoke of Judas the son of Simon Iscariot, for he, one of the twelve, was going to betray him.

Jesus at the Feast of Booths

7 After this Jesus went about in Galilee. He would not go about in Judea, because the Jews³ were seeking to kill him. [2] Now the Jews' Feast of Booths was at hand. [3] So his brothers⁴ said to him, "Leave here and go to Judea, that your disciples also may see the works you are doing. [4] For no one works in secret if he seeks to be known openly. If you do these things, show yourself to the world." [5] For not even his brothers believed in him. [6] Jesus said to them, "My time has not yet come, but your time is always here. [7] The world cannot hate you, but it hates me because I testify about it that its works are evil. [8] You go up to the feast. I am not⁵ going up to this feast, for my time has not yet fully come." [9] After saying this, he remained in Galilee.

---

¹ Greek lacks *the bread* ² Greek *He* ³ Or *Judeans*; Greek *Ioudaioi* probably refers here to Jewish religious leaders, and others under their influence, in that time ⁴ Or *brothers and sisters; also verses 5, 10* ⁵ Some manuscripts add *yet* ᵃIsa. 54:13

[10] But after his brothers had gone up to the feast, then he also went up, not publicly but in private. [11] The Jews were looking for him at the feast, and saying, "Where is he?" [12] And there was much muttering about him among the people. While some said, "He is a good man," others said, "No, he is leading the people astray." [13] Yet for fear of the Jews no one spoke openly of him.

[14] About the middle of the feast Jesus went up into the temple and began teaching. [15] The Jews therefore marveled, saying, "How is it that this man has learning,[1] when he has never studied?" [16] So Jesus answered them, "My teaching is not mine, but his who sent me. [17] If anyone's will is to do God's[2] will, he will know whether the teaching is from God or whether I am speaking on my own authority. [18] The one who speaks on his own authority seeks his own glory; but the one who seeks the glory of him who sent him is true, and in him there is no falsehood. [19] Has not Moses given you the law? Yet none of you keeps the law. Why do you seek to kill me?" [20] The crowd answered, "You have a demon! Who is seeking to kill you?" [21] Jesus answered them, "I did one work, and you all marvel at it. [22] Moses gave you circumcision (not that it is from Moses, but from the fathers), and you circumcise a man on the Sabbath. [23] If on the Sabbath a man receives circumcision, so that the law of Moses may not be broken, are you angry with me because on the Sabbath I made a man's whole body well? [24] Do not judge by appearances, but judge with right judgment."

Can This Be the Christ?

[25] Some of the people of Jerusalem therefore said, "Is not this the man whom they seek to kill? [26] And here he is, speaking openly, and they say nothing to him! Can it be that the authorities really know that this is the Christ? [27] But we know where this man comes from, and when the Christ appears, no one will know where he comes from." [28] So Jesus proclaimed, as he taught in the temple, "You know me, and you know where I come from. But I have not come of my own accord. He who sent me is true, and him you do not know. [29] I know him, for I come from him, and he sent me." [30] So they were seeking to arrest him, but no one laid a hand on him, because his hour had not yet come. [31] Yet many of the people believed in him. They said,

"When the Christ appears, will he do more signs than this man has done?"

Officers Sent to Arrest Jesus

[32] The Pharisees heard the crowd muttering these things about him, and the chief priests and Pharisees sent officers to arrest him. [33] Jesus then said, "I will be with you a little longer, and then I am going to him who sent me. [34] You will seek me and you will not find me. Where I am you cannot come." [35] The Jews said to one another, "Where does this man intend to go that we will not find him? Does he intend to go to the Dispersion among the Greeks and teach the Greeks? [36] What does he mean by saying, 'You will seek me and you will not find me,' and, 'Where I am you cannot come'?"

Rivers of Living Water

[37] On the last day of the feast, the great day, Jesus stood up and cried out, "If anyone thirsts, let him come to me and drink. [38] Whoever believes in me, as[3] the Scripture has said, 'Out of his heart will flow rivers of living water.'" [39] Now this he said about the Spirit, whom those who believed in him were to receive, for as yet the Spirit had not been given, because Jesus was not yet glorified.

Division Among the People

[40] When they heard these words, some of the people said, "This really is the Prophet." [41] Others said, "This is the Christ." But some said, "Is the Christ to come from Galilee? [42] Has not the Scripture said that the Christ comes from the offspring of David, and comes from Bethlehem, the village where David was?" [43] So there was a division among the people over him. [44] Some of them wanted to arrest him, but no one laid hands on him.

[45] The officers then came to the chief priests and Pharisees, who said to them, "Why did you not bring him?" [46] The officers answered, "No one ever spoke like this man!" [47] The Pharisees answered them, "Have you also been deceived? [48] Have any of the authorities or the Pharisees believed in him? [49] But this crowd that does not know the law is accursed." [50] Nicodemus, who had gone to him before, and who was one of them, said to them, [51] "Does our law judge a man without first giving him a hearing and learning what he does?" [52] They replied, "Are you from Galilee too? Search and see that no prophet arises from Galilee."

---

[1] Or this man knows his letters [2] Greek his [3] Or let him come to me, and let him who believes in me drink. As

[THE EARLIEST MANUSCRIPTS DO
NOT INCLUDE 7:53–8:11.][1]

The Woman Caught in Adultery

8 [53] [[They went each to his own house, [1] but Jesus went to the Mount of Olives. [2] Early in the morning he came again to the temple. All the people came to him, and he sat down and taught them. [3] The scribes and the Pharisees brought a woman who had been caught in adultery, and placing her in the midst [4] they said to him, "Teacher, this woman has been caught in the act of adultery. [5] Now in the Law, Moses commanded us to stone such women. So what do you say?" [6] This they said to test him, that they might have some charge to bring against him. Jesus bent down and wrote with his finger on the ground. [7] And as they continued to ask him, he stood up and said to them, "Let him who is without sin among you be the first to throw a stone at her." [8] And once more he bent down and wrote on the ground. [9] But when they heard it, they went away one by one, beginning with the older ones, and Jesus was left alone with the woman standing before him. [10] Jesus stood up and said to her, "Woman, where are they? Has no one condemned you?" [11] She said, "No one, Lord." And Jesus said, "Neither do I condemn you; go, and from now on sin no more."]]

I Am the Light of the World

[12] Again Jesus spoke to them, saying, "I am the light of the world. Whoever follows me will not walk in darkness, but will have the light of life." [13] So the Pharisees said to him, "You are bearing witness about yourself; your testimony is not true." [14] Jesus answered, "Even if I do bear witness about myself, my testimony is true, for I know where I came from and where I am going, but you do not know where I come from or where I am going. [15] You judge according to the flesh; I judge no one. [16] Yet even if I do judge, my judgment is true, for it is not I alone who judge, but I and the Father[2] who sent me. [17] In your Law it is written that the testimony of two people is true. [18] I am the one who bears witness about myself, and the Father who sent me bears witness about me." [19] They said to him therefore, "Where is your Father?" Jesus answered, "You know neither me nor my Father. If you knew me, you would know my Father also." [20] These words he spoke in the treasury, as he taught in the temple; but no one arrested him, because his hour had not yet come.

[21] So he said to them again, "I am going away, and you will seek me, and you will die in your sin. Where I am going, you cannot come." [22] So the Jews said, "Will he kill himself, since he says, 'Where I am going, you cannot come'?" [23] He said to them, "You are from below; I am from above. You are of this world; I am not of this world. [24] I told you that you would die in your sins, for unless you believe that I am he you will die in your sins." [25] So they said to him, "Who are you?" Jesus said to them, "Just what I have been telling you from the beginning. [26] I have much to say about you and much to judge, but he who sent me is true, and I declare to the world what I have heard from him." [27] They did not understand that he had been speaking to them about the Father. [28] So Jesus said to them, "When you have lifted up the Son of Man, then you will know that I am he, and that I do nothing on my own authority, but speak just as the Father taught me. [29] And he who sent me is with me. He has not left me alone, for I always do the things that are pleasing to him." [30] As he was saying these things, many believed in him.

The Truth Will Set You Free

[31] So Jesus said to the Jews who had believed him, "If you abide in my word, you are truly my disciples, [32] and you will know the truth, and the truth will set you free." [33] They answered him, "We are offspring of Abraham and have never been enslaved to anyone. How is it that you say, 'You will become free'?"

[34] Jesus answered them, "Truly, truly, I say to you, everyone who practices sin is a slave[3] to sin. [35] The slave does not remain in the house forever; the son remains forever. [36] So if the Son sets you free, you will be free indeed. [37] I know that you are offspring of Abraham; yet you seek to kill me because my word finds no place in you. [38] I speak of what I have seen with my Father, and you do what you have heard from your father."

You Are of Your Father the Devil

[39] They answered him, "Abraham is our father." Jesus said to them, "If you were Abraham's children, you would be doing the

---

[1] Some manuscripts do not include 7:53–8:11; others add the passage here or after 7:36 or after 21:25 or after Luke 21:38, with variations in the text [2] Some manuscripts *he* [3] For the contextual rendering of the Greek word *doulos*, see Preface; also verse 35

works Abraham did, ⁴⁰but now you seek to kill me, a man who has told you the truth that I heard from God. This is not what Abraham did. ⁴¹You are doing the works your father did." They said to him, "We were not born of sexual immorality. We have one Father—even God." ⁴²Jesus said to them, "If God were your Father, you would love me, for I came from God and I am here. I came not of my own accord, but he sent me. ⁴³Why do you not understand what I say? It is because you cannot bear to hear my word. ⁴⁴You are of your father the devil, and your will is to do your father's desires. He was a murderer from the beginning, and does not stand in the truth, because there is no truth in him. When he lies, he speaks out of his own character, for he is a liar and the father of lies. ⁴⁵But because I tell the truth, you do not believe me. ⁴⁶Which one of you convicts me of sin? If I tell the truth, why do you not believe me? ⁴⁷Whoever is of God hears the words of God. The reason why you do not hear them is that you are not of God."

Before Abraham Was, I Am

⁴⁸The Jews answered him, "Are we not right in saying that you are a Samaritan and have a demon?" ⁴⁹Jesus answered, "I do not have a demon, but I honor my Father, and you dishonor me. ⁵⁰Yet I do not seek my own glory; there is One who seeks it, and he is the judge. ⁵¹Truly, truly, I say to you, if anyone keeps my word, he will never see death." ⁵²The Jews said to him, "Now we know that you have a demon! Abraham died, as did the prophets, yet you say, 'If anyone keeps my word, he will never taste death.' ⁵³Are you greater than our father Abraham, who died? And the prophets died! Who do you make yourself out to be?" ⁵⁴Jesus answered, "If I glorify myself, my glory is nothing. It is my Father who glorifies me, of whom you say, 'He is our God.'¹ ⁵⁵But you have not known him. If I were to say that I do not know him, I would be a liar like you, but I do know him and I keep his word. ⁵⁶Your father Abraham rejoiced that he would see my day. He saw it and was glad." ⁵⁷So the Jews said to him, "You are not yet fifty years old, and have you seen Abraham?"² ⁵⁸Jesus said to them, "Truly, truly, I say to you, before Abraham was, I am." ⁵⁹So they picked up stones to throw at

him, but Jesus hid himself and went out of the temple.

Jesus Heals a Man Born Blind

9 As he passed by, he saw a man blind from birth. ²And his disciples asked him, "Rabbi, who sinned, this man or his parents, that he was born blind?" ³Jesus answered, "It was not that this man sinned, or his parents, but that the works of God might be displayed in him. ⁴We must work the works of him who sent me while it is day; night is coming, when no one can work. ⁵As long as I am in the world, I am the light of the world." ⁶Having said these things, he spit on the ground and made mud with the saliva. Then he anointed the man's eyes with the mud ⁷and said to him, "Go, wash in the pool of Siloam" (which means Sent). So he went and washed and came back seeing.

⁸The neighbors and those who had seen him before as a beggar were saying, "Is this not the man who used to sit and beg?" ⁹Some said, "It is he." Others said, "No, but he is like him." He kept saying, "I am the man." ¹⁰So they said to him, "Then how were your eyes opened?" ¹¹He answered, "The man called Jesus made mud and anointed my eyes and said to me, 'Go to Siloam and wash.' So I went and washed and received my sight." ¹²They said to him, "Where is he?" He said, "I do not know."

¹³They brought to the Pharisees the man who had formerly been blind. ¹⁴Now it was a Sabbath day when Jesus made the mud and opened his eyes. ¹⁵So the Pharisees again asked him how he had received his sight. And he said to them, "He put mud on my eyes, and I washed, and I see." ¹⁶Some of the Pharisees said, "This man is not from God, for he does not keep the Sabbath." But others said, "How can a man who is a sinner do such signs?" And there was a division among them. ¹⁷So they said again to the blind man, "What do you say about him, since he has opened your eyes?" He said, "He is a prophet."

¹⁸The Jews³ did not believe that he had been blind and had received his sight, until they called the parents of the man who had received his sight ¹⁹and asked them, "Is this your son, who you say was born blind? How then does he now see?" ²⁰His parents answered, "We know that this is our son and that he was born blind. ²¹But how he now sees we do not know, nor do we know who opened his eyes. Ask him; he is of age. He will speak for himself." ²²(His parents

---

¹ Some manuscripts *your God* ² Some manuscripts *has Abraham seen you?* ³ Greek *Ioudaioi* probably refers here to Jewish religious leaders, and others under their influence, in that time; also verse 22

said these things because they feared the Jews, for the Jews had already agreed that if anyone should confess Jesus[1] to be Christ, he was to be put out of the synagogue.) ²³ Therefore his parents said, "He is of age; ask him."

²⁴ So for the second time they called the man who had been blind and said to him, "Give glory to God. We know that this man is a sinner." ²⁵ He answered, "Whether he is a sinner I do not know. One thing I do know, that though I was blind, now I see." ²⁶ They said to him, "What did he do to you? How did he open your eyes?" ²⁷ He answered them, "I have told you already, and you would not listen. Why do you want to hear it again? Do you also want to become his disciples?" ²⁸ And they reviled him, saying, "You are his disciple, but we are disciples of Moses. ²⁹ We know that God has spoken to Moses, but as for this man, we do not know where he comes from." ³⁰ The man answered, "Why, this is an amazing thing! You do not know where he comes from, and yet he opened my eyes. ³¹ We know that God does not listen to sinners, but if anyone is a worshiper of God and does his will, God listens to him. ³² Never since the world began has it been heard that anyone opened the eyes of a man born blind. ³³ If this man were not from God, he could do nothing." ³⁴ They answered him, "You were born in utter sin, and would you teach us?" And they cast him out.

³⁵ Jesus heard that they had cast him out, and having found him he said, "Do you believe in the Son of Man?"[2] ³⁶ He answered, "And who is he, sir, that I may believe in him?" ³⁷ Jesus said to him, "You have seen him, and it is he who is speaking to you." ³⁸ He said, "Lord, I believe," and he worshiped him. ³⁹ Jesus said, "For judgment I came into this world, that those who do not see may see, and those who see may become blind." ⁴⁰ Some of the Pharisees near him heard these things, and said to him, "Are we also blind?" ⁴¹ Jesus said to them, "If you were blind, you would have no guilt;[3] but now that you say, 'We see,' your guilt remains.

I Am the Good Shepherd

10 "Truly, truly, I say to you, he who does not enter the sheepfold by the door but climbs in by another way, that man is a thief and a robber. ²But he who enters by the door is the shepherd of the sheep. ³To him the gate-keeper opens. The sheep hear his voice, and he calls his own sheep by name and leads them out. ⁴When he has brought out all his own, he goes before them, and the sheep follow him, for they know his voice. ⁵A stranger they will not follow, but they will flee from him, for they do not know the voice of strangers." ⁶This figure of speech Jesus used with them, but they did not understand what he was saying to them.

⁷So Jesus again said to them, "Truly, truly, I say to you, I am the door of the sheep. ⁸All who came before me are thieves and robbers, but the sheep did not listen to them. ⁹I am the door. If anyone enters by me, he will be saved and will go in and out and find pasture. ¹⁰The thief comes only to steal and kill and destroy. I came that they may have life and have it abundantly. ¹¹I am the good shepherd. The good shepherd lays down his life for the sheep. ¹²He who is a hired hand and not a shepherd, who does not own the sheep, sees the wolf coming and leaves the sheep and flees, and the wolf snatches them and scatters them. ¹³He flees because he is a hired hand and cares nothing for the sheep. ¹⁴I am the good shepherd. I know my own and my own know me, ¹⁵just as the Father knows me and I know the Father; and I lay down my life for the sheep. ¹⁶And I have other sheep that are not of this fold. I must bring them also, and they will listen to my voice. So there will be one flock, one shepherd. ¹⁷For this reason the Father loves me, because I lay down my life that I may take it up again. ¹⁸No one takes it from me, but I lay it down of my own accord. I have authority to lay it down, and I have authority to take it up again. This charge I have received from my Father."

¹⁹There was again a division among the Jews because of these words. ²⁰Many of them said, "He has a demon, and is insane; why listen to him?" ²¹Others said, "These are not the words of one who is oppressed by a demon. Can a demon open the eyes of the blind?"

I and the Father Are One

²²At that time the Feast of Dedication took place at Jerusalem. It was winter, ²³and Jesus was walking in the temple, in the colonnade of Solomon. ²⁴So the Jews gathered around him and said to him, "How long will you keep us in suspense? If you are the Christ, tell us plainly." ²⁵Jesus answered them, "I told you, and you do not believe. The works that I do in my Father's

---

[1] Greek him [2] Some manuscripts the Son of God [3] Greek you would not have sin

name bear witness about me, [26]but you do not believe because you are not among my sheep. [27]My sheep hear my voice, and I know them, and they follow me. [28]I give them eternal life, and they will never perish, and no one will snatch them out of my hand. [29]My Father, who has given them to me,[1] is greater than all, and no one is able to snatch them out of the Father's hand. [30]I and the Father are one."

[31]The Jews picked up stones again to stone him. [32]Jesus answered them, "I have shown you many good works from the Father; for which of them are you going to stone me?" [33]The Jews answered him, "It is not for a good work that we are going to stone you but for blasphemy, because you, being a man, make yourself God." [34]Jesus answered them, "Is it not written in your Law, "I said, you are gods'? [35]If he called them gods to whom the word of God came—and Scripture cannot be broken— [36]do you say of him whom the Father consecrated and sent into the world, 'You are blaspheming,' because I said, 'I am the Son of God'? [37]If I am not doing the works of my Father, then do not believe me; [38]but if I do them, even though you do not believe me, believe the works, that you may know and understand that the Father is in me and I am in the Father." [39]Again they sought to arrest him, but he escaped from their hands.

[40]He went away again across the Jordan to the place where John had been baptizing at first, and there he remained. [41]And many came to him. And they said, "John did no sign, but everything that John said about this man was true." [42]And many believed in him there.

The Death of Lazarus

11 Now a certain man was ill, Lazarus of Bethany, the village of Mary and her sister Martha. [2]It was Mary who anointed the Lord with ointment and wiped his feet with her hair, whose brother Lazarus was ill. [3]So the sisters sent to him, saying, "Lord, he whom you love is ill." [4]But when Jesus heard it he said, "This illness does not lead to death. It is for the glory of God, so that the Son of God may be glorified through it."

[5]Now Jesus loved Martha and her sister and Lazarus. [6]So, when he heard that Lazarus[2] was ill, he stayed two days longer in the place where he was. [7]Then after this he said to the disciples, "Let us go to Judea again." [8]The disciples said to him, "Rabbi, the Jews were just

now seeking to stone you, and are you going there again?" [9]Jesus answered, "Are there not twelve hours in the day? If anyone walks in the day, he does not stumble, because he sees the light of this world. [10]But if anyone walks in the night, he stumbles, because the light is not in him." [11]After saying these things, he said to them, "Our friend Lazarus has fallen asleep, but I go to awaken him." [12]The disciples said to him, "Lord, if he has fallen asleep, he will recover." [13]Now Jesus had spoken of his death, but they thought that he meant taking rest in sleep. [14]Then Jesus told them plainly, "Lazarus has died, [15]and for your sake I am glad that I was not there, so that you may believe. But let us go to him." [16]So Thomas, called the Twin,[3] said to his fellow disciples, "Let us also go, that we may die with him."

I Am the Resurrection and the Life

[17]Now when Jesus came, he found that Lazarus had already been in the tomb four days. [18]Bethany was near Jerusalem, about two miles[4] off, [19]and many of the Jews had come to Martha and Mary to console them concerning their brother. [20]So when Martha heard that Jesus was coming, she went and met him, but Mary remained seated in the house. [21]Martha said to Jesus, "Lord, if you had been here, my brother would not have died. [22]But even now I know that whatever you ask from God, God will give you." [23]Jesus said to her, "Your brother will rise again." [24]Martha said to him, "I know that he will rise again in the resurrection on the last day." [25]Jesus said to her, "I am the resurrection and the life.[5] Whoever believes in me, though he die, yet shall he live, [26]and everyone who lives and believes in me shall never die. Do you believe this?" [27]She said to him, "Yes, Lord; I believe that you are the Christ, the Son of God, who is coming into the world."

Jesus Weeps

[28]When she had said this, she went and called her sister Mary, saying in private, "The Teacher is here and is calling for you." [29]And when she heard it, she rose quickly and went to him. [30]Now Jesus had not yet come into the village, but was still in the place where Martha had met him. [31]When the Jews who were with her in the house, consoling her, saw Mary rise quickly and go out, they followed her, supposing that she was going to the tomb to weep

---

[1] Some manuscripts *What my Father has given to me* [2] Greek *he*; also verse 17 [3] Greek *Didymus* [4] Greek *fifteen stadia*; a *stadion* was about 607 feet or 185 meters [5] Some manuscripts omit *and the life* [a] Ps. 82:6

there. ³²Now when Mary came to where Jesus was and saw him, she fell at his feet, saying to him, "Lord, if you had been here, my brother would not have died." ³³When Jesus saw her weeping, and the Jews who had come with her also weeping, he was deeply moved[1] in his spirit and greatly troubled. ³⁴And he said, "Where have you laid him?" They said to him, "Lord, come and see." ³⁵Jesus wept. ³⁶So the Jews said, "See how he loved him!" ³⁷But some of them said, "Could not he who opened the eyes of the blind man also have kept this man from dying?"

Jesus Raises Lazarus

³⁸Then Jesus, deeply moved again, came to the tomb. It was a cave, and a stone lay against it. ³⁹Jesus said, "Take away the stone." Martha, the sister of the dead man, said to him, "Lord, by this time there will be an odor, for he has been dead four days." ⁴⁰Jesus said to her, "Did I not tell you that if you believed you would see the glory of God?" ⁴¹So they took away the stone. And Jesus lifted up his eyes and said, "Father, I thank you that you have heard me. ⁴²I knew that you always hear me, but I said this on account of the people standing around, that they may believe that you sent me." ⁴³When he had said these things, he cried out with a loud voice, "Lazarus, come out." ⁴⁴The man who had died came out, his hands and feet bound with linen strips, and his face wrapped with a cloth. Jesus said to them, "Unbind him, and let him go."

The Plot to Kill Jesus

⁴⁵Many of the Jews therefore, who had come with Mary and had seen what he did, believed in him, ⁴⁶but some of them went to the Pharisees and told them what Jesus had done. ⁴⁷So the chief priests and the Pharisees gathered the council and said, "What are we to do? For this man performs many signs. ⁴⁸If we let him go on like this, everyone will believe in him, and the Romans will come and take away both our place and our nation." ⁴⁹But one of them, Caiaphas, who was high priest that year, said to them, "You know nothing at all. ⁵⁰Nor do you understand that it is better for you that one man should die for the people, not that the whole nation should perish." ⁵¹He did not say this of his own accord, but being high priest that year

he prophesied that Jesus would die for the nation, ⁵²and not for the nation only, but also to gather into one the children of God who are scattered abroad. ⁵³So from that day on they made plans to put him to death.

⁵⁴Jesus therefore no longer walked openly among the Jews, but went from there to the region near the wilderness, to a town called Ephraim, and there he stayed with the disciples.

⁵⁵Now the Passover of the Jews was at hand, and many went up from the country to Jerusalem before the Passover to purify themselves. ⁵⁶They were looking for[2] Jesus and saying to one another as they stood in the temple, "What do you think? That he will not come to the feast at all?" ⁵⁷Now the chief priests and the Pharisees had given orders that if anyone knew where he was, he should let them know, so that they might arrest him.

Mary Anoints Jesus at Bethany

12 Six days before the Passover, Jesus therefore came to Bethany, where Lazarus was, whom Jesus had raised from the dead. ²So they gave a dinner for him there. Martha served, and Lazarus was one of those reclining with him at table. ³Mary therefore took a pound[3] of expensive ointment made from pure nard, and anointed the feet of Jesus and wiped his feet with her hair. The house was filled with the fragrance of the perfume. ⁴But Judas Iscariot, one of his disciples (he who was about to betray him), said, ⁵"Why was this ointment not sold for three hundred denarii[4] and given to the poor?" ⁶He said this, not because he cared about the poor, but because he was a thief, and having charge of the moneybag he used to help himself to what was put into it. ⁷Jesus said, "Leave her alone, so that she may keep it[5] for the day of my burial. ⁸For the poor you always have with you, but you do not always have me."

The Plot to Kill Lazarus

⁹When the large crowd of the Jews learned that Jesus[6] was there, they came, not only on account of him but also to see Lazarus, whom he had raised from the dead. ¹⁰So the chief priests made plans to put Lazarus to death as well, ¹¹because on account of him many of the Jews were going away and believing in Jesus.

---

¹ Or *was indignant; also verse 38* ² Greek *were seeking for* ³ Greek *litra; a litra* (or Roman pound) was equal to about 11 1/2 ounces or 327 grams ⁴ A *denarius* was a day's wage for a laborer ⁵ Or *Leave her alone; she intended to keep it* ⁶ Greek *he*

The Triumphal Entry

¹²The next day ᵃthe large crowd that had come to the feast heard that Jesus was coming to Jerusalem. ¹³So they took branches of palm trees and went out to meet him, crying out, "Hosanna! Blessed is he who comes in the name of the Lord, even the King of Israel!" ¹⁴And Jesus found a young donkey and sat on it, just as it is written,

¹⁵ ᵇ"Fear not, daughter of Zion;
  behold, your king is coming,
    sitting on a donkey's colt!"

¹⁶His disciples did not understand these things at first, but when Jesus was glorified, then they remembered that these things had been written about him and had been done to him. ¹⁷The crowd that had been with him when he called Lazarus out of the tomb and raised him from the dead continued to bear witness. ¹⁸The reason why the crowd went to meet him was that they heard he had done this sign. ¹⁹So the Pharisees said to one another, "You see that you are gaining nothing. Look, the world has gone after him."

Some Greeks Seek Jesus

²⁰Now among those who went up to worship at the feast were some Greeks. ²¹So these came to Philip, who was from Bethsaida in Galilee, and asked him, "Sir, we wish to see Jesus." ²²Philip went and told Andrew; Andrew and Philip went and told Jesus. ²³And Jesus answered them, "The hour has come for the Son of Man to be glorified. ²⁴Truly, truly, I say to you, unless a grain of wheat falls into the earth and dies, it remains alone; but if it dies, it bears much fruit. ²⁵Whoever loves his life loses it, and whoever hates his life in this world will keep it for eternal life. ²⁶If anyone serves me, he must follow me; and where I am, there will my servant be also. If anyone serves me, the Father will honor him.

The Son of Man Must Be Lifted Up

²⁷"Now is my soul troubled. And what shall I say? 'Father, save me from this hour'? But for this purpose I have come to this hour. ²⁸Father, glorify your name." Then a voice came from heaven: "I have glorified it, and I will glorify it again." ²⁹The crowd that stood there and heard it said that it had thundered. Others said, "An angel has spoken to him." ³⁰Jesus answered, "This voice has come for your sake, not mine.

³¹Now is the judgment of this world; now will the ruler of this world be cast out. ³²And I, when I am lifted up from the earth, will draw all people to myself." ³³He said this to show by what kind of death he was going to die. ³⁴So the crowd answered him, "We have heard from the Law that the Christ remains forever. How can you say that the Son of Man must be lifted up? Who is this Son of Man?" ³⁵So Jesus said to them, "The light is among you for a little while longer. Walk while you have the light, lest darkness overtake you. The one who walks in the darkness does not know where he is going. ³⁶While you have the light, believe in the light, that you may become sons of light."

The Unbelief of the People

When Jesus had said these things, he departed and hid himself from them. ³⁷Though he had done so many signs before them, they still did not believe in him, ³⁸so that the word spoken by the prophet Isaiah might be fulfilled:

ᶜ"Lord, who has believed what he heard
  from us,
    and to whom has the arm of the Lord
    been revealed?"

³⁹Therefore they could not believe. For again Isaiah said,

⁴⁰ ᵈ"He has blinded their eyes
    and hardened their heart,
  lest they see with their eyes,
    and understand with their heart, and
    turn,
    and I would heal them."

⁴¹Isaiah said these things because he saw his glory and spoke of him. ⁴²Nevertheless, many even of the authorities believed in him, but for fear of the Pharisees they did not confess it, so that they would not be put out of the synagogue; ⁴³for they loved the glory that comes from man more than the glory that comes from God.

Jesus Came to Save the World

⁴⁴And Jesus cried out and said, "Whoever believes in me, believes not in me but in him who sent me. ⁴⁵And whoever sees me sees him who sent me. ⁴⁶I have come into the world as light, so that whoever believes in me may not remain in darkness. ⁴⁷If anyone hears my words and does not keep them, I do not judge him; for I did not come to judge the world but to save the world. ⁴⁸The one who rejects me and does

ᵃFor 12:12-15 see parallels Matt. 21:4-9; Mark 11:7-10; Luke 19:35-38 ᵇZech. 9:9 ᶜIsa. 53:1 ᵈIsa. 6:10

not receive my words has a judge; the word that I have spoken will judge him on the last day. [49]For I have not spoken on my own authority, but the Father who sent me has himself given me a commandment—what to say and what to speak. [50]And I know that his commandment is eternal life. What I say, therefore, I say as the Father has told me."

Jesus Washes the Disciples' Feet

13 Now before the Feast of the Passover, when Jesus knew that his hour had come to depart out of this world to the Father, having loved his own who were in the world, he loved them to the end. [2]During supper, when the devil had already put it into the heart of Judas Iscariot, Simon's son, to betray him, [3]Jesus, knowing that the Father had given all things into his hands, and that he had come from God and was going back to God, [4]rose from supper. He laid aside his outer garments, and taking a towel, tied it around his waist. [5]Then he poured water into a basin and began to wash the disciples' feet and to wipe them with the towel that was wrapped around him. [6]He came to Simon Peter, who said to him, "Lord, do you wash my feet?" [7]Jesus answered him, "What I am doing you do not understand now, but afterward you will understand." [8]Peter said to him, "You shall never wash my feet." Jesus answered him, "If I do not wash you, you have no share with me." [9]Simon Peter said to him, "Lord, not my feet only but also my hands and my head!" [10]Jesus said to him, "The one who has bathed does not need to wash, except for his feet,[1] but is completely clean. And you[2] are clean, but not every one of you." [11]For he knew who was to betray him; that was why he said, "Not all of you are clean."

[12]When he had washed their feet and put on his outer garments and resumed his place, he said to them, "Do you understand what I have done to you? [13]You call me Teacher and Lord, and you are right, for so I am. [14]If I then, your Lord and Teacher, have washed your feet, you also ought to wash one another's feet. [15]For I have given you an example, that you also should do just as I have done to you. [16]Truly, truly, I say to you, a servant[3] is not greater than his master, nor is a messenger greater than the one who sent him. [17]If you know these things, blessed are you if you do them. [18]I am not speaking of all of you; I know whom I have

chosen. But the Scripture will be fulfilled,[4] [a]'He who ate my bread has lifted his heel against me.' [19]I am telling you this now, before it takes place, that when it does take place you may believe that I am he. [20]Truly, truly, I say to you, whoever receives the one I send receives me, and whoever receives me receives the one who sent me."

One of You Will Betray Me

[21]After saying these things, Jesus was troubled in his spirit, and testified, "Truly, truly, I say to you, one of you will betray me." [22]The disciples looked at one another, uncertain of whom he spoke. [23]One of his disciples, whom Jesus loved, was reclining at table at Jesus' side,[5] [24]so Simon Peter motioned to him to ask Jesus[6] of whom he was speaking. [25]So that disciple, leaning back against Jesus, said to him, "Lord, who is it?" [26]Jesus answered, "It is he to whom I will give this morsel of bread when I have dipped it." So when he had dipped the morsel, he gave it to Judas, the son of Simon Iscariot. [27]Then after he had taken the morsel, Satan entered into him. Jesus said to him, "What you are going to do, do quickly." [28]Now no one at the table knew why he said this to him. [29]Some thought that, because Judas had the moneybag, Jesus was telling him, "Buy what we need for the feast," or that he should give something to the poor. [30]So, after receiving the morsel of bread, he immediately went out. And it was night.

A New Commandment

[31]When he had gone out, Jesus said, "Now is the Son of Man glorified, and God is glorified in him. [32]If God is glorified in him, God will also glorify him in himself, and glorify him at once. [33]Little children, yet a little while I am with you. You will seek me, and just as I said to the Jews, so now I also say to you, 'Where I am going you cannot come.' [34]A new commandment I give to you, that you love one another: just as I have loved you, you also are to love one another. [35]By this all people will know that you are my disciples, if you have love for one another."

Jesus Foretells Peter's Denial

[36]Simon Peter said to him, "Lord, where are you going?" Jesus answered him, "Where I am going you cannot follow me now, but you will follow afterward." [37]Peter said to him, "Lord, why can I not follow you now? I will lay down

---

[1] Some manuscripts omit *except for his feet* [2] The Greek words for *you* in this verse are plural [3] Or *bondservant*, or *slave* (for the contextual rendering of the Greek word *doulos*, see Preface) [4] Greek *But in order that the Scripture may be fulfilled* [5] Greek *in the bosom of Jesus* [6] Greek lacks *Jesus* [a] Ps. 41:9

my life for you." [38]Jesus answered, "Will you lay down your life for me? Truly, truly, I say to you, the rooster will not crow till you have denied me three times.

I Am the Way, and the Truth, and the Life

14 "Let not your hearts be troubled. Believe in God;[1] believe also in me. [2]In my Father's house are many rooms. If it were not so, would I have told you that I go to prepare a place for you?[2] [3]And if I go and prepare a place for you, I will come again and will take you to myself, that where I am you may be also. [4]And you know the way to where I am going."[3] [5]Thomas said to him, "Lord, we do not know where you are going. How can we know the way?" [6]Jesus said to him, "I am the way, and the truth, and the life. No one comes to the Father except through me. [7]If you had known me, you would have known my Father also.[4] From now on you do know him and have seen him."

[8]Philip said to him, "Lord, show us the Father, and it is enough for us." [9]Jesus said to him, "Have I been with you so long, and you still do not know me, Philip? Whoever has seen me has seen the Father. How can you say, 'Show us the Father'? [10]Do you not believe that I am in the Father and the Father is in me? The words that I say to you I do not speak on my own authority, but the Father who dwells in me does his works. [11]Believe me that I am in the Father and the Father is in me, or else believe on account of the works themselves.

[12]"Truly, truly, I say to you, whoever believes in me will also do the works that I do; and greater works than these will he do, because I am going to the Father. [13]Whatever you ask in my name, this I will do, that the Father may be glorified in the Son. [14]If you ask me[5] anything in my name, I will do it.

Jesus Promises the Holy Spirit

[15]"If you love me, you will keep my commandments. [16]And I will ask the Father, and he will give you another Helper,[6] to be with you forever, [17]even the Spirit of truth, whom the world cannot receive, because it neither sees him nor knows him. You know him, for he dwells with you and will be[7] in you.

[18]"I will not leave you as orphans; I will come to you. [19]Yet a little while and the world will see me no more, but you will see me. Because I live, you also will live. [20]In that day you will know that I am in my Father, and you in me, and I in you. [21]Whoever has my commandments and keeps them, he it is who loves me. And he who loves me will be loved by my Father, and I will love him and manifest myself to him." [22]Judas (not Iscariot) said to him, "Lord, how is it that you will manifest yourself to us, and not to the world?" [23]Jesus answered him, "If anyone loves me, he will keep my word, and my Father will love him, and we will come to him and make our home with him. [24]Whoever does not love me does not keep my words. And the word that you hear is not mine but the Father's who sent me.

[25]"These things I have spoken to you while I am still with you. [26]But the Helper, the Holy Spirit, whom the Father will send in my name, he will teach you all things and bring to your remembrance all that I have said to you. [27]Peace I leave with you; my peace I give to you. Not as the world gives do I give to you. Let not your hearts be troubled, neither let them be afraid. [28]You heard me say to you, 'I am going away, and I will come to you.' If you loved me, you would have rejoiced, because I am going to the Father, for the Father is greater than I. [29]And now I have told you before it takes place, so that when it does take place you may believe. [30]I will no longer talk much with you, for the ruler of this world is coming. He has no claim on me, [31]but I do as the Father has commanded me, so that the world may know that I love the Father. Rise, let us go from here.

I Am the True Vine

15 "I am the true vine, and my Father is the vinedresser. [2]Every branch in me that does not bear fruit he takes away, and every branch that does bear fruit he prunes, that it may bear more fruit. [3]Already you are clean because of the word that I have spoken to you. [4]Abide in me, and I in you. As the branch cannot bear fruit by itself, unless it abides in the vine, neither can you, unless you abide in me. [5]I am the vine; you are the branches. Whoever abides in me and I in him, he it is that bears much fruit, for apart from me you can do nothing. [6]If anyone does not abide in me he is thrown away like a branch and withers; and the branches are gathered, thrown into the fire, and burned. [7]If you abide in me, and my words abide in you, ask whatever you wish, and it will be done for you. [8]By this my Father is glorified,

---

[1] Or You believe in God [2] Or In my Father's house are many rooms; if it were not so, I would have told you; for I go to prepare a place for you [3] Some manuscripts Where I am going you know, and the way you know [4] Or If you know me, you will know my Father also, or, If you have known me, you will know my Father also [5] Some manuscripts omit me [6] Or Advocate, or Counselor; also 14:26; 15:26; 16:7 [7] Some manuscripts and is

that you bear much fruit and so prove to be my disciples. [9]As the Father has loved me, so have I loved you. Abide in my love. [10]If you keep my commandments, you will abide in my love, just as I have kept my Father's commandments and abide in his love. [11]These things I have spoken to you, that my joy may be in you, and that your joy may be full.

[12]"This is my commandment, that you love one another as I have loved you. [13]Greater love has no one than this, that someone lay down his life for his friends. [14]You are my friends if you do what I command you. [15]No longer do I call you servants,[1] for the servant does not know what his master is doing; but I have called you friends, for all that I have heard from my Father I have made known to you. [16]You did not choose me, but I chose you and appointed you that you should go and bear fruit and that your fruit should abide, so that whatever you ask the Father in my name, he may give it to you. [17]These things I command you, so that you will love one another.

The Hatred of the World

[18]"If the world hates you, know that it has hated me before it hated you. [19]If you were of the world, the world would love you as its own; but because you are not of the world, but I chose you out of the world, therefore the world hates you. [20]Remember the word that I said to you: 'A servant is not greater than his master.' If they persecuted me, they will also persecute you. If they kept my word, they will also keep yours. [21]But all these things they will do to you on account of my name, because they do not know him who sent me. [22]If I had not come and spoken to them, they would not have been guilty of sin,[2] but now they have no excuse for their sin. [23]Whoever hates me hates my Father also. [24]If I had not done among them the works that no one else did, they would not be guilty of sin, but now they have seen and hated both me and my Father. [25]But the word that is written in their Law must be fulfilled: [a]'They hated me without a cause.'

[26]"But when the Helper comes, whom I will send to you from the Father, the Spirit of truth, who proceeds from the Father, he will bear witness about me. [27]And you also will bear witness, because you have been with me from the beginning.

16
"I have said all these things to you to keep you from falling away. [2]They will put you out of the synagogues. Indeed, the hour is coming when whoever kills you will think he is offering service to God. [3]And they will do these things because they have not known the Father, nor me. [4]But I have said these things to you, that when their hour comes you may remember that I told them to you.

The Work of the Holy Spirit

"I did not say these things to you from the beginning, because I was with you. [5]But now I am going to him who sent me, and none of you asks me, 'Where are you going?' [6]But because I have said these things to you, sorrow has filled your heart. [7]Nevertheless, I tell you the truth: it is to your advantage that I go away, for if I do not go away, the Helper will not come to you. But if I go, I will send him to you. [8]And when he comes, he will convict the world concerning sin and righteousness and judgment: [9]concerning sin, because they do not believe in me; [10]concerning righteousness, because I go to the Father, and you will see me no longer; [11]concerning judgment, because the ruler of this world is judged.

[12]"I still have many things to say to you, but you cannot bear them now. [13]When the Spirit of truth comes, he will guide you into all the truth, for he will not speak on his own authority, but whatever he hears he will speak, and he will declare to you the things that are to come. [14]He will glorify me, for he will take what is mine and declare it to you. [15]All that the Father has is mine; therefore I said that he will take what is mine and declare it to you.

Your Sorrow Will Turn into Joy

[16]"A little while, and you will see me no longer; and again a little while, and you will see me." [17]So some of his disciples said to one another, "What is this that he says to us, 'A little while, and you will not see me, and again a little while, and you will see me'; and, 'because I am going to the Father'?" [18]So they were saying, "What does he mean by 'a little while'? We do not know what he is talking about." [19]Jesus knew that they wanted to ask him, so he said to them, "Is this what you are asking yourselves, what I meant by saying, 'A little while and you will not see me, and again a little while and you will see me'? [20]Truly, truly, I say to you, you will weep and lament, but the world will rejoice. You will be sorrowful, but your sorrow will turn into joy. [21]When a woman is giving birth, she has sorrow because her hour has come, but when she has

---

[1] Or bondservants, or slaves (for the contextual rendering of the Greek word doulos, see Preface); likewise for servant later in this verse and in verse 20 [2] Greek they would not have sin; also verse 24 [a]Ps. 35:19 or 69:4

delivered the baby, she no longer remembers the anguish, for joy that a human being has been born into the world. ²²So also you have sorrow now, but I will see you again, and your hearts will rejoice, and no one will take your joy from you. ²³In that day you will ask nothing of me. Truly, truly, I say to you, whatever you ask of the Father in my name, he will give it to you. ²⁴Until now you have asked nothing in my name. Ask, and you will receive, that your joy may be full.

I Have Overcome the World

²⁵"I have said these things to you in figures of speech. The hour is coming when I will no longer speak to you in figures of speech but will tell you plainly about the Father. ²⁶In that day you will ask in my name, and I do not say to you that I will ask the Father on your behalf; ²⁷for the Father himself loves you, because you have loved me and have believed that I came from God.[1] ²⁸I came from the Father and have come into the world, and now I am leaving the world and going to the Father."

²⁹His disciples said, "Ah, now you are speaking plainly and not using figurative speech! ³⁰Now we know that you know all things and do not need anyone to question you; this is why we believe that you came from God." ³¹Jesus answered them, "Do you now believe? ³²Behold, the hour is coming, indeed it has come, when you will be scattered, each to his own home, and will leave me alone. Yet I am not alone, for the Father is with me. ³³I have said these things to you, that in me you may have peace. In the world you will have tribulation. But take heart; I have overcome the world."

The High Priestly Prayer

17 When Jesus had spoken these words, he lifted up his eyes to heaven, and said, "Father, the hour has come; glorify your Son that the Son may glorify you, ²since you have given him authority over all flesh, to give eternal life to all whom you have given him. ³And this is eternal life, that they know you, the only true God, and Jesus Christ whom you have sent. ⁴I glorified you on earth, having accomplished the work that you gave me to do. ⁵And now, Father, glorify me in your own presence with the glory that I had with you before the world existed.

⁶"I have manifested your name to the people whom you gave me out of the world. Yours they were, and you gave them to me, and they have kept your word. ⁷Now they know that everything that you have given me is from you. ⁸For I have given them the words that you gave me, and they have received them and have come to know in truth that I came from you; and they have believed that you sent me. ⁹I am praying for them. I am not praying for the world but for those whom you have given me, for they are yours. ¹⁰All mine are yours, and yours are mine, and I am glorified in them. ¹¹And I am no longer in the world, but they are in the world, and I am coming to you. Holy Father, keep them in your name, which you have given me, that they may be one, even as we are one. ¹²While I was with them, I kept them in your name, which you have given me. I have guarded them, and not one of them has been lost except the son of destruction, that the Scripture might be fulfilled. ¹³But now I am coming to you, and these things I speak in the world, that they may have my joy fulfilled in themselves. ¹⁴I have given them your word, and the world has hated them because they are not of the world, just as I am not of the world. ¹⁵I do not ask that you take them out of the world, but that you keep them from the evil one.[2] ¹⁶They are not of the world, just as I am not of the world. ¹⁷Sanctify them[3] in the truth; your word is truth. ¹⁸As you sent me into the world, so I have sent them into the world. ¹⁹And for their sake I consecrate myself,[4] that they also may be sanctified[5] in truth.

²⁰"I do not ask for these only, but also for those who will believe in me through their word, ²¹that they may all be one, just as you, Father, are in me, and I in you, that they also may be in us, so that the world may believe that you have sent me. ²²The glory that you have given me I have given to them, that they may be one even as we are one, ²³I in them and you in me, that they may become perfectly one, so that the world may know that you sent me and loved them even as you loved me. ²⁴Father, I desire that they also, whom you have given me, may be with me where I am, to see my glory that you have given me because you loved me before the foundation of the world. ²⁵O righteous Father, even though the world does not know you, I know you, and these know that you have sent me. ²⁶I made known to them your name, and I will continue to make it known, that the love with which you have loved me may be in them, and I in them."

---

[1] Some manuscripts *from the Father* [2] Or *from evil* [3] Greek *Set them apart* (for holy service to God) [4] Or *I sanctify myself*; or *I set myself apart* (for holy service to God) [5] Greek *may be set apart* (for holy service to God)

Betrayal and Arrest of Jesus

18 When Jesus had spoken these words, he went out with his disciples across the brook Kidron, where there was a garden, which he and his disciples entered. ²Now Judas, who betrayed him, also knew the place, for Jesus often met there with his disciples. ³ªSo Judas, having procured a band of soldiers and some officers from the chief priests and the Pharisees, went there with lanterns and torches and weapons. ⁴Then Jesus, knowing all that would happen to him, came forward and said to them, "Whom do you seek?" ⁵They answered him, "Jesus of Nazareth." Jesus said to them, "I am he."¹ Judas, who betrayed him, was standing with them. ⁶When Jesus² said to them, "I am he," they drew back and fell to the ground. ⁷So he asked them again, "Whom do you seek?" And they said, "Jesus of Nazareth." ⁸Jesus answered, "I told you that I am he. So, if you seek me, let these men go." ⁹This was to fulfill the word that he had spoken: "Of those whom you gave me I have lost not one." ¹⁰Then Simon Peter, having a sword, drew it and struck the high priest's servant³ and cut off his right ear. (The servant's name was Malchus.) ¹¹So Jesus said to Peter, "Put your sword into its sheath; shall I not drink the cup that the Father has given me?"

Jesus Faces Annas and Caiaphas

¹²So the band of soldiers and their captain and the officers of the Jews⁴ arrested Jesus and bound him. ¹³First they led him to Annas, for he was the father-in-law of Caiaphas, who was high priest that year. ¹⁴It was Caiaphas who had advised the Jews that it would be expedient that one man should die for the people.

Peter Denies Jesus

¹⁵Simon Peter followed Jesus, and so did another disciple. Since that disciple was known to the high priest, he entered with Jesus into the courtyard of the high priest, ¹⁶ᵇbut Peter stood outside at the door. So the other disciple, who was known to the high priest, went out and spoke to the servant girl who kept watch at the door, and brought Peter in. ¹⁷The servant girl at the door said to Peter, "You also are not one of this man's disciples, are you?" He said, "I am not." ¹⁸Now the servants⁵ and officers had made a charcoal fire, because it was cold, and they were standing and warming themselves. Peter also was with them, standing and warming himself.

The High Priest Questions Jesus

¹⁹The high priest then questioned Jesus about his disciples and his teaching. ²⁰Jesus answered him, "I have spoken openly to the world. I have always taught in synagogues and in the temple, where all Jews come together. I have said nothing in secret. ²¹Why do you ask me? Ask those who have heard me what I said to them; they know what I said." ²²When he had said these things, one of the officers standing by struck Jesus with his hand, saying, "Is that how you answer the high priest?" ²³Jesus answered him, "If what I said is wrong, bear witness about the wrong; but if what I said is right, why do you strike me?" ²⁴Annas then sent him bound to Caiaphas the high priest.

Peter Denies Jesus Again

²⁵ᶜNow Simon Peter was standing and warming himself. So they said to him, "You also are not one of his disciples, are you?" He denied it and said, "I am not." ²⁶One of the servants of the high priest, a relative of the man whose ear Peter had cut off, asked, "Did I not see you in the garden with him?" ²⁷Peter again denied it, and at once a rooster crowed.

Jesus Before Pilate

²⁸Then they led Jesus from the house of Caiaphas to the governor's headquarters.⁶ It was early morning. They themselves did not enter the governor's headquarters, so that they would not be defiled, but could eat the Passover. ²⁹ᵈSo Pilate went outside to them and said, "What accusation do you bring against this man?" ³⁰They answered him, "If this man were not doing evil, we would not have delivered him over to you." ³¹Pilate said to them, "Take him yourselves and judge him by your own law." The Jews said to him, "It is not lawful for us to put anyone to death." ³²This was to fulfill the word that Jesus had spoken to show by what kind of death he was going to die.

My Kingdom Is Not of This World

³³So Pilate entered his headquarters again and called Jesus and said to him, "Are you the King of the Jews?" ³⁴Jesus answered, "Do you say this of your own accord, or did others

---

¹ Greek I am; also verses 6, 8 ² Greek he ³ Or bondservant; twice in this verse ⁴ Greek Ioudaioi probably refers here to Jewish religious leaders, and others under their influence, in that time; also verses 14, 31, 36, 38 ⁵ Or bondservants; also verse 26 ⁶ Greek the praetorium ªFor 18:3-11 see parallels Matt. 26:47-56; Mark 14:43-50; Luke 22:47-53 ᵇFor 18:16-18 see parallels Matt. 26:69, 70; Mark 14:66-68; Luke 22:55-57 ᶜFor 18:25-27 see parallels Matt. 26:71-75; Mark 14:69-72; Luke 22:58-62 ᵈFor 18:29-38 see parallels Matt. 27:11-14; Mark 15:1-5; Luke 23:1-3

say it to you about me?" [35] Pilate answered, "Am I a Jew? Your own nation and the chief priests have delivered you over to me. What have you done?" [36] Jesus answered, "My kingdom is not of this world. If my kingdom were of this world, my servants would have been fighting, that I might not be delivered over to the Jews. But my kingdom is not from the world." [37] Then Pilate said to him, "So you are a king?" Jesus answered, "You say that I am a king. For this purpose I was born and for this purpose I have come into the world—to bear witness to the truth. Everyone who is of the truth listens to my voice." [38] Pilate said to him, "What is truth?"

After he had said this, he went back outside to the Jews and told them, "I find no guilt in him. [39] [a] But you have a custom that I should release one man for you at the Passover. So do you want me to release to you the King of the Jews?" [40] They cried out again, "Not this man, but Barabbas!" Now Barabbas was a robber.[1]

Jesus Delivered to Be Crucified

19 Then Pilate took Jesus and flogged him. [2] And the soldiers twisted together a crown of thorns and put it on his head and arrayed him in a purple robe. [3] They came up to him, saying, "Hail, King of the Jews!" and struck him with their hands. [4] Pilate went out again and said to them, "See, I am bringing him out to you that you may know that I find no guilt in him." [5] So Jesus came out, wearing the crown of thorns and the purple robe. Pilate said to them, "Behold the man!" [6] When the chief priests and the officers saw him, they cried out, "Crucify him, crucify him!" Pilate said to them, "Take him yourselves and crucify him, for I find no guilt in him." [7] The Jews[2] answered him, "We have a law, and according to that law he ought to die because he has made himself the Son of God." [8] When Pilate heard this statement, he was even more afraid. [9] He entered his headquarters again and said to Jesus, "Where are you from?" But Jesus gave him no answer. [10] So Pilate said to him, "You will not speak to me? Do you not know that I have authority to release you and authority to crucify you?" [11] Jesus answered him, "You would have no authority over me at all unless it had been given you from above. Therefore he who delivered me over to you has the greater sin."

[12] From then on Pilate sought to release him, but the Jews cried out, "If you release this man, you are not Caesar's friend. Everyone who makes himself a king opposes Caesar." [13] So when Pilate heard these words, he brought Jesus out and sat down on the judgment seat at a place called The Stone Pavement, and in Aramaic[3] Gabbatha. [14] Now it was the day of Preparation of the Passover. It was about the sixth hour.[4] He said to the Jews, "Behold your King!" [15] They cried out, "Away with him, away with him, crucify him!" Pilate said to them, "Shall I crucify your King?" The chief priests answered, "We have no king but Caesar." [16] So he delivered him over to them to be crucified.

The Crucifixion

So they took Jesus, [17] and he went out, bearing his own cross, to the place called The Place of a Skull, which in Aramaic is called Golgotha. [18] There they crucified him, and with him two others, one on either side, and Jesus between them. [19] Pilate also wrote an inscription and put it on the cross. It read, "Jesus of Nazareth, the King of the Jews." [20] Many of the Jews read this inscription, for the place where Jesus was crucified was near the city, and it was written in Aramaic, in Latin, and in Greek. [21] So the chief priests of the Jews said to Pilate, "Do not write, 'The King of the Jews,' but rather, 'This man said, I am King of the Jews.'" [22] Pilate answered, "What I have written I have written."

[23] When the soldiers had crucified Jesus, they took his garments and divided them into four parts, one part for each soldier; also his tunic.[5] But the tunic was seamless, woven in one piece from top to bottom, [24] so they said to one another, "Let us not tear it, but cast lots for it to see whose it shall be." This was to fulfill the Scripture which says,

> [b]"They divided my garments among them,
>   and for my clothing they cast lots."

So the soldiers did these things, [25] but standing by the cross of Jesus were his mother and his mother's sister, Mary the wife of Clopas, and Mary Magdalene. [26] When Jesus saw his mother and the disciple whom he loved standing nearby, he said to his mother, "Woman, behold, your son!" [27] Then he said to the disciple, "Behold, your mother!" And from that hour the disciple took her to his own home.

---

[1] Or *an insurrectionist* [2] Greek *Ioudaioi* probably refers here to Jewish religious leaders, and others under their influence, in that time; also verses 12, 14, 31, 38 [3] Or *Hebrew*; also verses 17, 20 [4] That is, about noon [5] Greek *chiton*, a long garment worn under the cloak next to the skin [a] For 18:39, 40 see parallels Matt. 27:15-18, 20-23; Mark 15:6-14; Luke 23:18-23 [b] Ps. 22:18

The Death of Jesus

[28] After this, Jesus, knowing that all was now finished, said (to fulfill the Scripture), "I thirst." [29] A jar full of sour wine stood there, so they put a sponge full of the sour wine on a hyssop branch and held it to his mouth. [30] When Jesus had received the sour wine, he said, "It is finished," and he bowed his head and gave up his spirit.

Jesus' Side Is Pierced

[31] Since it was the day of Preparation, and so that the bodies would not remain on the cross on the Sabbath (for that Sabbath was a high day), the Jews asked Pilate that their legs might be broken and that they might be taken away. [32] So the soldiers came and broke the legs of the first, and of the other who had been crucified with him. [33] But when they came to Jesus and saw that he was already dead, they did not break his legs. [34] But one of the soldiers pierced his side with a spear, and at once there came out blood and water. [35] He who saw it has borne witness—his testimony is true, and he knows that he is telling the truth—that you also may believe. [36] For these things took place that the Scripture might be fulfilled: [a] "Not one of his bones will be broken." [37] And again another Scripture says, [b] "They will look on him whom they have pierced."

Jesus Is Buried

[38] [c] After these things Joseph of Arimathea, who was a disciple of Jesus, but secretly for fear of the Jews, asked Pilate that he might take away the body of Jesus, and Pilate gave him permission. So he came and took away his body. [39] Nicodemus also, who earlier had come to Jesus[1] by night, came bringing a mixture of myrrh and aloes, about seventy-five pounds[2] in weight. [40] So they took the body of Jesus and bound it in linen cloths with the spices, as is the burial custom of the Jews. [41] Now in the place where he was crucified there was a garden, and in the garden a new tomb in which no one had yet been laid. [42] So because of the Jewish day of Preparation, since the tomb was close at hand, they laid Jesus there.

The Resurrection

20 Now on the first day of the week Mary Magdalene came to the tomb early, while it was still dark, and saw that the stone had been taken away from the tomb. [2] So she ran and went to Simon Peter and the other disciple, the one whom Jesus loved, and said to them, "They have taken the Lord out of the tomb, and we do not know where they have laid him." [3] So Peter went out with the other disciple, and they were going toward the tomb. [4] Both of them were running together, but the other disciple outran Peter and reached the tomb first. [5] And stooping to look in, he saw the linen cloths lying there, but he did not go in. [6] Then Simon Peter came, following him, and went into the tomb. He saw the linen cloths lying there, [7] and the face cloth, which had been on Jesus' head, not lying with the linen cloths but folded up in a place by itself. [8] Then the other disciple, who had reached the tomb first, also went in, and he saw and believed; [9] for as yet they did not understand the Scripture, that he must rise from the dead. [10] Then the disciples went back to their homes.

Jesus Appears to Mary Magdalene

[11] But Mary stood weeping outside the tomb, and as she wept she stooped to look into the tomb. [12] And she saw two angels in white, sitting where the body of Jesus had lain, one at the head and one at the feet. [13] They said to her, "Woman, why are you weeping?" She said to them, "They have taken away my Lord, and I do not know where they have laid him." [14] Having said this, she turned around and saw Jesus standing, but she did not know that it was Jesus. [15] Jesus said to her, "Woman, why are you weeping? Whom are you seeking?" Supposing him to be the gardener, she said to him, "Sir, if you have carried him away, tell me where you have laid him, and I will take him away." [16] Jesus said to her, "Mary." She turned and said to him in Aramaic,[4] "Rabboni!" (which means Teacher). [17] Jesus said to her, "Do not cling to me, for I have not yet ascended to the Father; but go to my brothers and say to them, 'I am ascending to my Father and your Father, to my God and your God.'" [18] Mary Magdalene went and announced to the disciples, "I have seen the Lord"—and that he had said these things to her.

Jesus Appears to the Disciples

[19] On the evening of that day, the first day of the week, the doors being locked where the disciples were for fear of the Jews,[5] Jesus came and stood among them and said to them, "Peace be with you." [20] When he had said this, he showed

[1] Greek him [2] Greek one hundred litras; a litra (or Roman pound) was equal to about 11 1/2 ounces or 327 grams [3] Greek his [4] Or Hebrew [5] Greek Ioudaioi probably refers here to Jewish religious leaders, and others under their influence, in that time [a] Ex. 12:46; Num. 9:12 [b] Zech. 12:10 [c] For 19:38-42 see parallels Matt. 27:57-61; Mark 15:42-47; Luke 23:50-56

them his hands and his side. Then the disciples were glad when they saw the Lord. ²¹Jesus said to them again, "Peace be with you. As the Father has sent me, even so I am sending you." ²²And when he had said this, he breathed on them and said to them, "Receive the Holy Spirit. ²³If you forgive the sins of any, they are forgiven them; if you withhold forgiveness from any, it is withheld."

Jesus and Thomas

²⁴Now Thomas, one of the twelve, called the Twin,¹ was not with them when Jesus came. ²⁵So the other disciples told him, "We have seen the Lord." But he said to them, "Unless I see in his hands the mark of the nails, and place my finger into the mark of the nails, and place my hand into his side, I will never believe." ²⁶Eight days later, his disciples were inside again, and Thomas was with them. Although the doors were locked, Jesus came and stood among them and said, "Peace be with you." ²⁷Then he said to Thomas, "Put your finger here, and see my hands; and put out your hand, and place it in my side. Do not disbelieve, but believe." ²⁸Thomas answered him, "My Lord and my God!" ²⁹Jesus said to him, "Have you believed because you have seen me? Blessed are those who have not seen and yet have believed."

The Purpose of This Book

³⁰Now Jesus did many other signs in the presence of the disciples, which are not written in this book; ³¹but these are written so that you may believe that Jesus is the Christ, the Son of God, and that by believing you may have life in his name.

Jesus Appears to Seven Disciples

21 After this Jesus revealed himself again to the disciples by the Sea of Tiberias, and he revealed himself in this way. ²Simon Peter, Thomas (called the Twin), Nathanael of Cana in Galilee, the sons of Zebedee, and two others of his disciples were together. ³Simon Peter said to them, "I am going fishing." They said to him, "We will go with you." They went out and got into the boat, but that night they caught nothing.

⁴Just as day was breaking, Jesus stood on the shore; yet the disciples did not know that it was Jesus. ⁵Jesus said to them, "Children, do you have any fish?" They answered him, "No." ⁶He said

to them, "Cast the net on the right side of the boat, and you will find some." So they cast it, and now they were not able to haul it in, because of the quantity of fish. ⁷That disciple whom Jesus loved therefore said to Peter, "It is the Lord!" When Simon Peter heard that it was the Lord, he put on his outer garment, for he was stripped for work, and threw himself into the sea. ⁸The other disciples came in the boat, dragging the net full of fish, for they were not far from the land, but about a hundred yards² off.

⁹When they got out on land, they saw a charcoal fire in place, with fish laid out on it, and bread. ¹⁰Jesus said to them, "Bring some of the fish that you have just caught." ¹¹So Simon Peter went aboard and hauled the net ashore, full of large fish, 153 of them. And although there were so many, the net was not torn. ¹²Jesus said to them, "Come and have breakfast." Now none of the disciples dared ask him, "Who are you?" They knew it was the Lord. ¹³Jesus came and took the bread and gave it to them, and so with the fish. ¹⁴This was now the third time that Jesus was revealed to the disciples after he was raised from the dead.

Jesus and Peter

¹⁵When they had finished breakfast, Jesus said to Simon Peter, "Simon, son of John, do you love me more than these?" He said to him, "Yes, Lord; you know that I love you." He said to him, "Feed my lambs." ¹⁶He said to him a second time, "Simon, son of John, do you love me?" He said to him, "Yes, Lord; you know that I love you." He said to him, "Tend my sheep." ¹⁷He said to him the third time, "Simon, son of John, do you love me?" Peter was grieved because he said to him the third time, "Do you love me?" and he said to him, "Lord, you know everything; you know that I love you." Jesus said to him, "Feed my sheep. ¹⁸Truly, truly, I say to you, when you were young, you used to dress yourself and walk wherever you wanted, but when you are old, you will stretch out your hands, and another will dress you and carry you where you do not want to go." ¹⁹(This he said to show by what kind of death he was to glorify God.) And after saying this he said to him, "Follow me."

Jesus and the Beloved Apostle

²⁰Peter turned and saw the disciple whom Jesus loved following them, the one who also

¹ Greek Didymus ² Greek two hundred cubits; a cubit was about 18 inches or 45 centimeters

had leaned back against him during the supper and had said, "Lord, who is it that is going to betray you?" 21 When Peter saw him, he said to Jesus, "Lord, what about this man?" 22 Jesus said to him, "If it is my will that he remain until I come, what is that to you? You follow me!" 23 So the saying spread abroad among the brothers[1] that this disciple was not to die; yet Jesus did not say to him that he was not to die, but, "If

it is my will that he remain until I come, what is that to you?"

24 This is the disciple who is bearing witness about these things, and who has written these things, and we know that his testimony is true.

25 Now there are also many other things that Jesus did. Were every one of them to be written, I suppose that the world itself could not contain the books that would be written.

THE
ACTS
OF THE APOSTLES

The Promise of the Holy Spirit

1 In the first book, O Theophilus, I have dealt with all that Jesus began to do and teach, ²until the day when he was taken up, after he had given commands through the Holy Spirit to the apostles whom he had chosen. ³He presented himself alive to them after his suffering by many proofs, appearing to them during forty days and speaking about the kingdom of God.

⁴And while staying[1] with them he ordered them not to depart from Jerusalem, but to wait for the promise of the Father, which, he said, "you heard from me; ⁵for John baptized with water, but you will be baptized with[2] the Holy Spirit not many days from now."

The Ascension

⁶So when they had come together, they asked him, "Lord, will you at this time restore the kingdom to Israel?" ⁷He said to them, "It is not for you to know times or seasons that the Father has fixed by his own authority. ⁸But you will receive power when the Holy Spirit has come upon you, and you will be my witnesses in Jerusalem and in all Judea and Samaria, and to the end of the earth." ⁹And when he had said these things, as they were looking on, he was lifted up, and a cloud took him out of their sight. ¹⁰And while they were gazing into heaven as he went, behold, two men stood by them in white robes, ¹¹and said, "Men of Galilee, why do you stand looking into heaven? This Jesus, who was taken up from you into heaven, will come in the same way as you saw him go into heaven."

Matthias Chosen to Replace Judas

¹²Then they returned to Jerusalem from the mount called Olivet, which is near Jerusalem, a Sabbath day's journey away. ¹³And when they had entered, they went up to the upper room, where they were staying, Peter and John and James and Andrew, Philip and Thomas, Bartholomew and Matthew, James the son of Alphaeus and Simon the Zealot and Judas the son of James. ¹⁴All these with one accord were devoting themselves to prayer, together with the women and Mary the mother of Jesus, and his brothers.[3]

¹⁵In those days Peter stood up among the brothers (the company of persons was in all about 120) and said, ¹⁶"Brothers, the Scripture had to be fulfilled, which the Holy Spirit spoke beforehand by the mouth of David concerning Judas, who became a guide to those who arrested Jesus. ¹⁷For he was numbered among us and was allotted his share in this ministry." ¹⁸(Now this man acquired a field with the reward of his wickedness, and falling headlong[4] he burst open in the middle and all his bowels gushed out. ¹⁹And it became known to all the inhabitants of Jerusalem, so that the field was called in their own language Akeldama, that is, Field of Blood.) ²⁰"For it is written in the Book of Psalms,

> [a]"'May his camp become desolate,
>   and let there be no one to dwell in it';

and

> [b]"'Let another take his office.'

²¹So one of the men who have accompanied us during all the time that the Lord Jesus went in and out among us, ²²beginning from the baptism of John until the day when he was taken up from us—one of these men must become with us a witness to his resurrection." ²³And they put forward two, Joseph called Barsabbas, who was also called Justus, and Matthias. ²⁴And they prayed and said, "You, Lord, who know the hearts of all, show which one of these two you have chosen ²⁵to take the place in this ministry and apostleship from which Judas turned aside to go to his own place." ²⁶And they cast lots for them, and the lot fell on Matthias, and he was numbered with the eleven apostles.

The Coming of the Holy Spirit

2 When the day of Pentecost arrived, they were all together in one place. ²And suddenly there came from heaven a sound like a mighty rushing wind, and it filled the entire house where they were sitting. ³And divided tongues as of fire appeared to them and rested[5] on each one of them. ⁴And they were all filled with the Holy Spirit and began to speak in other tongues as the Spirit gave them utterance.

---

[1] Or eating [2] Or in [3] Or brothers and sisters. In New Testament usage, depending on the context, the plural Greek word adelphoi (translated "brothers") may refer either to brothers or to brothers and sisters; also verse 15 [4] Or swelling up [5] Or And tongues as of fire appeared to them, distributed among them, and rested [a] Ps. 69:25 [b] Ps. 109:8

⁵ Now there were dwelling in Jerusalem Jews, devout men from every nation under heaven. ⁶ And at this sound the multitude came together, and they were bewildered, because each one was hearing them speak in his own language. ⁷ And they were amazed and astonished, saying, "Are not all these who are speaking Galileans? ⁸ And how is it that we hear, each of us in his own native language? ⁹ Parthians and Medes and Elamites and residents of Mesopotamia, Judea and Cappadocia, Pontus and Asia, ¹⁰ Phrygia and Pamphylia, Egypt and the parts of Libya belonging to Cyrene, and visitors from Rome, ¹¹ both Jews and proselytes, Cretans and Arabians— we hear them telling in our own tongues the mighty works of God." ¹² And all were amazed and perplexed, saying to one another, "What does this mean?" ¹³ But others mocking said, "They are filled with new wine."

Peter's Sermon at Pentecost

¹⁴ But Peter, standing with the eleven, lifted up his voice and addressed them: "Men of Judea and all who dwell in Jerusalem, let this be known to you, and give ear to my words. ¹⁵ For these people are not drunk, as you suppose, since it is only the third hour of the day.¹ ¹⁶ But this is what was uttered through the prophet Joel:

¹⁷ ᵃ " 'And in the last days it shall be, God declares,
that I will pour out my Spirit on all flesh,
and your sons and your daughters shall prophesy,
and your young men shall see visions,
and your old men shall dream dreams;
¹⁸ even on my male servants and female servants
in those days I will pour out my Spirit,
and they shall prophesy.
¹⁹ And I will show wonders in the heavens above
and signs on the earth below,
blood, and fire, and vapor of smoke;
²⁰ the sun shall be turned to darkness
and the moon to blood,
before the day of the Lord comes, the great and magnificent day.
²¹ And it shall come to pass that everyone who calls upon the name of the Lord shall be saved.'

²² "Men of Israel, hear these words: Jesus of Nazareth, a man attested to you by God with mighty works and wonders and signs that God did through him in your midst, as you yourselves know— ²³ this Jesus,² delivered up according to the definite plan and foreknowledge of God, you crucified and killed by the hands of lawless men. ²⁴ God raised him up, loosing the pangs of death, because it was not possible for him to be held by it. ²⁵ For David says concerning him,

ᵇ " 'I saw the Lord always before me,
for he is at my right hand that I may not be shaken;
²⁶ therefore my heart was glad, and my tongue rejoiced;
my flesh also will dwell in hope.
²⁷ For you will not abandon my soul to Hades,
or let your Holy One see corruption.
²⁸ You have made known to me the paths of life;
you will make me full of gladness with your presence.'

²⁹ "Brothers, I may say to you with confidence about the patriarch David that he both died and was buried, and his tomb is with us to this day. ³⁰ Being therefore a prophet, and knowing that God had sworn with an oath to him that he would set one of his descendants on his throne, ³¹ he foresaw and spoke about the resurrection of the Christ, that he was not abandoned to Hades, nor did his flesh see corruption. ³² This Jesus God raised up, and of that we all are witnesses. ³³ Being therefore exalted at the right hand of God, and having received from the Father the promise of the Holy Spirit, he has poured out this that you yourselves are seeing and hearing. ³⁴ For David did not ascend into the heavens, but he himself says,

ᶜ " 'The Lord said to my Lord,
"Sit at my right hand,
³⁵   until I make your enemies your footstool." '

³⁶ Let all the house of Israel therefore know for certain that God has made him both Lord and Christ, this Jesus whom you crucified."

³⁷ Now when they heard this they were cut to the heart, and said to Peter and the rest of the apostles, "Brothers, what shall we do?" ³⁸ And Peter said to them, "Repent and be baptized every one of you in the name of Jesus Christ for

¹ That is, 9 A.M. ² Greek *this one* ᵃ Joel 2:28-32 ᵇ Ps. 16:8-11 ᶜ Ps. 110:1

the forgiveness of your sins, and you will receive the gift of the Holy Spirit. [39] For the promise is for you and for your children and for all who are far off, everyone whom the Lord our God calls to himself." [40] And with many other words he bore witness and continued to exhort them, saying, "Save yourselves from this crooked generation." [41] So those who received his word were baptized, and there were added that day about three thousand souls.

The Fellowship of the Believers

[42] And they devoted themselves to the apostles' teaching and the fellowship, to the breaking of bread and the prayers. [43] And awe[1] came upon every soul, and many wonders and signs were being done through the apostles. [44] And all who believed were together and had all things in common. [45] And they were selling their possessions and belongings and distributing the proceeds to all, as any had need. [46] And day by day, attending the temple together and breaking bread in their homes, they received their food with glad and generous hearts, [47] praising God and having favor with all the people. And the Lord added to their number day by day those who were being saved.

The Lame Beggar Healed

3 Now Peter and John were going up to the temple at the hour of prayer, the ninth hour.[2] [2] And a man lame from birth was being carried, whom they laid daily at the gate of the temple that is called the Beautiful Gate to ask alms of those entering the temple. [3] Seeing Peter and John about to go into the temple, he asked to receive alms. [4] And Peter directed his gaze at him, as did John, and said, "Look at us." [5] And he fixed his attention on them, expecting to receive something from them. [6] But Peter said, "I have no silver and gold, but what I do have I give to you. In the name of Jesus Christ of Nazareth, rise up and walk!" [7] And he took him by the right hand and raised him up, and immediately his feet and ankles were made strong. [8] And leaping up, he stood and began to walk, and entered the temple with them, walking and leaping and praising God. [9] And all the people saw him walking and praising God, [10] and recognized him as the one who sat at the Beautiful Gate of the temple, asking for alms. And they were filled with wonder and amazement at what had happened to him.

Peter Speaks in Solomon's Portico

[11] While he clung to Peter and John, all the people, utterly astounded, ran together to them in the portico called Solomon's. [12] And when Peter saw it he addressed the people: "Men of Israel, why do you wonder at this, or why do you stare at us, as though by our own power or piety we have made him walk? [13] The God of Abraham, the God of Isaac, and the God of Jacob, the God of our fathers, glorified his servant[3] Jesus, whom you delivered over and denied in the presence of Pilate, when he had decided to release him. [14] But you denied the Holy and Righteous One, and asked for a murderer to be granted to you, [15] and you killed the Author of life, whom God raised from the dead. To this we are witnesses. [16] And his name—by faith in his name—has made this man strong whom you see and know, and the faith that is through Jesus[4] has given the man this perfect health in the presence of you all.

[17] "And now, brothers, I know that you acted in ignorance, as did also your rulers. [18] But what God foretold by the mouth of all the prophets, that his Christ would suffer, he thus fulfilled. [19] Repent therefore, and turn back, that your sins may be blotted out, [20] that times of refreshing may come from the presence of the Lord, and that he may send the Christ appointed for you, Jesus, [21] whom heaven must receive until the time for restoring all the things about which God spoke by the mouth of his holy prophets long ago. [22] Moses said, 'The Lord God will raise up for you [a]a prophet like me from your brothers. You shall listen to him in whatever he tells you. [23] And it shall be that every soul who does not listen to that prophet shall be destroyed from the people.' [24] And all the prophets who have spoken, from Samuel and those who came after him, also proclaimed these days. [25] You are the sons of the prophets and of the covenant that God made with your fathers, saying to Abraham, [b]'And in your offspring shall all the families of the earth be blessed.' [26] God, having raised up his servant, sent him to you first, to bless you by turning every one of you from your wickedness."

Peter and John Before the Council

4 And as they were speaking to the people, the priests and the captain of the temple and the Sadducees came upon them, [2] greatly annoyed because they were teaching the people

---

[1] Or fear [2] That is, 3 P.M. [3] Or child; also verse 26 [4] Greek him [a] Deut. 18:15, 18, 19 [b] Gen. 22:18

and proclaiming in Jesus the resurrection from the dead. [3] And they arrested them and put them in custody until the next day, for it was already evening. [4] But many of those who had heard the word believed, and the number of the men came to about five thousand.

[5] On the next day their rulers and elders and scribes gathered together in Jerusalem, [6] with Annas the high priest and Caiaphas and John and Alexander, and all who were of the high-priestly family. [7] And when they had set them in the midst, they inquired, "By what power or by what name did you do this?" [8] Then Peter, filled with the Holy Spirit, said to them, "Rulers of the people and elders, [9] if we are being examined today concerning a good deed done to a crippled man, by what means this man has been healed, [10] let it be known to all of you and to all the people of Israel that by the name of Jesus Christ of Nazareth, whom you crucified, whom God raised from the dead—by him this man is standing before you well. [11] This Jesus[1] is the stone that was rejected by you, the builders, which has become the cornerstone.[2] [12] And there is salvation in no one else, for there is no other name under heaven given among men[3] by which we must be saved."

[13] Now when they saw the boldness of Peter and John, and perceived that they were uneducated, common men, they were astonished. And they recognized that they had been with Jesus. [14] But seeing the man who was healed standing beside them, they had nothing to say in opposition. [15] But when they had commanded them to leave the council, they conferred with one another, [16] saying, "What shall we do with these men? For that a notable sign has been performed through them is evident to all the inhabitants of Jerusalem, and we cannot deny it. [17] But in order that it may spread no further among the people, let us warn them to speak no more to anyone in this name." [18] So they called them and charged them not to speak or teach at all in the name of Jesus. [19] But Peter and John answered them, "Whether it is right in the sight of God to listen to you rather than to God, you must judge, [20] for we cannot but speak of what we have seen and heard." [21] And when they had further threatened them, they let them go, finding no way to punish them, because of the people, for all were praising God for what had happened. [22] For the man on whom this sign of healing was performed was more than forty years old.

The Believers Pray for Boldness

[23] When they were released, they went to their friends and reported what the chief priests and the elders had said to them. [24] And when they heard it, they lifted their voices together to God and said, "Sovereign Lord, who made the heaven and the earth and the sea and everything in them, [25] who through the mouth of our father David, your servant,[4] said by the Holy Spirit,

[a] "'Why did the Gentiles rage,
      and the peoples plot in vain?
[26]   The kings of the earth set themselves,
      and the rulers were gathered together,
         against the Lord and against his
            Anointed'[5]—

[27] for truly in this city there were gathered together against your holy servant Jesus, whom you anointed, both Herod and Pontius Pilate, along with the Gentiles and the peoples of Israel, [28] to do whatever your hand and your plan had predestined to take place. [29] And now, Lord, look upon their threats and grant to your servants to continue to speak your word with all boldness, [30] while you stretch out your hand to heal, and signs and wonders are performed through the name of your holy servant Jesus." [31] And when they had prayed, the place in which they were gathered together was shaken, and they were all filled with the Holy Spirit and continued to speak the word of God with boldness.

They Had Everything in Common

[32] Now the full number of those who believed were of one heart and soul, and no one said that any of the things that belonged to him was his own, but they had everything in common. [33] And with great power the apostles were giving their testimony to the resurrection of the Lord Jesus, and great grace was upon them all. [34] There was not a needy person among them, for as many as were owners of lands or houses sold them and brought the proceeds of what was sold [35] and laid it at the apostles' feet, and it was distributed to each as any had need. [36] Thus Joseph, who was also called by the apostles Barnabas (which means son of encouragement), a Levite, a native of Cyprus, [37] sold a field that belonged to him and brought the money and laid it at the apostles' feet.

---

[1] Greek This one [2] Greek the head of the corner [3] The Greek word anthropoi refers here to both men and women [4] Or child; also verses 27, 30 [5] Or Christ [a] Ps. 2:1, 2

Ananias and Sapphira

5 But a man named Ananias, with his wife Sapphira, sold a piece of property, ² and with his wife's knowledge he kept back for himself some of the proceeds and brought only a part of it and laid it at the apostles' feet. ³ But Peter said, "Ananias, why has Satan filled your heart to lie to the Holy Spirit and to keep back for yourself part of the proceeds of the land? ⁴ While it remained unsold, did it not remain your own? And after it was sold, was it not at your disposal? Why is it that you have contrived this deed in your heart? You have not lied to man but to God." ⁵ When Ananias heard these words, he fell down and breathed his last. And great fear came upon all who heard of it. ⁶ The young men rose and wrapped him up and carried him out and buried him.

⁷ After an interval of about three hours his wife came in, not knowing what had happened. ⁸ And Peter said to her, "Tell me whether you[1] sold the land for so much." And she said, "Yes, for so much." ⁹ But Peter said to her, "How is it that you have agreed together to test the Spirit of the Lord? Behold, the feet of those who have buried your husband are at the door, and they will carry you out." ¹⁰ Immediately she fell down at his feet and breathed her last. When the young men came in they found her dead, and they carried her out and buried her beside her husband. ¹¹ And great fear came upon the whole church and upon all who heard of these things.

Many Signs and Wonders Done

¹² Now many signs and wonders were regularly done among the people by the hands of the apostles. And they were all together in Solomon's Portico. ¹³ None of the rest dared join them, but the people held them in high esteem. ¹⁴ And more than ever believers were added to the Lord, multitudes of both men and women, ¹⁵ so that they even carried out the sick into the streets and laid them on cots and mats, that as Peter came by at least his shadow might fall on some of them. ¹⁶ The people also gathered from the towns around Jerusalem, bringing the sick and those afflicted with unclean spirits, and they were all healed.

The Apostles Arrested and Freed

¹⁷ But the high priest rose up, and all who were with him (that is, the party of the Sadducees), and filled with jealousy ¹⁸ they arrested the apostles and put them in the public prison. ¹⁹ But during the night an angel of the Lord opened the prison doors and brought them out, and said, ²⁰ "Go and stand in the temple and speak to the people all the words of this Life." ²¹ And when they heard this, they entered the temple at daybreak and began to teach.

Now when the high priest came, and those who were with him, they called together the council, all the senate of the people of Israel, and sent to the prison to have them brought. ²² But when the officers came, they did not find them in the prison, so they returned and reported, ²³ "We found the prison securely locked and the guards standing at the doors, but when we opened them we found no one inside." ²⁴ Now when the captain of the temple and the chief priests heard these words, they were greatly perplexed about them, wondering what this would come to. ²⁵ And someone came and told them, "Look! The men whom you put in prison are standing in the temple and teaching the people." ²⁶ Then the captain with the officers went and brought them, but not by force, for they were afraid of being stoned by the people.

²⁷ And when they had brought them, they set them before the council. And the high priest questioned them, ²⁸ saying, "We strictly charged you not to teach in this name, yet here you have filled Jerusalem with your teaching, and you intend to bring this man's blood upon us." ²⁹ But Peter and the apostles answered, "We must obey God rather than men. ³⁰ The God of our fathers raised Jesus, whom you killed by hanging him on a tree. ³¹ God exalted him at his right hand as Leader and Savior, to give repentance to Israel and forgiveness of sins. ³² And we are witnesses to these things, and so is the Holy Spirit, whom God has given to those who obey him."

³³ When they heard this, they were enraged and wanted to kill them. ³⁴ But a Pharisee in the council named Gamaliel, a teacher of the law held in honor by all the people, stood up and gave orders to put the men outside for a little while. ³⁵ And he said to them, "Men of Israel, take care what you are about to do with these men. ³⁶ For before these days Theudas rose up, claiming to be somebody, and a number of men, about four hundred, joined him. He was killed, and all who followed him were dispersed and came to nothing. ³⁷ After him Judas the Galilean rose up in the days of the census and drew away some of the people after him. He too perished,

---

[1] The Greek for you is plural here

and all who followed him were scattered. [38] So in the present case I tell you, keep away from these men and let them alone, for if this plan or this undertaking is of man, it will fail; [39] but if it is of God, you will not be able to overthrow them. You might even be found opposing God!" So they took his advice, [40] and when they had called in the apostles, they beat them and charged them not to speak in the name of Jesus, and let them go. [41] Then they left the presence of the council, rejoicing that they were counted worthy to suffer dishonor for the name. [42] And every day, in the temple and from house to house, they did not cease teaching and preaching that the Christ is Jesus.

Seven Chosen to Serve

6 Now in these days when the disciples were increasing in number, a complaint by the Hellenists[1] arose against the Hebrews because their widows were being neglected in the daily distribution. [2] And the twelve summoned the full number of the disciples and said, "It is not right that we should give up preaching the word of God to serve tables. [3] Therefore, brothers,[2] pick out from among you seven men of good repute, full of the Spirit and of wisdom, whom we will appoint to this duty. [4] But we will devote ourselves to prayer and to the ministry of the word." [5] And what they said pleased the whole gathering, and they chose Stephen, a man full of faith and of the Holy Spirit, and Philip, and Prochorus, and Nicanor, and Timon, and Parmenas, and Nicolaus, a proselyte of Antioch. [6] These they set before the apostles, and they prayed and laid their hands on them.

[7] And the word of God continued to increase, and the number of the disciples multiplied greatly in Jerusalem, and a great many of the priests became obedient to the faith.

Stephen Is Seized

[8] And Stephen, full of grace and power, was doing great wonders and signs among the people. [9] Then some of those who belonged to the synagogue of the Freedmen (as it was called), and of the Cyrenians, and of the Alexandrians, and of those from Cilicia and Asia, rose up and disputed with Stephen. [10] But they could not withstand the wisdom and the Spirit with which he was speaking. [11] Then they secretly instigated men who said, "We have heard him speak blasphemous words against Moses and

God." [12] And they stirred up the people and the elders and the scribes, and they came upon him and seized him and brought him before the council, [13] and they set up false witnesses who said, "This man never ceases to speak words against this holy place and the law, [14] for we have heard him say that this Jesus of Nazareth will destroy this place and will change the customs that Moses delivered to us." [15] And gazing at him, all who sat in the council saw that his face was like the face of an angel.

Stephen's Speech

7 And the high priest said, "Are these things so?" [2] And Stephen said:

"Brothers and fathers, hear me. The God of glory appeared to our father Abraham when he was in Mesopotamia, before he lived in Haran, [3] and said to him, ᵃ'Go out from your land and from your kindred and go into the land that I will show you.' [4] Then he went out from the land of the Chaldeans and lived in Haran. And after his father died, God removed him from there into this land in which you are now living. [5] Yet he gave him no inheritance in it, not even a foot's length, but promised to give it to him as a possession and to his offspring after him, though he had no child. [6] And God spoke to this effect—that ᵇhis offspring would be sojourners in a land belonging to others, who would enslave them and afflict them four hundred years. [7] 'But I will judge the nation that they serve,' said God, 'and after that they shall come out and worship me in this place.' [8] And he gave him the covenant of circumcision. And so Abraham became the father of Isaac, and circumcised him on the eighth day, and Isaac became the father of Jacob, and Jacob of the twelve patriarchs.

[9] "And the patriarchs, jealous of Joseph, sold him into Egypt; but God was with him [10] and rescued him out of all his afflictions and gave him favor and wisdom before Pharaoh, king of Egypt, who made him ruler over Egypt and over all his household. [11] Now there came a famine throughout all Egypt and Canaan, and great affliction, and our fathers could find no food. [12] But when Jacob heard that there was grain in Egypt, he sent out our fathers on their first visit. [13] And on the second visit Joseph made himself known to his brothers, and Joseph's family became known to

---

[1] That is, Greek-speaking Jews [2] Or brothers and sisters ᵃGen. 12:1 ᵇGen. 15:13, 14

Pharaoh. ¹⁴And Joseph sent and summoned Jacob his father and all his kindred, seventy-five persons in all. ¹⁵And Jacob went down into Egypt, and he died, he and our fathers, ¹⁶and they were carried back to Shechem and laid in the tomb that Abraham had bought for a sum of silver from the sons of Hamor in Shechem.

¹⁷"But as the time of the promise drew near, which God had granted to Abraham, the people increased and multiplied in Egypt ¹⁸until there arose over Egypt another king who did not know Joseph. ¹⁹He dealt shrewdly with our race and forced our fathers to expose their infants, so that they would not be kept alive. ²⁰At this time Moses was born; and he was beautiful in God's sight. And he was brought up for three months in his father's house, ²¹and when he was exposed, Pharaoh's daughter adopted him and brought him up as her own son. ²²And Moses was instructed in all the wisdom of the Egyptians, and he was mighty in his words and deeds.

²³"When he was forty years old, it came into his heart to visit his brothers, the children of Israel. ²⁴And seeing one of them being wronged, he defended the oppressed man and avenged him by striking down the Egyptian. ²⁵He supposed that his brothers would understand that God was giving them salvation by his hand, but they did not understand. ²⁶And on the following day he appeared to them as they were quarreling and tried to reconcile them, saying, 'Men, you are brothers. Why do you wrong each other?' ²⁷But the man who was wronging his neighbor thrust him aside, saying, 'Who made you a ruler and a judge over us? ²⁸Do you want to kill me as you killed the Egyptian yesterday?' ²⁹At this retort Moses fled and became an exile in the land of Midian, where he became the father of two sons.

³⁰"Now when forty years had passed, an angel appeared to him in the wilderness of Mount Sinai, in a flame of fire in a bush. ³¹When Moses saw it, he was amazed at the sight, and as he drew near to look, there came the voice of the Lord: ³²ᵃ'I am the God of your fathers, the God of Abraham and of Isaac and of Jacob.' And Moses trembled and did not dare to look. ³³Then the Lord said to him, 'Take off the sandals from your feet, for the place where you are standing is holy ground. ³⁴I have surely seen

the affliction of my people who are in Egypt, and have heard their groaning, and I have come down to deliver them. And now come, I will send you to Egypt.'

³⁵"This Moses, whom they rejected, saying, 'Who made you a ruler and a judge?'—this man God sent as both ruler and redeemer by the hand of the angel who appeared to him in the bush. ³⁶This man led them out, performing wonders and signs in Egypt and at the Red Sea and in the wilderness for forty years. ³⁷This is the Moses who said to the Israelites, 'God will raise up for you ᵇa prophet like me from your brothers.' ³⁸This is the one who was in the congregation in the wilderness with the angel who spoke to him at Mount Sinai, and with our fathers. He received living oracles to give to us. ³⁹Our fathers refused to obey him, but thrust him aside, and in their hearts they turned to Egypt, ⁴⁰saying to Aaron, ᶜ'Make for us gods who will go before us. As for this Moses who led us out from the land of Egypt, we do not know what has become of him.' ⁴¹And they made a calf in those days, and offered a sacrifice to the idol and were rejoicing in the works of their hands. ⁴²But God turned away and gave them over to worship the host of heaven, as it is written in the book of the prophets:

ᵈ"'Did you bring to me slain beasts and sacrifices,
    during the forty years in the wilderness,
    O house of Israel?
⁴³ You took up the tent of Moloch
    and the star of your god Rephan,
    the images that you made to worship;
and I will send you into exile beyond
    Babylon.'

⁴⁴"Our fathers had the tent of witness in the wilderness, just as he who spoke to Moses directed him to make it, according to the pattern that he had seen. ⁴⁵Our fathers in turn brought it in with Joshua when they dispossessed the nations that God drove out before our fathers. So it was until the days of David, ⁴⁶who found favor in the sight of God and asked to find a dwelling place for the God of Jacob.ˡ ⁴⁷But it was Solomon who built a house for him. ⁴⁸Yet the Most High does not dwell in houses made by hands, as the prophet says,

---

ˡ Some manuscripts *for the house of Jacob* ᵃ Ex. 3:6 ᵇ Deut. 18:15 ᶜ Ex. 32:1, 23 ᵈ Amos 5:25-27

[49] [a]" 'Heaven is my throne,
    and the earth is my footstool.
  What kind of house will you build for me,
      says the Lord,
    or what is the place of my rest?
[50]   Did not my hand make all these things?'

[51] "You stiff-necked people, uncircumcised in heart and ears, you always resist the Holy Spirit. As your fathers did, so do you. [52] Which of the prophets did your fathers not persecute? And they killed those who announced beforehand the coming of the Righteous One, whom you have now betrayed and murdered, [53] you who received the law as delivered by angels and did not keep it."

The Stoning of Stephen

[54] Now when they heard these things they were enraged, and they ground their teeth at him. [55] But he, full of the Holy Spirit, gazed into heaven and saw the glory of God, and Jesus standing at the right hand of God. [56] And he said, "Behold, I see the heavens opened, and the Son of Man standing at the right hand of God." [57] But they cried out with a loud voice and stopped their ears and rushed together[1] at him. [58] Then they cast him out of the city and stoned him. And the witnesses laid down their garments at the feet of a young man named Saul. [59] And as they were stoning Stephen, he called out, "Lord Jesus, receive my spirit." [60] And falling to his knees he cried out with a loud voice, "Lord, do not hold this sin against them." And when he had said this, he fell asleep.

Saul Ravages the Church

8 And Saul approved of his execution.
  And there arose on that day a great persecution against the church in Jerusalem, and they were all scattered throughout the regions of Judea and Samaria, except the apostles. [2] Devout men buried Stephen and made great lamentation over him. [3] But Saul was ravaging the church, and entering house after house, he dragged off men and women and committed them to prison.

Philip Proclaims Christ in Samaria

[4] Now those who were scattered went about preaching the word. [5] Philip went down to the city[2] of Samaria and proclaimed to them the Christ. [6] And the crowds with one accord paid attention to what was being said by Philip, when they heard him and saw the signs that he did. [7] For unclean spirits, crying out with a loud voice, came out of many who had them, and many who were paralyzed or lame were healed. [8] So there was much joy in that city.

Simon the Magician Believes

[9] But there was a man named Simon, who had previously practiced magic in the city and amazed the people of Samaria, saying that he himself was somebody great. [10] They all paid attention to him, from the least to the greatest, saying, "This man is the power of God that is called Great." [11] And they paid attention to him because for a long time he had amazed them with his magic. [12] But when they believed Philip as he preached good news about the kingdom of God and the name of Jesus Christ, they were baptized, both men and women. [13] Even Simon himself believed, and after being baptized he continued with Philip. And seeing signs and great miracles[3] performed, he was amazed.

[14] Now when the apostles at Jerusalem heard that Samaria had received the word of God, they sent to them Peter and John, [15] who came down and prayed for them that they might receive the Holy Spirit, [16] for he had not yet fallen on any of them, but they had only been baptized in the name of the Lord Jesus. [17] Then they laid their hands on them and they received the Holy Spirit. [18] Now when Simon saw that the Spirit was given through the laying on of the apostles' hands, he offered them money, [19] saying, "Give me this power also, so that anyone on whom I lay my hands may receive the Holy Spirit." [20] But Peter said to him, "May your silver perish with you, because you thought you could obtain the gift of God with money! [21] You have neither part nor lot in this matter, for your heart is not right before God. [22] Repent, therefore, of this wickedness of yours, and pray to the Lord that, if possible, the intent of your heart may be forgiven you. [23] For I see that you are in the gall[4] of bitterness and in the bond of iniquity." [24] And Simon answered, "Pray for me to the Lord, that nothing of what you have said may come upon me."

[25] Now when they had testified and spoken the word of the Lord, they returned to Jerusalem, preaching the gospel to many villages of the Samaritans.

---

[1] Or rushed with one mind [2] Some manuscripts a city [3] Greek works of power [4] That is, a bitter fluid secreted by the liver; bile [a] Isa. 66:1, 2

Philip and the Ethiopian Eunuch

²⁶ Now an angel of the Lord said to Philip, "Rise and go toward the south¹ to the road that goes down from Jerusalem to Gaza." This is a desert place. ²⁷ And he rose and went. And there was an Ethiopian, a eunuch, a court official of Candace, queen of the Ethiopians, who was in charge of all her treasure. He had come to Jerusalem to worship ²⁸ and was returning, seated in his chariot, and he was reading the prophet Isaiah. ²⁹ And the Spirit said to Philip, "Go over and join this chariot." ³⁰ So Philip ran to him and heard him reading Isaiah the prophet and asked, "Do you understand what you are reading?" ³¹ And he said, "How can I, unless someone guides me?" And he invited Philip to come up and sit with him. ³² Now the passage of the Scripture that he was reading was this:

ᵃ"Like a sheep he was led to the slaughter
    and like a lamb before its shearer is
        silent,
    so he opens not his mouth.
³³ In his humiliation justice was denied
        him.
    Who can describe his generation?
    For his life is taken away from the earth."

³⁴ And the eunuch said to Philip, "About whom, I ask you, does the prophet say this, about himself or about someone else?" ³⁵ Then Philip opened his mouth, and beginning with this Scripture he told him the good news about Jesus. ³⁶ And as they were going along the road they came to some water, and the eunuch said, "See, here is water! What prevents me from being baptized?"² ³⁸ And he commanded the chariot to stop, and they both went down into the water, Philip and the eunuch, and he baptized him. ³⁹ And when they came up out of the water, the Spirit of the Lord carried Philip away, and the eunuch saw him no more, and went on his way rejoicing. ⁴⁰ But Philip found himself at Azotus, and as he passed through he preached the gospel to all the towns until he came to Caesarea.

The Conversion of Saul

9 But Saul, still breathing threats and murder against the disciples of the Lord, went to the high priest ² and asked him for letters to the synagogues at Damascus, so that if he found any belonging to the Way, men or women, he might bring them bound to Jerusalem. ³ Now as he went on his way, he approached Damascus, and suddenly a light from heaven shone around him. ⁴ And falling to the ground, he heard a voice saying to him, "Saul, Saul, why are you persecuting me?" ⁵ And he said, "Who are you, Lord?" And he said, "I am Jesus, whom you are persecuting. ⁶ But rise and enter the city, and you will be told what you are to do." ⁷ The men who were traveling with him stood speechless, hearing the voice but seeing no one. ⁸ Saul rose from the ground, and although his eyes were opened, he saw nothing. So they led him by the hand and brought him into Damascus. ⁹ And for three days he was without sight, and neither ate nor drank.

¹⁰ Now there was a disciple at Damascus named Ananias. The Lord said to him in a vision, "Ananias." And he said, "Here I am, Lord." ¹¹ And the Lord said to him, "Rise and go to the street called Straight, and at the house of Judas look for a man of Tarsus named Saul, for behold, he is praying, ¹²and he has seen in a vision a man named Ananias come in and lay his hands on him so that he might regain his sight." ¹³ But Ananias answered, "Lord, I have heard from many about this man, how much evil he has done to your saints at Jerusalem. ¹⁴ And here he has authority from the chief priests to bind all who call on your name." ¹⁵ But the Lord said to him, "Go, for he is a chosen instrument of mine to carry my name before the Gentiles and kings and the children of Israel. ¹⁶ For I will show him how much he must suffer for the sake of my name." ¹⁷ So Ananias departed and entered the house. And laying his hands on him he said, "Brother Saul, the Lord Jesus who appeared to you on the road by which you came has sent me so that you may regain your sight and be filled with the Holy Spirit." ¹⁸ And immediately something like scales fell from his eyes, and he regained his sight. Then he rose and was baptized; ¹⁹ and taking food, he was strengthened.

Saul Proclaims Jesus in Synagogues

For some days he was with the disciples at Damascus. ²⁰ And immediately he proclaimed Jesus in the synagogues, saying, "He is the Son of God." ²¹ And all who heard him were amazed and said, "Is not this the man who made havoc in Jerusalem of those who called upon this name? And has he not come here

¹ Or go at about noon ² Some manuscripts add all or most of verse 37: And Philip said, "If you believe with all your heart, you may." And he replied, "I believe that Jesus Christ is the Son of God." ᵃ Isa. 53:7, 8

for this purpose, to bring them bound before the chief priests?" ²²But Saul increased all the more in strength, and confounded the Jews who lived in Damascus by proving that Jesus was the Christ.

Saul Escapes from Damascus

²³When many days had passed, the Jews¹ plotted to kill him, ²⁴but their plot became known to Saul. They were watching the gates day and night in order to kill him, ²⁵but his disciples took him by night and let him down through an opening in the wall,² lowering him in a basket.

Saul in Jerusalem

²⁶And when he had come to Jerusalem, he attempted to join the disciples. And they were all afraid of him, for they did not believe that he was a disciple. ²⁷But Barnabas took him and brought him to the apostles and declared to them how on the road he had seen the Lord, who spoke to him, and how at Damascus he had preached boldly in the name of Jesus. ²⁸So he went in and out among them at Jerusalem, preaching boldly in the name of the Lord. ²⁹And he spoke and disputed against the Hellenists.³ But they were seeking to kill him. ³⁰And when the brothers learned this, they brought him down to Caesarea and sent him off to Tarsus.

³¹So the church throughout all Judea and Galilee and Samaria had peace and was being built up. And walking in the fear of the Lord and in the comfort of the Holy Spirit, it multiplied.

The Healing of Aeneas

³²Now as Peter went here and there among them all, he came down also to the saints who lived at Lydda. ³³There he found a man named Aeneas, bedridden for eight years, who was paralyzed. ³⁴And Peter said to him, "Aeneas, Jesus Christ heals you; rise and make your bed." And immediately he rose. ³⁵And all the residents of Lydda and Sharon saw him, and they turned to the Lord.

Dorcas Restored to Life

³⁶Now there was in Joppa a disciple named Tabitha, which, translated, means Dorcas.⁴ She was full of good works and acts of charity. ³⁷In those days she became ill and died, and when they had washed her, they laid her in an upper room. ³⁸Since Lydda was near Joppa, the dis-

ciples, hearing that Peter was there, sent two men to him, urging him, "Please come to us without delay." ³⁹So Peter rose and went with them. And when he arrived, they took him to the upper room. All the widows stood beside him weeping and showing tunics⁵ and other garments that Dorcas made while she was with them. ⁴⁰But Peter put them all outside, and knelt down and prayed; and turning to the body he said, "Tabitha, arise." And she opened her eyes, and when she saw Peter she sat up. ⁴¹And he gave her his hand and raised her up. Then, calling the saints and widows, he presented her alive. ⁴²And it became known throughout all Joppa, and many believed in the Lord. ⁴³And he stayed in Joppa for many days with one Simon, a tanner.

Peter and Cornelius

10 At Caesarea there was a man named Cornelius, a centurion of what was known as the Italian Cohort, ²a devout man who feared God with all his household, gave alms generously to the people, and prayed continually to God. ³About the ninth hour of the day⁶ he saw clearly in a vision an angel of God come in and say to him, "Cornelius." ⁴And he stared at him in terror and said, "What is it, Lord?" And he said to him, "Your prayers and your alms have ascended as a memorial before God. ⁵And now send men to Joppa and bring one Simon who is called Peter. ⁶He is lodging with one Simon, a tanner, whose house is by the sea." ⁷When the angel who spoke to him had departed, he called two of his servants and a devout soldier from among those who attended him, ⁸and having related everything to them, he sent them to Joppa.

Peter's Vision

⁹The next day, as they were on their journey and approaching the city, Peter went up on the housetop about the sixth hour⁷ to pray. ¹⁰And he became hungry and wanted something to eat, but while they were preparing it, he fell into a trance ¹¹and saw the heavens opened and something like a great sheet descending, being let down by its four corners upon the earth. ¹²In it were all kinds of animals and reptiles and birds of the air. ¹³And there came a voice to him: "Rise, Peter; kill and eat." ¹⁴But Peter said, "By no means, Lord; for I have never eaten anything that is

---

¹ The Greek word *Ioudaioi* refers specifically here to Jewish religious leaders, and others under their influence, who opposed the Christian faith in that time ² Greek *through the wall* ³ That is, Greek-speaking Jews ⁴ The Aramaic name *Tabitha* and the Greek name *Dorcas* both mean *gazelle* ⁵ Greek *chiton*, a long garment worn under the cloak next to the skin ⁶ That is, 3 P.M. ⁷ That is, noon

common or unclean." [15] And the voice came to him again a second time, "What God has made clean, do not call common." [16] This happened three times, and the thing was taken up at once to heaven.

[17] Now while Peter was inwardly perplexed as to what the vision that he had seen might mean, behold, the men who were sent by Cornelius, having made inquiry for Simon's house, stood at the gate [18] and called out to ask whether Simon who was called Peter was lodging there. [19] And while Peter was pondering the vision, the Spirit said to him, "Behold, three men are looking for you. [20] Rise and go down and accompany them without hesitation,[1] for I have sent them." [21] And Peter went down to the men and said, "I am the one you are looking for. What is the reason for your coming?" [22] And they said, "Cornelius, a centurion, an upright and God-fearing man, who is well spoken of by the whole Jewish nation, was directed by a holy angel to send for you to come to his house and to hear what you have to say." [23] So he invited them in to be his guests.

The next day he rose and went away with them, and some of the brothers from Joppa accompanied him. [24] And on the following day they entered Caesarea. Cornelius was expecting them and had called together his relatives and close friends. [25] When Peter entered, Cornelius met him and fell down at his feet and worshiped him. [26] But Peter lifted him up, saying, "Stand up; I too am a man." [27] And as he talked with him, he went in and found many persons gathered. [28] And he said to them, "You yourselves know how unlawful it is for a Jew to associate with or to visit anyone of another nation, but God has shown me that I should not call any person common or unclean. [29] So when I was sent for, I came without objection. I ask then why you sent for me."

[30] And Cornelius said, "Four days ago, about this hour, I was praying in my house at the ninth hour,[2] and behold, a man stood before me in bright clothing [31] and said, 'Cornelius, your prayer has been heard and your alms have been remembered before God. [32] Send therefore to Joppa and ask for Simon who is called Peter. He is lodging in the house of Simon, a tanner, by the sea.' [33] So I sent for you at once, and you have been kind enough to come. Now therefore we are all here in the presence of God to hear all that you have been commanded by the Lord."

Gentiles Hear the Good News

[34] So Peter opened his mouth and said: "Truly I understand that God shows no partiality, [35] but in every nation anyone who fears him and does what is right is acceptable to him. [36] As for the word that he sent to Israel, preaching good news of peace through Jesus Christ (he is Lord of all), [37] you yourselves know what happened throughout all Judea, beginning from Galilee after the baptism that John proclaimed: [38] how God anointed Jesus of Nazareth with the Holy Spirit and with power. He went about doing good and healing all who were oppressed by the devil, for God was with him. [39] And we are witnesses of all that he did both in the country of the Jews and in Jerusalem. They put him to death by hanging him on a tree, [40] but God raised him on the third day and made him to appear, [41] not to all the people but to us who had been chosen by God as witnesses, who ate and drank with him after he rose from the dead. [42] And he commanded us to preach to the people and to testify that he is the one appointed by God to be judge of the living and the dead. [43] To him all the prophets bear witness that everyone who believes in him receives forgiveness of sins through his name."

The Holy Spirit Falls on the Gentiles

[44] While Peter was still saying these things, the Holy Spirit fell on all who heard the word. [45] And the believers from among the circumcised who had come with Peter were amazed, because the gift of the Holy Spirit was poured out even on the Gentiles. [46] For they were hearing them speaking in tongues and extolling God. Then Peter declared, [47] "Can anyone withhold water for baptizing these people, who have received the Holy Spirit just as we have?" [48] And he commanded them to be baptized in the name of Jesus Christ. Then they asked him to remain for some days.

Peter Reports to the Church

11 Now the apostles and the brothers[3] who were throughout Judea heard that the Gentiles also had received the word of God. [2] So when Peter went up to Jerusalem, the circumcision party[4] criticized him, saying, [3] "You went to uncircumcised men and ate with them." [4] But Peter began and explained it to them in order: [5] "I was in the city of Joppa praying, and in a trance I saw a vision, something like a great sheet descending, being let down from heaven

---

[1] Or accompany them, making no distinction [2] That is, 3 P.M. [3] Or brothers and sisters [4] Or Jerusalem, those of the circumcision

by its four corners, and it came down to me. [6] Looking at it closely, I observed animals and beasts of prey and reptiles and birds of the air. [7] And I heard a voice saying to me, 'Rise, Peter; kill and eat.' [8] But I said, 'By no means, Lord; for nothing common or unclean has ever entered my mouth.' [9] But the voice answered a second time from heaven, 'What God has made clean, do not call common.' [10] This happened three times, and all was drawn up again into heaven. [11] And behold, at that very moment three men arrived at the house in which we were, sent to me from Caesarea. [12] And the Spirit told me to go with them, making no distinction. These six brothers also accompanied me, and we entered the man's house. [13] And he told us how he had seen the angel stand in his house and say, 'Send to Joppa and bring Simon who is called Peter; [14] he will declare to you a message by which you will be saved, you and all your household.' [15] As I began to speak, the Holy Spirit fell on them just as on us at the beginning. [16] And I remembered the word of the Lord, how he said, 'John baptized with water, but you will be baptized with the Holy Spirit.' [17] If then God gave the same gift to them as he gave to us when we believed in the Lord Jesus Christ, who was I that I could stand in God's way?" [18] When they heard these things they fell silent. And they glorified God, saying, "Then to the Gentiles also God has granted repentance that leads to life."

The Church in Antioch

[19] Now those who were scattered because of the persecution that arose over Stephen traveled as far as Phoenicia and Cyprus and Antioch, speaking the word to no one except Jews. [20] But there were some of them, men of Cyprus and Cyrene, who on coming to Antioch spoke to the Hellenists[1] also, preaching the Lord Jesus. [21] And the hand of the Lord was with them, and a great number who believed turned to the Lord. [22] The report of this came to the ears of the church in Jerusalem, and they sent Barnabas to Antioch. [23] When he came and saw the grace of God, he was glad, and he exhorted them all to remain faithful to the Lord with steadfast purpose, [24] for he was a good man, full of the Holy Spirit and of faith. And a great many people were added to the Lord. [25] So Barnabas went to Tarsus to look for Saul, [26] and when he had found him, he brought him to Antioch. For a whole year they met with the church and taught a great many people. And in Antioch the disciples were first called Christians.

[27] Now in these days prophets came down from Jerusalem to Antioch. [28] And one of them named Agabus stood up and foretold by the Spirit that there would be a great famine over all the world (this took place in the days of Claudius). [29] So the disciples determined, every one according to his ability, to send relief to the brothers[2] living in Judea. [30] And they did so, sending it to the elders by the hand of Barnabas and Saul.

James Killed and Peter Imprisoned

12 About that time Herod the king laid violent hands on some who belonged to the church. [2] He killed James the brother of John with the sword, [3] and when he saw that it pleased the Jews, he proceeded to arrest Peter also. This was during the days of Unleavened Bread. [4] And when he had seized him, he put him in prison, delivering him over to four squads of soldiers to guard him, intending after the Passover to bring him out to the people. [5] So Peter was kept in prison, but earnest prayer for him was made to God by the church.

Peter Is Rescued

[6] Now when Herod was about to bring him out, on that very night, Peter was sleeping between two soldiers, bound with two chains, and sentries before the door were guarding the prison. [7] And behold, an angel of the Lord stood next to him, and a light shone in the cell. He struck Peter on the side and woke him, saying, "Get up quickly." And the chains fell off his hands. [8] And the angel said to him, "Dress yourself and put on your sandals." And he did so. And he said to him, "Wrap your cloak around you and follow me." [9] And he went out and followed him. He did not know that what was being done by the angel was real, but thought he was seeing a vision. [10] When they had passed the first and the second guard, they came to the iron gate leading into the city. It opened for them of its own accord, and they went out and went along one street, and immediately the angel left him. [11] When Peter came to himself, he said, "Now I am sure that the Lord has sent his angel and rescued me from the hand of Herod and from all that the Jewish people were expecting."

---

[1] Or Greeks (that is, Greek-speaking non-Jews) [2] Or brothers and sisters

[12] When he realized this, he went to the house of Mary, the mother of John whose other name was Mark, where many were gathered together and were praying. [13] And when he knocked at the door of the gateway, a servant girl named Rhoda came to answer. [14] Recognizing Peter's voice, in her joy she did not open the gate but ran in and reported that Peter was standing at the gate. [15] They said to her, "You are out of your mind." But she kept insisting that it was so, and they kept saying, "It is his angel!" [16] But Peter continued knocking, and when they opened, they saw him and were amazed. [17] But motioning to them with his hand to be silent, he described to them how the Lord had brought him out of the prison. And he said, "Tell these things to James and to the brothers."[1] Then he departed and went to another place.

[18] Now when day came, there was no little disturbance among the soldiers over what had become of Peter. [19] And after Herod searched for him and did not find him, he examined the sentries and ordered that they should be put to death. Then he went down from Judea to Caesarea and spent time there.

The Death of Herod

[20] Now Herod was angry with the people of Tyre and Sidon, and they came to him with one accord, and having persuaded Blastus, the king's chamberlain,[2] they asked for peace, because their country depended on the king's country for food. [21] On an appointed day Herod put on his royal robes, took his seat upon the throne, and delivered an oration to them. [22] And the people were shouting, "The voice of a god, and not of a man!" [23] Immediately an angel of the Lord struck him down, because he did not give God the glory, and he was eaten by worms and breathed his last.

[24] But the word of God increased and multiplied.

[25] And Barnabas and Saul returned from[3] Jerusalem when they had completed their service, bringing with them John, whose other name was Mark.

Barnabas and Saul Sent Off

13 Now there were in the church at Antioch prophets and teachers, Barnabas, Simeon who was called Niger,[4] Lucius of Cyrene, Manaen a lifelong friend of Herod the tetrarch,

and Saul. [2] While they were worshiping the Lord and fasting, the Holy Spirit said, "Set apart for me Barnabas and Saul for the work to which I have called them." [3] Then after fasting and praying they laid their hands on them and sent them off.

Barnabas and Saul on Cyprus

[4] So, being sent out by the Holy Spirit, they went down to Seleucia, and from there they sailed to Cyprus. [5] When they arrived at Salamis, they proclaimed the word of God in the synagogues of the Jews. And they had John to assist them. [6] When they had gone through the whole island as far as Paphos, they came upon a certain magician, a Jewish false prophet named Bar-Jesus. [7] He was with the proconsul, Sergius Paulus, a man of intelligence, who summoned Barnabas and Saul and sought to hear the word of God. [8] But Elymas the magician (for that is the meaning of his name) opposed them, seeking to turn the proconsul away from the faith. [9] But Saul, who was also called Paul, filled with the Holy Spirit, looked intently at him [10] and said, "You son of the devil, you enemy of all righteousness, full of all deceit and villainy, will you not stop making crooked the straight paths of the Lord? [11] And now, behold, the hand of the Lord is upon you, and you will be blind and unable to see the sun for a time." Immediately mist and darkness fell upon him, and he went about seeking people to lead him by the hand. [12] Then the proconsul believed, when he saw what had occurred, for he was astonished at the teaching of the Lord.

Paul and Barnabas at Antioch in Pisidia

[13] Now Paul and his companions set sail from Paphos and came to Perga in Pamphylia. And John left them and returned to Jerusalem, [14] but they went on from Perga and came to Antioch in Pisidia. And on the Sabbath day they went into the synagogue and sat down. [15] After the reading from the Law and the Prophets, the rulers of the synagogue sent a message to them, saying, "Brothers, if you have any word of encouragement for the people, say it." [16] So Paul stood up, and motioning with his hand said:

"Men of Israel and you who fear God, listen. [17] The God of this people Israel chose our fathers and made the people great during their stay in the land of Egypt, and with uplifted arm he led

---

[1] Or brothers and sisters [2] That is, trusted personal attendant [3] Some manuscripts to [4] Niger is a Latin word meaning black, or dark

them out of it. ¹⁸And for about forty years he put up with¹ them in the wilderness. ¹⁹And after destroying seven nations in the land of Canaan, he gave them their land as an inheritance. ²⁰All this took about 450 years. And after that he gave them judges until Samuel the prophet. ²¹Then they asked for a king, and God gave them Saul the son of Kish, a man of the tribe of Benjamin, for forty years. ²²And when he had removed him, he raised up David to be their king, of whom he testified and said, ᵃ'I have found in David the son of Jesse ᵇa man after my heart, who will do all my will.' ²³Of this man's offspring God has brought to Israel a Savior, Jesus, as he promised. ²⁴Before his coming, John had proclaimed a baptism of repentance to all the people of Israel. ²⁵And as John was finishing his course, he said, 'What do you suppose that I am? I am not he. No, but behold, after me one is coming, the sandals of whose feet I am not worthy to untie.'

²⁶"Brothers, sons of the family of Abraham, and those among you who fear God, to us has been sent the message of this salvation. ²⁷For those who live in Jerusalem and their rulers, because they did not recognize him nor understand the utterances of the prophets, which are read every Sabbath, fulfilled them by condemning him. ²⁸And though they found in him no guilt worthy of death, they asked Pilate to have him executed. ²⁹And when they had carried out all that was written of him, they took him down from the tree and laid him in a tomb. ³⁰But God raised him from the dead, ³¹and for many days he appeared to those who had come up with him from Galilee to Jerusalem, who are now his witnesses to the people. ³²And we bring you the good news that what God promised to the fathers, ³³this he has fulfilled to us their children by raising Jesus, as also it is written in the second Psalm,

ᶜ"'You are my Son,
    today I have begotten you.'

³⁴And as for the fact that he raised him from the dead, no more to return to corruption, he has spoken in this way,

"'I will give you ᵈthe holy and sure blessings of David.'

³⁵Therefore he says also in another psalm,

ᵉ"'You will not let your Holy One see corruption.'

³⁶For David, after he had served the purpose of God in his own generation, fell asleep and was laid with his fathers and saw corruption, ³⁷but he whom God raised up did not see corruption. ³⁸Let it be known to you therefore, brothers, that through this man forgiveness of sins is proclaimed to you, ³⁹and by him everyone who believes is freed² from everything from which you could not be freed by the law of Moses. ⁴⁰Beware, therefore, lest what is said in the Prophets should come about:

⁴¹ᶠ"'Look, you scoffers,
    be astounded and perish;
    for I am doing a work in your days,
        a work that you will not believe, even if
            one tells it to you.'"

⁴²As they went out, the people begged that these things might be told them the next Sabbath. ⁴³And after the meeting of the synagogue broke up, many Jews and devout converts to Judaism followed Paul and Barnabas, who, as they spoke with them, urged them to continue in the grace of God.

⁴⁴The next Sabbath almost the whole city gathered to hear the word of the Lord. ⁴⁵But when the Jews³ saw the crowds, they were filled with jealousy and began to contradict what was spoken by Paul, reviling him. ⁴⁶And Paul and Barnabas spoke out boldly, saying, "It was necessary that the word of God be spoken first to you. Since you thrust it aside and judge yourselves unworthy of eternal life, behold, we are turning to the Gentiles. ⁴⁷For so the Lord has commanded us, saying,

ᵍ"'I have made you a light for the Gentiles,
    that you may bring salvation to the
        ends of the earth.'"

⁴⁸And when the Gentiles heard this, they began rejoicing and glorifying the word of the Lord, and as many as were appointed to eternal life believed. ⁴⁹And the word of the Lord was spreading throughout the whole region. ⁵⁰But the Jews incited the devout women of high standing and the leading men of the city, stirred up persecution against Paul and Barnabas, and drove them out of their district. ⁵¹But they shook off the dust from their feet against them and went to Iconium. ⁵²And the disciples were filled with joy and with the Holy Spirit.

¹ Some manuscripts he carried (compare Deuteronomy 1:31) ² Greek justified; twice in this verse ³ Greek loudaioi probably refers here to Jewish religious leaders, and others under their influence, in that time; also verse 50 ᵈPs. 89:20 ᵇ1 Sam. 13:14 ᶜPs. 2:7 ᵈIsa. 55:3 ᵉPs. 16:10 ᶠHab. 1:5 ᵍIsa. 49:6

Paul and Barnabas at Iconium

14 Now at Iconium they entered together into the Jewish synagogue and spoke in such a way that a great number of both Jews and Greeks believed. [2] But the unbelieving Jews stirred up the Gentiles and poisoned their minds against the brothers.[1] [3] So they remained for a long time, speaking boldly for the Lord, who bore witness to the word of his grace, granting signs and wonders to be done by their hands. [4] But the people of the city were divided; some sided with the Jews and some with the apostles. [5] When an attempt was made by both Gentiles and Jews, with their rulers, to mistreat them and to stone them, [6] they learned of it and fled to Lystra and Derbe, cities of Lycaonia, and to the surrounding country, [7] and there they continued to preach the gospel.

Paul and Barnabas at Lystra

[8] Now at Lystra there was a man sitting who could not use his feet. He was crippled from birth and had never walked. [9] He listened to Paul speaking. And Paul, looking intently at him and seeing that he had faith to be made well,[2] [10] said in a loud voice, "Stand upright on your feet." And he sprang up and began walking. [11] And when the crowds saw what Paul had done, they lifted up their voices, saying in Lycaonian, "The gods have come down to us in the likeness of men!" [12] Barnabas they called Zeus, and Paul, Hermes, because he was the chief speaker. [13] And the priest of Zeus, whose temple was at the entrance to the city, brought oxen and garlands to the gates and wanted to offer sacrifice with the crowds. [14] But when the apostles Barnabas and Paul heard of it, they tore their garments and rushed out into the crowd, crying out, [15] "Men, why are you doing these things? We also are men, of like nature with you, and we bring you good news, that you should turn from these vain things to a living God, who made the heaven and the earth and the sea and all that is in them. [16] In past generations he allowed all the nations to walk in their own ways. [17] Yet he did not leave himself without witness, for he did good by giving you rains from heaven and fruitful seasons, satisfying your hearts with food and gladness." [18] Even with these words they scarcely restrained the people from offering sacrifice to them.

Paul Stoned at Lystra

[19] But Jews came from Antioch and Iconium, and having persuaded the crowds, they stoned Paul and dragged him out of the city, supposing that he was dead. [20] But when the disciples gathered about him, he rose up and entered the city, and on the next day he went on with Barnabas to Derbe. [21] When they had preached the gospel to that city and had made many disciples, they returned to Lystra and to Iconium and to Antioch, [22] strengthening the souls of the disciples, encouraging them to continue in the faith, and saying that through many tribulations we must enter the kingdom of God. [23] And when they had appointed elders for them in every church, with prayer and fasting they committed them to the Lord in whom they had believed.

Paul and Barnabas Return to Antioch in Syria

[24] Then they passed through Pisidia and came to Pamphylia. [25] And when they had spoken the word in Perga, they went down to Attalia, [26] and from there they sailed to Antioch, where they had been commended to the grace of God for the work that they had fulfilled. [27] And when they arrived and gathered the church together, they declared all that God had done with them, and how he had opened a door of faith to the Gentiles. [28] And they remained no little time with the disciples.

The Jerusalem Council

15 But some men came down from Judea and were teaching the brothers, "Unless you are circumcised according to the custom of Moses, you cannot be saved." [2] And after Paul and Barnabas had no small dissension and debate with them, Paul and Barnabas and some of the others were appointed to go up to Jerusalem to the apostles and the elders about this question. [3] So, being sent on their way by the church, they passed through both Phoenicia and Samaria, describing in detail the conversion of the Gentiles, and brought great joy to all the brothers.[3] [4] When they came to Jerusalem, they were welcomed by the church and the apostles and the elders, and they declared all that God had done with them. [5] But some believers who belonged to the party of the Pharisees rose up and said, "It is necessary to circumcise them and to order them to keep the law of Moses."

[6] The apostles and the elders were gathered together to consider this matter. [7] And after

---

[1] Or brothers and sisters [2] Or be saved [3] Or brothers and sisters; also verse 22

there had been much debate, Peter stood up and said to them, "Brothers, you know that in the early days God made a choice among you, that by my mouth the Gentiles should hear the word of the gospel and believe. [8] And God, who knows the heart, bore witness to them, by giving them the Holy Spirit just as he did to us, [9] and he made no distinction between us and them, having cleansed their hearts by faith. [10] Now, therefore, why are you putting God to the test by placing a yoke on the neck of the disciples that neither our fathers nor we have been able to bear? [11] But we believe that we will be saved through the grace of the Lord Jesus, just as they will."

[12] And all the assembly fell silent, and they listened to Barnabas and Paul as they related what signs and wonders God had done through them among the Gentiles. [13] After they finished speaking, James replied, "Brothers, listen to me. [14] Simeon has related how God first visited the Gentiles, to take from them a people for his name. [15] And with this the words of the prophets agree, just as it is written,

[16] [a] "'After this I will return,
and I will rebuild the tent of David that has fallen;
I will rebuild its ruins,
and I will restore it,
[17] that the remnant[1] of mankind may seek the Lord,
and all the Gentiles who are called by my name,
says the Lord, who makes these things
[18] known from of old.'

[19] Therefore my judgment is that we should not trouble those of the Gentiles who turn to God, [20] but should write to them to abstain from the things polluted by idols, and from sexual immorality, and from what has been strangled, and from blood. [21] For from ancient generations Moses has had in every city those who proclaim him, for he is read every Sabbath in the synagogues."

The Council's Letter to Gentile Believers

[22] Then it seemed good to the apostles and the elders, with the whole church, to choose men from among them and send them to Antioch with Paul and Barnabas. They sent Judas called Barsabbas, and Silas, leading men among the brothers, [23] with the following letter: "The brothers, both the apostles and the elders, to the brothers[2] who are of the Gentiles in Antioch and Syria and Cilicia, greetings. [24] Since we have heard that some persons have gone out from us and troubled you[3] with words, unsettling your minds, although we gave them no instructions, [25] it has seemed good to us, having come to one accord, to choose men and send them to you with our beloved Barnabas and Paul, [26] men who have risked their lives for the name of our Lord Jesus Christ. [27] We have therefore sent Judas and Silas, who themselves will tell you the same things by word of mouth. [28] For it has seemed good to the Holy Spirit and to us to lay on you no greater burden than these requirements: [29] that you abstain from what has been sacrificed to idols, and from blood, and from what has been strangled, and from sexual immorality. If you keep yourselves from these, you will do well. Farewell."

[30] So when they were sent off, they went down to Antioch, and having gathered the congregation together, they delivered the letter. [31] And when they had read it, they rejoiced because of its encouragement. [32] And Judas and Silas, who were themselves prophets, encouraged and strengthened the brothers with many words. [33] And after they had spent some time, they were sent off in peace by the brothers to those who had sent them.[4] [35] But Paul and Barnabas remained in Antioch, teaching and preaching the word of the Lord, with many others also.

Paul and Barnabas Separate

[36] And after some days Paul said to Barnabas, "Let us return and visit the brothers in every city where we proclaimed the word of the Lord, and see how they are." [37] Now Barnabas wanted to take with them John called Mark. [38] But Paul thought best not to take with them one who had withdrawn from them in Pamphylia and had not gone with them to the work. [39] And there arose a sharp disagreement, so that they separated from each other. Barnabas took Mark with him and sailed away to Cyprus, [40] but Paul chose Silas and departed, having been commended by the brothers to the grace of the Lord. [41] And he went through Syria and Cilicia, strengthening the churches.

Timothy Joins Paul and Silas

16 Paul[5] came also to Derbe and to Lystra. A disciple was there, named Timothy, the son of a Jewish woman who was a believer, but

---

[1] Or rest [2] Or brothers and sisters; also verses 32, 33, 36 [3] Some manuscripts some persons from us have troubled you [4] Some manuscripts insert verse 34: But it seemed good to Silas to remain there [5] Greek He [a] Amos 9:11, 12

his father was a Greek. [2] He was well spoken of by the brothers[1] at Lystra and Iconium. [3] Paul wanted Timothy to accompany him, and he took him and circumcised him because of the Jews who were in those places, for they all knew that his father was a Greek. [4] As they went on their way through the cities, they delivered to them for observance the decisions that had been reached by the apostles and elders who were in Jerusalem. [5] So the churches were strengthened in the faith, and they increased in numbers daily.

The Macedonian Call

[6] And they went through the region of Phrygia and Galatia, having been forbidden by the Holy Spirit to speak the word in Asia. [7] And when they had come up to Mysia, they attempted to go into Bithynia, but the Spirit of Jesus did not allow them. [8] So, passing by Mysia, they went down to Troas. [9] And a vision appeared to Paul in the night: a man of Macedonia was standing there, urging him and saying, "Come over to Macedonia and help us." [10] And when Paul[2] had seen the vision, immediately we sought to go on into Macedonia, concluding that God had called us to preach the gospel to them.

The Conversion of Lydia

[11] So, setting sail from Troas, we made a direct voyage to Samothrace, and the following day to Neapolis, [12] and from there to Philippi, which is a leading city of the[3] district of Macedonia and a Roman colony. We remained in this city some days. [13] And on the Sabbath day we went outside the gate to the riverside, where we supposed there was a place of prayer, and we sat down and spoke to the women who had come together. [14] One who heard us was a woman named Lydia, from the city of Thyatira, a seller of purple goods, who was a worshiper of God. The Lord opened her heart to pay attention to what was said by Paul. [15] And after she was baptized, and her household as well, she urged us, saying, "If you have judged me to be faithful to the Lord, come to my house and stay." And she prevailed upon us.

Paul and Silas in Prison

[16] As we were going to the place of prayer, we were met by a slave girl who had a spirit of divination and brought her owners much gain by fortune-telling. [17] She followed Paul and us,

crying out, "These men are servants of the Most High God, who proclaim to you the way of salvation." [18] And this she kept doing for many days. Paul, having become greatly annoyed, turned and said to the spirit, "I command you in the name of Jesus Christ to come out of her." And it came out that very hour.

[19] But when her owners saw that their hope of gain was gone, they seized Paul and Silas and dragged them into the marketplace before the rulers. [20] And when they had brought them to the magistrates, they said, "These men are Jews, and they are disturbing our city. [21] They advocate customs that are not lawful for us as Romans to accept or practice." [22] The crowd joined in attacking them, and the magistrates tore the garments off them and gave orders to beat them with rods. [23] And when they had inflicted many blows upon them, they threw them into prison, ordering the jailer to keep them safely. [24] Having received this order, he put them into the inner prison and fastened their feet in the stocks.

The Philippian Jailer Converted

[25] About midnight Paul and Silas were praying and singing hymns to God, and the prisoners were listening to them, [26] and suddenly there was a great earthquake, so that the foundations of the prison were shaken. And immediately all the doors were opened, and everyone's bonds were unfastened. [27] When the jailer woke and saw that the prison doors were open, he drew his sword and was about to kill himself, supposing that the prisoners had escaped. [28] But Paul cried with a loud voice, "Do not harm yourself, for we are all here." [29] And the jailer[4] called for lights and rushed in, and trembling with fear he fell down before Paul and Silas. [30] Then he brought them out and said, "Sirs, what must I do to be saved?" [31] And they said, "Believe in the Lord Jesus, and you will be saved, you and your household." [32] And they spoke the word of the Lord to him and to all who were in his house. [33] And he took them the same hour of the night and washed their wounds; and he was baptized at once, he and all his family. [34] Then he brought them up into his house and set food before them. And he rejoiced along with his entire household that he had believed in God.

[35] But when it was day, the magistrates sent the police, saying, "Let those men go." [36] And the jailer reported these words to Paul, saying, "The

---

[1] Or brothers and sisters; also verse 40 [2] Greek he [3] Or that [4] Greek he

magistrates have sent to let you go. Therefore come out now and go in peace." [37] But Paul said to them, "They have beaten us publicly, uncondemned, men who are Roman citizens, and have thrown us into prison; and do they now throw us out secretly? No! Let them come themselves and take us out." [38] The police reported these words to the magistrates, and they were afraid when they heard that they were Roman citizens. [39] So they came and apologized to them. And they took them out and asked them to leave the city. [40] So they went out of the prison and visited Lydia. And when they had seen the brothers, they encouraged them and departed.

Paul and Silas in Thessalonica

17 Now when they had passed through Amphipolis and Apollonia, they came to Thessalonica, where there was a synagogue of the Jews. [2] And Paul went in, as was his custom, and on three Sabbath days he reasoned with them from the Scriptures, [3] explaining and proving that it was necessary for the Christ to suffer and to rise from the dead, and saying, "This Jesus, whom I proclaim to you, is the Christ." [4] And some of them were persuaded and joined Paul and Silas, as did a great many of the devout Greeks and not a few of the leading women. [5] But the Jews[1] were jealous, and taking some wicked men of the rabble, they formed a mob, set the city in an uproar, and attacked the house of Jason, seeking to bring them out to the crowd. [6] And when they could not find them, they dragged Jason and some of the brothers before the city authorities, shouting, "These men who have turned the world upside down have come here also, [7] and Jason has received them, and they are all acting against the decrees of Caesar, saying that there is another king, Jesus." [8] And the people and the city authorities were disturbed when they heard these things. [9] And when they had taken money as security from Jason and the rest, they let them go.

Paul and Silas in Berea

[10] The brothers[2] immediately sent Paul and Silas away by night to Berea, and when they arrived they went into the Jewish synagogue. [11] Now these Jews were more noble than those in Thessalonica; they received the word with all eagerness, examining the Scriptures daily to see if these things were so. [12] Many of them therefore believed, with not a few Greek women of high standing as well as men. [13] But when the Jews from Thessalonica learned that the word of God was proclaimed by Paul at Berea also, they came there too, agitating and stirring up the crowds. [14] Then the brothers immediately sent Paul off on his way to the sea, but Silas and Timothy remained there. [15] Those who conducted Paul brought him as far as Athens, and after receiving a command for Silas and Timothy to come to him as soon as possible, they departed.

Paul in Athens

[16] Now while Paul was waiting for them at Athens, his spirit was provoked within him as he saw that the city was full of idols. [17] So he reasoned in the synagogue with the Jews and the devout persons, and in the marketplace every day with those who happened to be there. [18] Some of the Epicurean and Stoic philosophers also conversed with him. And some said, "What does this babbler wish to say?" Others said, "He seems to be a preacher of foreign divinities"—because he was preaching Jesus and the resurrection. [19] And they took him and brought him to the Areopagus, saying, "May we know what this new teaching is that you are presenting? [20] For you bring some strange things to our ears. We wish to know therefore what these things mean." [21] Now all the Athenians and the foreigners who lived there would spend their time in nothing except telling or hearing something new.

Paul Addresses the Areopagus

[22] So Paul, standing in the midst of the Areopagus, said: "Men of Athens, I perceive that in every way you are very religious. [23] For as I passed along and observed the objects of your worship, I found also an altar with this inscription: 'To the unknown god.' What therefore you worship as unknown, this I proclaim to you. [24] The God who made the world and everything in it, being Lord of heaven and earth, does not live in temples made by man,[3] [25] nor is he served by human hands, as though he needed anything, since he himself gives to all mankind life and breath and everything. [26] And he made from one man every nation of mankind to live on all the face of the earth, having determined allotted periods and the boundaries of their

---

[1] Greek *Ioudaioi* probably refers here to Jewish religious leaders, and others under their influence, in that time; also verse 13 [2] Or *brothers and sisters*; also verse 14 [3] Greek *made by hands*

dwelling place, [27] that they should seek God, and perhaps feel their way toward him and find him. Yet he is actually not far from each one of us, [28] for

> " 'In him we live and move and have our
>   being';[1]

as even some of your own poets have said,

> " 'For we are indeed his offspring.'[2]

[29] Being then God's offspring, we ought not to think that the divine being is like gold or silver or stone, an image formed by the art and imagination of man. [30] The times of ignorance God overlooked, but now he commands all people everywhere to repent, [31] because he has fixed a day on which he will judge the world in righteousness by a man whom he has appointed; and of this he has given assurance to all by raising him from the dead."

[32] Now when they heard of the resurrection of the dead, some mocked. But others said, "We will hear you again about this." [33] So Paul went out from their midst. [34] But some men joined him and believed, among whom also were Dionysius the Areopagite and a woman named Damaris and others with them.

Paul in Corinth

18 After this Paul[3] left Athens and went to Corinth. [2] And he found a Jew named Aquila, a native of Pontus, recently come from Italy with his wife Priscilla, because Claudius had commanded all the Jews to leave Rome. And he went to see them, [3] and because he was of the same trade he stayed with them and worked, for they were tentmakers by trade. [4] And he reasoned in the synagogue every Sabbath, and tried to persuade Jews and Greeks.

[5] When Silas and Timothy arrived from Macedonia, Paul was occupied with the word, testifying to the Jews that the Christ was Jesus. [6] And when they opposed and reviled him, he shook out his garments and said to them, "Your blood be on your own heads! I am innocent. From now on I will go to the Gentiles." [7] And he left there and went to the house of a man named Titius Justus, a worshiper of God. His house was next door to the synagogue. [8] Crispus, the ruler of the synagogue, believed in the Lord, together with his entire household. And many of the Corinthians hearing Paul believed and

were baptized. [9] And the Lord said to Paul one night in a vision, "Do not be afraid, but go on speaking and do not be silent, [10] for I am with you, and no one will attack you to harm you, for I have many in this city who are my people." [11] And he stayed a year and six months, teaching the word of God among them.

[12] But when Gallio was proconsul of Achaia, the Jews[4] made a united attack on Paul and brought him before the tribunal, [13] saying, "This man is persuading people to worship God contrary to the law." [14] But when Paul was about to open his mouth, Gallio said to the Jews, "If it were a matter of wrongdoing or vicious crime, O Jews, I would have reason to accept your complaint. [15] But since it is a matter of questions about words and names and your own law, see to it yourselves. I refuse to be a judge of these things." [16] And he drove them from the tribunal. [17] And they all seized Sosthenes, the ruler of the synagogue, and beat him in front of the tribunal. But Gallio paid no attention to any of this.

Paul Returns to Antioch

[18] After this, Paul stayed many days longer and then took leave of the brothers[5] and set sail for Syria, and with him Priscilla and Aquila. At Cenchreae he had cut his hair, for he was under a vow. [19] And they came to Ephesus, and he left them there, but he himself went into the synagogue and reasoned with the Jews. [20] When they asked him to stay for a longer period, he declined. [21] But on taking leave of them he said, "I will return to you if God wills," and he set sail from Ephesus.

[22] When he had landed at Caesarea, he went up and greeted the church, and then went down to Antioch. [23] After spending some time there, he departed and went from one place to the next through the region of Galatia and Phrygia, strengthening all the disciples.

Apollos Speaks Boldly in Ephesus

[24] Now a Jew named Apollos, a native of Alexandria, came to Ephesus. He was an eloquent man, competent in the Scriptures. [25] He had been instructed in the way of the Lord. And being fervent in spirit,[6] he spoke and taught accurately the things concerning Jesus, though he knew only the baptism of John. [26] He began to speak boldly in the synagogue, but when Priscilla and Aquila heard him, they took him aside and explained to him the way of God

---

[1] Probably from Epimenides of Crete [2] From Aratus's poem "Phainomena" [3] Greek *he* [4] Greek *Ioudaioi* probably refers here to Jewish religious leaders, and others under their influence, in that time; also verses 14 (twice), 28 [5] Or *brothers and sisters*; also verse 27 [6] Or *in the Spirit*

more accurately. [27] And when he wished to cross to Achaia, the brothers encouraged him and wrote to the disciples to welcome him. When he arrived, he greatly helped those who through grace had believed, [28] for he powerfully refuted the Jews in public, showing by the Scriptures that the Christ was Jesus.

Paul in Ephesus

19 And it happened that while Apollos was at Corinth, Paul passed through the inland[1] country and came to Ephesus. There he found some disciples. [2] And he said to them, "Did you receive the Holy Spirit when you believed?" And they said, "No, we have not even heard that there is a Holy Spirit." [3] And he said, "Into what then were you baptized?" They said, "Into John's baptism." [4] And Paul said, "John baptized with the baptism of repentance, telling the people to believe in the one who was to come after him, that is, Jesus." [5] On hearing this, they were baptized in[2] the name of the Lord Jesus. [6] And when Paul had laid his hands on them, the Holy Spirit came on them, and they began speaking in tongues and prophesying. [7] There were about twelve men in all.

[8] And he entered the synagogue and for three months spoke boldly, reasoning and persuading them about the kingdom of God. [9] But when some became stubborn and continued in unbelief, speaking evil of the Way before the congregation, he withdrew from them and took the disciples with him, reasoning daily in the hall of Tyrannus.[3] [10] This continued for two years, so that all the residents of Asia heard the word of the Lord, both Jews and Greeks.

The Sons of Sceva

[11] And God was doing extraordinary miracles by the hands of Paul, [12] so that even handkerchiefs or aprons that had touched his skin were carried away to the sick, and their diseases left them and the evil spirits came out of them. [13] Then some of the itinerant Jewish exorcists undertook to invoke the name of the Lord Jesus over those who had evil spirits, saying, "I adjure you by the Jesus whom Paul proclaims." [14] Seven sons of a Jewish high priest named Sceva were doing this. [15] But the evil spirit answered them, "Jesus I know, and Paul I recognize, but who are you?" [16] And the man in whom was the evil spirit leaped on them, mastered all[4] of them and overpowered them,

so that they fled out of that house naked and wounded. [17] And this became known to all the residents of Ephesus, both Jews and Greeks. And fear fell upon them all, and the name of the Lord Jesus was extolled. [18] Also many of those who were now believers came, confessing and divulging their practices. [19] And a number of those who had practiced magic arts brought their books together and burned them in the sight of all. And they counted the value of them and found it came to fifty thousand pieces of silver. [20] So the word of the Lord continued to increase and prevail mightily.

A Riot at Ephesus

[21] Now after these events Paul resolved in the Spirit to pass through Macedonia and Achaia and go to Jerusalem, saying, "After I have been there, I must also see Rome." [22] And having sent into Macedonia two of his helpers, Timothy and Erastus, he himself stayed in Asia for a while.

[23] About that time there arose no little disturbance concerning the Way. [24] For a man named Demetrius, a silversmith, who made silver shrines of Artemis, brought no little business to the craftsmen. [25] These he gathered together, with the workmen in similar trades, and said, "Men, you know that from this business we have our wealth. [26] And you see and hear that not only in Ephesus but in almost all of Asia this Paul has persuaded and turned away a great many people, saying that gods made with hands are not gods. [27] And there is danger not only that this trade of ours may come into disrepute but also that the temple of the great goddess Artemis may be counted as nothing, and that she may even be deposed from her magnificence, she whom all Asia and the world worship."

[28] When they heard this they were enraged and were crying out, "Great is Artemis of the Ephesians!" [29] So the city was filled with the confusion, and they rushed together into the theater, dragging with them Gaius and Aristarchus, Macedonians who were Paul's companions in travel. [30] But when Paul wished to go in among the crowd, the disciples would not let him. [31] And even some of the Asiarchs,[5] who were friends of his, sent to him and were urging him not to venture into the theater. [32] Now some cried out one thing, some another, for the assembly was in confusion, and most of them did not know why they had come

---

[1] Greek *upper* (that is, highland)　[2] Or *into*　[3] Some manuscripts add *from the fifth hour to the tenth* (that is, from 11 A.M. to 4 P.M.)　[4] Or *both*　[5] That is, high-ranking officers of the province of Asia

together. [33] Some of the crowd prompted Alexander, whom the Jews had put forward. And Alexander, motioning with his hand, wanted to make a defense to the crowd. [34] But when they recognized that he was a Jew, for about two hours they all cried out with one voice, "Great is Artemis of the Ephesians!"

[35] And when the town clerk had quieted the crowd, he said, "Men of Ephesus, who is there who does not know that the city of the Ephesians is temple keeper of the great Artemis, and of the sacred stone that fell from the sky?[1] [36] Seeing then that these things cannot be denied, you ought to be quiet and do nothing rash. [37] For you have brought these men here who are neither sacrilegious nor blasphemers of our goddess. [38] If therefore Demetrius and the craftsmen with him have a complaint against anyone, the courts are open, and there are proconsuls. Let them bring charges against one another. [39] But if you seek anything further,[2] it shall be settled in the regular assembly. [40] For we really are in danger of being charged with rioting today, since there is no cause that we can give to justify this commotion." [41] And when he had said these things, he dismissed the assembly.

Paul in Macedonia and Greece

20 After the uproar ceased, Paul sent for the disciples, and after encouraging them, he said farewell and departed for Macedonia. [2] When he had gone through those regions and had given them much encouragement, he came to Greece. [3] There he spent three months, and when a plot was made against him by the Jews[3] as he was about to set sail for Syria, he decided to return through Macedonia. [4] Sopater the Berean, son of Pyrrhus, accompanied him; and of the Thessalonians, Aristarchus and Secundus; and Gaius of Derbe, and Timothy; and the Asians, Tychicus and Trophimus. [5] These went on ahead and were waiting for us at Troas, [6] but we sailed away from Philippi after the days of Unleavened Bread, and in five days we came to them at Troas, where we stayed for seven days.

Eutychus Raised from the Dead

[7] On the first day of the week, when we were gathered together to break bread, Paul talked with them, intending to depart on the next day, and he prolonged his speech until midnight. [8] There were many lamps in the upper room where we were gathered. [9] And a young man named Eutychus, sitting at the window, sank into a deep sleep as Paul talked still longer. And being overcome by sleep, he fell down from the third story and was taken up dead. [10] But Paul went down and bent over him, and taking him in his arms, said, "Do not be alarmed, for his life is in him." [11] And when Paul had gone up and had broken bread and eaten, he conversed with them a long while, until daybreak, and so departed. [12] And they took the youth away alive, and were not a little comforted.

[13] But going ahead to the ship, we set sail for Assos, intending to take Paul aboard there, for so he had arranged, intending himself to go by land. [14] And when he met us at Assos, we took him on board and went to Mitylene. [15] And sailing from there we came the following day opposite Chios; the next day we touched at Samos; and[4] the day after that we went to Miletus. [16] For Paul had decided to sail past Ephesus, so that he might not have to spend time in Asia, for he was hastening to be at Jerusalem, if possible, on the day of Pentecost.

Paul Speaks to the Ephesian Elders

[17] Now from Miletus he sent to Ephesus and called the elders of the church to come to him. [18] And when they came to him, he said to them:

"You yourselves know how I lived among you the whole time from the first day that I set foot in Asia, [19] serving the Lord with all humility and with tears and with trials that happened to me through the plots of the Jews; [20] how I did not shrink from declaring to you anything that was profitable, and teaching you in public and from house to house, [21] testifying both to Jews and to Greeks of repentance toward God and of faith in our Lord Jesus Christ.[5] [22] And now, behold, I am going to Jerusalem, constrained by[6] the Spirit, not knowing what will happen to me there, [23] except that the Holy Spirit testifies to me in every city that imprisonment and afflictions await me. [24] But I do not account my life of any value nor as precious to myself, if only I may finish my course and the ministry that I received from the Lord Jesus, to testify to the gospel of the grace of God. [25] And now, behold, I know that none of you among whom I have gone about proclaiming the kingdom

---

[1] The meaning of the Greek is uncertain [2] Some manuscripts *seek about other matters* [3] Greek *Ioudaioi* probably refers here to Jewish religious leaders, and others under their influence, in that time; also verse 19 [4] Some manuscripts add *after remaining at Trogyllium* [5] Some manuscripts omit *Christ* [6] Or *bound in*

will see my face again. ²⁶ Therefore I testify to you this day that I am innocent of the blood of all, ²⁷ for I did not shrink from declaring to you the whole counsel of God. ²⁸ Pay careful attention to yourselves and to all the flock, in which the Holy Spirit has made you overseers, to care for the church of God,¹ which he obtained with his own blood.² ²⁹ I know that after my departure fierce wolves will come in among you, not sparing the flock; ³⁰ and from among your own selves will arise men speaking twisted things, to draw away the disciples after them. ³¹ Therefore be alert, remembering that for three years I did not cease night or day to admonish every one with tears. ³² And now I commend you to God and to the word of his grace, which is able to build you up and to give you the inheritance among all those who are sanctified. ³³ I coveted no one's silver or gold or apparel. ³⁴ You yourselves know that these hands ministered to my necessities and to those who were with me. ³⁵ In all things I have shown you that by working hard in this way we must help the weak and remember the words of the Lord Jesus, how he himself said, 'It is more blessed to give than to receive.'"

³⁶ And when he had said these things, he knelt down and prayed with them all. ³⁷ And there was much weeping on the part of all; they embraced Paul and kissed him, ³⁸ being sorrowful most of all because of the word he had spoken, that they would not see his face again. And they accompanied him to the ship.

Paul Goes to Jerusalem

21 And when we had parted from them and set sail, we came by a straight course to Cos, and the next day to Rhodes, and from there to Patara.³ ² And having found a ship crossing to Phoenicia, we went aboard and set sail. ³ When we had come in sight of Cyprus, leaving it on the left we sailed to Syria and landed at Tyre, for there the ship was to unload its cargo. ⁴ And having sought out the disciples, we stayed there for seven days. And through the Spirit they were telling Paul not to go on to Jerusalem. ⁵ When our days there were ended, we departed and went on our journey, and they all, with wives and children, accompanied us until we were outside the city. And kneeling down on the beach, we prayed ⁶ and said farewell to one another. Then we went on board the ship, and they returned home.

⁷ When we had finished the voyage from Tyre, we arrived at Ptolemais, and we greeted the brothers⁴ and stayed with them for one day. ⁸ On the next day we departed and came to Caesarea, and we entered the house of Philip the evangelist, who was one of the seven, and stayed with him. ⁹ He had four unmarried daughters, who prophesied. ¹⁰ While we were staying for many days, a prophet named Agabus came down from Judea. ¹¹ And coming to us, he took Paul's belt and bound his own feet and hands and said, "Thus says the Holy Spirit, 'This is how the Jews⁵ at Jerusalem will bind the man who owns this belt and deliver him into the hands of the Gentiles.'" ¹² When we heard this, we and the people there urged him not to go up to Jerusalem. ¹³ Then Paul answered, "What are you doing, weeping and breaking my heart? For I am ready not only to be imprisoned but even to die in Jerusalem for the name of the Lord Jesus." ¹⁴ And since he would not be persuaded, we ceased and said, "Let the will of the Lord be done."

¹⁵ After these days we got ready and went up to Jerusalem. ¹⁶ And some of the disciples from Caesarea went with us, bringing us to the house of Mnason of Cyprus, an early disciple, with whom we should lodge.

Paul Visits James

¹⁷ When we had come to Jerusalem, the brothers received us gladly. ¹⁸ On the following day Paul went in with us to James, and all the elders were present. ¹⁹ After greeting them, he related one by one the things that God had done among the Gentiles through his ministry. ²⁰ And when they heard it, they glorified God. And they said to him, "You see, brother, how many thousands there are among the Jews of those who have believed. They are all zealous for the law, ²¹ and they have been told about you that you teach all the Jews who are among the Gentiles to forsake Moses, telling them not to circumcise their children or walk according to our customs. ²² What then is to be done? They will certainly hear that you have come. ²³ Do therefore what we tell you. We have four men who are under a vow; ²⁴ take these men and purify yourself along with them and pay their expenses, so that they may shave their heads. Thus all will know that there is nothing in what they have been told about you, but that you yourself also live in

---

¹ Some manuscripts *of the Lord* ² Or *with the blood of his Own* ³ Some manuscripts add *and Myra* ⁴ Or *brothers and sisters*; also verse 17 ⁵ Greek *Ioudaioi* probably refers here to Jewish religious leaders, and others under their influence, in that time

observance of the law. 25 But as for the Gentiles who have believed, we have sent a letter with our judgment that they should abstain from what has been sacrificed to idols, and from blood, and from what has been strangled,[1] and from sexual immorality." 26 Then Paul took the men, and the next day he purified himself along with them and went into the temple, giving notice when the days of purification would be fulfilled and the offering presented for each one of them.

Paul Arrested in the Temple

27 When the seven days were almost completed, the Jews from Asia, seeing him in the temple, stirred up the whole crowd and laid hands on him, 28 crying out, "Men of Israel, help! This is the man who is teaching everyone everywhere against the people and the law and this place. Moreover, he even brought Greeks into the temple and has defiled this holy place." 29 For they had previously seen Trophimus the Ephesian with him in the city, and they supposed that Paul had brought him into the temple. 30 Then all the city was stirred up, and the people ran together. They seized Paul and dragged him out of the temple, and at once the gates were shut. 31 And as they were seeking to kill him, word came to the tribune of the cohort that all Jerusalem was in confusion. 32 He at once took soldiers and centurions and ran down to them. And when they saw the tribune and the soldiers, they stopped beating Paul. 33 Then the tribune came up and arrested him and ordered him to be bound with two chains. He inquired who he was and what he had done. 34 Some in the crowd were shouting one thing, some another. And as he could not learn the facts because of the uproar, he ordered him to be brought into the barracks. 35 And when he came to the steps, he was actually carried by the soldiers because of the violence of the crowd, 36 for the mob of the people followed, crying out, "Away with him!"

Paul Speaks to the People

37 As Paul was about to be brought into the barracks, he said to the tribune, "May I say something to you?" And he said, "Do you know Greek? 38 Are you not the Egyptian, then, who recently stirred up a revolt and led the four thousand men of the Assassins out into the wilderness?" 39 Paul replied, "I am a Jew, from Tarsus in Cilicia, a citizen of no obscure city. I beg you, permit me to speak to the people." 40 And when he had given him permission, Paul, standing on the steps, motioned with his hand to the people. And when there was a great hush, he addressed them in the Hebrew language,[2] saying:

22 "Brothers and fathers, hear the defense that I now make before you."

2 And when they heard that he was addressing them in the Hebrew language,[3] they became even more quiet. And he said:

3 "I am a Jew, born in Tarsus in Cilicia, but brought up in this city, educated at the feet of Gamaliel[4] according to the strict manner of the law of our fathers, being zealous for God as all of you are this day. 4 I persecuted this Way to the death, binding and delivering to prison both men and women, 5 as the high priest and the whole council of elders can bear me witness. From them I received letters to the brothers, and I journeyed toward Damascus to take those also who were there and bring them in bonds to Jerusalem to be punished.

6 "As I was on my way and drew near to Damascus, about noon a great light from heaven suddenly shone around me. 7 And I fell to the ground and heard a voice saying to me, 'Saul, Saul, why are you persecuting me?' 8 And I answered, 'Who are you, Lord?' And he said to me, 'I am Jesus of Nazareth, whom you are persecuting.' 9 Now those who were with me saw the light but did not understand[5] the voice of the one who was speaking to me. 10 And I said, 'What shall I do, Lord?' And the Lord said to me, 'Rise, and go into Damascus, and there you will be told all that is appointed for you to do.' 11 And since I could not see because of the brightness of that light, I was led by the hand by those who were with me, and came into Damascus.

12 "And one Ananias, a devout man according to the law, well spoken of by all the Jews who lived there, 13 came to me, and standing by me said to me, 'Brother Saul, receive your sight.' And at that very hour I received my sight and saw him. 14 And he said, 'The God of our fathers appointed you to know his will, to see the Righteous One and to hear a voice from his mouth; 15 for you will be a witness for him to everyone of what you have seen and heard.

---

[1] Some manuscripts omit *and from what has been strangled* [2] Or *the Hebrew dialect* (probably Aramaic) [3] Or *the Hebrew dialect* (probably Aramaic) [4] Or *city at the feet of Gamaliel, educated* [5] Or *hear with understanding*

[16] And now why do you wait? Rise and be baptized and wash away your sins, calling on his name.'

[17] "When I had returned to Jerusalem and was praying in the temple, I fell into a trance [18] and saw him saying to me, 'Make haste and get out of Jerusalem quickly, because they will not accept your testimony about me.' [19] And I said, 'Lord, they themselves know that in one synagogue after another I imprisoned and beat those who believed in you. [20] And when the blood of Stephen your witness was being shed, I myself was standing by and approving and watching over the garments of those who killed him.' [21] And he said to me, 'Go, for I will send you far away to the Gentiles.'"

Paul and the Roman Tribune

[22] Up to this word they listened to him. Then they raised their voices and said, "Away with such a fellow from the earth! For he should not be allowed to live." [23] And as they were shouting and throwing off their cloaks and flinging dust into the air, [24] the tribune ordered him to be brought into the barracks, saying that he should be examined by flogging, to find out why they were shouting against him like this. [25] But when they had stretched him out for the whips,[1] Paul said to the centurion who was standing by, "Is it lawful for you to flog a man who is a Roman citizen and uncondemned?" [26] When the centurion heard this, he went to the tribune and said to him, "What are you about to do? For this man is a Roman citizen." [27] So the tribune came and said to him, "Tell me, are you a Roman citizen?" And he said, "Yes." [28] The tribune answered, "I bought this citizenship for a large sum." Paul said, "But I am a citizen by birth." [29] So those who were about to examine him withdrew from him immediately, and the tribune also was afraid, for he realized that Paul was a Roman citizen and that he had bound him.

Paul Before the Council

[30] But on the next day, desiring to know the real reason why he was being accused by the Jews, he unbound him and commanded the chief priests and all the council to meet, and he brought Paul down and set him before them.

23 And looking intently at the council, Paul said, "Brothers, I have lived my life before God in all good conscience up to this day." [2] And the high priest Ananias commanded those who stood by him to strike him on the mouth. [3] Then Paul said to him, "God is going to strike you, you whitewashed wall! Are you sitting to judge me according to the law, and yet contrary to the law you order me to be struck?" [4] Those who stood by said, "Would you revile God's high priest?" [5] And Paul said, "I did not know, brothers, that he was the high priest, for it is written, [a]'You shall not speak evil of a ruler of your people.'"

[6] Now when Paul perceived that one part were Sadducees and the other Pharisees, he cried out in the council, "Brothers, I am a Pharisee, a son of Pharisees. It is with respect to the hope and the resurrection of the dead that I am on trial." [7] And when he had said this, a dissension arose between the Pharisees and the Sadducees, and the assembly was divided. [8] For the Sadducees say that there is no resurrection, nor angel, nor spirit, but the Pharisees acknowledge them all. [9] Then a great clamor arose, and some of the scribes of the Pharisees' party stood up and contended sharply, "We find nothing wrong in this man. What if a spirit or an angel spoke to him?" [10] And when the dissension became violent, the tribune, afraid that Paul would be torn to pieces by them, commanded the soldiers to go down and take him away from among them by force and bring him into the barracks.

[11] The following night the Lord stood by him and said, "Take courage, for as you have testified to the facts about me in Jerusalem, so you must testify also in Rome."

A Plot to Kill Paul

[12] When it was day, the Jews made a plot and bound themselves by an oath neither to eat nor drink till they had killed Paul. [13] There were more than forty who made this conspiracy. [14] They went to the chief priests and elders and said, "We have strictly bound ourselves by an oath to taste no food till we have killed Paul. [15] Now therefore you, along with the council, give notice to the tribune to bring him down to you, as though you were going to determine his case more exactly. And we are ready to kill him before he comes near."

[16] Now the son of Paul's sister heard of their ambush, so he went and entered the barracks and told Paul. [17] Paul called one of the centurions and said, "Take this young man to the tribune, for he has something to tell him." [18] So

[1] Or when they had tied him up with leather strips   [a] Ex. 22:28

he took him and brought him to the tribune and said, "Paul the prisoner called me and asked me to bring this young man to you, as he has something to say to you." [19] The tribune took him by the hand, and going aside asked him privately, "What is it that you have to tell me?" [20] And he said, "The Jews have agreed to ask you to bring Paul down to the council tomorrow, as though they were going to inquire somewhat more closely about him. [21] But do not be persuaded by them, for more than forty of their men are lying in ambush for him, who have bound themselves by an oath neither to eat nor drink till they have killed him. And now they are ready, waiting for your consent." [22] So the tribune dismissed the young man, charging him, "Tell no one that you have informed me of these things."

Paul Sent to Felix the Governor

[23] Then he called two of the centurions and said, "Get ready two hundred soldiers, with seventy horsemen and two hundred spearmen to go as far as Caesarea at the third hour of the night.[1] [24] Also provide mounts for Paul to ride and bring him safely to Felix the governor." [25] And he wrote a letter to this effect:

[26] "Claudius Lysias, to his Excellency the governor Felix, greetings. [27] This man was seized by the Jews and was about to be killed by them when I came upon them with the soldiers and rescued him, having learned that he was a Roman citizen. [28] And desiring to know the charge for which they were accusing him, I brought him down to their council. [29] I found that he was being accused about questions of their law, but charged with nothing deserving death or imprisonment. [30] And when it was disclosed to me that there would be a plot against the man, I sent him to you at once, ordering his accusers also to state before you what they have against him."

[31] So the soldiers, according to their instructions, took Paul and brought him by night to Antipatris. [32] And on the next day they returned to the barracks, letting the horsemen go on with him. [33] When they had come to Caesarea and delivered the letter to the governor, they presented Paul also before him. [34] On reading the letter, he asked what province he was from. And when he learned that he was from Cilicia, [35] he said, "I will give you a hearing when your accusers arrive." And he commanded him to be guarded in Herod's praetorium.

Paul Before Felix at Caesarea

24 And after five days the high priest Ananias came down with some elders and a spokesman, one Tertullus. They laid before the governor their case against Paul. [2] And when he had been summoned, Tertullus began to accuse him, saying:

"Since through you we enjoy much peace, and since by your foresight, most excellent Felix, reforms are being made for this nation, [3] in every way and everywhere we accept this with all gratitude. [4] But, to detain[2] you no further, I beg you in your kindness to hear us briefly. [5] For we have found this man a plague, one who stirs up riots among all the Jews throughout the world and is a ringleader of the sect of the Nazarenes. [6] He even tried to profane the temple, but we seized him.[3] [8] By examining him yourself you will be able to find out from him about everything of which we accuse him."

[9] The Jews also joined in the charge, affirming that all these things were so.

[10] And when the governor had nodded to him to speak, Paul replied:

"Knowing that for many years you have been a judge over this nation, I cheerfully make my defense. [11] You can verify that it is not more than twelve days since I went up to worship in Jerusalem, [12] and they did not find me disputing with anyone or stirring up a crowd, either in the temple or in the synagogues or in the city. [13] Neither can they prove to you what they now bring up against me. [14] But this I confess to you, that according to the Way, which they call a sect, I worship the God of our fathers, believing everything laid down by the Law and written in the Prophets, [15] having a hope in God, which these men themselves accept, that there will be a resurrection of both the just and the unjust. [16] So I always take pains to have a clear conscience toward both God and man. [17] Now after several years I came to bring alms to my nation and to present offerings. [18] While I was doing this, they found me purified in the temple, without any crowd or tumult. But some Jews from Asia— [19] they ought to be here before you and to make an accusation, should they have anything against me. [20] Or else let these men themselves say what wrongdoing they found when I stood before the council, [21] other than this one thing

---

[1] That is, 9 P.M. [2] Or weary [3] Some manuscripts add and we would have judged him according to our law. [7] But the chief captain Lysias came and with great violence took him out of our hands, [8] commanding his accusers to come before you.

that I cried out while standing among them: 'It is with respect to the resurrection of the dead that I am on trial before you this day.'"

Paul Kept in Custody

²² But Felix, having a rather accurate knowledge of the Way, put them off, saying, "When Lysias the tribune comes down, I will decide your case." ²³ Then he gave orders to the centurion that he should be kept in custody but have some liberty, and that none of his friends should be prevented from attending to his needs.

²⁴ After some days Felix came with his wife Drusilla, who was Jewish, and he sent for Paul and heard him speak about faith in Christ Jesus. ²⁵ And as he reasoned about righteousness and self-control and the coming judgment, Felix was alarmed and said, "Go away for the present. When I get an opportunity I will summon you." ²⁶ At the same time he hoped that money would be given him by Paul. So he sent for him often and conversed with him. ²⁷ When two years had elapsed, Felix was succeeded by Porcius Festus. And desiring to do the Jews a favor, Felix left Paul in prison.

Paul Appeals to Caesar

25 Now three days after Festus had arrived in the province, he went up to Jerusalem from Caesarea. ² And the chief priests and the principal men of the Jews laid out their case against Paul, and they urged him, ³ asking as a favor against Paul[1] that he summon him to Jerusalem—because they were planning an ambush to kill him on the way. ⁴ Festus replied that Paul was being kept at Caesarea and that he himself intended to go there shortly. ⁵ "So," said he, "let the men of authority among you go down with me, and if there is anything wrong about the man, let them bring charges against him."

⁶ After he stayed among them not more than eight or ten days, he went down to Caesarea. And the next day he took his seat on the tribunal and ordered Paul to be brought. ⁷ When he had arrived, the Jews who had come down from Jerusalem stood around him, bringing many and serious charges against him that they could not prove. ⁸ Paul argued in his defense, "Neither against the law of the Jews, nor against the temple, nor against Caesar have I committed any offense." ⁹ But Festus, wishing to do the Jews a favor, said to Paul, "Do you wish to go up to Jerusalem and there be tried on these charges

before me?" ¹⁰ But Paul said, "I am standing before Caesar's tribunal, where I ought to be tried. To the Jews I have done no wrong, as you yourself know very well. ¹¹ If then I am a wrongdoer and have committed anything for which I deserve to die, I do not seek to escape death. But if there is nothing to their charges against me, no one can give me up to them. I appeal to Caesar." ¹² Then Festus, when he had conferred with his council, answered, "To Caesar you have appealed; to Caesar you shall go."

Paul Before Agrippa and Bernice

¹³ Now when some days had passed, Agrippa the king and Bernice arrived at Caesarea and greeted Festus. ¹⁴ And as they stayed there many days, Festus laid Paul's case before the king, saying, "There is a man left prisoner by Felix, ¹⁵ and when I was at Jerusalem, the chief priests and the elders of the Jews laid out their case against him, asking for a sentence of condemnation against him. ¹⁶ I answered them that it was not the custom of the Romans to give up anyone before the accused met the accusers face to face and had opportunity to make his defense concerning the charge laid against him. ¹⁷ So when they came together here, I made no delay, but on the next day took my seat on the tribunal and ordered the man to be brought. ¹⁸ When the accusers stood up, they brought no charge in his case of such evils as I supposed. ¹⁹ Rather they had certain points of dispute with him about their own religion and about a certain Jesus, who was dead, but whom Paul asserted to be alive. ²⁰ Being at a loss how to investigate these questions, I asked whether he wanted to go to Jerusalem and be tried there regarding them. ²¹ But when Paul had appealed to be kept in custody for the decision of the emperor, I ordered him to be held until I could send him to Caesar." ²² Then Agrippa said to Festus, "I would like to hear the man myself." "Tomorrow," said he, "you will hear him."

²³ So on the next day Agrippa and Bernice came with great pomp, and they entered the audience hall with the military tribunes and the prominent men of the city. Then, at the command of Festus, Paul was brought in. ²⁴ And Festus said, "King Agrippa and all who are present with us, you see this man about whom the whole Jewish people petitioned me, both in Jerusalem and here, shouting that he ought not to live any longer. ²⁵ But I found that he

---

[1] Greek *him*

had done nothing deserving death. And as he himself appealed to the emperor, I decided to go ahead and send him. [26] But I have nothing definite to write to my lord about him. Therefore I have brought him before you all, and especially before you, King Agrippa, so that, after we have examined him, I may have something to write. [27] For it seems to me unreasonable, in sending a prisoner, not to indicate the charges against him."

Paul's Defense Before Agrippa

26 So Agrippa said to Paul, "You have permission to speak for yourself." Then Paul stretched out his hand and made his defense:

[2] "I consider myself fortunate that it is before you, King Agrippa, I am going to make my defense today against all the accusations of the Jews, [3] especially because you are familiar with all the customs and controversies of the Jews. Therefore I beg you to listen to me patiently.

[4] "My manner of life from my youth, spent from the beginning among my own nation and in Jerusalem, is known by all the Jews. [5] They have known for a long time, if they are willing to testify, that according to the strictest party of our religion I have lived as a Pharisee. [6] And now I stand here on trial because of my hope in the promise made by God to our fathers, [7] to which our twelve tribes hope to attain, as they earnestly worship night and day. And for this hope I am accused by Jews, O king! [8] Why is it thought incredible by any of you that God raises the dead?

[9] "I myself was convinced that I ought to do many things in opposing the name of Jesus of Nazareth. [10] And I did so in Jerusalem. I not only locked up many of the saints in prison after receiving authority from the chief priests, but when they were put to death I cast my vote against them. [11] And I punished them often in all the synagogues and tried to make them blaspheme, and in raging fury against them I persecuted them even to foreign cities.

Paul Tells of His Conversion

[12] "In this connection I journeyed to Damascus with the authority and commission of the chief priests. [13] At midday, O king, I saw on the way a light from heaven, brighter than the sun, that shone around me and those who journeyed with me. [14] And when we had all fallen to the ground, I heard a voice saying to me in the Hebrew language,[1] 'Saul, Saul, why are you persecuting me? It is hard for you to kick against the goads.' [15] And I said, 'Who are you, Lord?' And the Lord said, 'I am Jesus whom you are persecuting. [16] But rise and stand upon your feet, for I have appeared to you for this purpose, to appoint you as a servant and witness to the things in which you have seen me and to those in which I will appear to you, [17] delivering you from your people and from the Gentiles—to whom I am sending you [18] to open their eyes, so that they may turn from darkness to light and from the power of Satan to God, that they may receive forgiveness of sins and a place among those who are sanctified by faith in me.'

[19] "Therefore, O King Agrippa, I was not disobedient to the heavenly vision, [20] but declared first to those in Damascus, then in Jerusalem and throughout all the region of Judea, and also to the Gentiles, that they should repent and turn to God, performing deeds in keeping with their repentance. [21] For this reason the Jews seized me in the temple and tried to kill me. [22] To this day I have had the help that comes from God, and so I stand here testifying both to small and great, saying nothing but what the prophets and Moses said would come to pass: [23] that the Christ must suffer and that, by being the first to rise from the dead, he would proclaim light both to our people and to the Gentiles."

[24] And as he was saying these things in his defense, Festus said with a loud voice, "Paul, you are out of your mind; your great learning is driving you out of your mind." [25] But Paul said, "I am not out of my mind, most excellent Festus, but I am speaking true and rational words. [26] For the king knows about these things, and to him I speak boldly. For I am persuaded that none of these things has escaped his notice, for this has not been done in a corner. [27] King Agrippa, do you believe the prophets? I know that you believe." [28] And Agrippa said to Paul, "In a short time would you persuade me to be a Christian?"[2] [29] And Paul said, "Whether short or long, I would to God that not only you but also all who hear me this day might become such as I am—except for these chains."

[30] Then the king rose, and the governor and Bernice and those who were sitting with them. [31] And when they had withdrawn, they said to one another, "This man is doing nothing to

---

[1] Or the Hebrew dialect (probably Aramaic) [2] Or In a short time you would persuade me to act like a Christian!

deserve death or imprisonment." [32] And Agrippa said to Festus, "This man could have been set free if he had not appealed to Caesar."

Paul Sails for Rome

27 And when it was decided that we should sail for Italy, they delivered Paul and some other prisoners to a centurion of the Augustan Cohort named Julius. [2] And embarking in a ship of Adramyttium, which was about to sail to the ports along the coast of Asia, we put to sea, accompanied by Aristarchus, a Macedonian from Thessalonica. [3] The next day we put in at Sidon. And Julius treated Paul kindly and gave him leave to go to his friends and be cared for. [4] And putting out to sea from there we sailed under the lee of Cyprus, because the winds were against us. [5] And when we had sailed across the open sea along the coast of Cilicia and Pamphylia, we came to Myra in Lycia. [6] There the centurion found a ship of Alexandria sailing for Italy and put us on board. [7] We sailed slowly for a number of days and arrived with difficulty off Cnidus, and as the wind did not allow us to go farther, we sailed under the lee of Crete off Salmone. [8] Coasting along it with difficulty, we came to a place called Fair Havens, near which was the city of Lasea.

[9] Since much time had passed, and the voyage was now dangerous because even the Fast[1] was already over, Paul advised them, [10] saying, "Sirs, I perceive that the voyage will be with injury and much loss, not only of the cargo and the ship, but also of our lives." [11] But the centurion paid more attention to the pilot and to the owner of the ship than to what Paul said. [12] And because the harbor was not suitable to spend the winter in, the majority decided to put out to sea from there, on the chance that somehow they could reach Phoenix, a harbor of Crete, facing both southwest and northwest, and spend the winter there.

The Storm at Sea

[13] Now when the south wind blew gently, supposing that they had obtained their purpose, they weighed anchor and sailed along Crete, close to the shore. [14] But soon a tempestuous wind, called the northeaster, struck down from the land. [15] And when the ship was caught and could not face the wind, we gave way to it and were driven along. [16] Running under the lee of a small island called Cauda,[2] we managed with difficulty to secure the ship's boat. [17] After hoisting it up, they used supports to undergird the ship. Then, fearing that they would run aground on the Syrtis, they lowered the gear,[3] and thus they were driven along. [18] Since we were violently storm-tossed, they began the next day to jettison the cargo. [19] And on the third day they threw the ship's tackle overboard with their own hands. [20] When neither sun nor stars appeared for many days, and no small tempest lay on us, all hope of our being saved was at last abandoned.

[21] Since they had been without food for a long time, Paul stood up among them and said, "Men, you should have listened to me and not have set sail from Crete and incurred this injury and loss. [22] Yet now I urge you to take heart, for there will be no loss of life among you, but only of the ship. [23] For this very night there stood before me an angel of the God to whom I belong and whom I worship, [24] and he said, 'Do not be afraid, Paul; you must stand before Caesar. And behold, God has granted you all those who sail with you.' [25] So take heart, men, for I have faith in God that it will be exactly as I have been told. [26] But we must run aground on some island."

[27] When the fourteenth night had come, as we were being driven across the Adriatic Sea, about midnight the sailors suspected that they were nearing land. [28] So they took a sounding and found twenty fathoms.[4] A little farther on they took a sounding again and found fifteen fathoms.[5] [29] And fearing that we might run on the rocks, they let down four anchors from the stern and prayed for day to come. [30] And as the sailors were seeking to escape from the ship, and had lowered the ship's boat into the sea under pretense of laying out anchors from the bow, [31] Paul said to the centurion and the soldiers, "Unless these men stay in the ship, you cannot be saved." [32] Then the soldiers cut away the ropes of the ship's boat and let it go.

[33] As day was about to dawn, Paul urged them all to take some food, saying, "Today is the fourteenth day that you have continued in suspense and without food, having taken nothing. [34] Therefore I urge you to take some food. For it will give you strength,[6] for not a hair is to perish from the head of any of you." [35] And when he had said these things, he took bread, and giving thanks to God in the presence of all he broke it and began to eat. [36] Then they all were encour-

---

[1] That is, the Day of Atonement [2] Some manuscripts *Clauda* [3] That is, the sea-anchor (or possibly the mainsail) [4] About 120 feet; a fathom (Greek *orguia*) was about 6 feet or 2 meters [5] About 90 feet (see previous note) [6] Or *For it is for your deliverance*

aged and ate some food themselves. [37](We were in all 276[1] persons in the ship.) [38] And when they had eaten enough, they lightened the ship, throwing out the wheat into the sea.

The Shipwreck

[39] Now when it was day, they did not recognize the land, but they noticed a bay with a beach, on which they planned if possible to run the ship ashore. [40] So they cast off the anchors and left them in the sea, at the same time loosening the ropes that tied the rudders. Then hoisting the foresail to the wind they made for the beach. [41] But striking a reef,[2] they ran the vessel aground. The bow stuck and remained immovable, and the stern was being broken up by the surf. [42] The soldiers' plan was to kill the prisoners, lest any should swim away and escape. [43] But the centurion, wishing to save Paul, kept them from carrying out their plan. He ordered those who could swim to jump overboard first and make for the land, [44] and the rest on planks or on pieces of the ship. And so it was that all were brought safely to land.

Paul on Malta

28 After we were brought safely through, we then learned that the island was called Malta. [2] The native people[3] showed us unusual kindness, for they kindled a fire and welcomed us all, because it had begun to rain and was cold. [3] When Paul had gathered a bundle of sticks and put them on the fire, a viper came out because of the heat and fastened on his hand. [4] When the native people saw the creature hanging from his hand, they said to one another, "No doubt this man is a murderer. Though he has escaped from the sea, Justice[4] has not allowed him to live." [5] He, however, shook off the creature into the fire and suffered no harm. [6] They were waiting for him to swell up or suddenly fall down dead. But when they had waited a long time and saw no misfortune come to him, they changed their minds and said that he was a god.

[7] Now in the neighborhood of that place were lands belonging to the chief man of the island, named Publius, who received us and entertained us hospitably for three days. [8] It happened that the father of Publius lay sick with fever and dysentery. And Paul visited him and prayed, and putting his hands on him, healed him. [9] And when this had taken place,

the rest of the people on the island who had diseases also came and were cured. [10] They also honored us greatly,[5] and when we were about to sail, they put on board whatever we needed.

Paul Arrives at Rome

[11] After three months we set sail in a ship that had wintered in the island, a ship of Alexandria, with the twin gods[6] as a figurehead. [12] Putting in at Syracuse, we stayed there for three days. [13] And from there we made a circuit and arrived at Rhegium. And after one day a south wind sprang up, and on the second day we came to Puteoli. [14] There we found brothers[7] and were invited to stay with them for seven days. And so we came to Rome. [15] And the brothers there, when they heard about us, came as far as the Forum of Appius and Three Taverns to meet us. On seeing them, Paul thanked God and took courage. [16] And when we came into Rome, Paul was allowed to stay by himself, with the soldier who guarded him.

Paul in Rome

[17] After three days he called together the local leaders of the Jews, and when they had gathered, he said to them, "Brothers, though I had done nothing against our people or the customs of our fathers, yet I was delivered as a prisoner from Jerusalem into the hands of the Romans. [18] When they had examined me, they wished to set me at liberty, because there was no reason for the death penalty in my case. [19] But because the Jews objected, I was compelled to appeal to Caesar—though I had no charge to bring against my nation. [20] For this reason, therefore, I have asked to see you and speak with you, since it is because of the hope of Israel that I am wearing this chain." [21] And they said to him, "We have received no letters from Judea about you, and none of the brothers coming here has reported or spoken any evil about you. [22] But we desire to hear from you what your views are, for with regard to this sect we know that everywhere it is spoken against."

[23] When they had appointed a day for him, they came to him at his lodging in greater numbers. From morning till evening he expounded to them, testifying to the kingdom of God and trying to convince them about Jesus both from the Law of Moses and from the Prophets. [24] And some were convinced by what he said,

---

[1] Some manuscripts *seventy-six*, or *about seventy-six* [2] Or *sandbank*, or *crosscurrent*; Greek *place between two seas* [3] Greek *barbaroi* (that is, non-Greek speakers); also verse 4 [4] Or *justice* [5] Greek *honored us with many honors* [6] That is, the Greek gods Castor and Pollux [7] Or *brothers and sisters*; also verses 15, 21

but others disbelieved. [25] And disagreeing among themselves, they departed after Paul had made one statement: "The Holy Spirit was right in saying to your fathers through Isaiah the prophet:

[26] [a] "'Go to this people, and say,
  "You will indeed hear but never under-
        stand,
      and you will indeed see but never per-
        ceive."
[27]   For this people's heart has grown dull,
      and with their ears they can barely
        hear,

and their eyes they have closed;
  lest they should see with their eyes
      and hear with their ears
  and understand with their heart
      and turn, and I would heal them.'

[28] Therefore let it be known to you that this salvation of God has been sent to the Gentiles; they will listen."[1]

[30] He lived there two whole years at his own expense,[2] and welcomed all who came to him, [31] proclaiming the kingdom of God and teaching about the Lord Jesus Christ with all boldness and without hindrance.

---

[1] Some manuscripts add verse 29: *And when he had said these words, the Jews departed, having much dispute among themselves* [2] Or *in his own hired dwelling* [a] Isa. 6:9, 10

THE LETTER OF PAUL TO THE

ROMANS

Greeting

1 Paul, a servant[1] of Christ Jesus, called to be an apostle, set apart for the gospel of God, [2] which he promised beforehand through his prophets in the holy Scriptures, [3] concerning his Son, who was descended from David[2] according to the flesh [4] and was declared to be the Son of God in power according to the Spirit of holiness by his resurrection from the dead, Jesus Christ our Lord, [5] through whom we have received grace and apostleship to bring about the obedience of faith for the sake of his name among all the nations, [6] including you who are called to belong to Jesus Christ,

[7] To all those in Rome who are loved by God and called to be saints:

Grace to you and peace from God our Father and the Lord Jesus Christ.

Longing to Go to Rome

[8] First, I thank my God through Jesus Christ for all of you, because your faith is proclaimed in all the world. [9] For God is my witness, whom I serve with my spirit in the gospel of his Son, that without ceasing I mention you [10] always in my prayers, asking that somehow by God's will I may now at last succeed in coming to you. [11] For I long to see you, that I may impart to you some spiritual gift to strengthen you— [12] that is, that we may be mutually encouraged by each other's faith, both yours and mine. [13] I do not want you to be unaware, brothers,[3] that I have often intended to come to you (but thus far have been prevented), in order that I may reap some harvest among you as well as among the rest of the Gentiles. [14] I am under obligation both to Greeks and to barbarians,[4] both to the wise and to the foolish. [15] So I am eager to preach the gospel to you also who are in Rome.

The Righteous Shall Live by Faith

[16] For I am not ashamed of the gospel, for it is the power of God for salvation to everyone who believes, to the Jew first and also to the Greek. [17] For in it the righteousness of God is revealed from faith for faith,[5] [a] as it is written, "The righteous shall live by faith."[6]

God's Wrath on Unrighteousness

[18] For the wrath of God is revealed from heaven against all ungodliness and unrighteousness of men, who by their unrighteousness suppress the truth. [19] For what can be known about God is plain to them, because God has shown it to them. [20] For his invisible attributes, namely, his eternal power and divine nature, have been clearly perceived,[7] ever since the creation of the world,[8] in the things that have been made. So they are without excuse. [21] For although they knew God, they did not honor him as God or give thanks to him, but they became futile in their thinking, and their foolish hearts were darkened. [22] Claiming to be wise, they became fools, [23] and exchanged the glory of the immortal God for images resembling mortal man and birds and animals and creeping things.

[24] Therefore God gave them up in the lusts of their hearts to impurity, to the dishonoring of their bodies among themselves, [25] because they exchanged the truth about God for a lie and worshiped and served the creature rather than the Creator, who is blessed forever! Amen.

[26] For this reason God gave them up to dishonorable passions. For their women exchanged natural relations for those that are contrary to nature; [27] and the men likewise gave up natural relations with women and were consumed with passion for one another, men committing shameless acts with men and receiving in themselves the due penalty for their error.

[28] And since they did not see fit to acknowledge God, God gave them up to a debased mind to do what ought not to be done. [29] They were filled with all manner of unrighteousness, evil, covetousness, malice. They are full of envy, murder, strife, deceit, maliciousness. They are gossips, [30] slanderers, haters of God, insolent, haughty, boastful, inventors of evil, disobedient to parents, [31] foolish, faithless, heartless, ruthless. [32] Though they know God's righteous decree that those who practice such things deserve to die, they not only do them but give approval to those who practice them.

[1] For the contextual rendering of the Greek word *doulos*, see Preface [2] Or *who came from the offspring of David* [3] Or *brothers and sisters*. In New Testament usage, depending on the context, the plural Greek word *adelphoi* (translated "brothers") may refer either to *brothers* or to *brothers and sisters*. [4] That is, non-Greeks [5] Or *beginning and ending in faith* [6] Or *The one who by faith is righteous shall live* [7] Or *clearly perceived from the creation of the world* [a] Hab. 2:4

God's Righteous Judgment

2 Therefore you have no excuse, O man, every one of you who judges. For in passing judgment on another you condemn yourself, because you, the judge, practice the very same things. [2] We know that the judgment of God rightly falls on those who practice such things. [3] Do you suppose, O man—you who judge those who practice such things and yet do them yourself—that you will escape the judgment of God? [4] Or do you presume on the riches of his kindness and forbearance and patience, not knowing that God's kindness is meant to lead you to repentance? [5] But because of your hard and impenitent heart you are storing up wrath for yourself on the day of wrath when God's righteous judgment will be revealed.

[6] He will render to each one according to his works: [7] to those who by patience in well-doing seek for glory and honor and immortality, he will give eternal life; [8] but for those who are self-seeking[1] and do not obey the truth, but obey unrighteousness, there will be wrath and fury. [9] There will be tribulation and distress for every human being who does evil, the Jew first and also the Greek, [10] but glory and honor and peace for everyone who does good, the Jew first and also the Greek. [11] For God shows no partiality.

God's Judgment and the Law

[12] For all who have sinned without the law will also perish without the law, and all who have sinned under the law will be judged by the law. [13] For it is not the hearers of the law who are righteous before God, but the doers of the law who will be justified. [14] For when Gentiles, who do not have the law, by nature do what the law requires, they are a law to themselves, even though they do not have the law. [15] They show that the work of the law is written on their hearts, while their conscience also bears witness, and their conflicting thoughts accuse or even excuse them [16] on that day when, according to my gospel, God judges the secrets of men by Christ Jesus.

[17] But if you call yourself a Jew and rely on the law and boast in God [18] and know his will and approve what is excellent, because you are instructed from the law; [19] and if you are sure that you yourself are a guide to the blind, a light to those who are in darkness, [20] an instructor of the foolish, a teacher of children, having in the law the embodiment of knowledge and truth—

[21] you then who teach others, do you not teach yourself? While you preach against stealing, do you steal? [22] You who say that one must not commit adultery, do you commit adultery? You who abhor idols, do you rob temples? [23] You who boast in the law dishonor God by breaking the law. [24] For, [a] as it is written, "The name of God is blasphemed among the Gentiles because of you."

[25] For circumcision indeed is of value if you obey the law, but if you break the law, your circumcision becomes uncircumcision. [26] So, if a man who is uncircumcised keeps the precepts of the law, will not his uncircumcision be regarded[2] as circumcision? [27] Then he who is physically[3] uncircumcised but keeps the law will condemn you who have the written code[4] and circumcision but break the law. [28] For no one is a Jew who is merely one outwardly, nor is circumcision outward and physical. [29] But a Jew is one inwardly, and circumcision is a matter of the heart, by the Spirit, not by the letter. His praise is not from man but from God.

God's Righteousness Upheld

3 Then what advantage has the Jew? Or what is the value of circumcision? [2] Much in every way. To begin with, the Jews were entrusted with the oracles of God. [3] What if some were unfaithful? Does their faithlessness nullify the faithfulness of God? [4] By no means! Let God be true though every one were a liar, as it is written,

[b] "That you may be justified in your words,
        and prevail when you are judged."

[5] But if our unrighteousness serves to show the righteousness of God, what shall we say? That God is unrighteous to inflict wrath on us? (I speak in a human way.) [6] By no means! For then how could God judge the world? [7] But if through my lie God's truth abounds to his glory, why am I still being condemned as a sinner? [8] And why not do evil that good may come?—as some people slanderously charge us with saying. Their condemnation is just.

No One Is Righteous

[9] What then? Are we Jews[5] any better off?[6] No, not at all. For we have already charged that all, both Jews and Greeks, are under sin, [10] as it is written:

---

[1] Or contentious [2] Or counted [3] Or is by nature [4] Or the letter [5] Greek Are we [6] Or at any disadvantage? [a] Isa. 52:5 [b] Ps. 51:4 (Gk.)

[a]"None is righteous, no, not one;
11   no one understands;
          no one seeks for God.
12   All have turned aside; together they have
                become worthless;
          no one does good,
                not even one."
13   [b]"Their throat is an open grave;
          they use their tongues to deceive."
      [c]"The venom of asps is under their lips."
14   [d]"Their mouth is full of curses and bitter-
                ness."
15   [e]"Their feet are swift to shed blood;
16   in their paths are ruin and misery,
17   and the way of peace they have not
                known."
18   [f]"There is no fear of God before their
                eyes."

[19] Now we know that whatever the law says it speaks to those who are under the law, so that every mouth may be stopped, and the whole world may be held accountable to God. [20] For by works of the law no human being[1] will be justified in his sight, since through the law comes knowledge of sin.

The Righteousness of God Through Faith

[21] But now the righteousness of God has been manifested apart from the law, although the Law and the Prophets bear witness to it— [22] the righteousness of God through faith in Jesus Christ for all who believe. For there is no distinction: [23] for all have sinned and fall short of the glory of God, [24] and are justified by his grace as a gift, through the redemption that is in Christ Jesus, [25] whom God put forward as a propitiation by his blood, to be received by faith. This was to show God's righteousness, because in his divine forbearance he had passed over former sins. [26] It was to show his righteousness at the present time, so that he might be just and the justifier of the one who has faith in Jesus.

[27] Then what becomes of our boasting? It is excluded. By what kind of law? By a law of works? No, but by the law of faith. [28] For we hold that one is justified by faith apart from works of the law. [29] Or is God the God of Jews only? Is he not the God of Gentiles also? Yes, of Gentiles also, [30] since God is one—who will justify the circumcised by faith and the uncircumcised through faith. [31] Do we then overthrow the law by this faith? By no means! On the contrary, we uphold the law.

Abraham Justified by Faith

4 What then shall we say was gained by Abraham, our forefather according to the flesh? [2] For if Abraham was justified by works, he has something to boast about, but not before God. [3] For what does the Scripture say? [g]"Abraham believed God, and it was counted to him as righteousness." [4] Now to the one who works, his wages are not counted as a gift but as his due. [5] And to the one who does not work but believes in[2] him who justifies the ungodly, his faith is counted as righteousness, [6] just as David also speaks of the blessing of the one to whom God counts righteousness apart from works:

[7]   [h]"Blessed are those whose lawless deeds are
                forgiven,
          and whose sins are covered;
[8]   blessed is the man against whom the Lord
                will not count his sin."

[9] Is this blessing then only for the circumcised, or also for the uncircumcised? For we say that faith was counted to Abraham as righteousness. [10] How then was it counted to him? Was it before or after he had been circumcised? It was not after, but before he was circumcised. [11] He received the sign of circumcision as a seal of the righteousness that he had by faith while he was still uncircumcised. The purpose was to make him the father of all who believe without being circumcised, so that righteousness would be counted to them as well, [12] and to make him the father of the circumcised who are not merely circumcised but who also walk in the footsteps of the faith that our father Abraham had before he was circumcised.

The Promise Realized Through Faith

[13] For the promise to Abraham and his offspring that he would be heir of the world did not come through the law but through the righteousness of faith. [14] For if it is the adherents of the law who are to be the heirs, faith is null and the promise is void. [15] For the law brings wrath, but where there is no law there is no transgression.

[16] That is why it depends on faith, in order that the promise may rest on grace and be guaranteed to all his offspring—not only to the adherent of the law but also to the one who shares the faith of Abraham, who is the father of us all, [17] as it is written, [i]"I have made you the father of many nations"—in the presence

---

[1] Greek flesh [2] Or but trusts; compare verse 24 [a] Ps. 14:1-3; 53:1-3 [b] Ps. 5:9 [c] Ps. 140:3 [d] Ps. 10:7 (Gk.) [e] Prov. 1:16; 3:15-17; Isa. 59:7, 8 [f] Ps. 36:1 [g] Gen. 15:6 (Gk.) [h] Ps. 32:1, 2 [i] Gen. 17:5

of the God in whom he believed, who gives life to the dead and calls into existence the things that do not exist. [18] In hope he believed against hope, that he should become the father of many nations, as he had been told, [a] "So shall your offspring be." [19] He did not weaken in faith when he considered his own body, which was as good as dead (since he was about a hundred years old), or when he considered the barrenness[1] of Sarah's womb. [20] No unbelief made him waver concerning the promise of God, but he grew strong in his faith as he gave glory to God, [21] fully convinced that God was able to do what he had promised. [22] That is why his faith was "counted to him as righteousness." [23] But the words "it was counted to him" were not written for his sake alone, [24] but for ours also. It will be counted to us who believe in him who raised from the dead Jesus our Lord, [25] who was delivered up for our trespasses and raised for our justification.

Peace with God Through Faith

5 Therefore, since we have been justified by faith, we[2] have peace with God through our Lord Jesus Christ. [2] Through him we have also obtained access by faith[3] into this grace in which we stand, and we[4] rejoice[5] in hope of the glory of God. [3] Not only that, but we rejoice in our sufferings, knowing that suffering produces endurance, [4] and endurance produces character, and character produces hope, [5] and hope does not put us to shame, because God's love has been poured into our hearts through the Holy Spirit who has been given to us.

[6] For while we were still weak, at the right time Christ died for the ungodly. [7] For one will scarcely die for a righteous person— though perhaps for a good person one would dare even to die— [8] but God shows his love for us in that while we were still sinners, Christ died for us. [9] Since, therefore, we have now been justified by his blood, much more shall we be saved by him from the wrath of God. [10] For if while we were enemies we were reconciled to God by the death of his Son, much more, now that we are reconciled, shall we be saved by his life. [11] More than that, we also rejoice in God through our Lord Jesus Christ, through whom we have now received reconciliation.

Death in Adam, Life in Christ

[12] Therefore, just as sin came into the world through one man, and death through sin, and so death spread to all men[6] because all sinned— [13] for sin indeed was in the world before the law was given, but sin is not counted where there is no law. [14] Yet death reigned from Adam to Moses, even over those whose sinning was not like the transgression of Adam, who was a type of the one who was to come.

[15] But the free gift is not like the trespass. For if many died through one man's trespass, much more have the grace of God and the free gift by the grace of that one man Jesus Christ abounded for many. [16] And the free gift is not like the result of that one man's sin. For the judgment following one trespass brought condemnation, but the free gift following many trespasses brought justification. [17] For if, because of one man's trespass, death reigned through that one man, much more will those who receive the abundance of grace and the free gift of righteousness reign in life through the one man Jesus Christ.

[18] Therefore, as one trespass[7] led to condemnation for all men, so one act of righteousness[8] leads to justification and life for all men. [19] For as by the one man's disobedience the many were made sinners, so by the one man's obedience the many will be made righteous. [20] Now the law came in to increase the trespass, but where sin increased, grace abounded all the more, [21] so that, as sin reigned in death, grace also might reign through righteousness leading to eternal life through Jesus Christ our Lord.

Dead to Sin, Alive to God

6 What shall we say then? Are we to continue in sin that grace may abound? [2] By no means! How can we who died to sin still live in it? [3] Do you not know that all of us who have been baptized into Christ Jesus were baptized into his death? [4] We were buried therefore with him by baptism into death, in order that, just as Christ was raised from the dead by the glory of the Father, we too might walk in newness of life.

[5] For if we have been united with him in a death like his, we shall certainly be united with him in a resurrection like his. [6] We know that our old self[9] was crucified with him in order that the body of sin might be brought to nothing, so that we would no longer be enslaved to

---

[1] Greek deadness [2] Some manuscripts let us [3] Some manuscripts omit by faith [4] Or let us; also verse 3 [5] Or boast; also verses 3, 11 [6] The Greek word anthropoi refers here to both men and women; also twice in verse 18 [7] Or the trespass of one [8] Or the act of righteousness of one [9] Greek man [a] Gen. 15:5

sin. [7] For one who has died has been set free[1] from sin. [8] Now if we have died with Christ, we believe that we will also live with him. [9] We know that Christ, being raised from the dead, will never die again; death no longer has dominion over him. [10] For the death he died he died to sin, once for all, but the life he lives he lives to God. [11] So you also must consider yourselves dead to sin and alive to God in Christ Jesus.

[12] Let not sin therefore reign in your mortal body, to make you obey its passions. [13] Do not present your members to sin as instruments for unrighteousness, but present yourselves to God as those who have been brought from death to life, and your members to God as instruments for righteousness. [14] For sin will have no dominion over you, since you are not under law but under grace.

Slaves to Righteousness

[15] What then? Are we to sin because we are not under law but under grace? By no means! [16] Do you not know that if you present yourselves to anyone as obedient slaves,[2] you are slaves of the one whom you obey, either of sin, which leads to death, or of obedience, which leads to righteousness? [17] But thanks be to God, that you who were once slaves of sin have become obedient from the heart to the standard of teaching to which you were committed, [18] and, having been set free from sin, have become slaves of righteousness. [19] I am speaking in human terms, because of your natural limitations. For just as you once presented your members as slaves to impurity and to lawlessness leading to more lawlessness, so now present your members as slaves to righteousness leading to sanctification.

[20] For when you were slaves of sin, you were free in regard to righteousness. [21] But what fruit were you getting at that time from the things of which you are now ashamed? For the end of those things is death. [22] But now that you have been set free from sin and have become slaves of God, the fruit you get leads to sanctification and its end, eternal life. [23] For the wages of sin is death, but the free gift of God is eternal life in Christ Jesus our Lord.

Released from the Law

7 Or do you not know, brothers[3]—for I am speaking to those who know the law—that the law is binding on a person only as long as he lives? [2] For a married woman is bound by law to her husband while he lives, but if her husband dies she is released from the law of marriage.[4] [3] Accordingly, she will be called an adulteress if she lives with another man while her husband is alive. But if her husband dies, she is free from that law, and if she marries another man she is not an adulteress.

[4] Likewise, my brothers, you also have died to the law through the body of Christ, so that you may belong to another, to him who has been raised from the dead, in order that we may bear fruit for God. [5] For while we were living in the flesh, our sinful passions, aroused by the law, were at work in our members to bear fruit for death. [6] But now we are released from the law, having died to that which held us captive, so that we serve in the new way of the Spirit and not in the old way of the written code.[5]

The Law and Sin

[7] What then shall we say? That the law is sin? By no means! Yet if it had not been for the law, I would not have known sin. For I would not have known what it is to covet if [a] the law had not said, "You shall not covet." [8] But sin, seizing an opportunity through the commandment, produced in me all kinds of covetousness. For apart from the law, sin lies dead. [9] I was once alive apart from the law, but when the commandment came, sin came alive and I died. [10] The very commandment that promised life proved to be death to me. [11] For sin, seizing an opportunity through the commandment, deceived me and through it killed me. [12] So the law is holy, and the commandment is holy and righteous and good.

[13] Did that which is good, then, bring death to me? By no means! It was sin, producing death in me through what is good, in order that sin might be shown to be sin, and through the commandment might become sinful beyond measure. [14] For we know that the law is spiritual, but I am of the flesh, sold under sin. [15] For I do not understand my own actions. For I do not do what I want, but I do the very thing I hate. [16] Now if I do what I do not want, I agree with the law, that it is good. [17] So now it is no longer I who do it, but sin that dwells within me. [18] For I know that nothing good dwells in me, that is, in my flesh. For I have the desire to do what is right, but not the ability to carry it out. [19] For I do not do the good I want, but the evil I do not want is what I keep on doing. [20] Now if I do

---

[1] Greek *has been justified* [2] For the contextual rendering of the Greek word *doulos*, see Preface; twice in this verse; also verses 17, 19 (twice), 20 [3] Or *brothers and sisters*; also verse 4 [4] Greek *law concerning the husband* [5] Greek *of the letter* [a] Ex. 20:17; Deut. 5:21

what I do not want, it is no longer I who do it, but sin that dwells within me.

²¹ So I find it to be a law that when I want to do right, evil lies close at hand. ²² For I delight in the law of God, in my inner being, ²³ but I see in my members another law waging war against the law of my mind and making me captive to the law of sin that dwells in my members. ²⁴ Wretched man that I am! Who will deliver me from this body of death? ²⁵ Thanks be to God through Jesus Christ our Lord! So then, I myself serve the law of God with my mind, but with my flesh I serve the law of sin.

Life in the Spirit

8 There is therefore now no condemnation for those who are in Christ Jesus.[1] ² For the law of the Spirit of life has set you[2] free in Christ Jesus from the law of sin and death. ³ For God has done what the law, weakened by the flesh, could not do. By sending his own Son in the likeness of sinful flesh and for sin,[3] he condemned sin in the flesh, ⁴ in order that the righteous requirement of the law might be fulfilled in us, who walk not according to the flesh but according to the Spirit. ⁵ For those who live according to the flesh set their minds on the things of the flesh, but those who live according to the Spirit set their minds on the things of the Spirit. ⁶ For to set the mind on the flesh is death, but to set the mind on the Spirit is life and peace. ⁷ For the mind that is set on the flesh is hostile to God, for it does not submit to God's law; indeed, it cannot. ⁸ Those who are in the flesh cannot please God.

⁹ You, however, are not in the flesh but in the Spirit, if in fact the Spirit of God dwells in you. Anyone who does not have the Spirit of Christ does not belong to him. ¹⁰ But if Christ is in you, although the body is dead because of sin, the Spirit is life because of righteousness. ¹¹ If the Spirit of him who raised Jesus from the dead dwells in you, he who raised Christ Jesus[4] from the dead will also give life to your mortal bodies through his Spirit who dwells in you.

Heirs with Christ

¹² So then, brothers,[5] we are debtors, not to the flesh, to live according to the flesh. ¹³ For if you live according to the flesh you will die, but if by the Spirit you put to death the deeds of the body, you will live. ¹⁴ For all who are led by the Spirit of God are sons[6] of God. ¹⁵ For you did not receive the spirit of slavery to fall back into fear, but you have received the Spirit of adoption as sons, by whom we cry, "Abba! Father!" ¹⁶ The Spirit himself bears witness with our spirit that we are children of God, ¹⁷ and if children, then heirs—heirs of God and fellow heirs with Christ, provided we suffer with him in order that we may also be glorified with him.

Future Glory

¹⁸ For I consider that the sufferings of this present time are not worth comparing with the glory that is to be revealed to us. ¹⁹ For the creation waits with eager longing for the revealing of the sons of God. ²⁰ For the creation was subjected to futility, not willingly, but because of him who subjected it, in hope ²¹ that the creation itself will be set free from its bondage to corruption and obtain the freedom of the glory of the children of God. ²² For we know that the whole creation has been groaning together in the pains of childbirth until now. ²³ And not only the creation, but we ourselves, who have the firstfruits of the Spirit, groan inwardly as we wait eagerly for adoption as sons, the redemption of our bodies. ²⁴ For in this hope we were saved. Now hope that is seen is not hope. For who hopes for what he sees? ²⁵ But if we hope for what we do not see, we wait for it with patience.

²⁶ Likewise the Spirit helps us in our weakness. For we do not know what to pray for as we ought, but the Spirit himself intercedes for us with groanings too deep for words. ²⁷ And he who searches hearts knows what is the mind of the Spirit, because[7] the Spirit intercedes for the saints according to the will of God. ²⁸ And we know that for those who love God all things work together for good,[8] for those who are called according to his purpose. ²⁹ For those whom he foreknew he also predestined to be conformed to the image of his Son, in order that he might be the firstborn among many brothers. ³⁰ And those whom he predestined he also called, and those whom he called he also justified, and those whom he justified he also glorified.

God's Everlasting Love

³¹ What then shall we say to these things? If God is for us, who can be[9] against us? ³² He who did not spare his own Son but gave him up for us all, how will he not also with him

---

[1] Some manuscripts add who walk not according to the flesh (but according to the Spirit) [2] Some manuscripts me [3] Or and as a sin offering [4] Some manuscripts lack Jesus [5] Or brothers and sisters; also verse 29 [6] See discussion on "sons" in the Preface [7] Or that [8] Some manuscripts God works all things together for good, or God works in all things for the good [9] Or who is

graciously give us all things? [33] Who shall bring any charge against God's elect? It is God who justifies. [34] Who is to condemn? Christ Jesus is the one who died—more than that, who was raised—who is at the right hand of God, who indeed is interceding for us.[1] [35] Who shall separate us from the love of Christ? Shall tribulation, or distress, or persecution, or famine, or nakedness, or danger, or sword? [36] As it is written,

> [a]"For your sake we are being killed all the
>   day long;
>   we are regarded as sheep to be slaugh-
>   tered."

[37] No, in all these things we are more than conquerors through him who loved us. [38] For I am sure that neither death nor life, nor angels nor rulers, nor things present nor things to come, nor powers, [39] nor height nor depth, nor anything else in all creation, will be able to separate us from the love of God in Christ Jesus our Lord.

God's Sovereign Choice

9 I am speaking the truth in Christ—I am not lying; my conscience bears me witness in the Holy Spirit— [2] that I have great sorrow and unceasing anguish in my heart. [3] For I could wish that I myself were accursed and cut off from Christ for the sake of my brothers,[2] my kinsmen according to the flesh. [4] They are Israelites, and to them belong the adoption, the glory, the covenants, the giving of the law, the worship, and the promises. [5] To them belong the patriarchs, and from their race, according to the flesh, is the Christ, who is God over all, blessed forever. Amen.

[6] But it is not as though the word of God has failed. For not all who are descended from Israel belong to Israel, [7] and not all are children of Abraham because they are his offspring, but [b]"Through Isaac shall your offspring be named." [8] This means that it is not the children of the flesh who are the children of God, but the children of the promise are counted as offspring. [9] For this is what the promise said: [c]"About this time next year I will return, and Sarah shall have a son." [10] And not only so, but also when Rebekah had conceived children by one man, our forefather Isaac, [11] though they were not yet born and had done nothing either good or bad—in order that God's purpose of election might

continue, not because of works but because of him who calls— [12] she was told, [d]"The older will serve the younger." [13] As it is written, [e]"Jacob I loved, but Esau I hated."

[14] What shall we say then? Is there injustice on God's part? By no means! [15] For he says to Moses, [f]"I will have mercy on whom I have mercy, and I will have compassion on whom I have compassion." [16] So then it depends not on human will or exertion,[3] but on God, who has mercy. [17] For the Scripture says to Pharaoh, [g]"For this very purpose I have raised you up, that I might show my power in you, and that my name might be proclaimed in all the earth." [18] So then he has mercy on whomever he wills, and he hardens whomever he wills.

[19] You will say to me then, "Why does he still find fault? For who can resist his will?" [20] But who are you, O man, to answer back to God? Will what is molded say to its molder, "Why have you made me like this?" [21] Has the potter no right over the clay, to make out of the same lump one vessel for honorable use and another for dishonorable use? [22] What if God, desiring to show his wrath and to make known his power, has endured with much patience vessels of wrath prepared for destruction, [23] in order to make known the riches of his glory for vessels of mercy, which he has prepared beforehand for glory— [24] even us whom he has called, not from the Jews only but also from the Gentiles? [25] As indeed he says in Hosea,

> [h]"Those who were not my people I will call
>   'my people,'
>   and her who was not beloved I will call
>   'beloved.'"
> [26] [i]"And in the very place where it was said to
>   them, 'You are not my people,'
>   there they will be called 'sons of the liv-
>   ing God.'"

[27] And Isaiah cries out concerning Israel: [j]"Though the number of the sons of Israel[4] be as the sand of the sea, only a remnant of them will be saved, [28] for the Lord will carry out his sentence upon the earth fully and without delay." [29] And as Isaiah predicted,

> [k]"If the Lord of hosts had not left us off-
>   spring,
>   we would have been like Sodom
>   and become like Gomorrah."

[1] Or Is it Christ Jesus who died . . . for us? [2] Or brothers and sisters [3] Greek not of him who wills or runs [4] Or children of Israel [a] Ps. 44:22 [b] Gen. 21:12 [c] Gen. 18:10, 14 [d] Gen. 25:23 [e] Mal. 1:2, 3 [f] Ex. 33:19 [g] Ex. 9:16 [h] Hos. 2:23 [i] Hos. 1:10 [j] Isa. 10:22, 23 [k] Isa. 1:9

Israel's Unbelief

30 What shall we say, then? That Gentiles who did not pursue righteousness have attained it, that is, a righteousness that is by faith; **31** but that Israel who pursued a law that would lead to righteousness[1] did not succeed in reaching that law. **32** Why? Because they did not pursue it by faith, but as if it were based on works. They have stumbled over the stumbling stone, **33** as it is written,[a]

> [a]"Behold, I am laying in Zion a stone of
>   stumbling, and a rock of offense;
>   and whoever believes in him will not be
>   put to shame."

10 Brothers,[2] my heart's desire and prayer to God for them is that they may be saved. **2** For I bear them witness that they have a zeal for God, but not according to knowledge. **3** For, being ignorant of the righteousness of God, and seeking to establish their own, they did not submit to God's righteousness. **4** For Christ is the end of the law for righteousness to everyone who believes.[3]

The Message of Salvation to All

5 For Moses writes about the righteousness that is based on the law, that the person who does the commandments shall live by them. **6** But the righteousness based on faith says, "Do not say in your heart, 'Who will ascend into heaven?'" (that is, to bring Christ down) **7** "or 'Who will descend into the abyss?'" (that is, to bring Christ up from the dead). **8** But what does it say? [b]"The word is near you, in your mouth and in your heart" (that is, the word of faith that we proclaim); **9** because, if you confess with your mouth that Jesus is Lord and believe in your heart that God raised him from the dead, you will be saved. **10** For with the heart one believes and is justified, and with the mouth one confesses and is saved. **11** For the Scripture says, "Everyone who believes in him will not be put to shame." **12** For there is no distinction between Jew and Greek; for the same Lord is Lord of all, bestowing his riches on all who call on him. **13** For [c]"everyone who calls on the name of the Lord will be saved."

14 How then will they call on him in whom they have not believed? And how are they to believe in him of whom they have never heard?[4] And how are they to hear without someone preaching? **15** And how are they to preach unless they are sent? As it is written, [d]"How beautiful are the feet of those who preach the good news!" **16** But they have not all obeyed the gospel. For Isaiah says, [e]"Lord, who has believed what he has heard from us?" **17** So faith comes from hearing, and hearing through the word of Christ.

18 But I ask, have they not heard? Indeed they have, for

> [f]"Their voice has gone out to all the earth,
>   and their words to the ends of the
>   world."

19 But I ask, did Israel not understand? First Moses says,

> [g]"I will make you jealous of those who are
>   not a nation;
>   with a foolish nation I will make you
>   angry."

20 Then Isaiah is so bold as to say,

> [h]"I have been found by those who did not
>   seek me;
>   I have shown myself to those who did
>   not ask for me."

21 But of Israel he says, [i]"All day long I have held out my hands to a disobedient and contrary people."

The Remnant of Israel

11 I ask, then, has God rejected his people? By no means! For I myself am an Israelite, a descendant of Abraham,[5] a member of the tribe of Benjamin. **2** God has not rejected his people whom he foreknew. Do you not know what the Scripture says of Elijah, how he appeals to God against Israel? **3** [j]"Lord, they have killed your prophets, they have demolished your altars, and I alone am left, and they seek my life." **4** But what is God's reply to him? [k]"I have kept for myself seven thousand men who have not bowed the knee to Baal." **5** So too at the present time there is a remnant, chosen by grace. **6** But if it is by grace, it is no longer on the basis of works; otherwise grace would no longer be grace.

7 What then? Israel failed to obtain what it was seeking. The elect obtained it, but the rest were hardened, **8** as it is written,

---

[1] Greek a law of righteousness [2] Or Brothers and sisters [3] Or end of the law, that everyone who believes may be justified [4] Or him whom they have never heard [5] Or one of the offspring of Abraham   [a] Isa. 28:16 [b] Deut. 30:14 [c] Joel 2:32 [d] Isa. 52:7 [e] Isa. 53:1 [f] Ps. 19:4 [g] Deut. 32:21 [h] Isa. 65:1 [i] Isa. 65:2 [j] 1 Kgs. 19:10, 14 [k] 1 Kgs. 19:18

"God gave them a spirit of stupor,
　　eyes that would not see
　　and ears that would not hear,
　　down to this very day."

[9] And David says,

[a]"Let their table become a snare and a
　　trap,
　　a stumbling block and a retribution
　　for them;
[10]　let their eyes be darkened so that they can-
　　not see,
　　and bend their backs forever."

Gentiles Grafted In

[11] So I ask, did they stumble in order that they might fall? By no means! Rather, through their trespass salvation has come to the Gentiles, so as to make Israel jealous. [12] Now if their trespass means riches for the world, and if their failure means riches for the Gentiles, how much more will their full inclusion[1] mean!

[13] Now I am speaking to you Gentiles. Inasmuch then as I am an apostle to the Gentiles, I magnify my ministry [14] in order somehow to make my fellow Jews jealous, and thus save some of them. [15] For if their rejection means the reconciliation of the world, what will their acceptance mean but life from the dead? [16] If the dough offered as firstfruits is holy, so is the whole lump, and if the root is holy, so are the branches.

[17] But if some of the branches were broken off, and you, although a wild olive shoot, were grafted in among the others and now share in the nourishing root[2] of the olive tree, [18] do not be arrogant toward the branches. If you are, remember it is not you who support the root, but the root that supports you. [19] Then you will say, "Branches were broken off so that I might be grafted in." [20] That is true. They were broken off because of their unbelief, but you stand fast through faith. So do not become proud, but fear. [21] For if God did not spare the natural branches, neither will he spare you. [22] Note then the kindness and the severity of God: severity toward those who have fallen, but God's kindness to you, provided you continue in his kindness. Otherwise you too will be cut off. [23] And even they, if they do not continue in their unbelief, will be grafted in, for God has the power to graft them in again. [24] For if you were cut from what is by nature a wild olive tree, and grafted, contrary to nature, into a cultivated olive tree, how much more will these, the natural branches, be grafted back into their own olive tree.

The Mystery of Israel's Salvation

[25] Lest you be wise in your own sight, I do not want you to be unaware of this mystery, broth-ers:[3] a partial hardening has come upon Israel, until the fullness of the Gentiles has come in. [26] And in this way all Israel will be saved, as it is written,

[b]"The Deliverer will come from Zion,
　　he will banish ungodliness from Jacob";
[27]　"and this will be my covenant with them
　　when I take away their sins."

[28] As regards the gospel, they are enemies for your sake. But as regards election, they are beloved for the sake of their forefathers. [29] For the gifts and the calling of God are irrevo-cable. [30] For just as you were at one time dis-obedient to God but now have received mercy because of their disobedience, [31] so they too have now been disobedient in order that by the mercy shown to you they also may now[4] receive mercy. [32] For God has consigned all to disobedience, that he may have mercy on all.

[33] Oh, the depth of the riches and wisdom and knowledge of God! How unsearchable are his judgments and how inscrutable his ways!

[34]　"For who has known the mind of the
　　Lord,
　　or who has been his counselor?"
[35]　"Or who has given a gift to him
　　that he might be repaid?"

[36] For from him and through him and to him are all things. To him be glory forever. Amen.

A Living Sacrifice

12 I appeal to you therefore, brothers,[5] by the mercies of God, to present your bodies as a living sacrifice, holy and accept-able to God, which is your spiritual worship.[6] [2] Do not be conformed to this world,[7] but be transformed by the renewal of your mind, that by testing you may discern what is the will of God, what is good and acceptable and perfect.[8]

---

[1] Greek their fullness [2] Greek root of richness; some manuscripts richness [3] Or brothers and sisters [4] Some manuscripts omit now [5] Or brothers and sisters [6] Or your rational service [7] Greek age [8] Or what is the good and acceptable and perfect will of God [a] Ps. 69:22, 23 [b] Isa. 59:20, 21

Gifts of Grace

[3]For by the grace given to me I say to everyone among you not to think of himself more highly than he ought to think, but to think with sober judgment, each according to the measure of faith that God has assigned. [4]For as in one body we have many members,[1] and the members do not all have the same function, [5]so we, though many, are one body in Christ, and individually members one of another. [6]Having gifts that differ according to the grace given to us, let us use them: if prophecy, in proportion to our faith; [7]if service, in our serving; the one who teaches, in his teaching; [8]the one who exhorts, in his exhortation; the one who contributes, in generosity; the one who leads,[2] with zeal; the one who does acts of mercy, with cheerfulness.

Marks of the True Christian

[9]Let love be genuine. Abhor what is evil; hold fast to what is good. [10]Love one another with brotherly affection. Outdo one another in showing honor. [11]Do not be slothful in zeal, be fervent in spirit,[3] serve the Lord. [12]Rejoice in hope, be patient in tribulation, be constant in prayer. [13]Contribute to the needs of the saints and seek to show hospitality.

[14]Bless those who persecute you; bless and do not curse them. [15]Rejoice with those who rejoice, weep with those who weep. [16]Live in harmony with one another. Do not be haughty, but associate with the lowly.[4] Never be wise in your own sight. [17]Repay no one evil for evil, but give thought to do what is honorable in the sight of all. [18]If possible, so far as it depends on you, live peaceably with all. [19]Beloved, never avenge yourselves, but leave it[5] to the wrath of God, for it is written, [a]"Vengeance is mine, I will repay, says the Lord." [20]To the contrary, [b]"if your enemy is hungry, feed him; if he is thirsty, give him something to drink; for by so doing you will heap burning coals on his head." [21]Do not be overcome by evil, but overcome evil with good.

Submission to the Authorities

13 Let every person be subject to the governing authorities. For there is no authority except from God, and those that exist have been instituted by God. [2]Therefore whoever resists the authorities resists what God has appointed, and those who resist will incur judgment. [3]For rulers are not a terror to good conduct, but to bad. Would you have no fear of the one who is in authority? Then do what is good, and you will receive his approval, [4]for he is God's servant for your good. But if you do wrong, be afraid, for he does not bear the sword in vain. For he is the servant of God, an avenger who carries out God's wrath on the wrongdoer. [5]Therefore one must be in subjection, not only to avoid God's wrath but also for the sake of conscience. [6]For because of this you also pay taxes, for the authorities are ministers of God, attending to this very thing. [7]Pay to all what is owed to them: taxes to whom taxes are owed, revenue to whom revenue is owed, respect to whom respect is owed, honor to whom honor is owed.

Fulfilling the Law Through Love

[8]Owe no one anything, except to love each other, for the one who loves another has fulfilled the law. [9]For the commandments, [c]"You shall not commit adultery, You shall not murder, You shall not steal, You shall not covet," and any other commandment, are summed up in this word: [d]"You shall love your neighbor as yourself." [10]Love does no wrong to a neighbor; therefore love is the fulfilling of the law.

[11]Besides this you know the time, that the hour has come for you to wake from sleep. For salvation is nearer to us now than when we first believed. [12]The night is far gone; the day is at hand. So then let us cast off the works of darkness and put on the armor of light. [13]Let us walk properly as in the daytime, not in orgies and drunkenness, not in sexual immorality and sensuality, not in quarreling and jealousy. [14]But put on the Lord Jesus Christ, and make no provision for the flesh, to gratify its desires.

Do Not Pass Judgment on One Another

14 As for the one who is weak in faith, welcome him, but not to quarrel over opinions. [2]One person believes he may eat anything, while the weak person eats only vegetables. [3]Let not the one who eats despise the one who abstains, and let not the one who abstains pass judgment on the one who eats, for God has welcomed him. [4]Who are you to pass judgment on the servant of another? It is before his own master[6] that he stands or falls. And he will be upheld, for the Lord is able to make him stand.

[5]One person esteems one day as better than another, while another esteems all days alike.

---

[1] Greek parts; also verse 5 [2] Or gives aid [3] Or fervent in the Spirit [4] Or give yourselves to humble tasks [5] Greek give place [6] Or lord [a] Deut. 32:35 [b] Prov. 25:21, 22 [c] Ex. 20:13-17; Deut. 5:17-21 [d] Lev. 19:18

Each one should be fully convinced in his own mind. [6] The one who observes the day, observes it in honor of the Lord. The one who eats, eats in honor of the Lord, since he gives thanks to God, while the one who abstains, abstains in honor of the Lord and gives thanks to God. [7] For none of us lives to himself, and none of us dies to himself. [8] For if we live, we live to the Lord, and if we die, we die to the Lord. So then, whether we live or whether we die, we are the Lord's. [9] For to this end Christ died and lived again, that he might be Lord both of the dead and of the living.

[10] Why do you pass judgment on your brother? Or you, why do you despise your brother? For we will all stand before the judgment seat of God; [11] for it is written,

[a]"As I live, says the Lord, every knee shall
    bow to me,
  and every tongue shall confess[1] to
    God."

[12] So then each of us will give an account of himself to God.

Do Not Cause Another to Stumble

[13] Therefore let us not pass judgment on one another any longer, but rather decide never to put a stumbling block or hindrance in the way of a brother. [14] I know and am persuaded in the Lord Jesus that nothing is unclean in itself, but it is unclean for anyone who thinks it unclean. [15] For if your brother is grieved by what you eat, you are no longer walking in love. By what you eat, do not destroy the one for whom Christ died. [16] So do not let what you regard as good be spoken of as evil. [17] For the kingdom of God is not a matter of eating and drinking but of righteousness and peace and joy in the Holy Spirit. [18] Whoever thus serves Christ is acceptable to God and approved by men. [19] So then let us pursue what makes for peace and for mutual upbuilding.

[20] Do not, for the sake of food, destroy the work of God. Everything is indeed clean, but it is wrong for anyone to make another stumble by what he eats. [21] It is good not to eat meat or drink wine or do anything that causes your brother to stumble.[2] [22] The faith that you have, keep between yourself and God. Blessed is the one who has no reason to pass judgment on himself for what he approves. [23] But whoever has doubts is condemned if he eats, because the

eating is not from faith. For whatever does not proceed from faith is sin.[3]

The Example of Christ

15 We who are strong have an obligation to bear with the failings of the weak, and not to please ourselves. [2] Let each of us please his neighbor for his good, to build him up. [3] For Christ did not please himself, but as it is written, [b]"The reproaches of those who reproached you fell on me." [4] For whatever was written in former days was written for our instruction, that through endurance and through the encouragement of the Scriptures we might have hope. [5] May the God of endurance and encouragement grant you to live in such harmony with one another, in accord with Christ Jesus, [6] that together you may with one voice glorify the God and Father of our Lord Jesus Christ. [7] Therefore welcome one another as Christ has welcomed you, for the glory of God.

Christ the Hope of Jews and Gentiles

[8] For I tell you that Christ became a servant to the circumcised to show God's truthfulness, in order to confirm the promises given to the patriarchs, [9] and in order that the Gentiles might glorify God for his mercy. As it is written,

[c]"Therefore I will praise you among the
    Gentiles,
  and sing to your name."

[10] And again it is said,

[d]"Rejoice, O Gentiles, with his people."

[11] And again,

[e]"Praise the Lord, all you Gentiles,
  and let all the peoples extol him."

[12] And again Isaiah says,

[f]"The root of Jesse will come,
  even he who arises to rule the
    Gentiles;
  in him will the Gentiles hope."

[13] May the God of hope fill you with all joy and peace in believing, so that by the power of the Holy Spirit you may abound in hope.

Paul the Minister to the Gentiles

[14] I myself am satisfied about you, my brothers,[4] that you yourselves are full of goodness, filled with all knowledge and able to instruct

---

[1] Or shall give praise [2] Some manuscripts add or be hindered or be weakened [3] Some manuscripts insert here 16:25–27 [4] Or brothers and sisters; also verse 30 [a] Isa. 45:23 [b] Ps. 69:9 [c] 2 Sam. 22:50; Ps. 18:49 [d] Deut. 32:43 [e] Ps. 117:1 [f] Isa. 11:10

one another. [15] But on some points I have written to you very boldly by way of reminder, because of the grace given me by God [16] to be a minister of Christ Jesus to the Gentiles in the priestly service of the gospel of God, so that the offering of the Gentiles may be acceptable, sanctified by the Holy Spirit. [17] In Christ Jesus, then, I have reason to be proud of my work for God. [18] For I will not venture to speak of anything except what Christ has accomplished through me to bring the Gentiles to obedience—by word and deed, [19] by the power of signs and wonders, by the power of the Spirit of God—so that from Jerusalem and all the way around to Illyricum I have fulfilled the ministry of the gospel of Christ; [20] and thus I make it my ambition to preach the gospel, not where Christ has already been named, lest I build on someone else's foundation, [21] but as it is written,

[a]"Those who have never been told of him
　　will see,
　　and those who have never heard will
　　　understand."

Paul's Plan to Visit Rome

[22] This is the reason why I have so often been hindered from coming to you. [23] But now, since I no longer have any room for work in these regions, and since I have longed for many years to come to you, [24] I hope to see you in passing as I go to Spain, and to be helped on my journey there by you, once I have enjoyed your company for a while. [25] At present, however, I am going to Jerusalem bringing aid to the saints. [26] For Macedonia and Achaia have been pleased to make some contribution for the poor among the saints at Jerusalem. [27] For they were pleased to do it, and indeed they owe it to them. For if the Gentiles have come to share in their spiritual blessings, they ought also to be of service to them in material blessings. [28] When therefore I have completed this and have delivered to them what has been collected,[1] I will leave for Spain by way of you. [29] I know that when I come to you I will come in the fullness of the blessing[2] of Christ.

[30] I appeal to you, brothers, by our Lord Jesus Christ and by the love of the Spirit, to strive together with me in your prayers to God on my behalf, [31] that I may be delivered from the unbelievers in Judea, and that my service for Jerusalem may be acceptable to the saints, [32] so that by God's will I may come to you with joy and be refreshed in your company. [33] May the God of peace be with you all. Amen.

Personal Greetings

16 I commend to you our sister Phoebe, a servant[3] of the church at Cenchreae, [2] that you may welcome her in the Lord in a way worthy of the saints, and help her in whatever she may need from you, for she has been a patron of many and of myself as well.

[3] Greet Prisca and Aquila, my fellow workers in Christ Jesus, [4] who risked their necks for my life, to whom not only I give thanks but all the churches of the Gentiles give thanks as well. [5] Greet also the church in their house. Greet my beloved Epaenetus, who was the first convert[4] to Christ in Asia. [6] Greet Mary, who has worked hard for you. [7] Greet Andronicus and Junia,[5] my kinsmen and my fellow prisoners. They are well known to the apostles,[6] and they were in Christ before me. [8] Greet Ampliatus, my beloved in the Lord. [9] Greet Urbanus, our fellow worker in Christ, and my beloved Stachys. [10] Greet Apelles, who is approved in Christ. Greet those who belong to the family of Aristobulus. [11] Greet my kinsman Herodion. Greet those in the Lord who belong to the family of Narcissus. [12] Greet those workers in the Lord, Tryphaena and Tryphosa. Greet the beloved Persis, who has worked hard in the Lord. [13] Greet Rufus, chosen in the Lord; also his mother, who has been a mother to me as well. [14] Greet Asyncritus, Phlegon, Hermes, Patrobas, Hermas, and the brothers[7] who are with them. [15] Greet Philologus, Julia, Nereus and his sister, and Olympas, and all the saints who are with them. [16] Greet one another with a holy kiss. All the churches of Christ greet you.

Final Instructions and Greetings

[17] I appeal to you, brothers, to watch out for those who cause divisions and create obstacles contrary to the doctrine that you have been taught; avoid them. [18] For such persons do not serve our Lord Christ, but their own appetites,[8] and by smooth talk and flattery they deceive the hearts of the naive. [19] For your obedience is known to all, so that I rejoice over you, but I want you to be wise as to what is good and innocent as to what is

---

[1] Greek *sealed to them this fruit* [2] Some manuscripts insert *of the gospel* [3] Or *deaconess* [4] Greek *firstfruit* [5] Or *Junias* [6] Or *messengers* [7] Or *brothers and sisters*; also verse 17 [8] Greek *their own belly* [a] Isa. 52:15

evil. **20** The God of peace will soon crush Satan under your feet. The grace of our Lord Jesus Christ be with you.

21 Timothy, my fellow worker, greets you; so do Lucius and Jason and Sosipater, my kinsmen.

22 I Tertius, who wrote this letter, greet you in the Lord.

23 Gaius, who is host to me and to the whole church, greets you. Erastus, the city treasurer, and our brother Quartus, greet you.[1]

Doxology

25 Now to him who is able to strengthen you according to my gospel and the preaching of Jesus Christ, according to the revelation of the mystery that was kept secret for long ages **26** but has now been disclosed and through the prophetic writings has been made known to all nations, according to the command of the eternal God, to bring about the obedience of faith— **27** to the only wise God be glory forevermore through Jesus Christ! Amen.

---

[1] Some manuscripts insert verse 24: *The grace of our Lord Jesus Christ be with you all. Amen*

1 CORINTHIANS

Greeting

1 Paul, called by the will of God to be an apostle of Christ Jesus, and our brother Sosthenes,

² To the church of God that is in Corinth, to those sanctified in Christ Jesus, called to be saints together with all those who in every place call upon the name of our Lord Jesus Christ, both their Lord and ours:

³ Grace to you and peace from God our Father and the Lord Jesus Christ.

Thanksgiving

⁴ I give thanks to my God always for you because of the grace of God that was given you in Christ Jesus, ⁵ that in every way you were enriched in him in all speech and all knowledge— ⁶ even as the testimony about Christ was confirmed among you— ⁷ so that you are not lacking in any gift, as you wait for the revealing of our Lord Jesus Christ, ⁸ who will sustain you to the end, guiltless in the day of our Lord Jesus Christ. ⁹ God is faithful, by whom you were called into the fellowship of his Son, Jesus Christ our Lord.

Divisions in the Church

¹⁰ I appeal to you, brothers,[1] by the name of our Lord Jesus Christ, that all of you agree, and that there be no divisions among you, but that you be united in the same mind and the same judgment. ¹¹ For it has been reported to me by Chloe's people that there is quarreling among you, my brothers. ¹² What I mean is that each one of you says, "I follow Paul," or "I follow Apollos," or "I follow Cephas," or "I follow Christ." ¹³ Is Christ divided? Was Paul crucified for you? Or were you baptized in the name of Paul? ¹⁴ I thank God that I baptized none of you except Crispus and Gaius, ¹⁵ so that no one may say that you were baptized in my name. ¹⁶ (I did baptize also the household of Stephanas. Beyond that, I do not know whether I baptized anyone else.) ¹⁷ For Christ did not send me to baptize but to preach the gospel, and not with words of eloquent wisdom, lest the cross of Christ be emptied of its power.

Christ the Wisdom and Power of God

¹⁸ For the word of the cross is folly to those who are perishing, but to us who are being saved it is the power of God. ¹⁹ For it is written,

> ᵃ"I will destroy the wisdom of the wise,
>   and the discernment of the discerning I
>   will thwart."

²⁰ Where is the one who is wise? Where is the scribe? Where is the debater of this age? Has not God made foolish the wisdom of the world? ²¹ For since, in the wisdom of God, the world did not know God through wisdom, it pleased God through the folly of what we preach[2] to save those who believe. ²² For Jews demand signs and Greeks seek wisdom, ²³ but we preach Christ crucified, a stumbling block to Jews and folly to Gentiles, ²⁴ but to those who are called, both Jews and Greeks, Christ the power of God and the wisdom of God. ²⁵ For the foolishness of God is wiser than men, and the weakness of God is stronger than men.

²⁶ For consider your calling, brothers: not many of you were wise according to worldly standards,[3] not many were powerful, not many were of noble birth. ²⁷ But God chose what is foolish in the world to shame the wise; God chose what is weak in the world to shame the strong; ²⁸ God chose what is low and despised in the world, even things that are not, to bring to nothing things that are, ²⁹ so that no human being[4] might boast in the presence of God. ³⁰ And because of him[5] you are in Christ Jesus, who became to us wisdom from God, righteousness and sanctification and redemption, ³¹ so that, as it is written, "Let the one who boasts, boast in the Lord."

Proclaiming Christ Crucified

2 And I, when I came to you, brothers,[6] did not come proclaiming to you the testimony[7] of God with lofty speech or wisdom. ² For I decided to know nothing among you except Jesus Christ and him crucified. ³ And I was with you in weakness and in fear and much trem-

---

[1] Or brothers and sisters. In New Testament usage, depending on the context, the plural Greek word adelphoi (translated "brothers") may refer either to brothers or to brothers and sisters; also verses 11, 26 [2] Or the folly of preaching [3] Greek according to the flesh [4] Greek no flesh [5] Greek And from him [6] Or brothers and sisters [7] Some manuscripts mystery (or secret) ᵃ Isa. 29:14

bling, [4] and my speech and my message were not in plausible words of wisdom, but in demonstration of the Spirit and of power, [5] so that your faith might not rest in the wisdom of men[1] but in the power of God.

Wisdom from the Spirit

[6] Yet among the mature we do impart wisdom, although it is not a wisdom of this age or of the rulers of this age, who are doomed to pass away. [7] But we impart a secret and hidden wisdom of God, which God decreed before the ages for our glory. [8] None of the rulers of this age understood this, for if they had, they would not have crucified the Lord of glory. [9] But, as it is written,

"What no eye has seen, nor ear heard,
     nor the heart of man imagined,
  what God has prepared for those who love
     him"—

[10] these things God has revealed to us through the Spirit. For the Spirit searches everything, even the depths of God. [11] For who knows a person's thoughts except the spirit of that person, which is in him? So also no one comprehends the thoughts of God except the Spirit of God. [12] Now we have received not the spirit of the world, but the Spirit who is from God, that we might understand the things freely given us by God. [13] And we impart this in words not taught by human wisdom but taught by the Spirit, interpreting spiritual truths to those who are spiritual.[2]

[14] The natural person does not accept the things of the Spirit of God, for they are folly to him, and he is not able to understand them because they are spiritually discerned. [15] The spiritual person judges all things, but is himself to be judged by no one. [16] "For who has understood the mind of the Lord so as to instruct him?" But we have the mind of Christ.

Divisions in the Church

3 But I, brothers,[3] could not address you as spiritual people, but as people of the flesh, as infants in Christ. [2] I fed you with milk, not solid food, for you were not ready for it. And even now you are not yet ready, [3] for you are still of the flesh. For while there is jealousy and strife among you, are you not of the flesh and behaving only in a human way? [4] For when one says, "I follow Paul," and another, "I follow Apollos," are you not being merely human?

[5] What then is Apollos? What is Paul? Servants through whom you believed, as the Lord assigned to each. [6] I planted, Apollos watered, but God gave the growth. [7] So neither he who plants nor he who waters is anything, but only God who gives the growth. [8] He who plants and he who waters are one, and each will receive his wages according to his labor. [9] For we are God's fellow workers. You are God's field, God's building.

[10] According to the grace of God given to me, like a skilled[4] master builder I laid a foundation, and someone else is building upon it. Let each one take care how he builds upon it. [11] For no one can lay a foundation other than that which is laid, which is Jesus Christ. [12] Now if anyone builds on the foundation with gold, silver, precious stones, wood, hay, straw— [13] each one's work will become manifest, for the Day will disclose it, because it will be revealed by fire, and the fire will test what sort of work each one has done. [14] If the work that anyone has built on the foundation survives, he will receive a reward. [15] If anyone's work is burned up, he will suffer loss, though he himself will be saved, but only as through fire.

[16] Do you not know that you[5] are God's temple and that God's Spirit dwells in you? [17] If anyone destroys God's temple, God will destroy him. For God's temple is holy, and you are that temple.

[18] Let no one deceive himself. If anyone among you thinks that he is wise in this age, let him become a fool that he may become wise. [19] For the wisdom of this world is folly with God. For it is written, [b] "He catches the wise in their craftiness," [20] and again, "The Lord knows the thoughts of the wise, that they are futile." [21] So let no one boast in men. For all things are yours, [22] whether Paul or Apollos or Cephas or the world or life or death or the present or the future—all are yours, [23] and you are Christ's, and Christ is God's.

The Ministry of Apostles

4 This is how one should regard us, as servants of Christ and stewards of the mysteries of God. [2] Moreover, it is required of stewards that they be found faithful. [3] But with me it is a very small thing that I should be judged by you or by any human court. In fact, I do not even judge myself. [4] For I am not aware of anything against myself, but I am not thereby acquitted. It is the Lord who judges me. [5] Therefore do not pronounce judgment before the time, before

---

[1] The Greek word *anthropoi* can refer to both men and women [2] Or *interpreting spiritual truths in spiritual language,* or *comparing spiritual things with spiritual* [3] Or *brothers and sisters* [4] Or *wise* [5] The Greek for *you* is plural in verses 16 and 17 [a] Isa. 40:13 [b] Job 5:13 [c] Ps. 94:11

the Lord comes, who will bring to light the things now hidden in darkness and will disclose the purposes of the heart. Then each one will receive his commendation from God.

[6] I have applied all these things to myself and Apollos for your benefit, brothers,[1] that you may learn by us not to go beyond what is written, that none of you may be puffed up in favor of one against another. [7] For who sees anything different in you? What do you have that you did not receive? If then you received it, why do you boast as if you did not receive it?

[8] Already you have all you want! Already you have become rich! Without us you have become kings! And would that you did reign, so that we might share the rule with you! [9] For I think that God has exhibited us apostles as last of all, like men sentenced to death, because we have become a spectacle to the world, to angels, and to men. [10] We are fools for Christ's sake, but you are wise in Christ. We are weak, but you are strong. You are held in honor, but we in disrepute. [11] To the present hour we hunger and thirst, we are poorly dressed and buffeted and homeless, [12] and we labor, working with our own hands. When reviled, we bless; when persecuted, we endure; [13] when slandered, we entreat. We have become, and are still, like the scum of the world, the refuse of all things.

[14] I do not write these things to make you ashamed, but to admonish you as my beloved children. [15] For though you have countless[2] guides in Christ, you do not have many fathers. For I became your father in Christ Jesus through the gospel. [16] I urge you, then, be imitators of me. [17] That is why I sent[3] you Timothy, my beloved and faithful child in the Lord, to remind you of my ways in Christ,[4] as I teach them everywhere in every church. [18] Some are arrogant, as though I were not coming to you. [19] But I will come to you soon, if the Lord wills, and I will find out not the talk of these arrogant people but their power. [20] For the kingdom of God does not consist in talk but in power. [21] What do you wish? Shall I come to you with a rod, or with love in a spirit of gentleness?

Sexual Immorality Defiles the Church

5 It is actually reported that there is sexual immorality among you, and of a kind that is not tolerated even among pagans, for a man has his father's wife. [2] And you are arrogant!

Ought you not rather to mourn? Let him who has done this be removed from among you.

[3] For though absent in body, I am present in spirit; and as if present, I have already pronounced judgment on the one who did such a thing. [4] When you are assembled in the name of the Lord Jesus and my spirit is present, with the power of our Lord Jesus, [5] you are to deliver this man to Satan for the destruction of the flesh, so that his spirit may be saved in the day of the Lord.[5]

[6] Your boasting is not good. Do you not know that a little leaven leavens the whole lump? [7] Cleanse out the old leaven that you may be a new lump, as you really are unleavened. For Christ, our Passover lamb, has been sacrificed. [8] Let us therefore celebrate the festival, not with the old leaven, the leaven of malice and evil, but with the unleavened bread of sincerity and truth.

[9] I wrote to you in my letter not to associate with sexually immoral people— [10] not at all meaning the sexually immoral of this world, or the greedy and swindlers, or idolaters, since then you would need to go out of the world. [11] But now I am writing to you not to associate with anyone who bears the name of brother if he is guilty of sexual immorality or greed, or is an idolater, reviler, drunkard, or swindler—not even to eat with such a one. [12] For what have I to do with judging outsiders? Is it not those inside the church[6] whom you are to judge? [13] God judges[7] those outside. "Purge the evil person from among you."

Lawsuits Against Believers

6 When one of you has a grievance against another, does he dare go to law before the unrighteous instead of the saints? [2] Or do you not know that the saints will judge the world? And if the world is to be judged by you, are you incompetent to try trivial cases? [3] Do you not know that we are to judge angels? How much more, then, matters pertaining to this life! [4] So if you have such cases, why do you lay them before those who have no standing in the church? [5] I say this to your shame. Can it be that there is no one among you wise enough to settle a dispute between the brothers, [6] but brother goes to law against brother, and that before unbelievers? [7] To have lawsuits at all with one another is already a defeat for you. Why not rather suffer wrong? Why not rather be defrauded? [8] But you yourselves wrong and defraud—even your own brothers![8]

---

[1] Or brothers and sisters [2] Greek you have ten thousand [3] Or am sending [4] Some manuscripts add Jesus [5] Some manuscripts add Jesus [6] Greek those inside [7] Or will judge
[8] Or brothers and sisters

[9] Or do you not know that the unrighteous[1] will not inherit the kingdom of God? Do not be deceived: neither the sexually immoral, nor idolaters, nor adulterers, nor men who practice homosexuality,[2] [10] nor thieves, nor the greedy, nor drunkards, nor revilers, nor swindlers will inherit the kingdom of God. [11] And such were some of you. But you were washed, you were sanctified, you were justified in the name of the Lord Jesus Christ and by the Spirit of our God.

Flee Sexual Immorality

[12] "All things are lawful for me," but not all things are helpful. "All things are lawful for me," but I will not be dominated by anything. [13] "Food is meant for the stomach and the stomach for food"—and God will destroy both one and the other. The body is not meant for sexual immorality, but for the Lord, and the Lord for the body. [14] And God raised the Lord and will also raise us up by his power. [15] Do you not know that your bodies are members of Christ? Shall I then take the members of Christ and make them members of a prostitute? Never! [16] Or do you not know that he who is joined[3] to a prostitute becomes one body with her? For, as it is written, [a]"The two will become one flesh." [17] But he who is joined to the Lord becomes one spirit with him. [18] Flee from sexual immorality. Every other sin[4] a person commits is outside the body, but the sexually immoral person sins against his own body. [19] Or do you not know that your body is a temple of the Holy Spirit within you, whom you have from God? You are not your own, [20] for you were bought with a price. So glorify God in your body.

Principles for Marriage

7 Now concerning the matters about which you wrote: "It is good for a man not to have sexual relations with a woman." [2] But because of the temptation to sexual immorality, each man should have his own wife and each woman her own husband. [3] The husband should give to his wife her conjugal rights, and likewise the wife to her husband. [4] For the wife does not have authority over her own body, but the husband does. Likewise the husband does not have authority over his own body, but the wife does. [5] Do not deprive one another, except perhaps by agreement for a limited time, that you may devote yourselves to prayer; but then come

together again, so that Satan may not tempt you because of your lack of self-control. [6] Now as a concession, not a command, I say this.[5] [7] I wish that all were as I myself am. But each has his own gift from God, one of one kind and one of another.

[8] To the unmarried and the widows I say that it is good for them to remain single, as I am. [9] But if they cannot exercise self-control, they should marry. For it is better to marry than to burn with passion.

[10] To the married I give this charge (not I, but the Lord): the wife should not separate from her husband [11] (but if she does, she should remain unmarried or else be reconciled to her husband), and the husband should not divorce his wife.

[12] To the rest I say (I, not the Lord) that if any brother has a wife who is an unbeliever, and she consents to live with him, he should not divorce her. [13] If any woman has a husband who is an unbeliever, and he consents to live with her, she should not divorce him. [14] For the unbelieving husband is made holy because of his wife, and the unbelieving wife is made holy because of her husband. Otherwise your children would be unclean, but as it is, they are holy. [15] But if the unbelieving partner separates, let it be so. In such cases the brother or sister is not enslaved. God has called you[6] to peace. [16] For how do you know, wife, whether you will save your husband? Or how do you know, husband, whether you will save your wife?

Live as You Are Called

[17] Only let each person lead the life[7] that the Lord has assigned to him, and to which God has called him. This is my rule in all the churches. [18] Was anyone at the time of his call already circumcised? Let him not seek to remove the marks of circumcision. Was anyone at the time of his call uncircumcised? Let him not seek circumcision. [19] For neither circumcision counts for anything nor uncircumcision, but keeping the commandments of God. [20] Each one should remain in the condition in which he was called. [21] Were you a bondservant[8] when called? Do not be concerned about it. (But if you can gain your freedom, avail yourself of the opportunity.) [22] For he who was called in the Lord as a bondservant is a freedman of the Lord. Likewise he who was free when called is a

---

[1] Or *wrongdoers* [2] The two Greek terms translated by this phrase refer to the passive and active partners in consensual homosexual acts [3] Or *who holds fast* (compare Genesis 2:24 and Deuteronomy 10:20); also verse 17 [4] Or *Every sin* [5] Or *I say this:* [6] Some manuscripts *us* [7] Or *each person walk in the way* [8] For the contextual rendering of the Greek word *doulos*, see Preface; also verses 22 (twice), 23 [a] Gen. 2:24

bondservant of Christ. [23] You were bought with a price; do not become bondservants of men. [24] So, brothers,[1] in whatever condition each was called, there let him remain with God.

The Unmarried and the Widowed

[25] Now concerning[2] the betrothed,[3] I have no command from the Lord, but I give my judgment as one who by the Lord's mercy is trustworthy. [26] I think that in view of the present[4] distress it is good for a person to remain as he is. [27] Are you bound to a wife? Do not seek to be free. Are you free from a wife? Do not seek a wife. [28] But if you do marry, you have not sinned, and if a betrothed woman[5] marries, she has not sinned. Yet those who marry will have worldly troubles, and I would spare you that. [29] This is what I mean, brothers: the appointed time has grown very short. From now on, let those who have wives live as though they had none, [30] and those who mourn as though they were not mourning, and those who rejoice as though they were not rejoicing, and those who buy as though they had no goods, [31] and those who deal with the world as though they had no dealings with it. For the present form of this world is passing away.

[32] I want you to be free from anxieties. The unmarried man is anxious about the things of the Lord, how to please the Lord. [33] But the married man is anxious about worldly things, how to please his wife, [34] and his interests are divided. And the unmarried or betrothed woman is anxious about the things of the Lord, how to be holy in body and spirit. But the married woman is anxious about worldly things, how to please her husband. [35] I say this for your own benefit, not to lay any restraint upon you, but to promote good order and to secure your undivided devotion to the Lord.

[36] If anyone thinks that he is not behaving properly toward his betrothed,[6] if his[7] passions are strong, and it has to be, let him do as he wishes: let them marry—it is no sin. [37] But whoever is firmly established in his heart, being under no necessity but having his desire under control, and has determined this in his heart, to keep her as his betrothed, he will do well. [38] So then he who marries his betrothed does well, and he who refrains from marriage will do even better.

[39] A wife is bound to her husband as long as he lives. But if her husband dies, she is free to be married to whom she wishes, only in the Lord. [40] Yet in my judgment she is happier if she remains as she is. And I think that I too have the Spirit of God.

Food Offered to Idols

8 Now concerning[8] food offered to idols: we know that "all of us possess knowledge." This "knowledge" puffs up, but love builds up. [2] If anyone imagines that he knows something, he does not yet know as he ought to know. [3] But if anyone loves God, he is known by God.[9]

[4] Therefore, as to the eating of food offered to idols, we know that "an idol has no real existence," and that "there is no God but one." [5] For although there may be so-called gods in heaven or on earth—as indeed there are many "gods" and many "lords"— [6] yet for us there is one God, the Father, from whom are all things and for whom we exist, and one Lord, Jesus Christ, through whom are all things and through whom we exist.

[7] However, not all possess this knowledge. But some, through former association with idols, eat food as really offered to an idol, and their conscience, being weak, is defiled. [8] Food will not commend us to God. We are no worse off if we do not eat, and no better off if we do. [9] But take care that this right of yours does not somehow become a stumbling block to the weak. [10] For if anyone sees you who have knowledge eating[10] in an idol's temple, will he not be encouraged,[11] if his conscience is weak, to eat food offered to idols? [11] And so by your knowledge this weak person is destroyed, the brother for whom Christ died. [12] Thus, sinning against your brothers[12] and wounding their conscience when it is weak, you sin against Christ. [13] Therefore, if food makes my brother stumble, I will never eat meat, lest I make my brother stumble.

Paul Surrenders His Rights

9 Am I not free? Am I not an apostle? Have I not seen Jesus our Lord? Are not you my workmanship in the Lord? [2] If to others I am not an apostle, at least I am to you, for you are the seal of my apostleship in the Lord.

[3] This is my defense to those who would examine me. [4] Do we not have the right to eat and drink? [5] Do we not have the right to take along a believing wife,[13] as do the other

---

[1] Or brothers and sisters; also verse 29 [2] The expression Now concerning introduces a reply to a question in the Corinthians' letter; see 7:1 [3] Greek virgins [4] Or impending [5] Greek virgin; also verse 34 [6] Greek virgin; also verses 37, 38 [7] Or her [8] The expression Now concerning introduces a reply to a question in the Corinthians' letter; see 7:1 [9] Greek him [10] Greek reclining at table [11] Or fortified; Greek built up [12] Or brothers and sisters [13] Greek a sister as wife

apostles and the brothers of the Lord and Cephas? [6] Or is it only Barnabas and I who have no right to refrain from working for a living? [7] Who serves as a soldier at his own expense? Who plants a vineyard without eating any of its fruit? Or who tends a flock without getting some of the milk?

[8] Do I say these things on human authority? Does not the Law say the same? [9] For it is written in the Law of Moses, [a] "You shall not muzzle an ox when it treads out the grain." Is it for oxen that God is concerned? [10] Does he not certainly speak for our sake? It was written for our sake, because the plowman should plow in hope and the thresher thresh in hope of sharing in the crop. [11] If we have sown spiritual things among you, is it too much if we reap material things from you? [12] If others share this rightful claim on you, do not we even more?

Nevertheless, we have not made use of this right, but we endure anything rather than put an obstacle in the way of the gospel of Christ. [13] Do you not know that those who are employed in the temple service get their food from the temple, and those who serve at the altar share in the sacrificial offerings? [14] In the same way, the Lord commanded that those who proclaim the gospel should get their living by the gospel.

[15] But I have made no use of any of these rights, nor am I writing these things to secure any such provision. For I would rather die than have anyone deprive me of my ground for boasting. [16] For if I preach the gospel, that gives me no ground for boasting. For necessity is laid upon me. Woe to me if I do not preach the gospel! [17] For if I do this of my own will, I have a reward, but if not of my own will, I am still entrusted with a stewardship. [18] What then is my reward? That in my preaching I may present the gospel free of charge, so as not to make full use of my right in the gospel.

[19] For though I am free from all, I have made myself a servant to all, that I might win more of them. [20] To the Jews I became as a Jew, in order to win Jews. To those under the law I became as one under the law (though not being myself under the law) that I might win those under the law. [21] To those outside the law I became as one outside the law (not being outside the law of God but under the law of Christ) that I might win those outside the law. [22] To the weak I became weak, that I might win the weak. I have become all things to all people, that by all means I might save some. [23] I do it all for the sake of the gospel, that I may share with them in its blessings.

[24] Do you not know that in a race all the runners run, but only one receives the prize? So run that you may obtain it. [25] Every athlete exercises self-control in all things. They do it to receive a perishable wreath, but we an imperishable. [26] So I do not run aimlessly; I do not box as one beating the air. [27] But I discipline my body and keep it under control, [1] lest after preaching to others I myself should be disqualified.

Warning Against Idolatry

10 For I do not want you to be unaware, brothers, [2] that our fathers were all under the cloud, and all passed through the sea, [2] and all were baptized into Moses in the cloud and in the sea, [3] and all ate the same spiritual food, [4] and all drank the same spiritual drink. For they drank from the spiritual Rock that followed them, and the Rock was Christ. [5] Nevertheless, with most of them God was not pleased, for they were overthrown[3] in the wilderness.

[6] Now these things took place as examples for us, that we might not desire evil as they did. [7] Do not be idolaters as some of them were; as it is written, [b] "The people sat down to eat and drink and rose up to play." [8] We must not indulge in sexual immorality as some of them did, and twenty-three thousand fell in a single day. [9] We must not put Christ[4] to the test, as some of them did and were destroyed by serpents, [10] nor grumble, as some of them did and were destroyed by the Destroyer. [11] Now these things happened to them as an example, but they were written down for our instruction, on whom the end of the ages has come. [12] Therefore let anyone who thinks that he stands take heed lest he fall. [13] No temptation has overtaken you that is not common to man. God is faithful, and he will not let you be tempted beyond your ability, but with the temptation he will also provide the way of escape, that you may be able to endure it.

[14] Therefore, my beloved, flee from idolatry. [15] I speak as to sensible people; judge for yourselves what I say. [16] The cup of blessing that we bless, is it not a participation in the blood of Christ? The bread that we break, is it not a participation in the body of Christ? [17] Because there is one bread, we who are many are one body, for

---

[1] Greek *I pummel my body and make it a slave* [2] Or *brothers and sisters* [3] Or *were laid low* [4] Some manuscripts *the Lord* [a] Deut. 25:4 [b] Ex. 32:6

we all partake of the one bread. [18] Consider the people of Israel:[1] are not those who eat the sacrifices participants in the altar? [19] What do I imply then? That food offered to idols is anything, or that an idol is anything? [20] No, I imply that what pagans sacrifice they offer to demons and not to God. I do not want you to be participants with demons. [21] You cannot drink the cup of the Lord and the cup of demons. You cannot partake of the table of the Lord and the table of demons. [22] Shall we provoke the Lord to jealousy? Are we stronger than he?

Do All to the Glory of God

[23] "All things are lawful," but not all things are helpful. "All things are lawful," but not all things build up. [24] Let no one seek his own good, but the good of his neighbor. [25] Eat whatever is sold in the meat market without raising any question on the ground of conscience. [26] For "the earth is the Lord's, and the fullness thereof." [27] If one of the unbelievers invites you to dinner and you are disposed to go, eat whatever is set before you without raising any question on the ground of conscience. [28] But if someone says to you, "This has been offered in sacrifice," then do not eat it, for the sake of the one who informed you, and for the sake of conscience— [29] I do not mean your conscience, but his. For why should my liberty be determined by someone else's conscience? [30] If I partake with thankfulness, why am I denounced because of that for which I give thanks?

[31] So, whether you eat or drink, or whatever you do, do all to the glory of God. [32] Give no offense to Jews or to Greeks or to the church of God, [33] just as I try to please everyone in everything I do, not seeking my own advantage, but that of many, that they may be saved.

11 Be imitators of me, as I am of Christ.

Head Coverings

[2] Now I commend you because you remember me in everything and maintain the traditions even as I delivered them to you. [3] But I want you to understand that the head of every man is Christ, the head of a wife[2] is her husband,[3] and the head of Christ is God. [4] Every man who prays or prophesies with his head covered dishonors his head, [5] but every wife[4] who prays or prophesies with her head uncov-

ered dishonors her head, since it is the same as if her head were shaven. [6] For if a wife will not cover her head, then she should cut her hair short. But since it is disgraceful for a wife to cut off her hair or shave her head, let her cover her head. [7] For a man ought not to cover his head, since he is the image and glory of God, but woman is the glory of man. [8] For man was not made from woman, but woman from man. [9] Neither was man created for woman, but woman for man. [10] That is why a wife ought to have a symbol of authority on her head, because of the angels.[5] [11] Nevertheless, in the Lord woman is not independent of man nor man of woman; [12] for as woman was made from man, so man is now born of woman. And all things are from God. [13] Judge for yourselves: is it proper for a wife to pray to God with her head uncovered? [14] Does not nature itself teach you that if a man wears long hair it is a disgrace for him, [15] but if a woman has long hair, it is her glory? For her hair is given to her for a covering. [16] If anyone is inclined to be contentious, we have no such practice, nor do the churches of God.

The Lord's Supper

[17] But in the following instructions I do not commend you, because when you come together it is not for the better but for the worse. [18] For, in the first place, when you come together as a church, I hear that there are divisions among you. And I believe it in part,[6] [19] for there must be factions among you in order that those who are genuine among you may be recognized. [20] When you come together, it is not the Lord's supper that you eat. [21] For in eating, each one goes ahead with his own meal. One goes hungry, another gets drunk. [22] What! Do you not have houses to eat and drink in? Or do you despise the church of God and humiliate those who have nothing? What shall I say to you? Shall I commend you in this? No, I will not.

[23] For I received from the Lord what I also delivered to you, that the Lord Jesus on the night when he was betrayed took bread, [24] and when he had given thanks, he broke it, and said, "This is my body, which is for[7] you. Do this in remembrance of me." [25] In the same way also he took the cup, after supper, saying, "This cup is the new covenant in my blood. Do this, as often as you drink it, in remembrance of me." [26] For as

---

[1] Greek Consider Israel according to the flesh [2] Greek gunē. This term may refer to a woman or a wife, depending on the context. [3] Greek anēr. This term may refer to a man or a husband, depending on the context [4] In verses 5–13, the Greek word gunē is translated wife in verses that deal with wearing a veil, a sign of being married in first-century culture [5] Or messengers, that is, people sent to observe and report [6] Or I believe a certain report [7] Some manuscripts broken for [8] Or as my memorial; also verse 25 [a] Ps. 24:1

often as you eat this bread and drink the cup, you proclaim the Lord's death until he comes. [27] Whoever, therefore, eats the bread or drinks the cup of the Lord in an unworthy manner will be guilty concerning the body and blood of the Lord. [28] Let a person examine himself, then, and so eat of the bread and drink of the cup. [29] For anyone who eats and drinks without discerning the body eats and drinks judgment on himself. [30] That is why many of you are weak and ill, and some have died.[1] [31] But if we judged[2] ourselves truly, we would not be judged. [32] But when we are judged by the Lord, we are disciplined[3] so that we may not be condemned along with the world.

[33] So then, my brothers,[4] when you come together to eat, wait for[5] one another— [34] if anyone is hungry, let him eat at home—so that when you come together it will not be for judgment. About the other things I will give directions when I come.

Spiritual Gifts

12 Now concerning[6] spiritual gifts,[7] brothers,[8] I do not want you to be uninformed. [2] You know that when you were pagans you were led astray to mute idols, however you were led. [3] Therefore I want you to understand that no one speaking in the Spirit of God ever says "Jesus is accursed!" and no one can say "Jesus is Lord" except in the Holy Spirit.

[4] Now there are varieties of gifts, but the same Spirit; [5] and there are varieties of service, but the same Lord; [6] and there are varieties of activities, but it is the same God who empowers them all in everyone. [7] To each is given the manifestation of the Spirit for the common good. [8] For to one is given through the Spirit the utterance of wisdom, and to another the utterance of knowledge according to the same Spirit, [9] to another faith by the same Spirit, to another gifts of healing by the one Spirit, [10] to another the working of miracles, to another prophecy, to another the ability to distinguish between spirits, to another various kinds of tongues, to another the interpretation of tongues. [11] All these are empowered by one and the same Spirit, who apportions to each one individually as he wills.

One Body with Many Members

[12] For just as the body is one and has many members, and all the members of the body, though many, are one body, so it is with Christ.

[13] For in one Spirit we were all baptized into one body—Jews or Greeks, slaves[9] or free—and all were made to drink of one Spirit.

[14] For the body does not consist of one member but of many. [15] If the foot should say, "Because I am not a hand, I do not belong to the body," that would not make it any less a part of the body. [16] And if the ear should say, "Because I am not an eye, I do not belong to the body," that would not make it any less a part of the body. [17] If the whole body were an eye, where would be the sense of hearing? If the whole body were an ear, where would be the sense of smell? [18] But as it is, God arranged the members in the body, each one of them, as he chose. [19] If all were a single member, where would the body be? [20] As it is, there are many parts,[10] yet one body.

[21] The eye cannot say to the hand, "I have no need of you," nor again the head to the feet, "I have no need of you." [22] On the contrary, the parts of the body that seem to be weaker are indispensable, [23] and on those parts of the body that we think less honorable we bestow the greater honor, and our unpresentable parts are treated with greater modesty, [24] which our more presentable parts do not require. But God has so composed the body, giving greater honor to the part that lacked it, [25] that there may be no division in the body, but that the members may have the same care for one another. [26] If one member suffers, all suffer together; if one member is honored, all rejoice together.

[27] Now you are the body of Christ and individually members of it. [28] And God has appointed in the church first apostles, second prophets, third teachers, then miracles, then gifts of healing, helping, administrating, and various kinds of tongues. [29] Are all apostles? Are all prophets? Are all teachers? Do all work miracles? [30] Do all possess gifts of healing? Do all speak with tongues? Do all interpret? [31] But earnestly desire the higher gifts.

And I will show you a still more excellent way.

The Way of Love

13 If I speak in the tongues of men and of angels, but have not love, I am a noisy gong or a clanging cymbal. [2] And if I have prophetic powers, and understand all mysteries and all knowledge, and if I have all faith, so as to remove mountains, but have not love, I am nothing. [3] If I give away all I have, and if I

---

[1] Greek *have fallen asleep* (as in 15:6, 20)   [2] Or *discerned*   [3] Or *when we are judged we are being disciplined by the Lord*   [4] Or *brothers and sisters*   [5] Or *share with*   [6] The expression *Now concerning* introduces a reply to a question in the Corinthians' letter; see 7:1   [7] Or *spiritual persons*   [8] Or *brothers and sisters*   [9] For the contextual rendering of the Greek word *doulos*, see Preface   [10] Or *members*; also verse 22

deliver up my body to be burned,[1] but have not love, I gain nothing.

[4] Love is patient and kind; love does not envy or boast; it is not arrogant [5] or rude. It does not insist on its own way; it is not irritable or resentful;[2] [6] it does not rejoice at wrongdoing, but rejoices with the truth. [7] Love bears all things, believes all things, hopes all things, endures all things.

[8] Love never ends. As for prophecies, they will pass away; as for tongues, they will cease; as for knowledge, it will pass away. [9] For we know in part and we prophesy in part, [10] but when the perfect comes, the partial will pass away. [11] When I was a child, I spoke like a child, I thought like a child, I reasoned like a child. When I became a man, I gave up childish ways. [12] For now we see in a mirror dimly, but then face to face. Now I know in part; then I shall know fully, even as I have been fully known.

[13] So now faith, hope, and love abide, these three; but the greatest of these is love.

Prophecy and Tongues

14 Pursue love, and earnestly desire the spiritual gifts, especially that you may prophesy. [2] For one who speaks in a tongue speaks not to men but to God; for no one understands him, but he utters mysteries in the Spirit. [3] On the other hand, the one who prophesies speaks to people for their upbuilding and encouragement and consolation. [4] The one who speaks in a tongue builds up himself, but the one who prophesies builds up the church. [5] Now I want you all to speak in tongues, but even more to prophesy. The one who prophesies is greater than the one who speaks in tongues, unless someone interprets, so that the church may be built up.

[6] Now, brothers,[3] if I come to you speaking in tongues, how will I benefit you unless I bring you some revelation or knowledge or prophecy or teaching? [7] If even lifeless instruments, such as the flute or the harp, do not give distinct notes, how will anyone know what is played? [8] And if the bugle gives an indistinct sound, who will get ready for battle? [9] So with yourselves, if with your tongue you utter speech that is not intelligible, how will anyone know what is said? For you will be speaking into the air. [10] There are doubtless many different languages in the world, and none is without meaning, [11] but if I do not know the meaning of the language, I will be a foreigner to the speaker and the speaker a foreigner to me. [12] So with yourselves, since you are eager for manifestations of the Spirit, strive to excel in building up the church.

[13] Therefore, one who speaks in a tongue should pray that he may interpret. [14] For if I pray in a tongue, my spirit prays but my mind is unfruitful. [15] What am I to do? I will pray with my spirit, but I will pray with my mind also; I will sing praise with my spirit, but I will sing with my mind also. [16] Otherwise, if you give thanks with your spirit, how can anyone in the position of an outsider[4] say "Amen" to your thanksgiving when he does not know what you are saying? [17] For you may be giving thanks well enough, but the other person is not being built up. [18] I thank God that I speak in tongues more than all of you. [19] Nevertheless, in church I would rather speak five words with my mind in order to instruct others, than ten thousand words in a tongue.

[20] Brothers, do not be children in your thinking. Be infants in evil, but in your thinking be mature. [21] In the Law it is written, [a]"By people of strange tongues and by the lips of foreigners will I speak to this people, and even then they will not listen to me, says the Lord." [22] Thus tongues are a sign not for believers but for unbelievers, while prophecy is a sign[5] not for unbelievers but for believers. [23] If, therefore, the whole church comes together and all speak in tongues, and outsiders or unbelievers enter, will they not say that you are out of your minds? [24] But if all prophesy, and an unbeliever or outsider enters, he is convicted by all, he is called to account by all, [25] the secrets of his heart are disclosed, and so, falling on his face, he will worship God and declare that God is really among you.

Orderly Worship

[26] What then, brothers? When you come together, each one has a hymn, a lesson, a revelation, a tongue, or an interpretation. Let all things be done for building up. [27] If any speak in a tongue, let there be only two or at most three, and each in turn, and let someone interpret. [28] But if there is no one to interpret, let each of them keep silent in church and speak to himself and to God. [29] Let two or three prophets speak, and let the others weigh what is said. [30] If a revelation is made to another sitting there, let the first be silent. [31] For you can all prophesy one

---

[1] Some manuscripts deliver up my body [to death] that I may boast [2] Greek irritable and does not count up wrongdoing [3] Or brothers and sisters; also verses 20, 26, 39 [4] Or of him that is without gifts [5] Greek lacks a sign [a] Isa. 28:11, 12

by one, so that all may learn and all be encouraged, [32] and the spirits of prophets are subject to prophets. [33] For God is not a God of confusion but of peace.

As in all the churches of the saints, [34] the women should keep silent in the churches. For they are not permitted to speak, but should be in submission, as the Law also says. [35] If there is anything they desire to learn, let them ask their husbands at home. For it is shameful for a woman to speak in church.

[36] Or was it from you that the word of God came? Or are you the only ones it has reached? [37] If anyone thinks that he is a prophet, or spiritual, he should acknowledge that the things I am writing to you are a command of the Lord. [38] If anyone does not recognize this, he is not recognized. [39] So, my brothers, earnestly desire to prophesy, and do not forbid speaking in tongues. [40] But all things should be done decently and in order.

The Resurrection of Christ

15 Now I would remind you, brothers,[1] of the gospel I preached to you, which you received, in which you stand, [2] and by which you are being saved, if you hold fast to the word I preached to you—unless you believed in vain.

[3] For I delivered to you as of first importance what I also received: that Christ died for our sins in accordance with the Scriptures, [4] that he was buried, that he was raised on the third day in accordance with the Scriptures, [5] and that he appeared to Cephas, then to the twelve. [6] Then he appeared to more than five hundred brothers at one time, most of whom are still alive, though some have fallen asleep. [7] Then he appeared to James, then to all the apostles. [8] Last of all, as to one untimely born, he appeared also to me. [9] For I am the least of the apostles, unworthy to be called an apostle, because I persecuted the church of God. [10] But by the grace of God I am what I am, and his grace toward me was not in vain. On the contrary, I worked harder than any of them, though it was not I, but the grace of God that is with me. [11] Whether then it was I or they, so we preach and so you believed.

The Resurrection of the Dead

[12] Now if Christ is proclaimed as raised from the dead, how can some of you say that there is no resurrection of the dead? [13] But if there is no resurrection of the dead, then not even Christ has been raised. [14] And if Christ has not been raised, then our preaching is in vain and your faith is in vain. [15] We are even found to be misrepresenting God, because we testified about God that he raised Christ, whom he did not raise if it is true that the dead are not raised. [16] For if the dead are not raised, not even Christ has been raised. [17] And if Christ has not been raised, your faith is futile and you are still in your sins. [18] Then those also who have fallen asleep in Christ have perished. [19] If in Christ we have hope[2] in this life only, we are of all people most to be pitied.

[20] But in fact Christ has been raised from the dead, the firstfruits of those who have fallen asleep. [21] For as by a man came death, by a man has come also the resurrection of the dead. [22] For as in Adam all die, so also in Christ shall all be made alive. [23] But each in his own order: Christ the firstfruits, then at his coming those who belong to Christ. [24] Then comes the end, when he delivers the kingdom to God the Father after destroying every rule and every authority and power. [25] For he must reign until he has put all his enemies under his feet. [26] The last enemy to be destroyed is death. [27] For [a] "God[3] has put all things in subjection under his feet." But when it says, "all things are put in subjection," it is plain that he is excepted who put all things in subjection under him. [28] When all things are subjected to him, then the Son himself will also be subjected to him who put all things in subjection under him, that God may be all in all.

[29] Otherwise, what do people mean by being baptized on behalf of the dead? If the dead are not raised at all, why are people baptized on their behalf? [30] Why are we in danger every hour? [31] I protest, brothers, by my pride in you, which I have in Christ Jesus our Lord, I die every day! [32] What do I gain if, humanly speaking, I fought with beasts at Ephesus? If the dead are not raised, [b] "Let us eat and drink, for tomorrow we die." [33] Do not be deceived: "Bad company ruins good morals."[4] [34] Wake up from your drunken stupor, as is right, and do not go on sinning. For some have no knowledge of God. I say this to your shame.

The Resurrection Body

[35] But someone will ask, "How are the dead raised? With what kind of body do they come?" [36] You foolish person! What you sow does not come to life unless it dies. [37] And what you sow is not the body that is to be, but a bare kernel,

---

[1] Or brothers and sisters; also verses 6, 31, 50, 58 [2] Or we have hoped [3] Greek he [4] Probably from Menander's comedy Thais [a] Ps. 8:6 [b] Isa. 22:13

perhaps of wheat or of some other grain. ³⁸But God gives it a body as he has chosen, and to each kind of seed its own body. ³⁹For not all flesh is the same, but there is one kind for humans, another for animals, another for birds, and another for fish. ⁴⁰There are heavenly bodies and earthly bodies, but the glory of the heavenly is of one kind, and the glory of the earthly is of another. ⁴¹There is one glory of the sun, and another glory of the moon, and another glory of the stars; for star differs from star in glory.

⁴²So is it with the resurrection of the dead. What is sown is perishable; what is raised is imperishable. ⁴³It is sown in dishonor; it is raised in glory. It is sown in weakness; it is raised in power. ⁴⁴It is sown a natural body; it is raised a spiritual body. If there is a natural body, there is also a spiritual body. ⁴⁵Thus it is written, ᵃ"The first man Adam became a living being";¹ the last Adam became a life-giving spirit. ⁴⁶But it is not the spiritual that is first but the natural, and then the spiritual. ⁴⁷The first man was from the earth, a man of dust; the second man is from heaven. ⁴⁸As was the man of dust, so also are those who are of the dust, and as is the man of heaven, so also are those who are of heaven. ⁴⁹Just as we have borne the image of the man of dust, we shall² also bear the image of the man of heaven.

Mystery and Victory

⁵⁰I tell you this, brothers: flesh and blood cannot inherit the kingdom of God, nor does the perishable inherit the imperishable. ⁵¹Behold! I tell you a mystery. We shall not all sleep, but we shall all be changed, ⁵²in a moment, in the twinkling of an eye, at the last trumpet. For the trumpet will sound, and the dead will be raised imperishable, and we shall be changed. ⁵³For this perishable body must put on the imperishable, and this mortal body must put on immortality. ⁵⁴When the perishable puts on the imperishable, and the mortal puts on immortality, then shall come to pass the saying that is written:

ᵇ"Death is swallowed up in victory."
⁵⁵ "O death, where is your victory?
     O death, where is your sting?"

⁵⁶The sting of death is sin, and the power of sin is the law. ⁵⁷But thanks be to God, who gives us the victory through our Lord Jesus Christ. ⁵⁸Therefore, my beloved brothers, be stead-

fast, immovable, always abounding in the work of the Lord, knowing that in the Lord your labor is not in vain.

The Collection for the Saints

16 Now concerning³ the collection for the saints: as I directed the churches of Galatia, so you also are to do. ²On the first day of every week, each of you is to put something aside and store it up, as he may prosper, so that there will be no collecting when I come. ³And when I arrive, I will send those whom you accredit by letter to carry your gift to Jerusalem. ⁴If it seems advisable that I should go also, they will accompany me.

Plans for Travel

⁵I will visit you after passing through Macedonia, for I intend to pass through Macedonia, ⁶and perhaps I will stay with you or even spend the winter, so that you may help me on my journey, wherever I go. ⁷For I do not want to see you now just in passing. I hope to spend some time with you, if the Lord permits. ⁸But I will stay in Ephesus until Pentecost, ⁹for a wide door for effective work has opened to me, and there are many adversaries.

¹⁰When Timothy comes, see that you put him at ease among you, for he is doing the work of the Lord, as I am. ¹¹So let no one despise him. Help him on his way in peace, that he may return to me, for I am expecting him with the brothers.

Final Instructions

¹²Now concerning our brother Apollos, I strongly urged him to visit you with the other brothers, but it was not at all his will⁴ to come now. He will come when he has opportunity.

¹³Be watchful, stand firm in the faith, act like men, be strong. ¹⁴Let all that you do be done in love.

¹⁵Now I urge you, brothers⁵—you know that the household⁶ of Stephanas were the first converts in Achaia, and that they have devoted themselves to the service of the saints— ¹⁶be subject to such as these, and to every fellow worker and laborer. ¹⁷I rejoice at the coming of Stephanas and Fortunatus and Achaicus, because they have made up for your absence, ¹⁸for they refreshed my spirit as well as yours. Give recognition to such people.

---

¹ Greek *a living soul* ² Some manuscripts *let us* ³ The expression *Now concerning* introduces a reply to a question in the Corinthians' letter; see 7:1; also verse 12 ⁴ Or *God's will for him* ⁵ Or *brothers and sisters; also verse 20* ⁶ Greek *house* ᵃGen. 2:7 ᵇIsa. 25:8

Greetings

[19] The churches of Asia send you greetings. Aquila and Prisca, together with the church in their house, send you hearty greetings in the Lord. [20] All the brothers send you greetings. Greet one another with a holy kiss.

[21] I, Paul, write this greeting with my own hand. [22] If anyone has no love for the Lord, let him be accursed. Our Lord, come![1] [23] The grace of the Lord Jesus be with you. [24] My love be with you all in Christ Jesus. Amen.

---

[1] Greek *Maranatha* (a transliteration of Aramaic)

2 CORINTHIANS

Greeting

1 Paul, an apostle of Christ Jesus by the will of God, and Timothy our brother,

To the church of God that is at Corinth, with all the saints who are in the whole of Achaia:

2 Grace to you and peace from God our Father and the Lord Jesus Christ.

God of All Comfort

3 Blessed be the God and Father of our Lord Jesus Christ, the Father of mercies and God of all comfort, **4** who comforts us in all our affliction, so that we may be able to comfort those who are in any affliction, with the comfort with which we ourselves are comforted by God. **5** For as we share abundantly in Christ's sufferings, so through Christ we share abundantly in comfort too.[1] **6** If we are afflicted, it is for your comfort and salvation; and if we are comforted, it is for your comfort, which you experience when you patiently endure the same sufferings that we suffer. **7** Our hope for you is unshaken, for we know that as you share in our sufferings, you will also share in our comfort.

8 For we do not want you to be unaware, brothers,[2] of the affliction we experienced in Asia. For we were so utterly burdened beyond our strength that we despaired of life itself. **9** Indeed, we felt that we had received the sentence of death. But that was to make us rely not on ourselves but on God who raises the dead. **10** He delivered us from such a deadly peril, and he will deliver us. On him we have set our hope that he will deliver us again. **11** You also must help us by prayer, so that many will give thanks on our behalf for the blessing granted us through the prayers of many.

Paul's Change of Plans

12 For our boast is this, the testimony of our conscience, that we behaved in the world with simplicity[3] and godly sincerity, not by earthly wisdom but by the grace of God, and supremely so toward you. **13** For we are not writing to you anything other than what you read and understand and I hope you will fully understand— **14** just as you did partially understand us—that on the day of our Lord Jesus you will boast of us as we will boast of you.

15 Because I was sure of this, I wanted to come to you first, so that you might have a second experience of grace. **16** I wanted to visit you on my way to Macedonia, and to come back to you from Macedonia and have you send me on my way to Judea. **17** Was I vacillating when I wanted to do this? Do I make my plans according to the flesh, ready to say "Yes, yes" and "No, no" at the same time? **18** As surely as God is faithful, our word to you has not been Yes and No. **19** For the Son of God, Jesus Christ, whom we proclaimed among you, Silvanus and Timothy and I, was not Yes and No, but in him it is always Yes. **20** For all the promises of God find their Yes in him. That is why it is through him that we utter our Amen to God for his glory. **21** And it is God who establishes us with you in Christ, and has anointed us, **22** and who has also put his seal on us and given us his Spirit in our hearts as a guarantee.[4]

23 But I call God to witness against me—it was to spare you that I refrained from coming again to Corinth. **24** Not that we lord it over your faith, but we work with you for your joy, for you stand firm in your faith.

2 For I made up my mind not to make another painful visit to you. **2** For if I cause you pain, who is there to make me glad but the one whom I have pained? **3** And I wrote as I did, so that when I came I might not suffer pain from those who should have made me rejoice, for I felt sure of all of you, that my joy would be the joy of you all. **4** For I wrote to you out of much affliction and anguish of heart and with many tears, not to cause you pain but to let you know the abundant love that I have for you.

Forgive the Sinner

5 Now if anyone has caused pain, he has caused it not to me, but in some measure—not to put it too severely—to all of you. **6** For such a one, this punishment by the majority is enough, **7** so you should rather turn to forgive and comfort him, or he may be overwhelmed by excessive sorrow. **8** So I beg you to reaffirm

---

[1] Or For as the sufferings of Christ abound for us, so also our comfort abounds through Christ [2] Or brothers and sisters. In New Testament usage, depending on the context, the plural Greek word adelphoi (translated "brothers") may refer either to brothers or to brothers and sisters [3] Some manuscripts holiness [4] Or down payment

your love for him. [9] For this is why I wrote, that I might test you and know whether you are obedient in everything. [10] Anyone whom you forgive, I also forgive. Indeed, what I have forgiven, if I have forgiven anything, has been for your sake in the presence of Christ, [11] so that we would not be outwitted by Satan; for we are not ignorant of his designs.

Triumph in Christ

[12] When I came to Troas to preach the gospel of Christ, even though a door was opened for me in the Lord, [13] my spirit was not at rest because I did not find my brother Titus there. So I took leave of them and went on to Macedonia.

[14] But thanks be to God, who in Christ always leads us in triumphal procession, and through us spreads the fragrance of the knowledge of him everywhere. [15] For we are the aroma of Christ to God among those who are being saved and among those who are perishing, [16] to one a fragrance from death to death, to the other a fragrance from life to life. Who is sufficient for these things? [17] For we are not, like so many, peddlers of God's word, but as men of sincerity, as commissioned by God, in the sight of God we speak in Christ.

Ministers of the New Covenant

3 Are we beginning to commend ourselves again? Or do we need, as some do, letters of recommendation to you, or from you? [2] You yourselves are our letter of recommendation, written on our[1] hearts, to be known and read by all. [3] And you show that you are a letter from Christ delivered by us, written not with ink but with the Spirit of the living God, not on tablets of stone but on tablets of human hearts.[2]

[4] Such is the confidence that we have through Christ toward God. [5] Not that we are sufficient in ourselves to claim anything as coming from us, but our sufficiency is from God, [6] who has made us sufficient to be ministers of a new covenant, not of the letter but of the Spirit. For the letter kills, but the Spirit gives life.

[7] Now if the ministry of death, carved in letters on stone, came with such glory that the Israelites could not gaze at Moses' face because of its glory, which was being brought to an end, [8] will not the ministry of the Spirit have even more glory? [9] For if there was glory in the ministry of condemnation, the ministry of righteousness must far exceed it in glory. [10] Indeed, in this case, what once had glory has come to have no glory at all, because of the glory that surpasses it. [11] For if what was being brought to an end came with glory, much more will what is permanent have glory.

[12] Since we have such a hope, we are very bold, [13] not like Moses, who would put a veil over his face so that the Israelites might not gaze at the outcome of what was being brought to an end. [14] But their minds were hardened. For to this day, when they read the old covenant, that same veil remains unlifted, because only through Christ is it taken away. [15] Yes, to this day whenever Moses is read a veil lies over their hearts. [16] But when one[3] turns to the Lord, the veil is removed. [17] Now the Lord[4] is the Spirit, and where the Spirit of the Lord is, there is freedom. [18] And we all, with unveiled face, beholding the glory of the Lord,[5] are being transformed into the same image from one degree of glory to another.[6] For this comes from the Lord who is the Spirit.

The Light of the Gospel

4 Therefore, having this ministry by the mercy of God,[7] we do not lose heart. [2] But we have renounced disgraceful, underhanded ways. We refuse to practice[8] cunning or to tamper with God's word, but by the open statement of the truth we would commend ourselves to everyone's conscience in the sight of God. [3] And even if our gospel is veiled, it is veiled to those who are perishing. [4] In their case the god of this world has blinded the minds of the unbelievers, to keep them from seeing the light of the gospel of the glory of Christ, who is the image of God. [5] For what we proclaim is not ourselves, but Jesus Christ as Lord, with ourselves as your servants[9] for Jesus' sake. [6] For God, who said, "Let light shine out of darkness," has shone in our hearts to give the light of the knowledge of the glory of God in the face of Jesus Christ.

Treasure in Jars of Clay

[7] But we have this treasure in jars of clay, to show that the surpassing power belongs to God and not to us. [8] We are afflicted in every way, but not crushed; perplexed, but not driven to despair; [9] persecuted, but not forsaken; struck down, but not destroyed;

---

[1] Some manuscripts your [2] Greek fleshly hearts [3] Greek he [4] Or this Lord [5] Or reflecting the glory of the Lord [6] Greek from glory to glory [7] Greek having this ministry as we have received mercy [8] Greek to walk in [9] Or slaves (for the contextual rendering of the Greek word doulos, see Preface)

[10] always carrying in the body the death of Jesus, so that the life of Jesus may also be manifested in our bodies. [11] For we who live are always being given over to death for Jesus' sake, so that the life of Jesus also may be manifested in our mortal flesh. [12] So death is at work in us, but life in you.

[13] Since we have the same spirit of faith according to what has been written, [a]"I believed, and so I spoke," we also believe, and so we also speak, [14] knowing that he who raised the Lord Jesus will raise us also with Jesus and bring us with you into his presence. [15] For it is all for your sake, so that as grace extends to more and more people it may increase thanksgiving, to the glory of God.

[16] So we do not lose heart. Though our outer self[1] is wasting away, our inner self is being renewed day by day. [17] For this light momentary affliction is preparing for us an eternal weight of glory beyond all comparison, [18] as we look not to the things that are seen but to the things that are unseen. For the things that are seen are transient, but the things that are unseen are eternal.

Our Heavenly Dwelling

5 For we know that if the tent that is our earthly home is destroyed, we have a building from God, a house not made with hands, eternal in the heavens. [2] For in this tent we groan, longing to put on our heavenly dwelling, [3] if indeed by putting it on[2] we may not be found naked. [4] For while we are still in this tent, we groan, being burdened—not that we would be unclothed, but that we would be further clothed, so that what is mortal may be swallowed up by life. [5] He who has prepared us for this very thing is God, who has given us the Spirit as a guarantee.

[6] So we are always of good courage. We know that while we are at home in the body we are away from the Lord, [7] for we walk by faith, not by sight. [8] Yes, we are of good courage, and we would rather be away from the body and at home with the Lord. [9] So whether we are at home or away, we make it our aim to please him. [10] For we must all appear before the judgment seat of Christ, so that each one may receive what is due for what he has done in the body, whether good or evil.

The Ministry of Reconciliation

[11] Therefore, knowing the fear of the Lord, we persuade others. But what we are is known to God, and I hope it is known also to your conscience. [12] We are not commending ourselves to you again but giving you cause to boast about us, so that you may be able to answer those who boast about outward appearance and not about what is in the heart. [13] For if we are beside ourselves, it is for God; if we are in our right mind, it is for you. [14] For the love of Christ controls us, because we have concluded this: that one has died for all, therefore all have died; [15] and he died for all, that those who live might no longer live for themselves but for him who for their sake died and was raised.

[16] From now on, therefore, we regard no one according to the flesh. Even though we once regarded Christ according to the flesh, we regard him thus no longer. [17] Therefore, if anyone is in Christ, he is a new creation.[3] The old has passed away; behold, the new has come. [18] All this is from God, who through Christ reconciled us to himself and gave us the ministry of reconciliation; [19] that is, in Christ God was reconciling[4] the world to himself, not counting their trespasses against them, and entrusting to us the message of reconciliation. [20] Therefore, we are ambassadors for Christ, God making his appeal through us. We implore you on behalf of Christ, be reconciled to God. [21] For our sake he made him to be sin who knew no sin, so that in him we might become the righteousness of God.

6 Working together with him, then, we appeal to you not to receive the grace of God in vain. [2] For he says,

> [b]"In a favorable time I listened to you,
>   and in a day of salvation I have helped
>   you."

Behold, now is the favorable time; behold, now is the day of salvation. [3] We put no obstacle in anyone's way, so that no fault may be found with our ministry, [4] but as servants of God we commend ourselves in every way: by great endurance, in afflictions, hardships, calamities, [5] beatings, imprisonments, riots, labors, sleepless nights, hunger; [6] by purity, knowledge, patience, kindness, the Holy Spirit, genuine love; [7] by truthful speech, and the power of God; with the weapons of righteousness for the right hand and for the left; [8] through honor and dishonor, through slander and praise. We are treated as impostors, and yet are true; [9] as unknown, and yet well known; as dying, and behold, we live; as punished, and yet not killed;

---

[1] Greek man [2] Some manuscripts putting it off [3] Or creature [4] Or God was in Christ, reconciling [a] Ps. 116:10 [b] Isa. 49:8

[10] as sorrowful, yet always rejoicing; as poor, yet making many rich; as having nothing, yet possessing everything.

[11] We have spoken freely to you,[1] Corinthians; our heart is wide open. [12] You are not restricted by us, but you are restricted in your own affections. [13] In return (I speak as to children) widen your hearts also.

The Temple of the Living God

[14] Do not be unequally yoked with unbelievers. For what partnership has righteousness with lawlessness? Or what fellowship has light with darkness? [15] What accord has Christ with Belial?[2] Or what portion does a believer share with an unbeliever? [16] What agreement has the temple of God with idols? For we are the temple of the living God; as God said,

[a]"I will make my dwelling among them and
　　walk among them,
　　and I will be their God,
　　and they shall be my people.
[17]　Therefore [b] go out from their midst,
　　and be separate from them, says the
　　　Lord,
　　and touch no unclean thing;
　　　then I will welcome you,
[18]　and I will be a father to you,
　　and you shall be sons and daughters to
　　　me,
　　says the Lord Almighty."

7 Since we have these promises, beloved, let us cleanse ourselves from every defilement of body[3] and spirit, bringing holiness to completion in the fear of God.

Paul's Joy

[2] Make room in your hearts[4] for us. We have wronged no one, we have corrupted no one, we have taken advantage of no one. [3] I do not say this to condemn you, for I said before that you are in our hearts, to die together and to live together. [4] I am acting with great boldness toward you; I have great pride in you; I am filled with comfort. In all our affliction, I am overflowing with joy.

[5] For even when we came into Macedonia, our bodies had no rest, but we were afflicted at every turn—fighting without and fear within. [6] But God, who comforts the downcast, comforted us by the coming of Titus, [7] and not only by his coming but also by the comfort with which he was comforted by you, as he told us of your longing, your mourning, your zeal for me, so that I rejoiced still more. [8] For even if I made you grieve with my letter, I do not regret it—though I did regret it, for I see that that letter grieved you, though only for a while. [9] As it is, I rejoice, not because you were grieved, but because you were grieved into repenting. For you felt a godly grief, so that you suffered no loss through us.

[10] For godly grief produces a repentance that leads to salvation without regret, whereas worldly grief produces death. [11] For see what earnestness this godly grief has produced in you, but also what eagerness to clear yourselves, what indignation, what fear, what longing, what zeal, what punishment! At every point you have proved yourselves innocent in the matter. [12] So although I wrote to you, it was not for the sake of the one who did the wrong, nor for the sake of the one who suffered the wrong, but in order that your earnestness for us might be revealed to you in the sight of God. [13] Therefore we are comforted.

And besides our own comfort, we rejoiced still more at the joy of Titus, because his spirit has been refreshed by you all. [14] For whatever boasts I made to him about you, I was not put to shame. But just as everything we said to you was true, so also our boasting before Titus has proved true. [15] And his affection for you is even greater, as he remembers the obedience of you all, how you received him with fear and trembling. [16] I rejoice, because I have complete confidence in you.

Encouragement to Give Generously

8 We want you to know, brothers,[5] about the grace of God that has been given among the churches of Macedonia, [2] for in a severe test of affliction, their abundance of joy and their extreme poverty have overflowed in a wealth of generosity on their part. [3] For they gave according to their means, as I can testify, and beyond their means, of their own accord, [4] begging us earnestly for the favor[6] of taking part in the relief of the saints— [5] and this, not as we expected, but they gave themselves first to the Lord and then by the will of God to us. [6] Accordingly, we urged Titus that as he had started, so he should complete among you this act of grace. [7] But as you excel in everything—in faith, in speech, in knowledge, in all

---

[1] Greek *Our mouth is open to you* [2] Greek *Beliar* [3] Greek *flesh* [4] Greek lacks *in your hearts* [5] Or *brothers and sisters* [6] The Greek word *charis* can mean *favor* or *grace* or *thanks*, depending on the context [a] Lev. 26:12 [b] Isa. 52:11

earnestness, and in our love for you[1]—see that you excel in this act of grace also.

[8] I say this not as a command, but to prove by the earnestness of others that your love also is genuine. [9] For you know the grace of our Lord Jesus Christ, that though he was rich, yet for your sake he became poor, so that you by his poverty might become rich. [10] And in this matter I give my judgment: this benefits you, who a year ago started not only to do this work but also to desire to do it. [11] So now finish doing it as well, so that your readiness in desiring it may be matched by your completing it out of what you have. [12] For if the readiness is there, it is acceptable according to what a person has, not according to what he does not have. [13] For I do not mean that others should be eased and you burdened, but that as a matter of fairness [14] your abundance at the present time should supply their need, so that their abundance may supply your need, that there may be fairness. [15] As it is written, [a]"Whoever gathered much had nothing left over, and whoever gathered little had no lack."

Commendation of Titus

[16] But thanks be to God, who put into the heart of Titus the same earnest care I have for you. [17] For he not only accepted our appeal, but being himself very earnest he is going[2] to you of his own accord. [18] With him we are sending[3] the brother who is famous among all the churches for his preaching of the gospel. [19] And not only that, but he has been appointed by the churches to travel with us as we carry out this act of grace that is being ministered by us, for the glory of the Lord himself and to show our good will. [20] We take this course so that no one should blame us about this generous gift that is being administered by us, [21] for we aim at what is honorable not only in the Lord's sight but also in the sight of man. [22] And with them we are sending our brother whom we have often tested and found earnest in many matters, but who is now more earnest than ever because of his great confidence in you. [23] As for Titus, he is my partner and fellow worker for your benefit. And as for our brothers, they are messengers[4] of the churches, the glory of Christ. [24] So give proof before the churches of your love and of our boasting about you to these men.

The Collection for Christians in Jerusalem

[9] Now it is superfluous for me to write to you about the ministry for the saints, [2] for I know your readiness, of which I boast about you to the people of Macedonia, saying that Achaia has been ready since last year. And your zeal has stirred up most of them. [3] But I am sending[5] the brothers so that our boasting about you may not prove empty in this matter, so that you may be ready, as I said you would be. [4] Otherwise, if some Macedonians come with me and find that you are not ready, we would be humiliated—to say nothing of you—for being so confident. [5] So I thought it necessary to urge the brothers to go on ahead to you and arrange in advance for the gift[6] you have promised, so that it may be ready as a willing gift, not as an exaction.[7]

The Cheerful Giver

[6] The point is this: whoever sows sparingly will also reap sparingly, and whoever sows bountifully[8] will also reap bountifully. [7] Each one must give as he has decided in his heart, not reluctantly or under compulsion, for God loves a cheerful giver. [8] And God is able to make all grace abound to you, so that having all sufficiency[9] in all things at all times, you may abound in every good work. [9] As it is written,

> [b]"He has distributed freely, he has given to the poor;
> his righteousness endures forever."

[10] He who supplies seed to the sower and bread for food will supply and multiply your seed for sowing and increase the harvest of your righteousness. [11] You will be enriched in every way to be generous in every way, which through us will produce thanksgiving to God. [12] For the ministry of this service is not only supplying the needs of the saints but is also overflowing in many thanksgivings to God. [13] By their approval of this service, they[10] will glorify God because of your submission that comes from your confession of the gospel of Christ, and the generosity of your contribution for them and for all others, [14] while they long for you and pray for you, because of the surpassing grace of God upon you. [15] Thanks be to God for his inexpressible gift!

Paul Defends His Ministry

[10] I, Paul, myself entreat you, by the meekness and gentleness of Christ—I who am humble when face to face with you, but

---

[1] Some manuscripts *in your love for us* [2] Or *he went* [3] Or *we sent; also verse 22* [4] Greek *apostles* [5] Or *I have sent* [6] Greek *blessing; twice in this verse* [7] Or *a gift expecting something in return;* Greek *greed* [8] Greek *with blessings; twice in this verse* [9] Or *all contentment* [10] Or *you* [a] Ex. 16:18 [b] Ps. 112:9

bold toward you when I am away!— ²I beg of you that when I am present I may not have to show boldness with such confidence as I count on showing against some who suspect us of walking according to the flesh. ³For though we walk in the flesh, we are not waging war according to the flesh. ⁴For the weapons of our warfare are not of the flesh but have divine power to destroy strongholds. ⁵We destroy arguments and every lofty opinion raised against the knowledge of God, and take every thought captive to obey Christ, ⁶being ready to punish every disobedience, when your obedience is complete.

⁷Look at what is before your eyes. If anyone is confident that he is Christ's, let him remind himself that just as he is Christ's, so also are we. ⁸For even if I boast a little too much of our authority, which the Lord gave for building you up and not for destroying you, I will not be ashamed. ⁹I do not want to appear to be frightening you with my letters. ¹⁰For they say, "His letters are weighty and strong, but his bodily presence is weak, and his speech of no account." ¹¹Let such a person understand that what we say by letter when absent, we do when present. ¹²Not that we dare to classify or compare ourselves with some of those who are commending themselves. But when they measure themselves by one another and compare themselves with one another, they are without understanding.

¹³But we will not boast beyond limits, but will boast only with regard to the area of influence God assigned to us, to reach even to you. ¹⁴For we are not overextending ourselves, as though we did not reach you. For we were the first to come all the way to you with the gospel of Christ. ¹⁵We do not boast beyond limit in the labors of others. But our hope is that as your faith increases, our area of influence among you may be greatly enlarged, ¹⁶so that we may preach the gospel in lands beyond you, without boasting of work already done in another's area of influence. ¹⁷"Let the one who boasts, boast in the Lord." ¹⁸For it is not the one who commends himself who is approved, but the one whom the Lord commends.

Paul and the False Apostles

11 I wish you would bear with me in a little foolishness. Do bear with me! ²For I feel a divine jealousy for you, since I betrothed you to one husband, to present you as a pure virgin to Christ. ³But I am afraid that as the serpent deceived Eve by his cunning, your thoughts will be led astray from a sincere and pure devotion to Christ. ⁴For if someone comes and proclaims another Jesus than the one we proclaimed, or if you receive a different spirit from the one you received, or if you accept a different gospel from the one you accepted, you put up with it readily enough. ⁵Indeed, I consider that I am not in the least inferior to these super-apostles. ⁶Even if I am unskilled in speaking, I am not so in knowledge; indeed, in every way we have made this plain to you in all things.

⁷Or did I commit a sin in humbling myself so that you might be exalted, because I preached God's gospel to you free of charge? ⁸I robbed other churches by accepting support from them in order to serve you. ⁹And when I was with you and was in need, I did not burden anyone, for the brothers who came from Macedonia supplied my need. So I refrained and will refrain from burdening you in any way. ¹⁰As the truth of Christ is in me, this boasting of mine will not be silenced in the regions of Achaia. ¹¹And why? Because I do not love you? God knows I do!

¹²And what I am doing I will continue to do, in order to undermine the claim of those who would like to claim that in their boasted mission they work on the same terms as we do. ¹³For such men are false apostles, deceitful workmen, disguising themselves as apostles of Christ. ¹⁴And no wonder, for even Satan disguises himself as an angel of light. ¹⁵So it is no surprise if his servants, also, disguise themselves as servants of righteousness. Their end will correspond to their deeds.

Paul's Sufferings as an Apostle

¹⁶I repeat, let no one think me foolish. But even if you do, accept me as a fool, so that I too may boast a little. ¹⁷What I am saying with this boastful confidence, I say not as the Lord would¹ but as a fool. ¹⁸Since many boast according to the flesh, I too will boast. ¹⁹For you gladly bear with fools, being wise yourselves! ²⁰For you bear it if someone makes slaves of you, or devours you, or takes advantage of you, or puts on airs, or strikes you in the face. ²¹To my shame, I must say, we were too weak for that!

But whatever anyone else dares to boast of—I am speaking as a fool—I also dare to boast of that. ²²Are they Hebrews? So am I. Are they Israelites? So am I. Are they offspring

¹ Greek not according to the Lord

of Abraham? So am I. **23** Are they servants of Christ? I am a better one—I am talking like a madman—with far greater labors, far more imprisonments, with countless beatings, and often near death. **24** Five times I received at the hands of the Jews the forty lashes less one. **25** Three times I was beaten with rods. Once I was stoned. Three times I was shipwrecked; a night and a day I was adrift at sea; **26** on frequent journeys, in danger from rivers, danger from robbers, danger from my own people, danger from Gentiles, danger in the city, danger in the wilderness, danger at sea, danger from false brothers; **27** in toil and hardship, through many a sleepless night, in hunger and thirst, often without food,[1] in cold and exposure. **28** And, apart from other things, there is the daily pressure on me of my anxiety for all the churches. **29** Who is weak, and I am not weak? Who is made to fall, and I am not indignant?

30 If I must boast, I will boast of the things that show my weakness. **31** The God and Father of the Lord Jesus, he who is blessed forever, knows that I am not lying. **32** At Damascus, the governor under King Aretas was guarding the city of Damascus in order to seize me, **33** but I was let down in a basket through a window in the wall and escaped his hands.

Paul's Visions and His Thorn

12 I must go on boasting. Though there is nothing to be gained by it, I will go on to visions and revelations of the Lord. **2** I know a man in Christ who fourteen years ago was caught up to the third heaven—whether in the body or out of the body I do not know, God knows. **3** And I know that this man was caught up into paradise—whether in the body or out of the body I do not know, God knows—**4** and he heard things that cannot be told, which man may not utter. **5** On behalf of this man I will boast, but on my own behalf I will not boast, except of my weaknesses— **6** though if I should wish to boast, I would not be a fool, for I would be speaking the truth; but I refrain from it, so that no one may think more of me than he sees in me or hears from me. **7** So to keep me from becoming conceited because of the surpassing greatness of the revelations,[2] a thorn was given me in the flesh, a messenger of Satan to harass me, to keep me from becoming conceited. **8** Three times I pleaded with the Lord

about this, that it should leave me. **9** But he said to me, "My grace is sufficient for you, for my power is made perfect in weakness." Therefore I will boast all the more gladly of my weaknesses, so that the power of Christ may rest upon me. **10** For the sake of Christ, then, I am content with weaknesses, insults, hardships, persecutions, and calamities. For when I am weak, then I am strong.

Concern for the Corinthian Church

11 I have been a fool! You forced me to it, for I ought to have been commended by you. For I was not at all inferior to these super-apostles, even though I am nothing. **12** The signs of a true apostle were performed among you with utmost patience, with signs and wonders and mighty works. **13** For in what were you less favored than the rest of the churches, except that I myself did not burden you? Forgive me this wrong!

14 Here for the third time I am ready to come to you. And I will not be a burden, for I seek not what is yours but you. For children are not obligated to save up for their parents, but parents for their children. **15** I will most gladly spend and be spent for your souls. If I love you more, am I to be loved less? **16** But granting that I myself did not burden you, I was crafty, you say, and got the better of you by deceit. **17** Did I take advantage of you through any of those whom I sent to you? **18** I urged Titus to go, and sent the brother with him. Did Titus take advantage of you? Did we not act in the same spirit? Did we not take the same steps?

19 Have you been thinking all along that we have been defending ourselves to you? It is in the sight of God that we have been speaking in Christ, and all for your upbuilding, beloved. **20** For I fear that perhaps when I come I may find you not as I wish, and that you may find me not as you wish—that perhaps there may be quarreling, jealousy, anger, hostility, slander, gossip, conceit, and disorder. **21** I fear that when I come again my God may humble me before you, and I may have to mourn over many of those who sinned earlier and have not repented of the impurity, sexual immorality, and sensuality that they have practiced.

Final Warnings

13 This is the third time I am coming to you. Every charge must be established by the evidence of two or three witnesses.

---

[1] Or often in fasting [2] Or hears from me, even because of the surpassing greatness of the revelations. So to keep me from becoming conceited

[2] I warned those who sinned before and all the others, and I warn them now while absent, as I did when present on my second visit, that if I come again I will not spare them—[3] since you seek proof that Christ is speaking in me. He is not weak in dealing with you, but is powerful among you. [4] For he was crucified in weakness, but lives by the power of God. For we also are weak in him, but in dealing with you we will live with him by the power of God.

[5] Examine yourselves, to see whether you are in the faith. Test yourselves. Or do you not realize this about yourselves, that Jesus Christ is in you?—unless indeed you fail to meet the test! [6] I hope you will find out that we have not failed the test. [7] But we pray to God that you may not do wrong—not that we may appear to have met the test, but that you may do what is right, though we may seem to have failed. [8] For we cannot do anything against the truth, but only for the truth. [9] For we are glad when we are weak and you are strong. Your restoration is what we pray for. [10] For this reason I write these things while I am away from you, that when I come I may not have to be severe in my use of the authority that the Lord has given me for building up and not for tearing down.

Final Greetings

[11] Finally, brothers,[1] rejoice. Aim for restoration, comfort one another,[2] agree with one another, live in peace; and the God of love and peace will be with you. [12] Greet one another with a holy kiss. [13] All the saints greet you.

[14] The grace of the Lord Jesus Christ and the love of God and the fellowship of the Holy Spirit be with you all.

---

[1] Or brothers and sisters [2] Or listen to my appeal

GALATIANS

Greeting

1 Paul, an apostle—not from men nor through man, but through Jesus Christ and God the Father, who raised him from the dead— [2] and all the brothers[1] who are with me,

To the churches of Galatia:

[3] Grace to you and peace from God our Father and the Lord Jesus Christ, [4] who gave himself for our sins to deliver us from the present evil age, according to the will of our God and Father, [5] to whom be the glory forever and ever. Amen.

No Other Gospel

[6] I am astonished that you are so quickly deserting him who called you in the grace of Christ and are turning to a different gospel— [7] not that there is another one, but there are some who trouble you and want to distort the gospel of Christ. [8] But even if we or an angel from heaven should preach to you a gospel contrary to the one we preached to you, let him be accursed. [9] As we have said before, so now I say again: If anyone is preaching to you a gospel contrary to the one you received, let him be accursed.

[10] For am I now seeking the approval of man, or of God? Or am I trying to please man? If I were still trying to please man, I would not be a servant[2] of Christ.

Paul Called by God

[11] For I would have you know, brothers, that the gospel that was preached by me is not man's gospel.[3] [12] For I did not receive it from any man, nor was I taught it, but I received it through a revelation of Jesus Christ. [13] For you have heard of my former life in Judaism, how I persecuted the church of God violently and tried to destroy it. [14] And I was advancing in Judaism beyond many of my own age among my people, so extremely zealous was I for the traditions of my fathers. [15] But when he who had set me apart before I was born,[4] and who called me by his grace, [16] was pleased to reveal his Son to[5] me, in order that I might preach him among the Gentiles, I did not immediately consult with anyone;[6] [17] nor did I go up to Jerusalem to those who were apostles before me, but I went away into Arabia, and returned again to Damascus.

[18] Then after three years I went up to Jerusalem to visit Cephas and remained with him fifteen days. [19] But I saw none of the other apostles except James the Lord's brother. [20] (In what I am writing to you, before God, I do not lie!) [21] Then I went into the regions of Syria and Cilicia. [22] And I was still unknown in person to the churches of Judea that are in Christ. [23] They only were hearing it said, "He who used to persecute us is now preaching the faith he once tried to destroy." [24] And they glorified God because of me.

Paul Accepted by the Apostles

2 Then after fourteen years I went up again to Jerusalem with Barnabas, taking Titus along with me. [2] I went up because of a revelation and set before them (though privately before those who seemed influential) the gospel that I proclaim among the Gentiles, in order to make sure I was not running or had not run in vain. [3] But even Titus, who was with me, was not forced to be circumcised, though he was a Greek. [4] Yet because of false brothers secretly brought in—who slipped in to spy out our freedom that we have in Christ Jesus, so that they might bring us into slavery— [5] to them we did not yield in submission even for a moment, so that the truth of the gospel might be preserved for you. [6] And from those who seemed to be influential (what they were makes no difference to me; God shows no partiality)—those, I say, who seemed influential added nothing to me. [7] On the contrary, when they saw that I had been entrusted with the gospel to the uncircumcised, just as Peter had been entrusted with the gospel to the circumcised [8] (for he who worked through Peter for his apostolic ministry to the circumcised worked also through me for mine to the Gentiles), [9] and when James and Cephas and John, who seemed to be pillars, perceived the grace that was given to me, they gave the right hand of fellowship to Barnabas and me, that we should go to the Gentiles and they to the circumcised. [10] Only, they asked us to remember the poor, the very thing I was eager to do.

[1] Or brothers and sisters. In New Testament usage, depending on the context, the plural Greek word adelphoi (translated "brothers") may refer either to brothers or to brothers and sisters; also verse 11 [2] For the contextual rendering of the Greek word doulos, see Preface [3] Greek not according to man [4] Greek set me apart from my mother's womb [5] Greek in [6] Greek with flesh and blood

Paul Opposes Peter

[11] But when Cephas came to Antioch, I opposed him to his face, because he stood condemned. [12] For before certain men came from James, he was eating with the Gentiles; but when they came he drew back and separated himself, fearing the circumcision party.[1] [13] And the rest of the Jews acted hypocritically along with him, so that even Barnabas was led astray by their hypocrisy. [14] But when I saw that their conduct was not in step with the truth of the gospel, I said to Cephas before them all, "If you, though a Jew, live like a Gentile and not like a Jew, how can you force the Gentiles to live like Jews?"

Justified by Faith

[15] We ourselves are Jews by birth and not Gentile sinners; [16] yet we know that a person is not justified[2] by works of the law but through faith in Jesus Christ, so we also have believed in Christ Jesus, in order to be justified by faith in Christ and not by works of the law, because by works of the law no one will be justified.

[17] But if, in our endeavor to be justified in Christ, we too were found to be sinners, is Christ then a servant of sin? Certainly not! [18] For if I rebuild what I tore down, I prove myself to be a transgressor. [19] For through the law I died to the law, so that I might live to God. [20] I have been crucified with Christ. It is no longer I who live, but Christ who lives in me. And the life I now live in the flesh I live by faith in the Son of God, who loved me and gave himself for me. [21] I do not nullify the grace of God, for if righteousness[3] were through the law, then Christ died for no purpose.

By Faith, or by Works of the Law?

3 O foolish Galatians! Who has bewitched you? It was before your eyes that Jesus Christ was publicly portrayed as crucified. [2] Let me ask you only this: Did you receive the Spirit by works of the law or by hearing with faith? [3] Are you so foolish? Having begun by the Spirit, are you now being perfected by[4] the flesh? [4] Did you suffer[5] so many things in vain—if indeed it was in vain? [5] Does he who supplies the Spirit to you and works miracles among you do so by works of the law, or by hearing with faith— [6] just as [a] Abraham "believed God, and it was counted to him as righteousness"?

[7] Know then that it is those of faith who are the sons of Abraham. [8] And the Scripture, foreseeing that God would justify[6] the Gentiles by faith, preached the gospel beforehand to Abraham, saying, [b] "In you shall all the nations be blessed." [9] So then, those who are of faith are blessed along with Abraham, the man of faith.

The Righteous Shall Live by Faith

[10] For all who rely on works of the law are under a curse; for it is written, [c] "Cursed be everyone who does not abide by all things written in the Book of the Law, and do them." [11] Now it is evident that no one is justified before God by the law, for [d] "The righteous shall live by faith."[7] [12] But the law is not of faith, rather [e] "The one who does them shall live by them." [13] Christ redeemed us from the curse of the law by becoming a curse for us—for it is written, [f] "Cursed is everyone who is hanged on a tree"— [14] so that in Christ Jesus the blessing of Abraham might come to the Gentiles, so that we might receive the promised Spirit[8] through faith.

The Law and the Promise

[15] To give a human example, brothers:[9] even with a man-made covenant, no one annuls it or adds to it once it has been ratified. [16] Now the promises were made to Abraham and to his offspring. It does not say, "And to offsprings," referring to many, but referring to one, "And to your offspring," who is Christ. [17] This is what I mean: the law, which came 430 years afterward, does not annul a covenant previously ratified by God, so as to make the promise void. [18] For if the inheritance comes by the law, it no longer comes by promise; but God gave it to Abraham by a promise.

[19] Why then the law? It was added because of transgressions, until the offspring should come to whom the promise had been made, and it was put in place through angels by an intermediary. [20] Now an intermediary implies more than one, but God is one.

[21] Is the law then contrary to the promises of God? Certainly not! For if a law had been given that could give life, then righteousness would indeed be by the law. [22] But the Scripture imprisoned everything under sin, so that the promise by faith in Jesus Christ might be given to those who believe.

---

[1] Or fearing those of the circumcision [2] Or counted righteous (three times in verse 16); also verse 17 [3] Or justification [4] Or now ending with [5] Or experience [6] Or count righteous; also verses 11, 24 [7] Or The one who by faith is righteous will live [8] Greek receive the promise of the Spirit [9] Or brothers and sisters [a] Gen. 15:6 [b] Gen. 12:3 [c] Deut. 27:26 [d] Hab. 2:4 [e] Lev. 18:5 [f] Deut. 21:23

[23] Now before faith came, we were held captive under the law, imprisoned until the coming faith would be revealed. [24] So then, the law was our guardian until Christ came, in order that we might be justified by faith. [25] But now that faith has come, we are no longer under a guardian, [26] for in Christ Jesus you are all sons of God, through faith. [27] For as many of you as were baptized into Christ have put on Christ. [28] There is neither Jew nor Greek, there is neither slave[1] nor free, there is no male and female, for you are all one in Christ Jesus. [29] And if you are Christ's, then you are Abraham's offspring, heirs according to promise.

Sons and Heirs

4 I mean that the heir, as long as he is a child, is no different from a slave,[2] though he is the owner of everything, [2] but he is under guardians and managers until the date set by his father. [3] In the same way we also, when we were children, were enslaved to the elementary principles[3] of the world. [4] But when the fullness of time had come, God sent forth his Son, born of woman, born under the law, [5] to redeem those who were under the law, so that we might receive adoption as sons. [6] And because you are sons, God has sent the Spirit of his Son into our hearts, crying, "Abba! Father!" [7] So you are no longer a slave, but a son, and if a son, then an heir through God.

Paul's Concern for the Galatians

[8] Formerly, when you did not know God, you were enslaved to those that by nature are not gods. [9] But now that you have come to know God, or rather to be known by God, how can you turn back again to the weak and worthless elementary principles of the world, whose slaves you want to be once more? [10] You observe days and months and seasons and years! [11] I am afraid I may have labored over you in vain.

[12] Brothers,[4] I entreat you, become as I am, for I also have become as you are. You did me no wrong. [13] You know it was because of a bodily ailment that I preached the gospel to you at first, [14] and though my condition was a trial to you, you did not scorn or despise me, but received me as an angel of God, as Christ Jesus. [15] What then has become of your blessedness? For I testify to you that, if possible, you would have gouged out your eyes and given them to me. [16] Have I then

become your enemy by telling you the truth? [17] They make much of you, but for no good purpose. They want to shut you out, that you may make much of them. [18] It is always good to be made much of for a good purpose, and not only when I am present with you, [19] my little children, for whom I am again in the anguish of childbirth until Christ is formed in you! [20] I wish I could be present with you now and change my tone, for I am perplexed about you.

Example of Hagar and Sarah

[21] Tell me, you who desire to be under the law, do you not listen to the law? [22] For it is written that Abraham had two sons, one by a slave woman and one by a free woman. [23] But the son of the slave was born according to the flesh, while the son of the free woman was born through promise. [24] Now this may be interpreted allegorically: these women are two covenants. One is from Mount Sinai, bearing children for slavery; she is Hagar. [25] Now Hagar is Mount Sinai in Arabia;[6] she corresponds to the present Jerusalem, for she is in slavery with her children. [26] But the Jerusalem above is free, and she is our mother. [27] For it is written,

> [a]"Rejoice, O barren one who does not bear;
>   break forth and cry aloud, you who are
>   not in labor!
> For the children of the desolate one will be
>   more
>   than those of the one who has a husband."

[28] Now you,[7] brothers, like Isaac, are children of promise. [29] But just as at that time he who was born according to the flesh persecuted him who was born according to the Spirit, so also it is now. [30] But what does the Scripture say? [b]"Cast out the slave woman and her son, for the son of the slave woman shall not inherit with the son of the free woman." [31] So, brothers, we are not children of the slave but of the free woman.

Christ Has Set Us Free

5 For freedom Christ has set us free; stand firm therefore, and do not submit again to a yoke of slavery.

[2] Look: I, Paul, say to you that if you accept circumcision, Christ will be of no advantage to you. [3] I testify again to every man who accepts circumcision that he is obligated to keep the

---

[1] For the contextual rendering of the Greek word *doulos*, see Preface [2] For the contextual rendering of the Greek word *doulos*, see Preface; also verse 7 [3] Or *elemental spirits*; also verse 9 [4] Or *Brothers and sisters*; also verses 28, 31 [5] Or *by dealing truthfully with you* [6] Some manuscripts *For Sinai is a mountain in Arabia* [7] Some manuscripts *we* [a] Isa. 54:1 [b] Gen. 21:10

whole law. [4] You are severed from Christ, you who would be justified[1] by the law; you have fallen away from grace. [5] For through the Spirit, by faith, we ourselves eagerly wait for the hope of righteousness. [6] For in Christ Jesus neither circumcision nor uncircumcision counts for anything, but only faith working through love.

[7] You were running well. Who hindered you from obeying the truth? [8] This persuasion is not from him who calls you. [9] A little leaven leavens the whole lump. [10] I have confidence in the Lord that you will take no other view, and the one who is troubling you will bear the penalty, whoever he is. [11] But if I, brothers,[2] still preach[3] circumcision, why am I still being persecuted? In that case the offense of the cross has been removed. [12] I wish those who unsettle you would emasculate themselves!

[13] For you were called to freedom, brothers. Only do not use your freedom as an opportunity for the flesh, but through love serve one another. [14] For the whole law is fulfilled in one word: [a]"You shall love your neighbor as yourself." [15] But if you bite and devour one another, watch out that you are not consumed by one another.

Keep in Step with the Spirit

[16] But I say, walk by the Spirit, and you will not gratify the desires of the flesh. [17] For the desires of the flesh are against the Spirit, and the desires of the Spirit are against the flesh, for these are opposed to each other, to keep you from doing the things you want to do. [18] But if you are led by the Spirit, you are not under the law. [19] Now the works of the flesh are evident: sexual immorality, impurity, sensuality, [20] idolatry, sorcery, enmity, strife, jealousy, fits of anger, rivalries, dissensions, divisions, [21] envy,[4] drunkenness, orgies, and things like these. I warn you, as I warned you before, that those who do[5] such things will not inherit the kingdom of God. [22] But the fruit of the Spirit is love, joy, peace, patience, kindness, goodness, faithfulness, [23] gentleness, self-control; against such things there is no law. [24] And those who belong to Christ Jesus have crucified the flesh with its passions and desires.

[25] If we live by the Spirit, let us also keep in step with the Spirit. [26] Let us not become conceited, provoking one another, envying one another.

Bear One Another's Burdens

6 Brothers,[6] if anyone is caught in any transgression, you who are spiritual should restore him in a spirit of gentleness. Keep watch on yourself, lest you too be tempted. [2] Bear one another's burdens, and so fulfill the law of Christ. [3] For if anyone thinks he is something, when he is nothing, he deceives himself. [4] But let each one test his own work, and then his reason to boast will be in himself alone and not in his neighbor. [5] For each will have to bear his own load.

[6] Let the one who is taught the word share all good things with the one who teaches. [7] Do not be deceived: God is not mocked, for whatever one sows, that will he also reap. [8] For the one who sows to his own flesh will from the flesh reap corruption, but the one who sows to the Spirit will from the Spirit reap eternal life. [9] And let us not grow weary of doing good, for in due season we will reap, if we do not give up. [10] So then, as we have opportunity, let us do good to everyone, and especially to those who are of the household of faith.

Final Warning and Benediction

[11] See with what large letters I am writing to you with my own hand. [12] It is those who want to make a good showing in the flesh who would force you to be circumcised, and only in order that they may not be persecuted for the cross of Christ. [13] For even those who are circumcised do not themselves keep the law, but they desire to have you circumcised that they may boast in your flesh. [14] But far be it from me to boast except in the cross of our Lord Jesus Christ, by which[7] the world has been crucified to me, and I to the world. [15] For neither circumcision counts for anything, nor uncircumcision, but a new creation. [16] And as for all who walk by this rule, peace and mercy be upon them, and upon the Israel of God.

[17] From now on let no one cause me trouble, for I bear on my body the marks of Jesus.

[18] The grace of our Lord Jesus Christ be with your spirit, brothers. Amen.

---

[1] Or counted righteous [2] Or brothers and sisters; also verse 13 [3] Greek proclaim [4] Some manuscripts add murder [5] Or make a practice of doing [6] Or Brothers and sisters; also verse 18 [7] Or through whom [a] Lev. 19:18

THE LETTER OF PAUL TO THE
EPHESIANS

Greeting

1 Paul, an apostle of Christ Jesus by the will of God,

To the saints who are in Ephesus, and are faithful[1] in Christ Jesus:

[2] Grace to you and peace from God our Father and the Lord Jesus Christ.

Spiritual Blessings in Christ

[3] Blessed be the God and Father of our Lord Jesus Christ, who has blessed us in Christ with every spiritual blessing in the heavenly places, [4] even as he chose us in him before the foundation of the world, that we should be holy and blameless before him. In love [5] he predestined us[2] for adoption to himself as sons through Jesus Christ, according to the purpose of his will, [6] to the praise of his glorious grace, with which he has blessed us in the Beloved. [7] In him we have redemption through his blood, the forgiveness of our trespasses, according to the riches of his grace, [8] which he lavished upon us, in all wisdom and insight [9] making known[3] to us the mystery of his will, according to his purpose, which he set forth in Christ [10] as a plan for the fullness of time, to unite all things in him, things in heaven and things on earth.

[11] In him we have obtained an inheritance, having been predestined according to the purpose of him who works all things according to the counsel of his will, [12] so that we who were the first to hope in Christ might be to the praise of his glory. [13] In him you also, when you heard the word of truth, the gospel of your salvation, and believed in him, were sealed with the promised Holy Spirit, [14] who is the guarantee[4] of our inheritance until we acquire possession of it,[5] to the praise of his glory.

Thanksgiving and Prayer

[15] For this reason, because I have heard of your faith in the Lord Jesus and your love[6] toward all the saints, [16] I do not cease to give thanks for you, remembering you in my prayers, [17] that the God of our Lord Jesus Christ, the Father of glory, may give you the Spirit of wisdom and of revelation in the knowledge of him, [18] having the eyes of your hearts enlightened, that you may know what is the hope to which he has called you, what are the riches of his glorious inheritance in the saints, [19] and what is the immeasurable greatness of his power toward us who believe, according to the working of his great might [20] that he worked in Christ when he raised him from the dead and seated him at his right hand in the heavenly places, [21] far above all rule and authority and power and dominion, and above every name that is named, not only in this age but also in the one to come. [22] And he put all things under his feet and gave him as head over all things to the church, [23] which is his body, the fullness of him who fills all in all.

By Grace Through Faith

2 And you were dead in the trespasses and sins [2] in which you once walked, following the course of this world, following the prince of the power of the air, the spirit that is now at work in the sons of disobedience— [3] among whom we all once lived in the passions of our flesh, carrying out the desires of the body[7] and the mind, and were by nature children of wrath, like the rest of mankind.[8] [4] But[9] God, being rich in mercy, because of the great love with which he loved us, [5] even when we were dead in our trespasses, made us alive together with Christ—by grace you have been saved— [6] and raised us up with him and seated us with him in the heavenly places in Christ Jesus, [7] so that in the coming ages he might show the immeasurable riches of his grace in kindness toward us in Christ Jesus. [8] For by grace you have been saved through faith. And this is not your own doing; it is the gift of God, [9] not a result of works, so that no one may boast. [10] For we are his workmanship, created in Christ Jesus for good works, which God prepared beforehand, that we should walk in them.

One in Christ

[11] Therefore remember that at one time you Gentiles in the flesh, called "the uncircumcision" by what is called the circumcision, which is made in the flesh by hands— [12] remember that you were at that time separated from Christ, alienated from the commonwealth of Israel and strangers to the covenants of promise, having no hope and without God in the

---

[1] Some manuscripts *saints who are also faithful* (omitting *in Ephesus*) [2] Or *before him in love,* [3] *having predestined us* [3] Or *he lavished upon us in all wisdom and insight, making known . . .* [4] Or *down payment* [5] Or *until God redeems his possession* [6] Some manuscripts omit *your love* [7] Greek *flesh* [8] Greek *like the rest* [9] Or *And*

world. [13]But now in Christ Jesus you who once were far off have been brought near by the blood of Christ. [14]For he himself is our peace, who has made us both one and has broken down in his flesh the dividing wall of hostility [15]by abolishing the law of commandments expressed in ordinances, that he might create in himself one new man in place of the two, so making peace, [16]and might reconcile us both to God in one body through the cross, thereby killing the hostility. [17]And he came and preached peace to you who were far off and peace to those who were near. [18]For through him we both have access in one Spirit to the Father. [19]So then you are no longer strangers and aliens,[1] but you are fellow citizens with the saints and members of the household of God, [20]built on the foundation of the apostles and prophets, Christ Jesus himself being the cornerstone, [21]in whom the whole structure, being joined together, grows into a holy temple in the Lord. [22]In him you also are being built together into a dwelling place for God by[2] the Spirit.

The Mystery of the Gospel Revealed

3 For this reason I, Paul, a prisoner of Christ Jesus on behalf of you Gentiles— [2]assuming that you have heard of the stewardship of God's grace that was given to me for you, [3]how the mystery was made known to me by revelation, as I have written briefly. [4]When you read this, you can perceive my insight into the mystery of Christ, [5]which was not made known to the sons of men in other generations as it has now been revealed to his holy apostles and prophets by the Spirit. [6]This mystery is[3] that the Gentiles are fellow heirs, members of the same body, and partakers of the promise in Christ Jesus through the gospel.

[7]Of this gospel I was made a minister according to the gift of God's grace, which was given me by the working of his power. [8]To me, though I am the very least of all the saints, this grace was given, to preach to the Gentiles the unsearchable riches of Christ, [9]and to bring to light for everyone what is the plan of the mystery hidden for ages in[4] God, who created all things, [10]so that through the church the manifold wisdom of God might now be made known to the rulers and authorities in the heavenly places. [11]This was according to the eternal purpose that he has realized in Christ Jesus our Lord, [12]in whom

we have boldness and access with confidence through our faith in him. [13]So I ask you not to lose heart over what I am suffering for you, which is your glory.

Prayer for Spiritual Strength

[14]For this reason I bow my knees before the Father, [15]from whom every family[5] in heaven and on earth is named, [16]that according to the riches of his glory he may grant you to be strengthened with power through his Spirit in your inner being, [17]so that Christ may dwell in your hearts through faith—that you, being rooted and grounded in love, [18]may have strength to comprehend with all the saints what is the breadth and length and height and depth, [19]and to know the love of Christ that surpasses knowledge, that you may be filled with all the fullness of God.

[20]Now to him who is able to do far more abundantly than all that we ask or think, according to the power at work within us, [21]to him be glory in the church and in Christ Jesus throughout all generations, forever and ever. Amen.

Unity in the Body of Christ

4 I therefore, a prisoner for the Lord, urge you to walk in a manner worthy of the calling to which you have been called, [2]with all humility and gentleness, with patience, bearing with one another in love, [3]eager to maintain the unity of the Spirit in the bond of peace. [4]There is one body and one Spirit—just as you were called to the one hope that belongs to your call— [5]one Lord, one faith, one baptism, [6]one God and Father of all, who is over all and through all and in all. [7]But grace was given to each one of us according to the measure of Christ's gift. [8]Therefore it says,

[a]"When he ascended on high he led a host of captives,
and he gave gifts to men."[6]

[9](In saying, "He ascended," what does it mean but that he had also descended into the lower regions, the earth?[7] [10]He who descended is the one who also ascended far above all the heavens, that he might fill all things.) [11]And he gave the apostles, the prophets, the evangelists, the shepherds[8] and teachers,[9] [12]to equip the saints for the work of ministry, for building

[1] Or sojourners [2] Or in [3] The words This mystery is are inferred from verse 4 [4] Or by [5] Or from whom all fatherhood; the Greek word patria in verse 15 is closely related to the word for Father in verse 14 [6] The Greek word anthropoi can refer to both men and women [7] Or the lower parts of the earth? [8] Or pastors [9] Or the shepherd-teachers [a] Ps. 68:18

up the body of Christ, [13] until we all attain to the unity of the faith and of the knowledge of the Son of God, to mature manhood,[1] to the measure of the stature of the fullness of Christ, [14] so that we may no longer be children, tossed to and fro by the waves and carried about by every wind of doctrine, by human cunning, by craftiness in deceitful schemes. [15] Rather, speaking the truth in love, we are to grow up in every way into him who is the head, into Christ, [16] from whom the whole body, joined and held together by every joint with which it is equipped, when each part is working properly, makes the body grow so that it builds itself up in love.

The New Life

[17] Now this I say and testify in the Lord, that you must no longer walk as the Gentiles do, in the futility of their minds. [18] They are darkened in their understanding, alienated from the life of God because of the ignorance that is in them, due to their hardness of heart. [19] They have become callous and have given themselves up to sensuality, greedy to practice every kind of impurity. [20] But that is not the way you learned Christ!— [21] assuming that you have heard about him and were taught in him, as the truth is in Jesus, [22] to put off your old self,[2] which belongs to your former manner of life and is corrupt through deceitful desires, [23] and to be renewed in the spirit of your minds, [24] and to put on the new self, created after the likeness of God in true righteousness and holiness.

[25] Therefore, having put away falsehood, let each one of you speak the truth with his neighbor, for we are members one of another. [26] Be angry and do not sin; do not let the sun go down on your anger, [27] and give no opportunity to the devil. [28] Let the thief no longer steal, but rather let him labor, doing honest work with his own hands, so that he may have something to share with anyone in need. [29] Let no corrupting talk come out of your mouths, but only such as is good for building up, as fits the occasion, that it may give grace to those who hear. [30] And do not grieve the Holy Spirit of God, by whom you were sealed for the day of redemption. [31] Let all bitterness and wrath and anger and clamor and slander be put away from you, along with all malice. [32] Be kind to one another, tenderhearted, forgiving one another, as God in Christ forgave you.

Walk in Love

5 Therefore be imitators of God, as beloved children. [2] And walk in love, as Christ loved us and gave himself up for us, a fragrant offering and sacrifice to God.

[3] But sexual immorality and all impurity or covetousness must not even be named among you, as is proper among saints. [4] Let there be no filthiness nor foolish talk nor crude joking, which are out of place, but instead let there be thanksgiving. [5] For you may be sure of this, that everyone who is sexually immoral or impure, or who is covetous (that is, an idolater), has no inheritance in the kingdom of Christ and God. [6] Let no one deceive you with empty words, for because of these things the wrath of God comes upon the sons of disobedience. [7] Therefore do not become partners with them; [8] for at one time you were darkness, but now you are light in the Lord. Walk as children of light [9] (for the fruit of light is found in all that is good and right and true), [10] and try to discern what is pleasing to the Lord. [11] Take no part in the unfruitful works of darkness, but instead expose them. [12] For it is shameful even to speak of the things that they do in secret. [13] But when anything is exposed by the light, it becomes visible, [14] for anything that becomes visible is light. Therefore it says,

> "Awake, O sleeper,
>   and arise from the dead,
>   and Christ will shine on you."

[15] Look carefully then how you walk, not as unwise but as wise, [16] making the best use of the time, because the days are evil. [17] Therefore do not be foolish, but understand what the will of the Lord is. [18] And do not get drunk with wine, for that is debauchery, but be filled with the Spirit, [19] addressing one another in psalms and hymns and spiritual songs, singing and making melody to the Lord with your heart, [20] giving thanks always and for everything to God the Father in the name of our Lord Jesus Christ, [21] submitting to one another out of reverence for Christ.

Wives and Husbands

[22] Wives, submit to your own husbands, as to the Lord. [23] For the husband is the head of the wife even as Christ is the head of the church, his body, and is himself its Savior. [24] Now as the church submits to Christ, so also wives should submit in everything to their husbands.

[1] Greek to a full-grown man [2] Greek man; also verse 24

[25] Husbands, love your wives, as Christ loved the church and gave himself up for her, [26] that he might sanctify her, having cleansed her by the washing of water with the word, [27] so that he might present the church to himself in splendor, without spot or wrinkle or any such thing, that she might be holy and without blemish.[1] [28] In the same way husbands should love their wives as their own bodies. He who loves his wife loves himself. [29] For no one ever hated his own flesh, but nourishes and cherishes it, just as Christ does the church, [30] because we are members of his body. [31] [a] "Therefore a man shall leave his father and mother and hold fast to his wife, and the two shall become one flesh." [32] This mystery is profound, and I am saying that it refers to Christ and the church. [33] However, let each one of you love his wife as himself, and let the wife see that she respects her husband.

Children and Parents

6 Children, obey your parents in the Lord, for this is right. [2] [b] "Honor your father and mother" (this is the first commandment with a promise), [3] "that it may go well with you and that you may live long in the land." [4] Fathers, do not provoke your children to anger, but bring them up in the discipline and instruction of the Lord.

Bondservants and Masters

[5] Bondservants,[2] obey your earthly masters[3] with fear and trembling, with a sincere heart, as you would Christ, [6] not by the way of eye-service, as people-pleasers, but as bondservants of Christ, doing the will of God from the heart, [7] rendering service with a good will as to the Lord and not to man, [8] knowing that whatever good anyone does, this he will receive back from the Lord, whether he is a bondservant or is free. [9] Masters, do the same to them, and stop your threatening, knowing that he who is both their Master[4] and yours is in heaven, and that there is no partiality with him.

The Whole Armor of God

[10] Finally, be strong in the Lord and in the strength of his might. [11] Put on the whole armor of God, that you may be able to stand against the schemes of the devil. [12] For we do not wrestle against flesh and blood, but against the rulers, against the authorities, against the cosmic powers over this present darkness, against the spiritual forces of evil in the heavenly places. [13] Therefore take up the whole armor of God, that you may be able to withstand in the evil day, and having done all, to stand firm. [14] Stand therefore, having fastened on the belt of truth, and having put on the breastplate of righteousness, [15] and, as shoes for your feet, having put on the readiness given by the gospel of peace. [16] In all circumstances take up the shield of faith, with which you can extinguish all the flaming darts of the evil one; [17] and take the helmet of salvation, and the sword of the Spirit, which is the word of God, [18] praying at all times in the Spirit, with all prayer and supplication. To that end, keep alert with all perseverance, making supplication for all the saints, [19] and also for me, that words may be given to me in opening my mouth boldly to proclaim the mystery of the gospel, [20] for which I am an ambassador in chains, that I may declare it boldly, as I ought to speak.

Final Greetings

[21] So that you also may know how I am and what I am doing, Tychicus the beloved brother and faithful minister in the Lord will tell you everything. [22] I have sent him to you for this very purpose, that you may know how we are, and that he may encourage your hearts.

[23] Peace be to the brothers,[5] and love with faith, from God the Father and the Lord Jesus Christ. [24] Grace be with all who love our Lord Jesus Christ with love incorruptible.

---

[1] Or holy and blameless [2] For the contextual rendering of the Greek word doulos, see Preface; also verse 6; likewise for bondservant in verse 8 [3] Or your masters according to the flesh [4] Greek Lord [5] Or brothers and sisters [a] Gen. 2:24 [b] Ex. 20:12

PHILIPPIANS

Greeting

1 Paul and Timothy, servants[1] of Christ Jesus,

To all the saints in Christ Jesus who are at Philippi, with the overseers[2] and deacons:[3]

[2] Grace to you and peace from God our Father and the Lord Jesus Christ.

Thanksgiving and Prayer

[3] I thank my God in all my remembrance of you, [4] always in every prayer of mine for you all making my prayer with joy, [5] because of your partnership in the gospel from the first day until now. [6] And I am sure of this, that he who began a good work in you will bring it to completion at the day of Jesus Christ. [7] It is right for me to feel this way about you all, because I hold you in my heart, for you are all partakers with me of grace,[4] both in my imprisonment and in the defense and confirmation of the gospel. [8] For God is my witness, how I yearn for you all with the affection of Christ Jesus. [9] And it is my prayer that your love may abound more and more, with knowledge and all discernment, [10] so that you may approve what is excellent, and so be pure and blameless for the day of Christ, [11] filled with the fruit of righteousness that comes through Jesus Christ, to the glory and praise of God.

The Advance of the Gospel

[12] I want you to know, brothers,[5] that what has happened to me has really served to advance the gospel, [13] so that it has become known throughout the whole imperial guard[6] and to all the rest that my imprisonment is for Christ. [14] And most of the brothers, having become confident in the Lord by my imprisonment, are much more bold to speak the word[7] without fear.

[15] Some indeed preach Christ from envy and rivalry, but others from good will. [16] The latter do it out of love, knowing that I am put here for the defense of the gospel. [17] The former proclaim Christ out of selfish ambition, not sincerely but thinking to afflict me in my imprisonment. [18] What then? Only that in every way, whether in pretense or in truth, Christ is proclaimed, and in that I rejoice.

To Live Is Christ

Yes, and I will rejoice, [19] for I know that through your prayers and the help of the Spirit of Jesus Christ this will turn out for my deliverance, [20] as it is my eager expectation and hope that I will not be at all ashamed, but that with full courage now as always Christ will be honored in my body, whether by life or by death. [21] For to me to live is Christ, and to die is gain. [22] If I am to live in the flesh, that means fruitful labor for me. Yet which I shall choose I cannot tell. [23] I am hard pressed between the two. My desire is to depart and be with Christ, for that is far better. [24] But to remain in the flesh is more necessary on your account. [25] Convinced of this, I know that I will remain and continue with you all, for your progress and joy in the faith, [26] so that in me you may have ample cause to glory in Christ Jesus, because of my coming to you again.

[27] Only let your manner of life be worthy[8] of the gospel of Christ, so that whether I come and see you or am absent, I may hear of you that you are standing firm in one spirit, with one mind striving side by side for the faith of the gospel, [28] and not frightened in anything by your opponents. This is a clear sign to them of their destruction, but of your salvation, and that from God. [29] For it has been granted to you that for the sake of Christ you should not only believe in him but also suffer for his sake, [30] engaged in the same conflict that you saw I had and now hear that I still have.

Christ's Example of Humility

2 So if there is any encouragement in Christ, any comfort from love, any participation in the Spirit, any affection and sympathy, [2] complete my joy by being of the same mind, having the same love, being in full accord and of one mind. [3] Do nothing from selfish ambition or conceit, but in humility count others more significant than yourselves. [4] Let each of you look not only to his own interests, but also to the interests of others. [5] Have this mind among yourselves, which is yours in Christ Jesus,[9] [6] who, though he was in the form of God, did not count equality with God a thing to be grasped,[10] [7] but emptied himself, by taking the form of

---

[1] For the contextual rendering of the Greek word *doulos*, see Preface [2] Or *bishops*; Greek *episkopoi* [3] Or *servants*, or *ministers*; Greek *diakonoi* [4] Or *you all have fellowship with me in grace* [5] Or *brothers and sisters*. In New Testament usage, depending on the context, the plural Greek word *adelphoi* (translated "brothers") may refer either to *brothers* or to *brothers and sisters*; also verse 14 [6] Greek *in the whole praetorium* [7] Some manuscripts add *of God* [8] Greek *Only behave as citizens worthy* [9] Or *which was also in Christ Jesus* [10] Or *a thing to be held on to for advantage*

a servant,[1] being born in the likeness of men. [8] And being found in human form, he humbled himself by becoming obedient to the point of death, even death on a cross. [9] Therefore God has highly exalted him and bestowed on him the name that is above every name, [10] so that at the name of Jesus every knee should bow, in heaven and on earth and under the earth, [11] and every tongue confess that Jesus Christ is Lord, to the glory of God the Father.

Lights in the World

[12] Therefore, my beloved, as you have always obeyed, so now, not only as in my presence but much more in my absence, work out your own salvation with fear and trembling, [13] for it is God who works in you, both to will and to work for his good pleasure.

[14] Do all things without grumbling or disputing, [15] that you may be blameless and innocent, children of God without blemish in the midst of a crooked and twisted generation, among whom you shine as lights in the world, [16] holding fast to the word of life, so that in the day of Christ I may be proud that I did not run in vain or labor in vain. [17] Even if I am to be poured out as a drink offering upon the sacrificial offering of your faith, I am glad and rejoice with you all. [18] Likewise you also should be glad and rejoice with me.

Timothy and Epaphroditus

[19] I hope in the Lord Jesus to send Timothy to you soon, so that I too may be cheered by news of you. [20] For I have no one like him, who will be genuinely concerned for your welfare. [21] For they all seek their own interests, not those of Jesus Christ. [22] But you know Timothy's[2] proven worth, how as a son[3] with a father he has served with me in the gospel. [23] I hope therefore to send him just as soon as I see how it will go with me, [24] and I trust in the Lord that shortly I myself will come also.

[25] I have thought it necessary to send to you Epaphroditus my brother and fellow worker and fellow soldier, and your messenger and minister to my need, [26] for he has been longing for you all and has been distressed because you heard that he was ill. [27] Indeed he was ill, near to death. But God had mercy on him, and not only on him but on me also, lest I should have sorrow upon sorrow. [28] I am the more eager to send him, therefore, that you may rejoice at see-

ing him again, and that I may be less anxious. [29] So receive him in the Lord with all joy, and honor such men, [30] for he nearly died[4] for the work of Christ, risking his life to complete what was lacking in your service to me.

Righteousness Through Faith in Christ

3 Finally, my brothers,[5] rejoice in the Lord. To write the same things to you is no trouble to me and is safe for you.

[2] Look out for the dogs, look out for the evildoers, look out for those who mutilate the flesh. [3] For we are the circumcision, who worship by the Spirit of God[6] and glory in Christ Jesus and put no confidence in the flesh— [4] though I myself have reason for confidence in the flesh also. If anyone else thinks he has reason for confidence in the flesh, I have more: [5] circumcised on the eighth day, of the people of Israel, of the tribe of Benjamin, a Hebrew of Hebrews; as to the law, a Pharisee; [6] as to zeal, a persecutor of the church; as to righteousness under the law,[7] blameless. [7] But whatever gain I had, I counted as loss for the sake of Christ. [8] Indeed, I count everything as loss because of the surpassing worth of knowing Christ Jesus my Lord. For his sake I have suffered the loss of all things and count them as rubbish, in order that I may gain Christ [9] and be found in him, not having a righteousness of my own that comes from the law, but that which comes through faith in Christ, the righteousness from God that depends on faith— [10] that I may know him and the power of his resurrection, and may share his sufferings, becoming like him in his death, [11] that by any means possible I may attain the resurrection from the dead.

Straining Toward the Goal

[12] Not that I have already obtained this or am already perfect, but I press on to make it my own, because Christ Jesus has made me his own. [13] Brothers, I do not consider that I have made it my own. But one thing I do: forgetting what lies behind and straining forward to what lies ahead, [14] I press on toward the goal for the prize of the upward call of God in Christ Jesus. [15] Let those of us who are mature think this way, and if in anything you think otherwise, God will reveal that also to you. [16] Only let us hold true to what we have attained.

[17] Brothers, join in imitating me, and keep your eyes on those who walk according to the example you have in us. [18] For many, of whom I

---

[1] Or slave (for the contextual rendering of the Greek word *doulos*, see Preface) [2] Greek *his* [3] Greek *child* [4] Or *he drew near to the point of death*; compare verse 8 [4] Or *brothers and sisters*; also verses 13, 17 [5] Some manuscripts *God in spirit* [6] Greek *in the law*

have often told you and now tell you even with tears, walk as enemies of the cross of Christ. [19] Their end is destruction, their god is their belly, and they glory in their shame, with minds set on earthly things. [20] But our citizenship is in heaven, and from it we await a Savior, the Lord Jesus Christ, [21] who will transform our lowly body to be like his glorious body, by the power that enables him even to subject all things to himself.

4 Therefore, my brothers,[1] whom I love and long for, my joy and crown, stand firm thus in the Lord, my beloved.

Exhortation, Encouragement, and Prayer

[2] I entreat Euodia and I entreat Syntyche to agree in the Lord. [3] Yes, I ask you also, true companion,[2] help these women, who have labored[3] side by side with me in the gospel together with Clement and the rest of my fellow workers, whose names are in the book of life.

[4] Rejoice in the Lord always; again I will say, rejoice. [5] Let your reasonableness[4] be known to everyone. The Lord is at hand; [6] do not be anxious about anything, but in everything by prayer and supplication with thanksgiving let your requests be made known to God. [7] And the peace of God, which surpasses all understanding, will guard your hearts and your minds in Christ Jesus.

[8] Finally, brothers, whatever is true, whatever is honorable, whatever is just, whatever is pure, whatever is lovely, whatever is commendable, if there is any excellence, if there is anything worthy of praise, think about these things. [9] What you have learned[5] and received and heard and seen in me—practice these things, and the God of peace will be with you.

God's Provision

[10] I rejoiced in the Lord greatly that now at length you have revived your concern for me. You were indeed concerned for me, but you had no opportunity. [11] Not that I am speaking of being in need, for I have learned in whatever situation I am to be content. [12] I know how to be brought low, and I know how to abound. In any and every circumstance, I have learned the secret of facing plenty and hunger, abundance and need. [13] I can do all things through him who strengthens me.

[14] Yet it was kind of you to share[6] my trouble. [15] And you Philippians yourselves know that in the beginning of the gospel, when I left Macedonia, no church entered into partnership with me in giving and receiving, except you only. [16] Even in Thessalonica you sent me help for my needs once and again. [17] Not that I seek the gift, but I seek the fruit that increases to your credit.[7] [18] I have received full payment, and more. I am well supplied, having received from Epaphroditus the gifts you sent, a fragrant offering, a sacrifice acceptable and pleasing to God. [19] And my God will supply every need of yours according to his riches in glory in Christ Jesus. [20] To our God and Father be glory forever and ever. Amen.

Final Greetings

[21] Greet every saint in Christ Jesus. The brothers who are with me greet you. [22] All the saints greet you, especially those of Caesar's household.

[23] The grace of the Lord Jesus Christ be with your spirit.

---

[1] Or brothers and sisters; also verses 8, 21 [2] Or loyal Syzygus; Greek true yokefellow [3] Or strived (see 1:27) [4] Or gentleness [5] Or these things—[5] which things you have also learned [6] Or have fellowship in [7] Or I seek the profit that accrues to your account

Greeting

1 Paul, an apostle of Christ Jesus by the will of God, and Timothy our brother,

[2] To the saints and faithful brothers[1] in Christ at Colossae:

Grace to you and peace from God our Father.

Thanksgiving and Prayer

[3] We always thank God, the Father of our Lord Jesus Christ, when we pray for you, [4] since we heard of your faith in Christ Jesus and of the love that you have for all the saints, [5] because of the hope laid up for you in heaven. Of this you have heard before in the word of the truth, the gospel, [6] which has come to you, as indeed in the whole world it is bearing fruit and increasing—as it also does among you, since the day you heard it and understood the grace of God in truth, [7] just as you learned it from Epaphras our beloved fellow servant.[2] He is a faithful minister of Christ on your[3] behalf [8] and has made known to us your love in the Spirit.

[9] And so, from the day we heard, we have not ceased to pray for you, asking that you may be filled with the knowledge of his will in all spiritual wisdom and understanding, [10] so as to walk in a manner worthy of the Lord, fully pleasing to him: bearing fruit in every good work and increasing in the knowledge of God; [11] being strengthened with all power, according to his glorious might, for all endurance and patience with joy; [12] giving thanks[4] to the Father, who has qualified you[5] to share in the inheritance of the saints in light. [13] He has delivered us from the domain of darkness and transferred us to the kingdom of his beloved Son, [14] in whom we have redemption, the forgiveness of sins.

The Preeminence of Christ

[15] He is the image of the invisible God, the firstborn of all creation. [16] For by[6] him all things were created, in heaven and on earth, visible and invisible, whether thrones or dominions or rulers or authorities—all things were created through him and for him. [17] And he is before all things, and in him all things hold together. [18] And he is the head of the body, the church. He is the beginning, the firstborn from the dead, that in everything he might be preeminent. [19] For in him all the fullness of God was pleased to dwell, [20] and through him to reconcile to himself all things, whether on earth or in heaven, making peace by the blood of his cross.

[21] And you, who once were alienated and hostile in mind, doing evil deeds, [22] he has now reconciled in his body of flesh by his death, in order to present you holy and blameless and above reproach before him, [23] if indeed you continue in the faith, stable and steadfast, not shifting from the hope of the gospel that you heard, which has been proclaimed in all creation[7] under heaven, and of which I, Paul, became a minister.

Paul's Ministry to the Church

[24] Now I rejoice in my sufferings for your sake, and in my flesh I am filling up what is lacking in Christ's afflictions for the sake of his body, that is, the church, [25] of which I became a minister according to the stewardship from God that was given to me for you, to make the word of God fully known, [26] the mystery hidden for ages and generations but now revealed to his saints. [27] To them God chose to make known how great among the Gentiles are the riches of the glory of this mystery, which is Christ in you, the hope of glory. [28] Him we proclaim, warning everyone and teaching everyone with all wisdom, that we may present everyone mature in Christ. [29] For this I toil, struggling with all his energy that he powerfully works within me.

2 For I want you to know how great a struggle I have for you and for those at Laodicea and for all who have not seen me face to face, [2] that their hearts may be encouraged, being knit together in love, to reach all the riches of full assurance of understanding and the knowledge of God's mystery, which is Christ, [3] in whom are hidden all the treasures of wisdom and knowledge. [4] I say this in order that no one may delude you with plausible arguments. [5] For though I am absent in body, yet I am with you in spirit, rejoicing to see your good order and the firmness of your faith in Christ.

[1] Or brothers and sisters. In New Testament usage, depending on the context, the plural Greek word adelphoi (translated "brothers") may refer either to brothers or to brothers and sisters [2] For the contextual rendering of the Greek word sundoulos, see Preface [3] Some manuscripts our [4] Or patience, with joy giving thanks [5] Some manuscripts us [6] That is, by means of; or in [7] Or to every creature

Alive in Christ

[6] Therefore, as you received Christ Jesus the Lord, so walk in him, [7] rooted and built up in him and established in the faith, just as you were taught, abounding in thanksgiving.

[8] See to it that no one takes you captive by philosophy and empty deceit, according to human tradition, according to the elemental spirits[1] of the world, and not according to Christ. [9] For in him the whole fullness of deity dwells bodily, [10] and you have been filled in him, who is the head of all rule and authority. [11] In him also you were circumcised with a circumcision made without hands, by putting off the body of the flesh, by the circumcision of Christ, [12] having been buried with him in baptism, in which you were also raised with him through faith in the powerful working of God, who raised him from the dead. [13] And you, who were dead in your trespasses and the uncircumcision of your flesh, God made alive together with him, having forgiven us all our trespasses, [14] by canceling the record of debt that stood against us with its legal demands. This he set aside, nailing it to the cross. [15] He disarmed the rulers and authorities[2] and put them to open shame, by triumphing over them in him.[3]

Let No One Disqualify You

[16] Therefore let no one pass judgment on you in questions of food and drink, or with regard to a festival or a new moon or a Sabbath. [17] These are a shadow of the things to come, but the substance belongs to Christ. [18] Let no one disqualify you, insisting on asceticism and worship of angels, going on in detail about visions,[4] puffed up without reason by his sensuous mind, [19] and not holding fast to the Head, from whom the whole body, nourished and knit together through its joints and ligaments, grows with a growth that is from God.

[20] If with Christ you died to the elemental spirits of the world, why, as if you were still alive in the world, do you submit to regulations— [21] "Do not handle, Do not taste, Do not touch" [22] (referring to things that all perish as they are used)— according to human precepts and teachings? [23] These have indeed an appearance of wisdom in promoting self-made religion and asceticism and severity to the body, but they are of no value in stopping the indulgence of the flesh.

Put On the New Self

3 If then you have been raised with Christ, seek the things that are above, where Christ is, seated at the right hand of God. [2] Set your minds on things that are above, not on things that are on earth. [3] For you have died, and your life is hidden with Christ in God. [4] When Christ who is your[5] life appears, then you also will appear with him in glory.

[5] Put to death therefore what is earthly in you:[6] sexual immorality, impurity, passion, evil desire, and covetousness, which is idolatry. [6] On account of these the wrath of God is coming.[7] [7] In these you too once walked, when you were living in them. [8] But now you must put them all away: anger, wrath, malice, slander, and obscene talk from your mouth. [9] Do not lie to one another, seeing that you have put off the old self[8] with its practices [10] and have put on the new self, which is being renewed in knowledge after the image of its creator. [11] Here there is not Greek and Jew, circumcised and uncircumcised, barbarian, Scythian, slave,[9] free; but Christ is all, and in all.

[12] Put on then, as God's chosen ones, holy and beloved, compassionate hearts, kindness, humility, meekness, and patience, [13] bearing with one another and, if one has a complaint against another, forgiving each other; as the Lord has forgiven you, so you also must forgive. [14] And above all these put on love, which binds everything together in perfect harmony. [15] And let the peace of Christ rule in your hearts, to which indeed you were called in one body. And be thankful. [16] Let the word of Christ dwell in you richly, teaching and admonishing one another in all wisdom, singing psalms and hymns and spiritual songs, with thankfulness in your hearts to God. [17] And whatever you do, in word or deed, do everything in the name of the Lord Jesus, giving thanks to God the Father through him.

Rules for Christian Households

[18] Wives, submit to your husbands, as is fitting in the Lord. [19] Husbands, love your wives, and do not be harsh with them. [20] Children, obey your parents in everything, for this pleases the Lord. [21] Fathers, do not provoke your children, lest they become discouraged. [22] Bondservants, obey in everything those who are your earthly masters,[10] not by way of eye-service, as people-pleasers, but with sincerity of heart, fearing the

---

[1] Or elementary principles; also verse 20 [2] Probably demonic rulers and authorities [3] Or in it (that is, the cross) [4] Or about the things he has seen [5] Some manuscripts our [6] Greek therefore your members that are on the earth [7] Some manuscripts add upon the sons of disobedience [8] Greek man; also as supplied in verse 10 [9] For the contextual rendering of the Greek word doulos, see Preface; likewise for Bondservants in verse 22 [10] Or your masters according to the flesh

Lord. ²³ Whatever you do, work heartily, as for the Lord and not for men, ²⁴ knowing that from the Lord you will receive the inheritance as your reward. You are serving the Lord Christ. ²⁵ For the wrongdoer will be paid back for the wrong he has done, and there is no partiality.

4 Masters, treat your bondservants¹ justly and fairly, knowing that you also have a Master in heaven.

Further Instructions

² Continue steadfastly in prayer, being watchful in it with thanksgiving. ³ At the same time, pray also for us, that God may open to us a door for the word, to declare the mystery of Christ, on account of which I am in prison— ⁴ that I may make it clear, which is how I ought to speak.

⁵ Walk in wisdom toward outsiders, making the best use of the time. ⁶ Let your speech always be gracious, seasoned with salt, so that you may know how you ought to answer each person.

Final Greetings

⁷ Tychicus will tell you all about my activities. He is a beloved brother and faithful minister and fellow servant² in the Lord. ⁸ I have sent him to you for this very purpose, that you may know how we are and that he may encourage your hearts, ⁹ and with him Onesimus, our faithful and beloved brother, who is one of you. They will tell you of everything that has taken place here.

¹⁰ Aristarchus my fellow prisoner greets you, and Mark the cousin of Barnabas (concerning whom you have received instructions—if he comes to you, welcome him), ¹¹ and Jesus who is called Justus. These are the only men of the circumcision among my fellow workers for the kingdom of God, and they have been a comfort to me. ¹² Epaphras, who is one of you, a servant of Christ Jesus, greets you, always struggling on your behalf in his prayers, that you may stand mature and fully assured in all the will of God. ¹³ For I bear him witness that he has worked hard for you and for those in Laodicea and in Hierapolis. ¹⁴ Luke the beloved physician greets you, as does Demas. ¹⁵ Give my greetings to the brothers³ at Laodicea, and to Nympha and the church in her house. ¹⁶ And when this letter has been read among you, have it also read in the church of the Laodiceans; and see that you also read the letter from Laodicea. ¹⁷ And say to Archippus, "See that you fulfill the ministry that you have received in the Lord."

¹⁸ I, Paul, write this greeting with my own hand. Remember my chains. Grace be with you.

---

¹ For the contextual rendering of the Greek word *doulos*, see Preface; likewise for *servant* in verse 12 ² For the contextual rendering of the Greek word *sundoulos*, see Preface
³ Or *brothers and sisters*

1 THESSALONIANS

Greeting

1 Paul, Silvanus, and Timothy,

To the church of the Thessalonians in God the Father and the Lord Jesus Christ:

Grace to you and peace.

The Thessalonians' Faith and Example

² We give thanks to God always for all of you, constantly[1] mentioning you in our prayers, ³ remembering before our God and Father your work of faith and labor of love and steadfastness of hope in our Lord Jesus Christ. ⁴ For we know, brothers[2] loved by God, that he has chosen you, ⁵ because our gospel came to you not only in word, but also in power and in the Holy Spirit and with full conviction. You know what kind of men we proved to be among you for your sake. ⁶ And you became imitators of us and of the Lord, for you received the word in much affliction, with the joy of the Holy Spirit, ⁷ so that you became an example to all the believers in Macedonia and in Achaia. ⁸ For not only has the word of the Lord sounded forth from you in Macedonia and Achaia, but your faith in God has gone forth everywhere, so that we need not say anything. ⁹ For they themselves report concerning us the kind of reception we had among you, and how you turned to God from idols to serve the living and true God, ¹⁰ and to wait for his Son from heaven, whom he raised from the dead, Jesus who delivers us from the wrath to come.

Paul's Ministry to the Thessalonians

2 For you yourselves know, brothers,[3] that our coming to you was not in vain. ² But though we had already suffered and been shamefully treated at Philippi, as you know, we had boldness in our God to declare to you the gospel of God in the midst of much conflict. ³ For our appeal does not spring from error or impurity or any attempt to deceive, ⁴ but just as we have been approved by God to be entrusted with the gospel, so we speak, not to please man, but to please God who tests our hearts. ⁵ For we never came with words of flattery,[4] as you know, nor with a pretext for greed—God is witness. ⁶ Nor did we seek glory from people, whether from you or from others, though we could have made demands as apostles of Christ. ⁷ But we were gentle[5] among you, like a nursing mother taking care of her own children. ⁸ So, being affectionately desirous of you, we were ready to share with you not only the gospel of God but also our own selves, because you had become very dear to us.

⁹ For you remember, brothers, our labor and toil: we worked night and day, that we might not be a burden to any of you, while we proclaimed to you the gospel of God. ¹⁰ You are witnesses, and God also, how holy and righteous and blameless was our conduct toward you believers. ¹¹ For you know how, like a father with his children, ¹² we exhorted each one of you and encouraged you and charged you to walk in a manner worthy of God, who calls you into his own kingdom and glory.

¹³ And we also thank God constantly[6] for this, that when you received the word of God, which you heard from us, you accepted it not as the word of men[7] but as what it really is, the word of God, which is at work in you believers. ¹⁴ For you, brothers, became imitators of the churches of God in Christ Jesus that are in Judea. For you suffered the same things from your own countrymen as they did from the Jews,[8] ¹⁵ who killed both the Lord Jesus and the prophets, and drove us out, and displease God and oppose all mankind ¹⁶ by hindering us from speaking to the Gentiles that they might be saved—so as always to fill up the measure of their sins. But wrath has come upon them at last![9]

Paul's Longing to See Them Again

¹⁷ But since we were torn away from you, brothers, for a short time, in person not in heart, we endeavored the more eagerly and with great desire to see you face to face, ¹⁸ because we wanted to come to you—I, Paul, again and again—but Satan hindered us. ¹⁹ For what is our hope or joy or crown of boasting before our Lord Jesus at his coming? Is it not you? ²⁰ For you are our glory and joy.

3 Therefore when we could bear it no longer, we were willing to be left behind at Athens alone, ² and we sent Timothy, our brother and God's coworker[10] in the gospel of Christ, to

---

[1] Or without ceasing [2] Or brothers and sisters. In New Testament usage, depending on the context, the plural Greek word adelphoi (translated "brothers") may refer either to brothers or to brothers and sisters [3] Or brothers and sisters; also verses 9, 14, 17 [4] Or with a flattering speech [5] Some manuscripts infants [6] Or without ceasing [7] The Greek word anthropoi can refer to both men and women [8] The Greek word Ioudaioi can refer to Jewish religious leaders, and others under their influence, who opposed the Christian faith in that time [9] Or completely, or forever [10] Some manuscripts servant

establish and exhort you in your faith, [3] that no one be moved by these afflictions. For you yourselves know that we are destined for this. [4] For when we were with you, we kept telling you beforehand that we were to suffer affliction, just as it has come to pass, and just as you know. [5] For this reason, when I could bear it no longer, I sent to learn about your faith, for fear that somehow the tempter had tempted you and our labor would be in vain.

Timothy's Encouraging Report

[6] But now that Timothy has come to us from you, and has brought us the good news of your faith and love and reported that you always remember us kindly and long to see us, as we long to see you— [7] for this reason, brothers,[1] in all our distress and affliction we have been comforted about you through your faith. [8] For now we live, if you are standing fast in the Lord. [9] For what thanksgiving can we return to God for you, for all the joy that we feel for your sake before our God, [10] as we pray most earnestly night and day that we may see you face to face and supply what is lacking in your faith?

[11] Now may our God and Father himself, and our Lord Jesus, direct our way to you, [12] and may the Lord make you increase and abound in love for one another and for all, as we do for you, [13] so that he may establish your hearts blameless in holiness before our God and Father, at the coming of our Lord Jesus with all his saints.

A Life Pleasing to God

4 Finally, then, brothers,[2] we ask and urge you in the Lord Jesus, that as you received from us how you ought to walk and to please God, just as you are doing, that you do so more and more. [2] For you know what instructions we gave you through the Lord Jesus. [3] For this is the will of God, your sanctification:[3] that you abstain from sexual immorality; [4] that each one of you know how to control his own body[4] in holiness and honor, [5] not in the passion of lust like the Gentiles who do not know God; [6] that no one transgress and wrong his brother in this matter, because the Lord is an avenger in all these things, as we told you beforehand and solemnly warned you. [7] For God has not called us for impurity, but in holiness. [8] Therefore

whoever disregards this, disregards not man but God, who gives his Holy Spirit to you.

[9] Now concerning brotherly love you have no need for anyone to write to you, for you yourselves have been taught by God to love one another, [10] for that indeed is what you are doing to all the brothers throughout Macedonia. But we urge you, brothers, to do this more and more, [11] and to aspire to live quietly, and to mind your own affairs, and to work with your hands, as we instructed you, [12] so that you may walk properly before outsiders and be dependent on no one.

The Coming of the Lord

[13] But we do not want you to be uninformed, brothers, about those who are asleep, that you may not grieve as others do who have no hope. [14] For since we believe that Jesus died and rose again, even so, through Jesus, God will bring with him those who have fallen asleep. [15] For this we declare to you by a word from the Lord,[5] that we who are alive, who are left until the coming of the Lord, will not precede those who have fallen asleep. [16] For the Lord himself will descend from heaven with a cry of command, with the voice of an archangel, and with the sound of the trumpet of God. And the dead in Christ will rise first. [17] Then we who are alive, who are left, will be caught up together with them in the clouds to meet the Lord in the air, and so we will always be with the Lord. [18] Therefore encourage one another with these words.

The Day of the Lord

5 Now concerning the times and the seasons, brothers,[6] you have no need to have anything written to you. [2] For you yourselves are fully aware that the day of the Lord will come like a thief in the night. [3] While people are saying, "There is peace and security," then sudden destruction will come upon them as labor pains come upon a pregnant woman, and they will not escape. [4] But you are not in darkness, brothers, for that day to surprise you like a thief. [5] For you are all children[7] of light, children of the day. We are not of the night or of the darkness. [6] So then let us not sleep, as others do, but let us keep awake and be sober. [7] For those who sleep, sleep at night, and those who get drunk, are drunk at night. [8] But since we belong to the day, let us be sober, having put

---

[1] Or brothers and sisters [2] Or brothers and sisters; also verses 10, 13 [3] Or your holiness [4] Or how to take a wife for himself; Greek how to possess his own vessel [5] Or by the word of the Lord [6] Or brothers and sisters; also verses 4, 12, 14, 25, 26, 27 [7] Or sons; twice in this verse

on the breastplate of faith and love, and for a helmet the hope of salvation. [9] For God has not destined us for wrath, but to obtain salvation through our Lord Jesus Christ, [10] who died for us so that whether we are awake or asleep we might live with him. [11] Therefore encourage one another and build one another up, just as you are doing.

Final Instructions and Benediction

[12] We ask you, brothers, to respect those who labor among you and are over you in the Lord and admonish you, [13] and to esteem them very highly in love because of their work. Be at peace among yourselves. [14] And we urge you, brothers, admonish the idle,[1] encourage the fainthearted, help the weak, be patient with them all. [15] See that no one repays anyone evil for evil, but always seek to do good to one another and to everyone. [16] Rejoice always, [17] pray without ceasing, [18] give thanks in all circumstances; for this is the will of God in Christ Jesus for you. [19] Do not quench the Spirit. [20] Do not despise prophecies, [21] but test everything; hold fast what is good. [22] Abstain from every form of evil.

[23] Now may the God of peace himself sanctify you completely, and may your whole spirit and soul and body be kept blameless at the coming of our Lord Jesus Christ. [24] He who calls you is faithful; he will surely do it.

[25] Brothers, pray for us.

[26] Greet all the brothers with a holy kiss.

[27] I put you under oath before the Lord to have this letter read to all the brothers.

[28] The grace of our Lord Jesus Christ be with you.

---

[1] Or disorderly, or undisciplined

2 THESSALONIANS

Greeting

1 Paul, Silvanus, and Timothy,
To the church of the Thessalonians in God our Father and the Lord Jesus Christ:

² Grace to you and peace from God our Father and the Lord Jesus Christ.

Thanksgiving

³ We ought always to give thanks to God for you, brothers,[1] as is right, because your faith is growing abundantly, and the love of every one of you for one another is increasing. ⁴ Therefore we ourselves boast about you in the churches of God for your steadfastness and faith in all your persecutions and in the afflictions that you are enduring.

The Judgment at Christ's Coming

⁵ This is evidence of the righteous judgment of God, that you may be considered worthy of the kingdom of God, for which you are also suffering— ⁶ since indeed God considers it just to repay with affliction those who afflict you, ⁷ and to grant relief to you who are afflicted as well as to us, when the Lord Jesus is revealed from heaven with his mighty angels ⁸ in flaming fire, inflicting vengeance on those who do not know God and on those who do not obey the gospel of our Lord Jesus. ⁹ They will suffer the punishment of eternal destruction, away from[2] the presence of the Lord and from the glory of his might, ¹⁰ when he comes on that day to be glorified in his saints, and to be marveled at among all who have believed, because our testimony to you was believed. ¹¹ To this end we always pray for you, that our God may make you worthy of his calling and may fulfill every resolve for good and every work of faith by his power, ¹² so that the name of our Lord Jesus may be glorified in you, and you in him, according to the grace of our God and the Lord Jesus Christ.

The Man of Lawlessness

2 Now concerning the coming of our Lord Jesus Christ and our being gathered together to him, we ask you, brothers,[3] ² not to be quickly shaken in mind or alarmed, either by a spirit or a spoken word, or a letter seeming to be from us, to the effect that the day of the Lord has come. ³ Let no one deceive you in any way. For that day will not come, unless the rebellion comes first, and the man of lawlessness[4] is revealed, the son of destruction,[5] ⁴ who opposes and exalts himself against every so-called god or object of worship, so that he takes his seat in the temple of God, proclaiming himself to be God. ⁵ Do you not remember that when I was still with you I told you these things? ⁶ And you know what is restraining him now so that he may be revealed in his time. ⁷ For the mystery of lawlessness is already at work. Only he who now restrains it will do so until he is out of the way. ⁸ And then the lawless one will be revealed, whom the Lord Jesus will kill with the breath of his mouth and bring to nothing by the appearance of his coming. ⁹ The coming of the lawless one is by the activity of Satan with all power and false signs and wonders, ¹⁰ and with all wicked deception for those who are perishing, because they refused to love the truth and so be saved. ¹¹ Therefore God sends them a strong delusion, so that they may believe what is false, ¹² in order that all may be condemned who did not believe the truth but had pleasure in unrighteousness.

Stand Firm

¹³ But we ought always to give thanks to God for you, brothers beloved by the Lord, because God chose you as the firstfruits[6] to be saved, through sanctification by the Spirit and belief in the truth. ¹⁴ To this he called you through our gospel, so that you may obtain the glory of our Lord Jesus Christ. ¹⁵ So then, brothers, stand firm and hold to the traditions that you were taught by us, either by our spoken word or by our letter.

¹⁶ Now may our Lord Jesus Christ himself, and God our Father, who loved us and gave us eternal comfort and good hope through grace, ¹⁷ comfort your hearts and establish them in every good work and word.

---

[1] Or brothers and sisters. In New Testament usage, depending on the context, the plural Greek word adelphoi (translated "brothers") may refer either to brothers or to brothers and sisters [2] Or destruction that comes from [3] Or brothers and sisters; also verses 13, 15 [4] Some manuscripts sin [5] Greek the son of perdition (a Hebrew idiom) [6] Some manuscripts chose you from the beginning

Pray for Us

3 Finally, brothers,[1] pray for us, that the word of the Lord may speed ahead and be honored,[2] as happened among you, 2 and that we may be delivered from wicked and evil men. For not all have faith. 3 But the Lord is faithful. He will establish you and guard you against the evil one.[3] 4 And we have confidence in the Lord about you, that you are doing and will do the things that we command. 5 May the Lord direct your hearts to the love of God and to the steadfastness of Christ.

Warning Against Idleness

6 Now we command you, brothers, in the name of our Lord Jesus Christ, that you keep away from any brother who is walking in idleness and not in accord with the tradition that you received from us. 7 For you yourselves know how you ought to imitate us, because we were not idle when we were with you, 8 nor did we eat anyone's bread without paying for it, but with toil and labor we worked night and day, that we might not be a burden to any of you. 9 It was not because we do not have that right, but to give you in ourselves an example to imitate. 10 For even when we were with you, we would give you this command: If anyone is not willing to work, let him not eat. 11 For we hear that some among you walk in idleness, not busy at work, but busybodies. 12 Now such persons we command and encourage in the Lord Jesus Christ to do their work quietly and to earn their own living.[4]

13 As for you, brothers, do not grow weary in doing good. 14 If anyone does not obey what we say in this letter, take note of that person, and have nothing to do with him, that he may be ashamed. 15 Do not regard him as an enemy, but warn him as a brother.

Benediction

16 Now may the Lord of peace himself give you peace at all times in every way. The Lord be with you all.

17 I, Paul, write this greeting with my own hand. This is the sign of genuineness in every letter of mine; it is the way I write. 18 The grace of our Lord Jesus Christ be with you all.

---

[1] Or brothers and sisters; also verses 6, 13 [2] Or glorified [3] Or evil [4] Greek to eat their own bread

1 TIMOTHY

Greeting

1 Paul, an apostle of Christ Jesus by command of God our Savior and of Christ Jesus our hope,

[2] To Timothy, my true child in the faith:

Grace, mercy, and peace from God the Father and Christ Jesus our Lord.

Warning Against False Teachers

[3] As I urged you when I was going to Macedonia, remain at Ephesus so that you may charge certain persons not to teach any different doctrine, [4] nor to devote themselves to myths and endless genealogies, which promote speculations rather than the stewardship[1] from God that is by faith. [5] The aim of our charge is love that issues from a pure heart and a good conscience and a sincere faith. [6] Certain persons, by swerving from these, have wandered away into vain discussion, [7] desiring to be teachers of the law, without understanding either what they are saying or the things about which they make confident assertions.

[8] Now we know that the law is good, if one uses it lawfully, [9] understanding this, that the law is not laid down for the just but for the lawless and disobedient, for the ungodly and sinners, for the unholy and profane, for those who strike their fathers and mothers, for murderers, [10] the sexually immoral, men who practice homosexuality, enslavers,[2] liars, perjurers, and whatever else is contrary to sound[3] doctrine, [11] in accordance with the gospel of the glory of the blessed God with which I have been entrusted.

Christ Jesus Came to Save Sinners

[12] I thank him who has given me strength, Christ Jesus our Lord, because he judged me faithful, appointing me to his service, [13] though formerly I was a blasphemer, persecutor, and insolent opponent. But I received mercy because I had acted ignorantly in unbelief, [14] and the grace of our Lord overflowed for me with the faith and love that are in Christ Jesus. [15] The saying is trustworthy and deserving of full acceptance, that Christ Jesus came into the world to save sinners, of whom I am the foremost. [16] But I received mercy for this reason, that in me, as the foremost, Jesus Christ might display his perfect patience as an example to those who were to believe in him for eternal life. [17] To the King of the ages, immortal, invisible, the only God, be honor and glory forever and ever.[4] Amen.

[18] This charge I entrust to you, Timothy, my child, in accordance with the prophecies previously made about you, that by them you may wage the good warfare, [19] holding faith and a good conscience. By rejecting this, some have made shipwreck of their faith, [20] among whom are Hymenaeus and Alexander, whom I have handed over to Satan that they may learn not to blaspheme.

Pray for All People

2 First of all, then, I urge that supplications, prayers, intercessions, and thanksgivings be made for all people, [2] for kings and all who are in high positions, that we may lead a peaceful and quiet life, godly and dignified in every way. [3] This is good, and it is pleasing in the sight of God our Savior, [4] who desires all people to be saved and to come to the knowledge of the truth. [5] For there is one God, and there is one mediator between God and men, the man[5] Christ Jesus, [6] who gave himself as a ransom for all, which is the testimony given at the proper time. [7] For this I was appointed a preacher and an apostle (I am telling the truth, I am not lying), a teacher of the Gentiles in faith and truth.

[8] I desire then that in every place the men should pray, lifting holy hands without anger or quarreling; [9] likewise also that women should adorn themselves in respectable apparel, with modesty and self-control, not with braided hair and gold or pearls or costly attire, [10] but with what is proper for women who profess godliness—with good works. [11] Let a woman learn quietly with all submissiveness. [12] I do not permit a woman to teach or to exercise authority over a man; rather, she is to remain quiet. [13] For Adam was formed first, then Eve; [14] and Adam was not deceived, but the woman was deceived and became a transgressor. [15] Yet she will be saved through childbearing—if they continue in faith and love and holiness, with self-control.

---

[1] Or good order [2] That is, those who take someone captive in order to sell him into slavery [3] Or healthy [4] Greek to the ages of ages [5] men and man render the same Greek word that is translated people in verses 1 and 4

Qualifications for Overseers

3 The saying is trustworthy: If anyone aspires to the office of overseer, he desires a noble task. ²Therefore an overseer¹ must be above reproach, the husband of one wife,² sober-minded, self-controlled, respectable, hospitable, able to teach, ³not a drunkard, not violent but gentle, not quarrelsome, not a lover of money. ⁴He must manage his own household well, with all dignity keeping his children submissive, ⁵for if someone does not know how to manage his own household, how will he care for God's church? ⁶He must not be a recent convert, or he may become puffed up with conceit and fall into the condemnation of the devil. ⁷Moreover, he must be well thought of by outsiders, so that he may not fall into disgrace, into a snare of the devil.

Qualifications for Deacons

⁸Deacons likewise must be dignified, not double-tongued,³ not addicted to much wine, not greedy for dishonest gain. ⁹They must hold the mystery of the faith with a clear conscience. ¹⁰And let them also be tested first; then let them serve as deacons if they prove themselves blameless. ¹¹Their wives likewise⁴ must be dignified, not slanderers, but sober-minded, faithful in all things. ¹²Let deacons each be the husband of one wife, managing their children and their own households well. ¹³For those who serve well as deacons gain a good standing for themselves and also great confidence in the faith that is in Christ Jesus.

The Mystery of Godliness

¹⁴I hope to come to you soon, but I am writing these things to you so that, ¹⁵if I delay, you may know how one ought to behave in the household of God, which is the church of the living God, a pillar and buttress of the truth. ¹⁶Great indeed, we confess, is the mystery of godliness:

> He⁵ was manifested in the flesh,
>   vindicated⁶ by the Spirit,⁷
>   seen by angels,
>   proclaimed among the nations,
>   believed on in the world,
>   taken up in glory.

Some Will Depart from the Faith

4 Now the Spirit expressly says that in later times some will depart from the faith by devoting themselves to deceitful spirits and teachings of demons, ²through the insincerity of liars whose consciences are seared, ³who forbid marriage and require abstinence from foods that God created to be received with thanksgiving by those who believe and know the truth. ⁴For everything created by God is good, and nothing is to be rejected if it is received with thanksgiving, ⁵for it is made holy by the word of God and prayer.

A Good Servant of Christ Jesus

⁶If you put these things before the brothers,⁸ you will be a good servant of Christ Jesus, being trained in the words of the faith and of the good doctrine that you have followed. ⁷Have nothing to do with irreverent, silly myths. Rather train yourself for godliness; ⁸for while bodily training is of some value, godliness is of value in every way, as it holds promise for the present life and also for the life to come. ⁹The saying is trustworthy and deserving of full acceptance. ¹⁰For to this end we toil and strive,⁹ because we have our hope set on the living God, who is the Savior of all people, especially of those who believe.

¹¹Command and teach these things. ¹²Let no one despise you for your youth, but set the believers an example in speech, in conduct, in love, in faith, in purity. ¹³Until I come, devote yourself to the public reading of Scripture, to exhortation, to teaching. ¹⁴Do not neglect the gift you have, which was given you by prophecy when the council of elders laid their hands on you. ¹⁵Practice these things, immerse yourself in them,¹⁰ so that all may see your progress. ¹⁶Keep a close watch on yourself and on the teaching. Persist in this, for by so doing you will save both yourself and your hearers.

Instructions for the Church

5 Do not rebuke an older man but encourage him as you would a father, younger men as brothers, ²older women as mothers, younger women as sisters, in all purity.

³Honor widows who are truly widows. ⁴But if a widow has children or grandchildren, let them first learn to show godliness to their own household and to make some return to

---

¹ Or *bishop*; Greek *episkopos*; a similar term occurs in verse 1 ² Or *a man of one woman*; also verse 12 ³ Or *devious in speech* ⁴ Or *Wives likewise*, or *Women likewise* ⁵ Greek *Who*; some manuscripts *God*; others *Which* ⁶ Or *justified* ⁷ Or *vindicated in spirit* ⁸ Or *brothers and sisters*. In New Testament usage, depending on the context, the plural Greek word *adelphoi* (translated "brothers") may refer either to *brothers* or to *brothers and sisters* ⁹ Some manuscripts *and suffer reproach* ¹⁰ Greek *be in them*

their parents, for this is pleasing in the sight of God. [5] She who is truly a widow, left all alone, has set her hope on God and continues in supplications and prayers night and day, [6] but she who is self-indulgent is dead even while she lives. [7] Command these things as well, so that they may be without reproach. [8] But if anyone does not provide for his relatives, and especially for members of his household, he has denied the faith and is worse than an unbeliever.

[9] Let a widow be enrolled if she is not less than sixty years of age, having been the wife of one husband,[1] [10] and having a reputation for good works: if she has brought up children, has shown hospitality, has washed the feet of the saints, has cared for the afflicted, and has devoted herself to every good work. [11] But refuse to enroll younger widows, for when their passions draw them away from Christ, they desire to marry [12] and so incur condemnation for having abandoned their former faith. [13] Besides that, they learn to be idlers, going about from house to house, and not only idlers, but also gossips and busybodies, saying what they should not. [14] So I would have younger widows marry, bear children, manage their households, and give the adversary no occasion for slander. [15] For some have already strayed after Satan. [16] If any believing woman has relatives who are widows, let her care for them. Let the church not be burdened, so that it may care for those who are truly widows.

[17] Let the elders who rule well be considered worthy of double honor, especially those who labor in preaching and teaching. [18] For the Scripture says, [a]"You shall not muzzle an ox when it treads out the grain," and, "The laborer deserves his wages." [19] Do not admit a charge against an elder except on the evidence of two or three witnesses. [20] As for those who persist in sin, rebuke them in the presence of all, so that the rest may stand in fear. [21] In the presence of God and of Christ Jesus and of the elect angels I charge you to keep these rules without prejudging, doing nothing from partiality. [22] Do not be hasty in the laying on of hands, nor take part in the sins of others; keep yourself pure. [23] (No longer drink only water, but use a little wine for the sake of your stomach and your frequent ailments.) [24] The sins of some people are conspicuous, going before them to judgment, but the sins of others appear later. [25] So also good works are conspicuous, and even those that are not cannot remain hidden.

6 Let all who are under a yoke as bondservants[2] regard their own masters as worthy of all honor, so that the name of God and the teaching may not be reviled. [2] Those who have believing masters must not be disrespectful on the ground that they are brothers; rather they must serve all the better since those who benefit by their good service are believers and beloved.

False Teachers and True Contentment

Teach and urge these things. [3] If anyone teaches a different doctrine and does not agree with the sound[3] words of our Lord Jesus Christ and the teaching that accords with godliness, [4] he is puffed up with conceit and understands nothing. He has an unhealthy craving for controversy and for quarrels about words, which produce envy, dissension, slander, evil suspicions, [5] and constant friction among people who are depraved in mind and deprived of the truth, imagining that godliness is a means of gain. [6] But godliness with contentment is great gain, [7] for we brought nothing into the world, and[4] we cannot take anything out of the world. [8] But if we have food and clothing, with these we will be content. [9] But those who desire to be rich fall into temptation, into a snare, into many senseless and harmful desires that plunge people into ruin and destruction. [10] For the love of money is a root of all kinds of evils. It is through this craving that some have wandered away from the faith and pierced themselves with many pangs.

Fight the Good Fight of Faith

[11] But as for you, O man of God, flee these things. Pursue righteousness, godliness, faith, love, steadfastness, gentleness. [12] Fight the good fight of the faith. Take hold of the eternal life to which you were called and about which you made the good confession in the presence of many witnesses. [13] I charge you in the presence of God, who gives life to all things, and of Christ Jesus, who in his testimony before[5] Pontius Pilate made the good confession, [14] to keep the commandment unstained and free from reproach until the appearing of our Lord Jesus Christ, [15] which he will display at the proper time—he who is the blessed and only

---

[1] Or *a woman of one man*   [2] For the contextual rendering of the Greek word *doulos*, see Preface   [3] Or *healthy*   [4] Greek *for*; some manuscripts insert [it is] *certain* [that]   [5] Or *in the time of*   [a] Deut. 25:4

Sovereign, the King of kings and Lord of lords, [16] who alone has immortality, who dwells in unapproachable light, whom no one has ever seen or can see. To him be honor and eternal dominion. Amen.

[17] As for the rich in this present age, charge them not to be haughty, nor to set their hopes on the uncertainty of riches, but on God, who richly provides us with everything to enjoy. [18] They are to do good, to be rich in good works, to be generous and ready to share, [19] thus storing up treasure for themselves as a good foundation for the future, so that they may take hold of that which is truly life.

[20] O Timothy, guard the deposit entrusted to you. Avoid the irreverent babble and contradictions of what is falsely called "knowledge," [21] for by professing it some have swerved from the faith.

Grace be with you.[1]

2 TIMOTHY

Greeting

1 Paul, an apostle of Christ Jesus by the will of God according to the promise of the life that is in Christ Jesus,

[2] To Timothy, my beloved child:

Grace, mercy, and peace from God the Father and Christ Jesus our Lord.

Guard the Deposit Entrusted to You

[3] I thank God whom I serve, as did my ancestors, with a clear conscience, as I remember you constantly in my prayers night and day. [4] As I remember your tears, I long to see you, that I may be filled with joy. [5] I am reminded of your sincere faith, a faith that dwelt first in your grandmother Lois and your mother Eunice and now, I am sure, dwells in you as well. [6] For this reason I remind you to fan into flame the gift of God, which is in you through the laying on of my hands, [7] for God gave us a spirit not of fear but of power and love and self-control.

[8] Therefore do not be ashamed of the testimony about our Lord, nor of me his prisoner, but share in suffering for the gospel by the power of God, [9] who saved us and called us to[1] a holy calling, not because of our works but because of his own purpose and grace, which he gave us in Christ Jesus before the ages began,[2] [10] and which now has been manifested through the appearing of our Savior Christ Jesus, who abolished death and brought life and immortality to light through the gospel, [11] for which I was appointed a preacher and apostle and teacher, [12] which is why I suffer as I do. But I am not ashamed, for I know whom I have believed, and I am convinced that he is able to guard until that day what has been entrusted to me.[3] [13] Follow the pattern of the sound[4] words that you have heard from me, in the faith and love that are in Christ Jesus. [14] By the Holy Spirit who dwells within us, guard the good deposit entrusted to you.

[15] You are aware that all who are in Asia turned away from me, among whom are Phygelus and Hermogenes. [16] May the Lord grant mercy to the household of Onesiphorus, for he often refreshed me and was not ashamed of my chains, [17] but when he arrived in Rome he searched for me earnestly and found me— [18] may the Lord grant him to find mercy from the Lord on that day!—and you well know all the service he rendered at Ephesus.

A Good Soldier of Christ Jesus

2 You then, my child, be strengthened by the grace that is in Christ Jesus, [2] and what you have heard from me in the presence of many witnesses entrust to faithful men,[5] who will be able to teach others also. [3] Share in suffering as a good soldier of Christ Jesus. [4] No soldier gets entangled in civilian pursuits, since his aim is to please the one who enlisted him. [5] An athlete is not crowned unless he competes according to the rules. [6] It is the hard-working farmer who ought to have the first share of the crops. [7] Think over what I say, for the Lord will give you understanding in everything.

[8] Remember Jesus Christ, risen from the dead, the offspring of David, as preached in my gospel, [9] for which I am suffering, bound with chains as a criminal. But the word of God is not bound! [10] Therefore I endure everything for the sake of the elect, that they also may obtain the salvation that is in Christ Jesus with eternal glory. [11] The saying is trustworthy, for:

> If we have died with him, we will also live
>   with him;
> [12] if we endure, we will also reign with
>   him;
> if we deny him, he also will deny us;
> [13] if we are faithless, he remains faithful—

for he cannot deny himself.

A Worker Approved by God

[14] Remind them of these things, and charge them before God[6] not to quarrel about words, which does no good, but only ruins the hearers. [15] Do your best to present yourself to God as one approved,[7] a worker who has no need to be ashamed, rightly handling the word of truth. [16] But avoid irreverent babble, for it will lead people into more and more ungodliness, [17] and their talk will spread like gangrene. Among them are Hymenaeus and Philetus,

---

[1] Or *with* [2] Greek *before times eternal* [3] Or *what I have entrusted to him*; Greek *my deposit* [4] Or *healthy* [5] The Greek word *anthropoi* can refer to both men and women, depending on the context [6] Some manuscripts *the Lord* [7] That is, one approved after being tested

[18] who have swerved from the truth, saying that the resurrection has already happened. They are upsetting the faith of some. [19] But God's firm foundation stands, bearing this seal: "The Lord knows those who are his," and, "Let everyone who names the name of the Lord depart from iniquity."

[20] Now in a great house there are not only vessels of gold and silver but also of wood and clay, some for honorable use, some for dishonorable. [21] Therefore, if anyone cleanses himself from what is dishonorable,[1] he will be a vessel for honorable use, set apart as holy, useful to the master of the house, ready for every good work. [22] So flee youthful passions and pursue righteousness, faith, love, and peace, along with those who call on the Lord from a pure heart. [23] Have nothing to do with foolish, ignorant controversies; you know that they breed quarrels. [24] And the Lord's servant[2] must not be quarrelsome but kind to everyone, able to teach, patiently enduring evil, [25] correcting his opponents with gentleness. God may perhaps grant them repentance leading to a knowledge of the truth, [26] and they may come to their senses and escape from the snare of the devil, after being captured by him to do his will.

Godlessness in the Last Days

3 But understand this, that in the last days there will come times of difficulty. [2] For people will be lovers of self, lovers of money, proud, arrogant, abusive, disobedient to their parents, ungrateful, unholy, [3] heartless, unappeasable, slanderous, without self-control, brutal, not loving good, [4] treacherous, reckless, swollen with conceit, lovers of pleasure rather than lovers of God, [5] having the appearance of godliness, but denying its power. Avoid such people. [6] For among them are those who creep into households and capture weak women, burdened with sins and led astray by various passions, [7] always learning and never able to arrive at a knowledge of the truth. [8] Just as Jannes and Jambres opposed Moses, so these men also oppose the truth, men corrupted in mind and disqualified regarding the faith. [9] But they will not get very far, for their folly will be plain to all, as was that of those two men.

All Scripture Is Breathed Out by God

[10] You, however, have followed my teaching, my conduct, my aim in life, my faith, my patience, my love, my steadfastness, [11] my persecutions and sufferings that happened to me at Antioch, at Iconium, and at Lystra—which persecutions I endured; yet from them all the Lord rescued me. [12] Indeed, all who desire to live a godly life in Christ Jesus will be persecuted, [13] while evil people and impostors will go on from bad to worse, deceiving and being deceived. [14] But as for you, continue in what you have learned and have firmly believed, knowing from whom[3] you learned it [15] and how from childhood you have been acquainted with the sacred writings, which are able to make you wise for salvation through faith in Christ Jesus. [16] All Scripture is breathed out by God and profitable for teaching, for reproof, for correction, and for training in righteousness, [17] that the man of God[4] may be complete, equipped for every good work.

Preach the Word

4 I charge you in the presence of God and of Christ Jesus, who is to judge the living and the dead, and by his appearing and his kingdom: [2] preach the word; be ready in season and out of season; reprove, rebuke, and exhort, with complete patience and teaching. [3] For the time is coming when people will not endure sound[5] teaching, but having itching ears they will accumulate for themselves teachers to suit their own passions, [4] and will turn away from listening to the truth and wander off into myths. [5] As for you, always be sober-minded, endure suffering, do the work of an evangelist, fulfill your ministry.

[6] For I am already being poured out as a drink offering, and the time of my departure has come. [7] I have fought the good fight, I have finished the race, I have kept the faith. [8] Henceforth there is laid up for me the crown of righteousness, which the Lord, the righteous judge, will award to me on that day, and not only to me but also to all who have loved his appearing.

Personal Instructions

[9] Do your best to come to me soon. [10] For Demas, in love with this present world, has deserted me and gone to Thessalonica. Crescens has gone to Galatia,[6] Titus to Dalmatia. [11] Luke alone is with me. Get Mark and bring him with you, for he is very useful to me for ministry. [12] Tychicus I have sent to Ephesus. [13] When you come, bring the cloak that I left with Carpus at

---

[1] Greek *from these things* [2] For the contextual rendering of the Greek word *doulos*, see Preface [3] The Greek for *whom* is plural [4] That is, a messenger of God (the phrase echoes a common Old Testament expression) [5] Or *healthy* [6] Some manuscripts *Gaul*

Troas, also the books, and above all the parchments. **14** Alexander the coppersmith did me great harm; the Lord will repay him according to his deeds. **15** Beware of him yourself, for he strongly opposed our message. **16** At my first defense no one came to stand by me, but all deserted me. May it not be charged against them! **17** But the Lord stood by me and strengthened me, so that through me the message might be fully proclaimed and all the Gentiles might hear it. So I was rescued from the lion's mouth. **18** The Lord will rescue me from every evil deed and bring me safely into his heavenly kingdom. To him be the glory forever and ever. Amen.

Final Greetings

19 Greet Prisca and Aquila, and the household of Onesiphorus. **20** Erastus remained at Corinth, and I left Trophimus, who was ill, at Miletus. **21** Do your best to come before winter. Eubulus sends greetings to you, as do Pudens and Linus and Claudia and all the brothers.[1]

22 The Lord be with your spirit. Grace be with you.[2]

---

[1] Or *brothers and sisters*. In New Testament usage, depending on the context, the plural Greek word *adelphoi* (translated "brothers") may refer either to *brothers* or to *brothers and sisters* [2] The Greek for *you* is plural

TITUS

Greeting

1 Paul, a servant[1] of God and an apostle of Jesus Christ, for the sake of the faith of God's elect and their knowledge of the truth, which accords with godliness, [2] in hope of eternal life, which God, who never lies, promised before the ages began[2] [3] and at the proper time manifested in his word[3] through the preaching with which I have been entrusted by the command of God our Savior;

[4] To Titus, my true child in a common faith:

Grace and peace from God the Father and Christ Jesus our Savior.

Qualifications for Elders

[5] This is why I left you in Crete, so that you might put what remained into order, and appoint elders in every town as I directed you— [6] if anyone is above reproach, the husband of one wife,[4] and his children are believers[5] and not open to the charge of debauchery or insubordination. [7] For an overseer,[6] as God's steward, must be above reproach. He must not be arrogant or quick-tempered or a drunkard or violent or greedy for gain, [8] but hospitable, a lover of good, self-controlled, upright, holy, and disciplined. [9] He must hold firm to the trustworthy word as taught, so that he may be able to give instruction in sound[7] doctrine and also to rebuke those who contradict it.

[10] For there are many who are insubordinate, empty talkers and deceivers, especially those of the circumcision party.[8] [11] They must be silenced, since they are upsetting whole families by teaching for shameful gain what they ought not to teach. [12] One of the Cretans,[9] a prophet of their own, said, "Cretans are always liars, evil beasts, lazy gluttons."[10] [13] This testimony is true. Therefore rebuke them sharply, that they may be sound in the faith, [14] not devoting themselves to Jewish myths and the commands of people who turn away from the truth. [15] To the pure, all things are pure, but to the defiled and unbelieving, nothing is pure; but both their minds and their consciences are defiled. [16] They profess to know God, but they deny him by their works. They are detestable, disobedient, unfit for any good work.

Teach Sound Doctrine

2 But as for you, teach what accords with sound[11] doctrine. [2] Older men are to be sober-minded, dignified, self-controlled, sound in faith, in love, and in steadfastness. [3] Older women likewise are to be reverent in behavior, not slanderers or slaves to much wine. They are to teach what is good, [4] and so train the young women to love their husbands and children, [5] to be self-controlled, pure, working at home, kind, and submissive to their own husbands, that the word of God may not be reviled. [6] Likewise, urge the younger men to be self-controlled. [7] Show yourself in all respects to be a model of good works, and in your teaching show integrity, dignity, [8] and sound speech that cannot be condemned, so that an opponent may be put to shame, having nothing evil to say about us. [9] Bondservants[12] are to be submissive to their own masters in everything; they are to be well-pleasing, not argumentative, [10] not pilfering, but showing all good faith, so that in everything they may adorn the doctrine of God our Savior.

[11] For the grace of God has appeared, bringing salvation for all people, [12] training us to renounce ungodliness and worldly passions, and to live self-controlled, upright, and godly lives in the present age, [13] waiting for our blessed hope, the appearing of the glory of our great God and Savior Jesus Christ, [14] who gave himself for us to redeem us from all lawlessness and to purify for himself a people for his own possession who are zealous for good works.

[15] Declare these things; exhort and rebuke with all authority. Let no one disregard you.

Be Ready for Every Good Work

3 Remind them to be submissive to rulers and authorities, to be obedient, to be ready for every good work, [2] to speak evil of no one, to avoid quarreling, to be gentle, and to show perfect courtesy toward all people. [3] For we ourselves were once foolish, disobedient, led astray, slaves to various passions and pleasures, passing our days in malice and envy, hated by others and hating one another. [4] But when the goodness and loving kindness of God our

---

[1] For the contextual rendering of the Greek word *doulos*, see Preface [2] Greek *before times eternal* [3] Or *manifested his word* [4] Or *a man of one woman* [5] Or *are faithful* [6] Or *bishop*; Greek *episkopos* [7] Or *healthy*; also verse 13 [8] Or *especially those of the circumcision* [9] Greek *One of them* [10] Probably from Epimenides of Crete [11] Or *healthy*; also verses 2, 8 [12] For the contextual rendering of the Greek word *doulos*, see Preface

Savior appeared, [5] he saved us, not because of works done by us in righteousness, but according to his own mercy, by the washing of regeneration and renewal of the Holy Spirit, [6] whom he poured out on us richly through Jesus Christ our Savior, [7] so that being justified by his grace we might become heirs according to the hope of eternal life. [8] The saying is trustworthy, and I want you to insist on these things, so that those who have believed in God may be careful to devote themselves to good works. These things are excellent and profitable for people. [9] But avoid foolish controversies, genealogies, dissensions, and quarrels about the law, for they are unprofitable and worthless. [10] As for a person who stirs up division, after warning him once and then twice, have nothing more to do with him, [11] knowing that such a person is warped and sinful; he is self-condemned.

Final Instructions and Greetings

[12] When I send Artemas or Tychicus to you, do your best to come to me at Nicopolis, for I have decided to spend the winter there. [13] Do your best to speed Zenas the lawyer and Apollos on their way; see that they lack nothing. [14] And let our people learn to devote themselves to good works, so as to help cases of urgent need, and not be unfruitful.

[15] All who are with me send greetings to you. Greet those who love us in the faith.

Grace be with you all.

PHILEMON

Greeting

1 Paul, a prisoner for Christ Jesus, and Timothy our brother,

To Philemon our beloved fellow worker **2** and Apphia our sister and Archippus our fellow soldier, and the church in your house:

3 Grace to you and peace from God our Father and the Lord Jesus Christ.

Philemon's Love and Faith

4 I thank my God always when I remember you in my prayers, **5** because I hear of your love and of the faith that you have toward the Lord Jesus and for all the saints, **6** and I pray that the sharing of your faith may become effective for the full knowledge of every good thing that is in us for the sake of Christ.¹ **7** For I have derived much joy and comfort from your love, my brother, because the hearts of the saints have been refreshed through you.

Paul's Plea for Onesimus

8 Accordingly, though I am bold enough in Christ to command you to do what is required, **9** yet for love's sake I prefer to appeal to you— I, Paul, an old man and now a prisoner also for Christ Jesus— **10** I appeal to you for my child, Onesimus,² whose father I became in my imprisonment. **11** (Formerly he was useless to you, but now he is indeed useful to you and to me.) **12** I am sending him back to you, sending my very heart. **13** I would have been glad to keep him with me, in order that he might serve me on your behalf during my imprisonment for the gospel, **14** but I preferred to do nothing without your consent in order that your goodness might not be by compulsion but of your own accord. **15** For this perhaps is why he was parted from you for a while, that you might have him back forever, **16** no longer as a bondservant³ but more than a bondservant, as a beloved brother—especially to me, but how much more to you, both in the flesh and in the Lord.

17 So if you consider me your partner, receive him as you would receive me. **18** If he has wronged you at all, or owes you anything, charge that to my account. **19** I, Paul, write this with my own hand: I will repay it—to say nothing of your owing me even your own self. **20** Yes, brother, I want some benefit from you in the Lord. Refresh my heart in Christ.

21 Confident of your obedience, I write to you, knowing that you will do even more than I say. **22** At the same time, prepare a guest room for me, for I am hoping that through your prayers I will be graciously given to you.

Final Greetings

23 Epaphras, my fellow prisoner in Christ Jesus, sends greetings to you, **24** and so do Mark, Aristarchus, Demas, and Luke, my fellow workers.

25 The grace of the Lord Jesus Christ be with your spirit.

---

¹ Or for *Christ's service* ² *Onesimus* means *useful* (see verse 11) or *beneficial* (see verse 20) ³ For the contextual rendering of the Greek word *doulos*, see Preface; twice in this verse

THE LETTER TO THE
HEBREWS

The Supremacy of God's Son

1 Long ago, at many times and in many ways, God spoke to our fathers by the prophets, [2] but in these last days he has spoken to us by his Son, whom he appointed the heir of all things, through whom also he created the world. [3] He is the radiance of the glory of God and the exact imprint of his nature, and he upholds the universe by the word of his power. After making purification for sins, he sat down at the right hand of the Majesty on high, [4] having become as much superior to angels as the name he has inherited is more excellent than theirs.

[5] For to which of the angels did God ever say,

[a]"You are my Son,
　　today I have begotten you"?

Or again,

[b]"I will be to him a father,
　　and he shall be to me a son"?

[6] And again, when he brings the firstborn into the world, he says,

[c]"Let all God's angels worship him."

[7] Of the angels he says,

[d]"He makes his angels winds,
　　and his ministers a flame of fire."

[8] But of the Son he says,

[e]"Your throne, O God, is forever and ever,
　　the scepter of uprightness is the scepter
　　　of your kingdom.
[9]　You have loved righteousness and hated
　　　wickedness;
　　therefore God, your God, has anointed you
　　　with the oil of gladness beyond your
　　　companions."

[10] And,

[j]"You, Lord, laid the foundation of the earth
　　　in the beginning,
　　and the heavens are the work of your
　　　hands;
[11]　they will perish, but you remain;
　　they will all wear out like a garment,
[12]　like a robe you will roll them up,
　　like a garment they will be changed.[1]
　　But you are the same,
　　　and your years will have no end."

[13] And to which of the angels has he ever said,

[g]"Sit at my right hand
　　until I make your enemies a footstool
　　　for your feet"?

[14] Are they not all ministering spirits sent out to serve for the sake of those who are to inherit salvation?

Warning Against Neglecting Salvation

2 Therefore we must pay much closer attention to what we have heard, lest we drift away from it. [2] For since the message declared by angels proved to be reliable, and every transgression or disobedience received a just retribution, [3] how shall we escape if we neglect such a great salvation? It was declared at first by the Lord, and it was attested to us by those who heard, [4] while God also bore witness by signs and wonders and various miracles and by gifts of the Holy Spirit distributed according to his will.

The Founder of Salvation

[5] For it was not to angels that God subjected the world to come, of which we are speaking. [6] It has been testified somewhere,

[h]"What is man, that you are mindful of him,
　　or the son of man, that you care for
　　　him?
[7]　You made him for a little while lower than
　　　the angels;
　　you have crowned him with glory and
　　　honor,[2]
[8]　putting everything in subjection under
　　　his feet."

Now in putting everything in subjection to him, he left nothing outside his control. At present, we do not yet see everything in subjection to him. [9] But we see him who for a little while was made lower than the angels, namely Jesus, crowned with glory and honor because of the suffering of death, so that by the grace of God he might taste death for everyone.

---

[1] Some manuscripts omit *like a garment* [2] Some manuscripts insert *and set him over the works of your hands* [a] Ps. 2:7 [b] 2 Sam. 7:14 [c] Deut. 32:43 (Gk.) [d] Ps. 104:4 [e] Ps. 45:6, 7 [f] Ps. 102:25-27 [g] Ps. 110:1 [h] Ps. 8:4-6

[10] For it was fitting that he, for whom and by whom all things exist, in bringing many sons to glory, should make the founder of their salvation perfect through suffering. [11] For he who sanctifies and those who are sanctified all have one source.[1] That is why he is not ashamed to call them brothers,[2] [12] saying,

> [a]"I will tell of your name to my brothers;
>   in the midst of the congregation I will
>   sing your praise."

[13] And again,

> "I will put my trust in him."

And again,

> [b]"Behold, I and the children God has given
>   me."

[14] Since therefore the children share in flesh and blood, he himself likewise partook of the same things, that through death he might destroy the one who has the power of death, that is, the devil, [15] and deliver all those who through fear of death were subject to lifelong slavery. [16] For surely it is not angels that he helps, but he helps the offspring of Abraham. [17] Therefore he had to be made like his brothers in every respect, so that he might become a merciful and faithful high priest in the service of God, to make propitiation for the sins of the people. [18] For because he himself has suffered when tempted, he is able to help those who are being tempted.

Jesus Greater Than Moses

3 Therefore, holy brothers,[3] you who share in a heavenly calling, consider Jesus, the apostle and high priest of our confession, [2] who was faithful to him who appointed him, just as Moses also was faithful in all God's[4] house. [3] For Jesus has been counted worthy of more glory than Moses—as much more glory as the builder of a house has more honor than the house itself. [4] (For every house is built by someone, but the builder of all things is God.) [5] Now Moses was faithful in all God's house as a servant, to testify to the things that were to be spoken later, [6] but Christ is faithful over God's house as a son. And we are his house, if indeed we hold fast our confidence and our boasting in our hope.[5]

A Rest for the People of God

[7] Therefore, as the Holy Spirit says,

> [c]"Today, if you hear his voice,
> [8]   do not harden your hearts as in the rebel-
>   lion,
>   on the day of testing in the wilder-
>   ness,
> [9]   where your fathers put me to the test
>   and saw my works for forty years.
> [10]   Therefore I was provoked with that gen-
>   eration,
>   and said, 'They always go astray in their
>   heart;
>   they have not known my ways.'
> [11]   As I swore in my wrath,
>   'They shall not enter my rest.'"

[12] Take care, brothers, lest there be in any of you an evil, unbelieving heart, leading you to fall away from the living God. [13] But exhort one another every day, as long as it is called "today," that none of you may be hardened by the deceitfulness of sin. [14] For we have come to share in Christ, if indeed we hold our original confidence firm to the end. [15] As it is said,

> [d]"Today, if you hear his voice,
>   do not harden your hearts as in the rebel-
>   lion."

[16] For who were those who heard and yet rebelled? Was it not all those who left Egypt led by Moses? [17] And with whom was he provoked for forty years? Was it not with those who sinned, whose bodies fell in the wilderness? [18] And to whom did he swear that they would not enter his rest, but to those who were disobedient? [19] So we see that they were unable to enter because of unbelief.

4 Therefore, while the promise of entering his rest still stands, let us fear lest any of you should seem to have failed to reach it. [2] For good news came to us just as to them, but the message they heard did not benefit them, because they were not united by faith with those who listened.[6] [3] For we who have believed enter that rest, as he has said,

> [e]"As I swore in my wrath,
>   'They shall not enter my rest,'"

[1] Greek *all are of one* [2] Or *brothers and sisters*. In New Testament usage, depending on the context, the plural Greek word *adelphoi* (translated "brothers") may refer either to brothers or to brothers and sisters; also verse 12 [3] Or *brothers and sisters*; also verse 12 [4] Greek *his*; also verses 5, 6 [5] Some manuscripts insert *firm to the end* [6] Some manuscripts *it did not meet with faith in the hearers* [a] Ps. 22:22 [b] Isa. 8:18 [c] Ps. 95:7-11 [d] Ps. 95:7, 8 [e] Ps. 95:11

although his works were finished from the foundation of the world. ⁴For he has somewhere spoken of the seventh day in this way: ᵃ"And God rested on the seventh day from all his works." ⁵And again in this passage he said,

ᵇ"They shall not enter my rest."

⁶Since therefore it remains for some to enter it, and those who formerly received the good news failed to enter because of disobedience, ⁷again he appoints a certain day, "Today," saying through David so long afterward, in the words already quoted,

ᶜ"Today, if you hear his voice,
    do not harden your hearts."

⁸For if Joshua had given them rest, God¹ would not have spoken of another day later on. ⁹So then, there remains a Sabbath rest for the people of God, ¹⁰for whoever has entered God's rest has also rested from his works as God did from his.

¹¹Let us therefore strive to enter that rest, so that no one may fall by the same sort of disobedience. ¹²For the word of God is living and active, sharper than any two-edged sword, piercing to the division of soul and of spirit, of joints and of marrow, and discerning the thoughts and intentions of the heart. ¹³And no creature is hidden from his sight, but all are naked and exposed to the eyes of him to whom we must give account.

Jesus the Great High Priest

¹⁴Since then we have a great high priest who has passed through the heavens, Jesus, the Son of God, let us hold fast our confession. ¹⁵For we do not have a high priest who is unable to sympathize with our weaknesses, but one who in every respect has been tempted as we are, yet without sin. ¹⁶Let us then with confidence draw near to the throne of grace, that we may receive mercy and find grace to help in time of need.

5 For every high priest chosen from among men is appointed to act on behalf of men in relation to God, to offer gifts and sacrifices for sins. ²He can deal gently with the ignorant and wayward, since he himself is beset with weakness. ³Because of this he is obligated to offer sacrifice for his own sins just as he does for those of the people. ⁴And no one takes this honor for himself, but only when called by God, just as Aaron was.

⁵So also Christ did not exalt himself to be made a high priest, but was appointed by him who said to him,

ᵈ"You are my Son,
    today I have begotten you";

⁶as he says also in another place,

ᵉ"You are a priest forever,
    after the order of Melchizedek."

⁷In the days of his flesh, Jesus² offered up prayers and supplications, with loud cries and tears, to him who was able to save him from death, and he was heard because of his reverence. ⁸Although he was a son, he learned obedience through what he suffered. ⁹And being made perfect, he became the source of eternal salvation to all who obey him, ¹⁰being designated by God a high priest after the order of Melchizedek.

Warning Against Apostasy

¹¹About this we have much to say, and it is hard to explain, since you have become dull of hearing. ¹²For though by this time you ought to be teachers, you need someone to teach you again the basic principles of the oracles of God. You need milk, not solid food, ¹³for everyone who lives on milk is unskilled in the word of righteousness, since he is a child. ¹⁴But solid food is for the mature, for those who have their powers of discernment trained by constant practice to distinguish good from evil.

6 Therefore let us leave the elementary doctrine of Christ and go on to maturity, not laying again a foundation of repentance from dead works and of faith toward God, ²and of instruction about washings,³ the laying on of hands, the resurrection of the dead, and eternal judgment. ³And this we will do if God permits. ⁴For it is impossible, in the case of those who have once been enlightened, who have tasted the heavenly gift, and have shared in the Holy Spirit, ⁵and have tasted the goodness of the word of God and the powers of the age to come, ⁶and then have fallen away, to restore them again to repentance, since they are crucifying once again the Son of God to their own harm and holding him up to contempt. ⁷For land that has drunk the rain that often falls on it, and produces a crop useful to those for whose sake it is cultivated, receives a blessing from God. ⁸But if it bears thorns and thistles,

---

¹ Greek he ² Greek he ³ Or baptisms (that is, cleansing rites) ᵃGen. 2:2 ᵇPs. 95:11 ᶜPs. 95:7, 8 ᵈPs. 2:7 ᵉPs. 110:4

it is worthless and near to being cursed, and its end is to be burned.

[9] Though we speak in this way, yet in your case, beloved, we feel sure of better things—things that belong to salvation. [10] For God is not unjust so as to overlook your work and the love that you have shown for his name in serving the saints, as you still do. [11] And we desire each one of you to show the same earnestness to have the full assurance of hope until the end, [12] so that you may not be sluggish, but imitators of those who through faith and patience inherit the promises.

The Certainty of God's Promise

[13] For when God made a promise to Abraham, since he had no one greater by whom to swear, he swore by himself, [14] saying, a "Surely I will bless you and multiply you." [15] And thus Abraham,[1] having patiently waited, obtained the promise. [16] For people swear by something greater than themselves, and in all their disputes an oath is final for confirmation. [17] So when God desired to show more convincingly to the heirs of the promise the unchangeable character of his purpose, he guaranteed it with an oath, [18] so that by two unchangeable things, in which it is impossible for God to lie, we who have fled for refuge might have strong encouragement to hold fast to the hope set before us. [19] We have this as a sure and steadfast anchor of the soul, a hope that enters into the inner place behind the curtain, [20] where Jesus has gone as a forerunner on our behalf, having become a high priest forever after the order of Melchizedek.

The Priestly Order of Melchizedek

7 For this Melchizedek, king of Salem, priest of the Most High God, met Abraham returning from the slaughter of the kings and blessed him, [2] and to him Abraham apportioned a tenth part of everything. He is first, by translation of his name, king of righteousness, and then he is also king of Salem, that is, king of peace. [3] He is without father or mother or genealogy, having neither beginning of days nor end of life, but resembling the Son of God he continues a priest forever.

[4] See how great this man was to whom Abraham the patriarch gave a tenth of the spoils! [5] And those descendants of Levi who receive the priestly office have a commandment in the law to take tithes from the people, that is, from their brothers,[2] though these also are descended from Abraham. [6] But this man who does not have his descent from them received tithes from Abraham and blessed him who had the promises. [7] It is beyond dispute that the inferior is blessed by the superior. [8] In the one case tithes are received by mortal men, but in the other case, by one of whom it is testified that he lives. [9] One might even say that Levi himself, who receives tithes, paid tithes through Abraham, [10] for he was still in the loins of his ancestor when Melchizedek met him.

Jesus Compared to Melchizedek

[11] Now if perfection had been attainable through the Levitical priesthood (for under it the people received the law), what further need would there have been for another priest to arise after the order of Melchizedek, rather than one named after the order of Aaron? [12] For when there is a change in the priesthood, there is necessarily a change in the law as well. [13] For the one of whom these things are spoken belonged to another tribe, from which no one has ever served at the altar. [14] For it is evident that our Lord was descended from Judah, and in connection with that tribe Moses said nothing about priests.

[15] This becomes even more evident when another priest arises in the likeness of Melchizedek, [16] who has become a priest, not on the basis of a legal requirement concerning bodily descent, but by the power of an indestructible life. [17] For it is witnessed of him,

> b "You are a priest forever,
> 　　after the order of Melchizedek."

[18] For on the one hand, a former commandment is set aside because of its weakness and uselessness [19] (for the law made nothing perfect); but on the other hand, a better hope is introduced, through which we draw near to God.

[20] And it was not without an oath. For those who formerly became priests were made such without an oath, [21] but this one was made a priest with an oath by the one who said to him:

> c "The Lord has sworn
> 　　and will not change his mind,
> 　'You are a priest forever.'"

[22] This makes Jesus the guarantor of a better covenant.

[23] The former priests were many in number, because they were prevented by death from continuing in office, [24] but he holds his priesthood

permanently, because he continues forever. [25]Consequently, he is able to save to the uttermost[1] those who draw near to God through him, since he always lives to make intercession for them.

[26]For it was indeed fitting that we should have such a high priest, holy, innocent, unstained, separated from sinners, and exalted above the heavens. [27]He has no need, like those high priests, to offer sacrifices daily, first for his own sins and then for those of the people, since he did this once for all when he offered up himself. [28]For the law appoints men in their weakness as high priests, but the word of the oath, which came later than the law, appoints a Son who has been made perfect forever.

Jesus, High Priest of a Better Covenant

8 Now the point in what we are saying is this: we have such a high priest, one who is seated at the right hand of the throne of the Majesty in heaven, [2]a minister in the holy places, in the true tent[2] that the Lord set up, not man. [3]For every high priest is appointed to offer gifts and sacrifices; thus it is necessary for this priest also to have something to offer. [4]Now if he were on earth, he would not be a priest at all, since there are priests who offer gifts according to the law. [5]They serve a copy and shadow of the heavenly things. For when Moses was about to erect the tent, he was instructed by God, saying, [a]"See that you make everything according to the pattern that was shown you on the mountain." [6]But as it is, Christ[3] has obtained a ministry that is as much more excellent than the old as the covenant he mediates is better, since it is enacted on better promises. [7]For if that first covenant had been faultless, there would have been no occasion to look for a second.

[8]For he finds fault with them when he says:[4]

[b]"Behold, the days are coming, declares the
    Lord,
  when I will establish a new covenant
    with the house of Israel
  and with the house of Judah,
[9] not like the covenant that I made with
    their fathers
  on the day when I took them by the
    hand to bring them out of the
    land of Egypt.

For they did not continue in my cov-
    enant,
  and so I showed no concern for them,
    declares the Lord.
[10] For this is the covenant that I will make
    with the house of Israel
  after those days, declares the Lord:
I will put my laws into their minds,
  and write them on their hearts,
and I will be their God,
  and they shall be my people.
[11] And they shall not teach, each one his
    neighbor
  and each one his brother, saying, 'Know
    the Lord,'
for they shall all know me,
  from the least of them to the greatest.
[12] For I will be merciful toward their iniqui-
    ties,
  and I will remember their sins no
    more."

[13]In speaking of a new covenant, he makes the first one obsolete. And what is becoming obsolete and growing old is ready to vanish away.

The Earthly Holy Place

9 Now even the first covenant had regulations for worship and an earthly place of holiness. [2]For a tent[5] was prepared, the first section, in which were the lampstand and the table and the bread of the Presence.[6] It is called the Holy Place. [3]Behind the second curtain was a second section[7] called the Most Holy Place, [4]having the golden altar of incense and the ark of the covenant covered on all sides with gold, in which was a golden urn holding the manna, and Aaron's staff that budded, and the tablets of the covenant. [5]Above it were the cherubim of glory overshadowing the mercy seat. Of these things we cannot now speak in detail.

[6]These preparations having thus been made, the priests go regularly into the first section, performing their ritual duties, [7]but into the second only the high priest goes, and he but once a year, and not without taking blood, which he offers for himself and for the unintentional sins of the people. [8]By this the Holy Spirit indicates that the way into the holy places is not yet opened as long as the first section is still standing [9](which is symbolic for the present age).[8] According to this arrangement, gifts and sacrifices are offered that cannot perfect the

[1] That is, completely; or at all times [2] Or tabernacle; also verse 5 [3] Greek he [4] Some manuscripts For finding fault with it he says to them [5] Or tabernacle; also verses 11, 21
[6] Greek the presentation of the loaves [7] Greek tent; also verses 6, 8 [8] Or which is symbolic for the age then present [a] Ex. 25:40 [b] Jer. 31:31-34

conscience of the worshiper, [10] but deal only with food and drink and various washings, regulations for the body imposed until the time of reformation.

Redemption Through the Blood of Christ

[11] But when Christ appeared as a high priest of the good things that have come,[1] then through the greater and more perfect tent (not made with hands, that is, not of this creation) [12] he entered once for all into the holy places, not by means of the blood of goats and calves but by means of his own blood, thus securing an eternal redemption. [13] For if the blood of goats and bulls, and the sprinkling of defiled persons with the ashes of a heifer, sanctify[2] for the purification of the flesh, [14] how much more will the blood of Christ, who through the eternal Spirit offered himself without blemish to God, purify our[3] conscience from dead works to serve the living God.

[15] Therefore he is the mediator of a new covenant, so that those who are called may receive the promised eternal inheritance, since a death has occurred that redeems them from the transgressions committed under the first covenant.[4] [16] For where a will is involved, the death of the one who made it must be established. [17] For a will takes effect only at death, since it is not in force as long as the one who made it is alive. [18] Therefore not even the first covenant was inaugurated without blood. [19] For when every commandment of the law had been declared by Moses to all the people, he took the blood of calves and goats, with water and scarlet wool and hyssop, and sprinkled both the book itself and all the people, [20] saying, [a] "This is the blood of the covenant that God commanded for you." [21] And in the same way he sprinkled with the blood both the tent and all the vessels used in worship. [22] Indeed, under the law almost everything is purified with blood, and without the shedding of blood there is no forgiveness of sins.

[23] Thus it was necessary for the copies of the heavenly things to be purified with these rites, but the heavenly things themselves with better sacrifices than these. [24] For Christ has entered, not into holy places made with hands, which are copies of the true things, but into heaven itself, now to appear in the presence of God on our behalf. [25] Nor was it to offer himself repeatedly, as the high priest enters the holy places every year with blood not his own, [26] for then he would have had to suffer repeatedly since the foundation of the world. But as it is, he has appeared once for all at the end of the ages to put away sin by the sacrifice of himself. [27] And just as it is appointed for man to die once, and after that comes judgment, [28] so Christ, having been offered once to bear the sins of many, will appear a second time, not to deal with sin but to save those who are eagerly waiting for him.

Christ's Sacrifice Once for All

10 For since the law has but a shadow of the good things to come instead of the true form of these realities, it can never, by the same sacrifices that are continually offered every year, make perfect those who draw near. [2] Otherwise, would they not have ceased to be offered, since the worshipers, having once been cleansed, would no longer have any consciousness of sins? [3] But in these sacrifices there is a reminder of sins every year. [4] For it is impossible for the blood of bulls and goats to take away sins.

[5] Consequently, when Christ[5] came into the world, he said,

> [b] "Sacrifices and offerings you have not
> 　　desired,
> 　　but a body have you prepared for
> 　　　me;
> [6]　in burnt offerings and sin offerings
> 　　you have taken no pleasure.
> [7]　Then I said, 'Behold, I have come to do
> 　　　your will, O God,
> 　　as it is written of me in the scroll of the
> 　　　book.'"

[8] When he said above, "You have neither desired nor taken pleasure in sacrifices and offerings and burnt offerings and sin offerings" (these are offered according to the law), [9] then he added, "Behold, I have come to do your will." He does away with the first in order to establish the second. [10] And by that will we have been sanctified through the offering of the body of Jesus Christ once for all.

[11] And every priest stands daily at his service, offering repeatedly the same sacrifices, which can never take away sins. [12] But when Christ[6] had offered for all time a single sacrifice for sins,

---

[1] Some manuscripts *good things to come*. [2] Or *For if the sprinkling of defiled persons with the blood of goats and bulls and with the ashes of a heifer sanctifies* [3] Some manuscripts *your* [4] The Greek word means both *covenant* and *will*; also verses 16, 17 [5] Greek *he* [6] Greek *this one* [a] Ex. 24:8 [b] Ps. 40:6-8

he sat down at the right hand of God, [13] waiting from that time until his enemies should be made a footstool for his feet. [14] For by a single offering he has perfected for all time those who are being sanctified.

[15] And the Holy Spirit also bears witness to us; for after saying,

[16] [a] "This is the covenant that I will make with them
after those days, declares the Lord:
I will put my laws on their hearts,
and write them on their minds,"

[17] then he adds,

[b] "I will remember their sins and their lawless deeds no more."

[18] Where there is forgiveness of these, there is no longer any offering for sin.

The Full Assurance of Faith

[19] Therefore, brothers,[1] since we have confidence to enter the holy places by the blood of Jesus, [20] by the new and living way that he opened for us through the curtain, that is, through his flesh, [21] and since we have a great priest over the house of God, [22] let us draw near with a true heart in full assurance of faith, with our hearts sprinkled clean from an evil conscience and our bodies washed with pure water. [23] Let us hold fast the confession of our hope without wavering, for he who promised is faithful. [24] And let us consider how to stir up one another to love and good works, [25] not neglecting to meet together, as is the habit of some, but encouraging one another, and all the more as you see the Day drawing near.

[26] For if we go on sinning deliberately after receiving the knowledge of the truth, there no longer remains a sacrifice for sins, [27] but a fearful expectation of judgment, and a fury of fire that will consume the adversaries. [28] Anyone who has set aside the law of Moses dies without mercy on the evidence of two or three witnesses. [29] How much worse punishment, do you think, will be deserved by the one who has trampled underfoot the Son of God, and has profaned the blood of the covenant by which he was sanctified, and has outraged the Spirit of grace? [30] For we know him who said, [c] "Vengeance is mine; I will repay." And again, [d] "The Lord will judge his people." [31] It is a fearful thing to fall into the hands of the living God.

[32] But recall the former days when, after you were enlightened, you endured a hard struggle with sufferings, [33] sometimes being publicly exposed to reproach and affliction, and sometimes being partners with those so treated. [34] For you had compassion on those in prison, and you joyfully accepted the plundering of your property, since you knew that you yourselves had a better possession and an abiding one. [35] Therefore do not throw away your confidence, which has a great reward. [36] For you have need of endurance, so that when you have done the will of God you may receive what is promised. [37] For,

"Yet a little while,
and [e] the coming one will come and
will not delay;
[38] but my righteous one shall live by faith,
and if he shrinks back,
my soul has no pleasure in him."

[39] But we are not of those who shrink back and are destroyed, but of those who have faith and preserve their souls.

By Faith

11 Now faith is the assurance of things hoped for, the conviction of things not seen. [2] For by it the people of old received their commendation. [3] By faith we understand that the universe was created by the word of God, so that what is seen was not made out of things that are visible.

[4] By faith Abel offered to God a more acceptable sacrifice than Cain, through which he was commended as righteous, God commending him by accepting his gifts. And through his faith, though he died, he still speaks. [5] By faith Enoch was taken up so that he should not see death, and he was not found, because God had taken him. Now before he was taken he was commended as having pleased God. [6] And without faith it is impossible to please him, for whoever would draw near to God must believe that he exists and that he rewards those who seek him. [7] By faith Noah, being warned by God concerning events as yet unseen, in reverent fear constructed an ark for the saving of his household. By this he condemned the world and became an heir of the righteousness that comes by faith.

[8] By faith Abraham obeyed when he was called to go out to a place that he was to receive

---

[1] Or brothers and sisters   [a] Jer. 31:33   [b] Jer. 31:34   [c] Deut. 32:35   [d] Deut. 32:36   [e] Hab. 2:3, 4

as an inheritance. And he went out, not knowing where he was going. [9] By faith he went to live in the land of promise, as in a foreign land, living in tents with Isaac and Jacob, heirs with him of the same promise. [10] For he was looking forward to the city that has foundations, whose designer and builder is God. [11] By faith Sarah herself received power to conceive, even when she was past the age, since she considered him faithful who had promised. [12] Therefore from one man, and him as good as dead, were born descendants as many as the stars of heaven and as many as the innumerable grains of sand by the seashore.

[13] These all died in faith, not having received the things promised, but having seen them and greeted them from afar, and having acknowledged that they were strangers and exiles on the earth. [14] For people who speak thus make it clear that they are seeking a homeland. [15] If they had been thinking of that land from which they had gone out, they would have had opportunity to return. [16] But as it is, they desire a better country, that is, a heavenly one. Therefore God is not ashamed to be called their God, for he has prepared for them a city.

[17] By faith Abraham, when he was tested, offered up Isaac, and he who had received the promises was in the act of offering up his only son, [18] of whom it was said, *a*"Through Isaac shall your offspring be named." [19] He considered that God was able even to raise him from the dead, from which, figuratively speaking, he did receive him back. [20] By faith Isaac invoked future blessings on Jacob and Esau. [21] By faith Jacob, when dying, blessed each of the sons of Joseph, bowing in worship over the head of his staff. [22] By faith Joseph, at the end of his life, made mention of the exodus of the Israelites and gave directions concerning his bones.

[23] By faith Moses, when he was born, was hidden for three months by his parents, because they saw that the child was beautiful, and they were not afraid of the king's edict. [24] By faith Moses, when he was grown up, refused to be called the son of Pharaoh's daughter, [25] choosing rather to be mistreated with the people of God than to enjoy the fleeting pleasures of sin. [26] He considered the reproach of Christ greater wealth than the treasures of Egypt, for he was looking to the reward. [27] By faith he left Egypt, not being afraid of the anger of the king, for he endured as seeing him who is invisible. [28] By

faith he kept the Passover and sprinkled the blood, so that the Destroyer of the firstborn might not touch them.

[29] By faith the people crossed the Red Sea as on dry land, but the Egyptians, when they attempted to do the same, were drowned. [30] By faith the walls of Jericho fell down after they had been encircled for seven days. [31] By faith Rahab the prostitute did not perish with those who were disobedient, because she had given a friendly welcome to the spies.

[32] And what more shall I say? For time would fail me to tell of Gideon, Barak, Samson, Jephthah, of David and Samuel and the prophets— [33] who through faith conquered kingdoms, enforced justice, obtained promises, stopped the mouths of lions, [34] quenched the power of fire, escaped the edge of the sword, were made strong out of weakness, became mighty in war, put foreign armies to flight. [35] Women received back their dead by resurrection. Some were tortured, refusing to accept release, so that they might rise again to a better life. [36] Others suffered mocking and flogging, and even chains and imprisonment. [37] They were stoned, they were sawn in two,[1] they were killed with the sword. They went about in skins of sheep and goats, destitute, afflicted, mistreated— [38] of whom the world was not worthy—wandering about in deserts and mountains, and in dens and caves of the earth.

[39] And all these, though commended through their faith, did not receive what was promised, [40] since God had provided something better for us, that apart from us they should not be made perfect.

Jesus, Founder and Perfecter of Our Faith

12 Therefore, since we are surrounded by so great a cloud of witnesses, let us also lay aside every weight, and sin which clings so closely, and let us run with endurance the race that is set before us, [2] looking to Jesus, the founder and perfecter of our faith, who for the joy that was set before him endured the cross, despising the shame, and is seated at the right hand of the throne of God.

Do Not Grow Weary

[3] Consider him who endured from sinners such hostility against himself, so that you may not grow weary or fainthearted. [4] In your struggle against sin you have not yet resisted to the

---

[1] Some manuscripts add *they were tempted*　*a* Gen. 21:12

point of shedding your blood. ⁵ And have you forgotten the exhortation that addresses you as sons?

> ᵃ"My son, do not regard lightly the discipline of the Lord,
>   nor be weary when reproved by him.
> ⁶   For the Lord disciplines the one he loves,
>   and chastises every son whom he receives."

⁷ It is for discipline that you have to endure. God is treating you as sons. For what son is there whom his father does not discipline? ⁸ If you are left without discipline, in which all have participated, then you are illegitimate children and not sons. ⁹ Besides this, we have had earthly fathers who disciplined us and we respected them. Shall we not much more be subject to the Father of spirits and live? ¹⁰ For they disciplined us for a short time as it seemed best to them, but he disciplines us for our good, that we may share his holiness. ¹¹ For the moment all discipline seems painful rather than pleasant, but later it yields the peaceful fruit of righteousness to those who have been trained by it.

¹² Therefore lift your drooping hands and strengthen your weak knees, ¹³ and make straight paths for your feet, so that what is lame may not be put out of joint but rather be healed. ¹⁴ Strive for peace with everyone, and for the holiness without which no one will see the Lord. ¹⁵ See to it that no one fails to obtain the grace of God; that no "root of bitterness" springs up and causes trouble, and by it many become defiled; ¹⁶ that no one is sexually immoral or unholy like Esau, who sold his birthright for a single meal. ¹⁷ For you know that afterward, when he desired to inherit the blessing, he was rejected, for he found no chance to repent, though he sought it with tears.

A Kingdom That Cannot Be Shaken

¹⁸ For you have not come to what may be touched, a blazing fire and darkness and gloom and a tempest ¹⁹ and the sound of a trumpet and a voice whose words made the hearers beg that no further messages be spoken to them. ²⁰ For they could not endure the order that was given, ᵇ"If even a beast touches the mountain, it shall be stoned." ²¹ Indeed, so terrifying was the sight that Moses said, "I tremble with fear." ²² But you have come to Mount Zion and to the city of the living God, the heavenly Jerusalem,

and to innumerable angels in festal gathering, ²³ and to the assembly¹ of the firstborn who are enrolled in heaven, and to God, the judge of all, and to the spirits of the righteous made perfect, ²⁴ and to Jesus, the mediator of a new covenant, and to the sprinkled blood that speaks a better word than the blood of Abel.

²⁵ See that you do not refuse him who is speaking. For if they did not escape when they refused him who warned them on earth, much less will we escape if we reject him who warns from heaven. ²⁶ At that time his voice shook the earth, but now he has promised, ᶜ"Yet once more I will shake not only the earth but also the heavens." ²⁷ This phrase, "Yet once more," indicates the removal of things that are shaken—that is, things that have been made— in order that the things that cannot be shaken may remain. ²⁸ Therefore let us be grateful for receiving a kingdom that cannot be shaken, and thus let us offer to God acceptable worship, with reverence and awe, ²⁹ for our God is a consuming fire.

Sacrifices Pleasing to God

13 Let brotherly love continue. ² Do not neglect to show hospitality to strangers, for thereby some have entertained angels unawares. ³ Remember those who are in prison, as though in prison with them, and those who are mistreated, since you also are in the body. ⁴ Let marriage be held in honor among all, and let the marriage bed be undefiled, for God will judge the sexually immoral and adulterous. ⁵ Keep your life free from love of money, and be content with what you have, for he has said, ᵈ"I will never leave you nor forsake you." ⁶ So we can confidently say,

> ᵉ"The Lord is my helper;
>   I will not fear;
>   what can man do to me?"

⁷ Remember your leaders, those who spoke to you the word of God. Consider the outcome of their way of life, and imitate their faith. ⁸ Jesus Christ is the same yesterday and today and forever. ⁹ Do not be led away by diverse and strange teachings, for it is good for the heart to be strengthened by grace, not by foods, which have not benefited those devoted to them. ¹⁰ We have an altar from which those who serve the tent² have no right to eat. ¹¹ For the bodies of those animals whose blood is brought into the

holy places by the high priest as a sacrifice for sin are burned outside the camp. [12] So Jesus also suffered outside the gate in order to sanctify the people through his own blood. [13] Therefore let us go to him outside the camp and bear the reproach he endured. [14] For here we have no lasting city, but we seek the city that is to come. [15] Through him then let us continually offer up a sacrifice of praise to God, that is, the fruit of lips that acknowledge his name. [16] Do not neglect to do good and to share what you have, for such sacrifices are pleasing to God.

[17] Obey your leaders and submit to them, for they are keeping watch over your souls, as those who will have to give an account. Let them do this with joy and not with groaning, for that would be of no advantage to you.

[18] Pray for us, for we are sure that we have a clear conscience, desiring to act honorably in all things. [19] I urge you the more earnestly to do this in order that I may be restored to you the sooner.

Benediction

[20] Now may the God of peace who brought again from the dead our Lord Jesus, the great shepherd of the sheep, by the blood of the eternal covenant, [21] equip you with everything good that you may do his will, working in us[1] that which is pleasing in his sight, through Jesus Christ, to whom be glory forever and ever. Amen.

Final Greetings

[22] I appeal to you, brothers,[2] bear with my word of exhortation, for I have written to you briefly. [23] You should know that our brother Timothy has been released, with whom I shall see you if he comes soon. [24] Greet all your leaders and all the saints. Those who come from Italy send you greetings. [25] Grace be with all of you.

---

[1] Some manuscripts you [2] Or brothers and sisters

THE LETTER OF
JAMES

Greeting

1 James, a servant[1] of God and of the Lord Jesus Christ,

To the twelve tribes in the Dispersion:

Greetings.

Testing of Your Faith

2 Count it all joy, my brothers,[2] when you meet trials of various kinds, 3 for you know that the testing of your faith produces steadfastness. 4 And let steadfastness have its full effect, that you may be perfect and complete, lacking in nothing.

5 If any of you lacks wisdom, let him ask God, who gives generously to all without reproach, and it will be given him. 6 But let him ask in faith, with no doubting, for the one who doubts is like a wave of the sea that is driven and tossed by the wind. 7 For that person must not suppose that he will receive anything from the Lord; 8 he is a double-minded man, unstable in all his ways.

9 Let the lowly brother boast in his exaltation, 10 and the rich in his humiliation, because like a flower of the grass[3] he will pass away. 11 For the sun rises with its scorching heat and withers the grass; its flower falls, and its beauty perishes. So also will the rich man fade away in the midst of his pursuits.

12 Blessed is the man who remains steadfast under trial, for when he has stood the test he will receive the crown of life, which God has promised to those who love him. 13 Let no one say when he is tempted, "I am being tempted by God," for God cannot be tempted with evil, and he himself tempts no one. 14 But each person is tempted when he is lured and enticed by his own desire. 15 Then desire when it has conceived gives birth to sin, and sin when it is fully grown brings forth death.

16 Do not be deceived, my beloved brothers. 17 Every good gift and every perfect gift is from above, coming down from the Father of lights, with whom there is no variation or shadow due to change.[4] 18 Of his own will he brought us forth by the word of truth, that we should be a kind of firstfruits of his creatures.

Hearing and Doing the Word

19 Know this, my beloved brothers: let every person be quick to hear, slow to speak, slow to anger; 20 for the anger of man does not produce the righteousness of God. 21 Therefore put away all filthiness and rampant wickedness and receive with meekness the implanted word, which is able to save your souls.

22 But be doers of the word, and not hearers only, deceiving yourselves. 23 For if anyone is a hearer of the word and not a doer, he is like a man who looks intently at his natural face in a mirror. 24 For he looks at himself and goes away and at once forgets what he was like. 25 But the one who looks into the perfect law, the law of liberty, and perseveres, being no hearer who forgets but a doer who acts, he will be blessed in his doing.

26 If anyone thinks he is religious and does not bridle his tongue but deceives his heart, this person's religion is worthless. 27 Religion that is pure and undefiled before God the Father is this: to visit orphans and widows in their affliction, and to keep oneself unstained from the world.

The Sin of Partiality

2 My brothers,[5] show no partiality as you hold the faith in our Lord Jesus Christ, the Lord of glory. 2 For if a man wearing a gold ring and fine clothing comes into your assembly, and a poor man in shabby clothing also comes in, 3 and if you pay attention to the one who wears the fine clothing and say, "You sit here in a good place," while you say to the poor man, "You stand over there," or, "Sit down at my feet," 4 have you not then made distinctions among yourselves and become judges with evil thoughts? 5 Listen, my beloved brothers, has not God chosen those who are poor in the world to be rich in faith and heirs of the kingdom, which he has promised to those who love him? 6 But you have dishonored the poor man. Are not the rich the ones who oppress you, and the ones who drag you into court? 7 Are they not the ones who blaspheme the honorable name by which you were called?

[1] For the contextual rendering of the Greek word *doulos*, see Preface [2] Or *brothers and sisters*. In New Testament usage, depending on the context, the plural Greek word *adelphoi* (translated "brothers") may refer either to *brothers* or to *brothers and sisters*; also verses 16, 19 [3] Or *a wild flower* [4] Some manuscripts *variation due to a shadow of turning* [5] Or *brothers and sisters*; also verses 5, 14

[8] If you really fulfill the royal law according to the Scripture, [a]"You shall love your neighbor as yourself," you are doing well. [9] But if you show partiality, you are committing sin and are convicted by the law as transgressors. [10] For whoever keeps the whole law but fails in one point has become guilty of all of it. [11] For he who said, [b]"Do not commit adultery," also said, [c]"Do not murder." If you do not commit adultery but do murder, you have become a transgressor of the law. [12] So speak and so act as those who are to be judged under the law of liberty. [13] For judgment is without mercy to one who has shown no mercy. Mercy triumphs over judgment.

Faith Without Works Is Dead

[14] What good is it, my brothers, if someone says he has faith but does not have works? Can that faith save him? [15] If a brother or sister is poorly clothed and lacking in daily food, [16] and one of you says to them, "Go in peace, be warmed and filled," without giving them the things needed for the body, what good[1] is that? [17] So also faith by itself, if it does not have works, is dead.

[18] But someone will say, "You have faith and I have works." Show me your faith apart from your works, and I will show you my faith by my works. [19] You believe that God is one; you do well. Even the demons believe—and shudder! [20] Do you want to be shown, you foolish person, that faith apart from works is useless? [21] Was not Abraham our father justified by works when he offered up his son Isaac on the altar? [22] You see that faith was active along with his works, and faith was completed by his works; [23] and the Scripture was fulfilled that says, [d]"Abraham believed God, and it was counted to him as righteousness"—and he was called a friend of God. [24] You see that a person is justified by works and not by faith alone. [25] And in the same way was not also Rahab the prostitute justified by works when she received the messengers and sent them out by another way? [26] For as the body apart from the spirit is dead, so also faith apart from works is dead.

Taming the Tongue

3 Not many of you should become teachers, my brothers, for you know that we who teach will be judged with greater strictness. [2] For we all stumble in many ways. And if anyone does not stumble in what he says, he is a perfect man, able also to bridle his whole body. [3] If we put bits into the mouths of horses so that they obey us, we guide their whole bodies as well. [4] Look at the ships also: though they are so large and are driven by strong winds, they are guided by a very small rudder wherever the will of the pilot directs. [5] So also the tongue is a small member, yet it boasts of great things.

How great a forest is set ablaze by such a small fire! [6] And the tongue is a fire, a world of unrighteousness. The tongue is set among our members, staining the whole body, setting on fire the entire course of life,[2] and set on fire by hell.[3] [7] For every kind of beast and bird, of reptile and sea creature, can be tamed and has been tamed by mankind, [8] but no human being can tame the tongue. It is a restless evil, full of deadly poison. [9] With it we bless our Lord and Father, and with it we curse people who are made in the likeness of God. [10] From the same mouth come blessing and cursing. My brothers,[4] these things ought not to be so. [11] Does a spring pour forth from the same opening both fresh and salt water? [12] Can a fig tree, my brothers, bear olives, or a grapevine produce figs? Neither can a salt pond yield fresh water.

Wisdom from Above

[13] Who is wise and understanding among you? By his good conduct let him show his works in the meekness of wisdom. [14] But if you have bitter jealousy and selfish ambition in your hearts, do not boast and be false to the truth. [15] This is not the wisdom that comes down from above, but is earthly, unspiritual, demonic. [16] For where jealousy and selfish ambition exist, there will be disorder and every vile practice. [17] But the wisdom from above is first pure, then peaceable, gentle, open to reason, full of mercy and good fruits, impartial and sincere. [18] And a harvest of righteousness is sown in peace by those who make peace.

Warning Against Worldliness

4 What causes quarrels and what causes fights among you? Is it not this, that your passions[5] are at war within you?[6] [2] You desire and do not have, so you murder. You covet and cannot obtain, so you fight and quarrel. You do not have, because you do not ask. [3] You ask and do not receive, because you ask wrongly, to spend it on your passions. [4] You adulterous people![7] Do

---

[1] Or benefit [2] Or wheel of birth [3] Greek Gehenna [4] Or brothers and sisters; also verse 12 [5] Greek pleasures; also verse 3 [6] Greek in your members [7] Or You adulteresses! [a] Lev. 19:18 [b] Ex. 20:14 [c] Ex. 20:13 [d] Gen. 15:6

you not know that friendship with the world is enmity with God? Therefore whoever wishes to be a friend of the world makes himself an enemy of God. [5] Or do you suppose it is to no purpose that the Scripture says, "He yearns jealously over the spirit that he has made to dwell in us"? [6] But he gives more grace. Therefore it says, [a] "God opposes the proud but gives grace to the humble." [7] Submit yourselves therefore to God. Resist the devil, and he will flee from you. [8] Draw near to God, and he will draw near to you. Cleanse your hands, you sinners, and purify your hearts, you double-minded. [9] Be wretched and mourn and weep. Let your laughter be turned to mourning and your joy to gloom. [10] Humble yourselves before the Lord, and he will exalt you.

[11] Do not speak evil against one another, brothers.[1] The one who speaks against a brother or judges his brother, speaks evil against the law and judges the law. But if you judge the law, you are not a doer of the law but a judge. [12] There is only one lawgiver and judge, he who is able to save and to destroy. But who are you to judge your neighbor?

Boasting About Tomorrow

[13] Come now, you who say, "Today or tomorrow we will go into such and such a town and spend a year there and trade and make a profit"— [14] yet you do not know what tomorrow will bring. What is your life? For you are a mist that appears for a little time and then vanishes. [15] Instead you ought to say, "If the Lord wills, we will live and do this or that." [16] As it is, you boast in your arrogance. All such boasting is evil. [17] So whoever knows the right thing to do and fails to do it, for him it is sin.

Warning to the Rich

5 Come now, you rich, weep and howl for the miseries that are coming upon you. [2] Your riches have rotted and your garments are motheaten. [3] Your gold and silver have corroded, and their corrosion will be evidence against you and will eat your flesh like fire. You have laid up treasure in the last days. [4] Behold, the wages of the laborers who mowed your fields, which you kept back by fraud, are crying out against you, and the cries of the harvesters have reached the ears of the Lord of hosts. [5] You have lived on the earth in luxury and in self-indulgence. You have fattened your hearts in a day of slaughter. [6] You have condemned and murdered the righteous person. He does not resist you.

Patience in Suffering

[7] Be patient, therefore, brothers,[2] until the coming of the Lord. See how the farmer waits for the precious fruit of the earth, being patient about it, until it receives the early and the late rains. [8] You also, be patient. Establish your hearts, for the coming of the Lord is at hand. [9] Do not grumble against one another, brothers, so that you may not be judged; behold, the Judge is standing at the door. [10] As an example of suffering and patience, brothers, take the prophets who spoke in the name of the Lord. [11] Behold, we consider those blessed who remained steadfast. You have heard of the steadfastness of Job, and you have seen the purpose of the Lord, how the Lord is compassionate and merciful.

[12] But above all, my brothers, do not swear, either by heaven or by earth or by any other oath, but let your "yes" be yes and your "no" be no, so that you may not fall under condemnation.

The Prayer of Faith

[13] Is anyone among you suffering? Let him pray. Is anyone cheerful? Let him sing praise. [14] Is anyone among you sick? Let him call for the elders of the church, and let them pray over him, anointing him with oil in the name of the Lord. [15] And the prayer of faith will save the one who is sick, and the Lord will raise him up. And if he has committed sins, he will be forgiven. [16] Therefore, confess your sins to one another and pray for one another, that you may be healed. The prayer of a righteous person has great power as it is working.[3] [17] Elijah was a man with a nature like ours, and he prayed fervently that it might not rain, and for three years and six months it did not rain on the earth. [18] Then he prayed again, and heaven gave rain, and the earth bore its fruit.

[19] My brothers, if anyone among you wanders from the truth and someone brings him back, [20] let him know that whoever brings back a sinner from his wandering will save his soul from death and will cover a multitude of sins.

---

[1] Or brothers and sisters [2] Or brothers and sisters; also verses 9, 10, 12, 19 [3] Or The effective prayer of a righteous person has great power [a] Prov. 3:34

1 PETER

Greeting

1 Peter, an apostle of Jesus Christ,

To those who are elect exiles of the Dispersion in Pontus, Galatia, Cappadocia, Asia, and Bithynia, ²according to the foreknowledge of God the Father, in the sanctification of the Spirit, for obedience to Jesus Christ and for sprinkling with his blood:

May grace and peace be multiplied to you.

Born Again to a Living Hope

³Blessed be the God and Father of our Lord Jesus Christ! According to his great mercy, he has caused us to be born again to a living hope through the resurrection of Jesus Christ from the dead, ⁴to an inheritance that is imperishable, undefiled, and unfading, kept in heaven for you, ⁵who by God's power are being guarded through faith for a salvation ready to be revealed in the last time. ⁶In this you rejoice, though now for a little while, if necessary, you have been grieved by various trials, ⁷so that the tested genuineness of your faith—more precious than gold that perishes though it is tested by fire—may be found to result in praise and glory and honor at the revelation of Jesus Christ. ⁸Though you have not seen him, you love him. Though you do not now see him, you believe in him and rejoice with joy that is inexpressible and filled with glory, ⁹obtaining the outcome of your faith, the salvation of your souls.

¹⁰Concerning this salvation, the prophets who prophesied about the grace that was to be yours searched and inquired carefully, ¹¹inquiring what person or time¹ the Spirit of Christ in them was indicating when he predicted the sufferings of Christ and the subsequent glories. ¹²It was revealed to them that they were serving not themselves but you, in the things that have now been announced to you through those who preached the good news to you by the Holy Spirit sent from heaven, things into which angels long to look.

Called to Be Holy

¹³Therefore, preparing your minds for action,² and being sober-minded, set your hope fully on the grace that will be brought to you at the revelation of Jesus Christ. ¹⁴As obedient children, do not be conformed to the passions of your former ignorance, ¹⁵but as he who called you is holy, you also be holy in all your conduct, ¹⁶since it is written, ᵃ"You shall be holy, for I am holy." ¹⁷And if you call on him as Father who judges impartially according to each one's deeds, conduct yourselves with fear throughout the time of your exile, ¹⁸knowing that you were ransomed from the futile ways inherited from your forefathers, not with perishable things such as silver or gold, ¹⁹but with the precious blood of Christ, like that of a lamb without blemish or spot. ²⁰He was foreknown before the foundation of the world but was made manifest in the last times for the sake of you ²¹who through him are believers in God, who raised him from the dead and gave him glory, so that your faith and hope are in God.

²²Having purified your souls by your obedience to the truth for a sincere brotherly love, love one another earnestly from a pure heart, ²³since you have been born again, not of perishable seed but of imperishable, through the living and abiding word of God; ²⁴for

ᵇ"All flesh is like grass
and all its glory like the flower of
    grass.
The grass withers,
    and the flower falls,
²⁵ but the word of the Lord remains forever."

And this word is the good news that was preached to you.

A Living Stone and a Holy People

2 So put away all malice and all deceit and hypocrisy and envy and all slander. ²Like newborn infants, long for the pure spiritual milk, that by it you may grow up into salvation—³if indeed you have tasted that the Lord is good.

⁴As you come to him, a living stone rejected by men but in the sight of God chosen and precious, ⁵you yourselves like living stones are being built up as a spiritual house, to be a holy priesthood, to offer spiritual sacrifices acceptable to God through Jesus Christ. ⁶For it stands in Scripture:

---

¹ Or what time or circumstances ² Greek girding up the loins of your mind ᵃ Lev. 11:44 ᵇ Isa. 40:6, 8

^a"Behold, I am laying in Zion a stone,
 a cornerstone chosen and precious,
and whoever believes in him will not be
 put to shame."

⁷So the honor is for you who believe, but for
those who do not believe,

^b"The stone that the builders rejected
 has become the cornerstone,"¹

⁸and

^c"A stone of stumbling,
 and a rock of offense."

They stumble because they disobey the word,
as they were destined to do.
 ⁹But you are a chosen race, a royal priesthood,
a holy nation, a people for his own possession,
that you may proclaim the excellencies of him
who called you out of darkness into his marvelous light. ¹⁰Once you were not a people, but now
you are God's people; once you had not received
mercy, but now you have received mercy.
 ¹¹Beloved, I urge you as sojourners and exiles
to abstain from the passions of the flesh, which
wage war against your soul. ¹²Keep your conduct among the Gentiles honorable, so that
when they speak against you as evildoers, they
may see your good deeds and glorify God on
the day of visitation.

Submission to Authority

¹³Be subject for the Lord's sake to every human
institution,² whether it be to the emperor³ as
supreme, ¹⁴or to governors as sent by him to punish those who do evil and to praise those who do
good. ¹⁵For this is the will of God, that by doing
good you should put to silence the ignorance of
foolish people. ¹⁶Live as people who are free, not
using your freedom as a cover-up for evil, but liv-
ing as servants⁴ of God. ¹⁷Honor everyone. Love
the brotherhood. Fear God. Honor the emperor.
 ¹⁸Servants, be subject to your masters with
all respect, not only to the good and gentle but
also to the unjust. ¹⁹For this is a gracious thing,
when, mindful of God, one endures sorrows
while suffering unjustly. ²⁰For what credit is
it if, when you sin and are beaten for it, you
endure? But if when you do good and suffer
for it you endure, this is a gracious thing in the
sight of God. ²¹For to this you have been called,
because Christ also suffered for you, leaving you
an example, so that you might follow in his

steps. ²²He committed no sin, neither was deceit
found in his mouth. ²³When he was reviled,
he did not revile in return; when he suffered,
he did not threaten, but continued entrusting
himself to him who judges justly. ²⁴He himself
bore our sins in his body on the tree, that we
might die to sin and live to righteousness. By
his wounds you have been healed. ²⁵For you
were straying like sheep, but have now returned
to the Shepherd and Overseer of your souls.

Wives and Husbands

3 Likewise, wives, be subject to your own
 husbands, so that even if some do not obey
the word, they may be won without a word by
the conduct of their wives, ²when they see your
respectful and pure conduct. ³Do not let your
adorning be external—the braiding of hair and
the putting on of gold jewelry, or the clothing
you wear— ⁴but let your adorning be the hidden person of the heart with the imperishable
beauty of a gentle and quiet spirit, which in
God's sight is very precious. ⁵For this is how the
holy women who hoped in God used to adorn
themselves, by submitting to their own husbands, ⁶as Sarah obeyed Abraham, calling him
lord. And you are her children, if you do good
and do not fear anything that is frightening.
 ⁷Likewise, husbands, live with your wives
in an understanding way, showing honor to
the woman as the weaker vessel, since they are
heirs with you⁵ of the grace of life, so that your
prayers may not be hindered.

Suffering for Righteousness' Sake

⁸Finally, all of you, have unity of mind,
sympathy, brotherly love, a tender heart, and
a humble mind. ⁹Do not repay evil for evil or
reviling for reviling, but on the contrary, bless,
for to this you were called, that you may obtain
a blessing. ¹⁰For

^d"Whoever desires to love life
 and see good days,
 let him keep his tongue from evil
 and his lips from speaking deceit;
¹¹ let him turn away from evil and do good;
 let him seek peace and pursue it.
¹² For the eyes of the Lord are on the righ-
 teous,
 and his ears are open to their prayer.
 But the face of the Lord is against those
 who do evil."

[13] Now who is there to harm you if you are zealous for what is good? [14] But even if you should suffer for righteousness' sake, you will be blessed. Have no fear of them, nor be troubled, [15] but in your hearts honor Christ the Lord as holy, always being prepared to make a defense to anyone who asks you for a reason for the hope that is in you; yet do it with gentleness and respect, [16] having a good conscience, so that, when you are slandered, those who revile your good behavior in Christ may be put to shame. [17] For it is better to suffer for doing good, if that should be God's will, than for doing evil.

[18] For Christ also suffered[1] once for sins, the righteous for the unrighteous, that he might bring us to God, being put to death in the flesh but made alive in the spirit, [19] in which[2] he went and proclaimed[3] to the spirits in prison, [20] because[4] they formerly did not obey, when God's patience waited in the days of Noah, while the ark was being prepared, in which a few, that is, eight persons, were brought safely through water. [21] Baptism, which corresponds to this, now saves you, not as a removal of dirt from the body but as an appeal to God for a good conscience, through the resurrection of Jesus Christ, [22] who has gone into heaven and is at the right hand of God, with angels, authorities, and powers having been subjected to him.

Stewards of God's Grace

4 Since therefore Christ suffered in the flesh,[5] arm yourselves with the same way of thinking, for whoever has suffered in the flesh has ceased from sin, [2] so as to live for the rest of the time in the flesh no longer for human passions but for the will of God. [3] For the time that is past suffices for doing what the Gentiles want to do, living in sensuality, passions, drunkenness, orgies, drinking parties, and lawless idolatry. [4] With respect to this they are surprised when you do not join them in the same flood of debauchery, and they malign you; [5] but they will give account to him who is ready to judge the living and the dead. [6] For this is why the gospel was preached even to those who are dead, that though judged in the flesh the way people are, they might live in the spirit the way God does.

[7] The end of all things is at hand; therefore be self-controlled and sober-minded for the sake of your prayers. [8] Above all, keep loving one another earnestly, since love covers a multitude of sins. [9] Show hospitality to one another without grumbling. [10] As each has received a gift, use it to serve one another, as good stewards of God's varied grace: [11] whoever speaks, as one who speaks oracles of God; whoever serves, as one who serves by the strength that God supplies—in order that in everything God may be glorified through Jesus Christ. To him belong glory and dominion forever and ever. Amen.

Suffering as a Christian

[12] Beloved, do not be surprised at the fiery trial when it comes upon you to test you, as though something strange were happening to you. [13] But rejoice insofar as you share Christ's sufferings, that you may also rejoice and be glad when his glory is revealed. [14] If you are insulted for the name of Christ, you are blessed, because the Spirit of glory[6] and of God rests upon you. [15] But let none of you suffer as a murderer or a thief or an evildoer or as a meddler. [16] Yet if anyone suffers as a Christian, let him not be ashamed, but let him glorify God in that name. [17] For it is time for judgment to begin at the household of God; and if it begins with us, what will be the outcome for those who do not obey the gospel of God? [18] And

> "If the righteous is scarcely saved,
> 　　what will become of the ungodly and
> 　　　　the sinner?"[7]

[19] Therefore let those who suffer according to God's will entrust their souls to a faithful Creator while doing good.

Shepherd the Flock of God

5 So I exhort the elders among you, as a fellow elder and a witness of the sufferings of Christ, as well as a partaker in the glory that is going to be revealed: [2] shepherd the flock of God that is among you, exercising oversight,[8] not under compulsion, but willingly, as God would have you;[9] not for shameful gain, but eagerly; [3] not domineering over those in your charge, but being examples to the flock. [4] And when the chief Shepherd appears, you will receive the unfading crown of glory. [5] Likewise, you who are younger, be subject to the elders. Clothe yourselves, all of you, with humility toward one another, for "God opposes the proud but gives grace to the humble."

---

[1] Some manuscripts *died* [2] Or *the Spirit, in whom* [3] Or *preached* [4] Or *when* [5] Some manuscripts add *for us; some for you* [6] Some manuscripts insert *and of power* [7] Greek *where will the ungodly and sinner appear?* [8] Some manuscripts omit *exercising oversight* [9] Some manuscripts omit *as God would have you*

⁶ Humble yourselves, therefore, under the mighty hand of God so that at the proper time he may exalt you, ⁷ casting all your anxieties on him, because he cares for you. ⁸ Be sober-minded; be watchful. Your adversary the devil prowls around like a roaring lion, seeking someone to devour. ⁹ Resist him, firm in your faith, knowing that the same kinds of suffering are being experienced by your brotherhood throughout the world. ¹⁰ And after you have suffered a little while, the God of all grace, who has called you to his eternal glory in Christ, will himself restore, confirm, strengthen, and establish you. ¹¹ To him be the dominion forever and ever. Amen.

Final Greetings

¹² By Silvanus, a faithful brother as I regard him, I have written briefly to you, exhorting and declaring that this is the true grace of God. Stand firm in it. ¹³ She who is at Babylon, who is likewise chosen, sends you greetings, and so does Mark, my son. ¹⁴ Greet one another with the kiss of love.

Peace to all of you who are in Christ.

2 PETER

Greeting

1 Simeon[1] Peter, a servant[2] and apostle of Jesus Christ,

To those who have obtained a faith of equal standing with ours by the righteousness of our God and Savior Jesus Christ:

[2] May grace and peace be multiplied to you in the knowledge of God and of Jesus our Lord.

Confirm Your Calling and Election

[3] His divine power has granted to us all things that pertain to life and godliness, through the knowledge of him who called us to[3] his own glory and excellence,[4] [4] by which he has granted to us his precious and very great promises, so that through them you may become partakers of the divine nature, having escaped from the corruption that is in the world because of sinful desire. [5] For this very reason, make every effort to supplement your faith with virtue,[5] and virtue with knowledge, [6] and knowledge with self-control, and self-control with steadfastness, and steadfastness with godliness, [7] and godliness with brotherly affection, and brotherly affection with love. [8] For if these qualities[6] are yours and are increasing, they keep you from being ineffective or unfruitful in the knowledge of our Lord Jesus Christ. [9] For whoever lacks these qualities is so nearsighted that he is blind, having forgotten that he was cleansed from his former sins. [10] Therefore, brothers,[7] be all the more diligent to confirm your calling and election, for if you practice these qualities you will never fall. [11] For in this way there will be richly provided for you an entrance into the eternal kingdom of our Lord and Savior Jesus Christ.

[12] Therefore I intend always to remind you of these qualities, though you know them and are established in the truth that you have. [13] I think it right, as long as I am in this body,[8] to stir you up by way of reminder, [14] since I know that the putting off of my body will be soon, as our Lord Jesus Christ made clear to me. [15] And I will make every effort so that after my departure you may be able at any time to recall these things.

Christ's Glory and the Prophetic Word

[16] For we did not follow cleverly devised myths when we made known to you the power and coming of our Lord Jesus Christ, but we were eyewitnesses of his majesty. [17] For when he received honor and glory from God the Father, and the voice was borne to him by the Majestic Glory, "This is my beloved Son,[9] with whom I am well pleased," [18] we ourselves heard this very voice borne from heaven, for we were with him on the holy mountain. [19] And we have the prophetic word more fully confirmed, to which you will do well to pay attention as to a lamp shining in a dark place, until the day dawns and the morning star rises in your hearts, [20] knowing this first of all, that no prophecy of Scripture comes from someone's own interpretation. [21] For no prophecy was ever produced by the will of man, but men spoke from God as they were carried along by the Holy Spirit.

False Prophets and Teachers

2 But false prophets also arose among the people, just as there will be false teachers among you, who will secretly bring in destructive heresies, even denying the Master who bought them, bringing upon themselves swift destruction. [2] And many will follow their sensuality, and because of them the way of truth will be blasphemed. [3] And in their greed they will exploit you with false words. Their condemnation from long ago is not idle, and their destruction is not asleep.

[4] For if God did not spare angels when they sinned, but cast them into hell[10] and committed them to chains[11] of gloomy darkness to be kept until the judgment; [5] if he did not spare the ancient world, but preserved Noah, a herald of righteousness, with seven others, when he brought a flood upon the world of the ungodly; [6] if by turning the cities of Sodom and Gomorrah to ashes he condemned them to extinction, making them an example of what is going to happen to the ungodly;[12] [7] and if he rescued righteous Lot, greatly distressed by the sensual conduct of the wicked [8] (for as that

[1] Some manuscripts *Simon* [2] For the contextual rendering of the Greek word *doulos*, see Preface [3] Or *by* [4] Or *virtue* [5] Or *excellence*; twice in this verse [6] Greek *these things*; also verses 9, 10, 12 [7] Or *brothers and sisters*. In New Testament usage, depending on the context, the plural Greek word *adelphoi* (translated "brothers") may refer either to *brothers* or to *brothers and sisters* [8] Greek *tent*; also verse 14 [9] Or *my Son, my (or the) Beloved* [10] Greek *Tartarus* [11] Some manuscripts *pits* [12] Some manuscripts *an example to those who were to be ungodly*

righteous man lived among them day after day, he was tormenting his righteous soul over their lawless deeds that he saw and heard); [9] then the Lord knows how to rescue the godly from trials,[1] and to keep the unrighteous under punishment until the day of judgment, [10] and especially those who indulge[2] in the lust of defiling passion and despise authority.

Bold and willful, they do not tremble as they blaspheme the glorious ones, [11] whereas angels, though greater in might and power, do not pronounce a blasphemous judgment against them before the Lord. [12] But these, like irrational animals, creatures of instinct, born to be caught and destroyed, blaspheming about matters of which they are ignorant, will also be destroyed in their destruction, [13] suffering wrong as the wage for their wrongdoing. They count it pleasure to revel in the daytime. They are blots and blemishes, reveling in their deceptions,[3] while they feast with you. [14] They have eyes full of adultery,[4] insatiable for sin. They entice unsteady souls. They have hearts trained in greed. Accursed children! [15] Forsaking the right way, they have gone astray. They have followed the way of Balaam, the son of Beor, who loved gain from wrongdoing, [16] but was rebuked for his own transgression; a speechless donkey spoke with human voice and restrained the prophet's madness.

[17] These are waterless springs and mists driven by a storm. For them the gloom of utter darkness has been reserved. [18] For, speaking loud boasts of folly, they entice by sensual passions of the flesh those who are barely escaping from those who live in error. [19] They promise them freedom, but they themselves are slaves[5] of corruption. For whatever overcomes a person, to that he is enslaved. [20] For if, after they have escaped the defilements of the world through the knowledge of our Lord and Savior Jesus Christ, they are again entangled in them and overcome, the last state has become worse for them than the first. [21] For it would have been better for them never to have known the way of righteousness than after knowing it to turn back from the holy commandment delivered to them. [22] What the true proverb says has happened to them: "The dog returns to its own vomit, and the sow, after washing herself, returns to wallow in the mire."

The Day of the Lord Will Come

3 This is now the second letter that I am writing to you, beloved. In both of them I am stirring up your sincere mind by way of reminder, [2] that you should remember the predictions of the holy prophets and the commandment of the Lord and Savior through your apostles, [3] knowing this first of all, that scoffers will come in the last days with scoffing, following their own sinful desires. [4] They will say, "Where is the promise of his coming? For ever since the fathers fell asleep, all things are continuing as they were from the beginning of creation." [5] For they deliberately overlook this fact, that the heavens existed long ago, and the earth was formed out of water and through water by the word of God, [6] and that by means of these the world that then existed was deluged with water and perished. [7] But by the same word the heavens and earth that now exist are stored up for fire, being kept until the day of judgment and destruction of the ungodly.

[8] But do not overlook this one fact, beloved, that with the Lord one day is as a thousand years, and a thousand years as one day. [9] The Lord is not slow to fulfill his promise as some count slowness, but is patient toward you,[6] not wishing that any should perish, but that all should reach repentance. [10] But the day of the Lord will come like a thief, and then the heavens will pass away with a roar, and the heavenly bodies[7] will be burned up and dissolved, and the earth and the works that are done on it will be exposed.[8]

[11] Since all these things are thus to be dissolved, what sort of people ought you to be in lives of holiness and godliness, [12] waiting for and hastening the coming of the day of God, because of which the heavens will be set on fire and dissolved, and the heavenly bodies will melt as they burn! [13] But according to his promise we are waiting for new heavens and a new earth in which righteousness dwells.

Final Words

[14] Therefore, beloved, since you are waiting for these, be diligent to be found by him without spot or blemish, and at peace. [15] And count the patience of our Lord as salvation, just as our beloved brother Paul also wrote to you according to the wisdom given him, [16] as he does in all his letters when he speaks in them of these

---

[1] Or temptations [2] Greek who go after the flesh [3] Some manuscripts love feasts [4] Or eyes full of an adulteress [5] For the contextual rendering of the Greek word doulos, see Preface [6] Some manuscripts on your account [7] Or elements; also verse 12 [8] Greek found; some manuscripts will be burned up

matters. There are some things in them that are hard to understand, which the ignorant and unstable twist to their own destruction, as they do the other Scriptures. **17** You therefore, beloved, knowing this beforehand, take care that you are not carried away with the error of lawless people and lose your own stability. **18** But grow in the grace and knowledge of our Lord and Savior Jesus Christ. To him be the glory both now and to the day of eternity. Amen.

1 JOHN

The Word of Life

1 That which was from the beginning, which we have heard, which we have seen with our eyes, which we looked upon and have touched with our hands, concerning the word of life— ²the life was made manifest, and we have seen it, and testify to it and proclaim to you the eternal life, which was with the Father and was made manifest to us— ³that which we have seen and heard we proclaim also to you, so that you too may have fellowship with us; and indeed our fellowship is with the Father and with his Son Jesus Christ. ⁴And we are writing these things so that our¹ joy may be complete.

Walking in the Light

⁵This is the message we have heard from him and proclaim to you, that God is light, and in him is no darkness at all. ⁶If we say we have fellowship with him while we walk in darkness, we lie and do not practice the truth. ⁷But if we walk in the light, as he is in the light, we have fellowship with one another, and the blood of Jesus his Son cleanses us from all sin. ⁸If we say we have no sin, we deceive ourselves, and the truth is not in us. ⁹If we confess our sins, he is faithful and just to forgive us our sins and to cleanse us from all unrighteousness. ¹⁰If we say we have not sinned, we make him a liar, and his word is not in us.

Christ Our Advocate

2 My little children, I am writing these things to you so that you may not sin. But if anyone does sin, we have an advocate with the Father, Jesus Christ the righteous. ²He is the propitiation for our sins, and not for ours only but also for the sins of the whole world. ³And by this we know that we have come to know him, if we keep his commandments. ⁴Whoever says "I know him" but does not keep his commandments is a liar, and the truth is not in him, ⁵but whoever keeps his word, in him truly the love of God is perfected. By this we may know that we are in him: ⁶whoever says he abides in him ought to walk in the same way in which he walked.

The New Commandment

⁷Beloved, I am writing you no new commandment, but an old commandment that you had from the beginning. The old commandment is the word that you have heard. ⁸At the same time, it is a new commandment that I am writing to you, which is true in him and in you, because² the darkness is passing away and the true light is already shining. ⁹Whoever says he is in the light and hates his brother is still in darkness. ¹⁰Whoever loves his brother abides in the light, and in him³ there is no cause for stumbling. ¹¹But whoever hates his brother is in the darkness and walks in the darkness, and does not know where he is going, because the darkness has blinded his eyes.

¹² I am writing to you, little children,
      because your sins are forgiven for his
         name's sake.
¹³ I am writing to you, fathers,
      because you know him who is from the
         beginning.
   I am writing to you, young men,
      because you have overcome the evil
         one.
   I write to you, children,
      because you know the Father.
¹⁴ I write to you, fathers,
      because you know him who is from the
         beginning.
   I write to you, young men,
      because you are strong,
      and the word of God abides in you,
      and you have overcome the evil one.

Do Not Love the World

¹⁵Do not love the world or the things in the world. If anyone loves the world, the love of the Father is not in him. ¹⁶For all that is in the world—the desires of the flesh and the desires of the eyes and pride of life⁴—is not from the Father but is from the world. ¹⁷And the world is passing away along with its desires, but whoever does the will of God abides forever.

Warning Concerning Antichrists

¹⁸Children, it is the last hour, and as you have heard that antichrist is coming, so now many antichrists have come. Therefore we

¹ Some manuscripts your ² Or that ³ Or it ⁴ Or pride in possessions

know that it is the last hour. [19] They went out from us, but they were not of us; for if they had been of us, they would have continued with us. But they went out, that it might become plain that they all are not of us. [20] But you have been anointed by the Holy One, and you all have knowledge.[1] [21] I write to you, not because you do not know the truth, but because you know it, and because no lie is of the truth. [22] Who is the liar but he who denies that Jesus is the Christ? This is the antichrist, he who denies the Father and the Son. [23] No one who denies the Son has the Father. Whoever confesses the Son has the Father also. [24] Let what you heard from the beginning abide in you. If what you heard from the beginning abides in you, then you too will abide in the Son and in the Father. [25] And this is the promise that he made to us[2]—eternal life.

[26] I write these things to you about those who are trying to deceive you. [27] But the anointing that you received from him abides in you, and you have no need that anyone should teach you. But as his anointing teaches you about everything, and is true, and is no lie—just as it has taught you, abide in him.

Children of God

[28] And now, little children, abide in him, so that when he appears we may have confidence and not shrink from him in shame at his coming. [29] If you know that he is righteous, you may be sure that everyone who practices righteousness has been born of him.

3 See what kind of love the Father has given to us, that we should be called children of God; and so we are. The reason why the world does not know us is that it did not know him. [2] Beloved, we are God's children now, and what we will be has not yet appeared; but we know that when he appears[3] we shall be like him, because we shall see him as he is. [3] And everyone who thus hopes in him purifies himself as he is pure.

[4] Everyone who makes a practice of sinning also practices lawlessness; sin is lawlessness. [5] You know that he appeared in order to take away sins, and in him there is no sin. [6] No one who abides in him keeps on sinning; no one who keeps on sinning has either seen him or

known him. [7] Little children, let no one deceive you. Whoever practices righteousness is righteous, as he is righteous. [8] Whoever makes a practice of sinning is of the devil, for the devil has been sinning from the beginning. The reason the Son of God appeared was to destroy the works of the devil. [9] No one born of God makes a practice of sinning, for God's[4] seed abides in him; and he cannot keep on sinning, because he has been born of God. [10] By this it is evident who are the children of God, and who are the children of the devil: whoever does not practice righteousness is not of God, nor is the one who does not love his brother.

Love One Another

[11] For this is the message that you have heard from the beginning, that we should love one another. [12] We should not be like Cain, who was of the evil one and murdered his brother. And why did he murder him? Because his own deeds were evil and his brother's righteous. [13] Do not be surprised, brothers,[5] that the world hates you. [14] We know that we have passed out of death into life, because we love the brothers. Whoever does not love abides in death. [15] Everyone who hates his brother is a murderer, and you know that no murderer has eternal life abiding in him. [16] By this we know love, that he laid down his life for us, and we ought to lay down our lives for the brothers. [17] But if anyone has the world's goods and sees his brother in need, yet closes his heart against him, how does God's love abide in him? [18] Little children, let us not love in word or talk but in deed and in truth.

[19] By this we shall know that we are of the truth and reassure our heart before him; [20] for whenever our heart condemns us, God is greater than our heart, and he knows everything. [21] Beloved, if our heart does not condemn us, we have confidence before God; [22] and whatever we ask we receive from him, because we keep his commandments and do what pleases him. [23] And this is his commandment, that we believe in the name of his Son Jesus Christ and love one another, just as he has commanded us. [24] Whoever keeps his commandments abides in God,[6] and God[7] in him. And by this we know that he abides in us, by the Spirit whom he has given us.

---

[1] Some manuscripts *you know everything* [2] Some manuscripts *you* [3] Or *when it appears* [4] Greek *his* [5] Or *brothers and sisters*. In New Testament usage, depending on the context, the plural Greek word *adelphoi* (translated "brothers") may refer either to *brothers* or to *brothers and sisters*; also verses 14, 16 [6] Greek *him* [7] Greek *he*

Test the Spirits

4 Beloved, do not believe every spirit, but test the spirits to see whether they are from God, for many false prophets have gone out into the world. [2] By this you know the Spirit of God: every spirit that confesses that Jesus Christ has come in the flesh is from God, [3] and every spirit that does not confess Jesus is not from God. This is the spirit of the antichrist, which you heard was coming and now is in the world already. [4] Little children, you are from God and have overcome them, for he who is in you is greater than he who is in the world. [5] They are from the world; therefore they speak from the world, and the world listens to them. [6] We are from God. Whoever knows God listens to us; whoever is not from God does not listen to us. By this we know the Spirit of truth and the spirit of error.

God Is Love

[7] Beloved, let us love one another, for love is from God, and whoever loves has been born of God and knows God. [8] Anyone who does not love does not know God, because God is love. [9] In this the love of God was made manifest among us, that God sent his only Son into the world, so that we might live through him. [10] In this is love, not that we have loved God but that he loved us and sent his Son to be the propitiation for our sins. [11] Beloved, if God so loved us, we also ought to love one another. [12] No one has ever seen God; if we love one another, God abides in us and his love is perfected in us.

[13] By this we know that we abide in him and he in us, because he has given us of his Spirit. [14] And we have seen and testify that the Father has sent his Son to be the Savior of the world. [15] Whoever confesses that Jesus is the Son of God, God abides in him, and he in God. [16] So we have come to know and to believe the love that God has for us. God is love, and whoever abides in love abides in God, and God abides in him. [17] By this is love perfected with us, so that we may have confidence for the day of judgment, because as he is so also are we in this world. [18] There is no fear in love, but perfect love casts out fear. For fear has to do with punishment, and whoever fears has not been perfected in love. [19] We love because he first loved us. [20] If anyone says, "I love God," and hates his brother, he is a liar; for he who does not love his brother whom he has seen cannot[1] love God whom he has not seen. [21] And this commandment we have from him: whoever loves God must also love his brother.

Overcoming the World

5 Everyone who believes that Jesus is the Christ has been born of God, and everyone who loves the Father loves whoever has been born of him. [2] By this we know that we love the children of God, when we love God and obey his commandments. [3] For this is the love of God, that we keep his commandments. And his commandments are not burdensome. [4] For everyone who has been born of God overcomes the world. And this is the victory that has overcome the world—our faith. [5] Who is it that overcomes the world except the one who believes that Jesus is the Son of God?

Testimony Concerning the Son of God

[6] This is he who came by water and blood—Jesus Christ; not by the water only but by the water and the blood. And the Spirit is the one who testifies, because the Spirit is the truth. [7] For there are three that testify: [8] the Spirit and the water and the blood; and these three agree. [9] If we receive the testimony of men, the testimony of God is greater, for this is the testimony of God that he has borne concerning his Son. [10] Whoever believes in the Son of God has the testimony in himself. Whoever does not believe God has made him a liar, because he has not believed in the testimony that God has borne concerning his Son. [11] And this is the testimony, that God gave us eternal life, and this life is in his Son. [12] Whoever has the Son has life; whoever does not have the Son of God does not have life.

That You May Know

[13] I write these things to you who believe in the name of the Son of God, that you may know that you have eternal life. [14] And this is the confidence that we have toward him, that if we ask anything according to his will he hears us. [15] And if we know that he hears us in whatever we ask, we know that we have the requests that we have asked of him.

[16] If anyone sees his brother committing a sin not leading to death, he shall ask, and God[2] will give him life—to those who commit sins that do not lead to death. There is sin that leads to death; I do not say that one should pray for that. [17] All wrongdoing is sin, but there is sin that does not lead to death.

---

[1] Some manuscripts *how can he* [2] Greek *he*

[18]We know that everyone who has been born of God does not keep on sinning, but he who was born of God protects him, and the evil one does not touch him.

[19]We know that we are from God, and the whole world lies in the power of the evil one.

[20]And we know that the Son of God has come and has given us understanding, so that we may know him who is true; and we are in him who is true, in his Son Jesus Christ. He is the true God and eternal life. [21]Little children, keep yourselves from idols.

2 JOHN

Greeting

¹The elder to the elect lady and her children, whom I love in truth, and not only I, but also all who know the truth, ²because of the truth that abides in us and will be with us forever:

³Grace, mercy, and peace will be with us, from God the Father and from Jesus Christ the Father's Son, in truth and love.

Walking in Truth and Love

⁴I rejoiced greatly to find some of your children walking in the truth, just as we were commanded by the Father. ⁵And now I ask you, dear lady—not as though I were writing you a new commandment, but the one we have had from the beginning—that we love one another. ⁶And this is love, that we walk according to his commandments; this is the commandment, just as you have heard from the beginning, so that you should walk in it. ⁷For many deceivers have gone out into the world, those who do not confess the coming of Jesus Christ in the flesh. Such a one is the deceiver and the antichrist. ⁸Watch yourselves, so that you may not lose what we[1] have worked for, but may win a full reward. ⁹Everyone who goes on ahead and does not abide in the teaching of Christ, does not have God. Whoever abides in the teaching has both the Father and the·Son. ¹⁰If anyone comes to you and does not bring this teaching, do not receive him into your house or give him any greeting, ¹¹for whoever greets him takes part in his wicked works.

Final Greetings

¹²Though I have much to write to you, I would rather not use paper and ink. Instead I hope to come to you and talk face to face, so that our joy may be complete.

¹³The children of your elect sister greet you.

[1] Some manuscripts *you*

3 JOHN

Greeting

[1] The elder to the beloved Gaius, whom I love in truth.

[2] Beloved, I pray that all may go well with you and that you may be in good health, as it goes well with your soul. [3] For I rejoiced greatly when the brothers[1] came and testified to your truth, as indeed you are walking in the truth. [4] I have no greater joy than to hear that my children are walking in the truth.

Support and Opposition

[5] Beloved, it is a faithful thing you do in all your efforts for these brothers, strangers as they are, [6] who testified to your love before the church. You will do well to send them on their journey in a manner worthy of God. [7] For they have gone out for the sake of the name, accepting nothing from the Gentiles. [8] Therefore we ought to support people like these, that we may be fellow workers for the truth.

[9] I have written something to the church, but Diotrephes, who likes to put himself first, does not acknowledge our authority. [10] So if I come, I will bring up what he is doing, talking wicked nonsense against us. And not content with that, he refuses to welcome the brothers, and also stops those who want to and puts them out of the church.

[11] Beloved, do not imitate evil but imitate good. Whoever does good is from God; whoever does evil has not seen God. [12] Demetrius has received a good testimony from everyone, and from the truth itself. We also add our testimony, and you know that our testimony is true.

Final Greetings

[13] I had much to write to you, but I would rather not write with pen and ink. [14] I hope to see you soon, and we will talk face to face.

[15] Peace be to you. The friends greet you. Greet the friends, each by name.

---

[1] Or *brothers and sisters*. In New Testament usage, depending on the context, the plural Greek word *adelphoi* (translated "brothers") may refer either to *brothers* or to *brothers and sisters*; also verses 5, 10

THE LETTER OF
JUDE

Greeting

[1] Jude, a servant[1] of Jesus Christ and brother of James,

To those who are called, beloved in God the Father and kept for[2] Jesus Christ:

[2] May mercy, peace, and love be multiplied to you.

Judgment on False Teachers

[3] Beloved, although I was very eager to write to you about our common salvation, I found it necessary to write appealing to you to contend for the faith that was once for all delivered to the saints. [4] For certain people have crept in unnoticed who long ago were designated for this condemnation, ungodly people, who pervert the grace of our God into sensuality and deny our only Master and Lord, Jesus Christ.

[5] Now I want to remind you, although you once fully knew it, that Jesus, who saved[3] a people out of the land of Egypt, afterward destroyed those who did not believe. [6] And the angels who did not stay within their own position of authority, but left their proper dwelling, he has kept in eternal chains under gloomy darkness until the judgment of the great day— [7] just as Sodom and Gomorrah and the surrounding cities, which likewise indulged in sexual immorality and pursued unnatural desire,[4] serve as an example by undergoing a punishment of eternal fire.

[8] Yet in like manner these people also, relying on their dreams, defile the flesh, reject authority, and blaspheme the glorious ones. [9] But when the archangel Michael, contending with the devil, was disputing about the body of Moses, he did not presume to pronounce a blasphemous judgment, but said, "The Lord rebuke you." [10] But these people blaspheme all that they do not understand, and they are destroyed by all that they, like unreasoning animals, understand instinctively. [11] Woe to them! For they walked in the way of Cain and abandoned themselves for the sake of gain to Balaam's error and perished in Korah's rebellion. [12] These are hidden reefs[5] at your love feasts, as they feast with you without fear, shepherds feeding themselves; waterless clouds, swept along by winds; fruitless trees in late autumn, twice dead, uprooted; [13] wild waves of the sea, casting up the foam of their own shame; wandering stars, for whom the gloom of utter darkness has been reserved forever.

[14] It was also about these that Enoch, the seventh from Adam, prophesied, saying, "Behold, the Lord comes with ten thousands of his holy ones, [15] to execute judgment on all and to convict all the ungodly of all their deeds of ungodliness that they have committed in such an ungodly way, and of all the harsh things that ungodly sinners have spoken against him." [16] These are grumblers, malcontents, following their own sinful desires; they are loud-mouthed boasters, showing favoritism to gain advantage.

A Call to Persevere

[17] But you must remember, beloved, the predictions of the apostles of our Lord Jesus Christ. [18] They[6] said to you, "In the last time there will be scoffers, following their own ungodly passions." [19] It is these who cause divisions, worldly people, devoid of the Spirit. [20] But you, beloved, building yourselves up in your most holy faith and praying in the Holy Spirit, [21] keep yourselves in the love of God, waiting for the mercy of our Lord Jesus Christ that leads to eternal life. [22] And have mercy on those who doubt; [23] save others by snatching them out of the fire; to others show mercy with fear, hating even the garment[7] stained by the flesh.

Doxology

[24] Now to him who is able to keep you from stumbling and to present you blameless before the presence of his glory with great joy, [25] to the only God, our Savior, through Jesus Christ our Lord, be glory, majesty, dominion, and authority, before all time[8] and now and forever. Amen.

---

[1] For the contextual rendering of the Greek word *doulos*, see Preface [2] Or by [3] Some manuscripts *although you fully knew it, that the Lord who once saved* [4] Greek *different flesh*
[5] Or *are blemishes* [6] Or *Christ, because they* [7] Greek *chiton*, a long garment worn under the cloak next to the skin [8] Or *before any age*

THE
REVELATION
TO JOHN

Prologue

1 The revelation of Jesus Christ, which God gave him to show to his servants[1] the things that must soon take place. He made it known by sending his angel to his servant John, [2] who bore witness to the word of God and to the testimony of Jesus Christ, even to all that he saw. [3] Blessed is the one who reads aloud the words of this prophecy, and blessed are those who hear, and who keep what is written in it, for the time is near.

Greeting to the Seven Churches

[4] John to the seven churches that are in Asia:

Grace to you and peace from him who is and who was and who is to come, and from the seven spirits who are before his throne, [5] and from Jesus Christ the faithful witness, the first-born of the dead, and the ruler of kings on earth.

To him who loves us and has freed us from our sins by his blood [6] and made us a kingdom, priests to his God and Father, to him be glory and dominion forever and ever. Amen. [7] Behold, he is coming with the clouds, and every eye will see him, even those who pierced him, and all tribes of the earth will wail[2] on account of him. Even so. Amen.

[8] "I am the Alpha and the Omega," says the Lord God, "who is and who was and who is to come, the Almighty."

Vision of the Son of Man

[9] I, John, your brother and partner in the tribulation and the kingdom and the patient endurance that are in Jesus, was on the island called Patmos on account of the word of God and the testimony of Jesus. [10] I was in the Spirit on the Lord's day, and I heard behind me a loud voice like a trumpet [11] saying, "Write what you see in a book and send it to the seven churches, to Ephesus and to Smyrna and to Pergamum and to Thyatira and to Sardis and to Philadelphia and to Laodicea."

[12] Then I turned to see the voice that was speaking to me, and on turning I saw seven golden lampstands, [13] and in the midst of the lampstands one like a son of man, clothed with a long robe and with a golden sash around his chest. [14] The hairs of his head were white, like white wool, like snow. His eyes were like a flame of fire, [15] his feet were like burnished bronze, refined in a furnace, and his voice was like the roar of many waters. [16] In his right hand he held seven stars, from his mouth came a sharp two-edged sword, and his face was like the sun shining in full strength.

[17] When I saw him, I fell at his feet as though dead. But he laid his right hand on me, saying, "Fear not, I am the first and the last, [18] and the living one. I died, and behold I am alive forevermore, and I have the keys of Death and Hades. [19] Write therefore the things that you have seen, those that are and those that are to take place after this. [20] As for the mystery of the seven stars that you saw in my right hand, and the seven golden lampstands, the seven stars are the angels of the seven churches, and the seven lampstands are the seven churches.

To the Church in Ephesus

2 "To the angel of the church in Ephesus write: 'The words of him who holds the seven stars in his right hand, who walks among the seven golden lampstands.

[2] "'I know your works, your toil and your patient endurance, and how you cannot bear with those who are evil, but have tested those who call themselves apostles and are not, and found them to be false. [3] I know you are enduring patiently and bearing up for my name's sake, and you have not grown weary. [4] But I have this against you, that you have abandoned the love you had at first. [5] Remember therefore from where you have fallen; repent, and do the works you did at first. If not, I will come to you and remove your lampstand from its place, unless you repent. [6] Yet this you have: you hate the works of the Nicolaitans, which I also hate. [7] He who has an ear, let him hear what the Spirit says to the churches. To the one who conquers I will grant to eat of the tree of life, which is in the paradise of God.'

To the Church in Smyrna

[8] "And to the angel of the church in Smyrna write: 'The words of the first and the last, who died and came to life.

---

[1] For the contextual rendering of the Greek word *doulos*, see Preface; likewise for *servant* later in this verse [2] Or *mourn*

[9] "'I know your tribulation and your poverty (but you are rich) and the slander[1] of those who say that they are Jews and are not, but are a synagogue of Satan. [10]Do not fear what you are about to suffer. Behold, the devil is about to throw some of you into prison, that you may be tested, and for ten days you will have tribulation. Be faithful unto death, and I will give you the crown of life. [11]He who has an ear, let him hear what the Spirit says to the churches. The one who conquers will not be hurt by the second death.'

To the Church in Pergamum

[12]"And to the angel of the church in Pergamum write: 'The words of him who has the sharp two-edged sword.

[13]"'I know where you dwell, where Satan's throne is. Yet you hold fast my name, and you did not deny my faith[2] even in the days of Antipas my faithful witness, who was killed among you, where Satan dwells. [14]But I have a few things against you: you have some there who hold the teaching of Balaam, who taught Balak to put a stumbling block before the sons of Israel, so that they might eat food sacrificed to idols and practice sexual immorality. [15]So also you have some who hold the teaching of the Nicolaitans. [16]Therefore repent. If not, I will come to you soon and war against them with the sword of my mouth. [17]He who has an ear, let him hear what the Spirit says to the churches. To the one who conquers I will give some of the hidden manna, and I will give him a white stone, with a new name written on the stone that no one knows except the one who receives it.'

To the Church in Thyatira

[18]"And to the angel of the church in Thyatira write: 'The words of the Son of God, who has eyes like a flame of fire, and whose feet are like burnished bronze.

[19]"'I know your works, your love and faith and service and patient endurance, and that your latter works exceed the first. [20]But I have this against you, that you tolerate that woman Jezebel, who calls herself a prophetess and is teaching and seducing my servants to practice sexual immorality and to eat food sacrificed to idols. [21]I gave her time to repent, but she refuses to repent of her sexual immorality. [22]Behold, I will throw her onto a sickbed, and those who commit adultery with her I will throw into great tribulation, unless they repent of her works, [23]and I will strike her children dead. And all the churches will know that I am he who searches mind and heart, and I will give to each of you according to your works. [24]But to the rest of you in Thyatira, who do not hold this teaching, who have not learned what some call the deep things of Satan, to you I say, I do not lay on you any other burden. [25]Only hold fast what you have until I come. [26]The one who conquers and who keeps my works until the end, to him I will give authority over the nations, [27]and he will rule[3] them with a rod of iron, as when earthen pots are broken in pieces, even as I myself have received authority from my Father. [28]And I will give him the morning star. [29]He who has an ear, let him hear what the Spirit says to the churches.'

To the Church in Sardis

3 "And to the angel of the church in Sardis write: 'The words of him who has the seven spirits of God and the seven stars.

"'I know your works. You have the reputation of being alive, but you are dead. [2]Wake up, and strengthen what remains and is about to die, for I have not found your works complete in the sight of my God. [3]Remember, then, what you received and heard. Keep it, and repent. If you will not wake up, I will come like a thief, and you will not know at what hour I will come against you. [4]Yet you have still a few names in Sardis, people who have not soiled their garments, and they will walk with me in white, for they are worthy. [5]The one who conquers will be clothed thus in white garments, and I will never blot his name out of the book of life. I will confess his name before my Father and before his angels. [6]He who has an ear, let him hear what the Spirit says to the churches.'

To the Church in Philadelphia

[7]"And to the angel of the church in Philadelphia write: 'The words of the holy one, the true one, who has the key of David, who opens and no one will shut, who shuts and no one opens.

[8]"'I know your works. Behold, I have set before you an open door, which no one is able to shut. I know that you have but little power, and yet you have kept my word and have not denied my name. [9]Behold, I will make those of the synagogue of Satan who say that they are Jews and are not, but lie—behold, I

---

[1] Greek blasphemy [2] Or your faith in me [3] Greek shepherd

will make them come and bow down before your feet, and they will learn that I have loved you. [10]Because you have kept my word about patient endurance, I will keep you from the hour of trial that is coming on the whole world, to try those who dwell on the earth. [11]I am coming soon. Hold fast what you have, so that no one may seize your crown. [12]The one who conquers, I will make him a pillar in the temple of my God. Never shall he go out of it, and I will write on him the name of my God, and the name of the city of my God, the new Jerusalem, which comes down from my God out of heaven, and my own new name. [13]He who has an ear, let him hear what the Spirit says to the churches.'

To the Church in Laodicea

[14]"And to the angel of the church in Laodicea write: 'The words of the Amen, the faithful and true witness, the beginning of God's creation.

[15]"'I know your works: you are neither cold nor hot. Would that you were either cold or hot! [16]So, because you are lukewarm, and neither hot nor cold, I will spit you out of my mouth. [17]For you say, I am rich, I have prospered, and I need nothing, not realizing that you are wretched, pitiable, poor, blind, and naked. [18]I counsel you to buy from me gold refined by fire, so that you may be rich, and white garments so that you may clothe yourself and the shame of your nakedness may not be seen, and salve to anoint your eyes, so that you may see. [19]Those whom I love, I reprove and discipline, so be zealous and repent. [20]Behold, I stand at the door and knock. If anyone hears my voice and opens the door, I will come in to him and eat with him, and he with me. [21]The one who conquers, I will grant him to sit with me on my throne, as I also conquered and sat down with my Father on his throne. [22]He who has an ear, let him hear what the Spirit says to the churches.'"

The Throne in Heaven

4 After this I looked, and behold, a door standing open in heaven! And the first voice, which I had heard speaking to me like a trumpet, said, "Come up here, and I will show you what must take place after this." [2]At once I was in the Spirit, and behold, a throne stood in heaven, with one seated on the throne. [3]And he who sat there had the appearance of jasper

and carnelian, and around the throne was a rainbow that had the appearance of an emerald. [4]Around the throne were twenty-four thrones, and seated on the thrones were twenty-four elders, clothed in white garments, with golden crowns on their heads. [5]From the throne came flashes of lightning, and rumblings[1] and peals of thunder, and before the throne were burning seven torches of fire, which are the seven spirits of God, [6]and before the throne there was as it were a sea of glass, like crystal.

And around the throne, on each side of the throne, are four living creatures, full of eyes in front and behind: [7]the first living creature like a lion, the second living creature like an ox, the third living creature with the face of a man, and the fourth living creature like an eagle in flight. [8]And the four living creatures, each of them with six wings, are full of eyes all around and within, and day and night they never cease to say,

"Holy, holy, holy, is the Lord God Almighty,
who was and is and is to come!"

[9]And whenever the living creatures give glory and honor and thanks to him who is seated on the throne, who lives forever and ever, [10]the twenty-four elders fall down before him who is seated on the throne and worship him who lives forever and ever. They cast their crowns before the throne, saying,

[11] "Worthy are you, our Lord and God,
to receive glory and honor and power,
for you created all things,
and by your will they existed and were created."

The Scroll and the Lamb

5 Then I saw in the right hand of him who was seated on the throne a scroll written within and on the back, sealed with seven seals. [2]And I saw a mighty angel proclaiming with a loud voice, "Who is worthy to open the scroll and break its seals?" [3]And no one in heaven or on earth or under the earth was able to open the scroll or to look into it, [4]and I began to weep loudly because no one was found worthy to open the scroll or to look into it. [5]And one of the elders said to me, "Weep no more; behold, the Lion of the tribe of Judah, the Root of David, has conquered, so that he can open the scroll and its seven seals."

[1] Or voices, or sounds

⁶And between the throne and the four living creatures and among the elders I saw a Lamb standing, as though it had been slain, with seven horns and with seven eyes, which are the seven spirits of God sent out into all the earth. ⁷And he went and took the scroll from the right hand of him who was seated on the throne. ⁸And when he had taken the scroll, the four living creatures and the twenty-four elders fell down before the Lamb, each holding a harp, and golden bowls full of incense, which are the prayers of the saints. ⁹And they sang a new song, saying,

"Worthy are you to take the scroll
　　and to open its seals,
for you were slain, and by your blood you
　　ransomed people for God
　　from every tribe and language and
　　people and nation,
¹⁰ and you have made them a kingdom and
　　priests to our God,
　　and they shall reign on the earth."

¹¹Then I looked, and I heard around the throne and the living creatures and the elders the voice of many angels, numbering myriads of myriads and thousands of thousands, ¹²saying with a loud voice,

"Worthy is the Lamb who was slain,
　　to receive power and wealth and wisdom
　　　　and might
　　and honor and glory and blessing!"

¹³And I heard every creature in heaven and on earth and under the earth and in the sea, and all that is in them, saying,

"To him who sits on the throne and to the
　　Lamb
be blessing and honor and glory and
　　might forever and ever!"

¹⁴And the four living creatures said, "Amen!" and the elders fell down and worshiped.

The Seven Seals

6 Now I watched when the Lamb opened one of the seven seals, and I heard one of the four living creatures say with a voice like thunder, "Come!" ²And I looked, and behold, a white horse! And its rider had a bow, and a crown was given to him, and he came out conquering, and to conquer.

³When he opened the second seal, I heard the second living creature say, "Come!" ⁴And out came another horse, bright red. Its rider was permitted to take peace from the earth, so that people should slay one another, and he was given a great sword.

⁵When he opened the third seal, I heard the third living creature say, "Come!" And I looked, and behold, a black horse! And its rider had a pair of scales in his hand. ⁶And I heard what seemed to be a voice in the midst of the four living creatures, saying, "A quart¹ of wheat for a denarius,² and three quarts of barley for a denarius, and do not harm the oil and wine!"

⁷When he opened the fourth seal, I heard the voice of the fourth living creature say, "Come!" ⁸And I looked, and behold, a pale horse! And its rider's name was Death, and Hades followed him. And they were given authority over a fourth of the earth, to kill with sword and with famine and with pestilence and by wild beasts of the earth.

⁹When he opened the fifth seal, I saw under the altar the souls of those who had been slain for the word of God and for the witness they had borne. ¹⁰They cried out with a loud voice, "O Sovereign Lord, holy and true, how long before you will judge and avenge our blood on those who dwell on the earth?" ¹¹Then they were each given a white robe and told to rest a little longer, until the number of their fellow servants and their brothers³ should be complete, who were to be killed as they themselves had been.

¹²When he opened the sixth seal, I looked, and behold, there was a great earthquake, and the sun became black as sackcloth, the full moon became like blood, ¹³and the stars of the sky fell to the earth as the fig tree sheds its winter fruit when shaken by a gale. ¹⁴The sky vanished like a scroll that is being rolled up, and every mountain and island was removed from its place. ¹⁵Then the kings of the earth and the great ones and the generals and the rich and the powerful, and everyone, slave⁴ and free, hid themselves in the caves and among the rocks of the mountains, ¹⁶calling to the mountains and rocks, "Fall on us and hide us from the face of him who is seated on the throne, and from the wrath of the Lamb, ¹⁷for the great day of their wrath has come, and who can stand?"

The 144,000 of Israel Sealed

7 After this I saw four angels standing at the four corners of the earth, holding back the four winds of the earth, that no wind might blow on earth or sea or against any tree. ²Then I saw another angel ascending from the rising

---

¹ Greek *choinix*, a dry measure equal to about a quart　² A *denarius* was a day's wage for a laborer　³ Or *brothers and sisters*. In New Testament usage, depending on the context, the plural Greek word *adelphoi* (translated "brothers") may refer either to *brothers* or to *brothers and sisters*　⁴ For the contextual rendering of the Greek word *doulos*, see Preface

of the sun, with the seal of the living God, and he called with a loud voice to the four angels who had been given power to harm earth and sea, ³saying, "Do not harm the earth or the sea or the trees, until we have sealed the servants of our God on their foreheads." ⁴And I heard the number of the sealed, 144,000, sealed from every tribe of the sons of Israel:

⁵   12,000 from the tribe of Judah were sealed,
      12,000 from the tribe of Reuben,
      12,000 from the tribe of Gad,
⁶   12,000 from the tribe of Asher,
      12,000 from the tribe of Naphtali,
      12,000 from the tribe of Manasseh,
⁷   12,000 from the tribe of Simeon,
      12,000 from the tribe of Levi,
      12,000 from the tribe of Issachar,
⁸   12,000 from the tribe of Zebulun,
      12,000 from the tribe of Joseph,
      12,000 from the tribe of Benjamin were
         sealed.

A Great Multitude from Every Nation

⁹After this I looked, and behold, a great multitude that no one could number, from every nation, from all tribes and peoples and languages, standing before the throne and before the Lamb, clothed in white robes, with palm branches in their hands, ¹⁰and crying out with a loud voice, "Salvation belongs to our God who sits on the throne, and to the Lamb!" ¹¹And all the angels were standing around the throne and around the elders and the four living creatures, and they fell on their faces before the throne and worshiped God, ¹²saying, "Amen! Blessing and glory and wisdom and thanksgiving and honor and power and might be to our God forever and ever! Amen."

¹³Then one of the elders addressed me, saying, "Who are these, clothed in white robes, and from where have they come?" ¹⁴I said to him, "Sir, you know." And he said to me, "These are the ones coming out of the great tribulation. They have washed their robes and made them white in the blood of the Lamb.

¹⁵   "Therefore they are before the throne of
            God,
        and serve him day and night in his
            temple;
        and he who sits on the throne will shel-
            ter them with his presence.

¹⁶   They shall hunger no more, neither thirst
            anymore;
        the sun shall not strike them,
        nor any scorching heat.
¹⁷   For the Lamb in the midst of the throne
            will be their shepherd,
        and he will guide them to springs of liv-
            ing water,
        and God will wipe away every tear from
            their eyes."

The Seventh Seal and the Golden Censer

8 When the Lamb opened the seventh seal, there was silence in heaven for about half an hour. ²Then I saw the seven angels who stand before God, and seven trumpets were given to them. ³And another angel came and stood at the altar with a golden censer, and he was given much incense to offer with the prayers of all the saints on the golden altar before the throne, ⁴and the smoke of the incense, with the prayers of the saints, rose before God from the hand of the angel. ⁵Then the angel took the censer and filled it with fire from the altar and threw it on the earth, and there were peals of thunder, rumblings,¹ flashes of lightning, and an earthquake.

The Seven Trumpets

⁶Now the seven angels who had the seven trumpets prepared to blow them.

⁷The first angel blew his trumpet, and there followed hail and fire, mixed with blood, and these were thrown upon the earth. And a third of the earth was burned up, and a third of the trees were burned up, and all green grass was burned up.

⁸The second angel blew his trumpet, and something like a great mountain, burning with fire, was thrown into the sea, and a third of the sea became blood. ⁹A third of the living creatures in the sea died, and a third of the ships were destroyed.

¹⁰The third angel blew his trumpet, and a great star fell from heaven, blazing like a torch, and it fell on a third of the rivers and on the springs of water. ¹¹The name of the star is Wormwood.² A third of the waters became wormwood, and many people died from the water, because it had been made bitter.

¹²The fourth angel blew his trumpet, and a third of the sun was struck, and a third of the moon, and a third of the stars, so that a third of their light might be darkened, and a third

¹ Or voices, or sounds ² Wormwood is the name of a plant and of the bitter-tasting extract derived from it

of the day might be kept from shining, and likewise a third of the night.

[13] Then I looked, and I heard an eagle crying with a loud voice as it flew directly overhead, "Woe, woe, woe to those who dwell on the earth, at the blasts of the other trumpets that the three angels are about to blow!"

9 And the fifth angel blew his trumpet, and I saw a star fallen from heaven to earth, and he was given the key to the shaft of the bottomless pit.[1] [2] He opened the shaft of the bottomless pit, and from the shaft rose smoke like the smoke of a great furnace, and the sun and the air were darkened with the smoke from the shaft. [3] Then from the smoke came locusts on the earth, and they were given power like the power of scorpions of the earth. [4] They were told not to harm the grass of the earth or any green plant or any tree, but only those people who do not have the seal of God on their foreheads. [5] They were allowed to torment them for five months, but not to kill them, and their torment was like the torment of a scorpion when it stings someone. [6] And in those days people will seek death and will not find it. They will long to die, but death will flee from them.

[7] In appearance the locusts were like horses prepared for battle: on their heads were what looked like crowns of gold; their faces were like human faces, [8] their hair like women's hair, and their teeth like lions' teeth; [9] they had breastplates like breastplates of iron, and the noise of their wings was like the noise of many chariots with horses rushing into battle. [10] They have tails and stings like scorpions, and their power to hurt people for five months is in their tails. [11] They have as king over them the angel of the bottomless pit. His name in Hebrew is Abaddon, and in Greek he is called Apollyon.[2]

[12] The first woe has passed; behold, two woes are still to come.

[13] Then the sixth angel blew his trumpet, and I heard a voice from the four horns of the golden altar before God, [14] saying to the sixth angel who had the trumpet, "Release the four angels who are bound at the great river Euphrates." [15] So the four angels, who had been prepared for the hour, the day, the month, and the year, were released to kill a third of mankind. [16] The number of mounted troops was twice ten thousand times ten thousand; I heard their number. [17] And this is how I saw the horses in my vision and those who rode them: they wore breastplates the color of fire and of sapphire[3] and of sulfur, and the heads of the horses were like lions' heads, and fire and smoke and sulfur came out of their mouths. [18] By these three plagues a third of mankind was killed, by the fire and smoke and sulfur coming out of their mouths. [19] For the power of the horses is in their mouths and in their tails, for their tails are like serpents with heads, and by means of them they wound.

[20] The rest of mankind, who were not killed by these plagues, did not repent of the works of their hands nor give up worshiping demons and idols of gold and silver and bronze and stone and wood, which cannot see or hear or walk, [21] nor did they repent of their murders or their sorceries or their sexual immorality or their thefts.

The Angel and the Little Scroll

10 Then I saw another mighty angel coming down from heaven, wrapped in a cloud, with a rainbow over his head, and his face was like the sun, and his legs like pillars of fire. [2] He had a little scroll open in his hand. And he set his right foot on the sea, and his left foot on the land, [3] and called out with a loud voice, like a lion roaring. When he called out, the seven thunders sounded. [4] And when the seven thunders had sounded, I was about to write, but I heard a voice from heaven saying, "Seal up what the seven thunders have said, and do not write it down." [5] And the angel whom I saw standing on the sea and on the land raised his right hand to heaven [6] and swore by him who lives forever and ever, who created heaven and what is in it, the earth and what is in it, and the sea and what is in it, that there would be no more delay, [7] but that in the days of the trumpet call to be sounded by the seventh angel, the mystery of God would be fulfilled, just as he announced to his servants the prophets.

[8] Then the voice that I had heard from heaven spoke to me again, saying, "Go, take the scroll that is open in the hand of the angel who is standing on the sea and on the land." [9] So I went to the angel and told him to give me the little scroll. And he said to me, "Take and eat it; it will make your stomach bitter, but in your mouth it will be sweet as honey." [10] And I took the little scroll from the hand of the angel and ate it. It was sweet as honey in my mouth, but when I had eaten it my stomach was made bitter.

[1] Greek the abyss; also verses 2, 11 [2] Abaddon means destruction; Apollyon means destroyer [3] Greek hyacinth

[11] And I was told, "You must again prophesy about many peoples and nations and languages and kings."

The Two Witnesses

11 Then I was given a measuring rod like a staff, and I was told, "Rise and measure the temple of God and the altar and those who worship there, [2] but do not measure the court outside the temple; leave that out, for it is given over to the nations, and they will trample the holy city for forty-two months. [3] And I will grant authority to my two witnesses, and they will prophesy for 1,260 days, clothed in sackcloth."

[4] These are the two olive trees and the two lampstands that stand before the Lord of the earth. [5] And if anyone would harm them, fire pours from their mouth and consumes their foes. If anyone would harm them, this is how he is doomed to be killed. [6] They have the power to shut the sky, that no rain may fall during the days of their prophesying, and they have power over the waters to turn them into blood and to strike the earth with every kind of plague, as often as they desire. [7] And when they have finished their testimony, the beast that rises from the bottomless pit[1] will make war on them and conquer them and kill them, [8] and their dead bodies will lie in the street of the great city that symbolically[2] is called Sodom and Egypt, where their Lord was crucified. [9] For three and a half days some from the peoples and tribes and languages and nations will gaze at their dead bodies and refuse to let them be placed in a tomb, [10] and those who dwell on the earth will rejoice over them and make merry and exchange presents, because these two prophets had been a torment to those who dwell on the earth. [11] But after the three and a half days a breath of life from God entered them, and they stood up on their feet, and great fear fell on those who saw them. [12] Then they heard a loud voice from heaven saying to them, "Come up here!" And they went up to heaven in a cloud, and their enemies watched them. [13] And at that hour there was a great earthquake, and a tenth of the city fell. Seven thousand people were killed in the earthquake, and the rest were terrified and gave glory to the God of heaven.

[14] The second woe has passed; behold, the third woe is soon to come.

The Seventh Trumpet

[15] Then the seventh angel blew his trumpet, and there were loud voices in heaven, saying, "The kingdom of the world has become the kingdom of our Lord and of his Christ, and he shall reign forever and ever." [16] And the twenty-four elders who sit on their thrones before God fell on their faces and worshiped God, [17] saying,

> "We give thanks to you, Lord God Almighty,
>   who is and who was,
> for you have taken your great power
>   and begun to reign.
> [18] The nations raged,
>   but your wrath came,
>   and the time for the dead to be
>   judged,
> and for rewarding your servants, the
>   prophets and saints,
>   and those who fear your name,
>   both small and great,
> and for destroying the destroyers of the
>   earth."

[19] Then God's temple in heaven was opened, and the ark of his covenant was seen within his temple. There were flashes of lightning, rumblings,[3] peals of thunder, an earthquake, and heavy hail.

The Woman and the Dragon

12 And a great sign appeared in heaven: a woman clothed with the sun, with the moon under her feet, and on her head a crown of twelve stars. [2] She was pregnant and was crying out in birth pains and the agony of giving birth. [3] And another sign appeared in heaven: behold, a great red dragon, with seven heads and ten horns, and on his heads seven diadems. [4] His tail swept down a third of the stars of heaven and cast them to the earth. And the dragon stood before the woman who was about to give birth, so that when she bore her child he might devour it. [5] She gave birth to a male child, one who is to rule[4] all the nations with a rod of iron, but her child was caught up to God and to his throne, [6] and the woman fled into the wilderness, where she has a place prepared by God, in which she is to be nourished for 1,260 days.

Satan Thrown Down to Earth

[7] Now war arose in heaven, Michael and his angels fighting against the dragon. And

---

[1] Or the abyss [2] Greek spiritually [3] Or voices, or sounds [4] Greek shepherd

the dragon and his angels fought back, [8] but he was defeated, and there was no longer any place for them in heaven. [9] And the great dragon was thrown down, that ancient serpent, who is called the devil and Satan, the deceiver of the whole world—he was thrown down to the earth, and his angels were thrown down with him. [10] And I heard a loud voice in heaven, saying, "Now the salvation and the power and the kingdom of our God and the authority of his Christ have come, for the accuser of our brothers[1] has been thrown down, who accuses them day and night before our God. [11] And they have conquered him by the blood of the Lamb and by the word of their testimony, for they loved not their lives even unto death. [12] Therefore, rejoice, O heavens and you who dwell in them! But woe to you, O earth and sea, for the devil has come down to you in great wrath, because he knows that his time is short!"

[13] And when the dragon saw that he had been thrown down to the earth, he pursued the woman who had given birth to the male child. [14] But the woman was given the two wings of the great eagle so that she might fly from the serpent into the wilderness, to the place where she is to be nourished for a time, and times, and half a time. [15] The serpent poured water like a river out of his mouth after the woman, to sweep her away with a flood. [16] But the earth came to the help of the woman, and the earth opened its mouth and swallowed the river that the dragon had poured from his mouth. [17] Then the dragon became furious with the woman and went off to make war on the rest of her offspring, on those who keep the commandments of God and hold to the testimony of Jesus. And he stood[2] on the sand of the sea.

The First Beast

13 And I saw a beast rising out of the sea, with ten horns and seven heads, with ten diadems on its horns and blasphemous names on its heads. [2] And the beast that I saw was like a leopard; its feet were like a bear's, and its mouth was like a lion's mouth. And to it the dragon gave his power and his throne and great authority. [3] One of its heads seemed to have a mortal wound, but its mortal wound was healed, and the whole earth marveled as they followed the beast. [4] And they worshiped the dragon, for he had given his authority to

the beast, and they worshiped the beast, saying, "Who is like the beast, and who can fight against it?"

[5] And the beast was given a mouth uttering haughty and blasphemous words, and it was allowed to exercise authority for forty-two months. [6] It opened its mouth to utter blasphemies against God, blaspheming his name and his dwelling,[3] that is, those who dwell in heaven. [7] Also it was allowed to make war on the saints and to conquer them.[4] And authority was given it over every tribe and people and language and nation, [8] and all who dwell on earth will worship it, everyone whose name has not been written before the foundation of the world in the book of life of the Lamb who was slain. [9] If anyone has an ear, let him hear:

[10]   If anyone is to be taken captive,
           to captivity he goes;
       if anyone is to be slain with the sword,
           with the sword must he be slain.

Here is a call for the endurance and faith of the saints.

The Second Beast

[11] Then I saw another beast rising out of the earth. It had two horns like a lamb and it spoke like a dragon. [12] It exercises all the authority of the first beast in its presence,[5] and makes the earth and its inhabitants worship the first beast, whose mortal wound was healed. [13] It performs great signs, even making fire come down from heaven to earth in front of people, [14] and by the signs that it is allowed to work in the presence of[6] the beast it deceives those who dwell on earth, telling them to make an image for the beast that was wounded by the sword and yet lived. [15] And it was allowed to give breath to the image of the beast, so that the image of the beast might even speak and might cause those who would not worship the image of the beast to be slain. [16] Also it causes all, both small and great, both rich and poor, both free and slave,[7] to be marked on the right hand or the forehead, [17] so that no one can buy or sell unless he has the mark, that is, the name of the beast or the number of its name. [18] This calls for wisdom: let the one who has understanding calculate the number of the beast, for it is the number of a man, and his number is 666.[8]

[1] Or brothers and sisters [2] Some manuscripts *And I stood*, connecting the sentence with 13:1 [3] Or *tabernacle* [4] Some manuscripts omit this sentence [5] Or *on its behalf* [6] Or on behalf of [7] For the contextual rendering of the Greek word *doulos*, see Preface [8] Some manuscripts *616*

The Lamb and the 144,000

14 Then I looked, and behold, on Mount Zion stood the Lamb, and with him 144,000 who had his name and his Father's name written on their foreheads. [2] And I heard a voice from heaven like the roar of many waters and like the sound of loud thunder. The voice I heard was like the sound of harpists playing on their harps, [3] and they were singing a new song before the throne and before the four living creatures and before the elders. No one could learn that song except the 144,000 who had been redeemed from the earth. [4] It is these who have not defiled themselves with women, for they are virgins. It is these who follow the Lamb wherever he goes. These have been redeemed from mankind as firstfruits for God and the Lamb, [5] and in their mouth no lie was found, for they are blameless.

The Messages of the Three Angels

[6] Then I saw another angel flying directly overhead, with an eternal gospel to proclaim to those who dwell on earth, to every nation and tribe and language and people. [7] And he said with a loud voice, "Fear God and give him glory, because the hour of his judgment has come, and worship him who made heaven and earth, the sea and the springs of water."

[8] Another angel, a second, followed, saying, "Fallen, fallen is Babylon the great, she who made all nations drink the wine of the passion[1] of her sexual immorality."

[9] And another angel, a third, followed them, saying with a loud voice, "If anyone worships the beast and its image and receives a mark on his forehead or on his hand, [10] he also will drink the wine of God's wrath, poured full strength into the cup of his anger, and he will be tormented with fire and sulfur in the presence of the holy angels and in the presence of the Lamb. [11] And the smoke of their torment goes up forever and ever, and they have no rest, day or night, these worshipers of the beast and its image, and whoever receives the mark of its name."

[12] Here is a call for the endurance of the saints, those who keep the commandments of God and their faith in Jesus.[2]

[13] And I heard a voice from heaven saying, "Write this: Blessed are the dead who die in the Lord from now on." "Blessed indeed," says the Spirit, "that they may rest from their labors, for their deeds follow them!"

The Harvest of the Earth

[14] Then I looked, and behold, a white cloud, and seated on the cloud one like a son of man, with a golden crown on his head, and a sharp sickle in his hand. [15] And another angel came out of the temple, calling with a loud voice to him who sat on the cloud, "Put in your sickle, and reap, for the hour to reap has come, for the harvest of the earth is fully ripe." [16] So he who sat on the cloud swung his sickle across the earth, and the earth was reaped.

[17] Then another angel came out of the temple in heaven, and he too had a sharp sickle. [18] And another angel came out from the altar, the angel who has authority over the fire, and he called with a loud voice to the one who had the sharp sickle, "Put in your sickle and gather the clusters from the vine of the earth, for its grapes are ripe." [19] So the angel swung his sickle across the earth and gathered the grape harvest of the earth and threw it into the great winepress of the wrath of God. [20] And the winepress was trodden outside the city, and blood flowed from the winepress, as high as a horse's bridle, for 1,600 stadia.[3]

The Seven Angels with Seven Plagues

15 Then I saw another sign in heaven, great and amazing, seven angels with seven plagues, which are the last, for with them the wrath of God is finished.

[2] And I saw what appeared to be a sea of glass mingled with fire—and also those who had conquered the beast and its image and the number of its name, standing beside the sea of glass with harps of God in their hands. [3] And they sing the song of Moses, the servant of God, and the song of the Lamb, saying,

"Great and amazing are your deeds,
     O Lord God the Almighty!
Just and true are your ways,
     O King of the nations![4]
[4]   Who will not fear, O Lord,
     and glorify your name?
For you alone are holy.
     All nations will come
     and worship you,
for your righteous acts have been
     revealed."

[5] After this I looked, and the sanctuary of the tent[5] of witness in heaven was opened, [6] and out of the sanctuary came the seven angels

with the seven plagues, clothed in pure, bright linen, with golden sashes around their chests. [7] And one of the four living creatures gave to the seven angels seven golden bowls full of the wrath of God who lives forever and ever, [8] and the sanctuary was filled with smoke from the glory of God and from his power, and no one could enter the sanctuary until the seven plagues of the seven angels were finished.

The Seven Bowls of God's Wrath

16 Then I heard a loud voice from the temple telling the seven angels, "Go and pour out on the earth the seven bowls of the wrath of God."

[2] So the first angel went and poured out his bowl on the earth, and harmful and painful sores came upon the people who bore the mark of the beast and worshiped its image.

[3] The second angel poured out his bowl into the sea, and it became like the blood of a corpse, and every living thing died that was in the sea.

[4] The third angel poured out his bowl into the rivers and the springs of water, and they became blood. [5] And I heard the angel in charge of the waters[1] say,

"Just are you, O Holy One, who is and who was,
    for you brought these judgments.
[6]   For they have shed the blood of saints and prophets,
        and you have given them blood to drink.
It is what they deserve!"

[7] And I heard the altar saying,

"Yes, Lord God the Almighty,
    true and just are your judgments!"

[8] The fourth angel poured out his bowl on the sun, and it was allowed to scorch people with fire. [9] They were scorched by the fierce heat, and they cursed[2] the name of God who had power over these plagues. They did not repent and give him glory.

[10] The fifth angel poured out his bowl on the throne of the beast, and its kingdom was plunged into darkness. People gnawed their tongues in anguish [11] and cursed the God of heaven for their pain and sores. They did not repent of their deeds.

[12] The sixth angel poured out his bowl on the great river Euphrates, and its water was dried up, to prepare the way for the kings from the east. [13] And I saw, coming out of the mouth of the dragon and out of the mouth of the beast and out of the mouth of the false prophet, three unclean spirits like frogs. [14] For they are demonic spirits, performing signs, who go abroad to the kings of the whole world, to assemble them for battle on the great day of God the Almighty. [15] ("Behold, I am coming like a thief! Blessed is the one who stays awake, keeping his garments on, that he may not go about naked and be seen exposed!") [16] And they assembled them at the place that in Hebrew is called Armageddon.

The Seventh Bowl

[17] The seventh angel poured out his bowl into the air, and a loud voice came out of the temple, from the throne, saying, "It is done!" [18] And there were flashes of lightning, rumblings,[3] peals of thunder, and a great earthquake such as there had never been since man was on the earth, so great was that earthquake. [19] The great city was split into three parts, and the cities of the nations fell, and God remembered Babylon the great, to make her drain the cup of the wine of the fury of his wrath. [20] And every island fled away, and no mountains were to be found. [21] And great hailstones, about one hundred pounds[4] each, fell from heaven on people; and they cursed God for the plague of the hail, because the plague was so severe.

The Great Prostitute and the Beast

17 Then one of the seven angels who had the seven bowls came and said to me, "Come, I will show you the judgment of the great prostitute who is seated on many waters, [2] with whom the kings of the earth have committed sexual immorality, and with the wine of whose sexual immorality the dwellers on earth have become drunk." [3] And he carried me away in the Spirit into a wilderness, and I saw a woman sitting on a scarlet beast that was full of blasphemous names, and it had seven heads and ten horns. [4] The woman was arrayed in purple and scarlet, and adorned with gold and jewels and pearls, holding in her hand a golden cup full of abominations and the impurities of her sexual immorality. [5] And on her forehead was written a name of mystery: "Babylon the great, mother of prostitutes and of earth's abominations." [6] And I saw the woman, drunk

---

[1] Greek angel of the waters [2] Greek blasphemed; also verses 11, 21 [3] Or voices, or sounds [4] Greek a talent in weight

with the blood of the saints, the blood of the martyrs of Jesus.[1]

When I saw her, I marveled greatly. [7] But the angel said to me, "Why do you marvel? I will tell you the mystery of the woman, and of the beast with seven heads and ten horns that carries her. [8] The beast that you saw was, and is not, and is about to rise from the bottomless pit[2] and go to destruction. And the dwellers on earth whose names have not been written in the book of life from the foundation of the world will marvel to see the beast, because it was and is not and is to come. [9] This calls for a mind with wisdom: the seven heads are seven mountains on which the woman is seated; [10] they are also seven kings, five of whom have fallen, one is, the other has not yet come, and when he does come he must remain only a little while. [11] As for the beast that was and is not, it is an eighth but it belongs to the seven, and it goes to destruction. [12] And the ten horns that you saw are ten kings who have not yet received royal power, but they are to receive authority as kings for one hour, together with the beast. [13] These are of one mind, and they hand over their power and authority to the beast. [14] They will make war on the Lamb, and the Lamb will conquer them, for he is Lord of lords and King of kings, and those with him are called and chosen and faithful."

[15] And the angel[3] said to me, "The waters that you saw, where the prostitute is seated, are peoples and multitudes and nations and languages. [16] And the ten horns that you saw, they and the beast will hate the prostitute. They will make her desolate and naked, and devour her flesh and burn her up with fire, [17] for God has put it into their hearts to carry out his purpose by being of one mind and handing over their royal power to the beast, until the words of God are fulfilled. [18] And the woman that you saw is the great city that has dominion over the kings of the earth."

The Fall of Babylon

18 After this I saw another angel coming down from heaven, having great authority, and the earth was made bright with his glory. [2] And he called out with a mighty voice,

"Fallen, fallen is Babylon the great!
　　She has become a dwelling place for
　　　demons,

a haunt for every unclean spirit,
　　a haunt for every unclean bird,
　　a haunt for every unclean and detestable beast.
[3]　For all nations have drunk[4]
　　the wine of the passion of her sexual immorality,
and the kings of the earth have committed immorality with her,
　　and the merchants of the earth have grown rich from the power of her luxurious living."

[4] Then I heard another voice from heaven saying,

"Come out of her, my people,
　　lest you take part in her sins,
lest you share in her plagues;
[5]　for her sins are heaped high as heaven,
　　and God has remembered her iniquities.
[6]　Pay her back as she herself has paid back others,
　　and repay her double for her deeds;
　　mix a double portion for her in the cup she mixed.
[7]　As she glorified herself and lived in luxury,
　　so give her a like measure of torment and mourning,
since in her heart she says,
　'I sit as a queen,
I am no widow,
　　and mourning I shall never see.'
[8]　For this reason her plagues will come in a single day,
　　death and mourning and famine,
and she will be burned up with fire;
　　for mighty is the Lord God who has judged her."

[9] And the kings of the earth, who committed sexual immorality and lived in luxury with her, will weep and wail over her when they see the smoke of her burning. [10] They will stand far off, in fear of her torment, and say,

"Alas! Alas! You great city,
　　you mighty city, Babylon!
For in a single hour your judgment has come."

[11] And the merchants of the earth weep and mourn for her, since no one buys their cargo anymore, [12] cargo of gold, silver, jewels, pearls, fine linen, purple cloth, silk, scarlet cloth, all

[1] Greek *the witnesses to Jesus* [2] Greek *the abyss* [3] Greek *he* [4] Some manuscripts *fallen by*

kinds of scented wood, all kinds of articles of ivory, all kinds of articles of costly wood, bronze, iron and marble, [13] cinnamon, spice, incense, myrrh, frankincense, wine, oil, fine flour, wheat, cattle and sheep, horses and chariots, and slaves, that is, human souls.[1]

[14] "The fruit for which your soul longed
 has gone from you,
  and all your delicacies and your splendors
 are lost to you,
  never to be found again!"

[15] The merchants of these wares, who gained wealth from her, will stand far off, in fear of her torment, weeping and mourning aloud,

[16] "Alas, alas, for the great city
  that was clothed in fine linen,
   in purple and scarlet,
  adorned with gold,
   with jewels, and with pearls!
[17] For in a single hour all this wealth has
   been laid waste."

And all shipmasters and seafaring men, sailors and all whose trade is on the sea, stood far off [18] and cried out as they saw the smoke of her burning,

 "What city was like the great city?"

[19] And they threw dust on their heads as they wept and mourned, crying out,

 "Alas, alas, for the great city
  where all who had ships at sea
  grew rich by her wealth!
 For in a single hour she has been laid
  waste.
[20] Rejoice over her, O heaven,
  and you saints and apostles and prophets,
 for God has given judgment for you
  against her!"

[21] Then a mighty angel took up a stone like a great millstone and threw it into the sea, saying,

 "So will Babylon the great city be thrown
  down with violence,
  and will be found no more;
[22] and the sound of harpists and musicians,
   of flute players and trumpeters,
  will be heard in you no more,
 and a craftsman of any craft
  will be found in you no more,

and the sound of the mill
 will be heard in you no more,
[23] and the light of a lamp
  will shine in you no more,
 and the voice of bridegroom and bride
  will be heard in you no more,
 for your merchants were the great ones of
  the earth,
  and all nations were deceived by your
   sorcery.
[24] And in her was found the blood of prophets and of saints,
  and of all who have been slain on earth."

Rejoicing in Heaven

19 After this I heard what seemed to be the loud voice of a great multitude in heaven, crying out,

 "Hallelujah!
 Salvation and glory and power belong to
  our God,
[2] for his judgments are true and just;
 for he has judged the great prostitute
  who corrupted the earth with her
   immorality,
 and has avenged on her the blood of his
  servants."

[3] Once more they cried out,

 "Hallelujah!
 The smoke from her goes up forever and
  ever."

[4] And the twenty-four elders and the four living creatures fell down and worshiped God who was seated on the throne, saying, "Amen. Hallelujah!" [5] And from the throne came a voice saying,

 "Praise our God,
  all you his servants,
 you who fear him,
  small and great."

The Marriage Supper of the Lamb

[6] Then I heard what seemed to be the voice of a great multitude, like the roar of many waters and like the sound of mighty peals of thunder, crying out,

 "Hallelujah!
 For the Lord our God
  the Almighty reigns.

[1] Or and slaves, and human lives

7.   Let us rejoice and exult
        and give him the glory,
    for the marriage of the Lamb has come,
        and his Bride has made herself ready;
8   it was granted her to clothe herself
        with fine linen, bright and pure"—

for the fine linen is the righteous deeds of the saints.

⁹ And the angel said¹ to me, "Write this: Blessed are those who are invited to the marriage supper of the Lamb." And he said to me, "These are the true words of God." ¹⁰ Then I fell down at his feet to worship him, but he said to me, "You must not do that! I am a fellow servant with you and your brothers who hold to the testimony of Jesus. Worship God." For the testimony of Jesus is the spirit of prophecy.

The Rider on a White Horse

¹¹ Then I saw heaven opened, and behold, a white horse! The one sitting on it is called Faithful and True, and in righteousness he judges and makes war. ¹² His eyes are like a flame of fire, and on his head are many diadems, and he has a name written that no one knows but himself. ¹³ He is clothed in a robe dipped in² blood, and the name by which he is called is The Word of God. ¹⁴ And the armies of heaven, arrayed in fine linen, white and pure, were following him on white horses. ¹⁵ From his mouth comes a sharp sword with which to strike down the nations, and he will rule³ them with a rod of iron. He will tread the winepress of the fury of the wrath of God the Almighty. ¹⁶ On his robe and on his thigh he has a name written, King of kings and Lord of lords.

¹⁷ Then I saw an angel standing in the sun, and with a loud voice he called to all the birds that fly directly overhead, "Come, gather for the great supper of God, ¹⁸ to eat the flesh of kings, the flesh of captains, the flesh of mighty men, the flesh of horses and their riders, and the flesh of all men, both free and slave,⁴ both small and great." ¹⁹ And I saw the beast and the kings of the earth with their armies gathered to make war against him who was sitting on the horse and against his army. ²⁰ And the beast was captured, and with it the false prophet who in its presence⁵ had done the signs by which he deceived those who had received the mark of the beast and those who worshiped its image. These two were thrown alive into the lake of fire that burns with sulfur. ²¹ And the rest were slain by the sword that came from the mouth of him who was sitting on the horse, and all the birds were gorged with their flesh.

The Thousand Years

20 Then I saw an angel coming down from heaven, holding in his hand the key to the bottomless pit⁶ and a great chain. ² And he seized the dragon, that ancient serpent, who is the devil and Satan, and bound him for a thousand years, ³ and threw him into the pit, and shut it and sealed it over him, so that he might not deceive the nations any longer, until the thousand years were ended. After that he must be released for a little while.

⁴ Then I saw thrones, and seated on them were those to whom the authority to judge was committed. Also I saw the souls of those who had been beheaded for the testimony of Jesus and for the word of God, and those who had not worshiped the beast or its image and had not received its mark on their foreheads or their hands. They came to life and reigned with Christ for a thousand years. ⁵ The rest of the dead did not come to life until the thousand years were ended. This is the first resurrection. ⁶ Blessed and holy is the one who shares in the first resurrection! Over such the second death has no power, but they will be priests of God and of Christ, and they will reign with him for a thousand years.

The Defeat of Satan

⁷ And when the thousand years are ended, Satan will be released from his prison ⁸ and will come out to deceive the nations that are at the four corners of the earth, Gog and Magog, to gather them for battle; their number is like the sand of the sea. ⁹ And they marched up over the broad plain of the earth and surrounded the camp of the saints and the beloved city, but fire came down from heaven⁷ and consumed them, ¹⁰ and the devil who had deceived them was thrown into the lake of fire and sulfur where the beast and the false prophet were, and they will be tormented day and night forever and ever.

Judgment Before the Great White Throne

¹¹ Then I saw a great white throne and him who was seated on it. From his presence earth and sky fled away, and no place was found for

---

¹ Greek *he said* ² Some manuscripts *sprinkled with* ³ Greek *shepherd* ⁴ For the contextual rendering of the Greek word *doulos*, see Preface ⁵ Or *on its behalf* ⁶ Greek *the abyss*; also verse 3 ⁷ Some manuscripts *from God, out of heaven*, or *out of heaven from God*

them. [12] And I saw the dead, great and small, standing before the throne, and books were opened. Then another book was opened, which is the book of life. And the dead were judged by what was written in the books, according to what they had done. [13] And the sea gave up the dead who were in it, Death and Hades gave up the dead who were in them, and they were judged, each one of them, according to what they had done. [14] Then Death and Hades were thrown into the lake of fire. This is the second death, the lake of fire. [15] And if anyone's name was not found written in the book of life, he was thrown into the lake of fire.

The New Heaven and the New Earth

21 Then I saw a new heaven and a new earth, for the first heaven and the first earth had passed away, and the sea was no more. [2] And I saw the holy city, new Jerusalem, coming down out of heaven from God, prepared as a bride adorned for her husband. [3] And I heard a loud voice from the throne saying, "Behold, the dwelling place[1] of God is with man. He will dwell with them, and they will be his people,[2] and God himself will be with them as their God.[3] [4] He will wipe away every tear from their eyes, and death shall be no more, neither shall there be mourning, nor crying, nor pain anymore, for the former things have passed away."

[5] And he who was seated on the throne said, "Behold, I am making all things new." Also he said, "Write this down, for these words are trustworthy and true." [6] And he said to me, "It is done! I am the Alpha and the Omega, the beginning and the end. To the thirsty I will give from the spring of the water of life without payment. [7] The one who conquers will have this heritage, and I will be his God and he will be my son. [8] But as for the cowardly, the faithless, the detestable, as for murderers, the sexually immoral, sorcerers, idolaters, and all liars, their portion will be in the lake that burns with fire and sulfur, which is the second death."

The New Jerusalem

[9] Then came one of the seven angels who had the seven bowls full of the seven last plagues and spoke to me, saying, "Come, I will show you the Bride, the wife of the Lamb." [10] And he carried me away in the Spirit to a great, high mountain, and showed me the holy city Jerusalem coming down out of heaven from

God, [11] having the glory of God, its radiance like a most rare jewel, like a jasper, clear as crystal. [12] It had a great, high wall, with twelve gates, and at the gates twelve angels, and on the gates the names of the twelve tribes of the sons of Israel were inscribed— [13] on the east three gates, on the north three gates, on the south three gates, and on the west three gates. [14] And the wall of the city had twelve foundations, and on them were the twelve names of the twelve apostles of the Lamb.

[15] And the one who spoke with me had a measuring rod of gold to measure the city and its gates and walls. [16] The city lies foursquare, its length the same as its width. And he measured the city with his rod, 12,000 stadia.[4] Its length and width and height are equal. [17] He also measured its wall, 144 cubits[5] by human measurement, which is also an angel's measurement. [18] The wall was built of jasper, while the city was pure gold, like clear glass. [19] The foundations of the wall of the city were adorned with every kind of jewel. The first was jasper, the second sapphire, the third agate, the fourth emerald, [20] the fifth onyx, the sixth carnelian, the seventh chrysolite, the eighth beryl, the ninth topaz, the tenth chrysoprase, the eleventh jacinth, the twelfth amethyst. [21] And the twelve gates were twelve pearls, each of the gates made of a single pearl, and the street of the city was pure gold, like transparent glass.

[22] And I saw no temple in the city, for its temple is the Lord God the Almighty and the Lamb. [23] And the city has no need of sun or moon to shine on it, for the glory of God gives it light, and its lamp is the Lamb. [24] By its light will the nations walk, and the kings of the earth will bring their glory into it, [25] and its gates will never be shut by day—and there will be no night there. [26] They will bring into it the glory and the honor of the nations. [27] But nothing unclean will ever enter it, nor anyone who does what is detestable or false, but only those who are written in the Lamb's book of life.

The River of Life

22 Then the angel[6] showed me the river of the water of life, bright as crystal, flowing from the throne of God and of the Lamb [2] through the middle of the street of the city; also, on either side of the river, the tree of life[7] with its twelve kinds of fruit, yielding its fruit each month. The leaves of the tree were for the

---

[1] Or tabernacle [2] Some manuscripts peoples [3] Some manuscripts omit as their God [4] About 1,380 miles; a stadion was about 607 feet or 185 meters [5] A cubit was about 18 inches or 45 centimeters [6] Greek he [7] Or the Lamb. In the midst of the street of the city, and on either side of the river, was the tree of life

healing of the nations. ³No longer will there be anything accursed, but the throne of God and of the Lamb will be in it, and his servants will worship him. ⁴They will see his face, and his name will be on their foreheads. ⁵And night will be no more. They will need no light of lamp or sun, for the Lord God will be their light, and they will reign forever and ever.

Jesus Is Coming

⁶And he said to me, "These words are trustworthy and true. And the Lord, the God of the spirits of the prophets, has sent his angel to show his servants what must soon take place."

⁷"And behold, I am coming soon. Blessed is the one who keeps the words of the prophecy of this book."

⁸I, John, am the one who heard and saw these things. And when I heard and saw them, I fell down to worship at the feet of the angel who showed them to me, ⁹but he said to me, "You must not do that! I am a fellow servant with you and your brothers the prophets, and with those who keep the words of this book. Worship God."

¹⁰And he said to me, "Do not seal up the words of the prophecy of this book, for the time is near. ¹¹Let the evildoer still do evil, and the filthy still be filthy, and the righteous still do right, and the holy still be holy."

¹²"Behold, I am coming soon, bringing my recompense with me, to repay each one for what he has done. ¹³I am the Alpha and the Omega, the first and the last, the beginning and the end."

¹⁴Blessed are those who wash their robes,[1] so that they may have the right to the tree of life and that they may enter the city by the gates. ¹⁵Outside are the dogs and sorcerers and the sexually immoral and murderers and idolaters, and everyone who loves and practices falsehood.

¹⁶"I, Jesus, have sent my angel to testify to you about these things for the churches. I am the root and the descendant of David, the bright morning star."

¹⁷The Spirit and the Bride say, "Come." And let the one who hears say, "Come." And let the one who is thirsty come; let the one who desires take the water of life without price.

¹⁸I warn everyone who hears the words of the prophecy of this book: if anyone adds to them, God will add to him the plagues described in this book, ¹⁹and if anyone takes away from the words of the book of this prophecy, God will take away his share in the tree of life and in the holy city, which are described in this book.

²⁰He who testifies to these things says, "Surely I am coming soon." Amen. Come, Lord Jesus!

²¹The grace of the Lord Jesus be with all.[2] Amen.

¹ Some manuscripts *do his commandments* ² Some manuscripts *all the saints*

TABLE OF
WEIGHTS AND MEASURES
AND MONETARY UNITS

The following table is based on the best generally accepted information available for biblical weights, measures, and monetary units. All equivalents are approximate. Weights and measures also varied somewhat in different times and places in the ancient world. Most weights, measures, and monetary units are also explained in footnotes on the pages where they occur in the ESV text.

Biblical Unit	Approximate American and Metric Equivalents	Biblical Equivalent
bath	A *bath* was about 6 gallons or 22 liters	1 ephah
beka	A *beka* was about 1/5 ounce or 5.5 grams	10 gerahs
cor	A *cor* was about 6 bushels or 220 liters	10 ephahs
cubit	A *cubit* was about 18 inches or 45 centimeters	6 handbreadths
daric	A *daric* was a coin of about 1/4 ounce or 8.5 grams	
denarius	A *denarius* was a day's wage for a laborer	
ephah	An *ephah* was about 3/5 bushel or 22 liters	10 omers
gerah	A *gerah* was about 1/50 ounce or 0.6 gram	1/10 beka
handbreadth	A *handbreadth* was about 3 inches or 7.5 centimeters	1/6 cubit
hin	A *hin* was about 4 quarts or 3.5 liters	1/6 bath
homer	A *homer* was about 6 bushels or 220 liters	10 ephahs
kab	A *kab* was about 1 quart or 1 liter	1/22 ephah
lethech	A *lethech* was about 3 bushels or 110 liters	5 ephahs
log	A *log* was about 1/3 quart or 0.3 liter	1/72 bath
mina	A *mina* was about 1 1/4 pounds or 0.6 kilogram	50 shekels
omer	An *omer* was about 2 quarts or 2 liters	1/10 ephah
pim	A *pim* was about 1/3 ounce or 7.5 grams	2/3 shekel
seah	A *seah* was about 7 quarts or 7.3 liters	1/3 ephah
shekel	A *shekel* was about 2/5 ounce or 11 grams	2 bekas
span	A *span* was about 9 inches or 22 centimeters	3 handbreadths
stadion	A *stadion* was about 607 feet or 185 meters	
talent	A *talent* was about 75 pounds or 34 kilograms	60 minas

CONCORDANCE

Introduction

As an essentially literal, word-for-word translation, the ESV Bible is ideally suited for use with a concordance. This is true because the ESV uses the same English word, as far as possible, to translate important recurring words in the original languages, and because the ESV retains key theological terms that have been of central importance for Christian doctrine through the centuries—thereby enabling the reader to locate specific words and texts and facilitating the reading and study of the Bible.

Using the ESV Concordance

The concordance in the ESV Thinline Bible contains more than 2,400 word entries and nearly 10,000 Scripture references. Each word entry is followed by a selected list of brief phrases showing the contexts in which each entry occurs, followed by the Scripture references. To conserve space, only the first letter of the word entry is used in the phrase; these letters appear in bold for easy recognition.

ABBREVIATIONS

Abbreviations for the books of the Bible as used in the concordance.

THE OLD TESTAMENT

Genesis	Gn	Ecclesiastes	Eccl
Exodus	Ex	Song of Solomon	Sg
Leviticus	Lv	Isaiah	Is
Numbers	Nm	Jeremiah	Jer
Deuteronomy	Dt	Lamentations	Lam
Joshua	Jos	Ezekiel	Ezk
Judges	Jgs	Daniel	Dn
Ruth	Ru	Hosea	Hos
1 Samuel	1 Sm	Joel	Jl
2 Samuel	2 Sm	Amos	Am
1 Kings	1 Kgs	Obadiah	Ob
2 Kings	2 Kgs	Jonah	Jon
1 Chronicles	1 Chr	Micah	Mi
2 Chronicles	2 Chr	Nahum	Na
Ezra	Ezr	Habakkuk	Hab
Nehemiah	Neh	Zephaniah	Zep
Esther	Est	Haggai	Hg
Job	Jb	Zechariah	Zec
Psalms	Ps	Malachi	Mal
Proverbs	Prv		

THE NEW TESTAMENT

Matthew	Mt	1 Timothy	1 Tm
Mark	Mk	2 Timothy	2 Tm
Luke	Lk	Titus	Ti
John	Jn	Philemon	Phlm
Acts	Acts	Hebrews	Heb
Romans	Rom	James	Jas
1 Corinthians	1 Cor	1 Peter	1 Pt
2 Corinthians	2 Cor	2 Peter	2 Pt
Galatians	Gal	1 John	1 Jn
Ephesians	Eph	2 John	2 Jn
Philippians	Phil	3 John	3 Jn
Colossians	Col	Jude	Jude
1 Thessalonians	1 Thes	Revelation	Rv
2 Thessalonians	2 Thes		

AARON

Moses and he said, "Is there not **A**, ... Ex 4:14
So **A** said to them, "Take off the rings ..... Ex 32:2
And the staff of **A** was among their ..... Nm 17:6
called by God, just as **A** was. .... Heb 5:4

ABADDON

Sheol and **A** lie open before the .... Prv 15:11
His name in Hebrew is **A**, and in Greek .. Rv 9:11

ABANDON

For you will not **a** my soul to Sheol, ... Ps 16:10
The LORD will not **a** him to .... Ps 37:33
he will not **a** his heritage; .... Ps 94:14
For you will not **a** my soul to Hades, ... Acts 2:27

ABANDONED

for having **a** their former faith. .... 1 Tm 5:12
you have **a** the love you had at first. ...... Rv 2:4

ABBA

"**A**, Father, all things are possible for ... Mk 14:36
sons, by whom we cry, "**A**! Father!" ... Rom 8:15
into our hearts, crying, "**A**! Father!" .... Gal 4:6

ABEL

"Where is **A** your brother?" .... Gn 4:9
By faith **A** offered to God a more .... Heb 11:4
a better word than the blood of **A**. .... Heb 12:24

ABHOR

they **a** him who speaks the truth. .... Am 5:10
A what is evil; hold fast to what is ...... Rom 12:9

ABIATHAR

A, escaped and fled after David. .... 1 Sm 22:20
son of Zeruiah and with **A** the priest. ..... 1 Kgs 1:7

ABIDE

His soul shall **a** in well-being, ... Ps 25:13
righteousness **a** in the fruitful field. .... Is 32:16
"If you **a** in my word, you are truly .... Jn 8:31
A in me, and I in you. As the branch .... Jn 15:4
so have I loved you. **A** in my love. ...... Jn 15:9
By this we know that we **a** in him and .... 1 Jn 4:13

ABIDES

says he **a** in him ought to walk. .... 1 Jn 2:6
who **a** in him keeps on sinning; .... 1 Jn 3:6
whoever **a** in love **a** in God, ... 1 Jn 4:16

ABIGAIL

When **A** saw David, she hurried and .... 1 Sm 25:23

ABIJAH

At that time **A** the son of Jeroboam ....1 Kgs 14:1
and **A** his son reigned in his place. ..... 2 Chr 12:16

ABILITY

Spirit of God, with **a** and intelligence, ... Ex 31:3
another one, to each according to his **a**.... Mt 25:15
is right, but not the **a** to carry it out. ..... Rom 7:18

ABIMELECH

prayed to God, and God healed **A**, ... Gn 20:17
A said, "What is this you have done to .. Gn 26:10

ABISHAI

and to Joab's brother **A** the son of .... 1 Sm 26:6
So Joab and **A** his brother killed Abner, .. 2 Sm 3:30
Zeruiah: **A**, Joab, and Asahel, three.... 1 Chr 2:16

ABLE

Every man shall give as he is **a**, ... Dt 16:17
But who is **a** to build him a house, ... 2 Chr 2:6
silver and gold are not **a** to deliver. ...... Ezk 7:19
our God whom we serve is **a** .... Dn 3:17
convinced that God was **a** to do what .... Rom 4:21
will be **a** to separate us from the love.... Rom 8:39
Now to him who is **a** to strengthen you . Rom 16:25
Now to him who is **a** to do far more .... Eph 3:20
him who was **a** to save him from death,.... Heb 5:7
Now to him who is **a** to keep you from ... Jude 24

ABNER

of his army was **A** the son of Ner, ...1 Sm 14:50
A was making himself strong in the .... 2 Sm 3:6

ABOLISH

I have not come to **a** them but to fulfill .... Mt 5:17

ABOLISHED

Jesus, who **a** death and brought life .... 2 Tm 1:10

ABOMINATION

Lying lips are an **a** to the LORD, ... Prv 12:22
shall set up the **a** that makes desolate. .. Dn 11:31
"So when you see the **a** of desolation .. Mt 24:15
what is exalted among men is an **a** in .. Lk 16:15

ABOUND

continue in sin that grace may **a**? .... Rom 6:1
you may **a** in every good work. .... 2 Cor 9:8
make you increase and **a** in love for .... 1 Thes 3:12

ABOUNDED

that one man Jesus Christ **a** for many.... Rom 5:15
sin increased, grace **a** all the more, ... Rom 5:20

ABOUNDING

LORD is slow to anger and **a** in .... Nm 14:18
slow to anger and **a** in steadfast love. .. Ps 103:8
and **a** in steadfast love; and he .... Jl 2:13
slow to anger and **a** in steadfast love, ... Jon 4:2

ABOVE

the LORD is God in heaven **a** .... Dt 4:39
Be exalted, O God, **a** the heavens! ...... Ps 57:5
He who comes from **a** is **a** all. .... Jn 3:31
"You are from below; I am from **a**. .... Jn 8:23
unless it had been given you from **a**. ..... Jn 19:11
far **a** all rule and authority and .... Eph 1:21
the name that is **a** every name, ... Phil 2:9
and every perfect gift is from **a**, ... Jas 1:17

ABRAHAM

Abram, but your name shall be **A**, ... Gn 17:5
After these things God tested **A** .... Gn 22:1
"I am the God of **A** your father. .... Gn 26:24
'We have **A** as our father,' .... Mt 3:9
to **A** and to his offspring forever." .... Lk 1:55
"**A** believed God, and it was counted .... Rom 4:3
just as **A** "believed God, and it was ..... Gal 3:6
By faith **A** obeyed when he was called .. Heb 11:8

ABRAHAM'S

carried by the angels to **A** side. .... Lk 16:22
"If you were **A** children, you .... Jn 8:39
are Christ's, then you are **A** offspring, ... Gal 3:29

ABRAM

LORD said to **A**, "Go from your .... Gn 12:1
"Fear not, **A**, I am your shield; .... Gn 15:1
LORD made a covenant with **A**, ... Gn 15:18

ABSALOM

A, David's son, had a beautiful .... 2 Sm 13:1
So **A** stole the hearts of the men of .... 2 Sm 15:6
"O my son **A**, O **A**, my son, ... 2 Sm 19:4

ABSTAIN

A from every form of evil. .... 1 Thes 5:22
to **a** from the passions of the flesh, ... 1 Pt 2:11

ABUNDANCE

But I, through the **a** of your steadfast .... Ps 5:7
according to the **a** of his steadfast love; . Lam 3:32
will be given, and he will have an **a**, ... Mt 13:12
contributed out of their **a**, but she ..... Mk 12:44
out of the **a** of the heart his mouth ...... Lk 6:45
so that their **a** may supply your need, .. 2 Cor 8:14

ABUNDANTLY

may have life and have it **a**. .... Jn 10:10
For as we share **a** in Christ's sufferings, .. 2 Cor 1:5
because your faith is growing **a**, ... 2 Thes 1:3

ACCENT

one of them, for your **a** betrays you." ... Mt 26:73

ACCEPT

A my freewill offerings of praise, ... Ps 119:108
Hear, my son, and **a** my words, ... Prv 4:10
to **a** his lot and rejoice in his toil— ..... Eccl 5:19
hear the word and **a** it and bear fruit, ... Mk 4:20

ACCEPTABLE

meditation of my heart be **a** .... Ps 19:14
lips of the righteous know what is **a**, ... Prv 10:32
holy and **a** to God, which is .... Rom 12:1
thus let us offer to God **a** worship, ... Heb 12:28

ACCEPTANCE

but the upright enjoy **a**. .... Prv 14:9
what will their **a** mean but life from ... Rom 11:15
is trustworthy and deserving of full **a**, .. 1 Tm 1:15

ACCEPTED

If you do well, will you not be **a**? .... Gn 4:7
the LORD **a** Job's prayer. .... Jb 42:9
you **a** it not as the word of men but ... 1 Thes 2:13

ACCESS

we both have **a** in one Spirit. .... Eph 2:18

ACCOMPLISH

but it shall **a** that which I purpose, ... Is 55:11
which he was about to **a** at Jerusalem. .. Lk 9:31
works that the Father has given me to **a**, .. Jn 5:36

ACCOMPLISHED

Son of Man by the prophets will be **a**.... Lk 18:31
having **a** the work that you gave me to .. Jn 17:4
except what Christ has **a** through me .. Rom 15:18

ACCORD

I have not come of my own **a**. .... Jn 7:28
I lay it down of my own **a**. .... Jn 10:18
being in full **a** and of one mind. .... Phil 2:2

ACCOUNT

of evil against you falsely on my **a**. .... Mt 5:11
people will give **a** for every careless ..... Mt 12:36
each of us will give an **a** .... Rom 14:12
eyes of him to whom we must give **a**. ... Heb 4:13
but they will give **a** to him .... 1 Pt 4:5

ACCOUNTABLE

whole world may be held **a** to God. ..... Rom 3:19

ACCURSED

wish that I myself were **a** .... Rom 9:3
no love for the Lord, let him be **a**. .... 1 Cor 16:22
No longer will there be anything **a**, ... Rv 22:3

ACCUSATION

"What **a** do you bring against .... Jn 18:29

ACCUSE

evil for good **a** me because I follow .... Ps 38:20
In return for my love they **a** me, ... Ps 109:4
so that they might **a** him. .... Mt 12:10

ACCUSER

lest your **a** hand you over to the judge, .. Mt 5:25
for the **a** of our brothers has been .... Rv 12:10

ACKNOWLEDGE

In all your ways **a** him, and he .... Prv 3:6
and you who are near, **a** my might. ...... Is 33:13
We **a** our wickedness, O LORD, ... Jer 14:20
I also will **a** before my Father .... Mt 10:32
not see fit to **a** God, God gave them up . Rom 1:28
the fruit of lips that **a** his name. .... Heb 13:15

ACQUAINTED

lying down and are **a** with all my ways. . Ps 139:3
a man of sorrows and **a** with grief; .... Is 53:3

ACT

trust in him, and he will **a**. .... Ps 37:5
forgive. O Lord, pay attention and **a**....... Dn 9:19

ACTED

We have **a** very corruptly .... Neh 1:7
done wrong and **a** wickedly and .... Dn 9:5

ADAM

for **A** there was not found a helper .... Gn 2:20
to **A** he said, "Because you have .... Gn 3:17
But like **A** they transgressed the .... Hos 6:7
Yet death reigned from **A** .... Rom 5:14
For as in **A** all die, so also .... 1 Cor 15:22
"The first man **A** became a living .... 1 Cor 15:45
For **A** was formed first, then Eve; .... 1 Tm 2:13

ADD

You shall not a to the word that I .... Dt 4:2
Do not a to his words, lest he .... Prv 30:6
God will a to him the plagues .... Rv 22:18

ADMONISH

but to a you as my beloved children. ... 1 Cor 4:14
a the idle, encourage the fainthearted, 1 Thes 5:14

ADOPTION

received the Spirit of a as sons, ... Rom 8:15
are israelites, and to them belong the a, Rom 9:4
law, so that we might receive a as sons. .. Gal 4:5
he predestined us for a to himself .... Eph 1:5

ADORN

women should a themselves in .... 1 Tm 2:9
women who hoped in God used to a .... 1 Pt 3:5

ADULTERERS

against the sorcerers, against the a, ... Mal 3:5
unjust, a, or even like this tax collector. .. Lk 18:11

ADULTERESS

both the adulterer and the a shall ...... Lv 20:10
from the a with her smooth words, ... Prv 2:16
and embrace the bosom of an a? .... Prv 5:20

ADULTEROUS

my words in this a and sinful generation, Mk 8:38
You a people! Do you not know that ...... Jas 4:4

ADULTERY

"You shall not commit a. .... Ex 20:14
He who commits a lacks sense; .... Prv 6:32
'You shall not commit a.' .... Mt 5:27
heart come evil thoughts, murder, a, ... Mt 15:19
marries another, commits a." .... Mt 19:9
been caught in the act of a. .... Jn 8:4
They have eyes full of a, insatiable ...... 2 Pt 2:14

ADVANTAGE

it is to your a that I go away, ... Jn 16:7
Christ will be of no a to you. .... Gal 5:2
boasters, showing favoritism to gain a. ... Jude 16

ADVERSARIES

Give me not up to the will of my a; ...... Ps 27:12
will destroy all the a of my soul, ... Ps 143:12
LORD takes vengeance on his a .... Na 1:2
which none of your a will be able .... Lk 21:15
fury of fire that will consume the a. .... Heb 10:27

ADVERSARY

'Give me justice against my a.' .... Lk 18:3
give the a no occasion for slander. ...... 1 Tm 5:14
Your a the devil prowls around like .... 1 Pt 5:8

ADVERSITY

and a brother is born for a. .... Prv 17:17
and in the day of a consider: .... Eccl 7:14
the Lord give you the bread of a .... Is 30:20

ADVICE

but a wise man listens to a. .... Prv 12:15
but with those who take a is wisdom. ... Prv 13:10
Listen to a and accept instruction, ... Prv 19:20

ADVOCATE

does sin, we have an a with the Father, ... 1 Jn 2:1

AFFECTION

Love one another with brotherly a. .... Rom 12:10
for you all with the a of Christ Jesus. ..... Phil 1:8
and brotherly a with love. .... 2 Pt 1:7

AFFLICT

taskmasters over them to a them .... Ex 1:11
repay with affliction those who a you, .. 2 Thes 1:6

AFFLICTED

He delivers the a by their affliction ...... Jb 36:15
gracious to me, for I am lonely and a. ... Ps 25:16
glad for as many days as you have a us, .. Ps 90:15
him stricken, smitten by God, and a. ...... Is 53:4
If we are a, it is for your comfort .... 2 Cor 1:6
We are a in every way, but not .... 2 Cor 4:8

AFFLICTION

"I have surely seen the a of my people .... Ex 3:7
Consider my a and my trouble, ... Ps 25:18
because you have seen my a; .... Ps 31:7
I have tried you in the furnace of a....... Is 48:10
In all their a he was afflicted, and the ...... Is 63:9
healing every disease and every a. ...... Mt 9:35
who comforts us in all our a, so .... 2 Cor 1:4
light momentary a is preparing .... 2 Cor 4:17

AFFLICTIONS

Many are the a of the righteous, but ... Ps 34:19
by great endurance, in a, hardships, ... 2 Cor 6:4
what is lacking in Christ's a for the ...... Col 1:24
that no one be moved by these a. .... 1 Thes 3:3

AFRAID

and I was a, because I was naked, ... Gn 3:10
the LORD, and they shall be a of you.... Dt 28:10
"Do not be a or dismayed; be strong .... Jos 10:25
of my life; of whom shall I be a? .... Ps 27:1
When I am a, I put my trust in you. ...... Ps 56:3
He is not a of bad news; .... Ps 112:7
Fear not, nor be a; have I not told .... Is 44:8
Do not be a of them, for I am with .... Jer 1:8
"Why are you a, O you of little faith?" ... Mt 8:26
"Take heart; it is I. Do not be a." .... Mt 14:27
Jesus said to them, "Do not be a; .... Mt 28:10
"Do not be a, Mary, for you have .... Lk 1:30
Jesus said to Simon, "Do not be a; .... Lk 5:10
be troubled, neither let them be a. ...... Jn 14:27
But if you do wrong, be a, for he .... Rom 13:4

AGE

They still bear fruit in old a; .... Ps 92:14
either in this a or in the a to .... Mt 12:32
The harvest is the end of the a, ... Mt 13:39
coming and of the end of the a?" .... Mt 24:3
with you always, to the end of the a." .. Mt 28:20
although it is not a wisdom of this a, ... 1 Cor 2:6
to deliver us from the present evil a, ... Gal 1:4
not only in this a but also in the one to .. Eph 1:21

AGES

renown, O LORD, throughout all a. ..... Ps 135:13
the mystery hidden for a in God, ... Eph 3:9
mystery hidden for a and generations .... Col 1:26
us in Christ Jesus before the a began, ... 2 Tm 1:9
never lies, promised before the a .... Ti 1:2

AGONY

Being in a he prayed more .... Lk 22:44

AGREE

if two of you a on earth about .... Mt 18:19
him, but their testimony did not a. ...... Mk 14:56
a with one another, live in peace; .... 2 Cor 13:11
and the blood; and these three a. ...... 1 Jn 5:8

AHAB

A did more to provoke the LORD, ... 1 Kgs 16:33
Elijah went to show himself to A. ...... 1 Kgs 18:2

AHAZ

A the son of Jotham, king of Judah, ... 2 Kgs 16:1
Again the LORD spoke to A: .... Is 7:10

AHAZIAH

A the son of Ahab began to reign over .. 1 Kgs 22:51
A the son of Jehoram, king of Judah, ... 2 Kgs 8:25

AIM

we a at what is honorable not only ..... 2 Cor 8:21
A for restoration, comfort one .... 2 Cor 13:11
The a of our charge is love that issues ... 1 Tm 1:5
my teaching, my conduct, my a in life, ... 2 Tm 3:10

AIR

I do not box as one beating the a. ...... 1 Cor 9:26
to meet the Lord in the a, ... 1 Thes 4:17
angel poured out his bowl into the a, ... Rv 16:17

ALABASTER

him with a flask of very expensive .... Mt 26:7

ALIENATED

a from the commonwealth of Israel ...... Eph 2:12
a from the life of God because of .... Eph 4:18
who once were a and hostile in mind, ... Col 1:21

ALIVE

He presented himself a to them after ...... Acts 1:3
also in Christ shall all be made a. .... 1 Cor 15:22
made us a together with Christ— .... Eph 2:5
as if you were still a in the world, ... Col 2:20
I died, and behold I am a forevermore, ... Rv 1:18

ALMIGHTY

"I am God A; walk before me, ... Gn 17:1
"I am God A: be fruitful and.............. Gn 35:11
to Isaac, and to Jacob, as God A, ... Ex 6:3
"Shall a faultfinder contend with the A? .. Jb 40:2
who was and who is to come, the A." ..... Rv 1:8
For the Lord our God the A reigns. .... Rv 19:6
the Lord God the A and the Lamb. .... Rv 21:22

ALMS

give as a those things that are within, ... Lk 11:41
prayers and your a have ascended as ... Acts 10:4

ALONE

not good that the man should be a; .... Gn 2:18
that you, O LORD, are God a." .... 2 Kgs 19:19
LORD, you a. You have made heaven, ... Neh 9:6
good? No one is good except God a. .... Mk 10:18
justified by works and not by faith a. ..... Jas 2:24

ALPHA

"I am the A and the Omega," .... Rv 1:8
"It is done! I am the A and the Omega, ... Rv 21:6
I am the A and the Omega, ... Rv 22:13

ALTAR

Isaac his son and laid him on the a, ... Gn 22:9
"You shall make the a of acacia wood, ... Ex 27:1
David built there an a .... 2 Sm 24:25
And he repaired the a of the LORD ... 1 Kgs 18:30
'If anyone swears by the a, ... Mt 23:18
an a with this inscription: 'To the ...... Acts 17:23
I saw under the a the souls of those .... Rv 6:9

ALWAYS

I am with you a, to the end of the age." .. Mt 28:20
a abounding in the work of the Lord, .. 1 Cor 15:58
Christ a leads us in triumphal .... 2 Cor 2:14
giving thanks a and for everything ...... Eph 5:20
Rejoice in the Lord a; .... Phil 4:4
a being prepared to make a defense ... 1 Pt 3:15

AMAZED

And all the people were a, ... Mt 12:23
they were all a and glorified God, ... Mk 2:12
heard him were a at his understanding. ... Lk 2:47
And they were a and astonished, ... Acts 2:7

AMAZIAH

A the son of Joash, king of Judah, ... 2 Kgs 14:1

AMBASSADOR

for which I am an a in chains, ... Eph 6:20

AMBASSADORS

we are a for Christ, God .... 2 Cor 5:20

AMBITION

I make it my a to preach the gospel, ... Rom 15:20
jealousy and selfish a in your hearts, ... Jas 3:14

AMEN

we utter our A to God for his glory. ...... 2 Cor 1:20
'The words of the A, the faithful and ..... Rv 3:14
"A! Blessing and glory and wisdom .... Rv 7:12
"Surely I am coming soon." A. .... Rv 22:20

AMON

and A his son reigned in his place. ..... 2 Kgs 21:18
A was twenty-two years old when he 2 Chr 33:21

ANCHOR

as a sure and steadfast a of the soul, ... Heb 6:19

ANCIENT

lifted up, O a doors, that the King .... Ps 24:7
Do not move an a landmark or .... Prv 23:10
and the A of Days took his seat; .... Dn 7:9

ANDREW

and A his brother, casting a net .... Mt 4:18
who is called Peter, and A his brother; .... Mt 10:2
John speak and followed Jesus was A, ... Jn 1:40
Peter and John and James and A, ... Acts 1:13

ANGEL

the a of the LORD called to him .... Gn 22:11
the a of the LORD appeared .... Ex 3:2
The a of the LORD encamps .... Ps 34:7
My God sent his a and shut the lions' .... Dn 6:22
an a of the Lord appeared to him in ..... Mt 1:20
earthquake, for an a of the Lord .... Mt 28:2
the sixth month the a Gabriel was .... Lk 1:26
during the night an a of the Lord .... Acts 5:19
Now an a of the Lord said to Philip, ... Acts 8:26
disguises himself as an a of light. ..... 2 Cor 11:14

ANGELS

the a of God were ascending and .... Gn 28:12
end of the age, and the reapers are a. ... Mt 13:39
one knows, not even the a of heaven, ... Mt 24:36
me more than twelve legions of a? ...... Mt 26:53
the a were ministering to him. .... Mk 1:13
send out the a and gather his elect ..... Mk 13:27
"He will command his a concerning ...... Lk 4:10
a of God over one sinner who repents. ... Lk 15:10
not know that we are to judge a? .... 1 Cor 6:3
on asceticism and worship of a, ... Col 2:18
for a little while lower than the a; ...... Heb 2:7
some have entertained a unawares. ..... Heb 13:2
things into which a long to look. .... 1 Pt 1:12
For if God did not spare a when .... 2 Pt 2:4

ANGER

LORD is slow to a and abounding ...... Nm 14:18
is slow to a has great understanding, ... Prv 14:29
wrath, but a harsh word stirs up a. ...... Prv 15:1
Wrath is cruel, a is overwhelming, ... Prv 27:4
He does not retain his a forever, ... Mi 7:18
is slow to a and great in power, ... Na 1:3
jealousy, a, hostility, slander, ... 2 Cor 12:20
not let the sun go down on your a, ... Eph 4:26
all away: a, wrath, malice, slander, ... Col 3:8
lifting holy hands without a .... 1 Tm 2:8
to hear, slow to speak, slow to a; ...... Jas 1:19

ANGRY

LORD said to Cain, "Why are you a, ... Gn 4:6
Be a, and do not sin; ponder in your ..... Ps 4:4
O LORD? Will you be a forever? .... Ps 79:5
and a backbiting tongue, causes. ...... Prv 25:23
not quick in your spirit to become a, ... Eccl 7:9
forever, nor will I always be a; .... Is 57:16
I will not be a forever. .... Jer 3:12
"Do you do well to be a?" .... Jon 4:4
is a with his brother will be liable ...... Mt 5:22
Be a and do not sin; do not let the sun ... Eph 4:26

ANGUISH

My heart is in a within me; the terrors .... Ps 55:4
a day of distress and a, a day .... Zep 1:15
sorrow and unceasing a in my heart. .... Rom 9:2
People gnawed their tongues in a ..... Rv 16:10

ANIMALS

Take with you seven pairs of all clean a, ... Gn 7:2
In it were all kinds of a and reptiles ... Acts 10:12
one kind for humans, another for a, ... 1 Cor 15:39
by all that they, like unreasoning a, ... Jude 10

ANOINT

"Arise, a him, for this is he." .... 1 Sm 16:12
I a you king over Israel.' .... 2 Kgs 9:3
fast, a your head and wash your face, ... Mt 6:17
You did not a my head with oil, but she ... Lk 7:46

ANOINTED

LORD a you king over Israel. .... 1 Sm 15:17
my lord, for he is the LORD's a.' ...... 1 Sm 24:10
the LORD and against his A, ... Ps 2:2
It was Mary who a the Lord with .... Jn 11:2
the feet of Jesus and wiped his feet ..... Jn 12:3
your holy servant Jesus, whom you a, ... Acts 4:27
how God a Jesus of Nazareth with .... Acts 10:38
But you have been a by the Holy One, ... 1 Jn 2:20

ANOINTING

a him with oil in the name of the Lord.... Jas 5:14
But the a that you received from .... 1 Jn 2:27

ANSWER

A me when I call, O God of my .... Ps 4:1
Attend to me, and a me; I am restless .... Ps 55:2
In your faithfulness a me, in·your .... Ps 143:1
A soft a turns away wrath, ... Prv 15:1
a of the tongue is from the LORD. .... Prv 16:1
Before they call I will a; .... Is 65:24
"Have you no a to make? .... Mt 26:62
not to meditate beforehand how to a, ... Lk 21:14
But Jesus gave him no a. .... Jn 19:9
are you, O man, to a back to God? ..... Rom 9:20
that you may be able to a those .... 2 Cor 5:12
know how you ought to a each person. ... Col 4:6

ANSWERED

"You have a correctly; do this, and...... Lk 10:28

ANTICHRIST

heard that a is coming, so now many ... 1 Jn 2:18
This is the a, he who denies the Father ... 1 Jn 2:22
This is the spirit of the a, which you ..... 1 Jn 4:3

ANTIOCH

in A the disciples were first called...... Acts 11:26
them and send them to A with Paul .... Acts 15:22
when Cephas came to A, I opposed ...... Gal 2:11
sufferings that happened to me at A, ... 2 Tm 3:11

ANXIETIES

I want you to be free from a. .... 1 Cor 7:32
casting all your a on him, because he ... 1 Pt 5:7

ANXIETY

A in a man's heart weighs him down, ... Prv 12:25
eat bread by weight and with a, ... Ezk 4:16

ANXIOUS

an a heart, "Be strong; fear not! ...... Is 35:4
I tell you, do not be a about your life, ... Mt 6:25
"Therefore do not be a about tomorrow, .. Mt 6:34
do not be a how you are to speak or ... Mt 10:19
Martha, you are a troubled about ..... Lk 10:41
which of you by being a can add a ...... Lk 12:25
married man is a about worldly .... 1 Cor 7:33
do not be a about anything, but in ...... Phil 4:6

ANYTHING

Is a too hard for the LORD? .... Gn 18:14
God of all flesh. Is a too hard for me? .... Jer 32:27
If you ask me a in my name, I will .... Jn 14:14
Owe no one a, except to love .... Rom 13:8
and do not fear a that is frightening. ..... 1 Pt 3:6

APART

LORD has set a the godly for himself; ..... Ps 4:3
I have no good a from you." .... Ps 16:2
"Set a for me Barnabas and Saul for ... Acts 13:2
For a from the law, sin lies dead. .... Rom 7:8
for honorable use, set a as holy, ... 2 Tm 2:21
that faith a from works is useless? ..... Jas 2:20

APOLLOS

Now a Jew named A, a native of....... Acts 18:24
or "I follow A," or "I follow .... 1 Cor 1:12
I planted, A watered, but God gave ..... 1 Cor 3:6

APOSTASY

you, and your a will reprove you. .... Jer 2:19
I will heal their a; I will love them ...... Hos 14:4

APOSTLE

then as I am an a to the Gentiles, ... Rom 11:13
Am I not an a? Have I not seen Jesus ... 1 Cor 9:1
I was appointed a preacher and an a ... 1 Tm 2:7
a and high priest of our confession, ... Heb 3:1

APOSTLES

The names of the twelve a are these:...... Mt 10:2
'I will send them prophets and a, ... Lk 11:49
The a and the elders were gathered .... Acts 15:6
has appointed in the church first a, ... 1 Cor 12:28
the foundation of the a and prophets, ... Eph 2:20
And he gave the a, the prophets, ... Eph 4:11
who call themselves a are not, ... Rv 2:2
names of the twelve a of the Lamb. ..... Rv 21:14

APOSTLES'

devoted themselves to the a teaching ... Acts 2:42
through the laying on of the a hands, ... Acts 8:18

APOSTLESHIP

have received grace and a to bring ...... Rom 1:5
you are the seal of my a in the Lord. ... 1 Cor 9:2

APPEAL

think that I cannot a to my Father, ... Mt 26:53
I was compelled to a to Caesar—...... Acts 28:19
God making his a through us. .... 2 Cor 5:20
as an a to God for a good conscience, ... 1 Pt 3:21

APPEAR

When shall I come and a before God? ... Ps 42:2
a righteous to others, but within you .... Mt 23:28
we must all a before the judgment ..... 2 Cor 5:10
you also will a with him in glory. .... Col 3:4
to a in the presence of God on our ...... Heb 9:24

APPEARANCE

man looks on the outward a, but .... 1 Sm 16:7
his a was so marred, beyond human .... Is 52:14
His a was like lightning, and his .... Mt 28:3
boast about outward a and not .... 2 Cor 5:12

APPEARANCES

for you are not swayed by a. .... Mt 22:16
Do not judge by a, but judge with ...... Jn 7:24

APPEARED

Then the LORD a to Abram .... Gn 12:7
glory of the LORD a in the cloud. ...... Ex 16:10
went into the holy city and a to many. ... Mt 27:53
to one untimely born, he a also to me. . 1 Cor 15:8
he has a once for all at the end of the ... Heb 9:26

APPEARING

from reproach until the a of our Lord ... 1 Tm 6:14
also to all who have loved his a. .... 2 Tm 4:8
blessed hope, the a of the glory of our ..... Ti 2:13

APPEARS

each one a before God in Zion. .... Ps 84:7
and who can stand when he a? .... Mal 3:2
"When the Christ a, will he do more ... Jn 7:31
that when he a we shall be like him, ... 1 Jn 3:2

APPETITE

righteous has enough to satisfy his a, ... Prv 13:25
A worker's a works for him; .... Prv 16:26
for his mouth, yet his a is not satisfied.... Eccl 6:7

APPETITES

our Lord Christ, but their own a, ... Rom 16:18

APPLE

he kept him as the a of his eye. .... Dt 32:10
Keep me as the a of your eye; .... Ps 17:8
my teaching as the a of your eye; .... Prv 7:2
touches you touches the a of his eye:..... Zec 2:8

APPOINT

Now a for us a king to judge us like all ... 1 Sm 8:5
to a you as a servant and witness to ... Acts 26:16

APPOINTED

for it refers to a time of the end. ...... Dn 8:19
For you also, O Judah, a harvest is a. ... Hos 6:11

this child is a for the fall and rising of ..... Lk 2:34
this the Lord a seventy-two others and ... Lk 10:1
but I chose you and a you that you ...... Jn 15:16
as many as were a to eternal life ...... Acts 13:48
the authorities resists what God has a, .. Rom 13:2

APPROVAL
what is good, and you will receive his a, Rom 15:7
For am I now seeking the a of man, ... Gal 1:10

APPROVED
is acceptable to God and a by men. ... Rom 14:18
commends himself who is a, but ..... 2 Cor 10:18
to present yourself to God as one a, ... 2 Tm 2:15

APT
To make an a answer is a joy to a man, .. Prv 15:23

AQUILA
Syria, and with him Priscilla and A. .. Acts 18:18
A and Prisca, together with the church 1 Cor 16:19

ARABIA
but I went away into A, and returned .... Gal 1:17

ARAMAIC
The letter was written in A and ...... Ezr 4:7
the Chaldeans said to the king in A, ... Dn 2:4
near the city, and it was written in A, ... Jn 19:20

ARARAT
ark came to rest on the mountains of A. ... Gn 8:4

ARCHANGEL
of command, with the voice of an a, . 1 Thes 4:16
But when the a Michael, contending ...... Jude 9

AREOPAGUS
Paul, standing in the midst of the A, .. Acts 17:22

ARGUE
A your case with your neighbor .... Prv 25:9

ARGUMENT
If a wise man has an a with a fool, the .. Prv 29:9
An a arose among them as to which of ... Lk 9:46

ARGUMENTATIVE
they are to be well-pleasing, not a, ... Ti 2:9

ARGUMENTS
We destroy a and every lofty opinion .2 Cor 10:5
no one may delude you with plausible a.... Col 2:4

ARIMATHEA
Joseph, from the Jewish town of A..... Lk 23:50
Joseph of A, who was a disciple of ...... Jn 19:38

ARISE
A, shine, for your light has come, ... Is 60:1
"Little girl, I say to you, a." .... Mk 5:41
"Young man, I say to you, a." .... Lk 7:14
"Tabitha, a." And she opened her eyes, .. Acts 9:40
a from the dead, and Christ will shine .. Eph 5:14

ARK
Make yourself an a of gopher wood. ... Gn 6:14
went into the a to escape the waters ...... Gn 7:7
"They shall make an a of acacia wood... Ex 25:10
"As soon as you see the a of the .... Jos 3:3
And the a of God was captured, ... 1 Sm 4:11
"The a of the covenant of the LORD." ... Jer 3:16
constructed an a for the saving of ...... Heb 11:7
Noah, while the a was being prepared, .. 1 Pt 3:20
the a of his covenant was seen within ... Rv 11:19

ARM
by a mighty hand and an outstretched a, . Dt 4:34
has the a of the LORD been revealed? ... Is 53:1
has the a of the Lord been revealed? ... Jn 12:38
a yourselves with the same way .... 1 Pt 4:1

ARMAGEDDON
at the place that in Hebrew is called A. .. Rv 16:16

ARMOR
Then Saul clothed David with his a. .. 1 Sm 17:38
and put on the a of light. .... Rom 13:12
Put on the whole a of God, ... Eph 6:11

ARMS
and underneath are the everlasting a. .. Dt 33:27
snapped the ropes off his a like a thread. Jgs 16:12
he will gather the lambs in his a; .... Is 40:11
of fine gold, its chest and a of silver, ... Dn 2:32
took them in his a and blessed them, .. Mk 10:16
him up in his a and blessed God and .... Lk 2:28

ARMY
Though an a encamp against me, my .... Ps 27:3
The king is not saved by his great a; .... Ps 33:16
LORD utters his voice before his a, ... Jl 2:11
sitting on the horse and against his a... Rv 19:19

AROMA
LORD smelled the pleasing a, ... Gn 8:21
For we are the a of Christ to God ...... 2 Cor 2:15

ARREST
together in order to a Jesus by stealth .. Mt 26:4
the Jews, he proceeded to a Peter also.... Acts 12:3

ARRESTED
when he heard that John had been a, ... Mt 4:12
officers of the Jews a Jesus and bound ... Jn 18:12
And they a them and put them in ...... Acts 4:3
they a the apostles and put them in ...... Acts 5:18
came up and a him and ordered ...... Acts 21:33

ARROGANCE
Pride and a and the way of evil .... Prv 8:13
As it is, you boast in your a. .... Jas 4:16

ARROGANT
Everyone who is a in heart is .... Prv 16:5
love does not envy or boast; it is not a .. 1 Cor 13:4
above reproach. He must not be a or ...... Ti 1:7

ARROW
night, nor the a that flies by day, ... Ps 91:5
he hid me; he made me a polished a; .... Is 49:2
Their tongue is a deadly a; it speaks .... Jer 9:8
bow and set me as a target for his a. .... Lam 3:12

ARROWS
For the a of the Almighty are in me; .... Jb 6:4
For your a have sunk into me, ... Ps 38:2
who aim bitter words like a, ... Ps 64:3
against you the deadly a of famine, ... Ezk 5:16

ARTAXERXES
associates wrote to A king of Persia. ..... Ezr 4:7
Nisan, in the twentieth year of King A, ... Neh 2:1

ASA
A did what was right in the eyes ...... 1 Kgs 15:11
A cried to the LORD his God, ... 2 Chr 14:11

ASCEND
"Who will a to heaven for us and bring .. Dt 30:12
Who shall a the hill of the LORD? .... Ps 24:3
If I a to heaven, you are there! .... Ps 139:8
said in your heart, 'I will a to heaven; .... Is 14:13
For David did not a into the heavens, ... Acts 2:34
"Who will a into heaven?" (that is, ... Rom 10:6

ASCENDED
Who has a to heaven and come down? .. Prv 30:4
No one has a into heaven except he ....Jn 3:13
for I have not yet a to the Father; .... Jn 20:17
"When he a on high he led a host of .... Eph 4:8

ASCENDING
the angels of God a and descending on .. Jn 1:51
were to see the Son of Man a to where ... Jn 6:62

ASCETICISM
insisting on a and worship of angels, ... Col 2:18
self-made religion and a and severity .... Col 2:23

ASCRIBE
a greatness to our God! .... Dt 32:3
A to the LORD the glory due .... Ps 29:2
A to the LORD the glory due his name; .... Ps 96:8

ASHAMED
All my enemies shall be a and .... Ps 6:10

radiant, and their faces shall never be a. .. Ps 34:5
For whoever is a of me and of my .... Mk 8:38
For I am not a of the gospel, for it is ...... Rom 1:16
things of which you are now a? ...... Rom 6:21
to do with him, that he may be a ..... 2 Thes 3:14
a worker who has no need to be a, ... 2 Tm 2:15
why he is not a to call them brothers, ... Heb 2:11
God is not a to be called their God, ... Heb 11:16
let him not be a, but let him glorify ..... 1 Pt 4:16

ASHES
I who am but dust and a. .... Gn 18:27
despise myself, and repent in dust and a." .. Jb 42:6
For I eat a like bread and mingle tears .. Ps 102:9
people, put on sackcloth, and roll in a; ... Jer 6:26
himself with sackcloth, and sat in a. ...... Jon 3:6
sprinkling of defiled persons with the a .. Heb 9:13

ASIA
the Holy Spirit to speak the word in A..... Acts 16:6
of the affliction we experienced in A...... 2 Cor 1:8
to the seven churches that are in A; ...... Rv 1:4

ASIDE
But you have turned a from the way. ...... Mal 2:8
All have turned a; together they have ... Rom 3:12

ASK
"A a sign of the LORD your God; .... Is 7:11
"A, and it will be given to you; seek, ... Mt 7:7
And whatever you a in prayer, you will .. Mt 21:22
the Holy Spirit to those who a him!" ..... Lk 11:13
If you a me anything in my name, I ...... Jn 14:14
a whatever you wish, and it will be done .. Jn 15:7
A, and you will receive, that your joy ...... Jn 16:24
abundantly than all that we a or think, .. Eph 3:20
You do not have, because you do not a.... Jas 4:2
that he hears us in whatever we a, ... 1 Jn 5:15

ASLEEP
And he fell a and dreamed a second ...... Gn 41:5
ship and had lain down and was fast a. ..... Jon 1:5
swamped by the waves; but he was a. .... Mt 8:24
"Our friend Lazarus has fallen a, ... Jn 11:11
firstfruits of those who have fallen a. .. 1 Cor 15:20
we are awake or a we might live ...... 1 Thes 5:10
For ever since the fathers fell a, all ...... 2 Pt 3:4

ASSIGNED
as my Father a to me, a kingdom, ... Lk 22:29
to the area of influence God a to us, .. 2 Cor 10:13

ASSURANCE
all the riches of full a of understanding ..... Col 2:2
to have the full a of hope until the end, .. Heb 6:11
with a true heart in full a of faith, ... Heb 10:22
Now faith is the a of things hoped for, .. Heb 11:1

ASSYRIA
the king of A captured Samaria, ... 2 Kgs 17:6
shall be carried to A as tribute to the .... Hos 10:6

ASTONISHED
the crowds were a at his teaching, ... Mt 7:28
uneducated, common men, they were a. Acts 4:13

ASTRAY
make me understand how I have gone a. .. Jb 6:24
All we like sheep have gone a; .... Is 53:6
go in search of the one that went a? .... Mt 18:12
to lead a, if possible, the elect. ...... Mk 13:22
"See that you are not led a. .... Lk 21:8
sins and led a by various passions, ... 2 Tm 3:6
They always go a in their heart; .... Heb 3:10
the right way, they have gone a. .... 2 Pt 2:15

ATE
one wise, she took of its fruit and a, ... Gn 3:6
Your words were found, and I a them, ... Jer 15:16
I a it, and it was in my mouth as sweet .. Ezk 3:3
I a no delicacies, no meat or wine ...... Dn 10:3
not like the bread the fathers a, and died. .. Jn 6:58

ATHENS
"Men of A, I perceive that in every ...... Acts 17:22

willing to be left behind at **A** alone, ... 1 Thes 3:1

ATHLETE

Every **a** exercises self-control .... 1 Cor 9:25
a is not crowned unless he competes .... 2 Tm 2:5

ATONE

you **a** for our transgressions................. Ps 65:3
a for our sins, for your name's sake! .... Ps 79:9
put an end to sin, and to **a** for iniquity, ... Dn 9:24

ATONED

love and faithfulness iniquity is a for, ... Prv 16:6
guilt is taken away, and your sin **a** for." ... Is 6:7

ATONEMENT

shall offer a bull as a sin offering for **a** .. Ex 29:36
of this seventh month is the Day of **A**.... Lv 23:27
the sin offerings to make **a** for Israel, ... Neh 10:33

ATTAIN

for me; it is high; I cannot **a** it. .... Ps 139:6
until we all **a** to the unity of the faith .... Eph 4:13
possible I may **a** the resurrection from .... Phil 3:11

ATTENTION

Give **a** to the sound of my cry, my.......... Ps 5:2
your flocks, and give **a** to your herds, ... Prv 27:23
Therefore we must pay much closer **a** ..... Heb 2:1
will do well to pay **a** as to a lamp .... 2 Pt 1:19

AUTHOR

and you killed the **A** of life, whom .... Acts 3:15

AUTHORITIES

many even of the **a** believed in him, ... Jn 12:42
taxes, for the **a** are ministers of God, ... Rom 13:6
be made known to the rulers and **a** .... Eph 3:10
be submissive to rulers and **a**, ... Ti 3:1

AUTHORITY

teaching them as one who had **a**, ... Mt 7:29
Son of Man has **a** on earth to forgive ..... Mt 9:6
"All in heaven and on earth has been .... Mt 28:18
"To you I will give all this **a** and ....!....... Lk 4:6
For I too am a man set under **a**, with ...... Lk 7:8
"Tell us by what **a** you do these things, ... Lk 20:2
For there is no **a** except from God, ... Rom 13:1
to have a symbol of **a** on her head, ... 1 Cor 11:10
be glory, majesty, dominion, and **a**, ... Jude 25
to him I will give **a** over the nations, ... Rv 2:26

AVENGE

may the LORD **a** me against you, ... 1 Sm 24:12
never **a** yourselves, but leave it to ...... Rom 12:19
you will judge and **a** our blood on .... Rv 6:10

AVENGER

to them, but an **a** of their wrongdoings.... Ps 99:8
an **a** who carries out God's wrath on .... Rom 13:4
because the Lord is an **a** in all these .... 1 Thes 4:6

AVOID

A the irreverent babble .... 1 Tm 6:20
denying its power. A such people......... 2 Tm 3:5
But **a** foolish controversies, genealogies, ... Ti 3:9

AWAKE

when I **a**, I shall be satisfied with .... Ps 17:15
My eyes are **a** before the watches of . Ps 119:148
I **a**, and I am still with you. .... Ps 139:18
A, **a**, put on strength, O arm .... Is 51:9
sleep in the dust of the earth shall **a**, ... Dn 12:2
stay **a**, for you do not know .... Mt 24:42
"**A**, O sleeper, and arise from the dead, .. Eph 5:14
that whether we are **a** or asleep we .. 1 Thes 5:10
Blessed is the one who stays **a**, ... Rv 16:15

AWE

the ends of the earth are in **a** at your .... Ps 65:8
of Jacob and will stand in **a** of the God ... Is 29:23
He stood in **a** of my name. .... Mal 2:5
glorified God and were filled with **a**, ... Lk 5:26
And **a** came upon every soul, ... Acts 2:43

AWESOME

"How **a** is this place! This is none other . Gn 28:17

---

for it is a thing that I will do with .... Ex 34:10
God is in your midst, a great and **a** .... Dt 7:21
"How **a** are your deeds! So great is ...... Ps 66:3
When you did **a** things that we .... Is 64:3
"O Lord, the great and **a** God, ... Dn 9:4
day of the LORD is great and very **a**; ..... Jl 2:11
great and **a** day of the LORD comes.... Mal 4:5

AXE

his **a** head fell into the water, ... 2 Kgs 6:5
Even now the **a** is laid to the root. .... Mt 3:10

AZARIAH

king of Israel, **A** the son of Amaziah, .. 2 Kgs 15:1
the prophecy of **A** the son of Oded, ... 2 Chr 15:8

BAAL

So Israel yoked himself to **B** of Peor. .... Nm 25:3
Thus Jehu wiped out **B** from Israel..... 2 Kgs 10:28
no longer will you call me 'My **B**.' ...... Hos 2:16
who have not bowed the knee to **B**." .. Rom 11:4

BAASHA

between Asa and **B** king of Israel ..... 1 Kgs 15:16
B king of Israel went up against........ 2 Chr 16:1

BABEL

The beginning of his kingdom was **B**, .. Gn 10:10
Therefore its name was called **B**, ... Gn 11:9

BABY

of Mary, the **b** leaped in her womb. ..... Lk 1:41
you will find a **b** wrapped in swaddling .. Lk 2:12

BABYLON

By the waters of **B**, there we sat down .. Ps 137:1
To **B** you shall go, and there .... Jer 20:6
carried into exile to **B** the rest of the .... Jer 39:9
Do not fear the king of **B**, ... Jer 42:11
"Is not this great **B**, which I have built ... Dn 4:30
"Fallen, fallen is **B** the great, she who ... Rv 14:8

BACK

away my hand, and you shall see my **b**, .. Ex 33:23
he brought the shadow **b** ten steps, .. 2 Kgs 20:11
cast your law behind their **b** and killed .. Neh 9:26
I gave my **b** to those who strike, ... Is 50:6
forgotten me and cast me behind your **b**, Ezk 23:35
to the plow and looks **b** is fit for the ..... Lk 9:62
the disciples went **b** to their homes. .... Jn 20:10
that whoever brings **b** a sinner from .... Jas 5:20

BACKSLIDING

but he went on **b** in the way of his ...... Is 57:17
people turned away in perpetual **b**? ..... Jer 8:5

BAD

but if your eye is **b**, your whole body ... Mt 6:23
"For no good tree bears **b** fruit, nor ..... Lk 6:43
impostors will go on from **b** to worse, .. 2 Tm 3:13

BAG

transgression would be sealed up in a **b**, .. Jb 14:17
does so to put them into a **b** with holes. .. Hg 1:6

BAKER

the chief cupbearer-and the chief **b**, ... Gn 40:2

BALAAM

And **B** said to the donkey, "Because .... Nm 22:29
They have followed the way of **B**, the .. 2 Pt 2:15
some there are who hold the teaching of **B**, ... Rv 2:14

BALANCE

(Let me be weighed in a just **b**, ... Jb 31:6
false **b** is an abomination to the .... Prv 11:1

BALANCES

You shall have just **b**, just weights, ... Lv 19:36
weighed in the **b** and found wanting; ... Dn 5:27

BALM

Is there no **b** in Gilead? Is there no ..... Jer 8:22

BANNER

name of it, The LORD Is My **B**, ... Ex 17:15
You have set up a **b** for those who fear .. Ps 60:4
and his **b** over me was love. .... Sg 2:4

BAPTISM

The **b** of John, from where did it come? . Mt 21:25
I have a **b** to be baptized with, ... Lk 12:50
he knew only the **b** of John............ Acts 18:25
therefore with him by **b** into death, ... Rom 6:4
one Lord, one faith, one **b**, ... Eph 4:5
having been buried with him in **b**, ... Col 2:12
B, which corresponds to this, ... 1 Pt 3:21

BAPTIST

"This is John the **B**. He has been raised .. Mt 14:2
For John the **B** has come eating no .... Lk 7:33

BAPTIZE

He will **b** you with the Holy Spirit .... Mt 3:11
John answered them, "I **b** with water, ... Jn 1:26
did not send me to **b** but to preach ..... 1 Cor 1:17

BAPTIZED

to the Jordan to John, to be **b** by him. .... Mt 3:13
John **b** with water, but you will be **b** ..... Acts 1:5
"Repent and be **b** every one of you in .... Acts 2:38
into Christ Jesus were **b** into his death? .. Rom 6:3
Or were you **b** in the name of Paul? ... 1 Cor 1:13
we were all **b** into one body— .... 1 Cor 12:13
by being **b** on behalf of the dead? ... 1 Cor 15:29
of you as were **b** into Christ have put ... Gal 3:27

BAPTIZING

b them in the name of the Father and .. Mt 28:19
for this purpose I came **b** with water, ... Jn 1:31
withhold water for **b** these people, ... Acts 10:47

BARAK

She sent and summoned **B** .... Jgs 4:6
tell of Gideon, **B**, Samson, Jephthah, ... Heb 11:32

BARE

so that its foundation will be laid **b**. .... Ezk 13:14
the body that is to be, but a **b** kernel, 1 Cor 15:37

BARN

but gather the wheat into my **b**."'" ...... Mt 13:30
they have neither storehouse nor **b**, ... Lk 12:24

BARNABAS

called by the apostles **B** (which means .. Acts 4:36
"Set apart for me **B** and Saul for the ... Acts 13:2
B took Mark with him and sailed ......Acts 15:39
Or is it only **B** and I who have no .... 1 Cor 9:6

BARNS

the blessing on you in your **b** and in all ... Dt 28:8
then your **b** will be filled with plenty, ... Prv 3:10
will tear down my **b** and build larger ..... Lk 12:18

BARREN

Sarai was **b**; she had no child. .... Gn 11:30
He gives the **b** woman a home, ... Ps 113:9
"Sing, O **b** one, who did not bear; .... Is 54:1
had no child, because Elizabeth was **b**, ... Lk 1:7
'Blessed are the **b** and the wombs .... Lk 23:29
"Rejoice, O **b** one who does not bear; ... Gal 4:27

BARTHOLOMEW

Philip and **B**; Thomas and Matthew .... Mt 10:3
Philip and Thomas, **B** and Matthew, ... Acts 1:13

BARTIMAEUS

B, a blind beggar, the son of ....Mk 10:46

BASHAN

"Hear this word, you cows of **B**, who .... Am 4:1
let them graze in **B** and Gilead as in the .. Mi 7:14

BASKET

she took for him a **b** made of bulrushes .. Ex 2:3
One **b** had very good figs, like first-ripe ... Jer 24:2
"A **b** of summer fruit." .... Am 8:2
in the wall, lowering him in a **b**. .... Acts 9:25

BASKETS

there were three cake **b** on my head, ... Gn 40:16
they took up twelve **b** full of the broken Mt 14:20
the broken pieces left over, seven **b** full.... Mk 8:8

BATHSHEBA
"Is this not **B**, the daughter of .... 2 Sm 11:3
B the mother of Solomon, ... 1 Kgs 1:11

BATTLE
For the **b** is the LORD's, ... 1 Sm 17:47
for the **b** is not yours but God's. .... 2 Chr 20:15
the LORD, mighty in **b**! .... Ps 24:8
not to the swift, nor the **b** to the strong. . Eccl 9:11
all the nations against Jerusalem to **b**, ... Zec 14:2
assemble them for **b** on the great day .... Rv 16:14

BEAR
On their hands they will **b** you up, ... Ps 91:12
but a crushed spirit who can **b**? .... Prv 18:14
and he shall **b** their iniquities. .... Is 53:11
another beast, a second one, like a **b**. ..... Dn 7:5
upon them like a **b** robbed of her cubs; .. Hos 13:8
She will **b** a son, and you shall call his .... Mt 1:21
to **b** witness about the light, ... Jn 1:7
in order that we may **b** fruit for God. ..... Rom 7:4
for I **b** on my body the marks of Jesus. .. Gal 6:17
offered once to **b** the sins of many, ... Heb 9:28

BEARS
but the root of the righteous **b** fruit. ..... Prv 12:12
he it is that **b** much fruit, for apart .... Jn 15:5
Love **b** all things, believes all things, ... 1 Cor 13:7
the Holy Spirit also **b** witness to us; ..... Heb 10:15

BEAST
has regard for the life of his **b**, ... Prv 12:10
his mind was made like that of a **b**, ... Dn 5:21
the **b** had four heads, and dominion ...... Dn 7:6
and they worshiped the **b**, ... Rv 13:4
had not worshiped the **b** or its image .... Rv 20:4

BEASTS
He gives to the **b** their food, and to the .. Ps 147:9
I fought with **b** at Ephesus? .... 1 Cor 15:32

BEAT
up his eyes to heaven, but **b** his breast, .. Lk 18:13
they **b** them and charged them not to .... Acts 5:40

BEATING
I do not box as one **b** the air. .... 1 Cor 9:26

BEATINGS
b, imprisonments, riots, labors, ... 2 Cor 6:5
imprisonments, with countless **b**, ... 2 Cor 11:23

BEAUTIFUL
you are a woman **b** in appearance, ... Gn 12:11
He has made everything **b** in its time. ... Eccl 3:11
You are altogether **b**, my love; .... Sg 4:7
branch of the LORD shall be **b** .... Is 4:2
How **b** upon the mountains are the feet ... Is 52:7
For she has done a **b** thing to me. ...... Mt 26:10
that is called the **B** Gate to ask alms ...... Acts 3:2
"How **b** are the feet of those who ..... Rom 10:15

BEAUTY
to gaze upon the **b** of the LORD .... Ps 27:4
strength and **b** are in his sanctuary. ...... Ps 96:6
Charm is deceitful, and **b** is vain, ... Prv 31:30
no **b** that we should desire him. .... Is 53:2
imperishable **b** of a gentle and quiet .... 1 Pt 3:4

BED
when I remember you upon my **b**, ... Ps 63:6
brought to him a paralytic, lying on a **b**.... Mt 9:2
"Get up, take up your **b**, and walk." .... Jn 5:8
and let the marriage **b** be undefiled, ... Heb 13:4

BEERSHEBA
with all that he had and came to **B**, ... Gn 46:1
Israel and over Judah, from Dan to **B**." . 2 Sm 3:10

BEFOREHAND
which he promised **b** through his .... Rom 1:2
which he has prepared **b** for glory— .... Rom 9:23
good works, which God prepared **b**, ... Eph 2:10

BEG
"Teacher, I **b** you to look at my son, ... Lk 9:38

enough to dig, and I am ashamed to **b**. .... Lk 16:3
the man who used to sit and **b**?" .... Jn 9:8

BEGINNING
In the **b**, God created the heavens and .... Gn 1:1
The fear of the LORD is the **b** .... Prv 1:7
Better is the end of a thing than its **b**, ... Eccl 7:8
In the **b** was the Word, and the Word .... Jn 1:1
He was in the **b** with God. .... Jn 1:2
Jesus knew from the **b** who those were ... Jn 6:64
He is the **b**, the firstborn from the dead, .. Col 1:18
having neither **b** of days nor end of life, ... Heb 7:3
That which was from the **b**, which we .... 1 Jn 1:1
first and the last, the **b** and the end." .... Rv 22:13

BEGOTTEN
"You are my Son, today I have **b** you"? .. Heb 1:5

BEHOLD
"**B**, I am the servant of the Lord; .... Lk 1:38
"**B**, the Lamb of God, who takes away ... Jn 1:29
"**B**, the dwelling place of God is with .... Rv 21:3
"**B**, I am making all things new." .... Rv 21:5
"**B**, I am coming soon, bringing my ...... Rv 22:12

BEING
sing praise to my God while I have **b**. ... Ps 104:33
sing and make melody with all my **b**! .... Ps 108:1
praises to my God while I have my **b**. .... Ps 146:2
My inmost **b** will exult when your lips ... Prv 23:16
cut short, no human **b** would be saved. ... Mt 24:22
for joy that a human **b** has been born .... Jn 16:21
we live and move and have our **b**'; .... Acts 17:28
for every human **b** who does evil, ... Rom 2:9
in the law of God, in my inner **b**, ... Rom 7:22
so that no human **b** might boast in ..... 1 Cor 1:29
through his Spirit in your inner **b**, ... Eph 3:16

BELIEVE
"that they may **b** that the LORD, ... Ex 4:5
how long will they not **b** in me, ... Nm 14:11
B in the LORD your God, ... 2 Chr 20:20
I **b** that I shall look upon the goodness ... Ps 27:13
that you may know and **b** me .... Is 43:10
"Do you **b** that I am able to do this?" ...... Mt 9:28
or 'There he is!' do not **b** it. .... Mt 24:23
at hand; repent and **b** in the gospel." .... Mk 1:15
"Do not fear, only **b**." .... Mk 5:36
"I **b**; help my unbelief!" .... Mk 9:24
But these have no root; they **b** for a ...... Lk 8:13
unless you **b** that I am he you will die .... Jn 8:24
you do not **b** me, **b** the works, ... Jn 10:38
I **b** that you are the Christ, ... Jn 11:27
B in God; **b** also in me. .... Jn 14:1
in my side. Do not disbelieve, but **b**." .... Jn 20:27
"**B** in the Lord Jesus, and you will be ... Acts 16:31
will be counted to us who **b** in him ...... Rom 4:24
we **b** that we will also live with him. ...... Rom 6:8
that Jesus is Lord and **b** in your heart .... Rom 10:9
greatness of his power toward us who **b**, Eph 1:19
For since we **b** that Jesus died and ..... 1 Thes 4:14
all people, especially of those who **b**, ... 1 Tm 4:10
Though you do not now see him, you **b** .. 1 Pt 1:8

BELIEVED
And he **b** the LORD, and he counted .... Gn 15:6
and they **b** in the LORD and .... Ex 14:31
Who has **b** what he has heard from us? ... Is 53:1
And the people of Nineveh **b** God, ... Jon 3:5
many **b** in his name when they saw .... Jn 2:23
who have not seen and yet have **b**." ...... Jn 20:29
And all who **b** were together and had ... Acts 2:44
receive the Holy Spirit when you **b**?" .... Acts 19:2
nearer to us now than when we first **b**. .. Rom 13:11
Abraham "**b** God, and it was counted ..... Gal 3:6
I know whom I have **b**, ... 2 Tm 1:12
For we who have **b** enter that rest, ... Heb 4:3
"Abraham **b** God, and it was counted ..... Jas 2:23

BELIEVER
what portion does a **b** share with an ... 2 Cor 6:15

BELIEVERS
And more than ever **b** were added to .... Acts 5:14
and his children are **b** and not open to ..... Ti 1:6

BELIEVES
All things are possible for one who **b**." .. Mk 9:23
not doubt in his heart, but **b** that what .. Mk 11:23
whoever **b** in him should not perish .... Jn 3:16
Whoever **b** in me, as the Scripture has .... Jn 7:38
who lives and **b** in me shall never die. ... Jn 11:26
b in him receives forgiveness of sins ... Acts 10:43
God for salvation to everyone who **b**, ... Rom 1:16
not work but **b** in him who justifies .... Rom 4:5
b in him will not be put to shame." .... Rom 9:33
Everyone who **b** that Jesus is the Christ . 1 Jn 5:1

BELIEVING
the Jews were going away and **b** in Jesus. Jn 12:11
and that by **b** you may have life in his .... Jn 20:31

BELLY
on your **b** you shall go, and dust you .... Gn 3:14
end is destruction, their god is their **b**, .. Phil 3:19

BELONG
"The secret things **b** to the LORD .... Dt 29:29
The plans of the heart **b** to man, but ...... Prv 16:1
It shall **b** to those who walk on the way; .. Is 35:8
To the Lord our God **b** mercy and .... Dn 9:9
To him **b** glory and dominion forever .... 1 Pt 4:11
and glory and power **b** to our God, ... Rv 19:1

BELONGS
I heard this: that power **b** to God, ... Ps 62:11
For our shield **b** to the LORD, ... Ps 89:18
but the victory **b** to the LORD. .... Prv 21:31
Salvation **b** to the LORD!" .... Jon 2:9
for to such **b** the kingdom of God. .... Mk 10:14
"Salvation **b** to our God who sits .... Rv 7:10

BELOVED
My **b** is mine, and I am his; he .... Sg 2:16
Let me sing for my **b** my love song .... Is 5:1
"This is my **b** Son, with whom .... Mt 3:17
who was not **b** I will call '**b**.'" .... Rom 9:25
he has blessed us in the **B**. .... Eph 1:6
the Majestic Glory, "This is my **b** Son, . 2 Pt 1:17
B, let us love one another, for love is .... 1 Jn 4:7

BELT
Righteousness shall be the **b** of his .... Is 11:5
he took Paul's **b** and bound his own ... Acts 21:11
having fastened on the **b** of truth, ... Eph 6:14

BENJAMIN
but his father called him **B**. .... Gn 35:18
of the people of Israel, of the tribe of **B**, . Phil 3:5

BEREFT
repay me evil for good; my soul is **b**. .... Ps 35:12
my soul is **b** of peace; I have forgotten . Lam 3:17

BESIDES
LORD is God; there is no other **b** .... Dt 4:35
and there is no God **b** you, ... 1 Chr 17:20
And there is no other god **b** me, a .... Is 45:21
no eye has seen a God **b** you, ... Is 64:4
but me, and **b** me there is no savior. ...... Hos 13:4
he is one, and there is no other **b** him. .. Mk 12:32

BETHANY
Jesus was at **B** in the house of Simon ... Mt 26:6
certain man was ill, Lazarus of **B**, ... Jn 11:1
Passover, Jesus therefore came to **B**, ... Jn 12:1

BETHEL
on the east of **B** and pitched his tent, ... Gn 12:8
He called the name of that place **B**, ... Gn 28:19

BETHLEHEM
a man of **B** in Judah went to sojourn ..... Ru 1:1
LORD commanded and came to **B**. ...... 1 Sm 16:4
O **B** Ephrathah, who are too little .... Mi 5:2
"In **B** of Judea, for so it is written .... Mt 2:5
city of David, which is called **B**, ... Lk 2:4

offspring of David, and comes from **B**, ... Jn 7:42

BETRAY

b the Son of Man with a kiss?" .... Lk 22:48
For he knew who was to **b** him; .... Jn 13:11

BETROTHED

his mother Mary had been **b** to Joseph, ... Mt 1:18
Now concerning the **b**, I have no ...... 1 Cor 7:25

BETTER

your steadfast love is **b** than life, ... Ps 63:3
good name is **b** than precious ointment, .. Eccl 7:1
For it is **b** that you lose one of .... Mt 5:29
It would be **b** for him if a millstone .... Lk 17:2

BEWARE

B lest you say in your heart, 'My power ...... Dt 8:17
"**B** of practicing your righteousness .... Mt 6:1
"**B** of the scribes, who like to walk ... Mk 12:38

BIND

You shall **b** them as a sign on your .... Dt 6:8
B them on your heart always, tie ...... Prv 6:21
and whatever you **b** on earth .... Mt 16:19

BINDS

He heals the brokenhearted and **b** up .... Ps 147:3
unless he first **b** the strong man......... Mk 3:27
put on love, which **b** everything .... Col 3:14

BIRDS

Look at the **b** of the air: they .... Mt 6:26
much more value are you than the **b**! .... Lk 12:24

BIRTH

the **b** of Jesus Christ took place in .... Mt 1:18
gladness, and many will rejoice at his **b**, .. Lk 1:14
passed by, he saw a man blind from **b**. .... Jn 9:1

BIRTHRIGHT

Jacob said, "Sell me your **b** now." ...... Gn 25:31
Esau, who sold his **b** for a single meal. Heb 12:16

BITTER

made their lives **b** with hard service, ... Ex 1:14
the water of Marah because it was **b**; .... Ex 15:23
But if you have **b** jealousy and selfish ... Jas 3:14

BITTERNESS

The heart knows its own **b**, ... Prv 14:10
Let all **b** and wrath and anger and ...... Eph 4:31
that no "root of **b**" springs up and ...... Heb 12:15

BLAMELESS

Almighty; walk before me, and be **b**, ... Gn 17:1
May my heart be **b** in your statutes, ... Ps 119:80
be holy and **b** before him. .... Eph 1:4
be pure and **b** for the day of Christ, ... Phil 1:10
kept **b** at the coming of our Lord .... 1 Thes 5:23
present you **b** before the presence ...... Jude 24

BLASPHEME

and **b** the glorious ones. .... Jude 8

BLASPHEMED

name of God is **b** among the Gentiles ... Rom 2:24
of them the way of truth will be **b**. .... 2 Pt 2:2

BLASPHEMES

but the one who **b** against the Holy ..... Lk 12:10

BLASPHEMY

every sin and **b** will be forgiven people, . Mt 12:31
but the **b** against the Spirit will not be ... Mt 12:31

BLEMISH

lamb shall be without **b**, ... Ex 12:5
like that of a lamb without **b** or spot.... 1 Pt 1:19

BLESS

I will **b** those who **b** you, ... Gn 12:3
I will surely **b** you, and I .... Gn 22:17
The LORD **b** you and keep you; .... Nm 6:24
I **b** the LORD who gives me counsel; ...... Ps 16:7
I will **b** the LORD at all times; .... Ps 34:1
B the LORD, O my soul, ... Ps 103:1
b those who curse you, pray for .... Lk 6:28

B those who persecute you; .... Rom 12:14

BLESSED

all the families of the earth shall be **b**." ... Gn 12:3
B is the man who walks not in .... Ps 1:1
B be the name of the LORD .... Ps 113:2
"**B** are the poor in spirit, for .... Mt 5:3
"**B** are those who mourn, for .... Mt 5:4
"**B** are the meek, for they shall .... Mt 5:5
"**B** are those who hunger and .... Mt 5:6
"**B** are the merciful, for they .... Mt 5:7
"**B** are the pure in heart, for .... Mt 5:8
"**B** are the peacemakers, for .... Mt 5:9
"**B** are those who are persecuted for ...... Mt 5:10
"**B** are you when others revile you .... Mt 5:11
"**B** are you among women, ... Lk 1:42
'**B** is he who comes in the name of ...... Lk 13:35
B are those who have not seen and yet .. Jn 20:29
shall all the families of the earth be **b**.' ... Acts 3:25
'It is more **b** to give than to receive.' .. Acts 20:35
b is the man against whom the Lord ...... Rom 4:8
who has **b** us in Christ with every ...... Eph 1:3
waiting for our **b** hope, the appearing ...... Ti 2:13
B is the man who remains steadfast ...... Jas 1:12
B are those who wash their robes, ... Rv 22:14

BLESSING

name great, so that you will be a **b**. ...... Gn 12:2
before you today a **b** and a curse: ...... Dt 11:26
yet our God turned the curse into a **b**. ... Neh 13:2
Whoever brings **b** will be enriched, ... Prv 11:25
to the Lamb be **b** and honor and glory ... Rv 5:13
B and glory and wisdom and .... Rv 7:12

BLESSINGS

And all these **b** shall come upon you ...... Dt 28:2
A faithful man will abound with **b**, ... Prv 28:20

BLIND

anyone who misleads a **b** man on the .... Dt 27:18
LORD opens the eyes of the **b**. ...... Ps 146:8
Then the eyes of the **b** shall be opened, ... Is 35:5
to open the eyes that are **b**, to bring out ... Is 42:7
the **b** receive their sight and the lame .... Mt 11:5
"Can a **b** man lead a **b** man?" .... Lk 6:39
a **b** man was sitting by the roadside .... Lk 18:35
that though I was **b**, now I see." ...... Jn 9:25
wretched, pitiable, poor, **b**, and naked. .... Rv 3:17

BLOOD

"Whoever sheds the **b** of man, by man..... Gn 9:6
all the water in the Nile turned into **b**. .... Ex 7:20
when I see the **b**, I will pass over ...... Ex 12:13
life of every creature is its **b**: .... Lv 17:14
I do not delight in the **b** of bulls, ... Is 1:11
we have now been justified by his **b**, ... Rom 5:9
"This cup is the new covenant in my **b**, .. 1 Cor 11:25
we have redemption through his **b**, ... Eph 1:7
been brought near by the **b** of Christ. .... Eph 2:13
making peace by the **b** of his cross. .... Col 1:20
sanctify the people through his own **b**. .. Heb 13:12
Christ and for sprinkling with his **b**: ...... 1 Pt 1:2
and the **b** of Jesus his Son cleanses us .... 1 Jn 1:7
has freed us from our sins by his **b** ...... Rv 1:5

BLOT

"I will **b** out man whom I have created .... Gn 6:7
I will **b** out of my book. .... Ex 32:33
and **b** out all my iniquities. .... Ps 51:9
and I will never **b** his name out .... Rv 3:5

BLOTS

I am he who **b** out your transgressions ... Is 43:25

BLOTTED

I have **b** out your transgressions like a ... Is 44:22
turn back, that your sins may be **b** out, .. Acts 3:19

BOAST

My soul makes its **b** in the LORD; ...... Ps 34:2
Do not **b** about tomorrow, for .... Prv 27:1
but let him who boasts **b** in this, ... Jer 9:24
he has something to **b** about, ... Rom 4:2

the one who boasts, **b** in the Lord." .... 1 Cor 1:31
love does not envy or **b**; .... 1 Cor 13:4
be it from me to **b** except in the cross .... Gal 6:14
a result of works, so that no one may **b**. ... Eph 2:9
do not **b** and be false to the truth........ Jas 3:14

BOAT

they left the **b** and their father .... Mt 4:22
Peter got out of the **b** and walked on ...... Mt 14:29
the waves were breaking into the **b**, ... Mk 4:37
down and taught the people from the **b**.... Lk 5:3

BOAZ

So **B** took Ruth, and she became his ...... Ru 4:13
and **B** the father of Obed by Ruth, ... Mt 1:5

BODIES

dishonoring their **b** among .... Rom 1:24
life to your mortal **b** through his Spirit ... Rom 8:11
you not know that your **b** are members. 1 Cor 6:15
There are heavenly **b** and earthly...... 1 Cor 15:40
should love their wives as their own **b**. ... Eph 5:28

BODILY

strong, but his **b** presence is weak, ... 2 Cor 10:10
the whole fullness of deity dwells **b**, ... Col 2:9
for while **b** training is of some value, ... 1 Tm 4:8

BODY

"Take, eat; this is my **b**." .... Mt 26:26
will deliver me from this **b** .... Rom 7:24
For as in one **b** we have many........... Rom 12:4
though absent in **b**, I am present .... 1 Cor 5:3
not know that your **b** is a temple of .... 1 Cor 6:19
we who are many are one **b**, ... 1 Cor 10:17
"This is my **b**, which is for you. .... 1 Cor 11:24
For just as the **b** is one and has .... 1 Cor 12:12
Now you are the **b** of Christ .... 1 Cor 12:27
There is one **b** and one Spirit— .... Eph 4:4
because we are members of his **b**, ... Eph 5:30
will transform our lowly **b** to be like ...... Phil 3:21
has now reconciled in his **b** of flesh ...... Col 1:22
the offering of the **b** of Jesus Christ..... Heb 10:10

BOLD

but the righteous are **b** as a lion. .... Prv 28:1
we have such a hope, we are very **b**, ... 2 Cor 3:12
are much more **b** to speak the word ...... Phil 1:14

BOLDNESS

to speak the word of God with **b**........ Acts 4:31
Christ with all **b** and without .... Acts 28:31
in whom we have **b** and access with ..... Eph 3:12

BONE

"This at last is **b** of my bones and flesh . Gn 2:23
and a soft tongue will break a **b**. .... Prv 25:15

BONES

the **b** of Joseph, which the people .... Jos 24:32
like water, and all my **b** are out of joint; . Ps 22:14
my **b** wasted away through my .... Ps 32:3
but a crushed spirit dries up the **b**. ...... Prv 17:22
dry **b**, hear the word of the LORD......... Ezk 37:4
For a spirit does not have flesh and **b** .... Lk 24:39
"Not one of his **b** will be broken." ...... Jn 19:36

BOOK

"Take this **B** of the Law and .... Dt 31:26
This **B** of the Law shall not depart ...... Jos 1:8
"I have found the **B** of the Law in the . 2 Kgs 22:8
name shall be found written in the **b**..... Dn 12:1
whose names are in the **b** of life, ... Phil 4:3
not found written in the **b** of life, ... Rv 20:15
who are written in the Lamb's **b** of life. ... Rv 21:27

BOOKS

Of making many **b** there is no end, ... Eccl 12:12
sat in judgment, and the **b** were opened. . Dn 7:10
could not contain the **b** that would be .... Jn 21:25

BOOTHS

You shall dwell in **b** for seven days. ...... Lv 23:42
palm, and other leafy trees to make **b**, .. Neh 8:15
Now the Jews' Feast of **B** was at hand. ..... Jn 7:2

BORE
yet he **b** the sin of many, and makes ..... Is 53:12
took our illnesses and **b** our diseases." .. Mt 8:17
He himself **b** our sins in his body on .... 1 Pt 2:24

BORN
man is **b** to trouble as the sparks fly .... Jb 5:7
For unto you is **b** this day in the city of ... Lk 2:11
unless one is **b** again he cannot .... Jn 3:3
this purpose I was **b** and for this .... Jn 18:37
Last of all, as to one untimely **b**, he ..... 1 Cor 15:8
set me apart before I was **b**, ... Gal 1:15
servant, being **b** in the likeness of men. ... Phil 2:7
since you have been **b** again, not of ..... 1 Pt 1:23
No one **b** of God makes a practice of .... 1 Jn 3:9

BORNE
Surely he has **b** our griefs and .... Is 53:4
And I have seen and have **b** witness .... Jn 1:34

BORROW
not refuse the one who would **b** from you.. Mt 5:42

BORROWER
the **b** is the slave of the lender............ Prv 22:7

BOUGHT
you were **b** with a price. So glorify ..... 1 Cor 6:20

BOW
I have set my **b** in the cloud, ... Gn 9:13
You shall not **b** down to them or serve ... Ex 20:5
let us worship and **b** down; let .... Ps 95:6
'To me every knee shall **b**, every .... Is 45:23
every knee shall **b** to me, and every ... Rom 14:11
the name of Jesus every knee should **b**, .. Phil 2:10

BRANCH
the **b** of the LORD shall be beautiful .... Is 4:2
and a **b** from his roots shall bear fruit. ... Is 11:1
I will raise up for David a righteous **B**, ... Jer 23:5
a righteous **B** to spring up for David, ... Jer 33:15
behold, I will bring my servant the **B**. ..... Zec 3:8
and every **b** that does bear fruit he .... Jn 15:2

BRANCHES
the birds of the air made nests in its **b**." .. Lk 13:19
I am the vine; you are the **b**. .... Jn 15:5
and if the root is holy, so are the **b**. ..... Rom 11:16

BREAD
king of Salem brought out **b** and wine.. Gn 14:18
I am about to rain **b** from heaven .... Ex 16:4
and the **b** of the Presence; .... Ex 35:13
that man does not live by **b** alone, ... Dt 8:3
ravens brought him **b** and meat in ...... 1 Kgs 17:6
and gave them **b** from heaven in .... Ps 105:40
"'Man shall not live by **b** alone, ... Mt 4:4
Jesus took **b**, and after blessing it ...... Mt 26:26
Give us each day our daily **b**, ... Lk 11:3
"I am the **b** of life; whoever .... Jn 6:35
to the breaking of **b** and the prayers. .... Acts 2:42
The **b** that we break, is it not a........ 1 Cor 10:16
as you eat this **b** and drink the cup, ... 1 Cor 11:26

BREAKING
sins that people commit by **b** faith .... Nm 5:6
the law dishonor God by **b** the law..... Rom 2:23

BREASTPLATE
put on righteousness as a **b**, ... Is 59:17
having put on the **b** of righteousness, ... Eph 6:14
having put on the **b** of faith and love, ... 1 Thes 5:8

BREATH
everything that has the **b** of life, ... Gn 1:30
breathed into his nostrils the **b** of life, ... Gn 2:7
"Remember that my life is a **b**; .... Jb 7:7
Surely all mankind stands as a mere **b**! .. Ps 39:5
Man is like a **b**; his days are like a ...... Ps 144:4
everything that has **b** praise the............ Ps 150:6
gives **b** to the people on it and spirit .... Is 42:5
gives to all mankind life and **b** .... Acts 17:25

BREATHED
Jesus uttered a loud cry and **b** his last... Mk 15:37
b on them and said to them, "Receive ... Jn 20:22

BRIBE
And you shall take no **b**, ... Ex 23:8
partiality, and you shall not accept a **b**, ... Dt 16:19
does not take a **b** against the innocent. ... Ps 15:5
The wicked accepts a **b** in secret to ..... Prv 17:23
and a **b** corrupts the heart. .... Eccl 7:7
Everyone loves a **b** and runs after gifts. .. Is 1:23

BRIDE
captivated my heart, my sister, my **b**; ..... Sg 4:9
forget her ornaments, or a **b** her attire? .. Jer 2:32
one who has the **b** is the bridegroom. ..... Jn 3:29
and his **B** has made herself ready; .... Rv 19:7
"Come, I will show you the **B**, ... Rv 21:9
The Spirit and the **B** say, "Come." .... Rv 22:17

BRIDEGROOM
comes out like a **b** leaving his chamber, .. Ps 19:5
took their lamps and went to meet the **b**.. Mt 25:1
guests fast while the **b** is with them? ..... Mk 2:19

BROKE
the tablets out of his hands and **b** them .. Ex 32:19
land of Egypt, my covenant that they **b**, .. Jer 31:32
and she **b** the flask and poured it over ... Mk 14:3
after blessing it **b** it and gave it .... Mk 14:22

BROKEN
"My spirit is **b**; my days are extinct; ...... Jb 17:1
a threefold cord is not quickly **b**. .... Eccl 4:12
b cisterns that can hold no water........... Jer 2:13
and Scripture cannot be **b**— .... Jn 10:35
"Not one of his bones will be **b**," .... Jn 19:36
"Branches were **b** off so that I might .. Rom 11:19

BROKENHEARTED
The LORD is near to the **b** .... Ps 34:18
He heals the **b** and binds up their .... Ps 147:3
he has sent me to bind up the **b**, to ...... Is 61:1

BROKENNESS
LORD binds up the **b** of his people, ... Is 30:26

BROTHER
"I am your **b**, Joseph, whom you sold .... Gn 45:4
is a friend who sticks closer than a **b**. ... Prv 18:24
who is nearer than a **b** who is far away... Prv 27:10
First be reconciled to your **b**, ... Mt 5:24
b will deliver **b** over to death, ... Mt 10:21
"If your **b** sins against you, go and tell ... Mt 18:15
he is my **b** and sister and mother." .... Mk 3:35
for this your **b** was dead, and is alive; ... Lk 15:32
If your **b** sins, rebuke him, ... Lk 17:3
been here, my **b** would not have died." .. Jn 11:32
do you pass judgment on your **b**? ..... Rom 14:10
but **b** goes to law against **b**, ... 1 Cor 6:6
and wrong his **b** in this matter, ... 1 Thes 4:6
If a **b** or sister is poorly clothed and ..... Jas 2:15
loves God must also love his **b**. .... 1 Jn 4:21

BROTHER'S
"I do not know; am I my **b** keeper?" ...... Gn 4:9
do not go to your **b** house in the day of .. Prv 27:10
you see the speck that is in your **b** eye,... Lk 6:41

BROTHERS
And his **b** were jealous of him, ... Gn 37:11
pleasant it is when **b** dwell in unity! ...... Ps 133:1
who sows discord among **b**. .... Prv 6:19
And are not his **b** James and Joseph .... Mt 13:55
did it to one of the least of these my **b**, .. Mt 25:40
left house or wife or **b** or parents or ..... Lk 18:29
For not even his **b** believed in him. .... Jn 7:5
Mary the mother of Jesus, and his **b**. .... Acts 1:14
be the firstborn among many **b**. .... Rom 8:29
why he is not ashamed to call them **b**, ... Heb 2:11

BRUISED
a **b** reed he will not break, ... Is 42:3
a **b** reed he will not break, ... Mt 12:20

BUILD
David my father to **b** a house for the ... 1 Kgs 8:17
and on this rock I will **b** my church, ... Mt 16:18
and in three days I will **b** another, ... Mk 14:58
'This man began to **b** and was not able .. Lk 14:30
What kind of house will you **b** for me; .... Acts 7:49
which is able to **b** you up and to give .... Acts 20:32
are lawful," but not all things **b** up.... 1 Cor 10:23
one another and **b** one another up, ... 1 Thes 5:11

BUILDER
like a skilled master **b** I laid a .... 1 Cor 3:10
whose designer and **b** is God. .... Heb 11:10

BUILDING
like a man **b** a house, who dug deep .... Lk 6:48
You are God's field, God's **b**. .... 1 Cor 3:9
strive to excel in **b** up the church. ..... 1 Cor 14:12
for **b** up the body of Christ, ... Eph 4:12

BUILDS
Unless the LORD **b** the house, ... Ps 127:1
"Woe to him who **b** his house by .... Jer 22:13
each one take care how he **b** upon it. .. 1 Cor 3:10
body grow so that it **b** itself up in love... Eph 4:16

BUILT
In him you also are being **b** together ..... Eph 2:22
(For every house is **b** by someone, but ... Heb 3:4

BURDEN
Cast your **b** on the LORD, ... Ps 55:22
For my yoke is easy, and my **b** is light." .. Mt 11:30
lay on you no greater **b** than these .... Acts 15:28

BURDENS
you load people with **b** hard to bear, ... Lk 11:46
Bear one another's **b**, and so fulfill the .... Gal 6:2

BURIAL
she has done it to prepare me for **b**..... Mt 26:12
potter's field as a **b** place for strangers.. Mt 27:7
spices, as is the **b** custom of the Jews.... Jn 19:40

BURIED
The rich man also died and was **b**, ... Lk 16:22
We were **b** therefore with him by .... Rom 6:4
that he was **b**, that he was raised on .. 1 Cor 15:4
having been **b** with him in baptism, ... Col 2:12

BURNED
to his chest and his clothes not be **b**? ... Prv 6:27
gathered, thrown into the fire, and **b**. ..... Jn 15:6
If anyone's work is **b** up, he will....... 1 Cor 3:15
and if I deliver up my body to be **b**,.... 1 Cor 13:3
heavenly bodies will be **b** up and .... 2 Pt 3:10

BURNING
bush was **b**, yet it was not consumed........ Ex 3:2
in his hand a **b** coal that he had taken ..... Is 6:6
for action and keep your lamps **b**,.......Lk 12:35
He was a **b** and shining lamp, and you ...Jn 5:35

BUSINESS
It is an unhappy **b** that God has given ..... Eccl 1:13
I rose and went about the king's **b**, ... Dn 8:27
off, one to his farm, another to his **b**, ... Mt 22:5
'Engage in **b** until I come.' .... Lk 19:13

BUSYBODIES
in idleness, not busy at work, but **b**. ... 2 Thes 3:11
only idlers, but also gossips and **b**, ... 1 Tm 5:13

BUY
B truth, and do not sell it; **b** wisdom, ... Prv 23:23
that we may **b** the poor for silver and ..... Am 8:6

BUYS
She considers a field and **b** it; .... Prv 31:16
sells all that he has and **b** that field. ..... Mt 13:44

BYWORD
and a **b** among all the peoples .... Dt 28:37
a proverb and a **b** among all peoples. ... 1 Kgs 9:7
"He has made me a **b** of the peoples, ... Jb 17:6
you have been a **b** of cursing among .... Zec 8:13

CAESAR
it lawful to pay taxes to **C**, ... Mk 12:14
I appeal to **C**." .... Acts 25:11

CAIAPHAS
the high priest, whose name was **C**, ... Mt 26:3

CAIN
C spoke to Abel his brother. .... Gn 4:8
a more acceptable sacrifice than **C**, ... Heb 11:4
We should not be like **C**, who was of ... 1 Jn 3:12
the way of **C** and abandoned .... Jude 11

CALAMITY
who is glad at **c** will not go unpunished . Prv 17:5
hardens his heart will fall into **c**. .... Prv 28:14

CALEB
C, because he has a different spirit .... Nm 14:24
he gave Hebron to **C** the son of .... Jos 14:13

CALF
with a graving tool and made a golden **c**. . Ex 32:4
And bring the fattened **c** and kill it, ... Lk 15:23

CALL
people began to **c** upon the name of the . Gn 4:26
I **c** upon the LORD, who is .... Ps 18:3
to all who **c** on him in truth. .... Ps 145:18
c upon his name, make known his deeds .. Is 12:4
c upon him while he is near; .... Is 55:6
Before they I will answer; while they .... Is 65:24
C to me and I will answer you, and will ... Jer 33:3
and you shall **c** his name Jesus, ... Mt 1:21
I have not come to **c** the righteous but ...... Lk 5:32
How then will they **c** on him .... Rom 10:14
prize of the upward **c** of God in Christ... Phil 3:14

CALLED
And whatever the man **c** every living ...... Gn 2:19
if my people who are **c** by my name ...... 2 Chr 7:14
I have **c** you by name, you are mine. ..... Is 43:1
The LORD **c** me from the womb, ... Is 49:1
for they shall be **c** sons of God. .... Mt 5:9
For many are **c**, but few are chosen." ... Mt 22:14
and those whom he **c** he also justified, .. Rom 8:30
For you were **c** to freedom, ... Gal 5:13
who saved us and **c** us to a holy .... 2 Tm 1:9
For to this you have been **c**, ... 1 Pt 2:21
c us to his own glory and excellence, ... 2 Pt 1:3

CALLING
wash away your sins, **c** on his name.' .. Acts 22:16
For the gifts and the **c** of God are ...... Rom 11:29
For consider your **c**, brothers: not ...... 1 Cor 1:26
in a manner worthy of the **c** to which .... Eph 4:1
you worthy of his **c** and may fulfill .... 2 Thes 1:11
diligent to confirm your **c** and election, .. 2 Pt 1:10

CALLS
When he **c** to me, I will answer him; ..... Ps 91:15
and he **c** his own sheep by name .... Jn 10:3
who **c** upon the name of the Lord shall . Acts 2:21
whom the Lord our God **c** to himself." .. Acts 2:39
For "everyone who **c** on the name of .. Rom 10:13
who **c** you into his own kingdom .... 1 Thes 2:12
He who **c** you is faithful; .... 1 Thes 5:24

CAMEL
easier for a **c** to go through the eye of .: Mt 19:24
out a gnat and swallowing a **c**! .... Mt 23:24

CAMP
"This is God's **c**!" So he called the .... Gn 32:2
your God walks in the midst of your **c**, .. Dt 23:14
to him outside the **c** and bear the ...... Heb 13:13

CANA
day there was a wedding at **C** .... Jn 2:1
So he came again to **C** in .... Jn 4:46

CANAAN
Abram settled in the land of **C**, ... Gn 13:12
"Send men to spy out the land of **C**, ... Nm 13:2
I will give the land of **C**, ... 1 Chr 16:18

CANAANITE
a **C** woman from that region came out .. Mt 15:22

CAPTIVE
he carried the people **c** to Assyria, ... 2 Kgs 15:29
of Babylon brought **c** to Babylon all .. 2 Kgs 24:16
died to that which held us **c**, ... Rom 7:6
take every thought to **c** to obey Christ, ... 2 Cor 10:5
we were held **c** under the law, ... Gal 3:23
no one takes you **c** by philosophy and .... Col 2:8

CAPTIVES
leading a host of **c** in your train .... Ps 68:18
to proclaim liberty to the **c**, ... Is 61:1
to proclaim liberty to the **c** and .... Lk 4:18
ascended on high he led a host of **c**, ... Eph 4:8

CAPTIVITY
into **c** from Jerusalem to Babylon. ...... 2 Kgs 24:15
plead with you in the land of their **c**, ... 2 Chr 6:37
that time those who had come from **c**, ... Ezr 8:35

CARE
"Only take **c**, and keep your soul .... Dt 4:9
and the son of man that you **c** for him? .... Ps 8:4
overseers, to **c** for the church .... Acts 20:28
have the same **c** for one another. ...... 1 Cor 12:25
or the son of man, that you **c** for him? ... : Heb 2:6

CAREFUL
O Israel, and be **c** to do them, that it ...... Dt 6:3
being **c** to do according to all the law ..... Jos 1:7
to devote themselves to good works. ...... Ti 3:8

CARELESS
from evil, but a fool is reckless and **c**. .. Prv 14:16
account for every **c** word they speak, ... Mt 12:36

CARES
When the **c** of my heart are many, ... Ps 94:19
LORD of hosts **c** for his flock, ... Zec 10:3
anxieties on him, because he **c** for you... 1 Pt 5:7

CARPENTER'S
Is not this the **c** son? Is not his mother .. Mt 13:55

CARRIED
how the LORD your God **c** you, ... Dt 1:31
borne our griefs and **c** our sorrows; ...... Is 53:4
from them and was **c** up into heaven. .. Lk 24:51
God as they were **c** along by the Holy .. 2 Pt 1:21
And he **c** me away in the Spirit to a .... Rv 21:10

CASE
and I desire to argue my **c** with God. ...... Jb 13:3
one who states his **c** first seems right, ... Prv 18:17
Set forth your **c**, says the LORD; .... Is 41:21

CAST
them, and for my clothing they **c** lots. ..... Ps 22:18
Why are you **c** down, O my soul, ... Ps 42:11
C me not away from your presence, ... Ps 51:11
C your burden on the LORD, ... Ps 55:22
You will **c** all our sins into the depths ..... Mi 7:19
by the Spirit of God that I **c** out .... Mt 12:28
"How can Satan **c** out Satan? .... Mk 3:23
they **c** lots to divide his garments. ...... Lk 23:34
comes to me I will never **c** out. .... Jn 6:37
let us **c** off the works of darkness ...... Rom 13:12

CASTING
his garments among them by **c** lots. ..... Mt 27:35
c all your anxieties on him, because he .. 1 Pt 5:7

CATTLE
is mine, the **c** on a thousand hills. .... Ps 50:10

CAUGHT
that this man was **c** up into paradise— .. 2 Cor 12:3
will be **c** up together with .... 1 Thes 4:17

CAUSE
Who has wounds without **c**? .... Prv 23:29
to the fatherless, plead the widow's **c**. ..... Is 1:17
pleads my **c** and executes judgment ...... Mi 7:9
fulfilled: 'They hated me without a **c**.' ..... Jn 15:25

CAUSES
If your right eye **c** you to sin, ... Mt 5:29
but whoever **c** one of these little ones... Mt 18:6
or do anything that **c** your brother to .. Rom 14:21

CEASE
and winter, day and night, shall not **c**." .. Gn 8:22
they never **c** to say, "Holy, holy, holy, ... Rv 4:8

CEASES
love of the LORD never **c**; .... Lam 3:22

CENSER
each took his **c** and put fire in it .... Lv 10:1
and stood at the altar with a golden **c**, ... Rv 8:3

CENTURION
And when the **c**, who stood facing...... Mk 15:39
When the **c** heard about Jesus, he sent...... Lk 7:3
But the **c**, wishing to save Paul, kept ...Acts 27:43

CEPHAS
You shall be called **C**" .... Jn 1:42

CHAFF
but are like **c** that the wind drives away. .... Ps 1:4
but the **c** he will burn with .... Mt 3:12

CHAINS
"Get up quickly." And the **c** fell off ..... Acts 12:7
I am an ambassador in **c**, ... Eph 6:20
Remember my **c**. Grace be .... Col 4:18
bound with **c** as a criminal. .... 2 Tm 2:9
and even **c** and imprisonment. .... Heb 11:36
committed them to **c** of gloomy .... 2 Pt 2:4

CHANGE
that he should **c** his mind. .... Nm 23:19
has sworn and will not **c** his mind, ... Ps 110:4
"For I the LORD do not **c**; .... Mal 3:6
has sworn and will not **c** his mind, ... Heb 7:21
no variation or shadow due to **c**. .... Jas 1:17

CHANGED
not all sleep, but we shall all be **c**, ... 1 Cor 15:51
like a garment they will be **c**. .... Heb 1:12

CHARACTER
and endurance produces **c**, ... Rom 5:4
promise the unchangeable **c** of his ...... Heb 6:17

CHARGE
Job did not sin or **c** God with wrong. ...... Jb 1:22
him no answer, not even to a single **c**,... Mt 27:14
Who shall bring any **c** against God's .. Rom 8:33
Every **c** must be established .... 2 Cor 13:1
not domineering over those in your **c**, ... 1 Pt 5:3

CHARIOT
he makes the clouds his **c**; .... Ps 104:3
to Philip, "Go over and join this **c**." ...... Acts 8:29

CHARIOTS
returned and covered the **c** and the...... Ex 14:28
c of fire and horses of fire separated... 2 Kgs 2:11
Some trust in **c** and some in horses, but .. Ps 20:7

CHEEK
But if anyone slaps you on the right **c**, ... Mt 5:39

CHEERFUL
A glad heart makes a **c** face, ... Prv 15:13
the **c** of heart has a continual feast. ..... Prv 15:15
for God loves a **c** giver. .... 2 Cor 9:7
Is anyone **c**? Let him sing praise. .... Jas 5:13

CHERUB
Make one **c** on the one end, ... Ex 25:19
was the length of one wing of the **c**, ... 1 Kgs 6:24

CHERUBIM
of Eden he placed the **c** and a flaming .... Gn 3:24
the mercy seat were the faces of the **c**... Ex 37:9
The **c** spread out their wings over the ... 2 Chr 5:8
God of Israel, enthroned above the **c**, ... Is 37:16
Above it were the **c** of glory .... Heb 9:5

CHILD

Even a **c** makes himself known by his ... Prv 20:11
Train up a **c** in the way he should go;.... Prv 22:6
Do not withhold discipline from a **c**; .... Prv 23:13
but a **c** left to himself brings shame ..... Prv 29:15
For to us a **c** is born, to us a son .... Is 9:6
and a little **c** shall lead them................. Is 11:6
Whoever humbles himself like this **c** .... Mt 18:4
the hand he called, saying, "**C**, arise." ... Lk 8:54
I was a **c**, I spoke like a **c**,............... 1 Cor 13:11

CHILDREN

shall teach them diligently to your **c**, ... Dt 6:7
As a father shows compassion to his **c** .. Ps 103:13
c are a heritage from the LORD,............. Ps 127:3
blessed are his **c** after him!................... Prv 20:7
Her **c** rise up and call her blessed; ...... Prv 31:28
the **c** of the desolate one will be more .... Is 54:1
know how to give good gifts to your **c**, ... Mt 7:11
unless you turn and become like **c**, ... Mt 18:3
"Let the **c** come to me, and do not .... Lk 18:16
he gave the right to become **c** of God, ... Jn 1:12
with our spirit that we are **c** of God, ... Rom 8:16
and not all are **c** of Abraham because ... Rom 9:7
be imitators of God, as beloved **c**. .... Eph 5:1
Fathers, do not provoke your **c** to anger,.. Eph 6:4
C, obey your parents in everything, ... Col 3:20
know how, like a father with his **c**, ... 1 Thes 2:11
For you are all **c** of light,.................. 1 Thes 5:5
women to love their husbands and **c**,......... Ti 2:4
Beloved, we are God's **c** now, and what ... 1 Jn 3:2

CHOOSE

Therefore **c** life, that you and .... Dt 30:19
c this day whom you will serve, ... Jos 24:15
Blessed is the one you **c** and bring near, ... Ps 65:4
You did not **c** me, but I chose you .... Jn 15:16

CHOSE

LORD set his love on you and **c** .... Dt 7:7
But I **c** David to be over my people .... 1 Kgs 8:16
elect, whom he **c**, he shortened the days. .. Mk 13:20
his disciples and **c** from them twelve, ... Lk 6:13
but I **c** you out of the world, ... Jn 15:19
God **c** what is low and despised in .... 1 Cor 1:28
even as he **c** us in him before .... Eph 1:4
because God **c** you as the firstfruits.... 2 Thes 2:13

CHOSEN

The LORD your God has **c** you to .... Dt 7:6
A good name is to be **c** rather than .... Prv 22:1
and Israel my **c**, I call you by .... Is 45:4
For many are called, but few are **c**." ..... Mt 22:14
Mary has **c** the good portion,.............. Lk 10:42
I know whom I have **c**. .... Jn 13:18
Put on then, as God's **c** ones, holy .... Col 3:12
loved by God, that he has **c** you, ... 1 Thes 1:4
has not God **c** those who are poor in .... Jas 2:5
But you are a **c** race, a royal priesthood, ... 1 Pt 2:9

CHRIST

Peter replied, "You are the **C**,............... Mt 16:16
that the **C** should suffer and on the ..... Lk 24:46
I believe that you are the **C**, ... Jn 11:27
God has made him both Lord and **C**,..... Acts 2:36
still sinners, **C** died for us. .... Rom 5:8
for those who are in **C** Jesus. .... Rom 8:1
C died for our sins in accordance .... 1 Cor 15:3
But in fact **C** has been raised from .... 1 Cor 15:20
For we are the aroma of **C** .... 2 Cor 2:15
if anyone is in **C**, he is a new .... 2 Cor 5:17
insight into the mystery of **C**, ... Eph 3:4
For to me to live is **C**, and to .... Phil 1:21
When **C** who is your life appears, ... Col 3:4
But when **C** had offered,for all time a ... Heb 10:12
For **C** also suffered once for sins, ... 1 Pt 3:18
C, and he shall reign forever and ever." ... Rv 11:15

CHRIST'S

We are fools for **C** sake;.................... 1 Cor 4:10
we share abundantly in **C** sufferings, ... 2 Cor 1:5
If anyone is confident that he is **C**,......... 2 Cor 10:7

And if you are **C**, then you ....*....... Gal 3:29

CHRISTIAN

would you persuade me to be a **C**?" ... Acts 26:28
Yet if anyone suffers as a **C**, ... 1 Pt 4:16

CHURCH

tell it to the **c**. And if he refuses to .... Mt 18:17
fear came upon the whole **c** .... Acts 5:11
persecution against the **c** in Jerusalem, ... Acts 8:1
strive to excel in building up the **c**..... 1 Cor 14:12
him as head over all things to the **c**, ... Eph 1:22
through the **c** the manifold wisdom .... Eph 3:10
Christ is the head of the **c**, ... Eph 5:23
Christ loved the **c** and gave himself .... Eph 5:25
sake of his body, that is, the **c**, ... Col 1:24
how will he care for God's **c**? .... 1 Tm 3:5

CHURCHES

give proof before the **c** of your love .... 2 Cor 8:24
hear what the Spirit says to the **c**. .... Rv 2:7
to you about these things for the **c**. .... Rv 22:16

CIRCLE

He has inscribed a **c** on the face of .... Jb 26:10
he drew a **c** on the face of the deep, ... Prv 8:27
It is he who sits above the **c** of the earth, ... Is 40:22

CIRCUMCISE

your God will **c** your heart and the ....*.. Dt 30:6

CIRCUMCISED

Every male among you shall be **c**.......... Gn 17:10
who will justify the **c** by faith .... Rom 3:30
of all who believe without being **c**, ... Rom 4:11
For even those who are **c** do not .... Gal 6:13
In him also you were **c** with .... Col 2:11

CIRCUMCISION

and **c** is a matter of the heart, ... Rom 2:29
He received the sign of **c** as a seal .... Rom 4:11
For neither **c** counts for anything, ... Gal 6:15
For we are the **c**, who worship by .... Phil 3:3

CIRCUMSTANCES

In all I have put on the shield of faith, ... Eph 6:16
give thanks in all **c**; for this is the ..... 1 Thes 5:18

CISTERN

Drink water from your own **c**, flowing ..... Prv 5:15
put Jeremiah into the **c**—the king was ..... Jer 38:7

CITIZENS

but you are fellow **c** with the saints....... Eph 2:19

CITIZENSHIP

But our **c** is in heaven, and .... Phil 3:20

CITY

streams make glad the **c** of God, ... Ps 46:4
greatly to be praised in the **c** of our .... Ps 48:1
blessing of the upright a **c** is exalted, ... Prv 11:11
A **c** set on a hill cannot be hidden,......... Mt 5:14
God, for he has prepared for them a **c**. .. Heb 11:16
we seek the **c** that is to come. .... Heb 13:14
And I saw the holy **c**, new Jerusalem, ... Rv 21:2
while the **c** was pure gold, like clear .... Rv 21:18

CLAP

C your hands, all peoples! .... Ps 47:1
Let the rivers **c** their hands; let the hills .... Ps 98:8
the trees of the field shall **c** their hands.... Is 55:12

CLAY

Does the **c** say to him who forms it, ... Is 45:9
we are the **c**, and you are our potter; .... Is 64:8
like the **c** in the potter's hand, ... Jer 18:6
its feet partly of iron and partly of **c**....... Dn 2:33
Has the potter no right over the **c**, ... Rom 9:21
But we have this treasure in jars of **c**, ... 2 Cor 4:7
but also of wood and **c**, ... 2 Tm 2:20

CLEAN

Create in me a **c** heart, O God,............. Ps 51:10
"Lord, if you will, you can make me **c**." ..... Mt 8:2
"What God has made **c**,................. Acts 10:15
our hearts sprinkled **c** from an evil .... Heb 10:22

CLEANSE

and **c** me from my sin! .... Ps 51:2
let us **c** ourselves from every .... 2 Cor 7:1
C your hands, you sinners, and purify .... Jas 4:8
to **c** us from all unrighteousness. .... 1 Jn 1:9

CLEANSED

having **c** their hearts by faith.............. Acts 15:9
having **c** her by the washing of water .... Eph 5:26
having once been **c**, would no longer .... Heb 10:2
forgotten that he was **c** from his former ... 2 Pt 1:9

CLEFT

by I will put you in a **c** of the rock,......... Ex 33:22

CLOAK

take your neighbor's **c** in pledge, ... Ex 22:26
let him have your **c** as well.................. Mt 5:40
stripped him of the purple **c** .... Mk 15:20

CLOTHE

how much more will he **c** you, ... Lk 12:28
C yourselves, all of you, with humility ...... 1 Pt 5:5

CLOTHED

his wife garments of skins and **c** them.... Gn 3:21
You **c** me with skin and flesh, ... Jb 10:11
c me with the garments of salvation; .... Is 61:10
in the city until you are **c** with power .... Lk 24:49

CLOTHES

But if God so **c** the grass of the field, ... Mt 6:30
sun, and his **c** became white as light..... Mt 17:2

CLOTHING

why are you anxious about **c**? .... Mt 6:28
who come to you in sheep's **c** but .... Mt 7:15
than food, and the body more than **c** .... Lk 12:23

CLOUD

them by day in a pillar of **c** to lead......... Ex 13:21
a little **c** like a man's hand is rising ...... 1 Kgs 18:44
and a voice came out of the **c**, ... Mk 9:7
Son of Man coming in a **c** with power .... Lk 21:27
a **c** took him out of their sight. .... Acts 1:9

CLOUDS

the heavens, your faithfulness to the **c**..... Ps 57:10
c of heaven there came one like a son ..... Dn 7:13
and the **c** are the dust of his feet......... Na 1:3
Son of Man coming on the **c** of heaven .. Mt 24:30
in the **c** to meet the Lord in the air, ... 1 Thes 4:17
Behold, he is coming with the **c**, and .... Rv 1:7

COALS

His breath kindles **c**, and a flame comes .. Jb 41:21
for you will heap burning **c** on his head, .. Prv 25:22
you will heap burning **c** on his head." ... Rom 12:20

COIN

Show me the **c** for the tax." .... Mt 22:19
ten silver coins, if she loses one **c**, ... Lk 15:8

COINS

put in two small copper **c**, ... Mk 12:42
poured out the **c** of the money-changers ... Jn 2:15

COLD

increased, the love of many will grow **c**. .. Mt 24:12
Would that you were either **c** or hot! ...... Rv 3:15

COLLECTION

Now concerning the **c** for the saints: ... 1 Cor 16:1

COLLECTORS

he was eating with sinners and tax **c**, ... Mk 2:16
Tax **c** also came to be baptized and .... Lk 3:12

COLT

on a **c**, the foal of a donkey. .... Zec 9:9
and throwing their cloaks on the **c**, ... Lk 19:35
is coming, sitting on a donkey's **c**!" .... Jn 12:15

COME

Oh **c**, let us worship and bow down; .... Ps 95:6
C into his presence with singing! .... Ps 100:2
"**C**, everyone who thirsts, **c** to the .... Is 55:1
all flesh shall **c** to worship before me, ... Is 66:23

"**C**, let us return to the LORD;............ Hos 6:1
C to me, all who labor and are heavy.... Mt 11:28
"Let the children **c** to me; do not .... Mk 10:14
do not know when the time will **c**....... Mk 13:33
"Are you the one who is to **c**,............ Lk 7:19
will **c** in my name, saying, 'I am he!'.... Lk 21:8
I will **c** again and will take you .... Jn 14:3
"Father, the hour has **c**; .... Jn 17:1
that Jesus Christ has **c** in the flesh is ..... 1 Jn 4:2
who is and who was and who is to **c**,..... Rv 1:4
coming soon. Amen. **C**, Lord Jesus! .... Rv 22:20

COMES

Blessed is he who **c** in the name of .... Ps 118:26
Blessed is he who **c** in the name of the .. Mk 11:9
Nevertheless, when the Son of Man **c**,.... Lk 18:8
But we know where this man **c**,...... Jn 7:27
No one **c** to the Father except through .... Jn 14:6
When the Spirit of truth, **c**, he will .... Jn 16:13
proclaim the Lord's death until he **c**.... 1 Cor 11:26
when he **c** on that day to be glorified . 2 Thes 1:10

COMFORT

your rod and your staff, they **c** me......... Ps 23:4
Let your steadfast love **c** me .... Ps 119:76
C, **c** my people, says your .... Is 40:1
mother comforts, so I will **c** you;......... Is 66:13
the Father of mercies and God of all **c**, . 2 Cor 1:3
so that we may be able to **c** those who . 2 Cor 1:4
c one another, agree with one .... 2 Cor 13:11
and gave us eternal **c** and good hope . 2 Thes 2:16

COMFORTED

LORD has **c** his people and will............ Is 49:13
she refused to be **c**, because they are no .. Mt 2:18
those who mourn, for they shall be **c**.... Mt 5:4

COMFORTS

I am he who **c** you; who are .... Is 51:12
who **c** us in all our affliction, ... 2 Cor 1:4
God, who **c** the downcast, ... 2 Cor 7:6

COMING

and the time is **c** to gather all nations .... Is 66:18
But who can endure the day of his **c**,...... Mal 3:2
so will be the **c** of the Son of Man. ...... Mt 24:27
not know on what day your Lord is **c**. .... Mt 24:42
foreboding of what is **c** on the world. .... Lk 21:26
at his **c** those who belong to Christ. .. 1 Cor 15:23
account of these the wrath of God is **c**. .... Col 3:6
c of our Lord Jesus with all his saints. . 1 Thes 3:13
who are left until the **c** of the Lord, ... 1 Thes 4:15
Now concerning the **c** of our Lord .... 2 Thes 2:1
"Where is the promise of his **c**? .... 2 Pt 3:4
"Behold, I am **c** soon, bringing my .... Rv 22:12

COMMAND

For he will **c** his angels concerning you ... Ps 91:11
"'He will **c** his angels concerning you, ... Lk 4:10
are my friends if you do what I **c** .... Jn 15:14
C and teach these things. .... 1 Tm 4:11

COMMANDMENT

the **c** of the LORD is pure, ... Ps 19:8
For the **c** is a lamp and the teaching a .. Prv 6:23
This is the great and first **c**................ Mt 22:38
"This is my **c**, that you love one another . Jn 15:12
Beloved, I am writing you no new **c**, ... 1 Jn 2:7

COMMANDMENTS

the words of the covenant, the Ten **C**. .. Ex 34:28
but let your heart keep my **c**, ... Prv 3:1
Fear God and keep his **c**, for this is ..... Eccl 12:13
those who love him and keep his **c**, ... Dn 9:4
teaching as doctrines the **c** of men.'" .... Mt 15:9
On these two **c** depend all the Law and . Mt 22:40
Whoever has my **c** and keeps them, ... Jn 14:21
And his **c** are not burdensome. .... 1 Jn 5:3

COMMANDS

He **c** even the unclean spirits, and they .. Mk 1:27
that he **c** even winds and water, ... Lk 8:25

COMMENDED

A man is **c** according to his good sense,.. Prv 12:8
though **c** through their faith, ... Heb 11:39

COMMIT

c your way to the LORD; trust .... Ps 37:5

COMMITTED

lustful intent has already **c** adultery ...... Mt 5:28
if he has **c** sins, he will be forgiven. ...... Jas 5:15
He **c** no sin, neither was deceit found in . 1 Pt 2:22

COMMON

distinguish between the holy and the **c**, .. Lv 10:10
were together and had all things in **c**. .... Acts 2:44
God has made clean, do not call **c**.' ..... Acts 11:9
manifestation of the Spirit for **c** good. . 1 Cor 12:7

COMPANION

who forsakes the **c** of her youth .... Prv 2:17
though she is your **c** and your wife ...... Mal 2:14

COMPANY

"Bad **c** ruins good morals." .... 1 Cor 15:33

COMPARE

none can **c** with you! .... Ps 40:5
liken God, or what likeness **c** with him? .. Is 40:18

COMPASSION

As a father shows **c** to his children, ... Ps 103:13
everlasting love I will have **c** on you," ..... Is 54:8
my **c** grows warm and tender. .... Hos 11:8
he saw the crowds, he had **c** for them, ... Mt 9:36
his father saw him and felt **c**, and ran .... Lk 15:20
I will have **c** on whom I have **c**." .... Rom 9:15
For you had **c** on those in prison, ... Heb 10:34

COMPASSIONATE

if he cries to me, I will hear, for I am **c** .. Ex 22:27
c hearts, kindness, humility, ... Col 3:12
how the Lord is **c** and merciful. .... Jas 5:11

COMPETENT

an eloquent man, **c** in the Scriptures. .. Acts 18:24

COMPLACENCY

and the **c** of fools destroys them; .... Prv 1:32
against me and your **c** has come to my ... Is 37:29

COMPLAINT

"Today also my **c** is bitter; my hand ...... Jb 23:2
I am restless in my **c** and I moan, ... Ps 55:2
I pour out my **c** before him; .... Ps 142:2
if one has a **c** against another, ... Col 3:13

COMPLETE

For he will **c** what he appoints for me, ... Jb 23:14
c my joy by being of the same mind, ... Phil 2:2
that you may be perfect and **c**, ... Jas 1:4
so that our joy may be **c**. .... 1 Jn 1:4

COMPLETION

bringing holiness to **c** in the fear of ..... 2 Cor 7:1
work in you will bring it to **c** .... Phil 1:6

CONCEAL

he will **c** me under the cover of his tent; .. Ps 27:5
It is the glory of God to **c** things, but .... Prv 25:2

CONCEIT

slander, gossip, **c**, and disorder. .... 2 Cor 12:20
Do nothing from selfish ambition or **c**,.... Phil 2:3
he is puffed up with **c** and understands .. 1 Tm 6:4

CONCEITED

Let us not become **c**, provoking one .... Gal 5:26

CONCEIVE

the virgin shall **c** and bear a son, ... Is 7:14
the virgin shall **c** and bear a son, ... Mt 1:23
you will **c** in your womb and bear a son, .. Lk 1:31

CONCEIVED

for that which is **c** in her is from the .... Mt 1:20
Then desire when it has **c** gives birth .... Jas 1:15

CONDEMN

c not, and you will not be condemned; .... Lk 6:37

his Son into the world to **c** the world, ... Jn 3:17
And Jesus said, "Neither do I **c** you;...... Jn 8:11
Who is to **c**? Christ Jesus is the one .... Rom 8:34
if our heart does not **c** us, we .... 1 Jn 3:21

CONDEMNATION

C is ready for scoffers, and beating for .. Prv 19:29
as one trespass led to **c** for all men, ... Rom 5:18
There is therefore now no **c** for those .... Rom 8:1
Their **c** from long ago is not idle, ... 2 Pt 2:3

CONDEMNED

and by your words you will be **c**." .... Mt 12:37
rulers delivered him up to be **c** to death, . Lk 24:20
Whoever believes in him is not **c**, ... Jn 3:18
for sin, he **c** sin in the flesh, ... Rom 8:3
By this he **c** the world and became an .. Heb 11:7

CONDEMNS

for whenever our heart **c** us, God is...... 1 Jn 3:20

CONDUCT

but the **c** of the pure is upright. .... Prv 21:8
For rulers are not a terror to good **c**,..... Rom 13:3
By his good **c** let him show his works .... Jas 3:13
is holy, you also be holy in all your **c**, ... 1 Pt 1:15

CONFESS

"I will **c** my transgressions to the LORD,".. Ps 32:5
if you **c** with your mouth that Jesus ..... Rom 10:9
c your sins to one another .... Jas 5:16
If we **c** our sins, he is faithful and just .... 1 Jn 1:9

CONFESSES

c and forsakes them will obtain mercy. .. Prv 28:13
Whoever **c** that Jesus is the Son of God, .. 1 Jn 4:15

CONFESSION

Now then make **c** to the LORD, ... Ezr 10:11
that comes from your **c** of the gospel ... 2 Cor 9:13
you made the good **c** in the presence . 1 Tm 6:12
hold fast the **c** of our hope without .... Heb 10:23

CONFIDENCE

for the LORD will be your **c** .... Prv 3:26
we have boldness and access with **c**...... Eph 3:12
Let us then with **c** draw near .... Heb 4:16
since we have **c** to enter the holy .... Heb 10:19
appears we may have **c** and not shrink .. 1 Jn 2:28
not condemn us, we have **c** before God; . 1 Jn 3:21

CONFORMED

he also predestined to be **c** to the ...... Rom 8:29
Do not be **c** to this world, but be .... Rom 12:2
do not be **c** to the passions of your .... 1 Pt 1:14

CONQUERORS

we are more than **c** through him .... Rom 8:37

CONSCIENCE

a clear **c** toward both God and man. ... Acts 24:16
their **c**, being weak, is defiled............ 1 Cor 8:7
any question on the ground of **c**....... 1 Cor 10:25
the mystery of the faith with a clear **c** .. 1 Tm 3:9
but as an appeal to God for a good **c**, .. 1 Pt 3:21

CONSCIENCES

insincerity of liars whose **c** are seared, .. 1 Tm 4:2
both their minds and their **c** are defiled.... Ti 1:15

CONSECRATE

C yourselves, therefore, and be holy, ... Lv 20:7
C a fast; call a solemn assembly. .... Jl 1:14
And for their sake I **c** myself, that .... Jn 17:19

CONSIDER

For what great things he has done ...... 1 Sm 12:24
let them **c** the steadfast love of the .... Ps 107:43
C the lilies, how they grow: they .... Lk 12:27
c him who endured from sinners such .. Heb 12:3

CONSUME

"Zeal for your house will **c** me." .... Jn 2:17

CONSUMING

For the LORD your God is a **c** fire, ... Dt 4:24
for our God is a **c** fire. .... Heb 12:29

CONTEMPT

and some to shame and everlasting c. .... Dn 12:2
and treated others with c: .... Lk 18:9
treated him with c and mocked him. .... Lk 23:11
own harm and holding him up to c. .... Heb 6:9

CONTENT

and be c with your wages." .... Lk 3:14
then, I am c with weaknesses, ... 2 Cor 12:10
in whatever situation I am to be c. ...... Phil 4:11
and clothing, with these we will be c. ..... 1 Tm 6:8
and be c with what you have, ... Heb 13:5

CONTENTMENT

there is great gain in godliness with c, ... 1 Tm 6:6

CONTINUE

but c in the fear of the LORD .... Prv 23:17
Are we to c in sin that grace may .... Rom 6:1
c in what you have learned .... 2 Tm 3:14

CONTRARY

preach to you a gospel c to the one .... Gal 1:8
Is the law then c to the promises of God? . Gal 3:21

CONTRIBUTION

pleased to make some c for the poor . Rom 15:26
the generosity of your c for them ...... 2 Cor 9:13

CONTRITE

a broken and c heart, O God, ... Ps 51:17
with him who is of a c and lowly .... Is 57:15
who is humble and c in spirit .... Is 66:2

CONTROL

my body and keep it under c, ... 1 Cor 9:27
how to c his own body in holiness ...... 1 Thes 4:4

CONTROLS

For the love of Christ c us, ... 2 Cor 5:14

CONVICT

he will c the world concerning sin .... Jn 16:8
to c all the ungodly of all their deeds .... Jude 15

CONVICTION

hoped for, the c of things not seen. ...... Heb 11:1

COPY

They serve a c and shadow of .... Heb 8:5

CORNELIUS

Caesarea there was a man named C, ... Acts 10:1

CORNERSTONE

the builders rejected has become the c. . Ps 118:22
a precious c, of a sure foundation: .... Is 28:16
the builders rejected has become the c; . Mt 21:42
which has become the c. .... Acts 4:11
Jesus himself being the c, ... Eph 2:20
the builders rejected has become the c," . 1 Pt 2:7

CORRECTION

for teaching, for reproof, for c, ... 2 Tm 3:16

CORRUPT

Now the earth was c in God's sight, ... Gn 6:11

CORRUPTION

or let your holy one see c. .... Ps 16:10
or let your Holy One see c. .... Acts 2:27
but they themselves are slaves of c. ..... 2 Pt 2:19

COUNSEL

You guide me with your c, ... Ps 73:24
Without c plans fail, but with many ..... Prv 15:22
no c can avail against the LORD. .... Prv 21:30
all things according to the c of his will, .. Eph 1:11

COUNSELOR

shall be called Wonderful C, ... Is 9:6

COUNT

does not first sit down and c the cost, ... Lk 14:28
whom the Lord will not c his sin." .... Rom 4:8
I c everything as loss because .... Phil 3:8
C it all joy, my brothers, when .... Jas 1:2

COUNTED

he c it to him as righteousness. .... Gn 15:6
it was c to him as righteousness"? .... Gal 3:6
I c as loss for the sake of Christ. .... Phil 3:7

COUNTENANCE

the LORD lift up his c upon you .... Nm 6:26

COURAGE

Be strong, and let your heart take c, ... Ps 31:24
be strong and of good c." .... Dn 10:19
"Take c, for as you have testified ...... Acts 23:11

COURAGEOUS

Be strong and c. Do not fear or .... Dt 31:6
Be strong and c, for you shall .... Jos 1:6

COURT

c sat in judgment, and the books .... Dn 7:10
while you are going with him to c, ... Mt 5:25
and the ones who drag you into c? .... Jas 2:6

COURTS

For a day in your c is better than a ...... Ps 84:10
and his c with praise! Give thanks ...... Ps 100:4

COVENANT

I establish my c with you .... Gn 9:9
the LORD made a c with Abram, ... Gn 15:18
So shall my c be in your flesh an .... Gn 17:13
he has made with me an everlasting c, . 2 Sm 23:5
I will make with you an everlasting c, ... Is 55:3
I will make a new c with the house of ... Jer 31:31
for this is my blood of the c, ... Mt 26:28
"This cup is the new c in my blood, ... 1 Cor 11:25
read the old c, that same veil remains . 2 Cor 3:14
makes Jesus the guarantor of a better c. . Heb 7:22
new c, he makes the first one obsolete. . Heb 8:13
and to Jesus, the mediator of a new c, . Heb 12:24
the ark of his c was seen within his ...... Rv 11:19

COVER

I did not c my iniquity; .... Ps 32:5
He will c you with his pinions, and .... Ps 91:4
death and will c a multitude of sins. ..... Jas 5:20

COVERED

trustworthy in spirit keeps a thing c. .... Prv 11:13
Nothing is c up that will not be .... Lk 12:2
are forgiven, and whose sins are c; ...... Rom 4:7

COVERS

Whoever c an offense seeks love, ... Prv 17:9
since love c a multitude of sins. .... 1 Pt 4:8

COVET

"You shall not c your neighbor's .... Ex 20:17
You shall not c," and any other .... Rom 13:9
You c and cannot obtain, so you fight .... Jas 4:2

COVETOUSNESS

be on your guard against all c, ... Lk 12:15
produced in me all kinds of c. .... Rom 7:8
all impurity or c must not even be .... Eph 5:3
impurity, passion, evil desire, and c, ... Col 3:5

CREATE

C in me a clean heart, O God, ... Ps 51:10
I c new heavens and a new earth, ... Is 65:17
that he might c in himself one new man . Eph 2:15

CREATED

God c the heavens and the earth. .... Gn 1:1
So God c man in his own image, ... Gn 1:27
the LORD, who c the heavens and .... Is 42:5
of the creation that God c until now, ... Mk 13:19
c in Christ Jesus for good works, ... Eph 2:10
hidden for ages in God, who c all things, . Eph 3:9
For by him all things were c, in heaven .. Col 1:16
For everything c by God is good, ... 1 Tm 4:4
the universe was c by the word of God, . Heb 11:3
honor and power, for you c all things, ... Rv 4:11
who c heaven and what is in it, ... Rv 10:6

CREATION

his work that he had done in c. .... Gn 2:3

beginning of c, 'God made them male .... Mk 10:6
For the c waits with eager longing ...... Rom 8:19
in Christ, he is a new c. The old .... 2 Cor 5:17
nor uncircumcision, but a new c, ... Gal 6:15
invisible God, the firstborn of all c. ..... Col 1:15
they were from the beginning of c." ..... 2 Pt 3:4

CREATOR

Remember also your C in the days ...... Eccl 12:1
God, the C of the ends of the earth. ..... Is 40:28
served the creature rather than the C; . Rom 1:25
in knowledge after the image of its c. ... Col 3:10
souls to a faithful C while doing good. .. 1 Pt 4:19

CREATURE

whatever the man called every living c, ... Gn 2:19
For the life of every c is its blood: .... Lv 17:14
And no c is hidden from his sight, but .. Heb 4:13

CREATURES

forth living c according to their kinds .... Gn 1:24
the earth is full of your c. .... Ps 104:24
should be a kind of firstfruits of his c. ... Jas 1:18
c of instinct, born to be caught .... 2 Pt 2:12

CRIED

I c to you for help, and you .... Ps 30:2

CRIPPLED

better for you to enter life c .... Mt 18:8
a good deed done to a c man, ... Acts 4:9

CROOKED

The way of the guilty is c, ... Prv 21:8
the c shall become straight, ... Lk 3:5
without blemish in the midst of a c ..... Phil 2:15

CROPS

for I have nowhere to store my c?' ...... Lk 12:17
ought to have the first share of the c. ... 2 Tm 2:6

CROSS

whoever does not take his c and follow . Mt 10:38
lest the c of Christ be emptied of its ... 1 Cor 1:17
boast except in the c of our Lord .... Gal 6:14
point of death, even death on a c. ...... Phil 2:8
making peace by the blood of his c. ..... Col 1:20
set aside, nailing it to the c. .... Col 2:14
that was set before him endured the c, .. Heb 12:2

CROWN

You shall be a c of beauty in the hand .. Is 62:3
wearing the c of thorns and the purple ... Jn 19:5
whom I love and long for, my joy and c, . Phil 4:1
laid up for me the c of righteousness, .. 2 Tm 4:8
the test he will receive the c of life, ... Jas 1:12
receive the unfading c of glory. .... 1 Pt 5:4
and I will give you the c of life. .... Rv 2:10

CROWNED

heavenly beings and c him with glory ..... Ps 8:5
An athlete is not c unless he competes .. 2 Tm 2:5
Jesus, crowned with glory and honor because .... Heb 2:9

CRUCIFIED

mocked and flogged and c, ... Mt 20:19
I know that you seek Jesus who was c... Mt 28:5
is called The Skull, there they c him, ... Lk 23:33
of sinful men and be c and on the third .. Lk 24:7
this Jesus whom you c." .... Acts 2:36
know that our old self was c with him .. Rom 6:6
but we preach Christ c, ... 1 Cor 1:23
I have been c with Christ. .... Gal 2:20
belong to Christ Jesus have c the flesh .. Gal 5:24
by which the world has been c to me, ... Gal 6:14

CRUCIFYING

since they are c once again the Son of ... Heb 6:6

CRUSH

the will of the LORD to c him; .... Is 53:10
when it falls on anyone, it will c him." .. Mt 21:44
The God of peace will soon c Satan ... Rom 16:20

CRUSHED

brokenhearted and saves the c in spirit. . Ps 34:18

CRY

but a c spirit dries up the bones. .... Prv 17:22
but not c; perplexed, but not .... 2 Cor 4:8

CRY

he inclined to me and heard my c. .... Ps 40:1
They do not c to me from the heart, ... Hos 7:14
He will not quarrel or c aloud, ... Mt 12:19
silent, the very stones would c out." ..... Lk 19:40

CUP

is my chosen portion and my c; .... Ps 16:5
head with oil; my c overflows. .... Ps 23:5
little ones even a c of cold water. .... Mt 10:42
you clean the outside of the c .... Mt 23:25
if it be possible, let this c pass .... Mt 26:39
shall I not drink the c that the Father .... Jn 18:11
"This c is the new covenant .... 1 Cor 11:25

CURSE

"I will never again c the ground .... Gn 8:21
before you today a blessing and a c: ..... Dt 11:26
bless those who c you, pray for .... Lk 6:28
of the law by becoming a c for us— ...... Gal 3:13
with it we c people who are made in ...... Jas 3:9

CURSED

c is the ground because of you; .... Gn 3:17
The fig tree that you c has withered." ... Mk 11:21
"C is everyone who is hanged on a" ..... Gal 3:13

CURTAIN

length of each c shall be twenty-eight ... Ex 26:2
who stretches out the heavens like a c, ... Is 40:22
the c of the temple was torn in two, ... Mt 27:51
that he opened for us through the c, ... Heb 10:20

CYMBAL

I am a noisy gong or a clanging c. ...... 1 Cor 13:1

CYRUS

"Thus says C king of Persia, ... 2 Chr 36:23
In the first year of C king of Persia, ... Ezr 1:1
was there until the first year of King C. ... Dn 1:21

DAILY

Blessed be the Lord, who d bears us up; .. Ps 68:19
Give us this day our d bread, ... Mt 6:11
and take up his cross d and follow me. ... Lk 9:23
examining the Scriptures d to see if ... Acts 17:11

DAMASCUS

him for letters to the synagogues at D, ..Acts 9:2

DAN

Therefore she called his name D. .... Gn 30:6
And the people of D set up the carved .. Jgs 18:30

DANCE

Praise him with tambourine and d; ...... Ps 150:4
a time to mourn, and a time to d; .... Eccl 3:4
for you, and you did not d; we sang a ... Mt 11:17

DANCING

the camp and saw the calf and the d, ... Ex 32:19
turned for me my mourning into d; ...... Ps 30:11
Let them praise his name with d, ... Ps 149:3
our d has been turned to mourning. .... Lam 5:15

DANGER

The prudent sees d and hides himself, ... Prv 27:12
famine, or nakedness, or d, or sword? ... Rom 8:35

DANIEL

even if Noah, D, and Job were in it, ... Ezk 14:20
And God gave D favor and compassion .... Dn 1:9
Then this D became distinguished .... Dn 6:3
D was brought and cast into the den .... Dn 6:16
desolation spoken of by the prophet D, .. Mt 24:15

DARIUS

even until the reign of D king of Persia. .. Ezr 4:5
And D the Mede received the kingdom, ... Dn 5:31
In the second year of D the king, in the ... Hg 1:1

DARK

even the darkness is not d to you; ...... Ps 139:12
body is full of light, having no part d, ... Lk 11:36

whatever you have said in the d shall .... Lk 12:3
as to a lamp shining in a d place, ... 2 Pt 1:19

DARKENED

the whole land, so that the land was d, ... Ex 10:15
that tribulation, the sun will be d, ... Mk 13:24
and their foolish hearts were d. .... Rom 1:21
They are d in their understanding, ... Eph 4:18

DARKNESS

who walked in d have seen a great .... Is 9:2
the people dwelling in d have seen ...... Mt 4:16
bad, your whole body will be full of d. ... Mt 6:23
will be thrown into the outer d. .... Mt 8:12
loved the d rather than the light .... Jn 3:19
Whoever follows me will not walk in d, ... Jn 8:12
Or what fellowship has light with d? ... 2 Cor 6:14
for at one time you were d, but now ...... Eph 5:8
God is light, and in him is no d at all. ... 1 Jn 1:5

DAUGHTER

shall transfer his inheritance to his d. .... Nm 27:8
year to lament the d of Jephthah the .... Jgs 11:40
Rejoice greatly, O d of Zion! Shout. ...... Zec 9:9
"My d has just died, but come and .... Mt 9:18
his father, and a d against her mother, ... Mt 10:35
"D, your faith has made you well; .... Mk 5:34

DAVID

was the father of Jesse, the father of D... Ru 4:17
Spirit of the LORD rushed upon D ..... 1 Sm 16:13
and there they anointed D king over .... 2 Sm 2:4
D said to Nathan, "I have sinned ...... 2 Sm 12:13
And D built there an altar to the ...... 2 Sm 24:25
D said to Solomon, "My son, I had .... 1 Chr 22:7
anointed, to D and his offspring forever. .. Ps 18:50
covenant, my steadfast, sure love for D... Is 55:3
the son of D, the son of Abraham. .... Mt 1:1
"Have mercy on us, Son of D." .... Mt 9:27
city of D, which is called Bethlehem, ... Lk 2:4
Christ comes from the offspring of D, ... Jn 7:42
risen from the dead, the offspring of D, .. 2 Tm 2:8
of Judah, the Root of D, has conquered, ... Rv 5:5
I am the root and the descendant of D, .. Rv 22:16

DAY

God called the light D, and the .... Gn 1:5
for it is a D of Atonement, to make ...... Lv 23:28
in a pillar of cloud by d and in a pillar ... Nm 14:14
This is the d that the LORD has .... Ps 118:24
you do not know what a d may bring. .... Prv 27:1
for the d of the LORD is near; .... Is 13:6
For the d of the LORD is great. .... Jl 2:1
The great d of the LORD is near, ... Zep 1:14
And there shall be a unique d, ... Zec 14:7
who can endure the d of his coming, ... Mal 3:2
do not know on what d your Lord is .... Mt 24:42
given me, but raise it up on the last d. .... Jn 6:39
manifest, for the D will disclose it, ... 1 Cor 3:13
spirit may be saved in the d of the Lord. . 1 Cor 5:5
were sealed for the d of redemption. ..... Eph 4:30
it to completion at the d of Jesus Christ. .. Phil 1:6
d of the Lord will come like a thief ...... 1 Thes 5:2
that he is able to guard until that d ...... 2 Tm 1:12
more as you see the D drawing near. .... Heb 10:25
with the Lord one d is as a thousand ..... 2 Pt 3:8
battle on the great d of God the .... Rv 16:14

DAYS

for he is flesh: his d shall be 120 years." ... Gn 6:3
in six d the Lord made heaven and ..... Ex 31:17
in those d I will pour out my Spirit. ...... Jl 2:29
be killed, and after three d rise again. ... Mk 8:31
use of the time, because the d are evil. ... Eph 5:16
that in the last d there will come times ... 2 Tm 3:1
but in these last d he has spoken to us ... Heb 1:2
scoffers will come in the last d with ..... 2 Pt 3:3

DEACONS

at Philippi, with the overseers and d: ..... Phil 1:1
D likewise must be dignified, not .... 1 Tm 3:8

Let d each be the husband of one ...... 1 Tm 3:12

DEAD

Your d shall live; their bodies shall rise. .. Is 26:19
leave the d to bury their own d." .... Mt 8:22
disciples that he has risen from the d, ... Mt 28:7
He is not God of the d, but of the living. . Mk 12:27
do you seek the living among the d? ..... Lk 24:5
But God raised him from the d, ... Acts 13:30
Christ to suffer and to rise from the d, .. Acts 17:3
who raised from the d Jesus our Lord, ... Rom 4:24
consider yourselves d to sin. .... Rom 6:11
For if the d are not raised, ... 1 Cor 15:16
And you were d in the trespasses .... Eph 2:1
may attain the resurrection from the d.... Phil 3:11
of God, who raised him from the d. ...... Col 2:12
And the d in Christ will rise first. ..... 1 Thes 4:16
who is to judge the living and the d, ... 2 Tm 4:1
faith apart from works is d. .... Jas 2:26
ready to judge the living and the d, ... 1 Pt 4:5
And the d were judged by what was ..... Rv 20:12

DEAF

Who makes him mute, or d, or seeing, ... Ex 4:11
In that day the d shall hear the words .... Is 29:18
"You mute and d spirit, I command ..... Mk 9:25

DEATH

The murderer shall be put to d. .... Nm 35:16
that I have set before you life and d, ... Dt 30:19
through the valley of the shadow of d, ... Ps 23:4
you have delivered my soul from d, ... Ps 56:13
the LORD is the d of his saints. .... Ps 116:15
to a man, but its end is the way to d. .... Prv 14:12
upon your arm, for love is strong as d, ... Sg 8:6
He will swallow up d forever; .... Is 25:8
I have no pleasure in the d of anyone, ... Ezk 18:32
O D, where are your plagues? .... Hos 13:14
who will not taste d until they see the .... Mt 16:28
but has passed from d to life. .... Jn 5:24
keeps my word, he will never see d." ..... Jn 8:51
so d spread to all men because all ...... Rom 5:12
For the wages of sin is d, but the free ... Rom 6:23
Christ Jesus from the law of sin and d. ... Rom 8:2
I am sure that neither d nor life, ... Rom 8:38
"O d, where is your victory? .... 1 Cor 15:55
point of d, even d on a cross. .... Phil 2:8
sufferings, becoming like him in his d, ... Phil 3:10
Put to d therefore what is earthly in .... Col 3:5
through d he might destroy the one .... Heb 2:14
when it is fully grown brings forth d. ..... Jas 1:15
we have passed out of d into life, ... 1 Jn 3:14
There is sin that leads to d; .... 1 Jn 5:16
they loved not their lives even unto d. ... Rv 12:11
Over such the second d has no power, ... Rv 20:6
This is the second d, the lake of fire. .... Rv 20:14
from their eyes, and d shall be no more, ... Rv 21:4

DEBAUCHERY

and not open to the charge of d .... Ti 1:6
do not join them in the same flood of d, . 1 Pt 4:4

DEBORAH

Now D, a prophetess, the wife .... Jgs 4:4

DEBT

I forgave you all that d because you ..... Mt 18:32
by canceling the record of d that stood .. Col 2:14

DEBTORS

"A certain moneylender had two d. ...... Lk 7:41
summoning his master's d one by one, ... Lk 16:5
we are d, not to the flesh, to live ...... Rom 8:12

DEBTS

"Go, sell the oil and pay your d, ... 2 Kgs 4:7
and forgive us our d, as we also have ..... Mt 6:12

DECEIT

and in whose spirit there is no d. .... Ps 32:2
D is in the heart of those who devise ... Prv 12:20
and there was no d in his mouth. .... Is 53:9
d, sensuality, envy, slander, ... Mk 7:22

full of envy, murder, strife, **d**, ... Rom 1:29
neither was **d** found in his mouth. .... 1 Pt 2:22

DECEITFUL

Charm is **d**, and beauty is vain, but a ... Prv 31:30
The heart is **d** above all things, ... Jer 17:9

DECEITFULNESS

cares of the world and the **d** of riches .. Mt 13:22
may be hardened by the **d** of sin. .... Heb 3:13

DECEIVE

Let no one **d** himself. If anyone .... 1 Cor 3:18
Let no one **d** you with empty words, ... Eph 5:6
we **d** ourselves, and the truth .... 1 Jn 1:8
will come out to **d** the nations that .... Rv 20:8

DECEIVED

"The serpent **d** me, and I ate." .... Gn 3:13
Take care lest your heart be **d**, ... Dt 11:16
Do not be **d**: God is not mocked, ... Gal 6:7
Adam was not **d**, but the woman .... 1 Tm 2:14
bad to worse, deceiving and being **d**... 2 Tm 3:13

DECEIVER

Such a one is the **d** and the antichrist. ..... 2 Jn 7
Satan, the **d** of the whole world— .... Rv 12:9

DECEIVERS

empty talkers and **d**, especially .... Ti 1:10
For many **d** have gone out into the .... 2 Jn 7

DECEIVES

when he is nothing, he **d** himself. .... Gal 6:3
not bridle his tongue but **d** his heart, ... Jas 1:26

DECISION

but it every **d** is from the LORD. .... Prv 16:33
LORD is near in the valley of **d**. .... Jl 3:14

DECLARE

The heavens **d** the glory of God, ... Ps 19:1
to **d** your steadfast love in the morning, .. Ps 92:2
D his glory among the nations, his .... Ps 96:3
and new things I now **d**; before they ...... Is 42:9
d how much God has done for you." ...... Lk 8:39
D these things; exhort and rebuke .... Ti 2:15

DECREASE

He must increase, but I must **d**." .... Jn 3:30

DECREED

Whatever is **d** by the God of heaven, ... Ezr 7:23
God **d** before the ages for our glory. ...... 1 Cor 2:7

DEED

God will bring every **d** into judgment, ... Eccl 12:14
what good **d** must I do to have eternal .. Mt 19:16
Lord will rescue me from every evil **d** .... 2 Tm 4:18
let us not love in word or talk but in **d** ... 1 Jn 3:18

DEEDS

awesome in glorious **d**, doing wonders?. Ex 15:11
make known his **d** among the peoples! .. Ps 105:1
all our righteous **d** are like a polluted .... Is 64:6
They do all their **d** to be seen by .... Mt 23:5
are receiving the due reward of our **d**; ... Lk 23:41
d in keeping with their repentance. ..... Acts 26:20
impartially according to each one's **d**, ... 1 Pt 1:17
may see your good **d** and glorify God .... 1 Pt 2:12
linen is the righteous **d** of the saints. ..... Rv 19:8

DEEP

and darkness was over the face of the **d**.... Gn 1:2
the fountains of the great **d** burst forth, ...Gn 7:11
D calls to **d** at the roar of your .... Ps 42:7
to draw water with, and the well is **d**.....Jn 4:11

DEER

As a **d** pants for flowing streams, ... Ps 42:1

DEFEND

d the rights of the poor and needy. ...... Prv 31:9
they do not **d** the rights of the needy. .... Jer 5:28
how you should **d** yourself or what you .. Lk 12:11

DEFENSE

I am put here for the **d** of the gospel. .... Phil 1:16

being prepared to make a **d** to anyone .. 1 Pt 3:15

DEFILE

resolved that he would not **d** himself .... Dn 1:8
These are what **d** a person. .... Mt 15:20

DEFRAUDED

And if I have **d** anyone of anything, I ...... Lk 19:8
suffer wrong? Why not rather be **d**? ...... 1 Cor 6:7

DELAY

not far off, and my salvation will not **d**; ... Is 46:13
Will he **d** long over them? .... Lk 18:7
upon the earth fully and without **d**." ...... Rom 9:28
coming one will come and will not **d**;... Heb 10:37
that there would be no more **d**, ... Rv 10:6

DELIGHT

his **d** is in the law of the LORD, ... Ps 1:2
D yourself in the LORD, ... Ps 37:4
For you will not **d** in sacrifice, or I .... Ps 51:16
For I **d** in the law of God, in my inner ... Rom 7:22

DELIGHTS

them drink from the river of your **d**. .... Ps 36:8
you are, O loved one, with all your **d**! ...... Sg 7:6
my chosen, in whom my soul **d**; .... Is 42:1
forever, because he **d** in steadfast love. ... Mi 7:18

DELILAH

So **D** said to Samson, "Please tell me ... Jgs 16:6

DELIVER

I have come down to **d** them out of the ... Ex 3:8
"He trusts in the LORD; let him **d** .... Ps 22:8
but **d** us from evil. .... Mt 6:13
He trusts in God; let God **d** him now, ... Mt 27:43
gave himself for our sins to **d** us .... Gal 1:4

DELIVERANCE

you surround me with shouts of **d**. .... Ps 32:7
this will turn out for my **d**, ... Phil 1:19

DELIVERED

For you have **d** my soul from death, ... Ps 56:13
Son of Man will be **d** up to be crucified." .. Mt 26:2
who was **d** up for our trespasses .... Rom 4:25
He **d** us from such a deadly peril, ... 2 Cor 1:10
He has **d** us from the domain of .... Col 1:13
and that we may be **d** from wicked ..... 2 Thes 3:2

DELIVERER

my rock and my fortress and my **d**, ... Ps 18:2
"The **D** will come from Zion, ... Rom 11:26

DELIVERS

the LORD hears and **d** them out .... Ps 34:17
but righteousness **d** from death. .... Prv 10:2
when he **d** the kingdom to God .... 1 Cor 15:24
d us from the wrath to come. .... 1 Thes 1:10

DELUSION

those of high estate are a **d**; .... Ps 62:9
Behold, they are all a **d**; their works ...... Is 41:29
God sends them a strong **d**, ... 2 Thes 2:11

DEMON

And when the **d** had been cast out, ... Mt 9:33
daughter is severely oppressed by a **d**." .. Mt 15:22
man who had the spirit of an unclean **d**, .. Lk 4:33
he was casting out a **d** that was mute. ... Lk 11:14
Can a **d** open the eyes of the blind?"..... Jn 10:21

DEMON-OPPRESSED

a **d** man who was mute was brought ...... Mt 9:32
Then a **d** man who was blind .... Mt 12:22

DEMON-POSSESSED

two **d** men met him, coming out .... Mt 8:28
how the **d** man had been healed. .... Lk 8:36

DEMONS

And if I cast out **d** by Beelzebul, by ...... Mt 12:27
they cast out many **d** and anointed ...... Mk 6:13
and authority over all **d** and to cure ...... Lk 9:1
Even the **d** believe—and shudder! .... Jas 2:19

DEN

become a **d** of robbers in your eyes? ..... Jer 7:11
brought and cast into the **d** of lions. ...... Dn 6:16
but you make it a **d** of robbers." .... Mt 21:13

DENARIUS

Bring me a **d** and let me look at it." .... Mk 12:15

DENIED

Peter again **d** it, and at once a rooster ... Jn 18:27
he has **d** the faith and is worse than an .. 1 Tm 5:8
kept my word and have not **d** my name. ... Rv 3:8

DENIES

but whoever **d** me before men, I also ..... Mt 10:33
No one who **d** the Son has the Father.... 1 Jn 2:23

DENY

let him **d** himself and take up his cross .... Lk 9:23
you will **d** me three times." .... Lk 22:61
if we **d** him, he also will **d** us; .... 2 Tm 2:12
profess to know God, but they **d** him ...... Ti 1:16
into sensuality and **d** our only Master .... Jude 4
my name, and you did not **d** my faith ...... Rv 2:13

DENYING

of godliness, but **d** its power. Avoid .... 2 Tm 3:5
even **d** the Master who bought them, ... 2 Pt 2:1

DEPART

lest they **d** from your heart all the days.... Dt 4:9
d from me, you workers of lawlessness.'... Mt 7:23
say to those on his left, '**D** from me, ... Mt 25:41
"**D** from me, for I am a sinful man, ... Lk 5:8
later times some will **d** from the faith ..... 1 Tm 4:1

DEPARTURE

appeared in glory and spoke of his **d**, ... Lk 9:31
and the time of my **d** has come. .... 2 Tm 4:6
so that after my **d** you may be able .... 2 Pt 1:15

DEPENDS

That is why it **d** on faith, in order .... Rom 4:16
righteousness from God that **d** on faith ... Phil 3:9

DEPRAVED

are **d** in mind and deprived of the truth, .. 1 Tm 6:5

DEPRIVE

or to **d** the righteous of justice. .... Prv 18:5
Do not **d** one another, except perhaps .. 1 Cor 7:5

DEPTH

sprang up, since they had no **d** of soil, ... Mt 13:5
nor height nor **d**, nor anything else in ..... Rom 8:39
Oh, the **d** of the riches and wisdom ..... Rom 11:33

DEPTHS

In his hand are the **d** of the earth; the .... Ps 95:4
name, O LORD, from the **d** of the pit; .... Lam 3:55
cast all our sins into the **d** of the sea. ..... Mi 7:19
everything, even the **d** of God. .... 1 Cor 2:10

DESCEND

"I saw the Spirit **d** from heaven like a ..... Jn 1:32
"'Who will **d** into the abyss?'" .... Rom 10:7

DESCENDED

because the Lord had **d** on it in fire. ...... Ex 19:18
an angel of the Lord **d** from heaven ...... Mt 28:2
and the Holy Spirit **d** on him in bodily .... Lk 3:22
For not all who are **d** from Israel .... Rom 9:6
He who **d** is the one who also ascended .. Eph 4:10

DESERT

He turns a **d** into pools of water, ... Ps 107:35
the **d** shall rejoice and blossom like the ... Is 35:1
in the wilderness, and streams in the **d**; ... Is 35:6

DESIRE

Its **d** is contrary to you, but you must .....Gn 4:7
had sought him with their whole **d**, ... 2 Chr 15:15
you hear the **d** of the afflicted; .... Ps 10:17
grant you your heart's **d** and fulfill .... Ps 20:4
He fulfills the **d** of those who fear .... Ps 145:19
and nothing you **d** can compare with ..... Prv 3:15
the **d** of the righteous will be granted. .... Prv 10:24

A **d** fulfilled is sweet to the soul, ... Prv 13:19
D without knowledge is not good, ... Prv 19:2
I am my beloved's, and his **d** is for me. ..... Sg 7:10
and satisfy the **d** of the afflicted, ... Is 58:10
For I **d** steadfast love and not sacrifice, ... Hos 6:6
"I **d** mercy, and not sacrifice." .... Mt 9:13
but having his **d** under control, ... 1 Cor 7:37
My **d** is to depart and be with Christ, ... Phil 1:23
a better country, that is, a heavenly .. Heb 11:16
lured and enticed by his own **d**. .... Jas 1:14

DESIRED

More to be **d** are they than gold, ... Ps 19:10
many prophets and kings **d** to see what. .. Lk 10:24

DESIRES

he will give you the **d** of your heart. .... Ps 37:4
For the **d** of the flesh are against .... Gal 5:17
who **d** all people to be saved .... 1 Tm 2:4
d of the flesh and the **d** of the eyes .. 1 Jn 2:16
world is passing away along with its **d**, . 1 Jn 2:17
following their own sinful **d**; .... Jude 16
let the one who **d** take the water of life .. Rv 22:17

DESOLATE

set up the abomination that makes **d**. .... Dn 11:31
he would withdraw to **d** places and pray. .. Lk 5:16

DESOLATION

see the abomination **d** spoken of by ... Mt 24:15
then know that its **d** has come near. ...... Lk 21:20

DESOLATIONS

how he has brought **d** on the earth. .... Ps 46:8
there shall be war. **D** are decreed. .... Dn 9:26

DESPAIR

broken my heart, so that I am in **d**. .... Ps 69:20
crushed; perplexed, but not driven to **d**; . 2 Cor 4:8

DESPISE

therefore I **d** myself, and repent in dust..... Jb 42:6
Let no one **d** you for your youth, ... 1 Tm 4:12

DESPISED

He was **d** and rejected by men, ... Is 53:3
d the day of small things shall rejoice, ... Zec 4:10
chose what is low and **d** in the world, . 1 Cor 1:28

DESPISES

Whoever **d** his neighbor is a sinner, ... Prv 14:21
A fool **d** his father's instruction, ... Prv 15:5
but a foolish man **d** his mother. .... Prv 15:20

DESTINED

know that we are **d** for this. .... 1 Thes 3:3
For God has not **d** us for wrath, ... 1 Thes 5:9

DESTITUTE

the right of the afflicted and the **d**. .... Ps 82:3
regards the prayer of the **d** .... Ps 102:17
d, afflicted, mistreated— .... Heb 11:37

DESTROY

Behold, I will **d** them with the earth. ...... Gn 6:13
fear him who can **d** both soul and ...... Mt 10:28
thief comes only to steal and kill and **d**... Jn 10:10
but have divine power to **d** strongholds. . 2 Cor 10:4
was to **d** the works of the devil. .... 1 Jn 3:8

DESTROYED

set up a kingdom that shall never be **d**, ... Dn 2:44
ark, and the flood came and **d** them all... Lk 17:27
earthly home is **d**, we have a building .. 2 Cor 5:1

DESTROYS

lacks sense; he who does it **d** himself. .... Prv 6:32
but one sinner **d** much good. .... Eccl 9:18
no thief approaches and no moth **d**...... Lk 12:33
If anyone **d** God's temple, God will ..... 1 Cor 3:17

DESTRUCTION

Pride goes before **d**, and a haughty ..... Prv 16:18
and the way is easy that leads to **d**, ... Mt 7:13
vessels of wrath prepared for **d**, ... Rom 9:22
peace and security," then sudden **d** ... 1 Thes 5:3
suffer the punishment of eternal **d**, ... 2 Thes 1:9

bringing upon themselves swift **d**. .... 2 Pt 2:1

DETERMINED

"'Have you not heard that I **d** it long ...... Is 37:26
of the earth, having **d** allotted periods .. Acts 17:26

DETESTABLE

They are **d**, disobedient, unfit for any ...... Ti 1:16
as for the cowardly, the faithless, the **d**, ... Rv 21:8

DEVIL

the wilderness to be tempted by the **d**. .... Mt 4:1
the enemy who sowed them is the **d**. ... Mt 13:39
fire prepared for the **d** and his angels... Mt 25:41
then the **d** comes and takes away .... Lk 8:12
give no opportunity to the **d**. .... Eph 4:27
to stand against the schemes of the **d**... Eph 6:11
fall into disgrace, into a snare of the **d**... 1 Tm 3:7
Your adversary the **d** prowls around ...... 1 Pt 5:8
makes a practice of sinning is of the **d**, ... 1 Jn 3:8
the **d** who had deceived them was .... Rv 20:10

DEVOTE

But we will **d** ourselves to prayer .... Acts 6:4
that you may **d** yourselves to prayer; .... 1 Cor 7:5
d yourself to the public reading of ...... 1 Tm 4:13
learn to **d** themselves to good works, ... Ti 3:14

DEVOTED

he will be **d** to the one and despise ...... Mt 6:24
And they **d** themselves to the .... Acts 2:42
have **d** themselves to the service of ... 1 Cor 16:15

DEVOTION

secure your undivided **d** to the Lord .... 1 Cor 7:35
from a sincere and pure **d** to Christ. ..... 2 Cor 11:3

DEVOUR

to Joab, "Shall the sword **d** forever? ..... 2 Sm 2:26
who **d** widows' houses .... Mk 12:40
But if you bite and **d** one another, ... Gal 5:15
roaring lion, seeking someone to **d**. .... 1 Pt 5:8

DEVOUT

d men are taken away, while no one ..... Is 57:1
and this man was righteous and **d**, ... Lk 2:25
dwelling in Jerusalem Jews, **d** men .... Acts 2:5

DEW

as the rain, my speech distill as the **d**, ... Dt 32:2
If there is **d** on the fleece alone, ... Jgs 6:37
I will be like the **d** to Israel; he shall ..... Hos 14:5

DIE

that you eat of it you shall surely **d**." ...... Gn 2:17
fast your integrity? Curse God and **d**." ...... Jb 2:9
to be born, and a time to **d**; a time to ..... Eccl 3:2
"Even if I must **d** with you, I will .... Mt 26:35
and believes in me shall never **d**. .... Jn 11:26
that one man should **d** for the people, ... Jn 11:50
good person one would dare even to **d**. .... Rom 5:7
For as in Adam all **d**, so also in .... 1 Cor 15:22
to live is Christ, and to **d** is gain. .... Phil 1:21
it is appointed for man to **d** once, ... Heb 9:27

DIED

And all flesh that moved on the earth, .. Gn 7:21
the right time Christ **d** for the ungodly.... Rom 5:6
How can we who **d** to sin still live in it?.. Rom 6:2
Christ **d** for our sins in accordance ...... 1 Cor 15:3
For through the law I **d** to the law, so .... Gal 2:19
If with Christ you **d** to the elemental ...... Col 2:20
we believe that Jesus **d** and rose ...... 1 Thes 4:14
If we have **d** with him, we will also ..... 2 Tm 2:11
and the last, who **d** and came to life. ...... Rv 2:8

DIES

For when he **d** he will carry nothing ...... Ps 49:17
but if it **d**, it bears much fruit. .... Jn 12:24
does not come to life unless it **d**...... 1 Cor 15:36

DIGNITY

Strength and **d** are her clothing, ... Prv 31:25
in your teaching show integrity, **d**, ... Ti 2:7

DIGS

He who **d** a pit will fall into................ Eccl 10:8

DILIGENT

The plans of the **d** lead surely to .... Prv 21:5
all the more **d** to confirm your calling ... 2 Pt 1:10
be **d** to be found by him without spot ... 2 Pt 3:14

DIRGE

sang a **d**, and you did not weep.' .... Lk 7:32

DISASTER

D pursues sinners, but the righteous ..... Prv 13:21
I will relent of the **d** that I intended....... Jer 18:8
D after **d**! Behold, it comes. .... Ezk 7:5
in steadfast love, and relenting from **d**... Jon 4:2

DISCERN

Who can **d** his errors? Declare me ...... Ps 19:12
you **d** my thoughts from afar. .... Ps 139:2
may **d** what is the will of God, ... Rom 12:2
to **d** what is pleasing to the Lord .... Eph 5:10

DISCERNING

The **d** sets his face toward wisdom, ... Prv 17:24
whoever is **d**, let him know them; .... Hos 14:9
and of marrow, the thoughts and .... Heb 4:12

DISCERNMENT

the **d** of the discerning I will thwart." ... 1 Cor 1:19
who have their powers of **d** trained .... Heb 5:14

DISCIPLE

"A **d** is not above his teacher, ... Mt 10:24
even his own life, he cannot be my **d**, ... Lk 14:26
his mother and the **d** whom he loved... Jn 19:26

DISCIPLES

his twelve **d** and gave them authority ...... Mt 10:1
Go therefore and make **d** of all nations, .. Mt 28:19
abide in my word, you are truly my **d**, ... Jn 8:31
all people will know that you are my **d**, .. Jn 13:35

DISCIPLINE

consider the **d** of the LORD your........... Dt 11:2
Blessed is the man whom you **d**, ... Ps 94:12
Whoever loves **d** loves knowledge, ... Prv 12:1
he who loves him is diligent to **d** him... Prv 13:24
Do not withhold **d** from a child; .... Prv 23:13
D your son, and he will give you rest;.... Prv 29:17
But I **d** my body and keep it under ...... 1 Cor 9:27
do not regard lightly the **d** of the Lord, ... Heb 12:5
For the moment all **d** seems painful .... Heb 12:11
Those whom I love, I reprove and **d**, ... Rv 3:19

DISCIPLINED

The LORD has **d** me severely, ... Ps 118:18
we are **d** so that we may not be ...... 1 Cor 11:32
self-controlled, upright, holy, and **d**...... Ti 1:8
had earthly fathers who **d** us and we .... Heb 12:9

DISCIPLINES

son, the LORD your God **d** you. .... Dt 8:5
For the Lord **d** the one he loves, ... Heb 12:6
but he **d** us for our good, ... Heb 12:10

DISCLOSED

the secrets of his heart are **d**,........ 1 Cor 14:25

DISCOURAGED

He will not grow faint or be **d** till he ...... Is 42:4
your children, lest they become **d**......... Col 3:21

DISCRETION

may the LORD grant you **d** .... 1 Chr 22:12
is a beautiful woman without **d**. .... Prv 11:22
Daniel replied with prudence and **d**....... Dn 2:14

DISEASES

all your iniquity, who heals all your **d**, ... Ps 103:3
those afflicted with various **d** and pains, .. Mt 4:24

DISGRACE

inherit honor, but fools get **d**. .... Prv 3:35
When pride comes, then comes **d**, ... Prv 11:2
Poverty and **d** come to him who .... Prv 13:18
so that he may not fall into **d**, ... 1 Tm 3:7

DISGUISES
Whoever hates **d** himself with his lips ... Prv 26:24
for even Satan **d** himself as an angel . 2 Cor 11:14

DISHONEST
A **d** man spreads strife, and a whisperer . Prv 16:28
who is **d** in a very little is also .... Lk 16:10
to much wine, not greedy for **d** gain. .... 1 Tm 3:8

DISHONOR
shame and **d** who seek after my life! ...... Ps 35:4
It is sown in **d**; it is raised in glory. .... 1 Cor 15:43

DISHONORABLE
some for honorable use, some for **d** .... 2 Tm 2:20

DISHONORS
"'Cursed be anyone who **d** his father ... Dt 27:16

DISMAYED
Do not be frightened, and do not be **d**, ... Jos 1:9
Fear not; do not be **d**. .... 1 Chr 22:13
be not **d**, for I am your God; .... Is 41:10

DISOBEDIENCE
by the one man's **d** the many were ..... Rom 5:19
For God has consigned all to **d**, ... Rom 11:32
that is now at work in the sons of d—... Eph 2:2
or **d** received a just retribution, ... Heb 2:2

DISOBEDIENT
boastful, inventors of evil, **d** to parents, . Rom 1:30
you were at one time **d** to God but .... Rom 11:30
abusive, to their parents, ungrateful, . 2 Tm 3:2
detestable, **d**, unfit for any good work. ..... Ti 1:16

DISORDER
slander, gossip, conceit, and **d**. .... 2 Cor 12:20
there will be **d** and every vile practice. .... Jas 3:16

DISPERSED
people of the whole earth were **d**. ...... Gn 9:19
So the LORD **d** them from there .... Gn 11:8

DISPUTE
A **d** also arose among them, as to ...... Lk 22:24
to settle a **d** between the brothers, ... 1 Cor 6:5

DISQUALIFIED
preaching to others I myself should be **d**. 1 Cor 9:27
corrupted in mind and **d** regarding ...... 2 Tm 3:8

DISSENSIONS
fits of anger, rivalries, **d**, divisions, ... Gal 5:20
genealogies, **d**, and quarrels about .... Ti 3:9

DISTINCTION
see the **d** between the righteous and .... Mal 3:18
and he made no **d** between us and ..... Acts 15:9
for all who believe. For there is no **d**: .... Rom 3:22
For there is no **d** between Jew and .... Rom 10:12

DISTINGUISH
the ability to **d** between spirits, ... 1 Cor 12:10
constant practice to **d** good from evil. ... Heb 5:14

DISTRESS
In my **d** I called upon the LORD; .... Ps 18:6
called out to the LORD, out of my **d**, ... Jon 2:2
will be great **d** upon the earth and ...... Lk 21:23

DISTRIBUTED
and it was **d** to each as any had need. .. Acts 4:35
"He has **d** freely, he has given to the .... 2 Cor 9:9

DIVIDED
"Every kingdom **d** against itself is laid .. Mt 12:25
"They **d** my garments among them, ... Jn 19:24
Is Christ **d**? Was Paul crucified .... 1 Cor 1:13

DIVINATION
anyone who practices **d** or tells fortunes . Dt 18:10

DIVINE
because in his **d** forbearance he had ... Rom 3:25
not of the flesh but have **d** power to .. 2 Cor 10:4
His **d** power has granted to us all things . 2 Pt 1:3

DIVISION
No, I tell you, but rather **d**. .... Lk 12:51
that there may be no **d** in the body, ... 1 Cor 12:25
piercing to the **d** of soul and of spirit, ... Heb 4:12

DIVISIONS
watch out for those who cause **d** ...... Rom 16:17
and that there be no **d** among you, ... 1 Cor 1:10
It is these who cause **d**, worldly people, ... Jude 19

DIVORCE
"Is it lawful to **d** one's wife for any ...... Mt 19:3
the husband should not **d** his wife. ..... 1 Cor 7:11
live with her, she should not **d** him. ..... 1 Cor 7:13

DIVORCES
who does not love his wife but **d** her, ... Mal 2:16
I say to you that everyone who **d** his ..... Mt 5:32
whoever **d** his wife, except for sexual ..... Mt 19:9

DOCTRINE
create obstacles contrary to the **d** ...... Rom 16:17
carried about by every wind of **d**, ... Eph 4:14
not to teach any different **d**, ... 1 Tm 1:3
whatever else is contrary to sound **d**, .. 1 Tm 1:10
the good **d** that you have followed. ..... 1 Tm 4:6
anyone teaches a different **d** .... 1 Tm 6:3
to give instruction in sound **d** .... Ti 1:9
teach what accords with sound **d**. .... Ti 2:1
d of Christ and go on to maturity, ... Heb 6:1

DOERS
But be **d** of the word, and not hearers .... Jas 1:22

DOMINION
fill the earth and subdue it, and have **d** ... Gn 1:28
You have given him **d** over the works ...... Ps 8:6
for his **d** is an everlasting **d**, ... Dn 4:34
death no longer has **d** over him. .... Rom 6:9
all rule and authority and power and **d**, ... Eph 1:21

DONKEY
humble and mounted on a **d**, ... Zec 9:9
humble, and mounted on a **d**, ... Mt 21:5
a speechless **d** spoke with human voice . 2 Pt 2:16

DOOR
sin is crouching at the **d**. .... Gn 4:7
"Strive to enter through the narrow **d** .... Lk 13:24
I am the **d**. If anyone enters by me, ... Jn 10:9
behold, the Judge is standing at the **d**. ... Jas 5:9
Behold, I stand at the **d** and knock. If ... Rv 3:20

DOUBLE-MINDED
he is a **d** man, unstable in all his ways. ... Jas 1:8
sinners, and purify your hearts, you **d**. .... Jas 4:8

DOUBT
"O you of little faith, why did you **d**?" ... Mt 14:31
to you, if you have faith and do not **d**, ... Mt 21:21
and does not **d** in his heart, ... Mk 11:23
And have mercy on those who **d**; .... Jude 22

DOUBTS
why do **d** arise in your hearts? .... Lk 24:38
one who is like a wave of the sea ...... Jas 1:6

DOVE
And the **d** came back to him .... Gn 8:11
Spirit of God descending like a **d** .... Mt 3:16

DRAGON
and he will slay the **d** that is in the sea. . Is 27:1
and his angels fighting against the **d**. .... Rv 12:7
And they worshiped the **d**, for he .... Rv 13:4
he seized the **d**, that ancient serpent, ... Rv 20:2

DRAW
D near to my soul, redeem me; .... Ps 69:18
a man of understanding will **d** it out. ..... Prv 20:5
With joy you will **d** water from the wells .. Is 12:3
the earth, will **d** all people to myself." ... Jn 12:32
let us **d** near with a true heart in full .. Heb 10:22
for whoever would **d** near to God .... Heb 11:6
D near to God, and he will **d** near .... Jas 4:8

DRAWING
because your redemption is **d** near." ..... Lk 21:28

DRAWS
unless the Father who sent me **d** him. .... Jn 6:44

DREAM
Joseph had a **d**, and when he told .... Gn 37:5
Lord appeared to Joseph in a **d** .... Mt 2:13
and your old men shall **d** dreams; .... Acts 2:17

DRINK
D water from your own cistern, ... Prv 5:15
Wine is a mocker, strong **d** a brawler, ... Prv 20:1
Jesus said to her, "Give me a **d**." .... Jn 4:7
thirsts, let him come to me and **d**. .... Jn 7:37
shall I not **d** the cup that the Father ..... Jn 18:11
and all were made to **d** of one Spirit. 1 Cor 12:13
being poured out as a **d** offering, ... 2 Tm 4:6

DRUNK
For these people are not **d**, as you ...... Acts 2:15
And do not get **d** with wine, for that .... Eph 5:18
those who get **d**, are **d** at night. .... 1 Thes 5:7

DRUNKARD
d and the glutton will come to poverty, . Prv 23:21
d, or swindler—not even to eat with .. 1 Cor 5:11
not a **d**, not violent but gentle, not .... 1 Tm 3:3

DRUNKARDS
Be not among **d** or among gluttonous . Prv 23:20
nor thieves, nor the greedy, nor **d**, ... 1 Cor 6:10

DRUNKENNESS
weighed down with dissipation and **d** .... Lk 21:34
as in the daytime, not in orgies and **d**, .. Rom 13:13
d, orgies, and things like these. .... Gal 5:21
passions, **d**, orgies, drinking parties, ... 1 Pt 4:3

DRY
may go through the sea on **d** ground. .... Ex 14:16
on **d** ground in the midst of the Jordan, ... Jos 3:17

DULL
Make the heart of this people **d**, and .... Is 6:10
For this people's heart has grown **d**, ... Mt 13:15

DUST
LORD God formed the man of **d** .... Gn 2:7
are **d**, and to **d** you shall return." .... Gn 3:19
he remembers that we are **d**. .... Ps 103:14
All are from the **d**, and to **d** all .... Eccl 3:20
town shake off the **d** from your feet as .... Lk 9:5

DUTY
for this is the whole **d** of man. .... Eccl 12:13
we have only done what was our **d**.'" .... Lk 17:10

DWELL
"But will God indeed **d** with man on ... 2 Chr 6:18
and I shall **d** in the house of the .... Ps 23:6
I **d** in the midst of a people of unclean .. Is 6:5
so that Christ may **d** in your hearts ...... Eph 3:17
fullness of God was pleased to **d**, ... Col 1:19
the spirit that he has made to **d** in us"? .. Jas 4:5

DWELLING
The eternal God is your **d** place, ... Dt 33:27
How lovely is your **d** place, O .... Ps 84:1
been our **d** place in all generations. ..... Ps 90:1
longing to put on our heavenly **d**, ... 2 Cor 5:2
"I will make my **d** among them .... 2 Cor 6:16
built together into a **d** place for God .... Eph 2:22
the **d** place of God is with man. .... Rv 21:3

DWELLS
He who **d** in the shelter of the Most ...... Ps 91:1
if in fact the Spirit of God **d** in you. ...... Rom 8:9
temple and that God's Spirit **d** in you? . 1 Cor 3:16
whole fullness of deity **d** bodily, ... Col 2:9
By the Holy Spirit who **d** within us, ... 2 Tm 1:14

DWELT
Word became flesh and **d** among us, ... Jn 1:14

EAGLE'S
so that your youth is renewed like the e. . . Ps 103:5

EAGLES'
I bore you on e wings and brought you . . . . Ex 19:4

EAR
Give e to my words, O LORD; . . . . Ps 5:1
no one has heard or perceived by the e, ... Is 64:4
of the high priest and cut off his e. . . . . . Mt 26:51
And if the e should say, "Because I . . . 1 Cor 12:16

EARN
quietly and to e their own living. . . . . . . .2 Thes 3:12

EARNESTLY
O God, you are my God; e I seek you; . . . . . Ps 63:1
my spirit within me e seeks you. . . . . Is 26:9
Therefore pray e to the Lord . . . . Lk 10:2
Above all, keep loving one another e, ... 1 Pt 4:8

EARS
He who has e to hear, let him hear. . . . . . . Mt 11:15
but having itching e they will . . . . 2 Tm 4:3
and his e are open to their prayer. . . . . . 1 Pt 3:12

EARTH
God called the dry land E, ... Gn 1:10
Everything that is on the e shall die. . . . . . .Gn 6:17
is no God like you, in heaven or on e, . .2 Chr 6:14
the void and hangs the e on nothing. . . . . Jb 26:7
how majestic is your name in all the e! . . . . Ps 8:1
The e is the LORD's and the fullness . . . . . . Ps 24:1
He set the e on its foundations, so that . . Ps 104:5
LORD by wisdom founded the e; . . . . Prv 3:19
the whole e is full of his glory!" . . . . Is 6:3
I made the e and created man on it; . . . . . Is 45:12
heavens and the new e that I make shall . . Is 66:22
let all the e keep silence before him." . . . Hab 2:20
until heaven and e pass away, not an . . . . Mt 5:18
your will be done, on e as it is in . . . . Mt 6:10
you, Father, Lord of heaven and e, ... Lk 10:21
For "the e is the Lord's, and the . . . . . 1 Cor 10:26
descended into the lower regions, the e? . Eph 4:9
heaven and on e and under the e, ... Phil 2:10

EARTHLY
are heavenly bodies and e bodies, . . . 1 Cor 15:40
if the tent that is our e home is . . . . 2 Cor 5:1
with minds set on e things. . . . . Phil 3:19
to death therefore what is e in you: . . . . . . Col 3:5

EARTHQUAKE
but the LORD was not in the e. . . . . .1 Kgs 19:11
And behold, there was a great e, for an . . Mt 28:2
and suddenly there was a great e, so . . .Acts 16:26
and behold, there was a great e, ... Rv 6:12
thousand people were killed in the e, ... Rv 11:13

EARTHQUAKES
will be famines and e in various places. . . . Mt 24:7
There will be great e, and in various . . . . . Lk 21:11

EASE
I was at e, and he broke me apart; . . . . . . Jb 16:12
Tremble, you women who are at e, ... Is 32:11

EAST
as far as the e is from the west, ... Ps 103:12
behold, wise men from the e came . . . . . . Mt 2:1
as the lightning comes from the e . . . . . . Mt 24:27

EASY
gate is wide and the way is e that leads . . Mt 7:13
For my yoke is e, and my burden is . . . . . Mt 11:30

EAT
day that you e of it you shall surely die." . . Gn 2:17
your life, what you will e or what . . . . Mt 6:25
"Take, e; this is my body." . . . . Mt 26:26
"I have food to e that you do not know . . . Jn 4:32
brother stumble, I will never e meat, . . . 1 Cor 8:13
For as often as you e this bread . . . . . . 1 Cor 11:26
is not willing to work, let him not e. . . . . 2 Thes 3:10
I will come in to him and e with him, ... Rv 3:20

EATING
The Son of Man came e and drinking, ... Mt 11:19
kingdom of God is not a matter of e . . . . Rom 14:17
as to the e of food offered to idols, ... 1 Cor 8:4

EATS
man receives sinners and e with them." . . . Lk 15:2
If anyone e of this bread, he will live . . . . . Jn 6:51
For anyone who e and drinks without . . 1 Cor 11:29

EBENEZER
and called its name E; . . . . 1 Sm 7:12

EDEN
LORD God planted a garden in E, ... Gn 2:8
settled in the land of Nod, east of E. . . . . . Gn 4:16
makes her wilderness like E, her desert . . . Is 51:3
You were in E, the garden of God; . . . . . . Ezk 28:13

EFFECT
the e of righteousness will be peace, ... Is 32:17
For a will takes e only at death, since . . . Heb 9:17
And let steadfastness have its full e, ... Jas 1:4

EGYPT
They took Joseph to E. . . . . Gn 37:28
into E, Jacob and all his offspring . . . . Gn 46:6
the children of Israel, out of E." . . . . Ex 3:10
of Israel lived in E was 430 years. . . . . . Ex 12:40
"Behold, a people has come out of E, . . . Nm 22:11
the child and his mother, and flee to E, . . Mt 2:13
"Out of E I called my son." . . . . Mt 2:15
By faith he left E, not being afraid of . . . Heb 11:27
symbolically is called Sodom and E, ... Rv 11:8

ELDER
the youth will be insolent to the e, ... Is 3:5
a charge against an e except on the . . . 1 Tm 5:19

ELDERS
they had appointed e for them in . . . . . Acts 14:23
Let the e who rule well be considered . . 1 Tm 5:17
into order, and appoint e in every town . . . Ti 1:5
Let him call for the e of the church, ... Jas 5:14
So I exhort the e among you, ... 1 Pt 5:1
who are younger, be subject to the e. . . . . 1 Pt 5:5
on the thrones were twenty-four e, ... Rv 4:4

ELECT
But for the sake of the e those days . . . . Mt 24:22
angels and gather his e from the four . . . Mk 13:27
And will not God give justice to his e, ... Lk 18:7
shall bring any charge against God's e? . .Rom 8:33
The e obtained it, but the rest were . . . . Rom 11:7
Christ Jesus and of the e angels . . . . 1 Tm 5:21
endure everything for the sake of the e, . . 2 Tm 2:10
for the sake of the faith of God's e . . . . Ti 1:1

ELECTION
God's purpose of e might continue, ... Rom 9:11
But as regards e, they are beloved for . Rom 11:28
diligent to confirm your calling and e, ... 2 Pt 1:10

ELIJAH
Now E the Tishbite, of . . . . .1 Kgs 17:1
E took the child and brought him . . . . . 1 Kgs 17:23
Then E said to the prophets of Baal, . . . 1 Kgs 18:25
E passed by him and cast his cloak . . . 1 Kgs 19:19
And E went up by a whirlwind into . . . . . 2 Kgs 2:11
"Behold, I will send you E the prophet . . . Mal 4:5
there appeared to them Moses and E, . . . Mt 17:3
But I tell you that E has already come, . . . Mt 17:12
spirit and power of E, to turn the hearts . . Lk 1:17
many widows in Israel in the days of E, . . Lk 4:25
Are you E?" He said, "I am not." . . . . Jn 1:21
not know what the Scripture says of E, . . Rom 11:2
E was a man with a nature like ours, ... Jas 5:17

ELISHA
found E the son of Shaphat, who was . . 1 Kgs 19:19
"The spirit of Elijah rests on E." . . . . 2 Kgs 2:15
and chariots of fire all around E. . . . . . . 2 Kgs 6:17
all the great things that E has done." . . . 2 Kgs 8:4
So E died, and they buried him. Now . . . 2 Kgs 13:20

in Israel in the time of the prophet E, ... Lk 4:27

ELIZABETH
had no child, because E was barren, ... Lk 1:7
when E heard the greeting of Mary, ... Lk 1:41

EMMAUS
were going to a village named E, ... Lk 24:13

EMPTY
it shall not return to me e, but . . . . Is 55:11
captive by philosophy and e deceit, ... Col 2:8
insubordinate, e talkers and deceivers, ... Ti 1:10

ENCAMPS
The angel of the LORD e around . . . . Ps 34:7

ENCOURAGE
Therefore e one another and build . . . . 1 Thes 5:11
admonish the idle, e the fainthearted, . 1 Thes 5:14

ENCOURAGED
so that all may learn and all be e, ... 1 Cor 14:31
that their hearts may be e, being knit . . . . Col 2:2

ENCOURAGEMENT
Barnabas (which means son of e), ... Acts 4:36
through the e of the Scriptures . . . . Rom 15:4
upbuilding and e and consolation. . . . . . 1 Cor 14:3
So if there is any e in Christ, any . . . . Phil 2:1

END
determined to make an e of all flesh, ... Gn 6:13
"O LORD, make me know my . . . . Ps 39:4
we bring our years to an e like a sigh. . . . . Ps 90:9
The e of the matter; all has been heard. . Eccl 12:13
declaring the e from the beginning and . . Is 46:10
one who endures to the e will be saved. . Mt 10:22
to all nations, and then the e will come. . Mt 24:14
and of his kingdom there will be no e." . . . Lk 1:33
to sanctification and its e, eternal life. . . Rom 6:22
For Christ is the e of the law . . . . Rom 10:4
will sustain you to the e, guiltless . . . . . 1 Cor 1:8
Then comes the e, when he delivers . 1 Cor 15:24
your years will have no e." . . . . Heb 1:12
The e of all things is at hand; . . . . 1 Pt 4:7
keeps my works until the e, to him I . . . . . Rv 2:26

ENDURANCE
By your e you will gain your lives. . . . . . . Lk 21:19
knowing that suffering produces e, ... Rom 5:3
by great e, in afflictions, hardships, ... 2 Cor 6:4
his glorious might, for all e and . . . . Col 1:11
For you have need of e, so that when . . Heb 10:36
you have kept my word about patient e, . . Rv 3:10
Here is a call for the e of the saints, ... Rv 14:12

ENDURE
May the glory of the LORD e forever; . . . Ps 104:31
we bless; when persecuted, we e; . . . . . 1 Cor 4:12
always be open-minded, e suffering, ... 2 Tm 4:5
It is for discipline that you have to e, ... Heb 12:7
you do good and suffer for it you e, ... 1 Pt 2:20

ENDURES
The steadfast love of God e all the day. . . . Ps 52:1
for his steadfast love e forever. . . . . Ps 136:1
LORD is good, for his steadfast love e . . . . Jer 33:11
your throne e to all generations. . . . . Lam 5:19
But the one who e to the end will be . . . . Mt 24:13
things, hopes all things, e all things. . . . . 1 Cor 13:7
when, mindful of God, one e sorrows . . . . 1 Pt 2:19

ENDURING
fear of the LORD is clean, e . . . . Ps 19:9
for he is the living God, e forever, ... Dn 6:26
and in the afflictions that you are e, ... 2 Thes 1:4
I know you are e patiently and bearing . . . Rv 2:3

ENEMIES
table before me in the presence of my e; . Ps 23:5
he makes even his e to be at peace . . . . . Prv 16:7
Love your e and pray for those . . . . Mt 5:44
a person's e will be those of his own . . . Mt 10:36
until I make your e your footstool.'" . . . . Lk 20:43

ENEMY

while we were **e** we were reconciled ...... Rom 5:10
he has put all his **e** under his feet. .... 1 Cor 15:25
until I make your **e** a footstool .... Heb 1:13

ENEMY

my refuge, a strong tower against the **e**. .... Ps 61:3
Do not rejoice when your **e** falls, ... Prv 24:17
If your **e** is hungry, give him bread ...... Prv 25:21
his **e** came and sowed weeds .... Mt 13:25
and over all the power of the **e**, ... Lk 10:19
To the contrary, "if your **e** is hungry, ... Rom 12:20
The last **e** to be destroyed is death. ... 1 Cor 15:26
Do not regard him as an **e**, but warn . 2 Thes 3:15
the world makes himself an **e** of God. ..... Jas 4:4

ENGRAVED

I have **e** you on the palms of my hands; .. Is 49:16

ENJOY

E life with the wife whom you love, ... Eccl 9:9
my chosen shall long **e** the work of ...... Is 65:22
provides us with everything to **e**. .... 1 Tm 6:17

ENLARGE

you would bless me and **e** my border, .. 1 Chr 4:10
when you **e** my heart! .... Ps 119:32
"**E** the place of your tent, and let the ...... Is 54:2

ENLIGHTENED

having the eyes of your hearts **e**, ... Eph 1:18
those who have once been **e**, ... Heb 6:4

ENMITY

I will put **e** between you and the .... Gn 3:15
idolatry, sorcery, **e**, strife, jealousy, fits ... Gal 5:20
friendship with the world is **e** with God? ... Jas 4:4

ENOCH

E walked with God, and he was not, ... Gn 5:24
By faith **E** was taken up so that he .... Heb 11:5

ENOUGH

never satisfied; four never say, "**E**": .... Prv 30:15
It is **e**; the hour has come. .... Mk 14:41

ENRICHED

Whoever brings blessing will be **e**, ... Prv 11:25
trusts in the LORD will be **e**. .... Prv 28:25
in every way you were **e** in him in all ... 1 Cor 1:5

ENSLAVED

that we would no longer be **e** to sin. ...... Rom 6:6
we were children, were **e** to the .... Gal 4:3
overcomes a person, to that he is **e**. .... 2 Pt 2:19

ENTANGLED

No soldier gets **e** in civilian pursuits, ... 2 Tm 2:4
are again **e** in them and overcome, ... 2 Pt 2:20

ENTER

E his gates with thanksgiving, ... Ps 100:4
Pharisees, you will never **e** the .... Mt 5:20
"**E** by the narrow gate. For the gate is ... Mt 7:13
than for a rich person to **e** the kingdom ... Lk 18:25
have confidence to **e** the holy places ... Heb 10:19
may **e** the city by the gates. .... Rv 22:14

ENTERED

for whoever has **e** God's rest has also ... Heb 4:10
he **e** once for all into the holy places, ... Heb 9:12

ENTERS

since it **e** not his heart but his stomach, .. Mk 7:19
I am the door. If anyone **e** by me, ... Jn 10:9

ENTERTAINED

some have **e** angels unawares. .... Heb 13:2

ENTHRONED

Yet you are holy, **e** on the praises .... Ps 22:3
God of Israel, **e** above the cherubim, ... Is 37:16

ENTICE

My son, if sinners **e** you, do not .... Prv 1:10
insatiable for sin. They **e** unsteady souls. . 2 Pt 2:14

ENTREATED

he **e** the favor of the LORD his .... 2 Chr 33:12

yet we have not **e** the favor of the .... Dn 9:13

ENTRUST

who will **e** to you the true riches? .... Lk 16:11
on his part did not **e** himself to them, ... Jn 2:24
suffer according to God's will **e** their ..... 1 Pt 4:19

ENTRUSTED

saw that I had been **e** with the gospel ... Gal 2:7
approved by God to be **e** with the ...... 1 Thes 2:4
until that day what has been **e** to me. ... 2 Tm 1:12
guard the good deposit **e** to you. .... 2 Tm 1:14

ENVIOUS

For I was **e** of the arrogant when I saw ... Ps 73:3
Be not **e** of evil men, nor desire to be ... Prv 24:1

ENVY

but **e** makes the bones rot. .... Prv 14:30
Let not your heart **e** sinners, ... Prv 23:17
e, slander, pride, foolishness. .... Mk 7:22
love does not **e** or boast; it .... 1 Cor 13:4
e, drunkenness, orgies, and things like ... Gal 5:21
preach Christ from **e** and rivalry, ... Phil 1:15

EPHESUS

I fought with beasts at **E**? .... 1 Cor 15:32
"To the angel of the church in **E** write: ...... Rv 2:1

EQUAL

will you liken me and make me **e**, ... Is 46:5
are **e** to angels and are sons of God, ... Lk 20:36
Father, making himself **e** with God. .... Jn 5:18

EQUALITY

form of God, did not count **e** with God .... Phil 2:6

EQUIP

to **e** the saints for the work of ministry, ... Eph 4:12
e you with everything good that you ...... Heb 13:21

EQUIPPED

may be complete, **e** for every good ...... 2 Tm 3:17

ERROR

not carried away with the **e** of lawless ... 2 Pt 3:17
the Spirit of truth and the spirit of **e**. ...... 1 Jn 4:6

ESAU

Thus **E** despised his birthright. .... Gn 25:34
But **E** ran to meet him and embraced .... Gn 33:4
unholy like **E**, who sold his birthright ... Heb 12:16

ESCAPE

may have strength to **e** all these things ... Lk 21:36
that you will **e** the judgment of God? ...... Rom 2:3
he will also provide the way of **e**, ... 1 Cor 10:13
e from the snare of the devil, ... 2 Tm 2:26
how shall we **e** if we neglect such .... Heb 2:3
much less will we **e** if we reject him ..... Heb 12:25

ESTABLISH

I will **e** his kingdom forever if he .... 1 Chr 28:7
and **e** the work of our hands upon us; ..... Ps 90:17
of God, and seeking to **e** their own, ... Rom 10:3
E your hearts, for the coming of the .... Jas 5:8

ESTABLISHED

The steps of a man are **e** by the .... Ps 37:23
by understanding he **e** the heavens; ...... Prv 3:19
No one is **e** by wickedness, but the .... Prv 12:3
Who has **e** all the ends of the earth? ..... Prv 30:4
who **e** the world by his wisdom, ... Jer 10:12
and built up in him and **e** in the faith, ... Col 2:7

ETERNAL

The **e** God is your dwelling place, ... Dt 33:27
because man is going to his **e** home, ... Eccl 12:5
but the righteous into **e** life." .... Mt 25:46
what must I do to inherit **e** life?" .... Mk 10:17
should not perish but have **e** life. .... Jn 3:16
a spring of water welling up to **e** life." ...... Jn 4:14
believes him who sent me has **e** life. ...... Jn 5:24
as were appointed to **e** life believed. .... Acts 13:48
righteousness leading to **e** life through .... Rom 5:21
This was according to the **e** purpose .... Eph 3:11
blood, thus securing an **e** redemption. ... Heb 9:12

you an entrance into the **e** kingdom ... 2 Pt 1:11
you may know that you have **e** life. ...... 1 Jn 5:13

ETERNITY

he has put **e** into man's heart, yet .... Eccl 3:11
who inhabits **e**, whose name is Holy: ..... Is 57:15

EVANGELIST

we entered the house of Philip the **e**, ... Acts 21:8
endure suffering, do the work of an **e**, ... 2 Tm 4:5

EVANGELISTS

gave the apostles, the prophets, the **e**, ... Eph 4:11

EVE

The man called his wife's name **E**, ... Gn 3:20
as the serpent deceived **E** by his .... 2 Cor 11:3
For Adam was formed first, then **E**; ...... 1 Tm 2:13

EVERLASTING

see it and remember the **e** covenant .... Gn 9:16
generations for an **e** covenant, ... Gn 17:7
from **e** to **e** you are God. .... Ps 90:2
way in me, and lead me in the way **e**! ... Ps 139:24
e joy shall be upon their heads; .... Is 35:10
the **e** God, the Creator of the ends .... Is 40:28
I will make with you an **e** covenant, ... Is 55:3
a double portion; they shall have **e** joy. ... Is 61:7
I have loved you with an **e** love; .... Jer 31:3
I will make with them an **e** covenant, ... Jer 32:40
His kingdom is an **e** kingdom, ... Dn 4:3
of the earth shall awake, some to **e** life, ... Dn 12:2

EVERYONE

let **e** who is godly offer prayer .... Ps 32:6
e whose name shall be found written .... Dn 12:1
Let **e** turn from his evil way and from ...... Jon 3:8
"Not **e** who says to me, 'Lord, Lord,' ...... Mt 7:21
So it is with **e** who is born of the Spirit." ... Jn 3:8
e whose name has not been written .... Rv 13:8

EVERYTHING

And God saw **e** that he had made, ... Gn 1:31
Let **e** that has breath praise the .... Ps 150:6
made **e** for its purpose, even the .... Prv 16:4
to land, they left **e** and followed him. ..... Lk 5:11
and **e** that is written about the Son of ..... Lk 18:31
as having nothing, yet possessing **e**. ... 2 Cor 6:10
in order that in **e** God may be glorified ... 1 Pt 4:11

EVIDENCE

On the **e** of two witnesses or of three .... Dt 17:6
be established by the **e** of two or three . 2 Cor 13:1
This is **e** of the righteous judgment of . 2 Thes 1:5

EVIDENT

Now it is **e** that no one is justified .... Gal 3:11
By this it is **e** who are the children .... 1 Jn 3:10

EVIL

will be like God, knowing good and **e**." .... Gn 3:5
intention of man's heart is **e** from his ..... Gn 8:21
I will fear no **e**, for you are with me; .... Ps 23:4
Turn away from **e** and do good; .... Ps 34:14
no **e** shall be allowed to befall you, ... Ps 91:10
an **e** person will not go unpunished, ... Prv 11:21
Woe to those who call **e** good and .... Is 5:20
into temptation, but deliver us from **e**. ..... Mt 6:13
The weeds are the sons of the **e** one, ... Mt 13:38
Depart from me, all you workers of **e**!' .... Lk 13:27
the light because their works were **e**. ...... Jn 3:19
but that you keep them from the **e** one. ... Jn 17:15
the good I want, but the **e** I do not .... Rom 7:19
Repay no one **e** for **e**, but .... Rom 12:17
"Purge the **e** person from among ...... 1 Cor 5:13
use of the time, because the days are **e**. ... Eph 5:16
speak **e** of no one, to avoid quarreling, ... Ti 3:2
for God cannot be tempted with **e**, ... Jas 1:13
Do not speak **e** against one another, ... Jas 4:11
using your freedom as a cover-up for **e**, . 1 Pt 2:16
because you have overcome the **e** one. ... 1 Jn 2:13
and the **e** one does not touch him. .... 1 Jn 5:18
Beloved, do not imitate **e** but imitate .... 3 Jn 11

EXALT

LORD with me, and let us e his name .... Ps 34:3
my God; I will e you; I will praise .... Is 25:1
So also Christ did not e himself to be ... Heb 5:5
before the Lord, and he will e you, ... Jas 4:10
at the proper time he may e you, ... 1 Pt 5:6

EXALTED

Be e, O God, above the heavens! .... Ps 108:5
the blessing of the upright a city is e, ... Prv 11:11
The LORD is e, for he dwells on high; ..... Is 33:5
whoever humbles himself will be e, ... Mt 23:12
For what is e among men is an .... Lk 16:15
Being therefore e at the right hand of ... Acts 2:33
Therefore God has highly e him and ..... Phil 2:9

EXALTS

Righteousness e a nation, but sin is .... Prv 14:34
Whoever e himself will be humbled, ... Mt 23:12

EXAMINE

Let us test and e our ways, and return ... Lam 3:40
Let a person e himself, ... 1 Cor 11:28
E yourselves, to see whether you are .. 2 Cor 13:5

EXAMPLE

For I have given you an e, that you ...... Jn 13:15
things happened to them as an e, ... 1 Cor 10:11
give you in ourselves an e to imitate. .. 2 Thes 3:9
display his perfect patience as an e .... 1 Tm 1:16
also suffered for you, leaving you an e, .. 1 Pt 2:21

EXCEL

strive to e in building up the church. .. 1 Cor 14:12
But as you e in everything—in faith, ... 2 Cor 8:7

EXCELLENT

I will show you a still more e way. .... 1 Cor 12:31
so that you may approve what is e, ... Phil 1:10
These things are e and profitable ...... Ti 3:8
that is as much more e than the old ..... Heb 8:6

EXCHANGED

They e the glory of God for the image .. Ps 106:20
and e the glory of the immortal God .... Rom 1:23

EXCUSE

but now they have no e for their sin. ..... Jn 15:22
So they are without e. .... Rom 1:20

EXHORT

reprove, rebuke, and e, with complete .. 2 Tm 4:2
e and rebuke with all authority. .... Ti 2:15
So I e the elders among you, as a fellow .. 1 Pt 5:1

EXIST

are all things and for whom we e, ... 1 Cor 8:6
for whom and by whom all things e, ... Heb 2:10
earth that now e are stored up for fire, .. 2 Pt 3:7

EXPOSED

to the light, lest his works should be e. .. Jn 3:20
the works that are done on it will be e. .. 2 Pt 3:10

EXTOL

I will e you, my God and King, ... Ps 145:1
and let all the peoples e him." .... Rom 15:11

EXULT

he will e over you with loud singing. .... Zep 3:17
Let us rejoice and e and give him the ..... Rv 19:7

EYE

e for e, tooth for tooth, ... Ex 21:24
He who formed the e, does he not see? ... Ps 94:9
it was said, 'An e for an e .... Mt 5:38
first take the log out of your own e, ... Mt 7:5
And if your e causes you to sin, tear ...... Mt 18:9
Your e is the lamp of your body. .... Lk 11:34
"What no e has seen, nor ear heard, ... 1 Cor 2:9
in a moment, in the twinkling of an e, .. 1 Cor 15:52
the clouds, and every e will see him, ... Rv 1:7

EYES

eat of it your e will be opened, ... Gn 3:5
For the e of the LORD run to .... 2 Chr 16:9

Open my e, that I may behold .... Ps 119:18
I lift up my e to the hills. From where ... Ps 121:1
Let your e look directly forward, ... Prv 4:25
e of the LORD are in every place, ... Prv 15:3
for my e have seen the King, ... Is 6:5
But blessed are your e, for they see, ... Mt 13:16
"Lord, let our e be opened." .... Mt 20:33
for my e have seen your salvation ...... Lk 2:30
For the e of the Lord are on the .... 1 Pt 3:12
heard, which we have seen with our e, .. 1 Jn 1:1
wipe away every tear from their e, ... Rv 21:4

EYEWITNESSES

from the beginning were e and .... Lk 1:2
Christ, but we were e of his majesty. ... 2 Pt 1:16

EZEKIEL

word of the LORD came to E .... Ezk 1:3

EZRA

While E prayed and made confession, ... Ezr 10:1
And they told E the scribe to bring .... Neh 8:1

FACE

"For I have seen God f to f, ... Gn 32:30
But," he said, "you cannot see my f, ... Ex 33:20
LORD make his f to shine upon .... Nm 6:25
Moses, whom the LORD knew f to f, ... Dt 34:10
angels always see the f of my Father .... Mt 18:10
mirror dimly, but then f to f, ... 1 Cor 13:12
of the glory of God in the f of Jesus .... 2 Cor 4:6
intently at his natural f in a mirror. ..... Jas 1:23
They will see his f, and his name will ...... Rv 22:4

FADE

For they will soon f like the grass ...... Ps 37:2
will the rich man f away in the midst ..... Jas 1:11

FAIL

My flesh and my heart may f, but God .. Ps 73:26
for you that your faith may not f. ...... Lk 22:32
unless indeed you f to meet the test! ... 2 Cor 13:5

FAILS

See to it that no one f to obtain .... Heb 12:15
keeps the whole law but f in one point... Jas 2:10
knows the right thing to do and f to ..... Jas 4:17

FAINT

they shall walk and not f. .... Is 40:31

FAITH

righteous shall live by his f. .... Hab 2:4
"According to your f be it done .... Mt 9:29
if you have f like a grain .... Mt 17:20
"Daughter, your f has made you well; ... Mk 5:34
Jesus answered them, "Have f in God. .. Mk 11:22
not even in Israel have I found such f." ... Lk 7:9
to the Lord, "Increase our f!" .... Lk 17:5
Man comes, will he find f on earth?" ... Lk 18:8
prayed for you that your f may not fail. .. Lk 22:32
having cleansed their hearts by f ...... Acts 15:9
"The righteous shall live by f." .... Rom 1:17
since we have been justified by f, ... Rom 5:1
righteousness that is by f; .... Rom 9:30
So f comes from hearing, ... Rom 10:17
f might not rest in the wisdom of men .. 1 Cor 2:5
So now f, hope, and love abide, ... 1 Cor 13:13
for we walk by f, not by sight. .... 2 Cor 5:7
to see whether you are in the f. .... 2 Cor 13:5
we might be justified by f. .... Gal 3:24
grace you have been saved through f. .. Eph 2:8
one Lord, one f, one baptism, ... Eph 4:5
some have made shipwreck of their f, .. 1 Tm 1:19
disqualified regarding the f. .... 2 Tm 3:8
but my righteous one shall live by f, ... Heb 10:38
Now f is the assurance of things hoped . Heb 11:1
But let him ask in f, with no doubting, ... Jas 1:6
and I will show you my f by my works. ... Jas 2:18
so that your f and hope are in God. .... 1 Pt 1:21
those who have obtained a f of equal .. 2 Pt 1:1
effort to supplement your f with virtue, .. 2 Pt 1:5
that has overcome the world—our f. ... 1 Jn 5:4

FAITHFUL

LORD your God is God, the f God .... Dt 7:9
love, but a f man who can find? .... Prv 20:6
'Well done, good and f servant. .... Mt 25:21
who is f in a very little is also f .... Lk 16:10
God is f, and he will not let you be .... 1 Cor 10:13
He who calls you is f; he will surely ... 1 Thes 5:24
But the Lord is f. He will establish .... 2 Thes 3:3
if we are faithless, he remains f— ..... 2 Tm 2:13
for he who promised is f. .... Heb 10:23
Be f unto death, and I will give you ..... Rv 2:10
one sitting on it is called F and True, ... Rv 19:11

FAITHFULNESS

A God of f and without iniquity, ... Dt 32:4
I will make known your f to all .... Ps 89:1
his f is a shield and buckler. .... Ps 91:4
Let not steadfast love and f forsake you; .. Prv 3:3
belt of his waist, and f the belt of ...... Is 11:5
new every morning; great is your f. .... Lam 3:23
their faithlessness nullify the f of God? .. Rom 3:3

FAITHLESS

if we are f, he remains faithful— ...... 2 Tm 2:13

FALL

though he f, he shall not be cast. ...... Ps 37:24
all have sinned and f short of the glory. . Rom 3:23
that he stands take heed lest he f. .... 1 Cor 10:12
these qualities you will never f. .... 2 Pt 1:10

FALLEN

law; you have f away from grace. ...... Gal 5:4
firstfruits of those who have f asleep. . 1 Cor 15:20
with him those who have f asleep. .... 1 Thes 4:14

FALSE

"You shall not bear f witness .... Ex 20:16
And many f prophets will arise and .... Mt 24:11
Do not steal, Do not bear f witness, ... Mk 10:19
For f christs and f prophets will .... Mk 13:22
For such men are f apostles, ... 2 Cor 11:13
all power and f signs and wonders, ... 2 Thes 2:9

FALSEHOOD

Therefore, having put away f, let ...... Eph 4:25

FALSELY

you shall not deal f; .... Lv 19:11
all kinds of evil against you f on my .... Mt 5:11
to those of old, 'You shall not swear f, ... Mt 5:33

FAMILIES

all the f of the earth shall be blessed." .. Gn 12:3
shall all the f of the earth be blessed.' .. Acts 3:25

FAMILY

from whom every f in heaven and on ... Eph 3:15

FAMINE

there will arise seven years of f, ... Gn 41:30
not a f of bread, nor a thirst for water, ... Am 8:11
sword and with f and with pestilence ..... Rv 6:8

FAMINES

and there will be f and earthquakes in .. Mt 24:7

FAST

"Is not this the f that I choose: to loose ... Is 58:6
"And when you f, do not look gloomy ... Mt 6:16
but your disciples do not f?" .... Mk 2:18
I f twice a week; I give tithes of all ..... Lk 18:12
test everything; hold f what is good. .... 1 Thes 5:21

FASTING

And after f forty days and forty nights, ... Mt 4:2
they were worshiping the Lord and f, ... Acts 13:2

FATHER

shall be the f of a multitude of nations. .. Gn 17:4
"Honor your f and your mother, that.... Ex 20:12
Is not he your f, who created you, ... Dt 32:6
how you left your f and mother and .... Ru 2:11
For my f and my mother have forsaken .. Ps 27:10
F of the fatherless and protector of ..... Ps 68:5
As a f shows compassion to his .... Ps 103:13

He who loves wisdom makes his f glad,.. Prv 29:3
you are our F; we are the clay, ... Is 64:8
son suffer for the iniquity of the f?' ...... Ezk 18:19
If then I am a F, where is my honor?'.... Mal 1:6
"Our F in heaven, hallowed be .... Mt 6:9
acknowledge before my F who is in ..... Mt 10:32
Whoever loves f or mother more than .. Mt 10:37
a man shall leave his f and his mother ... Mt 19:5
And call no man your f on earth, for ..... Mt 23:9
What f among you, if his son asks for ... Lk 11:11
They will be divided, f against son and .. Lk 12:53
his f saw him and felt compassion, ... Lk 15:20
And Jesus said, "F, forgive them, for .... Lk 23:34
"F, into your hands I commit my .... Lk 23:46
I and the F are one." .... Jn 10:30
No one comes to the F except through .... Jn 14:6
whatever you ask of the F in my name, ... Jn 16:23
to make him the f of all who believe .... Rom 4:11
and I will be a f to you, and you shall .. 2 Cor 6:18
our hearts, crying, "Abba! F!" .... Gal 4:6
both have access in one Spirit to the F.... Eph 2:18
"Honor your f and mother" .... Eph 6:2
how, like a f with his children, ... 1 Thes 2:11
whom his f does not discipline? .... Heb 12:7
See what kind of love the F has given ... 1 Jn 3:1

FATHER'S
know that I must be in my F house?" ..... Lk 2:49
to snatch them out of the F hand. ...... Jn 10:29
In my F house are many rooms. .... Jn 14:2

FATHERLESS
He executes justice for the f and the .... Dt 10:18
Father of the f and protector of widows .. Ps 68:5
he upholds the widow and the f, ... Ps 146:9

FATHERS
and the glory of children is their f. ..... Prv 17:6
turn the hearts of f to their children .... Mal 4:6
F, do not provoke your children, lest .... Col 3:21
have had earthly f who disciplined us ... Heb 12:9

FAVOR
Noah found f in the eyes of the LORD. ..... Gn 6:8
the LORD bestows f and honor. .... Ps 84:11
good man obtains f from the LORD, ... Prv 12:2
the year of the LORD's f, ... Is 61:2
And the f of God was upon him. .... Lk 2:40
to proclaim the year of the Lord's f." .... Lk 4:19

FEAR
the LORD your God you shall f. .... Dt 6:13
"Now therefore the LORD .... Jos 24:14
Serve the LORD with f, ... Ps 2:11
the f of the LORD is clean, ... Ps 19:9
light and my salvation; whom shall I f? ... Ps 27:1
f of the LORD is the beginning .... Prv 1:7
The f of man lays a snare, but .... Prv 29:25
F God and keep his commandments, ... Eccl 12:13
"F not, I am the one who helps you." .... Is 41:13
And do not f those who kill the body .... Mt 10:28
"Do not f, only believe." .... Mk 5:36
"F not, little flock, for it is your .... Lk 12:32
So do not become proud, but f. ...... Rom 11:20
no f of the one who is in authority? .... Rom 13:3
holiness to completion in the f of God. .. 2 Cor 7:1
God gave us a spirit not of f but of .... 2 Tm 1:7
F God. Honor the emperor. .... 1 Pt 2:17
Have no f of them, nor be troubled, ... 1 Pt 3:14
but perfect love casts out f. .... 1 Jn 4:18

FEARS
and delivered me from all my f. .... Ps 34:4
Blessed is the one who f the LORD .... Prv 28:14

FEAST
shall observe the F of Unleavened ...... Ex 12:17
king who gave a wedding f for his son, .. Mt 22:2
But when you give a f, invite the poor, .. Lk 14:13

FEED
the ravens to f you there." .... 1 Kgs 17:4
The lips of the righteous f many, but ... Prv 10:21

desolate place to f so great a crowd?" .. Mt 15:33
when did we see you hungry and f you, . Mt 25:37
Jesus said to him, "F my sheep. .... Jn 21:17

FEET
you have put all things under his f, ... Ps 8:6
made my f like the f of a deer .... Ps 18:33
miry bog, and set my f upon a rock, ... Ps 40:2
its f partly of iron and partly of clay. .... Dn 2:33
until I put your enemies under your f." ... Mt 22:44
she began to wet his f with her tears .... Lk 7:38
he showed them his hands and his f.... Lk 24:40
wash the disciples' f and to wipe them .... Jn 13:5
will soon crush Satan under your f. .... Rom 16:20
all things in subjection under his f." ... 1 Cor 15:27
he put all things under his f .... Eph 1:22

FELLOWSHIP
you were called into the f of his Son, .. 1 Cor 1:9
the love of God and the f of the Holy . 2 Cor 13:14
If we say we have f with him while we ... 1 Jn 1:6
he is in the light, we have f with one .... 1 Jn 1:7

FEMALE
male and f he created them. .... Gn 1:27
creation, 'God made them male and f.' .. Mk 10:6

FIELD
The f is the world, and the good seed ... Mt 13:38
Then two men will be in the f; one .... Mt 24:40
You are God's f, God's building. .... 1 Cor 3:9

FIG
And they sewed f leaves together .... Gn 3:7
And seeing a f tree by the wayside, he .. Mt 21:19
"From the f tree learn its lesson: as .... Mt 24:32
Can a f tree, my brothers, bear olives, ... Jas 3:12

FIGHT
The LORD will f for you, ... Ex 14:14
Our God will f for us." .... Neh 4:20
F the good f of the faith. .... 1 Tm 6:12
I have fought the good f, ... 2 Tm 4:7

FIGS
from thornbushes, or f from thistles? ... Mt 7:16

FILL
I will f this house with glory, ... Hg 2:7
The God of hope f you with all joy ..... Rom 15:13
the heavens, that he might f all things.) .. Eph 4:10

FILLED
and he will be f with the Holy Spirit, ... Lk 1:15
they were all f with the Holy Spirit ..... Acts 2:4
but be f with the Spirit, ... Eph 5:18
f with the fruit of righteousness .... Phil 1:11

FILTHINESS
Let there be no f nor foolish talk nor ... Eph 5:4
Therefore put away all f and rampant .... Jas 1:21

FIND
be sure your sin will f you out. .... Nm 32:23
loses his life for my sake will f it. ...... Mt 16:25

FINDS
Blessed is the one who f wisdom, ... Prv 3:13
He who f a wife f a good .... Prv 18:22
and the one who seeks f, ... Mt 7:8
Whoever f his life will lose it, ... Mt 10:39
after the one that is lost, until he f it? ... Lk 15:4

FINISHED
And on the seventh day God f his work ... Gn 2:2
When Moses had f writing the words .... Dt 31:24
"It is f," and he bowed his head .... Jn 19:30
fought the good fight, I have f the race, .. 2 Tm 4:7

FIRE
night in a pillar of f to give them light, .. Ex 13:21
LORD your God is a consuming f, ... Dt 4:24
Then the f of the LORD fell .... 1 Kgs 18:38
and chariots of f all around Elisha. .... 2 Kgs 6:17
can dwell with the consuming f? .... Is 33:14
Is not my word like f, declares the ...... Jer 23:29

unbound, walking in the midst of the f, .. Dn 3:25
For he is like a refiner's f and like ...... Mal 3:2
to be thrown into the hell of f. .... Mt 18:9
into the eternal f prepared for the devil .. Mt 25:41
to go to hell, to the unquenchable f. .... Mk 9:43
And divided tongues as of f appeared .... Acts 2:3
f will test what sort of work each one .. 1 Cor 3:13
though it is tested by f—may be found .. 1 Pt 1:7
earth that now exist are stored up for f, ... 2 Pt 3:7
the heavens will be set on f and .... 2 Pt 3:12
others by snatching them out of the f; ... Jude 23
This is the second death, the lake of f." .. Rv 20:14

FIRM
said to the people, "Fear not, stand f, .. Ex 14:13
heart is f, trusting in the LORD. .... Ps 112:7
your joy, for you stand f in your faith. .. 2 Cor 1:24
day, and having done all, to stand f. .... Eph 6:13

FIRST
"I am the f and I am the last; .... Is 44:6
But seek f the kingdom of God .... Mt 6:33
But many who are f will be last, ... Mt 19:30
disciples were f called Christians. ..... Acts 11:26
covenant, he makes the f one obsolete. . Heb 8:13
We love because he f loved us. .... 1 Jn 4:19

FIRSTBORN
every f in the land of Egypt shall die, ... Ex 11:5
order that he might be the f among .... Rom 8:29
the invisible God, the f of all creation. ... Col 1:15
the faithful witness, the f of the dead, ... Rv 1:5

FIRSTFRUITS
the f of those who have fallen asleep. .. 1 Cor 15:20
God chose you as the f to be saved, .. 2 Thes 2:13
should be a kind of f of his creatures. ..... Jas 1:18

FISH
Or if he asks for a f, will give him a ..... Mt 7:10
three nights in the belly of the great f, .. Mt 12:40
have only five loaves here and two f." ... Mt 14:17
haul it in, because of the quantity of f. ... Jn 21:6

FISHERS
and I will make you f of men." .... Mt 4:19

FIXED
You have f all the boundaries .... Ps 74:17
day and night and the f order of heaven.. Jer 33:25
us and you a great chasm has been f, ... Lk 16:26

FLAME
tongue, for I am in anguish in this f.' .... Lk 16:24
you to fan into f the gift of God, ... 2 Tm 1:6

FLATTERS
For he f himself in his own eyes .... Ps 36:2
A man who f his neighbor spreads a .... Prv 29:5

FLATTERY
and by smooth talk and f they deceive . Rom 16:18
For we never came with words of f, ... 1 Thes 2:5

FLEE
where shall I f from your presence? .... Ps 139:7
The wicked f when no one pursues, ... Prv 28:1
F from sexual immorality. .... 1 Cor 6:18
my beloved, f from idolatry. .... 1 Cor 10:14
So f youthful passions and pursue ..... 2 Tm 2:22
Resist the devil, and he will f from you. ... Jas 4:7

FLEECE
let me test just once more with the f. .... Jgs 6:39

FLESH
bone of my bones and f of my f; .... Gn 2:23
wife, and they shall become one f. ...... Gn 2:24
yet in my f I shall see God, ... Jb 19:26
not be afraid. What can f do to me? .... Ps 56:4
"What shall I cry?" All f is grass, ... Is 40:6
So they are no longer two but one f. .... Mt 19:6
willing, but the f is weak." .... Mt 26:41
the Word became f and dwelt among ... Jn 1:14
who are in the f cannot please God. .... Rom 8:8
and make no provision for the f, ... Rom 13:14

Now the works of the **f** are evident: ...... Gal 5:19
wife, and the two shall become one **f**." .. Eph 5:31
we do not wrestle against **f** and blood, ... Eph 6:12
"All **f** is like grass and all its glory ...... 1 Pt 1:24
the desires of the **f** and the desires of ... 1 Jn 2:16

FLOCK
keeping watch over their **f** by night. .... Lk 2:8
So there will be one **f**, one shepherd. .... Jn 10:16
shepherd the **f** of God that is among ...... 1 Pt 5:2

FLOG
some you will **f** in your synagogues ...... Mt 23:34
"is it lawful for you to **f** a man who ....Acts 22:25

FLOOD
For behold, I will bring a **f** of waters ..... Gn 6:17
never again become a **f** to destroy all .... Gn 9:15
as in those days before the **f** they were .. Mt 24:38
when he brought a **f** upon the world ...... 2 Pt 2:5

FLOW
for from it **f** the springs of life. .... Prv 4:23
'Out of his heart will **f** rivers of ....Jn 7:38

FLOWER
he flourishes like a **f** of the field; .... Ps 103:15
The grass withers, the **f** fades, but .... Is 40:8
like a **f** of the grass he will pass away .... Jas 1:10
The grass withers, and the **f** falls, ... 1 Pt 1:24

FLOWING
The water was **f** down from below .... Ezk 47:1
f from the throne of God and of the ...... Rv 22:1

FLY
wings like a dove! I would **f** away .... Ps 55:6
they are soon gone, and we **f** away. .... Ps 90:10

FOLLOW
If the LORD is God, **f** him; .... 1 Kgs 18:21
"**F** me, and I will make you fishers of ...... Mt 4:19
and take up his cross and **f** me. .... Mt 16:24
he goes before them, and the sheep **f** .... Jn 10:4
If anyone serves me, he must **f** me; .... Jn 12:26
F the pattern of the sound words .... 2 Tm 1:13

FOLLY
her cubs rather than a fool in his **f**. ...... Prv 17:12
word of the cross is **f** to those who ...... 1 Cor 1:18
wisdom of this world is **f** with God. ...... 1 Cor 3:19
for their **f** will be plain to all, ... 2 Tm 3:9

FOOD
I have given every green plant for **f**." ..... Gn 1:30
not defile himself with the king's **f**, ... Dn 1:8
Is not life more than **f**, and .... Mt 6:25
"My **f** is to do the will of him who sent .... Jn 4:34
Do not work for the **f** that perishes, ...Jn 6:27
F will not commend us to God. .... 1 Cor 8:8
But if we have **f** and clothing, with ...... 1 Tm 6:8
poorly clothed and lacking in daily **f**, ... Jas 2:15

FOODS
(Thus he declared all **f** clean.) .... Mk 7:19
abstinence from **f** that God created ...... 1 Tm 4:3
to be strengthened by grace, not by **f**, ... Heb 13:9

FOOL
The **f** says in his heart, "There is no ...... Ps 14:1
way of a **f** is right in his own eyes, ... Prv 12:15
so honor is not fitting for a **f**. .... Prv 26:1
A **f** gives full vent to his spirit, but ...... Prv 29:11
whoever says, 'You **f**!' will be liable. ...... Mt 5:22

FOOLISH
my people are **f**; they know me not; .... Jer 4:22
like a man who built his house .... Mt 7:26
But God chose what is **f** in the world ... 1 Cor 1:27
Therefore do not be **f**, but understand ... Eph 5:17
For we ourselves were once **f**, ... Ti 3:3

FOOLISHNESS
For the **f** of God is wiser than men, ... 1 Cor 1:25

FOOLS
f despise wisdom and instruction. .... Prv 1:7

Claiming to be wise, they became **f**, ... Rom 1:22
We are **f** for Christ's sake, but you ...... 1 Cor 4:10

FOOT
He will not let your **f** be moved; .... Ps 121:3
And if your **f** causes you to sin, ... Mk 9:45
lest you strike your **f** against a stone.'" ... Lk 4:11
If the **f** should say, "Because I am .... 1 Cor 12:15

FOOTSTOOL
is my throne, and the earth is my **f**; ...... Is 66:1
until I make your enemies your **f**."' .... Lk 20:43
is my throne, and the earth is my **f**. ...... Acts 7:49

FORBEARANCE
In your **f** take me not away; .... Jer 15:15
riches of his kindness and **f** and .... Rom 2:4
because in his divine **f** he had passed ... Rom 3:25

FOREFATHERS
are beloved for the sake of their **f**. ...... Rom 11:28
the futile ways inherited from your **f**, ... 1 Pt 1:18

FOREKNEW
those whom he **f** he also predestined .... Rom 8:29
has not rejected his people whom he **f**. .. Rom 11:2

FOREKNOWLEDGE
to the definite plan and **f** of God, ... Acts 2:23
according to the **f** of God the Father, ... 1 Pt 1:2

FOREKNOWN
He was **f** before the foundation of ...... 1 Pt 1:20

FORERUNNER
Jesus has gone as a **f** on our behalf, ... Heb 6:20

FORETOLD
had made, as the LORD had **f**. .... 2 Kgs 24:13
But what God **f** by the mouth of all ...... Acts 3:18

FOREVER
tree of life and eat, and live **f**—" .... Gn 3:22
This is my name **f**, and thus I am to ...... Ex 3:15
dwell in the house of the LORD **f**. .... Ps 23:6
his steadfast love endures **f**, ... Ps 100:5
but the word of our God will stand **f**. .... Is 40:8
but my salvation will be **f**, and my .... Is 51:6
eats of this bread, he will live **f**. ....Jn 6:51
you another Helper, to be with you **f**, ... Jn 14:16
"You are a priest **f**, after the order of ... Heb 5:6
word of the Lord remains **f**." .... 1 Pt 1:25
whoever does the will of God abides **f**. ... 1 Jn 2:17
Christ, and he shall reign **f** and ever." .... Rv 11:15

FORFEIT
gain the whole world and **f** his soul? ...... Mk 8:36

FORGAVE
released him and **f** him the debt. .... Mt 18:27
one another, as God in Christ **f** you. ...... Eph 4:32

FORGET
take care lest you **f** the LORD, ... Dt 6:12
O my soul, and **f** not all his benefits, ... Ps 103:2
these may **f**, yet I will not **f** you. .... Is 49:15

FORGETTING
But one thing I do: **f** what lies behind ... Phil 3:13

FORGIVE
But you are a God ready to **f**, gracious ... Neh 9:17
my trouble, and **f** all my sins. .... Ps 25:18
For I will **f** their iniquity, ... Jer 31:34
and **f** us our debts, as we also............. Mt 6:12
Who can **f** sins but God alone?" .... Mk 2:7
who is in heaven may **f** you your .... Mk 11:25
f, and you will be forgiven; .... Lk 6:37
Jesus said, "Father, **f** them, for .... Lk 23:34
has forgiven you, so you also must **f**. ..... Col 3:13
he is faithful and just to **f** us our sins .... 1 Jn 1:9

FORGIVEN
is the one whose transgression is **f**, ... Ps 32:1
'Your sins are **f**,' or to say, ... Mt 9:5
against the Son of Man will be **f**, ... Mt 12:32
But he who is **f** little, loves little." .... Lk 7:47

alive together with him, having **f** us ...... Col 2:13
if he has committed sins, he will be **f**. .... Jas 5:15
because your sins are **f** for his name's ... 1 Jn 2:12

FORGIVENESS
the Lord our God belong mercy and **f**, ... Dn 9:9
poured out for many for the **f** of sins.... Mt 26:28
a baptism of repentance for the **f** .... Mk 1:4
of Jesus Christ for the **f** of your sins, ... Acts 2:38
we have redemption, the **f** of sins. .... Col 1:14
shedding of blood there is no **f** of sins. .. Heb 9:22

FORGIVES
who **f** all your iniquity, who heals all..... Ps 103:3
"Who is this, who even **f** sins?" .... Lk 7:49

FORGIVING
f iniquity and transgression and sin, ... Ex 34:7
you, O Lord, are good and **f**,.............. Ps 86:5

FORGOTTEN
failed me, my close friends have **f** me..... Jb 19:14
God, my rock: "Why have you **f** me? ..... Ps 42:9
former troubles are **f** and are hidden .... Is 65:16
And not one of them is **f** before God. .... Lk 12:6
having **f** that he was cleansed from .... 2 Pt 1:9

FORM
emptied himself, by taking the **f** of a ...... Phil 2:7

FORMED
then the LORD God **f** the man .... Gn 2:7
For you **f** my inward parts; .... Ps 139:13
and **f** the spirit of man within him: ...... Zec 12:1
and the earth was **f** out of water and ... 2 Pt 3:5

FORSAKE
He will not leave you or **f** you." .... Dt 31:6
Do not **f** the work of your hands.......... Ps 138:8
let the wicked **f** his way, and .... Is 55:7
"I will never leave you nor **f** you." .... Heb 13:5

FORSAKEN
my God, why have you **f** me? .... Ps 22:1
yet I have not seen the righteous **f** .... Ps 37:25
my God, why have you **f** me?" .... Mt 27:46
persecuted, but not **f**; struck down, ... 2 Cor 4:9

FORTRESS
is my rock and my **f** and my deliverer, .. 2 Sm 22:2
For you are my rock and my **f**; .... Ps 31:3

FORTY
rain on the earth **f** days and **f** .... Gn 7:4
people of Israel ate the manna **f** years, ... Ex 16:35
Moses was on the mountain **f** days and **f** .. Ex 24:18
after fasting **f** days and **f** nights, ... Mt 4:2
appearing to them during **f** days and ... Acts 1:3

FOUND
If you seek him, he will be **f** by you, ... 2 Chr 15:2
"Seek the LORD while he may be **f**; ...... Is 55:6
f by those who did not seek me. .... Is 65:1
he was lost, and is **f**.'" .... Lk 15:32

FOUNDATION
a precious cornerstone, of a sure **f**: ...... Is 28:16
For no one can lay a **f** other than .... 1 Cor 3:11
chose us in him before the **f** of the ...... Eph 1:4
But God's firm **f** stands, bearing this .... 2 Tm 2:19
was foreknown before the **f** of the .... 1 Pt 1:20

FRAGRANCE
spreads the **f** of the knowledge of him . 2 Cor 2:14

FRAGRANT
gave himself up for us, a **f** offering ...... Eph 5:2

FRAME
For he knows our **f**; he remembers ...... Ps 103:14
My **f** was not hidden from you, ... Ps 139:15

FREE
and the truth will set you **f**." ....Jn 8:32
But the **f** gift is not like the trespass..... Rom 5:15
you have been set **f** from sin .... Rom 6:22
Spirit of life has set you **f** in Christ ...... Rom 8:2

Live as people who are **f**, not using ...... 1 Pt 2:16

FREED
everyone who believes is **f** from .... Acts 13:39
To him who loves us and has **f** us .... Rv 1:5

FREEDOM
obtain the **f** of the glory of the .... Rom 8:21
the Spirit of the Lord is, there is **f**.......... 2 Cor 3:17
For **f** Christ has set us free; .... Gal 5:1
They promise them **f**, but they .... 2 Pt 2:19

FRIEND
face to face, as a man speaks to his **f**...... Ex 33:11
A **f** loves at all times, and a brother..... Prv 17:17
but there is a **f** who sticks closer .... Prv 18:24
gracious, will have the king as his **f**...... Prv 22:11
Faithful are the wounds of a **f**; .... Prv 27:6
a **f** of tax collectors and sinners!' .... Mt 11:19

FRIENDS
a whisperer separates close **f**. .... Prv 16:28
lay down his life for his **f**. .... Jn 15:13

FRIENDSHIP
The **f** of the LORD is for those .... Ps 25:14
Make no **f** with a man given to anger... Prv 22:24
Do you not know that **f** with the world ... Jas 4:4

FRUIT
yielding seed, and **f** trees bearing **f** in ... Gn 1:11
one wise, she took of its **f** and ate, ... Gn 3:6
Blessed shall be the **f** of your womb .... Dt 28:4
of water that yields its **f** in its season, ... Ps 1:3
The **f** of the righteous is a tree of life, ... Prv 11:30
salvation and righteousness may bear **f**; ... Is 45:8
leaves will not wither, nor their **f** fail, ... Ezk 47:12
Bear **f** in keeping with repentance. ...... Mt 3:8
healthy tree bears good **f**, ... Mt 7:17
branch that does bear **f** he prunes,........ Jn 15:2
But the **f** of the Spirit is love, ... Gal 5:22
(for the **f** of light is found in .... Eph 5:9
filled with the **f** of righteousness .... Phil 1:11

FRUITFUL
"Be **f** and multiply and fill the earth ...... Gn 1:28
I will make you exceedingly **f**, ... Gn 17:6
Your wife will be like a **f** vine .... Ps 128:3

FRUITS
You will recognize them by their **f**....... Mt 7:16

FULFILL
your heart's desire and **f** all your plans! ... Ps 20:4
If you really **f** the royal law according ... Jas 2:8

FULFILLED
A desire **f** is sweet to the soul, ... Prv 13:19
Prophets and the Psalms must be **f**." ..... Lk 24:44
one who loves another has **f** the law. ...... Rom 13:8
law is **f** in one word: "You shall love ..... Gal 5:14

FULL
earth shall be **f** of the knowledge .... Is 11:9
Jesus, **f** of the Holy Spirit, returned ...... Lk 4:1
And Stephen, **f** of grace and power, ... Acts 6:8

FULLNESS
The earth is the LORD's and the **f** .... Ps 24:1
until the **f** of the Gentiles has come .... Rom 11:25
But when the **f** of time had come, ... Gal 4:4
may be filled with all the **f** of God....... Eph 3:19
For in him all the **f** of God was .... Col 1:19

FUTILE
but they became **f** in their thinking, ... Rom 1:21
thoughts of the wise, that they are **f**." ... 1 Cor 3:20
has not been raised, your faith is **f** .... 1 Cor 15:17

FUTILITY
For the creation was subjected to **f**, ... Rom 8:20
Gentiles do, in the **f** of their minds. ...... Eph 4:17

FUTURE
for there is a **f** for the man of peace. ..... Ps 37:37
not for evil, to give you a **f** and a hope. ... Jer 29:11
a good foundation for the **f**, ... 1 Tm 6:19

GABRIEL
"**G**, make this man understand the .... Dn 8:16
the angel answered him, "I am **G**. .... Lk 1:19

GAIN
What does man **g** by all the toil........... Eccl 1:3
does it profit a man to **g** the whole ...... Mk 8:36
but have not love, I **g** nothing. .... 1 Cor 13:3
in order that I may **g** Christ .... Phil 3:8
godliness with contentment is great **g**, ... 1 Tm 6:6

GALILEE
beyond the Jordan, **G** of the nations. .... Is 9:1
I will go before you to **G**." .... Mt 26:32
"Men of **G**, why do you stand looking ... Acts 1:11

GALL
wine to drink, mixed with **g**, ... Mt 27:34

GARDEN
LORD God planted a **g** in Eden, ... Gn 2:8
and you shall be like a watered **g**, ... Is 58:11
where he was crucified there was a **g**, ... Jn 19:41

GARMENT
woman shall not wear a man's **g**, nor ...... Dt 22:5
the earth will wear out like a **g**, ... Is 51:6
piece of unshrunk cloth on an old **g**, ... Mt 9:16
they will all wear out like a **g**, ... Heb 1:11

GARMENTS
for Adam and for his wife **g** of skins ...... Gn 3:21
they divide my **g** among them, ... Ps 22:18
clothed me with the **g** of salvation; .... Is 61:10
Jesus, they took his **g** and divided .... Jn 19:23

GATE
"Enter by the narrow **g**. For.................. Mt 7:13

GATES
Enter his **g** with thanksgiving, ... Ps 100:4
build my church, and the **g** of hell .... Mt 16:18
that they may enter the city by the **g**. ...... Rv 22:14

GATHER
time is coming to **g** all nations and ..... Is 66:18
LORD, and all nations shall **g** to it, ... Jer 3:17
whoever does not **g** with me scatters. ..... Mt 12:30
will **g** his elect from the four winds, ... Mt 24:31

GATHERED
where two or three are **g** in my name, ... Mt 18:20
How often would I have **g** your .... Mt 23:37
Before him will be **g** all the nations, ... Mt 25:32

GAVE
The LORD **g**, and the LORD has taken .... Jb 1:21
whom you **g** me I have lost not one." ...... Jn 18:9
For they **g** according to their means, ... 2 Cor 8:3
who loved me and **g** himself for me...... Gal 2:20
g himself for our sins to deliver us .... Gal 1:4
as Christ loved us and **g** himself up ...... Eph 5:2
who **g** himself as a ransom for all, ... 1 Tm 2:6

GENEALOGIES
to myths and endless **g**, ... 1 Tm 1:4

GENEALOGY
people to be enrolled by **g**. .... Neh 7:5
The book of the **g** of Jesus .... Mt 1:1

GENERATION
One **g** shall commend your works to...... Ps 145:4
"But to what shall I compare this **g**? .... Mt 11:16
An evil and adulterous **g** seeks for a ...... Mt 16:4

GENERATIONS
have been our dwelling place in all **g**, ... Ps 90:1
from now on all **g** will call me blessed; ... Lk 1:48

GENEROUS
but the righteous is **g** and gives; .... Ps 37:21
blessed is he who is **g** to the poor....... Prv 14:21
their food with glad and **g** hearts, ... Acts 2:46
to be **g** and ready to share, ... 1 Tm 6:18

GENEROUSLY
He is ever lending **g**, and his children .... Ps 37:26

It is well with the man who deals **g** .... Ps 112:5
ask God, who gives **g** to all without .... Jas 1:5

GENTILES
a light for revelation to the **G**, ... Lk 2:32
until the times of the **G** are fulfilled. ...... Lk 21:24
Is he not the God of **G** also? Yes, ... Rom 3:29
salvation has come to the **G**, so as to ... Rom 11:11
block to Jews and folly to **G**, ... 1 Cor 1:23
that God would justify the **G** by faith, ... Gal 3:8

GENTLE
learn from me, for I am **g** and lowly ..... Mt 11:29
imperishable beauty of a **g** and quiet ...... 1 Pt 3:4

GENTLENESS
by the meekness and **g** of Christ .... 2 Cor 10:1
g, self-control; against such................ Gal 5:23
restore him in a spirit of **g**.................... Gal 6:1
with all humility and **g**, with patience, ... Eph 4:2
correcting his opponents with **g**. .... 2 Tm 2:25

GETHSEMANE
went with them to a place called **G**, ... Mt 26:36

GIDEON
"A sword for the LORD and for **G**!" .... Jgs 7:20
For time would fail me to tell of **G**, ... Heb 11:32

GIFT
A man's **g** makes room for him and...... Prv 18:16
who boasts of a **g** he does not give. ...... Prv 25:14
pleasure in all his toil—this is God's **g** .... Eccl 3:13
brother, and then come and offer your **g**. ... Mt 5:24
"If you knew the **g** of God, and who ...... Jn 4:10
will receive the **g** of the Holy Spirit. ...... Acts 2:38
justified by his grace as a **g**, ... Rom 3:24
sin is death, but the free **g** of God is ...... Rom 6:23
But each has his own **g** from God, ... 1 Cor 7:7
be to God for his inexpressible **g**! .... 2 Cor 9:15
not your own doing; it is the **g** of God, ... Eph 2:8
Do not neglect the **g** you have, ... 1 Tm 4:14
you to fan into flame the **g** of God, ... 2 Tm 1:6
Every good and every perfect **g** is .... Jas 1:17
each has received a **g**, use it to serve ... 1 Pt 4:10

GIFTS
Having **g** that differ according to the ..... Rom 12:6
Now concerning spiritual **g**,............... 1 Cor 12:1
and earnestly desire the spiritual **g**,..... 1 Cor 14:1
by **g** of the Holy Spirit distributed .... Heb 2:4

GILEAD
Is there no balm in **G**? Is there no ...... Jer 8:22

GIVE
my glory I **g** to no other, nor my praise ... Is 42:8
But when you **g** to the needy, do not ...... Mt 6:3
G us this day our daily bread, ... Mt 6:11
For what can a man **g** in return for .... Mk 8:37
g, and it will be given to you. .... Lk 6:38
'It is more blessed to **g** than to .... Acts 20:35
So then each of us will **g** an account ...... Rom 14:12
If I **g** away all I have, and if .... 1 Cor 13:3
Each one must **g** as he has decided ...... 2 Cor 9:7

GIVEN
"This is my body, which is **g** for you...... Lk 22:19
Holy Spirit who has been **g** to us. .... Rom 5:5
the things freely **g** us by God. .... 1 Cor 2:12
But grace was **g** to each one of us ...... Eph 4:7

GIVES
One **g** freely, yet grows all the richer; ..... Prv 11:24
Whoever **g** to the poor will not want, ... Prv 28:27
letter kills, but the Spirit **g** life............ 2 Cor 3:6

GLAD
Therefore my heart is **g**, and my .... Ps 16:9
a river whose streams make **g** the city..... Ps 46:4
I was **g** when they said to me, "Let ...... Ps 122:1
A **g** heart makes a cheerful face, ... Prv 15:13

GLADNESS
Let me hear joy and **g**; let the .... Ps 51:8
Serve the LORD with **g**! Come .... Ps 100:2

the oil of **g** instead of mourning, ... Is 61:3
and give them **g** for sorrow. .... Jer 31:13

GLORIFIED

Jesus said, "Now is the Son of Man **g**, ... Jn 13:31
those whom he justified he also **g**........ Rom 8:30
on that day to be **g** in his saints, ... 2 Thes 1:10

GLORIFY

Father, **g** your name." Then a voice .... Jn 12:28
g your Son that the Son may **g** you, ... Jn 17:1
with a price. So **g** God in your body. .... 1 Cor 6:20
see your good deeds and **g** God .... 1 Pt 2:12

GLORIOUS

G things of you are spoken, O city of ...... Ps 87:3
to the praise of his **g** grace, with which .. Eph 1:6
lowly body to be like his **g** body, ... Phil 3:21

GLORY

The **g** of the LORD dwelt on .... Ex 24:16
Moses said, "Please show me your **g**." ... Ex 33:18
Ichabod, saying, "The **g** has departed .. 1 Sm 4:21
for the **g** of the LORD filled the .... 1 Kgs 8:11
Declare his **g** among the nations, ... Ps 96:3
Let your **g** be over all the earth! .... Ps 108:5
not to us, but to your name give **g**, ... Ps 115:1
It is the **g** of God to conceal things, ... Prv 25:2
the whole earth is full of his **g**!" .... Is 6:3
And the **g** of the LORD shall be revealed,... Is 40:5
My **g** I will not give to another. .... Is 48:11
"When the Son of Man comes in his **g**, .. Mt 25:31
"**G** to God in the highest, and on earth ... Lk 2:14
with the **g** that I had with you before .... Jn 17:5
not worth comparing with the **g** .... Rom 8:18
you do, do all to the **g** of God. .... 1 Cor 10:31
since he is the image and **g** of God, ... 1 Cor 11:7
eternal weight of **g** beyond all .... 2 Cor 4:17
Christ might be to the praise of his **g**. .... Eph 1:12
according to his riches in **g** in Christ .... Phil 4:19
then you also will appear with him in **g**. .. Col 3:4
on in the world, taken up in **g**. .... 1 Tm 3:16
for the **g** of God gives it light, ... Rv 21:23

GLUTTON

g will come to poverty, and slumber ..... Prv 23:21
A **g** and a drunkard, a friend of tax .... Lk 7:34

GLUTTONS

a companion of **g** shames his father...... Prv 28:7
are always liars, evil beasts, lazy **g**." .... Ti 1:12

GNASHING

will be weeping and **g** of teeth." .... Mt 8:12

GO

'Let my people **g**, ... Ex 5:1
God is with you wherever you **g**." .... Jos 1:9
For where you **g** I will **g**, ... Ru 1:16
Where shall I **g** from your Spirit? .... Ps 139:7
G therefore and make disciples of all .... Mt 28:19
But if I **g**, I will send him to you. .... Jn 16:7
"that it may **g** well with you and that .... Eph 6:3
Never shall he **g** out of it, and I will .... Rv 3:12

GOD

G sent him out from the garden of .... Gn 3:23
the sons of **G** saw that the daughters ...... Gn 6:2
"For I have seen **G** face to face, ... Gn 32:30
against me, but **G** meant it for good, ... Gn 50:20
G said to Moses, "I am who I am." .... Ex 3:14
to be my people, and I will be your **G**, ... Ex 6:7
no one like the LORD our **G**. .... Ex 8:10
do not let **G** speak to us, lest we die."... Ex 20:19
serve the LORD, for he is our **G**." .... Jos 24:18
defy the armies of the living **G**?" .... 1 Sm 17:26
there is no **G** like you, in heaven .... 1 Kgs 8:23
G who answers by fire, he is **G**." .... 1 Kgs 18:24
sinned against the LORD their **G**, ... 2 Kgs 17:7
cherubim, you are the **G**, you alone, ... 2 Kgs 19:15
for our **G** is greater than all gods. .... 2 Chr 2:5
Shall we receive good from **G**, and .... Jb 2:10
My **G**, my **G**, why have you .... Ps 22:1

G is our refuge and strength, a very ...... Ps 46:1
"Be still, and know that I am **G**. .... Ps 46:10
Your way, O **G**, is holy. What **g** .... Ps 77:13
my fortress, my **G**, in whom I trust." .... Ps 91:2
Be exalted, O **G**, above the heavens! .... Ps 108:5
you are the **G**, you alone, of all the .... Is 37:16
I am the last; besides me there is no **g**... Is 44:6
But the LORD is the true **G**; .... Jer 10:10
And I will be their **G**, and they shall .... Jer 31:33
'Ah, Lord **G**! It is you who have made .... Jer 32:17
is proud, and you have said, 'I am a **g**, .. Ezk 28:2
our **G** whom we serve is able to deliver ... Dn 3:17
I am the LORD your **G** and there .... Jl 2:27
Who is a **G** like you, pardoning iniquity .. Mi 7:18
one Father? Has not one **G** created us?.. Mal 2:10
Caesar's, and to **G** the things that are ... Mt 22:21
that is, "My **G**, my **G**, why .... Mt 27:46
The Lord our **G**, the Lord is one. .... Mk 12:29
But if it is by the finger of **G** that I cast .. Lk 11:20
answered him, "My Lord and my **G**!" .... Jn 20:28
G raised him up, loosing the pangs of .... Acts 2:24
For **G** shows no partiality. .... Rom 2:11
"Abraham believed **G**, and it was .... Rom 4:3
If **G** is for us, who can be against us? ... Rom 8:31
do all to the glory of **G**. .... 1 Cor 10:31
is not a **G** of confusion but of peace. .. 1 Cor 14:33
one **G** and Father of all, who is over ...... Eph 4:6
though he was in the form of **G**, ... Phil 2:6
proclaiming himself to be **G**. .... 2 Thes 2:4
to fall into the hands of the living **G**. .... Heb 10:31
for our **G** is a consuming fire. .... Heb 12:29
"Abraham believed **G**, and it was .... Jas 2:23
G is light, and in him is no darkness .... 1 Jn 1:5
G is love, and whoever abides in love ... 1 Jn 4:16
which he is called is The Word of **G**. ...... Rv 19:13

GODLINESS

But **g** with contentment is great gain, ... 1 Tm 6:6
the appearance of **g**, but denying .... 2 Tm 3:5
of the truth, which accords with **g**,......... Ti 1:1
us all things that pertain to life and **g**, .. 2 Pt 1:3
and steadfastness with **g**, ... 2 Pt 1:6

GODLY

let everyone who is **g** offer prayer to .... Ps 32:6
a peaceful and quiet life, **g** and .... 1 Tm 2:2
who desire to live a **g** life in Christ. .... 2 Tm 3:12

GODS

"You shall have no other **g** before me. .... Ex 20:3
g made with hands are not **g**. .... Acts 19:26

GOLD

More to be desired are they than **g**, ... Ps 19:10
I love your commandments above **g**, .. Ps 119:127
a man wearing a **g** ring and fine .... Jas 2:2
Your **g** and silver have corroded, ... Jas 5:3
more precious than **g** that perishes .... 1 Pt 1:7
and the street of the city was pure **g**, ... Rv 21:21

GOLGOTHA

came to a place called **G** .... Mt 27:33
of a Skull, which in Aramaic is called **G**. .. Jn 19:17

GOLIATH

a champion named **G** of Gath, ... 1 Sm 17:4

GOOD

had made, and behold, it was very **g**.... Gn 1:31
LORD God said, "It is not **g** that .... Gn 2:18
evil against me, but God meant it for **g**, .. Gn 50:20
there is none who does **g**. .... Ps 14:1
For you, O Lord, are **g** and forgiving, ... Ps 86:5
The Lord is **g** to all, and his mercy .... Ps 145:9
For it is **g** to sing praises to our God; .... Ps 147:1
Do not withhold **g** from those to .... Prv 3:27
G sense makes one slow to anger, ... Prv 19:11
Woe to those who call evil **g** and .... Is 5:20
He has told you, O man, what is **g**; .... Mi 6:8
are evil, know how to give **g** gifts to ...... Mt 7:11
"Why do you ask me about what is **g**?.. Mt 19:17
Love your enemies, do **g** to .... Lk 6:27

The **g** person out of the **g** treasure .... Lk 6:45
all things work together for **g**,............ Rom 8:28
Let no one seek his own **g**, but the ..... 1 Cor 10:24
he who began a **g** work in you .... Phil 1:6
For everything created by God is **g**, ... 1 Tm 4:4
So also **g** works are conspicuous, ... 1 Tm 5:25
They are to do **g**, to be rich in **g** works, .. 1 Tm 6:18
but he disciplines us for our **g**, ... Heb 12:10
you have tasted that the Lord is **g**......... 1 Pt 2:3

GOODNESS

will make all my **g** pass before you .... Ex 33:19
Surely **g** and mercy shall follow .... Ps 23:6
But when the **g** and loving kindness .... Ti 3:4

GOSPEL

For I am not ashamed of the **g**, for ...... Rom 1:16
I do it all for the sake of the **g**, ... 1 Cor 9:23
even if our **g** is veiled, it is veiled ...... 2 Cor 4:3
and are turning to a different **g**— .... Gal 1:6
to proclaim the mystery of the **g**, ... Eph 6:19
before in the word of the truth, the **g**, ... Col 1:5
by God to be entrusted with the **g**, ... 1 Thes 2:4
share in suffering for the **g** by the .... 2 Tm 1:8

GOSSIP

g, conceit, and disorder. .... 2 Cor 12:20

GOSSIPS

deceit, maliciousness. They are **g**, ... Rom 1:29
not only idlers, but also **g** .... 1 Tm 5:13

GRACE

from the Father, full of **g** and truth. .... Jn 1:14
be saved through the **g** of the Lord ..... Acts 15:11
obtained access by faith into this **g** ...... Rom 5:2
but where sin increased, **g** abounded .... Rom 5:20
you are not under law but under **g**. .... Rom 6:14
otherwise **g** would no longer be **g**. .... Rom 11:6
differ according to the **g** given to us, ... Rom 12:6
But by the **g** of God I am what I am, .. 1 Cor 15:10
God is able to make all **g** abound to .... 2 Cor 9:8
"My **g** is sufficient for you, for my .... 2 Cor 12:9
I do not nullify the **g** of God, ... Gal 2:21
by **g** you have been saved— .... Eph 2:5
be strengthened by the **g** that is in .... 2 Tm 2:1
For the **g** of God has appeared, ... Ti 2:11
so that being justified by his **g** we .... Ti 3:7
draw near to the throne of **g**, ... Heb 4:16
opposes the proud but gives **g** to the .... Jas 4:6
as good stewards of God's varied **g**. .... 1 Pt 4:10
The **g** of the Lord Jesus be with all....... Rv 22:21

GRACIOUS

And I will be **g** to whom I will be .... Ex 33:19
to shine upon you and be **g** to you; ...... Nm 6:25
The LORD is merciful and **g**, ... Ps 103:8
The LORD is **g** and merciful, ... Ps 145:8
G words are like a honeycomb, ... Prv 16:24
the LORD waits to be **g** to you, ... Is 30:18
yes, Father, for such was your **g** will. ...... Mt 11:26
and marveled at the **g** words that were ... Lk 4:22

GRAFT

for God has the power to **g** them in ... Rom 11:23

GRAIN

began to pluck heads of **g** and to eat... Mt 12:1
choked it, and it yielded no **g**. .... Mk 4:7
I say to you, unless a **g** of wheat falls .. Jn 12:24

GRANDCHILDREN

G are the crown of the aged, and the ... Prv 17:6
But if a widow has children or **g**, let ..... 1 Tm 5:4

GRASS

As for man, his days are like **g**; .... Ps 103:15
The **g** withers, the flower fades, but........ Is 40:8
But if God so clothes the **g**, which .... Lk 12:28
"All flesh is like **g** and all its glory .... 1 Pt 1:24

GRAVE

And they made his **g** with the wicked ... Is 53:9
"Their throat is an open **g**; they use ...... Rom 3:13

GREAT

G is the LORD and greatly to be .... Ps 48:1
so **g** is his steadfast love toward .... Ps 103:11
g is your faithfulness. .... Lam 3:23
in darkness have seen a **g** light, ... Mt 4:16
This is the **g** and first commandment. .... Mt 22:38
But whoever would be **g** among you ... Mk 10:43
least among you all is the one who is **g**." . Lk 9:48
us and you a **g** chasm has been fixed, ... Lk 16:26

GREATER

G love has no one than this, ... Jn 15:13
condemns us, God is **g** than our heart, .. 1 Jn 3:20
for he who is in you is **g** than he .... 1 Jn 4:4

GREATEST

humbles himself like this child is the **g** ... Mt 18:4
but the **g** of these is love. .... 1 Cor 13:13

GREATNESS

O LORD, is the **g** and the power .... 1 Chr 29:11
praise him according to his excellent **g**! .. Ps 150:2
immeasurable **g** of his power .... Eph 1:19

GREED

but inside they are full of **g** .... Mt 23:25
nor with a pretext for **g**— .... 1 Thes 2:5
And in their **g** they will exploit you .... 2 Pt 2:3

GREEDY

Whoever is **g** for unjust gain troubles ... Prv 15:27
nor thieves, nor the **g**, nor drunkards, ... 1 Cor 6:10
up to sensuality, **g** to practice every .... Eph 4:19
or a drunkard or violent or **g** for gain, ... Ti 1:7

GREEN

He makes me lie down in **g** pastures. ...... Ps 23:2
righteous will flourish like a **g** leaf. ...... Prv 11:28

GREW

For he **g** up before him like a young ..... Is 53:2
And the child **g** and became strong, ... Lk 2:40

GRIEF

in distress; my eye is wasted from **g**; ...... Ps 31:9
g is upon me; my heart is sick .... Jer 8:18
man of sorrows and acquainted with **g**; ... Is 53:3
For you felt a godly **g**, so that you ...... 2 Cor 7:9

GRIEFS

Surely he has borne our **g** .... Is 53:4

GRIEVANCE

When one of you has a **g** against .... 1 Cor 6:1

GRIEVE

And do not **g** the Holy Spirit .... Eph 4:30
that you may not **g** as others do .... 1 Thes 4:13

GRIEVED

made man on the earth, and it **g** him to ... Gn 6:6
But they rebelled and **g** his Holy Spirit; ... Is 63:10
with anger, **g** at their hardness of heart, ... Mk 3:5
you have been **g** by various trials, ... 1 Pt 1:6

GRIEVOUS

And see if there be any **g** way in me, .. Ps 139:24

GROAN

For in this tent we **g**, longing to put .... 2 Cor 5:2

GROANING

And God heard their **g**, and God .... Ex 2:24
whole creation has been **g** together ..... Rom 8:22

GROUND

cursed is the **g** because of you; .... Gn 3:17
Other seeds fell on rocky **g**, where they ... Mt 13:5
place where you are standing is holy **g** .. Acts 7:33

GROW

Let both **g** together until the harvest, ... Mt 13:30
Consider the lilies, how they **g**: .... Lk 12:27
truth in love, we are to **g** up in every ... Eph 4:15
by it you may **g** up into salvation— ...... 1 Pt 2:2
But **g** in the grace and knowledge ...... 2 Pt 3:18

GRUMBLE

nor **g**, as some of them did and were .. 1 Cor 10:10
Do not **g** against one another, ... Jas 5:9

GRUMBLED

And the people **g** against Moses, ... Ex 15:24
Pharisees and their scribes **g** at his .... Lk 5:30
So the Jews **g** about him, because he ...... Jn 6:41

GRUMBLING

Do all things without **g** or disputing, ... Phil 2:14
hospitality to one another without **g**. ...... 1 Pt 4:9

GUARANTEE

Spirit in our hearts as a **g**. .... 2 Cor 1:22
who has given us the Spirit as a **g**. ...... 2 Cor 5:5
who is the **g** of our inheritance .... Eph 1:14

GUARANTEED

promise may rest on grace and be **g** .... Rom 4:16
of his purpose, he **g** it with an oath, ... Heb 6:17

GUARANTOR

This makes Jesus the **g** of a better ...... Heb 7:22

GUARD

Oh, my soul, and deliver me! .... Ps 25:20
understanding will **g** you, ... Prv 2:11
God of Israel will be your rear **g**, ... Is 52:12
But be on **g**; I have told you all .... Mk 13:23
will **g** your hearts and your minds .... Phil 4:7
and **g** you against the evil one. .... 2 Thes 3:3
O Timothy, **g** the deposit entrusted ..... 1 Tm 6:20

GUARDS

Whoever **g** his mouth preserves his life; . Prv 13:3
whoever **g** his soul will keep far from ... Prv 22:5

GUIDANCE

Where there is no **g**, a people falls, ... Prv 11:14

GUIDE

You **g** me with your counsel, ... Ps 73:24
of truth comes, he will **g** you into all..... Jn 16:13

GUILT

lambs and offer it for a **g** offering, ... Lv 14:12
pardon my **g**, for it is great. .... Ps 25:11
your **g** is taken away, and your sin .... Is 6:7
acknowledge their **g** and seek my face, .. Hos 5:15
I have found in him no **g** deserving ...... Lk 23:22

GUILTY

The way of the **g** is crooked, but .... Prv 21:8
in one point has become **g** of all of it. ... Jas 2:10

HADES

and in **H**, being in torment, he lifted ..... Lk 16:23
and I have the keys of Death and **H**. ...... Rv 1:18
Then Death and **H** were thrown into .... Rv 20:14

HAIR

you cannot make one **h** white or black. ... Mt 5:36
not a **h** of your head will perish. .... Lk 21:18
ointment and wiped his feet with her **h**, ... Jn 11:2
but if a woman has long **h**, it is her ... 1 Cor 11:15
braiding of **h** and the putting on of gold .. 1 Pt 3:3

HAIRS

But even the **h** of your head are all ..... Mt 10:30

HALLELUJAH

in heaven, crying out, "**H**! Salvation ...... Rv 19:1
"**H**! For the Lord our God the Almighty .... Rv 19:6

HALLOWED

"Our Father in heaven, **h** be your name. ... Mt 6:9
"Father, **h** be your name. Your .... Lk 11:2

HAND

My times are in your **h**; rescue me ...... Ps 31:15
Whatever your **h** finds to do, do it .... Eccl 9:10
I will take you by the **h** and keep you; .... Is 42:6
potter; we are all the work of your **h**. ..... Is 64:8
fingers of a human **h** appeared and .... Dn 5:5
needy, do not let your left **h** know .... Mt 6:3
a man was there with a withered **h**. ...... Mt 12:10
no one will snatch them out of my **h**...... Jn 10:28

Jesus standing at the right **h** of God. ..... Acts 7:55
"Because I am not a **h**,.................. 1 Cor 12:15
seated him at his right **h** in the .... Eph 1:20

HANDS

He who has clean **h** and a pure .... Ps 24:4
a little folding of the **h** to rest, ... Prv 6:10
"Father, into your **h** I commit my........ Lk 23:46
they prayed and laid their **h** on them. ..... Acts 6:6
and to work with your **h**,.............. 1 Thes 4:11
should pray, lifting holy **h** without......... 1 Tm 2:8
to fall into the **h** of the living God. ...... Heb 10:31

HARD

Is anything too **h** for the LORD? .... Gn 18:14
and the way is **h** that leads to life, ... Mt 7:14

HARDENED

But Pharaoh **h** his heart this time .... Ex 8:32
blinded their eyes and **h** their heart, ... Jn 12:40
elect obtained it, but the rest were **h**, ... Rom 11:7
But their minds were **h**. .... 2 Cor 3:14
that none of you may be **h** by the .... Heb 3:13

HARDENS

but whoever **h** his heart will fall .... Prv 28:14
and he **h** whomever he wills. .... Rom 9:18

HARDNESS

"Because of your **h** of heart Moses .... Mt 19:8
with anger, grieved at their **h** of heart, ... Mk 3:5
in them, due to their **h** of heart. .... Eph 4:18

HARM

She does him good, and not **h**, ... Prv 31:12
Now who is there to **h** you if you .... 1 Pt 3:13

HARMONY

Live in **h** with one another................ Rom 12:16
everything together in perfect **h**. .... Col 3:14

HARSH

but a **h** word stirs up anger. .... Prv 15:1
wives, and do not be **h** with them. .... Col 3:19

HARVEST

the earth remains, seedtime and **h**, ... Gn 8:22
"The **h** is plentiful, but the laborers .... Mt 9:37
and see that the fields are white for **h**. .... Jn 4:35
And a **h** of righteousness is sown in ...... Jas 3:18
for the **h** of the earth is fully ripe." .... Rv 14:15

HATE

"You shall not **h** your brother .... Lv 19:17
H evil, and love good, and establish .... Am 5:15
betray one another and **h** one another. .. Mt 24:10
do good to those who **h** you, ... Lk 6:27

HATED

You will be **h** by all for my name's .... Lk 21:17
it has **h** me before it **h** you. .... Jn 15:18
For no one ever **h** his own flesh, but ..... Eph 5:29

HATES

six things that the LORD **h**, ... Prv 6:16
Whoever **h** me my Father .... Jn 15:23
Whoever says he is in the light and **h** .... 1 Jn 2:9

HAUGHTY

before destruction, and a **h** spirit .... Prv 16:18
Do not be **h**, but associate with the..... Rom 12:16

HEAD

Son of Man has nowhere to lay his **h**." ... Mt 8:20
that the **h** of every man is Christ, ... 1 Cor 11:3
gave him as **h** over all things .... Eph 1:22
he is the **h** of the body, the church. ...... Col 1:18

HEAL

forgive their sin and **h** their land. ...... 2 Chr 7:14
h me, for I have sinned against you!" ...... Ps 41:4
H the sick, raise the dead, cleanse .... Mt 10:8
"'Physician, **h** yourself." .... Lk 4:23
heart and turn, and I would **h** them.' .. Acts 28:27

HEALED

with their hearts, and turn and be **h**." .... Is 6:10

and with his wounds we are **h**. ...... Is 53:5
compassion on them and **h** their sick. .. Mt 14:14
And he **h** many who were sick .... Mk 1:34
on physicians, she could not be **h** ...... Lk 8:43
for one another, that you may be **h**. ... Jas 5:16
By his wounds you have been **h**. ...... 1 Pt 2:24

HEALING
the tongue of the wise brings **h**. ..... Prv 12:18
for food, and their leaves for **h**." .... Ezk 47:12
shall rise with **h** in its wings. .... Mal 4:2
gospel of the kingdom and **h** every .... Mt 4:23
to another gifts of **h** by the one Spirit, . 1 Cor 12:9
the tree were for the **h** of the nations. ... Rv 22:2

HEALS
iniquity, who **h** all your diseases, ... Ps 103:3
He **h** the brokenhearted and binds up ... Ps 147:3

HEALTH
no **h** in my bones because of my sin. ..... Ps 38:3
in his illness you restore him to full **h**. ... Ps 41:3
sweetness to the soul and **h** to the body. Prv 16:24
with you and that you may be in good **h**, .. 3 Jn 2

HEALTHY
So, if your eye is **h**, your whole body ... Mt 6:22
A **h** tree cannot bear bad fruit, ... Mt 7:18

HEAR
"**H**, O Israel: The LORD our .... Dt 6:4
Be gracious to me and **h** my prayer! ..... Ps 4:1
or his ear dull, that it cannot **h**; .... Is 59:1
who has ears to **h**, let him **h**. .... Mt 11:15
will indeed **h** but never understand, ... Mt 13:14
And how are they to **h** without .... Rom 10:14
let every person be quick to **h**, ... Jas 1:19

HEARD
The Lord has **h** my plea .... Ps 6:9
he inclined to me and **h** my cry. .... Ps 40:1
those who had **h** the word believed, ... Acts 4:4
which we have seen and **h** we proclaim . 1 Jn 1:3

HEARERS
For it is not the **h** of the law who are ... Rom 2:13
be doers of the word, and not **h** only, ... Jas 1:22

HEARING
"Keep on **h**, but do not understand; ..... Is 6:9
do not see, and **h** they do not hear, ... Mt 13:13
So faith comes from **h**, and **h** ...... Rom 10:17

HEARS
For the LORD **h** the needy and .... Ps 69:33
If one gives an answer before he **h**, ... Prv 18:13
"Everyone then who **h** these words of ... Mt 7:24
Whoever is of God **h** the words of ...... Jn 8:47
anything according to his will he **h** us. . 1 Jn 5:14
If anyone **h** my voice and opens the door, Rv 3:20

HEART
your God with all your **h** and with all ..... Dt 6:5
to serve him with all your **h** and with .... Jos 22:5
sought out a man after his own **h**, ... 1 Sm 13:14
but the LORD looks on the **h**." .... 1 Sm 16:7
will give you the desires of your **h**. .... Ps 37:4
My **h** overflows with a pleasing theme; ... Ps 45:1
I have stored up your word in my **h**, ... Ps 119:11
Keep your **h** with all vigilance, for ..... Prv 4:23
A joyful **h** is good medicine, ... Prv 17:22
face, so the **h** of man reflects the man. . Prv 27:19
Do not take to **h** all the things that .... Eccl 7:21
and to revive the **h** of the contrite. ..... Is 57:15
The **h** is deceitful above all things, ... Jer 17:9
I will give you a new **h**, ... Ezk 36:26
"Blessed are the pure in **h**, ... Mt 5:8
treasure is, there your **h** will be .... Mt 6:21
of the abundance of the **h** the mouth ... Mt 12:34
their lips, but their **h** is far from me; .... Mt 15:8
your God with all your **h** and with all ... Mt 22:37
ought always to pray and not lose **h**. .... Lk 18:1
they heard this they were cut to the **h**, .. Acts 2:37
will disclose the purposes of the **h**. .... 1 Cor 4:5

for whenever our **h** condemns us, God .. 1 Jn 3:20
I am he who searches mind and **h**, ... Rv 2:23

HEARTLESS
foolish, faithless, **h**, ruthless. .... Rom 1:31
h, unappeasable, slanderous, without .. 2 Tm 3:3

HEARTS
I will write it on their **h**. .... Jer 31:33
before men, but God knows your **h**. .... Lk 16:15
"Did not our **h** burn within us while ... Lk 24:32
"Let not your **h** be troubled. .... Jn 14:1
work of the law is written on their **h**, ... Rom 2:15
And he who searches **h** knows what ... Rom 8:27
of stone but on tablets of human **h**. ... 2 Cor 3:3
sent the Spirit of his Son into our **h**, ... Gal 4:6
Christ may dwell in your **h** through ..... Eph 3:17

HEAVEN
God called the expanse **H**. .... Gn 1:8
highest **h** cannot contain you; .... 1 Kgs 8:27
"**H** is my throne, and the earth is my ..... Is 66:1
behold, with the clouds of **h** there ..... Dn 7:13
bind on earth shall be bound in **h**, ... Mt 16:19
H and earth will pass away, but my ..... Mt 24:35
Power and coming on the clouds of **h**." ... Mt 26:64
"All authority in **h** and on earth .... Mt 28:18
will be more joy in **h** over one sinner ... Lk 15:7
poor, and you will have treasure in **h**; ... Lk 18:22
same way as you saw him go into **h**." .... Acts 1:11
wrath of God is revealed from **h** ...... Rom 1:18
caught up to the third **h**—whether in .. 2 Cor 12:2
But our citizenship is in **h**, ... Phil 3:20
of the hope laid up for you in **h**. .... Col 1:5
and unfading, kept in **h** for you, ... 1 Pt 1:4
Then I saw a new **h** and a new earth, ... Rv 21:1

HEAVENLY
can you believe if I tell you **h** things? ... Jn 3:12
bring me safely into his **h** kingdom. ... 2 Tm 4:18
better country, that is, a **h** one. ...... Heb 11:16

HEAVENS
God created the **h** and the earth. .... Gn 1:1
When I look at your **h**, the work of .... Ps 8:3
The **h** declare the glory of God, ... Ps 19:1
steadfast love is great above the **h**; ... Ps 108:4
For as the **h** are higher than the earth, ... Is 55:9
his splendor covered the **h**, and .... Hab 3:3
behold, the **h** were opened to him, ... Mt 3:16
and the powers of the **h** be shaken. .. Mt 24:29
who also ascended far above all the **h**, .. Eph 4:10
and the **h** are the work of your hands; .. Heb 1:10
we are waiting for new **h** and a new .... 2 Pt 3:13

HEAVY
and night your hand was **h** upon me; ..... Ps 32:4
to me, all who labor and are **h** laden, ... Mt 11:28
They tie up **h** burdens, hard to bear, ... Mt 23:4

HEEL
your head, and you shall bruise his **h**." ... Gn 3:15
my bread has lifted his **h** against me.' ... Jn 13:18

HEIGHT
nor **h** nor depth, nor anything else in ... Rom 8:39
breadth and length and **h** and depth, ... Eph 3:18

HEIR
very own son shall be your **h**." .... Gn 15:4
and if a son, then an **h** through God. .... Gal 4:7
whom he appointed the **h** of all things, .. Heb 1:2

HEIRS
h of God and fellow **h** .... Rom 8:17
are Abraham's offspring, **h** according ..... Gal 3:29
mystery is that the Gentiles are fellow **h**, . Eph 3:6
by his grace we might become **h** .... Ti 3:7

HELL
can destroy both soul and body in **h** ... Mt 10:28
course of life, and set on fire by **h**. ..... Jas 3:6
when they sinned, but cast them into **h** .. 2 Pt 2:4

HELMET
as a breastplate, and a **h** of salvation ...... Is 59:17
and take the **h** of salvation, ... Eph 6:17

HELP
LORD, there is none like you to **h**, ... 2 Chr 14:11
to my God I cried for **h**. .... Ps 18:6
From where does my **h** come? .... Ps 121:1
I will strengthen you, I will **h** you, ... Is 41:10
knelt before him, saying, "Lord, **h** me." .. Mt 15:25
the fainthearted, **h** the weak, ... 1 Thes 5:14
tempted, he is able to **h** those .... Heb 2:18

HELPED
"Till now the LORD has **h** us." .... 1 Sm 7:12
in a day of salvation I have **h** you." .... 2 Cor 6:2

HELPER
alone; I will make him a **h** fit for him." ... Gn 2:18
you have been the **h** of the fatherless. ... Ps 10:14
Father, and he will give you another **H**, ... Jn 14:16
confidently say, "The Lord is my **h**; ..... Heb 13:6

HERESIES
who will secretly bring in destructive **h**, .. 2 Pt 2:1

HEROD
For **H** had seized John and bound him ... Mt 14:3
governor of Judea, and **H** being .... Lk 3:1
jurisdiction, he sent him over to **H**, ... Lk 23:7

HEZEKIAH
fourteenth year of King **H**, ... 2 Kgs 18:13
In the fourteenth year of King **H**, ... Is 36:1

HID
and the man and his wife **h** .... Gn 3:8
Moses **h** his face, for he was afraid ...... Ex 3:6
shall live, because she **h** the messengers .. Jos 6:17

HIDDEN
Declare me innocent from **h** faults. ..... Ps 19:12
Better is open rebuke than **h** love. ..... Prv 27:5
your sins have **h** his face from you .... Is 59:2
he reveals deep and **h** things; .... Dn 2:22
have **h** these things from the wise ..... Mt 11:25
kingdom of heaven is like a treasure **h** .. Mt 13:44
For nothing is **h** except to be made .... Mk 4:22
died, and your life is **h** with Christ ..... Col 3:3

HIDE
h me in the shadow of your wings, ... Ps 17:8
H your face from my sins, and blot out ... Ps 51:9

HIGH
For as **h** as the heavens are above ..... Ps 103:11
he makes me tread on my **h** places. ..... Hab 3:19

HILL
A city set on a **h** cannot be hidden. ..... Mt 5:14
brought him to the brow of the **h** ...... Lk 4:29

HILLS
is mine, the cattle on a thousand **h**. .... Ps 50:10
I lift up my eyes to the **h**. .... Ps 121:1

HINDER
children come to me and do not **h** .... Mt 19:14

HINDERED
You were running well. Who **h** you ..... Gal 5:7
so that your prayers may not be **h**. ..... 1 Pt 3:7

HOLD
h fast to what is good. .... Rom 12:9
H fast what you have, so that no one ..... Rv 3:11

HOLINESS
Who is like you, majestic in **h**, ... Ex 15:11
the LORD in the splendor of **h**. .... Ps 29:2
bringing **h** to completion in the fear ... 2 Cor 7:1
not called us for impurity, but in **h**. .... 1 Thes 4:7
and for the **h** without which no one ... Heb 12:14
ought you to be in lives of **h** and ...... 2 Pt 3:11

HOLY
blessed the seventh day and made it **h**, .. Gn 2:3
which you are standing is **h** ground." .... Ex 3:5

HOME

the Sabbath day, to keep it **h**. .... Ex 20:8
be **h**, for I the LORD your God am **h**. ..... Lv 19:2
"There is none **h** like the LORD: .... 1 Sm 2:2
And who shall stand in his **h** place? ...... Ps 24:3
"**H**, **h**, **h** is the LORD .... Is 6:3
conceived in her is from the **H** Spirit. ..... Mt 1:20
blasphemes against the **H** Spirit never .... Mk 3:29
and the **H** Spirit descended on him in ..... Lk 3:22
Father give the **H** Spirit to those who ..... Lk 11:13
But the Helper, the **H** Spirit, whom ..... Jn 14:26
receive power when the **H** Spirit has .... Acts 1:8
For God's temple is **h**, and you are .... 1 Cor 3:17
in order to present you **h** and blameless . Col 1:22
upright, **h**, and disciplined. .... Ti 1:8
a high priest, **h**, innocent, unstained, .. Heb 7:26
"You shall be **h**, for I am **h**." .... 1 Pt 1:16
"**H**, **h**, **h**, is the Lord God .... Rv 4:8

HOME

God settles the solitary in a **h**; .... Ps 68:6
Even the sparrow finds a **h**, ... Ps 84:3
because man is going to his eternal **h**, . Eccl 12:5
come to him and make our **h** with him. .. Jn 14:23
that while we are at **h** in the body we . 2 Cor 5:6
self-controlled, pure, working at **h**, ... Ti 2:5

HOMELESS

and bring the **h** poor into your house; .... Is 58:7
are poorly dressed and buffeted and **h**, . 1 Cor 4:11

HOMES

"See, we have left our **h** and followed ... Lk 18:28

HOMOSEXUALITY

adulterers, nor men who practice **h**, ... 1 Cor 6:9
men who practice **h**, enslavers, ... 1 Tm 1:10

HONEST

Whoever gives an **h** answer kisses ...... Prv 24:26
hold it fast in an **h** and good heart, ... Lk 8:15
rather let him labor, doing **h** work. ...... Eph 4:28

HONEY

a land flowing with milk and **h**, ... Ex 3:8
much fine gold; sweeter also than **h** ..... Ps 19:10
his waist and ate locusts and wild **h**. .... Mk 1:6

HONOR

"**H** your father and your mother, ... Ex 20:12
those who **h** me I will **h**, ... 1 Sm 2:30
and humility comes before **h**. .... Prv 15:33
For God commanded, '**H** your father .... Mt 15:4
knew God, they did not **h** him .... Rom 1:21
h to whom **h** is owed. .... Rom 13:7
"**H** your father and mother" (this is .... Eph 6:2
H everyone. Love the brotherhood. ...... 1 Pt 2:17
to the Lamb be blessing and **h** .... Rv 5:13

HONORABLE

whatever is true, whatever is **h**, ... Phil 4:8
a vessel for **h** use, set apart as holy, ... 2 Tm 2:21

HONORS

who is generous to the needy **h** him. ..... Prv 14:31
"This people **h** me with their lips, but ... Mt 15:8

HOPE

Though he slay me, I will **h** in him; .... Jb 13:15
for what do I wait? My **h** is in you. .... Ps 39:7
H in God; for I shall again praise him, ... Ps 42:5
H deferred makes the heart sick, ... Prv 13:12
I call to mind, and therefore I have **h**; .. Lam 3:21
and in his name the Gentiles will **h**." .... Mt 12:21
and **h** does not put us to shame, ... Rom 5:5
Now **h** that is seen is not **h**. .... Rom 8:24
Rejoice in **h**, be patient in tribulation, .. Rom 12:12
So now faith, **h**, and love abide, ... 1 Cor 13:13
may know what is the **h** to which he .... Eph 1:18
is Christ in you, the **h** of glory. .... Col 1:27
waiting for our blessed **h**, the appearing . Ti 2:13
hold fast the confession of our **h** .... Heb 10:23
to be born again to a living **h** .... 1 Pt 1:3
so that your faith and **h** are in God. ..... 1 Pt 1:21

HOPES

not hope. For who **h** for what he sees? .. Rom 8:24
believes all things, **h** all things, ... 1 Cor 13:7

HORSE

the **h** and his rider he has thrown .... Ex 15:1
delight is not in the strength of the **h**, .. Ps 147:10
heaven opened, and behold, a white **h**! . Rv 19:11

HOSANNA

name of the Lord! **H** in the highest!" ..... Mt 21:9

HOSEA

says in **H**, "Those who were not my ..... Rom 9:25

HOSHEA

H the son of Elah began to reign in .... 2 Kgs 17:1

HOSPITABLE

respectable, **h**, able to teach, ... 1 Tm 3:2
but **h**, a lover of good, ... Ti 1:8

HOSPITALITY

of the saints and seek to show **h**. ...... Rom 12:13
brought up children, has shown **h**, ... 1 Tm 5:10
Do not neglect to show **h** to strangers, . Heb 13:2
Show **h** to one another without .... 1 Pt 4:9

HOSTILE

mind that is set on the flesh is **h** to God, . Rom 8:7
once were alienated and **h** in mind, ... Col 1:21

HOUR

of Man is coming at an **h** you do not .... Mt 24:44
"The **h** has come for the Son of Man ... Jn 12:23
"Father, the **h** has come; glorify your ... Jn 17:1

HOUSE

But as for me and my **h**, we will serve ... Jos 24:15
dwell in the **h** of the Lord forever. .... Ps 23:6
I may dwell in the **h** of the LORD .... Ps 27:4
Unless the LORD builds the **h**, ... Ps 127:1
By wisdom a **h** is built, and by .... Prv 24:3
h shall be called a **h** of prayer .... Is 56:7
wise man who built his **h** on the rock. .. Mt 7:24
enter a strong man's **h** and plunder ..... Mt 12:29
h shall be called a **h** of prayer,' .... Mt 21:13
divided against itself, that **h** will not ..... Mk 3:25
not make my Father's **h** a **h** of trade." .. Jn 2:16
In my Father's **h** are many rooms. .... Jn 14:2

HOUSEHOLD

enemies will be those of his own **h**. ..... Mt 10:36
to those who are of the **h** of faith. .... Gal 6:10
He must manage his own **h** well, ... 1 Tm 3:4
judgment to begin at the **h** of God; .... 1 Pt 4:17

HOW

H can we know the way?" .... Jn 14:5
"**H** are the dead raised? .... 1 Cor 15:35
h much more will the blood of Christ, ... Heb 9:14

HUMAN

"Whoever takes a **h** life shall .... Lv 24:17
And being found in **h** form, he .... Phil 2:8

HUMBLE

are called by my name **h** themselves, ... 2 Chr 7:14
He leads the **h** in what is right, ... Ps 25:9
scornful, but to the **h** he gives favor. ..... Prv 3:34
he who is **h** and contrite in spirit .... Is 66:2
the proud but gives grace to the **h**." ...... Jas 4:6
H yourselves before the Lord, ... Jas 4:10
H yourselves, therefore, under the .... 1 Pt 5:6

HUMBLED

he **h** himself by becoming obedient to .... Phil 2:8

HUMBLES

Whoever **h** himself like this child is ...... Mt 18:4
whoever **h** himself will be exalted. .... Mt 23:12

HUMILITY

or conceit, but in **h** count others .... Phil 2:3
kindness, **h**, meekness, and patience, ... Col 3:12

HUNGER

"Blessed are those who **h** and thirst for .. Mt 5:6

HUNGRY

the **h** soul he fills with good things. ...... Ps 107:9
For I was **h** and you gave me food, ... Mt 25:35
"Blessed are you who are **h** now, for .... Lk 6:21
"if your enemy is **h**, feed him; .... Rom 12:20

HURT

the enemy, and nothing shall **h** you. ..... Lk 10:19
conquers will not be **h** by the second ..... Rv 2:11

HUSBAND

Your desire shall be contrary to your **h**, ." . Gn 3:16
An excellent wife is the crown of her **h**, . Prv 12:4
For your Maker is your **h**, the .... Is 54:5
Jesus said to her, "Go, call your **h**, ... Jn 4:16
wife should not separate from her **h** .... 1 Cor 7:10
and the **h** should not divorce his wife. . 1 Cor 7:11
For the **h** is the head of the wife even ... Eph 5:23
be above reproach, the **h** of one wife, .. 1 Tm 3:2
prepared as a bride adorned for her **h**. .. Rv 21:2

HUSBANDS

H, love your wives, as Christ loved .... Eph 5:25
women to love their **h** and children, ." ..... Ti 2:4
wives, be subject to your own **h**, ... 1 Pt 3:1
Likewise, **h**, live with your wives in an .... 1 Pt 3:7

HYMNS

praying and singing **h** to God, ... Acts 16:25
in psalms and **h** and spiritual songs, ... Eph 5:19

HYPOCRISY

but within you are full of **h** and .... Mt 23:28
malice and all deceit and **h** and envy .... 1 Pt 2:1

HYPOCRITES

you pray, you must not be like the **h**. ..... Mt 6:5
h! For you shut the kingdom of heaven . Mt 23:13

HYSSOP

Take a bunch of **h** and dip it in the ...... Ex 12:22
the sour wine on a **h** branch and held .... Jn 19:29

IDLE

an **i** person will suffer hunger. .... Prv 19:15
sing **i** songs to the sound of the harp ...... Am 6:5
'Why do you stand here **i** all day?' .... Mt 20:6
brothers, admonish the **i**, encourage .. 1 Thes 5:14

IDLENESS

does not eat the bread of **i**. .... Prv 31:27
some among you walk in **i**, ... 2 Thes 3:11

IDOL

An **i**! A craftsman casts it, and a .... Is 40:19
know that "an **i** has no real existence," .. 1 Cor 8:4
is anything, or that an **i** is anything? .. 1 Cor 10:19

IDOLATER

or greed, or is an **i**, reviler, ... 1 Cor 5:11
covetous (that is, an **i**), has no .... Eph 5:5

IDOLATRY

and presumption is as iniquity and **i**. .. 1 Sm 15:23
Therefore, my beloved, flee from **i**. .. 1 Cor 10:14

IDOLS

Do not turn to **i** or make for .... Lv 19:4
Now concerning food offered to **i**: we .. 1 Cor 8:1
That food offered to **i** is anything, or .. 1 Cor 10:19
Little children, keep yourselves from **i**. . 1 Jn 5:21

IGNORANCE

The times of **i** God overlooked, but .... Acts 17:30
the life of God because of the **i** .... Eph 4:18
should put to silence the **i** of foolish .... 1 Pt 2:15

IGNORANT

being **i** of the righteousness of God, ... Rom 10:3
to do with foolish, **i** controversies; ..... 2 Tm 2:23
about matters of which they are **i**, ... 2 Pt 2:12

ILL

is why many of you are weak and **i**, .. 1 Cor 11:30

IMAGE

"Let us make man in our **i**, ... Gn 1:26
shed, for God made man in his own **i**. ..... Gn 9:6
shall not make for yourself a carved **i**, ... Ex 20:4
to be conformed to the **i** of his Son, ... Rom 8:29
since he is the **i** and glory of God, ... 1 Cor 11:7
also bear the **i** of the man of heaven. 1 Cor 15:49
He is the **i** of the invisible God, ... Col 1:15

IMAGES

All worshipers of **i** are put to shame, ... Ps 97:7
immortal God for **i** resembling mortal ... Rom 1:23

IMITATE

of their way of life, and **i** their faith. ...... Heb 13:7
do not **i** evil but **i** good. .... 3 Jn 11

IMITATORS

Be **i** of me, as I am of Christ. .... 1 Cor 11:1
Therefore be **i** of God, as beloved .... Eph 5:1
And you became **i** of us and .... 1 Thes 1:6
may not be sluggish, but **i** .... Heb 6:12

IMMANUEL

bear a son, and shall call his name **I**. ...... Is 7:14
call his name **I**" (which means, ... Mt 1:23

IMMORAL

not to associate with sexually **i** people .. 1 Cor 5:9
but the sexually **i** person sins against ... 1 Cor 6:18
the sexually **i**, sorcerers, idolaters, ... Rv 21:8

IMMORALITY

wife, except on the ground of sexual **i**, .. Mt 5:32
of man, come evil thoughts, sexual **i**, ... Mk 7:21
not in sexual **i** and sensuality, ... Rom 13:13
The body is not meant for sexual **i**, ... 1 Cor 6:13
But sexual **i** and all impurity .... Eph 5:3

IMMORTAL

exchanged the glory of the **i** God .... Rom 1:23
To the King of the ages, **i**, invisible, ... 1 Tm 1:17

IMMORTALITY

seek for glory and honor and **i**, ... Rom 2:7
and this mortal body must put on **i**. ... 1 Cor 15:53
who alone has **i**, who dwells in .... 1 Tm 6:16
and brought life and **i** to light through . 2 Tm 1:10

IMPERISHABLE

perishable body must put on the **i**, ... 1 Cor 15:53
to an inheritance that is **i**, undefiled, ... 1 Pt 1:4

IMPOSSIBLE

move, and nothing will be **i** for you." .. Mt 17:20
"With man this is **i**, but with God all ... Mt 19:26
in which it is **i** for God to lie, ... Heb 6:18
And without faith it is **i** to please him, .. Heb 11:6

IMPURITY

in the lusts of their hearts to **i**, ... Rom 1:24
as slaves to **i** and to lawlessness .... Rom 6:19
have not repented of the **i**, ... 2 Cor 12:21
sexual immorality, **i**, sensuality, ... Gal 5:19
For God has not called us for **i**, ... 1 Thes 4:7

INCENSE

the cloud of the **i** may cover the mercy . Lv 16:13
my prayer be counted as **i** before you, .. Ps 141:2
having the golden altar of **i** and the ark .. Heb 9:4
i, which are the prayers of the saints. .... Rv 5:8

INCREASE

Of the **i** of his government and of peace .... Is 9:7
run to and fro, and knowledge shall **i**." ... Dn 12:4
apostles said to the Lord, "**I** our faith!" ... Lk 17:5
He must **i**, but I must decrease." .... Jn 3:30
And the word of God continued to **i**, ... Acts 6:7
i the harvest of your righteousness. ...... 2 Cor 9:10
may the Lord make you **i** and abound . 1 Thes 3:12

INCREASED

And because lawlessness will be **i**, the .. Mt 24:12
And Jesus **i** in wisdom and in stature .... Lk 2:52
But the word of God **i** and multiplied. .. Acts 12:24
but where sin **i**, grace abounded all ..... Rom 5:20

INCREASES

the wicked increase, transgression **i**, ... Prv 29:16
to him who has no might he **i** strength. ... Is 40:29

INDESTRUCTIBLE

but by the power of an **i** life. .... Heb 7:16

INDIGNATION

prosper till the **i** is accomplished; .... Dn 11:36
Who can stand before his **i**? .... Na 1:6

INFANTS

Out of the mouth of babies and **i**, ... Ps 8:2
"Out of the mouth of **i** and nursing ..... Mt 21:16
as people of the flesh, as **i** in Christ. ... 1 Cor 3:1
Be **i** in evil, but in your thinking .... 1 Cor 14:20
Like newborn **i**, long for the pure .... 1 Pt 2:2

INHERIT

offspring, and they shall **i** it forever.'" .. Ex 32:13
The righteous shall **i** the land .... Ps 37:29
his own household will **i** the wind, ... Prv 11:29
LORD will **i** Judah as his portion .... Zec 2:12
are the meek, for they shall **i** the earth. ... Mt 5:5
what must I do to **i** eternal life?" .... Mk 10:17
unrighteous will not **i** the kingdom of .. 1 Cor 6:9
flesh and blood cannot **i** the kingdom . 1 Cor 15:50
such things will not **i** the kingdom of .... Gal 5:21

INHERITANCE

of Egypt, to be a people of his own **i**, ... Dt 4:20
indeed, I have a beautiful **i**. .... Ps 16:6
A good man leaves an **i** to his .... Prv 13:22
Wisdom is good with an **i**, an .... Eccl 7:11
"This shall be their **i**: I am their **i**: ...... Ezk 44:28
tell my brother to divide the **i** with me." .. Lk 12:13
For if the **i** comes by the law, it no ...... Gal 3:18
In him we have obtained an **i**, ... Eph 1:11
you to share in the **i** of the saints .... Col 1:12
from the Lord you will receive the **i** ...... Col 3:24
may receive the promised eternal **i**, ... Heb 9:15
to an **i** that is imperishable, undefiled, ... 1 Pt 1:4

INIQUITIES

my sins, and blot out all my **i**. .... Ps 51:9
nor repay us according to our **i**. .... Ps 103:10
The **i** of the wicked ensnare him, ... Prv 5:22
he was crushed for our **i**; upon him .... Is 53:5
righteous, and he shall bear their **i**. ...... Is 53:11
but your **i** have made a separation .... Is 59:2
he will tread our **i** underfoot. .... Mi 7:19
For I will be merciful toward their **i**, ... Heb 8:12

INIQUITY

A God of faithfulness and without **i**, ... Dt 32:4
sin to you, and I did not cover my **i**; ...... Ps 32:5
Wash me thoroughly from my **i**, ... Ps 51:2
who forgives all your **i**, who heals all .... Ps 103:3
and let no **i** get dominion over me. .... Ps 119:133
the LORD has laid on him the **i** .... Is 53:6
Who is a God like you, pardoning **i** ...... Mi 7:18
I have taken your **i** away from you, ... Zec 3:4
the name of the Lord depart from **i**." .... 2 Tm 2:19

INJUSTICE

"You shall do no **i** in court. .... Lv 19:15
for there is no **i** with the LORD .... 2 Chr 19:7
Whoever sows **i** will reap calamity, ... Prv 22:8
plowed iniquity; you have reaped **i**; ...... Hos 10:13
Is there **i** on God's part? By no means! .. Rom 9:14

INNOCENT

Declare me **i** from hidden faults. .... Ps 19:12
so be wise as serpents and **i** as doves. .. Mt 10:16
"Certainly this man was **i**!" .... Lk 23:47
what is good and **i** as to what is evil... Rom 16:19
such a high priest, holy, **i**, unstained, ... Heb 7:26

INSIGHT

the knowledge of the Holy One is **i**....... Prv 9:10
lavished upon us, in all wisdom and **i** ...... Eph 1:8

INSOLENT

slanderers, haters of God, **i**, ... Rom 1:30

persecutor, and **i** opponent. But I .... 1 Tm 1:13

INSTRUCT

I will **i** you and teach you in .... Ps 32:8
the mind of the Lord so as to **i** him?" .. 1 Cor 2:16
with my mind in order to **i** others, ... 1 Cor 14:19

INSTRUCTED

when a wise man is **i**, he gains .... Prv 21:11
because you are **i** from the law; .... Rom 2:18

INSTRUCTION

Whoever heeds **i** is on the path to life, . Prv 10:17
Whoever ignores **i** despises himself, ... Prv 15:32
in former days was written for our **i**, ... Rom 15:4
but they were written down for our **i**, . 1 Cor 10:11
so that he may be able to give **i** .... Ti 1:9

INSTRUCTS

in the night also my heart **i** me. .... Ps 16:7
therefore he **i** sinners in the way......... Ps 25:8

INSULT

but the prudent ignores an **i**. .... Prv 12:16
in saying these things you **i** us also." .... Lk 11:45

INSULTS

oppresses a poor man **i** his Maker, ... Prv 14:31
whoever **i** his brother will be liable .... Mt 5:22

INTEGRITY

away from evil? He still holds fast his **i**, ... Jb 2:3
May **i** and uprightness preserve me, ... Ps 25:21
I will walk with **i** of heart .... Ps 101:2
he is a shield to those who walk in **i**, ... Prv 2:7
Whoever walks in **i** walks securely, ... Prv 10:9
works, and in your teaching show **i**, ... Ti 2:7

INTELLIGENT

when he closes his lips, he is deemed **i**. . Prv 17:28
An **i** heart acquires knowledge, and .... Prv 18:15

INTERCEDES

but the Spirit himself **i** for us .... Rom 8:26

INTERCESSION

the sin of many, and makes **i** for the ...... Is 53:12
he always lives to make **i** for them. ...... Heb 7:25

INTERESTS

his **i** are divided. And the unmarried .... 1 Cor 7:34
look not only to his own **i**, ... Phil 2:4

INTERPRET

and understanding to **i** dreams, ... Dn 5:12
Do all speak with tongues? Do all **i**? . 1 Cor 12:30
But if there is no one to **i**, let .... 1 Cor 14:28

INTERPRETATION

a tongue, or an **i**. Let all things be .... 1 Cor 14:26
from someone's own **i**. .... 2 Pt 1:20

INVISIBLE

For his **i** attributes, namely, ... Rom 1:20
in heaven and on earth, visible and **i**, ... Col 1:16
immortal, **i**, the only God, ... 1 Tm 1:17

INVITE

the main roads and **i** to the wedding ..... Mt 22:9
But when you give a feast, **i** the poor, ... Lk 14:13

INWARD

you delight in truth in the **i** being, ... Ps 51:6
the **i** mind and heart of a man are deep. .. Ps 64:6
For you formed my **i** parts; .... Ps 139:13

IRON

them with a rod of **i** and dash them in ...... Ps 2:9
i sharpens **i**, and one man .... Prv 27:17
and he will rule them with a rod of **i**. ...... Rv 19:15

IRREVERENT

Have nothing to do with **i**, silly myths. .. 1 Tm 4:7
But avoid **i** babble, for it will lead .... 2 Tm 2:16

IRREVOCABLE

the gifts and the calling of God are **i**. .. Rom 11:29

ISAAC

a son, and you shall call his name I. ..... Gn 17:19
for through I shall your offspring be ..... Gn 21:12
wood in order and bound I his son ..... Gn 22:9
God of Abraham, the God of I, ... Ex 3:6
children by one man, our forefather I, ... Rom 9:10
when he was tested, offered up I, ... Heb 11:17
he offered up his son I on the altar? ..... Jas 2:21

ISAIAH

sackcloth, to the prophet I .... 2 Kgs 19:2
I the prophet the son of Amoz wrote. ..... 2 Chr 26:22
And the LORD said to I, "Go out .... Is 7:3
I when he said, "The voice of one .... Mt 3:3
prophet I: "He took our illnesses and ..... Mt 8:17
Well did I prophesy of you, when he ...... Mt 15:7
I cries out concerning Israel: "Though .. Rom 9:27
Then I is so bold as to say, "I have .... Rom 10:20

ISHMAEL

You shall call his name I, because .... Gn 16:11
The sons of Abraham: Isaac and I. ..... 1 Chr 1:28

ISRAEL

"Hear, O I: The LORD our God, ... Dt 6:4
"The glory has departed from I, ... 1 Sm 4:22
I was holy to the LORD, ... Jer 2:3
new covenant with the house of I and .. Jer 31:31
ruler who will shepherd my people I." .... Mt 2:6
no one in I have I found such faith. ...... Mt 8:10
to the lost sheep of the house of I. ..... Mt 10:6
Gentiles, and for glory to your people I." .. Lk 2:32
at this time restore the kingdom to I? .....Acts 1:6
in this way all I will be saved, ... Rom 11:26

JACOB

Esau's heel, so his name was called J. .. Gn 25:26
J said, "Sell me your birthright now." .... Gn 25:31
J was left alone. And a man wrestled .. Gn 32:24
Now the sons of J were twelve. .... Gn 35:22
Egypt, and all his offspring with him, ... Gn 46:6
As it is written, "J I loved, but Esau I .. Rom 9:13
By faith J, when dying, blessed each ... Heb 11:21

JAMES

J the son of Zebedee and John .... Mt 4:21
And are not his brothers J and Joseph .. Mt 13:55
Jesus took with him Peter and J, and .... Mt 17:1
After they finished speaking, J replied, ..Acts 15:13
the other apostles except J the Lord's ... Gal 1:19

JAPHETH

Noah fathered Shem, Ham, and J. .... Gn 5:32

JAR

handful of flour in a j and a little oil .. 1 Kgs 17:12
nothing in the house except a j of oil." .. 2 Kgs 4:2

JARS

empty j, with torches inside the j. .... Jgs 7:16
But we have this treasure in j of clay, .. 2 Cor 4:7

JEALOUS

I the LORD your God am a j God, ... Ex 20:5
name is J, is a j God), ... Ex 34:14
your God is a consuming fire, a j God. .... Dt 4:24
"I have been very j for the LORD, ... 1 Kgs 19:10
and I will be j for my holy name. ..... Ezk 39:25
I am exceedingly j for Jerusalem .... Zec 1:14
"I will make you j of those who are .... Rom 10:19

JEALOUSY

but who can stand before j? .... Prv 27:4
For while there is j and strife .... 1 Cor 3:3
For I feel a divine j for you, since ...... 2 Cor 11:2
strife, j, fits of anger, rivalries, ... Gal 5:20
For where j and selfish ambition exist, ... Jas 3:16

JEHOAHAZ

J the son of Jehu began to reign over .. 2 Kgs 13:1
J was twenty-three years old when .... 2 Kgs 23:31

JEHOIACHIN

And he carried away J to Babylon. ..... 2 Kgs 24:15
graciously freed J king of Judah ..... 2 Kgs 25:27

So J put off his prison garments. .... Jer 52:33

JEHOIADA

to all that J the priest commanded, ... 2 Kgs 11:9
But J grew old and full of days, and .. 2 Chr 24:15

JEHOIAKIM

father, and changed his name to J. ..... 2 Kgs 23:34
says the LORD concerning J .... Jer 22:18
In the fourth year of J the son of Josiah, .. Jer 36:1
year of the reign of J king of Judah, ... Dn 1:1

JEHOSHAPHAT

in the third year J the king of Judah .. 1 Kgs 22:2
The LORD was with J, because .... 2 Chr 17:3

JEHU

And J the son of Nimshi you shall .... 1 Kgs 19:16
Then J mounted his chariot and went.. 2 Kgs 9:16
Thus J wiped out Baal from Israel. ... 2 Kgs 10:28

JEPHTHAH

Now J the Gileadite was a mighty .... Jgs 11:1
And J made a vow to the LORD .... Jgs 11:30

JEREMIAH

LORD by the mouth of J, ... 2 Chr 36:21
by the mouth of J might be fulfilled, ... Ezr 1:1
word of the LORD came to J .... Jer 37:6
word of the LORD to J the .... Dn 9:2
what was spoken by the prophet J: ...... Mt 2:17
had been spoken by the prophet J, ... Mt 27:9

JERICHO

When Joshua was by J, he lifted up ..... Jos 5:13
By faith the walls of J fell .... Heb 11:30

JEROBOAM

Solomon sought therefore to kill J. .... 1 Kgs 11:40
all Israel heard that J had returned, ... 1 Kgs 12:20
upon the house of J and will cut off .. 1 Kgs 14:10

JERUSALEM

at J he reigned over all Israel and Judah .. 2 Sm 5:5
Solomon desired to build in J, ... 1 Kgs 9:19
"In J I will put my name." .... 2 Kgs 21:4
He carried away all J and all the ..... 2 Kgs 24:14
Pray for the peace of J! .... Ps 122:6
The LORD builds up J. .... Ps 147:2
Speak tenderly to J, and cry to her .... Is 40:2
I create J to be a joy, and her people to .. Is 65:18
the holy land, and will again choose J." .. Zec 2:12
J shall dwell in security. .... Zec 14:11
"O J, J, the city that kills .... Mt 23:37
the boy Jesus stayed behind in J, ... Lk 2:43
when you see J surrounded by armies, .. Lk 21:20
name to all nations, beginning from J. .... Lk 24:47
but you say that in J is the place where .. Jn 4:20
she corresponds to the present J, for ..... Gal 4:25
city of the living God, the heavenly J, .. Heb 12:22
city of my God, the new J, which .... Rv 3:12
showed me the holy city J coming .... Rv 21:10

JESSE

And I said to David his son, "Take .. 1 Sm 17:17
forth a shoot from the stump of J, ... Is 11:1
Isaiah says, "The root of J will come, .. Rom 15:12

JESUS

Then J was led up by the Spirit .... Mt 4:1
These twelve J sent out, instructing ...... Mt 10:5
together in order to arrest J by stealth ... Mt 26:4
seeking false testimony against J .... Mt 26:59
But J remained silent. .... Mt 26:63
"This man was with J of Nazareth." ...... Mt 26:71
"This is J, the King of the Jews." .... Mt 27:37
"J, Son of David, have mercy on me!" ... Mk 10:47
And at the ninth hour J cried with a .... Mk 15:34
He drew near to J to kiss him, ... Lk 22:47
them once more, desiring to release J, .. Lk 23:20
"J, remember me when you come into .. Lk 23:42
J wept. .... Jn 11:35
prophesied that J would die for the .... Jn 11:51
that he might take away the body of J, ... Jn 19:38

I have dealt with all that J began to do ... Acts 1:1
This J God raised up, and of .... Acts 2:32
"I am J, whom you are persecuting. ...... Acts 9:5
saved through the grace of the Lord J, .. Acts 15:11
'I am J of Nazareth, whom you are ...... Acts 22:8
J Christ, through whom are all things. .... 1 Cor 8:6
is not ourselves, but J Christ as Lord, .. 2 Cor 4:5
do everything in the name of the Lord J, .. Col 3:17
consider J, the apostle and high priest. ... Heb 3:1
J, the Son of God, let us hold fast our .. Heb 4:14
This makes J the guarantor of a better .. Heb 7:22
Whoever confesses that J is the Son ... 1 Jn 4:15
The revelation of J Christ, ... Rv 1:1
"I, J, have sent my angel to testify ...... Rv 22:16

JEW

take hold of the robe of a J, ... Zec 8:23
the J first and also to the Greek. .... Rom 1:16
But a J is one inwardly, and .... Rom 2:29
no distinction between J and Greek; .. Rom 10:12
To the Jews I became as a J, ... 1 Cor 9:20
There is neither J nor Greek, ... Gal 3:28

JEWELS

She is more precious than j, ... Prv 3:15
for wisdom is better than j, and all ..... Prv 8:11
like the j of a crown they shall shine ... Zec 9:16

JEWS

he who has been born king of the J? ..... Mt 2:2
"Are you the King of the J?" .... Mt 27:11
for salvation is from the J. .... Jn 4:22
Or is God the God of J only? .... Rom 3:29
For J demand signs and Greeks ...... 1 Cor 1:22
into one body—J or Greeks, slaves .. 1 Cor 12:13
you force the Gentiles to live like J?" .... Gal 2:14

JEZEBEL

J cut off the prophets of the LORD, ... 1 Kgs 18:4
Ahab, whom J his wife incited. .... 1 Kgs 21:25

JOASH

took J the son of Ahaziah and stole .. 2 Kgs 11:2
And J did what was right in the eyes .. 2 Chr 24:2

JOB

land of Uz whose name was J, ... Jb 1:1
J, that there is none like him on the earth, .. Jb 1:8
Noah, Daniel, and J, were in it, ... Ezk 14:14
have heard of the steadfastness of J, ... Jas 5:11

JOHN

In those days J the Baptist .... Mt 3:1
when he heard that J had been arrested, .. Mt 4:12
son of Zebedee, and J his brother; ...... Mt 10:2
"Go and tell J what you hear and see: .. Mt 11:4
He sent and had J beheaded .... Mt 14:10
"Some say J the Baptist, ... Mt 16:14
was the baptism of J from heaven or .. Lk 20:4
Now Peter and J were going .... Acts 3:1
they saw the boldness of Peter and J, .. Acts 4:13
to take with them J called Mark. ...... Acts 15:37

JOINED

What therefore God has j together, ... Mt 19:6
But he who is j to the Lord becomes ... 1 Cor 6:17
being j together, grows into a holy ...... Eph 2:21

JOINTS

of j and of marrow, and discerning ...... Heb 4:12

JOKING

neighbor and says, "I am only j!" .... Prv 26:19
nor foolish talk nor crude j, ... Eph 5:4

JONAH

appointed a great fish to swallow up J. .. Jon 1:17
I prayed to the LORD his God .... Jon 2:1
to it except the sign of the prophet J. .. Mt 12:39
something greater than J is here. ...... Lk 11:32

JONATHAN

And Saul and J his son .... 1 Sm 13:16
And J spoke well of David to Saul .. 1 Sm 19:4
"J lies slain on your high places. .... 2 Sm 1:25

JORDAN

of you will pass over the **J** .... Nm 32:21
dry ground in the midst of the **J**, ... Jos 3:17
"Go and wash in the **J** seven times, .. 2 Kgs 5:10
baptized by him in the river **J**, ... Mt 3:6

JOSEPH

sons of Rachel: **J** and Benjamin. .... Gn 35:24
Now Israel loved **J** more than .... Gn 37:3
And **J** stored up grain in great .... Gn 41:49
So **J** went up to bury his father. .... Gn 50:7
king over Egypt, who did not know **J**... Ex 1:8
Moses took the bones of **J** with him, ... Ex 13:19
Mary had been betrothed to **J**, ... Mt 1:18
Lord appeared in a dream to **J** in Egypt, .. Mt 2:19
And **J** took the body and wrapped it .... Mt 27:59

JOSHUA

Moses said to **J**, "Choose for us men, ... Ex 17:9
And **J** the son of Nun, the assistant of .. Nm 11:28
J the son of Nun, who stands before .... Dt 1:38
J said, "Alas, O Lord GOD, ... Jos 7:7
So **J** made a covenant with the people .. Jos 24:25

JOSIAH

J was eight years old when he began .. 2 Kgs 22:1
J kept a Passover to the LORD .... 2 Chr 35:1
word of the LORD came in the days of **J** ... Jer 1:2

JOY

the **j** of the LORD is your strength." ...... Neh 8:10
You have put more **j** in my heart .... Ps 4:7
but **j** comes with the morning. .... Ps 30:5
works of your hands I sing for **j**. .... Ps 92:4
"For you shall go out in **j** and be led ..... Is 55:12
take **j** in the God of my salvation. .... Hab 3:18
from the tomb with fear and great **j**, ... Mt 28:8
I bring you good news of great **j** .... Lk 2:10
and that your **j** may be full. .... Jn 15:11
no one will take your **j** from you. .... Jn 16:22
fill you with all **j** and peace in .... Rom 15:13
fruit of the Spirit is love, **j**, peace .... Gal 5:22
complete my **j** by being of the same ..... Phil 2:2
Count it all **j**, my brothers, ... Jas 1:2
things so that our **j** may be complete. ... 1 Jn 1:4

JOYFUL

Make a **j** noise to the LORD, ... Ps 100:1
A **j** heart is good medicine, ... Prv 17:22
make them **j** in my house of prayer; ...... Is 56:7

JUDAH

she called his name **J**. .... Gn 29:35
The scepter shall not depart from **J**, ... Gn 49:10
But the house of **J** followed David. ...... 2 Sm 2:10
are too little to be among the clans of **J**, .. Mi 5:2
no means least among the rulers of **J**, ... Mt 2:6
that our Lord was descended from **J**, ... Heb 7:14
the Lion of the tribe of **J**, the Root ...... Rv 5:5

JUDAISM

I was advancing in **J** beyond many of .... Gal 1:14

JUDAS

and **J** Iscariot, who betrayed him. .... Mt 10:4
dipped the morsel, he gave it to **J**, ... Jn 13:26

JUDGE

Shall not the **J** of all the earth do ...... Gn 18:25
for he comes to **j** the earth. .... 1 Chr 16:33
he will **j** the peoples with equity." .... Ps 96:10
"**J** not, that you be not judged. .... Mt 7:1
on the way, lest he drag you to the **J**, ... Lk 12:58
for I did not come to **j** the world but ..... Jn 12:47
know that the saints will **j** the world? ... 1 Cor 6:2
who is to **j** the living and the dead, ... 2 Tm 4:1
There is only one lawgiver and **j**, ... Jas 4:12
behold, the **J** is standing at the door. .... Jas 5:9
to him who is ready to **j** the living and .. 1 Pt 4:5
whom the authority to **j** was committed. ... Rv 20:4

JUDGED

But if we **j** ourselves truly, we .... 1 Cor 11:31
we who teach will be **j** with greater ...... Jas 3:1

JUDGES

Then the LORD raised up **j**, ... Jgs 2:16
surely there is a God who **j** on earth." ... Ps 58:11
God **j** the secrets of men by Christ ...... Rom 2:16
It is the Lord who **j** me. .... 1 Cor 4:4
call on him as Father who **j** impartially .. 1 Pt 1:17

JUDGMENT

wicked will not stand in the **j**, nor .... Ps 1:5
but it is God who executes **j**, ... Ps 75:7
God will bring every deed into **j**, ... Eccl 12:14
day of **j** people will give account .... Mt 12:36
but has given all **j** to the Son, ... Jn 5:22
concerning sin and righteousness and **j**: .. Jn 16:8
God's righteous **j** will be revealed. .... Rom 2:5
all stand before the **j** seat of God; ...... Rom 14:10
eats and drinks **j** on himself. .... 1 Cor 11:29
we must all appear before the **j** .... 2 Cor 5:10
man to die once, and after that comes **j**, .. Heb 9:27
a fearful expectation of **j**, and a fury ... Heb 10:27
Mercy triumphs over **j**. .... Jas 2:13
For it is time for **j** to begin at .... 1 Pt 4:17
day of **j** and destruction of the ungodly. .. 2 Pt 3:7

JUDGMENTS

LORD of hosts, Render true **j**, ... Zec 7:9
the Almighty, true and just are your **j**!" .. Rv 16:7

JUST

without iniquity, **j** and upright is he. .... Dt 32:4
The thoughts of the righteous are **j**; ..... Prv 12:5
sends rain on the **j** and on the unjust. ... Mt 5:45
so that he might be **j** and the justifier .. Rom 3:26
disobedience received a **j** retribution, ... Heb 2:2
J and true are your ways, O King .... Rv 15:3

JUSTICE

You shall not pervert **j**. .... Dt 16:19
For the LORD loves **j**; he will .... Ps 37:28
As I have done, it is a joy to the **j** ...... Prv 21:15
Evil men do not understand **j**, ... Prv 28:5
By a **j** king builds up the land, but he ... Prv 29:4
do good; seek **j**, correct oppression; ..... Is 1:17
And I will make **j** the line, ... Is 28:17
For the LORD is a God of **j**; .... Is 30:18
he will bring forth **j** to the nations. ..... Is 42:1
and I will set my **j** for a light .... Is 51:4
But let **j** roll down like waters, ... Am 5:24
LORD require of you but to do **j**, ... Mi 6:8
every morning he shows forth his **j**; ...... Zep 3:5
Or by asking, "Where is the God of **j**?" .. Mal 2:17
and he will proclaim **j** to the Gentiles. ... Mt 12:18
and neglect **j** and the love of God. .... Lk 11:42
And will not God give **j** to his elect, ... Lk 18:7

JUSTIFICATION

for our trespasses and raised for our **j**. .. Rom 4:25
one act of righteousness leads to **j** ...... Rom 5:18

JUSTIFIED

and are **j** by his grace as a gift, ... Rom 3:24
For we hold that one is **j** by faith apart .. Rom 3:28
For if Abraham was **j** by works, he ...... Rom 4:2
since we have been **j** by faith, ... Rom 5:1
whom he called he also **j**, and those ..... Rom 8:30
with the heart one believes and is **j**, ... Rom 10:10
you were **j** in the name of the Lord .... 1 Cor 6:11
in order to be **j** by faith in Christ .... Gal 2:16
in order that we might be **j** by faith. ..... Gal 3:24
You see that a person is **j** by works .... Jas 2:24

JUSTIFIER

he might be just and the **j** of the one .... Rom 3:26

JUSTIFIES

He who **j** the wicked and he who .... Prv 17:15
work but believes in him who **j** the ...... Rom 4:5
against God's elect? It is God who **j**. ..... Rom 8:33

JUSTIFY

who will **j** the circumcised by faith ...... Rom 3:30
foreseeing that God would **j** the Gentiles .. Gal 3:8

JUDGMENT (continued)
And the dead were **j** by what............ Rv 20:12

KEEP

love me and **k** my commandments. .... Ex 20:6
The Lord bless you and **k** you; .... Nm 6:24
K back your servant also from .... Ps 19:13
nor will he **k** his anger forever. .... Ps 103:9
The LORD will **k** your going out and ..... Ps 121:8
K your heart with all vigilance, for .... Prv 4:23
a time to **k**, and a time to cast away; ..... Eccl 3:6
enter life, **k** the commandments." .... Mt 19:17
"If you love me, you will **k** my .... Jn 14:15
Holy Father, **k** them in your name, ... Jn 17:11
of God, that we **k** his commandments. ... 1 Jn 5:3
I will **k** you from the hour of trial .... Rv 3:10
and with those who **k** the words of this .. Rv 22:9

KEEPER

"I do not know; am I my brother's **k**?" ... Gn 4:9
The LORD is your **k**; .... Ps 121:5
the LORD, am its **k**; .... Is 27:3

KEEPS

the faithful God who **k** covenant and .... Dt 7:9
he who **k** you will not slumber. .... Ps 121:3
if anyone **k** my word, he will never ...... Jn 8:51
and **k** them, he it is who loves me... .... Jn 14:21
Blessed is the one who **k** the words ...... Rv 22:7

KEPT

and your sins have **k** good from you. .... Jer 5:25
"All these I have **k**. What do I still ...... Mt 19:20
I have **k** the faith. .... 2 Tm 4:7

KEYS

I will give you the **k** of the kingdom .... Mt 16:19
and I have the **k** of Death and Hades. ... Rv 1:18

KILL

and they will **k** him, and he will be ..... Mt 17:23
do not fear those who **k** the body, ... Lk 12:4
Why do you seek to **k** me?" .... Jn 7:19

KILLED

sake we are being **k** all the day long; .... Rom 8:36
they were **k** with the sword. .... Heb 11:37

KILLS

whoever **k** a person shall be put to ...... Lv 24:21
For the letter **k**, but the Spirit gives .... 1 Cor 3:6

KIND

is their seed, each according to its **k**, ... Gn 1:11
all his words and **k** in all his works. ..... Ps 145:13
A man who is **k** benefits himself, but ... Prv 11:17
for he is **k** to the ungrateful and the evil. .. Lk 6:35
Love is patient and **k**; love does not ... 1 Cor 13:4
Be **k** to one another, tenderhearted, ... Eph 4:32
not be quarrelsome but **k** to everyone, ... 2 Tm 2:24
pure, working at home, **k**, and........... Ti 2:5

KINDNESS

the teaching of **k** is on her tongue. ...... Prv 31:26
I led them with cords of **k**, with the ..... Hos 11:4
show **k** and mercy to one another, ... Zec 7:9
but God's **k** to you, provided you........ Rom 11:22
patience, **k**, the Holy Spirit, genuine . .. 2 Cor 6:6
of his grace in **k** toward us in Christ .... Eph 2:7
the goodness and loving **k** of God our ... Ti 3:4

KING

"Give us a **k** to judge us." And Samuel ... 1 Sm 8:6
LORD your God was your **k**. .... 1 Sm 12:12
Who is this **K** of glory? .... Ps 24:8
is the living God and the everlasting **K**. .. Jer 10:10
Behold, your **k** is coming to you; .... Zec 9:9
he who has been born **k** of the Jews? .... Mt 2:2
'Behold, your **k** is coming to you, ... Mt 21:5
"Are you the **K** of the Jews?" .... Mt 27:11
"Blessed is the **K** who comes in .... Lk 19:38
Son of God! You are the **K** of Israel!" ... Jn 1:49
"We have no **k** but Caesar." .... Jn 19:15
the **K** of the ages, immortal, invisible, .. 1 Tm 1:17
the **K** of kings and Lord of lords, ... 1 Tm 6:15
written, **K** of kings and Lord of lords. .... Rv 19:16

KINGDOM

and you shall be to me a **k** of priests ..... Ex 19:6
establish the throne of his **k** forever. ... 2 Sm 7:13
Yours is the **k**, O LORD, and .... 1 Chr 29:11
The scepter of your **k** is a scepter of ...... Ps 45:6
His **k** is an everlasting **k**, ... Dn 4:3
Your **k** come, your will be done, on .... Mt 6:10
is least in the **k** of heaven is greater ..... Mt 11:11
"The **k** of heaven may be compared to .. Mt 13:24
'than for a rich person to enter the **k** ... Mt 19:24
against nation, and **k** against **k**, ... Mt 24:7
'The **k** of God has come near to you.' ..... Lk 10:9
"My **k** is not of this world. If my **k** .... Jn 18:36
For the **k** of God is not a matter of ..... Rom 14:17
For the **k** of God does not consist ..... 1 Cor 4:20
blood cannot inherit the **k** of God, ... 1 Cor 15:50
receiving a **k** that cannot be shaken, ... Heb 12:28
"The **k** of the world has become the ...... Rv 11:15

KINGS

The **k** of the earth set themselves, ... Ps 2:2
By me **k** reign, and rulers decree .... Prv 8:15
out of this kingdom ten **k** shall arise, ... Dn 7:24
before governors and **k** for my sake, ... Mt 10:18
The **k** of the earth set themselves, and ... Acts 4:26

KISS

K the Son, lest he be angry, and you .... Ps 2:12
"The one I will **k** is the man; seize ...... Mt 26:48
she has not ceased to **k** my feet. .... Lk 7:45
you betray the Son of Man with a **k**?" ... Lk 22:48
Greet one another with a holy **k**........ Rom 16:16

KNEE

'To me every **k** shall bow, every tongue .. Is 45:23
the Lord, every **k** shall bow to me, ... Rom 14:11
the name of Jesus every **k** should bow, ... Phil 2:10

KNEES

and make firm the feeble **k**. .... Is 35:3
For this reason I bow my **k** before the ...Eph 3:14
and strengthen your weak **k**, ... Heb 12:12

KNEW

"Before I formed you in the womb I **k** ..... Jer 1:5
for I **k** that you are a gracious God ....Jon 4:2
'I never **k** you; depart from me, ... Mt 7:23
But he **k** their thoughts, and he said ...... Lk 6:8

KNIT

and **k** me together with bones and ...... Jb 10:11
being **k** together in love, ... Col 2:2

KNOCK

seek, and you will find; **k**, and it will ...... Mt 7:7
k at the door, saying, 'Lord, open .... Lk 13:25

KNOW

For I **k** that my Redeemer lives, and ...... Jb 19:25
"I **k** that you can do all things, and that ...Jb 42:2
Make me to **k** your ways, O .... Ps 25:4
For I **k** my transgressions, and my sin ... Ps 51:3
And I applied my heart to **k** wisdom .....Eccl 1:17
a heart to **k** that I am the LORD, ... Jer 24:7
saying, '**K** the LORD,' for they .... Jer 31:34
him, yet the world did not **k** him. ....Jn 1:10
I **k** my own and my own **k** me, ... Jn 10:14
life, that they **k** you, the only true God,.. Jn 17:3
"It is not for you to **k** times or seasons ... Acts 1:7
we **k** that for those who love God .... Rom 8:28
k in part; then I shall **k** fully, ... 1 Cor 13:12
that I may **k** him and the power of his ... Phil 3:10
Whoever says "I **k** him" but does not ... 1 Jn 2:4
you may **k** that you have eternal life. .... 1 Jn 5:13
"'I **k** your works, your toil and your .... Rv 2:2
and you will not **k** at what hour I will ...... Rv 3:3

KNOWING

be like God, **k** good and evil." .... Gn 3:5
Jesus, **k** all that would happen to him, ...Jn 18:4
surpassing worth of **k** Christ Jesus my ... Phil 3:8

KNOWLEDGE

and the tree of the **k** of good and evil. .... Gn 2:9

out speech, and night to night reveals **k**. .. Ps 19:2
Such **k** is too wonderful for me; it is ..... Ps 139:6
The wise lay up **k**, but the mouth of ..... Prv 10:14
Every prudent man acts with **k**, ... Prv 13:16
shall be full of the **k** of the LORD .... Is 11:9
My people are destroyed for lack of **k**; ..... Hos 4:6
will be filled with the **k** of the glory ...... Hab 2:14
riches and wisdom and **k** of God! ...... Rom 11:33
This "**k**" puffs up, but love builds up. ... 1 Cor 8:1
the love of Christ that surpasses **k**, ... Eph 3:19
all the treasures of wisdom and **k**, ... Col 2:3
your faith with virtue, and virtue with **k**, ... 2 Pt 1:5
But grow in the grace and **k** of our ..... 2 Pt 3:18

KNOWN

Make them **k** to your children .... Dt 4:9
you have searched me and **k** me! ..... Ps 139:1
Have you not **k**? Have you not heard?... Is 40:28
for the tree is **k** by its fruit. .... Mt 12:33
For what can be **k** about God is plain ... Rom 1:19
"For who has **k** the mind of the Lord, .. Rom 11:34
if anyone loves God, he is **k** by God, ... 1 Cor 8:3
better for them never to have **k** the .... 2 Pt 2:21

KNOWS

But he **k** the way that I take; .... Jb 23:10
LORD **k** the way of the righteous, ... Ps 1:6
righteous man **k** the rights of the poor; ... Prv 29:7
he **k** what is in the darkness, ... Dn 2:22
he **k** those who take refuge in him. .... Na 1:7
your Father **k** what you need before .... Mt 6:8
that day and hour no one **k**, ... Mt 24:36
k what is the mind of the Spirit, ... Rom 8:27
imagines that he **k** something, he ...... 1 Cor 8:2
"The Lord **k** those who are his," .... 2 Tm 2:19
So whoever **k** the right thing to do and ... Jas 4:17
loves has been born of God and **k** God... 1 Jn 4:7

LABAN

Arise, flee to **L** my brother in Haran ...... Gn 27:43
Then Jacob said to **L**, "Give me my ...... Gn 29:21

LABOR

Six days you shall **l**, and do all your .... Ex 20:9
your **l** for that which does not satisfy?..... Is 55:2
Come to me, all who **l** and are heavy .... Mt 11:28
receive his wages according to his **l**. .... 1 Cor 3:8
in the Lord your **l** is not in vain. .... 1 Cor 15:58
respect those who **l** among you and ... 1 Thes 5:12

LABORER

for the **l** deserves his wages. .... Lk 10:7
"The **l** deserves his wages." .... 1 Tm 5:18

LABORERS

harvest is plentiful, but the **l** are few; ..... Mt 9:37

LACK

who seek the LORD **l** no good thing..... Ps 34:10
these I have kept. What do I still **l**?" ..... Mt 19:20

LACKS

follows worthless pursuits **l** sense. .... Prv 12:11
For whoever **l** these qualities is so ...... 2 Pt 1:9

LADDER

there was a **l** set up on the earth, ... Gn 28:12

LAID

LORD has **l** on him the iniquity .... Is 53:6
love, that he **l** down his life for us, ... 1 Jn 3:16

LAKE

Hades were thrown into the **l** of fire..... Rv 20:14

LAMB

provide for himself the **l** for a burnt .... Gn 22:8
to your clans, and kill the Passover **l**. .... Ex 12:21
The wolf shall dwell with the **l**, ... Is 11:6
like a **l** that is led to the slaughter, ... Is 53:7
"Behold, the **L** of God, who takes away ... Jn 1:29
like a **l** before its shearer is silent, ... Acts 8:32
For Christ, our Passover **l**, has been ... 1 Cor 5:7
like that of a **l** without blemish or spot. .. 1 Pt 1:19
among the elders I saw a **L** standing, ... Rv 5:6

"Worthy is the **L** who was slain,........... Rv 5:12
God gives it light, and its lamp is the **L**... Rv 21:23

LAMBS

I am sending you out as **l** in the midst..... Lk 10:3
He said to him, "Feed my **l**."............... Jn 21:15

LAME

then shall the **l** man leap like a deer, ... Is 35:6
blind receive their sight and the **l** walk,.... Mt 11:5
for you to enter life **l** than with two feet .. Mk 9:45

LAMP

For you are my **l**, O LORD, ... 2 Sm 22:29
For it is you who light my **l**; .... Ps 18:28
Your word is a **l** to my feet and a ..... Ps 119:105
Nor do people light a **l** and put it .... Mt 5:15
"The eye is the **l** of the body. So, if...... Mt 6:22

LAMPS

virgins who took their **l** and went to ..... Mt 25:1
for action and keep your **l** burning, ... Lk 12:35

LAND

God called the dry **l** Earth, ... Gn 1:10
a **l** flowing with milk and honey, ... Ex 3:8
he was cut off out of the **l** of the living, ... Is 53:8
and that you may live long in the **l**." ...... Eph 6:3
faith he went to live in the **l** of promise, . Heb 11:9

LANGUAGE

LORD confused the **l** of all the earth........ Gn 11:9
was hearing them speak in his own **l**. ..... Acts 2:6

LANGUAGES

peoples, nations, and **l** should serve him;.. Dn 7:14
all tribes and peoples and **l**, standing .....Rv 7:9

LAST

"I am the first and I am the **l**; .... Is 44:6
But many who are first will be **l**, ... Mt 19:30
he must be **l** of all and servant of all." ... Mk 9:35
I will raise him up on the **l** day." .... Jn 6:40
the **l** Adam became a life-giving ...... 1 Cor 15:45
in the **l** days there will come times .... 2 Tm 3:1
You have laid up treasure in the **l** days.... Jas 5:3
ready to be revealed in the **l** time. ...... 1 Pt 1:5
"In the **l** time there will be scoffers, ...Jude 18
"Fear not, I am the first and the **l**, ... Rv 1:17

LAUGH

time to weep, and a time to **l**; .... Eccl 3:4
are you who weep now, for you shall **l** .... Lk 6:21

LAUGHTER

Sarah said, "God has made **l** for me; ......Gn 21:6
Even in **l** the heart may ache, and the ... Prv 14:13
Sorrow is better than **l**, for by sadness ... Eccl 7:3
Let your **l** be turned to mourning and........ Jas 4:9

LAW

Then Moses wrote this **l** and gave it ...... Dt 31:9
his delight is in the **l** of the LORD, ... Ps 1:2
The **l** of the LORD is perfect, ... Ps 19:7
Oh how I love your **l**! It is my .... Ps 119:97
for this is the **L** and the Prophets. .... Mt 7:12
depend all the **L** and the Prophets." ..... Mt 22:40
for one dot of the **L** to become void.... Lk 16:17
the **l** was given through Moses; grace ..... Jn 1:17
by faith apart from works of the **l**. ...... Rom 3:28
For the **l** brings wrath, but where .... Rom 4:15
Now the **l** came in to increase the ...... Rom 5:20
So the **l** is holy, and the commandment ... Rom 7:12
For Christ is the end of the **l** for .... Rom 10:4
therefore love is the fulfilling of the **l**. ... Rom 13:10
To those under the **l** I became as........ 1 Cor 9:20
is sin, and the power of sin is the **l**..... 1 Cor 15:56
not justified by works of the **l** but .... Gal 2:16
by the Spirit, you are not under the **l**. ..... Gal 5:18
(for the **l** made nothing perfect); but ..... Heb 7:19
the perfect **l**, the **l** of liberty, ...Jas 1:25

LAWLESS

And then the **l** one will be revealed, ... 2 Thes 2:8
not laid down for the just but for the **l** ... 1 Tm 1:9

righteous soul over their l deeds that ......2 Pt 2:8

LAWLESSNESS
and the man of l is revealed, ... 2 Thes 2:3
For the mystery of l is already at work. . 2 Thes 2:7
sinning also practices l; sin is l. .... 1 Jn 3:4

LAY
and I I down my life for the sheep......... Jn 10:15
I down his life for his friends. .... Jn 15:13
and we ought to l down our lives for .... 1 Jn 3:16

LAYING
Do not be hasty in the l on of hands, ... 1 Tm 5:22
in you through the l on of my hands, ... 2 Tm 1:6

LAZARUS
his gate was laid a poor man named L, . Lk 16:20
a certain man was ill, L of Bethany, ...Jn 11:1

LEAD
L me in your truth and teach me, ... Ps 25:5
And l us not into temptation, ... Mt 6:13
And if the blind l the blind, both .... Mt 15:14
perform signs and wonders, to l astray, . Mk 13:22

LEADS
He l me beside still waters. .... Ps 23:2
The fear of the LORD l to life, ... Prv 19:23
"See that no one l you astray. .... Mk 13:5

LEAH
he loved Rachel more than L, ... Gn 29:30

LEAN
do not l on your own understanding. .... Prv 3:5

LEARN
l to do good; seek justice, correct .... Is 1:17
l from me, for I am gentle .... Mt 11:29

LEARNED
for I have l in whatever situation I am .... Phil 4:11

LEARNING
always l and never able to arrive at ...... 2 Tm 3:7

LEAST
Yet the one who is l in the kingdom .... Mt 11:11
it to one of the l of these my brothers, . Mt 25:40
For I am the l of the apostles, ... 1 Cor 15:9

LEAVEN
day you shall remove l out of your ...... Ex 12:15
of heaven is like l that a woman took .. Mt 13:33
and beware of the l of the Pharisees ..... Mt 16:6
A little l leavens the whole lump. ....Gal 5:9

LED
I have l you in the paths of uprightness.. Prv 4:11
Jesus was l up by the Spirit into the .... Mt 4:1
For all who are l by the Spirit of God .... Rom 8:14

LEFT
on his right, but the goats on the l. ...... Mt 25:33

LEGION
He replied, "My name is L, ... Mk 5:9

LEND
him and l him sufficient for his need, ... Dt 15:8
love your enemies, and do good, and l, ... Lk 6:35
'Friend, l me three loaves, ... Lk 11:5

LENDS
the man who deals generously and l; ..... Ps 112:5
generous to the poor l to the LORD, ... Prv 19:17

LENGTH
for l of days and years of life and peace ... Prv 3:2
all the saints what is the breadth and l . Eph 3:18

LEPER
a l came to him and knelt before him, ... Mt 8:2
at Bethany in the house of Simon the l, . Mt 26:6

LEPERS
these l came to the edge of the camp, .. 2 Kgs 7:8
Heal the sick, raise the dead, cleanse l, ... Mt 10:8
And there were many l in Israel in the ..... Lk 4:27

entered a village, he was met by ten l, .. Lk 17:12

LEPROSY
Therefore the l of Naaman shall cling ...2 Kgs 5:27
And immediately his l was cleansed. .... Mt 8:3

LETTER
For the l kills, but the Spirit gives life... 2 Cor 3:6
does not obey what we say in this l, .. 2 Thes 3:14

LETTERS
For they say, "His l are weighty and .. 2 Cor 10:10
as he does in all his l when he speaks .. 2 Pt 3:16

LEVEL
the path of the upright is a l highway... Prv 15:19
The path of the righteous is l; .... Is 26:7

LEVI
Therefore his name was called L. .... Gn 29:34
And L made him a great feast in his .... Lk 5:29

LIAR
and a poor man is better than a l. .... Prv 19:22
for he is a l and the father of lies. .... Jn 8:44
God be true though every one were a l, .. Rom 3:4
have not sinned, we make him a l, ... 1 Jn 1:10

LIBERTY
to proclaim l to the captives, ... Is 61:1
For why should my l be determined ... 1 Cor 10:29
the law of l, and perseveres, being no ....Jas 1:25

LIE
you shall not l to one another. .... Lv 19:11
God is not man, that he should l, ... Nm 23:19
A faithful witness does not l, ... Prv 14:5
filled your heart to l to the Holy Spirit ....Acts 5:3
truth about God for a l and worshiped .. Rom 1:25
Do not l to one another, seeing ....Col 3:9
it is impossible for God to l, ... Heb 6:18

LIES
he who breathes out l will not escape. ... Prv 19:5
of eternal life, which God, who never l, ...Ti 1:2

LIFE
into his nostrils the breath of l, ... Gn 2:7
Therefore choose l, that you and your .... Dt 30:19
shall follow me all the days of my l, ... Ps 23:6
The years of our l are seventy, ... Ps 90:10
Long l is in her right hand; .... Prv 3:16
For whoever finds me finds l and ...... Prv 8:35
will find l, righteousness, and honor. ..... Prv 21:21
do not be anxious about your l, ... Mt 6:25
Whoever finds his l will lose it, ... Mt 10:39
to give his l as a ransom for many." ..... Mt 20:28
In him was l, and the l was the light......... Jn 1:4
"I am the bread of l; whoever comes .....Jn 6:35
whoever believes has eternal l. ....Jn 6:47
It is the Spirit who gives l; ....Jn 6:63
"I am the resurrection and the l .... Jn 11:25
"I am the way, and the truth, and the l....Jn 14:6
this is eternal l, that they know you, ... Jn 17:3
were appointed to eternal l believed. ...Acts 13:48
who gives l to the dead and calls .... Rom 4:17
gift of God is eternal l in Christ .... Rom 6:23
I am sure that neither death nor l, ... Rom 8:38
lead the l that the Lord has assigned ... 1 Cor 7:17
If in Christ we have hope in this l .... 1 Cor 15:19
And the l I now live in the flesh I .... Gal 2:20
holding fast to the word of l, ... Phil 2:16
When Christ who is your l appears, ... Col 3:4
we may lead a peaceful and quiet l, ... 1 Tm 2:2
Take hold of the eternal l to .... 1 Tm 6:12
desire to live a godly l in Christ .... 2 Tm 3:12
in hope of eternal l, which God, who ....Ti 1:2
heirs according to the hope of eternal l......Ti 3:7
What is your l? For you are a mist ....Jas 4:14
"Whoever desires to love l and see ...... 1 Pt 3:10
granted to us all things that pertain to l .. 2 Pt 1:3
we have passed out of death into l, ... 1 Jn 3:14
Whoever has the Son has l; .... 1 Jn 5:12
was opened, which is the book of l. ...... Rv 20:12

are written in the Lamb's book of l........Rv 21:27

LIFT
To you, O LORD, I l up my soul. .... Ps 25:1

LIFTED
he shall be high and l up, and shall be ... Is 52:13
so must the Son of Man be l up, ...Jn 3:14
And I, when I am l up from the earth, ... Jn 12:32

LIGHT
And God said, "Let there be l," .... Gn 1:3
Lift up the l of your face upon us, ... Ps 4:6
I may walk before God in the l of life. ... Ps 56:13
a lamp to my feet and a l to my path. . Ps 119:105
let us walk in the l of the LORD. .... Is 2:5
walked in darkness have seen a great l; ..... Is 9:2
I will make you as a l for the nations, ... Is 49:6
Arise, shine, for your l has come, ... Is 60:1
the LORD will be your everlasting l, ... Is 60:20
in darkness have seen a great l, ... Mt 4:16
"You are the l of the world. A city .... Mt 5:14
let your l shine before others, ... Mt 5:16
The l shines in the darkness, and the .... Jn 1:5
the l has come into the world, ...Jn 3:19
"I am the l of the world. ....Jn 8:12
"I have made you a l for the Gentiles, .Acts 13:47
Walk as children of l .... Eph 5:8
who dwells in unapproachable l, ... 1 Tm 6:16
out of darkness into his marvelous l. ...... 1 Pt 2:9
loves his brother abides in the l, ... 1 Jn 2:10
or sun, for the Lord God will be their l, ... Rv 22:5

LIGHTNING
his face like the appearance of l, ... Dn 10:6
For as the l comes from the east .... Mt 24:27
His appearance was like l, ... Mt 28:3

LIGHTS
"Let there be l in the expanse of the .... Gn 1:14
whom you shine as l in the world, ... Phil 2:15

LIKENESS
he made him in the l of God. .... Gn 5:1
carved image, or any l of anything .... Ex 20:4
liken God, or what l compare with him? .. Is 40:18
his own Son in the l of sinful flesh .... Rom 8:3
created after the l of God in true .... Eph 4:24
a servant, being born in the l of men. ..... Phil 2:7

LILIES
Consider the l of the field, how they ......Mt 6:28

LINTEL
sees the blood on the l and on the two .. Ex 12:23

LION
the honey from the carcass of the l. .....Jgs 14:9
And when there came a l, or a bear, ... 1 Sm 17:34
and the l shall eat straw like the ox. .... Is 11:7
first was like a l and had eagles' wings. ... Dn 7:4
devil prowls around like a roaring l, ... 1 Pt 5:8
behold, the L of the tribe of Judah, ... Rv 5:5

LIPS
In all this Job did not sin with his l ....Jb 2:10
for I am a man of unclean l, and l .... Is 6:5
fruit of l that acknowledge his name... Heb 13:15

LISTEN
to my prayer; l to my plea for grace. ...... Ps 86:6
To draw near to l is better than to .... Eccl 5:1
whom I am well pleased; l to him." ...... Mt 17:5
and they will l to my voice. .... Jn 10:16

LISTENS
The ear that l to life-giving reproof ...... Prv 15:31
who is of the truth l to my voice." ...... Jn 18:37
Whoever knows God l to us; .... 1 Jn 4:6

LITTLE
Better is the l that the righteous has .... Ps 37:16
more clothe you, O you of l faith? .... Mt 6:30
"Let the l children come to me .... Mt 19:14
should cause one of these l ones to sin.... Lk 17:2
L children, keep yourselves from idols. ... 1 Jn 5:21

LIVE

the tree of life and eat, and I forever—" . . . Gn 3:22
for man shall not see me and I." . . . . Ex 33:20
keep my commandments, and I. . . . . Prv 4:4
but the righteous shall I by his faith. . . . . . Hab 2:4
"'Man shall not I by bread alone, ... Mt 4:4
though he die, yet shall he I, ... Jn 11:25
does not I in temples made by man, ... Acts 17:24
"'in him we I and move and have . . . . . Acts 17:28
"The righteous shall I by faith." . . . . Rom 1:17
depends on you, I peaceably with all. . . . Rom 12:18
For if we I, we I to the Lord, ... Rom 14:8
might no longer I for themselves . . . . 2 Cor 5:15
It is no longer I who I, but Christ . . . . Gal 2:20
If we I by the Spirit, let us also keep in . . . Gal 5:25
For to me to I is Christ, ... Phil 1:21
I as people who are free, not using . . . . . . 1 Pt 2:16
so that we might I through him. . . . . 1 Jn 4:9

LIVES

For I know that my Redeemer I, ... Jb 19:25
The LORD I, and blessed be my rock, ... Ps 18:46
but the life he I he I to God. . . . . Rom 6:10
I who live, but Christ who I in me. . . . . Gal 2:20
since he always I to make intercession . . . Heb 7:25

LIVING

My soul thirsts for God, for the I God. . . . . Ps 42:2
On that day I waters shall flow out . . . . . . Zec 14:8
not God of the dead, but of the I." . . . . . . Mt 22:32
do you seek the I among the dead? . . . . . . Lk 24:5
to present your bodies as a I sacrifice, . . . Rom 12:1
proclaim the gospel should get their I . . . 1 Cor 9:14
For we are the temple of the I God; . . . . . 2 Cor 6:16
we have our hope set on the I God, ... 1 Tm 4:10
For the word of God is I and active, ... Heb 4:12
like I stones are being built up as a . . . . . . 1 Pt 2:5

LOAVES

command these stones to become I . . . . . . Mt 4:3
only five I here and two fish." . . . . Mt 14:17
but because you ate your fill of the I. . . . . Jn 6:26

LOCKED

Although the doors were I, Jesus came . . . Jn 20:26
the prison securely I and the guards . . . . Acts 5:23

LOCUST

years that the swarming I has eaten, ... Jl 2:25

LOCUSTS

The I came up over all the land of . . . . . . Ex 10:14
and his food was I and wild honey. . . . . . . Mt 3:4

LONELY

gracious to me, for I am I and afflicted. . . Ps 25:16
I am like a I sparrow on the housetop. . . . Ps 102:7
How I sits the city that was full of . . . . Lam 1:1

LONG

that your days may be I in the land . . . . . Ex 20:12
I life is in her right hand; . . . . Prv 3:16
how I before you will judge and . . . . Rv 6:10

LONGING

O Lord, all my I is before you; . . . . Ps 38:9
For he satisfies the I soul, ... Ps 107:9
creation waits with eager I for the . . . . . Rom 8:19
For in this tent we groan, I to put on . . . . 2 Cor 5:2

LOOK

Let your eyes I directly forward, ... Prv 4:25
is to come, or shall we I for another?" . . . . Mt 11:3
says to you, 'L, here is the Christ!' . . . . . . Mk 13:21
as we I not to the things that are seen . . . 2 Cor 4:18
Let each of you I not only to his own . . . . Phil 2:4

LORD (LORD; Hb. Yahweh)

day that the L God made the earth and . . . Gn 2:4
And he believed the L, and he counted . . . Gn 15:6
the L hardened the heart of Pharaoh, ... Ex 9:12
"I am the L your God, who brought . . . . . . Ex 20:2
shall be filled with the glory of the L, . . . Nm 14:21
If the L is God, follow him; but if . . . . 1 Kgs 18:21

But the L was gracious to them . . . . 2 Kgs 13:23
"You are the L, you alone. You have . . . . . . Neh 9:6
The L is my chosen portion and my cup; . . . Ps 16:5
For who is God, but the L? . . . . Ps 18:31
The L is my shepherd; I shall not . . . . Ps 23:1
the L, the Most High, is to be feared, ... Ps 47:2
"I am the L, and there is no other. . . . . . . Is 45:18
"I the L search the heart . . . . Jer 17:10
to you who desire the day of the L! . . . . . Am 5:18
The L is slow to anger and great in . . . . . . Na 1:3
But the L is in his holy temple; let all . . . Hab 2:20
great and awesome day of the L comes. . . Mal 4:5

LORD (Lord; Hb. 'Adonay)

to you, O L, belongs steadfast love. . . . . . Ps 62:12
For you, O L, are good and forgiving, ... Ps 86:5
Great is our L, and abundant in power; . . . Ps 147:5
I saw the L sitting upon a throne, high . . . Is 6:1

LORD (Lord; Gk. Kyrios)

who says to me, 'L, L,' . . . . Mt 7:21
"You shall love the L your God with . . . . . Mt 22:37
The L our God, the L is one. . . . . Mk 12:29
"Why do you call me 'L, L,' and not . . . . . Lk 6:46
be L both of the dead and of the living. . . Rom 14:9
"Jesus is L" except in the Holy Spirit. . . . 1 Cor 12:3
Finally, my brothers, rejoice in the L. . . . . Phil 3:1
heartily, as for the L and not for men, . . . Col 3:23
without which no one will see the L. . . . . . Heb 12:14
written, King of kings and L of lords. . . . . . Rv 19:16

LORD'S (LORD's; Hb. Yahweh)

But the L portion is his people, ... Dt 32:9
The earth is the L and the fullness . . . . . . Ps 24:1
do not despise the L discipline or be . . . . Prv 3:11

LORD'S (Lord's; Gk. Kyrios)

live or whether we die, we are the L. . . . . Rom 14:8
you proclaim the L death until he . . . . . 1 Cor 11:26

LOSE

For it is better that you I one of your . . . . Mt 5:29
to Christ will by no means I his reward. . . Mk 9:41
that I should I nothing of all that he . . . . . Jn 6:39
So we do not I heart. Though our . . . . . . 2 Cor 4:16

LOSES

and whoever I his life for my sake will . . . Mt 10:39
ten silver coins, if she I one coin, ... Lk 15:8

LOSS

burned up, he will suffer I, though . . . . . 1 Cor 3:15

LOST

For I am I; for I am a man of unclean . . . . . Is 6:5
"My people have been I sheep. . . . . Jer 50:6
I will seek the I, and I will bring . . . . . . Ezk 34:16
"I was sent only to the I sheep of . . . . . . Mt 15:24
hundred sheep, if he has I one of them, . . Lk 15:4
and is alive; he was I, and is found.'" . . . . Lk 15:32
came to seek and to save the I." . . . . Lk 19:10
whom you gave me I have I not one." . . . . Jn 18:9

LOT

L chose for himself all the Jordan . . . . Gn 13:11
The L is cast into the lap, but its every . . . Prv 16:33
So they cast lots, and the L fell on Jonah. . . Jon 1:7
and if he rescued righteous L, greatly . . . . 2 Pt 2:7

LOTS

and for my clothing they cast I. . . . . Ps 22:18
garments among them by casting I. . . . . . . Mt 27:35

LOVE

but showing steadfast I to thousands . . . . Ex 20:6
to anger, and abounding in steadfast I . . . Ex 34:6
but you shall I your neighbor as . . . . Lv 19:18
I I you, O LORD, my strength. . . . . Ps 18:1
Your steadfast I, O LORD, extends . . . . Ps 36:5
I I the LORD, because he has . . . . Ps 116:1
but my steadfast I shall not depart. . . . . . Is 54:10
The steadfast I of the LORD never . . . . Lam 3:22
Hate evil, and I good, and establish . . . . . Am 5:15
you who hate the good and I the evil, ... Mi 3:2

But I say to you, L your enemies . . . . Mt 5:44
"You shall I the Lord your God with . . . . . Mt 22:37
even sinners I those who I . . . . Lk 6:32
Greater I has no one than this, ... Jn 15:13
"Simon, son of John, do you I me?" . . . . . Jn 21:16
but God shows his I for us in that . . . . Rom 5:8
Let I be genuine. Abhor what is evil; . . . . Rom 12:9
L does no wrong to a neighbor; . . . . Rom 13:10
L is patient and kind; . . . . 1 Cor 13:4
three; but the greatest of these is I. . . . . 1 Cor 13:13
Let all that you do be done in I. . . . . 1 Cor 16:14
For the I of Christ controls us, ... 2 Cor 5:14
but only faith working through I. . . . . Gal 5:6
the fruit of the Spirit is I, joy, peace, ... Gal 5:22
speaking the truth in I, we are to grow . . . Eph 4:15
my prayer that your I may abound more . . Phil 1:9
but of power and I and self-control. . . . . . 2 Tm 1:7
how to stir up one another to I and . . . . Heb 10:24
Let brotherly I continue. . . . . Heb 13:1
"You shall I your neighbor as yourself," . . Jas 2:8
since I covers a multitude of sins. . . . . 1 Pt 4:8
See what kind of I the Father has given . . . 1 Jn 3:1
let us not I in word or talk but in deed . . . 1 Jn 3:18
Beloved, let us I one another, for I . . . . . . 1 Jn 4:7
God is I, and whoever abides in I . . . . . . 1 Jn 4:16
but perfect I casts out fear. . . . . 1 Jn 4:18
keep yourselves in the I of God, ... Jude 21
have abandoned the I you had at first. . . . Rv 2:4
Those whom I I, I reprove and . . . . Rv 3:19

LOVED

I have I you with an everlasting love; . . . . Jer 31:3
"For God so I the world, that he gave . . . . Jn 3:16
just as I have I you, you also are to . . . . . Jn 13:34
As the Father has I me, so have I I you. . . . Jn 15:9
than conquerors through him who I us. . . . Rom 8:37
who I me and gave himself for me. . . . . . . Gal 2:20
of the great love with which he I us, ... Eph 2:4
who I us and gave us eternal comfort . . . 2 Thes 2:16
We love because he first I us. . . . . 1 Jn 4:19

LOVELY

How I is your dwelling place, ... Ps 84:1
whatever is pure, whatever is I, ... Phil 4:8

LOVER

therefore hear this, you I of pleasures, . . . Is 47:8
but hospitable, a I of good, ... Ti 1:8

LOVERS

be I of self, I of money, proud, ... 2 Tm 3:2
I of pleasure rather than I of God, ... 2 Tm 3:4

LOVES

but it is because the Lord I you . . . . Dt 7:8
the LORD reproves him whom he I, ... Prv 3:12
He who I money will not be satisfied . . . . Eccl 5:10
Whoever I father or mother more than . . . Mt 10:37
But he who is forgiven little, I little." . . . . Lk 7:47
And he who I me will be loved by my . . . Jn 14:21
But if anyone I God, he is known by . . . . 1 Cor 8:3
for God I a cheerful giver. . . . . 2 Cor 9:7
He who I his wife I himself. . . . . Eph 5:28
For the Lord disciplines the one he I, ... Heb 12:6
the world, the love of the Father is not . . . 1 Jn 2:15
whoever I God must also love his . . . . 1 Jn 4:21

LOW

God chose what is I and despised. . . . . . 1 Cor 1:28
I know how to be brought I, ... Phil 4:12

LOWLY

the LORD is high, he regards the I, ... Ps 138:6
Better to be I and have a servant than . . . Prv 12:9
he who is I in spirit will obtain honor. . . . Prv 29:23
Let the I brother boast in his exaltation, . . Jas 1:9

LUKE

L the beloved physician greets you, as . . . Col 4:14
L alone is with me. Get Mark and . . . . 2 Tm 4:11

LUKEWARM

So, because you are I, and neither hot . . . . Rv 3:16

LUST

treacherous are taken captive by their **l**... Prv 11:6
not in the passion of **l** like the Gentiles . 1 Thes 4:5

LUSTFUL

looks at a woman with **l** intent............. Mt 5:28

LUXURY

It is not fitting for a fool to live in **l**,...... Prv 19:10
on the earth in **l** and in self-indulgence.... Jas 5:5

LYING

You search out my path and my **l** down .. Ps 139:3
L lips are an abomination to the LORD, .. Prv 12:22

MACEDONIA

"Come over to **M** and help us." .... Acts 16:9

MADE

in six days the Lord **m** heaven and .... Ex 31:17
In wisdom have you **m** them all; the ... Ps 104:24
for I am fearfully and wonderfully **m**.... Ps 139:14
All these things my hand has **m**, and ...... Is 66:2
It is you who have **m** the heavens .... Jer 32:17
All things were **m** through him, and .... Jn 1:3
Christ Jesus has **m** me his own. .... Phil 3:12

MAGNIFY

Oh, **m** the LORD with me, and let .... Ps 34:3
I will **m** him with thanksgiving............ Ps 69:30

MAGOG

I will send fire on **M** and on those .... Ezk 39:6
four corners of the earth, Gog and **M**,... Rv 20:8

MAJESTIC

how **m** is your name in all the earth!...... Ps 8:1
was borne to him by the **M** Glory,........ 2 Pt 1:17

MAJESTY

"Adorn yourself with **m** and dignity; ...... Jb 40:10
On the glorious splendor of your **m**, ... Ps 145:5
he had no form or **m** that we should ...... Is 53:2
all were astonished at the **m** of God. ...... Lk 9:43
hand of the throne of the **M** in heaven, .. Heb 8:1
but we were eyewitnesses of his **m**. ..... 2 Pt 1:16
be glory, **m**, dominion, and authority, ... Jude 25

MAKE

"You shall not **m** for yourself a carved .. Ex 20:4
how will you **m** it salty again? .... Mk 9:50
and take him by force to **m** him king,...... Jn 6:15
come to him and **m** our home with him. . Jn 14:23
m every effort to supplement your faith .. 2 Pt 1:5

MAKER

kneel before the LORD, our **M**! .... Ps 95:6
the LORD is the **M** of them all. .... Prv 22:2
say of its **m**, "He did not make me"; ...... Is 29:16
forgotten the LORD, your **M**, ... Is 51:13
For its **m** trusts in his own creation ...... Hab 2:18

MALE

m and female he created them. .... Gn 1:27
If a man lies with a **m** as with .... Lv 20:13
beginning made them **m** and female, ... Mt 19:4
nor free, there is no **m** and female, ... Gal 3:28

MALICE

covetousness, **m**. They are full of envy, .. Rom 1:29
put away from you, along with all **m**...... Eph 4:31
anger, wrath, **m**, slander, and obscene .. Col 3:8
So put away all **m** and all deceit and .... 1 Pt 2:1

MAN

God said, "Let us make **m** in our image, . Gn 1:26
because she was taken out of **M**." .... Gn 2:23
sought out a **m** after his own heart, ... 1 Sm 13:14
what is **m** that you are mindful of him, ... Ps 8:4
a cool spirit is a **m** of understanding. ... Prv 17:27
nest is a **m** who strays from his home... Prv 27:8
that a **m** should rejoice in his work ...... Eccl 3:22
heaven there came one like a son of **m**,.. Dn 7:13
for the Son of **M** is coming at an hour ... Mt 24:44
'**M** shall not live by bread alone.'" .... Lk 4:4
and descending on the Son of **M**." .... Jn 1:51

came into the world through one **m**, ... Rom 5:12
each **m** should have his own wife ...... 1 Cor 7:2
the head of every **m** is Christ, ... 1 Cor 11:3
When I became a **m**, I gave up .... 1 Cor 13:11
that the **m** of God may be complete, ... 2 Tm 3:17
as it is appointed for **m** to die once, ... Heb 9:27
I will not fear; what can **m** do to me?".. Heb 13:6

MANAGE

not know how to **m** his own household, . 1 Tm 3:5
bear children, **m** their households, ... 1 Tm 5:14

MANASSEH

the name of the firstborn **M**. .... Gn 41:51
"Because **M** king of Judah has ...... 2 Kgs 21:11

MANGER

in swaddling cloths and laid him in a **m**, ... Lk 2:7

MANIFEST

is hidden that will not be made **m**, ... Lk 8:17
but was made **m** in the last times ...... 1 Pt 1:20
life was made **m**, and we have seen ...... 1 Jn 1:2

MANIFESTED

He was **m** in the flesh, vindicated by .. 1 Tm 3:16
and at the proper time **m** in his word ...... Ti 1:3

MANNA

house of Israel called its name **m**. ...... Ex 16:31
is nothing at all but this **m** to look at.".. Nm 11:6
Our fathers ate the **m** in the wilderness; .. Jn 6:31
I will give some of the hidden **m**, ... Rv 2:17

MANNER

in an unworthy **m** will be guilty ...... 1 Cor 11:27
urge you to walk in a **m** worthy of ...... Eph 4:1
Only let your **m** of life be worthy of ..... Phil 1:27
as to walk in a **m** worthy of the Lord, ... Col 1:10

MARK

And the LORD put a **m** on Cain, ... Gn 4:15
Barnabas took **M** with him and ...... Acts 15:39
Get **M** and bring him with you, for he .. 2 Tm 4:11
can buy or sell unless he has the **m**, ... Rv 13:17

MARKS

for I bear on my body the **m** of Jesus. .... Gal 6:17

MARRIAGE

they neither marry nor are given in, ... Mt 22:30
drinking, marrying and giving in **m**, ... Mt 24:38
he who refrains from **m** will do even .. 1 Cor 7:38
Let **m** be held in honor among all, ... Heb 13:4
for the **m** of the Lamb has come, ... Rv 19:7

MARRIED

For a **m** woman is bound by law to ...... Rom 7:2
To the **m** I give this charge (not I, ... 1 Cor 7:10
But the **m** man is anxious about .... 1 Cor 7:33

MARRY

with his wife, it is better not to **m**." ...... Mt 19:10
resurrection they neither **m** nor are ...... Mt 22:30
For it is better to **m** than to burn ...... 1 Cor 7:9
Yet those who **m** will have worldly...... 1 Cor 7:28
So I would have younger widows **m**, ... 1 Tm 5:14

MARTHA

But **M** was distracted with much ...... Lk 10:40
M said to him, "I know that he will rise .. Jn 11:24

MARTYRS

the saints, the blood of the **m** of Jesus.... Rv 17:6

MARVELOUS

a new song, for he has done **m** things! .. Ps 98:1
with things too great and too **m** for me. . Ps 131:1
Lord's doing, and it is **m** in our eyes'? ... Mt 21:42

MARY

they saw the child with **M** his mother, ... Mt 2:11
among whom were **M** Magdalene and ... Mt 27:56
he appeared first to **M** Magdalene, ... Mk 16:9
And the virgin's name was **M**.............. Lk 1:27
M, for you have found favor with God. ... Lk 1:30
M said, "My soul magnifies the .... Lk 1:46

M treasured up all these things, ... Lk 2:19
M has chosen the good portion, ... Lk 10:42
M therefore took a pound of expensive .... Jn 12:3
M stood weeping outside the tomb, ... Jn 20:11
M the mother of Jesus, and his brothers. .. Acts 1:14

MASTER

nor a servant above his **m**................. Mt 10:24
M, we are perishing!" And he awoke ...... Lk 8:24
It is before his own **m** that he .... Rom 14:4
he who is both their **M** and yours is ...... Eph 6:9
you also have a **M** in heaven.............. Col 4:1

MASTERS

"No one can serve two **m**, for either ...... Mt 6:24
M, do the same to them, and stop your .. Eph 6:9
earthly **m**, not by way of eye-service, ... Col 3:22
be subject to your **m** with all respect, ... 1 Pt 2:18

MATTHEW

a man called **M** sitting at the tax booth, ... Mt 9:9

MATURE

Yet among the **m** we do impart .... 1 Cor 2:6
but in your thinking be **m**. .... 1 Cor 14:20
to **m** manhood, to the measure of ...... Eph 4:13
Let those of us who are **m** think this ..... Phil 3:15
we may present everyone **m** in Christ. ... Col 1:28
But solid food is for the **m**, for those ..... Heb 5:14

MEASURE

a full and fair **m** you shall have, ... Dt 25:15
what is the **m** of my days; .... Ps 39:4
and with the **m** you use it will be ...... Mt 7:2
for he gives the Spirit without **m**. .... Jn 3:34
the **m** of faith that God has assigned. ... Rom 12:3
us according to the **m** of Christ's gift. .... Eph 4:7

MEAT

"Oh that we had **m** to eat!" .... Nm 11:4
brother stumble, I will never eat **m**, ... 1 Cor 8:13
sold in the **m** market without raising . 1 Cor 10:25

MEDIATES

the covenant he **m** is better, since it ...... Heb 8:6

MEDIATOR

and there is one **m** between God and .. 1 Tm 2:5
Therefore he is the **m** of a new .... Heb 9:15
Jesus, the **m** of a new covenant, ... Heb 12:24

MEDITATE

but you shall **m** on it day and night,...... Jos 1:8
I **m** on all that you have done;.......... Ps 143:5

MEDITATION

of my mouth and the **m** of my heart be .. Ps 19:14
May my **m** be pleasing to him, for I ...... Ps 104:34
I love your law! It is my **m** all the day. .. Ps 119:97

MEDIUM

woman who is a **m** or a necromancer ... Lv 20:27
"Behold, there is a **m** at En-dor." .... 1 Sm 28:7

MEEK

Now the man Moses was very **m**, ... Nm 12:3
But the **m** shall inherit the land and ..... Ps 37:11
"Blessed are the **m**, for they shall .... Mt 5:5

MEEKNESS

kindness, humility, and patience, ... Col 3:12
and receive with **m** the implanted word, . Jas 1:21

MEET

Steadfast love and faithfulness **m**; ...... Ps 85:10
prepare to **m** your God, ... Am 4:12
not neglecting to **m** together, as is ...... Heb 10:25

MELCHIZEDEK

And **M** king of Salem brought out ...... Gn 14:18
a priest forever after the order of **M**." .... Ps 110:4
For this **M**, king of Salem, priest of the ... Heb 7:1

MELODY

I will sing and make **m** to the LORD........ Ps 27:6
singing and making **m** to the Lord .... Eph 5:19

MELT
heavenly bodies will m as they burn! ...... 2 Pt 3:12

MEMBERS
For as in one body we have many m, ... Rom 12:4
that your bodies are m of Christ? ...... 1 Cor 6:15
God arranged the m in the body, ... 1 Cor 12:18
for we are m one of another. ...... Eph 4:25

MEN
was life, and the life was the light of m ...... Jn 1:4
"We must obey God rather than m. ...... Acts 5:29
spread to all m because all sinned— ...... Rom 5:12
stand firm in the faith, act like m, ... 1 Cor 16:13
not as the word of m but as what it .. 1 Thes 2:13
Older m are to be sober-minded, ... Ti 2:2
the younger m to be self-controlled. ...... Ti 2:6
but m spoke from God as they were ...... 2 Pt 1:21

MERCIES
ceases; his m never come to an end; ...... Lam 3:22
the Father of m and God of all comfort, . 2 Cor 1:3

MERCIFUL
For the LORD your God is a m ...... Dt 4:31
The LORD is m and gracious, ... Ps 103:8
"Blessed are the m, for they shall ...... Mt 5:7
Be m, even as your Father is m. ...... Lk 6:36
For I will be m toward their iniquities, ... Heb 8:12
how the Lord is compassionate and m. .. Jas 5:11

MERCY
"You shall make a m seat of pure gold. . Ex 25:17
Have m on me, O God, according to ...... Ps 51:1
'I desire m, and not sacrifice.' ...... Mt 12:7
because of the tender m of our God, .. Lk 1:78
have m on whom I have m, ... Rom 9:15
But God, being rich in m, because ...... Eph 2:4
but according to his own m, by the ...... Ti 3:5
of glory overshadowing the m seat. ...... Heb 9:5
M triumphs over judgment. ...... Jas 2:13
According to his great m, he has ...... 1 Pt 1:3
but now you have received m. ...... 1 Pt 2:10

MESSAGE
entrusting to us the m of reconciliation. .... 2 Cor 5:19
through me the m might be fully ...... 2 Tm 4:17
This is the m we have heard from him .. 1 Jn 1:5

MESSIAH
"We have found the M" ...... Jn 1:41
"I know that M is coming ...... Jn 4:25

METHUSELAH
Thus all the days of M were 969 years, ... Gn 5:27

MICHAEL
withstood me twenty-one days, but M, .. Dn 10:13
"At that time shall arise M, the great ... Dn 12:1
But when the archangel M, contending .. Jude 9
Now war arose in heaven, M and his ...... Rv 12:7

MIGHT
with all your soul and with all your m. ...... Dt 6:5
But I say that wisdom is better than m, . Eccl 9:16
Not by m, nor by power, but by my ...... Zec 4:6

MIGHTY
with a m hand and redeemed ...... Dt 7:8
How the m have fallen! ...... 2 Sm 1:19
who is m as you are, O LORD, ... Ps 89:8
Wonderful Counselor, M God, ... Is 9:6
a m one who will save; ...... Zep 3:17
under the m hand of God so that at .... 1 Pt 5:6

MILE
And if anyone forces you to go one m, . Mt 5:41

MILK
I fed you with m, not solid food, for .. 1 Cor 3:2
You need m, not solid food, ... Heb 5:12
long for the pure spiritual m, that by it .. 1 Pt 2:2

MIND
that he should change his m. ...... Nm 23:19

peace whose m is stayed on you, ... Is 26:3
with all your soul and with all your m. . Mt 22:37
serve the law of God with my m, ... Rom 7:25
but to set the m on the Spirit is life ...... Rom 8:6
who has known the m of the Lord, ... Rom 11:34
transformed by the renewal of your m, . Rom 12:2
But we have the m of Christ. ...... 1 Cor 2:16
spirit, but I will pray with my m also; . 1 Cor 14:15
Have this m among yourselves, ... Phil 2:5
quietly, and to m your own affairs, .. 1 Thes 4:11
has sworn and will not change his m, ... Heb 7:21

MINDFUL
what is man that you are m of him, ... Ps 8:4
"What is man, that you are m of him, ... Heb 2:6

MINDS
set their m on the things of the Spirit. ... Rom 8:5
has blinded the m of the unbelievers, .. 2 Cor 4:4
to be renewed in the spirit of your m, . Eph 4:23
Set your m on things that are above, ... Col 3:2
I will put my laws into their m, and ...... Heb 8:10
preparing your m for action, ... 1 Pt 1:13

MINISTRY
to prayer and to the m of the word." ...... Acts 6:4
and gave us the m of reconciliation; .. 2 Cor 5:18
work of an evangelist, fulfill your m, ... 2 Tm 4:5
Christ has obtained a m that is as much .. Heb 8:6

MIRACLES
works that he has done, his m, ... Ps 105:5
seeing signs and great m performed, . Acts 8:13
to another the working of m, to ...... 1 Cor 12:10
to you and works m among you do so .... Gal 3:5
wonders and various m and by gifts ...... Heb 2:4

MIRIAM
M sang to them: "Sing to the LORD, ... Ex 15:21
M and Aaron spoke against Moses ...... Nm 12:1

MIRROR
For now we see in a m dimly, but .. 1 Cor 13:12
looks intently at his natural face in a m. . Jas 1:23

MISERY
and remember their m no more. ...... Prv 31:7
in their paths are ruin and m, ... Rom 3:16

MISLEADS
"'Cursed be anyone who m a blind ...... Dt 27:18
Whoever m the upright into an evil ...... Prv 28:10

MIST
For you are a m that appears for a little .. Jas 4:14

MOCK
All who see me m me; they make ...... Ps 22:7
Fools m at the guilt offering, but ...... Prv 14:9
And they will m him and spit on him, .. Mk 10:34

MOCKED
m him, saying, "Hail, King of the ...... Mt 27:29
Do not be deceived: God is not m, ... Gal 6:7

MOCKER
Wine is a m, strong drink a brawler, ... Prv 20:1

MOCKS
Whoever m the poor insults his Maker; .. Prv 17:5
The eye that m a father and scorns to . Prv 30:17

MODESTY
parts are treated with greater m, .. 1 Cor 12:23
apparel, with m and self-control, ... 1 Tm 2:9

MOMENT
his anger is but for a m, and his favor . Ps 30:5
a nation be brought forth in one m? ...... Is 66:8
in a m, in the twinkling of an eye, .. 1 Cor 15:52

MONEY
He who loves m will not be satisfied .... Eccl 5:10
he who has no m, come, buy and eat! ...... Is 55:1
You cannot serve God and m. ...... Mt 6:24
no staff, nor bag, nor bread, nor m; ...... Lk 9:3
could obtain the gift of God with m! .. Acts 8:20

not quarrelsome, not a lover of m. ...... 1 Tm 3:3
For the love of m is a root of all kinds .. 1 Tm 6:10
Keep your life free from love of m, ... Heb 13:5

MONEY-CHANGERS
he overturned the tables of the m and .. Mt 21:12

MOON
of your fingers, the m and the stars, ... Ps 8:3
He made the m to mark the seasons; .. Ps 104:19
and the m will not give its light, ... Mt 24:29
turned to darkness and the m to blood, . Acts 2:20
the sun, and another glory of the m, . 1 Cor 15:41

MORALS
"Bad company ruins good m." ...... 1 Cor 15:33

MORNING
when the m stars sang together and ...... Jb 38:7
O LORD, in the m you hear my voice; ...... Ps 5:3
take the wings of the m and dwell in .... Ps 139:9
In the m sow your seed, and at evening . Eccl 11:6
they are new every m; great is your ...... Lam 3:23
the m star rises in your hearts, ... 2 Pt 1:19
of David, the bright m star." ...... Rv 22:16

MORTAL
'Can m man be in the right before God? .. Jb 4:17
give life to your m bodies through his ...... Rom 8:11
and the m puts on immortality, ... 1 Cor 15:54
so that what is m may be swallowed ... 2 Cor 5:4

MOSES
She named him M, "Because," ...... Ex 2:10
God said to M, "I AM WHO I AM." ...... Ex 3:14
So M and Aaron went to Pharaoh ...... Ex 7:10
M implored the LORD his God ...... Ex 32:11
M would put the veil over his face ...... Ex 34:35
M sent them to spy out the land of ...... Nm 13:17
So M made a bronze serpent and set it . Nm 21:9
there appeared to them M and Elijah, ... Mt 17:3
For the law was given through M; ...... Jn 1:17
Yet death reigned from Adam to M, ... Rom 5:14
all were baptized into M in the cloud . 1 Cor 10:2
Now M was faithful in all God's house ... Heb 3:5
they sing the song of M, the servant ...... Rv 15:3

MOTH
where m and rust destroy and where ...... Mt 6:19

MOTHER
Eve, because she was the m of all living. . Gn 3:20
"Honor your father and your m, that ...... Ex 20:12
but a foolish son is a sorrow to his m, ... Prv 10:1
"Who is my m, and who are my ...... Mt 12:48
Honor your father and m, and, You ...... Mt 19:19
And his m treasured up all these ...... Lk 2:51
His m said to the servants, "Do ...... Jn 2:5
said to the disciple, "Behold, your m!" ... Jn 19:27
leave his father and m and hold fast to . Eph 5:31

MOTHER'S
"Naked I came from my m womb, ... Jb 1:21
his m womb he shall go again, naked .. Eccl 5:15

MOUNTAIN
"Come, let us go up to the m of the ...... Is 2:3
to a very high m and showed him all ...... Mt 4:8
will say to this m, 'Move from here ...... Mt 17:20
for we were with him on the holy m ... 2 Pt 1:18

MOUNTAINS
The waters prevailed above the m, ... Gn 7:20
Before the m were brought forth, ... Ps 90:2
How beautiful upon the m are the feet ... Is 52:7
the m and the hills before you ...... Is 55:12
if I have all faith, so as to remove m, .. 1 Cor 13:2

MOURN
a time to laugh; a time to m, ... Eccl 3:4
of our God; to comfort all who m; ...... Is 61:2
have pierced, they shall m for him, ... Zec 12:10
"Blessed are those who m, for they ...... Mt 5:4
then all the tribes of the earth will m, ... Mt 24:30
Be wretched and m and weep. Let ...... Jas 4:9

MOURNING

have turned for me my **m** into dancing; .. Ps 30:11
better to go to the house of **m** than to .... Eccl 7:2
and your days of **m** shall be ended. .... Is 60:20
ashes, the oil of gladness instead of **m**, ... Is 61:3
I will turn their **m** into joy; I will .... Jer 31:13
m, nor crying, nor pain anymore, ... Rv 21:4

MOUTH

Let the words of my **m** and .... Ps 19:14
He put a new song in my **m**, a song of ... Ps 40:3
My **m** is filled with your praise, and .... Ps 71:8
with my **m** I will make known .... Ps 89:1
Whoever guards his **m** preserves his ...... Prv 13:3
A fool's **m** is his ruin, and his lips are ... Prv 18:7
was afflicted, yet he opened not his **m**; ... Is 53:7
there was no deceit in his **m**. .... Is 53:9
word that comes from the **m** of God.'" .... Mt 4:4
abundance of the heart the **m** speaks. .... Mt 12:34
a person, but what comes out of the **m**; .. Mt 15:11
if you confess with your **m** that Jesus .. Rom 10:9
From the same **m** come blessing and ..... Jas 3:10

MULTIPLY

"Be fruitful and **m** and fill the waters ..... Gn 1:22
"Be fruitful and **m** and fill the earth. .... Gn 9:1
He will love you, bless you, and **m** you. .. Dt 7:13
so I will **m** the offspring of David .... Jer 33:22
"Surely I will bless you and **m** you." ...... Heb 6:14

MULTITUDE

will cover a **m** of sins. .... Jas 5:20
love covers a **m** of sins. .... 1 Pt 4:8
a great **m** that no one could number, ... Rv 7:9

MULTITUDES

M, m, in the valley of decision! .... Jl 3:14

MURDER

"You shall not **m**. .... Ex 20:13
"'You shall not **m**. .... Dt 5:17
said to those of old, 'You shall not **m**, ... Mt 5:21
commit adultery, You shall not **m**, ... Rom 13:9
also said, "Do not **m**." If you .... Jas 2:11

MURDERED

are sons of those who **m** the prophets. .. Mt 23:31
whom you have now betrayed and **m**, .. Acts 7:52

MURDERER

The **m** shall be put to death. .... Nm 35:16
He was a **m** from the beginning, ... Jn 8:44
Everyone who hates his brother is a **m**, . 1 Jn 3:15

MURDERERS

strike their fathers and mothers, for **m**, .. 1 Tm 1:9
the faithless, the detestable, as for **m**, ... Rv 21:8

MUSTARD

is like a grain of **m** seed that a man ... Mt 13:31
you have faith like a grain of **m** seed, ... Mt 17:20

MYRRH

him gifts, gold and frankincense and **m**... Mt 2:11
they offered him wine mixed with **m**, ... Mk 15:23
bringing a mixture of **m** and aloes, ... Jn 19:39

MYSTERY

not want you to be unaware of this **m**, .. Rom 11:25
the revelation of the **m** that was kept ... Rom 16:25
I tell you a **m**. We shall not all sleep, .. 1 Cor 15:51
This **m** is profound, and I am saying .... Eph 5:32
the **m** hidden for ages and generations .. Col 1:26
we confess, is the **m** of godliness: .... 1 Tm 3:16

MYTHS

nothing to do with irreverent, silly **m**. .. 1 Tm 4:7
follow cleverly devised **m** when we ..... 2 Pt 1:16

NADAB

and **N** his son reigned in his place. ... 1 Kgs 14:20

NAILING

This he set aside, **n** it to the cross. .... Col 2:14

NAILS

I see in his hands the mark of the **n**, ... Jn 20:25

NAKED

and they knew that they were **n**. .... Gn 3:7
"N I came from my mother's .... Jb 1:21
when you see the **n**, to cover him, ... Is 58:7
I was **n** and you clothed me, I was sick .. Mt 25:36
putting it on we may not be found **n**. ..... 2 Cor 5:3
wretched, pitiable, poor, blind, and **n**. .... Rv 3:17

NAME

Abram called upon the **n** of the .... Gn 13:4
This is my **n** forever, and thus I am to ..... Ex 3:15
"You shall not take the **n** of the .... Ex 20:7
fear this glorious and awesome **n**, ... Dt 28:58
place, that shall build the house for my **n**.' .. 1 Kgs 5:5
and let us exalt his **n** together! .... Ps 34:3
all that is within me, bless his holy **n**! ...... Ps 103:1
n of the LORD is a strong tower; .... Prv 18:10
A good **n** is to be chosen rather than ...... Prv 22:1
host by number, calling them all by **n**; ..... Is 40:26
I am the LORD; that is my **n**; .... Is 42:8
But I had concern for my holy **n**, ... Ezk 36:21
who calls on the **n** of the LORD .... Jl 2:32
They will call upon my **n**, and I will .... Zec 13:9
sun to its setting my **n** will be great ...... Mal 1:11
receives this child in my **n** receives me, ... Lk 9:48
Whatever you ask in my **n**, this I will ..... Jn 14:13
by believing you may have life in his **n**. ... Jn 20:31
for there is no other **n** under heaven .... Acts 4:12
who calls on the **n** of the Lord will ...... Rom 10:13
bestowed on him the **n** that is above ..... Phil 2:9
do everything in the **n** of the Lord Jesus, .. Col 3:17
Yet you hold fast my **n**, and you did ...... Rv 2:13
and he has a **n** written that no one .... Rv 19:12
And if anyone's **n** was not found .... Rv 20:15

NAME'S

in paths of righteousness for his **n** sake. ... Ps 23:3
For your **n** sake, O LORD, ... Ps 143:11
you will be hated by all for my **n** sake. ... Mt 10:22
your sins are forgiven for his **n** sake. ... 1 Jn 2:12
bearing up for my **n** sake, and you .... Rv 2:3

NAMES

the stars; he gives to all of them their **n**.. Ps 147:4
but rejoice that your **n** are written in ... Lk 10:20
whose **n** are in the book of life. .... Phil 4:3

NAOMI

Elimelech and the name of his wife **N**, ... Ru 1:2
"A son has been born to **N**." .... Ru 4:17

NATHAN

word of the LORD came to **N**, ... 2 Sm 7:4
N said to David, "You are the man! .. 2 Sm 12:7

NATHANAEL

N said to him, "Can anything good ...... Jn 1:46
N of Cana in Galilee, the sons of .... Jn 21:2

NATION

I will make of you a great **n**, ... Gn 12:2
me a kingdom of priests and a holy **n**.' .. Ex 19:6
Blessed is the **n** whose God is the .... Ps 33:12
Righteousness exalts a **n**, but sin is a .... Prv 14:34
here I am," to a **n** that was not called ... Is 65:1
For **n** will rise against **n**, ... Mt 24:7
for he loves our **n**, and he is the one ...... Lk 7:5
a royal priesthood, a holy **n**, ... 1 Pt 2:9
tribe and language and people and **n**, ... Rv 5:9

NATIONS

shall be the father of a multitude of **n**. ... Gn 17:4
Let the **n** be glad and sing for joy, ... Ps 67:4
Declare his glory among the **n**, ... Ps 96:3
the hills; and all the **n** shall flow to it, ... Is 2:2
the **n** are like a drop from a bucket, ... Is 40:15
praise to sprout up before all the **n**. ...... Is 61:11
n will know that I am the LORD, ... Ezk 36:23
n, and languages should serve him; ..... Dn 7:14
And many **n** shall join themselves to ..... Zec 2:11

Then all **n** will call you blessed, for .... Mal 3:12
and make disciples of all **n**, ... Mt 28:19
must first be proclaimed to all **n**. .... Mk 13:10
"In you shall all the **n** be blessed." .... Gal 3:8
By its light will the **n** walk, and the ...... Rv 21:24

NATURAL

if God did not spare the **n** branches, ... Rom 11:21
The **n** person does not accept the ...... 1 Cor 2:14
If there is a **n** body, there is also a ... 1 Cor 15:44

NATURE

his eternal power and divine **n**, ... Rom 1:20
mind, and were by **n** children of wrath, ... Eph 2:3
of God and the exact imprint of his **n**, ... Heb 1:3
may become partakers of the divine **n**, .. 2 Pt 1:4

NAZARETH

he went and lived in a city called **N**, ... Mt 2:23
anything good come out of **N**?" .... Jn 1:46
It read, "Jesus of **N**, the King of the ... Jn 19:19
And he said to me, 'I am Jesus of **N**, .. Acts 22:8

NAZIRITE

makes a special vow, the vow of a **N**, ... Nm 6:2

NEAR

Be not far from me, for trouble is **n**, ... Ps 22:11
LORD is **n** to the brokenhearted .... Ps 34:18
LORD is **n** to all who call on him, ... Ps 145:18
all these things, you know that he is **n**, .. Mt 24:33
kingdom of God has come **n** to you.' .... Lk 10:9
"The word is **n** you, in your mouth, ... Rom 10:8
far off and peace to those who were **n**. .. Eph 2:17
what is written in it, for the time is **n**. ..... Rv 1:3

NEARER

For salvation is **n** to us now than ...... Rom 13:11

NEBUCHADNEZZAR

In his days, **N** king of Babylon came ... 2 Kgs 24:1
Jerusalem into exile by the hand of **N**.. 1 Chr 6:15
Then King **N** fell upon his face and .... Dn 2:46
Now I, **N**, praise and extol and honor the .. Dn 4:37

NECESSARY

Was it not **n** that the Christ should ...... Lk 24:26
proving that it was **n** for the Christ to ... Acts 17:3

NEED

you a blessing until there is no more **n**. .. Mal 3:10
Father knows what you **n** before you ..... Mt 6:8
it was distributed to each as any had **n**.. Acts 4:35
will supply every **n** of yours according ... Phil 4:19
and find grace to help in time of **n**. .... Heb 4:16
world's goods and sees his brother in **n**, .. 1 Jn 3:17

NEEDS

Contribute to the **n** of the saints and .. Rom 12:13
not only supplying the **n** of the saints ... 2 Cor 9:12

NEEDY

As for me, I am poor and **n**, but the ...... Ps 40:17
and reaches out her hands to the **n**. ..... Prv 31:20
to turn aside the **n** from justice .... Is 10:2
silver, and the **n** for a pair of sandals— .. Am 2:6
"Thus, when you give to the **n**, ... Mt 6:2
There was not a **n** person among them, .. Acts 4:34

NEGLECT

instruction and be wise, and do not **n** it. . Prv 8:33
and **n** justice and the love of God. .... Lk 11:42
escape if we **n** such a great salvation? ... Heb 2:3
Do not **n** to do good and to share .... Heb 13:16

NEHEMIAH

with Zerubbabel, Jeshua, **N**, Seraiah, ... Ezr 2:2
in the days of **N** the governor and ...... Neh 12:26

NEIGHBOR

but you shall love your **n** as yourself: ..... Lv 19:18
Better is a **n** who is near than a .... Prv 27:10
was said, 'You shall love your **n** and ...... Mt 5:43
said to Jesus, "And who is my **n**?" .... Lk 10:29
Love does no wrong to a **n**; .... Rom 13:10
his own good, but the good of his **n**. .. 1 Cor 10:24

"You shall love your **n** as yourself." .... Gal 5:14

NEIGHBOR'S

shall not covet your **n** house; .... Ex 20:17
be seldom in your **n** house, lest he .... Prv 25:17

NET

kingdom of heaven is like a **n** that .... Mt 13:47
"Cast the **n** on the right side of the .... Jn 21:6

NEVER

and **n** again shall there be a flood to .... Gn 9:11
steadfast love of the LORD **n** ceases; .... Lam 3:22
I will give him will **n** be thirsty again. ... Jn 4:14
whoever comes to me I will **n** cast out. ... Jn 6:37
eternal life, and they will **n** perish, ... Jn 10:28
Love **n** ends. .... 1 Cor 13:8
I will **n** blot his name out of the book .... Rv 3:5

NEW

Oh sing to the LORD a **n** song; .... Ps 96:1
I create **n** heavens and a **n** earth, ... Is 65:17
I will give you a **n** heart, and a .... Ezk 36:26
Neither is **n** wine put into old wineskins. . Mt 9:17
for you is the **n** covenant in my blood. .. Lk 22:20
A **n** commandment I give to you, that .... Jn 13:34
create in himself one **n** man in place .... Eph 2:15
and have put on the **n** self, which is .... Col 3:10
the **n** and living way that he opened .. Heb 10:20
with a **n** name written on the stone .... Rv 2:17
"Behold, I am making all things **n**." ..... Rv 21:5

NEWS

publishes peace, who brings good **n** .... Is 52:7
and the poor have good **n** preached to ... Mt 11:5
I bring you good **n** of great joy that ...... Lk 2:10
anointed me to proclaim good **n** to the .. Lk 4:18
preaching good **n** of peace through .... Acts 10:36
And this word is the good **n** that was .. 1 Pt 1:25

NICODEMUS

was a man of the Pharisees named **N**, ... Jn 3:1
N, who had gone to him before, and ...... Jn 7:50
N also, who earlier had come to Jesus .. Jn 19:39

NIGHT

and the darkness he called **N**. .... Gn 1:5
and on his law he meditates day and **n**. .... Ps 1:2
love, and at **n** his song is with me, ... Ps 42:8
You will not fear the terror of the **n**, ... Ps 91:5
This **n** your soul is required of you, ... Lk 12:20
n is coming, when no one can work. .... Jn 9:4
We are not of the **n** or of the darkness. 1 Thes 5:5
And **n** will be no more. .... Rv 22:5

NOAH

But **N** found favor in the eyes of the .... Gn 6:8
They went into the ark with **N**, too .... Gn 7:15
"This is like the days of **N** to me: as I .... Is 54:9
if these three men, **N**, Daniel, and Job, . Ezk 14:14
until the day when **N** entered the ark, .. Mt 24:38
By faith **N**, being warned by God .... Heb 11:7
God's patience waited in the days of **N**, . 1 Pt 3:20
the ancient world, but preserved **N**, ... 2 Pt 2:5

NOBLE

Hear, for I will speak **n** things, ... Prv 8:6
he who is in **n** plans in things, ... Is 32:8
powerful, not many were of **n** birth. .... 1 Cor 1:26
office of overseer, he desires a **n** task. .. 1 Tm 3:1

NOISE

let us make a joyful **n** to the rock of our ... Ps 95:1
Make a joyful **n** to the LORD, ... Ps 100:1

NONE

For there is **n** like you, and there is no .. 2 Sm 7:22
no other; I am God, and there is **n** like .... Is 46:9
There is **n** like you, O LORD; .... Jer 10:6
"**N** is righteous, no, not one; .... Rom 3:10

NOTHING

there is **n** new under the sun. .... Eccl 1:9
N is too hard for you. .... Jer 32:17
n is covered that will not be revealed, ... Mt 10:26

For **n** will be impossible with God." .... Lk 1:37
"I can do **n** on my own. .... Jn 5:30
for apart from me you can do **n**. .... Jn 15:5
but have not love, I am **n**. .... 1 Cor 13:2
for we brought **n** into the world, ... 1 Tm 6:7
be perfect and complete, lacking in **n**. .... Jas 1:4

NULLIFY

Does their faithlessness **n** the .... Rom 3:3
I do not **n** the grace of God, for if .... Gal 2:21

NUMBER

"Look toward heaven, and **n** the stars, .. Gn 15:5
So teach us to **n** our days that we may .. Ps 90:12
He determines the **n** of the stars; ...... Ps 147:4

OATH

keeping the **o** that he swore to your .... Dt 7:8
But I say to you, Do not take an **o** .... Mt 5:34
heaven or by earth or by any other **o**, ... Jas 5:12

OBEDIENCE

to bring about the **o** of faith for the ...... Rom 1:5
so by the one man's **o** the many will .... Rom 5:19
he learned **o** through what he suffered. .. Heb 5:8
purified your souls by your **o** to .... 1 Pt 1:22

OBEDIENT

himself by becoming **o** to the point .... Phil 2:8
to rulers and authorities, to be **o**, ... Ti 3:1
As **o** children, do not be conformed .... 1 Pt 1:14

OBEY

Be careful to **o** all these words that I .... Dt 12:28
Behold, to **o** is better than sacrifice, ... 1 Sm 15:22
'O my voice, and I will be your God, ... Jer 7:23
"We must **o** God rather than men. ...... Acts 5:29
you are slaves of the one whom you **o**, .. Rom 6:16
Children, **o** your parents in everything, .. Col 3:20
of eternal salvation to all who **o** him, ... Heb 5:9
O your leaders and submit to them, ... Heb 13:17
when we love God and **o** his .... 1 Jn 5:2

OBEYED

because you have **o** my voice." .... Gn 22:18
By faith Abraham **o** when he was ...... Heb 11:8
as Sarah **o** Abraham, calling him lord. .. 1 Pt 3:6

OBLIGATION

I am under **o** both to Greeks and to .... Rom 1:14
o to bear with the failings of the weak, .. Rom 15:1

OBSERVE

ruler, **o** carefully what is before you, ... Prv 23:1
teaching them to **o** all that I have .... Mt 28:20

OBSOLETE

new covenant, he makes the first one **o**. .. Heb 8:13

OBTAIN

they shall **o** gladness and joy, ... Is 35:10
but to **o** salvation through our Lord .... 1 Thes 5:9
may **o** the salvation that is in Christ .. 2 Tm 2:10
that no one fails to **o** the grace of God . Heb 12:15

OBTAINED

Through him we have also **o** access by .. Rom 5:2
Not that I have already **o** this or .... Phil 3:12

OFFENDED

A brother **o** is more unyielding than .... Prv 18:19
blessed is the one who is not **o** by me." .. Mt 11:6

OFFENSE

Whoever covers an **o** seeks love, but .... Prv 17:9
and it is his glory to overlook an **o**. ...... Prv 19:11

OFFENSES

stirs up strife, but love covers all **o**. .... Prv 10:12
for calmness will lay great **o** to rest. .... Eccl 10:4

OFFERED

o without blemish to God, ... Heb 9:14
But when Christ had **o** for all time .... Heb 10:12

OFFERING

the lamb for a burnt **o**, ... Gn 22:8
you will not be pleased with a burnt **o**. .. Ps 51:16

when his soul makes an **o** for guilt, ... Is 53:10
So if you are **o** your gift at the altar .... Mt 5:23
For by a single **o** he has perfected for .. Heb 10:14

OFFERINGS

than all whole burnt **o** and sacrifices." .. Mk 12:33
"Sacrifices and **o** you have not desired, . Heb 10:5

OFFSPRING

between your **o** and her **o**; .... Gn 3:15
"To your **o** I will give this land." .... Gn 12:7
an offering for guilt, he shall see his **o**; .. Is 53:10
"'For we are indeed his **o**.' .... Acts 17:28
of the promise are counted as **o**. .... Rom 9:8
Christ's, then you are Abraham's **o**, ... Gal 3:29

OIL

Then the **o** stopped flowing. .... 2 Kgs 4:6
wind or to grasp **o** in one's right hand. .. Prv 27:16
'Give us some of your **o**, ... Mt 25:8
You did not anoint my head with **o**, but . . Lk 7:46
has anointed you with the **o** of gladness . Heb 1:9
anointing him with **o** in the name of .... Jas 5:14

OINTMENT

In pouring this **o** on my body, she has .. Mt 26:12
Mary who anointed the Lord with **o** .... Jn 11:2

OLD

even when he is **o** he will not depart .... Prv 22:6
The **o** has passed away; behold, the .. 2 Cor 5:17
have put off the **o** self with its practices . . Col 3:9
than the **o** as the covenant he mediates . Heb 8:6

OLIVE

And there are two **o** trees by it, one on .. Zec 4:3
off, and you, although a wild **o** shoot, .. Rom 11:17
These are the two **o** trees and the two .... Rv 11:4

OLIVES

the Mount of **O** shall be split in two ...... Zec 14:4
As he sat on the Mount of **O**, the .... Mt 24:3
hymn, they went out to the Mount of **O**. . Mt 26:30

OLIVET

out and lodged on the mount called **O**. .. Lk 21:37
to Jerusalem from the mount called **O**, .. Acts 1:12

ONCE

death he died he died to sin, **o** for all, .. Rom 6:10
since he did this **o** for all when he ...... Heb 7:27
just as it is appointed for man to die **o**, .. Heb 9:27
For Christ also suffered **o** for sins, ... 1 Pt 3:18

ONE

wife, and they shall become **o** flesh. ...... Gn 2:24
our God, the LORD is **o**. .... Dt 6:4
O thing have I asked of the LORD ...... Ps 27:4
Two are better than **o**, because they ...... Eccl 4:9
"Are you the **o** who is to come, or ...... Mt 11:3
his wife, and the two shall become **o** ..... Mt 19:5
No **o** can come to me unless the Father .. Jn 6:44
I and the Father are **o**." .... Jn 10:30
though many, are **o** body in Christ, ... Rom 12:5
that **o** has died for all, therefore all .... 2 Cor 5:14
o Lord, **o** faith, **o** baptism, ... Eph 4:5
You believe that God is **o**; you do well. .... Jas 2:19

OPEN

O your mouth wide, and I will fill it. ...... Ps 81:10
You **o** your hand; you satisfy the .... Ps 145:16
He shall **o**, and none shall shut; .... Is 22:22
I have set before you an **o** door, ... Rv 3:8
"Who is worthy to **o** the scroll and ...... Rv 5:2

OPENED

when you eat of it your eyes will be **o**, ... Gn 3:5
and was praying, the heavens were **o**, ... Lk 3:21
Then he **o** their minds to understand .... Lk 24:45
that anyone **o** the eyes of a man born .... Jn 9:32
I see the heavens **o**, and the Son of .... Acts 7:56
living way that he **o** for us through .... Heb 10:20

OPINIONS

go limping between two different **o**? . 1 Kgs 18:21
but not to quarrel over **o**. .... Rom 14:1

OPPORTUNITY

your freedom as an **o** for the flesh, ... Gal 5:13
So then, as we have **o**, let us do good ... Gal 6:10
and give no **o** to the devil. .... Eph 4:27

OPPRESS

"You shall not **o** a sojourner. .... Ex 23:9
"You shall not **o** your neighbor. .... Lv 19:13
do not **o** the widow, the fatherless, ... Zec 7:10

OPPRESSED

But the more they were **o**, the more ...... Ex 1:12
who executes justice for the **o**, who ..... Ps 146:7
He was **o**, and he was afflicted, yet he ... Is 53:7
him all who were sick or **o** by demons. ... Mk 1:32

ORDER

'Set your house in **o**, for you shall ...... 2 Kgs 20:1
"If this fixed **o** departs from before me, .. Jer 31:36
should be done decently and in **o**. ... 1 Cor 14:40
to see your good **o** and the firmness ...... Col 2:5
high priest after the **o** of Melchizedek. .. Heb 5:10

ORGIES

not in **o** and drunkenness, ... Rom 13:13
envy, drunkenness, **o**, and things like ..... Gal 5:21

ORION

who made the Bear and **O**, the Pleiades ... Jb 9:9
He who made the Pleiades and **O**, and ..... Am 5:8

ORPHANS

"I will not leave you as **o**; I will come ... Jn 14:18
visit **o** and widows in their affliction, ... Jas 1:27

OUTSIDERS

For what have I to do with judging **o**? . 1 Cor 5:12
Walk in wisdom toward **o**, ... Col 4:5
walk properly before **o** and be .... 1 Thes 4:12
he must be well thought of by **o**, ... 1 Tm 3:7

OUTSTRETCHED

redeem you with an **o** arm and with ...... Ex 6:6
with a strong hand and an **o** arm, ... Ps 136:12

OUTWARD

man looks on the **o** appearance, ... 1 Sm 16:7
who boast about **o** appearance .... 2 Cor 5:12

OVERCOME

and the darkness has not **o** it. .... Jn 1:5
But take heart; I have **o** the world." ...... Jn 16:33
Do not be **o** by evil, but **o** evil with .... Rom 12:21
and you have **o** the evil one. .... 1 Jn 2:14

OVERCOMES

o a person, to that he is enslaved. ...... 2 Pt 2:19
who has been born of God **o** the world. .. 1 Jn 5:4

OVERFLOWS

you anoint my head with oil; my cup **o**. .. Ps 23:5

OVERSEER

If anyone aspires to the office of **o**, ... 1 Tm 3:1
For an **o**, as God's steward, must be .... Ti 1:7
to the Shepherd and **O** of your souls. .... 1 Pt 2:25

OVERSEERS

the Holy Spirit has made you **o**, ... Acts 20:28
at Philippi, with the **o** and deacons: ...... Phil 1:1

OVERWHELM

through the rivers, they shall not **o** you; .. Is 43:2

OWE

choke him, saying, 'Pay what you **o**.' ..... Mt 18:28
'How much do you **o** my master?' .... Lk 16:5
O no one anything, except to love ...... Rom 13:8

OWED

One **o** five hundred denarii, and the .... Lk 7:41
Pay to all what is **o** to them: taxes to .... Rom 13:7

OWN

did what was right in his **o** eyes. .... Jgs 17:6
sought out a man after his **o** heart, ... 1 Sm 13:14
But everyone shall die for his **o** iniquity. .. Jer 31:30
He came to his **o**, and his **o** people .... Jn 1:11

I know my **o** and my **o** know me, ... Jn 10:14
having loved his **o** who were in the .... Jn 13:1
By sending his **o** Son in the likeness ..... Rom 8:3
You are not your **o**, ... 1 Cor 6:19
Christ Jesus has made you his **o**. .... Phil 3:12

OX

"You shall not muzzle the **o** when it is .... Dt 25:4
the face of an **o** on the left side, ... Ezk 1:10
the Sabbath untie his **o** or his donkey ... Lk 13:15
"You shall not muzzle an **o** when it ...... 1 Cor 9:9
the second living creature like an **o**, ... Rv 4:7

PAGANS

that is not tolerated even among **p**, ... 1 Cor 5:1
No, I imply that what **p** sacrifice ...... 1 Cor 10:20
that when you were **p** you were led ...... 1 Cor 12:2

PAIN

in **p** you shall bring forth children. .... Gn 3:16
and my **p** is ever before me. .... Ps 38:17
nor crying, nor **p** anymore, for the .... Rv 21:4

PALMS

engraved you on the **p** of my hands; ..... Is 49:16

PANTS

As a deer **p** for flowing streams, so ...... Ps 42:1

PARABLE

I will open my mouth in a **p**; .... Ps 78:2
"Hear then the **p** of the sower: .... Mt 13:18

PARADISE

today you will be with me in **p**." .... Lk 23:43
was caught up into **p**—whether in .... 2 Cor 12:3
tree of life, which is in the **p** of God.' ... Rv 2:7

PARALYTIC

bringing to him a **p** carried by four men. .. Mk 2:3

PARDON

and **p** our iniquity and our sin, ... Ex 34:9
O LORD, **p** my guilt, for it is great. ...... Ps 25:11
to our God, for he will abundantly **p**. ..... Is 55:7

PARENTS

delivered up even by **p** and brothers ..... Lk 21:16
to save up for their **p**, but **p** for ...... 2 Cor 12:14
Children, obey your **p** in the Lord, ... Eph 6:1

PARTAKERS

and **p** of the promise in Christ Jesus ...... Eph 3:6
for you are all **p** with me of grace, ... Phil 1:7
may become **p** of the divine nature, ... 2 Pt 1:4

PARTIALITY

You shall not show **p**, and .... Dt 16:19
P in judging is not good. .... Prv 24:23
I understand that God shows no **p**, ... Acts 10:34
But if you show **p**, you are committing .... Jas 2:9

PARTICIPATION

is it not a **p** in the blood of Christ? ... 1 Cor 10:16
comfort from love, any **p** in the Spirit, ... Phil 2:1

PASS

when I see the blood, I will **p** over you, .. Ex 12:13
Heaven and earth will **p** away, but my ... Lk 21:33
perfect comes, the partial will **p** away. .. 1 Cor 13:10
and then the heavens will **p** away with .. 2 Pt 3:10

PASSED

The LORD **p** before him and .... Ex 34:6
LORD **p** by, and a great and strong .... 1 Kgs 19:11
forbearance he had **p** over former sins. .. Rom 3:25
We know that we have **p** out of death .. 1 Jn 3:14
heaven and the first earth had **p** away, ... Rv 21:1

PASSION

better to marry than to burn with **p**. .... 1 Cor 7:9
immorality, impurity, **p**, evil desire, ... Col 3:5
lust of defiling **p** and despise authority. .. 2 Pt 2:10

PASSIONS

God gave them up to dishonorable **p**. ... Rom 1:26
we were living in the flesh, our sinful **p**, ... Rom 7:5
crucified the flesh with its **p** and .... Gal 5:24

---

to renounce ungodliness and worldly **p**, ... Ti 2:12
do not be conformed to the **p** of your ... 1 Pt 1:14

PASSOVER

eat it in haste. It is the LORD's **P**. .... Ex 12:11
directed them, and they prepared the **P**. .. Mt 26:19
For Christ, our **P** lamb, has been .... 1 Cor 5:7

PASTURE

God, and we are the people of his **p**, ... Ps 95:7
are his people, and the sheep of his **p**. .. Ps 100:3
saved and will go in and out and find **p**. .. Jn 10:9

PASTURES

He makes me lie down in green **p**. .... Ps 23:2

PATH

You make known to me the **p** of life; ..... Ps 16:11
lead me on a level **p** because of my ...... Ps 27:11
a lamp to my feet and a light to my **p**... Ps 119:105
But the **p** of the righteous is like the ...... Prv 4:18
p of life leads upward for the prudent, ... Prv 15:24
he sowed, some seeds fell along the **p**, ... Mt 13:4

PATHS

He leads me in **p** of righteousness .... Ps 23:3
O LORD; teach me your **p**. .... Ps 25:4
and make them straight your **p**. .... Prv 3:6
have made known to me the **p** of life; .. Acts 2:28
and make straight **p** for your feet, so ... Heb 12:13

PATIENCE

With **p** a ruler may be persuaded, ... Prv 25:15
and good heart, and bear fruit with **p**. ... Lk 8:15
to those who by **p** in well-doing seek ... Rom 2:7
endured with much **p** vessels of wrath ... Rom 9:22
of the Spirit is love, joy, peace, **p**, ... Gal 5:22
with all humility and gentleness, with **p**, .. Eph 4:2
display his perfect **p** as an example ...... 1 Tm 1:16
when God's **p** waited in the days of .... 1 Pt 3:20
And count the **p** of our Lord as .... 2 Pt 3:15

PATIENT

Rejoice in hope, be **p** in tribulation, ... Rom 12:12
Love is **p** and kind; love does not envy . 1 Cor 13:4
help the weak, be **p** with them all. ..... 1 Thes 5:14
Be **p**, therefore, brothers, until the .... Jas 5:7
but is **p** toward you, not wishing that ... 2 Pt 3:9

PAUL

who was also called **P**, filled with the ... Acts 13:9
they stoned **P** and dragged him out of . Acts 14:19
the Jews a favor, Felix left **P** in prison. ... Acts 24:27
then is Apollos? What is **P**? Servants ... 1 Cor 3:5
as our beloved brother **P** also wrote ... 2 Pt 3:15

PAY

wicked borrows but does not **p** back, ... Ps 37:21
Is it lawful to **p** taxes to Caesar; .... Mt 22:17
P to all what is owed to them: taxes ... Rom 13:7
you will do well to **p** attention .... 2 Pt 1:19

PEACE

I will give **p** in the land, and you .... Lv 26:6
countenance upon you and give you **p**... Nm 6:26
for he will speak **p** to his people, ... Ps 85:8
You keep him in perfect **p** whose mind ... Is 26:3
the effect of righteousness will be **p**, ... Is 32:17
your **p** would have been like a river, ... Is 48:18
no **p**," says my God, "for the wicked." ... Is 57:21
'**P**, **p**,' when there is no **p**. .... Jer 6:14
and he shall speak **p** to the nations; .... Zec 9:10
not come to bring **p**, but a sword. .... Mt 10:34
"**P**! Be still!" And the wind ceased, ... Mk 4:39
go in **p**, and be healed of your disease." .. Mk 5:34
to God in the highest, and on earth **p** ..... Lk 2:14
you enter, first say, '**P** be to this house!' .. Lk 10:5
P I leave with you; my **p** I give .... Jn 14:27
in me you may have **p**. In the world ...... Jn 16:33
"**P** be with you," .... Jn 20:26
we have **p** with God through our Lord ... Rom 5:1
God has called you to **p**. .... 1 Cor 7:15
is not a God of confusion but of **p**. .... 1 Cor 14:33
For he himself is our **p**, who has made ... Eph 2:14

And the **p** of God, which surpasses all .... Phil 4:7
making **p** by the blood of his cross. .... Col 1:20
And let the **p** of Christ rule in your .... Col 3:15
Strive for **p** with everyone, ... Heb 12:14
righteousness is sown in **p** by those .... Jas 3:18
do good; let him seek **p** and pursue it. ... 1 Pt 3:11
was permitted to take **p** from the earth, ... Rv 6:4

PEACEFUL
My people will abide in a **p** habitation, ... Is 32:18
that we may lead a **p** and quiet life, ... 1 Tm 2:2
it yields the **p** fruit of righteousness ..... Heb 12:11

PEACEMAKERS
"Blessed are the **p**, for they shall be ...... Mt 5:9

PEARL
who, on finding one **p** of great value, ... Mt 13:46
each of the gates made of a single **p**, ... Rv 21:21

PEARLS
and do not throw your **p** before pigs, ... Mt 7:6

PENALTY
A man of great wrath will pay the **p**, ... Prv 19:19
in themselves the due **p** for their error. ... Rom 1:27

PENNY
get out until you have paid the last **p**.... Mt 5:26
Are not two sparrows sold for a **p**? ...... Mt 10:29

PENTECOST
When the day of **P** arrived, they were .... Acts 2:1

PEOPLE
the God of Israel, 'Let my **p** go, ... Ex 5:1
the burden of all this **p** on me? .... Nm 11:11
God has chosen you to be a **p** for his ...... Dt 7:6
Your **p** shall be my **p**, ... Ru 1:16
if my **p** who are called by my name ..... 2 Chr 7:14
God restores the fortunes of his **p**, ... Ps 53:6
blows on it; surely the **p** are grass. ...... Is 40:7
my **p** shall know my name. .... Is 52:6
But my **p** have forgotten me; .... Jer 18:15
be my **p** and I will be their God, ... Jer 24:7
My **P**, for you are not my **p**, ... Hos 1:9
p honors me with their lips, but their ..... Mk 7:6
make ready for the Lord a **p** prepared." ... Lk 1:17
the earth, will draw all **p** to myself." ... Jn 12:32
has God rejected his **p**? By no means! ... Rom 11:1
desires all **p** to be saved and to .... 1 Tm 2:4
propitiation for the sins of the **p**. .... Heb 2:17
be mistreated with the **p** of God than .. Heb 11:25
with them, and they will be his **p**, ... Rv 21:3

PEOPLES
kingdom, that all **p**, nations, ... Dn 7:14
above the hills; and **p** shall flow to it, ... Mi 4:1
from all tribes and **p** and languages, ... Rv 7:9

PERFECT
My dove, my **p** one, is the only one, ... Sg 6:9
p, as your heavenly Father is perfect. .... Mt 5:48
but when the **p** comes, the partial .... 1 Cor 13:10
for my power is made in weakness." .. 2 Cor 12:9
of their salvation **p** through suffering, .. Heb 2:10
that you may be **p** and complete, ... Jas 1:4

PERFECTER
Jesus, the founder and **p** of our faith, .. Heb 12:2

PERFECTION
I have seen a limit to all **p**, but your .... Ps 119:96
Now if **p** had been attainable through .. Heb 7:11

PERISH
is against the law, and if I **p**, I **p**." .... Est 4:16
but the way of the wicked will **p**. .... Ps 1:6
take the sword will **p** by the sword. .... Mt 26:52
you repent, you will all likewise **p**. .... Lk 13:3
should not **p** but have eternal life. .... Jn 3:16
eternal life, and they will never **p**; .... Jn 10:28
they will **p**, but you remain; .... Heb 1:11
not wishing that any should **p**, ... 2 Pt 3:9

PERISHABLE
What is sown is **p**; what is raised is .... 1 Cor 15:42
not with **p** things such as silver .... 1 Pt 1:18

PERPLEXED
crushed; **p**, but not driven to despair; ... 2 Cor 4:8

PERSECUTE
and pray for those who **p** you, ... Mt 5:44
persecuted me, they will also **p** you. ..... Jn 15:20
Bless those who **p** you; bless and do .. Rom 12:14

PERSECUTED
for so they **p** the prophets .... Mt 5:12
reviled, we bless; when **p**, we endure; ... 1 Cor 4:12
p, but not forsaken; struck down, but... 2 Cor 4:9
a godly life in Christ Jesus will be **p**, ... 2 Tm 3:12

PERSECUTION
when tribulation or **p** arises on .... Mt 13:21
Shall tribulation, or distress, or **p**, or .... Rom 8:35

PERSECUTIONS
faith in all your **p** and in the afflictions . 2 Thes 1:4
p I endured; yet from them all........... 2 Tm 3:11

PERSEVERANCE
To that end, keep alert with all **p**, ... Eph 6:18

PERSIST
P in this, for by so doing you will .... 1 Tm 4:16
As for those who **p** in sin, rebuke .... 1 Tm 5:20

PERSUADE
the fear of the Lord, we **p** others. .... 2 Cor 5:11

PERSUASIVENESS
and sweetness of speech increases **p**. ... Prv 16:21
his speech judicious and adds **p**. .... Prv 16:23

PERVERSE
A **p** heart shall be far from me; .... Ps 101:4
the mouth of the wicked, what is **p**. .... Prv 10:32

PERVERT
bribe in secret to **p** the ways of justice. .. Prv 17:23
who **p** the grace of our God into .... Jude 4

PESTILENCE
LORD sent a **p** on Israel from .... 2 Sm 24:15
nor the **p** that stalks in darkness, ... Ps 91:6

PETER
So **P** got out of the boat and walked .... Mt 14:29
I tell you, you are **P**, and on this rock .... Mt 16:18
Jesus took with him **P** and James, and .... Mt 17:1
But **P** rose and ran to the tomb;.......... Lk 24:12
P again denied it, and at once a rooster ... Jn 18:27
But **P**, standing with the eleven, lifted ... Acts 2:14
Then **P**, filled with the Holy Spirit, ... Acts 4:8
P was sleeping between two soldiers, ... Acts 12:6
through **P** for his apostolic ministry to ..... Gal 2:8

PHARISEE
You blind **P**! First clean the inside ...... Mt 23:26
The **P**, standing by himself, prayed ...... Lk 18:11
Hebrew of Hebrews; as to the law, a **P**; .. Phil 3:5

PHARISEES
exceeds that of the scribes and **P**, ... Mt 5:20
P cleanse the outside of the cup .... Lk 11:39

PHILIP
P and Bartholomew; Thomas and .... Mt 10:3
found **P** and said to him, "Follow me." .... Jn 1:43
P said to him, "Lord, show us the .... Jn 14:8
So **P** ran to him and heard him .... Acts 8:30

PHILOSOPHY
you captive by **p** and empty deceit, ... Col 2:8

PHYLACTERIES
For they make their **p** broad and their .... Mt 23:5

PHYSICIAN
who are well have no need of a **p**, ... Mt 9:12
to me this proverb, '"**P**, heal yourself.'" .... Lk 4:23
Luke the beloved **p** greets you, ... Col 4:14

PIECE
No one puts a **p** of unshrunk cloth on .... Mt 9:16

PIERCED
they have **p** my hands and feet— .... Ps 22:16
look on me, on him whom they have **p**, .. Zec 12:10
But one of the soldiers **p** his side .... Jn 19:34
will look on him whom they have **p**." .... Jn 19:37
eye will see him, even those who **p** him, ... Rv 1:7

PIGS
a herd of many **p** was feeding at some .... Mt 8:30
to be fed with the pods that the **p** ate; ... Lk 15:16

PILATE
delivered him over to **P** the governor...... Mt 27:2
P answered, "What I have written I .... Jn 19:22
and denied in the presence of **P**, ... Acts 3:13
in his testimony before Pontius **P** .... 1 Tm 6:13

PILLAR
by day in a **p** of cloud to lead .... Ex 13:21
God, a **p** and buttress of the truth. .... 1 Tm 3:15

PIT
He drew me up from the **p** of .... Ps 40:2
redeems your life from the **p**, ... Ps 103:4
lead the blind, both will fall into a **p**." ... Mt 15:14
and threw him into the **p**, and shut it .... Rv 20:3

PITIED
we are of all people most to be **p**. .... 1 Cor 15:19

PLACE
"Surely the LORD is in this **p**, ... Gn 28:16
and caused the dawn to know its **p**, ... Jb 38:12
You are a hiding **p** for me; you .... Ps 32:7
that I go to prepare a **p** for you? .... Jn 14:2
the dwelling **p** of God is with man. ...... Rv 21:3

PLAGUE
"Yet one **p** more I will bring .... Ex 11:1
to befall you, no **p** come near your tent. .. Ps 91:10
strike the earth with every kind of **p**, ... Rv 11:6

PLAN
but those who **p** peace have joy. .... Prv 12:20
to the definite **p** and foreknowledge of .. Acts 2:23
as a **p** for the fullness of time, to unite ... Eph 1:10
what is the **p** of the mystery hidden ...... Eph 3:9

PLANS
heart's desire and fulfill all your **p**! .... Ps 20:4
The heart of man **p** his way, but .... Prv 16:9
P are established by counsel; by wise ... Prv 20:18
p formed of old, faithful and sure. .... Is 25:1
But he who is noble **p** noble things, ... Is 32:8
For I know the **p** I have for you, ... Jer 29:11

PLANTED
Father has not **p** will be rooted up. .... Mt 15:13
tree, 'Be uprooted and **p** in the sea,' ..... Lk 17:6
I **p**, Apollos watered, but God gave ..... 1 Cor 3:6

PLEAD
to the Lord I **p** for mercy; .... Ps 30:8
P my cause and redeem me; give .... Ps 119:154
for the LORD will **p** their cause .... Prv 22:23

PLEADED
Three times I **p** with the Lord about .... 2 Cor 12:8

PLEASANT
The lines have fallen for me in **p** places; ... Ps 16:6
how good and **p** it is when brothers ..... Ps 133:1
Light is sweet, and it is **p** for the eyes ... Eccl 11:7

PLEASE
who are in the flesh cannot **p** God. ...... Rom 8:8
Let each of us **p** his neighbor for his .... Rom 15:2
things of the Lord, how to **p** the Lord... 1 Cor 7:32
just as I try to **p** everyone in .... 1 Cor 10:33
we make it our aim to **p** him. .... 2 Cor 5:9
how you ought to walk and to **p** God, ... 1 Thes 4:1
without faith it is impossible to **p** ...... Heb 11:6

PLEASED

beloved Son, with whom I am well p." .... Mt 3:17
it p God through the folly of what ...... 1 Cor 1:21
beloved Son, with whom I am well p," .. 2 Pt 1:17

PLEASES

Whatever the LORD p, he does, ... Ps 135:6
commandments and do what p him. ...... 1 Jn 3:22

PLEASING

a sacrifice acceptable and p to God. .... Phil 4:18
worthy of the Lord, fully p to him: .... Col 1:10
for such sacrifices are p to God.......... Heb 13:16

PLEASURE

Whoever loves p will be a poor man; ... Prv 21:17
for it is your Father's good p to give .... Lk 12:32
both to will and to work for his good p.. Phil 2:13
lovers of p rather than lovers of God, .. 2 Tm 3:4

PLEASURES

at your right hand are p forevermore. .. Ps 16:11
by the cares and riches and p of life, ... Lk 8:14
than to enjoy the fleeting p of sin, ... Heb 11:25

PLOW

hand to the p and looks back is fit........ Lk 9:62
the plowman should p in hope and .... 1 Cor 9:10

PLOWSHARES

shall beat their swords into p, ... Is 2:4
Beat your p into swords, and .... Jl 3:10

PLUNDER

So you shall p the Egyptians." .... Ex 3:22
strong man's house and p his goods, .. Mt 12:29

POINT

obedient to the p of death, ... Phil 2:8
but fails in one p has become .... Jas 2:10

POISON

have turned justice into p and the fruit ... Am 6:12
It is a restless evil, full of deadly p. ...... Jas 3:8

POLLUTE

You shall not p the land in which ...... Nm 35:33

POLLUTED

they p the house of the LORD .... 2 Chr 36:14
and the land was p with blood. .... Ps 106:38
to abstain from the things p by idols, .. Acts 15:20

PONDER

Be angry, and do not sin; p in .... Ps 4:4
P the path of your feet; then all your .... Prv 4:26

POOR

But there will be no p among you; .... Dt 15:4
never cease to be p in the land. .... Dt 15:11
You shall not be partial to the p or ...... Lv 19:15
The LORD makes p and makes .... 1 Sm 2:7
distributed freely; he has given to the p .. Ps 112:9
Better is a p person who walks in .... Prv 19:1
closes his ear to the cry of the p will .... Prv 21:13
anointed me to bring good news to the p; .. Is 61:1
"Blessed are the p in spirit, for theirs .... Mt 5:3
sell what you possess and give to the p .. Mt 19:21
For you always have the p with you, ... Mt 26:11
and he saw a p widow put in two small .. Lk 21:2
for your sake he became p, ... 2 Cor 8:9
who are p in the world to be rich in faith .. Jas 2:5

PORTION

But the LORD's p is his people, ... Dt 32:9
let there be a double p of your spirit .... 2 Kgs 2:9
strength of my heart and my p forever. .. Ps 73:26
The LORD is my p; I promise .... Ps 119:57
their land they shall possess a double p; .. Is 61:7
"The LORD is my p," says my soul, ... Lam 3:24

POSSESS

to give you this land to p." .... Gn 15:7
LORD your God is giving you to p.'" ...... Jos 1:11
and p the kingdom forever, ... Dn 7:18

POSSESSION

land of Canaan, for an everlasting p, ... Gn 17:8
I will give it to you for a p................... Ex 6:8
our inheritance until we acquire p of it, .. Eph 1:14
people for his own p who are zealous ...... Ti 2:14

POSSESSIONS

away sorrowful, for he had great p... ... Mt 19:22
not consist in the abundance of his p." .. Lk 12:15
were selling their p and belongings .... Acts 2:45

POSSIBLE

but with God all things are p." .... Mt 19:26
impossible with man is p with God." ...... Lk 18:27

POT

a smoking fire p and a flaming torch .... Gn 15:17
man of God, there is death in the p!" .. 2 Kgs 4:40

POTTER

we are the clay, and you are our p; ...... Is 64:8
as it seemed good to the p to do.......... Jer 18:4
Has the p no right over the clay, to .... Rom 9:21

POUR

p out your heart before him; .... Ps 62:8
I will p my Spirit upon your offspring, ... Is 44:3
that I will p out my Spirit on all flesh; .... Jl 2:28
that I will p out my Spirit on all flesh, .. Acts 2:17

POURED

the covenant, which is p out for many. .. Mk 14:24
Spirit was p out even on the Gentiles. .. Acts 10:45
God's love has been p into our hearts .... Rom 5:5
For I am already being p out as a drink .. 2 Tm 4:6
whom he p out on us richly through Jesus .. Ti 3:6

POVERTY

Love not sleep, lest you come to p; .... Prv 20:13
who is hasty comes only to p. .... Prv 21:5
give me neither p nor riches; .... Prv 30:8
she out of her p has put in everything .. Mk 12:44
so that you by his p might become rich. .. 2 Cor 8:9

POWER

I have raised you up, to show you my p, .. Ex 9:16
Great is our Lord, and abundant in p; .. Ps 147:5
He gives p to the faint, and to him ...... Is 40:29
"It is he who made the earth by his p, .. Jer 51:15
And the p of the Lord was with him .... Lk 5:17
for I perceive that p has gone out from .. Lk 8:46
you are clothed with p from on high." .. Lk 24:49
But you will receive p when the Holy .... Acts 1:8
gospel, for it is the p of God for .... Rom 1:16
who are being saved it is the p of God.. 1 Cor 1:18
will also raise us up by his p. .... 1 Cor 6:14
that the surpassing p belongs to God .... 2 Cor 4:7
being strengthened with all p, ... Col 1:11
Salvation and glory and p belong to ...... Rv 19:1

POWERFUL

The voice of the LORD is p; .... Ps 29:4
worldly standards, not many were p, .. 1 Cor 1:26
through faith in the p working of God, .. Col 2:12

POWERS

present nor things to come, nor p, ... Rom 8:38
against the cosmic p over this present .. Eph 6:12

PRACTICE

For they preach, but do not p.... .... Mt 23:3
P these things, immerse yourself .... 1 Tm 4:15
No one born of God makes a p of .... 1 Jn 3:9

PRACTICING

break off your sins by p righteousness, .. Dn 4:27
"Beware of p your righteousness before .. Mt 6:1

PRAISE

this is my God, and I will p him, ... Ex 15:2
O you righteous! P befits the upright. .... Ps 33:1
p shall continually be in my mouth. ...... Ps 34:1
my mouth will declare your p .... Ps 51:15
Let the peoples p you, O God; .... Ps 67:3
Let the heavens p your wonders, ... Ps 89:5

and his courts with p! Give thanks .... Ps 100:4
I p you, for I am fearfully and .... Ps 139:14
P the LORD! P the LORD, ... Ps 146:1
Let everything that has breath p the .... Ps 150:6
Let another p you, and not your .... Prv 27:2
and a man is tested by his p................ Prv 27:21
let her works p her in the gates. .... Prv 31:31
garment of p instead of a faint spirit; .... Is 61:3
I will sing p with my spirit, ... 1 Cor 14:15
to the p of his glorious grace, ... Eph 1:6
anything worthy of p, think .... Phil 4:8
offer up a sacrifice of p to God, ... Heb 13:15
Is anyone cheerful? Let him sing p ...... Jas 5:13
be found to result in p and glory .... 1 Pt 1:7
"P our God, all you his servants, ... Rv 19:5

PRAISED

LORD, who is worthy to be p, ... Ps 18:3
and greatly to be p in the city of our .... Ps 48:1
streets, that they may be p by others. .... Mt 6:5
saw what had taken place, he p God, .. Lk 23:47

PRAISES

nations, and sing p to your name. ...... 2 Sm 22:50
will shout for joy, when I sing p to you; .. Ps 71:23
"Sing p to the LORD, for he has .... Is 12:5

PRAISING

p and giving thanks to the LORD, ... Ezr 3:11
healed, turned back, p God with a ...... Lk 17:15
p God and having favor with all .... Acts 2:47
walking and leaping and p God. .... Acts 3:8

PRAY

the LORD by ceasing to p for you, ... 1 Sm 12:23
Love your enemies and p for .... Mt 5:44
P then like this: "Our Father in .... Mt 6:9
p for those who abuse you. .... Lk 6:28
ought always to p and not lose heart. .... Lk 18:1
do not know what to p for as we .... Rom 8:26
For if I p in a tongue, my spirit prays .. 1 Cor 14:14
p without ceasing, ... 1 Thes 5:17
the men should p, lifting holy hands ...... 1 Tm 2:8
and p for one another, ... Jas 5:16

PRAYED

I p to the LORD my God .... Dn 9:4
a little farther he fell on his face and p, .. Mt 26:39
Pharisee, standing by himself, p thus: .... Lk 18:11

PRAYER

O God, hear my p; give ear to .... Ps 54:2
be called a house of p for all peoples." .... Is 56:7
'My house shall be called a house of p,' .. Mt 21:13
And whatever you ask in p, you will .... Mt 21:22
were devoting themselves to p, ... Acts 1:14
in tribulation, be constant in p. .... Rom 12:12
You also must help us by p, so .... 2 Cor 1:11
anything, but in everything by p .... Phil 4:6
Continue steadfastly in p, being .... Col 4:2
made holy by the word of God and p. .. 1 Tm 4:5
The p of a righteous person has great .. Jas 5:16

PRAYERS

for a pretense make long p. .... Mk 12:40
granted us through the p of many........ 2 Cor 1:11
know that through your p and the help .. Phil 1:19
that supplications, intercessions, ... 1 Tm 2:1
so that your p may not be hindered. .... 1 Pt 3:7
incense, which are the p of the saints. .. Rv 5:8

PRAYING

And whenever you stand p, forgive, ... Mk 11:25
and Silas were p and singing hymns .... Acts 16:25
p at all times in the Spirit, ... Eph 6:18

PREACH

For they p, but do not practice. .... Mt 23:3
And how are they to p unless they .... Rom 10:15
folly of what we p to save those .... 1 Cor 1:21
Woe to me if I do not p the gospel! .. 1 Cor 9:16
I might p him among the Gentiles, ... Gal 1:16
to p to the Gentiles the unsearchable .... Eph 3:8

p the word; be ready in season and ...... 2 Tm 4:2

PREACHED
he p good news to the people............... Lk 3:18
And he came and p peace to you ,..... Eph 2:17
through those who p the good news .. 1 Pt 1:12

PREACHING
not cease teaching and p that the Christ ..Acts 5:42
are they to hear without someone p? ... Rom 10:14
not been raised, then our p is in vain .. 1 Cor 15:14
if anyone is p to you a gospel contrary ....Gal 1:9
those who labor in p and teaching. ..... 1 Tm 5:17

PRECEPTS
the p of the LORD are right, rejoicing .... Ps 19:8
I will meditate on your p and fix my .... Ps 119:15
I give you good p; do not forsake my .... Prv 4:2

PRECIOUS
How p is your steadfast love, ... Ps 36:7
P in the sight of the LORD is the .... Ps 116:15
your faith—more p than gold that ..... 1 Pt 1:7
but with the p blood of Christ, ... 1 Pt 1:19

PREDESTINED
and your plan had p to take place. ...... Acts 4:28
he foreknew he also p to be conformed .Rom 8:29
p us for adoption to himself as sons .... Eph 1:5
having been p according to the .... Eph 1:11

PREEMINENT
that in everything he might be p. .... Col 1:18

PREPARE
You p a table before me in the .... Ps 23:5
"In the wilderness p the way of the ..... Is 40:3
to you, to meet your God, ... Am 4:12
'P the way of the Lord; .... Mt 3:3
And if I go and p a place for you, I .....Jn 14:3

PREPARED
which he has p beforehand for glory— .. Rom 9:23
what God has p for those who love .. 1 Cor 2:9
He who has p us for this very thing ... 2 Cor 5:5
good works, which God p beforehand, ...Eph 2:10
always being p to make a defense to .. 1 Pt 3:15

PRESENCE
set the bread of the P on the table .... Ex 25:30
Let us come into his p with .... Ps 95:2
Or where shall I flee from your p? ... Ps 139:7
and bring us with you into his p. ...... 2 Cor 4:14
away from the p of the Lord .... 2 Thes 1:9
appear in the p of God on our behalf. ... Heb 9:24

PRESENT
but p yourselves to God as those .... Rom 6:13
absent in body, I am p in spirit; .... 1 Cor 5:3
so that he might p the church to .... Eph 5:27
in order to p you holy and blameless ... Col 1:22

PRESERVE
but the lips of the wise will p them. ..... Prv 14:3
Whoever seeks to p his life will lose ...... Lk 17:33
who have faith and p their souls. .... Heb 10:39

PRESERVES
The LORD p the faithful but .... Ps 31:23
wisdom p the life of him who has it. ... Eccl 7:12

PRESS
let us p on to know the LORD; .... Hos 6:3
I p on toward the goal for the prize ... Phil 3:14

PRESSED
Good measure, p down, shaken .... Lk 6:38

PRICE
for you were bought with a p........... 1 Cor 6:20
You were bought with a p; do not .... 1 Cor 7:23
desires take the water of life without p .. Rv 22:17

PRIDE
P goes before destruction, ... Prv 16:18
sensuality, envy, slander, p, foolishness. .. Mk 7:22
desires of the eyes and p of life— .... 1 Jn 2:16

PRIEST
"You are a p forever after the order ...". Ps 110:4
For we do not have a high p who is ... Heb 4:15
"You are a p forever, after the order ... Heb 5:6
have such a high p, holy, innocent, ... Heb 7:26
we have such a high p, one who is .... Heb 8:1

PRIESTHOOD
but he holds his p permanently, ... Heb 7:24
a chosen race, a royal p, a holy nation, .. 1 Pt 2:9

PRIESTS
a kingdom of p and a holy nation.' ..... Ex 19:6
a kingdom and p to our God, ... Rv 5:10
but they will be p of God and .... Rv 20:6

PRINCE
Everlasting Father, P of Peace. .... Is 9:6
following the p of the power of the air, .. Eph 2:2

PRISON
I was in p and you came to me.' .... Mt 25:36
Lord opened the p doors and brought ... Acts 5:19
Christ, on account of which I am in p— .. Col 4:3
Remember those who are in p, ... Heb 13:3
went and proclaimed to the spirits in p, . 1 Pt 3:19
Satan will be released from his p .... Rv 20:7

PRISONER
For this reason I, Paul, a p of Christ ... Eph 3:1

PRISONERS
The LORD sets the p free; .... Ps 146:7
to bring out the p from the dungeon, ... Is 42:7

PRIZE
run, but only one receives the p? .... 1 Cor 9:24
for the p of the upward call of God ... Phil 3:14

PROCLAIM
hear whispered, p on the housetops. .... Mt 10:27
"Go into all the world and p the gospel .. Mk 16:15
to p the year of the Lord's favor." .... Lk 4:19
drink the cup, you p the Lord's death . 1 Cor 11:26
For what we p is not ourselves, but ..... 2 Cor 4:5

PROCLAIMS
and the sky above p his handiwork. .... Ps 19:1

PRODUCES
For godly grief p a repentance that ... 2 Cor 7:10
and p a crop useful to those .... Heb 6:7
testing of your faith p steadfastness. .... Jas 1:3

PROFANE
you shall not p my holy name, ... Lv 22:32

PROFIT
Riches do not p in the day of wrath, ... Prv 11:4
In all toil there is p, but mere talk ...... Prv 14:23
For what will it p a man if he gains ..... Mt 16:26

PROFITABLE
out by God and p for teaching, ... 2 Tm 3:16
are excellent and p for people. .... Ti 3:8

PROMISE
I am sending the p of my Father upon ... Lk 24:49
but to wait for the p of the Father, ... Acts 1:4
in order that the p may rest on grace ... Rom 4:16
so that the p by faith in Jesus Christ ...... Gal 3:22
the first commandment with a p), ... Eph 6:2
God according to the p of the life .... 2 Tm 1:1
The Lord is not slow to fulfill his p .... 2 Pt 3:9
according to his p we are waiting. .... 2 Pt 3:13
And this is the p that he made to us— .. 1 Jn 2:25

PROMISED
your God will bless you, as he p you, ... Dt 15:6
will do this thing that he has p: .... Is 38:7
God was able to do what he had p. ..... Rom 4:21
receive the p Spirit through faith. .... Gal 3:14
were sealed with the p Holy Spirit, ... Eph 1:13
for he who p is faithful. .... Heb 10:23
God has p to those who love him. ....Jas 1:12

PROMISES
Not one word of all the good p .... Jos 21:45
of the law, the worship, and the p....... Rom 9:4
For all the p of God find their Yes ..... 2 Cor 1:20
Since we have these p, beloved, let ...... 2 Cor 7:1
to us his precious and very great p, ... 2 Pt 1:4

PROPERTY
accepted the plundering of your p, ... Heb 10:34

PROPHECIES
As for p, they will pass away; .... 1 Cor 13:8
Do not despise p, ... 1 Thes 5:20

PROPHECY
working of miracles, to another p, ... 1 Cor 12:10
while p is a sign not for unbelievers .. 1 Cor 14:22
For no p was ever produced by the will . 2 Pt 1:21
keeps the words of the p of this book." .. Rv 22:7

PROPHESY
your sons and your daughters shall p, ... Jl 2:28
Lord, did we not p in your name, ... Mt 7:22
pour out my Spirit, and they shall p ..... Acts 2:18
For we know in part and we p in part, . 1 Cor 13:9
gifts, especially that you may p, ... 1 Cor 14:1
So, my brothers, earnestly desire to p, .. 1 Cor 14:39

PROPHET
I will raise up for them a p like you ...... Dt 18:18
when the word of that p comes to pass, .. Jer 28:9
send you Elijah the p before the great .... Mal 4:5
The one who receives a p because he .. Mt 10:41
no p is acceptable in his hometown....... Lk 4:24
"Sir, I perceive that you are a p .... Jn 4:19

PROPHETIC
through the p writings has been .... Rom 16:26
the p word more fully confirmed, ... 2 Pt 1:19

PROPHETS
my anointed ones, do my p no harm!" .. Ps 105:15
abolish the Law or the P; I have not ..... Mt 5:17
"Beware of false p, who come to you .... Mt 7:15
believe all that the p have spoken! ...... Lk 24:25
To him all the p bear witness ....Acts 10:43
apostles, second p, third teachers, ... 1 Cor 12:28
the spirits of p are subject to p........ 1 Cor 14:32
the apostles, the p, the evangelists, ... Eph 4:11
God spoke to our fathers by the p, ... Heb 1:1
p who prophesied about the grace ...... 1 Pt 1:10
for many false p have gone out into ..... 1 Jn 4:1

PROPITIATION
God put forward as a p by his blood, ... Rom 3:25
to make p for the sins of the people. .... Heb 2:17
He is the p for our sins, and .... 1 Jn 2:2
sent his Son to be the p for our sins. .... 1 Jn 4:10

PROSPER
His ways p at all times; your .... Ps 10:5
conceals his transgressions will not p, ... Prv 28:13
for you do not know which will p, ... Eccl 11:6
the will of the LORD shall p .... Is 53:10

PROSPERS
not wither. In all that he does, he p. ......Ps 1:3

PROSPERITY
when I saw the p of the wicked. .... Ps 73:3
In the day of p be joyful, and in .... Eccl 7:14

PROSTITUTE
For a p is a deep pit; an adulteress is .. Prv 23:27
make them members of a p? Never! .. 1 Cor 6:15
also Rahab the p justified by works .... Jas 2:25

PROSTITUTES
but a companion of p squanders his ... Prv 29:3
tax collectors and the p believed him. ... Mt 21:32
devoured your property with p, you .... Lk 15:30

PROTECT
I will deliver him; I will p him, ... Ps 91:14

PROTECTS

the LORD **p** him and keeps him .... Ps 41:2
but he who was born of God **p** him, ... 1 Jn 5:18

PROUD

tears down the house of the **p** but...... Prv 15:25
patient in spirit is better than the **p** ..... Eccl 7:8
So do not become **p**, but fear, ... Rom 11:20
lovers of money, **p**, arrogant, abusive, ... 2 Tm 3:2
"God opposes the **p** but gives grace ....Jas 4:6

PROVE

P me, O LORD, and try me; test .... Ps 26:2
much fruit and so **p** to be my disciples....Jn 15:8
if they **p** themselves blameless........... 1 Tm 3:10

PROVIDE

"The Lord will **p**"; .... Gn 22:14
he will also **p** the way of escape, ... 1 Cor 10:13
if anyone does not **p** for his relatives, ... 1 Tm 5:8

PROVIDED

O God, you **p** for the needy................. Ps 68:10
there will be richly **p** for you an .... 2 Pt 1:11

PROVOKE

your God, so as to **p** him to anger, ... Dt 4:25
Shall we **p** the Lord to jealousy? ...... 1 Cor 10:22

PRUDENCE

to give **p** to the simple, knowledge .... Prv 1:4
Daniel replied with **p** and discretion to .... Dn 2:14

PRUDENT

but whoever restrains his lips is **p**. ...... Prv 10:19
at once, but the **p** ignores an insult. ..... Prv 12:16
A **p** man conceals knowledge, ... Prv 12:23
but the **p** gives thought to his steps. ..... Prv 14:15
but whoever heeds reproof is **p**, ... Prv 15:5
Therefore he who is **p** will keep silent .... Am 5:13

PSALMS

addressing one another in **p** and hymns .... Eph 5:19
singing **p** and hymns and spiritual ...... Col 3:16

PUFFS

"knowledge" **p** up, but love builds ...... 1 Cor 8:1

PUNISH

I will **p** the world for its evil, ... Is 13:11
being ready to **p** every disobedience, .. 2 Cor 10:6
as sent by him to **p** those who do evil ... 1 Pt 2:14

PUNISHMENT

Cain said to the LORD, "My **p** is .... Gn 4:13
What will you do on the day of **p**, ... Is 10:3
And these will go away into eternal **p**, .. Mt 25:46
will suffer the **p** of eternal destruction, .. 2 Thes 1:9
How much worse **p**, do you think, ... Heb 10:29
For fear has to do with **p**, and whoever .. 1 Jn 4:18
by undergoing a **p** of eternal fire. .... Jude 7

PURE

The words of the LORD are **p** .... Ps 12:6
with the purified you show yourself **p**; .. Ps 18:26
How can a young man keep his way **p**? .. Ps 119:9
are **p** in his own eyes, but the Lord ...... Prv 16:2
"Blessed are the **p** in heart, for they ...... Mt 5:8
present you as a **p** virgin to Christ. .... 2 Cor 11:2
whatever is just, whatever is **p**, ... Phil 4:8
the sins of others; keep yourself **p**...... 1 Tm 5:22
who call on the Lord from a **p** heart. .... 2 Tm 2:22
To the **p**, all things are **p**, but .... Ti 1:15
But the wisdom from above is first **p**, ...Jas 3:17
love one another earnestly from a **p** ..... 1 Pt 1:22
hopes in him purifies himself as he is **p**... 1 Jn 3:3

PURGE

P me with hyssop, and I shall be clean; ... Ps 51:7
"**P** the evil person from among you." ... 1 Cor 5:13

PURIFY

Many shall **p** themselves and make ..... Dn 12:10
to **p** for himself a people for his own ...... Ti 2:14
p our conscience from dead works ...... Heb 9:14

PURITY

He who loves **p** of heart, and whose... Prv 22:11
by **p**, knowledge, patience, kindness, ... 2 Cor 6:6
younger women as sisters, in all **p**........ 1 Tm 5:2

PURPOSE

and that no **p** of yours can be thwarted. ...Jb 42:2
The LORD will fulfill his **p** for me; .... Ps 138:8
LORD has made everything for its **p**, ... Prv 16:4
but it shall accomplish that which I **p**, ... Is 55:11
who are called according to his **p**. ...... Rom 8:28
mystery of his will, according to his **p**, ... Eph 1:9
but because of his own **p** and grace, ... 2 Tm 1:9

PURSUE

do good; seek peace and **p** it. .... Ps 34:14
So then let us **p** what makes for peace .. Rom 14:19
P love, and earnestly desire the .... 1 Cor 14:1
P righteousness, godliness, faith, ... 1 Tm 6:11
do good; let him seek peace and **p** it. .... 1 Pt 3:11

QUARREL

Whoever meddles in a **q** not his own .... Prv 26:17
but not to **q** over opinions. .... Rom 14:1
before God not to **q** about words, ... 2 Tm 2:14
and cannot obtain, so you fight and **q**. ....Jas 4:2

QUARRELING

where there is no whisperer, **q** ceases. .... Prv 26:20
and sensuality, not in **q** and jealousy. .. Rom 13:13
lifting holy hands without anger or **q**; .... 1 Tm 2:8
evil of no one, to avoid **q**, to be gentle, ... Ti 3:2

QUARRELS

for controversy and for **q** about words, ... 1 Tm 6:4
you know that they breed **q**............... 2 Tm 2:23
What causes **q** and what causes fights ....Jas 4:1

QUARRELSOME

than in a house shared with a **q** wife. .... Prv 21:9
but gentle, not **q**, not a lover of money. ... 1 Tm 3:3
servant must not be **q** but kind to .... 2 Tm 2:24

QUENCH

Many waters cannot **q** love, neither .... Sg 8:7
Do not **q** the Spirit. .... 1 Thes 5:19

QUENCHED

shall not die, their fire shall not be **q**, ... Is 66:24
worm does not die and the fire is not **q**. .. Mk 9:48

QUICK

A man of **q** temper acts foolishly, ... Prv 14:17
let every person be **q** to hear, slow to ....Jas 1:19

QUIET

with **q** than a house full of feasting ...... Prv 17:1
he will **q** you by his love; .... Zep 3:17
beauty of a gentle and **q** spirit, ... 1 Pt 3:4

QUIETLY

spirit, but a wise man **q** holds it back. .... Prv 29:11
and to aspire to live **q**, and to mind ... 1 Thes 4:11
Let a woman learn **q** with all .... 1 Tm 2:11

QUIETNESS

in **q** and in trust shall be your strength." .. Is 30:15
result of righteousness, **q** and trust ...... Is 32:17

QUIVER

is the man who fills his **q** with them! .... Ps 127:5

RACE

the **r** is not to the swift, ... Eccl 9:11
know that in a **r** all the runners run, ... 1 Cor 9:24
the good fight, I have finished the **r**, ... 2 Tm 4:7
run with endurance the **r** that is set ..... Heb 12:1

RACHEL

So Jacob served seven years for **R**, ... Gn 29:20
R weeping for her children; .... Mt 2:18

RADIANCE

He is the **r** of the glory of God .... Heb 1:3
having the glory of God, its **r** like a ...... Rv 21:11

RADIANT

Those who look to him are **r**, ... Ps 34:5

REBUKE

Better is open **r** than hidden love......... Prv 27:5

My beloved is **r** and ruddy, ... Sg 5:10
Then you shall see and be **r**; .... Is 60:5
and his clothes became **r**, intensely .... Mk 9:3

RAIN

I will send **r** on the earth forty days and ... Gn 7:4
May my teaching drop as the **r**, my ...... Dt 32:2
shall be neither dew nor **r** these years, .. 1 Kgs 17:1
let the clouds **r** down righteousness; .... Is 45:8
and sends **r** on the just and on the .... Mt 5:45
he prayed fervently that it might not **r**, ...Jas 5:17

RAISE

temple, and in three days I will **r** it up." ....Jn 2:19
and I will **r** him up on the last day." .... Jn 6:40
and will also **r** us up by his power. .... 1 Cor 6:14
he who raised the Lord Jesus will **r** us .. 2 Cor 4:14
was able even to **r** him from the dead, .. Heb 11:19
who is sick, and the Lord will **r** him up..... Jas 5:15

RAISED

be killed, and on the third day be **r**. ...... Mt 16:21
Lazarus, whom he had **r** from the dead. ....Jn 12:9
This Jesus God **r** up, and of that we all .. Acts 2:32
trespasses and **r** for our justification. ..... Rom 4:25
he who **r** Christ Jesus from the dead ..... Rom 8:11
that he was **r** on the third day in .... 1 Cor 15:4
what is **r** is imperishable. .... 1 Cor 15:42
and **r** us up with him and seated us .... Eph 2:6
If then you have been **r** with Christ, ... Col 3:1
who **r** him from the dead and gave him . 1 Pt 1:21

RANSOM

and to give his life as a **r** for many." .... Mt 20:28
who gave himself as a **r** for all, ... 1 Tm 2:6

RANSOMED

the **r** of the Lord shall return and come .. Is 51:11
knowing that you were **r** from the futile. . 1 Pt 1:18
and by your blood you **r** people for God .... Rv 5:9

RAVENS

And the **r** brought him bread and ...... 1 Kgs 17:6
Consider the **r**: they neither sow nor : .... Lk 12:24

READ

the Covenant and **r** it in the hearing....... Ex 24:7
They **r** from the book, from the Law ...... Neh 8:8
our hearts, to be known and **r** by all. .... 2 Cor 3:2

READY

But you are a God **r** to forgive, ... Neh 9:17
I was **r** to be sought by those who........ Is 65:1
Therefore you also must be **r**, for the .... Mt 24:44
obedient, to be **r** for every good work, ... Ti 3:1

REAP

sow in tears shall **r** with shouts of joy! ... Ps 126:5
deposit, and **r** what you did not sow.' .... Lk 19:21
sows bountifully will also **r** bountifully. .. 2 Cor 9:6
whatever one sows, that he will also **r**. ... Gal 6:7
for the hour to **r** has come, ... Rv 14:15

REAPERS

end of the age, and the **r** are angels. .... Mt 13:39

REASON

"Come now, let us **r** together, ... Is 1:18
pure, then peaceable, gentle, open to **r**, ...Jas 3:17
a **r** for the hope that is in you; .... 1 Pt 3:15

REBEKAH

And **R** lifted up her eyes, and when ..... Gn 24:64
But Jacob said to **R** his mother,.......... Gn 27:11

REBELLION

An evil man seeks only **r**, ... Prv 17:11
not come, unless the **r** comes first, ... 2 Thes 2:3
do not harden your hearts as in the **r**, ... Heb 3:8

REBELLIOUS

but the **r** dwell in a parched land.......... Ps 68:6
GOD has opened my ear, and I was not **r**; .. Is 50:5
this people has a stubborn and **r** heart; ... Jer 5:23

better for a man to hear the **r** of the ...... Eccl 7:5
If your brother sins, **r** him, ... Lk 17:3
Do not **r** an older man but encourage ... 1 Tm 5:1
in sin, **r** them in the presence of all, ... 1 Tm 5:20
exhort and **r** with all authority. .... Ti 2:15

RECEIVE
But to all who did **r** him, who believed .....Jn 1:12
'It is more blessed to give than to **r**.' ...Acts 20:35
so that we might **r** the promised Spirit ... Gal 3:14
You ask and do not **r**, because you ask ..... Jas 4:3
God, to **r** glory and honor and power, ... Rv 4:11

RECEIVED
I say to you, they have **r** their reward. ...... Mt 6:2
in prayer, believe that you have **r** it, ... Mk 11:24
Therefore, as you **r** Christ Jesus the .... Col 2:6

RECEIVES
For everyone who asks **r**, ... Mt 7:8
"Whoever **r** you **r** me, and .... Mt 10:40
"Whoever **r** one such child in my name ... Mt 18:5

RECKONING
I will require a **r** for the life of man. .... Gn 9:5

RECOMPENSE
Vengeance is mine, and **r**, for the time ... Dt 32:35
is with him, and his **r** before him. .... Is 40:10

RECONCILE
and might **r** us both to God in one ...... Eph 2:16
and through him to **r** to himself all .... Col 1:20

RECONCILED
First be **r** to your brother, and then .... Mt 5:24
were enemies we were **r** to God by ...... Rom 5:10
or else be **r** to her husband), ... 1 Cor 7:11
you on behalf of Christ, be **r** to God. ... 2 Cor 5:20

RECONCILIATION
whom we have now received **r**. .... Rom 5:11
rejection means the **r** of the world, ... Rom 11:15
himself and gave us the ministry of **r**; ... 2 Cor 5:18
entrusting to us the message of **r**. ...... 2 Cor 5:19

RED
though they are **r** like crimson, ... Is 1:18
'It will be fair weather, for the sky is **r**.' ... Mt 16:2

REDEEM
I will **r** you with an outstretched arm .... Ex 6:6
God went to **r** to be his people, ... 2 Sm 7:23
R us for the sake of your steadfast love! ... Ps 44:26
Is my hand shortened, that it cannot **r**? .... Is 50:2
to **r** those who were under the law, so ... Gal 4:5
gave himself for us to **r** us from all .... Ti 2:14

REDEEMED
Let the **r** of the LORD say so, ... Ps 107:2
return to me, for I have **r** you. ....Is 44:22
and you shall be **r** without money." .... Is 52:3
for he has visited and **r** his people .... Lk 1:68
Christ **r** us from the curse of the law ...... Gal 3:13

REDEEMER
For I know that my **R** lives, and at........ Jb 19:25
O Lord, my rock and my **r**. .... Ps 19:14
Our **R**—the Lord of hosts is his name— ... Is 47:4
Holy One of Israel is your **R**, ... Is 54:5

REDEEMS
LORD **r** the life of his servants; .... Ps 34:22
who **r** your life from the pit, ... Ps 103:4

REDEMPTION
heads, because your **r** is drawing near." ... Lk 21:28
adoption as sons, the **r** of our bodies. .... Rom 8:23
righteousness and sanctification and **r**, . 1 Cor 1:30
In him we have **r** through his blood, ... Eph 1:7
in whom we have **r**, the forgiveness of ... Col 1:14
own blood, thus securing an eternal **r**. .... Heb 9:12

REFUGE
select cities to be cities of **r** for you, ... Nm 35:11
Blessed are all who take **r** in him. .... Ps 2:12
God is our **r** and strength, a very .... Ps 46:1

"My **r** and my fortress, my God, ... Ps 91:2
But the LORD is a **r** to his .... Jl 3:16

REIGN
The LORD will **r** forever, ... Ps 146:10
Behold, a king will **r** in righteousness, ... Is 32:1
Let not sin therefore **r** in your mortal ...... Rom 6:12
For he must **r** until he has put all ...... 1 Cor 15:25
if we endure, we will also **r** with him;... 2 Tm 2:12
Christ, and he shall **r** forever and ever." ... Rv 11:15
they will **r** with him for a thousand .... Rv 20:6

REIGNED
death **r** through that one man, ... Rom 5:17
so that, as sin **r** in death, grace also ...... Rom 5:21

REIGNS
LORD **r**; he is robed in majesty; .... Ps 93:1
The LORD **r**, let the earth rejoice; .... Ps 97:1
says to Zion, "Your God **r**." .... Is 52:7
For the Lord our God the Almighty **r**. ...... Rv 19:6

REJECTED
that the builders **r** has become the ...... Ps 118:22
He was despised and **r** by men, ... Is 53:3
Jesus is the stone that was **r** by you, ... Acts 4:11
God has not **r** his people whom he ...... Rom 11:2
nothing is to be **r** if it is received .... 1 Tm 4:4
a living stone **r** by men but in the sight ... 1 Pt 2:4

REJECTS
one who **r** me **r** him who sent me." ...... Lk 10:16
one who **r** me and does not receive ...... Jn 12:48

REJOICE
those who seek the LORD **r**! .... 1 Chr 16:10
my heart shall **r** in your salvation. .... Ps 13:5
has made; let us **r** and be glad in it. ...... Ps 118:24
the righteous increase, the people **r**, ... Prv 29:2
bride, so shall your God **r** over you. .... Is 62:5
he will **r** over you with gladness; .... Zep 3:17
R and be glad, for your reward is .... Mt 5:12
but **r** that your names are written in ...... Lk 10:20
More than that, we **r** in our sufferings, ... Rom 5:3
R with those who **r**, weep .... Rom 12:15
R in the Lord always; again I will say, ... Phil 4:4
In this you **r**, though now for a little .... 1 Pt 1:6

REJOICES
my heart is glad, and my whole being **r**; .... Ps 16:9
and my spirit **r** in God my Savior, ... Lk 1:47

REJOICING
r that they were counted worthy to ...... Acts 5:41
as sorrowful, yet always **r**; as poor, ... 2 Cor 6:10

RELENT
God may turn and **r** and turn from his ...... Jon 3:9

RELENTED
LORD **r** from the calamity and .... 2 Sm 24:16

RELIGION
promoting self-made **r** and asceticism ... Col 2:23
R that is pure and undefiled before God ...Jas 1:27

RELY
LORD our God, for we **r** on you, ... 2 Chr 14:11
make us **r** not on ourselves but on God . 2 Cor 1:9
For all who **r** on works of the law are .... Gal 3:10

REMAIN
Each one should **r** in the condition in ... 1 Cor 7:20
But to **r** in the flesh is more necessary ... Phil 1:24
they will perish, but you **r**; .... Heb 1:11

REMEMBER
I will see it and **r** the everlasting .... Gn 9:16
You shall **r** the LORD your God, ... Dt 8:18
R the wondrous works that he has ...... 1 Chr 16:12
R not the sins of my youth or my............ Ps 25:7
R how short my time is! .... Ps 89:47
R also your Creator in the days of ....Eccl 12:1
own sake, and I will not **r** your sins........ Is 43:25
and I will **r** their sin no more." .... Jer 31:34
R Lot's wife. .... Lk 17:32

Only, they asked us to **r** the poor, ... Gal 2:10
r that you were at that time separated ... Eph 2:12
and I will **r** their sins no more." .... Heb 8:12

REMEMBERS
our frame; he **r** that we are dust. .... Ps 103:14
He **r** his covenant forever, the word .... Ps 105:8

REMEMBRANCE
is given for you. Do this in **r** of me." .... Lk 22:19
which is for you. Do this in **r** of me." . 1 Cor 11:24

REMNANT
A **r** will return, the **r** of Jacob, ...Is 10:21
I will gather the **r** of Israel; .... Mi 2:12
there is a **r**, chosen by grace. .... Rom 11:5

REMOVE
And I will **r** the heart of stone .... Ezk 36:26
R this cup from me. .... Mk 14:36

REND
Oh that you would **r** the heavens and ...... Is 64:1
and **r** your hearts and not your .... Jl 2:13

RENDER
What shall I **r** to the LORD .... Ps 116:12
"Therefore **r** to Caesar the things that ... Mt 22:21
He will **r** to each one according to his ... Rom 2:6

RENEW
and **r** a right spirit within me. .... Ps 51:10
the LORD shall **r** their strength; .... Is 40:31

RENEWED
so that your youth is **r** like the eagle's. .... Ps 103:5
inner self is being **r** day by day............ 2 Cor 4:16
and to be **r** in the spirit of your minds, ... Eph 4:23
new self, which is being **r** in .... Col 3:10

RENOUNCE
Why does the wicked **r** God .... Ps 10:13
does not **r** all that he has cannot be my ... Lk 14:33

REPAY
nor **r** us according to our iniquities. ...... Ps 103:10
then he will **r** each person according ..... Mt 16:27
R no one evil for evil, but give.......... Rom 12:17
"Vengeance is mine; I will **r**." .... Heb 10:30
Do not **r** evil for evil or reviling for .... 1 Pt 3:9
to **r** each one for what he has done. ...... Rv 22:12

REPENT
despise myself, and **r** in dust and ashes." ... Jb 42:6
"**R**, for the kingdom of heaven is at .... Mt 3:2
unless you **r**, you will all likewise perish. ... Lk 13:3
Peter said to them, "**R** and be baptized . Acts 2:38
R therefore, and turn back, ... Acts 3:19
all people everywhere to **r**,................Acts 17:30

REPENTANCE
Bear fruit in keeping with **r**....................... Mt 3:8
to call the righteous but sinners to **r**." ...... Lk 5:32
kindness is meant to lead you to **r**?....... Rom 2:4
godly grief produces a **r** that leads to... 2 Cor 7:10
but that all should reach **r**. .... 2 Pt 3:9

REPROACH
blameless and above **r** before him, ... Col 1:22
an overseer must be above **r**, ... 1 Tm 3:2

REPROOF
who rejects **r** leads others astray. .... Prv 10:17
who listens to **r** gains intelligence. .... Prv 15:32
and profitable for teaching, for **r**, ... 2 Tm 3:16

REPROVE
r, rebuke, and exhort, with complete ...... 2 Tm 4:2
Those whom I love, I **r** and discipline, ... Rv 3:19

REQUESTS
let your **r** be made known to God. .... Phil 4:6
we have the **r** that we have asked ...... 1 Jn 5:15

REQUIRE
does the LORD your God **r** of you, ... Dt 10:12
what does the LORD **r** of you ....Mi 6:8

RESCUE

righteousness deliver me and **r** me; .... Ps 71:2
The Lord will **r** me from every evil .... 2 Tm 4:18
Lord knows how to **r** the godly from ...... 2 Pt 2:9

RESCUED

yet from them all the Lord **r** me. .... 2 Tm 3:11

RESIST

Do not **r** the one who is evil. .... Mt 5:39
R the devil, and he will flee from you. ...... Jas 4:7
R him, firm in your faith, knowing .... 1 Pt 5:9

RESPECT

r to whom **r** is owed, honor to whom ... Rom 13:7
to **r** those who labor among .... 1 Thes 5:12
be subject to your masters with all **r**, ... 1 Pt 2:18

REST

seventh day is a Sabbath of solemn **r**, ... Ex 31:15
a dove! I would fly away and be at **r**; ..... Ps 55:6
a little folding of the hands to **r**, ... Prv 6:10
Spirit of the LORD shall **r** upon .... Is 11:2
"In returning and **r** you shall be saved; .. Is 30:15
walk in it, and find **r** for your souls. ...... Jer 6:16
heavy laden, and I will give you **r**. .... Mt 11:28
For we who have believed enter that **r**, .. Heb 4:3
"that they may **r** from their labors, ... Rv 14:13

RESTITUTION

shall make **r** from the best in his own ..... Ex 22:5
make full **r** for his wrong, ... Nm 5:7

RESTORATION

Aim for **r**, comfort one another, ... 2 Cor 13:11

RESTORE

R to me the joy of your salvation, ... Ps 51:12
I will lead him and **r** comfort to him ...... Is 57:18
I will **r** to you the years that the .... Jl 2:25
"Elijah does come first to **r** all things. .... Mk 9:12
at this time **r** the kingdom to Israel?" .... Acts 1:6
are spiritual should **r** him in a spirit ...... Gal 6:1
will himself **r**, confirm, strengthen, ... 1 Pt 5:10

RESTORES

He **r** my soul. He leads me in paths .... Ps 23:3

RESURRECTION

For in the **r** they neither marry nor .... Mt 22:30
you will be repaid at the **r** of the just." ... Lk 14:14
"I am the **r** and the life. .... Jn 11:25
that there will be a **r** of both the just .... Acts 24:15
be united with him in a **r** like his. .... Rom 6:5
So is it with the **r** of the dead. .... 1 Cor 15:42
may know him and the power of his **r**, .. Phil 3:10
living hope through the **r** of Jesus .... 1 Pt 1:3
years were ended. This is the first **r**. ...... Rv 20:5

RETURN

but if you **r** to me and keep my .... Neh 1:9
my mouth; it shall not **r** to me empty, ... Is 55:11
"**r** to me with all your heart, ... Jl 2:12
R to me, and I will **r** to you, ... Mal 3:7
what shall a man give in **r** for his soul? .. Mt 16:26
and lend, expecting nothing in **r**, ... Lk 6:35

REVEALED

but the things that are **r** belong to us .... Dt 29:29
the glory of the LORD shall be **r**, ... Is 40:5
nothing is covered that will not be **r**, ... Mt 10:26
flesh and blood has not **r** this to you, ... Mt 16:17
righteousness of God is **r** from faith ...... Rom 1:17
when the Lord Jesus is **r** from heaven .. 2 Thes 1:7
a salvation ready to be **r** in the last time . 1 Pt 1:5

REVELATION

light for **r** to the Gentiles, and for glory ... Lk 2:32
but I received it through a **r** of Jesus ..... Gal 1:12
brought to you at the **r** of Jesus Christ.. 1 Pt 1:13

REVERENCE

to one another out of **r** for Christ. .... Eph 5:21
acceptable worship, with **r** and awe, ... Heb 12:28

REVILE

"Blessed are you when others **r** you ...... Mt 5:11
he was reviled, he did not **r** in return; ... 1 Pt 2:23
those who **r** your good behavior in ...... 1 Pt 3:16

REVILED

When **r**, we bless; when persecuted, ...1 Cor 4:12
that the word of God may not be **r**. .... Ti 2:5

REVIVE

you who seek God, let your hearts **r**. ..... Ps 69:32
Will you not **r** us again, that your .... Ps 85:6
to **r** the spirit of the lowly, ... Is 57:15

REWARD

shield; your **r** shall be very great." .... Gn 15:1
in keeping them there is great **r**. .... Ps 19:11
the fruit of the womb a **r**. .... Ps 127:3
who sows righteousness gets a sure **r**. .. Prv 11:18
be glad, for your **r** is great in heaven, ... Mt 5:12
they have received their **r**. .... Mt 6:5
he will by no means lose his **r**." .... Mt 10:42
are receiving the due **r** of our deeds; .... Lk 23:41
will receive the inheritance as your **r**. .... Col 3:24
for he was looking to the **r**. .... Heb 11:26

RICH

blessing of the LORD makes **r**, ... Prv 10:22
The **r** and the poor meet together; ...... Prv 22:2
only with difficulty will a **r** person ...... Mt 19:23
"But woe to you who are **r**, for you...... Lk 6:24
for himself and is not **r** toward God." .... Lk 12:21
as poor, yet making many **r**; .... 2 Cor 6:10
you by his poverty might become **r**, ... 2 Cor 8:9
are to do good, to be **r** in good works, .. 1 Tm 6:18
For you say, I am **r**, I have prospered, ... Rv 3:17

RICHES

if **r** increase, set not your heart on them. . Ps 62:10
I delight as much as in all **r**. .... Ps 119:14
Whoever trusts in his **r** will fall, ... Prv 11:28
his eyes are never satisfied with **r**, ... Eccl 4:8
deceitfulness of **r** choke the word, ... Mt 13:22
who will entrust to you the true **r**? .... Lk 16:11
to make known the **r** of his glory .... Rom 9:23
bestowing his **r** on all who call on ...... Rom 10:12
show the immeasurable **r** of his grace .... Eph 2:7
that according to the **r** of his glory he .... Eph 3:16
to reach all the **r** of full assurance of ..... Col 2:2
on the uncertainty of **r**, but on God, ... 1 Tm 6:17
Your **r** have rotted and your garments ... Jas 5:2

RIGHT

And you shall do what is **r** and good .... Dt 6:18
Everyone did what was **r** in his own .... Jgs 17:6
how can a man be in the **r** before God? .. Jb 9:2
the precepts of the LORD are **r**, ... Ps 19:8
my Lord: "Sit at my **r** hand, until I .... Ps 110:1
Do not swerve to the **r** or to the left; .... Prv 4:27
There is a way that seems **r** to a man, ... Prv 14:12
gave the **r** to become children of God, ... Jn 1:12
I want to do **r**, evil lies close at hand.... Rom 7:21
found in all that is good and **r** and true), .. Eph 5:9
"Sit at my **r** hand until I make your .... Heb 1:13

RIGHTEOUS

Noah was a **r** man, blameless .... Gn 6:9
LORD knows the way of the **r**, ... Ps 1:6
Let the **r** one rejoice in the .... Ps 64:10
The **r** flourish like the palm tree .... Ps 92:12
Your testimonies are **r** forever; give .... Ps 119:144
the good and keep to the paths of the **r**. . Prv 2:20
but he hears the prayer of the **r**. .... Prv 15:29
When the **r** increase, the people rejoice, .. Prv 29:2
but a man sings and rejoices. .... Prv 29:6
our **r** deeds are like a polluted garment, .. Is 64:6
but the **r** shall live by his faith. .... Hab 2:4
For I came not to call the **r**, but sinners." .. Mt 9:13
separate the evil from the **r** .... Mt 13:49
punishment, but the **r** into eternal life." .. Mt 25:46
"The **r** shall live by faith." .... Rom 1:17
wrath when God's **r** judgment will be .... Rom 2:5

it is written: "None is **r**, no, not one; .... Rom 3:10
for "The **r** shall live by faith." .... Gal 3:11
This is evidence of the **r** judgment ...... 2 Thes 1:5
but my **r** one shall live by faith, ... Heb 10:38
For the eyes of the Lord are on the **r**, ... 1 Pt 3:12

RIGHTEOUSNESS

and he counted it to him as **r**. .... Gn 15:6
I hold fast my **r** and will not let it go; ..... Jb 27:6
he judges the world with **r**; .... Ps 9:8
dealt with me according to my **r**; .... Ps 18:20
R and justice are the foundation .... Ps 89:14
I walk in the way of **r**, in the paths .... Prv 8:20
R exalts a nation, but sin is a reproach .. Prv 14:34
R shall be the belt of his waist, ... Is 11:5
And the effect of **r** will be peace, ... Is 32:17
He put on **r** as a breastplate, ... Is 59:17
be called: 'The LORD is our **r**.' .... Jer 23:6
for iniquity, to bring in everlasting **r**, ... Dn 9:24
those who turn many to **r**, like the stars .. Dn 12:3
the sun of **r** shall rise with healing in .... Mal 4:2
unless your **r** exceeds that of the .... Mt 5:20
seek first the kingdom of God and his **r**, .. Mt 6:33
For in it the **r** of God is revealed .... Rom 1:17
the **r** of God through faith in Jesus ...... Rom 3:22
God, and it was counted to him as **r**." ... Rom 4:3
faith was counted to Abraham as **r**. ...... Rom 4:9
r leading to eternal life through Jesus .... Rom 5:21
of sin, the Spirit is life because of **r**. .... Rom 8:10
him we might become the **r** of God. .... 2 Cor 5:21
if **r** were through the law, then Christ .... Gal 2:21
God, and it was counted to him as **r**"? ... Gal 3:6
not having a **r** of my own .... Phil 3:9
anger of man does not produce the **r** ... Jas 1:20
way of **r** than after knowing it to turn ... 2 Pt 2:21
Whoever practices **r** is righteous, ... 1 Jn 3:7

RIPE

Put in the sickle, for the harvest is **r**. ...... Jl 3:13
But when the grain is **r**, at once he puts .. Mk 4:29
for the harvest of the earth is fully **r**." ... Rv 14:15

RISE

know when I sit down and when I **r** up; .. Ps 139:2
their bodies shall **r**. .... Is 26:19
are forgiven,' or to say, '**R** and walk'? .... Mt 9:5
and children will **r** against parents .... Mt 10:21
'After three days I will **r**.' .... Mt 27:63
Scripture, that he must **r** from the dead. .. Jn 20:9
And the dead in Christ will **r** first. ..... 1 Thes 4:16
so that they might **r** again to a better .. Heb 11:35

RISEN

glory of the LORD has **r** upon you. .... Is 60:1
'He has **r** from the dead,' .... Mt 27:64
He has **r**; he is not here. See the place ... Mk 16:6
"The Lord has **r** indeed, and has .... Lk 24:34
Christ, **r** from the dead, the offspring .... 2 Tm 2:8

RIVER

A **r** flowed out of Eden to water the ...... Gn 2:10
There is a **r** whose streams make glad .... Ps 46:4
enrich it; the **r** of God is full of water; ..... Ps 65:9
I will extend peace to her like a **r**, ... Is 66:12
on the bank of the **r** very many trees .... Ezk 47:7
were baptized by him in the **r** Jordan, ... Mt 3:6
r of the water of life, bright as crystal, ... Rv 22:1

ROAD

the crowd spread their cloaks on the **r**, .. Mt 21:8
chance a priest was going down that **r**, .. Lk 10:31
within us while he talked to us on the **r**, .. Lk 24:32
how on the **r** he had seen the Lord, ... Acts 9:27

ROB

Do not **r** the poor, because he is poor, ... Prv 22:22
Will man **r** God? Yet you are robbing .... Mal 3:8
who abhor idols, do you **r** temples? ...... Rom 2:22

ROBBERS

by my name, become a den of **r** .... Jer 7:11
And with him they crucified two **r**, ... Mk 15:27
but you have made it a den of **r**." .... Lk 19:46

who came before me are thieves and r, ...Jn 10:8

ROBE
And he made him a r of many colors. ....Gn 37:3
and the train of his r filled the temple. ......Is 6:1
covered me with the r of righteousness, ...Is 61:10
his servants, 'Bring quickly the best r, ...Lk 15:22
each given a white r and told to rest ....Rv 6:11

ROCK
and you shall strike the r, and water .....Ex 17:6
by I will put you in a cleft of the r, ...Ex 33:22
and struck the r with his staff twice, ...Nm 20:11
besides you; there is no r like our God. ...1 Sm 2:2
LORD lives, and blessed be my r, ...2 Sm 22:47
The LORD is my r and my fortress ......Ps 18:2
Lead me to the r that is higher than I, ...Ps 61:2
a joyful noise to the r of our salvation! ...Ps 95:1
not remembered the R of your refuge; ...Is 17:10
me? There is no R; I know not any." ......Is 44:8
wise man who built his house on the r. ...Mt 7:24
on this r I will build my church, ...Mt 16:18
And some fell on the r, and as it grew ....Lk 8:6
and the R was Christ. ....1 Cor 10:4

ROCKS
He split r in the wilderness and gave ...Ps 78:15
the earth shook, and the r were split, ...Mt 27:51

ROD
your r and your staff, they comfort .....Ps 23:4
Whoever spares the r hates his son, ...Prv 13:24
I come to you with a r, or with love ...1 Cor 4:21

ROME
commanded all the Jews to leave R. .....Acts 18:2
And when we came into R, Paul was ...Acts 28:16
To all those in R who are loved by God ...Rom 1:7

ROOF
them up to the r and hid them with ......Jos 2:6
Through sloth the r sinks in, and ......Eccl 10:18
crowd, they removed the r above him, ...Mk 2:4

ROOM
into your r and shut the door and pray ....Mt 6:6
entered, they went up to the upper r, ...Acts 1:13
Make r in your hearts for us. ....2 Cor 7:2

ROOT
In that day the r of Jesse, who shall ....Is 11:10
like a r out of dry ground; ....Is 53:2
And since they had no r, they withered ...Mt 13:6
"The r of Jesse will come, ...Rom 15:12
love of money is a r of all kinds ......1 Tm 6:10
of the tribe of Judah, the R of David, ...Rv 5:5
I am the r and the descendant of David, ..Rv 22:16

ROOTED
that you, being a r and grounded in love, ..Eph 3:17
r and built up in him and established .....Col 2:7

ROUGH
become level, and the r places a plain. ...Is 40:4
the r places shall become level ways, ...Lk 3:5

ROYAL
If you really fulfill the r law ....Jas 2:8
you are a chosen race, a r priesthood, ...1 Pt 2:9

RUDE
or r. It does not insist on its own ......1 Cor 13:5

RUIN
many companions may come to r, ...Prv 18:24
A foolish son is r to his father, ...Prv 19:13
and the r of that house was great." ......Lk 6:49
plunge people into r and destruction. ...1 Tm 6:9

RUINS
the house of our God, to repair its r, ...Ezr 3:1
how Jerusalem lies in r with its gates. ...Neh 2:17
And your ancient r shall be rebuilt; .....Is 58:12
all our pleasant places have become r. ...Is 64:11
I will make Jerusalem a heap of r, ...Jer 9:11
fallen; I will rebuild its r, and I will ....Acts 15:16

does no good, but only r the hearers.... 2 Tm 2:14

RULE
to r over the day and over the night, ...Gn 1:18
desire is contrary to you, but you must r ...Gn 4:7
Can you establish their r on the earth? ...Jb 38:33
the sun to r over the day, for his ......Ps 136:8
The hand of the diligent will r, while.... Prv 12:24
far above all r and authority and power ...Eph 1:21
who is the head of all r and authority, ...Col 2:10
let the peace of Christ r in your hearts, ...Col 3:15
Let the elders who r well be considered ..1 Tm 5:17
and he will r them with a rod of iron, ...Rv 2:27

RULER
A r who lacks understanding is a ....Prv 28:16
Many seek the face of a r, but it is ......Prv 29:26
shall come a r who will shepherd my ....Mt 2:6
now will the r of this world be cast .....Jn 12:31
'Who made you a r and a judge over ....Acts 7:27

RULERS
a land transgresses, it has many r, ...Prv 28:2
and makes the r of the earth as ......Is 40:23
"You know that the r of the Gentiles ....Mt 20:25
by, watching, but the r scoffed at him, ...Lk 23:35
For r are not a terror to good conduct, ...Rom 13:3
None of the r of this age understood ....1 Cor 2:8
or dominions or r or authorities— ......Col 1:16

RULES
LORD, and he r over the nations. ......Ps 22:28
heavens, and his kingdom r over all. ...Ps 103:19
and he who r his spirit than he who ....Prv 16:32
know not the r of the LORD. ....Jer 8:7
to keep these r without prejudging, ...1 Tm 5:21
unless he competes according to the r....2 Tm 2:5

RUMORS
will hear of wars and r of wars. ....Mt 24:6

RUN
they shall r and not be weary; ....Is 40:31
So r that you may obtain it. ....1 Cor 9:24
So I do not r aimlessly; I do not ....1 Cor 9:26
I was not running or had not r in vain. ...Gal 2:2

RUNNING
pressed down, shaken together, r over, ...Lk 6:38
You were r well. Who hindered you .....Gal 5:7

RUST
where moth and r destroy ....Mt 6:19

RUTH
and the name of the other R. ....Ru 1:4
Also R the Moabite, the widow ....Ru 4:10
and Boaz the father of Obed by R, ...Mt 1:5

SABBATH
"Remember the S day, to keep it holy. ...Ex 20:8
For the Son of Man is lord of the S." ....Mt 12:8
"Is it lawful on the S to do good or .....Mk 3:4
there remains a S rest for the people ....Heb 4:9

SACKCLOTH
his garments and put s on his loins .....Gn 37:34
have repented long ago in s and ashes. ..Mt 11:21

SACRIFICE
and Jacob offered a s in the ....Gn 31:54
'It is the s of the LORD's Passover, ...Ex 12:27
to obey is better than s, ...1 Sm 15:22
For you will not delight in s, or I ......Ps 51:16
I desire steadfast love and not s, ...Hos 6:6
'I desire mercy, and not s.' ....Mt 9:13
present your bodies as a living s, ...Rom 12:1
a fragrant offering and s to God. ......Eph 5:2
a s acceptable and pleasing to God. ....Phil 4:18
to put away sin by the s of himself. ....Heb 9:26

SACRIFICED
on which the Passover lamb had to be s... Lk 22:7
Christ, our Passover lamb, has been s.... 1 Cor 5:7

SACRIFICES
Offer right s, and put your trust in the ...Ps 4:5
The s of God are a broken spirit; ......Ps 51:17
to God, to offer gifts and s for sins. ....Heb 5:1
have, for such s are pleasing to God. ...Heb 13:16
to offer spiritual s acceptable to God .....1 Pt 2:5

SADDUCEES
Pharisees and S coming to his baptism, ...Mt 3:7
of the leaven of the Pharisees and S." ...Mt 16:6
The same day S came to him, who say ...Mt 22:23

SAFE
righteous man runs into it and is s. .....Prv 18:10
whoever trusts in the LORD is s. ......Prv 29:25

SAFETY
enemies around, so that you live in s, ...Dt 12:10
O LORD, make me dwell in s. ....Ps 4:8
He redeems my soul in s from the battle ..Ps 55:18
an abundance of counselors there is s. ..Prv 11:14

SAINTS
Love the LORD, all you his s! ....Ps 31:23
He preserves the lives of his s; ....Ps 97:10
of the LORD is the death of his s. .....Ps 116:15
But the s of the Most High shall receive ..Dn 7:18
locked up many of the s in prison after ..Acts 26:10
are loved by God and called to be s: ....Rom 1:7
intercedes for the s according to the ....Rom 8:27
Contribute to the needs of the s and ....Rom 12:13
in the Lord in a way worthy of the s, ...Rom 16:2
not know that the s will judge the .....1 Cor 6:2
not only supplying the needs of the s ....2 Cor 9:12
his glorious inheritance in the s, ...Eph 1:18
to equip the s for the work of ministry, ...Eph 4:12
generations but now revealed to his s ...Col 1:26
on that day to be glorified in his s, ...2 Thes 1:10
incense, which are the prayers of the s. ..Rv 5:8
linen is the righteous deeds of the s. ...Rv 19:8

SAKE
Yet for your s we are killed all the day ...Ps 44:22
deal on my behalf for your name's s; ...Ps 109:21
Delay not, for your own s, O my God, ...Dn 9:19
For our s he made him to be sin who ....2 Cor 5:21
I counted as loss for the s of Christ. ....Phil 3:7
suffer for righteousness' s, ...1 Pt 3:14

SALT
she became a pillar of s. ....Gn 19:26
"You are the s of the earth, but if s ....Mt 5:13
always be gracious, seasoned with s, ...Col 4:6

SALVATION
he has become my s; ....Ex 15:2
Tell of his s from day to day. ....1 Chr 16:23
LORD is my light and my s; ....Ps 27:1
He alone is my rock and my s, ...Ps 62:2
tell of his s from day to day. ....Ps 96:2
my song, and he has become my s." .....Is 12:2
but my s will be forever, ...Is 51:6
clothed me with the garments of s; .....Is 61:10
wait quietly for the s of the LORD. .....Lam 3:26
S belongs to the LORD!" ....Jon 2:9
for my eyes have seen your s ....Lk 2:30
"Today s has come to this house, ...Lk 19:9
what we know, for s is from the Jews. ...Jn 4:22
And there is s in no one else, for ......Acts 4:12
behold, now is the day of s. ....2 Cor 6:2
work out your own s with fear and .....Phil 2:12
has appeared, bringing s for all people, ...Ti 2:11
we escape if we neglect such a great s? ..Heb 2:3
Concerning this s, the prophets who.... 1 Pt 1:10
count the patience of our Lord as s, ...2 Pt 3:15
"S belongs to our God who sits on .....Rv 7:10
S and glory and power belong to our ....Rv 19:1

SAMARITAN
But a S, as he journeyed, came to.... Lk 10:33
giving him thanks. Now he was a S. ....Lk 17:16
The S woman said to him, "How is it ....Jn 4:9

SAMSON

bore a son and called his name **S**. .... Jgs 13:24
And **S** said, "With the jawbone .... Jgs 15:16
to tell of Gideon, Barak, **S**, Jephthah, .. Heb 11:32

SAMUEL

and she called his name **S**,............... 1 Sm 1:20
Therefore Eli said to **S**, "Go, lie down, ... 1 Sm 3:9
When **S** became old, he made his sons ... 1 Sm 8:1
the LORD had revealed to **S**: .... 1 Sm 9:15
with fear because of the words of **S**, .. 1 Sm 28:20
of David and **S** and the prophets— ..... Heb 11:32

SANCTIFICATION

slaves to righteousness leading to **s**. .... Rom 6:19
For this is the will of God, your **s**: ..... 1 Thes 4:3
through **s** by the Spirit and belief in .. 2 Thes 2:13
of God the Father, in the **s** of the Spirit, ... 1 Pt 1:2

SANCTIFIED

inheritance among all those who are **s**. . Acts 20:32
be acceptable, **s** by the Holy Spirit. ..... Rom 15:16
But you were washed, you were **s**, ... 1 Cor 6:11
we have been **s** through the offering ..... Heb 10:10
for all time those who are being **s**. ..... Heb 10:14

SANCTIFIES

I am the LORD who **s** you. .... Lv 20:8
For he who **s** and those who are .... Heb 2:11

SANCTIFY

S them in the truth; your word is truth. .... Jn 17:17
that he might **s** her, having cleansed .... Eph 5:26
may the God of peace himself **s** you .. 1 Thes 5:23
to **s** the people through his own blood. .. Heb 13:12

SANCTUARY

And let them make me a **s**, that I may ..... Ex 25:8
Arise and build the **s** of the LORD ..... 1 Chr 22:19
Praise God in his **s**; praise him in his ..... Ps 150:1

SAND

stars of heaven and as the **s** that is on .. Gn 22:17
man who built his house on the **s**. .... Mt 7:26
sons of Israel be as the **s** of the sea, ... Rom 9:27

SANDALS

not come near; take your **s** off your feet, ... Ex 3:5
Joshua, "Take off your **s** from your .... Jos 5:15
whose **s** I am not worthy to carry." .... Mt 3:11

SANG

when the morning stars **s** together .... Jb 38:7
s a new song, saying, "Worthy .... Rv 5:9

SARAH

S, who is ninety years old, bear a .... Gn 17:17
So **S** laughed to herself, saying, ... Gn 18:12
By faith **S** herself received power to .... Heb 11:11
as **S** obeyed Abraham, calling him lord. ... 1 Pt 3:6

SATAN

and **S** also came among them. .... Jb 1:6
And the LORD said to **S**, "The .... Zec 3:2
"Be gone, **S**! For it is written, "You .... Mt 4:10
And if **S** casts out **S**, he is divided ..... Mt 12:26
to Peter, "Get behind me, **S**! You are .... Mt 16:23
forty days, being tempted by **S**. .... Mk 1:13
will soon crush **S** under your feet. ...... Rom 16:20
S disguises himself as an angel .... 2 Cor 11:14
flesh, a messenger of **S** to harass me, ... 2 Cor 12:7
serpent, who is called the devil and **S**,.... Rv 12:9
who is the devil and **S**, and bound him ... Rv 20:2
S will be released from his prison .... Rv 20:7

SATISFIED

with treasure; they are **s** with children, ... Ps 17:14
Three things are never **s**; four never .... Prv 30:15
anguish of his soul he shall see and be **s**; . Is 53:11
for righteousness, for they shall be **s**. .... Mt 5:6

SATISFIES

s you with good so that your youth ...... Ps 103:5
For he **s** the longing soul, ... Ps 107:9

SATISFY

S us in the morning with your steadfast .. Ps 90:14
your labor for that which does not **s**? ..... Is 55:2
For I will **s** the weary soul, and every ... Jer 31:25

SAUL

a son whose name was **S**, ... 1 Sm 9:2
there they made **S** king before the ... 1 Sm 11:15
"I regret that I have made **S** king, ... 1 Sm 15:11
And **S** approved of his execution. .... Acts 8:1
"**S**, **S**, why are you persecuting me?" .... Acts 9:4
But **S**, who was also called Paul, ... Acts 13:9

SAVE

S me according to your steadfast love! .. Ps 109:26
hand is not shortened, that it cannot **s**, ... Is 59:1
I am with you to **s** you and deliver you, .. Jer 15:20
for he will **s** his people from their sins." ... Mt 1:21
"**S** us, Lord; we are perishing." .... Mt 8:25
to sink he cried out, "Lord, **s** me." .... Mt 14:30
For whoever would **s** his life will lose .... Mt 16:25
Man came to seek and to **s** the lost." .... Lk 19:10
to judge the world but to **s** the world: .... Jn 12:47
all people, that by all means I might **s** ... 1 Cor 9:22
Jesus came into the world to **s** sinners, .. 1 Tm 1:15
he is able to **s** to the uttermost .... Heb 7:25
to **s** those who are eagerly waiting ...... Heb 9:28
not have works? Can that faith **s** him? ..... Jas 2:14

SAVED

"Turn to me and be **s**, all the ends of ... Is 45:22
on the name of the LORD shall be **s**. ...... Jl 2:32
"Who then can be **s**?" .... Mt 19:25
to the woman, "Your faith has **s** you; .... Lk 7:50
that the world might be **s** through him. .... Jn 3:17
among men by which we must be **s**." ..... Acts 4:12
what must I do to be **s**?" .... Acts 16:30
on the name of the Lord will be **s**." .... Acts 10:13
loss, though he himself will be **s**, ... 1 Cor 3:15
For by grace you have been **s** through ..... Eph 2:8
desires all people to be **s** and to come ... 1 Tm 2:4
he **s** us, not because of works .... Ti 3:5

SAVES

the LORD **s** not with sword .... 1 Sm 17:47
Now I know that the LORD **s** .... Ps 20:6
now **s** you, not as a removal of dirt ...... 1 Pt 3:21

SAVIOR

my stronghold and my refuge, my **s**; .. 2 Sm 22:3
O **S** of those who seek refuge from .... Ps 17:7
he will send them a **s** and defender, ... Is 19:20
and besides me there is no **s**. .... Is 43:11
I, the LORD, am your **S** and .... Is 60:16
but me, and besides me there is no **s**. .... Hos 13:4
my spirit rejoices in God my **S**, ... Lk 1:47
born this day in the city of David a **S**, ... Lk 2:11
that this is indeed the **S** of the world." .... Jn 4:42
church, his body, and is himself its **S**. ..... Eph 5:23
living God, who is the **S** of all people, .. 1 Tm 4:10
loving kindness of God our **S** appeared, ... Ti 3:4
sent his Son to be the **S** of the world. ... 1 Jn 4:14
to the only God, our **S**, through Jesus ..... Jude 25

SCALES

and false **s** are not good. .... Prv 20:23
the mountains in **s** and the hills .... Is 40:12
And its rider had a pair of **s** in his hand. ... Rv 6:5

SCARLET

though your sins are like **s**, they shall .... Is 1:18

SCATTERED

"He who **s** Israel will gather him, ... Jer 31:10
and the sheep of the flock will be **s**.' ..... Mt 26:31
who were **s** went about preaching .... Acts 8:4

SCEPTER

The **s** shall not depart from Judah, ... Gn 49:10
uprightness is the **s** of your kingdom. .... Heb 1:8

SCHEMES

by craftiness in deceitful **s**. .... Eph 4:14
stand against the **s** of the devil. .... Eph 6:11

SCOFFER

but a **s** does not listen to rebuke. .... Prv 13:1
Drive out a **s**, and strife will go out,..... Prv 22:10
the **s** is an abomination to mankind..... Prv 24:9

SCOFFERS

way of sinners, nor sits in the seat of **s**; .... Ps 1:1
S set a city aflame, but the wise turn .... Prv 29:8
s will come in the last days .... 2 Pt 3:3
"In the last time there will be **s**,........... Jude 18

SCORCHING

neither **s** wind nor sun shall strike .... Is 49:10
shall not strike them, nor any **s** heat. ...... Rv 7:16

SCORPION

if he asks for an egg, will give him a **s**? .. Lk 11:12
like the torment of a **s** when it stings .... Rv 9:5

SCRIPTURE

"Today this **S** has been fulfilled in your ... Lk 4:21
S must be fulfilled in me: 'And he was ... Lk 22:37
Whoever believes in me, as the **S** has .... Jn 7:38
God came—and **S** cannot be broken— .. Jn 10:35
S says, "They will look on him whom .... Jn 19:37
And the **S**, foreseeing that God would ..... Gal 3:8
yourself to the public reading of **S**, ... 1 Tm 4:13
All **S** is breathed out by God and .... 2 Tm 3:16
that no prophecy of **S** comes from .... 2 Pt 1:20

SCRIPTURES

you know neither the **S** nor the power .. Mt 22:29
he interpreted to them in all the **S** .... Lk 24:27
opened their minds to understand the **S**, .. Lk 24:45
You search the **S** because you think ..... Jn 5:39
he reasoned with them from the **S**, ... Acts 17:2
examining the **S** daily to see if these .... Acts 17:11
showing by the **S** that the Christ was .... Acts 18:28
through his prophets in the holy **S**, ... Rom 1:2
encouragement of the **S** we might ...... Rom 15:4
for our sins in accordance with the **S**, .. 1 Cor 15:3
own destruction, as they do the other **S**.. 2 Pt 3:16

SCROLL

rot away, and the skies roll up like a **s**. .... Is 34:4
And he rolled up the **s** and gave it .... Lk 4:20
"Who is worthy to open the **s** and .... Rv 5:2

SEA

and the LORD drove the **s** back .... Ex 14:21
The **s** is his, for he made it, ... Ps 95:5
dwell in the uttermost parts of the **s**, ... Ps 139:9
when he assigned to the **s** its limit, so.... Prv 8:29
all our sins into the depths of the **s**. ...... Mi 7:19
And I saw a beast rising out of the **s**, ... Rv 13:1
beside the **s** of glass with harps of God ... Rv 15:2

SEAL

Set me as a **s** upon your heart, as a ...... Sg 8:6
For on him God the Father has set his **s**." .. Jn 6:27
and who has also put his **s** on us .... 2 Cor 1:22
When the Lamb opened the seventh **s**, ... Rv 8:1

SEALED

were **s** with the promised Holy Spirit, ... Eph 1:13
by whom you were **s** for the day of ...... Eph 4:30

SEALS

the Lamb opened one of the seven **s**, ... Rv 6:1

SEARCH

if you **s** after him with all your heart ...... Dt 4:29
S me, O God, and know my heart! ...... Ps 139:23
"I the LORD **s** the heart and test .... Jer 17:10
You **s** the Scriptures because you think .... Jn 5:39

SEARCHED

O LORD, you have **s** me and known ...... Ps 139:1

SEARCHES

LORD **s** all hearts and understands .... 1 Chr 28:9
And he who **s** hearts knows what is .... Rom 8:27
For the Spirit **s** everything, even .... 1 Cor 2:10
that I am he who **s** mind and heart, ... Rv 2:23

SEASON

For everything there is a **s**, and a time ..... Eccl 3:1
doing good, for in due **s** we will reap, ... Gal 6:9
be ready in **s** and out of **s**; .... 2 Tm 4:2

SEASONS

And let them be for signs and for **s**, ... Gn 1:14
He made the moon to mark the **s**; ...... Ps 104:19
He changes times and **s**; he removes .... Dn 2:21
Now concerning the times and the **s**, ... 1 Thes 5:1

SEAT

nor sits in the **s** of scoffers; .... Ps 1:1
you love the best **s** in the synagogues .. Lk 11:43
stand before the judgment **s** of God; .. Rom 14:10
before the judgment **s** of Christ, ... 2 Cor 5:10

SEATED

see the Son of Man **s** at the right hand .. Mt 26:64
s us with him in the heavenly places .... Eph 2:6
Christ is, **s** at the right hand of God. .... Col 3:1
high priest, one who is **s** at the right .... Heb 8:1

SECOND

appear a **s** time, not to deal with sin .... Heb 9:28
Over such the **s** death has no power, ... Rv 20:6

SECRET

"The **s** things belong to the LORD .... Dt 29:29
you teach me wisdom in the **s** heart. ..... Ps 51:6
our **s** sins in the light of your presence. .. Ps 90:8
when i was being made in **s**, ... Ps 139:15
and do not reveal another's **s**, ... Prv 25:9
so that your giving may be in **s**. .... Mt 6:4
mystery that was kept **s** for long ages . Rom 16:25
But we impart a **s** and hidden wisdom .. 1 Cor 2:7
I have learned the **s** of facing plenty .... Phil 4:12

SECRETS

For he knows the **s** of the heart. .... Ps 44:21
given to know the **s** of the kingdom .... Lk 8:10
God judges the **s** of men by Christ .... Rom 2:16
the **s** of his heart are disclosed, and .. 1 Cor 14:25

SECURE

feet upon a rock, making my steps **s**. ...... Ps 40:2
in a peaceful habitation, in **s** dwellings, ... Is 32:18

SECURELY

Whoever walks in integrity walks **s**, ... Prv 10:9

SECURITY

"There will be peace and **s** in my days." ... Is 39:8
"There is peace and **s**," then sudden . 1 Thes 5:3

SEE

face, for man shall not **s** me and live." .... Ex 33:20
yet in my flesh I shall **s** God, ... Jb 19:26
lest they **s** with their eyes, and hear ...... Is 6:10
and all flesh shall **s** it together, ... Is 40:5
the pure in heart, for they shall **s** God. ..... Mt 5:8
people longed to **s** what you **s**, ... Mt 13:17
that though I was blind, now I **s**." .... Jn 9:25
whom no one has ever seen or can **s**. .. 1 Tm 6:16
without which no one will **s** the Lord. .. Heb 12:14
because we shall **s** him as he is. .... 1 Jn 3:2
They will **s** his face, and his name .... Rv 22:4

SEED

a man who sowed **s** in his field, ... Mt 13:24
"A sower went out to sow his **s**. .... Lk 8:5
He who supplies **s** to the sower .... 2 Cor 9:10
not of perishable **s** but of imperishable, . 1 Pt 1:23
for God's **s** abides in him; .... 1 Jn 3:9

SEEING

the lame walking, and the blind **s**. .... Mt 15:31
to keep them from **s** the light of the .... 2 Cor 4:4

SEEK

If you **s** him, he will be found by you, ... 1 Chr 28:9
pray and **s** my face and turn from ...... 2 Chr 7:14
With my whole heart I **s** you; .... Ps 119:10
those who **s** me diligently find me. ...... Prv 8:17
"**S** the LORD while he may be .... Is 55:6

SEEKS

to be found by those who did not **s** me. .... Is 65:1
when you **s** me with all your heart. ...... Jer 29:13
I will **s** the lost, and I will bring back .... Ezk 34:16
But **s** first the kingdom of God .... Mt 6:33
s, and you will find; knock, ... Mt 7:7
Son of Man came to **s** and to save .... Lk 19:10
found by those who did not **s** me; ...... Rom 10:20
with Christ, **s** the things that are above, ... Col 3:1
that he rewards those who **s** him. .... Heb 11:6
city, but we **s** the city that is to come. .. Heb 13:14

SEEKS

asks receives, and the one who **s** finds, ... Mt 7:8
no one understands; no one **s** for God. .. Rom 3:11

SEEN

no eye has **s** a God besides you, ... Is 64:4
No one has ever **s** God; the only God, ... Jn 1:18
Whoever has **s** me has **s** the Father. .... Jn 14:9
For the things that are **s** are transient, .. 2 Cor 4:18
for, the conviction of things not **s**. .... Heb 11:1
Though you have not **s** him, you love .... 1 Pt 1:8

SEES

For the LORD **s** not as man **s**: .... 1 Sm 16:7
heaven; he **s** all the children of man; .... Ps 33:13
And whoever **s** me **s** him .... Jn 12:45

SELF

We know that our old **s** was crucified ... Rom 6:6
Though our outer **s** is wasting away, ... 2 Cor 4:16
and to put on the new **s**, created after .. Eph 4:24
have put off the old **s** with its practices .... Col 3:9

SELF-CONTROL

A man without **s** is like a city broken .. Prv 25:28
Every athlete exercises **s** in all things. .. 1 Cor 9:25
gentleness, **s**; against such things .... Gal 5:23
not of fear but of power and love and **s**. .. 2 Tm 1:7
and knowledge with **s**, and .... 2 Pt 1:6

SELF-CONTROLLED

a lover of good, **s**, upright, holy, ... Ti 1:8
Likewise, urge the younger men to be **s**. .... Ti 2:6
therefore be **s** and sober-minded .... 1 Pt 4:7

SELF-INDULGENCE

but inside they are full of greed and **s**. .. Mt 23:25
lived on the earth in luxury and in **s**. .... Jas 5:5

SELF-SEEKING

who are **s** and do not obey the truth .... Rom 2:8

SELFISH

For where jealousy and **s** ambition ...... Jas 3:16

SEND

"Here I am! **S** me." .... Is 6:8
of the harvest to **s** out laborers into his .. Mt 9:38
But if I go, I will **s** him to you. .... Jn 16:7

SENDING

"Behold, I am **s** you out as sheep .... Mt 10:16
has sent me, even so I am **s** you." .... Jn 20:21

SENSUALITY

deceit, **s**, envy, slander, pride, ... Mk 7:22
not in sexual immorality and **s**, ... Rom 13:13
impurity, sexual immorality, and **s** .... 2 Cor 12:21
evident: sexual immorality, impurity, **s**, ... Gal 5:19
given themselves up to **s**, greedy .... Eph 4:19
living in **s**, passions, drunkenness, ... 1 Pt 4:3
And many will follow their **s**, ... 2 Pt 2:2
pervert the grace of our God into **s** .... Jude 4

SENT

receives me receives him who **s** me. ..... Mt 10:40
believes not in me but in him who **s** me. .. Jn 12:44
are they to preach unless they are **s**? .... Rom 10:15
that had come, God **s** forth his Son, ... Gal 4:4

SEPARATE

and let it **s** the waters from the waters." .... Gn 1:6
God has joined together, let not man **s**." .. Mt 19:6
Who shall **s** us from the love of .... Rom 8:35
and be **s** from them, says the Lord, ... 2 Cor 6:17

SEPARATED

at that time **s** from Christ, alienated ...... Eph 2:12
unstained, **s** from sinners, and exalted .. Heb 7:26

SEPARATES

who repeats a matter **s** close friends. ..... Prv 17:9
But if the unbelieving partner **s**, ... 1 Cor 7:15

SERPENT

Now the **s** was more crafty than any ...... Gn 3:1
So Moses made a bronze **s** and set it .... Nm 21:9
if he asks for a fish, will give him a **s**? .... Mt 7:10
And as Moses lifted up the **s** in the .... Jn 3:14
And he seized the dragon, that ancient **s**, .. Rv 20:2

SERVANT

"Speak, for your **s** hears." .... 1 Sm 3:10
Behold, my **s** shall act wisely; he .... Is 52:13
"Behold, my **s** whom I have chosen, ... Mt 12:18
be great among you must be your **s**, ... Mt 20:26
"Who then is the faithful and wise **s**, ... Mt 24:45
'Well done, good and faithful **s**. .... Mt 25:21
"Behold, I am the **s** of the Lord; .... Lk 1:38
No **s** can serve two masters, ... Lk 16:13
'A **s** is not greater than his master.' .... Jn 15:20
I have made myself a **s** to all, ... 1 Cor 9:19
emptied himself, by taking the form of a **s**, .. Phil 2:7

SERVANTS

wished to settle accounts with his **s**. ..... Mt 18:23
'We are unworthy **s**; we have only .... Lk 17:10
Calling ten of his **s**, he gave them ten .... Lk 19:13
No longer do I call you **s**, for the .... Jn 15:15
cover-up for evil, but living as **s** of God. . 1 Pt 2:16

SERVE

to **s** the LORD your God with all .... Dt 10:12
my house, we will **s** the LORD." .... Jos 24:15
S the LORD with gladness! .... Ps 100:2
your God and him only shall you **s**.'" .... Mt 4:10
of Man came not to be served but to **s**, .. Mt 20:28
You cannot **s** God and money." .... Lk 16:13
we **s** in the new way of the Spirit .... Rom 7:6
but with my flesh I **s** the law of sin. ..... Rom 7:25
but through love **s** one another. .... Gal 5:13
from dead works to **s** the living God. .... Heb 9:14
received a gift, use it to **s** one another, . 1 Pt 4:10

SERVES

If anyone **s** me, he must follow me; ...... Jn 12:26
Whoever thus **s** Christ is acceptable .... Rom 14:18
as one who **s** by the strength that God .. 1 Pt 4:11

SERVICE

if **s**, in our serving; the one .... Rom 12:7
there are varieties of **s**, but the .... 1 Cor 12:5
rendering **s** with a good will as to the .... Eph 6:7

SEVEN

Take with you **s** pairs of all clean .... Gn 7:2
march around the city **s** times, ... Jos 6:4
I will leave **s** thousand in Israel, ... 1 Kgs 19:18
there shall be **s** weeks. Then .... Dn 9:25
I forgive him? As many as **s** times?" ...... Mt 18:21
Then it goes and brings **s** other spirits .... Lk 11:26
John to the **s** churches that are in Asia: ... Rv 1:4
who holds the **s** stars in his right .... Rv 2:1
the Lamb opened one of the **s** seals, ... Rv 6:1
and **s** trumpets were given to them. .... Rv 8:2
"Seal up what the **s** thunders have said, .. Rv 10:4
s angels **s** golden bowls full .... Rv 15:7

SEVENTH

And on the **s** day God finished his .... Gn 2:2
but on the **s** day you shall rest; .... Ex 23:12

SEVENTY

of Jacob who came into Egypt were **s**. .. Gn 46:27
it kept Sabbath, to fulfill **s** years. .... 2 Chr 36:21
The years of our life are **s**, or even .... Ps 90:10
Then after **s** years are completed, I .... Jer 25:12
"**S** weeks are decreed about your .... Dn 9:24

SEXUAL

Flee from **s** immorality. Every other ...... 1 Cor 6:18
We must not indulge in **s** immorality. .. 1 Cor 10:8
that you abstain from **s** immorality; ... 1 Thes 4:3

SHADE

LORD is your **s** on your right .... Ps 121:5
birds of the air can make nests in its **s**." . Mk 4:32

SHADOW

through the valley of the **s** of death, ... Ps 23:4
take refuge in the **s** of your wings. ...... Ps 36:7
will abide in the **s** of the Almighty. ...... Ps 91:1
shall return and dwell beneath my **s**; .... Hos 14:7
These are a **s** of the things to come, ... Col 2:17
law has but a **s** of the good things to ... Heb 10:1

SHAKEN

salvation, my fortress; I shall not be **s**...... Ps 62:6
they were gathered together was **s**, ... Acts 4:31
receiving a kingdom that cannot be **s**, .. Heb 12:28

SHALLUM

S the son of Jabesh began to reign in .. 2 Kgs 15:13

SHAME

in you I trust; let me not be put to **s**; ...... Ps 25:2
but the wicked brings **s** and disgrace...... Prv 13:5
hope does not put us to **s**, because ...... Rom 5:5
believes in him will not be put to **s**." .. Rom 10:11
is foolish in the world to **s** the wise; ... 1 Cor 1:27
endured the cross, despising the **s**, ... Heb 12:2
believes in him will not be put to **s**." .. 1 Pt 2:6
not shrink from him in **s** at his coming.. 1 Jn 2:28

SHARE

Is it not to **s** your bread with the hungry ... Is 58:7
has two tunics is to **s** with him who ...... Lk 3:11
give me the **s** of property that is .... Lk 15:12
not wash you, you have no **s** with me." ...Jn 13:8
Let the one who is taught the word **s** all ... Gal 6:6
something to **s** with anyone in need. ..... Eph 4:28
to do good and to **s** what you have, ... Heb 13:16
But rejoice insofar as you **s** Christ's ...... 1 Pt 4:13
God will take away his **s** in the tree of ... Rv 22:19

SHARES

for he **s** his bread with the poor. .... Prv 22:9
to the one who **s** the faith of Abraham, ..Rom 4:16

SHARON

I am a rose of **S**, a lily of the valleys......... Sg 2:1

SHARPER

s than any two-edged sword, ... Heb 4:12

SHEAVES

shouts of joy, bringing his **s** with him. .... Ps 126:6

SHEBA

Now when the queen of **S** heard of....1 Kgs 10:1

SHED

by man shall his blood be **s**, for God ...... Gn 9:6
s from the foundation of the world, ... Lk 11:50
"Their feet are swift to **s** blood; .... Rom 3:15
For they have **s** the blood of saints........ Rv 16:6

SHEDDING

and without the **s** of blood there is no ... Heb 9:22

SHEEP

his people, and the **s** of his pasture. ...... Ps 100:3
All we like **s** have gone astray; .... Is 53:6
"My people have been lost **s**. .... Jer 50:6
will search for my **s** and will seek ...... Ezk 34:11
helpless, like **s** without a shepherd. .... Mt 9:36
out as **s** in the midst of wolves, ... Mt 10:16
man has a hundred **s**, and one of them .. Mt 18:12
shepherd separates the **s** from the. ...... Mt 25:32
The **s** hear his voice, and he calls........... Jn 10:3
I lay down my life for the **s**. .... Jn 10:15
"Like a **s** he was led to the slaughter.... Acts 8:32
are regarded as **s** to be slaughtered." ... Rom 8:36
you were straying like **s**, but have ...... 1 Pt 2:25

SHELTER

He who dwells in the **s** of the Most ...... Ps 91:1
for a refuge and a **s** from the storm ...... Is 4:6
throne will **s** them with his presence. ...... Rv 7:15

SHEM

Noah fathered **S**, Ham, and Japheth....... Gn 5:32

SHEOL

For you will not abandon my soul to **S**, ... Ps 16:10
If I make my bed in **S**, you are there! ...... Ps 139:8
out of the belly of **S** I cried, and you ...... Jon 2:2

SHEPHERD

The LORD is my **s**; I shall not .... Ps 23:1
He will tend his flock like a **s**; .... Is 40:11
As a **s** seeks out his flock when he ...... Ezk 34:12
"Strike the **s**, and the sheep will .... Zec 13:7
helpless, like sheep without a **s**. .... Mt 9:36
For it is written, 'I will strike the **s**, ... Mt 26:31
I am the good **s**. The good **s** lays ...... Jn 10:11
Lord Jesus, the great **s** of the sheep, ... Heb 13:20
returned to the **S** and Overseer of ... 1 Pt 2:25
And when the chief **S** appears, you ...... 1 Pt 5:4
of the throne will be their **s**, and he ...... Rv 7:17

SHEPHERDS

"Woe to the **s** who destroy and scatter ... Jer 23:1
region there were **s** out in the field, ... Lk 2:8
evangelists, the **s** and teachers, ... Eph 4:11

SHIELD

"Fear not, Abram, I am your **s**; .... Gn 15:1
LORD is my strength and my **s**; .... Ps 28:7
take up the **s** of faith, with which you ... Eph 6:16

SHINE

LORD make his face to **s** upon .... Nm 6:25
are wise shall **s** like the brightness .... Dn 12:3
let your light **s** before others, so that ...... Mt 5:16
Then the righteous will **s** like the sun .. Mt 13:43
"Let light **s** out of darkness," .... 2 Cor 4:6
the dead, and Christ will **s** on you." ...... Eph 5:14
you **s** as lights in the world, ... Phil 2:15

SHINES

which **s** brighter and brighter until .... Prv 4:18
The light **s** in the darkness, and the .... Jn 1:5

SHIPWRECK

some have made **s** of their faith, ... 1 Tm 1:19

SHONE

of his face **s** because he had been ...... Ex 34:29
his face **s** like the sun, and his clothes ... Mt 17:2
and the glory of the Lord **s** around ...... Lk 2:9
out of darkness," has **s** in our hearts ... 2 Cor 4:6

SHORT

of the elect those days will be cut **s**. ... Mt 24:22
sinned and fall **s** of the glory of God, ... Rom 3:23

SHOULDER

government shall be upon his **s**,............... Is 9:6

SHOW

Moses said, "Please **s** me your glory." ... Ex 33:18
"Lord, **s** us the Father, and it is enough ...Jn 14:8
I will **s** you my faith by my works. .... Jas 2:18
and I will **s** you what must take place ...... Rv 4:1

SHREWD

this world are more **s** in dealing with ...... Lk 16:8

SHRINK

not of those who **s** back and are .... Heb 10:39

SHROUD

body and wrapped it in a clean linen **s**. . Mt 27:59

SICK

Hope deferred makes the heart **s**, ... Prv 13:12
and healed all who were **s**. .... Mt 8:16
s and in prison and you did not visit ... Mt 25:43
Is anyone among you **s**? Let him call ... Jas 5:14

SIDE

"Who is on the LORD's **s**? Come to ...... Ex 32:26

the soldiers pierced his **s** with a spear, .. Jn 19:34
he showed them his hands and his **s**...... Jn 20:20
striving **s** by **s** for the faith ....Phil 1:27

SIGHT

I sinned and done what is evil in your **s**, .. Ps 51:4
Precious in the **s** of the LORD is .... Ps 116:15
for we walk by faith, not by **s**. .... 2 Cor 5:7
and it is pleasing in the **s** of God our ... 1 Tm 2:3
in us that which is pleasing in his **s**, ... Heb 13:21

SIGN

the Lord himself will give you a **s**. .... Is 7:14
what will be the **s** of your coming........ Mt 24:3

SIGNS

arise and perform great **s** and wonders, .. Mt 24:24
Now Jesus did many other **s** in the ...... Jn 20:30
the heavens above and **s** on the earth... Acts 2:19
while God also bore witness by **s** and .... Heb 2:4

SILAS

midnight Paul and **S** were praying ..... Acts 16:25
When **S** and Timothy arrived from ...... Acts 18:5

SILENCE

For God alone my soul waits in **s**; .... Ps 62:1
a time to keep **s**, and a time to speak; ...... Eccl 3:7
let all the earth keep **s** before him." ...... Hab 2:20
put to **s** the ignorance of foolish people. .. 1 Pt 2:15
there was **s** in heaven for about half an .... Rv 8:1

SILENT

For when I kept **s**, my bones wasted ...... Ps 32:3
a fool who keeps **s** is considered wise; .. Prv 17:28
like a sheep that before its shearers is **s** ... Is 53:7
Be **s** before the Lord GOD! .... Zep 1:7
But Jesus remained **s**. .... Mt 26:63
like a lamb before its shearer is **s**, ... Acts 8:32
women should keep **s** in the churches. ...1 Cor 14:34

SILVER

The **s** is mine, and the gold is mine, ... Hg 2:8
they paid him thirty pieces of **s**. .... Mt 26:15
Peter said, "I have no **s** and gold, but .....Acts 3:6
builds on the foundation with gold, **s**, .. 1 Cor 3:12

SIMEON

And she called his name **S**. .... Gn 29:33
And **S** blessed them and said to Mary ... Lk 2:34

SIMON

S Peter replied, "You are the Christ, ... Mt 16:16
Bethany in the house of **S** the leper, ... Mt 26:6
found a man of Cyrene, **S** by name. ...... Mt 27:32
and **S** who was called the Zealot, ... Lk 6:15
He is lodging with one **S**, a tanner, ... Acts 10:6

SIMPLE

of the LORD is sure, making wise the **s**; ... Ps 19:7
The **s** believes everything, but the ...... Prv 14:15

SIN

s is crouching at the door. .... Gn 4:7
and be sure your **s** will find you out. ...... Nm 32:23
Be angry, and do not **s**; ponder in .... Ps 4:4
no health in my bones because of my **s**. .. Ps 38:3
and my **s** is ever before me. .... Ps 51:3
that I might not **s** against you. .... Ps 119:11
is taken away, and your **s** atoned for." ...... Is 6:7
little ones who believe in me to **s**, ... Mt 18:6
"Temptations to **s** are sure to come, ... Lk 17:1
"Let him who is without **s** among you ...... Jn 8:7
made him to be **s** who knew no **s**, ... 2 Cor 5:21
As for those who persist in **s**, rebuke ... 1 Tm 5:20
been tempted as we are, yet without **s**. .. Heb 4:15
when it has conceived gives birth to **s**, ..Jas 1:15
to do and fails to do it, for him it is **s**. ... Jas 4:17
He committed no **s**, neither was deceit .. 1 Pt 2:22
If we say we have no **s**, we deceive ..... 1 Jn 1:8

SINCERE

with a **s** heart, as you would Christ, ... Eph 6:5
a good conscience and a **s** faith. .... 1 Tm 1:5
mercy and good fruits, impartial and **s**. ... Jas 3:17

SINFUL

"Depart from me, for I am a **s** man, ... Lk 5:8
into the hands of **s** men and be crucified .. Lk 24:7
were living in the flesh, our **s** passions, ... Rom 7:5
scoffing, following their own **s** desires. .. 2 Pt 3:3

SING

"I will **s** to the LORD, ... Ex 15:1
S to him a new song; play skillfully .... Ps 33:3
I will **s** of the steadfast love of the .... Ps 89:1
at the works of your hands I **s** for joy. .... Ps 92:4
S for joy, O heavens, and exult, O earth; .. Is 49:13
I will **s** praise with my spirit, but I .... 1 Cor 14:15
Is anyone cheerful? Let him **s** praise. ...... Jas 5:13

SINGING

Come into his presence with **s**! .... Ps 100:2
shall return and come to Zion with **s**; ..... Is 35:10
were praying and **s** hymns to God, ... Acts 16:25
s psalms and hymns and spiritual .... Col 3:16

SINGLE

it is good for them to remain **s**, as I am.... 1 Cor 7:8

SINNED

have I **s** and done what is evil in your ..... Ps 51:4
we have **s** and done wrong and acted ...... Dn 9:5
I have **s** against heaven and before you.. Lk 15:18
For all who have **s** without the law .... Rom 2:12
all have **s** and fall short of the glory ..... Rom 3:23
who **s** earlier and have not repented .. 2 Cor 12:21
If we say we have not **s**, we make him .. 1 Jn 1:10

SINNER

but one **s** destroys much good. .... Eccl 9:18
angels of God over one **s** who repents." .. Lk 15:10
'God, be merciful to me, a **s**!' .... Lk 18:13
will become of the ungodly and the **s**?".. 1 Pt 4:18

SINNERS

therefore he instructs **s** in the way. .... Ps 25:8
I came not to call the righteous, but **s**." .. Mt 9:13
of Man is betrayed into the hands of **s**.. Mt 26:45
For even **s** do the same. .... Lk 6:33
We know that God does not listen to **s**, .. Jn 9:31
that while we were still **s**, Christ died ... Rom 5:8
in Christ, we too were found to be **s**, ... Gal 2:17
s, of whom I am the foremost. .... 1 Tm 1:15

SINNING

as is right, and do not go on **s**. .... 1 Cor 15:34
For if we go on **s** deliberately after ... Heb 10:26
No one who abides in him keeps on **s**; .. 1 Jn 3:6
makes a practice of **s** is of the devil, ... 1 Jn 3:8

SINS

your servant also from presumptuous **s**; .. Ps 19:13
not deal with us according to our **s**, ... Ps 103:10
I will not remember your **s**. .... Is 43:25
your **s** have hidden his face from .... Is 59:2
the soul who **s** shall die. .... Ezk 18:4
You will cast all our **s** into the depths ..... Mi 7:19
heart; my son; your **s** are forgiven." ...... Mt 9:2
"If your brother **s** against you, go .... Mt 18:15
out for many for the forgiveness of **s**. .. Mt 26:28
and forgive us our **s**, for we ourselves .. Lk 11:4
If you forgive the **s** of any, they........... Jn 20:23
you were dead in the trespasses and **s** .. Eph 2:1

SIT

"**S** at my right hand, until I .... Ps 110:1
but to **s** at my right hand and at my left .. Mt 20:23
feast, do not **s** down in a place of honor,.. Lk 14:8
said to my Lord, "**S** at my right hand, ... Acts 2:34
"You **s** here in a good place," while .... Jas 2:3

SKIN

I have escaped the **s** of my teeth. .... Jb 19:20
after my **s** has been thus destroyed, ... Jb 19:26
Can the Ethiopian change his **s** or .... Jer 13:23

SKULL

Golgotha (which means Place of a **S**), ... Mt 27:33

SKY

how to interpret the appearance of the **s**, .. Mt 16:3
The **s** vanished like a scroll that is being .. Rv 6:14

SLACK

A **s** hand causes poverty, but the hand .. Prv 10:4
Whoever is **s** in his work is a brother .... Prv 18:9

SLAIN

"Worthy is the Lamb who was **s**, ... Rv 5:12
of those who had been **s** for the word ..... Rv 6:9

SLANDER

and whoever utters **s** is a fool. .... Prv 10:18
s, gossip, conceit, and disorder. .... 2 Cor 12:20
anger and clamor and **s** be put away .... Eph 4:31
give the adversary no occasion for **s**. .. 1 Tm 5:14
deceit and hypocrisy and envy and all **s**, .. 1 Pt 2:1

SLANDERED

when **s**, we entreat. We have become,.. 1 Cor 4:13
when you are **s**, those who revile your .. 1 Pt 3:16

SLANDERERS

s, haters of God, insolent, haughty, ... Rom 1:30
be dignified, not **s**, but sober-minded, .. 1 Tm 3:11
not **s** or slaves to much wine. .... Ti 2:3

SLAUGHTER

us like sheep for **s** and have scattered ... Ps 44:11
he was led to the **s** and like a lamb ..... Acts 8:32

SLAVE

be first among you must be your **s**, ... Mt 20:27
everyone who practices sin is a **s** to sin. .. Jn 8:34
So you are no longer a **s**, but a son, ... Gal 4:7
s, free; but Christ is all, and in all. ...... Col 3:11

SLAVERY

not receive the spirit of **s** fo fall back ... Rom 8:15
do not submit again to a yoke of **s**. ...... Gal 5:1
fear of death were subject to lifelong **s**. .. Heb 2:15

SLAVES

you are **s** of the one whom you obey, ... Rom 6:16
from sin and have become **s** of God, ... Rom 6:22
but they themselves are **s** of corruption. .. 2 Pt 2:19

SLAY

Though he **s** me, I will hope in him; .... Jb 13:15

SLEEP

God caused a deep **s** to fall upon .... Gn 2:21
keeps Israel will neither slumber nor **s**. .. Ps 121:4
A little, a little slumber, a little .... Prv 6:10
Sweet is the **s** of a laborer, whether he .. Eccl 5:12
And many of those who **s** in the dust ..... Dn 12:2
We shall not all **s**, but we shall all .... 1 Cor 15:51
So then let us not **s**, as others do, but .. 1 Thes 5:6

SLOTHFUL

while the **s** will be put to forced labor. .... Prv 12:24
'You wicked and **s** servant! You knew .... Mt 25:26
Do not be **s** in zeal, be fervent in spirit .. Rom 12:11

SLOW

a God merciful and gracious, **s** to anger, .. Ex 34:6
s to anger and abounding in steadfast .. Neh 9:17
s to anger and abounding in steadfast .. Ps 103:8
If it seems, **s**, wait for it; it will surely... Hab 2:3
to hear, **s** to speak, **s** to anger; .... Jas 1:19
The Lord is not **s** to fulfill his promise .. 2 Pt 3:9

SLUGGARD

Go to the ant, O **s**; consider her ways, .. Prv 6:6
The **s** says, "There is a lion outside! I .... Prv 22:13
on its hinges, so does a **s** on his bed. ..... Prv 26:14

SMALL

"Behold, I am of **s** account; what shall .... Jb 40:4
living things both **s** and great. .... Ps 104:25
the day of **s** things shall rejoice, ... Zec 4:10
So also the tongue is a **s** member, ... Jas 3:5

SMALLEST

It is the **s** of all seeds, but when it ...... Mt 13:32

SNARE

deliver you from the **s** of the fowler .... Ps 91:3
escape from the **s** of the devil, ... 2 Tm 2:26

SNOW

wash me, and I shall be whiter than **s**. .... Ps 51:7
like scarlet, they shall be as white as **s**; .. Is 1:18
his clothing was white as **s**, and the hair .. Dn 7:9
lightning, and his clothing white as **s**. ..... Mt 28:3

SOBER

but to think with **s** judgment,............. Rom 12:3
we belong to the day, let us be **s**, ... 1 Thes 5:8

SOBER-MINDED

but **s**, faithful in all things. .... 1 Tm 3:11
As for you, always be **s**, endure .... 2 Tm 4:5
Older men are to be **s**, dignified, ... Ti 2:2
your minds for action, and being **s**, ... 1 Pt 1:13

SODOM

LORD rained on **S** and Gomorrah sulfur .. Gn 19:24
we would have been like **S** .... Rom 9:29
turning the cities of **S** and Gomorrah to .. 2 Pt 2:6

SOJOURNERS

The LORD watches over the **s**; .... Ps 146:9
I urge you as **s** and exiles to abstain .... 1 Pt 2:11

SOLDIER

Who serves as a **s** at his own expense? .. 1 Cor 9:7
in suffering as a good **s** of Christ Jesus. .. 2 Tm 2:3
No **s** gets entangled in civilian .... 2 Tm 2:4

SOLITARY

God settles the **s** in a home; he leads ..... Ps 68:6

SOLOMON

King David had made **S** king, ... 1 Kgs 1:43
S loved the LORD, walking .... 1 Kgs 3:3
The proverbs of **S**, son of David, ... Prv 1:1
yet I tell you, even **S** in all his glory ...... Mt 6:29
something greater than **S** is here. .... Mt 12:42

SON

"Take your **s**, your only Isaac, ... Gn 22:2
behold, I will kill your firstborn **s**."" ...... Ex 4:23
said to me, "You are my **S**; today I .... Ps 2:7
A wise **s** hears his father's instruction, ... Prv 13:1
Discipline your **s**, for there is hope; ...... Prv 19:18
out of Egypt I called my **s**. .... Hos 11:1
no one knows the **S** except the Father, .. Mt 11:27
the Christ, the **S** of the living God." ...... Mt 16:16
"Truly this was the **S** of God!" .... Mt 27:54
"You are my beloved **S**; with you I am ... Lk 3:22
divided, father against **s** and **s** .... Lk 12:53
when the **S** of Man comes, will he find .. Lk 18:8
For the **S** of Man came to seek and to ... Lk 19:10
his mother, "Woman, behold, your **s**!" .. Jn 19:26
not spare his own **S** but gave him up ..... Rom 8:32
S himself will also be subjected .... 1 Cor 15:28
but a **s**, and if a **s**, then an heir .... Gal 4:7
how as a **s** with a father he has served .. Phil 2:22
last days he has spoken to us by his **S**, ... Heb 1:2
God sent his only **S** into the world, ... 1 Jn 4:9
Whoever has the **S** has life; .... 1 Jn 5:12
'The words of the **S** of God, who has ..... Rv 2:18
seated on the cloud one like a **s** of man .. Rv 14:14

SONG

LORD is my strength and my **s**, ... Ex 15:2
He put a new **s** in my mouth, ... Ps 40:3
Sing to the LORD a new **s**, ... Ps 149:1
LORD GOD is my strength and my **s**, ... Is 12:2
they sang a new **s**, saying, "Worthy .... Rv 5:9

SONGS

Shout to God with loud **s** of joy! .... Ps 47:1
Whoever sings **s** to a heavy heart is .... Prv 25:20
psalms and hymns and spiritual **s**, ... Eph 5:19

SONS

for they shall be called **s** of God. .... Mt 5:9
"What do you think? A man had two **s**.. Mt 21:28
"The **s** of this age marry and are given .. Lk 20:34

that you may become **s** of light." .... Jn 12:36
led by the Spirit of God are **s** of God.... Rom 8:14
and you shall be **s** and daughters to .... 2 Cor 6:18
so that we might receive adoption as **s**... Gal 4:5
have to endure. God is treating you as **s**.. Heb 12:7

SOON

for **s** my salvation will come, and my .... Is 56:1
The God of peace will **s** crush Satan ... Rom 16:20
"Surely I am coming **s**." Amen............. Rv 22:20

SORROW

My soul melts away for **s**; .... Ps 119:28
who increases knowledge increases **s**.... Eccl 1:18
S is better than laughter, for by sadness ... Eccl 7:3
joy, and **s** and sighing shall flee away. ... Is 35:10
but your **s** will turn into joy.............. Jn 16:20
I have great **s** and unceasing anguish .... Rom 9:2

SORROWS

Many are the **s** of the wicked, but .... Ps 32:10
and rejected by men, a man of **s** .... Is 53:3
borne our griefs and carried our **s**; yet .... Is 53:4
one endures **s** while suffering unjustly. .. 1 Pt 2:19

SORRY

I confess my iniquity; I am **s** for my sin. .. Ps 38:18

SOUGHT

I **s** the LORD, and he answered .... Ps 34:4

SOUL

with all your **s** and with all your .... Dt 6:5
LORD is perfect, reviving the **s**; .... Ps 19:7
Why are you cast down, O my **s**, ... Ps 42:11
My **s** longs, yes, faints for the courts ..... Ps 84:2
Bless the LORD, O my **s**, and all .... Ps 103:1
But I have calmed and quieted my **s**, ... Ps 131:2
your works; my **s** knows it very well.... Ps 139:14
The **s** who sins shall die. .... Ezk 18:20
who kill the body but cannot kill the **s**... Mt 10:28
with all your **s** and with all your........... Mt 22:37
This night your **s** is required of you, ... Lk 12:20
good health, as it goes well with your **s**. .. 3 Jn 2

SOULS

walk in it, and find rest for your **s** .... Jer 6:16
heart, and you will find rest for your **s**. .. Mt 11:29
word, which is able to save your **s**........ Jas 1:21
Having purified your **s** by your .... 1 Pt 1:22
entrust their **s** to a faithful Creator ...... 1 Pt 4:19

SOUND

if the bugle gives an indistinct **s**, ... 1 Cor 14:8
For the trumpet will **s**, and the .... 1 Cor 15:52
people will not endure **s** teaching, ... 2 Tm 4:3

SOURCE

who are sanctified all have one **s**. .... Heb 2:11
s of eternal salvation to all who obey..... Heb 5:9

SOVEREIGN

to God and said, "**S** Lord, who made .... Acts 4:24
"O **S** Lord, holy and true, how long .... Rv 6:10

SOW

Those who **s** in tears shall reap with .... Ps 126:5
S for yourselves righteousness; reap .... Hos 10:12
they neither **s** nor reap nor gather .... Mt 6:26
"A sower went out to **s**.................. Mt 13:3
deposit, and reap what you did not **s**.' .. Lk 19:21

SOWS

Whoever **s** injustice will reap calamity, ... Prv 22:8
"The one who **s** the good seed is .... Mt 13:37
The sower **s** the word. .... Mk 4:14
'One **s** and another reaps.'.................. Jn 4:37
whoever **s** bountifully will also reap...... 2 Cor 9:6
God is not mocked, for whatever one **s**, ... Gal 6:7

SPARE

He who did not **s** his own Son but ...... Rom 8:32
if God did not **s** the natural branches, . Rom 11:21
For if God did not **s** angels when they .... 2 Pt 2:4

SPARES

Whoever **s** the rod hates his son, ... Prv 13:24

SPEAK

Behold, I do not know how to **s**, for I .... Jer 1:6
the wilderness, and **s** tenderly to her. ... Hos 2:14
how you are to **s** or what you are .... Mt 10:19
"I who **s** to you am he." .... Jn 4:26
let each one of you **s** the truth with his .. Eph 4:25
So **s** and so act as those who are to be ... Jas 2:12

SPEECH

but I am slow of **s** and of tongue." ...... Ex 4:10
drop as the rain, my **s** distill as the dew, .. Dt 32:2
Day to day pours out **s**, and night to ...... Ps 19:2
whose **s** is gracious, will have the king .. Prv 22:11
excel in everything—in faith, in **s**, ... 2 Cor 8:7
Let your **s** always be gracious, ... Col 4:6
and sound **s** that cannot be condemned, ... Ti 2:8

SPIRIT

"My **S** shall not abide in man forever, ... Gn 6:3
I have filled him with the **S** of God, ... Ex 31:3
a harmful **s** from God is tormenting .... 1 Sm 16:15
be a double portion of your **s** on me." .... 2 Kgs 2:9
You gave your good **S** to instruct .... Neh 9:20
The **S** of God has made me, ... Jb 33:4
Into your hand I commit my **s**; .... Ps 31:5
own eyes, but the LORD weighs the **s**. .... Prv 16:2
and the **s** returns to God who gave it. .... Eccl 12:7
I have put my **S** upon him; .... Is 42:1
that I will pour out my **S** on all flesh; ...... Jl 2:28
by might, nor by power, but by my **S**, ... Zec 4:6
I will put my **S** upon him, and he will .... Mt 12:18
with a loud voice and yielded up his **s**. .. Mt 27:50
child grew and became strong in **s**, ... Lk 1:80
"The **S** of the Lord is upon me, ... Lk 4:18
into your hands I commit my **s**!"......... Lk 23:46
unless one is born of water and the **S**, ... Jn 3:5
God is **s**, and those who worship him .... Jn 4:24
It is the **S** who gives life; .... Jn 6:63
set their minds on the things of the **S**... Rom 8:5
are varieties of gifts, but the same **S**; .. 1 Cor 12:4
the **S** of the Lord is, there is freedom. .. 2 Cor 3:17
But the fruit of the **S** is love, joy, ... Gal 5:22
Do not quench the **S**................... 1 Thes 5:19
I was in the **S** on the Lord's day, ... Rv 1:10

SPIRITS

he cast out the **s** with a word .... Mt 8:16
the **s** are subject to you, but rejoice...... Lk 10:20
the evil **s** came out of them. .... Acts 19:12
all ministering **s** sent out to serve .... Heb 1:14
proclaimed to the **s** in prison, ... 1 Pt 3:19
God of the **s** of the prophets, has sent .... Rv 22:6

SPIRITUAL

to God, which is your **s** worship. .... Rom 12:1
s truths to those who are **s**. .... 1 Cor 2:13
Now concerning **s** gifts, ... 1 Cor 12:1
a natural body; it is raised a **s** body. ... 1 Cor 15:44
with every **s** blessing in the heavenly .... Eph 1:3
will in all **s** wisdom and understanding, ... Col 1:9

SPLENDOR

Worship the LORD in the **s** of .... Ps 96:9
You are clothed with **s** and majesty, ... Ps 104:1
present the church to himself in **s**, ... Eph 5:27

SPOT

without **s** or wrinkle or any such .... Eph 5:27
be found by him without **s** or blemish, .. 2 Pt 3:14

SPRING

in him a **s** of water welling up to eternal ... Jn 4:14
To the thirsty I will give from the **s** .... Rv 21:6

STAFF

Moses took the **s** of God in his hand. .... Ex 4:20
your rod and your **s**, they comfort .... Ps 23:4

STAND

said to the people, "Fear not, **s** firm, ... Ex 14:13
"Who is able to **s** before the LORD, ... 1 Sm 6:20

the wicked will not **s** in the judgment, ... Ps 1:5
glorify him, and **s** in awe of him, ... Ps 22:23
but the house of the righteous will **s**..... Prv 12:7
the wall and **s** in the breach before .... Ezk 22:30
by faith into this grace in which we **s**, ... Rom 5:2
For we will all **s** before the judgment .... Rom 14:10
S therefore, having fastened on the belt.. Eph 6:14
is the true grace of God. **S** firm in it. .... 1 Pt 5:12

STANDING

on which you are **s** is holy ground." .... Ex 3:5
great and small, **s** before the throne, ... Rv 20:12

STANDS

thinks that he **s** take heed lest he fall. .. 1 Cor 10:12

STAR

a **s** shall come out of Jacob, ... Nm 24:17
When they saw the **s**, they rejoiced .... Mt 2:10
morning **s** rises in your hearts, ... 2 Pt 1:19
I saw a **s** fallen from heaven to earth, ... Rv 9:1
of David, the bright morning **s**." .... Rv 22:16

STARS

lesser light to rule the night—and the **s**... Gn 1:16
heaven, and number the **s**, if you are .... Gn 15:5
when the morning **s** sang together and .... Jb 38:7
to righteousness, like the **s** forever ...... Dn 12:3
as many as the **s** of heaven and as ...... Heb 11:12
In his right hand he held seven **s**, from .... Rv 1:16

STEADFAST

but showing **s** love to thousands .... Dt 5:10
s love surrounds the one who trusts ...... Ps 32:10
O God, according to your **s** love; .... Ps 51:1
What is desired in a man is **s** love, ... Prv 19:22
The **s** love of the LORD never .... Lam 3:22
be **s**, immovable, always abounding .. 1 Cor 15:58
continue in the faith, stable and **s**, ... Col 1:23
who remains **s** under trial, for when ...... Jas 1:12

STEADFASTNESS

testing of your faith produces **s**. .... Jas 1:3
and self-control with **s**, and **s** .... 2 Pt 1:6

STEAL

"You shall not **s**................... Ex 20:15.
and where thieves break in and **s**, ... Mt 6:19
You shall not murder, You shall not **s**,.... Rom 13:9
Let the thief no longer **s**, but rather ...... Eph 4:28

STEPHEN

And **S**, full of grace and power, was ...... Acts 6:8
And as they were stoning **S**, he called ... Acts 7:59

STEPS

The **s** of a man are established by the .... Ps 37:23
but the prudent gives thought to his **s**. .. Prv 14:15
so that you might follow in his **s**. .... 1 Pt 2:21

STEWARDS

Moreover, it is required of **s** that they .... 1 Cor 4:2
as good **s** of God's varied grace: .... 1 Pt 4:10

STEWARDSHIP

I am still entrusted with a **s**.............. 1 Cor 9:17
heard of the **s** of God's grace .... Eph 3:2
according to the **s** from God that .... Col 1:25
rather than the **s** from God that .... 1 Tm 1:4

STIFF-NECKED

and behold, it is a **s** people. .... Ex 32:9
"You **s** people, uncircumcised in heart ... Acts 7:51

STILL

Be **s** before the LORD and wait .... Ps 37:7
"Be **s**, and know that I am God. .... Ps 46:10
s do right, and the holy **s** be holy." ...... Rv 22:11

STING

O Sheol, where is your **s**? .... Hos 13:14
O death, where is your **s**?" .... 1 Cor 15:55
The **s** of death is sin, and the power ... 1 Cor 15:56

STONE

this **s** shall be a witness against us, ... Jos 24:27
Philistine with a sling and with a **s**, ... 1 Sm 17:50

lest you strike your foot against a **s**. ...... Ps 91:12
The **s** that the builders rejected has ..... Ps 118:22
foundation in Zion, a **s**, a tested **s**, ... Is 28:16
I will remove the heart of **s** from .... Ezk 11:19
a **s** was cut out by no human hand, ... Dn 2:34
asks him for bread, will give him a **s**? ...... Mt 7:9
"The **s** that the builders rejected .... Mt 21:42
command this **s** to become bread." .... Lk 4:3
be the first to throw a **s** at her." .... Jn 8:7
This Jesus is the **s** that was rejected ..... Acts 4:11
I am laying in Zion a **s** of stumbling, ... Rom 9:33
a living **s** rejected by men but in the ..... 1 Pt 2:4

STONES

chose five smooth **s** from the brook .. 1 Sm 17:40
God is able from these **s** to raise up .... Mt 3:9
were silent, the very **s** would cry out." ... Lk 19:40

STORM

He made the **s** be still, and the waves .. Ps 107:29
a shelter from the **s** and a shade from ..... Is 25:4
there arose a great **s** on the sea, ... Mt 8:24

STRAIGHT

make your way **s** before me. .... Ps 5:8
and he will make **s** your paths. .... Prv 3:6
and your gaze be **s** before you. .... Prv 4:25
of the blameless keeps his way **s**, ... Prv 11:5
make in the desert a highway for our ..... Is 40:3

STRANGER

I was a **s** and you welcomed me, ... Mt 25:35
A **s** they will not follow, but they will ..... Jn 10:5

STRANGERS

So then you are no longer **s** and aliens, .. Eph 2:19
they were **s** and exiles on .... Heb 11:13
Do not neglect to show hospitality to **s**, . Heb 13:2

STREAMS

He is like a tree planted by **s** of water ..... Ps 1:3
As a deer pants for flowing **s**, ... Ps 42:1
in the wilderness, and **s** in the desert; ..... Is 35:6

STREET

Wisdom cries aloud in the **s**, in the ..... Prv 1:20
and the **s** of the city was pure gold, ... Rv 21:21

STRENGTH

equipped me with **s** for the battle; ... 2 Sm 22:40
Seek the LORD and his **s**; .... 1 Chr 16:11
joy of the LORD is your **s**." .... Neh 8:10
LORD is my **s** and my shield; .... Ps 28:7
but God is the **s** of my heart and my ... Ps 73:26
Blessed are those whose **s** is in you, ... Ps 84:5
A wise man is full of **s**, and a man ..... Prv 24:5
the Lord shall renew their **s**; .... Is 40:31
all your mind and with all your **s**.' ..... Mk 12:30
may have **s** to comprehend with all ..... Eph 3:18

STRENGTHEN

I will **s** you, I will help you, I will .... Is 41:10
have turned again, **s** your brothers." ..... Lk 22:32
hands and **s** your weak knees, ... Heb 12:12

STRENGTHENED

You then, my child, be **s** by the grace .. 2 Tm 2:1
Lord stood by me and **s** me, ... 2 Tm 4:17
it is good for the heart to be **s** by grace, .. Heb 13:9

STRENGTHENS

do all things through him who **s** me. ..... Phil 4:13

STRIFE

By insolence comes nothing but **s**, ... Prv 13:10
A hot-tempered man stirs up **s**, but ..... Prv 15:18
They are full of envy, murder, **s**, ... Rom 1:29
there is jealousy and **s** among you, ... 1 Cor 3:3

STRIKE

and you shall **s** the rock, and water .... Ex 17:6
lest you **s** your foot against a stone.'" ..... Lk 4:11

STRONG

Be **s** and courageous. Do not fear .... Dt 31:6
Be **s** and courageous, for you shall .... Jos 1:6

We who are **s** have an obligation to ..... Rom 15:1
is weak in the world to shame the **s**; ... 1 Cor 1:27
firm in the faith, act like men, be **s**. .. 1 Cor 16:13
For when I am weak, then I am **s**. ..... 2 Cor 12:10
Finally, be **s** in the Lord .... Eph 6:10

STRONGHOLD

The LORD is a **s** for the .... Ps 9:9
he is their **s** in the time of trouble. ...... Ps 37:39
The LORD is good, a **s** in .... Na 1:7

STRUGGLE

In your **s** against sin you have not yet ... Heb 12:4

STUDY

Ezra had set his heart to **s** the Law of ... Ezr 7:10
and much **s** is a weariness .... Eccl 12:12

STUMBLE

nothing can make them **s**. .... Ps 119:165
straight path in which they shall not **s**, ... Jer 31:9
walks in the day, he does not **s**, ... Jn 11:9
that causes your brother to **s**. .... Rom 14:21
eat meat, lest I make my brother **s**. ..... 1 Cor 8:13
For we all **s** in many ways. And if .... Jas 3:2
They **s** because they disobey .... 1 Pt 2:8

STUMBLING

and a rock of **s** to both houses .... Is 8:14
They have stumbled over the **s** stone, ... Rom 9:32
never to put a **s** block or hindrance .... Rom 14:13
s block to Jews and folly to Gentiles, ... 1 Cor 1:23
become a **s** block to the weak. .... 1 Cor 8:9
and in him there is no cause for **s**. ...... 1 Jn 2:10
to keep you from **s** and to present ..... Jude 24

SUBDUE

fill the earth and **s** it, and have dominion .Gn 1:28

SUBJECT

Let every person be **s** to the governing .. Rom 13:1
enables him even to **s** all things to ..... Phil 3:21
we not much more be **s** to the Father ... Heb 12:9
Be **s** for the Lord's sake to every ...... 1 Pt 2:13

SUBJECTED

For the creation was **s** to futility, ... Rom 8:20
that God **s** the world to come, ... Heb 2:5
and powers having been **s** to him. ..... 1 Pt 3:22

SUBJECTION

Therefore one must be in **s**, not only .... Rom 13:5
put all things in **s** under his feet." ... 1 Cor 15:27
putting everything in **s** under his feet." ... Heb 2:8

SUBMISSION

to speak, but should be in **s**, as the ... 1 Cor 14:34
because of your **s** that comes from ..... 2 Cor 9:13

SUBMISSIVE

with all dignity keeping his children **s**, ... 1 Tm 3:4
kind, and **s** to their own husbands, ... Ti 2:5
Remind them to be **s** to rulers .... Ti 3:1

SUBMIT

flesh is hostile to God, for it does not **s** .. Rom 8:7
Wives, **s** to your own husbands, ... Col 5:22
Wives, **s** to your husbands, as is fitting .. Col 3:18
Obey your leaders and **s** to them, for .. Heb 13:17
S yourselves therefore to God. .... Jas 4:7

SUBMITS

Now as the church **s** to Christ, so also ... Eph 5:24

SUBMITTING

s to one another out of reverence for .... Eph 5:21
by **s** to their own husbands, ... 1 Pt 3:5

SUCCEED

believe his prophets, and you will **s**." .. 2 Chr 20:20
fail, but with many advisers they **s**. ...... Prv 15:22
but wisdom helps one to **s**. .... Eccl 10:10

SUCCESS

that you may have good **s** wherever .... Jos 1:7
O LORD, we pray, give us **s**! .... Ps 118:25

SUFFER

he must go to Jerusalem and **s** many ..... Mt 16:21
of Man will certainly **s** at their hands." .. Mt 17:12
the prophets, that his Christ would **s**, ... Acts 3:18
counted worthy to **s** dishonor for the .... Acts 5:41
With Christ, provided we **s** with him ...... Rom 8:17
endure the same sufferings that we **s**. .. 2 Cor 1:6
believe in him but also **s** for his sake, ... Phil 1:29
that we were to **s** affliction, ... 1 Thes 3:4
For it is better to **s** for doing good, ... 1 Pt 3:17
Do not fear what you are about to **s**. ...... Rv 2:10

SUFFERED

he himself has **s** when tempted, ... Heb 2:18
because Christ also **s** for you, ... 1 Pt 2:21
For Christ also **s** once for sins, the ..... 1 Pt 3:18
whoever has **s** in the flesh has ceased .... 1 Pt 4:1

SUFFERING

knowing that **s** produces endurance, ... Rom 5:3
but share in **s** for the gospel by .... 2 Tm 1:8
of their salvation perfect through **s**. ..... Heb 2:10
Is anyone among you **s**? Let him pray. ..... Jas 5:13
one endures sorrows while **s** unjustly. .. 1 Pt 2:19
s wrong as the wage for their .... 2 Pt 2:13

SUFFERINGS

For I consider that the **s** of this present . Rom 8:18
as we share abundantly in Christ's **s**, ... 2 Cor 1:5
his resurrection, and may share his **s**, ... Phil 3:10
Now I rejoice in my **s** for your sake, ... Col 1:24
when he predicted the **s** of Christ and .. 1 Pt 1:11

SUFFERS

If one member **s**, all suffer together; .. 1 Cor 12:26
Yet if anyone **s** as a Christian, let .... 1 Pt 4:16

SUFFICIENT

S for the day is its own trouble. .... Mt 6:34
"My grace is **s** for you, for my power .. 2 Cor 12:9

SUN

And the **s** stood still, and the moon .... Jos 10:13
In them he has set a tent for the **s**, ... Ps 19:4
from the rising of the **s** to its setting. ...... Ps 50:1
The **s** shall not strike you by day, ... Ps 121:6
So the **s** turned back on the dial the ten .. Is 38:8
The **s** shall be no more your light by day, ... Is 60:19
For he makes his **s** rise on the evil and .... Mt 5:45
of those days the **s** will be darkened, ... Mt 24:29
do not let the **s** go down on your anger, . Eph 4:26
need no light of lamp or **s**, for .... Rv 22:5

SUPPER

rose from **s**. He laid aside his outer .... Jn 13:4
it is not the Lord's **s** that you eat. ..... 1 Cor 11:20
invited to the marriage **s** of the Lamb." ... Rv 19:9

SUPPLICATION

making **s** for all the saints, ... Eph 6:18
by prayer and **s** with thanksgiving let ...... Phil 4:6

SUPPLICATIONS

I urge that **s**, prayers, intercessions, ... 1 Tm 2:1
Jesus offered up prayers and **s**, ... Heb 5:7

SUPPLY

And my God will **s** every need .... Phil 4:19

SURE

For I am **s** that neither death nor life, ... Rom 8:38

SURPASSES

the love of Christ that **s** knowledge, ... Eph 3:19
of God, which **s** all understanding, ... Phil 4:7

SURPASSING

show that the **s** power belongs to God .. 2 Cor 4:7
because of the **s** grace of God upon .. 2 Cor 9:14

SURROUNDED

Therefore, since we are **s** by so great a .. Heb 12:1

SUSTAIN

on the LORD, and he will **s** you; .... Ps 55:22
who will **s** you to the end, guiltless in .. 1 Cor 1:8

SWALLOWED

"Death is **s** up in victory." .... 1 Cor 15:54
what is mortal may be **s** up by life. .... 2 Cor 5:4

SWEAR

to those of old, 'You shall not **s** falsely, ... Mt 5:33
But above all, my brothers, do not **s**, ... Jas 5:12

SWEAT

By the **s** of your face you shall eat .... Gn 3:19
and his **s** became like great drops .... Lk 22:44

SWEET

into the water, and the water became **s**. .. Ex 15:25
How **s** are your words to my taste, ... Ps 119:103
lie down, your sleep will be **s**. .... Prv 3:24
A desire fulfilled is **s** to the soul, but .... Prv 13:19
It was **s** as honey in my mouth, but ...... Rv 10:10

SWORD

a flaming **s** that turned every way to ..... Gn 3:24
I have not come to bring peace, but a **s**.. Mt 10:34
For all who take the **s** will perish by .... Mt 26:52
for he does not bear the **s** in vain. ...... Rom 13:4
of salvation, and the **s** of the Spirit, ... Eph 6:17
active, sharper than any two-edged **s**, ... Heb 4:12
his mouth came a sharp two-edged **s**, ... Rv 1:16

SWORDS

Beat your plowshares into **s**, ... Jl 3:10
they shall beat their **s** into plowshares, ... Mi 4:3

SYMPATHY

in the Spirit, any affection and **s**, ... Phil 2:1
unity of mind, **s**, brotherly love, ...1 Pt 3:8

SYNAGOGUE

he went to the **s** on the Sabbath day, ... Lk 4:16
named Jairus, who was a ruler of the **s**. .. Lk 8:41
that they would not be put out of the **s**; .Jn 12:42

TABERNACLE

you concerning the pattern of the **t**, ... Ex 25:9
glory of the LORD filled the **t**. .... Ex 40:34

TABITHA

turning to the body he said, "**T**, arise." .. Acts 9:40

TABLE

You prepare a **t** before me in .... Ps 23:5
"Can God spread a **t** in the wilderness? . Ps 78:19
crumbs that fall from their masters' **t**." .. Mt 15:27

TABLET

write them on the **t** of your heart. .... Prv 7:3

TABLETS

that I may give you the **t** of stone, ... Ex 24:12
The **t** were the work of God, and the .... Ex 32:16
mountain and put the **t** in the ark .... Dt 10:5
not on **t** of stone but on **t** .... 2 Cor 3:3

TAKE

You shall not add to it or **t** from it. ...... Dt 12:32
"**T**, eat; this is my body." .... Mt 26:26
deny himself and **t** up his cross .... Mk 8:34
down my life that I may **t** it up again. ... Jn 10:17
we cannot **t** anything out of the world... 1 Tm 6:7
T hold of the eternal life to which you .. 1 Tm 6:12

TAKES

Blessed is the man who **t** refuge in him! . Ps 34:8
who **t** away the sin of the world! .... Jn 1:29
and if anyone **t** away from the words .... Rv 22:19

TALENTS

To one he gave five **t**, to another two, .. Mt 25:15

TALK

and shall **t** of them when you sit in .... Dt 6:7
but mere **t** tends only to poverty. .... Prv 14:23
does not consist in **t** but in power. .... 1 Cor 4:20
Let no corrupting **t** come out of .... Eph 4:29
nor foolish **t** nor crude joking, ... Eph 5:4

TAME

no human being can **t** the tongue. .... Jas 3:8

TASTE

Oh, **t** and see that the LORD is .... Ps 34:8
of the earth, but if salt has lost its **t**, ... Mt 5:13
here who will not **t** death until they ..... Mt 16:28
keeps my word, he will never **t** death.' ... Jn 8:52
Do not handle, Do not **t**, Do not touch ... Col 2:21
of God he might **t** death for everyone..... Heb 2:9

TASTED

who have **t** the heavenly gift, and have .. Heb 6:4
if indeed you have **t** that the Lord is ...... 1 Pt 2:3

TAUGHT

he **t** them as one who had authority, ... Mk 1:22
'And they will all be **t** by God.' .... Jn 6:45
in words not **t** by human wisdom .... 1 Cor 2:13
Let the one who is **t** the word share all ... Gal 6:6
t by God to love one another, ... 1 Thes 4:9
the traditions that you were **t** by us, ... 2 Thes 2:15
hold firm to the trustworthy word as **t**, ... Ti 1:9

TAX

"Does your teacher not pay the **t**?" ..... Mt 17:24
Show me the coin for the **t**." .... Mt 22:19

TAXES

Is it lawful to pay **t** to Caesar, or not?" . Mt 22:17
to whom **t** are owed, ... Rom 13:7

TEACH

You shall **t** them diligently to your .... Dt 6:7
T me your way, O LORD, ... Ps 27:11
So **t** us to number our days that we .... Ps 90:12
T me to do your will, for you .... Ps 143:10
no longer shall each one **t** his .... Jer 31:34
"Lord, **t** us to pray, ... Lk 11:1
he will **t** you all things and bring to ...... Jn 14:26
I do not permit a woman to **t** or to .... 1 Tm 2:12
who will be able to **t** others also. .... 2 Tm 2:2
t what accords with sound doctrine. .... Ti 2:1
have no need that anyone should **t** you... 1 Jn 2:27
we who **t** will be judged with .... Jas 3:1

TEACHER

"A disciple is not above his **t**, nor a ...... Mt 10:24
"**T**, what good deed must I do to have . Mt 19:16

TEACHERS

Are all **t**? Do all work miracles? ...... 1 Cor 12:29
evangelists, the shepherds and **t**, ... Eph 4:11
accumulate for themselves **t** to suit ...... 2 Tm 4:3
by this time you ought to be **t**, ... Heb 5:12
Not many of you should become **t**, ... Jas 3:1
just as there will be false **t** among you, .. 2 Pt 2:1

TEACHES

the one who **t**, in his teaching; .... Rom 12:7
all good things with the one who **t**. .... Gal 6:6
If anyone **t** a different doctrine and ...... 1 Tm 6:3

TEACHING

forsake not your mother's **t**, ... Prv 1:8
"What is this? A new **t** with authority! .. Mk 1:27
he will know whether the **t** is from God .. Jn 7:17
t and admonishing one another in all ..... Col 3:16
and in your **t** show integrity, dignity, ... Ti 2:7
Whoever abides in the **t** has both the ...... 2 Jn 9

TEACHINGS

according to human precepts and **t**? .... Col 2:22
be led away by diverse and strange **t**, ... Heb 13:9

TEAR

a time to **t**, and a time to sew; .... Eccl 3:7
He will wipe away every **t** from their..... Rv 21:4

TEARS

every night I flood my bed with **t**; .... Ps 6:6
My **t** have been my food day and night, .. Ps 42:3
put my **t** in your bottle. .... Ps 56:8
Those who sow in **t** shall reap .... Ps 126:5
but folly with her own hands **t** it down. .. Prv 14:1
GOD will wipe away **t** from .... Is 25:8

TEETH

sour grapes, his **t** shall be set on edge. .. Jer 31:30
gave you cleanness of **t** in all your .... Am 4:6
will be weeping and gnashing of **t**." .... Mt 8:12

TELL

t of his salvation from day to day. .... Ps 96:2
t of all his wondrous works! .... Ps 105:2
When he comes, he will **t** us all things." .... Jn 4:25
If you are the Christ, **t** us plainly." .... Jn 10:24

TEMPER

A man of quick **t** acts foolishly, ... Prv 14:17
but he who has a hasty **t** exalts folly. .... Prv 14:29

TEMPLE

Solomon purposed to build a **t** for the ... 2 Chr 2:1
The LORD is in his holy **t**; .... Ps 11:4
But the LORD is in his holy **t**; .... Hab 2:20
and set him on the pinnacle of the **t** .... Mt 4:5
something greater than the **t** is here. .... Mt 12:6
Jesus answered them, "Destroy this **t**, ... Jn 2:19
that you are God's **t** and that God's .... 1 Cor 3:16
your body is a **t** of the Holy Spirit .... 1 Cor 6:19
grows into a holy **t** in the Lord. .... Eph 2:21
for its **t** is the Lord God the Almighty ..... Rv 21:22

TEMPLES

does not live in **t** made by man, ... Acts 17:24

TEMPT

so that Satan may not **t** you .... 1 Cor 7:5

TEMPTATION

And lead us not into **t**, but deliver us .... Mt 6:13
pray that you may not enter into **t**. ...... Mt 26:41
No **t** has overtaken you that is not ..... 1 Cor 10:13
those who desire to be rich fall into **t**, ... 1 Tm 6:9

TEMPTATIONS

For it is necessary that **t** come, but .... Mt 18:7
"**T** to sin are sure to come, but woe .... Lk 17:1

TEMPTED

into the wilderness to be **t** by the devil. .. Mt 4:1
not let you be **t** beyond your ability, . 1 Cor 10:13
watch on yourself, lest you too be **t**. ...... Gal 6:1
he is able to help those who are being **t**. .. Heb 2:18
in every respect has been **t** as we are, ... Heb 4:15
But each person is **t** when he is lured .... Jas 1:14

TEN

the covenant, the **T** Commandments. ...... Ex 34:28
and give it to him who has the **t** talents. .. Mt 25:28
Jesus answered, "Were not **t** cleansed? .. Lk 17:17

TENDER

because of the **t** mercy of our God, ... Lk 1:78
sympathy, brotherly love, a **t** heart, ... 1 Pt 3:8

TENDERHEARTED

Be kind to one another, **t**, forgiving .... Eph 4:32

TENDS

Whoever **t** a fig tree will eat its fruit, ... Prv 27:18
Or who **t** a flock without getting some .. 1 Cor 9:7

TENT

moving about in a **t** for my dwelling. ..... 2 Sm 7:6
"Enlarge the place of your **t**, and let ...... Is 54:2
My **t** is destroyed, and all my cords ..... Jer 10:20
For we know that if the **t** that is our .... 2 Cor 5:1
and more perfect **t** (not made with .... Heb 9:11
and the sanctuary of the **t** of witness in .. Rv 15:5

TENTH

Abram gave him a **t** of everything. .... Gn 14:20
Abraham apportioned a **t** part of.......... Heb 7:2

TENTMAKERS

for they were **t** by trade. .... Acts 18:3

TERRIFIED

they fell on their faces and were **t**......... Mt 17:6
hear of wars and tumults, do not be **t**, ... Lk 21:9

TERROR

whispering of many—**t** on every side! .... Ps 31:13

You will not fear the **t** of the night, ... Ps 91:5

TEST

not put the LORD your God to the **t**, ... Dt 6:16
try me; **t** my heart and my mind. .... Ps 26:2
Let us **t** and examine our ways, ... Lam 3:40
not put the Lord your God to the **t**." .... Mt 4:7
T yourselves. Or do you not .... 2 Cor 13:5
But let each one **t** his own work, ... Gal 6:4
but **t** everything; hold fast what is .... 1 Thes 5:21
trial when it comes upon you to **t** you, .. 1 Pt 4:12
but **t** the spirits to see whether they ...... 1 Jn 4:1

TESTED

After these things God **t** Abraham .... Gn 22:1
For you, O God, have **t** us; .... Ps 66:10
and a man is **t** by his praise. .... Prv 27:21
t first; then let them serve as deacons .. 1 Tm 3:10
By faith Abraham, when he was **t**, ... Heb 11:17

TESTIFY

And we have seen and **t** that the Father . 1 Jn 4:14

TESTIMONY

world as a **t** to all nations, and then .... Mt 24:14
and we know that his **t** is true. .... Jn 21:24
not be ashamed of the **t** about our Lord . 2 Tm 1:8
And this is the **t**, that God gave us .... 1 Jn 5:11

TESTING

For the LORD your God is **t** you, ... Dt 13:3
for a while, and in time of **t** fall away. ... Lk 8:13
by **t** you may discern what is the will ... Rom 12:2
for you know that the **t** of your faith .... Jas 1:3

TESTS

The LORD **t** the righteous, ... Ps 11:5
for gold, and the LORD **t** hearts. .... Prv 17:3
but to please God who **t** our hearts. .. 1 Thes 2:4

THANK

And now we **t** you, our God, and .... 1 Chr 29:13
Let them **t** the LORD for his .... Ps 107:8
Jesus declared, "I **t** you, ... Mt 11:25
'God, I **t** you that I am not like other ... Lk 18:11
I **t** my God in all my remembrance .... Phil 1:3
We always **t** God, the Father of our .... Col 1:3

THANKS

his saints, and give **t** to his holy name. .... Ps 30:4
Oh give **t** to the LORD, for he .... Ps 118:1
All your works shall give **t** to you, ... Ps 145:10
and when he had given **t** he gave it ...... Mt 26:27
on his face at Jesus' feet, giving him **t**. .. Lk 17:16
the loaves, and when he had given **t**, ... Jn 6:11
not honor him as God or give **t** to him, .. Rom 1:21
But **t** be to God, who gives us the ..... 1 Cor 15:57
But **t** be to God, who in Christ always .. 2 Cor 2:14
T be to God for his inexpressible gift! . 2 Cor 9:15
giving **t** always and for everything .... Eph 5:20
give **t** in all circumstances; for this .... 1 Thes 5:18
give glory and honor and **t** to him .... Rv 4:9

THANKSGIVING

I will magnify him with **t**. .... Ps 69:30
Sing to the LORD with **t**; .... Ps 147:7
through us will produce **t** to God. ...... 2 Cor 9:11
but instead let there be **t**. .... Eph 5:4
with **t** let your requests be made .... Phil 4:6
as you were taught, abounding in **t**. ...... Col 2:7
For what **t** can we return to God for ... 1 Thes 3:9
received with **t** by those who believe ... 1 Tm 4:3
glory and wisdom and **t** and honor and ... Rv 7:12

THIEF

if the **t** is found, he shall pay double. ... Ex 22:7
night the **t** was coming, he would .... Mt 24:43
where no **t** approaches and no moth ...... Lk 12:33
The **t** comes only to steal and kill .... Jn 10:10
Lord will come like a **t** in the night. ... 1 Thes 5:2
the day of the Lord will come like a **t**, .. 2 Pt 3:10
I am coming like a **t**! Blessed is the ...... Rv 16:15

THIEVES

rust destroys and where **t** do not break ... Mt 6:20
nor **t**, nor the greedy, nor drunkards, .. 1 Cor 6:10

THINGS

"I know that you can do all **t**, ... Jb 42:2
living **t** both small and great. .... Ps 104:25
LORD has done great **t** for us; .... Ps 126:3
and all these **t** will be added to you. ...... Mt 6:33
but with God all **t** are possible." .... Mt 19:26
All **t** were made through him, and .... Jn 1:3
fullness of time, to unite all **t** in him, ... Eph 1:10
and in him all **t** hold together. .... Col 1:17

THINK

you not to **t** of himself more highly ...... Rom 12:3
worthy of praise, **t** about these things. ...... Phil 4:8
T over what I say, for the Lord will .... 2 Tm 2:7

THINKING

but they became futile in their **t**, ... Rom 1:21
do not be children in your **t**. .... 1 Cor 14:20
arm yourselves with the same way of **t**, .. 1 Pt 4:1

THINKS

If anyone among you **t** that he is wise . 1 Cor 3:18
For if anyone **t** he is something, ... Gal 6:3
If anyone **t** he is religious and does not ... Jas 1:26

THIRST

who hunger and **t** for righteousness, ... Mt 5:6
whoever believes in me shall never **t**. ...... Jn 6:35
said (to fulfill the Scripture), "I **t**." .... Jn 19:28
hunger no more, neither **t** anymore; ...... Rv 7:16

THIRSTS

My soul **t** for God, for the living God. ...... Ps 42:2
earnestly I seek you; my soul **t** for you; ... Ps 63:1
my soul **t** for you like a parched land. .. Ps 143:6
"Come, everyone who **t**, come to the ...... Is 55:1
Jesus stood up and cried out, "If anyone **t** . Jn 7:37

THIRSTY

I was **t** and you gave me drink, ... Mt 25:35
drinks of this water will be **t** again, ... Jn 4:13
And let the one who is **t** come; .... Rv 22:17

THOMAS

T said to him, "Lord, we do not know ...... Jn 14:5
Then he said to **T**, "Put your finger ...... Jn 20:27

THORN

a **t** was given me in the flesh, ... 2 Cor 12:7

THORNS

t and thistles it shall bring forth for ...... Gn 3:18
Other seeds fell among **t**, and the **t**..... Mt 13:7
and twisting together a crown of **t**, ... Mt 27:29

THOUGHT

needy, but the Lord takes **t** for me. ...... Ps 40:17
Whoever gives **t** to the word will .... Prv 16:20
I speak like a child, I **t** like a child, ... 1 Cor 13:11
take every **t** captive to obey Christ, ... 2 Cor 10:5

THOUGHTS

every intention of the **t** of his heart .... Gn 6:5
knows the **t** of man, that they are .... Ps 94:11
precious to me are your **t**, O God! .... Ps 139:17
Try me and know my **t**! .... Ps 139:23
Even in your **t**, do not curse the king, .. Eccl 10:20
For my **t** are not your **t**, ... Is 55:8
For out of the heart come evil **t**, ... Mt 15:19
knows a person's **t** except the spirit .. 1 Cor 2:11
"The Lord knows the **t** of the wise, ... 1 Cor 3:20

THOUSAND

For a **t** years in your sight are but as ...... Ps 90:4
with the Lord one day is as a **t** years, ... 2 Pt 3:8
Satan, and bound him for a **t** years, ... Rv 20:2

THREE

For just as Jonah was **t** days and **t** .... Mt 12:40
For where two or **t** are gathered .... Mt 18:20
'After **t** days I will rise.' .... Mt 27:63
faith, hope, and love abide, these **t**; .. 1 Cor 13:13

THRONE

Your **t** shall be established forever.'" .... 2 Sm 7:16
Your **t**, O God, is forever and ever. .... Ps 45:6
I saw the Lord sitting upon a **t**, ... Is 6:1
"Heaven is my **t**, and the earth is .... Is 66:1
either by heaven, for it is the **t** of God, ... Mt 5:34
then he will sit on his glorious **t**. .... Mt 25:31
seated at the right hand of the **t** of God. . Heb 12:2
They cast their crowns before the **t**, ... Rv 4:10
Then I saw a great white **t** and him who . Rv 20:11
but the **t** of God and of the Lamb will ... Rv 22:3

THROW

be the first to **t** a stone at her." .... Jn 8:7
do not **t** away your confidence, which .. Heb 10:35

THUNDER

and God answered him in **t**. .... Ex 19:19
name Boanerges, that is, Sons of **T**); ...... Mk 3:17
waters and like the sound of loud **t**. ...... Rv 14:2

TIE

heart always; **t** them around your neck. . Prv 6:21
They **t** up heavy burdens, hard to bear, .. Mt 23:4

TIME

to the kingdom for such a **t** as this?" .... Est 4:14
For man does not know his **t**. .... Eccl 9:12
shut up and sealed until the **t** of the end. . Dn 12:9
for it is the **t** to seek the LORD, ... Hos 10:12
at the right **t** Christ died for the .... Rom 5:6
But when the fullness of **t** had come, ... Gal 4:4
making the best use of the **t**, because ... Eph 5:16
outsiders, making the best use of the **t**. ... Col 4:5
"In the last **t** there will be scoffers, ... Jude 18

TIMES

"It is not for you to know **t** or seasons ... Acts 1:7
Now concerning the **t** and the seasons, .. 1 Thes 5:1
last days there will come **t** of difficulty. .. 2 Tm 3:1

TIMOTHY

A disciple was there, named **T**, ... Acts 16:1
T, my fellow worker, greets you; ...... Rom 16:21
that our brother **T** has been released, .. Heb 13:23

TITHE

within your towns the **t** of your grain .... Dt 12:17
in abundantly the **t** of everything. ...... 2 Chr 31:5
Bring the full **t** into the storehouse, ... Mal 3:10
For you **t** mint and dill and cumin, ... Mt 23:23

TITHES

to the LORD from all your **t**, ... Nm 18:28
'How have we robbed you?' In your **t** ... Mal 3:8
twice a week; I give **t** of all that I get.' .. Lk 18:12

TITUS

As for **T**, he is my partner and fellow .. 2 Cor 8:23
has gone to Galatia, **T** to Dalmatia. ...... 2 Tm 4:10
To **T**, my true child in a common faith: ...... Ti 1:4

TODAY

T, if you hear his voice, ... Ps 95:7
"**T** this Scripture has been fulfilled .... Lk 4:21
"**T** salvation has come to this house, ... Lk 19:9
t you will be with me in paradise." ...... Lk 23:43
as long as it is called "**t**," that none ...... Heb 3:13
the same yesterday and **t** and forever. ...... Heb 13:8

TOGETHER

be revealed, and all flesh shall see it **t**, ... Is 40:5
all things, and in him all things hold **t**. ... Col 1:17

TOIL

how they grow: they neither **t** nor spin, .. Mt 6:28
remember, brothers, our labor and **t**: .... 1 Thes 2:9
For to this end we **t** and strive, ... 1 Tm 4:10

TOMB

and laid it in his own new **t**, which he... Mt 27:60
found the stone rolled away from the **t**, ... Lk 24:2

Mary Magdalene came to the t early, ... Jn 20:1

TOMBS

For you are like whitewashed t, ... Mt 23:27
The t also were opened. And many ...... Mt 27:52
He lived among the t. And no one .... Mk 5:3

TOMORROW

Do not boast about t, for you do not .... Prv 27:1
"Let us eat and drink, for t we die." ...... Is 22:13
"Therefore do not be anxious about t, ... Mt 6:34
"Let us eat and drink, for t we die." .. 1 Cor 15:32
yet you do not know what t will bring. ... Jas 4:14

TONGUE

Keep your t from evil and your lips .... Ps 34:13
but the t of the wise brings healing. ..... Prv 12:18
Death and life are in the power of the t, . Prv 18:21
and every t shall confess to God." ...... Rom 14:11
For one who speaks in a t speaks not . 1 Cor 14:2
than ten thousand words in a t. .... 1 Cor 14:19
every t confess that Jesus Christ is .... Phil 2:11
does not bridle his t but deceives his ... Jas 1:26
but no human being can tame the t. ...... Jas 3:8
let him keep his t from evil and his ... 1 Pt 3:10

TONGUES

speak in other t as the Spirit gave .... Acts 2:4
them speaking in t and extolling God. .. Acts 10:46
began speaking in t and prophesying. .. Acts 19:6
Do all speak with t? Do all interpret? . 1 Cor 12:30
If I speak in the t of men and of .... 1 Cor 13:1
Now I want you all to speak in t, but... 1 Cor 14:5
Thus t are a sign not for believers .... 1 Cor 14:22
and do not forbid speaking in t. .... 1 Cor 14:39

TOOTH

eye for eye, t for t, hand .... Ex 21:24
'An eye for an eye and a t for a t.' ...... Mt 5:38

TORMENTED

they will be t day and night forever ...... Rv 20:10

TORN

the curtain of the temple was t in two, .. Mt 27:51

TORTURED

Some were t, refusing to accept .... Heb 11:35

TOUCH

"T not my anointed ones, ... Ps 105:15
T me, and see. For a spirit does not ..... Lk 24:39
the Lord, and t no unclean thing; ...... 2 Cor 6:17
Do not taste, Do not t" .... Col 2:21
and the evil one does not t him. .... 1 Jn 5:18

TOUCHED

whose hearts God had t. .... 1 Sm 10:26
And as many as t it were made well. ..... Mt 14:36
"Who was it that t me?" .... Lk 8:45

TOWER

ourselves a city and a t with its top ...... Gn 11:4
refuge, a strong t against the enemy. ..... Ps 61:3
name of the LORD is a strong t; .... Prv 18:10

TRADITION

So for the sake of your t you have ...... Mt 15:6
empty deceit, according to human t, ... Col 2:8
in accord with the t that you received . 2 Thes 3:6

TRADITIONS

maintain the t even as I delivered ...... 1 Cor 11:2
hold to the t that you were taught ..... 2 Thes 2:15

TRAIN

T up a child in the way he should go; .... Prv 22:6
Rather t yourself for godliness; .... 1 Tm 4:7

TRAINED

being t in the words of the faith and .... 1 Tm 4:6
to those who have been t by it. .... Heb 12:11

TRAINING

for while bodily t is of some value, ... 1 Tm 4:8
and for t in righteousness, ... 2 Tm 3:16
t us to renounce ungodliness and .... Ti 2:12

TRANCE

they were preparing it, he fell into a t .. Acts 10:10

TRANSFIGURED

And he was t before them, and his face ... Mt 17:2

TRANSFORM

who will t our lowly body .... Phil 3:21

TRANSFORMED

but be t by the renewal of your mind, ... Rom 12:2
are being t into the same image from .. 2 Cor 3:18

TRANSGRESSION

Blessed is the one whose t is forgiven, ... Ps 32:1
stricken for the t of my people? .... Is 53:8
but where there is no law there is no t. .. Rom 4:15

TRANSGRESSIONS

For I know my t, and my sin is ever ..... Ps 51:3
so far does he remove our t from us. .. Ps 103:12
Whoever conceals his t will not .... Prv 28:13
who blots out your t for my own sake, ... Is 43:25
But he was pierced for our t; .... Is 53:5
It was added because of t, until the ..... Gal 3:19

TRANSGRESSORS

to death and was numbered with the t; .. Is 53:12
'And he was numbered with the t.' ...... Lk 22:37

TREAD

it is he who will t down our foes. .... Ps 60:12
he will t our iniquities underfoot. .... Mi 7:19
He will t the winepress of the fury of .... Rv 19:15

TREASURE

You fill their womb with t; .... Ps 17:14
house of the righteous there is much t, .. Prv 15:6
fear of the LORD is Zion's t. .... Is 33:6
For where your t is, there your heart ..... Mt 6:21
out of his good t brings forth good, ... Mt 12:35
poor, and you will have t in heaven; .... Mt 19:21
But we have this t in jars of clay, ... 2 Cor 4:7
thus storing up t for themselves as ..... 1 Tm 6:19
You have laid up t in the last days. ...... Jas 5:3

TREASURED

to be a people for his t possession, ... Dt 7:6
But Mary t up all these things, ... Lk 2:19

TREASURES

T gained by wickedness do not profit, ... Prv 10:2
but lay up for yourselves t in heaven, ... Mt 6:20
in whom are hidden all the t of wisdom .. Col 2:3

TREAT

You shall t the stranger who .... Lv 19:34
Masters, t your slaves justly .... Col 4:1

TREE

The t of life was in the midst of the .... Gn 2:9
but of the t of the knowledge of good .. Gn 2:17
shall not remain all night on the t, ... Dt 21:23
He is like a t planted by streams of .... Ps 1:3
The fruit of the righteous is a t of life, .. Prv 11:30
Every t therefore that does not bear .... Mt 3:10
for the t is known by its fruit. .... Mt 12:33
bore our sins in his body on the t, ... 1 Pt 2:24
I will grant to eat of the t of life, ... Rv 2:7
have the right to the t of life and .... Rv 22:14

TREES

shall not destroy its t by wielding an .... Dt 20:19
Then shall all the t of the forest sing ... Ps 96:12
The t of the LORD are watered .... Ps 104:16
fruitless in late autumn, twice dead, ... Jude 12

TREMBLE

The LORD reigns; let the peoples t! ...... Ps 99:1
T, O earth, at the presence of the Lord, .. Ps 114:7
they do not t as they blaspheme the .... 2 Pt 2:10

TREMBLING

how you received him with fear and t. . 2 Cor 7:15
your own salvation with fear and t, ... Phil 2:12

TRESPASS

But the free gift is not like the t. .... Rom 5:15
For if, because of one man's t, death .... Rom 5:17
Rather, through their t salvation has ... Rom 11:11

TRESPASSES

For if you forgive others their t, your ...... Mt 6:14
not counting their t against them, ... 2 Cor 5:19
we were dead in our t, made us alive .... Eph 2:5
having forgiven us all our t, ... Col 2:13

TRIAL

man who remains steadfast under t, ... Jas 1:12
surprised at the fiery t when it comes ... 1 Pt 4:12

TRIALS

when you meet t of various kinds, ... Jas 1:2
you have been grieved by various t, ... 1 Pt 1:6
knows how to rescue the godly from t, .. 2 Pt 2:9

TRIBES

All these are the twelve t of Israel. ...... Gn 49:28
thrones, judging the twelve t of Israel. ... Mt 19:28
all the t of the earth will mourn, ... Mt 24:30
from all t and peoples .... Rv 7:9

TRIBULATION

and when t or persecution arises on ..... Mt 13:21
For then there will be great t, such ..... Mt 24:21
In the world you will have t. .... Jn 16:33
Shall t, or distress, or persecution, or .. Rom 8:35
Rejoice in hope, be patient in t, ... Rom 12:12
are the ones coming out of the great t. ... Rv 7:14

TRIUMPHAL

always leads us in t procession, ... 2 Cor 2:14

TRIUMPHING

to open shame, by t over them in him. ... Col 2:15

TROUBLE

a very present help in t. .... Ps 46:1
For he has delivered me from every t, ... Ps 54:7
Though I walk in the midst of t, ... Ps 138:7
I tell my t before him. .... Ps 142:2
The righteous is delivered from t, ... Prv 11:8
even the wicked for the day of t. .... Prv 16:4
morning, our salvation in the time of t. .. Is 33:2
is good, a stronghold in the day of t; .... Na 1:7
Sufficient for the day is its own t. .... Mt 6:34

TROUBLED

"Let not your hearts be t. Believe in ...... Jn 14:1
Let not your hearts be t, neither let ...... Jn 14:27
Have no fear of them, nor be t, ... 1 Pt 3:14

TRUE

word does not come to pass or come t, .. Dt 18:22
held in honor; all that he says comes t. .. 1 Sm 9:6
The t light, which gives light to everyone, ... Jn 1:9
that they know you, the only t God, ... Jn 17:3
Let God be t though every one .... Rom 3:4
Finally, brothers, whatever is t, ... Phil 4:8
He is the t God and eternal life. .... 1 Jn 5:20
for these words are trustworthy and t." ... Rv 21:5

TRUMPET

send out his angels with a loud t call, .. Mt 24:31
the twinkling of an eye, at the last t. . 1 Cor 15:52
and with the sound of the t of God. .. 1 Thes 4:16

TRUST

but we t in the name of the LORD .... Ps 20:7
O my God, in you I t; let me not be ..... Ps 25:2
T in the LORD, and do good; .... Ps 37:3
and put their t in the LORD. .... Ps 40:3
T in him at all times, O people; .... Ps 62:8
T in the LORD with all your .... Prv 3:5
I will t, and will not be afraid; .... Is 12:2
T in the LORD forever, ... Is 26:4
and in t shall be your strength." .... Is 30:15
"I will put my t in him." .... Heb 2:13

TRUSTED

But I have t in your steadfast love; .... Ps 13:5

I have **t** in the LORD without............. Ps 26:1
delivered his servants, who **t** in him, ... Dn 3:28

TRUSTS

blessed is the one who **t** in you! .... Ps 84:12
Whoever **t** in his riches will fall, ... Prv 11:28
blessed is he who **t** in the LORD. .... Prv 16:20
is stayed on you, because he **t** in you. ...... Is 26:3
"Blessed is the man who **t** in the .... Jer 17:7

TRUSTWORTHY

Your decrees are very **t**; holiness .... Ps 93:5
but he who is **t** in spirit keeps a thing .... Prv 11:13
The saying is **t**, for: If we have died ..... 2 Tm 2:11
"These words are **t** and true. .... Rv 22:6

TRUTH

Behold, you delight in **t** in the inward .... Ps 51:6
I may walk in your **t**; unite my heart ..... Ps 86:11
I the LORD speak the **t**; .... Is 45:19
not accept discipline; **t** has perished; ..... Jer 7:28
Speak the **t** to one another; .... Zec 8:16
will worship the Father in spirit and **t**, ... Jn 4:23
and the **t** will set you free." .... Jn 8:32
"I am the way, and the **t**, and the .... Jn 14:6
to you from the Father, the Spirit of **t**, ... Jn 15:26
When the Spirit of **t** comes, he will ...... Jn 16:13
Sanctify them in the **t**; your word is ...... Jn 17:17
Pilate said to him, "What is **t**? .... Jn 18:38
their unrighteousness suppress the **t**. .... Rom 1:18
wrongdoing, but rejoices with the **t**. .... 1 Cor 13:6
so that the **t** of the gospel might be ...... Gal 2:5
the **t** in love, we are to grow up in .... Eph 4:15
refused to love the **t** and so be saved. 2 Thes 2:10
to come to the knowledge of the **t**. ..... 1 Tm 2:4
God, a pillar and buttress of the **t**. ..... 1 Tm 3:15
after receiving the knowledge of the **t**, . Heb 10:26
we lie and do not practice the **t**. .... 1 Jn 1:6

TRUTHFUL

T lips endure forever, but a lying ...... Prv 12:19
A **t** witness saves lives, but one who ..... Prv 14:25

TRUTHS

interpreting spiritual **t** to those who .... 1 Cor 2:13

TRY

Prove me, O LORD, and **t** me; .... Ps 26:2
T me and know my thoughts! .... Ps 139:23
to **t** those who dwell on the earth....... Rv 3:10

TUNIC

would sue you and take your **t**, let him .... Mt 5:40

TURN

Do not **t** from it to the right hand or .... Jos 1:7
remember and **t** to the LORD, ... Ps 22:27
fear the LORD, and **t** away from .... Prv 3:7
You **t** things upside down! Shall .... Is 29:16
"**T** to me and be saved, all the ends .... Is 45:22
but that the wicked **t** from his way ..... Ezk 33:11
And he will **t** the hearts of fathers to ..... Mal 4:6
unless you **t** and become like children, ... Mt 18:3
to **t** the hearts of the fathers to the ...... Lk 1:17
so that they may **t** from darkness to ... Acts 26:18
and will **t** away from listening to the .... 2 Tm 4:4
let him **t** away from evil and do good; .... 1 Pt 3:11

TURNED

number who believed **t** to the Lord..... Acts 11:21
All have **t** aside; together they .... Rom 3:12
and how you **t** to God from idols .... 1 Thes 1:9

TWELVE

All these are the **t** tribes of Israel. ...... Gn 49:28
And Joshua set up **t** stones in the midst ... Jos 4:9
And he called to him his **t** disciples .... Mt 10:1
And they took up **t** baskets full of the .... Mt 14:20
followed me will also sit on **t** thrones, ... Mt 19:28
"Did I not choose you, the **t**? .... Jn 6:70
the tree of life with its **t** kinds of fruit, ... Rv 22:2

TYPE

who was a **t** of the one who was to .... Rom 5:14

UNAPPROACHABLE

who dwells in **u** light, ... 1 Tm 6:16

UNBELIEF

mighty works there, because of their **u**. ... Mt 13:58
"I believe; help my **u**!" .... Mk 9:24
were broken off because of their **u**, ... Rom 11:20
they were unable to enter because of **u**. .. Heb 3:19

UNBELIEVER

If any brother has a wife who is an **u**, .. 1 Cor 7:12
does a believer share with an **u**? ...... 2 Cor 6:15

UNBELIEVERS

world has blinded the minds of the **u**, ... 2 Cor 4:4
Do not be unequally yoked with **u**...... 2 Cor 6:14

UNBELIEVING

For the **u** husband is made holy .... 1 Cor 7:14
there be in any of you an evil, **u** heart, ... Heb 3:12

UNBORN

his righteousness to a people yet **u**, ... Ps 22:31
might know them, the children yet **u**, ... Ps 78:6

UNCHANGEABLE

heirs of the promise the **u** character .... Heb 6:17

UNCIRCUMCISED

been entrusted with the gospel to the **u**, .. Gal 2:7
circumcised and **u**, barbarian, ... Col 3:11

UNCIRCUMCISION

counts for anything nor **u**, but keeping . 1 Cor 7:19
nor **u** counts for anything, but only ...... Gal 5:6

UNCLEAN

For I am lost; for I am a man of **u** lips, ... Is 6:5
We have all become like one who is **u**, ... Is 64:6
and gave them authority over **u** spirits, ... Mt 10:1
Lord Jesus that nothing is **u** in itself, ... Rom 14:14

UNDEFILED

let the marriage bed be **u**, ... Heb 13:4
that is imperishable, **u**, and unfading, ... 1 Pt 1:4

UNDERSTAND

I have uttered what I did not **u**, ... Jb 42:3
and desperately sick; who can **u** it? ..... Jer 17:9
but those who are wise shall **u**. .... Dn 12:10
opened their minds to **u** the Scriptures, ... Lk 24:45
"Do you **u** what you are reading?" ..... Acts 8:30
For I do not **u** my own actions. .... Rom 7:15
but **u** what the will of the Lord is. ...... Eph 5:17
By faith we **u** that the universe was ..... Heb 11:3
things in them that are hard to **u**, ... 2 Pt 3:16

UNDERSTANDING

his **u** is beyond measure. .... Ps 147:5
and do not lean on your own **u**. .... Prv 3:5
Whoever is slow to anger has great **u**, ... Prv 14:29
u is to be chosen rather than silver. ..... Prv 16:16
peace of God, which surpasses all **u**, ... Phil 4:7
the Lord will give you **u** in everything. .... 2 Tm 2:7
of God has come and has given us **u**, ... 1 Jn 5:20

UNDERSTANDS

boast in this, that he **u** and knows me, ... Jer 9:24
the one who hears the word and **u** it. .... Mt 13:23
no one **u**; no one seeks for God. ...... Rom 3:11

UNDIVIDED

to secure your **u** devotion to the Lord... 1 Cor 7:35

UNEQUALLY

Do not be **u** yoked with .... 2 Cor 6:14

UNFADING

undefiled, and **u**, kept in heaven .... 1 Pt 1:4
you will receive the **u** crown of glory. .... 1 Pt 5:4

UNFRUITFUL

Take no part in the **u** works of .... Eph 5:11
help cases of urgent need, and not be **u**. ... Ti 3:14
keep you from being ineffective or **u** .... 2 Pt 1:8

UNGODLINESS

against all **u** and unrighteousness........ Rom 1:18

lead people into more and more **u**, ... 2 Tm 2:16
training us to renounce **u** and worldly ...... Ti 2:12

UNGODLY

at the right time Christ died for the **u**. ... Rom 5:6
what will become of the **u** and the ...... 1 Pt 4:18
brought a flood upon the world of the **u**; .. 2 Pt 2:5

UNITED

For if we have been **u** with him in a .... Rom 6:5
but that you be **u** in the same mind .... 1 Cor 1:10

UNITY

pleasant it is when brothers dwell in **u**! .. Ps 133:1
eager to maintain the **u** of the Spirit .... Eph 4:3
have **u** of mind, sympathy, brotherly .... 1 Pt 3:8

UNIVERSE

and he upholds the **u** by the word .... Heb 1:3
understand that the **u** was created ...... Heb 11:3

UNJUST

resurrection of both the just and the **u**. .. Acts 24:15
For God is not **u** so as to overlook ...... Heb 6:10

UNKNOWN

with this inscription: 'To the **u** god.'.... Acts 17:23

UNLEAVENED

shall observe the Feast of **U** Bread, ... Ex 12:17

UNRIGHTEOUS

for sins, the righteous for the **u**, ... 1 Pt 3:18
and to keep the **u** under punishment .... 2 Pt 2:9

UNRIGHTEOUSNESS

who by their **u** suppress the truth. ...... Rom 1:18
But if our **u** serves to show the .... Rom 3:5
the truth but had pleasure in **u**. .... 2 Thes 2:12
us our sins and to cleanse us from all **u**. .. 1 Jn 1:9

UNSEARCHABLE

How **u** are his judgments and how .... Rom 11:33
to the Gentiles the **u** riches of Christ, ... Eph 3:8

UNSEEN

but the things that are **u** are eternal. ... 2 Cor 4:18

UNSTABLE

double-minded man, **u** in all his ways. ...... Jas 1:8
which the ignorant and **u** twist to their .. 2 Pt 3:16

UNSTAINED

and to keep oneself **u** from the world. ..... Jas 1:27

UNVEILED

And we all, with **u** face, beholding .... 2 Cor 3:18

UPHOLD

and **u** me with a willing spirit. .... Ps 51:12
On the contrary, we **u** the law. .... Rom 3:31

UPHOLDS

but the LORD **u** the righteous. .... Ps 37:17
clings to you; your right hand **u** me. ..... Ps 63:8
The LORD **u** all who are falling .... Ps 145:14

UPRIGHT

Job, and that man was blameless and **u**, ... Jb 1:1
the **u** shall behold his face. .... Ps 11:7
self-controlled, **u**, holy, and .... Ti 1:8

URGE

u you to walk in a manner worthy ...... Eph 4:1
Teach and **u** these things. .... 1 Tm 6:2
I **u** you as sojourners and exiles .... 1 Pt 2:11

USEFUL

as holy, **u** to the master of the house, .. 2 Tm 2:21

UTTER

heart be hasty to **u** a word before God, ... Eccl 5:2
I will **u** what has been hidden since the .. Mt 13:35

UTTERANCE

other tongues as the Spirit gave them **u**... Acts 2:4
through the Spirit the **u** of wisdom, ... 1 Cor 12:8

UTTERMOST

to save to the **u** those who draw near ... Heb 7:25

Antes de que llegaras

Lisa Wingate

Antes de que llegaras

Traducción de
Laura Vidal

Título original: *Before We Were Yours*

Primera edición: abril de 2018

© 2017, Wingate Media, LLC
Todos los derechos reservados
© 2018, de la presente edición en castellano para todo el mundo:
Penguin Random House Grupo Editorial, S. A. U.
Travessera de Gràcia, 47-49. 08021 Barcelona
© 2018, de la presente edición en castellano:
Penguin Random House Grupo Editorial USA, LLC.,
8950 SW 74th Court, Suite 2010
Miami, FL 33156

© 2018, Laura Vidal, por la traducción

Portada: Adaptación del diseño original de Lynn Andreozzi:
Penguin Random House Grupo Editorial
Imagen de cubierta: Alan Ayers, basado en imágenes
de © Krasimira Petrova Shishkova / Trevillion Images
© Cristina Iranzo / Getty Images

Printed in USA – Impreso en Estados Unidos

ISBN: 978-1-947783-52-2

Penguin
Random House
Grupo Editorial

A los cientos que desaparecieron y a los miles que no.
Que vuestras historias no se olviden nunca

A aquellos que ayudan hoy a los
huérfanos a encontrar un hogar definitivo.
No olvidéis nunca el valor de vuestro
trabajo y de vuestro amor

«¿Sabían ustedes que en esta tierra de la libertad y hogar de los valientes hay un gran mercado de niños? Y las mercancías que cambian de manos... no son meros trozos de papel impreso que prometen unos dividendos económicos determinados, sino bebés de carne y hueso, que se mueven y respiran».

Del artículo «El mercado de niños»,
The Saturday Evening Post, 1 de febrero de 1930

«Son, dijo [Georgia Tann] varias veces, pizarras en blanco. Nacen sin contaminar y, si los adoptan de pequeños y los rodean de belleza y cultura, llegarán a ser lo que queramos que sean».

Barbara Bisantz Raymond,
The Baby Thief (La ladrona de niños)

Preludio

BALTIMORE, MARYLAND

3 de agosto de 1939

Mi historia empieza una sofocante noche del mes de agosto, en un lugar que nunca veré. La habitación cobra vida solo en mi imaginación. Casi siempre que la evoco es grande. Las paredes son blancas y limpias, las sábanas tienen el apresto de una hoja seca. La *suite* privada tiene de todo y de la mejor calidad. Fuera, la brisa es perezosa y las chicharras palpitan en las copas de los árboles, sus escondites frondosos justo debajo de las ventanas. Las mosquiteras se comban hacia dentro mientras el ventilador traquetea en el techo, haciendo circular un aire húmedo que no tiene deseo alguno de moverse.

Entra el aroma de los pinos y los gritos de la mujer aumentan mientras las enfermeras la sujetan con fuerza a la cama. El sudor se le acumula en la piel y le baja por la cara, los brazos y las piernas. Si fuera consciente de ello, estaría horrorizada.

Es bonita. Un alma buena, frágil. No de las que desencadenarían de manera intencionada la serie de desgracias que van a sucederse a partir de este momento. En mis muchos días de vida he aprendido que la mayoría de las personas hacen lo que pueden. Su intención no es hacer daño a los demás. Cuando esto ocurre, no es más que una consecuencia del impulso de sobrevivir.

No es culpa suya todo lo que pasará después de un último y violento empujón. Ha dado a luz lo último que querría. Asoma un cuerpo mudo: una niña diminuta y rubia, bonita como una muñeca, pero azul e inmóvil.

La mujer no tiene manera de conocer el destino de su hija y, si lo hace, para mañana la medicación habrá convertido ese recuerdo en algo borroso. Deja de luchar y se rinde a un sueño narcótico, arrullada por las dosis de morfina y escopolamina que le administran para combatir el dolor.

Para ayudarla a olvidar. Y eso hará.

Mientras los médicos suturan y las enfermeras limpian los restos, intercambian comentarios compasivos.

—Es una pena cuando pasan estas cosas. Qué injusto cuando una criatura no llega viva a este mundo...

—Es difícil de entender a veces... por qué... cuando es un niño tan deseado...

Una mortaja cubre los ojos diminutos. Ojos que nunca verán.

La mujer oye, pero no entiende. Las palabras vienen y van. Es como si intentara atrapar la marea, que se le escapa entre los dedos agarrotados hasta que por fin se deja arrastrar por ella.

Un hombre espera muy cerca, quizá en el pasillo a la salida de la habitación. Su actitud es solemne, digna. No está acostumbrado a sentirse tan impotente. Hoy iba a convertirse en abuelo.

La maravillosa ilusión se ha transformado en angustia desgarradora.

—Señor, lo siento muchísimo —dice el médico al salir de la habitación—. No dude que hicimos todo lo humanamente posible por su hija y por salvar al bebé. Entiendo lo difícil que es esto. Por favor, transmita nuestro pésame al padre cuando consigan ponerse en contacto con él. Después de tantas decepciones, su familia debía de estar muy ilusionada.

—¿Podrá tener más hijos?

—No es aconsejable.

—Esto la matará. Y a su madre también, cuando lo sepa. Christine es nuestra única hija, ¿sabe usted? El correteo de unos piececitos... El principio de una nueva generación...

—Lo entiendo, señor.

—¿Qué riesgo habría si...?

—Podría morir. Y es muy poco probable que su hija lleve otro embarazo a término. Si lo intentara, los resultados podrían ser...

—Entiendo.

El médico apoya una mano en el hombre con el corazón roto para consolarlo, o al menos eso es lo que imagino. Sus miradas se encuentran.

El médico se vuelve para asegurarse de que las enfermeras no pueden oírle.

—Señor, ¿me permite una sugerencia? —dice con voz queda y seria—. Conozco a una mujer en Memphis...

1

AVERY STAFFORD

Aiken, Carolina del Sur, época actual

Respiro hondo, me acerco al borde del asiento y me estiro la chaqueta mientras la limusina se detiene en el asfalto recalentado. A lo largo de la calle hay aparcadas furgonetas de televisión, lo que subraya la importancia de la en apariencia rutinaria reunión de esta mañana.

Pero hoy no habrá ningún momento dejado al azar. Estos últimos dos meses en Carolina del Sur han estado dedicados a garantizar que los matices son los indicados, a moldear los mensajes de manera que sugieran, pero nada más.

No habrá declaraciones definitivas.

Al menos no de momento.

Y, si de mí depende, no en mucho tiempo.

Me encantaría poder olvidarme de por qué he vuelto a casa, pero el simple hecho de que mi padre no esté leyendo sus notas ni revisando el informe de Leslie, su ultraeficiente jefa de prensa, me sirve de recordatorio ineludible. No hay forma de escapar del enemigo que viaja en silencio en el coche con nosotros. Está ahí, en el asiento trasero, agazapado detrás del traje sastre gris de mi padre que le queda ligeramente holgado a la altura de sus anchos hombros.

Papá mira por la ventana con la cabeza ladeada. Ha mandado a sus asistentes y a Leslie al otro coche.

—¿Te encuentras bien?

Sacudo un cabello rubio largo, mío, del asiento para que no se le pegue a los pantalones cuando salga. Si mi madre estuviera aquí, sacaría un cepillito quitapelusas, pero se ha quedado en casa preparándose para el segundo compromiso del día, una fotografía familiar navideña que hay que hacer con meses de antelación..., no sea que el pronóstico de papá empeore.

Él se endereza más en el asiento, levanta la cabeza. La electricidad estática le ha erizado un poco el pelo y quiero alisárselo, pero no lo hago. Sería saltarse el protocolo.

Si mi madre se implica íntimamente en microaspectos de nuestras vidas tales como quitar pelusas u organizar la fotografía navideña familiar en julio, mi padre es lo contrario. Es distante, una isla de masculinidad acérrima en una casa de mujeres. Sé que nos quiere mucho a mi madre, a mis dos hermanas y a mí, pero rara vez expresa ese sentimiento de viva voz. También sé que soy su favorita, pero también la que más lo desconcierta. Mi padre proviene de una época en que las mujeres iban a la universidad para encontrar marido. No sabe muy bien qué hacer con una hija de treinta años que fue la primera de su promoción en la Facultad de Derecho de Columbia y que ahora disfruta trabajando en el rudo ambiente de la oficina de un fiscal general.

Sea cual sea la razón —quizá porque los puestos de hija perfeccionista e hija cariñosa ya estaban cogidos—, siempre he sido la hija lista. Me encantaba estudiar y había un acuerdo tácito de que sería la abanderada de la familia, la sustituta del hijo, la que sucedería a mi padre. No sé por qué, pero siempre supuse que cuando eso ocurriera sería mayor y estaría preparada.

Ahora miro a mi padre y pienso: *¿Cómo puedes no quererlo, Avery? Es para lo que ha trabajado tu padre toda su vida. Para lo que han trabajado generaciones de Staffords desde la guerra de Independencia, por amor del cielo.* Nuestra familia siempre se ha asido con fuerza al timón de la administración pública. Papá no es una excepción. Desde que se graduó en West Point y sirvió en la aviación, antes de que yo naciera, ha llevado el apellido familiar con dignidad y determinación.

Pues claro que lo quieres, me digo. *Siempre lo has querido. No esperaba que fuera tan pronto, ni de esta manera. Eso es todo.*

Pero, en secreto, me aferro con uñas y dientes al mejor pronóstico: que los enemigos serán derrotados en ambos frentes, el político y el médico. Mi padre se curará gracias a la combinación de la cirugía que lo obligó a volver a casa antes de que terminara la sesión estival del Congreso y la bomba de quimioterapia que debe llevar sujeta a una pierna cada tres semanas. Mi vuelta a Aiken será solo temporal.

El cáncer ya no será parte de nuestras vidas.

Puede vencerse. Otras personas lo han derrotado y, si otros pueden, el senador Wells Stafford también.

No hay en ninguna parte un hombre más fuerte ni mejor que mi padre.

—¿Preparada? —me pregunta mientras se estira el traje. Me siento aliviada cuando se alisa la cresta del pelo. No estoy preparada para cruzar la línea que separa a la hija de la cuidadora.

—Cuando tú quieras.

Haría cualquier cosa por él, pero confío en que falten muchos años aún hasta que tengamos que invertir los papeles de padre e hija. He aprendido lo difícil que es viendo a mi padre obligado a tomar decisiones sobre su madre.

Mi en otro tiempo ingeniosa y divertida abuela Judy es ahora una sombra de lo que fue. Por doloroso que esto resulte, papá no puede hablar con nadie de ello. Si los medios de comunicación se enteran de que la hemos llevado a una residencia, sobre todo a una de lujo, en una finca preciosa a unos escasos quince kilómetros de aquí, sería un desastre desde el punto de vista político. Después del gran rechazo público que despertaron una serie de homicidios por negligencia y malos tratos en varios centros de mayores propiedad de corporaciones en nuestro estado, los enemigos políticos de papá se apresurarían a señalar que solo las personas con dinero pueden permitirse cuidados de calidad. Eso o lo acusarían de internar a su madre porque es un miserable sin corazón al que no le importan las personas mayores. Dirían que está dispuesto a hacer la vista gorda con las necesidades de los desvalidos si con ello beneficia a sus amigos y a los contribuyentes a su campaña.

La realidad es que las decisiones que tomó mi padre respecto a la abuela Judy no tenían nada de políticas. Somos como cualquier otra familia. Cada camino posible está pavimentado de culpa, lleno de dolor y marcado por la vergüenza. Nos avergonzamos de la abuela Judy. Tememos por ella. Nos duele el corazón cuando pensamos adónde puede llevarla este cruel descenso hacia la demencia. Antes de que la trasladáramos a la residencia, mi abuela se escapó de su cuidadora y del personal de servicio de su casa. Llamó a un taxi y estuvo un día entero desaparecida hasta que la encontraron deambulando por un complejo de negocios que había sido en otro tiempo su centro comercial favorito. Cómo consiguió hacer eso cuando ni siquiera recordaba nuestros nombres es un misterio.

Esta mañana llevo puesta una de sus joyas preferidas. Soy vagamente consciente de ella en la muñeca antes de bajar de la limusina. Simulo haber elegido la pulsera de las libélulas en su honor, pero lo cierto es que está ahí a modo de recordatorio silencioso de que las mujeres Stafford cumplen con su deber, incluso cuando no quieren. El lugar donde se celebra hoy el acto me hace sentir incómoda. Nunca me han gustado los hogares de ancianos.

No es más que llegar y saludar, me digo. *La prensa ha venido a cubrir el acto, no a hacer preguntas.* Estrecharemos manos, visitaremos el edificio, nos uniremos a los residentes en la celebración del cumpleaños de una mujer que cumple los cien. Su marido tiene noventa y nueve. Toda una hazaña.

En el pasillo huele como si alguien hubiera dejado sueltos a los trillizos de mi hermana con botes de espray desinfectante. Un aroma a jazmín artificial llena el aire. Leslie lo olisquea y a continuación asiente con la cabeza en un gesto de aprobación mientras se coloca, acompañada de un fotógrafo y varios becarios y asistentes, a nuestro lado. En esta ocasión no llevamos guardaespaldas. Sin duda han ido a prepararlo todo para el acto de esta tarde en el Ayuntamiento. A lo largo de los años mi padre ha recibido amenazas de muerte de grupos radicales y anticomunistas, así como de toda clase de trastornados que afirman ser francotiradores, bioterroristas y secuestradores. Rara vez se toma las amenazas en serio, pero su personal de seguridad sí lo hace.

Cuando doblamos la esquina, nos reciben la directora de la residencia y dos reporteros con cámaras. Hacemos la visita. Nos graban. Mi padre despliega su encanto. Estrecha manos, posa para fotografías, dedica tiempo a charlar con los presentes, se inclina delante de sillas de ruedas y da las gracias a las enfermeras por el trabajo tan duro y difícil al que se entregan cada día.

Yo le sigo y hago lo mismo. Un caballero mayor y elegante con bombín de *tweed* coquetea conmigo. Con un encantador acento británico, me dice que tengo unos ojos azules preciosos.

—Hace cincuenta años habría conseguido que aceptara salir conmigo.

—Y ahora también —le digo y reímos a la vez.

Una de las enfermeras me advierte de que el señor McMorris es un donjuán de pelo cano. Él le guiña un ojo a modo de confirmación.

Mientras vamos por el pasillo camino de la fiesta de la mujer centenaria, me doy cuenta de que en realidad lo estoy pasando bien. Las personas aquí parecen contentas. No es tan lujosa como la residencia de la abuela Judy, pero está muy lejos de los centros mal gestionados que citaron los abogados en la última oleada de demandas judiciales. Lo más probable es que ninguno de esos abogados llegue a ver un centavo, con independencia de los daños y perjuicios que sean reconocidos por los tribunales. Los que controlan el dinero detrás de las cadenas de centros de mayores utilizan holdings empresariales y sociedades instrumentales que pueden llevar a la quiebra en cualquier momento para así evitar pagar indemnizaciones. Por eso, que se hayan descubierto vínculos entre una de esas cadenas y un viejo amigo y uno de los principales donantes de las campañas de mi padre ha sido tan potencialmente devastador. Mi padre es muy conocido y, por tanto, un blanco fácil en el que concentrar las iras del público y las acusaciones políticas.

La ira y la culpa son armas poderosas. La oposición lo sabe.

En la sala común han instalado un estrado pequeño. Me siento en una esquina, con el séquito, cerca de las puertas acristaladas que dan a un jardín umbroso donde un caleidoscopio de flores sobrevive al brutal calor del verano.

En uno de los senderos en sombra del jardín hay una mujer sola. Está de espaldas y parece ajena a la fiesta, con la mirada fija en algún punto lejano. Sus manos descansan en un bastón. Lleva un vestido sencillo de algodón color crema y un jersey blanco, a pesar de lo caluroso del día. La espesa melena gris está trenzada y enroscada alrededor de la cabeza y eso, unido al vestido claro, le da una apariencia casi fantasmal, de vestigio de un pasado remoto. Una brisa agita la glicinia, pero no parece tocarla, lo que aumenta la sensación de que no está realmente allí.

Vuelvo a concentrarme en lo que dice la directora de la residencia. Da la bienvenida a todos, explica el motivo de la reunión: al fin y al cabo no todos los días se cumple un siglo de vida. Haber estado casada casi todo ese tiempo y conservar a la persona que quieres a tu lado es aún más notable. Es, de hecho, un acontecimiento digno de la visita de un senador.

Por no mencionar que esta pareja se cuenta entre los seguidores de mi padre desde que trabajaba en el gobierno estatal de Carolina del Sur. Técnicamente lo conocen desde hace más tiempo que yo y lo quieren casi tanto como yo. La homenajeada y su marido levantan sus finas manos unidas y aplauden con furia cuando se menciona el nombre de mi padre.

La directora cuenta la historia de estos dos adorables enamorados sentados en la mesa de honor. Luci nació en Francia cuando por las calles aún circulaban coches de caballos. Cuesta incluso imaginarlo. Trabajó en la Resistencia francesa durante la Segunda Guerra Mundial. Su marido, Frank, piloto de guerra, fue derribado en combate. Su historia parece salida de una película, un romance cautivador. Luci formaba parte de una cadena de evacuación y ayudó a Frank a disfrazarse y a salir herido del país. Terminada la guerra, volvió a buscarla. Seguía viviendo en la misma granja con su familia, todos apiñados en el sótano, la única parte de la casa que seguía en pie.

Las adversidades que ha superado esta pareja me maravillan. Estas cosas son posibles cuando el amor es verdadero y fuerte, cuando las personas están entregadas la una a la otra, cuando lo sacrifican todo por estar juntas. Es lo que quiero para mí, pero a veces me pregunto si es algo posible para mi generación. Estamos tan ensimismados, tan... ocupados.

Miro mi anillo de compromiso y pienso: *Elliot y yo sí podemos. Nos conocemos muy bien. Siempre nos hemos apoyado...*

La cumpleañera se levanta despacio y se coge del brazo de su marido. Avanzan juntos, encorvados y torcidos y apoyados el uno en el otro. Verlos es bonito y enternecedor, espero que mis padres vivan hasta esa etapa de la vida. Espero que puedan disfrutar de una larga jubilación... algún día... Dentro de muchos años, cuando mi padre por fin se decida a bajar el ritmo. La enfermedad no puede llevárselo con solo cincuenta y siete años. Es demasiado joven. Se le necesita demasiado, tanto en casa como en el mundo. Todavía le queda trabajo por hacer y, después de eso, mis padres se merecen una jubilación y una vida tranquila, con tiempo para estar juntos.

Un sentimiento de ternura se instala en mi pecho y ahuyento estos pensamientos. *Nada de muestras excesivas de emoción en público,* es lo que me recuerda siempre Leslie. *En el mundo de la política las mujeres no pueden permitírselo. Se ve como signo de incompetencia, de debilidad.*

Como si no lo supiera. Un tribunal no es muy diferente. Las mujeres que ejercen la abogacía estamos sometidas a un juicio constante. Nos regimos por reglas distintas.

Mi padre saluda a Frank cuando se reúne con él cerca del estrado. Este se detiene, se yergue y le devuelve el saludo con precisión militar. Sus miradas se encuentran y el momento es genuino. Puede que quede perfecto en la pantalla, pero no está pensado para las cámaras. Mi padre aprieta los labios. Intenta no desmoronarse.

Es raro en él que se le note tanto algo.

Supero otro momento de emoción. Reprimo un suspiro. Bajo los hombros, miro para otro lado, hacia la ventana, y me pongo a estudiar a la mujer en el jardín. Sigue allí, con la mirada perdida. ¿Quién es? ¿Qué busca?

El ruidoso coro que canta el *Cumpleaños feliz* traspasa el cristal y la hace volverse despacio hacia el edificio. Soy consciente de que la canción sube de volumen y sé que es probable que las cámaras me enfoquen y que pareceré distraída, pero soy incapaz de apartar los ojos del camino del jardín, quiero verle la cara a la mujer, por lo menos. ¿Será tan inescrutable como el cielo de verano? ¿Estará simplemente deambulando, confusa? ¿O habrá huido a propósito de la celebración?

Leslie me tira de la chaqueta desde detrás y me enderezo igual que una colegiala a la que han regañado por hablar en la fila.

—Cumpleaños fe... Céntrate —me canta al oído y asiento mientras ella se aleja para tener mejor ángulo en las fotos que está sacando con el móvil y que después colgará en la cuenta de Instagram de mi padre. El senador está en todas las redes sociales, aunque no sabe usar ninguna. Su *community manager* es un lince.

La ceremonia prosigue. Hay flashes de cámaras. Familiares felices se enjugan lágrimas y graban vídeos cuando mi padre hace entrega de una carta de felicitación enmarcada.

Llega la tarta en una mesa con ruedas, cien velas encendidas.

Leslie está encantada. La habitación está tan llena de felicidad y emoción que se hincha igual que un globo de helio. Un gramo más de alegría y saldremos flotando.

Alguien me toca la mano y la muñeca, unos dedos me sujetan tan inesperadamente que me sobresalto y al instante me controlo para no llamar la atención. El tacto es frío, huesudo y tembloroso, pero sorprendentemente fuerte. Me vuelvo y veo a la mujer del jardín. Endereza la espalda encorvada y me mira con unos ojos del color de las hortensias del jardín de casa, en Drayden Hill. Un azul suave y claro con un asomo de bruma en los bordes. Los labios rodeados de arrugas le tiemblan.

Antes de que me dé tiempo a recobrarme del susto, viene una enfermera a llevársela, cogiéndola con firmeza.

—May —dice, y me mira como pidiendo disculpas—. Venga conmigo. No debe molestar a los invitados.

En lugar de soltarme la muñeca, la mujer se aferra más fuerte. Parece desesperada, como si necesitara algo, pero no tengo idea de qué puede ser.

Me mira a la cara. Alarga el cuello.

—¿Fern? —susurra.

$\mathscr{2}$

MAY CRANDALL

Aiken, Carolina del Sur, época actual

A veces es como si los goznes de mis recuerdos se hubieran oxidado y gastado. Las puertas se abren y cierran cuando quieren. Un atisbo aquí. Un espacio vacío allí. Un lugar oscuro al que me da miedo asomarme.

Nunca sé lo que me voy a encontrar.

No hay forma de predecir cuándo se abrirá, o por qué, una barrera.

Detonantes. Es como los llaman los psicólogos en los programas de televisión. Detonantes... Como si la pólvora prendiera e impulsara un proyectil por el cañón de una escopeta. Es una metáfora apropiada.

Verle la cara ha detonado alguna cosa.

Se abre una puerta al pasado. Cruzo el umbral inconscientemente primero, preguntándome qué puede haber encerrado dentro de la habitación. En cuanto la llamo Fern, sé que no estoy pensando en Fern. He retrocedido más en el tiempo. A quien veo es a Queenie.

Queenie, nuestra madre, una mujer fuerte cuyos preciosos rizos dorados todos heredamos. Todos menos la pobre Camellia.

Mis pensamientos viajan ligeros como plumas sobre copas de árboles y lechos de valles. Llego hasta una orilla en pendiente del Misisipi, a la última vez que vi a Queenie. El aire cálido y suave de aquella noche de verano en Memphis sopla en remolinos sobre mi cabeza, pero la noche es una impostora.

No es clemente. No perdona.

Después de esta noche no habrá vuelta atrás.

Doce años, aún delgada y fibrosa como la columna de un porche. Balanceo las piernas debajo de la barandilla de nuestra casa flotante a la espera de ver los ojos de un caimán en el parpadeo ámbar del farol. No debería haber caimanes a esta altura del Misisipi, pero se rumorea que alguien ha visto uno hace poco. Eso convierte buscarlos en una suerte de juego. Los niños que viven en el río se divierten como pueden.

Y ahora mismo necesitamos más que nunca una distracción.

A mi lado, Fern se sube a la barandilla y busca luciérnagas entre los árboles. Con casi cuatro años, está aprendiendo a contarlas. Señala con un dedo gordezuelo y se asoma, sin pensar en los caimanes.

—¡He visto una, Rill! ¡La he visto!

Le agarro el vestido y tiro de ella.

—Si te caes a esta hora no pienso tirarme a sacarte.

Lo cierto es que no le vendría mal caerse al agua. Le serviría de lección. El barco está amarrado en un agradable remanso cruzando el río desde la isla de Mud. A la altura de la popa del *Arcadia,* el agua solo me llega a la cadera. Fern podría tocar el fondo de puntillas, pero, en cualquier caso, los cinco nadamos como renacuajos, incluso el pequeño Gabion, que aún no sabe decir una frase entera. Cuando naces en el río, este se vuelve algo tan natural como respirar. Conoces sus sonidos, sus formas y sus criaturas. Para habitantes del río como nosotros, el agua es un hogar. Un lugar seguro.

Pero ahora mismo hay algo en el aire..., algo que no va bien. Un escalofrío me sube por los brazos y me aguijonea las mejillas. Una parte de mí siempre ha presentido cosas. Nunca se lo he contado a nadie, pero así es. Es una sofocante noche de verano y tengo frío. El cielo está cubierto. Las nubes, maduras como melones a punto de reventar. Se acerca una tormenta, pero eso por sí solo no explica cómo me siento.

Dentro de la casa, los suaves gemidos de Queenie se aceleran, ajenos a la voz espesa como la melaza de la partera.

—A ver, señora Foss, tiene usted que dejar de empujar, y ahora mismo. Si este niño sale mal colocado, no estará mucho tiempo en este mundo, y usted tampoco. Tiene que tranquilizarse. Cálmese.

Queenie emite un sonido grave y abrupto como el de una bota despegándose del espeso cieno del pantano. Nos ha dado a luz a los cinco con apenas un jadeo, pero esta vez está tardando mucho más. Me seco el sudor frío de los brazos y tengo la impresión de que hay algo entre los árboles. Una presencia maligna. Nos está mirando. ¿Qué hace aquí? ¿Ha venido a llevarse a Queenie?

Quiero bajar la pasarela, correr por la orilla y gritar: «¡Largo de aquí! ¡Vete! ¡No te vas a llevar a mi madre!».

Lo haría. No me asusta que pueda haber caimanes. Pero en lugar de ello me quedo quieta igual que un chorlito en su nido. Escucho lo que dice la partera. Habla tan alto que la oigo como si estuviera dentro.

—Por Dios santo, que el cielo se apiade de nosotros. Tiene más de un niño dentro. ¡Desde luego que sí!

Mi padre murmura algo que no consigo oír. Sus botas cruzan la habitación, vacilan, cruzan otra vez.

—Señor Foss —continúa la partera—, no puedo hacer nada. Si no lleva enseguida a esta mujer a un médico, estos niños no llegarán a ver el mundo y su mamá morirá también.

Briny tarda en contestar. Golpea con fuerza los puños contra la pared y hace temblar los marcos de las fotografías de Queenie. Algo se desprende, se oye un sonido de metal chocando contra madera y sé qué es por dónde cae y cómo suena. Veo la cruz de hojalata con el hombre de aspecto triste y quiero entrar corriendo y cogerla y arrodillarme junto a la cama y susurrar palabras polacas misteriosas, como hace Queenie cuando Briny no está en la casa y el agua de lluvia cae a chorros por el tejado y las olas golpean el casco del barco.

Pero no conozco ese lenguaje extraño y seco que Queenie aprendió de la familia que dejó atrás cuando huyó para irse a vivir en el río con Briny. Si juntara en una frase las pocas palabras polacas que sé, no formarían más que una tontería sin sentido. Aun así, si pudiera coger la cruz de Queenie ahora mismo, se las diría al hombre de hojalata al que ella besa cada vez que hay tormenta.

Haría casi cualquier cosa por que terminara el parto y por ver a Queenie sonreír de nuevo.

Al otro lado de la puerta, la bota de Briny araña los tablones y oigo la cruz rodar por el suelo. Briny mira por la ventana empañada sacada de la casa que derribó para construir el barco antes de que yo naciera. Con la madre de Briny en el lecho de muerte y una nueva sequía, el banco se iba a quedar la granja de todos modos. Briny decidió que lo mejor era irse a vivir al río. Y acertó. Para cuando llegó la Depresión, a Queenie y a él les iba bien. *Ni siquiera la Depresión puede matar de hambre al río*, dice cada vez que cuenta la historia. *El río tiene su propia magia. Cuida de su gente. Siempre lo hará.*

Pero esta noche la magia ha salido mal.

—¡Señor! ¿Me oye? —La partera se deja de cortesías—. No pienso cargar con sus muertes. Lleve a su mujer al hospital. Ya.

Al otro lado del cristal, Briny arruga el semblante. Cierra los ojos con fuerza. Con un puño se golpea la frente y a continuación la pared.

—Con esta tormenta...

—Por mí como si está el demonio ahí fuera, señor Foss. No puedo hacer nada por esta mujer. Nada. Y no pienso cargar con su muerte en mi conciencia.

—Nunca ha tenido problemas... Con ninguno de los otros. Les...

Queenie suelta un chillido fuerte y agudo y el sonido se pierde en la noche como el aullido de un gato salvaje.

—A no ser que se le olvidara contármelo, nunca ha tenido dos bebés a la vez.

Me levanto, cojo a Fern y la dejo en el porche con Gabion, que tiene dos años, y Lark, que tiene seis. Camellia sigue mis movimientos desde donde está mirando, junto a la ventana delantera. Cierro la cancela que hay en el arranque de la pasarela para encerrarlos a todos en el porche y le digo a Camellia que no deje a los pequeños subirse. Camellia me contesta frunciendo el ceño. A sus diez años, ha heredado la obstinación de mi padre y también su pelo y sus ojos oscuros. No le gusta que le digan lo que tiene que hacer. Es terca como un tocón de ciprés y a veces el doble de dura. Si los pequeños se ponen a armar jaleo, tendremos un problema todavía más gordo.

—Todo va a salir bien —prometo y les acaricio las cabezas suaves y doradas como si fueran cachorros—. Queenie está pasando un mal rato, nada más. No conviene que nadie la moleste ahora. Quedaos aquí. El rugarú anda suelto esta noche, le he oído respirar hace un minuto. No es seguro salir.

Ahora que tengo doce años, no creo ni en el hombre lobo ni en el hombre del saco ni tampoco en Jack, el capitán loco de los piratas del río. Por lo menos no mucho. Dudo de que Camellia se tragara alguna vez las historias llenas de imaginación de Briny.

Agarra el picaporte.

—No —le digo en un susurro—. Voy yo.

Nos han ordenado que nos quedemos fuera, algo que Briny no dice nunca sin motivo. Pero ahora Briny habla como si no tuviera ni idea de qué hacer y me preocupan Queenie y mi nuevo hermanito o hermanita. Todos hemos estado esperando a ver qué era. Aunque se suponía que no tenía que llegar tan pronto. Es pronto, más pronto incluso que cuando nació Gabion, que era tan poquita cosa que salió antes de que a Briny le diera tiempo a llevar el barco a la orilla y encontrar a una mujer que ayudara en el parto.

Este nuevo bebé no parece demasiado dispuesto a poner las cosas tan fáciles. Quizá cuando nazca se parezca a Camellia y sea igual de terco.

Bebés, me corrijo. Caigo en la cuenta de que viene más de uno, como pasa con los cachorros, y que no es normal. Detrás de la cortina que cosió Queenie con cuatro sacos de harina Golden Heart hay tres vidas. Tres cuerpos que intentan separarse los unos de los otros, pero que no pueden.

Abro la puerta y, antes de que me dé tiempo a decidir si entro o no, tengo a la partera encima. Me agarra el brazo con una mano. Es como si sus dedos dieran dos veces la vuelta alrededor de mi brazo. Bajo la vista y veo el círculo de piel oscura contra mi piel pálida. Si quisiera, podría partirme en dos. ¿Por qué no puede salvar a mi hermanito o hermanita? ¿Por qué no puede sacarlo del cuerpo de mi madre y traerlo a este mundo?

La mano de Queenie se aferra a la cortina y chilla y tira, arqueándose en la cama. Se desprenden media docena de arandelas. Veo la cara de mi madre; su pelo largo rubio y sedoso como el maíz pegado a la cara; sus ojos azules, esos preciosos ojos celestes que nos distinguen a todos menos a Camellia, desorbitados. La piel de las mejillas está tan tirante que la recorren arañas de venillas como alas de libélula.

—¿Papá?

Mi susurro llega una vez ha terminado el grito de Queenie, pero aun así parece alterar el aire de la habitación. Jamás llamo a Briny «papá» ni a Queenie «mamá», a no ser que algo vaya muy mal. Eran tan jóvenes cuando me tuvieron que creo que ni se les ocurrió enseñarme las palabras «mamá» y «papá». Siempre hemos sido como amigos de la misma edad. Pero de vez en cuando necesito que sean mis padres. La última vez fue hace semanas, cuando vimos a un hombre colgado de un árbol, muerto, con el cuerpo hinchado.

¿Tendrá Queenie ese aspecto cuando muera? ¿Morirá ella primero y después los bebés? ¿O será al revés?

Tengo el estómago tan encogido que ni siquiera siento ya la manaza de la partera en el brazo. Quizá incluso me alegro de que esté ahí, sosteniéndome, impidiendo que me mueva. Me da miedo acercarme más a Queenie.

—¡Díselo! —La partera me sacude como si fuera una muñeca de trapo y me hace daño. Le brillan los dientes a la luz de la lámpara.

No muy lejos retumba el trueno y una ráfaga de viento golpea la popa y la partera da un traspiés hacia delante llevándome con ella. Los ojos de Queenie encuentran los míos. Me mira como mira un niño pequeño, como si pensara que puedo ayudarla y suplicándome que lo haga.

Trago con dificultad e intento sacar mi voz.

—¿P-papá? —tartamudeo otra vez, pero Briny sigue con la vista perdida. Está paralizado como un conejo cuando presiente peligro cerca.

Por la ventana veo a Camellia con la cara pegada al cristal. Los pequeños se han subido al banco para mirar. A Lark le ruedan gruesas lágrimas por las mejillas regordetas. No soporta ver sufrir a ninguna criatura. Si puede, tira al río los peces que usamos de cebo. Cada vez que Briny caza comadrejas, patos, ardillas o ciervos se comporta como si acabaran de matar a su mejor amigo delante de sus ojos.

Me mira para que salve a Queenie. Todos lo hacen.

De algún lugar lejano llega el fogonazo de un relámpago. Hace retroceder el resplandor amarillo de la lámpara de aceite, luego se apaga. Intento contar los segundos antes de oír el trueno, para saber a qué distancia está la tormenta, pero estoy demasiado nerviosa.

Si Briny no lleva pronto a Queenie al médico, será demasiado tarde. Como siempre, estamos fondeados en la orilla virgen. Memphis está al otro lado del ancho y oscuro río Misisipi.

Toso para expulsar el nudo de la garganta y enderezo el cuello para que no se me vuelva a formar.

—Briny, tienes que llevarla a la otra orilla.

Se vuelve hacia mí despacio. Su expresión sigue siendo perpleja, pero da la impresión de que estaba esperando algo así, que alguien que no fuera la partera le dijera lo que tiene que hacer.

—Briny, tienes que llevarla en el esquife ahora, antes de que llegue la tormenta.

Sé que mover el barco llevaría demasiado tiempo. Briny también lo sabría, si fuera capaz de pensar con claridad.

—¡Díselo! —La partera me espolea. Se vuelve hacia Briny y me empuja hacia él—. Como no baje a esta mujer del barco, para mañana esta niña se habrá quedado sin madre.

3

AVERY STAFFORD

Aiken, Carolina del Sur, época actual

*A*very, baja! ¡Te necesitamos!

Nada te hace retroceder más deprisa de los treinta a los trece años que la voz de tu madre resonando en las escaleras como una pelota de tenis después de un buen saque.

—¡Bajo ahora mismo!

Elliot ríe al otro lado del teléfono. El sonido me resulta a la vez familiar y reconfortante. Me devuelve a un camino de recuerdos que llega hasta mi infancia. Con la madre de Elliot y la mía que no nos quitaban ojo, nunca teníamos ocasión de pasarnos de la raya y mucho menos de hacer esas travesuras que otros adolescentes sí hacían. Estábamos más o menos predestinados a ser buenos. Juntos.

—Parece que te reclaman, cariño.

—Es la foto familiar de Navidad. —Me inclino hacia el espejo y me retiro bucles rubios de la frente que, de inmediato, vuelven a caer. Mi rápida visita al establo a la vuelta de la residencia ha hecho aflorar los rizos que heredé de la abuela Judy.

Sabía que pasaría, pero una yegua de cría parió anoche y no puedo resistirme a un potrillo recién nacido. Ahora estoy pagando por ello. No hay alisador de pelo hecho por la mano del hombre que pueda competir con la brisa húmeda del río Edisto.

—¿Foto de Navidad en julio? —Elliot tose y me doy cuenta de cuánto le echo de menos. Esto de vivir separados es duro y solo llevamos así dos meses.

—A mi madre le preocupa la quimio. Le dijeron que papá no se quedaría sin pelo con el tipo de quimio que le están dando, pero le da miedo que pueda pasar.

En realidad no hay médico en todo el planeta capaz de tranquilizar a mi madre sobre el diagnóstico de cáncer de colon de mi padre. Mamá siempre ha estado a cargo del mundo y está decidida a no abdicar ahora. Si dice que papá va a perder pelo, es probable que así sea.

—Genio y figura. —Elliot vuelve a reír. Sabe de lo que habla. Su madre, Bitsy, y la mía están cortadas por el mismo patrón.

—Lo que pasa es que le da mucho miedo perder a papá.

Me cuesta terminar la frase. Estos últimos meses nos han dejado en carne viva, cada uno sangrando en silencio por dentro.

—Lógico. —Elliot calla y la pausa se me hace eterna. Oigo sonido de teclas de ordenador. Me recuerdo a mí misma que está dirigiendo una agencia nueva de corretaje y que el éxito de esta es lo más importante para él ahora mismo. Lo último que necesita es a su prometida llamándolo en plena jornada laboral y sin un motivo concreto—. Está bien que hayas ido, Aves.

—Espero estar ayudando. A veces me parece que estoy empeorando el estrés en lugar de reducirlo.

—Tienes que estar allí. Necesitas pasar un año en Carolina del Sur para restablecer allí tu residencia, por si acaso...

—Elliot me recuerda lo mismo cada vez que hablamos de esto,

cada vez que me entran ganas de coger un vuelo a Maryland y volver a mi antiguo despacho en la oficina del fiscal general, donde no tenía que preocuparme de tratamientos para el cáncer, fotos de Navidad hechas con meses de antelación, votantes y personas como aquella mujer de aspecto desesperado que me cogió del brazo en la residencia de mayores.

—Oye, Aves, espera. Perdona. Esta mañana está siendo una locura. —Elliot me pone en espera para atender una llamada y mis pensamientos retroceden a esta mañana.

Veo a la mujer, May, en el jardín con su jersey blanco. Luego está a mi lado, la cara le llega apenas a la altura de mi hombro, con sus manos delgadísimas aferradas a mi muñeca y el bastón colgado de su brazo. La expresión de sus ojos me resulta inolvidable incluso ahora. Transmite tanta certeza... Está convencida de que me conoce.

¿Fern?

¿Perdón?

Fernie, soy yo. Tiene lágrimas en los ojos. *Cariño, cómo te he echado de menos. Me dijeron que te habías ido. Sabía que no romperías tu promesa.*

Durante un segundo quise ser Fern, solo por hacerla feliz, para que pudiera dejar de estar sola en el jardín mirando la glicinia. Parecía tan desvalida. Tan perdida.

Me salvan de tener que decirle que no soy la persona que busca. Interviene la auxiliar, roja de vergüenza y claramente alterada. «Perdón», me susurra. «La señora Crandall es nueva». Le pasa un brazo con firmeza por los hombros a la señora Crandall y le suelta las manos de mi muñeca. La anciana es sorprendentemente fuerte. Se rinde centímetro a centímetro y la enfermera dice con voz queda: «Venga, May. La voy a llevar a su habitación».

La miro ir con la sensación de que debería hacer algo para ayudar, pero no sé qué.

Elliot vuelve a ponerse al teléfono y mis pensamientos regresan al presente.

—Y, en cualquier caso, al mal tiempo buena cara. Tú puedes. Te he visto ganar a los mejores abogados defensores del país. Aiken no puede suponerte un problema.

—Ya lo sé. —Suspiro—. Siento interrumpirte. Es que... necesitaba oír tu voz, supongo. —Me empiezo a ruborizar. Por lo general no soy tan dependiente emocionalmente. Quizá es consecuencia de la salud de papá y de los problemas con la abuela Judy, pero no me quito de encima una dolorosa sensación de mortalidad. Es espesa y persistente como la niebla del río. Lo único que puedo hacer es avanzar a tientas por ella sin ver lo que puede estar acechando.

He tenido una vida muy afortunada. Es posible que nunca haya sido consciente de ello hasta ahora.

—No seas tan dura contigo. —La voz de Elliot es tierna ahora—. Son muchas cosas a la vez. Date tiempo. Preocupándote demasiado no vas a solucionar nada.

—Tienes razón. Sé que la tienes.

—¿Podrías ponerlo por escrito?

La broma de Elliot me arranca una carcajada.

—Jamás.

Cojo el bolso de encima del secreter y busco algo con que recogerme el pelo. Cuando lo vuelco en la cama aparecen dos pasadores plateados. Servirán. Me recojo los mechones delanteros y me los sujeto formando ondas. A la abuela Judy le encantará esta foto. Después de todo, tengo su mismo pelo y ella siempre lo llevaba rizado.

—Esa es mi Aves.

Elliot saluda a alguien que acaba de entrar en su despacho y nos despedimos deprisa mientras me peino y me miro por última vez en el espejo, alisando el vestido verde de tubo que he elegido para la fotografía. Espero que la estilista de mi madre no se ponga a comprobar marcas. El vestido me lo compré en unos grandes almacenes. El pelo, en cambio, me ha quedado bien. Incluso a la estilista le gustará..., si está aquí..., y probablemente está. Leslie y ella coinciden en que necesito «trabajar un poquito el *look*», tal y como lo expresan ellas.

Llaman a la puerta suavecito.

—No pases, ¡tengo un pulpo gigante encerrado en el armario! —aviso.

Mi sobrina de diez años, Courtney, asoma su cabeza de rizos rubios por la puerta. También ella es un calco de la abuela Judy.

—La última vez dijiste que tenías un oso —se queja y pone los ojos en blanco para hacerme saber que mi chiste podía hacerle gracia cuando tenía nueve años, pero no ahora, que ha alcanzado oficialmente las dos cifras.

—Perdona, pero era un oso mutante que cambia de forma —digo haciendo alusión a un videojuego que la tiene demasiado obsesionada. Con la llegada inesperada de los trillizos, Courtney pasa mucho tiempo sola. No parece que su nueva libertad le moleste, pero a mí me preocupa.

Apoya una mano en la cadera y me mira con desparpajo.

—Si no bajas, te va a hacer falta ese oso, porque Honeybee te va a soltar los perros.

Honeybee, abejita, es el apodo cariñoso que usa mi padre con mi madre.

—Huy, ahora sí que me has asustado.

Los terrier escoceses de Drayden Hill están tan mimados que probablemente esperan que un intruso llegue con chucherías gourmet compradas en una pastelería para mascotas.

Le revuelvo el pelo a Courtney cuando paso a su lado.

—¡Allison! —grito hacia las escaleras y echo a correr—. ¡Tu hija está retrasando la fotografía familiar!

Courtney chilla y echamos una carrera hasta el piso de abajo. Gana ella porque es pequeña y menuda y yo llevo tacones. No necesito los centímetros de más, pero a mi madre no le gustaría que posara para el retrato familiar de Navidad con zapato plano.

En el salón para las visitas, el personal y el fotógrafo están embarcados en una misión. Empieza el frenesí fotográfico. Para cuando hemos terminado, los hijos adolescentes de mi hermana mayor están furiosos y yo necesito una siesta. En lugar de ello cojo a uno de los pequeños y me pongo a hacerle cosquillas en el sofá. Los otros no tardan en unirse a la refriega.

—¡Avery, por amor del cielo! —protesta mi madre—. Tienes la ropa hecha un higo y tienes que salir con tu padre en veinte minutos. —Leslie me mira con un solo ojo, una demostración de su habilidad de iguana para mirar en dos direcciones a la vez. Señala el vestido verde.

—Es demasiado elegante para el encuentro en el Ayuntamiento y lo que llevabas esta mañana es demasiado informal. Ponte el traje pantalón azul con el bajo de cordoncillo. Muy senatorial, pero también discreto. ¿Sabes cuál te digo?

—Sí.

Preferiría quedarme a luchar con los trillizos o hablar con los hijos de Missy sobre sus planes de hacerse monitores de campamento de verano, pero nadie me ofrece esas opciones.

Beso a mis sobrinos y corro escaleras arriba a cambiarme. Al poco estoy otra vez en la limusina con mi padre.

Este saca el móvil y repasa el dosier de la agenda de esta tarde. Entre Leslie, sus numerosos ayudantes y becarios, el personal de aquí y de Washington y los periódicos, siempre está bien informado. Necesita estarlo. Con el clima político actual hay riesgo real de que el equilibrio en la Cámara se vea alterado si el cáncer lo obliga a dejar el escaño. Papá se moriría antes de dejar que eso ocurra. Que estuviera tanto tiempo ignorando los síntomas y se quedara en Washington durante la sesión del Congreso es prueba de ello, como lo es el hecho de que yo haya tenido que volver a casa para recuperar mi residencia, tal y como dice Elliot, por si acaso.

En Carolina del Sur, el apellido Stafford siempre ha estado por encima de ideologías políticas, pero la publicidad generada por el escándalo del centro de mayores nos tiene a todos sudando como turistas en una tarde de verano en Charleston. Cada semana se publica algo nuevo; residentes que murieron porque no les trataban las escaras, centros que contrataban personal no cualificado, otros que no cumplían ni de lejos las regulaciones federales, que exigen al menos 1,3 horas de cuidados a cada paciente y que, aun así, facturaban a Medicare y Medicaid. Familias destrozadas que creían que sus seres queridos estaban en manos competentes. Es desgarrador y horrible, y la ligera conexión con mi padre ha proporcionado a sus enemigos políticos munición de fuerte carga emocional. Quieren que todos crean que, con personas dispuestas a dejarse sobornar, mi padre usaría su influencia para ayudar a un amigo a beneficiarse del sufrimiento humano y luego evitar ser procesado por ello.

Cualquiera que conozca a mi padre sabe que esto es imposible. No está en posición de insistir en que quienes apoyan y financian las campañas políticas enseñen sus balances, y, aunque lo estuviera, la verdad quedaría oculta bajo capa tras capa de entidades corporativas que a primera vista parecen perfectamente legales.

—Será mejor que nos preparemos —dice papá y pulsa el botón del *play* en su agenda de voz. Sostiene el teléfono entre los dos y se inclina hacia mí, y de pronto vuelvo a tener siete años. Me invade esa sensación de cálida emoción que tenía cada vez que mamá me llevaba por los sacrosantos pasillos del Capitolio, se detenía delante de la puerta de mi padre y me dejaba entrar sola. Muy en silencio y con gran solemnidad, yo iba hasta la mesa de la secretaria y anunciaba que tenía una cita con el senador.

«Muy bien, déjeme confirmarlo», decía siempre la señora Dennison mientras levantaba una ceja y contenía una sonrisa pulsando el intercomunicador. «Senador, está aquí una tal señorita Stafford. ¿La hago pasar?».

Después de ser admitida, mi padre me recibía con un apretón de manos y decía: «Señorita Stafford, buenos días. Qué alegría que haya venido. ¿Está preparada para saludar al público?».

«¡Sí, señor!».

Siempre le brillaban los ojos de orgullo cuando yo me giraba para enseñarle cómo me había vestido para la ocasión. Una de las mejores cosas que puede hacer un padre por su hija es hacerle saber que está a la altura de sus expectativas. Mi padre lo hizo conmigo y, por mucho que haga, nunca podré pagar la deuda que tengo con él. Haría cualquier cosa por él y también por mi madre.

Ahora estamos hombro con hombro escuchando los pormenores de las actividades que nos quedan hoy, los temas a tratar y las preguntas a evitar. Se nos dan respuestas cuidadosamente argumentadas a preguntas sobre maltrato en centros de mayores, intentos de demanda y sociedades instrumentales que entran en bancarrota por arte de magia antes de poder pagar indemnizaciones. ¿Qué tiene intención de hacer mi padre al respecto? ¿Ha estado pidiendo favores, protegiendo a contribuyentes a su campaña y viejos amigos del largo brazo de la justicia? ¿Usará ahora su cargo para ayudar a las miles de personas mayores que tienen problemas para encontrar cuidados de calidad? ¿Y qué pasa con los que siguen viviendo en sus casas, sufriendo las consecuencias de la última e histórica inundación, obligados a elegir entre costear las reparaciones, comer, pagar las facturas de la luz o su medicación? ¿Qué cree mi padre que habría que hacer para ayudarlas?

Las preguntas no se terminan nunca. Cada una viene con al menos una respuesta perfectamente redactada. En muchas hay varias opciones que podemos usar en función del contexto, además de notas para refutarlas. El encuentro de esta tarde en el Ayuntamiento será una comparecencia para la prensa cuidadosamente orquestada, pero siempre existe la posibilidad remota de que un topo se haga con el micrófono. El ambiente podría caldearse.

Nos dicen incluso cómo reaccionar en caso de que alguien saque a relucir la cuestión de la abuela Judy. ¿Por qué pagamos una residencia que cuesta unas siete veces la cantidad por día que asigna Medicaid a los mayores de renta baja?

¿Por qué? Porque el médico de la abuela Judy nos dijo que Magnolia Manor era nuestra mejor opción, puesto que la abuela ya estaba familiarizada con el lugar. Una de sus amigas de infancia vivía en la propiedad antes de que fuera reconvertida, así que para ella es como ir a casa. Queremos que tenga todo lo que le proporcione consuelo, pero también nos preocupa su seguridad. Al igual que muchas familias, nos enfrentamos a un dilema complejo y delicado para el que no existe una respuesta sencilla.

Dilema complejo y delicado... No hay respuesta sencilla...

Me aprendo esas frases de memoria palabra por palabra por si me preguntan. En temas tan personales no me conviene improvisar.

—Muy buen trabajo en la residencia esta mañana, Wells —comenta Leslie cuando se sube al coche durante una parada para comprar café a unas manzanas de donde es el acto—. Nos queda poco para atajar esto de raíz. —Está más intensa de lo habitual—. Que Cal Fortner y su equipo intenten aprovecharse del tema de los cuidados a los mayores. Terminarán ahorcados con su propia soga.

—Cuerda no les falta, desde luego. —El comentario de papá tiene poco de chistoso. Hay un plan de ataque muy bien pensado, una estrategia sistemática para retratar a mi padre como un elitista alejado de las necesidades de los ciudadanos, un político de Washington cuyos años en la capital le han vuelto ciego a los problemas de su estado natal.

—Más a nuestro favor —dice Leslie con convencimiento—. Una cosa: ha habido un pequeño cambio de planes. Vamos a entrar en el edificio por la puerta de atrás, hay una protesta frente a la entrada principal.

A continuación se dirige a mí:

—Avery, esta vez te vamos a sacar. Para el encuentro, el senador estará sentado frente al entrevistador, así le damos un aire informal a la cosa. Tú te sentarás al lado de tu padre en el sofá, a su derecha, la hija preocupada que ha vuelto a casa para cuidar de su salud y ocuparse de los asuntos familiares. Eres la hija soltera y sin niños que educar; tienes planeado casarte aquí, en Aiken, etcétera, etcétera. Ya sabes cómo va esto. No hagas un discurso político, pero que tampoco te dé miedo demostrar que conoces los temas a debatir y los aspectos legales. Lo que buscamos es una charla relajada, sin guion, que dé pie a que te hagan alguna pregunta de tipo más personal. Solo habrá programas de noticias locales, así que es la oportunidad perfecta de darte un poco de visibilidad sin demasiada presión.

—Muy bien. —Me he pasado los cinco últimos años con un jurado escrutando cada uno de mis movimientos y abogados defensores respirándome en el cuello. Los participantes en un encuentro cuidadosamente supervisado en el Ayuntamiento no me asustan.

O eso me digo a mí misma. Por alguna razón, tengo el pulso acelerado y noto la garganta rasposa y seca.

—Ya sabes, cariño. Cara de «aquí estoy yo». —Mi padre me dedica lo que en ocasiones llamamos «el guiño del millón de dólares». Rezuma confianza, como miel caliente, espesa e irresistible.

Si yo tuviera la mitad del carisma de mi padre...

Leslie sigue con el programa. Para cuando llegamos al Ayuntamiento, no ha dejado de hablar. A diferencia de la visita a la residencia de mayores de la mañana, aquí hay seguridad, incluidos agentes del Departamento de Seguridad Pública. Oigo la algarabía delante del edificio y al final de la calle trasera veo un coche de la policía.

Cuando nos bajan de la limusina, Leslie parece dispuesta a enzarzarse con alguien a puñetazos. Yo empiezo a sudar dentro de mi conservador traje de chaqueta azul marino.

—¿Honrarás a tu padre y a tu madre? —grita un manifestante por encima del bullicio.

Quiero dar media vuelta, ir hasta la acera y preguntarle a estas personas cómo se atreven.

—¡Fuera los campos de concentración para mayores! —Esta nos sigue mientras entramos.

—¿Qué son? ¿Locos? —murmuro, y Leslie me dedica una mirada de advertencia y a continuación hace un gesto con los hombros señalando a los agentes de policía. Me está diciendo que me guarde mis opiniones en público, a no ser que hayan sido previamente aprobadas. Pero ahora estoy furiosa..., lo que quizá sea bueno. El pulso se me normaliza poco a poco y noto que se me empieza a poner la cara de «aquí estoy yo».

En cuanto se cierra la puerta, las cosas se tranquilizan. Nos recibe Andrew Moore, el coordinador del programa para los anfitriones del debate de hoy. Andrew, miembro de un CAP, un comité de acción política en defensa de los mayores, parece sorprendentemente joven para un puesto así. No puede tener más de veinticinco años. El traje de chaqueta gris sin una arruga combinado con una corbata ligeramente torcida y una camisa que parece elegida al azar le dan aspecto de niño al que han dejado la ropa preparada por la mañana, pero ha tenido que ponérsela solo. Nos cuenta que lo criaron sus abuelos, que hicieron enormes sacrificios por él. Es su manera de pagarles su esfuerzo. Cuando alguien menciona que he sido fiscal federal, me mira y comenta que al comité de acción política le vendría bien tener un buen abogado en plantilla.

—Lo tendré en cuenta —bromeo.

Mientras esperamos, charlamos de esto y lo otro. Parece agradable, sincero, enérgico y comprometido. Mi confianza en que tengamos un debate justo sobre los temas a tratar aumenta.

Enseguida nos presentan a más personas. Conocemos al periodista local que hará las veces de moderador. Nos meten micrófonos debajo de las chaquetas, nos los enganchan a las solapas y nos sujetan los transmisores a la cintura con una banda.

Esperamos entre bastidores hasta que el presentador entra en el plató, da las gracias a los organizadores y recuerda a todos el formato del debate de hoy antes de presentarnos. El público aplaude y entramos en el plató saludando con alegría. Todos se portan bien aunque, cuando miro hacia el público, veo unas cuantas caras que parecen mostrar preocupación, escepticismo y cierta antipatía. Otras miran al senador con lo que podría considerarse adoración.

Mi padre se las arregla razonablemente bien para contestar preguntas y desviar las pocas que no pueden responderse con una frase jugosa. No hay soluciones sencillas al problema de la financiación de la jubilación, que ahora es mucho más larga que en generaciones pasadas, o a la cuestión de las familias fracturadas y el cambio de tendencia a recurrir a los cuidados profesionales en lugar de ocuparse de los parientes ancianos en casa.

A pesar de sus cuidadas respuestas, me doy cuenta de que mi padre no está hoy en plena forma. Tarda un poco en reaccionar cuando un joven le dice:

—Me gustaría oír qué tiene que decir de la acusación de
Cal Fortner de que el objetivo de la cadena de residencias propiedad de una corporación es almacenar a la población mayor
de la manera más barata posible y así aumentar los beneficios,
y que su aceptación en repetidas ocasiones de contribuciones
de L. R. Lawton y sus socios de inversión prueba que apoya
este modelo de supeditar a las personas a los beneficios. ¿Admite que estos centros de mayores estaban atendidos por trabajadores con el salario mínimo y poca o nula formación, y eso
en el mejor de los casos? La oposición pide que haya una legislación federal que haga responsable a cualquiera que saque
beneficios de un centro de asistencia o al holding de empresas
propietario de los cuidados que se proporcionan, así como de
los daños que se reconozcan en los tribunales. Fortner también
pide impuestos para ciudadanos ricos como usted para costear
un aumento de las prestaciones de nuestros ciudadanos más
pobres. A la vista de los últimos acontecimientos, ¿apoyaría
esta propuesta en el Congreso y por qué? En caso contrario,
¿por qué no?

Casi me parece oír rechinar los dientes de Leslie detrás
de la cortina. Este tipo de preguntas no estaban en el guion y
sin duda no están escritas en la tarjeta que sostiene el joven.

Mi padre duda y parece momentáneamente desconcertado. *Vamos,* pienso. El sudor me baja por la espalda. Se me
tensan los músculos y me agarro al reposabrazos de la silla
para tener las manos ocupadas.

El silencio es una tortura. Parece que pasan minutos, pero
sé que no es así.

Mi padre se embarca por fin en una larga explicación
sobre la existencia de regulaciones federales de las residencias
de mayores y sobre los impuestos y los fideicomisos federales que financian Medicaid. Parece competente y sereno. Al
mando una vez más. Deja claro que no está en situación de

modificar él solo el sistema de financiación de Medicaid, el código impositivo o el estado actual del cuidado de los mayores, pero que son cuestiones prioritarias para él de cara a la próxima sesión del Congreso.

El encuentro vuelve entonces al guion previsto.

Por fin me hacen una pregunta y el presentador me mira indulgente. Contesto lo acordado a si me están preparando o no para ocupar el escaño de mi padre en el Congreso. No digo que sí ni tampoco digo: «Ni en un millón de años». En lugar de eso, termino con: «En cualquier caso, es prematuro pensar siquiera en ello... A no ser que quiera presentarme como su contrincante. ¿Y quién estaría tan loco para hacer algo así?».

El público ríe y remato la faena con el guiño que he heredado de mi padre. Está tan complacido que parece medir dos metros mientras contesta unas cuantas preguntas sencillas más y se termina el encuentro.

Al salir del plató, me preparo para que Leslie me dé palmaditas en la espalda. En lugar de eso, me detiene con cara de preocupación y se pega mucho a mí mientras salimos.

—Han llamado de la residencia. Al parecer te dejaste una pulsera.

—¿Qué? ¿Una pulsera?

De pronto recuerdo haberme puesto una esta mañana. Noto que me falta algo en la muñeca y, sí, la pulsera ha desaparecido.

—La llevaba puesta una de las residentes. La directora ha mirado las fotos del acto y ha comprobado que era tuya.

La mujer de la residencia..., la que me cogió la mano...

Ahora recuerdo las diminutas patas de oro de tres libélulas arañándome la muñeca mientras se llevaban a May Crandall. Debió de quedarse con la pulsera.

—Aaah, ya sé lo que pasó.

—La directora se ha disculpado muchísimo. La paciente es nueva y le está costando adaptarse. La encontraron hace dos semanas en una casa junto al río con el cuerpo muerto de su hermana y una docena de gatos.

—Qué horror. —Mis pensamientos vuelan y, sin poder evitarlo, imagino lo deprimente y espantoso de una escena así—. Seguro que fue un accidente. Lo de la pulsera, quiero decir. Me cogió de la mano mientras hablaba papá. La enfermera casi tuvo que soltarla a la fuerza.

—No debería haber ocurrido algo así.

—No pasa nada, Leslie. No tiene importancia.

—Mandaré a alguien a recogerla.

Recuerdo los ojos azules de May Crandall, la desesperación con la que me miraba. La imagino marchándose con mi pulsera, examinándola sola en su habitación, encajándosela en la muñeca y admirándola, feliz.

Si no fuera una herencia, dejaría que se la quedara.

—¿Sabes qué? Creo que voy a ir yo a buscarla. La pulsera era de mi abuela. —La agenda del día requiere que mi padre y yo nos separemos. Él estará un rato en su despacho antes de cenar con uno de sus electores, mientras mi madre hace de anfitriona de una reunión de un comité de acción política en Drayden Hill—. ¿Puede llevarme alguien? ¿O puedo coger uno de los coches?

Leslie me mira furiosa. Parecemos a punto de embestirnos la una a la otra, así que añado otra excusa, más convincente.

—Además tendría que pasarme a tomar el té con la abuela Judy ahora que estoy libre un rato. Y le gustará ver la pulsera.

El encuentro en el Ayuntamiento me ha dejado sintiéndome culpable por llevar casi una semana sin visitar a mi abuela.

A Leslie le tiembla la mandíbula cuando accede, dejando claro que mi capricho le parece inquietantemente poco profesional.

No puedo evitarlo. No dejo de pensar en May Crandall y en los numerosos artículos en la prensa sobre maltrato en las residencias de mayores. Quizá solo quiero asegurarme de que no acudió a mí porque tiene algún problema.

Quizá su historia triste y macabra ha despertado mi curiosidad. *La encontraron hace dos semanas en una casa junto al río con el cuerpo muerto de su hermana...*

¿Sería Fern el nombre de su hermana?

4

RILL FOSS

Memphis, Tennessee, 1939

Queenie está pálida como la leche descremada, con el cuerpo tenso y rígido, cuando Briny la deja en el borde del porche y va a buscar el esquife, que está amarrado a un pilote río abajo. Queenie llora y grita, fuera de sí, con la mejilla apoyada en la madera suave y húmeda.

Lark se refugia en las sombras de la noche junto a la pared de la casa, pero los pequeños, Fern y Gabion, se acercan gateando. Nunca han visto a un adulto actuar de esta manera.

Gabion se inclina para mirar, no está seguro de que esa cosa que lleva el vestido floreado rosa de Queenie sea ella. Queenie es luz y risa y todas las viejas canciones que nos canta mientras navegamos de una ciudad a otra. Esta mujer que enseña los dientes y jura y gime y llora no puede ser ella, pero lo es.

—*Dil, Dil* —dice Gabion, porque tiene solo dos años y no sabe pronunciar mi nombre, Rill. Me agarra el borde de la falda y tira de él mientras yo me arrodillo para sujetarle la cabeza a Queenie—. ¿*Quini* pupa?

—¡A callar!

Camellia pega a los pequeños en la mano cuando Fern intenta acariciar los rizos largos y dorados de Queenie. Su pelo es lo primero que llamó la atención de Briny y le hizo fijarse en ella. *¿A que tu madre parece una princesa de cuento?*, me pregunta a veces. *Reina del reino de Arcadia, esa es tu madre. Eso te convierte a ti en princesa, ¿verdad?*

Pero mi madre no está guapa ahora, con la cara sucia de sudor y la boca abierta en una mueca de dolor. Estos bebés la van a romper. El estómago se le encoge y crece debajo del vestido. Me coge y no me suelta, mientras, dentro de la casa, la partera se limpia las manos y guarda su instrumental en una cesta verde.

—¡Tiene que ayudarnos! —grito—. ¡Se está muriendo!

—No quiero tener nada que ver con este asunto —dice la mujer y su cuerpo voluminoso hace mecerse el barco y que la lámpara oscile y chisporrotee—. Se acabó. Sois unos locos, escoria del río.

Está como un perro rabioso porque Briny no ha querido darle dinero. Briny dice que prometió traer al mundo a un niño, cosa que no ha hecho, y que debería darse por satisfecha con los dos gruesos bagres que soltó del espinel esta mañana, además de algo de aceite de carbón para la lámpara que ha traído con ella. Se vengaría de nosotros si pudiera, pero es más negra que el alquitrán y nosotros blancos, y sabe lo que podría pasar si nos hace algo.

Se suponía que los bagres iban a ser nuestra cena, lo que nos deja con nada excepto una torta de maíz para los cinco. Es lo que se me pasa por la cabeza junto con media docena de cosas más.

¿Debería coger algo de ropa para Queenie? ¿Su cepillo de pelo? ¿Sus zapatos?

¿Tendrá Briny dinero suficiente para pagar a un médico de verdad? ¿Qué pasará si no es así?

¿Y si lo detienen? Una vez, cuando nos dedicábamos a trapichear en billares de las ciudades a orillas del río, lo pillaron. Briny es un buen jugador. Nadie le gana a un juego de bola ocho y toca el piano lo bastante bien para que le paguen por ello, pero con la Depresión el dinero en metálico escasea. Ahora juega al billar y toca y le pagan con cosas que luego podemos cambiar por lo que necesitamos.

¿Habrá dinero escondido en alguna parte? ¿Debería preguntarle a Briny cuando vuelva? ¿Recordarle que quizá lo necesite?

¿Cómo cruzará el río en la oscuridad con la tormenta que ha empezado ya a levantar olas?

La partera se vuelve hacia la puerta y la cesta le golpea el trasero. Hay algo rojo que sobresale y, a pesar de la escasa luz, sé lo que es: el sombrero de terciopelo rojo rematado con plumas de Queenie, el que ganó Briny en una partida de billar en un pueblo pequeño y mugriento llamado Boggyfield.

—¡Devuelve eso! —le digo—. ¡Es de mi madre!

La mujer cierra sus ojos oscuros y me mira levantando la barbilla.

—He estado aquí todo el día y no pienso conformarme con dos pescados. Tengo pescados de sobra. Me llevo el sombrero. —Mira a su alrededor en busca de Briny y a continuación se dirige hacia la pasarela en uno de los laterales del porche.

Quiero detenerla, pero no puedo. En mi regazo, Queenie grita y se revuelve. Su cabeza aterriza en la cubierta con un golpe hueco, como de una sandía. La sujeto con las dos manos.

Camellia adelanta corriendo a la mujer y le cierra el paso, con sus brazos delgados abiertos y extendidos sobre la barandilla.

—No vas a ir a ninguna parte con el sombrero de mi madre.

La mujer da un paso más, pero, si conociera a Camellia, no lo habría hecho. Puede que mi hermana no tenga más que diez años, pero no solo ha heredado el pelo negro y espeso de Briny, también su temperamento. Cuando Briny se enfada, se *vuelve loco*, tal y como dice el viejo Zede. *Alguien que se vuelve loco puede acabar matándote.* Zede ha advertido a mi padre de ello en más de una ocasión cuando nuestros barcos han estado amarrados uno junto al otro, y eso ha sido muchas veces. Zede es amigo de Briny desde que Briny se fue a vivir al río. Le ha enseñado cómo son las cosas.

—Mocosa insolente. Eres una desvergonzada.

Un brazo grande y oscuro aferra el de Camellia y la mujer tira de ella y Camellia se agarra tan fuerte a la barandilla que creo que se le va a salir el hueso del hombro. No han pasado dos segundos cuando Camellia se gira y le hinca los dientes. La mujer aúlla y retrocede, zarandeando el barco.

Queenie chilla.

A lo lejos, retumba el trueno.

Brilla un relámpago, la noche se convierte en día y vuelve a cubrirse con su velo negro.

¿Dónde está Briny? ¿Por qué tarda tanto?

Me viene un pensamiento aterrador. ¿Y si el esquife se ha soltado y Briny no lo encuentra? ¿Y si ha ido a pedir prestado otro a alguien del campamento? Por una vez me gustaría que Briny no fuera tan independiente. Nunca fondea en los campamentos del río y quienes reconocen nuestro barco jamás vienen por aquí a no ser que hayan sido invitados. Briny dice que en el río hay buenas y malas personas y que es mejor identificarlas de lejos.

Queenie patalea y hace caer a Gabion, que se golpea el brazo y suelta un alarido largo y agudo. Lark entra corriendo en la casa ahora que ya no está la partera. Queenie se está muriendo en mis brazos. Estoy segura.

En el arranque de la pasarela, Camellia sigue sin moverse. Su expresión de desdén desafía a la mujer a que intente enfrentarse a ella otra vez. Camellia se pelea con una facilidad pasmosa. Es capaz de coger serpientes con la mano o enzarzarse con muchachos de la orilla sin pensárselo dos veces.

—¡Deja el sombrero de mi madre! —grita haciéndose oír por encima del llanto de Gabion—. ¡Y tampoco te vas a llevar el pescado! Bájate de nuestro barco antes de que avisemos a la policía de que una mujer de color ha intentado matar a nuestra madre y robarnos. Te van a colgar de un árbol, ya lo verás. —Echa la cabeza hacia atrás, saca la lengua y a mí se me pone un nudo en el estómago. Hace dos miércoles vimos a un hombre ahorcado río abajo. Un tipo grande, de color, con pantalón de peto. No había una casa en kilómetros a la redonda y llevaba tanto tiempo allí que los buitres ya la habían emprendido con él.

Solo Camellia usaría algo así para salirse con la suya. Solo de pensarlo, me pongo enferma.

Quizá por eso está mal Queenie, me susurra una voz dentro de mi cabeza. *Quizá es porque Briny no se paró a descolgar a aquel hombre y buscar a su familia para que pudieran enterrarlo. Quizá nos está mirando desde el bosque.*

Queenie le suplicó a Briny que fueran hasta la orilla y se ocuparan del cuerpo, pero Briny se negó. «Tenemos que pensar en los niños, Queenie», dijo. «No sabemos quién lo ha hecho ni quién puede estar vigilando. Es mejor que sigamos navegando».

La partera saca el sombrero rojo de Queenie de la cesta, lo tira y pasa por encima de él, haciendo balancearse el barco al bajar la pasarela. Luego coge la lámpara que había dejado en la orilla. Lo último que decide es llevarse el portapeces con los dos bagres. A continuación se aleja sin dejar de maldecirnos.

—¡Que el diablo te lleve a ti también! —le responde Camellia asomada a la baranda del porche—. ¡Te estará bien empleado, por ladrona! —Está a punto de repetir las palabras soeces de la mujer. A sus diez años, Camellia ha comido jabón suficiente para lavar el estómago de una ballena. Prácticamente se ha criado con él. Es un milagro que no le salgan pompas por las orejas—. Viene alguien. Gabion, calla. —Coge a Gabby, le tapa la boca con una mano y escucha en la noche. Yo también oigo un motor.

—Mira a ver si es Briny —le digo a Fern, y esta se dispone a ir, pero Camellia le pasa a Gabby.

—Que se esté callado. —Camellia cruza el porche y se inclina sobre la barandilla que da al agua y, por primera vez, oigo alivio en su voz—. Parece que trae a Zede.

El consuelo me envuelve como una manta. Si hay alguien capaz de arreglar las cosas es el viejo Zede. Yo ni siquiera sabía que andaba por la isla de Mud, pero Briny seguramente sí. Siempre se siguen la pista el uno al otro río abajo o río arriba. Lo último que supe de Zede es que estaba en tierra firme cuidando de una hermana que había tenido que ingresar en el hospital por tuberculosis.

—Ha venido Zede —le susurro a Queenie, inclinándome hacia ella. Parece que me oye y también que se tranquiliza un poco. Zede sabrá qué hacer. Calmará a Briny, le quitará la nube de los ojos que le impide ver y conseguirá que piense—. Ha venido Zede, Queenie. Todo va a salir bien. Todo va a salir bien... —repito una y otra vez hasta que cogen el cabo que les ha tirado Camellia y suben por la pasarela.

Briny cruza el porche de dos zancadas, se arrodilla al lado de Queenie y la incorpora con la cara cerca de la suya. Noto cómo el peso de mi madre me abandona, cómo su calor se esfuma de mi piel. Cae el rocío de la noche y, de pronto, tengo frío. Me pongo de pie, levanto más la lámpara y me abrazo.

Zede se agacha, mira a Queenie a los ojos, retira un poco la sábana que la envuelve y está llena de sangre. Le apoya una mano en el vientre, donde una mancha roja acuosa le sube por el vestido.

—¿Señora Foss? —Su voz es serena y clara—. Señora Foss, ¿me oye?

Queenie emite algo que podría ser un «sí», pero el sonido muere entre sus dientes apretados y pega la cara al pecho de Briny.

Detrás de la espesa barba gris, la boca de Zede forma una mueca de preocupación. Los ojos con el filo encarnado parecen bailarle en las cuencas. Toma aire por su nariz ancha y peluda y lo expulsa por entre los labios apretados. Desprende un fuerte olor a whisky y a tabaco, pero es un consuelo. Es lo único esta noche que sigue siendo como siempre.

Mira a Briny a los ojos y niega un poco con la cabeza.

—Queenie, niña, vamos a sacarte del barco, ¿me oyes? Tenemos que llevarte al hospital en el *Jenny*. Va a ser un viaje duro, cruzando el río. Pero vas a ser valiente, ¿a que sí?

Ayuda a Briny a levantarla del suelo y los gritos de Queenie rasgan el aire igual que las mujeres rasgan velos en un funeral en Nueva Orleans. Antes de que consigan llevarla al bote, ya está inerte en brazos de Briny.

—Sujétala —le dice Zede a Briny, y a continuación me mira y me señala con ese dedo torcido que se rompió en la guerra con España—. Llévate a los pequeños dentro y acuéstalos, niña. Quedaos dentro. Yo volveré antes de que amanezca si no hay tormenta, pero, si no, el *Lizzy Mae* está amarrado río abajo, muy cerca de aquí. Allí está vuestro esquife. Tengo a un chico en el *Lizzy* conmigo. No tiene buena pinta ahora mismo, intentó subirse a un tren de polizón y los matones del ferrocarril lo cogieron. Pero no os hará daño. Le he dicho que se acerque por la mañana si no ha tenido noticias mías.

Enciende el motor del fueraborda y este ruge, y miro fijamente el lodo que levanta la hélice a la luz del candil. No quiero ver a Queenie con los ojos cerrados y la boca abierta de esa manera.

Camellia tira el cabo, que aterriza limpiamente en la popa de la lancha. Zede la señala con el dedo.

—Y tú, mocosa, haz caso a tu hermana. No hagas nada sin pedirle permiso antes a Rill, ¿me has oído?

Camellia arruga tanto la nariz que se le juntan las pecas de las mejillas.

—¿Me has oído? —vuelve a preguntar Zede. Sabe cuál de nosotros suele dar problemas.

—¡Mellia! —Las nubes de Briny se despejan por un momento.

—Sí, señor. —Camellia accede, pero no está contenta.

Entonces Briny se vuelve hacia mí, pero es como si me suplicara algo en lugar de decírmelo.

—Cuida de los pequeños, Rill. Cuida de todos hasta que volvamos... Queenie y yo.

—Nos portaremos bien, te lo prometo. Cuidaré de todos. No iremos a ninguna parte.

Zede tira de la caña del timón, acelera y la lancha se interna con mi madre en la oscuridad. Los cinco corremos a la barandilla y nos quedamos allí juntos mirando hasta que la negrura engulle el *Jenny* por completo. Escuchamos el casco golpear contra la cresta de las olas, subiendo y bajando, el motor fueraborda que ruge y calla y vuelve a rugir. Su voz suena un poco más lejos cada vez. Un contramaestre toca el silbato. Ladra un perro.

La noche se vuelve silenciosa.

Fern se enrosca en mi pierna como un mono y Gabby se mete en la casa con Lark, porque es su preferida. Ahora no hay más que hacer que entrar y ver qué podemos comer. Solo tenemos la torta de maíz y unas peras que cambió Briny en Wilson, Arkansas, donde estuvimos tres meses y fuimos a la escuela hasta que llegó el verano. Para entonces, Briny tenía de nuevo el gusanillo y quería navegar otra vez.

En circunstancias normales, nunca nos habría acercado tanto a la orilla de una ciudad grande como Memphis, pero Queenie llevaba quejándose de dolores desde antes de ayer. Aunque era un poco temprano, después de haber tenido cinco hijos sabía que lo sensato era amarrar el barco y quedarnos donde estábamos.

Dentro del *Arcadia* todos están llorosos y preocupados, y acalorados y de mal humor. Camellia se queja porque he cerrado la puerta en lugar de solo la mosquitera y el calor húmedo es agobiante, incluso con las ventanas abiertas.

—Calla —la regaño y preparo la cena y nos sentamos en círculo en el suelo porque no nos parece bien sentarnos a la mesa cuando van a quedar dos sitios vacíos.

—*Teno hambe.* —Gabby hace un puchero cuando se termina la comida. Come más deprisa que un gato callejero.

Corto un pedazo de mi porción de torta de maíz y lo muevo delante de su boca.

—Comes demasiado deprisa.

Abre la boca como un pájaro cada vez que se lo acerco y por fin se lo meto en la boca.

—Ñam —dice y se frota la barriga.

Fern me sigue en el juego y lo mismo hace Lark. Para cuando hemos terminado, Gabby se ha comido la ración de todos excepto la de Camellia, que se come la suya entera.

—Mañana pondré los espineles —comenta, como si eso compensara su egoísmo.

—Zede nos ha dicho que no salgamos —contesto.

—Lo haré cuando vuelva Zede. O cuando venga el chico.

No puede poner un espinel sola y lo sabe.

—Ni siquiera tenemos el esquife. Briny lo ha amarrado al barco de Zede.

—Pero mañana lo tendremos.

—Mañana habrá vuelto Briny con Queenie y los bebés.

Entonces nos miramos, solo Camellia y yo. Noto que Lark y Fern están pendientes, pero las dos somos las únicas lo bastante mayores para estar preocupadas y compartirlo. Camellia mira hacia la puerta y yo también. Las dos sabemos que esta noche no la cruzará nadie. Nunca antes hemos estados solos de noche. Siempre estaba Queenie, incluso cuando Briny se había ido a cazar, o a trapichear en los billares o a pescar ranas.

Gabion se tumba en la estera trenzada de Queenie con los ojos cerrados y las largas pestañas castaño claro tocándole las mejillas. Todavía necesita pañal por las noches, pero esperaré a que esté dormido para ponérselo, como hace Queenie. Ahora que ha aprendido a usar el orinal durante el día, se enfada cuando nos ve acercarnos con un pañal.

Fuera, el trueno ruge y los relámpagos centellean y el cielo empieza a escupir bruma. *¿Habrán conseguido Zede y Briny llegar a la orilla con nuestra madre?*, me pregunto. *¿Estará en algún sitio donde los médicos puedan curarla como hicieron con Camellia cuando se puso mala del apéndice?*

—Atranca las ventanas que dan al río. Para que no entre la lluvia —le digo a Camellia y ni siquiera me discute. Por primera vez en su vida, está perdida. No está segura de qué conviene hacer. El problema es que yo tampoco.

Gabion abre la boca y empieza a roncar. Por lo menos uno de los pequeños no dará la lata esta noche. Lark y Fern son otra cosa. Los enormes ojos azules de Lark se llenan de lágrimas y susurra:

—Quiero a Queenie, *teno* miedo.

Yo también quiero a Queenie, pero eso no puedo decírselo.

—A callar, que ya tienes seis años. No eres un bebé. Cerrad las ventanas antes de que se levante viento y poneos el pijama. Vamos a cambiar las sábanas de la cama grande y a dormir ahí. Como cuando no está Briny.

Siento el cuerpo débil y exhausto, pero la cabeza me va a mil por hora. No puede pensar con claridad, se limita a producir palabras sin sentido, igual que el motor fueraborda girando en el bajío, levantando hojas y ramas y gusanos de cebo y barro.

Así sigue, de manera que no me deja oír los llantos y quejas y los resoplidos y el sorber de narices y a Camellia empeorando las cosas llamando gallina a Fern y a Lark bebé y otra palabra fea que ni siquiera debería conocer.

Por fin, cuando todos están acostados en la cama grande y apago las lámparas, recojo la cruz con el hombre de hojalata del suelo y vuelvo a colgarla en su sitio en la pared. A Briny no le gusta, pero a Queenie sí y es el único que está aquí para cuidarnos esta noche.

Antes de meterme en la cama, me arrodillo y susurro todas las palabras polacas que me sé.

5

AVERY

*V*uelvo enseguida —digo a Ian, el becario de Leslie, cuando aparca bajo el soportal de la residencia de mayores.

Se detiene cuando se disponía a bajar del coche.

—Ah..., vale. Entonces espero aquí mientras contesto unos correos.

Parece decepcionarle que no necesite acompañante. Noto cómo su mirada curiosa me acompaña mientras bajo del coche y voy hacia el vestíbulo.

La directora me espera en su despacho. La pulsera de la abuela Judy está en su mesa. Los ojos hechos de piedras preciosas de las libélulas centellean cuando me pongo mi tesoro recuperado en la muñeca.

Charlamos un rato sobre el acto de unas horas antes y a continuación la directora se disculpa por las molestias causadas.

—Hemos tenido bastantes problemas con la señora Crandall —reconoce—. Pobre mujer. Casi nunca habla con nadie. No hace más que... deambular por los pasillos y el jardín hasta que cerramos, por la noche. Luego se queda en su habitación, a no ser que hayan venido voluntarios a tocar el piano. Parece que le encanta la música, pero ni siquiera cuando hacemos karaoke hemos conseguido convencerla de que cante con los otros residentes. El duelo y el cambio de casa a veces son más de lo que la cabeza y el cuerpo pueden soportar.

De inmediato imagino a alguien diciendo lo mismo de la abuela Judy. Sufro por esta pobre mujer, May.

—Espero que no se haya disgustado. Estoy segura de que no se quedó la pulsera a propósito. Se la regalaría, lo que pasa es que lleva mucho tiempo en mi familia.

—Por favor, no. Es mejor que la devuelva. Una de las cosas que les cuesta más aceptar a nuestros residentes es que muchas de sus pertenencias no han venido con ellos. Tienden a ver cosas por aquí y a creerse que son suyas y que alguien se las ha quitado. Lo de tener que devolver objetos sustraídos es bastante frecuente. La señora Crandall todavía se está adaptando a haber dejado su casa. Ahora mismo está confusa y agitada, pero es normal.

—Sé que el cambio es duro. —La propiedad de mi abuela en la calle Lagniappe sigue cerrada con todas sus cosas dentro. No estamos preparados para decidir qué hacer con una vida de recuerdos e innumerables objetos familiares. Con el tiempo, la casa pasará a la siguiente generación, como ha ocurrido siempre. Con suerte una de mis hermanas se instalará en ella y así conservará la mayoría de las antigüedades—. ¿Tiene la señora Crandall familiares que la visiten? —Evito mencionar la historia de la hermana muerta. Me siento culpable hablando de esta mujer como si fuera una especie de... objeto de estudio. Es una persona. Igual que la abuela Judy.

La directora niega con la cabeza y frunce el ceño.

—Aquí no. Su hijo murió hace años. Tiene nietos, pero es una familia con matrimonios de segundas nupcias e hijos de padres distintos y ninguno vive cerca, así que es complicado.

Hacen lo que pueden y, a decir verdad, la señora Crandall no ha colaborado nada. Al principio la llevaron a una residencia más cerca de su casa e intentó escaparse. La familia la trasladó aquí pensando que le vendría bien algo de distancia. En dos semanas ha tratado de irse tres veces. Que los residentes nuevos estén algo desorientados y sean poco colaboradores no es raro. Con un poco de suerte, mejorará cuando se haya aclimatado un poco. No me gustaría tener que trasladarla a la unidad de pacientes con alzhéimer, pero... —Cierra la boca antes de terminar la frase, al parecer porque se ha dado cuenta de que no debería estar contándome nada de esto.

—Lo siento mucho. —No puedo evitar tener la impresión de que he empeorado una situación ya mala de por sí—. ¿Podría verla... solo para darle las gracias por devolver la pulsera?

—No la devolvió... exactamente. La enfermera vio que la tenía.

—Por lo menos me gustaría decirle que agradezco haberla recuperado. —En realidad lo que me preocupa es que la directora parece tomarse todo esto de un modo tan... clínico. ¿Y si le he buscado problemas a May?—. Esta pulsera era una de las favoritas de mi abuela. —Bajo la vista a las libélulas doradas de ornada montura con granates a modo de ojos y cuerpo multicolor.

—Aquí no restringimos las visitas, pero quizá sería mejor que no lo hiciera. Además, lo más probable es que la señora Crandall no quiera hablar con usted. Le haremos saber que hemos devuelto la pulsera y que está todo solucionado.

Terminamos la conversación con una charla agradable sobre la fiesta de cumpleaños y nos despedimos en la puerta de su despacho. De camino a la salida veo un cartel en el pasillo con nombres y números de habitación dispuestos ordenadamente en ranuras metálicas.

May Crandall, 107. Doblo la esquina.

La habitación 107 se encuentra al final del pasillo. La puerta está abierta. La cama de la primera mitad de la habitación está vacía. La cortina del centro está echada. Entro, susurro:

—¿Hola? ¿Señora Crandall?

El aire huele a cargado, las luces están apagadas, pero oigo el sonido ronco de una respiración.

—¿Señora Crandall?

Un paso más y veo unos pies que asoman de las mantas de la segunda cama. Son unos pies encogidos y curvos. Como si llevaran mucho tiempo sin soportar peso. No debe de ser ella.

Examino la mitad de la habitación que sin duda es de la señora Crandall. Es pequeña e impersonal y un poco deprimente. El apartamentito donde vive ahora la abuela Judy está amueblado con un sofá, una silla y una mesita y adornado con todas sus fotografías preferidas que pudimos meter; esta habitación dice que su ocupante no tiene intención de quedarse. Hay un único objeto personal en la mesilla de noche: un marco de fotos con un pie de terciopelo desgastado y polvoriento en la parte de atrás.

Sé que no debo ser cotilla, pero no me quito de la cabeza la imagen de May mirándome con sus ojos azules como el huevo de un petirrojo con expresión de necesitar algo. Desesperadamente. ¿Y si ha intentado escapar de aquí porque alguien la maltrata? Como fiscal federal, no puedo ignorar los horribles casos de maltrato a personas mayores. Los delitos federales como estafas por teléfono, suplantación de identidad o robo de cheques de la seguridad social entran dentro de nuestra jurisdicción. Hay demasiados casos de gente joven esperando echar el guante al dinero de sus parientes de mayor edad. Es posible que los nietos de la señora Crandall sean maravillosos, pero es difícil entender que, en su estado, la hayan dejado aquí en lugar de en un sitio donde puedan supervisar sus cuidados.

Solo quiero cerciorarme, me digo. El sentido del deber de los Stafford es algo innato en mí. Me hace sentirme responsable del bienestar de los desconocidos, en especial de los indefensos o marginados. Las ONG son el segundo empleo a tiempo completo y no oficial de mi madre.

Por desgracia, el marco está vuelto contra la pared. Está hecho de esa celulosa nacarada que imita el marfil y que hacía juego con polveras, cepillos y abotonadores que usaban las mujeres en las décadas de 1930 y 1940. Ni siquiera inclinándome consigo ver la fotografía.

Al final lo hago y ya está. Le doy la vuelta al marco. Sepia y blanquecina en los bordes, es la fotografía de una pareja joven a la orilla de un lago o un estanque. El hombre lleva un sombrero de fieltro gastado y sostiene una caña de pescar. Es difícil distinguir sus facciones: ojos oscuros, pelo oscuro. Es guapo y la manera en que posa, con un pie apoyado en un tronco caído y los hombros delgados hacia atrás, transmite confianza, desafío incluso. Es como si retara al fotógrafo a que lo retrate.

La mujer está embarazada. El viento le atrapa el vestido de flores y dibuja los contornos de un vientre que parece demasiado grande para sus piernas largas y delgadas. La espesa melena rubia le llega formando espirales hasta casi la cintura. Lleva la parte delantera sujeta con un lazo desaliñado, como las niñas pequeñas. Es lo primero que me llama la atención de ella, que parece una adolescente disfrazada para una obra de teatro del instituto. *Las uvas de la ira*, quizá.

Lo segundo que pienso es que me recuerda a mi abuela. Parpadeo, me acerco más, pienso en las fotografías que colgamos con esmero en la habitación de la abuela Judy no hace mucho. Hay una en concreto, del viaje de fin de curso de su último año en el instituto; está sentada en un embarcadero de Coney Island y sonríe a la cámara.

Seguro que el parecido son imaginaciones mías. A juzgar por las ropas, esta fotografía es demasiado antigua para ser de la abuela Judy. Mi siempre estilosa abuela nunca habría vestido así, pero ahora mismo, mientras escudriño el cristal, solo me viene a la cabeza: *Podría ser ella*. También veo un parecido con mi sobrina Courtney, y, por supuesto, conmigo.

Saco el móvil e intento enfocar la cámara en la escasa luz.

El encuadre de la cámara viene y va. Saco una fotografía. Sale borrosa. Me acerco a la cama y pruebo otra vez. Por alguna razón, encender la lámpara me parece una intrusión y, si uso el flash, con el cristal no saldrá más que un destello blanco. Pero quiero una foto. Tal vez mi padre reconozca a alguna de estas personas... o quizá, una vez que llegue a casa y la mire de nuevo, me daré cuenta de que he exagerado el parecido. La fotografía es vieja y no demasiado nítida.

—Invadir el espacio de alguien sin haber sido invitado es de mala educación.

Me incorporo con un respingo mientras la cámara dispara otra vez y el teléfono se me resbala. Se cae dando vueltas y parezco un dibujo animado que intenta atraparlo en el aire a cámara lenta.

May Crandall entra en la habitación mientras rescato el móvil de debajo de la cama.

—Lo siento muchísimo. Quería... —No hay explicación posible a mi comportamiento. No la hay.

—¿Qué está haciendo exactamente? —Cuando me doy la vuelta se aparta, sorprendida. Pega la barbilla al cuello y a continuación la saca, despacio—. Has vuelto. —Mira el marco de fotos, indicándome que sabe que lo han movido—. ¿Eres uno de ellos?

—¿Ellos?

—Esta gente. —Mueve una mano en el aire indicando al personal de la residencia. Se acerca—. Me tienen encarcelada aquí.

Pienso en lo que me contó Leslie: la casa, el cadáver de la hermana. Quizá hay algo más que duelo y desorientación. En realidad no sé nada de esta mujer.

—Veo que lleva mi pulsera. —Señala mi muñeca.

Me vienen a la cabeza las palabras de la directora. *Casi nunca habla con nadie... No hace más que deambular por los pasillos y el jardín...*

Pero a mí me está hablando.

Sin poder evitarlo, pego la pulsera con fuerza a mi pecho cubriéndola con una mano.

—Lo siento, la pulsera era mía. Debió de caérseme cuando me cogió de la muñeca antes..., hoy..., en la fiesta de cumpleaños.

Parpadea como si no tuviera ni idea de lo que le hablo. ¿Quizá es que ha olvidado ya la fiesta?

—¿Tenía usted una igual? —pregunto.

—¿Una fiesta? No, claro que no.

El rencor asoma a su voz, potente y cáustico.

Tal vez la directora de la residencia ha valorado mal el estado de salud de esta mujer. He oído que la demencia senil y el alzhéimer pueden manifestarse en forma de paranoia y agitación. Lo que pasa es que nunca lo he visto. La abuela Judy está desorientada y en ocasiones impaciente consigo misma, pero sigue tan encantadora y cariñosa como siempre.

—Lo que quería decir es si ha tenido una pulsera como esta.

—Pues sí..., hasta que se la dieron a usted.

—No. Yo la llevaba cuando vine aquí esta mañana. Es un regalo de mi abuela. Una de sus joyas preferidas. De otro modo, se la... —Me interrumpo antes de decir: «De otro modo se la regalaría a usted». Me parece que sería ofensivo, como tratarla igual que a una niña pequeña.

Me mira largo rato. De pronto parece completamente lúcida, sagaz incluso.

—Quizá pueda presentarme a su abuela y así aclaramos esto. ¿Vive cerca de aquí?

Hay un cambio brusco en la atmósfera de la habitación. Lo noto, y no tiene nada que ver con el ventilador encendido en el techo. Esta mujer quiere algo de mí.

—Me temo que no es posible. Me gustaría, pero no puede ser. —En realidad jamás expondría a mi abuela a esta mujer extraña, implacable. Cuanto más habla, menos me cuesta imaginarla encerrada con el cadáver de su hermana.

—¿Está muerta, entonces? —De pronto parece abatida, vulnerable.

—No, pero tuvimos que sacarla de su casa y llevarla a una residencia.

—¿Hace poco?

—Hace aproximadamente un mes.

—Ah..., vaya, qué lástima. ¿Está contenta allí, por lo menos? —Una mirada implorante, desesperada, acompaña sus palabras y me invade una penetrante tristeza por May. ¿Qué vida habrá tenido? ¿Dónde están los amigos, los vecinos, los compañeros de trabajo..., las personas que deberían venir a verla ahora, aunque solo sea por sentido del deber? La abuela Judy al menos tiene una visita al día, en ocasiones dos o tres.

—Creo que sí. Para serle sincera, en su casa se sentía sola. Ahora que está en la residencia tiene gente con quien hablar, y todos los días hay juegos y reuniones. Hacen manualidades y tienen una biblioteca con muchos libros. —Sin duda aquí también habrá alguna de esas cosas. Quizá consiga despertar un poco el interés de May, animarla a probar su nueva vida y a dejar de resistirse a las enfermeras. El rumbo que ha tomado nuestra conversación me está haciendo sospechar que no está tan desorientada como ha estado haciendo creer.

Ignora hábilmente mi insinuación y cambia de tema.

—Creo que la conocí. A su abuela. Me parece que íbamos al mismo club de bridge. —Me señala con un dedo torcido y arrugado—. Se parece bastante a ella.

—Eso dicen. Sí, tengo su pelo. Mis hermanas no, pero yo sí.

—Y sus ojos.

La conversación se ha vuelto íntima. Su mirada parece penetrarme hasta el tuétano.

¿Qué está pasando?

—Le..., le hablaré de usted cuando la vea. Pero es posible que no se acuerde. Tiene días buenos y malos.

—Como todos, ¿no? —May curva los labios hacia arriba y yo río nerviosa sin poder evitarlo.

Al cambiar de posición, rozo la lámpara de la mesilla con el codo y al sujetarla le doy al marco. Lo cojo antes de que se caiga, lo sostengo e intento resistirme a mirarlo de cerca.

—Siempre lo están tirando. Las chicas que trabajan aquí.

—Podría ponerlo en la cómoda.

—Lo quiero cerca.

—Ah..., vale. —Ojalá pudiera hacerle otra foto con el móvil. Desde este ángulo no habría destello y la cara se parece aún más a la de mi abuela. ¿Podría ser ella..., quizá vestida para una obra de teatro? En el curso de preparación a la universidad fue presidenta del club de teatro—. Precisamente cuando llegó usted me estaba preguntando... —Ahora que hemos tenido una charla amistosa, me parece que puedo preguntar—. La mujer de la fotografía me recuerda a mi abuela. Un poco.

Me vibra el teléfono, aún lo tengo en silencio del encuentro en el Ayuntamiento. Me acuerdo de que tengo a Ian esperando en el coche. Pero el mensaje es de mi madre. Quiere que la llame.

—Tienen el mismo pelo —admite May Crandall sin entusiasmo—. Pero eso no es nada raro.

—No, supongo que no.

No me da más información. Devuelvo de mala gana el marco a su sitio en la mesilla de noche. May mira mi teléfono cuando vibra por segunda vez, es un mensaje de mi madre que quiere saber si he leído el otro. Sé que más me vale contestar.

—Me ha encantado conocerla —intento despedirme.

—¿Tiene que irse?

—Me temo que sí. Pero le preguntaré a mi abuela si se acuerda de su nombre.

Se humedece los labios y los chasquea un poco al separarlos.

—Vuelva y le contaré la historia de la fotografía. —Se gira con agilidad inesperada y, sin apoyarse en el bastón, se dirige hacia la puerta, añadiendo—: Tal vez.

Antes de que me dé tiempo a contestar, se ha ido.

Saco una fotografía mejor de la foto y me voy corriendo.

En el vestíbulo, Ian está revisando correos en el móvil. Al parecer se ha cansado de esperarme en el coche.

—Siento haber tardado tanto —digo.

—No pasa nada. Así he tenido tiempo de limpiar mi bandeja de entrada.

La directora de la residencia pasa cerca y frunce el ceño, preguntándose probablemente por qué sigo aquí. De no ser yo una Stafford, seguramente se habría parado para interrogarme. Pero como lo soy, aparta la vista y sigue su camino. Llevo dos meses de vuelta en Carolina del Sur y me sigue extrañando que me traten como a una estrella del rock solo por mi apellido. En Maryland he tratado a personas durante meses antes de que cayeran en la cuenta de que mi padre es senador. Era agradable tener la ocasión de demostrar quién soy por mí misma.

Ian y yo vamos al coche y enseguida quedamos atrapados en el atasco producido por unas obras en la carretera, así que aprovecho para llamar a mi madre. En casa no podré hablar

con ella, con la reunión de las Hijas de la Revolución Americana celebrándose allí. Y después de eso estará ocupada asegu-
rándose de que cada plato de porcelana y cada vaso de ponche
está guardado en el sitio que le corresponde. Así es Honeybee,
un as de la organización.

Y además nunca se le olvida un nombre.

—¿Conocemos a una tal May Crandall? —le pregunto
después de que me pida que «me pase un momento» por la
reunión de las Hijas de la Revolución Americana para causar
buena impresión, estrechar unas cuantas manos y ganar puntos
con las mujeres adecuadas. *Id a las mujeres y tendréis los votos*,
dice siempre mi padre. *Solo los hombres poco inteligentes me-
nosprecian su poder.*

—No creo —responde mi madre pensativa—. Crandall...
Crandall...

—May Crandall. Tendrá la edad de la abuela Judy. ¿Puede ser que fueran compañeras de bridge?

—Huy, imposible. La abuela Judy solo jugaba al bridge
con amigas. —Por «amigas» se refiere a conocidas de la familia
desde hace muchos años, en su mayoría con vínculos de generaciones. Gente de nuestro círculo social—. Lois Heartstein,
Dot Greeley, Mini Clarkson... Tú las conoces.

—Vale.

Quizá May Crandall no es más que una anciana desorientada con la cabeza llena de recuerdos mezclados que tienen
poco que ver con la realidad. Aunque eso no explica la fotografía de la mesilla.

—¿Por qué?

—Por nada especial. La he conocido hoy en la residencia
de mayores.

—Qué bien. Ha sido muy amable por tu parte charlar con
ella. Algunas de esas personas están muy solas. Lo más seguro es
que sepa quiénes somos, Avery. Le pasa a mucha gente.

Me horrorizo y confío en que Ian no haya oído la última frase de mi madre. Es embarazoso.

La fotografía no se me va de la cabeza.

—¿Quién va esta noche a ver a la abuela Judy?

—Tenía intención de ir yo. Después de la reunión de las Hijas de la Revolución Americana, si no se me hace muy tarde. —Mamá suspira—. Tu padre no podrá. —Como siempre, Honeybee se hace cargo de las responsabilidades familiares cuando el trabajo de papá le impide a él hacerlo.

—¿Por qué no te quedas en casa y descansas? —sugiero—. Ya voy yo.

—Pero ¿primero te pasarás por la reunión? —insiste mi madre—. Bitsy ha vuelto ya del lago Tahoe. Se muere de ganas de verte.

De pronto me invade la sensación horrible, desesperante, que debe de tener un animal salvaje cuando se cierra la puerta de su jaula. No me extraña que mi madre quiera que vaya a la reunión de las Hijas de la Revolución Americana. Bitsy está en la ciudad. Dada la lista de invitadas, no me voy a librar de un interrogatorio múltiple acerca de si Elliot y yo hemos fijado ya la fecha de la boda, elegido vajilla y cubertería, hablado de dónde y cuándo: a cubierto o al aire libre, en invierno o en primavera.

«No tenemos ninguna prisa. Ahora mismo estamos los dos muy ocupados. Queremos esperar a cuando nos apetezca» no es lo que Bitsy quiere oír. Una vez que ella y las damas de la HRA me tengan acorralada, no me dejarán ir hasta que hayan usado todas las armas de su arsenal para obtener las respuestas que buscan.

Tengo el triste presentimiento de que, después de todo, no me va a dar tiempo a ir a Magnolia Manor esta noche a preguntarle a mi abuela por la fotografía.

6

RILL

En mi sueño navegamos por el río. El motor modelo T que puso Briny en la popa del barco nos permite remontar la corriente con facilidad, como si no pesáramos nada. Queenie está sentada sobre el techo de la casa igual que si viajara en elefante. Lleva la cabeza echada hacia atrás y el pelo le ondea bajo el sombrero rojo de plumas. Canta una canción que aprendió de un viejo irlandés en un campamento.

—¿No es bonita como una reina? —pregunta Briny.

El sol calienta, los gorriones cantores trinan y róbalos gordos saltan en el agua. Una bandada de pelícanos blancos vuela formando una flecha que apunta hacia el norte, lo que significa que tenemos todo el verano por delante. No se ven barcos de vapor de ruedas, barcazas ni remolcadores por ninguna parte. El río es nuestro.

Solo nuestro.

—¿Y en qué te convierte eso? —me pregunta Briny en mi sueño.

—¡En la princesa Rill del reino de Arcadia! —grito.

Briny me pone una corona de madreselva en la cabeza y me nombra princesa, como hacen los reyes en los cuentos.

Por la mañana, cuando me despierto, conservo un sabor dulce en la boca. Me dura hasta que abro los ojos y me acuerdo de por qué estamos los cinco en la cama de Queenie y Briny, atravesados en el colchón igual que el contenido de la red de un pescador, brillantes de sudor.

Queenie no está. Pienso en ello justo antes de darme cuenta de lo que me ha despertado.

Alguien llama a la puerta.

El corazón me da un salto y yo también. Me pongo uno de los chales de Queenie por encima del camisón para ir a ver quién es. Al otro lado de la puerta está Zede y a pesar del cristal veo que su cara con largos bigotes blancos está larga y triste. Se me hace un nudo en el estómago.

Fuera, la tormenta ha amainado. El aire de la mañana se ha vuelto cálido y húmedo, pero abro la puerta y, cuando salgo, noto cómo el frío penetra el viejo camisón de algodón al que Queenie tuvo que coser un volante porque he crecido mucho. Dijo que una chica de mi edad no debía enseñar tanto las piernas.

Me cierro más el chal, no por Zede o porque tenga un cuerpo de mujer que ocultar —dice Queenie que ya llegará el momento, todavía no toca—, sino porque hay un muchacho en su bote. Es muy flaco, pero alto. Tiene la piel oscura como un cajún o como un indio. Aún no es un hombre, pero creo que es mayor que yo. Tendrá unos quince años. Zede siempre está adoptando a alguien; tiene prohijado a medio río.

El chico esconde su cara bajo una gorra raída y tiene la vista fija en el fondo de la barca y no en mí. Zede no nos presenta.

Sé lo que significa eso, pero me gustaría que no fuera así.

La mano de Zede me pesa en el hombro. Busca consolarme, pero quiero escapar de ella, salir corriendo a algún lugar de la orilla, corriendo tan deprisa que mis pies apenas dejen huella en la arena mojada.

Me suben lágrimas por la garganta y trago con fuerza. A mi espalda, Fern pega la cara al cristal. Era de esperar que se levantara y me siguiera. Nunca me deja alejarme demasiado.

—Los bebés de Queenie no han sobrevivido. —Zede no es de los que se andan por las ramas.

Algo se muere dentro de mí, un hermanito o una hermanita con el que tenía intención de jugar como si fuera una muñeca de porcelana nueva.

—¿Ninguno de los dos?

—El médico dijo que no. Que no pudo salvar a ninguno. Dijo que habría dado igual que Briny hubiera llevado antes a vuestra madre al hospital. Que los bebés no estaban destinados a vivir y eso es todo.

Sacudo la cabeza con fuerza en un intento de sacar esas palabras de mis oídos, como cuando te entra agua después de nadar. No puede ser verdad. No en el reino de Arcadia. El río es nuestro amuleto. Briny prometió que siempre nos protegería.

—¿Qué dijo Briny?

—Está destrozado. Lo he dejado allí con vuestra madre. Tenían que firmar unos papeles en el hospital y no sé qué más. Todavía no le habían contado a tu madre lo de los bebés. Supongo que Briny se lo dirá cuando esté mejor. Se pondrá bien, ha dicho el médico.

Pero conozco a Queenie. No estará bien. Nada la hace más feliz que tener un nuevo bebé en brazos.

Zede me dice que tiene que volver al hospital, que Briny no estaba bien esta mañana.

—He ido a ver si encontraba alguna mujer en el campamento del río que pudiera echaros un ojo, pero casi no había nadie. Ha habido líos con la policía y casi todos los del campamento se han echado al río. He traído a Silas para que os cuide hasta que pueda traer a vuestro padre del hospital. —Hace un gesto en dirección al chico que está en la lancha, el cual levanta la vista, sorprendido. Supongo que no sabía que Zede tenía intención de dejarlo aquí.

—Podemos cuidarnos solos.

Yo lo que quiero es que Queenie y Briny regresen a casa y volvamos a navegar río abajo. Lo quiero tanto que me duele por dentro, debajo del nudo que tengo en el estómago.

—No tenemos para darle de comer. —Camellia está en la puerta haciendo su aportación.

—Buenos días, señorita Rayo de Sol. —Zede llama siempre así a Camellia porque es justo lo opuesto de un rayo de sol.

—Pensaba coger unas ranas. —Lo dice como si acabaran de nombrarla capitana del *Arcadia*.

—De eso nada —le contesto—. No debemos salir del barco. Ninguno.

Zede señala a mi hermana con el dedo.

—No os mováis de aquí. —Mira el río de reojo—. No sé qué es lo que ha echado a la gente del campamento de la isla de Mud, pero es mejor que estéis aquí en este remanso, solos. Lo importante es que no hagáis ruido, no llaméis la atención ni nada de eso.

Algo me presiona el pecho. Algo pesado. La preocupación se hace un nido dentro de mí y se instala. No quiero que Zede se vaya.

Fern se acerca y se agarra a mi pierna. La cojo en brazos y acerco la barbilla a sus rizos despeinados. Es un consuelo.

Sale Gabion y lo cojo también a él y el peso de los dos no me deja moverme. El chal de Queenie se me tensa alrededor de los hombros y me aprieta.

Zede me pone de nuevo al mando y trae al chico, Silas, a bordo del *Arcadia*. Silas es más alto de lo que pensaba. Está flaco como una estaca, pero sería guapo si no tuviera el labio roto y un ojo amoratado. Si es verdad lo que Zede dijo de que viajaba de polizón en los trenes, ha tenido suerte de que los matones del ferrocarril no lo hayan dejado en peor estado.

Se sienta en la baranda del porche como si tuviera intención de quedarse ahí.

—Cuídalos —le dice Zede.

Silas asiente con la cabeza, pero salta a la vista que no está contento. Un azor pasa volando en busca de una presa y Silas lo mira. Luego se queda con la cara vuelta en dirección a Memphis.

Zede deja comida: un saco de harina de maíz, un puñado de zanahorias, diez huevos y algo de pescado salado.

Silas mira a Zede subirse al bote y desaparecer.

—¿Tienes hambre? —le pregunto.

Se vuelve a mirarme y entonces es cuando me acuerdo de que voy en camisón. Siento el aire húmedo tocándome la piel donde tengo el escote abierto por el peso de mis dos hermanos en brazos.

Silas aparta la vista como si se hubiera dado cuenta.

—Algo. —Tiene los ojos oscuros como la medianoche en el agua. Reflejan todo lo que mira: una garza que pesca cerca, ramas que cuelgan de un árbol quebrado, el cielo de la mañana con sus nubes blancas como la espuma... A mí—. ¿Sabes cocinar?

Por la manera en que lo dice parece que ha decidido ya que no sé.

Levanto la barbilla y me pongo recta. El chal de Queenie me aprieta aún más. Me parece que Silas no me gusta demasiado.

—Sí, sé cocinar.

—Buah —suelta Camellia.

—Tú te callas. —Dejo a los pequeños en el suelo y los empujo en su dirección—. Y cuídalos. ¿Dónde está Lark?

—Sigue acostada.

—Pues cuídala a ella también.

Lark puede escabullirse tan veloz y silenciosa como un susurro. Una vez se tumbó en un pequeño claro junto a un arroyo y se quedó dormida. Tardamos un día y media noche en encontrarla. Queenie casi se volvió loca de preocupación.

—Será mejor que me asegure de que no quemas el barco —refunfuña Silas.

Entonces lo decido: este chico no me gusta nada.

Pero cuando cruzamos la puerta, me mira, y una de las comisuras del labio partido sube y pienso que igual no es tan malo.

Encendemos la estufa y cocino lo mejor que sé. Ni Silas ni yo tenemos demasiada idea. La estufa es territorio de Queenie y nunca me he interesado por ella. Siempre he preferido estar fuera mirando el río y sus animales y escuchando a Briny contar historias sobre caballeros y castillos e indios del oeste, en lugares lejanos. Yo creo que Briny ha estado casi en todas partes.

Silas también ha visto mundo. Mientras cocinamos y nos sentamos a comer, habla de cómo ha viajado de polizón por cinco estados, de cómo ha arañado comida en campamentos y vivido de la tierra como un indio salvaje.

—¿Por qué no tienes mamá? —pregunta Camellia cuando se termina una tortita solo un poco quemada por los bordes.

Lark asiente en silencio porque también quiere saberlo, pero es demasiado tímida para preguntar.

Silas agita un elegante tenedor de plata que Briny encontró en la arena junto a los restos de un viejo barco abandonado.

—La tuve. Y la quería y eso, hasta los nueve años. Luego me fui y no he vuelto a verla.

—¿Y eso? —Miro muy seria a Silas, para ver si habla en broma. Con todo lo que estoy echando ya de menos a Queenie, no me cabe en la cabeza que alguien se aleje de su madre a propósito.

—Se casó con un tipo al que le gustaba beber whisky y pegar zurras. Aguanté un año y decidí que era mejor hacer mi vida. —El brillo de sus ojos se apaga un instante y no queda más que oscuridad. Pero con la misma rapidez se encoge de hombros y sonríe y entonces reaparecen los hoyuelos de las mejillas—. Me fui con unos recolectores que buscaban trabajo. Subimos hasta Canadá recogiendo manzanas y cosechando trigo. Cuando eso se terminó, volví al sur y trabajé en lo que podía.

—¿Con solo diez años? —Camellia chasquea los labios para hacerle saber que no se cree una palabra—. ¿Todo eso has hecho? Apuesto a que no.

Silencioso como un gato, Silas se gira en la silla, se levanta la falda de la gastada camisa y nos enseña las cicatrices que tiene en la espalda. Los cinco nos separamos de un salto de la mesa. Ni siquiera Camellia tiene una de sus respuestas de listilla preparada.

—Dad gracias de tener padre y madre. —Silas la mira con dureza—. No se os ocurra nunca abandonarlos si son buenos con vosotros. Los hay que no lo son.

Todos nos callamos durante un minuto y a Lark se le llenan los ojos de lágrimas. Silas rebaña los restos de su huevo y bebe un sorbo de agua. Nos mira por encima del borde de la taza de hojalata y frunce el ceño como si no entendiera por qué tenemos esas caras tan largas.

—Tú, peque. —Le pellizca la nariz a Lark y las pestañas de esta aletean como dos alas de mariposa—. ¿Te he contado lo que me pasó cuando conocí a Banjo Bill y a Henry, su perro bailarín?

Y así, de repente, ya está contando otra historia y luego otra más. El tiempo pasa volando mientras terminamos de comer y recogemos los platos sucios.

—No cocinas nada mal. —Silas se pasa la lengua por los labios cuando terminamos de fregar los platos en el cubo en el porche. Para entonces Fern lleva el vestido del revés porque se lo ha puesto ella sola y Gabion corretea medio desnudo buscando a alguien que lo limpie después de haber ido solo al retrete, que está en la parte trasera del barco. Menos mal que no se ha caído al río. El retrete no tiene suelo, solo agua.

Le digo a Camellia que lo saque al porche, le remoje el trasero en el río y se lo seque. Será lo más fácil.

A Camellia se le hinchan las aletas de la nariz. La única cosa en el mundo que le da miedo es la caca. Y esa es precisamente la razón por la que la obligo a limpiar a Gabby. Se lo merece. Esta mañana no ha ayudado en nada.

—¡Mellia! ¡Mellia! —grita nuestro hermano pequeño tambaleándose sobre sus piernas gordezuelas hacia la puerta, con el culo al aire—. *¡Toi susio!*

Mi hermana me mira con desdén, abre la puerta mosquitera y saca a Gabion, cogiéndolo de un brazo de manera que este queda de puntillas.

—Ya lo hago yo —susurra Lark con la esperanza de poner fin a la discusión.

—Deja que se ocupe Camellia. Tú eres demasiado pequeña.

Silas y yo nos miramos y sonríe un poco.

—¿No piensas vestirte en todo el día?

Me miro y me doy cuenta de que ni me he cambiado ni he pensado siquiera en ello, tan distraída estaba con las historias de Silas.

—Debería —contesto y me río de mí misma mientras descuelgo el vestido de su gancho y me quedo con él en la mano—. Pero tienes que salir, y nada de espiar.

Me ha venido un pensamiento raro a la cabeza mientras Silas y yo cocinábamos y cuidábamos de los pequeños. He estado jugando a que soy la mamá y Silas el papá y que esta es nuestra casa. Me ayudaba a no pensar en que Queenie y Briny siguen fuera.

Pero no pienso desnudarme delante de él, ni de nadie. Este último año he crecido tanto que ahora siempre me visto detrás de la cortina, como hace Queenie. Prefiero que me azoten con un látigo y me dejen señales a que alguien me vea desnuda.

—Sí, claro —dice Silas y pone los ojos en blanco—. ¿Y qué voy a ver? Si eres una niña.

Me quema la piel de la cabeza a los pies y me arden las mejillas.

Al otro lado de la puerta mosquitera, Camellia se ríe.

Me sonrojo aún más. Si pudiera, los tiraría a ella y a Silas al agua ahora mismo.

—Y llévate a los niños —ordeno cortante—. Las mujeres necesitan intimidad.

—¿Y tú cómo vas a saberlo? No eres una mujer. No eres más que un muñeco pelón solo que con pelo —bromea Silas, pero no me hace gracia, sobre todo porque Camellia le está oyendo. Está en el porche con Fern y Lark disfrutando del espectáculo.

Se me tensa hasta el último músculo del cuerpo. No me enfado con facilidad, pero cuando lo hago es como si tuviera fuego dentro.

—Pues tú no eres más que... ¡un palillo! Un niño palillo. Como haga un poco de viento, saldrás volando, de lo flaco que estás. —Le hago frente con toda la cara de odio que soy capaz de poner y los brazos en jarras.

—Por lo menos no tengo un pelo que parece un trapo para fregar el suelo. —Coge la gorra del gancho y se va furioso hacia la puerta. Desde algún punto de la pasarela grita—: Deberías unirte al circo, eso es lo que deberías hacer. ¡Podrías trabajar de payaso!

Me miro en el espejo de la pared y veo rizos rubios apuntando en todas las direcciones y la cara roja como la cabeza de un pájaro carpintero. Antes de que me dé tiempo a asimilar mi aspecto, ya estoy corriendo a la puerta y gritando:

—Silas... Silas como te llames. Si es que tienes apellido. No te necesitamos y...

En la orilla, de pronto se agacha y me hace un gesto con la mano. No puedo verle la cara debajo de la gorra, pero está claro que algo malo pasa. Ha visto algo en el bosque.

El calor de mi piel cambia de dirección, se vuelve interno.

—¡Eso, sigue andando! —grita Camellia inmiscuyéndose en la pelea—. Lárgate de nuestro barco, so palillo.

Silas nos mira y nos hace un gesto de nuevo con la palma de la mano. Los arbustos se cierran detrás de él cuando se interna en la espesura.

—No te has escondido. ¡Te estoy viendo!

—¡Cállate, Camellia! —Abro la puerta mosquitera y meto a Fern y a Lark.

Camellia me mira con el ceño fruncido. Está inclinada sobre la barandilla sujetando a Gabion por los brazos. El trasero de este se balancea en el agua mientras da patadas y ríe. Camellia simula dejarlo caer, luego le tira de los brazos y Gabion grita antes de que me dé tiempo a llegar.

—Vamos dentro. —Me asomo e intento coger a mi hermano del brazo, pero Camellia me aparta y lo sostiene por una mano.

—Se lo está pasando bien —dice— y dentro hace calor. —La melena espesa y oscura le cae hacia delante, las puntas llegan hasta el agua y la tocan como tinta derramada—. ¿Quieres ir a nadar? —le pregunta a Gabby. Por un momento creo que se va a tirar al agua con él.

En la orilla, Silas se asoma entre los arbustos y se lleva un dedo a los labios en un intento por hacernos callar.

—Algo pasa. —Cojo la mano de Gabion y lo levanto como si fuera un hueso de los deseos, tirando de mi hermana con él.

—Auuuu —protesta esta cuando se golpea el hombro contra la barandilla.

—¡Meteos dentro! —En la orilla se abren las hojas y veo algo negro, quizá un sombrero de hombre—. Hay alguien ahí.

Camellia resopla.

—Lo que pasa es que quieres que vuelva el chico. —No ve a Silas, pero este debe de estar a menos de tres metros de donde se rompe una rama y un cuervo echa a volar mientras grazna enfadado.

—Ahí, ¿lo ves?

Camellia ve la mancha negra. Es alguien que viene, eso seguro, pero, en lugar de entrar, Camellia va al otro lado del barco.

—Voy a bajar por la parte de atrás a ver quién es.

—No —susurro, pero lo cierto es que no estoy segura de qué hacer. Me gustaría soltar las amarras y sacar el *Arcadia* de la arena y navegar. El río está quieto y en calma esta mañana, así que nos resultaría fácil sacarlo, solo que no me atrevo. Con solo Camellia y yo y quizá Silas para evitar que el *Arcadia* encalle en un banco de arena o que lo arrollen una barcaza o un vapor de ruedas, no hay forma de saber lo que puede pasarnos en el río.

—Vamos dentro —digo—. Igual se piensa que el barco está vacío y sigue su camino.

Pero ¿qué puede traer a alguien a este remanso solitario?

—Tal vez es un cazador de ardillas —comenta Camellia esperanzada—. Y nos da una para cenar, si somos amables. —Sabe ser encantadora cuando quiere, por ejemplo, cuando alguien tiene caramelos para regalar o tortitas fritas para compartir alrededor de una hoguera.

—Zede nos dijo que no hiciéramos ruido. Y Briny nos dará una buena zurra si se entera. —Briny no nos ha zurrado a ninguno jamás, pero en ocasiones nos amenaza. La idea preocupa a Camellia lo suficiente para cruzar el porche hasta reunirse conmigo y entramos.

Atrancamos las puertas, nos subimos a la cama grande y corremos la cortina. Esperamos y escuchamos. Me parece oír al hombre en la orilla. Luego decido que ha debido de marcharse. Quizá no era más que un cazador o un vagabundo.

—¡Ah del barco!

—Chsss. —Me tiembla la voz. Ojos grandes y preocupados me miran. Cuando creces en el río, aprendes a desconfiar de desconocidos. El río es un sitio en el que terminan personas huyendo de cosas malas que han hecho en otra parte.

Camellia se me acerca.

—No es Zede. —Su susurro me eriza los pelos de la nuca.

El barco se mece un poco. Alguien ha puesto un pie en la pasarela.

Lark se arrima más a mí y Fern se acurruca en mi regazo, con la mejilla pegada a mi corazón.

El *Arcadia* se inclina hacia la orilla por efecto del peso del hombre. Es corpulento. Sea quien sea, Silas no es rival para él.

Me llevo un dedo a los labios. Los cinco nos quedamos paralizados como un cervatillo cuando su madre se aleja para alimentarse.

El hombre ya está en el porche.

—¡Ah del barco! —repite.

Vete... Aquí no hay nadie.

Intenta abrir la puerta y el pomo gira despacio.

—¿Ah del barco?

La puerta choca con la tranca y no se abre más.

Una sombra se dibuja en el cuadrado de la luz de la ventana en el suelo. Una cabeza de hombre. Los contornos de un sombrero. En la mano lleva un palo o un bate. Golpetea el cristal con él.

¿Un policía? Me temo que sí. La policía viene a por la gente que vive en barcos cuando les parece. Peinan los campamentos, dan palizas a los habitantes del río, se llevan lo que quieren y nos echan. Por eso siempre fondeamos solos, a no ser que Briny necesite estar con otras personas por algún motivo especial.

—¿Puedo ayudarlo, agente? —Silas interrumpe al desconocido cuando este se dirige a la otra ventana para ver el interior del barco. Sus sombras se alargan juntas en el suelo, una le saca una cabeza a la otra.

—¿Vives aquí, hijo?

—No. Estoy cazando. Mi padre está por aquí cerca.

—¿Viven aquí niños? —La voz no es despectiva, pero sí seria. ¿Y si detienen a Silas por mentir?

—No lo sé. No había visto el barco hasta ahora.

—No me digas. Me parece que me estás contando una patraña, golfillo del río. Te he oído hablar con alguien en este barco.

—No, señor. —Silas habla seguro como el amanecer—. Los he visto irse en un esquife hará... un par de horas quizá. Usted debe de haber oído a alguien del campamento. El sonido en el río viaja muy deprisa.

El hombre da un paso rápido hacia Silas.

—No me des lecciones, chico. Este es mi río y llevo media mañana buscando a esos niños. Haz que salgan, para que pueda llevármelos a la ciudad con su padre y su madre. —Cuando Silas no contesta, el agente se acerca más a él y las sombras de ambos se unen a la altura de las caras—. Mira, hijo, estoy seguro de que no quieres buscarte problemas con la ley. Además, ¿quién te ha puesto así el ojo? ¿No habrás estado metido en algo? ¿Tienes familia o eres un vagabundo?

—Tengo a mi tío Zede. Me cuida.

—Creía que me habías dicho que estabas cazando por aquí con tu padre.

—También tengo a mi padre.

—Si mientes a un agente de policía, terminarás en la cárcel, golfillo del río.

—No estoy mintiendo.

Oigo otras voces que se acercan. Hombres gritar en el bosque y un perro ladrar.

—Di a los niños que salgan. Nos han mandado sus padres a buscarlos.

—Dígame entonces cómo se llama su padre.

Camellia y yo nos miramos. Tiene los ojos grandes como dos avellanas. Niega con la cabeza. Está pensando lo mismo que yo. *Briny no mandaría a la policía aquí y, si lo hubiera hecho, habrían sabido llegar al barco.*

¿Qué quiere este hombre de nosotros?

Miramos por la rendija de la cortina cómo la sombra grande levanta a la pequeña por el cuello de la camisa. Silas tose y se atraganta.

—No me seas insolente, chico. No he venido en tu busca, pero, como sigas dándome problemas, te llevaremos con nosotros. Ya verás dónde terminan los arrapiezos como tú en esta ciudad.

Antes de que a Camellia le dé tiempo a sujetarme, me he bajado de la cama.

—No, Rill. ¡No!

Me agarra del camisón, pero se le desliza entre los dedos. Cuando abro la puerta, lo primero que veo son los pies de Silas suspendidos a quince centímetros del suelo. Tiene la cara morada. Intenta dar un puñetazo y el policía se ríe.

—¿Quieres pegarme, chico? Voy a meterte un minuto debajo del agua a ver si te tranquilizas.

—¡Pare, no! —Oigo llegar a más hombres. Hay algunos en la orilla y por estribor se acerca una embarcación a motor.

No sé qué hemos hecho mal —aparte de vivir en el río—, pero no hay duda de que nos han cogido. A Silas no le servirá de nada que lo maten o que se lo lleven con nosotros.

El agente lo suelta tan bruscamente que aterriza contra la pared de la casa y se golpea fuerte contra la madera.

—Vamos, Silas —digo, pero me tiembla tanto la voz que apenas se me oye—. Vete a casa. Ni siquiera deberías estar aquí. Queremos ir a ver a papá y a mamá.

Imagino que será mejor que colaboremos. De estar yo sola, podría quizá saltar del barco y llegar al bosque antes de que los hombres me cogieran, pero con mis hermanas pequeñas y Gabion es imposible. Si una cosa tengo clara es que Briny quiere que permanezcamos juntos pase lo que pase.

Me pongo recta, miro al agente de policía y trato de parecer lo mayor posible.

Este sonríe.

—Buena chica.

—¿Está bien mi padre?

—Pues claro que sí.

—¿Y mi madre?

—Perfectamente. Quiere que vayáis a visitarla.

Ni siquiera tengo que mirarle a los ojos para saber que miente. Es imposible que Queenie esté perfectamente ahora mismo. Esté donde esté, tendrá el corazón roto por los bebés.

Trago saliva y la noto bajar como una esquirla de hielo que se acabara de desprender de un témpano.

—Voy por los demás.

El agente se acerca, me coge del brazo y hace ademán de detenerme.

—Tú eres una listilla, me parece. —Se pasa la lengua por los dientes y por primera vez lo tengo lo bastante cerca para verle la cara debajo del ala brillante del sombrero. Tiene ojos grises y mezquinos, pero no fríos, como habría imaginado. Están interesados en algo, aunque no sé en qué. Baja la mirada de mi cara por el cuello y hasta el hombro que ahora mismo asoma del camisón—. Alguien debería darte de comer.

Detrás de él, Silas se pone de pie vacilante, parpadea y se tambalea. Pone una mano en un hacha que hay junto a la pila de leña.

No, intento decirle sin hablar. ¿Es que no oye a los hombres en la orilla y la lancha a motor que se acerca?

De dentro de la casa llega un chirrido suave y agudo lo bastante alto para que pueda oírlo. La puerta del retrete. Camellia está intentando escapar por la parte de atrás.

Haz algo.

—Mi hermanito está aprendiendo a dejar el orinal. Tengo que limpiarle antes de irnos o habrá caca por todas partes. A no ser que quiera hacerlo usted.

Es lo único que se me ocurre. A los hombres no les gustan los niños sucios.

Briny no los toca si no es para meterlos en el río, y eso es si no estamos Queenie o Camellia o yo para hacerlo.

El agente frunce los labios, me suelta y se vuelve para escuchar. Silas levanta la mano del hacha y cierra los puños con los flacos brazos estirados.

—Será mejor que te des prisa. —Los labios del policía esbozan una sonrisa, pero no hay amabilidad en ella—. Tu mamá espera.

—Silas, vamos. Vete. —Me detengo en la puerta, le miro pensando: *Vete, ¡corre!*

El agente mira a Silas y después a mí. Se echa la mano al cinturón, donde lleva el arma, la porra, las esposas de metal negro. ¿Qué piensa hacer?

—¡Vamos, vete! —grito y le doy a Silas un empujón—. ¡Briny y Zede no te querrían aquí!

Nos miramos. Niega ligeramente con la cabeza. Yo hago una inclinación con la mía. Cierra los ojos muy despacio, luego los abre y echa a correr por la pasarela.

—¡Hay uno en el agua! —grita otro policía desde la orilla. Los hombres de la lancha chillan y el motor acelera.

¡Camellia! Me giro y entro corriendo, con las pisadas pesadas del policía siguiéndome. Me empuja y aterrizo contra la estufa, él corre hasta la parte de atrás, donde la puerta de popa está abierta. Fern, Lark y Gabion están muy juntos, pegados a la barandilla. El hombre los obliga a entrar, con violencia, y aterrizan en un revoltijo, gritando y llorando.

—¡Mellia! ¡Mellia! —gime Gabion y señala el retrete, donde mi hermana ha bajado por el agujero de la letrina al agua. Ahora se dirige hacia la orilla, con el camisón mojado pegado a sus piernas largas y bronceadas. Un agente corre detrás de ella y los hombres de la lancha los siguen desde el río.

Se sube a una madera a la deriva, veloz y ágil como una liebre.

Gabion deja escapar un chillido.

El agente del porche trasero desenfunda su pistola.

—¡No!

Intento abalanzarme sobre él, pero tengo a Fern abrazada a las piernas. Nos caemos, llevándonos a Lark con nosotras. Esta grita fuerte y lo último que veo antes de que el cajón de leña me tape la vista es al hombre de la orilla que salta por encima de una rama, alarga una mano y sujeta a Camellia por la melena.

Cuando consigo levantarme, está resistiéndose como una loca, dando patadas, chillando y gruñendo. Agita brazos y piernas mientras el policía la sujeta lejos de sí.

Los hombres de la lancha motora echan la cabeza atrás y ríen como borrachos en una pelea en los billares.

Hacen falta tres de ellos para subir a mi hermana a la lancha y dos para sujetarla una vez allí. Cuando se dirigen al *Arcadia*, tienen a Camellia inmovilizada en el suelo. Están sucios de barro y furiosos porque huele a letrina y ahora ellos también.

El agente que está a bordo del *Arcadia* se ha quedado en la puerta con los brazos cruzados y apoyado en el quicio, como si se encontrara cómodo ahí.

—Ahora os vais a vestir... donde yo pueda veros. No queremos que se escape nadie más.

No pienso vestirme delante de él, así que me ocupo primero de Gabion, Lark y Fern. Por fin me pongo el vestido encima del camisón, aunque hace demasiado calor para ello.

El policía ríe.

—Muy bien. Si es lo que quieres... Ahora vais a estar muy calladitos y educados y os llevaremos a ver a vuestros padres.

Obedezco y lo seguimos fuera de la casa y cierro la puerta a mi espalda. No puedo tragar, ni respirar, ni pensar.

—Menos mal que los otros cuatro no han dado tanta guerra —dice uno de los agentes. Tiene a Camellia inmoviliza-da en el suelo de la lancha con los brazos detrás del cuerpo—. Esta es un gato salvaje.

—Pues huele más bien a jabalí —bromea el otro agente. Nos ayuda a acomodarnos. Coge a Gabion, a Fern y luego a Lark y les dice que se sienten en el suelo. Camellia me mira mal cuando yo hago lo mismo.

Cree que es mi culpa, que debería haberme resistido y haber impedido esto de alguna manera.

Tal vez debería haberlo hecho.

—Estos le van a gustar —grita uno de los hombres mien-tras el motor arranca y nos aleja del *Arcadia*. Pone su manaza en la cabeza de Lark y esta se aparta y gatea hasta pegarse a mí. Fern hace lo mismo. Solo Gabion es demasiado pequeño para saber que debería estar asustado.

—Le gustan rubios, ¿verdad? —El agente que subió a bordo del *Arcadia* ríe—. Lo que no sé es qué va a hacer con esta apestosa. —Señala con el mentón a Camellia y esta hace acopio de saliva y le escupe. El hombre hace ademán de abofetearla, pero luego se limita a reír y a limpiarse los pantalones.

—¿Al almacén Dawson entonces? —pregunta el hombre que lleva el motor.

—Eso dijeron.

No sé cuánto tiempo estamos en el agua. Cruzamos el río, luego el canal por el que el Wolf desemboca en el Misisipi. Cuando rodeamos el extremo de la isla de Mud, vemos Memphis. Edificios que se alargan hacia el cielo como monstruos esperando para engullirnos enteros. Pienso en saltar al agua. Pienso en escapar. Pienso en pelear. Veo pasar barcos: remolcadores, barcos de vapor de ruedas, lanchas de pesca y barcazas. Incluso una casa flotante. Pienso en gritar, agitar los brazos y pedir ayuda.

Pero ¿quién nos iba a ayudar?

Estos hombres son policías.

¿Nos llevan a la cárcel?

Una mano se posa en mi hombro como si alguien hubiera estado leyéndome los pensamientos. Se queda ahí hasta que llegamos a un embarcadero. Colina arriba veo más edificios.

—Ahora vas a ser muy buenecita y a no dejar que tus hermanos se porten mal —me susurra al oído el agente del *Arcadia*. A continuación les dice a los otros hombres que sujeten al gato salvaje un momento, hasta que «ella» nos haya visto a los cuatro.

Recorremos la pasarela en fila india, yo con Gabion a la cadera. Los tintineos y chasquidos de las máquinas y el olor a alquitrán caliente me atrapan y pierdo los aromas del río. Cruzamos una calle y oigo a una mujer cantar, a un hombre gritar, un martillo golpear metal. Las pelusas de las balas de algodón flotan en el aire como nieve.

En un arbusto escuálido de un extremo de un aparcamiento un cardenal emite su agudo canto: güip, güip, güip.

Hay un automóvil cerca. Un automóvil grande. Un hombre uniformado se baja de él y lo rodea hasta la puerta trasera y la abre para dejar salir a una mujer. Se queda mirándonos, parpadeando en la luz del sol. Es una mujer ni joven ni vieja, sino algo entremedias. Es gruesa y corpulenta, su cuerpo forma pliegues de grasa dentro del vestido de flores. Lleva el pelo corto; parte de él es castaño, parte gris.

Su cara me recuerda a una garza. Por cómo nos mira mientras los agentes nos colocan en fila. Sus ojos grises se mueven veloces y nerviosos, registrando todo lo que ocurre.

—Debería haber cinco —dice.

—Ahora viene la otra, señorita Tann —responde uno de los agentes—. Ha dado algo más de guerra. Intentó escaparse por el río.

La mujer chasquea la lengua contra los dientes, tch, tch, tch.

—Vosotros no haríais eso, ¿verdad? —Apoya un dedo en la barbilla de Fern y se inclina hasta que las narices de las dos casi se tocan—. Tú no eres una niña mala, ¿verdad?

Fern abre mucho sus ojos azules y dice que no con la cabeza.

—Qué huerfanitos tan encantadores —comenta la mujer, la señorita Tann—. Cinco preciosos niños de rizos rubios. Es perfecto. —Junta las palmas y se las lleva debajo de la barbilla. Se le arrugan las comisuras de los ojos y cierra la boca con fuerza, de manera que sonríe, pero le desaparecen los labios.

—Solo cuatro. —El agente hace un gesto con la cabeza en dirección a Camellia, que viene del río con un policía que la tiene sujeta por la nuca. No sé qué le habrán dicho, pero ha dejado de resistirse.

La señorita Tann frunce el ceño.

—Esa... no ha salido al resto de la familia, me parece. Es bastante vulgar. Aunque supongo que encontraremos quien se la quede. Casi siempre lo hacemos. —Retrocede y se tapa la nariz con una mano—. Santo cielo, ¿qué es ese olor?

La señorita Tann no parece contenta cuando ve a Camellia de cerca y toda sucia. Les dice a los agentes que la dejen en el suelo del automóvil y a nosotros en el asiento. En el suelo hay otros dos niños, una niñita rubia que tendrá la edad de Lark y un niño un poco mayor que Gabion. Los dos me miran con ojos castaños grandes y asustados. No dicen una palabra ni se mueven un milímetro.

La señorita Tann intenta quitarme a Gabion cuando voy a subirme. Cuando me resisto, frunce el ceño.

—Pórtate bien —dice y suelto a mi hermano.

Una vez que estamos en el coche, se coloca a Gabion en el regazo y le pone de pie para que pueda mirar por la ventana. Gabion salta, señala y parlotea, nervioso. Es la primera vez que viaja en automóvil.

—Qué maravilla de rizos. —Desliza los dedos por la cabeza de mi hermanito, levantándole el pelo color trigo de manera que forme picos igual que el de los muñecos de la feria del condado.

Gabion señala la ventana y grita contento:

—¡Caballito! ¡Caballito!

Ha visto a una niña pequeña fotografiándose a lomos de un potrillo moteado delante de una casa grande.

—En cuanto te quitemos la peste del río, serás un niñito muy guapo.

La señorita Tann arruga la nariz.

Me pregunto a qué se refiere. ¿Quién nos va a lavar y por qué?

Quizá es que no nos dejan entrar así en el hospital, me digo. *Quizá tenemos que lavarnos antes... ¿de ver a Queenie?*

—Se llama Gabion —aclaro, para que sepa cómo llamarlo—. O Gabby.

Gira deprisa la cabeza igual que hace un gato que ha visto un ratón en la despensa. Me mira como si hubiera olvidado que viajaba en el coche.

—Abstente de contestar preguntas que no te han hecho.

Alarga un brazo, carnoso y pálido, y coge a Lark y la separa de mí.

Miro a los dos niños muy juntos y asustados en el suelo y a continuación a Camellia. Los ojos de mi hermana me dicen que ya ha adivinado todo lo que yo ya sé, aunque no quiero reconocerlo.

No vamos al hospital a ver a mamá y a papá.

7

AVERY

Una suave luz matutina baña la residencia de mayores. Incluso con el aparcamiento recién construido en lo que antes era un jardín delantero, Magnolia Manor recuerda a otra época, a la elegancia de los tés vespertinos, a espléndidos bailes de cotillón y a cenas formales alrededor de la larga mesa de caoba que hay en el comedor. Es fácil imaginar a Escarlata O'Hara abanicándose debajo de los robles cubiertos de musgo que dan sombra al porche de columnas blancas.

Recuerdo lo que fue este sitio en otro tiempo, un poco al menos. Mi madre me trajo a una fiesta de una amiga suya que esperaba un bebé cuando yo tenía nueve o diez años. Por el camino me contó que había asistido a una importante recepción de un primo que se presentaba a gobernador de Carolina del Sur. Por entonces mi madre era una estudiante universitaria y no le interesaba en absoluto la política. No llevaba ni media hora en Magnolia Manor cuando se fijó en mi padre, al otro lado de la habitación. Se propuso averiguar quién era. Cuando supo que era un Stafford, decidió que se casaría con él.

El resto es historia. Un matrimonio entre dos dinastías políticas. El abuelo de mi madre había sido miembro de la cámara de representantes antes de jubilarse y su padre tenía un cargo político.

Esta historia me hace sonreír mientras subo los escalones de mármol e inserto el código en el inesperadamente moderno teclado que hay junto a la puerta principal. Aquí siguen viviendo personas importantes. No se permite entrar a cualquiera. Por desgracia, tampoco salir. Detrás de la mansión, los extensos jardines han sido cuidadosamente vallados con una ornada verja de hierro demasiado alta para que se pueda saltar. Las puertas están cerradas. Se puede mirar el lago y el espejo de agua, pero no acercarse a ellos... ni tampoco caerse.

A muchos de los residentes hay que protegerlos de sí mismos, esa es la triste realidad. A medida que su estado se deteriora, los van trasladando de un ala a otra. Acercándolos poco a poco a niveles más altos de cuidados delicadamente proporcionados. Es innegable que Magnolia Manor es un centro más exclusivo que la residencia en que vive May Crandall, pero ambos lugares se enfrentan a la misma compleja tarea, la de proporcionar dignidad, cuidados y consuelo cuando la vida entra en los años más difíciles.

Me dirijo a la Unidad de la Memoria, a la que nadie aquí se atrevería a llamar directamente Unidad de Alzhéimer. Cruzo otra puerta cerrada y llego a una sala de estar con un televisor que retransmite a gran volumen capítulos viejos de *La ley del revólver.*

Una mujer junto a la ventana me mira pasar con cara inexpresiva. Al otro lado del cristal, las rosas trepan frescas y cubiertas de rocío, de color rosa y llenas de vida.

Las rosas que hay al otro lado de la ventana de la abuela Judy son de un amarillo alegre. Está sentada en el sillón de orejas mirándolas cuando entro. Me detengo nada más cruzar el umbral y me preparo mentalmente antes de decir su nombre.

Me preparo para que me mire como me acaba de mirar la mujer de la salita, sin reconocerme en absoluto.

Espero que no sea así. Nunca se sabe.

—¡Hola, abuela Judy!

Pronuncio las palabras con tono animado, alto y alegre. Pero, incluso así, tardan en provocar una reacción.

Se vuelve despacio, hojea las páginas desperdigadas en su cabeza y, a continuación, con su dulzura acostumbrada, dice:

—Hola, cielo, buenas tardes.

Es por la mañana, claro. Tal y como me había temido, la reunión de las Hijas de la Revolución Americana anoche se alargó y no me libré del interrogatorio acerca de mis planes de boda. Me sentí como un desventurado saltamontes atrapado en un gallinero. Ahora tengo la cabeza llena de sugerencias, fechas con las que no puedo contar porque alguien importante estará fuera de la ciudad y ofrecimientos de préstamos de vajillas, cuberterías, cristalerías y mantelerías.

—Fenomenal, gracias —le digo a la abuela Judy y cruzo la habitación para abrazarla con la esperanza de que ese momento de cercanía le despierte algún recuerdo.

Por un instante parece que es así. Me mira fijamente a los ojos y por fin suspira y habla:

—Qué guapa eres. Tienes un pelo precioso.

Me lo acaricia y sonríe. La tristeza invade mi pecho. He venido con la esperanza de encontrar respuestas sobre May Crandall y la vieja fotografía de su mesilla de noche. No parece que vaya a ser posible.

—Había una niñita que tenía un ricito que le caía justo sobre la frente.

Mi abuela me sonríe y unos dedos frescos con piel fina como el papel me acarician la mejilla.

—Y cuando era buena, era muy buena —añado. La abuela Judy siempre me recibía con este poema cuando la visitaba de pequeña en su casa de la calle Lagniappe.

—Pero cuando era mala, era malísima —termina, y sonríe y me guiña un ojo y reímos juntas. Es como en los viejos tiempos.

Me siento en la butaca que hay al otro lado de la mesita redonda.

—Me encantaba cuando me recitabas ese poema.

En casa de Honeybee, de las niñas pequeñas se esperaba que fueran cualquier cosa menos malísimas, pero la abuela Judy siempre fue famosa por una vena de rebeldía que rayaba en la incorrección. Se había manifestado sobre cuestiones como los derechos civiles y la educación femenina mucho antes de que resultara aceptable que las mujeres tuvieran opinión.

Me pregunta si he visto a Welly, como le gusta llamar a mi padre, Wells.

Le cuento la sesión con la prensa de ayer y el encuentro en el Ayuntamiento, luego la interminable reunión de las Hijas de la Revolución Americana en Drayden Hill. Por supuesto, me salto las conversaciones sobre la boda.

La abuela Judy mueve la cabeza en señal de aprobación mientras hablo, entrecerrando un ojo y haciendo comentarios inteligentes sobre el encuentro en el Ayuntamiento.

—Wells no debe dejar que esa gente lo amilane. Les encantaría arrastrar a un Stafford por el barro, pero no lo conseguirán.

—Pues claro que no. Lo gestionó de maravilla, como hace siempre.

No menciono su aspecto cansado ni el lapsus mental que pareció sufrir durante las preguntas.

—Ese es mi chico. Un muchacho estupendo. No sé cómo ha podido tener una hija tan malísima.

—Pues ya ves, abuela. —Pongo una mano sobre una de las suyas y le doy un apretón. Está haciendo bromas y sabe quién es quién. Es un buen día—. Creo que en eso ha habido un salto generacional.

Espero una réplica ingeniosa, pero, en lugar de ello, se limita a decir:

—Bueno, pasa con muchas cosas. —Vuelve a recostarse en la butaca y me suelta la mano. Siento que el momento se escapa.

—Abuela Judy, quería preguntarte una cosa.

—Ah, ¿sí?

—Ayer conocí a una mujer que dice que te conoce. May Crandall. ¿Te suena?

Mi abuela suele recordar los nombres de viejas amistades y conocidos. Es como si el libro de sus recuerdos hubiera caído abierto y un viento persistente hubiera arrancado primero las páginas más recientes. Cuanto más antiguos son los recuerdos, más probable es que sigan intactos.

—May Crandall. —En cuanto repite el nombre, me doy cuenta de que lo reconoce. Me dispongo a sacar el teléfono para enseñarle la fotografía, cuando dice—: No, no me suena. —Levanto la vista del bolso y me está mirando con fijeza, con las pestañas blancas entrecerradas sobre sus ojos color aguamarina que, de pronto, han adquirido una extraña intensidad. Me temo que vamos a tener uno de esos momentos en que se detiene en medio de una conversación y, sin avisar, te saluda como si acabaras de llegar diciendo algo del tipo: «No esperaba verte hoy. ¿Qué tal estás?». Pero en lugar de eso añade—: ¿Por qué me lo preguntas?

—La conocí ayer... en una residencia de mayores.

—Sí, ya me lo has dicho. Pero mucha gente conoce a los Stafford de nombre, cielo. Debemos andarnos con cuidado. La gente siempre anda a la búsqueda de un escándalo.

—¿Escándalo? —La palabra me sobresalta.

—Pues claro.

De pronto noto el teléfono frío entre los dedos.

—No sabía que tuviéramos ningún secreto oscuro en la familia.

—Por favor. Pues claro que no lo tenemos.

Busco la fotografía y miro la cara de una mujer que me recuerda aún más a mi abuela, ahora que la tengo delante.

—Tenía esta fotografía. ¿Sabes quién es esta persona?

Quizá son ovejas negras de la familia. Parientes que mi abuela no quiere incluir en el árbol genealógico. Todos los clanes deben tener alguno. ¿Quizá hubo una prima que se fugó con un hombre que no debía y se quedó embarazada?

Le enseño la pantalla y espero a ver cómo reacciona.

—Queen... —murmura y se acerca el teléfono—. Ay...

Los ojos se le humedecen. La humedad forma lágrimas que rebosan y dibujan dos surcos en sus mejillas.

—Abuela Judy...

Está a miles de kilómetros de distancia.

De kilómetros no, de años. Está recordando algo. Sabe quién es la mujer de la fotografía. *Queen.* ¿Qué significa eso?

—¿Abuela Judy?

—Queenie. —Acaricia la imagen con la yema del dedo. Luego se vuelve hacia mí con una intensidad que me deja clavada en la silla—. No puede enterarse nadie... —dice en voz baja. Mira hacia la puerta, se inclina hacia mí y añade en un susurro—: Nunca deben saber lo del *Arcadia.*

Tardo un poco en responder. No hago más que pensar: ¿le he oído antes esa palabra?

—¿Qué? Abuela Judy, ¿qué es Arcadia?

—Chsss. —Lo dice tan fuerte que escupe una pequeña rociada de saliva en la mesa—. Si lo descubren...

—¿Quiénes?

Se mueve el pomo de la puerta y la abuela se recuesta de nuevo en la butaca y apoya una mano encima de la otra con cuidado. Con una mirada rápida, me indica que haga lo mismo.

Simulo tranquilizarme, pero tengo la cabeza repleta de hipótesis que van desde un encubrimiento tipo Watergate que involucre a mi abuelo a una especie de sociedad secreta de mujeres de políticos que ejercieran de espías durante la Guerra Fría. ¿En qué ha estado metida mi abuela?

Una amable auxiliar entra con café y galletas. En Magnolia Manor, a los residentes no solo se les da de comer, también tentempiés entre horas.

Mi abuela tapa enseguida mi teléfono con la mano mientras vuelve la cabeza hacia la camarera.

—¿Qué quiere?

La auxiliar no se inmuta ante un recibimiento tan brusco.

—El café de la mañana, señora Stafford.

—Ah, sí, claro. —La abuela Judy me hace un gesto discreto para indicarme que debo esconder el teléfono—. Nos vendrá bien una taza.

Miro la hora. Es más tarde de lo que pensaba. Se supone que tengo que reunirme con mi padre para un almuerzo y una inauguración en Columbia. «Una oportunidad de oro para que se os vea hombro con hombro en vuestro estado natal», como lo define Leslie. Estará la prensa y también el gobernador. Con los recientes rifirrafes entre Washington y la oposición, estos actos locales son importantes. Y lo entiendo, pero lo que en realidad me apetece es quedarme con la abuela Judy el tiempo suficiente para ver si consigo sacar algo en claro sobre May Crandall y qué tiene que ver Arcadia con ello.

¿Igual está hablando de un lugar? ¿De Arcadia, California? ¿De Arcadia, Florida?

—Tengo que irme, abuela. Tengo que acompañar a papá a una inauguración.

—Vaya por Dios, entonces no debería entretenerte.

La auxiliar entra y sirve dos tazas de café.

—Por si acaso —dice.

—Deberías llevártelo para el camino —bromea mi abuela. Nos han servido el café en tazas de porcelana.

—Me parece que no debo beber más esta mañana o me voy a poner a dar saltos. Solo he pasado para hablarte de May...

—Chsss. —El siseo y el dedo levantado me impiden terminar de decir el nombre. La abuela me fulmina con la mirada, como si hubiera dicho una palabrota en la iglesia.

La auxiliar, con buen criterio, recoge el carrito y se va. La abuela Judy susurra:

—Ten cuidado, Rill.

—¿C-cómo? —La intensidad me ha sobresaltado de nuevo. ¿Qué le pasa por la cabeza? *Rill.* ¿Es eso un nombre?

—Las paredes oyen. —La abuela señala una pared.

Su estado de ánimo cambia con idéntica velocidad. Suspira, coge la jarrita de porcelana y se echa una gota de leche en el café.

—¿Leche?

—No puedo quedarme.

—Vaya, cuánto lo siento. Ojalá tuvieras más tiempo. Me ha encantado que vengas.

Llegado este momento, llevamos charlando media hora por lo menos. Pero ya se le ha olvidado. Arcadia, sea lo que sea, ha desaparecido en la bruma.

Me regala una sonrisa tan limpia como una página en blanco. Es completamente sincera. No está segura de quién soy, pero intenta ser educada.

—Vuelve otro día que tengas más tiempo.

—Lo haré. —La beso en la mejilla y salgo de la habitación sin respuestas y con más preguntas de las que tenía.

Ahora sí que estoy decidida a seguir investigando. Necesito averiguar de qué va todo esto. Voy a necesitar otra fuente de información y sé dónde empezar a buscarla.

RILL

La sombra de la gran casa blanca envuelve el coche hasta engullirlo por completo. Altos magnolios se alinean en la acera formando un muro verde frondoso que me recuerda al castillo de la Bella Durmiente. Nos oculta de la calle, donde niños juegan en jardines y madres empujan carritos de bebé por las aceras. En el porche delantero de esta casa también hay un cochecito de niño. Es viejo y le falta una rueda, así que está torcido. Si alguien metiera en él un bebé, lo más seguro es que se caería.

Un niñito está acuclillado debajo de uno de los magnolios igual que un mono. Será de grande como Lark, unos cinco o seis años. Nos mira llegar con el automóvil pero no nos sonríe, ni saluda ni se mueve. Cuando el automóvil se detiene, desaparece entre las hojas.

Un segundo después lo veo salir a gatas de debajo del árbol y colarse por debajo de una alta valla de hierro que encierra el jardín trasero de esta casa y de la propiedad de al lado. El pequeño edificio contiguo tiene aspecto de haber sido en otro tiempo una escuela o una iglesia. Hay algunos niños jugando en los balancines y columpios del jardín, pero las puertas y ventanas están tapiadas y en la madera apenas queda rastro de pintura. Delante del porche crecen zarzas, lo que me hace pensar de nuevo en la Bella Durmiente.

Camellia se levanta del suelo del automóvil para mirar.

—¿Esto es el hospital? —Dirige a la señorita Tann una mirada que le deja claro que no se lo cree. Mi hermana ha descansado durante el trayecto y está preparada para seguir peleando.

La señorita Tann se vuelve hacia ella y cambia de postura a Gabion, que se ha quedado dormido como un tronco en su regazo. Se le cae el bracito y los dedos gordezuelos se abren y cierran. Mueve los labios como si estuviera lanzando besos en sueños.

—¿Cómo vais a ir al hospital así? Apestando a río e infestados de parásitos. La señora Murphy se ocupará de vosotros y luego, si sois muy buenos, ya veremos lo del hospital.

Una chispa de esperanza trata de prender en mí, pero no encuentro yesca con que alimentarla. Se apaga en cuanto la señorita Tann me mira.

Fern trepa por mi pecho y me clava las rodillas en el vientre.

—Quiero con Briny —susurra llorosa.

—Bajad. Ya hemos llegado. Aquí vais a estar muy bien —nos dice la señorita Tann—. Siempre que seáis buenos, ¿entendido?

—Sí, señora. —Intento contestar por todos, pero Camellia no piensa rendirse tan fácilmente.

—¿Dónde está Briny? —No le gusta nada de lo que está pasando y está a punto de ponerse como una fiera. Noto cómo se acerca la tormenta.

—¡Calla, Camellia! —la regaño—. Obedece.

La señorita Tann sonríe un poco.

—Muy bien. ¿Veis? Todo esto puede ser muy fácil. La señora Murphy os cuidará.

Espera a que el chófer rodee el automóvil y abra la portezuela. Luego sale la primera, con mi hermanito en brazos y Lark de la mano. Lark me mira con los ojos muy abiertos, pero, como de costumbre, no se va a resistir. Es mansa como una gatita.

—Ahora tú. —La mujer me reclama, así que salgo del coche y mis rodillas chocan con el niño y la niña de ojos castaños que están en el suelo. Fern me echa los brazos al cuello, por lo que apenas puedo respirar.

—Ahora vosotros dos.

Los niños que estaban en el coche antes que nosotros salen al camino de entrada.

—Y ahora tú. —La señorita Tann baja la voz cuando mira a Camellia. Me da a Gabion y a Lark y se sitúa junto a la portezuela, con las piernas separadas y bloqueando la salida con el cuerpo. No es una mujer menuda. Es más alta que yo y parece fuerte.

—Vamos, Camellia. —Le estoy suplicando que se porte bien y ella lo sabe. Hasta el momento no se ha movido un milímetro. Tiene una mano detrás de la espalda y me temo que esté planeando intentar salir por la otra puerta. ¿De qué serviría? No sabemos dónde estamos ni cómo volver al río o llegar al hospital. Nuestra única esperanza es que, como dice la señorita Tann, si nos portamos bien, consigamos ver a Queenie y a Briny.

O que Silas les cuente lo que ha pasado y vengan a buscarnos.

El hombro de Camellia se mueve un poco y oigo moverse el picaporte. La puerta no se abre y se le hinchan las aletas de la nariz. Se gira para empujar, y la señorita Tann suspira y mete la cabeza dentro del coche.

Cuando la saca, arrastra a Camellia por la ropa.

—¡Ya está bien de tonterías! Ahora vas a obedecer y a portarte bien.

—¡Camellia, para! —grito.

—¡Mellia, no, no! —La voz de Fern es como un eco.

Gabion echa la cabeza hacia atrás y chilla, el sonido rebota en la casa y se adentra flotando entre los árboles.

La señorita Tann cambia de posición el brazo, de manera que tiene bien sujeta a Camellia.

—¿Nos estamos entendiendo? —Tiene las mejillas redondas rojas y sudorosas. Detrás de las gafas, sus ojos grises son saltones.

Cuando Camellia aprieta los labios pienso que la señorita Tann la va a abofetear, pero no es así. En lugar de ello le susurra algo al oído y luego se endereza.

—Vas a ser buena, ¿a que sí?

Camellia sigue teniendo la boca como si acabara de chupar un limón.

El instante se balancea igual que una botella en el borde de la cubierta del *Arcadia* antes de caer al agua y que la arrastre el río.

—¿A que sí? —repite la señorita Tann.

Los ojos oscuros de Camellia echan chispas, pero asiente con la cabeza.

—Así me gusta.

La señorita Tann nos hace formar una fila y Camellia sube los peldaños del porche con nosotros. Desde detrás de la verja de hierro nos miran niños y niñas de todas las edades. Ni uno solo de ellos sonríe.

Dentro, la casona huele mal. Todas las cortinas están echadas y hay penumbra. En el vestíbulo delantero hay una escalera ancha. Dos niños están sentados en el escalón de arriba. Uno de ellos me recuerda a Silas en grande, solo que tiene un pelo tan rojo como la piel de un zorro. Estos niños no se parecen nada a los del jardín o al del árbol. No pueden ser todos hermanos.

¿Quiénes son? ¿Cuántos hay? ¿Viven aquí? ¿Los han traído a todos para lavarlos antes de llevarlos a visitar a sus mamás y papás en el hospital?

¿Qué es este sitio?

Nos llevan a una habitación donde una mujer espera detrás de un escritorio. Es menuda, comparada con la señorita Tann, con unos brazos tan delgados que se le ven los huesos y las venas. La nariz le sobresale entre las gafas, ganchuda como el pico de una lechuza. Se le arruga cuando nos mira. Luego sonríe, se pone de pie y saluda a la señorita Tann.

—¿Cómo está, Georgia?

—Muy bien, gracias, señora Murphy. La verdad es que he tenido una mañana muy productiva.

—Ya lo veo. —La señora Murphy pasa los dedos por la superficie del escritorio y dibuja caminos en el polvo mientras se acerca a nosotros. Se le levanta una de las comisuras de la boca dejando ver un colmillo—. Cielo santo. ¿De dónde ha sacado a estos pobres desgraciados?

Los pequeños se arremolinan a mi alrededor, incluso los dos que no conozco. Tengo a Fern apoyada en una cadera y a Gabion en la otra. Se me están empezando a dormir los brazos, pero no pienso soltarlos.

—¿No dan muchísima lástima? —dice la señorita Tann—. Creo que los hemos rescatado justo a tiempo. ¿Tiene sitio para todos? No le causaría demasiado trastorno, espero trasladar a algunos enseguida.

—Pero ¡qué pelo! —La señora Murphy se acerca más y la señorita Tann la sigue. Su grueso cuerpo oscila de un lado a otro cuando se mueve. Por primera vez me doy cuenta de que es coja.

—Una maravilla, ¿verdad? Cuatro rubios con el pelo rizado de la misma familia y luego... esa. —Resopla y mira a Camellia.

—Pero esa no es de la misma camada. —La señora Murphy me mira—. ¿Es hermana tuya?

—S-sí —digo.

—¿Y cómo se llama?

—C-Camellia.

—Un nombre muy elegante para una niña tan vulgar. Y esas ridículas pecas. Me parece que la cigüeña se equivocó de nido contigo.

—No es nada colaboradora —le advierte la señorita Tann—. Ya nos ha dado problemas. Es la ovejita negra, en más de un sentido.

La señora Murphy entrecierra los ojos.

—Vaya por Dios. Bueno, pues en esta casa exijo buen comportamiento. Los que no cumplan mis exigencias no podrán dormir arriba en compañía de los otros niños. —Se pasa la lengua por los dientes.

Me quedo helada. Fern y Gabion me abrazan más fuerte del cuello. Lo que quiere decir la señora Murphy está muy claro. Si Camellia la hace enfadar, se la llevará y la dejará... en otro sitio.

Camellia asiente, pero sé que no tiene ninguna intención de obedecer.

—A estos otros dos, con el pelo castaño claro..., los encontré por el camino—. La señorita Tann obliga a acercarse al niño y la niña que han ido en el suelo del coche con Camellia. Ambos tienen el cabello largo y liso, de un tono pajizo, y grandes ojos marrones. Por cómo se aferra el niño a la niña, estoy segura de que ella es la hermana mayor—. También son vagabundos del río, claro, aunque cuando llegué el campamento estaba casi vacío. Alguien debió de correr la voz.

—Qué caritas tan encantadoras.

—Desde luego. Estos de los rizos son casi angelicales. Creo que van a estar muy solicitados.

La señora Murphy se aleja.

—¡Por el amor de Dios! Apestan a río. Así no puedo tenerlos en casa. Tendrán que quedarse en el jardín hasta la hora del baño.

—No los deje salir sin asegurarse de que entienden perfectamente las reglas de esta casa. —La señorita Tann le pone una mano en el hombro a Camellia y esta se retuerce, por eso sé que la mujer le está clavando los dedos con fuerza—. A esta le gusta escaparse. ¡Pero si hasta intentó bajarse del automóvil, nada menos! Esa escoria que vive en el río sabe cómo hacer niños, pero no cómo enseñarles modales. Me temo que esta tanda le va a dar trabajo.

—Pues como todas. —La señora Murphy asiente con la cabeza. De nuevo me mira a mí—: ¿Cómo te llamas?

—Rill. Rill Foss. —Trato de no decir nada más, pero las palabras salen de mi boca. No entiendo de qué están hablando y el corazón me late con fuerza. Me tiemblan las rodillas por el peso de mis hermanitos, pero no solo por eso. Estoy muerta de miedo. ¿Tiene la señorita Tann intención de dejarnos aquí? ¿Cuánto tiempo?—. ¿Cuándo podremos ir a ver a nuestros padres? Están en el hospital. Mamá ha tenido un bebé y...

—A callar —dice la señora Murphy—. Lo primero es lo primero. Saca a todos al vestíbulo y que se sienten junto a la escalera pegados a la pared, de menor a mayor. Esperad ahí y nada de hacer ruido ni travesuras. ¿Entendido?

—Pero...

Esta vez la señorita Tann me pone a mí la mano en el hombro. Sus dedos me pellizcan la carne alrededor del hueso.

—De ti no espero problemas. Estoy segura de que eres más lista que tu hermana.

Me baja el dolor por el brazo y noto que Gabion se me escurre.

—S-sí, señora. S-sí, señora.

Me suelta. Me coloco a Gabion de nuevo en la cadera. Quiero frotarme el hombro, pero no lo hago.

—Y..., Rill, ¿qué clase de nombre es ese?

—Es del río. Me lo puso mi padre. Dice que suena tan bonito como una canción.

—Pues te pondremos un nombre como Dios manda. Un nombre de verdad para una niña de carne y hueso. May, por ejemplo. May Weathers.

—Pero soy...

—May. —Me indica la puerta y los otros niños me siguen. A Camellia vuelven a advertirle que no haga nada más que sentarse en silencio en el vestíbulo.

Los pequeños gimen y lloriquean como cachorros cuando intento despegarlos de mí y dejarlos en el suelo. Los dos niños que estaban al final de las escaleras se han ido. Fuera, los niños juegan a martín pescador. Conozco el juego de cuando hemos ido a la escuela. Cuando empieza el curso, Queenie y Briny suelen fondear cerca de alguna población para que Camellia y yo, y ahora también Lark, podamos ir. El resto del tiempo leemos libros y Briny nos enseña aritmética. Es capaz de calcular casi cualquier cosa. Camellia es una maga de los números. Incluso Fern se sabe ya el alfabeto y eso que es demasiado pequeña para ir a la escuela. El otoño próximo Lark irá a primer curso...

Lark me está mirando con sus grandes ojos de ratoncito asustado y una sensación de angustia brota dentro de mí como un remolino de aguas negras. No lleva a ninguna parte. Se limita a girar una y otra vez en círculos.

—¿Nos van a llevar a la cárcel? —susurra la niñita. Esa cuyo nombre ni siquiera sé.

—No. Claro que no —digo—. No se mete en la cárcel a niños pequeños.

¿O sí? La mirada de Camellia viaja hacia la puerta principal. Se está preguntando si puede echar a correr y conseguir escapar.

—Ni se te ocurra —le susurro indignada. La señora Murphy nos ha dicho que no hagamos ruido. Cuanto mejor nos portemos, más probabilidades tendremos de que nos lleven a donde queremos ir, o eso supongo—. Tenemos que estar juntos. Briny vendrá a buscarnos en cuanto sepa que no estamos en el *Arcadia.* En cuanto Silas le cuente lo que ha pasado. Tenemos que estar todos en el mismo sitio cuando llegue. ¿Me oyes? —Hablo como Queenie cuando hay que romper hielo en la superficie del río y no nos deja subirnos a la barandilla, no sea que un témpano golpee el barco y nos haga caer al agua. En momentos como esos quiere que entendamos que no es no. No lo hace muy a menudo.

Todos asienten con la cabeza excepto Camellia. Incluso la niña y el niño.

—¿Mellia?

Camellia emite un murmullo de asentimiento. Se rinde, se pega las rodillas al pecho, cruza los brazos y baja la cabeza hasta golpeársela para dejarnos claro que no está contenta en absoluto.

Les pregunto sus nombres a los otros niños y ninguno de los dos dice una palabra. Por las mejillas del niñito ruedan gruesas lágrimas y su hermana lo abraza con fuerza.

Un pájaro choca contra el cristal de la puerta principal y todos nos sobresaltamos. Me estiro para ver si ha conseguido levantarse y remontar el vuelo. Es un petirrojo pequeñito. Quizá es el mismo que solemos oír en el río, que nos ha seguido. Ahora se tambalea y sus alas despiden destellos en la luz lenta y perezosa de la tarde. Me gustaría poder rescatarlo antes de que lo atrape un gato —al entrar aquí hemos visto al menos tres entre los arbustos—, pero no me atrevo. La señorita Tann podría pensar que intento escaparme.

Lark se pone de rodillas para mirar, le tiemblan los labios.

—No le ha pasado nada —susurro—. Siéntate. Pórtate bien.

Obedece.

El pájaro se aleja tambaleándose hacia los peldaños de manera que tengo que separarme un poco de la pared para verlo. *Vuela*, pienso. *Date prisa. Echa a volar antes de que te cojan.*

Pero se queda allí, con el pico abierto y jadeando con todo el cuerpo.

Vuela. Vuelve a casa.

Estoy atenta. Si viene un gato, quizá pueda espantarlo desde la ventana.

Llegan palabras de debajo de la puerta al otro lado del vestíbulo. Me levanto muy despacio y me acerco de puntillas.

Capto palabras sueltas de lo que dicen la señorita Tann y la señora Murphy, pero no entiendo nada.

—... papeles de renuncia de la patria potestad de los cinco hermanos en el hospital mismo. Así de fácil. Es la mejor manera de cortar lazos. Lo más complicado fue encontrar la localización exacta del barco. Estaba fondeado solo frente a la isla de Mud, según me dijo la policía. La pecosa intentó escapar nadando por el retrete. Así que no huele solo a río.

Se oyen risas, pero son siniestras, como el graznido del cuervo.

—¿Y los otros dos?

—Los encontré cogiendo flores cerca de donde estaban fondeados varios barcos de vagabundos del río. Enseguida tendremos papeles para ellos. No darán ningún problema. También parecen dóciles. Mmm..., Sherry y Stevie. Se pueden llamar así. Es mejor que los acostumbremos a estos nombres cuanto antes. Son una monería, ¿verdad? Y pequeños. Es probable que no estén aquí mucho tiempo. Tenemos planeada una visita para el mes que viene. Espero que estén preparados para entonces.

—Pues claro que sí.

—Para los otros cinco, May, Iris, Bonnie..., Beth... y Robby, creo. Weathers puede servir de apellido. May Weathers, Iris Weathers, Bonnie Weathers... Suena bien.

De nuevo risas. Suben tanto de volumen que me tengo que separar de la puerta.

Las últimas palabras que oigo son de la señora Murphy.

—Yo me ocupo. Puede estar segura de que estarán bien preparados.

Para cuando salen, he vuelto a mi sitio y comprobado que todos están bien pegados a la pared. Incluso Camellia levanta la cabeza y se sienta a lo indio, como hacemos en la escuela.

Esperamos, quietos como estatuas, mientras la señora Murphy acompaña a la señorita Tann a la puerta. Solo nuestros ojos se giran para verlas hablar en el porche.

El petirrojo ha llegado dando saltitos hasta los escalones, pero sigue allí, indefenso. Ninguna de las dos lo ha visto.

Vete.

Pienso en el sombrero rojo de Queenie. *Vete volando a buscar a Queenie y dile dónde estamos.*

Vete.

La señorita Tann da unos pasos cojeando y está a punto de pisar el pájaro. Me quedo sin respiración y Lark da un respingo. Entonces la señorita Tann se detiene para añadir alguna cosa.

Cuando echa a andar de nuevo, el petirrojo por fin se aleja volando.

Le hará saber a Briny que estamos aquí.

La señora Murphy entra en la casa, pero no sonríe. Regresa a la habitación al otro lado del vestíbulo y cierra la puerta.

Esperamos sentados. Camellia vuelve a esconder la cara entre las piernas.

Fern recuesta la cabeza en mi hombro. La niñita —la señorita Tann la ha llamado Sherry— coge la mano de su hermano.

—Tengo hambre —susurra este.

—*Teno hambe* —le imita Gabion en voz demasiado alta.

—Chsss. —Su pelo es suave al tacto cuando le acaricio la cabeza—. Tenemos que estar callados. Como en el escondite. Como si fuera un juego.

Gabion cierra fuerte la boca y se esfuerza. Como solo tiene dos años, nunca le dejamos jugar con nosotros a «Vamos a jugar a que éramos...», así que está contento de poder participar por una vez.

Me gustaría que fuera un juego de verdad. Me gustaría conocer las reglas y cuál es el premio si ganamos.

Pero ahora mismo lo único que podemos hacer es esperar a ver qué ocurre.

Esperamos, esperamos y esperamos.

Parece que ha transcurrido una eternidad cuando sale la señora Murphy. Yo también estoy hambrienta, pero, por la expresión de su cara, sé que es mejor no decir nada.

Se acerca a nosotros con los brazos en jarras, los puños cerrados y las caderas que sobresalen bajo su vestido negro floreado.

—Siete más —dice, frunciendo el ceño y mirando escaleras arriba. De su boca sale un aliento espeso como la niebla. Huele mal—. Claro que tampoco tenemos mucha elección, puesto que vuestros padres no pueden ocuparse de vosotros.

—¿Dónde está Briny? ¿Dónde está Queenie? —salta Camellia.

—¡A callar ahora mismo! —La señora Murphy se tambalea mientras nos pasa revista y ahora sé a qué le olía el aliento. A whisky. He visitado los suficientes billares para reconocerlo.

La señora Murphy señala a Camellia con el dedo.

—Tú tienes la culpa de que tengan que estar todos aquí en lugar de fuera, jugando. —Recorre el vestíbulo a grandes zancadas y sus pasos dibujan una línea torcida.

Seguimos esperando. Los pequeños por fin se han quedado dormidos y Gabion está tumbado en el suelo. Pasan por allí unos cuantos críos, mayores y menores, niños y niñas. La mayoría llevan ropas que les quedan grandes o pequeñas. Ni uno solo nos mira. Pasan a nuestro lado como si no nos hubieran visto. Mujeres vestidas de blanco se mueven apresuradas por el vestíbulo. Tampoco ellas nos ven.

Me rodeo los tobillos con los dedos y aprieto con fuerza, para asegurarme de que aún estoy aquí. Casi tengo la impresión de que me he convertido en el Hombre Invisible, ese sobre el que escribió el señor H. G. Wells. A Briny le encanta esa historia. Nos la ha leído un montón de veces y Camellia y yo jugamos a ella con los niños de los campamentos. Nadie puede ver al Hombre Invisible.

Cierro los ojos y finjo durante un rato.

Fern necesita un orinal y, antes de que se me ocurra una solución, se ha hecho pis encima. Una mujer uniformada de pelo oscuro pasa a nuestro lado y ve la mancha en el suelo. Coge a Fern del brazo.

—Eso aquí no se hace. Hay que saber pedir ir al retrete. —Se saca un paño del delantal y lo tira sobre la mancha—. Límpialo —me dice—. La señora Murphy se va a poner furiosa.

Se lleva a Fern y yo hago lo que me ordena. Cuando vuelve Fern, ha lavado las bragas y el vestido y los lleva mojados. La señora nos dice al resto que también podemos ir al retrete, pero que nos demos prisa y volvamos luego junto a las escaleras.

No llevamos mucho tiempo en nuestros sitios cuando fuera alguien toca un silbato. Oigo niños corretear. Muchos. No hablan, pero el eco de sus pisadas traspasa la puerta al final del vestíbulo. Se quedan allí un rato y a continuación hay un estruendo, como si subieran corriendo unas escaleras, pero no las que tenemos nosotros al lado.

En el piso de arriba, los tablones del suelo crujen y rechinan como hacen la borda y el entablado del *Arcadia.* Es un sonido familiar y cierro los ojos para escuchar y fingir que puedo trasladarnos de vuelta sanos y salvos a bordo de nuestro barquito.

Mi deseo se esfuma enseguida. Una mujer de vestido blanco se detiene y dice:

—Venid por aquí.

Nos ponemos de pie para seguirla. Camellia va la primera y yo cierro la fila de los niños más pequeños, incluidos Sherry y Stevie.

La señora nos hace cruzar la puerta al final del vestíbulo y allí todo tiene un aspecto distinto. Es feo y viejo. De la pared cuelgan tiras de papel y estopilla. En uno de los lados hay una cocina y dos mujeres de color tienen algo al fuego. Espero que nos den de comer pronto. Tengo la sensación de que el estómago se me ha encogido y es del tamaño de un cacahuete.

De solo pensar eso, me entran unas ganas horribles de comer cacahuetes.

Del otro lado de la cocina arranca una escalera grande. Se le ha borrado casi toda la pintura, como si la hubieran subido y bajado muchas veces. A la barandilla le faltan la mitad de los balaústres. Hay un par sueltos que cuelgan igual que los pocos dientes que se le ven al viejo Zede cada vez que sonríe.

La mujer del uniforme blanco nos lleva al piso de arriba y nos coloca de espaldas a la pared de un pasillo. Otros niños hacen fila cerca y oigo correr el agua de una bañera en alguna parte.

—No se habla —dice la mujer—. Esperaréis aquí en silencio hasta que os toque el turno de bañaros. Ahora quitaos la ropa y dejadla bien doblada en un montón a vuestros pies. Toda.

El rubor me escuece en la piel, caliente y pegajoso, y miro a mi alrededor y veo a los otros niños, grandes y pequeños, haciendo lo mismo que nos han ordenado hacer a nosotros.

9

AVERY

*M*ay Crandall. ¿Estáis seguros de que no os suena el nombre? —Voy en la limusina con mi madre y mi padre de camino a una inauguración en Columbia—. Es la mujer que encontró mi pulsera en la residencia ayer. —Digo «encontró» porque suena mejor que «me la quitó de la muñeca»—. La del diseño Greer con las libélulas de granate, la que me regaló la abuela Judy. Creo que esta mujer la reconoció.

—Tu abuela se ponía mucho esa pulsera. Cualquiera que la viera con ella puede recordarla. Es bastante singular. —Mamá bucea en sus archivos de recuerdos con los labios perfectamente delineados muy cerrados—. No, ese nombre no me suena. ¿Igual es de los Crandall de Asheville? Cuando era joven salí con un chico de esa familia..., antes de conocer a tu padre, claro. ¿Le preguntaste de dónde es su familia?

Para Honeybee, al igual que para todas las sureñas de buena familia de su generación, es una pregunta de lo más normal cuando se conoce a alguien. *Encantada de conocerte. Qué buen día hace, ¿verdad? Y, dime, tu familia ¿de dónde es?*

—No se me ocurrió preguntarle.

—De verdad, Avery, que no sé qué vamos a hacer contigo.

—¿Encerrarme en el cobertizo?

Mi padre ríe y levanta la vista de un maletín lleno de documentos que ha estado leyendo.

—A ver, Honeybee. La he tenido bastante ocupada. Y a nadie se le da tan bien reunir información como a ti.

Mamá le da una palmada cariñosa.

—Cállate.

Mi padre le coge la mano y se la besa. Estoy atrapada entre los dos y me siento como si tuviera trece años.

—A ver, chicos, que estamos en público.

Desde mi regreso a casa he vuelto a adoptar expresiones como «chicos», que en el norte había eliminado de mi vocabulario. Son buenas palabras, he decidido. Muy agradecidas, igual que el humilde cacahuete cocido.

—¿Te suena una tal May Crandall, Wells, que fuera amiga de tu madre? —Honeybee recupera el hilo de la conversación.

—Creo que no. —Mi padre hace ademán de rascarse la cabeza y entonces se acuerda de que le han rociado generosamente con laca. Los actos al aire libre exigen preparación extra. Nada peor que terminar en un periódico con aspecto de haber metido los dedos en un enchufe.

Leslie se aseguró de que yo me recogía el pelo. De hecho, Honeybee y yo vamos a juego. Hoy toca moño francés.

—Arcadia —suelto de pronto, solo para ver si la palabra suscita alguna reacción—. ¿Puede ser el nombre de uno de los clubes de la abuela..., o quizá de un grupo de bridge...? ¿O quizá conocía a alguien que vivía en Arcadia?

Ni mi madre ni mi padre parecen reaccionar de forma inusual a la palabra.

—¿Arcadia, Florida? —pregunta mi madre.

—No estoy segura. Salió en la conversación sobre sus grupos de bridge. —No le digo que la manera en que pronunció la palabra la abuela Judy me dejó inquieta—. ¿Cómo puedo averiguar más?

—Te veo preocupadísima con este asunto.

Estoy a punto de sacar el teléfono para enseñarle la foto. A punto. Mi mano se detiene a medio camino y, en lugar de meterla en el bolso, me aliso la falda. La expresión de mi madre muestra claramente un asomo de nueva preocupación. Lo último que le hace falta ahora es otro motivo de estrés. Si le enseño la fotografía, pensará que hay en marcha algún plan malvado y que May Crandall quiere sacarnos algo. Mi madre es una profesional de la preocupación.

—No estoy preocupada, mamá, es solo curiosidad. La mujer parecía muy sola.

—Pues es muy amable por tu parte, pero la abuela Judy no le haría demasiada compañía, aunque se conocieran. Acabo de tener que pedir a las chicas de las reuniones de los lunes que dejen de ir a Magnolia Manor. Tener tantas visitas de viejos amigos agobia a tu abuela. Le da vergüenza no poder situar nombres ni caras. Es más duro cuando no son familia. Le preocupa ser objeto de habladurías.

—Ya lo sé.

Tal vez debería olvidarme de este asunto. Pero me persigue. Me susurra, me asedia, me provoca. No me deja tranquila en toda la tarde. Charlamos, socializamos, aplaudimos cuando mi padre corta la cinta. Estamos un rato en la sala VIP del club de campo local, charlando con el gobernador y hablando con directivos de corporaciones. Incluso tengo ocasión de asesorar gratuitamente sobre la fracturación hidráulica y la legislación actual que podría levantar la veda para Carolina del Norte. Economía frente a medio ambiente..., a menudo las cuestiones se reducen a esos dos pesos pesados enfrentados en el cuadrilátero de la opinión pública y, por supuesto, de la nueva legislación.

Hasta cuando estoy discutiendo cuestiones relativas a costes-beneficios, algo que de verdad me interesa, una parte de mí sigue pensando en el móvil que llevo en el bolso y en la reacción de la abuela Judy a la fotografía.

Sé que reconoció a la mujer. *Queen... o Queenie.*

No es una coincidencia. Lo sé.

Arcadia. ¿Arcadia qué más?

En el coche de vuelta a la oficina de mi padre en Aiken, me invento una excusa inocente para escabullirme un rato de mis padres... Recados y esas cosas. Lo cierto es que voy a volver a ver a May Crandall. Si hay algo detrás de todo esto, será mejor que me entere. Así podré decidir lo que hay que hacer.

Papá parece algo desilusionado por que nos separemos. Tiene una reunión con su equipo para discutir estrategia antes de ir a casa a cenar. Tenía la esperanza de que yo también fuera.

—Por el amor del cielo, Wells. Avery tiene derecho a su vida privada —interviene mi madre—. Tiene un guapo prometido al que hacer caso. ¿Te acuerdas? —Levanta los delgados hombros y me sonríe con complicidad—. También una boda que organizar. No pueden prepararla si no hablan. —Termina la frase con entonación ascendente, llena de ilusión. Me da una palmadita en la rodilla y se acerca. Me dirige una mirada llena de significado: *Vamos a poner esto ya en marcha,* es lo que quiere decir. Rebusca un rato en su bolso, deja que pasen unos instantes y simula cambiar de tema de conversación de forma natural—. El jardinero trajo el otro día un mantillo nuevo..., para las azaleas..., una recomendación del paisajista de Bitsy. Lo usaron el otoño pasado y sus azaleas crecieron el doble que las nuestras. La primavera próxima los jardines de Drayden Hill serán la envidia de..., bueno..., de todos. Hacia finales de marzo. Va a ser... celestial.

Las palabras no dichas, *perfecto para una boda,* flotan en el aire. Cuando anunciamos nuestro compromiso, Elliot hizo prometer a Bitsy y a Honeybee que no entrarían a saco y empezarían a tomar decisiones. Y la verdad es que lo están pasando fatal. Si las dejáramos, ya lo tendrían todo atado y bien atado, pero estamos decididos a planear las cosas cuando creamos que es el momento y de la manera que consideremos mejor. Ahora mismo, mi padre y Honeybee deberían estar totalmente centrados en la salud de él y no organizando mi boda.

Pero eso no puedo decírselo a Honeybee.

Simulo no haber captado la indirecta.

—Jason sería capaz de cultivar rosas en el desierto.

Jason se ocupa de los jardines de Drayden Hill desde mucho antes de que yo me fuera a la universidad. Le encantaría tener ocasión de presumir de ellos, pero Elliot nunca aceptará una boda ideada por nuestras madres. Elliot quiere a su madre, pero, como es hijo único, le agota su continua obsesión por organizarle la vida.

Cada cosa a su tiempo, me digo. *Papá, cáncer, política.* Esos son ahora los tres grandes objetivos.

Nos detenemos delante de la oficina. El conductor nos abre la puerta y me bajo, contenta de tener tiempo libre.

Una última y sutil indirecta me acompaña mientras bajo del coche.

—Dile a Elliot que le dé las gracias a su madre por la sugerencia de las azaleas.

—Lo haré —le prometo, y me apresuro a ir a mi coche, donde telefoneo a Elliot. No me lo coge. Es probable que esté en una reunión, aunque son más de las cinco. Sus clientes son internacionales, así que le llegan consultas las veinticuatro horas del día.

Le dejo un mensaje breve sobre las azaleas. Le hará reír y a menudo necesita algo así después de un día especialmente estresante.

Cuando he recorrido una manzana, me llama mi hermana mediana, Allison.

—Hola, Allie, ¿qué tal todo? —digo.

Allison ríe, pero suena agotada. Oigo a los trillizos armando jaleo al fondo.

—¿Crees que podrías recoger a Courtney de clase de ballet? Tengo a los niños malos y hoy ya los he tenido que cambiar tres veces de ropa y..., sí, ahora mismo estamos desnudos otra vez, los cuatro. Lo más seguro es que Court esté a la puerta de la academia preguntándose dónde me he metido.

Cambio de sentido y me dirijo al estudio de la señorita Hannah, donde en su momento fui bailarina y *majorette* fracasada. Por suerte, Court tiene verdadero talento. En la función de primavera estuvo increíble.

—Pues claro. Yo la recojo. No estoy muy lejos, llego en diez minutos.

Allison contesta con un suspiro de alivio.

—Gracias, eres mi salvadora. Hoy eres mi hermana favorita.

Es una broma que compartimos desde niñas, quién es la hermana favorita de Allison. En calidad de hija mediana, tenía derecho a elegir. Missy era mayor y más interesante, pero yo era más pequeña y me podía mangonear.

Río con suavidad.

—Solo eso compensa cruzar otra vez la ciudad.

—Y, por favor, no le digas a mamá que los niños están malos. Vendrá corriendo y no quiero arriesgarme a que papá se exponga a un virus. Deja a Courtney en casa de Shellie, ahora te pongo un mensaje con la dirección. Ya he llamado a la madre de Shellie y me ha dicho que no hay problema con que Courtney se quede a dormir.

—Muy bien. —De las tres hermanas, Allison es la que más se parece a Honeybee. Funciona como un general de cuatro estrellas, pero desde que llegaron los trillizos se ha visto abrumada por un ejército invasor—. Estoy llegando a la academia. Te escribo cuando haya rescatado a tu hija.

Colgamos y a los pocos minutos detengo el coche delante de la escuela de la señorita Hannah. Courtney está en la puerta. Se alegra cuando ve que no la han abandonado.

—¡Hola, tía Aves! —dice mientras sube al coche.

—Hola, tú.

—¿Mamá se ha vuelto a olvidar de mí? —Pone los ojos en blanco y deja caer la cabeza a un lado, un gesto que la hace parecer mayor de diez años.

—No..., es que tenía ganas de estar contigo. He pensado que podíamos hacer algo juntas. Ir al parque, tirarnos por el tobogán, subirnos al fuerte, esa clase de cosas.

—Sí, claro. En serio, tía Aves...

Me molesta la rapidez con que rechaza mi propuesta. Es demasiado madura para su edad. Hace nada me tiraba de la pernera del pantalón y me suplicaba que trepara con ella a un árbol en Drayden Hill.

—Vale, tu madre me ha pedido que te recoja, pero solo porque los trillizos están malos. Se supone que tengo que llevarte a casa de Shellie.

Se le ilumina la cara y se endereza en el asiento.

—¡Ah, genial! —La miro mal y añade—: A ver, lo de que los trillizos estén malos no.

Ofrezco parar a tomar un helado, algo que en otro tiempo fue nuestra actividad preferida, pero me dice que no tiene hambre. Solo le interesa llegar cuanto antes a casa de Shellie, así que enciendo el GPS y meto la dirección.

Ella saca su móvil para escribir a Shellie y mis pensamientos cambian de rumbo. Arcadia y May Crandall eclipsan las punzadas de tristeza que me produce ver a mi sobrina precipitarse a la adolescencia. ¿Cuál será la reacción de May cuando le pregunte por esa palabra, «Arcadia»?

No parece probable que consiga hacérsela hoy. Para cuando deje a Courtney, será la hora de cenar en la residencia. El personal estará ocupado, y May también.

Me salgo de la avenida principal y me adentro por calles arboladas flanqueadas por casas de principios del siglo xx rodeadas de céspedes y jardines perfectamente cuidados. Recorremos varias manzanas antes de que caiga en la cuenta de por qué el viaje a casa de Shellie me resulta tan familiar. La casa de la abuela Judy en Lagniappe no está lejos.

—Oye, Court, ¿quieres venir un momento a casa de la abuela Judy antes de que te deje con Shellie? —No me apetece ir sola, pero se me acaba de ocurrir que a lo mejor entre las cosas de la abuela puedo encontrar respuestas a algunas preguntas.

Courtney baja el móvil y me mira desconcertada.

—Me parece un poco siniestro, tía Aves. La casa está vacía, pero todas las cosas de la abuela siguen allí. —Saca el labio inferior. Sus grandes ojos azules me miran con franqueza. A los niños les resulta difícil aceptar el cambio tan drástico que ha sufrido la abuela Judy. Es su primer encuentro real con la mortalidad—. Te acompaño si de verdad lo necesitas.

—No, no pasa nada. —Me salto el desvío. En realidad no hay necesidad de meter a Courtney en esto. Me acercaré a Lagniappe después de dejarla en casa de su amiga.

Su alivio salta a la vista.

—Vale. Gracias por venir a buscarme, tía Aves.

—Es un placer, peque.

Minutos después sube corriendo el camino de entrada a la casa de Shellie y yo me dirijo a la casa de la calle Lagniappe en busca del pasado.

Un mazazo de dolor me golpea en cuanto aparco en el camino de entrada y bajo del coche. Mire donde mire, encuentro un recuerdo. Las rosas que ayudaba a mi abuela a cuidar, el sauce donde jugaba a las casitas con la niña que vivía calle abajo, la ventana salediza del castillo de Cenicienta en el piso de arriba, el amplio porche que hacía de fondo para las fotos de graduación, el jardín acuático donde los koi multicolor cabeceaban a la espera de migas de galleta.

Casi puedo sentir a mi abuela en el pórtico que recorre el lateral de la casa. Cuando subo las escaleras, estoy medio esperando encontrarla. Me duele que no sea así. Nunca más volveré a este lugar para ser recibida por mi abuela.

En el jardín trasero, el aire en el invernadero está viciado y huele a polvo. El aroma a tierra húmeda ha desaparecido. Tampoco están los estantes y las macetas. Sin duda mi madre se los dio a alguien que pudiera utilizarlos.

La llave escondida sigue donde siempre. Atrapa un rayo de luz del atardecer cuando levanto el ladrillo suelto cerca de los cimientos. A partir de ahí, entrar y quitar la alarma es tarea fácil. Luego me quedo en la sala de estar y pienso: *¿Y ahora qué?*

La madera del suelo cruje bajo mis pies y me sobresalto, aunque se trate de un sonido muy familiar. Courtney tenía razón. La casa parece vacía y tétrica, ya no tiene nada del segundo hogar que siempre fue para mí. A partir de los trece años y durante el curso, vivía aquí siempre que mis padres estaban en Washington para poder ir a clase en Aiken con mis amigos.

Ahora me siento como un ladrón entrando a hurtadillas.

Además, esto es absurdo. Ni siquiera sabes lo que estás buscando.

¿Fotografías, quizá? ¿Estará la mujer de la mesilla de May Crandall en alguno de los viejos álbumes? La abuela Judy siempre ha sido la historiadora de la familia, la guardiana del linaje de los Stafford, la que escribe infatigable etiquetas en su vieja máquina de escribir manual y las pega a objetos. No hay un solo mueble, cuadro, pieza de arte o fotografía en esta casa que no esté cuidadosamente etiquetado con sus orígenes y el nombre de sus anteriores dueños. Sus objetos personales —los que le importan— también los guarda así. La pulsera de las libélulas me llegó en una caja muy gastada con una nota amarillenta pegada a la parte de abajo.

Julio, 1966. Un regalo. Piedras de luna por las primeras fotografías enviadas desde la Luna por la sonda espacial estadounidense *Surveyor*. Granates porque simbolizan el amor. Libélulas por el agua. Zafiros y ónices a modo de evocación. Hecho por encargo en Greer Designs, Damon Greer, diseñador.

Debajo de esto había añadido:

Para Avery:
Porque eres quien soñará nuevos sueños que abrirán nuevos caminos. Que las libélulas te lleven a lugares más allá de tu imaginación.
Tu abuela, Judy

Es extraño, ahora me doy cuenta, que no especificara de quién era el regalo. Me pregunto si encontraré esa información en alguno de sus dietarios. No pasaba una semana sin que documentara con precisión los detalles de su día a día, dejando constancia de todas las personas a las que veía, la ropa que vestía, lo que se servía en las comidas. Si May Crandall y ella fueron amigas o compartieron grupo de bridge, su nombre seguramente figurará ahí.

«Algún día los leerás y sabrás todos mis secretos», me dijo una vez cuando le pregunté por qué era tan meticulosa poniendo todo por escrito.

El comentario me parece ahora una autorización, pero, mientras cruzo la casa en penumbra, la culpa me atormenta.

No es como si mi abuela hubiera ya muerto. Sigue aquí. Lo que estoy haciendo es husmear y, sin embargo, no logro quitarme de encima la sensación de que quiere que comprenda algo, de que esto es importante, de alguna manera, para las dos.

En su pequeño despacho junto a la biblioteca, su último dietario sigue sobre el escritorio. Está abierto por el día que desapareció durante ocho horas y terminó perdida y desorientada en el antiguo centro comercial. Un jueves.

La letra es apenas legible. Tiembla y se curva hacia abajo. No se parece en nada a la caligrafía bonita y redondeada de mi abuela. «Trent Turner, Edisto» es la única anotación del día.

¿Edisto? ¿Es eso lo que pasó cuando desapareció? Pensaba que iba a ir a la casa de la isla de Edisto a... ¿reunirse con alguien? ¿Quizá esa noche había tenido un sueño y se había despertado creyendo que era real? ¿Tal vez estaba reviviendo algo ocurrido en el pasado?

¿Quién es Trent Turner?

Sigo pasando las hojas.

En los compromisos sociales de mi abuela de los últimos meses no hay mención alguna de May Crandall. Y, sin embargo, May me dio a entender que se habían visto hacía poco.

Cuanto más retrocedo, más clara se vuelve la escritura. Me sumerjo en rutinas familiares en las que en otro tiempo acompañé a mi abuela, actos del Club de la Federación de Mujeres, el consejo de la biblioteca, las Hijas de la Revolución Americana, el Club de Jardinería en primavera... Me resulta doloroso darme cuenta de que hace solo siete meses, antes de su súbita espiral descendente, siguiera funcionando razonablemente bien, mantuviera su calendario social, aunque un par de amigas les habían comentado a mis padres que había tenido algún que otro lapsus.

Sigo pasando hojas haciéndome preguntas, recordando, pensando en este año decisivo. La vida te puede cambiar de un día para otro. El dietario me hace ser más consciente aún de esto. Planificamos nuestros días, pero no los controlamos.

Las notas de enero de mi abuela empiezan con una única línea garabateada al azar en el margen justo antes del día de Año Nuevo. «Edisto y Trent Turner», ha vuelto a escribir. Debajo hay apuntado un número de teléfono.

¿Quizá estaba hablando con alguien sobre algún arreglo que había que hacer en la casa? Es difícil de creer. La secretaria personal de mi padre lleva ocupándose de los asuntos de la abuela Judy desde que murió mi abuelo, hace siete años. De haber sido necesario algún arreglo, lo habría gestionado ella.

Solo hay una forma de averiguarlo, supongo.

Saco el móvil y marco el número.

El teléfono suena una, dos veces.

Empiezo a preguntarme qué voy a decir si alguien contesta. *Esto... No estoy muy segura de por qué llamo. Encontré su nombre en una libreta vieja en casa de mi abuela y...*

Y... ¿qué?

Salta un contestador. «Inmobiliaria Turner. Soy Trent. Ahora no podemos atenderle, pero si deja un mensaje...».

¿Inmobiliaria? Estoy atónita. ¿Estaba la abuela Judy pensando en vender la casa de Edisto? Es difícil de creer. Esa casa lleva en su familia desde antes de que se casara con mi abuelo. Le encanta.

Mis padres me lo habrían dicho si estuvieran pensando en vender el lugar. Tiene que haber otra explicación, pero, puesto que no tengo manera de averiguarlo, sigo buscando.

En el armario encuentro el resto de dietarios, guardados en una gastada estantería acristalada, donde siempre habían estado. Están cuidadosamente ordenados a partir del año en que se casó con mi abuelo hasta el presente. Solo por curiosidad, saco el más antiguo. La tapa de cuero color blanco lechoso está seca y atravesada por grietas marrones, de manera que parece una pieza de porcelana antigua. En el interior, la escritura es sinuosa y aniñada. Llenan las páginas notas sobre fiestas de la universidad, exámenes, despedidas de soltera, modelos para vajillas y citas vespertinas con mi abuelo.

En uno de los márgenes, aparecen ensayos de firmas con el que pronto sería su nuevo nombre de casada. Las florituras de las letras dan testimonio del atolondramiento del primer amor.

«Visita a los padres de Harold en Drayden Hill», dice una de las entradas. «Monté a caballo. Salté unas cuantas vallas. Harold me dijo que no se lo contara a su madre. Nos quiere ilesos en la boda. He encontrado a mi príncipe. No tengo la más mínima duda».

Una emoción me llena la garganta. Es agridulce.

No tengo la más mínima duda.

¿De verdad sentía eso? ¿De verdad supo que había encontrado al hombre de su vida cuando conoció a mi abuelo? ¿Deberíamos haber experimentado Elliot y yo algún tipo de... descarga eléctrica en lugar de la relajada transición de compañeros de aventuras infantiles a una amistad adulta y de las citas informales al compromiso porque, después de seis años saliendo, parece que ya toca? ¿Debería preocuparnos no haber sido más impetuosos, no tener prisa?

Me suena el móvil y contesto, deseando que sea él.

La voz al otro lado de la línea es masculina y cordial, pero no es de Elliot.

—Hola, soy Trent Turner. He recibido una llamada de este número. Siento no haber contestado. ¿En qué puedo ayudarla?

—Eh... Esto.... —No se me ocurre ninguna frase con que romper el hielo, así que suelto sin más—: Encontré su número en la agenda de mi abuela.

Oigo ruido de papeles.

—¿Teníamos una cita aquí en Edisto? ¿Para ver alguna casa? ¿O es para un alquiler?

—No sé para qué es. De hecho esperaba que me lo dijera usted. Mi abuela ha tenido problemas de salud y estoy intentando poner orden en su agenda.

—¿Para qué día era la cita?

—No estoy segura de que la tuviera. He pensado que quizá lo llamó para hablar de la venta de una propiedad. La casa Myers. —Por aquí es costumbre conocer las propiedades por el nombre de quienes fueron sus dueños hace décadas. Los padres de mi abuela construyeron la casa de Edisto como un refugio para escapar de los veranos calurosos y húmedos del interior—. Stafford, Judy Stafford. —Me preparo para el cambio de tono que acompaña casi siempre el anuncio del nombre. En todo el estado la gente o nos quiere o nos odia, pero por lo general nos conoce.

—Staff... for... Stafford... —murmura. Quizá no es de por aquí. Ahora que lo pienso, en su acento no hay ni asomo de Charleston. No es del sur del estado, pero sí que arrastra las palabras. ¿Texas quizá? Al haber pasado gran parte de mi infancia con niños de otros lugares se me dan bien los acentos, tanto extranjeros como nacionales.

Hay una pausa extraña. Cuando vuelve a hablar, su tono es más cauto.

—Solo llevo aquí nueve meses, pero le prometo que nadie me ha llamado nunca para vender o alquilar la casa Myers. Siento no poder serle de más ayuda. —De pronto está intentando colgarme. ¿Por qué?—. Si fue antes de primeros de año probablemente hablaría con mi abuelo, Trent I. Pero falleció hace seis meses.

—Vaya, lo siento mucho. —De inmediato siento una afinidad que va más allá del hecho de que ese hombre me hable desde un lugar que siempre he amado profundamente—. ¿Tiene alguna idea de por qué estaba mi abuela en contacto con él?

Hay otro silencio incómodo, como si estuviera sopesando sus palabras.

—La verdad es que sí. Tenía unos papeles para ella. Es todo lo que le puedo decir.

Sale mi abogado interior. He detectado a un testigo reticente que se está guardando información.

—¿Qué clase de papeles?

—Lo siento. Se lo prometí a mi abuelo.

—¿Qué le prometió?

—Si viene ella en persona podré darle el sobre que le dejó.

Se dispara una alarma dentro de mi cabeza. ¿Qué está pasando aquí?

—No puede viajar.

—Entonces no puedo ayudarla. Lo siento.

Y, sin más, cuelga.

10

RILL

*E*n la habitación hay silencio y huele a humedad. Abro los ojos, los cierro muy fuerte, los abro de nuevo muy despacio. La bruma del sueño no me deja ver demasiado claro. Es como la niebla del río que trepa por las ventanas de la casa flotante por la noche.

Nada está donde se supone que debe estar. En lugar de las puertas y ventanas del *Arcadia* hay gruesas paredes de piedra seca. El aire huele igual que en los compartimentos cerrados donde guardamos las cajas de víveres y el combustible. El hedor a moho y a tierra húmeda me entra en la nariz y ahí se queda.

Oigo a Lark gemir en sueños. Se oye un rechinar de muelles en lugar del susurro de los camastros abatibles donde Lark y Fern duermen.

Parpadeo, levanto la vista y distingo un ventanuco muy alto, cerca del techo. La luz de la mañana entra por él, pero es pálida y tenebrosa.

Un arbusto araña el cristal. Sus ramas emiten un suave gemido. Una rosa marchita de color rosa cuelga, medio rota.

De repente lo recuerdo todo. Recuerdo acostarme en el camastro que huele a humedad, mirar por la ventana la rosa hasta que la luz del día se apaga y la respiración de mis hermanos que duermen a mi alrededor se vuelve rítmica y tranquila.

Recuerdo a la empleada con uniforme blanco que nos condujo escaleras abajo y junto al cuarto de la caldera y las pilas de carbón hasta esta habitación diminuta.

«Dormiréis aquí hasta que sepamos si os vais a quedar definitivamente. Nada de ruido ni de charlas. Tenéis que estar callados. No podéis levantaros de la cama». Señaló cinco camas plegables, como las que usan los soldados en los campamentos de prácticas que hay a veces cerca del río.

Luego salió y cerró la puerta detrás de ella.

Nos acostamos en silencio, también Camellia. Yo me alegraba de que estuviéramos solos otra vez los cinco. Sin empleadas, sin otros niños mirándonos con ojos curiosos, preocupados, tristes, mezquinos, ojos vacíos que están muertos, endurecidos.

Revivo todo lo ocurrido ayer como si fuera una película. Veo el *Arcadia,* a la policía, a Silas, el automóvil de la señorita Tann, la cola para el baño en el piso de arriba. Una náusea me recorre de la cabeza a los pies. Me engulle como una ola de agua estancada, caliente por el sol de verano, envenenada por todo lo que ha arrastrado.

Me siento sucia por dentro. No tiene nada que ver con el agua turbia marrón por la arena y el jabón de todos los niños que se habían bañado en ella antes que yo, incluidas mis hermanas y Gabion.

Veo a la empleada de pie junto a mí mientras me meto en la bañera, dándole la espalda para protegerme.

—Lávate —me dice. Señala el jabón y un trapo—. No tenemos tiempo para tonterías. Y además, los que vivís en el río no tenéis fama de pudorosos, precisamente. ¿No te parece?

No sé qué quiere decir ni qué contestarle. Quizá no deba hacerlo.

—¡He dicho que te laves! —grita—. ¿Te crees que tengo todo el día?

Ya sé que no lo tiene. Le he oído gritarle lo mismo a otros niños. He oído gimoteos y sollozos y balbuceos cuando empujaban cabezas bajo el agua para enjuagarlas. Por suerte, a ninguno de los Foss nos molestan las aguadillas. Los pequeños e incluso Camellia han pasado por el baño sin armar demasiado jaleo. Yo quiero hacer lo mismo, pero la mujer parece tenerla tomada conmigo, quizá porque soy la mayor.

Me acuclillo en el agua porque está sucia y fría.

Se acerca para verme mejor y me dedica una mirada que me pone la carne de gallina.

—Parece que después de todo no eres demasiado mayor para estar con las pequeñas. Aunque no falta mucho, y entonces tendremos que trasladarte a otro sitio.

Le doy la espalda todavía más y me lavo lo más deprisa que puedo.

Esta mañana me siento sucia por el hecho de que alguien me haya mirado así. Espero que nos vayamos de aquí antes de que nos toque bañarnos otra vez.

Quiero que la pequeña rosa color rosa desaparezca. Quiero que la ventana cambie, que las paredes se vuelvan de madera, que el suelo de cemento se marche, se transforme, se evapore. Quiero tablones gastados por nuestros pies y el río meciéndonos bajo nuestras camas y el suave arrullo de Briny tocando la armónica en el porche.

Durante la noche me he despertado al menos diez veces. En la madrugada, Fern se acurrucó a mi lado y la lona hundida por el peso nos obligaba a estar tan juntas que es un milagro que pudiera respirar y aún más dormir.

Cada vez que me rindo al sueño, vuelvo a estar en el *Arcadia*. Cada vez que me despierto, estoy aquí, en este lugar, y me esfuerzo en comprender qué significa.

Dormiréis aquí hasta que sepamos si os vais a quedar definitivamente...

¿Qué significa eso de «definitivamente»? ¿No van a llevarnos al hospital a ver a Briny y a Queenie ahora que hemos pasado aquí la noche y estamos limpios? ¿Vamos a ir todos o solo algunos? No puedo dejar aquí a los pequeños. ¿Y si estas personas les hacen daño?

Tengo que proteger a mis hermanos, pero ni siquiera puedo protegerme a mí misma.

Las lágrimas me ponen la boca pegajosa. Me he dicho a mí misma que no voy a llorar. Solo asustaría a los pequeños. Les he prometido que todo saldrá bien y de momento me creen, incluso Camellia.

Cierro los ojos, abrazo a Fern, dejo que broten las lágrimas y le empapen el pelo. Los sollozos me suben por el estómago y me oprimen el pecho y los trago como si fueran hipidos. Fern no se despierta. Quizá en sus sueños no es más que el río meciendo su litera.

No te duermas, me digo. Tengo que devolver a Fern a su catre antes de que venga alguien. Pueden regañarnos por mi culpa. La mujer dijo que no debíamos levantarnos de nuestras camas.

Solo dos minutos más. Solo dos minutos más, luego me levantaré y me aseguraré de que todos están en su sitio.

Me adormezco y me despierto una y otra vez. El corazón se me desboca cuando oigo a alguien respirar cerca. No es ninguno de nosotros, es alguien más grande. Un hombre. Quizá es Briny.

En cuanto pienso eso, un olor a grasa vieja y hierba verde y carbonilla llena la habitación. No es Briny. Briny huele a agua del río y a cielo. A niebla de la mañana en verano y a escarcha y humo de leña en invierno.

Se me despeja la cabeza y escucho. Unos pies dan un par de pasos, a continuación se paran. Briny no camina así.

Le tapo la cabeza a Fern con las mantas, espero que no se despierte y se mueva precisamente ahora. Aún está muy oscuro, por la ventana entra la misma luz tenue. Quizá no se dé cuenta de que Fern no está en su catre.

Cuando vuelvo la cabeza, apenas alcanzo a verlo de reojo. Es mucho más grande, alto y grueso que Briny, pero es todo lo que puedo distinguir. Es una sombra de pie. No se mueve ni dice nada. Se limita a mirar.

Me moquea la nariz de tanto llorar, pero no me la limpio ni me la sorbo. No quiero que sepa que estoy despierta. ¿Qué hace aquí?

Camellia cambia de postura.

No, pienso. Chsss. ¿Está el hombre mirándola? ¿Ve si tiene los ojos abiertos?

Se adentra en la habitación. Avanza, se detiene, avanza otra vez, se detiene. Se inclina sobre el catre de Lark, toca la almohada. Se tambalea un poco y tropieza con la estructura de madera.

Lo miro con los ojos entrecerrados. A continuación viene hasta mi catre, me mira un segundo. La almohada cruje cerca de mi cabeza. La toca dos veces con mucha suavidad.

Luego se detiene junto a las otras camas y por fin sale y cierra la puerta.

Dejo de contener la respiración, tomo aire de nuevo y entonces huelo el aroma a caramelo de menta. Cuando retiro las sábanas y despierto a Fern, veo que hay dos pastillas blancas en la almohada. Enseguida me recuerdan a Briny. Cuando Briny saca dinero en los billares o trabaja en un barco con espectáculo, siempre vuelve al *Arcadia* con un cucurucho de pastillas de menta Beech-Nut Luster en el bolsillo. Son las mejores. Briny nos hace adivinanzas y, si acertamos las respuestas, nos da un caramelo. *Si hay dos petirrojos en un árbol y uno en el suelo y tres azulejos en un arbusto y cuatro en el suelo y un búho grande en una cerca y otro en el establo, ¿cuántos pájaros hay en el suelo?*

Cuanto mayor eres, más difíciles son las preguntas. Cuanto más difíciles las preguntas, mejor saben los caramelos.

El olor a menta me da ganas de correr hacia la puerta y ver si Briny está fuera. Pero estos caramelos son de otra clase. Los noto raros cuando los cojo y llevo a Fern a su cama.

Junto a la puerta, Camellia se mete el suyo en la boca y lo mastica.

Considero dejar los caramelos en las almohadas de los pequeños, pero decido que es mejor cogerlos. Me preocupa que, si entran las empleadas, nos metamos en un lío por tenerlos.

—¡Ladrona! —Es lo primero que me dice Camellia desde que hicimos la cola para el baño anoche. Está sentada en su cama y la manga del camisón que le queda demasiado grande le deja el hombro al descubierto. Después del baño, una de las empleadas rebuscó en una pila de camisones y nos dio unos—. Nos ha dejado una pastilla para cada uno. No te las puedes quedar todas. No es justo.

—Chsss. —Habla tan alto que casi espero ver la puerta abrirse y a nosotros metidos en un lío—. Se las estoy guardando para después.

—Las estás robando.

—De eso nada.

Sin duda Camellia vuelve a ser ella hoy, pero, como casi todas las mañanas, está de mal humor. La mayoría de las veces le planto cara, pero hoy estoy demasiado cansada.

—Ya te he dicho que las estoy guardando para luego. No quiero que nos metamos en un lío.

Los delgados hombros de mi hermana se caen.

—En un lío ya estamos. —El pelo negro le cae hacia delante en marañas, como la crin de un caballo—. ¿Qué vamos a hacer, Rill?

—Vamos a portarnos bien para que estas personas nos lleven con Briny. No puedes volver a intentar escaparte, Camellia. No puedes enfrentarte a ellos, ¿de acuerdo? Si se enfadan con nosotros, no nos llevarán.

Me mira con intensidad, con sus ojos castaños tan entrecerrados que recuerda a los chinos que hacen la colada en enormes calderos de agua hirviendo en las orillas del río.

—¿De verdad crees que nos van a llevar? ¿Hoy?

—Si nos portamos bien.

Espero que no sea mentira, pero igual lo es.

—¿Por qué nos han traído aquí? —Está a punto de llorar—. ¿Por qué no nos dejan tranquilos?

Mis pensamientos trabajan tratando de entender. Necesito una explicación para mí misma tanto como para Camellia.

—Debe de ser un error. Habrán pensado que Briny no iba a venir a buscarnos. Pero Briny hablará con ellos en cuanto se entere de que no estamos. Les dirá que todo esto es una equivocación y nos llevará a casa.

—Pero ¿hoy? —Le tiembla la barbilla y saca el labio inferior con determinación, como hace cuando se dispone a pelearse con un chico.

—Apuesto a que hoy. Estoy segura.

Se sorbe la nariz y se limpia los mocos con el brazo.

—No pienso dejar que esas mujeres me metan otra vez en la bañera, Rill. No pienso.

—¿Por qué? ¿Qué te van a hacer, Camellia?

—Nada. —Levanta el mentón—. Pero no van a meterme otra vez, eso es todo. —Alarga una mano y la abre—. Si no vas a dar caramelos a todos, dámelos a mí. Estoy muerta de hambre.

—Los vamos a guardar para más tarde... Si nos llevan a donde estaban los niños ayer. Entonces los sacaré.

—Has dicho que Briny vendría luego.

—No sé cuándo. Solo sé que vendrá.

Arruga los labios hacia un lado como si no me creyera en absoluto y luego se vuelve hacia la puerta.

—Igual ese hombre nos puede ayudar a escapar. El que nos ha traído los caramelos. Es nuestro amigo.

Eso ya lo he pensado. Pero ¿quién era ese hombre? ¿A qué ha entrado aquí? Es la primera persona que es amable con nosotros en casa de la señora Murphy.

—Esperaremos a Briny —digo—. Lo único que tenemos que hacer es portarnos bien y...

Se agita el pomo de la puerta. Camellia y yo nos metemos en nuestras camas a la vez y fingimos dormir. El corazón me late con fuerza bajo la sábana áspera. ¿Quién está ahí? ¿Será nuestro nuevo amigo u otra persona? ¿Nos habrán oído hablar?

No necesito esperar mucho. Una mujer de pelo castaño vestida de blanco entra en la habitación. La observo por una rendija en la manta. Es robusta como un leñador y tiene la cintura gruesa. No es ninguna de las mujeres que vimos ayer.

Desde la puerta frunce el ceño, mira nuestras camas y luego las llaves que lleva en la mano.

—Todos *fuerra* de la cama. —Habla igual que la familia noruega que tuvo el barco fondeado junto al nuestro un mes el verano pasado. La palabra «fuera» la pronuncia rara, pero yo la entiendo. No parece enfadada, solo muy cansada—. De pie y doblad las mantas.

Nos levantamos todos excepto Gabion. Tengo que levantarlo del catre y una vez en el suelo se tambalea y se cae de culo mientras me ocupo de las mantas.

—Ha entrado alguien más en la habitación *durrante* la noche, ¿sí?

Sostiene una llave entre los dedos.

¿Deberíamos hablarle del hombre de las pastillas de menta? ¿Quizá no debía entrar en nuestra habitación? Igual nos metemos en un lío si no lo contamos.

—No, señora. No ha entrado nadie. Hemos estado solo nosotros —contesta Camellia antes de que me dé tiempo a mí.

—Tú *erres* la revoltosa, me han dicho. —Mira a Camellia con dureza y esta se encoge un poco.

—No, señora.

—No ha entrado nadie. —Tengo que mentir también. ¿Qué otra cosa puedo hacer si Camellia ha contado una patraña?—. A no ser que fuera cuando estábamos dormidos.

La mujer tira de la cadenilla de la bombilla del techo. Esta parpadea y pestañeamos, deslumbrados.

—Esta *puerrta* tenía que *estarr* cerrada. Lo estaba, ¿sí?

—No lo sabemos —contesta Camellia—. No nos hemos movido de nuestras camas.

La mujer me mira y asiento con la cabeza, luego empiezo a ordenar la habitación. Quiero deshacerme de los caramelos de menta, pero me da demasiado miedo, así que sigo con ellos en la mano, lo que hace que me cueste doblar las mantas, pero la mujer no se da cuenta. Tiene demasiada prisa por sacarnos de allí.

Cuando salimos, veo al hombre corpulento en el sótano, apoyado en el mango de una escoba junto a la gran estufa negra con rendijas que recuerdan a la boca de una calabaza de Halloween. El hombre nos mira pasar. Camellia le sonríe y él le devuelve la sonrisa. Tiene los dientes gastados y feos y el pelo castaño y fino le cuelga a ambos lados de la cara en mechones húmedos de sudor, pero su sonrisa es agradable.

Puede que después de todo tengamos un amigo aquí dentro.

—*Señorr* Riggs, si no tiene nada que *hacerr*, ocúpese de la rama que se ha caído esta noche en el *jarrdín* —dice la mujer—. Antes de que salgan los niños.

—Sí, señora Pulnik. —Se le curvan las comisuras de los labios y mueve un poco la escoba cuando la señora Pulnik empieza a subir las escaleras seguida por nosotros, pero no barre.

Camellia se vuelve para mirarlo y él le guiña un ojo. El guiño me recuerda a Briny, así que puede que el señor Riggs me guste un poco.

En el piso de arriba, la señora Pulnik nos lleva al cuarto de la lavandería y nos da cosas de una pila de ropa. Las llama «ropas de jugar», pero en realidad son poco más que andrajos. Nos dice que nos vistamos y vayamos al cuarto de baño y eso hacemos, y el desayuno se parece mucho a la cena que nos dieron anoche después del baño: una cucharadita de gachas de maíz. Llegamos tarde a la mesa. Los otros niños ya han salido a jugar. Cuando hemos dejado los tazones bien limpios, nos dicen que salgamos y que no intentemos ir más allá del jardín ni del cementerio. O de lo contrario...

—Y tampoco os *acerrquéis* a la valla. —La señora Pulnik coge a Camellia y a Lark del brazo antes de que nos dé tiempo a cruzar la puerta. Se inclina hacia nosotros con las mejillas gordezuelas sudorosas y brillantes—. *Ayerr* un niño intentó colarse *porr* debajo. La señora Murphy lo ha mandado al *arrmario*. Que te manden al *arrmario* es malo, muy malo. En el *arrmario* está muy oscuro. ¿Lo entendéis?

—Sí, señora —respondo con un hilo de voz mientras cojo en brazos a Gabby y le tiendo la mano a Lark para llevármela. Está quieta como un tocón de árbol, inmóvil, pero por las mejillas le corren gruesos lagrimones—. Me aseguraré de que obedecen las reglas hasta que podamos ir a ver a nuestros papás.

La señora Pulnik aprieta y curva sus gruesos labios.

—Bien —dice—. Es una decisión sensata. *Parra* todos.

—Sí, señora.

Salimos lo más rápido que podemos. El sol es como un regalo, y el cielo se extiende entre chopos y arces, y la tierra desnuda al final de los escalones es fresca y suave. Me siento a salvo y cierro los ojos, y escucho hablar a las hojas y cantar a los pájaros sus canciones matutinas. Una a una reconozco sus voces. El chochín de Carolina, el petirrojo, el pinzón. Los mismos pájaros que estaban ayer por la mañana cuando nos despertamos en nuestro viejo barco.

Las niñas pequeñas se aferran a mi falda y Gabby se retuerce en mis brazos para que le deje en el suelo y Camellia se queja porque estamos quietos. Abro los ojos y está mirando la valla negra de hierro que cierra el jardín. Está cubierta en gran parte por madreselva, acebo espinoso y azaleas que crecen espesas y es más alta que nuestras cabezas. Hay una única puerta, por lo que veo, y lleva a un jardín detrás de la iglesia medio en ruinas contigua. Que rodea la misma valla.

Camellia es demasiado grande para pasar por debajo, pero tiene aspecto de estar buscando la mejor manera de intentarlo.

—Por lo menos vamos hasta los columpios —gimotea—. Desde allí podemos ver el camino... para cuando venga Briny a buscarnos.

Cruzamos el jardín; llevo a Gabion en brazos y mis hermanas forman un apretado nudo a mi espalda, incluso Camellia, que por lo general se enzarza en una pelea en menos que canta un gallo en cada nueva escuela a la que vamos. Los niños nos miran porque somos nuevos. Fingimos no darnos cuenta. Este juego se nos da bien: no mostrarnos demasiado simpáticos, cuidar los unos de los otros, hacerles saber que si se meten con uno de nosotros tendrán que vérselas con el resto. Pero esta vez es distinta. No conocemos las reglas de este lugar. No hay una profesora vigilando. No se ve a un solo adulto. Solo hay niños que dejan de saltar a la comba y de jugar al martín pescador para mirarnos fijamente.

No veo a la niñita que vino con nosotros del río ayer. Su hermano pequeño —al que la señorita Tann puso el nombre de Stevie— está sentado en el suelo con un camión de juguete al que le faltan la pintura y una de las ruedas.

—¿Dónde está tu hermana? —Me acuclillo a su lado. El peso de Gabion me hace perder el equilibrio, así que tengo que apoyar una mano en el suelo para evitar caerme.

Los hombros de Stevie suben y bajan y sus grandes ojos castaños se llenan de lágrimas.

—Puedes venir con nosotros —le digo.

Camellia protesta.

—No es problema nuestro.

La mando callar.

Stevie hace un puchero, asiente con la cabeza y levanta los dos brazos. En uno de ellos tiene una mordedura de gran tamaño y me pregunto quién se la habrá hecho. Lo cojo en brazos y me pongo de pie. Es mayor que Gabion, pero pesa más o menos lo mismo. Es una cosita delgaducha.

Dos niñas que juegan con platos de latón abollados nos miran. Han reunido hojas secas y montado una cocinita a la sombra de la caseta del pozo, como hacemos a veces Camellia y yo en el bosque.

—¿Queréis jugar? —pregunta una de ellas.

—Déjanos en paz —salta Camellia—. No tenemos tiempo. Vamos al cementerio a esperar a nuestro padre.

—Pues no deberíais. —Las niñas vuelven a su juego y nosotros seguimos caminando.

En la puerta del cementerio, un niño mayor sale de detrás del acebo. Ahora veo que hay una abertura en los arbustos. Hay cuatro o cinco niños con una baraja de cartas. Uno está tallando una lanza con una navaja. Me mira con ojos entrecerrados y prueba la punta afilada con la yema del dedo.

El niño mayor pelirrojo está en la puerta con los brazos cruzados.

—Tú, ven aquí —me dice, como si estuviera a sus órdenes—. Los otros se pueden ir a jugar.

Es evidente lo que quiere. Quiere que me meta entre los arbustos con los cuatro chicos. De otra manera mis hermanos no podrán entrar en el cementerio.

Me arde la cara. Noto que me estoy ruborizando. *¿Qué tiene pensado hacer?*

Camellia dice lo que estoy pensando.

—No vamos a ir a ninguna parte contigo. —Separa las piernas y saca pecho y barbilla—. Tú no nos mandas.

—No te estoy hablando a ti, lagartija. Eres más fea que un chucho callejero, ¿no te lo han dicho nunca? Estoy hablando con tu hermana la guapa.

A Camellia se le salen los ojos de las órbitas. Está a punto de ponerse furiosa.

—No soy tan fea como tú, pelo de zanahoria. ¿Lloró tu madre cuando naciste? ¡Seguro que sí!

Le doy a Gabby a Fern. El pequeño Stevie no quiere soltarse. Sigue con los brazos alrededor de mi cuello. Si vamos a pelearnos, no puedo tener a un niño colgado del cuello. El chico pelirrojo seguramente podrá con Camellia y conmigo, y, si además salen sus amigos, vamos a tener problemas. No se ven empleadas por ninguna parte y uno de esos matones tiene una navaja.

Al pelirrojo se le hinchan las aletas de la nariz y descruza los brazos. Se va a armar una buena. Esta vez Camellia ha hecho una apuesta que no podemos pagar. El chico me saca al menos treinta centímetros y eso que soy alta.

Mis pensamientos corren igual que una ardilla que salta de rama en rama. *Piensa. Piensa en algo.*

Usa siempre la cabeza, Rill, oigo a Briny decirme, *y enseguida encontrarás la salida de un atolladero.*

—Tengo pastillas de menta —suelto y meto la mano en el bolsillo de mi vestido prestado—. Os las damos todas si nos dejáis pasar.

El chico mete la barbilla y me mira parpadeando.

—¿De dónde has sacado pastillas de menta?

—No estoy mintiendo. —Me cuesta decir esas tres palabras porque tengo a Stevie agarrado a mí con fuerza—. ¿Nos dejáis pasar o no?

—Dame los caramelos. —Los otros bravucones han empezado a salir de su escondrijo para coger su parte del botín.

—¡Son nuestros! —protesta Camellia.

—Cállate. —Saco los caramelos. Están algo sucios de llevarlos en la mano toda la mañana, pero no creo que a estos chicos les importe.

El pelirrojo abre la mano y le pongo un caramelo en ella. Se lo acerca tanto a la cara que se pone bizco y parece aún más estúpido que antes. Una sonrisa lenta y mezquina se dibuja en sus labios. Tiene mellado uno de los dientes delanteros.

—¿Te los ha dado el viejo Riggs?

No quiero causar problemas al hombre del sótano. Es la única persona que ha sido amable con nosotros hasta el momento.

—No es asunto tuyo.

—¡Es nuestro amigo! —Camellia es incapaz de tener la boca cerrada. Igual cree que asustará a estos chicos si creen que le caemos bien a un hombre mayor.

Pero el chico pelirrojo se limita a sonreír. Se acerca a mi oreja, tanto que huelo su aliento apestoso y noto su calor en mi piel. Susurra:

—No dejes que Riggs se quede a solas contigo. Los amigos como él no te convienen.

11

AVERY

El musgo español gotea de los árboles, tan delicadamente hilado como el encaje de un velo de novia. Una garza azul alza el vuelo desde la marisma, sobresaltada por el paso de mi coche. Al principio vuela con torpeza, como si necesitara un momento para sentirse cómoda en el aire, para usar las alas. Bate con fuerza y por fin flota hacia lo lejos, sin prisa por volver a la tierra.

Conozco la sensación. Llevo dos semanas intentando escabullirme para ir a la isla de Edisto. Entre las reuniones y los encuentros con la prensa que ya estaban previstos y las complicaciones inesperadas de la salud de papá, me ha sido imposible.

He pasado los últimos seis días en despachos de médicos, cogiéndole la mano a mi madre mientras tratábamos de comprender por qué, cuando se suponía que la cirugía había curado el cáncer y la hemorragia intestinal, papá volvía a estar anémico y tan débil que apenas podía sostenerse en pie. Después de interminables pruebas, creemos que han encontrado la causa. La solución era fácil: cirugía laparoscópica para sellar los vasos sanguíneos rotos de su aparato digestivo, un problema que no tenía relación con el cáncer. Paciente ambulatorio. Rápido y sencillo.

Excepto que nada es sencillo cuando estás intentando esconderte del mundo exterior y papá insiste en no contar a nadie que ha sufrido un pequeño percance de salud. Leslie está completamente de acuerdo. Está diciendo que mi padre ha sufrido una intoxicación alimentaria; que retomará su agenda en unos pocos días.

Mi hermana mayor, Missy, echó una mano en un par de actos benéficos que no se podían cancelar.

—Te veo agotada, Aves —me comentó—. ¿Por qué no te vas unos días, aprovechando que Leslie ha despejado casi toda la agenda? Ve a ver a Elliot. Allison y yo estaremos pendientes de Drayden Hill.

—Gracias, pero... ¿estás segura?

—Ve. Hablad de la boda. Igual puedes convencerlo de que ceda a las presiones de mamá.

No le dije que, aparte de unas pocas conversaciones apresuradas, Elliot y yo no hemos hecho planes de boda. Tenemos demasiadas cosas de que ocuparnos.

—Elliot ha tenido que ir a Milán a reunirse con un cliente, pero creo que me voy a ir a la casa de Edisto. ¿Ha estado alguien hace poco?

—Scott y yo llevamos a los niños unos días..., esto..., creo que la primavera pasada. Los guardeses se ocupan muy bien de la propiedad. Seguro que lo tienen todo perfecto. Vete y descansa unos días.

Antes de que le diera tiempo a decirme que saludara a la playa de su parte, ya estaba haciendo la maleta. Antes de salir de la ciudad, hice una visita que debía desde hacía tiempo a la residencia de May Crandall. Una auxiliar me dijo que May estaba ingresada por una infección respiratoria. No sabía si era grave ni cuándo volvería.

Lo que significa que el misterioso paquete de documentos de Edisto es mi única pista, al menos de momento. Trent Turner no me coge el teléfono. Punto. Mi única opción es hacerle una visita. El sobre que tiene ha empezado a ocupar todos mis pensamientos. Estoy un poco obsesionada, invento historias en las que Trent Turner interpreta distintos papeles según la escena. A veces es un chantajista que ha descubierto un secreto horrible sobre mi familia y vendido la información a los enemigos políticos de mi padre; por eso no contesta mis llamadas. En otras es el hombre de la fotografía de May Crandall. La mujer embarazada que está a su lado es mi abuela, que tuvo alguna clase de vida secreta antes de casarse con mi abuelo. Un amor de adolescencia. Un escándalo silenciado durante generaciones.

Dio al niño en adopción y ha vivido en otra parte todo este tiempo. Ahora el heredero desposeído quiere la parte que le corresponde del dinero familiar. O de lo contrario...

Todas mis hipótesis me parecen descabelladas, pero no carecen por completo de fundamentos. Leyendo entre líneas los dietarios de mi abuela, me he enterado de cosas. Mi pulsera de libélulas tiene algún tipo de vínculo con Edisto. *Un regalo encantador de un día encantador en Edisto,* decía la entrada. *A solas.*

Ese «a solas» es lo que me tiene intrigada. Solo una página antes anotó haber recibido carta de mi abuelo, que se había llevado a los niños a pescar a las montañas toda la semana.

A solas...

¿Quiénes? ¿Quién le regalaba cosas a mi abuela en Edisto en 1966?

Mi abuela a menudo venía aquí sola, pero muchas veces no estaba sola una vez llegaba a la isla. Eso queda claro de sus dietarios.

¿Es posible que tuviera una aventura?

Se me revuelve el estómago mientras veo el puente Dawhoo carretera adelante. No puede ser. A pesar de la presión de una vida pública, mi familia siempre se ha caracterizado por los matrimonios muy estables. Mi abuela quería a mi abuelo con toda su alma. Aparte de eso, la abuela Judy es una de las personas más rectas que conozco. Es un pilar de la comunidad y un referente en la Iglesia metodista. Nunca, jamás le ocultaría algo a su familia.

A no ser que fuera algo que pudiera hacernos daño.

Y eso es precisamente lo que me da miedo.

Es también la razón por la que hay un sobre con el nombre de mi abuela escrito y alguna clase de información clandestina en el interior.

—Estés o no preparado, aquí vengo —susurro al aire salobre—. ¿Qué es lo que querías de mi abuela, Trent Turner?

Mientras esperaba en coches y en salas de espera de médicos estas últimas semanas he tratado de averiguar cosas sobre Trent Turner I y II, abuelo y padre respectivamente del Trent con el que hablé por teléfono, que es Trent Turner III. He buscado vínculos políticos, antecedentes penales o cualquier cosa que pueda explicar su relación con mi abuela. He usado mis mejores trucos de fiscal. Por desgracia no hay nada evidente. Según una necrológica publicada hace siete meses en el diario de Charleston, Trent Turner I residió toda su vida en Charleston y en la isla de Edisto y era propietario de la inmobiliaria Turner. Un hombre como cualquier otro. Normal y corriente. Su hijo, Trent Turner II, está casado y vive en Texas, donde tiene una agencia inmobiliaria.

Trent Turner III no parece ser tampoco nadie extraordinario. Jugó a baloncesto en Clemson y era bastante bueno. Se dedicaba al negocio inmobiliario hasta hace poco, sobre todo en Nueva York. Una noticia en la prensa local de hace unos meses informa de que dejó la ciudad para hacerse cargo del negocio de su abuelo en Edisto.

¿Por qué, no puedo evitar preguntarme, *un hombre que se dedica a comprar y vender rascacielos se muda a un lugar perdido como Edisto a trabajar con casas de playa y alquileres vacacionales?*

Pronto lo sabré, he buscado la dirección de su oficina. De una manera u otra, mi intención es salir de las oficinas de la inmobiliaria Turner con el sobre de mi abuela y todo su contenido, sea el que sea.

A pesar del nerviosismo que siento, Edisto empieza a ejercer su magia cuando salgo del puente y conduzco por la autopista ya del lado de la isla, dejando atrás casitas curtidas por el mar y unas cuantas tiendas escondidas entre pinos y robles de Virginia. Arriba, el cielo es de un color azul perfecto.

Este sitio sigue casi igual a como lo recordaba. Se respira una atmósfera apacible, elegante, virgen. No en vano los habitantes la llaman «la isla tranquila». Los robles centenarios se inclinan sobre la carretera como si buscaran protegerla del mundo exterior. Árboles recubiertos de musgo proyectan sombras oscuras en el pequeño todoterreno que he birlado del garaje de Drayden Hill para hacer este viaje. Las carreteras secundarias de Edisto pueden ser algo rústicas y, además, presentarme en un BMW no parecía una buena idea considerando que no sé si el contenido del sobre puede ser algo relacionado con un chantaje.

El edificio de la inmobiliaria Turner es fácil de encontrar. Es original, pero no necesariamente imponente, de esa clase de construcciones que se contentan con ser lo que son, un chalé tradicional de color azul marino en la calle Jungle, a un par de manzanas de la playa. Ahora que estoy aquí, me resulta vagamente familiar, claro que de niña no tenía ninguna razón para entrar en un sitio así.

Mientras aparco y cruzo el aparcamiento salpicado de arena, siento por un momento celos del hombre que he venido a ver. Yo podría trabajar en un sitio así. Podría incluso vivir aquí. Levantarme cada mañana en el paraíso. Llegan risas y sonidos de la playa cercana. Cometas de vivos colores sobrevuelan las copas de los árboles, la brisa marina las sostiene en lo alto.

Dos niñas pequeñas corren calle abajo tirando de cintas rojas atadas a un palo. Pasan tres mujeres en bicicleta, riendo. Una vez más siento envidia y entonces pienso: *¿Por qué no vengo aquí más a menudo? ¿Por qué no llamo nunca a mis hermanas o a mi madre y les digo: «Venga, vámonos unos días a tomar el sol. Nos vendrá bien un descanso haciendo planes de chicas, ¿no?»?*

¿Por qué no hemos venido nunca Elliot y yo?

La respuesta tiene un sabor amargo, así que no la mastico demasiado. Nuestras agendas están siempre llenas de otras cosas. Esa es la razón.

¿Quién decide nuestras agendas? Nosotros, supongo.

Aunque a menudo da la impresión de que no tenemos elección. Si no pintamos continuamente las murallas, el viento y el clima se colarán y erosionarán los logros de doce generaciones previas. Una buena vida exige mucho mantenimiento.

Cuando subo los peldaños del porche de la inmobiliaria Turner, respiro hondo para coger fuerzas. El letrero dice: «Pase, estamos abiertos...», y eso hago. El tintineo de una campana anuncia mi entrada, pero detrás del mostrador no hay nadie.

La habitación delantera es un vestíbulo con sillas de vinilo de colores alineadas contra las paredes. Hay un dispensador de agua con vasos de papel. En los estantes hay innumerables folletos. Una máquina de palomitas me recuerda que no he comido. Cubren las paredes atractivas fotografías de la isla. La base del mostrador al fondo está decorada con dibujos infantiles y fotografías de familias felices posando delante de sus nuevas casas en la playa. Algunas, en blanco y negro, parecen ser de principios de la década de 1950. Me pongo a mirarlas, buscando a mi abuela. No hay rastro de ella.

—¿Hola? —digo, puesto que de las habitaciones del pasillo no sale nadie—. ¿Hola?

Tal vez han salido un momento. El lugar está en completo silencio.

Me ruge el estómago, pidiendo palomitas.

Estoy a punto de asaltar la máquina cuando se abre la puerta trasera. Dejo la bolsa de papel de las palomitas y me vuelvo.

—Hola, no sabía que había alguien.

Reconozco a Trent Turner III de la fotografía de internet, pero esa imagen estaba sacada de lejos, un plano de cuerpo entero delante de un edificio. Llevaba gorra deportiva y barba. No le hacía justicia. Ahora está recién afeitado. Vestido con pantalones caqui, mocasines muy gastados sin calcetines y un polo entallado y favorecedor, parece salido de un almuerzo al aire libre o de un anuncio de muebles de jardín. Es rubio pajizo y de ojos azules, lleva el pelo algo descuidado, lo justo para dar a entender: *Vivo al lado de la playa*.

Avanza por el pasillo con un par de bolsas de comida para llevar y una bebida. No puedo evitar que se me vayan los ojos a las bolsas. Me parece oler gambas y patatas fritas. Mi estómago vuelve a protestar de forma audible.

—Perdón... No había nadie. —Señalo con el pulgar hacia la puerta.

—He salido a comprar algo de comer. —Deja la comida en el mostrador, busca una servilleta y se conforma con un papel de la impresora para limpiarse de salsa rosa. El apretón de manos que nos damos es pegajoso, pero cordial.

—Trent Turner —dice con naturalidad—. ¿En qué puedo ayudarla?

Su sonrisa me hace querer sentir simpatía por él. Es la clase de sonrisa que da por hecho que gusta a la gente. Parece... sincero, supongo.

—Lo llamé hace un par de semanas. —No tiene sentido empezar diciendo nombres.

—¿Para alquiler o compraventa?

—¿Cómo?

—La casa. ¿Busca para alquilar o para comprar?

Es evidente que está intentando hacer memoria. Pero hay alguna cosa más que le interesa de mí. Siento una chispa de..., de algo.

Me doy cuenta de que le estoy devolviendo la sonrisa.

Al instante me remuerde la conciencia. ¿Debería una mujer prometida —por sola que se sienta— reaccionar así? Quizá es porque Elliot y yo apenas hemos hablado desde hace casi dos semanas. Ha estado en Milán. Con la diferencia horaria es difícil. Está centrado en su trabajo. Yo estoy centrada en los asuntos familiares.

—Ninguna de las dos cosas. —Supongo que no tiene sentido seguir posponiéndolo. El hecho de que este hombre sea atractivo y simpático no cambia la realidad—. Lo llamé en relación con algo que encontré en casa de mi abuela. —Mi naciente amistad con Trent Turner está sin duda destinada a ser fugaz—. Soy Avery Stafford. Me dijo que tenía un sobre dirigido a mi abuela, Judy Stafford. He venido a recogerlo.

Su actitud cambia de inmediato. Unos antebrazos musculosos se cruzan delante del pecho y el mostrador se convierte instantáneamente en una mesa de negociación. De negociación hostil.

Parece disgustado. Mucho.

—Siento que haya hecho un viaje en balde. Ya le dije que no puedo darle esos documentos a nadie salvo a las personas a las que van dirigidos. Ni siquiera a un familiar.

—Tengo un poder notarial. —Empiezo a sacarlo de mi bolso tamaño gigante. Al ser la abogada de la familia y con mi madre y mi padre centrados en la salud de este, soy la persona designada para representar a la abuela Judy. Despliego los papeles y empiezo a pasar hojas mientras él levanta la mano en señal de protesta—. No está en situación de llevar sus propios asuntos y estoy autorizada a...

Rechaza el ofrecimiento sin mirar siquiera los documentos.

—No es un asunto legal.

—Sí, si es correo dirigido a ella.

—No es correo. Es más... la limpieza de algunos cabos sueltos de los archivos de mi abuelo. —Aparta la vista y mira las palmeras agitadas por la brisa al otro lado de la ventana, esquivando mi curiosidad.

—Entonces, ¿es sobre la casa de Edisto? Después de todo, esto es una agencia inmobiliaria, pero ¿por qué tanto secreto con los papeles de una propiedad?

—No.

La respuesta es decepcionante en su brevedad. Por lo general, cuando haces una suposición incorrecta sobre un testigo, este reacciona dándote involuntariamente al menos algo de información veraz.

Es evidente que Trent Turner tiene mucha experiencia en negociaciones. De hecho, tengo la impresión de que ya ha tenido esta misma negociación. Ha dicho: «documentos» y «personas», en plural. ¿Hay otras familias a las que se niega a dar información?

—No pienso irme hasta descubrir la verdad.

—Hay palomitas. —Su intento de bromear no consigue más que encenderme más.

—Esto no es ninguna broma.

—Ya lo sé. —Por primera vez, parece compadecerse ligeramente de mi situación. Descruza los brazos. Se pasa una mano por el pelo con brusquedad. Cierra los ojos de espesas pestañas marrones. Se le forman en las comisuras unas arrugas que sugieren que no siempre ha llevado una vida tan relajada—. Mire, se lo prometí a mi abuelo... en su lecho de muerte. Y créame, es mejor así.

No le creo. Esa es la cuestión.

—Los solicitaré por la vía legal, si es necesario.

—¿Los archivos de mi abuelo? —Una risa sardónica me dice que no le gustan demasiado las amenazas—. Pues buena suerte. Eran propiedad suya. Y ahora mía. Tendrá que aceptarlo.

—No si es algo que puede perjudicar a mi familia.

La expresión de su cara me dice que me he acercado a la verdad. Se me pone mal cuerpo. Así que, después de todo, mi familia tiene un secreto profundo, oscuro. ¿Qué es?

Trent deja escapar un largo suspiro.

—Es... De verdad que es mejor así. Es todo lo que puedo decirle.

Suena el teléfono y lo contesta, según parece con la esperanza de que la interrupción me haga marcharme de allí. La persona que llama tiene un millón de preguntas sobre alquiler de casas de playa y sobre las actividades que se pueden hacer en la isla. Trent se toma tiempo para hablar de todo, desde la pesca de corvina negra hasta la búsqueda de fósiles de mastodonte y puntas de flecha en la playa. Le da a su interlocutor una encantadora lección de historia sobre familias acaudaladas que vivían en Edisto antes de la guerra entre estados. Habla de cangrejos violinistas, de cieno salino y del cultivo de ostras.

Se mete gambas fritas en la boca, las saborea mientras escucha. Me está dando la espalda, apoyado en el mostrador.

Regreso a mi asiento original junto a la puerta, me quedo en el borde de la silla y le miro la espalda mientras recita su letanía interminable sobre la bahía de Botany. Parece estar describiendo las mil seiscientas veinte hectáreas de parque nacional centímetro a centímetro. Golpeo el suelo con el pie y tamborileo con los dedos. Simula no darse cuenta, pero lo sorprendo mirándome por el rabillo del ojo.

Saco el teléfono y miro los correos. En el peor de los casos, me meteré en Instagram o echaré un vistazo a las ideas que mi madre y Bitsy quieren que mire en Pinterest.

Trent Turner se inclina sobre un ordenador de mesa, busca información, habla de alquileres y fechas.

El cliente por fin se decide por un lugar y unas fechas para unas vacaciones ideales. Trent le confiesa que él no se ocupa de hacer las reservas. Tiene a su secretaria en casa con un niño malo, pero le enviará un correo y ella se encargará de las confirmaciones.

Por fin, después de lo que me ha parecido al menos media hora de conversación, se endereza y mira hacia donde estoy. Sigue un duelo de miradas. Es muy posible que este hombre sea tan obstinado como yo. Por desgracia, él puede resistir más tiempo. Tiene comida.

Cuando cuelga el teléfono, se lleva un nudillo a los labios, menea la cabeza y suspira.

—Puede quedarse aquí todo el tiempo que quiera. Eso no va a cambiar nada.

Empieza a notársele que está irritado. He conseguido alterarlo.

Con toda tranquilidad, voy hasta la máquina de palomitas y el dispensador de agua y me sirvo.

Pertrechada ya para la espera, vuelvo a mi silla.

Él coloca con brusquedad una silla delante del ordenador, se sienta y desaparece tras un archivador de cuatro cajones.

Cuando me como la primera palomita, mi estómago deja escapar un rugido de lo menos discreto.

De pronto en el mostrador aparece un cesto con gambas. Unos dedos de hombre lo empujan en mi dirección, pero no dice una palabra. La amabilidad del detalle me hace sentir culpable, más aún cuando, con un gesto resuelto, añade un refresco. Sin duda estoy echando a perder su día perfecto.

Cojo unas pocas gambas y vuelvo a mi sitio. Resulta que el sentimiento de culpa y las gambas fritas casan bien.

Sonido de teclas de ordenador. De detrás del archivador sale otro suspiro. Pasa el tiempo. La silla de escritorio rechina a modo de protesta, como si se estuviera columpiando en ella.

—¿Los Stafford no tienen a gente que se ocupe de estas cosas?

—A veces, pero no en este caso.

—Seguro que están acostumbrados a salirse con la suya.

Esa insinuación me hace daño. Llevo toda la vida luchando por demostrar que soy algo más que una rubia guapa que lleva el apellido Stafford. Ahora, con las crecientes especulaciones sobre mi futuro en la política, estoy más que harta de oírlo. No me gradué con honores en la Facultad de Derecho de Columbia gracias a mi apellido.

—Lo que tengo lo consigo trabajando, si no le importa.

—Sí, ya...

—Nunca pido trato de favor y tampoco lo espero.

—Entonces, ¿puedo llamar a la policía para que se la lleven de mi sala de espera, como haría con cualquier otra persona que se instalara aquí y se negara a irse?

Las gambas y las palomitas forman una bola justo debajo de mi esternón. No haría algo así... ¿O sí? No quiero ni imaginarme lo que saldría en los periódicos. Leslie me cortaría la cabeza.

—¿Le pasa a menudo?

—No, a no ser que alguien se haya pasado con las cervezas en la playa. Y realmente Edisto no es ese tipo de lugares. No tenemos demasiadas emociones aquí.

—Lo sé. Y tengo la sensación de que es una de las razones por las que no quiere que venga la policía.

—¿Una de las razones?

—Dudo mucho que no sepa que hay personas que no habrían dudado en amenazar a mi familia con información que pudiera ser perjudicial... si es que tal información existe. Y esa clase de comportamiento es ilegal.

Al momento Trent Turner se ha levantado de la silla y yo de la mía. Nos miramos como dos generales desde lados opuestos de una mesa de operaciones.

—Está usted a punto de conocer a la policía de la playa de Edisto.

—¿Qué quería su abuelo de mi abuela?

—No era chantaje, si es lo que quiere insinuar. Mi abuelo era un hombre honrado.

—¿Por qué tenía un sobre para ella?

—Tenían asuntos comunes.

—¿Qué asuntos? ¿Por qué no le habló a nadie de ello?

—Quizá pensó que era lo mejor.

—¿Mi abuela venía aquí... a encontrarse con alguien? ¿Eso fue lo que descubrió su abuelo?

Retrocede y tuerce el gesto.

—¡No!

—Entonces, cuéntemelo. —Me he puesto en modo interrogatorio, centrada en un único objetivo: llegar a la verdad—. ¡Deme el sobre!

Da una palmada en el mostrador que hace vibrar todo lo que hay encima y a continuación lo rodea y sale. Da unos cuantos pasos y estamos cara a cara. Me pongo lo más alta que puedo y, aunque sigue superándome en estatura, no me dejo intimidar. Vamos a solucionar esto. Aquí y ahora.

Suena la campanilla de la puerta y al principio casi ni me doy cuenta. Estoy concentrada en unos ojos azules sobre un fondo blanco y unos dientes apretados.

—Madre mía, qué calor hace fuera. ¿Hay palomitas?

—Cuando miro por encima del hombro, veo a un hombre

uniformado, un empleado del servicio de parques o quizá un guarda de caza, en la puerta, mirándonos a Trent Turner y a mí alternativamente—. Ah, no sabía que tenías visita...

—Pasa y coge unas cuantas, Ed. —Trent Turner recibe al recién llegado con una simpatía entusiasta que se esfuma en cuanto se vuelve de nuevo hacia mí y añade—: Avery ya se iba.

12

RILL

Pasan dos semanas hasta que me entero de que los niños aquí somos tutelados de la Asociación de Hogares Infantiles de Tennessee. No sé lo que significa «tutelado» la primera vez que se lo oigo decir a la señora Murphy por teléfono. Tampoco puedo preguntar, puesto que se supone que no estoy escuchando. He descubierto que, si me cuelo entre las azaleas que hay a lo largo de la pared de la casa, me puedo acercar lo bastante para oír a través de las mosquiteras de las ventanas de su despacho.

—Por supuesto que todos los niños son tutelados de la Asociación de Hogares Infantiles de Tennessee, Dortha. Entiendo la situación de su nuera. Cuando son infelices, los hombres recurren a la bebida y a... la haraganería. Para una mujer es muy duro. Tener un niño en casa puede animar un poco el ambiente y solucionar el problema por completo. La paternidad transforma a los hombres. Estoy segura de que no habrá problemas, puesto que pueden pagar los costes. Sí..., sí..., enseguida, por supuesto. Una sorpresa por su aniversario. Qué bonito. Si pudiera darle uno de estos, Dortha, sin duda lo haría.

Ahora mismo tengo unos angelitos encantadores. Pero la señorita Tann es quien toma las decisiones, a mí solo me pagan por hospedar a los niños y...

De la conversación deduzco enseguida el significado de la palabra. «Tutelado» quiere decir que los padres de estos niños no han vuelto a buscarlos. Los niños de aquí dicen que, si tus padres no vienen a buscarte, la señorita Tann te da a otras personas que te llevan a casa con ellas. A veces se quedan contigo, pero a veces no. Me da miedo hacer demasiadas preguntas porque se supone que no tenemos que hablar de ello, pero tengo la sensación de que por eso no hemos vuelto a ver a la hermana mayor de Stevie desde que llegamos. La señorita Tann se la dio a alguien. Sherry era una tutelada.

Nosotros tenemos suerte de no serlo. Nosotros somos de Briny y pronto vendrá a buscarnos, en cuanto Queenie esté bien. Está tardando más de lo que pensaba y por eso he empezado a escuchar debajo de la ventana de la señora Murphy, porque tengo la esperanza de oír algo sobre Briny. Cuando pregunto a las empleadas de aquí, me dicen que me porte bien o tendré que quedarme más tiempo. No imagino qué puede ser peor que eso, así que hago todo lo posible por asegurarme de que todos nos portamos bien.

Estoy corriendo un riesgo acercándome así a la ventana y lo sé. No nos dejan acercarnos a los parterres de la señora Murphy. Si supiera que estoy oyendo sus conversaciones telefónicas y las que tiene en el porche delantero cuando vienen visitas... Tengo cierta idea de lo que podría pasarme.

Se acerca a la mosquitera y entre las hojas de azalea veo salir humo de cigarrillo. Se queda suspendido en la humedad del aire como el genio flotando sobre la lámpara de Aladino y me pica la nariz por las ganas de estornudar. Me cubro la cara con la mano y las ramas se mueven. El corazón me golpea con fuerza las costillas.

—¡Señora Pulnik! —grita—. ¡Señora Pulnik!

Me quedo helada. *No salgas corriendo. No salgas corriendo,* me digo.

Unos pasos rápidos resuenan en el vestíbulo dentro de la casa.

—¿Qué ocurre, señora Murphy?

—Dígale a Riggs que eche veneno esta noche debajo de las azaleas. Esos conejos endemoniados han vuelto a meterse en mis parterres.

—Se lo *dirré* enseguida.

—Y que arregle el jardín delantero y limpie las malas hierbas. Dígale que ponga a los niños mayores a ayudarlo como crea conveniente. Que la señorita Tann viene mañana y que más le vale tener el lugar presentable. De lo contrario...

—Sí, señora Murphy.

—¿Qué ha pasado con los que estaban en la enfermería? Concretamente con el niño pequeño de ojos violeta oscuro. La señorita Tann quiere verlo. Lo tiene comprometido para un pedido de Nueva York.

—Está *aletarrgado,* me temo. Es que está muy flaco. Solo come unas pocas gachas de maíz. No creo que pueda *viajarr.*

—Pues a la señorita Tann no le va a gustar. Y a mí tampoco. Uno habría esperado que, después de haber crecido en callejones y zanjas, estos pequeños pordioseros serían más resistentes.

—Eso es verdad. La niña de la *enferrmería* también está empeorando. Desde hace dos días se niega a *comerr.* Deberíamos *llamarr* al médico, ¿sí?

—Por supuesto que no. ¿Por qué en nombre del cielo vamos a llamar al médico por una simple descomposición? Los niños andan siempre con la tripa suelta. Denle raíz de jengibre. Con eso se le pasará.

—Lo que usted diga.

—¿Qué tal está el pequeño Stevie? Es más o menos del mismo tamaño que el niño de la enfermería. Mayor, pero eso lo podemos cambiar. ¿De qué color tiene los ojos?

—Castaños. Pero sigue mojando la cama todas las noches. Y se niega a *decirr* una palabra. No creo que le guste a ningún cliente.

—Pues no lo vamos a permitir. Átenlo a la cama y déjenlo ahí si vuelve a mojarse. Una ampolla o dos le enseñarán la lección. En cualquier caso, los ojos castaños no nos sirven para este pedido. Tienen que ser azules, verdes o violetas. Es lo que han especificado. No castaños.

—¿Y Robby?

Se me cierra la garganta. Robby es como llaman a mi hermanito. No hay otro Robby en la casa.

—Me temo que no. A esos cinco los estamos reservando para una visita especial.

Me trago el nudo de la garganta, lo empujo hasta el estómago. *Una visita especial.* Creo que sé lo que eso significa. He visto venir padres aquí unas cuantas veces. Esperan en el porche y las empleadas les sacan a los niños, limpios, vestidos y repeinados. Los padres traen regalos y los abrazan y lloran cuando se tienen que ir. Eso deben de ser las visitas especiales.

Briny vendrá pronto a vernos.

Pero eso también me preocupa. La semana pasada se presentó un hombre a ver a su hijito y la señora Murphy le dijo que no estaba aquí. «Ha sido dado en adopción. Lo siento mucho». Eso fue lo que dijo.

«Tiene que estar aquí», insistió el hombre. «Lonnie Kemp. Es mío. No lo he dado en adopción. Solo lo dejé en el hogar infantil hasta que pudiera hacerme cargo de él».

La señora Murphy no pareció preocupada, ni siquiera cuando el hombre se desmoronó y se echó a llorar. «Sea como sea, no está. El juzgado de familia decidió que era lo mejor. Se lo han llevado unos padres que lo cuidarán muy bien».

«Pero es mi hijo».

«No debe usted ser egoísta, señor Kemp. Lo hecho hecho está. Piense en el niño. Tendrá lo que usted nunca podría darle».

«Es mi hijo...».

El hombre cayó de rodillas y se puso a llorar allí en el porche.

La señora Murphy entró en la casa y cerró la puerta sin más.

Al cabo de un rato, el señor Riggs hizo levantarse al hombre y lo acompañó a la calle y a su camioneta. Estuvo allí todo el día mirando el jardín, buscando a su hijo.

Me preocupa que Briny venga y tenga el mismo problema. Solo que Briny no se quedará llorando sin hacer nada. Entrará por la fuerza y ocurrirá algo horrible. El señor Riggs es un hombre grande. La señorita Tann conoce a la policía.

—Extremen los cuidados con el niñito de la enfermería —está diciendo ahora la señora Murphy—. Denle un buen baño y un poco de helado. Quizá una galleta de jengibre. Estimúlenlo un poco. Voy a preguntarle a la señorita Tann si puede retrasar el pedido un día o dos. Quiero que esté lo bastante bien para viajar. ¿Me ha entendido?

—Sí, señora Murphy. —La señora Pulnik pronuncia las palabras entre dientes, lo que me dice que no me conviene que me encuentre hoy debajo de las azaleas. Cuando está de ese humor, más te vale correr y esconderte bien, porque está buscando con quien pagarlo.

Lo último que oigo es a la señora Murphy cruzando la habitación y gritando en dirección al vestíbulo:

—¡Y no se olvide de envenenar a los conejos!

Cojo una rama rota y froto con las hojas sobre las huellas de mis rodillas para que el señor Riggs no sepa que he estado aquí. No quiero que se lo cuente a la señora Pulnik.

Pero eso no es lo que más miedo me da. Lo que más me asusta es que el señor Riggs sepa que alguien se mete entre los arbustos. Para llegar hasta las azaleas hay que deslizarse por delante de las puertas del sótano. El señor Riggs las deja abiertas y, siempre que puede, se trae a algún niño. Nadie habla de lo que ocurre ahí abajo, ni siquiera los chicos mayores. «Si hablas de ello», dicen, «el señor Riggs te cogerá, te retorcerá el pescuezo y dirá que te has caído de un árbol o tropezado con los peldaños del porche. Luego se llevarán tu cuerpo en un carro al pantano y se lo comerán los caimanes y nadie volverá a saber de ti».

James, el pelirrojo alto, lleva aquí el tiempo suficiente para haberlo visto. Le damos caramelos de menta y él nos cuenta lo que necesitamos saber para sobrevivir aquí, en la casa de la señora Murphy. No somos amigos, pero los caramelos sirven para comprar muchas cosas aquí. Cada mañana, cuando nos levantamos, hay un paquetito de pastillas de menta que nos han metido por debajo de la puerta de nuestra habitación. De noche oigo al señor Riggs acercarse. Prueba con el picaporte, pero la puerta está cerrada, y las empleadas siempre se llevan las llaves después de acostarnos. Mejor. A veces, después de que el señor Riggs venga a nuestra habitación, le oigo subir las escaleras de la casa. No sé adónde va, pero me alegro de que estemos en el sótano. Hace frío y los catres militares son ásperos y huelen mal, y tenemos que usar un orinal, pero al menos cuando estamos aquí nadie puede venir a por nosotros.

Espero que Briny venga antes de que se queden camas libres arriba y nos trasladen.

Riggs se dirige a la puerta del sótano justo cuando llego al final del seto de azaleas. Casi no me da tiempo a esconderme detrás de las ramas.

Mira hacia donde estoy antes de bajar las escaleras, pero no puede verme. Soy otra vez como el Hombre Invisible. La Niña Invisible. Esa soy yo.

Espero hasta estar segura de que se ha ido y entonces salgo de mi escondrijo tan sigilosa como un lince. Un lince puede estar a menos de un metro de ti sin que lo sepas. Cojo aire profundamente y paso corriendo delante de la puerta del sótano hasta rodear la higuera. Una vez hecho esto, estás a salvo. Riggs sabe que las empleadas se asoman mucho a las ventanas de la cocina. No hace nada donde otros puedan verlo.

Camellia me espera en el montículo detrás del jardín de la iglesia. Lark y Fern están subidas en el balancín con Gabion en el centro. Stevie está sentado en el suelo al lado de Camellia. En cuanto me siento, trepa a mi regazo.

—Qué bien —dice Camellia—. Quítamelo de encima. Apesta a pis.

—No es culpa suya. —Stevie me echa los brazos al cuello y se recuesta contra mi pecho. Está pegajoso y es verdad que huele mal. Le paso la mano por el pelo y gime y se aparta. Tiene un chichón en la cabeza. A las empleadas de aquí les gusta pegar a los niños donde no se vea.

—Sí es culpa suya. Y también podría hablar si quisiera. Lo único que está consiguiendo es buscarse líos con las empleadas. Le he dicho que más le vale parar. De lo contrario...

Mira quién fue a hablar. Si alguno de nosotros termina en el armario mientras estamos aquí será Camellia. Sigo sin saber con seguridad lo que pasa dentro de ese armario, pero debe de ser malo. Hace solo un par de días la señora Murphy se acercó a la mesa del desayuno y dijo: «Cuando pillemos al ladrón de comida, irá al armario, y no solo por un día».

Desde entonces no falta nada en la cocina.

—Stevie está asustado, eso es todo. Echa de menos... —me interrumpo antes de decir el nombre. Si hablo de su hermana, se pondrá más triste. A veces se me olvida que, aunque ya no habla, sí entiende todo lo que decimos.

—¿Qué has oído en la ventana? —Camellia odia que no deje a nadie más esconderse entre las azaleas. Siempre me mira de arriba abajo y me olisquea para ver si he encontrado caramelos de menta mientras estaba allí. Cree que los chicos mayores mienten cuando hablan del señor Riggs. Si no la vigilo, intentará escabullirse allí cuando salimos a jugar. No puedo perderla de vista un momento, si no es para dejarla a cargo de los pequeños.

—No ha dicho nada de Briny. —Sigo intentando encontrar sentido a lo que oí debajo de la ventana de la señora Murphy. No estoy segura de cuánto debo contarle a Camellia.

—No va a venir. Lo han metido en la cárcel o algo y no puede salir. Queenie está muerta.

Me pongo de pie con Stevie en brazos.

—¡De eso nada! ¡No digas eso, Mellia! ¡No lo digas nunca!

En el parque, los balancines se detienen y los pies arañan la tierra para parar los columpios. Hay niños mirándonos. Están acostumbrados a ver a los niños mayores pelear, rodar por el suelo y darse patadas y puñetazos. Con las niñas no suele pasar.

—¡Es verdad!

Camellia se pone de pie a la velocidad del rayo con el mentón levantado y los brazos largos y flacos en jarras. Los remolinos de pecas le achican los ojos hasta casi hacerlos desaparecer y arruga la nariz. Parece un cerdo moteado.

—¡No lo es!

—¡Claro que sí!

Stevie gime y se revuelve para soltarse. Decido que es mejor dejarlo en el suelo. Corre hasta el balancín, donde Lark lo coge en brazos.

Camellia saca un puño. No sería la primera vez que terminamos enredadas en un combate de escupitajos y tirones de pelo.

—¡Eh, parad ahora mismo!

Antes de que me dé cuenta, James ha salido del escondrijo de los chicos mayores y viene hacia nosotras.

Camellia duda el tiempo justo para que llegue hasta ella. Saca una manaza, la coge del vestido y la empuja al suelo con brusquedad.

—Quédate ahí —gruñe y la amenaza con el dedo.

Camellia no obedece, por supuesto. Se pone de pie más furiosa que una avispa a la que han intentado aplastar. James vuelve a tirarla al suelo.

—¡Oye! —grito—. ¡Para!

Es mi hermana, aunque estuviera a punto de dejarme inconsciente de un puñetazo.

James me mira y sonríe, el diente mellado deja ver la punta rosada de su lengua.

—¿Quieres que pare?

Camellia hace ademán de pegarle y él le coge un brazo y la sujeta lejos de él de manera que no pueda darle patadas. Camellia parece una araña que se ha enganchado una pata en una puerta. James la aprieta tan fuerte que se le amorata la piel. Tiene los ojos llenos de lágrimas a punto de brotar, pero sigue resistiéndose.

—¡Para! —grito—. ¡Déjala en paz!

—Si quieres que pare tienes que ser mi novia, chica guapa —dice. Y añade—: De lo contrario, que gane el mejor.

Camellia ruge y chilla y se pone como loca.

—¡Suéltala! —Intento pegarle, pero James me coge de la muñeca y ahora nos tiene a las dos. Me crujen los huesos. Los pequeños vienen corriendo de los columpios, también Stevie, y empiezan a pegar a James en las piernas. Él zarandea a Camellia y la usa para derribar a Fern y a Gabion. De la nariz de Fern sale sangre y grita, llevándose las manos a la cara.

—¡De acuerdo! ¡De acuerdo! —digo. ¿Qué otra cosa puedo hacer? Miro a mi alrededor en busca de adultos y, como siempre, no hay ninguno.

—¿De acuerdo qué, chica guapa? —pregunta James.

—De acuerdo, seré tu novia. Pero no pienso besarte.

Parece contentarse con eso. Deja caer a Camellia al suelo y le dice que más le vale quedarse ahí. Me hace seguirlo ladera arriba y rodear un antiguo retrete que está tapiado para que nadie pueda entrar y le muerda una serpiente. Por segunda vez en el mismo día, el corazón me martillea.

—No pienso besarte —le repito.

—Cállate —dice.

Una vez detrás del retrete me empuja al suelo y se tira a mi lado sin dejar de apretarme el brazo. Mi respiración se acelera y se me queda atrapada en la garganta. Me sabe la boca a bilis.

¿Qué piensa hacer conmigo? Al haber crecido en un barco y visto nacer a cuatro niños, sé un poco sobre lo que hacen hombres y mujeres cuando están juntos. No quiero que alguien me lo haga a mí. Nunca. No me gustan los chicos y nunca me gustarán. A James le huele el aliento a patata podrida y el único chico al que pensé que podría dejarle besarme fue Silas, y eso fue solo durante un minuto o dos.

Las cancioncillas de su panda nos llegan desde la casa: «James tiene novia. James y May. En un árbol sentaditos, se van a dar besitos...».

Pero James no intenta besarme. Se limita a estar a mi lado mientras unas manchas rojas le suben por el cuello hasta las mejillas.

—Eres guapa. —La voz le sale chillona como la de un lechón. Es gracioso, pero no me río. Estoy demasiado asustada.

—No lo soy.

—Eres muy guapa. —Me suelta la muñeca e intenta cogerme la mano. La retiro y me abrazo las rodillas formando una bola apretada.

—No me gustan los chicos —digo.

—Un día me casaré contigo.

—No quiero casarme con nadie. Voy a construirme un barco y navegar río abajo. Cuidarme sola.

—Igual me subo yo también al barco.

—De eso nada.

Nos quedamos sentados un rato. Los chicos canturrean colina abajo: «James tiene novia... Besitos».

Apoya los codos en las rodillas y me mira.

—¿De ahí venís? ¿Del río?

—Sí.

Hablamos de barcos. James es de una pequeña granja del condado de Shelby. La señorita Tann los recogió un día a él y a su hermano cuando iban camino de la escuela. Entonces estaba en cuarto curso. Lleva aquí desde entonces y no ha ido a la escuela ni un solo día. Su hermano se fue hace mucho. Lo adoptaron.

James levanta la barbilla.

—No quiero padres nuevos —dice—. Dentro de poco seré demasiado mayor y saldré de aquí. Voy a necesitar una esposa. Podemos ir a vivir al río, si quieres.

—Va a venir mi padre a buscarnos. —Me siento mal diciendo esto. James me da pena. Más que ninguna otra cosa, parece estar muy solo. Solo y triste—. Vendrá pronto.

James se limita a encogerse de hombros.

—Mañana te traeré bollos de pasas. Pero tienes que seguir siendo mi novia.

No contesto. La boca se me hace agua de pensar en los bollos. Me parece que ya sé quién ha estado rondando por la cocina de noche.

—No deberías. Te pueden mandar al armario.

—No me da miedo. —Pone una mano encima de la mía.

La dejo estar.

Quizá no me moleste tanto, después de todo.

Pronto me doy cuenta de que no está tan mal ser novia de James. Es fácil hablar con él y lo único que quiere es cogerme la mano. Durante el resto del día nadie me molesta. Nadie se porta mal con Camellia, con Lark o con los pequeños. James y yo paseamos de la mano y me cuenta más cosas que me interesa saber sobre la casa de la señora Murphy. Me promete otra vez los bollos. Me explica cómo se colará en la cocina esta noche a cogerlos.

Le digo que no me gustan los bollos de pasas.

En la cola para el baño, los chicos mayores no me miran. Saben que no les conviene.

Pero al día siguiente James no está en el desayuno. La señora Pulnik se acerca a la mesa dándose golpecitos en la palma de la mano grande y carnosa con una cuchara de madera. Dice que han enviado a James a un sitio donde los chicos tienen que ganarse el sustento en lugar de recibirlo gratis gracias a la amabilidad de la Asociación de Hogares Infantiles de Tennessee.

—Un chico que es lo bastante *mayorr* para *andarr* detrás de las chicas es lo bastante *mayorr* para trabajar y demasiado para que lo quiera una buena familia. La señora Murphy no tiene intención de *tolerarr* este tipo de *comporrtamiento* entre chicos y chicas aquí. Todos conocéis las reglas. —Golpea fuerte el cucharón contra la mesa, respira en largas bocanadas que le hinchan las aletas de la nariz ancha y chata. Nos ponemos rectos como marionetas con un hilo en la cabeza. Se inclina hacia el lado de la mesa donde se sientan los chicos. Estos bajan la mirada y la fijan en sus cuencos vacíos—. Y en cuanto a las chicas —el cucharón y el brazo que se agita vienen ahora en nuestra dirección—, debería daros vergüenza *meterr* a los chicos en líos. Se acabó el *levantarrse* la falda, comportaos como señoritas. —Esa última palabra la acompaña con una mirada dura hacia mí—. De lo contrario, no quiero ni *pensarr* en lo que puede pasaros.

El rubor me sube por el cuello y las mejillas me arden. Me siento mal por haber hecho que se lleven a James. No debería haber sido su novia. No lo sabía.

Las empleadas tampoco traen a Stevie a desayunar hoy. No está en los columpios. Los otros niños me dicen que se ha tenido que quedar en la cama porque anoche volvió a mojarla. Lo veo más tarde detrás de la ventana del piso de arriba con la nariz pegada a la mosquitera. Me acerco y le susurro:

—Pórtate bien, ¿de acuerdo? Tú pórtate bien y ya está.

Después, esa misma tarde, las empleadas nos hacen formar fila en el porche y reúno a mis hermanos a mi alrededor porque tengo miedo. Ni siquiera los otros niños saben lo que pasa.

La señora Pulnik y las empleadas nos hacen pasar uno a uno por el barril con agua de lluvia. Lavan caras, brazos y rodillas sucias con trapos mojados, nos peinan y nos hacen lavarnos las manos. Algunos niños tienen que cambiarse de ropa allí mismo, en el porche. Algunos reciben ropa limpia o delantales que deben ponerse encima de sus ropas de juego.

La señora Murphy sale y se detiene en el primer peldaño para inspeccionarnos. Del brazo le cuelga una palmeta de sacudir alfombras hecha de alambre. Nunca he visto a las mujeres de la cocina usarla para quitar la suciedad de las alfombras, pero sí las he visto emplearla con niños muchas veces. Los niños la llaman la «bruja de alambre».

—Hoy va a pasar algo muy especial —anuncia la señora Murphy—, pero solo para los niños que sean buenos. Quien no se comporte hoy perfectamente no podrá participar. ¿Lo entendéis?

—Sí, señora —digo junto al resto de los niños.

—Muy bien. —Sonríe, pero la sonrisa me hace retroceder un paso—. Hoy viene la biblioteca móvil. Las amables damas de la Sociedad de Beneficencia van a dedicar su tiempo a ayudaros a escoger libros. Es muy importante que demos buena impresión. Si sois buenos, cada uno tendréis un libro para leer.

—Sigue hablando recordándonos que debemos tener buenos modales, decir «sí, señora» o «no, señora», no coger ni tocar todos los libros y, si las empleadas nos preguntan si somos felices aquí, debemos decir que estamos muy agradecidos a la señorita Tann por encontrarnos y a la señora Murphy por recogernos en su casa.

El resto me lo pierdo. En lo único que puedo pensar es en que vamos a tener la oportunidad de coger un libro, y pocas cosas hay en el mundo que me gusten más que los libros. Y al ser cinco, tendremos cinco libros.

Pero cuando las empleadas abren las puertas del jardín y empezamos a salir en fila, la señora Murphy nos detiene a Camellia, a mí y a los pequeños.

—Vosotros no —dice—. Puesto que aún no estáis en el piso de arriba, no tenéis dónde meter los libros y no puedo arriesgarme a que la propiedad de la biblioteca se estropee.

—Los trataremos con mucho cuidado, lo prometo —se me escapa. En condiciones normales jamás le habría contestado a la señora Murphy, pero esta vez no puedo evitarlo—. Por favor, ¿podemos coger aunque sea uno? ¿Y se lo puedo leer a mis hermanos? Queenie siempre... —Aprieto los labios antes de buscarme más problemas. Aquí tenemos prohibido hablar de nuestros padres.

Con un suspiro, la señora Murphy cuelga la palmeta de un clavo de una de las columnas del porche.

—Muy bien. Pero los pequeños no tienen por qué ir. Ve tú sola. Y date prisa.

Tardo un segundo en decidir si dejo o no a los pequeños. Camellia los coge de los brazos y los acerca a ella.

—Ve. —Me mira con los ojos muy abiertos—. Tráenos algo bueno.

Los miro por última vez antes de salir disparada por la verja. Tengo que hacer un esfuerzo por no echar a correr por el jardín y entre los magnolios. Aquí fuera huele a libertad. Huele bien. Tengo que obligarme a hacer cola y a seguir a los otros niños por la acera de manera ordenada.

Al otro lado de la pared que forman los árboles hay un gran camión negro. Aparcan dos automóviles más. De uno de ellos sale la señorita Tann y, del otro, un hombre con una cámara de fotos. Se estrechan la mano y el hombre se saca del bolsillo una libreta y una estilográfica.

El camión negro grande lleva escrito «Bibliotecas del condado de Shelby» en uno de los lados y, cuando nos acercamos, veo que de la parte trasera sobresalen estantes. Y los estantes están llenos de libros. Los niños se arremolinan alrededor de ellos y tengo que sujetarme las manos detrás de la espalda y enlazar con fuerza los dedos para no tocar nada mientras espero mi turno.

—Como puede ver usted mismo, nos gusta proporcionar a estos niños oportunidades estimulantes —explica la señorita Tann y el hombre escribe en su libreta como si las palabras fueran a escaparse si no las atrapa a tiempo—. Algunos de nuestros pequeños no conocían el lujo de la lectura antes de venir aquí. En todos nuestros hogares tenemos libros y juguetes maravillosos.

Agacho la cabeza, me impaciento y me pongo a desear que haya menos gente. Si la señorita Tann tiene otros sitios como este, no sé cómo serán, pero en casa de la señora Murphy no hay un solo libro y todos los juguetes están rotos. Nadie se molesta en arreglarlos. La señorita Tann ha estado aquí las veces suficientes para saber eso.

—Pobres criaturas —le dice al hombre—. Las acogemos cuando nadie las quiere y están abandonadas. Les damos todo lo que sus padres no quieren o no pueden darles.

Clavo la vista en el suelo y cierro los puños detrás de la espalda. *Es mentira*, me gustaría poder gritarle al hombre. *Mi madre y mi padre no nos han abandonado. Nos quieren. Lo mismo que el padre que vino a ver a aquel niñito, Lonnie, y terminó roto en el porche llorando como un crío cuando le dijeron que lo habían adoptado.*

—¿Cuánto tiempo de media se queda un niño en la asociación? —pregunta el hombre.

—Bueno, no tenemos una media. —La señorita Tann fuerza una risita—. Cada niño es especial. Algunos pueden quedarse más tiempo que otros, dependiendo de las condiciones en que nos lleguen. Algunos están débiles y famélicos, tan apagados que no pueden ni siquiera correr o jugar. Les devolvemos la energía con tres nutritivas comidas al día. Los niños necesitan una buena alimentación para crecer adecuadamente. Fruta y verdura en abundancia y carne roja les devuelven el brillo a las mejillas.

No en casa de la señora Murphy. En casa de la señora Murphy se comen gachas de maíz, un tazón pequeño por la mañana y otro por la noche. Siempre estamos hambrientos. Gabby está pálido como la leche y Lark y Fern tienen los brazos tan flacos que se les ven los músculos y los huesos.

—Supervisamos todos nuestros hogares para asegurarnos de que los niños están bien alimentados y cuidados.

Se comporta como si dijera la verdad y nada más que la verdad.

El hombre asiente con la cabeza y dice «Ajá», como si estuviera tragándoselo todo y le supiera la mar de bien.

Mira en el jardín trasero, quiero decirle. *Mira en la cocina. Verás cómo es en realidad.* Me muero de ganas de decirlo. Pero sé que si lo hago, no me darán un libro. Y me mandarán al armario.

—Los niños están muy agradecidos. Los sacamos del arroyo y...

Alguien me toca el brazo y no puedo evitar sobresaltarme. Una señora con un vestido azul me mira. Tiene una sonrisa tan radiante como un rayo de sol.

—Y a ti ¿qué te gusta leer? —pregunta—. ¿Qué clase de libros? Llevas esperando mucho rato y has sido muy paciente.

—Sí, señora.

Me conduce hacia los estantes y los ojos se me salen de las órbitas. Me olvido de la señorita Tann y solo pienso en libros. He ido a bibliotecas en pueblos a lo largo del río antes, pero es que antes también teníamos libros en el *Arcadia*. Ahora no tenemos nada y, cuando no tienes un solo libro, la idea de tocar uno es como Navidad y tu cumpleaños juntos.

—Me... me gustan todos —balbuceo. Solo mirar los estantes y ver todos esos colores y palabras me hace sonreír de oreja a oreja. Por primera vez desde que llegué aquí, me siento feliz—. Quizá uno largo estaría bien, como solo podemos coger uno...

—Chica lista. —La mujer me guiña un ojo—. ¿Lees mucho?

—Sí, mucho. En el... —Agacho la cabeza porque he estado a punto de decir: «En el *Arcadia* Queenie nos hacía leer todo el rato».

Hay una empleada a menos de un metro de mí y la señorita Tann tampoco está lejos. Si me oyera, me echaría de aquí en un abrir y cerrar de ojos.

—Muy bien —dice la señora—. Pues vamos a ver...

—Me gustan las aventuras. Las historias de aventuras.

—Mmm. Aventuras ¿sobre qué?

—Sobre reinas y princesas e indios salvajes. De todo tipo. —La cabeza se me llena de fantasías.

—¿Una del oeste entonces?

—O del río. ¿Tienen alguna de aventuras en el río?

Leer un libro sobre el río sería como volver a casa. Nos consolaría hasta que Briny nos lleve de vuelta al *Arcadia*.

La mujer junta las manos.

—Pues sí, sí tenemos. —Levanta un dedo—. Tengo el libro perfecto para ti.

Después de buscar un minuto, me da *Las aventuras de Huckleberry Finn*, de Mark Twain, y me parece que es un libro pensado especialmente para mí. Nunca lo hemos tenido, pero Briny nos ha contado historias de Tom Sawyer y Huckleberry Finn y Joe el indio. Mark Twain es uno de los autores preferidos de Briny. Leía sus libros cuando era pequeño. Es casi como si Tom Sawyer y él hubieran sido amigos de verdad.

La señora del vestido azul escribe mi nuevo nombre, May Weathers, en la tarjeta. Cuando pone un sello con la fecha en el libro, me doy cuenta de que ayer fue el cumpleaños de Fern. Ya tiene cuatro años. Si estuviéramos en el *Arcadia*, Queenie le haría un pastelito y todos le daríamos regalos hechos a mano o encontrados en la orilla del río. Aquí, en casa de la señora Murphy, tendremos que conformarnos con el libro. Cuando vuelva al jardín, le diré a Fern que es su sorpresa de cumpleaños, pero que solo podrá quedársela un tiempo. Haremos un pastel de barro y usaremos flores como si fueran glaseado y velas hechas de palitos con hojitas en la parte superior, para que Fern pueda jugar a soplarlas.

La señora de la biblioteca me da un abrazo de despedida y me siento tan bien que quiero quedarme allí y agarrarme a ella y oler los libros, pero no puedo.

Me pego *Huckleberry Finn* al pecho y cruzo el jardín. Ahora podemos olvidarnos de este sitio siempre que queramos. Nos basta con unirnos a Huckleberry Finn. En su balsa cabemos los cinco. Quizá nos encontremos con el *Arcadia*.

Aunque tengo que volver a casa de la señora Murphy, me parece un sitio completamente distinto.

Ahora tiene un río.

Esa misma noche, antes de acostarnos, abrimos el libro de cumpleaños de Fern y empezamos nuestras aventuras con Huck Finn. Llevamos viajando río abajo con él casi una semana cuando el automóvil negro reluciente de la señorita Tann sube una tarde por el camino de entrada. Es un día soleado y la casa está recalentada igual que la grasa de freír, así que la señora Murphy y ella se sientan a hablar en el porche. Me escabullo, rodeo la higuera y me escondo debajo de las azaleas para escuchar.

—Sí, sí. Los anuncios han salido ya en todos los periódicos —está diciendo la señorita Tann—. Tengo que reconocer que he estado de lo más inspirada. «Querubines de cabello rubio para el claro verano. ¡Solo tienen que pedirlos!». ¿A que es perfecto? Todos esos niñitos rubios.

—Como una reunión de ninfas del bosque. Duendecillos y hadas —se muestra de acuerdo la señora Murphy.

—Es casi tan atractivo como el programa de Un Bebé para Navidad. Los clientes ya han empezado a llamar. En cuanto vean a estos niños, se van a pelear por ellos.

—Sin duda.

—¿Los tendrá a todos preparados el sábado por la mañana, entonces? Doy por hecho que irán bien vestidos, con trajecitos tiroleses, lazos y todos los detalles. Todos bañados y restregados a base de bien. Nada de uñas mugrientas o de porquería detrás de las orejas. Asegúrese de que saben lo que se espera de ellos y lo que les pasará si me avergüenzan en público. Castigue a alguno a modo de ejemplo antes y que los otros lo vean. Esta fiesta representa una oportunidad importante de aumentar nuestra reputación de ofrecer lo mejor de lo mejor. Con los nuevos anuncios tendremos a las mejores familias de Tennessee y de una docena de estados más. Vendrán todos a ver a nuestros niños y cuando los vean no podrán resistirse. Querrán uno por encima de todo.

—Nos aseguraremos de que los niños están preparados como corresponde. Déjeme repasar la lista otra vez. —Dejan de hablar. Ruido de papeles. El viento cambia y agita las ramas de las azaleas y veo la cabeza de la señorita Tann. Su pelo corto gris atrapa la brisa y se le pone de punta cuando se inclina hacia la señora Murphy.

Me pego a la pared y me quedo muy quieta, por miedo a que me oigan y se asomen a la barandilla. El viento me trae el olor de algo muerto. No puedo verlo, pero probablemente se ha comido el veneno que puso el señor Riggs. Cuando el mal olor vaya a más, encontrará el cuerpo y lo enterrará en alguna parte.

—¿May también? —pregunta la señora Murphy y aguzo los oídos—. Tiene poco de querubín.

La señorita Tann suelta una risita aguda.

—Ayudará con los más pequeños y, por lo que recuerdo, es una chica bonita.

—Supongo que sí. —La señora Murphy no parece contenta—. Desde luego no da problemas.

—Mandaré los automóviles a buscarlos a la una del sábado. Que no vayan hambrientos ni con sueño ni con ganas de ir al retrete. Espabilados, contentos y con buen comportamiento garantizado. Es lo que espero.

—Por supuesto.

—¿Se puede saber qué es ese olor horrible?

—Conejos. Hemos tenido problemas con ellos este verano.

Me escabullo antes de que decidan salir a mirar. El señor Riggs no está por ninguna parte, así que no tardo en rodear la higuera y estar de vuelta en la colina. A Camellia no le digo nada de la fiesta ni de que mañana toca bañarse. No tiene sentido que se lleve un berrinche antes de tiempo.

Tengo el presentimiento de que, en cualquier caso, ella no va a tener que bañarse.

Camellia no es rubia.

Resulta que tengo razón. El sábado después del desayuno, compruebo que Camellia no está en la lista. Donde sea que vayamos, ella no viene.

—No me importa que no me quieran, me alegro de no tenerme que dar otro baño. —Cuando intento darle un abrazo de despedida, me empuja.

—Pórtate bien mientras no estemos, Mellia. No te metas en líos con nadie y no te acerques a los chicos mayores y no vayas más lejos de la higuera ni...

—No necesito que nadie me cuide. —Camellia levanta la barbilla, pero el labio inferior le tiembla un poco. Está asustada.

—¡May! —ladra una de las empleadas—. ¡A la fila, ya! Ya tienen reunidos a todos los niños de la lista.

—Enseguida volvemos —le susurro a Camellia—. No tengas miedo.

—No tengo miedo. —Pero a continuación me abraza, después de todo.

La empleada vuelve a gritarme y corro a la fila. Durante la hora y media siguiente nos frotan con jabón, nos peinan, nos recogen el pelo, nos cepillan debajo de las uñas, nos ponen lazos y ropas nuevas con encaje. Nos probamos zapatos de un armario lleno de ellos hasta encontrar unos que nos quedan bien.

Para cuando las empleadas nos llevan a los automóviles que esperan a la puerta, no parecemos los mismos niños. Estamos nosotros cuatro, otras tres niñas, un niño de cinco años, dos niños pequeñitos y Stevie, a quien le han dicho que si vuelve a mojarse en los pantalones le darán una azotaina.

En el automóvil no nos dejan hablar. Por el camino, quien habla es la empleada:

—Niñas, os sentaréis educadamente con las piernas juntas como señoritas. No habléis si no os hablan primero. Seréis corteses con los invitados de casa de la señorita Tann. Solo diréis cosas buenas de vuestra estancia en casa de la señora Murphy. Hoy en la fiesta habrá juguetes y lápices de colores, pasteles y galletas. Tendréis...

Dejo de escuchar en cuanto el automóvil sube una colina y se ve el río. May desaparece como una mota de sol en el agua y sale Rill. Se estira hasta la rendija de la parte superior de la ventana, aspira el aire y capta todos los aromas familiares.

Durante un minuto ha vuelto a casa.

Entonces el automóvil dobla una esquina y el río desaparece. Algo pesado y triste se instala en mí. Reclino la cabeza en el asiento y la empleada me dice que no lo haga; me estoy aplastando el lazo del pelo.

En mi regazo, Gabion se queda dormido y lo estrecho contra mí; dejo que su pelo me haga cosquillas en la barbilla y consigo estar otra vez en casa. Estas personas pueden controlar todo lo que hago, pero no dónde viajo con la imaginación.

Pero mi visita al *Arcadia* dura demasiado poco. Muy pronto el automóvil se detiene delante de una gran casa blanca que es incluso mayor que la de la señora Murphy.

—El que no se comporte como es debido lo lamentará y mucho —dice la empleada y nos señala con un dedo a la cara antes de dejarnos bajar—. Sed amables con los invitados de la fiesta. Si os lo piden, sentaos en su regazo. Sonreíd. Demostradles que sois unos niños buenos.

Entramos y la casa está llena de gente. Hay más niños, y bebés. Todos llevan ropas bonitas y hay pasteles y galletas para comer. Para los niños pequeños hay juguetes y, cuando quiero darme cuenta, Fern, Gabion e incluso Lark se han alejado de mi lado.

Un hombre saca a Gabion a jugar al jardín con una pelota azul. Una mujer de pelo oscuro se sienta con Lark y juntas colorean un libro. Fern se ríe y juega a cucú-tras con una señora bonita de pelo rubio que está sentada sola con aspecto cansado y triste. Fern la hace reír y muy pronto la mujer empieza a llevarla en brazos de un juguete a otro como si Fern no supiera caminar sola.

Por fin se sientan juntas a leer un libro y se me encoge el corazón. Pienso en Queenie y en cómo nos leía. Quiero que la mujer suelte a Fern, que me la devuelva.

Entra un hombre y le hace cosquillas a Fern en la barriga y la mujer sonríe y dice:

—Darren, ¡es perfecta! Amelia tendría ahora su edad. —Da un golpecito en el brazo de la butaca—. Siéntate a leer con nosotras.

—Hazlo tú. —La besa en la mejilla—. Yo tengo que hablar con unas personas.

Y sale de la habitación.

Fern y la mujer van por el segundo cuento cuando vuelve el hombre. Están tan concentradas que ni siquiera se dan cuenta de que él se ha sentado a mi lado en el sofá.

—¿Sois hermanas? —pregunta.

—Sí, señor —contesto tal y como me han dicho. «Señor» y «señora» siempre.

Se aparta y me mira con atención.

—Sí que os parecéis.

—Sí, señor. —Me miro las manos. Se me acelera el corazón, me salta dentro del pecho como un gorrión atrapado en el interior de la casa flotante. ¿Qué es lo que quiere?

El hombre me pone una mano en la espalda. Cierro las escápulas alrededor de ella. Los pelillos de la base de la nuca me dan tirones. El sudor me baja por el áspero vestido.

—¿Y tú —pregunta el hombre— cuántos años tienes?

13

AVERY

*L*a casa está silenciosa y bañada por la luz de la luna cuando abro la puerta. Busco a tientas el interruptor de la luz y sujeto el móvil con el hombro mientras espero a que el tío Clifford me conteste a lo que le acabo de preguntar. Me ha puesto en espera mientras pide comida para llevar desde el coche.

Me asalta el recuerdo especialmente intenso de llegar aquí en una ocasión después de oscurecido, mi abuela y yo solas. La casa estaba igual que ahora, con haces de luna proyectados sobre el suelo en forma de hojas de palma, el aire oliendo a sal y a alfombras con arena, a aceite de limón y muebles que han vivido mucho tiempo junto al mar.

Muevo los dedos. Casi puedo sentir su mano cogiendo la mía. Yo debía de tener once o doce años, esa edad tonta en la que dejas de dar la mano en público, pero aquí, en nuestro rincón mágico, no pasaba nada.

Detenida ahora en la entrada, busco esa sensación de bienestar, pero esta visita está intensamente marcada por dos sabores opuestos: amargo y dulce. Familiar y desconocido. Los sabores de la vida.

El tío Clifford vuelve al teléfono. Después de un largo paseo por la playa y de cenar en el restaurante Waterfront, he decidido que mi tío puede ser el único medio de hacer progresos en mi búsqueda, de momento. Trent Turner me dejó plantada y se marchó en un jeep con el tipo uniformado. Lo esperé en el coche, pero la inmobiliaria Trent Turner siguió cerrada toda la tarde.

De momento, este viaje está resultando un fracaso.

—¿Qué me estabas diciendo, Avery? ¿Qué pasa con la casa de Edisto? —pregunta el tío Clifford.

—Bueno, quería saber si papá y tú veníais mucho de pequeños aquí con la abuela Judy. Quiero decir, cuando erais pequeños. —Intento hablar con naturalidad. Que no sospeche nada. El tío Clifford fue agente federal de joven—. ¿Tenía la abuela Judy amigos aquí o personas a las que venía a visitar?

—Pues... déjame pensar. —Piensa un rato y al cabo se limita a decir—: Creo que no íbamos mucho, ahora que lo mencionas. Cuando era pequeño, sí fuimos más. Luego, cuando nos hicimos mayores, preferíamos la casa de la abuela Stafford en la isla Pawleys. Era más grande y estaba el velero y la mayoría de las veces teníamos otros primos con quienes jugar. Lo normal era que mamá fuera sola a Edisto. Le gustaba escribir allí. Ya sabes que cultivaba un poco la poesía y durante un tiempo llevó la columna de sociedad.

Por un momento me quedo boquiabierta.

—¿Que la abuela Judy escribía una columna de sociedad? —Que es lo mismo que decir de cotilleos.

—Bueno, no firmaba con su nombre, claro.

—¿Cómo firmaba?

—Si te lo contara, tendría que matarte.

—¡Tío Clifford!

Frente a lo convencional de mi padre, el tío Clifford siempre ha sido rebelde y algo provocador. La tía Diana tiene por su culpa completamente gris el pelo, que, como toda dama sureña que se precie, se tiñe con regularidad.

—Mira, deja estar los secretos de tu abuela. —Por un momento pienso que hay un mensaje oculto en esa frase, pero entonces me doy cuenta de que me está tomando el pelo—. ¿Así que estás en la casa Myers?

—Sí. He decidido escaparme unos días.

—Bueno, pues echa la caña al agua por mí.

—Ya sabes que no pesco. Puaj.

Con tres hijas, mi pobre padre se esforzó mucho por convertirnos al menos a una en una ávida pescadora. Pero incluso el tío Clifford sabe que fue una causa perdida.

—Pues desde luego en eso no has salido a tu abuela. Le encantaba pescar, sobre todo en Edisto. Cuando tu padre y yo éramos pequeños, nos llevaba mucho a ver a alguien que tenía una barquita de pesca. Navegábamos río arriba y pasábamos la mitad del día pescando. No recuerdo quién era. Un amigo, supongo. Tenía un niño rubio con el que me gustaba jugar. Su nombre empezaba por T... Tommy, Timmie..., no, Tr... Puede que fuera Trey o Travis.

—¿Trent? ¿Trent Turner?

El Trent Turner actual es Trent III, su padre se llama Trent también y tendrá la edad de mi tío.

—Puede ser. ¿Lo preguntas por algo en especial? ¿Pasa algo?

De pronto me doy cuenta de que he hecho una pregunta de más y, sin querer, he abierto la puerta al detective.

—No, por nada. Al llegar a Edisto me he puesto a pensar en cosas. Me gustaría haber venido más a menudo con la abuela Judy. También me gustaría haberle hecho más preguntas cuando todavía recordaba las cosas.

—Bueno, es una de las paradojas de la vida. No se puede tener todo. Puedes tener un poco de esto y un poco de aquello o todo de esto y nada de aquello. Hacemos elecciones que en el momento nos parecen las mejores. Tú has conseguido mucho para una chica, quiero decir, para una mujer de treinta años.

A veces me pregunto si mi familia no ve más en mí de lo que hay en realidad.

—Gracias, tío Clifford.

—Son cinco dólares por la sesión.

—Te mando el cheque por correo.

Después de colgar, repaso la conversación mientras saco la compra que he hecho en BI-LO, que cuando yo era pequeña era todavía un Piggly Wiggly.

¿Hay alguna pista en lo que me ha contado el tío Clifford?

Nada me viene a la cabeza. Nada que lleve a alguna parte. Si el niño de la barca se llamaba Trent, eso indica que mi abuela tenía alguna clase de relación personal con Trent Turner I, algo que yo ya imaginaba. Pero si pasaban tiempo juntos pescando con los niños, eso desarma mi teoría del chantaje. Uno no se va de pesca con quien le está chantajeando, y mucho menos se lleva a niños pequeños. Tampoco llevas niños si estás viviendo una aventura amorosa extramatrimonial. Sobre todo niños lo bastante mayores para acordarse de la excursión.

Quizá Trent no era más que un viejo amigo. Quizá el sobre no contenga más que fotografías..., algo por completo inocente. Pero, entonces, ¿a qué viene la promesa entre nieto y abuelo en el lecho de muerte de este de que el paquete no sería entregado más que a su propietaria?

Formulo teorías mientras llevo mis cosas al dormitorio, abro la maleta y me instalo. Lanzo dardos a las teorías, igual que haría si estuviera en una reunión de estrategia en mi despacho. Los dardos dan en la diana y no queda nada. En cualquier caso, ha sido un día muy largo. Necesito una ducha y dormir. Quizá mañana me venga la inspiración... o consiga pillar a Trent Turner III y sacarle la verdad.

Las dos posibilidades me parecen igual de remotas.

Hasta que no abro el grifo y me doy cuenta de que no hay agua caliente en la casa, no caigo en la cuenta de algo que ha dicho el tío Clifford. Mi abuela venía aquí a escribir.

¿Podrían estar aquí algunos de sus escritos? ¿Contendrán alguna pista?

Al momento he vuelto a vestirme. En cualquier caso, lo de la ducha fría no era muy tentador.

Fuera, las uniolas se mecen sobre las dunas y la luna brilla sobre las palmeras enanas. Las olas golpetean la orilla mientras busco en cajones y registro armarios y cómodas llenas de mantas y guardarropas. Estoy a punto de rendirme al hecho obvio de que no hay nada que encontrar, cuando después de mirar debajo del colchón de mi abuela me doy cuenta de que el mueblecito junto a la cama no es un escritorio ni un tocador, sino la mesa de una máquina de escribir. Hay una vieja máquina de escribir negra colgando boca abajo por debajo del panel central. Al haber crecido en hogares familiares llenos de muebles antiguos, más o menos sé cómo funciona. No tardo demasiado en conseguir abrir los cierres ni en girar los pivotes. La máquina de escribir se abre con un golpetazo contundente.

Paso un dedo por las teclas. Casi me parece oír a mi abuela pulsándolas. Me inclino y estudio el rodillo negro en el que se engancha la página. Las teclas han dejado en él muescas diminutas. Si esto fuera un ordenador, quizá podría sacar algo del disco duro, pero aquí no quedan palabras legibles. Es imposible saber lo que se ha escrito en esta máquina o cuándo.

—¿Qué sabes tú que yo no sé? —le susurro mientras rebusco en los cajones. En el mueble no hay más que plumas y lápices, papel de escribir amarillento, una caja de papel carbón y tiras de cinta correctora, blanco tiza por un lado y adhesivas por el otro. En la primera hoja hay huellas de letras. La sostengo a la luz y enseguida descifro las palabras mal escritas y luego corregidas: «Bulevar Palmetto, Isla de Edisto...».

Al parecer, mi abuela escribía aquí cartas, pero, ya fuera por accidente o a propósito, limpiaba después las huellas. No hay papeles a medio escribir y las hojas de papel carbón están prístinas, sin fantasmas de palabras. Es raro, porque en su escritorio de casa siempre había una carpeta con papel que podía reciclarse para trabajos manuales o dibujos de los niños.

Pulso una tecla de la máquina de escribir y el martillo sube y golpea el rodillo dejando solo la impresión tenue y trémula de una K. La tinta de la cinta está seca.

La cinta...

Al momento estoy inclinada sobre el armazón negro de metal de la máquina, desmontándolo para acceder al rodillo. Es sorprendentemente fácil. Por desgracia, la cinta entintada está casi sin usar. Solo unos pocos centímetros podrían contener la impresión de lo último que fue escrito. La desenrollo, la sostengo a la luz y entrecierro los ojos para desentrañarlo.

yduJ ,etnematnetA .someesed ol euq etnemadarpsesed rop ,tnerT ,acnun somapes ol on zev laT .eessenneT ed selitnafnI seragoH ed nóicaicosA al ed sovihcra sol ne rebah aírdop sám éuq emodnátnugerp y adaduarfed...

Al principio es un galimatías, pero he pasado tiempo suficiente con la abuela Judy para saber cómo funciona la cinta de una máquina de escribir. Va avanzando a medida que la golpean las teclas. Las letras tienen que seguir alguna clase de orden.

Las primeras letras de la línea de arriba de pronto adquieren significado: «Judy». El nombre de mi abuela escrito al revés, de derecha a izquierda, resultado de haber sido mecanografiado. De la confusión surge una nueva palabra: «Asociación», hacia la mitad del texto.

La preceden tres palabras más con mayúscula inicial: «Hogares Infantiles de Tennessee».

Cojo papel y lápiz y descifro el resto.

... defraudada y preguntándome qué más podría haber en los archivos de la Asociación de Hogares Infantiles de Tennessee. Tal vez no lo sepamos nunca, Trent, por desesperadamente que lo deseemos.

Atentamente,

Judy

Leo lo que he escrito tratando de recomponer el resto de la historia. Los hogares infantiles son para huérfanos y niños dados en adopción. La mujer joven de la foto de May Crandall estaba embarazada. ¿Sería pariente de mi abuela, una chica que se vio metida en un apuro?

Me vienen a la cabeza situaciones: una muchacha ingenua de buena familia, un hombre de dudosa reputación, una fuga envuelta en escándalo o, peor aún, nada de boda. Un embarazo fuera del matrimonio. ¿Quizá su enamorado la abandonó y tuvo que volver con su familia?

En aquellos días se enviaba a las jóvenes fuera a que tuvieran el niño y lo dieran en adopción. Incluso ahora, las mujeres del círculo social de mi madre murmuran de cuando en cuando sobre alguien que se ha ido a pasar una temporada a casa de su tía. Quizá eso es lo que me oculta Trent Turner.

Una cosa sí tengo clara. La última nota escrita con esta máquina de escribir estaba dirigida a Trent Turner y, aunque no sé cómo es de reciente, no hay duda de que el misterioso sobre contestará un montón de preguntas.

O planteará más.

Sin pensarlo dos veces, cruzo la casa corriendo, cojo el teléfono y marco el número de Trent Turner que ya me sé de memoria.

El teléfono suena tres veces antes de que se me ocurra mirar el reloj y vea que es casi medianoche. Una hora poco apropiada para llamar a un casi desconocido. Mi madre estaría horrorizada.

Me acaba de venir a la cabeza lo que me diría: *Si quieres conseguir la cooperación de ese hombre, esa no es la manera, Avery,* cuando un pastoso: «Dígame, soy Nrent Nurner», me confirma que lo he sacado de la cama. Probablemente por eso ha contestado el teléfono sin mirar antes quién llamaba.

—Asociación de Hogares Infantiles de Tennessee —suelto, porque calculo que dispongo de unos dos segundos y medio antes de que se espabile y me cuelgue.

—¿Qué?

—La Asociación de Hogares Infantiles de Tennessee. ¿Qué tiene que ver con su abuelo y mi abuela?

—¿Señorita Stafford? —A pesar de que se dirige a mí de manera formal, el tono pastoso, adormilado, convierte el saludo en algo íntimo, como de conversación entre enamorados. Sigue un suspiro profundo y oigo crujir ropa de cama.

—Avery. Por favor, llámame Avery. Tienes que contármelo. He encontrado algo. Necesito saber qué significa.

Otro suspiro largo. Carraspea, pero la voz sigue siendo profunda y adormilada.

—¿Sabes qué hora es?

Miro tímidamente el reloj, como si eso pudiera disculpar mi mal comportamiento.

—Perdón. No me di cuenta hasta que ya había marcado.

—Podrías haber colgado.

—Me da miedo que no vuelvas a cogerme el teléfono.

Una risita me dice que he acertado.

—En eso tienes razón.

—Por favor, escúchame. Por favor. Llevo toda la noche buscando por la casa y he encontrado algo, y eres el único que puede contarme lo que significa. Solo... solo necesito saber lo que pasa y lo que debería hacer al respecto. —Si hay un escándalo en nuestra familia, es muy posible que ya dé igual, excepto quizá a unos pocos miembros conservados en salmuera de la Vieja Brigada de los Chismorreos, pero no hay manera de averiguarlo hasta que no sepa a qué me enfrento.

—De verdad que no puedo contártelo.

—Entiendo que se lo prometiste a tu abuelo, pero...

—No. —De pronto suena muy despierto, completamente despierto y dueño de la situación—. Es que no puedo decírtelo. No he abierto ninguno de los sobres. Ayudé a mi abuelo a hacerlos llegar a sus destinatarios. Eso es todo.

¿Está diciendo la verdad? Me resulta difícil de creer. Soy de esas personas que despega con cuidado el celo del papel de envolver y fisga los regalos de Navidad en cuanto aparecen en el árbol. No me gustan las sorpresas.

—Pero ¿de qué eran los sobres? ¿Qué tenían que ver con la Asociación de Hogares Infantiles de Tennessee? Los hogares infantiles son para huérfanos. ¿Podría mi abuela haber estado buscando a alguien dado en adopción?

En cuanto lo sugiero, me preocupa haber hablado demasiado.

—Eso es solo una teoría mía —añado—. No tengo razón ninguna para creer que sea verdad.

Será mejor que no abra la puerta a un escándalo en potencia. No sé si puedo fiarme de Trent Turner, aunque un hombre que guarda durante meses unos sobres sin abrir tiene que ser íntegro. Trent Turner I debía de saber que su nieto estaba hecho de buena pasta.

El teléfono se queda en silencio y sigue así tanto rato que me pregunto si Trent Turner se ha ido. Me da miedo hablar, me da miedo decir algo que incline la balanza a un lado o a otro.

No estoy demasiado acostumbrada a suplicar, pero por fin susurro:

—Por favor, sé que esta tarde hemos empezado con mal pie, pero no sé por dónde seguir.

Coge aire, casi puedo ver su pecho hincharse.

—Ven.

—¿Cómo?

—Que vengas aquí antes de que cambie de opinión.

Solo puedo responder con un silencio atónito. No estoy segura de si estoy contenta o muerta de miedo..., o incluso loca por considerar siquiera ir a casa de un desconocido en plena noche.

Por otra parte, es un hombre de negocios respetable y conocido en la isla.

Un hombre de negocios que ahora sabe que he desenterrado al menos parte de un secreto.

Un secreto que su abuelo se llevó al lecho de muerte.

¿Y si detrás de esta invitación nocturna hay una intención siniestra? Nadie sabrá nunca mi paradero. ¿A quién se lo puedo contar?

No se me ocurre nadie a quien quiera contarle esto ahora mismo.

Dejaré una nota... Aquí, en la casa.

No..., mejor me mandaré a mí misma un correo electrónico. Si desaparezco, es lo que mirarán primero.

La idea se me antoja melodramática y tonta, pero en realidad no lo es tanto.

—Cojo las llaves y...

—No te hace falta el coche. Estoy a cuatro casas bajando la calle.

—¿Vives por aquí? —Separo las cortinas de la cocina e intento ver algo a través de la pared de robles y acebo de yaupon. ¿Todo este tiempo estaba aquí al lado?

—Se llega antes por la playa. Encenderé la luz del porche trasero.

—Voy ahora mismo.

Recorro la casa en busca de una linterna y pilas. Por suerte, los familiares que han estado aquí dejaron las cosas básicas. Me suena el teléfono mientras me estoy enviando un correo a mí misma, documentando mi paradero y la hora de salida. Doy un salto de casi un metro de alto y aterrizo en un pozo de terror. *Trent ha cambiado de idea...*

Pero el número es del teléfono de Elliot. Estoy demasiado nerviosa para calcular qué hora es en Milán, pero sin duda está trabajando.

—Ayer cuando me llamaste estaba liado, perdona —dice.

—Ya me imaginé. ¿Mucho trabajo?

—Bastante —responde sin especificar, como acostumbra. En su familia, a las mujeres no les interesan los negocios—. ¿Qué tal por Edisto?

El radio macuto familiar es más eficaz que el rastreo de microchips.

—¿Cómo has sabido que estaba aquí?

—Me lo dijo mi madre. —Suspira—. Ha estado en Drayden Hill para quitarse el mono de bebé, porque están allí tu hermana y Courtney y los niños. Y ya ha empezado otra vez con la tabarra de los nietos. —Es comprensible que Elliot esté molesto—. Me recordó que tengo ya treinta y un años y ella cincuenta y siete y que no quiere ser una abuela anciana.

—Ya... —A veces me pregunto cómo será tener a Bitsy de suegra. La quiero y su intención es buena, pero a su lado Honeybee es una mujer sutil.

—Podríamos contratar a tu hermana y los trillizos para que vayan a pasar unos días con mi madre —sugiere Elliot con tono lastimero—. Igual así se le pasan las ganas.

Aunque entiendo que es una broma, me duele. Adoro a los trillizos, aunque son unos trastos.

—Se lo puedes preguntar.

Aunque Elliot y yo solo hemos hablado de tener hijos como parte posible de nuestro plan de vida futura, le inquieta la abundancia de embarazos múltiples en mi familia. No se cree capaz de tener más de uno a la vez. De cuando en cuando, a mí me preocupa que tener hijos algún día se convierta en nunca con Elliot. Sé que iremos solucionando estas cosas sobre la marcha. ¿No es lo que hacen la mayoría de las parejas?

—Entonces, ¿cuánto tiempo te vas a quedar en la playa? —dice, cambiando de tema.

—Solo un par de días. Si me quedo más, Leslie mandará a alguien a buscarme.

—Bueno, Leslie mira por tu bien. Necesitas dejarte ver. Para eso has vuelto a tu casa.

He vuelto a mi casa a cuidar de mi padre, quiero decirle, pero con Elliot todo es un paso para conseguir algo. Es la persona más competitiva que conozco.

—Ya lo sé. Pero es agradable darme un pequeño respiro. Y me da la impresión de que a ti también te vendría bien. Descansa un poco en Milán, ¿vale? Y no te preocupes por tu madre y lo de los niños. Mañana ya estará distraída con otra cosa.

Nos despedimos y termino el correo cautelar dirigido a mí misma. Si no se vuelve a saber nada de mí, alguien terminará por buscar aquí. *Medianoche del martes. Voy cuatro casas más abajo de la casa de Edisto a hablar con Trent Turner sobre algo relacionado con la abuela Judy. Debería estar de vuelta en una hora más o menos. Dejo este mensaje por si acaso.*

Queda estúpido, pero lo mando antes de salir.

Fuera, la noche es serena y oscura mientras recorro el sendero entre las dunas alumbrándome con la linterna por si hay serpientes. A lo largo de la orilla, la mayoría de las casas están ya a oscuras y solo quedan el resplandor de la luna y unas lucecillas que parecen flotar sobre el horizonte de agua. Las hojas y las hierbas de la playa susurran y los cangrejos corretean de lado por la arena. Los ilumino con la linterna y cuido de no interrumpir su tráfico frenético pisando alguno.

La brisa me acaricia el cuello y se me mete por el pelo y quiero caminar relajada y disfrutar del arrullo del mar. Tengo música para meditar que suena así, pero pocas veces me tomo tiempo para disfrutar de la experiencia auténtica. Ahora que lo pienso, me parece una lástima. Me había olvidado de lo maravilloso que es este sitio, el encuentro perfecto entre tierra y mar, libre de rascacielos gigantes, de hogueras y de campistas.

Llego a la casa de Trent Turner antes de lo que me gustaría. Se me acelera el pulso mientras recorro un sendero desgastado a través de arbustos y cruzo una corta pasarela de madera hasta una cancela inclinada. Esta casa tiene más o menos los mismos años que la de mi abuela. Un camino de piedra conduce a los escalones del porche. Arriba, polillas aletean en círculos alrededor de una única bombilla.

Trent Turner abre la puerta antes de que me dé tiempo a llamar. Viste una camiseta descolorida con un desgarrón en el cuello y un pantalón de chándal que le queda grande. Lleva los pies morenos descalzos y no puede tener el pelo más revuelto.

Se cruza de brazos y se apoya en el marco de la puerta, estudiándome.

De pronto me siento todo piernas y brazos, igual que una adolescente en su primera cita para el baile de fin de curso. No sé qué hacer ni cómo ponerme.

—Empezaba a dudar —dice.

—¿De si iba a venir?

—De si la llamada no había sido más que un mal sueño. —Pero las comisuras de los labios se curvan hacia arriba y deduzco que está de broma.

Aun así, me ruborizo un poco. La verdad es que todo esto es un abuso.

—Lo siento. Lo que pasa es que... necesito saber. ¿Qué relación tenía tu abuelo con mi abuela?

—Lo más probable es que trabajara para ella.

—¿Haciendo qué?

Mira detrás de mí hacia una cabaña diminuta escondida bajo los árboles a uno de los lados de la casa. Percibo sus dudas. Está intentando decidir si está traicionando o no la promesa hecha en el lecho de muerte.

—Mi abuelo se dedicaba a buscar.

—¿A buscar qué?

—Personas.

14

RILL

Empieza a oscurecer para cuando la fiesta toca a su fin y las empleadas comienzan a reunir a los niños para meterlos en los automóviles y llevarlos de vuelta. Para entonces casi no quiero marcharme. Durante toda la tarde ha habido galletas y helado y tiras de regaliz y tarta y leche y emparedados y libros para colorear y cajas sin abrir de lápices de colores Crayola y muñecas para las niñas y automóviles de hojalata en miniatura para los niños.

Estoy tan llena que casi no puedo moverme. Después de tres semanas de pasar hambre, este sitio sabe a gloria.

Me siento mal porque Camellia se lo esté perdiendo, pero tampoco sé si habría aguantado aquí. No soporta que le hagan mimos..., ni siquiera que la toquen. Robo una galleta para dársela y me la guardo en el bolsillo delantero de mi delantal con la esperanza de que nadie nos registre antes de irnos.

Estas personas nos llaman «cariñín», «cielito» y «monada». Lo mismo hace la señorita Tann mientras estamos aquí. Igual que en la biblioteca ambulante, cuenta cosas que no son ciertas. Le brillan los ojos y sonríe, como si disfrutara engañando a todos.

Igual que en la biblioteca ambulante, mantengo la boca cerrada sobre la verdad.

—Son absolutamente perfectos —les repite una y otra vez a los invitados—. Especímenes maravillosos y además mentalmente avanzados para su edad. Muchos han tenido padres con talento para la música y el arte. Son pizarras en blanco esperando a ser llenadas. Pueden llegar a ser lo que ustedes quieran que sean.

»Es una monería, ¿verdad? —le pregunta a un matrimonio que lleva todo el día con Gabion en brazos. Han jugado a la pelota y con los automóviles en miniatura y el hombre ha lanzado a Gabby al aire mientras este reía.

Ahora que tenemos que irnos, la señora no quiere devolver a Gabby. Viene con él hasta la puerta principal y mi hermano pequeño se le agarra al cuello igual que Fern está agarrada al mío.

—No me *quiedo* ir —gimotea Gabby.

—Tenemos que irnos. —Me paso a Fern a la otra cadera mientras la señora Pulnik trata de empujarnos hacia el porche. No culpo a Gabby por resistirse. Yo también odio tener que volver a la casa de la señora Murphy. Preferiría ver a Fern leer algún libro más con esa señora tan simpática, pero se marchó hace un rato con su marido. Le dio un beso a Fern en la cabeza y le dijo: «Hasta muy pronto, cariñín», antes de devolvérmela.

—Gab... —Me interrumpo justo antes de decir el nombre que me costará un papirotazo en casa de la señora Murphy si me oye la señora Pulnik—. Robby, aquí no te puedes quedar. Venga. Tenemos que averiguar lo que les pasa a Huckleberry Finn y a Jim cuando bajan por el río hasta Arkansas, ¿no te acuerdas? —Le tiendo un brazo porque con el otro estoy sujetando a Fern. Gabby no quiere venirse conmigo y la mujer tampoco quiere soltarlo—. Lo leeremos cuando lleguemos a casa de la señora Murphy. Di adiós a esta señora tan buena.

—¡Silencio! —La señorita Tann me mira con fuego en los ojos y retrocedo y dejo caer el brazo tan deprisa que me golpeo sonoramente la pierna.

La señorita Tann sonríe a la mujer y luego se enrosca un mechón del pelo de Gabby en el dedo.

—¿A que nuestro pequeño Robby es adorable? Un encanto. —Con la misma rapidez con que se volvió cruel, ahora es simpática—. Me parece que los dos han hecho buenas migas.

—Sí, mucho.

El marido se acerca. Se tira del cuello del traje para que esté recto y pulcro.

—Quizá deberíamos hablar. Podríamos llegar a un acuerdo para que...

—Es muy posible. —La señorita Tann no le deja terminar—. Pero debo advertirles de que este pequeñín es muy popular. Ya he tenido varias peticiones. Esos ojos azules tan bonitos con las pestañas oscuras y los rizos dorados. Una rareza. Es como un angelito. Enamoraría a cualquier madre.

Todos miran a mi hermano. El hombre le pellizca una mejilla y Gabby deja escapar su encantadora risa de bebé. Lleva sin reír así desde que la policía nos sacó del *Arcadia*. Me alegro de que esté contento, aunque sea por un día.

—Lleve fuera a los otros niños. —La voz de la señorita Tann se vuelve grave y sin entonación. Se acerca a la señora Pulnik y le susurra entre dientes—: Métalos en los automóviles. Espere cinco minutos antes de decirle al conductor que arranque. —En voz aún más baja, añade—: Pero no creo que la necesitemos.

La señora Pulnik carraspea y pone una voz alegre y cariñosa que nunca le hemos oído en casa de la señora Murphy.

—Todos a los automóviles. Vamos.

Lark, Stevie y los otros niños corren al porche. Fern me da patadas en la pierna y se revuelve contra mi cadera como si estuviera intentando hacer salir del establo a un caballo testarudo.

—Pero Ga... Robby. —Me han salido raíces en los pies y al principio ni siquiera estoy segura de por qué. Estas personas solo quieren abrazar y besar a Gabby un poco más. Les gusta jugar con niños pequeños. Llevo todo el día vigilando a Gabby, Lark y Fern cada vez que conseguía escapar de dos señores que querían saber quién soy y qué hacía allí puesto que soy mayor que el resto de los niños. He corrido de habitación en habitación, de ventana en ventana para asegurarme de que sabía dónde estaban mis hermanos y que nadie les hacía daño.

Pero en mi fuero interno he estado pensando en la hermana de Stevie. Que dejó la casa de la señora Murphy y no volvió. Sé lo que les pasa a los huérfanos como Sherry y Stevie, pero nosotros no lo somos. Tenemos una madre y un padre que van a venir a buscarnos.

¿Sabe eso la mujer que ha estado jugando con Gabion? ¿Se lo ha dicho alguien? No pensará que es huérfano, ¿verdad?

Doy otro paso hacia mi hermano.

—Deme. Ya lo cojo yo.

La mujer me da la espalda.

—Aquí está bien.

—¡*Fuerra!* —Los dedos de la señora Pulnik se cierran con fuerza alrededor de mi brazo y sé lo que va a pasar si no obedezco.

Le toco la rodilla a Gabby y digo:

—No pasa nada. Esta señora quiere decirte adiós.

Él levanta una manita y la agita.

—Adiós —repite. Tiene la sonrisa llena de dientes de leche. Recuerdo cuándo le salió cada uno de ellos.

—Al coche. —La uña afilada de la señora Pulnik se me clava en la carne. Me empuja, tropiezo en el umbral y salgo dando traspiés al porche; casi se me cae Fern.

—Ay, Dios mío, ¿es su hermana? —dice preocupada la señora que tiene a Gabion.

—Pues claro que no —contesta la señorita Tann mintiendo de nuevo—. En el hogar infantil los más pequeños se encariñan con los mayores, eso es todo. No se puede evitar. Pero los olvidan con la misma facilidad. La única familia que tiene este pequeñín es una niñita. Recién nacida. Adoptada por una familia ilustre, nada menos. Así que, como puede ver, no es un niño corriente. Ha escogido usted el mejor. La madre estudió en la universidad, era una joven de lo más inteligente. Por desgracia murió dando a luz y el padre abandonó a los niños. Pero no han sufrido ningún daño. ¿Y no resultaría adorable este niño en las playas de California? Claro que las adopciones entre estados tienen una tarifa especial...

Son las últimas palabras que oigo antes de que la señora Pulnik me arrastre por los escalones del porche diciéndome en voz baja lo que me hará la señora Murphy si no obedezco. Me aprieta tanto el brazo que estoy segura de que me lo va a romper.

Me da igual. No siento nada, ni la hierba seca de verano que cruje bajo mis pies, ni los zapatos tan duros que me dieron esta mañana las empleadas. Ni el aire caliente y pegajoso de la noche o el vestido demasiado apretado que me tira cuando Fern patalea y se retuerce y mira por encima de mi hombro gimoteando:

—Gabby... Gabby...

Estoy fría por fuera. Como si me hubiera caído al río en pleno invierno y se me hubiera ido toda la sangre muy dentro para impedir que muera congelada. Los brazos y las piernas no me parecen míos. Se mueven, pero solo porque saben lo que deben hacer, no porque yo se lo diga.

La señora Pulnik nos empuja a Fern y a mí al interior del automóvil con el resto de los niños y se sienta a mi lado. Yo estoy rígida con la mirada fija en la casa blanca, esperando a que alguien abra la puerta, cruce el jardín y me traiga a Gabion. Lo deseo tanto que me duele.

—¿Dónde está Gabby? —me susurra Fern al oído y Lark me mira con sus ojos tristes y callados. No ha dicho gran cosa desde que llegamos a casa de la señora Murphy y ahora tampoco, pero yo la oigo igual. *Tienes que rescatar a Gabion*, me está diciendo.

Lo imagino cruzando el jardín.

Espero.

Miro.

Trato de pensar.

¿Qué debería hacer?

El reloj de pulsera de la señora Pulnik marca los segundos. Tic-tac, tic-tac.

Las palabras de la señorita Tann me revolotean dentro de la cabeza, salen disparadas igual que hacen los zapateros cuando alguien tira una piedra al río. Cada una en una dirección.

Murió dando a luz...

¿Está muerta mi madre?

... abandonó a los niños...

¿Briny no va a venir a buscarnos?

La única familia que tiene este pequeñín es una niñita. Recién nacida.

¿Uno de los niños no llegó a morir en el hospital? ¿Tengo una hermanita nueva? ¿La señorita Tann se la ha dado a alguien? ¿Es una mentira? ¿Es todo mentira? La señorita Tann cuenta patrañas con tal facilidad que parece hasta creérselas ella. Gabby no tiene una madre que estudió en la universidad. Queenie es lista, pero solo hizo hasta octavo curso antes de conocer a Briny y marcharse con él al río.

Son mentiras, me digo. *Todo lo que dice es mentira. Tiene que serlo.*

Está intentando agradar a las personas de la fiesta, pero van a tener que devolver a Gabion porque la señorita Tann sabe que papá va a venir a buscarnos en cuanto pueda. Briny nunca nos abandonaría. Jamás dejaría que una mujer como la señorita Tann se llevara a mi hermanita recién nacida, si es que la tengo. Nunca. Jamás. Antes preferiría la muerte.

¿Está muerto Briny? ¿Por eso no ha venido a buscarnos?

El automóvil arranca y salto hacia la ventana quitándome a Fern del regazo. Se acomoda en el asiento y yo cojo la manilla de la puerta. Correré hasta la casa y les diré la verdad a esas personas. Les diré que la señorita Tann es una mentirosa. Me da igual lo que me hagan después.

Antes de que pueda pasar nada, la señora Pulnik me está sujetando por el enorme lazo con que me adornaron las empleadas esta mañana. Fern se retuerce entre las dos y termina en el suelo con Stevie y Lark.

—*Pórrtate* bien. —La señora Pulnik pega la boca a mi oreja y su aliento es caliente y acre. Huele al whisky de la señora Murphy—. Si no te *porrtas* bien, la señora Murphy te meterá en el armario. Y no solo eso. Os ataremos a todas y os dejaremos allí, colgadas como zapatos de los *corrdones.* En el armario hace frío. Y está oscuro. ¿Crees que a tus *herrmanitas* les gustará la oscuridad?

El corazón me late con fuerza cuando me tira de la cabeza hacia atrás. El cuello me cruje y me chasca. Se me desprende pelo de las raíces. Un fogonazo blanco de dolor me ciega.

—¿Has entendido?

Intento asentir con la cabeza.

Me empuja contra la puerta y me rebota la cabeza en el cristal.

—No pensaba que *fuerras* a *serr* tú la que diera problemas.

Se me llenan los ojos de lágrimas y pestañeo con fuerza para contenerlas. *No pienso llorar. No pienso.*

El asiento se hunde y me acerca al grueso cuerpo de la señora Pulnik. Esta suspira con un ronroneo, igual que un gato al sol.

—*Chóferr*, llévenos a casa. Es la hora.

Me aparto de ella y miro por la ventana hasta que la casa blanca con grandes columnas desaparece.

En el automóvil nadie dice una palabra. Fern trepa de nuevo a mi regazo y nos quedamos todos quietos como estatuas.

De camino a casa de la señora Murphy busco el río. Una pequeña fantasía se cuela en mi cabeza con Fern agarrada a mi cuello y Lark apoyada en mi rodilla y Stevie acurrucado entre mis pies, cogido de las hebillas de mis zapatos. Imagino que cuando pasemos junto al río, el *Arcadia* estará allí y Briny verá el automóvil.

En mi ensueño, corre por la orilla y obliga al conductor a detenerse. Briny abre la portezuela y nos saca a todos, incluso a Stevie. Cuando la señora Pulnik intenta impedirlo, le da un puñetazo en la nariz, como haría con cualquiera que intentara robarle una bola en los billares. Briny nos secuestra igual que hace el padre de Huck Finn en el libro, pero el padre de Huck era un hombre malo y Briny es bueno.

Vuelve a la casa, le quita a Gabion a la señorita Tann y nos lleva a un lugar muy lejos de aquí.

Pero mi sueño no es real. El río viene y va. No hay rastro del *Arcadia* y muy pronto la sombra de la casa de la señora Murphy envuelve el automóvil. Debajo de la piel me noto vacía y fría, como las cuevas indias a las que nos llevó Briny una vez que fuimos de excursión por los riscos. En las cuevas había huesos. Huesos muertos de personas que ya no están. Dentro de mí hay huesos muertos.

Rill Foss no puede respirar aquí. No vive aquí. Aquí solo vive May Weathers. Rill Foss vive río abajo. Es la princesa del reino de Arcadia.

Hasta que no cruzamos la acera hacia la casa de la señora Murphy no pienso en Camellia. Me siento culpable por imaginar que Briny nos rescataba del automóvil y se nos llevaba sin Camellia.

Me da miedo lo que dirá cuando le cuente que Gabion no ha vuelto con nosotras, que esperamos que venga más tarde. Camellia dirá que tendría que haberme resistido más, que tendría que haber mordido y arañado y chillado como habría hecho ella. Y puede que sea verdad. Puede que me merezca oírlo. Es posible que sea demasiado cobarde, pero no quiero ir al armario. Y tampoco quiero que metan allí a mis hermanas pequeñas.

El miedo se apodera de mí cuando entramos. Es de esa clase de miedo que te asalta en un río crecido cuando llega el deshielo de primavera y ves un témpano que se dirige hacia el barco. A veces el hielo es tan grande que sabes que no se puede empujar con un remo. Va a golpear el barco y con fuerza, y, si el borde raja el casco, lo hundirá.

Tengo que esforzarme por no soltar a los pequeños, darme la vuelta y salir corriendo de la casa de la señora Murphy antes de que se cierre la puerta a nuestra espalda. La casa apesta a moho y a letrina y al perfume de la señora Murphy y a whisky. Los olores se me pegan a la garganta y no puedo respirar y me alegro cuando nos mandan salir porque aún no es la hora de la cena.

—¡Y nada de *ensuciarr* la ropa! —nos grita la señora Pulnik.

Busco a Camellia en los sitios donde le dije que se quedara, los sitios seguros. No está en ninguno. Los chicos mayores no contestan cuando les pregunto. Se limitan a encogerse de hombros y a seguir jugando a chocar castañas que cogen junto a la valla trasera y atan a un cordel.

Camellia no está escarbando en la tierra ni columpiándose ni jugando a las casitas en la sombra bajo los árboles. Todos los otros niños están, menos Camellia.

Por segunda vez en un día, me parece que el corazón me va a estallar. ¿Y si se la han llevado? ¿Y si tuvo una pataleta cuando nos fuimos y se ha metido en un lío?

—¡Camellia! —grito y a continuación presto atención, pero solo oigo las voces de otros niños. Mi hermana no contesta—. ¡Camellia!

Me dispongo a ir al lateral de la casa, a los arbustos de azaleas, cuando la veo. Está sentada en una esquina del porche con las piernas pegadas al pecho y la cara tapada. Su pelo oscuro y su piel están cubiertos de un polvo gris. Parece que se ha peleado con alguien mientras yo no estaba. Tiene arañazos en un brazo y una rodilla desollada.

Tal vez por eso los chicos mayores no han querido decirme dónde estaba. Probablemente se ha peleado con ellos.

Dejo a los pequeños junto a los caquis y les digo que no se muevan de allí, subo las escaleras y recorro el largo porche hasta donde está Camellia. Mis zapatos rígidos resuenan contra la madera, clac, clac, clac, pero mi hermana no se mueve.

—Camellia. —Si me siento, me mancharé el vestido, así que me acuclillo a su lado. Quizá está dormida—. Camellia, te he traído algo, lo llevo en el bolsillo. Vamos a la colina donde no nos vean y te lo doy.

No contesta. Le toco el pelo y se aparta. Cuando mi mano se desliza hacia su hombro, se levanta una nubecilla gris. Huele a ceniza, pero no de chimenea. Conozco el olor, solo que no consigo situarlo.

—¿En qué lío te has metido mientras hemos estado fuera?

Vuelvo a tocarla y retira el hombro, pero levanta la cabeza. Tiene el labio inflamado y cuatro magulladuras redondas en la mejilla. Tiene los ojos hinchados y rojos, como si hubiera estado llorando, pero lo que más me preocupa es la expresión que hay en ellos. Es como mirar por una ventana a una habitación vacía. Dentro no hay nada más que oscuridad.

Me viene de nuevo el olor y entonces lo reconozco. Carbonilla. Siempre que amarrábamos el *Arcadia* cerca de unas vías de ferrocarril, cogíamos el carbón que se había caído de los trenes. Para calentarnos y cocinar. Y gratis, decía siempre Briny.

¿Ha estado aquí Briny?

En cuanto lo pienso, me doy cuenta de lo equivocada que estoy. Pero muy equivocada. Mientras estábamos fuera, ha sucedido algo muy malo.

—¿Qué ha pasado? —Me dejo caer en el suelo del porche, demasiado asustada para preocuparme por el vestido. En las piernas se me clavan pequeñas astillas—. Camellia, ¿qué ha pasado?

Entreabre los labios, pero no emite ningún sonido. De uno de los ojos le brota una lágrima que traza un río rosa entre la carbonilla.

—Cuéntamelo. —Me inclino para verla mejor, pero se gira y mira para el otro lado. Tiene la mano cerrada en un puño. Se la cojo, le abro los dedos para ver qué está sujetando y, en cuanto lo hago, las galletas y el helado que he comido en la fiesta me suben por la garganta. En la palma de mi hermana hay unas pastillas de menta redondas y sucias tan pegadas que se le han fundido con la piel.

Cierro los ojos, meneo la cabeza e intento no saber, pero sé. Mis pensamientos me llevan contra mi voluntad al sótano de la señora Murphy, al rincón oscuro detrás de las escaleras donde las cenizas recubren el cubo del carbón y la caldera. Veo brazos flacos y fuertes peleando, piernas dando patadas. Veo una manaza tapar la boca que chilla, los dedos sucios y grasientos apretando tan fuerte que dejan cuatro marcas redondas.

Quiero entrar corriendo en la casa, aullar y gritar. Quiero pegar a Camellia por ser testaruda e ir a las azaleas cuando le dije que no lo hiciera. Quiero cogerla y estrecharla contra mí y que esto se pase. No sé exactamente lo que le ha hecho

Riggs, pero sé que es algo malo. También sé que, si lo cuento, hará que mi hermana se caiga de un árbol y se golpee la cabeza. Tal vez incluso me haga lo mismo a mí. Y entonces ¿quién cuidará de las pequeñas? ¿Quién estará esperando a Gabion cuando vuelva?

Cojo la mano de mi hermana, sacudo las pastillas de menta y las dejo que reboten en el porche y caigan en el arriate, donde desaparecen debajo de una enredadera.

Cuando la hago ponerse de pie, no se resiste.

—Vamos. Si te ven así cuando suene la campana, pensarán que te has metido en una pelea y te llevarán al armario.

Tiro de ella y la hago bajar del porche como si fuera un saco de trigo y la llevo hasta el barril de lluvia y, poco a poco, le voy echando agua y la lavo lo mejor que puedo.

—Diles que te has caído de un columpio. —Aunque le tengo cogida la cara con las manos, no me mira—. ¿Me oyes? Si alguien te pregunta por las desolladuras, les dices que te has caído del columpio y ya está.

En los escalones nos esperan Fern, Lark y Stevie, callados como tumbas.

—Quedaos donde estáis y dejad tranquila a Camellia —les ordeno—. No se encuentra bien.

—¿Te duele la tripa?

Fern se acerca sigilosamente y lo mismo hace Lark, y Camellia las aparta con brusquedad. Lark me mira, confusa. Por lo general es la única con la que Camellia es cariñosa.

—He dicho que la dejéis tranquila.

—¡Se te ven las bragas! —grita uno de los chicos mayores a medio camino desde el jardín. Siempre empiezan a acercarse a esta hora para ponerse los primeros en la fila para cenar. No sé por qué. Siempre nos dan lo mismo. En todas las comidas.

—Cállate, Danny Boy —siseo y le bajo a Camellia la falda del vestido hasta las rodillas. Las empleadas le llaman

Danny Boy por la balada irlandesa y porque es irlandés. Pelirrojo y con mil pecas, igual que James. Es el jefe de los mayores, ahora que James ya no está. Pero Danny Boy no es como el chico de la canción, es una mala persona.

Se acerca y se lleva las manos a la cuerda con la que se sujeta unos pantalones que le quedan grandes.

—Míralas, todas finas y elegantes. Apuesto a que ni con esa ropa tan bonita habéis encontrado un papá y una mamá nuevos.

—No necesitamos padres nuevos. Ya tenemos.

—De todas maneras, ¿quién os iba a querer? —Repara en el brazo y la pierna llenos de rasguños de Camellia y se acerca para mirar—. ¿Qué le ha pasado? Parece que se ha peleado con alguien.

Le planto cara a Danny Boy. Si tengo que ir al armario para proteger a mi hermana, lo haré.

—Se ha caído y se ha hecho un poco de daño, nada más. ¿Te molesta?

Suena la campana de la cena y nos ponemos en fila antes de que pase nada más.

Y al final esta noche la que acaba en el armario no soy yo, sino Camellia. Durante la cena está callada y no se come su ración, pero, cuando llega la hora del baño, se espabila y monta una pataleta. Chilla igual que un animal y araña y da patadas y le deja a la señora Pulnik unas marcas rojas alargadas en el brazo con sus uñas.

Hacen falta tres empleadas para sujetar a Camellia y llevarla a rastras al cuarto de baño. Para entonces, la señora Pulnik ya me tiene a mí también sujeta del pelo.

—Calladita. Ni una palabra o *sufrirrás* las consecuencias.

Fern, Lark y Stevie se aferran los unos a los otros pegados a la pared.

En el cuarto de baño, Camellia ruge y grita. Hay ruido de salpicaduras. Una botella que se hace añicos. Cepillos de cerdas caen al suelo. La puerta tiembla en el marco.

—¡Riggs! —grita la señora Pulnik por el hueco de las escaleras—. Venga y tráigame la *cuerrda*. ¡Tráigame la *cuerrda* para el *arrmario!*

Y, sin más, Camellia desaparece. Lo último que veo de ella es a una empleada que la arrastra por el pasillo envuelta como una oruga en una sábana para que no pueda pegar y dar patadas.

Esta noche solo somos tres. No saco el libro, y mis hermanitas no me piden que les siga leyendo la historia. Lark, Fern y yo nos acurrucamos en uno de los catres y tarareo una de las viejas canciones de Queenie hasta que se duermen. Por fin yo también lo hago.

En algún momento, antes de que salga el sol, Fern moja la cama por primera vez desde que tenía dos años y medio. Ni siquiera la regaño. Me limito a limpiarlo lo mejor que puedo y a abrir todo lo posible el ventanuco del sótano. Enrollo la sábana y las bragas de Fern y las meto debajo de los arbustos, donde espero que nadie las encuentre. Luego iré a las azaleas y las tenderé para que se sequen antes de esta noche.

Cuando estoy extendiendo la sábana sobre las ramas, el viento atrapa las hojas y estas se levantan lo suficiente para dejarme ver algo. Debajo de la farola de la calle hay personas mirando la casa. En la penumbra del amanecer no distingo ni caras ni ropa, solo la silueta de un hombre encorvado y un chico alto y flaco.

Se parecen a Zede y a Silas.

Con la misma rapidez con la que han aparecido, las hojas vuelven a su sitio y los tapan.

15

AVERY

El sobre es sorprendentemente normal. De esos de estraza que se usan en las oficinas. El contenido es delgado, quizá unas cuantas hojas dobladas en tres. Está cerrado y lleva el nombre de mi abuela escrito en el reverso en una letra temblorosa que se sale del margen y cae hacia una esquina.

—El párkinson del abuelo se le agravó un poco al final —explica Trent. Se frota la frente y mira el sobre con el ceño fruncido, como replanteándose si debería haber roto el juramento dándomelo.

Sé que lo mejor sería abrirlo antes de que se arrepienta, pero me remuerde la conciencia. Trent parece sentirse como si hubiera fracasado en algo y la culpa de eso es mía.

Entiendo muy bien lo que es la lealtad a la familia. De hecho, es lo que me ha traído hasta aquí en plena noche.

—Gracias —le digo, como si eso fuera a ayudar.

Se frota una ceja con las yemas de los dedos y asiente con la cabeza de mala gana.

—Solo para que lo sepas, esto puede empeorar las cosas. Hay una razón por la que mi abuelo dedicaba tanto tiempo a ayudar a localizar personas. Después de casarse con mi abuela y hacerse cargo del negocio familiar en Charleston, se matriculó en Derecho para poder llevar sus propios contratos inmobiliarios..., pero también por otro motivo. Cuando cumplió dieciocho años descubrió que era adoptado. Nadie se lo había dicho nunca. Su padre adoptivo era sargento en el departamento de policía de Memphis y, que yo sepa, nunca estuvieron muy unidos, pero que mi abuelo se enterara de que habían estado mintiéndole toda su vida fue la gota que colmó el vaso. Se alistó en el ejército y no volvió a hablar a sus padres adoptivos. Estuvo años buscando a su familia biológica, pero nunca la encontró. Mi abuela siempre pensó que le habría ido mejor si no hubiera encontrado sus papeles de adopción. Para serte sincero, a ella le habría gustado que los padres adoptivos los hubieran destruido.

—Los secretos siempre acaban por salir a la luz.

Es una reflexión que me ha hecho mi padre muchas veces. «Los secretos también te hacen vulnerable ante tus enemigos, políticos o de otra clase».

Haya lo que haya dentro de este sobre, prefiero saberlo.

Aun así, me tiemblan los dedos cuando los deslizo bajo la solapa.

—Entiendo que tu abuelo quisiera dedicarse a ayudar a otras personas a encontrar información y a familiares perdidos. *Pero ¿qué tiene que ver mi abuela con eso?*

La tira adhesiva se desprende un poco cuando tiro. Voy con cuidado, igual que mi madre cuando abre un regalo de cumpleaños, evitando que el papel se rasgue.

—No dejes para mañana lo que puedas hacer hoy —digo. Muy despacio, saco un sobre más pequeño que ha sido abierto ya en algún momento. Los papeles que hay dentro están doblados como un folleto o una factura de la luz, pero no distingo si son documentos oficiales o de otra clase.

Al otro lado de la mesa, Trent se mira las manos mientras saco el contenido del sobre.

—De verdad... —No tiene sentido darle las gracias otra vez. No le quitará el cargo de conciencia—. Quiero que sepas que puedes contar conmigo para hacer con esto lo que sea mejor. No pienso dejar que te cause problemas con tu familia. Respeto la preocupación de tu abuelo, dada la clase de investigación a la que se dedicaba.

—Sabía por experiencia propia lo que podía pasar.

Un ruido en la casa nos hace volvernos justo cuando estoy alisando los papeles en la mesa. Identifico el sonido de unos pequeños pies recién salidos de la cama en un suelo con restos de arena. Casi espero ver a uno de mis sobrinos en el pasillo, pero quien aparece es un niño rubio de tres o cuatro años con ojos azules adormilados y un adorable hoyuelo en la barbilla. Sé de dónde lo ha sacado.

Trent Turner tiene un hijo. ¿Habrá una señora Turner durmiendo en una de las habitaciones de la casa? Una extraña punzada de desilusión tiñe este pensamiento de un tono verdoso. Inconscientemente, busco una alianza en el dedo de Trent antes de volver a mirar al niño y pensar: *Ya está bien, Avery Stafford, ¿se puede saber qué te pasa?*

En momentos como este me pregunto qué problema tengo. ¿Por qué no me siento como una mujer que se ha comprometido con su alma gemela para siempre jamás, fin de la historia? Mis dos hermanas se enamoraron perdidamente de sus maridos y, que yo sepa, nunca tuvieron dudas. Mi madre igual. Y mi abuela.

El niñito me mira mientras rodea la mesa bostezando y frotándose la frente con el dorso de un brazo. Lo hace de manera muy teatral. Parece la actriz de una película muda practicando un desmayo exagerado.

—¿No deberías estar en la cama, Jonah? —pregunta su padre.

—*Zí...*

—¿Y por qué te has levantado, a ver? —Puede que Trent pretenda parecer severo, pero su expresión es de lo más blandengue. Jonah apoya las dos manos en la rodilla de su padre, levanta una pierna y empieza a trepar por él como un mono en la jungla.

Trent lo levanta y Jonah se acerca a él para susurrar:

—Hay un *peterodáctil* en mi *armadio*.

—¿Un pterodáctilo?

—*Zí.*

—Jonah, en tu armario no hay nada. Eso es por la película que te dejaron ver los primos mayores el otro día en casa de la tía Lou, ¿te acuerdas? Ya tuviste otra pesadilla con ello. Un dinosaurio ni siquiera cabría en tu armario. Aquí no hay dinosaurios.

—*Zí* hay. —Jonah se sorbe la nariz. Agarrado a la camiseta de su padre, se gira lo bastante para examinarme con la boca abierta en un enorme bostezo.

No debería meterme, igual empeoro las cosas. Sin embargo, he vivido este asunto de los dinosaurios algunas noches en Drayden Hill y en vacaciones, con los hijos de mis hermanas.

—A mis sobrinos también les pasaba. Les daban miedo los dinosaurios, pero ¿sabes lo que hicimos?

Jonah niega con la cabeza y Trent me mira intrigado, con las cejas rubias muy juntas. Tiene una frente muy flexible.

Dos pares de ojos azules idénticos me están invitando a que dé mi solución al problema de los dinosaurios.

Por suerte la tengo.

—Al día siguiente fuimos a comprar linternas, unas linternas alucinantes. Si tienes una linterna muy buena en la cama, cuando te despiertas por la noche y te parece ver algo, puedes encenderla, enfocarla y mirar. ¿Y sabes lo que pasa cada vez que enciendes la linterna?

Jonah aguarda mi respuesta conteniendo la respiración, su boquita perfecta abierta, pero está claro que su padre conoce la respuesta. Tiene aspecto de querer darse una palmada en la frente como queriendo decir: *¿Cómo no se me había ocurrido?*

—Cada vez que enciendes la linterna, no hay nada.

—¿Cada *ves?* —Jonah no está convencido.

—Siempre. Te lo prometo.

Jonah se vuelve a su padre buscando confirmación y se intercambian una dulce mirada de confianza. Salta a la vista que es un padre entregado. De los que matan monstruos y meten a sus hijos en la cama.

—Mañana iremos a BI-LO a compra una linterna. ¿Te parece bien?

Me fijo en que no dice: «Mamá te llevará mañana a comprar una linterna». También en que no le dice al pobre niño que ya es mayor ni lo manda de vuelta a la cama. En lugar de eso, se lo coloca contra su hombro y apoya una mano en la mesa señalando los documentos que estoy tapando con la mano.

Jonah se mete un pulgar en la boca y se acurruca contra el pecho de su padre.

Miro los papeles, sorprendida por el hecho de haberme olvidado de ellos por un momento.

La primera hoja es una fotocopia borrosa de algún tipo de formulario oficial. *Hoja de historial,* dice el encabezamiento en letras negritas. Abajo hay un número de expediente: *7501. Edad: recién nacido. Sexo: varón.* El nombre del bebé que figura es *Shad Arthur Foss, religión: desconocida.* En la esquina del formulario hay estampada una fecha de octubre de 1939 y al parecer se cumplimentó en un hospital de Memphis, Tennessee. *Nombre de la madre: Mary Anne Anthony. Nombre del padre: B. A. Foss.* En la dirección de ambos padres dice: *indigentes, campamento del río.* Tanto el padre como la madre tenían menos de treinta años cuando nació el niño.

La funcionaria responsable del formulario, la señorita Eugenia Carter, expone en pocas palabras la situación del niño en apartados que recuerdan un informe clínico: *Motivo de entrega a la Asociación H. I. T.: Nacido fuera del matrimonio – imposibilidad de manutención. Forma de entrega: Renuncia de patria potestad firmada por el padre y la madre en el momento del nacimiento.*

—No reconozco estos nombres —murmuro separando estas hojas del resto y dejándolas con cuidado en la mesa. De acuerdo, tenemos muchos parientes, pero nunca he visto un Foss ni un Anthony en una invitación de boda ni los he conocido en un funeral—. No sé qué relación puede tener nada de esto con mi abuela. Supongo que es más o menos del año en que nació. —La edad de la abuela Judy cambia cada vez que se la preguntan. Nunca admite nada y además le parece una pregunta poco elegante—. ¿Puede ser Shad Arthur Foss alguien a quien conociera después, en la escuela? ¿Es posible que estuviera ayudando a un amigo a rastrear información?

La siguiente página es una copia del expediente del niño Foss.

FECHA DE NACIMIENTO: 1 de septiembre de 1939

PESO AL NACER: prematuro — 1,8 kg

PESO ACTUAL: 3,1 kg

NIÑO: El niño nació prematuro, con solo un kilo ochocientos gramos de peso. Se ha desarrollado con normalidad en todos los aspectos. Kahn negativo. Wasserman y frotis de la madre negativos. Sin enfermedades ni vacunaciones infantiles.

MADRE: 28 años de edad, nacida en Estados Unidos, de origen polaco-holandés. Estudios medios, ojos azules, pelo rubio, altura aproximada 1,70 m. Peso: 52 kg. De religión protestante. Considerada muy atractiva e inteligente.

PADRE: 29 años de edad, nacido en Estados Unidos, de
origen escocés-irlandés y cajún-francés. Estudios
medios, ojos castaños, pelo negro, 1,80 m aproximadamente de estatura. Unos 80 kg de peso. Sin
afiliación religiosa.

No existen enfermedades hereditarias por parte de
ninguna de las dos familias, y a pesar de los des-
lices extramaritales de estos jóvenes individuos,
tanto la familia materna como la paterna son tra-
bajadoras y respetadas en sus comunidades respectivas. Ninguna está interesada en hacerse cargo de
la custodia del niño.

Le paso el segundo documento a Trent, que está leyendo
el primero. La tercera hoja dice:

Padres o Tutores
CEDEN LA PATRIA POTESTAD
A la Asociación de Hogares Infantiles de Tennessee

———

NUESTRO LEMA ES: AYUDA A UN NIÑO
A ENCONTRAR UNA FAMILIA

La triste historia del niño Shad está contada de nuevo en
letras mal mecanografiadas sobre fondo rayado al lado de preguntas del tipo: *¿Saludable? ¿Robusto? ¿Deforme? ¿Lisiado?
¿Hernias? ¿Retraso mental?*
¿Apto para la adopción?
El niño Shad es firmado, sellado, testificado y despacha-
do. Lo transfieren a la casa de acogida de Memphis para su
observación y adopción.
—No tengo ni idea de qué significa todo esto. —Pero sí
sé que es imposible que mi abuela viniera varias veces a Edisto

a reunirse con Trent Turner I si no se tratara de algo importante. También me cuesta creer que llegara tan lejos para ayudar a un amigo. Tenía algún tipo de interés personal en esto—. ¿Hay más paquetes? ¿Dejó tu abuelo algo más?

Trent aparta la mirada como si estuviera intentando decidir si contármelo o no, luchando otra vez con su conciencia. Por fin dice:

—Solo más sobres con nombres escritos, igual que este. Mi abuelo consiguió entregar la mayoría de los documentos a sus dueños antes de morir. Los paquetes que quedaron suponía que pertenecían a personas que habían muerto sin que él lo supiera. —Hace una pausa para cambiar de postura a Jonah, que se está quedando dormido apoyado en su hombro—. Hubo casos que guardó durante cincuenta o sesenta años, desde que empezó las investigaciones. Lo que no sé es cómo decidía cuáles aceptar. Nunca se lo pregunté. Tengo un vago recuerdo de clientes que venían a verlo con fotografías y que se sentaban en la mesa que hay fuera de la casa a llorar y hablar, pero no era muy a menudo. Casi todo el trabajo lo hacía en la oficina de Charleston. La única razón de que yo lo viera es que venía a Edisto cada vez que tenía ocasión. De vez en cuando se reunía aquí con personas, supongo que para tener más intimidad. Tengo la sensación de que a veces trataba con clientes de perfil alto. —Me mira con expresión cómplice y sé que me está incluyendo en esa categoría. De pronto me pica la piel y me retuerzo debajo de la camiseta.

—Sigo sin entender qué tiene que ver esto con mi abuela. ¿Hay algo en los papeles de tu abuelo que tenga que ver con una mujer llamada May Crandall? ¿O quizá con alguien llamada Fern... o Queenie? Creo que es posible que fueran amigas de mi abuela.

Apoya la barbilla en la cabeza rubia de Jonah.

—No me suenan esos nombres, pero, como ya te he dicho, cuando mi abuelo murió, no leí ninguno de esos documentos. Cerré su despacho con llave y no he vuelto a entrar desde entonces. —Señala con un gesto del hombro una cabaña diminuta iluminada por el resplandor de una farola del jardín—. Me hice cargo de los sobres, como me pidió, y nada más. Lo que haya quedado allí supongo que no lo consideró importante. Respetaba mucho la intimidad de estas personas, después de lo mucho que sufrió él cuando se enteró de la verdad sobre sus padres. Nunca quiso ser responsable de alterar el pasado de alguien de esa manera. A no ser que solicitaran la información.

—Entonces, ¿eso significa que fue mi abuela quien acudió a él?

—Basándome en lo que sé del trabajo de mi abuelo, sí. —Se acaricia el labio inferior pensativo. Cuando quiero darme cuenta, lo estoy mirando fijamente casi sin escuchar lo que me dice—. Si alguien hubiera estado buscando a tu abuela, por ejemplo, un familiar desaparecido, mi abuelo le habría dado los documentos y cerrado el expediente una vez que la hubiera localizado. Siempre dejaba a sus clientes la decisión última sobre si ponerse o no en contacto. El hecho de que no cerrara este caso y que lo dejara marcado con el nombre «Judy Stafford» quiere decir que tu abuela estaba buscando a alguien..., alguien a quien no consiguió localizar.

Mis pensamientos van a toda velocidad, a pesar de la hora que es.

—¿Podría ver el resto? —Sé que es muy atrevido pedir esto ahora, pero me da miedo que Trent cambie de idea si tiene tiempo de pensárselo. Es una lección que he aprendido de mi experiencia en los juicios. Si quieres que tu testigo cambie de idea, pide un receso. De lo contrario, sigue derecha hacia donde quieres llegar.

—Créeme, no es un sitio para ir de noche. El edificio es una antigua cabaña de esclavos que se trajo a la propiedad, así que no está muy bien aislado. Puede haber cualquier cosa dentro.

—He crecido rodeada de establos. No tengo miedo de casi nada.

Tuerce la boca y le sale un hoyuelo.

—¿Por qué será que no me sorprende? —Se cambia de hombro a Jonah otra vez—. Déjame que lo acueste.

Nuestros ojos se encuentran y por un instante... nos miramos. Quizá es la luz tenue de las lámparas retro o el silencio íntimo de la casa, pero siento algo que no quiero sentir. Me recorre, lánguido y cálido, visible como el charco que deja la marea una tarde de verano cuando el aire ha refrescado.

Meto un dedo del pie en el agua, río para mis adentros, noto que me ruborizo, bajo la vista y luego vuelvo a mirar a Trent de reojo. La otra comisura de la boca se le tuerce en una sonrisa y una extraña sensación me recorre entera. Es como un relámpago sobre el agua, algo impredecible y peligroso.

Por un instante me aturde y me olvido de dónde estoy y de a qué he venido.

Entonces Jonah separa la cabeza del hombro de su padre y se rompe el hechizo. Me despierto igual que un paciente recién salido de la anestesia. Tengo la cabeza perdida. Tardo un momento en pensar con claridad y entonces aparto la mirada. En algún instante del proceso me miro el dedo anular, en el que ahora mismo no llevo el anillo de compromiso porque, antes de que la noche tomara este rumbo tan inesperado, me lo quité para no mancharlo de crema después de ducharme.

¿Qué es esto? Nunca en la vida me había pasado algo así. Jamás he tenido lapsus mentales. No me dejo seducir con facilidad por las personas, no me comporto de forma inapropiada con desconocidos. La tremenda importancia de no hacer esas cosas me ha sido inculcada desde que nací y la Facultad de Derecho ha sido un buen refuerzo en ese sentido.

—Tengo que irme. —Como si me hubiera oído, en ese momento me vibra el móvil en el bolsillo, la irrupción del mundo real. Mi silla rechina cuando la empujo. El sonido parece detener inesperadamente a Trent. ¿De verdad iba a dejarme entrar en el taller esta noche? ¿O estaba pensando en algo... más íntimo?

Ignoro el teléfono y le doy las gracias por darme el sobre y a continuación añado:

—¿Nos podríamos ver mañana? —*En la clara luz del día*—. Para mirar si queda algo más. —Haga lo que haga, me estoy arriesgando. Para mañana es posible que Trent haya cambiado de opinión. Pero aquí, esta noche, los riesgos son de otra clase—. Ya te he dado bastante la lata. Ha sido de muy mala educación llamar tan tarde. Perdóname... Es que estaba desesperada... por descifrar todo esto.

Suprime un bostezo y se obliga a abrir los ojos.

—No pasa nada. Soy noctámbulo.

—Ya lo veo —bromeo y se ríe.

—Mañana. —Pronuncia la palabra como si fuera una promesa—. Tendrá que ser después del trabajo. Tengo un día muy ocupado. A ver si la tía Lou se puede quedar con Jonah un par de horas más.

Que se comprometa me alivia. Espero que se sienta igual después de pensar en todo esto.

—Entonces te veo mañana por la noche. Ya me dirás a qué hora. Ah, y no dejes a Jonah con su tía por mí. Tengo sobrinos trillizos de dos años. Me encantan los niños pequeños. —Recojo los papeles de la abuela Judy y la linterna, doy un paso en dirección a la puerta y entonces me paro y busco un lápiz y algo donde escribir—. Debería darte mi número de teléfono.

—Lo tengo. —Hace una mueca—. En el móvil..., como unas doscientas veces. —Debería resultar violento, pero en lugar de eso nos reímos. Se vuelve hacia el pasillo—. Déjame que acueste a Jonah y te acompaño a la playa y espero a que llegues a tu casa.

Mi cabeza dice no, pero tengo que obligarme a pronunciar las palabras:

—No hace falta, conozco el camino.

Al otro lado de la ventana, la noche está iluminada por el resplandor de la luna, el mar reluce entre las palmeras que rodean el jardín trasero de la casa. Las rosas y el jazmín se mecen en la brisa marina. Es la combinación perfecta. De las que solo son posibles en esta costa.

Trent me mira.

—Es muy de noche. Déjame por lo menos que sea un caballero.

Espero a que acueste a Jonah; después cruzamos el porche trasero juntos y bajamos los escalones. La brisa que llega del mar me atrapa el pelo y me lo revuelve, me acaricia la piel y se me cuela por la camiseta. Al llegar al final de las escaleras, miro la pequeña cabaña de esclavos, examino las viejas ventanas con marcos de madera, seis en total, que dan al porche delantero. ¿Habrá respuestas ocultas detrás del vidrio turbio por la sal?

—Es de alrededor de 1850. —Trent parece estar buscando temas de conversación. Quizá los dos notamos la presión de una situación que parece pedir algo más que una conversación intrascendente—. Mi abuelo la trajo cuando compró la propiedad. Al principio la usaba de despacho. Este solar fue su primera operación inmobiliaria. Compró el terreno adyacente a la casa Myers y lo dividió para hacer esta casa y las dos que hay en medio.

Otro vínculo entre Trent Turner I y mi abuela. Es evidente que se trataron durante muchos años. ¿Lo reclutaría ella para que la ayudara a buscar a alguien porque sabía que se ocupaba de esas cosas? ¿O fueron sus investigaciones las que lo condujeron hasta mi abuela? ¿Le sugirió ella que comprara el terreno contiguo a la casa? ¿Es el Trent Turner actual realmente tan ajeno a estos vínculos como yo? ¿Ha llevado una generación de nuestras familias unas vidas inextricablemente ligadas que después han ocultado, por alguna razón, a la generación siguiente?

Las preguntas se ensartan unas con otras en mi cabeza cuando nos detenemos en el sendero de la playa, donde las uniolas brillan como filamentos de fibra de vidrio a la luz de la luna.

—Bonita noche —dice.

—Sí.

—Cuidado. Está subiendo la marea. Te vas a mojar los pies. —Hace un gesto con la cabeza en dirección al mar y no puedo evitar mirar. Un camino de olas relucientes conduce a la luna y una alfombra de estrellas centellea radiante en el cielo. ¿Cuánto tiempo hace que no me siento en la oscuridad a disfrutar de una noche así? Estoy hambrienta de agua, de cielo y de días que no estén divididos en recuadros de una agenda.

¿Se sentiría así mi abuela? ¿Es esa la razón de que viniera aquí tan a menudo?

—Gracias otra vez... por dejarme interrumpir tu velada. —Retrocedo y piso la arena. Algo me pasa corriendo al lado del pie y grito.

—Será mejor que enciendas la linterna.

Lo último que veo antes de rodearme de una esfera de luz artificial es a Trent sonriéndome.

Me doy la vuelta y me alejo, consciente de que me está mirando.

Me vuelve a vibrar el móvil y cuando me lo saco del bolsillo es como abrir una puerta a otro mundo. Cruzo el umbral enseguida. Necesito algo familiar y seguro en lo que centrarme después de ese momento tan extraño en la playa con Trent.

Pero ¿Abby? ¿Desde la oficina de Baltimore? ¿Por qué me llama de madrugada?

Cuando contesto, está sin aliento.

—Avery, por fin te localizo. ¿Estás bien? Me ha llegado un e-mail rarísimo tuyo hace un rato.

Me río.

—Ay, Abby, perdona. La idea era enviármelo a mí misma.

—¿Tienes que recordarte a ti misma dónde vas? ¿Así es como te sienta la vida de niña rica en Carolina del Sur?

Abby es una chica de Washington D. C. sin pájaros en la cabeza, una trabajadora nata que pasó de vivir en una casa de protección oficial a estudiar en la Facultad de Derecho. También es una excelente fiscal. Echo de menos comer con ella e intercambiar ideas sobre los casos que llevamos.

Si hay alguien a quien pueda confiar la información sobre la abuela Judy es Abby, pero es más seguro hablar de cómo va todo en la oficina, así que eso hago.

—Es una larga historia. ¿Qué haces despierta a esta hora?

—Trabajar. Mañana tenemos presentación de pruebas documentales. Blanqueo de dinero y fraude cibernético. Un caso gordo. Han contratado a Bracken y Thompson.

—Vaya... Artillería pesada. —La conversación sobre leyes me devuelve enseguida a Baltimore. Lo que fuera esa tontería que se apoderó de mí en casa de Trent se eclipsa y me alegro, porque así es como debe ser—. Cuéntame cómo está la cosa.

Mis sentidos se agudizan de una manera que no tiene nada que ver con la noche o con el hecho de que al volver la cabeza haya visto a Trent, que sigue mirándome.

Abby empieza a contarme los detalles de la investigación y me concentro. Una cosa sí es innegable.

Echo de menos mi vida de antes.

16

RILL

*A*rriba todo el mundo! ¡Parece que por fin ha salido el sol! —dice la señorita Dodd mientras abre con llave la habitación del sótano. La señorita Dodd es nueva aquí, lleva dos días. Es más joven que las demás y también más simpática. Si consigo pillarla a solas, voy a preguntarle por Camellia. Nadie quiere decirme dónde está mi hermana. La señora Pulnik me dijo que cerrara la boca y dejara de molestar a las empleadas.

Danny Boy asegura que Camellia está muerta. Dice que se despertó y oyó a la señora Murphy contarle a Riggs que Camellia murió después de que la metieran en el armario y le dio instrucciones sobre lo que hacer con ella. Danny Boy dice que Riggs llevó su cuerpo a la camioneta para tirarlo en el pantano. Que lo vio todo con sus propios ojos. Asegura que mi hermana está muerta y que adiós muy buenas.

No me creo una sola palabra de lo que dice Danny Boy. Es la persona más odiosa del mundo.

La señorita Dodd me contará la verdad.

Ahora mismo está preocupada por lo mal que huele en la habitación. Cuando llueve, hay moho y goteras y encima

Fern lleva mojando la cama desde que se llevaron a Camellia y a Gabion. Le digo que no lo haga, pero no sirve de nada.

—¡Madre mía, qué olor! —La señorita Dodd nos mira preocupada—. Este no es sitio para que duerman unos niños.

Me acerco a ella desde el catre mojado. Lo he tapado con mantas porque no se me ocurre otra manera de esconderlo.

—Se..., se me ha volcado el orinal.

Mira al rincón. Debajo del orinal, el cemento está seco.

—¿Ha tenido alguno un accidente en la cama?

Se me llenan los ojos de lágrimas y Lark se refugia en un rincón llevándose a Fern con ella. Agarro a la señorita Dodd del delantal al tiempo que agacho la cabeza porque estoy esperando una bofetada. Aun así, tengo que evitar que suba a contárselo a la señora Pulnik.

—No se lo diga a nadie.

Las pestañas de la señorita Dodd aletean sobre sus amables ojos gris verdoso.

—¿Y por qué no, por san Francisco de Asís? Lo limpiamos y ya está.

—Castigarán a Fern.

Supongo que la señorita Dodd no sabe todavía lo que les pasa a los niños que mojan la cama.

—Por el amor del cielo, pues claro que no.

—Por favor. —El pánico me inunda como una marea que sube—. Por favor, no lo diga.

No puedo perder a Fern y a Lark. No estoy segura de lo que le ha pasado a Camellia, y después de cuatro días imagino que las personas que se llevaron a Gabby no lo van a devolver. He perdido a mi hermano. Camellia ha desaparecido. Lark y Fern son todo lo que tengo.

La señorita Dodd me coge la cara con las manos y me abraza con mucha amabilidad.

—Chsss, tranquila. Yo me ocupo. No te preocupes, tesoro. Será nuestro secreto.

Lloro más fuerte. Nadie me ha abrazado así desde Queenie.

—Y ahora, a tranquilizarse todos. —La señorita Dodd mira a su alrededor nerviosa—. Será mejor que subamos antes de que vengan a buscarnos.

Asiento con la cabeza y digo entre lágrimas:

—Sí, señora.

Meter en un lío a la señorita Dodd sería lo peor que podría hacer. La oí contarle a la cocinera que su padre murió el año pasado, que su madre está enferma de hidropesía y que tiene cuatro hermanos pequeños viviendo en una granja en el condado de Shelby, en el norte. La señorita Dodd vino a Memphis andando y con quien se ofreciera a llevarla para encontrar trabajo y así poder mandarles dinero.

La señorita Dodd necesita este trabajo.

Nosotros necesitamos a la señorita Dodd.

Cojo a Lark y a Fern y salimos por la puerta delante de la señorita Dodd. Riggs anda cerca de la caldera, husmeando igual que un perro en una cocina. Como siempre, mantengo la cabeza baja y lo miro por el rabillo del ojo.

—Señor Riggs —dice la señorita Dodd antes de que lleguemos a la escalera—, ¿me haría usted un favor? No hace falta que se lo cuente a nadie.

—Sí, señora.

Antes de que me dé tiempo a detenerla, le pregunta:

—¿Podría mezclar un poco de agua y lejía y limpiar el catre que está junto a la puerta? Cuando termine déjeme el cubo, que luego ya limpiaré yo el resto.

—Sí, señora, claro que sí. —Los dientes torcidos le asoman al sonreír, largos y amarillos como los de un castor—. Creo que estas niñas se irán pronto al piso de arriba. —Nos saluda con el asa de la pala.

—Cuanto antes mejor. —La señorita Dodd no sabe lo equivocada que está. Una vez arriba, no habrá puertas cerradas con llave entre nosotras y Riggs—. Ningún niño debería dormir en una habitación del sótano.

—No, señora.

—Y si hubiera un incendio, quedarían atrapados.

—Si hubiera un incendio, yo echaría la puerta abajo. No lo dude.

—Es usted un buen hombre, señor Riggs.

La señorita Dodd no sabe la verdad sobre Riggs. No la sabe.

—Gr-gracias, señora.

—Y no le cuente a nadie lo de limpiar la cama —le recuerda—. Será nuestro secreto.

Riggs se limita a sonreír y a mirarnos, con los ojos blancos alrededor de las comisuras y más desquiciados que un oso en invierno. Si te encuentras a un oso en invierno, más te vale tener cuidado. Está hambriento y busca algo con que saciar esa hambre. Le dará igual qué.

La mirada de Riggs me persigue durante el desayuno e incluso más tarde ese día, cuando el jardín está por fin lo bastante seco para que salgamos a jugar. Al cruzar el porche, miro hacia el rincón, pienso en Camellia y me pregunto: *¿Estaría Danny Boy diciendo la verdad? ¿Es posible que mi hermana esté muerta?*

Sería mi culpa. Soy la mayor. Se suponía que tenía que cuidar de todos. Fue lo último que me dijo Briny antes de irse corriendo al otro lado del río. *Cuida de los pequeños, Rill. Cuida de todos hasta que volvamos.*

Incluso el nombre me suena raro ya. Todo el mundo me llama May. Quizá Rill sigue en algún lugar del río con Camellia y Lark y Fern y Gabion. Quizá están flotando en las perezosas y suaves corrientes de verano, viendo barcos y barcazas pasar y azores de Cooper sobrevolar el agua en amplios y lentos círculos en busca de peces que cazar.

Quizá Rill es solo una historia que he leído, como la de Huck Finn y Jim. Quizá ni siquiera soy Rill y nunca lo fui.

Me vuelvo, bajo corriendo las escaleras y cruzo el jardín con el vestido pegado alrededor de las piernas. Extiendo los brazos, echo la cabeza atrás para crear mi propia brisa y durante un minuto recupero a Rill, soy de nuevo ella. Estoy en el *Arcadia,* nuestro trocito de cielo.

No me paro al llegar a la verja donde tienen su túnel los chicos mayores. Están ocupados metiéndose con dos niños nuevos que llegaron ayer mientras llovía. Hermanos, creo. En cualquier caso, me da igual. Si Danny Boy tratara de detenerme, le daría un puñetazo y lo tumbaría, igual que haría Camellia. Lo tiraría al suelo de espaldas justo al lado de la valla y lo usaría para trepar por ella y escapar.

No dejaría de correr hasta llegar a la orilla del río.

Rodeo el viejo retrete corriendo lo más deprisa que puedo y salto hacia los barrotes de hierro intentando subir lo bastante para llegar al otro lado, pero no puedo. Solo consigo trepar unos centímetros antes de resbalar y golpearme contra el suelo. Me agarro de los barrotes y grito y aúllo igual que una criatura salvaje encerrada en una jaula.

Así sigo hasta que los barrotes resbalan por el sudor y las lágrimas y están manchados de sangre. Los barrotes no ceden tampoco ante eso. No se mueven. Siguen donde estaban mientras yo me dejo caer al suelo y me abandono al llanto.

De algún lugar fuera de mis propios sonidos oigo decir a Danny Boy:

—La chica guapa ha perdido un tornillo.

Oigo a Fern y a Stevie llorar y a Fern llamándome y a los chicos mayores metiéndose con ellos y empujándolos cada vez que quieren llegar a la puerta. Tengo que ir. Tengo que ayudar-los, pero, más que nada, lo que quiero es desaparecer. Quiero estar sola en un sitio donde nadie me encuentre. Donde no me puedan quitar a las personas que quiero.

Danny Boy le retuerce el brazo a Stevie detrás de la espalda y lo obliga a decir «me rindo». Luego sigue hasta que el grito de Stevie es como un puñal en mi vientre. Se me clava justo en el lugar que quiero tener duro como una piedra. Igual que la espada de Arturo, el grito de Stevie me atraviesa.

Antes de darme cuenta de lo que hago, he cruzado el cementerio y tengo a Danny Boy sujeto por los pelos.

—¡Suéltalo! —Tiro con fuerza y le doblo la cabeza hacia atrás—. Suéltalo y no vuelvas a ponerle un dedo encima o te rompo el pescuezo igual que a un pollo. Te lo digo en serio. —Sin Camellia aquí para pelearse por todos, de pronto me he transformado en ella—. Te partiré el pescuezo y te tiraré al pantano.

Uno de los otros chicos suelta a Fern y retrocede. Me mira con los ojos muy abiertos. Entiendo por qué. Tengo el pelo erizado y apuntando en todas las direcciones. Parezco la Medusa de las fábulas griegas.

—¡Pelea! ¡Pelea! —gritan los niños y vienen corriendo a mirar.

Danny Boy suelta a Stevie. No quiere que le peguen delante de todo el mundo. Stevie cae de cara al suelo y se levanta con la boca llena de tierra. Escupe y llora y yo empujo a Danny Boy y cojo a Stevie y a Fern de la mano. Ya estamos en la colina cuando me doy cuenta de que nos falta alguien.

El corazón me da un vuelco.

—¿Dónde está Lark?

Fern se lleva un puño a la boca como si temiera que la vaya a regañar. Tal vez me tiene miedo después de verme como me ha visto.

—¿Queréis responder? ¿Dónde está Lark?

—*Ñora.* —Stevie balbucea la primera palabra que le oigo decir desde que llegamos aquí—. *Ñora.*

Me arrodillo en la hierba húmeda y los miro a los dos a la cara.

—¿Qué señora? ¿Qué señora, Fern?

—Una señora la cogió en el porche —susurra Fern con la mano todavía en la boca. Tiene lágrimas en los ojos—. Así. —Coge a Stevie del brazo y tira de él, arrastrándolo unos cuantos pasos. Stevie asiente para decirme que también él lo ha visto.

—¿Una señora? ¿No era Riggs? ¿No se la ha llevado Riggs? Ambos niegan con la cabeza.

—*Ñora* —repite Stevie.

Sigo aturdida de lágrimas secas y restos de odio. ¿Se habrá metido Lark en un lío? ¿Estará enferma? No puede ser. Cuando bajamos a desayunar estaba como siempre. No se llevan a los niños a la enfermería a no ser que tengan fiebre o estén vomitando.

Mando a Stevie y a Fern a los columpios.

—Id allí, al balancín, y no os bajéis pase lo que pase hasta que vaya yo a buscaros o suene la campana. ¿Entendido?

Los dos parecen muertos de miedo, pero asienten con la cabeza y se dan la mano. Me aseguro de que llegan al balancín y me dirijo a la casa. Cuando paso junto a la puerta, le hago saber a Danny Boy que, si los molesta, tendrá que vérselas conmigo.

El valor me flaquea mientras cruzo el jardín. No le quito ojo a la casa con la esperanza de ver a la señorita Dodd. Cuando subo al porche de puntillas y voy al cuarto de lavar, el corazón me late tan fuerte que me martillea los oídos. Dependiendo de quién me vea allí, puedo meterme en un buen lío. Alguien puede pensar que quiero robar comida.

Las mujeres de color están lavando y escurriendo ropa cuando paso. ¿Saben qué le ha pasado a Lark? ¿Me lo dirían si así fuera? Por lo general, cuando nos cruzamos, hacemos como si no nos conviniera vernos.

No me miran, así que no pregunto. En la cocina no hay nadie y la cruzo corriendo para que no me pillen allí.

La puerta batiente rechina un poco cuando asomo la cabeza en el vestíbulo delantero de la señora Murphy. Casi no me da tiempo a ocultarme cuando oigo su voz y veo la puerta de su despacho abierta.

—Creo que les va a encantar. —La señorita Tann también está en la habitación. Su voz suena empalagosa, así que sé que está hablando con alguien más aparte de la señora Murphy—. Es perfecta en todos los sentidos. Su madre incluso llegó a ir a la universidad antes de la Depresión. Una joven muy inteligente y con fama de hermosa. Claramente su hija ha salido a ella. Esta pequeña es igualita que Shirley Temple y ni siquiera necesita una permanente. Es un poco callada, pero se porta bien y tiene buenos modales. No les dará ninguna guerra en público, que sé que es algo muy importante, dada su profesión. Me habría gustado que nos hubiesen permitido llevársela a casa. Que los padres vengan a los hogares infantiles no es el procedimiento habitual.

—Le agradezco que hayan hecho una excepción. —La voz del hombre es profunda. Suena a capitán del ejército—. Nos resulta complicado ir a ningún sitio sin que nos reconozcan.

—Lo comprendemos muy bien. —Nunca he oído a la señora Murphy hablar con tanta amabilidad—. Es un honor que nos visiten. ¡Aquí en mi propia casa!

—Han elegido a uno de los mejores niños que tenemos. —La señorita Tann se acerca a la puerta—. ¿Y te vas a portar muy bien, verdad que sí, Bonnie? Harás todo lo que te digan tu mamá y tu papá nuevos. Eres una niña muy afortunada. Y vas a dar las gracias por ello, ¿verdad?

Bonnie es el nuevo nombre de Lark.

Intento oír si Lark contesta, pero no consigo saberlo.

—Así que supongo que tenemos que dejarte marchar, aunque te echaremos mucho de menos —añade la señorita Tann.

Un hombre y una mujer salen al vestíbulo llevando a Lark con ellos. El hombre es apuesto, como un príncipe de cuento. La mujer es hermosa, con un peinado elegante y los labios pintados de un color bonito. Lark lleva un vestido blanco de volantes. Parece una bailarina en miniatura.

El aire se me espesa en la garganta. Abro de par en par la puerta de la cocina. *Tienes que detenerlos,* me digo. *Tienes que explicarles que Lark es tuya y que no se la pueden quedar.*

Una mano me coge del brazo y tira de mí y la puerta se cierra de golpe. Doy un traspiés y me tambaleo mientras alguien me lleva a rastras cruzando la cocina y el lavadero hasta el porche. Ni siquiera sé quién es hasta que la señorita Dodd me hace girarme y me ayuda a enderezarme sujetándome por los hombros.

—¡No deberías estar aquí, May! —Tiene los ojos muy abiertos y está pálida. Parece casi tan asustada como lo estoy yo—. Conoces las reglas. Si molestas a la señora Murphy y a la señorita Tann te castigarán a base de bien.

La bola que tengo en la garganta se rompe como un huevo de gallina recién puesto. Gotea, pegajosa, caliente y espesa.

—M-mi hermana...

La señorita Dodd me coge la cara.

—Ya lo sé, cariño, pero tienes que pensar en lo que es mejor para ella. Va a tener unos padres que son estrellas de cine. —Toma aliento como si acabara de ganar un premio en la feria de carnaval—. Ya sé que estarás triste un tiempo, pero es lo mejor que le podía pasar. Va a tener unos papás y un hogar nuevo. Una vida nueva.

—¡Tenemos madre y padre!

—Chsss. A callar. —La señorita Dodd empieza a tirar de mí por el porche, a alejarme de la puerta. Intento soltarme, pero no me deja—. Calla. Deja ya de protestar. Ya sé que te gustaría que tus padres vinieran a buscaros, pero no pueden. Os cedieron a la Asociación de Hogares Infantiles de Tennessee. Ahora sois huérfanos.

—¡No lo somos! —protesto. No lo puedo evitar. La verdad me sale a borbotones, le cuento todo sobre el *Arcadia* y Queenie y Briny y mis hermanos. Hablo de Camellia y el armario, y de las distintas versiones de las empleadas sobre lo que le ha pasado y lo de Danny Boy diciéndome que la habían tirado al pantano.

La señorita Dodd abre la boca y así se queda. Me tiene sujeta por los hombros tan fuerte que la piel se me irrita y me escuece.

—¿Me estás diciendo la verdad? —me pregunta cuando me quedo sin nada que decir.

Cierro con fuerza los ojos, asiento con la cabeza y trago lágrimas y mocos.

—Chsss —susurra y me abraza fuerte—. No digas nada más ahora. A nadie. Ve con los otros niños. Pórtate bien y estate tranquila. Voy a ver de qué puedo enterarme.

Cuando me suelta, le cojo la mano.

—No se lo diga a la señora Murphy. Me quitará a Fern. Fern es lo único que me queda.

—No se lo diré. Tampoco te voy a abandonar. Me enteraré de lo que le ha pasado a tu hermana. A Dios pongo por testigo de que vamos a solucionar esto, pero tienes que ser muy fuerte. —Me mira a los ojos y hay fuego en su mirada. El fuego es un consuelo, pero sé lo que acabo de pedirle que haga. Si la señora Murphy puede hacer desaparecer a Camellia, puede hacer lo mismo con la señorita Dodd.

—¡N-no deje que la cojan, señorita Dodd!

—Soy más inteligente de lo que la gente cree. —Me empuja hacia el jardín y de pronto tenemos una amiga aquí. Por fin alguien nos escucha.

Esa noche Fern llora y se queja sin parar preguntando por Lark. Incluso pruebo a leerle un poco el libro, pero no se calla y al final no lo puedo soportar. La cojo, le estrujo los brazos con fuerza, la levanto y pego mi cara a la suya.

—¡Ya está bien! —Mi voz resuena en la diminuta habitación—. ¡Ya está bien, niña estúpida! ¡Lark se ha ido! ¡No es culpa mía! Como no pares, te vas a ganar una azotaina.

Alzo la mano y, hasta que mi hermana no pestañea varias veces, no me doy cuenta de lo que estoy haciendo.

La dejo en la cama y le doy la espalda y me tiro del pelo hasta que me duele. Me lo quiero arrancar todo. Hasta el último cabello. Quiero sentir un dolor que pueda entender en lugar de uno que no. Quiero un dolor que tenga un principio y un final, no uno interminable que te llega hasta el tuétano.

Este dolor me está convirtiendo en una niña a la que ni siquiera conozco.

Me está convirtiendo en una de ellas. En una de las personas que trabajan aquí. Lo veo en la cara de mi hermana. Eso es lo que más me duele.

Me dejo caer en el catre que la señorita Dodd consiguió que nos limpiaran. Ahora huele a lejía. De debajo de la sucia almohada salen tres pastillas de menta y las tiro al orinal.

Fern viene a sentarse a mi lado y me da palmaditas en la espalda, como haría una madre para tranquilizar a un niño pequeño. Este día, este lugar y todo lo que ha ocurrido aquí me pasa por la cabeza. Lo veo como si fuera una película, de esas que vemos por cinco centavos cuando el carnaval llega a las ciudades a orilla del río y enfocan un proyector a la pared de una casa o un granero. Pero la película que tengo en la cabeza es entrecortada y borrosa y pasa demasiado rápido.

Por fin me hundo aún más y todo se vuelve oscuro y silencioso.

Me despierto en plena noche y Fern está acurrucada a mi lado. Una manta nos tapa a las dos. Está retorcida y sin desdoblar bien, así que sé que la ha puesto Fern.

Entonces la abrazo y sueño con el *Arcadia* y es un buen sueño. Estamos todos juntos otra vez y hace tan buen día que sabe como las gotas de sirope de una mata de madreselva. Saco la lengua y lo saboreo una y otra vez.

Me pierdo en el olor a humo de leña y bruma de la mañana, tan espesa que tapa la orilla opuesta y convierte el río en un mar. Corro por los bancos de arena con mis hermanas y me escondo entre la hierba y espero a que me encuentren. Sus voces serpentean atenuadas entre la niebla, así que no puedo saber a qué distancia están.

A bordo del *Arcadia,* Queenie canta una canción. Me quedo muy quieta en la hierba y escucho la voz de mi madre.

Cuando el mirlo en primavera
en el sauce
se meció, le oí cantar.
Cantaba Aura Lee.
Aura Lee, Aura Lee,
doncella de pelo dorado.
Contigo llega el sol...

Estoy tan absorta en la canción que ni siquiera oigo abrirse la puerta del sótano hasta que no gira el pomo. Me levanto de un salto y veo que ya es por la mañana. Hilillos de sol se cuelan entre las azaleas y entran oblicuos en la habitación.

En el rincón, Fern se está levantando del orinal y subiéndose las bragas. Después de anoche quizá está demasiado asustada para volver a mojar la cama.

—Buena chica —le susurro y me apresuro a hacer la cama.

—No hace falta. Hoy no vais a ninguna parte.

La voz desde la puerta no es la de la señorita Dodd, sino la de la señora Murphy. Me golpea como un látigo y me estremezco entera. Nunca había bajado aquí.

—¡Cómo te atreves! —Tensa la boca de manera que los pómulos sobresalen. El aire sale siseando por entre sus dientes torcidos. Da tres pasos y me coge del pelo—. ¿Cómo te atreves a usar mi hospitalidad, mi bondad, para contar mentiras sobre mí? ¿De verdad pensabas que esa palurda, esa inútil, te iba a ayudar? Por supuesto que es tan tonta como para creerse tus mentiras. Pero lo que has hecho le ha costado el empleo y la señorita Tann pronto estará recogiendo a los hermanitos y hermanitas Dodd. Los hemos denunciado a la Agencia del Bienestar del condado de Shelby y ya han empezado con el papeleo. ¿Es eso lo que querías? ¿Es eso lo que tenías en mente cuando le llenaste la cabeza de cuentos espeluznantes sobre el pobre señor Riggs? ¡Que es primo mío, nada menos! ¡Mi primo, que limpia la porquería que dejáis en el jardín vosotros, sanguijuelas, y os arregla los juguetes y cuida de la caldera para que sus queridos pequeñines no se acatarren en las noches frías! —Mira con una mueca de odio a Fern, que se ha pegado todo lo que puede al rincón.

—Yo... no...

¿Qué puedo hacer? ¿Dónde puedo ir? Podría intentar escapar y correr hacia la puerta, pero tiene a Fern.

—No te molestes en negarlo. Debería darte vergüenza. ¡Vergüenza! Haber contado semejantes mentiras. Os he dado mucho más de lo que merecéis, escoria del río. Veremos qué tal estás cuando hayas pasado un tiempo a solas y reflexiones sobre lo equivocado de tu comportamiento. —Me empuja con fuerza y caigo de espaldas en el catre. Antes de que pueda levantarme, coge a Fern.

Mi hermana aúlla y trata de agarrarse a mí.

—¡No! —grito poniéndome de pie—. ¡Le está haciendo daño!

—Tienes suerte de que no le haga nada peor. Igual debería pagar ella por tus faltas. —La señora Murphy me da un empujón para apartarme de su camino—. Como me sigas dando problemas, lo haré.

Quiero pelear, pero me contengo. Sé que si lo hago solo perjudicaré a Fern.

—Pórtate bien —le digo a mi hermanita—. Sé buena chica.

Lo último que veo son sus pies deslizándose por la carbonilla mientras la señora Murphy la arrastra hacia la puerta. Gira la cerradura y oigo los gritos de Fern cada vez más lejos. Por fin desaparecen.

Me tiro en el catre y cojo la manta que conserva aún el calor de Fern y el mío y lloro hasta que no me queda una sola lágrima y lo único que puedo hacer es mirar al techo.

Espero todo el día, pero nadie viene a buscarme. Abro el ventanuco y oigo a los niños jugar fuera. El sol gana altura y luego empieza a marcharse hacia el oeste. Al cabo, suena la campana de la cena.

Pasado un rato, la madera del techo tiembla cuando todos suben a acostarse.

Tengo hambre y sed, pero sobre todo echo de menos a Fern. No la pondrán a dormir en otro sitio, ¿verdad? ¿Por lo que dije?

Pero sí lo hacen.

Cuando la casa está en silencio, vuelvo a tumbarme. El estómago me ruge y me duele como si tuviera una rata mordiéndome por dentro. Tengo la garganta como si alguien me la hubiera arañado hasta dejarla en carne viva.

Duermo y me despierto, duermo y me despierto.

Por la mañana viene la señora Pulnik y me trae un cubo con agua y un cazo.

—Bebe de poco en poco. Pasarás un tiempo sin *verr* a nadie. Estás con racionamiento.

Pasan tres días hasta que me traen comida. Tengo tanta hambre que he empezado a comerme las pastillas de menta que me mete Riggs por debajo de la puerta, aunque me odio por ello.

Un día se confunde con el siguiente y el siguiente y el siguiente. Llego al final de *Huckleberry Finn*, cuando Huck decide que prefiere huir a territorio indio antes que ser adoptado.

Cierro los ojos e imagino que también huyo a territorio indio. Tengo un caballo rojo grande y bonito, con calcetines blancos y un cordón en la testuz, como Tony el Caballo Maravilla y Tom Mix. Mi caballo es más rápido que nada y corremos, corremos sin parar.

Vuelvo a empezar el libro y estoy otra vez en Misuri, a orillas del gran río. Paso los días viajando en balsa con Huckleberry Finn.

De noche, cuando la brisa agita las ramas, miro por la ventana, buscando a Zede, a Silas o a Briny bajo la luz de la farola. En una ocasión en que hace viento los veo. Hay una mujer con ellos. Es demasiado robusta para ser Queenie. Creo que es la señorita Dodd.

Con la misma velocidad con la que aparecen, se van. Me pregunto si lo que me pasa es que me estoy volviendo loca.

Viene la señora Pulnik y me quita el libro y me dice que las señoras de la biblioteca ambulante han llamado la atención a la señora Murphy. Me llama ladrona y me abofetea con fuerza por no recordarle que tenía un libro de la biblioteca.

No sé muy bien cómo voy a sobrevivir sin *Huckleberry Finn*.

Me preocupa Fern y cómo estará, sola en el piso de arriba.

Pasan días y más días. Pierdo la cuenta de cuántos, pero pasa mucho tiempo hasta que por fin la señora Pulnik me saca de la habitación y me lleva al despacho de la señora Murphy.

Huelo casi tan mal como el orinal y tengo el pelo anudado en un gran amasijo sucio. La luz del piso de arriba es tan fuerte que doy traspiés y me choco con cosas y tengo que avanzar a tientas.

La señora Murphy no es más que una sombra borrosa detrás de la mesa. Guiño los ojos para verla mejor y entonces me doy cuenta de que no es la señora Murphy. Es la señorita Tann. La señora Murphy está detrás de ella, junto a la ventana.

La señora Pulnik me da un empujón para que avance. Me fallan las piernas y caigo de rodillas. La señora Pulnik me agarra del vestido y del pelo para sujetarme.

La señorita Tann se levanta y se inclina sobre la mesa.

—Así es exactamente como debes estar. De rodillas y pidiendo perdón por todos los problemas que has causado. Por todas las mentiras que has contado sobre la pobre señora Murphy. Eres una niña mezquina y desagradecida, ¿no te parece?

—S-sí, señora —digo en un susurro. Estoy dispuesta a decir casi cualquier cosa con tal de salir de esa habitación.

La señora Murphy apoya los puños en las caderas.

—Contar esas mentiras sobre mi primo. Niña horrible y de mente calentu...

—Chsss. —La señorita Tann levanta una mano y la señora Murphy cierra la boca—. Creo que May sabe muy bien lo que ha hecho. Creo que solo quería llamar la atención. ¿Es eso lo que te pasa, May? ¿Quieres llamar la atención?

No sé qué decir, así que sigo arrodillada con el estómago encogido y el mentón tembloroso. La señora Pulnik me empuja para clavarme más en el suelo. El dolor me viene de las raíces del pelo y sube de las rodillas. Tengo lágrimas en los ojos, pero no las dejo salir.

—¡Contesta! —La voz de la señorita Tann llena la habitación como un trueno. Rodea la mesa cojeando y me mira agitando un dedo delante de mi cara. Sus ojos son del color azul grisáceo de una tormenta de invierno.

—S-sí, se... N-no, señora.

—¿En qué quedamos? ¿Sí o no?

Abro la boca, pero no sale nada.

Me coge la barbilla. Me obliga a estirar el cuello y se acerca. Huele a polvos de talco y a mal aliento.

—Ahora ya no estás tan parlanchina, ¿verdad? ¿Quizá es que te has dado cuenta de lo mal que te has portado?

Consigo asentir un poquito con la cabeza.

Se le curva la boca en una sonrisa y sus ojos brillan hambrientos, como si notara mi miedo y le gustara.

—Quizá deberías haberlo pensado antes de inventar una historia ridícula sobre tu hermana ficticia y el pobre señor Riggs.

Me late la sangre dentro de la cabeza. Intento encontrarle sentido a lo que dice, pero no puedo.

—Nunca ha existido ninguna Camellia... Tú y yo lo sabemos, ¿verdad, May? Cuando vinisteis erais solo cuatro. Dos hermanas pequeñas y un hermanito. Solo cuatro. Y hasta el momento hemos hecho un maravilloso trabajo encontrándoles un hogar. Un buen hogar. Y por eso nos estás muy agradecida, ¿verdad? —Le hace un gesto a la señora Pulnik. Ya no tengo su peso en los hombros. La señorita Tann me tira de la barbilla hasta que estoy de pie delante de ella—. Se han acabado las tonterías, ¿entendido?

Digo que sí con la cabeza y me odio al mismo tiempo. Está mal. Todo lo que le conté a la señorita Dodd era cierto. Pero no puedo volver al sótano. Tengo que encontrar a Fern y asegurarme de que no le han hecho daño. Fern es todo lo que me queda.

—Bien. —La señorita Tann me suelta. Dobla una mano sobre la otra y gira sobre sus talones; la falda le revolotea alrededor de las rodillas.

La señora Murphy ríe bajito.

—Bueno, parece que estos pequeños palurdos tienen algo de seso dentro de la cabeza, después de todo.

Los labios de la señorita Tann se curvan hacia arriba, pero es una de esas sonrisas que te dan frío cuando las ves.

—Incluso los más rebeldes terminan aprendiendo. Es solo cuestión de encontrar la manera adecuada de enseñarles la lección. —Parpadea y me mira de arriba abajo antes de que el reloj de la repisa de la chimenea dé la hora y capte su atención—. Tengo que volver a mi trabajo.

Pasa a mi lado dejando su olor a talco en la habitación. Intento no olerlo, pero se me pega a la nariz.

La señora Murphy se sienta a su mesa y coge unos papeles como si se hubiera olvidado de que estoy ahí.

—A partir de ahora nos darás las gracias por nuestra hospitalidad.

—S-sí. ¿Puedo ver a Fern, señora Murphy? —Apenas me atrevo a preguntarlo, pero debo hacerlo.

No levanta la vista.

—Tu hermana ya no está. La han adoptado. No volverás a verla. Ahora puedes salir a jugar con los otros niños. —Ordena los papeles y saca una estilográfica—. Señora Pulnik, por favor, asegúrese de que May se baña antes de trasladarla al piso de arriba a su nueva cama esta noche. No soporto lo mal que huele.

—Me *ocuparré* de que así sea.

La señora Pulnik me coge del brazo, pero casi ni lo siento. Cuando me deja fuera, me quedo sentada largo rato en los escalones del porche. Los otros niños se acercan y me miran como si fuera un animal del zoológico.

No les hago caso.

Stevie viene e intenta subirse a mi regazo, pero ni siquiera soporto tenerlo cerca. Me recuerda a Fern.

—Ve a jugar con los camiones —le digo y luego cruzo el jardín, hasta la valla detrás de la iglesia, y trepo a una parra para esconderme.

Miro entre las hojas hacia las ventanas del dormitorio donde duermen las niñas y me pregunto: *Si salto por una esta noche, ¿me mataré?*

No puedo vivir sin Fern. Llevamos unidas por el corazón desde que nació.

Y ahora me he quedado sin corazón.

Dejo caer la cabeza y siento los pinchacitos del sol en el cuello y dejo que el sueño se apodere de mí y deseo no despertarme nunca.

Cuando lo hago, alguien me está tocando el brazo. Doy un salto y me quedo acuclillada, creyendo que es Riggs. Pero la cara que me mira me hace pensar que sigo soñando.

Tiene que ser un sueño.

—¿Silas?

Se lleva un dedo a los labios.

—Chsss —susurra.

Meto las manos temblorosas entre los barrotes. Necesito saber si es real.

Sus dedos se cierran alrededor de los míos. Me los aprieta.

—Por fin averiguamos dónde estabais —dice—. Una señora del hospital obligó a tus padres a firmar unos papeles justo después de que nacieran los bebés. Le dijeron a tu padre que, si los firmaba todos, le pagarían la factura del médico y que los niños tendrían un buen entierro. Pero los papeles no eran para eso. Les daban permiso para ir a buscaros al *Arcadia*. Cuando Briny y Zede fueron a la policía, les dijeron que Briny os había cedido a la Asociación de Hogares Infantiles de Tennessee, que no se podía hacer nada y que fin de la historia. Llevamos semanas buscándoos. Esa señora, la señorita Dodd, nos encontró y nos dijo dónde estabais. He estado viniendo aquí a vigilar cada vez que podía, esperando a ver si seguíais aquí.

—Me han tenido encerrada. Me han castigado. —Miro a mi alrededor, a las enredaderas. Todavía no me puedo creer lo que está pasando. Deben de ser imaginaciones mías—. ¿Dónde están Queenie y Briny?

—Cuidando del *Arcadia*. Preparándolo para navegar otra vez. Ha estado mucho tiempo amarrado.

Me dejo caer sobre los barrotes. Me arde la piel y estoy colorada. El sudor me corre debajo del camisón raído que llevo puesto desde hace semanas. ¿Qué pensará Briny de mí cuando sepa la verdad?

—Se han llevado a todos. Se han llevado a todos menos a mí. No pude hacer lo que me dijo Briny. No pude mantenernos juntos.

—No pasa nada —susurra Silas. Me acaricia el pelo mientras lloro y se le enredan los dedos en los mechones sucios—. Te voy a sacar de aquí. Esta noche vendré y cortaré uno de los barrotes... Aquí, debajo de las bayas de acebo, donde los arbustos son más espesos. ¿Puedes venir aquí esta noche? ¿Podrás escaparte?

Hipo, me sorbo los mocos y asiento con la cabeza. Si James podía bajar a la cocina a robar comida, yo también conseguiré llegar a la cocina. Si puedo llegar a la cocina, podré llegar hasta el cementerio.

Silas estudia la valla.

—Dame un rato. Espera un par de horas después de que haya anochecido para que me dé tiempo a venir y cortar el barrote. Luego baja. Cuanto menos tiempo te echen de menos, mejor.

Repasamos el plan y luego me dice que me vaya antes de que alguien lo descubra. Tengo que hacer un esfuerzo por soltarlo, salir de debajo de la enredadera y alejarme.

Solo unas horas más, me digo. *Lo que queda del día, luego la cena, un baño y estaré en casa. Estaré de vuelta en el Arcadia.*

Danny Boy viene a meterse con Stevie a la puerta del cementerio.

—Déjalo en paz. —Me interpongo entre los dos y le planto cara a Danny Boy. Creo que en el sótano me he hecho mayor. El puño que agito delante de la cara de Danny Boy es tan huesudo que parece sacado de una tumba.

—No pienso pelear contigo, apestas demasiado. —Danny Boy traga saliva. Tal vez piensa que, si he resistido semanas en el sótano, soy demasiado dura para enfrentarse a mí. Tal vez tiene miedo de que, si se mete en una pelea, le hagan lo mismo a él.

Durante el resto del día no nos molesta ni a Stevie ni a mí.

Cuando anochece y formamos una fila para entrar en la casa, Stevie y yo nos ponemos los primeros. A Danny Boy no le hace gracia, pero no tiene arrestos para impedírmelo. Se conforma con burlarse de mi pelo y de lo mal que huelo.

—Me han dicho que mañana traen de vuelta a la idiota de tu hermanita —me dice a la espalda cuando entramos—. He oído que no quieren quedarse con ella porque es tan tonta que no sabe dormir sin mojar la cama.

Es probable que sea una mentira más de las suyas, pero aun así se enciende en mí una llamita de esperanza. No la apago; en lugar de ello, la avivo soplando con mucho cuidado. Después de cenar, reúno valor para preguntarle a una de las empleadas si es verdad que Fern va a volver. Me dice que sí. Durante todo el tiempo que ha estado fuera, Fern no ha dejado de llorar, de preguntar por mí y de orinarse encima.

—Parece que la terquedad es de familia —comenta la empleada—. Es una pena, porque ya no encontrará otros padres.

Intento no parecer contenta, pero lo estoy. Cuando Fern vuelva, podremos escapar las dos, pero tengo que conseguir que Silas espere un día más. Esta noche saldré a escondidas y se lo diré.

Solo tengo que pensar en cómo hacerlo sin que las empleadas me descubran. Puede que me vigilen de cerca porque es la primera noche que duermo arriba. Pero las empleadas no son lo que más me preocupa, sino Riggs. También él tiene que saber dónde duermo esta noche.

Y sabe que esa puerta no tiene cerradura.

17

AVERY

Si necesitas matar el tiempo, la isla de Edisto no es un mal lugar para hacerlo.

La brisa del mar se cuela por las mosquiteras y levanta la falda del sencillo vestido cruzado que me he puesto después de un día sin hacer nada. Antes de salir de casa, se me olvidó coger el cargador del teléfono. Ahora tengo la batería baja y en toda la isla no hay un cargador compatible. En lugar de contestar correos o peinar internet en busca de algo relacionado con las revelaciones de anoche, me he visto obligada a entretenerme a la manera tradicional.

El paseo en kayak por la reserva ACE Basin ha compensado una segunda ducha con agua apenas templada y una mancha imposible de quitar en unos pantalones cortos de la mezcla negruzca de rocío y cieno salino del asiento de la canoa. Me siento como si hubiera redescubierto mi yo infantil.

Remar me devolvió recuerdos olvidados hace tiempo de una excursión en sexto curso a Edisto con mi padre. Yo había estado trabajando en un proyecto sobre ecosistemas para el concurso de ciencias. Como era tan perfeccionista, quería coger mis propias muestras y hacer fotografías en lugar de sacar las cosas de libros. Mi padre había accedido a ayudarme. Nuestra visita de una noche aquí hizo posible uno de esos momentos padre-hija que no estaba relacionado con una exhibición ecuestre o un posado para la prensa. Es un recuerdo que sigo atesorando, a pesar de todos los años transcurridos.

También recuerdo que fue Elliot quien me ayudó a preparar el fondo sobre el que montar el trabajo. Habíamos sacado cosas de un armario lleno de materiales de acampada viejos, luego hecho los carteles y discutido largo rato sobre cómo conseguir que las enormes cartulinas se sostuvieran solas. A ninguno se nos daban muy bien las manualidades.

«No sé por qué no compraste algo hecho y ya está», se quejó después de nuestro segundo y épico fracaso. Para entonces era ya de noche y seguíamos en el granero de la casa de mi padre, hasta las cejas de manchas de pintura y maderos mal clavados.

«Porque quiero poner en mi redacción que mi trabajo se hizo con materiales reciclados. Quiero poder decir que lo hice sola».

«No veo la diferencia...».

El resto de la discusión, por fortuna, se ha perdido en las arenas del tiempo. Sí recuerdo que, cuando empezamos a subir la voz, el jefe de establos de papá entró con un conjunto de obstáculos de madera para hacer saltar a los caballos. Añadió una caja grande de bridas y cinta aislante. Elliot y yo entendimos la indirecta.

Acordarme del concurso de ciencias me hace reír. Miro el reloj pensando en llamar a Elliot y contárselo, pero no quiero estar comunicando cuando me llame Trent Turner. Me asalta la preocupación y pienso en la hora. Son más de las cinco y no he sabido nada de él. ¿Tal vez tiene que quedarse trabajando hasta tarde?

Quizá ha cambiado de opinión sobre dejarme ver el resto de los archivos de su abuelo.

Pasa otra media hora. Estoy tan nerviosa como un hámster en una jaula pequeña. Me siento. Me pongo de pie. Camino por la casa comprobando el móvil, para ver si tiene cobertura.

Por fin sucumbo a la tentación de bajar a la playa y buscar subrepticiamente indicios de que hay alguien en su casa. Cuando suena el teléfono, estoy ya a medio camino, escudriñando entre las dunas y las uniolas.

El tono de llamada me coge tan desprevenida que salto, doy un traspiés en la arena y termino pescando el teléfono en el aire.

—Ya estaba a punto de darme por vencido —dice Trent cuando por fin contesto—. He llamado tres veces a la puerta y no ha contestado nadie. Pensé que igual habías cambiado de opinión.

Intento no parecer ansiosa, pero no lo consigo.

—No, estoy aquí. En la parte de atrás. —*¿Dice que ha llamado? ¿Está a la puerta de mi casa?*

—Voy por atrás entonces.

Miro hacia la casa Myers y me doy cuenta de lo lejos que estoy. Va a saber lo que he estado haciendo.

—Creo que la cancela trasera está cubierta de hiedra venenosa.

—No. No parece.

Me giro y echo a correr hacia el jardín. Corro sobre la arena con el vestido largo pegado a las piernas, las chanclas haciendo chasquidos. Atisbo un trozo de camisa azul cerca del arbusto de palmito de mi abuela justo a tiempo de echar el freno y subir por la pasarela de madera con aire de naturalidad.

Aun así, Trent reacciona mirándome un poco perplejo.

—Te veo un poco demasiado elegante... para rebuscar en el cobertizo de mi abuelo. Te dije que estaba hecho una pena por dentro, ¿verdad? Y hace calor.

—Ah, ¿esto? —Me miro el vestido—. Es lo último que me quedaba limpio en la maleta. Esta mañana he estado haciendo kayak y me he destrozado la ropa. Soy un desastre.

—Pues nadie lo diría. —Intento descifrar si está simplemente siendo amable o coqueteando. Entiendo que se le dé tan bien el negocio inmobiliario. Destila encanto por todos sus poros—. ¿Preparada? —añade.

—Sí.

Cierro la cancela trasera y bajamos juntos hacia la playa. Pide disculpas por llegar tan tarde a casa.

—Hoy hemos vivido momentos de emoción en casa de la tía Lou. No sabemos cómo, ninguno de los primos ha querido confesar, Jonah terminó con un chocokrispi dentro de la nariz. He tenido que quedarme para ayudar a sacárselo.

—¿Y habéis podido? ¿Está bien?

Trent sonríe.

—Pimienta negra. La obstrucción se solucionó con aire comprimido desde el interior del tracto nasal. En otras palabras, estornudó. Ahora queda saber si la tía Lou conseguirá que alguno de los primos confiese quién ha sido. Son siete. Todos chicos y Jonah es el más pequeño, con tres años de diferencia, así que está aprendiendo lo que es la vida por la vía rápida.

—Pobrecito. Le comprendo. Ser el más pequeño no es fácil. En mi familia somos solo chicas y eso ya era bastante duro. Si tienes que ir a buscarlo...

—¿Estás de broma? Si fuera me enfrentaría a un motín. Le encanta estar ahí. Dos de las hermanas de mi madre y una prima viven en la misma calle, y mis padres suelen pasar aquí parte del año, así que siempre hay acción y comida, y alguien con quien jugar. Esa fue la razón principal por la que me vine a vivir aquí y compré la agencia inmobiliaria después de que muriera la madre de Jonah. Necesitaba trabajar menos horas, tener un horario más razonable, pero también quería que Jonah tuviera familia cerca. No quería que creciera en un apartamento solo conmigo.

Se me llena la cabeza de preguntas. La mayoría parecen demasiado personales.

—¿Dónde vivíais antes?

Conozco la respuesta. Estuve investigándolo cuando contemplaba la teoría del chantaje.

—Nueva York. —Con los pantalones chinos, el polo, los zapatos náuticos y ese ligero acento de Texas es difícil imaginarlo con el traje oscuro propio del profesional neoyorquino—. En el negocio inmobiliario.

Siento una afinidad inesperada con Trent Turner. Los dos nos estamos adaptando a un nuevo entorno, a una vida nueva. Envidio la suya.

—Qué cambio tan grande, ¿no? ¿Te gusta vivir aquí?

Hay un atisbo de algo, cierta nostalgia.

—El ritmo es mucho más lento..., pero sí. Está bien.

—Siento lo de tu mujer. —Me intrigan los detalles, pero no voy a preguntar. Lo que he creído que podía ser coqueteo por su parte es probablemente un sentimiento de soledad lógico cuando solo han pasado unos meses desde una pérdida tan importante. Y no quiero que se lleve una impresión equivocada. Llevo puesto el anillo de compromiso, pero es una esmeralda de talla princesa, así que no todo el mundo se da cuenta de que no es una joya sin más.

—No estábamos casados.

Me ruborizo al instante, sintiéndome una tonta por sacar conclusiones. Estos días nunca se sabe con estas cosas.

—Ah, lo siento... Quiero decir...

Sonríe para tranquilizarme.

—No pasa nada. Es que es complicado. Éramos colegas... y amigos. Después de su divorcio cruzamos alguna raya que no deberíamos haber cruzado. Yo sospechaba que Jonah era hijo mío, pero Laura decía que no. Decidió mudarse al norte del estado para dar una nueva oportunidad a su matrimonio. Lo dejé estar. No supe la verdad sobre Jonah hasta después del accidente de tráfico. Jonah tenía lesiones internas y necesitaba un donante de hígado. La hermana de su madre se puso en contacto conmigo con la esperanza de que fuera compatible. Lo era y ya está.

—Ah... —Es todo lo que acierto a decir.

Me mira. Nos paramos antes de enfilar el camino hasta su casa y sé que va a contarme el resto de la historia.

—Jonah tiene dos medio hermanos a los que ya casi no recuerda. No parece que vaya a tener ocasión de conocerlos a no ser que, ya de adultos, decidan ponerse en contacto. Después del juicio por la custodia, su padre no quiso que tuvieran ninguna relación con Jonah, ni conmigo. No es lo que yo habría querido, pero así están las cosas. Comprendo a las personas a las que ayudaba mi abuelo mejor de lo que crees.

—Ya veo por qué. —Su franqueza me sorprende. Lo profundo de su dolor y su decepción son evidentes. Ni siquiera intenta ocultar el hecho de que tiene sentimientos encontrados sobre algunas de sus decisiones o por la posibilidad de que un error de juicio del pasado pueda afectar a Jonah toda su vida.

Vengo de un mundo donde nadie reconocería abiertamente cosas así, desde luego no a alguien que es prácticamente un desconocido. En el mundo en que yo vivo, una apariencia pulcra y una reputación sin mácula son fundamentales. Trent me hace preguntarme si no me he acostumbrado demasiado a las constricciones que lleva consigo estar siempre guardando las apariencias.

¿Qué haría yo si me enfrentara a una situación así?

—Jonah parece un niño estupendo —digo.

—Lo es. Ahora ya no imagino otra clase de vida. Supongo que a todos los padres les pasa lo mismo.

—Seguro que sí.

Espera a que enfile el camino y me sigue. Cuando entramos en el jardín, una telaraña se me pega a la cara y luego otra. Ahora me acuerdo de por qué mis primos y yo nos peleábamos siempre por quién saldría el primero cuando montábamos a caballo en Hitchcock Woods, en casa. Me quito la seda de la cara y arranco una hoja seca de palmera para agitarla en el aire delante de mí.

Trent se ríe.

—No eres tan urbanita como pareces.

—Ya te dije que crecí rodeada de establos.

—La verdad es que no te creí. Pensaba que el estudio del abuelo te asustaría en cuanto lo vieras.

—Eso es imposible. —Cuando me vuelvo a mirar, está sonriendo—. ¿Tenías la esperanza de que fuera así?

El camino termina en el jardín y Trent deja de sonreír cuando llegamos a la cabaña de techo bajo y subimos los escalones.

—No sé... Me gustaría que mi abuelo estuviera aquí y tomara él las decisiones.

La preocupación le dibuja profundas arrugas en la frente bronceada mientras busca las llaves en un bolsillo y se inclina para mirarlas.

—Te comprendo, lo digo en serio. Yo también me he preguntado más de una vez si debería estar escarbando en el pasado de mi abuela, pero no puedo evitarlo. Tengo la sensación de que la verdad es más importante.

Mete la llave en la cerradura de seguridad y descorre el cerrojo.

—Esas palabras son más propias de un periodista que de un político. Será mejor que tengas cuidado, Avery Stafford. Esa clase de idealismo puede volverse en tu contra en el mundo de la política.

Enseguida me pongo a la defensiva.

—Me parece que has tratado con la clase equivocada de políticos. —No está diciendo nada que no me haya dicho ya Leslie. Le preocupa que sea demasiado escrupulosa y demasiado poco realista sobre lo que significaría presentarme al Senado. Olvida que me he pasado la vida oyendo a desconocidos brindándonos sus opiniones sobre todo, desde la ropa que usamos hasta lo que cuestan los colegios privados a los que fuimos. De hecho, no solo desconocidos, también amigos—. En mi familia, el servicio público sigue significando servicio público.

Su expresión es impenetrable, así que no sé si está de acuerdo conmigo o no.

—Entonces no te va a gustar lo que estás a punto de descubrir sobre la Asociación de Hogares Infantiles de Tennessee. La mires por donde la mires, no es una historia bonita.

—¿Por qué?

—Era un sitio con mucha reputación y la mujer que lo dirigía, Georgia Tann, se movía en círculos poderosos, sociales y políticos. Estaba muy bien considerada. La gente admiraba lo que hacía. Cambió la percepción pública de que los huérfanos eran mercancía defectuosa. Pero la realidad es que la Asociación de Hogares Infantiles de Tennessee de Memphis estaba corrompida hasta el tuétano. No me extraña que mi abuelo nunca quisiera hablar de lo que hacía en esta casita. Las historias son tristes y atroces, y hay literalmente miles. Se comerciaba con niños. Georgia Tann ganaba dinero cobrando precios altísimos por adopción, transporte, entregas fuera del estado. Les quitaba a familias pobres sus hijos y se los vendía a famosos y a personas con influencia en la política. Tenía comprados a la policía y a los jueces. Embaucaba a mujeres en las maternidades de los hospitales para que firmaran documentos renunciando a sus hijos mientras estaban bajo los efectos de la sedación. Le decía a la gente que los padres de los niños habían muerto cuando no era verdad. —Se saca un papel doblado del bolsillo y me lo da—. Hay bastantes más cosas. Esto te lo he impreso hoy en un momento que he tenido libre en el trabajo.

Es un artículo escaneado de un viejo periódico. El titular no se anda con rodeos. Dice: «La benefactora de los huérfanos pudo ser en realidad una prolífica asesina en serie».

Trent se detiene con la mano en el pomo de la puerta. Está esperando a que lea el artículo.

—Nadie entraba aquí salvo mi abuelo y, de vez en cuando, algún cliente. Ni siquiera mi abuela. Pero es que ella tampoco compartía su interés por este asunto. Ya te conté que mi abuela opinaba que no hay que remover el pasado. Quizá tenía razón. Al final mi abuelo también debió de decidir lo mismo. Me pidió que limpiara este sitio y destruyera todo lo que había. Para que estés avisada antes de entrar, no tengo ni idea de lo que hay al otro lado de esta puerta.

—Lo entiendo. Pero soy..., he sido fiscal federal en Maryland. No hay muchas cosas que me asusten.

Y sin embargo solo el título del artículo ya me ha conmocionado. Me doy cuenta de que Trent no va a dejarme entrar hasta que no me lea el artículo, hasta que esté sobre aviso. Quiere que entienda que lo que hay dentro de la casa no son historias tiernas y bonitas sobre huerfanitos solitarios que encuentran un hogar.

Vuelvo al artículo y empiezo a leer:

Saludada en otro tiempo como la «madre de la adopción moderna» y consultada por personalidades como Eleanor Roosevelt en los esfuerzos por reformar las leyes sobre adopción en

Estados Unidos, Georgia Tann hizo posible la adopción de miles de niños entre las décadas de 1920 y 1950. También dirigió una organización que, bajo su dirección férrea, permitió o causó deliberadamente la muerte de hasta quinientos niños y bebés.

«Muchos de los niños no eran huérfanos», declaró Mary Sykes, quien, junto con su hermana, una niña de pecho, fue robada del porche de la casa de su madre, soltera, con solo cuatro años y puesta bajo la tutela de la Asociación de Hogares Infantiles de Tennessee. «Muchos tenían padres que los querían y querían criarlos. Los niños eran a menudo secuestrados literalmente en pleno día y, por mucho que lucharan sus padres por recuperarlos en un tribunal, no se les permitía ganar el juicio». La señora Sykes vivió tres años en una gran casa blanca gestionada por Georgia Tann y su red de ayudantes.

La hermana pequeña de Mary, que tenía solo seis meses cuando una mujer que decía ser enfermera de los servicios sociales se las llevó a las dos del porche de la casa familiar, solo pasaría dos meses en el hogar de la asociación.

«Los bebés no recibían ni alimentación ni atención médica adecuada», dice Mary Sykes. «Recuerdo estar sentada en el suelo en una habitación llena de cunas, acariciando a través de las barras el brazo de mi hermana. Estaba demasiado deshidratada y débil incluso para llorar. Nadie la ayudaba. Una vez que quedó claro que estaba demasiado enferma para recuperarse, una empleada la metió en una caja de cartón y se la llevó. No volví a verla. Más tarde supe que a los bebés que estaban muy enfermos o lloraban mucho los abandonaban en un cochecito al sol. Yo ahora tengo hijos, nietos y bisnietos. No concibo que alguien pudiera hacer eso con unos niños, pero así fue. Nos ataban a las camas y a las sillas, nos pegaban, nos hacían aguadillas en la bañera; sufríamos abusos. Era la casa de los horrores».

Al parecer, en el curso de tres décadas desaparecieron numerosos niños al cuidado de la Asociación de Hogares Infantiles de Tennessee. A menudo su documentación desaparecía también y, con ella, todo rastro de sus vidas. Si miembros de su familia biológica se presentaban allí en busca de información o elevaban una petición en los tribunales, se les decía sin más que los niños habían sido adoptados y que los expedientes eran secretos.

Al operar bajo la protección de Edward Hull Crump, conocido como «Jefe Crump», el tristemente influyente político de Memphis, parece que la red de Georgia Tann era intocable.

El resto del artículo proporciona detalles sobre la venta de niños a padres adinerados y famosos de Hollywood, el dolor de las familias biológicas y las acusaciones de abusos psicológicos y sexuales. Las últimas líneas citan las palabras de un hombre que mantiene una página web llamada «Los corderos perdidos».

«La rama de Memphis de la Asociación de Hogares Infantiles de Tennessee tenía ojeadores en todas partes, en las oficinas de los servicios sociales, en consultas médicas rurales, en vecindarios pobres y en campamentos. A menudo los niños eran entregados a trabajadores sociales y funcionarios que habrían podido entorpecer la carrera de Georgia Tann. En ocasiones se chantajeaba a los padres adoptivos amenazándolos con quitarles a los niños si no daban más dinero. Georgia Tann se ganó la protección del Jefe Crump y de los tribunales de familia. Tenía el poder para alterar vidas como se le antojaba. Jugaba a ser Dios, al parecer sin remordimiento alguno. Georgia Tann murió de cáncer antes de que tuviera que rendir cuentas. Había personas poderosas que querían ver el caso cerrado, y así fue».

—Esto es... —Hago una pausa en busca de una palabra. Estoy a punto de decir «increíble», pero no es el término adecuado—. Es espantoso. Cuesta imaginar que algo así pudiera pasar, y a semejante escala..., durante años.

—La Asociación de Hogares Infantiles no fue obligada a cerrar hasta 1950.

Está claro que Trent comparte mi mezcla de espanto, perplejidad y furia. Lo que cuenta Mary Sykes de acariciar a su hermanita moribunda me hace pensar en mis sobrinos y en lo unidos que están a sus hermanos. Courtney se subía a la cuna de los trillizos y se dormía con ellos si los oía llorar de noche.

—No puedo... Es que no me lo puedo imaginar. —He sido fiscal en casos de abusos sexuales y de corrupción, pero este es a gran escala. Docenas y docenas de personas tenían que saber que esto estaba pasando—. ¿Cómo pudieron ignorarlo?

Entonces caigo en la cuenta. Yo tengo familia de Tennessee. Pertenecían al mundo de la política, eran influyentes. Tenían diversos cargos en las administraciones estatal y federal, en la judicatura. ¿Conocían estos hechos? ¿Miraron para otro lado? ¿Fue esa la razón por la que la abuela Judy se puso en contacto con Trent Turner I? ¿Estaba intentando expiar las malas acciones de la familia?

Quizá no quería que se supiera que su familia había cooperado en estas acciones monstruosas, que las había apoyado incluso.

Me mareo y apoyo una mano en la pared para recuperar el equilibrio. Siento las mejillas heladas a pesar del calor del verano.

La cara de Trent es de preocupación mientras sigue de pie sujetando la puerta.

—¿Estás segura?

Él no parece mucho más convencido que yo. Somos como dos niños reuniendo valor para aventurarse en territorio prohibido. ¿Estará esperando que cambie de opinión y así ahorrarnos a los dos los detalles que nos esperan, sean cuales sean?

—La verdad tarde o temprano termina por salir. Soy de las que creen que es mejor saberla cuanto antes.

Pero, mientras lo digo, no estoy tan segura. Toda mi vida he estado convencida de que los Stafford somos irreprochables. De que mi familia es un libro abierto. Quizá ha sido ingenuo por mi parte. ¿Y si, después de todos estos años, resulta que me equivoco?

Trent se mira los zapatos, da una patada a una concha que hay en el suelo del porche. Choca con un tractor rojo de juguete que en este momento resulta especialmente enternecedor.

—Me da miedo descubrir que la adopción de mi abuelo fue como las que salen en el artículo, cuando habla de que daban niños a funcionarios para que tuvieran la boca cerrada. El padre adoptivo de mi abuelo era sargento de la policía de Memphis. No eran personas que pudieran permitirse una adopción cara... —Se interrumpe como si no quisiera añadir más palabras a la historia, pero en sus ojos veo reflejado mi propio miedo. ¿Cargamos con la culpa de nuestros antepasados? Y, si es así, ¿seremos capaces de soportar ese peso?

Trent abre la puerta y con ella, quizá, el misterio.

Por dentro, la casita tiene techos bajos y está en penumbra. Las paredes de madera blanca están agrietadas y desvaídas, y los marcos de madera de las ventanas están combados. El aire huele a polvo, a moho y a algo más que tardo un instante en identificar. Tabaco de pipa. El olor me recuerda automáticamente al abuelo Stafford. Su despacho en la casa de Lagniappe olía siempre así, aún huele.

Trent enciende la luz y la bombilla parpadea obstinada en una lámpara art déco que desentona con el entorno.

Entramos en la única habitación. Contiene un escritorio grande que parece comprado en el mercadillo de una biblioteca, dos muebles archivadores, una mesa pequeña de madera y un par de sillas desparejadas. Encima del escritorio hay un teléfono negro, antiguo, de disco. Hay un bote con lápices, una grapadora, un perforador de tres agujeros, un cenicero sucio, un flexo, una máquina de escribir eléctrica de color verde oliva apagado. Las estanterías de la pared están abarquilladas bajo el peso de cajas archivadoras, carpetas viejas, papeles sueltos y libros.

Trent suspira y se pasa una mano por el pelo. Parece demasiado grande para un espacio tan estrecho. La cabeza le queda a pocos centímetros de las vigas, que veo que están labradas a mano y tienen muescas; probablemente están hechas de madera recuperada de los naufragios.

—¿Estás bien? —pregunto.

Niega con la cabeza y a continuación se encoge de hombros mientras señala un sombrero, un paraguas anticuado con un dragón tallado en el mango y unos zapatos náuticos azules. Las tres cosas aguardan junto al perchero, se diría que con la esperanza de que su dueño regrese.

—Es como si estuviera aquí, ¿sabes? Casi siempre olía igual que este sitio.

Abre las contraventanas y se iluminan los corchos que llenan las paredes.

—Mira —susurro y el polvo me irrita la garganta.

Hay docenas de fotografías, algunas con los colores intensos de la fotografía moderna, otras con los tonos apagados de las viejas polaroids, algunas en tonos de negro y gris enmarcadas en recuadros blancos con fechas escritas: «julio de 1941, diciembre de 1936, abril de 1952...».

Miramos juntos la pared, cada uno perdido en sus pensamientos, fascinados y horrorizados a la vez. Comparo imágenes de niños yuxtapuestas a rostros de adultos. Los parecidos son evidentes. Son padres e hijos, supongo que familias biológicas a las que separaron. Las fotografías de los hijos están colgadas junto a retratos recientes de los adultos en que se convirtieron.

Miro los ojos de una hermosa mujer de vibrante sonrisa con un bebé apoyado en la cadera. Lleva un vestido y un delantal que le quedan grandes y le dan aspecto de una niña disfrazada con ropas de mayor. No puede tener más de quince o dieciséis años.

¿Qué me contarías?, me pregunto. *¿Qué te pasó?*

A mi lado, Trent levanta algunas de las fotografías. Debajo hay más, capa tras capa de imágenes. Trent Turner I fue muy meticuloso con su trabajo.

—En los reversos no pone nada —comenta—. Supongo que por eso no se molestó en pedirme que me ocupara de estas. Es imposible saber quiénes son estas personas a no ser que las conozcas de algo.

La tristeza tiñe mis pensamientos, pero es un sentimiento impreciso. Estoy concentrada en la fotografía de cuatro mujeres que posan cogidas del brazo en la playa. Aunque es en blanco y negro, imagino los colores vivos de los vestidos veraniegos y los sombreros de ala ancha de los años sesenta. Veo el destello dorado del sol en sus largos rizos rubios.

Una de las mujeres es mi abuela. Está sujetándose el sombrero. En la muñeca lleva la pulsera de las libélulas.

Las otras tres mujeres se parecen a mi abuela. Los mismos rizos rubios, los mismos ojos claros, probablemente azules. Podrían ser familia mía perfectamente, pero no reconozco a ninguna.

Todas llevan una pulsera de libélulas idéntica a la de mi abuela.

Al fondo, un poco desenfocados, hay unos niños pequeños acuclillados en la orilla, las rodillas apuntando hacia arriba mientras trabajan con cubo y pala haciendo torres de arena.

¿Es uno de ellos mi padre?

Levanto la mano para intentar alcanzar la fotografía y Trent se estira para separarla del corcho y dármela. Cuando quita la chincheta, cae algo pequeño y blanco que revolotea como una cometa sin viento que la impulse. Antes de agacharme a cogerlo, ya sé lo que es.

Hay una versión ampliada en un marco nacarado en la habitación de la residencia de May Crandall.

Una voz rompe el silencio, pero estoy tan absorta que casi ni me doy cuenta de que la que habla soy yo:

—Esta foto ya la he visto.

18

RILL

Por dentro, la casa está oscura como boca de lobo. No queda encendida ninguna luz y las cortinas no dejan entrar la luna por la ventana del dormitorio. A mi alrededor, las niñas se revuelven en sus camas, gimen y rechinan los dientes en sueños. Después de tanto tiempo encerrada en el sótano a solas, estar acompañada me resulta un consuelo, pero lo cierto es que aquí no hay lugar seguro. Estas niñas cuentan cosas. Cuentan que Riggs a veces viene de noche y se lleva a quien quiere..., casi siempre niñas pequeñas, que pesan poco.

Yo soy demasiado grande para que me lleven en brazos. Espero. Pero no quiero tener que comprobarlo.

Silenciosa como una sombra, me deslizo de debajo de la manta y cruzo la habitación de puntillas. Ya la he recorrido con mucha atención antes de acostarme en mi nueva cama. Sé dónde están los tablones que rechinan, sé cuántos pasos hay hasta la puerta, cuántos hasta las escaleras, la forma más segura de pasar junto al cuartito contiguo a la cocina donde las empleadas estarán dormitando en sus sillas. James me explicó cómo bajar a la cocina de noche para robar bizcochos a la señora Murphy. Sé cómo lo conseguía sin ser descubierto.

Pero todas las cosas que sabía James no lo salvaron, así que he de tener mucho cuidado cuando me escabulla para decirle a Silas que debo esperar a que vuelva Fern. En cuanto lo haga, la cogeré en brazos y nos iremos cuando esté oscuro y Silas nos llevará de vuelta al río, y estos días horribles se habrán terminado.

¿Y si Briny y Queenie no me quieren de vuelta después de lo que he hecho? Quizá me odien tanto como me odio a mí misma. Quizá miren a la chica flaca y triste en que me he convertido y vean a alguien a quien nadie quiere.

Acallo mis pensamientos porque la cabeza puede echarlo todo a perder si la dejas. Tengo que prestar atención, hacerlo todo bien para que no me descubran.

No es tan difícil como había pensado. Enseguida he bajado las escaleras. Del cuarto contiguo a la cocina llega un pequeño círculo de luz. Dentro, alguien ronca sonoramente. Cerca de la puerta, unos pies enfundados en unos zapatones blancos se asoman como las alas de una polilla. Ni siquiera miro a ver de quién son. Me pego a la pared al otro lado de los fogones cuidando de quedarme en las sombras, como decía James. Tanteo cada tablón del suelo con la punta del pie, con mucho cuidado. El bajo raído de mi camisón roza contra la superficie áspera de hierro del horno. Imagino que está haciendo ruido, pero en realidad no es así.

La puerta mosquitera del lavadero chirría un poco cuando tiro de ella para abrirla. Me paro, contengo la respiración, aguzo el oído para ver si algo se mueve en la casa.

Nada.

Sigilosa como un suspiro, salgo. La madera del suelo del porche está húmeda de rocío, igual que la cubierta del *Arcadia*. En lo alto, saltamontes y grillos hacen palpitar el cielo y un millón de estrellas brillan como fogatas lejanas. La media luna está acostada, meciéndose de espaldas. Su gemela arruga el agua del barril de agua de lluvia cuando paso junto a él.

De pronto estoy de vuelta en casa. Envuelta en la manta de la noche y las estrellas. La manta es parte de mí y yo soy parte de ella. Nadie puede tocarme. Somos indistinguibles la una de la otra.

Croan las ranas y pájaros oscuros graznan cuando cruzo el jardín con el delgado camisón blanco pegado a las piernas, ligera como la semilla de la asclepia. Cuando estoy cerca de la valla trasera, me pego a los arbustos de acebo y silbo imitando al chotacabras.

Me contesta otro silbido, sonrío, aspiro el olor dulce e intenso del jazmín y corro hacia el sonido, cruzando el túnel de los chicos mayores hasta que llego a la valla. Silas está al otro lado. En las sombras de la noche no le veo la cara, solo el contorno de su gorra de visera y sus piernas huesudas dobladas como ancas de rana. Mete la mano entre los barrotes.

—Vámonos —susurra y agarra uno de los barrotes como si pensara arrancarlo con las manos—. He aserrado este casi entero. Debería...

Le cojo la mano para detenerlo. Si abre un hueco, los chicos mayores lo verán por la mañana, cuando vengan a su escondite.

—No puedo ir. — Todo en mi interior grita: *¡Vete! ¡Corre!*—. No puedo irme aún, Fern va a volver. Las personas que se la llevaron no la quieren. Tengo que esperar a mañana por la noche para poder traerla conmigo.

—Tienes que salir ahora. Yo volveré a por Fern.

Las dudas empiezan a asaltar mis pensamientos, a derrapar de un lado a otro de mi cabeza.

—No. Si se enteran de que me he ido, si ven el hueco en la valla, nunca lograremos sacarla de aquí. Mañana por la noche puedo escaparme otra vez. Y hay otro niñito, Stevie. También es del río. No puedo dejarlo aquí. —¿Cómo lo haré? Sé dónde duerme Stevie, pero sacarlo del cuarto de los pequeños y traer también a Fern sin que nadie nos vea...

Ni siquiera parece posible.

Aun así, que Silas esté aquí me da seguridad. Me da valor. Me siento capaz de cualquier cosa. Encontraré la manera. No puedo dejar aquí a Fern y a Stevie. Su sitio es el río. Su sitio es con nosotros. La señora Murphy y la señorita Tann ya me han quitado bastante. Quiero recuperarlo. Quiero volver a ser Rill Foss.

Antes de que esto termine, encontraré a todas mis hermanas y a mi hermanito y me los llevaré al *Arcadia*. Eso es lo que haré.

Silas se acerca y sus brazos delgados y largos me rodean. Me inclino hacia él y se le cae la gorra. Apoya la frente en mi mejilla y su pelo como ala de cuervo me hace cosquillas.

—No quiero que vuelvas ahí.

Me pasa la mano por el pelo, con suavidad y cuidado. Se me acelera el corazón.

Tengo que hacer un esfuerzo para no colarme por la valla.

—Es solo un día.

—Estaré aquí mañana por la noche —promete Silas.

Me besa en la mejilla. Algo nuevo me recorre de pies a cabeza y cierro los ojos con fuerza para ahuyentar el sentimiento.

Dejarlo allí es de lo más difícil que he hecho en mi vida. Mientras me alejo a gatas, él tapa los barrotes con barro para que nadie vea los cortes en el metal. Espero que no cedan si uno de los chicos mayores se apoya en la valla mientras están en el túnel.

Estoy de vuelta en la casa y subiendo las escaleras sin que me haya dado tiempo a respirar, o al menos esa es la sensación que tengo. Una vez en el piso de arriba, me quedo en el pasillo y compruebo que no hay ningún ruido antes de rodear la barandilla donde hacemos fila para el baño. No hay nada salvo las sombras de la luna que entran por la ventana de la escalera y los ruidos de los que duermen. Un niño pequeño habla en sueños. Me paro inmediatamente, pero enseguida se calla.

Quince pasos más y estaré en mi habitación. Lo he conseguido. Nadie sabrá dónde he ido. Mañana será incluso más fácil ahora que ya lo he hecho. James tenía razón. Aquí no es tan difícil conseguir hacer las cosas si eres listo.

Puedo engañarlos a todos. La idea se apodera de mí. Me hace sentirme como si les hubiera quitado algo, algo que me robaron y que era mío. Poder. Ahora soy poderosa. Cuando estemos a salvo en el *Arcadia* y el río nos lleve lejos de aquí, me olvidaré de este lugar. Será como si nunca hubiera ocurrido.

Un mal sueño lleno de personas malvadas.

Tan entusiasmada estoy con la idea que piso donde no debo. Una tabla del suelo cruje bajo mi pie. Contengo un grito, miro al suelo y decido que lo mejor es darme prisa, no sea que aparezca una de las empleadas. Si estoy en la cama, no podrá saber quién...

Casi no veo al señor Riggs hasta que lo tengo encima. Viene del dormitorio de los niños pequeños. Pierde el equilibrio y yo también. Se golpea el hombro con la pared y susurra:

—Uf.

Me doy la vuelta para echar a correr, pero me agarra del camisón y del pelo. Su manaza me tapa la boca y la nariz. Huelo sudor y whisky, tabaco y cenizas de carbón. Me dobla la cabeza hacia atrás de tal manera que pienso: *Me va a partir el cuello aquí mismo. Me va a partir el cuello y a tirarme por las escaleras y dirá que me caí. Es el fin...*

Fuerzo los ojos para enfocarlo. Mira a su alrededor, tratando de decidir dónde llevarme. No puedo dejar que me lleve al sótano. Si lo hace, estoy muerta, lo sé. Fern volverá mañana y yo no estaré.

Cuando tantea las escaleras, tropieza. Me pisa el dedo del pie con la bota y veo las estrellas y gimo. Aprieta la mano que me tapa la boca y no puedo respirar. Oigo cómo me cruje la espalda, me retuerzo e intento soltarme, pero me aplasta más contra él, levantándome del suelo y arrastrándome por el pasillo hasta las sombras junto al cuarto de baño. Busca a tientas el picaporte para abrirla. Gimo, me resisto y tiro hasta que con un gruñido me sujeta contra la pared para poder abrir la puerta. Me está aplastando el pecho con la barriga y se me empieza a nublar la vista, no me queda aire en los pulmones.

Acerca la cara a mi oreja.

—T-tú y yo p-podemos ser amigos. P-puedo darte pastillas de m-menta y ga-galletas. —Me restriega la mejilla por la barbilla y el hombro y me araña con su bigote cuando me huele el pelo, luego mete la cara por el cuello de mi camisón—. Hueles a aire li-libre. ¿Has es-estado con alguno de los chicos m-mayores ahí fuera? ¿Y-ya tienes otro novio?

Su voz parece llegar de muy lejos, convertida en un eco, como las sirenas de niebla de los barcos en las mañanas frías del río. Me tiemblan las rodillas. Siento un hormigueo en los pies, los tengo entumecidos. No siento ni la pared ni a él. Me palpitan los costados del cuerpo igual que las agallas de un pez colgando del anzuelo.

Veo chispas como las que salen de las varitas de las hadas. Bailan en la oscuridad.

¡No!, me digo. ¡No! Pero no me queda con qué luchar. No tengo cuerpo. Tal vez me asfixie y muera. Ojalá.

Entonces, de pronto me suelta y donde antes estaba su cuerpo ahora entra aire frío y puedo volver a respirar. Me deslizo por la pared y aterrizo hecha un guiñapo, mareada, parpadeando y tratando de levantarme del suelo.

—¿Señor Riggs? —La voz cortante de una empleada llega desde las escaleras—. ¿Qué hace aquí a estas horas?

Se me aclara la visión y veo que Riggs me tapa, así que la empleada no me ve. Me refugio en las sombras, me pego mucho a la pared. Si me cogen, seré yo la que tenga un problema, no él. Me encerrarán otra vez... O algo peor.

—He-he oído truenos hace un rato. T-tengo que cerrar las v-ventanas.

La empleada se acerca a la barandilla. La luz de la luna la ilumina y veo que es la nueva que vino cuando se marchó la señorita Dodd. No sé gran cosa de ella ni si es mala. Habla como si fuera mala. No le gusta que Riggs esté aquí arriba, eso está claro. Como se meta con él, no durará mucho tiempo en casa de la señora Murphy.

—No he oído nada. —Se vuelve a un lado y a otro, comprobando las puertas de los dormitorios.

—E-estaba fuera c-cuando lo he oído. Eran u-unos gatos v-vagabundos maullando. He c-cogido la escopeta para m-matarlos.

—Cielo santo, habría despertado a toda la casa. No creo que los gatos estén haciendo daño a nadie.

—A-a la prima Ida no le gusta que nadie merodee por a-aquí.

Cuando dice Ida se refiere a la señora Murphy. También lo dice para recordarle a la nueva empleada cuál es su sitio.

—Ya cierro yo las ventanas. —La empleada no retrocede y no sé si alegrarme de ello o no. Como se siga acercando, me verá. Si se va, Riggs me meterá en el cuarto de baño—. No hay necesidad de que se levante usted de la cama, señor Riggs, cuando a mí me pagan por vigilar a los niños de noche.

Riggs se aparta de mí y se acerca a ella con paso inseguro y tambaleante. Cuando llega a la esquina de la barandilla, le corta el paso. Las dos sombras se funden. Riggs susurra alguna cosa.

—¡Señor Riggs! —La mano de la mujer sale y entra de la sombra. Piel que abofetea piel—. ¿Ha bebido?

—He-he visto cómo me mira.

—Usted no ha visto nada.

—P-pórtese bien o se lo contaré a la prima Ida. N-no le gusta que se porten mal c-conmigo.

La empleada se pega a la pared para zafarse de él y él la deja.

—No... no vuelva a acercarse a mí o... o seré yo quien hable con ella. Le diré que ha bebido y ha sido descarado conmigo.

Riggs camina despacio hacia las escaleras.

—D-debería entrar a mirar... p-primero a los niños pequeños. A-alguno se ha caído de la cama.

Baja las escaleras con ruidosas pisadas. La madera del suelo cruje y silba.

La empleada lo mira marcharse con los brazos cruzados alrededor del cuerpo antes de ir al cuarto de los pequeños. Me pongo de pie con piernas temblorosas, corro a mi cama, me tapo con las mantas y me envuelvo bien en ellas. Hago bien, porque la empleada entra a continuación en nuestro dormitorio, quizá pensando que encontró a Riggs más cerca de él.

Pasea entre las camas, levanta las mantas y nos mira a todos como si quisiera comprobar alguna cosa. Cuando llega a mi cama, respiro pausada y profundamente para no temblar cuando aparta las mantas y me toca. Quizá le extraña que esté tan tapada con el calor que hace. Quizá huele la noche en mí, como hizo Riggs.

Se queda un rato junto a mi cama.

Por fin se marcha y me quedo despierta mirando la oscuridad. *Un día más,* me digo. *Solo tienes que aguantar un día más.*

Me lo repito una y otra vez, como una promesa. Tengo que hacerlo. De otro modo, encontraría la manera de arrancar la mosquitera de esa ventana y saltaría confiando en que esté lo bastante alta para matarme.

No puedo vivir así.

Me duermo convencida de ello.

La mañana llega a trompicones. Dormito a ratos mientras espero a oír las voces de las empleadas ordenándonos levantarnos y vestirnos. Sé que antes de eso no debo moverme. La señora Pulnik se aseguró de explicarme las reglas del piso de arriba antes de enseñarme mi cama y la caja debajo de ella para guardar mi ropa.

Pero no la voy a necesitar mucho tiempo. Esta noche saldremos de aquí, los tres —Fern, Stevie y yo— como sea. *Si tengo que coger un cuchillo de la cocina y clavárselo a alguien para que nos deje pasar, lo haré*, me digo. *No dejaré que nadie me detenga.*

Hasta que no hemos bajado a desayunar, no me entero de que he hecho promesas que me resultará difícil cumplir. De entrada, la señora Pulnik ha visto esta mañana pisadas con arena en la cocina. Están secas, así que sabe que son de anoche. Desaparecen antes de llegar a las escaleras, lo que significa que no sabe dónde terminan, pero como son grandes está convencida de que pertenecen a uno de los chicos mayores. Les ha hecho formar una fila y está haciéndoles pisar uno a uno las huellas para ver cuál coincide.

Aún no se ha dado cuenta de que tengo los pies grandes. De pie junto a mi sitio en la mesa de las chicas, doblo los dedos y confío en que no me mire.

Quizá uno de los chicos tiene un pie que encaja en las huellas, me digo y sé que no está bien porque castigarán a alguien por mi culpa. Un castigo muy feo. La señora Murphy también está y parece un perro rabioso. Lleva un paraguas con la lona toda rota. Tiene intención de pegar a alguien con él. Después, seguramente lo mandarán al armario.

Yo no puedo ir al armario.

Pero no puedo dejar que metan a otra persona cuando es mi culpa. Sería lo mismo que pegarle yo misma con el paraguas.

Miro hacia el lavadero y veo a Riggs al otro lado de la puerta mosquitera. Está mirando el espectáculo. Me saluda con la cabeza y sonríe y me entra frío.

La empleada nueva mira desde un rincón, los ojos oscuros nerviosos.

—Es... es posible que haya sido yo —balbucea—. El señor Riggs me dijo que había gatos sueltos fuera y fui a echarlos.

La señora Murphy apenas la oye.

—¡No se entrometa! —chilla—. Y sus pies son demasiado pequeños. ¿A quién está encubriendo? ¿A quién?

—A nadie. —Sus ojos miran en mi dirección.

La señora Murphy y la señora Pulnik tratan de seguirlos. El tiempo empieza a pasar muy despacio.

No te muevas. No te muevas. Me quedo muy quieta.

—P-puede que est-tuvieran ya anoche. Hay barro cerca del barril de agua. —Riggs interviene, ahora que todos están mirando a mi lado de la mesa. Al principio creo que Riggs quiere ayudarme y entonces comprendo que lo que busca es que no me encierren esta noche donde no pueda entrar a buscarme.

La señora Murphy le manda callar con un gesto de la mano.

—Chsss. De verdad que eres demasiado bueno con estos pequeños ingratos. Les das una mano y te cogen el brazo. —Se golpea la palma de la mano con el paraguas mientras estudia mi lado de la mesa—. Bien, y si no ha sido uno de los chicos..., entonces ¿quién?

La niña que durmió anoche en la cama frente a la mía, Dora, inclina la cabeza hacia atrás, se tambalea y cae al suelo inconsciente.

Nadie se mueve.

—Ella no, supongo —dice la señora Murphy—. Y si no fue ella, ¿quién?

El paraguas traza un círculo como una varita mágica.

—Apartaos de la mesa, niñas. —Los ojos le echan chispas—. Veamos quién es nuestra Cenicienta.

Suena el teléfono y todos damos un respingo. Luego nos quedamos muy quietos, incluso las empleadas, mientras la señora Murphy decide si contestar o no. Cuando lo hace, casi arranca el teléfono de la pared, pero, en cuanto oye quién está al otro lado de la línea, su voz se vuelve dulce como la miel.

—Pues claro que sí. Buenos días, Georgia. Qué alegría oírla tan temprano. —Hace una pausa y a continuación dice—: Sí, sí. Por supuesto. Llevo horas levantada. Déjeme que vaya al despacho para que podamos hablar en privado.

Las palabras que salen del teléfono son rápidas como el ratatatá de los rifles de repetición en las películas del oeste.

—Ah, entiendo. Pues claro. —La señora Murphy deja el paraguas y se lleva la palma de la mano a la frente y enseña los dientes en un gesto que me recuerda a Queenie la última noche que la vi—. Bueno, sí, podremos estar allí a las diez, pero no me parece aconsejable. Es que...

Salen más palabras del teléfono, sonoras y veloces.

—Sí, lo entiendo. No llegaremos tarde —dice la señora Murphy entre dientes y, cuando cuelga con violencia el auricular del teléfono en la horquilla, me señala con los ojos entrecerrados y la boca apretada—. Llévensela y vístanla de domingo. Algo azul que le haga juego con los ojos... y un delantal. La señorita Tann la quiere en el hotel del centro a las diez.

La cara de la señora Pulnik es como la de la señora Murphy. Lo último que quieren hacer conmigo ahora mismo es lavarme, peinarme y ponerme un vestido.

—Pero si ha...

—¡No me lleve la contraria! —aúlla la señora Murphy y a continuación pega con fuerza a Danny Boy en la cabeza porque es el que tiene más cerca. Todos nos encogemos mientras nos va señalando con el dedo—. ¿Se puede saber qué miráis?

Los niños no saben si sentarse o quedarse donde están. Esperan a que la señora Murphy salga furiosa por las puertas batientes. Luego se sientan a hurtadillas mientras las bisagras aún chirrían.

—Me voy a *ocuparr* de ti personalmente.

La señora Pulnik me coge del brazo y aprieta con fuerza. Sé que va a vengarse de mí de una manera u otra.

Pero también sé que, sea lo que sea lo que tiene planeado la señorita Tann, puede ser peor. Circulan historias sobre lo que les pasa a los niños cuando las empleadas los llevan a un hotel.

—¡Y no le dejen cardenales! —La orden de la señora Murphy llega como un eco desde el pasillo.

Así que me he salvado. Pero no. La señora Pulnik me tira del pelo y me hace darme la vuelta. Durante la hora siguiente hace lo posible por que sufra al máximo y lo consigue. Para cuando me subo al automóvil donde me espera la señora Murphy, me estalla la cabeza y tengo los ojos rojos de las lágrimas que me han dicho que más me vale no derramar.

En el automóvil, la señora Murphy no dice una palabra y me alegro. Me pego a la puerta y miro por la ventana, asustada, preocupada y dolorida. No sé lo que me va a pasar, pero sé que no será bueno. Aquí nunca pasa nada bueno.

De camino al centro pasamos junto al río. Veo remolcadores y barcazas y un barco con espectáculo a bordo. La música de organillo entra en el coche y recuerdo cómo bailaba Gabion en la cubierta del *Arcadia* cuando pasaban los barcos con espectáculo. Nos hacía reír sin parar. Mi corazón viaja hacia el agua, con la esperanza de ver el *Arcadia* o el barco del viejo Zede o cualquier casa flotante, pero no hay nada. En la otra orilla hay un campamento abandonado. Solo quedan hogueras apagadas, círculos de hierba pisoteada y una pila de madera de deriva que alguien reunió, pero no llegó a quemar. Todos los barcos han desaparecido.

Por primera vez caigo en la cuenta de que ya debe de ser octubre. Muy pronto los arces y los gomeros cambiarán de color y el rojo y el amarillo se asomarán a sus hojas. Los habitantes del río han emprendido ya su viaje hacia el sur, donde los inviernos son cálidos y el agua rebosa de gruesos bagres.

Briny no se ha ido, me digo; pero de pronto tengo la sensación de que no volveré a verlo, ni a él ni a Fern ni a ninguno de mis seres queridos. El sentimiento me engulle por completo y lo único que puedo hacer es dejar que mis pensamientos abandonen mi cuerpo. Cuando el conductor aparca delante de un edificio alto, ya no estoy. Apenas oigo a la señora Murphy amenazándome con lo que me pasará si no me comporto. Casi no me duele cuando me pellizca a través del vestido y me retuerce la piel sobre las costillas y me dice que más me vale hacer lo que me ordenen cuando entremos y que no diga que no a nada, ni llore, ni proteste.

—Vas a ser encantadora como una gatita. —Me pellizca más fuerte y acerca mi cara a la suya—. O lo lamentarás... Lo mismo que tu amiguito, Stevie. No quieres que le pase nada malo, ¿verdad?

Sale a la acera y me arrastra con ella. A nuestro lado pasan hombres vestidos de traje. Las mujeres pasean con paquetes de colores brillantes. Una mamá con abrigo rojo empujando un cochecito de bebé sale del hotel y nos mira al pasar. Tiene una cara muy amable y quiero correr hacia ella. Quiero aferrarme a su abrigo y contárselo todo.

Ayúdeme, le diré.

Pero no puedo hacerlo. Sé que, si lo hago, castigarán a Stevie. Y probablemente también a Fern, una vez esté de vuelta en casa de la señora Murphy. Pase lo que pase, hoy tengo que ser buena. Tengo que hacer todo lo que me digan para que no me encierren cuando volvamos a casa esta noche.

Enderezo la espalda y me digo que es la última vez. *Esta es la última vez que podrán obligarme a hacer nada.*

Sea lo que sea, lo haré.

Pero tengo el corazón acelerado y el estómago cerrado como un puño. Un hombre uniformado abre la puerta. Parece un soldado o un príncipe. Quiero que me rescate igual que hacen los príncipes en los cuentos.

—Buenos días. —La señora Murphy sonríe, levanta la nariz y echa a andar con paso firme.

Dentro del hotel, la gente ríe, charla y almuerza. Es un sitio bonito, como un castillo, solo que hoy no parece bonito. Parece una trampa.

El ascensorista es como una estatua al lado de los botones. Ni siquiera parece respirar mientras la cabina sube y sube y sube. Cuando salimos, me dirige una mirada triste. ¿Sabrá dónde me llevan, lo que está a punto de pasarme?

La señora Murphy me lleva por el pasillo y llama a una puerta con los nudillos.

—Adelante —dice una mujer y, cuando entramos, la señorita Tann está recostada en el sofá igual que un gato descansando al sol. A su espalda, las cortinas están descorridas y un gran ventanal deja ver todo Memphis. Estamos tan altos que se ven los tejados a nuestros pies. Nunca he estado en un sitio tan alto.

Cierro los puños, los escondo en el pichi de volantes e intento no moverme.

La señorita Tann sostiene un vaso lleno hasta la mitad. Tiene aspecto de llevar aquí un rato. ¿Igual es que vive en el hotel?

Hace girar la bebida marrón, la levanta en dirección a una puerta que hay frente al sofá.

—Métala en el dormitorio y luego puede irse, señora Murphy. Cierre la puerta al salir... y dígale que se esté sentada y en silencio a no ser que se le ordene otra cosa. Primero hablaré con él aquí, para asegurarme de que... de que está todo en orden.

—No me importa quedarme, Georgia.

—Si lo prefiere. —Me mira mientras cruzamos la puerta; la señora Murphy me sujeta por la axila, así que no puedo evitar andar torcida—. La verdad es que hay mejores opciones, pero entiendo por qué quiere a esta —dice la señorita Tann.

—Yo no entiendo que pueda quererla nadie.

Cuando entramos en el dormitorio, la señora Murphy me sienta en la cama y despliega la falda de volantes de manera que parezco una muñeca de esas que se ponen de adorno encima de las camas. Me tira del pelo para que me caiga por delante de los hombros en largos rizos y luego me dice que no me mueva ni un milímetro.

—Ni uno solo —es lo último que dice mientras va hacia la puerta. La cierra al salir.

Las oigo a ella y a la señorita Tann hablar en la otra habitación. Charlan sobre las vistas y beben juntas. Luego solo se oye silencio y los sonidos lejanos de la ciudad. Bocinas de automóviles. La campana de un tranvía. Los gritos de un niño vendedor de periódicos.

No sé cuánto tiempo ha pasado cuando llaman a la puerta de la habitación. Abre la señorita Tann y habla con voz melosa y oigo una voz de hombre, pero no entiendo lo que dicen hasta que se acercan.

—Por supuesto, es toda suya..., si está seguro de que aún la quiere, claro —dice la señorita Tann.

—Sí, y agradezco que haya alterado su procedimiento habitual y con tan poca antelación. Mi mujer ha sufrido mucho estos últimos años, hasta el punto de que ha pasado semanas en cama y sin querer hablar conmigo. ¿Qué otra cosa puedo hacer?

—Desde luego. Entiendo que la chica responda a sus necesidades, pero disponemos de otras niñas más... tratables —sugiere la señorita Tann—. Tenemos muchas niñas mayorcitas. Puede elegir la que quiera.

Por favor, pienso. *Escoja a otra.* Y entonces me doy cuenta de que eso está mal, de que no debería desear cosas malas a los otros niños.

—No. La quiero a ella.

Pellizco la colcha de la cama. El sudor que me cubre las palmas de las manos empapa la tela. Clavo las uñas.

Pórtate bien. Sea lo que sea, pórtate bien.

Esta noche viene Silas...

—¿Qué otra cosa puedo hacer? —pregunta de nuevo el hombre—. Mi mujer está muy frágil. La niña no deja de llorar, no puedo tener ese jaleo y ese ruido constantes en casa. Soy compositor y eso interfiere en mi trabajo. Tengo que terminar varias bandas sonoras para películas que se estrenan en Navidad y me estoy quedando sin tiempo.

—Pero, señor, le aseguro que esta niña le va a dar problemas, no a quitárselos —interviene la señora Murphy—. Pensé... Había dado por hecho que solo la quería para... No tenía ni idea de que tenía intención de quedársela para siempre; de lo contrario habría dicho algo antes.

—Eso no viene al caso, señora Murphy —dice la señorita Tann, cortante—. La niña es lo bastante mayor para hacer cualquier cosa que el señor Sevier desee.

—Sí..., sí, por supuesto, Georgia. Perdone la interrupción.

—La niña es perfecta en todos los sentidos, se lo aseguro, señor. Nadie la ha tocado.

El hombre dice algo que no logro entender y entonces vuelve a hablar la señorita Tann.

—Entonces ya está. Tengo sus papeles para dárselos y, por supuesto, como en su otra adopción, pasará un año hasta que el proceso se decrete como definitivo, pero no creo que haya ningún problema en ese sentido, sobre todo con un cliente de su... categoría.

La conversación decae. Hay ruido de papeles.

—Solo quiero que Victoria vuelva a ser feliz. Quiero mucho a mi mujer y estos últimos años han sido un tormento. Los médicos dicen que la única posible solución a sus ataques de tristeza es darle una razón poderosa para mirar hacia delante y no hacia atrás.

—Situaciones como estas son, por supuesto, la razón misma de nuestra existencia, señor Sevier. —A la señorita Tann le tiembla la voz como si estuviera a punto de llorar—. Estos pobres niños perdidos y las familias que los necesitan son mi acicate y mi inspiración en mi incansable labor. Cada día me enfrento a mi ardua tarea y a la triste vida de estos pequeñines para poder rescatarlos y darles una vida a ellos y a tantos hogares vacíos. Claro que, al ser yo de buena familia, sin duda podría haber elegido un camino más fácil, pero alguien debe sacrificarse para proteger a los que no pueden hacerlo solos. Es una vocación. Es mi vocación y la acepto de buena gana sin esperar méritos ni beneficio personal.

El hombre suspira y parece impaciente.

—Le estoy muy agradecido, por supuesto. ¿Hace falta alguna cosa más para cerrar este asunto?

—Ninguna. —Se oyen pisadas, pero que se alejan del dormitorio en lugar de acercarse—. Todos los papeles están en orden. Ha hecho el abono correspondiente y es suya, señor Sevier. Le está esperando ahí, en el dormitorio, así que los dejamos a solas para que se conozcan... o hagan lo que usted considere.

—Le aconsejo que tenga mano dura con ella. Es...

—Vamos, señora Murphy.

Entonces se van y me quedo muy quieta en la cama, atenta al hombre. Viene hasta la puerta y se detiene. Le oigo coger aire y expulsarlo.

Me pego con fuerza el vestido a las rodillas, estoy temblando de pies a cabeza.

Se abre la puerta y el hombre se queda allí, a solo unos metros de mí.

Lo conozco. Se sentó a mi lado en el sofá en la fiesta y me preguntó cuántos años tenía.

Su mujer era la que le leía cuentos a Fern.

19

AVERY

El coche de delante reduce la velocidad, pero estoy tan concentrada mirando a dos chicas adolescentes montar a caballo a uno de los lados de la carretera que no piso el freno hasta que es casi demasiado tarde. El coche toma el desvío que lleva al centro de actividades ecuestres. Me pregunto si allí es donde irán las chicas con sus caballos. Es la época de los derbys. Cuando era más joven yo también habría estado allí, de espectadora o compitiendo, pero estos días apenas tengo tiempo de lamentarme de que la vida adulta no me deje tiempo para actividades que en otro tiempo me apasionaban, como la equitación.

Ahora mismo mis pensamientos van varios kilómetros por delante, entrando ya en la habitación de May Crandall en la residencia. Ian, el becario simpático, ha hecho unas cuantas llamadas discretas para comprobar dónde y cómo se encuentra ahora mismo. Ha vuelto a la residencia y está lo bastante restablecida para traer de cabeza a las cuidadoras.

Detrás de mí, Trent toca el claxon y levanta una mano, como para decirme: «Ve con cuidado», pero detrás de las gafas de sol está sonriendo.

Si no fuera en un coche separado le diría: «Has insistido en venir. Ya te dije que las cosas podían ser impredecibles».

Probablemente se reiría y diría que no tiene intención de perderse esto.

Somos como un par de niños de sexto curso que hacen novillos por primera vez. Ninguno estamos donde deberíamos estar esta mañana, pero después de descubrir esa foto anoche en el estudio de su abuelo, no hemos podido resistirnos a hacer este viaje. Ni siquiera una llamada a primera hora de Leslie y media docena de consultas de nuevos clientes en la agencia de Trent han podido cambiar el plan que anoche hicimos llevados por un impulso. De una manera u otra vamos a descubrir lo que ocultaban nuestros abuelos y cómo mi vida y la suya están relacionadas... y qué tiene que ver May Crandall con ello.

Yo he ignorado adrede las llamadas de Leslie, Trent ha puesto una nota en la puerta de la agencia y nos hemos dado a la fuga a primera hora de la mañana.

Poco más de dos horas después, estamos en Aiken. Nuestra idea es ver a May Crandall después de que desayune. Dependiendo de lo que nos diga, es posible que después vayamos a la casa de mi abuela en Lagniappe.

Intento concentrarme en conducir mientras recorremos bonitas calles serpenteantes y arboladas, con magnolias somnolientas y enormes pinos que proyectan su sombra apacible en el todoterreno y parecen decir: *¿A qué viene tanta prisa? Tranquilízate. Disfruta del día.*

Por un momento me relajo, me convenzo de que esta no es más que otra mañana de verano. Pero en cuanto la residencia aparece al doblar una esquina, la ilusión se desvanece. Como para subrayar este hecho, me suena el teléfono y el nombre de Leslie aparece en la pantalla por cuarta vez. Esta llamada tan inoportuna me recuerda que, cuando termine mi visita a May

Crandall —dé el resultado que dé—, tendré que dar señales de vida. El mundo de los asuntos del día me llama. Literalmente.

Por lo menos sé que, si las llamadas tuvieran algo que ver con la salud de mi padre, serían mis hermanas las que me estarían buscando, no Leslie. Así que sin duda es algo del trabajo. Algo ha surgido desde que hablé anoche con Ian, o de lo contrario este lo habría mencionado entonces. Seguro que Leslie tiene un posible encuentro con la prensa que no hay que dejar escapar y quiere que vuelva antes de tiempo de mis minivacaciones en Edisto. Ni se imagina que ya he vuelto.

La idea de regresar al hervidero político me incomoda un tanto. La verdad es que no quiero pensar en ello. Pongo el teléfono en modo vibración y lo meto en el bolso sin mirar los mensajes que tengo acumulados. Seguramente también tengo correos electrónicos. A Leslie no le gusta nada que la ignoren.

Dejo de pensar en Leslie en cuanto aparco, cojo la carpeta donde están las fotos viejas del corcho y los papeles del sobre de la abuela Judy y salgo del coche.

Trent se reúne conmigo en la acera.

—Si alguna vez hacemos un viaje campo a través, yo conduzco.

—¿Por qué? ¿No te fías de mí?

Un extraño cosquilleo me baja por la espalda y enseguida sacudo los hombros para ahuyentarlo. Estar de nuevo en Aiken me recuerda ineludiblemente que, por muy agradable que me resulte Trent Turner, lo nuestro nunca pasará de una amistad.

Me aseguré de mencionar a mi prometido antes de salir de Edisto, para ser justa con todas las partes comprometidas.

—De ti sí me fío. De tu manera de conducir... no tanto.

—Pero si ni lo he rozado.

Seguimos bromeando mientras recorremos la acera y para cuando llegamos a la puerta estoy riéndome sin poder evitarlo.

El aroma a ambientador y el silencio opresivo nos devuelven a la realidad.

La expresión de Trent se transforma casi de manera instantánea. Su sonrisa se desvanece.

—Esto me trae recuerdos.

—¿Has estado aquí?

—No, pero se parece mucho a donde llevamos a mi abuela después de que tuviera el ictus. No había elección, pero para el abuelo fue duro. No habían pasado más de una o dos noches separados en sesenta años.

—Es muy difícil cuando llegas a ese punto en que no hay solución buena.

Sabe lo de mi abuela Judy. El tema surgió anoche cuando estábamos sentados en el porche de la casita hablando de las fotografías y de lo que podrían significar.

Nos cruzamos con una cuidadora vestida con un pijama de colores alegres. Nos saluda y parece preguntarse si me conoce de algo. Luego sigue su camino. Me alegro. Lo último que me apetece ahora es que alguien sepa que estoy aquí. Si se enteran Leslie y mi padre, habrá un interrogatorio intenso y no tengo ni idea de qué decir.

En la puerta de la habitación de May Crandall, de pronto me doy cuenta de que tampoco estoy segura de lo que voy a decirle. Me pregunto si debo entrar con las fotografías y preguntarle sin más: *¿Qué relación tenía usted con mi abuela? ¿Qué tenía que ver en ella Trent Turner I?*

¿Debería empezar de forma más sutil? Con lo poco que he tratado a May, no tengo ni idea de cómo reaccionará a nuestra visita. Tengo la esperanza de que la presencia de Trent ayude un poco. Después de todo, es muy probable que May conociera a su abuelo.

¿Y si que nos presentemos los dos resulta ser demasiado para ella? Lo cierto es que ha estado enferma. No quiero causarle más problemas. De hecho, estar aquí me hace darme cuenta de que debería hacer algo para ayudarla. Igual podría hablar con Andrew Moore, del comité de defensa de los derechos de las personas mayores. Quizá me pueda dar algunos nombres de organizaciones que ayuden a ancianos que, como May, tienen lejos a sus familias.

Trent se para en la puerta y señala la placa con el nombre.

—Parece que es aquí.

—Estoy nerviosa —confieso—. Sé que ha estado enferma. No sé si estará lo bastante fuerte para...

—¿Quién anda ahí? —May ataja mi inseguridad antes de que me dé tiempo a ponerla en palabras—. ¡Largo! No necesito nada. ¡No quiero chismorreos sobre mí!

Por la abertura entre la puerta y el marco sale volando una zapatilla y a continuación un cepillo, que aterriza con estrépito en el suelo.

Trent recupera los objetos arrojados.

—Tiene buen saque.

—Dejadme en paz —insiste May.

Trent y yo nos miramos inseguros y me acerco a la puerta evitando ponerme en la línea de fuego, por si May tiene más munición a mano.

—May, escuche un minuto, ¿de acuerdo? Soy Avery Stafford, ¿se acuerda de mí? Nos conocimos hace unas semanas. Le gustó mi pulsera de las libélulas. ¿Se acuerda?

Silencio.

—Me dijo que mi abuela era amiga suya. Judy. Judy Myers Stafford. Hablamos de la fotografía que tenía en la mesilla.

Tengo la sensación de que desde ese día mi mundo entero ha cambiado.

—¿Y entonces? —dice May al cabo de un instante—. ¿Vas a pasar o no?

Al otro lado de la puerta se oye un cuerpo moviéndose y también ruido de ropa de cama. No sé si se está preparando para recibirnos o para lanzarnos algún otro objeto.

—¿Ha terminado de tirar cosas?

—Si sigo tirando, imagino que te irás —dice.

Pero esta vez en su voz hay expectación. Está invitándome a entrar, así que lo hago, dejando a Trent a salvo en el pasillo.

Está recostada en la cama, con una bata azul que le hace juego con los ojos. Incluso así, apoyada en varias almohadas, hay un aire de realeza en su forma de mirarme, como si estuviera acostumbrada a que le llevaran el desayuno a la cama antes de vivir en una residencia de mayores.

—Tenía la esperanza de que hoy se encontrara lo bastante bien para hablar conmigo —me atrevo a decir—. Le pregunté por usted a mi abuela. Mencionó algo como Queen... o Queenie, pero era todo lo que recordaba.

May parece desolada.

—¿Tan mal está?

—Eso me temo. —Me siento fatal por ser portadora de esta noticia—. La abuela Judy no sufre. Simplemente no se acuerda de cosas. Es difícil para ella.

—Y supongo que para ti también.

La repentina perspicacia de May me deja temblando emocionalmente.

—Pues sí. Mi abuela y yo siempre estuvimos muy unidas.

—¿Y aun así nunca te habló de las personas de mi fotografía? —Detrás de la pregunta está la insinuación de que esta mujer conoce mejor a mi abuela que yo. No estoy segura de que consiga resignarme si nunca llego a conocer la verdad... Si May no me la cuenta.

—Sospecho que la abuela Judy me la contaría ahora, si pudiera. Pero, puesto que no puede, tengo la esperanza de que lo haga usted.

—No tiene nada que ver contigo. —May se vuelve de lado, como si temiera que la mire a la cara.

—Tengo la sensación de que sí lo tiene. Y a lo mejor...

Mira hacia la puerta.

—¿Quién está ahí? ¿Quién más está escuchando?

—He venido con alguien. Ha estado ayudándome a intentar descubrir lo que mi abuela no ha podido contarme. Es un amigo.

Trent entra y cruza la habitación con la mano extendida y una sonrisa que podría vender nieve a un esquimal.

—Soy Trent —se presenta—. Encantado de conocerla, señora Crandall.

Esta acepta la mano y la retiene entre las suyas, obligándolo a inclinarse un poco sobre la cama mientras se vuelve hacia mí.

—¿Un amigo, dices? Lo dudo.

Retrocedo un poco.

—Trent y yo nos hemos conocido hace unos días, cuando fui a Edisto.

—Precioso lugar, Edisto. —Se concentra en Trent con los ojos entrecerrados.

—Sí lo es —digo. *¿Por qué lo estudia así?*—. Mi abuela pasó bastante tiempo allí a lo largo de los años. Mi tío Clifford me ha contado que le gustaba escribir en la casa. Parece que ella y el abuelo de Trent hicieron..., colaboraron en algo allí.

Igual que si May fuera un testigo en el estrado, me fijo en si hay algún cambio en su expresión. Intenta disimularlos, pero los hay, y son evidentes. Más con cada frase que digo.

Se está preguntando cuánto sé.

—Creo que no he oído tu apellido. —Mira a Trent pestañeando.

El aire en la habitación parece tensarse mientras espera su respuesta, pero, cuando Trent se presenta de manera más formal, May asiente con la cabeza y sonríe.

—Mmm —dice—. Sí, tienes sus ojos.

Siento el mismo cosquilleo que cuando presiento que un testigo está a punto de hablar. A menudo es algo así lo que lo desencadena: la aparición por sorpresa de una cara que les resulta familiar, un vínculo con algo enterrado en el pasado, el indicio de un secreto guardado durante demasiado tiempo.

Los dedos temblorosos de May sueltan la mano de Trent. Se toca el mentón. Tiene las pestañas húmedas.

—Te pareces a él. También era guapísimo.

Esboza una sonrisa con los labios cerrados que me dice que en su día fue bastante coqueta, una mujer que no tenía dificultades para desenvolverse en un mundo de hombres.

Trent incluso se pone un poco colorado. Qué mono. La verdad es que disfruto mirándolos a los dos.

May me señala con el dedo.

—Este chico es una joya, tú hazme caso.

Ahora me toca a mí ponerme colorada.

—Por desgracia ya estoy comprometida.

—Pues no veo ninguna alianza todavía. —May me coge la mano y examina con ostentación mi anillo de compromiso—. Y detecto la chispa entre dos personas cuando la veo. Más me vale. He sobrevivido a tres maridos.

Una carcajada se escapa de los labios de Trent; baja la cabeza y el pelo rubio pajizo le cae hacia delante.

—Y no tuve nada que ver con sus muertes, por si os lo estabais preguntando —nos informa May—. Los quise a todos mucho. Uno era profesor, otro predicador y el último un artista que descubrió su vocación ya mayor. Uno me enseñó a pensar, otro a aprender y el tercero a ver. Todos fueron una inspiración para mí. Yo me dedicaba a la música, ¿sabéis? Trabajé en Hollywood y también hice giras con grandes orquestas. Eso fue en la época dorada del cine, antes de toda esta tontería digital.

Me vibra el teléfono en el bolso y lo mira con el ceño fruncido.

—Esos chismes infernales. El mundo sería mejor si nunca los hubieran inventado.

Apago el móvil. Si May por fin se decide a contarme la historia de la fotografía de su mesilla, no quiero que nada nos distraiga. De hecho, lo que tengo que hacer ahora es conseguir que la testigo se centre en los hechos.

Abro el sobre y saco las fotografías que encontramos en la cabaña de Trent.

—Hemos estado preguntándonos qué son estas fotografías. Eso y la Asociación de Hogares Infantiles de Tennessee.

Al instante su expresión se endurece. Me mira con ojos encendidos.

—Me gustaría no volver a oír ese nombre en la vida.

Trent le coge la mano entre las suyas y mira los dedos entrelazados.

—Lo siento, señora Crandall..., si estamos desenterrando recuerdos dolorosos. Pero mi abuelo nunca me habló de ello. Quiero decir, me enteré de que lo habían adoptado cuando era bastante joven y que, cuando lo supo, dejó de hablarse con sus padres adoptivos. Pero no sabía gran cosa sobre la Asociación de Hogares Infantiles de Tennessee... hasta hace poco. Quizá había oído hablar de ella de pasada a personas que venían a ver a mi abuelo. Yo sabía que mi abuelo ayudaba a esas personas de alguna forma y que sentía la necesidad de tener esas reuniones en privado..., en su estudio o en el barco. A mi abuela nunca le gustó que se hablara de trabajo dentro de la casa, de asuntos inmobiliarios o de ninguna otra clase. Yo no sabía nada de la afición, o de la segunda ocupación de mi abuelo o lo que fuera hasta que lo ayudé a enviar los expedientes que le quedaban antes de que se muriera. Me pidió que no leyera los documentos y no lo he hecho. Hasta que Avery llegó a Edisto hace unos días.

May abre la boca. Se le llenan los ojos de lágrimas.

—Entonces, ¿ha muerto? Sabía que estaba muy enfermo.

Trent le confirma que perdió a su abuelo meses atrás y May lo atrae hacia ella para besarlo en la mejilla.

—Era un buen hombre y un amigo muy querido.

—¿Lo adoptaron a través de la Asociación de Hogares Infantiles de Tennessee? —pregunta Trent—. ¿Por eso le interesaba?

May responde con un gesto sombrío de cabeza.

—Claro que sí. Y a mí también. Así nos conocimos. Claro que él entonces solo tenía tres años. Era una monada y muy cariñoso. Entonces no se llamaba Trent. Se cambió el nombre años después, cuando se enteró de quién era en realidad. Tenía una hermana de la que lo separaron mientras estábamos en el hogar infantil. Era dos o tres años mayor que él y creo que siempre tuvo la esperanza de que usar su verdadero nombre le ayudaría a encontrarla. Pero eso es lo triste. El hombre que ayudó a tantas personas a reencontrarse nunca consiguió localizar a su hermana. Quizá fue de los que no sobrevivieron. Fueron tantos...

La voz se le quiebra y se apaga. Se sienta más recta en la cama, carraspea.

—Nací en el río Misisipi en una casa flotante que construyó mi padre. Mi madre se llamaba Queenie y mi padre, Briny. Tenía tres hermanas pequeñas, Camellia, Lark y Fern, y un hermano, Gabion. Gabion era el pequeño...

Cierra los ojos, pero los veo moverse detrás de los párpados delgados y recorridos por venillas azules mientras prosigue su relato. Es como si soñara y viera las imágenes pasar flotando delante de ella. Cuenta que la policía se los llevó del barco y terminaron en un hogar infantil. Habla de semanas de incertidumbre y miedo, de empleadas crueles, de la separación de sus hermanos, de horrores como aquellos sobre los que hemos leído Trent y yo.

La historia que nos cuenta es desgarradora, pero fascinante. Estamos cada uno a un lado de la cama, escuchando casi sin respirar.

—En la casa perdí la pista de mis otros tres hermanos —dice por fin—, pero Fern y yo tuvimos suerte. Nos dejaron vivir juntas. Adoptadas.

Mira por la ventana y por un momento me pregunto si ya nos ha contado todo lo que tiene intención de contarnos. Por fin vuelve la vista a Trent.

—La última vez que vi a tu abuelo de niño me temí que fuera a ser de esos que no sobrevivían en el hogar. Era muy tímido. Siempre se metía en problemas con las empleadas sin que fuera su intención. Para cuando me fui, era para mí casi como un hermano pequeño. Pensé que no volvería a verlo. Cuando un hombre llamado Trent Turner se puso en contacto conmigo años más tarde, di por hecho que era un impostor. Porque no reconocí el nombre, claro. Georgia Tann acostumbraba a cambiar los nombres a los niños, sin duda para impedir que sus familias biológicas los localizaran. La recuerdo como una mujer horrible y cruel y creo que la dimensión de sus crímenes nunca llegará a conocerse del todo. Pocas de sus víctimas fueron capaces de hacer lo que hizo tu abuelo, reclamar su certificado de nacimiento y su verdadera ascendencia. Incluso llegó a conocer a su madre biológica antes de que muriera y también se reunió con otros familiares. Volvió a ser Trent, pero yo lo conocí como Stevie.

Vuelve a distraerse y sus pensamientos parecen viajar con ella. Cambio un poco de sitio la fotografía de las cuatro mujeres y hago algunas suposiciones. En un tribunal, esto equivaldría a guiar al testigo, aquí solo ayuda a desenterrar una historia.

—¿Las que salen en esta fotografía con usted y mi abuela son sus hermanas?

Sé que las otras tres mujeres tienen que ser hermanas o primas. Es evidente, aunque los sombreros les ocultan parcialmente la cara. Sigue intrigándome lo mucho que se parecen a mi abuela. El color de pelo. Los ojos claros que dan la impresión de traspasar la fotografía. Pero la forma de la cara, al menos lo que puedo ver de ella, es distinta. Los rasgos de las tres hermanas son llamativos, perfectamente cincelados. Tienen barbillas amplias y cuadradas, narices rectas y ojos almendrados un poco rasgados en las comisuras. Son muy hermosas. Mi abuela también es guapa, pero sus rasgos son más delgados y recuerdan un poco a un pájaro, y los ojos azules casi parecen demasiado grandes para su cara. Son luminosos, incluso en blanco y negro.

May coge la foto y la sostiene con manos temblorosas. Parece estudiarla durante una eternidad. Tengo que contenerme para no preguntar. *¿Qué le pasa por la cabeza? ¿En qué está pensando? ¿Qué está recordando?*

—Sí, las tres... Lark, Fern y yo. Las bellas nadadoras. —Suelta una risa breve y traviesa y le da una palmadita a Trent en la mano—. Me parece que tu abuela se inquietaba un poco cuando aparecíamos. Pero no tenía razón para ello. Trent la quería con toda su alma. Le estábamos muy agradecidas por ayudarnos a encontrarnos. Edisto era un lugar especial para nosotras. Fue donde nos reunimos por primera vez.

—¿Fue allí donde conoció a mi abuela? —Necesito una respuesta sencilla a todo esto. Una con la que pueda vivir. No quiero enterarme de que mi abuela estaba cumpliendo una penitencia por la participación de mi familia en la Asociación de Hogares Infantiles de Tennessee, que mis abuelos fueron de los muchos políticos que protegieron a Georgia Tann y su red, que ignoraron las atrocidades porque había familias poderosas que no querían que se hicieran públicos sus delitos o declaradas nulas sus adopciones—. ¿Fue allí donde se hicieron amigas?

Recorre con los dedos el recuadro blanco de la fotografía. Está mirando a mi abuela. Ojalá pudiera meterme dentro de su cabeza o, mejor aún, dentro de la fotografía.

—Sí, fue allí. Coincidimos en actos sociales antes incluso de tratarnos, aunque debo decir que antes de conocerla tenía una impresión completamente equivocada de ella. Llegó a ser una amiga muy querida. Y fue muy generosa prestándonos a mis hermanas y a mí la casa de Edisto de vez en cuando para que pudiéramos pasar unos días juntas. Esa foto se hizo durante una de nuestras visitas. Tu abuela se reunió con nosotras allí. Pasamos un día precioso de finales de verano en la playa.

Esta información me tranquiliza y me gustaría parar aquí, pero no explica por qué estaban las palabras «Asociación de Hogares Infantiles de Tennessee» en la cinta de la máquina de escribir de mi abuela... O por qué se puso Trent Turner I en contacto con mi abuela.

—El abuelo de Trent dejó un sobre para mi abuela Judy —digo—. A juzgar por su dietario, creo que tenía intención de ir a buscarlo antes de caer enferma. Dentro del sobre había documentos de la Asociación de Hogares Infantiles de Tennessee. Certificados médicos y documentos de cesión de un recién nacido llamado Shad Arthur Foss. ¿Para qué querría esos papeles mi abuela?

Ahora he pillado a May desprevenida. Hay más cosas que contar, pero no parece muy dispuesta a hacerlo.

Parpadea y cierra los ojos.

—De repente me encuentro... muy cansada. Y tanta charla... Es más de lo que hablo en una semana entera.

—¿Tenía mi abuela algo que ver con la Asociación de Hogares Infantiles de Tennessee? ¿Estaba mi familia implicada?

Tengo la sensación de que, si no lo averiguo hoy, nunca lo haré.

—Eso tendrías que preguntárselo a ella.

May se recuesta en las almohadas y suspira de forma exagerada.

—No puedo. Ya se lo he dicho. Ya no recuerda esas cosas. Por favor, sea lo que sea dígame la verdad. Arcadia. ¿Tiene algo que ver con esto?

Agarro con fuerza los barrotes de la cama. Trent pone una mano encima de la mía.

—Tal vez sea mejor si lo dejamos por hoy.

Pero veo que May se está encerrando en sí misma y que la historia se desvanece como un dibujo a tiza en un día de lluvia.

Corro detrás de los colores que se van.

—Solo quiero saber si mi familia fue... responsable de alguna manera. ¿Por qué tenía mi abuela tanto interés en todo esto?

May palpa la barandilla hasta encontrar mi mano y me la aprieta en un gesto para tranquilizarme.

—Pues claro que no, querida. No te angusties. Durante un tiempo, Judy me estuvo ayudando a escribir mi historia, eso es todo. Pero luego me lo pensé mejor. En la vida he descubierto que los tiempos pasados son un poco como la berza. Tienden a tener un sabor amargo. Es mejor no masticarlos demasiado tiempo. Tu abuela era una estupenda escritora, pero le resultaba duro hablar de nuestras vivencias en el hogar infantil. Creo que su talento estaba hecho para relatos más alegres.

—¿La estaba ayudando a escribir su historia? ¿Eso es todo?

¿Podría ser esta la explicación? ¿Nada de secreto familiar? ¿Solo la abuela Judy usando su talento para ayudar a una amiga, para arrojar luz sobre una vieja injusticia, cuyas consecuencias aún perviven? Un inmenso alivio se apodera de mí.

Tiene todo el sentido del mundo.

—Eso es todo —confirma May—. Ojalá pudiera contarte más.

Esta última parte despierta mi curiosidad como la repentina bocanada de humo de un fuego supuestamente extinto. A los testigos que no están diciendo la verdad les cuesta trabajo atenerse a un sí o un no tajantes.

¿Qué es lo que le gustaría poder contarme? ¿Es que hay más?

May encuentra la mano de Trent, se la aprieta y la suelta.

—Siento mucho lo de tu abuelo. Para muchos de nosotros fue como un regalo caído del cielo. Antes de que el estado hiciera públicos los expedientes de adopción en el 96, teníamos pocos medios para buscar a nuestras familias..., a nuestras verdaderas familias. Pero tu abuelo sabía cómo hacerlo. Sin él, Fern y yo nunca habríamos encontrado a nuestra hermana. Las dos han muerto ya, claro, Lark y Fern. Os agradecería que no molestaseis a sus familias..., ni a la mía tampoco, la verdad. Para cuando nos reencontramos éramos mujeres jóvenes con maridos y con hijos. Decidimos no interferir en nuestras vidas respectivas. Nos bastaba con saber que las otras estaban bien. Tu abuelo lo entendió. Espero que respetéis sus deseos. —Abre los ojos y me mira—. Los dos.

De pronto, todo indicio de agotamiento ha desaparecido. La mirada que me dirige es intensa, exigente.

—Por supuesto —dice Trent. Pero yo me doy cuenta de que no es la suya la respuesta que le interesa a May.

—No he empezado esto con intención de molestar a nadie. —Ahora soy yo la que se va por las ramas... y por eso no debería hacer promesas que no puedo cumplir—. Solo quería saber cuál era la participación de mi abuela en esto.

—Y ahora lo sabes, así que asunto terminado. —May asiente con la cabeza para dar énfasis. No estoy segura de a cuál de las dos nos está intentando convencer, si a mí o a ella—. Me he reconciliado con mi pasado. Es una historia que espero no tener que volver a contar. Como ya he dicho, me pensé mejor lo de contarlo todo, aunque fuera a tu abuela. ¿Por qué hacer públicas cosas tan feas hoy? Todos tenemos problemas. Los míos pueden ser distintos de los de algunos, pero los he superado, lo mismo que Lark y Fern y supongo que, aunque nunca conseguimos encontrarlo, mi hermano también. Prefiero pensar que así fue. Él era la única razón por la que quería poner mi historia por escrito, hace años, cuando convencí a tu abuela de que me ayudara con el proyecto. Supongo que pensé que un libro o un artículo en un periódico podría llegarle si seguía vivo, y que si era de los muchos que desaparecieron estando al cuidado de la Asociación de Hogares Infantiles de Tennessee, podría al menos servir de homenaje. Quizá también para mis padres biológicos. No hay lápidas en las que poner flores. Por lo menos yo no las encontré.

—Siento..., siento mucho todo por lo que ha pasado.

Asiente con la cabeza y vuelve a cerrar los ojos, pidiéndome que me calle.

—Ahora necesito descansar. Enseguida vendrán a molestarme, a moverme o a llevarme a esa sala de rehabilitación infernal. Tengo casi noventa años. ¿Se puede saber para qué quiero ganar tono muscular?

Trent ríe.

—Eso mismo decía mi abuelo. De haber sido por él, lo habríamos dejado en una barca a la deriva en el río Edisto.

—Me parece un plan maravilloso. ¿Serías tan amable de buscarme un barco? Así podré volver a Augusta y bajar por el río hasta Savannah.

Cierra los ojos y sonríe un poco. A los pocos instantes, su respiración se alarga y los párpados aletean en sus arrugados ojos. La sonrisa permanece. Me pregunto si vuelve a ser la niñita que navega las aguas turbias del Misisipi a bordo de la casa flotante que construyó su padre.

Trato de imaginar una historia como la suya, haber vivido dos vidas, haber sido, de hecho, dos personas distintas. No soy capaz. Para mí solo ha existido el amparo incondicional del apellido Stafford y una familia que me apoyó, me crio, me dio amor. ¿Cómo sería la vida de May con sus padres adoptivos? Caigo en la cuenta de que no me ha contado esa parte de la historia. Solo ha dicho que, después de una estancia desgarradora en un hogar infantil, su hermana y ella habían sido entregadas a una familia.

¿Por qué se interrumpió ahí? ¿Era el resto demasiado personal?

Aunque ha contestado a la pregunta que vine aquí a hacer y nos ha pedido que no sigamos indagando, no puedo evitar querer saber más.

Trent parece sentir lo mismo. Lógico. El pasado de su familia está vinculado al de May.

Nos quedamos unos minutos junto a la cama mirándola, los dos perdidos en nuestros pensamientos. Luego recogemos las fotografías y salimos de la habitación de mala gana. Ninguno hablamos hasta que estamos donde nadie puede oírnos.

—No sabía eso de mi abuelo —dice.

—Tiene que ser duro enterarse.

Trent frunce el entrecejo.

—Se me hace raro pensar que mi abuelo pasó por una cosa así de niño. Me hace admirarlo aún más, lo que hizo con su vida, la clase de persona que era. Pero también me pone furioso. No puedo evitar preguntarme cómo habría sido su vida si no hubiera estado en el lugar equivocado en el momento equivocado, si sus padres no hubieran sido pobres, si alguien hubiera intervenido en la Asociación de Hogares Infantiles de Tennessee antes de que se lo llevaran. De haber crecido con la familia en la que nació, ¿habría sido la misma persona? ¿Le gustaba tanto el río porque venía de él o porque el padre que lo crio iba a pescar los fines de semana? May dijo que conoció a algunos de sus parientes biológicos. ¿Cómo se sentiría al respecto? ¿Por qué nunca nos presentó a ninguno? Son tantas las preguntas que tengo ahora mismo...

Nos detenemos justo después de cruzar la puerta principal, los dos reacios a separarnos e ir a nuestros respectivos coches. La historia de May nos ha dejado sin excusa para estar juntos. Deberíamos despedirnos, pero tengo la sensación de que hemos formado vínculos y que no deberíamos cortarlos.

—¿Crees que intentarás localizar a alguien de la familia de tu abuelo?

Se mete las manos en los bolsillos del pantalón vaquero y baja la vista a la acera.

—Hace tanto tiempo de eso que no le veo sentido. A estas alturas ya serían familia lejana. Igual por eso mi abuelo no se molestó en intentarlo. Aunque quizá investigue un poco. Me gustaría conocer detalles..., aunque solo sea por Jonah y mis sobrinos. Puede que algún día pregunten y no quiero más secretos.

La conversación decae. Trent se pasa la lengua por el labio como si quisiera decir algo, pero no acabara de decidirse si debe hacerlo o no.

Entonces hablamos los dos a la vez.

—Gracias...

—Avery, sé que...

Por alguna razón a los dos nos hace gracia. La risa afloja un poco la tensión.

—Las damas primero. —Me hace un gesto, como para darme la entrada a lo que estoy a punto de decir. Lo cierto es que no encuentro las palabras adecuadas. Después de lo que hemos vivido estos últimos días, casi me parece inconcebible que esto sea el final. Algo nos une, o al menos eso siento yo.

Quizá estoy siendo una tonta.

—Iba a darte las gracias por todo esto. Por no mandarme a casa con las manos vacías. Sé que romper la promesa que le habías hecho a tu abuelo fue difícil. No... —Nuestras miradas se encuentran. El resto de la frase se desvanece. Me arden las mejillas. Una vez más soy consciente de la química inesperada que hay entre los dos. Pensé que era la emoción de resolver el misterio, pero ahora el misterio está resuelto y el cosquilleo de la fascinación sigue ahí.

Me viene un pensamiento aleatorio, en absoluto buscado, ni deseado. *Igual me estoy equivocando... con Elliot.* Y entonces me doy cuenta de que no es tan aleatorio como parece. Hasta ahora no he estado más que evitando hacerme la pregunta. ¿Estamos Elliot y yo enamorados o simplemente... hemos cumplido los treinta y tenemos la sensación de que ya toca? ¿Lo nuestro es una profunda amistad de muchos años o es pasión? Aunque nos hemos estado diciendo a nosotros mismos que no vamos a dejarnos avasallar por nuestras familias, ¿no lo hemos hecho al final? Me viene a la cabeza un consejo político de Leslie. De pronto me parece la demostración de todo. *Si necesitamos darte un perfil más público, Avery, un anuncio de boda bien organizado nos puede venir muy bien. Aparte de eso, a una mujer joven y guapa no le supone ninguna ventaja estar soltera en Washington, da igual lo mucho que cuide su lenguaje corporal en situaciones sociales. Los lobos necesitan saber que no está disponible oficialmente.*

Intento ahuyentar el pensamiento, pero es como una espiga en la crin de un caballo. Las agujas se enredan en cada mechón. A estas alturas no imagino cambiar de rumbo. Todos, absolutamente todos están esperando un anuncio de boda de un momento a otro. Una ruptura sería... inimaginable. A Honeybee y Bitsy se les rompería el corazón. Social y políticamente yo parecería una veleta, alguien incapaz de decidirse, que no sabe lo que quiere.

¿Es así?

—¿Avery? —Trent entrecierra los ojos y ladea la cabeza. Se está preguntando en qué pienso.

No se lo puedo decir.

—Te toca a ti.

No me atrevo a decir nada más, considerando lo descabellado de mis últimos pensamientos.

—Ya da igual.

—No es justo. En serio, ¿qué ibas a decir?

Se rinde sin resistirse demasiado.

—Siento que empezáramos con mal pie el primer día. No suelo hablar así a los clientes.

—Bueno, yo no era en realidad un cliente, así que tenías disculpa.

Lo cierto es que se portó bastante bien, teniendo en cuenta lo exigente que estuve yo. Soy una Stafford de los pies a la cabeza. Tiendo a dar por hecho que siempre voy a conseguir lo que quiero.

Algo que, ahora me doy cuenta con un escalofrío, me asemeja inquietantemente a los padres adoptivos que financiaron sin saberlo el negocio de Georgia Tann. Sin duda, algunos eran personas decentes y algunos de los niños sí necesitaban un hogar, pero otros, sobre todo aquellos que sabían que se estaban pagando sumas exorbitantes por hijos de encargo, alguna idea debían de tener de lo que ocurría. Pero supusieron que el dinero, el poder y su posición social les daban derecho.

Al pensar esto, me siento culpable. Pienso en todos los privilegios que he tenido, incluido un escaño en el Senado prácticamente regalado.

¿Tengo derecho a todas estas cosas solo por la familia de la que provengo?

Trent vuelve a meterse las manos en los bolsillos, incómodo. Mira su coche y luego a mí otra vez.

—No desaparezcas. Dame un toque la próxima vez que estés en Edisto.

La idea me recuerda al sonido del clarín al comienzo de una cacería campestre, cuando tu caballo tensa los músculos y sabes que, si aflojas las riendas, toda esa energía en potencia se desatará en una dirección.

—Me encantará saber qué más descubres sobre la familia de tu abuelo... Quiero decir, si es que encuentras algo. Pero sin agobios, no quiero parecer entrometida.

—A buenas horas.

Toso, haciéndome la ofendida, pero los dos sabemos que tiene razón.

—Perdóname. Es la abogada que llevo dentro.

—Seguro que es muy buena.

—Lo intento. —Me lleno del orgullo que me produce oír a otra persona hacerme un cumplido sobre algo que me importa. Algo que me he ganado a base de trabajo—. Me gusta que se haga justicia.

—Se nota.

Un coche aparca junto a nosotros. La intrusión nos recuerda que no podemos quedarnos ahí para siempre.

Trent mira por última vez la residencia.

—Da la sensación de que ha vivido mucho.

—Sí, desde luego.

Me duele pensar en May, la amiga de mi abuela, languideciendo día tras día en este sitio. Sin visitas. Sin nadie con quien hablar. Con los nietos viviendo lejos, en una situación familiar compleja. Decididamente voy a ponerme en contacto con Andrew Moore, del comité, a ver si me puede sugerir alguna organización que la ayude.

Suena un claxon y se cierra la portezuela de un coche. El mundo sigue moviéndose y Trent y yo también deberíamos.

El pecho se le hincha y a continuación se le relaja. Su respiración me acaricia el oído cuando se acerca para besarme en la mejilla.

—Gracias, Avery. Me alegro de haber descubierto la verdad.

Su cara sigue cerca de la mía. Huelo aire salobre, champú infantil y una pizca de cieno salino. O quizá son imaginaciones mías.

—Yo también.

—No desaparezcas —repite.

—No lo haré.

Por el rabillo del ojo veo a una mujer que se acerca por la acera. Blusa blanca, tacones, falda negra. Sus pisadas veloces se me antojan inoportunas, fuera de lugar en un día así. Me empiezan a arder las mejillas y me separo de Trent tan bruscamente que me mira desconcertado.

Leslie me ha localizado. No debería haberle pedido a Ian que preguntara por el estado de salud de May por mí. Leslie mete la barbilla mientras nos mira a Trent y a mí. Imagino lo que estará pensando. En realidad no necesito imaginarlo. Lo veo. La escena que acaba de presenciar era íntima.

—Gracias otra vez, Trent. —Intento borrar la impresión que debe de haberse llevado—. Conduce con cuidado.

Doy un paso atrás, junto las manos.

Sus ojos buscan los míos.

—Sí —murmura ladeando la cabeza y mirándome con los ojos entrecerrados. No tiene ni idea de que hay alguien detrás de él o de que el mundo real acaba de irrumpir igual que una galerna.

—Te hemos estado buscando. —Leslie hace notar su presencia sin perder el tiempo en cortesías—. ¿No te funciona el teléfono o es que te estás escondiendo?

Trent se hace a un lado, mira a la jefa de prensa de mi padre y luego a mí.

—Estaba de vacaciones —digo—. Todo el mundo sabía dónde localizarme.

—¿En Edisto? —contesta Leslie con un matiz de sarcasmo. Es evidente que ahora mismo no estoy en Edisto. Dirige otra mirada desconfiada a Trent.

—Sí, bueno... He... —Intento pensar. Estoy sudando debajo del vestido playero de flores que me compré para tener algo limpio que ponerme hoy—. Es una larga historia.

—Bueno, pues me temo que no tenemos tiempo para que me la cuentes. Te necesitan en casa. —Quiere hacer saber a Trent que tenemos trabajo y que su presencia sobra. Funciona. Me dedica una última mirada perpleja y a continuación se disculpa diciendo que tiene que visitar a alguien en Aiken.

—Cuídate, Avery —se despide mientras se dirige hacia su coche.

—Trent... Gracias —le digo. Levanta una mano y saluda sin volverse como queriendo decir que, pase lo que pase aquí, no quiere tener nada que ver.

Me gustaría poder correr detrás de él y al menos disculparme por la intromisión tan brusca de Leslie, pero sé que no debo. No hará más que provocar más preguntas.

—Creo que tenía el móvil apagado —le digo a Leslie antes de que empiece su interrogatorio—. Lo siento. ¿Qué es lo que pasa?

Parpadea despacio, levanta la barbilla.

—Ahora te lo cuento. Primero quiero hablar de lo que he visto cuando venía por esta acera. —Levanta una mano en dirección a Trent y confío en que este se haya alejado ya lo bastante para no oírla—. Porque me ha parecido preocupante.

—Leslie, es un amigo. Me estaba ayudando a localizar información sobre la historia de mi familia, nada más.

—Información sobre tu familia. ¿De verdad? ¿Aquí? —Levanta el mentón y resopla, irritada—. ¿De qué tipo?

—Prefiero no contártelo.

Le relampaguean los ojos. Aprieta los labios hasta que forman una delgada línea. Respira hondo, vuelve a parpadear y me mira furiosa.

—Pues déjame que te diga una cosa. Lo que he visto aquí es exactamente la clase de escena que no te puedes permitir. Nada que pueda ser manipulado, usado o malinterpretado, Avery. Nada. Tienes que ser pura como la nieve virgen y de lejos no me has parecido nada pura. ¿Te imaginas cómo habría quedado algo así en una fotografía? Todos nosotros, el equipo entero, estamos dándolo todo por ti. Por si llega el momento...

—Lo sé. Lo entiendo.

—Lo último que necesita esta familia es abrir otro frente.

—Tomo nota. —Digo las palabras con confianza, pero en mi interior estoy confusa; estoy avergonzada; me humilla tener que vérmelas con Leslie ahora mismo. Me debato entre apaciguarla y salir corriendo detrás de Trent. Me da miedo hasta levantar la vista para comprobar si ha llegado ya al coche.

El motor arranca y eso contesta a mi pregunta. Lo oigo salir marcha atrás y alejarse. *Probablemente es lo mejor,* me digo. *Por supuesto que lo es.* Tenía mi vida entera planeada antes de ir a Edisto. ¿Por qué iba a querer ponerla en peligro por... el pasado remoto de mi familia, cosas que ya no importan, un hombre al que no me une nada excepto una historia que hasta quienes la vivieron prefieren olvidar?

—Hay novedades. —Tardo un momento en asimilar las palabras de Leslie, a pesar de que la estoy mirando—. *The Sentinel* acaba de publicar un reportaje larguísimo sobre centros de mayores propiedad de corporaciones y exención de responsabilidades. Es cuestión de tiempo que los medios de comunicación nacionales se hagan eco. El artículo hacía hincapié en los casos de Carolina del Sur. Tienen costes comparativos entre Magnolia Manor y la clase de centros que se han mencionado en algunas demandas por daños y perjuicios. Tienen fotografías de las víctimas y sus familiares. Lo han titulado «Envejecer en desigualdad de condiciones» y el artículo empieza con una fotografía de lejos de tu padre y tu abuela paseando por los jardines de Magnolia Manor.

La miro boquiabierta mientras una furia febril me enciende por dentro.

—¿Cómo se atreven? ¿Cómo se atreve nadie? No tienen ningún derecho a acosar a mi abuela.

—Es política, Avery. Política y sensacionalismo. Aquí no hay terreno vedado.

20

RILL

El hombre se llama Darren y la mujer, Victoria, pero nos han dicho que los llamemos papá y mamá, no Darren y Victoria, ni señor y señora Sevier. No me molesta demasiado. Nunca he llamado papá o mamá a nadie, así que esas palabras no ocupan ningún lugar en mí. Son solo palabras. Nada más.

Queenie y Briny siguen siendo nuestros padres y vamos a volver con ellos, en cuanto sepa cómo. No será tan difícil como pensé que podría ser. La casa de los Sevier es grande y está llena de habitaciones que nadie usa, y en la parte de atrás hay un porche amplio que da a campos de altos árboles y hierba verde, y todo forma una pendiente que conduce a lo mejor de todo: el agua. No es el río; es un brazo muerto largo y delgado que termina en un lago llamado Dedmen's Slough..., y Dedmen's Slough llega hasta el Misisipi. Esto lo sé porque le pregunté a Zuma, que limpia la casa y cocina y vive encima de la vieja cochera donde el señor Sevier aparca sus automóviles. Tiene tres. Nunca he conocido a nadie que tenga tres automóviles.

El marido de Zuma, Hoy, y su hija, Hootsie, viven ahí con ella. Hoy cuida el jardín y el gallinero, los perros de caza del señor Sevier que ladran y aúllan toda la noche y un poni que la señora Sevier lleva diciéndonos ya dos semanas que podemos montar si queremos. Le dije que no nos gustan los ponis, aunque no es verdad. Le advertí a Fern que no dijera lo contrario.

El marido de Zuma da miedo, es grande y negro como el betún y después de vivir en casa de la señora Murphy no quiero que ningún jardinero nos lleve a Fern o a mí a ninguna parte. No quiero que estemos solas con el señor Sevier. También él ha intentado llevarnos a montar en poni, pero solo porque la señora Sevier lo obligó. Él hará cualquier cosa con tal de evitar que la señora Sevier se vaya por el camino del jardín donde los dos niños que nacieron muertos y tres que no llegaron a nacer tienen sus tumbas adornadas con corderitos de piedra. Cuando la señora Sevier va allí, se tumba en el suelo y llora. Luego vuelve a la casa y se mete en la cama y no se levanta. Tiene cicatrices en las muñecas. Yo sé por qué las tiene, pero no se lo cuento a Fern, claro.

—Tú siéntate en su regazo y déjala que te peine y juegue contigo a las muñecas. Asegúrate de que es feliz —le digo a Fern—. Nada de llorar ni de mojar la cama, ¿me oyes?

Esa es la única razón por la que los Sevier me trajeron aquí, porque Fern no dejaba de llorar, de mojar la cama y de quejarse.

Hasta ahora y en general, Fern lo está haciendo bastante bien. Pero algunos días no hay nada que ayude a la señora Sevier. Algunos días no quiere que la toque absolutamente nadie. Solo quiere a los muertos.

Cuando se tumba en la cama a llorar por los hijos que perdió, el señor Sevier se esconde en su sala de música y nosotras tenemos que estar con Zuma, que piensa que tenernos en la casa le supone demasiado trabajo. La señora Sevier antes le compraba cosas a la hijita de Zuma, Hootsie, que tiene diez años, dos menos que yo. Pero ahora la señora Sevier nos compra cosas a nosotras. A Zuma eso no le hace ninguna gracia. Le ha sonsacado información suficiente a Fern para saber de dónde somos y no entiende para qué quieren unas personas tan finas como el señor y la señora Sevier a unas vagabundas del río como nosotras. Nos lo dice bien claro, pero nunca cuando la señora Sevier pueda oírla, claro.

Zuma no se atreve a pegarnos, pero le gustaría. Cuando Hootsie se porta mal, Zuma le da una buena zurra. A veces, cuando nadie nos ve, Zuma nos mira agitando el cucharón largo de madera y nos dice: «Deberíais estar agradecidas. Deberíais estar besándole los pies a la señora por dejaros estar en esta casa tan buena. Pero yo sé quiénes sois, eso no lo olvidéis. Estáis aquí solo hasta que la señora tenga su propio hijo. El señor cree que, si deja de preocuparse tanto, lo tendrá. Cuando lo tenga, vosotras, alimañas del río, os largaréis. Con el resto de escoria blanca. Solo estáis aquí de momento. No os acostumbréis. Solo para que lo sepáis, esto yo ya lo he vivido. No os vais a quedar mucho tiempo».

Tiene razón, así que no veo motivos para llevarle la contraria. Por lo menos aquí hay comida, y mucha. Hay vestidos de volantes, aunque pican y están tiesos, y cintas para el pelo, y lápices de colores y libros y zapatos merceditas nuevos y relucientes. Hay un juego de té pequeñito para jugar a tomar té con pastas por las tardes. Nunca habíamos jugado a tomar el té, así que la señora Sevier nos tiene que enseñar.

No hay que hacer cola para bañarse. No tenemos que desnudarnos mientras otras personas nos miran. Nadie nos da pescozones. Nadie nos amenaza con atarnos ni dejarnos en un armario. A nadie lo encierran en el sótano. Al menos no de momento, y, como dice Zuma, no estaremos aquí el tiempo suficiente para saber si lo harán una vez que se haya pasado la novedad.

De lo único que estoy segura es de que, cuando los Sevier se cansen de nosotras, no vamos a volver a casa de la señora Murphy. Por las noches, cuando estoy a salvo en mi dormitorio, contiguo al de Fern, miro hacia los prados y veo el agua a través de los árboles. Busco faros en el brazo muerto y veo algunos. A veces veo luces, incluso a lo lejos, en el lago, flotando como estrellas fugaces. Lo único que tengo que hacer es conseguir llegar a uno de los barcos y luego podremos cruzar Dedmen's Slough hasta el gran río. Una vez allí, será fácil bajar hasta donde el Wolf se encuentra con el Misisipi en la isla de Mud, y allí es donde nos estarán esperando Queenie y Briny.

Solo necesito conseguir una barca y lo haré. Cuando nos hayamos ido, los Sevier no tendrán la más mínima idea de lo que nos ha pasado. La señorita Tann no les dijo que somos del río y me apuesto a que Zuma tampoco. Nuestros nuevos padres creen que nuestra madre de verdad era una universitaria y nuestro padre, un profesor. Creen que ella enfermó de neumonía y se murió y él se quedó sin trabajo y no podía mantenernos. También creen que Fern no tiene más que tres años, pero tiene cuatro.

No les cuento a los Sevier la verdad. Lo único que hago es intentar portarme bien para que no pase nada antes de que Fern y yo podamos escapar.

—Ahí estáis —dice la señora Sevier cuando nos encuentra sentadas a la mesa esperando para desayunar. Frunce el ceño al ver que ya nos hemos puesto la ropa que nos dejaron preparada anoche. Fern lleva unos pantalones de cuadros azules con una blusita que se abrocha en la espalda. Tiene las mangas abullonadas y le deja a la vista la barriguita debajo del encaje del borde inferior. Yo llevo un vestido violeta lleno de puntillas y un poco estrecho por la parte de arriba. Tuve que contener la respiración para abrochármelo, y no debería, pero estoy creciendo, supongo. Queenie dice que los niños Foss damos estirones de un día para otro.

Así que o he dado un estirón o es que aquí comemos muchas más cosas que gachas de maíz. Cada mañana nos sentamos todos a una mesa llena de comida y para el almuerzo Zuma nos sirve emparedados en una bandeja. Por la noche también cenamos mucho, a no ser que el señor Sevier esté ocupado en su sala de música. Cuando pasa eso, volvemos a comer emparedados en una bandeja y la señora Sevier juega con nosotras a juegos de mesa, que a Fern le encantan.

—May, te dije que no tienes por qué madrugar tanto y vestir también a la pequeña Beth. —Cruza los brazos sobre la bata de seda, que parece una túnica de las que lleva Cleopatra. Fern y yo tenemos batas a juego. Nuestra nueva mamá le mandó a Zuma que nos las hiciera especialmente. No nos las hemos puesto. Creo que es mejor que no nos acostumbremos a las cosas elegantes, puesto que no nos vamos a quedar mucho tiempo.

Aparte de que me están saliendo dos bultitos en el pecho y las batas son tan brillantes y finas que se me marcan y no quiero que nadie los vea.

—Hemos esperado… un rato. —Me miro el regazo. No entiende que llevamos toda la vida levantándonos al amanecer. No se puede vivir de otra manera en un barco. Cuando el río se despierta, tú también. Los pájaros hablan y los barcos silban y las olas rompen una detrás de otra si el barco está fondeado cerca de un canal grande. También hay que vigilar los sedales y los peces que pican y hay que encender la estufa. Hay cosas que hacer.

—Ya es hora de que aprendáis a dormir hasta una hora decente. —La señora Sevier me mira moviendo la cabeza y no sé si está bromeando o si no le gusto demasiado—. Ya no estáis en un orfanato, May. Esta es vuestra casa.

—Sí, señora.

—Sí, mamá. —Me pone una mano en la cabeza y se inclina para besar a Fern en la mejilla, luego hace como que le come la oreja. Fern se ríe y suelta un gritito.

—Sí, mamá —repito. No me sale natural, pero voy mejorando. La próxima vez lo recordaré.

Se sienta en el extremo de la mesa y mira hacia el largo pasillo mientras apoya la barbilla en una mano y frunce el ceño.

—¿No habéis visto a papá esta mañana?

—No..., mamá.

Fern se encoge en su silla y mira el ceño fruncido de nuestra nueva mamá con preocupación. Todos sabemos dónde está el señor Sevier. Oímos la música que llega por el pasillo. Se supone que no debe meterse en la sala de música antes del desayuno. Los hemos oído discutir por eso.

—¡Darreeeeen! —grita tamborileando en la mesa con las uñas.

Fern se tapa los oídos y Zuma llega corriendo con una salsera de porcelana con tapa que le tiembla en las manos. La tapa casi se cae al suelo antes de que le dé tiempo a cogerla. Tiene los ojos muy abiertos y se le ve mucho el blanco, hasta que se da cuenta de que la señora Sevier no está enfadada con ella.

—Voy a llamarlo, señora. —Deja la salsera en la mesa y grita en dirección a la cocina—: ¡Hootsie, trae las fuentes antes de que se enfríen!

Pasa junto a la mesa tiesa como un palo de escoba y me mira furiosa cuando nuestra nueva mamá no la ve. Antes de que viniéramos, Zuma no tenía que manchar tantos platos para desayunar. Solo tenía que preparar una bandeja y llevarla al dormitorio de la señora Sevier. Me lo ha contado Hootsie. Antes de que viniéramos, a veces Hootsie se pasaba la mañana entera en el piso de arriba con la señora, hojeando la revista *Life* y libros con dibujos tratando de distraerla para que el señor Sevier pudiera trabajar.

Ahora Hootsie tiene que ayudar en la cocina y es culpa nuestra.

Cuando viene a traer los huevos, mete un pie debajo de la mesa y me pisa los dedos.

Al cabo de un minuto viene Zuma con el señor Sevier. Es la única que consigue sacarlo de la sala de música cuando tiene la puerta cerrada. Crio al señor Sevier cuando era un niño y sigue cuidándolo como si todavía lo fuera. Él la obedece más que a la señora Sevier.

—¡Tiene que comer! —dice mientras lo sigue por el pasillo agitando las manos en las sombras de la mañana—. He hecho un montón de comida y ahora se está quedando fría.

—Me he despertado temprano con una melodía en la cabeza. Tenía que ponerme a trabajar antes de que se me fuera. —El señor Sevier se detiene al final del pasillo, se lleva una mano al estómago y sube la otra. Da unos pasos de baile, como si fuera un actor subido a un escenario. Luego nos hace una reverencia—. Buenos días, señoras.

El ceño de la señora Sevier se frunce un poco más.

—Ya sabes en qué quedamos, Darren. No antes de desayunar y las comidas se hacen a la mesa, todos juntos. ¿Cómo van a aprender las niñas a ser una familia si te pasas el día encerrado y solo?

El señor Sevier no se para en su silla, sino que rodea la mesa y la besa en los labios.

—¿Cómo está mi musa esta mañana?

—No empieces —se queja ella—. Ya estás intentando engatusarme.

—¿Y lo estoy consiguiendo?

Le guiña un ojo a Fern y esta ríe, yo hago como que no he visto nada. Algo me oprime dentro del pecho y me pongo a mirar mi plato y veo a Briny besando a Queenie de esa misma manera cuando cruzaba el barco para ir a la cubierta de popa.

De pronto la comida no huele tan bien, aunque el estómago me ruge de hambre. No quiero comerme el desayuno de estas personas ni reírme con sus chistes ni llamarlas «mamá» y «papá». Yo ya tengo mamá y papá y quiero irme a casa con ellos.

Y Fern no debería reírse ni seguir la corriente a estas personas. No está bien.

Le pellizco la pierna debajo de la mesa y da un pequeño aullido.

Nuestros nuevos mamá y papá nos miran tratando de averiguar qué ha pasado. Fern no se lo dice.

Zuma y Hootsie traen el resto de la comida y desayunamos mientras el señor Sevier nos habla de su nueva música y de cómo le llegó la melodía en mitad de la noche. Habla de partituras y notas y de muchas otras cosas. La señora Sevier suspira y mira por la ventana, pero yo no puedo evitar escuchar. Nunca he oído nada sobre cómo se escribe música en un papel. Las canciones que me sé son de escuchar a Briny tocar la guitarra o la armónica o incluso a veces el piano en unos billares. La música siempre me llega muy adentro y me hace sentir de una manera especial.

Ahora me pregunto si Briny sabía que hay personas que escriben melodías en un papel como si fuera un libro de cuentos y luego salen en películas, como explica el señor Sevier. Su música nueva es para una película. Sentado a la cabecera de la mesa, agita las manos en el aire y habla nervioso y emocionado de una escena en que los guerrilleros confederados de William Quantrill cruzan Kansas a caballo y queman una ciudad entera.

Tararea la melodía y usa la mesa de tambor y los platos tiemblan y me imagino los caballos galopando y el estruendo de los rifles.

—¿Qué te parece, cariño? —le dice a la señora Sevier cuando termina.

Esta aplaude y lo mismo hace Fern.

—Una obra maestra —responde la señora Sevier—. Por supuesto que es una obra maestra. ¿A que sí, Bethie?

No consigo acostumbrarme a que llamen a Fern «Beth», que creen que es su verdadero nombre, claro.

—*Oba maeta.* —Fern intenta decir «obra maestra» con la boca llena de gachas.

Los tres ríen y yo me limito a bajar la vista al plato.

—Qué alegría verla tan contenta. —Nuestra nueva mamá se inclina sobre la mesa y le retira a Fern el pelo de la cara para que no se lo manche de gachas.

—Desde luego. —El señor Sevier está mirando a su mujer, pero ella no lo sabe. Está ocupada haciendo carantoñas a Fern.

La señora Sevier se enrosca el pelo de Fern en el dedo uniendo mechones rizados hasta formar tirabuzones grandes como los de Shirley Temple. Así es como le gusta que lo lleve. La mayoría de los días yo me hago una trenza a la espalda para no darle ideas y que no quiera hacer lo mismo conmigo.

—Me preocupaba que no llegáramos a este punto —le dice a su marido.

—Estas cosas llevan tiempo.

—Tenía tanto miedo de no llegar nunca a ser madre...

El señor Sevier levanta la vista al cielo, como si estuviera contento. Mira hacia la mesa.

—Es nuestra.

¡No lo es!, quiero gritar. *No eres nuestra madre. Tus hijos son esos niños muertos del cementerio.* Odio a la señora Sevier por querer quedarse a Fern. Odio a esos niños por haberse

muerto. Odio al señor Sevier por traernos aquí. Si nos hubiera dejado tranquilas, a estas alturas estaríamos de vuelta en el *Arcadia* Fern y yo. Nadie estaría haciéndole tirabuzones a lo Shirley Temple ni la llamaría Beth.

Aprieto tanto los dientes que el dolor me sube hasta la cabeza. Me alegro. Es un dolor pequeño y sé de dónde viene. Puedo pararlo cuando quiera. El dolor de mi corazón es mucho más grande. No puedo quitármelo por mucho que lo intente. Me da tanto miedo que no me deja ni respirar.

¿Y si Fern decide que le gustan más estas personas que yo? ¿Y si se olvida de Briny y de Queenie y del Arcadia? Allí no teníamos vestidos bonitos ni juguetes de cuerda en el porche, ni osos de peluche, lápices de colores y juegos de té en miniatura. Solo teníamos el río, pero el río nos alimentaba y nos hacía libres.

Tengo que asegurarme de que Fern no se olvida. No puede convertirse en Beth por dentro.

—¿May? —La señora Fern me está hablando y no la he oído. Pongo cara alegre y la miro.

—¿Sí..., mamá?

—Decía que voy a llevarme a Beth a Memphis para que le hagan unos zapatos especiales. Es importante que le corrijamos la pierna que mete hacia dentro antes de que crezca más. Una vez que un niño crece, es demasiado tarde, me han dicho. Y sería una pena, cuando es algo que tiene remedio. —Ladea un poco la cabeza, parece un águila buscando peces. Bonita, pero a los peces más les vale tener cuidado. Me alegro de tener los pies debajo de la mesa porque así no me puede ver la pierna derecha. Todos tenemos un pie un poco torcido hacia dentro. Lo hemos heredado de Queenie. Briny dice que es la marca de linaje del reino de *Arcadia*.

Ahora lo enderezo, no sea que a la señora Sevier se le ocurra mirar.

—Por la noche tendrá que dormir con un aparato ortopédico —me dice la señora Sevier. A su lado, el señor Sevier abre el periódico y lo lee por encima mientras se come el tocino.

—Ah —murmuro. *Por la noche se lo quitaré. Eso haré.*

—Había pensado llevarla yo sola. —La señora Sevier habla muy despacio y sus ojos azul intenso me miran fijamente bajo unos rizos rubios que me recuerdan a Queenie aunque no quiera. Claro que Queenie es muchísimo más guapa. Lo es—. Beth tiene que acostumbrarse a pasar tiempo con su nueva mamá, las dos solas..., sin protestar.

Sonríe a mi hermana, que está ocupada intentando pescar una de las fresas en conserva de Zuma en el plato con un tenedorcito de plata. A los Sevier no les gusta que nadie coma con los dedos.

La señora Sevier da una palmada para llamar la atención del señor Sevier y este baja un poco el periódico y asoma la nariz.

—Darren. Pero, Darren, ¡mírala! ¡Mira qué monería!

—Sigue así, soldado —dice el señor Sevier—. Cuando captures esa, te daremos otra.

Fern pincha la fresa, se la mete entera en la boca y sonríe mientras le chorrea jugo por las comisuras de la boca.

Nuestros nuevos papás se ríen. La señora Sevier le limpia el carrillo a Fern con una servilleta para que no se estropee la blusa.

Intento decidir si debo suplicar que me lleven al médico de los zapatos o no. Me da miedo que se lleve a Fern. Le comprará cosas y Fern se encariñará con ella. Pero no quiero ir a Memphis. Mi último recuerdo de Memphis es cuando la señora Murphy me llevó al centro y me entregó a mi nuevo papá en la habitación de un hotel.

Si me quedo en casa cuando no esté la señora Sevier, seguramente podré salir y explorar un poco. Casi nunca nos deja salir. Le da miedo que cojamos hiedra venenosa o que nos muerda una serpiente. No puede saber que los niños del río aprendemos todas esas cosas desde que somos lo bastante mayores para caminar.

—Pronto empezarás el colegio. —A nuestra nueva mamá no le ha gustado que no le haya contestado sobre lo de llevarse a Fern al médico—. Beth es demasiado pequeña, claro. Pasará dos años en casa antes de ir al jardín de infancia..., si es que va. Igual me la quedo un año más. Dependerá... —Se lleva una mano esbelta al estómago y se lo acaricia despacio. No lo dice, pero espera que haya un niño dentro.

Intento no pensar en eso. E intento no pensar tampoco en el colegio. Cuando vaya, la señora Sevier tendrá todo el día a Fern para ella. Fern la querrá más a ella que a mí, estoy segura. Tenemos que irnos de aquí antes de que eso pase.

La señora Sevier carraspea y su marido vuelve a dejar el periódico.

—¿Qué planes tienes para hoy, cariño? —le pregunta ella.

—Componer, por supuesto. Quiero terminar la partitura nueva mientras la tengo fresca en la cabeza. Luego llamaré a Stanley y le tocaré un trozo por teléfono..., a ver si le gusta para la película.

La señora Sevier suspira y le salen arrugas alrededor de los ojos.

—Había pensado que tal vez podías decirle a Hoy que enganchara al poni y así salíais los dos a dar un paseo. —Nos mira a mí y al señor Sevier—. ¿Te gustaría, May? Si papá te acompaña no te dará miedo el poni. Es hembra y es muy buena. Yo tuve una como ella cuando era pequeña, en Augusta. Era lo que más me gustaba del mundo entero.

Se me tensan los músculos y se me enfría la cara. No me da miedo el poni. Me da miedo el señor Sevier. No porque me haya hecho nada, sino porque después de vivir en casa de la señora Murphy sé lo que puede pasar.

—No quiero dar trabajo.

Me sudan las manos y me las seco en el vestido.

—Hum... —El señor Sevier baja las cejas. La idea le gusta tan poco como a mí y me alegro—. Veremos cómo se me da el día, cariño. La producción de la película va tan retrasada que me han dado menos plazo del normal y con el caos que ha habido en casa estas últimas semanas por... —Su mujer levanta la barbilla, hace un ligero movimiento de negación con la cabeza y el señor Sevier se interrumpe—. Veremos cómo va el día.

Me miro el regazo y no vuelve a hablarse del paseo en poni. Terminamos de desayunar y el señor Sevier desaparece en su sala de música lo más deprisa que puede. Muy pronto Fern y la señora Sevier se han ido también. Cojo los lápices de colores y un libro y me siento en el amplio porche que da a los árboles y al lago. Del estudio del señor Sevier sale música de piano. Se mezcla con el canto de los pájaros y cierro los ojos y espero a que Zuma y Hootsie se vayan a la cochera para escabullirme y echar un vistazo por los alrededores...

Me quedo dormida y sueño que Fern y yo estamos en el muelle de pesca del señor Sevier. Estamos sentadas en una de esas maletas grandes que guardan en la despensa, cerca de los cepillos y escobas de Zuma, y la hemos llenado de juguetes para Camellia, Lark y Gabion. Estamos esperando a que Queenie y Briny vengan a recogernos.

El *Arcadia* aparece al final del brazo muerto. Avanza contra corriente muy despacio. Entonces, de pronto, el viento lo impulsa y lo aleja. Me vuelvo y veo un automóvil negro que cruza traqueteando el prado a nuestra espalda. La cara de la señorita Tann está pegada al cristal de la ventanilla. Le hierven los ojos de furia. Cojo a Fern e intentamos llegar al agua para escapar nadando.

Echamos a correr, pero, cuanto más corremos, más lejos está el embarcadero.

El automóvil se detiene en el muelle justo detrás de nosotras. Una mano me coge por el vestido y por el pelo.

«Eres una sinvergüenza y una ingrata», dice la señorita Tann.

Me despierto de un salto y veo a Hootsie con un vaso de té y un plato de comida para mí. Los deja con brusquedad en la mesa de mimbre. La bebida salpica la bandeja y el plato.

—Ahora estará como la comida del río, ¿verdad? Bien remojadita.

Me sonríe guiñando los ojos.

Cojo el emparedado mojado, doy un mordisco grande y le devuelvo la sonrisa. Hootsie no tiene ni idea de cómo vivíamos antes de venir aquí. Puedo comer gachas de maíz con gorgojos sin pensármelo dos veces. Un emparedado mojado de té no me va a hacer perder los estribos. Ni tampoco Hootsie, por mucho que lo intente. No es dura. Yo sí que conozco chicos duros.

Resopla y levanta la nariz, y se va. Cuando termino de comer, tapo el plato con una servilleta para que no vengan moscas. Luego voy por el largo porche hasta la sala de música. Ahora hay silencio, pero tengo cuidado cuando llego al final de la casa y doblo la esquina. No hay ni rastro del señor Sevier. Antes de acercarme, miro bien.

Cuando cruzo la puerta mosquitera, su sala de música está en penumbra, con las cortinas completamente echadas. En un rincón, un proyector dibuja un cuadrado blanco de luz en la pared. Me hace pensar en los espectáculos de cine ambulante que ponían en los pueblos junto al río. Me acerco y veo mi sombra, larga y delgada, con pedacitos rizados de luz que brillan a través del pelo. Pienso en cuando a veces Briny hacía sombras chinescas en la luz de la ventana del *Arcadia*. Intento hacer una, pero no me sale.

Junto al proyector, una aguja se mueve atrás y adelante sobre un disco de un fonógrafo. Un sonido suave, áspero, sale del lado del armario en que se encuentra. Voy hasta él, bajo la vista y miro el círculo negro dar vueltas. Durante un tiempo tuvimos uno de estos en el porche trasero del barco, pero era de manivela. Briny lo encontró en una casa vieja junto al río donde ya no vivía nadie.

Poco después lo cambió por leña.

Me digo que no debería tocarlo, pero no puedo evitarlo. Es la cosa más bonita que he visto en mi vida. Tiene que ser nuevecito.

Cojo la bola plateada que sujeta la aguja y la muevo hacia atrás solo un poquito, de manera que vuelve a sonar el último trocito de música. Luego la muevo otra vez, y otra. Está puesto bajito, así que supongo que no lo oirá nadie más.

Al cabo de un minuto voy hasta el piano y pienso en cuando Briny y yo nos sentábamos en los billares o en los barcos con espectáculo cuando no había nadie. Me enseñaba a tocar melodías. De todos los hermanos, yo era a la que se le daba mejor aprenderlas; eso decía Briny.

La música del fonógrafo se termina y la aguja araña el disco.

Encuentro las notas del piano sin hacer nada de ruido. Solo pulso las teclas un poco. Descifrar la música no es muy difícil. Me gusta, así que vuelvo a mover la aguja y toco un poco más. Esa parte es más difícil, así que tengo que esforzarme más, pero al final también lo consigo.

—¡Bravo!

Salto y veo al señor Sevier con una mano en la puerta mosquitera. La suelta y aplaude. Me levanto enseguida de la banqueta del piano y busco un sitio donde esconderme.

—Perdón. No tenía... —Se me forman lágrimas en la garganta. ¿Y si le he hecho enfadar y se lo cuenta a la señora Sevier y se desembarazan de mí antes de que Fern y yo podamos llegar al río y volver a casa?

Entra y cierra la puerta.

—No te preocupes. No vas a hacer daño al piano. Pero Victoria estaba decidida a que saliéramos con el poni mientras no está. Le he pedido a Hoy que lo enganche. Van a venir unas personas a construir una casita junto al lago, un sitio tranquilo donde pueda trabajar cuando haya demasiado barullo en la casa. Iremos en el coche, echaremos un vistazo y luego daremos un paseo por la finca. Cuando volvamos, te enseñaré a...

Se adentra unos pasos más en la habitación.

—Aunque, ¿sabes qué? Ahora que lo pienso, al poni no le importará esperar. Es muy paciente. —El señor Sevier hace un gesto con la mano en dirección al piano—. Repite eso.

Las lágrimas se me van secando en la garganta. Me trago lo que queda de ellas mientras el señor Sevier va hasta el fonógrafo.

—A ver, lo pongo otra vez. ¿Cuánto puedes tocar?

Me encojo de hombros.

—No lo sé. No mucho. Primero lo tengo que escuchar fijándome mucho.

Pone el disco un poco antes de lo que lo había puesto yo, pero pienso rápido y lo acierto casi todo.

—¿Has tocado antes? —pregunta.

—No, señor.

Retrocede más con la aguja y lo repetimos. Solo me equivoco en un trocito de la parte nueva.

—Impresionante —dice.

No lo es, pero me gusta mucho oírselo decir. Al mismo tiempo me pregunto: *¿Qué quiere? No necesita que le toque el piano. Ya lo toca él muy bien. Mejor incluso que el disco del fonógrafo.*

—Otra vez. —Gira la mano una vez más—. Pero toca de memoria.

Lo hago, pero algo sale mal.

—Ups —dice—. ¿Te has dado cuenta?

—Sí, señor.

—Porque es un sostenido. —Señala el piano—. Si quieres, te lo enseño.

Asiento con la cabeza, me vuelvo hacia el piano y pongo los dedos en las teclas.

—No, así. —Se inclina hacia mí a mi espalda y me enseña a extender la mano—. El do con el pulgar. Tienes dedos delgados y largos. Manos de pianista.

Son las manos de Briny, pero eso el señor Sevier no lo sabe.

Me toca los dedos uno a uno. Las teclas tocan la melodía. Me enseña cómo tocar el sostenido en el que me equivocaba.

—Es así —explica—. ¿Oyes la diferencia?

Digo que sí con la cabeza.

—¡Sí! Sí lo oigo.

—Y ahora ¿sabes dónde va esa nota? —pregunta—. Quiero decir en la melodía.

—Sí, señor.

—Muy bien. —Antes de que me dé tiempo a pensar, se ha sentado a mi lado—. Tú vas a tocar la melodía y yo los acordes. Verás cómo combinan. Así es como se compone una pieza, como la que has oído en el disco.

Hago lo que dice y él toca las teclas de su lado ¡y sonamos igual que en el disco! Siento cómo la música sale del piano y se desliza a través de mi cuerpo. Ahora ya sé lo que sienten los pájaros cuando cantan.

—¿Podemos tocarla otra vez? —digo cuando llegamos al final—. ¿Un trozo más largo?

Quiero más y más y más.

Pone el disco y me ayuda a encontrar las teclas y luego tocamos juntos. Cuando terminamos, se está riendo y yo también.

—Deberíamos pensar en buscarte unas clases —dice—. Tienes talento.

Le miro con mucha atención para ver si está bromeando. *¿Talento? ¿Yo?*

Me tapo la sonrisa con la mano, bajo la vista a las teclas y me arden las mejillas. *¿Lo dice de verdad?*

—No lo diría si no fuera verdad, May. Puede que no sepa mucho de criar a niñas pequeñas, pero de música sí entiendo. —Se acerca a mí para intentar verme la cara—. Entiendo que debe de ser difícil para ti venir a una casa nueva, a tu edad..., pero creo que tú y yo podemos ser amigos.

De pronto estoy de vuelta en la casa de la señora Murphy, en la oscuridad como boca de lobo, y el señor Riggs me tiene atrapada entre él y la pared y se pega mucho contra mí, dejándome sin aire, sin sensación en el cuerpo. El olor a whisky y a carbonilla me sube por la nariz y susurra: *T-tú y yo p-podemos ser amigos. P-puedo darte pastillas de m-menta y ga-galletas. L-lo que quieras. P-podemos ser muy b-buenos amigos...*

Salto de la banqueta y golpeo las teclas tan fuerte que unas cuantas suenan a la vez. El ruido se mezcla con el sonido de mis zapatos chocando contra el suelo.

No dejo de correr hasta que estoy en el piso de arriba hecha un ovillo dentro de mi armario con los pies contra la puerta para que no pueda entrar nadie.

21

AVERY

Cuando el clan Stafford cierra filas somos una fuerza formidable. Durante casi tres semanas ya, nos hemos parapetado y repelido los ataques de la prensa, cuyo objetivo es retratarnos como unos elitistas delincuentes porque hemos elegido una residencia de mayores de lujo para mi abuela, quien, por cierto, puede permitírselo. No estamos pidiendo a los ciudadanos que paguen los recibos..., que es lo que me entran ganas de decir a cada reportero que nos acosa con un micrófono cuando vamos a actos públicos, reuniones, compromisos sociales..., incluso a la iglesia.

De vuelta de acompañar a mis padres a misa seguida de *brunch* dominical, veo a mis hermanas en uno de los *paddocks* de las yeguas de cría con los trillizos de Allison. Courtney va a lomos de Doughboy, un hermoso rucio que lleva a medio galope. Monta a pelo y, mientras aparco, imagino el ritmo del caballo. Los músculos que se tensan y relajan, el ancho lomo que sube y baja.

—¡Hola, tía Aves! ¿Te vienes a dar una vuelta? —me pregunta Courtney esperanzada mientras camino hacia la cerca—. Luego me llevas a casa.

Estoy a punto de decir: «Déjame ir a por unos vaqueros», pero la madre de Courtney se me adelanta:

—¡Court, tienes que prepararte para el campamento!

—Jooo, mamá —se queja mi sobrina, y a continuación se aleja al trote.

Entro en el *paddock* y cruzo el pasto con mis tacones altos. En la parte opuesta de la cerca, los niños lo pasan en grande metiendo flores y briznas de hierba entre los listones de madera para que los potrillos nuevos los olisqueen. Allison y Missy sacan fotografías sin parar con sus iPhones. Los pantalones cortos de lino y las pajaritas de los chicos no están tan prístinos como en la iglesia.

Missy se agacha y achucha a uno de los niños mientras lo ayuda a arrancar una flor silvestre.

—Ay... Echo de menos esto —dice soñadora. Sus adolescentes están ya en el campamento de verano de Asheville al que fuimos durante toda nuestra infancia. Court se va mañana para una estancia más corta.

—Pues te alquilo a estos tres gamberros cuando quieras. —Allison abre los ojos esperanzada mientras se sujeta la melena caoba detrás de la oreja—. Cuando quieras, de verdad. Ni siquiera tienes que llevarte a los tres. Con uno o dos me conformo.

Reímos las tres. Es un momento agradable, sin estrés. Las últimas semanas nos han tenido a todos hechos un manojo de nervios.

—¿Qué tal papá en el *brunch*?

Como de costumbre, Missy vuelve a los asuntos prácticos.

—Bien, creo. Se han quedado hablando con unos amigos. Espero que mamá le haga echarse un rato en cuanto llegue a casa. Más tarde tenemos una cena.

Mi padre está decidido a seguir con el ritmo de siempre, pero la polémica sobre la abuela Judy lo está desgastando. Que su madre se haya convertido en blanco de las últimas refriegas políticas le resulta difícil de sobrellevar. El senador Stafford sabe defenderse cuando lo atacan a él, pero, cuando su familia queda atrapada en el fuego cruzado, la presión sanguínea se le dispara.

Los días en que tiene que llevar la bomba de quimioterapia sujeta a la pierna da la impresión de que el peso añadido va a derribarlo en cualquier momento.

—Pues nos iremos pronto, antes de que lleguen. —Allison mira hacia el camino de entrada—. Solo quería sacar unas fotos de los potrillos y los niños con la ropa de los domingos. Leslie piensa que un posado de niños Stafford con crías de animal en las noticias de sociedad puede gustar a la prensa. Algo inocente y mono.

—A mí, si fuera periodista, desde luego me encantaría.

Beso a uno de mis sobrinos en la cabeza y me acaricia cariñoso la cara con las manitas sucias de hierba.

—Eh, tía Aves. ¡Mira esto! —Courtney hace saltar un pequeño obstáculo a Doughboy.

—¡Courtney, sin silla ni casco no! —grita Allison.

—Esa chica se parece a mí —digo.

—Sí. Demasiado. —Missy me empuja suavemente con el hombro.

—No tengo ni idea de a qué te refieres.

La nariz recta de Allison se arruga.

—Claro que lo sabes.

—Vamos, Al. Déjala quedarse y montar un rato. —No puedo evitar intervenir a favor de Court. Además, tengo algo de tiempo libre y dar una vuelta a caballo suena apetecible—. Te la llevo a casa en una hora... o dos. Luego ya puede hacer el equipaje para el campamento.

Court hace saltar de nuevo a Doughboy.

—¡Courtney Lynne! —la reprende Allison.

Estoy a punto de decir que no son más que obstáculos pequeñitos y que además Courtney monta a caballo igual que un nómada mongol, pero me distrae un coche que está aparcando frente al establo. Reconozco enseguida el BMW plateado descapotable. Un peso de diez kilos se instala en mi pecho.

—¿Qué hace aquí Bitsy? —pregunta Missy.

—Esto no puede ser bueno.

No debería decir algo así, y menos de mi futura suegra, pero lo último que me apetece hoy es que Bitsy venga a agobiarme con sus planes de boda. Su intención es buena, pero me persigue en cuanto tiene ocasión.

Se me quita el peso de encima cuando es otra persona la que baja del coche, alguien alto, moreno y decididamente guapo.

—Anda, mira quién ha venido a ver a su enamorada. No sabía que estaba aquí tu chico. —Missy me sonríe y saluda con la mano hacia el establo—. ¡Hola, Elliot!

Estoy atónita.

—No... No me ha dicho que venía a Aiken. Cuando hablamos ayer, estaba en Washington porque tenía una reunión y hoy volaba a California.

—Pues supongo que ha cambiado de opinión. Qué romántico, ¿no? —Allison me empuja hacia la cerca—. Ya puedes ir a darle un abrazo.

—Y un beso —añade Missy—. Y algo más que se te ocurra.

—Ya vale. —Quizá son los años de infancia que Elliot y yo pasamos soportando las bromas de mis hermanas sobre que éramos novios cuando no lo éramos, pero me pongo colorada mientras Elliot saluda y echa a andar hacia el *paddock*. Está muy atractivo con un traje gris que le queda como un guante. Desde luego lleva ropa de trabajo. ¿Qué hace aquí?

De pronto me muero de ganas de saberlo. Me quito los zapatos, echo a correr por la hierba y me tiro a sus brazos. Me levanta del suelo y luego vuelve a dejarme y me da un beso rápido. Todo en el gesto me encanta. Es una sensación familiar, bonita, tranquilizadora, y me doy cuenta de es precisamente lo que necesito ahora.

—¿Qué haces en Aiken? —Sigo desconcertada por su aparición repentina. Feliz, pero desconcertada.

Sus ojos marrón intenso centellean. Está encantado de haberme dado una sorpresa.

—Cambié el vuelo para poder pasar aquí unas horas antes de seguir a Los Ángeles.

—¿Vuelas hoy a Los Ángeles? —Odio parecer decepcionada, pero ya había empezado a hacer planes mentalmente.

—Esta noche —contesta—. Siento no poder quedarme más. Pero, oye, es mejor que nada, ¿no?

Oigo un coche que se acerca por el camino y tiro de Elliot hacia el establo. Podrían ser papá o Honeybee que vuelven del *brunch*. Si nos ven, no tendremos tiempo para estar solos.

—Vamos a dar un paseo. Te quiero todo para mí.

Con un poco de suerte, mis padres ni se fijarán en el coche aparcado junto al de Allison.

Elliot me mira los pies descalzos con el ceño fruncido.

—¿No necesitas zapatos?

—Cogeré unas botas de goma en el cobertizo. Si subo a casa, todos se enterarán de que estás aquí y mamá querrá que te quedes a charlar. —Apenas acabo de decir estas palabras cuando la realidad se impone—. ¿Sabe tu madre que has venido?

Bitsy nos matará a los dos si Elliot no pasa tiempo con ella mientras está aquí.

—Tranquila. Ya he pasado a verla. Hemos desayunado juntos.

Eso explica por qué Bitsy no estaba en el *brunch*.

—¿Tu madre sabía que venías pero a mí no me lo dijiste?

Odio tener celos, pero así es. Elliot se presenta en la ciudad y la primera persona que va a ver es Bitsy.

Elliot me acerca a él y me besa de una manera que me deja claro a quién de las dos prefiere.

—Quería darte una sorpresa. —Recorremos despacio y muy juntos el pasillo del establo—. Y además quería quitarme a mamá de en medio. Ya sabes cómo es.

—Tienes razón. —Como siempre, ha manejado la cuestión de Bitsy de la mejor manera posible. Y nos ha evitado tener que ir a visitarla juntos y una intensa conversación sobre la boda—. ¿Te ha dado la murga con lo de los planes de boda?

—Un poco —reconoce—. Le dije que tú y yo lo íbamos a hablar.

Me abstengo de comentar que «lo vamos a hablar» significa «sí, haremos lo que tú quieras» en el lenguaje particular de Bitsy. Lo último que nos apetece a ninguno de los dos en este momento es hablar de su madre.

Me abre la puerta del cobertizo y cuelga su chaqueta en un gancho.

—¿Cómo está tu padre?

Le pongo al día de las últimas novedades de la salud de papá mientras encuentro unas botas de goma de mi número, me las pongo y me meto los pantalones por dentro.

—Muy guapa —bromea, inspeccionando mi atuendo cuando he terminado. Elliot no es de los de botas de goma con pantalones metidos por dentro.

—Si quieres voy a casa y me pongo algo más adecuado mientras hablas con Honeybee sobre lo bonitas que resultan las bodas en primavera...

Ríe, se frota los ojos y me doy cuenta de que está cansado. Eso hace que el hecho de que haya dado un rodeo para venir a verme sea aún más adorable.

—Es tentador, pero... no. Vamos a caminar un rato e igual luego podemos dar una vuelta en coche.

—Me parece perfecto. Voy a escribir a Allison y a Missy para que no les digan a mis padres que estás aquí. —Mando un mensaje rápido mientras echamos a andar por el sendero. Como siempre, tenemos mucho que contarnos. Elliot me coge de la mano y charlamos de trabajo, de la familia, de su viaje a Milán, de política. Nos ponemos al día de todo lo que no hemos tenido tiempo de hablar por teléfono. Es agradable, como volver a casa después de un largo viaje.

Los ritmos de conversación y movimiento son los que hemos ido aprendiendo con el tiempo. Ambos sabemos dónde vamos, hacia un pequeño lago natural donde podemos sentarnos en un cenador rodeado de pinos que lleva allí desde que tengo uso de razón. Hemos casi llegado cuando, sin habérmelo propuesto, he empezado a contarle la historia de May Crandall, la Asociación de Hogares Infantiles de Tennessee y la extraña advertencia que me hizo la abuela Judy sobre Arcadia.

Elliot se detiene junto a las escaleras del cenador. Se recuesta en un poste, cruza los brazos y me mira como si me acabaran de salir cuernos.

—Avery, ¿a qué viene todo esto?

—¿Todo el qué?

—Todo esto..., no sé... Escarbar en cosas que han pasado hace mucho tiempo. Cosas que no tienen nada que ver contigo. ¿No tienes bastante con tu padre, el revuelo que se ha montado por los centros de mayores y Leslie que no deja de regañarte?

No sé muy bien si ofenderme o tomarme la protesta de Elliot como la voz de la razón.

—Es que esa es la cuestión. ¿Y si tuviera algo que ver con nosotros? ¿Y si la abuela Judy estuviera tan interesada en la Asociación de Hogares Infantiles de Tennessee porque nuestra familia tenía alguna vinculación con ella? ¿Y si tuvieron algo que ver en la legislación que hizo legítimas todas esas adopciones y protegió los expedientes?

—Si así fuera, ¿por qué querrías saberlo? ¿Qué importancia tiene ahora, décadas después? —Frunce el ceño y se le juntan las cejas formando un nudo oscuro.

—Porque..., bueno..., en primer lugar porque a la abuela Judy le importaba.

—Por eso precisamente tienes que andarte con cuidado.

Por un momento estoy perpleja. Siento calor debajo de la blusa de seda sin mangas que me he puesto para ir a la iglesia. De pronto mi prometido habla como su madre. Incluso la entonación de la frase me recuerda a Bitsy. En el pasado, mi abuela y ella han estado en lados opuestos en varias cuestiones relativas a la ciudad, a menudo con Honeybee en medio, haciendo de árbitro.

—Y eso ¿qué significa?

Quizá Elliot solo está cansado, o puede que Bitsy lo irritara durante el desayuno, pero me quedo atónita cuando agita una mano en el aire y se da una palmada en la pierna.

—Avery, sabes que Judy Stafford nunca se ha caracterizado por su discreción. No es ningún secreto. Así que no me mires como si nadie lo hubiera dicho antes. —Me mira a los ojos con una expresión tan tranquila que me irrita—. Estuvo a punto de arruinar la carrera política de tu abuelo varias veces... y la de tu padre también.

Me ofendo al instante.

—Creía que cuando algo no estaba bien había que decirlo.

—A tu abuela le encantaba ser polémica.

—De eso nada. —Noto el pulso en el cuello, tengo ganas de llorar. Me siento un poco traicionada por esta opinión hasta ahora disimulada sobre mi familia, pero por encima de todo estoy pensando: *Elliot por fin viene a verme ¿y nos ponemos a discutir?*

Me acaricia el brazo y me coge la mano.

—Oye, Aves... —Su tono es conciliador, me tranquiliza—. No quiero discutir. Solo te estoy dando mi opinión sincera. Y eso es porque te quiero y quiero lo mejor para ti.

Nos miramos y es como si pudiera verle el corazón. Está diciendo la verdad. Me quiere. Y está en su derecho de tener su opinión.

—Yo tampoco quiero discutir.

La pelea termina donde lo hacen todas, en el punto en que cada uno cede un poco.

Se lleva mi mano a los labios y la besa.

—Te quiero.

Le miro a los ojos y veo todos los años, los kilómetros y las experiencias que hemos compartido. Veo al niño que era mi amigo y hoy es un hombre.

—Lo sé. Yo también te quiero.

—Supongo que deberíamos hablar de la boda. —Me guiña un ojo y tengo la sensación de que su desayuno no ha sido fácil. Saca el móvil y comprueba la hora—. Se lo prometí a mamá.

Vamos a nuestro rincón preferido del cenador y estamos sentados un rato, pero hace demasiado calor, por lo menos para hablar de detalles. Terminamos por ir a nuestro restaurante preferido de la ciudad para hacer lo que hacíamos en nuestra infancia, en nuestra adolescencia, durante la universidad: entresacar lo que queremos y tratar de separarlo de lo que los demás quieren para nosotros.

Para cuando Elliot tiene que volverse al aeropuerto, no hemos llegado a ninguna conclusión, pero nos hemos puesto al día de nuestras vidas y nos llevamos bien, que es lo que de verdad importa.

Cuando vuelvo a casa, me encuentro a Honeybee en la puerta. Hace ademán de salir al camino de entrada. No sé cómo se ha enterado de la visita de Elliot y le ha decepcionado que no haya entrado conmigo en la casa.

—Está muy ocupado, mamá —le digo para disculparlo—. Tenía que coger un avión.

—Podría haberse quedado en uno de los cuartos de invitados. Nos encanta tenerlo aquí.

—Lo sabe, mamá.

Tamborilea con un dedo mientras sostiene la puerta abierta y mira pensativa el camino. Para cuando la cierra y renuncia a Elliot, probablemente el aire acondicionado ha llegado a toda la finca.

—Ha llamado Bitsy. Dice que ha comentado vuestros planes de boda, o la ausencia de ellos, con Elliot esta mañana y que este le prometió que lo hablaríais. Así que supuse que, después de pasar un rato juntos, vendríais aquí.

—Hemos hablado de algunas posibilidades. Pero no hemos tomado aún ninguna decisión.

Se muerde el labio con el ceño fruncido.

—No quiero que todo lo que está pasando... interfiera en vuestros planes. No quiero que penséis que tenéis que poner vuestro futuro en espera.

—Mamá, no nos sentimos así.

—¿Estás segura?

La decepción y desesperación en su cara me duelen. Un anuncio de boda sería una noticia feliz, una razón para mirar hacia delante. También transmitiría el mensaje de que los Stafford están tranquilos y siguen adelante con sus vidas.

Tal vez Elliot y yo estamos siendo egoístas manteniendo a todo el mundo en vilo. ¿Tan malo sería fijar una fecha y un lugar, quizá incluso en el jardín de las azaleas en primavera? Eso haría muy feliz a toda la familia. Y si se supone que te vas a casar con la persona adecuada, ¿por qué importa tanto cuándo y dónde sea?

—Pronto decidiremos algo, te lo prometo. —Pero en lo más recóndito de mis pensamientos están estas palabras: *Avery, sabes que Judy Stafford nunca se ha caracterizado por su discreción. No es ningún secreto.* De lo que Elliot no se da cuenta (quizá porque no quiere reconocerlo) es de que mi abuela y yo nos parecemos mucho.

—Estupendo. —Las arrugas de preocupación alrededor de los ojos de Honeybee se suavizan—. Pero no te estoy presionando.

—Lo sé.

Me coge la cara con sus manos frías y me mira con adoración.

—Te quiero, garbancita.

El apelativo de mi infancia me hace sonrojar.

—Yo también te quiero, mamá.

—Elliot es un hombre afortunado. Estoy segura de que se da cuenta cada vez que estáis juntos. —Está algo llorosa y me contagia. Me siento bien viéndola... tan feliz—. Y ahora cámbiate o vamos a llegar tarde a la gala benéfica del coro infantil de África. Tengo entendido que son maravillosos.

—Sí, mamá.

Me hago la firme promesa de hablar con Elliot de la boda en cuanto vuelva de Los Ángeles. El hecho de que mañana sea mi día de visita a la abuela Judy en Magnolia Manor no hace más que reforzar mi determinación. Quiero que mi abuela esté en la celebración. Desde que soy pequeña, he imaginado ese día con ella en él. Y no hay forma de saber cuánto tiempo nos queda.

Doy vueltas a varias ideas durante la velada. Intento imaginarme una boda en un jardín, Elliot y yo, varios centenares de amigos y conocidos, un precioso día de primavera. La verdad es que podría ser muy bonito, la versión moderna de una tradición antigua. La abuela Judy y el abuelo se casaron en los jardines de Drayden Hill.

Elliot accederá, por mucho que se resista instintivamente a que mi madre o la suya nos organicen la vida. Si una boda en un jardín es de verdad lo que quiero, también lo querrá él.

Por la mañana voy a Magnolia Manor con un nuevo propósito en la cabeza. Le preguntaré a la abuela Judy por los detalles de su boda. Igual tiene momentos preferidos que podemos recrear.

Como si presintiera que esta vez vengo para hablar de algo importante, me recibe con una sonrisa radiante que me dice que me reconoce.

—¡Has venido! Siéntate aquí a mi lado, tengo que contarte una cosa. —Intenta acercar un sillón de orejas al suyo, pero no puede. Lo empujo un poco y me siento en el borde de manera que nuestras rodillas se tocan.

Me coge la mano y me mira con tal intensidad que me quedo muy quieta.

—Quiero que destruyas todo lo que hay en el armario de mi despacho. El de la casa de Lagniappe. —Sus ojos me taladran—. No creo que vaya a salir de aquí, así que no podré hacerlo yo. No me gustaría que nadie leyera mis dietarios cuando ya no esté.

Me resisto a la inevitable punzada de dolor.

—No digas eso, abuela Judy. Te vi el otro día en clase de gimnasia. La profesora dijo que estabas estupenda. —Me hago la tonta respecto a los dietarios. No puedo soportar la idea. Sería como decir adiós a la ajetreada activista que siempre ha sido mi abuela.

—Hay nombres y números de teléfono. No quiero que caigan en las manos equivocadas. Haz una fogata en el jardín y quémalos.

Ahora me pregunto si no se le ha ido otra vez la cabeza, pero el caso es que parece lúcida. Hacer un fuego en el jardín..., ¿en una calle llena de casas históricas meticulosamente conservadas? Los vecinos tardarían dos segundos y medio en llamar a la policía.

Me imagino lo que dirían los periódicos.

—Pensarán que estás quemando hojarasca. —Sonríe y me hace un guiño cómplice—. No te preocupes, Beth.

De pronto queda muy claro que no estamos en el mismo sitio. No tengo ni idea de quién es Beth. Casi me siento aliviada de que la abuela Judy no sepa con quién está hablando. Me da una excusa para ignorar su petición sobre la limpieza del armario.

—Claro que sí, abuela —digo.

—Maravilloso. Qué buena has sido siempre conmigo.

—Eso es porque te quiero.

—Lo sé. No abras las cajas. Quémalas directamente.

—¿Las cajas?

—En las que están mis antiguas columnas de sociedad. No conviene que se me recuerde como la señorita Chief. —Se tapa la boca y simula avergonzarse de su época de columnista de cotilleos, pero en realidad no lo hace. Su expresión no deja lugar a dudas.

—Nunca me contaste que escribías ecos de sociedad. —Muevo un dedo simulando regañarla.

Se hace la inocente en eso de tener secretos.

—Ah, ¿no? Bueno, fue hace ya mucho tiempo.

—Pero en esas columnas no dirías nada que no fuera verdad, ¿no es cierto? —bromeo.

—Pues claro que no. Pero la gente no siempre se toma bien la verdad.

Con la misma velocidad con la que nos hemos puesto a hablar de la señorita Chief, abandonamos el tema. La abuela se pone a hablar de personas que llevan años muertas, pero que en su cabeza es como si hubiera almorzado ayer con ellas.

Le pregunto por su boda. Como respuesta, me ofrece un revoltijo de recuerdos de su ceremonia y de otras a las que ha asistido a lo largo de los años, incluidas las de mis hermanas. A la abuela Judy le encantan las bodas.

De la mía ni se acordará.

La conversación me deja triste y vacía. Siempre hay suficientes fogonazos de lucidez para hacerme albergar esperanzas, pero las olas de la demencia enseguida se las llevan mar adentro.

Para cuando la beso y me despido y le digo que mi padre seguramente irá a verla hoy, estamos flotando muy lejos de la orilla.

—Ah, ¿y quién es tu padre?

—Tu hijo Wells.

—Creo que te equivocas. Yo no tengo ningún hijo.

Cuando salgo del edificio, necesito desesperadamente hablar con alguien y contarle todo esto. Abro mi lista de favoritos y me detengo antes de pulsar el nombre de Elliot. Después de lo que dijo ayer sobre la abuela, casi me parece desleal contarle lo mucho que se le va la cabeza.

No soy consciente hasta que suena el teléfono y veo el nombre en la pantalla de que sí hay alguien con quien me apetece hablar. Pienso en la expresión de su cara cuando me habló de esas últimas y difíciles promesas que le hizo a su abuelo, las promesas que tenían que ver con los secretos de May Crandall y de mi abuela, y de forma instintiva sé que él me va a comprender.

Algo dentro de mí me impulsa instintivamente hacia él, a pesar de que no hemos hablado desde aquel día en la residencia de mayores, hace ya varias semanas. Entonces me dije que no debía volver a ponerme en contacto con él, que era mejor dejar las cosas como estaban y seguir con mi vida.

En cuanto contesto, parece no estar muy seguro de por qué me ha llamado. Me pregunto si ha estado pensando lo mismo que yo, que entre nosotros la amistad no tiene cabida. Nuestro encuentro con Leslie en el aparcamiento fue la demostración.

—Quería... —dice por fin—. He visto algo en la prensa de lo de las residencias de mayores. Solo quería decirte que he pensado en ti.

Una sensación cálida y agradable se apodera de mí. Me coge totalmente por sorpresa. No se me puede notar en la voz.

—Ay, no me lo recuerdes. Como sigamos así mucho tiempo, voy a tener que ponerme en plan tortuga Ninja con alguien.

—No lo creo.

—Yo tampoco, supongo. Pero me gustaría. Es tan... irritante. Entiendo que mi padre tiene un cargo público, pero seguimos siendo humanos. Se supone que determinados temas no deberían estar encima de la mesa, por ejemplo el cáncer. Y luego está lo de ver a mi abuela esforzarse por recordar quién es. Parece que la gente está sedienta de sangre estos días. Cuando era pequeña no era así. Incluso en política la gente tenía... —Busco la palabra adecuada, pero la única que se me ocurre es «decencia».

—Vivimos en la sociedad del entretenimiento —dice Trent serio—. Todo vale.

Abro la boca para seguir despotricando de los ataques a mi familia, pero me lo pienso mejor.

—Perdona, no quería desahogarme contigo. Tal vez necesito otro viaje a la playa.

Hasta que no las pronuncio, no me doy cuenta de que las palabras han sonado a coquetería.

—¿Qué te parece una comida?

—¿Qué?

—Te he llamado porque pensé que quizá tenías tiempo, es que estoy en Aiken. He estado investigando un poco sobre los papeles de mi abuelo y hablando con gente que lo ayudó en sus búsquedas. Uno es un hombre que fue funcionario de juzgado en el condado de Shelby, Tennessee, cuando los expedientes de adopción seguían siendo confidenciales. Por lo que he visto, le pasó bastante información a mi abuelo.

Al momento me siento transportada. Los olores de la diminuta cabaña de Edisto despiertan mis sentidos. Huelo a tabaco de pipa, a recortes de periódicos viejos, a tablones de corcho resecos, a pintura desconchada, a fotografías antiguas.

—¿Para que pudiera ayudar a las personas adoptadas a encontrar a sus familiares, quieres decir? Entonces, ¿estás continuando con lo que él empezó?

—En realidad no. Estaba curioseando sobre May Crandall. Pensando que igual descubría algo sobre el hermanito que no llegó a encontrar, Gabion.

Por un momento estoy perpleja. Este chico es genuino hasta la médula. También es mejor persona que yo. He estado tan obsesionada con los problemas familiares que he retrasado la llamada al comité por los derechos de los mayores para hablar de la situación de May. Ahora me he dado cuenta de que he dejado este asunto de lado a propósito. Me da miedo que me relacionen con ella después de toda la controversia que suscitó el artículo sobre «Envejecer en desigualdad de condiciones». Si se supiera que la estoy ayudando, nuestros enemigos políticos me acusarían de utilizarla para lavar nuestra magullada imagen.

Tampoco pueden verme comiendo con Trent. No puedo ir de ninguna manera, pero no consigo decirle que no, así que continúo yéndome por las ramas.

—Qué detalle por tu parte. ¿Y qué has encontrado?

—De momento nada importante. En los papeles del juzgado había una dirección en California. Escribí para ver si sabían algo de un niño de dos años adoptado a través de la Asociación de Hogares Infantiles de Tennessee en 1939... o al menos que vivió en esa dirección a finales de la década de 1930. Claro que era bastante improbable.

—¿Y has venido hasta aquí para decírselo a May?

—No... No quiero darle esperanzas si no averiguo algo. En realidad he venido a buscar mermelada. La última vez que te vi fui a visitar a mi tía, a las afueras de Aiken. Estaba haciendo mermelada de moras y ya está lista.

Se me escapa una risita.

—Dos horas y media de coche para recoger mermelada son muchas horas.

—Lo dices porque no has probado las conservas de mora de mi tía. Además a Jonah le encanta ir. El tío Bobby tiene una mula.

—¿Así que has traído a Jonah? —De pronto quedar a comer se convierte en una posibilidad, si vamos a estar los tres. Incluso si nos ven, nadie sacaría conclusiones equivocadas estando Jonah. Repaso a toda prisa mi agenda para la tarde y trato de calcular cómo cambiar algunas cosas para poder escaparme un rato—. ¿Sabes qué? Que me encantaría comer con vosotros.

—Creo que podré arrancar a Jonah del tío Bobby y de la mula. Dime dónde y a qué hora. ¿Te apetece algún sitio en especial? Somos muy flexibles..., siempre que no sea a la hora de la siesta. A esa hora las cosas pueden ponerse feas.

Este comentario me hace reír otra vez.

—¿A qué hora es la siesta?

—Sobre las dos.

—Muy bien. Entonces, ¿qué te parece si comemos pronto? ¿Sobre las once? ¿Es demasiado temprano? —No tengo ni idea de lo lejos del centro que está la casa de su tía, pero, si tienen una mula, entonces no puede estar cerca de donde estoy yo ahora. Hace años que no se crían animales en Magnolia Manor, los jardines están prístinos—. Elige tú el sitio y nos vemos allí. Pero que no sea demasiado elegante, ¿vale? Estaría bien algo sin mucha gente.

Trent ríe.

—Nosotros no vamos a sitios elegantes. Somos más de cafeterías con zona infantil. ¿No conocerás alguna?

Mis pensamientos retroceden y aterrizan en un recuerdo agradable.

—Pues mira, sí. Hay una hamburguesería de toda la vida con un pequeño parque infantil no lejos de la casa de mi abuela. Nos llevaba cuando éramos pequeñas. —Le explico cómo llegar y está decidido. Lo mejor de todo es que, si quedamos a las once, en casa ni siquiera me echarán de menos.

Soy una persona adulta, razono mientras cambio de sentido y me dirijo hacia el vecindario de la abuela Judy. *No debería sentirme como una adolescente saliendo a hurtadillas solo porque he quedado a comer con..., con un amigo.*

Tengo derecho a mi propia vida, ¿no?

Paso un rato centrada en mi debate interior, mis pensamientos trazando curvas igual que el coche en la carretera. Quizá es que en Maryland me malacostumbré, al llevar una vida anónima, con un trabajo que era mío y solo mío y no vinculado a un equipo de apoyo, a un despacho de Washington y a mi estado natal, a los electores, contribuyentes y a toda una red política.

Quizá es que nunca fui consciente de hasta qué punto ser una Stafford es algo tan exigente, sobre todo aquí, en territorio nativo. La identidad colectiva resulta tan abrumadora que no queda espacio para la individual.

En otro tiempo eso me gustaba..., ¿o no? Disfrutaba de las ventajas que traía consigo. Siempre con alguien que me allanaba cualquier camino que tomara.

Pero ahora tengo ganas de escalar mis propias montañas y a mi manera.

¿Me he cansado de esta vida?

La idea me parte en dos y una mitad de mi identidad se queda en uno de los lados. ¿Soy la hija de mi padre o soy simplemente yo? ¿Tengo que sacrificar una cosa por la otra?

Sin duda esto no es más que... una reacción a todo el estrés de estas últimas semanas.

Me detengo en un stop, miro hacia la calle de la abuela Judy, más allá de la hondonada donde de niños chapoteábamos en charcos que se formaban al llover, más allá del seto pulcramente podado y del buzón de correos con una cabeza de caballo de hierro en la parte de arriba.

Hay un taxi en el camino de entrada a la casa de mi abuela. En una ciudad del tamaño de Aiken, no es una imagen habitual.

En la intersección, vacilo y me fijo un momento en el taxi. No da marcha atrás y se va. ¿Igual el conductor no sabe que ya no vive nadie allí? Debe de haberse equivocado de casa.

Cuando tuerzo por la calle doy por hecho que se irá mientras llego yo, pero lo cierto es que el conductor está... ¿dormitando? Cuando le adelanto y salgo del coche, no se mueve.

Parece joven, adolescente casi, pero debe de tener edad suficiente para conducir. En el asiento de atrás no hay nadie y tampoco en los alrededores de la casa, hasta donde puedo ver. Lo lógico sería pensar que tiene algo que ver con otra campaña de difamación de la prensa, un reportero husmeando para sacar fotografías de cómo viven los ricos, pero ¿por qué iba a coger un taxi alguien así?

El conductor da un salto en el sentido estricto de la palabra cuando toco en la ventanilla entreabierta. Tiene la boca abierta mientras intenta enfocar la vista.

—Eh... Me parece que me he quedado dormido —se disculpa—. Perdón, señora.

—Me parece que se ha equivocado de casa —le digo.

Mira a su alrededor, suprime un bostezo, agita sus pestañas oscuras y espesas contra la luz brillante de plena mañana.

—No..., no, señora. La reserva es para las diez y media.

Consulto mi reloj.

—¿Lleva aquí... casi una hora, esperando en la puerta? —*¿Quién puede haber enviado un taxi a casa de mi abuela?*—. Deben de haberle dado mal la dirección.

En algún sitio debe de haber un pobre cliente esperando impaciente.

El taxista no parece en absoluto preocupado. Se endereza en el asiento y mira en la guantera.

—No, señora. Es una reserva semanal. Cada jueves a las diez y media. Está prepagada, así que mi padre..., quiero decir, mi jefe dice que tengo que venir aquí y esperar, puesto que lo hemos cobrado.

—¿Cada jueves? —Repaso la agenda, o lo que recuerdo de ella, de cuando la abuela Judy aún vivía aquí con una cuidadora a tiempo completo. El día que terminó perdida y confusa en un centro comercial iba en un taxi—. ¿Cuánto tiempo lleva haciendo esto? ¿Lo de venir cada jueves?

—Pues... igual debería... llamar a la oficina y hablar...

—No. No pasa nada. —Me temo que en la oficina no contestarán mis preguntas. El chico al volante del taxi tampoco parece saber nada—. Cuando recogía a mi abuela los jueves, ¿dónde la llevaba?

—A Augusta. A un sitio que hay en el río. Yo solo la llevé unas cuantas veces, pero mi padre y mi abuelo lo hicieron durante... quizá un par de años. Somos una empresa familiar. Cuatro generaciones.

La última parte la pronuncia con cuidado, como si la hubiera arrancado directamente de una valla publicitaria.

—¿Años?

Confusión es una palabra que se queda corta para describir cómo me siento ahora mismo. Las agendas de mi abuela no decían nada de una cita cada jueves. Es más, mi abuela no tenía compromisos semanales a excepción del club de bridge o las visitas a centros de belleza. ¿Y en Augusta? Eso es media hora de ida y otra media de vuelta. ¿A quién podía tener que ir a ver todas las semanas en Augusta? Y en taxi. Y durante años.

—¿Y siempre iba al mismo sitio? —pregunto.

—Sí, señora. Por lo que yo sé.

Ahora parece muy incómodo. Por un lado se da cuenta de que le estoy interrogando. Por otra, no quiere quedarse sin lo que obviamente ha sido una carrera de muchos años. No quiero ni imaginar lo que cuesta un viaje de ida y vuelta a Augusta.

Apoyo la mano encima de su ventanilla. Parecerá una tontería, pero quiero asegurarme de que no se escapa mientras proceso esta avalancha de información. *Un sitio que hay en el río...*

—Con lo del sitio en el río, ¿se refiere en la orilla?

Me viene a la cabeza algo del todo inesperado. El río Savannah atraviesa Augusta. Cuando Trent y yo hablamos con May, mencionó Augusta. Algo sobre volver a casa y navegar sin rumbo por el río Savannah.

—Bueno, podría ser. La valla está... cubierta de maleza. Yo la dejo allí y espero. No sé lo que pasa luego.

—¿Cuánto tiempo suele quedarse?

—Unas horas. Mientras esperaba, mi padre solía ir al puente a pescar. A ella no le importaba. Cuando quería irse, venía al taxi y tocaba el claxon.

Le miro con la boca abierta. No sé cómo casar toda esta información con la abuela que conozco. Con la abuela que creía conocer.

¿Será verdad que estaba escribiendo la historia de May Crandall? ¿O hay algo más?

—¿Puede llevarme? —le digo de sopetón.

El taxista se encoge de hombros. Empieza a bajar del coche para abrirme la puerta trasera.

—Sí, claro. La carrera está ya pagada.

Se me acelera el pulso. Tengo la carne de gallina. *Si me subo a este coche, ¿dónde terminaré?*

Me vibra el teléfono recordándome que iba a alguna parte antes de dar este rodeo. Es un mensaje de Trent diciéndome que Jonah y él han cogido una mesa. El puesto de hamburguesas ya está lleno a esta hora.

En lugar de escribirle otro mensaje, me separo del taxista y lo llamo. Me disculpo por no estar allí y le pregunto:

—¿Puedes..., podrías venir conmigo a hacer una cosa? —La explicación de dónde estoy y lo que pasa suena todavía más rara dicha en voz alta.

Por suerte, Trent no piensa que estoy loca. De hecho está intrigado. Acordamos que el taxi parará en el restaurante para que Jonah y él puedan seguirnos en el coche.

—Te cojo una hamburguesa —me ofrece Trent—. Los batidos aquí al parecer son famosos. Jonah está encantado. ¿Quieres uno?

—Genial. Gracias. —Aunque no estoy segura de poder comer nada ahora mismo.

Durante el corto trayecto al restaurante, casi no puedo pensar de lo nerviosa que estoy. Trent me espera en el aparcamiento con Jonah ya sentado y con el cinturón puesto. Me da una bolsa de papel y un batido y me dice que nos sigue.

—¿Estás bien? —pregunta. Nuestras miradas se encuentran un momento y me pierdo en el azul intenso de sus ojos. Me tranquilizo, pienso: *Está aquí Trent. Todo saldrá bien.*

Ese pensamiento casi ahuyenta el miedo gigantesco que se está apoderando de mí. Casi.

Por desgracia conozco la sensación lo bastante bien para saber que no debo ignorarla. Es el sexto sentido que se me despierta cuando estoy a punto de descubrir algo casi impensable sobre los implicados en el caso en que estoy trabajando: el vecino de confianza que resulta ser el responsable de la desaparición de un niño; el alumno de octavo curso y aspecto inocente que tiene una colección de bombas de fabricación casera; el pulcro padre de cuatro hijos con el ordenador lleno de fotografías repugnantes. Ese sexto sentido me está preparando para algo. Solo que no sé qué es.

—Estoy bien —digo—, pero me asusta dónde nos va a llevar este taxi... y lo que vayamos a encontrar.

Trent me pone una mano en el brazo y parece que se me calienta la piel al contacto con sus dedos.

—¿Quieres venir con nosotros? Podemos seguir al taxi.

Hace un gesto en dirección a su coche, donde Jonah saluda como loco desde su sillita de niño, tratando de captar mi atención. Quiere compartir conmigo sus patatas fritas.

—Te lo agradezco, pero no. Quiero aprovechar para seguir hablando con el taxista por el camino. —La realidad es que creo que me ha dicho todo lo que sabe, pero quiero mantenerlo ocupado para que no se ponga en contacto con su oficina. Es posible que su padre tenga una opinión distinta sobre que yo use el taxi de la abuela para que me transporte a un destino misterioso. Quizá sea lo bastante espabilado para darse cuenta de que puede tratarse de un asunto privado—. Y no quiero arriesgarme a que se nos escape.

Los dedos de Trent me recorren el brazo antes de soltarme... o quizá es que me lo imagino.

—Pues entonces te seguimos, ¿vale?

Asiento con la cabeza y saludo con la mano a Jonah, que me sonríe con la boca llena de patatas fritas, y nos vamos. El tráfico de esta carrera de treinta y cinco minutos a media mañana es fluido, así que al taxista le resulta fácil charlar. Me cuenta que se llama Oz y que, cuando llevaba a mi abuela, esta siempre le daba galletas, chocolatinas o dulces que habían sobrado de fiestas y reuniones. Por eso la recuerda tan bien. Siente que esté en una residencia. Es evidente que no se ha enterado de todo lo que ha salido en los periódicos ni de la polémica. Ha estado ocupado trabajando después de hacerse cargo casi a tiempo completo del taxi de su padre, que tiene problemas de salud.

—La última vez que la traje me quedé preocupado —reconoce cuando dejamos la autopista y circulamos por carreteras rurales, se supone que acercándonos ya a nuestro destino. Muros de arbustos abajeños, parras y altos pinos se espesan a nuestro alrededor, cerrándose más a medida que tomamos una curva y luego otra—. Se manejaba bien, pero parecía un poco confusa. Le pregunté si quería que la acompañara hasta la verja, pero no quiso. Dijo que habría un coche de golf esperándola al otro lado, como siempre, y que no me preocupara. Así que la dejé ir sola. Fue la última vez que la llevé.

Callada en el asiento trasero, trato de visualizar lo que me está contando Oz, pero no consigo imaginar nada de lo que me describe.

—A la semana siguiente operaron a mi padre del corazón. Tuvimos un sustituto durante un mes más o menos. El primer jueves después de reincorporarme fui a la casa, pero no había nadie. Y así desde entonces. El conductor sustituto no tenía ni idea de lo que había pasado. La última vez que la vio la dejó en un centro comercial y se despidió de él hasta el jueves siguiente. Hemos intentado llamar al número que sale en su factura, pero no lo coge nadie, y, cuando voy, nadie me abre tampoco la puerta. Nos preguntábamos si le había pasado algo. Siento si hemos causado alguna molestia.

—No es culpa suya. Sus cuidadoras no deberían haberla dejado salir sola. —Estos días es difícil encontrar buen servicio doméstico, pero además a mi abuela se le daba extremadamente bien convencer a sus cuidadoras de que era perfectamente competente y de que la tenían demasiado controlada. Es evidente que la dejaban coger un taxi los jueves. Claro que mi abuela era quien las pagaba, y lo sabían. No tenía reparos a la hora de despedir a los empleados domésticos que le llevaban la contraria.

El coche cruza traqueteando un viejo puente construido durante la Gran Depresión con pasamanos de cemento desconchado y arcos cubiertos de musgo. El taxista reduce la velocidad, pero no veo indicios de casas ni de buzones de correo. Por lo que parece, estamos en mitad de ninguna parte.

Menos mal que Oz sabe dónde va. Otra persona se habría pasado el desvío. Los restos apenas visibles de un sendero de grava dibujan dos caminos entrecortados a través de la hierba y de una acequia. Al final, una enorme entrada de piedra está escondida entre enredaderas de jazmín de Virginia y zarzamoras. Unas gruesas puertas de hierro, de unos dos metros y medio de altura, cuelgan torcidas, el peso amortiguado por hojas y raíces, las bisagras oxidadas hace tiempo. Una cadena y un candado en estado de desintegración casi parecen una broma. Hace décadas que un coche no cruza esta puerta. Justo al otro lado hay un sicomoro, a unos quince centímetros, cuyos brazos musculosos se cuelan entre los barrotes y levantan ligeramente una de las puertas.

—La entrada es por ahí. —Oz señala un estrecho sendero que conduce a una cancela más pequeña al lado de la principal. Está claro que es la usada, porque el suelo bajo ella está lo suficientemente pisado como para que la hierba de verano no lo haya cubierto aún del todo—. Por ahí iba siempre ella.

Detrás de nosotros se cierra una portezuela de coche. Doy un respingo y me vuelvo antes de acordarme de que es Trent.

Cuando me giro otra vez, me sobreviene la poderosa sensación de que la puerta va a desaparecer. Zas. Me despertaré en mi cama de Drayden Hill pensando: *Qué sueño tan raro...*

Pero la puerta no ha desaparecido y el camino sigue esperando.

22

RILL

Fern se queda paralizada en medio del cuarto de estar. Está tan rígida que le veo cada músculo. Un segundo después, se hace pis encima por primera vez en semanas.

—¡Fern! —la reprendo en voz baja porque no quiero que la señora Sevier me oiga y venga a ver lo que acaba de hacer. Nuestra nueva mamá está tan orgullosa de Fern que nos lleva al cine y habla de viajes que haremos juntos y de cómo veremos a Papá Noel y los regalos que nos traerá. Incluso se le ha metido en la cabeza que deberíamos ir en automóvil a Augusta a visitar a su madre. Yo no quiero ir a Augusta, pero tampoco quiero problemas, ahora que la señora Sevier nos deja un poco más de libertad.

Cruzo corriendo la habitación y le quito a Fern el vestido, los zapatos y los calcetines, que uso para secar el charco.

—Sube antes de que te vea.

Oigo a la señora Sevier hablar con alguien en la salita de la entrada.

A Fern le tiembla la boca y se le llenan los ojos de lágrimas. Se queda quieta mientras hago una bola con las ropas mojadas y la escondo detrás de una papelera; ya me ocuparé de ella luego.

De pronto entiendo por qué no se mueve Fern. Hay otra voz en la salita. Cuanto más me acerco, más escalofríos me produce y me llegan hasta el tuétano.

—Ve a esconderte debajo de la cama —le susurro de nuevo a Fern al oído y la empujo hacia las escaleras.

Fern corre al piso de arriba y desaparece. La respiración sale y entra en mi nariz en pequeños jadeos cuando me pego contra la pared de la escalera y me acerco con cuidado a la puerta abierta de la salita. En la cocina, Zuma enciende la batidora eléctrica. Por un instante no oigo las voces, pero luego sí.

—... una situación muy desafortunada, pero puede darse —está diciendo la señorita Tann—. No me gusta llevarme a los niños una vez hemos encontrado buenos hogares para ellos.

—Pero mi marido..., los papeles... Se nos prometió que podríamos quedarnos con las niñas. —La voz de la señora Sevier tiembla y se quiebra.

Una taza de té tintinea al contacto con un plato. La respuesta de la señorita Tann parece tardar una eternidad en llegar.

—Y así debería ser. —Habla como si nos compadeciera—. Pero las adopciones no son definitivas hasta que no ha pasado un año. La abuela de estos niños ha elevado una solicitud para recuperar su custodia.

Se me escapa un grito ahogado y entonces me doy cuenta de que he hecho ruido y me tapo la boca con la mano. Ni siquiera tenemos abuela. Por lo menos que yo sepa. Los padres de Briny están muertos y Queenie lleva sin ver a los suyos desde que se fugó con él.

—Eso no puede... —La señora Sevier deja escapar un sollozo que parece que la va a partir en dos. Se sorbe la nariz, tose y por fin vuelve a hablar—: No, no podemos permitir...

D-Darren volverá a la hora de comer. Por favor..., por favor, espere. Él sabrá..., él sabrá qué hacer.

—Ay, me temo que la he disgustado más de la cuenta. —La voz de la señorita Tann es de lo más cariñosa, pero me imagino su cara. Tiene la misma sonrisa mezquina que cuando la señora Pulnik me tenía sujeta de rodillas. A la señorita Tann le gusta el aspecto que tienen las personas asustadas—. No era mi intención llevarme a las niñas hoy. Por supuesto pueden oponerse a esta locura. De hecho deberían. La abuela no tiene en realidad medios para mantener a las pequeñas. Llevarían una vida horrorosa. May y la pequeña Beth dependen de ustedes, de su protección. Pero debe entender que... los trámites legales... pueden ser costosos.

—¿C-costosos?

—Para personas de posibles como ustedes, eso no debería suponer ninguna dificultad, ¿verdad? No cuando el destino de dos niñas está en juego. Dos niñas a las que quieren mucho.

—Sí, pero...

—Tres mil dólares, un poco más quizá. Eso debería bastar para empezar a resolver los problemas legales.

—¿Tres..., tres mil dólares?

—Quizá cuatro.

—Pero ¿qué me está diciendo?

Otra pausa y a continuación:

—Nada es más importante que su familia, ¿no le parece?

Oigo esa horrible sonrisa en la voz de la señorita Tann. Quiero entrar corriendo y contar la verdad. Quiero señalarla con el dedo y gritar: *¡Mentirosa! ¡Ni siquiera tenemos abuela! Y yo tenía tres hermanas, no dos. Y un hermanito, y se llamaba Gabion, no Robby. Y usted se lo llevó, igual que se llevó a mis hermanas.*

Quiero contarlo todo. Paladeo las palabras, pero no puedo decirlas. Si lo hago, sé lo que pasará. La señorita Tann volverá a llevarnos al hogar infantil. Le dará a Fern a otras personas y ya no estaremos juntas.

La señora Sevier vuelve a sorberse la nariz y a toser.

—Sí, claro... Estoy de acuerdo, pero... —Rompe a llorar de nuevo sin dejar de disculparse.

Una silla cruje y gime y unas pisadas decididas cruzan la habitación.

—Hable con su marido. Exprésele sus sentimientos sinceros sobre el asunto. Dígale lo mucho que necesita a las niñas y lo mucho que la necesitan ellas a usted. Hoy ni siquiera voy a verlas, estoy segura de que están bien cuidadas. Estupendamente incluso.

Sus pisadas se acercan más a las puertas del otro extremo de la habitación. Me separo de la pared y corro escaleras arriba. Lo último que oigo es la voz de la señorita Tann resonando en toda la casa.

—No se moleste en levantarse. Ya salgo sola. Espero tener noticias suyas mañana. No hay tiempo que perder.

Una vez arriba, corro a la habitación de Fern. Ni siquiera la saco de debajo de la cama. Me meto yo también. Estamos tumbadas con las caras juntas, igual que hacíamos en el *Arcadia*.

—No pasa nada —susurro—. No dejaré que se nos lleve, lo prometo. Pase lo que pase.

Oigo a la señora Sevier en el pasillo. Las paredes de madera y el alto techo con los remates dorados devuelven el eco de sus sollozos. La puerta al final del pasillo se cierra y la oigo tumbarse en la cama y llorar, llorar y llorar, como hacía cuando vinimos a vivir aquí. Zuma sube y llama a la puerta, pero está cerrada con llave y la señora Sevier no quiere dejar entrar a nadie. Sigue en la cama cuando el señor Sevier viene a comer. Para entonces he aseado a Fern y le he leído un cuento y está dormida con el pulgar en la boca y el oso de peluche al que llama Gabby, como nuestro hermanito.

Escucho mientras el señor Sevier abre la puerta del dormitorio. Cuando entra, salgo de puntillas al pasillo para oír mejor. No tengo que acercarme mucho para oír lo furioso que está el señor Sevier después de que su mujer le cuente lo que ha pasado.

—¡Esto es chantaje! —grita—. ¡Esto es un chantaje descarado!

—No podemos dejar que se lleve a las niñas, Darren —suplica la señora Sevier—. No podemos.

—No pienso dejarme chantajear por esta mujer. Ya pagamos los costes de adopción que, por cierto, fueron exorbitantes, sobre todo la segunda vez.

—Darren, por favor te lo pido.

—Victoria, estas cosas cuando empiezan ya no tienen fin. —Algo metálico cae y hace ruido contra el suelo—. ¿Cuándo se terminará? Dímelo.

—No lo sé. No lo sé, pero tenemos que hacer algo.

—No te preocupes, que algo voy a hacer. Esa mujer no sabe con quién está tratando.

Suena el picaporte y corro a mi habitación.

—Darren, por favor. Por favor, escúchame —suplica la señora Sevier—. Podríamos ir a casa de mamá en Augusta. En Bellegrove hay sitio de sobra, y, ahora que papá no está, la casa le resulta demasiado grande. Las niñas tendrán tíos y tías y a todos mis amigos. Nos llevaríamos a Hoy y a Zuma y a Hootsie. Podemos quedarnos todo el tiempo que sea necesario. Para siempre incluso. Mamá se encuentra sola y Bellegrove House necesita una familia. Para un niño es un sitio maravilloso donde crecer.

—Vamos a ver, Victoria, nuestra casa está aquí. Por fin he conseguido hacerme el estudio junto al lago. Los McCamey no es que trabajen muy rápido, pero ya han puesto los cimientos y el suelo y están avanzando con las paredes. No podemos permitir que Georgia Tann nos eche de nuestra casa, de la casa de mi familia, por el amor del cielo.

—Bellegrove tiene muchísimas hectáreas junto al río Savannah. Te puedes hacer otro estudio. Más grande. Como más te guste. —La señora Sevier habla tan deprisa que casi no distingo las palabras—. Por favor, Darren, ¡no puedo vivir aquí sabiendo que esa mujer puede venir en cualquier momento a llevarse a nuestras hijas!

El señor Sevier no contesta. Cierro los ojos y clavo las uñas en el mullido papel rosa de la pared, esperando, confiando.

—No nos precipitemos —dice por fin el señor Sevier—. Esta noche tengo una reunión en la ciudad. Le haré una visita a la señorita Tann y arreglaré este asunto cara a cara, de una vez por todas. Veremos si sigue igual de exigente.

La señora Sevier no sigue discutiendo. La oigo llorar bajito y luego la cama crujir y al señor Sevier consolarla.

—Vamos, cariño. No llores más. Todo se arreglará y, si quieres llevarte a las niñas unos días a Augusta, también lo podemos organizar.

Me bulle la cabeza con cien pensamientos, pero logro concentrarme en uno. Sé lo que tengo que hacer. No hay tiempo que perder. Voy a mi cómoda, saco lo que necesito y corro escaleras abajo.

En la cocina, Zuma tiene el almuerzo preparado, pero está en un rincón con la cabeza metida en el conducto de la ropa sucia para enterarse de lo que les pasa a los Sevier. Hootsie está probablemente dentro del conducto contándole lo que oye. En la tabla de cortar hay una cesta con comida preparada para llevársela a los McCamey a la obra. Normalmente Zuma haría a Hootsie llevársela: Hootsie los odia y Zuma también. Zuma dice que los McCamey no son más que escoria blanca y que están esperando a que el señor Sevier se dé la vuelta para robarle. Lo único bueno de esto es que Zuma y Hootsie ahora nos odian menos, porque están ocupadas odiando a los chicos McCamey y a su padre.

Cojo la cesta y salgo por la puerta mientras grito:

—Llevo yo esto a la obra. Tengo un folleto para el chico.

Me voy antes de que Zuma pueda decirme que voy a llegar tarde a comer.

Salgo corriendo por la parte de atrás, salto la barandilla del porche y cruzo el jardín lo más deprisa que me permiten las piernas sin dejar de mirar por encima del hombro para ver si Hootsie me sigue. Es un alivio que no sea así.

Junto al lago, el señor McCamey está a punto de sentarse a la sombra de un árbol cuando aparezco con la cesta. A mí me parece que siempre está deseando dejar de trabajar. La única razón por la que hoy ha sudado es que sus dos hijos mayores han ido a la casa de un vecino a ayudar a talar un árbol que tiró un rayo encima del granero y arreglar el tejado. No volverán hasta dentro de un día o dos, cuando hayan terminado el trabajo. La única ayuda que tiene el señor McCamey ahora mismo es su hijo menor. Se llama Arney, pero el señor McCamey le llama «chico».

Saludo con la cabeza a Arney y me sigue por el sendero hasta un sauce donde nos hemos sentado y charlado otras veces. Me meto debajo de las ramas y le doy a Arney un emparedado, una manzana y dos galletas de azúcar que llevo escondidos en el bolsillo. Arney está bastante raquítico, así que siempre que vengo le traigo comida que no tenga que compartir con los demás McCamey. Creo que la necesita. Tiene un año más que yo, pero ni siquiera es igual de alto.

—Hoy te he traído otra cosa además. —Le doy el folleto del cinematógrafo.

Mira el dibujo de un vaquero a lomos de un gran caballo palomino y da un largo silbido en voz baja.

—Seguro que era buena. Cuéntame cómo era la historia. ¿Había muchos tiros?

Se sienta y me siento con él. Quiero contarle todo sobre la película a la que nos llevó la señora Sevier y sobre la sala del cinematógrafo con sus butacas de terciopelo rojo y unas torres altas que parecían del castillo de un rey. Pero no tenemos tiempo de hablar de esas cosas. Hoy no. No con lo que ha pasado. Tengo que conseguir que Arney me diga que sí a lo que le pedí ayer.

Hoy habrá luna llena y el río estará casi tan claro como a mediodía. Ahora que no están los hermanos de Arney, no hay momento mejor. No puedo permitir que la señora Sevier nos lleve con ella a Augusta. No puedo permitir que la señorita Tann nos lleve de vuelta al hogar infantil. Y además de todo eso, Fern está empezando a pensar en la señora Sevier como su mamá. Poco a poco se está olvidando de nuestra verdadera madre. Por las noches me cuelo en su habitación y le hablo de Queenie y Briny, pero ya no sirve de nada. Fern se está olvidando del río y del reino de Arcadia. Se está olvidando de quiénes somos.

Es hora de irnos.

—Entonces, sobre lo que hablamos ayer. Nos vas a llevar, ¿verdad? —le pregunto a Arney—. Esta noche. La luna saldrá pronto y la noche será larga. —Una no ha vivido toda su vida en el río sin saber cómo viaja la luna. El río y sus criaturas deciden sus estados de ánimo en función de la luna.

Arney se aparta como si lo hubiera abofeteado. Se pellizca los ojos marrones cerrados. Un mechón de pelo fino castaño rojizo le cae sobre la frente y se separa encima de su nariz larga y huesuda. Niega con la cabeza, nervioso. Quizá nunca fue su intención ayudarnos. Quizá solo quería presumir cuando dijo que sabía guiar el barco de su padre y llegar por el brazo muerto hasta Dedmen's Slough y el gran río.

Pero le conté la verdad sobre Fern y sobre mí. La historia entera. Incluso le dije nuestros verdaderos nombres. Pensé que comprendía por qué necesitábamos ayuda.

Apoya los codos en el sucio pantalón de peto con agujeros en las rodillas.

—Te voy a echar de menos cuando os vayáis. Eres lo único bueno que he encontrado aquí.

—Puedes venir con nosotras. El viejo Zede ha recogido a muchos chicos. Apuesto a que te dejaría quedarte, estoy segura. No tendrías que volver a ver este sitio. Podrías ser libre. Como lo vamos a ser nosotras. —El padre de Arney se emborracha por las noches, hace trabajar a sus hijos como mulas de carga y les pega todo el tiempo, sobre todo a Arney. Hootsie le vio pegar a Arney en la cabeza con el mango de un martillo solo por haberle llevado los clavos equivocados—. Y, en cualquier caso, las perlas son tuyas, como te prometí.

Me meto la mano en el bolsillo, las saco y las sostengo donde Arney pueda verlas. Me siento mal por lo de las perlas. La señora Sevier me las dio la noche después de llevarse a Fern a hacerse los zapatos especiales. Pensaba que era mi cumpleaños por lo que dicen los papeles de la Asociación de Hogares Infantiles de Tennessee. Los Sevier creyeron que me había olvidado de que era mi día especial y me sorprendieron con una cena de cumpleaños. Ya lo creo que me sorprendieron. Mi cumpleaños fue hace cinco meses y medio y soy un año mayor de lo que creen. Claro que tampoco me llamo May Weathers, así que me dio bastante igual celebrar mi cumpleaños en otoño.

Estas perlas son de las cosas más bonitas que he tenido, pero renunciaré a ellas a cambio de Queenie, Briny y el río. Renunciaré sin pensármelo dos veces.

Además, Arney necesita el dinero que cuestan más que yo. La mayoría de las veces en el campamento tienen whisky, pero no comida.

Arney toca las perlas, luego retira la mano y se pellizca una costra del nudillo.

—Bah... No quiero dejar a mi familia. A mis hermanos y eso.

—Piénsalo bien. Lo de quedarte con nosotros en el río, quiero decir. —Lo cierto es que los hermanos de Arney ya son casi mayores y casi tan malos como el padre. Cuando se cansen de trabajar como mulas y decidan irse, es probable que Arney se muera de hambre o de las palizas que le da su padre—. Briny y Queenie te encontrarán un hogar, te lo prometo. Estarán tan contentos de que nos hayas llevado a Fern y a mí de vuelta que te encontrarán un buen hogar. Si Zede no está ya en la isla de Mud, te puedes quedar con nosotros en el *Arcadia* hasta que volvamos a encontrárnoslo.

Siento una punzada de preocupación. Lo cierto es que no puedo estar segura de que Briny y Queenie sigan amarrados en el sitio de siempre..., pero el caso es que lo sé. Esperarían para siempre si hiciera falta, aunque las noches se estén haciendo frías y los árboles estén perdiendo sus hojas y sea ya hora de poner rumbo sur hacia un condado más cálido.

Lo que me temo que no será fácil es conseguir que Briny y Queenie zarpen una vez Fern y yo estemos de vuelta en el *Arcadia*.

¿Les habrá contado Silas que solo quedamos Fern y yo, que Camellia ha desaparecido y que Lark y Gabion están lejos? ¿Lo sabrán?

No puedo pensar demasiado en eso porque me duele. *No te preocupes por lo que aún está a la vuelta de la esquina*, dice siempre Briny. Ahora mismo tengo que concentrarme en llegar por el lago hasta el gran río. A partir de ahí nos quedaremos cerca de la costa y tendremos cuidado con las estelas de los barcos y barcazas..., y estaremos atentos a la madera de deriva, ramas de árbol y esas cosas. Son muchas las noches en que he subido a la buhardilla de la casa de los Sevier y mirado hacia el horizonte. No puedo ver el río, pero sí sentirlo. Estoy convencida de oír las sirenas y los silbatos, a lo lejos. Al final del cielo veo las luces de Memphis. Por lo que me ha dicho Arney, supongo que el pantano en el que desemboca el brazo muerto debe de unirse al Misisipi en algún punto entre los acantilados de Chickasaw y los bancos de arena río arriba, pasada la isla de Mud. Arney no está seguro, pero yo creo que, si estoy equivocada, es por poco.

Arney asiente con la cabeza y es un alivio.

—De acuerdo. Os llevo. Pero tiene que ser esta noche. No hay manera de saber cuándo van a volver mis hermanos.

—Muy bien. Fern y yo vendremos aquí en cuanto la luna esté más alta que las copas de los árboles. Nos encontraremos en el bote. Asegúrate de que tu padre empieza a beber pronto esta noche. Déjale también que coma mucho, eso le dará sueño. Yo me ocupo de que Hootsie os traiga comida de sobra para la cena.

Eso no será difícil. Solo tengo que decirle a nuestra nueva mamá que el chico del campamento tiene hambre y no ha comido lo suficiente a mediodía. Le dirá a Zuma que prepare muchas cosas.

La señora Sevier tiene el corazón blando como el vilano de un diente de león. Lo malo es que también es frágil. No quiero ni pensar en cómo saldrá adelante cuando nos hayamos ido. No puedo pensar en ello. Queenie y Briny también nos necesitan y son nuestros padres. Es así de sencillo. No hay otra manera de verlo.

Es hora de irnos.

Arney asiente de nuevo con la cabeza.

—De acuerdo. Estaré en el bote, pero, si vamos a bajar juntos por el río, hay algo que debes saber primero. Igual cambia algunas cosas.

—¿El qué? —Se me corta un poco la respiración.

Los hombros delgados como huesos de Arney suben y bajan y me mira con los ojos entornados antes de decir:

—No soy un chico. —Se desabrocha el cuello de la camisa, que en realidad es poco más que un harapo. Una tira de muselina sucia que parece el vendaje de un doctor le envuelve el pecho y Arney no es un chico—. Arney es diminutivo de Arnelle, pero padre no quiere que nadie se entere. La gente no me dejaría trabajar si lo supiera.

Ahora estoy más convencida que nunca de que Arney tiene que quedarse en el río con nosotras. Además del hecho de que sea una chica, y de que esta no es vida para una chica, tiene cardenales por todo su cuerpo flacucho.

Pero ¿qué opinará Zede de tener una chica en su barco?

Quizá Briny y Queenie nos dejen tener a Arney en el *Arcadia*. Encontraré la manera de solucionarlo.

—Da igual que seas una chica, Arney. Te encontraremos un hogar. Tú estate preparada esta noche cuando la luna esté sobre los árboles.

Nos lo prometemos enlazando el dedo meñique y luego el padre de Arney la llama a gritos desde el otro lado de los árboles. Se terminó el almuerzo.

Me paso la tarde preguntándome si Arney estará esta noche en la barca cuando Fern y yo lleguemos allí. Pero supongo que sí, porque, si lo piensa, se dará cuenta de que no hay gran cosa que la retenga aquí. Necesita irse río abajo tanto como nosotras.

Los Sevier vuelven a hablar en su dormitorio antes de que el señor Sevier se vaya a Memphis a su reunión. Cuando bajan, lleva una bolsa de viaje pequeña.

—Si la reunión termina tarde, igual me quedo en la ciudad —dice y a continuación besa a Fern en la frente y a mí también, algo que no ha hecho nunca antes.

Aprieto los dientes e intento estarme muy quieta cuando se inclina sobre mí. Solo puedo pensar en el señor Riggs.

—Cuidaos las tres. —Mira a la señora Sevier—. No te preocupes. Todo va a salir bien.

Zuma le da su sombrero cuando sale por la puerta y ya estamos las mujeres solas. La señora Sevier les dice a Zuma y a Hootsie que pueden irse al cuarto de la cochera a descansar. No merece la pena ponerse a cocinar. Las chicas cenaremos emparedados en una bandeja.

Zuma prepara una bandeja muy bonita antes de irse.

—Vamos a hacer una fiesta de pijamas. Esta noche tenemos *Capitán Midnight* en la radio —dice la señora Sevier—. Y también cacao caliente. A ver si me asienta el estómago.

Se pasa la lengua por los labios y se apoya una mano en el vientre.

—Yo tampoco tengo muy bien la barriga —comento.

Estoy deseando subir y recoger algunas cosas. No me llevaré más que lo imprescindible de lo que nos han comprado los Sevier. No estaría bien. Y además en el *Arcadia* tenemos cosas. No son elegantes, como las de aquí, pero nos bastan y nos sobran. ¿Para qué querría una niña que vive en el río vestidos de volantes y zapatos de piel reluciente? Además, el ruido de las suelas ahuyentaría a los peces.

—Subid a poneros los pijamas, niñas. May, te encontrarás mejor cuando tomemos un poco de cacao y cosas ricas. —La señora Sevier se seca la frente con el dorso de la mano, luego se obliga a sonreír—. Venga. Lo vamos a pasar muy bien esta noche. Las chicas solas.

Cojo a Fern de la mano y subimos.

Fern está tan ilusionada con la fiesta de la señora Sevier que se lava y se cambia en un periquete, aunque se pone el camisón al revés.

Se lo arreglo y le pongo la bata y me la pongo yo también, pero encima de la ropa. Si la señora Sevier se da cuenta, le diré que tenía frío. Últimamente ha empezado a refrescar en la casa de noche. Un recordatorio más de que tenemos que volver al río antes de que llegue el invierno.

Intento parecer contenta por nuestra fiesta, pero estoy nerviosa como un gato mientras nos comemos los emparedados. Se me cae uno en la bata y la mancha, y la señora Sevier me lo limpia.

Me toca la frente para ver si tengo fiebre.

—¿Cómo te encuentras ahora que has comido?

En lo único que puedo pensar es en que ojalá fuera Queenie. Me gustaría que esta gran casa fuera de Queenie y Briny y me gustaría que la señora Sevier pudiera tener un hijo detrás de otro como Queenie para que no estuviera tan sola cuando nos vayamos.

Niego con la cabeza y susurro:

—Me gustaría irme a la cama. Puedo llevarme a Fern y acostarla.

—No hace falta. —Me pasa una mano por el pelo cogiéndomelo con los dedos y separándomelo de la nuca igual que hacía Queenie—. Ya la subo yo luego. A fin y al cabo soy su mamá.

Dentro de mí todo se vuelve otra vez frío y duro. Casi ni la siento cuando me besa en la mejilla y me pregunta si quiero que venga a arroparme.

—No..., mamá.

Salgo de la habitación lo más deprisa que puedo y no me vuelvo ni una sola vez.

Una vez arriba, el tiempo se me hace eterno hasta que la señora Sevier sube a acostar a Fern. A través de la pared la oigo cantar una nana y me tapo los oídos con las manos.

Queenie y yo les cantábamos mucho esa canción a mis hermanitos.

Duerme, niñito,
no llores más.

Bonitos caballos
mañana tendrás.

Todo se enreda dentro de mi cabeza. El *Arcadia* y esta casa. Mis padres verdaderos y el señor y la señora Sevier. Queenie y mamá y Briny y papá. El gran río. El brazo muerto. El pantano. Porches blancos alargados y otros pequeños que navegan sin rumbo, sin ningún rumbo, por el río, sin pintar.

Me hago la dormida cuando la señora Sevier entra en mi habitación y vuelve a tocarme la frente. Me da miedo que quiera despertarme y preguntarme cómo me encuentro, pero se va. La puerta del final del pasillo se cierra y por fin puedo respirar tranquila.

La luna está saliendo justo cuando me levanto y me pongo el abrigo y los zapatos. Me cuelgo una bolsa pequeña a la espalda y voy al cuarto de Fern y la cojo en brazos.

—Chsss, no hagas ruido. Vamos a ir hasta el río a ver luciérnagas. Si alguien nos oye, no nos dejarán ir.

Envuelvo a mi hermanita en una manta y, para cuando hemos bajado las escaleras y salido al porche, ya se ha dormido encima de mi hombro. Fuera está oscuro y hay sombras, y oigo algo arañar el suelo del jardín cerca de la casa, un mapache o una mofeta, quizá. Los perros de caza del señor Sevier ladran cuando salgo al césped, pero se callan cuando ven que soy yo. En la cochera nadie enciende la luz. El rocío salpica y me moja las piernas mientras sujeto con fuerza a Fern y corro hacia los árboles. Por encima de las ramas, la luna brilla alta y llena, tan radiante como el farol que Briny cuelga siempre en el *Arcadia* por las noches. Hay luz de sobra para ver por dónde voy y eso es todo lo que necesito. Enseguida llegamos a la orilla del lago. Arney nos está esperando, como prometió.

Hablamos en susurros, aunque me dice que su padre duerme como un tronco por el whisky, como de costumbre.

—Si se despierta y quiere algo de mí, no podrá levantarse para ir a buscarme.

Pero, por si acaso, Arney nos hace subir deprisa a la barca. Sus ojos son dos grandes círculos blancos en su carita delgada cuando se vuelve a mirar el campamento.

Está quieta con una mano sobre el pequeño bote y los dos pies en la orilla. Tengo la sensación de que lleva una eternidad vuelta hacia el campamento, mirando.

—Sube —susurro. En el suelo del bote, Fern se está empezando a despertar; bosteza, se estira y mira a su alrededor. Tengo miedo de que, si se entera de lo que está pasando, arme un escándalo.

Los dedos de Arney se van separando del bote hasta apoyar solo las puntas.

—Arney. —¿Estará pensando en mandarnos solas? No tengo ni idea de cómo llevar el bote y tampoco conozco el pantano. Nos perderemos y no saldremos vivas—. Arney, tenemos que irnos.

Pasadas las copas de los árboles, las sombras sobre el césped cambian y me parece ver haces de luz moviéndose sobre la hierba. Para cuando me levanto para mirar, han desaparecido. Igual estaban solo en mi imaginación... O quizá el señor Sevier ha decidido volver a casa esta noche en lugar de quedarse en la ciudad. Podría estar aparcando el automóvil y entrando en la casa en este momento. Mirará en nuestros dormitorios y verá que nos hemos ido.

Me inclino como puedo sobre la borda y cojo a Arney del brazo, y ella da un salto, como si se hubiera olvidado de que estoy allí. A la luz de la luna, sus ojos se clavan en los míos.

—No sé si hago bien —dice—. Nunca volveré a ver a mi familia.

—Te tratan mal, Arney. Tienes que irte. Tienes que venir con nosotras. Ahora somos tu familia. Fern y yo y Briny y Queenie y el viejo Zede.

Nos miramos largo rato. Por fin asiente con la cabeza y empuja el bote de manera que pierdo el equilibrio y me caigo encima de Fern. Cogemos los remos y nos alejamos, dejando que el viento y la corriente nos impulsen hacia el pantano hasta que estamos lejos de la orilla.

—¿Dónde están... las luciérnagas? —murmura Fern cuando me acerco a gatas a ella.

—Chsss. Primero tenemos que llegar hasta el río. Puedes dormir otro rato. —La tapo bien con la manta, le pongo los zapatos para que no se le enfríen los pies y dejo que use la bolsa de almohada—. Te despertaré para que las veas.

No habrá caimanes, pero, cuando Fern vea por fin el *Arcadia*, no le importará.

Arney arranca el motor y se sienta en la popa para pilotar. Yo cojo un remo y me coloco en la parte de delante por si hay troncos a la deriva.

—Enciende la lámpara —dice Arney—. En esa caja de ahí hay cerillas.

Hago lo que me dice y minutos después navegamos por el ancho y claro lago despertando a las criaturas de la noche que se escabullen de la luz de la lámpara. Me siento libre como los gansos del Canadá que nos sobrevuelan, llamándose a graznidos y tapando las estrellas. Se dirigen al mismo lugar que nosotras. Al sur del río. Los veo pasar y deseo poder atrapar uno y dejar que me lleve volando a casa.

—Estate atenta. —Arney reduce la velocidad cuando el brazo se estrecha y los árboles se cierran—. Si ves troncos, apártalos. No dejes que choquemos con ninguno.

—Ya.

El aire de la noche se enfría, se espesa y huele a pantano. Me abotono el abrigo hasta el cuello. Los árboles tapan el cielo, sus troncos son anchos, retorcidos y nudosos. Las ramas nos buscan como dedos. Algo araña la quilla y nos levanta por uno de los lados.

—Apártalas —ladra Arney—. Si una rompe el bote, se acabó.

Estoy atenta a troncos, a nudos de ramas de ciprés y a cualquier madera a la deriva. La empujo con el remo y avanzamos muy despacio. Aquí y allí hay esquifes amarrados en la orilla y casas flotantes con faroles que parpadean, pero estamos prácticamente solas. No hay nada excepto kilómetros de tierra baja y cenagosa donde viven nutrias y linces y el musgo cuelga espeso de las ramas altas. Los árboles forman siluetas que parecen monstruos en la oscuridad.

Grita una lechuza y Arney y yo nos agachamos. La oímos pasar volando sobre nuestras cabezas.

Fern se revuelve en sueños, el ruido la ha molestado.

Pienso en las historias de Briny sobre el rugarú, el hombre lobo que se lleva a los niños al pantano. Un escalofrío me recorre el cuerpo, pero no dejo que Arney se dé cuenta. No hay aquí monstruos peores que los que nos esperan en casa de la señora Murphy si nos mandan de vuelta.

Pase lo que pase, no pueden cogernos a Fern y a mí.

Me concentro en el agua e intento no pensar en lo que puede haber en el pantano. Arney vira a un lado y a otro encontrando siempre la manera de avanzar, tal y como dijo que haría.

Por fin nos quedamos sin luz de luna y se termina el queroseno de la lámpara. La llama chisporrotea hasta que solo arde la mecha. La brisa la apaga cuando nos acercamos a la orilla y atamos la guía a la rama de un árbol. Las piernas y los brazos me pesan igual que los troncos empapados que he estado apartando con el remo. Me duelen y me crujen cuando gateo hasta el centro del bote para meterme debajo de la manta al lado de Fern, que ha estado dormida casi todo el rato.

Arney hace lo mismo.

—Desde aquí, el final del pantano no está lejos —dice y las tres nos hacemos un ovillo, ateridas y mojadas y con ganas de dormir. Me parece oír música procedente de alguna parte y me digo que es un barco con espectáculo a bordo y que eso quiere decir que el río está cerca, pero podría ser mi imaginación, que me engaña. A medida que me quedo dormida, estoy más convencida de que es el sonido de barcas y barcazas a lo lejos. Las sirenas y los silbidos viajan en la noche. Escucho con atención, intento decidir si sé cuáles son. El *Benny Slade*, el *General P.* y un vapor de ruedas con su inconfundible chuuuu, chas chas, chuuuu.

Estoy en casa. Me envuelve una nana que conozco de memoria. Dejo que la oscuridad y los sonidos de la noche entren en mí y ahuyenten los malos sueños y las preocupaciones. Mamá agua me mece con suavidad y dulzura hasta que no me rodea nada más.

Duermo el sueño profundo de los habitantes del río.

Por la mañana unas voces me sacan de la calma... Voces... y madera que choca contra madera. Retiro la manta y Arney se endereza enseguida al otro lado de Fern. Nos miramos un minuto mientras recordamos dónde estamos y lo que hemos hecho. Entre las dos, Fern se gira y mira el cielo pestañeando.

—Ya te dije que había alguien en el bote, Remley. —Tres chiquillos de color nos miran subidos a raíces de ciprés; sus pantalones de peto enrollados dejan ver piernas flacas y sucias de barro.

—¡Ese es una chica! —dice el niño mayor de todos levantando el mentón para verme mejor y golpeando el bote con el garfio de un palo para coger ranas—. ¡Y también hay una niña pequeña! ¡Son blancas!

Los otros retroceden, pero el niño mayor —no puede tener más de nueve o diez años— se queda donde está apoyado en el palo.

—¿Qué hacéis aquí? ¿Os habéis perdido?

Arney se pone de pie y los ahuyenta con la mano.

—¡Fuera de aquí! Largo si sabéis lo que os conviene. —Su voz es más profunda, como la que usaba antes de que supiera que es una chica—. Hemos salido a pescar y estamos esperando a que sea de día para volver, ya está. Que uno de vosotros suelte esa amarra para que podamos irnos.

Los niños se quedan donde están sin dejar de mirarnos con los ojos muy abiertos.

—¡Deprisa! ¿Es que no me oís? —Arney agita un remo en dirección a la rama a la que está atado el bote. El agua nos ha hecho dar vueltas mientras dormíamos y la cuerda está enganchada. Será difícil que consigamos soltarla nosotras solas.

Rebusco en la bolsa y saco una galleta. En casa de los Sevier no es difícil birlar algún dulce de los que hace Zuma. En los últimos días he estado escondiendo algunos en previsión para nuestro viaje. Ahora nos vendrán bien.

—Si lo hacéis, os doy una galleta.

Fern se frota los ojos y susurra:

—¿Dónde está mamá?

—Calla —le digo—. Estate muy callada. Nada de preguntas.

Sostengo la galleta para que la vean los niños. El más pequeño sonríe, luego suelta el palo y se sube a la rama con la agilidad de una lagartija. Tarda un poco, pero consigue soltar el nudo. Antes de alejarnos, tiro tres galletas a la orilla.

—No tenías que darles ninguna —protesta Arney.

Fern se acerca a mí y se pasa la lengua por los labios.

Les doy las dos últimas galletas.

—Cuando lleguemos al *Arcadia,* tendremos comida de sobra. Queenie y Briny estarán tan contentos de vernos que prepararán tal barbaridad de comer que te parecerá mentira.

Desde que empezó este viaje, he estado prometiendo cosas a Arney para animarla a seguir. Me doy cuenta de que sigue queriendo volver con su familia. Es curioso como aquello a lo que estás acostumbrado te parece bien aunque esté mal.

—Verás —le digo—. Cuando estemos en el *Arcadia,* nos iremos río abajo donde nadie nos moleste. Iremos hacia el sur y el viejo Zede nos seguirá.

No dejo de repetirme eso a mí misma mientras arrancamos el motorcillo y navegamos hacia la desembocadura del pantano, pero es como si tuviera dentro una cuerda que sigue atada a lo que dejo atrás. Se va tensando cada vez más, incluso después de doblar un recodo y de que los árboles se espacien y vea el río, esperando para llevarnos a casa. Hay una preocupación que crece en mi interior y no tiene nada que ver con las estelas de los barcos grandes que nos mecen y zarandean mientras nos dirigimos traqueteando hacia Memphis.

Cuando por fin vemos la isla de Mud, la preocupación me impide respirar y casi deseo que una barcaza a la deriva nos hunda mientras cruzamos hacia el remanso. ¿Qué dirán Briny y Queenie cuando vean que Fern es la única que queda además de mí?

La pregunta me pesa más y más cuando dejamos atrás el viejo campamento, que ahora está casi vacío, y mientras guío a Arney hacia el remanso que he cruzado cien veces en mi imaginación. He viajado aquí desde el automóvil de la señorita Tann, desde el sótano de la señora Murphy, desde el sofá de la fiesta para padres adoptivos y desde el dormitorio decorado con puntillas rosas de la mansión de los Sevier.

Me cuesta creer, incluso cuando doblamos el recodo y el *Arcadia* está esperándonos, que esto es real. Que no es otro sueño más.

La casa flotante de Zede está amarrada un poco más abajo, pero, a medida que me acerco, me doy cuenta de que algo le pasa al *Arcadia*. La baranda del porche está rota. El techo está cubierto de ramas y hojas caídas. Los afilados colmillos de cristal de una ventana hecha añicos centellean en la luz del sol cerca de la chimenea de la estufa. El *Arcadia* está escorado y tiene el casco tan encallado en la orilla que me pregunto cómo lo vamos a soltar.

—¡El *Arcadia*! ¡El *Arcadia*! —Fern chilla, aplaude y señala; sus tirabuzones dorados como el sol suben y bajan. Se pone de pie en el centro del bote como solo una niña del río sabría—. ¡*Arcadia*! ¡Queenie! ¡Queenie! —vuelve a gritar mientras nos acercamos.

No parece haber nadie. *¿Habrán salido a primera hora a pescar o cazar? ¿O quizá están con Zede?*

Pero Queenie no suele dejar el barco. Le gusta quedarse en casa a no ser que tenga alguna amiga cerca a la que visitar. Y por aquí no hay nadie.

—¿Es este? —pregunta Arney dudosa.

—Deben de haber salido. —Trato de parecer tranquila, pero no lo estoy. Un sentimiento espeso y negro se apodera de mí. Queenie y Briny nunca permitirían que el *Arcadia* tuviera este aspecto. A Briny le gustaba presumir de su barco. Lo tenía siempre muy cuidado. Incluso con cinco niños, Queenie tenía nuestro hogar inmaculado. «Impoluto», decía.

El *Arcadia* no está nada impoluto ahora mismo. La cosa empeora cuando Arney nos acerca a la pasarela y apaga el motor para que podamos llegar flotando. Cuando agarro la barandilla para impulsarnos, me quedo con un trozo en la mano y estoy a punto de caerme al agua.

Acabamos de echar la amarra cuando veo a Silas correr por la orilla, sus largas piernas abriéndose paso en la arena. Salta un montón de maleza, ágil como un zorro. Me acuerdo de Camellia escabulléndose cuando vino la policía.

Parece que hace años de eso y no solo meses.

Silas se encuentra conmigo cuando bajo del barco. Me da un abrazo de oso y me mece y me levanta en volandas mientras hunde los pies en la arena. Luego me deja a la entrada de la pasarela.

—¡Qué alegría! —dice—. Pensaba que no volvería a verte.

—Yo tampoco estaba segura. —A mi espalda, oigo a Arney ayudar a Fern, pero no puedo apartar los ojos de Silas. Yo sí que me alegro de verlo—. Estoy en casa. He vuelto a casa.

—Claro que sí. Y además traes a Fern. ¡Espera a que se entere Zede!

Vuelve a abrazarme y esta vez no me quedo con los brazos pegados al cuerpo. Le devuelvo el abrazo.

Hasta que no habla Fern, no me acuerdo de que hay alguien más con nosotros.

—¿Dónde está Queenie? —pregunta.

En cuanto me separo de Silas y doy un paso atrás para mirarlo a la cara, sé que algo va mal. Nadie ha salido del barco, y eso que hemos hecho ruido.

—Silas, ¿dónde está Queenie? ¿Dónde está Briny?

Silas me coge por los hombros. Sus ojos oscuros se clavan con intensidad en los míos. Le tiembla un poco una de las comisuras de la boca.

—Tu madre murió hace tres semanas, Rill. El médico dijo que de envenenamiento de la sangre, pero Zede me dijo que tenía el corazón roto. Os echaba mucho de menos.

La noticia me destripa igual que a un pez. Estoy vacía por dentro. *¿Que mi madre ya no está en este mundo? ¿No está en este mundo y no volveré a verla?*

—¿Dónde..., dónde está Briny? —pregunto.

Silas me sujeta más fuerte. Me doy cuenta de que tiene miedo de que, si me suelta, me caiga al suelo como una muñeca de trapo. Durante un segundo creo que lo voy a hacer.

—No está bien, Rill. Empezó a beber después de perderos a todos. Y desde que murió Queenie, está aún peor. Mucho peor.

23

Trent y yo estamos uno junto al otro mirando las viejas columnas que cierran el perímetro de unos cimientos de cemento y piedra en mal estado. Se alzan como centinelas, de porte militar, los pies perdidos en la hiedra y la hierba crecida, las gorras coronadas con volutas y querubines.

Transcurren unos instantes antes de que nos demos cuenta de que Jonah ha subido los peldaños para investigar lo que debió de ser en otro tiempo un porche de varias alturas. Sobre nuestras cabezas, las oxidadas barandillas del segundo piso se intercalan serpenteantes con las columnas, uniéndolas como mechones desvaídos de una trenza dorada.

—Oye, vuelve aquí, peque —le dice Trent a Jonah. La piedra parece sólida, pero no hay manera de saber si este lugar es seguro.

Esto fue en otro tiempo la casa de una plantación, asentada sobre una suave colina a orillas del río Savannah, no lejos de Augusta. ¿De quién era? En las inmediaciones, un nevero y otras construcciones exentas se alzan desvalidas, sus techumbres de tejas rojas deteriorándose despacio, con maderos rotos asomando como huesos astillados.

—¿A qué vendría aquí mi abuela?

Me resulta imposible imaginarme a la abuela Judy, una mujer que me regañaba si entraba en casa procedente del establo con pelo de caballo en los pantalones y se me ocurría sentarme en algún mueble, en un lugar como este.

Y cada jueves durante años. ¿Por qué?

—Una cosa es segura. Aquí no la molestaba nadie. Dudo de que alguien sepa siquiera que este sitio existe. —Trent va hacia los escalones y le tiende la mano a Jonah mientras este salta alegremente—. No te separes de papá, cariño. Ya sé que esto es alucinante, pero puede haber serpientes.

Jonah se pone de puntillas para ver más allá de la entrada.

—¿Dónde está la serpiente?

—He dicho que puede haber una.

—Ah...

Por un momento me distraigo mirándolos. Parecen la fotografía de una revista. El radiante sol de mediodía se cuela a raudales por entre los árboles centenarios y se posa en ellos, resaltando su pelo rubio pajizo y el parecido de sus facciones.

Por fin me vuelvo hacia la casa en ruinas. En su día debió de ser una gran mansión.

—Bueno, a juzgar por el hecho de que venía en taxi y no en su coche con su chófer, no quería que nadie supiera dónde estaba.

Quiero que la verdad sea así de inocente, pero no me engaño. Es demasiada coincidencia que May Crandall mencionara Augusta y que mi abuela viniera aquí de forma regular. Esto es algo que tiene que ver con las dos. Esta casa es de May, lo sé. Su relación con la abuela Judy va más allá de trabajar juntas en una historia trágica de adopción ocurrida hace tiempo.

—Parece que la carretera sigue por allí. —Trent señala el camino que hemos recorrido desde la verja de entrada. Con hierba crecida en la parte central y las inflorescencias que se doblan tapando los surcos hechos por neumáticos, apenas puede llamarse carretera, pero es evidente que desde la estación pasada alguien ha conducido por ella y ha segado la hierba. Alguien ha estado cuidando este lugar hasta hace relativamente poco.

—Supongo que deberíamos ver a dónde lleva.

Pero parte de mí, una parte muy grande, no quiere saberlo.

Echamos a andar por la carretera después de cruzar lo que en otro tiempo fue el césped delantero. Jonah levanta mucho las piernas a cada paso que da, vadeando la hierba sin segar como si estuviera tanteando las olas en la orilla del mar. Trent lo levanta y lo sujeta con un brazo cuando la hierba se espesa y el camino se acerca a los árboles.

Jonah señala pájaros y ardillas y flores haciendo que nuestro paseo parezca algo inocente, una excursión por la naturaleza con amigos. Quiere que tanto su padre como yo comentemos lo que ve. Lo intento, pero mis pensamientos corren colina abajo a un millón de kilómetros por hora. Por entre los árboles veo agua. El sol la ilumina y una brisa arruga ligeramente su superficie. Es el río, sin duda.

Jonah me llama *Ei-ver-vi.* Su padre lo corrige:

—Se llama señorita Stafford. —Me sonríe mirándome de reojo—. Mi familia es de la vieja escuela. A los adultos se les llama por su apellido.

—Está muy bien. —A mí también me educaron así. Honeybee me mandaba a mi habitación si no usaba «señor» o «señora» para dirigirme a las personas mayores. La norma estuvo vigente hasta que me fui a la universidad, ya adulta.

Más adelante, el camino rodea lo que parecen ser los restos de una verja de hierro oxidado. Está tan cubierta de matas de jazmín de Virginia que no me doy cuenta de que encierra un jardín hasta que la tenemos casi encima. Por entre las rosas trepadoras rojas y los pétalos blancos como la nieve del mirto asoma una pulcra casita. Situada en una colina baja que da al río, parece la cabaña encantada de un cuento infantil, donde podría refugiarse una princesa o un sabio ermitaño que en otro tiempo fue rey. Desde la verja del jardín delantero, una pasarela conduce colina abajo a un embarcadero inclinado sobre el agua.

Aunque los jardines que rodean la casa están ahora descuidados, es evidente que se hicieron con cariño. Hay cenadores, bancos y bebederos de pájaros junto a cuidados caminos de piedra. A juzgar por lo gastado de los marcos de madera de las ventanas y el tejado de chapa, diría que lleva décadas aquí.

Así que aquí era donde venía mi abuela. Es fácil imaginar que disfrutara haciéndolo. Es un sitio donde podría dejar atrás sus obligaciones, preocupaciones, deberes, la reputación de la familia, el ojo público..., todo lo que llenaba esos dietarios cuidadosamente llevados.

—Quién iba a decir que había aquí un sitio así. —Trent admira el pequeño refugio mientras nos encaminamos a la parte delantera, donde un amplio porche cerrado se adivina entre los árboles. Las ventanas tienen visillos de encaje. Un viento entona la música dulce y suave del mediodía. Ramitas y hojas en los peldaños confirman que nadie ha barrido desde las últimas tormentas.

—Desde luego.

¿Es esta la casa de May Crandall? ¿Donde la encontraron haciendo compañía al cuerpo sin vida de su hermana?

Trent abre la verja torcida para que podamos entrar. Los hierros arañan el suelo de piedra, quejándose de nuestra intrusión.

—Está muy silenciosa. Vamos a ver si hay alguien.

Subimos juntos los peldaños y Trent deja a Jonah en el porche mientras la puerta mosquitera se cierra a nuestra espalda con un chirrido.

Llamamos y esperamos y por fin miramos por entre los visillos de encaje. Dentro, un sofá canapé con tapicería de flores y rodeado de mesas estilo reina Ana y lámparas Tiffany parece fuera de lugar en una sencilla casa de campo. Cuadros y fotografías llenan las paredes del pequeño cuarto de estar, pero desde donde estoy no los veo bien. Al fondo hay una cocina. Hay dos puertas en la habitación principal que parecen conducir a dormitorios y a un porche cerrado, al fondo.

Me he ido a la otra ventana para ver mejor, cuando oigo a Trent girar el pomo de la puerta.

—¿Qué haces? —Me vuelvo a mirar por encima de mi hombro medio esperando una sirena de policía, o incluso una escopeta apuntándonos.

Trent me guiña un ojo; su mirada es traviesa cuando el pomo hace clic.

—Estoy inspeccionando una posible venta. Creo recordar que me llamaron para que hiciera un informe de la casa.

Entra antes de que me dé tiempo a llevarle la contraria. Y tampoco sé si quiero hacerlo. No puedo irme sin saber más, sin descubrir lo que ha estado ocurriendo aquí. Me cuesta imaginar cómo alguien en el estado de May Crandall haya podido vivir en este lugar tan aislado.

—Jonah, tú quédate en el porche. Nada de bajar al jardín. —Trent se gira y lo mira con autoridad.

—Vale. —Jonah está ocupado cogiendo bellotas que ha debido de ir acumulando alguna ardilla a través de la esquina rota de la puerta mosquitera. Cuando entro detrás de Trent, las está contando—: Una, dos, *tes*... siete... ocho... *cuadenta y cuato*.

Su voz se pierde cuando piso una pequeña alfombra en el umbral y paseo la vista por la habitación. No es lo que me esperaba. No hay capa de polvo, ni insectos muertos en los antepechos de las ventanas. Todo está impoluto. Se nota que la casa está habitada, pero los únicos sonidos son el silbido del viento, los pájaros, las hojas, la voz susurrada de Jonah y el canto de un ave desde el río.

Trent toca un sobre que hay en la encimera de la cocina y se inclina para mirarlo.

—May Crandall.

Me está presentando una prueba, pero solo la veo a medias.

Estoy concentrada en un cuadro que hay sobre la repisa de la chimenea. Las pamelas de colores brillantes, los vestidos sesenteros bien almidonados, las sonrisas, los rizos dorados que agita la brisa marina, la risa que ves aunque no la oigas...

Reconozco la escena, aunque la he visto en otra versión. En esta, las cuatro mujeres se miran y se ríen. Los niños que juegan en la arena han desaparecido del fondo. La fotografía que encontré en el estudio del abuelo de Trent era en blanco y negro y las mujeres sonreían a la cámara. La instantánea que inspiró este cuadro debió de hacerse un momento antes o después de la otra. El artista que pintó el retrato añadió los colores vivos. No existe un color para pintar la risa y, sin embargo, el momento capturado irradia alegría. Las mujeres están cogidas del brazo a la altura del codo y con la cabeza echada hacia atrás. Una de ellas está dando una patada a unas algas para lanzárselas al fotógrafo.

Me acerco al cuadro para leer la firma en la esquina inferior: «Fern», dice.

Una placa metálica en el marco lleva el título de la obra: «Día de las hermanas».

Mi abuela está a la izquierda. Las otras tres, a juzgar por lo que nos contaron en la residencia, son May, Lark y Fern.

Con las cabezas hacia atrás y el sol que les da en la cara, estas mujeres parecen claramente hermanas.

También mi abuela.

—No es el único retrato. —Trent se gira para inspeccionar la habitación. Hay fotografías por todas partes. Distintas décadas, distintas localizaciones, variedad de marcos y tamaños, pero siempre las mismas cuatro mujeres. En el embarcadero del río, con los tejanos remangados y una caña de pescar en la mano, tomando el té junto al rosal trepador detrás de esta casita; en canoas color rojo empuñando remos.

Trent se inclina sobre una mesa, abre un álbum de fotografías negro gastado y lo hojea.

—Han pasado mucho tiempo aquí.

Doy un paso hacia él.

De pronto ladra un perro fuera. Los dos nos quedamos paralizados mientras el sonido se acerca. Ruido de pezuñas que suben los escalones del porche. En solo cuatro zancadas, Trent ha cruzado la habitación y salido a la puerta, pero no ha sido lo bastante rápido. Un enorme perro negro nos gruñe desde el otro lado de la puerta mosquitera y Jonah se queda muy quieto.

—Tranquilo, colega... —Trent avanza, coge a Jonah de un brazo y me lo pasa.

El perro levanta la cabeza y ladra, luego araña la parte inferior de la puerta intentando meter el hocico por la esquina rota.

No muy lejos, ruge un motor de alguna clase. Una cortadora de césped, quizá. Viene hacia nosotros. Trent y yo no tenemos más remedio que esperar. Ni siquiera me atrevo a cerrar la puerta principal de la casa a nuestra espalda. Si el perro entra en el porche, necesitaremos un refugio.

Somos como delincuentes pillados con las manos en la masa. No, somos delincuentes pillados con las manos en la masa. Sin el como.

Solo Jonah, que no ha cometido ningún delito, está pasándolo bien. Mantengo una mano en su hombro mientras da saltitos intentando averiguar de qué es el sonido de motor.

—Ah. ¡Un tractor!... ¡Un tractor! —saluda cuando un hombre con pantalón de peto y sombrero de paja aparece subido a un tractor rojo y gris del año de la polca. Lleva a remolque un carro viejo de dos ruedas con una desbrozadora y unas cuantas ramas dentro. El sol dibuja motas en la piel marrón lustrosa del hombre cuando se detiene cerca de la verja y apaga el motor.

Cuando lo miro con atención, veo que es más joven de lo que su indumentaria hace pensar. Debe de tener la edad de mis padres... ¿Unos sesenta y algo?

—¡Sammy! —dice con voz profunda y autoritaria mientras se baja del tractor y llama al perro—. ¡Quieto ahora mismo! ¡A callar! ¡Ven aquí!

A Sammy no le gusta que le digan lo que tiene que hacer. Espera casi hasta que el hombre está a su lado para obedecerle.

El desconocido se detiene en la mitad de la escalera del porche, pero es tan alto que ya estamos casi a la misma altura.

—¿Querían algo? —pregunta.

Trent y yo nos miramos. Está claro que ninguno de los dos tenía este momento planeado.

—Estuvimos hablando con May en la residencia. —Trent es un vendedor muy listo. Hace que la frase parezca una explicación, aunque en realidad no lo sea.

—¿Es... es suya esta casa? —balbuceo yo haciéndonos parecer todavía más culpables.

—¡Tienes un tractor! —De los tres, Jonah es el que hace el comentario más inteligente.

—Sí, señor, sí lo tengo, hombrecito. —El hombre apoya las manos en las rodillas para hablar con Jonah—. Era el tractor de mi padre. Lo compró nuevecito en 1958. Cuando tengo un rato vengo a arrancarlo. Limpio la maleza de la granja, recojo las ramas y veo a mi madre. A los nietos les encanta venir conmigo. Tengo allí a uno que debe de ser como tú de mayor.

—Ah —dice Jonah convenientemente impresionado—. Tengo *tes* años. —Con mucho esfuerzo, levanta los tres dedos del medio de una mano y dobla el pulgar y el meñique.

—Pues Bart es de tu edad, entonces —contesta el hombre—. Tres y medio. Se llama como su abuelo, que soy yo. —Bart I se endereza y nos estudia a Trent y a mí.

—¿Son parientes de May? ¿Qué tal está? Me dijo mi madre que su hermana murió y que tuvieron que meterla en una residencia. Dice que sus nietos se la llevaron hasta Aiken pensando que sería mejor que no estuviera demasiado cerca de su casa. Una lástima. Le encantaba este sitio.

—Pues está todo lo bien que puede esperarse, supongo —le digo—. No le gusta mucho estar allí. Y después de ver esta casa, lo entiendo.

—¿Es usted sobrina o nieta? —Se concentra en mí, le veo repasar su catálogo mental tratando de decidir quién puedo ser.

Me da miedo mentirle. No sé ni siquiera si May tiene una nieta. Quizá Bart me está poniendo a prueba.

Y, en cualquier caso, una mentira no solucionará nada.

—Si le soy sincera, no lo sé exactamente. ¿Ha dicho que su madre vive cerca de aquí? Me pregunto si sabrá algo sobre... —*sobre el secreto de mi abuela*— sobre las fotografías que hay en la casa y el cuadro que está encima de la chimenea. Mi abuela es una de las mujeres que está retratada.

Bart mira la casa con expresión de despiste.

—No sabría decirle. Hace años que no entro. Mi madre es la que cuida la casa desde hace mucho tiempo. Desde antes de que un rayo derribara la casa grande en el 82 incluso.

—¿Sería posible... hablar con ella? ¿Cree que la molestaría?

Se retira el sombrero y sonríe.

—Por Dios, ¡en absoluto! Le encanta tener visitas. Solo asegúrense de que tienen tiempo. A mi madre le gusta mucho hablar. —Se inclina hacia atrás y se asoma detrás de la casa—. ¿Han venido andando desde la casa grande? Hay un camino más fácil por ahí. Un sendero que lleva a la granja. May aparcaba su coche al lado de la casa de mi madre.

—Ah, no lo sabía. —Pero eso explica unas cuantas cosas, como lo descuidado de la entrada principal y el camino de cabras por el que hemos llegado hasta aquí—. Hemos entrado por la puerta de hierro.

—Mecachis, pues mañana van a estar llenos de picaduras de ácaros rojos. Recuérdeme que luego les dé un poco del jabón para ácaros de mi madre. Lo hace ella.

Enseguida empieza a picarme todo.

—Súbanse al remolque y los acerco a casa de mi madre. ¿O prefieren ir andando?

Miro el terreno que tenemos que cruzar y no veo más que millones de ácaros rojos esperando a pegarse a mí y causarme picazón para toda la eternidad.

Jonah ya tiembla y le tira a su padre de la pernera del pantalón señalando el tractor.

—Mejor vamos con usted —decide Trent.

Jonah aplaude y vitorea para secundar la moción.

—Vamos, hombrecito. —Bart abre la puerta mosquitera y Jonah le da la mano como si fuera un amigo de toda la vida. Bart lo coge en volandas y baja las escaleras; está claro que tiene experiencia en estas cosas. Se ve que es un abuelo entregado.

Jonah está en la gloria cuando subimos a la pequeña cabina de madera de dos ruedas que me recuerda al vagón para el estiércol que usan los mozos de cuadra en Drayden Hill. Sospecho incluso que este vehículo también ha tenido ese uso. De debajo de las ramas saltan de vez en cuando sustancias de aspecto sospechoso. A Jonah no le importa en absoluto. Parece feliz como un pato en una charca mientras cruzamos la maleza del borde del jardín y seguimos lo que es claramente un camino transitado, quizá por un *quad* o un cochecito de golf.

Nuestra ruta se aleja del río y nos lleva por un camino rural, donde cogemos el primer desvío. La casa azul recién

pintada parece de esos lugares donde habitaría una vieja gran-
jera. Hay gallinas picoteando en el corral. Una vaca lechera
moteada descansa a la sombra de un árbol. La colada tendi-
da ondea perezosa. Sammy se adelanta ladrando y aullando
para anunciar nuestra llegada.

La madre de Bart sale al porche vestida con una bata de
colores vivos, zapatillas de estar en casa y un pañuelo amarillo
intenso. Una flor de seda del mismo color adorna un moño de
rosca gris en lo alto de la cabeza. Cuando nos ve en el remolque del tractor, retrocede y se coloca una mano sobre los ojos
a modo de visera.

—¿A quién traes ahí, Bartholomew?

Dejo que su hijo le dé una explicación, puesto que yo no
tengo ninguna.

—Estaban en casa de la señora Crandall. Dicen que la han
visitado en la residencia.

La barbilla de la mujer desaparece entre los pliegues cur-
tidos y color canela de su cuello.

—¿Cómo dicen que se llaman?

Bajo del remolque antes de que le dé tiempo a decirle a
su hijo que nos lleve adonde nos encontró.

—Avery. —En dos pasos estoy en el porche y me apresuro a darle la mano—. Le he preguntado a su hijo por los
cuadros y las fotografías que hay en casa de May. Mi abuela
está en ellos.

La anciana nos mira alternativamente a mí y a Trent, que
espera al pie de los escalones mientras Jonah investiga el tractor
con ayuda de Bart. De un granero vecino sale un niño de aproximadamente su misma estatura y cruza corriendo el jardín
para unirse a ellos. No hacen falta presentaciones, pero aun así
nos las dan. Es el pequeño Bart.

La mujer vuelve a fijarse en mí. Alarga el cuello y me
inspecciona largo rato y con intensidad, como si estuviera car-

tografiando los contornos de mi cara, comparándolos con algo. ¿Son imaginaciones mías o parece reconocerme?

—¿Cómo me ha dicho que se llama?

—Avery —repito esta vez más alto.

—¿Avery qué más?

—Stafford.

No le he dado esa información hasta ahora a propósito. Pero no quiero irme de aquí sin respuestas y haré lo que sea necesario.

—¿Es hija de la señorita Judy?

El corazón empieza a latirme tan fuerte que noto el latido en los oídos.

—Nieta.

El tiempo parece detenerse, pierdo toda conciencia de los niños que hablan y de Bart I, del cloqueo de las gallinas y la vaca espantando moscas y el canto interminable de un sinsonte.

—Quiere preguntarme por la casa de al lado. Saber por qué venía.

No es una pregunta, sino una afirmación, como si esta mujer llevara años sabiendo que tarde o temprano alguien aparecería haciendo preguntas.

—Sí, señora. Se lo preguntaría a mi abuela, pero, si le digo la verdad, mentalmente no está muy bien. Se olvida de las cosas.

Mueve despacio la cabeza mientras chasquea la lengua. Cuando se concentra de nuevo en mí, dice:

—Lo que la cabeza no recuerda el corazón lo sigue sabiendo. El amor es lo más fuerte que existe. Más fuerte que todas las demás cosas. Quiere saber de las hermanas.

—Por favor —susurro—. Sí, por favor. Cuéntemelo.

—No puedo contar un secreto que no es mío.

Se gira y echa a andar hacia la casa y por un momento pienso que da por concluida la conversación, pero una rápida mirada de reojo me dice lo contrario. Me está pidiendo que entre con ella.

Me lo está ordenando.

Me detengo nada más cruzar el umbral y espero mientras abre la puerta inclinada de un secreter de roble y saca una cruz de hojalata abollada. De debajo saca tres hojas de papel arrugado arrancadas de un bloc amarillo. Aunque han sido arrugadas y estiradas después, no parecen demasiado viejas, desde luego no son de la misma época que la cruz.

—Lo cogí para que no les pasara nada —dice la mujer. Me da la cruz y los papeles por separado—. La cruz fue de Queenie, hace mucho tiempo. Lo otro lo escribió la señorita Judy. Es su historia, pero nunca la terminó. Han decidido llevársela a la tumba con ellas, supongo. Pero imaginaba que algún día aparecería alguien preguntando. Los secretos no son buenos, por muchos años que tengan. A veces los secretos más viejos son los peores. Lleve a su abuela a ver a la señorita May. Su corazón la reconocerá. Sigue sabiendo a quién quiere.

Miro la cruz, le doy la vuelta y a continuación despliego las hojas amarillas. Reconozco la letra. Es la de mi abuela. He leído lo bastante de sus dietarios para estar segura.

—Siéntate, niña. —La madre de Bart me guía hasta un sillón de orejas. Más que sentarme, me dejo caer. La primera página empieza:

PRELUDIO

Baltimore, Maryland
3 de agosto de 1939

La fecha del cumpleaños de mi abuela y el lugar donde nació.

Mi historia empieza una sofocante noche del mes de agosto, en un lugar que nunca veré. La habitación cobra vida solo en mi imaginación. Casi siempre que la evoco es grande. Las paredes son blancas y limpias, las sábanas crujen como una hoja seca. La *suite* privada tiene de todo...

Floto a través del tiempo, retrocedo años y décadas, me desplazo hasta una habitación de hospital en agosto de 1939, a una vida diminuta que sale al mundo y lo abandona de inmediato, a sangre y dolor y a una joven madre exhausta que se sume en un sueño clemente.

Hay hombres poderosos que hablan en susurros. Un abuelo que, a pesar de su fortuna y su posición social, no puede salvar a su nietecita.

Es un hombre importante... ¿Un congresista tal vez?

No puede ayudar a su hija. ¿O igual sí?

Conozco a una mujer en Memphis...

Se toma una decisión desesperada.

Aquí es donde termina la historia escrita.

Y donde empieza otra. La vida de una niñita de pelo rubio que, como otros protagonistas de la sórdida historia de Georgia Tann, es separada de su madre nada más nacer. Se firman documentos falsificados o quizá se le dice simplemente a la madre exhausta que la niña ha nacido muerta. Georgia se lleva a la pequeña y la entrega en secreto a una familia que dirá que es suya y enterrará así su doloroso secreto.

La niñita se convierte en Judy Myers Stafford.

Esta es la verdad que lleva buscando mi corazón desde el día que vi aquella fotografía borrosa en la mesilla de May y me llamó la atención el parecido.

La fotografía de la residencia es de Queenie y Briny. No son dos personas cualquiera del pasado de May. Son mis bisabuelos. Habitantes del río.

Yo podría haberlo sido también, de no haber dado el destino un giro impensable.

La madre de Bart se coloca a mi lado. Se sienta en el brazo del sillón y me frota la espalda, me da un pañuelo cuando empiezo a llorar.

—Ay, cariño. Niña mía. Es mejor saber. Yo lo digo siempre, es mejor ser quien eres. Lo que eres de verdad. No hay otra manera buena de vivir. Pero es una decisión que no me corresponde a mí tomar.

No estoy segura de cuánto tiempo sigo allí con la anciana dándome palmaditas y consolándome mientras contemplo todas las cosas que separaron a los niños del *Arcadia* los unos de los otros. Pienso en cómo explicó May sus decisiones: *Para cuando nos reencontramos éramos mujeres jóvenes con maridos y con hijos. Decidimos no interferir en nuestras vidas respectivas. Nos bastaba con saber que las otras estaban bien...*

Pero lo cierto es que no bastaba. Ni siquiera las barreras de la reputación y la ambición, la posición social pudieron borrar el amor de hermanas, los lazos que las unían. De pronto, los obstáculos que impusieron la necesidad de llevar vidas ocultas y reunirse en lugares secretos parecen casi tan crueles como las adopciones amañadas, los papeles falsificados y las separaciones forzosas.

—Lleva a tu abuela a ver a su hermana. —Una mano temblorosa aprieta la mía—. Solo quedan ellas dos. De las hermanas. Diles que Hootsie ha dicho que es el momento de ser quienes de verdad son.

24

RILL

El canto del chotacabras trata de arrancarme de mi sueño, pero lo ahuyento y me aferro al sueño. Estamos todos a bordo del *Arcadia*... Briny y Lark y Fern y Gabion. Navegamos por el centro del ancho Misisipi como si fuéramos dueños y señores del río. Hace un día despejado y hermoso y no se ve un remolque ni una barcaza ni un vapor de ruedas.

Somos libres. Somos libres y dejamos que el río nos lleve hacia el sur. Lejos, muy lejos de la isla de Mud y de todo lo que ocurrió allí.

Silas y Zede también están. Y Camellia y Queenie.

Por eso sé que es un sueño.

Abro los ojos, aparto la manta y, por un momento, el sol me ciega y no sé dónde estoy. Es pleno día, no de noche. Entonces me doy cuenta de que estoy hecha un ovillo en el esquife con Fern y que estamos arrebujadas bajo una lona, no una manta. El esquife está amarrado a la popa del *Arcadia* y no va a ninguna parte. Es el único sitio en el que podemos descansar durante el día sin tener que preocuparnos de que nos encuentre Briny.

El chotacabras canta otra vez. Es Silas, lo sé. Le busco entre los arbustos, pero está escondido.

Me retuerzo bajo la lona y Fern se despierta y me coge del tobillo. Desde que hemos vuelto al *Arcadia* le da miedo estar sola. Nunca sabe cuándo puede darle Briny un empujón que la haga caer al suelo o abrazarla tan fuerte que no pueda respirar.

Contesto a la llamada del pájaro y Fern se incorpora tratando de ver algo en el bosque.

—Chsss —susurro. Cuando nos fuimos a hurtadillas al esquife esta mañana, Briny andaba dando tumbos con una botella de whisky en la mano. Lo más probable es que a estas alturas se haya quedado dormido en el porche. Pero no puedo saberlo con seguridad—. Mejor que Briny no se entere de que ha venido Silas.

Fern asiente con la cabeza y se pasa la lengua por los labios. Le rugen las tripas. Probablemente sabe que Silas nos traerá algo de comer. Si no fuera por Silas, el viejo Zede y Arney, nos habríamos muerto de hambre en las tres semanas que llevamos en el *Arcadia*. Briny no necesita mucha comida. Se alimenta casi solo de whisky.

Levanto la lona y le digo a Fern:

—Quédate ahí un minuto.

Si Briny ve a Silas y se pone furioso, no quiero que Fern esté por medio.

Tengo que soltármela del cuello para ponerla otra vez debajo de la lona, pero después se queda quieta.

Silas me espera en los arbustos. Me abraza fuerte y tengo que morderme el labio para no llorar. Nos alejamos un poco más del río, pero no tanto como para que no pueda oír a Fern si me llama.

—¿Estáis bien? —me pregunta Silas cuando nos sentamos en un claro debajo de un árbol.

Asiento con la cabeza.

—Aunque esta mañana la pesca no se nos ha dado bien. —No quiero pedir, pero tengo la esperanza de que eso que lleva en un hatillo sea comida.

Me da un bulto que no es más grande que dos puños, pero significa mucho. Zede se está quedando sin provisiones y ahora también tiene que dar de comer a Arney. Se ha ido a su barco, donde estará segura. Zede quería que Fern y yo nos fuéramos también, pero yo sé que Briny no nos hará daño.

—Tortas de avena y un poco de pescado salado. Y una manzana que podéis compartir. —Silas se inclina hacia atrás apoyado en las manos, toma aire y mira entre las zarzas en dirección al río.

—¿Está Briny mejor hoy? ¿Más sereno?

—Un poco. —No estoy segura de si es cierto. Quiero que lo sea. Todo lo que hace Briny es deambular por el barco y beber y gritar por las noches. Por el día duerme la mona.

—Zede dice que esta tarde va a llover.

Yo también he visto las señales de lluvia. Me preocupa.

—No volváis a intentar soltar amarras, ¿de acuerdo? Todavía no. Quizá dentro de unos días. En unos cuantos días creo que Briny estará preparado.

Llevamos dos semanas en la orilla opuesta a la isla de Mud mientras el tiempo se vuelve cada vez más frío. Aunque Silas y Zede advirtieron a Briny de que la policía nos encontraría enseguida si venían a buscarnos aquí, Briny no nos deja soltar amarras. Casi le vuela una mano a Silas de un disparo por intentarlo. Y estuvo a punto de disparar también a la pobre Arney. Le di algo de ropa de Queenie y Briny decidió que era Queenie y se puso furioso con ella por haberse muerto.

—Solo un poquito más —le suplico a Silas.

Silas se frota la oreja como si no fuera eso lo que quiere oír.

—Deberías coger a Fern y veniros conmigo al barco de Zede. Lo sacaremos al río y ya verás como Briny nos sigue.

—Solo unos días más. Briny se pondrá mejor. Ha perdido la cabeza, pero se le pasará.

Esa es mi esperanza, pero lo cierto es que Briny no quiere dejar a Queenie y Queenie está enterrada en la espesa tierra del Misisipi no lejos de aquí. Un sacerdote católico dijo allí una última oración por ella, me contó Zede. Yo ni siquiera sabía que Queenie era católica. Hasta que me fui a vivir con los Sevier, ni siquiera sabía lo que significaba eso. Zuma llevaba una crucecita como la de la pared de nuestro barco. A veces la cogía y le hablaba, igual que hacía Queenie, solo que no en polaco. A los Sevier no les hacía mucha gracia porque son baptistas.

Supongo que, sea como sea, es un consuelo saber que a mi madre la enterraron como es debido y con un predicador que dijera unas plegarias en su tumba.

—Zede quiere que le digas a Briny que dentro de cuatro días se va, que se lleva nuestro barco y que, si no quiere venir, os sacará a Fern y a ti del *Arcadia*. Os llevamos río abajo con nosotros.

—¿Quién *essshtá* ahí? —La voz de Briny retumba desde algún lugar cerca de la orilla. Arrastra las palabras por efecto del alcohol. Ha debido de oír a Silas—. ¿Quién *eresshh?*

Briny aparece dando tumbos entre los arbustos y la maleza.

Cojo el hatillo, me lo meto debajo del vestido y le hago una señal a Silas para que se marche. Briny se tambalea mientras me escabullo hasta el esquife, cojo a Fern y la llevo al barco.

Cuando por fin vuelve, Briny nos encuentra ahí. Hago como que acabo de freír las tortas de avena. Ni siquiera se da cuenta de que la estufa no está encendida.

—Ya casi está la cena. —Empiezo a sacar platos con gran despliegue—. ¿Tienes hambre?

Parpadea, coge a Fern en brazos y se sienta a la mesa mientras la abraza con fuerza. Fern me mira, pálida y asustada.

Me siento como si me estrangularan. ¿Cómo voy a decirle a Briny que Zede solo piensa esperar unos días más? No puedo, así que digo:

—Tortas de avena, pescado salado y gajos de manzana.

Pongo la comida en la mesa y Briny deja a Fern en su sitio. Se diría que hemos comido juntos como las personas normales todos los días. Durante un rato, todo es como debería. Briny me sonríe con ojos oscuros y cansados que me recuerdan a Camellia.

Echo de menos a mi hermana, aunque nos peleáramos todo el rato. Echo de menos lo dura y terca que era. Cómo no se rendía nunca.

—Dice Zede que en cuatro días las corrientes serán buenas y que es el momento de echarse al río. Navegar hacia el sur, donde hay pesca y las aguas son cálidas. Dice que ha llegado el momento.

Briny apoya un codo en la mesa y se frota los ojos mientras mueve la cabeza despacio atrás y adelante. Se le traban las palabras, pero consigo oír las últimas.

—... no sin Queenie.

Se levanta y va hacia la puerta cogiendo la botella vacía de whisky por el camino. Un minuto después, oigo cómo se aleja remando en el esquife.

Espero a que se haya ido y en el silencio que deja atrás me parece que el mundo se me cae encima. Cuando estaba en casa de la señora Murphy y luego con los Sevier pensaba que si conseguía volver al *Arcadia* todo iría bien. Que yo estaría bien. Pero ahora me doy cuenta de que solo me estaba engañando para darme fuerzas un día y otro más.

La verdad es que, en lugar de arreglar nada, haber vuelto al *Arcadia* lo hace todo real. Camellia se ha ido, Lark y Gabion están lejos. Queenie está enterrada en una tumba anónima y con ella el corazón de Briny. Briny se ha refugiado en el whisky y no quiere volver.

Ni siquiera por mí. Ni por Fern. No somos suficiente para él.

Fern trepa a mi regazo y la abrazo con fuerza. Pasamos el resto de la tarde atentas a que vuelva Briny, pero no viene nadie. Lo más seguro es que haya ido a la ciudad a trapichear en los billares para conseguir dinero con que seguir bebiendo.

Por fin acuesto a Fern en su litera, me acuesto en la mía y trato de conciliar el sueño. Ni siquiera tengo un libro que me acompañe. Todo lo que podía servir para comprar whisky se ha vendido.

La lluvia llega antes de que me duerma y Briny sigue sin aparecer.

Lo encuentro en mi sueño. Estamos la familia al completo y todo es como debería. Briny toca la armónica mientras almorzamos en la arena de la orilla. Cogemos margaritas y chupamos madreselva. Gabion y Lark cazan ranas pequeñas hasta que tienen un frasco lleno.

«¿A que tu madre es bonita como una reina?», pregunta Briny. «Y eso, ¿en qué te convierte a ti? Pues en la princesa Rill del reino de Arcadia, claro está».

Cuando me despierto, oigo a Briny fuera, pero no hay música. Está gritándole a la creciente tormenta. El sudor me pega la sábana a la piel, así que tengo que despegármela para sentarme. Tengo la boca pastosa y seca y me cuesta enfocar la vista. El aire alrededor es oscuro como boca de lobo. La lluvia repiquetea en el techo. Alguien ha llenado la estufa y el tiro debe de estar abierto del todo porque chisporrotea y silba y en la habitación hace un calor infernal.

En cubierta, Briny suelta un juramento. Hay un destello de una lámpara en la ventana. Saco los pies para levantarme, pero el barco se inclina bruscamente y me devuelve a la litera. El *Arcadia* se balancea a un lado y a otro.

Fern rueda por encima de la barandilla de su litera y cae al suelo hecha un ovillo.

De pronto lo entiendo... Ya no estamos fondeados. Estamos navegando.

Silas y Zede han venido y soltado las amarras antes de que volviera Briny. Es lo primero que pienso. *Y Briny grita porque está furioso con ellos.*

Pero enseguida me doy cuenta de que no nos dejarían a la deriva de noche. Es demasiado peligroso, con los maderos y bancos de arena y las estelas de los barcos grandes y las barcazas. Silas y Zede lo saben.

Briny también, pero está en cubierta, fuera de sí. No está intentando volver a la orilla. Está desafiando al río a que se nos lleve.

—¡Vamos, canalla! —aúlla como el capitán Ahab en *Moby Dick*—. ¡Plántame cara! A ver si puedes conmigo, ¡vamos!

Ruge el trueno. Centellea un relámpago. Briny insulta al río. Se ríe.

La lámpara desaparece de la ventana y a continuación cabecea por la escalera cuando Briny se sube al techo.

Voy como puedo a ver cómo está Fern y a devolverla a su litera.

—Quédate aquí. Quédate hasta que yo te diga.

Me agarra del camisón y gime con voz ronca:

—Nooo.

Desde que estamos de vuelta en el *Arcadia,* le tiene un miedo atroz a la noche.

—No pasa nada. Creo que se han soltado las amarras, nada más. Seguramente Briny está llevándonos otra vez a la orilla.

Echo a correr dejándola en la cama. El *Arcadia* se escora mientras avanzo a tumbos y un remolque hace sonar la sirena y oigo los crujidos y silbidos de cascos de barcazas y sé que vienen estelas más grandes. La madera se desliza bajo mis dedos y me clava astillas bajo la piel. Caigo de bruces, aterrizo en el porche, en el frío. El barco apunta en la otra dirección, se vira hasta colocarse en paralelo al agua.

¡No, no! ¡No, por favor!

Como si me hubiera oído, el *Arcadia* se endereza. Capea la siguiente ola con limpieza y agilidad.

—¿Crees que puedes conmigo? ¿Crees que puedes conmigo? —grita Briny desde arriba. Una botella se estrella y del techo del porche bajan cristales que centellean a la luz de la lluvia nocturna y del faro del remolcador. Parecen caer despacio. Luego desaparecen con un destello en las negras aguas.

—¡Briny, tenemos que volver a la orilla! —grito—. ¡Briny, tenemos que amarrar el barco!

Pero la sirena del remolcador y la tormenta ahogan mi voz.

En alguna parte, un hombre grita insultos y advertencias. Suena un silbato de emergencia. Una fuerte estela levanta el *Arcadia,* que se mantiene en equilibrio igual que una bailarina de puntillas.

Al bajar, la proa se hunde. Agua fría cubre el porche.

El barco vira hasta quedar atravesado en el río.

La luz de un remolcador nos atrapa.

Un madero a la deriva se dirige hacia nuestra proa, un tronco gigantesco con las raíces y la tierra aún unidas a él. Lo veo justo antes de que la luz se mueva. Busco a tientas el bichero para apartarlo, pero no está donde debería. Lo único que puedo hacer es abrazarme a uno de los postes del porche y gritarle a Fern que aguante y ver cómo el árbol nos golpea y sus raíces envuelven al *Arcadia* como si fueran dedos, cogiéndome de un tobillo, retorciéndomelo, tirando con fuerza.

Dentro de la casa, Fern me llama a gritos.

—¡Agárrate! ¡Agárrate fuerte! —chillo.

El árbol tira y rasga, haciendo girar el *Arcadia* igual que una peonza, zarandeándolo y luego soltándolo y dejándonos a merced de la corriente. Viene una fuerte estela que inunda el camarote.

Empiezo a resbalar.

El *Arcadia* gime. Clavos que se sueltan. Maderas que se astillan.

El casco choca contra algo duro, el poste al que estoy agarrada se me escapa y, cuando quiero darme cuenta, estoy volando bajo la lluvia. Se me quedan los pulmones sin aire. Todo se vuelve negro.

Dejo de oír la madera que se astilla y las voces que gritan y el trueno a lo lejos.

El agua está fría, pero tengo calor. Hay una luz y dentro de ella veo a mi madre. Queenie me tiende la mano y yo busco la suya y, antes de que pueda cogerla, el río tira de mí cogiéndome por la cintura.

Pataleo y me resisto y subo a la superficie. Veo el *Arcadia* a la luz del faro del remolcador. Veo un esquife que viene hacia nosotros. Oigo silbidos y gritos. Tengo las piernas rígidas y la piel fría como el hielo.

El *Arcadia* está encajado en un gran montón de madera a la deriva. El Misisipi arremete contra él como la boca de un gigantesco dragón, engullendo poco a poco su popa.

—¡Fern! —Mi voz se pierde en el agua y el ruido. Nado con todas mis fuerzas, noto los remolinos y las corrientes que tiran de mí mientras voy hacia el montón de madera. El remolino intenta tirar de mí, pero me resisto, me subo a las maderas y trepo haciendo equilibrios hasta la cubierta y asciendo hasta la puerta de la casa.

La puerta cede y se desprende cuando la abro.

—¡Fern! ¡Fern! —grito—. ¡Fern, contesta!

El humo ahoga mi voz. La estufa está volcada y abierta. Hay brasas por el suelo, chisporrotean en la cubierta mojada y silban bajo mis pies.

Todo está del revés y no veo nada. Me equivoco de camino y termino en la mesa en lugar de en la litera de Fern. La colcha hecha de sacos de harina cosidos de la cama de Briny y Queenie nada como una ballena de colores transportando una lengua de fuego. Muy cerca, el fuego sube por las cortinas.

—¡Fern!

¿Es que no está? ¿Se ha caído al río? ¿La ha sacado Briny?

Entra una ola, atrapa las brasas rojas y se las lleva con ella. Chisporrotean y gimen al morir.

—¡Riiiiill! ¡Ven! ¡Ven!

El reflector nos ilumina entrando por la ventana en un círculo lento y alargado. Veo la cara de mi hermana, con los ojos muy abiertos y aterrada debajo de la litera. Me tiende la mano y al segundo siguiente la tengo cogida y estoy intentando tirar de ella, pero el agua nos alcanza a las dos. Una silla se desliza a gran velocidad y me golpea la espalda con fuerza, tirándome al suelo. El agua me cubre la cara y los oídos. Me agarro a Fern con todas mis fuerzas.

La silla se cae. Cojo a mi hermana y cruzo como puedo y a gatas la casa hasta la puerta lateral.

Entra de nuevo la luz del reflector. Veo la fotografía de Briny y Queenie colgada en la pared con la cruz de Queenie debajo.

No debería, pero después de sujetar a Fern en el sitio con la pierna, cojo la fotografía y la cruz de mi madre y me las meto por el cuello del camisón y dentro de las bragas. Me golpean la piel y se me clavan mientras salimos y trepamos por la barandilla y cruzamos hasta el montón de maderos, abriéndonos paso entre una maraña de ramas, tablones y árboles. Ágiles como ratones. Llevamos haciendo esto toda la vida.

Pero las dos sabemos lo bastante para comprender que un montón de maderos de deriva no es lugar seguro. Incluso desde el otro extremo, noto el calor del fuego. Cojo la mano de Fern, me vuelvo a mirar el *Arcadia* y levanto un brazo para protegerme los ojos. Las llamas se rizan y se estiran hacia arriba, quemando el techo y las paredes y la cubierta, dejando el *Arcadia* en los huesos, despojándolo de su belleza. Pedazos de él flotan en el aire. Suben y suben y giran hasta volar en el cielo como un millón de estrellas nuevas.

Cuando la lluvia los enfría, caen y se posan sobre nuestra piel. Fern grita cuando uno aterriza todavía caliente. La sujeto por el cuello del camisón, me agacho y la meto en el agua. Le digo que se agarre muy fuerte a las ramas enmarañadas. Hay demasiada corriente para que podamos nadar hasta la orilla. Le castañetean los dientes y se pone muy pálida.

La madera de deriva está empezando a arder. El fuego no tardará en alcanzarnos.

—¡Briny! —grito desesperada. Tiene que estar por aquí. Seguro que ha bajado del barco. Nos salvará.

¿Verdad?

—¡Aguanta! —grita alguien, pero no es la voz de Briny—. ¡Aguanta, no te muevas!

Explota uno de los tanques del *Arcadia*. Cenizas salen despedidas y caen por todas partes. Una aterriza en mi pie; chillo y pataleo y meto la pierna en el agua y sujeto más fuerte a Fern.

El montón de madera se mueve. Ya humea por varias partes.

—¡Ya llegamos! —grita una voz de hombre.

Un bote pequeño sale de la oscuridad, a bordo hay dos hombres encapuchados que reman con fuerza.

—¡No os soltéis! ¡No os soltéis!

La ramas crujen. Los leños gimen y silban. La pila entera se desplaza unos centímetros río abajo. Uno de los hombres del bote salvavidas advierte al otro de que se hundirán si los maderos se sueltan.

Pero aun así vienen, nos suben al bote, nos tapan con mantas y reman con brío.

—¿Había alguien más en el barco? ¿Nadie? —quieren saber.

—Mi padre —digo entre toses—. Briny. Briny Foss.

La orilla me parece un lugar maravilloso cuando nos dejan en ella y vuelven a buscar a Briny. Abrazo a Fern por debajo de la manta; la fotografía y la cruz están entre las dos. Tiritamos y temblamos y vemos arder el *Arcadia* hasta que el montón de maderos se suelta y se lleva lo que queda de él.

Fern y yo nos ponemos de pie y vamos hasta el borde del agua y miramos el reino de Arcadia desaparecer poco a poco. Al cabo de un rato ya no queda nada. Ni rastro. Es como si nunca hubiera existido.

En la luz gris del alba que llega del este miro a los hombres y las barcas. No dejan de buscar. Llaman a gritos, mueven las lámparas y reman.

Me parece ver a alguien orilla abajo. Un impermeable le aletea a la altura de las rodillas. No se mueve ni grita ni hace gestos en dirección a las luces. Se limita a mirar el río, donde la vida que conocía ha sido engullida.

¿Es Briny?

Pongo las manos en forma de bocina y lo llamo. La niebla de la mañana transporta mi voz y el eco la repite una y otra vez.

Uno de los hombres de los botes mira hacia donde estoy.

Cuando vuelvo a mirar hacia la orilla, apenas veo al hombre del impermeable. Se vuelve y se dirige hacia los árboles hasta que las sombras lo envuelven.

Tal vez nunca estuvo allí.

Me acerco unos pasos y vuelvo a gritar.

Mi voz resuena y muere.

—¡Rill! —Cuando por fin llega la respuesta, no viene de río abajo. No es la voz de Briny.

Una lancha motora se acerca al banco de la orilla y Silas salta antes de que el *Jenny* se haya detenido. Ata deprisa el cabo, corre hacia mí y me abraza. Me aferro a él y lloro.

—¡Estás bien! ¡Estás bien! —Me respira en el pelo apretándome tan fuerte que la fotografía y la cruz de Queenie se me clavan más en la carne—. Zede, Arney y yo casi nos morimos de miedo cuando vimos que el *Arcadia* no estaba.

—Briny soltó las amarras anoche. Me desperté y estábamos navegando. —Le cuento el resto entre sollozos: Briny subido al techo diciendo cosas sin sentido, la barcaza con la que casi chocamos, la pila de madera, el incendio, mi caída al agua, mi visión de Queenie, cómo salí luego a la superficie y trepé al *Arcadia* mientras el río se lo tragaba entero—. Unos hombres nos rescataron de la madera flotante antes de que se deshiciera —digo para terminar nuestra triste historia tiritando de frío—. Han ido a buscar a Briny.

No le cuento a Silas que me parece haberlo visto y que, en lugar de venir a buscarnos, se alejó.

Si no se lo cuento a nadie, no será verdad. No será así como terminó el reino de Arcadia.

Entonces Silas me obliga a apartarme un poco para mirarme.

—Pero estás bien. Las dos estáis sanas y salvas. Gracias al cielo. Zede y Arney traerán el barco de Zede en cuanto puedan. Y encontraremos a Briny. Vendréis todos con nosotros. Nos iremos a donde haga calor y haya pesca y...

Sigue hablando de cómo Zede y Briny recogerán madera de la orilla y nos construirán un barco nuevo. Un nuevo *Arcadia*. Empezaremos de nuevo y de ahora en adelante viajaremos siempre juntos.

Mi cabeza quiere colorear esas imágenes, pero no puede. El barco de Zede es demasiado pequeño para todos y Briny no está. Zede es demasiado mayor para seguir viviendo mucho más tiempo en el río. Es demasiado mayor para criar a Fern. Fern es muy pequeña aún.

Agarrada a mi pierna, escarba debajo de la manta y me tira del camisón.

—Quiero con mi mamá —gimotea. Sus dedos casi tocan el borde de la fotografía de Queenie, pero sé que no se refiere a ella.

Miro a Silas a la cara, que le iluminan los primeros rayos del sol. Tengo el corazón tan encogido que me duele. Ojalá fuéramos mayores. Ojalá fuéramos lo bastante mayores. Quiero a Silas, lo sé.

Pero también quiero a Fern. A Fern la quise primero. Es la única familia que me queda.

Río adentro, la búsqueda de Briny baja de intensidad a medida que el sol de la mañana proyecta su resplandor en el río. En cualquier momento los hombres se darán cuenta de que no hay esperanza de encontrar más supervivientes. Volverán a por Fern y a por mí.

—Silas, tienes que sacarnos de aquí. Tienes que sacarnos ahora mismo.

Me separo de él y voy hacia la lancha mientras tiro de Fern.

—Pero... Briny... —dice Silas.

—Tenemos que irnos. Antes de que vengan los hombres. Nos llevarán otra vez al hogar infantil.

Entonces Silas comprende. Sabe que tengo razón. Nos sube a la lancha y nos marchamos sin hacer ruido hasta estar lo bastante lejos como para que nadie oiga el motor cuando Silas lo arranca. Nos quedamos cerca de la orilla, lejos de los almacenes de algodón, los muelles, la isla de Mud y Memphis en general. Cuando llegamos al remanso, le digo a Silas que no quiero subir al barco de Zede más que para despedirnos.

Tengo que llevar de nuevo a Fern río arriba y confiar en que los Sevier la acepten. No es culpa suya que nos escapáramos. No fue idea suya robar cosas. Fue mía. Lo que ha pasado no es cosa de Fern.

Si tenemos suerte, la dejarán volver..., si es que no tienen ya otra niñita del hogar infantil. Pero, incluso si la tienen, se quedarán con Fern. Quizá prometan quererla y mantenerla a salvo de la señorita Tann.

Lo que será de mí después ya no lo sé. Los Sevier no me querrán, eso seguro. No querrán a una mentirosa y una ladrona. No puedo dejar que la señorita Tann me encuentre otra vez. Igual consigo trabajo en algún sitio cerca, pero son tiempos difíciles. No volveré al río. El viejo Zede no puede alimentar más bocas, aunque esa no es la verdadera razón por la que no puedo quedarme.

La verdadera razón es que tengo que estar cerca de mi hermana. Hemos vivido cosidas por el corazón desde que nació. No puedo respirar en un mundo en el que no la tenga cerca.

Le digo a Silas lo que quiero que haga por nosotras. Niega con la cabeza y, cuanto más hablo, más triste es su expresión.

—Cuida de Arney —le digo por fin—. No tiene adonde ir. Su familia la trataba muy mal. Encuéntrale un sitio, ¿de acuerdo? No le importa trabajar duro.

Silas mira correr el agua.

—Sí.

Quizá Silas y Arney se casen dentro de unos años, pienso. Se me encoge otra vez el corazón.

Mi vida ya no será como siempre he querido que fuera. El camino que me trajo hasta aquí está anegado. No hay marcha atrás. Esa es la verdadera razón por la que, cuando llegamos al barco de Zede, le digo que los Sevier estarán encantados de volver a acogernos a Fern y a mí.

—Solo necesito que Silas nos lleve río arriba.

No quiero que Zede venga también. Me da miedo que no nos deje ir cuando llegue el momento.

Zede mira por la puerta abierta al interior de su casa como si estuviera intentando decidir si puede hacerse cargo de todos nosotros.

—En casa de los Sevier Fern tiene un montón de vestidos bonitos y de juguetes. Y lápices de colores. Y yo pronto empezaré el colegio. —Me tiembla la voz y trago saliva para tranquilizarme.

Cuando Zede vuelve sus ojos hacia mí, tengo la sensación de que ve en mi interior.

Fern le busca y él la coge en brazos y apoya la cabeza en la suya.

—Pequeñuela —dice emocionado y a continuación tira de mí y nos abraza a las dos con fuerza. Huele a ceniza, a pez, a aceite de carbón y al gran río. A cosas que conozco.

—Si alguna vez me necesitáis, decidlo en el río.

Asiento con la cabeza, pero cuando nos suelta ambos sabemos que este adiós es para siempre. El río es muy grande.

Tiene el rostro teñido de tristeza. La borra antes de asentir con la cabeza. Luego levanta el mentón y pone a Fern en el *Jenny* para que podamos irnos.

—Tengo que acompañaros, no conocéis el pantano —dice Arney—. Pero cuando lleguemos no pienso quedarme. Llevaré la lancha de mi padre y la dejaré atada por allí. Dile dónde puede encontrarla. No quiero nada suyo.

Sin esperar respuesta, va a buscar la lancha. A pesar de lo mal que la ha tratado siempre su familia, ha estado preocupada por cómo se las arreglarán sin la lancha.

Cuando nos alejamos, no lloro. El motor fueraborda tiene que luchar contra la corriente, pero conseguimos llegar a la desembocadura del pantano. Cuando doblamos el recodo, los árboles empiezan a cerrarse y me vuelvo una sola vez y dejo que el río se lleve algo de mí con él.

Se lleva lo que queda de Rill Foss.

Rill Foss, la princesa del reino de Arcadia. El rey ha muerto y con él, el reino.

Rill Foss tiene que morir también.

Ahora soy May Weathers.

25

Y aquí termina mi historia. —Los ojos azules de May, brumosos y húmedos, me estudian desde el otro lado de la mesita redonda en un rincón de la residencia de mayores—. ¿Te alegras de conocerla? ¿O te pesa? Siempre me he preguntado cómo os sentiríais los jóvenes. Pensaba que nunca llegaría a saberlo.

—Creo que... las dos cosas.

Aunque he dedicado una semana a pensar en ello desde nuestra visita a la casita del río y la granja de Hootsie, me sigue costando asimilar que esta historia es la historia de mi familia.

He sopesado una y otra vez las advertencias de Elliot de que estoy jugando con fuego, de que no hay que remover el pasado. Ni siquiera las sorprendentes revelaciones que le hice después de mi visita a la casita junto al río Savannah le hicieron cambiar de opinión. «Piensa en las repercusiones, Avery. Hay personas que ya no... volverían a mirar a tu familia con los mismos ojos».

Cuando dice «personas» creo que se refiere a Bitsy.

Lo triste es que Bitsy no sería la única. Si todo esto se supiera, es imposible predecir cómo afectaría al futuro político, a la reputación, al nombre de los Stafford.

Los tiempos han cambiado, pero las viejas convenciones siguen vigentes.

Si el mundo se enterara de que los Stafford no son en realidad quienes afirman ser, las consecuencias...

No quiero ni imaginarlas.

Eso me asusta tanto que no quiero ni pensar en ello, pero lo cierto es que no soporto la idea de que mi abuela y su hermana pasen separadas lo que les queda de vida. Lo que más me importa es saber que hice lo mejor para la abuela Judy.

—En un par de ocasiones consideré la posibilidad de contárselo a mis nietos —dice May—. Pero están demasiado instalados en sus vidas. Su madre se casó con un hombre con hijos después de que muriera mi hijo. Son unos jóvenes estupendos que están criando a sus hijos rodeados de un grupo de tías, tíos y primos. Con las familias de mis hermanas pasa más o menos lo mismo. Lark se casó con un empresario que levantó un imperio de grandes almacenes. Fern se casó con un reputado médico de Atlanta. Entre las dos tuvieron ocho hijos y dos docenas de nietos y, por supuesto, también bisnietos. A todos les va bien, son felices... y están muy ocupados. ¿Qué puede ofrecerles una historia del pasado remoto que no tengan ya?

May me mira con intensidad, me ve haciendo equilibrios sobre la línea divisoria que separa su generación de la mía.

—¿Se lo vas a contar a tu familia? —pregunta.

Trago saliva, en guerra conmigo misma.

—Se lo voy a contar a mi padre. Es una decisión que le corresponde tomar a él, más que a mí. La abuela Judy es su madre. —No tengo ni idea de cómo reaccionará mi padre a la información ni lo que hará con ella—. Parte de mí piensa que

Hootsie tiene razón. La verdad sigue siendo la verdad. Tiene valor en sí misma.

—Hootsie —gruñe May—. Así es como me agradece que le vendiera el terreno junto a la casa de mi abuela para que ella y Ted pudieran tener su granja. Después de todos estos años se pone a contar mis secretos.

—Creo que pensaba que te estaba haciendo un favor. Quería que comprendiera la relación entre tú y mi abuela. Estaba pensando en vosotras.

May espanta la idea como si fuera una mosca revoloteándole cerca de la cara.

—Bah. A Hootsie es que le gusta echar leña al fuego. Siempre ha sido así. ¿Sabes? Gracias a ella me quedé con los Sevier. Para cuando llegamos a la casa, Silas casi me había convencido de que me volviera al río con él. Se paró en la orilla, me cogió por los hombros y me besó. Era la primera vez que me besaba un chico. —Ríe, las mejillas se le encienden y en sus ojos hay un brillo infantil. Por un instante veo a esa niña de doce años a orillas del lago—. «Te quiero, Rill Foss», me dijo. «Te esperaré una hora. Esperaré a que vuelvas. Puedo cuidar de ti, Rill. Ya lo verás». Sabía que estaba haciendo promesas que no podía cumplir. Solo unos meses antes era un vagabundo que viajaba de polizón en trenes tratando de sobrevivir. Si una cosa había aprendido yo de vivir con Queenie y Briny, es que el amor por sí solo no pone comida en la mesa. No mantiene a una familia a salvo.

Asiente con la cabeza a su propia conclusión, con el ceño fruncido.

—Querer y poder son dos cosas distintas. Supongo que en el fondo sabía que Silas y yo no estábamos destinados a estar juntos. Al menos no tan jóvenes. Pero cuando eché a andar por el camino con Fern, lo único que quería era volver corriendo con aquel chico de pelo oscuro y al río. Puede que lo hubiera hecho de no ser por Hootsie. Decidió por mí antes de que pudiera hacerlo yo. Mi plan era llegar hasta el final del bosque, esconderme allí y asegurarme de que los Sevier acogían de nuevo a Fern. Me daba pánico que, si me encontraban, me mandaran de vuelta al hogar infantil o a alguna clase de correccional para niñas, incluso a la cárcel. Pero Hootsie estaba buscando raíces para su madre cuando nos vio cerca del jardín y empezó a gritar. Al minuto siguiente, Zuma, Hoy y el señor y la señora Sevier corrían ladera abajo con los perros delante. No podía escapar, así que me quedé allí y me preparé para lo peor.

Hace una pausa y me deja al borde de un precipicio.

—¿Y qué pasó?

—Aprendí que no hace falta haber nacido en una familia para que te quieran.

—Así que os recibieron bien.

Asoma una sonrisa a las comisuras de su boca.

—Sí. Papá Sevier y Hoy y los otros hombres habían estado semanas buscándonos por los pantanos. Sabían que nos habíamos ido en la lancha con Arney. Para cuando volvimos, habían perdido la esperanza de encontrarnos. —Ríe con suavidad—. Incluso Zuma y Hootsie nos abrazaron, de lo contentas que estaban de vernos.

—Y después de aquello ¿fuisteis felices con los Sevier?

—Fueron comprensivos con lo que habíamos hecho. Quiero decir, después de que les contara la verdad sobre el *Arcadia*. O al menos toda la verdad de la que fui capaz. Decidí que nunca sabrían que había otros hermanos aparte de Fern y de mí. Supongo que en mi corazón de doce años me seguía avergonzando no haber podido proteger a Camellia, a Lark y a Gabion. Me daba miedo que los Sevier no me quisieran si sabían eso de mí. Los Sevier eran buenas personas, pacientes y cariñosas. Me enseñaron a encontrar la música.

—¿La música?

Se acerca a mí por encima de la mesa.

—Sí, tesoro, la música. Hay una cosa que aprendí de seguir los pasos de papá Sevier. La vida se parece al cine. Cada escena tiene su propia música y la música se crea para esa escena, las dos cosas están entretejidas de maneras que no comprendemos. Da igual lo mucho que nos guste la melodía de un día pasado o imaginemos la canción de uno futuro; tenemos que bailar la música del hoy, de lo contrario perderemos el paso y haremos algo que no le corresponde a ese momento. Yo dejé atrás la música del río y encontré la de aquella casa. Encontré sitio para una nueva vida, una nueva madre que me quería, un nuevo padre que me enseñó no solo a hacer música, también a confiar. Era el mejor hombre que he conocido. De acuerdo, nunca fue como vivir en el *Arcadia,* pero fue una buena vida. Nos sentíamos queridas, valoradas y protegidas.

Un suspiro le hace levantar los hombros, luego los relaja.

—Viéndome ahora, nadie diría que llegué a comprender el secreto. Esta música de la vejez... no está hecha para bailar. Es demasiado... solitaria. Te conviertes en una carga para todo el mundo.

Pienso en mi abuela, en su casa vacía, en su cuarto de la residencia, en su incapacidad de reconocerme la mayor parte de los días. Se me llenan los ojos de lágrimas. La música de la vejez es difícil de oír cuando suena por alguien a quien quieres. Me pregunto si mi abuela reconocerá a May cuando por fin se reúnan. ¿Accederá May a venir conmigo? Aún no se lo he preguntado. Trent me espera en el pasillo. Ha venido desde Edisto. Después de estudiar las distintas posibilidades, decidimos que era mejor que hablara yo sola con May primero.

—¿Volviste a ver a Silas?

La pregunta surge y al principio no entiendo por qué la he hecho. Luego me doy cuenta de que estoy pensando en

Trent... y en lo que me ha contado May de su primer amor. Es extraño, pero no me lo quito de la cabeza últimamente. La sonrisa de Trent, sus chistes tontos, su cercanía, incluso su voz al teléfono despiertan algo dentro de mí. El hecho de que le importe un bledo cuál sea mi historia familiar o las decisiones que tome al respecto me conmueve de una manera para la que no estoy preparada. No sé cómo categorizarla o encajarla en mi vida.

Solo sé que no puedo ignorarla.

La expresión de May me taladra. Es como si estuviera escarbando en mi interior y siguiendo los pasillos que conducen a mi alma.

—Me habría gustado, pero no todos los deseos se hacen realidad. Papá Sevier nos llevó a Augusta para protegernos de Georgia Tann. Nuestra familia era bastante conocida allí, así que imagino que pensó que no se atrevería a chantajearle, desde otro estado, además. Silas y el viejo Zede no habrían sabido dónde buscarnos. Nunca supe lo que fue de ellos. La última vez que vi a Silas fue entre los mechones de pelo de mi nueva madre mientras me abrazaba fuerte. Estaba en el lindero del bosque, donde yo había estado momentos antes, y luego se dio la vuelta y volvió al lago. Nunca volví a verlo.

Niega despacio con la cabeza.

—Siempre me pregunté qué habría sido de él. Quizá es mejor no saberlo. Yo crecí en una vida distinta, un mundo distinto y con un nombre distinto. De Arney sí supe, años más tarde. Llegó una carta de repente. Mi madre me la dio cuando fui a casa durante unas vacaciones de la universidad. Siempre había imaginado que tal vez Arney y Silas se casarían, pero no había sido así. Zede le encontró trabajo a Arney en una vaquería poco después de que yo me marchara. Arney estaba hecha para el trabajo duro, pero aquellas personas la trataron bien. Con el tiempo encontró trabajo en una fábrica de aviones de guerra y se casó con un militar. Cuando me escribió, vivían en el extranjero y estaba disfrutando de conocer mundo. Nunca imaginó que la vida le daría una oportunidad así.

Aunque sé que han pasado ya muchos años, la historia me hace sonreír.

—Me alegra que las cosas le fueran bien después de una infancia tan dura.

Dado que May tiene noventa años y Arney era mayor que ella, es poco probable que siga viva, pero me siento reconfortada. Después de oír la historia de May, tengo la sensación de conocer a Arney, a Silas y a todos los habitantes del río.

—Sí. —May asiente con la cabeza—. Me hizo concienciarme de la situación de todas esas mujeres jóvenes e ingenuas que terminaban en manos de los playboys de Hollywood. Conocí a muchas durante mis años allí y me hice el propósito de ayudarlas, de proporcionarles un lugar donde dormir o un hombre en el que apoyarse. Pasaba a menudo, muchachas que terminaban en unas situaciones terribles. Siempre recordaba las palabras de Arney al final de su carta.

—¿Qué decía?

—Decía que yo la había salvado. —May se seca una pequeña lágrima cerca del ojo—. Claro que no es verdad. Nos salvamos mutuamente. Si Arney no me hubiera llevado de vuelta al río, si no hubiera ocurrido lo del *Arcadia,* yo habría seguido aferrada a Briny, a Queenie y al río. Me habría pasado la vida buscando esa música. Al llevarme de vuelta, Arney me ayudó a pasar página. Eso le dije cuando respondí a su carta.

—Supongo que se emocionaría mucho.

—Las personas no llegan a nuestras vidas por accidente.

—Desde luego.

De nuevo pienso en Trent. De nuevo siento el dilema entre mis sentimientos y las esperanzas y planes que siempre ha tenido mi familia para mí. Unos planes que siempre creí compartir.

—Arney y yo mantuvimos el contacto —continúa diciendo May y trato de concentrarme otra vez en lo que me está contando, de dejar atrás la preocupación por cómo será el resto del día—. Era una mujer muy estimulante. Cuando volvieron a Estados Unidos su marido y ella, montaron una constructora. Trabajó con él hombro con hombro, una mujer entre hombres, haciéndose valer. Estoy segura de que los hogares que construyeron son unos edificios de lo más sólidos. Nos sobrevivirán a todos.

—Claro que sí.

May se vuelve hacia mí con expresión cómplice, se acerca en un gesto íntimo, como si fuera a contarme un secreto.

—El pasado de una mujer no tiene por qué determinar su futuro. Puede elegir bailar otra música distinta. Su propia música. Para oír la melodía, solo necesita dejar de hablar. Consigo misma, quiero decir. Nos pasamos la vida intentando convencernos de cosas.

Me impacta la profundidad de lo que me está diciendo. ¿Estará notando que desde que fuimos a la casita junto al río, desde que supe la verdad sobre mi abuela, me estoy replanteando mi vida?

No quiero hacer daño a nadie, pero quiero encontrar mi propia música. May me ha ayudado a creer que es posible. Lo que me trae a la razón por la que he venido a verla hoy.

—Me preguntaba si querrías venir conmigo esta tarde a un sitio —digo por fin.

—¿Puedo preguntar dónde?

Pero ya se está poniendo de pie, apoyando las manos en los brazos de la butaca.

—¿Querrás venir aunque no te diga adónde?

—¿Es un sitio fuera de estas aburridísimas paredes?

—Sí.

Se levanta sorprendentemente rápido.

—Entonces me da igual a dónde vayamos. Soy toda tuya. Siempre que no me lleves a un acto político, quiero decir. Odio la política.

Me río.

—No es un acto político.

—Estupendo.

Salimos juntas al pasillo. May se impulsa a una velocidad sorprendente con el andador. No me extrañaría que lo tirara y echara a correr hacia la puerta.

—Trent nos está esperando para llevarnos en su coche.

—¿El guapo de ojos azules?

—Ese mismo.

—Esto cada vez pinta mejor. —Se mira la camisa y los pantalones tipo pijama—. No voy muy bien vestida. Tal vez debería cambiarme.

—Vas muy bien.

Cuando llegamos a su habitación no me lleva la contraria. De hecho, entra solo a coger el bolso.

Trent se levanta cuando salimos al vestíbulo de entrada. Sonríe y me hace a escondidas un gesto triunfal con los pulgares cuando May le dice a la auxiliar que nos la llevamos a pasar la tarde fuera. Ella me da el andador y elige cogerse del brazo de Trent para salir. Me toca doblarlo y meterlo en el maletero mientras Trent ayuda a May a subir al coche. Por suerte tengo experiencia con estos trastos.

Por el camino, May le cuenta a Trent su historia. Toda, no solo las partes que nos contó después de nuestra primera incursión en el estudio de detrás de la casa de Trent en Edisto. Trent me mira por el espejo retrovisor varias veces, mueve la cabeza con un gesto como de triste asombro. Es difícil creer que no hace tantos años los niños huérfanos fueran tratados como mercancía.

May está tan absorta en su relato o tan fascinada con Trent que no se fija en adónde vamos. Hasta que no estamos cerca de Augusta, no inclina la cabeza hacia la ventana y suspira.

—Me lleváis a casa. Deberíais habérmelo dicho. Me habría puesto las deportivas.

Trent mira las zapatillas planas que lleva May.

—No pasa nada. Su vecino ha cortado el césped.

—Hootsie ha tenido unos hijos encantadores. Parece mentira. Con el mal genio que gastaba. Me peleé más con ella de lo que me peleé nunca con ninguna de mis hermanas.

Trent sonríe.

—Después de conocerla un poco, me lo creo. —Ha estado hablando con Hootsie de la visita de hoy. Bart y ella han removido cielo y tierra para ayudarnos a organizarla.

May se fija en los cambios cuando pasamos delante de la casa de Hootsie por el camino de la granja y ve que el sendero del bosque hasta la casa está limpio. Aparcamos en grava nueva cerca de la puerta.

—¿Quién ha hecho todo esto? —May mira la hierba recién segada, el jardín con las plantas podadas, el porche con sillas esperando detrás de las puertas mosquiteras.

—Me preocupaba que no pudieras llegar andando hasta aquí —le digo—. Así que eso me pareció lo mejor. Espero que no te importe.

Se limita a secarse los ojos y a apretar los labios, que le tiemblan.

—He pensado que quizá te gustaría venir aquí más a menudo después de esto. Mi abuela tiene contratado un taxi con una compañía. Conocen el camino.

—No sé si... si me van a dejar. —Solo acierta a susurrar—. En la residencia. Y no quiero que llamen a mis nietos y los molesten.

—He hablado de eso con un amigo, un hombre que lleva un grupo por los derechos de los mayores. Creo que podremos ayudarte en algunas cosas. No eres prisionera de la residencia, May, solo quieren asegurarse de que no te pasa nada.

De momento le dejo que vaya asimilando esta información. Más tarde podemos hablar de las sugerencias que me ha hecho Andrew Moore, incluida la de que May podría sentirse útil colaborando de voluntaria en el comité. Andrew es una persona increíble, llena de ideas. Creo que a May le gustará.

Ahora mismo está demasiado hipnotizada con el paisaje para hablar de otra cosa. Se acerca al parabrisas y se echa a llorar.

—Estoy en casa... Pensé que nunca volvería a verla.

—Hootsie y su nieta se han ocupado de mantenerla limpia.

—Pero... No he podido pagarles... desde... —Las lágrimas no la dejan seguir—. Desde que se me llevaron.

—Dice que no le importa. —Abro mi puerta mientras Trent rodea el coche—. Te quiere mucho, no sé si lo sabes.

—¿Eso dijo?

—Bueno, no. Pero salta a la vista.

May resopla escéptica y de nuevo veo en ella la precocidad de una habitante del río.

—Me habías preocupado. Por un momento he pensado que Hootsie había perdido la chaveta. —Me sonríe irónica y deja que Trent la ayude a bajar del coche—. Hootsie y yo siempre nos hemos ayudado la una a la otra a mantenernos lúcidas. Sería una pena estropearlo poniéndonos sentimentales ahora.

Miro entre los árboles a las ruinas de la mansión mientras me desperezo. Me resulta difícil asimilar los matices de la relación entre estas dos mujeres a lo largo de los años.

—Puedes decírselo en persona. Ha dicho que luego se acercará. Le he pedido que nos deje primero estar un rato solas.

May me mira suspicaz mientras cruza la puerta de entrada con la mano cogida del hombro de Trent.

—¿Qué estáis planeando? Esta vez os lo he contado todo. Sabéis toda la historia.

Oigo a lo lejos un coche que sube por el camino de la granja. May aún no se ha dado cuenta y quizá sea mejor así. Mi idea era llevarla a la casita e instalarla allí primero. Pero igual no nos da tiempo. Es muy propio de mi madre llegar a las citas con antelación, aunque no tiene ni idea de a dónde viene ni a qué.

—Les he pedido a mis padres que vengan.

No se me ocurre otra manera mejor de conseguir que se crean todo esto que enseñándoselo directamente. Me preocupa que, si no, piensen que me he vuelto loca.

—¿Al senador? —May pone cara de horrorizada y empieza a peinarse con la mano.

Trent intenta que May entre en la casa, pero esta se agarra al poste y se aferra a él como un colegial al que intentan llevar a poner una inyección.

—¡Por el amor de Dios! Te pregunté si necesitaba cambiarme de ropa. No puedo conocerlos vestida así.

Siento que mis buenas intenciones se dan de bruces con las barreras de la corrección. Son unas barreras que no caen para nadie. Conseguir que mis padres cooperaran con mi misterioso plan para esta tarde de domingo ha sido casi imposible. Les he dicho que es un favor para una amiga, pero a mi madre no hay quien la engañe. Cuando llegue, estará de lo más alerta, sobre todo teniendo en cuenta lo extraño de la petición y lo remoto de la localización.

Pero esto va a pasar, con independencia de que las partes implicadas lo quieran o no, y en mi fuero interno sé que lo he organizado así a propósito. Me daba miedo perder el impulso de seguir adelante, ahora que he cogido carrerilla.

—¡Venga, deprisa! —May echa a andar hacia la casa haciendo perder el equilibrio a Trent—. Tengo ropa en los armarios. Algo habrá que pueda ponerme.

Por entre los árboles veo la limusina blanca de la compañía de taxis.

—No da tiempo. Ya están aquí.

A May se le hinchan las aletas de la nariz.

—¿Sabía esto Hootsie?

—Sí y no, pero la idea ha sido mía. Por favor, confía en mí. De verdad creo que es lo mejor.

Después de hoy, May y yo estaremos más unidas o no volverá a dirigirme la palabra. Una de las dos cosas.

—Creo que me voy a desmayar —dice May apoyándose en Trent. No sé si está actuando.

Trent la rodea con un brazo, listo para sostenerla.

—¿Y si la llevo hasta la casa?

May se deja llevar, demasiado aturdida para protestar.

Yo espero en la puerta. Cuando la limusina se detiene, mamá sale por su lado sin esperar a que Oz le abra la puerta. Honeybee está furiosa.

—Avery Judith Stafford, ¿se puede saber qué pasa aquí? Estaba convencida de que o el conductor se había perdido o nos estaban secuestrando. —Por su cara enrojecida y ligeramente brillante, se ve que lleva kilómetros enfadadísima, probablemente quejándose a mi padre o agobiando al pobre Oz, que ha sido reclutado para esta operación solo porque se conoce el camino—. Te he llamado al móvil por lo menos quince veces. ¿Por qué no lo has cogido?

—Me parece que aquí no hay cobertura.

No sé si es verdad. Llevo toda la mañana con el teléfono apagado. Si Honeybee no podía ponerse en contacto conmigo para cancelar o cambiar los planes, entonces no tendría más elección que venir. Honeybee nunca falta a un compromiso.

—Vamos, chicas.

Mi padre está de mucho mejor humor. A diferencia de mamá, le encanta salir al campo. Le han curado la hemorragia con cirugía laparoscópica, le ha subido la hemoglobina y está recuperando las fuerzas. Ahora que está casi en plenas facultades, puede hacer frente a sus detractores respecto al asunto de los hogares de mayores. Y lo que ha hecho es ignorarlo sistemáticamente. Al mismo tiempo está recabando apoyos para una propuesta de ley que impida a los dueños de estos centros escudarse en empresas fantasma para evitar demandas judiciales.

Mira interesado hacia el río.

—Ha sido un viaje muy agradable. Hacía tiempo que no veníamos a Augusta. Ojalá hubiera traído la caña y los aparejos de pesca. —Me sonríe y al instante nuestra vida juntos me pasa por la cabeza, desde las visitas cuando era niña a su despacho o las excursiones de pesca en las que no pescábamos nada hasta bailes de fin de curso, cotillones, ceremonias de graduación..., y, más recientemente, reuniones y sesiones para debatir estrategias y actos públicos—. No nos pide cosas muy a menudo, Honeybee. —Me guiña el ojo—. Esta hija no.

Quiere hacerme saber que, sea lo que sea lo que he planeado para hoy, está conmigo, pero lo único que consigue es recordarme todo lo que tengo que perder, sobre todo y entre otras cosas mi relación especial con mi padre. Soy su preferida. Siempre he sido su hija adorada.

¿Cómo le sentará enterarse de que llevo semanas hurgando a escondidas en información que mi abuela había ocultado para proteger el legado Stafford?

¿Qué pasará después, cuando le explique que este viaje me ha cambiado? Que no quiero vivir la vida que vivió mi abuela. Que quiero ser quien soy de verdad. Eso puede significar que la dinastía política Stafford se termine con mi padre. O no. Es posible que su salud le permita seguir en el cargo un tiempo. Con salud, podrá gestionar esta controversia sobre las residencias de mayores de manera que salga algo positivo. De eso estoy segura.

Yo estaré ahí para ayudarlo en todo lo que pueda, pero lo cierto es que no me siento preparada aún para entrar en política. No tengo la experiencia suficiente. No debería ser elegida para ese cargo solo por ser quien soy. Quiero ganármelo de la manera tradicional. Quiero estudiar las cuestiones sobre las que hay que gobernar —no todas, solo unas pocas— y después decidir cuál es mi postura respecto a cada una. Y si alguna vez me llega el turno, me presentaré con mis propios méritos, no como hija de mi padre. Mientras tanto, Andrew Moore me dijo que su comité para los derechos de los mayores necesita un buen abogado. El salario es indudablemente bajo, pero esa no es la cuestión. Si quiero meter el pie en las procelosas aguas de la política, es la clase de trabajo por la que empezaría una persona corriente, y yo soy buena abogada.

¿Lo entenderá mi padre?

¿Seguirá queriéndome?

Pues claro. Pues claro que lo hará. Siempre ha sido padre ante todo. Sé que es así. Sí. Cuando informe a mis padres de mis planes, habrá decepción. Sí, habrá algún desencuentro, pero sobreviviremos. Siempre lo hacemos.

—Avery, no pienso sacar a tu abuela del coche aquí. —Honeybee inspecciona la casita, el río colina abajo, los árboles sin podar con las ramas que cuelgan sobre el tejado del porche. Se abraza y se frota los brazos con las manos.

—Honeybee. —Mi padre intenta aplacar a mi madre mientras me sonríe indulgente—. Avery no nos habría traído aquí si no tuviera una buena razón. —Se acerca, coge a Honeybee por la cintura y le hace cosquillas en un sitio que solo él conoce. Es su arma secreta.

Mi madre se esfuerza por no sonreír.

—Para. —La mirada que me dirige no es tan alegre—. Avery, por favor, ¿hacía falta todo este teatro? ¿A qué viene tanto misterio? ¿Y se puede saber por qué hemos tenido que venir en limusina, por el amor del cielo? ¿Y traer a tu abuela? Salir de Magnolia Manor la afecta mucho. Luego le cuesta mucho recuperar sus rutinas.

—Quería ver si recuerda algo —digo.

Honeybee chasquea los labios.

—Dudo que recuerde este sitio.

—Quería decir a alguien.

—Tu abuela no conoce a nadie que viva aquí, Avery. Creo que sería mejor que...

—Entra conmigo, mamá, por favor. La abuela Judy ya ha estado aquí. Tengo el presentimiento de que lo va a saber.

—¿No va a sacarme nadie de aquí? —protesta mi abuela desde el coche.

Oz nos mira pidiendo permiso. Mi padre dice que sí con la cabeza. Tiene miedo de que, si suelta a Honeybee, salga disparada.

Cojo a mi abuela del brazo y enfilamos juntas el camino de entrada. A pesar de su deterioro mental, la abuela Judy solo tiene setenta y ocho años y está bastante ágil. Eso hace que la demencia parezca todavía más injusta.

La miro mientras caminamos. A cada paso se va animando. Su vista se posa en todas partes, en las rosas trepadoras y las azaleas, en el banco junto al río, en la vieja cerca de madera, una espaldera con glicinia, una mata de jazmín de Virginia, un bebedero de pájaros hecho de bronce con esculturas de dos niñas pequeñas jugando en el agua.

—Ay —susurra—. Ay, cómo me gusta este sitio. Hace mucho que no venía, ¿verdad?

—Me parece que sí —contesto.

—Lo he echado de menos —susurra—. Lo he echado mucho de menos.

Mis padres se han detenido al llegar al porche y nos miran pestañeando a mi abuela y a mí, atónitos. Honeybee se encuentra en una situación que no puede controlar y por esa razón ya la odia, con independencia de qué se trate.

—Avery Judith, será mejor que empieces a explicar qué es todo esto.

—¡Mamá! —le digo cortante y da un paso atrás. Nunca le he hablado así a mi madre. En mis treinta años de vida—. Deja que la abuela Judy vea de qué se acuerda.

Pongo una mano en el hombro de mi abuela y la acompaño al umbral de la casita. Se para un momento mientras sus ojos se acostumbran al cambio de luz.

La miro examinar la habitación, las fotografías, el cuadro sobre la repisa de la vieja chimenea.

Tarda un momento en darse cuenta de que hay alguien.

—Pero... ¡May! —dice con naturalidad, como si se hubieran visto ayer.

—Judy. —May intenta levantarse del sofá, pero está hundido y no consigue ponerse de pie, así que extiende los brazos. Trent, que se disponía a ayudarla, se aparta.

Mi abuela cruza la habitación. La dejo hacer el viaje sola. A May se le llenan los ojos de lágrimas, levanta los brazos y abre y cierra los dedos para recibir a su hermana. La abuela Judy, que estos días no conoce a casi nadie, no muestra vacilación alguna. Como si fuera lo más normal del mundo, se inclina hacia el sofá y los brazos de May. Se funden en el tembloroso abrazo propio de dos personas mayores. May cierra los ojos y apoya la barbilla en el hombro de su hermana. Se aferran la una a la otra hasta que por fin mi abuela se deja caer exhausta en una butaca que está junto al sofá. Ella y su hermana se cogen de la mano por encima de una mesa que hay entre las dos. Se miran como si no hubiera nadie más en la habitación.

—No creía que fuera a volver a verte —reconoce May.

La sonrisa radiante de mi abuela parece ignorar todos los obstáculos que las han mantenido separadas.

—Ya sabes que siempre vengo. Los jueves. El Día de las hermanas. —Señala con un gesto la mecedora que está junto a la ventana—. ¿Dónde ha ido Fern?

May levanta las manos entrelazadas de las dos y las agita un poco.

—Fern ya no está con nosotros, tesoro. Murió mientras dormía.

—¿Fern? —Mi abuela hunde los hombros y se le llenan los ojos de lágrimas. Una lágrima se desprende y le baja pegada a la nariz—. Ay, Fern...

—Solo quedamos nosotras dos.

—Tenemos a Lark.

—Lark murió hace cinco años. De cáncer, ¿no te acuerdas?

La abuela Judy se hunde un poco más, se seca otra lágrima.

—Dios santo, se me había olvidado. Si es que ya casi no me queda memoria.

—Da igual. —May cubre las manos entrelazadas con la que le queda libre—. ¿Te acuerdas de la primera semana que pasamos en Edisto? —Señala con la cabeza el cuadro que está sobre la chimenea—. ¿No fue maravilloso? ¿Las cuatro juntas? A Fern le encantaba ese sitio.

—Sí lo fue —se muestra de acuerdo la abuela Judy. No sé si se acuerda de verdad o simplemente intenta ser educada, pero sonríe mirando el cuadro y de pronto su expresión es de lucidez—. Nos regalaste las pulseras de las libélulas. Tres libélulas para recordar a los hermanos que nunca volvimos a ver. Camellia, Gabion y mi gemelo. La tarde que nos las diste estábamos celebrando el cumpleaños de Camellia, ¿verdad? Camellia era la libélula con el ónice. —La luz de la memoria brilla en los ojos de mi abuela. El amor de hermanas vuelve cálida su sonrisa—. Anda que no éramos guapas entonces, ¿verdad?

—Desde luego. Todas teníamos el pelo tan bonito de mamá, pero tú eras la única que había heredado también su preciosa cara. De no saber que eres tú, diría que la mujer del cuadro que está con nosotras es nuestra madre.

A mi espalda, mi madre susurra entre dientes:

—¿Se puede saber qué es todo esto?

Noto el calor que irradia su cuerpo. Está sudando y Honeybee no suda nunca.

—Tal vez deberíamos salir. —Intento reunir a mis padres y sacarlos al porche. Mi padre parece casi reacio a abandonar la habitación. Está ocupado mirando las fotografías, tratando de encontrarle un sentido a todo esto. ¿Hay una parte de él que recuerda las ausencias inexplicadas de su madre? ¿Recuerda salir en el fondo de la fotografía tomada en Edisto? ¿Ha sospechado siempre que su madre es algo más que la mujer que conoció?

Cuando me dispongo a cerrar la puerta, Trent me hace un gesto con la cabeza desde el otro lado de la habitación. Los ánimos que me transmite me hacen sentir fuerte, capaz, confiada. Es un defensor de contar la verdad sea cual sea. Tiene eso en común con Hootsie.

—Es mejor que oigáis sentados lo que os voy a contar —les digo a mis padres.

Honeybee se sienta de mala gana en el borde de una mecedora. Mi padre elige el balancín para dos y su postura me da a entender que espera oír algo serio y desagradable. Se inclina hacia delante con los pies bien plantados en el suelo, los codos apoyados en las rodillas, los dedos juntos. Sea cual sea la situación, está preparado para analizarla y controlar los daños.

—Dejadme que os lo cuente todo —les pido—. No hagáis preguntas hasta que haya terminado, ¿vale?

Sin esperar respuesta, tomo aire profundo y empiezo a hablar.

Mi padre escucha desde detrás de su habitual máscara de estoicismo. Mi madre termina por recostarse en el respaldo de la mecedora con una muñeca pegada a la frente.

Cuando termino, se hace el silencio. Nadie sabe qué decir. Es evidente que ni siquiera mi padre tenía idea de nada de esto, aunque algo en su expresión me dice que ahora se explica determinados comportamientos de su madre.

—¿Cómo... cómo sabes que todo esto es verdad? Igual... igual esta mujer... —Mi madre se calla, mira por la ventana de la casita. Está pensando en lo que ha oído ahí dentro, en las fotografías de las paredes—. Es que me parece imposible.

Mi padre respira por encima de los dedos juntos y sus cejas grises se juntan. Sabe que es posible, aunque le gustaría que no fuera así. Pero le he contado lo que descubrimos Trent y yo sobre la Asociación de Hogares Infantiles de Tennessee y me he dado cuenta de que la información no es nueva ni para él ni para mi madre. Sin duda han oído hablar del escándalo, quizá han visto alguno de los programas de televisión que recrean los hechos del infame orfanato de Tann.

—No puedo... ¿Mi madre? —murmura mi padre—. ¿Lo sabía mi padre?

—No creo que lo supiera nadie. La abuela Judy y sus hermanas eran mujeres adultas para cuando se reencontraron. May me dijo que no quisieron interferir las unas en las vidas de las otras. Teniendo en cuenta que los documentos se prepararon expresamente para evitar que las familias biológicas se encontraran, es un milagro que cuatro hermanas consiguieran reunirse.

—Dios mío. —Niega con la cabeza como si estuviera tratando de ordenar los pensamientos de forma que tengan algún sentido—. ¿Mi madre tiene un hermano gemelo?

—Nació con un hermano gemelo. Investigó durante años, pero nunca llegó a saber qué fue de él. Si murió o sobrevivió y lo adoptaron.

Mi padre apoya la barbilla en las manos. Levanta la vista hacia los árboles.

—Dios bendito que estás en los cielos.

Sé lo que está pensando. Yo llevo dando vueltas a las mismas cosas desde el día que supe la verdad. Toda la semana me he debatido entre llevarme el secreto conmigo a la tumba... y liberar la verdad, sean cuales sean las consecuencias. Al final mi conclusión es esta: mi padre se merece saber quién es. Mi abuela se merece pasar con su hermana el tiempo que le quede.

Los cinco niños del río que sufrieron a manos de la Asociación de Hogares Infantiles de Tennessee se merecen que sus verdaderas historias pervivan. De no ser por un giro del destino, la madre de mi padre habría crecido en un barco, entre personas humildes y rodeada de la pobreza de la Gran Depresión.

Al ser de esa clase social, no habría conocido a mi abuelo y, desde luego, no se habría casado con él.

No seríamos Stafford.

Mi madre recupera un poco la compostura y le coge una de las manos a mi padre.

—Eso pasó hace mucho tiempo. No tiene sentido atormentarse ahora con ello, Wells. No tiene sentido ni siquiera contarlo.

Me mira de reojo, es una advertencia. Me resisto al impulso de acobardarme. Para mí no hay vuelta atrás.

—Papá, lo que decidas hacer ahora es elección tuya. Lo único que pido es que la abuela Judy pueda pasar tiempo, el que le quede, con su hermana... Se han pasado toda la vida escondiéndose del mundo por nosotros, para no perjudicarnos. Ahora se merecen un poco de paz.

Mi padre besa los dedos a mi madre, los coge entre sus manos y asiente con la cabeza. Sin hablar, nos está diciendo a las dos que reflexionará sobre esto y tomará una decisión.

Honeybee se inclina hacia mí.

—¿Y qué me dices de ese..., del hombre que está ahí dentro? ¿Podemos estar seguros de que no..., de que no querrá...

usar esta información? Con las elecciones al Senado el año que viene, nada le gustaría más a Cal Fortner que un escándalo personal para alejar el debate de los verdaderos problemas.

Me alivia que mire automáticamente a mi padre y no a mí cuando habla de las elecciones al Senado. Tengo la sensación de que la vida está volviendo a ser como era y me alegro. Así será más fácil decirles que no habrá una boda ventajosa desde el punto de vista político en nuestro jardín cuando florezcan las azaleas. No estoy preparada para abordar aún el tema, pero ya llegará.

Estar aquí, ver a May y a mi abuela juntas me reafirma en mi decisión. Mucho.

—Por Trent no tienes que preocuparte. No haría algo así. Es un amigo. De no ser por su abuelo, las hermanas de la abuela nunca la habrían encontrado. No habría sabido la verdad sobre su pasado.

La expresión de mi madre da a entender que no está convencida de que eso no hubiera sido mejor.

La de mi padre dice otra cosa.

—Me gustaría hablar un ratito con la señora Crandall.

Honeybee abre un poco la boca. Luego la cierra, se endereza y asiente con la cabeza. Sea cual sea el camino que elija mi padre, lo recorrerá a su lado. Es lo que han hecho siempre mis padres.

—Creo que a May le gustará. Podemos dejaros solos a los cuatro para que pueda contártelo todo.

Oír lo ocurrido de boca de May, en sus propias palabras, convencerá a mi padre, creo. Es la historia de nuestra familia.

—Puedes quedarte —dice mi madre, vacilante.

—Prefiero daros un poco de tiempo.

Lo que quiero en realidad es estar a solas con Trent. Sé que se muere por preguntarme cómo se han tomado mis padres la noticia sobre la abuela Judy. No hace más que mirarme por la ventana de la casa.

Cuando nos levantamos y entramos en la casa, su alivio salta a la vista. Mi abuela está hablando de una excursión en barca por el río. Habla de ello como si hubiera pasado ayer. Al parecer, en algún momento May compró una lancha. La abuela Judy ríe al recordar a las cuatro flotando por el río Savannah porque el motor no arrancaba.

Mi padre se acerca despacio a una silla; mira a su madre como si fuera la primera vez que la ve. En cierto modo es así. La mujer que recuerda era una actriz interpretando un papel, al menos en parte. Durante todos los años transcurridos desde que sus hermanas la encontraron, en el cuerpo de Judy Stafford han vivido dos personas. Una de ellas es la mujer de un senador. La otra tiene sangre de los nómadas del río.

En esta casita, en el Día de las hermanas, las dos se funden en una.

Trent está encantado de salir conmigo.

—Vamos a subir la colina —sugiero—. Quiero sacar algunas fotos de la casa grande..., por si esto sale mal y nunca volvemos aquí.

Trent sonríe mientras cruzamos la verja y dejamos atrás el jardín de la casa.

—No creo que eso pase.

Recorremos el camino hasta los árboles. Pienso en Rill Foss convirtiéndose en May Weathers hace todos esos años.

¿Imaginaría entonces la vida que le esperaba?

La luz del sol me calienta mientras cruzamos el prado y empezamos a subir. Hace un día precioso, de esos que anuncian un cambio de estación. La sombra de la antigua mansión se proyecta en la hierba y hace que no parezca en ruinas. Mientras saco el teléfono y hago fotografías, me tiemblan las manos. En realidad no quería venir aquí para eso. Hay una razón por la que sentía la necesidad de venir con Trent adonde no pudieran vernos —ni oírnos— desde la casa.

Pero ahora no doy con las palabras... ni con el valor. Así que saco una cantidad absurda de fotografías. Llega un momento en que se me agota la excusa.

Me trago una repentina avalancha de mariposas y trato de reunir el valor suficiente.

Trent se me adelanta.

—No llevas el anillo —dice con los ojos llenos de preguntas cuando me vuelvo hacia él.

Me miro la mano, pienso en todo lo que he aprendido desde que acepté la proposición de matrimonio de Elliot y vine a Carolina del Sur a hacer lo que se esperaba de mí. Todo eso me parece ahora una vida distinta, la música de una mujer que no soy yo.

—Elliot y yo hemos hablado. No está de acuerdo con mi decisión sobre la abuela Judy y May y probablemente no lo estará nunca. Pero es más que eso. Creo que desde hace un tiempo los dos sabemos que funcionamos mejor como amigos que como pareja. Llevamos muchos años juntos, compartimos muchos recuerdos bonitos, pero... falta algo. Lo de casarnos fue algo que decidimos más por nuestras familias que por nosotros. Quizá en el fondo siempre lo hemos sabido.

Miro a Trent estudiar nuestras sombras en la hierba, con el ceño fruncido y expresión pensativa.

Mi corazón se agita, luego se desboca. Los segundos parecen tofe, pegajosos y eternos. *¿Siente Trent lo mismo que yo? ¿Y si no es así?*

Al fin y al cabo, primero tiene que pensar en su hijo.

Y en cuanto a mí, no sé exactamente hacia dónde va mi vida. Trabajar con el comité me dará tiempo para descubrir quién quiero ser. Creo que por eso he indagado tanto en el pasado de May, por eso he traído a mi abuela aquí esta tarde.

Hoy se ha reparado una injusticia de hace muchos años, en la medida en que algo así es posible cuando ha pasado ya tanto tiempo.

Eso me produce satisfacción, pero ahora las preguntas que me hago sobre Trent me hacen olvidarme de ella. *¿Cómo encaja él en este futuro que no he hecho más que empezar a imaginar? Su familia y la mía son muy diferentes.*

Cuando me mira, sus ojos atrapan la luz. Son del color azul intenso de las aguas profundas y, por primera vez, me doy cuenta de que quizá no somos tan distintos como parece. Compartimos un rico legado. Los dos descendemos del río.

—¿Quiere decir esto que puedo cogerte de la mano? —Mientras dice estas palabras, sonríe, levanta una ceja y espera.

—Sí. Creo que sí.

Me ofrece una palma y pongo mi mano en ella.

Sus dedos se cierran sobre los míos, en un círculo cálido, fuerte, y subimos la colina alejándonos de las ruinas de una vida que fue.

Hacia una vida que puede ser.

26

MAY CRANDALL

Época actual

Nuestra historia empieza una sofocante noche de agosto en una habitación blanca, estéril, en la que se toma una decisión fatídica fruto del egoísmo que causa el dolor. Pero nuestra historia no termina aquí. No ha terminado aún.

¿Cambiaría el curso de nuestras vidas si pudiera? ¿Preferiría haber pasado mi vida tocando el piano en un barco o arando la tierra como mujer de un granjero o esperando a que mi marido vuelva del río y se siente conmigo delante de la chimenea?

¿Cambiaría el hijo que tuve por otro, por más hijos, por una hija que me consolara en mi vejez? ¿Cambiaría los maridos que amé y enterré, la música, las sinfonías, las luces de Hollywood, los nietos y los bisnietos que viven lejos de mí pero tienen mis ojos?

En esto pienso sentada en el banco de madera, con la mano de Judy en la mía, las dos compartiendo otro Día de las hermanas. Aquí, en los jardines de Magnolia Manor, podemos tener un Día de las hermanas siempre que queremos. Es tan fácil como salir de mi habitación, cruzar al otro pasillo y decirle a la auxiliar: «Creo que voy a llevarme a mi amiga Judy a dar un paseo. Sí, por supuesto, yo me ocupo de traerla de vuelta a la Unidad de Trastornos de la Memoria. Ya sabe que lo hago siempre».

A veces mi hermana y yo nos reímos de nuestra triquiñuela.

—En realidad somos hermanas, no amigas —le recuerdo—. Pero eso no se lo digas. Es nuestro secreto.

—No lo diré. —Me sonríe con esa dulzura tan suya—. Pero las hermanas también son amigas. Las hermanas son amigas especiales.

Evocamos las muchas aventuras de los Días de las hermanas pasados y me pide que le cuente lo que recuerdo de Queenie y Briny y nuestra vida en el río. Le hablo de los años y estaciones que viví con Camellia y Lark y Fern y Gabion y Silas y el viejo Zede. Le hablo de remansos y de fuertes corrientes, del baile de las luciérnagas en verano y del hielo que permitía a los hombres caminar por el río. Juntas navegamos por el río que fluye. Volvemos la cara al sol y volamos una y otra vez al reino de Arcadia.

Otros días, para mi hermana no soy más que una vecina de esta vieja casa de campo. Pero el amor entre hermanas no necesita palabras. No requiere recuerdos, ni memoria ni pruebas. Es tan profundo como el latido de un corazón. Está tan presente como el pulso sanguíneo.

—¿No son adorables? —Judy señala una joven pareja que pasea de la mano por los jardines cerca del lago. Forman una estampa muy bonita.

Doy una palmadita cariñosa a Judy en la mano.

—Es tu nieta. Supongo que ha venido a visitarte. Y se ha traído a su enamorado. Es un bombón. Se lo dije la primera vez

que los vi juntos, que no lo dejara escapar. Reconozco un fle-
chazo cuando lo veo.

—Pues claro que es mi nieta. —Judy simula haberlo sabido desde el principio. Algunos días así habría sido, pero no
hoy—. Y su enamorado. —Mira hacia el camino con los ojos
entrecerrados—. Lo que pasa es que no me salen los nombres.
Ya sabes, mi memoria.

—Avery.

—Ah, sí... Avery.

—Y Trent.

—Conocimos un Trent, ¿verdad? Era un encanto de
hombre. Vendía los terrenos que estaban contiguos a nuestra
casa de Edisto, me parece.

—Sí. Pues el que viene con Avery es su nieto.

—Mira tú. —Judy saluda con entusiasmo y Avery le devuelve el saludo. Luego su novio y ella desaparecen detrás del
cenador. No reaparecen tan pronto como cabría esperar.

Judy se tapa la boca con una mano, riendo.

—¡Ahí va!

—Pues sí. —Recuerdo amores perdidos y amores que no
llegaron a ser—. Nosotros los Foss siempre hemos sido apa-
sionados. Y no creo que eso cambie.

—Creo que no debería cambiar.

Judy está de acuerdo conmigo y nos damos un cariñoso
abrazo de hermanas mientras nos reímos de los secretos que
compartimos.

Nota de la autora

Llegado el final del libro, seguramente el lector se está preguntando: ¿cuánto hay de verdad en esta historia? Es una pregunta hasta cierto punto difícil de contestar. Quien quiera saber más de la historia real de granjas de niños, orfanatos, adopciones irregulares, Georgia Tann y el escándalo que rodeó a la Asociación de Hogares Infantiles de Tennessee en Memphis encontrará información excelente en *Pricing the Priceless Child*, de Viviana A. Zelizer (1985); *Babies For Sale: The Tennessee Children's Home Adoption Scandal*, de Linda Tollett Austin (1993); *Alone In the World: Orphans and Orphanages in America*, de Catherine Reef (2005), y *The Baby Thief: The Untold Story of Georgia Tann, the Baby Seller Who Corrupted Adoption*, de Barbara Bisantz Raymond (2007), que incluye entrevistas con varias de las víctimas de Georgia Tann. Para saber cómo saltó el escándalo, se recomienda leer el informe original presentado al gobernador Gordon Browning llamado *Report to Governor Gordon Browning on Shelby County Branch, Tennessee Children's Home Society*, disponible en bibliotecas públicas. También hay artículos de periódicos y revistas sobre el escándalo y sobre la reunión de familias años más tarde, así como episodios dedicados al caso en los programas de televisión *60 Minutes* y *Unsolved Mysteries* y el documental *Deadly Women*. Todas estas fuentes me fueron de gran valor en mi trabajo de documentación.

Los niños Foss y el *Arcadia* cobraron forma en el polvo de la imaginación y en las aguas terrosas del río Misisipi. Aunque Rill y sus hermanos existen solo en estas páginas, sus experiencias reflejan las de otros niños que fueron arrancados de sus familias entre las décadas de 1920 y 1950.

La verdadera historia de Georgia Tann y la rama de Memphis de la Asociación de Hogares Infantiles de Tennessee es una paradoja extraña y triste. Sin duda la organización rescató a muchos niños de circunstancias deplorables y peligrosas, o simplemente acogió a niños que no eran queridos y los colocó en buenos hogares. Tampoco hay duda de que hubo muchos niños separados de sus padres sin motivo y sin trámites legales y de que sus familias biológicas, para su dolor, nunca los volvieron a ver. Los testimonios de supervivientes revelan que hubo madres que sufrieron durante décadas la ausencia de sus hijos robados al nacer y que muchos de esos niños se alojaron en centros donde sufrieron abandono, maltrato, abusos sexuales y fueron tratados como mercancías.

Madres solteras, padres indigentes, mujeres ingresadas en pabellones psiquiátricos y aquellas que recurrían a la beneficencia y a clínicas de maternidad fueron los blancos principales. Se obligaba a las madres biológicas a firmar papeles cuando estaban bajo los efectos de la sedación y se les decía que ceder temporalmente la custodia de sus hijos era necesario para asegurar que estos recibían tratamiento médico. Otras veces se les decía que sus hijos habían muerto. Niños que pasaron periodos en el hogar infantil —los que tenían edad suficiente para recordar su vida anterior— afirman haber sido secuestrados del porche de su casa, de la carretera camino a la escuela, de barcos donde vivían en el río. En esencia, si eras pobre y vivías en o pasabas cerca de Memphis, tus hijos estaban en peligro.

Los niños rubios como los Foss eran especialmente populares en la red de Georgia Tann y a menudo eran detectados por «espías» que trabajaban en hospitales y en clínicas de la beneficencia. Los residentes de la ciudad, aunque ignoraban los métodos, no eran ajenos a su trabajo. Durante años vieron anuncios de periódico con fotografías de niños de aspecto adorable con pies de foto del tipo: «Puede ser suyo», «¿Busca un regalo de Navidad de carne y hueso?» y «George quiere jugar a la pelota, pero necesita un papá». Georgia Tann era saludada como la «madre de la adopción moderna» y la misma Eleanor Roosevelt le pidió consejo sobre cuestiones relativas a la atención a la infancia. Para el gran público, no era más que una señora respetable y con buenas intenciones que dedicaba su vida a rescatar a niños necesitados. Su defensa de que estos niños fueran adoptados por familias ricas y conocidas ayudó a popularizar la idea de la adopción en general y a ahuyentar la creencia, muy extendida, de que los huérfanos eran niños indeseables y con problemas irreversibles. Entre los padres adoptivos famosos que recurrieron a Georgia Tann hubo políticos como el gobernador de Nueva York Herbert Lehman y estrellas de Hollywood como June Allyson y su marido Dick Powell, y Joan Crawford. Antiguos empleados del orfanato de Tann en Memphis hablaban de hasta siete niños transportados al mismo tiempo durante la noche a «hogares adoptivos» en California, Nueva York y otros estados. Cuando le preguntaban por sus métodos, Tann alababa con total descaro las virtudes de separar a niños de padres de baja extracción social que no podían criarlos como es debido y colocarlos en hogares de «clase social alta».

Desde una perspectiva actual, cuesta imaginar cómo Georgia Tann y su red consiguió actuar sin ningún tipo de control durante décadas o dónde encontró empleados dispuestos a mirar hacia otro lado ante el trato inhumano que se dispensaba a los niños en los hogares de la organización o en centros de acogida sin licencia, como aquel en el que Rill y sus hermanos fueron a parar. Sin embargo, sucedió. En un determinado momento, la Oficina para la Infancia de Estados Unidos envió a un investigador a Memphis para indagar sobre el elevado índice de mortalidad infantil en la ciudad. En 1945 una epidemia de disentería causó la muerte de entre cuarenta y cincuenta niños en un centro de la red de Georgia Tann, pese a los esfuerzos de un médico que ofreció sus servicios de forma voluntaria. Tann, no obstante, insistió en que solo se había perdido a dos niños. Bajo presión, la asamblea legislativa del estado aprobó una ley que exigía la posesión de una licencia a todos los hogares de acogida de Tennessee. La nueva legislación aprobada incluía un artículo que eximía de su cumplimiento a todos los hogares de acogida contratados por la agencia de Georgia Tann.

Aunque la señora Murphy y su hogar infantil son ficticios, las vivencias de Rill se inspiran en testimonios de supervivientes. También hubo muchos que, debido a los abusos, el abandono, la enfermedad o la atención médica inadecuada, no vivieron para contar su historia. Son las víctimas silenciosas de un sistema no regulado, alimentado por la avaricia y los beneficios económicos. Se calcula que el número de niños que desaparecieron a manos de la organización de Georgia Tann puede ascender a seiscientos. Otros varios miles fueron dados en adopción previo pago y se alteraron sus nombres, fechas y partidas de nacimiento para evitar que sus familias biológicas los encontraran.

Cabría suponer, dado lo terrible de las cifras, que el reinado de Georgia Tann terminó con una avalancha de acusaciones públicas, investigación policial y acciones legales. Si *Antes de que llegaras* fuera solo ficción, habría escrito un final en el que la justicia se impone. Por desgracia, la realidad no fue esa. Los muchos años de Tann dedicados al negocio de la adopción no terminaron hasta 1950. En una rueda de prensa de septiembre de ese año, el gobernador Gordon Browning evitó abordar la terrible tragedia humana que había detrás y se centró en el dinero. La señorita Tann, informó, había ganado ilegalmente un millón de dólares (el equivalente aproximado a diez millones de dólares hoy) cuando trabajaba para la Asociación de Hogares Infantiles de Tennessee. A pesar de la divulgación de sus crímenes, para entonces Georgia Tann estaba a salvo de cualquier acción legal. A los pocos días de la rueda de prensa murió en su casa a consecuencia de un cáncer de útero para el que se había negado a recibir tratamiento. Un periódico local publicó un reportaje que denunciaba sus acciones junto a su necrológica, en portada. Se cerró su hogar infantil y se designó un investigador, que pronto se vio frenado por personas poderosas con secretos, reputaciones y, en algunos casos, adopciones que había que proteger.

Aunque el cierre del hogar infantil dio esperanzas a las familias biológicas, pronto se apagaron. Legisladores y agentes políticos enseguida aprobaron medidas para legalizar incluso la más dudosa de las adopciones y clasificar los expedientes. De los veintidós niños que seguían bajo la tutela de Tann cuando esta murió, solo dos —que ya habían sido rechazados por sus familias adoptivas— fueron devueltos a sus padres biológicos. Miles de familias no llegarían a saber lo que había sido de sus hijos. El sentimiento público más extendido era que, al haber sido sacados de la pobreza para ser criados en familias acomodadas, habían resultado beneficiados, con independencia de las circunstancias en que se hubiera producido su adopción.

Aunque algunos niños adoptados, hermanos separados y familias biológicas consiguieron encontrarse uniendo recuerdos, recuperando documentos de los archivos de juzgados y con la ayuda de detectives privados, las víctimas de Georgia Tann no tuvieron acceso a sus archivos hasta 1995. Para muchos padres biológicos e hijos adoptados, que habían llorado por sus seres queridos toda su vida, ya era demasiado tarde. Para otros fue el principio de una reunión familiar esperada durante mucho tiempo y la oportunidad, por fin, de contar su historia.

Si hay una lección que se puede extraer de la historia de los Foss y de la verdad sobre el escándalo de la Asociación de Hogares Infantiles de Tennesee, es que los niños, con independencia del rincón del mundo del que provengan, no son mercancías ni objetos, ni tampoco pizarras en blanco, como a menudo describía Georgia Tann a sus tutelados. Son seres humanos con recuerdos, necesidades, deseos y sueños propios.

Agradecimientos

Los personajes de ficción se parecen un poco a las personas de carne y hueso: con independencia de sus orígenes, sus vidas las conforman la familia, los amigos, los vecinos, los colegas y los conocidos en general. Algunos de estos los animan, algunos los guían, algunos les brindan amor incondicional, algunos les enseñan, otros los impulsan a ser mejores. Esta historia, como la mayoría de las historias, debe su existencia a un conjunto de individuos únicos y generosos.

En primer lugar, estoy agradecida a mi familia por apoyarme todos estos años que he dedicado a escribir, incluso cuando ello implicaba noches sin dormir, horarios imposibles y neveras vacías. Este año quiero dar las gracias en particular a mi hijo mayor por enamorarse y añadir por fin una chica a la familia. Una boda no solo te distrae de corregir, reescribir y volver a corregir, ahora por fin tengo a alguien con quien ir a las presentaciones de libros y con quien charlar en el camino de ida y de vuelta.

Gracias a mi madre por ser mi ayudante oficial y también una excelente primera lectora. No todos tienen la suerte de contar con un ayudante que te diga cuándo necesitas ir a la peluquería o que tu último capítulo necesita un retoque. Gracias a mi encantadora suegra por ayudarme con las listas de envíos y por querer a mis chicos, que han crecido demasiado deprisa, y a Paw-Paw por asegurarse de que la próxima generación de Wingate sabe contar como es debido una historia a la hora de la cena. Gracias también a familiares y amigos de aquí y de allí por quererme y ayudarme y acogerme en sus casas cuando viajo. Sois los mejores.

Estoy agradecida a algunos amigos especiales que son como de la familia, en concreto a Ed Stevens por su ayuda con la documentación y sus constantes ánimos, y a Steve y Rosemary Fitts por ser nuestros anfitriones en la isla de Edisto. Si existe un lugar más agradable donde investigar, aún no lo conozco. Gracias también al maravilloso equipo que me ayudó con las primeras lecturas en público y las presentaciones: Duane Davis, Mary Davis, Virginia Rush, y, por último, aunque no menos importante, a mi tía Sandy, que tiene un gran talento para los argumentos y un sentido del humor igual de grande. A Kathie Bennett y Susan Zurenda de Magic Time Literary, gracias por haberme organizado tan bien viajes de promoción en el pasado, por apoyar este libro desde sus primeras fases y por el entusiasmo que habéis puesto en ayudarlo a nacer.

En el lado editorial, estoy eternamente en deuda con mi fabulosa agente, Elisabeth Weed, por animarme a escribir esta novela y a continuación trabajar como la profesional que es para asegurarse de que encontraba la editorial idónea. Gracias a la extraordinaria editora Susanna Porter por insistirme en que desarrollara más las vivencias de los niños Foss y el viaje de Avery al pasado secreto de su familia. Gracias al magnífico equipo editorial que hay detrás de este libro: Kara Welsh, Kim Hovey, Jennifer Hershey, Scott Shannon, Susan Corcoran, Melanie DeNardo, Kristin Fassler, Debbie Aroff, Lynn Andreozzi,

Toby Ernst, Beth Pearson y Emily Hartley. No hay palabras que expresen lo mucho que agradezco a cada uno de vosotros el amor que habéis puesto a la hora de lanzar este libro. Estoy en deuda también con los equipos de diseño, producción, marketing, publicidad y ventas. Gracias por aportar vuestro increíble talento. Sin vuestro trabajo, las novelas se quedarían ignoradas y sin leer en un estante. Vosotros conectáis los libros con los lectores y, al hacerlo, conectáis a unas personas con otras. Si los libros pueden cambiar el mundo, los que ayudáis a los libros a nacer sois los artífices del cambio.

Por último, estoy agradecida a los muchos lectores que habéis compartido viajes anteriores conmigo y que ahora os embarcáis en este. Os valoro mucho. Valoro el tiempo que pasamos juntos a través de mis historias. Gracias por recomendar mis otros libros a amigos, por proponerlos en clubes de lectura y por tomaros tiempo de enviarme mensajes de apoyo por correo electrónico, Facebook y Twitter. Estoy en deuda con todos los que leéis mis historias y también con los libreros que las venden con tanta devoción. Tal y como dijo Fred Rogers: «Buscad a los que ayudan. Siempre encontraréis personas dispuestas a ayudar».

Vosotros, amigos míos, sois quienes me ayudáis a mí.

Y os estoy muy agradecida.

Lisa Wingate trabajó como periodista y actualmente es conferenciante y autora de más de veinte novelas de gran éxito en Estados Unidos. Sus obras han ganado o han sido nominadas a numerosos premios, incluyendo el Pat Conroy Southern Book Prize, el Oklahoma Book Award, el Carol Award, el Christy Award y el RT Reviewers' Choice Award. Wingate vive en las Montañas Ouachita del suroeste de Arkansas.